The
International
Directory of
Little Magazines
& Small Presses

35th Edition, 1999–00

Len Fulton, Editor

★ Dustbooks ★

CONTENTS

Dustbooks would like to thank the many people who by advice and criticism have helped make this Directory a more useful and readable publication.

PAPER: $34.95/copy ISBN 0-916685-73-X
$116.00/4-year subscription
CLOTH: $55.00/copy ISBN 0-916685-74-8
$140.00/4-year subscription

email: dustbooks@telis.org
len@dustbooks.com
website: http://www.dustbooks.com

Published annually by Dustbooks, P.O. Box 100, Paradise, CA 95967, also publishers of the Directory of Editors, Small Press Record of Books in Print, Directory of Poetry Publishers and the Small Press Review/Small Magazine Review (bimonthly). Systems design, typesetting format and computer programming by Neil McIntyre, 3135 Prince Henry Drive, Sacramento, CA 95833.

Pressure sensitive or cheshire labels are available from the International Directory data base. These can be sorted alphabetically or by Zip Code.

SMALL PRESS INFORMATION LIBRARY
1999–2000

Gives you three annual volumes plus the CD plus a subscription to the monthly *Small Press Review/Small Magazine Review*.

This offer gets you this year's or next year's editions of our four annual directories at lower prices, saving you $30.85 for the `99 volumes and $29.85 on the `00 volumes (the Information Library price of $150.00 is $30.85 below the total of the individual `99 cover prices and subscription to the bi-monthly *Small Press Review/Small Magazine Review*, and $29.85 below the projected '00 volumes). It also assures you of receiving next year's volumes automatically.

Second, the Dustbooks Small Press Information Library gives you the single largest and most up-to-date collection of small press and magazine information available in the world -- magazines, presses, editors, publishers, books, pamphlets, broadsides, prices, discounts, editorial policies, news, reviews, articles -- it's almost endless!

The information Library ('99 prices shown) consists of:

»International Directory of Little Magazines and Small Presses (reg. $34.95)
»Directory of Small Magazine/Press Editors and Publishers (reg. $23.95)
»Small Press Record of Books in Print (reg. $55.00/ CD-ROM format only)
»Directory of Poetry Publishers (reg. $22.95)
»Small Press Review (bi-monthly) subscription for four years ($39.00)

Please use the order blank below -- and be sure to specify if you want the 1999 or 2000 Library.

- -

To: Dustbooks, PO Box 100, Paradise, CA 95967

Send_____1999 (Sept.`99)\\_____2000(Sept.`00) Info Library.
        ($150)   ($155)
   $_____Enclosed (Californians add 7.25% sales tax)

NAME_____

ADDRESS_____

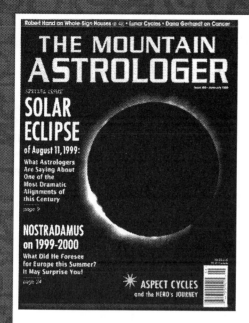

Free *issue!*

1-800-247-6463

Science of **Mind**® magazine has helped thousands of people improve their lives in every way—physically, mentally, spiritually, emotionally, financially. It will do the same for you.

- Since 1927, *Science of* **Mind**® magazine has been addressing such issues as personal growth, individual and business success, true abundance, health, wealth, prosperity, and happiness. We spotlight practical approaches to living well as we explore methods of tapping the wisdom of the ages. We interview best-selling authors and leading sacred explorers, sharing their insights with you. *Science of* **Mind**® magazine helps you to embrace that wisdom and release the genius that lies within you.

Science of **Mind**® magazine helps you think broader, smile wider, love deeper, grow faster, live better. Take advantage of this opportunity today and order your free issue **right now.** You'll be well on your way to becoming all you were meant to be!

You deserve it!

PALANQUIN PRESS
DEPARTMENT OF ENGLISH
UNIVERSITY OF SOUTH CAROLINA AIKEN
AIKEN, SC 29801

POETRY CHAPBOOK CONTESTS:

Manuscripts: 20-25 pages of poetry plus bio and acknowledgments.

$10.00 reading fee (includes copy of winning chapbook).
(checks payable to Palanquin Press)

SASE (results only)

Postmark Deadlines:
Oct. 15 & May 1 annually.

Winning manuscript to be published by Palanquin Press.
Winner gets $100.00 and 50 copies.

SASE: Results only.

SPRING 1999 CONTEST WINNERS:

Michelle Holland: *Love in the Real World*
Robert Parham: *What Part Motion Plays in the Equation of Love*
Dana Wildsmith: *Annie*

SEND SUBMISSIONS TO:

Phebe Davidson, Editor
Palanquin Press
Department of English
University of South Carolina Aiken
Aiken, SC 29801

MASTER OF PROFESSIONAL WRITING PROGRAM

Faculty Includes:

Shelley Berman-- Humor Writing, *Up in the Air*
Lee Blessing -- Playwriting, *A Walk in the Woods*
Noel Riley Fitch -- Nonfiction, *Julia Child: An Appetite for Life*
Donald Freed -- Playwriting, *Secret Honor*
Sy Gomberg-- Screenwriting, *When Willie Comes Marching Home*
Richard Lid-- Non-Fiction, *Ford Madox Ford*
Shelly Lowenkopf-- Editor, *The Harrad Experiment*
James Ragan -- Poetry, *Lusions*
Tristine Rainer-- Non-fiction, *Your Life as Story*
John Rechy -- Fiction, *City of Night*
Aram Saroyan -- Fiction, *The Romantic*
Hubert Selby, Jr. -- Fiction, *Last Exit to Brooklyn*
Mel Shavelson -- Screenwriting, *Houseboat*
Jason Squire-- Screenwriting, *The Movie Business Book*
S.L. Stebel -- Screenwriting, *Picnic at Hanging Rock*
Gay Talese -- Nonfiction, *The Kingdom and the Power*
Shirley Thomas -- Technical Writing, *Men of Space*
Kenneth Turan-- Film Critic, *Los Angeles Times*
Paul Zindel -- Playwriting, *The Effects of Gamma Rays on Man-In-The-Moon Marigolds*

Recent Visiting Writers:

Edward Albee - Shana Alexander - Marvin Bell - Robert Bly - Betty Freidan - William Gaddis - William Gass - Galway Kinnell - Dale Pollock - Kurt Vonnegut - Alice Walker

Alumni Include:

Mark Andrus (screenwriter, *As Good as it Gets*), novelist **Catherine Davidson** (*The Priest Fainted*), **Judith Freeman** (*Family Attractions*), NPR's **Sandra Tsing Loh,** poet **Charles Webb** (Samuel French Morse prize), Pulitzer nominated novelist **Gina Nahai** (*Cry of the Peacock*), author **Margaret Leslie Davis** (*Rivers in the Desert)*, and **Ehrich Van Lowe** (executive producer/writer *The Cosby Show*).

For more information, please write:

James Ragan, Director
The Professional Writing Program - WPH 404
University of Southern California
Los Angeles, CA 90089-4034
Telephone: (213) 740-3252

USC
UNIVERSITY
OF SOUTHERN
CALIFORNIA

Bilingual Spanish-English and Multilingual Four-color Books on Nature

Natural Puerto Rico / *Puerto Rico natural* (Young Adult / Adult)

"What differentiates this book from others is a Spanish/English format and intense color photos throughout, which provide a rich multicultural travel exploration . . .." MIDWEST BOOK REVIEW

"This showy volume is...something unquestionably necessary in Puerto Rico today." EL NUEVO DÍA (San Juan)

Natural Patagonia / *Patagonia natural*

"Even if you never read a word of the text, you can respond to the photographs with both a sense of wonder that is beckoning and a feeling of imaginative engagement that is intimate. However . . . reading it will help make the reader an educated traveler, one who will go gently and preserve it." INDEPENDENT PUBLISHER

Natural Cuba / *Cuba natural*

"Naturally, it was much needed—a work that gathered, for posterity, the diverse Cuban flora and fauna, one warning what could be lost in the future, if not preserved in the present." MIAMI HERALD / EL NUEVO HERALD

Patagonia Wilderness / *Patagonia sylvestre*

"Few regions lie farther away or bear an odder name than Patagonia, the southern extremity of South America. Patagonia Wilderness gives a better idea of what the place is like than any other books." WASHINGTON POST

Books on Children's and Cultural Issues

ROBBED OF HUMANITY Lives of Guatemalan Street Children

"The book's originality lies in its ability to let the children speak for themselves." MULTICULTURAL REVIEW

"If you care about children, or your government's respect for human rights, read this book." URBAN LATINO

"A powerful and disturbing work . . . it will hopefully outrage and compel concerned citizens." WORLDVIEW

EAGLE DOCTOR Soaring on the Wings of Others NEW 1999

There are those who hear the voiceless child. Breaking the silence of the multiply-disabled, Stephen shares his young life through his nurse Chrissy, who came to be his Mother. An unforgettable tribute to all caregivers.

Coquí y sus amigos / *Coquí & His Friends* (Children 8-12)
Los animales de Puerto Rico / *The Animals of Puerto Rico* NEW 1999

Natural Iguassu / *Iguaçu* / Iguazú natural NEW 1999

Natural Pantanal & Iberá / *Pantanal & Iberá natural* NEW 2000

Natural Venezuela / *Venezuela natural* NEW 2000

226 WHEELER ST S ST PAUL, MN 55105-1927 USA TEL 651.690-3320 FAX 651.690-1485 INFO@PANGAEA.ORG WEB PANGAEA.ORG

Independent Publishers,

Do your titles have international potential?

But are you too busy for book fairs?
Inexperienced at negotiating foreign rights deals?
Uncertain about overseas distribution possibilities?
Looking to maximize exposure for your titles worldwide?

Frankfurt Prague Warsaw London
Australia Taipei BookExpo America

International Titles/Harry Smith provides at major fairs
- cover-out display at our busy, prominent stand
- extensive listing in our fully illustrated catalogues
- individual representation at foreign rights meetings
- individual pursuit of your distribution objectives
- individual detailed reports on all show contacts & requests

The Frankfurt fair, by far the world's largest, is our most important marketing event. Because of our many years of experience and the host of overseas contacts we've built up, we're quite successful in selling foreign rights across the whole fabulous range of independent publishing. We enjoy equal success at obtaining non-U.S. distribution contracts for our clients. We also sell translation rights year-round to our regular customers overseas and at other major trade shows.

Contact us for a free information kit

International Titles/Harry Smith
931 East 56th Street/ Austin, TX 78751-1724
(512) 451-2221/ fax (512) 467-1330
email: leint@eden.com

Keep Your Directory Updated!
With
Small Press Review
Bi-Monthly

The bi-monthly **Small Press Review**, now including the **Small Magazine Review**, is published in an expanded format with two sections, one for books, one for magazines. All the features of both periodicals are still included – news and notes on editorial needs and contests, reviews, guest editorials, copious listings of new publishers, letters, columns by Laurel Speer, Bob Grumman and others. Also every issue: the popular "Free Sample Mart," offering free copies of some thirty books and magazines.

$25 / yr.❖ $33 / 2 yrs❖ $36 / 3yrs

DUSTBOOKS
THE LEADER IN THE SMALL PRESS INFORMATION FIELD
P.O. Box 100, Paradise, CA 95967-0100

Listings are of three basic kinds: those for **magazines** (periodicals, printed in all caps), those for **presses** (book publishers), and **cross-references.**

The **cross-references** are simply publisher imprints (usually presses but sometimes magazines) which have no listing data of their own but which are designed to lead you to a listing for that publisher which does have such data.

A complete **magazine** listing would include, in the following order: Name of magazine, name of press, name(s) of editor(s), address, phone number, founding year, type of material used, additional comments by editors including recent contributors, circulation, frequency of publication, number of issues published in 1998, expected in 1999 and 2000, one-year subscription price, single copy price, sample copy price, back issues price, discount schedules, average number of pages, page size, production method (mi-mimeo, lo or of - offset; lp-letterpress), length of reporting time on manuscripts, payment rates, rights purchased and/or copyright arrangements, number of reviews published in 1998, areas of interest for review materials, ad rates (page/half page) and membership in small mag/press organizations.

A complete **press** listing would include, in the following order: Name of press, name of magazine (if any), names(s) of editor(s), address, founding year, type of material used, additional comments by editors including recent contributors, average press run, number of titles published in 1998, expected in 1999 and 2000, average copy price, in cloth, paperback and "other," discount schedules, average number of pages, average page size, printing method (mi-mimeo, lo or of-offset; lp-letterpress), length of reporting time on manuscripts, payment or royalty arrangements, rights purchased and/or copyright arrangements, number of titles listed in the current edition of the **Small Press Record of Books in Print**, and membership in publishing organizations.

Certain special abbreviations apply to listings from the United Kingdom: px-postage is extra; pf-postage is free; pp-pages; p-pence.

Listings preceded by a bullet (●) are new in this edition. In some cases in this edition we received no report by press time but had a reasonable sense that the magazine or press was still going. In such cases a ‡ is used before the name. Query before sending money or material, however.

The following additional indicators are used in this edition to simplify yes or no in the listings: † means the magazine or press does its own printing; § before a listing of areas of interest for review materials indicates the magazine wishes to receive materials for review.

For those who wish to list a magazine or press in future editions of this **Directory** or our **Directory of Poetry Publishers**, Dustbooks provides a special form. Please write to us for it. Write to us also for a form to list books, pamphlets, broadsides, posters, and poem-cards (i.e. *non*-periodicals) in our annual **Small Press Record of Books in Print** (now in CD-ROM format). However, once a report form has been filled out for the **Directory**, further forms and requests for information will be sent automatically. A "proof-sheet" is sent in February of each year for updating **Directory** listings, and for updating **Record** listings. Deadline is July 1st of each year.

A

A & M Books, Anyda Marchant, PO Box 283, Rehoboth Beach, DE 19971, 302-227-2893; 800-489-7662. 4 titles listed in the *Small Press Record of Books in Print* (28th Edition, 1999-00).

A & U AMERICA'S AIDS MAGAZINE, David Waggoner, Editor-in-Chief, 25 Monroe Street, Suite 205, Albany, NY 12210, 518-426-9010, fax 518-436-5354, mailbox@aumag.org. 1991. Poetry, fiction, articles, art, photos, cartoons, interviews, satire, criticism, reviews, music, letters, plays, news items, non-fiction, parts-of-novels, long-poems, collages, plays. "Recent contributors: John Ashbery, Gwendolyn Brooks, Michael Lassell, Mark Doty, Mark O'Donnell, Edward Field, Eve Ensler, David Bergman, Walter Holland, Leslea Newman, Paula Martinac, Diamanda Galas, William Parker, Assoto Saint, etc." circ. 150M. 12/yr. Pub'd 8 issues 1998; expects 12 issues 1999, 12 issues 2000. sub. price: $24.95, $80.00 Library; per copy: $3.50; sample: $5. Back issues: $10 for all back issues, except 1991 fall premiere $30.00. Discounts: bulk schedule: one year rate is $1.75 for 1-25 copies, $1.25 for 26-50 copies, $1 for 50+ copies. 80pp; 8⅛×10½; of. Reporting time: 6 months to 1 year. Simultaneous submissions accepted: yes. Publishes 5% of manuscripts submitted. Payment: 5 complimentary copies and negotiable honorariums. Copyrighted, reverts to author. Pub's reviews: 60 in 1998. §Anything AIDS-related, especially the arts and AIDS. Ads: Back cover/$18,247, 8 all page/$12,850, half page/ $8,738, all rates for color. Gay & Lesbian Press Association.

A G M Enterprises, Inc., Jean French, Editor-in-Chief, 3232 Cobb Parkway, Suite 203, Atlanta, GA 30339, 404-951-1603; 800-645-1323. 1993. "We will be primarily in music related area." Expects 1 title 1999, 2 titles 2000. 1 title listed in the *Small Press Record of Books in Print* (28th Edition, 1999-00). avg. price, cloth: $18.95; paper: $14.95. Discounts: 20% libraries. 195pp; 6×9. Copyrights for author.

A. Borough Books, Evan Griffin, Editorial Director, PO Box 15391, Charlotte, NC 28211, 704-364-1788; 800-843-8490 (orders only). 1994. Non-fiction. "Non-fiction book proposals only (no manuscripts), 200 pages or less. Topics: recent history, how-to, humor" avg. press run 1M-3M. Pub'd 2 titles 1998; expects 2 titles 1999, 2 titles 2000. 9 titles listed in the *Small Press Record of Books in Print* (28th Edition, 1999-00). avg. price, paper: $10.95. Discounts: 20% library (2 or more), 20% academic (10 or more), 40% bookseller (5 or more), 55% jobber. 128pp; 6×9, 5½×8½; of. Reporting time: 2 months. Simultaneous submissions accepted: yes. Publishes 30% of manuscripts submitted. Payment: negotiable. Does not copyright for author. PMA.

A.L.I., Daniel Richardson, T. Chatterton, 20 Byron Place, Bristol, B58 1JT, England, E-mail: DSR@maths.bath.ac.uk. 1990. Poetry, fiction, reviews. "Aspiring to the odd life of overheard conversations in which a great deal is revealed and almost everything is left out." circ. 200. 4/yr. Pub'd 4 issues 1998; expects 4 issues 1999, 4 issues 2000. sub. price: $10; per copy: $5; sample: $5. Discounts: none. 12pp; 8×11½; †photocopy. Reporting time: 6 weeks. Simultaneous submissions accepted: no. Publishes 10% of manuscripts submitted. Payment: none. Rights revert to author on publication. Pub's reviews: 6 in 1998. §Poetry, short stories. Ads: $50/$25. ALP.

A.R.A. JOURNAL, American Romanian Academy, Dr. Ion Manea, Dr. Ion Manea-Manoliu, 3328 Monte Vista Avenue, Davis, CA 95616, 916-758-7720. 1975. "Yearly publication that contains Romanian studies of interest to American intellectuals." circ. 500. 1/yr. Pub'd 1 issue 1998; expects 1 issue 1999, 1 issue 2000. price per copy: $20; sample: $20. Back issues: $20. Discounts: 10%. 300pp; 5½×8½. Reporting time: 3 months. Simultaneous submissions accepted: yes. Publishes 30% of manuscripts submitted. Payment: none. Copyrighted, does not revert to author. Pub's reviews: 3 in 1998. §East-Central Europe, Romania. Ads: no.

A.R.E. Press, Jon Robertson, Editor-in-Chief, PO Box 656, Virginia Beach, VA 23451, 804-428-3588. 1931. Non-fiction, fiction. "We publish books, fiction and nonfiction, that deal with some aspect of the information and the concepts found in the work of Edgar Cayce, well-known American psychic. Manuscripts should run approximately 65,000 words, although length is not a strict criterium. We do not accept unsolicited mss. SASE for author's guidelines, query first" avg. press run 5M. Pub'd 13 titles 1998; expects 14 titles 1999, 15 titles 2000. avg. price, cloth: $19.95; paper: $12.95. Discounts: 1-4 20%, 5-14 40%, 15-24 42%, 25-49 45%, 50-99 48%, 100+ 50%. 240pp; 5½×8¼. Reporting time: 4-6 weeks. Publishes 4% of manuscripts submitted. Payment: advance up to $2,000, 10% of net on first 10,000, 12.5% on next 10,000, 15% on all else. Copyrights for author. ABA, NAPRA.

AABYE (formerly New Hope International Writing), New Hope International, Gerald England, 20 Werneth Avenue, Gee Cross, Hyde, Cheshire SK14 5NL, United Kingdom, 061-351 1878. 1970. Poetry, long-poems, art, photos. "Founded as Headland in 1970. Partner stole the name Headland (and all the money in the bank a/c) in 1980 so New Hope International started up. Publish poetry (including translations). Reviews published separately. Guidelines for contributors available for IRC, or by e-mail from newhope@iname.com" circ. 500-1M. 2/yr. Pub'd 1 issue 1998; expects 2 issues 1999, 2 issues 2000. sub. price: £10 for 3 issues (UK); £13 sterling only; per copy: £5. Back issues: on application. Discounts: 33% to shops (cash with order). 60pp; size A5; offset/litho. Reporting time: up to 6 months, but usually only 4-6 weeks. Simultanous submissions not encouraged. Publishes 1% of manuscripts submitted. Payment: copies. Not copyrighted. Association of Little Presses.

AAIMS Publishers, Edward Torrey, 11000 Wilshire Boulevard, PO Box 241777, Los Angeles, CA 90024-9577, 213-968-1195; 888-490-2276; fax 213-931-7217; email aaims1@aol.com. 1969. avg. press run 4M. Pub'd 1 title 1998; expects 1 title 1999, 2 titles 2000. 10 titles listed in the *Small Press Record of Books in Print* (28th Edition, 1999-00). avg. price, paper: $16.95. Discounts: 1 copy 30%, 2 35%, 3 40%, 4 41%, 15 45%, 30 47%, 45 49%, 200+ 50%. 250pp; webb. Reporting time: 3 weeks. Copyrights for author. Assoc. of American Publishers, American Booksellers Assoc., Canadian Booksellers Association, Australian Booksellers Association.

Aardvark Enterprises (A Division of Speers Investments Ltd.), J. Alvin Speers, 204 Millbank Drive S.W., Calgary, Alta T2Y 2H9, Canada, 403-256-4639. 1977. Poetry, fiction, articles, photos, cartoons, interviews, reviews, letters, news items, non-fiction. "Open to proposals. We publish for hire at reasonable rates, which is advantageous for special short run projects, or other. Over 59 books with successful results." avg. press run varies. Pub'd 6 titles 1998; expects 6 titles 1999, 6 titles 2000. 63 titles listed in the *Small Press Record of Books in Print* (28th Edition, 1999-00). avg. price, paper: $8.95; other: $4.95 booklets. Discounts: inquiries invited - quantity discounts only. 100pp; 5½×8½; †quality photocopying. Reporting time: fast, return mail usually. Publishes 50% of manuscripts submitted. Payment: by arrangement on individual project. Copyrights for author.

AAS HISTORY SERIES, Univelt, Inc., Donald C. Elder, Series Editor, PO Box 28130, San Diego, CA 92198, 760-746-4005; Fax 760-746-3139; 76121.1532@compuserve.com; www.univelt.staigerland.com. 1977. Non-fiction. "History of Science (esp. Space Science and Technology). Science Fiction and Space Futures. An irregular serial. Standing orders accepted. Vols 1-22 published." circ. 400. Irregular. Pub'd 3 issues 1998; expects 2 issues 1999, 2 issues 2000. sub. price: varies. Back issues: no. Discounts: 20% and more by arrangement; reduced prices for classroom use. 200-500pp; 7×9½; of. Reporting time: 90 days. Payment: 10% (if the volume author). Copyrighted, authors may republish material with appropriate credits given and authorization from publishers. Ads: none.

aatec publications, Christina Bych, PO Box 7119, Ann Arbor, MI 48107, 800-995-1470 (phone & fax), e-mail aatecpub@aol.com. 1980. Non-fiction. "We specialize in the sustainable energies, with an emphasis on photovoltaics. *aatec* books offer background and working knowledge to actual and aspiring renewable energy users." avg. press run 5M. Pub'd 1 title 1998; expects 2 titles 1999, 2 titles 2000. 3 titles listed in the *Small Press Record of Books in Print* (28th Edition, 1999-00). avg. price, paper: $16.95. Discounts: contact for schedules. 200+pp; 6×9; of. Reporting time: 2-3 weeks. Simultaneous submissions accepted: yes. Payment: 15% of monies received, annual. Copyrights for author.

ABBEY, White Urp Press, David Greisman, 5360 Fallriver Row Court, Columbia, MD 21044. 1971. Poetry, articles, art, interviews, criticism, reviews, letters. "*Abbey* is the Molson's Ale of Small Press rags. Recent contributors: Ann Menebroker, Gretchen Johnsen, Peter Wild, John Elsberg, Ron Androla, Richard Peabody, Harry Calhoun, Cheryl Townsend, Vera Bergstrom, Wayne Hogan, Joan Payne Kincaid, and Sister Mary Ann Henn" circ. 200. 3-4/yr. Pub'd 4 issues 1998; expects 4 issues 1999, 4 issues 2000. sub. price: $2; per copy: 50¢; sample: 50¢. Back issues: 50¢. 18pp; 8½×11; of. Reporting time: 2 minutes-2 years. Payment: nothing. Copyrighted, reverts to author. Pub's reviews: 12-20 in 1998. §Poetry, running. Ads: $10/$5.

ABE Press, Ruth Williams, Editor & Publisher, PO Box 521, Alta Loma, CA 91701. 1 title listed in the *Small Press Record of Books in Print* (28th Edition, 1999-00).

ABELexpress, Ken Abel, PO Box 668, Carnegie, PA 15106-0668, 412-279-0672; fax 412-279-5012; email ken@abelexpress.com. 1983. Non-fiction. avg. press run 5M. Pub'd 1 title 1998; expects 3 titles 1999. 1 title listed in the *Small Press Record of Books in Print* (28th Edition, 1999-00). avg. price, paper: $5.95. Discounts: varies. 128pp; 6×9, 5½×8½, 3½×4¾; of. Reporting time: 15 days. Simultaneous submissions accepted: yes. Publishes 5-10% of manuscripts submitted. Payment: 10% of selling price, monthly payments. Copyright for author if requested. PMA.

ABERRATIONS, Richard Blair, Editor; Eric Turowski, Art Editor, PO Box 460430, San Francisco, CA 94146, 415-648-3908. 1991. Fiction, articles, art, cartoons, interviews, satire, criticism, long-poems, non-fiction, reviews. "All must be horror, science fiction, fantasy" circ. 1.5M. 12/yr. Pub'd 5 issues 1998; expects 12 issues 1999, 12 issues 2000. sub. price: $31; per copy: $3.50; sample: $4.48 ppd. Discounts: 50% bookstores, 40% libraries or classrooms. 64pp; 5½×8½; web. Reporting time: 2-16 weeks. Simultaneous

2

submissions accepted: no. Publishes 2-1/2-5% of manuscripts submitted. Payment: 1/2¢ per word. Copyrighted, reverts to author. Pub's reviews: 10 in 1998. Ads: $40/$21/$8 2¼ X 2"/$15 4½ X 2"

●**Abiding Mystery Press**, PO Box 138, Independence, MO 64051. "Abiding Mystery is a new and rather small press, primarily interested in mystery fiction." 1 title listed in the *Small Press Record of Books in Print* (28th Edition, 1999-00).

Abiko Literary Press (ALP) (see also THE ABIKO QUARTERLY WITH JAMES JOYCE FW STUDIES), Laurel Sicks, Tatsuo Hamada, 8-1-8 Namiki, Abiko, Chiba 270-1165, Japan, 0471-84-7904; alp@db3.so-net.or.jp. 1988. Poetry, fiction, articles, art, photos, cartoons, interviews, satire, criticism, reviews, letters, parts-of-novels, long-poems, collages, plays, concrete art, non-fiction. "We specialize in James Joyce *Finnegans Wake*." avg. press run 500. Pub'd 1 title 1998; expects 1 title 1999, 1 title 2000. avg. price, paper: $15. Discounts: to be negotiated. 800pp. Reporting time: 2 weeks. Simultaneous submissions accepted: no. Publishes 10% of manuscripts submitted. Payment: 1 free copy, you must pay $15 for postage. Does not copyright for author. Small Press Center.

THE ABIKO QUARTERLY WITH JAMES JOYCE FW STUDIES, Abiko Literary Press (ALP), Anna Livia Plurabelle, Managing Editor; Tatsuo Hamada, Fiction & Poetry Editor, 8-1-8 Namiki, Abiko-shi, Chiba-ken 270-1165, Japan, 0471-84-7904; alp@db3.so-net.or.jp. 1989. Poetry, fiction, art, photos, interviews, criticism, reviews, long-poems, collages, plays, non-fiction. "All types of fiction considered. Fiction contest in Fall. First prize $1000 Especially want essays on Joyce w/emphasis on Finnegans Wake. We receive most of our submissions from contests. We do not retype manuscripts for publication. Send camera ready copy designed as creatively or experimentally as you want." circ. 500. Irregular. Pub'd 1 issue 1998; expects 1 issue 1999, 1 issue 2000. sub. price: $100; per copy: $35 (personal check to: Laurel Sicks); sample: $35. Back issues: $35. Discounts: to be negotiated. 800pp; size B5; of. Reporting time: 2 weeks. Simultaneous submissions accepted: no. Publishes 10% of manuscripts submitted. Payment: 1 free copy, you must pay postage $15. Copyrighted, reverts to author. Pub's reviews: 10 in 1998. §Books relating to the analysis of Finnegan's Wake. Ads: $100/$50/$25. James Joyce Foundation, Small Press Center.

ABILITY NETWORK, Spencer Bevan-John, Lucia Dutton, PO Box 24045, Dartmouth, Nova Scotia B3A 4T4, Canada, 902-461-9009; FAX 902-461-9484; e-Mail: anet@fox.nstn.ca. 1992. Poetry, articles, art, photos, cartoons, interviews, letters, news items, non-fiction. "Submissions should not exceed 1,200 words. Most articles/material are submitted by people with disabilities, since magazine is a cross disability magazine with an emphasis on the philosophy of independent living. Regular features on children and disabilities, philosophy, international stories, sex, technology with emphasis on human interest editorial." circ. 35M-50M. 4/yr. Pub'd 6 issues 1998; expects 4 issues 1999, 4 issues 2000. sub. price: $15; per copy: $5; sample: free. Back issues: $5. 48-64pp; 8½×10⅞; web press and electronic version available on internet. Reporting time: 3 months. Simultaneous submissions accepted: yes. Publishes 20% of manuscripts submitted. Payment: $25-$50. Copyrighted, reverts to author. Pub's reviews: 6 in 1998. §Issues of interest to people with disabilities. Ads: $995/$770/n/a (price in Canadian dollars).

ABRAXAS, Ingrid Swanberg, Editor-in-Chief; Warren Woessner, Senior Editor, PO Box 260113, Madison, WI 53726-0113, 608-238-0175; irmarkha@students.wisc.edu; www.litline.org/html/abraxas.html; www.geocities.com/paris/4614. 1968. Poetry, articles, art, satire, criticism, letters, collages, concrete art. "Address for exchanges and large packages: 2518 Gregory Street, Madison, WI 53711. *Abraxas* is no longer considering unsolicited poetry except for special projects. We will announce submission policies as projects arise. See our websites for reading periods. We are particularly interested in lyric poetry, and contemporary poetry in translation. *Abraxas Press* has published an anthology of Jazz Poetry, *Bright Moments* ($4.00), and a new translation of Cesar Vallejo's *Trilce*, based on the only authorized edition. Inquiries should be sent to Ingrid Swanberg at above address or to Warren Woessner, (34 W. Minnehaha Parkway, Minneapolis, MN 55419). We have recently published Cesar Vallejo, Denise Levertov, William Stafford, Ivan Arguelles, Andrei Codrescu, John Perlman, Andrea Moorhead, prospero saiz." circ. 500+. Irregular. Expects 2 issues 1999, 2 issues 2000. sub. price: $16/4 issues, $20/4 issues foreign; per copy: $4; sample: $8 double issues, $4 single issue. Back issues: catalog on request, SASE please. Discounts: 20% 1-4 copies; 40% 5-9 copies; 50% on orders of more than 10 copies. 80pp, 144pp double issues; 6×9; of. Reporting time: 2-5 months, sometimes longer; we currently have a very great backlog of unsolicited mss. Simultaneous submissions accepted: no. Publishes 2% of manuscripts submitted. Payment: copies; 40% author's discount on additional copies. Copyrighted, reverts to author. Ads: $60/$35. CLMP.

ABSOLUTE MAGNITUDE, DNA Publications, Inc., Warren Lapine, PO Box 2988, Radford, VA 24143-2988, 413-772-0725; Wilder@shaysnet.com. 1993. Poetry, fiction, interviews, letters. "1,000 to 25,000 words. Looking for character driven action adventure oriented technical science fiction. Recent contributors: C.J. Cherryh, Barry B. Longyear, Allen Steele, Chris Bunch, Harlen Elison, Allen Dean Foster." circ. 9M. 4/yr. Pub'd 4 issues 1998; expects 4 issues 1999, 4 issues 2000. sub. price: $14; per copy: $5; sample: $5. Discounts: none. 96pp; 8½×11; web press. Reporting time: 2 weeks. Simultaneous submissions accepted: yes. Publishes

.5% of manuscripts submitted. Payment: 3¢-5¢ per word on publications. Copyrighted, reverts to author. Pub's reviews: 75 in 1998. §Science fiction, fantasy, horror. Ads: $225/$115/$78.

AC, Alternating Crimes Publishing, Danie L. Gallant, Editor-in-Chief; Danielle Nation, Assistant Extraodinair, 306 Parham Street, Suite 200, Raleigh, NC 27601, 919-834-5433; Fax 919-834-2449; E-mail gstudios@mindspring.com. 1985. Poetry, fiction, articles, art, photos, cartoons, interviews, reviews, parts-of-novels, long-poems, plays, non-fiction. circ. 2M. 2/yr. Pub'd 1 issue 1998; expects 2 issues 1999, 2 issues 2000. sub. price: $7/postage; per copy: $2.95; sample: $3.50 w/postage. Back issues: Number 5 @ $5, Number 6 @ $5, for AC $3.95. Discounts: 40%, negotiate with distributors on individual basis. 32pp; 6¾×10; of. Reporting time: 16 weeks. Simultaneous submissions accepted: yes. Publishes 10% of manuscripts submitted. Payment: contributor's copies. Copyrighted, reverts to author. Pub's reviews: none yet in 1998. §Art, design film, fiction and non-fiction, graphic novel, comics, fiction, poetry, music, magazines. Ads: $300 inside covers/$200 full page/$75 1/2 page, inquire for other sizes. N.C. Writer's Network.

AC Projects, Inc., 7111 Sweetgum Drive SW #B, Fairview, TN 37062-9384, 615-646-3757. 1977. "Not accepting ms until further notice" avg. press run 3M-25M. Pub'd 1 title 1998; expects 1 title 2000. 5 titles listed in the *Small Press Record of Books in Print* (28th Edition, 1999-00). avg. price, cloth: $9.95-$35; paper: $9.95. Discounts: inquire please. 44-691pp.

Acada Books, 1850 Union Street, Suite 1236, San Francisco, CA 94123, 415-776-2325. 1996. Non-fiction. "Current college professor and previous writing credits relevant to subject" avg. press run 3M. Pub'd 2 titles 1998; expects 2 titles 1999, 3 titles 2000. 4 titles listed in the *Small Press Record of Books in Print* (28th Edition, 1999-00). avg. price, paper: $17. 176pp; 6×9; of. Reporting time: 4 weeks. Simultaneous submissions accepted: yes. Publishes 5% of manuscripts submitted. Payment: negotiable. Does not copyright for author.

ACCCA Press, Milli Janz, 149 Cannongate III, Nashua, NH 03063-1953. 1978. Articles. "*Culture Without Pain or Money* is now in a new 2nd edition, and is being distributed in Haiti, Japan, The Philippines and Egypt. It is being used currently in many parts of the U.S. as a blueprint for initiating, developing and continuing cultural centers in communities. (Especially where art services are exchanged in lieu of money). Because the book is in a smaller edition, the price for the book and mailing will remain at $4 each. For the newest edition, $39.95 and $5 p/h = $44.95." 1 title listed in the *Small Press Record of Books in Print* (28th Edition, 1999-00). avg. price, paper: $3.00 plus postage ($4.00). Discounts: 10%. 8½×11. Payment: when other writers will join me, I will offer a per page fee.

Accent on Music, Mark Hanson, Greta Pedersen, 19363 Willamette Drive #252, West Linn, OR 97068, 503-699-1814; FAX 503-699-1813; e-mail accentm@teleport.com. 1985. Music. avg. press run 5M. Pub'd 3 titles 1998; expects 3 titles 1999, 3 titles 2000. 10 titles listed in the *Small Press Record of Books in Print* (28th Edition, 1999-00). avg. price, other: $19.95 with instruction cassette. Discounts: 50% distr. 40% retail, 20% college bookstores (texts). 96pp; 9×12; of. Reporting time: 4-6 weeks. Payment: royalties paid semi-annually; contract negotiable. Copyrights for author.

Access Multimedia (see also MULTIMEDIA REVIEWS FOR EDUCATION, MULTIMEDIA REVIEWS FOR INDUSTRY), Carol J. Anderson, PO Box 5182, Bellingham, WA 98227, 360-733-2155. 1985. Fiction, non-fiction. "Access Multimedia is dedicated to provide educational materials for able students. (i.e., gifted, advanced, excellerated). Interested in multimedia science materials" avg. press run 5M-10M. Pub'd 1 title 1998; expects 5 titles 1999, 5-10 titles 2000. avg. price, cloth: $27.95; paper: $19.95. Pages vary; 8½×11. Reporting time: 2 months. Payment: 10%. Copyrights for author if requested. PMA.

Acclaim Publishing Co. Inc., David L. Brothers, PO Box 3918, Grand Junction, CO 81502-3918, 719-784-3712. 1992. Poetry, fiction, articles, photos, interviews, satire, criticism, letters, plays, news items, non-fiction. "Look for *After the Crash* to be released in August." avg. press run 50M. Pub'd 3 titles 1998; expects 4 titles 1999, 7 titles 2000. 8 titles listed in the *Small Press Record of Books in Print* (28th Edition, 1999-00). avg. price, cloth: $29.95; paper: $12.95. Discounts: 50% orders of 300 or more (most instances), 50% direct to bookstores. 375pp; 5½×8½, 8½×11; webb press. Reporting time: 4 months. Simultaneous submissions accepted: yes. Publishes 10% of manuscripts submitted. Payment: 10%. Copyrights for author. Quality Paperback Book Club, Fortune Book Club, ABA, International Assn. of Independent Publishers.

●**Achievement Publications,** 1920-125 Centerville Tnpk, PMB 140, Virginia Beach, VA 23464-6800, 757-474-7955; fax 757-474-9154; achievepubs@mindspring.com. 1 title listed in the *Small Press Record of Books in Print* (28th Edition, 1999-00).

ACM (ANOTHER CHICAGO MAGAZINE), Barry Silesky, 3709 N. Kenmore, Chicago, IL 60613, 312-248-7665. 1976. Poetry, fiction, articles, art, photos, cartoons, interviews, satire, criticism, reviews, long-poems. "Recent contributors have included Albert Goldbarth, Diane Wakoski, Wanda Coleman, Alan Cheuse, Bonita Friedman, Perry Glasser, Sterling Plumpp." circ. 2.5M. 1/yr. Pub'd 2 issues 1998; expects 2 issues 1999, 2 issues 2000. sub. price: $15; per copy: $8; sample: $8. Back issues: $7. Discounts: 10% on 10 or more. 220pp; 8½×5½; of. Reporting time: 10 weeks. Simultaneous submissions accepted: yes. Publishes 2% of manuscripts submitted. Payment: minimum of $5 + copy + 1 year subscription. Copyrighted, reverts to author. Pub's reviews: 20 in 1998. §Small press poetry, fiction, literary reviews or criticism. Ads: $250/$125. CLMP.

ACME Press, PO Box 1702, Westminster, MD 21158, 410-848-7577. 1991. Fiction, satire. "Our basic requirement is that a work be funny. We prefer comic novels (60K-90K words)" avg. press run 10M. Pub'd 1 title 1998; expects 1 title 1999, 1 title 2000. 4 titles listed in the *Small Press Record of Books in Print* (28th Edition, 1999-00). avg. price, cloth: $16; paper: $10. Discounts: standard. 250pp; 5½×8½. Reporting time: 4 weeks. Simultaneous submissions accepted: yes. Payment: varies. Copyrights for author. PMA.

THE ACORN, Hot Pepper Press, J.K. Colvin, Judith T. Graham, Harlan Stafford, Joy Burris, PO Box 1266, El Dorado, CA 95623, 916-621-1833. 1993. Poetry, fiction, articles, satire, non-fiction. "We seek to publish quality fiction, non-fiction, essays, and poetry. No porn, erotica, or articles of prejudice. Our focus is on the western slope of the Sierra Nevada. Length: 4000 words maximum for prose; poems to 30 lines (shorter poems have a better chance)." circ. 250. 4/yr. Pub'd 5 issues 1998; expects 5 issues 1999, 5 issues 2000. sub. price: $12; per copy: $4; sample: $4. Discounts: 5-9 20%, 10+ 40%. 48pp; 5¼×8½; Desktop publishing - Commercial of. Reporting time: 3 months (1 month after deadlines of 2/1, 5/1, 8/11, 11/1). We accept simultaneous submissions if so informed. Publishes 35% of manuscripts submitted. Payment: 2 free copies. Copyrighted, reverts to author. Ads: none. El Dorado Writers' Guild.

●**Acorn Books,** Jami Parkison, 7337 Terrace, Suite 200, Kansas City, MO 64114-1256, 816-523-8321; fax 816-333-3843; e-mail jami.parkison@micro.com. 1997. Non-fiction. "Biographies for children about well-known midwesterners. Submissions through agents only." avg. press run 1M. Pub'd 2 titles 1998; expects 3 titles 1999, 3 titles 2000. 3 titles listed in the *Small Press Record of Books in Print* (28th Edition, 1999-00). avg. price, paper: $8.95/$10.95. Discounts: 15/25%. 125pp; 5¼×7¾; of.

Acorn Publishing, Richard Mansfield, 4431 Lehigh Road #288, College Park, MD 20740-3127. 1985. Non-fiction. "Distributed by Alan Hood, Inc. PO Box 775, Chambersburg, PA 17201, 717-267-0867" avg. press run 3M. Pub'd 1 title 1998; expects 2 titles 1999, 2 titles 2000. 7 titles listed in the *Small Press Record of Books in Print* (28th Edition, 1999-00). avg. price, paper: $15. Discounts: 1 (prepaid) 20%, 2-4 books 30%, 5-24 40%, 25-99 45%, 100+ 50%. 176pp; 6×9; of. Reporting time: 4 weeks. Publishes 5% of manuscripts submitted. Payment: on case by case basis. Does not copyright for author.

ACORN WHISTLE, Fred Burwell, 907 Brewster Avenue, Beloit, WI 53511. 1994. Poetry, fiction, articles, art, photos, long-poems, interviews, non-fiction. "We publish high quality, accessible work that appeals to readers on both emotional and intellectual levels. *Acorn Whistle* is open to writers and artists of all backgrounds and experiences. Apart from traditional literary fare, we also seek autobiography/reminiscences, slice of life sketches, oral histories, vivid travel and nature writing." circ. 500. 1-2/yr. Pub'd 1 issue 1998; expects 1 issue 1999, 2 issues 2000. sub. price: $14 for 2 issues; per copy: $7; sample: $7. 75-100pp; 8½×11; of. Reporting time: 1 week to 3 months. Simultaneous submissions accepted: yes. Publishes 1-2% of manuscripts submitted. Payment: 2 copies. Copyrighted, reverts to author.

Acre Press (see also FELL SWOOP), Joel Dailey, 3003 Ponce De Leon Street, New Orleans, LA 70119. 1980. Poetry. "Have seen the light of day: *New Sky* by Gordon Anderson; *Red Hats* by Mark Chadwick; *Arthur Zen Comes To America* by Robb Jackson; *Between The Eyes* by Richard Martin; *Angry Red Blues* translations from the Martian poet, S. Zivvit 57; *Minigolf* by Anselm Hollo; *The Nolan Anthology of Poetry* by Pat Nolan. You are welcome to submit after you purchase a title; three bucks American. New title in 94: *You're Out of My Mind (But So Am I)* by Dan Nielsen" avg. press run 200. Pub'd 1 title 1998; expects 2 titles 1999, 3 titles 2000. 9 titles listed in the *Small Press Record of Books in Print* (28th Edition, 1999-00). avg. price, paper: $3 all titles. Discounts: 50%. 20pp; 5½×8½; of. Reporting time: fast. Payment: copies, % of run. Does not copyright for author.

Acrobat Books, Tony Cohan, PO Box 870, Venice, CA 90294, 310-578-1055, Fax 310-823-8447. 1975. Fiction, art, photos, non-fiction. "Non fiction books in the creative arts. *Kirsch's Handbook of Publishing Law* by Jonathan Kirsch; *Directing the Film* by Eric Sherman; *Nine Ships, A Book of Tales* by Tony Cohan; *Outlaw Visions* ed. by Tony Cohan/Gordon Beam; *Frame By Frame* by Eric Sherman." avg. press run 4M. Pub'd 3 titles 1998; expects 4 titles 1999, 5 titles 2000. 8 titles listed in the *Small Press Record of Books in Print* (28th Edition, 1999-00). avg. price, cloth: $19.95; paper: $16.95. Discounts: 1-5 copies 20%, 6-49 40%. 196pp; 5¼×8¼; of. Reporting time: 60 days. Payment: negotiable. Copyrights for author.

ACS Publications (see also ASTROFLASH), Maritha Pottenger, Editorial Director, PO Box 34487, San Diego, CA 92163, 619-492-9919. 1982. Articles, interviews, reviews. "Please submit OUTLINE only. An imprint of Astro Communications Services, Inc." avg. press run 3M. Pub'd 4 titles 1998; expects 4 titles 1999, 4 titles 2000. 47 titles listed in the *Small Press Record of Books in Print* (28th Edition, 1999-00). avg. price, paper: $15.95. Discounts: trade. 300pp; 5⅜×8⅜, 8½×11, 6×9; of/lo. Reporting time: 1-3 months. Simultaneous submissions accepted: yes. Publishes 5% of manuscripts submitted. Payment: usual. Copyrights for author.

5

Acting World Books (see also THE HOLLYWOOD ACTING COACHES AND TEACHERS DIRECTORY; THE AGENCIES-WHAT THE ACTOR NEEDS TO KNOW), Lawrence Parke, PO Box 3044, Hollywood, CA 90078, 818-905-1345/Fax 800-210-1197. 1981. "Publications and career guidance for the acting community. Publishes books and periodicals of career and acting methodology natures. Typical is the six-volume 'seminars to go' series on six different 'how to' topics involved in the actor's career building processes. In-house publishing and waiting." avg. press run 2M. Expects 1 title 1999, 2 titles 2000. 4 titles listed in the *Small Press Record of Books in Print* (28th Edition, 1999-00). avg. price, paper: $10-$15. Discounts: trade, 40% booksellers. 40pp; 8½×11; †photocopy. Payment: none. Copyrights for author.

Actium Publishing, Inc., Dan Brown, 1375 Coney Island Ave., Ste. 122, Brooklyn, NY 11230, 718-382-2129; fax 718-621-0402; email home@actium1.com. 1996. avg. press run 5M. Pub'd 3 titles 1998. 2 titles listed in the *Small Press Record of Books in Print* (28th Edition, 1999-00). Discounts: 55% wholesalers, 20% stop orders. 250pp. Reporting time: 4-12 weeks. Simultaneous submissions accepted: yes. Publishes 1% of manuscripts submitted.

Acton Circle Publishing Company, Thomas E. Anderson, PO Box 1564, Ukiah, CA 95482, 707-463-3921, 707-462-2103, Fax 707-462-4942; actoncircle@pacific.net. 1992. Non-fiction. "The company was started to publish guides fortarting and running popular small business enterprises. Although it will publish in other subject areas, that is the main thrust of its activity." avg. press run 3-5M. Pub'd 1 title 1998; expects 2 titles 1999, 2+ titles 2000. 4 titles listed in the *Small Press Record of Books in Print* (28th Edition, 1999-00). avg. price, paper: $18. Discounts: dealers 1-2 net, 3-9 30%, 10-49 40%, 50-299 50%. 200pp; 7×10; lp. Reporting time: 2 months. Simultaneous submissions accepted: yes. Payment: 10%. Copyrights for author.

Adams-Blake Publishing, Paul Raymond, 8041 Sierra Street, Fair Oaks, CA 95628, 916-962-9296. 1992. Non-fiction. "As a small publisher, we do not market 'me-too' books. We look for titles that either the big houses won't do, or are too stupid not to do! We like titles that help people either start their own business or help run an existing business. One area we are very interested in is finding information or data that can be packaged and sold to a select industry for a high price. Our goal is to publish books that will sell respectfully year after year. We don't look for a blockbuster. We spend a lot of time and effort choosing what we will publish and we put a lot of resources into marketing our books. We like to market direct to the customer but we also publish to the bookstore trade." avg. press run 5M. Expects 7 titles 1999, 10 titles 2000. 4 titles listed in the *Small Press Record of Books in Print* (28th Edition, 1999-00). avg. price, paper: $25. Discounts: 40-50% industry standard. 300pp; 6×9; of. Reporting time: 3-4 weeks. Simultaneous submissions accepted: yes. Publishes 5% of manuscripts submitted. Payment: 10% net. Copyrights for author. PMA.

Adams-Hall Publishing, Sue Ann Bacon, Marketing Director, PO Box 491002, Los Angeles, CA 90049, 310-826-1851; 800-888-4452. "Only interested in business or finance titles." Pub'd 3 titles 1998; expects 1 title 1999, 1 title 2000. 5 titles listed in the *Small Press Record of Books in Print* (28th Edition, 1999-00). Reporting time: 1 month. Simultaneous submissions accepted: yes. PMA.

ADAPTED PHYSICAL ACTIVITY QUARTERLY (APAQ), Human Kinetics Pub. Inc., Claudine Sherrill, Ph.D., Box 5076, Champaign, IL 61825-5076, 217-351-5076. 1984. Articles, reviews. "Study of physical activity for special populations of all ages" circ. 1M. 4/yr. Pub'd 4 issues 1998; expects 4 issues 1999, 4 issues 2000. sub. price: $42 individual, $100 institution, $26 student; per copy: $12 indiv., $26 instit.; sample: free. Back issues: $12 indiv., $26 instit. Discounts: 5% agency. 106pp; 6×9; of. Reporting time: 2 months. Payment: none. Copyrighted, does not revert to author. Pub's reviews: 4 in 1998. §Sport, sport science, and physical education related to disabilities and rehabilation. Ads: $300/$200. Midwest Publishers Association, American Booksellers Association.

Adaptive Living, Angela Van Etten, 4922 SE Pompano Terrace, Stuart, FL 34997, 561-781-6153; Fax 561-781-9179. 1988. avg. press run 4M. 1 title listed in the *Small Press Record of Books in Print* (28th Edition, 1999-00). avg. price, paper: $15.95. Discounts: 2-20%; 5-30%; 10-40%; 25-42%; 50-44%; 100-48%. 200pp; 8 inches; desk-top, laser print, camera-ready. Payment: negotiable. Copyrights for author.

Adastra Press, Gary Metras, 16 Reservation Road, Easthampton, MA 01027-1227. 1978. Poetry. "All books are hand-set letterpress printed and hand-sewn with flat spine paper wrapper. Each book is individually designed with the poetry in mind. I pay attention to the craft and art of printing and expect poets to pay attention to their art. Interested authors should query first. The poetry should have some bite to it and be grounded in experience. Poem cycles, thematic groups and long poems are always nice to produce in chapbook format. Reading period for manuscripts is during the month of February only. Send queries with samples in the fall; if I like the sample, I'll ask you to send the manuscript in February. Manuscripts should have 12 to 18 pages; nothing longer; no full-length manuscripts will be considered. Accepted authors can expect to help with publicity. Payment is copies. *Adastra Press* is a one man operation, paying for itself as it goes without grants of any kind, and I am always overworked and booked in advance. Chances of acceptance are slim, but there's no harm in trying. Some titles to date are: *Pocuahontas Discovers America*, Miriam Sagan; *The Distance We*

Travel, W. D. Ehrhart; *Niagara Falls*, Jim Daniels. Send $6 for a sample chapbook.'' avg. press run 200. Pub'd 4 titles 1998; expects 4 titles 1999, 3 titles 2000. 24 titles listed in the *Small Press Record of Books in Print* (28th Edition, 1999-00). avg. price, cloth: $25; paper: $7-$10; other: $10-$30, signed and numbered. Discounts: bookstores 30%, distributors 40%, more than 1 copy, 20% on cl/signed editions. 18pp; 5×8; †1p. Reporting time: up to 3 months. Simultaneous submissions accepted: yes. Publishes less than 1% of manuscripts submitted. Payment: usually percent of print run, but each arrangement made individually. Does not copyright for author.

Addicus Books, Inc., Rod Colvin, PO Box 45327, Omaha, NE 68145, 402-330-7493. 1994. ''We publish high-quality non-fiction books with a focus on health, self-help, business, and true crime.'' avg. press run 3M-5M. Pub'd 6 titles 1998; expects 6 titles 1999, 10 titles 2000. 19 titles listed in the *Small Press Record of Books in Print* (28th Edition, 1999-00). avg. price, paper: $14.95. Discounts: Retailers 40%, wholesalers, distributors 55%. STOP 40%, plus shipping. 275pp; 5½×8½. Reporting time: 1 month. Simultaneous submissions accepted: yes. Publishes 2-3% of manuscripts submitted. Payment: royalty contract based on list price. Copyrights for author. NAIP, PMA.

ADIRONDAC, Adirondack Mountain Club, Inc., Neal S. Burdick, Editor, 814 Goggins Road, Lake George, NY 12845-4117, 518-668-4447; e-mail ADKinfo@adk.org. 1922. Poetry, articles, art, photos, interviews, reviews, letters, news items, non-fiction. ''Avg. length: 1000-3000 words, with conservation, education, and recreation focus, representing different stances on issues of concern to the Adirondack and Catskill constitutionally-protected Forest Preserves. Contributors include ADK members, state authorities, Forest Preserve historians, outdoor recreationists, etc.'' circ. 14M. 6/yr. Pub'd 7 issues 1998; expects 6 issues 1999, 6 issues 2000. sub. price: $20; per copy: $2.95; sample: $2.95. Back issues: $4.95. Discounts: retailers 40% (min. 10 copies); libraries $15/yr. 52pp; 8½×11; of. Reporting time: 3 months. Payment: none. Copyrighted, does not revert to author. Pub's reviews: approx. 36 in 1998. §Natural history, conservation, ''muscle-powered'' recreation, Adirondack or Catskill history and lore. Ads: 1x: $540, 3x: $480/1x: $285, 3x: $250/request rate sheet for other sizes.

Adirondack Mountain Club, Inc. (see also ADIRONDAC), Andrea Masters, Publications Director; Neal Burdick, Editor of Adirondac, 814 Goggins Road, Lake George, NY 12845-4117, 518-668-4447; FAX 518-668-3746; e-mail pubs@adk.org. 1922. Articles, non-fiction. ''We publish guidebooks—hiking, canoeing, climbing, skiing, and biking guides—as well as natural and cultural histories about the Forest Preserve of New York State (which comprises the Adirondack and Catskill parks). We also publish a history of the Adirondack Park for young people (ages 10+), trail maps, and an annual calendar of Adirondack nature photography.'' avg. press run 2.5M. Pub'd 2 titles 1998; expects 3 titles 1999, 3 titles 2000. 26 titles listed in the *Small Press Record of Books in Print* (28th Edition, 1999-00). avg. price, cloth: $23; paper: trade $15; other: $6 maps, $10 calendar. Discounts: retail 1-5 20%, 6-99 40%, 100+ 42%, STOP 40%; schools & libraries 25%; wholesalers, 10-49 40%, 50-99 46%, 100+ 50%, and free freight. 200pp; 4⅞×6⅜ (guidebooks only); of. Reporting time: 3 weeks to 3 months (decided by Committee). We accept simultaneous submissions (must be disclosed). Publishes 1% of manuscripts submitted. Payment: typical is 7½% royalty on gross. Copyrights for author. NEBA.

Ad-Lib Publications, Marie Kiefer, 51-1/2 West Adams, Fairfield, IA 52556, 515-472-6617. 1982. Non-fiction. ''Length of material: 96-360 pages. We are primarily into illusions, fairytales, fables, and anything to do with words and writing and publishing'' avg. press run 3M. Pub'd 5 titles 1998; expects 4 titles 1999, 4-6 titles 2000. avg. price, cloth: $19.95; paper: $14.95. Discounts: 2-4 books 20%, 5-24 40%, 25-49 43%, 50-99 45%, over 100 50%. 200pp; 8½×11; of. Reporting time: 2 weeks. Payment: 8%, no advance. Copyrights for author. PMA, American Booksellers Association, Mid-America Publisher Group, Upper Midwest Booksellers Association, Minnesota Independent Publishers Association.

Admiral House Publishing, John Gilhart, PO Box 8176, Naples, FL 34101, email AdmHouse@aol.com. 1997. Fiction. ''Currently publishing *Walking K* by Wes DeMott. Absolutely no unsolicited manuscripts.'' avg. press run 15M. Pub'd 1 title 1998; expects 3 titles 1999, 5 titles 2000. 4 titles listed in the *Small Press Record of Books in Print* (28th Edition, 1999-00). avg. price, cloth: $23.95. Discounts: from 20% (short discount) to 55% (distributor). 300pp; 6⅛×9¼. Reporting time: 2 months. Simultaneous submissions accepted: no. Publishes 1% of manuscripts submitted. Payment: 10-15%. Copyrights for author. PMA.

ADOLESCENCE, Libra Publishers, Inc., 3089C Clairemont Dr., Suite 383, San Diego, CA 92117, 619-571-1414. 1960. Articles. circ. 3M. 4/yr. Pub'd 4 issues 1998; expects 4 issues 1999, 4 issues 2000. sub. price: $115; per copy: $25; sample: free. Back issues: $25. Discounts: 10% to subscriber agents. 256pp; 6×9; of. Reporting time: 6 weeks. Payment: none. Copyrighted, does not revert to author. Pub's reviews: 60 in 1998. §Behavioral sciences. Ads: $300/$175.

Adolfo Street Publications, Gene A. Valdes, PO Box 490, Santa Fe, NM 87504, 505-986-2010, Fax 505-986-1353, toll free order line 800-526-2010; email adolfostr@aol.com. 1992. Non-fiction. ''Additional address: 2104 Calle Tecolote, Santa Fe, NM 87505 (returns only). We specialize in straightforward, easy-to-use books on community relations and interaction among people - especially those people who are trying to make this a better world." avg. press run 3M-5M. Pub'd 2 titles 1998; expects 1 title 1999, 1 title 2000. 6 titles listed in the *Small Press Record of Books in Print* (28th Edition, 1999-00). avg. price, paper: $14.50. Discounts: trade 1-4 20%, 1-4 STOP 30%, 5-24 40%, 25-49 42%, 50-99 44%, 100+ 50%; wholesaler 50%; write for classroom and special schedule for nonprofits. 150pp; 5½×8½; of. Reporting time: 30-60 days. Simultaneous submissions accepted: yes. Publishes 4% of manuscripts submitted. Payment: 10% of cover price for each book sold; advance equal to projected 1st year royalties. Copyrights for author. PMA.

AD/VANCE, Vance Philip Hedderel, Editor-in-Chief, 1581 Colonial Terrace, Suite 101, Arlington, VA 22209-1428. 1992. Articles, interviews, music, letters, news items. circ. 250. 3/yr. Pub'd 3 issues 1998; expects 3 issues 1999, 3 issues 2000. sub. price: $5; per copy: $2; sample: $1. Back issues: negotiable, however back issues are not generally available. Discounts: none. 8pp; 5½×8½. Reporting time: usually within 3 weeks. Simultaneous submissions accepted: no. Publishes less than 30% of manuscripts submitted. Payment: 2 sample issues. Not copyrighted. Pub's reviews: 4 in 1998. §Art, Brontes, Dada, surrealism, film, gays, poetry, music, lesbianism, London, Post Modernism, tapes and records. Ads: none.

ADVANCES IN THE ASTRONAUTICAL SCIENCES, Univelt, Inc., R.H. Jacobs, Series Editor, PO Box 28130, San Diego, CA 92198, 760-746-4005; Fax 760-746-3139; 76121.1532@compuserve.com; www.univelt.staigerland.com. 1957. "Space and related fields. An irregular serial. Publishers for the American Atronautical Society. Vols. 1-100 published. Standing orders accepted." circ. 400. Irregular. Pub'd 2 issues 1998; expects 4 issues 1999, 5 issues 2000. sub. price: varies. Back issues: no. Discounts: normally 20% but more by arrangement; discounts for classroom use. 400-700pp; 7×9½; of. Reporting time: 60 days. Payment: none. Copyrighted, authors may republish material with appropriate credits given and authorization from publishers. Ads: none.

ADVENTURE CYCLIST, Daniel D'Ambrosio, PO Box 8308, Missoula, MT 59807, 406-721-1776. 1974. Fiction, articles, cartoons, interviews, news items, non-fiction. circ. 30M. 9/yr. Pub'd 9 issues 1998; expects 9 issues 1999, 9 issues 2000. sub. price: $25; sample: 9x12 SASE w/$1 postage. 32pp; 8⅜×10⅞; of. Reporting time: 1 month. Payment: negotiable. Copyrighted, reverts to author. Ads: $1420/$925/$75 for 30 words.

Advisory Press, Inc., Charles H. Green, 5600 Roswell Road, Suite 210N, Atlanta, GA 30342, 404-250-1991; FAX 404-705-8249. 1996. Articles, non-fiction. avg. press run varies. Expects 1 title 1999, 2 titles 2000. 1 title listed in the *Small Press Record of Books in Print* (28th Edition, 1999-00). avg. price, paper: $19.95. Discounts: trade 40%+. 200pp; 8×11; lp. Reporting time: 90 days. Simultaneous submissions accepted: no.

The Advocado Press (see also THE DISABILITY RAG & RESOURCE), Eric Francis, PO Box 145, Louisville, KY 40201, 502-459-5343. 1981. Non-fiction. "We publish chiefly books but also some shorter monographs and educational materials on disability related civil rights issues. Our books are generally very practical and action oriented. *Making News* is chiefly directed toward disability groups to use in training themselves how to work with the media to get appropriate coverage of disability issues; another book tells how small businesses can economically adapt to ADA accommodation requirements. Our newest title, *The Ragged Edge*, is an anthology from the first 15 year of *The Disability Rag"* avg. press run 3M. Pub'd 2 titles 1998; expects 1 title 1999, 1 title 2000. 4 titles listed in the *Small Press Record of Books in Print* (28th Edition, 1999-00). avg. price, paper: $13.95. Discounts: contact office for schedule. 170pp; 5¼×8¼; of. Reporting time: 1-2 months. Payment: royalty negotiable. Copyrights for author.

THE ADVOCATE, Mavis Belisle, HCR 2, Box 25, Panhandle, TX 79068, 806-335-1715. 1986. Poetry, articles, photos, cartoons, reviews, letters. circ. 1M. 4/yr. sub. price: $5; per copy: $1; sample: $1. Back issues: pay postage. 4pp; 8½×11; of. Payment: none. Not copyrighted. Pub's reviews: 1 in 1998. §Peace and justice, social change, disarmament, ecology. Ads: $75/$50/$10 business card.

Aegean Publishing Company, PO Box 6790, Santa Barbara, CA 93160, 805-964-6669. 1993. Non-fiction. "Technology-oriented popular books. Current title in press: *Set Phasers on Stun and Other True Tales of Design, Technology, and Human Error* (second edition)." avg. press run 5M. Expects 1 title 1999, 1 title 2000. 1 title listed in the *Small Press Record of Books in Print* (28th Edition, 1999-00). avg. price, cloth: $29. Discounts: schedules available on request. 256pp; 6×9; of. Reporting time: contact publisher. Payment: contact publisher. Copyrights for author. PMA.

Aegina Press, Inc., Ira Herman, Managing Editor, 1905 Madison Avenue, Huntington, WV 25704, 304-429-7204; fax 304-429-7234. 1984. Poetry, fiction, non-fiction. "Publishes fiction, strongly encourages new authors. Also publishes poetry and nonfiction originals and reprints, in perfect-bound paperbacks and hardcovers. Manuscripts should be book-length (45-400 page typescript). Will consider all types of fiction, nonfiction and poetry, as long as quality is high. No racist, sexist, or hate materials. Primarily interested in novels, short story collections, and volumes of poetry. Enclose SASE for return of material. Reports in about one month. Simultaneous and photocopied submissions are acceptable. A 1-2 page synopsis is helpful.

Presently reading in all categories for upcoming list. Often publishes material by new writers. Recent authors include Richard Ashton, Richard Nelson, and Shirley Campbell. During next year, at least, we will be doing primarly subsidized publication. On susidized books, author receives all sales proceeds until breakeven point. Then, a 40% royalty begins. Attempts to help and establish new authors'' avg. press run 500-1M. Pub'd 30 titles 1998; expects 35 titles 1999, 45 titles 2000. 5 titles listed in the *Small Press Record of Books in Print* (28th Edition, 1999-00). avg. price, cloth: $16.95; paper: $6. Discounts: 40% to libraries, bookstores and jobbers on orders of 5 or more copies. Free examination copies to potential adopters and distributors. 64-300pp; 5½x8½; of. Reporting time: 1 month. Payment: depends on author and subject matter; up to 15% royalty on nonsubsidized books. Copyrights for author.

Aegis Publishing Group, Ltd., Robert Mastin, 796 Aquidnect Avenue, Newport, RI 02842, 401-849-4200; FAX 401-849-4231. 1987. Non-fiction. ''*Strictly* telecommunications books written for non-technical end-users such as telecommuters, entrepreneurs, and the Soho market.'' avg. press run 5M. Pub'd 6 titles 1998; expects 4 titles 1999, 5 titles 2000. 13 titles listed in the *Small Press Record of Books in Print* (28th Edition, 1999-00). avg. price, paper: $19.95. Discounts: per distributor - NBN. 336pp; 5½x8½; of. Reporting time: 2 months. Simultaneous submissions accepted: yes. Payment: 12% net proceeds. Copyrights for author. PMA.

Aeolus Press, Inc. (see also KITE LINES), Valerie Govig, Publisher & Editor, PO Box 466, Randallstown, MD 21133-0466, 410-922-1212; fax 410-922-4262. 1977. Articles, art, photos, interviews, reviews, letters, news items. ''All material is about *Kites*'' avg. press run 13M. Expects 4 titles 1999. 3 titles listed in the *Small Press Record of Books in Print* (28th Edition, 1999-00). avg. price, paper: $4.50. Discounts: $2.55 each + shipping to kite and bookstores (10 minimum). 72pp; 8⅜x10⅞; of. Reporting time: 2 weeks to 3 months. May consider simultaneous submissions but must be informed as such. Publishes about 15% of manuscripts submitted. Payment: varies + copies. Does not copyright for author. PMA.

AERIAL, Rod Smith, P.O. Box 25642, Washington, DC 20007, 202-362-6418; aerialedge@aol.com. 1984. Poetry, fiction, articles, art, photos, cartoons, interviews, satire, criticism, reviews, music, letters, parts-of-novels, long-poems, collages, plays, concrete art, news items, non-fiction. ''*Aerial* #9, just published, is a special issue on the work of Bruce Andrews.'' circ. 1M. Irregular. sub. price: $25/2 issues; per copy: varies; sample: $15.00. Back issues: #6/7 is $15, #5 is $7.50. Discounts: 40% to retailers. 200pp; 6x9; of. Reporting time: 1 week-6 months. Payment: contributors copies. Copyrighted, reverts to author. Pub's reviews. §Lit. mags, poetry, fiction, criticism, art. Ads: $100/$60/will consider exchanges. CLMP.

AERO-GRAMME, Jerry Mintz, 417 Roslyn Road, Roslyn Heights, NY 11577, 516-621-2195. 1989. Letters, non-fiction. ''This is a networking magazine for alternative educators (including homeschoolers).'' circ. 5M. 3-4/yr. Pub'd 3 issues 1998; expects 3 issues 1999, 4 issues 2000. sub. price: $15; per copy: $5. Back issues: $5. 27pp; 8½x11; †of. Payment: none. Pub's reviews: 6-8 in 1998. §Only alternative education. Ads: subscription. EWA.

Afcom Publishing, Greg Cook, PO Box H, Harbor City, CA 90710-0330, 213-326-7589. 1988. Collages, non-fiction. avg. press run 5M-10M. Pub'd 2 titles 1998. 7 titles listed in the *Small Press Record of Books in Print* (28th Edition, 1999-00). avg. price, cloth: $20; paper: $10. Discounts: 50% wholesalers/distributors; 40% bookstores; 40% libraries. 200pp; 5½x8½. Reporting time: 90 days. Publishes 5% of manuscripts submitted. Payment: 7-15% royalty. Copyrights for author. PMA.

AFFABLE NEIGHBOR, Affable Neighbor Press, Joel Henry-Fisher, Editor in Chief; Leigh Chalmers, Poetry Editor; Marshall Stanley, Assistant Editor, PO Box 3635, Ann Arbor, MI 48106. 1994. Poetry, fiction, articles, art, photos, cartoons, interviews, satire, criticism, reviews, music, letters, parts-of-novels, collages, concrete art, news items, non-fiction. ''*Affable Neighbor* has no set format, so it is hard to generalize. Most issues are unsuitable for children, nudity, graphic language, etc. But also has contained puzzles, 'serious' literature, etc., 'arts of all kinds.' Recently published a ''Weak Stomach''issue that was, suitable for children.'' circ. 25-1M. Irregular. Pub'd 6 issues 1998. sub. price: $20(includes prizes and extras); per copy: $2 (or less). Back issues: #1-3 $2, #4 $1, #5-7 $2, #6 $1.50. Discounts: selective trades, otherwise individually bargained. 50pp; 8½x11; †xerox/hand printing/photography. Reporting time: as soon as we get around to it. Simultaneous submissions accepted: yes. Payment: free copies. Not copyrighted. Pub's reviews. §Unique, outspoken, offensive, stretching the definitions of magazines and censorship ''art '' too. Ads: $1,000/$500/all negotiable.

Affable Neighbor Press (see also AFFABLE NEIGHBOR), Joel Henry-Fisher, Editor in Chief; Leigh Chalmers, poetry editor; Marshall Stanley, Assistant editor, PO Box 3635, Ann Arbor, MI 48106. 1994. Poetry, fiction, articles, art, photos, cartoons, interviews, satire, criticism, reviews, music, letters, parts-of-novels, long-poems, collages, plays, concrete art, news items, non-fiction. ''Normally geared only for small print runs, although open to anything.'' avg. press run 100. Pub'd 1 title 1998. avg. price, other: varies. Pages vary; size varies; †xerox/hand printing/photography. Reporting time: as soon as we get around to it. Simultaneous submissions accepted: yes. Payment: per individual. Does not copyright for author.

AFFAIR OF THE MIND: A Literary Quarterly, Tracy Lyn Rottkamp, Editor, 8 Mare Lane, Commack, NY 11725, 516-864-5135. 1997. Poetry, fiction, articles, art, photos, interviews, satire, criticism, reviews, letters, parts-of-novels, long-poems, plays, concrete art, non-fiction. "We are a literary quarterly, highly interested in over 70 diverse subjects, ranging from humor, historical-based work, religion, medical-based work and thesis, interviews with prominent poets and writers, classical studies, translations, genocide, memoirs, satire, erotica, personal narrative poems, politics, plays, vignettes, short stories/essays re: history, Holocaust, the era of French writers and French Impressionism, the Russian Revolution, etc. Poetry has no specific line limit, stories, essays not to exceed 40 pages. We publish both established and unpublished writers. SASE is a must and cover letters are very much appreciated. We have recently published work by B.Z. Niditch, Ruth Wildes Schuler, Michael Estabrook, Simon Perchik, David M. Wright, David Castleman, John Cox, Dick Reynolds, Robert Robinson, Ward Kelly, Hugh Fox, Michele Mitchell Weal, Robert Cooperman, Paul Haugh, Richard Alan Bunch, etc. Please refer to Subject Index Codes of the Directory or SASE for our 8 page Subject Themes lists and other information. (Please affix 2-33¢ stamps to SASE.) Each issue is accompanied by a 40p. 'Advertising & Book Review Supplement,' which is sent to over 20 countries world-wide. All accepted writers are entitled to 1 (one) year of free advertising, reviews of their books, and publicity." circ. 1.8M. 30/yr plus several limited editions. Pub'd 20 issues 1998; expects 25 issues 1999, 30 issues 2000. sub. price: $28; $24 gift subscriptions (please make checks, etc. payable to Tracy Lyn Rottkamp); per copy: $9; sample: $9. Back issues: $10 (limited editions). 125-150+pp, Limited Editions 400+pp; size varies; †desktop/computer. Reporting time: 1 day to 2 weeks max. No simultaneous/previously published work accepted. We publish less than 1% out of every 8,000+ submissions we receive. Payment: varies, contributors always receive 1-5 copies. Copyrighted, reverts to author. Pub's reviews: 30 in 1998. §Any of the subjects listed, please send books for review consideration. Ads: $20/$9.50/others query with SASE.

THE AFFILIATE, Reveal, Peter Riden, Publisher, Conceptor, Editor, 777 Barb Road, #257, Vankleek Hill, Ontario K0B 1R0, Canada, 613-678-3453. 1987. Poetry, articles, art, photos, cartoons, interviews, reviews, music, letters, news items, non-fiction. "To be an Affiliate means the scope is universal. The desire is to be a participant to a global dialogue with others of the same scope. The attitude is one of reciprocity and understanding. Traveling distances by way of correspondence or hosting one another. A requisite for excellence in conduct and expression. An aim at cleaning up our act for our planet Earth. The recognition of one's talent(s) in their achievements, be it music, art and all other laudable efforts. An obvious open mind through the desire to pride rather than shame our body. A communal strength in our international friendship. If this is part of what you feel deep inside—join in! Subscribe! Become an *Affiliate*." circ. as requested, can be as much as 10M. 12/yr. Pub'd 12 issues 1998; expects 12 issues 1999, 12 issues 2000. sub. price: $75 US/North America, $100 anywhere else; per copy: $10; sample: $10. Back issues: as collectors items they may turn to be more costly. Discounts: complimentary to contributors and traders. 40pp; 8½x11; †photocopy, color and b/w. Reporting time: must be received prior to the 15th preceding the current issue. Payment: complimentary issue and undeniably an opportunity to become better known. Copyrighted, rights revert to author by mutual agreement if to be reprinted. Pub's reviews: few in 1998. §We definitely have an extended section for the most pioneering and cohesive publications. Ads: Contact for ad rates.

Affinity Publishers Services, A. Doyle, Founder, c/o Continuous, PO Box 416, Denver, CO 80201-0416, 303-575-5676. 1981. avg. press run 55. Expects 2 titles 2000. avg. price, cloth: $18.95; paper: $18.95. Discounts: standard. 70pp; 8½x11.

African American Audio Press (see also AFRICAN AMERICAN AUDIOBOOK REVIEW), Corinne Butler, 138 Palm Coast Parkway NE #217, Palm Coast, FL 32137-8241. 1995. avg. press run 2.5M. Pub'd 1 title 1998; expects 4 titles 1999, 6 titles 2000. avg. price, cloth: $19.95; paper: $5.95. 120pp; 6x9. Reporting time: 2 months. Simultaneous submissions accepted: yes. Publishes 5% of manuscripts submitted. Payment: on publication. Copyrights for author. Black Women in Publishing, APA.

AFRICAN AMERICAN AUDIOBOOK REVIEW, African American Audio Press, Corinne Butler, 138 Palm Coast Parkway NE #217, Palm Coast, FL 32137-8241. 1995. "We are particularly interested in audiobooks; mss. that could and will be translated into audio books welcome." circ. 1M. 12/yr. Expects 12 issues 1999, 12 issues 2000. sub. price: $26.95; per copy: $3; sample: $3.50. Back issues: none. 20-30pp; 8x11; lp. Reporting time: 2 months. Simultaneous submissions accepted: yes. Publishes 5% of manuscripts submitted. Payment: on publication. Not copyrighted. Pub's reviews: 36 in 1998. §Fiction, non-fiction, mystery, romance, science fiction, poetry, juvenile fiction. Ads: on request. ABA, Black Women in Publishing.

African American Images, Jawanza Kunjufu, 1909 West 95th Street, Chicago, IL 60643-1105, 312-445-0322; FAX 312-445-9844. 1980. Non-fiction. avg. press run 5M. Pub'd 10 titles 1998. 56 titles listed in the *Small Press Record of Books in Print* (28th Edition, 1999-00). avg. price, paper: $14.95. Discounts: 5-100 40%, 101-199 46%, 200+ 50%. 125pp; 5½x8½; of. Reporting time: 2 months. Publishes 10% of manuscripts submitted. Payment: 10% net. Copyrights for author.

AFRICAN AMERICAN REVIEW, Joe Weixlmann, Indiana State University, Dept. of English, Terre Haute, IN 47809, 812-237-2968. 1967. Poetry, fiction, articles, art, photos, interviews, criticism, reviews, non-fiction. circ. 4068. 4/yr. Pub'd 4 issues 1998; expects 4 issues 1999, 4 issues 2000. sub. price: $24 individuals, $48 institutions (foreign add $7); per copy: $10; $12 institutions (foreign add $2); sample: $8. Back issues: $10. Discounts: 40%. 176pp; 7×10; of. Reporting time: 3 months. Simultaneous submissions accepted: no. Publishes 15% of manuscripts submitted. Payment: 1 copy, plus offprints; honorarium. Indiana State Univ. holds copyright on entire issue, author on individual article or poem. Pub's reviews: 31 in 1998. §African-American literature. Ads: $200/$120. CLMP, Society for Scholarly Publishing.

THE AFRICAN BOOK PUBLISHING RECORD, Hans Zell Publishers, Hans M. Zell, Editor; Cecile Lomer, Ass. Editor (US office), PO Box 56, Oxford 0X13EL, England, +44-(0)1865-511428; fax +44-1865-311534. 1975. Articles, interviews, criticism, reviews, news items. "Largely a bibliographic tool, providing information on new and forthcoming African published materials; plus 'Notes & News', 'Magazines', 'Reports', 'Reference Sources' sections and interviews; normally one major article on aspects of publishing and book development in Africa per issue. Major book review section. (Ca. 40-60 reviews per issue). US Office, PO Box 130, Flagstaff, AZ 86002-0130'' circ. 800. 4/yr. Pub'd 4 issues 1998; expects 4 issues 1999, 4 issues 2000. sub. price: £130/£215 institution; £65/£107.50 individual; per copy: £32.50; sample: gratis. Discounts: 15% to adv. agents/10% to subs. agents. 84pp; size A4; of/li. Reporting time: 6-8 weeks. Simultaneous submissions accepted: no. Publishes 25% of manuscripts submitted. Copyrighted. Pub's reviews: 192 in 1998. §Books published in Africa only, with an emphasis on scholarly books, creative writing, reference tools, and children's books. Ads: $200 ($330)/ £140 ($230)/ £220 ($360).

THE AFRICAN HERALD, Good Hope Enterprises, Inc., Dr. Richard O. Nwachukwu, PO Box 2394, Dallas, TX 75221. 1989. Articles, photos, interviews, news items, non-fiction. "Additional address: 4300 N. Central Expressway, Suite 201, Dallas, TX 75206.'' circ. 15M. 12/yr. Pub'd 12 issues 1998; expects 12 issues 1999, 12 issues 2000. sub. price: $15 corps, libraries; $12 individuals; per copy: $1; sample: free. Back issues: $1.50. Discounts: 30% to 40%. 32pp; tabloid. Publishes 95% of manuscripts submitted. Payment: none. Copyrighted, does not revert to author. Pub's reviews: 6 in 1998. §African/African-American Books. Ads: $1365/$725/$475/$295/$155 business card size. Texas Publishers Association.

‡**AFRICAN STUDIES, Witwatersrand University Press**, W.D. Hammond-Tooke, WITS, 2050 Johannesburg, Republic of South Africa. 1921. Articles, criticism, reviews. "(Former title: *Bantu Studies*). African anthropology and linguistics.'' circ. 800. 2/yr. Pub'd 2 issues 1998; expects 2 issues 1999, 2 issues 2000. sub. price: individual R15, institutions R35; per copy: individual R8.00; insititutions R18.00; sample: on application. Back issues: on application. Discounts: 10% to booksellers and agents. 100pp; 21×15cm (A5); of. Reporting time: 3 months. Payment: none. Copyrighted, does not revert to author. Pub's reviews: 19 in 1998. §African anthropology and linguistics. Ads: R100/R50.

●**African Ways Publishing**, Lynn D. Casto, Publisher, 33 Hansen Court, Moraga, CA 94556-1580, 925-631-0630; Fax 925-376-1926. 1996. Non-fiction. "Publish history, political, biographical books about Africa.'' avg. press run 3M. Pub'd 1 title 1998; expects 1 title 1999, 1 title 2000. 1 title listed in the *Small Press Record of Books in Print* (28th Edition, 1999-00). avg. price, cloth: $25; paper: $15. Discounts: retail 1-2 books 20%, 3-4 30%, 5+ 40%; wholesale 55%. 300pp. Reporting time: 6 weeks. Payment: trade standard. Copyrights for author. PMA.

Afrimax, Inc., Emmanuel Nnadozie, PO Box 946, Kirksville, MO 63501-0946, 660-665-0757; Fax 660-665-8778; email afrimax@afrmimax.com; www.afrimax.com. 1996. "Publishes materials relating to international business, especially US-African business.'' avg. press run 3M. Pub'd 2 titles 1998; expects 2 titles 1999, 3 titles 2000. 1 title listed in the *Small Press Record of Books in Print* (28th Edition, 1999-00). avg. price, paper: $19.95. 200pp; 5½×8½. Reporting time: 1 month. Simultaneous submissions accepted: no. PMA.

AFRO-HISPANIC REVIEW, Marvin A. Lewis, Edward J. Mullen, Romance Languages, Univ. of Missouri, 143 Arts & Science Building, Columbia, MO 65211, 573-882-5040 or 573-882-5041. 1982. Poetry, fiction, articles, interviews, criticism, reviews, letters, news items. "We also publish translations.'' circ. 500. 2/yr. Pub'd 2 issues 1998; expects 2 issues 1999, 2 issues 2000. sub. price: $15 indiv., $20 instit.; per copy: $7.50; sample: $7.50. Back issues: $7.50. Discounts: 40%. 60pp; 8½×11; of. Reporting time: 60 days. Simultaneous submissions accepted: no. Publishes 40% of manuscripts submitted. Payment: 3 copies of issue containing contribution. Copyrighted, does not revert to author. Pub's reviews: 3 in 1998. §Afro-Hispanic history, literature and sociology. Ads: $100/$50/50¢.

AFTERIMAGE, Visual Studies Workshop, Grant H. Kester, Senior Editor; Lynn Love, Managing Editor, 31 Prince Street, Rochester, NY 14607, 716-442-8676. 1972. Articles, photos, interviews, criticism, reviews, letters, news items. "*Afterimage* welcomes unsolicited manuscripts. Manuscripts must be typed double-spaced and cannot be returned unless a SASE is included. Features, reviews, news, notices of exhibitions. Recent contributors: Paul Byers, Howard Becker, Michael Lesy, A.D. Coleman, Les Krims, Nam June Paik, Richard Rudisill'' circ. 4.2M. 10/yr. Pub'd 10 issues 1998; expects 10 issues 1999, 10 issues 2000. sub. price: $30; per copy: $3; sample: gratis. Back issues: $3. Discounts: classrooms (10 or more subscriptions) 20%, trade 40%. 24pp; 11×17; †of. Reporting time: 2-3 weeks. Copyrighted, reverts to author. Pub's reviews: 54 long, 248 short in 1998. §Photography, film, video, and visual books. No advertising. CLMP.

AFTERTHOUGHTS, Andreas Gripp, 1100 Commissioners Rd. E, PO Box 41040, London, ON N5Z 4Z7, Canada. 1994. Poetry. ''Poems up to 3 pages (single-spaced). Vegan editorial stance. Open to all types of poetry. Recent contributors include: John Grey, Nancy Berg, Daniel Green, Fredrick Zydek, Kenneth Salzmann, Claire Litton, Wesley Britton, Lyn Lifshin, C. David Hay'' circ. 500. 2/yr. Pub'd 3 issues 1998; expects 3 issues 1999, 2 issues 2000. sub. price: $13 US; per copy: $4; sample: $5 includes p/h. Back issues: $4. Discounts: retail 40%, library 40%, jobber 40%, educational/bulk 40%. 92pp; 5⅜×8⅜; of. Reporting time: 1 month. Simultaneous submissions accepted: yes. Publishes 5% of manuscripts submitted. Payment: complimentary copy. Copyrighted, rights revert to author, but we reserve right to reprint. Pub's reviews: 1 in 1998. Ads: $25/$15.

AFTERTOUCH: New Music Discoveries, Ronald A. Wallace, 1024 West Willcox Avenue, Peoria, IL 61604, 309-685-4843. 1987. ''Includes audio CD with music samples.'' 1/yr. Pub'd 2 issues 1998; expects 2 issues 1999, 1 issue 2000. sub. price: $10/2 issues USA, additional foreign, $5/1 issue USA; per copy: $5; sample: $5. Discounts: none. 250pp; 5½×8½; of. Publishes 0% of manuscripts submitted. §Music.

AGADA, Reuven Goldfarb, Editor; Yehudit Goldfarb, Associate Editor, 2020 Essex Street, Berkeley, CA 94703, 510-848-0965. 1981. Poetry, fiction, articles, art, interviews, criticism, parts-of-novels. ''We have a limit of 6M words on our fiction and articles but also print much shorter pieces. We publish as much poetry as prose and like a spiritual point of view. We generally select for publication work whose subject matter is in some way related to the Jewish experience, its values and aspirations. We publish fiction, poetry, commentary, calligraphy, photography, and illustrated graphic art. We draw from Classical sources—Scriptural, Rabbinic, Kabbalistic, and Chassidic—for translations and for inspiration but cultivate a contemporary sensibility in regard to how we shape these material. Recent contributors: Thomas Friedmann, Daniel Spicehandler, Marcia Tager, Florence Wallach Freed, Julie Heifetz, Yael Mesinai, Robert Stern and Roger White. The magazine is illustrated with graphic art'' circ. 1M. 1/yr. Pub'd 1 issue 1998; expects 1 issue 1999, 1 issue 2000. sub. price: $12/double issue; per copy: $6.50; sample: $6.50. Back issues: $6/$5/$4—inquire for more details. Discounts: bookstores 40% ($3.90 each), agents $3.25 each on orders of 25 or more. 64pp; 7×10; of. Reporting time: 3-4 months, more or less. Simultaneous submissions accepted if so notified. Publishes a minimal % of manuscripts submitted. Payment: only to illustrators, at present. Copyrighted, reverts to author. Pub's reviews: 0 in 1998. Ads: query for ad rates. CLMP.

Agathon Books, Allen A. Huemer, PO Box 630, Lander, WY 82520-0630, 307-332-5252; Fax 307-332-5888; agathon@rmisp.com; www.rmisp.com/agathon/. 1998. ''Issues in philosophy and related areas, using a clearly-reasoned, good-spirited approach.'' avg. press run 3M. Expects 3 titles 1999, 4+ titles 2000. 1 title listed in the *Small Press Record of Books in Print* (28th Edition, 1999-00). avg. price, paper: $19.95. Discounts: trade 40%, colleges and libraries 25%, bulk and jobber 60% max. 300pp; 5½×8½. Reporting time: 6 months. Simultaneous submissions accepted: yes. Publishes 25% of manuscripts submitted. Payment: arranged individually. Copyrights for author.

Ageless Press, Iris Forrest, PO Box 5915, Sarasota, FL 34277-5915, 941-952-0576, e-Mail irishope@home.com. 1992. Fiction, articles, non-fiction. ''First book is an anthology of experiences of dealing with computers. Fiction & nonfiction.'' avg. press run 5M. Expects 1 title 1999, 1 title 2000. 2 titles listed in the *Small Press Record of Books in Print* (28th Edition, 1999-00). avg. price, paper: $9.95. 160pp; 5½×8½. Reporting time: 2 weeks. Simultaneous submissions accepted: yes. Payment: negotiable. Does not copyright for author. PMA.

THE AGENCIES-WHAT THE ACTOR NEEDS TO KNOW, Acting World Books, Lawrence Parke, PO Box 3044, Hollywood, CA 90078, 818-905-1345. 1981. ''Articles in every issue by and or about subject material people, orgns, currently recommended procedures, etc.'' circ. 1.5M. 12/yr. Pub'd 12 issues 1998; expects 12 issues 1999, 12 issues 2000. sub. price: $50; per copy: $10. Back issues: not available. Discounts: 40% bookstore. 56pp; 8½×11; †of. Reporting time: 2 weeks. Payment: as and if negotiated. Copyrighted, reverts to author. Ads: $500 1/2 page/special 6 months in both pub's, rate $800.

Ages Publications, Lynne Shuttleworth, Liba Berry, Phyllis Schwager, 8391 Beverly Blvd., Suite 323-DS, Los Angeles, CA 90048, 800-652-8574. 1994. Non-fiction. ''Not accepting submissions until the end of 1997. Unsolicited materials not accepted, only through AAR member literary agents queries. Contact person: Al Daniels. Also produce audio-tapes of books. Branch office: 1054-2 Centre Street, Suite 153-DS, Thornhill, Ontario, L4J 8E5, Canada'' avg. press run varies. Expects 3 titles 1999, 4 titles 2000. 2 titles listed in the *Small Press Record of Books in Print* (28th Edition, 1999-00). avg. price, paper: $14.95. Discounts: Retail trade 40%,

12

wholesalers 55%, please call 1-800-263-1991 for list of wholesalers. 200pp; 6×9. Reporting time: 9-18 months. Payment: as per contract. Copyrights as per contract. NAPRA, New Editions International.

AGNI, Askold Melnyczuk, Editor; Colette Kelso, Managing Editor, Boston University, 236 Bay State Road, Boston, MA 02215, 617-353-7135. 1972. Poetry, fiction, parts-of-novels, long-poems. "Derek Walcott, Leslie Epstein, Seamus Heaney, Marilynne Robinson, Ai, Ginger Adcock, Sven Birkerts, Olena Kayhiak Davis, Joe Osterhaus, Eavan Boland, Jessica Treadway, Robert Pinsky, Ha Jin are among past contributors. We expect you to buy a sample copy before submitting your work." circ. 1.5M. 2/yr. Pub'd 2 issues 1998; expects 2 issues 1999. sub. price: $18; per copy: $8.95; sample: $9. Back issues: varies, usually $5. 200-270pp; 5⅜×8½; of. Reporting time: 1-4 months, reading period October 1 to April 30 only (check magazine for shortened reading period dates). Payment: $10 per page ($150 max, $20 minimum). Copyrighted, reverts to author. Pub's reviews: 4+ in 1998. §Politics & literature. Ads: $330/$250. CLMP, AWP.

AGRICULTURAL HISTORY, University of California Press, Doug Hurt, Shellie Orngard, Assistant Editor, University of California Press, 2120 Berkeley Way, Berkeley, CA 94720, 510-643-7154. 1926. Articles, reviews, non-fiction. "Editorial address: Center for Agricultural History and Rural Studies, 618 Ross Hall, Iowa State University, Ames, IA 50011. Copyrighted by Agricultural History Society." circ. 1.2M. 4/yr. Pub'd 4 issues 1998; expects 4 issues 1999, 4 issues 2000. sub. price: $34 indiv., $82 instit., $19 students; per copy: $10 indiv.; $20 instit., $10 students. Back issues: $8 indiv.; $16 instit., $8 students. Discounts: foreign subs. agent 10%, one-time orders 10+ 30%, standing orders (bookstores): 1-99 40%, 100+ 50%. 112pp; 6×9; of. Reporting time: 2-3 weeks. Payment: varies. Copyrighted, does not revert to author. Pub's reviews: 100 in 1998. §Agricultural history and economics. Ads: $275/$200.

THE AGUILAR EXPRESSION, Xavier F. Aguilar, 1329 Gilmore Avenue, Donora, PA 15033, 412-379-8019. 1986. Poetry, fiction, art, reviews, letters. circ. 150. 2/yr. Pub'd 2 issues 1998; expects 2 issues 1999, 2 issues 2000. sub. price: $11; per copy: $6; sample: $6. 8-14pp; 8½×11; mi. Reporting time: 1 month. Simultaneous submissions accepted: no. Publishes 10% of manuscripts submitted. Payment: free copy, byline. Not copyrighted. Pub's reviews: 2 in 1998. §Poetry books and short story collections. Ads: by request.

AHA Books, Jane Reichhold, Werner Reichhold, PO Box 767, Gualala, CA 95445, 707-882-2226. 1986. "Since this summer (1996) we have been working to establish a place for poets on the Internet with a Web site. We are in the final phases of completing that work. Through this new venture we have decided not to publish, for a time, any more paper books. Through our web site we offer authors several options about how to share what they have written. We hope that here you can pick out the method that is best for your book." avg. press run 200-1M. Pub'd 7 titles 1998; expects 8 titles 1999, 8 titles 2000. 20 titles listed in the *Small Press Record of Books in Print* (28th Edition, 1999-00). avg. price, cloth: $12; paper: $10. Discounts: distributors 40%; bookstores 25%. 125-400pp; 5×8; of. Reporting time: 2 weeks. Simultaneous submissions accepted: yes. Payment: individually arranged. Copyrights for author.

Ahsahta, T. Trusky, Boise State University, Department of English, Boise, ID 83725, 208-426-1999; orders 1-800-526-6522; www.bsubkst.idbsu.edu/. 1975. Poetry. "We publish only work by Western poets—this does not mean paeans to the pommel or songs of the sage, but quality verse which clearly indicates its origin in the West. Samplers (15 poems) sent SASE read Jan-Mar. Not reading samplers until 2000" avg. press run 500. Pub'd 3 titles 1998; expects 3 titles 1999, 3 titles 2000. 54 titles listed in the *Small Press Record of Books in Print* (28th Edition, 1999-00). avg. price, paper: $9.95 postpaid; other: $9 Ahsahta Cassette Sampler, postpaid. Discounts: 40% to trade, bulk, jobber, classroom; no returns. 60pp; 6×8½; †of. Reporting time: 2 months. Simultaneous submissions accepted: yes. Publishes 1% of manuscripts submitted. Payment: copies of book; royalties begin on third printing; titles in-print eternally. Copyrights for author.

AIM MAGAZINE, Ruth Apilado, Editor; Myron Apilado, Managing Editor, PO Box 1174, Maywood, IL 60153-8174. 1973. "AIM is a national magazine that uses the written word to help purge racism from the human bloodstream. A consistent theme that winds its way through the prose poetry of the magazine is one that depicts how people from one ethnic group, usually through some personal experience, come to realize the common humanity of all ethnic groups. We're looking for compelling, well-written pieces with lasting social significance. The story should not moralize. Maximum length is 4,000 words" circ. 7M. 4/yr. Pub'd 4 issues 1998; expects 4 issues 1999, 4 issues 2000. sub. price: $12; per copy: $4; sample: $5. Back issues: $6. Discounts: 30%. 48pp; 8½×11. Reporting time: 2 months. Simultaneous submissions accepted: yes. Publishes 70% of manuscripts submitted. Payment: $15-$25 articles and stories. Not copyrighted. Pub's reviews: 2 in 1998. §Black and Hispanic life. Ads: $250/$150/$90 1/4 page.

Aircraft Owners Group (see also CESSNA OWNER MAGAZINE; PIPERS MAGAZINE), Jodi Lindquist, Editor, PO Box 5000, Iola, WI 54945, 800-331-0038; e-mail cessna@aircraftownergroup.com or piper@aircraftownergroup.com. 1974. Articles, photos, interviews, reviews, letters. avg. press run 3M-5M.

Airplane Books, Barbara Richter, PO Box 111, Glenview, IL 60025. 1994. Art, cartoons, non-fiction. "*Eat Like A Horse* treats the serious subject of dieting in a light-hearted and humorous fashion. 150 recipes, 80 of which are vegetarian. Each recipe original and tested" Pub'd 1 title 1998; expects 3 titles 1999, 5 titles 2000. 2 titles listed in the *Small Press Record of Books in Print* (28th Edition, 1999-00). avg. price, paper: $11.95. Discounts: standard. 192pp; 5½×8; of.

AK Press, Ramsey Kanaan, PO Box 40682, San Francisco, CA 94140, 415-864-0892; FAX 415-864-0893; akpress@org.org. 1994. Fiction, art, criticism, long-poems, non-fiction. "Most of what we publish is solicited. However we have published the occasional unsolicited work. We largely publish non-fiction of a radical nature, in the fields of anarchism, art & culture" avg. press run 2M-10M. Pub'd 15 titles 1998; expects 18 titles 1999, 25 titles 2000. 71 titles listed in the *Small Press Record of Books in Print* (28th Edition, 1999-00). avg. price, paper: $6-15. Discounts: normal discounts to trade, depending on whether it's to a retailer, distributor, library, etc. 100-400pp; 5½×8½, 6×9, 8½×11; of. Reporting time: a couple of months. Publishes 2% of manuscripts submitted. Payment: usually 10% of net sales, no advance.

ALABAMA DOGSHOE MOUSTACHE, Ge(of Huth), po.ed.t, 875 Central Parkway, Schenectady, NY 12309. 1987. Poetry, cartoons, collages, concrete art. "*Alabama Dogshoe Moustache (ADM)* is an irregularly published poetry magazine publishing mostly visual and language poetry. Subscriptions can be of any amount—cost (which varies) per issue will be subtracted when mailed." circ. 100. 4/yr. Pub'd 4 issues 1998; expects 4 issues 1999, 4 issues 2000. sub. price: varies by complexity of issue—about $5 per year; per copy: 40¢-$2.75; sample: 40¢-$2.75. Discounts: none. 5pp; size varies; †photocopy, rubberstamp printing, of, linoleum block printing. Reporting time: 2 weeks. Payment: at least 2 copies; 1/4 of press run is divided among contributors. Copyrighted, reverts to author.

ALABAMA LITERARY REVIEW, Theron E. Montgomery III, Editor; James G. Davis, Fiction Editor; Ed Hicks, Poetry Editor; Steve Cooper, Prose Editor, Smith 253, Troy State University, Troy, AL 36082, 334-670-3307;FAX 334-670-3519. 1987. Poetry, fiction, articles, art, photos, cartoons, interviews, criticism, reviews, parts-of-novels, long-poems, plays. "No bias against style or length of poetry, fiction or drama. First issue included Eve Shelnutt and Elise Sanguinetti." circ. 800+. 1/yr. Pub'd 1 issue 1998; expects 1 issue 1999, 1 issue 2000. sub. price: $10; per copy: $10; sample: $5. 100pp; 7×10; of, hand spine. Reporting time: 2-3 months. Publishes 5-10% of manuscripts submitted. Payment: copies and honorarium when available; $5-10 per printed page. Copyrighted, reverts to author. Pub's reviews: 5 in 1998. §All kinds, particularly poetry and fiction by new authors and/or smaller presses. Ads: $25.

ALABAMA REVIEW, Sarah Woolfolk Wiggins, Editor, 1306 Overlook Road, N, Tuscaloosa, AL 35406-2176. 1947. "Published in cooperation with the Alabama Historical Assn. The journal includes articles on Alabama history and culture and book reviews on Alabama and Southern history and culture." circ. 2M. 4/yr. Pub'd 4 issues 1998; expects 4 issues 1999, 4 issues 2000. sub. price: $15; per copy: $5.50. 80pp. Payment: none. Copyrighted, does not revert to author. Pub's reviews: 75 in 1998. §Alabama history.

ALADDIN'S WINDOW, J.R. Molloy, Box 399, Shingletown, CA 96088, 916-474-1385. 1991. Articles, interviews, satire, reviews, letters, non-fiction. "Articles, essays 800-1200 words. Subjects *not* considered: anything androphobic. Subjects considered include men's rights, men's issues, men's studies with an emphasis on spiritual awakening." circ. 250. 4/yr. Pub'd 6 issues 1998; expects 4 issues 1999, 4 issues 2000. sub. price: $30; per copy: $8; sample: $8. Back issues: available on request. Discounts: over 10 copies $4. 100pp; 8½×11; †liquid toner transfer. Reporting time: 6 weeks. Simultaneous submissions accepted: yes. Publishes 20% of manuscripts submitted. Payment: none at present. Copyrighted, reverts to author. Pub's reviews: 12 in 1998. §Psychology, men's issues, population control. Ads: By arrangement. Directory of Men's Organizations & Periodicals (DMOP).

Alamo Square Press, Bert Herrman, 103 FR 321, Tajique, NM 87057, 503-384-9766; alamosquare@earth-link.net. 1988. Non-fiction. "Book length, gay, non-pornographic, social or spiritual importance only." avg. press run 5M. Pub'd 1 title 1998; expects 2 titles 1999, 2 titles 2000. 16 titles listed in the *Small Press Record of Books in Print* (28th Edition, 1999-00). avg. price, cloth: $19.95; paper: $11.95. Discounts: 40% retail, 55% distributor. 144pp; 5½×8½; of. Reporting time: 2 weeks. Simultaneous submissions accepted: no. Publishes 20% of manuscripts submitted. Payment: negotiable. Copyrights for author.

Alan Wofsy Fine Arts, Milton J. Goldbaum, Zeke Greenberg, Adios Butler, PO Box 2210, San Francisco, CA 94126, 415-986-3030. 1969. Art, cartoons. "Art reference books only." avg. press run 500. Pub'd 4 titles 1998; expects 4 titles 1999, 5+ titles 2000. 35 titles listed in the *Small Press Record of Books in Print* (28th Edition, 1999-00). avg. price, cloth: $125. Discounts: 20-40. 300pp; 9×12; of. Payment: varies. Copyrights for author.

Al-Anon Family Group Headquarters, Inc. (see also THE FORUM), Patrick Quiggle, Editor; Caryn Johnson, Director, 1600 Corporate Parkway, Virginia Beach, VA 23454-0862, 757-563-1600. 1951. Non-fiction. "Articles and stories of personal recovery in Al-Anon from the effects of alcoholism in a spouse, lover, friend, parent, child or other individual. We often require the services of freelance writers/editors, copy editors and proofers who are Al-Anon members." avg. press run 40M. Pub'd 12 titles 1998; expects 12 titles 1999, 12 titles 2000. 24 titles listed in the *Small Press Record of Books in Print* (28th Edition, 1999-00). avg.

price, paper: $10; other: $1. 320-400pp; 5⅜×8⅛. Reporting time: 8 weeks. Simultaneous submissions accepted: no. We own copyright. ASAE, PMA, PM.

ALARM CLOCK, Allen Salyer, PO Box 1551, Royal Oak, MI 48068, 313-593-9677. 1990. Music. "Women in alternative music." circ. 200. 4/yr. Pub'd 5 issues 1998; expects 4 issues 1999, 4 issues 2000. sample price: $2. 32pp; 5½×8½; of. Payment: contributor's copy. Copyrighted, reverts to author. Pub's reviews: 10-15 per issue in 1998. §Music, science fiction, fashion, women's issues.

Alaska Geographic Society, Penny Rennick, Editor, PO Box 93370, Anchorage, AK 99509, 907-562-0164, Fax 907-562-0479, e-mail akgeo@aol.com. 1968. Photos, news items, non-fiction. "Pictoral geography of Alaska regions." avg. press run 12M. Pub'd 4 titles 1998; expects 4 titles 1999, 4 titles 2000. 76 titles listed in the *Small Press Record of Books in Print* (28th Edition, 1999-00). avg. price, paper: $19.95-$21.95. Discounts: library 20%. 112pp; 11×8½. Reporting time: 1 month. Simultaneous submissions accepted: no. Publishes 40% of manuscripts submitted. Payment: purchase 1 time rights to publish. Does not copyright for author. ABA, PNBA, RMPBA, PMA.

Alaska Native Language Center, Tom Alton, University of Alaska, PO Box 757680, Fairbanks, AK 99775-7680, 907-474-7874, fax 907-474-6586. 1972. Non-fiction. "We publish materials in or about Alaska Native languages only" avg. press run 500-1M. Pub'd 2 titles 1998; expects 5 titles 1999, 6 titles 2000. 41 titles listed in the *Small Press Record of Books in Print* (28th Edition, 1999-00). avg. price, cloth: $40; paper: $15. Discounts: wholesalers 40% on 5 each or more; 20% on fewer than 5 each. 300pp; 8½×11, 6×9, 8½×7, 5½×8½; of. Sometimes copyrights for author—joint copyright or ANLC alone. Alaska Association of Small Presses (AASP).

Alaska Northwest Books, Ellen Wheat, Editor, 203 West 15th Avenue, Ste. 108, Anchorage, AK 99501-5128, 907-278-8838. 1959. Non-fiction. "We do not want to receive unsolicited manuscripts—query letters and proposals only, please. We publish primarily regional nonfiction in the following subject areas: nature and the environment, travel, Native heritage, cooking, essays of place, regional history, and adventure literature. Our books are centered on Alaska and the Pacific Northwest. We publish some children's books, most of which are targeted to the geographic regions and subject areas in which we publish books for an adult audience. Some recent authors are Nick Jans (*A Place Beyond*) and Wayne Mergler (*Last New Land*). Manuscript submission guidelines available with SASE. No poetry please." avg. press run 8M. Pub'd 8 titles 1998; expects 8 titles 1999, 10 titles 2000. 21 titles listed in the *Small Press Record of Books in Print* (28th Edition, 1999-00). avg. price, cloth: $24.95; paper: $14.95. Discounts: standard discounts described in catalog. computer-generated to disk. Reporting time: 3-6 months. Simultaneous submissions accepted: no. Publishes 3% of manuscripts submitted. Payment: royalty on net; payments twice annually. Copyrights for author. ABA, PNBA, RMBPA, NCBPA, ACB.

ALASKA QUARTERLY REVIEW, Ronald Spatz, Fiction Editor, Executive Editor, University of Alaska-Anchorage, 3211 Providence Drive, Anchorage, AK 99508, 907-786-6916. 1981. Poetry, fiction, criticism, reviews, parts-of-novels. "We are looking for high quality traditional and unconventional fiction, poetry, short plays, and literary nonfiction. Unsolicited manuscripts welcome between August 15 and May 15." circ. 2.2M. 2/yr. Expects 2 issues 2000. 1 title listed in the *Small Press Record of Books in Print* (28th Edition, 1999-00). sub. price: $10; per copy: $5.95; sample: $5. Back issues: $5 and up. 264pp; 6×9; of. Reporting time: 6-12 weeks. Publishes less than 1% of manuscripts submitted. Payment: 1 contributor's copy and a one-year subscription; additional payment depends on terms of grants. Copyrighted, reverts to author. CLMP.

ALBATROSS, Anabiosis Press, Richard Smyth, Richard Brobst, PO Box 7787, North Port, FL 34287-0787. 1986. Poetry, art, interviews, long-poems. "Continuous deadline. Send 3-5 poems, 200 line max. 1 issues/year. $3/issue; $5/2 issues. Recent contributors: Duane Niatum, Peter Huggins, Lenny Emmanuel, Errol Miller. Tend to be biased towards ecological concerns." circ. 300. 1/yr. Pub'd 1 issue 1998; expects 1 issue 1999, 1 issue 2000. sub. price: $5; per copy: $3; sample: $3. Back issues: $2. Discounts: $2/copy if 10 or more ordered. 36pp; 5½×8½; of. Reporting time: up to 6 months. Simultaneous submissions accepted: no. Publishes 3% of manuscripts submitted. Payment: 1 copy. Copyrighted, rights revert to author (credit given to *Albatross*).

ALBERTA HISTORY, Historical Society of Alberta, Hugh A. Dempsey, 95 Holmwood Ave NW, Calgary Alberta T2K 2G7, Canada, 403-289-8149. 1953. Articles, reviews, non-fiction. "3.5M to 5M word articles on Western Canadian History" circ. 1.6M. 4/yr. Pub'd 4 issues 1998; expects 4 issues 1999. sub. price: $25; per copy: $5.50; sample: free. Back issues: $5.50. Discounts: 33%. 28pp; 8½×11; of. Reporting time: 2 months. Simultaneous submissions accepted: no. Publishes 50% of manuscripts submitted. Payment: nil. Copyrighted. Pub's reviews: 12 in 1998. §In our field-Western Canadian History. No ads. AASLH, CHA.

●**Albion Press,** 9701 Twincrest Drive, St. Louis, MO 63126, 888-787-4477; fax 314-962-7808; e-mail albionpr@stlnet.com. 1 title listed in the *Small Press Record of Books in Print* (28th Edition, 1999-00).

ALCATRAZ, Alcatraz Editions, Stephen Kessler, Hollis deLancey, 133 Towne Terrace, Santa Cruz, CA

95060. 1978. Articles, art, photos, interviews, criticism, reviews, letters, long-poems. "No unsolicited mss. until further notice." circ. 1M. Irregular. price per copy: varies; sample: free to writers. Discounts: 40% to booksellers on orders of 3 or more. 300pp; 6×9; of. Payment: copies. Copyrighted, reverts to author. Pub's reviews: 5 in 1998. §Poetry, translations, cultural commentary, criticism, biography. No ads.

Alcatraz Editions (see also ALCATRAZ), Hollis deLancey, 325 Kramaur Lane, Santa Cruz, CA 95060. 1978. Poetry, fiction, articles, art, photos, cartoons, satire, criticism, reviews, music, long-poems, collages. "See *Alcatraz 3* for current biases. No new books until further notice." avg. press run 500. Pub'd 1 title 1998. 4 titles listed in the *Small Press Record of Books in Print* (28th Edition, 1999-00). avg. price, paper: $6.00. Discounts: 40% to trade on orders of 3 or more. 80-120pp; of.

Alchemist/Light Publishing, Bil Paul, P.O. Box 1275, Belmont, CA 94002-6275, 650-345-6812; email bbp@alchemist-light.com; http://www.alchemist-light.com. 1973. Fiction, non-fiction. "Most of our books have been bicycle touring guides." avg. press run 2M. Expects 1 title 1999. 2 titles listed in the *Small Press Record of Books in Print* (28th Edition, 1999-00). avg. price, paper: $12. Discounts: 40% bookstores. 200pp; 5×8; of. Reporting time: 2 weeks. Simultaneous submissions accepted: yes. Payment: varies. Copyrights for author.

The Aldine Press, Ltd. (see also HELLAS: A Journal of Poetry & the Humanities), Gerald Harnett, Erika Harnett, Barry Baldwin, William Kerrigan, Christopher Clausen, 304 South Tyson Avenue, Glenside, PA 19038. 1988. Poetry. avg. press run 2M. Expects 1 title 1999, 2 titles 2000. 1 title listed in the *Small Press Record of Books in Print* (28th Edition, 1999-00). avg. price, cloth: $22; paper: $16. Discounts: 10 or more 40%. 150pp; 6×9; of. Reporting time: 2 months. Payment: variable. Copyrights for author. CLMP.

Alef Design Group, Jane Golub, 4423 Fruitland Avenue, Los Angeles, CA 90058, 800-845-0662; Fax 213-585-0327; misrad@alefdesign.com; www.alefdesign.com. 1990. Fiction, non-fiction. "We publish books of Judaic interest only." avg. press run 2M. Pub'd 7 titles 1998; expects 8-10 titles 1999, 8-10 titles 2000. avg. price, cloth: $14.95; paper: $8.95. Discounts: call for information. 150pp; 6×9; †of. Reporting time: 6 months. Simultaneous submissions accepted: yes. Publishes 5-10% of manuscripts submitted. Payment: 10% min/max royalty. Copyrights for author.

Alegra House Publishers, Robert C. Peters, Managing Editor; Linda Marado, Co-Editor; Edward Amicucci, Co-Editor, PO Box 1443-D, Warren, OH 44482, 216-372-2951. 1985. Non-fiction. "Major goals/objectives: 1) Provide self-help adult and childrens' books(divorce, war, learning, relaxation), 2) self-help cassette tape (divorce, learning, relaxation)" avg. press run 5M. Pub'd 4 titles 1998; expects 6 titles 1999, 2 titles 2000. 11 titles listed in the *Small Press Record of Books in Print* (28th Edition, 1999-00). avg. price, cloth: $14.95; paper: $9.95. Discounts: bookstores 40%, distributors 50%, 20% STOP. 224pp; 8½×5½, 6×9. Does not copyright for author. PMA.

THE ALEMBIC, Department of English, Providence College, Providence, RI 02918-0001. 1920. Poetry, fiction, articles, art, photos, interviews, reviews, long-poems, collages, plays, concrete art. "Recent contributors include Mark Rudman, James Merrill, Ai, C.D. Wright, Jane Lunin Perel, Martha Collins, William Matthews, Bruce Smith. Looking for exploratory poetry, fiction, art in black and white, and reviews" circ. 4M. 1/yr. Pub'd 1 issue 1998; expects 1 issue 1999, 1 issue 2000. sub. price: $15/2 years; per copy: $8. 200pp; 7×9. Reporting time: 4 months. Simultaneous submissions accepted: no. Publishes 15% of manuscripts submitted. Payment: copies. Copyrighted, reverts to author. Pub's reviews: 5 in 1998. §Poetry, fiction, literary criticism. Ads: $75. AWP.

Aletheia Publications, Inc., Carolyn D. Smith, Publisher; Guy J. Smith, Managing Editor, 46 Bell Hollow Road, Putnam Valley, NY 10579-1426, 914-526-2873, Fax 914-526-2905. 1993. Non-fiction. "Short-run (1M-2M) paperbacks for tightly targeted markets, especially works dealing with the attitudes and experiences of expatriate and repatriate Americans and with running a freelance business" avg. press run 1M. Pub'd 2 titles 1998; expects 4 titles 1999, 2 titles 2000. 8 titles listed in the *Small Press Record of Books in Print* (28th Edition, 1999-00). avg. price, paper: $15.95. Discounts: 4-5 25%, 6-99 40%, 100+ 50%. 150-250pp; 5½×8½, 6×9; of. Reporting time: 2-3 months. Simultaneous submissions accepted: yes. Publishes very small % of manuscripts submitted. Payment: 10%. Copyrights for author. Small Press Center.

Al-Galaxy Publishing Company, Martin Mathias, PO Box 2591, Wichita, KS 67201, 316-651-0072; Fax 316-651-2790. 1994. Reviews, non-fiction. avg. press run 100M. Pub'd 1 title 1998; expects 3 titles 1999, 5 titles 2000. 1 title listed in the *Small Press Record of Books in Print* (28th Edition, 1999-00). avg. price, paper: $19.95. Discounts: 2-4 books 20%, 5-9 30%, 10-24 40%, 25-49 42%, 50-74 44%, 75-99 46%, 100-199 48%, 20-499 50%, 500+ 52%. 180pp; 5½×8½; of. Reporting time: 60 days. Simultaneous submissions accepted: yes. Publishes 5% of manuscripts submitted. Payment: 8-10% of net (agreed fraction paid in advance). Copyrights for author if author so desires. PMA.

Algol Press (see also SCIENCE FICTION CHRONICLE), Andrew Porter, Editor & Publisher, PO Box

022730, Brooklyn, NY 11202-0056, 718-643-9011; fax 718-522-3308; sf-chronicle@compuserve.com. 1963. Articles, art, photos, reviews, letters, news items, non-fiction. "Not soliciting material." avg. press run 2M. Expects 1 title 1999, 1 title 2000. 2 titles listed in the *Small Press Record of Books in Print* (28th Edition, 1999-00). avg. price, cloth: $30; paper: $15; other: *S.F. Chronicle* $3.95. Discounts: 40% trade, write publisher. 196pp; 5½×8½; of. Reporting time: 1-3 weeks. Simultaneous submissions accepted: no. Payment: royalties percentage of gross cover price. Copyrights for author.

Alice James Books, Peg Peoples, Program Director, University of Maine at Farmington, 98 Main Street, Farmington, ME 04938-1911. 1973. Poetry. "Alice James Books is a non-profit poetry press emphasizing the work of New England poets. The cooperative was founded in 1973 by five women and two men who'd formed a writer's workshop and a reading series in Cambridge in the early '70's, and who decided to launch a poetry publishing venture at a time when they felt women's literature was not being recognized by male dominated publishing houses. After 25 years, the cooperative has grown into a national community of poets who have participated as past members as well as those who are actively engaged in the publishing process. AJB award-winning poets include B.H. Fairchild, 1998 National Book Award Finalist, 1999 William Carlos Williams Award & 1999 Kingsley Tufts Poetry Award for *The Art of the Lathe*; Timothy Liu, Norma Farber First Book Award for *Vox Angelica*; Jean Valentine, Maurice Poetry award for *River at Wolf*; and Doug Anderson, Kate Tufts Discovery Award for Poetry for *Moon Reflected Fire*. Known for its commitment to both emerging and early career poets, AJB has published books by Jane Kenyon, Robin Becker, Betsy Sholl, Joyce Peseroff, Forrest Hamer, Richard McCann, Erica Funkhouser and Laura Kasischke." avg. press run 1.2M. Pub'd 4 titles 1998; expects 5 titles 1999, 4 titles 2000. 1 titles listed in the *Small Press Record of Books in Print* (28th Edition, 1999-00). avg. price, paper: $9.95. Discounts: bookstores 2-4 books 20%, 5+ 40%; distributors 50%; no discounts to libraries and jobbers. 72pp; 5½×8½; of. Reporting time: 3 months. We accept simultaneous submissions if notified. Publishes 1% of manuscripts submitted. Payment: no royalties; author receives 100 books as part of cooperative's contract with author. Copyrights for author.

Alicubi Publications, Martin Downs, Zara Steinman, 1658 N. Milwaukee Avenue, Box 380, Chicago, IL 60647, e-mail alicubi@earthlink.net. 1998. Fiction, art, photos, non-fiction. "We are looking for exciting gift and coffee-table book ideas. Query first, please. We specialize in publishing fine editors. Also send romance-novel manuscripts." avg. press run 3M. Expects 1-3 titles 2000. avg. price, cloth: $19.95. Discounts: trade 20% short; 60% max. 30pp; 8½×5½; of. Reporting time: varies. Simultaneous submissions accepted: yes. Copyrights for author. Publisher's Marketing Association.

Alioth Press, Mark Dominik, PO Box 1554, Beaverton, OR 97075, 503-644-2927. 1987. "Alioth Press specializes in works on English literature—criticism and reprints of early editions. We regret we cannot accept unsolicited submissions." avg. press run 500. Expects 2 titles 1999, 1 title 2000. 3 titles listed in the *Small Press Record of Books in Print* (28th Edition, 1999-00). avg. price, cloth: $22.50. Discounts: 20% to library wholesalers. 2-300pp; 5½×8½.

Alive Books (see also ALIVE: Canadian Journal of Health and Nutrition), PO Box 80055, Burnaby, BC V5H 3X1, Canada, 604-435-1919; FAX 604-435-4888. Photos, non-fiction. "Alternative health, natural health, natural diet and recipe books." avg. press run 7M. Pub'd 3 titles 1998; expects 6 titles 1999, 10 titles 2000. 14 titles listed in the *Small Press Record of Books in Print* (28th Edition, 1999-00). avg. price, paper: $12.95. Pages vary. Simultaneous submissions accepted: yes. Publishes 30% of manuscripts submitted. Does not copyright for author.

ALIVE: Canadian Journal of Health and Nutrition, Alive Books, Siegfried Gursche, Rhody Lake, PO Box 80055, Burnaby, BC V5H 3X1, Canada, 604-435-1919; FAX 604-435-4888; editorial@ultranet.ca. 1975. Articles, art, photos, cartoons, reviews, letters, news items, non-fiction. "Alternative medicine and natural health." circ. 205M. 12/yr. Pub'd 12 issues 1998; expects 12 issues 1999, 12 issues 2000. sub. price: $34. Back issues: $3 each. 80pp; 8½×11. Reporting time: 2 months. Simultaneous submissions accepted: yes. Publishes 30% of manuscripts submitted. Payment: 18¢ per word. Copyrighted, does not revert to author.

ALLA TIDERS BODER, Tryckeriforlaget, Leif Lindberg, Tumstocksvagen 19, Taby S-18304, Sweden, 08-7567445. 1993. Non-fiction. "Book collecting" circ. 15M. 4/yr. Pub'd 4 issues 1998; expects 4 issues 1999, 4 issues 2000. sub. price: SEK 225; per copy: SEK 52; sample: free. Back issues: SEK 25. 37pp; 210×297mm; of. Pub's reviews: 20 in 1998. Ads: SEK 900/500/200.

ALLEGHENY REVIEW, Brooke Balta, Senior Editor, Box 32, Allegheny College, Meadville, PA 16335, 814-332-6553. 1983. Poetry, fiction, photos, criticism, long-poems, plays. "Editorial staff changes yearly. Publish work by undergraduate college students only, from across the country. *Allegheny Review* has been used as a classroom text. National edition founded 1983; a local version under similar names has been published since 1983" circ. 1M. 1/yr. Pub'd 1 issue 1998; expects 1 issue 1999, 1 issue 2000. sub. price: $6; per copy: $7.50; sample: $5. Back issues: $5. Discounts: 25 copies, $3.00 each for use in classroom. 100pp; 6×9; of. Reporting time: 2 months after deadline. Simultaneous submissions accepted: no. Publishes 5% of manuscripts submitted. Payment: in copies (2), $50 to contest winners (best submission each genre; poetry, fiction). Copyrighted, rights revert to author upon request.

Allergy Publications, Gale Alpin, 1259 El Camino #254, Menlo Park, CA 94025, 415-322-1663, e-mail: alergyaid@aol.com. 1976. Articles. avg. press run 3M. Pub'd 1 title 1998; expects 4 titles 1999. 5 titles listed in the *Small Press Record of Books in Print* (28th Edition, 1999-00). avg. price, paper: $28. Discounts: trade 20%, bulk 40%, agent 12%. 236pp; 5½×8½, 8½×11; of. Reporting time: 6 weeks. Payment: 10% of money received. Copyrights for author.

Allworth Press, Tad Crawford, Publisher, 10 East 23rd Street, Suite 400, New York, NY 10010, 212-777-8395; FAX 212-777-8261; E-mail Pub@allworth.com. 1989. Non-fiction. "Allworth Press publishes guides giving practical legal and business information to creative professionals in the art world and others in book, tape and disk formats." avg. press run 4M. Pub'd 14 titles 1998; expects 26 titles 1999, 26 titles 2000. 53 titles listed in the *Small Press Record of Books in Print* (28th Edition, 1999-00). avg. price, paper: $16.95; other: $14.95 disk. Discounts: mostly 50% plus shipping. 200pp; 6×9; of. Reporting time: 6 weeks. Simultaneous submissions accepted: yes. Publishes 2% of manuscripts submitted. Payment: 10% of retail. Copyrights for author. PMA.

Ally Press, Paul Feroe, 524 Orleans St., St. Paul, MN 55107, 651-291-2652; pferoc@pclink.com; www.catalog.com/ally. 1973. Poetry. "The Ally Press is a publisher and distributor of books and tapes by Robert Bly. It will seek to maintain a blacklist of all Bly material in print through its mail-order service. In addition it publishes a quarterly newsletter detailing Bly's current reading schedule. Those desiring these free mailings can write care of the press. Ally Press is not accepting any manuscripts at this time." avg. press run 1.5M. Expects 2 titles 2000. 14 titles listed in the *Small Press Record of Books in Print* (28th Edition, 1999-00). avg. price, paper: $6.50. Discounts: 1-4, 20%; 4-49, 40%. 60pp; 5¼×8; of, lp. Payment: in copies. Copyrights for author.

Alms House Press, Alana Sherman, Lorraine S. DeGennaro, PO Box 217, Pearl River, NY 10965-0217. 1985. Poetry. "16-24 pages of poetry that works as a collection. We seek variety and excellence in many styles. Each year we publish one or two chapbooks. Costs: $9 handling/reading fee. Chapbook sent to each contributor. Recent winners include Lenore Balliro, and William Vernon." avg. press run 200. Pub'd 4 titles 1998; expects 3-4 titles 1999, 3-4 titles 2000. 11 titles listed in the *Small Press Record of Books in Print* (28th Edition, 1999-00). avg. price, paper: $5. Discounts: 50% bookstores; $10 set of five. 20pp; 5½×8½. Reporting time: 4 months. We prefer not to accept simultaneous submissions. Payment: 15 copies to the author. Copyrights for author.

Alpha Beat Press (see also ALPHA BEAT SOUP; BOUILLABAISSE), Dave Christy, Ana Christy, 31 Waterloo Street, New Hope, PA 18938, 215-862-0299. 1987. Poetry, fiction, articles, art, photos, interviews, long-poems. avg. press run 500. Expects 4 titles 1999, 6 titles 2000. 59 titles listed in the *Small Press Record of Books in Print* (28th Edition, 1999-00). avg. price, paper: $10; other: $5. 75-150pp; size varies; †IBM-PS2. Reporting time: immediately. Simultaneous submissions accepted: yes. Publishes 35% of manuscripts submitted. Payment: copies. Copyrights for author. Index of American Periodical Verse.

ALPHA BEAT SOUP, Alpha Beat Press, Dave Christy, Alpha Beat Press, 31 Waterloo Street, New Hope, PA 18938. 1987. Poetry, fiction, articles, art. "Steve Richmond, Joseph Verrilli, Daniel Crocker, Ralph Haselmann, Kevin Hibshman, Al Aronowitz, Wayne Wilkinson are recent contributors. *ABS* features beat generation, post-beat independent and other international writings." circ. 600. 2+. Expects 2 issues 1999, 2 issues 2000. sub. price: $15; per copy: $10; sample: $10. Back issues: $10. Discounts: 1/2 of cover price to dealers. 75pp; 7×8½; †IBM-PS2. Reporting time: immediately. Simultaneous submissions accepted: yes. Publishes 35% of manuscripts submitted. Payment: copies. Copyrighted, rights remain with author. Pub's reviews: 2 in 1998. §Beat literature. Index of American Periodical Verse.

Alpha Omega Press, John R. Broyles, Morjorie Kinnee, 3198 Brookshear Circle, Auburn Hills, MI 48326-2208, 910-245-3560. 1994. 1 title listed in the *Small Press Record of Books in Print* (28th Edition, 1999-00).

AlphaBooks, Inc., Edward Wallace, 30765 Pacific Coast Hwy #355, Malibu, CA 90265, 310-317-4855, Fax 310-589-9523, e-Mail: alphabooks@aol.com. 1994. Non-fiction. "AlphaBooks, Inc. publishes 'how-to' books, tapes, CD-ROMS , and self-help kits in the areas of healthcare, psychology, preventative medicine, and human potential. It's current feature is a reprint of Dr. David Bresler's classic book *Free Yourself From Pain*, originally published by Simon and Schuster" avg. press run 5M. Pub'd 5 titles 1998; expects 5 titles 1999, 10 titles 2000. avg. price, cloth: $22.50; paper: $12.95. Discounts: quantity discounts available. 150pp; 5½×8½; lp. Reporting time: 2 months. Payment: varies. Copyrights for author. PMA.

Alpine Guild, Inc., PO Box 4846, Dillon, CO 80435, fax 970-262-9378, e-Mail ALPINEGLD@aol.com. 1977. Non-fiction. "Publish books only, aimed at specific identifiable, reachable audiences. The book must provide information of value to the audience." Pub'd 3 titles 1998; expects 5 titles 1999, 3 titles 2000. 12 titles listed in the *Small Press Record of Books in Print* (28th Edition, 1999-00). avg. price, cloth: $29.95; paper: $12.95. Discounts: standard. of. Reporting time: within 30 days. Payment: depends on book, audience, etc. Copyrights for author. PMA, RMBPA.

Alpine Press, S.F. Achenbach, PO Box 1930, Mills, WY 82644, 307-234-1990. 1985. Non-fiction. *"How To Be Your Own Veterinarian (Sometimes)*, by Ruth B. James, D.V.M. We do not read unsolicited manuscripts." avg. press run 15M. Pub'd 2 titles 1998; expects 1 title 1999, 2 titles 2000. 3 titles listed in the *Small Press Record of Books in Print* (28th Edition, 1999-00). avg. price, paper: $19.95. Discounts: 1-2 copies 20%, 3-9 25%, 10+ 30%, freight paid with prepaid orders. 300pp; 8½×11; of. Reporting time: long. Payment: negotiated individually on merits of book. Copyrights for author.

Alpine Publications, Inc., Betty McKinney, Managing Editor, 225 S. Madison Avenue, Loveland, CO 80537, 970-667-9317; Fax 970-667-9157; alpinepubl@aol.com; www.alpinepub.com. 1975. Non-fiction. "We publish nonfiction hardback & trade paperback how-to books for the dog, horse, and pet markets. About half of our sales are by mail order. Our books are high quality, in-depth, thorough coverage of a specific subject or breed. Authors must know their field and be able to provide useful, how-to information with illustrations." avg. press run 2M. Pub'd 7 titles 1998; expects 10 titles 1999, 10 titles 2000. 63 titles listed in the *Small Press Record of Books in Print* (28th Edition, 1999-00). avg. price, cloth: $35; paper: $19. Discounts: 1-4 20%; 5-20 35%; 21-74 40%; 75-99 42%. 200pp; 6×9, 8½×11; of. Reporting time: 8-12 weeks. Payment: royalty. Copyrights for author. ABA, SPAN, PMA.

Alpine Publishing Inc., Tim Anders, 991 Lomas Santa Fe, Ste. C-195, Solana Beach, CA 92075, 619-591-8001, 619-794-7302. 1994. Non-fiction. "Additional address: 6965 El Camino Real, Ste. 105-107, Carlsbad, CA 92009" avg. press run 5M. Pub'd 1 title 1998; expects 3 titles 1999, 6 titles 2000. 2 titles listed in the *Small Press Record of Books in Print* (28th Edition, 1999-00). avg. price, paper: $17. 200pp; 5½×8½; of. Reporting time: 30 days. Publishes 10% of manuscripts submitted. Payment: individual negotiations. Copyrights for author.

Alta Research, Reed White, 131 NW 4th Street #290, Corvallis, OR 97330-4702, 500-288-ALTA; 541-929-5738; alta@alta-research.com. 1983. Photos, non-fiction. "Desire write-ups and information on recreation within easy access of airports in the western states." avg. press run 10M. Pub'd 4 titles 1998; expects 3 titles 1999, 3 titles 2000. 2 titles listed in the *Small Press Record of Books in Print* (28th Edition, 1999-00). avg. price, cloth: $18; other: $26.95. Discounts: 2 books 20%, 3-25%, 6-30%, 12-35%, 24-40%, 48-50%. 500pp; 4×6; of. Reporting time: 30 days. Payment: negotiable. Does not copyright for author.

●**Altair Publications**, Edmond Wollmann, Marsha Kalfsbeck, PO Box 221000, San Diego, CA 92192-1000, e-mail altair@astroconsalting.com. 1995. Art, photos, interviews. "Mostly academically oriented texts." avg. press run 5M. Pub'd 1 title 1998; expects 2 titles 1999, 3 titles 2000. 1 title listed in the *Small Press Record of Books in Print* (28th Edition, 1999-00). avg. price, paper: $20. 300pp; 6×9. Reporting time: 6-8 weeks. Simultaneous submissions accepted: no. Payment: negotiated. Copyrights for author. PMA.

AltaMira Press, Allen Mitchell, Publisher, 1630 N. Main Street, Suite 367, Walnut Creek, CA 94596, 510-938-7243; FAX 510-933-9720. 1995. Non-fiction. "AltaMira Press, a division of Sage Publications, Inc., entered into a publishing agreement with the American Association for State and Local History Press in September, 1995. Under this agreement, AltaMira has assumed marketing, publishing, distributing, and selling of all book titles previously published by American Association for State and Local History Press." avg. press run 2M. Pub'd 22 titles 1998; expects 26 titles 1999, 32 titles 2000. 25 titles listed in the *Small Press Record of Books in Print* (28th Edition, 1999-00). avg. price, cloth: $42; paper: $22.95. Discounts: AASLH members 20%; trade 20%; museum stores, historical sites, book services for museums and related fields 20% 1-4 books, 5-49 30%, 50+ 40% nonreturnable. 200-300pp; 6×9; of. Reporting time: 3-4 months. Payment: every 12 months. Copyrights for author.

Altamont Press, Inc. (see also FIBERARTS), Rob Pulleyn, Publisher, 50 College Street, Asheville, NC 28801, 704-253-0468. 1973. Art, photos. "Looking for a broad spectrum of high quality crafts/arts books." avg. press run 7.5M. Pub'd 50 titles 1998; expects 50 titles 1999, 50 titles 2000. 31 titles listed in the *Small Press Record of Books in Print* (28th Edition, 1999-00). avg. price, cloth: $25; paper: $15. Discounts: all depend on volume, college and university bookstores, foreign; all other wholesale books through Random House and Sterling Publishing Co. 150+pp; 8½×10; of. Reporting time: 1-2 months. Payment: 5%+. Copyrights for author. Publishers Assn. of the South.

The Alternate Press (see also NATURAL LIFE), Wendy Priesnitz, 272 Highway 5, RR 1, St. George, Ont. N0E 1N0, Canada, 519-448-4001; fax 519-448-4411; e-mail natural@life.ca. 1976. Cartoons, news items, non-fiction. "We are not currently accepting manuscripts. We focus on sustainable living and self-reliance issues and the environment and health. Books to date deal with home business and homeschooling." avg. press run 5M. Pub'd 3 titles 1998; expects 3 titles 1999, 3 titles 2000. 3 titles listed in the *Small Press Record of*

Books in Print (28th Edition, 1999-00). avg. price, paper: $15. Discounts: retail 40%. 150pp; size varies; of. Reporting time: 1 month. Simultaneous submissions accepted: no. Publishes 2% of manuscripts submitted. Payment: varies. Does not copyright for author.

Alternating Crimes Publishing (see also AC), Daniel Gallant, Editor in Chief; Danielle Nation, Assistant Extraoridinair, 306 Parham St. Ste 200, Raleigh, NC 27601, 919-834-5433; fax 919-834-2449; e-mail 6studios@mindspring.com. 1985. Poetry, fiction, art, cartoons, long-poems, non-fiction. "Comicbooks, essays, short experimental pieces." avg. press run 2M. Pub'd 1 title 1998; expects 1 title 1999, 2 titles 2000. avg. price, cloth: n/a; paper: $2.95. Discounts: 40%, negotiate with distributors on individual basis. 32pp; 6½x10; of. Reporting time: 16 weeks. Simultaneous submissions accepted: yes. Publishes 10% of manuscripts submitted. Payment: contributor's copies. Copyrights for author. N.C. Writer's Network, Carolina Crime Writer's Assoc.

●**ALTERNATIVE HARMONIES LITERARY & ARTS MAGAZINE, New Dawn Unlimited**, Jerri Hardesty, 1830 Marvel Road, Brierfield, AL 35035, 205-665-7904; fax 205-665-2500; e-mail wytrabbit1@aol.com. 1997. Poetry, fiction, art, photos, cartoons, long-poems, plays, non-fiction. "Any length is fine. Recent contributors: Errol Miller, Susan S. Hahn, Iris Schwartz." circ. 300. 4/yr. Pub'd 4 issues 1998; expects 4 issues 1999, 4 issues 2000. sub. price: $15; per copy: $4; sample: $3. Back issues: $2 or free if one sends postage ($1). Discounts: $1 each for 20 or more. Also considers this rate for worthwhile causes. 40pp; 5½x8½; †of. Reporting time: 3-6 months. Simultaneous submissions accepted: yes. Publishes 15% of manuscripts submitted. Payment: copies. Not copyrighted. Ads: trade only. ASPS.

ALTERNATIVE LIFESTYLES DIRECTORY, HAIR TO STAY, Pam Winter, PO Box 80667, Dartmouth, MA 02748, 508-999-0078. 1994. Reviews. "A comprehensive directory of alternative lifestyle publications. Listings include name/address, phone/fax, ad/issue cost, format/# of pages, and a review of contents by the publisher" circ. 3M. 1/yr. Pub'd 1 issue 1998; expects 1 issue 1999, 1 issue 2000. price per copy: $14.95 + $3.05 p/h; sample: same. Back issues: none. Discounts: 50%. 130pp; 8½x11; web press. Copyrighted. Pub's reviews: 550 in 1998. §Alternatives lifestyles. Ads: $300/$175.

ALTERNATIVE PRESS INDEX, Collective, Alternative Press Center, Inc., PO Box 33109, Baltimore, MD 21218, 410-243-2471. 1969. "The *Alternative Press Index* is a quarterly subject index to alternative and radical publications. Fourth issue is cumulative for year" circ. 700. 4/yr. Pub'd 4 issues 1998; expects 4 issues 1999, 4 issues 2000. sub. price: $225 libraries, $50 individuals; sample: free. Back issues: 50% discount if 3 or more back volumes are purchased. Discounts: $50 individuals, high schools, movement groups. 160pp; 8½x11; of. Copyrighted, reverts to author. No ads accepted.

ALTERNATIVE PRESS REVIEW, Columbia Alternative Library, Jason McQuinn, PO Box 1446, Columbia, MO 65205, 573-442-4352. 1980. Articles, art, photos, cartoons, interviews, satire, criticism, reviews, letters, collages, news items, non-fiction. "Reprints from alternative press magazines, tabloids, newsletter & zines, plus original material covering the entire alternative press/alternative media scene, with an emphasis on periodical reviews & other media reviews." circ. 7M. 4/yr. Pub'd 1 issue 1998; expects 3 issues 1999, 4 issues 2000. sub. price: $16; per copy: $4.95; sample: $6. Discounts: wholesale 5-19 copies 20%, 20-59 40%, 60-99 45%, 100-249 50%, 250+ 55%. 84pp; 8¼x10¾; web offset. Reporting time: 2-3 months. Simultaneous submissions accepted: yes. Publishes 5% of manuscripts submitted. Payment: 2.5¢/word for original contributions, or 1.25¢/word for reprints. Not copyrighted. Pub's reviews: 200 in 1998. §Alternative press, alternative media, alternative social issues & movements, critiques of mainstream media. Ads: $300/$187.50/$135 1/4 page/$120 1/6 page. Independent Press Association.

ALT-J: Association for Learning Technology Journal, University Of Wales Press, Gabriel Jacobs, 6 Gwennyth Street, Cathays, Cardiff CF2 4YD, Wales. 1993. "An international journal devoted to research and good practice in the use of learning technologies within higher education." 2/yr. sub. price: £60 institutions, £40 individuals. Discounts: 10%. 80pp; 17x24.

ALWAYS JUKIN', *Always Jukin'*, Mike Baute, Richard Leatham, 1952 1st Avenue S #6, Seattle, WA 98134-1406. 1985. Articles, photos, interviews, reviews, music, letters, news items, non-fiction. *"Always Jukin'* is a hobby magazine. It is read by a few thousand people in 27 countries who own, collect, repair, buy, sell & trade all vintages of jukeboxes and jukebox parts & related items (records). Each issue averages 10-15 pages of letters, photos, stories, technical tips, and general jukebox related information. Each issue also contains 20-30 pages of ads for all of the above. 90% of the articles are written by the subscribers. The current issue has 12 contributors. All articles must relate to the general area of 'jukeboxes & music.'" circ. 3M. 12/yr. Pub'd 12 issues 1998; expects 12 issues 1999, 12 issues 2000. sub. price: $33 US, $44 foreign; per copy: $3; sample: $3. Discounts: $1 per issue, net cost. 40pp; 10x16; web. Reporting time: same day received. Payment: as negotiated. Copyrighted, rights reverting to author negotiable. Pub's reviews: 12 in 1998. §Books and mags relating to jukeboxes and records. Ads: $200 10x16/$110 7½x10/10¢ classified, $5 min.

Always Jukin' (see also ALWAYS JUKIN'), Mike Baute, Richard Leatham, 1952 1st Avenue S #6, Seattle, WA 98134-1406. 1986. Photos, non-fiction. "We publish books & booklets relating to jukeboxes. In 1988 we published the first *Guide to Collectible Jukeboxes* with over 300 pictures and prices for same. We are now putting together 'How To Repair' manuals for specific jukeboxes. We will do as many manuals as are submitted each year and will do a yearly update of the *Guide to Collectible Jukeboxes*. We also plan to do a 250 page 'Coffee Table' book on the history of jukeboxes: 4 colors and hundreds of photos'' avg. press run 5M. Pub'd 1 title 1998; expects 1 title 1999, 2 titles 2000. 1 title listed in the *Small Press Record of Books in Print* (28th Edition, 1999-00). avg. price, cloth: $14.95-34.95; paper: $14.95. Discounts: 40/45/50. 60pp; 8½×11; web. Reporting time: 2 weeks. Payment: 50% of net profit. Does not copyright for author.

Alyson Publications, Inc. (see also Alyson Wonderland), Scott Brassert, Assistant Publisher; Greg Constante, Publisher, PO Box 4371, Los Angeles, CA 90078-4371, 213-860-6065, Fax 213-467-0173. 1980. "We publish books for and about gay men and lesbians and their children." avg. press run 6M. Pub'd 32 titles 1998; expects 38 titles 1999, 40 titles 2000. 86 titles listed in the *Small Press Record of Books in Print* (28th Edition, 1999-00). avg. price, cloth: $21.95; paper: $11.95; other: children's $15.95. Discounts: standard 40% trade. 200-350pp; 5½×8½; of. Reporting time: 8-10 weeks average. Simultaneous submissions accepted: yes. Publishes unsolicited 5%, agented 50% of manuscripts submitted. Payment: 8-15% net. Copyrights for author. ABA..

Alyson Wonderland (see also Alyson Publications, Inc.), PO Box 4371, Los Angeles, CA 90078-4371, 213-871-1225; Fax 213-467-6805. 1990. "Books for children of gay and lesbian parents." avg. press run 6M. Pub'd 4 titles 1998; expects 3 titles 1999, 4 titles 2000. avg. price, cloth: $15.95; paper: $8.95. 32pp; 8½×11; of. Reporting time: 8-10 weeks. Publishes 5% of manuscripts submitted. Copyrights for author. ABA, NEBA.

Amador Publishers, Adela Amador, Proprietor; Harry Willson, Editor-in-Chief, PO Box 12335, Albuquerque, NM 87195, 505-877-4395, 800-730-4395, Fax 505-877-4395, harry@nmia.com, www.amadorbooks.com. 1986. Fiction. "Not open for submissions of new material until after 2000." avg. press run 3M. Pub'd 2 titles 1998; expects 2 titles 2000. 24 titles listed in the *Small Press Record of Books in Print* (28th Edition, 1999-00). avg. price, cloth: $17; paper: $10; other: $4. Discounts: bookstores 40%, wholesalers 50%. 176-250pp; 5½×8½; lp. Reporting time: varies. Publishes less than 1% of manuscripts submitted. Payment: varies. Copyrights for author. Poets & Writers, RGWA, Rocky Mtn. Book Publishers Ass'n, New Mexico Book Ass'n, Southwest Writer's Workshop.

AMARANTH, Becky Rodia, Christopher Sanzeni, PO Box 184, Trumbull, CT 06611, 203-452-9652. 1995. Poetry, reviews. "Recent contributors: Denise Duhamel, Charles H. Webb, Gary Young, Walt McDonald. Would like to see well-crafted free and formal verse. Dislike Beat work. We run occasional contests with monetary awards. We nominate our best poets for Pushcart Prizes. We're not responsible for correspondence that arrives without a SASE." circ. 1M. 2/yr. Pub'd 2 issues 1998; expects 2 issues 1999, 2 issues 2000. sub. price: $10; per copy: $6; sample: $6. Back issues: $4. Discounts: classroom discounts or even freebies are negotiable. 40pp; 5½×8½; of. Reporting time: 3-6 months for serious contenders. We accept simultaneous submissions if notified. Publishes 10% of manuscripts submitted. Payment: 2 free copies, with option to buy more at 1/3 discount. Copyrighted, reverts to author. Pub's reviews: 2 in 1998. §Would like to receive poetry books and chapbooks for in-house review consideration.

AMBASSADOR REPORT, John Trechak, PO Box 60068, Pasadena, CA 91116, 626-799-3754, E-mail mejhlp@aol.com. 1976. Articles, photos, interviews, reviews, letters, news items. "ISSN: 0882-2123. We are a Christian ministry that is primarily a publisher of exposes dealing with the following subjects: Armstrongism, The Worldwide Church of God, Ambassador University, and the problem of religious cults." circ. 1.5M. 4/yr. Pub'd 4 issues 1998; expects 4 issues 1999, 4 issues 2000. sub. price: $20 (contribution); per copy: $5.00; sample: $5.00. Back issues: varies; send for catalog. Discounts: negotiable. 12pp; 8½×14; of. Reporting time: 1 month maximum. Simultaneous submissions accepted: no. Publishes 5% of manuscripts submitted. Payment: usually in copies, but will negotiate for quality research. Copyrighted, rights revert to author if requested. Pub's reviews: 4 in 1998. §Anything on mind control and cults. Ads: negotiable (We do not usually run ads).

AMBIT, Martin Bax, 17 Priory Gardens, London, N6 5QY, England, 0181-340-3566. 1959. Poetry, fiction, art, photos, reviews, long-poems. "Always looking for material which excites and interests. Suggest contributors read the magazine before they submit." circ. 3M. 4/yr. Pub'd 4 issues 1998; expects 4 issues 1999, 4 issues 2000. sub. price: £22 UK, £24 ($48) USA and overseas; per copy: £6 UK, £8 overseas; sample: £6 UK, £8 overseas. Back issues: recent back nos. £6 UK, £8 overseas; Archival issues £10. Discounts: bookstores 1-11 25%, 12+ 33%. 96pp; 9½×7½; of. Reporting time: 4 months. Publishes less than 5% of manuscripts submitted. Payment: by arrangement. Copyrighted, reverts to author. Pub's reviews: 30+ in 1998. §Poetry. Ads: b&w: £325/£190/£115 1/4 page; colour £500/£280; serial ad discount 20% for 4 issues. ALP.

AMELIA, Amelia Press, Frederick A. Raborg, Jr., Editor, 329 'E' Street, Bakersfield, CA 93304, 805-323-4064. 1983. Poetry, fiction, articles, art, photos, cartoons, interviews, satire, criticism, reviews, parts-of-novels, long-poems, plays, non-fiction. "Fiction to 5M words, occasionally longer; poetry to 100 lines, any form; strong satire; belles lettres to 1M words; criticism to 2M words; translations of both fiction and poetry, same lengths; reviews of small press interest; pen and ink sketches and line drawings; b/w photos with artistic merit. We welcome newcomers and have published the first works in both fiction and poetry of several new writers. *Amelia* sponsors the following annual contests: The Amelia Awards (poetry of all types to 100 lines); The Reed Smith Fiction Prize; The Willie Lee Martin Short Story Award; The Bernard Ashton Raborg Prize for Criticism; The Charles Katzman Journalism Award; The Frank McClure One-Act Play Award; The Hildegarde Janzen Prize for Oriental Forms of Poetry; The Lucille Sandberg Haiku Award; The Eugene Smith Prize for Sonnets; The Charles William Duke Longpoem Award; The Georgie Starbuck Galbraith Prize for Light/Humorous Verse; The Amelia Chapbook Awards. When submitting to *Amelia* be professional in your approach; it is a high quality magazine which uses the very best material available to it. Neatness is always appreciated. More important, have something to say, say it well and economically. Contributors include Pattiann Rogers, Florri McMillan, David Ray, Gary Fincke, Ben Brooks, Lawrence P. Spingarn, Larry Rubin, Maxine Kumin, Merrill Joan Gerber, Knute Skinner, James Steel Smith, Fredrick Zydek, Bruce Michael Gans, Charles Bukowski, Stuart Friebert, Matt Mulhern, Thomas F. Wilson and many others.'' circ. 1.75M. 4/yr. Pub'd 2 issues 1998; expects 4 issues 1999, 4 issues 2000. sub. price: $30; per copy: $9.95 ppd.; sample: $9.95 ppd. Back issues: first four years are sold out. Discounts: contributors 20% on 5 or more copies; classroom 25%. 204pp; 5½×8½; of. Reporting time: 2 weeks-3 months (the latter if under serious consideration). We accept simultaneous submissions with reluctance. Publishes 1% of manuscripts submitted. Payment: $35 for fiction; $2-$25 for poetry on acceptance (also contests). Copyrighted, reverts to author. Pub's reviews: 8 in-depth, plus many brief in 1998. §Poetry and fiction, drama, photography, essays, videos, cassetts, CD's. Will consider university press and small press (quality) ads on exchange basis or $300/$175. Will consider other outside quality ads and reading notices (80¢ per word, payable with copy). CLMP.

Amelia Press (see also AMELIA; CICADA; SPSM&H), 329 'E' Street, Bakersfield, CA 93304, 805-323-4064. 1983. Poetry, fiction, articles, art, photos, cartoons, interviews, satire, criticism, reviews, parts-of-novels, long-poems, plays, concrete art. avg. press run 500-1.75M. Pub'd 2 titles 1998; expects 3 titles 1999, 4 titles 2000. 18 titles listed in the *Small Press Record of Books in Print* (28th Edition, 1999-00). avg. price, paper: $4.95-$8.95. Discounts: bookstore 40%. 20-176pp; 5½×8; of. Reporting time: 2 weeks to 3 months. Simultaneous submissions are rarely accepted. Publishes 1% of manuscripts submitted. Payment: varies. Copyrights for author. CLMP.

AMERICA, Thomas J. Reese, Editor-in-Chief; Robert Collins, Managing Editor; Paul Mariani, Poetry Editor, 106 West 56th Street, New York, NY 10019, 212-581-4640. 1909. *''America* is a journal of opinion that publishes about 10 poems a year.'' circ. 40M. 41/yr. Pub'd 41 issues 1998; expects 41 issues 1999, 41 issues 2000. sub. price: $43; per copy: $2.25; sample: $2.25. Back issues: $2.25. Discounts: call for details. 32pp; 8¼×10½; of. Reporting time: indeterminate. Simultaneous submissions accepted: no. Payment: yes. Copyrighted, reverts to author. Pub's reviews: 200+ in 1998. §General interest. Ads: call for ad brochure or ads@americapress.org. CPA (Catholic Press Association).

America West Publishers, George Green, Desiree Stevens, Marketing Director, PO Box 2208, Carson City, NV 89702, 800-729-4131. 1985. Non-fiction. ''New Age, new science & technology, new spirituality, metaphysics. Some recent contributors: Dr. Taki Anagoston, Dr. Eva Snead, and John Coleman, PhD.'' avg. press run 5M. Pub'd 14 titles 1998; expects 10 titles 1999. 13 titles listed in the *Small Press Record of Books in Print* (28th Edition, 1999-00). avg. price, paper: $16.95. Discounts: bookstores 40%, distributors 50-60%, bulk (over 500) 50%, libraries 20%. 250pp; 5¼×8¼; of. Reporting time: 4-6 weeks. Payment: twice yearly—10% of wholesale net, 5% of retail price. Copyrights for author. PMA.

AMERICAN AMATEUR JOURNALIST, Micheal J. O'Conner, P.O.Box 18117, Fountain Hills, AZ 85269. 1937. Articles, interviews, reviews, news items, non-fiction. ''The editor and address change yearly, in October. 'Official Editor' is an elective office in the publishing organization (American Amateur Press Association)'' circ. 340. 6/yr. Pub'd 6 issues 1998; expects 6 issues 1999, 6 issues 2000. sub. price: $15. 20pp; 5½×8½; of. Reporting time: 1 month. Payment: none. Not copyrighted. Pub's reviews: 1 in 1998. §Amateur (hobby) journalism, printing history, letterpress techniques, desktop publishing, hints on writing. No ads. AAPA.

American & World Geographic Publishing, Barbara Fifer, Special Projects Editor, PO Box 5630, Helena, MT 59601, 406-443-2842. 1970. Photos, non-fiction. ''We are now emphasizing packaging.'' avg. press run 10M. Pub'd 16 titles 1998; expects 18 titles 1999, 15 titles 2000. avg. price, cloth: $29.95; paper: $16.95. Discounts: available upon request. 104pp; 11×8½; of. Reporting time: 12 weeks. We accept simultaneous submissions if marked as such. Publishes 5% of manuscripts submitted. Payment: varies, we have photo-editorial mix. Does not copyright for author. PNBA, RMBPA, UMBA.

American Audio Prose Library (non-print), Kay Bonetti, Director, PO Box 842, Columbia, MO 65205, 573-443-0361; 800-447-2275; FAX 573-499-0579. 1980. Fiction, interviews, parts-of-novels, non-fiction. ''The *American Audio Prose Library* records an annual series of distinguished American prose artists who read from their own work and discuss their life, work, and related matters in a thoroughly researched, in-depth interview conducted by Director Kay Bonetti. Tapes are then distributed nationally for mail order sale to appropriate individuals and institutions. Some tapes are also edited for public radio broadcast (The American Prose Series). A cross section of published writers are invited by *AAPL* to record each year, chosen for balance as to venerability, prominence, region, racial or ethnic background, and gender. *AAPL*'s ultimate goal: comprehensiveness. All *AAPL* materials are deposited with the Western Manuscript Collection of the State Historical Society of Missouri, which serves as *AAPL*'s official listening facility." Pub'd 3 titles 1998; expects 2 titles 1999, 2 titles 2000. avg. price, other: $13.95 for the reading cassette, $13.95 for the interview cassette, $25 for the two cassette set. Discounts: for retail outlets only: 40% for AAPL tapes only. audio recordings of the writer. Payment: royalty 8% of net receipts. AAPL retains copyright of the *recording* (not the work read from).

THE AMERICAN BOOK REVIEW, Ronald Sukenick, Publisher; Charles Harris, Publisher; Rebecca Kaiser, Editor; Rochelle Ratner, John Tytell, Unit for Contemporary Literature, IL State Univ., Campus Box 4241, Normal, IL 61790-4241, 309-438-3026, Fax 309-438-3523. 1977. Reviews. "Length: ideally, 750-1.5M words. Reviewers should be primarily writers. We would like to see more reviews, or review articles, departing from the traditional review form—more innovative material. Contributors: Jamie Gordon, Fanny Howe, Seymour Krim, Andrei Codrescu, etc." circ. 15M. 6/yr. Pub'd 6 issues 1998; expects 6 issues 1999, 6 issues 2000. sub. price: $30 libraries & institutions, $35 foreign, $24 individuals, $40/2 years individuals; per copy: $4; sample: $4. Back issues: $3 (check w/office). 32pp; 11½×16; desktop. Reporting time: 1-2 months. Payment: $50 honorarium per review, or subscription. Copyrighted. Pub's reviews: 250 in 1998. §Literary or closely allied fields. Ads: check w/advertising manager.

American Canadian Publishers, Inc., Arthur Goodson, Editorial Director; Herman Zaage, Art Director, PO Box 4595, Santa Fe, NM 87502-4595, 505-983-8484, fax 505-983-8484. 1972. Poetry, fiction, articles, art, photos, interviews, satire, criticism, reviews, music, letters, parts-of-novels, long-poems, collages, plays, concrete art, news items, non-fiction. "We are categorically against realism in the novel simply because it is by now a bankrupt form. We reject orthodox "story" because it generally tortures the truth to fit the formula. We support the novel that investigates "inner consciousness," that is multi-dimensional and open-structured in language and thought: the novel for the year 2000. Interested? Send SASE for free Catalog full of new examples. *No unsolicited manuscripts.*" avg. press run 1.5M-3M. Pub'd 2 titles 1998; expects 2 titles 1999, 6 titles 2000. 11 titles listed in the *Small Press Record of Books in Print* (28th Edition, 1999-00). avg. price, cloth: $22.95; paper: $15; other: $10-$100. Discounts: 40% to dealers; 50% bulk-class adoptions: rates negotiable. 200pp; 6×9; of. Payment: negotiable. Copyrights for author. Santa Fe Writers Coop.

American Cooking Guild, Doug Greenhut, President, 3600-K South Congress Avenue, Boyton Beach, FL 33426, 561-732-8111; Fax 561-732-8183. 1981. "We specialize in the publication of small cookbooks and will accept manuscripts in that area." avg. press run 10K. Pub'd 7 titles 1998; expects 5 titles 1999, 5 titles 2000. 34 titles listed in the *Small Press Record of Books in Print* (28th Edition, 1999-00). avg. price, paper: $3.95-$14.95. Discounts: 50% or better to trade. 64-96pp; 5½×8½, 8¼×9; of. Reporting time: 2-3 months. Payment: upon request. Copyrights for author.

The American Dissident, G. Tod Slone, 1837 Main Street, Concord, MA 01742, e-mail; members. theglobe.com/enmarge@hotmail.com. Poetry, articles, cartoons, criticism, reviews, non-fiction. "One page max. for poems, 900 words max. for essays. Material should be critical of America, academe, politics, general life, etc. Material should be NEGATIVE, CONTROVERSIAL & CONFRONTATIONAL." circ. 200. bi-annual. sub. price: $14; per copy: $7; sample: $7. Discounts: 10 copies for $50. 56pp; 5½×8½; professional. Reporting time: 1 week - 1 month. Simultaneous submissions accepted: Y. Publishes 5-10% of manuscripts submitted. Payment: 1 copy. Copyrighted, reverts to author. Pub's reviews. §criticism, dissidence, politics. Ads: $60/$30.

AMERICAN FORESTS, Michelle Robbins, Editor, PO Box 2000, Washington, DC 20013, 202-955-4500. 1895. Articles, art, photos, interviews, reviews, news items, non-fiction. "We are looking for factual articles that are well written, well illustrated, and will inform, entertain, and perhaps inspire. *We rarely accept fiction or poetry*. We welcome informative news stories on controversial topics as long as they are well documented and present the issue fairly. Feature stories have a better chance when quotes and anecdotes liven the text. Articles should be neither too elementary nor too technical. A written query is suggested. Manuscripts should be on disc in Microsoft Word or convertible software, accompanied by double-spaced hard copy, and should not exceed 1,200 words. Include SASE with submissions." circ. 25M. 4/yr. Pub'd 4 issues 1998; expects 4 issues 1999, 4 issues 2000. sub. price: $25 membership; per copy: $3; sample: $2 postage w/SASE. 40pp; 8×10⅞; web. Reporting time: 8 weeks. Payment: full length feature articles, *with photo or other illustrative support* ranges from $300 to $1,000; cover photos $400. Copyrighted, reverts to author. Pub's reviews: 10 in 1998. §Trees, forests, forest policy, nature guides, forestry. Ads: available on request.

AMERICAN HIKER, American Hiking Society, Gwyn Hicks, 1422 Fenwick Lane, Silver Spring, MD 20910-2160, 301-565-6704. 1977. Articles, photos, cartoons, interviews, reviews, news items. circ. 10M. 6/yr. Pub'd 6 issues 1998; expects 6 issues 1999, 6 issues 2000. sub. price: $25; sample: $2. Back issues: $4 if available. 32pp; 10×13½; web. Reporting time: 6 weeks. Publishes 5-10% of manuscripts submitted. Payment: $25-$50 for briefs, $75-$125 for lectures. Pub's reviews: 20 in 1998. §Books on the outdoors.

American Hiking Society (see also AMERICAN HIKER), Gwyn Hicks, 1422 Fenwick Lane, Silver Spring, MD 20910-2160, 301-565-6704. 1977. Articles, photos, interviews, reviews, news items. avg. press run 10M. Pub'd 6 titles 1998; expects 6 titles 1999, 6 titles 2000. 2 titles listed in the *Small Press Record of Books in Print* (28th Edition, 1999-00). Discounts: please inquire. 28pp; 10×13¼; web. Reporting time: 6 weeks. Publishes 5% of manuscripts submitted. Payment: none. Does not copyright for author.

American Homeowners Foundation Press, Bruce Hahn, 6776 Little Falls Road, Arlington, VA 22213, 703-536-7776. 1984. Non-fiction. "Booklets through books." avg. press run 3-10M. Pub'd 2 titles 1998; expects 3 titles 1999, 3 titles 2000. 3 titles listed in the *Small Press Record of Books in Print* (28th Edition, 1999-00). avg. price, paper: $12.95; other: $7.95. Discounts: standard. 160pp; 5½×8½. Reporting time: varies. Payment: varies. We can copyright for author. PMA.

AMERICAN INDIAN CULTURE AND RESEARCH JOURNAL, American Indian Studies Center, Duane Champagne, 3220 Campbell Hall, Box 951548, Los Angeles, CA 90095-1548, 310-825-7315; Fax 310-206-7060; www.sscnet.ucla.edu/esp/aisc/index.html. 1972. Poetry, fiction, articles, criticism, reviews. "*AICRJ* is a multidisciplinary journal that focuses on historical and contemporary issues as they pertain to American Indians. Some poetry and fiction are also published." circ. 1.2M. 4/yr. Pub'd 4 issues 1998; expects 4 issues 1999, 4 issues 2000. sub. price: $25 individuals, $60 institutions; per copy: $12. Back issues: $7 (varies by year). Discounts: bookstores and jobbers 20%, 40% if 10+. 300pp; 6×9; of. Reporting time: 4 months (articles are refereed). Simultaneous submissions accepted: no. Publishes 10% of manuscripts submitted. Payment: none. Copyrighted, rights don't revert to author, but authors have permission to reprint free. Pub's reviews: 80 in 1998. Ads: $150/$75.

American Indian Studies Center (see also AMERICAN INDIAN CULTURE AND RESEARCH JOURNAL), Duane Champagne, 3220 Campbell Hall, Box 951548, UCLA, Los Angeles, CA 90095-1548, 310-825-7315; Fax 310-206-7060; www.sscnet.ucla.edu/esp/aisc/index.html. 1969. Poetry, fiction, articles, non-fiction. "AISC publishes books of interest to scholars and the general public that address contemporary and historical issues as they pertain to American Indians in addition to the quarterly *American Indian Culture and Research Journal*." avg. press run 1M-2M. Pub'd 1 title 1998; expects 4 titles 1999, 2-3 titles 2000. 5 titles listed in the *Small Press Record of Books in Print* (28th Edition, 1999-00). avg. price, cloth: $25; paper: $15. Discounts: bookstores and jobbers 20%, 10+ 40%. 300pp; 6×9; of. Reporting time: 6 months. Simultaneous submissions accepted: no. Publishes 5% of manuscripts submitted. Payment: varies per project. Does not copyright for author.

AMERICAN JONES BUILDING & MAINTENANCE, Missing Spoke Press, Von G. Binuia, Editor, PO Box 9569, Seattle, WA 98109, 206-443-4693; von@singspeak.com. 1997. Poetry, fiction, art, photos, interviews, satire, parts-of-novels, long-poems, non-fiction. "No line limits. No word limits. Send query with or regarding works of 9,000 or more words. Poetry, short fiction, essays, and interviews that address the interests and concerns of the working class—unionized or not—and what constitutes the 'middle class' in *American Jones Building & Maintenance*." circ. 400. 4/yr. Expects 4 issues 1999, 4 issues 2000. sub. price: $12; per copy: $6; sample: $3. Back issues: $6. 128pp; 5½×8½. Reporting time: 4 months. Simultaneous submissions accepted: yes. Publishes 2% of manuscripts submitted. Payment: $2/page and 1 copy. Copyrighted, reverts to author. Ads: $40 full page.

THE AMERICAN JOURNAL OF PSYCHOANALYSIS, Human Sciences Press, Inc., Mario Rendon, 233 Spring Street, New York, NY 10013, 212-620-8000. 1941. Articles, reviews, non-fiction. "*The American Journal of Psychoanalysis* was founded by Dr. Karen Horney, and is sponsored by the Association for the Advancement of Psychoanalysis of the Karen Horney Psychoanalytic Institute and Center. Its purpose is to communicate modern concepts of psychoanalytic theory and practice, and related investigations in allied fields. All correspondence concerning subscriptions should be addressed to: American Journal of Psychoanalysis, Journal Subscription Dept. Address manuscripts, editorial correspondence, and books for review to: Mario Rendon, M.D., Editor, The American Journal of Psychoanalysis, 329 East 62nd Street, New York, NY 10021" circ. 1M. 4/yr. Pub'd 4 issues 1998; expects 4 issues 1999, 4 issues 2000. sub. price: indiv. $34, instit. $135. Back issues: Contact: J.S. Canner & Co., Inc., 10 Charles St, Needham Hts, MA 02194. Discounts: 5% to subscription agents. 96pp; 6½×9½; of. Reporting time: 3 months. Payment: none. Copyrighted, does not revert to author. Pub's reviews: 3 in 1998. §Books on psychology, psychoanalysis, and psychoanalysts.

AMERICAN JOURNALISM REVIEW, Rem Rieder, Editor; Jean Cobb, Managing Editor, 8701 Adelphi Road, Adelphi, MD 20783-1716. 1977. Non-fiction. "Please read the magazine before submitting queries or manuscripts." circ. 25M. 10/yr. Pub'd 10 issues 1998; expects 10 issues 1999, 10 issues 2000. sub. price: $24.95; per copy: $2.95; sample: $4.50. Back issues: $4.50 each. 52pp; 8½×11¼; web of. Reporting time: 3-4 weeks. We sometimes accept simultaneous submissions. Publishes (unsolicited) 10% of manuscripts submitted.

Payment: $1 flat fee for front-of-the-book section, "Free Press" Copyrighted, rights revert to author 1 year after publication. Pub's reviews: 15 in 1998. §Journalism. Ads: $5980 B&W; $7445 Color.

AMERICAN LETTERS & COMMENTARY, Anna Rabinowitz, Jeanne Marie Beaumont, 850 Park Avenue, Suite 5B, New York, NY 10021, fax 212-327-0706; email rabanna@aol.com; amleters.org. 1988. Poetry, fiction, articles, art, criticism, reviews, non-fiction. "AL&C is an eclectic literary magazine featuring innovative and challenging writing in all forms. Past contributors include Michael Heller, Stephen Dixon, Barbara Guest, Paul Hoover, Clayton Eshleman, Ann Lauterbach, David Lehman, Donald Revell, Diane Glancy, C.D. Wright, Denise Duhamel. Particularly interested in creative non-fiction and the personal essay, literary but not academic in tone. Recent examples include Kathleen Norris on "Deserts" and Suzanne Fox on the domestic side of Sherlock Holmes. Open to new and lively voices in all genres." circ. 850. 1/yr. Pub'd 1 issue 1998; expects 1 issue 1999, 1 issue 2000. sub. price: $6; per copy: $6; sample: $6. Back issues: $5. Discounts: 2 year sub. $10; 3 year sub $15. 144pp; 7×8; of. Reporting time: 2 weeks-4 months. We accept simultaneous submissions if advised. Payment: copies. Copyrighted, reverts to author. Pub's reviews: 1 in 1998. §Poetry, literary fiction and nonfiction (biography, essays, memoirs, letters, etc.). Ads: $50/$30/exchange ads.

American Literary Press Inc./Noble House, Kimberly Barker, Managing Editor, 8019 Belair Road #10, Baltimore, MD 21236, 410-882-7700; fax 410-882-7703; e-mail amerlit@erols.com; www.erols.com/amerlit. 1991. Poetry, fiction, long-poems, non-fiction. avg. press run 500-1M. Pub'd 50 titles 1998; expects 60 titles 1999, 70 titles 2000. 129 titles listed in the *Small Press Record of Books in Print* (28th Edition, 1999-00). avg. price, cloth: $19.95; paper: $9.95; other: saddle $6.95. Discounts: 1-5 40%, 6-25 43%, 26-50 46%. 200pp; 5½×8½; of. Reporting time: 3-4 weeks. Simultaneous submissions accepted: yes. Publishes 20% of manuscripts submitted. Payment: 40%-50%. Copyrights for author. Baltimore's Publishers Association (BPA), North American Bookdealers Exchange (NABE), Mid-Atlantic Publishers Association (MAPA), SPAN.

AMERICAN LITERARY REVIEW, Lee Martin, Editor, Dept of English, University of North Texas, Denton, TX 76203-6827, 817-565-2127. 1990. Poetry, fiction. "Recent contributors: Erin Page, Gordon Weaver, David St. John, Patricia Goedicke, Lex Williford, Charles Wyatt, Mark Jacobs, Miller Williams, Steve Heller, Debra Monroe." circ. 900. 2/yr. Pub'd 2 issues 1998; expects 2 issues 1999, 2 issues 2000. sub. price: $15 individual, $25 institution; per copy: $8; sample: $8. Back issues: $8, if available. Discounts: standard. 128pp; 7×10; of. Reporting time: 8-12 weeks. Simultaneous submissions accepted: yes. Publishes 5% of manuscripts submitted. Payment: 2 copies. Copyrighted, reverts to author. Pub's reviews: 2 in 1998. §Contemporary poetry, short story collections. Ads: $150/$75/$50 must be camera ready. AWP.

AMERICAN LITERATURE, Duke University Press, Cathy N. Davidson, Editor; Michael Moon, Associate Editor, Box 90660, Duke University, Durham, NC 27708-0660, 919-684-3948. 1929. Articles, criticism, reviews. "American literature *only*. This journal of literary history, criticism, and bibliography reaches academics worldwide in literature, history, and American studies. Send review copies to Carol Rigsby, 304E Allen Building, Box 90020, Duke University, Durham, NC 27708-0020." circ. 5.5M. 4/yr. Pub'd 4 issues 1998; expects 4 issues 1999, 4 issues 2000. sub. price: $34 individuals, $80 institutions, $17 students with photocopy of current ID, foreign add $12 postage; per copy: $18. Back issues: single $18; volume $72. 250pp; 6×9; lp. Reporting time: 3 months. Simultaneous submissions accepted: no. Publishes 7% of manuscripts submitted. Payment: 50 reprints. Copyrighted, rights optional with author. Pub's reviews: 175 in 1998. §American literary criticism, scholarship, bibliography. Ads: $325/$225.

AMERICAN LITERATURE SECTION, Duke University Press, Susan Belasco Smith, Executive Coordinator, Box 90660, Duke University, Durham, NC 27708-0660. "The American Literature Section of the Modern Language Association is the sponsoring organization of *American Literature*. (Note: ALS members do not receive *American Literature* as a benefit of membership, but are entitled to a 25% discount on the journal.) In addition to regular membership privileges, ALS members receive an annual hardbound copy of *American Literary Scholarship*." circ. 1M. 1/yr. Pub'd 1 issue 1998; expects 1 issue 1999, 1 issue 2000. sub. price: $20 individuals, $10 students, additional $4 foreign. Ads: $100/$50.

American Living Press (see also WEIRD POETRY), Michael Shores, Angela Mark, PO Box 901, Allston, MA 02134, 617-522-6196. 1982. Poetry, art, collages. "Currently not accepting submissions." avg. press run 250-500. Pub'd 3 titles 1998; expects 2 titles 1999. 10 titles listed in the *Small Press Record of Books in Print* (28th Edition, 1999-00). avg. price, paper: $3.50. 40pp; 5½×8½; †xerox. Reporting time: 2-6 weeks. Payment: 1-10 copies, sometimes pay $5-$10 for work. Does not copyright for author.

American Malacologists, Inc., Cecelia White Abbott, President, 2208 Colonial Drive, Melbourne, FL 32901-5315, 407-725-2260. 1974. Articles, non-fiction. "Publish books on shells and conchology. Latest *Compendium of Landshells*." avg. press run 5M. Pub'd 2 titles 1998; expects 2 titles 1999, 2 titles 2000. 8 titles listed in the *Small Press Record of Books in Print* (28th Edition, 1999-00). avg. price, cloth: $38; paper: $4.95. Discounts: 35-50%. 250pp; size varies; of. Copyrights for author.

AMERICAN MODELER, The Newspaper of Scale Modeling, Robert Thomason, PO Box 273, Whitsett,

NC 27377-0273, 336-449-0809; Fax 336-222-6294; fotodroid@aol.com. 1992. Articles, art, photos, cartoons, interviews, satire, music, news items, non-fiction. *"American Modeler* reports on projects and events of interest to people that are involved in the hobby of scale model construction. This includes plastic manufactured kits and scratchbuilding projects. Submitted material for text should be an average of 14 column inches for events coverage. Length can be longer for interviews and project accounts. Photos submitted should be no larger than 8x10 inches. They can be color or black & white. Photo for cover consideration should be a 35mm color slide." circ. 5M. 6/yr. Pub'd 2 issues 1998; expects 6 issues 1999, 6 issues 2000. sub. price: $14.95; per copy: $2.50; sample: $2.50 + $1 p/h. Back issues: same. Discounts: 55% off retail price to periodical wholesalers and hobby shops. 20-40pp; 11¼×13½; †of. Reporting time: 1 day to 1 month. Payment: photos/art $10 b&w or alone art; $50 color front cover; text $25 unsolicited material; $50 solicited material. Copyrighted, rights reverting to author negotiable. Pub's reviews: 36 in 1998. §Aircraft, armor (military tanks), ships, science fiction/fantasy (movie/TV special effects), automobiles (civilian), model hobby books and publications. Ads: $658/$511/$285 1/4 page/$60 1/16 page.

AMERICAN PHYSICIANS ART ASSOCIATION NEWSLETTER, JB Press, James S. Benedict, Editor, 1130 North Cabrillo, San Pedro, CA 90731, 310-832-7024. 1939. Art, news items. "Articles and information about the American Physicians Art Assn." circ. 300. 2/yr. Pub'd 2 issues 1998; expects 2 issues 1999, 2 issues 2000. sample price: free. 15pp; 8½×11; camera-ready copy. Reporting time: 2-3 months. Payment: none. Not copyrighted.

AMERICAN POETRY MONTHLY, David L. Moore, Editor; Justin Martino, Associate Editor, PO Box 187, Sapulpa, OK 74067. 1996. Poetry. "We consider all styles, lengths and subject matter. Recent contributors include: George Scarbrough, Peter Meinke, Meredith Hasemann, Turner Cassity and Jon Powell." circ. 150. 13/yr. Pub'd 13 issues 1998; expects 13 issues 1999, 13 issues 2000. sub. price: $22; sample: $2.50. Discounts: 15% 25+ copies. 28pp; 5½×8½; laser print. Reporting time: 3-6 weeks. Simultaneous submissions accepted: yes. Publishes less than 1% of manuscripts submitted. Payment: 1 copy. Copyrighted, reverts to author. Ads: $24/$14/$7 50-word classified.

AMERICAN POETRY REVIEW, Stephen Berg, David Bonanno, Arthur Vogelsang, 1721 Walnut St., Philadelphia, PA 19103, 215-496-0439. 1972. Poetry, fiction, articles, art, photos, cartoons, interviews, satire, criticism, reviews, music, letters, parts-of-novels, long-poems, collages, plays, concrete art, news items, non-fiction. circ. 18M. 6/yr. Pub'd 6 issues 1998; expects 6 issues 1999. sub. price: $18; per copy: $3.95; sample: $3.95. Back issues: $5. Discounts: through Eastern News for stores and newsstands. 52pp; 9¾×13¾; of. Reporting time: 10 weeks. Simultaneous submissions accepted: no. Publishes less than 1% of manuscripts submitted. Payment: $1/line for poetry; $60/tabloid page for prose. Copyrighted, reverts to author. Pub's reviews: 30 in 1998. §Literary. Ads: $855/$520. CLMP.

●**American Research Press,** Dr. M.L. Perez, Box 141, Rehoboth, NM 87322, e-mail arp@cia-g.com; website http://www.gallup.unm.edu/~smarandache/. 10 titles listed in the *Small Press Record of Books in Print* (28th Edition, 1999-00).

American Romanian Academy (see also A.R.A. JOURNAL), Dr. Ion Manea, University of California, Dept. of French & Italian, Davis, CA 95616, 916-758-7720. 1975. "Presents scholarly essays of Romanian-American relations and interactions since the beginning of the diplomatic recognition of the Romanian principalities, economic, diplomatic, literary, etc" avg. press run 30-40. Pub'd 2 titles 1998; expects 2 titles 1999. avg. price, cloth: $20; paper: $20. Discounts: 10%. 300pp; 6×9; Private printing Schythian Books, Oakland, CA. Reporting time: 3 months. Simultaneous submissions accepted: no. Publishes 60% of manuscripts submitted. Payment: none. Does not copyright for author.

THE AMERICAN SCHOLAR, Lancaster Press, Anne Fadiman, 1811 Q Street NW, Washington, DC 20009, 202-265-3808. 1932. Poetry, articles, criticism, reviews, letters. "3,000 to 4,000 words best." circ. 25M. 4/yr. Pub'd 4 issues 1998; expects 4 issues 1999, 4 issues 2000. sub. price: $25; per copy: $6.95; sample: $6.95. Back issues: $6.95 and up. Discounts: vary. 160pp; 5½×8; of. Reporting time: 4-8 weeks. Publishes .5% of manuscripts submitted. Payment: $500 per article. Copyrighted. Pub's reviews: 25 in 1998. §Literary, cultural, contemporary. Ads: $695/$555.

AMERICAN SHORT FICTION, Joseph Kruppa, Parlin 108 English Department, University of Texas-Austin, Austin, TX 78712-1164, 512-471-1772. 1990. Fiction. circ. 2M. 4/yr. Pub'd 4 issues 1998; expects 4 issues 1999, 4 issues 2000. sub. price: $24; per copy: $9.95; sample: $9.95. Back issues: $9.95. Discounts: agent 10%, trade 1 20%, 3 40%, 25 42%, 100 44%, 250 46%, 750 47%. 128pp; 5¾×9¼. Reporting time: 3 months. We accept simultaneous submissions, but please notify in cover letter. Publishes less than 1% of manuscripts submitted. Payment: $400. Copyrighted, reverts to author. Ads: $250/$150. AAUP.

American Source Books, a division of Impact Publishers, Robert E. Alberti, Publisher, PO Box 6016, Atascadero, CA 93423-6016, 805-466-5917; Fax 805-466-5919. 1988. Non-fiction. avg. press run 5M. Pub'd 2 titles 1998; expects 2 titles 1999, 3 titles 2000. 4 titles listed in the *Small Press Record of Books in Print* (28th

Edition, 1999-00). avg. price, paper: $13. Discounts: 1-4 25% ppd., 5-49 40%, 50-99 42%, 100+ 44%. 150pp; 6×9; of. Reporting time: 2 months. We accept simultaneous submissions with notification. Publishes 1% of manuscripts submitted. Payment: 10% royalty on net. Copyrights for author. PMA.

AMERICAN TANKA, Laura Maffei, PO Box 120-024, Staten Island, NY 10312-0024, email editor@americantanka.com; web site www.americantanka.com. 1996. Poetry. "This journal is dedicated exclusively to English-language tanka poetry" circ. 100. 2/yr. Pub'd 1 issue 1998; expects 2 issues 1999, 2 issues 2000. sub. price: $16; per copy: $8; sample: $8. 80pp; 5½×8½; of. Reporting time: 4-6 weeks. Simultaneous submissions accepted: no. Publishes 15-20% of manuscripts submitted. Payment: 1 copy. Copyrighted, reverts to author. Ads: none.

THE AMERICAN VOICE, Frederick Smock, 332 West Broadway, #1215, Louisville, KY 40202, 502-562-0045. 1985. Poetry, fiction, articles, photos, interviews, criticism. "We publish daring new writers, and the more radical work of established writers from Canada, the U.S., *and* South America. At least half of our contributors are women. Recent contributors include Marge Piercy, Sergio Ramirez, Isabel Allende, Joan Givner, Jamake Highwater, Wendell Berry, Bienvenido Santos, Ernesto Cardenal, Chaim Potok, Key Boyle, Sharon Doubiago, Linda Hogan, Olga Broumas. We are open to all forms." circ. 2M. 3/yr. Pub'd 3 issues 1998; expects 3 issues 1999, 3 issues 2000. sub. price: $15; per copy: $5; sample: $7. Back issues: $7. 150pp; 6×9; of. Reporting time: 6 weeks. Payment: varies. Copyrighted, reverts to author. Pub's reviews: 1 in 1998. Ads: swap full-page ads only. CLMP.

AMERICAN WRITING: A Magazine, Nierika Editions, Alexandra Grilikhes, 4343 Manayunk Avenue, Philadelphia, PA 19128. 1990. Poetry, fiction, articles, interviews, criticism, letters, parts-of-novels, long-poems, collages, plays, concrete art, non-fiction. "We are open to all forms. We encourage experimentation in writing and welcome the innovative idea. We are more interested in the new work itself than in the fame or publication credits of the writers. The subtext of much of what we publish has to do with the powers of intuition. It's a good idea to look at an issue before submitting- but certainly not required. 3000 word max for prose." circ. 1M. 2/yr. Pub'd 2 issues 1998; expects 2 issues 1999, 2 issues 2000. sub. price: $10/yr. individual; $18/yr. institutions; per copy: $6; sample: $6. Back issues: $6. Discounts: negotiable. 80pp; 5⅜×8½; of. Reporting time: 2 months average, sometimes 3-4; depends on volume of submissions which is very high. Publishes 2% of manuscripts submitted. Payment: copies; discount to contributors on additional copies. Copyrighted, reverts to author. Ads: none.

Americana Books, David G. MacLean, PO Box 14, Decatur, IN 46733, 219-728-2810; Fax 219-724-9755; E-mail maclean@amerbook.com. 1968. "Our focus is bibliographies and material of interest to the antiquarian book trade. Most of our publications have been centered on a regional author, Gene Stratton-Porter. Not seeking submissions." avg. press run 1M hardback, 2M paperback. Expects 1 title 1999, 1 title 2000. 4 titles listed in the *Small Press Record of Books in Print* (28th Edition, 1999-00). avg. price, cloth: $18.95; paper: $6.95. Discounts: 1-2 20%, 3-9 40%, 10+ 50%. 175pp; 5½×8½; of. Payment: negotiable. Copyrights for author.

Americans for the Arts/ACA Books (see also ARTSLINK), J.R. Wells, Director of Sales, One East 53rd Street, New York, NY 10022-4201, 212-223-2787; fax 212-753-1325. 1968. Articles, news items. "Interested in material on arts administration, legislation affecting all the arts, news on all art forms. Arts research & policy studies. No submissions accepted at this time." avg. press run 3M. Pub'd 3 titles 1998; expects 5 titles 1999, 5 titles 2000. 21 titles listed in the *Small Press Record of Books in Print* (28th Edition, 1999-00). avg. price, paper: $18.95. Discounts: discounts for members; all othr orders are 5+ with non-return only. 200pp; 6×9, 8½×11. Simultaneous submissions accepted: no. Payment: varies. Copyrights for author.

AMERICAS REVIEW, Gerald Gray, Karen Joy Fowler, Mary Hower, Glenn Keyser, Kieran Ridge, Hannah Stein, PO Box 72466, Davis, CA 95617. 1985. Poetry, fiction, art, cartoons, satire, long-poems, plays. "Poems range from one page to twelve pages. Stories vary in length. Content generally has a political sense, dealing with events in the U.S. since the Civil Rights Movement and the countries in Europe and Latin America since about the same time." circ. 1M. 1/yr. Pub'd 1 issue 1998; expects 1 issue 1999, 1 issue 2000. sub. price: $7 individual, $10 institution; per copy: same; sample: $5 indiv., $7 institution. Back issues: $5 individual, $7 institution. Discounts: 40/60. 75pp; 6×9; photo offset. Reporting time: 5 months. Simultaneous submissions accepted: yes. Publishes 5% of manuscripts submitted. Payment: 1 copy of magazine in which their work appears. Copyrighted, reverts to author. Ads: $100/$50.

Amethyst & Emerald, Cathyann Ortiz, Editor-Publisher, 1556 Halford Avenue, Suite 124, Santa Clara, CA 95051-2661, 408-296-5483; fax 408-249-7646. 1997. Poetry, non-fiction. avg. press run 500. Pub'd 1 title 1998; expects 3 titles 1999, 3 titles 2000. 3 titles listed in the *Small Press Record of Books in Print* (28th Edition, 1999-00). avg. price, paper: $14. 150pp; 5½×8½; of. Reporting time: 2 months. Simultaneous submissions accepted: yes.

THE AMETHYST REVIEW, Penny Ferguson, Lenora Steele, 23 Riverside Avenue, Truro, N.S. B2N 4G2, Canada, 902-895-1345. 1992. Poetry, fiction, art, long-poems, plays. "Primarily uses poetry & fiction. Poetry to

200 lines each. Submit 3-5 poems. Fiction to 5,000 words. Contemporary, unpublished work. Black ink art work only. Will consider other written creative forms if within length limits. No manuscripts responded to without SASE. Americans must use IRCs or Canadian postage—not US postage." circ. 150-200. 2/yr. Pub'd 2 issues 1998; expects 2 issues 1999, 2 issues 2000. sub. price: $12CAN; per copy: $6CAN; sample: $6CAN. Back issues: $4CAN. Discounts: individually negotiated. 84pp; 6¾x8½; of. Reporting time: 6 months max. Simultaneous submissions accepted: no. Publishes 10% of manuscripts submitted. Payment: 1 copy. Copyrighted, reverts to author. Pub's reviews: 1 in 1998. §We only publish reviews about books by authors we've published. Ads: $80/$40/$20 1/4 page.

Amherst Media, Inc., Craig Alesse, P.O. Box 586, Amherst, NY 14226, 716-874-4450. 1976. "We publish how-to photography books. We distribute for 50 other presses into photo retailers." avg. press run 5M. Pub'd 6 titles 1998; expects 6 titles 1999, 9 titles 2000. avg. price, paper: $29.95. Discounts: 40% stores, 20% schools. 160pp; 8½x11; of. Reporting time: 6 weeks. Publishes 40% of manuscripts submitted. Payment: negotiable. Copyrights for author.

Amherst Press, Ed Gahona, Publisher, Fiction Editor; Susan Mason, Non-Fiction Editor, 3380 Sheridan Drive, Suite 365, Amherst, NY 14226, 716-633-5434 phone/fax. 1995. "Fiction and non-fiction-all categories and genres. Prefered submission is outline with complete manuscript. Queries and sample chapters are not wanted. SASE is required or else material is recycled. Please, no phone calls. Prefer 300-400 pages max. No poetry, no children's." avg. press run 5M. Expects 2 titles 1999, 5 titles 2000. avg. price, cloth: $20-25; paper: $6.95. Discount returns: 1-4 copies 20%, 5-24 40%, 25-49 42%, 50-99 45%, 100-249 48%, 250-999 50%; libraries: 1-9 copies 10%, 10+ 15%. 325pp; 5½x8½. Reporting time: 3 weeks. Publishes a variable % of manuscripts submitted. Payment: Std. paperback/hardcover 10-12½%. Copyrights for author.

Amherst Writers & Artists Press, Inc. (see also PEREGRINE), Pat Schneider, Editor; Nancy Rose, Managing Editor, PO Box 1076, Amherst, MA 01004, 413-253-7764 phone/fax; e-mail awapress@javan-et.com. 1981. Poetry, fiction, reviews. "Annual contests in poetry and fiction: $500 prizes and publication in *Peregrine*. Send for guidelines." avg. press run 500-1M. Pub'd 3 titles 1998; expects 3 titles 1999, 3 titles 2000. 15 titles listed in the *Small Press Record of Books in Print* (28th Edition, 1999-00). avg. price, paper: $8 chapbook, $12 book. Discounts: 40%. 34-90pp; 6x9; of. Simultaneous submissions accepted: yes. Copyrights for author.

THE AMICUS JOURNAL, Kathrin Day Lassila, Editor; Brian Swann, Poetry Editor, 40 West 20th Street, New York, NY 10011, 212-727-2700. 1979. Poetry, articles. "We are a quarterly environmental magazine of ideas." circ. 250M. 4/yr. Pub'd 4 issues 1998; expects 4 issues 1999, 4 issues 2000. sub. price: $10; per copy: $2.50; sample: $4.00. Back issues: $4. Discounts: none. 56pp; 7½x10½; of. Reporting time: 2 months. Simultaneous submissions accepted: no. Publishes prose 10%, poetry 2% of manuscripts submitted. Payment: $50 on publication for poetry. Copyrighted, reverts to author. Pub's reviews: 10 in 1998. §Environment, energy, pollution; water, air; land conservation. Ads: none.

Ammons Communications, Ltd., 55 Woody Hampton Road, Sylva, NC 28779, 704-631-0414 phone/FAX. 1995. avg. press run 1M. Pub'd 2 titles 1998; expects 2 titles 1999, 2 titles 2000. 4 titles listed in the *Small Press Record of Books in Print* (28th Edition, 1999-00). avg. price, paper: $9.95. 175pp; 5 1/2x8. Reporting time: 1 month.

AMNESIA, Monica Rex, PO Box 661441, Los Angeles, CA 90066. 1989. "Emphasize shorter literary pieces, poetry, good quality graphic work." circ. 500. 2/yr. Pub'd 2 issues 1998; expects 2 issues 1999, 2 issues 2000. price per copy: $3 U.S., $4 overseas; sample: $3 U.S., $4 overseas. Back issues: $4 U.S., $5 overseas. 50pp; 8x11; †of. Payment: 1 copy. Copyrighted, reverts to author. Pub's reviews. §Art, underground music, new writers. Ads: $50/$25/$12.50 listing.

Amnos Publications, Ann Lampros, 2501 South Wolf Road, Westchester, IL 60154, 312-562-2744. 1984. Non-fiction. "We publish historical studies of the early Christian Church, based upon the teachings of the Eastern Orthodox Church." avg. press run 7M. Pub'd 2 titles 1998; expects 2 titles 1999, 2 titles 2000. 3 titles listed in the *Small Press Record of Books in Print* (28th Edition, 1999-00). avg. price, paper: $7.95. Discounts: trade. 175pp; 6x9. Does not copyright for author.

AMSTERDAM CHRONICLE, Grace Hogan, Michael Hogan, Kanaalstraat 66 huis, 1054XK Amsterdam, Holland. 1997. Articles, criticism, letters, news items, non-fiction. circ. 200. Pub'd 4 issues 1998; expects 3 issues 1999. sub. price: $25 for 6 issues; per copy: $5; sample: $5. Discounts: none. 60pp; †xerography. Payment: none. Copyrighted. Pub's reviews. §Politics, current events, philosophy, sociology, economics, etc. Ads: $100 US, f200(gulden)/$50 US, f100/$25 US, f50 1/4 page/$200 US, f400 inside or back cover.

AMUSING YOURSELF TO DEATH, Ruel Gaviola, PO Box 91934, Santa Barbara, CA 93190-1934, E-mail rgaviola@aol.com. 1997. Articles, art, cartoons, interviews, criticism, reviews, letters, news items, non-fiction. "*AYTD* reviews, reports on and promotes zines. Send a stamp/IRC for the *AYTD* mailorder catalog." circ. 5M.

6/yr. Pub'd 9 issues 1998; expects 6 issues 1999, 6 issues 2000. sub. price: $18 US only; per copy: $3, $4 Canada/Mexico, $5 world; sample: same. 48pp; 8½×11; web. Reporting time: 2 months. Simultaneous submissions accepted: yes. Publishes 10% of manuscripts submitted. Payment: copy. Copyrighted, reverts to author. Pub's reviews: 1000 in 1998. §Zines only with circulation under 5,000. Ads: inquire.

Ana Libri Press, PO Box 5961, Bellingham, WA 98227-5961, 360-715-1836; Fax 360-715-1869; ana-libri@themysterybox.com; web themysterybox.com. 1996. Fiction, non-fiction. "Ana Libri Press seeks to publish artful combinations of fictional entertainment and creative non-fiction that explore the realms of history, art, and the humanities." avg. press run to be determined. Pub'd 1 title 1998; expects 1 title 1999, 2 titles 2000. 1 title listed in the *Small Press Record of Books in Print* (28th Edition, 1999-00). avg. price, cloth: $24.95; paper: $16.95. Discounts: 2-9 copies 20%, 10-99 40%, 100-199 45%, 200+ 50%. 240pp; 6×9. Reporting time: within 2 months. Payment: to be determined. Copyrights for author. PMA, Book Publishers Northwest (BPNW).

Anabiosis Press (see also ALBATROSS), Richard Smyth, Richard Brobst, PO Box 7787, North Port, FL 34287-0787. 1991. "Send chapbook ms with name, address, and phone number on title page. 16-24 pages of poetry. $7 reading fee, for which entrants receive one copy of winner's chapbook. Deadline is May 31 of each year. Winners gets $100 and 25 copies. Send ms to Chapbook Contest, R. Brobst, Editor, at above address." avg. press run 1M. Pub'd 1 title 1998; expects 1 title 1999, 1 title 2000. 6 titles listed in the *Small Press Record of Books in Print* (28th Edition, 1999-00). avg. price, paper: $3.50. 16-24pp; 5½×8½; OF. Payment: $100 to winner and 25 copies. Copyrights for author.

Anacus Press, Inc., Christian Glazar, Publisher, PO Box 4544, Warren, NJ 07059-0544, 908-748-0400; email anacus@worldnet.att.net. 1985. Non-fiction. "We publish a series of books on bicycling." avg. press run 2M. Pub'd 2 titles 1998; expects 5 titles 1999, 5 titles 2000. 9 titles listed in the *Small Press Record of Books in Print* (28th Edition, 1999-00). avg. price, paper: $14.95. Discounts: 40%-50% retail, 55% wholesale. 160pp; 5¼×8¼; of. Reporting time: 1 month. Payment: 10% of net first 2,000 copies, 15% of net on balance; bid twice a year; usually $500 advance. Copyrights for author. Small Press Association.

ANAIS: An International Journal, Gunther Stuhlmann, PO Box 276, Becket, MA 01223, 413-623-5170. 1983. Poetry, fiction, articles, art, photos, criticism, reviews, letters. "Most material is assigned but we invite critical, biographical essays on Anais Nin, Henry Miller, Otto Rank, et al." circ. 1M. 1/yr. Pub'd 1 issue 1998; expects 1 issue 1999, 1 issue 2000. sub. price: $8, $9 outside US., $12.50 libraries (foreign $14); per copy: same; sample: $8, $9 outside US. Back issues: same. 136pp; 6×9. Reporting time: 4 weeks (SASE required). Simultaneous submissions accepted: no. Copyrighted, reverts to author. Pub's reviews: 12 in 1998. §Diaries, feminism, psychoanalysis, surrealism, literary life Paris 1930-1940s, French, Japanese lit. Ads: none. CELJ.

Anamnesis Press, Keith Allen Daniels, Toni L. Montealegre, PO Box 51115, Palo Alto, CA 94303-0688, 415-244-8366; fax 415-255-3190; web site ourworld.compuserve.com/homepages/anamnesis/ E-mail:anamnesis@compuserve.com. 1990. Poetry, art, photos, non-fiction. "Anamnesis Press is a small, independent publisher of unusual nonfiction and poetry. We publish 2-3 books per year, but hope to expand in the future. In addition to science fiction, fantasy and horror poetry by established names in the field, we publish nonfiction on topics ranging from education to telecommunications. Not currently seeking unsolicited manuscripts." avg. press run 500. Pub'd 3 titles 1998; expects 4 titles 1999, 3 titles 2000. 11 titles listed in the *Small Press Record of Books in Print* (28th Edition, 1999-00). avg. price, cloth: $29.95; paper: $12.95; other: $3 per book on disk. Discounts: available on request. 5½×8½; PC-based desktop publishing, electronic publishing on the Internet and on disk. Reporting time: 2 weeks or less. Simultaneous submissions accepted: no. Publishes 2% of manuscripts submitted. Payment: $100-$200 advance against royalties; royalties typically 10% of cover price. Copyrights for author. PMA.

Ananse Press, Esther Mumford, PO Box 22565, Seattle, WA 98122, 206-325-8205. 1980. Non-fiction. "We do not accept unsolicited manuscripts." avg. press run 5M. Pub'd 1 title 1998; expects 2 titles 1999, 2 titles 2000. 1 title listed in the *Small Press Record of Books in Print* (28th Edition, 1999-00). avg. price, cloth: $12; paper: $8.95. Discounts: 40% trade. 158pp; 5½×8¼; of. Simultaneous submissions accepted: no. Payment: by contract; twice yearly royalty payments; occasionally work-for-hire. Copyrights for author.

Anaphase II, Lily Splane, 2739 Wightman Street, San Diego, CA 92104-3526, 619-688-1959. 1987. Art, satire, non-fiction. "Main publishing interests are handbooks and manuals by previously unpublished authors who are considered experts in their fields. We have 3 books in print: *Nutritional Self Defense* by Lily Splane, *Fiction Writer's Companion* by L.M. Shubailey, and *Quantum Consciousness* by Lily Splane. We are planning to publish more titles this year. Other interests include books for young adults (13-18 years) written *by* young adults." avg. press run 500. Pub'd 1 title 1998; expects 3 titles 1999, 5 titles 2000. 4 titles listed in the *Small Press Record of Books in Print* (28th Edition, 1999-00). avg. price, paper: $15. Discounts: distributors 55%, bookstores 40%, special interest groups 25%. 100-250pp; 8½×11, 5½×8½; of, xerox. Reporting time: 4 weeks. Simultaneous submissions accepted: yes. Payment: negotiable. Copyrights for author.

ANARCHIST AGE MONTHLY REVIEW, ANARCHIST AGE WEEKLY REVIEW, Editorial Collective - Libertarian Workers for a Self-Managed Society, PO Box 20, Parkville, Melbourne, Victoria 3052, Australia, 03/8282856; FAX 03/4824371. 1990. Articles, reviews, letters, news items. circ. 500. 12/yr. Pub'd 12 issues 1998; expects 12 issues 1999, 12 issues 2000. sub. price: $40; sample: postage only. Discounts: 1/3 off. 36pp; size A4; †mi. Reporting time: 1 month. Payment: nil. Not copyrighted. Pub's reviews: 6 in 1998. §Anarchism, non-authoritarian movement. Ads: none. Anarchist Associated Press (AAP).

ANARCHIST AGE WEEKLY REVIEW, ANARCHIST AGE MONTHLY REVIEW, Editorial Collective - Libertarian Workers for a Self-Managed Society, PO Box 20, Parkville, Melbourne, Victoria 3052, Australia, 03/8282856; FAX 03/4844371. 1990. Articles, reviews, letters, news items. circ. 100. 50/yr. Pub'd 50 issues 1998; expects 50 issues 1999, 50 issues 2000. sub. price: $70 (includes p/h); sample: postage only. Discounts: 1/3 off. 4pp; size A4; †mi. Reporting time: 1 month. Payment: nil. Not copyrighted. Pub's reviews: 6 in 1998. §Anarchism, non-authoritarian movement. Ads: none. Anarchist Associated Press (AAP).

ANARCHIST STUDIES, Thomas V. Cahill, 10 High Street, Knapwell, Cambridge CB3 8NR, United Kingdom. 1993. "A refereed journal covering all aspects of contemporary anarchist research and theory." 2/yr. Expects 2 issues 1999, 2 issues 2000. sub. price: £32, $55 US institutions; £16, $30 US individuals; per copy: £16, $30. Discounts: trade terms - less 10% for cash with order, or payment before start of year of publication. 96pp; Crown quarto; of. Reporting time: 3 months. Simultaneous submissions accepted: no. Publishes 25% of manuscripts submitted. Payment: none. Copyrighted, does not revert to author. Pub's reviews: 20 in 1998. §Anarchist, libertarian, politics, history. Ads: £100/£50.

Ancient City Press, Mary A. Powell, President; Marta Weigle, Secretary-Treasurer, Editor, PO Box 5401, Santa Fe, NM 87502, 505-982-8195. 1961. Non-fiction. "Booklets through book-length." avg. press run 2M-5M. Pub'd 5 titles 1998; expects 6 titles 1999, 5 titles 2000. 59 titles listed in the *Small Press Record of Books in Print* (28th Edition, 1999-00). avg. price, cloth: $32; paper: $17; other: $15. Discounts: 40% trade; standard for individuals; 50% distributors. 48pp booklet, 300pp book; 6×9. Reporting time: 1-4 months. Payment: contracts negotiated individually, royalties paid once a year. Copyrights for author. Rocky Mountain Book Publishers Association, New Mexico Book Assn.

and books, Janos Szebedinszky, Editor, 702 South Michigan, Suite 836, South Bend, IN 46601. 1978. Art, photos, non-fiction. "Encourage non-fiction mss on computers, alternative materials, Blues music. Please query first with outline" avg. press run 2M. Pub'd 10 titles 1998; expects 10 titles 1999, 15 titles 2000. 12 titles listed in the *Small Press Record of Books in Print* (28th Edition, 1999-00). avg. price, paper: $12. Discounts: 1-4 copies 10%, 5-14 30%, 15+ $40%. 200pp; 6×9; of. Reporting time: 3 months. Payment: 6%-10%. Copyrights for author.

Anderson Press, Barbara S. Anderson, President; Martin B. Tittle, Administrative Assistant, 706 West Davis, Ann Arbor, MI 48103, 734-995-0125; 734-994-6182; fax 734-994-5207. 1987. Photos, criticism, reviews, music, non-fiction. "Specialized music books welcome." avg. press run 1M. Pub'd 2 titles 1998; expects 2 titles 1999, 2 titles 2000. 2 titles listed in the *Small Press Record of Books in Print* (28th Edition, 1999-00). avg. price, cloth: $14.95; paper: $9.95. Discounts: Regular: 1-2 net; 3-99, 40%; 100, 45%; returnable; for non-returnable, 5% add'l Short: 1-2 net; 3, 20%; returnable; no add'l disc for non-returnable; both schedules + shipping. 32-400pp; 5×7, 9×12; of/lo. Reporting time: 3 months. Payment: royalties accrue on sales but are not paid until our out-of-pocket costs are recovered. Copyrights for author.

●**Andmar Press,** John M. Gist, PO Box 217, Mills, WY 82644, e-mail fjozwik@csi.com; www.andmar-press.com. 1982. Articles, non-fiction. avg. press run 5M. Expects 4 titles 1999, 4 titles 2000. 3 titles listed in the *Small Press Record of Books in Print* (28th Edition, 1999-00). avg. price, cloth: $60; paper: $25. Discounts: contact for guidelines. 300pp; 5½×8½. Reporting time: 1 month. Simultaneous submissions accepted: yes. Publishes 5% of manuscripts submitted. Copyrights for author. PMA, National Publishers Exchange.

●**Andrew Scott Publishers,** E.S. Lev, 15023 Tierra Alta, Del Mar, CA 92014, 619-755-0715; e-mail andrewscottpublishers@juno.com. 1998. Fiction. "Dedicated to advance informative, realistic mysteries. Prescription for terror is our debut novel." avg. press run 2M. Expects 2 titles 1999, 1 title 2000. 1 title listed in the *Small Press Record of Books in Print* (28th Edition, 1999-00). avg. price, paper: $11.95. Discounts: 50% non-returnable, 40% returnable plus freight. 240pp; 5½×8½; camera ready. Reporting time: 2 weeks. Simultaneous submissions accepted: no. Publishes 5% of manuscripts submitted. Copyrights for author. PMA.

Androgyne Books, Ken Weichel, 930 Shields, San Francisco, CA 94132, 415-586-2697. 1971. Poetry, fiction, articles, art, photos, criticism, collages, plays. avg. press run 500. Pub'd 2 titles 1998; expects 4 titles 1999. 27 titles listed in the *Small Press Record of Books in Print* (28th Edition, 1999-00). avg. price, cloth: $12; paper: $12. Discounts: 40% bookstores, 50% wholesalers. 65pp; 5×7½; of. Reporting time: 3 weeks. Payment: 10% of press run. Copyrights for author.

Angel City Press, Paddy Calistro, 2118 Wilshire Blvd., Suite 880, Santa Monica, CA 90403, 310-395-9982;

fax 310-395-3353; angelcitypress@aol.com. 1992. Photos, non-fiction. "Submit complete proposal. Limit topics to food & history, Hollywood & history, film & television & history (all with photos)" avg. press run 5M. Pub'd 3 titles 1998; expects 3 titles 1999, 3 titles 2000. avg. price, cloth: $22.95. Discounts: depends on quantity 40-55%; stop orders 20%. 128pp. Reporting time: 12 weeeks. Simultaneous submissions accepted: no. Publishes 2% of manuscripts submitted. Payment: 10% of revenues. Copyrights for author. ABA, PMA.

ANGELFLESH, Angelflesh Press, Jim Buchanan, PO Box 141123, Grand Rapids, MI 49514. 1994. Poetry, fiction, art, reviews, long-poems. "I like writing that comes alive on the page-the kind that sticks in your head like a bad dream, or a great fantasy. Recent contributors: Catfish McDaris, Michael Estabrook, Elizabeth Florio, John Sweet, Cheryl A. Townsend" circ. 100-200. 3/yr. Pub'd 1 issue 1998; expects 3 issues 1999, 4-5 issues 2000. 1 title listed in the *Small Press Record of Books in Print* (28th Edition, 1999-00). sub. price: $10 for 3 issues; per copy: $4; sample: $4. Back issues: $4. Discounts: contact editor. 50pp; 5½x8½; †xerox. Reporting time: 1 month. Simultaneous submissions accepted: yes. Publishes 2%-5% of manuscripts submitted. Payment: 1 copy. Copyrighted, reverts to author. Ads: $50/$30/$.10 per word.

Angelflesh Press (see also ANGELFLESH), Jim Buchanan, PO Box 141123, Grand Rapids, MI 49514. 1994. Poetry, fiction, art, cartoons, reviews, parts-of-novels, long-poems. avg. press run 100. Pub'd 3 titles 1998; expects 4 titles 1999, 4-6 titles 2000. 1 title listed in the *Small Press Record of Books in Print* (28th Edition, 1999-00). avg. price, other: $3-5. 50pp; 5½x8½; †xerox. Reporting time: usually within 1 month. We accept simultaneous submissions but prefer not to. Publishes 2%-5% of manuscripts submitted. Payment: negotiable. Copyrights for author if requested.

ANGLE, Brian Lucas, PO BOX 220027, Brooklyn, NY 11222-0027, 415-864-3228. 1996. Poetry, long-poems. "Innovative work by younger unknown poets as well as more established poets. Recent contributors include Clark Coolidge, Paul Vangelisti, Bernadette Mayer, Garrett Caples, Ray DiPalma, John Yau, Wayne E. Ludvickson, John Godfrey, Albert Mobilio, Sheila E. Murphy, et al." circ. 100. 2-4/yr. Expects 2-4 issues 1999, 2-4 issues 2000. sub. price: $10; per copy: $3.50; sample: $3.50. Approx. 40pp; 8×11; †xerox. Reporting time: 1 month. Simultaneous submissions accepted: no. Publishes 80% of manuscripts submitted. Payment: copies. Copyrighted, reverts to author. Ads: none.

THE ANGRY THOREAUAN, Rev. Randall Tin-ear, PO Box 3478, Hollywood, CA 90078-3478. 1987. Articles, photos, interviews, satire, criticism, reviews, music, letters, non-fiction. "For more than ten years, the Rev. Randall Tin-ear has been publishing: first a fanzine, and now a MagaZine. During this first ten-year tenure, he has long since burned the envelope of literary device, and yet for all the burgeoning slickness of his single-handedly helmed, internationally distributed magazine, his concepts retain a raw approach that is as intimidating as it is intimate in its onionesque style." circ. 3M+. 3/yr. Pub'd 3 issues 1998; expects 4 issues 1999, 4 issues 2000. sub. price: $15; per copy: $4; sample: $4. Back issues: *AT* #11-18, 20: $4 each. Discounts: selective trades with zines only. 72pp; 8½×11; of. Simultaneous submissions accepted: no. Publishes 3% of manuscripts submitted. Payment: maybe. Copyrighted, reverts to author. Pub's reviews: 1000+ in 1998. §Anything interesting. Ads: send SASE for current rate sheet.

Angst World Library, Thomas Carlisle, Kathleen Carlisle, PO Box 593, Selma, OR 97538-0593. 1974. Fiction, parts-of-novels, non-fiction. "Please query prior to submitting ms. and *always* enclose SASE. *Tragedy of the Moisty Morning* by Jessica Salmonson." avg. press run 100-500. Expects 2 titles 1999, 3 titles 2000. 5 titles listed in the *Small Press Record of Books in Print* (28th Edition, 1999-00). avg. price, paper: $5.95. Discounts: 40% on purchases over 5 copies; 40% to retailers. Pages vary; 5×8; of. Reporting time: 1-2 months. Payment: 25% of net profit + 5 copies, and/or outright purchase. Copyrights for author.

Anhinga Press, Van K. Brock, Rick Campbell, Director, PO Box 10595, Tallahassee, FL 32302, 850-521-9920; Fax 850-442-6323; info@anhinga.org; www.anhinga.org. 1973. Poetry. "The Anhinga Prize is open to all poets writing in English who have not yet published a second full-length book of poetry, carries an award of $2000 plus publication, requires an entry fee of $20US, and is judged anonymously. Send SASE for complete details. Aside from the contest, we publish 1 to 2 manuscripts per year" avg. press run 2M. Pub'd 2 titles 1998; expects 3 titles 1999, 3 titles 2000. 24 titles listed in the *Small Press Record of Books in Print* (28th Edition, 1999-00). avg. price, cloth: $21; paper: $11. Discounts: 40%. 96pp; 6×9; of. Reporting time: varies greatly, contest submissions 10 months. Simultaneous submissions accepted: yes. Publishes 1% of manuscripts submitted. Payment: varies. Copyrights for author.

ANIMAL ACTION, ANIMAL LIFE, Michaela Miller, RSPCA, Causeway, Horsham, West Sussex RH12 1HG, England, 01403-64181. "Material originated and written in house. Animal welfare-orientated." circ. 70M. 6/yr. Pub'd 6 issues 1998; expects 6 issues 1999, 6 issues 2000. sub. price: £5.50, £6.50 overseas; per copy: £1.25; sample: free. Discounts: bulk orders. 32pp; size A4; web (heat set). Not copyrighted. Pub's reviews: 24 in 1998. §Animals, animal welfare.

ANIMAL LIFE, ANIMAL ACTION, Amanda Bailey, RSPCA, Causeway, Horsham, West Sussex RH12 1HG, England, 0403-64181. Fiction, articles, photos, interviews, reviews, letters, news items, non-fiction. "All material originated and written in house.'' circ. 29M-35M. 4/yr. Pub'd 4 issues 1998; expects 4 issues 1999, 4 issues 2000. sub. price: £5, £6 overseas; per copy: £1; sample: free. Discounts: bulk orders. 32pp; size A4; web (heat set). Not copyrighted. Pub's reviews: 6 in 1998. §Animals, animal welfare. Ads: £610/£370/£200 1/4/£130 1/8 page.

ANIMAL PEOPLE, Merritt Clifton, Editor; Kim Bartlett, Publisher, PO Box 960, Clinton, WA 98236-0960. 1992. News items, non-fiction. ''Stressing original investigative reporting, *Animal People* encourages, empowers, and honors cat and dog rescuers, vegetarians who feed the hungry, caring shelter and animal control workers, wildlife rehabilitators, humane educators; everyone who does whatever she or he can, personally, to prevent suffering and set an example of kindness. Coming out 10 times a year, we bring you unprecedentedly prompt, wide-ranging coverage of all the issues and events of concern to animal people. And we keep close tabs on how the national groups spend your donations, routinely publishing budget and salary information obtained from tax filings via the Freedom of Information Act.'' circ. 15M. 10/yr. Pub'd 10 issues 1998; expects 10 issues 1999, 10 issues 2000. sub. price: $24; per copy: $3; sample: send free sample on request. Back issues: $3. 24pp; 10×17; of. Reporting time: 1 week maximum. Simultaneous submissions accepted: no. Payment: none for opinion pieces; 10¢ a word for features. Copyrighted, reverts to author. Pub's reviews: 40 in 1998. §Animals. Ads: $1,155/$578/50¢ per word classified.

THE ANIMALS' AGENDA, Kim Stallwood, Editor, PO Box 25881, Baltimore, MD 21224-0581, 410-675-4566; FAX 410-675-0066. 1979. Articles, photos, interviews, criticism, reviews, letters, news items, non-fiction. ''News + discussion concerning animal rights and environmental issues—hunting, fur-trapping, food animals, lab animals. *Clearing House* magazine for animal rights movement supporters also presents ideas, strategies, & tactics for political change.'' circ. 20M. 6/yr. Pub'd 5 issues 1998; expects 6 issues 1999, 6 issues 2000. sub. price: $24 US, $30 Canada and Mexico, $37 other foreign; per copy: $3.95 US, $4.45 Canada and Mexico, $35 other foreign; sample: $3. Back issues: $3. Discounts: write for bulk rates. 48pp; 8⅛×10⅞; of. Reporting time: 8 weeks. Publishes 10% of manuscripts submitted. Payment: on application. Copyrighted. Pub's reviews: 10 in 1998. §Animals, environmental, general progressive. Ads: $625/$365/$1.

THE ANNALS OF IOWA, Marvin Bergman, 402 Iowa Avenue, Iowa City, IA 52240, 319-335-3931; fax 319-335-3935; e-mail mbergman@blue.weeg.uiowa.edu. 1863. Articles, reviews. circ. 1M. 4/yr. Pub'd 4 issues 1998; expects 4 issues 1999, 4 issues 2000. sub. price: $20; per copy: $6; sample: none. Discounts: 20% for resale. 120pp; 6×9. Reporting time: 90 days. Simultaneous submissions accepted: no. Publishes 25% of manuscripts submitted. Payment: none. Copyrighted, does not revert to author. Pub's reviews: c. 80 in 1998. §History of Iowa and the Midwest; other relevant state and local history. Conference of Historical Journals.

Annedawn Publishing, Don Langevin, PO Box 247, Norton, MA 02766, 508-222-9069. 1992. Non-fiction. ''I now accept unsolicited manuscripts, both of a horticultural and birdwatching nature, from writers in search of publishers.'' avg. press run 10M. Pub'd 2 titles 1998; expects 2 titles 1999. 4 titles listed in the *Small Press Record of Books in Print* (28th Edition, 1999-00). avg. price, paper: $14.95-19.95. Discounts: 1-4 25%, 5-23 40%, 24+ 45%. 128pp; 8¼×10¾; of. Reporting time: 1 month. Publishes 10% of manuscripts submitted. Payment: negotiable. Copyrights for author. PMA.

Annick Press Ltd., Anne W. Millyard, Rick Wilks, 15 Patricia Avenue, Willowdale, Ontario M2M 1H9, Canada, 416-221-4802. 1975. Fiction. ''We cannot accept unsolicited manuscripts any longer.'' avg. press run 10M. Pub'd 28 titles 1998; expects 26 titles 1999, 28 titles 2000. 312 titles listed in the *Small Press Record of Books in Print* (28th Edition, 1999-00). avg. price, cloth: $15.95; paper: $5.95; other: 99¢ (Annikins - 3 X 3). Discounts: order from Firefly Books Ltd., 3680 Victoria Park Avenue, Willowdale,Ont. M2H 3K1, or your favorite supplier. 24-32pp; 8×8, 8¼×10½; of. Reporting time: 3 months. We accept simultaneous submissions if identified as such. Payment: twice a year. Copyrights for author. ACP, Children's Book Centre.

ANQ: A Quarterly Journal of Short Articles, Notes, and Reviews, Dr. Arthur Wrobel, Heldref Publications, 1319 18th Street, NW, Washington, DC 20036-1802, 202-296-5149. Articles, criticism, reviews. ''*ANQ*, formerly titled *American Notes and Queries* is a medium of exchange for bibliographers, biographers, editors, lexicographers, and textual scholars. From sources and analogues to the identification of allusions, from variant manuscript readings to previously neglected archives, from Old English word studies to *OED* supplements, from textual emendations to corrections of bibliographies and other scholarly reference works, *ANQ* provides a needed outlet for short factual research concerning the language and literature of the English-speaking world. We publish signed reviews of critical studies, new editions, and recently published bibliographies. Manuscripts offering only explication de textes are not appropriate. Manuscript length should not exceed 1,600 words in length; must be accompanied by loose stamps and a self-addressed envelope for the return mailings; and must follow the MLA documentation style that includes parenthetical citations in the text and an alphabetized list of Works Cited as described in *The MLA Style Manual* by Walter S. Achtert and Joseph Gibaldi (specifically chapters 4-5.6). *ANQ* also publishes queries related to scholarly research; replies to queries should be sent to the editor for publication in future issues. Authors are responsible for reading and correcting proofs.'' circ. 650. 4/yr. Pub'd 4 issues 1998; expects 4 issues 1999, 4 issues 2000. sub. price: $38 individual, $67 institution; per copy: $16.75; sample: same. Back issues: contact publisher for back issue prices. 64pp; 6×9; desktop. Reporting time: 1 month. Simultaneous submissions accepted: no. Payment: 2 copies of the issue in which the author's contribution appears. Copyrighted, rights revert to author only upon request. Pub's reviews: 25 in 1998. §Bibliographies, new scholarly editions of the major poets, novelists, essayists, and men-of-letters of the English-speaking world, critical studies. Ads: $125.

ANT ANT ANT ANT ANT, Chris Gordon, PO Box 16177, Oakland, CA 94610. 1994. Poetry, art, photos, collages, concrete art. "A haiku-biased collusion of words and images preoccupied with fragmentary investigations into the secret meanings of everyday life. Mostly poems 1-5 lines in length, some up to 10 lines, a few longer (sequences, assemblages, microscopy, etc.), photographs, collages, colligraphy, abstract art, text as image, varying format. Magazine as art rather than magazine about art: no articles, letters, reviews, table of contents, index, or page numbers." circ. 200. 1/yr. Pub'd 1 issue 1998; expects 1 issue 1999, 1 issue 2000. sub. price: $5; per copy: $5; sample: $5. 68pp; 5½×8½; †mi, of, handstamp. Reporting time: 1-3 months. Simultaneous submissions accepted: yes. Publishes 5% of manuscripts submitted. Payment: none. Not copyrighted.

Anteater Press (see also ON PARAGUAY), Lynn Van Houten, PO Box 750745, Petaluma, CA 94975-0745, 707-763-6835; E-mail paraguay@wco.com. 1997. Photos, non-fiction. "Interested in Paraguay and South America." avg. press run 1M. Expects 2 titles 1999, 3 titles 2000. 1 title listed in the *Small Press Record of Books in Print* (28th Edition, 1999-00). avg. price, paper: $16.95. Discounts: schedule available on request. 200pp; 5½×8½. Simultaneous submissions accepted: yes.

THE ANTHOLOGY OF NEW ENGLAND WRITERS, Frank Anthony, Editor; Richard Eberhart, Honorary Advisor; Susan Anthony, Associate Editor, PO Box 483, Windsor, VT 05089, 802-674-2315; newvtpoet@aol.com. 1989. Poetry, fiction. "Each issue a contest issue: *AnthNEW* includes three Robert Penn Warren Awards ($500, $200, $150) and ten each, Honorable Mentions, Commendables, Editor's Choice. Guidelines: Free Verse: Open to ALL poets (not just New England); reading fee $6 for each set of 3 poems (6 poems/$10: one year NEW membership; 9 poems/$15: membership and anthology); unpublished, original poems 30 lines or less; type each poem with title: one page/no name, address; include a 3x5 card with your name, address and poem titles. SASE for winner's list only, poems are not returned. Annual postmark date: June 15. Winners announced at New England Writers Conference, third or fourth Saturday of July. Published in November. Indexed in *The American Humanities Index* and *Index of American Periodical Verse*. Also Short Short Fiction Contest for original unpublished work (no more than 1,000 words) open to all. Postmark date June 15, $6 fee per entry, $500 Marjory Bartlett Sanger Award. Winner published in *The Anthology of New England Writers*. Winners announced at NEW Conference. Mail entries for both contests to Dr. Frank Anthony, New England Writers Contest, 151 Main Street, PO Box 483, Windsor, VT 05089-0483." circ. 400. 1/yr. Pub'd 1 issue 1998; expects 1 issue 1999, 1 issue 2000. sub. price: $3.95; per copy: $3.95; sample: $3.50. Back issues: $3. Discounts: 25%. 44pp; 5½×8½; of. Simultaneous submissions accepted: no. Publishes 10% of manuscripts submitted. Payment: 1 copy. Copyrighted, reverts to author.

Anti-Aging Press (see also SO YOUNG!), Julia Busch, Box 141489A, Coral Gables, FL 33114, 305-661-2802; 305-662-3928; Fax 305-661-4123; julia2@gate.net. 1992. Poetry, articles, cartoons, reviews, non-fiction. "Additional address: 4185 Pamona Avenue, Coconut Grove, FL 33133. Committed to erasing wrinkles on all levels—mental, emotional, physical via books, cassettes, newsletters. Imprint Kosmic Kuprints for spiritual, metaphysical, New Age titles." avg. press run 3M-5M. Pub'd 1 title 1998; expects 2 titles 1999, 2 titles 2000. 9 titles listed in the *Small Press Record of Books in Print* (28th Edition, 1999-00). avg. price, paper: $9.95-$14.95; other: $59.98 binder. Discounts: 1-2 copies 20%, 3-4 30%, 5-199 40%, 200+ 50%; payment with order; returns. 128-256pp; 8½×5½, 6×6; of. Payment: royalty on wholesale, or outright buy. We copyright for author, but depends on individual arrangement. SPAN, PMA, NAIP, FPA, NAPRA, ABA, NPA.

ANTIETAM REVIEW, Ann B. Knox, Fiction Editor; Crystal Brown, Poetry Editor; Susanne Kass, Executive Editor, 41 S. Potomac Street, Hagerstown, MD 21740-5512, 301-791-3132. 1982. Poetry, fiction, photos, interviews, parts-of-novels. "Our stories average about 3,000 words—min. 1,500, max. 5,000. We look for well-crafted literary work. In fiction we like relevant detail and significant emotional movement within the story—something happening to the characters. We expect dialogue, gesture, and image to carry emotional content without resorting to abstract language. Poems to 40 lines. We take work of natives or residents of MD, VA, WV, PA, DE and the District of Columbia, from Sept. 1 - Feb. 1" circ. 1.5M. 1/yr. Pub'd 1 issue 1998; expects 1 issue 1999, 2 issues 2000. sub. price: $5.25; per copy: $5.25; sample: $3.15/$5.25. Back issues: $3.15. 64pp; 8½×11; of. Reporting time: 4-12 weeks. Simultaneous submissions accepted: yes. Publishes 3% of manuscripts submitted. Payment: $50/story; $20/poem. Copyrighted, reverts to author. CLMP.

THE ANTIGONISH REVIEW, George S. Sanderson, St Francis Xavier University, PO Box 5000, Antigonish, Nova Scotia B2G 2W5, Canada. 1970. Poetry, fiction, articles, art, interviews, criticism, reviews. "All submissions from U.S. must be accompanied by Postal Reply Coupons; submissions accompanied by U.S. postage will not be returned." circ. 800. 4/yr. Pub'd 4 issues 1998; expects 4 issues 1999, 4 issues 2000. sub.

price: $22; per copy: $7; sample: $4 accompanied by postage. Back issues: $4. Discounts: 20%. 150pp; 9×6; of. Reporting time: 3 months. Payment: 2 copies only. Copyrighted. Pub's reviews: 40 in 1998. §Literary, biographies and autobiographies of poets, writers, artists. Ads: none. The Canadian Periodical Publishers Association.

THE ANTIOCH REVIEW, Robert Fogarty, Editor; Judith Hall, Poetry Editor; Jon Saari, Book Review Editor; Melinda Kanner, Book Review Editor; Nolan Miller, Associate Editor, PO Box 148, Yellow Springs, OH 45387, 937-767-6389. 1941. Poetry, fiction, articles, satire, criticism, reviews, long-poems, non-fiction. "Recent contributors: Stephen Dixon, Emile Capouya, Gordon Lish, Alan Cheuse, Carolyn Osborn, Lore Segal. No unsolicited reviews accepted." circ. 5M. 4/yr. Pub'd 4 issues 1998; expects 4 issues 1999. sub. price: $35 ($45 foreign), $60 institutional ($70 foreign); per copy: $6.50; sample: $6. Back issues: $6 plus postage. Discounts: 10% to agents. 128pp; 9×6; of. Reporting time: fiction 6-8 weeks, poetry 2-3 months. Simultaneous submissions accepted: no. Publishes 2% of manuscripts submitted. Payment: $10 per page (approx. 425 words). Copyrighted, reverts to author. Pub's reviews: 100 in 1998. Ads: $250/$150. CLMP, OAC, ABA.

Anubian Press, Margarete Saville, Managing Editor; Melanie Warren, Associate Editor, PO Box 12694, Centerville Station, Tallahassee, FL 32317-2694, 904-668-7414; anubis@polaris.net. 1995. Non-fiction. "Well-substantiated exposes and educational books on a variety of topics but geared toward a general audience. No technical books. Prefer lengths of 75,000-100,000 words. Most recently published: expose on historical accuracy of biographical materials using the life of Beethoven as a focus." avg. press run 1.5M+. Pub'd 1 title 1998; expects 3 titles 1999, 3 titles 2000. 1 title listed in the *Small Press Record of Books in Print* (28th Edition, 1999-00). avg. price, cloth: $25; paper: $18. Discounts: bulk up to 50%, distributor/wholesaler 55%, libraries 20%. 300pp; 6×9. Reporting time: 2 months. Simultaneous submissions accepted: yes. Publishes currently 50% of manuscripts submitted. Payment: no advance but 10% on all sales up to 1,000 copies, 20% on 1,001-10,000, 25% over 10,001. Copyrights for author. NABE.

Anvil Press (see also SUB-TERRAIN), Brian Kaufman, Managing Editor; Dennis E. Bolen, Associate Editor; Paul Pitre, Associate Editor, PO Box 1575, Bentall Centre, Vancouver, B.C. V6C 2P7, Canada. 1988. Fiction, plays. "We publish broadsheets, pamphlets and books. Submissions should be accompanied by a sample chapter and outline with query letter. Canadian authors *only*." avg. press run 1M. Pub'd 2 titles 1998; expects 2 titles 1999, 3 titles 2000. 21 titles listed in the *Small Press Record of Books in Print* (28th Edition, 1999-00). avg. price, paper: $12.95; other: $4.95 pamphlet. Discounts: bookstores 40% on orders of 4+ books; 20% to libraries/institutions. 100-200pp; 5¼×8; of, web. Publishes 2% of manuscripts submitted. Payment: 15%. Copyrights for author. Association of Book Publishers of B.C., Association of Canadian Publishers Literary Press Group.

APDG, Publishing, Lawrence Harte, James Harte, Manager of Direct Marketing; Judith Rourke-O'Briant, Manager of Publishing; Nancy Campbell, Project Manager, 4736 Shady Greens Drive, Suite D, Fuguay-Varina, NC 27526, 919-557-2260; fax 919-557-2261; toll free 800-277-9681; toll free fax 800-390-5507; email success@APDG-Inc.com; www.apdg-inc.com. 1994. Non-fiction. "We publish or recruit writers for and in the telecommunications field." avg. press run 2M. Pub'd 1 title 1998; expects 15 titles 1999, 30 titles 2000. 7 titles listed in the *Small Press Record of Books in Print* (28th Edition, 1999-00). avg. price, cloth: $80; paper: $35. Discounts: varies. 250-450pp; 6×9; of. Reporting time: 6 months. Simultaneous submissions accepted: yes. Publishes 5% of manuscripts submitted. Payment: varies. Copyrights for author.

APHRODITE GONE BERSERK, C. Esposito, E. Eccleston, 233 Guyon Avenue, Staten Island, NY 10306. 1995. Poetry, fiction, articles, art, photos, interviews, criticism, reviews, letters, parts-of-novels, long-poems, collages, non-fiction. "AGB is a semi-annual literary journal of erotic art dedicated to publishing the best work reflecting the homosexual, lesbian, heterosexual or bisexual experience. AGB publishes poetry, fiction, photography, memories, essays and art work. Please include a SASE for your work to be returned" circ. 250. 2/yr. Expects 2 issues 2000. sub. price: $12; per copy: $7; sample: $7. 48pp; 5 1/2×8 1/2. Reporting time: immediately to 2 month. Payment: 1 copy. Copyrighted, reverts to author. Pub's reviews. §Poetry, fiction, non-fiction, photography, video or artwork that deals with the erotic.

APKL Publications, Stephen Mark Rafalsky, 42-07 34th Ave., Apt. 4-D, Long Island City, NY 11101-1115. 1977. "APKL is an acronym of the Greek *apokalypsis*, which means uncovering or revelation. We find buried in the collective consciousness of the human race the central archetype of existence; we declare this to be Jesus Christ the resurrected and living Creator, and we publish those works that illuminate the human condition in this light. We are not religious, but creators of consciousness. No unsolicited manuscripts, please. Inquiries with SASE accepted." avg. press run 10-200. Pub'd 1 title 1998; expects 1 title 1999, 1 title 2000. avg. price, paper: $2. 4-100pp; 5½×8½; of. Payment: negotiable. Copyrights for author.

The Apostolic Press, Emily Mouzakis, 547 NW Coast Street, Newport, OR 97365, 503-265-4641. 1992. "We are seeking material for either books or a quarterly newsletter consisting of Biblical Greek subject matter only." avg. press run 1M. Expects 1 title 1999, 4 titles 2000. 1 title listed in the *Small Press Record of Books in*

Print (28th Edition, 1999-00). avg. price, paper: $9.95. Discounts: trade. 224pp; 5½×8½. Does not copyright for author.

APOSTROPHE: USCB Journal of the Arts, Sheila Tombe, 801 Carteret Street, Beaufort, SC 29902, 803-521-4158; FAX 803-522-9733; E-Mail ibfrt56@vm.sc.edu. 1996. Poetry, fiction, art, interviews, criticism, reviews, letters, parts-of-novels, plays. "'Eclectic excellence required.' Recent contributors: James Dickey and Charlton Ogburn. If books are submitted for review, we might review them." circ. 700. 2/yr. Expects 2 issues 1999, 2 issues 2000. sub. price: $15; per copy: $7.50; sample: $3. Back issues: $5. Discounts: student $5 per copy. 65pp; 5½×8; of. Reporting time: no deadlines; replies (as soon as) when can. Simultaneous submissions accepted: no. Publishes 5% of manuscripts submitted. Payment: 2 copies. Rights revert to author. Pub's reviews: 0 in 1998. §Outstanding fiction, criticism, or poetry.

APPALACHIA JOURNAL, Appalachian Mountain Club Books, Sandy Stott, 5 Joy Street, Boston, MA 02108, 617-523-0636. 1877. Poetry, fiction, articles, art, photos, interviews, reviews, letters, news items, non-fiction. "Most pieces in Appalachia are between 1,500-4,000 words. Poetry rarely exceeds 45 lines. Bias against 'I came, I saw, I conquered...' Interested in historical considerations of land, mountains, rivers and the people who sought them. Also interested in contemporary stories of relationships with landscapes. Recent contributors: Diane Morgan, Reg. Saner, Lynn Rogers, Guy and Laura Waterman, Justin Askins, Doug Peacock." circ. 13M. 2/yr. Pub'd 2 issues 1998; expects 2 issues 1999, 2 issues 2000. sub. price: $10; per copy: $5; sample: $5. Back issues: $5. Discounts: 10+ copies 20%. 160pp; 6×9; of. Reporting time: 1-3 months. Simultaneous submissions accepted: no. Payment: copies. Copyrighted, reverts to author. Pub's reviews: 20 in 1998. §Mountaineering, conservation, canoeing, walking, backpacking, cycling. ABA, NEBA.

Appalachian Consortium Press, A 14-member publications committee acts as editorial board, University Hall, Appalachian State University, Boone, NC 28608, 704-262-2064, fax 704-262-6564. 1971. Poetry, fiction, articles, art, photos, interviews, criticism, music, non-fiction. "We publish occasional works of poetry but, most often, *non-fiction* relating to the Appalachian region." avg. press run 2M. Pub'd 3 titles 1998; expects 5 titles 1999, 4 titles 2000. 20 titles listed in the *Small Press Record of Books in Print* (28th Edition, 1999-00). avg. price, cloth: $15.95; paper: $6.95. Discounts: on purchases for resale, 1-3 books 0%, 4+ 20%. 150pp; 6×9¼; of. Reporting time: at least 6 months. Payment: a negotiable 5-10% of sales. Copyrights for author.

APPALACHIAN HERITAGE, Sidney Saylor Farr, Appalachian Center, Berea College, Berea, KY 40404, 606-986-9341 ext. 5260; e-mail sidney-farr@berea.edu. 1973. Poetry, fiction, articles, art, photos, interviews, non-fiction. "1,500-2,000 words. Material must have Appalachian topics and the art work and/or photos should be scenic or have people and backgrounds similar to that found in Southern Appalachia." circ. 1050. 4/yr. Pub'd 4 issues 1998; expects 4 issues 1999, 4 issues 2000. sub. price: $18; per copy: $6; sample: $6. Back issues: $4. 80pp; 6×9; of. Reporting time: 4-6 weeks. Simultaneous submissions accepted: yes. Publishes 50% of manuscripts submitted. Payment: 3 copies. Copyrighted, reverts to author. Pub's reviews: 8-10 in 1998. §Appalachian subjects. Ads: $150/$85/$50 1/4 page.

Appalachian Log Publishing Company (see also THE SOUTHERN JOURNAL), Ron Gregory, PO Box 20297, Charleston, WV 25362, 304-342-5789. 1991. Poetry, fiction, articles, photos, cartoons, interviews, satire, non-fiction. "No religion, no profanity, regional only. No unsolicited mss., only letter and sample chapter" avg. press run 2M. Pub'd 2 titles 1998; expects 2 titles 1999, 10 titles 2000. 1 title listed in the *Small Press Record of Books in Print* (28th Edition, 1999-00). avg. price, paper: $6. Discounts: 40%. 2pp; 5½×8½; †of. Reporting time: 60 days. Publishes 1% of manuscripts submitted. Payment: contract in advance. Does not copyright for author.

Appalachian Mountain Club Books (see also APPALACHIA JOURNAL), Mark Russell, Editor, 5 Joy Street, Boston, MA 02108, 617-523-0636. 1897. Photos, non-fiction. "We publish nonfiction books and maps focusing on guidebooks for the Northeast and recreational how-to books. We usually contract authors for projects but we welcome unsolicited proposals." avg. press run 5M. Pub'd 6 titles 1998; expects 6 titles 1999, 8 titles 2000. 39 titles listed in the *Small Press Record of Books in Print* (28th Edition, 1999-00). avg. price, cloth: $29.95; paper: $12.95; other: $3.50 map. Discounts: 10-24 books 40%, 25-49 42%, 50-74 43%, 75-149 44%, 150-249 45%, 250-799 46%, 800+ 47%. 256pp; 6×9; of. Reporting time: 1-4 months. Simultaneous submissions accepted: yes. Payment: varies. Copyrights for author. NEBA.

Apples & Oranges, Inc., Gene S. Kira, PO Box 2296, Valley Center, CA 92082, 619-751-8868. 1988. Non-fiction. "Publish titles on sports" avg. press run 5M. Expects 3 titles 1999, 5 titles 2000. 3 titles listed in the *Small Press Record of Books in Print* (28th Edition, 1999-00). avg. price, cloth: $21.95; paper: $21.95. Discounts: please inquire, 1-3 20%, 4-39 40%, etc. 320pp; 8½×11; of. Copyrights for author. ABA.

Application Publishing, Inc., PO Box 4124, Great Neck, NY 11023, 516-482-5796; Fax 516-773-4743. 1995. Non-fiction. "Books relating to the practical aspects of using technology in business operations." avg. press run 5M. Expects 2 titles 1999, 2-4 titles 2000. 1 title listed in the *Small Press Record of Books in Print* (28th Edition, 1999-00). avg. price, paper: $15-$25. Discounts: per distributor - Assciated Publishers Group. 200pp;

7×10. Reporting time: 60-90 days. Simultaneous submissions accepted: yes. Payment: negotiation. Copyrights for author.

Applied Probability Trust (see also MATHEMATICAL SPECTRUM), D. W. Sharpe, School of Mathmathmatics and Statistics, The University, Sheffield S3 7RH, England. 1968. Articles, reviews, letters. 2 titles listed in the *Small Press Record of Books in Print* (28th Edition, 1999-00). of.

AQUARIUS, Eddie S. Lindẹn, Flat 4, Room B, 116 Sutherland Avenue, London W9, England. 1968. Poetry, fiction, articles, reviews. "Special all Irish issue forthcoming with Seamus Heaney. 1992 *Aquarius* will publish in late summer a special issue on women and women writers. It will contain poetry, fictional prose, essays, interviews and reviews. Hilary Davies is the guest editor and we are seeking contributions that will reflect the best of women's writing today. They may be sent to Hilary Davies, 70 Wargrave Avenue, Stanford Hill, London N15-6UB, England. Postage cost must be sent to cover the return of material." circ. 1.5M. 2/yr. sub. price: $40; per copy: $6; sample: £5 - $12. Back issues: $5. Discounts: 33% trade. 120pp; lp. Payment: special issues only. Pub's reviews: 40 in 1998. §Poetry, biography. Ads: £80/£40.

AQUATERRA, METAECOLOGY & CULTURE, Jacqueline Froelich, 5473 Highway 23N, Eureka Springs, AR 72631. 1986. Poetry, articles, art, cartoons, letters, interviews. "Water-related information particularly compost toilet information and innovative conservation." circ. 3M. 1/yr. Pub'd 1 issue 1998; expects 1 issue 1999, 1 issue 2000. sub. price: $9.95; per copy: $9.95; sample: $9.95. Back issues: $9.95. Discounts: inquire. 140pp; 8×5; †varies. Reporting time: varies. Simultaneous submissions accepted: yes. Publishes 50% of manuscripts submitted. Payment: none. Copyrighted, reverts to author. Pub's reviews: 1 in 1998. §Submissions related to technical and/or spiritual experiences with water articles, research, interviews, ceremonies, prose, poetry, artwork, summaries of water organizations. Ads: inquire. The Water Center.

ARARAT, Leo Hamalian, 55 E 59th Street, New York, NY 10022-1112. 1960. Poetry, fiction, articles, art, criticism, reviews, parts-of-novels. "We prefer material in some way pertinent to Armenian life and culture." circ. 2.2M. 4/yr. Pub'd 4 issues 1998; expects 4 issues 1999, 4 issues 2000. sub. price: $24; per copy: $7; sample: $4. Back issues: $4. Discounts: 15%. 74pp; 9×12; of. Reporting time: 4 months. Payment: $10 a printed page (roughly). Copyrighted, reverts to author. Pub's reviews: 30 in 1998. §Ethnic Armenian. Ads: $250/$125. CLMP.

ARBA SICULA, Legas, Gaetano Cipolla, c/o Modern Foreign Languages, St. John's University, Jamaica, NY 11439-0002. 1979. Poetry, fiction, articles, art, photos, reviews, music, letters, long-poems, collages, plays, news items, non-fiction. "Bilingual ethnic oriented material in the Sicilian language with a lyrical English translation." circ. 2M. 2/yr. Pub'd 2 issues 1998; expects 2 issues 1999, 2 issues 2000. sub. price: $20; per copy: $10; sample: $10. Back issues: we'll give you a quote. Discounts: ask for quote. 90pp; 5½×8½; laser, of. Reporting time: flexible. Payment: none. Copyrighted, does not revert to author. Pub's reviews: several in 1998. §Sicilian ethnic worldwide. Ads: $150/$75.

Arch Grove Press, Julia Surtshin, PO Box 2387, Lake Oswego, OR 97035, 503-624-7811 phone/fax. 1997. Fiction, non-fiction. avg. press run 3M. Expects 1 title 1999, 1 title 2000. 1 title listed in the *Small Press Record of Books in Print* (28th Edition, 1999-00). avg. price, paper: $14.95. Discounts: 55% to wholesalers, 40% to retailers. 300pp; 6×9. Reporting time: 60 days. Simultaneous submissions accepted: no. Publishes 1% of manuscripts submitted. Payment: to be arranged. Will possibly copyright for author. Northwest Book Publishers Association.

ARCHIPELAGO, Katherine McNamara, PO Box 2485, Charlottesville, VA 22902-2485, 804-979-5292; editor@archipelago.org. 1997. Poetry, fiction, articles, photos, interviews, criticism, reviews, letters, parts-of-novels. "Emphasis is on writing, not subject. Strong interest in international writers, Americans abroad or with critical (literary) insight, non-academic fiction and poetry. Recent contributors: Frederic Tuten, Anna Marie Ortese, Henry Martin, Fidelio, Benjamin H. Cheever, K. Callaway, Maria Negroni, Hubert Butler, Richard Jones, Ann Beattie." 4/yr. Expects 4 issues 1999, 4 issues 2000. 40-60pp; 8×11. Reporting time: 2 months. Copyrighted, reverts to author.

Archipelago Publishing, Steven C. Brandt, PO Box 1249, Friday Harbor, WA 98250, 800-360-6166; Fax 360-378-7097; info@gmex.com. 1996. Non-fiction. "Business books and regional history - Northwest & California" avg. press run 5M. Pub'd 2 titles 1998; expects 2 titles 1999, 2 titles 2000. 2 titles listed in the *Small Press Record of Books in Print* (28th Edition, 1999-00). avg. price, paper: $14.95. Discounts: trade 40%, bulk - call for quote. 200pp; 5½×8½; web. Reporting time: 60 days. Simultaneous submissions accepted: no. Publishes 100% of manuscripts submitted. Payment: varies. We will possibly copyright for author. PMA, IPG, BPNW, PNBA.

Arctos Press, CB Follett, PO Box 401, Sausalito, CA 94966, E-mail Runes@aol.com. 1996. Poetry, photos. "Anthologies, theme oriented, send only response to call for submissions. Looking for quality poems. Recent contributors: Robert Hass, Linda Gregg, Brenda Hillman, Jane Hirshfield, Kay Ryan, Rosalie Moore, Ellery

Akers." avg. press run 2M. Pub'd 1 title 1998; expects 3 titles 1999, 1-2 titles 2000. 3 titles listed in the *Small Press Record of Books in Print* (28th Edition, 1999-00). avg. price, paper: $15. Discounts: usual. 130pp; 6×9; of. Reporting time: 2-3 months. Simultaneous submissions accepted: yes. Publishes 30% of manuscripts submitted. Payment: in copies. Copyrights for author. SPAN, BAIPA.

Arden Press, Inc., Susan Conley, Editor, PO Box 418, Denver, CO 80201, 303-697-6766. 1980. Non-fiction. "We are actively pursuing women's topics of either historical or contemporary significance, reference works, nonfiction works including practical guides in all subject areas. No autobiographical works or memoirs are considered" avg. press run 3M. Pub'd 3 titles 1998; expects 4 titles 1999, 5 titles 2000. 14 titles listed in the *Small Press Record of Books in Print* (28th Edition, 1999-00). avg. price, cloth: $28; paper: $18. Discounts: 1-4 copies 20%, 5-49 40% to trade. 250pp; 6×9. Reporting time: 1 month. Simultaneous submissions accepted: yes. Payment: 8-15% according to number of copies sold; annual payments. Copyrights for author. Publishers Marketing Association.

AREOPAGUS, John G. LeMond, Editor, Tao Fong Shan Christian Centre, PO Box 33, Shatin, New Territories, Hong Kong, 952-269-1904; FAX 852-269-9885. 1987. Poetry, articles, art, photos, cartoons, interviews, criticism, reviews, letters, news items. "*Areopagus* is a full-color Christian magazine on interreligious dialog and mission. Writers analyze traditional and contemporary religious movements, including New Age. Religious news from all parts of the world is presented. Features include interviews, dialog, testimonies, personal reflections and experiences, and scholarly treatment of religious topics. *Areopagus* maintains a commitment to respect the integrity of all religious communities and people of faith." circ. 1M+ in 50 countries. 4/yr. Pub'd 4 issues 1998; expects 4 issues 1999, 4 issues 2000. sub. price: $24 US; $120 HK; 165 NOK; per copy: $6 US; sample: $4 US. Back issues: $4 US; $30 US complete set back issues. Discounts: Free or discount to certain Third World Countries. 56pp; 8¼×11¼; of. Reporting time: 2-4 weeks. Publishes 10% of manuscripts submitted. Payment: writers $50 US; photos $12.50 US. Copyrighted, reverts to author. Pub's reviews: 4 in 1998. §General religion, Christian mission, Christian analysis of religious movements and world events.

Argo Press, Michael E. Ambrose, PO Box 4201, Austin, TX 78765-4201. 1972. Fiction. "All submissions are by solicitation only" avg. press run 500. 4 titles listed in the *Small Press Record of Books in Print* (28th Edition, 1999-00). avg. price, paper: $14.95. Discounts: 5 or more, 40%. 200pp; size varies; of. Payment: individual terms. Copyrights for author.

Ariadne Press, Carol F. Hoover, Editor, 4817 Tallahassee Avenue, Rockville, MD 20853, 301-949-2514. 1976. Fiction. "Ellen Moore, *Lead Me to the Exit*, publication date 12-01-77. Michael Marsh, *The Rudelstein Affair*, publication date 6/1/81. Henry Alley, *The Lattice*, publication date 3/15/86. Writers Mentor Group, ed. Carol Hoover, *How to Write an Uncommonly Good Novel*, publication date 6/1/90. Paul Bourguignon, *The Greener Grass* 10/1/93, Eugene Jeffers, *A Rumor of Distant Tribes*, 1/15/94. Deborah Churchman, *Cross a Dark Bridge*, 1996. Eva Thaddeus, *Steps of the Sun*, 1997" avg. press run 1M. Expects 3 titles 1999. 8 titles listed in the *Small Press Record of Books in Print* (28th Edition, 1999-00). avg. price, cloth: $19.95; paper: $13.95. Discounts: 20-40% to booksellers or libraries ordering in quantity. 208pp; 5½×8½, 6×9; of. Reporting time: 2 months. We accept simultaneous submissions if indicated. Publishes about 1% of manuscripts submitted. Payment: 10% of list price. Copyrights for author. Writer's Center, Small Press Center.

ARIEL—A Review of International English Literature, V.J. Ramraj, The University of Calgary, 2500 University Drive NW, Calgary, Alberta T2N 1N4, Canada, 403-220-4657. 1970. Articles, reviews. "Critical and scholarly perspectives on literatures in English from around the world." circ. 925. 4/yr. Pub'd 4 issues 1998; expects 4 issues 1999, 4 issues 2000. sub. price: $33 institution, $23 individual; per copy: add G.S.T. in Canada; sample: G.S.T. Canada. Back issues: $30 indiv., $45 instit., payable in Cdn. funds, add G.S.T. in Canada; discount on 5 or more volumes. Discounts: $1 for agents, claim period is 6 months ($2 on p/h claims). 140pp; 6×9; of. Reporting time: 3 months. Simultaneous submissions accepted: no. Payment: none. Copyrighted, contact editor regarding rights reverting to author. Pub's reviews: 12-14 in 1998. §English literature. Ads: write for info. C.A.L.J.

Ariko Publications, Jonathan Musere, 12335 Santa Monica Blvd., Suite 155, Los Angeles, CA 90025. 1998. Articles, non-fiction. "We primarily deal with translation, oral, literary and field research work associated with personal names and proverbs from the central, Southern and Eastern African region." Expects 1 title 1999, 4 titles 2000. 3 titles listed in the *Small Press Record of Books in Print* (28th Edition, 1999-00). avg. price, paper: $12.50. Discounts: 60% on multiple copies. 200pp; 5½×8½. Reporting time: 1 month. Simultaneous submissions accepted: yes. Payment: 10% on retail price copies. Copyrights for author.

ARISTOS, Louis Torres, Editor; Michelle Marder Kamhi, Editor, PO Box 1105, Radio City Station, New York, NY 10101, aristos@aristos.org; www.aristos.org. 1982. Articles, photos, interviews, criticism, reviews, letters. "Publisher: The Aristos Foundation. *Aristos* is dedicated to the preservation and advancement of traditional values (as opposed to modernism and post-modernism) in the arts, and to objective standards in scholarship and criticism. Advocates positive humanistic values in literature; realism in the visual arts; melody and tonality in music; intelligibility in all the arts. Feature articles range from 1,500 to 7,000 words; other items vary in length. Indexed in *The American Humanities Index*, and abstracted in *ARTbibliographies Modern*. An annotated table of contents is available. 'The value is there, particularly as the point of view is unique' *Library Journal*. 'A scholarly but gutsy little periodical that vigorously challenges modernist scholars and critics'; 'its one long article per issue caries more weight than those found in more substantial periodicals' *(Magazines for Libraries*, 6th, 7th, and 8th eds.)'' Irregular, 2-6/yr. Expects 1 issue 1999, 3 issues 2000. sub. price: $25 (six issues) individuals, $35 (six issues) institutions; per copy: $4.50; sample: $3 individuals; free to institutions. Back issues: available to individual subscribers upon request. 6pp; 8½×11; of. Reporting time: 4-6 weeks. Payment: $25-$100 honorarium, paid upon publication. Copyrighted, does not revert to author. Pub's reviews: 0 in 1998. §Books on all the fine, literary, and performing arts, and the philosophy of art, if the treatment is compatible with our edirorial philosophy. No ads.

Arizona Master Gardener Press, Cathy L. Cromell, 4341 E. Broadway Road, Phoenix, AZ 85040-8807, 602-470-8086 ext. 312, FAX 602-470-8092. 1996. Non-fiction. ''We publish books that educate the public about appropriate strategies, materials, and methods primarily for arid, low-desert gardening. Non-fiction, any length.'' avg. press run 3M. Expects 1 title 1999, 1 title 2000. 2 titles listed in the *Small Press Record of Books in Print* (28th Edition, 1999-00). avg. price, paper: $10.95. 120pp; 5½×8½; of. Arizona Book Publishing Association.

Arjay Associates, Rodolfo Jacobson, PO Box 850251, Mesquite, TX 75185-0251, 972-226-0336 tel/fax; E-mail jake4@airmail.net. 1996. Non-fiction. ''Length: About 150-225pp. Biases: language, culture, travels, seniority, human relations, autobiographies, education. Recent contributors: Rodolfo Jacobson, *Diary of a Quite Unusual Tour*.'' Pub'd 1 title 1998; expects 1 title 1999, 1 title 2000. 1 title listed in the *Small Press Record of Books in Print* (28th Edition, 1999-00). avg. price, paper: $14.95. Discounts: 20-50% depending on quantities ordered. 150pp; 6×9; Camera-ready art. Reporting time: 3 months. Simultaneous submissions accepted: no. Publishes 20% of manuscripts submitted. Payment: 6% net. Copyrights for author. PMA.

Arjuna Library Press (see also JOURNAL OF REGIONAL CRITICISM), Count Prof. Joseph A. Uphoff Jr., Director, 1025 Garner Street, D, Space 18, Colorado Springs, CO 80905-1774. 1983. Fiction, art, photos, long-poems, non-fiction. ''The idea of preformance is developing by means of localized publication with repeated showings or extensive readings in open microphone, now proliferating. This is a team spirited, social movement in search of the proper audience; the key factor is economic adjustment. Longevity is approximately correlated to merit, science to art, and international to regional. The result is a sensitivity for literate means that will develope personal style in attractive, sociable ways.'' Pub'd 3 titles 1998; expects 3 titles 1999, 3 titles 2000. 28 titles listed in the *Small Press Record of Books in Print* (28th Edition, 1999-00). avg. price, paper: $2-$5; other: $1 if available. 30pp; 5×7; †xerography. Reporting time: indefinite. Payment: dependent on market, profit sharing. Does not copyright for author.

The Ark, Geoffrey Gardner, 115 Montebello Road, Jamaica Plain, MA 02130, 617-522-1922. 1970. Poetry, long-poems. ''This is a highly selective press.'' avg. press run 1.5M+. Pub'd 1 title 1998; expects 1 title 1999, 2 titles 2000. 2 titles listed in the *Small Press Record of Books in Print* (28th Edition, 1999-00). avg. price, cloth: $10; paper: $5. Discounts: 40% to bookstores only. 116pp; 5½×8½; of. Reporting time: at once to 3 months. Payment: unique to each project and by arrangement with each author. Copyrights for author.

Armadillo Books, Lawrence Simpson, PO Box 2052, Georgetown, TX 78627-2052, 512-863-8660. 1997. Poetry, fiction, art, non-fiction. ''Self-publishing production services for authors on all topics/Publishing for self. We produce 70-400 page paperback books in runs of 25-200; archive electronic files for future runs. Patsy McCleery/nonfiction, Don Snell/art & poetry, Larry Simpson/fiction.'' avg. press run +/- 100. Expects 7 titles 1999, 35+ titles 2000. 5 titles listed in the *Small Press Record of Books in Print* (28th Edition, 1999-00). avg. price, paper: $10. Discounts: 10% under 10 books, 40% over 100. 175pp; 5¼×8; †Hybrid laser. Reporting time: 1 week. Simultaneous submissions accepted: yes. Publishes 10% of manuscripts submitted. Does not copyright for author.

Armchair Publishing, Mark Eddlemon, 1121 South John, Springfield, MO 65804. 1996. Non-fiction. ''Book length, sports history, coaching sports, outdoor recreation.'' avg. press run 1.5M. Expects 1 title 1999, 1 title 2000. 1 title listed in the *Small Press Record of Books in Print* (28th Edition, 1999-00). avg. price, cloth: $29.95. 250pp; 8½×11. Reporting time: 6 months. Simultaneous submissions accepted: yes. Publishes 67% of manuscripts submitted. Payment: varies. Copyrights for author.

ARNAZELLA, Woody West, Advisor, 3000 Landerholm Circle SE, Bellevue, WA 98007, 206-641-2373. 1976. Poetry, fiction, art, photos, cartoons, satire, parts-of-novels, plays, non-fiction. circ. 300. 1/yr. Pub'd 1 issue 1998; expects 1 issue 1999, 1 issue 2000. price per copy: $10; sample: $10. Back issues: $3. 80pp; 8½×9. Reporting time: spring. Payment: copies. Copyrighted, reverts to author.

Arnold & Johnson, Publishers, Arnold, Johnson, 5024 College Acres Drive, Willington, NC 28403-1741.

1996. Poetry, plays. "We are new, trying to avoid large mistakes. Our first book, a volume of poems, entitled *Alone*, came out in March 1997. We have another volume, of plays, in the works. We plan a small output at first, and since we know many writers, we are *not* accepting submissions at this time. That policy may change at a later date." avg. press run 1M. Expects 2 titles 1999. 1 title listed in the *Small Press Record of Books in Print* (28th Edition, 1999-00). avg. price, paper: $10+. Discounts: 40% bookstores; for all prepaid purchases, we pay s+h. Payment: negotiated. Copyrights for author.

Arrowstar Publishing, R. Punley, 100134 University Park Station, Denver, CO 80210-0134, 303-231-6599. 1984. Non-fiction. avg. press run 10M. Expects 2 titles 1999, 50 titles 2000. 9 titles listed in the *Small Press Record of Books in Print* (28th Edition, 1999-00). avg. price, cloth: $25; paper: $20; other: $10. Discounts: variable. 350pp; 5½×8½; †of. Reporting time: 3 weeks. Simultaneous submissions accepted: no. Publishes 5% of manuscripts submitted. Payment: negotiable. Copyrights for author.

ART CALENDAR, Barbara Dougherty, PO Box 199, Upper Fairmount, MD 21867, 410-651-9150. 1985. Articles, art, photos, interviews, news items. "Marketing and career management journal for visual artists. Articles on marketing, art law, psychology of creativity; interviews with dealers, curators. Professional listings: grants, residencies, juried shows, museums, etc., reviewing portfolios." circ. 17M. 11/yr. Pub'd 11 issues 1998; expects 11 issues 1999, 11 issues 2000. sub. price: $32; per copy: $5; sample: $5. Back issues: book available of articles 1986-1990, $17.95 + $3 s/h. Discounts: inquire. 48pp; 8¼×10½; Quark/Macintosh. Reporting time: varies. Simultaneous submissions accepted: no. Publishes 10% of manuscripts submitted. Payment: yes. Copyrighted, rights revert to author if requested. Pub's reviews: 10 in 1998. §For visual artists, career management and marketing books. Ads: inquire.

ART PAPERS, Ruth Resnicow, Editor; Cathy Downey, Managing Editor, PO Box 5748, Atlanta, GA 31107-5748, 404-588-1837; FAX 404-588-1836. 1977. Articles, art, cartoons, interviews, criticism, parts-of-novels, news items, non-fiction. "Features: 8,000 words. Reviews: 800-1,000 words. *Art Papers* is primarily interested in reviews of contemporary and experimental artists' exhibitions. Call or write or e-mail ruth@pd.org for writers' guidelines. Shipping address: Atlanta Art Papers, Inc., Po Box 77348, Atlanta, GA 30357" circ. 90M. 6/yr. Pub'd 6 issues 1998; expects 6 issues 1999, 6 issues 2000. sub. price: $30; per copy: $5.50; sample: $1.24. Back issues: $5.50 per copy. Discounts: Group subscriptions to groups of 10 or more. 88pp; 10×13½; desktop. Reporting time: 6 weeks. Simultaneous submissions accepted: no. Publishes 75% of manuscripts submitted. Payment: copies, fees range from $35 to $100. Copyrighted, reverts to author. Pub's reviews: 8 in 1998. §Contemporary visual arts, dance, new music, theater, performance, video, film. Ads: $480/$260/40¢ per word (some classified listings are free; call for details).

ART TIMES, Raymond J. Steiner, PO Box 730, Mount Marion, NY 12456-0730, 914-246-6944; email arttimes@alster.net. 1984. "Other address: 16 Fite Road, Saugerties, NY 12477. *Art Times* is a monthly journal and resource for all of and for the arts. Although the bulk is written by Staff members, we solicit poetry and short stories from free-lancers around the world (we are listed in *Writer's Market, Literary Market, Poet's Market*, etc). Fiction: short stories up to 1,500 words. No excessive sex, violence or racist themes. High literary quality sought. Poetry: up to 20 lines. All topics; all forms. High literary quality sought. Readers of *Art Times* are generally over 40, affluent and art conscious. Articles in *Art Times* are general pieces on the arts written by staff *and are not solicited*. General tone of paper governed by literary essays on arts—no journalistic writing, press releases. *Always include SASE.* Guidelines: business size envelope, 1 first-class stamp." circ. 19M. 11/yr. Pub'd 11 issues 1998; expects 11 issues 1999, 11 issues 2000. sub. price: $15, $25 foreign; per copy: $1.75 on newsstands; sample: SASE + 3 first class stamps. Back issues: same. Discounts: bundles (25-100 copies) sent free to preforming art centers, galleries, museums and similar distribution points. 20pp; 10×14½; of. Reporting time: 6 months (24-48 months for publication). Simultaneous submissions accepted: yes. Publishes .01% of manuscripts submitted. Payment: poetry 6 free issues + 1 yr. sub.; short stories $25 + 1 yr. sub. Copyrighted, reverts to author. Pub's reviews: 75-100 in 1998. §We only review art books. Ads: $1174/$607/$325 1/4 page/$27 for 1st 15 words, 50¢ each additional word for classifieds.

ART-CORE, Patty Puke, PO Box 49324, Austin, TX 78765. 1989. Poetry, fiction, art, photos, cartoons, collages. "Uncensored open forum alternative art zine. We invite submissions from the underground, no mainstream material accepted. Graphics: 8x10" max., black and white. Written work one page or less. Photos: 8x10" max, screened. Theme issues, send SASE for guidelines and upcoming theme. New *Art-Core* video magazine aired monthly on ACTV" circ. 400. 3/yr. Pub'd 2 issues 1998; expects 2 issues 1999, 3 issues 2000. price per copy: $4 ppd; sample: $4 ppd. Back issues: $2 ppd, send SASE for product availability and price. Discounts: rates available for large quantities, free with trade. 24pp; 8×10. Reporting time: 6-8 weeks max. Payment: free copy. Not copyrighted. §New music and videos. Ads: $20 1/2 page/$6 for short listing.

Arte Publico Press, Nicolas Kanellos, Publisher, University of Houston, Houston, TX 77204-2090, 713-743-2841. 1980. Poetry, fiction, art, photos. avg. press run 3M. Pub'd 22 titles 1998; expects 20 titles 1999, 20 titles 2000. 129 titles listed in the *Small Press Record of Books in Print* (28th Edition, 1999-00). avg. price, paper: $5-$12. Discounts: 40% trade. 120pp; 5½×8½; of. Reporting time: 4 months. Payment: varies per type of book. Copyrights for author. CLMP.

ARTFUL DODGE, Daniel Bourne, Editor, Department of English, College of Wooster, Wooster, OH 44691. 1979. Poetry, fiction, articles, art, photos, cartoons, interviews, satire, criticism, reviews, parts-of-novels, long-poems, collages, plays. "According to *Library Journal*, our interviews (Borges, Sarraute, Milosz, Merwin, Michael Dorris, Lee Smith, William Matthews, Stanislaw Baranczak, Tim O'Brien, Vaclav Havel, Charles Simic, William Least Heat-Moon) are 'much more perceptive and informative than most.' Translations are heartily encouraged; we like to print special sections of contemporary writing (especially East European and Third World) beyond America's extensive, though not infinite, linguistic/cultural borders, and in general like to see work which accomplishes broader vision and breadth than is standard practice today, but which is grounded in an awareness of the accomplishment of contemporary poetics in the illumination of the particular. We also do a 'poet as translator' series, featuring the original poetry and translations of such prominent and emerging practitioners as William Stafford, Stuart Friebert, Khaled Mattawa, Nicholas Kolumban, Len Roberts, Mary Crow, Karen Kovacik, Jim Barnes, etc." circ. 1M. 1 double issue per year. Pub'd 1 issue 1998; expects 1 issue 1999, 1 issue 2000. sub. price: indiv. $7, instit. $16; per copy: $7; sample: recent issues are double ones available for $5. Older sample copies are $2.75 for one issue or $5 for 5 issues. Discounts: 20%. 150-200pp; 5½x8½; of. Reporting time: 6 months maximum. Simultaneous submissions accepted: no. Publishes less than 1% of manuscripts submitted. Payment: 2 copies, plus at least $5 per page honorarium, thanks to Ohio Arts Council. Copyrighted, reverts to author. Pub's reviews. §Poetry, fiction, plays, criticism, arts, social commentary, translation. Ads: $100/$60. CLMP.

The Arthritis Trust of America/The Rheumatoid Disease Foundation, 7111 Sweetgum Drive SW, Suite A, Fairview, TN 37062-9384, 615-799-1002. 6 titles listed in the *Small Press Record of Books in Print* (28th Edition, 1999-00).

ARTHUR'S COUSIN, Joshua Handley, 6811 Greycloud, Austin, TX 78745, 512-445-7065. 1993. Poetry, fiction, articles, art, photos, cartoons, satire, criticism, reviews, collages, news items. circ. 100. 4/yr. Expects 10 issues 1999, 4 issues 2000. price per copy: $1; sample: $1. Back issues: $1. 24-30pp; 8½x11; †xerox. Not copyrighted. Pub's reviews: 48 in 1998. §Poetry, fiction, articles, art, photos, cartoons, satire, criticism, reviews, collages, news-items. Ads: ads are free.

Artifact Press, Ltd., Connie Hershey, 900 Tanglewood Drive, Concord, MA 01742, 978-287-5296; Fax 978-287-5299; hershey@tiac.net. 1991. Poetry, fiction. "First title was an anthology of L.A. poetry" avg. press run 1M. Expects 1 title 1999, 1-2 titles 2000. 2 titles listed in the *Small Press Record of Books in Print* (28th Edition, 1999-00). avg. price, paper: $12.95. Discounts: standard. 215pp; 6x9; of. Reporting time: 4 weeks. Payment: not yet determined. PMA, NAIP, SPAN.

ARTISTAMP NEWS, Ed Varney, PO Box 3655, Vancouver, B.C. V6B 3Y8, Canada. 1991. Articles, art, criticism, reviews, letters, news items. "This newsletter's objective is to present current news of events and editions and history of artist use of the stamp format as a print medium, profiles of artists, and articles about techniques used in producing stamp art. Includes section of mail-art show & project listings, reviews of related books and publications." circ. 400. 1/yr. Pub'd 1 issue 1998; expects 1 issue 1999, 1 issue 2000. sub. price: $10/2 years; per copy: $5; sample: $4. Back issues: $4 each; not all issues available. Discounts: no wholesale. 12pp; 11x17 folded to 8½x11; of. Reporting time: 12 months. Publishes 75% of manuscripts submitted. Payment: 10 copies. Copyrighted, reverts to author. Pub's reviews: 23 brief-description in 1998. §Books or periodicals either about or utilizing stamps by artists or sheets of stamps by artists. Ads: 45¢/word.

ART/LIFE, Art/Life Limited Editions, Joe Cardella, Editor & Publisher, PO Box 23020, Ventura, CA 93002, 805-648-4331. 1981. Poetry, art, photos, collages, concrete art. "Poetry and prose should be sent to Poetry Editor, Art/Life" circ. 500-1M. 11/yr. Pub'd 11 issues 1998; expects 11 issues 1999, 11 issues 2000. sub. price: $450; per copy: $50; sample: $50. Back issues: $50. Discounts: 30% wholesale-minimum 2. 50pp; 8½x11. Reporting time: 1-6 weeks. Payment: each contributor receives a copy of the issue in which his work appears. Copyrighted, reverts to author. No ads.

Art/Life Limited Editions (see also ART/LIFE), Joe Cardella, Editor & Publisher, PO Box 23020, Ventura, CA 93002, 805-648-4331. 1981. Poetry, art, photos, collages, concrete art. "Poetry and prose should be sent to Poetry Editor" avg. press run 150. Pub'd 11 titles 1998; expects 11 titles 1999, 11 titles 2000. avg. price, other: $50 per copy. Discounts: 30% wholesale-minimum 2. 50pp; 8½x11. Reporting time: 1-6 weeks. Payment: each contributor receives a copy of the issue in which their work appears. Copyrights for author.

ART:MAG, Peter Magliocco, Editor, PO Box 70896, Las Vegas, NV 89170, 702-734-8121. 1984. Poetry, fiction, art, photos, cartoons, interviews, satire, parts-of-novels, long-poems. "Subscribers receive chapbooks & 'surprises' now and then" circ. 100+. 2/yr. Pub'd 2 issues 1998; expects 2 issues 1999, 2 issues 2000. sub. price: $10; per copy: $5; sample: $5. Back issues: query. Discounts: none. 35-90pp; 8½x11, 8½x7; †xerox. Reporting time: 1-3 months. Simultaneous submissions accepted: yes. Publishes 25% of manuscripts submitted. Payment: 1 copy of magazine. Not copyrighted. Pub's reviews: 1-2 in 1998. §Poetry, fiction. Ads: exchange

40

only.

Arts End Books (see also NOSTOC MAGAZINE), Marshall Brooks, Editor, Box 162, Newton, MA 02468. 1979. Poetry, fiction, music, parts-of-novels, long-poems, non-fiction. "Send a SASE for our catalog describing our subscription package program. No submissions please; queries okay." avg. press run varies. Pub'd 2 titles 1998; expects 2 titles 1999, 2 titles 2000. 11 titles listed in the *Small Press Record of Books in Print* (28th Edition, 1999-00). avg. price, cloth: $15; paper: $4. Discounts: on request. Pages vary; size varies; of, lp. Simultaneous submissions accepted: no. Publishes 1-5% of manuscripts submitted. Payment: worked out on an individual basis with each author, for each project. Copyrights for author.

ART'S GARBAGE GAZZETTE, Art Paul Schlosser, 1938 East Mifflin Street, Madison, WI 53704-4729, 608-249-0715. 1990. Poetry, fiction, articles, art, cartoons, satire, letters, news items, non-fiction. Irregular. Pub'd 6 issues 1998; expects -20 issues 1999, -20 issues 2000. sub. price: $25; per copy: $5; sample: $2. 14-20+pp; 5½×8½. Reporting time: 1 year, 6 months, or as soon as possible (the more money the sooner). Payment: they pay me. Copyrighted, reverts to author. Pub's reviews. §Music, fiction, strange news items, things that are bizarre. (people with money). Ads: (if I support the product) $20 a page.

ARTSLINK, Americans for the Arts/ACA Books, Jennifer Gottlieb, Editor, 1000 Vermont Avenue NW, 12th Floor, Washington, DC 20005, 212-223-2787. 1997. Articles. circ. 2.5M. 10/yr. Pub'd 10 issues 1998; expects 10 issues 1999, 10 issues 2000. sub. price: with Americans for the Arts membership only. 8pp; 8½×11. Payment: none. Copyrighted, does not revert to author. Ads: please call 202-371-2830.

ARTWORD QUARTERLY, Carol Robertshaw, 5273 Portland Avenue, White Bear Lake, MN 55110-2411, 612-426-7059; email artword@wavefront.com. 1995. Poetry. *"ArtWord Quarterly* seeks poetry which is image filled, metaphorical and written with precision, unity, clarity and depth. Submit up to five poems (no more than one poem per page, maximum length 33 lines per poem including stanza breaks, name and address on each page), plus brief bio and SASE with adequate postage." circ. 200. 4/yr. Pub'd 4 issues 1998; expects 4 issues 1999, 4 issues 2000. sub. price: $15; per copy: $4; sample: $4. Back issues: $2. 40pp; 5½×8½; of. Reporting time: 1-4 months. Simultaneous submissions accepted: no. Publishes 10% of manuscripts submitted. Payment: 1 copy. Copyrighted, reverts to author.

ASC NEWSLETTER, Roberta Faul-Zeitler, 1725 K Street NW, Suite 601, Washington, DC 20006-1401, 202-347-2850. 1972. Articles, photos, interviews, reviews, letters, news items. *"ASC Newsletter* carries articles, newsnotes, book reviews and job ads relevent to biologists in the broad field of systematic biology, or to those whose interests are peripheral to systematics. Articles are reviewed. Submissions detailing techniques applicable to systematics collections in general, museum computer projects, collection resources, etc., are encouraged." circ. 1.0M. 6/yr. Pub'd 6 issues 1998; expects 6 issues 1999, 6 issues 2000. 11 titles listed in the *Small Press Record of Books in Print* (28th Edition, 1999-00). sub. price: $28 indiv., $46 instit.; 2 yr. sub—$49 indiv., $82 instit.; per copy: n/a; sample: n/a. Back issues: $2 each copy 1998/1997; $7/copy prior to 1997. 12pp; 8½×11; †of. Reporting time: 3 weeks. Publishes 80% of manuscripts submitted. Payment: none. Copyrighted, does not revert to author. Pub's reviews: 9 in 1998. §Botany, zoology, natural history, museum management and conservation. write for rate/format sheet.

Ascension Publishing, Betsy Thompson, Box 3001-323, Burbank, CA 91508, 818-848-8145. 1990. "Approx. 190 pages. Work is generally concerned with proposing new possibilities for coping with modern living through ideas that offer greater serenity." avg. press run 3M. Expects 1 title 1999, 2 titles 2000. 4 titles listed in the *Small Press Record of Books in Print* (28th Edition, 1999-00). avg. price, paper: $11. Discounts: bookstore 40%; other 3-199 40%, 200-499 50%, 500+ 65%. 190pp; 5½×8½. Copyrights for author. NAPRA.

ASCENT, W. Scott Olsen, Department of English, Concordia College, Moorhead, MN 56562, E-mail Ascent@cord.edu. 1975. Poetry, fiction, letters, parts-of-novels, long-poems, non-fiction. circ. 500. 3/yr. Pub'd 3 issues 1998; expects 3 issues 1999, 3 issues 2000. sub. price: $9; per copy: $4; sample: $4. Back issues: $4. 85pp; 6×9. Reporting time: 1 week to 3 months. Simultaneous submissions accepted: yes. We accept 60 manuscripts out of 2,600 submitted each year. Payment: none. Copyrighted, reverts to author.

Ash Grove Press, Patricia Ouellette, Susan Boone, Carole Ann Camp, PO Box 365, Sunderland, MA 01375-0365, 413-665-1200. 1994. Non-fiction. "Ash Grove Press is a earth-conscious organization which publishes books in the fields of elementary school science curriculum (grades 3-5) and womens' spirituality." avg. press run 5M. Pub'd 8 titles 1998; expects 4 titles 1999, 4 titles 2000. 9 titles listed in the *Small Press Record of Books in Print* (28th Edition, 1999-00). avg. price, paper: $12. 150pp; 6×9. Reporting time: 3 weeks. Publishes 5-10% of manuscripts submitted. Payment: 7.5% of list price. Copyrights for author. PMA, Bookbuilders of Boston, New England Booksellers Association, Small Press Center.

Ash Lad Press, Bill Romey, PO Box 294, East Orleans, MA 02643, phone/fax 508-255-2301. 1975. Non-fiction. "No unsolicited submissions accepted." avg. press run 1.5M. Pub'd 1 title 1998; expects 2 titles 1999. 5 titles listed in the *Small Press Record of Books in Print* (28th Edition, 1999-00). avg. price, paper:

$19.95. Discounts: trade 40% for orders of over 5, 20% for 1-4, texts 20%, libraries 25%. 150pp; 6×9; of. Payment: cooperative sharing of costs and income. Copyrights for author.

Ash Tree Publishing, Susun Weed, PO Box 64, Woodstock, NY 12498, 914-246-8081. 1986. Non-fiction. "Women's health, women's spirituality" avg. press run 15M. Pub'd 1 title 1998; expects 2 titles 1999, 2 titles 2000. 9 titles listed in the *Small Press Record of Books in Print* (28th Edition, 1999-00). avg. price, paper: $11.95. Discounts: 20% 1-2 copies, 30% 3-9, 40% 10-51, 40% S.T.O.P. orders, 45% 1 case, 50% 2-4 cases, 55% 5 cases. 240pp; 5½×8½; of. Reporting time: 2-6 months. Publishes 1% of manuscripts submitted. Payment: standard. Copyrights for author. PMA, SPAN.

The Ashland Poetry Press, Robert McGovern, Editor; Stephen Haven, Associate Editor, Ashland University, Ashland, OH 44805, 419-289-5110; FAX 419-289-5329. 1969. Poetry. "Thematic anthologies and occasional individual books of poems by a single poet; series of lectures by AU annual writer-in-residence. Annual Richard Snyder publication Competition for full-length collection of poetry." avg. press run 1M. Pub'd 1 title 1998; expects 2 titles 1999, 2 titles 2000. 26 titles listed in the *Small Press Record of Books in Print* (28th Edition, 1999-00). avg. price, paper: $9. Discounts: 40% to book companies. 85pp; 8½×5; of. Reporting time: solicited manuscripts mainly; Annual Snyder publication competition. We accept solicited simultaneous submissions. Payment: 10%. Does not copyright for author.

Ashton Productions, Inc., Susan Phelps, Ph.D., Publisher; Gina Byrne, Marketing Director, 1014 Gay Street, Sevierville, TN 37862-4213, 423-774-0174; api@ssmagnolia.com. 1995. Satire, non-fiction. "We do not return or respond to unsolicited manuscripts. Queries invited through referrals." avg. press run 7.5M. Pub'd 3 titles 1998; expects 2 titles 1999, 4 titles 2000. 3 titles listed in the *Small Press Record of Books in Print* (28th Edition, 1999-00). avg. price, cloth: $15.95; paper: $12.95; other: $12 monographs, special events. Discounts: 40% on STOP orders, distributed to the trade by all major wholesalers. 5½×8½. Reporting time: 2 months. Simultaneous submissions accepted: no. Publishes 2% of manuscripts submitted. Payment: negotiate with each author. Copyrights for author. PMA, Writers & Publishers PEG-NSA.

THE ASIAN PACIFIC AMERICAN JOURNAL, Hanya Yanagihara, Editor; Jerome Chou, Editor, 37 Saint Marks Place, New York, NY 10003-7801, 212-228-6718. 1992. Poetry, fiction, art, photos, parts-of-novels, long-poems, plays, non-fiction. "Open to working with new writers. Interested in works from all segments of the Asian Pacific American community. Special interest in works by Americans of Southeast Asian and South Asian descent and gay/lesbian Asian Americans." circ. 2M. 2/yr. Pub'd 2 issues 1998; expects 2 issues 1999, 2 issues 2000. sub. price: $35, includes membership to the Asian American Writers' Workshop; per copy: $10; sample: $12. Back issues: $12. Discounts: call for special prices. 200pp; 7×8¼; of. Reporting time: 3 months. We accept simultaneous submissions but please let us know. Publishes 20% of manuscripts submitted. Payment: 2 free copies. Copyrighted, reverts to author. Pub's reviews: 6 in 1998. §Asian or Asian American. Ads: $250/$120/quarter page $60.

ASIAN SURVEY, University of California Press, Lowell Dittmer, Editor; Joyce Kallgren, Editor; Bonnie Dehler, Assistant Editor, University of California Press, 2120 Berkeley Way, Berkeley, CA 94720, 510-643-7154. 1960. Non-fiction. "Editorial address: Institute of East Asian Studies, 6701 San Pablo Avenue, Room 408, Marchant Bldg., Oakland, CA 94608." circ. 2.7M. 12/yr. Pub'd 12 issues 1998; expects 12 issues 1999, 12 issues 2000. sub. price: $60 indiv., $133 instit., $33 students ($11 foreign postage); per copy: $9 indiv., $14 instit., $9 student; sample: free. Back issues: $7 indiv., $10 instit.; $7 student. Discounts: 10% foreign agents, 30% 10+ one time orders, standing orders (bookstores): 1-99 40%, 100+ 50%. 96pp; 6×9; of. Reporting time: 1-2 months. Payment: varies. Copyrighted, does not revert to author. Ads: $275/$200.

Aspire Publishing Company, Dave McWilliam, Fiction; Marni Shepard, Non-fiction, 1008 E. Baseline Road #878, Tempe, AZ 85283, 602-225-1447. 1994. "Fiction and non-fiction - all genre and categories" avg. press run 5M. Pub'd 3 titles 1998; expects 5 titles 1999, 7 titles 2000. avg. price, cloth: $22.95; paper: $6.95. Discounts: Discount ret: 1-4 20%, 5-24 40%, 25-49 42%, 50-99 43%, 100-999 45%, 1M+ 46%. No ret: 10-49 45%, 50-249 48%, 250-999 50%. Libraries: 1-9 10%, 10+ 15%. 300pp; 5½×8½. Reporting time: 1-3 months. Payment: 10% 50M 12½ standard paperback & hardback royalty. Copyrights for author.

ASSEMBLAGE: A Critical Journal of Architecture and Design Culture, Alicia Kennedy, K. Michael Hays, PO Box 180299, Boston, MA 02118, email assmblag@gsd.harvard.edu. 1986. Articles, art, photos, interviews, criticism, reviews, letters, non-fiction. "Send editorial correspondence and books for review to Alicia Kennedy, PO Box 180299. Send subscriptions and address changes to MIT Press Journals, 5 Cambridge Center, Suite 4, Cambridge MA 02142-1493. *Assemblage's* project is the theorization of architecture—its histories, its criticisms, and its practices—along cultural fault lines. Cutting across disciplines, we promote experiments with forms of exegesis, commentary, and analysis. Among the journal's recurring sections, 'The Strictly Architectural' raises the question of what 'properly' belongs to architecture, 'New Babylons' charts out an urbanism of ideas, 'Re:view' engages books and conferences as jumping off points for longer investigations, and 'Re:assemblage' sends trajectories into previous issues and out toward emerging debates." circ. 2.3M. 3/yr.

Pub'd 3 issues 1998; expects 3 issues 1999, 3 issues 2000. sub. price: $62 individuals, $130 institutions, $40 students; per copy: $22; sample: free to libraries for review. Back issues: $22 for individuals, $44 for institutions. Discounts: trade—under 5 copies 25%, 5+ 40%; agency 10%. 114pp; 8½×10¼; of. Reporting time: 2 months. Simultaneous submissions accepted: no. Publishes 10% of manuscripts submitted. Payment: none, contributors receive 2 copies of the journal. Copyrighted, does not revert to author. Pub's reviews: 6 in 1998. §Avant-garde/experimental art and architecture, cultural criticism. Ads: $350/$250/$625 2-page spread/agency discount 15%.

ASSEMBLING, Assembling Press, Charles Doria, Publisher, Editor; Richard Kostelanetz, Editor, Box 444 Prince Street, New York, NY 10012-0008. 1970. Poetry. "*Assembling* is a collaborative magazine. Contributors print 1M copies of up to three 8½ x 11 pages of anything they wish at their own initiative and expense. Contribution is by invitation. Those wishing invitations are invited to send sample manuscripts. Acceptance comes in the form of an invitation. Editors of *Assembling* are really compilers. Fourteen *Assembling* annuals have collected an unprecedented variety of avant-garde printed art. Individual books extend the press. Send SASE for catalogue." circ. 200. 1/yr. Pub'd 1 issue 1998; expects 1 issue 1999, 1 issue 2000. sub. price: $30; per copy: variable; sample: $10 for a sample. Back issues: complete set of Assembling $1000. Discounts: 40% to retailers paying in advance, and incl. postage. We do not send consignments as past issues are scarce. No returns accepted. All sales final. 300pp; size varies; mi, of, lp. Reporting time: 1 month. Payment: copies only. Copyrighted.

Assembling Press (see also ASSEMBLING), Charles Doria, Richard Kostelanetz, Box 444 Prince Street, New York, NY 10012-0008. 1970. "Assembling Press, now in its thirtieth year, publishes and distributes poetry, fiction (experimental and otherwise), criticism, artists' books and anthologies. We sponsor readings and other events, and arrange for the publication of *The Annual Assembling*, a collective anthology of artists and writers. We also distribute records and tapes or any other interesting art object that we can conveniently handle. We work closely with our authors to insure that each book is as close to the original concept as possible, without needless editorial intervention. Our publications have been reviewed, exhibited and distributed around the world." avg. press run 700. Expects 3 titles 2000. 4 titles listed in the *Small Press Record of Books in Print* (28th Edition, 1999-00). avg. price, cloth: $10; paper: $8. Discounts: 40% to dealers paying in advance; no returns accepted, all sales final. Pages vary; size varies; variable. Reporting time: 1 month. Payment: 10% of edition. Copyrights for author.

ASSEMBLY, Liturgy Training Publications, Nathan Mitchell, Editor, 1800 N. Hermitage Avenue, Chicago, IL 60622-1101, 773-486-8970. 1979. Articles, photos. "Explores the tradition, meaning and practice of some aspect of the liturgical/worship event in order to help the community and its ministers enter more deeply into the spirit of Christian worship." circ. 1M. 6/yr. Pub'd 5 issues 1998; expects 6 issues 1999, 6 issues 2000. sub. price: $15 US, $17 Canada, $19 foreign; per copy: $3; sample: $3. Back issues: $3. 8pp; 8½×11; of. Reporting time: 5 weeks. Payment: contributors paid. Copyrighted, reverts to author. Catholic Book Publishing Assn.

Associated Writing Programs (see also WRITER'S CHRONICLE), D.W. Fenza, Tallwood House, Mail Stop 1E3, George Mason Umiversity, Fairfax, VA 22030-0079, 703-993-4301. 1967. Articles, interviews, criticism, news items. "Articles pertaining to contemporary literature, writing, and the teaching of writing welcome. Book reviews, news items, grants & awards, magazine submission notices. Occasional interviews." avg. press run 17M. Pub'd 6 titles 1998; expects 6 titles 1999, 6 titles 2000. avg. price, paper: $3.95/issue, $20/year. Discounts: none. 36pp; 10×15; web offset. Reporting time: 3 months. Simultaneous submissions accepted: no. Publishes 5% of manuscripts submitted. Payment: copies and honorarium, $5/100 words for accepted articles; no kill-fees.

The Association of Freelance Writers (see also FREELANCE MARKET NEWS), A Cox, Sevendale House, 7 Dale Street, Manchester, M1 1JB, England, 0161-228-2362; Fax 0161-228-3533. 1960. "We use articles of interest to freelance writers" avg. press run 3M. avg. price, paper: £2.50. 16pp; size A4. Reporting time: 1 month. Simultaneous submissions accepted: no. Publishes 50% of manuscripts submitted. Payment: £35 per 1000 words. Does not copyright for author.

ASSPANTS, Chad Lange, Michael Barnett, 2232 15th Street, San Francisco, CA 94114-1238, E-mail asspants@sirius.com. 1996. "*Asspants* does not adhere to any one style or theme. We also have no restrictions on length. We do ask that fiction contributors send manuscripts no longer than 5000 words in length; poetry submitters should send no more than five poems at one time. Artists should not send original works. We gladly accept online submissions. Simultaneous submissions are also accepted. Recent contributors include Jules Mann, Gini Savage, Karen Newcombe, Carey Lamprecht, Jim Nawrocki, and Robert P. Langdon." circ. 250. 2/yr. Pub'd 4 issues 1998; expects 4 issues 1999, 4 issues 2000. sub. price: $16; per copy: $6; sample: $7. Back issues: 1st and 4th episodes for $7. 70pp; 8½×8½; printed. Reporting time: 2-3 months. Simultaneous submissions accepted: yes. Publishes 5% of manuscripts submitted. Payment: 1 copy of episode in which author is published. Copyrighted, reverts to author. Ads: $300/$150/$75 1/4.

Astarte Shell Press, Eleanor H. Haney, HC 63 Box 89, Bath, ME 04530-9503, 207-828-1992. 1989. Poetry, non-fiction. "Purpose: publication of books and other materials on feminist, spiritual, politics and related themes." avg. press run 4M. Pub'd 1 title 1998; expects 4 titles 1999, 4 titles 2000. 15 titles listed in the *Small Press Record of Books in Print* (28th Edition, 1999-00). avg. price, paper: $11. Discounts: 55% for distributors, 40% bookstores, 20% libraries Inbook. 275pp; 6×9; of. Reporting time: 2 months. Simultaneous submissions accepted: no. Payment: varies, 8% of income. Copyrights for author. Feminist Bookstore News, 456 14th St. #6, PO Box 882554, San Francisco, CA 94188; Maine Writers and Publishers Alliance.

ASTERISM: The Journal of Science Fiction, Fantasy, and Space Music, Jeff Berkwits, 3525 Lebon Drive #201, San Diego, CA 92122-4547, 847-568-3957; FAX 847-568-3999; asterismsf@aol.com. 1995. Reviews. "Inquire before submitting, needs are limited and quite specific." circ. 2001. 4/yr. Pub'd 4 issues 1998; expects 4 issues 1999, 4 issues 2000. sub. price: $6; per copy: $2.00; sample: $2.50. Discounts: none. 28pp; 5½×8½; of. Simultaneous submissions accepted: Occaasionally. Payment: none at this time. Copyrighted, reverts to author. §Music (cd & vinyl only). Ads: $85/$50/$20 1/4 page.

Astrion Publishing, Warren Sanderson, PO Box 783, Champlain, NY 12919, 514-935-4097. 1993. Art, satire, criticism, non-fiction. "We publish books on art, architecture, science, science fiction, humor and will consider well written, informative, rather than essentially theoretical, book length manuscripts in other fields. We are also interested in translations of important works recognized in Europe and Asia but not yet known in North America." avg. press run varies. Expects 3 titles 1999, 3 titles 2000. 3 titles listed in the *Small Press Record of Books in Print* (28th Edition, 1999-00). avg. price, cloth: $45; paper: $22. Discounts: schedule sent upon inquiry on letterhead company stationery. 125-400pp; 9×7; of, lp. Simultaneous submissions accepted: no. Payment: royalty scale. Copyrights for author. PMA.

Astro Black Books, Charles Luden, P O Box 46, Sioux Falls, SD 57101, 605-338-0277. 1976. Poetry. "Our first book published is *Virgin Death* by Charles Luden (Feb. 1977). Will not be reading any new manuscripts." avg. press run 1M. Pub'd 1 title 1998; expects 1 title 1999, 1 title 2000. 4 titles listed in the *Small Press Record of Books in Print* (28th Edition, 1999-00). avg. price, cloth: $15; paper: $5; other: $25 signed, numbered edition. Discounts: 35% to trade (stores), 45% to jobbers. 75-130pp; 5½×8½; of. Reporting time: 1 month. Payment: negotiable. Copyrights for author.

ASTROFLASH, ACS Publications, Maritha Pottenger, Editorial Director, PO Box 34487, San Diego, CA 92163, 619-297-9203. 1982. Articles, interviews, reviews. circ. 5M. 4/yr. Pub'd 4 issues 1998; expects 4 issues 1999, 4 issues 2000. sub. price: free to customers. 16pp; 8½×11. Payment: none. Copyrighted, reverts to author. Pub's reviews: 4 in 1998. §Astrology.

Asylum Arts, Greg Boyd, 5847 Sawmill Rd., Paradise, CA 95969, 530-876-1454; asyarts@sunset.net. 1990. Poetry, fiction, photos, criticism, long-poems, collages, plays. "Manuscripts by invitation only. Asylum Arts publishes high-quality literary titles—fiction, plays, translations, essays, and poetry—in attractive trade paperback format. Recent books by Gerard de Nerval, Robert Peters, Charles Baudelaire, Kenneth Bernard, Geoffrey Clark, and Cynthia Hendershot, Eric Basso, Richard Martin, and Samuel Appelbaum." avg. press run 1M. Pub'd 2 titles 1998; expects 8 titles 1999, 6 titles 2000. 31 titles listed in the *Small Press Record of Books in Print* (28th Edition, 1999-00). avg. price, cloth: $20; paper: $12. 128pp; 5½×8½; of. Reporting time: 1-3 months. Simultaneous submissions accepted: no. Payment: varies from book to book. Copyrights for author. CLMP.

●**AT THE LAKE MAGAZINE, B & B Publishing, Inc.,** Andria Hayday, Barb Krause, PO Box 96, Walworth, WI 53184, 414-275-9474; Fax 414-275-9530; at-the-lake@idcnet.com. 1997. Articles, photos, non-fiction. "Regional magazine focusing on Southeastern Wisconsin." circ. 27M. 4/yr. Pub'd 4 issues 1998; expects 4 issues 1999, 4 issues 2000. sub. price: $11.95; per copy: $3; sample: free. Back issues: $3 each. 84pp; 8¼×10¾; web press. Reporting time: 6 weeks. Simultaneous submissions accepted: yes. Publishes 10% of manuscripts submitted. Payment: $300 per article. Not copyrighted. Ads: $1600/$1000 (color).

ATELIER, Sarah Jensen, 8 Holton Street, Allston, MA 02134-1337. 1990. Poetry, fiction, art, interviews, criticism, reviews, parts-of-novels, long-poems, concrete art. "Mostly poetry, some fiction - any length (will print serially if lengthy). Bias toward experimental, Olson-inspired, Duncan-inspired, contemporary. Recent contributors: Vincent Ferrini, Ed Sanders, Andrew Schelling, Susan Smith Nash, Spencer Selby" circ. 250. 4/yr. Pub'd 4 issues 1998; expects 4 issues 1999, 4 issues 2000. sub. price: $18; per copy: $5; sample: $5. Back issues: $5. 48pp; 5½×8½; of. Reporting time: 3 months. Simultaneous submissions accepted: yes. Publishes 10% of manuscripts submitted. Payment: copies. Copyrighted, reverts to author. Pub's reviews: 4 in 1998. §Experimental poetry, haiku.

Athanor Books (a division of ETX Seminars), Bruce Schaffenberger, P.O.Box 22201, Sacramento, CA 95820, 916-424-4355. 1993. Non-fiction. "We publish exclusively non-fiction books on paranormal and mystical topics such as sacred sites and truelife stories of otherworldly encounters. The works we publish are handbooks, directories, and case studies." avg. press run 5M. Pub'd 1 title 1998; expects 3 titles 1999, 4 titles

2000. 2 titles listed in the *Small Press Record of Books in Print* (28th Edition, 1999-00). avg. price, paper: $25; other: $10. Discounts: 2-4 copies 20%, 5-99 40%, 100+ 50%. 300pp; 8½×11; perfect bound, spiral bound. Reporting time: 4-6 weeks. Simultaneous submissions accepted: yes. Publishes 2% of manuscripts submitted. Payment: 8% to 500 copies; 10% over. Copyrights for author. ABA, PMA, NABDE.

ATHLETIC THERAPY TODAY (ATT), Human Kinetics Pub. Inc., Joseph J. Godek, MS, Box 5076, Champaign, IL 61825-5076, 217-351-5076. 1996. Articles, reviews. "Provides insights into professional practice issues; health care techniques, practical applications of current research." circ. 1M. 6/yr. Pub'd 6 issues 1998; expects 6 issues 1999, 6 issues 2000. sub. price: $30 individual, $70 institution, $20 student; per copy: $6 ind., $13 inst.; sample: free. Back issues: $6 ind., $13 inst. Discounts: 5% agency. 56pp; 8½×11; of. Reporting time: 2 months. Simultaneous submissions accepted: no. Payment: none. Copyrighted, does not revert to author. §Rehabilitation, equipment for therapy/rehab. Ads: $300/$200. Midwest Publishers Assn., American Booksellers Assn.

AT-HOME DAD, Peter Baylies, 61 Brightwood Avenue, North Andover, MA 01845, E-mail: athomedad@aol.com; www.athomedad.com. 1994. Articles, satire, letters, news items, non-fiction. "First-hand experiences of being an at-home dad preferred; plus experiences of running a home business while caring for children." circ. 800. 4/yr. Pub'd 4 issues 1998; expects 4 issues 1999, 4 issues 2000. sub. price: $15; per copy: $3; sample: $1. 12pp; 8½×11; of. Reporting time: 2-4 weeks. Simultaneous submissions accepted: yes. Publishes 20% of manuscripts submitted. Payment: free year subscription plus media exposure (newsletter sent to 500 media outlets). Copyrighted, reverts to author. Pub's reviews: 10 in 1998. §Any on fatherhood, parenting, recipes, kid publications or products. Ads: none.

ATL Press, Inc., Tom Kesh, PO Box 4563 T Station, Shrewsbury, MA 01545, 508-898-2290; FAX 508-898-2063; E-mail 104362.2523@compuserve.com; atlpress@compuserve.com. 1992. "First-time and established authors. Titles vary from 200-400 pages." avg. press run 2M-25M. Expects 8 titles 1999, 14 titles 2000. 6 titles listed in the *Small Press Record of Books in Print* (28th Edition, 1999-00). avg. price, cloth: $175 (profesional titles), $35 (trade titles); paper: $110 (profesional), $19 (trade titles). Discounts: 1-5 copies 5%, 6-15 15%, 16+ 25%. 200-400pp; 6×9. Reporting time: 2-4 weeks. Simultaneous submissions accepted: yes. Publishes 5% of manuscripts submitted. Payment: case by case. PMA, ABA.

ATLANTA REVIEW, Daniel Veach, PO Box 8248, Atlanta, GA 31106. 1994. Poetry, fiction, art, interviews, parts-of-novels, non-fiction. "Primarily devoted to quality poetry of genuine human appeal. Also interviews, short fiction and non-fiction. *Atlanta Review* has published Seamus Heaney, Derek Walcott, Maxine Kumin, Charles Simic, Naomi Shibab Nye, Stephen Dunn, Rachel Hadas, and Charles Wright. Each spring issue features a new country or region: Ireland, England, Africa, the Caribbean. Art in black and white." circ. 4M. 2/yr. Pub'd 2 issues 1998; expects 2 issues 1999, 2 issues 2000. sub. price: $10; per copy: $6; sample: $5. Back issues: $5. Discounts: negotiable. 120pp; 6×9. Reporting time: 1 month. Simultaneous submissions accepted: yes. Publishes 1% of manuscripts submitted. Payment: 2 free copies. Copyrighted, reverts to author. Ads: $250/$125/na. CLMP, AWP.

ATOM MIND, Gregory Smith, PO Box 22068, Albuquerque, NM 87154. 1992. Poetry, fiction, articles, art, photos, cartoons, interviews, satire, reviews, parts-of-novels, long-poems, collages. "Originally published from 1968-70; began publishing again under imprint of Mother Road Publications in 1992. Each issue contains a segment called The Living Poets Series, which focuses on the work and life of one American poet, someone who has devoted his life to his art, in most cases for little material reward or widespread recognition." circ. 1M+. 4/yr. Pub'd 4 issues 1998; expects 4 issues 1999. sub. price: $20; per copy: $6; sample: $6. Back issues: $10, $25 signed & numbered copies. Discounts: 1-5 copies 35%, 6+ 40%. 120pp; 8½×11; of. Reporting time: 1-2 months. Simultaneous submissions accepted: no. Publishes 5% of manuscripts submitted. Payment: contributor's copies, with some cash awards. Copyrighted, reverts to author. Ads: $80/$50/$30 1/4 page.

Atrium Society Publications/DBA Education For Peace Publications, Martha Nye, Managing Director, PO Box 816, Middlebury, VT 05753, 802-388-0922; fax 802-388-1027; e-mail atrium@sover.net; www.atrium-soc.org. 1984. Art. "We focus exclusively on understanding conflict in its many forms (internal, interpersonal, international) and helping readers—particularly young readers—learn to resolve their differences nonviolently. We publish no unsolicited written material but are often interested in seeing samples of illustrative work for our non-fiction children's books." avg. press run 5M. Pub'd 4 titles 1998; expects 2 titles 1999, 2 titles 2000. 15 titles listed in the *Small Press Record of Books in Print* (28th Edition, 1999-00). avg. price, cloth: $19.95; paper: $14.95. 150pp; of. Payment: none. Publishers Marketing Assoc. (PMA).

ATROCITY, Hank Roll, 2419 Greensburg Pike, Pittsburgh, PA 15221. 1976. Fiction, articles, art, cartoons, satire, reviews, letters, concrete art, news items. "Length of material: half page. Biases: funny. Recent contributor: Joe Lintner. Don't waste our time with long stories." circ. 250. 12/yr. Pub'd 12 issues 1998; expects 12 issues 1999, 12 issues 2000. sub. price: $10; per copy: $1; sample: $1. Back issues: $1. 7pp; 11×8½; †xerox. Reporting time: 1 month. Simultaneous submissions accepted: yes. Publishes 33% of manuscripts submitted. Payment: copies. Copyrighted, reverts to author. Pub's reviews: 4 in 1998. §Humor, satire, comics, parody. Ads: $100/$50/$15 business card/$5 one line.

ATS Publishing, Robert Jay Bentz, 996 Old Eagle School Road, Suite 1105, Wayne, PA 19087, 610-688-6000. 1989. Non-fiction. avg. press run 2M. Pub'd 1 title 1998; expects 1 title 1999, 1 title 2000. 1 title listed in the *Small Press Record of Books in Print* (28th Edition, 1999-00). avg. price, paper: $29.95. Discounts: available upon request. 160pp; 5×7; of. Copyrights for author.

AU NATUREL, Federation quebecoise de naturisme, 4545 Pierre-de-Coubertin, C.P. 1000 succ. M., Montreal, Quebec, H1V 3R2, Canada, 514-252-3014, 514-254-1363, legrand@generation.net. 1982. Articles. "No copyright, but citation of source requested. Exchange of material whenever possible. *Au Naturel* is the official publication of the Federation. The Federation is affiliated with the International Naturist Federation, Antwerp, Belgium, and is a member of the Quebec Leisure Regrouping of the provincial Government (Quebec)" circ. 4M. 1/yr. Pub'd 2 issues 1998; expects 2 issues 1999, 2-3 issues 2000. sub. price: membership only $20 to $35 Can.; per copy: $5; sample: $7Can, $9US. Back issues: USA $2 each plus $4 mailing; minimum $10, limited supply. Discounts: 50% FAB Montreal. 24pp; 8×10½; of. Publishes 5% of manuscripts submitted. Payment: none. Not copyrighted. Pub's reviews: 4 in 1998. §Natural sciences, self-esteem, body appreciation, naturism-nudism, alternative medicine. Ads: $200-$300/$125-$175.

THE AUCTION MAGAZINE, Barbara Joyce, PO Box 62101-411, Houston, TX 77205, 713-359-1200. 1989. Articles, photos, interviews, reviews, news items, non-fiction. "Articles currently desired and used are relatively short. They are always related to auctions, auctioneers, or items sold at auctions." circ. 10M. 24/yr. Pub'd 24 issues 1998; expects 24 issues 1999, 24 issues 2000. sub. price: $129.95. 60pp; 8½×11. Not copyrighted. Pub's reviews. §Auctions, cars, antiques, computers, all items sold at auction.

AUFBAU, Monika Ziegler, Editor; Andreas Irink, Editor, 2121 Broadway, New York, NY 10023, 212-873-7400, fax 212-496-5736. 1934. Art, interviews, criticism, reviews, music, plays, news items, non-fiction. "*AUFBAU* is mainly read by and published for the German-speaking Jewish refugees who came to this country during WWII. *AUFBAU* used to be the leading publication for German exile literature and was connected with names like Albert Einstein, Thomas Mann, Hannah Arendt et al. The bi-weekly tabloid covering cultural and political events in Europe and the U.S. is read mainly in the United States, Germany, and Israel." circ. 20M. 26/yr. Pub'd 26 issues 1998; expects 26 issues 1999, 26 issues 2000. sub. price: USA $58.50; per copy: $2.50; sample: free. Back issues: varies from $2.00 to $20.00 depending upon year and volume. Discounts: special discounts for teachers upon request. 24pp; 10½×13¼; †desktop. Reporting time: 2-4 weeks. Publishes 50% of manuscripts submitted. Payment: monthly for freelancers, bi-weekly for staff. Copyrighted, does not revert to author. Pub's reviews: 200 in 1998. §American literature (fiction, poetry), Judaica, German Literature, WWII, Holocaust. Ads: $1110/$555/$1.50 per 14 pica line.

Aunt Lute Books, Joan Pinkvoss, PO Box 410687, San Francisco, CA 94141, 415-826-1300; FAX 415-826-8300. 1978. Fiction, criticism, plays, non-fiction. "We publish only multicultural, feminist material. Recent authors: Audre Lorde, Gloria Anzaldua, Melanie Kaye-Kantrowitz, Cherry Muhanji. Aunt Lute Books is part of the Aunt Lute Foundation, which is the non-profit entity that grew out of the work of Spinsters/Aunt Lute Book Co." avg. press run 3M-5M. Pub'd 6 titles 1998; expects 7 titles 1999, 5 titles 2000. 23 titles listed in the *Small Press Record of Books in Print* (28th Edition, 1999-00). avg. price, cloth: $18.95; paper: $9.95. Discounts: bookstores 40% on 5+ books, 50+ mixed titles 45%; distributors 50-55%, classroom 20%, no rate for single orders from library, jobbers, etc. 40% on STOP orders, 2-5 copies 20%. 200pp; 5½×8; of. Reporting time: 3 months. Payment: 7% on first 30,000, increased thereafter. Copyrights for author. Bookbuilders West.

AURA LITERARY/ARTS REVIEW, David Good, Steven Smith, Box 76, University Center, Birmingham, AL 35294, 205-934-3216. 1974. Poetry, fiction, articles, art, photos, interviews, reviews, plays. "No limits as to poem length, 5,000 word limit on prose. Recent contributors include Andrew Glaze, Jon Silkin, Fred Bonnie, Steven Ford Brown" circ. 500. 2/yr. Pub'd 2 issues 1998; expects 2 issues 1999, 2 issues 2000. sub. price: $6; per copy: $3; sample: $2.50. Back issues: $3. 100pp; 6×9; lp. Reporting time: 5-12 weeks. Simultaneous submissions accepted: yes. Publishes 10% of manuscripts submitted. Payment: 2 copies. Copyrighted, reverts to author. Pub's reviews: 3 in 1998. §fiction, poetry.

Auromere Books and Imports, 2621 W. US Highway 12, Lodi, CA 95242-9200, 800-735-4691; 209-339-3710; FAX 209-339-3715; sasp@aol.com. 1974. "Sri Aurobindo Books, classical Indian Spiritual Texts, Children's Books, and Health books, including Ayurveda. Also carry a number of side lines including imported bookmarks and incense. We are the exclusive U.S. representative of a number of publishers from India and their titles are significantly more in number. Including: Ganesh & Co.; National Book Trust of India; Hemkunt Books; All India Press; Children's Book Trust of India. In addition we also represent Sri Aurobindo Books Distribution Agency and here in the U.S., list has over titles. We do not accept submissions, as we publish existent classical texts. A free catalog of our books is available on request" avg. press run 5M-10M. Pub'd 1 title 1998; expects 3 titles 1999. 14 titles listed in the *Small Press Record of Books in Print* (28th

46

Edition, 1999-00). avg. price, cloth: $14; paper: $5.95. Discounts: trade 40%, $50 minimum order after discount; jobbers, distributors by arrangement. 200pp; 5⅜×8⅜. Payment: variable. Does not copyright for author. AAIP.

●THE AUROREAN, A POETIC QUARTERLY, Encircle Publications, Cynthia Brackett-Vincent, PO Box 219, Sagamore Beach, MA 02562-0219, 508-833-0805 phone/fax, phone before faxing. 1995. Poetry. "One of 12 'Insider Reports' in 1999 *Poet's Market*. Request guidelines or sample! 36 lines max. I always send proofs, I always acknowledge receipt of manuscript. One Poet-of-the-Quarter each issue receives 10 copies, 100 word bio. and 1 year subscription. Have published: Errol Miller, B.Z. Niditch, Kathleen Gunton Deal and Jadene Felina Stevens." circ. 350-400. 4/yr. Pub'd 4 issues 1998; expects 4 issues 1999, 4 issues 2000. sub. price: $17,$21 international; per copy: $5,$6 international; sample: $5,$6 international. 33pp; 5½×8½; of. Reporting time: 3-12 months maximum. Simultaneous submissions accepted if noted up front; I discourage them. Publishes 15% of manuscripts submitted. Payment: 3 copies/50 word bio in issue. Copyrighted, reverts to author. Ads: will do ad and subscription swaps with other magazines.

Austen Press, Peggy Rosenthal, Walter Ching, 620 Park Avenue #119, Rochester, NY 14607, 716-271-8520. 1993. "Publishing 'graphic novel' genre cartoon narratives of high literary quality." avg. press run 1M. Expects 2 titles 1999, 3 titles 2000. 1 title listed in the *Small Press Record of Books in Print* (28th Edition, 1999-00). avg. price, paper: $12.95. 150pp; 6×9. Payment: co-publishing only.

Author's Partner in Publishing, Don Chivers, Darrell Jones, Suite 551-800-15355 24th Avenue, White Rock, B.C. V4A 2H9, Canada, 604-535-8558; 604-536-6627; dchivers@uniserve.com. 1996. Fiction, non-fiction. "Recent contributors: John Cleverly, Alexander Noble, and Don Chivers." avg. press run 5M-10M. Expects 3 titles 1999, 6 titles 2000. 1 title listed in the *Small Press Record of Books in Print* (28th Edition, 1999-00). avg. price, cloth: $27.95; paper: $18.95. Discounts: subject to negotiation depending on quantity. 300pp; 6×9. Reporting time: 90 days. Simultaneous submissions accepted: yes. Publishes 5% of manuscripts submitted. Payment: negotiable. Copyrights for author.

AUTO-FREE TIMES, Randy Ghent, Jan Lundberg, Publisher, PO Box 4347, Arcata, CA 95518, 707-826-7775. 1995. Poetry, articles, art, photos, cartoons, interviews, reviews. "Max: 2,000 words; average: 1,000 words. Our name says it all (re: bias)." circ. 10M. 4/yr. Pub'd 4 issues 1998; expects 4 issues 1999, 4 issues 2000. sub. price: $30 includes membership to the Alliance for a Paving Moratorium; per copy: $3; sample: free. Discounts: 40-60% off cover price for distributors. 30pp; 8½×11; web press. Reporting time: maximum 1 month. Simultaneous submissions accepted: yes. Publishes 70% of manuscripts submitted. Payment: none, yet. Copyrighted, reverts to author. Pub's reviews: 4 in 1998. §Alternative transporation, alternatives to automobile and sprawl. Ads: contact office for quotes.

Autonomedia, Inc. (see also SEMIOTEXT(E)), Jim Fleming, Lewanne Jones, PO Box 568, Brooklyn, NY 11211, 718-936-2603, e-Mail autonobook@aol.com. 1983. Fiction, criticism, non-fiction. "Essays. Post-Marxist theory, post-structuralist theory, philosophy, politics and culture" avg. press run 5M. Pub'd 7 titles 1998; expects 7 titles 1999, 10 titles 2000. 4 titles listed in the *Small Press Record of Books in Print* (28th Edition, 1999-00). avg. price, cloth: $21.95; paper: $9.95. Discounts: trade 40%, distributors 50%. 300pp; 6×9; of. Reporting time: 6 weeks. Payment: arranged per title for royalties. Copyrights for author. CLMP, PMA.

Autumn Publishing Group, LLC., Michael J. Matthews, PO Box 71604, Madison Heights, MI 48071, 810-589-5249; fax 810-585-5715; email TSMPublish@aol.com. 1995. Non-fiction. "Specializes in non-fiction and 'how-to' information books on work/family issues, human resources, seniors, family, parenting, and employment. We seek out non-traditional sales outlets for usable information. No manuscripts, query first with a SASE" avg. press run 5M-10M. Pub'd 1 title 1998; expects 3 titles 1999, 3 titles 2000. 1 title listed in the *Small Press Record of Books in Print* (28th Edition, 1999-00). avg. price, paper: $19.95. Discounts: 6-199 40%, 200-499 50%, 500+ 55%. 300pp; 7⅜×9¼; †of, web. Reporting time: 4 weeks. If we are notified, we will accept simultaneous submissions. Payment: negotiated, average 8% of list price. Copyrights for author. PMA.

Avalon Writing Center, Inc., Frances E. Hanson, PO Box 183, Mills, WY 82644, 307-235-6177; E-mail fehanson@juno.com. 1996. "We are boook doctors. We do ghost writing, revisions, and offer a full line of author services. Our publishing exists of projects done by in-house staff. We also do a workshop on writing, editing, proofing, and publishing." avg. press run 1M. Pub'd 1 title 1998; expects 1 title 1999, 1 title 2000. 3 titles listed in the *Small Press Record of Books in Print* (28th Edition, 1999-00). avg. price, cloth: $40; paper: $12.95. Discounts: 20/40 5-25 books, 55% 25+. 180pp; 8½×11, 5½×7½, 6½×9½; of, lp. Simultaneous submissions accepted: no. Publishes 1% of manuscripts submitted. Copyrights for author. PMA.

Averasboro Press (see also CAPE FEAR JOURNAL), John Hairr, Joey Powell, PO Box 482, Erwin, NC 28339, E-mail jpowell@nceye.net. 1992. News items, non-fiction. avg. press run 1M. Pub'd 2 titles 1998; expects 15 titles 1999, 10 titles 2000. 6 titles listed in the *Small Press Record of Books in Print* (28th Edition, 1999-00). avg. price, paper: $12.95. Discounts: 40% off orders of 10+. 150pp; 6×9; of. Reporting time: 6 months. Simultaneous submissions accepted: no. Publishes 25% of manuscripts submitted. Payment:

negotiable. Copyrights for author. SPAWN.

Avery Color Studios, Wells Chapin, 511 D Avenue, Gwinn, MI 49841, 800-722-9925. 1956. Fiction, photos, non-fiction. "History, folklore, shipwrecks, pictorials. Contributors: Frederick Stonehouse, Jerry Harju, Joan Bestwick, Neil Moran, Cully Gage, Wes Oleszewski." avg. press run 3M. Pub'd 2 titles 1998; expects 4 titles 1999, 2 titles 2000. 34 titles listed in the *Small Press Record of Books in Print* (28th Edition, 1999-00). avg. price, paper: $10.95-$17.95. Discounts: 40% trade. 185pp; 5½×8½, 7×10; of. Reporting time: 30 days. Payment: negotiable. Copyrights for author.

Avery Publishing Group, Inc., Rudy Shur, Managing Editor, 120 Old Broadway, Garden City Park, NY 11040, 516-741-2155. 1976. Non-fiction. avg. press run 10M-20M. Pub'd 35 titles 1998; expects 40 titles 1999, 40 titles 2000. avg. price, cloth: $25; paper: $9.95. Discounts: college 20%, trade 20% to 45%. 200pp; 6×9; of. Reporting time: 2 weeks. Simultaneous submissions accepted: yes. Publishes 2% of manuscripts submitted. Payment: 10% of net, paid semi-annually. Copyrights for author.

Aviation Book Company, Nancy Griffith, 7201 Perimeter Road South, Seattle, WA 98108-2999. 1964. Non-fiction. "Aviation only." avg. press run 3M. Expects 3 titles 1999. 2 titles listed in the *Small Press Record of Books in Print* (28th Edition, 1999-00). avg. price, cloth: $25; paper: $15. Discounts: distributor, dealer, school, public library. 192pp; 8×10; of. Reporting time: 90 days. Payment: usually 10% of list price. Copyrights for author.

Avisson Press, Inc., M.L. Hester, 3007 Taliaferro Road, Greensboro, NC 27408, 336-288-6989 phone/FAX. 1995. Non-fiction. "Book-length only; regional; helpful book for senior citizens or teens; young adult (age 12-18) biographies of famous people or historical period; writer's reference books. Additional address: PO Box 38816, Greensboro, NC 27438" avg. press run 1M-3M. Pub'd 8 titles 1998; expects 8 titles 1999, 8 titles 2000. avg. price, cloth: $23; paper: $12. Discounts: 20-40%. 144pp; 5½×8½; of. Reporting time: 2-4 weeks. Simultaneous submissions accepted: yes. Publishes 1% of manuscripts submitted. Payment: standard royalty (6-10%). Copyrights for author.

Avocet Press Inc., Melanie Kershaw, Cynthia Webb, 635 Madison Avenue, Suite 400, New York, NY 10022, 212-754-6300; email oopc@interport.net; www.avocetpress.com. 1997. Poetry, fiction. "Publishers of Renee Ashley's second book of poetry *The Various Reasons of Light*." avg. press run 3M. Pub'd 1 title 1998; expects 3 titles 1999, 6 titles 2000. 3 titles listed in the *Small Press Record of Books in Print* (28th Edition, 1999-00). avg. price, paper: $12.95. Reporting time: 6 months. Simultaneous submissions accepted: yes. Publishes 1% of manuscripts submitted. Copyrights for author. PMA.

AVON LITERARY INTELLIGENCER, Dan Richardson, T. Chatterton, 20 Byron Place, Bristol, BS8 1JT, United Kingdom, 44-225-826105. 1992. Poetry, fiction, satire, reviews, parts-of-novels. "Helen Dunmore, Fred Beake, Philip Gross, Pamela Gillilan, William Oxley. Fast talking, slow talking stories" circ. 200. 4/yr. Pub'd 4 issues 1998; expects 4 issues 1999, 4 issues 2000. sub. price: $10; per copy: $5; sample: $5. Back issues: $10. 10pp; 8½×11; photocopy. Reporting time: 2 weeks. Payment: none. Not copyrighted. Pub's reviews: 6 in 1998. §US/UK poetry, short fiction. Ads: $100/$50/free notices.

AXE FACTORY REVIEW, Cynic Press, Joseph Farley, PO Box 40691, Philadelphia, PA 19107. 1986. Poetry, fiction, articles, art, photos, cartoons, interviews, satire, criticism, reviews, music, letters, parts-of-novels, long-poems, collages, plays, concrete art, news items, non-fiction. "Poetry, black and white art, and book reviews have the best shot. Also read short stories. Recent contributors include Louis McKee, Taylor Graham, John Sweet, A.O. Winans, Xu Juan, Arthur Winfield Knight. Indexed in *Index of American Periodical Verse*." circ. 100. 2-3/yr. Expects 2 issues 1999, 2-3 issues 2000. sub. price: $20/5 issues; per copy: $5; sample: $3. Back issues: $3. Discounts: none. Pages vary; 8½×11; †mi. Reporting time: immediately. Simultaneous submissions accepted: yes. Publishes 10% of manuscripts submitted. Payment: 2 copies; more for featured poet. Copyrighted, reverts to author. Pub's reviews: 8 in 1998. §Poetry, sci-fi, martial arts, Asian literature and history, fiction, short stories, American history, Medieval history, sex, art history. Ads: $50/$25/trade. Cynic Poetry Circle.

Axelrod Publishing of Tampa Bay, Sally Axelrod, 1304 De Soto Avenue, PO Box 14248, Tampa, FL 33690, 813-251-5269. 1985. Non-fiction, fiction, art, satire. "May condsider other materials" avg. press run 1.5M-5M. Pub'd 3 titles 1998; expects 3 titles 1999, 3 titles 2000. avg. price, cloth: $25; paper: $17. Discounts: 40-55% net 30-60 to be determined at point of purchase. 300pp; 5½×8½, 6×9, 7×10, 8×10; sheetfed offset. Reporting time: 2-4 weeks, prefer cover letter, outline & SASE. We prefer not to receive simultaneous submissions. Publishes 20% of manuscripts submitted. Payment: author subsidizes cost of production; publisher is paid percentage of sales for marketing, sales and fulfillment. Copyrights for author. PMA, PAS.

Axiom Information Resources, Terry Robinson, PO Box 8015, Ann Arbor, MI 48107, 313-761-4842. 1987. Non-fiction. avg. press run 10M. Pub'd 1 title 1998; expects 1 title 1999, 5 titles 2000. 7 titles listed in the *Small Press Record of Books in Print* (28th Edition, 1999-00). avg. price, paper: $12.95. Discounts: 10 or more copies

40%. 182pp; 5½×8½. Copyrights for author. PMA.

Axiom Press, Publishers, Erik Jorgensen, PO Box L, San Rafael, CA 94913, 415-956-4859. 1977. Non-fiction. *"Successful Real Estate Sales Agreements* is the ultimate authoritative guide for Real Estate agents, brokers, and investors for structuring and understanding transactions, contracts, and negotiation. It is both a day-to-day realtor's handbook and an essential reference book for school and business libraries. It is an excellent second text for real estate and business courses. Additionally, this 4th Edition has been substantially revised and expanded to include discussion of and instruction about creative financing, new disclosures and comparison of printed forms in common use, etc. This Edition matches the diversity of the free-flowing and difficult investment market, and successfully decodes its complexities. Realtors across the country have found this book a "must" for each day's challenges, and many schools structure courses around the information it offers" avg. press run 5M. Pub'd 2 titles 1998; expects 2 titles 1999. 1 title listed in the *Small Press Record of Books in Print* (28th Edition, 1999-00). avg. price, paper: $17.95. Discounts: 2-4, 20%; 5-9, 30%;10-99, 40%; 100+, 50%. 370pp; 6×9; of. Reporting time: 2 weeks. Payment: royalty. Copyrights for author. PMA.

AXIOS, Axios Newletter, Inc., Daniel John Gorham, 30-32 Macaw Avenue, PO Box 279, Belmodan, Belize, 501-8-23284. 1981. Articles, art, photos, interviews, criticism, reviews, letters, parts-of-novels, non-fiction. *"Axios* is published for the purpose of explaining the world-wide Orthodox Catholic faith and religious practices to those who would wish to have a better understanding of it. *Axios* carries articles that help to give a religious solution to world and personal problems. We criticize the half-stupid ideas put forth by the 'reasonable men of this world'! Now read in 32 countries." circ. 8,462. 10/yr. Pub'd 12 issues 1998; expects 10 issues 1999, 6 issues 2000. sub. price: $10; per copy: $2; sample: $2. Back issues: $2. Discounts: 40%. 24pp; 8½×11; †of. Reporting time: 2-4 weeks. Payment: varies. Copyrighted. Pub's reviews: 15 in 1998. §Religion, all types! (Our book reviews are well read in religious book stores.). Ads: $85/$55. OCPA, ACP.

Axios Newletter, Inc. (see also AXIOS; GORHAM; THE VORTEX; Orthodox Mission in Belize; ORTHODOX MISSION), Daniel John Gorham, Joseph T. Magnin, 30-32 Macaw Avenue, PO Box 279, Belmopan, Belize, 501-8-23284. 1981. Articles, art, photos, cartoons, interviews, satire, criticism, reviews, letters, parts-of-novels, news items, non-fiction. "We publish Orthodox Christian books, art and pamphlets, also philosophy and historical books. Republish old out-of-print books, in some cases—would like to see some religious history of Russia, Greece, Albania, Bulgaria, Finland, Rumania, and also America, if it pertains to the Orthodox Christian." avg. press run varies. Pub'd 3 titles 1998; expects 5 titles 1999. 1 title listed in the *Small Press Record of Books in Print* (28th Edition, 1999-00). avg. price, cloth: $10.95; paper: $3.75-$6.95. Discounts: 40% trade. 355pp; size varies; †of. Reporting time: 2-4 weeks. Payment: negotiated. Copyrights for author. OCPA, ACP, Belize Publishers.

THE AZOREAN EXPRESS, Seven Buffaloes Press, Art Coelho, PO Box 249, Big Timber, MT 59011. 1985. Poetry, fiction, art, photos, cartoons, collages. "Although I have a strong focus on rural America and working people, I also consider non-rural material and everything of literary value. Spotlight is on poetry and fiction. Prefer fiction to be 5 or 6 double-space pages. Will accept stories up to 10 double-space pages." circ. 500. 2/yr. Pub'd 1 issue 1998; expects 2 issues 1999, 2 issues 2000. sub. price: $10; per copy: $8.75; sample: $7.75. Back issues: $2.50 p.p. 24-30pp; 5½×8½; †of. Reporting time: 1 day to 2 weeks. Payment: copies. Copyrighted, reverts to author. CLMP.

AZTLAN: A Journal of Chicano Studies, Chicano Studies Research Center Publications, Chon A. Noriega, University of California-Los Angeles, PO Box 951544, Los Angeles, CA 90095, 310-825-2642. 1970. Articles, criticism, reviews, news items. *"Aztlan* is the oldest continuously published journal focusing on the Chicano experience in the U.S. and Mexico." circ. 1M. 2/yr. Pub'd 2 issues 1998; expects 2 issues 1999, 2 issues 2000. sub. price: $25 individuals, $50 libraries & institutions. Discounts: classroom use. 200pp; 6×9; of. Reporting time: 6 months. Simultaneous submissions accepted: yes. Publishes 25% of manuscripts submitted. Payment: books in quantity. Copyrighted, reverts to author. Pub's reviews: 6 in 1998. §Chicano studies. Ads: none.

B

B & B Publishing, Inc. (see also AT THE LAKE MAGAZINE), PO Box 96, 820 Wisconsin Street, Walworth, WI 53184, 414-275-9474. 1990. Non-fiction. "We publish 7-10 titles per year. Titles include: *The Awesome Almanac Series* (WI, MI, MN, IL, IN, CA, FL, GA, TX, OH, NY). Looking for supplementary education material. Grades 1-10. We also publish a regional magazine for Southeastern Wisconsin tourists." avg. press run 5M. Pub'd 5 titles 1998; expects 3 titles 1999, 5 titles 2000. 13 titles listed in the *Small Press*

Record of Books in Print (28th Edition, 1999-00). avg. price, paper: $14.95. Discounts: call and request. 200pp; size varies; web press. Reporting time: varies. Publishes 1% of manuscripts submitted. Payment: varies. Copyrights for author. MAPA, PMA.

●**The B & R Samizdat Express,** Barbara Hartley Seltzer, Richard Seltzer, Robert Richard Seltzer, Heather Katherine Seltzer, Michael Richard Seltzer, Timothy Seltzer, PO Box 161, West Roxbury, MA 02132, 617-469-2269; E-mail seltzer@samizdat.com; www.samizdat.com. 1974. Fiction. "We publish two titles. 1) *The Lizard of Oz,* a fable for all ages 2) *Now & Then & Other Tales from Ome,* a short collection of children's stories. We publish electronic books on IBM diskettes. We do not solicit manuscripts" avg. press run 2M-6M. 37 titles listed in the *Small Press Record of Books in Print* (28th Edition, 1999-00). avg. price, cloth: $12.95; paper: $1.95-$4.50; other: $10-$40 electronic books. Discounts: trade 40% (orders of 5 or more copies) 20% (orders of less than 5). 64-128pp; 5½×8½; of. Copyrights for author.

B.A Cass Publishing, #1101-140 10th Avenue S.W., Calgary Alberta T2R 0A3, Canada, 403-264-9714; fax 403-261-3673; E-mail bacass@iul-ccs.com. 1 title listed in the *Small Press Record of Books in Print* (28th Edition, 1999-00).

B.A.D. Press (see also BREAKFAST ALL DAY), Philip Boxall, 43 Kingsdown House, Amhurst Road, London E8 2AS, United Kingdom, 0171-923-0734. 1995.

●**Baba Yoga Micropress,** 430 N. Main Street, Herkimer, NY 13350. 1994. Poetry, fiction, articles, art, photos, interviews, satire, criticism, reviews, music, letters, long-poems, collages, plays, concrete art, non-fiction. "Looking to publish the mature work of deceased women who in some way or other lived outside the dominant society." avg. press run 50. Expects 1 title 1999, 1 title 2000. avg. price, cloth: $50; paper: $20. Discounts: 5+ books 1/3 off. 80pp; 8×10; of. Reporting time: 2 months. Simultaneous submissions accepted: yes. Payment: 15% to author's heir or estate executor.

BabelCom, Inc., David Appell, Paul Balido, 231 W. 16th Street #5WR, New York, NY 10011-6015, 212-627-2074. 1994. Non-fiction. "Focus is on romance and social life in conjunction with travel" avg. press run 5M. Expects 6 titles 1999, 6 titles 2000. 5 titles listed in the *Small Press Record of Books in Print* (28th Edition, 1999-00). avg. price, paper: $9.95. Discounts: 55% wholesale, 40% bookstore. 160pp; 4¼×5½; of. ABA.

BABYSUE, BABYSUE MUSIC REVIEW, Don W. Seven, PO Box 8989, Atlanta, GA 31106, 404-320-1178. 1985. Poetry, cartoons, interviews, satire, reviews, music. "We mainly feature bizarre adult cartoons, although we feature poetry, interviews, and reviews as well." circ. 5M. 2/yr. Pub'd 2 issues 1998; expects 2 issues 1999, 2 issues 2000. sub. price: $12; per copy: $3; sample: $3. Back issues: $3. 32pp; 8½×11; †of. Reporting time: 1 month. Simultaneous submissions accepted: yes. Publishes 5% of manuscripts submitted. Payment: 1 free copy of magazine in which work appears. Copyrighted, reverts to author. Pub's reviews: 10 in 1998. §Cartoons, music magazines, cassettes, CDs and vinyl. Ads: $150/$75.

BABYSUE MUSIC REVIEW, BABYSUE, Don W. Seven, S. Fievet, PO Box 8989, Atlanta, GA 31106, 404-320-1178. 1985. Photos, cartoons, interviews, music, news items. "*babysue Music Review* consists mostly of music reviewS. We review all types of music on all formats (vinyl, CD, cassette)." circ. 5M. 4/yr. Pub'd 4 issues 1998; expects 4 issues 1999, 4 issues 2000. sub. price: $12; per copy: $3; sample: $3. Back issues: $3 per issue (if available). Discounts: varies. 32pp; 8½×11; of. Reporting time: 3 months. Payment: each contributor recieves 1 copy of the issue in which their contribution appears. Copyrighted, reverts to author. Pub's reviews: 25 in 1998. §Anything related to music. Ads: $150/$80/$50 quarter page.

The Bacchae Press, Robert Brown, c/o The Brown Financial Group, 10 Sixth Street, Astoria, OR 97103-5315, 503-325-7972; FAX 503-325-7959; 800-207-4358; E-mail brown@pacifier.com. 1992. Poetry, fiction. "We publish mostly poetry. In 1993, we published 5 books of poetry: 2 anthologies of local poets, 1 full-length collection of poetry, and two chapbooks. All of our books are professionally printed on high-quality paper. Chapbook contest deadline is April 15." avg. press run 500. Pub'd 3 titles 1998; expects 4 titles 1999, 4 titles 2000. 4 titles listed in the *Small Press Record of Books in Print* (28th Edition, 1999-00). avg. price, paper: $8; other: $5 chapbooks. Discounts: 40%. 70pp; 5½×8½; of. Reporting time: 3 months. Simultaneous submissions accepted: yes. Publishes less than 1% of manuscripts submitted. Payment: 10%. Copyrights for author.

Bacchus Press Ltd., James M. Gabler, 1751 Circle Road, Baltimore, MD 21204, 301-576-0762. 1983. Non-fiction. "We publish books on wine and wine-related subjects." avg. press run 5M. Pub'd 2 titles 1998. 3 titles listed in the *Small Press Record of Books in Print* (28th Edition, 1999-00). avg. price, cloth: $25; paper: $12.95. Discounts: 40% libraries; 40% booksellers; 55% wholesalers. 167-315pp; 7×10, 6×9; lp. Reporting time: 2 months. Simultaneous submissions accepted: no. Payment: 20%. Copyrights for author. PASCAL, ABA.

BACKBOARD, Backspace Ink, Joanne Shwed, 561 Paloma Avenue, Pacifica, CA 94044-2438, 650-355-4640; FAX 650-355-3630; joski@ix.netcom.com. 1986. Poetry, articles, art, interviews, reviews, music, news items. "Brief, newsworthy, creative." circ. 200. 1/yr. Expects 1 issue 2000. sub. price: free; per copy: free; sample: free. Back issues: free. 4-8pp; 8½×11; of. Reporting time: 1 month. Payment: client basis. Copyrighted, reverts to author. §All areas. No ads at present.

Backcountry Publishing, Michelle Riley, Editor; Matt Richards, Editor, PO Box 343, Rexford, MT 59930, 541-955-5650. 1997. Non-fiction. "Books and booklets (40-600 pages); Only interested in authors who want to take strong role in publicizing, publishing their own books. We are a publishing co-op that supports, shares and directs authors through collective publishing. Topics limited to primitive skills, wilderness living, and simple living. Backcountry Publishing is distributed by Partners Publishers Group." avg. press run 5K. Pub'd 1 title 1998; expects 3 titles 1999. 1 title listed in the *Small Press Record of Books in Print* (28th Edition, 1999-00). avg. price, paper: $14.95. Discounts: 3-20 40%, 20-199 40% + free shipping, 200-499 50%, 500+ 55%. 180pp; 5½×8½; of. Reporting time: 4-6 weeks. Simultaneous submissions accepted: yes. Payment: individual basis. Does not copyright for author. PMA.

BACKSPACE: A QUEER POETS JOURNAL, Kimberly J. Smith, Charlotte A. Stratton, 25 Riverside Avenue, Gloucester, MA 01930-2552, e-mail bkspqpj@aol.com. 1991. Poetry, fiction, art, photos, cartoons, collages. "Poetry up to 8 pieces, no longer than 50 lines each. We will spotlight one piece of fiction per issue, no longer than 2,500 words. Submissions by e-mail or snailmail. 3.5 floppy disk in Ms Word, QuarkXpress or Ascii formats." 3/yr. Pub'd 4 issues 1998; expects 4 issues 1999, 4 issues 2000. sub. price: $10 includes postage; per copy: $5 includes postage; sample: $2. 28+pp; 5½×8½; †Laser/Xerox. Reporting time: 2 month deadline, response to submission is immediate. Not copyrighted. Pub's reviews. §Alternative lifestyles. Ads: $12 2X/$10 2X.

Backspace Ink (see also BACKBOARD), Joanne Shwed, 561 Paloma Avenue, Pacifica, CA 94044-2438, 650-355-4640; FAX 650-355-3630; joski@ix.netcom.com. 1985. Poetry, art, music. "Recent contributors: Thomas A. Ekkens, San Francisco poet, artist and musician; Mark S. Johnson, Bay Area writer; Chappell Rose Holt, Bay Area artist." avg. press run 200. Expects 1 title 2000. 1 title listed in the *Small Press Record of Books in Print* (28th Edition, 1999-00). avg. price, cloth: $12. Discounts: trade. 96pp; 5½×8½; of. Reporting time: client basis. Payment: client basis. Copyrights for author.

●**The Backwaters Press**, Greg Kosmicki, 3502 North 52nd Street, Omaha, NE 68104-3506, 402-451-4052. 1997. Poetry, fiction. "Ms. by invitation only, except for annual Backwaters prize competition. Send SASE for prize details. Postmark deadline for ms. submission for Backwaters prize is May 30th." avg. press run 300-600. Pub'd 1 title 1998; expects 4 titles 1999, 4 titles 2000. 2 titles listed in the *Small Press Record of Books in Print* (28th Edition, 1999-00). avg. price, paper: $12. Discounts: libraries and bookstores, please query. 80pp; 5½×8½; of. Reporting time: Submissions by invitation only except for the Backwaters Prize annual competition, send SASE for prize details. Simultaneous submissions accepted for prize competition, if so noted. Publishes 1% of manuscripts submitted. Copyrights for author. CLMP.

THE BADGER STONE CHRONICLES, Seven Buffaloes Press, Art Coelho, PO Box 249, Big Timber, MT 59011. 1987. Poetry. "This literary newsletter is dedicated to the life and artistic times of the late Michael Lynn Coelho—pen name: Badger Stone. Each issue special theme. #2 issue, Family Farm." 2/yr. sub. price: $5. 8pp; 8½×11.

THE BAFFLER, Tom Frank, Matt Weiland, PO Box 378293, Chicago, IL 60637. 1988. Poetry, fiction, articles, art, photos, cartoons, interviews, satire, criticism, reviews, music, letters, parts-of-novels, long-poems, collages, non-fiction. "Emphasis on criticism of culture, media, art, etc. Have published cartoons, art poetry, critique, fiction, etc" circ. 30M. 3/yr. Pub'd 1 issue 1998; expects 2 issues 1999, 3 issues 2000. sub. price: $20/4 issues; per copy: $6; sample: $6. Back issues: All sold out (1-5) #6,7,8,9 $10 each. 128pp; 6×9; of. Reporting time: 4-6 months. Simultaneous submissions accepted: no. Publishes 5% of manuscripts submitted. Payment: yes. Copyrighted, does not revert to author. Pub's reviews: 30 in 1998. §Literature, politics, culture, media, sociology, business. Ads: $1000/600.

Bain-Dror International Travel, Inc. (BDIT), Eli Dror, Joseph H. Bain, PO Box 1405, Port Washington, NY 11050, 513-944-5508; fax 516-944-7540. 1984. Non-fiction. avg. press run 10M. Pub'd 1 title 1998; expects 2 titles 1999, 3 titles 2000. 2 titles listed in the *Small Press Record of Books in Print* (28th Edition, 1999-00). avg. price, paper: $27. Discounts: trade 40%, jobber 50%, distributors 55%. 600pp; 5½×8½.

BAJA SUN, Editorial El Sol De Baja, T. Michael Bircumshaw, 858 3rd Avenue #456, Chula Vista, CA 91911-1305, 1-800-WIN BAJA. 1990. Poetry, fiction, articles, photos, cartoons, interviews, satire, criticism, reviews, music, letters, parts-of-novels, news items, non-fiction. "*The Baja Sun* is the largest, most comprehensive, only English language publication in Baja California, Mexico. 500-1500 words—material to be related to Baja California, Mexico" circ. 250M. 12/yr. Pub'd 12 issues 1998; expects 12 issues 1999, 12 issues 2000. sub. price: $18; per copy: $2; sample: free. Back issues: $2. Discounts: negotiable. 40pp; 10×13; web press. Payment: negotiable. Copyrighted, reverts to author. Pub's reviews: 8 in 1998. §Baja California, doing business in Mexico, Mexico. Ads: $1000/550/.60 per word.

BAKER STREET GAZETTE, Baker Street Publications, Sharida Rizzuto, Harold Tollison, Ann Hoyt, Rose Dalton, 577 Central Avenue, Box 4, Jefferson, LA 70121-1400, E-mail sherlockian@mailcity.com, sherlockian@england.com, www2.cybercities.com/z/zines/. 1983. Poetry, fiction, articles, art, photos, cartoons, interviews, satire, criticism, reviews, letters, long-poems, collages, news items, non-fiction. circ. 500. 2/yr. Pub'd 2 issues 1998; expects 2 issues 1999, 2 issues 2000. sub. price: $13.80; per copy: $6.90; sample: $6.90. Back issues: $6.90. Discounts: trade with other like publications. 80pp; 8½×11; †of, excellent quality offset covers. Reporting time: 2-6 weeks. Simultaneous submissions accepted: yes. Publishes 30-35% of manuscripts submitted. Payment: free copies, fees paid to all contributors negotiable. Copyrighted, reverts to author. Pub's reviews: 24 in 1998. §Sherlock Holmes and Victorian Times, zines, books films, internet websites. Ads: free. NWC, HWA, MWA, Western Writers of America (WWA), Arizona Author Association (AAA), Small Press Genre Association.

Baker Street Publications (see also BAKER STREET GAZETTE; SLEUTH JOURNAL; JACK THE RIPPER GAZETTE; PEN & INK WRITERS JOURNAL), Sharida Rizzuto, Harold Tollison, Ann Hoyt, Rose Dalton, 577 Central Avenue, Box 4, Jefferson, LA 70121-1400, E-mail sherlockian@mailcity.com, sherlockian@england.com, www2.cybercities.com/z/zines/. 1983. Poetry, fiction, articles, art, photos, cartoons, interviews, satire, criticism, reviews, letters, long-poems, collages, plays, news items, non-fiction. "We plan to publish several poetry chapbooks and a few story anthologies this year. This year we are expanding to non-fiction books and novels. We are interested in published writers and talented newcomers." avg. press run 300-1M. Pub'd 35 titles 1998; expects 45 titles 1999, 45 titles 2000. 1 title listed in the *Small Press Record of Books in Print* (28th Edition, 1999-00). avg. price, paper: $5-12; other: card stock covers $5-10. Discounts: trades. 80-100pp; 8½×11; †of. Reporting time: 2-6 weeks. Simultaneous submissions accepted: yes. Publishes 30-40% of manuscripts submitted. Payment: 50% after printing costs for books; negotiable for non-fiction; free copy(s) for poetry and fiction. Copyrights for author. National Writers Club (NWC), Western Writers of America (WWA), Arizona Authors Associaiton (AAS), Small Press Genre Association, Horror Writers of America (HWA), Mystery Writers of America.

Walter H. Baker Company (Baker's Plays), John B. Welch, 100 Chauncy St., Boston, MA 02111, 617-482-1280; Fax 617-982-7613; E-mail http://www.ziplink.net/bakers.plays.html. 1845. Plays. "Seeking one-act, full length, musicals, chancel and children's plays." avg. press run 1M. Expects 18 titles 1999, 25 titles 2000. 3 titles listed in the *Small Press Record of Books in Print* (28th Edition, 1999-00). avg. price, paper: $3.25-$9.95. Discounts: 20-40%. 50pp. Reporting time: 3-4 months. Payment: varies, 50/50 split amateur rights; 80/20 split professional rights; 10% book royalty. Copyrights for author.

Balboa Books, PO Box 658, Newport Beach, CA 92661, 714-720-8464. 1987. avg. press run 5M. Expects 1 title 1999, 1 title 2000. 1 title listed in the *Small Press Record of Books in Print* (28th Edition, 1999-00). avg. price, cloth: $20. 200pp; 5½×8½; of. Reporting time: 3 months.

Balcony Press, 512 E. Wilson, #306, Glendale, CA 91206. 1994. Art, non-fiction. "Prefer art and architecture submissions with a focus on cultural importance as opposed to analytical or reference material. Authors must be able to provide all images and illustrations with permissions." avg. press run 5M. Pub'd 1 title 1998; expects 4 titles 1999, 5 titles 2000. 12 titles listed in the *Small Press Record of Books in Print* (28th Edition, 1999-00). avg. price, cloth: $40; paper: $25. Discounts: varies depending on quantity. 150pp; size varies; †of. Reporting time: 1 month. Simultaneous submissions accepted: yes. Publishes 10% of manuscripts submitted. Payment: 10% net, paid semi-annually. Copyrights for author. ABA.

BALL MAGAZINE, Douglas M. Kimball, Senior Editor, PO Box 775, Northampton, MA 01061, 413-584-3076. 1992. Poetry, fiction, articles, art, photos, cartoons, interviews, satire, reviews, music, long-poems, collages, non-fiction. "No material more than 8,000 words. Alternative magazine generally, but we have no biases. Will tend to avoid poets/writers/artists of the day; i.e., we will not publish work just because other publications like the artist." circ. 2M+. 2/yr. Pub'd 2 issues 1998; expects 2 issues 1999, 4 issues 2000. sub. price: $7; per copy: $5; sample: $4.95. Back issues: $6. Discounts: 10+ 30%, 20+ 40%. 80pp; 8½×11; web. Reporting time: varies—2 weeks to 2 months. Publishes 2-4% of manuscripts submitted. Payment: copies, some honoraries. Copyrighted, reverts to author. Pub's reviews: 5-10 in 1998. §Music, books, plays, or magazines—we are willing and able to review any and all. Ads: $150/$90/back cover $400/inside covers $300.

The Ballard Locks Publishing Co., Shirley S. Henry, PO Box C79005, Seattle, WA 98119-3185, 206-720-8337. 1 title listed in the *Small Press Record of Books in Print* (28th Edition, 1999-00).

Ballena Press, Sylvia Brakke Vane, President & General Editor; Lowell John Bean, Thomas C. Blackburn, 823 Valparaiso Avenue, Menlo Park, CA 94025, 650-323-9261; orders: 415-883-3530; fax 415-883-4280. 1973. Non-fiction. "We publish works on the anthropology of the western United States, especially California and the Southwest. We are interested only in books demonstrating the highest level of scholarship. Unsolicited manuscripts are not used and will not be returned to the author. Orders: P.O. Box 2510, Novato, CA 94948" avg. press run 1M. Pub'd 1 title 1998; expects 2 titles 1999. 14 titles listed in the *Small Press Record of Books* *in Print* (28th Edition, 1999-00). avg. price, cloth: $39.95; paper: $19.95. Discounts: resale only 20% for 1 book, 40% for more than 1 book, 55% by special arrangement. 100-400pp; 6×9, 8¼×10½; of. Reporting time: 1 month to 1 year. Simultaneous submissions accepted: no. Publishes a variable % of manuscripts submitted. Payment: varies. Copyrights for author.

BALLOT ACCESS NEWS, Richard Winger, PO Box 470296, San Francisco, CA 94147, 415-922-9779; fax 415-441-4268; e-Mail ban@igc.apc.org. 1985. News items. "Bias in favor of voter's right to vote for the party of his or her choice. Bias against laws which interfere with this right." circ. 1M. 13/yr. Pub'd 13 issues 1998; expects 13 issues 1999, 13 issues 2000. sub. price: $11; per copy: free; sample: free. Back issues: 50¢ per issue. 6.25pp; 8½×11; of. Publishes 25% of manuscripts submitted. Payment: none. Copyrighted, does not revert to author. Pub's reviews: 3 in 1998. §Political parties. Ads: none. Coalition for Free & Open Elections.

THE BALTIMORE REVIEW, Barbara Westwood Diehl, PO Box 410, Riderwood, MD 21139, 410-377-5265; Fax 410-377-4325; E-mail hdiehl@bcpl.net. 1996. Poetry, fiction. "Literary journal—entirely short stories and poems." 2/yr. Pub'd 2 issues 1998; expects 2 issues 1999, 2 issues 2000. sub. price: $14; per copy: $7.95; sample: $8 incl. p/h. Back issues: $7. Discounts: distributor—Ingram Periodicals 50%, libraries $7. 128pp; 6×9. Reporting time: 1-3 months. Simultaneous submissions accepted: yes. Payment: 2 copies and reduced rates on add'l copies. Copyrighted, reverts to author.

BAMBOO RIDGE, A HAWAI'I WRITERS JOURNAL, Bamboo Ridge Press, Eric Chock, Darrell Lum, PO Box 61781, Honolulu, HI 96839-1781. 1978. Poetry, fiction, articles, parts-of-novels, plays, non-fiction. "Particular interest in literature reflecting the multi-ethnic culture of the Hawaiian islands." circ. 600-1M. 2/yr. Pub'd 2 issues 1998; expects 2 issues 1999, 2 issues 2000. sub. price: $20 individual, $25 institutions; per copy: $8-15; sample: $8. Back issues: varies. Discounts: 40%. 125-200pp; 6×9; of. Reporting time: 6 months. Simultaneous submissions accepted: no. Payment: usually $10/poem, $20/prose piece. Copyrighted, reverts to author. Ads: $100/$60. CLMP.

Bamboo Ridge Press (see also BAMBOO RIDGE, A HAWAI'I WRITERS JOURNAL), Eric Chock, Darrell Lum, PO Box 61781, Honolulu, HI 96839-1781. 1978. Poetry, fiction, plays. "Particular interest in island writers and writing which reflects the multi-ethnic culture of Hawaii." avg. press run 1M. Pub'd 2 titles 1998; expects 2 titles 1999, 2 titles 2000. 20 titles listed in the *Small Press Record of Books in Print* (28th Edition, 1999-00). avg. price, paper: $10. Discounts: 40%. 125-200pp; 6×9; of. Reporting time: 6 months. Simultaneous submissions accepted: no. Copyrights for author. CLMP.

BANAL PROBE, Oyster Publications, Drucilla B. Blood, PO Box 4333, Austin, TX 78765. 1986. Articles, cartoons, interviews, satire, criticism, reviews, music, letters, news items, non-fiction. "True personal experiences that lead to thought" circ. 500. 4-6/yr. Pub'd 6 issues 1998; expects 6 issues 1999, 6 issues 2000. sub. price: $6; per copy: $2; sample: $2. 16pp; 11×8½; †xerox. Reporting time: 3-4 months. Payment: none. Not copyrighted. Pub's reviews: 100+ in 1998. §Music, poetry, political humor, comics. Ads: write for rates.

Banana Productions (see also INTERNATIONAL ART POST), Anna Banana, PO Box 2480, Sechelt, BC V0N 3A0, Canada, 604-885-7156; fax 604-885-7183. 1988. Art, photos. "This is a cooperatively published periodical. Contributors pay and get 1/2 the edition." avg. press run 1M. Pub'd 2 titles 1998; expects 2 titles 1999, 2 titles 2000. 3 titles listed in the *Small Press Record of Books in Print* (28th Edition, 1999-00). avg. price, other: *International Art Post* $20-varies by edition. Discounts: 40% on consignment, 50% wholesale. 8-12pp; 8½×11; of. Reporting time: 6-9 months depending on busy-level here. We publish 100% of art or photos submitted. Copyrights for author.

●**BANANAFISH,** Ellen Balber, Managing Editor; Robin Lippincott, Fiction Editor, PO Box 381332, Cambridge, MA 02238-1332, 617-868-0662 phone/Fax; bananafi@aol.com. 1997. Fiction. "Length: 25 pages (or less). Recent contributors: Lisa Borders, N. Nye, Sheila Cudahy, Gerald Green, Sena Jeter Naslund, and R.S. Steinberg." circ. 400. 2/yr. Pub'd 1 issue 1998; expects 2 issues 1999, 2 issues 2000. sub. price: $12.50; per copy: $7.50; sample: $7.50. Back issues: $6. Discounts: trade 40%, classroom (10 or more) 25%. 125pp; 5½×8½. Reporting time: less than 2 months. Simultaneous submissions accepted: yes. Publishes 2% of manuscripts submitted. Payment: 2 copies of magazine, beginning Fall '99 2¢/word. Copyrighted, reverts to author. Ads: $150/free for ad exchange. CLMP.

Bancroft Press, Bruce Bortz, Publisher; Sarah Azizi, Fiction Editor, PO Box 65360, Baltimore, MD 21209-9945, 410-358-0658; Fax 410-764-1967. 1991. Fiction, non-fiction. "We are a general interest trade publisher specializing in books by journalists. However, submissions are welcome from all serious writers." avg. press run 10M. Pub'd 4 titles 1998; expects 5 titles 1999, 4-6 titles 2000. 8 titles listed in the *Small Press Record of Books in Print* (28th Edition, 1999-00). avg. price, cloth: $24; paper: $18.95. Discounts: standard discounts apply. 300pp; 6×9. Reporting time: varies. Simultaneous submissions accepted: yes. Publishes 1-5% of manuscripts submitted. Payment: yes. Copyrights for author. PMA, NBN, NAIBA, ABA.

Bandanna Books (see also COLLEGIUM NEWSLETTER), Sasha Newborn, 319 Anacapa Street #B, Santa

Barbara, CA 93101, 805-564-3559; FAX 805-564-3278. 1975. Fiction, art, non-fiction. "Our market is college literature/humanities. Looking for useful, innovative, non-sexist English texts/supplements, and language-learning materials" avg. press run 2M. Expects 2 titles 1999, 2 titles 2000. 25 titles listed in the *Small Press Record of Books in Print* (28th Edition, 1999-00). avg. price, paper: $8. Discounts: Credits, textbooks 1-4 copies no discount; 5+ 20%; tradebooks: 1-4 copies no discount, 5+ 40%; credit is good for 2 years. 80pp; 5½×8½; of. Reporting time: 2 months. Simultaneous submissions accepted: yes. Publishes 1% of manuscripts submitted. Payment: by agreement. Copyrights for author. PMA.

Bank Street Press, Mary Bertschmann, Maurice Hart, 24 Bank Street, New York, NY 10014, 212-255-0692. 1984. Poetry, fiction, articles, art, long-poems, plays. avg. press run 1M. Pub'd 1 title 1998; expects 4 titles 1999, 8 titles 2000. 9 titles listed in the *Small Press Record of Books in Print* (28th Edition, 1999-00). avg. price, paper: $6; other: fine print editions $15-$20. Pages vary; 5½×8½; of. Reporting time: 6 weeks. Copyrights for author. ISBN, PAPL (Port Authority Poetry League), The Small Press Center, New York.

Banks Channel Books, PO Box 4446, Wilmington, NC 28406, phone/fax 910-762-4677; E-mail bankschan@aol.com. 1993. Fiction, art, photos, non-fiction. "We publish Carolina authors only." avg. press run 1M-5M. Pub'd 4 titles 1998; expects 3 titles 1999, 2 titles 2000. 9 titles listed in the *Small Press Record of Books in Print* (28th Edition, 1999-00). avg. price, cloth: $22; paper: $12. Discounts: retailers 1-2 copies 20%, 3 or more 40%, 10+ prepaid, nonreturnable 45%. 200pp; 5½×8½, 6×9. Simultaneous submissions accepted: no. Payment: 6-7% (based on retail price). Copyrights for author. PAS, SPAN, SEBA.

THE BANNER, CRC Publications, John Suk, 2850 Kalamazoo SE, Grand Rapids, MI 49560, 616-246-0819. 1865. Poetry, fiction, articles, photos, cartoons, interviews, reviews, letters, news items, non-fiction. "Religion-in the Reformed-Presbyterian tradition" circ. 41M. 45/yr. Pub'd 46 issues 1998; expects 46 issues 1999, 45 issues 2000. sub. price: $31; per copy: $1.50. Back issues: $2. 32pp; 8½×11; †of. Reporting time: 2 weeks. Copyrighted, reverts to author. Pub's reviews: 20 in 1998. §Religion. Ads: $1410/$805/$65 per column inch. ACP, EPA.

●**Banshee Press (see also ONE TRICK PONY),** Louis McKee, PO Box 11186, Philadelphia, PA 19136-6186. 1997. Poetry. "Some recent contributors: David Kirby, Philip Dacey, Denise Duhamel, Naomi Shihad Nye, W.D. Ehrhart" avg. press run 350. Expects 1 title 1999, 1 title 2000. 1 title listed in the *Small Press Record of Books in Print* (28th Edition, 1999-00). avg. price, paper: $6. 24pp; 5½×8½; †of. Reporting time: query first. Payment: copies. Copyrights for author.

Banyan Tree Books, 1963 El Dorado Avenue, Berkeley, CA 94707, 510-524-2690. 1975. "We are not accepting any mss. at present." avg. press run 1.5M. 3 titles listed in the *Small Press Record of Books in Print* (28th Edition, 1999-00). avg. price, paper: $8.95. Discounts: Bookpeople's. of.

Bard Press (see also WATERWAYS: Poetry in the Mainstream), Richard Spiegel, Editor, 393 St. Paul's Avenue, Staten Island, NY 10304-2127, 718-442-7429. 1974. Poetry, art, long-poems. "Chapbooks containing the work of one poet, most recently Ida Fasel and Joy Hewitt Mown. Most poets come to us through our magazine *Waterways*. Publication by invitation only." avg. press run 300. Pub'd 2 titles 1998; expects 2 titles 1999, 2 titles 2000. 6 titles listed in the *Small Press Record of Books in Print* (28th Edition, 1999-00). avg. price, paper: $3.50. Discounts: 40% to booksellers. 32pp; 4×5½; †xerox. Simultaneous submissions accepted: no. Payment: in copies. Copyrights for author. NYSWP.

BARDIC RUNES, Michael McKenny, 424 Cambridge Street South, Ottawa, Ontario K1S 4H5, Canada, 613-231-4311. 1990. Poetry, fiction, art. *"Traditional and high fantasy only.* Prefer short stories but use some poems. Setting must be pre-industrial, either historical or of author's invention. Length: 3,500 words or less. Art: only illustrations of stories, usually contracted from Ottawa fantasy artists." circ. 500. 2/yr. Pub'd 2 issues 1998; expects 3 issues 1999, 3 issues 2000. sub. price: $10/3 issues; per copy: $4; sample: $4. Back issues: $3.50. 64pp; digest. Reporting time: normally within 2 weeks. Payment: on acceptance, 1/2¢ per word. Copyrighted, reverts to author. Ads: none.

Bardsong Press, Ann Gilpin, PO Box 775396, Steamboat Springs, CO 80477, 970-870-1401; fax 970-879-2657. 1997. Poetry, fiction. "We specialize in historical fiction, especially Celtic/Medieval/Britain. Also Celtic history in non-fiction." avg. press run 3M. Pub'd 1 title 1998; expects 1 title 2000. 1 title listed in the *Small Press Record of Books in Print* (28th Edition, 1999-00). avg. price, cloth: $22.95. Discounts: 40% to stores, 55% to wholesalers. 400pp; 6×9. Reporting time: 4 weeks. Simultaneous submissions accepted: yes. Publishes 1% of manuscripts submitted. Payment: varies. Copyrights for author. SPAN, PMA.

THE BAREFOOT POET: Journal of Poetry, Fiction, Essays, & Art, Writers House Press, John-Paul Ignatius, LSM, PO Box 52, Pisgah, IA 51564-0052, 515-279-7804; Compuserve 76330,3325; Internet stmichael@commonlink.com. 1994. Poetry, fiction, art, photos, letters. "Not accepting manuscripts at this time. *The Barefoot Poet* publishes fiction, essays, and art as well as poetry. Photos should be black and white with high contrast, but it is best if it is line art (pen and ink). Unestablished and beginning writers are welcome to submit. We will respond to all submissions. Even if your manuscript is rejected at first, a 2nd or 3rd revision may be accepted. We provide critique to assist in revisions, thus offering writers a sort of mini writing workshop experience. No light verse or haiku. Barefoot Poet and Writers House Press has been acquired by St. Michael's Press'' 1/yr. Expects 1 issue 1999, 1 issue 2000. sub. price: $15; per copy: $15; sample: $15. 64pp; 5½x8½; †of. Reporting time: 3 weeks to 3 months. Copyrighted, reverts to author.

Barefoot Press, Kent Bailey, Director, 1856 Cherry Road, Annapolis, MD 21401. 1987. Fiction, art, photos. "We are concerned with publishing high quality, *lasting* graphics (posters and cards) and children's books. As such, we print on acid free paper wherever possible (as in our *California Girls* poster). Sorry, we do not accept submissions of any kind." avg. press run 5M. avg. price, other: $20 (California Girls poster). of.

Barking Dog Books, Michael Mercer, Editor; Michael Cope, Art Director, Centro De Mensajes, A.P. 48, Todos Santos, B.C.S. 23300, Mexico, fax 011-52-114-50288. 1996. Poetry, fiction, art, photos. "Partial to submissions by American expatriate and Mexican writers, poets, travelers, artists, and photographers dealing with life in Baja or other parts of Mexico; but open to anything outside the American mainstream if local angle can be found." avg. press run 1M. Pub'd 1 title 1998; expects 2 titles 1999, 3 titles 2000. avg. price, paper: $10-$15. 150pp; 5½x8½. Reporting time: 3-6 months. Simultaneous submissions accepted: yes. Payment: 10-15%, small advance.

BARNABE MOUNTAIN REVIEW, Gerald Fleming, PO Box 529, Lagunitas, CA 94938. 1995. Poetry, fiction, art, photos, interviews, photos, cartoons, reviews, letters, long-poems, concrete art, non-fiction. "Seeking only highest quality material. Direct, reflecting craft, music, passion. 50% writers of notoriety, 50% writers worth noting. Send no more than 5 poems; fiction length flexible. Looking for strong generalist essays as well. *Barnabe Mountain Review* will not exceed 500 copies, and will appear only five times, its last issue appearing December 1999'' circ. 500. 1/yr. Expects 1 issue 1999, 1 issue 2000. sub. price: $10; per copy: $10; sample: $10. Discounts: 20% Discounts over 10 copies to same address. 200+pp; 5½x8½; of, recycled, acid-free. Reporting time: 3 weeks. Simultaneous submissions accepted: no. Publishes 5-10% of manuscripts submitted. Payment: 2 copies. Copyrighted, reverts to author. Pub's reviews. §Poetry, fiction, literary criticism, essays. Ads: no ads at this time.

Barnegat Light Press/Pine Barrens Press, R. Marilyn Schmidt, Publisher, PO Box 607, 3959 Route 563, Chatsworth, NJ 08019-0607, 609-894-4415; Fax 609-894-2350. 1980. Non-fiction. avg. press run 1M. Pub'd 3 titles 1998; expects 6 titles 1999, 6 titles 2000. 19 titles listed in the *Small Press Record of Books in Print* (28th Edition, 1999-00). avg. price, paper: $8.95. Discounts: single copy 25%, wholesale 4 or more—40%. 80pp; 5½x8½; of. Reporting time: 14 days. Payment: variable. Copyrights for author.

Barney Press, Donna Litherland, 3807 Noel Place, Bakersfield, CA 93306, 805-871-9118. 1982. "How to books on speed reading, imaging, Jungian psychology, changing human energy patterns, development of women's consciousness. Books designed to help students with study habits." avg. press run 500. Pub'd 1 title 1998; expects 1 title 1999. 5 titles listed in the *Small Press Record of Books in Print* (28th Edition, 1999-00). avg. price, cloth: $13.95; paper: $14.95; other: heavy binder: $10.50. Discounts: 40/60, $5 for examination copy to schools. 128pp; 8½x11; printed in Santa Barbara. Reporting time: 6 weeks. Simultaneous submissions accepted: yes. Publishes 15% of manuscripts submitted. Payment: 15%. Copyrights for author. Small Press Center.

BARNWOOD, The Barnwood Press, Tom Koontz, Thom Tammaro, PO Box 146, Selma, IN 47383. 1980. Poetry, reviews. "Poetry, reviews. Each issue features five or six poems that we believe our readers will be very pleased to have received. Recent authors include Robert Bly, Grace Butcher, Jared Carter, Siv Cedering, Phyllis Janowitz, Lyn Lifshin, Marge Piercy, Paul Ramsey, William Stafford, Lewis Turco." circ. 500. 3/yr. 1 title listed in the *Small Press Record of Books in Print* (28th Edition, 1999-00). sub. price: $6; per copy: $2; sample: $2. 16pp; 8½x7; of. Reporting time: 1 month. Payment: $25/poem. Copyrighted, reverts to author. Pub's reviews. §Poetry.

The Barnwood Press (see also BARNWOOD), Tom Koontz, Thom Tammaro, PO Box 146, Selma, IN 47383. 1975. Poetry, reviews. "Our organization is a nonprofit cooperative in support of contemporary poetry. Criterion is artistic excellence. Recent authors include: Baker, Bly, Carter, Friman, Goedicke, Jerome, Mathis-Eddy, Robinson, Ronnow, Stafford." avg. press run 1M. 39 titles listed in the *Small Press Record of Books in Print* (28th Edition, 1999-00). avg. price, paper: $5; other: $2. Discounts: 40% to stores, 50% to members. 64pp; 6x9; of. Reporting time: varies from 2 weeks to 6 months. Payment: 10% of copies. Copyrights for author.

Barricade Books, Carole Stuart, Publisher, 150 5th Avenue #700, New York, NY 10011. 1991. Fiction, non-fiction. "We are a small trade publisher (hardcover and trade paperback). We publish books that are worth reading and even worth keeping. We publish almost exclusively non-fiction, primarily controversial subjects, celebrity bios, general interest—health, true crime." avg. press run 3.5M-10M. Pub'd 24 titles 1998; expects 35 titles 1999, 40 titles 2000. 2 titles listed in the *Small Press Record of Books in Print* (28th Edition, 1999-00).

avg. price, cloth: varies; paper: varies. Discounts: discount schedule varies per customer. Pages vary; 5½×8¼, 6×9; of. Reporting time: 8 weeks. Payment: standard royalties, cloth 10% first 10,000 sold, 12% thereafter; paper 7.5% first 10M, 8% thereafter. Copyrights for author.

BAST Media, Inc. (see also HELIOCENTRIC NET/STIGMATA; THE HELIOCENTRIC WRITER'S NETWORK), Lisa Jean Bothell, 17650 1st Avenue South, Box 291, Seattle, WA 98148. 1994. avg. press run 100. 2 titles listed in the *Small Press Record of Books in Print* (28th Edition, 1999-00). avg. price, paper: $4.95. Discounts: none. 44pp; 8½×11. Reporting time: 6-8 weeks. Simultaneous submissions accepted: no. Publishes .5% of manuscripts submitted. Copyrights for author.

BATH AVENUE NEWSLETTER (BATH), Vincent Laspina, Rhett Moran, 1980 65th Street #3D, Brooklyn, NY 11204, 718-331-5960; Fax 718-331-4997; E-mail Laspina@msn.con, VLaspina@wow.con. 1996. Poetry, fiction, art, photos, cartoons, interviews, satire, criticism, reviews, music, letters, news items, non-fiction. "A publication (free) distributed in Manhattan and Brooklyn which tries to bring writers to the attention of a literate audience." circ. 3M+. 12/yr. Expects 7 issues 1999, 12 issues 2000. sub. price: $24; per copy: $2.50; sample: $2.50. Discounts: sub agents standard discounts. 16pp; 8½×11; †of. Reporting time: 1 week to 1 month. Payment: copies; some honorariums when available. Copyrighted. Pub's reviews. §Politics, literature, poetry, mainstream fiction. Ads: rate card available on request.

BATHTUB GIN, Christopher Harter, Tom Maxedon, PO Box 2392, Bloomington, IN 47402, 812-323-2985. 1997. Poetry, fiction, art, photos, interviews, satire, reviews, letters, parts-of-novels, collages, plays. "No strict length limits, prose around 2,500 words preferred. Looking for work that has the kick of bathtub gin (could be strong imagery, feeling within the work, or attitude). No trite rhymes. Latest issue featured A.D. Winans, Errol Miller, Walt Phillips, Vincent Farnsworth and others." circ. 150. 2/yr. Pub'd 2 issues 1998; expects 2 issues 1999, 2 issues 2000. sub. price: $10; per copy: $6; sample: $6. Back issues: $6. Discounts: none. 52pp; 5½×8½; †laserprinter. Reporting time: 1-2 months. Simultaneous submissions accepted: yes. Publishes 10% of manuscripts submitted. Payment: 1 contributer's copy, plus discounts. Copyrighted, reverts to author. Pub's reviews: 6 in 1998. §Poetry chapbooks and broadsides, works from small presses. Ads: 2.5 x 4 inches $15/issue or $25/year; 2.5 X 2 $10/issue or $17/year; 2.25 X 1 $7/issue or $12/year.

The Battery Press, Inc., PO Box 198885, Nashville, TN 37219, 615-298-1401; E-mail battery@aol.com. 1976. "We reprint scarce military unit histories. Inquire for a list of reprints. No new projects at this time." avg. press run 1M. Pub'd 22 titles 1998; expects 22 titles 1999, 18 titles 2000. 31 titles listed in the *Small Press Record of Books in Print* (28th Edition, 1999-00). avg. price, cloth: $39.95. Discounts: 1-4 copies 20%, 5+ 40%. 350-500pp; size varies; various methods of production. Simultaneous submissions accepted: no. Payment: varies. Copyrights for author.

William L. Bauhan, Publisher, William L. Bauhan, PO Box 443, Dublin, NH 03444-0443, 603-563-8020. 1960. Poetry, art. "Specialize in New England regional books." avg. press run 1.5M-2.5M. Pub'd 6 titles 1998; expects 8 titles 1999, 8 titles 2000. 57 titles listed in the *Small Press Record of Books in Print* (28th Edition, 1999-00). avg. price, cloth: $25; paper: $8.95. Discounts: 40% off on 5 or more copies, flat 20% off on textbooks, ltd. editions. 150pp; 5½×8½; of, lp. Reporting time: a month or so. Payment: 10% of list price; less on poetry & small editions. Copyrights for author. NESPA.

Bay Area Poets Coalition (see also POETALK), POETALK, PO Box 11435, Berkeley, CA 94712-2435, 510-272-9176. 1974. Poetry. "1 will often be used from first-time contributors (revisions may be requested); payment in copy." avg. press run 275. Pub'd 1 title 1998; expects 1 title 1999, 1 title 2000. 1 title listed in the *Small Press Record of Books in Print* (28th Edition, 1999-00). Membership: $15/year (includes letter, *POETALK* & *BAPC Anthology*, etc.); subscription $6/year. of. Reporting time: 2-4 months. Simultaneous submissions accepted: yes. Publishes 20-30% of manuscripts submitted. Payment: none. Copyrights for author.

Bay Press, Kimberly Barnett, Sally Brunsman, 115 West Denny Way, Seattle, WA 98119, 206-284-5913. 1981. Criticism. "Contemporary cultural criticism." avg. press run 7M. Pub'd 2 titles 1998; expects 2 titles 1999, 2 titles 2000. 34 titles listed in the *Small Press Record of Books in Print* (28th Edition, 1999-00). avg. price, cloth: $17.95; paper: $16.95. Discounts: trade 20-50%. 192pp; 5¼×8; of. Reporting time: 6 weeks. Simultaneous submissions accepted: yes. Publishes 1% of manuscripts submitted. Payment: net receipts, payable bi-annually. Copyrights for author.

BAY WINDOWS, Rudy Kikel, Editor, 631 Tremont Street, Boston, MA 02118, 617-266-6670, X211. 1983. Poetry. "We're looking for short poems (1-36 lines) on themes of interest to gay men or lesbians." circ. 60M. 51/yr. Pub'd 51 issues 1998; expects 51 issues 1999, 51 issues 2000. sub. price: $50; per copy: 50¢; sample: $2.50 (includes postage). Back issues: not available. 80pp; 10⅛×15½. Reporting time: 2 months. We accept simultaneous submissions if so advised. Publishes 10% of manuscripts submitted. Payment: copies. Copyrighted, reverts to author. Pub's reviews: 51+ in 1998. §Gay or lesbian—fiction, non-fiction, poetry. Ads: $716.10/$346.50/$173.25 1/4 page/$92.40 1/8 page.

BAYBURY REVIEW, Janet St. John, 40 High Street, Highwood, IL 60040, email baybury@flash.net. 1997. Poetry, fiction, interviews, criticism, reviews, non-fiction. "Reading period is June 1-December 1 of every year. Submission guidelines 3-5 poems and no more than 5,000 words of prose. Include name and address on each work and include adequate SASE. We encourage quality submissions by emerging writers." circ. 300. 1/yr. sub. price: $7.25; per copy: $6; sample: $7.25. 80-100pp; 5½×8½; of. Reporting time: 1-2 months. Will accept simultaneous submissions if indicated as such in cover letter. Publishes 20-25% of manuscripts submitted. Payment: 2 copies. Copyrighted, reverts to author. Pub's reviews: 2 in 1998. §current poetry, fiction and non-fiction books. Ads: exchanges with other small press publications only.

Bayhampton Publications, Kelly Smith, Director of Marketing, PMB 264, 2900 Delk Road, Suite 700, Marietta, GA 30067-5320, 905-455-7331; FAX 905-455-0207. 1995. Fiction, non-fiction. "Not accepting at this time. Canadian address: Bayhampton Publications, 54 Mozart Crescent, Brampton, ON L6Y 2W7, 905-455-7331; fax 905-455-0207" avg. press run 5M. Expects 2 titles 1999, 3 titles 2000. 1 title listed in the *Small Press Record of Books in Print* (28th Edition, 1999-00). avg. price, paper: $14.95. Discounts: available on request; bookstores 5+, 40%; libraries, 20%. 250pp; 6×9. PMA.

Bayley & Musgrave, Trevor White, 4949 Trailridge Pass, Suite 230, Atlanta, GA 30338, 404-668-9738. 1992. "Children's, How-to and stories; adult, how-to and science texts." Pub'd 1 title 1998; expects 4 titles 1999, 5 titles 2000. 3 titles listed in the *Small Press Record of Books in Print* (28th Edition, 1999-00). avg. price, paper: $10. Reporting time: 6 weeks. Payment: by arrangement. Copyrights for author. PMA.

‡**BB Books (see also GLOBAL TAPESTRY)**, Dave Cunliffe, 1 Spring Bank, Longsight Road, Copster Green, Blackburn, Lancs BB1 9EU, England, 0254 249128. 1963. Poetry, fiction, articles, art, long-poems. "Mainly publish poetry collections, short novels, anarchic counter-culture theoretics & mystic tracts (zen,tantra, etc.)." avg. press run 800. Pub'd 4 titles 1998; expects 4 titles 1999, 4 titles 2000. 11 titles listed in the *Small Press Record of Books in Print* (28th Edition, 1999-00). avg. price, paper: $5. Discounts: 1/3 to trade. 44pp; 8×6; †of. Reporting time: soon. Payment: 10%. Copyrights for author. NWASP.

Beachway Press, Scott Adams, 9201 Beachway Lane, Springfield, VA 22153, 703-644-8544, e-mail smadate@beachway.com. 1993. Non-fiction. avg. press run 5M. Expects 2-4 titles 1999. 5 titles listed in the *Small Press Record of Books in Print* (28th Edition, 1999-00). avg. price, paper: $12.95; other: $14.95. 200-300pp; 6×9; of. Reporting time: 6-8 weeks. Simultaneous submissions accepted: yes. Publishes 20% of manuscripts submitted. Payment: 10% retail royalties; no advance 10%-12% net invoice price; $1000-$2000 advance. Copyrights for author.

Beacon Point Press, Tom Magness, Acquisitions Editor, PO Box 460, Junction City, OR 97448. 1992. Non-fiction. "We're interested in all types of books about spirituality. We're not interested in fundamentalist, evangelical or new age viewpoints. All manuscripts should include SASE for return of submission. Before submitting manuscripts, first write for our catalog to get an idea of our interests." avg. press run 5M. Pub'd 1 title 1998; expects 3 titles 1999, 2 titles 2000. 2 titles listed in the *Small Press Record of Books in Print* (28th Edition, 1999-00). avg. price, paper: $14.95. Discounts: full trade discounts. 250pp; 6×9; of. Reporting time: 2-3 months. Simultaneous submissions accepted: yes. Payment: negotiable royalty. Copyrights for author. PMA, CBPA.

Beacon Press, 25 Beacon Street, Boston, MA 02108, 617-742-2110. 1854. Non-fiction. "No original fiction, poetry inspirational books, or memoirs accepted. We publish books on scholarly topics that have an interest for the general reader, and trade books with potential scholarly uses. Subjects: women's studies, environmental studies, religious studies, gay and lesbian studies, African-Americanm Asian-American, Jewish, Latino, and Native American studies, anthropology, politics and current affairs, legal studies, child and family issues, Irish studies, history, philosophy, education. Submit 2 sample chapters (typed double-spaced) with table of contents, synopsis, and curriculum vitae." avg. press run varies widely. Pub'd 60 titles 1998; expects 50 titles 1999, 60 titles 2000. avg. price, cloth: $22.95; paper: $12.95. Discounts: trade, nonreturnable and returnable special bulk, text...all different. Reporting time: 6-8 weeks. Simultaneous submissions accepted: yes. Publishes less than 1% of manuscripts submitted. Payment: negotiated separately. Copyrights for author.

Bear & Company, Inc., John Nelson, Box 2860, Santa Fe, NM 87504, 505-983-5968; 1800-WE-BEARS. 1981. Non-fiction. avg. press run 7.5M. Pub'd 12 titles 1998; expects 10 titles 1999, 12 titles 2000. 41 titles listed in the *Small Press Record of Books in Print* (28th Edition, 1999-00). avg. price, cloth: $22.95; paper: $14. Discounts: 1-24 (30 day net) 20%; 1-24 (prepaid) 40%; 25+ 44%. 300pp; 5½×8½, 6×9; web, cameron belt. Reporting time: 8 weeks SASE only. Publishes 1% of manuscripts submitted. Payment: 8%-10% of net. Copyrights for author.

Bear Creek Publications, Kathleen Shea, Editor, 2507 Minor Avenue East, Seattle, WA 98102, 206-322-7604. 1985. Non-fiction. avg. press run 4M. Pub'd 1 title 1998; expects 1 title 1999, 1 title 2000. 2 titles listed in the *Small Press Record of Books in Print* (28th Edition, 1999-00). avg. price, paper: $5.50. Discounts: 2-4 20%, 5-24 40%, 25-49 43%, 50-99 46%, 100+ 50%. 72pp; 5½×8½; of. Reporting time: 3 months. Payment:

negotiable. PMA, PNBA, PNBPA, NWPC.

THE BEAR DELUXE, Thomas L. Webb, Editor, PO Box 10342, Portland, OR 97296, 503-242-1047; Fax 503-243-2645; bear@teleport.com. 1993. Poetry, fiction, articles, art, photos, cartoons, interviews, satire, criticism, reviews, music, letters, parts-of-novels, plays, news items, non-fiction. "Send most unique environmental story ideas in well-developed one-page query letter. Send clips and letter as initial contact. Follow-up with phone call and have patience. Non-fiction ideas are reviewed and assigned. Fiction, poetry and essay considered under open submission policy. Ideal word limit is 2,500 (up to 4,000 accepted)." circ. 17M. 4/yr. Pub'd 3 issues 1998; expects 4 issues 1999, 4 issues 2000. sub. price: $16; per copy: $3; sample: $3. Back issues: $5 if available. Discounts: possible trades. 52pp; 11×14; web press. Reporting time: 2 months. We accept simultaneous submissions, but must be noted. Publishes 5% of manuscripts submitted. Payment: 5¢/word, copies; $30 photographs. Copyrighted, reverts to author. Pub's reviews: 12 in 1998. §Environmental, social justice, media, popular culture. Ads: $750/$450/$30 and up.

Bear Star Press, Beth Spencer, 185 Hollow Oak Drive, Cohasset, CA 95973, 530-891-0360. 1996. Poetry. "poets/poetry from Western and Pacific states with no restrictions as to form. Annual contest — rules change year to year. Not for profit!" avg. press run 3-500. Pub'd 1 title 1998; expects 2 titles 1999, 1-2 titles 2000. 3 titles listed in the *Small Press Record of Books in Print* (28th Edition, 1999-00). avg. price, paper: $7-$12. Discounts: varies, stores usually take 1/3. Chapbooks 35-40pp; other books 60pp; 5½×8¼. Reporting time: 3-5 months. Simultaneous submissions accepted: yes. Payment: cash and copies to authors. We can copyright for author. CLMP.

The Bear Wallow Publishing Company, Jerry Gildemeister, 809 South 12th Street, La Grande, OR 97850, 541-962-7864. 1976. Art, photos, non-fiction. "Primarily, Bear Wallow is for in-house publishing projects; however, we work with authors wishing to self-publish; and consider special projects that fit our style. Specialize in one-of-a-kind, limited edition printing." avg. press run 1M-10M. Pub'd 1 title 1998; expects 1 title 1999, 1 title 2000. 5 titles listed in the *Small Press Record of Books in Print* (28th Edition, 1999-00). avg. price, cloth: $20-$45. Discounts: school, library 20%; trade 40%. 96-208pp; 9×8, 12×9, 11×11, varies by project; of. Reporting time: promptly. Payment: 5-10%, quarterly. Copyrights for author.

Bearhouse Publishing (see also LUCIDITY), Ted O. Badger, Editor, 398 Mundell Rd., Eureka Springs, AR 72631-9505, 501-253-9351, E-mail tbadger@ipa.net. 1985. Poetry, articles, criticism. "Contract Publication of chapbooks, write for prices and parameters" avg. press run 100-300. Pub'd 16 titles 1998; expects 17 titles 1999, 12 titles 2000. avg. price, paper: $5-6. Discounts: negotiable. 40-50pp; 5½×8½; †photocopy. Reporting time: 30 days or less. Publishes 90% of manuscripts submitted. Payment: primarily a press for self-publishing, but we do some promotion. Copyrights for author.

Beaudoin Publishing Co., 14222 Clearview Drive, Orland Park, IL 60462, 708-349-7140. 1 title listed in the *Small Press Record of Books in Print* (28th Edition, 1999-00).

Beekman Publishers, Inc., Stuart A. Ober, Po Box 888, Woodstock, NY 12498, 914-679-2300. 1972. Art, non-fiction. "Beekman is a distributor of titles published in North America, England and other European countries. We do not accept unsolicited manuscripts. Beekman publishes a small number of non-fiction and gift books. We are known for our music, homoeopathic, business & finance, medical and other technical lines. No unsolicated mss." avg. press run 2M. Pub'd 5 titles 1998; expects 10 titles 1999, 20 titles 2000. 24 titles listed in the *Small Press Record of Books in Print* (28th Edition, 1999-00). avg. price, cloth: $25; paper: $15. Discounts: 20%. 300pp; of. Reporting time: 6 months. Payment: 8-10%. Copyrights for author.

●BEGINNINGS - A Magazine for the Novice Writer, Jenine Boisits, PO Box 92-R, Shirley, NY 11967, 516-924-7826; scbeginnings@juno.com; www.scbeginnings.com. 1998. Poetry, fiction, articles, cartoons, long-poems, non-fiction. "3,000 words max. for short stories. Children's section written or drawn by children. Articles *only* about non-profit organizations. Need articles by published writers - how to get published, write better fiction, etc." circ. 500. 2/yr. Expects 2 issues 1999, 2-3 issues 2000. sub. price: $8; per copy: $4; sample: $4. Back issues: $2. 54pp; 8½×11; †lp. Reporting time: 4-6 weeks. Simultaneous submissions accepted: yes. Publishes 30% of manuscripts submitted. Payment: sample copy. Copyrighted, reverts to author. Ads: $50/$25/$15 business card.

Behavioral Sciences Research Press, Inc., Theresa Donia, 12803 Demetra Drive, Ste. 100, Dallas, TX 75234, 214-243-8543, fax 214-243-6349. 1979. Non-fiction. avg. press run 5M-25M. Pub'd 3 titles 1998; expects 2 titles 1999, 4 titles 2000. avg. price, cloth: $28.95; paper: $22.95. 350pp; 5½×8½; of. Reporting time: 60 days. Simultaneous submissions accepted: yes. Payment: by contract. Does not copyright for author. ABA.

BEHIND BARS, Stephanie Owen, PO Box 2975, Tempe, AZ 85280-2975. 1996. Poetry, fiction, art, photos, reviews. "Only interested in reading cover letters that are three lines or less. Accept any subject, any length, in any voice just as long as it's fresh, honest, and has strong and original images. Only want poets who are obsessed with their poetry to submit. Send 5 poems maximum and SASE. Recent contributors include Martha

Vertreace, William Greenway, Rane Arroyo, and Barbara Daniels.'' circ. 60-70. 2/yr. Pub'd 1 issue 1998; expects 2 issues 1999, 2 issues 2000. sub. price: $6; per copy: $3; sample: $3. Discounts: trade with other magazines. 40-50pp; 5½×8½. Reporting time: 2-3 months. Simultaneous submissions accepted: no. Publishes 10% of manuscripts submitted. Payment: 1 copy. Not copyrighted. Pub's reviews. §Poetry, fiction.

Belfry Books (see also Toad Hall, Inc.), A.P. Pinzow, RR 2 Box 2090, Laceyville, PA 18623, 717-869-2942; Fax 717-869-1031. 1995. avg. press run 4M. Pub'd 1 title 1998; expects 2 titles 1999, 2 titles 2000. avg. price, paper: $14.95. 224pp; 6×9; of. Reporting time: 3 months. Payment: $1000 advance and 10% royalty. Copyrights for author. PMA, SPAN, MABA, ABA.

Bell Publishing, Burton E. Lipman, 15 Surrey Lane, East Brunswick, NJ 08816, 201-257-7793. 1982. Non-fiction. ''We specialize in technical + semi-technical books, as well as 'self-improvement' books for business people'' avg. press run varies. Pub'd 2 titles 1998; expects 2 titles 1999, 2 titles 2000. 3 titles listed in the *Small Press Record of Books in Print* (28th Edition, 1999-00). avg. price, cloth: $38.50; paper: $24.95. Discounts: inquire. 200pp; 8½×11; of. Reporting time: 1 month. Payment: open. Copyrights for author.

Bell Springs Publishing, Bernard Bear Kamoroff, P.O. Box 1240, Willits, CA 95490, 707-459-6372, Fax 707-459-8614. 1976. ''Printing, sizes, page, prices vary. No submissions wanted.'' 6 titles listed in the *Small Press Record of Books in Print* (28th Edition, 1999-00). Discounts: bookstores 40%; wholesalers 50%. of.

Belle Terre Press, Inc., Roger Wunderlich, 655-74 Belle Terre Road, Port Jefferson, NY 11777, 516-473-7630; RWunder100@aol.com. 1995. Fiction, long-poems. avg. press run 1M. Pub'd 1 title 1998; expects 1 title 1999, 2 titles 2000. 6 titles listed in the *Small Press Record of Books in Print* (28th Edition, 1999-00). avg. price, cloth: $21; paper: $15. Discounts: trade 45%, libraries 33 1/3%, jobbers 50%. 6×9; of. Reporting time: 30 days. Simultaneous submissions accepted: no. Publishes 2% of manuscripts submitted. Payment: yes. Copyrights for author.

‡**BELLES LETTRES,** Janet Mullaney, Editor, Publisher, 1243 Maple View Drive, Charlottesville, VA 22902-6779, 301-294-0278. 1985. Poetry, fiction, articles, art, photos, cartoons, interviews, satire, criticism, reviews, letters, news items. ''We do reviews, interviews, retrospectives, and rediscoveries; personal essays will be published also. Contributors must query first. Recent contributors include Susan Koppelman, Merrill Joan Gerber, Dale Spender, and Faye Moskowitz. Reviews may be written by men, but only women-authored books are reviewed. Reviews run 90 days before print month. Multicultural and international work is especially solicited.'' circ. 8M. 3/yr. Pub'd 4 issues 1998; expects 3 issues 1999, 3 issues 2000. sub. price: $21/indiv. domestic, foreign add $20 to subscription; $40/institution, $15/student ID; per copy: $5; sample: $5. Back issues: write for price schedule. Discounts: classroom, 10+ copies @ $4 each. 96pp; 8½×11; of. Reporting time: 4-6 weeks. Payment: copies. Copyrighted, rights revert to author, except for rights to anthologies. Pub's reviews: 80 per issue in 1998. §Women-authored books—all genres (fiction and poetry predominate). Ads: $1000/600/500 (1/3)/400 (1/4)/200 (1/8). MLA.

THE BELLINGHAM REVIEW, Signpost Press Inc., Robin Hemley, Editor, Mail Stop 9053, WWU, Bellingham, WA 98225, 360-650-3209. 1977. Poetry, fiction, art, photos, reviews, parts-of-novels, long-poems, plays. ''No prose over 10M words.'' circ. 2.5M. 2/yr. Pub'd 2 issues 1998; expects 2 issues 1999, 2 issues 2000. sub. price: $10/2 issues, $19/4 issues, $25/6 issues; per copy: $5; sample: $5. Discounts: 25% on 5 + copies. 120pp; 5½×8½; of. Reporting time: 1-4 months. Simultaneous submissions accepted: yes. Payment: varies. Copyrighted, reverts to author. Pub's reviews: 4 in 1998. §Poetry volumes & books of fiction and nonfiction.

BELLOWING ARK, Bellowing Ark Press, Robert R. Ward, Editor, PO Box 55564, Shoreline, WA 98155, 206-440-0791. 1984. Poetry, fiction, art, photos, letters, parts-of-novels, long-poems, plays, non-fiction. ''*Bellowing Ark* publishes high-quality literary works that affirm the fact that life has meaning. We are interested in poetry, fiction, essays and work in other forms that extends the philosophical ground established by the American Romantics and the transcendentalists. Our belief is that the techniques developed in the last 60 years (and particularly the last 20) are just that, technique; for us polish is a secondary consideration and work in the ''modern'' vein need not apply (i.e. stories should have a plot; poetry should contain a grain of universal truth). Our desire is to expand the philosophical and literary marketplace of ideas, not to be its arbiters—but we have very definite ideas about what our mission entails. Please write for a sample copy or subscription if you have any doubts. While form is generally not a consideration for selection we have one regular feature, ''Literal Lives'', which presents well-developed autobiographical stories. Other work particularly featured in the past have been serializations and sequences; long and narrative poems; stories of childhood; and love, nature and erotic poetry. Our contributors over the past year have included Gene Armstrong, Margaret Hodge, Teresa Noelle Roberts, Elizabeth Biller Chapman, Muriel Karr, James Hobbs, L.L. Ollivier, and David Athey.'' circ. 1M+. 6/yr. Pub'd 6 issues 1998; expects 6 issues 1999, 6 issues 2000. sub. price: $15; per copy: $3; sample: SASE (9 X 12 please) with $1.25 postage, or $3. Back issues: varies: Some back issues are now quite rare, quotes on request. Discounts: negotiable. 32pp; 11½×16; of. Reporting time: 6-10 weeks. Simultaneous submissions accepted: no. Publishes less than 1% of manuscripts submitted. Payment: in copy at present. Copyrighted, rights revert to author on request only. Pub's reviews: 1 in 1998. §No unsolicited reviews. We review volumes of poetry that interest us. none.

Bellowing Ark Press (see also BELLOWING ARK), Robert R. Ward, Editor-in-Chief, PO Box 45637, Seattle, WA 98145, 206-545-8302. 1987. "As we are just beginning book publishing, we are not currently able to consider unsolicited manuscripts; however, we are interested in any work with a philosophical bent as described under the listing for the magazine we publish, *Bellowing Ark*. At this time the best approach would be to submit work to *Bellowing Ark* with a cover letter describing the complete project; also, *BA* has in the past published chapbook-length poetry manuscripts and has serialized complete book-length works." avg. press run 1M. Pub'd 4 titles 1998; expects 5 titles 1999, 5 titles 2000. 19 titles listed in the *Small Press Record of Books in Print* (28th Edition, 1999-00). avg. price, paper: $4-$20. Discounts: will negotiate. 48-192pp; 6×9; †of. Payment: negotiable (currently 10% of net). Copyrights for author.

BELOIT FICTION JOURNAL, Tenaya Darlington, Box 11, Beloit College, Beloit, WI 53511, 608-363-2308. 1984. Fiction. "We publish new contemporary short fiction. Theme and subject matter open, except we will not print pornography, political propaganda, or religious dogma. Length of stories ranges from about three to thirty pages. Recent contributors include Tony Ardizzone, Maura Stanton, Gary Fincke, Erin McGraw, David R. Young, William F. Van Wert, Alvin Greenberg, David Michael Kaplan, Scott Russell Sanders, T.M. McNally." circ. 700. 2/yr. Pub'd 2 issues 1998; expects 2 issues 1999, 2 issues 2000. sub. price: $14; per copy: $7; sample: $7. Back issues: $5 each, all issues available. 144pp; 6×9. Reporting time: varies, 2 weeks to 2 months. Payment: in copies. Copyrighted, reverts to author.

BELOIT POETRY JOURNAL, Marion K. Stocking, 24 Berry Cove Road, Lamoine, ME 04605, 207-667-5598. 1950. Poetry. "We publish the best of the poems submitted. No biases as to length, form, subject, or school. Occasional chapbooks on special themes, such as the recent chapbook of New Chinese. Some recent contributors: Albert Goldbarth, Sherman Alexie, Ursula K. Le Guin, Bei Dao, Lola Haskins" circ. 1.2M. 4/yr. Pub'd 4 issues 1998; expects 4 issues 1999, 4 issues 2000. sub. price: $15; per copy: $5; sample: $5. Back issues: $5 for recent issues, list available for others. Discounts: by arrangement. 48pp; 6×9; of. Reporting time: immediately to 4 months. Simultaneous submissions accepted: no. Publishes .7% of manuscripts submitted. Payment: 3 copies. Copyrighted, reverts to author. Pub's reviews: 24 in 1998. §Books by and about poets, mags with poetry. All reviews written by editor. CLMP.

Benchmark Publications Inc., Alice McElhone, 65 Locust Avenue, New Canaan, CT 06840-5328, 203-966-6653; FAX 203-972-7129; Benchpress@gnn.com. 1995. Cartoons, non-fiction. "Business and economy how-to books only (250 pages up)." avg. press run 5-10K. Expects 2-4 titles 1999, 6 titles 2000. 7 titles listed in the *Small Press Record of Books in Print* (28th Edition, 1999-00). avg. price, paper: $34.95. 320pp; 7×9; †of. Reporting time: 3 months. Simultaneous submissions accepted: no. Payment: to be determined (7-10%). Rights are assigned to BPI. PMA.

R.J. Bender Publishing, R.J. Bender, J.R. Angolia, D. Littlejohn, H.P. Taylor, PO Box 23456, San Jose, CA 95153, 408-225-5777; Fax 408-225-4739; order@bender-publishing.com. 1967. Non-fiction. avg. press run 5M. Expects 4 titles 1999, 4 titles 2000. 27 titles listed in the *Small Press Record of Books in Print* (28th Edition, 1999-00). avg. price, cloth: $44.95. Discounts: 33%-55%. 400pp; 6×9; of. Reporting time: 1-2 years. Payment: variable. Copyrights for author.

The Benefactory, Inc., 1 Post Road, Fairfield, CT 06430, 203-255-7744. 1991. "Children's book publisher: true animal stories from The Humane Society of the United States with accompanying audio tape narrated by Tom Chapin and plush animal bringing a character to life for the child. Published in 1997: *Cheesie, The Travelin' Man, Chocolate, A Glacier Grizzly, Caesar: On Deaf Ears, Condor Magic*. 1998: *Buster, Where Are You?* and *Rico's Hawk*." avg. press run 7.5M. Pub'd 5 titles 1998; expects 4 titles 1999, 6 titles 2000. 8 titles listed in the *Small Press Record of Books in Print* (28th Edition, 1999-00). avg. price, cloth: $12.95; paper: $5.95; other: $14.95. Discounts: yes. 32pp; 10×10, 7×7; †web, sheetfed. Simultaneous submissions accepted: yes. Publishes 10% of manuscripts submitted. Payment: yes. Copyrights for author.

Bennett & Kitchel, William Whallon, PO Box 4422, East Lansing, MI 48826. 1990. Poetry. "No free verse, off-rhyme, or blank verse." avg. press run 600. Pub'd 1 title 1998; expects 1 title 1999. 6 titles listed in the *Small Press Record of Books in Print* (28th Edition, 1999-00). avg. price, cloth: $10. Discounts: 40%. 68pp; 5½×8½; photolithography. Reporting time: 1 week on queries, 1 month on submissions. Publishes 2% of manuscripts submitted. Payment: negotiable. Copyrights for author.

Bennett Books, James Tomarelli, PO Box 1553, Santa Fe, NM 87504, 505-989-8381. 1988. Non-fiction. "High quality paperbacks. Occasional hardbacks. Spiritually oriented material, sacred traditions." avg. press run 3M. 9 titles listed in the *Small Press Record of Books in Print* (28th Edition, 1999-00). avg. price, cloth: $24; paper: $11. 128pp; 6×9; of. Payment: between 5-10% list price, quarterly. Does not copyright for author. Rocky Mountain Book Publishers Association.

●**THE BENT,** Tom Maxedon, Christopher Harter, 719 E. Main Street, Muncie, IN 47305, tomwhon@hotmail.com. 1999. Poetry, art, photos, reviews. "Eight pages total, including reviews, ads, and editorial." 2/yr. Expects 300 issues 1999, 500 issues 2000. sub. price: $5; per copy: $3; sample: $3. Back issues: $5. Discounts: 20% 1-4; 40% 5-10. 8pp; 5½×8½; †xerox/ink jet printer. Simultaneous submissions accepted: yes. Publishes 5% of manuscripts submitted. Payment: none. Not copyrighted. Pub's reviews. §Poetry, short drama, film, and music.

●**Bereshith Publishing,** Vincent Harper, Executive Editor, PO Box 2366, Centreville, VA 20122-2366, 703-222-9387; e-mail tempus@bereshith.com; website www.bereshith. 1998. Poetry, fiction, art. "Two imprints: ShadowLands Press and Final Frontier Books." avg. press run 1M. Pub'd 1 title 1998; expects 4 titles 1999, 6 titles 2000. 2 titles listed in the *Small Press Record of Books in Print* (28th Edition, 1999-00). avg. price, cloth: $40; paper: $8. 300pp; 5½×8½; of. Reporting time: 2-3 months. Simultaneous submissions accepted: yes. Payment: advance and royalties for novels. Copyrights for author. PMA, HWA.

Berkeley Hills Books, Robert Dobbin, John Strohmeier, PO Box 9877, Berkeley, CA 94709, 510-848-7303 phone/Fax; E-mail bhbsales@berkeleyhills.com. 1996. Fiction, non-fiction. "We follow the interests of our two editors. We are interested in trade paperback books of general interest." avg. press run 5M. Pub'd 1 title 1998; expects 4 titles 1999, 6 titles 2000. 4 titles listed in the *Small Press Record of Books in Print* (28th Edition, 1999-00). avg. price, paper: $15. Discounts: 40%-47.5%. 250pp; 6×9; of. Reporting time: 120 days. Simultaneous submissions accepted: yes. Payment: negotiable. Copyrights for author.

BERKELEY JOURNAL OF EMPLOYMENT AND LABOR LAW, University of California Press, Univ. of California at Berkeley Students of Boalt Hall School of Law, University of California Press, 2120 Berkeley Way, Berkeley, CA 94720, 510-643-7154. Articles, reviews, non-fiction. "Editorial address: 387 Simon Hall, University of CA, Berkeley, CA 94720. Copyrighted by Industrial Relations Law Journal." circ. 650. 2/yr. Pub'd 2 issues 1998; expects 2 issues 1999, 2 issues 2000. sub. price: $34 indiv., $40 instit. (+ $4 foreign postage); per copy: $17 indiv.; $20 instit. (+ $4 foreign postage); sample: free. Back issues: $17 indiv.; $20 instit. (+ $4 foreign postage). Discounts: foreign subs. agent 10%, one-time order 10+ 30%, standing orders (bookstores): 1-99 40%, 100+ 50%. 150pp; 7×10; of. Reporting time: 1-2 months. Payment: varies. Copyrighted, does not revert to author. Ads: $275/$200.

BERKELEY JOURNAL OF INTERNATIONAL LAW, University of California Press, Univ. of California at Berkeley Students of Boalt Hall School of Law, University of California Press, 2120 Berkeley Way, Berkeley, CA 94720, 410-643-7154. Articles, reviews, non-fiction. "Editorial address: 126 Boalt Hall School of Law, Berkeley, CA 94720. Copyrighted by International Tax and Business Lawyer." circ. 400. 2/yr. Pub'd 2 issues 1998; expects 2 issues 1999, 2 issues 2000. sub. price: $45 indiv., $45 instit., (+ $4 foreign postage); per copy: $23 (+ $4 foreign postage); sample: free. Back issues: $23 (+ $4 foreign postage). Discounts: foreign subs. agent 10%, one-time order 10+ 30%, standing orders (bookstores): 1-99 40%, 100+ 50%. 200pp; 7×10; of. Reporting time: 1-2 months. Payment: varies. Copyrighted, does not revert to author. Pub's reviews: 5 in 1998. Ads: $275/$200.

BERKELEY POETRY REVIEW, Patricia Johnson, Editor, 201 MLK Student Union, University of California, Berkeley, CA 94720. 1973. Poetry, art, photos, interviews, criticism, reviews, long-poems. "While the *BPR* is biased towards new poets and writers who reside in the San Francisco Bay Area, we are happy to consider all submissions. Please include a SASE, up to five poems and a short biography. Recent contributors: Thom Gunn, Robert Hass, Philip Levine, Ron Loewinsohn, Czeslaw Milosz, Leonard Nathan, Robert Pinsky, William Stafford, Gary Soto." circ. 750. 1/yr. Pub'd 2 issues 1998; expects 1 issue 1999, 1 issue 2000. sub. price: $10; per copy: issues $6. Back issues: 3.50. Discounts: 40% trade. 120-150pp; 5½×8½; of. Reporting time: 3-4 months. Payment: contributor's copy. Copyrighted, reverts to author. Pub's reviews: 0 in 1998. §Poetry, criticism, film, literature. Ads: $55/$30. CLMP.

THE BERKELEY REVIEW OF BOOKS, H.D. Moe, Florence Windfall, Publisher & Managing Editor, 1731 10th Street, Apt. A, Berkeley, CA 94710, 415-528-8713. 1988. Poetry, fiction, articles, art, photos, interviews, satire, criticism, reviews, music, letters, parts-of-novels, long-poems, collages, plays, concrete art, non-fiction. "We want reviews (200-300 words) of what isn't reviewed; art, poems, fiction that couldn't have been possibly written or drawn. Open to any kind of books, very interested in experimental writing, art (*not* the language prose/poetry sponsored by the university presses—'Our American professors like their literature clear, cold and very dead'—Sinclair Lewis). Recent contributors: Jenifer Stone, Ivan Arguelles, Lisa Chang, D. McNaughton, Larry Eigner, Mary Rudge, Hadassal Haskale, David Meltzer, Denise du Roi, Norman Moser." circ. 500-1M. 1/yr. Pub'd 1 issue 1998; expects 3 issues 1999, 4 issues 2000. sub. price: $20/4 issues; per copy: $10; sample: $10. Back issues: $9. Discounts: 30%-70%. 100-150pp; 8½×11; xerox, litho. Reporting time: 3-4 months. Simultaneous submissions accepted: yes. Publishes 1% of manuscripts submitted. Payment: none as of now. Copyrighted, reverts to author. Pub's reviews: 50 in 1998. §All subjects. Ads: $100/$60/$40 1/4 page/$25 1/8 page.

BERKELEY TECHNOLOGY LAW JOURNAL, University of California Press, Univ. of California at Berkeley Students of Boalt Hall School of Law, University of California Press, 2120 Berkeley Way, Berkeley, CA 94720, 510-643-7154. 1986. Articles. "Editorial address: 587 Simon Hall, University of CA, Berkeley, Ca 94720. Copyrighted by High Technology Law Journal." circ. 450. 2/yr. Pub'd 2 issues 1998; expects 2 issues 1999, 2 issues 2000. sub. price: $50 (+ $4 foreign postage); per copy: $27 (+ $4 foreign postage); sample: free. Back issues: $27 (+ $4 foreign postage). Discounts: foreign subs. agent 10%, one-time order 10+ 30%, standing orders (bookstores): 1-99 40%, 100+ 50%. 300pp; 7×10; of. Copyrighted, does not revert to author. Pub's reviews: 8 in 1998. Ads: $275/$200.

BERKELEY WOMEN'S LAW JOURNAL, University of California Press, Boalt Hall Students of the Univ. of Calif., 2 Boalt Hall, Univ. of Ca., School of Law, Berkeley, CA 94720, 510-642-6263. 1985. "*The Journal* is an interdisciplinary law journal focusing on the legal concerns of under represented women, such as women of color, lesbians, disabled women, and poor woman" circ. 450. 1/yr. Pub'd 1 issue 1998; expects 1 issue 1999, 1 issue 2000. sub. price: $18 individuals, $40 institutions, $9 students (+ $4 foreign postage); per copy: $18 indiv.; $40 instit.; $9 students; sample: free. Back issues: same. Discounts: call Univ of Calif Press Periodicals for info at 415-642-4191. 400pp; 6¾×10, 7×10; lp. Reporting time: 4-5 weeks during academic year. Simultaneous submissions accepted: yes. Publish 1 out of 200 manuscripts received. Payment: none. Copyrighted, does not revert to author. Pub's reviews: 3 in 1998. §Feminism, women's studies, gay/lesbian studies, disability issues. Ads: $275/$200.

Berry Hill Press, Doris Bickford, Douglas Swarthout, 2349 State Route 12-B, Deansboro, NY 13328, 315-821-6188 phone/fax. 1995. "Have manuscripts through 1997. Subjects: gardening, history, cinema, women authors and artists" avg. press run 5M. Expects 2 titles 1999, 4 titles 2000. 4 titles listed in the *Small Press Record of Books in Print* (28th Edition, 1999-00). avg. price, cloth: $35. Copyrights for author.

The Bess Press, Dr. Ann Louise Rayson, Reve Shapard, 3565 Harding Avenue, Honolulu, HI 96816, 808-734-7159. 1979. Non-fiction. "The Bess Press is a regional, educational and trade publisher seeking manuscript materials for the el-hi, college and trade markets. We are actively seeking regional materials, including Asian/Pacific history texts, and cookbooks, humor, and children's books dealing with Hawaii." avg. press run 5M. Pub'd 12 titles 1998; expects 12 titles 1999, 12 titles 2000. 129 titles listed in the *Small Press Record of Books in Print* (28th Edition, 1999-00). avg. price, cloth: $35; paper: $15. Discounts: standard. 200pp; 6×9, varies. Reporting time: usually less than 4-6 weeks. Simultaneous submissions accepted: yes. Publishes 3% of manuscripts submitted. Payment: standard 10%. Copyrights for author.

BEST OF MAUI, Sandwich Islands Publishing, Joe Harabin, PO Box 10669, Lahaina, HI 96761, 808-661-5844. 1984. Photos. "I seek beautiful photographs taken on Maui, preferably with descriptions written." circ. 20M. 1/yr. Pub'd 1 issue 1998; expects 1 issue 1999, 1 issue 2000. sub. price: $12; per copy: $12; sample: $12. Back issues: $12. Discounts: 5+ 50%. 108pp; 8½×11½; of. Reporting time: 1 week. Payment: $50/photo. Copyrighted, reverts to author. Ads: $9960/$5500/$3500 1/3 page.

Best Sellers Publishing, John Tschohl, Chairman, 9201 E. Bloomington Fwy, Minneapolis, MN 55420, 612-888-7672; FAX 612-884-8901; E-mail booker@bestsellerspub.com; www.bestsellerspub.com. 1992. Non-fiction. "Hardcover trade titles. Most authors are investors in company." avg. press run 5M. Pub'd 3 titles 1998; expects 6 titles 1999, 12 titles 2000. 6 titles listed in the *Small Press Record of Books in Print* (28th Edition, 1999-00). avg. price, cloth: $23; paper: $15. 350pp; 6×9. Reporting time: 2-3 weeks. Publishes 25% of manuscripts submitted. Copyrights for author. Publishers Marketing Association (PMA).

Betelgeuse Books, David Pelly, Glenna Munro, F24-122 St. Patrick St., Ste. 193, Toronto Ont. M5T 2X8, Canada. 1980. Fiction, non-fiction. "We are a small press specializing in 'northern wilderness literature.' No unsolicited manuscripts." avg. press run 3M. Expects 1 title 1999, 1 title 2000. 6 titles listed in the *Small Press Record of Books in Print* (28th Edition, 1999-00). avg. price, paper: $19.95. Discounts: 40% trade, 20% library. 192pp; 6×9; of. Payment: varies.

Between The Lines, Ruth Bradley-St-Cyr, Acquisitions & Managing Editor, 720 Bathurst Street, Suite 404, Toronto, Ontario M5S 2R4, Canada, 416-535-9914, fax 416-535-1484; btlbooks@web.net. 1977. Photos, interviews, criticism, non-fiction. "Popular non-fiction, national and international history, economics, politics, theory and practice, women, enviroment, Third World." avg. press run 2M. Pub'd 7 titles 1998; expects 11 titles 1999, 11 titles 2000. 66 titles listed in the *Small Press Record of Books in Print* (28th Edition, 1999-00). avg. price, cloth: $34.95; paper: $16.95. Discounts: for university bookstore course orders 20%, trade stores 5+ copies 40%, 20% libraries, except to library services. 240pp; 6×9, 5½×8½; of. Reporting time: 2-3 months. Payment: variable. Copyrights for author. ACP (Assoc. of Canadian Publishers).

Beynch Press Publishing Company, Alyce P. Cornyn-Selby, 1928 S.E. Ladd Avenue, Portland, OR 97214, 503-232-0433. 1986. Non-fiction. avg. press run 5M. Pub'd 2 titles 1998; expects 4 titles 1999, 4-6 titles 2000. 12 titles listed in the *Small Press Record of Books in Print* (28th Edition, 1999-00). avg. price, paper: $8.95-$12.95. 100pp; 4¼×5½. Reporting time: 1 month. Payment: each is different, money and number of copies. Copyrights for author. Pacific Northwest Book Publishers Assn., Willamette Writers, Oregon Writers Colony, PMA.

●**BEYOND DOGGEREL,** Claire T. Feild, 1141 Knollwood Court, Auburn, AL 36830-6126, e-mail feild@mindspring.com. 1996. Poetry. "I like 20-line max.story image poetry written by instructors (all levels). Submit five poems (on any subject) in Jan./Feb. only. The first four issues of *BD* were for school personnel poets K-12. The fall 1999 issue will target 4-year and community college instructors. The fall 2000 issue will be for all instructor poets. Do not submit poetry via e-mail. Submit poems snail mail with SASE. E-mail or write to order back or current issues." circ. 1. 1/yr. Pub'd 1 issue 1998; expects 1 issue 1999, 1 issue 2000. price per copy: $7; sample: $7. Back issues: $5. 35pp; 7×9; †Auburn University Printing. Reporting time: 2-4 months. Simultaneous submissions accepted: yes. Publishes 50-75% of manuscripts submitted. Payment: 1 copy. Copyrighted, reverts to author. AWF, APS.

Beyond Words Publishing, Inc., Cynthia Black, Editor, 20827 NW Cornell Road, Ste. 500, Hillsboro, OR 97124-9808, 503-693-8700, fax 503-693-6888, e-mail BeyondWord@aol.com. 1983. Photos, non-fiction. "Photo books contain 100-200 photos and text of 20,000 words. Softcover titles 200 pages of text. Children's picture books approx. 30-50 words of text and illustrations. Authors must be willing to do school and other programs" avg. press run 10M. Pub'd 10 titles 1998; expects 14 titles 1999, 12 titles 2000. 37 titles listed in the *Small Press Record of Books in Print* (28th Edition, 1999-00). avg. price, cloth: $22.95; paper: $12.95; other: $12.95 children's. Discounts: bookstore standard 40%-high volume up to 45%. 200pp; 10×12, 9×7; of. Reporting time: 90 days. Payment: 10% royalty. Copyrights for author if requested. ABA, PMA.

●**BGB Press, Inc. (see also THE PANNUS INDEX),** Vincent Bator, 14545 N. Frank Lloyd Wright Blvd., Suite 276, Scottsdale, AZ 85260, www.home.earthlink.net/~bgbpress. 1996. Poetry, fiction, criticism, non-fiction. "We accept very select projects of books that have potential for crossover into commercial markets. Poetry, fiction and non-fiction (psychology, linguistics are the few disciplines that we are looking to tap into). New books/forthcoming books: Hugh Fox, Richard Kostelanetz, Errol Miller, Mehmet Mizanoglu, Denn Saleh." avg. press run 500+. Expects 4 titles 1999, 2 titles 2000. 2 titles listed in the *Small Press Record of Books in Print* (28th Edition, 1999-00). avg. price, paper: $10.95. Discounts: 1-5 40%, 6+ 50%. 120pp; 5½×8½; of. Reporting time: 4-5 months. Simultaneous submissions accepted: no. Publishes 2% of manuscripts submitted. Payment: yes, contract with author. Copyrights for author.

BGS Press, Dan Nielsen, 1240 William Street, Racine, WI 53402, 414-639-2406. 1991. Poetry, fiction, art, collages. avg. press run 200. Pub'd 4 titles 1998; expects 4 titles 1999, 4 titles 2000. avg. price, other: $3 chapbook. 30pp; 5½×8½; †photocopy. Reporting time: 2 days to 3 months. Payment: varies. Does not copyright for author.

Biblio Press, Doris B. Gold, Editor and Publisher, PO Box 20195, London Terrace Station, New York, NY 10011-0008, 212-989-2755; E-mail bibook@aol.com. 1979. Non-fiction. "Jewish women's studies, (non-fiction) and significant reprint fiction; bibliographies, and reference materials on Jewish women. No poetry. Authors should not submit mss. Query first. Distributors: H & M Distribution, Trumbull, CT; Bookpeople, Oakland, CA; New Leaf Distribution, Lithia Springs, GA." avg. press run 1M-3M. Pub'd 3 titles 1998; expects 2 titles 1999, 1 title 2000. 15 titles listed in the *Small Press Record of Books in Print* (28th Edition, 1999-00). avg. price, cloth: $16; paper: $9.95-$14.95. Discounts: Women's bookstores get 40% plus other special discounts off; jobbers 25% or more, Judaica & religion bookstores 20% and up; our distributors generously discount. 150pp; 5¼×8¼, 6×9, 7×10, 8½×11; of. Reporting time: 3 weeks for queries. Publishes 10% of manuscripts submitted. Payment: flat fee for ms and limited royalty arrangement. Copyrights for author.

BIBLIOTHEQUE D'HUMANISME ET RENAISSANCE, Librairie Droz S.A., A. Dufour, M. Engammare, Librairie Droz S.A., 11r.Massot, 1211 Geneve 12, Switzerland. 1934. Articles, criticism, reviews. "History of 16th century." circ. 1M. 3/yr. Pub'd 3 issues 1998; expects 3 issues 1999. sub. price: 100 SW.FR ($73)-yr (indiv.); 140 SW.FR ($94)-yr (institutions); per copy: 40 SW.FR. ($24). 300pp; 16×24cm; typography. Pub's reviews: 100 in 1998. §15th and 16th Centuries.

Bicycle Books (Publishing) Inc., Rob Van der Plas, 1282 7th Avenue, San Francisco, CA 94122, 415-665-8214. 1985. Photos, news items, non-fiction. "Length of material: 200 pages. Biases: only bicycle related books. Recent contributors: Samuel Abt, Rob Van Der Pas, Tim Hughes, John Smith" avg. press run 8M. Pub'd 6 titles 1998; expects 5 titles 1999, 5 titles 2000. 26 titles listed in the *Small Press Record of Books in Print* (28th Edition, 1999-00). avg. price, cloth: $22.50; paper: $12. Discounts: 1-4 30%, 5-99 40%, 100-249 45%, 250 + 50%. 160pp; 6×9, 7⅜×9¼, 4¾×8½; Ventura publisher, linotype. Reporting time: 6 months. Simultaneous submissions accepted: no. Publishes 5% of manuscripts submitted. Payment: 15% of net. Copyrights for author. PMA, MSPA, ABA.

The Bieler Press, Gerald Lange, 4216-1/4 Glencoe Avenue, Marina del Rey, CA 90292. 1975. 19 titles listed in the *Small Press Record of Books in Print* (28th Edition, 1999-00). †letterpress.

63

Big Mouth Publications, Jon Bell, 284 Clay Street, Sonoma, CA 95476-7551. 1992. Music, non-fiction. "Big Mouth Publications publishes humorous motivational audiotapes featuring dynamic narration teams, music and sound effects." avg. press run 5M. Pub'd 1 title 1998; expects 1 title 1999. 1 title listed in the *Small Press Record of Books in Print* (28th Edition, 1999-00). avg. price, other: $12.95 audiocassette. Discounts: 55% wholesalers. digital recording. Bay Area Independent Publishers Assn. (BAIPA).

BIG SCREAM, Nada Press, David Cope, 2782 Dixie S.W., Grandville, MI 49418, 616-531-1442. 1974. Poetry, fiction, art. "We include 2-5 pages of each writer publ.- some longpoems tend to have imagist bias; prefer *personal* poems. Contributors: David Cope, Andy Clausen, Anne Waldman, Marcia Arrieta, Jim Cohn, Antler, Jeff Poniewaz, Allen Ginsberg. Poets and writers *must* include SASE with their submissions." circ. 100. 1/yr. Pub'd 1 issue 1998; expects 1 issue 1999, 1 issue 2000. sub. price: $5; per copy: $5; sample: $5. Back issues: $5 per copy. 35pp; 8½×11; photo offset. Reporting time: 1 week - 1 month. Payment: 1 copy, more if requested.

Big Sky Press, 3647 Kalsman Drive, Suite 4, Los Angeles, CA 90016-4447, 310-838-0807. 1987. 1 title listed in the *Small Press Record of Books in Print* (28th Edition, 1999-00). Copyrights for author.

Big Star Press, Lisa Radon, 1770 48th Avenue, #2-D, Capitola, CA 95010, 408-464-3625 ph/fax. 1996. Poetry, fiction, art, photos, long-poems. avg. press run 200. Expects 2-3 titles 1999, 2-3 titles 2000. 1 title listed in the *Small Press Record of Books in Print* (28th Edition, 1999-00). avg. price, paper: $6.95. Discounts: short: 20%, max: 43%. 36pp; 5½×8½; mi, of. Reporting time: 2 months. Simultaneous submissions accepted: yes. Payment: to be determined, varies. Copyrights for author.

BIG WORLD, Jim Fortney, PO Box 8743-DB, Lancaster, PA 17601, 717-569-0217; E-mail bigworld@big-world.com. 1994. Articles, art, photos, reviews, music, letters, news items, non-fiction. "Independent travel, on the cheap and down to earth" circ. 10M. 4/yr. Pub'd 6 issues 1998; expects 4 issues 1999, 4 issues 2000. sub. price: $15; per copy: $3.50; sample: $3.50. Discounts: bulk 50%. 64pp; 8½×11; of. Reporting time: 1-2 months. Simultaneous submissions accepted: yes. Publishes 5% of manuscripts submitted. Payment: varies. Copyrighted, reverts to author. Pub's reviews: 24 in 1998. §Travel, cultural, geopolitical, environmental. Ads: Ad rates available on request.

Bigwater Publishing, Freelance Editors, PO Box 170, Caledonia, MI 49316, 616-891-1113; Fax 616-891-8015. 1988. "Not accepting submissions" Pub'd 2 titles 1998; expects 2 titles 1999, 2 titles 2000. 11 titles listed in the *Small Press Record of Books in Print* (28th Edition, 1999-00). avg. price, paper: $8.95. 220pp.

Bilingual Review/Press (see also BILINGUAL REVIEW/Revista Bilingue), Gary D. Keller, General Editor; Karen S. Van Hooft, Managing Editor, Hispanic Research Center, Arizona State Univ., Box 872702, Tempe, AZ 85287-2702, 602-965-3867. 1976. Poetry, fiction, articles, criticism, plays. "We publish U.S. Hispanic creative literature (fiction, poetry, drama) and scholarly monographs and collections of articles in the following areas: U.S. Hispanic language and literature, Chicano and Puerto Rican studies, contemporary methods of literary analysis." avg. press run 1M cloth, 2M paper. Pub'd 10 titles 1998; expects 12 titles 1999, 12 titles 2000. 140 titles listed in the *Small Press Record of Books in Print* (28th Edition, 1999-00). avg. price, cloth: $20; paper: $12. Discounts: 20% for textbooks; trade—1-4 copies 20%, 5-24 42%, 25-99 43%, 100+ 44%. 256pp; 5½×8½; of. Reporting time: 8-10 weeks. Payment: varies from author subsidy with repayment to author from royalties on copies sold, to standard 10% royalty with no subsidy, depending on commercial prospects of book. We copyright in our name. CLMP.

BILINGUAL REVIEW/Revista Bilingue, Bilingual Review/Press, Gary D. Keller, Editor; Karen S. Van Hooft, Managing Editor, Hispanic Research Center, Arizona State Univ., Box 872702, Tempe, AZ 85287-2702, 602-965-3867. 1974. Poetry, fiction, articles, interviews, criticism, reviews. "Research and scholarly articles dealing with bilingualism, primarily but not exclusively Spanish-English; U.S.-Hispanic literature; English-Spanish contrastive linguistics; fiction, poetry, etc., concerning Hispanic life in the US." circ. 1M. 3/yr. Pub'd 3 issues 1998; expects 3 issues 1999, 3 issues 2000. sub. price: $21 individuals, $35 institutions; per copy: $13 institutions, $7 individuals; sample: $13 institutions; $7 individuals. Back issues: depends on issue. Discounts: none. 96pp; 7×10; of. Reporting time: 6-8 weeks. Payment: 2 complimentary copies of issue. Copyrighted, does not revert to author. Pub's reviews: 9 in 1998. §Books dealing with our primary areas of interest: bilingualism, U.S. Hispanic literature. Ads: $150/$90/2-pg spread $250, back cover $200, inside back cover $175. CLMP.

Bilingue Publications & Productions, Robert C. Medina, PO Box 1629, Las Cruces, NM 88004, 505-526-1557. 1975. Fiction, plays. avg. press run 1M. Pub'd 1 title 1998; expects 1 title 1999, 1 title 2000. 4 titles listed in the *Small Press Record of Books in Print* (28th Edition, 1999-00). avg. price, paper: $5. Discounts: 40%. 140pp; 6×8. Reporting time: 3 months. We help authors with copyright.

BIOLOGY DIGEST, Plexus Publishing, Inc., Mary Suzanne Hogan, 143 Old Marlton Pike, Medford, NJ 08055, 609-654-6500. 1977. Non-fiction. "*Biology Digest* is an abstracting journal with subject and author indexes. Each issue also contains a full-length original feature article on some life science subject of particular timely interest. We also publish an annual cumulative index." circ. 2M. 9/yr. Pub'd 9 issues 1998; expects 9 issues 1999, 9 issues 2000. 6 titles listed in the *Small Press Record of Books in Print* (28th Edition, 1999-00). sub. price: $139. Back issues: same. Discounts: call for pricing. 170pp; 8½×11; of. Reporting time: 60 days. Payment: feature article varies. Copyrighted, does not revert to author. Pub's reviews: 32 books in 1998. §Biology, life sciences, medicine, health, ecology.

Bio-Probe, Inc., Sam Ziff, PO Box 608010, Orlando, FL 32860-8010, Phone 407-290-9670; fax 407-299-4149. 1984. Non-fiction. "Most books deal with dental mercury and health." avg. press run 5M. Pub'd 5 titles 1998. 6 titles listed in the *Small Press Record of Books in Print* (28th Edition, 1999-00). avg. price, paper: $14.95. Discounts: universal. 64-448pp; 6×9. Payment: negotiated % on wholesale—every 6 months. Copyrights for author. National Association of Independent Publishers (NAIP), PO Box 850, Moore Haven, FL 33471; Florida Publishers Group (FPG), PO Box 20603, Bradenton, FL 64203.

Birch Brook Press, Tom Tolnay, PO Box 81, Delhi, NY 13753, 212-353-3326 messages; Phone & Fax orders & inquiries 607-746-7453. 1982. Poetry, fiction. "Birch Brook Press prefers inquiries with samples from manuscript, SASE required. BBP has its own complete letterpress print shop and uses monies from designing, printing, typesetting books for other publishers to do some original anthologies on a project-by-project basis, soliciting material for each. Our latest, for example, are *Baseball & The Game of Ideas, Fiction Flyfishing and the Search for Innocence, Editors in the Stream, The Romance of the Book, Magic & Madness in the Library,The Road Taken.* (These projects are now completed.) We sometimes do handcrafted books of unusual merit by individual writers on a co-op basis. Though popular culture is our main interest, we do three books of literary poetry/fiction each year. Recent titles include *Immigrant* by Stanley Nelson, *A Thing Among Things* by Carolyn Bennett, and *Life & Death of Peter Stubble* by Jesse Glass, *The Melancholy of Yorick* by Joel Chace, *In Foreign Parts* by Elisabeth Stevens, and *Kilimanjano Burning* by John B. Robinson. Some of our books are made entirely by hand, and these are sold as limited editions." avg. press run 250-1M. Pub'd 5 titles 1998; expects 6 titles 1999, 7 titles 2000. 26 titles listed in the *Small Press Record of Books in Print* (28th Edition, 1999-00). avg. price, cloth: $25-$35; paper: $13.50-$18; other: $40-$150 limited editions. Discounts: 1 copy 32%, 2-4 36%, 5-9 38%, 10-15 40%; these discounts do not apply to limited editions. 64-232pp; 5½×8½, 6×9; †lp. Reporting time: 2-6 weeks. We accept simultaneous submissions if indicated. Payment: 5-10%. Copyrights for author. Small Press Center.

Birdalone Books, Viola Roth, 9245 E. Woodview Drive, Bloomington, IN 47401-9101, 812-337-0118. 1988. Poetry, fiction, criticism, music, long-poems, non-fiction. "Primary interest is in the facsimile reprinting, via offset lithography, of obscure out-of-print literature (e.g. William Morris) and music. Specialty is in high-*quality* production, encompassing paper selection, design, and binding. Any volume is also available in half- or full-leather (goat or calf), completely hand-sewn and hand-bound, with authentic, *sewn* silk headbands. All acid-free papers and boards; skins are pared by hand (no bonded leather!). Bindery will also do repairs and restoration of customers' other books, at competitive prices. No unsolicited mss, please." avg. press run 750. Pub'd 1 title 1998; expects 1 title 1999, 1 title 2000. 3 titles listed in the *Small Press Record of Books in Print* (28th Edition, 1999-00). avg. price, cloth: $40-$150; other: $130 half goat; $175 half calf; $160 full goat; $205 full calf. Discounts: 1 copy: 10%, 2-5: 20%, 6-9: 30%, 10+: 40%. 400pp; size varies; of. Payment: 5% of net sales. Copyrights for author.

BIRMINGHAM POETRY REVIEW, Robert Collins, Co-Editor; Randy Blythe, Co-Editor, English Department, University of Alabama-Birmingham, Birmingham, AL 35294, 205-934-8573. 1988. Poetry. "Poetry of any length or style. We are interested in publishing work on the cutting edge of contemporary poetry." circ. 600. 2/yr. Pub'd 2 issues 1998; expects 2 issues 1999, 2 issues 2000. sub. price: $4; per copy: $1; sample: $2. Back issues: $2. 50pp; 6×9; of. Reporting time: 1-3 months. Simultaneous submissions accepted: no. Publishes 1% of manuscripts submitted. Payment: 2 copies, plus a one year subscription. Copyrighted, reverts to author. Pub's reviews: 4 in 1998. §Contemporary poetry. Ads: none.

Birth Day Publishing Company, PO Box 7722, San Diego, CA 92167, 619-296-3194. 1975. Poetry, articles, art, photos, interviews, reviews, letters, non-fiction. "We publish material dealing with spirituality in general and, in particular, the life and teachings of an Indian holy man named Sri Sathya Sai Baba. Published material has been book length, non-fiction. Recent contributors include Samuel H. Sandweiss, M.D., Dr. John S. Hislop, Ph.D, and Howard Murphet. Ms by invitation only." avg. press run 5M. Pub'd 2 titles 1998; expects 3 titles 1999, 3 titles 2000. 8 titles listed in the *Small Press Record of Books in Print* (28th Edition, 1999-00). avg. price, paper: $6.40/$9. Discounts: book trade 40%, bulk 50%, classroom/library 40%, jobber 50%. 225pp; 5½×8½; of. Payment: usually none. Copyrights for author. SSA.

BIRTHKIT NEWSLETTER, Jan Tritten, PO Box 2672, Eugene, OR 97402, 503-344-7438. 1994. "Birth information for midwives, childbirth educators and interested consumers. Photos, experiences, technical and non-technical articles." 4/yr. Expects 4 issues 1999, 4 issues 2000. sub. price: $20. Discounts: none. 12pp; 8½×11; †photocopy. Reporting time: 6 weeks. Simultaneous submissions accepted: no. Publishes 85% of manuscripts submitted. Copyrighted, both can use copyrights. Ads: none.

BITTER OLEANDER, Paul B. Roth, 4983 Tall Oaks Drive, Fayetteville, NY 13066-9776, FAX 315-637-5056; E-mail bones44@ix.netcom.com. 1974. Poetry, fiction. "Prefer the experimental and imaginative but not solipsistic. Interested in an international approach to writing. Recent contributions by Alan Britt, Steve Barfield, Duane Locke, Silvia Scheibli, Robert Bly, Charles Wright, and Marjorie Agosin." circ. 1500. 2/yr. Expects 2 issues 1999, 2 issues 2000. sub. price: $15; per copy: $8; sample: $8. Back issues: $8. Discounts: negotiable. 128pp; 6×9. Reporting time: 1-3 months. Simultaneous submissions accepted: yes. Publishes 1% of manuscripts submitted. Payment: 1 copy, some payment if available. Copyrighted, reverts to author. Ads: $125/$95.

●**BitterSweet Publishing Company,** James Imel, PO Box 30407, Bakersfield, CA 93385, 805-665-0326. 1992. Non-fiction. "I started out as a self-publisher but have since published four books by three different authors." avg. press run 1.5M. Pub'd 1 title 1998; expects 2 titles 1999, 2 titles 2000. avg. price, cloth: $21.95; paper: $13.45. Discounts: 40% to bookstores; 55% to agents. 160pp; 5½×8½; of. Reporting time: 4 weeks. Simultaneous submissions accepted: yes. Publishes 2% of manuscripts submitted. Payment: 10% for first 1500, 12% for more. Copyrights for author. VIP, CWC.

BkMk Press, James McKinley, Director, University of Missouri-Kansas City, 5100 Rockhill, University House, Kansas City, MO 64110, 816-235-2558; FAX 816-235-2611; freemank@smtpgate.ssb.umkc.edu. 1971. Poetry, fiction, long-poems, non-fiction. "*BkMk Press* ordinarily publishes non-commercial materials of high quality & cultural significance, poetry, fiction and essay collection, translations, etc." avg. press run 750. Pub'd 5 titles 1998; expects 6 titles 1999. 60 titles listed in the *Small Press Record of Books in Print* (28th Edition, 1999-00). avg. price, cloth: $12; paper: $9; other: $3 chapbooks. Discounts: trade 40%. 75pp; 5½×8½; of. Reporting time: 5 months. Payment: permission fees, 10% royalty. Copyrights for author.

THE BLAB, K. Engle, Editor, 3073 Rio Bonita Street, Indialantic, FL 32903. 1989. Articles, photos, cartoons, interviews, reviews, news items. "*The Blab* varies from issue to issue. Sometimes a holiday is lampooned. Usually man's inhumanity and fathomless capacity for stupidity is illustrated, often with news clippings and articles culled from mainstream and underground publications." circ. 2M+. 6/yr. Pub'd 10 issues 1998; expects 6 issues 1999, 6 issues 2000. sub. price: $10, $15 Canada and foreign; per copy: $1; sample: $1. Back issues: 6 for $5, all 30 for $20. Discounts: trade. 2pp; 11×17; of. Payment: issues. Copyrighted, reverts to author. Pub's reviews. Ads: negotiable.

Blacfax, Bob NcNeil, Midtown Station, PO Box 542, New York, NY 10018. Poetry, art, long-poems, non-fiction.

Black Bear Publications (see also BLACK BEAR REVIEW), Ave Jeanne, Ron Zettlemoyer, 1916 Lincoln Street, Croydon, PA 19021-8026. 1984. Poetry, articles, art, reviews. "Chapbook publications depends upon funding at present times. Usually no more than 3 per year. Manuscripts should reflect Black Bear image. Contributors should have a good knowledge of Black Bear and have worked with us before. Send complete manuscript. We have recently published America and other poems by A.D. Winans. We receive numerous chapbook submissions, so be prepared for competition. Follow guidelines. Samples available for $5 ppd. in the US and Canada. Illustrators receive cash payment on acceptance for illustrating our chapbooks. Query for current titles. Our main objective is to get more poets into print and off the streets. Enclose a $5 reading fee and SASE. Subsidy considered." avg. press run 500. Pub'd 3 titles 1998; expects 3 titles 1999, 3 titles 2000. 12 titles listed in the *Small Press Record of Books in Print* (28th Edition, 1999-00). avg. price, paper: $5. 34pp; 5½×8½; of. Reporting time: 2 weeks. Simultaneous submissions accepted: no. Publishes 5% of manuscripts submitted. Payment: in copies. Copyrights for author.

BLACK BEAR REVIEW, Black Bear Publications, Ave Jeanne, Poetry & Art Editor; Ron Zettlemoyer, Publisher, Black Bear Publications, 1916 Lincoln Street, Croydon, PA 19021, E-mail bbreview@aol.com; Website http://members.aol.com//bbreview/index.htm. 1984. Poetry, art, reviews, collages. "We like to see poetry that is puissant, and explosive. Forms used are avant-garde, free verse and haiku. No line limit. We would like to see artwork in black & white, (4x6—no larger, signed by author. Cover illustrations, cash on acceptance. Poets published: John Elsberg, Sherman Alexie, Ivan Arguelles, Andrew Gettler, John Grey, Jon Daunt, A. D. Winans. Artists published: Nancy Glazer, Mark Z., Kathryn DiLego, Ruth Richards, Walt Phillips, Ristau. E-mail submissions are encouraged. No attached files please." circ. 500. 2/yr. Expects 2 issues 1999, 2 issues 2000. sub. price: $10; per copy: $5; sample: $5. Back issues: $4. Discounts: 40%. 64pp; 5½×8½; of. Reporting time: 2 weeks. Simultaneous submissions accepted: no. Publishes 5% of manuscripts submitted. Payment: contributor copy. Copyrighted, reverts to author. §Social, political, ecological. Ads: $45/$25—barter.

Black Bile Press, Matthew Firth, 1315 Niagara Street #4, Windsor, Ont. N9A 3V8, Canada, 519-253-3237. 1994. Fiction. "Publish short books from contributors to magazine *Black Cat 115*." avg. press run 100-150. Pub'd 1 title 1998; expects 2 titles 1999, 2 titles 2000. 1 title listed in the *Small Press Record of Books in Print* (28th Edition, 1999-00). avg. price, paper: $4. 30pp; 5½×8½; mi. Simultaneous submissions accepted: no. Does not copyright for author.

BLACK BOUGH, Charles Easter, 188 Grove Street #1, Somerville, NJ 08876. 1991. Poetry, art. "We publish haiku, senryu, tanka, haibun, longer poems in the haiku or Japanese tradition. Accept news items about haiku. SASE required for return. Recent contributors include Emily Romano, Jim Kacian, and Michael Dylan Welch. Our name is taken from Pound's 'In a station at the Metro,' arguably one of the earliest haiku-like pooems in English. We emphasize haiku and related forms that exemplify the use of the eastern form in the western idiom and milieu." circ. 200. 3/yr. Pub'd 3 issues 1998; expects 3 issues 1999, 3 issues 2000. sub. price: $16.50; per copy: $6; sample: $6. Back issues: $6. Discounts: none. 30pp; 4¼×5½; chapbook style. Reporting time: 1-3 months. Simultaneous submissions accepted: no. Publishes 5% of manuscripts submitted. Payment: $1 for each verse, up to $4 for sequence/longer poem. No contributor's copies, except in cases of financial hardship. Copyrighted, reverts to author. Pub's reviews: 10 in 1998. §Haiku and related poetry. exchanges with similar magazines.

Black Buzzard Press (see also VISIONS-INTERNATIONAL, The World Journal of Illustrated Poetry; BLACK BUZZARD REVIEW), Bradley R. Strahan, 1007 Ficklen Road, Fredericksburg, VA 22405. 1979. Poetry, art. *"No unsolicited manuscripts! The Black Buzzard Illustrated Chapbook Series* currently has 3 volumes in print: *Dada Dog* by Larry Couch, and *Silvija, A Riga Nocturine* by Karlis Freivalds. *Cryptch* by Melissa Bell. The International *-Visions* series of full length poetry books (illustrated as all our materials are) has begun with *Speaking in Tongues* a collection of unique verse by linguists from all over the world and *Corday* by the great internationally known writer and biographer of Thomas Merton, Michael Mott. Our latest book is *Fabrications* by Lane Jennings (new and selected poems)." avg. press run 250-850. Expects 1 title 1999, 1 title 2000. 6 titles listed in the *Small Press Record of Books in Print* (28th Edition, 1999-00). avg. price, paper: $5.50. Discounts: 20 or more 40%. 32pp; 5½×8½; of. Reporting time: 2 weeks to 2 months. Payment: by arrangement. Copyrights for author.

BLACK BUZZARD REVIEW, Black Buzzard Press, Bradley R. Strahan, 1007 Ficklen Road, Fredericksburg, VA 22045. 1988. Poetry. "We decided to publish this informal journal as a supplement to our successful, long-running international magazine *Visions*, which has become more and more occupied with translations and special projects. *BBR* prints only original work in English (poetry), no translations, no reprints, *rarely* will do non-USA work. We are *wide open* to a wide variety of poems. All poems should be less than 30 lines, not previously published or submitted elsewhere and *must include a SASE* with adequate postage. Strongly suggest reading a sample before submitting work. A sample (only $4) is worth a thousand words of description." circ. 300. 1/yr. Pub'd 1 issue 1998; expects 1 issue 1999, 1 issue 2000. sub. price: $3.50 when added to a subscription to *Visions-International* (no separate subscription); per copy: $5; sample: $4. Discounts: none. 32pp; 8½×11; of. Reporting time: 2 days to 2 months. Publishes 5% of manuscripts submitted. Payment: copy. Not copyrighted. VIAS.

BLACK CROSS, Jim Guess, Erik Jensen, 3121 Corto Place #2, Long Beach, CA 90803, 562-987-4305; wstien@csulb.edu. 1995. Poetry, fiction, art, photos, cartoons, reviews, long-poems, plays. "Recent contributors: Gerald Locklin, T. Thrasher, Andrew Demcak, Ben Ohmart, Rick Lupert, Raindog." circ. 250-300. 2/yr. Pub'd 2 issues 1998; expects 2 issues 1999, 2 issues 2000. sub. price: $4; per copy: $2; sample: $2. 70pp; 4¼×5½; †laser. Reporting time: 1-6 months. Simultaneous submissions accepted: no. Publishes 7% of manuscripts submitted. Payment: 1 copy. Not copyrighted. Pub's reviews: 12 in 1998. §Poetry, short fiction, eroticism, politics, anti-religious material. Ads: none.

Black Diamond Book Publishing, N. Earle, PO Box 492299, Los Angeles, CA 90049-8299, 800-962-7622; fax 310-472-9833; E-mail 103615.1070@compuserve.com or nancy-shaffron@compuserve.com. 1994. Fiction. "New Age books and fiction, books on healing" avg. press run 5M. Pub'd 4 titles 1998; expects 4 titles 1999, 6 titles 2000. 4 titles listed in the *Small Press Record of Books in Print* (28th Edition, 1999-00). avg. price, paper: $12.95. Discounts: wholesale/distributors discounts available; contact publisher. 200+pp; 5×8. Reporting time: depends on complexity of submission. Simultaneous submissions accepted: no. Very few manuscripts are accepted for publication. Payment: available upon request. Copyrights for author. PMA, NAPRA, NEI.

BLACK DIRT, Black Dirt Press, Patrick Parks, Joanne Lowery, Rachael Tecza, ECC 1700 Spartan Drive, Elgin, IL 60123-7193. 1998. Poetry, fiction, art, photos, interviews, non-fiction. "Formerly *Farmer's Market.* We read and like a variety of writing, but we are especially taken by things that surprise us in some way. Recent contribuors include Philip Dacey, Michael Martone, William Heyen, Ken Pobo, Jesse Lee Kercheval, and Simone Muench." circ. 700. 2/yr. Pub'd 2 issues 1998; expects 2 issues 1999, 2 issues 2000. sub. price: $10; per copy: $6; sample: $5.50. Discounts: 40%. 100pp; 6×9; of. Reporting time: 4-6 weeks. We accept simultaneous submissions, but we don't encourage them. Publishes 15% of manuscripts submitted. Payment: 2 copies + 1 year subscription. Copyrighted, reverts to author. Ads: exchange only.

Black Dirt Press (see also BLACK DIRT), Patrick Parks, Joanne Lowery, Rachael Tecza, ECC 1700 Spartan Drive, Elgin, IL 60123-7193. 1997. Poetry. "At present, we are only publishing poetry chapbooks, either by invitation or through our chapbook contest." avg. press run 250. Pub'd 1 title 1998; expects 2 titles 1999, 2 titles 2000. 3 titles listed in the *Small Press Record of Books in Print* (28th Edition, 1999-00). avg. price, paper: $5. Discounts: 40%. 32pp; 6×6; of. Simultaneous submissions accepted: no. Payment: 50 copies. Does not copyright for author.

Black Dome Press Corp., Route 296, Box 422, Hensonville, NY 12439, 518-734-6357. 1990. Non-fiction. avg. press run 3M. Pub'd 4 titles 1998; expects 4 titles 1999, 5 titles 2000. 22 titles listed in the *Small Press Record of Books in Print* (28th Edition, 1999-00). avg. price, cloth: $30; paper: $13. Discounts: 40%. 200pp; 6×9. Reporting time: 3 months. Simultaneous submissions accepted: yes. Publishes 5% of manuscripts submitted. Payment: varies per contract. Copyrights for author. SPC.

Black Dress Press (see also SPINNING JENNY), C.E. Harrison, PO Box 213, Village Station, New York, NY 10014, website www.blackdresspress.com. 1994. Poetry, fiction, art, music, plays, non-fiction. avg. press run 1M. Expects 1 title 1999, 2 titles 2000. Discounts: write for details. of. Reporting time: 8 weeks. Simultaneous submissions accepted: no. Publishes 5% of manuscripts submitted. Copyrights for author.

Black Forest Press, Dahk Knox, Publisher, Editor-in-Chief; Mary Inbody, Senior Editor; Keith Pearson, Acquisitions Editor; Deborah Johnson, Marketing Director; Raul Espinosa, Art Director, 539 Telegraph Canyon Road #521, Chula Vista, CA 91910, 619-656-8048; FAX 619-482-8704; E-mail BFP@flash.net/~dbk. 1991. Poetry, fiction, satire, plays, non-fiction. "Kinder Books is an imprint for children's books. Black Forest Press is a small press which focuses on the publications of new authors who have difficulty obtaining large press publishers, but whose work has merit and is marketable. BFP also publishes books on professional growth and career development; i.e., Drs. Dahk and Jan Knox, noted resident experts in vocational guidance counseling and training. Psychology, business, management and fiction. Kinder Books-Imprint for Children's Books; Dichter Books (Poetry) and Abentenuer Books (Adventure) both are new imprints; Sonnenschein books (visionary)" avg. press run 2M-5M. Pub'd 20 titles 1998; expects 25 titles 1999, 35 titles 2000. 8 titles listed in the *Small Press Record of Books in Print* (28th Edition, 1999-00). avg. price, cloth: $18.95; paper: $11.95; other: $9.95 workbooks. Discounts: 20% to educational institutions who order quantities of 50 books/sets of books at a time; 15% on orders of 21-49; 10% on orders of 1-20; distributors/wholesalers regular discounts; 40% to bookstores. 200-250pp; 5½×8½, 6×9, 8½×11, 7×9, 4½×6; of, lp, desktop. Reporting time: 2 weeks. Simultaneous submissions are accepted, but no more than two by any one author at a time. Publishes 10% of manuscripts submitted. Payment: varies with promotion's agreement and terms. Copyrights for author. PMA.

Black Hat Press (see also RAG MAG), Beverly Voldseth, Editor & Publisher, Box 12, Goodhue, MN 55027, 651-923-4590. 1989. Poetry, fiction, articles, art, photos, cartoons, interviews, satire, criticism, reviews, letters, long-poems, plays, non-fiction. "Just send your best stuff. I am not reading any book length manuscripts until further notice." avg. press run 750. Pub'd 2 titles 1998; expects 2 titles 1999, 2 titles 2000. 14 titles listed in the *Small Press Record of Books in Print* (28th Edition, 1999-00). avg. price, paper: $9.95. Discounts: 40%. 80pp; 5½×8½; of. Reporting time: 2-3 months. Simultaneous submissions accepted: yes. Publishes 1% of manuscripts submitted. Payment: varies. Does not copyright for author.

Black Heron Press, Jerry Gold, PO Box 95676, Seattle, WA 98145. 1984. Fiction. "May do something other than fiction, if it appeals to us." avg. press run 1.2M. Pub'd 4 titles 1998; expects 4 titles 1999, 4 titles 2000. 27 titles listed in the *Small Press Record of Books in Print* (28th Edition, 1999-00). avg. price, cloth: $21; paper: $12. Discounts: trade 40% regardless of # of copies, 42% if order prepaid. 200pp; 5½×8½; of. Reporting time: 4-6 months. Simultaneous submissions accepted: yes. Publishes .003% of manuscripts submitted. Payment: 8% of retail price of book, payment semiannually. Copyrights for author. Rocky Mountain Book Publishers Assn.

BLACK ICE, Ronald Sukenick, Publisher; Michael Dorsey, Editor, English Dept., Publications Center, Box 494, University of Colorado, Boulder, CO 80309-0494, 303-492-8938. 1984. Fiction. "Fiction only. Guidelines: very innovative work only. We suggest familiarity with the magazine, as inappropriate work will be returned without comment. All submissions must be under 35 pages (total), with SASE. Computer print-outs OK. Contributors include: Steve Katz, Tom Glynn, Eurudice, Diane Glancy, Alain Arias-Misson, Erik Belgum, Harold Jaffe, Ricardo Cortez Cruz" circ. 1.2M. 2/yr. Pub'd 2 issues 1998; expects 2 issues 1999, 2 issues 2000. sub. price: 3 issues $18; per copy: $7; sample: $7. Back issues: $7. Discounts: standard to distributors. 100pp; 5½×8½; of. Reporting time: 6-12 months. We accept simultaneous submissions if noted as such. Publishes 7% of manuscripts submitted. Payment: 2 copies. Copyrighted, reverts to author. Ads: inquire. CLMP.

BLACK JACK & VALLEY GRAPEVINE, Seven Buffaloes Press, Art Coelho, Box 249, Big Timber, MT 59011. 1973. Poetry, fiction, art, photos, interviews, reviews, parts-of-novels, long-poems, collages. "*Black Jack*: rural poems & stories from anywhere in America, especially the West, the Appalachias, Oklahoma, and the Ozarks. Work that tells a story, a craft that shows experience, not only of the head (technique), but of the heart (passion and compassion). I'm more than prejudiced against poems that are made up or forced, even when they are concocted out of the supposed wisdom of some established school. A 'school' is nothing more than a group of individuals sitting in one communal literary lap. Give me a loner on his foggy mountaintop; at least the fog is from the mountain, not from his song or his tale to tell. *Valley Grapevine* takes material native to Central California...the San Joaquin and Sacramento Valleys. Especially want work from small town farming communities, but will look at non-rural city work too.focus on Okies, hoboes, ranch life, migrant labor, the Dustbowl era, and heritage and pride. Want writers and poets who write predominately of the valley of their birth. Contributors: Gerry Haslam, Wilma McDaniel, Richard Dokey, Dorothy Rose, Morine Stanley, Frank Cross, William Rintoul.'' circ. 750. 1/yr. Pub'd 1 issue 1998; expects 1 issue 1999, 1 issue 2000. price per copy: $8.75 postpaid; sample: $7.75. Back issues: none. Discounts: 1-4, 0%; 5 copies or over, 40%. 80pp; 5½×8½; †of. Reporting time: within a week, often a day or two. Payment: copies, often other free copies. Copyrighted, reverts to author. No ads. CLMP.

BLACK LACE, BLK Publishing Company, Alycee J. Lane, PO Box 83912, Los Angeles, CA 90083, 310-410-0808, fax 310-410-9250, e-mail newsroom@blk.com. 1991. Poetry, fiction, articles, art, photos, interviews, satire, criticism, reviews, letters, news items, non-fiction. ''Erotic black lesbian magazine.'' circ. 9M. 4/yr. Expects 4 issues 1999, 4 issues 2000. sub. price: $20; per copy: $5.95; sample: $7. Back issues: $7. 48pp; 8¼×10⅞; of. Reporting time: 4 weeks. Simultaneous submissions accepted: yes. Payment: varies. Copyrighted, rights reverting to author varies. Pub's reviews: 1 in 1998. §Black lesbian community. Ads: $420.

Black Light Fellowship, PO Box 5369, Chicago, IL 60680, 312-563-0081; fax 312-563-0086. 1976. Non-fiction. ''Street address: Black Light Fellowship, 128 Paulina St., Chicago, IL, 60612'' avg. press run 6M. Pub'd 2 titles 1998; expects 2+ titles 1999. 10 titles listed in the *Small Press Record of Books in Print* (28th Edition, 1999-00). avg. price, paper: $12. Discounts: 20% short, 40% trade, 50% distributors. 200pp; 5½×8½. Payment: yes. C.B.A.

BLACK LITERARY PLAYERS, Grace Adams, 829 Langdon Court, Rochester Hills, MI 48307, 810-556-7335. 1992. ''First Black Signatory Agent in Michigan and the world, Writers Guild of Amercia. Also literary agent for books.'' 8/yr. Pub'd 12 issues 1998; expects 12 issues 1999, 12 issues 2000. 4 titles listed in the *Small Press Record of Books in Print* (28th Edition, 1999-00). sub. price: $36; per copy: $3.50; sample: $3. 4-8pp; 8½×11. Reporting time: 4-6 weeks. Simultaneous submissions accepted: yes. Pub's reviews. §Black author books, all genre. Black Authors & Published Writer's Directory.

BLACK MOON, Alan Britt, Editor, Publisher; Silvia Scheibli, West Coast Editor, 233 Northway Road, Reisterstown, MD 21136, 410-833-9424. 1994. Poetry, articles, interviews, criticism, long-poems. ''Imagination: surrealism, deep image. Robert Bly, Louis Simpson, David Ray, David Ignatow, John Haines, Andrei Codrescu, Donald Hall, Michael Waters, Duane Locke, Paul Roth, Steve Barfield, Marjorie Agosin, Judy Ray, Steve Sleboda, Angel Gonzalez, Ira Sadoff, Gregory Orr, Daniel Comiskey, Colette Inez, Pierre Reverdy, Ray Gonzalez, Donald Ryburn, Nicomedes Suarez-Arauz, Thomas R. Smith.'' circ. 2M. 1/yr. Pub'd 1 issue 1998; expects 1 issue 1999, 1 issue 2000. sub. price: $8.95 + $1.75(S & H); per copy: $8.95 + $1.75(S & H); sample: $8.95 + $1.75(S & H). Back issues: $8.95 + $1.75(S & H). Discounts: 2-4 10%, 5-9 20%, 10+ 40%. 224pp; 6×9; of. Reporting time: 2 months. Simultaneous submissions accepted: yes. Publishes 5% of manuscripts submitted. Payment: contributor's copy. Copyrighted, reverts to author. Ads: $125/$75/$50 1/4 page.

BLACK MOON MAGAZINE, Black Moon Publishing, Armand Rosamilia, 1385 Route 35, Suite 169, Middletown, NJ 07748, 908-787-2445. 1995. Poetry, fiction, interviews, reviews, music. ''Looking for horror fiction (to 3000 words), band press kits, fanzines to review, books to review, dark poetry'' circ. 5M. 9/yr. Expects 9 issues 1999, 9 issues 2000. sub. price: $24; per copy: $3.95; sample: $3.95. Discounts: trade for like, distributor discounts. 44pp; 8½×11; of. Reporting time: 2-4 weeks. Payment: 1 free copy, discounts on more. Copyrighted, reverts to author. Pub's reviews. §Horror, mystery, true crime, science fiction, fantasy. Ads: $20/$15/$6 3½ X 2.

Black Moon Publishing (see also BLACK MOON MAGAZINE), Armand Rosamilia, 1385 Route 35, Suite 169, Middletown, NJ 07748, 908-787-2445. 1995. Poetry, fiction, interviews, reviews, music. ''Looking for novella length horror stories or short stories for inclusion in an upcoming book'' Expects 1 title 1999, 1+ titles 2000. 180pp; 5½×8½. Reporting time: 2-4 months. Payment: negotiable. Copyrights for author.

Black Rose Books Ltd., D. Roussopoulos, C.P. 1258, Succ. Place du Parc, Montreal, Quebec H2W 2R3, Canada, 514-844-4076. 1970. Non-fiction. ''USA address: 250 Sonwil Drive, Buffalo, NY 14225, (716) 683-4547. Published over 250 books.'' avg. press run 3M. Pub'd 10 titles 1998; expects 12 titles 1999, 10 titles 2000. 141 titles listed in the *Small Press Record of Books in Print* (28th Edition, 1999-00). avg. price, cloth: $29.95; paper: $14.95. Discounts: regular trade. 200pp; 6×9; of. Reporting time: 6 months. Payment: 10% of list price. Copyrights for author. Association of Canadian Publishers.

THE BLACK SCHOLAR: Journal of Black Studies and Research, Robert Chrisman, Editor; Robert L. Allen, Senior Editor, PO Box 2869, Oakland, CA 94609, 510-547-6633. 1969. Poetry, articles, art, photos, interviews, criticism, reviews, music. ''Manuscripts for full-length articles may range in length from 2M to 5M words, include brief biographical statement, typewritten, double spaced. Articles may be historical and documented, they may be analytic and theoretical; they may be speculative. However, an article should not simply be a 'rap'; it should present a solid point of view convincingly and thoroughly argued. Recent Contributors: Jesse Jackson, Manning Marable, Jayne Cortez, Sonia Sanchez, Henry Louis Gates'' circ. 10M. 4/yr. Pub'd 4 issues 1998; expects 4 issues 1999. sub. price: $30 individual, $75 institution; per copy: $6. Back issues: $6. Discounts: publishers 10% off above rates. 80pp; 7×10; of. Reporting time: 1-2 months. Payment: in contributors copies of magazine and 1 year subscription. Rights become property of the *Black Scholar*. Pub's reviews: 22 in 1998. §The black experience or black related books. Ads: $1,200/$725/$550 1/4 page/classified $200 for 50 words or less, over 50 words add $22 per line per 7 words. CLMP.

BLACK SHEETS MAGAZINE, Bill Brent, PO Box 31155, San Francisco, CA 94131-0155, 415-431-0173; Fax 415-431-0172; blacksheets@blackbooks.com. 1993. Fiction, articles, art, photos, reviews, letters, non-fiction. circ. 6M. 3/yr. Pub'd 3 issues 1998; expects 3 issues 1999, 3 issues 2000. sub. price: $20; per copy: $6; sample: $6. 60pp; 8½×11; of. Reporting time: 6 months. Simultaneous submissions accepted: yes. Publishes 5% of manuscripts submitted. Payment: minimal. Copyrighted, reverts to author. Pub's reviews: 50 in 1998. §Alternative sexuality. Ads: $250/$140/inquire.

Black Sparrow Press, 24 Tenth Street, Santa Rosa, CA 95401. 1966. Poetry, fiction, criticism, letters. ''See our publications.'' avg. press run 2.5M. Pub'd 11 titles 1998; expects 12 titles 1999, 12 titles 2000. 197 titles listed in the *Small Press Record of Books in Print* (28th Edition, 1999-00). avg. price, cloth: $20; paper: $12. Discounts: trade 20%-46%. 150-300pp; 6×9; of, lp. Reporting time: 60 days. Payment: royalty on sales. Copyrights for author.

BLACK TALENT NEWS (The Entertainment Industry Publication for African Americans), Tanya Kersey-Henley, Editor-in-Chief, 1620 Centinela Avenue, Ste. 204, Inglewood, CA 90302-1045. 1994. ''National trade publication for African Americans in the entertainment industry.'' circ. 40M. 12/yr. Pub'd 12 issues 1998; expects 12 issues 1999, 12 issues 2000. sub. price: $23.97; per copy: $2.95; sample: $3.50. Back issues: $5. Discounts: 40% bookstores, 50% newsstands. 40pp; 8½×11. Reporting time: 4 weeks. Simultaneous submissions accepted: yes. Publishes 75% of manuscripts submitted. Payment: varies, negotiable. Copyrighted, reverts to author. Minority Publishers Exchange.

Black Thistle Press, Hollis Melton, 491 Broadway, New York, NY 10012, 212-219-1898. 1990. Poetry, fiction. avg. press run 1M-5M. Pub'd 2 titles 1998; expects 4 titles 1999. 2 titles listed in the *Small Press Record of Books in Print* (28th Edition, 1999-00). avg. price, paper: $14. Discounts: 1-5 20%, 5+. 200pp; 7×9, varies; of. Reporting time: 2 months. Payment: individual arrangements made. Copyrights for author.

Black Tie Press, Peter Gravis, Publisher, Editor; John Dunivent, Art Consultant; Harry Burrus, Associate Editor & Designer, PO Box 440004, Houston, TX 77244-0004, 713-789-5119 fax. 1986. Poetry, art, photos, collages. ''We are not a magazine, we publish books. Send ms. with 30-60 poems. We like the unusual, the wild and rough, sensual and erotic. Narrative poems must provoke, startle. No rhymed material. We want writing that sits in the flame, that ignites the reader's imagination. Always include a cover letter'' avg. press run 300-2M. Pub'd 1 title 1998; expects 3 titles 1999, 3-4 titles 2000. 23 titles listed in the *Small Press Record of Books in Print* (28th Edition, 1999-00). avg. price, cloth: $19.95, limited editions are more; paper: $12.50; other: $28 signed and lettered. Discounts: available upon request; 20% bookstores, if prepaid; special discounts for libraries and foreign bookstores; much smaller discounts on limited editions. 40-112pp; 6×9, 5½×8½; offset, limited editions may be letter press. Reporting time: 2-12 weeks depending on material, time of year. Sometimes, due to the volume we receive, it may be several months before a writer hears from us regarding his ms. We acknowledge receipt straight away. Publishes less than 1% of manuscripts submitted. Payment: may depend on material and author, usually 20 copies. Copyrights for author. Small Press Center.

THE BLACK WARRIOR REVIEW, Laura Didyk, Editor; T.J. Beitelman, Managing Editor; Christopher Manlove, Fiction Editor; Susan Goslee, Poetry Editor, PO Box 862936, University of Alabama, Tuscaloosa, AL 35486-0027, 205-348-4518. 1974. Poetry, fiction, art, photos, interviews, reviews, parts-of-novels, long-poems, non-fiction. ''Publish high quality contemporary fiction and poetry. Recent contributors include Bob Hicok, C.D. Wright, Barry Hannah, William Tester, Janet Burroway, Pamela Ryder, W.S. Merwin, and Tomaz Salamun.'' circ. 1.5M. 2/yr. Pub'd 2 issues 1998; expects 2 issues 1999. sub. price: $14; per copy: $8; sample: $8. Back issues: $4-$6. Discounts: none at present. 180pp; 6×9; of. Reporting time: 2 weeks to 4 months. Simultaneous submissions accepted: yes. Publishes 1% of manuscripts submitted. Payment: varies, includes 2 copies of magazine, 2 annual $500 prizes; varies. Copyrighted, rights transferred to author on request. Pub's reviews: 8 in 1998. §Serious poetry and fiction. Ads: $150/$85. CLMP, AWP.

BlackBox, Bill Austin, Ellen Rosenburg, 77-44 Austin Street #3F, Forest Hills, NY 11375. 1996. Poetry, fiction, articles, art, photos, cartoons, interviews, satire, criticism, long-poems, collages, concrete art, non-fiction. ''BlackBox was created and funded by the above editors. Recent authors: Igor Satanovsky (editor of KOJA).'' circ. 100. 2/yr. Pub'd 1 issue 1998; expects 2 issues 1999, 2 issues 2000. price per copy: $6; sample: $6. Back issues: $5. Discounts: 30%; 40% over 5 issues. 25pp; 8×11; lp. Reporting time: 4 weeks.

Simultaneous submissions accepted: yes. Publishes 5% of manuscripts submitted. Payment: copies. Copyrighted, reverts to author. Ads: $30/$15.

BLACKFIRE, BLK Publishing Company, Alan Bell, PO Box 83912, Los Angeles, CA 90083, 310-410-0808, fax 310-410-9250, e-mail newsroom@blk.com. 1992. Poetry, fiction, articles, art, photos, interviews, long-poems, non-fiction. "Erotic black gay male magazine." circ. 12M. 6/yr. Expects 6 issues 2000. sub. price: $30; per copy: $5.95; sample: $7.00. Back issues: $7.00. 48pp; 8⅛×11⅞; of. Reporting time: 4 weeks. Simultaneous submissions accepted: yes. Payment: varies. Copyrighted, rights reverting to author varies. §Black gay community. Ads: $1800.

BLACKFLASH, Blackflash Editorial Committee, 2nd Floor, 12-23rd Street East, Saskatoon, Saskatchewan S7L 5E2, Canada, 306-244-8018; fax 306-665-6568; E-mail af248@sfn.saskatoon.sk.ca. 1982. Articles, art, photos, interviews, criticism, reviews. circ. 1.7M. 4/yr. Pub'd 4 issues 1998; expects 4 issues 1999, 4 issues 2000. sub. price: $14.95; per copy: $4.75; sample: free. Back issues: $1. Discounts: bulk. 24pp; 8½×11; of. Reporting time: 2 weeks. Payment: $250 Canadian for main article. Copyrighted, reverts to author. Pub's reviews: 1 in 1998. §Contemporary photography and critical writing on contemporary photography. CMPA.

BLACKJACK FORUM, R.G.E. Publishing, Arnold Snyder, 414 Santa Clara Avenue, Oakland, CA 94610, 510-465-6452; FAX 510-652-4330. 1981. Articles, news items. "All articles, items, etc., relate to casino blackjack and/or systems for beating the game. From short news items to 1.5M word max." circ. 3M. 4/yr. Pub'd 4 issues 1998; expects 4 issues 1999, 4 issues 2000. sub. price: $56, $64 Canada or 1st class; per copy: $12.50; sample: $12.50. Back issues: Vol. I #1-4, $3 each; Vol. II and III, $4.95 each; Vol. IV-VII, $6 each; Vol. V-VIII, $7.50 each, Vol. IX-XV $10 each. Discounts: 40% in quantities of 4 or more (same issue). 100pp; 5½×8½; of. Reporting time: 2-6 weeks. Simultaneous submissions accepted: yes. Publishes 65% of manuscripts submitted. Payment: $25-$100 for articles of 500 words to 1,500 words. Copyrighted, reverts to author. Pub's reviews: 15 in 1998. §Gambling in general, blackjack in particular. Ads: $600/$350/$1.50 classified word. PMA.

Blacksmith Corporation, Nancy J. Padua, PO Box 1752, Chino Valley, AZ 86323, 520-636-4456; Fax 520-636-4457. 1973. "Recently published: *Sea Officer*, a novel by Ken Waters pertaining to U.S. Civil War naval maneuvers; and *CCW - Carrying Concealed Weapons* by Jerry Ahern." avg. press run 3.5M. Pub'd 2 titles 1998; expects 2 titles 1999, 2 titles 2000. 2 titles listed in the *Small Press Record of Books in Print* (28th Edition, 1999-00). avg. price, cloth: $19.95; paper: $9.95. Discounts: STOP 30%, trade 40%. 160pp; 6×9; web. Reporting time: 8 weeks maximum. Simultaneous submissions accepted: yes. Publishes 10% of manuscripts submitted. Payment: 5%-10% of net sales price. Copyrights for author. ABA.

‡**BLACKWATER, Scopcraeft,** Cynthia Hendershot, Cheryll, & Scott, Antony Oldknow, PO Box 1091, Portales, NM 88130-1091, 505-359-0901. 1983. Poetry, fiction, articles, art, photos, reviews, parts-of-novels. "Surrealism, Tom McKeown, Kirpal Gordon, Larry Bogan, Rowena Runyan, Michael Shores" circ. 200. 4/yr. Pub'd 1 issue 1998; expects 4 issues 1999, 4 issues 2000. sub. price: $9; per copy: $5; sample: $4. 28pp; 5½×8; laser. Reporting time: 1 month. Payment: copies. Copyrighted, reverts to author. Ads: $50/$25/$10.

BLADES, Francis Poole, Poporo Press, 335 Paper Mill Road, Newark, DE 19711-2254. 1977. Poetry, fiction, art, satire, letters, collages, news items. "*Blades* is a tiny magazine, so send short poems (15 lines=one page). Occasionally we publish longer ones, 3 or 4 pages. We publish surrealism (drawings too), satire, humor, linguistically interesting work. Very short stories, dreams, and cultural documents also sought; prose should be short. We are interested in non-English poems, also. Editors like imagery and poems that examine the strange natural world." circ. 175. 2/yr. Pub'd 1 issue 1998; expects 2 issues 1999, 2 issues 2000. sub. price: $1 or exchange of publications, and SASE; per copy: $1 with SASE; sample: $1,or for exchange, enclose SASE. Back issues: $1. 36pp; 4¼×3¾; †offset or photocopy. Reporting time: 2 months. Payment: copies. Copyrighted, reverts to author. Pub's reviews: 0 in 1998. Ads: exchange ads free.

John F. Blair, Publisher, Carolyn Sakowski, 1406 Plaza Drive, Winston-Salem, NC 27103, 336-768-1374. 1954. Fiction, non-fiction. Pub'd 15 titles 1998; expects 17 titles 1999, 20 titles 2000. 49 titles listed in the *Small Press Record of Books in Print* (28th Edition, 1999-00). avg. price, cloth: $20; paper: $10-$20. Discounts: wholesalers 50%, libraries and schools 20%, trade schedule is according to quantity of books ordered. 100-300pp; size varies; of. Reporting time: 6-8 weeks. Simultaneous submissions accepted: yes. Publishes less than 1% of manuscripts submitted. Payment: % of net sales, bi-annual payments. Copyrights for author. PAS.

BLAST, Bill Tully, Craig Cormick, PO Box 3514, Manuka, Act. 2603, Australia. 1987. Poetry, fiction, articles, art, cartoons, satire, criticism, reviews, music, letters, parts-of-novels, collages, news items, non-fiction. circ. 1M. 4/yr. Pub'd 3 issues 1998; expects 4 issues 1999, 4 issues 2000. sub. price: $A30; per copy: $A2; sample: free. Back issues: $A3. Discounts: 40%. 30pp. Reporting time: 3-10 months. Simultaneous submissions accepted: no. Payment: if we are subsidized. Copyrighted, reverts to author. Pub's reviews: 4 in 1998. Ads: $A80/$A40.

Bleeding Heart Press (see also THE BLIND HORSE REVIEW), Noel Watson, Editor; Todd Kalinski, Assistant Editor, PO Box 15902, Beverly Hills, CA 90209-1902. 1992. Poetry, fiction, art, photos, parts-of-novels, non-fiction. "Bleeding Heart Press queries own submissions. *Septic Stick* by Todd Kalinski (1992); *New Dark Ages* by Kurt Nimo (1993); *Tangiers Nowhere* by Todd Kalinski (1995); and *The New Male* by Gerald Locklin (1995)." avg. press run 300. 4 titles listed in the *Small Press Record of Books in Print* (28th Edition, 1999-00). avg. price, paper: $6. †of. Simultaneous submissions accepted: no. Payment: copies. Copyrights for author.

Blind Beggar Press, Gary Johnston, C. D. Grant, Box 437 Williamsbridge Station, Bronx, NY 10467, 914-683-6792. 1976. Poetry, fiction, art, photos, parts-of-novels, long-poems, plays. "No length on material. Recent contributors: Judy Simmons, Fatisha, Sandra Maria Esteves, Louis Reyes Rivera, Askia Toure." avg. press run 1M. Pub'd 2 titles 1998; expects 3 titles 1999, 3 titles 2000. 17 titles listed in the *Small Press Record of Books in Print* (28th Edition, 1999-00). avg. price, paper: $4.95-$9.95. Discounts: 50% on bulk orders of 5 or more copies for retailers and distributors. 60-200pp; 5½×8½, 6×9; computer. Reporting time: 2-3 months. Payment: in copies. Copyrights for author. BCA.

THE BLIND HORSE REVIEW, Bleeding Heart Press, Todd Kalinski, PO Box 15902, Beverly Hills, CA 90209-1902. 1992. Poetry, reviews, long-poems, parts-of-novels. "Anything goes, but prefer 'gut' poetry & prose. Recent contributors: Steve Richmond, A.D. Winans, Hugh Fox, Barbara Peck, Chris Mortenson." circ. 200-300. Irregular. Pub'd 2 issues 1998; expects 2 issues 1999, 2 issues 2000. sub. price: $16; per copy: $6; sample: $6. Back issues: query to see what is still available. Discounts: trades okay. Pages vary - (46-54) about 15 writers an issue; size varies; †of. Reporting time: 0-2 months. Simultaneous submissions accepted: no. Publishes less than 10% of manuscripts submitted. Payment: 1 copy of magazine. Rights revert to author on publication. Ads: none.

BLIND SPOT, Kim Zorn Caputo, 210 11th Avenue FL 10, New York, NY 10001-1210, 212-633-1317. Fiction, art, photos, interviews. circ. 27M. 2/yr. Pub'd 2 issues 1998; expects 2 issues 1999, 2 issues 2000. sub. price: $24; per copy: $14. Back issues: $5. 70pp; 8½×10. Simultaneous submissions accepted: yes. Payment: none. Ads: $5,000/$2,500/$1,450 1/4 page.

Bliss Publishing Company, Inc., Stephen H. Clouter, PO Box 920, Marlboro, MA 01752, 508-779-2827. 1989. Non-fiction. "Booklength manuscripts" avg. press run 2M. Expects 4 titles 1999, 4 titles 2000. 3 titles listed in the *Small Press Record of Books in Print* (28th Edition, 1999-00). avg. price, paper: $16.50. Discounts: 40% trade. 220pp; 6×9. Reporting time: 8 weeks. Payment: negotiated. Copyrights for author.

BLITHE SPIRIT, Jackie Hardy, Farneley Gate Farmhouse, Riding Mill, Northumberland NE 44 6AA, England, (UK) 0434-682-465. 1991. Poetry. "Haiku, senryu, renku, tanka and articles on these, normally from members of British Haiku Society only. Recent contributors: James Kirkup, Dee Evetts, David Cobb, Kohjin Sakamoto, Jim Norton, George Marsh, Jackie Hardy, and Brian Tasker." circ. approx. 200. 4/yr. Pub'd 4 issues 1998; expects 4 issues 1999, 4 issues 2000. sub. price: £7, Britain and elsewhere £9; per copy: £1.50; sample: £1.50. Back issues: £1.50. Discounts: none. 32pp; 5½×8½; †photocopy. Reporting time: less than 2 months. Simultaneous submissions accepted: no. Publishes 30% of manuscripts submitted. Payment: none. Copyrighted, reverts to author. Pub's reviews: 6 in 1998. §Haiku, senryu, renku, tanka. Ads: none.

BLITZ, Mike McDowell, Editor & Publisher, PO Box 48124, Los Angeles, CA 90048-0124, 818-985-8618; e-mail blitzmed@aol.com. 1975. Articles, photos, interviews, criticism, reviews, music, letters, news items. "Magazine is billed as 'The Rock and Roll Magazine For Thinking People'. Emphasis is on artists who are not being afforded enough exposure via other forms of the media. Magazine covers all forms of aesthetically meritous rock and roll music, with slant towards the academic. Deadline for submissions is 15th day before publication." circ. 3M. 4/yr. Pub'd 6 issues 1998; expects 2 issues 1999, 4 issues 2000. sub. price: $14.50 for 6 issues; per copy: $2.75; sample: $2.75. Back issues: varies with each title, information supplied upon request. Discounts: $1.75 per copy on orders of 10 or more; overseas $2.25 per copy, US currency in advance only (cover lists price of 95p for U.K.). 28pp; 8½×11; of. Reporting time: 6 weeks. Payment: all submissions are non-solicited, no financial remuneration. Copyrighted, reverts to author. Pub's reviews: 25 in 1998. §Music, music related films and publications. Ads: $300/$160/$10 for insert any size.

BLK, BLK Publishing Company, Alan Bell, PO Box 83912, Los Angeles, CA 90083, 310-410-0808, fax 310-410-9250, e-mail newsroom@blk.com. 1988. Articles, photos, cartoons, interviews, criticism, reviews, music, letters, news items, non-fiction. "The news magazine of the black lesbian and gay community." circ. 22M. 12/yr. Pub'd 12 issues 1998; expects 12 issues 1999, 12 issues 2000. sub. price: $18; per copy: $4; sample: $2.95. Back issues: all $2.95 except #1 which is $10. 48pp; 8⅛×10⅞; of. Reporting time: 4 weeks. Simultaneous submissions accepted: yes. Payment: varies. Copyrighted, rights reverting to author varies. Pub's reviews: 0 in 1998. §Black lesbian and gay community. Ads: $1800/$1170/.40¢.

BLK Publishing Company (see also BLACK LACE; BLACKFIRE; KUUMBA; BLK), PO Box 83912, Los Angeles, CA 90083, 213-410-0808. 1988. Webb, of.

BLOCK'S MAGAZINE, Alan J. Block, 1419 Chapin Street, Beloit, WI 53511, 608-364-4893. 1993. Poetry, art, interviews, criticism, reviews, letters. "Prefer short poems, about 1 page. Recent contributors: Robert Bunzel, Corrine De Winter." circ. 100. 4/yr. Pub'd 4 issues 1998; expects 4 issues 1999, 4 issues 2000. sub. price: $20; per copy: $6; sample: $6. 60pp; 5½×8½; of. Reporting time: 3 months. Simultaneous submissions accepted: no. Publishes 3% of manuscripts submitted. Payment: 1 copy per poem. Copyrighted, reverts to author. Pub's reviews: 8 in 1998. §any poetry books, chapbooks, magazines. Ads: trade.

BLOOD & APHORISMS: A Journal of Literary Fiction, Mark Hickmott, Managing Editor; Tim Paleczny, Publisher; Dennis Bock, Fiction; Gabriella Skubincan, Features; Jake Klisivitch, Features, PO Box 702, Station P, Toronto, ON M5S 2Y4, Canada. 1990. Fiction, interviews, reviews. "Literary fiction (prose only) 500-4,000 words. Include a SASE in Canadian postage or International Reply Coupons, no U.S. postage. Please send a SASE with all correspondence, especially when requesting guidelines or sample/single copies at $6US each. B&A is Canada's best-selling fiction magazine based on sales through CMPA. US Distributor: Ingram, LaVergne, Tennessee." circ. 2.5M. 4/yr. Pub'd 4 issues 1998; expects 4 issues 1999, 4 issues 2000. sub. price: $18US; per copy: $6US; sample: $6US, plus SASE. Back issues: $10US each. Discounts: to be negotiated. 48pp; 8½×11; printed. Reporting time: 6 weeks. Payment: one-year subscription, plus $20 Cdn. per printed page. Copyrighted, reverts to author. Pub's reviews: 16-20 in 1998. §Fiction: novels or short story collections, anthologies, other journals. Ads: $375US/$195US. CMPA.

BLOOD & FEATHERS: Poems of Survival, Jennifer Helms, PO Box 55, Willoughby, OH 44096-0055, 440-951-1875. 1995. Poetry, art, photos, reviews. "*Blood & Feathers* is looking for poetry that reflects the beauty and sorrow that comes from everyday life. All subject matter open, poems no longer than 1 page typed. B&F is about 30 pgs. w/ card cover and b&w illos on the inside. We lean toward Victorian/Art Nouveau styles. Recently seen in our pages: Greg Watson, Lyn Lifshin, John Sweet, Leonard Cirino, art by Virgil Barfield. $12/4 issues. We are always looking for new chapbooks, magazines, and other poetry related publications for review." circ. 100. 4/yr. Pub'd 4 issues 1998; expects 4 issues 1999, 4 issues 2000. sub. price: $12; per copy: $3; sample: $3. Back issues: $2.50. 30pp; 5½×8; mi. Reporting time: 2 weeks to 1 month. Simultaneous submissions accepted: yes. Publishes 16% of manuscripts submitted. Payment: art—$15 front cover, copies or cash, agreed upon by editor and author. Copyrighted, reverts to author. Pub's reviews: 7 in 1998. §Poetry books, magazines, chapbooks. Ads: $10 - 3 issues/$5 - 3 issues.

BLOODJET LITERARY MAGAZINE, New World Press, Noni Ph.D Howard, Publisher, 20 Driftwood Trail, Half Moon Bay, CA 94019-2349, 650-726-5939; Fax 415-921-3730. 1977. Poetry, fiction, art, photos, letters, parts-of-novels, collages, long-poems. "Length 100-200 pages, women preferred but will consider men, Jennifer Stone is a recent contributor. Persons able to write grants or obtain other funding especially considered. Please send nothing by mail without calling mmy phone or fax number for a personal inquiry." circ. 1.2M. 1-2/yr. Expects 2 issues 1999, 2 issues 2000. price per copy: $10; sample: $10. Back issues: $7.50. Discounts: 40% to bulk or educational institutions. 100pp; 9×6; of. Reporting time: 60-90 days. Publishes less than 10% of manuscripts submitted. Payment: free copies. Copyrighted, reverts to author. CLMP, AAP.

Bloody Someday Press, T.H. Cornell, Stan Heleva, 3721 Midvale Avenue, Philadelphia, PA 19129, 610-667-6687; FAX 215-951-0342; E-mail poettes@erols.com; website http://www.libertynet.org/bsomeday. 1996. Poetry, long-poems. "Our editorial taste might be described as avant garde, but closer to a Modernist/Symbolist sensibility than the 'Ginsbergsonian' heat-without-light that so often passes for avant garde. Poets and readers bored with both pseudo-Zen and social relevance, who crave a poetry that is psycho/sexual, intellectually robust, and undomesticated by academic trends will find satisfaction in Bloody Someday. We publish the manuscripts of maverick 'poets of endurance,' and we are pioneering alternative approaches to their marketing. These approaches include our unique website on the internet and the touring of Poetry Theatre/Music ensembles." avg. press run 500-1M. Pub'd 1 title 1998; expects 1 title 1999. 3 titles listed in the *Small Press Record of Books in Print* (28th Edition, 1999-00). avg. price, paper: $10-12. Discounts: 15% for individuals if books are purchased at readings and appearances, or when orders are made in advance of publication. Retailers: 40-60% of list price if no returns. Option of return acceptance available at 20-80%. 70pp; 7×4¼, 8½×5½, 5⅜×8½. Reporting time: 3 months. Simultaneous submissions accepted: yes. Publishes roughly 3% of manuscripts submitted. Payment: generally 25% of list price after cost of printing. Does not copyright for author. CLMP, Small Press Center.

THE BLOOMSBURY REVIEW, Tom Auer, Publisher, Editor-in-Chief; Marilyn Auer, Editor & Associate Publisher, 1553 Platte Street, Suite 206, Denver, CO 80202, 303-455-3123, Fax 303-455-7039. 1980. Poetry, fiction, articles, art, photos, interviews, reviews, letters, long-poems, non-fiction. "We do not publish original fiction at this time." circ. 50M. 6/yr. Pub'd 6 issues 1998; expects 6 issues 1999, 6 issues 2000. sub. price: $16; per copy: $3; sample: $4.00. Back issues: $4. Discounts: inquiries about distribution are welcome. 24pp; 10½×15¼; of. Reporting time: 3 months. Payment: $10 per review, $5 poetry, $20 features. Copyrighted, reverts to author. Pub's reviews: 900 in 1998. §Literature, history, biography, poetry, autobiography, politics-All subject areas. Ads: $3,300/$1,800/$25 first 25 words, $1 each additional word.

THE BLOWFISH CATALOG, Blowfish Press, Annye Scherer, Christophe Pettus, 2261 Market Street #284, San Francisco, CA 94114, 415-864-0880; fax 1-415-864-1858; e-Mail blowfish@blowfish. rom. 1994. Poetry, fiction, art, photos, cartoons, interviews, letters, parts-of-novels. *"The Blowfish Catalog* is the mail-order catalog for Blowfish Press. We feature very short fiction (500-750 words) and photography as well as other material, in each issue" circ. 4M. 3/yr. Pub'd 2 issues 1998; expects 3 issues 1999, 3 issues 2000. sub. price: $10; per copy: $3; sample: $3. 48+pp; 8½×11; of. Reporting time: 1-2 months. Simultaneous submissions accepted: yes. Publishes 5% of manuscripts submitted. Payment: negotiated individually, $10-50 per piece used. Copyrighted, reverts to author. Pub's reviews: 5-15/issue in 1998. §Erotic and alternative sexuality materials of all kinds. Ads: $125/$70.

Blowfish Press (see also THE BLOWFISH CATALOG), Annye Scherer, Christophe Pettus, 2261 Market Street #284, San Francisco, CA 94114, 415-864-0880; fax 1-415-864-1858; e-Mail blowfish@blowfish. com. 1993. Poetry, fiction, art, photos, cartoons, parts-of-novels, long-poems. "Not accepting any submissions. Fiction to 5M words, poetry to 500 words. We specialize in erotica related to 'alternative sexuality,' freely defined" avg. press run 1.5M-3M. Expects 3 titles 1999, 5 titles 2000. avg. price, paper: $9.95. Discounts: trade schedules available. 100pp; 5½×8½; of. Reporting time: 1-2 months. Payment: advance and royalty available, negotiated individually. Copyrights for author.

●**BLU,** Pete Weeks, Peter Mommsen, Chris Meier, PO Box 517, New Paltz, NY 12561, 1-800-778-8461; e-mail revcenter@hotmail.com; website www.revolutioncenter.org. 1998. Poetry, fiction, articles, art, photos, cartoons, interviews, satire, criticism, reviews, music, long-poems, collages. "Mumia Abu-Jamal, Martin Espada, Desmond Tutu, Assata Shakur, Roberto Rodriguez, the Welfare poets, Fred Ho. We include a CD with music, poetry, and interviews.We accept submissions of art, poetry, music, and journalism—either on paper or in audio form. Those who wish to submit should be aware that poor audio, while it doesn't disqualify submissions, does make them more difficult to accept." circ. 4M. 6/yr. Expects 2 issues 1999, 6 issues 2000. sub. price: $27; per copy: $5; sample: free. Back issues: $2. Discounts: 1-5 copies 40%; 6-10 copies 50%; 11-20 copies 55%; 21+ negotiable. 24pp; 7½×13; of. Reporting time: 4 weeks. Simultaneous submissions accepted: yes. Publishes 5% of manuscripts submitted. Payment: no. Copyrighted, does not revert to author. Plough Publishing House, Independent Press Association.

Blue Arrow Books, Reyna Thera Lorele, PO Box 1669, Pacific Palisades, CA 90272, 310-216-1160 phone/Fax; goodbooks@compuserve.com. 1989. Fiction, non-fiction. "Our first book is a how-to related to the film and television industry, titled Reading For A Living, How to be a Professional Story Analyst for Film and Television. We do not accept submissions. Our first novel is forthcoming in Sept. 1999" avg. press run 3.5M. Expects 1 title 1999. 2 titles listed in the *Small Press Record of Books in Print* (28th Edition, 1999-00). avg. price, paper: $12.95. Discounts: contact SCB Distributors for *Reading for a Living.* 192pp; 5½×8½.

BLUE BEAT JACKET, Blue Jacket Press, Yusuke Keida, 1-5-54 Sugue-cho, Sanjo-shi, Niigata-ken 955, Japan, 0256-32-3301. 1971. Poetry, fiction, reviews, letters. "Recent contributors: Sam Hamill, Morgan Gibson, Michael Bullock, George K. Dowden, Michael Basinski, Pradip Choudhuri, Rod Anstee, Arthur W. Knight, Herschel Silverman. a.d. Winans, Robert Peters, Gerald Locklin, Mark Weber, Dave Moore." circ. 100. 1/yr. Pub'd 2 issues 1998; expects 2 issues 1999, 2 issues 2000. sub. price: $5; per copy: $5; sample: $2. Discounts: $3 each item over 2 copies. 50pp; 8.3×10.1; †of. Payment: no money but 2 copies. Not copyrighted. Pub's reviews: 5 in 1998. §Especially Beat and Post-Beat books, magazines and recordings.

Blue Bird Publishing, Cheryl Gorder, 2266 S. Dobson #275, Mesa, AZ 85202, 602-831-6063. 1985. Non-fiction. "Encouraging submission of manuscripts of non-fiction topics, both adult and juvenile levels. We specialize in home education topics, and are looking for good educational manuscripts for parents teaching their children. Also interested in manuscripts on current social issues, spirituality, and healing." Pub'd 10 titles 1998; expects 10 titles 1999, 12 titles 2000. 57 titles listed in the *Small Press Record of Books in Print* (28th Edition, 1999-00). avg. price, paper: $14.95. Discounts: usually 40%. 208pp; 5½×8½; of. Reporting time: 6-12 weeks. Payment: standard. Copyrights for author. PMA.

●**BLUE COLLAR REVIEW, Partisan Press,** Al Markowitz, Mary Franke, PO Box 11417, Norfolk, VA 23517, 757-627-0952; e-mail redart@pilot.infi.net. 1997. Poetry, fiction, art, photos, interviews, reviews, long-poems, non-fiction. "Poetry and writing of high quality with a progressive working class perspective. Abroad range of work, not polemic or screed. We have published work by Martin Espada, Robert Edwards, Tom McGrath, Sonia Sanchez. Please put name and address on every page, SASE for return of manuscript. For best results, see a sample issue." circ. 253. 4/yr. Pub'd 4 issues 1998; expects 4 issues 1999, 4 issues 2000. sub. price: $10 - to A. Markowitz (BCR); per copy: $5; sample: $5. Discounts: $3 in quantity. 40-60pp; 5½×8½; †of. Reporting time: 3-6 weeks. Simultaneous submissions accepted: yes. Publishes 25% of manuscripts submitted. Payment: copies. Copyrighted, reverts to author. Pub's reviews: 1 in 1998. §Working class issues or perspectives in fiction, novels, films...poetry. Ads: $60/$40.

Blue Crane Books, Ms. Alvart Badalian, Publisher, PO Box 0291, Cambridge, MA 02238, 617-926-8989.

1991. Fiction, non-fiction. "No submissions" avg. press run 1.2M. Pub'd 2 titles 1998; expects 2 titles 1999, 3 titles 2000. 18 titles listed in the *Small Press Record of Books in Print* (28th Edition, 1999-00). avg. price, cloth: $35; paper: $20. Discounts: available. 200pp; 6×9; of. Simultaneous submissions accepted: no. Publishes 0% of manuscripts submitted. Copyrights for author. PMA.

Blue Dolphin Publishing, Inc., Paul M. Clemens, PO Box 8, Nevada City, CA 95959, 916-265-6925. 1985. Non-fiction. "We publish books on comparative spiritual traditions, personal growth, self-help, and health. We offer high resolution computer output from our ECRM and accept both IBM and Macintosh. Call for price list. 10% discount to Dustbooks' users." avg. press run 3M-5M. Pub'd 10+ titles 1998; expects 12-15 titles 1999. 52 titles listed in the *Small Press Record of Books in Print* (28th Edition, 1999-00). avg. price, cloth: $24.95; paper: $12.95. Discounts: 40-55%. 200+pp; 5½×8½, 6×9; †of. Reporting time: 3-6 months, bids 1 week. Simultaneous submissions accepted: yes. Publishes less than 1% of manuscripts submitted. Payment: 10%. Copyrights for author.

Blue Dove Press, Jeff Blom, 4204 Sorrento Valley Blvd, Ste. K, San Diego, CA 92121, 619-623-3330; orders 800-691-1008; FAX 619-623-3325; bdp@bluedove.com; www.bluedove.com. 1993. Non-fiction. avg. press run 5M. Expects 7 titles 1999, 10 titles 2000. 19 titles listed in the *Small Press Record of Books in Print* (28th Edition, 1999-00). avg. price, paper: $14. Discounts: 40%, more in large quantities. 200pp; 6×9, 5½×8½; Commercial book printers. Reporting time: 4 weeks. Yes, we prefer to receive queries, not unsolicited manuscripts. Publishes .5% of manuscripts submitted. Payment: usually 8% of retail. Copyrights for author. PMA.

Blue Heron Publishing, Inc., Dennis Stovall, Publisher; Robyn Anders, Associate Publisher, 1234 SW Stark Street, Portland, OR 97205, 503-221-6841; Fax 503-221-6843; bhp@teleport.com; www.teleport.com/~bhp. 1985. "Additional address: 311 SW 104th Street, Seattle, WA; 206-762-6366. Books from Walt Morey (author of *Gentle Ben*); writing and publishing books; adult literary, left-wing mysteries, cookbooks, multicultural books for educational markets, NW regional subjects, poetry series." avg. press run 3M-5M. Pub'd 2 titles 1998; expects 7 titles 1999, 12 titles 2000. 32 titles listed in the *Small Press Record of Books in Print* (28th Edition, 1999-00). avg. price, cloth: $13.95; paper: $7.95-$18.95. Discounts: trade sales through Consortium Book Sales & Distribution; educators should contact the press for current discounts. 224pp; 5½×8½; of. Reporting time: 90 days. Simultaneous submissions accepted: yes. Publishes .5% of manuscripts submitted. Payment: royalty, no advance. Copyrights for author. Northwest Association of Book Publishers.

Blue Horizon Press, Clint Nangle, 397 NW 35th Place, Boca Raton, FL 33431-5847. 1992. Non-fiction. "We distribute self-help information to create positive change through 12 step recovery." avg. press run 3M. Pub'd 1 title 1998; expects 3 titles 1999, 5 titles 2000. 1 title listed in the *Small Press Record of Books in Print* (28th Edition, 1999-00). avg. price, paper: $14.95. Discounts: 40%. 160pp; 5½×8½; of. Reporting time: 1-2 months. Payment: royalty 7-10%. Does not copyright for author. PMA.

BLUE HORSE, Blue Horse Publications, Jacqueline T. Bradley, Editor & Publisher; Eugenia P. Mallory, Graphics Editor, P.O. Box 6061, Augusta, GA 30906, 706-798-5628. 1964. Poetry, fiction, satire. "*Blue Horse* is a magazine of satire, misanthropy and scurrilous language without regard to sex, religion, age, race, creed, or I.Q. *Blue Horse* is the periodical of Blue Horse Movement which recognizes the folly of human life and the inutility of politics. *Blue Horse* sees writers as the victims of their own art. Currently publishing only solicited chapbooks." circ. 500. Irregular. Expects 1 issue 2000. price per copy: $3.50; sample: $2. Back issues: $4 except Vol. 1, $8. Discounts: prisoners pay postage only. 36pp; 5½×8½; of. Reporting time: 30-60 days. Simultaneous submissions accepted: no. Payment: copies. Copyrighted. Exchange ads.

Blue Horse Publications (see also BLUE HORSE), Jacqueline Bradley, Editor & Publisher, PO Box 6061, Augusta, GA 30906, 706-798-5628. 1964. Poetry, fiction, satire. avg. press run 500. Expects 1 title 2000. 7 titles listed in the *Small Press Record of Books in Print* (28th Edition, 1999-00). avg. price, paper: $4. Discounts: 25%. 36pp; 5½×8½; of, lp. Reporting time: 30-60 days. Simultaneous submissions accepted: no. Payment: mutual agreement. Does not copyright for author.

Blue Jacket Press (see also BLUE BEAT JACKET), Yusuke Keida, 1-5-54 Sugue-cho, Sanjo-shi, Niigata-ken 955, Japan, 0256-32-3301. 1971. Poetry, fiction, reviews, letters. 2 titles listed in the *Small Press Record of Books in Print* (28th Edition, 1999-00). of.

BLUE MESA REVIEW, David Johnson, Editor; Patricia Lynn Sprott, Managing Editor, Department of English, Humanities Building, Albuquerque, NM 87131, 505-277-6347; fax 277-5573; e-Mail psprott@unm.edu. 1989. Poetry, fiction, photos, interviews, reviews. "Founded by Rudolfo Anaya. Please submit 2 copies, double spaced" circ. 1,200. 1/yr. Pub'd 1 issue 1998; expects 1 issue 1999, 1 issue 2000. sub. price: $10 + $2 postage; per copy: $10 + $2 postage; sample: $10+$2 postage. Back issues: $10 + $2 postage. Discounts: please contact UNM Press, 800-249-7737. 220pp; 6×9; of. Reporting time: 6 months. Simultaneous submissions accepted: no. Publishes 25% of manuscripts submitted. Payment: 2 copies. Copyrighted, reverts to author. Pub's reviews: 4 in 1998. §Poetry, S.W. literature, literary journals, S.W. non-fiction, multi-culture topics, Native American lit., Hispanic lit., etc. Council of Literary Magazines and Presses.

Blue Mouse Studio, Rex Schneider, Chris Buchman, 26829 37th Street, Gobles, MI 49055, 616-628-5160; fax 616-628-4970. 1980. Cartoons. "No unsolicited manuscripts." avg. press run 2M. Pub'd 1 title 1998; expects 1 title 1999, 1 title 2000. 1 title listed in the *Small Press Record of Books in Print* (28th Edition, 1999-00). avg. price, paper: $3.95. Discounts: wholesalers 50%; retailers 40%. 80pp; 5¼×7¼; of.

The Blue Oak Press, Morris Campbell, HC10 Box 621, Lakeview, OR 97630-9704, 916-994-3397. 1967. Poetry, fiction, criticism, long-poems. "Recent contributors: Cornel Lengyel, Edith Snow, William Everson, Robinson Jeffers, John Berutti, Bill Hotchkiss. Our bias would be toward the poetry of contemporary Western America, and we have drawn a significant focus on the work of Robinson Jeffers as the seminal figure of this developing tradition. We do not invite submissions" avg. press run 500. Pub'd 4 titles 1998; expects 3-4 titles 1999. 6 titles listed in the *Small Press Record of Books in Print* (28th Edition, 1999-00). avg. price, cloth: $20; paper: $15; other: special editions, cloth, $30-$500. Discounts: 40% to bookstores and dealers; 20% to libraries; 30% on consignment; short discounts on special editions. 80-100+pp; 6×9; †of, lp. Payment: no specific policy. Copyrights for author.

Blue Poppy Press Inc., Bob Flaws, Honora Lee Wolfe, 3450 Penrose Place, Suite 110, Boulder, CO 80301, 303-442-0796. 1981. Non-fiction. "Material is mostly translations from Chinese medical source texts." avg. press run 1M-5M. Pub'd 12+ titles 1998. 20 titles listed in the *Small Press Record of Books in Print* (28th Edition, 1999-00). avg. price, cloth: $35; paper: $12.95-$24.95. Discounts: 55% consignment to distributors; 40% to stores, other. 100-300pp; 6×9; of. Reporting time: 3 weeks. Publishes 5-7% of manuscripts submitted. Payment: 7-10% of all sales, paid biannually. Copyrights for author. ABI, SPAN, PMA, Small Press Center.

Blue Raven Publishing, Frances Colbert, 9 South Wenatchee Avenue, Wenatchee, WA 98801-2210, 509-665-8353. 1983. Photos. avg. press run 5M. Expects 1 title 1999. avg. price, other: $70. Discounts: all books are 40% of the retail price. 176pp; 11¼×9½; of. Payment: author fee. Does not copyright for author.

Blue Reef Publications, Inc., Keith A. Ellenbogen, PO Box 42, Newton Centre, MA 02159, 617-332-7965, fax 617-332-7967, e-mail Info@bluereef.com. 1995. Photos, non-fiction. avg. press run 10M. Pub'd 1 title 1998. 2 titles listed in the *Small Press Record of Books in Print* (28th Edition, 1999-00). avg. price, other: $14.95. 75pp; 8×5; of. Reporting time: 4 weeks. Simultaneous submissions accepted: yes. Payment: negotiable. Copyrights for author. PMA, ITPA.

Blue River Publishing Inc., Jim Scheetz, Editor, Publisher, PO Box 6786A, Colorado Springs, CO 80934-6786, 719-634-3918; FAX 719-634-7559. 1992. Non-fiction. "Publish both hard and softcover. Non-Fiction only. Looking for authoritative, well-written books on self-esteem, values and ethics without strong religious slant. Also motivational, inspirational and multi-cultural, socially liberal. Emphasis on quality of life. We only publish nonfiction with broad consumer appeal. It must be an interesting subject by an author whose credentials indicate he/she knows a lot about the subject, has personal experience, be well researched and most importantly, must have a certain uniqueness about it. Recent titles: *The Incredible Power of Cults*, *The Waco Cult, Inside and Out*, *Dystonia-Misguided Muscles*." avg. press run 5M. Pub'd 1 title 1998; expects 4 titles 1999, 5 titles 2000. avg. price, cloth: $20; paper: $10. Discounts: Universal Discount Schedule-Quantity of 1=0 discount; 2-4=20%; 5-99=40%; 100 up=50%. Review copies on request. Pages vary; size varies; lp. Reporting time: 1 month, query letter, outline & sample chapters. Payment: standard royalties (7-15%) on publisher's receipts. Copyrights for author.

Blue Rock Publishing (see also EBB AND FLOW), Pamela Sheffield, PO Box 5246, Niceville, FL 32578, 850-897-7267; e-mail bluerock@home.com. 1996. Non-fiction. avg. press run 800. Pub'd 50 titles 1998; expects 1,000 titles 1999, 2,000 (calendars) titles 2000. avg. price, other: $12.95. Reporting time: 30-60 days. Simultaneous submissions accepted: no. Payment: negotiable. Copyrights for author.

BLUE SATELLITE, The Sacred Beverage Press, Amelie Frank, Matthew Niblock, PO Box 10312, Burbank, CA 91510-0312, fax 818-780-1912; E-mail sacredbev@aol.com. 1994. Poetry, long-poems. "Any style, subject, length—*nothing* previously published. Will toss out anything with the word 'empower' in it. Editorial bias: eye for quality. Contributors: Laurel Ann Bogen, Scott Wannberg, FrancEyE, Ellyn Maybe, Marc Olmsted, Bill Mohr, Diane DiPrima, and Viggo Mortensen." circ. 250-300. 2/yr. Pub'd 2 issues 1998; expects 2 issues 1999, 2 issues 2000. sub. price: $20/2 years; per copy: $7; sample: $7. Back issues: $7. Discounts: 40% of retail/cover price. 60pp; 5½×8½; of. Reporting time: 2-3 months max. Simultaneous submissions accepted: no. Publishes 5% of manuscripts submitted. Payment: 1 copy of issue plus discount on extra copies. Copyrighted, reverts to author. Ads: none. CLMP, PSA.

Blue Sky Marketing, Inc., Vic Spadaccini, Editor, PO Box 21583, Saint Paul, MN 55121-0583, 651-456-5602. 1982. Non-fiction. avg. press run 5M. Pub'd 4 titles 1998; expects 1 title 1999, 3 titles 2000. 9 titles listed in the *Small Press Record of Books in Print* (28th Edition, 1999-00). avg. price, cloth: $14.95; paper: $9.70. Discounts: distributed by Adventure Publications. 116pp; size varies; of. Reporting time: 60 days.

Publishes 1% of manuscripts submitted. Payment: negotiable. Copyrights for author on request. PMA, MN Book Publishers Roundtable.

Blue Star Press, Deborah Ann Baker, PO Box 645, Oakville, WA 98568, 360-273-7656. 1995. Poetry, fiction. "Poetry: 60 pages max., poems 22 lines max. Fiction: Children's picture book, easy readers. Recently published *Forbidden Crossings* by Deborah Ann Baker, Diamond Homer Trophy Winner." avg. press run 500-2.5M. Pub'd 1 title 1998; expects 1 title 1999, 1+ titles 2000. 2 titles listed in the *Small Press Record of Books in Print* (28th Edition, 1999-00). avg. price, paper: $11.95. Discounts: 1-4 0%, 5-9 30%, 10+ 40%, prepaid orders we pay postage. 60pp; 6×9. Reporting time: 3 months. Simultaneous submissions accepted: yes. Payment: individual (copies). We send forms to authors to copyright in author's name.

BLUE UNICORN, Ruth G. Iodice, Martha E. Bosworth, Fred Ostrander, 22 Avon Road, Kensington, CA 94707, 510-526-8439. 1977. Poetry, art. "*Blue Unicorn* is a journal looking for excellence of the individual voice, whether that voice comes through in a fixed form or an original variation or in freer lines. We publish poets who are established and those who are less known but deserve to be known better, and we are also proud to welcome new talent to our pages. We like poems which communicate in a memorable way whatever is deeply felt by the poet, and we believe in an audience that is delighted, like us, by a lasting image, a unique twist of thought, and a haunting music. We also use a limited number of expert translations. Among recent contributors to our tri-quarterly are: Rosalie Moore, Charles Edward Eaton, James Schevill, John Ditsky, Don Welch, Barbara A. Holland, Lawrence Spingarn, A.D. Winans, William Dickey, Adrianne Marcus, Stuart Silverman. Please send only unpublished poems." circ. 500. 3/yr. Expects 3 issues 1999. 1 title listed in the *Small Press Record of Books in Print* (28th Edition, 1999-00). sub. price: $14, $20 foreign; per copy: $5; add $2 mailing for foreign copies; sample: $5; $7 foreign. Back issues: $4. 48-60pp; 4¼×5½; of. Reporting time: 1-3 months. Simultaneous submissions accepted: no. We publish .5% or less of manuscripts submitted. Payment: 1 copy. Copyrighted, reverts to author. §no reviews. Ads: none. CLMP.

●**Blue Unicorn Press, Inc.,** Wanda Z. Larson, PO Box 40300, Portland, OR 97240-3826, 503-775-9322. 1990. Poetry, long-poems, non-fiction. "Additional address: 4153 SE 39th Avenue, Suite 35, Portland, OR 97202-3176." avg. press run 200-300. Expects 4 titles 1999, 2 titles 2000. 1 title listed in the *Small Press Record of Books in Print* (28th Edition, 1999-00). avg. price, paper: $4.95-$16.99. Discounts: 1-3 books 0%, 4-9 30%, 10+ 40%, 100 (in year) specified terms. 64-300pp; 5½×8½; offset-bids. Reporting time: 1 month to 1 year. Simultaneous submissions accepted: yes. Publishes 1% of manuscripts submitted. Payment: 10% of wholesale price. Copyrights for author. Publishers Marketing Assn.

BLUE VIOLIN, Mary Agnes Dalrymple, PO Box 1175, Humble, TX 77347-1175. 1995. Poetry. "I accept free-verse poetry only. Do not want to see sexually explicit works, rhyming poetry or overly experimental poems (e.g. calligrams)." circ. very small, but growing. 2/yr. Expects 2 issues 1999, 2 issues 2000. sub. price: $10; per copy: $5; sample: $5. 40pp; 5½×8½; photocopy. Reporting time: 2-4 weeks. Simultaneous submissions accepted: yes. Publishes 1% of manuscripts submitted. Payment: 1 copy. Copyrighted, reverts to author.

BLUEBOOK, Michael Price, Editor; Kevin Opstedal, Editor, 766 Valencia Street, San Francisco, CA 94110, 415-437-3450; Fax 415-626-5541. 1998. circ. 400. 4/yr. Pub'd 4 issues 1998; expects 4 issues 1999, 4 issues 2000. sub. price: $15; per copy: $5; sample: $5. Back issues: order through SPD, Berkeley. 100pp; †mi, lp. Reporting time: 2 months or less. Simultaneous submissions accepted: yes. Publishes 50% of manuscripts submitted. Payment: copies. Copyrighted, reverts to author. Pub's reviews: 3 in 1998. §Poetry. Ads: none. CLMP.

BLUELINE, Richard Henry, Editor, State University College, English Dept., Potsdam, NY 13676, 315-267-2043. 1979. Poetry, fiction, articles, art, reviews, parts-of-novels, plays, non-fiction. "We are interested in material that has some relationship,to the Adirondack mountain region or to simular regions. Short fiction and essays should be no more than 3.5M words, poems 44 lines or less. Recent contributors include Paul Corrigan, Joanne Seltzer, Roger Mitchell, L.M. Rosenberg, Maurice Kenny, Annie Dawid, Eric Ormsby, and Joan Connor. We occasionally publish reviews." circ. 400. 1/yr. Pub'd 1 issue 1998. sub. price: $10; per copy: $10; sample: $10. Back issues: $6. Discounts: $7 per copy to distributors. 180-200pp; 6×9; photo, of. Reporting time: weeks. Simultaneous submissions accepted: no. Publishes 10% of manuscripts submitted. Payment: copies. Copyrighted, reverts to author. Pub's reviews: 3 in 1998. §Short fiction, novels, poetry, essays about the Adirondacks. No ads. CLMP.

Bluestocking Press, Jane A. Williams, PO Box 1014, Dept. D, Placerville, CA 95667-1014, 530-621-1123, Fax 530-642-9222, 1-800-959-8586 (orders only). 1987. Fiction, non-fiction. "UPS address: 3333 Gold Country Drive, El Dorado, CA 95623 Query with SASE for reply. Not accepting any new submissions until 2005" avg. press run 4M. Pub'd 2 titles 1998; expects 3 titles 1999, 2 titles 2000. 11 titles listed in the *Small Press Record of Books in Print* (28th Edition, 1999-00). avg. price, paper: $11.95 perfect. Discounts: quantity discounts available to booksellers, wholesalers, catalogers—query for schedule. 175pp; 5½×8½; desk top publishing. Simultaneous submissions accepted: no. Payment: by agreement. Does not copyright for author.

BOA Editions, Ltd., A. Poulin, Jr., 260 East Avenue, Rochester, NY 14604, 716-546-3410. 1976. Poetry. "Major poets invited to select and introduce new poets. Contributors include: W. D. Snodgrass, Anthony Piccione, Archibald MacLeish, William B. Patrick, John Logan, Isabella Gardner, Michael Waters, Richard Wilbur, Dorianne Laux, Peter Makuck, Emanuel di Pasquale, Carolyn Kizer, Lucille Clifton, Li-Young Lee, Bill Tremblay, Anne Hebert, Yannis Ritsos, Gerald Costanzo, Diann Blakely Shoaf, Robert Bly." avg. press run 500 cloth. Pub'd 6 titles 1998; expects 6 titles 1999, 6 titles 2000. 5 titles listed in the *Small Press Record of Books in Print* (28th Edition, 1999-00). avg. price, cloth: $20; paper: $12.50. Discounts: bookstores 40%, 20% for signed editions. 100pp; 6×9; of. Reporting time: 8 weeks. Payment: advance and royalty. Copyrights for author. American Booksellers Association.

●**Bob & Bob Publishing,** Robert O. Owolabi, PO Box 10246, Gaithersburg, MD 20898-0246, 301-977-3442; FAX 301-990-2393; Bobowo@aol.com; www.members.aol.com/bobowo. 2 titles listed in the *Small Press Record of Books in Print* (28th Edition, 1999-00).

BOGG, Bogg Publications, John Elsberg, USA Editor; George Cairncross, British Editor; Sheila Martindale, Canadian Editor; Wilga Rose, Australian Editor, 422 N Cleveland Street, Arlington, VA 22201. 1968. Poetry, articles, art, interviews, satire, reviews, letters. "U.K. Address: 31 Belle Vue St., Filey, N. Yorks, UK YO14 9HU. Canadian address: PO Box 23148, 380 Wellington St., London, Ontario N6A 5N9. Australian address: 13 Urara Road, Avalon Beach, NSW 2107. Poetry, prose poems and very short 'experimental' prose, interviews, plus essays on British and American small press history and experience; mainly short reviews. The magazine puts out a series of free (for postage) pamphlets of poetry. The magazine combines British/Canadian/Australian and American work. ISSN 0882-648X." circ. 850. 2-3/yr. Pub'd 1 issue 1998; expects 2 issues 1999, 2 issues 2000. sub. price: £5 ($12)/3 issues; per copy: £2 ($4.50); sample: $3.50. Back issues: negotiable. Discounts: 40% 10 copies or more. 68pp; 6×9; of. Reporting time: 1 week. Simultaneous submissions accepted: no. Publishes 1% of manuscripts submitted. Payment: 2 copies of issue. Copyrighted, reverts to author. Pub's reviews: 13 in 1998. §Small press publications, U.K., Commonwealth, and U.S. CLMP.

Bogg Publications (see also BOGG), John Elsberg, George Cairncross, Sheila Martindale, Wilga Rose, 422 North Cleveland Street, Arlington, VA 22201. 1968. Poetry, fiction, fiction. "Only solicited mss considered from writers who have appeared in *Bogg* magazine." avg. press run 300. Pub'd 2 titles 1998; expects 4 titles 1999, 2 titles 2000. 9 titles listed in the *Small Press Record of Books in Print* (28th Edition, 1999-00). avg. price, paper: free-for-postage (first printings); other: $3 (2nd and subsequent printings). 24pp; size varies; of. Reporting time: varies. Simultaneous submissions accepted: no. Payment: 25% of print run (in copies). Copyrights for author; author has to register. CLMP.

Bolchazy-Carducci Publishers, Inc., Ladislaus J. Bolchazy, Ph.D., 1000 Brown Street, Wauconda, IL 60084, 847-526-4344; fax 847-526-2867. 1981. "We are also interested in translations of classics from any language in addition to translations of Eastern European works of merit. Book-length proposals only: 25,000 word minimum. Prefer word-processed manuscripts available on diskettes. Any serious, intelligent work of non-fiction will be given a thorough, professional review." avg. press run 2M. Pub'd 10 titles 1998; expects 15 titles 1999, 15 titles 2000. 21 titles listed in the *Small Press Record of Books in Print* (28th Edition, 1999-00). avg. price, cloth: $35; paper: $20. Discounts: 20% bookstores, 40% to qualified distributors and representatives. Payment: negotiable. Copyrights for author. Publishers Marketing Association, Chicago Book Clinic.

Bold Productions, Mary Bold, PO Box 152281, Arlington, TX 76015, 817-468-9924; info@boldproductions.com. 1983. "Since 1997, emphasis has shifted to electronic publishing. We are not seeking submissions." Book Publishers of Texas.

The Bold Strummer Ltd., Nicholas Clarke, Mary Clarke, PO Box 2037, Westport, CT 06880-0037, 203-259-3021; Fax 203-259-7369; bstrummer@aol.com. 1974. Cartoons, interviews, music. "The Bold Strummer actively seeks and promotes music books for publication, with an emphasis on guitars and related instruments and equipment. Also importer and distributor of books of same." avg. press run 2M. Pub'd 4 titles 1998; expects 6 titles 1999, 8 titles 2000. 50 titles listed in the *Small Press Record of Books in Print* (28th Edition, 1999-00). avg. price, cloth: $24.95; paper: $13.95; other: $20. Discounts: 20-50%. 130pp; 8½×11; of. Reporting time: approx. 6 months (if this means from contest to publication). Publishes 60% of manuscripts submitted. Payment: royalty 10% of retail. We copyright for author if required. NAMM, AAP, ASIA, GAL, GFA, NEPA, WCC, WSRC.

Bolton Press, Amanda Bolton, 7671 121st Avenue, Largo, FL 33773, 813-535-4668. 1987. Fiction, non-fiction. "Hardbound and softbound books." avg. press run 5M. Pub'd 1-2 titles 1998. 2 titles listed in the *Small Press Record of Books in Print* (28th Edition, 1999-00). avg. price, cloth: $15; paper: $9. Discounts: 40% trade, 50% jobber. 250pp; 6×9; of. Reporting time: 6 weeks. Payment: negotiated. Copyrights for author.

BOMB MAGAZINE, Betsy Sussler, Editor-in-Chief; Minna Proctor, Managing Editor, 594 Broadway, Suite 905, New York, NY 10012, 212-431-3943, FAX 212-431-5880. 1981. Poetry, fiction, art, photos, interviews, parts-of-novels. circ. 60M. 4/yr. Pub'd 4 issues 1998; expects 4 issues 1999, 4 issues 2000. sub. price: $18; per copy: $4.95; sample: $6 (includes p/h). Back issues: #1, NY Film $10/#4 Painters & Writers $10/#6, Sculpture & Fiction $8/#8, Drawing $7. Discounts: trade 40%, classroom 30%. 112pp; 8⅞×10⅞; heatset. Reporting time: 3 months unsolicited. Payment: yes. Copyrighted, reverts to author. Ads: $1,485/$795/1/4 page $605.

Bombshelter Press (see also ONTHEBUS), Jack Grapes, P.O Box 481266, Bicentennial Station, Los Angeles, CA 90048, 213-651-5488. 1975. Poetry. "We publish books of California poets, most specifically poets from the Los Angeles area. Poets should not send manuscripts without sending a query letter first. Recent books by Macdonald Carey, Doraine Poretz, Michael Andrews, John Oliver Simon, Lee Rossi, Ko Wan, Jack Grapes, Bill Mohr, James Krusoe, and an anthology of *New Los Angeles Poets*. *Onthebus* is a biannual literary magazine—open to submissions from anyone." avg. press run 800. Pub'd 3 titles 1998; expects 3 titles 1999, 3 titles 2000. 11 titles listed in the *Small Press Record of Books in Print* (28th Edition, 1999-00). avg. price, paper: $10. Discounts: 40% consignment to bookstores, etc., 50% to distributors. 72pp; 5½×8½; of, mostly jobbed out, lp. Reporting time: 3-4 months. Simultaneous submissions accepted: no. Payment: free copies (usually 50) plus 10% of profits from sales. Copyrights for author.

●**BONDAGE FANTASIES**, Robert Dante, David Busch, 901 W. Victoria, Unit G, Compton, CA 90220, 310-631-1600; www.bondage.org. 1979. Fiction, articles, art, cartoons, interviews, reviews, news items, non-fiction. "BDSM stories, art, photos - all fiction." circ. 5M. 4/yr. Pub'd 4 issues 1998; expects 4 issues 1999, 4 issues 2000. sub. price: $22; per copy: $6.95; sample: $10. 44pp; 7¾×10¾; web. Reporting time: 1 month. Simultaneous submissions accepted: no. Publishes 25% of manuscripts submitted. Payment: $25-$50. Copyrighted, does not revert to author. Pub's reviews. §Sexuality, BDSM. Ads: $230/$125/$75 1/4 page/$45 business card.

BONE & FLESH, Lester Hirsh, Editor; Frederick Moe, Editor; Amy Shea, Editor; Monica Nagel, Managing Editor; Susan Bartlett, Editor, PO Box 349, Concord, NH 03302-0349. 1988. Poetry, fiction, articles, art, reviews, letters, long-poems. "We publish work that is thought provoking and aesthetic. All styles, prose poems, haiku, concrete, avant-garde, experimental are welcome. Themes should focus on the substance of our lives, or the link with other lives and times. We are oriented toward the literary, and interpersonal bend with a spiritual base. (Not any current vogue but the univeral message is paramount.) Poetry: length open. No more than 6 submissions per contributor. Fiction: to 2,000 words. Reviews/essays: to 1,000 words." circ. 350+. 2/yr. Pub'd 2 issues 1998; expects 2 issues 1999, 2 issues 2000. sub. price: $14(includes 1 main issue, 1 chapbook, occasional inserts or newsletter) or supplemental issue; per copy: $7; sample: $6. Back issues: Priced by issue. Discounts: 10% off orders of two or more publications. 50-70pp; 7×8, 8×10; of. Reporting time: 3-4 months. We prefer not to receive simultaneous submissions. Publishes 10-15% of manuscripts submitted. Payment: 1 contributors copy minimum. Copyrighted, reverts to author. Pub's reviews: 5 in 1998. §Literary magazines, chapbooks. Ads: $100/$50/$30 1/3 page/$25 1-4 page.

Bonus Books, Inc., Rachel Drzewicki, Managing Editor; Carey Spears-Millsap, Assistant Editor, 160 East Illinois Street, Chicago, IL 60611, 312-467-0580. 1985. Non-fiction. avg. press run 5M-10M. Pub'd 25 titles 1998; expects 28 titles 1999, 30 titles 2000. 113 titles listed in the *Small Press Record of Books in Print* (28th Edition, 1999-00). avg. price, cloth: $24.95; paper: $12.95. Discounts: please inquire. 240pp; 6×9; of. Reporting time: 2 months (send SASE). Simultaneous submissions accepted: yes. Publishes less than 5% of manuscripts submitted. Payment: standard scale. Copyrights for author.

Boog Literature (see also BOOGLIT), David Kirschenbaum, PO Box 20531, New York, NY 10011, e-mail dak@cunytimessqr.gc.cuny.edu. 1991. Poetry, fiction, interviews, non-fiction. "Query in advance on chap mss. Am open to any and all works, though poetry, politics and fiction mss are preferred. Recent chaps by Ed Sandess, Patrick McKinnon and Lee Ann Brown." avg. press run 300. Pub'd 5 titles 1998; expects 7 titles 1999, 5 titles 2000. avg. price, paper: $3. 32pp; 5½×8½; photocopy. Reporting time: within 2 months. Payment: 10% of print run in copies.

BOOGLIT, Boog Literature, David Kirschenbaum, PO Box 150570, Brooklyn, NY 11215-0570. 1994. Poetry, fiction, articles, art, photos, cartoons, interviews, criticism, reviews, parts-of-novels, long-poems, collages, non-fiction. "A monthly Litzine which seeks to link regional poetry/writing communities, and publish solid words from all over the place. The focus here is solely on literature, be it places to read, submit, stock your wares, or stay and eat cheap if you feel like stopping in that area to read your words on your way to visit friends elsewhere. As always, it'll include solid words from these and all regions. Past issues have featured the poetry of Barry Gifford and John Bennett and the prose of Anne Coletta." circ. 300. 12/yr. Expects 7 issues 1999, 12 issues 2000. sub. price: $12; per copy: $2; sample: $3. Back issues: limited supplies at $3ppd each. 20pp; 5½×8½; †photocopy. Reporting time: within 2 months. Publishes less than 10% of manuscripts submitted. Payment: 1 copy and clip. Copyrighted, reverts to author. Pub's reviews. §Zines, poetry, politics - especially American history and pop culture, fiction, poetics. Ads: $100/$60.

THE BOOK ARTS CLASSIFIED, Tom Bannister, PO Box 77167, Washington, DC 20013-7167, 800-821-6604; fax 800-538-7549; e-mail pagetwo@bookarts.com. 1993. "Free classified ads! We also publish the bi-annual *Book Arts Directory.*" circ. 5M. 6/yr. Pub'd 6 issues 1998; expects 6 issues 1999, 6 issues 2000. sub. price: $16; per copy: $2; sample: $2. 12pp; 11×15; web offset. Payment: none. Not copyrighted. Ads: $225/$125 discounts for multiple submissions/25¢/word classified.

BOOK DEALERS WORLD, North American Bookdealers Exchange, Al Galasso, Editorial Director; Russ von Hoelscher, Associate Editor, PO Box 606, Cottage Grove, OR 97424-0026. 1979. Articles, news items, non-fiction. "Articles of interest to self-publishers, writers, and mail order book dealers and information sellers. 1000-2000 words length." circ. 20M. 4/yr. Pub'd 4 issues 1998; expects 4 issues 1999, 4 issues 2000. sub. price: $40; per copy: $10; sample: $3. Back issues: 2 for $8. Discounts: 35% off 1 yr. sub. 32pp; 8½×11; of. Reporting time: 2 weeks. Publishes 30% of manuscripts submitted. Payment: ad space in exchange for contributions or $20 to $50 for articles depending on length. Copyrighted, reverts to author. Pub's reviews: 100+ in 1998. §Money-making and money-saving books of all types, how-to, male-female relationships, health & diet, computer-related, business, internet. Ads: $400/$220/$16-20 words.

The Book Department, Cylvia Lowe, 107 White Rock Drive, Windsor, CT 06095-4348. 1978. "Attn: Lowe" 1 title listed in the *Small Press Record of Books in Print* (28th Edition, 1999-00). avg. price, paper: $9 each. Discounts: 40% 3 or more books. 120pp; 8¼×5¼. Simultaneous submissions accepted: no.

Book Faith India, Chaitanya Nagar, Mgr. Editor, PO Box 3872, Kathmandu, Nepal, fax 977-1-424943; e-mail pilgrims@wlink.com.np. 1993. Non-fiction. avg. press run 1.5-3M. Pub'd 16 titles 1998; expects 14 titles 1999, 20 titles 2000. avg. price, cloth: $14.95; paper: $5.50. Discounts: 40%. 350pp; 6×9; of. Reporting time: 60 days. Publishes 25% of manuscripts submitted. Payment: 10% annually in July. Does not copyright for author.

BOOK MARKETING UPDATE, Open Horizons Publishing Company, John Kremer, PO Box 205, Fairfield, IA 52556-0205, 515-472-6130, Fax 515-472-1560, e-mail johnkremer@bookmarket.com. 1986. Articles, art, photos, cartoons, interviews, reviews, letters, news items, non-fiction. "News, stories, and resources to help other publishers market their books more effectively." circ. 3M. 40/yr. Pub'd 10 issues 1998; expects 40 issues 1999, 40 issues 2000. sub. price: $60; per copy: $2; sample: $2. 4-6pp; 8½×11; of. Reporting time: 1 week. Payment: none. Copyrighted, reverts to author. Pub's reviews: 3-4 in 1998. §Book publishing, marketing, direct mail, graphics, printing, publicity, directories. Ads: $350/$175/$125 1/4 page. PMA, MAP, MSPA, UMBA, ABA, MIPA.

BOOK NEWS & BOOK BUSINESS MART, Premier Publishers, Inc., Neal Michaels, Owen Bates, PO Box 330309, Fort Worth, TX 76163, 817-293-7030. 1971. Articles, reviews, news items. "Recent contributors: Lee Howard, author and president of *Selective Books*; Galen Stilson, consultant and publisher of *The Direct Response Specialist.* Character of circulation: distributed to mail order dealers, suppliers to mail order firms, new entrants to mail order and new opportunity seekers. Doubles as advertising forum for mail order distributors, news magazine and wholesale catalog" circ. 50M. 3/yr. Pub'd 3 issues 1998; expects 3 issues 1999, 3 issues 2000. sub. price: $8; per copy: $3; sample: $3. 80pp; 8½×11; of, web. Payment: negotiable. Copyrighted, reverts to author. Pub's reviews: 8 in 1998. §Self-improvement, do-it-yourself, how-to, success oriented how-to, or instruction manual how-to. Ads: $500/$275/$1.

Book Peddlers, Vicki Lansky, Editor & President, 15245 Minnetonka Boulevard, Minnetonka, MN 55345, 612-912-0036; fax 612-912-0105; e-Mail VickileeAol.com. 1983. Non-fiction. "Parenting area." avg. press run 10M. Pub'd 5 titles 1998; expects 2 titles 1999, 2 titles 2000. 19 titles listed in the *Small Press Record of Books in Print* (28th Edition, 1999-00). avg. price, paper: $6.95. Discounts: bookstore distribution—PGW. 132pp; size varies; Belt press. Reporting time: varies. Publishes 0% of manuscripts submitted. Payment: percent of net receipts. Copyrights for author. ABA.

THE BOOK REPORT: Journal for Junior & Senior High School Librarians, Linworth Publishing, Inc., Marlene Woo-Lun, Publisher; Cynthia Allen, Director of Marketing, 480 East Wilson Bridge Road #L, Worthington, OH 43085-2372. 1982. Articles, reviews. circ. 12.1M. 5/yr. Pub'd 5 issues 1998; expects 5 issues 1999, 5 issues 2000. sub. price: $49 US, $60 Canada; per copy: $9; sample: no charge. Back issues: $11. Discounts: 5%. 96pp; 8½×11. Copyrighted, does not revert to author. Pub's reviews: 900 in 1998. §Books suitable for school libraries, grades 6-12. Ads: $990/$640/$395 1/3 page (b/w); 1 time rate-add $875 for color. EDPress.

BOOK TALK, Carol A. Myers, 8632 Horacio Pl NE, Albuquerque, NM 87111, 505-299-8940; fax 505-294-8032. 1972. Articles, reviews. "300-1M words. All contributors actively engaged in a book-related field (editors, librarians, booksellers, publishers, authors (of books), etc.). ISSN: 0145 627X." circ. 500. 4/yr. Pub'd 4 issues 1998; expects 4 issues 1999, 4 issues 2000. sub. price: $15; per copy: $5; sample: free. Back issues: $3 for existing issues, $5 for issues needing reproduction. 16pp; 8½×11; of. Reporting time: 1 month. Payment: none - all donated by subscribers or interested bookpeople. Not copyrighted. Pub's reviews: 165 in 1998. §Southwestern non-fiction and fiction (area defined as TX, NM, AZ, CA, UT, CO and OK). Ads: $100/$50. New Mexico Book League.

Bookhaven Press, LLC, Dennis V. Damp, Victor Richards, PO Box 1243, Moon Township, PA 15108, 412-262-5578; Fax 412-262-5417; e-Mail bookhaven@aol.com; website http://federaljobs.net. 1985. Articles, non-fiction. "Looking for new career and job search titles from computer literate authors" avg. press run 5M. Pub'd 2 titles 1998; expects 3 titles 1999, 4 titles 2000. 6 titles listed in the *Small Press Record of Books in Print* (28th Edition, 1999-00). avg. price, paper: $18.95. Discounts: 1-4 20%, 5-9 30%, 10-24 40%, 25-49 42%, 50-74 44%, 75-99 46%, 100-199 48%, 200+ 50%; S.T.O.P. orders earn 40% discount CWO + $2 s/h. 224pp; 8½×11, 6×9. Reporting time: 8 weeks. Simultaneous submissions accepted: yes. Publishes 1% of manuscripts submitted. Payment: negotiable. Copyrights for author. Publishers Marketing Assoc. (PMA), Three Rivers Publishers' Group.

Bookhome Publishing/Panda Publishing, Scott Gregory, PO Box 5900, Navarre, FL 32566, E-mail bookhome@gte.net; www.bookhome.com. 1996. Non-fiction. "Nonfiction ms./proposals in areas of business, lifestyles, writing, publishing." avg. press run 2M. Pub'd 1 title 1998; expects 5 titles 1999, 7 titles 2000. 2 titles listed in the *Small Press Record of Books in Print* (28th Edition, 1999-00). avg. price, cloth: $22.95; paper: $14.95. 225pp; 6×9. Reporting time: 6-8 weeks. Simultaneous submissions accepted: no. Publishes 2% of manuscripts submitted. Payment: varies. We file the copyright in the name of the author. PMA.

The Bookman Press, Barbara Wersba, PO Box 1892, Sag Harbor, NY 11963, 516-725-1115. 1994. Poetry, fiction, criticism, letters. "No unsolicited manuscripts. Work only with established authors and books in the public domain. Signed, limited editions aimed at collectors, universities, and special bookstores." avg. press run 300. Expects 1 title 1999, 3 titles 2000. avg. price, paper: $35. Discounts: will sell through direct mail only. lp. Copyrights for author.

BOOK/MARK SMALL PRESS QUARTERLY REVIEW, Mindy Kronenberg, 9 Garden Avenue, Miller Place, NY 11764, 516-331-4118. 1994. Reviews. "Reviews run 500-750pp avg.. We look for objective assessments of books by writers who are empathetic with their material and connected to the genre of literature (poets, novelists) or have experience/interest in the subject/field of the books reviewed" circ. 500. 4/yr. Pub'd 4 issues 1998; expects 4 issues 1999, 4 issues 2000. sub. price: $12; per copy: $3.50 ppd.; sample: $2.50 ppd. Back issues: $2 ppd. 12pp; 8½×11; of. Reporting time: immediately, 1 week max. Simultaneous submissions accepted: yes. We publish 50-70% of manuscripts submitted. Many are solicited; we appreciate writers contacting us with ideas. Payment: copies/subscription at present. Copyrighted, reverts to author. Pub's reviews: 47-48 in 1998. §Poetry, fiction, the arts, sciences, popular culture, history—we're eclectic. Ads: $250/$135/$75 1/4 page.

BookPartners, Inc., Thorn Bacon, Editor-in-Chief; Ursula Bacon, Publisher; Ross Hawkins, President, PO Box 922, Wilsonville, OR 97070, 503-682-9821; FAX 503-682-8684; bpbooks@teleport.com. 1992. Non-fiction. "BookPartners, Inc. is a small publisher whose objective in trade book publishing is to earn a reputation that lives up to the responsibility that Eugene Fitch Ware innocently placed upon publishers when he wrote: 'Man builds no structure that outlives a book.' BookPartners occupies a unique middle ground in American trade book publishing with its partnership approach. It collaborates with authors in book development, preparation, marketing, financing and sales to provide more intense cooperation and equitable profit sharing. One rule of excellence governs the selection of BookPartner books. They must have the potential to be lifetime books that gain prestige as they develop reputation." avg. press run 2.5M-3M. Pub'd 15 titles 1998; expects 40 titles 1999, 40 titles 2000. 64 titles listed in the *Small Press Record of Books in Print* (28th Edition, 1999-00). avg. price, paper: $14.95. Discounts: 45%. 175pp; 6×9; of. Reporting time: 2 weeks. Simultaneous submissions accepted: yes. Publishes 25% of manuscripts submitted. Payment: quarterly. Copyrights for author. PMA, NWBPA, PNBA, IPN.

Books for All Times, Inc. (see also EDUCATION IN FOCUS), Joe David, PO Box 2, Alexandria, VA 22313, 703-548-0457; e-mail staff@bfat.com. 1981. Fiction, non-fiction. "Will only consider at a future date (always query) books of lasting quality (non-fiction and fiction). Modern classics of mentally healthy and efficacious characters achieving. Example: *Dodsworth* by Sinclair Lewis" avg. press run 3M. Pub'd 1 title 1998; expects 1 title 1999, 1 title 2000. 3 titles listed in the *Small Press Record of Books in Print* (28th Edition, 1999-00). avg. price, paper: $9.95. Discounts: 20% libaries; 40% bookstores; 50% wholesalers and distributors; write publisher for details. 250pp; 5¼×8½; of. Reporting time: query always, 4 weeks at the most. Payment: to be negotiated. Copyrights for author.

BOOKS FROM FINLAND, Jyrki Kiiskinen, Editor-in-Chief; Hildi Hawkins, Editor, PO Box 15 (Unioninkatu 36), FIN-00014 University of Helsinki, Finland, (358/g) 1357942; bff@helsinki.fi; http://linnea.helsinki.fi/bff. 1967. Poetry, fiction, articles, photos, interviews, satire, criticism, reviews, parts-of-novels, plays, news items, non-fiction. circ. 3.4M. 4/yr. Pub'd 4 issues 1998; expects 4 issues 1999, 4 issues 2000. sub. price: Fim120 Finland & Scandinavia, Fim160 other countries; per copy: Fim30. Back issues: Fim20/copy. 80pp; 170mm X 250mm; of. Reporting time: 2 months. Payment: approx Fim200 per page. All rights belong to authors/translators. Pub's reviews: 17 in 1998. §History, politics, arts, nature, folklore. Ads: Fim3500 full page.

BOOKS OF THE SOUTHWEST, Dr. Francine K. Ramsey Richter, Publisher; Rawlyn W. Richter, Editor, PO Box 398, Sabinal, TX 78881, e-mail books@peppersnet.com. 1957. Reviews. circ. 500. 4/yr. Pub'd 4 issues 1998; expects 4 issues 1999, 4 issues 2000. sub. price: $28 indiv., $36 instit., $60 foreign; per copy: $3; sample: free, when available. Back issues: ask for quote. Discounts: none. 18pp; 7×8½; of. Payment: none. Copyrighted. Pub's reviews: 600 in 1998. §Anything Southwest Americana. Ads: none.

Booksplus of Maine, Arthur H. Young, RR 2 Box 2568, Sabattus, ME 04280, 207-375-6251. 1991. Poetry, fiction, satire, criticism, non-fiction. "Organized 1991 as vehicle for writings of its founder. Projects 2-3 books per year focusing on satirical fantasy, poetry, and folk history. Publishes fiction and poetry under 'Profile' imprint. Folk legacy books published under 'Trail Blazer' and 'Bygone' imprints. Plans to solicit mss. from other authors once established. Inquiries welcome. Prefers short fiction, poetry, and brief mss. outlining innovations in American folk art. Emphasis on metaphysics, fantasy, and New Age. Contributors must be truly gifted." avg. press run 1M-2M. Pub'd 1 title 1998; expects 2 titles 1999, 2 titles 2000. 6 titles listed in the *Small Press Record of Books in Print* (28th Edition, 1999-00). avg. price, paper: $7.50. Discounts: 2-50 copies 40%, 50+ 50%. 75-100pp; 5¼×8¼; of. Payment: to be arranged individually with author. Does not copyright for author. Maine Writers & Publishers Alliance.

THE BOOKWATCH, Diane C. Donovan, Editor, 12424 Mill Street, Petaluma, CA 94952, 415-437-5731. 1980. Reviews. "*The Bookwatch* publishes short (approx. 100 words) reviews, bias towards titles which would appeal to a general readership. Reviews outline the scope of each title with notations on how it compares to similar publications. Only titles which are recommended are reviewed. The bulk of *The Bookwatch* lies in nonfiction, but other major sections include science fiction and fantasy and young adult fiction. A section is also devoted to audiocassettes." circ. 5M. 12/yr. Pub'd 12 issues 1998; expects 12 issues 1999, 12 issues 2000. sub. price: $12; per copy: $1.50; sample: $1.50. Back issues: $1.50 each. Discounts: 40% bookstores. 12pp; 8½×11; of. Reporting time: 4-6 weeks. Payment: 1 copy of issue in which review appears. Copyrighted, reverts to author. Pub's reviews: 800+ in 1998. §General-interest nonfiction (science, history/culture, health, travel), SF and Fantasy, Young adult fiction. Ads: $504/$327.60/write for smaller size rates.

Bookworm Publishing Company, Barbara Redin, Editor-In-Chief, PO Box 3037, Ontario, CA 91761. 1975. Non-fiction. "We publish books of interest in the fields of natural and social ecology, broadly defined. Current titles include *Earthworms For Ecology And Profit, Don't Call It Dirt!*, by Gordon Baker Lloyd. *House Plants and Crafts For Fun & Profit* by Derek Fell, *Living Off the Country For Fun & Profit* by John L. Parker. Other titles cover the fields of vermology, gardening, and botany. We are looking for well-written how-to-do-it type books on any topic related to gardening & agriculture, including business, and family self-sufficiency" Pub'd 4 titles 1998; expects 10 titles 1999. 9 titles listed in the *Small Press Record of Books in Print* (28th Edition, 1999-00). avg. price, cloth: $9.95; paper: $5.95; other: $6.95. Discounts: 1-5, 20%; 6-10, 33%; 11-25, 40%; 26-50, 44%; 51-100, 48%. 200pp; 5½×8½. Reporting time: 6 weeks. Payment: royalty, 5-10% of revenue. Copyrights for author. BPASC, BPSC.

BOOMERANG! MAGAZINE, Listen and Learn Home Education, Inc., David Strohm, Editor, PO Box 261, La Honda, CA 94020-0261, 415-747-0978. 1990. Fiction, articles, interviews, reviews, letters, parts-of-novels, news items, non-fiction. "70-minute magazine on audiocassette tape featuring current events, history, geography, economics, mysteries, author interviews, jokes, and more—all done in kids' metaphor and voices." circ. 34M. 12/yr. Pub'd 12 issues 1998; expects 12 issues 1999, 12 issues 2000. sub. price: $43.95; per copy: $7.95; sample: $3 p/h. Back issues: $5 each. Discounts: 40% retail, call for school, catalogs. 70 minutes; duplication. Reporting time: 1 month. Payment: variable. Copyrighted. Pub's reviews: 10 in 1998. §Children's books, news-related books.

THE BOOMERPHILE, Dan Culberson, Editor, Publisher, PO Box 17446, Boulder, CO 80308-0446, 303-444-3363. 1992. Poetry, articles, interviews, satire, criticism, reviews, music, letters, news items, non-fiction. "Additional address: 6359 Old Stage Road, Boulder, CO 80302. *The BoomerPhile* is for and about Baby Boomers, to counteract all the negative publicity they have received all their lives, to talk about things that interest them today (health, old age, mortgages, kids in college, nostalgia, music, etc.), and to allow them to make fun of themselves, for a change" circ. 150. 6/yr. Pub'd 3 issues 1998; expects 9 issues 1999, 6 issues 2000. sub. price: $20; per copy: $2.50; sample: $1. Back issues: $5. Discounts: standard rates. 8pp; 8½×11; †of. Reporting time: 1-2 weeks. Simultaneous submissions accepted: yes. Publishes 25-50% of manuscripts submitted. Payment: 1 copy for items of interest; 2 copies for original work. Copyrighted, reverts to author. Pub's reviews: 1 in 1998. §Americana, arts, entertainment, humor, politics, sex, singles, society, baby boomers, history. Ads: $25/column inch.

BOOTSTRAPPIN' ENTREPRENEUR: The Newsletter For Individuals With Great Ideas and a Little Bit of Cash, Kimberly Stansell, 6308 West 89th St, Suite 306-SPD, Los Angeles, CA 90045, 310-568-9861 emailibootstrap@aol.com. 1992. Articles, letters, news items. "Interested in low-cost marketing strategies, business building tips, business management and ideas for self-employed individuals. Recent contributors: Jay Conrad Levison ('Guerilla Marketing' series); Kate Kelly ('The Publicity Manual'); and more. Article length:

300-800 words." circ. 1M+. 4/yr. Pub'd 4 issues 1998; expects 4 issues 1999, 4-6 issues 2000. sub. price: $30; per copy: $8; sample: $8. Back issues: Back-issue bundler package for $15 for 4 issues. 12pp; 8½×11; of. Reporting time: 1-8 weeks; all inquiries should include a SASE. Payment: 1-year subscription. Copyrighted, reverts to author. Pub's reviews: 3 in 1998. §Material of interest to self-employed people. Ads: none. NAPW.

Borden Publishing Co., Joseph Campbell, 2623 San Fernando Road, Los Angeles, CA 90065, 213-223-4267. 1939. Art, non-fiction. "Only books non-fiction, reference, occult, metaphysical." avg. press run 2M-4M. Pub'd 2 titles 1998; expects 2 titles 1999, 5 titles 2000. 1 title listed in the *Small Press Record of Books in Print* (28th Edition, 1999-00). avg. price, cloth: $20; paper: $10. Discounts: trade 1-4 books 25%, 5+ 40%. of, lp. Payment: 10% royalty. Copyrights for author.

Borderland Sciences Research Foundation (see also BORDERLANDS: A Quarterly Journal Of Borderland Research), Michael Theroux, Editor in Chief, PO Box 220, Bayside, CA 95524-0220. 1945. Articles, photos, reviews, news items. "We publish research on alternate energy, alternate medicine, UFOs, fortean phenomenon, ether physics." avg. press run 2.5M. Pub'd 3 titles 1998; expects 6 titles 1999, 8 titles 2000. 12 titles listed in the *Small Press Record of Books in Print* (28th Edition, 1999-00). avg. price, paper: $9.95. Discounts: 40% to qualified retail outlets. 120pp; 5½×8½; web. Reporting time: 30-60 days. Payment: varies, average 10% of net. Copyrights for author.

BORDERLANDS: A Quarterly Journal Of Borderland Research, Borderland Sciences Research Foundation, Michael Tueroux, Editor in Chief, PO Box 220, Bayside, CA 95524-0220. 1945. Articles, photos, reviews, news items. "ISSN: 0897-0394. We print articles of research on alternative energy, medicine and health, Fortean phenomena, earth mysteries, and other Borderland subjects." circ. 1.2M. 4/yr. Pub'd 4 issues 1998; expects 4 issues 1999, 4 issues 2000. 3 titles listed in the *Small Press Record of Books in Print* (28th Edition, 1999-00). sub. price: $25; per copy: $6.95; sample: $6.95. Back issues: $6.95 each. 64pp; 8½×11; Web. Reporting time: 30-60 days on solicited, none on non-solicited. Payment: none. Copyrighted, rights revert if author desires it. Pub's reviews: 10 in 1998. §Alternative scientific and medical research, subtle energies. Ads: $600/$350/not available.

BORDERLANDS: Texas Poetry Review, Germaine Curry, Coordinator; Susan Marshall, Coordinator; Robert Lee, Poetry Editor; Ramona Cearley, Poetry Editor, PO BOX 33096, Austin, TX 78764, fax 512-499-0441; e-mail cemgilbert@earthlink.net; website http://www.fastair.com/borderlands. 1992. Poetry, articles, art, criticism, reviews, photos, interviews. "*Borderlands* provides a venue for contemporary American poetry that shows an awareness of the historical, social, political, ecological and spiritual. We have a special interest in poets of the southwest and bi-lingual poets. Past contributors include: William Stafford, Pattiann Rogers, Naomi Shihab Nye, David Romtvedt, Walter McDonald, James Ulmer, Wendy Barker." 2/yr. Pub'd 2 issues 1998; expects 2 issues 1999, 2 issues 2000. sub. price: $17 includes p/h; per copy: $10 includes p/h or $8.50 retail; sample: same. Back issues: same. Discounts: 50%. 100pp; 5½×8½; of. Reporting time: varies up to 4 months. Simultaneous submissions accepted: no. Publishes 5% of manuscripts submitted. Payment: 1 copy. Copyrighted, reverts to author. Pub's reviews: 8 in 1998. §Southwest and Texas writing, political poetry or poetry that addresses our general interests, multicultural poets, outwardly-directed poetry. Ads: exchange only. CLMP.

BORDERLINES, RESOURCE CENTER BULLETIN, George Kourous, Box 2178, Silver City, NM 88062, 505-388-0208; fax 505-388-0619; e-Mail info@ire-online.org. 1992. Reviews, non-fiction, articles, news items. circ. 1M. 11/yr. Pub'd 11 issues 1998; expects 11 issues 1999, 11 issues 2000. sub. price: $12; per copy: $3; sample: free upon request. Back issues: $3. 12pp; 8½×11; offset press. Reporting time: 1-2 months. Simultaneous submissions accepted: yes. Payment: by arrangement. Copyrighted, does not revert to author.

Borealis Press Limited (see also JOURNAL OF CANADIAN POETRY), Frank Tierney, Glenn Clever, 110 Bloomingdale Street, Ottawa, Ont. K2C 4A4, Canada, 613-798-9299; Fax 613-798-9747. 1976. Poetry, fiction, criticism, plays, non-fiction. "With few exceptions, publish only material Canadian in authorship or orientation. Query first." avg. press run 1M. Pub'd 10 titles 1998; expects 10 titles 1999, 8 titles 2000. 47 titles listed in the *Small Press Record of Books in Print* (28th Edition, 1999-00). avg. price, cloth: $30; paper: $15. Discounts: 40% to retail; 20% to jobbers. 150pp; 5½×8½; of. Reporting time: 6 months. Simultaneous submissions accepted: no. Publishes 2-3% of manuscripts submitted. Payment: 10% once yearly. Does not copyright for author. Canadian Booksellers Assn., Council of Editors of Learned Journals, Assn. of Canadian Studies in the United States.

The Borgo Press, Robert Reginald, Publisher; Mary Burgess, Associate Publisher; Michael Burgess, Editorial Director; Barbara Quarton, Editor; Richard Rogers, Business Manager, Box 2845, San Bernardino, CA 92406, 714-884-5813; 714-885-1161; Fax 714-888-4942. 1975. Criticism, non-fiction. "We publish and distribute scholarly books in the Humanities and Social Sciences for the library and academic markets. All of our books are published in open-ended, monographic series, including: The Milford Series: Popular Writers of Today; Stokvis Studies in Historical Chronology and Thought; I.O. Evans Studies in the Philosophy and Criticism of

Literature; Clipper Studies in the Theater; Borgo BioViews; Bibliographies of Modern Authors; etc. We do *not* publish fiction, poetry, children's books, or trade books." avg. press run 300. Pub'd 100 titles 1998; expects 100 titles 1999, 100 titles 2000. 16 titles listed in the *Small Press Record of Books in Print* (28th Edition, 1999-00). avg. price, cloth: $35; paper: $25. Discounts: 20% for trade sales, 50-99 copies 22%, 100-199 24%, 200+ 25%. Payment in advance required for all sales to bookstores and individuals. Pages vary; 5¼x8¼; of. Reporting time: 2 months minimum. Payment: royalty 10%, no advances; we pay once annually. Copyrights for author.

Bosck Publishing House, Kenya Williams, PO Box 42487, Atlanta, GA 30311-3246, 404-755-8170. 1991. Poetry, fiction, long-poems. "Additional address: 1474 Dodson Drive, Atlanta, GA 30311. We are committed through 1998." avg. press run 2M. Pub'd 1 title 1998; expects 1 title 1999, 1 title 2000. 1 title listed in the *Small Press Record of Books in Print* (28th Edition, 1999-00). avg. price, cloth: $14.95; paper: $9.95. Discounts: 40%-55% distributors. 85pp; 5⅜x8⅜; of. Reporting time: asap. Simultaneous submissions accepted: yes. Payment: negotiable. Copyrights for author.

THE BOSTON BOOK REVIEW, Theoharis C. Theoharis, 30 Brattle Street, 4th floor, Cambridge, MA 02138, 617-497-0344, BBR-info@BostonBookReview.org, www.BostonBookReview.org. 1993. Articles, art, photos, cartoons, interviews, satire, criticism, reviews, letters, news items, long-poems, collages, non-fiction. "Standard reviews are 800-1500 words, we now publish fiction and poetry" circ. 10M. 10/yr. Pub'd 10 issues 1998; expects 10 issues 1999, 10 issues 2000. sub. price: $24 domestic, $50 international; per copy: $3.25; sample: $5. Back issues: $10. 44-60pp; 11½x14½; of. Reporting time: 2 months. Simultaneous submissions accepted: yes. Publishes 5% of manuscripts submitted. Copyrighted, reverts to author. Pub's reviews: 400 in 1998. §We review books in all areas. Ads: $590/$350/30¢ word. NEBA, BEA, PEN, NBCC.

BOSTON REVIEW, Josh Cohen, Editor, 30 Wadsworth Street, MIT, Cambridge, MA 02139, 617-253-3642, fax 617-252-1549. 1975. Poetry, fiction, articles, art, photos, cartoons, interviews, criticism, reviews, parts-of-novels, non-fiction. "Bi-monthly publication of politics, culture, and the arts." circ. 20M. 6/yr. Pub'd 6 issues 1998; expects 6 issues 1999, 6 issues 2000. sub. price: $15 individuals, $18 institutions; per copy: $3; sample: $4.50. Back issues: $4.50 and up. Discounts: varies. 40pp; 11⅜x14½; of. Reporting time: up to 4 months. Payment: varies. Copyrighted, reverts to author. Pub's reviews: 40 in 1998. §Poetry, fiction, criticism, all the arts, politics, culture. Ads: $800/$450/Class: $1 per word, $10 minimum. CLMP.

BOTH COASTS BOOK REVIEW, Lucy Bernholz, Martha Bernholz, 882 14th Street, San Francisco, CA 94114, 415-252-7276 (phone & fax). 1995. Fiction, articles, art, photos, cartoons, interviews, reviews, news items. "Supplementary address: PO Box 263, Boston, MA 02117" circ. 5M. 6/yr. Pub'd 1 issue 1998; expects 6 issues 1999, 6 issues 2000. sub. price: $9; per copy: $2; sample: free with 9 X 12 SASE & 55¢ postage. 8pp; 8x11. Reporting time: 1 month. Simultaneous submissions accepted: yes. Publishes 1% of manuscripts submitted. Copyrighted, reverts to author. Pub's reviews: 11 in 1998. §Twentieth century fiction. Ads: $100 1/3 page/$150 1/2 page/$40 business card.

BOTH SIDES NOW, Free People Press, Elihu Edelson, Editor, 10547 State Highway 110 North, Tyler, TX 75704-9537, 903-592-4263. 1969. Poetry, fiction, articles, art, photos, cartoons, interviews, satire, criticism, reviews, music, letters, news items, non-fiction. ""An Alternative Journal of New Age/Aquarian Transformations." Articles on current events and thinkpieces with emphasis on alternatives which have implicit spiritual content. Unique spiritual/political synthesis related to such concepts as 'New Age politics' and 'the Aquarian conspiracy.' Editorial concerns include nonviolence, pacifism, decentralism, green politics, human rights, social justice, alternative lifestyles & institutions, healing, economics, appropriate technology, organic agriculture, philosophy, prophecy, psychic pheanomena, the occult, metaphysics, and religion. Reprints of important material which deserves wider circulation." circ. 200. Irregular. Pub'd 3 issues 1998; expects 4 issues 1999, 4+ issues 2000. sub. price: $9/10 issues, $5/5 issues; per copy: $1; sample: $1. Back issues: price list on request with SASE. Discounts: 30% on 10 or more copies. 10pp; 8½x11; †photocopied. Reporting time: erratic. Payment: copies. Copyrighted, reverts to author. Pub's reviews. §'New Age', spirituality, pacifism, anarchism, religion, the occult and metaphysics, radical and 'Green' politics, general alternatives. Ads: $50 (7½ X 10)/smaller sizes pro-rated/classifieds 20¢/word. APS.

Bottom Dog Press, Larry Smith, c/o Firelands College of BGSU, Huron, OH 44839, 419-433-5560. 1984. Poetry, fiction, parts-of-novels, long-poems. "We do books of fiction, poetry, personal essays as well as a combined poetry chapbook series (three-four chapbooks bound as one). A chapbook of poetry should be 30-40 poems with a unified theme and form. We are particularly interested in the work of Ohio writers—our Ohio Writers Series—and in the writing of the Midwest—Our Midwest Writers Series—and in the working class—Working Lives Series. We expect the writer to work with us on the book. Our slant is towards writing that is direct and human with clean, clear images and voice. We prefer the personal, but not the self-indulgent, simple but not simplistic, writing of value to us all. Our bias is towards sense of place writing—being who you are, where you are. And toward working class writing. Authors we've published: Robert Flanagan, Philip F. O'Connor, Jack Matthews, Robert Fox, Wendell Berry, Scott Sanders, David Shevin, Joe Napora, Chris

Llewellyn, Annabel Thomas, Kenneth Patchen." avg. press run 850 poetry, 1M fiction. Pub'd 3 titles 1998; expects 4 titles 1999, 4 titles 2000. 28 titles listed in the *Small Press Record of Books in Print* (28th Edition, 1999-00). avg. price, cloth: $19.95; paper: $6-$10. Discounts: 1-4 30%, 5-9 copies 35%, 40% 10+ copies. 160pp; 5½×8½, 6×9; of, lp. Reporting time: 1-6 months, query first. Payment: either through royalties, copies, or co-op arrangement. Copyrights for author. CLMP.

Bottom Line Pre$$, Joseph Peter Simini, PO Box 31420, San Francisco, CA 94131-0420. 1981. Non-fiction. "Not accepting submissions right now." avg. press run 2M. Expects 3 titles 1999, 3 titles 2000. 1 title listed in the *Small Press Record of Books in Print* (28th Edition, 1999-00). avg. price, cloth: $18.97; paper: $14.97. Discounts: as appropriate to relationship. 128pp; 5½×8½. PMA.

THE BOTTOM LINE PUBLICATIONS, Kay Weems, Editor, HCR-13, Box 21AA, Artemas, PA 17211-9405, 814-458-3102. 1988. "This is a huge market listing for poets and writers. Offers over 50 listings per month, complete with guidelines and entry forms when available. Guidelines given for writers and poets on contests, etc." circ. 100+. 12/yr. Pub'd 12 issues 1998; expects 12 issues 1999, 12 issues 2000. sub. price: $25; per copy: $3; sample: $3. 30-50pp; 8½×11; †Sharp copier. Reporting time: 3-5 weeks. Copyrighted. info furnished upon request. PA Poetry Society, Walt Whitman Guild, UAPAA, National Arts Society, National Federation of State Poetry Societies, New Horizons Poetry Club, Southern Poetry Assoc.

BOTTOMFISH, Randolph Splitter, 21250 Stevens Creek Blvd., De Anza College, Cupertino, CA 95014, Fax 408-864-5533; splitter@cruzio.com. 1976. Poetry, fiction, art, photos, interviews, non-fiction. "Recent contributors include Walter Griffin, Lyn Lifshin, Edward Kleinschmidt, Robert Cooperman, Chitra Divakaruni" circ. 500. 1/yr. Pub'd 1 issue 1998; expects 1 issue 1999, 1 issue 2000. sub. price: free to libraries, small press racks, schools, but is $5 per copy to individual requests; per copy: $5; sample: $5. Back issues: $2.50. Discounts: none, free on request to libraries, mags. 100pp; 6×9 (varies); †of. Reporting time: 2-4 months. Simultaneous submissions accepted: yes. Publishes 5-10% of manuscripts submitted. Payment: 2 copies of magazine. Copyrighted, reverts to author. Ads: $100/$50.

●**BOUDOIR NOIR,** Robert Dante, David Busch, 901 W. Victoria, Unit G, Compton, CA 90220, 310-631-1600; www.bondage.org. 1979. Fiction, articles, art, cartoons, interviews, reviews, news items, non-fiction. "Non-fiction mag about leather-fetish-consensual s&m lifestyles." circ. 5M. 4/yr. Pub'd 4 issues 1998; expects 4 issues 1999, 4 issues 2000. sub. price: $32; per copy: $9.95; sample: $10. 44pp; 7¾×10¾; web. Reporting time: 1 month. Simultaneous submissions accepted: no. Publishes 25% of manuscripts submitted. Payment: $25-$50. Copyrighted, does not revert to author. Pub's reviews. §Sexuality, BDSM. Ads: $230/$125/$75 1/4 page/$45 business card.

BOUILLABAISSE, Alpha Beat Press, Dave Christy, Ana Christy, 31 Waterloo Street, New Hope, PA 18938, 215-862-0299. 1991. Poetry, fiction, articles, photos, interviews, reviews, letters, long-poems, collages, news items, news items. "This magazine features modern, Beat Generation and post-Beat independent writings. A larger format than *Alpha Beat Soup*. Recent contributors: Fielding Dawson, Charles Plymell, elliott, Daniel Crocker, Joe Rochette, Wayne Wilkinson, and Joan Reid." circ. 700. 2/yr. Pub'd 2 issues 1998; expects 2 issues 1999, 2 issues 2000. sub. price: $17; per copy: $10; sample: $10. Back issues: $10. Discounts: 40%. 160pp; 8½×11. Reporting time: immediately. Publishes 35% of manuscripts submitted. Payment: copies. Copyrighted, reverts to author. Pub's reviews: 6 in 1998. §Relating to Beat Generation.

BOULEVARD, Richard Burgin, Editor, 4579 Laclede Avenue, #332, St. Louis, MO 63108-2103, 215-568-7062. 1985. Poetry, fiction, articles, art, photos, cartoons, interviews, criticism, music, parts-of-novels, long-poems, plays, non-fiction. "Contributors: John, Barth, W.S. Merwin, John Updike, Tess Gallagher, Kenneth Koch, Tom Disch, Allen Ginsberg, Joyce Carol Oates, Alice Adams, David Mamet, Donald Hall, John Ashbery, Phillip Lopate. *Boulevard* is committed to publishing the best of contemporary fiction, poetry, and non-fiction." circ. 3M. 3/yr. Pub'd 3 issues 1998; expects 3 issues 1999, 3 issues 2000. sub. price: $12; per copy: $7; sample: $8. Back issues: $10. Discounts: 50% agency. 200pp; 5⅜×8½; of. Reporting time: 8 weeks. Simultaneous submissions accepted: yes. Publishes 1% of manuscripts submitted. Payment: $25-$200 (poetry), $50-$250 (fiction), plus contributor's copies. Copyrighted, reverts to author. §Fiction, poetry, lit. criticism, art/music criticism. Ads: $150/$500 for back cover. CLMP.

Boulevard Books, Inc. Florida, Barbara Mulligan, Kay Judah, PO Box 16267, Panama City, FL 32406, 904-785-1922. 1992. Fiction, art. "We presently have nine freelance writers and illustrators who will be developing material for publication in the next two years. Our primary market will be supplement readers for alternative reading programs in public schools. Two titles are 'paired' to be marketed at one time; one title geared for the middle school interest level and one for the senior high school level where teachers need new approaches in their reading programs. We have twelve titles already developed for this market. The design of the books and format is new; i.e. we have not found anything like them in the marketplace. Several of our writers are certified public school educators. We also have planned a series of easy reading adult mystery novels of about 320 pages in 6 X 9 format." avg. press run 1M. Expects 6 titles 2000. 4 titles listed in the *Small Press*

Record of Books in Print (28th Edition, 1999-00). Discounts: 20% short or terms offered by a large distributor. Pages vary; 8½×11, 6×9; of. Payment: to be negotiated. Copyrights for author.

THE BOUND SPIRAL, Mr. M. Petrucci, 72 First Avenue, Bush Hill Park, Enfield, Middlesex, EN1 1BW, England. 1988. Poetry, articles, art, criticism, reviews, letters. "Generally poems any length, some short prose. All art received will be considered, but must be photo-copy tolerant." circ. 100-200. 2/yr. Pub'd 1 issue 1998; expects 2 issues 1999, 2 issues 2000. sub. price: £6; per copy: £3; sample: £2.50. Back issues: £2.50. Discounts: 10% for 5+. 35-40pp; 5¾×8¼; Xerox, high quality. Reporting time: 1-4 months (dependent on sub-editors). Simultaneous submissions accepted: yes. Publishes 1-5% of manuscripts submitted. Payment: 1 complimentary copy. Copyrighted, reverts to author. Pub's reviews: 6 in 1998. §Poetry, but available review space is limited. Ads: £20/£10/£1.50 per line (6 words).

BOUNDARY 2: An International Journal of Literature and Culture, Duke University Press, Paul A. Bove, Box 90660, Duke University, Durham, NC 27708-0660. "Extending beyond its previous concern with the postmodern, the new *boundary 2* approaches problems of literature and culture from a number of politically, historically, and theoretically informed perspectives. *boundary 2* remains committed to understanding the present and approaching the study of culture and politics (national and international) through literature, philosophy, and the human sciences. Send review copies to Paul A. Bove, Dept. of English, Univ. of Pittsburgh, 526 Cathedral of Learning, Fifth Avenue and Bigelow, Pittsburgh, PA 15260." circ. 850. 3/yr. Pub'd 3 issues 1998; expects 3 issues 1999, 3 issues 2000. sub. price: $75 institutions, $27 individuals, additional $9 foreign. Pub's reviews. Ads: $200/$125.

BOVINE GAZETTE, Mad Dog, PO Box 2263, Pasadena, CA 91102, e-Mail GREENHEART.COM. 1990. Cartoons, satire. 8/yr. Pub'd 8 issues 1998; expects 8 issues 1999, 8 issues 2000. sub. price: $5/6 issues; per copy: $1; sample: $1. Back issues: $1. 16pp; 5½×8½; †mi. Reporting time: 1-2 weeks. Payment: none. Copyrighted, reverts to author. Pub's reviews: 2 in 1998. §Anything. Ads: $2/$1.

Bowerdean Publishing Co. Ltd., Robert Dudley, 8 Abbotstone Road, London SW15 1QR, United Kingdom, Phone/Fax 44(0)181-7880938; E-mail 101467.1264@compuserve.com. 1989. Non-fiction. "We publish books on the application of digital technology. Series called 'Work in the Digital Age' edited by D. Bowen of the *Independent.* Also 'Bowerdean Briefings,' short books written by leading authorities to explain complex or controversial issues for the non-specialist." avg. press run 2M. Pub'd 10 titles 1998; expects 12 titles 1999, 15 titles 2000. avg. price, cloth: £20; paper: £10. Discounts: standard trade terms. 144pp; 145×210cm; litho. Reporting time: 2 months. Simultaneous submissions accepted: yes. Payment: by agreement. Copyrights for author. IPG.

Box Turtle Press (see also MUDFISH), Jill Hoffman, Poetry Editor, 184 Franklin Street, New York, NY 10013. 1983. avg. press run 1.2M. Pub'd 1 title 1998; expects 1 title 1999, 1 title 2000. avg. price, paper: $10. Discounts: 1983. 200pp; 6⅞×8¼. Reporting time: immediately to 2 months. Simultaneous submissions accepted: no. Publishes 5% of manuscripts submitted. Payment: 1 copy.

The Boxwood Press, Ralph Buchsbaum, Editor, 183 Ocean View Blvd, Pacific Grove, CA 93950, 408-375-9110; FAX 408-375-0430. 1952. Non-fiction. "Books: science & natural history, misc." avg. press run 1M. Pub'd 8 titles 1998; expects 8 titles 1999. 45 titles listed in the *Small Press Record of Books in Print* (28th Edition, 1999-00). avg. price, cloth: $25; paper: $9.95. Discounts: 20% on texts, 40% trade. 200pp; 5½×8½, 6×9; of, photo type setting-digital. Reporting time: 30 days. Payment: 10% royalty. Copyrights for author.

The Bradford Book Company, Inc., Cara Bailey, Barry Quiner, PO Box 818, Chester, NJ 07930, 908-879-1284; fax 908-879-1263. 1994. Photos, interviews, reviews, non-fiction. "We specialize in gymnastics products: books, calendars, and videos" avg. press run 10M. Pub'd 2 titles 1998; expects 2 titles 1999, 3 titles 2000. 3 titles listed in the *Small Press Record of Books in Print* (28th Edition, 1999-00). avg. price, paper: $11.95. Discounts: bookstores & libraries 1 book 20%; 2-3 30%; 4+ 40%; wholesaler 50%. 200pp; 5½×8½. Reporting time: 4-6 weeks. Publishes 10% of manuscripts submitted. Payment: varies. Copyrights for author.

The Bradford Press (see also Toad Hall, Inc.), RR 2 Box 2090, Laceyville, PA 18623, 717-869-2942; Fax 717-869-1031. 1995. Fiction. avg. press run 4M. Pub'd 1 title 1998; expects 2 titles 1999, 2 titles 2000. avg. price, cloth: $22.95; paper: $14.95. 224pp; 6×9; of. Reporting time: 3 months. Payment: $1000 advance and 10% royalty. Copyrights for author. PMA, SPAN, MABA, ABA.

Bradley Publishing, Judy Wilbourn, Susan Bradley, Matt Bradley, 15 Butterfield Lane, Little Rock, AR 72212, 501-224-0692; FAX 501-224-0762; 76503.1622@compuserve.com. 1981. Photos. "Currently not seeking unsolicited ideas. Mostly self-publish, but not exclusively." avg. press run 8M. Expects 1 title 1999, 1 title 2000. 1 title listed in the *Small Press Record of Books in Print* (28th Edition, 1999-00). avg. price, cloth: $55; other: $90 limited edition. 128pp; 12×9.

BRAIN/MIND BULLETIN, Bulletin of Breakthroughs, Interface Press, Marilyn Ferguson, Publisher &

Executive Editor, P O Box 42211, Los Angeles, CA 90042, 213-223-2500; 800-553-MIND. 1975. Articles, interviews, reviews, news items. "Except for 'Letters,' BMB is staff-written" circ. 5M. 12/yr. Pub'd 12 issues 1998; expects 12 issues 1999, 12 issues 2000. sub. price: $50 domestic, $55 foreign, $55 institutional; per copy: $4; sample: $1. Back issues: $45 for 12 in sequence — otherwise $4 each. Also BMB 'Collections' and BMB 'ThemePacks' Discounts: inquire. 8pp; 8½×11; of. Payment: none. Copyrighted. Pub's reviews: 50+ in 1998. §Psychology, psychiatry, consciousness, brain research, learning, human potential, creativity, health, etc. Ads: none.

Branch Redd Books (see also BRANCH REDD REVIEW), William Sherman, 9300 Atlantic Avenue, Apt. 218, Margate City, NJ 08402-2340. 1976. Poetry. "No unsolicited contributions please." avg. press run 400. Pub'd 1 title 1998; expects 1 title 1999. 10 titles listed in the *Small Press Record of Books in Print* (28th Edition, 1999-00). avg. price, paper: $10. Discounts: none. Pages vary; size varies. Copyrights for author.

BRANCH REDD REVIEW, Branch Redd Books, William David Sherman, 9300 Atlantic Ave, Apt 218, Margate City, NJ 08402-2340. 1976. Poetry. "No unsolicited contributions, please." circ. 400. Irregular. Expects 1 issue 1999. sub. price: No subscriptions available; per copy: $10; sample: none. Back issues: *Branch Redd* poetry chapbooks #1 & #3, still in-print: *The Leer* by Allen Fisher $2, *Four Poems* by John Lobb $2. Both for $3. *Branch Redd Review #4 & #5* still in-print, $10 each, both for $15. Discounts: none. Pages vary; size varies. Payment: copies. Copyrighted, reverts to author.

Branden Publishing Company, Adolph Caso, 17 Station Street, Box 843, Brookline Village, MA 02147, 617-734-2045; FAX 617-734-2046, E-mail: branden@usa1.com, Web page: http://www1.usa1.com/nbranden/. 1965. Fiction, art, music, letters, long-poems, plays, non-fiction. "See our latest catalogue. No manuscripts accepted, only queries with SASE." avg. press run 5M. Pub'd 15 titles 1998; expects 10 titles 1999, 15 titles 2000. 59 titles listed in the *Small Press Record of Books in Print* (28th Edition, 1999-00). avg. price, cloth: $20; paper: $14; other: $4 IPL Series. Discounts: from 1 copy 10% to 101+ copies 48%. 215pp; 6×9. Reporting time: 1 week. Simultaneous submissions accepted: no. Publishes 1% of manuscripts submitted. Payment: 10% on monies from sales; 50% on monies from sales of rights. Copyrights for author. ABA.

●**BRANDO'S HAT,** Sean Body, 14 Vine Street, Kersal, Salford M7 3PG, United Kingdom, e-mail tarantula-pubs@lineone.net. 1998. Poetry. "High quality modern poetry. We like to showcase poets, allowing room for a number of poems, a sequence, part sequence or longer poem." circ. 200. 3/yr. Pub'd 3 issues 1998; expects 3 issues 1999, 3 issues 2000. sub. price: £10; per copy: £4; sample: £4. Discounts: none. 42pp; 5½×8½; †laserprint. Reporting time: 2-3 months. Simultaneous submissions accepted: no. Publishes 10% of manuscripts submitted. Payment: free copy. Copyrighted, reverts to author.

Brandylane Publishers (see also PLEASANT LIVING), R.H. Pruett, PO Box 261, White Stone, VA 22578, 804-435-6900; Fax 804-435-9812. 1985. Poetry, fiction, non-fiction. "We publish fiction, non-fiction, poetry. Especially interested in working with unpublished writers." avg. press run 1.5M. Pub'd 7 titles 1998; expects 14 titles 1999, 24 titles 2000. avg. price, cloth: $23.95; paper: $13.95. Discounts: standard 40%, 55% distributors, 30% STOP orders. 200pp; 6×9; of. Reporting time: 4 weeks. Simultaneous submissions accepted: yes. Publishes 10% of manuscripts submitted. Payment: varies. Copyrights for author.

Brannon Enterprises, Inc., 1224 NE Walnut Street, #337, Roseburg, OR 97470-5106. 1 title listed in the *Small Press Record of Books in Print* (28th Edition, 1999-00).

Brason-Sargar Publications, Sondra Anice Barnes, Publisher, PO Box 872, Reseda, CA 91337, 818-994-0089; e-mail sonbar@bigfoot.com. 1978. Poetry, art. "We are primarily interested in gift books which express psychological truths. Must use as few words as possible. We publish thoughts, observations or statements expressing human truths written in a style which visually looks like poetry but is not poetry per se. If the poet reads our books *Life Is The Way It Is* or *We Are The Way We Are* and can write in this style, then we are interested and will negotiate payment." avg. press run 2M 1st printing, up to 20M subsequent printings. Pub'd 1 title 1998; expects 4 titles 1999, 6 titles 2000. 2 titles listed in the *Small Press Record of Books in Print* (28th Edition, 1999-00). avg. price, paper: $7.50. Discounts: 40% bookstores, 50% distributers. 96pp; 5½×8½; of. Reporting time: 30 days. Payment: to be negotiated. Copyrights for author. WNBA.

(THE) BRAVE NEW TICK, Paul N. Dion-Deitch, PO Box 24, S. Grafton, MA 01560, 508-799-3769. 1985. Poetry, fiction, articles, art, photos, cartoons, satire, reviews, music, letters, long-poems, collages, news items, non-fiction. "Formerly *The Bloated Tick*. No porn published at all." circ. 50+/-. 6/yr. Pub'd 6 issues 1998; expects 6 issues 1999, 6 issues 2000. price per copy: $1; sample: same. Back issues: same. Discounts: free in trade at editor's discretion. 10-15pp; 8½×11; †photocopy. Simultaneous submissions accepted: yes. Publishes 75%-80% of manuscripts submitted. Payment: copies. Copyrighted. Pub's reviews: 5 in 1998. §Anything. Ads: $10/$5.50/on request.

BRAVO, THE POET'S MAGAZINE, John Edwin Cowen/Bravo Editions, Jose Garcia Villa, Founding Editor; John Cowen, Current Editor, 1081 Trafalgar Street, Teaneck, NJ 07666, 201-836-5922. 1980. Poetry.

"*Bravo* believes that 1. poetry must have formal excellence; 2. poetry must be lyrical; 3. poetry is not prose. Recent contributors: Robert Levine, John Cowen, Gloria Potter, and Filipino poets: Nick Joaquin, Virginia Moreno, Alex Hufana, Jolico Cuadra, and Hilario Francia. ISSN 0275-6080." circ. 500. 1/yr. Pub'd 2 issues 1998; expects 1 issue 1999, 1 issue 2000. price per copy: $10; sample: $10. Back issues: $10. Discounts: 15%. 50pp; 6×9; of. Reporting time: 2 months. Payment: 2 copies of magazine. Copyrighted, reverts to author. NYSSPA.

BRB Publications, Inc. (see also Facts on Demand Press), Michael Sankey, PO Box 27869, Tempe, AZ 85285-7869, 800-929-3811; Fax 800-929-4981; brb@brbpub.com. 1989. Non-fiction. avg. press run 2.5M. Pub'd 5 titles 1998; expects 7 titles 1999, 7 titles 2000. 10 titles listed in the *Small Press Record of Books in Print* (28th Edition, 1999-00). avg. price, paper: $35. Discounts: 25% onesy-twosy, 45-55% for distributors. 400pp; 8½×11.

THE BREAD AND BUTTER CHRONICLES, Seven Buffaloes Press, Art Coelho, PO Box 249, Big Timber, MT 59011. 1986. Art, photos, news items. "Special three-page feature in every issue entitled 'Rural American Hall of Fame'; inductees taken from poets, writers, and artists in rural and working people. There's a farm column by Frank Cross where he covers rural American literature at large. I list contests, mags looking for special materials, special anthologies being sought. New publications just born. Events, etc. *New focus* is on *rural essays*." circ. 500. 2/yr. Expects 2 issues 1999, 2 issues 2000. sub. price: $6.75; per copy: $4.75; sample: $4.75. Back issues: none available. 8pp; 8½×11; †of. Reporting time: 1 day to 2 weeks. Payment: copies. Copyrighted, reverts to author. CLMP.

BREAKFAST ALL DAY, B.A.D. Press, Philip Boxall, 43 Kingsdown House, Amhurst Road, London E8 2AS, United Kingdom, 0171-923-0734. 1995. Poetry, fiction, articles, art, photos, cartoons, satire, letters, non-fiction. "Articles 1000-2000 words. Short stories 2000-3000 words. Strip cartoons, fillers. Interest in art, language, alternative/minority views, mental health." circ. 500. 4/yr. Pub'd 2 issues 1998; expects 4 issues 1999, 4 issues 2000. sub. price: £5; per copy: £1.50. 36pp; 8×11½; of. Payment: none. Copyrighted, reverts to author. Pub's reviews: 10 in 1998. §Art, cartoons, fiction, psychology, mental health. Ads: £25/£13. Small Press Group.

Breakout Productions, Michael Hoy, President; Vanessa McGrady, Chief Editor, PO Box 1643, Port Townsend, WA 98368. 1998. Non-fiction. "We specialize in 'how-to' books on outrageous subjects written in an authoritative style, and books about obscure-but-useful technologies. Our books are controversial and unusual. Manuscripts that we accept are usually at least 200 pages long" avg. press run 2M. Pub'd 15 titles 1998; expects 15 titles 1999, 15 titles 2000. 148 titles listed in the *Small Press Record of Books in Print* (28th Edition, 1999-00). avg. price, cloth: $24.95; paper: $14.95. Discounts: 5-9 20%, 10-49 40%, 50-99 45%, 100-199 50%, 200+ 55%. 120pp; 5½×8½, 8½×11; of. Reporting time: 3 months. Simultaneous submissions accepted: yes. Publishes 5% of manuscripts submitted. Payment: negotiable. Copyrights for author.

Brenner Information Group, Robert C. Brenner, Editor-in-Chief; Dawn M. Essman, Editor, PO Box 721000, San Diego, CA 92172-1000, 619-538-0093. 1988. Non-fiction. "50-300 pages published. How-to subjects (all categories including computers, engineering, and science)." avg. press run 2M. Pub'd 4 titles 1998; expects 2 titles 1999, 2 titles 2000. 8 titles listed in the *Small Press Record of Books in Print* (28th Edition, 1999-00). avg. price, paper: $16.95-$49; other: $49.95. Discounts: 0-55%. 300pp; 7×9, 8½×11, 5½×8½; of. Reporting time: 4-6 weeks. Simultaneous submissions accepted: yes. Publishes 10% of manuscripts submitted. Payment: 10%-12%. Copyrights for author. Publishers Marketing Ass. Small Publishers of North America, San Diego Writers/Editors Guild.

●**Briarwood Publications, Inc.**, Barbara Turner, 150 West College Street, Rocky Mount, VA 24151, 540-483-3606; website www.briarwoodva.com. 1998. Poetry, fiction, non-fiction. Pub'd 6 titles 1998; expects 6 titles 1999, 6 titles 2000. 1 title listed in the *Small Press Record of Books in Print* (28th Edition, 1999-00). avg. price, paper: $8; other: textbook $14. Discounts: max 40%; short 20%. 250pp. Simultaneous submissions accepted: yes. Publishes 2% of manuscripts submitted. Does not copyright for author.

Briarwood Publishing, Richard Smith, 1587 10th Street, Cuyahoga Falls, OH 44221-4635. 1991. Fiction, articles, art, photos, cartoons, non-fiction. avg. press run 5M-10M. avg. price, paper: $15. Reporting time: 60-90 days. Payment: varies. Copyrights for author.

Brick Row Publishing Co. Ltd. (see also POETRY NZ), Oswald Kraus, L., PO Box 100-057, North Shore Mail Centre, Auckland 1310, New Zealand, 64-9-410-6993. 1978. avg. press run 1M-2M. Pub'd 3 titles 1998; expects 4 titles 1999, 4 titles 2000. 9 titles listed in the *Small Press Record of Books in Print* (28th Edition, 1999-00). avg. price, paper: $16.95. Discounts: trade 35%. of. Reporting time: 4 weeks. Publishes 5% of manuscripts submitted. Payment: standard. Copyrights for author.

BrickHouse Books, Inc., Clarinda Harriss, Editor-in-Chief, 541 Piccadilly Road, Baltimore, MD 21204, 410-828-0724; 830-2938. 1970. Poetry. "BrickHouse Books averages 80 copies of poetry or prose. New Poets

Series, formerly the corporate name as well as its premier imprint, is for first collections only. Poetry by authors with previous books, as well as fiction (55-90 pages), goes directly to BrickHouse Books. Stonewall is specifically for mss. with a gay/lesbian perspective.'' avg. press run 1M. Pub'd 6 titles 1998; expects 6 titles 1999, 6 titles 2000. 49 titles listed in the *Small Press Record of Books in Print* (28th Edition, 1999-00). avg. price, cloth: $10; paper: $10. Discounts: 40% to bookstores; $10 retail depending on # of pages. 80pp; 6×9; of. Reporting time: 1 year. Simultaneous submissions accepted: yes. Publishes 5% of manuscripts submitted. Payment: all cash revenue from sales goes to publish the next issue; 25 copies free to author. Author holds own copyright. CLMP, Maryland State Arts Council, The Writers' Center, AWP.

BRIDAL CRAFTS, Clapper Publishing Co., Julie Stephani, 2400 Devon, Suite 375, Des Plaines, IL 60018, 847-635-5800. 1951. circ. 300M. 1/yr. Pub'd 1 issue 1998; expects 1 issue 1999, 1 issue 2000. price per copy: $3.95-$4.95. 106pp; 8½×11. Reporting time: 3 months. Simultaneous submissions accepted: yes. Payment: yes. Copyrighted, does not revert to author. Pub's reviews. §Craft books. MPA.

THE BRIDGE: A Journal of Fiction and Poetry, Jack Zucker, Editor; Helen Zucker, Fiction Editor; Mitzi Alvin, Poetry Editor, 14050 Vernon Street, Oak Park, MI 48237, 313-547-6823. 1990. Poetry, fiction, criticism, reviews, parts-of-novels, non-fiction. ''We like our fiction energetic and finished. We like our poetry expressive and professional. Reviews by query, non-fiction under 10 typed ds pages, stories under 7500 words, poems under 200 lines.'' circ. 700. 2/yr. Pub'd 2 issues 1998; expects 2 issues 1999, 2 issues 2000. sub. price: $10, $15/2 year; per copy: $5; sample: $5. Back issues: $5 for issue #2. Discounts: bookstore 40%. 192pp; 5½×8; desktop publishing. Reporting time: 1-4 months. Publishes 5% of manuscripts submitted. Payment: none right now. Copyrighted, reverts to author. Pub's reviews: 3 in 1998. §Books of real value. Ads: $50/$30. CLMP.

BRIDGES: A Journal for Jewish Feminists and Our Friends, Robin Bernstein, Debra Crespin, Sarah Jacobus, Clare Kinberg, Managing Editor; Ruth Kraut, Shlomit Segal, tova, Enid Dame, PO Box 24839, Eugene, OR 97402, 541-935-5720, E-mail: ckinberg@pond.net. 1990. Poetry, fiction, articles, art, photos, cartoons, interviews, reviews, music, letters, parts-of-novels, long-poems, plays, news items, non-fiction. ''*Bridges* seeks works of relevance to Jewish feminists which combines identity and social/political activism.'' circ. 3M. 2/yr. Pub'd 2 issues 1998; expects 2 issues 1999, 2 issues 2000. sub. price: $15; per copy: $7.50; sample: free. Back issues: $7.50. Discounts: must order through Small Changes, KOEN, ubiquity. 128pp; 7×10; of. Reporting time: 6 months. Simultaneous submissions accepted: no. Payment: 3 issues plus $50-75 per manuscript upon publication. Copyrighted, reverts to author. Pub's reviews: 10 in 1998. §Feminism, multi-cultural alliances, Jewish identity.

BRIDGES: An Interdisciplinary Journal of Theology, Philosophy, History, and Science, Robert S. Frey, Editor-Publisher, PO Box 186, Monkton, MD 21111-0186, 410-329-3055; Fax 410-472-3152; E-mail Bridges23@aol.com. 1988. Articles, photos, reviews. ''Each issue of *Bridges* provides a forum for interdisciplinary reflection on themes that share the common focus of values, humaneness, ethics, and meaning. Affiliated with St. Mary's University of Minnesota, Lebanon Valley College of Pennsylvania, and St. Mary's College of California.'' circ. 450. 2/yr. Pub'd 2 issues 1998; expects 2 issues 1999, 2 issues 2000. sub. price: $45 institutions, $30 individuals, $15 students; foreign: $50 instit., $35 indiv., $20 students; per copy: $15 (US); sample: $15 (US). Back issues: prices upon request. 175pp; 5½×8½; xerox docu tech. Reporting time: 1 month. Simultaneous submissions accepted: no. Publishes 80% of manuscripts submitted. Payment: none, complimentary copies of particular issue. Copyrighted, does not revert to author. Pub's reviews: 22 in 1998. §Theology, philosophy, history, science, cultural criticism, Holocaust. Ads: $50/$25. Conference of Editors of Learned Journals (CELJ).

Bright Hill Press, Bertha Rogers, PO Box 193, Treadwell, NY 13846, Fax 607-746-7274; E-mail wordthurs@aol.com. 1992. Poetry, fiction, art, photos, criticism, parts-of-novels, long-poems, collages, plays, non-fiction. ''We have 2 competitions per year: a chapbook (fiction even-numbered years, poetry odd-numbered years) and a full-length poetry book competition - both national. Full-length poetry book competition judged by nationally-known poets. We also publish anthologies with a theme. No unsolicited mss.'' avg. press run 700. Pub'd 1 title 1998; expects 3 titles 1999, 4-5 titles 2000. 9 titles listed in the *Small Press Record of Books in Print* (28th Edition, 1999-00). avg. price, paper: $10-$12. Discounts: trade 40%, bulk 40%, classroom 20-40%, jobber 40-55%, agent 20%. 70pp; 5⅛×8½; of. Reporting time: 3-6 months. We accept simultaneous submissions, with notification if accepted elsewhere. Publishes 5% of manuscripts submitted. Payment: cash payment for award winners and copies. Does not copyright for author. Small Press Center, CLMP.

Bright Moon Press, David Crowther, Editor, 584 Castro Street, Ste. 232, San Francisco, CA 94114. Pub'd 1 title 1998; expects 3 titles 1999, 5 titles 2000. 1 title listed in the *Small Press Record of Books in Print* (28th Edition, 1999-00).

Bright Mountain Books, Inc., Cynthia Bright, 138 Springside Road, Asheville, NC 28803, fax/phone 828-681-1790. 1983. Non-fiction. ''Length of material: booklength. Biases: regional, Southern Appalachians,

Carolinas, nonfiction. Imprint: Historical Images." avg. press run 4M. Pub'd 2 titles 1998; expects 4 titles 1999, 6 titles 2000. 19 titles listed in the *Small Press Record of Books in Print* (28th Edition, 1999-00). avg. price, cloth: $14.95; paper: $10.95; other: $22.95. Discounts: 40% trade, 20% libraries on 1-5 copies, 40% on 6+. 200pp; 6×9; of. Reporting time: 2 months. Simultaneous submissions accepted: yes. Publishes 10% of manuscripts submitted. Payment: 10% of retail price on actual sales, paid quarterly. Copyrights for author. PAS.

Bright Ring Publishing, Inc., MaryAnn F. Kohl, PO Box 31338, Bellingham, WA 98228-3338, 360-734-1601, 800-480-4278. 1985. Non-fiction. "We are looking for material for teachers using learning centers, individualized classrooms, and creative thinking. Preferrably early childhood and primary. Should transfer easily to use at home. Creative, independent, open-minded. First contribution, *Scribble Cookies And Other Independent Creative Art Experiences for Children*, 144 pages, black line drawings (120), 11 X 8½, suitable for teachers, parents, children, and others who work with children ages 2-forever. We do not publish poetry, fiction, picture books, or books with fill-ins or coloring. Books must mirror our format and design." avg. press run 20M. Pub'd 1 title 1998; expects 1 title 1999, 1 title 2000. 5 titles listed in the *Small Press Record of Books in Print* (28th Edition, 1999-00). avg. price, paper: $14.95. Discounts: bulk. 150pp; 11×8; of. Reporting time: 4 weeks. We accept simultaneous submissions if so designated. Payment: 4% of net, quarterly. Copyrights for author. PMA, Pacific Northwest Assoc. of Publishers.

Brighton Publications, Inc., Sharon E. Dlugosch, PO Box 120706, St. Paul, MN 55112-0706, 651-636-2220. 1977. Non-fiction. "Were'e developing party themes, games, celebration themes. We need authors who can convey their enthusiasm and knowledge of a subject, as well as willing to rewrite." Expects 3 titles 1999, 5 titles 2000. 20 titles listed in the *Small Press Record of Books in Print* (28th Edition, 1999-00). avg. price, paper: $9.95. 160pp; 5½×8½. Reporting time: 3 months. Payment: 10% of net. Copyrights for author.

BRILLIANT STAR, Pepper P. Oldziey, Managing Editor; Cindy Savage, Fiction Editor, Baha'i National Center, 1233 Central Street, Evanston, IL 60201. 1969. Poetry, fiction, articles, art, photos, cartoons, interviews, music, plays, non-fiction. "Material should not generally exceed 500 words. We do publish unpublished writers. Prefer articles & fiction which reflect racial and cultural diversity. Stories with moral or religious theme should not be 'preachy' or heavy-handed in conveying a lesson. Baha'i content a top priority. No Christmas material will be accepted. Send for guidelines, 2 year theme list and informational material on the Baha'i Faith" circ. 3M. 6/yr regular, 1 special edition. Pub'd 7 issues 1998; expects 7 issues 1999, 7 issues 2000. sub. price: $18; per copy: $3.50; sample: $3.00 with 9 X 12 SASE with postage for 5 oz. Back issues: $3.50. Discounts: Bulk (5 or more) $2.50. 33pp; 8½×11; †of. Reporting time: 8-12 weeks. Simultaneous submissions accepted: yes. Publishes 2% of manuscripts submitted. Payment: 2 copies. Copyrighted, rights revert to author if they specify that they are retaining copyright. No ads.

BRITISH JOURNAL OF AESTHETICS, Oxford University Press, Dr. T.J. Diffey, Journal Subscription Department, Pinkhill House, Southfield Road, Eynsham, Oxford, OX8 1JJ, United Kingdom. 1960. Articles, reviews, letters. "For ad rates write Oxford University Press, Oxford Journals, Production Department, Pinkhill House, Southfield Road, Eynsham, Oxford OX8 1JJ, United Kingdom. Discussions of general philosophical aesthetics and articles on the principles of appraisal which apply in the various arts severally, working towards a better understanding of them all and throwing light on the analogies and differences between them." circ. 1550. 4/yr. Pub'd 4 issues 1998; expects 4 issues 1999, 4 issues 2000. sub. price: $90; per copy: $27; sample: free. 100pp; 234×155mm; of. Reporting time: normally 3 months. Payment: 20 free offprints. Copyrighted, copyright held by Oxford U Press. Pub's reviews. §Aesthetics, philosophy of art, theory of art, theory of art and literary criticism; reviews are commissioned, unsolicited reviews not accepted. Ads: £205($370)/£120($215)/ £85($155) 1/4 page.

Brittain Communications, PO Box 2567, North Canton, OH 44720, phone/fax 330-497-2304; email brittainak@aol.com. 1989. Expects 1 title 1999, 1 title 2000. 1 title listed in the *Small Press Record of Books in Print* (28th Edition, 1999-00). avg. price, paper: $10.95. Discounts: available. 105pp; 8½×5½; various used. Reporting time: 3 months. Simultaneous submissions accepted: no. Publishes 10% of manuscripts submitted. Does not copyright for author.

THE BROBDINGNAGIAN TIMES, Giovanni Malito, 96 Albert Road, Cork, Ireland, (21 311227). 1996. Poetry, fiction, art, satire. "Format is a broadsheet - brevity is vital but that is not to say that we are looking for minimalist work. An annual magazine (40 pages) is also planned." circ. 500. 4/yr. Expects 2 issues 1999, 4 issues 2000. sub. price: £2.00; per copy: 50P/$1; sample: 2 IRC's for postage. Back issues: 2 IRC's. 8pp; 6×8½; †mi. Reporting time: 2 weeks to 2 months. Simultaneous submissions accepted: yes. Publishes 10-20% of manuscripts submitted. Payment: copies. Copyrighted, reverts to author. Ads: exchange.

Broken Boulder Press (see also NEOTROPE), Paul Silvia, Adam Powell, PO Box 172, Lawrence, KS 66044-0172, E-mail paulsilvia@hotmail.com; website www.brokenboulder.com. 1996. Poetry, fiction, art, long-poems, collages, plays. "*Gestalten*: Aggressively experimental poetry of all styles, send 5-25 poems with cover letter and SASE. *Neotrope*: Progressive fiction, drama, and visual art, 1-4 manuscripts with cover letter

90

and SASE.'' avg. press run 200. Pub'd 4 titles 1998; expects 6 titles 1999, 6 titles 2000. avg. price, paper: $3; other: $1 saddle stitch. Discounts: 30% for 10 or less copies for educational purposes. 20-80pp; 5½×8½; of, letterpress. Reporting time: 4 weeks. Simultaneous submissions accepted only for Neotrope. Publishes 10% of manuscripts submitted. Payment: negotiated case-by-case. Copyrights for author.

Broken Jaw Press (see also NEW MUSE OF CONTEMPT), Joe Blades, PO Box 596 Stn A, Canada, Fredericton, NB E3B 5A6, Canada, ph/fax 506-454-5127; e-mail jblades@nbnet.nb.ca; www.brokenjaw.com. 1985. Poetry, fiction, cartoons, non-fiction. ''Focus on Canadian, especially Canadian authors and/or subjects.'' avg. press run 700. Pub'd 15 titles 1998; expects 12 titles 1999, 12 titles 2000. 69 titles listed in the *Small Press Record of Books in Print* (28th Edition, 1999-00). avg. price, paper: $14; other: cassettes $12.00. Discounts: direct trade 40%, trade in U.S./Canada by General Distributions Services. 80pp; 6×9; of. Reporting time: 4-6 months. Simultaneous submissions accepted: no. Publishes 2% of manuscripts submitted. Payment: 10% of list price. Copyrights for author. Assoc. of Canadian Publishers (ACP), Small Press Assoc. of Canada (SPANC), Atlantic Publisher Marketing Association (APMA), Literary Press Group of Canada (LPG).

Broken Mirrors Press, Bryan Cholfin, PO Box 1110, New York, NY 10159-1110. 1988. Fiction. ''I am looking for science fiction and fantasy short stories, demonstrating the highest levels of imagination and style, prefer 3-8,000 words'' avg. press run 2500. Pub'd 1 title 1998; expects 4 titles 1999, 4 titles 2000. avg. price, paper: $4; other: $2-4 issue subscriptions-payement to Broken Mirrors Press. 6×9; of. Reporting time: less than 1 month. Publishes .1% of manuscripts submitted. Payment: 10¢ a word. We copyright for author if desired.

BROKEN PENCIL, Hal Niedzviecki, PO Box 203 Station P, Toronto, ON M5S 2S7, Canada, 416-538-2813; E-mail editor@brokenpencil.com. 1995. Fiction, articles, cartoons, interviews, criticism, reviews, letters, collages, news items, non-fiction, music, parts-of-novels. ''We use anything on the subject of alternative culture in Canada. Fiction by Canadians only. Our main capacity is as a review journal of canadian zines.'' circ. 2.5M. 2-3/yr. Pub'd 2 issues 1998; expects 3 issues 1999, 3 issues 2000. sub. price: $12/3 issues; per copy: $5; sample: $5. 88pp; 8½×11; lp. Reporting time: 2-3 months. Simultaneous submissions accepted: no. Payment: copy/$25-$200. Copyrighted, reverts to author. Pub's reviews: hundreds in 1998. §Anything published in Canada on an independent/small press basis. Ads: $200/$100. CMPA.

Broken Rifle Press, Gerald R. Gioglio, Publisher, 2 Rowland Place, Metuchen, NJ 08840-2534, 732-549-0631 e-mail: jerrkate@erols.com. 1987. Non-fiction. ''Focus on peace, antiwar movements, non-violent resistance.'' avg. press run 3.5M. Pub'd 1 title 1998; expects 1 title 1999, 1 title 2000. 2 titles listed in the *Small Press Record of Books in Print* (28th Edition, 1999-00). avg. price, cloth: $27.50; paper: $14.45. Discounts: 1-4 20%, 5-32 40%, 33-64 43%, 65-98 46%, 99+ 48%. 5½×8½; lo. Reporting time: 6-8 weeks. Payment: standard. Copyrights for author.

Broken Shadow Publications, Gail Ford, 472 44th Street, Oakland, CA 94609-2136, 510-450-0640. 1993. Poetry, fiction, non-fiction. ''Do not accept unsolicited manuscripts. Material we publish is honest, accessible, and deeply felt. Contributing authors place an emphasis on communication, and participate in regular peer reviews to ensure the clarity and power of their work'' avg. press run 500. Expects 2 titles 1999, 2 titles 2000. 2 titles listed in the *Small Press Record of Books in Print* (28th Edition, 1999-00). avg. price, paper: $10. 75pp; 5½×8¼; of. Simultaneous submissions accepted: no. Copyrights for author.

Brooding Heron Press, Samuel Green, Co-Publisher; Sally Green, Co-Publisher, Bookmonger Road, Waldron Island, WA 98297. 1984. Poetry. ''No unsolicited manuscripts. New work by James Laughlin, Hayden Carruth, and Ted Genoways. Forthcoming by David Lee, Judy Lightfoot, and Laurel Rust.'' avg. press run 300. Pub'd 3 titles 1998; expects 2 titles 1999, 3 titles 2000. 14 titles listed in the *Small Press Record of Books in Print* (28th Edition, 1999-00). avg. price, cloth: $25-$125; paper: $10; other: $40-$250 signed editions. Discounts: 30% to bookstores for trade copies. 36-54pp; size varies; †lp. Reporting time: 1-2 weeks. Simultaneous submissions accepted: no. Publishes 1% of manuscripts submitted. Payment: copies, 10% of run. Copyrights for author.

Brook Farm Books, Donn Reed, PO Box 246, Bridgewater, ME 04735. 1981. Fiction, cartoons, satire, non-fiction. ''Especially interested in home-school material.'' avg. press run 1M. Pub'd 2 titles 1998; expects 2 titles 1999, 2 titles 2000. 1 title listed in the *Small Press Record of Books in Print* (28th Edition, 1999-00). avg. price, paper: $15. Discounts: 1-9 30%, 10-49 40%, 50+ 50%, 40% STOP. 80-200pp; 7×8, 5×7, 8½×11; of. Reporting time: 2 months. Simultaneous submissions accepted: no. Payment: 10%; no advance. Copyrights for author.

The Brookdale Press, Ray Freiman, 566 E. Shore Rd., Jamestown, RI 02835, 203-322-2474. 1976. avg. press run as required. Pub'd 1 title 1998; expects 2 titles 1999, 1-3 titles 2000. 2 titles listed in the *Small Press Record of Books in Print* (28th Edition, 1999-00). Discounts: trade 1 copy 33%, 5+ 40%, jobbers 45% any quantity. Payment: negotiated. We copyright for author if asked.

Brooke-Richards Press, Audrey Bricker, Editor, 9420 Reseda Blvd., Suite 511, Northridge, CA 91324, 818-893-8126. 1989. ''Supplementary textbooks. Not accepting submissions at the present time.'' avg. press

91

run varies. Pub'd 2-3 titles 1998. 3 titles listed in the *Small Press Record of Books in Print* (28th Edition, 1999-00). avg. price, paper: $9.95. Discounts: 40%. 96pp; 8½×11.

The Brookfield Reader, Jason T. Freeman, Fiction Editor; Susan K. Baggette, Non-Fiction Editor; Ralph Scherer, Art Director, 137 Peyton Road, Sterling, VA 20165-5605, email info@brookfieldreader.com; prodir@erols.com. 1997. Fiction, art, photos, non-fiction. "For board and picture books: submit entire manuscript and photocopies of 3 sample illustrations. Fiction/non-fiction: submit 3 sample chapters, outline/synopsis. Wants: pre-school series books, American history, historical fiction, adventure, folktales, nature/environment, concept." avg. press run 10M. Pub'd 6 titles 1998; expects 1 title 1999, 3 titles 2000. 7 titles listed in the *Small Press Record of Books in Print* (28th Edition, 1999-00). avg. price, cloth: $16.95; other: $9.95 (board). Discounts: For information call 703-430-0202 or fax 703-430-7315. of. Reporting time: 6-8 weeks. We accept simultaneous submissions if indicated in cover letter. Payment: project-by-project basis. Copyrights for author. PMA, ABA, MPA.

Brooks Books (see also MAYFLY), Randy Brooks, Shirley Brooks, 4634 Hale Dr, Decatur, IL 62526-1117, 217-877-2966. 1976. Poetry, articles, reviews, concrete art. "High/Coo Press chapbooks are published on an irregular basis by invitation only. Indiv. prices are $3.50 for chapbooks and $2.00 for mini-chapbooks (cl editions are $10.00 and $7.00 respectively). High/Coo Press publishes manuscripts of short poetry including haiku, tanka, senryu, epigrams, visual poetry and others. Include a SASE for each submission. Sample our publications before submitting. Catalog for first class stamp or SASE" avg. press run 350. Pub'd 2 titles 1998; expects 2 titles 1999, 2 titles 2000. 45 titles listed in the *Small Press Record of Books in Print* (28th Edition, 1999-00). avg. price, cloth: $20; paper: $5 postpaid (chapbooks); other: $2 postpaid (mini-chapbooks). Discounts: 40% to authors of our titles; 40% to bookstores (minimum order 5 books). 24-48pp; 4¼×5½; †of, lp, laser. Reporting time: 5 months. Simultaneous submissions accepted: no. Publishes .01% of manuscripts submitted. Payment: copies and 15% after costs are met. Does not copyright for author.

Browder Springs, Billy Bob Hill, PO Box 823521, Dallas, TX 75382, 214-368-4360. 1996. Poetry, fiction, non-fiction. "We welcome proposals, not manuscripts. *Circling,* a collection of poetry released in 1996. In 1997, two books released: *Texas Short Stories* a short fiction anthology, and *Twenty Questions,* a how-to-get-in print book. *Texas Short Stories 2* is in progress." avg. press run 1M. Pub'd 1 title 1998; expects 2 titles 1999, 3 titles 2000. 2 titles listed in the *Small Press Record of Books in Print* (28th Edition, 1999-00). avg. price, cloth: $15.95; paper: $13.95. Discounts: jobber - standard split. 200pp; 5½×8½. Reporting time: 8 months. Simultaneous submissions accepted: yes. Publishes 5% of manuscripts submitted. Payment: varies. Copyrights for author.

BROWNBAG PRESS, Hyacinth House Publications/Caligula Editions, Randal Seyler, Fiction Editor; Shannon Frach, Poetry Editor & Editor-in-Chief, PO Box 120, Fayetteville, AR 72702-0120. 1989. Poetry, fiction, art, satire, cartoons. "We seek quality fiction of 2,00 words or less. We also use poetry. All of our publications are decidedly 'left of center'—we value edgy, hard-hitting writing for an audience which appreciates powerful, often 'disturbed' perspectives in literature. We like to see material reflecting a wide array of counter-culture viewpoints—occult, Dadaist, gay, Beat, psychedelic, etc. Recent contributors include Bill Eakin, Belinda Subraman, Kim Bright, Gomez Robespierce, and Kirsten Fox, Donna Y. Orme. We do *not* take romance, inspirational material. No rhyming poetry." circ. 200+. 2/yr. Pub'd 2 issues 1998; expects 3 issues 1999, 3 issues 2000. sub. price: $12; per copy: $4; sample: $4. 40pp; 8½×11; †mi. Reporting time: 1 week to 8 months; depends on backlog. Publishes 5-10% of manuscripts submitted. Payment: we do not pay. Copyrighted, reverts to author. Ads: negotiable; we occasionally trade ads.

Brownout Laboratories, Michael Hanna, RD 2, Box 5, Little Falls, NY 13365. 1994. Poetry, fiction, art, criticism, plays, non-fiction. "All submissions are seriously considered, and at least half the submissions which fit the profile of this press are published." avg. press run 100. Pub'd 1 title 1998; expects 3 titles 1999, 2 titles 2000. 4 titles listed in the *Small Press Record of Books in Print* (28th Edition, 1999-00). avg. price, cloth: $50; paper: $10. Discounts: 2-4 20%; 5+ 40%. 120pp; 5×8. Reporting time: 4 days to 4 months. Simultaneous submissions accepted: yes. Publishes less than 10% of manuscripts submitted. Payment: author receives 20% royalty on all copies sold. Author retains copyright.

PTOLEMY, THE BROWNS MILLS REVIEW, David Vajda, PO Box 252, Juliustown, NJ 08052. 1979. circ. 250. 1-4/year. Expects 1 issue 1999, 2 issues 2000. sub. price: $4; per copy: $4; sample: $2. Back issues: $2. 16pp; 5½×8½; of. Reporting time: 1-3 months. Payment: copies. Copyrighted, reverts to author.

THE BROWNS MILLS REVIEW (see also PTOLEMY), David Vajda, PO Box 252, Juliustown, NJ 08052. 1979. Poetry, fiction, art, satire, long-poems. "Too traditional, too conservative - not usually accepted..." avg. press run 250. Expects 1 title 1999, 2 titles 2000. avg. price, paper: $2; other: $4.50. 16pp; 5½×8½; of. Reporting time: 1-3 months. Publishes 10% - 15% of manuscripts submitted. Payment: copies. Copyrights for author.

THE BROWNSTONE REVIEW, Keith Dawson, Publisher; Laura Dawson, Fiction Editor; Aaron Scharf,

Poetry Editor, 335 Court St. #114, Brooklyn, NY 11231-4335. 1995. Poetry, fiction, criticism, parts-of-novels, long-poems. "Additional address: Aaron Scharf, 19 Wyckoff Street, Brooklyn, NY 11201." circ. 100. 2/yr. Pub'd 1 issue 1998; expects 2 issues 1999, 2 issues 2000. sub. price: $10; per copy: $6; sample: $6. 64pp; 5½×8½; †custom desktop output. Reporting time: 2 months max. Simultaneous submissions accepted: yes. Publishes less than 10% of manuscripts submitted. Payment: 2 copies. Copyrighted, reverts to author.

Brunswick Publishing Corporation, 1386 Lawrenceville Plank Road, Lawrenceville, VA 23868, 804-848-3865; Fax 804-848-0607; brunspub@jnent.com. 1973. Poetry, fiction, articles, parts-of-novels, long-poems, plays, non-fiction. "Most categories apply. We accept or reject upon examination on individual basis." avg. press run 500-5M. Pub'd 12 titles 1998; expects 15 titles 1999, 18 titles 2000. 29 titles listed in the *Small Press Record of Books in Print* (28th Edition, 1999-00). avg. price, cloth: $29.95; paper: $15. Discounts: jobber 40% trade books, 20% textbooks. 280pp; 5¼×8¼, 6×9, 8½×11; of. Reporting time: 2 weeks. Simultaneous submissions accepted: yes. Publishes 5% of manuscripts submitted. Payment: send for statement of philosophy and purpose. Copyrights for author. PMA.

BRUTARIAN, Dominik Salemi, PO Box 25222, Arlington, VA 22202-9222, 703-360-2514. 1991. Poetry, fiction, articles, art, photos, cartoons, interviews, satire, criticism, reviews, music, letters, parts-of-novels, long-poems, collages, plays, concrete art, news items, non-fiction. "Quality not quantity is the philosophy here. We have contributors who work for highbrow publications like Sally Ekhoff of the *Village Voice,* artists like Jarrett Huddleston whose paintings routinely fetch five figures and writers like myself (Salemi the editor) whose work has appeared primarily in underground publications." circ. 3M. 4/yr. Pub'd 4 issues 1998; expects 4 issues 1999, 4 issues 2000. sub. price: $12; per copy: $4; sample: $6. Back issues: $7 (cheap for works of such unsurpassed genius). Discounts: $2 per if order 10 copies or more. 84pp; 8½×11; professional printer. Reporting time: 30 days. Simultaneous submissions accepted: no. Publishes 10% of manuscripts submitted. Payment: features fetch 5¢/word, reviews $20, art $40 a page, cover illustration $100, 10¢/word for stories from established writers and for features. Copyrighted, reverts to author. Pub's reviews: 50+ in 1998. §Any area dealing with pop culture or offbeat controversial subject matter. Ads: $90/$50/$30/$175 inside cover/$500 back cover.

●**Buckhead Press,** Christy Hunt, 3777 Peachtree Road, Suite 1401, Atlanta, GA 30319, 404-949-0527; fax 404-949-0528; e-mail buckheadpress@worldnet.att.net. 1998. Fiction, criticism, reviews. avg. press run 2.5-5M. Expects 1 title 1999, 2 titles 2000. avg. price, cloth: $21; paper: $12. Discounts: trade and bulk. 200-300pp; 5¾×7¾. Reporting time: 3-6 months. Simultaneous submissions accepted: yes. We publish 1-2 manuscripts of those submitted per year. Payment: advance plus 10%. Copyrights for author. SPAN, ABA.

Buckhorn Books, 9330 B State Suite 257, Marysville, WA 98270, 360-658-0373. 1994. Non-fiction. avg. press run 5M. Pub'd 1 title 1998; expects 3 titles 1999, 1 title 2000. 1 title listed in the *Small Press Record of Books in Print* (28th Edition, 1999-00). avg. price, paper: $12.95. Discounts: 75% on all. 147pp; 9×12; of. Payment: yes. NABE.

Buddhist Study Center Press, Ruth M. Tabrah, 876 Curtis Street #3905, Honolulu, HI 96813, 808-597-8967. 1979. "We publish translations of Pure Land Buddhist texts and commentaries, also such biographical material as our 1991 title—*Memories of a Woman Buddhist Missionary in Hawaii* by Shigeo Kikuchi. We are not taking submissions at this time, but welcome query letters." avg. press run 3.5M. Pub'd 1 title 1998; expects 1 title 1999, 1-2 titles 2000. 17 titles listed in the *Small Press Record of Books in Print* (28th Edition, 1999-00). avg. price, cloth: $12.95; paper: $9.95; other: $9.95. Discounts: usual discounts for orders of more than 10 copies. 75-175pp; 6×9. Copyrights for author.

Buddhist Text Translation Society, Dharma Realm Buddhist Assn., 1777 Murchison Drive, Burlingame, CA 94010-4504, phone/fax 415-692-9286, e-mail drbabtts@jps.net. 1970. Poetry, fiction, articles, art, photos, interviews, non-fiction. "Buddhist Text Translation Society began publishing in 1972 with the goal of making the principles of Buddhist wisdom available to the American reader in a form that can be put directly into practice. BTTS translators are not only scholars but are practicing Buddhists who encounter every day the living meaning of the works they translate. Each translation is accompanied by a contemporary commentary. On the publishing list are standard Buddhist classics such as the *Shurangama Sutra,* the *Lotus Sutra,* and the *Vajra Sutra;* esoteric works such as the *Earth Store Bodhisattva Sutra* and the *Shurangama Mantra;* books of informal instruction in meditation; and books, including fiction, that have grown out of the American Buddhist experience. Beginning in 1979 the Society started publishing translations of Buddhist Scriptures bilingually (Chinese and English). Some of the works available bilingually include chapters from the *Avatamsaka Sutra, The Heart Sutra* and the *Brahma Net Sutra.* Extensive commentaries accompany each of these works in both languages. The Society also plans to publish more works in other languages in the future. In 1980 the Society published two translation works into Spanish and will be publishing works in other languages in the near future." avg. press run 2M. Pub'd 6 titles 1998; expects 8 titles 1999, 6 titles 2000. 113 titles listed in the *Small Press Record of Books in Print* (28th Edition, 1999-00). avg. price, cloth: $16; paper: $8. Discounts: retail stores 2-4 books 20%, 5+ 40%. 200pp; 5½×8½; of. Payment: none, non profit org. Copyrights for author.

BUENO, In One Ear Publications, Elizabeth Reid, 1700 Wagon Gap, Round Rock, TX 78681. 1991. Poetry, articles, cartoons, non-fiction. "All material *must* pertain to learning a foreign language or be *bilingual*: the same article in both English and another language. Articles are generally short." circ. 8M. 4/yr. Pub'd 4 issues 1998; expects 4 issues 1999, 4 issues 2000. sub. price: $10 US; $20 International; per copy: $3; sample: $1. Back issues: none available. Discounts: 65% on minimum of 10 copies. 16pp; 5½×8½; of. Reporting time: 1 month. Simultaneous submissions accepted: yes. Publishes 10% of manuscripts submitted. Payment: negotiated, usually 10 copies + $10.00. Copyrighted, reverts to author. Pub's reviews: 150 in 1998. §Must pertain to learning a foreign language or be bilingual or in a foreign language, preferably Spanish. Ads: none. PMA, SPAN, San Diego Publishers Alliance, Rocky Mtn Book Pub, SPAN.

BUFFALO SPREE, Johanna Van De Mark, 5678 Main Street, Buffalo, NY 14221-5563, 716-634-0820; fax 716-634-4659. 1967. Poetry, fiction, articles, non-fiction. circ. 21M. 4/yr. Pub'd 4 issues 1998; expects 4 issues 1999, 4 issues 2000. sub. price: $8; per copy: $2; sample: $2. Discounts: none. 80pp; 8⅜×10⅞; of. Reporting time: 1-3 months. Simultaneous submissions accepted: yes. Publishes 10% of manuscripts submitted. Payment: varies, payment upon publication. Copyrighted, authors must request permission for rights to revert. Pub's reviews.

Bull Publishing Co., James Bull, P O Box 208, Palo Alto, CA 94302, 415-322-2855. 1974. "Texts in health sciences; books in nutrition and health, child care and cancer patient education." avg. press run 7M. Pub'd 7 titles 1998; expects 4 titles 1999, 4 titles 2000. 30 titles listed in the *Small Press Record of Books in Print* (28th Edition, 1999-00). avg. price, cloth: $19.95; paper: $14.95. Discounts: trade distributor: Publishers Group West, 4065 Hollis St., Emeryville, Ca. 94608. 300pp; 5½×8½, 8½×11; web or sheet feed press-usually in the Midwest. Reporting time: 1 week. Copyrights for author. PMA, NCBPA, NCBA.

BULLETIN OF HISPANIC STUDIES, Liverpool University Press, Dorothy Sherman Severin, James Higgins, Dept. Of Hispanic Studies, The University, PO Box 147, Liverpool L69 3BX, England, 051 794 2774/5. 1923. Articles, reviews. "Specialist articles on the languages and literatures of Spain, Portugal and Latin America, in English, Spanish, Portuguese and Catalan." circ. 1M. 4/yr. Pub'd 4 issues 1998; expects 4 issues 1999, 4 issues 2000. sub. price: inland (European community) indiv. £29, instit. £75, overseas indiv. US $50, instit. US $155; per copy: £20. Back issues: £40 per volume. 112pp; metric crown quarto; of. Reporting time: 3 months max. Payment: none. Not copyrighted. Pub's reviews: 200 in 1998. §Languages and literatures of Spain, Portugal and Latin America. Ads: £250/£150/£80 1/4 page. CELJ.

The Bunny & The Crocodile Press/Forest Woods Media Productions, Inc, Grace Cavalieri, President; Robert Sargent, Vice Press; Cynthia Comitz, Senior editor, Chief of Production, PO Box 416, Hedgesville, WV 25427-0416, 304-754-8847. 1976. Poetry. "Other address: Suite 1102, 4200 Cathedral Ave. NW. Manuscripts by invitation only, no unsolicited mss." avg. press run 500-1M. Pub'd 2 titles 1998; expects 10 titles 1999, 10 titles 2000. 16 titles listed in the *Small Press Record of Books in Print* (28th Edition, 1999-00). avg. price, paper: $10. Discounts: 10% discount for orders of 12+. 77-100pp; 5½×8½; of. Simultaneous submissions accepted: no. Payment: to date authors obtain grants to publish, get 80% of sales; publisher supplies 20% funding. Author owns copyright. Small Press Center, Writers Center.

Burd Street Press, Harold E. Collier, Acquisitions Editor, PO Box 152, 63 W. Burd Street, Shippensburg, PA 17257, 717-532-2237; FAX 717-532-7704. 1992. Fiction, non-fiction. "A division of White Mane Publishing Co., Inc. Military history and some military fiction." avg. press run 1M-2M. Pub'd 4 titles 1998; expects 10 titles 1999, 15 titles 2000. 78 titles listed in the *Small Press Record of Books in Print* (28th Edition, 1999-00). avg. price, cloth: $24.95; paper: $12. Discounts: available on request. 150-250pp; 6×9; †lp. Reporting time: 60 days. Simultaneous submissions accepted: yes. Publishes 25% of manuscripts submitted. Payment: twice yearly. Copyrights for author.

BurnhillWolf, Kurt Palomaki, 321 Prospect Street, SW, Lenoir, NC 28645, 704-754-0287; FAX 707-754-8392. 1995. Poetry, fiction. "Collections of poetry and short stories, novels. Seeking writers with a new or different perspective on being alive, will accept science fiction." avg. press run 2M-3M. Pub'd 1 title 1998; expects 2 titles 1999, 2-3 titles 2000. 3 titles listed in the *Small Press Record of Books in Print* (28th Edition, 1999-00). avg. price, paper: $8-13. Discounts: trade and distributor discounts. Pages vary; 5½×8½; of. Reporting time: 1-3 months. Simultaneous submissions accepted: yes. Payment: standard 7.5-10%. Copyrights for author.

Burning Books, Melody Sumner Carnahan, Kathleen Burch, Michael Sumner, PO Box 2638, Santa Fe, NM 87504, Fax 505-820-6216; E-mail brnbx@nets.com. 1979. Poetry, fiction, art, interviews, music. "We are artists and writers who publish books that extend possibilities in literature, music, art, and ideas. We use volunteer labor, donated professional services, income from previous publications and advance sales to create our books." avg. press run 1M-3M. Pub'd 1 title 1998; expects 2 titles 1999, 2 titles 2000. 9 titles listed in the *Small Press Record of Books in Print* (28th Edition, 1999-00). avg. price, cloth: $25-$35; paper: $10-$25. Discounts: 40/60. 84-450pp; 8×10; of, lp. Reporting time: 6 weeks. Simultaneous submissions accepted: yes.

Publishes 0% of manuscripts submitted. Payment: varies. We sometimes copyright for author. PCBA (Pacific Center for the Book Arts, PO 6209, San Francisco, CA 94101).

Burning Bush Publications, Cheryl Williams, Coordinator, PO Box 9636, Oakland, CA 94613-0636, 510-482-9996; www.home.earthlink.net/~abbyb. 1996. Poetry, fiction, photos, non-fiction. "Burning Bush is a press committed to social and economic justice, highlighting the experiences of women, people of color, lesbians and gays, and Jews in a variety of genres available to a wide audience" avg. press run 1M. Pub'd 1 title 1998; expects 1 title 1999, 2 titles 2000. 4 titles listed in the *Small Press Record of Books in Print* (28th Edition, 1999-00). avg. price, paper: $13.95. Discounts: 40% to bookstores, 20% to libraries, 50% for 100 or more copies, 10% to contributors. 160pp; 5½×8½, 6×9; digital prepress. Reporting time: 2 months. Simultaneous submissions accepted: no. Payment: negotiable. Copyrights for author. WPLP.

BURNING CAR, Jesus Pinata Press, Jerry Rummonds, PO Box 26692, San Francisco, CA 94126, E-mail elfool@aol.com. 1995. Poetry, fiction, articles, art, photos, cartoons, interviews, satire, criticism, reviews, letters, long-poems, collages, plays, non-fiction. "Fiction & non-fiction: 5,000 words max. Art: Black & white only, camera ready. Recent contributors include: Joe R. Lansdale, Michael Burkand, Dean Young, Mark Cox" circ. 1M. 2/yr. Pub'd 1 issue 1998; expects 2 issues 1999, 2 issues 2000. sub. price: $12.50; per copy: $7.50; sample: $7.50. 100pp; 6×9; of. Reporting time: 60 days. Simultaneous submissions accepted: yes. Publishes 15-20% of manuscripts submitted. Payment: yes, a little more than beer money. Copyrighted, reverts to author. Pub's reviews: 1 in 1998. §We read everything. Ads: $275/$150/$75 1/4 page. NABE.

Burning Cities Press (see also VIETNAM GENERATION: A Journal of Recent History and Contemporary Issues), Kali Tal, PO Box 13746, Tucson, AZ 85732-3746. 1989. Poetry, fiction, non-fiction. "We publish poetry, fiction and non-fiction manuscripts related to the Vietnam war, Vietnam Generation and the 1960s. We are particularly interested in manuscripts by Vietnam veterans, especially vets who belong to minority groups. We also reprint classic literature about the Vietnam War. Recent publications: *Just for Laughs*, poetry by W.D. Ehrhart; *The Land of a Million Elephants*, Asa Baber; *Australia R & R; Australia's War in Viet Nam; Interrogations*, poetry by Leroy Quintana." avg. press run 1M. Pub'd 4-6 titles 1998; expects 6 titles 1999, 10 titles 2000. 10 titles listed in the *Small Press Record of Books in Print* (28th Edition, 1999-00). avg. price, paper: $15. Discounts: 20% for orders of over 10 books. 200pp; 6×9; of. Reporting time: 6-8 weeks. Payment: 10% of printed copies given to author, royalties only on 2nd printing. Does not copyright for author. SSP.

THE BURNING CLOUD REVIEW, Eric Andrew Rhinerson, 225 15th Avenue N, St. Cloud, MN 56303-4531, E-mail ERhinerson@aol.com. 1996. Poetry, fiction. "3-7 poems any length. 1-2 fiction pieces under 2,000 words. Seeks intelligent, well crafted works." circ. 150. 6/yr. Pub'd 6 issues 1998; expects 6 issues 1999, 6 issues 2000. sub. price: $18; per copy: $4.25 ppd.; sample: same. Discounts: write for details. 36pp; 8½×5½; mi. Reporting time: 4 months. We accept simultaneous submissions if notified. Publishes 1% of manuscripts submitted. Payment: 1 copy. Copyrighted, reverts to author. Pub's reviews: 2 in 1998. §Single poet collections. Ads: write for details.

Burning Deck Press (see also SERIE D'ECRITURE), Keith Waldrop, Rosmarie Waldrop, 71 Elmgrove Avenue, Providence, RI 02906. 1962. Poetry. "Order from Small Press Distribution." avg. press run 500-1M. Pub'd 5 titles 1998; expects 3 titles 1999, 2 titles 2000. 101 titles listed in the *Small Press Record of Books in Print* (28th Edition, 1999-00). avg. price, cloth: $20; paper: $10; other: LP Chapbook $10. Discounts: see schedule of Small Press Distribution. 40-80pp; 6×9; lp for chapbooks, offset for full books. Reporting time: 2 months. Payment: 10% of edition (copies). Does not copyright for author.

Burning Llama Press (see also THE IMPLODING TIE-DYED TOUPEE; THE NEW SOUTHERN SURREALIST REVIEW), Keith Higginbotham, Tracey R. Combs, 82 Ridge Lake Drive, Columbia, SC 29209-4213. 1993. Poetry, collages. "Biased toward avant-garde, surreal, experimental, and visual. We are especially interested in collages. Our magazines feature writers such as John M. Bennett, Jake Berry, Frank Cotolo, Sheila E. Murphy, Greg Evason, Richard Kostelanetz, John Elsberg. Prospective authors should query with 5-10 samples of work, along with brief biography and publication credits." avg. press run varies. Expects 1 title 1999, 2-3 titles 2000. Discounts: none as of yet. 1-40pp; size varies; †varies. Reporting time: immediate on queries, longer on mss. Publishes 1% of manuscripts submitted. Payment: varies. Copyrights for author.

BUS TOURS MAGAZINE, Transportation Trails, Larry Plachno, Editor; Joe Plachno, Assistant Editor, 9698 West Judson Road, Polo, IL 61064, 815-946-2341. 1979. "This magazine is a cross between a trade magazine and a travel magazine. It circulates primarily to individuals and companies in the US and Canada that plan motocoach tours. Most editorial 'scouts' potential destinations for motorcoach tour planners." circ. 8M. 6/yr. Pub'd 6 issues 1998; expects 6 issues 1999, 6 issues 2000. sub. price: $10; per copy: $2; sample: n/c (additional for foreign). Back issues: $2. Discounts: none. 56pp; 8½×11; of. Reporting time: 30 days. Payment: as agreed. Not copyrighted. Ads: $1,325/$695.

BUSINESPIRIT JOURNAL, The Message Company, James Berry, Lin Reams, Richard Auer, 4 Camino

Azul, Santa Fe, NM 87505, 505-474-7604; Fax 505-471-2584; message@nets.com; www.bizspirit.com. 1997. Articles, photos, cartoons, interviews, criticism, reviews, letters, news items, non-fiction. "We cover business topics: vision, values, leadership, spirituality in business, sustainability, integrity, etc." circ. 4M. 12/yr. Pub'd 4 issues 1998; expects 6 issues 1999, 12 issues 2000. sub. price: free online; sample: free. Back issues: $5. 16pp; 8½×11; online. Reporting time: 30 days. Simultaneous submissions accepted: yes. Publishes 70% of manuscripts submitted. Payment: none. Copyrighted, reverts to author. Pub's reviews: 10 in 1998. §Business topics. Ads: call for rates. SPAN, PMA.

Business By Phone, Inc., 13254 Stevens Street, Omaha, NE 68137, 402-895-9399, fax 402-896-3353. 2 titles listed in the *Small Press Record of Books in Print* (28th Edition, 1999-00).

BUSINESS CONSUMER GUIDE, Mie-Yun Lee, 125 Walnut Street, Watertown, MA 02172, Subscriptions 800-938-0088, editorial 617-924-0044; e-mail brg@buyrszone.com. 1992. Articles, criticism, news items. "National publication established to evaluate office products and services for the business community. Reports review the purchasing process and recommend brands and models offering the best combination of price, quality and service." 6/yr. Pub'd 10 issues 1998; expects 6 issues 1999, 6 issues 2000. sub. price: $159; per copy: $25; sample: free. Back issues: single copy is $15 for subscribers. 50pp; 8½×11; of. Copyrighted, does not revert to author. Ads: none. PMA.

Business Resource Publishing, Mark B. Gray, PO Box 526193-DS, Salt Lake City, UT 84152, Fax 801-273-0167. 1997. Non-fiction. "Contracted with business professionals. Not seeking new authors. We produce custom newsletters and work with a small group of authors in similar areas of business and sales." Pub'd 1 title 1998; expects 2 titles 1999, 5 titles 2000. 1 title listed in the *Small Press Record of Books in Print* (28th Edition, 1999-00). avg. price, paper: $14.95. Discounts: 20/65. 5½×8½; litho. Payment: by contract. Copyrights for author. Publishers Marketing Association.

Business Smarts, Inc., Dan Modderick, 3505 E. Royalton Road, #150, Broadview Heights, OH 44147, 808-639-4656, fax 216-526-1203, 102563134@compuserve.com. 1990. Fiction, non-fiction. "All material must encourage a renewal to traditional American values. These include: individualism, pride, patriotism, respect, integrity and honor." avg. press run varies. Expects 1 title 1999, 2 titles 2000. 1 title listed in the *Small Press Record of Books in Print* (28th Edition, 1999-00). avg. price, paper: $12.95. Discounts: varies. 5⅜×8½. Reporting time: 3 months. Simultaneous submissions accepted: yes. Payment: varies. Copyrights for author. PMA.

Butterfield Press, Keith Connes, 283 Carlo Drive, Goleta, CA 93117-2046, 805-964-8627. 1984. "Now seeking nonfiction material on topical sujects in addition to aviation fields." avg. press run 3M. Pub'd 1 title 1998; expects 2 titles 1999, 2 titles 2000. 3 titles listed in the *Small Press Record of Books in Print* (28th Edition, 1999-00). avg. price, paper: $18. Discounts: 1-4 25%, 5-24 40%, 25-49 43%, 50-99 46%, 100+ 50%. 300pp; 6×9. Reporting time: varies. Simultaneous submissions accepted: yes. Payment: 10% royalty. Copyrights for author.

THE BUTTERFLY CHRONICLES, A Literary Journal from the Butterfly Tree, In Between Books, Karla Andersdatter, Editor, PO Box 790, Sausalito, CA 94966, 415-383-8447. 1997. "We (actually I) are looking for poems, good jokes, lovely thoughts, and fiction or non-fiction which can be finished on one page, or continued in the next issue. Our (actually my) editorial policy is as follows: If I like it well enough to type it up, I'll print it. If not, I'll send it back. If you wish to use your nom de plume, it's fine with me, as long as you tell me what your real name is, and I will never reveal it (except under torture). I can tell you what I dont like, so you won't bother to send it: sick language unless it is in character, sick characters, unless they are funny and original, pornography, romance novels, and anal minds, unless in character with a character who later endears me with his uniqueness or her particular story. All material becomes copyrighted in the name of the author(s). Include SASE if you want submission returned." 6/yr. Pub'd 6 issues 1998; expects 6 issues 1999, 6 issues 2000. sub. price: $25; per copy: $5. 8pp; 8½×11. Publishes 50-70% of manuscripts submitted. Ads: $75 6X/$50 6X/$37.50 6X 1/4 page/free to all subscribers 2" ad space.

BUTTERFLY GARDENERS' QUARTERLY, Claire Hagen Dole, PO Box 30931, Seattle, WA 98103, 206-783-3924. 1994. "I do not seek freelance contributors." circ. 1M. 4/yr. Pub'd 4 issues 1998; expects 4 issues 1999, 4 issues 2000. sub. price: $8; sample: $1. Back issues: $2. Discounts: negotiable. 4pp; 11×17; newspaper. Copyrighted, reverts to author. Pub's reviews: 8 in 1998. §Gardening, natural history.

BUTTON, Sally Cragin, PO Box 26, Lunenburg, MA 01462, E-mail buttonx26@aol.com. 1993. Poetry, fiction, art, cartoons, music, parts-of-novels. "We like wit, brevity, the cleverly-conceived of essay/recipe, how-to's that people would actually do (a big nein to silver-polishing and deck-building), poetry that might have a rhyme scheme, but isn't a rhyme scheme that's abab or aabb or anything really obvious, true moments carefully preserved. We don't like whining, cheap sentimentality, egregious profanity, vampires, neuroses for neuroses' sake, most song lyrics passing as poetry, anything overlong, overdull or overreaching. Recent contributors include: William Corbett, Birdsongs of the Mesozoic, actress Shannen Dougherty, Sven Birkerts,

96

Stephen Sandys, They Might Be Giants, Brendan Galvin.'' circ. 1M. 2/yr. Pub'd 2 issues 1998; expects 2 issues 1999. sub. price: $5; per copy: $2; sample: $2. Back issues: same. Discounts: none - our prices are low, low, low; stores are 60/40 split. 28pp; 4×5; †of. Reporting time: 9 weeks. Simultaneous submissions accepted: no. Publishes 5-10% of manuscripts submitted. Payment: subscriptions for writer + 2 friends + $10. Copyrighted, reverts to author. Pub's reviews: 2 in 1998. §Fiction, fashion, poetry, manuals. Ads: $100/$60/$25 minimum.

BUZZARD, Stephen Beaupre, PO Box 576, Hudson, MA 01749, 508-568-0793. 1983. Cartoons. ''We are a comics anthology in the tradition of *Raw* and *Weirdo*.'' circ. 2M. 3/yr. Pub'd 3 issues 1998; expects 3 issues 1999, 3 issues 2000. sub. price: $12; per copy: $4; sample: $4. Back issues: $4. Discounts: stores 40%, distributors 60% (no returns). 36pp; 8⅜×10¾; of. Reporting time: 4 weeks. Simultaneous submissions accepted: yes. Publishes 10% of manuscripts submitted. Payment: $25/comic page. Copyrighted, reverts to author. Ads: $150/$80.

BWALO: A Forum for Social Development, S. Khaila, C. Hickey, M. Tsoka, PO Box 278, Zomba, Malawi, 265-522-916; Fax 265-522-578. 1997. ''*Bwalo* is an annual independent expression of considered yet controversial opinion on a broad range of human and social development issues. Articles are informed by professional interdisciplinary research, and where not, by judicious speculation and advocacy on the basis of fundamentals.'' circ. 500. 1/yr. Pub'd 1 issue 1998; expects 1 issue 1999, 1 issue 2000. sub. price: US$25; per copy: US$25. 164pp; 210×297mm; of. Reporting time: 3-4 months. Simultaneous submissions accepted: no. Payment: none. Copyrighted. Ads: negotiable.

BYLINE, Marcia Preston, Editor & Publisher; Sandra Soli, Poetry Editor, PO Box 130596, Edmond, OK 73013, 405-348-5591. 1981. Poetry, fiction, articles, interviews, non-fiction. circ. 3.5M. 11/yr. Pub'd 11 issues 1998; expects 11 issues 1999, 11 issues 2000. sub. price: $22; per copy: $4; sample: $4. Back issues: $4 (incl. p/h). 36pp; 8½×11; of. Reporting time: 6-8 weeks. Simultaneous submissions accepted: yes. Publishes 1% of manuscripts submitted. Payment: varies by department, approx. 5¢/word. Copyrighted, reverts to author. Ads: $300/$150/$1 word.

Byte Masters International, Bernard H. Browne, Jr., PO Box 3805, Clearwater, FL 33767, 727-593-3717; FAX 727-593-3605; Email BernieByte@aol.com. 1991. Non-fiction. avg. press run 5M. Pub'd 1 title 1998; expects 1 title 1999, 1 title 2000. 3 titles listed in the *Small Press Record of Books in Print* (28th Edition, 1999-00). avg. price, paper: $19.95. Discounts: trade, bulk and other. 500pp; 7¼×9¼; of. Simultaneous submissions accepted: no. Copyrights for author. Florida Publisher's Association (FPA), PO Box 430, Highland City, FL 33846-0430; National Association of Independent Publishers (NAIP).

By-The-Book Publishing, David Epp, Rhonda Lund, 2337 Roscomare Road, #2-218, Bel Air, CA 90077, 310-440-4809. 1986. Articles, news items, non-fiction. ''Must be well written, journalistic style, news, factual, and conservative viewpoint - health and religion. *Fax on Demand* for information 310-440-4859'' avg. press run 3-5M. Expects 2 titles 1999, 3 titles 2000. 1 title listed in the *Small Press Record of Books in Print* (28th Edition, 1999-00). avg. price, cloth: $26; paper: $18; other: $7 mini size. Discounts: 45% to retailer, 50-60% wholesale, library/school 25%, 20-50% for bulk. 250pp. Reporting time: 3-5 months. Payment: 5%.

C

C & T Publishing, Barbara Kuhn, Editor in Chief; Diane Pedersen, Production Director; Liz Aneloski, Editorial Scheduling Director, 1651 Challenge Drive, Concord, CA 94520-5206, 925-677-0377. 1983. Non-fiction. ''We publish how-to quilting books, most of which are softcover with an average of 44 pages. Most books are all color'' avg. press run 15M. Pub'd 13 titles 1998; expects 15 titles 1999, 18 titles 2000. 79 titles listed in the *Small Press Record of Books in Print* (28th Edition, 1999-00). avg. price, cloth: $34.95; paper: $22.95. Discounts: Total retail amount: $50 or less 20%, $51-300 40%, $301-600 45%, $601+ 50%. 112pp; 8½×11. Reporting time: 8 weeks. Simultaneous submissions accepted: yes. Publishes 10% of manuscripts submitted. Payment: 8% retail price, monthly. Copyrights for author. Northern Calif. Booksellers Assn. (NCBA), Publishers Marketing Association, Bookbuilders West.

C.S.P. WORLD NEWS, Edition Stencil, Guy F. Claude Hamel, Editor & Publisher, c/o Guy F. Claude Hamel, 1307 Bethamy Lane, Gloucester, Ont. K1J 8P3, Canada, 613-741-8675. 1962. Poetry, satire, reviews. ''Recent Contributors: Hundreds of poets. Best Book of the Year (1977) Contest: Wm. B. Eerdmans, publishers; Poet of the Year (1977) Teresa Peirinska, televised series *Poetry Ottawa* by Hamel Theatre Productions. C.S.P. World News Poet of the Year: 1975, Alexandre L. Amprimoz, Winnipeg, Man.; 1976, Lynda Rostad, Toronto, Ont.; 1977, Teresinka Pereira, Boulder, CO.; 1978, Sheila Sommer, Toronto, Ont.; 1979, Marilyn Carmen, Mechanicsburg, PA.; Book of the Year Contest Winners: 1977, Wm. B. Eerdmans,

Grand Rapids, MI.; 1978, Rasheed Mohammed, New York, NY. *Poet of the Year* 1980: Bluebell S. Phillips, Dorval, P. Que. Carl T. Endemann, *1981* Calistoga California. Eda Howink, *1982* St. Louis, Missouri. Ken Stone, *1983* Portland, NY, George Orwell (1984)-posthumously. Pope John Paul II (1985). Robert L.J. Zenik, Sudbury, Ontario (1986), Ida Fawers, Haifa, Israel (1987), Elsie M. Brien, Montreal (1988), H.H. Claudius I, universal patriarch of the Old Catholic churches, Ottawa (1989)'' circ. 2M. 12/yr. Pub'd 12 issues 1998; expects 12 issues 1999, 12 issues 2000. 1 title listed in the *Small Press Record of Books in Print* (28th Edition, 1999-00). sub. price: $15. 20pp; 8×14; †of. Reporting time: 2 weeks. Copyrighted. Pub's reviews: 312 in 1998. §All types books, LP's and tapes. Ads: not available. International News Registry.

Caddo Gap Press (see also EDUCATIONAL FOUNDATIONS; EDUCATIONAL LEADERSHIP & ADMINISTRATION; JOURNAL OF THOUGHT; MULTICULTURAL EDUCATION; NOTES AND ABSTRACTS IN AMERICAN AND INTERNATIONAL EDUCATION; SUMMER ACADEME: A Journal of Higher Education; TEACHER EDUCATION QUARTERLY; VITAE SCHOLASTICAE: The Journal of Educational Biography), Alan H. Jones, Publisher, 3145 Geary Boulevard, Suite 275, San Francisco, CA 94118, 415-922-1911. 1989. "Caddo Gap Press is primarily a publisher of educational books and journals, with particular interest in the fields of teacher education and the social foundations of education." avg. press run 2M. Pub'd 5 titles 1998; expects 5 titles 1999, 5 titles 2000. 33 titles listed in the *Small Press Record of Books in Print* (28th Edition, 1999-00). avg. price, paper: $19.95. Discounts: 20% to educational institutions; 40% to bookstores; other discounts based on quantity. 150pp; size varies; of. Reporting time: 1 month. Simultaneous submissions accepted: yes. Publishes 10% of manuscripts submitted. Payment: to be arranged, usually 10%. Copyrights for author. EDPRESS.

CADENCE: THE REVIEW OF JAZZ & BLUES: CREATIVE IMPROVISED MUSIC, Robert D. Rusch, Cadence Building, Redwood, NY 13679, 315-287-2852; Fax 315-287-2860. 1975. Articles, photos, interviews, criticism, reviews, music, news items. "We run about 24 interviews or oral histories a year. Have covered more than 35,000 record releases (reviews) since 1976. We also publish a yearly index." circ. 10M+. 12/yr. Pub'd 12 issues 1998; expects 12 issues 1999, 12 issues 2000. sub. price: $30; per copy: $3; sample: $3. Back issues: $5 each. Discounts: Distributors only 5-10 $2.09; 11-15 $1.92; 16-20 $1.86; 20-49 $1.74; 50 $1.61; 100 or more $1.50. 128pp; 5½×8½; of. Reporting time: 2 weeks. Payment: varies. Not copyrighted. Pub's reviews: 1.6M in 1998. §Jazz, blues and related areas. Ads: $200/$125/75¢.

Cadmus Editions, Jeffrey Miller, PO Box 126, Belvedere Tiburon, CA 94920-0126. 1979. Poetry, fiction, music, parts-of-novels. "Do not send unsolicited mss." avg. press run 2M. Pub'd 3 titles 1998; expects 3 titles 1999, 3 titles 2000. 21 titles listed in the *Small Press Record of Books in Print* (28th Edition, 1999-00). avg. price, paper: $15; other: $40 signed/ltd. Discounts: 1-4 20%, 5-24 42%, 25-49 44%, 50-99 46%, 100+ 50%; additional 2% on prepaid orders; always add estimated shipping; net 30 days. 150pp; 6×9; lp, of. Reporting time: 30 days. Simultaneous submissions accepted: no. Publishes .001% of manuscripts submitted. Payment: negotiable; paid annually. Copyrights for author.

CAESURA, Lequita Vance-Watkins, San Jose Museum of Art, 110 S. Market, San Jose, CA 95113, FAX 408-624-7432. 1976. Poetry, interviews, criticism, reviews. "No unsolicited material accepted. Contributors: Elisabeth Marshall, Anna Mortal, Maude Meehan. Publishes poetry of the very highest quality; reviews and interviews of poetry and literature that is important to the literary life of today." circ. 900. 4/yr. Pub'd 4 issues 1998; expects 4 issues 1999, 4 issues 2000. sub. price: $12; per copy: $3; sample: $2. Back issues: $2 when available. Discounts: negotiated on individual basis. 24pp; 8½×11; printed. Reporting time: 3 weeks. Simultaneous submissions accepted: no. Payment: 3 copies of publication. Rights revert to author on publication. Pub's reviews: 4 in 1998. §Poetry/literature.

THE CAFE REVIEW, Steve Luttrell, Publishing Editor; Wayne Atherton, Editor; Alex Fisher, Editor, c/o Yes Books, 20 Danforth Street, Portland, ME 04101, e-mail seegerlab@aol.com, www.thecapereview.com. 1989. Poetry, art, photos, interviews, criticism. "Send $1 handling fee per submission and SASE" circ. 300-500. 4/yr. Pub'd 4 issues 1998; expects 4 issues 1999, 4 issues 2000. sub. price: $24; per copy: $6 newsstand; sample: $6 includes p/h. Back issues: $5 includes p/h. Discounts: none. 60-70pp; 5½×8½; †off. Reporting time: 2-4 months. Simultaneous submissions accepted: no. Publishes 10% of manuscripts submitted. Payment: 1 copy. Copyrighted, reverts to author. Pub's reviews: a few in 1998. §Small press poetry and visual art (photography). Poets House, MWPA.

●**Cage Consulting, Inc.,** Cheryl Cage, Pam Ryan, Marcia Konegni, 13275 E. Fremont Place, Ste. 315, Englewood, CO 80112, 888-899-CAGE; Fax 303-799-1998; www.cageconsulting.com. Non-fiction. Pub'd 2 titles 1998; expects 2 titles 1999, 2 titles 2000. 5 titles listed in the *Small Press Record of Books in Print* (28th Edition, 1999-00). avg. price, paper: $16.95. Discounts: standard. 120pp; 5½×9.

CAK Publishing, PO Box 953, Broomfield, CO 80038, 303-469-3133; glen-hanket@stortek.com. 1 title listed in the *Small Press Record of Books in Print* (28th Edition, 1999-00).

CALAPOOYA, Jodi Varon, David Axelrod, School of Arts and Sciences, Eastern Oregon University, La

Grande, OR 97850, 541-962-3633. 1981. Poetry, fiction, articles, photos, interviews, reviews, non-fiction. "Sponsor of annual $1000 Carolyn Kizer Poetry Awards. Recent contributors: Robert Bly, Joseph Bruchac, Octavio Paz, Marge Piercy, William Stafford, Ursula K. LeGuin, Patricia Goedicke, Colleen J. McElroy, David Wagoner, Warren French, David Ray." circ. 1.5M. 1/yr. Pub'd 1 issue 1998; expects 1 issue 1999, 1 issue 2000. sub. price: $5; per copy: $5; sample: $5. Back issues: $5. 44pp; 11¼×17½; laser/offset. Reporting time: 4-8 weeks. Simultaneous submissions accepted: no. Publishes 3% of manuscripts submitted. Payment: copies. Copyrighted, reverts to author. Pub's reviews: 9 in 1998. §Poetry. Ads: gratis ads.

Caliban Press, Mark McMurray, Patricia McMurray, 14 Jay Steet, Canton, NY 13617-1414, 315-386-4923. 1985. Fiction, letters, plays. avg. press run 100-250. Pub'd 3 titles 1998; expects 2 titles 1999, 2 titles 2000. 8 titles listed in the *Small Press Record of Books in Print* (28th Edition, 1999-00). avg. price, other: $50-200. Discounts: 30-40%. 10-70pp; size varies; †lp. Reporting time: 6-9 months. Payment: 5-10% part cash, part copies. Copyrights for author.

Calibre Press, Inc., Charles Remsberg, President; Dennis Anderson, Vice President, 666 Dundee Road, Suite 1607, Northbrook, IL 60062-2760, 708-498-5680, fax 708-498-6869, e-mail calivrepr@aol.com. 1979. Non-fiction. avg. press run 5M. Pub'd 1 title 1998; expects 3 titles 1999, 2 titles 2000. 7 titles listed in the *Small Press Record of Books in Print* (28th Edition, 1999-00). avg. price, cloth: varies, over $25; paper: $14. Discounts: varies with book. 400pp; size varies; perfect bound. Reporting time: 1 month. Payment: varies with project, author. Nat'l Assn. of Independent Publishers; Nat'l Direct Mail Order Assn.; Assn. Midwest Publishers; Publishers Marketing Assn.

CALIFORNIA EXPLORER, Kay Graves, 1135 Terminal Way, Suite 209, Reno, NV 89502, E-mail 2xp1@metro.net. 1978. Articles, photos. "Stories on hiking to 1,500 words." circ. 5M. 6/yr. Pub'd 6 issues 1998; expects 6 issues 1999, 6 issues 2000. sub. price: $28.50; per copy: $5.95; sample: free. Back issues: $4. Discounts: 20%. 12pp; 8½×11; of. Reporting time: 2 months. Simultaneous submissions accepted: no. Publishes 90% of manuscripts submitted. Payment: $75-$175. Copyrighted, reverts to author. Ads: $350 1/3 page/$275 1/4 page.

CALIFORNIA LAW REVIEW, University of California Press, Univ. of California at Berkeley Students of Boalt Hall School of Law, University of California Press, 2120 Berkeley Way, Berkeley, CA 94720, 510-643-7154. 1912. Articles, reviews, non-fiction. "Editorial address: California Law Review, 592 Simon Hall, University of CA, Berkeley, CA 94720. Copyrighted by California Law Review, Inc." circ. 1.8M. 6/yr. Pub'd 6 issues 1998; expects 6 issues 1999, 6 issues 2000. sub. price: $40 (+ $20 foreign postage); per copy: $11; sample: free. Back issues: $15. Discounts: foreign subs. agent 10%, one-time order 10+ 30%, standing orders (bookstores): 1-99 40%, 100+ 50%. 300pp; 7×10; of. Reporting time: 1-2 months. Payment: none. Copyrighted, does not revert to author. Pub's reviews: 6 in 1998. Ads: $275/$200.

CALIFORNIA STATE POETRY QUARTERLY (CQ), Rotating Chief Editors, CSPS/CQ, PO Box 7126, Orange, CA 92863, 805-543-8255. 1973. Poetry. "Deadlines: 1/31, 4/30, 7/31, 10/31, all mss. considered at one time, after qtr. deadline" circ. 700. 4/yr. Pub'd 4 issues 1998; expects 4 issues 1999, 4 issues 2000. sub. price: $12 (4 issues); per copy: $4; sample: $4. Back issues: $2-3. Discounts: 50/50. 64pp; 5½×8½; of. Reporting time: 1-4 months. Simultaneous submissions accepted: yes. Publishes 2-5% of manuscripts submitted. Payment: 1 copy of magazine. Copyrighted, reverts to author.

CALLALOO, Charles H. Rowell, Editor, 2715 North Charles Street, Baltimore, MD 21218-4319, 301-338-6901. 1979. Poetry, fiction, articles, art, photos, interviews, criticism, reviews, parts-of-novels, long-poems, plays, news items, non-fiction. "Short one act plays. Journal is sponsored by The University of Virginia, but published by The John Hopkins University Press" circ. 1M. 4/yr. Pub'd 4 issues 1998; expects 4 issues 1999, 4 issues 2000. 4 titles listed in the *Small Press Record of Books in Print* (28th Edition, 1999-00). sub. price: $16; per copy: $8; sample: $8. Back issues: $8, $10 for photo copies of issues out-of-stock. 280pp; 6⅞×10; of. Reporting time: 3 months. Payment: 2 copies. Copyrighted, reverts to author. Pub's reviews: 5 in 1998. §Creative literature by Black writers and critical works about Black literature. Ads: $300/$150. CLMP.

Callawind Publications Inc., 2083 Hempstead Turnpike, Suite 355, East Meadow, NY 11554-1730, 514-685-9109, Fax: 514-685-7055, E-mail info@callawind.com. 1995. Non-fiction. "Accepting queries from authors, regarding cookbooks." Pub'd 2 titles 1998; expects 2 titles 1999, 2 titles 2000. 6 titles listed in the *Small Press Record of Books in Print* (28th Edition, 1999-00). avg. price, paper: $17. 250pp; size varies; of. SPAN, PMA.

CALLBOARD, Belinda Taylor, 657 Mission Street #402, San Francisco, CA 94105, 415-957-1557. 1976. Articles, photos, interviews. "Open to short articles (750-2,000 words) related to theatre. No reviews. Essays, features, interviews with theatre personalities. Emphasis on San Francisco Bay Area." circ. 10M. 12/yr. Pub'd 12 issues 1998; expects 12 issues 1999, 12 issues 2000. sub. price: $40; per copy: $5.25; sample: $6. Back issues: $6. 40pp; 8×10; of. Reporting time: 2 months. Simultaneous submissions accepted: no. Most ms. are assigned, unsolicited ms. are occasionally published. Payment: $150/article; $100/cover art. Copyrighted, reverts to author. Pub's reviews: 10 in 1998. §Theatre: production, administration, playwrighting, plays, acting, how to articles, etc. Ads: $720/$445/$6 line classified. Theatre Bay Area.

Calliope Press, Eileen Wyman, PO Box 2408, New York, NY 10108-2408, 212-564-5068. Non-fiction. avg. press run 2 M. 1 title listed in the *Small Press Record of Books in Print* (28th Edition, 1999-00). avg. price, cloth: $22.95.

CALLIOPE: World History for Young People, Cobblestone Publishing, Inc., Rosalie F. Baker, Editor, 7 School Street, Peterborough, NH 03458, 603-924-7209. 1990. Poetry, articles, art, photos, reviews, non-fiction. "The magazine will accept freelance articles related to themes covered. Write for guidelines." circ. 10.5M. 9/yr. Pub'd 5 issues 1998; expects 5 issues 1999, 9 issues 2000. sub. price: $26.95 + $8 foreign, Canadian subs add 7% GST; per copy: $4.50; sample: $4.50. Back issues: $4.50. Discounts: 15% for sub. agencies, bulk rate 3+ $15.95/year sub. each. 48pp; 7×9; of. Reporting time: queries sent well in advance of deadline may not be answered for several months. Go-aheads usually sent 5 months prior to publication date. Payment: on publication. Copyrighted, *Calliope* buys all rights. Pub's reviews: 39 in 1998. §Books pertaining to the issues' themes, and written for children ages 8-14. Ads: none. Classroom Publishers Assoc./EdPress.

●**Calypso Publications**, Susan Richardson, 5810 Osage Avenue #205, Cheyenne, WY 82009. 1989. Poetry, fiction, articles, criticism, reviews, parts-of-novels, long-poems, non-fiction. "Originally produced annual literary magazine but have shifted to occasional chapbooks and anthologies. Most recently put out *Dreaming in Chinese* by Tam Neville and *First Light: Poems, Stories & Essays of the Winter Holiday Season*. Contributors: Cherry, Nordhaus, William Dickey, Kloefkorn, Crooker, Ritchie, Lifshin, Cooperman, Glancy, Shelnutt, Milenski and many others. Do not accept submissions open-endedly. Please watch writers magazines for guidelines to upcoming projects." avg. press run 250-500. Pub'd 1 title 1998. 2 titles listed in the *Small Press Record of Books in Print* (28th Edition, 1999-00). avg. price, paper: $8. 80pp; 6×9; of. Reporting time: 3 months. Accepting simultaneous submissions depends on project. Publishes 5% of manuscripts submitted. Payment: copies. Copyrights for author.

CALYX: A Journal of Art and Literature by Women, Calyx Books, Margarita Donnelly, Director; Beverly McFarland, Senior Editor; Micki Reaman, Managing Editor, PO Box B, Corvallis, OR 97339, 541-753-9384. 1976. Poetry, fiction, art, photos, criticism, reviews, parts-of-novels, long-poems, non-fiction, interviews. "*Calyx* is the Major West Coast publication of its kind. Recently reviewed as 'undoubtedly...one of the best literary mags in the U.S.'—New Pages Press. (128 pages). Manuscript queries and submissions must be accompanied by a SASE. The journal is no longer open to submissions all year round. Open reading dates for journal submissions are usually 3/1-4/15 and 10/1-11/15, in 1998 and 1999 we will only be open for journal submissions 10/1-11/15 not in the spring. Be sure to include brief bio statement with all submissions. Please be aware we occasionally close for one submission period each year." circ. 3.5M. 2/yr. Pub'd 2 issues 1998; expects 2 issues 1999, 2 issues 2000. sub. price: $19.50 indiv., institutional & library $25 (subs are 3 issues but take 18 months to complete); per copy: $9.50 + $2 p/h; sample: $9.50 + $2 p/h. Back issues: Spring 86 & 87 double issues, $15.95 + $3 postage (supply limited). Discounts: trade 40%. 128pp; 6×8; of. Reporting time: 6-8 months. Simultaneous submissions accepted: yes. Publishes 5% of manuscripts submitted. Payment: in copies and subscriptions. Copyrighted, reverts to author. Pub's reviews: 20 in 1998. §Feminist criticism, reviews of books & films by women, autobiographies, literary or art books by woman. Ads: $550/$285/75¢. CLMP, WCA, COWO.

Calyx Books (see also CALYX: A Journal of Art and Literature by Women), Margarita Donnelly, Director; Micki Reaman, Managing Editor, PO Box B, Corvallis, OR 97339. 1986. Poetry, fiction, art, non-fiction. avg. press run 5M. Pub'd 3 titles 1998; expects 3 titles 1999, 3 titles 2000. 26 titles listed in the *Small Press Record of Books in Print* (28th Edition, 1999-00). avg. price, cloth: $23; paper: $12. Discounts: 20% 1-4 books, 40% 5-49, 43% 50-99, 45% 100+. 170pp; 6×9; of. Reporting time: 1 year. Publishes 1% of manuscripts submitted. Payment: individually contracted. Copyrights for author. CLMP, COWO.

CAMBRENSIS: THE SHORT STORY QUARTERLY MAGAZINE OF WALES, Arthur Smith, 41 Heol Fach, Cornelly, Bridgend, Mid-Glamorgan, CF334LN South Wales, United Kingdom, 01656-741-994. 1987. Fiction, art, cartoons. "Uses only short stories, under 2,500 words, by writers born or resident in Wales; no poetry used; cartoons/black & white artwork sharp-contrast used." circ. 500. 4/yr. Pub'd 4 issues 1998; expects 4 issues 1999, 4 issues 2000. sub. price: £6; per copy: £1.50; sample: IRC. Back issues: £1.25. Discounts: 20%. 72pp; size A4; of. Reporting time: by return. Payment: none at present time, copies given. Copyrighted, reverts to author. Pub's reviews: 30 in 1998. §literary. Ads: £40/£20/£10 1/4 page. ALP, BAPA, Welsh Academy.

Cambric Press dba Emerald House, Joel Rudinger, Publisher, 208 Ohio Street, Huron, OH 44839-1514, 419-433-5660; 419-929-4203. 1975. Poetry, fiction, non-fiction. "Self-publishing, book manufacturer." avg. press run 500-1M+. Pub'd 2 titles 1998; expects 2 titles 1999. 2 titles listed in the *Small Press Record of Books in Print* (28th Edition, 1999-00). avg. price, paper: $10. Discounts: 40% on bulk orders over 10; 30% under 10. 72+pp; 5½×8½, 4¼×6⅞; of. Reporting time: 4 weeks. Publishes 50% of manuscripts submitted. Payment:

100% to author first printing. Copyrights for author.

Camel Press (see also DUST (From the Ego Trip)), James Hedges, Editor, Box 212, Needmore, PA 17238, 717-573-4526. 1984. Poetry, fiction, articles, non-fiction. "Autobiography, 1-2.5M words." avg. press run 700. Exects 1 title 1999, 1 title 2000. 10 titles listed in the *Small Press Record of Books in Print* (28th Edition, 1999-00). avg. price, paper: $2. Discounts: on request. 20pp; 4¼×5¾; †1p. Reporting time: 2 weeks. Simultaneous submissions accepted: yes. Publishes 5% of manuscripts submitted. Payment: 50 free copies, page charges may be requested from author. Copyrights for author. NAPA, APA.

CAMERA OBSCURA: Feminism, Culture, and Media Studies, Phillip Harper, Constance Penley, Sasha Torres, Sharon Willis, Lynne Joyrich, Patty White, c/o Film Studies Program, University of California, Santa Barbara, CA 93106, 805-893-7069; fax 805-893-8630; e-Mail cameraob@humanitas.ucsb.edu. 1976. Articles, photos, interviews, criticism, reviews, letters. "Indiana University Press." circ. 3M. 3/yr. Pub'd 2 issues 1998; expects 3 issues 1999, 3 issues 2000. sub. price: individual $27, institution $50 (foreign postage: Canada & Mexico + $10, outside North America + $10), $20 airmail outside USA; per copy: varies; sample: $7.50. Back issues: No. 3/4 $9.50 individual, $15 institutions; No. 8/9/10 $11.50 individual, $17 institutions; No. 13/14 $9.50, $15 institutions. Discounts: 40% bookstores. 150-180pp; 5½×8½; of. Reporting time: 3-5 months. Payment: none. Copyrighted, does not revert to author. Ads: check with IUP, Journals Division, Indiana Univ. Press, 601 N. Morton Street, Bloomington, IN 47404.

Camino Bay Books, Ann Adams, PO Box 2487, Glen Rose, TX 76043-2487, 254-897-3016. 1997. Non-fiction. avg. press run 5M. Expects 1-2 titles 1999, 1-2 titles 2000. 1 title listed in the *Small Press Record of Books in Print* (28th Edition, 1999-00). avg. price, paper: $15. Discounts: 1-4 books 20%, 5-99 40%, 100+ 50%. 250pp; 5½×8½; of. Reporting time: 6 weeks. Payment: negotiable. Does not copyright for author. PMA, SPAN.

CANADIAN CHILDREN'S LITERATURE, Canadian Children's Press, Mary Rubio, Daniel Chouinard, Marie Davis, SLAPSIE, University of Guelph, Guelph, Ontario N1G 2W1, Canada, 519-824-4120 ext. 3189; FAX 519-837-1315; E-mail ccl@uoguelph.ca; http://www.uoguelph.ca/englit/ccl/. 1975. Articles, interviews, criticism, reviews. "*CCL* publishes critical articles and in-depth reviews of Canadian books and other media for children and adolescents." circ. 1.5M. 4/yr. Pub'd 4 issues 1998; expects 4 issues 1999, 4 issues 2000. sub. price: $29 indiv., schools; $36 Postsecondary & other instit. (plus $10 postage outside Canada); per copy: $10; sample: $10 (plus $2.50 postage outside Canada). Back issues: prices available upon request. Discounts: none. 96pp; 6×9; of. Reporting time: 2 months. Simultaneous submissions accepted: no. Payment: none. Copyrighted. Pub's reviews: 110 in 1998. §Canadian books, plays and videos written for children and adolescents. Ads: $250/$150/$85 1/4 page/$295 OBC/$275 IFC/20% discount for 4 consecutive ads. CMPA.

Canadian Children's Press (see also CANADIAN CHILDREN'S LITERATURE), SLAPSIE, University of Guelph, Guelph, Ontario N1G 2W1, Canada. 1975. Articles, interviews, criticism, reviews. 5 titles listed in the *Small Press Record of Books in Print* (28th Edition, 1999-00). avg. price, paper: $10.

Canadian Committee on Labour History (see also LABOUR/LE TRAVAIL), Bryan D. Palmer, History/CCLH, FM 2005, Memorial University, St. John's, NF A1C 5S7, Canada, 709-737-2144. 1971. Non-fiction. "Recent contributors: Jack Scott, Max Swerdlow, Gregory S. Kealey, Reg Whitaker, Lefty Morgan, Gail Pool" avg. press run 750. Pub'd 1 title 1998; expects 2 titles 1999, 2 titles 2000. 7 titles listed in the *Small Press Record of Books in Print* (28th Edition, 1999-00). avg. price, paper: $24.95. Discounts: 20% on orders over 5. 150-300pp; 6×9; of. Reporting time: 6 months. Simultaneous submissions accepted: no. Publishes 25% of manuscripts submitted. Payment: variable. Does not copyright for author. ACP, APA, CALJ, CMPA.

Canadian Educators' Press, S. Deonarine, 100 City Centre Drive, PO Box 2094, Mississauga, ON L5B 3C6, Canada, 905-826-0578. 1995. Non-fiction. avg. press run 800. Pub'd 2 titles 1998; expects 5 titles 1999, 5 titles 2000. 7 titles listed in the *Small Press Record of Books in Print* (28th Edition, 1999-00). avg. price, paper: $33. Discounts: depends on quantity. 250pp; 6×9; lp. Reporting time: 3 months. Simultaneous submissions accepted: no. Payment: 10% net sale. Copyrights for author.

CANADIAN JOURNAL OF APPLIED PHYSIOLOGY (CJAP), Human Kinetics Pub. Inc., Phillip Gardiner, Ph.D, Francois Perronet, Ph.D, PO Box 5076, Champaign, IL 61825-5076, 217-351-5076. 1976. Articles, reviews. "Articles concerning physiology applied to physical activity, fitness and health." circ. 1M. 6/yr. Pub'd 6 issues 1998; expects 6 issues 1999, 6 issues 2000. sub. price: $50 individual, $120 institution, $32 student; per copy: $9 indiv, $21 instit; sample: free. Back issues: $9 indiv, $21 instit. Discounts: 5% agency. 104pp; 6×9; of. Reporting time: 2 months. Payment: none. Copyrighted, does not revert to author. Pub's reviews: 36 in 1998. §Exercise physiology, applied physiology. Ads: $300/$200. Midwest Book Publishers Association, American Booksellers Association.

CANADIAN JOURNAL OF PHILOSOPHY, University of Calgary Press, T. Hurka, Board Coordinator,

University of Calgary Press, Univ. of Calgary, 2500 University Dr. N.W., Calgary, Alberta T2N 1N4, Canada, 403-220-7578; FAX 403-282-0085, e-mail 75003@aoss.ucalgary.ca. 1970. Articles, reviews. "Publishes philosophical work of high quality in any field of philosophy" circ. 1.1M. 4+. Pub'd 4 issues 1998; expects 4 issues 1999, 4 issues 2000. sub. price: $25 indiv., $50 instit., $15 student, add GST in Canada; other: $25US indiv., $50US instit., $15US student; per copy: $9 + GST. Canada, $9US. Back issues: back volume of 4 issues $30 + G.S.T. Canada, $30 US. 150pp; 6×9; of. Reporting time: 2 months. Payment: none. Copyrighted, does not revert to author. Pub's reviews: 8 in 1998. §Philosophy. write for info. BPAA, ACUP, CALJ.

CANADIAN JOURNAL OF PROGRAM EVALUATION/LA REVUE CANADIENNE D'EVALUA- TION DE PROGRAMME, University of Calgary Press, R. Segsworth, Editor, University of Calgary Press, Univ. of Calgary, 2500 University Dr. N.W., Calgary, Alberta T2N 1N4, Canada, 403-220-7578; FAX 403-282-0085; powell@ucalgary.ca. 1986. Articles, criticism, reviews. "Publishes all aspects of the theory and practice of evaluation including research and practice notes. Subscriptions: Canadian Evaluation Society, 582 Somerset Street West, Ottawa, Ont K1R 5K2" circ. 1.45M. 2/yr. Pub'd 3 issues 1998; expects 2 issues 1999, 2 issues 2000. sub. price: Indiv. $75. Canada; outside Canada price in U.S. dollars; libraries $95 Canada, outside Canada price in US dollars, $35 full time students; per copy: $11 + G.S.T. Canada. 200pp; 6×9; of. Reporting time: 3 months. Payment: none. Copyrighted, does not revert to author. Pub's reviews: 3 in 1998. §Evaluation of programs in all fields. write for info. BPAA, ACUP, CALJ.

Canadian Library Association (see also FELICITER), Elizabeth Morton, Editor, 200 Elgin Street, Suite 602, Ottawa, Ontario K2P 1L5, Canada, 613-232-9625 X322. 1946. Non-fiction. avg. press run 250. Pub'd 2 titles 1998; expects 2 titles 1999, 2 titles 2000. 7 titles listed in the *Small Press Record of Books in Print* (28th Edition, 1999-00). avg. price, paper: $20Cdn. Discounts: bulk only. 200pp; size varies; of. Reporting time: 6 months. Simultaneous submissions accepted: no. Publishes 75% of manuscripts submitted. Payment: 10%. Copyright varies.

CANADIAN LITERATURE, E.M. Kroller, University of British Columbia, 2029 West Mall, Vancouver, B.C. V6T 1Z2, Canada, 604-822-2780. 1959. Poetry, criticism, reviews. "Criticism and reviews focus primarily on Canadian writers." circ. 1.5M. 4/yr. Pub'd 3 issues 1998; expects 4 issues 1999, 4 issues 2000. sub. price: indiv. $40, institution $55 plus postage (outside Canada); per copy: $15; sample: $15-25. Back issues: may be obtained from Journal. Discounts: $2 for agencies. 176pp; 6×9; lp. Reporting time: 1 month. Publishes 10% of manuscripts submitted. Payment: $5 a page. Copyrighted. Pub's reviews: 83 in 1998. §Canadian writers and writing. Ads: $300/$400/$250.

CANADIAN MONEYSAVER, Dale L. Ennis, Box 370, Bath, Ontario K0H 1G0, Canada. 1981. Articles, interviews, non-fiction. circ. 32.8M. 11/yr. Pub'd 11 issues 1998; expects 11 issues 1999, 11 issues 2000. sub. price: Canada $19.95, Elsewhere: U.S. $36; per copy: $3; sample: $3. Back issues: $3. Discounts: up to 50% off for large orders (100+). 36pp; 8×10½; web. Reporting time: 3 weeks. Publishes 90% of manuscripts submitted. Payment: none. Copyrighted, reverts to author. Pub's reviews: 25-30 in 1998. §Finance, money management, investment, consumer savings. NIL.

CANADIAN PUBLIC POLICY- Analyse de Politiques, Charles Beach, Editor, School of Policy Studies, Queens University, Kingston, Ontario K7L 3N6, Canada, 613-533-6644; fax 613-533-6960. 1975. Articles, reviews. "A journal for the discussion of social and economic policy in Canada." circ. 1.3K. 4/yr. Pub'd 6 issues 1998; expects 5 issues 1999, 5 issues 2000. sub. price: $53 indiv., $43 members, $25 students, $80 institutions, includes GST in Canada, Rates in U.S. money outside of Canada.; per copy: $15; sample: free. Back issues: available on request. Discounts: can be arranged. 144pp; 7×10; of. Reporting time: 35 days. Simultaneous submissions accepted: no. Publishes 24% of manuscripts submitted. Payment: none. Copyrighted, does not revert to author. Pub's reviews: 37 in 1998. §Public policy. Ads: $295/$195/on request.

CANADIAN REVIEW OF AMERICAN STUDIES, University of Calgary Press, Stephen J. Randall, Editor; Christine Bold, Editor, University of Calgary Press, 2500 University Drive NW, Calgary, Alberta T2N 1N4, Canada, 403-220-7578, fax 403-282-0085, 75003@aoss.ucalgary.ca. 1970. Articles, criticism, reviews, non-fiction. "The journal publishes essays, review essays and shorter reviews whose purpose is the multi- and inter-disciplinary analysis and understanding of the culture, both past and present, of the United States - and of the relations between the cultures of the U.S. and Canada." circ. 475. 3/yr. Pub'd 3 issues 1998; expects 3 issues 1999, 3 issues 2000. sub. price: $40, institutions $50, student $20, in Canada add GST, outside Canada price in US dollars; per copy: $13 CDA, $10, US outside Canada + postage and handling. 230pp; 6×9; of. Reporting time: 2 months. Copyrighted, does not revert to author. Pub's reviews: 29 in 1998. §All fields of American studies. Ads: write for information. BPAA, ACUP, CALJ.

CANADIAN WOMAN STUDIES/les cahiers de la femme, Luciana Ricciutelli, 212 Founders College, York Univ., 4700 Keele Street, New York, Ontario M3J 1P3, Canada, 416-736-5356; fax 416-736-5765; e-mail cwscf@yorku.ca. 1978. Poetry, fiction, articles, art, photos, cartoons, interviews, reviews, non-fiction. "We do not publish sexist, racist, homophobic, or any other discriminatory material. Length of articles: 10 typed, double-spaced pages." circ. 3M. 4/yr. Pub'd 4 issues 1998; expects 4 issues 1999, 4 issues 2000. sub. price: $32.10 indiv. (Cdn), $42.80 instit. (Cdn), $42 indiv. outside Canada, $52 instit. outside Canada; per copy: $8; sample: $5. Back issues: usually $3 per issue unless out of print. 156pp; 8½x11; of. Reporting time: 3 months. Simultaneous submissions accepted: no. Publishes 10% of manuscripts submitted. Payment: complimentary copy of issue in which work appears. Copyrighted, reverts to author. Pub's reviews: 50 in 1998. §Women's studies, women's issues, feminism, literary works and criticism. Ads: $350/$200/$125 1/3 page/$75 1/6 page. CMPA.

CANDELABRUM POETRY MAGAZINE, Red Candle Press, M.L. McCarthy, 9 Milner Road, Wisbech PE13 2LR, England, tel: 01945 581067. 1970. Poetry. "Is one of the magazines providing an outlet for poets using traditional verse-forms. It is also open to good-quality free-verse. We believe that the purpose of poetry is to delight and exalt through the pattern of language & the beauty of imagery. As the English language is heavily accented, English poetry has developed as metrical verse; the disciplines imposed by the structure & accentuation of the language must be observed for sustained artistry to be possible in poetry. Authors keep the copyright. We send the usual British copyright copies." circ. 1M. 2/yr. Pub'd 2 issues 1998; expects 2 issues 1999, 2 issues 2000. sub. price: One year subs. no longer accepted. Subscription to volume 9 (1997-1998) £11.50 or $22 (bills only, don't accept checks); per copy: £2, US$4 in bills. Back issues: Back numbers before 1990, as available: £1 (US $2 in bills). 40pp; 8½x5½; of. Reporting time: 1-2 months. Simultaneous submissions accepted: no. Publishes 5% of manuscripts submitted. Payment: 1 free copy, no cash payment. Copyrighted, reverts to author. Ads: £20/£10 (US $40/$20 in bills).

Candlestick Publishing, David Alter, PO Box 39241, San Antonio, TX 78218-1241. 1988. Non-fiction. Pub'd 2 titles 1998; expects 2 titles 1999, 1 title 2000. 4 titles listed in the *Small Press Record of Books in Print* (28th Edition, 1999-00). avg. price, cloth: $30; paper: $10. Discounts: library editions 30%, paperbacks 50%. Simultaneous submissions accepted: yes. Publishes 3% of manuscripts submitted.

Canterbury Press, John Hurley, 5540 Vista Del Amigo, Anaheim, CA 92807, Fax 714-998-1929. 1979. Poetry, fiction, photos, plays, non-fiction. "We usually commission the work" avg. press run 300-1M. Pub'd 3 titles 1998; expects 3 titles 1999, 5 titles 2000. 1 title listed in the *Small Press Record of Books in Print* (28th Edition, 1999-00). avg. price, paper: $3-20. Discounts: 20% to wholesalers, libraries, bookstores. Pages vary; size varies. Reporting time: 8 weeks. Simultaneous submissions accepted: yes. Payment: standard 10% 1st 5000. Copyrights for author.

CAPE FEAR JOURNAL, Averasboro Press, John Hairr, Joey Powell, PO Box 482, Erwin, NC 28339, E-mail jpowell@nceye.net. 1992. Articles, news items, non-fiction. "Covers history and lore pertaining to the Cape Fear River Valley in North Carolina." circ. 30M. 12/yr. Expects 12 issues 1999, 12 issues 2000. sub. price: $15. Back issues: $3. 24pp; 8½x11; of. Reporting time: 3 months. Simultaneous submissions accepted: no. Publishes 25% of manuscripts submitted. Payment: negotiable. Copyrighted, reverts to author. Pub's reviews: 12 in 1998. §History, geography and travel relating to North Carolina. Ads: $100/$65/$35 1/4 page.

THE CAPE ROCK, Harvey Hecht, English Dept, Southeast Missouri State, Cape Girardeau, MO 63701, 314-651-2500. 1964. Poetry, photos. "Our criterion for selection is the quality of the work, not the bibliography of the author. We consider poems of almost any style on almost any subject and favor poems under 75 lines. Each submission should have the author's name and complete address, preferably in the upper right hand corner. A self-addressed, stamped envelope (SASE) is required to guarantee return. We do not read submissions April through August. We feature the work of a single photographer in each issue; submit 20-25 thematically organized 5 x 7 B & W glossies. Submissions, subscriptions, and queries should be addressed to *The Cape Rock*, Harvey Hecht, Editor." circ. 600. 2/yr. Pub'd 2 issues 1998; expects 2 issues 1999. sub. price: $7; per copy: $5; sample: $3. Back issues: $3. Discounts: 25% off on orders of 20 or more (our cost plus postage). 64pp; 5½x8¾; †of. Reporting time: 2-4 months. Payment: $100 for photography, $200 for best poem, in each issue; other payment in copies. Copyrighted, rights to contents released to authors and artists upon request, subject only to their giving credit to *The Cape Rock* whenever and wherever else the work is placed. *The Cape Rock* retains reprint rights. No ads. CLMP, NESPA.

THE CAPILANO REVIEW, Ryan Knighton, Editor; Carol Hamshaw, Managing Editor, 2055 Purcell Way, North Vancouver, B.C. V7J 3H5, Canada, 604-984-1712. 1972. Poetry, fiction, art, photos, interviews, parts-of-novels, long-poems, collages, plays. circ. 800. 3/yr. Pub'd 3 issues 1998; expects 3 issues 1999, 3 issues 2000. sub. price: $25; per copy: $9; sample: $9. Back issues: $7 for regular back issues, $10-20 for special issues. Discounts: 25% off. 120pp; 6x9; of. Reporting time: 4 months. Simultaneous submissions accepted: no. Payment: $50-200 maximum. Copyrighted, reverts to author. Ads: $150/$75/$50 1/3 page. CMPA.

Capital Communications, Todd L. Mayo, 10611 Fruitville Road, Sarasota, FL 34240, 941-342-9088; capital@investors.org. 1993. Articles, interviews, reviews, news items, non-fiction. avg. press run 7M. Pub'd 1 title 1998; expects 2 titles 1999, 2-4 titles 2000. 4 titles listed in the *Small Press Record of Books in Print* (28th

Edition, 1999-00). avg. price, cloth: $18; paper: $12.95. Discounts: 40-50%. 500pp; 6×9; of. PMA.

CAPITALISM, NATURE, SOCIALISM, Guilford Publications, Inc., James O'Connor, 72 Spring Street, New York, NY 10012, 212-431-9800. 1990. Poetry, articles, interviews, reviews, news items, non-fiction. *"CNS* publishes regular reports on red-green politics around the world, as well as articles, interviews, conference and research reports, debates, and reviews that locate their subject on the interface between history and nature, or society and environment. Publication of Italian and Spanish editions of *CNS*, the appearance of a new sibling journal in France, and a rich network of relations with like-minded magazines in the Third World testify to *CNS*'s widespread influence and appeal." circ. 1.5M. 4/yr. Pub'd 4 issues 1998; expects 4 issues 1999, 4 issues 2000. sub. price: $25.50 indiv., $90 instit.; per copy: $7.50; sample: free. Back issues: $10. Discounts: 5% subscription agents, 50% distributors. 144pp; 6×9; of. Payment: none. Copyrighted, does not revert to author. Pub's reviews. §Environmentalism. Ads: $212/$133/none.

A Cappela Publishing, PO Box 3691, Sarasota, FL 34230, 941-351-2050; fax 941-362-3481. 1996. Fiction, non-fiction. avg. press run 3M. Expects 1 title 1999, 1 title 2000. 1 title listed in the *Small Press Record of Books in Print* (28th Edition, 1999-00). avg. price, paper: $19.95. Discounts: 5-9 copies = 30%, 10-199 48%, 200+ 50%. 208pp; 5½×8½; of. Reporting time: 3 months. Simultaneous submissions accepted: no. Publishes 20% of manuscripts submitted. Payment: 6% on sales, bi-yearly. Copyrights for author.

A Cappella Books, Linda Matthews, 814 N. Franklin Avenue, Chicago, IL 60610, 312-337-0747; FAX 312-337-5985. 1990. Art, interviews, music, plays, non-fiction. avg. press run 3M. Pub'd 7 titles 1998; expects 6 titles 1999, 8 titles 2000. 29 titles listed in the *Small Press Record of Books in Print* (28th Edition, 1999-00). avg. price, cloth: $29.95; paper: $14.95. Discounts: 1-4 20%, 5-9 40%, 10-49 42%, 50-99 43%, 100-499 44%, 500-999 45%, 1000-1999 46%, 2000-4999 47%, 5000+ 48%. 196pp; 6×9; of. Reporting time: 6 months. Simultaneous submissions accepted: yes. Publishes 5% of manuscripts submitted. Payment: negotiated. Copyrights for author.

Capra Press, Noel Young, PO Box 2068, Santa Barbara, CA 93120, 805-966-4590; FAX 805-965-8020. 1969. Fiction, interviews, satire, criticism, letters, non-fiction. "A general trade press with a focus on the West. *No poetry."* avg. press run 5M. Pub'd 8 titles 1998. 22 titles listed in the *Small Press Record of Books in Print* (28th Edition, 1999-00). avg. price, cloth: $19; paper: $10.95. Discounts: distributors 1-4 20%, 5-249 45%, 250-499 46%. 96-300pp; 5½×8½, 6×9, 7⅜×9¼; of. Reporting time: 6 weeks average. Simultaneous submissions accepted: no. Publishes 10% of manuscripts submitted. Payment: royalties negotiated. Copyright in author's name. AAP, ABA.

Cardinal Press, Inc., Mary McAnally, 76 N Yorktown, Tulsa, OK 74110, 918-583-3651. 1978. Poetry, art, photos, long-poems. "Bias for Midwest/Southwest poets, for women, prisoners, minorities. Will not publish any racist or sexist material. Socialist/humanist orientation, no unsolicited manuscripts." avg. press run 300. Expects 1 title 1999, 2-4 titles 2000. 5 titles listed in the *Small Press Record of Books in Print* (28th Edition, 1999-00). avg. price, paper: $5. Discounts: 3-5 15%; 6-10 25%; 11+ 35%. 48pp; 6×9; of. Reporting time: 1-3 months. Simultaneous submissions accepted: no. Payment: copies. Does not copyright for author.

Cardoza Publishing, Rose Swann, 132 Hastings Street, Brooklyn, NY 11235, 718-743-5229; FAX 718-743-8284. Non-fiction. avg. press run 15M. Pub'd 10 titles 1998; expects 10 titles 1999, 10 titles 2000. 1 title listed in the *Small Press Record of Books in Print* (28th Edition, 1999-00). avg. price, paper: $9.95. 160pp; 6×9. Reporting time: 3 months. Simultaneous submissions accepted: yes. Publishes 5% of manuscripts submitted.

Career Advancement Center, Inc., Arthur VanDam, PO Box 436, Woodmere, NY 11598, 516-374-1387, Fax: 516-374-1175, E-mail: caradvctr@aol.com. 1991. Non-fiction. "Personal Finance, Business and career development; mass market appeal; user-friendly." avg. press run 2M. Pub'd 1 title 1998; expects 3 titles 1999, 3 titles 2000. 6 titles listed in the *Small Press Record of Books in Print* (28th Edition, 1999-00). avg. price, paper: $15.50. Discounts: competitive. 100pp; 8½×11, 5½×8½; web press. Reporting time: 3 months. Simultaneous submissions accepted: yes. Publishes 5% of manuscripts submitted. Payment: 6-10% of retail price. Copyrights for author. ABA, PMA.

Career Publishing, Inc., PO Box 5486, Orange, CA 92613-5486, 714-771-5155; 800-854-4014; fax 714-532-0180. 1972. Non-fiction. "Truck driving course, for commercial driver license, guidance material, medical office management, career guidance, HyperCard, CDL manuals, desktop publishing, clinical Allied HealthCare course ware" avg. press run 5M-10M. Pub'd 8 titles 1998; expects 6 titles 1999, 10 titles 2000. 17 titles listed in the *Small Press Record of Books in Print* (28th Edition, 1999-00). avg. price, paper: $25; other: guidance booklets $2.50 each, pack of 20 for $37.50, no discount. Discounts: classroom 20% textbooks, guides no discount. 350-500pp; 8½×11; of. Reporting time: 1 month or longer. Payment: 10%. Does not copyright for author. ABA, PMA.

THE CARETAKER GAZETTE, Thea K. Dunn, P.O. Box 5887, Carefree, AZ 85377-5887, 480-488-1970.

1983. Articles, photos, cartoons, interviews, reviews, letters, news items, non-fiction. "Articles about property caretaking, homesteading, organic farming, RV living, caretaker profiles." circ. 5M. 6/yr. Pub'd 6 issues 1998; expects 6 issues 1999, 6 issues 2000. sub. price: $27; per copy: $6; sample: $6. Back issues: $6. Discounts: $19/year. 16pp; 8½×11; 1p. Reporting time: 1 month. Simultaneous submissions accepted: yes. Publishes 50% of manuscripts submitted. Payment: yes. Copyrighted, reverts to author. Pub's reviews: 6 in 1998. §Conservation, environment, property caretaking, RV living. Ads: 50¢ per word classifieds.

CARIBBEAN NEWSLETTER, Box 20392, Park West Station, New York, NY 10025. 1981. Articles, cartoons, news items. "Length of material: 8-14 pages" circ. 500. 4/yr. Pub'd 4 issues 1998; expects 4 issues 1999, 4 issues 2000. sub. price: $15, made out to 'Friends For Jamaica'; per copy: $2; sample: $2. 10pp; 8½×11; of. Not copyrighted. Pub's reviews: 3 in 1998. §Caribbean issues or biographies.

THE CARIBBEAN WRITER, Erika J. Waters, RR 2, Box 10,000, Univ of Virgin Islands, Kingshill, St. Croix, VI 00850, 340-692-4152; fax 340-692-4026; e-mail ewaters@uvi.edu or qmars@uvi.edu. 1987. Poetry, fiction, interviews, reviews, parts-of-novels, plays, non-fiction. "*The Caribbean Writer* is an international literary magazine with a Caribbean focus. The Caribbean should be central to the work or the work should reflect a Caribbean heritage, experience or perspective." circ. 1M. 1/yr. Pub'd 1 issue 1998; expects 1 issue 1999, 1 issue 2000. sub. price: $10 + $1.50 postage; per copy: same; sample: $5 + $1.50 p/h. Back issues: same. Discounts: 12-24 copies 30%. 288pp; 6×9; of. Reporting time: authors of accepted mss are notified in December/January. Simultaneous submissions accepted: yes. Publishes 20% of manuscripts submitted. Payment: 2 copies. Copyrighted, reverts to author. Pub's reviews: 30 in 1998. §Caribbean fiction, poetry, or related reference materials. Ads: $250/$150/$100 1/4 page. Index of American Periodical Verse.

The Carnation Press, H.K. Henisch, B.A. Henisch, PO Box 101, State College, PA 16804, 814-238-3577. 1966. Plays, non-fiction. "1 facsimile reprint; 3 non-fiction; 1 play, 1 poetry. Among the contributors: Prof. Robert Lima, Dept. of Spanish, PSU; Prof. Robert Snetsinger, Dept. of Entymology, PSU." avg. press run 500-2.4M. Expects 1 title 2000. 4 titles listed in the *Small Press Record of Books in Print* (28th Edition, 1999-00). avg. price, cloth: $13; paper: $11. Discounts: 40% (10 copies or more); 30% (single copies). 150pp; 6×9, 5½×8½; of. Reporting time: 1 month. Simultaneous submissions accepted: no. Payment: no royalties to break even point; 25% of net receipts after that. Copyrights negotiable.

Carolina Academic Press, Keith Sipe, 700 Kent Street, Durham, NC 27701. 1976. "Legal, medical, and scholarly titles." avg. press run 1.5M. Pub'd 28 titles 1998; expects 30 titles 1999. avg. price, cloth: $39.95; paper: $20. Discounts: 33⅓%. 450pp; 6×9; of. Reporting time: 6 months. Payment: various. Copyrights for author.

THE CAROLINA QUARTERLY, Brian Carpenter, General Editor, CB# 3520 Greenlaw Hall, Univ of N. Carolina, Chapel Hill, NC 27599-3520, 919-962-0244; fax 919-962-3520. 1948. Poetry, fiction, art, photos, reviews, long-poems. "Looking for well-crafted poems and stories." circ. 1.1M. 3/yr. Pub'd 3 issues 1998; expects 3 issues 1999, 3 issues 2000. sub. price: $12 indiv., $15 instit.; per copy: $5; sample: $5 (postage paid). Back issues: $5. Discounts: 20% local stores, agent 10%. 88-100pp; 6×9; of. Reporting time: 2-4 months. Simultaneous submissions accepted: no. Publishes 1% of manuscripts submitted. Payment: 2 copies. Copyrighted, reverts to author. Pub's reviews: 8 in 1998. §Fiction, poetry, non-fiction. Ads: $80/$40. CLMP.

Carolina Wren Press/Lollipop Power Books, Elaine Goolsby, Editor-in-Chief; Shelley Day, Director; Mary Moore, Fiction Editor; Richard Morrison, Poetry Editor; Ruth Smullin, Children's Editor; Jacqueline K Ogburn, President; Claudia Kimbrough, Vice-president; Martha Scotford, Secretary and Art Director; Ruth Smullin, Lollipop Children's Editor, 120 Morris Street, Durham, NC 27701, 919-560-2738. 1976. Poetry, fiction, letters, long-poems, plays, non-fiction. "Our goal is to publish high-quality, non-stereotyping literature for adults and children that is both intellectually and artistically challenging. Our publishing priorities are: works which are written by women and/or minorities, works which deal with issues of concern to those same groups, works which are innovative." avg. press run 2.5M. Expects 4 titles 1999, 3 titles 2000. 28 titles listed in the *Small Press Record of Books in Print* (28th Edition, 1999-00). avg. price, paper: $9.95. Discounts: 40% to bookstores after 5 copies, (1-4 20%). 150pp; 6×9; of. Reporting time: 2-4 months. Payment: 10% of printrun. Copyrights for author. North Carolina Writers Network, Council of Literary Magazines and Presses.

Carousel Press, Carole T. Meyers, Editor & Publisher; Gene Howard Meyers, Sales Manager, PO Box 6038, Berkeley, CA 94706-0038, 510-527-5849; info@carousel-press.com; www.carousel-press.com. 1976. Non-fiction. "We are interested in family-oriented travel guides and related books as well asgeneral round-up travel guides. 200-300 pages. And we distribute family-oriented travel guides and travel game books from other publishers through our Internet catalog subsidary: *The Family Travel Guides Catalogue*." avg. press run 5-7M. Pub'd 1 title 1998; expects 1 title 1999, 1 title 2000. 6 titles listed in the *Small Press Record of Books in Print* (28th Edition, 1999-00). avg. price, paper: $17.95. Discounts: trade, bulk, jobber 40% 5-12 books; 41% 13-24; 42% 25-49; 43% 50-99; library 10% prepaid; STOP orders 20% disc. + $3.50 shipping prepaid. 300pp; 6×9; of, web. Reporting time: 4 weeks, include return postage. Simultaneous submissions accepted: no. Publishes 1% of manuscripts submitted. Payment: royalties. Copyrights for author. Northern California Book Publicists' Association, PMA, SPAN, BAIPA.

Carpe Diem Publishing (see also THIRST (CYBERTHIRST)), William A. Conner, Jessica E. Griffin, 1705 E. 17th Street, #400, The Dalles, OR 97058, 503-296-1552, waconner@aol.com. 1993. Fiction. avg. press run 3M-10M. Expects 1 title 1999, 6 titles 2000. avg. price, paper: $15. of. Reporting time: 3 months to 1 year. Simultaneous submissions accepted: yes. Payment: negotiable, upon acceptance. Copyrights for author. PMA.

Carpenter Press, Bob Fox, Publisher & Editor, PO Box 14387, Columbus, OH 43214. 1973. Poetry, fiction, art, photos. "Full-length fiction and poetry, chapbooks. Publish traditional as well as experimental fiction and poetry. Full-length fiction by Hugh Fox, Jerry Bumpus, and Curt Johnson; poetry by Steve Kowit and David Shevin. Tenth anniversary first novel competition winner, Jane Piirto's *The Three-Week Trance Diet*, published in 1985. Not considering new manuscripts." avg. press run 500-1.5M. 12 titles listed in the *Small Press Record of Books in Print* (28th Edition, 1999-00). avg. price, paper: $12.50; other: $3 chapbooks. Discounts: trade. Chapbooks 32pp, full-length poetry 96pp, full-length fictions 144pp; 6×9; of, lp. Reporting time: several months. Payment: by contract. Copyrights for author. AWP.

Carrefour Press, Michael P. Harris, Karl Orend, Saddle Fold, Hawkins Lane, Rainow, Macclesfield, Cheshire, England. 1929. Poetry, fiction, articles, interviews, criticism, letters, non-fiction. "Only surviving expatrist publishing house from Paris of the 1920s. Founded by Michael Fraenkel and now revived in assocation with Alyscamps Press of Paris. Authors include Fraenkel, Henry Miller, Walter Lowenfels, Gordon Harris, etc. New publishing program includes a bibliograpy of Carrefour Press, *The Genesis of the Tropic of Cancer*, and a renewed program of reprints and new literary work. Published in English, French and Italian. Additional address: 35 Rue de l'esperunce, 75013 Paris, France." avg. press run 500-1M. Pub'd 3 titles 1998; expects 5 titles 1999, 6 titles 2000. 4 titles listed in the *Small Press Record of Books in Print* (28th Edition, 1999-00). avg. price, cloth: $15; paper: $10. Discounts: 25-40% depending on quantity. 80-500pp; size varies; of, lp. Reporting time: 2 months. Payment: twice yearly. Copyrights for author.

Carrier Pigeon Press, Ramon Sender Barayon, PO Box 460141, San Francisco, CA 94146-0141, 415-821-2090. 1992. Non-fiction. "Books about intentional communities, religious sects, experimental social groups, memoirs of members and ex-members of such groups." avg. press run 600. Expects 4 titles 1999, 4 titles 2000. 5 titles listed in the *Small Press Record of Books in Print* (28th Edition, 1999-00). avg. price, paper: $17. Discounts: 40% trade or jobber. 350pp; 5½×8½; of, laserprinter. Reporting time: 6 weeks. Simultaneous submissions accepted: no. Publishes 1% of manuscripts submitted. Payment: 10-12%.

Carson Street Publishing Inc., Thomas Shaw, Publisher; Anita Klemke, Editor; Gayle Pyle, Editor, 205 East John Street, Carson City, NV 89701, 702-882-1528. 1992. Fiction, non-fiction. "Send query with SASE first; will do book packaging" avg. press run 2M. Pub'd 1 title 1998; expects 3 titles 1999, 3 titles 2000. 2 titles listed in the *Small Press Record of Books in Print* (28th Edition, 1999-00). avg. price, paper: $13.62. Discounts: bulk. 214pp. Reporting time: 1 month. Payment: depends. Copyrights for author. RMBPA, PMA.

Cartoon Books, PO Box 16973, Columbus, OH 43216, 614-224-4487, fax 614-224-4488. 1 title listed in the *Small Press Record of Books in Print* (28th Edition, 1999-00).

Cassandra Press, Inc., Gurudas, PO Box 150868, San Rafael, CA 94915, 415-382-8507. 1985. Non-fiction. "We publish New Age and metaphysical and political tyranny and holistic health books. I like to see the full manuscript before making a final decision, although this isn't necessarily true with an established author. We are now actively looking for new titles to expand next year. We are not accepting novels or children's books." avg. press run 8M-12M. Pub'd 3 titles 1998. 23 titles listed in the *Small Press Record of Books in Print* (28th Edition, 1999-00). avg. price, paper: $13.95. Discounts: 40% to stores, 1-3 copies 20%. 150-230pp; size varies. Reporting time: 1-2 months. Payment: varies. Copyrights for author if asked. PMA.

CASTAWAYS, Derek Davis, Ram Bhutani, Elaine Cox Clever, Dick Prior, Norma Zion, c/o Derek Davis, 3311 Baring Street, Philadelphia, PA 19104. 1996. Poetry, fiction, articles, art, photos, cartoons, satire, criticism, non-fiction. "Continues *Schuylkill Scallywag*. All but one of the editors are retired from various professions. We publish anything that takes our fancy. Always looking for new contributors." circ. 100+. 2/yr. Expects 3 issues 1999, 2 issues 2000. sub. price: $15 for 3 issues; per copy: $5; sample: $5. Back issues: none. Discounts: none. 60pp; 8½×11; xerox. Reporting time: 3 months. Payment: none. Copyrighted, reverts to author.

Castle Peak Editions, Mack Madison, Editor-in-Chief, PO Box 277, Murphy, OR 97533, 503-846-6152. 1971. Poetry, fiction, non-fiction. "We are a *book-length* publisher of poetry, fiction, criticism of a literary nature. We don not accept unsolicited manuscripts." avg. press run 500-1M. Pub'd 6 titles 1998; expects 8 titles 1999, 8 titles 2000. 2 titles listed in the *Small Press Record of Books in Print* (28th Edition, 1999-00). avg. price, cloth: $25; paper: $15; other: $15-$17 texts. Discounts: libraries 20%; 30 days; inquire for other schedules. 5×7, 7×9, 8×11; of, lp. Payment: 10%, publisher's net. Copyrights for author.

CATAMARAN SAILOR, Ram Press, Mary Wells, Rick White, PO Box 2060, Key Largo, FL 33037, 05-451-3287; FAX 305-453-0255; E-mail ram5@icanect.net; Website http://www.catsailor.com. 1995. Articles, photos, cartoons, interviews, satire, criticism, reviews, letters, news items, non-fiction. "40-60 pages - newsprint." circ. 20M. 10/yr. Pub'd 10 issues 1998; expects 10 issues 1999, 10 issues 2000. sub. price: $10; per copy: $1; sample: free. Back issues: $1. Discounts: none. 60pp; 8½×11. Reporting time: 60 days. Simultaneous submissions accepted: yes. Publishes 90% of manuscripts submitted. Payment: none. Copyrighted, reverts to author. Pub's reviews: 3 in 1998. §Catamaran, multihull sailing. Ads: $150$90/$75 1/3 page/$60 1/4 page/$25 business card/$10 classified.

Catamount Press (see also COTYLEDON), Georgette Perry, 2519 Roland Road SW, Huntsville, AL 35805, 205-536-9801. 1992. Poetry, art, long-poems. "Catamount Press is a small press publisher of poetry in anthologies and chapbooks. During 1995-96 we will concentrate on Cotyledon, miniature magazine. Send 3 unattached 33¢ stamps for a sample before submitting, or send no more than 6 poems for consideration. Recent contributors: Joe Salerno and Joy Dworkin (in *Witnessing Earth*, 76-page anthology of poems on nature and the sacred, $6 postpaid). Preferences: environmental awareness and concern. Short poems have a better chance. Sometimes use previously published. Give details in cover note and include SASE." avg. press run 200. Expects 2 titles 1999, 2 titles 2000. 3 titles listed in the *Small Press Record of Books in Print* (28th Edition, 1999-00). avg. price, paper: $3 chapbook, $5 anthology. Discounts: 40% for bookstores. Chapbooks 24pp, anthologies 75pp; 5½×8½; mi. Reporting time: 1 month. Simultaneous submissions accepted: yes. Publishes 5% of manuscripts submitted. Payment: for anthology contributors, payment in copies; for chapbook, 25 copies, extra payment if reprinted. Copyrights for author.

Catbird Press, Robert Wechsler, 16 Windsor Road, North Haven, CT 06473-3015, 203-230-2391; FAX 203-230-8029; e-Mail catbird@pipeline.com. 1987. Fiction, non-fiction. "Our specialties are upmarket prose humor. Central European literature in translation; literary American fiction." avg. press run 3M. Pub'd 4 titles 1998; expects 4 titles 1999, 4 titles 2000. 33 titles listed in the *Small Press Record of Books in Print* (28th Edition, 1999-00). avg. price, cloth: $21.95; paper: $13.95. Discounts: Independent Publishers Group schedule (our distributor). 250pp; of. Reporting time: 1 month. Publishes .03% of manuscripts submitted. Payment: up to 10% gross. Copyrights for author.

THE CATBIRD SEAT, Nancy Purnell, PO Box 506, Tolland, CT 06084-0506. 1997. Poetry, fiction, art. "Poetry: 30 lines or less preferred. Cat poem contest in each issue. Poetry and art about nature and the forces of the universe and humankind's ambivalent relationship with all of it. Connection—interconnection—disconnection. Recent contributers: Charlee Jacob, John Grey, Corrine Dewinter, Nancy Bennett, W. Gregory Stewart, Margaret B. Simon, and Cathy Buburuz. Fiction: prefer 500-1,500 words." circ. 150. 3/yr. Pub'd 3 issues 1998; expects 3 issues 1999, 3 issues 2000. sub. price: $13 US, $14 Canada, $18 overseas; per copy: $4.50 US & Canada, $6 overseas; sample: $4.50 US & Canada, $6 overseas. Back issues: none. 80pp; 5½×8½; †desktop publish—laser printer. Reporting time: 2-8 weeks. Simultaneous submissions accepted: no. Publishes 40% of manuscripts submitted. Payment: fiction and poetry: contributor's copy, art: stamp payment. Copyrighted, reverts to author. Pub's reviews: 20 in 1998. §Small press poetry chapbooks and magazines with similar subjects. Ads: ad exchange 3½ x 4"

CATECHUMENATE: A Journal of Christian Initiation, Liturgy Training Publications, Victoria M. Tufano, 1800 North Hermitage Avenue, Chicago, IL 60622, 312-486-8970. 1975. Articles, photos. "A magazine for all who are involved in the Christian initiation of adults, children and infants." circ. 6M. 6/yr. Pub'd 6 issues 1998; expects 6 issues 1999, 6 issues 2000. sub. price: $20; per copy: $3. Back issues: $3. Discounts: bulk 5+ $9/year. 48pp; 6×9; of. Reporting time: 6-8 weeks. Payment: yes. Copyrighted, does not revert to author. Catholic Book Publishers Assn.

Cattpigg Press, Cal Beauregard, Joedi Johnson, PO Box 565, Billings, MT 59103, 406-248-4875; e-mail starbase@mcn.net; website www.mcn.net/~starbase/dawn. 1994. Photos, non-fiction. avg. press run 1-2M. Pub'd 1 title 1998; expects 2 titles 1999, 1 title 2000. 1 title listed in the *Small Press Record of Books in Print* (28th Edition, 1999-00). avg. price, paper: $19.95. Discounts: 25% for 6+ copies. 100pp; 5½×8½; of. Reporting time: 3-5 weeks. Publishes 10% of manuscripts submitted. Copyrights for author.

Cave Books, Richard Watson, Editor, 756 Harvard Avenue, Saint Louis, MO 63130-3134, 314-862-7646. 1980. Fiction, non-fiction. "Only prose (adult non-fiction, fiction) concerning caves, karst, and speleology. Must be authentic, knowledgable, and realistic." avg. press run 1.5M. Pub'd 4 titles 1998; expects 4 titles 1999, 4 titles 2000. 5 titles listed in the *Small Press Record of Books in Print* (28th Edition, 1999-00). avg. price, cloth: $25; paper: $15. Discounts: 40% trade. 200pp; size varies; of, lp. Reporting time: 3 months. Simultaneous submissions accepted: yes. Publishes 5% of manuscripts submitted. Payment: 10%. Copyrights for author.

CAVEAT LECTOR, Christopher Bernard, Jamess Bybee, Andrew Towne, 400 Hyde Street, Apt. 606, San Francisco, CA 94109, 415-928-7431. 1989. Poetry, fiction, articles, art, photos, satire, criticism, music, collages, concrete art, non-fiction. "Poetry: 300 line max; Prose: 4,000 word max. We seek work of highly polished craft and strong emotional commitment, in classical and experimental forms. SASE's are a must. Recent contributors: Les Murray, R.T. Castleberry, Joanne Lowery, Paula Tetarumis, Jack Foley, and Deanne Bayer. We are not accepting new submissions until the fall of 1999." circ. 300. 2-3/yr. Pub'd 2 issues 1998; expects 2 issues 1999, 3 issues 2000. sub. price: $10; per copy: $2.50; sample: $3. 48pp; 4¼×11; mi. Reporting time: 1 month. Publishes 1% of manuscripts submitted. Payment: 5 copies. Copyrighted, reverts to author.

The Caxton Press, Wayne Cornell, General Editor, 312 Main Street, Caldwell, ID 83605, 208-459-7421. 1895. Non-fiction. "Books around 40,000 words up, unless largely photo" avg. press run 5M. Pub'd 5 titles 1998; expects 6 titles 1999, 6 titles 2000. 13 titles listed in the *Small Press Record of Books in Print* (28th Edition, 1999-00). avg. price, cloth: $24.95; paper: $14.95. Discounts: 1-9 40%, 10-24 42%, 25-49 43%, 50-99 44%, 100+ 45%, 1 title or assorted. 236pp; size varies; †of. Reporting time: 60-90 days. Simultaneous submissions accepted: yes. Payment: 10% of list. Copyrights for author. Rocky Mountain Book Publishers Assn., AAP, PMA.

Wm Caxton Ltd, Kubet Luchterhand, PO Box 220, Ellison Bay, WI 54210-0220, 414-854-2955. 1986. Poetry, criticism, letters, non-fiction. "We have 25 titles in print, 2 more in press now, and a total of 4 more in various stages of editing/typesetting/proofing. We publish book-length manuscripts, and reprint some books (9 of our titles so far); most titles so far are non-fiction, though we have published 4 books of poetry and are looking for more good poetry. We're especially interested in northern mid-West material of all kinds; we have two philosophy titles; one book about theatre technique (*Chamber Theatre* by Robert Breen); a reprint of a classic Wisconsin economic history book (*Empire In Pine* by Robert Fries). In a phrase, we will consider publishing any book that is actually *about* something." avg. press run 700-2M. Pub'd 2 titles 1998; expects 6 titles 1999, 6 titles 2000. 25 titles listed in the *Small Press Record of Books in Print* (28th Edition, 1999-00). avg. price, cloth: $25; paper: $12.95. Discounts: Trade bookstores 40%, returnable for credit only; textbooks 20% returnable for credit only for orders of five copies or more; returns must be in saleable condition, unmarked in any way, returned within 6 months of invoice date. 230pp; 5½×8½, 6×9, 8½×11; of. Reporting time: 1-6 months, depending upon season. Payment: varies widely; prefer subvention coupled with much higher than average royalty structure on first printing, guarantee to keep in print for 5 years, high but not as high as original on later printings. Copyrights for author.

CAYO, A MAGAZINE OF LIFE IN THE KEYS, Alyson Matley, P.O. Box 4516, Key West, FL 33040, 305-296-4286. 1995. Poetry, fiction, articles, photos, cartoons, interviews, reviews, non-fiction. circ. 1M. 4/yr. Pub'd 9 issues 1998; expects 4 issues 1999, 4 issues 2000. sub. price: $16; per copy: $3; sample: $4. Back issues: $4 when available. Discounts: Subscription $6/year to school libraries. 48pp; 8½×11; of. Reporting time: 4 months. Simultaneous submissions accepted: yes. Payment: fiction, nonfiction, and poetry copies; $10 for photos. Copyrighted, reverts to author. Pub's reviews: 1 in 1998. §Books, regional authors or topics, fiction and nonfiction. Ads: $800/$400/$200 1/4 page.

CBR (see also COMPUTER BOOK REVIEW), C. Char, 735 Ekekela Place, Honolulu, HI 96817, 808-595-7089. 1983.

CC. Marimbo Communications, Randy Fingland, PO Box 933, Berkeley, CA 94701-0933. 1996. Poetry. "CC. Marimbo is currently publishing minichaps which are 5½ X 4¼, handsewn, with a unique cover design/package. The object is to publish/promote underpublished writers in an accessible and artistic format." avg. press run 250+. Pub'd 1 title 1998; expects 2 titles 1999, 2 titles 2000. 4 titles listed in the *Small Press Record of Books in Print* (28th Edition, 1999-00). avg. price, paper: $4.95. Discounts: 1 copy, no discount; 2-5 copies, 30%; 6 or more copies, 40%. Wholesale terms available upon request. 40pp; 4¼×5½; of, photocopy. Reporting time: 4-6 weeks. Simultaneous submissions accepted as long as it's up front. Publishes 5% of manuscripts submitted. Payment: yes, generally 10% of cover price. Copyrights for author. East Bay Publishers Network.

CCM Publishing (see also CE CONNECTION COMMUNIQUE), PO Box 12624, Roanoke, VA 24027. 1986. avg. press run small. Pub'd 12 titles 1998; expects 12 titles 1999. avg. price, other: varies. Discounts: write for rates. Pages vary; 8½×11. Reporting time: 3 months. Simultaneous submissions accepted: yes. Publishes 25% of manuscripts submitted. Payment: write for information. Does not copyright for author.

CC600, Otto Katz, 7-9 Rantoul Street, Suite 206, Beverly, MA 01915, 978-927-5556; Fax 978-927-5558. 1997. Fiction, plays. "Query first" avg. press run 2M-4M. Expects 3 titles 1999, 3 titles 2000. 1 title listed in the *Small Press Record of Books in Print* (28th Edition, 1999-00). avg. price, cloth: $21.95. 320pp; 5½×8½. Reporting time: 3 months. Simultaneous submissions accepted: yes. Publishes 1% of manuscripts submitted. Payment: to be announced. Copyrights for author. SPAN, PMA.

CE CONNECTION COMMUNIQUE, CCM Publishing, Betty Robertson, PO Box 12624, Roanoke, VA 24027. 1996. Articles, reviews, news items. "Length of material: 100-600 words." 6/yr. Expects 6 issues 1999, 6 issues 2000. sub. price: $19.95; per copy: $3; sample: $3. 8pp; 8½×11. Reporting time: 3 months. Simultaneous submissions accepted: yes. Payment: varies. Copyrighted, reverts to author. Pub's reviews: 15 in

1998. §Christian education. Ads: write for rates.

Cedar Hill Publications (see also CEDAR HILL REVIEW), Gloria Doyle, Editor; Christopher Presfield, Editor, 3722 Highway 8 West, Mena, AR 71953, 501-394-7029. 1997. Poetry, art, photos. "Contributors: Leonard Cirino, John Taylor, Alan Britt, Michael McIrvin, Maggie Jaffe, William Doreski, James Doyle." avg. press run 300. Pub'd 6 titles 1998; expects 10 titles 1999, 10 titles 2000. 12 titles listed in the *Small Press Record of Books in Print* (28th Edition, 1999-00). avg. price, paper: $9. Discounts: to distributors. 80pp; 5½×8½; of, professionally printed with fully laminated covers. Reporting time: 60 days. Simultaneous submissions accepted: yes. Publishes 2% of manuscripts submitted. Payment: 50% press run. Copyrights for author.

CEDAR HILL REVIEW, Cedar Hill Publications, Gloria Doyle, Editor; Maggie Jaffe, Editor; David Geyette, Editor; Thom Hofman, Editor, 3722 Highway 8 West, Mena, AR 71953, 501-394-7029. 1997. Poetry, fiction, criticism, reviews. "Generally poems under 60 lines; open as to style, form, subject, but nothing racist, sexist or anti-environment. Recent contributers: Leonard J. Cirino, Hayden Carruth, David Budbill, Margaret Randall, Serena Fusek." circ. 300. 2/yr. Pub'd 4 issues 1998; expects 2 issues 1999, 2 issues 2000. sub. price: $10; per copy: $6; sample: $4. Back issues: $4. Discounts: 12 for $40. 80pp; 5½×8½; of. Reporting time: 60 days. Simultaneous submissions accepted: yes. Publishes 2% of manuscripts submitted. Payment: 1 copy. Copyrighted, reverts to author. Pub's reviews: 20 in 1998. §Poetry.

CELEBRATION, William J. Sullivan, 2707 Lawina Road, Baltimore, MD 21216-1608, 410-542-8785. 1975. Poetry. "All styles, we hope to be as unbiased as contributors will permit. Recent contributors: Terry Kennedy, Michael L. Johnson, Lisa Yount, Tim Houghton, Sheila E. Murphy, Ivan Arguelles." circ. 300. Occasional. Expects 1 issue 1999, 1 issue 2000. sub. price: $8/4 issues; per copy: $2; sample: $2. Back issues: $2. 30pp; 5½×8½; of. Reporting time: 12 weeks. Payment: copies.

Celebrity Profiles Publishing, Richard Grudens, PO Box 344, Stonybrook, NY 11790, 516-862-8555; FAX 862-0139. 1995. Interviews, music, non-fiction. avg. press run 5M. Pub'd 1 title 1998; expects 2 titles 1999, 2 titles 2000. 3 titles listed in the *Small Press Record of Books in Print* (28th Edition, 1999-00). avg. price, paper: $17.95. Discounts: 55%. 240pp; 6×9; lp. Reporting time: 3 months. Simultaneous submissions accepted: yes. Publishes 50% of manuscripts submitted. Payment: by agreement. Copyrights for author. Publishers Marketing Association.

Celestial Otter Press (see also MAGIC CHANGES), John Sennett, Editor, 237 Park Trail Court, Schaumburg, IL 60173. 1978. Poetry, fiction, art, photos, cartoons, interviews, satire, criticism, reviews, music, long-poems, plays. avg. press run 200. Expects 1 title 2000. avg. price, paper: $5. Discounts: inquire. 64pp; 5½×8½; †desktop laser. Reporting time: 2-3 months. Publishes 1% of manuscripts submitted. Payment: negotiable. Copyrights for author.

CELFAN Editions Monographs (see also REVUE CELFAN REVIEW), Dept. of French & Italian, Tulane University, New Orleans, LA 70118. 8 titles listed in the *Small Press Record of Books in Print* (28th Edition, 1999-00).

Celo Valley Books, Diana M. Donovan, 346 Seven Mile Ridge Road, Burnsville, NC 28714, 828-675-5918. 1989. Poetry, fiction, non-fiction. avg. press run 50-3M. Pub'd 5 titles 1998; expects 5 titles 1999, 5 titles 2000. 28 titles listed in the *Small Press Record of Books in Print* (28th Edition, 1999-00). avg. price, cloth: $18; paper: $10. 176pp; size varies; of. Reporting time: 1 month. Payment: so far all our titles are paid for by the author; within 5 years, though, we hope to do some titles in a more traditional way. Copyrights for author. NC Writers Network, Asheville Writers Workshop, Editorial Freelancers Association.

Celtic Heritage Books, PO Box 770637, Woodside, NY 11377-0637, 718-478-8162; 1-800-273-5281. 1985. Non-fiction. "Desired works are approximately 150 pages." Expects 1 title 1999, 1 title 2000. 4 titles listed in the *Small Press Record of Books in Print* (28th Edition, 1999-00). avg. price, paper: $7.95. Discounts: 30%. 90pp; 5½×4¼; of. Reporting time: 3 weeks. Payment: varies with each contributing author. Copyrights for author.

CELTIC HISTORY REVIEW, THE CELTIC PEN, Micheal Siochru, 216 Falls Road, Belfast, BT12, Ireland, 0232-232608. 1994. Articles, letters, non-fiction. circ. 500. 4/yr. Pub'd 1 issue 1998; expects 3 issues 1999, 4 issues 2000. sub. price: £7. 28pp; size A4; of. Reporting time: 7 weeks. Publishes 60% of manuscripts submitted. Pub's reviews: 1 in 1998. §Histories of the Celtic countries, social, economic, laguage. Ads: £55/£35/£20 1/4 page.

THE CELTIC PEN, CELTIC HISTORY REVIEW, Diarmuid Breaslain, 36 Fruithill Park, Belfast, BT11 8GE, Ireland, 01232-232608. 1993. Poetry, articles, reviews, letters, news items. circ. 900. 4/yr. Pub'd 4 issues 1998; expects 4 issues 1999, 4 issues 2000. sub. price: $15.00; per copy: $3; sample: $3. 28pp; of. Reporting time: 7 weeks. Publishes 60% of manuscripts submitted. Pub's reviews: 13 in 1998. §Celtic language, literature translations, histories. Ads: £55/£35/£20 1/4 page.

THE CENTENNIAL REVIEW, R.K. Meiners, Editor; Cheryllee Finney, Managing Editor, 312 Linton Hall, Mich. State Univ., E. Lansing, MI 48824-1044, 517-355-1905. 1955. Poetry, articles. "Topics cover English literature, soc. sci, sciences, humanities, 3M words, double-spaced. Contributors:Joseph Needham, Susan Fromberg Schaeffer." circ. 1M. 3/yr. Pub'd 3 issues 1998; expects 3 issues 1999. sub. price: $12; per copy: $6; sample: $6. Back issues: $6. 200pp; 6×9; of, linotype (metal). Reporting time: 3-6 months. Publishes 10% of manuscripts submitted. Payment: year's free subscription. Copyrighted, reprint rights granted on request of the author. Ads: $75/$50. CELJ.

Center for Japanese Studies, Bruce E. Willoughby, Executive Editor; Robert N. Mory, Assistant Editor, 202 S. Thayer Street, University of Michigan, Ann Arbor, MI 48104-1608, 734-998-7265; FAX 734-998-7982. 1947. Poetry, fiction, criticism, non-fiction. "We publish scholarly monographs, symposia, bibliographic and reference aids, language aids, literature in translation, and poetry on and about Japan." avg. press run 750-1.5M. Pub'd 10 titles 1998; expects 8 titles 1999, 8 titles 2000. 31 titles listed in the *Small Press Record of Books in Print* (28th Edition, 1999-00). avg. price, cloth: $35; paper: $15.95. Discounts: orders and customer service handled by The University of Michigan Press, 839 Greene St./P.O. Box 1104, Ann Arbor MI 48106-1104. 734-764-4392; fax 734-936-0456; e-mail um.press.bus@umich.edu. 250pp; 6×9, 8½×11; of. Reporting time: 2-6 months. Simultaneous submissions accepted: no. Payment: varies with series and book. We hold copyright.

Center for Public Representation, Nicole Graper, Editor, PO Box 260049, Madison, WI 53726-0049, 608-251-4008. 1974. Articles, non-fiction. "The Center for Public Representation (CPR) is a nonprofit, public interest law firm founded in 1974 to provide advocacy, research, and training on behalf of a broad range of citizen groups. Special areas of interest: rights of consumers, citizens, and the elderly; health care cost containment; and maternal and child health. Most of our publications are generated through our own organization, but we will also consider manuscripts on appropriate subjects. A copy of our free publications catalog is available on request. Please include stamped, self-addressed envelope when sending manuscript." avg. press run 1M. Pub'd 4 titles 1998; expects 2 titles 1999, 2 titles 2000. 8 titles listed in the *Small Press Record of Books in Print* (28th Edition, 1999-00). Discounts: 10-25% institutional on bulk orders of same title. 100-200pp; 8½×11, 5½×8½; of. Reporting time: 3 months. Payment: arrangements vary. Does not copyright for author.

Center For Self-Sufficiency, A.C. Doyle, Founder, PO Box 416, Denver, CO 80201-0416, 305-575-5676. 1982. avg. press run 2M. 10 titles listed in the *Small Press Record of Books in Print* (28th Edition, 1999-00). avg. price, cloth: $19.95; paper: $19.95. Discounts: 25% to libraries & bookstores. 60pp; 8½×11; †of.

Center for South and Southeast Asian Studies Publications, Hemalata Dandekar, Director, Center For South and Southeast Asain Studies, 130 Lane Hall, University of Michigan, Ann Arbor, MI 48109-1290, Editorial: 313-763-5790; distribution: 313-763-5408. 1970. "CSSEAS Publications publishes scholarly works on South and Southeast Asia. Since 1970, we have released more than forty monographs in our two series, *Michigan Papers on South and Southeast Asia* and the *Buddhist Literature Series*. The majority of our volumes are written by scholars and distributed to specialists, research libraries, and educational institutions, although the press occasionally publishes titles of more general interest. We have published an excellent Maharashtran Indian cookbook and are currently seeking a manuscript on the Southeast Asian cuisines of Thailand, Vietnam, Indonesia, and the Philippines that features recipes adapted for the Western kitchen." avg. press run 750-1M. Pub'd 2 titles 1998; expects 2 titles 1999, 2 titles 2000. avg. price, cloth: $31.95; paper: $16.95. Discounts: jobbers and bookstores: 20% for 1-4 copies of a single title; 30% for 5 or more of a single title. Examination copy policy for classroom use available upon request. 300pp; 6×9. Reporting time: 3-6 months; must be approved by our Publications Committee. Payment: we follow the conventions of scholarly publishing. Copyrights for author.

Center Press, Gabriella Stone, Publisher, PO Box 16452, Encino, CA 91416-6425. 1980. Poetry, fiction, photos, non-fiction. "We look for high quality manuscripts with a socially redeeming benefit. Very 'current' styles are preferred. We have strong liaisons in the entertainment industry and thusly we are media oriented. Only strong writers with some sort of track record should submit. We will not be reading unsolicited mss through 2001. We sponsor the 'Masters Literary Award', and publish the results, et al. Professionalism, style and quality are the keys to submission here." avg. press run 3M-10M poetry, 50M calendars. Pub'd 4 titles 1998; expects 5 titles 1999, 5 titles 2000. 6 titles listed in the *Small Press Record of Books in Print* (28th Edition, 1999-00). avg. price, cloth: $19.95; paper: $9.95. Discounts: trade 2-4 20%, 5-9 30%, 10-24 40%, 25-49 45%, 50-99 50%; schools and libraries less added 5%. 112pp; 5½×8½; of, lp. Reporting time: 2-6 months. Payment: 5-10% on sales + guarantee and expenses, see Standard Writers Union Contract. Copyrights for author.

The Center Press, Susan Artof, 30961 W. Agoura Road #223-B, Westlake Village, CA 91361, 818-889-7071; FAX 818-879-0806;. 1991. "Looking for clear writing and good concept. Electronic query ok. Will consider IBM-PC 5¾" disk on MSWORD or WordPerfect." avg. press run 3M. Pub'd 2 titles 1998; expects 3 titles

1999, 5 titles 2000. 11 titles listed in the *Small Press Record of Books in Print* (28th Edition, 1999-00). avg. price, paper: $9.95-$14.95; other: $18.95. Discounts: 2-19 books 38%, 20 books 40%, 21-100 42%, up to 67% if over 4 case orders; average distributors 55%, payment 60 days. 176-224pp; 5½×8½; WEB Press. Reporting time: 4-6 weeks. Publishes 10% of manuscripts submitted. Payment: to be arranged. Copyrights for author. ABA, Publishers Marketing Assoc.

Century Press (see also NORTHWOODS JOURNAL, A Magazine for Writers), PO Box 298, Thomaston, ME 04861, 207-354-0998; Fax 207-354-8953; cal@americanletters.org; www.americanletters.org. 1997. avg. press run 1M-2M. Expects 3 titles 1999, 12 titles 2000. 3 titles listed in the *Small Press Record of Books in Print* (28th Edition, 1999-00). avg. price, cloth: $24.95; paper: $15.95. Discounts: 1 copy 25%; 2-5 copies 20%; 6+ copies 40%. 200pp; 5½×8½; of. Reporting time: 2-3 weeks. Simultaneous submissions accepted: no. We publish virtually all submitted manuscripts, though some must be delayed until brought up to standards. Payment: royalty of 40% of cover price. Copyrights for author. CA.

Cerberus Books, 381 Casa Linda Plaza, Suite 179, Dallas, TX 75218, 214-324-0894. 1 title listed in the *Small Press Record of Books in Print* (28th Edition, 1999-00).

Ceres Press, David Goldbeck, Nikki Goldbeck, PO Box 87, Woodstock, NY 12498. 1977. "Unsolicited mss. cannot be returned unless S.A.S.E." avg. press run 5M. Pub'd 1 title 1998; expects 1 title 1999. 8 titles listed in the *Small Press Record of Books in Print* (28th Edition, 1999-00). avg. price, paper: $11.95. Discounts: normal trade. of. Reporting time: 2 months. Payment: as agreed.

CESSNA OWNER MAGAZINE, Aircraft Owners Group, Jodi Lindquist, Editor, PO Box 5000, Iola, WI 54945, 715-445-5000; E-mail cessna@aircraftownergroup.com. Articles, photos, interviews. "Aimed at owners and pilots of Cessna aircraft." circ. 6.3M. 12/yr. Pub'd 12 issues 1998; expects 12 issues 1999, 12 issues 2000. sub. price: $42, includes membership in Cessna Owner Organization; per copy: $4; sample: free on request. Back issues: $3. Discounts: subscription only. 64pp; 8½×11; desktop, litho. Reporting time: varies. Payment: 5¢/word and up, on publication; one-time rights + 30 days. Copyrighted, rights revert to author after 30 days. Pub's reviews: 6 in 1998. §Aviation, pilot's skills and experiences. Ads: call for media kit.

CHACHALACA POETRY REVIEW, Marty Lewis, Chip Dameron, Manuel Medrano, English Department, Univ. of Texas - Brownsville, Brownsville, TX 78520, 956-544-8239; Fax 956-544-8988; E-Mail mlewis@b1.utb.edu. 1997. Poetry. "Substance/craftmanship in lines, substance in theme no gratuitous typography, no intrusive rhymes, Susan Weston, Michael Blumenthal, Richard Cecil." circ. 500. 1-2/yr. Pub'd 2 issues 1998; expects 1-2 issues 1999, 1-2 issues 2000. sub. price: $15/2 issues; per copy: $8; sample: $3. Back issues: $3. 60pp; 6×9; of. Reporting time: 30-90 days. Simultaneous submissions accepted with notice. Publishes 3-5% of manuscripts submitted. Payment: 2 copies. Copyrighted, reverts to author. Ads: none.

●**CHAFFIN JOURNAL**, William Sutton, Department of English, 467 Case Annex, Eastern Kentucky University, Richmond, KY 40475-3140. 1998. Poetry, fiction. "Fiction up to 10,000 words, main interest is literary quality." circ. 500. 1/yr. Expects 1 issue 1999, 1 issue 2000. sub. price: $5. 100pp; 5½×8½; of. Reporting time: 1 month. Simultaneous submissions accepted: yes. Payment: $100 for best fiction and poetry each issue. Copyrighted, reverts to author.

CHALLENGE: A Journal of Faith and Action in the Americas, EPICA, Minor Sinclair, Scott Wright, 1470 Irving Street NW, Washington, DC 20010, 202-332-0292. 1989. Articles, interviews, non-fiction. "*Challenge* publishes original material predominently from Central American and Caribbean theologians and activists reflecting on their faith and vision for justice. Article length is from 1,000-7,500 words. Submissions in English or Spanish." circ. 2M. 3/yr. Pub'd 1 issue 1998; expects 3 issues 1999, 4 issues 2000. sub. price: $15 for individuals, $20 for institutions; per copy: $3.50; sample: $3.50. Back issues: $3.50 each. Discounts: 10 copies or more $2. 16pp; 8½×11; of. Reporting time: 3 weeks. Payment: none. Copyrighted, reverts to author. Pub's reviews: 2 in 1998. §Central American politics and faith, U.S. solidarity with Central America and the Caribbean. Ads: $100/$65/$40 1/4 page.

CHANCE MAGAZINE, Robert L. Penick, 3929 South Fifth Street, Louisville, KY 40214. 1991. Poetry. "I *strongly* urge writers to purchase a sample before submitting. Recent contributors include: Jim Wayne Miller, Cliff Wieck, and Thomas Michael McDade." circ. 200. 2/yr. Pub'd 2 issues 1998; expects 2 issues 1999, 2 issues 2000. sub. price: $4; per copy: $2; sample: $2. Back issues: $2. 32pp; 5½×8½; xerox. Reporting time: 4 weeks. We accept simultaneous submissions if stated where else it is. Publishes 2% of manuscripts submitted. Payment: 1 copy. Not copyrighted. Pub's reviews: 25 in 1998. §Any poetry that does not put me to sleep, no Lyn Lifshin.

Chandler & Sharp Publishers, Inc., Jonathan Sharp, 11A Commercial Blvd., Novato, CA 94949, 415-883-2353, FAX: 415-883-4280. 1972. "College-level books in anthropology and political science with both supplementary text and general-reader appeal" avg. press run 3M. Pub'd 4 titles 1998; expects 3 titles 1999, 3 titles 2000. 36 titles listed in the *Small Press Record of Books in Print* (28th Edition, 1999-00). avg.

price, cloth: $25; paper: $12.95. Discounts: trade books 40%, textbooks 20%, wholesalers 50%. 192pp; 6×9; of. Reporting time: 2-6 weeks. Simultaneous submissions accepted: yes. Payment: royalties. Copyrights for author on request. AAA, SWAA, WSSA.

CHANTEH, the Iranian Cross Cultural Qu'ly, Saideh Pakravan, PO Box 703, Falls Church, VA 22046, 703-533-1727. 1992. Poetry, fiction, articles, art, photos, cartoons, interviews, satire, criticism, music, letters, non-fiction. "Open to writers of all nationalities interested in the multicultural experience, in exile and adaptation to new environments. Any and all writing, including political. The only criteria are relevance and excellence in writing" circ. 1.2M. 4/yr. Pub'd 3 issues 1998; expects 4 issues 1999, 4 issues 2000. sub. price: $20; per copy: $5.95; sample: $5. Back issues: free. Discounts: none. 50pp; 8½×11; of. Reporting time: 4 weeks. We accept simultaneous submissions when notified. Payment: 2 copies. Copyrighted, reverts to author. Pub's reviews: 12 in 1998. §The exile and multicultural experience, culture shock, travel, politics in the Middle East. Ads: $350/$175.

CHAOS FOR THE CREATIVE MIND, Rich Carpenter, Steve Carpenter, Michele Arambula, PO Box 633, Tinley Park, IL 60477. 1998. Poetry, fiction, articles, reviews, music, letters, news items, non-fiction. "Short stories 3-4 pages, consider all story types. Poems 30-40 lines, all types. Don't let the name scare you. Focuses on new talent never seen before. Checks payable to Rich Carpenter." circ. 100. 12/yr. Expects 12 issues 1999, 12 issues 2000. sub. price: $9; per copy: $2; sample: free. Back issues: $1. 24pp; 8½×11; mi. Reporting time: 2-3 weeks. Simultaneous submissions accepted: yes. Publishes 75% of manuscripts submitted. Payment: 3 copies where work appears. Not copyrighted. Ads: $40/$25/5¢ per word, 10 word minimum.

Chaos Warrior Productions, Aaron Larson, Boghdan Csagha, PO Box 14407, University Station, Minneapolis, MN 55414, 612-788-4491. 1993. "Primary function is shareware-style distribution promotion of novel or anthology samples of computer diskette, and very occasional book publishing (1-2 titles/year)." avg. press run 2M. Expects 1 title 1999, 1 title 2000. 1 title listed in the *Small Press Record of Books in Print* (28th Edition, 1999-00). avg. price, cloth: $29.95; paper: $9.95; other: $12.95 cassettes, $19.95 cd-roms. Discounts: trade, bulk. 400pp; 6×9. Reporting time: variable. Payment: no advance; substantial royalty arranged. Does not copyright for author. PMA, MIPA.

CHAPMAN, Joy M. Hendry, 4 Broughton Place, Edinburgh EH1 3RX, Scotland, 0131-557-2207. 1970. Poetry, fiction, articles, art, interviews, criticism, reviews, long-poems. "Literary material, philosophical orientation, Scottish bias, but *not* exclusive. High standards." circ. 2M. 4/yr. Expects 4 issues 1999. 41 titles listed in the *Small Press Record of Books in Print* (28th Edition, 1999-00). sub. price: £15 (£20 overseas, US$34); per copy: £3.30 ($6); sample: £3.30 ($6). Back issues: list available. Discounts: variable. 104pp; 6×8½; of. Reporting time: 2 months. Simultaneous submissions accepted: no. Payment: copies of magazine. Copyrighted. Pub's reviews: 70 in 1998. §Literature (general), politics, culture. Ads: £75/£40. Scottish Publishers Association, Association of Little Presses.

Chardon Press (see also GRASSROOTS FUNDRAISING JOURNAL), Kim Klein, Publisher; Stephanie Roth, Publisher; Nancy Adess, Editor, 3781 Broadway, Oakland, CA 94611, 510-596-8160; Fax 510-596-8822; chardon@chardonpress.com; www.chardonpress.com. Criticism, non-fiction. "Fundraising, grant writing, community organizing, anti-racism" avg. press run 5M. Pub'd 6 titles 1998; expects 3 titles 1999, 3 titles 2000. avg. price, paper: $25. Discounts: 40% for bulk or prepaid STOP. 100-250pp; 6×9. Reporting time: 3 months. Simultaneous submissions accepted: yes. Publishes 10% of manuscripts submitted. Payment: varies. Copyrights for author.

THE CHARIOTEER, Pella Publishing Co, Carmen Capri-Karka, 337 West 36 Street, New York, NY 10018, 212-279-9586. 1960. Poetry, fiction, articles, art, criticism, reviews, letters, plays. "Purpose: to bring to English-speaking readers information on, appreciation of, and translations from modern Greek literature, with criticism and reproductions of modern Greek art and sculpture." circ. 1M. 1/yr. Pub'd 1 issue 1998; expects 1 issue 1999, 1 issue 2000. sub. price: $15 US indiv., $20 US instit., $20 foreign indiv., $25 foreign instit.; per copy: $15; sample: free. Back issues: $9-single; $15-double. Discounts: jobbers 20%, bookstores 20%. 160pp; 5½×8½; †lp. Reporting time: 1 year. Payment: 20 offprints. Copyrighted, rights revert to author if requested. Pub's reviews: 0 in 1998. §Modern Greek Literature & Poetry. Ads: $125/$75/Outside Back Cover-$250/Inside Covers-$200.

CHARITON REVIEW, Jim Barnes, Truman University, Kirksville, MO 63501, 660-785-4499. 1975. Poetry, fiction, art, photos, reviews. "We try to keep open minds, but admit a bias to work that relies more on strong imagery than talkiness. We are very interested in translation, particularly translations of modern poets and especially those from languages other than French or Spanish though we have used numerous translations from those two languages. Recent contributors include Gordon Weaver, Steve Heller, Elizabeth Moore, Lynn Thorsen, Lucien Stryk, Brian Bedard, Greg Johnson, Lewis Horne, David Ray, Quinton Duval, James Welch, Paul Zimmer, translations of Belli, Koteski, Huchel, Paulovski, Sabines, Aleixandre, Elytis, Nick. No xerox or carbons or dot matrix." circ. 650+. 2/yr. Pub'd 2 issues 1998; expects 2 issues 1999. sub. price: $9/yr, $15 2/yr;

112

per copy: $5; sample: $5. Back issues: Vol. 1 No. 1 $100; Vol. 1 No. 2 $50; Vol. 2 No. 1 $50; Vol. 2 No. 2 $50; others $5. Discounts: on request. 104pp; 6×9; electronic type. Reporting time: 1 month or less. Payment: $5/page up to $50 and 1 copy. Copyrighted, rights returned to author on request. Pub's reviews: 0 in 1998. §Modern poetry, fiction, translation, mags. Ads: $100/$50. CLMP.

Deborah Charles Publications (see also INTERNATIONAL JOURNAL FOR THE SEMIOTICS OF LAW; LAW AND CRITIQUE; LIVERPOOL LAW REVIEW; FEMINIST LEGAL STUDIES; RES PUBLICA), B.S. Jackson, 173 Mather Avenue, Liverpool L18 6JZ, United Kingdom, fax 441-151-729-0371 from outside UK. 1986. Non-fiction. "Mainly legal theory" avg. press run 300. 9 titles listed in the *Small Press Record of Books in Print* (28th Edition, 1999-00). Discounts: 5% subscription agents, 25% bookshops. 112pp; royal octavo; desktop publishing Macintosh. IPG.

CHASQUI, David William Foster, Dept of Languages and Literature, Arizona State University, Tempe, AZ 85207-0202. 1971. Fiction, articles, interviews, criticism, reviews, parts-of-novels. circ. 500. 2/yr. Pub'd 2 issues 1998; expects 2 issues 1999, 2 issues 2000. sub. price: $15. Discounts: none. 130pp; 6×9; laser. Reporting time: 3 months. Payment: none. Copyrighted, reverts to author. Pub's reviews: 65 in 1998. §Brazilian and Spanish American literature, literary criticism, theory. Ads: none. CLMP.

THE CHATTAHOOCHEE REVIEW, Jo Ann Yeager Adkins, Managing Editor; Larence Hetrick, Editor; Collie Owens, Poetry Editor; J. Steven Beauchamp, Poetry Editor; Kate Roddy, Fiction Editor, Georgia Perimeter College, 2101 Womack Road, Dunwoody, GA 30338-4497, 404-551-3019. 1980. Poetry, fiction, art, interviews, reviews, non-fiction. "We publish a number of Southern writers, but *CR* is not by design a regional magazine. We prefer fiction marked by a distinctive voice and powered by innovative language, not gimmicks, which invites the reader's imagination to work along side of well-wrought characters. Recent contributors: Larry Brown, Lisa Koger, Lewis Nordan, Patrick Ryan, Janet Peery, Andrew Depthereos. In poetry we look for vivid imagery, unique point of view and voice, freshness of figurative language, and attention to craft. Recent contributors: Peter Meinke, David Kirby, Allan Peterson, Bin Ramke, Peter Wild, Cory Brown. All themes, forms, and styles are considered as long as they impact the whole person: heart, mind, intuition, and imagination." circ. 1.3M. 4/yr. Pub'd 4 issues 1998; expects 4 issues 1999, 4 issues 2000. sub. price: $16/yr or $30/2 yrs; per copy: $6; sample: $6. Back issues: $6. Discounts: 30% to retailers. 120pp; 6×9; of. Reporting time: 3-4 months. Simultaneous submissions accepted: no. Payment: $50 per poem, $20 per page fiction, $15 per page essays, $100 per omni review, $50 single book review, $100 per interview, upon publication. Copyrighted, reverts to author. Pub's reviews: 6 in 1998. §Poetry, fiction and literary magazines. Ads: $150. CLMP, CELJ.

CHELSEA, Richard Foerster, Editor; Alfredo de Palchi, Senior Associate Editor; Andrea Lockett, Associate Editor; Eric Miles Williamson, Associate Editor, PO Box 773, Cooper Station, New York, NY 10276-0773. 1958. Poetry, fiction, articles, art, photos, interviews, criticism, parts-of-novels, long-poems, concrete art, non-fiction. "Stress on quality, originality, style, variety...superior translations. No special biases, no requirements but prefer fiction under 25 pages. Flexible attitudes, eclectic material. Recent contributors: Kim Addonizio, W.S. DiPiero, Laurie Foos, Bob Hicok, Valerio Magrelli, Lisel Mueller, Carl Phillips, A. Poulin Jr., Laura Riding, Reginald Shepherd, Karen Volkman, Michael Waters." circ. 1.8M. 2/yr. Pub'd 2 issues 1998; expects 2 issues 1999, 2 issues 2000. sub. price: $13/2 consecutive issues as published or one double issue, $16 foreign; per copy: $8 (500-page *Retrospective* double issue—$10); sample: $7. Back issues: prices range from $3 to $25 if rare. Discounts: agency 30%, bookstores 30%. 192pp; 6×9; of. Reporting time: 3 weeks to 3 months. Simultaneous submissions accepted: no. Publishes less than 1% of manuscripts submitted. Payment: 2 copies plus $20 per printed page. Copyrighted, reverts to author. Pub's reviews: 30 in 1998. §poetry, translations, fiction from small presses. Ads: $125/$75/exchange ads with other literary mags. CLMP.

Chelsea Green Publishing Company, Morris Stephen, Publisher; Jim Schley, Editor-in-Chief, PO Box 428, White River Junction, VT 05001-0428, 802-295-6300. 1984. Non-fiction. "Emphasis on non-fiction: nature, environment, outdoors. Books for sustainable Living" avg. press run 5M. Pub'd 7 titles 1998; expects 10 titles 1999, 12 titles 2000. 16 titles listed in the *Small Press Record of Books in Print* (28th Edition, 1999-00). avg. price, cloth: $22; paper: $18. Discounts: under 5 35% prepaid, 5+ 45% returnable, 10+ 50% non-returnable. 200pp; size varies; of, desktop through prepress. Reporting time: 2-3 months. Payment: varies. Copyrights for author. NEBA, BEA.

●**Chelsey Press,** 441 N. Oakhurst Drive #205, Beverly Hills, CA 90210, 310-275-0803; fax 310-271-6634; e-mail chelseyink@aol.com. 1998. Fiction, non-fiction. "Chelsey Press is dedicated to publishing fine cultural literature for children. New York office: 750 Park Ave. #10C, New York, NY 10021. Phone/fax 212-879-0089" avg. press run 1.5M. Expects 1 title 1999, 1 title 2000. 1 title listed in the *Small Press Record of Books in Print* (28th Edition, 1999-00). avg. price, paper: $24.95. Discounts: varies. 200pp; 7×10. Reporting time: 6 weeks. Simultaneous submissions accepted: yes. Payment: 4-6%. Copyrights for author. PMA.

Cherokee Publishing Company, Alexa Selph, PO Box 1730, Marietta, GA 30061, 404-467-4189. 1968.

"Additional address: 764 Miami Circle NE #206, Atlanta, GA 30324." avg. press run 3M. Pub'd 5 titles 1998; expects 5 titles 1999. avg. price, cloth: $24.95; paper: $14.95. Discounts: 1-4 books 35%, 5-24 40%, 25-199 42%, 200+ 45%, STOP 40%. Pages vary; size varies; of. Reporting time: 3 months. Simultaneous submissions accepted: yes. Publishes 1% of manuscripts submitted. Payment: usually 10% of net. Copyrights for author. PMA, ABA, PAS, GA Pub Assoc-President.

THE CHEROTIC (r)EVOLUTIONARY, Frank Moore, Editor; Linda Mac, Editor; Michael LaBash, Art Editor, PO Box 11445, Berkeley, CA 94712, 510-526-7858; FAX 510-524-2053. 1975. Poetry, fiction, articles, art, photos, cartoons, interviews, satire, criticism, reviews, music, letters, parts-of-novels, long-poems, collages, plays, concrete art, news items, non-fiction. "Recent contributors: Annie Sprinkle, LaBash, John Seabury, Carol A. Queen, Frank Moore, Jesse Beagle, Veronica Vera, James David Audlin, Linda Montano, Robert W. Howington, JoAnna Pettit, Ana Christy, H.R. Giger, and Mapplethorpe." circ. 500. Irregular. Expects 1 issue 1999, 1 issue 2000. price per copy: $5; sample: $5. Back issues: $5. Discounts: trade ok, consignment 40%. 28pp; 8½×11; xerox. Reporting time: 1-2 months. Simultaneous submissions accepted: yes. Publishes 30% of manuscripts submitted. Payment: free copy of issue. Copyrighted, reverts to author. Pub's reviews: 0 in 1998. Ads: inquire for rates.

Cherubic Press, Bill Morgan, Art Coordinator; Juliette Gray, Senior Editor; Robert Gratton, Submissions Editor, PO Box 5036, Johnstown, PA 15904-5036, 814-535-4300, Fax: 814-535-4580. 1995. Art, cartoons, non-fiction. "For our children's picture books we use art copiously-length of book is usually 32 pages size 9 X 10 and 8 X 11 or so. Older juvenile fiction and adult non-fiction variy in length and subject matter, size 6 X 9 and 8 X 11" avg. press run 2M. Pub'd 4 titles 1998; expects 4 titles 1999, 4 titles 2000. 8 titles listed in the *Small Press Record of Books in Print* (28th Edition, 1999-00). avg. price, paper: $10-20; other: $24.95. 32pp children's and 375 children's story book, adult books vary; 6×9, 9×10, 8×11; of. Reporting time: 3-5 months. Simultaneous submissions accepted: yes. Payment: varies. Copyright for author if necessary.

Chess Enterprises (see also EN PASSANT), B.G. Dudley, Owner, 107 Crosstree Road, Coraopolis, PA 15108, 412-262-2138; fax 412-262-2138. 1977. Non-fiction. "Only chess; no beginner text." avg. press run 1.2M. Pub'd 8 titles 1998; expects 8 titles 1999, 8 titles 2000. 23 titles listed in the *Small Press Record of Books in Print* (28th Edition, 1999-00). avg. price, paper: $7.50. Discounts: trade 25%, 25+ copies 45%. 100pp; 5×8; of. Reporting time: 30 days. Simultaneous submissions accepted: no. Publishes 50% of manuscripts submitted. Payment: flat fee up front. Copyrights for author.

CHESS LIFE, U.S. Chess Federation, Glenn Petersen, United States Chess Federation, 186 Route 9W, New Windsor, NY 12553, (914) 562-8350. 1939. Articles, photos, cartoons, interviews, reviews, news items, non-fiction. "Incorporates *Chess Review*; until 1960 name was *Chess Life & Review*. Chess must be central to all material submitted. Very little fiction used." circ. 61M. 12/yr. Pub'd 12 issues 1998; expects 12 issues 1999, 12 issues 2000. sub. price: $40; per copy: $3.75; sample: free with req. for writer guidelines. 84pp; 8¼×10¾; of. Reporting time: 1 month. Payment: on publication. Copyrighted, does not revert to author. Pub's reviews: 8-10 in 1998. Ads: $3200/$1770/$1 per word, min. $15.

CHICAGO REVIEW, Andrew Rathmann, Editor, 5801 South Kenwood, Chicago, IL 60637, 773-702-0887. 1946. Poetry, fiction, articles, art, photos, interviews, criticism, reviews, parts-of-novels, plays, non-fiction. "*CR* has an international readership; submissions from unknown writers are welcome. *CR* looks for poetry and fiction which participates in and tests the bounds of these respective traditions. It seeks essays, reviews and interviews which address contemporary literary and cultural questions and problems. SASE expected (including subs. from agents)." circ. 2900. 4/yr. Pub'd 4 issues 1998; expects 4 issues 1999, 4 issues 2000. sub. price: $18 individuals, $42 institutions, add $5/yr postage to foreign countries; per copy: $6; sample: $6. Back issues: yes, on inquiry, usually $5. Discounts: agency 15% subscription. 144pp; 6×9; of. Reporting time: 3 months with fiction, 2 months for other submissions. Simultaneous submissions accepted: yes. Publishes 1% of manuscripts submitted. Payment: 3 copies plus volume subscription. Copyrighted, rights revert to author only on request. Pub's reviews: 20 in 1998. §Literature, the arts, cultural studies. Ads: $150/$75. CLMP, CELJ.

Chicago Review Press, Cynthia Sherry, Editorial Director, 814 North Franklin Street, Chicago, IL 60610, 312-337-0747. 1973. Art, non-fiction-interviews. avg. press run 5M-7.5M. Pub'd 25 titles 1998. avg. price, cloth: $21.95; paper: $11.95. Discounts: distributed by Independent Publishers Group. 200pp. Reporting time: 1-2 months (if submission includes SASE). Simultaneous submissions accepted: yes. Publishes 5% of manuscripts submitted. Payment: royalty 7.5%-10% of retail price is our standard. Copyrights for author.

Chicago Spectrum Press, Dorothy Kavka, Senior Editor, 4848 Brownsboro Center, Louisville, KY 40207-2342, 502-899-1919; Fax 502-896-0246; evanstonpb@aol.com. 1993. avg. press run 2M. Pub'd 5 titles 1998; expects 10 titles 1999, 24 titles 2000. 21 titles listed in the *Small Press Record of Books in Print* (28th Edition, 1999-00). avg. price, cloth: $25; paper: $15. Discounts: 2-4 20%, 5-99 40%, 100+ 50%. 224pp; 6×9. Reporting time: 1 month. Simultaneous submissions accepted: no. Publishes 10% of manuscripts submitted. Payment: standard small press agreement. Copyrights for author. PMA, ABPA, Small Press Assoc.

CHICAGO STUDIES, Liturgy Training Publications, Reverend George Dyer, 1800 North Hermitage Avenue, Chicago, IL 60622, 312-486-8970. 1962. Articles, photos. "A magazine designed for all who work in pastoral ministry, it is the country's leading journal in which theologians write for non-theologians on issues of current and ongoing interest" circ. 4M. 3/yr. Pub'd 3 issues 1998; expects 3 issues 1999, 3 issues 2000. sub. price: $17.50; per copy: $7.50. Back issues: $7.50. Discounts: bulk 5+ $12/year. 6×9; of. Reporting time: 6-8 weeks. Simultaneous submissions accepted: no. Publishes 10% of manuscripts submitted. Payment: yes. Copyrighted, does not revert to author. Catholic Book Publishers Assn.

Chicano Studies Research Center Publications (see also AZTLAN: A Journal of Chicano Studies), Chon A. Noriega, University of California-Los Angeles, PO Box 951544, Los Angeles, CA 90095, 310-825-2642. 1970. Articles, criticism, reviews, news items. "Original research and analysis related to Chicanos." avg. press run 1M. Pub'd 1 title 1998; expects 2 titles 1999. 14 titles listed in the *Small Press Record of Books in Print* (28th Edition, 1999-00). avg. price, cloth: $20. Discounts: for classroom use only. 200pp; 6×9; of. Reporting time: 6 months. Simultaneous submissions accepted: yes. Publishes 25% of manuscripts submitted. Payment: books in quantity. Copyrights for author.

Chicken Soup Press, Inc., Margaret S. Campilonga, PO Box 164, Circleville, NY 10919, 914-692-6320; fax 914-692-7574; e-mail poet@warwick.net. 1995. avg. press run 2.5M. Pub'd 3 titles 1998; expects 2 titles 1999, 2 titles 2000. 8 titles listed in the *Small Press Record of Books in Print* (28th Edition, 1999-00). avg. price, cloth: $9.95; paper: $6.95. Discounts: industry standard. Young adult 160pp, children's 32pp. Simultaneous submissions accepted: no. Payment: 10%. Copyrights for author. PMA, SPAN.

Chicory Blue Press, Inc., 795 East Street North, Goshen, CT 06756, 860-491-2271; FAX 860-491-8619. 1987. Poetry, fiction, art, interviews, letters, parts-of-novels, non-fiction. "Chicory Blue Press specializes in writing by women, with a current focus on women poets past 60." avg. press run 500-1M. Pub'd 3 titles 1998; expects 1 title 1999, 1 title 2000. 16 titles listed in the *Small Press Record of Books in Print* (28th Edition, 1999-00). avg. price, paper: $16.95; other: $10 chapbooks. Discounts: 3-199 40%, 200-499 50%, 500+ 55%. 6×9; printer. Reporting time: 3-5 months. Simultaneous submissions accepted: yes. Publishes 2-3% of manuscripts submitted. Payment: negotiable. Copyrights for author. Small Press Center.

The Chicot Press, Randall P. Whatley, Box 53198, Atlanta, GA 30355, 770-640-9918; fax 770-640-9819. 1978. Non-fiction. avg. press run 2M. Expects 3 titles 1999, 5 titles 2000. 2 titles listed in the *Small Press Record of Books in Print* (28th Edition, 1999-00). avg. price, paper: $10. Discounts: 1-4 copies 20%, 5-9 30%, 10-99 40%, 100-499 45%, 500+ 50%. 100pp; 6×9; of. Reporting time: 60 days. Payment: percentage of profits. Copyrights for author.

CHILDREN, CHURCHES AND DADDIES, A Non Religious, Non Familial Literary Magazine, Scars Publications, Janet Kuypers, 8830 W. 120th Place, Palos Park, IL 60464-1203, E-ail ccandd96@aol.com; www.members.aol.com/scarspub/scras.html. 1993. Poetry, fiction, art, photos, letters, long-poems, non-fiction. "CC & D is a magazine for contemporary poetry, short prose and art. I'm a computer artist, and a feminist specializing in acquaintance rape education. Anything about pertinent issues will be given attention. No sappy rhyme, rhyme for rhyme's sake. Try under 5 pp per piece. No racist/sexist/homophobic material. Need editor's name on address. SASE necessary. I primarily accept work on disk (Mac Preferred).E-mail submissions accepted. Submit as many pieces as you like, but no originals. I'm collecting works from the magazines into perfect bound paperback books as time goes on, so if you're published. For more information, look under Scars Publications. Permanent address 8830 West 120th Place, Palos Park Illinois 60464, attn: Janet Kuypers. *CC&D* also runs book, chapbook, and calender contests. Contact *CC&D* for more information. Issues available in print (paid only), electronic format, and on the internet at above address" circ. varies. 12/yr. Pub'd 12 issues 1998; expects 12 issues 1999, 12 issues 2000. sub. price: $36; per copy: $3; sample: $4.25, $3. Back issues: write to request information. Discounts: write for more information. Pages vary; 8½×11; †mimeo. Reporting time: I'll get back to you in a week if there is a SASE; otherwise, you'll never hear from me. Simultaneous submissions accepted: yes. Publishes 40% of manuscripts submitted. Payment: none. Copyrighted. Ads: contact CC&D.

Children Of Mary (see also FIDELIS ET VERUS), Ella McBride, PO Box 350333, Ft. Lauderdale, FL 33335. 1981. Non-fiction. "Orthodox Roman Catholic views reflected in commentary apparitions of Jesus and Mary in Bayside, NY (1970-85) are completely recorded in two volumes *Roses* and also published in *Fidelis et Verus*, a Catholic quarterly newspaper, $10/yr." avg. press run 2M (newspaper) and 15K for books. Pub'd 3 titles 1998; expects 4 titles 1999, 4 titles 2000. 3 titles listed in the *Small Press Record of Books in Print* (28th Edition, 1999-00). avg. price, cloth: $9; paper: $8-$9. Discounts: 40% trade, bulk, classroom, agent, jobber, etc. 592pp; 8½×11; of. Reporting time: 3 months. Payment: voluntary. Does not copyright for author.

Children's Book Press, Harriet Rohmer, 246 First Street, Suite 101, San Francisco, CA 94105-1028, 415-995-2200, FAX: 415-995-2222; cbookpress@cbookpress.org. 1975. "We prefer for authors to write to us for our editorial guidelines, rather than inquire by phone. We publish legends, folklore and contemporary stories of the different peoples who live in America today. Most of our books are bilingual in Spanish, Chinese,

Korean or Vietnamese. We do not solicit manuscripts." avg. press run 7.5M. Pub'd 2 titles 1998; expects 6 titles 1999, 8 titles 2000. 52 titles listed in the *Small Press Record of Books in Print* (28th Edition, 1999-00). avg. price, cloth: $15.95; paper: $6.95; other: $9.95 tapes. Discounts: 40% trade, other rates on request. 32pp; 9×9½; of. Reporting time: up to 4 months. Simultaneous submissions accepted: yes. Payment: yes. Copyrights for author.

CHILDREN'S LITERATURE IN EDUCATION, Human Sciences Press, Inc., Anita Moss, US & Canada; Geoff Fox, United Kingdom, 233 Spring Street, New York, NY 10013, 212-620-8000. 1970. Articles, interviews, criticism, reviews. *"Children's Literature in Education* features interviews with noted children's authors, literary criticism of both classic and contemporary writing for children, and articles about successful classroom reading projects. All correspondence concerning subscriptions should be addressed to: Subscription Dept., Human Sciences Press, Inc., PO Box 735, Canal St. Station, New York, NY 10013-1578. All editorial correspondence, manuscript submissions, and review copies should be addressed as follows: In North America, to Anita Moss, English Dept., Univ. of N. Carolina at Charlotte, UNCC Station, Charlotte, NC 28223; In the UK and elsewhere outside North America, to Geoff Fox, Exeter Univ. School of Education, St. Luke's, Exeter EX1 2LU, Devon, England" circ. 2.5M. 4/yr. Pub'd 4 issues 1998; expects 4 issues 1999, 4 issues 2000. sub. price: ind. & schools K-12 $27, inst. $95; sample: free. Back issues: Contact: J.S. Canner, Inc., 10 Charles St, Needham Heights, MA 02194. Discounts: 5% to subscription agents. 64pp; 7×10; of. Reporting time: 3 months. Payment: none. Copyrighted, does not revert to author. Pub's reviews: 1 in 1998. §Recent titles of professional interest to educators on reading-related topics.

Child's Play, Paul J. Gardner, 64 Wellington Avenue, West Orange, NJ 07052, 201-731-3777. 1972. Fiction, art, music. "Head office: Ashworth Road, Bridgemead, Swindon SN5 7YD England. Child's Play was the first publisher to encourage children to 'learn through play.' It's product line of educational books, toys, games and audio/video materials looks to stimulate the whole child—the senses, the imagination, and the intellect—through an interactive process involving the parent and/or teacher. Our aim is to help children develop a vision of the world for themselves that includes concepts of fundamental value." avg. press run 5M. Pub'd 25 titles 1998; expects 25 titles 1999, 25 titles 2000. avg. price, cloth: $9.95; paper: $5.95. Discounts: trade and wholesale 50%, classroom 0% to 25%, agent and jobber 50-55%. 32pp. ABA, ALA, NSSEA, EDSA, IRA.

Chili Verde, Cynthia J. Harper, 736 E. Guenther Street, San Antonio, TX 78210, 210-532-8384. 1993. Poetry. "A poetry press with an ongoing chapbook series (just published #6). Not currently accepting manuscripts for full size books. Currently have 2 titles in that category. Annual chapbook contest." avg. press run 300. Pub'd 5 titles 1998; expects 4 titles 1999, 5 titles 2000. avg. price, paper: $5-7. Discounts: none. 30pp; 5½×11. Reporting time: 1 month. Publishes 1% of manuscripts submitted. Payment: in copies. Copyrights for author.

China Books & Periodicals, Inc., Greg Jones, Editor, 2929 24th Street, San Francisco, CA 94110, 415-282-2994; info@chinabooks.com. 1960. Fiction, photos, non-fiction. "China Books publishes only books relating to China, including history, language, culture, children, art, music, and other topics. We are less interested in Chinese American topics, but will consider the right books for our market. Recent authors include Peter Uhlmann, Jeannette Faurot, Stefan Verstappen, Tony Gallagher, and Elizabeth Chiu King. We also distribute books for other publishers to bookstores around the world, have an active web site, and retail bookstore." avg. press run 3M-5M. Pub'd 5 titles 1998; expects 6 titles 1999, 10 titles 2000. 3 titles listed in the *Small Press Record of Books in Print* (28th Edition, 1999-00). avg. price, cloth: $29.95; paper: $14.95; other: $9.95 calendars, $1 cards. Discounts: trade 1-4 20%, 5-50 40%, 51-100 42%, 101-250 43%. 250pp; size varies; of. Reporting time: 1-3 months. Simultaneous submissions accepted: yes. Publishes 3% of manuscripts submitted. Payment: 10-12% of net income. Copyrights for author. Bookbuilders West, American Booksellers Association (ABA), Publishing Marketing Association (PMA).

CHINA REVIEW INTERNATIONAL, Roger T. Ames, Executive Editor; Daniel Cole, Managing Editor, 1890 East-West Road, Rm. 417, Honolulu, HI 96822-2318, 808-956-8891; fax 808-956-2682. 1994. Reviews. "For subscriptions, contact: University of Hawaii Press Journals Department, 2840 Kolowalu Street, Honolulu, HI 96822, telephone (808) 956-8833. Reviews are commissioned, generally; however, unsolicited reviews are occasionally accepted." 2/yr. Expects 2 issues 1999, 2 issues 2000. sub. price: $30; per copy: $18. Discounts: for one-time orders: 20% on 10-19 copies, and 30% on 20 or more. 300pp; 7×10; of. Reporting time: 1 month. Payment: complimentary copy of book to reviewers. Copyrighted, does not revert to author. Pub's reviews: 140 in 1998. §Any field in Chinese studies. Ads: $200/$125.

CHINESE LITERATURE, Chinese Literature Press, He Jingzhi, 24 Baiwanzhuang Road, Beijing 100037, People's Republic of China, 892554. 1951. circ. 50M. 4/yr. Pub'd 4 issues 1998; expects 4 issues 1999, 4 issues 2000. sub. price: $10.50. 200pp; 21.5×14cm; †photo of. Copyrighted. Pub's reviews: 4 in 1998. §Chinese literature and art areas.

Chinese Literature Press (see also CHINESE LITERATURE), Tang Jialong, 24 Baiwanzhuang Road,

Beijing 100037, People's Republic of China. 1951. avg. press run 50M. Pub'd 4 titles 1998; expects 4 titles 1999, 4 titles 2000. 110 titles listed in the *Small Press Record of Books in Print* (28th Edition, 1999-00). 200pp; 21.5×14cm; †li. Payment: in Chinese and foreign currency. Copyrights for author.

Chiron Press (see also CHIRON REVIEW), Michael Hathaway, 702 North Prairie, St. John, KS 67576-1516, 316-549-6156; chironreview@hotmail.com; www.geocities.com/soho/nook/1748. 1987. Poetry, fiction, non-fiction. "We are always on the lookout for excellent manuscripts" avg. press run 100-200. Pub'd 3 titles 1998; expects 2 titles 1999, 3 titles 2000. 9 titles listed in the *Small Press Record of Books in Print* (28th Edition, 1999-00). avg. price, paper: $10. Discounts: 20% bookstores & distributors. Pages vary; 8½×5½; of. Reporting time: quick—between 1 week and 1 month. Simultaneous submissions accepted: no. Publishes 5% of manuscripts submitted. Payment: 25% of press run, no royalties. Copyrights for author.

CHIRON REVIEW, Chiron Press, Michael Hathaway, Editor; Jane Hathaway, Assistant Editor; Gerald Locklin, Contributing Editor (Poetry); Ray Zapeda, Contributing Editor (Fiction), 702 North Prairie, St. John, KS 67576-1516, 316-549-6156; 316-786-4955; chironreview@hotmail.com; www.geocities.com/soho/nook/ 1748. 1982. Poetry, fiction, articles, art, photos, interviews, satire, criticism, reviews, letters, long-poems, collages, concrete art, news items, non-fiction. "Presents the widest possible range of contemporary creative writing—fiction and non-fiction, traditional and off-beat—in an attractive, professional tabloid format, including artwork and photographs of featured writers. All submissions are invited; no taboos. Recent contributors include Charles Bukowski, Robert Peters, Edward Field, William Stafford, Lyn Lifshin, Will Inman, Janice Eidus, Antler, Marge Piercy, Leslea Newman and a host of others, both well-known and new. Also, about a quarter of each issue is devoted to news, views, and reviews of interest to writers and the literary community. We are always on the lookout for intelligent non-fiction, as well as talented reviewers who wish to write in-depth, analytical reviews of literary books and magazines (500-1000 words). Artwork suitable for cover and/or illustrations also needed. *Be sure to include self-addressed, stamped envelope with all correspondence and submissions.* Make all checks payable to Michael Hathaway." circ. 2.5M. 4/yr. Pub'd 4 issues 1998; expects 4 issues 1999, 4 issues 2000. sub. price: $12 ($24 overseas), $28 instit.; per copy: $4 ($8 overseas), $7 instit.; sample: $4 ($6 overseas), $7 instit. Back issues: $4. Discounts: 20%. 48pp; 10×13; photocomposition, of. Reporting time: 1-4 weeks. Simultaneous submissions accepted: no. Publishes 10% of manuscripts submitted. Payment: 1 copy. Copyrighted, reverts to author. Pub's reviews: 79 in 1998. §Literary magazines, poetry, fiction, essays—all areas. Ads: SASE for rates.

THE CHRISTIAN LIBRARIAN, Ron Jordahl, Southern Evangelical Seminary, 4298 McKee Road, Charlotte, NC 28270. 1957. Articles, interviews, reviews, letters, non-fiction. "1,500-3,500 words. Looking for articles of Christian interpretation of librarianship; philosophy, theory, and practice of library science; bibliographic essays." circ. 525. 3/yr. Pub'd 3 issues 1998; expects 3 issues 1999, 3 issues 2000. sub. price: $25; per copy: $8.50; sample: same. 36pp; 8½×11; of. Reporting time: 2 weeks. Simultaneous submissions accepted: yes. Payment: none. Not copyrighted. Pub's reviews: 26 in 1998. §Library science, reference, religion. Ads: $72/$36/$1 per line, minimum $5. EPA (Evangelical Press Association).

●**Christian Martyrs' Press**, Margaret E. Stucki, Ph.D., Director, 1050 E. Center Street, Pocatello, ID 83201. 5 titles listed in the *Small Press Record of Books in Print* (28th Edition, 1999-00).

Christian Traditions Publishing Co., 7728 Springborn Road, Casco, MI 48064-3910, 810-765-4805; searcher@in-gen.net. 1997. Non-fiction. avg. press run 1M. Expects 1 title 1999. 1 title listed in the *Small Press Record of Books in Print* (28th Edition, 1999-00). avg. price, paper: $14.95. 276pp; 6×9.

CHRISTIANITY & THE ARTS, Marci Whitney-Schenck, PO Box 118088, Chicago, IL 60611, 312-642-8606. 1994. Poetry, articles, art, photos, interviews, criticism, reviews, music, collages, news items, non-fiction. "Prefer manuscripts of less than 2M words. Interests: Christian expression in the arts, see a sample copy." circ. 5M. 4/yr. Expects 4 issues 1999, 4 issues 2000. sub. price: $21; per copy: $7; sample: $7. Discounts: $3 per issue over 10 copies. 72pp; 8½×11; of. Reporting time: 4 weeks. Simultaneous submissions accepted: yes. Publishes 10% of manuscripts submitted. Payment: 1 copy and 1 year's subscription. Copyrighted, reverts to author. Pub's reviews: 20 in 1998. §Christian expression, art, dance, music, literature, film, drama. Ads: $470/$295. Associated Church Press, Evangelical Press Assn., Catholic Press Assn.

CHRISTIAN*NEW AGE QUARTERLY, Catherine Groves, PO Box 276, Clifton, NJ 07011. 1989. Articles, art, cartoons, reviews, letters, news items, non-fiction. "*Christian*New Age Quarterly* is a lively forum exploring the similarities and distinctions between Christianity and the New Age movement. Essentially a vehicle for communication—to draw the two ideological groups into genuine dialogue—articles must quickly cut through superficial divisions to explore the substance of our unity and differences. Pertinent controversy is fine. Garbage thinking (ie., 'I'm right - you're wrong') makes the editor frown. Submissions should sparkle with both insight and creativity. Article lengths vary from 400 to 1500 words (longer pieces accepted if excellent). Guidelines available." 4/yr. Pub'd 4 issues 1998; expects 4 issues 1999, 4 issues 2000. sub. price: $12.50; per copy: $3.50; sample: $3.50. Back issues: $3.50. Discounts: prepaid orders only; on 5 or more

117

copies, 30%. 24pp; 7×8½; photocopy. Reporting time: 6 weeks (and we always respond, if SASE enclosed). Simultaneous submissions accepted: no. Publishes 20% of manuscripts submitted. Payment: in subscription or copies (depending on nature of article). Copyrighted, reverts to author. Pub's reviews: 4 in 1998. §Books which address both Christian and New Age issues. Before sending review copies, write for reviewer's address. Ads: $45/$35/$25 1/4 page/$15 1/6 page/cheap classifieds!

CHRONICLE OF COMMUNITY, Don Snow, Sarah Van de Wetering, PO Box 8291, Missoula, MT 59807-8291, 406-721-7415; Fax 406-721-7416; chronicle@bigsky.net; www.batesinfo.com/chronicle. 1996. Articles, art, photos, reviews, letters, non-fiction. "Writers' and artists' guidelines are available at our website, or by calling our office and requesting them." circ. 1M. 3/yr. Pub'd 3 issues 1998; expects 3 issues 1999, 3 issues 2000. sub. price: $24; per copy: $8; sample: free. Back issues: inquire. Discounts: inquire. 48pp; 8×10½; web offset. Reporting time: 3 months. Simultaneous submissions accepted: yes. Payment: 10¢/word, $25/inside art, $175/cover art. Copyrighted, reverts to author. Pub's reviews: 2 in 1998. §Public resource management, community conservation, sustainability. Ads: inquire.

CHRONICLES OF DISORDER, Thomas Christian, 20 Edie Road, Saratoga Springs, NY 12866-5425. 1996. Poetry, fiction, articles, art, photos, interviews, music, long-poems, collages, non-fiction. "*Chronicles of Disorder* is a semi-annual publication accepting submissions of all types as it relates to the specific topic of focus, which changes with each issue. It also accepts submissions on prior topics which are issued as 'updates.' Issue #1 was Patti Smith issue; issue #2 was Jack Kerouac issue; issue #3 was Beat Generation; issue #4 James Joyce, future topics include: William S. Burroughs; Loureed; Arthur Rimbaud." circ. 500. 2/yr. Pub'd 2 issues 1998; expects 2 issues 1999, 2 issues 2000. price per copy: $2.95 ppd; sample: $2.95. Back issues: $2.95. Discounts: 40% to bookstores, record stores. 48pp; 5½×8½; †mi, xerox. Reporting time: 2 weeks. Simultaneous submissions accepted: yes. Publishes 20% of manuscripts submitted. Payment: 2 copies of issue that it appears in. Copyrighted, reverts to author. Pub's reviews: 12 in 1998. §Contemporary Literature. Ads: $40/$25/none.

CHRYSALIS: The Journal of Transgressive Gender Identities, Sullivan Press, Dallas Denny, PO Box 33724, Decatur, GA 30033, 770-939-2128; Fax 770-939-1770; aegis@gender.org. 1990. Poetry, fiction, articles, art, photos, cartoons, interviews, satire, criticism, reviews, letters, parts-of-novels, long-poems, plays, news items, non-fiction. "Material is related to gender roles and especially to transgender roles." circ. 1M. 2/yr. Pub'd 2 issues 1998; expects 2 issues 1999, 2 issues 2000. price per copy: $9; sample: $9. Back issues: varies by scarcity. Discounts: 40% to wholesalers. 56pp; 8½×11; of. Reporting time: 1 month. We occasionally accept simultaneous submissions; ask us. Publishes 50% of manuscripts submitted. Payment: copies. Copyrighted, reverts to author. Pub's reviews: 3 in 1998. §Gender roles. Ads: $100/$50.

CICADA, Amelia Press, Frederick A. Raborg, Jr., Editor, 329 'E' Street, Bakersfield, CA 93304, 805-323-4064. 1985. Poetry, fiction, articles, art, cartoons, reviews. "Haiku, senryu and other Japanese forms, traditional or experimental; fiction to 3,000 words which in some way uses the haiku form or pertains to Japanese culture; essays to 2,000 words on the history and techniques of the forms; pen & ink sketches and line drawings as well as well-perceived cartoons with oriental themes. We welcome newcomers. Sponsors the annual Lucille Sandberg Haiku Awards and The Hildegarde Janzen Prizes for Oriental Forms of Poetry. Reviews collections of haiku and books about the forms. Contributors include: H.F. Noyes, David Ray, Ryokufu Ishizaki, Alexis Rotella, Michael Dylan Welch, Francine Porad, Elizabeth St Jacques and many others." circ. 600. 4/yr. Pub'd 4 issues 1998; expects 4 issues 1999, 4 issues 2000. sub. price: $14; per copy: $4.95 ppd; sample: $4.95 ppd. Back issues: $4 when available. Discounts: contributor's discount, 20% on five or more copies. 20pp; 5½×8½; of. Reporting time: 2 weeks. We reluctantly accept simultaneous submissions. Publishes 12% of manuscripts submitted. Payment: none, except three *best of issue* poets each receive $10 on publication, plus copy and 20% discount on subscriptions. Copyrighted. Pub's reviews: 12 and many brief in 1998. §Collections of haiku and books on the form. Ads: will consider ads based on $60/$40/$25.

Cider Mill Press, Napoleon St. Cyr, P O Box 211, Stratford, CT 06497. 1966. "CMP does not consider unsolicited mss. It selects its authors, and publishes only once in a while." 7 titles listed in the *Small Press Record of Books in Print* (28th Edition, 1999-00).

CIMARRON REVIEW, E.P. Walkiewicz, Editor; Todd Fuller, Associate Editor; Jennifer Schell, Associate Editor; James Cooper, Poetry Editor; Todd Fuller, Poetry Editor; Lisa Lewis, Poetry Editor; Doug Martin, Poetry Editor; Gordon Weaver, Fiction Editor; Peter Donahue, Fiction Editor; Brian Evenson, Fiction Editor; Philip Heldrich, Fiction Editor; Grant Holt, Fiction Editor; Linda Austin, NonFiction Editor; Thomas E. Kennedy, European Editor, 205 Morrill Hall, Oklahoma State University, Stillwater, OK 74078-0135, 405-744-9476. 1967. Poetry, fiction, articles, satire, criticism, reviews, long-poems, non-fiction. circ. 500. 4/yr. Pub'd 4 issues 1998; expects 4 issues 1999, 4 issues 2000. sub. price: $16 ($20 in Canada), $45/3 years ($55 Canada); per copy: $5; sample: $5. Back issues: $3. Discounts: none. 96-128pp; 6×9; †of. Reporting time: 3 months. Simultaneous submissions accepted: no. Publishes under 3% of manuscripts submitted. Payment: 1-year subscriptions and $50 per short story or essay, $15 per poem. Copyrighted, does not revert to author. Pub's reviews: 18 in 1998. §Poetry, fiction, articles, art, satire, nonfiction. No ads. CLMP, MLA.

CIN-DAV, Inc., David L. Dodge, Route 1, Box 778, Starke, FL 32091, 904-964-5370; Fax: 904-964-4917. 1990. Photos, interviews, criticism, reviews, music, non-fiction. "Also available on audio cassette for $24.95" avg. press run 3M. Pub'd 1 title 1998; expects 1 title 1999, 2 titles 2000. 1 title listed in the *Small Press Record of Books in Print* (28th Edition, 1999-00). avg. price, paper: $14.95. Discounts: bulk. 384pp; 6×9. Copyrights for author. PMA.

CINEASTE MAGAZINE, Gary Crowdus, Dan Georgakas, Roy Grundmann, Cynthia Lucia, Richard Porton, Leonard Quart, Barbara Saltz, Advertising Rep., 200 Park Avenue South, New York, NY 10003, 212-982-1241; fax 212-982-1241. 1967. Articles, photos, interviews, satire, criticism, reviews, letters. "Offers a social & political perspective on the cinema—everything from the latest hollywood flicks & the American independent scene to political thrillers from Europe and revolutionary cinema from the Third World. Query before submitting." circ. 10M. 4/yr. Pub'd 4 issues 1998; expects 4 issues 1999, 4 issues 2000. sub. price: $20 (institutions $35); per copy: $6; sample: $6. Back issues: $4 to subscribers/$5 to others. Discounts: 25%. 68pp; 8½×11; of. Reporting time: 2-3 weeks. Payment: reviews $50, articles $100 and up. Not copyrighted. Pub's reviews: 60 in 1998. §Social, political perspective on all aspects of movies. Ads: $400/$300.

Circa Press, Robert Brooks, PO Box 5856, Eugene, OR 97405, 541-465-9111. 1985. Fiction, non-fiction. "We are looking for nonfiction titles that are written on serious subjects for adults. We are especially interested in new ideas, new information and works that make difficult, but important, topics more easily understood." avg. press run 2M. Pub'd 2 titles 1998; expects 3 titles 1999, 4 titles 2000. 6 titles listed in the *Small Press Record of Books in Print* (28th Edition, 1999-00). avg. price, cloth: $14.95; paper: $9.95. Discounts: trade: prepaid 1-10 copies 40%; 2-5 25%, 6-10 30%, 11-25 40%, 26-75 45%, 76-99 50%, 100+ 55%. 200pp; 5½×8½; of. Reporting time: 2 months. Payment: no advance; royalty about 10% of list price, terms negotiable. Copyrights for author. NWABP.

Circlet Press, Inc., Cecilia Tan, 1770 Mass Avenue #278, Cambridge, MA 02140, 617-864-0492; Fax 617-864-0663; circlet-info@circlet.com. 1992. Fiction, non-fiction. "We publish anthologies of short stories of erotic science fiction and fantasy. We accept manuscripts only between April 15 and August 31. Jan. 1 each year we announce specific anthology topics. Write for complete, very specific guidelines. *No horror! No novels!* We have added an imprint of erotic nonfiction and sex how-to books also. Writer/SASE for query instructions." avg. press run 2M-5M. Pub'd 6 titles 1998; expects 6 titles 1999, 8 titles 2000. 21 titles listed in the *Small Press Record of Books in Print* (28th Edition, 1999-00). avg. price, paper: $14.95. Discounts: retail 40%-48%, short 20%. 192pp; 5½×8½; depends on the book. Reporting time: 2-12 months. Simultaneous submissions accepted: yes. Publishes 5% of manuscripts submitted. Payment: varies by book. Copyrights for author. SFWA, NEBA.

Circumpolar Press, Jane Niebergall, Box 221955, Anchorage, AK 99522, 907-248-7323. 1990. Fiction, articles, non-fiction. "We focus upon Alaskan educational materials. We will produce a broader scope of titles (Early Action (pre-school) and Old Believer Cookbook). We are looking for Alaskan material for teachers and student level K-12." avg. press run 1M-5M. Expects 4 titles 1999, 10 titles 2000. 8 titles listed in the *Small Press Record of Books in Print* (28th Edition, 1999-00). avg. price, paper: $7-$12. Discounts: 10%-20%-30%-40%. 100-300pp; 5×7, 8½×11; †of. Reporting time: within 1 quarter. Payment: per individual contract. Copyrights for author.

Citeaux Commentarii Cistercienses (see also CITEAUX: COMMENTARII CISTERCIENSES), Dr. Terryl N. Kinder, Editor-in-Chief, 17 rue Rabe, 89230 Pontigny, France, Pontigny, France, fax (33) 86.47.58.64. 1950. Articles, art, photos, reviews, non-fiction. "Publishes scholarly books pertaining to the history, art, law, etc. of the Cistercian monastic order. French address: 17, rue Rabe, 89230 Pontgny, France" avg. press run 600-1M. Pub'd 1 title 1998; expects 2 titles 1999, 2 titles 2000. avg. price, other: subscription price: $48 per year. 250-400pp; of. Reporting time: 6 months or less. Simultaneous submissions accepted: no.

CITEAUX: COMMENTARII CISTERCIENSES, Citeaux Commentarii Cistercienses, Dr. Terryl N. Kinder, Editor-in-Chief, 17, rue Rabe, 89230 Pontigny France, Pontigny, France, e-mail 104124.3655@compuserve.com. 1950. Articles, art, photos, reviews, non-fiction. "Scholarly journal, publishing articles, notes, book reviews on all aspects of Cistercian monastic life. French address: 17 r. Rabe, 89230 Pontigny, France" circ. 500+. 2/yr. Pub'd 1 issue 1998; expects 2 issues 1999, 2 issues 2000. sub. price: $48. Back issues: 15. 200pp; 15.5×23.5cm; of. Reporting time: depends on when submitted; editorial board meets winter & summer. Simultaneous submissions accepted: no. Publishes 40-50% of manuscripts submitted. Payment: none. Copyrighted, reverts to author. Pub's reviews: 1996 was a special issue and had no reviews. Normally there are 20-25 reviews per year. in 1998. §All aspects of Cistercian life, history, literature, law, arts, etc.

CITIES AND ROADS: A Collection of Short Stories for North Carolina Readers and Writers., Tom Kealey, PO Box 10886, Greensboro, NC 27404. E-mail cities@nr.infi.net. 1995. Fiction. "*Cities and Roads* features the fiction of North Carolina writers. We are looking for quality work without regard to genre or past experience. There are two slots open in every issue for previously unpublished writers. There is a 7000 word limit." circ. 200. 2/yr. Pub'd 2 issues 1998; expects 2 issues 1999, 2 issues 2000. sub. price: $18/3 issues; per copy: $5-6; sample: $2. Back issues: $5. 100pp; 6×8½; of. Reporting time: 1 month. Simultaneous submissions accepted: yes. Publishes 8-15% of manuscripts submitted. Payment: 2 copies of issues. Copyrighted, reverts to author.

‡City Lights Books (see also CITY LIGHTS JOURNAL), Lawrence Ferlinghetti, Nancy J. Peters, Robert Sharrard, Attn: Bob Sharrard, Editor, 261 Columbus Avenue, San Francisco, CA 94133, 415-362-8193. 1955. Poetry, fiction, articles, non-fiction. avg. press run 3M. Pub'd 5 titles 1998; expects 5 titles 1999. 73 titles listed in the *Small Press Record of Books in Print* (28th Edition, 1999-00). avg. price, cloth: $10.95; paper: $4.00. 100pp; size varies; of. Reporting time: 4 weeks. Payment: varies. Copyrights for author.

‡CITY LIGHTS JOURNAL, City Lights Books, Lawrence Ferlinghetti, Nancy J. Peters, Robert Sharrard, 261 Columbus Avenue, San Francisco, CA 94133, 415-362-8193. "1 issue every 2 years, infrequent." No subscriptions available.

CITY PRIMEVAL, David Ross, PO Box 30064, Seattle, WA 98103, 206-440-0791. 1995. Poetry, fiction, art, photos. "*City Primeval* seeks narrative writing - fiction or poetry - that addresses the nature and activity of men and women contending in, and with, the evolving urban environment: the breaking down of social structures and their re-creation, the on-going redefinition of male and female roles; family structures and the individual's responsibilities within those structures. The individuals may be marginalized but will ultimately find satisfaction and meaning in their engagement with their environment. Since our requirements are very sepcific, we recommend reading our guidelines - available for an SASE - or a sample copy. Recent contributors include J. Bernhard, Diane Trzcinski, Robert R. Ward, Paula Milligan, Susan Montag, Dave Roberts. Submissions without SASE will be discarded." circ. 100+. 4/yr. Pub'd 4 issues 1998; expects 4 issues 1999, 4 issues 2000. sub. price: $16; per copy: $5 + postage; sample: $5 + $1.01 postage. 64pp; 6×9; †photocopy. Reporting time: 2-3 months. Simultaneous submissions accepted: no. Publishes .5% of manuscripts submitted. Payment: 1 copy of issue with contributor's material. Copyrighted, reverts to author.

THE CIVIL ABOLITIONIST, Civitas, Bina Robinson, Box 26, Swain, NY 14884, 607-545-6213. 1983. Articles, art, photos, cartoons, interviews, criticism, reviews, letters, news items, non-fiction. circ. 1M. 4/yr. Pub'd 4 issues 1998; expects 4 issues 1999, 4 issues 2000. sub. price: $5, foreign $7; per copy: $1; sample: $1. Back issues: $1. 10pp; 8½×11; of. Payment: none. Not copyrighted. Pub's reviews: 9 in 1998. §Human health in relation to animal experimentation.

THE CIVIL WAR NEWS, C. Peter Jorgensen, RR 1 Box 36, Tunbridge, VT 05077, 802-889-3500. 1974. Articles, photos, interviews, reviews, letters, news items. "Articles and photos on authors, collectors, book reviews, research and preservation projects, coming events listing related to American Civil War. We are a current events newspaper. Most 'submissions' are press releases, no pay. News/feature articles by query" circ. 10M. 11/yr. Pub'd 11 issues 1998; expects 11 issues 1999, 11 issues 2000. sub. price: $27, $50 overseas air; per copy: $4; sample: free on request. Back issues: $4. 96pp; 10×16; of. Payment: minimal. Not copyrighted. Pub's reviews: 100+ in 1998. §American Civil War Era. Ads: $12.45 col.inch, SAU column widths, volume and frequency discounts.

Civitas (see also THE CIVIL ABOLITIONIST), Bina Robinson, Box 26, Swain, NY 14884, 607-545-6213. 1983. Poetry, articles, art, photos, cartoons, interviews, criticism, reviews, letters, news items, non-fiction. "We are a special interest organization promoting human and environmental health. We are a non-profit organization devoted to education. We do not solicit manuscripts because we are unable to pay for them, but voluntary submissions are welcome." avg. press run 1M. Pub'd 2 titles 1998; expects 2 titles 1999. 2 titles listed in the *Small Press Record of Books in Print* (28th Edition, 1999-00). avg. price, paper: $1. Discounts: none. 40pp; 8½×11, booklets 5½×8½; of.

CJE NEWS (Newsletter of the Coalition for Jobs & the Environment), PO Box 645, Abingdon, VA 24210-0645, 703-628-8996. 1990. Articles, interviews, letters, news items, non-fiction. "We are a small, heavily-edited bi-monthly. We have regular columns entitled 'Action Needed,' 'Calendar,' 'Reports from Member Groups,' 'Resources,' which take up most of the space. We are always interested in hearing of successful methods for sustanable economics" circ. 500. 6/yr. Pub'd 6 issues 1998; expects 6 issues 1999, 6 issues 2000. sub. price: $6 individuals, $12 groups, free w/membership; per copy: $1; sample: one 32¢ stamp. Back issues: $1 per issue. Discounts: on request, depends who asks. 8pp; 8½×11; high-speed xerox. Reporting time: 4 weeks. Payment: none, low budget, volunteer organization. Not copyrighted. Pub's reviews: 25 in 1998. §Alternative economics, pollution reduction and elimination. Ads: none.

CLACKAMAS LITERARY REVIEW, Jeff Knorr, Tim Schell, 19600 South Molalla Avenue, Oregon City, OR 97045. 1996. "The *Clackamas Literary Review* is a nationally distributed magazine that publishes quality literature. It is an annual magazine produced at Clackamas Community College under the direction of the English Department. *CLR* promotes the work of emerging writers and established writers of fiction, poetry, and creative nonfiction. Submission deadline (postmark) for Spring issue: September 25th. Submissions received after the posted deadlines will not be held for the next issue. Manuscripts must be typed or produced on a letter-quality printer—clean photocopies are acceptable. Send poetry and prose separately. Submissions are limited to 6 poems, 1 story, or 1 essay per submission. We cannot respond to submissions unless they are accompanied by a SASE. We have previously published work by Ron Carlson, Naomi Shihab Nye, Pamela Uschuk, Melissa Pritchard, George Kalamaras, H. Lee Barnes, and Greg Sellers.'' circ. 1M. 1-2/yr. Expects 1 issue 1999, 2 issues 2000. sub. price: $10; per copy: $6. 128pp; 6×9. Reporting time: 8 weeks. Simultaneous submissions okay, please inform us if accepted elsewhere. Payment: copies. Ads: trade space.

Claitor's Law Books & Publishing Division, Inc., Robert G. Claitor, PO Box 261333, Baton Rouge, LA 70826-1333, 504-344-0476; FAX 504-344-0480; claitors@claitors.com; www.claitors.com. 1922. Non-fiction. "Unsolicited manuscripts not desired." avg. press run 1M. Pub'd 100 titles 1998; expects 110 titles 1999, 120 titles 2000. avg. price, cloth: $45; paper: $30. Discounts: trade 1 copy 20%, 2-4 33%, 5+ 40%. 500pp; 8×10¼ and others; †of. Reporting time: 90 days. Simultaneous submissions accepted: no. Publishes 1% of manuscripts submitted. Payment: 6-10%. Copyrights for author.

●**Clamp Down Press,** Joshua Bodwell, PO Box 7270, Cape Porpoise, ME 04014, 207-967-2605. 1997. Poetry, fiction, long-poems. "Recently published book of poems by Mark Weber. All CD Press books are handcrafted, limited editions, using different formats and stitch techniques. May start a broadside series this year. Upcoming projects: Hemingway Homage, Fred Voss/Joan Jobe Smith and Todd Moore, David Mason Heminway'' avg. press run 200-500. Pub'd 3 titles 1998; expects 4 titles 1999. 1 title listed in the *Small Press Record of Books in Print* (28th Edition, 1999-00). avg. price, cloth: $16-20; paper: $5-8; other: $20+ limited editions. 32-50pp; 5½×8½ and others; of, lp. Reporting time: varies. Simultaneous submissions accepted: yes.

Clamshell Press, D.L. Emblen, 160 California Avenue, Santa Rosa, CA 95405. 1973. "We do not read unsolicited mss." avg. press run 250-500. Pub'd 1 title 1998; expects 2 titles 1999, 2 titles 2000. 13 titles listed in the *Small Press Record of Books in Print* (28th Edition, 1999-00). avg. price, paper: $15. 48pp; 5½×8½; †lp. Copyrights for author.

Clapper Publishing Co. (see also BRIDAL CRAFTS; CRAFTS 'N THINGS; THE CROSS STITCHER; PACK-O-FUN; PAINTING), Julie Stephani, 2400 Devon, Suite 375, Des Plaines, IL 60018, 847-635-5800. 1 title listed in the *Small Press Record of Books in Print* (28th Edition, 1999-00).

Clarity Press, Inc., 3277 Roswell Road NE, Suite 469, Atlanta, GA 30305, 404-231-0649; FAX 404-231-3899; 1-800-533-0301; clarity@islandnet.com; www.bookmaster.com/clarity. 1984. Fiction, non-fiction. "Prefer nonfiction on political, social, minority, and human rights issues." avg. press run 3M. Pub'd 2 titles 1998; expects 2 titles 1999, 4 titles 2000. 16 titles listed in the *Small Press Record of Books in Print* (28th Edition, 1999-00). Discounts: Discount schedule established by distributor, LDC Group. 104-512pp; 5½×8½, 6×9; of. Reporting time: 2 months—send query letter first (we will respond only if interested, so SASE not necessary). Simultaneous submissions accepted: yes. Payment: negotiable. Copyrights for author. PMA.

Arthur H. Clark Co., Robert A. Clark, PO Box 14707, Spokane, WA 99214, 509-928-9540. 1902. "Documentary source material and non-fiction dealing with the history of the Western U.S." avg. press run 750-1.5M. Pub'd 7 titles 1998; expects 10 titles 1999, 9 titles 2000. 30 titles listed in the *Small Press Record of Books in Print* (28th Edition, 1999-00). avg. price, cloth: $30. Discounts: 1-2 copies 15%, 3-4 25%, 5-25 40%, 26+ 45%. 250pp; 6¼×9½; of, lp. Reporting time: 2 months. Payment: 10% generally. Copyrights for author.

CLASS ACT, Susan Thurman, PO Box 802, Henderson, KY 42419. 1993. Articles, non-fiction. "We are interested in English/language arts articles. We publish ready-to-use study sheets for the junior/senior high classroom, as well as teaching tips and classroom ideas. Our readers are concerned with all facets of language arts education, including articles that are interdisciplinary with English. Grammar, writing, spelling, speech, literature, creative thinking, cooperative learning-you name it, an English teacher can use it. We don't want articles not written for our audience (Please, no master's theses). Articles from 1/2-4 pages (double spaced)'' circ. 200. 9/yr. Pub'd 9 issues 1998; expects 9 issues 1999, 9 issues 2000. sub. price: $20; per copy: $3; sample: $3. Back issues: $3. 6pp; 8½×11; †photocopy. Reporting time: usually less than 1 month. We would rather not accept simultaneous submissions. Publishes 40% of manuscripts submitted. Payment: $10-$40. Copyrighted, does not revert to author. Pub's reviews: 0 in 1998. §English, grammar, literature. Ads: ad rates being established for future issues.

CLASSICAL ANTIQUITY, University of California Press, Ralph Hexter, Editorial Board Chair, Univ of California Press, 2120 Berkeley Way, Berkeley, CA 94720, 510-643-7154. 1981. Non-fiction. "Editorial address: Department of Classics, 358B Duinelle Hall 2520, Univ. of CA, Berkeley, CA 94720." circ. 650. 2/yr. Pub'd 2 issues 1998; expects 2 issues 1999, 2 issues 2000. sub. price: $35 indiv.; $82 instit. (+ $4 foreign postage); $18 students; per copy: $19 indiv.; $41 instit.; $19 students; sample: free. Back issues: $18 indiv.; $36 instit.; $18 students. Discounts: 10% foreign subs., 30% one-time orders 10+, standing orders (bookstores): 1-99 40%, 100+ 50%. 200pp; 7×10; of. Reporting time: 3 months. Payment: none. Copyrighted, does not revert to author. Ads: $275/$200.

THE CLASSICAL OUTLOOK, Richard A. LaFleur, Department of Classics, The University of Georgia, Athens, GA 30602, 706-542-9257, fax 706-542-8503; mricks@arches.uga.edu. 1923. Poetry, articles, criticism, reviews. circ. 4M. 4/yr. Pub'd 4 issues 1998; expects 4 issues 1999, 4 issues 2000. sub. price: $35 ($37 Canada, $40 overseas); per copy: $10; sample: $10. Back issues: same. 40pp; 8½x11; †1p. Reporting time: 6 months. Simultaneous submissions accepted: no. Publishes 15% of manuscripts submitted. Payment: 2 complimentary copies. Copyrighted, does not revert to author. Pub's reviews: 55 in 1998. §Latin, classical Greek, classical studies. Ads: $265/$175/$120 1/4 page. American Classical League.

Clay Press, Inc. (see also LLAMAS MAGAZINE), PO Box 250, Jackson, CA 95642.

ClearPoint Press, Christiane Buchet, PO Box 170658, San Francisco, CA 94117, 415-386-5377 phone/Fax. 1991. Non-fiction. "We publish books on meditation and spiritual development. We do not accept unsolicited material." avg. press run 3M. Pub'd 1 title 1998; expects 2 titles 1999, 2 titles 2000. 10 titles listed in the *Small Press Record of Books in Print* (28th Edition, 1999-00). avg. price, paper: $12.45. Discounts: standard industry. 136pp; 5½x7½. Payment: 10%. Does not copyright for author.

Clearwater Publishing Co., PO Box 778, Broomfield, CO 80038-0778, 303-436-1982; fax 303-465-2741; e-mail wordguise@aol.com. 1990. "Readable, entertaining introduction to subjects taught in schools." Pub'd 1 title 1998; expects 1 title 1999. 4 titles listed in the *Small Press Record of Books in Print* (28th Edition, 1999-00). avg. price, paper: $14. 260pp; 5½x8½. Rocky Mt. Book Publishers Assoc., Colorado Independent Publishers Assoc., Small Publishers of North America, Colorado Authors League, Rocky Mountain Fiction Writers.

Cleis Press, Frederique Delacoste, Acquisitions Editor; Felice Newman, Marketing Director, PO Box 14684, San Francisco, CA 94114-0684, cleis@aol.com; www.cleispress.com. 1980. Fiction, non-fiction. "Full-length book manuscripts only. Please include SASE w/complete ms. or sample chapter(s). Welcome manuscripts or query letters from progressive women and men writers. Cleis Press is committed to publishing progressive nonfiction and fiction by women and men, especially gay and lesbian." avg. press run 5M. Pub'd 5 titles 1998; expects 7 titles 1999, 7 titles 2000. 46 titles listed in the *Small Press Record of Books in Print* (28th Edition, 1999-00). avg. price, cloth: $24.95; paper: $9.95. Discounts: standard bookstore & distributor, please write for terms. 150-300pp; 5½x8½; of. Reporting time: 2-3 months. Payment: please write us for information on royalty. Copyrights for author.

Cleveland State Univ. Poetry Center, Ted Lardner, Co-Director; Ruth Schwartz, Co-Director; David Evett, Editorial Committee; Rita Grabowski, Coordinator; Bonnie Jacobson, Editorial Committee, 1983 East 24th Street, Cleveland, OH 44115-2400, 216-687-3986; Fax 216-687-6943; poetrycenter@popmail.csuohio.edu. 1962. Poetry, concrete art. "1 local (Ohio) poetry series—51 published since 1971, 24-100pp. 2 national series, 61 published since 1971, most 72-120pp. Other additional titles also published. Among authors published: David Breskin, Jared Carter, Chrystos, Beckian Fritz Goldberg, Marilyn Krysl, Robert Hill Long, Frankie Paino, Caludia Rankine, Tim Seibles, Sandra Stone, Anthony Vigil, Judith Vollmer, Jeanne Murray Walker. Submit only Nov. 1st-Feb. 1st, $20 reading fee for national series, $1,000 prize for best booklength ms. (50-100pp). Send SASE for complete guidelines, $2 for 64 page catalogue." avg. press run 600 local series, 1.3M-1.5M national series. Pub'd 4 titles 1998; expects 4 titles 1999, 4 titles 2000. 103 titles listed in the *Small Press Record of Books in Print* (28th Edition, 1999-00). avg. price, cloth: $17.50; paper: $10; other: $5 chapbooks. Discounts: 40% to retail bookstores, 50% to wholesalers/jobbers. Distributed through Partners Book Distributing (800-336-3137) and Ingram (615-793-5000) and Spring Church Book Co., PO Box 127, Spring Church, PA 15686. 32-100pp; size varies; †of. Reporting time: 5-7 months. We accept simultaneous submissions, but identify as such. Publishes .5% of manuscripts submitted. Payment: local series 100 copies, national series 50 copies + $300. Copyrights for author.

THE CLIMBING ART, Ron Morrow, Editor, 6390 E. Floyd Dr., Denver, CO 80222-7638. 1986. Poetry, fiction, articles, art, photos, cartoons, interviews, satire, criticism, reviews, letters, parts-of-novels, long-poems, collages, news items, non-fiction. "We will consider material of any length, and will even serialize book-length mss. We publish only material that is well written and of interest to those who live in, travel in, or climb mountains. Recent contributors include Reg Saner, David Craig and Grant McConnell" circ. 1M. 2/yr. sub. price: $18; per copy: $4.50; sample: $4.50. Back issues: inquire. Discounts: 1-4 copies 20%, 5-24 40%, 25-49 43%, 50-99 46%, 100+ 50%; jobbers up to 55%. 160pp; 7½x5½; of. Reporting time: 2 months. Simultaneous submissions accepted: yes. Publishes 20% of manuscripts submitted. Payment: up to $200. Copyrighted, reverts to author. Pub's reviews: 20 in 1998. §The mountains, mountaineering and rock-climbing, mountain-area histories, biographies of figures associated with the mountains. Ads: $100/$50/$30.

CLOCKWATCH REVIEW, James Plath, Zarina Mullan Plath, James Plath, English Department, Illinois Wesleyan University, Bloomington, IL 61702, 309-556-3352; http://titan.iwu.edu/~jplath/clockwatch.html. 1983. Poetry, fiction, art, interviews, music. "*Clockwatch* wants poetry to 32 lines, fiction to 4M words. In any case, we look for strong voice and characterization which is believable and colorful without being cliched. We seek material which can straddle two worlds: the literary and the popular. Recent contributors include Albert Goldbarth, Bob Shacochis, Martin Espada, Jamaica Kincaid and Ronald J. Rindo. Our emphasis is on excellence, but we prefer upbeat and the offbeat, or things which do what all art attempts: to leave a lingering shadow of learning within a work which entertains." circ. 1.4M. 1 volume (2 issues/1 double issue) per year. Pub'd 1 issue 1998; expects 2 issues 1999, 2 issues 2000. sub. price: $8-$10 (U.S-Foreign); per copy: $4-$5 (U.S.-Foreign); sample: $4-$5 (U.S.-Foreign). Back issues: $5 each. Discounts: Wholesalers, 50% plus shipping; Retailers, 40%. 51-80pp, double issue 176pp; 5½×8½; of. Reporting time: 6 months. Simultaneous submissions accepted if declared. Publishes 3% of manuscripts submitted. Payment: 3 copies, small cash awards—presently $25 fiction, $5 poetry. Copyrighted, rights don't revert to author, but we reassign rights if asked. Pub's reviews: 8 in 1998. §Fiction, poetry, literary criticism, art, music, creative non-fiction. Ads: $300/$150. CLMP.

ClockWorks Press (see also IN PRINT), Nancy A. Frank, PO Box 1699, Shingle Springs, CA 95682, 916-676-0701. 1991. Articles, non-fiction. "Material of interest to clock and watch collectors, repairers and related areas such as jewelry repair, how to repair, etc." avg. press run 4M. Pub'd 1 title 1998; expects 6 titles 1999, 8 titles 2000. avg. price, cloth: $24.95; paper: $9.95. Discounts: trade. 225pp; of. Reporting time: 1 month. Payment: negotiable - flat fee. Copyrights for author.

Clover Park Press, Geraldine Kennedy, Publisher, PO Box 5067, Santa Monica, CA 90409-5067, 310-452-7657; cloverparkpr@loop.com. 1990. Non-fiction. "Non-fiction, send letter first. Interested in multi-cultural, literary travel, biography, California history, translations of Third-World writers especially women: excellent writing that illuminates life's wonders and wanderings. Book length. All production details customized to individual book and market." Pub'd 1 title 1998; expects 2-3 titles 1999, 5 titles 2000. 2 titles listed in the *Small Press Record of Books in Print* (28th Edition, 1999-00). Discounts: upon request. of. Reporting time: 4-6 weeks. Simultaneous submissions accepted: yes. Payment: as per contract. Does not copyright for author. PMA.

CLUBHOUSE, Krista Hainey, Your Story Hour, PO Box 15, Berrien Springs, MI 49103, (616) 471-9009. 1951. Poetry, fiction, cartoons, non-fiction. "Not currently accepting material. Try again in the Spring of 1999. 1,200 word limit, psychologically 'up', can-do, kids-are-neat philosophy. No Halloween, Santa-elves, Easter-bunny-eggs, etc. material. Prefer action-oriented stories in which kids are clever, wise, kind, etc. Religious backdrop, but not overtly stated. Age group 9-14 years old." circ. 4M. 12/yr. Pub'd 5 issues 1998; expects 6 issues 1999, 6 issues 2000. sub. price: $5; sample: free with SASE for 3 oz. Discounts: none. 8pp; 8½×11. Reporting time: 4-8 weeks. Payment: $30-$35 stories, $10-$12 cartoons, puzzles, poems. Copyrighted, reverts to author. No ads.

CLUTCH, Dan Hodge, Lawrence Oberc, 147 Coleridge Street, San Francisco, CA 94110. 1991. Poetry, fiction, art, photos, interviews, satire, letters, long-poems, non-fiction. "Recent contributors: John Bennett, Charles Bukowski, Mitchel Cohen, Denise Dee, Lorri Jackson, Jon Longhi, Todd Moore, Kurt Nimmo, Nicole Panter, Simon Perchik, Robert Peters, Carl Watson. Non-academic/writing with an edge. Both tried and unheard-from voices. ISSN 1061-737X. Writers: please do not submit work more than once a year. Work accepted for publication may take up to two years for printing. A *Clutch* supplement series is planned beginning 1999. All work submitted to *Clutch* will be considered for the regular/annual issue and for the supplement series unless we are told otherwise." circ. 400-500. 1/yr + 1 supplement issue. Pub'd 1 issue 1998; expects 1 issue 1999, 1 issue 2000. sub. price: $5/issue, payment must be made in cash or check payable to Dan Hodge. Subscribers receive supplements at no extra charge.; per copy: $5 annual issue, $2 supplement; sample: $5 annual issue, $2 supplement. Discounts: $4 in bookstores; $4 for libraries; $1 for supplements. Annual issues 65pp, supplements 12pp; 5½×8½; determined issue by issue. Reporting time: approx. 1-6 months. Simultaneous submissions accepted: yes. Publishes 7% of manuscripts submitted. Payment: free copy. Copyrighted, reverts to author. Pub's reviews. §Underground press publications.

CLWN WR, Bob Heman, PO Box 2165 Church Street Station, New York, NY 10008-2165. 1972. Poetry. "We invite visual poetry and related forms (including poetry objects, conceptual poetry, etc.). Black and white only. Send high quality photocopies (no originals). Recent contributors include: Spencer Selby, A.F. Caldiero, John M.Bennett, Richard Kostelanetz, David Cole, Scott Helmes, Hannah Weiner, Dick Higgins, etc. We also sometimes do prose poem issues, for which we invite work that stretches the boundaries of the form." circ. 300-500. Irregular. Pub'd 1 issue 1998; expects 3 issues 1999, 3 issues 2000. sample price: #10 SASE w/2oz. postage. 10-14pp; 8½×11; high-quality photocopy. Reporting time: 1-9 months. Simultaneous submissions accepted: no. Payment: copies. Copyrighted, reverts to author. Pub's reviews. §Visual poetry and related works, prose poems.

CNW Publishing (see also FREELANCE WRITER'S REPORT), Dana K. Cassell, PO Box A, North Stratford, NH 03590-0167, 603-922-8338, fax 603-922-8339; danakcnw@ncia.net; www.writers-editors.com. 1977. "Not currently publishing book titles by outside authors" Expects 1 title 1999, 2 titles 2000. 3 titles listed in the *Small Press Record of Books in Print* (28th Edition, 1999-00). Florida Publishers Assn., NAIP.

COALITION FOR PRISONERS' RIGHTS NEWSLETTER, Mara Taub, PO Box 1911, Santa Fe, NM 87504, 505-982-9520. 1976. Articles, cartoons, interviews, letters, news items, non-fiction. "Length of material: 250+/- words. Politically progressive. Half of each issue is excerpts of letters from prisoners" circ. 2.5M-4.5M. 12/yr. Pub'd 12 issues 1998; expects 12 issues 1999, 12 issues 2000. sub. price: $12 individuals, $25 to institutions, free to prisoners and their families; per copy: free; sample: free. Back issues: $1 an issue to non-prisoners. 8pp; 7×8½; lp. Reporting time: 6 weeks. Payment: none. Not copyrighted. Ads: none.

Cobblestone Publishing, Inc. (see also COBBLESTONE: The History Magazine for Young People; FACES: The Magazine About People; CALLIOPE: World History for Young People; ODYSSEY: Science Adventures in Science), Denise Babcock, Managing Editor, 7 School Street, Peterborough, NH 03458, 603-924-7209. avg. press run 22M. 4 titles listed in the *Small Press Record of Books in Print* (28th Edition, 1999-00). 40-48pp; 7×9; of. Reporting time: queries sent well in advance of deadline may not be answered for several months. Go-aheads usually sent 5 months prior to publication date. Payment: upon publication. We own copyright. Classroom Publishers Assoc., EdPress.

COBBLESTONE: The History Magazine for Young People, Cobblestone Publishing, Inc., Margaret E. Chorlian, Editor, 7 School Street, Peterborough, NH 03458, 603-924-7209. 1980. Poetry, fiction, articles, art, photos, interviews, reviews, music, plays, non-fiction. "Material must be written for children ages 8-14. Most articles do not exceed 1M words, write Editor for guidelines as we focus each issue on a particular theme." circ. 36M. 9/yr. Pub'd 9 issues 1998; expects 9 issues 1999, 9 issues 2000. sub. price: $26.95 + $8/yr for foreign and Canada, Canadian subs add 7% GST; per copy: $4.50; sample: $4.50. Back issues: $4.50, annual set $46.95, includes slipcase and cumulative index. Discounts: 15% to agency, bulk rate 3 subs @ $15.95 each/year. 48pp; 7×9; of. Reporting time: queries sent well in advance of deadline may not be answered for several months. Go-aheads usually sent 5 months prior to publication date. Payment: on publication. Copyrighted, *Cobblestone* buys all rights. Pub's reviews: 89 in 1998. §History books for children, ages 8-14, American history related only. No ads. Classroom Publishers Assoc., EdPress.

Cobra Publishing, Caralee Roberts, PO Box 217, Antelope, OR 97001, 503-244-0805; e-mail bbeas10010@aol.com. 1997. Non-fiction. ""How to" and business books." avg. press run 5M. Expects 2 titles 1999, 3 titles 2000. avg. price, paper: $35. 200pp; of. Reporting time: varies. Simultaneous submissions accepted: yes. Publishes 10% of manuscripts submitted. Payment: varies. Copyrights for author.

CODA: The Jazz Magazine, Bill Smith, PO Box 1002, Station O, Toronto, Ont. M4A 2N4, Canada, 416-593-7230. 1958. Articles, photos, interviews, criticism, reviews, news items. "Our emphasis is on the art rather than the commerce of the music (i.e. we concentrate on non-commercialism) and we cover jazz of all styles and areas." circ. 4M. 6/yr. Expects 6 issues 1999. sub. price: $24 Canada & US, elsewhere $30 Can.; per copy: $4; sample: $4. Back issues: $15 for 10. Discounts: agency discount (subscriptions only) 20%. 40pp; 8¼×10⅜; of. Reporting time: 1 month to 2 years. Payment: small. Rights revert to author on publication. Pub's reviews: 22 in 1998. §Jazz, blues. Ads: $300/$160/75¢ (min. $15).

Coffee House Press, Allan Kornblum, 27 N. 4th Street, Minneapolis, MN 55401, 612-338-0125; Fax 612-338-4004. 1984. Poetry, fiction, art, long-poems. "Books may be ordered directly from publisher." avg. press run 2M. Pub'd 6 titles 1998; expects 10 titles 1999, 10 titles 2000. 94 titles listed in the *Small Press Record of Books in Print* (28th Edition, 1999-00). avg. price, cloth: $19.95; paper: $9.95; other: $10 handsewn chapbooks. Discounts: paperback: 2-5 copies, 25%; 6-9 copies, 35%, 10-49, 40%; 42% for 50 or more books (bookstores); libraries, standing orders 10%. 150pp; poetry 6×9, fiction 5½×8½; lp, of. Reporting time: 6-8 months. Payment: 8% of list for trade books, 10% of run for chapbooks. Copyrights for author. CBA MCBA.

COKEFISH, Cokefish Press, Ana Christy, 31 Waterloo Street, New Hope, PA 18938. 1990. Poetry, art, cartoons. "Limit poems to one page. Do not want to see violence, religion, or rhyme. Recent contributors are Wayne Wilkinson, Steve Richmond, Margaret Crocker, Joseph Verrilli." circ. 500. 6/yr. Pub'd 6 issues 1998; expects 6 issues 1999, 8 issues 2000. sub. price: $17; per copy: $6; sample: $6. Back issues: $6. 50-60pp; 8½×11; computer. Reporting time: immediate to 1 week. Simultaneous submissions accepted: yes. Publishes 50% of manuscripts submitted. Payment: copy. Copyrighted. Pub's reviews: 20 in 1998. §Poetry, modern culture. Ads: $15/$10/$5 by line.

Cokefish Press (see also COKEFISH), Ana Christy, 31 Waterloo Street, New Hope, PA 18938. 1990. Poetry. "Cokefish Press is seeking manuscripts for publishing: poetry avant garde modern. Length of manuscript: 30 poems. We're interested in unpublished as well as recognized poets. We also do co-operative publishing" avg. press run 100. Pub'd 2 titles 1998; expects 6 titles 1999, 6 titles 2000. 11 titles listed in the *Small Press Record of Books in Print* (28th Edition, 1999-00). avg. price, paper: $5. Discounts: 40%. 30-50pp; 5×8½; of & photocopied. Reporting time: immediately to 1 week. Simultaneous submissions accepted: yes. Publishes 50% of manuscripts submitted. Payment: varies. Copyrights for author.

Coker Publishing House, Editorial Board, PO BOX 81017, Chicago, IL 60681-0017. 1970. Fiction, non-fiction. avg. press run 5M. Pub'd 4 titles 1998; expects 6-10 titles 1999, 10-12 titles 2000. 5 titles listed in the *Small Press Record of Books in Print* (28th Edition, 1999-00). avg. price, cloth: $12.95; paper: $6.95. Discounts: 20% to retailers, 50% to jobbers. 150pp; 5½×8½. Reporting time: 4-6 weeks. Payment: negotiable. Copyrights for author.

COLD-DRILL, Cold-Drill Books, Mitch Wieland, Faculty Editor, 1910 University Drive, Boise, ID 83725, 208-426-3862. 1970. Poetry, fiction, articles, art, photos, cartoons, parts-of-novels, plays, concrete art, non-fiction. "Submission deadline: December 1st for March 1 issue. Send xerox, SASE (we notify by Jan. 15 only if accepted). Open to literary and innovative forms of high quality." circ. 500. 1/yr. Pub'd 1 issue 1998; expects 1 issue 1999, 1 issue 2000. sub. price: $15 (inc. p/h); per copy: $15 (inc. p/h); sample: $15 (inc. p/h). Back issues: same. Discounts: none. 150pp; 6×9; †of. Reporting time: by January 1 of each year. Payment: copy of magazine. Copyrighted, reverts to author. CSPA, CMA.

Cold-Drill Books (see also COLD-DRILL), Tom Trusky, Dept. of English, Boise State University, Boise, ID 83725. 1980. "Prior publication in *Cold-Drill Magazine* required. Interested in multiple artist's books editions." avg. press run 50-1M. Pub'd 1 title 1998; expects 1 title 1999. 5 titles listed in the *Small Press Record of Books in Print* (28th Edition, 1999-00). avg. price, cloth: varies; paper: varies. Discounts: 40%, no returns. Pages vary; size varies; †varies. Reporting time: 4 months. Payment: 25% on third printing. Copyrights for author.

Coldwater Press, Neila A. Petrick, 9806 Coldwater Circle, Dallas, TX 75228, 214-328-7612. 1991. Fiction, plays. "We publish *no* adult fiction. We are interested in books Texas and the Southwest for 4-7 grades (juveniles). *Must query. No* unsolicited manuscripts due to small staff. We are interested in good Texana for juveniles. Moving toward more videos." avg. press run 2.5M. Pub'd 1 title 1998; expects 2 titles 1999, 2 titles 2000. 4 titles listed in the *Small Press Record of Books in Print* (28th Edition, 1999-00). avg. price, paper: $8.95. Discounts: standard. 94-150pp; 5¼×7½; of. Reporting time: 3 months. Payment: negotiated. We can copyright for author. Book Pub. of Texas (BPT).

Cole Publishing Group, Inc., Annette Gooch, VP Product Development, PO Box 4089, Santa Rosa, CA 95402-4089, 707-526-2682. 1988. Non-fiction. avg. press run 10M. Expects 6 titles 1999, 13 titles 2000. 37 titles listed in the *Small Press Record of Books in Print* (28th Edition, 1999-00). avg. price, paper: $7.95-$18.95; other: $14.95-$29.95. Discounts: trade. 8×8, 8¼×11, 5×8¼, 7¾×7¾, 7¼×10, 9×10, 5×8½; of. Payment: variable.

COLLECTORS CLUB PHILATELIST, E.E. Fricks, Editor, 22 East 35th Street, New York, NY 10016, 212-683-0559. 1922. Articles, photos, interviews, reviews, news items, non-fiction. "Average single article 15 pages. Some extended articles continued to suceeding issues" circ. 3M. 6/yr. Pub'd 6 issues 1998; expects 6 issues 1999, 6 issues 2000. sub. price: $42; per copy: $7; sample: $7. Back issues: $7. Discounts: 40% to the trade for 5 or more. 80pp; 6½×9; of. Reporting time: 2-6 weeks. Simultaneous submissions accepted: no. Publishes 80% of manuscripts submitted. Payment: varies with length, content; average $200. Copyrighted, rights revert to author by special arrangement only. Pub's reviews: 40 in 1998. §Stamp collecting (philately), history. Ads: $225/$125/ask for rate card. AAP.

Collectors Press, Inc., Lisa Perry, Editor-in-Chief, PO Box 230986, Portland, OR 97281, 503-684-3030, fax 503-684-3777. 1990. Art, photos, non-fiction. "Our focus is American Illustration, art, price guides, nostalgia." avg. press run 7.5M. Pub'd 6 titles 1998; expects 10 titles 1999, 15 titles 2000. 27 titles listed in the *Small Press Record of Books in Print* (28th Edition, 1999-00). avg. price, cloth: $35; paper: $16.95; other: $75 limited editions. Trade discounts. 150pp; 9×12; of. Reporting time: standard. Simultaneous submissions accepted: yes. Publishes 5% of manuscripts submitted. Payment: confidential. Copyrights for author. PMA, PNBA.

COLLEGE ENGLISH, Louise Z. Smith, Dept. of English, U Mass/Boston, 100 Morrissey Boulevard, Boston, MA 02125-3393. 1939. Poetry, articles, criticism, reviews, letters. circ. 16M. 8/yr. Pub'd 8 issues 1998; expects 8 issues 1999, 8 issues 2000. sub. price: $40, includes membership in NCTE, student rate $10.50; per copy: $6, $5 members; sample: $6, $6.25 from NCTE in Urbana, IL. Back issues: $6. 100pp; 7½×9½; of. Reporting time: 16 weeks. Simultaneous submissions accepted: no. Publishes 12% of manuscripts submitted. Payment: none. Copyrighted, reverts to author. Pub's reviews: 16 in 1998. §Literary theory, linguistic theory, theory of learning and pedagogy, history of English studies, studies of works of literature. Ads: phone NCTE for most recent rates (800-369-6283).

COLLEGIUM NEWSLETTER, Bandanna Books, Sasha Newborn, 319-B Anacapa Street, Santa Barbara, CA 93101, fax 805-564-3278; website bandannabooks.com. 1998. Fiction, articles, cartoons, reviews, letters, parts-of-novels, news items, non-fiction. "This is an electronic weekly newsletter for college freshmen/women, their teachers, their parents and anyone interested in the freshman year. Special emphases: distance learning, self-education, writing, languages, college fiction." circ. 500. Weekly during school year. Pub'd 20 issues 1998; expects 40 issues 1999, 40 issues 2000. sub. price: free; per copy: free; sample: free. Back issues: not available. 20pp. Reporting time: 2 weeks. Simultaneous submissions accepted: yes. Publishes 10% of manuscripts submitted. Payment: none. Not copyrighted. Pub's reviews: 4 in 1998. §Writing, language, self-education, fiction, puzzles, surveys, must be college related. PMA.

Colophon House, Mary Dodson Wade, 17522 Brushy River Court, Houston, TX 77095, 218-304-9502; Fax 281-256-3442. 1992. Fiction, non-fiction. "No picture books. No YA. Prefer non-fiction. No unsolicited submissions." avg. press run 1K-2K. Expects 1 title 1999, 1 title 2000. 8 titles listed in the *Small Press Record of Books in Print* (28th Edition, 1999-00). avg. price, cloth: $11.95; paper: $5.95; other: $14.95 full color. Discounts: bulk (over 500 copies)=50%; jobber (21-499)=45%; (1-20)-20%. 32-64pp; 6×9; lp. Simultaneous submissions accepted: no. Payment: flat fee. Does not copyright for author. Assoc. of Authors and Publishers; Small Publishers Association of North America.

COLORADO REVIEW: A Journal of Contemporary Literature, David Milofsky, Fiction & General Editor, 359 Eddy, English Dept., Colorado State University, Fort Collins, CO 80523, 303-491-5449. 1966. Poetry, fiction, articles, interviews, criticism, reviews, parts-of-novels, long-poems. "We publish three issues per year including fiction, poetry, translations, interviews, reviews, and articles on contemporary literary culture. Our readers will consider mss. from Sept. 1 to April 30 each year. Allow until end of reading period for reply. *Colorado Review* is listed in both the *American Humanities Index* and the *Index of American Periodical Verse*. It is distributed nationally by Ingram Periodicals, Inc. Libraries may use Faxon or Ebsco or Readmore." circ. 1.8M. 3/yr. Pub'd 2 issues 1998; expects 2 issues 1999, 3 issues 2000. sub. price: $24/1 year, $45/2 years, $65/3 years; per copy: $10; sample: $10. Back issues: same. Discounts: 50% to distributors, 30% to bookstores, classes, other orders of 10 or more copies. 200pp; 6⅛×9¼; of. Reporting time: 3 months. Simultaneous submissions accepted: no. Publishes a variable % of manuscripts submitted. Payment: 1 copy; $5 per printed page of poetry; $5 fiction. Copyrighted, reverts to author. Pub's reviews: 6 in 1998. §Contemporary fiction & poetry. CLMP.

●**COLORLINES,** Bob Wing, 4096 Piedmont Avenue, PMB 319, Oakland, CA 94611, 510-653-3415; Fax 510-653-3427; colorlines@arc.org; www.colorlines.com. 1998. Articles, art, photos, cartoons, interviews, criticism, reviews, music, news items, non-fiction. "Recent contributors: Angela Davis, Robin D.G. Kelley, Mike Davis, Gloria Anzaldua, William 'Upski' Wimsatt, Michael Omi, June Jordan, Angela Oh. Material: 3,000-4,000 words per article. Biases: welcome articles with race angle or community organizing/activism angle." circ. 20M. 4/yr. Pub'd 3 issues 1998; expects 4 issues 1999, 4 issues 2000. sub. price: $15/6 issues; per copy: $5 publisher, $2.95 newsstand; sample: free. Back issues: $5. Discounts: please contact publisher for bulk prices; trades are free. 45pp; 7⅜×10⅞. Reporting time: 1-2 months. Simultaneous submissions accepted: yes. Publishes 10% of manuscripts submitted. Payment: none. Copyrighted, rights negotiable. Pub's reviews: 5 in 1998. §Politics, race/ethnicity non-fiction/fiction, sociology, gender/feminist studies. Ads: $700/$350/$160 1/4 page. IPA, PNS.

Columbia Alternative Library (see also ALTERNATIVE PRESS REVIEW), Jason McQuinn, PO Box 1446, Columbia, MO 65205-1446, 573-442-4352. 1989. avg. press run 5M. Pub'd 1 title 1998; expects 3 titles 1999, 4 titles 2000. 1 title listed in the *Small Press Record of Books in Print* (28th Edition, 1999-00). avg. price, paper: $4.95. Discounts: Same as Alternative Press Review. 84pp; 8¼×10¾; web of. Reporting time: 2-3 months. Simultaneous submissions accepted: yes. Publishes 5% of manuscripts submitted. Payment: copies. Does not copyright for author. IPA.

Columbine Publishing Group, Lee Ellison, PO Box 456, Angel Fire, NM 87710, 505-377-3474, 800-996-9783, FAX 505-377-3526, publish@intriguepress.com. 1994. Non-fiction. avg. press run 3-10M. Pub'd 1 title 1998; expects 2 titles 1999, 2 titles 2000. 2 titles listed in the *Small Press Record of Books in Print* (28th Edition, 1999-00). avg. price, cloth: $24.95; paper: $18.95. Discounts: 40% stores, 55% wholesalers. 200+pp; 6×9; of. Reporting time: 4-5 weeks. Simultaneous submissions accepted: yes. Publishes less than 1% of manuscripts submitted. Payment: varies. Copyrights for author. PMA, SPAN.

THE COMICS JOURNAL, Fantagraphics Books, Gary Groth, Tom Spurgeon, 7563 Lake City Way, Seattle, WA 98115. 1976. Articles, cartoons, interviews, criticism, reviews, letters, news items. "*The Comics Journal* is a monthly magazine devoted to news and reviews of the comic book trade, both mainstream and independent publishing" circ. 10M. 10/yr. Pub'd 10 issues 1998; expects 10 issues 1999, 10 issues 2000. sub. price: $35 USA; per copy: $4.95; sample: $4.95. 120pp; 8½×11; of. Reporting time: 1-2 months. Simultaneous submissions accepted: yes. Publishes 1% of manuscripts submitted. Payment: 1½¢ per word. Copyrighted, reverts to author. Pub's reviews: 100 in 1998. §Comics, comics-related publications and products. Ads: $200/$120.

COMICS REVUE, Manuscript Press, Rick Norwood, PO Box 336 -Manuscript Press, Mountain Home, TN 37684-0336, 432-926-7495. 1984. Cartoons. "We publish syndicated comic strips: Tarzan, Flash Gordon, Krazy Kat, Buz Sawyer, Modesty Blaise, The Phantom, Alley Oop, Buz Sawyer, Gasoline Alley, and B.C. We are not interested in looking at submissions unless they are better than what is available from the syndicates. No submissions can be returned. Submissions are discouraged, but if you must submit a comic strip, send xerox copies only and include a SASE for a reply." circ. 4M. 12/yr. Pub'd 14 issues 1998; expects 12 issues 1999, 12 issues 2000. sub. price: $45; per copy: $6; sample: same. Back issues: $6 for single copies, $45 for 12 copies, current or old. Discounts: 10-99 copies 40% off, 100-499 copies 50% off, 500+ copies 60% off. 64pp; 8½×11; of. Reporting time: indefinite. Simultaneous submissions accepted: no. Publishes 0% of manuscripts submitted. Payment: $5 per page. Copyrighted, reverts to author. Pub's reviews: 10-12 in 1998. §Comic strip reprints. Ads: $125/$70.

COMMON BOUNDARY MAGAZINE, Anne Simpkinson, 7005 Florida Street, Chevy Chase, MD 20815, 301-652-9495; FAX 301-652-0579; e-mail connect@commonboundary.org; website www.commonboundary.org. 1980. Articles, art, photos, interviews, criticism, reviews, letters, news items, non-fiction. "1,500-3,000 average article. Prefer journalistic style when writing about spiritual/psychotherapeutic experiences." circ. 30M. 6/yr. Pub'd 6 issues 1998; expects 6 issues 1999, 6 issues 2000. sub. price: $24.95; per copy: $4.95, $6.40 Canada; sample: $5. Back issues: $5. Discounts: 15% for teachers who sign up 10 students (all receive discount). 72pp; 8½×11; of, Web press. Reporting time: 2 months. We accept simultaneous submissions if indicated as such. Publishes 5% of manuscripts submitted. Payment: $50-$4000. Copyrighted, reverts to author. Pub's reviews: 20 in 1998. §Psychology, spirituality, religion, creativity, mythology, storytelling, meditation practice. Ads: $1240/$700/$505 1/3 page/$400 1/4/$305 1/6/$205 1/12. American Society of Magazine Editors.

Common Courage Press, Box 702, Monroe, ME 04951, 207-525-0900. 1991. Non-fiction. "Politics, alternative, social justice, feminism, race and gender issues, ecology, economics." avg. press run 5M. Pub'd 10 titles 1998; expects 10 titles 1999, 10 titles 2000. 9 titles listed in the *Small Press Record of Books in Print* (28th Edition, 1999-00). avg. price, cloth: $29.95; paper: $14.95. Discounts: trade 5-99 40%, 100+ 50%. 250pp; 5×7⅝. Reporting time: 30 days. Simultaneous submissions accepted: yes. Publishes 5% of manuscripts submitted. Payment: 10% net. Copyrights for author.

COMMON LIVES / LESBIAN LIVES, 1802 7th Ave. Ct., Iowa City, IA 52240-6436. 1981. Poetry, fiction, articles, art, photos, cartoons, interviews, satire, criticism, reviews, music, letters, parts-of-novels, plays, non-fiction. "Journal entries, diaries, correspondence etc. The everyday writings of ordinary lesbians, oral history." circ. 3M. 4/yr. Pub'd 4 issues 1998; expects 4 issues 1999, 4 issues 2000. 1 title listed in the *Small Press Record of Books in Print* (28th Edition, 1999-00). sub. price: $15; per copy: $5; sample: $5. Back issues: $3.50 + $1 p/h. Discounts: 40% to bookstores. 128pp; 5½×8½; of. Reporting time: maximum 90 days. Payment: 2 copies of issue in which her piece appears. Copyrighted, reverts to author. Pub's reviews: 10-15 in 1998. §Lesbian-authored work, esp. small press. Ads: $100/$50/20¢.

Commonwealth Press Virginia (see also THE LYRIC), Bonnie Clark, 415 First Street, Box 3547, Radford, VA 24141. 1954. "General fiction & nonfiction. Recent books: *Appalachian Heritage cookbook, Hold 'Em Poker Bible, There Will Never Be Another You, Murder On The Appalachian Trail*. Reprints on special arrangement." avg. press run 2M. Pub'd 16 titles 1998; expects 14 titles 1999. avg. price, cloth: $12.95; paper: $6.95. Discounts: 5 copies 40%, 100-249 45%, Bulk shipments to wholesalers (1,000 copies and up) 50%. 176pp; 5½×8½; †of. Payment: some of our books are done on contract with historical societies, others on royalty, still more on coop with other publishers.

Commune-A-Key Publishing, Inc., Caryn L. Summers, Editor-in-Chief; Nancy Lang, Managing Editor, PO Box 58637, Salt Lake City, UT 84158, 801-581-9191, Fax 801-581-9196, 800-983-0600. 1992. Non-fiction. avg. press run 10M. Pub'd 2 titles 1998; expects 2 titles 1999, 2 titles 2000. 11 titles listed in the *Small Press Record of Books in Print* (28th Edition, 1999-00). avg. price, cloth: $19.95; paper: $9.95-$14.95. Discounts: 1-4 books 20% off, 5-9 books 30% off, 10-24 40% off, 25-74 44% off, 200 or more books 50% off. 250pp; 6×9. Reporting time: 4-6 weeks. Publishes 10% of manuscripts submitted. Payment: on contract 4-8%. Copyrights for author. PMA, PW, ABA.

Communication Creativity, Ann Markham, 425 Cedar, PO Box 909, Buena Vista, CO 81211, 719-395-8659; span@spannet.org; www.spannet.org/cc. 1977. Non-fiction. "Communication Creativity books are designed to be both entertaining and informational. They deal primarily with subjects in the fields of business. Not soliciting submissions" avg. press run 5M. Pub'd 3 titles 1998; expects 3 titles 1999, 4 titles 2000. 9 titles listed in the *Small Press Record of Books in Print* (28th Edition, 1999-00). avg. price, cloth: $24.95; paper: $16.95. Discounts: from 20% to 50%. 224pp; 5½×8½, 6×9; cameron belt, of. PMA, CIPA, SPAN.

The Communication Press, Randall Harrison, PO Box 22541, San Francisco, CA 94122, 415-386-0178. 1977. Cartoons. "Our focus is on humorous how-to, such as our *How To Cut Your Water Use—and Still Stay Sane and Sanitary*. We also are interested in art, psychology and communication. We're probably a poor market for freelancers as we already have as many projects as we can handle for the next few years; and we hope to stay small and quality oriented." avg. press run 5M. Pub'd 1-2 titles 1998. 11 titles listed in the *Small Press Record of Books in Print* (28th Edition, 1999-00). avg. price, cloth: $7.50; paper: $3.50. Discounts: 40% trade. 96-128pp; 5×8; of. Reporting time: 6-8 weeks. Payment: variable. Copyrights for author.

Communicom Publishing Company, Donna Matrazzo, 19300 NW Sauvie Island Road, Portland, OR 97231,

503-621-3049. 1984. Non-fiction. "We publish and distribute books (and other items) related to business communications, specializing in writing and audio visual work. Title published: *The Corporate Scriptwriting Book*, Donna Matrazzo; Titles distributed: *Organizational TV News*, Tom Thompson; *Editing Your Newsletter*, Mark Beach, *Getting It Printed*, Mark Beach, *Thinking on Your Feet*, Marian Woodall, *Speaking to a Group*, Marian Woodall." avg. press run 5M. Expects 2 titles 2000. 1 title listed in the *Small Press Record of Books in Print* (28th Edition, 1999-00). avg. price, paper: $20. Discounts: 20% to schools, bookstore discount varies by volume. 250pp; 5½×8½. Reporting time: no specification. Payment: arrangements made on book-by-book basis. Copyrights for author. Northwest Association of Book Publishers.

COMMUNITIES, Diana Christain, Editor, 290 McEntire Road, Tryon, NC 28782-9764, 828-863-4425; e-mail communities@ic.org. 1972. Articles, art, photos, interviews, reviews, letters. "Bias: limited to contributions relating to aspects of intentioned communities cooperative living" circ. 4.4M. 4/yr. Pub'd 4 issues 1998; expects 4 issues 1999, 4 issues 2000. sub. price: $18/4 issues; per copy: $6; sample: $6. Back issues: full available set (approx. 85) $300. Discounts: 3-4 copies 25%, 5-9 30%, 10-24 35%, 25-49 40%, 50+ 50%. 76pp; 8½×11; of. Reporting time: 60 days. Simultaneous submissions accepted: yes. Publishes 1% of manuscripts submitted. Payment: free copies, or 1 year subscription. Copyrighted, reverts to author. Pub's reviews: 12 in 1998. §Intentional communities, alternative culture, worker-owned co-ops. Ads: $250/$145/proportionals. Fellowship for Intentional Community.

COMMUNITY DEVELOPMENT JOURNAL, Oxford University Press, Gary Craig, Foldyard House, Naburn, York YO1 4RU, England, 0904-87329. 1966. Articles, photos, cartoons, reviews, news items, non-fiction. "Articles (should be sent) to Editorial address above. For subs, advertising, back nos., write Journal Manager, Oxford Univ. Press, Pinkhill House, Southfield Road, Eynsham, Oxford OX8 1JJ, United Kingdom. Copyright held by Oxford University Press." circ. 1.4M. 4/yr. Pub'd 4 issues 1998; expects 4 issues 1999, 4 issues 2000. sub. price: $70; per copy: $21; sample: free of charge. Back issues: negotiable. Discounts: on request for more than 20 copies. 80pp; 23×15cm; cold metal/photosetting. Reporting time: 8 weeks approx. Payment: none, except one copy of journal and eight off-prints free. Copyrighted. Pub's reviews: 45 in 1998. §Community problems, politics, policy making, planning, programming, participation, action. Ads: £205($370)/£120($215)/£85($155) 1/4 page.

Community Resource Institute Press (see also OPEN EXCHANGE MAGAZINE), Bart Brodsky, 1442-A Walnut #51, Berkeley, CA 94709, 415-526-7190. 1972. Non-fiction. Pub'd 2 titles 1998. 3 titles listed in the *Small Press Record of Books in Print* (28th Edition, 1999-00). Discounts: call for schedule. 225pp; size varies; of. Payment: call.

Community Service, Inc. (see also COMMUNITY SERVICE NEWSLETTER), Marianne MacQueen, Director & Editor, P.O. Box 243, Yellow Springs, OH 45387, 513-797-2161. 1940. Articles, reviews, letters, non-fiction, interviews, criticism, news items. avg. press run 400 for newsletter, 1M for pamphlets. Pub'd 2 titles 1998; expects 1 title 1999. 32 titles listed in the *Small Press Record of Books in Print* (28th Edition, 1999-00). avg. price, paper: $5. Discounts: write for them 40% off for 10. 35pp. Reporting time: 4-6 weeks. Simultaneous submissions accepted: yes. Publishes 66% of manuscripts submitted. Payment: none. Does not copyright for author.

COMMUNITY SERVICE NEWSLETTER, Community Service, Inc., Marianne MacQueen, Director & Editor, P.O. Box 243, Yellow Springs, OH 45387, 513-767-2161. 1940. Articles, reviews, letters, non-fiction. circ. 325. 4/yr. Pub'd 4 issues 1998; expects 4 issues 1999, 4 issues 2000. sub. price: $25 includes membership; per copy: $3; sample: free. Back issues: $2. Discounts: write for 40% on 10 or more. 16pp; 7×8½; of. Reporting time: 2 weeks. Simultaneous submissions accepted: yes. Publishes 66% of manuscripts submitted. Payment: copies. Copyrighted, reverts to author. Pub's reviews: 6 in 1998. §Community, alternatives in community, society, economy, education, land trusts and land reform, ecologreal concerns, family, simple living. exchange ads.

Compact Clinicals, 7205 NW Waukomis Drive, Kansas City, MO 64151, 816-587-0044 or 800-408-8830; Fax 816-587-7198. 1996. Non-fiction. "Psychology books - condensed reviews of assessment and treatment of mental disorders. A series produced for mental health professionals and educated lay public. Please contact before submitting." avg. press run 2M. Pub'd 2 titles 1998; expects 4 titles 1999, 6 titles 2000. 6 titles listed in the *Small Press Record of Books in Print* (28th Edition, 1999-00). avg. price, paper: $14.95. Discounts: Retail: 1-3 0%, 4+ 20%; wholesalers/distrib. up to 24 books 35%, 25+ 50%. 96pp; 7×10; †of. Simultaneous submissions accepted: yes. Payment: 7% royalty. Does not copyright for author. PMA.

A COMPANION IN ZEOR, Karen Litman, 307 Ashland Ave., Egg Harbor Township, NJ 08234-5568, 609-645-6938; fax 609-645-8084; E-mail Klitman323@aol.com; website http://www.geocities.com/~rmgiroux/cz; http://www.simegen-com/index.html. 1978. Poetry, fiction, art, cartoons, interviews, letters, news items. "Contributions based on the universes of Jacqueline Lichtenberg. Any and all universes she has created or worked in. Preferred, nothing obscene—no homosexuality unless relevant to story line. Science-fiction oriented.

128

Limited only to creations based on Lichtenberg works. None other considered." circ. 100. Irregular. Expects 1 issue 1999, 2 issues 2000. price per copy: issues are different prices, SASE for flyer, can negotiate for free issues on occasion. Discounts: willing to discuss and arrange. 60pp; 8½×11; †mi, of, photocopy. Reporting time: 1 month. Payment: contributor copy, possibly more than one if arranged. Copyrighted, rights revert to author after 5 years to the contributor. Pub's reviews: 1 in 1998. §Almost anything but romance type, science fiction preferred for my own reading. free at present.

Companion Press, Jim Fredrickson, PO Box 2575, Laguna Hills, CA 92654, 949-362-9726. 1990. Non-fiction, fiction. "Specialize in gay erotic books. Recently published *The Best of Gay Adult Video-1998*, by Mickey Skee." avg. press run 10M. Pub'd 6 titles 1998; expects 8 titles 1999, 10 titles 2000. 11 titles listed in the *Small Press Record of Books in Print* (28th Edition, 1999-00). avg. price, paper: $12.95. Discounts: standard. 250pp; of. Reporting time: 30-60 days. Simultaneous submissions accepted: no. Publishes 5% of manuscripts submitted. Payment: 7½% to 8½% royalties, advance varies. Flat fee for short stories/anthologies. Copyrights for author. PMA.

THE COMPANY NORTH AMERICA, Eric Brooks, President; B.T. Tumey, Production Chief, PO Box 20766, Castro Valley, CA 94546, 510-888-1485. 1993. Articles, photos, interviews, music, letters, poetry, art, cartoons, reviews, news items. "Fanzine for Fish ex-lead singer from the prog-rock band 'Marillion.'" circ. 450+. 4/yr. Pub'd 4 issues 1998; expects 4 issues 1999, 4 issues 2000. sub. price: $15; per copy: $5; sample: $5. Back issues: $4 #1-4, $5 #6. 48+pp; 5½×8½; xerox. Publishes 90% of manuscripts submitted. Payment: none. Copyrighted, does not revert to author. Pub's reviews: 12+ in 1998. §Progressive rock music. Ads: Inquire. NACF.

Company of Words Publishing, Manuel Araujo, Editior; Silvana Batista, President, 2082 Shannon Lakes Blvd., Kissimmee, FL 34743-3648, 617-492-7930; FAX 617-354-3392; e-mail wordspub@aol.com; web page www.wordspublishing.com. 1996. Fiction, non-fiction. avg. press run 3M. Expects 3 titles 1999, 10 titles 2000. 2 titles listed in the *Small Press Record of Books in Print* (28th Edition, 1999-00). avg. price, paper: $12. 220pp; 5½×8½. Simultaneous submissions accepted: yes. Publishes 30% of manuscripts submitted. Payment: 10%. Copyrights for author. PMA.

Comparative Sedimentology Lab., R.N. Ginsburg, University of Miami, RSMAS/MGG, 4600 Rickenbacker Cswy., Miami, FL 33149. 1972. 14 titles listed in the *Small Press Record of Books in Print* (28th Edition, 1999-00). avg. price, paper: $10-15. Discounts: 10% discounts on orders of 10 copies or more of any one issue. offsel.

The Compass Press, W.D. Howells, Box 9546, Washington, DC 20016, 202-333-2182; orders 212-564-3730. 1988. Articles, interviews, non-fiction. "Contemporary history with special interest in institutional biography and generational change. Current public and political affairs with special interest in decision process" avg. press run 3M. Pub'd 2 titles 1998; expects 4 titles 1999, 4 titles 2000. 3 titles listed in the *Small Press Record of Books in Print* (28th Edition, 1999-00). avg. price, paper: $17. Discounts: standard. 250pp; 6×9; of. Payment: possible, modest advance for completed mss only 15% net. Copyrights for author. SSP, PMA.

THE COMPLEAT NURSE, Dry Bones Press, J. R.N. Rankin, PO Box 640345, San Francisco, CA 94164, 415-252-7371; fax 415-292-7314. 1991. Poetry, fiction, articles, cartoons, interviews, satire, criticism, reviews, letters, news items, non-fiction. "*TCN* only became monthly in late 1992. A 4 pager, occasionally longer. Any matter of interest to nurses, their patients or colleagues. Great interest in law, social policy affecting health care/health care delivery. Support single-payer health care. Welcome idea pieces, controversial pieces to trigger discussion" circ. 500. 12/yr. Pub'd 12 issues 1998; expects 12 issues 1999, 12 issues 2000. sub. price: $12; per copy: offering; sample: SASE. Back issues: SASE, if available. Discounts: Bulk arrangement, usually cost of printing and shipping extra amount requested. 4-6pp; 8½×11; †of. Reporting time: we will respond briefly at once. Simultaneous submissions accepted: yes. Payment: copies, diskette in desired format, glory, being published. Copyrighted, reverts to author. Pub's reviews: 3 in 1998. §Nursing, patient-authored books, economics, arts and letters, health care. Ads: $50/$30/$10 per column inch, $10 business card.

COMPUTER BOOK REVIEW, CBR, Carlene Char, Editor & Publisher, 735 Ekekela Place, Honolulu, HI 96817, 808-595-7089. 1983. "Recommends books for the computer - based professional" 6/yr. Pub'd 6 issues 1998; expects 6 issues 1999, 6 issues 2000. sub. price: $30; per copy: $5; sample: $5. 6pp; 8½×11; of. Copyrighted, does not revert to author. Pub's reviews: 600 in 1998. §Computer-related books. No ads.

Computer Press, 4101 Winners Circle, #126, Sarasota, FL 34238-5554. 1990. avg. press run 1M. Pub'd 1-2 titles 1998; expects 1-2 titles 1999, 1-2 titles 2000. 4 titles listed in the *Small Press Record of Books in Print* (28th Edition, 1999-00). avg. price, paper: $6-20. 130pp; 8½×11; web. Copyrights for author. PMA.

Comstock Bonanza Press, 18919 William Quirk Drive, Grass Valley, CA 95945-8611, 530-273-6220. 1979. Non-fiction. avg. press run 2M. Pub'd 2 titles 1998; expects 2 titles 1999, 1 title 2000. 15 titles listed in the *Small Press Record of Books in Print* (28th Edition, 1999-00). avg. price, cloth: $19.50; paper: $13; other:

$17.50. Discounts: 40% trade and wholesale; 15% schools and libraries. 120-400pp; size standard; of. Reporting time: 45 days. Simultaneous submissions accepted: yes. Publishes 5% of manuscripts submitted. Payment: 10%. Copyrights for author.

THE COMSTOCK REVIEW, Jennifer B. MacPherson, Editor, Comstock Writers' Group, Inc., 907 Comstock Avenue, Syracuse, NY 13210. 1987. Poetry. "Formerly *Poetpourri.*" circ. 500. 2/yr. Pub'd 2 issues 1998; expects 2 issues 1999, 2 issues 2000. sub. price: $15/2 issues; per copy: $8; sample: $6. Back issues: $5. 105pp; 5½x8½. Reporting time: 2-3 months. Simultaneous submissions accepted: no. Publishes less than 10% of manuscripts submitted. Payment: contributor's copy only. Copyrighted, reverts to author.

Conari Press, Mary Jane Ryan, Executive Editor; Nancy Margolis, Editorial Associate, 2550 Ninth Street, Suite 101, Berkeley, CA 94710, 501-649-7175, 1-800-685-9595. 1987. Non-fiction. "Distribution: Publishers Group West, Ingram, Raincoast Books (Canada)" avg. press run 10M-30M. Pub'd 25 titles 1998; expects 25 titles 1999, 25 titles 2000. 17 titles listed in the *Small Press Record of Books in Print* (28th Edition, 1999-00). avg. price, cloth: $21.95; paper: $10.95. Discounts: standard. Pages vary; size varies; litho. Reporting time: 6 weeks. Simultaneous submissions accepted: yes. Publishes 1-2% of manuscripts submitted. Payment: varies. Copyrights for author. PMA, ABA, NCIBA Bookpublishers West, San Francisco Bay Area Book Council.

CONCHO RIVER REVIEW, James A. Moore, English Department, Angelo State University, San Angelo, TX 76909, 915-942-2273; james.moore@angelo.edu. 1986. Poetry, fiction, articles, criticism, reviews, non-fiction. "Fiction and non-fiction: 1500-5000 words; poetry open. We read all submissions carefully but generally publish only material by writers of Texas and the Southwest or about Texas and the Southwest. Circulation office: Fort Concho Museum Press, 630 S. Oakes, San Angelo, TX 76903." circ. 300. 2/yr. Pub'd 2 issues 1998; expects 2 issues 1999, 2 issues 2000. sub. price: $14; per copy: $8; sample: $5. Back issues: $5. Discounts: query. 115pp; 6x9; of. Reporting time: 2-6 months. Simultaneous submissions accepted: yes. Publishes 10-15% of manuscripts submitted. Payment: copies. Copyrighted, reverts to author. Pub's reviews: 10 in 1998. §Fiction, poetry, nonfiction by writers of Texas and the Southwest or about Texas and the Southwest. Ads: query.

CONFLICT OF INTEREST, Proper PH Publications, Pam Hartney, 4701 East National Road, Springfield, OH 45505-1847, 330-630-5646 phone/Fax; E-mail PHartney@aol.com. 1994. Poetry, articles, art, photos, cartoons, interviews, reviews, long-poems. "Editor would like to see: Poetry and artwork should be radical, concise, deliberate, unabashed, deadly if ingested. I want my readers to be pulled down and drowned in an explosive whirlpool of emotion. No rhyming, nature, or kissy, kissy poetry. SASE a must for return of poems or response from editor. Magazines, chapbooks, etc. are welcome for reviews. No limit on length or number of submissions. No taboos! No rules! Previously published work is OK if it is noted when and where." circ. 250+. 4/yr. Pub'd 4 issues 1998; expects 4 issues 1999, 4 issues 2000. sub. price: $20; per copy: $5; sample: $5. Discounts: bulk rates, trades OK. 100pp; 11x17; †mi. Reporting time: 4-6 months backlog. Simultaneous submissions accepted: yes. Publishes 20% of manuscripts submitted. Payment: copy. Copyrighted, reverts to author. Pub's reviews: 12+ in 1998. §Poetry, feminist, gay and lesbian.

CONFLUENCE, Daniel Born, Fiction Editor; James S. Bond, Poetry Editor; David B. Prather, Poetry Editor, PO Box 336, Belpre, OH 45714, 304-422-3112; e-mail dbprather@prodigy.net. 1989. Poetry, fiction, art, photos, interviews, satire, criticism, reviews, parts-of-novels, non-fiction. "Poetry of any length or general literary style. Fiction shouldn't exceed 3,000 words; no dot matrix due to scanner equipment; SASE required. Prefer no simultaneous submissions. Work displays knowledge of language, its flexibilities. Contributors include Richard Hague, Pamela Kircher, Walt McDonald, and Valerie Martinez." circ. 500. 1/yr. Pub'd 1 issue 1998; expects 1 issue 1999, 1 issue 2000. sub. price: $5 + $1.24 S&H; per copy: $5 + $1.24 S&H; sample: $4 + $1.24 S&H. Back issues: none. Discounts: 5 or more 20%. 112pp; 5½x8½; lp. Reporting time: 1-3 months max. Simultaneous submissions accepted: no. Publishes 1-2% of manuscripts submitted. Payment: copies. Copyrighted, reverts to author. Ads: dna.

Confluence Press, Inc., James Hepworth, Director, Lewis-Clark State College, 500 8th Avenue, Lewiston, ID 83501-2698, 208-799-2336. 1975. Poetry, fiction, articles, art, photos, interviews, criticism, music, non-fiction. "Poetry, fiction, literary criticism" avg. press run 1M-3M. Pub'd 4 titles 1998; expects 4 titles 1999, 4 titles 2000. 36 titles listed in the *Small Press Record of Books in Print* (28th Edition, 1999-00). avg. price, cloth: $14.95; paper: $8.95; other: chapbooks (limited editions) pa $20, cl $50. Discounts: 20% libraries, 47% bookstores, 50% jobbers and wholesalers. 96-200pp; 5½x8½, 6x9; of. Reporting time: 1-3 months. Simultaneous submissions accepted: yes. Publishes 1-2% of manuscripts submitted. Payment: cash advance against standard trade royalties. Copyrights for author.

CONFRONTATION, Martin Tucker, English Department, C.W. Post of Long Island Univ., Greenvale, NY 11548, 516-299-2391. 1968. Poetry, fiction, articles, interviews, parts-of-novels, long-poems, plays. circ. 2M. 2/yr. Expects 2 issues 1999. 11 titles listed in the *Small Press Record of Books in Print* (28th Edition, 1999-00). sub. price: $10; per copy: $7; sample: $3. Back issues: $8. Discounts: 20% on orders of 10 or more copies.

295pp; 6×9; lp. Reporting time: 6-8 weeks. We accept simultaneous submissions, but not preferred. Publishes 10-15% of manuscripts submitted. Payment: $20-$150 stories, $10-$75 poetry. Copyrighted, reverts to author. Pub's reviews: 40 in 1998. §Fiction, poetry, criticism. CLMP.

CONJUNCTIONS, Bradford Morrow, Editor, 21 East 10th Street #3E, New York, NY 10003-5924. 1981. Poetry, fiction. "Contributing editors include: Walter Abish, Mei-mei Berssenbrugge, Guy Davenport, William H. Gass, Chinua Achebe, Ann Lauterbach, Nathaniel Tarn, Quincy Troupe, John Edgar Wideman, and Susan Howe. Among most recently published authors are: David Foster Wallace, John Hawkes, Harry Mathews, Paul West, Chinua Achebe, Juan Goytisolo, Joanna Scott, Lydia Davis, Kathy Acker, Can Xue, and Jorie Graham." circ. 7.5M. 2/yr. Pub'd 2 issues 1998; expects 2 issues 1999, 2 issues 2000. sub. price: $18 indiv., $25 instit. and overseas; $32/2 yrs indiv., $45/2 yrs instit. and overseas; per copy: $12; sample: $12. Back issues: $12. Discounts: special rates to distributors. 400pp; 6×9; of, lp covers—2 colors + four color. Reporting time: solicited mss. immediately, unsolicited 4-6 weeks. Simultaneous submissions accepted: no. Payment: $175 plus copies. Copyrighted, reverts to author. Ads: $350/$250.

THE CONNECTICUT POETRY REVIEW, J. Claire White, Co-Editor; Harley More, Co-Editor, PO Box 818, Stonington, CT 06378. 1981. Poetry, interviews, satire, criticism, reviews. "Reviews: 700 words. Poems: 10-40 lines. But we do make exceptions. We look for poetry of quality which is both genuine and original in content. That is all we seek. We will consider any new and interesting book of poems mailed to us for a review. Some past and recent contributors: Cornelia Veenendaal, Nikki Giovanni, Walter MacDonald, Laurel Speer, John Updike, Dona Stein, James Sallis, Celia Gilbert, Diane Wakoski, Stuart Friebert, Felice Picano, Joseph Bruchac, W.D. Ehrhart, Joel Chace, Anna Maxwell, James Chichetto, Marge Piercy, Steve Abbott, Rochelle Ratner, Dan Duffy, A.R. Ammons, Mark Johnson, Jefferson Peters, Greg Kuzma, Diane Kruchkow, Daniel Langton, M. Marcuss Oslander, Robert Peters, Philip Fried, Emily Glen, Andrew Holleran, Edwin Honig, Rudy Kikel, F.D. Reeve, Dennis Cooper, Richard Kostelanetz, Charles Edward Eaton, Clifton Snider, Wm. Virgil Davis, John Tagliabue, Edward Butscher, Allen Ginsberg, Margaret Randall, Barry Spacks, J. Kates, Eugenio de Andrade, Susan Fromberg Schaeffer, Claudia Buckholts, Simon Perchik, Odysseus Elytis, Peter Wild, Gabriela Mistral, and William Reichard." circ. 400. 1/yr. Pub'd 1 issue 1998; expects 1 issue 1999, 1 issue 2000. 3 titles listed in the *Small Press Record of Books in Print* (28th Edition, 1999-00). sub. price: $3; per copy: $3; sample: $3. Back issues: $25 first issue. Discounts: none. 40-45pp; 4¼×8½; lp. Reporting time: 3 months. Payment: $5 per poem, $10 per review. Copyrighted, reverts to author. Pub's reviews. §Poetry, poetry, poetry. CLMP.

CONNECTICUT REVIEW, Dr. Vivian Shipley, SCSU, 501 Crescent Street, New Haven, CT 06515, 203-392-6737; FAX 203-392-5355. 1967. Poetry, fiction, articles, art, photos, interviews, non-fiction. "2000-4000 words; 3-5 poems, photograph or art work. Send 2 copies of typed work. Recent contributors: Denise Levertov, Syd Lea, David Baker, Maige Piercy, Maria Gillan" circ. 3M. 2/yr. Pub'd 2 issues 1998; expects 2 issues 1999, 2 issues 2000. sub. price: $12; per copy: $6. 160pp; 6×9. Reporting time: 2-4 months. Simultaneous submissions accepted: no. Publishes 10% of manuscripts submitted. Payment: 2 copies. Copyrighted, reverts to author

CONNECTICUT RIVER REVIEW: A National Poetry Journal, Kevin Carey, Editor, PO Box 4053, Waterbury, CT 06704-0053. 1978. Poetry. "Looking for original, honest, diverse, vital, well-crafted poetry. Poetry, poetry translations, long-poems. No simultaneous submissions. Recent contributors: Walt McDonald, Alvin Laster, Fileman Waitts, Thomas Michael McDade, Kathryn Rantala, and Lewis K. Parker." circ. 500. 2/yr. Pub'd 2 issues 1998; expects 2 issues 1999, 2 issues 2000. sub. price: $11; per copy: $6; sample: $5. Back issues: $5 + $1 postage. 35-50pp; 6×9; of. Reporting time: 6-8 weeks. Simultaneous submissions accepted: no. Publishes 5% of manuscripts submitted. Payment: 1 copy. Copyrighted, reverts to author. Ads: none. CLMP.

CONNEXIONS DIGEST, Connexions Information Services, Inc., Ulli Diemer, PO Box 158, Station D, Toronto, Ontario M6P 3J8, Canada, 416-537-3949; connex@sources.com; www.connexions.org. 1976. Articles, art, photos, cartoons, interviews, criticism, reviews, letters, news items. "A digest linking groups working for social justice—we are interested in materials that include reflection, analysis, report on action." circ. 1.2M. 4/yr. Pub'd 4 issues 1998; expects 4 issues 1999, 4 issues 2000. sub. price: $15.50 Canada, $18 foreign; per copy: $30 for directory issue; sample: $1. Back issues: $1. Discounts: 40% for resale; other negotiable. 48pp; 8½×11; of. Reporting time: 3 months maximum. Payment: none. Not copyrighted. Pub's reviews: 200 in 1998. §Social justice struggles/analysis. Ads: $175/$100/25¢.

Connexions Information Services, Inc. (see also CONNEXIONS DIGEST), Ulli Diemer, Managing Editor, PO Box 158, Station D, Toronto, Ontario M6P 3J8, Canada, 416-537-3949. 1975. avg. press run 2M. Pub'd 1 title 1998; expects 2 titles 1999. 2 titles listed in the *Small Press Record of Books in Print* (28th Edition, 1999-00). avg. price, paper: $30. 224pp; 8½×11.

CONSCIENCE, M. Hume, 1436 U Street NW, Washington, DC 20009. 1980. Poetry, articles, cartoons, interviews, criticism, reviews, news items, non-fiction. circ. 10M. 4/yr. Pub'd 3 issues 1998; expects 4 issues

1999, 4 issues 2000. sub. price: $10; per copy: $3.50; sample: free to writers w/$1.01 9x12 SASE. Back issues: $1 depending on availability. Discounts: by negotiation. 40pp; 8×10½; web press. Reporting time: 2 months. Publishes 55% of manuscripts submitted. Payment: up to $125. Copyrighted, rights usually revert to author. Pub's reviews: 4 in 1998. §Women's studies, Catholic church, abortion/family planning.

Conscious Living (see also HEALTH MASTER), Dr. Tim Lowenstein, PO Box 9, Drain, OR 97435. 1976. Articles, music, non-fiction. avg. press run 3M. Pub'd 2 titles 1998; expects 3 titles 1999, 5 titles 2000. 2 titles listed in the *Small Press Record of Books in Print* (28th Edition, 1999-00). avg. price, paper: $9.95. 96pp; 8½×11; of. Copyrights for author.

Conservatory of American Letters (see also NORTHWOODS JOURNAL, A Magazine for Writers), Robert Olmsted, Executive Director; Richard S. Danbury III, Senior Editor, PO Box 298, Thomaston, ME 04861-0298, 207-354-0998; Fax 207-354-8953; cal@americanletters.org; www.americanletters.org. 1986. "CAL is the owner of Dan River Press and Northwoods Press, who offer publication of poetry, fiction, local history. We don't charge a reading fee, but require a donation, whatever you can afford. If you can afford nothing, convince us and we'll read free. We use anything *not* seditious, pornographic." avg. press run 2M. Pub'd 2 titles 1998; expects 6 titles 1999, 6 titles 2000. avg. price, cloth: $29.95; paper: $12.95; other: collector's $100. Discounts: 2% X No. of paperback books ordered to maximum of 50% for 25 or more. No discount on hardcovers, or collectors. 150pp; 5½×8½; †of. Reporting time: 1 week to 1 month. Simultaneous submissions accepted: no. Publishes 10% of manuscripts submitted. Payment: minimum advance on books - $250 payable on contracting, minimum 10% royalties from first sale; for anthologies, minimum is $4 per page (pro-rated). Copyrights for author.

THE CONSTANTIAN, Randall J. Dicks, The Constantian Society, 840 Old Washington Rd, MCMurray, PA 15317-3228, 724-942-5374. 1970. Articles, photos, interviews, letters, news items, non-fiction. "The Constantian Society is a monarchist organization with educational goals and activities. Our journal, *The Constantian*, published four times a year or more, offers news, historical articles, genealogical information, interviews, profiles, book reviews, and commentaries on *monarchy* and *royalty*. Format is tabloid, 8 1/2 X 11, 12-16 pages per issue. Black and white illustrations used, also maps, drawings, heraldry, ornaments. ISSN 0270-532X. Our journal is produced on a Macintosh computer. Recent articles include monarchist developments in Eastern Europe, interview with Crown Prince of Nepal, African monarchies." circ. 550. 4/yr. Pub'd 4 issues 1998; expects 4 issues 1999, 4 issues 2000. sub. price: $8 (membership $20); per copy: $3; sample: $1. Back issues: $3 each generally (list available). 15pp; 8½×11; of. Reporting time: generally 2 weeks. Simultaneous submissions accepted: no. Publishes 60% of manuscripts submitted. Payment: limited funds available for honoraria. Copyrighted, rights revert to author in general. Pub's reviews: 15 in 1998. §Monarchs, royalty, historical subjects related to monarchy/royalty, biography, political theory of monarchy. Ads: $50/$30/no classifieds.

Construction Trades Press, Chris Forhan, PO Box 953, Clinton, NC 28328, 919-592-1310. 1989. Non-fiction. "*Pipe Fitter's Math Guide*, 1995." avg. press run 2M. Expects 2 titles 1999, 2 titles 2000. 1 title listed in the *Small Press Record of Books in Print* (28th Edition, 1999-00). avg. price, paper: $25. Discounts: distributors, wholesalers and bookstores - 1 0%, 2-4 20%, 5-99 40%, 100+ 50%; schools 20%; libraries 1-4 0%, 5+ 10%. 240pp; 8½×11; of. Reporting time: 12 months. Payment: 4-8%. Copyrights for author.

The Consultant Press, Ltd., Robert S. Persky, 163 Amsterdam Avenue, New York, NY 10023, 212-838-8640. 1983. "Our orientation is information concerning fine art photography and picture resources. We do not publish books of pictures. Titles of general interest to artists are also considered—e.g. *The Artist's Guide To Getting/Having A Successful Exhibition.*" avg. press run 5M. Pub'd 6 titles 1998; expects 6 titles 1999, 6 titles 2000. 13 titles listed in the *Small Press Record of Books in Print* (28th Edition, 1999-00). avg. price, cloth: $39.95; paper: $24.95. Discounts: 35% on stop-40% on multiple copy order. No invoicing for anyone except libraries and schools. 125-400pp; 5×8, 8½×11. Reporting time: 30 days. Payment: varies with estimated market for book and production costs. Copyrights for author. PMA, The Small Press Center.

Consumer Education Research Center, Robert L. Berko, 1980 Springfield Ave, Maplewood, NJ 07040, 201-275-3955, Fax 201-275-3980. 1969. Non-fiction. "Books that will aid consumers in coping with the marketplace and modern society" avg. press run 10M-20M. Pub'd 6 titles 1998; expects 6 titles 1999, 6 titles 2000. 1 title listed in the *Small Press Record of Books in Print* (28th Edition, 1999-00). avg. price, paper: $18. Discounts: 25-60% depending on amount and payment arrangements. 240pp; 8½×10, 4½×7½; web. Payment: subject to negotiation. Copyrights for author. CERC.

Consumer Press, Joseph Pappas, 13326 SW 28th Street, Ste. 102, Fort Lauderdale, FL 33330, 954-370-9153, Fax 954-370-5722; e-mail bookguest@aol.com. 1989. Non-fiction. avg. press run 5M. Pub'd 2 titles 1998; expects 2 titles 1999, 3 titles 2000. 3 titles listed in the *Small Press Record of Books in Print* (28th Edition, 1999-00). avg. price, paper: $12.95. Discounts: trade, bulk, jobber. 150pp; 5½×8½. Reporting time: varies. Publishes 10% of manuscripts submitted. Payment: standard. Copyrights for author. PMA.

132

CONTACT!, Michael C. Myal, 2900 East Weymouth, Tucson, AZ 85716-1249, 602-881-2232. 1990. Articles. "Experimental aircraft and power plants" circ. 1M+. 6/yr. Pub'd 6 issues 1998; expects 6 issues 1999, 6 issues 2000. sub. price: $20, $27 Can, $29/$36 overseas; per copy: $4; sample: $4. Back issues: write for back issue list. Discounts: none. 20pp; 8½×11; of. Reporting time: varies. Publishes 98% of manuscripts submitted. Payment: none. Copyrighted, does not revert to author. Ads: no ads.

Contemax Publishers, Warren R. Freeman, Griebel, Karin R., 17815 24th Ave N. Suite 100, Minneapolis, MN 55447, phone/fax 612-473-6436. 1995. "We publish how to books" Expects 2 titles 1999. 170pp; 5½×8½. MIPA.

CON-TEMPORAL, S. Mitchel Merritt, 5202 Tacoma Drive, Arlington, TX 76017-1866, 817-467-0681; Fax 817-467-5346. 1974. "Lists science fiction, gaming, media and comics conventions happening around the world." sub. price: $15/quarterly ($23 foreign), $20/bimonthly ($30 foreign), $30/monthly ($45 foreign). Ads: $60/$35/$20 1/4 page.

CONTEMPORARY LITERATURE, Thomas Schaub, 7141 Helen C. White Hall, University of Wisconsin, 600 N. Park St. Madison, WI 53706. 1960. Criticism, reviews. "Scholarly literary criticism" circ. 2.3M. 4/yr. Pub'd 4 issues 1998. sub. price: individuals $25/yr, institutions $63; per copy: varies. Back issues: write for details. Discounts: 5% subscription agency. 136pp; 6×9; of. Reporting time: varies. Simultaneous submissions accepted: no. Publishes 10% of manuscripts submitted. Payment: none. Copyrighted, does not revert to author. Pub's reviews. §All reviews commissioned. Ads: $150/$80. CELJ.

CONTEMPORARY WALES, University Of Wales Press, G. Day, D. Thomas, 6 Gwennyth Street, Cathays, Cardiff CF2 4YD, Wales, 44-1222-231919; Fax 44-1222-230908; press@press.wales.ac.uk. 1987. Articles. circ. 500. 1/yr. Pub'd 1 issue 1998; expects 1 issue 1999, 1 issue 2000. sub. price: £6.50; per copy: £7.50; sample: £7.50. Discounts: booksellers 10%. 100pp; size A5; of. Payment: none. Copyrighted. Ads: £75/£37.50. UWP.

Content Communications, Jacalyn Mindell, PO Box 4763, Topeka, KS 66604, 913-233-9066. 1985. "Publishes, primarily, books and newspapers dealing with race, class, color and ethnicity issues for a diverse and general audience. Material should be readily accessible to lay readers, although it may be based on academic research or expertise. Publications are varied in topic and approach and focus on all (or any) racial or ethnic group. Material varies in length. We believe that we can all do more than just get along - we can understand each other and make this world a better place for all. We have published only non-fiction material to date, but would consider great fiction that meets the guidelines above. Biography, autobiography, sociology, psychology, education, ethnic studies are among wide range of non-fiction topics we look at." avg. press run 3M. Expects 3 titles 1999, 6 titles 2000. 1 title listed in the *Small Press Record of Books in Print* (28th Edition, 1999-00). avg. price, paper: $15. Discounts: call or write for schedules. 150pp; of. Reporting time: 8-12 weeks. Copyrights for author.

Context Publications, Ron Kennedy, PO Box 2909, Rohnert Park, CA 94927, 707-576-1700. 1979. Non-fiction. avg. press run 10M Pub'd 6 titles 1998; expects 7 titles 1999, 8 titles 2000. 9 titles listed in the *Small Press Record of Books in Print* (28th Edition, 1999-00). avg. price, cloth: $19.90; paper: $15. Discounts: 40% over 20 copies, 20% 1-9 copies, 30% 10-19 copies. 250pp; 6×9. Payment: royalties only (10%). Copyrights for author.

CONTEXT SOUTH, David Breeden, Poetry Editor; Craig Taylor, Fiction; Paul Hadella, Assistant Poetry Editor, Box 4504, Schreiner College, Kerrville, TX 78028, 512-896-7945. 1989. Poetry, fiction, art, photos, interviews, criticism, reviews, concrete art, non-fiction. "Make art. Recent contributors: Wayne Dodd, William Greenway, Andrea Budy" circ. 500. 2-3/yr. Pub'd 1 issue 1998; expects 1 issue 1999, 2 issues 2000. sub. price: $10; per copy: $5; sample: $5. 65pp; 4¼×5½; of. Reporting time: 4-6 weeks. Publishes 1% of manuscripts submitted. Payment: 1 copy. Copyrighted, reverts to author. Pub's reviews. §Small press, contemporary poets, aesthetics. Ads: $50/$25. CLMP.

Continuing Education Press, Alba Scholz, Portland State University, PO Box 1394, Portland, OR 97207. 1968. Non-fiction. avg. press run 5M. Pub'd 2 titles 1998; expects 2 titles 1999, 2 titles 2000. 7 titles listed in the *Small Press Record of Books in Print* (28th Edition, 1999-00). avg. price, paper: $15. Discounts: 2-5 20%, 6-49 40%, 50+ 50%. 100pp; 8½×11; of. Reporting time: 2 months. Payment: contract terms by arrangement. Can copyright for author. Northwest Association of Book Publishers (NWABP), PEMA.

COOKING CONTEST CHRONICLE, Karen Martis, PO Box 10792, Merrillville, IN 46411-0792. 1985. circ. 2.5M. 12/yr. Pub'd 12 issues 1998; expects 12 issues 1999, 12 issues 2000. sub. price: $19.95; per copy: $3; sample: $3. Back issues: $3. Discounts: none. 8pp; 8½×11; of. Not copyrighted. Pub's reviews: 12 in 1998. §Cookbooks. Ads: $100/$75/must be food related and approved by editor.

THE COOL TRAVELER, bob Moore, Editor & Publisher, 196 Bowery Street, Frostburg, MD 21532-2255, 215-440-0592. 1988. Poetry, fiction, articles, art, photos, cartoons, interviews, letters, news items, non-fiction.

"Recent contributors include Andre Nelson, Catherine Rooney, and Jack Lindeman. We like material about 'place' including diaries written when travelling, and letters, info, articles about where one lives." circ. 1M. 6/yr. Pub'd 4 issues 1998; expects 6 issues 1999, 6 issues 2000. sub. price: $10; per copy: $2; sample: $2. Back issues: $3. Discounts: negotiable. 12pp; 8½×11; of. Reporting time: 4 weeks. Publishes 10% of manuscripts submitted. Payment: sometimes—well written articles or unique info about places. Copyrighted, reverts to author. Pub's reviews: 4 in 1998. §Travel, art shows happening internationally (cultural events), what is a cool traveler? Ads: $100/$200 inside covers/$250 back cover.

THE COOPERATOR, Vicki Chesler, 301 East 45th Street, New York, NY 10017, 212-697-1318. 1980. Articles, photos, cartoons, interviews, news items. "Query first or send written outline with article proposal" circ. 60M. 10/yr. Pub'd 10 issues 1998; expects 10 issues 1999, 10 issues 2000. sub. price: free; per copy: free; sample: free. Back issues: $2. 48pp; 10½×14; web offset. Reporting time: 1-2 months. Publishes 50% of manuscripts submitted. Payment: $150-250. Copyrighted, does not revert to author. Ads: $2450/$1525.

COPING WITH TURBULENT TIMES, Reynolds Griffith, PO Box 4630, Nacogdoches, TX 75962, e-mail iii2k@yahoo.com. 1993. Articles, reviews. "Maximum length 4-5 pages (typed, double spaced)." 4/yr. Pub'd 4 issues 1998; expects 4 issues 1999, 4 issues 2000. sub. price: $5; per copy: $2; sample: $2. 10pp; 8½×11; of. Reporting time: 2 weeks. Payment: none. Copyrighted, rights revert to author on request. Pub's reviews: 4-8 in 1998. §Self-sufficiency, personal finances, survival, economic/social trends. Ads: no advertising.

Copper Beech Press, M.K. Blasing, Director; Randy Blasing, Editor, P O Box 2578, English Department, Providence, RI 02906, 401-351-1253. 1973. Poetry, fiction, long-poems. avg. press run 1M. Pub'd 4 titles 1998; expects 3 titles 1999, 3 titles 2000. 18 titles listed in the *Small Press Record of Books in Print* (28th Edition, 1999-00). avg. price, paper: $9.95. Discounts: bookstores, jobbers, etc. 1-5 20%; 6-9 33%; 10+ 40%. 64pp; size varies; of. Reporting time: ASAP, usually within 1 month. Payment: copies, 5%. Does not copyright for author.

Copper Canyon Press, Sam Hamill, Editor; Bailey Thatcher, Publisher; Michael Wiegers, Managing Editor, P.O. Box 271, Port Townsend, WA 98368. 1972. Poetry, long-poems. "We no longer read unsolicited mss. Queries should include SASE. Books distributed to the trade by Consortium, 1045 Westgate Drive, St. Paul, MN 55114-0165, 800-283-3572" avg. press run 2.5M. Pub'd 8 titles 1998; expects 9 titles 1999, 10 titles 2000. 51 titles listed in the *Small Press Record of Books in Print* (28th Edition, 1999-00). avg. price, cloth: $22; paper: $12. Discounts: standard 40%, returnable, short 20% on cloth. 80pp; 6×9; of. Reporting time: 1 month. Simultaneous submissions accepted: no. Payment: 7% of edition. Copyrights for author.

Coreopsis Books, Lee Passarella, 1384 Township Drive, Lawrenceville, GA 30243, 404-995-9475. 1993. Poetry, fiction, non-fiction. "Seeking well-crafted poetry, no biases, although excellent nature/environmental poetry is appreciated. Also interested in quality fiction and non-fiction in the areas of literature, biography, history, self-help, and psychology." avg. press run 500. Expects 2-3 titles 2000. 2 titles listed in the *Small Press Record of Books in Print* (28th Edition, 1999-00). avg. price, paper: $7. Discounts: 40% to bookstores. of. Reporting time: 1 month for queries, 2-3 months for manuscripts. Payment: varies. Copyrights for author.

Cornell Maritime Press, Inc., Charlotte Kurst, Managing Editor, PO Box 456, Centreville, MD 21617, 301-758-1075. 1938. "We publish books for the merchant marine, recreational boating books, regional adult nonfiction, children's regional fiction and nonfiction." avg. press run 3M. Pub'd 10 titles 1998; expects 12 titles 1999, 12 titles 2000. 26 titles listed in the *Small Press Record of Books in Print* (28th Edition, 1999-00). avg. price, cloth: $47.95; paper: $13.95. Discounts: on request. 330pp; of. Reporting time: 1 month. Simultaneous submissions accepted: no. Copyrights for author.

CORNERSTONE, Jon Trott, Editor in Chief; Eric Pement, Senior Editor; Dawn Mortimer, Editorial Director; Chris Wiitala, Music Editor, 939 W. Wilson Avenue, Chicago, IL 60640, 773-561-2450 ext. 2080; fax 773-989-2076. 1972. Poetry, fiction, articles, art, photos, cartoons, interviews, satire, criticism, reviews, music, letters, news items, non-fiction. "Call publication." circ. 38M. 3-4/yr. Pub'd 2 issues 1998; expects 3 issues 1999, 4 issues 2000. sub. price: donation; per copy: donation; sample: SASE with 5 first class stamps. Back issues: call publication. Discounts: call for info. 64-72pp; 8½×11; web, of. Reporting time: 3-6 months, respond only if we wish to use work. Simultaneous submissions accepted: yes. Publishes 2% of manuscripts submitted. Payment: varies. Copyrighted, reverts to author. Pub's reviews: 14 in 1998. §Religious, social, political. Ads: $1,300/$840/50¢ classified. EPA.

CORONA, Lynda Sexson, Co-Editor; Michael Sexson, Co-Editor; Sarah Merrill, Managing Editor, Dept. of Hist. & Phil., Montana State University, Bozeman, MT 59717, 406-994-5200. 1980. Poetry, fiction, articles, art, photos, cartoons, satire, music, collages, plays, non-fiction. "Journal of arts and ideas; imaginative treatment of cultural issues. Looking particularly for work that transcends categories. We are interested in everything from the speculative essay to recipes for the construction or revision of things; we publish art and ideas that surprise with their quality and content. Recent contributors: Frederick Turner, William Irwin Thompson, James Hillman, Rhoda Lerman, Philip Dacey, Ivan Doig, Donald Hall, A.B. Guthrie, Jr., Richard Hugo, William Matthews, Stephen Dixon, James Dickey, Rayna Green, Fritjof Capra, Wendy Battin, Charles Edward Eaton, Nick

Johnson.'' circ. 2M. Occasional. Expects 1 issue 2000. sub. price: $7; per copy: $7; sample: $7. Back issues: $7. Discounts: trade, classroom, 20% (orders of 10 or more). 130pp; 10×7; of. Reporting time: 1 week to 6 months. Payment: nominal honorarium, 2 copies. Copyrighted. Pub's reviews: 10 in 1998. §All aspects of current thought, technology & the imagination, metaphor, art, religion. Ads: $150/$95/$65/back cover (inside) $200.

Corona Publishing Co., David Bowen, PO Drawer 12407, San Antonio, TX 78212, 210-341-7525. 1977. Poetry, fiction, non-fiction. ''We are a regional, independent, trade publishing house...operated for profit'' avg. press run 2.5M-3.5M. Pub'd 4 titles 1998; expects 3 titles 1999, 5 titles 2000. 5 titles listed in the *Small Press Record of Books in Print* (28th Edition, 1999-00). avg. price, cloth: $15.95; paper: $8.95. Discounts: 30-45% to retail; 50% wholesale. 200pp; size varies; of. Reporting time: 6 weeks. Payment: 10% of net and up. Copyrights for author. Book Publishers of Texas, 3404 S. Ravinia Dr., Dallas, TX 75233.

CORRECTIONS TODAY, Kurt Olsson, Managing Editor, American Correctional Association, 4380 Forbes Boulevard, Lanham, MD 20706-4322, 301-918-1800. 1938. Fiction, articles, art, photos, interviews, reviews, letters, news items, non-fiction. ''We accept manuscripts from members of the American Correctional Association on topics related to the field of corrections. Manuscripts should be submitted to the attention of Linda Acorn at the above address and should be no longer than 10 double-spaced, typed pages. We accept well-written pieces on new and informative programs and issues that would be of interest to our members.'' circ. 20M. 7/yr. Pub'd 7 issues 1998; expects 7 issues 1999, 7 issues 2000. sub. price: free sub. with membership to the American Correctional Assn.; per copy: $4.50; sample: free. Back issues: $4.50 per issue. 200pp; 8⅜×10⅞; of. Reporting time: 4-6 weeks. Payment: none, we are a non-profit organization. Copyrighted, does not revert to author. Pub's reviews: 25 in 1998. §Anything related to the corrections field of on criminal justice issues. Ads: b/w $1,233/b/w $960/2-color and 4-color fees apply, call for rates, frequency rates available.

Cosmic Concepts, George W. Fisk, 2531 Dover Lane, St. Joseph, MI 49085, 616-428-2792. 1988. ''Cosmic Concepts seeks to produce books for all ages which will enhance spiritual enlightenment and planetary unity. In accord with these goals, believing that the Creator is moving through all humanity, Cosmic Concepts is open to review manuscripts from other countries and other cultures. Submissions should be limited to a three page summary, mailed, not faxed.'' avg. press run 3M. Pub'd 2 titles 1998; expects 2 titles 1999, 2 titles 2000. 4 titles listed in the *Small Press Record of Books in Print* (28th Edition, 1999-00). avg. price, paper: $9.95. Discounts: wholesale 50%, distributors 55%, bookstores 40% (4 or more). 175pp; 6×9; beltpress. Reporting time: 6 weeks. Simultaneous submissions accepted: yes. Payment: 10% on profits. We sometimes copyright for author. MAPA.

Cosmic Trend (see also PARA*PHRASE), Jiri Jirasek, George Le Grand, Tedy Asponsen, Sheridan Mall, Box 47014, Mississauga, Ontario L5K 2R2, Canada. 1984. Poetry, art, reviews, music. ''Cosmic Trend produces anthologies of contemporary poetry and publishes approximately two chapbooks accompanied with audio cassettes, where some of the corresponding items are dramatized to original Cosmic Trend music. In addition, some special projects, dedicated to most compatible authors, are also published. Some recent published poets: Susan Benischek, Joanna Nealon, Heather Fraser'' avg. press run 100. Pub'd 3 titles 1998; expects 3 titles 1999, 3 titles 2000. 27 titles listed in the *Small Press Record of Books in Print* (28th Edition, 1999-00). avg. price, paper: $12 (incl. audio cassette). Discounts: $6 plus $3 shipping per item. 70pp; 8½×11; †photocopy. Reporting time: usually less than 1 month. Simultaneous submissions accepted: yes. Publishes 20% of manuscripts submitted. Payment: discount copy of book, discount on cassettes. Does not copyright for author.

Cosmoenergetics Publications, Rick Blanchard, PO Box 12011, Prescott, AZ 86304-2011, 520-778-0867. 1981. Non-fiction. ''Biases: *Interrelationships*, metaphysics and science, symbolism and language, psychology and health, mind and healing'' avg. press run 5M. Expects 1 title 2000. 1 title listed in the *Small Press Record of Books in Print* (28th Edition, 1999-00). avg. price, paper: $9.95. Discounts: bookstores-40%; wholesalers-55%; 2-4 books-20%; 5-9 30%; 10-24 40%. 250pp; 5½×8½. Reporting time: 2-3 weeks. Payment: 10% quarterly. Copyrights for author. PMA.

Coteau Books, Geoffrey Ursell, Publisher, 401-2206 Dewdney Avenue, Regina, Sask. S4R 1H3, Canada, 306-777-0170; e-Mail coteau@coteau.unibase.com. 1975. Poetry, fiction, interviews, criticism, long-poems, plays, non-fiction. ''Coteau Books was established to publish prairie and Canadian writing: poetry, fiction, songs, plays, children's books and literary criticism. We do *not* consider manuscripts from non-Canadian writers. Coteau Books is committed to publishing the work of new as well as established writers and two series of books are devoted to new writers' work'' avg. press run 1.5M. Pub'd 12 titles 1998; expects 13 titles 1999, 12 titles 2000. 95 titles listed in the *Small Press Record of Books in Print* (28th Edition, 1999-00). avg. price, cloth: $21.95; paper: $11.95; other: $6.95 mass market format. Discounts: 40% retail, 20% to schools and universities on 10 or more of same title. 80-325pp; 6×9, 4¼×7, 8×8, 8½×11; of. Reporting time: 2-6 months. Simultaneous submissions accepted: no. Publishes 4% of manuscripts submitted. Payment: normally 12%

royalties. Copyrights for author. Sask. Publishers Group (SPG), Association of Canadian Publishers (ACP), Literary Press Group (LPG), Can. Book Information Centre (CBIC), Can. Telebook Agency (CTA), Can. Booksellers Association (CBA).

Cottage Publications, Inc., Don Wright, 24396 Pleasant View Drive, Elkhart, IN 46517, 219-293-7553. 1986. Articles, photos, non-fiction. avg. press run 20M. Pub'd 2 titles 1998; expects 3 titles 1999, 4 titles 2000. 7 titles listed in the *Small Press Record of Books in Print* (28th Edition, 1999-00). avg. price, paper: $14.95. Discounts: standard trade. 250-600pp; 5½×8½, 8½×11; of. Reporting time: 3 months. Publishes 1% of manuscripts submitted. Payment: negotiable. Copyrights for author.

Cottontail Publications (see also THE PRESIDENTS' JOURNAL), Ellyn R. Kern, 79 Drakes Ridge, Bennington, IN 47011, 812-427-3921. 1979. News items, non-fiction. avg. press run 1M. Pub'd 1 title 1998; expects 2 titles 1999, 1 title 2000. 1 title listed in the *Small Press Record of Books in Print* (28th Edition, 1999-00). avg. price, paper: $9. Discounts: 2-50 40%, short discount under $10 cover price. 90pp; 8½×11, 5½×7; of. Reporting time: 6 weeks or less. Payment: to be negotiated. Copyrights for author. NWA.

COTTONWOOD, Cottonwood Press, Tom Lorenz, Editor; Amy Stuber, Fiction Editor; Philip Wedge, Poetry Editor; Denise Low, Review Editor, 400 Kansas Union, Box J, University of Kansas, Lawrence, KS 66045, 785-864-2528. 1965. Poetry, fiction, art, photos, interviews, reviews. "We publish a wide variety of styles of poetry, fiction, and nonfiction. Poetry submissions should be limited to the five best, fiction to one story. Past issues have included interviews with William Burroughs, Gwendolyn Brooks and Scott Heim. We have published recent work by Gerald Early, Wanda Coleman, Patricia Traxler, William Stafford, Jared Carter, Victor Contoski, Robert Day, W.S. Merwin, Antonya Nelson, Connie May Fowler, Oakley Hall, and Luci Tapahonso. We welcome submissions of photos, graphics, short fiction, poetry, and reviews from new as well as established writers." circ. 500-600. 2/yr. Pub'd 1 issue 1998; expects 2 issues 1999, 2 issues 2000. sub. price: $15, $18 overseas; per copy: $8.50; sample: $4. Back issues: $3. Discounts: 30% trade, bulk negotiable. 112pp; 9×6; computer, of. Reporting time: 2-5 months. Simultaneous submissions accepted: yes. Publishes 1% of manuscripts submitted. Payment: 1 copy, eligibility for yearly Alice Carter Awards in poetry and fiction. Copyrighted. Pub's reviews: 2 in 1998. §national, midwest poetry or fiction chapbooks. Ads: none. CLMP.

Cottonwood Press (see also COTTONWOOD), Tom Lorenz, Editor, 400 Kansas Union, Box J, Univ. of Kansas, Lawrence, KS 66045, 785-864-2528. 1965. "We generally solicit material for the press" avg. press run 500-1M. Pub'd 1 title 1998; expects 1 title 1999, 1 title 2000. 16 titles listed in the *Small Press Record of Books in Print* (28th Edition, 1999-00). avg. price, paper: $10. Discounts: 30% to bookstores. 80pp; 9×6; computer, of. Copyrights for author. CLMP.

Cottonwood Press, Inc., Cheryl Thurston, 305 West Magnolia, Suite 398, Fort Collins, CO 80521, 970-204-0715. 1986. Poetry, plays, non-fiction. "We are interested primarily in practical books for language arts teachers, grades 5-12" avg. press run 2M. Pub'd 3 titles 1998; expects 3 titles 1999, 3-5 titles 2000. 29 titles listed in the *Small Press Record of Books in Print* (28th Edition, 1999-00). avg. price, paper: $15.95. Discounts: available upon request. 100pp; 8½×11. Reporting time: 2-4 weeks. We accept simultaneous submissions only if notified. Payment: royalties of 10% of net sales. Copyrights for author.

COTYLEDON, Catamount Press, Georgette Perry, Editor, 2519 Roland Road SW, Huntsville, AL 35805, 205-536-9801. 1997. "I welcome imagistic nature poems and the mysterious and cryptic. Surprise me!" 5/yr. Pub'd 5 issues 1998; expects 5 issues 1999, 5 issues 2000. sub. price: $3; per copy: $1 ppd.; sample: $1 or 3 unattached 33¢ stamps. 12 or 16pp; 3½×4¼; photocopy. Reporting time: 1 month. Simultaneous submissions accepted: no. Publishes 5% of manuscripts submitted. Payment: copies. Copyrighted, reverts to author.

Cougar Books, Ruth Pritchard, Editorial Director, 1228 N Street, Suite 10, Sacramento, CA 95814, 916-442-1434. 1973. Non-fiction. "Publish books primarily on health & parenting" avg. press run 5M. 3 titles listed in the *Small Press Record of Books in Print* (28th Edition, 1999-00). avg. price, paper: $7.95. Discounts: 1-4, 20; 5-49, 40%; 50-99, 42%. 160pp; 5½×8½; of. Reporting time: 2 months. Payment: 5% to 10%. Copyrights for author. AAP, NCBPA, WBPA.

Cougar Imprints, PO Box 1573, Rawlins, WY 82301-1573, 307-864-3328, fax 307-864-5279, e-mail CougarBook@AOL.com. avg. press run 1. 1 title listed in the *Small Press Record of Books in Print* (28th Edition, 1999-00). Discounts: 2-4 20%, 5-99-40%, non-return on5 or more extra discount to wholesale and retailers. To bookstores for prepaid only on 1 book 10% off. Reporting time: 3 months. Simultaneous submissions accepted: yes. Copyrights for author.

Michael E. Coughlin, Publisher (see also THE DANDELION), Michael E. Coughlin, PO Box 205, Cornucopia, WI 54827. 1978. avg. press run 1M. Pub'd 1 title 1998; expects 1 title 1999, 1 title 2000. 6 titles listed in the *Small Press Record of Books in Print* (28th Edition, 1999-00). avg. price, cloth: $25; paper: $5.95. Discounts: 40% to bookstores ordering 3 or more copies. 300pp; 6×9; †lp. Reporting time: 2 months. Payment: negotiated. Copyrights for author.

Council For Indian Education, Hap Gilliland, 2032 Woody Drive, Billings, MT 59102-2852, 406-252-7451. 1963. Fiction, non-fiction. "Small books on themes related to American Indian life and culture, both fiction and non-fiction, also Indian crafts, and small books on teaching. Book ordering address: PO Box 31215, Billings, MT 59107" avg. press run 1M. Pub'd 4 titles 1998; expects 4 titles 1999, 4 titles 2000. 70 titles listed in the *Small Press Record of Books in Print* (28th Edition, 1999-00). avg. price, cloth: $14.95; paper: $7.95. Discounts: 1 20%, 2-10 30%, 11+ 40% to bookstores only. 100pp; 6×9; of. Reporting time: 2-8 months. Simultaneous submissions accepted: yes. Publishes 3% of manuscripts submitted. Payment: 10% of wholesale price or 2¢ per word. We furnish author with copyright forms.

Council Oak Books, Kevin Bentley, Editor; Paulette Millichap, Publisher, 1350 East 15th Street, Tulsa, OK 74120, 918-587-6454; Fax 918-583-4995; oakie@ionet.net. 1984. Non-fiction. "We accept unsolicited queries" avg. press run 4M. Pub'd 11 titles 1998; expects 8 titles 1999, 12 titles 2000. 65 titles listed in the *Small Press Record of Books in Print* (28th Edition, 1999-00). avg. price, cloth: $18.95; paper: $10.95. Discounts: trade 1-3 20%, 4-49 43%, 50-99 44%, 100-249 45%, 250-499 46%, 500+ 47%; wholesale 50%. 250pp; size varies. Reporting time: varies. Simultaneous submissions accepted: yes. Publishes 1% of manuscripts submitted. Payment: standard percentages of net sales. Copyrights for author. ABA, Oklahoma Booksellers Association, South Central Booksellers Assn., Rocky Mountain Book Publishers Association.

COUNTERMEASURES, Greg Glazner, Editor; Jon Davis, Editor, Creative Writing Program, College of Santa Fe, St. Michael's Drive, Santa Fe, NM 87505. 1994. Poetry, letters. "We publish only ten or twelve poems per year, so the poems we publish get a lot of attention. We favor ambitious poems which exhibit passion, scope, craft, and intelligent attention to form (usually free verse form). We're partial to long poems, but we have also published a six line poem. We are discovering a group of poets with whose work we are unfamiliar" circ. 2M. 2/yr. Pub'd 1 issue 1998; expects 2 issues 1999, 2 issues 2000. sub. price: $5; per copy: $2.50; sample: $2.50. Back issues: $2.50. Discounts: 10%-50%. 40pp; 8½×11. Reporting time: 30 days, submission period September through April. Payment: copies. Copyrighted, reverts to author. Ads: none.

COUNTERPOISE: For Social Responsibilities, Liberty and Dissent, Charles Willett, 1716 SW Williston Road, Gainesville, FL 32608-4049, 352-335-2200. 1997. Articles, criticism, reviews, letters. "A review journal for alternative publications; alternatives in print Task Force of the Social Responsibilities Round Table of the American Library Association. No unsolicited reviews or essays." circ. 200. 4/yr. Pub'd 4 issues 1998; expects 4 issues 1999, 4 issues 2000. sub. price: $25 indiv.; $35 institution; per copy: $9 + $3 S&H; sample: free. Back issues: $9 + $3 S&H. Discounts: none. 65pp; 8½×11. Payment: none. Copyrighted, does not revert to author. Pub's reviews: 322 in 1998. §Alternative press. Ads: $275/$165. Independent Press Association.

COUNTRY CHARM MAGAZINE, Denise Friedel, Box 696, Palmerston, ON N0G 2P0, Canada, 519-343-3059. 1993. Poetry, fiction, articles, art, photos, cartoons, interviews, satire, news items, non-fiction. "500-1000 words preferred; eg. 'Saps Runni' by Lorne Parker (alias Ole Bent Knees); Dear Dave (humour), 'Let's Eat Out,' by Ruth Latta" circ. 1.5M. 12/yr. Pub'd 12 issues 1998; expects 12 issues 1999, 12 issues 2000. sub. price: $14; per copy: $1; sample: $1. Back issues: $1. 24pp; 8½×11; of. Reporting time: 1-2 months. Simultaneous submissions accepted: yes. Publishes 50-60% of manuscripts submitted. Payment: $10 per article; smaller items (poems, recipes) paid in copies. Copyrighted, reverts to author. Pub's reviews: 1 in 1998. §Humour, rural, agricultural, food, health, crafts, cartoons. Ads: $300/$160/$85 1/4 page/$48 1/4 page.

Courtyard Publishing Company, David Schorr, 3725 May Street, Los Angeles, CA 90066. 1992. Non-fiction. "We specialize in self-help books." avg. press run 2M. Pub'd 2 titles 1998; expects 2 titles 1999, 4 titles 2000. 1 title listed in the *Small Press Record of Books in Print* (28th Edition, 1999-00). avg. price, paper: $12.95. Discounts: usual trade 25% to 50%. 160pp; 5½×8½. Reporting time: 2-3 months. Payment: to be arranged. Copyrights for author.

Cove View Press, Mereda Kaminski, 2165 Carlmont #205, Belmont, CA 94002. 1977. avg. press run 500. Pub'd 2 titles 1998; expects 2 titles 1999. 12 titles listed in the *Small Press Record of Books in Print* (28th Edition, 1999-00). Discounts: 1 30%, 2+ 40%, no returns. of. Reporting time: 1-4 weeks. Payment: 10% of net. Copyrights for author.

COVER MAGAZINE, Hard Press, Jeffrey C. Wright, 632 East 14th Street, #18, New York, NY 10009, 212-673-1152; Fax 212-253-7614. 1987. Poetry, articles, art, photos, interviews, criticism, reviews, music. "*Cover* is the only magazine that covers all the arts exclusively. Recent poems by John Ashbery, Anne Waldman and Allen Ginsberg. Recent interviews with Lou Reed, Alex Katz, Wim Wenders, Kyle MacClachlan, Sandra Bernhard, Richard Linklater. Recent art by Eric Drooker and Judy Rifka. $5 reading and comment fee for submission." circ. 25M. 6/yr. Pub'd 9 issues 1998; expects 6 issues 1999, 6 issues 2000. sub. price: $10; per copy: $5; sample: $5 with submission also. Back issues: rare. Discounts: the best. 64pp; 10×11½; web press. Reporting time: 2-4 months. Simultaneous submissions accepted: no. Publishes 4% of manuscripts submitted. Payment: nothing, not even a copy. Copyrighted, reverts to author. Pub's reviews: 36 in 1998. §Poetry, fiction, essays, autobiography, nonfiction arts related. Ads: $1,100/$600/$350 1/4 page/$225 1/6 page/$175 1/8 page.

John Edwin Cowen/Bravo Editions (see also BRAVO, THE POET'S MAGAZINE), Jose Garcia Villa, Founding Editor; John Cowen, Editor, 1081 Trafalgar Street, Teaneck, NJ 07666. 1977. "Biases: (1) Poetry must have formal excellence, (2) Poetry must be lyrical, (3) Poetry is not prose. Mss. by invitation only" avg. press run 1.5M. Pub'd 1 title 1998; expects 1 title 1999, 1 title 2000. 3 titles listed in the *Small Press Record of Books in Print* (28th Edition, 1999-00). avg. price, cloth: $20; paper: $10. Discounts: 40%. 96pp; 6¼×9½; lp. Reporting time: 2 months (send inquiry with no more than 6 poem submission). Payment: by arrangement with author. Copyrights for author. NYSSPA.

Coyote Books, James Koller, PO Box 629, Brunswick, ME 04011. 1964. avg. press run varies 200-5000. Expects 1 title 1999. 2 titles listed in the *Small Press Record of Books in Print* (28th Edition, 1999-00). avg. price, paper: $10-$15. Discounts: 40% to retail. 100-300pp; 5½×8½; all. Reporting time: varies. Query before sending simultaneous submissions. Publishes a small % of manuscripts submitted. Payment: copies - percentage. Copyright varies.

Coyote Publishing, Shari Ficck, PO Box 1854, Yreka, CA 96097, 916-842-5788. 1991. Cartoons, non-fiction. "Parent company, Shari and Associates, established 1968, is a public relation agency. Coyote Publishing was identified to sell/market *Family Reunions & Clan Gatherings*, a how-to guide and celebration for organizing events. Since the first book, various projects have been completed addressing a wide variety of publishing needs: children's illustrated books, poetry anthology, phonic dictionary, and art book, health guide to native plants are in process." avg. press run depends on client and marketing potential. Pub'd 1 title 1998; expects 3 titles 1999, 4 titles 2000. 9 titles listed in the *Small Press Record of Books in Print* (28th Edition, 1999-00). avg. price, paper: $10-$15. Discounts: STOP. Pages vary; 5½×8½. Payment: our company helps authors publish and market their labors. Copyright for author if asked. NWC.

COZY DETECTIVE MYSTERY MAGAZINE, Meager Ink Press, David Workman, Charlie Bradley, 686 Jakes Court, McMinnville, OR 97128, 503-435-1212; Fax 503-472-4896; e-mail papercapers@yahoo.com. 1993. Fiction, articles, art, photos, cartoons, interviews, criticism, reviews, parts-of-novels, news items, non-fiction. "Length of material: 6,000 words or less." circ. 500. 4/yr. Pub'd 4 issues 1998; expects 5 issues 1999, 5 issues 2000. sub. price: $10.50; per copy: $2.95; sample: $2.95 + $1.50 p/h. 68pp; 5½×8½; mi. Reporting time: 3-6 months. Simultaneous submissions accepted: yes. Payment: in copies. Copyrighted, reverts to author. Pub's reviews: 5 in 1998. §Crime, mystery, author related or cases. Ads: $100/$50/$25 1/4 page.

CPG Publishing Company, PO Box 50062, Phoenix, AZ 85076, 800-578-5549. 1992. Non-fiction. "Publish practical guides for early childhood program administrators and early childhood consultants." avg. press run 3M-5M. Expects 4 titles 1999, 25 titles 2000. 3 titles listed in the *Small Press Record of Books in Print* (28th Edition, 1999-00). avg. price, paper: $15.95. 175pp; 5½×8½, 8½×11; of. Simultaneous submissions accepted: yes. Payment: negotiated with each author. Copyrights for author. North American Bookdealers Exchange.

CPHC Press and Products, 861 Main Street, Baton Rouge, LA 70802-5529, 504-383-3013; 800-445-8026; FAX 504-383-0030; email ssd720@aol.com; itoldson@premier.net. 2 titles listed in the *Small Press Record of Books in Print* (28th Edition, 1999-00).

CRAB CREEK REVIEW, Kimberly Allison, Harris Levinson, Laura Sinai, Terri Stone, 7265 S. 128th St., Seattle, WA 98178, 206-772-8489; http://www.drizzle.net/nccr. 1983. Poetry, fiction, art, satire, non-fiction. "After releasing Volume XI in August 1997, *CCR* is now a biannual publication again. They publish an eclectic mix of energetic poems, free or formal, and remain more interested in powerful imagery than obscure literary allusion. Like work that reads well aloud, has an authentic voice, presents clear and effective images, and poems that display a sense of wit and word-play. Recent contributors include: David Lee, Yehuda Amichai, Naomi Shihab Nye, Olga Popova, and Kevin Miller. Translations are welcome—please submit with a copy of the poem in its original language, if possible. Send up to 5 poems. *CCR* also seeks submissions of short fiction. They accept stories up to 3500 words, with an admitted predilection for dynamic prose of distinct voice and strong images. Offer a compelling view of the world in which we live and let us revel in your telling of it. Art is cover only." circ. 400. 2/yr. Pub'd 1 issue 1998; expects 2 issues 1999, 2 issues 2000. sub. price: $15 per anthology 1996; $10-2 semiannual issues; per copy: $6 Vol. XI forward; sample: $6; $5 for anniversary 1994, $5 for Bread for the Hunger (1996). Back issues: $3. 80pp; 6×9; of. Reporting time: 10-12 weeks. Simultaneous submissions accepted: no. Publishes 5% of manuscripts submitted. Payment: 2 copies. Copyrighted, rights revert to author but request mention of *Crab Creek Review* with subsequent printings. Ads: $120/$65. CLMP.

CRAB ORCHARD REVIEW, Jon Tribble, Managing Editor, Dept. of English, Southern Illinois University, Carbondale, IL 62901, 618-453-6833. 1995. Poetry, fiction, interviews, reviews, parts-of-novels, long-poems, non-fiction. "Journal of creative works publishing fiction, poetry, creative non-fiction, interviews, novel excerpts, and book reviews. Recent contributors include Pete Fromm, William Matthews, Yusef Komunyakaa, Cathy Song, and Judy Juanita." circ. 1M. 2/yr. Pub'd 2 issues 1998; expects 2 issues 1999, 2 issues 2000. sub. price: $10; per copy: $6; sample: $6. 280pp; 5½×8½. Reporting time: 3 weeks to 5 months. We accept

138

simultaneous submissions when informed. Publishes 5% of manuscripts submitted. Payment: $50 min. for poetry, $100 min. for prose, plus a year's subscription and 2 copies. Copyrighted, reverts to author. Pub's reviews: 10 in 1998. §Small press and university press titles only (poetry, fiction, creative nonfiction); book reviews are done in-house by staff. Writers may send books for review to the Managing Editor. Ads: none. CLMP.

Beverly Cracom Publications, Barbara E. Norwitz, Publisher and Editorial Director, 12685 Dorsett Road, #179, Maryland Heights, MO 63043-2100, 314-291-0880; fax 314-291-3829. 1993. Non-fiction. "Edditorial office 27 Danbury Rd. Wilton, CT 06897 203-834-6077 Fax 203-834-6079" avg. press run 5000-10,000. Pub'd 2 titles 1998; expects 6 titles 1999, 6 titles 2000. 4 titles listed in the *Small Press Record of Books in Print* (28th Edition, 1999-00). avg. price, cloth: varies; paper: varies. Discounts: varies. Pages vary; size varies. Reporting time: 2-3 months. Simultaneous submissions accepted: yes. Publishes 25% of manuscripts submitted. Payment: 10-13%. Does not copyright for author. PMA.

CRAFTS 'N THINGS, Clapper Publishing Co., Julie Stephani, 2400 Devon, Suite 375, Des Plaines, IL 60018, 847-635-5800. 1951. circ. 300M. 10/yr. Pub'd 10 issues 1998; expects 10 issues 1999, 10 issues 2000. price per copy: $3.95-$4.95. 106pp; 8½×11. Reporting time: 3 months. Simultaneous submissions accepted: yes. Payment: yes. Copyrighted, does not revert to author. Pub's reviews. §Craft books. MPA.

Craftsman Book Company, Gary Moselle, Publisher; Laurence Jacobs, Editor, 6058 Corte Del Cedro, Carlsbad, CA 92009, 619-438-7828. 1952. Non-fiction. "Craftsman Book Company publishes *practical references for professional builders.* Craftsman books are loaded with step-by-step instructions, illustrations, charts, reference data, checklists, forms, samples, cost estimates, rules of thumb, and examples that solve actual problems in the builder's office or in the field. Every book covers a limited construction subject fully, becomes the builder's primary reference on that subject, has a high utility-to-cost ratio, and will help the builder make a better living in his profession. Length is variable but should be at least 500 manuscript pages including illustrations and charts. We seek queries and outlines and will consider material in nearly all construction areas and trades, including electrical, heating and air conditioning, lath and plaster, painting, prefab housing construction, heavy construction, estimating, and costing" avg. press run 5M. Pub'd 10 titles 1998; expects 12 titles 1999, 12 titles 2000. 16 titles listed in the *Small Press Record of Books in Print* (28th Edition, 1999-00). avg. price, paper: $35. Discounts: trade 1-4 copies 33%, 5-49 copies 40%, 50+ copies 45%. 297pp; 8½×11. Reporting time: 3 weeks. Simultaneous submissions accepted: yes. Publishes 10% of manuscripts submitted. Payment: 12½% of net of all books sold, 7½% for discounts of 50% or more. Copyrights for author. Publishers Marketing Assn.

The F. Marion Crawford Memorial Society (see also THE ROMANTIST), John C. Moran, Editor; Steve Eng, Co-Editor; Jesse F. Knight, Co-Editor; Don Herron, Contributing Editor, Saracinesca House, 3610 Meadowbrook Avenue, Nashville, TN 37205. 1975. Poetry, articles, art, photos, interviews, criticism, reviews, music, letters, long-poems, collages. "Recent contributions on: Russell Kirk, H. Warner Munn, Algernon Blackwood, J. Sheridan LeFanu, H.P. Lovecraft, Arthur Machen, and kindred authors. Purview is modern romanticism, ca. 1850 - ca. 1950 especially imaginative literature (emphasis upon fantasy) ; contains a regular section on F. Marion Crawford (1854-1909). Publishes mostly traditional (rimed) poetry. No fiction" avg. press run 300 (limited and numbered). Pub'd 1 title 1998; expects 1 title 1999, 1 title 2000. 3 titles listed in the *Small Press Record of Books in Print* (28th Edition, 1999-00). avg. price, paper: $15.00 incl postage. Discounts: 20% to 40% depending upon quantity. 160pp; 8½×11; of, lp. Reporting time: within 1 month (query on all articles). Payment: 1 copy (at present). Does not copyright for author.

CRAZYHORSE, Ralph Burns, Editor; Dennis Vannatta, Review and Criticism Editor, 2801 S. University, Dept. of English, Univ. of Arkansas-Little Rock, Little Rock, AR 72204, 501-569-3161. 1960. Poetry, interviews, criticism, reviews, long-poems. "Past Contributors include James Wright, Louis Simpson, Richard Hugo, Philip Levine, Maura Stanton, Jorie Graham, William Matthews, Yusef Komunyakaa, Marianne Boruch, Galway Kinnell, Stephen Dunn, David Wojahn. We regret we are no longer publishing fiction." circ. 1M. 2/yr. Pub'd 2 issues 1998; expects 2 issues 1999, 2 issues 2000. sub. price: $10; per copy: $5; sample: $5. Back issues: $1-$5. Discounts: agencies, 30%; bookstores, 40%. 150pp; 6×9; of. Reporting time: 2-12 weeks. Simultaneous submissions accepted: no. Publishes less than 1% of manuscripts submitted. Payment: $10 per printed page, also $500 awards for best poem and story we publish each year. Copyrighted. Pub's reviews: 2 in 1998. §Contemporary poetry and criticism of the same. Ads: $85/$50. CLMP.

CRC Publications (see also THE BANNER), Harvey Smit, John Suk, 2850 Kalamazoo SE, Grand Rapids, MI 49560. 1979. Poetry, fiction, articles, art, photos, cartoons, interviews, criticism, reviews, music, letters, news items, non-fiction. "Religion-in the Reformed-Presbyterian tradition" avg. press run *Banner* 41M. Pub'd 40 titles 1998; expects 50 titles 1999, 60 titles 2000. avg. price, paper: $9. Discounts: 15-30% to qualified bookstores/distributors. Pages vary; †of. Reporting time: varies. Does not always copyright for author. PCPA, CBA.

CRCS Publications, Barbara McEnerney, PO Box 1460, Sebastopol, CA 95473-1460. 1975. Non-fiction. "We are specializing in the production of high-quality, aesthetically-pleasing astrological books, with a psychological and spiritual slant, & books on health." avg. press run 5M. Expects 1 title 1999, 1 title 2000. 25 titles listed in the *Small Press Record of Books in Print* (28th Edition, 1999-00). avg. price, paper: $9.95-$14.95. Discounts: 40% off orders of 5 or more books to dealers; 25% off all pre-paid orders from dealers, in any quantity; 10% to libraries if requested. Free shipping on pre-paid orders for 25 or more books. 200+pp; size varies; of. Reporting time: 8 weeks, must inquire before sending ms. Simultaneous submissions accepted: no. Publishes 1% of manuscripts submitted. Payment: royalties plus large discounts on books. Copyrights for author.

THE CREAM CITY REVIEW, Kate Ranft, Editor, PO Box 413, English Dept, Curtin Hall, Univ. of Wisconsin, Milwaukee, WI 53201, 414-229-4708. 1975. Poetry, fiction, art, photos, interviews, criticism, reviews, parts-of-novels, long-poems, plays, non-fiction. "We publish a variety of writers and writings, offering a range of perspectives, styles, and contents from new and well-known writers. We prefer prose of 25 pages or less, though we'll consider longer pieces. Please submit no more than one work of prose, or up to five poems. Short, small press book reviews are especially welcome, as are b/w camera-ready art and photos. Recent contributors: Marge Piercy, Maxine Kumin, Ted Kooser, William Matthews, Stuart Dybek, Amy Clampitt, Houston Baker, F.D. Reeve, Tess Gallagher, Robley Wilson, Jr., Lawrence Ferlinghetti, Denise Levertov, Alicia Ostriker, Cathy Song, Russell Edson, William Kittredge, Audre Lorde, Donald Hall, Albert Goldbarth, Adrienne Rich" circ. 2M. 2/yr. Pub'd 2 issues 1998; expects 2 issues 1999, 2 issues 2000. sub. price: $12; per copy: $7; sample: $5. Back issues: varies per issue (average $1.50-$5); request a back-issue order blank. Discounts: schools send SASE for rates. 200pp; 5½x8½; †of. Reporting time: 4 months, we read from Sept. 1st - April 30th only. Simultaneous submissions acceptable with notification. Payment: subscriptions or contributor copies. Copyrighted, reverts to author. Pub's reviews: 5 in 1998. §Poetry, fiction, creative non-fiction, autobiography. Ads: $50/$25/no classified word rate. CLMP.

Creative Arts & Science Enterprises (see also STARBURST), Charles J. Palmer, Jacqueline Palmer, 341 Miller Street, Abilene, TX 79605-1903. 1989. Poetry, fiction, non-fiction. "Contest Deadlines: Feb 28/April 30/June 30/Aug 31/Oct 31/Dec 31 Poetry: 32 lines or less. Prose: 400 words or less. Any subject suitable for a general reading audience. Winners of contest and other selected works of high quality, produced in one of three hardcover anthologies each year. (No reading fees, no purchase necessary to enter and win contest.) Guidelines available, send SASE." avg. press run 1M. Pub'd 4 titles 1998; expects 3 titles 1999, 3 titles 2000. 12 titles listed in the *Small Press Record of Books in Print* (28th Edition, 1999-00). avg. price, cloth: $39.95. 230pp; 8½x11; †of. Reporting time: final selection 45 days from end of each contest. Payment: cash to winners 45 days after end of contest. Authors retain own rights.

Creative Concern Publications, Richard Hughes, Editor, 12066 Suellen Circle, West Palm Beach, FL 33414, 407-793-5854. 1984. Fiction, non-fiction. "General office: 3208 East Mayaguana Lane, Lantana, FL 33462" avg. press run 5M. Pub'd 2 titles 1998; expects 2 titles 1999, 2 titles 2000. 3 titles listed in the *Small Press Record of Books in Print* (28th Edition, 1999-00). avg. price, paper: $3.95. Discounts: 40% wholesalers, 30% bookstores. 250pp; 5½x8¾; of. Reporting time: 6 months. Payment: subsidize press. Copyrights for author. NWC, FFWA.

Creative Consortium, Inc., 4850 Marieview Court, Ste. 101, Cincinnati, OH 45236-2012, 513-984-0614, 800-320-8631; Fax 513-984-0635; creatcon@fuse.net. 2 titles listed in the *Small Press Record of Books in Print* (28th Edition, 1999-00).

CREATIVE NONFICTION, Lee Gutkind, 5501 Walnut St., #202, Pittsburgh, PA 15232-2329, 412-688-0304; fax 412-683-9173. 1993. Interviews, reviews, non-fiction. circ. 4.5M. 3/yr. Pub'd 3 issues 1998; expects 3 issues 1999, 3 issues 2000. sub. price: $22.50; per copy: $10; sample: $10. Back issues: $10. 164pp; 5½x8¼; of. Reporting time: 3-5 months. Simultaneous submissions accepted: yes. Publishes 1% of manuscripts submitted. Payment: varies. Copyrighted, reverts to author. Pub's reviews: 8 in 1998. §Creative nonfiction. Ads: $250/$175.

Creative Roots, Inc., Lloyd deMause, 140 Riverside Drive, New York, NY 10024, 212-799-2294. 1975. Non-fiction. "Book publishing" avg. press run 2M. Pub'd 1 title 1998; expects 2 titles 1999, 5 titles 2000. 2 titles listed in the *Small Press Record of Books in Print* (28th Edition, 1999-00). avg. price, cloth: $25; paper: $10. Discounts: 2 or more-20%. 350pp; 6x9; of. Reporting time: 1 month. Payment: variable. Copyrights for author.

●**Creative With Words Publications (CWW) (see also THEECLECTICS)**, Brigitta Geltrich, Editor & Publisher; Bert Hower, Editor, PO Box 223226, Carmel, CA 93922-3226, Fax: 831-655-8627; e-mail: cwwpub@usa.net; http://members.tripod.com/~creativewithwords. 1975. Poetry, fiction, cartoons, satire. "On any topic, written by all ages (poetry and prose)." Pub'd 14 titles 1998; expects 12-14 titles 1999, 12-14 titles 2000. 64 titles listed in the *Small Press Record of Books in Print* (28th Edition, 1999-00). avg. price, paper:

$10-$20; other: varies. Discounts: schools & libraries 10%; authors receive 20% off; on orders 10 or more an additional 10% off. There are no free copies, except for winner of "Best of the Month" (1 free copy). Pages vary (approx. 60+pp); 7×8½; mi, xerox, laser printer. Reporting time: 1-2 months, SASE is always a must; if a seasonal anthology, reporting time is 2 months after set deadline. Simultaneous submissions accepted: no. Publishes 90% of manuscripts submitted. Payment: 20% reduction of regular cost to participants, no payment in copies; small fee for guest artists, readers, and guest editors. Copyrights for author. SCBW.

THE CREATIVE WOMAN, Margaret A. Choudhury, 126 East Wing Street #288, Arlington Heights, IL 60004, 708-255-1232; FAX 708-255-1243. 1977. Poetry, fiction, articles, art, photos, interviews, criticism, reviews, letters, news items, non-fiction. circ. 1M. 4/yr. Pub'd 4 issues 1998; expects 4 issues 1999, 4 issues 2000. sub. price: $16; per copy: $5; sample: $5. Back issues: $5. Discounts: 40%. 52pp; 8½×11; †of. Reporting time: 6 months or less. Payment: 3 copies. Copyrighted, reverts to author. Pub's reviews: 16 in 1998. §Women's involvement in creative endeavors, any aspect of creativity in any field applied to women. Ads: $350/$200/$50 per inch.

CREATIVITY CONNECTION, Marshall J. Cook, Room 622 Lowell Hall, 610 Langdon Street, Madison, WI 53703, 608-262-4911. 1990. Articles, photos, cartoons, interviews, reviews, news items, non-fiction, letters. "We publish articles and art of interest to writers and small press publishers" circ. 500. 4/yr. Pub'd 4 issues 1998; expects 4 issues 1999, 4 issues 2000. sub. price: $18/$34 for 2 years; sample: $1. Back issues: $1. Discounts: we negotiate with classrooms and writers' groups. 16pp; 8½×11; †of. Reporting time: 2 weeks. Simultaneous submissions accepted: no. Publishes 50% of manuscripts submitted. Payment: 5 copies, 1 year subscription. Copyrighted, reverts to author. Pub's reviews: 50 in 1998. §Creativity, writing (how-to), writers (auto & bio), small presses/ publishers. Ads: none.

Creatures At Large Press, John Stanley, PO Box 687, 1082 Grand Teton Drive, Pacifica, CA 94044, 415-355-READ; fax 415-355-4863. 1981. Fiction, reviews. avg. press run 5M-10M. Pub'd 1 title 1998. 3 titles listed in the *Small Press Record of Books in Print* (28th Edition, 1999-00). avg. price, cloth: $40; paper: $12. Discounts: available on request. 400-500pp; size varies; of. PMA.

CREEPY MIKE'S OMNIBUS OF FUN, Michael Ruspantini, PO Box 401026, San Francisco, CA 94140-1026, aueplayer@aol.com. 1995. Art, photos, cartoons, interviews, reviews, music. "*CMOOF* does fairly short reviews of comics, zines, music and interviews (humorous) of comics creators, music figures, interesting characters. Also review videos. Likes alt. comics, punk/noise music and weird news." circ. 1M+. 4/yr. Pub'd 1 issue 1998; expects 4 issues 1999, 4 issues 2000. sub. price: n/a; per copy: $2; sample: $2. Back issues: $2. Discounts: selective trades, bulk/agent rates available on request. 30pp; 5½×8; †mi. Simultaneous submissions accepted: no. Publishes 0% of manuscripts submitted. Payment: courtesy copies. Not copyrighted. Pub's reviews: 7 in 1998. §Punk/noise music, comix/mini-comics, alternative/underground/psychotronic movies/videos. Ads: $40/$20/$75 back cover/$10 1/4 page.

Creighton-Morgan Publishing Group, Fay Faron, Po Box 470862, San Francisco, CA 94147-0862. 1989. "Do not submit" avg. press run 5M. Pub'd 1 title 1998; expects 3 titles 1999. 1 title listed in the *Small Press Record of Books in Print* (28th Edition, 1999-00). avg. price, cloth: $0; paper: $29.95. Discounts: 40%. 300pp; 8½×11; OF. Does not copyright for author.

Crescent Moon (see also PAGAN AMERICA; PASSION), Jeremy Robinson, Cassidy Hughes, PO Box 393, Maidstone, Kent ME14 5XU, United Kingdom. 1988. Poetry, articles, art, photos, interviews, criticism, reviews, music, letters, parts-of-novels, news items. "We prefer a letter and sample first, not a whole manuscript. Return postage and envelope. We are open to many ideas for books" avg. press run 100-200. Pub'd 15 titles 1998; expects 15 titles 1999, 20 titles 2000. 4 titles listed in the *Small Press Record of Books in Print* (28th Edition, 1999-00). avg. price, paper: $9.99. Discounts: Trade: single order 20%, 2+ 35%, add $1.50 postage. 120pp; mi. Reporting time: 2 months. Simultaneous submissions accepted: yes. Publishes 5% of manuscripts submitted. Payment: to be negotiated. Copyrights for author. Small Press Group.

THE CRESCENT REVIEW, J.T. Holland, Editor, PO Box 15069, Chevy Chase, MD 20825. 1982. Fiction. "*The Crescent Review* is a short-story journal. SASE for guidelines. No submissions in May-June or November-December. Maximum word count is 12,000" circ. 2M. 3-4/yr. Pub'd 3 issues 1998; expects 3 issues 1999, 4 issues 2000. sub. price: $21; per copy: u8 next issue; sample: $8 + shipping ($1.40). Back issues: $9 + shipping ($1.40). 160pp; 6×9; of. Reporting time: 90% in 8 weeks; 10% in 3 months. Simultaneous submissions accepted: yes. Payment: 2 contributor copies. Copyrighted, reverts to author. Ads: $200/$100. CLMP.

The Cresset Press, Inc., John M. Schofield, PO Box 2578, Sarasota, FL 34230, 813-371-8544. 1992. Satire, criticism, non-fiction. avg. press run 1M-2M. Pub'd 1 title 1998; expects 1 title 1999. 3 titles listed in the *Small Press Record of Books in Print* (28th Edition, 1999-00). avg. price, paper: $9.95. Discounts: 40% (30% to bookstore on 3 or less copies); 55% wholesalers. 160pp; 5½×8½; of. Reporting time: 6 weeks. Payment: 10%. Copyrights for author.

CRICKET, Marianne Carus, Editor-in-Chief; Deborah Vetter, Editor, PO Box 300, Peru, IL 61354, 815-224-6656. 1973. Poetry, fiction, articles, art, photos, interviews, music, plays, non-fiction. "Word limit for fiction: 2000 words; for non-fiction: 1500 words. SASE is required for response." circ. 71M. 12/yr. Pub'd 12 issues 1998; expects 12 issues 1999, 12 issues 2000. sub. price: $35.97; per copy: $5; sample: $5. Back issues: $5. 64pp; 8×10; of. Reporting time: approximately 3 months. Please indicate that it's a simultaneous submission. Publishes 1% of manuscripts submitted. Payment: stories and articles up to 25¢ per word (2000 max), poems up to $3 per line. Copyrighted, reverts to author. Pub's reviews: 60 one-paragraph reviews in 1998. §Any good children's or young adult books: fiction or non-fiction. Magazine Publishers Assn.

●**Crime and Again Press**, Bill Gluck, 245 Eighth Avenue, Ste. 283, New York, NY 10011, 212-727-0151; crimepress@aol.com. 1998. Fiction. "40,000 to 75,000 words. Mystery only, will consider true crime." avg. press run 3M-5M. Expects 3 titles 1999, 3-5 titles 2000. 1 title listed in the *Small Press Record of Books in Print* (28th Edition, 1999-00). avg. price, paper: $13.95. Discounts: 20%-55%. 240pp; 5½×8½. Reporting time: 4-6 months. Simultaneous submissions accepted: no. Payment: negotiable. Copyrights for author. PMA.

CRIMINAL JUSTICE ABSTRACTS, Criminal Justice Press, Willow Tree Press, Inc., Richard S. Allinson, PO Box 249, Monsey, NY 10952, 914-354-9139. 1968. circ. 1M. 4/yr. Pub'd 4 issues 1998; expects 4 issues 1999, 4 issues 2000. sub. price: $185; per copy: $46.25. 180pp; 6×9. Reporting time: 2 months. Simultaneous submissions accepted: no. Payment: none. Copyrighted, reverts to author. Ads: $350 full page. SSP.

Criminal Justice Press (see also CRIMINAL JUSTICE ABSTRACTS), Richard S. Allinson, PO Box 249, Monsey, NY 10952, 914-362-8376 fax. 1983. Pub'd 4 titles 1998. 10 titles listed in the *Small Press Record of Books in Print* (28th Edition, 1999-00). avg. price, cloth: $47.50; paper: $30. 6×9.

CRIPES!, James Tolan, Aimee Record, 110 Bemont Avenue, Staten Island, NY 10310, 718-273-9447. 1994. Poetry, fiction, art, photos, cartoons, interviews, reviews, parts-of-novels, collages, plays, non-fiction. "We want stuff with passion, 'duende', divine frenzy—stuff that chills you or blows the top of your head off. But we also want it to be real and well-made—no uncrafted impulses played for shock. All checks should be made out to James Tolan" circ. 300. 1-2/yr. Pub'd 2 issues 1998; expects 1 issue 1999, 2 issues 2000. sub. price: $13/3 issues; per copy: $5; sample: $5. 48-60pp; 5½×8½; of. Reporting time: 2 weeks to 2 months. Simultaneous submissions accepted: yes. Publishes 2% of manuscripts submitted. Payment: copies. Not copyrighted. Pub's reviews: 0 in 1998. §Poetry, fiction, zines, art, culture.

CRITICAL REVIEW, Jeffrey M. Friedman, PO Box 10, Newtown, CT 06470-0010, 203-270-8103; fax 203-270-8105; e-mail info@criticalreview.com. 1987. Articles, reviews. "Uniquely, *Critical Review* offers its contributors the opportunity to explore, develop and criticize neo-liberal political and social theory at length. It welcomes extended scholarly essays and review essays that conform to its style sheet (available on request). Of particular interest are developments and criticisms of ideas informed by classical liberalism, including public choice theory, Austrian-school economics, and spontaneous order analysis. *CR* is the only journal in the world that confronts such ideas in every field with the most sophisticated scholarship drawn from other intellectual traditions." circ. 3M. 4/yr. Pub'd 4 issues 1998; expects 4 issues 1999, 4 issues 2000. sub. price: $29, libraries $59; per copy: $7.25; sample: $7.25. Back issues: $10-$20, indiv/$15-$30 libraries. 160pp; 5½×8½; of. Reporting time: 2 months. Payment: none. Copyrighted, rights revert to author if arranged. Pub's reviews: 14 in 1998. §Economics, anthropology, jurisprudence, political science, history, philosophy, sociology. Ads: $75 full page.

CRONE CHRONICLES: A Journal of Conscious Aging, Ann Kreilkamp, PO Box 81, Kelly, WY 83011, 307-733-5409. 1989. Poetry, articles, art, photos, cartoons, interviews, reviews, letters, collages, news items, non-fiction. circ. 6M. 4/yr. Pub'd 4 issues 1998; expects 4 issues 1999, 4 issues 2000. sub. price: $21; per copy: $6.95; sample: $6.50. Back issues: $6 per issue, order 3 issues get 1 free. Discounts: On contract, case by case. 80pp; 8½×11; cold web. Reporting time: varies. Simultaneous submissions not desirable. Publishes 30% of manuscripts submitted. Payment: none at this time. Copyrighted, reverts to author. Pub's reviews: 20-30 in 1998. §Aging, metaphysics, consciousness, community, spirituality. Ads: $300/$150/$1 word classified.

CROSS CURRENTS, Kenneth Arnold, Editor; Joseph Cunneen, Founding Editor; Shelley Schiff, Managing Editor, College of New Rochelle, New Rochelle, NY 10805-2339, 914-235-1439; fax: 914-235-1584; aril@ecunet.org. 1950. Poetry, articles, reviews, letters, non-fiction, interviews. "Relation of religion and ethics to contemporary intellectual, political, cultural, philosophical questions. Published by the Association for Religion and Intellectual Life." circ. 4.5M. 4/yr. Pub'd 4 issues 1998; expects 4 issues 1999, 4 issues 2000. 1 title listed in the *Small Press Record of Books in Print* (28th Edition, 1999-00). sub. price: $40, libraries $50, outside US $5 additional postage; per copy: $7.50; sample: $7.50. Back issues: $7.50. 144pp; 6×9; computer. Reporting time: 1 month. Payment: none. Copyrighted, reverts to author. Pub's reviews: 52 in 1998. §Theology, philosophy, world politics, literature, and arts. Ads: $400/$250/$150 1/4 pg.

CROSS ROADS, Damita Brown, Linda Burnham, Max Elbaum, Arnoldo Garcia, Mike Greer, Steven Hiatt,

Elizabeth Martinez, Nancy Stein, Irwin Silber, Ethan Young, PO Box 2809, Oakland, CA 94609, 510-843-7495. 1990. Poetry, articles, art, photos, cartoons, interviews, satire, criticism, reviews, letters, news items. "Articles range from 500-3.5M words, most issues have theme packages of 1/2 - 2/3 of each issue. Recent contributors include: Clarence Lusane, Kim Moody, Frances M. Beal, Harry Hay, Tahan Jones, Mirium Chiney Louie, Jeremy Cronin, Dave Dyson, Diane Green" circ. 2.5M. 10/yr. Pub'd 10 issues 1998; expects 10 issues 1999, 10 issues 2000. sub. price: $26; per copy: $4; sample: $1.50. Back issues: $2 for 5 or more. Discounts: 55% discount, 50 or more, 40% dicount bookstores, 50% classroom discount. 32pp; 8½×11; of. Reporting time: 1 month. Payment: none. Not copyrighted. Pub's reviews: 10 in 1998. §Politics. Ads: $300/$185-150/$70-100 1/4 page, $125 1/3 page.

THE CROSS STITCHER, Clapper Publishing Co., Julie Stephani, 2400 Devon, Suite 375, Des Plaines, IL 60018, 847-635-5800. 1951. circ. 300M. 10/yr. Pub'd 10 issues 1998; expects 10 issues 1999, 10 issues 2000. price per copy: $3.95-$4.95. 106pp; 8½×11. Reporting time: 3 months. Simultaneous submissions accepted: yes. Payment: yes. Copyrighted, does not revert to author. Pub's reviews. §Craft books. MPA.

CROSSCURRENTS, Bob Fink, 516 Ave K South, Saskatoon, Saskatchewan, Canada, fax: 306-244-0795; e-mail: green@webster.sk.ca; http://www.webster.sk.ca/greenwich/xc.htm. 1975. Art, criticism, music. "*Crosscurrents* was a left-wing quarterly newsletter emphasizing environment, history and the arts. There will still be commentary issues but the focus will now be on publishing original music in classical styles, like Bach, Mozart, etc., and it will publish computer-composed music, and deal with other musicology issues." circ. 500-5M depending upon the subject and reprints. 4+. Pub'd 4 issues 1998; expects 4 issues 1999, 4 issues 2000. sub. price: $10 quarterly; per copy: $1.50 ppd; sample: $1 + $.50 postage ($1.50 postpaid). Back issues: $5 for 10 from 1975 to present + $1 postage. Discounts: none. 4-8pp; 7×8½, 8½×11, varies; †varies. Reporting time: forever. Payment: zip. Copyrighted, reverts to author. Pub's reviews: 1 in 1998. §Arts and musicology.

‡CROSSCURRENTS, A QUARTERLY, Linda Brown Michelson, Editor-in-Chief, 2200 Glastonbury Road, Westlake Village, CA 91361, 818-991-1694. 1980. Fiction, art, photos. "Fiction to 6M words: no heavy erotica, science fiction or western. Xerox O.K., but no simultaneous submission. We no longer review unsolicited manuscripts. Recent contributors: Alice Adams, Joyce Carol Oates, John Updike, Josephine Jacobsen, Margaret Atwood, Saul Bellow. Please note: Re poetry, *Crosscurrents* no longer regularly uses poetry. We will, however, feature special issues devoted to in-depth looks at poetry, from time to time. I do want to stem the voluminous flow of poetry submissions, as I hate to waste submittor's postage when there is little to no chance of acceptance." circ. 3M. Irregular. Pub'd 2 issues 1998; expects 2 issues 2000. 1 title listed in the *Small Press Record of Books in Print* (28th Edition, 1999-00). price per copy: $6; sample: $6. Back issues: $6. Discounts: wholesale and retail. 176pp; 6×9; of. Reporting time: 6 weeks. Payment: 1 contributors copy, fiction $35, graphics $10-$25. Copyrighted, reverts to author. Ads: $70/$35. CLMP, PMA, AWP, PSA.

Crossgar Press, Joseph E. Murphy, 2116 W. Lake Isles Parkway, Minneapolis, MN 55405, 612-867-5837. "No unsolicited manuscripts." avg. press run 500. Pub'd 2 titles 1998; expects 4 titles 1999. 7 titles listed in the *Small Press Record of Books in Print* (28th Edition, 1999-00). Discounts: 40%.

The Crossing Press, Brigid Fuller, Rights Manager; Linda Gunnarson, Editor; Elaine Gill, Publisher; Jane Somers, Marketing Director; Karen Narita, Publicity, PO Box 1048, Freedom, CA 95019-1048, 408-722-0711 e-mail crossing@aol.com. 1966. Non-fiction. avg. press run 5M-10M. Pub'd 36 titles 1998; expects 24-30 titles 1999, 30-36 titles 2000. 16 titles listed in the *Small Press Record of Books in Print* (28th Edition, 1999-00). avg. price, cloth: $18.95; paper: $14.95. Discounts: 1-4 books, 25%, 5-24 40%, 25-49 42% and free freight, wholesale-jobbers negotiable. 64-300pp; 8½×5½, 6×9, 8¼×9; of. Reporting time: 4-6 weeks. Payment: royalties. Copyrights for author.

Crossroads Communications, D. Ray Wilson, Editor, PO Box 7, Carpentersville, IL 60110. 1980. Non-fiction. "Interested in American history 50M-100M words in length. Must be well researched. Some biographies. Recent contributors: Ira Morton, (Red Grange biography), A. Richard Crabb (Everett Mitchell memoirs)" avg. press run 3M. Pub'd 3 titles 1998; expects 3 titles 1999, 3 titles 2000. 22 titles listed in the *Small Press Record of Books in Print* (28th Edition, 1999-00). avg. price, cloth: $19.95; paper: $12.95. Discounts: 40% bulk, to the trade. 320pp; 5½×8½; of. Reporting time: 4 weeks. Payment: each separate, negotiable. Does not copyright for author.

Crossway Books, Marvin Padgett, Vice President Editorial, 1300 Crescent Street, Wheaton, IL 60187, 630-682-4300. 1979. Fiction, non-fiction. "Publish books with an orthodox Christian perspective, including novels, contemporary issues, theology, and the family." avg. press run 7M. Pub'd 60 titles 1998; expects 65 titles 1999, 60 titles 2000. avg. price, cloth: $19.99; paper: $12.99. Discounts: trade, jobber. 192pp; 5½×8½; of. Reporting time: 6 months. Simultaneous submissions accepted: yes. Publishes 2-3% of manuscripts submitted. Payment: based on net receipts. Copyrights for author. CBA, ECPA.

CRUCIBLE, Terrence L. Grimes, English Department, Barton College, Wilson, NC 27893, 919-399-6456. 1964. Poetry, fiction. "Short stories should not exceed 8,000 words." circ. 300. 1/yr. Pub'd 1 issue 1998;

expects 1 issue 1999, 1 issue 2000. sub. price: $6; per copy: $6; sample: $6. Back issues: $6. Discounts: none. 70pp; 6×9; of. Reporting time: 2-4 months. Simultaneous submissions accepted: no. Publishes 10% of manuscripts submitted. Payment: none. Copyrighted, reverts to author.

●**Crystal Clarity, Publishers**, Sean Meshorer, 14618 Tyler Foote Road, Nevada City, CA 95959, 1-800-424-1055; 530-478-7600; fax 530-478-7610. 1969. 50 titles listed in the *Small Press Record of Books in Print* (28th Edition, 1999-00).

Crystal Publishers, Inc., Frank Leanza, 4947 Orinda Court, Las Vegas, NV 89120, 702-434-3037 phone/Fax. 1985. Music. avg. press run 5M. Pub'd 2 titles 1998; expects 2 titles 1999, 5 titles 2000. 20 titles listed in the *Small Press Record of Books in Print* (28th Edition, 1999-00). avg. price, paper: $19.95. Discounts: 46-55% wholesaler. 224pp; 6×9; of. Reporting time: 6-8 weeks. Payment: semi-annual. Copyrights for author.

Cucumber Island Storytellers, PO Box 158544, Nashville, TN 37215-8544, 800-730-3030. 1995. Poetry, art, music, long-poems, plays. avg. press run 5M. Expects 8 titles 1999, 6 titles 2000. 7 titles listed in the *Small Press Record of Books in Print* (28th Edition, 1999-00). avg. price, cloth: $15.95. Discounts: Bookstores 40%, general wholesalers/distributors 55%. 32pp; 8½×11; of. Reporting time: 1 month. Publishes 5% of manuscripts submitted. Payment: advance against royalty. Copyrights for author. MABA.

Culinary Arts Ltd., Cheryl Long, PO Box 2157, Lake Oswego, OR 97035, 503-639-4549; FAX 503-620-4933. 1979. "Published magazine prior to 1983. Changed to books in that year. Special culinary areas are our forte; unusual subjects, hard-to-find, or new concepts, specialty in microwave area, and gourmet food hobbies." avg. press run 3M. Pub'd 2 titles 1998; expects 3 titles 1999, 3-4 titles 2000. 8 titles listed in the *Small Press Record of Books in Print* (28th Edition, 1999-00). avg. price, paper: $7. Discounts: 40% trade with 6 book minimum, titles can be mixed, etc. 96pp; 5½×8½, 6×9; of. Reporting time: approx. 1 month, query first! Simultaneous submissions accepted: no. Payment: quarterly. We do not copyright for author, but will assist. Northwest Assoc. of Book Publishers (NWABP), Publishers Marketing Assn. (PMA).

●**Cultivated Underground Press (see also THE CUP)**, Tony H. Webb, PO Box 7610, Tacoma, WA 98407-0610. 1999. Poetry, fiction, non-fiction. "We work with the author on a true cooperative basis-meaning we share the risk as well as the profit. Especially interested in manuscripts concerning: self-help/self-improvement, regional guidebooks, how-to/instructional, and general nonfiction. Query with sample. In English, SASE." avg. press run 100. Expects 12 titles 2000. avg. price, cloth: $10-20; paper: $7-12. Discounts: negotiable. 50-400pp; 6×9; professionally printed. Reporting time: ASAP. Simultaneous submissions accepted: no. Payment: negotiable-competitive. Copyrights for author.

CULTUREFRONT, Jay Kaplan, Editor; Mel Rosenthal, Photography Editor; Philip Katz, Associate Editor, 150 Broadway, Room #1700, New York, NY 10038-4401, 212-233-1131; fax 212-233-4607; e-mail hum@echonyc.com. 1992. Poetry, fiction, articles, photos, interviews, reviews, letters, non-fiction. "Articles are generally commissioned." circ. 2M. 4/yr. Pub'd 3 issues 1998; expects 4 issues 1999, 4 issues 2000. sub. price: $15; $25 for libraries; per copy: $5; sample: $5. Back issues: $7 per issue. Discounts: contact publisher for discounts. 100pp; 8½×11; web. Reporting time: 3 weeks. Simultaneous submissions accepted: no. Payment: authors donate their articles. Copyrighted, *Culturefront* retains copyright unless other arrangements are made. Pub's reviews: 24 in 1998. §The humanities, the production and interpretation of culture. Ads: $750/$400/$250 1/4 page; back cover $1250/inside cover $1000/1/3 page $325/1-6 page $175.

Cumberland, 7652 Sawmill Road, Suite 194, Dublin, OH 43017. 1976. Poetry, fiction. *"No unsolicited manuscripts."* avg. press run 500. 6 titles listed in the *Small Press Record of Books in Print* (28th Edition, 1999-00). avg. price, paper: $5; other: $5. 104pp; 5×8; of. Reporting time: 2 weeks. Copyrights for author.

CUMBERLAND POETRY REVIEW, Editorial board, Poetics, Inc., PO Box 120128 Acklen Station, Nashville, TN 37212, 615-373-8948. 1981. Poetry, reviews. "Translations, poetry criticism. Recent contributors include Laurence Lerner, Dana Gioia, Seamus Heaney, X.J. Kennedy and Emily Grosholz. *CPR* presents poets of diverse origins to a widespread audience. Our aim is to support the poet's effort to keep up the language" circ. 500. 2/yr. Pub'd 2 issues 1998; expects 2 issues 1999, 2 issues 2000. sub. price: $18 (individuals), $24 (institutions), $28 (overseas); per copy: $10; sample: $10. Back issues: Vol. I, #1 and Vol XII, #1 unavailable; all others $7. Discounts: 30% to bookstores. 75-100pp; 6×9; lp. Reporting time: 3-6 months. Simultaneous submissions accepted: no. Payment: 2 copies. Copyrighted, rights revert to author on request. §Review on a poet's entire work. No ads. CLMP.

Cune Press, Scott C. Davis, PO Box 31024, 911-N 67th Street, Seattle, WA 98103, 206-782-1433. 1994. Art. avg. press run 2M. Expects 1 title 1999, 3 titles 2000. 2 titles listed in the *Small Press Record of Books in Print* (28th Edition, 1999-00). avg. price, cloth: $19.95; paper: $14.95. Discounts: trade 40%. 256pp; 6×8¼; of. Reporting time: 3 months. Publishes 2% of manuscripts submitted. Payment: 5% royalty on cover price. Copyrights for author.

●**THE CUP, Cultivated Underground Press**, Tony H. Webb, PO Box 7610, Tacoma, WA 98407-0610. 1999.

Poetry, fiction, reviews, letters. *"The Cup* is a members only publication. Prefer popular forms and subject matter, under 40 lines. Short-short fiction. No vulgarity. SASE. Invest heart and soul into several drafts before submitting. We wish not to reject a piece, instead offering suggestion when requesting revision. The Cup offers poets the opportunity to share their literary voice with the world." circ. 1M. 2/yr. Expects 2 issues 2000. sub. price: $10; per copy: $5; sample: $5. Discounts: negotiable. 40pp; 6×9; Professionally printed. Reporting time: ASAP. Simultaneous submissions accepted: no. Publishes 50% of manuscripts submitted. Payment: membership includes biannual copies. Not copyrighted. Pub's reviews. §literary publication reviews for members. Ads: $100/$50/$10 business card.

CURARE, Venom Press, Jan Schmidt, J.D. Rage, c/o Whalen, 20 Clinton Street #1G, New York, NY 10002, 212-533-7167. 1993. Poetry, fiction, art, photos. "Length of material: 2pp single-spaced. Biases in favor of women and minority writers. Recent contributors: Susan Sherman, David Huberman, Katherine Arnoldi, Mike Halchin, Will Inman, and Charlene Cambridge." circ. 200. 2/yr. Pub'd 1 issue 1998; expects 4 issues 1999, 4 issues 2000. price per copy: $3..50pp; 8½×11; †laser printer. Reporting time: at least 3 months. Publishes 30% of manuscripts submitted. Payment: 1 copy. Copyrighted, reverts to author. Ads: none.

Curbstone Press, Alexander Taylor, Judy Doyle, 321 Jackson Street, Willimantic, CT 06226, 203-423-5110; fax 203-423-9242; e-Mail TAYLORAL@ECSUC.CTSTATEV.EDU. 1975. "Curbstone Press is a non-profit publishing house dedicated to literature that reflects a commitment to social change, with an emphasis on writing from Latin America and Latino communities in the United States. Curbstone presents writers who give voice to the unheard in language that goes beyond denunciation to celebrate, honor and teach. Curbstone builds bridges between writers directly engaged in social struggle and the reading public, ranging from colleges to community centers, children to adults, a public increasingly eager to be educated about the cultures these writers represent. Curbstone seeks out the highest aesthetic expression of the dedication to human rights: poetry, stories, novels, testimonials, photography. Curbstone Press combines editorial integrity with painstaking craft in the creation of books, books of passion and purpose." avg. press run 3M. Pub'd 4 titles 1998; expects 9 titles 1999, 6 titles 2000. 83 titles listed in the *Small Press Record of Books in Print* (28th Edition, 1999-00). avg. price, cloth: $19.95; paper: $11; other: $25-$50 signed, limited. Discounts: all trade orders are handled by Consortium Book Sales & Distribution. Poetry 96pp, prose 200pp; 6×9, 5½×8½; of. Reporting time: not accepting unsolicited ms. at present. Publishes 1% of manuscripts submitted. Payment: we pay a royalty of 10-12% of net sales. Copyrights for author, the author retains all rights. CLMP.

‡**CURMUDGEON,** Erik McKelvey, 3420 Earlwood Drive, Columbia, SC 29201-1422, 803-736-1449. 1992. Poetry, fiction, articles, art, photos, cartoons, satire, parts-of-novels, long-poems, collages. "The length can really vary - the only bias that I have, is that the stuff submitted should be real and heartfelt. I really like to hear people's stories. I want sweat and blood on the submissions. Curmudgeon #1 was a huge success. #2 and all others will have a color cover. Poets Keith Higginbother, Walter Kuchinsky, Michael Estubrook, John M. Bennett, Edmond Conti, Lori Ann Larkin, Chris A. Stafford, Ericka Meinter, elliot, etc" circ. 1-100. 2/yr. Pub'd 2 issues 1998; expects 2 issues 1999, 2 issues 2000. sub. price: $6; per copy: $3; sample: $3. Back issues: $3. Discounts: hey if you want some - sell at cost plus postage. 40-60pp; 8×11½; mi. Reporting time: 2-3 weeks. Publishes 25% of manuscripts submitted. Payment: hey, I'm broke - my eternal gratitude, copy. Copyrighted, reverts to author. Pub's reviews. §Small press chapbooks. Ads: $5/$2.50.

CURRENT ACCOUNTS, Rod Riesco, 16 Mill Lane, Horwich, Bolton BL6 6AT, England, 01204 669858 tel/fax; e-mail 100417.37226@compuserve.com. 1994. Poetry, fiction, articles, non-fiction. "Most contributors are members of our writers group 'Bank Street Writers.' Guest contributions and unsolicited. Contributions also used. Enclose S.A.E with all submissions." circ. 25-30. 2/yr. Pub'd 2 issues 1998; expects 2 issues 1999, 2 issues 2000. sub. price: £3; per copy: £1.50; sample: £1.50. 10pp; size A4; †xerox. Simultaneous submissions accepted: yes. Publishes 10-20% of manuscripts submitted. Payment: none. Not copyrighted. Pub's reviews: 1 in 1998. §Creative writing.

CURRENTS, Greg Moore, National Organization for Rivers, 212 W. Cheyenne Mountain Blvd., Colorado Springs, CO 80906, 719-579-5759. 1979. Articles, photos, cartoons, reviews, letters, news items, non-fiction. "Subscription includes membership in NORS. We have a writer's guideline sheet, which includes info for photogrpahers too" circ. 5M. 4/yr. Pub'd 3 issues 1998; expects 4 issues 1999, 4 issues 2000. sub. price: $20; per copy: $1; sample: $1. Back issues: $1 plus 9X12 SASE (75¢ p/h). 24pp; 8×10½; of. Reporting time: 10-30 days. Simultaneous submissions must be indicated. Publishes 30% of manuscripts submitted. Payment: $10-$90, $20-$150. Copyrighted, reverts to author. Pub's reviews: 10 in 1998. §Whitewater river running, kayaking, canoeing, rafting. Ads: $329/$257/$15 - 3 lines.

Curtis/Strongmen Publishing, David Lolic, Richard Perry, Antonio M. Monaco, 70 Barker Street #603, Mount Kisco, NY 10549-1703. 1996. Fiction, interviews, non-fiction. "Publishing the best in quality masculine gay fiction and non-fiction." avg. press run 5M-10M anticipated. Expects 11 titles 2000. avg. price, paper: $11.95. Discounts: none. 6×9. Reporting time: 4 weeks. Payment: negotiable. Copyrights for author. PMA.

Custom Services, Pam Brown, PO Box 3311, Montrose, CO 81402. avg. press run 500. Expects 1 title 1999, 2 titles 2000. 1 title listed in the *Small Press Record of Books in Print* (28th Edition, 1999-00). avg. price, paper: $16.95. Discounts: 40% dealer discount. 300pp; 5½×8½. Reporting time: 1-2 months. Simultaneous submissions accepted: yes. NABE.

CUTBANK, English Dept., University of Montana, Missoula, MT 59812. 1973. Poetry, fiction, articles, art, photos, interviews, criticism, reviews, long-poems. "All correspondence should be addressed to 'editor(s)-in-chief'. All submissions should be addressed to either the 'poetry editor' or the 'fiction editor. Recent contributors include James Tate, Mary Blew, Dara Wier, Jim Harrison, Norman Dubie, James Welch." circ. 600. 2/yr. Pub'd 2 issues 1998; expects 2 issues 1999, 2 issues 2000. sub. price: $12; per copy: $6.95; sample: $4. Back issues: write for current information. Discounts: trade rates for bulk orders. 120+pp; 5½×8½; of, perfect bound. Reporting time: 8-12 weeks. We prefer not to receive simultaneous submissions. Payment: 2 issues. Copyrighted, rights revert to author with provision that *CutBank* is credited. Pub's reviews: none in 1998. §Poetry, fiction, creative non-fiction. Ads: $90/$45. CLMP.

CYBERCOPYWRITER, Brian S. Konradt, Editor-in-Chief, PO Box 554, Oradell, NJ 07649, 201-262-3277; Fax 201-599-2635; bskcom@tiac.net; www.tiac.net/users/bskcom. 1998. "*CyberCopywriter* helps writers write commercial copy for the 'Wired World' and other interactive media such as CD-ROMS, Web sites, software, compact disks, audio tapes, MARCOM and technical materials. Writer's guidelines for #10 SASE or free at web site." 6/yr. Expects 6 issues 1999, 6 issues 2000. sub. price: $72; per copy: $12; sample: $12. 8½×11. Reporting time: 2 weeks on queries, 1 month on mss. Payment: pays on acceptance for columnists, pays on publication for contributors.

Cyclone Books, Melany Shapiro, Jonathan Shapiro, 420 Pablo Lane, Nipomo, CA 93444, 805-929-4430 phone/Fax; cyclone@utech.net. 1997. Non-fiction. "Query and SASE. Sample chapter or outline would be helpful also. Especially interested in 'self-help' topics i.e. marriage, money, fatherhood, etc." avg. press run 5M. Expects 1 title 1999, 3-4 titles 2000. 1 title listed in the *Small Press Record of Books in Print* (28th Edition, 1999-00). avg. price, paper: $20. Discounts: 10-100 copies 30%, 101-499 40%, 500-999 50%, 1000+ 60%. 192pp; 8½×11; of. Reporting time: 3 weeks. Simultaneous submissions accepted: yes. Payment: advance against royalties. Copyrights for author. PMA.

Cygnet Trumpeter, 11661 San Vicente Blvd., Ste. 615, Los Angeles, CA 90049, 310-442-0102/Fax 310-442-9011. 1 title listed in the *Small Press Record of Books in Print* (28th Edition, 1999-00).

Cynic Press (see also AXE FACTORY REVIEW), Joseph Farley, PO Box 40691, Philadelphia, PA 19107. 1996. Poetry, fiction, articles, art, photos, cartoons, interviews, satire, criticism, reviews, music, letters, parts-of-novels, long-poems, collages, plays, concrete art, news items. "At this point, books are by invitation or by contest only." avg. press run varies. Expects 1 title 2000. 4 titles listed in the *Small Press Record of Books in Print* (28th Edition, 1999-00). avg. price, paper: varies. Pages vary; size varies; of. Reporting time: immediate. Simultaneous submissions accepted: yes. Payment: copies. Copyrights for author.

Cypress House, John Fremont, Senior Editor, 155 Cypress Street, Fort Bragg, CA 95437, 707-964-9520, Fax 707-964-7531; E-mail publishing@cypresshouse.com. 1986. Fiction, art, non-fiction. "Cypress House titles focus on biography, autobiography, self-help and how-to books. Our current list also includes quality fiction and poetry titles." avg. press run 2M. Pub'd 5 titles 1998; expects 5 titles 1999, 5 titles 2000. 16 titles listed in the *Small Press Record of Books in Print* (28th Edition, 1999-00). avg. price, cloth: $19.95; paper: $14.95; other: $22.95. Discounts: 1-2 books 0%, 3-5 33%, 6+ 40%. 224pp; 5½×8½; of. Reporting time: 3 months. Simultaneous submissions accepted: yes. Copyrights for author. Marin Self-Publishers Assoc., Northern California Book Publicists Assoc., Pacific Northwest Booksellers Assoc., American Booksellers Assoc., PMA.

Cypress Publishing Group, Inc., Carl Heintz, 11835 Roe #187, Leawood, KS 66211, 913-681-9875. 1976. Fiction, non-fiction. "Looking for how to business and economics texts, especially good computer, marketing, finance and entrepreneur texts" avg. press run 2.5M. Pub'd 2 titles 1998; expects 3 titles 1999, 8 titles 2000. 3 titles listed in the *Small Press Record of Books in Print* (28th Edition, 1999-00). avg. price, paper: $28. 200pp; 6×9; of. Reporting time: 1 week Payment: negotiable percentages. Copyrights for author. PMA, MPA.

D

D.B.A. Books, Mark Hetherington, D.M. Bellavance, 291 Beacon Street #8, Boston, MA 02116, 617-262-0411. 1980. Non-fiction. avg. press run 5M. Pub'd 3 titles 1998; expects 4 titles 1999, 4 titles 2000. 3 titles listed in the *Small Press Record of Books in Print* (28th Edition, 1999-00). avg. price, paper: $15.95. Discounts: 2-5

10%, 6-9 15%, 10+ 20%, also 10% for prepayment. 100pp; 6×8½; of. Reporting time: 2 weeks. Simultaneous submissions accepted: no. Payment: by contract. Does not copyright for author.

D.D.B. Press, k. Margaret Grossman, Editor, 401 N.E. Ravenna Blvd., Ste. 152, Seattle, WA 98115, 904-224-0478. 1972. Poetry, fiction, articles, satire, criticism, long-poems, plays. "We are not accepting manuscripts for publication at the present time. Because of funding problems, we are limited to local work and *The Apalachee Quarterly.*" avg. press run varies. Pub'd 2 titles 1998. avg. price, paper: $2.50. 100pp; 6×8; of. Payment: to be discussed. Copyrights for author. CCLM.

Daedal Press, Dorothy Keesecker, Ernest Walters, 2315 Belair Road, Fallston, MD 21047. 1968. Fiction, art. "High literary merit fiction. Works about art and artists a plus. Must be suitable (sellable) to a strong targeting audience with direct mail. No present use of distributors or bookstores except with advance purchases or author's locale. Highly selected original artist made printmaking (lithos, etchings, acquatint, reduction relief)." avg. press run 2M. Pub'd 1 title 1998; expects 3-5 titles 1999, 3-5 titles 2000. 4 titles listed in the *Small Press Record of Books in Print* (28th Edition, 1999-00). avg. price, cloth: $24; paper: $16. Discounts: 10-50% by number bought, returns acceptable if perfect. 265pp; 6×9. Reporting time: 1 month or less, query and 1-page synopsis. Simultaneous submissions accepted: yes. Payment: 10-20% on net sale. Copyrights for author.

DAEDALUS, Journal of the American Academy of Arts and Sciences, Stephen R. Graubard, Editor, American Academy of Arts and Sciences, 136 Irving Street, Cambridge, MA 02138, 617-491-2600; fax 617-576-5088; e-mail daedalus@amacad.org. 1958. Articles. "No unsolicited mss." circ. 20M. 4/yr. Pub'd 4 issues 1998; expects 4 issues 1999, 4 issues 2000. sub. price: individual—$33, $55/2 yrs, $82.50/3 yrs; institution—$49.50, $82.50/2 yrs, $110/3 yrs; Canada - individual $42/1 yr; institution $60/1yr; per copy: $7.95 + p/h; sample: same. Back issues: $7.95 + p/h. 256pp; 6×9; of. Copyrighted, does not revert to author. No ads.

Daedalus Publishing Company, 584 Castro Street, Suite 518, San Francisco, CA 94114, office 415-626-1867; fax 415-487-1137; e-Mail DPCBooks@aol.com. 1992. "Do not accept manuscripts, send letter first." avg. press run 3M-5M. Pub'd 1 title 1998; expects 4 titles 1999, 4 titles 2000. 8 titles listed in the *Small Press Record of Books in Print* (28th Edition, 1999-00). avg. price, paper: $13.95. Discounts: 1 no discount; 2-25 40%; 26-250 50%; 250+ 55%; stop 40% + $2.00. 200pp; 5½×8½. Payment: 10% quarterly. Copyrights for author. PMA.

DAILY WORD, Unity Books, Colleen Zuck, Unity Village, MO 64065, 816-524-3550, fax 816-251-3553. 1924. Poetry, articles, photos, non-fiction. "Types of materials presented spiritual, Christian, motiviational. Daily affirmations and lessons" circ. 1.5K. 12/yr. Pub'd 12 issues 1998; expects 12 issues 1999, 12 issues 2000. sub. price: $6.95; per copy: $1; sample: free. 48pp; 4⅛×5½; web. Reporting time: 6 weeks. Simultaneous submissions accepted: no. Payment: upon acceptance. Copyrighted, reverts to author. Ads: none.

Dakota Books, PO Box 1551, Santa Cruz, CA 95061, 408-464-9636. 1992. Poetry. "On recovery." avg. press run 2M. Expects 1 title 1999, 2 titles 2000. 2 titles listed in the *Small Press Record of Books in Print* (28th Edition, 1999-00). avg. price, cloth: $7.95. Discounts: 40%. 64pp; 6×9; typeset. Reporting time: 1 month. Payment: 10% royalties, paid monthly. Copyrights for author. Assoc. of Amer. Publ., Independent Publishers Guild.

THE DALHOUSIE REVIEW, Ronald Huebert, Editor, Dalhousie University, Halifax, Nova Scotia B3H 3J5, Canada, 902-494-2541; fax 902-494-3561; email dalhousie.review@dal.ca. 1921. Poetry, fiction, articles, criticism, reviews. "Authors change with each issue." circ. 750. 4/yr. Pub'd 3 issues 1998; expects 4 issues 1999, 4 issues 2000. sub. price: institutional: $32.10 within Canada, outside $40 includes GST; individual: $22.50 within Canada, $28 outside; per copy: $10 + mailing, handling (double issue $12); sample: $10 + mailing and handling ($12 double issue). Back issues: vary from $10 to $25. Discounts: none. 144pp; 9×6; desktop. Reporting time: 1-3 months. Simultaneous submissions accepted: yes. Publishes 10% of manuscripts submitted. Payment: 2 complimentary copies of issue and 10 offprints. Copyrighted, rights are held by both publisher and author. Pub's reviews: 30-40 in 1998. §All areas would be examined. Ads: $300/$150. Canadian Association of Learned Journals.

Dalkey Archive Press (see also THE REVIEW OF CONTEMPORARY FICTION), John O'Brien, 4241 Illinois State University, Normal, IL 61790-4241, 309-438-7555. 1984. Fiction. "No unsolicited manuscripts." avg. press run 6M. Pub'd 23 titles 1998; expects 28 titles 1999, 25 titles 2000. avg. price, cloth: $20; paper: $13. Discounts: 47% to bookstores with a minimum of 5 units. 180pp; 5×8, 6×9; of. Reporting time: 1 month. Payment: 10%. Copyrights for author. CLMP, IBPA (Illinois Book Publishers Association).

Dalrymple Publishing Company, Ron Dalrymple, P.O. Box 170133, Boise, ID 83717-0133, 208-333-0488. 1976. Fiction, satire. "Not presently accepting unsolicited manuscripts." avg. press run 5M. Pub'd 1 title 1998; expects 2 titles 1999, 2 titles 2000. 3 titles listed in the *Small Press Record of Books in Print* (28th Edition, 1999-00). avg. price, paper: $10. Discounts: standard industry. 100-200pp; 5×8; of. Copyrights for author. ABA, PMA.

147

Dan River Press (see also NORTHWOODS JOURNAL, A Magazine for Writers), Richard S. Danbury III, Editor, PO Box 298, Thomaston, ME 04861-0298, 207-354-0998; Fax 207-354-8953; cal@americanletters.org; www.americanletters.org. 1978. "Request 15 point program, SASE-2 stamps. Anything except porn. No reading fee." avg. press run 2M. Pub'd 2 titles 1998; expects 4 titles 1999, 4 titles 2000. 21 titles listed in the *Small Press Record of Books in Print* (28th Edition, 1999-00). avg. price, cloth: $32.50; paper: $13.95; other: $100 collector's. Discounts: no. of paperback books ordered X2%. Maximum 50% for 25 or more copies. No discount on hardcovers, or collectors or single copy. 145-180pp; 5½×8½; †of. Reporting time: 1-4 weeks. Simultaneous submissions accepted: no. Publishes anthology 40%, books 5% of manuscripts submitted. Payment: minimum advance $250, payable on contracting; minimum royalty 10% from first sale. Copyrights for author.

THE DANDELION, Michael E. Coughlin, Publisher, Michael E. Coughlin, Cornucopia, WI 54827. 1977. Articles, cartoons, satire, criticism, reviews, letters. "*The Dandelion* is an occasional journal of philosophical anarchism which welcomes a wide variety of articles, cartoons, reviews, satire, criticism and news items. Prefers shorter articles, but will consider major pieces if appropriate. A sample copy is available at no cost to prospective authors" circ. about 400. 0/yr. Pub'd 1 issue 1998; expects 2 issues 1999, 1 issue 2000. sub. price: $6/4 issues; per copy: $1.50; sample: 50¢. Back issues: $1.50. Discounts: 25% off listed price for bulk orders. 28pp; 4½×6¾; †lp. Reporting time: 1 month. Payment: copies of the magazine. Not copyrighted. Pub's reviews: 0 in 1998. §Anarchist/libertarian history, biographies, philosophy. Ads: none.

DANDELION ARTS MAGAZINE, Joaquina Gonzalez-Marina, Casa Alba, 24 Frosty Hollow, E. Hunsbury, Northants NN4 0SY, England, 01604-701730. 1978. Poetry, articles, art, photos, interviews, criticism, reviews, music, collages. circ. 1M. 2/yr. Pub'd 2 issues 1998; expects 2 issues 1999, 2 issues 2000. sub. price: £8 UK, £18 Europe incl. postage + packing, £24 USA and the rest of the world (money could be sent in dollars but add extra for transaction); per copy: £5 UK, £10 Europe incl. postage + packing, £14 USA and the rest of the world; sample: £5 UK, £10 Europe incl. postage + packing, £14 USA and the rest of the world. Back issues: £5 UK, £10 Europe incl. postage + packing, £14 USA and the rest of the world. 20-30pp; size A4; †lp. Reporting time: by return of post provided an International Reply Coupon is attached. Simultaneous submissions accepted: yes. Publishes 20% of manuscripts submitted. Payment: it is an international non-profit magazine. Copyrighted, reverts to author. Pub's reviews: 12 in 1998. §Nature, history, travel, arts, poetry, music biographies. Ads: £50/£25/£15 1/4 page. JGM, ATAL, SM, FP, REA.

DANGER!, Dan Kelly, Editor-in-Chief, 1573 N. Milwaukee Avenue, #481, Chicago, IL 60622-2029. 1994. Articles, art, cartoons, interviews, reviews, news items, non-fiction. "Letters describing article ideas are preferred to mss." circ. 200+. 4/yr. Expects 4 issues 1999, 4 issues 2000. sub. price: no subs; per copy: $3ppd; sample: same. Back issues: none. 40pp; digest; †mi. Payment: free copy of issue they appear in. Copyrighted, reverts to author. Pub's reviews: 20+ in 1998. §True crime, occult themes, anything having to do with extremes in human behavior. Ads: $30/$15/$8/$5/$1 for 30 word classified ad.

John Daniel and Company, Publishers, John Daniel, Publisher; Susan Daniel, Sales Manager, PO Box 21922, Santa Barbara, CA 93121, 805-962-1780; fax 805-962-8835; email dand@danielpublishing.com. 1980. Poetry, fiction, non-fiction. "We will look at anything, but we specialize in belles lettres, primarily literary memoir. Our current best-selling authors are Nancy Huddleston Packer, Al Capp, John Espey and Charles Champlin, T.A. Roberts, and Artie Shaw." avg. press run 2M. Pub'd 4 titles 1998; expects 4 titles 1999, 4 titles 2000. avg. price, cloth: $22.95; paper: $10.95. Discounts: trade 1-4 20%, 5+ 47%; library 20%; jobber 1-9 20%, 10+ 50%. 176pp; 5½×8½; of. Reporting time: 2 months. Simultaneous submissions accepted: yes. Publishes less than 1% of manuscripts submitted. Payment: no advance, 10% of net receipts. Copyrights for author. Publishers Marketing Assn.

The Daniels Publishing Company, 10443 Shelley Road, Thornville, OH 43076. 1 title listed in the *Small Press Record of Books in Print* (28th Edition, 1999-00).

Danrus Publishers, Albert Scharf, 1233 Siler Road, #A, Santa Fe, NM 87505-3132, 505-474-5858; FAX 505-474-6100. 1 title listed in the *Small Press Record of Books in Print* (28th Edition, 1999-00).

Danzon Press, Myra S. Gann, 14 Hamilton Street, Potsdam, NY 13676, 315-265-3466. 1994.

Dark Regions Press (see also DARK REGIONS: The Years Best Fantastic Fiction; THE GENRE WRITER'S NEWS), Mike Olson, Joe Morey, PO Box 6301, Concord, CA 94524. 1 title listed in the *Small Press Record of Books in Print* (28th Edition, 1999-00).

DARK REGIONS: The Years Best Fantastic Fiction, Dark Regions Press, Joe Morey, PO Box 6301, Concord, CA 94524. 1987. Fiction, articles, art, reviews. circ. 3M. 2-4/yr. Pub'd 1-2 issues 1998; expects 4 issues 1999. sub. price: $14/3 issues; per copy: $4.95; sample: $4 first time sample copy. Back issues: sold out. Discounts: 40% for 5 or more copies. 80-150pp; 11×17; of. Reporting time: 1 month. Simultaneous submissions accepted: no. Payment: 1¢-6¢ per word. Copyrighted, reverts to author. Pub's reviews. §Science fiction, fantasy and horror. Ads: $100/$60/1/4 page $35. The Genre Writer's Association/HWA.

DARK STARR, Marjorie Navarro, Editor; Richard LeJose Navarro, Executive Editor, PO Box 1107, Blythe, CA 92226-1107. "Horror, sci-fi, fantasy, mystery, occult/paranormal. Poetry to 45 lines. Short stories to 8,500 words. Refundable reading fee of $3 per 6 poems, $4 per short story." circ. 200+. Pub'd 1 issue 1998; expects 3 issues 1999, 4 issues 2000. price per copy: $7.

DAUGHTERS OF SARAH, Elizabeth Anderson, 2121 Sheridan Road, Evanston, IL 60201. 1974. Poetry, fiction, articles, art, photos, cartoons, interviews, satire, criticism, reviews, music, letters, news items, non-fiction. "Must be Christian feminist. No more than 2,000 words; mostly nonfiction articles." circ. 5M. 4/yr. Pub'd 4 issues 1998; expects 4 issues 1999, 4 issues 2000. sub. price: $22; per copy: $6.25; sample: $6.25. Back issues: $3.50-$5 plus p/h. Discounts: 20% off 10+ issues. 64pp; 5½×8½; of, sheet fed. Reporting time: 1-2 months. Simultaneous submissions accepted: no. Publishes 10% of manuscripts submitted. Payment: approx. $15 per printed page. Copyrighted, reverts to author. Pub's reviews: 25-35 in 1998. §On Christian feminism. Ads: $250/$125/50¢. ACP (Assoc. Church Press), SMPG (Small Mag Publishing Group).

Dava Books, 513 Bankhead Avenue, Suite 194, Carrollton, GA 30117, 770-214-1764. 1994. 1 title listed in the *Small Press Record of Books in Print* (28th Edition, 1999-00). Discounts: 2-4, 20%; 5-99, 40%; 100-up, 50%. Publishers Marketing Association.

Dawn Publications, 14618 Tyler Foote Road, Nevada City, CA 95959, 530-292-7540; toll free 800-545-7475; fax 530-478-7541; email dawnpub@oro.net. 1979. avg. press run 10M. Pub'd 6 titles 1998; expects 6 titles 1999, 6 titles 2000. 31 titles listed in the *Small Press Record of Books in Print* (28th Edition, 1999-00). avg. price, cloth: $16.95; paper: $7.95. Discounts: 1-9 40%; 10+ 45% returnable; 10+ 50% nonreturnable. 10½×9. Reporting time: 2 month. Simultaneous submissions accepted: yes. Publishes less than 1/10% of manuscripts submitted. Payment: yes. Copyrights for author.

Dawn Sign Press, Joe Dannis, 6130 Nancy Ridge Drive, San Diego, CA 92121-3223. 1983. Fiction, parts-of-novels, plays, non-fiction. "We are a specialty publisher for instructional sign language and educational deaf culture materials for both children and adults." avg. press run 5M-20M. Pub'd 7 titles 1998; expects 4 titles 1999, 4 titles 2000. 23 titles listed in the *Small Press Record of Books in Print* (28th Edition, 1999-00). avg. price, paper: $20; other: games $15.95. Discounts: write for details. 100pp; 10½×8; of. Reporting time: 120 days. Payment: varies. Copyrights for author.

Dawnwood Press, Bette Gahres, 387 Park Avenue South, 5th Floor, New York, NY 10016-8810, 212-532-7160; fax 212-213-2495; 800-367-9692. 1983. Fiction. "Recent contributor: Paul Kuttner. More to come. No unsolicited mss." avg. press run 2.5M. Pub'd 1 title 1998; expects 1 title 1999, 1 title 2000. 5 titles listed in the *Small Press Record of Books in Print* (28th Edition, 1999-00). avg. price, cloth: $14.95. Discounts: 42% - books returnable after six months by trade; 20% - to schools and libraries; 50% - to jobbers - returnable after one year. 250-500pp; 6×9 (average); of. Reporting time: agents' submissions - 6 weeks. Payment: yes - outright, depends on sales appeal of novel. Copyrights for author.

DAYS AND NIGHTS OF A SMALL PRESS PUBLISHER, Full Moon Publications, Sharida Rizzuto, 577 Central Avenue, Box 4, Jefferson, LA 70121-1400, e-mail popculture@popmail.com, publisher@mailex-cite.com; www2.cybercities.com/z/zines/. 1983. Poetry, fiction, articles, art, photos, cartoons, interviews, satire, criticism, reviews, letters, long-poems, news items, non-fiction. circ. 500. 3/yr. Pub'd 3 issues 1998; expects 3 issues 1999, 3 issues 2000. sub. price: $12; per copy: $4; sample: $4. Back issues: $4. Discounts: trade with other like publications. 40-50pp; 8½×11; †of. Reporting time: 2-6 weeks. Simultaneous submissions accepted: yes. Publishes 30-35% of manuscripts submitted. Payment: free copies, fees paid to all contributors negotiable. Copyrighted, reverts to author. Pub's reviews: 30 in 1998. §Zines and books about women's issues, relationships, society's problems, multi-cultural, writing, small press publishing, gothic-vampire, horror, scifi/fantasy, occult/paranormal, mystery. Ads: free. NWC, HWA, MWA, Western Writers of America (WWA), Arizona Author Assn. (AAA), Small Press Genre Assn.

DAYSPRING, John C. Brainerd, 18600 West 58 Avenue, Golden, CO 80403-1070, 303-279-2462. 1983. Poetry, fiction, articles, art, photos, cartoons, interviews, satire, criticism, reviews, music, letters, parts-of-novels, long-poems, collages, plays, concrete art, non-fiction. circ. 980. 12/yr. Pub'd 12 issues 1998; expects 12 issues 1999, 12 issues 2000. sub. price: $50; per copy: $5; sample: $5. Back issues: $5. 40pp; 5½×8½; †photo offset. Reporting time: 30-90 days. Payment: 1/2 net. Copyrighted, does not revert to author. Pub's reviews: 12 in 1998. §Theology, philosophy, history, education. Ads: $35//$5 per inch. Int. Pub. Assn.

dbS Productions, Bob Adams, PO Box 1894, University Station, Charlottesville, VA 22903, 800-745-1581; 804-296-6172; Fax 804-293-5502. 1990. Non-fiction. "Outdoor skill related, first-aid, survival; biology skills; video production." avg. press run 10M. Pub'd 3 titles 1998; expects 4 titles 1999, 5 titles 2000. 4 titles listed in the *Small Press Record of Books in Print* (28th Edition, 1999-00). avg. price, cloth: $29; paper: $19. Discounts: 20% bulk, 40% retail. 60pp; 4×7. Reporting time: 1 month. Payment: 10% biannual. Copyrights for author.

●**DEAD FUN**, Kelli, PO Box 752, Royal Oak, MI 48068-0752. 1998. Poetry, fiction, art, photos, reviews, music, collages, non-fiction. "Please limit short stories to 2000 words, anything above that relates to gothic or horror genre, need pen and ink art contributions badly." 2/yr. Pub'd 2 issues 1998; expects 2 issues 1999, 2 issues 2000. price per copy: $3.75. Discounts: Will trade single copy and give discounts on bulk. 48pp; 5×8; †xerox. Reporting time: 2-4 weeks. Simultaneous submissions accepted: yes. Publishes 50% of manuscripts submitted. Payment: 1 copy. Not copyrighted. Pub's reviews: 6 in 1998. §gothic, horror. Ads: $13/$8/ 1/4 pg $5.

Dead Metaphor Press, Richard Wilmarth, PO Box 2076, Boulder, CO 80306, 303-417-9398. 1985. Poetry, art, criticism, long-poems. "Send for information on yearly contest. Some recent contibutors: Aimee Grunberger, Jack Collom, Donald Guravich, Anselm Hollo, Jane Dalrymple-Hollo, Tree Bernstein, Richard Wilmarth, Tracy Davis, Bill Morgan." avg. press run 100-500. Pub'd 2 titles 1998; expects 2 titles 1999, 2-4 titles 2000. 8 titles listed in the *Small Press Record of Books in Print* (28th Edition, 1999-00). avg. price, paper: $4.95; other: $7.95. 24-60pp; 6×9, 7×9; of. Simultaneous submissions accepted: yes. Payment: varies. Does not copyright for author.

S. Deal & Assoc., Shirley Herd Deal, 5128 Neeper Valley Road, Manitou Springs, CO 80829-3862. 1977. Pub'd 1 title 1998; expects 1 title 1999, 3 titles 2000. 5 titles listed in the *Small Press Record of Books in Print* (28th Edition, 1999-00). avg. price, paper: $15; other: poly vinyl notebook $18. Discounts: 5 books-40%; classroom-20%; wholesaler-55% for 100 or more. 255pp.

DEANOTATIONS, Dean Blehert, Pam Blehert, 11919 Moss Point Lane, Reston, VA 20194, 703-471-7907; fax 703-471-6446; e-mail blehert@aol.com; website www.blehert.com. 1984. Poetry, art, satire, long-poems, articles. "*Deanotations* publishes only work by poets named Dean Blehert." circ. 300. 6/yr. Pub'd 6 issues 1998; expects 6 issues 1999, 6 issues 2000. sub. price: $10, $17.50/2 yrs, $35/3 yrs; per copy: $1.75; sample: free with SASE. Back issues: $1.75 or issues 1-88 ringbound for $112. Discounts: will exchange for other publications; students and retirees, $5/yr (U.S.A. only). 4pp; 8½×11; †of. Copyrighted, reverts to author. PMA.

Dearborn Business Press, D. Winslow, 2878 Bridgeway Drive, Ste. 200, West Lafayette, IN 47906, 765-583-2422. 1984. avg. press run 1.2M. 1 title listed in the *Small Press Record of Books in Print* (28th Edition, 1999-00). avg. price, cloth: $49.95. Discounts: STOP 30%.

December Press, Curt Johnson, Box 302, Highland Park, IL 60035. 1958. "Publishes special issues for December Press, which see: publishes them as books. Can still be subscribed for these at $35/4 issues. Has suspended publication as a magazine of shorter pieces. Chiefly fiction, very little poetry" avg. press run 2M. Pub'd 1 title 1998; expects 2 titles 1999, 1 title 2000. 27 titles listed in the *Small Press Record of Books in Print* (28th Edition, 1999-00). avg. price, paper: $14.95 (trade). Discounts: 20% 1-5; 40% 6+. 176pp; 6×9; of. Reporting time: 12 weeks. Simultaneous submissions accepted: no. Publishes .025% of manuscripts submitted. Payment: 10% net. Copyrights for author. PMA.

DeeMar Communications, Diane Tait, 6325-9 Falls of Neuse Road, #320, Raleigh, NC 27615, 919-870-6423; deemar@aol.com; www.deemarcommunications.com; www.deemar.com. 1995. Poetry, non-fiction. "Interested in material which deals with social issues, particularly minority and special populations viewpoints. Interested in mss. less than 100 pages which have literary merit but not necessarily mass market appeal needed to attract 'big' publishers. Quality most important." avg. press run 100. Pub'd 2 titles 1998; expects 1 title 1999. 4 titles listed in the *Small Press Record of Books in Print* (28th Edition, 1999-00). avg. price, paper: $8. Discounts: libraries 20%, bookstores 55%. 50pp; 5½×8½; varies with project. Reporting time: 2 months (Jan-April of each year only). Simultaneous submissions accepted: no. Publishes 50% of manuscripts submitted. Payment: varies with mss., average 10% net sales and 10 copies. Copyrights for author. PMA.

Deep In Lingo, Inc., James C. Perin, PO Box 6491, Bloomington, IN 47407, 812-339-2072. 1994. 1 title listed in the *Small Press Record of Books in Print* (28th Edition, 1999-00).

Deerbridge Books, Charles Gonyea, PO Box 2266, Pittsfield, MA 01201, 413-499-2255; Fax 413-442-5025; riverd@vgernet.net. 1998. Fiction, non-fiction. "Novel or novella-length fiction in which social and spiritual issues facing new millennium are explored but in which the telling of a story is of primary importance." avg. press run 3M. Expects 1-2 titles 2000. 1 title listed in the *Small Press Record of Books in Print* (28th Edition, 1999-00). avg. price, cloth: $26; paper: $15. 275pp; 6×9; of. Reporting time: 2 months. Simultaneous submissions accepted: no. Payment: to be negotiated. Does not copyright for author. SPAN, PMA.

DeerTrail Books, Jack Campbell, 637 Williams Court, PO Box 171, Gurnee, IL 60031, 312-367-0014. 1988. Non-fiction. "Interested in non-fiction m.s.—books only—of approx. 40-100,000 words. Subjects are open, but no poetry, religious tracts, personal life philosophies, autobiographies, and other subjects of interest only to the writer. We *don't* want to see a ms. first. Write a one-page letter (if you can) describing your subject, your reader, and your thrust and treatment. We are currently interested only in subjects that are aimed to fill the needs of a specific audience. An audience hot on a readily - identified subject. In other words, a book that might sell well to a group through mailorder promotion. We are getting good at reaching narrow - interest audiences'' avg. press run 2M-5M. Pub'd 1 title 1998; expects 3-4 titles 1999, 4-5 titles 2000. 1 title listed in the *Small Press Record of Books in Print* (28th Edition, 1999-00). avg. price, cloth: $17; paper: $12. Discounts: standard trade. 144-250pp; size varies; of. Reporting time: 90 days. Payment: negotiable. Copyrights for author. Heartland Press Association, MidAmerica Publishers Group.

THE DEFENDER - RUSH UTAH'S NEWSLETTER, Eborn Books, Rush Utah, Bret Brooks, PO Box 559, Dept. RU, Roy, UT 84067, 801-393-6699. 1993. Poetry, fiction, articles, art, photos, cartoons, satire, criticism, reviews, letters, news items, non-fiction. "Defends Mormonism against anti-Mormon claims" circ. 5M. 4/yr. Pub'd 4 issues 1998; expects 4 issues 1999, 4 issues 2000. sub. price: $14.95; per copy: $4.95; sample: $4.95. 20pp; 8½×11. Payment: none. Not copyrighted. Pub's reviews: 8 in 1998. §Anti-Mormon. Ads: $100/$75.

Manya DeLeon Booksmith, 940 Royal Street, Suite 201, New Orleans, LA 70116, 504-895-2357. 1993. Poetry, fiction, criticism. "The production and dissemination of high quality works in high quality editions are the main focus of Manya DeLeon Booksmith, New Orleans' newest literary publishing company. Following the publication of *Little Puddles*—scheduled for Spring, 1994—translations of contemporary international literature will be incorporated into the first line of books, a line of poetry and fiction which will marry literary and art worlds in unique and handsome volumes. Based in the heart of Southern literary heritage and culture, Manya DeLeon Booksmith will maintain offices in New Orleans, Louisiana. Manya DeLeon Booksmith is interested in learning of new international works and contemporary translators. Manya DeLeon BrockSmith just released Pen America Center/South's premier edition of its literary review, *Southern Lights*" avg. press run 600-2M. Expects 2 titles 1999, 4 titles 2000. 2 titles listed in the *Small Press Record of Books in Print* (28th Edition, 1999-00). avg. price, cloth: $17; paper: $10. Discounts: std. bookseller discount; individuals 1-4 30%, 5-9 35%, 10-25 40%, 725 50%. 100pp; 8½×6½; varies. Reporting time: 4-6 weeks. Payment: negotiable; expect standard royalty after costs met; authors to receive maximum possible authors' copies of works, no advances on royalties at this time. Copyrights for author. New Orleans Gulf South Booksellers Association, RHINO Contemporary Crafts Collective, Friend of Pen.

Delta-West Publishing, Inc., S.B. Thompson, John van Geldern, President, 2720 Wrondel Way, Reno, NV 89502, 775-828-9398; 888-921-6788 (outside of NV); fax 775-828-9163; info@deltawest.com. 1990. Fiction, satire, non-fiction. "We prefer full-length novels which have unusual story lines and characters and in which there is a strong philosophical message. We also entertain non-fiction book-length writings and political satire. Presently 3 years backlogged." avg. press run 15M. Pub'd 3 titles 1998. 4 titles listed in the *Small Press Record of Books in Print* (28th Edition, 1999-00). avg. price, cloth: $22 or less; paper: $10. Discounts: conventional quantity trade discounts, STOP orders and wholesale distributor discounts. 300pp; 6½×9; of. Reporting time: 60 days. Publishes 1% of manuscripts submitted. Payment: industry standard but we encourage author participation in pub. work for greater royalties. Copyrights for author. ABA, PMA.

Deltiologists of America (see also POSTCARD CLASSICS), Dr. James Lewis Lowe, PO Box 8, Norwood, PA 19074, 610-485-8572. 1960. "We publish books about picture postcards only." avg. press run 1.5M. Expects 3 titles 1999, 3 titles 2000. 7 titles listed in the *Small Press Record of Books in Print* (28th Edition, 1999-00). avg. price, cloth: $15; paper: $10. Discounts: quantity discounts to booksellers. Reporting time: 60 days. Payment: by arrangement. Does not copyright for author.

The Denali Press, Alan Edward Schorr, Editorial Director and Publisher, PO Box 021535, Juneau, AK 99802, 907-586-6014; FAX 907-463-6780; e-mail denalipr@alaska.net. 1986. Non-fiction. "Firm publishes only reference and scholarly publications oriented toward library (academic and public) market, with modest sales directly to stores and individuals. Principally interested in: directories, guides, handbooks, indexes/abstracts as well as scholarly academic works, principally in the area of cultural diversity, ethnic and minority groups as well as occasional titles on Alaskana. Emphasis on books about ethnic groups and refugees. Exclusive distributor in US for Hull University Press, Libris, and Meridian Books. Recent titles include national resource directories for Hispanics and refugees/immigrants, as well as books on Jewish refugee children, US policy in Micronesia, Southern social justice organizations" avg. press run 2M. Pub'd 4 titles 1998; expects 4 titles 1999, 4 titles 2000. 18 titles listed in the *Small Press Record of Books in Print* (28th Edition, 1999-00). avg. price, paper: $35. Discounts: 20%. 320pp; 8½×11, 5⅛×8½, 6×9; of. Reporting time: 1 month. Simultaneous submissions accepted: yes. Publishes 1% of manuscripts submitted. Payment: 10%. Does not copyright for author. PMA, American Library Assn., Small Press Center of NY, Pen Center USA West.

DENVER QUARTERLY, Bin Ramke, Editor; Joie Holmberg, Managing Editor, University of Denver, Denver, CO 80208, 303-871-2892. 1966. Poetry, fiction, articles, interviews, satire, criticism, reviews, parts-of-novels, long-poems, non-fiction. "Essays: Carl Dennis, David Wojahn, Lee Upton, James Longenbach. Fiction: Charles Baxter. Poems: James Tate, Philip Booth, Jane Miller, Ann Lauterbach" circ. 1M. 4/yr. Pub'd 4 issues 1998; expects 4 issues 1999, 4 issues 2000. sub. price: $24/institutions, $20/individuals; per copy: $6; sample: $6. Back issues: cost is based on cover price of the individual issue; usually $6 to $10. Discounts:

individual: 1 yr $20, 2 yrs $37, 3 yrs $50. 144pp; 6×9; of. Reporting time: 4-5 months. We accept simultaneous submissions if told. Publishes 5% of manuscripts submitted. Payment: $5 per page. Copyrighted, reverts to author. Pub's reviews: 6 in 1998. §Literature of last 100 years and contemporary fiction and poetry. Ads: $150/$75. CLMP, Council of Editors of Learned Journals.

Department of Romance Languages, Floyd Gray, University of Michigan, 4108 MLB, Ann Arbor, MI 48109-1275, 734-764-5344; fax 734-764-8163; e-mail kojo@umich.edu. 1980. Articles. "We publish literary criticism in the Romance Languages. Manuscripts by invitation only." avg. press run 500. 16 titles listed in the *Small Press Record of Books in Print* (28th Edition, 1999-00). avg. price, paper: $15; other: Vol. X-XIV $10, Vol. V-IX $9, Vol. I-IV $8. Discounts: 20% off to book wholesalers. 250pp; 6×9; desk top preparation of camera-ready copy. Simultaneous submissions accepted: no. Copyrights for author.

Depth Charge (see also THE JOURNAL OF EXPERIMENTAL FICTION), Matthew Sonnenberg, Editor; Eckhard Gerdes, Senior Editor, PO Box 7037, Evanston, IL 60201-7037, 708-733-9554;800-639-0008; fax 708-733-0928. 1986. Poetry, fiction, parts-of-novels, long-poems, concrete art. "We publish 'Fiction that Explodes Beneath the Surface.' We are interested in innovative novels that maximize, rather than minimize, adventuring in technique as well as content. We're looking for the best in subterficial fiction" avg. press run 2M. Pub'd 1 title 1998; expects 2 titles 1999, 4 titles 2000. 7 titles listed in the *Small Press Record of Books in Print* (28th Edition, 1999-00). avg. price, paper: $9.95-$16.95. Discounts: 1 book: no discount; 2-4 20%; 5-9 30%; 10-24 40%; 25-49 42%; 50-74 44%; 75-99 46%; 100-199 48%; 200 or more 50%. STOP orders earn 40%, please add $1.75 per book for shipping. Distributors: By contract. Class adoptions: 20%. 100-300pp; 5½×8½; of. Reporting time: 6-8 weeks, query first. Payment: 8% of list price. Copyrights for author.

Derrynane Press, Henry Berry, Peter Cherici, PO Box 93, Hampton, CT 06247, 860-455-0039; Fax 860-455-9198. 1995. Non-fiction. "Publish material on Irish and Celtic history and culture." avg. press run 2M. Expects 2 titles 1999, 3 titles 2000. 1 title listed in the *Small Press Record of Books in Print* (28th Edition, 1999-00). avg. price, cloth: $24; paper: $16. Discounts: bookstore 45%, jobber 55%. 325pp; 6×9; of. Reporting time: 3 weeks. Simultaneous submissions accepted: yes. Publishes 2% of manuscripts submitted. Payment: semi-annual 10%. Copyrights for author. PMA.

DESCANT, Neil Easterbrook, Stanley Trachtenberg, Steve Sherwood, English Department, TCU, Box 297270, Fort Worth, TX 76129. 1955. Poetry, fiction. "*Descant* does not publish poetry volumes or essays." circ. 500. 2/yr. sub. price: $12, $18 foreign; per copy: $6.50; sample: $6. Back issues: $6. 64pp; 6×9; †of. Reporting time: 6 weeks. Simultaneous submissions accepted: no. Publishes .5% of manuscripts submitted. Payment: in copies. We retain copyright. No ads.

DESCANT, Karen Mulhallen, PO Box 314, Station P, Toronto, Ontario M5S 2S8, Canada. 1970. Poetry, fiction, articles, art, photos, interviews, long-poems, plays. circ. 1M. 4/yr. Pub'd 4 issues 1998; expects 4 issues 1999, 4 issues 2000. sub. price: Ind.: $25 - one year $40 two years instit.: $35 one year $70 two years add $6 per year outside Canada; per copy: $13; sample: $8.50 + $2 outside Canada. Back issues: inquire. 120pp; 6×8; of. Reporting time: 8-12 weeks. Simultaneous submissions accepted: no. Publishes 2% of manuscripts submitted. Payment: $100. Copyrighted, reverts to author. §Poetry, quality fiction, arts and letters. Ads: inquire. CPPA, CMPA.

Desert Oasis Publishing Co., Gene B. Williams, PO Box 1805, Moses Lake, WA 98837, 509-766-0477. 1992. Non-fiction. avg. press run 1M. Expects 1 title 1999, 1+ titles 2000. 1 title listed in the *Small Press Record of Books in Print* (28th Edition, 1999-00). avg. price, cloth: $17.95. Discounts: resale (agent, jobber, etc.) 1-up 55% direct use (school, etc.) 1-up 40%. 208pp; 6×9. Reporting time: 1 month. Payment: negotiable. Copyrighting negotiable. Northwest Association of Book Publishers (NWABP), Pacific Northwest Booksellers Association (PNBA).

DESIGN BOOK REVIEW, Mitchell Schwarzer, Executive Editor; William Littmann, Associate Editor; Rita Huang, Assistant Editor; John Loomis, Editorial Advisor; Barry Katz, Editorial Advisor, 720 Channing Way, Berkeley, CA 94710, 415-486-1956; fax 415-644-3930; e-mail DBReview@ix.netcom.com. 1983. Articles, art, photos, criticism, reviews, letters. "*Design Book Review* is a leading magazine of ideas in the design field. Each quarter we provide our readers with essays, interviews, design criticism, and reviews of the latest and most significant books and exhibitions on architecture, design, urbanism, and landscape architecture." circ. 7M. 4/yr. Pub'd 3 issues 1998; expects 4 issues 1999. sub. price: $34 indiv., $98 instit., outside US add $16 per year; per copy: $9. Back issues: $18, $36 for double issues. Discounts: schedules on request. 96pp; 8½×11; sheetfed offset. Reporting time: 2 months. Simultaneous submissions accepted: no. Payment: in copies and books they review. Copyrighted, reverts to author. Pub's reviews: 25/30 per issue in 1998. §Architecture, design, landscape architecture, urban design, decorative arts. Ads: write for rates.

The Design Image Group Inc., 231 S. Frontage Road, Suite 17, Burr Ridge, IL 60521, 630-789-8991; Fax 630-789-9013. 1984. Fiction. avg. press run 3M-9M. Expects 6 titles 1999, 6 titles 2000. 5 titles listed in the *Small Press Record of Books in Print* (28th Edition, 1999-00). avg. price, paper: $15.95. Discounts: 50/free ship. 262pp; 5½×8½; of. Reporting time: 60 days. Simultaneous submissions accepted: yes. Publishes 1-2% of manuscripts submitted. Payment: competitive advances and royalties. Copyrights for author. PMA, Horror Writers Association.

DESIRE STREET, Jonathan Laws, Editor; Daniel Lonzo, Publisher; Andrea S. Gereighty, President, New Orleans Poetry Forum, 257 Bonnabel Boulevard, Metairie, LA 70005-3738, 504-833-0641; Fax 504-834-2005; ager80@worldnet.att.net. 1984. Poetry. circ. 1.2M. 12/yr. Pub'd 12 issues 1998; expects 4 issues 1999, 4 issues 2000. sub. price: $15; per copy: $5; sample: $3. Back issues: $3. 8pp; 8½×11; †of. Reporting time: 3 months. Simultaneous submissions accepted: yes. Publishes 45% of manuscripts submitted. Payment: seeing their work in publication and 1 copy. Copyrighted, reverts to author. Ads: $100/$75. New Orleans Poetry Forum.

THE DESK, PO Box 50376, Washington, DC 20091. 1996. Reviews, non-fiction. "Focus: reviews of spoken word, poet's audio, video and theater, and other non-printed dimensions of poetic practice." circ. 350. 4/yr. Expects 4 issues 1999, 4 issues 2000. sub. price: free. Back issues: $5/4 issues. 8pp; 8×11; mi. Reporting time: varies. Simultaneous submissions accepted: yes. Publishes 80% of manuscripts submitted. Payment: copies. Copyrighted, reverts to author. Ads: none.

●**Desk-Drawer Micropress**, Editorial Board, 209 W. Ann Street, Milford, PA 18337. 1997. Poetry, fiction, articles, art, photos, cartoons, interviews, satire, criticism, reviews, music, letters, parts-of-novels, long-poems, collages, plays, concrete art, news items, non-fiction. avg. press run 10. Expects 2 titles 1999, 2 titles 2000. avg. price, paper: $10. Discounts: 5+ copies 25%. 5×8. Reporting time: 2 weeks-2 months. Simultaneous submissions accepted: yes. Publishes 70% of manuscripts submitted. Payment: 10% in copies. Copyrights for author.

Desktop, Ink., Claudia Bravo, Editor, PO Box 548, Archer, FL 32618-0548, 352-486-6570 phone/Fax; E-mail dktop@aol.com. Poetry, fiction, non-fiction. "We are a small book and newsletter publisher. At this time we publish and print strictly 'desktop' books with laminate card cover. We welcome fiction, non-fiction, poetry and Christian works. Also, we have been soliciting Christian input to compile a newsletter. In return the contributor will receive a free issue, month of print, and a subscription offer." 1 title listed in the *Small Press Record of Books in Print* (28th Edition, 1999-00).

●**DEVIL BLOSSOMS**, John C. Erianne, PO Box 5122, Seabrook, NJ 08302. 1997. Poetry, fiction. "No upward limit for poetry, 2500 words for short stories. I like works which focus on the dark side of human nature. Recent contributors include Patricia Garfinkel and A.D. Winans." circ. 500. 1-2/yr. Expects 2 issues 1999, 1-2 issues 2000. sub. price: $8/3 issues; checks payable to John C. Erianne; per copy: $3; sample: $3. Discounts: 1-25 copies 35%, 26+ 45%. 24pp; 8½×11; of. Reporting time: 1-2 weeks. Simultaneous submissions accepted if so stated. Publishes 1% of manuscripts submitted. Payment: 1 copy. Copyrighted, reverts to author.

Devil Mountain Books, Clark Sturges, PO Box 4115, Walnut Creek, CA 94596, 925-939-3415; Fax 925-937-4883; devlmtn@aol.com. 1984. Fiction, articles, non-fiction. avg. press run 1.5M. 4 titles listed in the *Small Press Record of Books in Print* (28th Edition, 1999-00). avg. price, paper: $12.95. 100-175pp; 5½×8½. Copyrights for author.

THE DEVIL'S MILLHOPPER, The Devil's Millhopper Press (TDM Press), Stephen Gardner, Editor, USC - Aiken, 471 University Parkway, Aiken, SC 29801-6399, Fax/Phone 803-641-3239 e-mail Gardner@vm.sc.edu. 1976. Poetry, art, photos. "Submission periods: Sept. 1 to Oct. 31 of each year" circ. 600. 1/yr. Pub'd 1 issue 1998; expects 1 issue 1999, 1 issue 2000. sub. price: $6, $10 for 2 years; sample: $4.50. Back issues: $4.50. 40pp; 5½×8½; of. Reporting time: 3 months. Simultaneous submissions accepted: no. Publishes 1% of manuscripts submitted. Payment: 2 copies of issue containing author's work; 3 cash prizes—$150, $100, $50 (Kudzu contest). Copyrighted, reverts to author.

The Devil's Millhopper Press (TDM Press) (see also THE DEVIL'S MILLHOPPER), Stephen Gardner, Editor; Jannette Giles, Assistant Editor, USC - Aiken, 471 University Parkway, Aiken, SC 29801-6399, phone/fax 803-641-3239; e-Mail gardner@vm.sc.edu. 1984. Poetry. "The chapbook and many of the poems in our magazine issue are received and published as the results of our yearly contests. Send SASE for guidelines. Submission periods: Chapbooks-January 1 to February 28 of each year; Magazine-Sept. 1 to Oct. 31 of each year." avg. press run 600. Pub'd 2 titles 1998; expects 2 titles 1999, 2 titles 2000. 7 titles listed in the *Small Press Record of Books in Print* (28th Edition, 1999-00). avg. price, paper: $5 (chapbook). Discounts: for 5 copies or more, $1 off per copy price. 28-40pp; 5½×8½; of. Reporting time: 3 months. Simultaneous submissions acceptable for chapbook contest only. Publishes less than 1% of manuscripts submitted. Payment: chapbook $50 + 50 copies; contests variable. Copyrights for author.

Devin-Adair Publishers, Inc., Jane Andrassi, PO Box A, Old Greenwich, CT 06870. 1911. Photos, cartoons, criticism, non-fiction. "Publishing in these areas exclusively: 1) Political and national affairs, 2) Health and ecology, 3) Irish topics, 4) Americana, 5) Cooking and gardening, 6) Photography." avg. press run 4M. Pub'd 14 titles 1998; expects 16 titles 1999, 22 titles 2000. 8 titles listed in the *Small Press Record of Books in Print*

(28th Edition, 1999-00). avg. price, cloth: $16.95; paper: $12.95. Discounts: 3-5 books 20%, 6-9 40%, 10-24 41%, 25-99 42%, 100+ individual discounts arranged 50%+. 220pp; size varies; web printing, internal typesetting, w/freelance designers. Reporting time: 1-2 months. We accept simultaneous submissions, but we would prefer this practice be stopped. Publishes 2% of manuscripts submitted. Payment: 10% royalty. Copyrights for author. APA, ABA, SWGA, SACIA, Small Press Center.

DHARMA BEAT, Attila Gyenis, Mark Hemenway, Box 1753, Lowell, MA 01853-1753. 1993. Articles, photos, interviews, criticism, reviews, letters, parts-of-novels, news items, non-fiction. "*Dharma beat* is dedicated to Jack Kerouac events, activities, organizations and ideas. We need book reviews, reviews of events and activities, news of organizations/events related to Jack Kerouac. We will consider 500-1M word articles on Kerouac or Kerouac related places. First person articles on your connection to Kerouac are great. Typewritten ms, Wordperfect or ASCII disks are better. SASE for return. Please no poetry/fiction. First edition included articles on Jack Kerouac in Florida and North Carolina" circ. 750. 2/yr. Pub'd 2 issues 1998; expects 2 issues 1999, 2 issues 2000. sub. price: $7; sample: $3. Discounts: on request. 12pp; 8x11; of. Reporting time: 1 month. Payment: copies. Copyrighted, reverts to author. Pub's reviews: 1 in 1998. §Kerouac, Ginsberg, Beat related. Ads: $200.

Dharma Publishing (see also GESAR-Buddhism in the West), Tarthang Tulku, President; Margaret Mitchell, Publisher's contact, 2910 San Pablo Avenue, Berkeley, CA 94702. 1972. Articles, art, photos, interviews, reviews, news items. "91 titles currently in print; over 200 reproductions of Tibetan art in full color. Sepcializes in books on Buddhism. We have our own photo-typesetting and offset printing facilities." avg. press run 5M. Pub'd 4 titles 1998; expects 10 titles 1999, 10 titles 2000. 89 titles listed in the *Small Press Record of Books in Print* (28th Edition, 1999-00). avg. price, cloth: $21.95-$108; paper: $9.95-$25; other: $3.50 Gesar, $12 Tibetan art prints. Discounts: bookstores 1 book 0%, 2-4 20%, 5-25 40%, 26-49 42%, 50-99 43%, 100-250 45%; 40% maximum on returnable books; distributors by contract; libraries 20%; class adoptions 20%. 32-400pp; 5½x8½, 8½x11, 7x10; †of. Reporting time: 2 months. Publishes very small % of manuscripts submitted. Payment: subject to individual arrangement. Copyright is held by Dharma Publishing. ABA, PMA.

DIALOGOS: Hellenic Studies Review, Michael Silk, David Ricks, Dept. of Byzantine & Modern Greek, Attn: David Ricks, King's College, London WC2R 2LS, United Kingdom, fax 0171-873-2830. 1994. Poetry, articles, reviews. "*Dialogos* considers any material related to the Greek world and Greek culture, of any period. Articles max. 8000 words, review articles max. 3500 words. Previous contributors include Edmund Keeley, Oliver Taplin, Robin Osborne, Stephen Halliwell and G.E.R. Lloyd. Translations from Greek literature of any period are particularly welcome." circ. 500. 1/yr. Expects 1 issue 1999, 1 issue 2000. sub. price: $40; per copy: $40; sample: $40. Back issues: none. Discounts: none. 140pp; 5¾x8½; desktop. Reporting time: average 3 months. Simultaneous submissions accepted: yes. Publishes 20% of manuscripts submitted. Payment: none. Copyrighted, reverts to author. Pub's reviews: 2 in 1998. §Greek world and Greek culture from ancient times to the present. Ads: inquire.

DIAMOND INSIGHT, Guido Giovannini-Torelli, 790 Madison Avenue, New York, NY 10021, 212-570-4180; FAX 212-772-1286. 1988. Articles, photos, interviews, reviews, news items, non-fiction. "Publisher: Tryon Mercantile, Inc." 11/yr. Pub'd 11 issues 1998; expects 11 issues 1999, 11 issues 2000. sub. price: $325; sample: free. 12pp; 8½x11½; mi. Reporting time: 4 weeks. Payment: copies. Copyrighted, reverts to author. Pub's reviews: 5 in 1998. §Diamonds, precious stones, jewelry.

DIARIST'S JOURNAL, Ed Gildea, 209 E. 38th Street, Covington, KY 41015, 717-645-4692. 1988. "We print excerpts from diaries people are keeping today. Articles about diaries and diarists, reviews of books relating to diaries. 'True things happening to ordinary people.'" circ. 800. 4/yr. Pub'd 12 issues 1998; expects 4 issues 1999, 4 issues 2000. sub. price: $12; per copy: $3; sample: $3. Back issues: $1 each for 10 or more. 32pp; 11x13; of. Reporting time: 1 month. Payment: copies. Not copyrighted. Pub's reviews: 10 in 1998. §Diaries, diarists, journals. Ads: $180/$90/$5 per column inch.

●**The Dibble Fund for Marriage Education**, Catherine M. Reed, PO Box 7881, Berkeley, CA 94707-0881, 800-695-7975; Fax: 510-528-1956; e-mail: dibblefund@aol.com. 1991. Non-fiction. "We focus exclusively on materials which help adolescents learn relationship skills" avg. press run 1M+. Pub'd 1 title 1998; expects 1 title 2000. 2 titles listed in the *Small Press Record of Books in Print* (28th Edition, 1999-00). avg. price, other: curriculum package. Discounts: 40% trade. 100pp; 8½x11; †of. Reporting time: 2 months. Simultaneous submissions accepted: no. Payment: negotiable. Copyrights for author. SPAN, BAIPA.

DIE YOUNG, Skip Fox, Jesse Glass Jr., English Department, Univ of Southwestern Louisiana, Lafayette, LA 70504-4691. 1990. "We believe in poetry. Fiction is foreplay. (But then some fiction is poetry.) We've published both traditional (formal) poetry and poetry in open forms. Even though our preference is for poetry in open forms (experimental, avant-garde, free verse), our primary criterion is quality (based on entheos, intelligence, music, grace of the line, energy, etc.). We are not interested in simple minded poetry nor in poetry written in the period syle. The sentimental is, as Stevens wrote, a "failure of feeling." We would like to see an

154

ambitious poetry. William Carlos Williams has it, "A poet thinks with his poem. If he is to be profound, therein lies his profundity."Olson's "Projective Verse" holds as well, and is necessary, today as in 1951." circ. varies. 2/yr. Pub'd 2 issues 1998; expects 2 issues 1999, 2-3 issues 2000. sub. price: $9/3 issues; per copy: $3; sample: $3. Back issues: $3 per issue—but most are out of print. 48pp; 7×8; xerox. Reporting time: varies. Payment: 2 issues. Not copyrighted. Pub's reviews: 0 in 1998. §Poetry, poetry, poetry, etc.

DIET & HEALTH MAGAZINE, Lifetime Books, Inc., Brain Feinblum, Editor-in-Chief, 2131 Hollywood Boulevard, Hollywood, FL 33020, 305-925-5242. 1943. Non-fiction. "We are the leading publisher of one-shot magazines in the United States. We have four categories in which we publish. These are diet & health, health, cookbook series and financial planning series. We are looking for full manuscripts that would lend themselves to these areas." circ. 50M. 8/yr. Pub'd 8 issues 1998; expects 8 issues 1999, 8 issues 2000. price per copy: $2.95. Back issues: cover price. 128pp; 5-3/16×7⅝; of. Reporting time: 3 months. Payment: negotiated. Copyrighted, reverts to author. Ads: $2,000. PBAA, ACIDA.

Paul Dilsaver, Publisher, PO Box 1621, Pueblo, CO 81002. 1974. Poetry, fiction. "Have published limited edition chapbooks under the imprints of Blue Light Books, Rocky Mountain Creative Arts, Academic & Arts Press. Authors published include Pulitzer winner Yusef Komunyakaa, John Sweet, John Garmon, Clifton Snider, Elinor Meiskey, John Calderazzo, Howard McCord, Victoria McCabe, Bim Angst, Kirk Robertson, R.P. Dickey, Richard F. Fleck, and many others. Most current imprint: Scrooge's Ledger. New titles by Richard Houff and Peter Maglioggo. Submissions by open call for specific projects only." avg. press run 100-150. Pub'd 1 title 1998; expects 2 titles 1999, 2 titles 2000. avg. price, paper: varies. Pages vary; size varies; varies. Payment: copies. Does not copyright for author.

Dimension Engineering Press, C.L. Briones, 1620 Beacon Place, Oxnard, CA 93033, 805-487-2248; FAX 805-486-2491. 1995. Non-fiction. avg. press run 6M-10M. Expects 1 title 1999, 2-3 titles 2000. 1 title listed in the *Small Press Record of Books in Print* (28th Edition, 1999-00). avg. price, paper: $29.95. Discounts: distributors, e.g. Baker & Taylor 55%. 250pp; 5×8. Reporting time: 30-45 days. Simultaneous submissions accepted: no. Publishes 25% of manuscripts submitted. Payment: 15-20%. Copyrights for author.

Dimi Press, Dick Lutz, 3820 Oak Hollow Lane, SE, Salem, OR 97302, 503-364-7698; fax 503-364-9727. 1981. Non-fiction. "We now publish books about unusual things in nature, such as animals, natural distasters, etc. Also interested in related subjects that could fit as nature/travel/environment. No travel guides." avg. press run 1.5M. Pub'd 1 title 1998; expects 2 titles 1999, 3 titles 2000. 14 titles listed in the *Small Press Record of Books in Print* (28th Edition, 1999-00). avg. price, paper: $15; other: $9.95 cassette. Discounts: 1-4 20%, 5+ 40%; libraries 20%, 10+ 50%. 130pp; 5½×8½; of. Reporting time: 1 month. Simultaneous submissions accepted: yes. Publishes 5% of manuscripts submitted. Payment: 10% royalties, no advance. Copyrights for author. PMA, NWABP.

Timothy A. Dimoff/SACS Consulting, Timothy A. Dimoff, David B. Nicholson, 143 Northwest Avenue, Bldg. B-102, Tallmadge, OH 44278, 330-633-9551; Fax 330-633-5862. 1990. Non-fiction. "Focus on business topics, especially entrepreneurship, human resources" avg. press run 3M. Pub'd 3 titles 1998; expects 1 title 1999, 2 titles 2000. 1 title listed in the *Small Press Record of Books in Print* (28th Edition, 1999-00). avg. price, paper: $15. Discounts: 40% to bookstores, 50% wholesale/distributors, 20% libraries & schools, 2-4 quantities 20%, 5-99 40%, 100+ 50%. 125pp; 5½×8½; of. Simultaneous submissions accepted: yes. Payment: negotiable. Copyrights for author.

DIONYSIA, Angie Magill, Box 1500, Capital University, Columbus, OH 43209, 614-236-6563. 1980. Poetry, fiction, art, photos. "Prefer 3-5 poems, fiction no longer than 1,000 words" circ. 500. 1/yr. Pub'd 1 issue 1998; expects 1 issue 1999, 1 issue 2000. sub. price: distributed free. 20pp; 5½×8½; of. Reporting time: 2 months. Payment: 1 copy. Not copyrighted.

THE DIPLOMAT, Katherine B. Holmes, 111 Conduit Street, Annapolis, MD 21401-2603. 1990. Articles. "The newsletter for international business and protocol." circ. 2M. 5/yr. Pub'd 5 issues 1998; expects 5 issues 1999, 5 issues 2000. sub. price: $50; per copy: $10; sample: free. Back issues: $3. 10-20pp; 8½×11; of. Publishes 0% of manuscripts submitted. Copyrighted, reverts to author.

DIRECT RESPONSE, Craig A. Huey, Publisher, 1815 West 213th Street, Ste. 210, Torrance, CA 90501, 310-212-5727; cdms@earthlink.net. 1977. Reviews, news items, non-fiction. circ. 1M. 12/yr. Pub'd 12 issues 1998; expects 12 issues 1999, 12 issues 2000. sub. price: $79; per copy: $10; sample: same. Back issues: $10, 12/$100. 8pp; of. Not copyrighted. Pub's reviews: 10 in 1998. §Marketing, advertising, business.

DIRIGIBLE, David Todd, Editor; Cynthia Conrad, Co-Editor, 101 Cottage Street, New Haven, CT 06511, email dirigibl@javanet.com. 1994. Poetry, fiction, criticism. "We seek language-centered, *controlled* experiments, fiction that is postmodern, paraliterary, nonlinear or subjective, and work that breaks with genre, convention, or form. Hybrid forms of writing and essays on aesthetics, poetics, reader experience and writing processes are also of interest to us. We are inspired by the continental avant-garde tradition (pataphysiquian,

155

surrealist, absurdist, futurist, dada) and by theory-based literature (writerly, abstract, analytical, phenomenological, textual). Recent contributors: Sheila E. Murphy, W.B. Keckler, John Grey, Ron Padgett, Simon Perchik, Barbara Lefcowitz, Richard Kostelanetz, and J.M. Bennett.'' circ. 500. 4/yr. Pub'd 4 issues 1998; expects 4 issues 1999, 4 issues 2000. sub. price: $7 ppd, $10 outside US; per copy: $3 ppd; sample: $3 ppd. Back issues: $2 ppd. Discounts: we are interested in selective swaps with similar magazines, 50% to bookstores. 40-48pp; 4¼×7; of. Reporting time: 1-4 months. Simultaneous submissions accepted: no. Publishes less than 10% of manuscripts submitted. Payment: 2 copies. Copyrighted, reverts to author. Pub's reviews: 0 in 1998. §Avant-garde, experimental, literary books and magazines. Ads: negotiable, will swap with similar magazines.

THE DIRTY GOAT, Host Publications, Inc., Elzbieta Szoka, Joe W. Bratcher III, 2717 Wooldridge, Austin, TX 78703, 512-482-8229; E-mail jbhost@cerf.net. 1988. Poetry, fiction, art, photos, interviews, criticism, parts-of-novels, long-poems, plays. ''Maximum length 20 pages. Will consider anything. Recent contributors: Mel Clay, David Ohle, Alfred Leslie, Gerald Nicosia. Artwork done in b/w and color.'' circ. 300. 2/yr. Pub'd 4 issues 1998; expects 2 issues 1999, 2 issues 2000. sub. price: $20; per copy: $10; sample: $2. Back issues: none. Discounts: 1 copy 20%, 2-9 30%, 10-24 40%, 25-49 43%. 100pp; 8×10; of. Reporting time: indeterminate. Payment: free copy. Copyrighted, reverts to author. Ads: none. Small Press Center, Book Publishers of Texas (BPT).

DIRTY LINEN, Paul Hartman, Editor-Publisher, PO Box 66600, Baltimore, MD 21239-6600, 410-583-7973; fax 410-337-6763. 1983. Articles, photos, interviews, reviews, music, news items, non-fiction. ''Folk, world music. Record and concert reviews: preferably 200-300 words, max. 400 words. Feature articles and interviews: 1,000-2,000+ words depending on topic. No unsolicited manuscripts.'' circ. 20M. 6/yr. Pub'd 6 issues 1998; expects 6 issues 1999, 6 issues 2000. sub. price: $22; per copy: $5; sample: $4. Back issues: $4 plus postage. Discounts: distributors 55%, retail stores 40%. 116pp; 8⅜×10⅜; sheet. Simultaneous submissions accepted: no. Publishes 5% of manuscripts submitted. Payment: $50 for major articles, $0 for reviews, etc. Copyrighted, rights revert to author upon request. Pub's reviews: 30 in 1998. §Music. Ads: b&w: $1050/$585/$325 1/4 page/$220 for 1/6 page/$90 business card; color: $1475/$875/$490 1/4 page. AFIM.

THE DISABILITY RAG & RESOURCE, The Advocado Press, Eric Francis, Anne Finger, Fiction and Poetry, PO Box 145, Louisville, KY 40201, 502-459-5343. 1980. Poetry, fiction, articles, art, photos, cartoons, interviews, satire, criticism, reviews, letters, news items, non-fiction. ''Street Address: 1962 Roanoke Ave, Louisville, KY 40205. Lengths vary, short to medium; types of articles include analysis, investigative reporting, first-person narratives, informational pieces. Emphasis on civil rights perspective. No pity pieces, no hero stories. Book reviews, media analysis, satire, humor. Poetry regularly, fiction occasionally. Some recent contributors: John Woodward, Marta Russell, Kathi Wolfe, Jean Stewart, Arthur Jacobs'' circ. 4M. 6/yr. Pub'd 6 issues 1998; expects 6 issues 1999, 6 issues 2000. sub. price: $17.50 individuals; $35 organizations; $42 international; per copy: $3.95; sample: free. Back issues: $4.50 if available, list on request. Discounts: agent 20%, others contact office for schedule. 48pp; 8×10½; of. Reporting time: 1-2 months. Publishes 25% of manuscripts submitted. Payment: articles $25 per page; $25 per poem. Copyrighted, we reserve 1st North American Serial Rights. Pub's reviews: 10 in 1998. §Disability issues, particularly from civil rights perspective. Ads: $875/$545/$650 2/3 page, $350 1/3 page, $95 1/6 page, IFC full color $1095, IBC $1050.

DISC GOLF JOURNAL, Tom Schlueter, Publisher; Kathleen Ignowski, Managing Editor, PO Box 3577, Champaign, IL 61826-3577, 217-398-7880;fax 217-398-7881; e-mail kathyig@aol.com. 1991. Articles, photos, interviews, reviews, letters. ''Disc evaluations, player profiles, city and course closeups as well as a wide variety of special features relevant to disc golf.'' circ. 2.5M. 6/yr. Pub'd 6 issues 1998; expects 6 issues 1999, 6 issues 2000. sub. price: $17.97; per copy: $5. 48pp; 8½×11 newsletter; of. Reporting time: 1 month. Publishes 75% of manuscripts submitted. Payment: yes. Ads: $175/$90.

DISC GOLF WORLD NEWS, Rick Rothstein, Editor-Publisher, Disc Golf World, PO Box 025678, Kansas City, MO 64102-5678, 816-471-3472; fax 816-471-4653, email RickdGwn@aol.com. 1984. Articles, photos, cartoons, interviews, reviews, letters, news items, non-fiction. circ. 5M. 4/yr. Pub'd 4 issues 1998; expects 4 issues 1999, 4 issues 2000. sub. price: $18 US ($30 1st class), $26 Can., $31 Europe, $34 Australia & Japan; per copy: $6N. America, $8 rest; sample: same. 76pp; 8½×11; of. Reporting time: 1-2 weeks. Simultaneous submissions are not usually accepted. Publishes 50-60% of manuscripts submitted. Payment: rarely; in kind (merchandise). Copyrighted, reverts to author. Pub's reviews: 1 in 1998. §New sports and games, psychology of individual sports (especially golf), flying disc subjects. Ads: $280/$170.

Discovery Enterprises, Ltd., Kenneth M. Deitch, JoAnne W. Deitch, 31 Laurelwood Drive, Carlisle, MA 01741-1205. 1990. Plays, non-fiction. ''Nonfiction for ages 10-adult. Series of biographies and history series. Length: 60-220 pages. Also, Discovery Enterprises, Ltd. supplies book design and production to other small publishers as well as full service marketing and advertising.'' avg. press run 2M-3M. Pub'd 15 titles 1998; expects 25 titles 1999, 12 titles 2000. 86 titles listed in the *Small Press Record of Books in Print* (28th Edition, 1999-00). avg. price, cloth: $14.95; paper: $5.95 and $25; other: $10. Discounts: 3-6 20%, 7-20 40%, 21+ 40%, returns by 120 days, 90% credit toward future orders only; prepaid orders over 100 books 45%. 60-96pp; 8½×11, 5½×7½, 6×9; of. Reporting time: 6 weeks, to queries only. Simultaneous submissions accepted: no. Publishes 2% of manuscripts submitted. Payment: negotiable; co-publishing for new authors. We occasionally copyright for author. ABA, PMA, NCTE, NCSS, NELMS, ASCD, NCHE.

DISSONANCE MAGAZINE, Leif Hunneman, 1315 NW 185TH Ave. #220, Beaverton, OR 97006-1947, 802-860-6285. 1990. Art, photos, interviews, satire, criticism, reviews, music, letters. "Focused primarily on independent (read: non-corporate) thought, music, and action. Futurist slant, concentrating on discussion of action-oriented ideas to empower the individual. Attempting to document media transmissions helpful to new concepts of thought. Dedicated to connecting previously unjoined subcultures and individuals with similar goals. Science/technology oriented with roots in punk and industrial culture." circ. 3M. 4/yr. Pub'd 4 issues 1998; expects 4 issues 1999, 4 issues 2000. price per copy: $2. Discounts: trade for comparable publication. 32pp; 8½×11; †of. Payment: none. Copyrighted, reverts to author. Pub's reviews: 70+ in 1998. §Along the lines of science, technology, futurism, punk/industrial culture, cyberpunk, fortean. Ads: $100/$60/$35 quarter page (discount for indiemedia).

DISTURBED GUILLOTINE, Fredrik Hausmann, PO Box 14871, University Station, Minneapolis, MN 55414-0871. Poetry, fiction, art, photos, criticism, parts-of-novels, long-poems, collages, concrete art, non-fiction. "Recent contributors: Nick Piombino, Hannah Weiner, Robert Kelly, Bruce Andrews, Will Alexander, Fiona Templeton, John Yau, Spencer Selby, Katie Yates, Lisa Cooper, Gene Frumkin, Ray DiPalma, Raymond Federman, Robert Grenier, and Aaron Shurin." circ. 200. 1/yr. Pub'd 1 issue 1998; 1 issue 1999, 1 issue 2000. price per copy: $7; sample: $4. Back issues: $4. Discounts: none. 130pp; 6×9; of. Reporting time: 2-3 weeks. Simultaneous submissions accepted: no. Publishes 40% of manuscripts submitted. Payment: copies. Not copyrighted. Ads: none.

Divina (A MacMurray & Beck imprint) (see also MacMurray & Beck), Leslie Koffler, Associate Editor, 1490 Lafayette Street, Suite #108, Denver, CO 80218-2391. 1998. Non-fiction. Expects 3 titles 1999, 3 titles 2000. 2 titles listed in the *Small Press Record of Books in Print* (28th Edition, 1999-00). avg. price, paper: $14.95. Discounts: distributed to the trade through Words Distributing, 510-632-1281. 314pp; 6×9; of. Reporting time: 2-3 months. Simultaneous submissions accepted: yes. Payment: negotiated. Copyrights for author. Rocky Mountain Book Publishers Assn. (RMBPA).

DIVINATION FOR DECISION-MAKERS, Iris K. Barratt, PO Box 80, Bellevue, ID 83313, phone/fax 208-788-8585; e-mail visionpb@micron.net. 1998.

DNA Publications, Inc. (see also ABSOLUTE MAGNITUDE; DREAMS OF DECADENCE: Vampire Poetry and Fiction; PIRATE WRITINGS), Warren Lapine, Angela Kessler, PO Box 2988, Radford, VA 24143-2988, 413-772-0725; wilder@shaysnet.com. 1993. Poetry, fiction. "We publish a trade paperback of Roger Zelazny's poetry book, *A Hymn to the Sun.*" avg. press run 2M. Expects 1 title 1999, 3 titles 2000. 1 title listed in the *Small Press Record of Books in Print* (28th Edition, 1999-00). avg. price, paper: $6.95. Pages vary; 8×5; of. Reporting time: 2 weeks. Simultaneous submissions accepted: yes. Payment: 8-15% plus advance. Copyrights for author.

Doctor Jazz Press, A.J. Wright, 119 Pintail Drive, Pelham, AL 35124, 205-663-3403. 1979. Poetry, art. "DJ Press continues to issue poetry broadsides. No submissions, please; I am still overstocked. Until next time, this is Doctor Jazz signing off." avg. press run 100. Pub'd 2 titles 1998; expects 8 titles 1999. 10 titles listed in the *Small Press Record of Books in Print* (28th Edition, 1999-00). avg. price, paper: $1; other: $2.50, 3 broadsides. 1 page; 8½×11; of. Reporting time: less than a month. Payment: 25 copies. Copyrights for author.

Doctors Press, Inc., Gretchen Welsh, PO Box 2200, Angleton, TX 77516, 409-848-2704. 1996. avg. press run 20M. Pub'd 4 titles 1998; expects 4 titles 1999, 4 titles 2000. 4 titles listed in the *Small Press Record of Books in Print* (28th Edition, 1999-00). avg. price, cloth: $24.99. 50pp; 8½×11. Reporting time: 6 months. NAIP, ALA, PMA.

Dog-Eared Publications, Nancy Field, Publisher, PO Box 620863, Middleton, WI 53562-0863, 608-831-1410. 1978. Art, non-fiction. "Dog-Eared Publications creates and produces materials about nature and the environment for children. To date we have not accepted others' work." avg. press run 4M-10M. Pub'd 3 titles 1998; expects 3 titles 1999, 3 titles 2000. 15 titles listed in the *Small Press Record of Books in Print* (28th Edition, 1999-00). avg. price, paper: $5.95. Discounts: 2-5 20%, 6-10 25%, 11-199 40%, 200+ 45%. 32-40pp; 8½×11; of. Reporting time: 2 weeks. Copyrights for author.

Doggerel Press, Raymond Meliza, PO Box 985, Salem, OR 97308, 503-588-2926. 1990. Cartoons, satire. "We publish offbeat/mainstream, mass-market humor, visual (illus. cartoon books). Recent contributors: Irene Turk, Mark McCoin" avg. press run 5M-10M. Pub'd 1 title 1998; expects 1 title 1999, 3 titles 2000. 1 title listed in the *Small Press Record of Books in Print* (28th Edition, 1999-00). avg. price, paper: $6.95. 100pp; 8¼×5½; full web. Reporting time: 2-3 months (SASE). Payment: per agreement. Copyrights for author.

Dolphin Books, Inc., Michael Fearheiley, Maryvonne Fuentes, PO Box 2877, Decatur, IL 62524, 217-876-1232, fax 217-876-9210. 1995. Fiction. "We are looking for serious science fiction novels, between 30,000 and 50,000 words, written for 4th graders up to young adults. We prefer to see completed manuscripts, but will accept outlines/synopses" avg. press run 4M. Pub'd 1 title 1998; expects 2 titles 1999, 3 titles 2000. 1 title listed in the *Small Press Record of Books in Print* (28th Edition, 1999-00). avg. price, cloth: $15.95. 192pp; 5½×8½; of. Reporting time: 1 month. Simultaneous submissions accepted: yes. Publishes a variable % of manuscripts submitted. Payment: royalty on retail price. Copyrights for author. PMA.

Dolphin-Moon Press, James Taylor, President, PO Box 22262, Baltimore, MD 21203. 1973. Poetry, fiction, art, photos, cartoons. "Books and chapbooks with unusual design formats by poets, fiction writers and dramatists. In addition, anthologies, record albums, cassette tapes, note cards, and other art objects have also been published by the press. The press also publishes a comic book series" avg. press run 750. Pub'd 1 title 1998; expects 7 titles 1999, 7 titles 2000. 40 titles listed in the *Small Press Record of Books in Print* (28th Edition, 1999-00). avg. price, cloth: $16; paper: $8; other: $1.50 (pamphlets, etc.). Discounts: negotiable. 60-100pp; size varies; of. Reporting time: 1 month. Payment: percentage of print run. Copyrights for author.

Doone Publications, 7950 Hwy 72 W. #G106, Madison, AL 35758. 3 titles listed in the *Small Press Record of Books in Print* (28th Edition, 1999-00).

DOOR COUNTY ALMANAK, Fred Johnson, 10905 Bay Shore Drive, Sister Bay, WI 54234, 414-854-2742. 1982. Poetry, fiction, articles, art, photos, cartoons, interviews, parts-of-novels, long-poems, non-fiction. "The *Door County Almanak* is an occasional regional magazine/book covering a different topic each issue. It covers history, people, and events in N.E. Wisconsin, especially Door County. Open to writers from any area. Guidelines available with SASE. There is no issue planned for the near future." Irregular. Expects 1 issue 1999, 1 issue 2000. price per copy:.$9.95; sample: $9.95. Back issues: #1-$4.95, #2-#4 $9.95 each. Discounts: 40% to trade. 300pp; 6×9; of. Reporting time: 2-8 weeks. Payment: copies, plus payment. Copyrighted, reverts to author. Pub's reviews. Ads: rate sheet available.

●**DOPE FRIENDS**, Emmett Taylor, Ivy Shields, Ballagh, Bushypark, Galway, Ireland, e-mail mmtaylor@iol.ie. 1998. Art, cartoons, reviews, letters. "Ongoing comic book series." Pub'd 2 issues 1998; expects 4 issues 1999, 4 issues 2000. price per copy: $2. Discounts: 5-10 copies $1.80; 11-19 copies $1.65; 20 or more $1.50. 24pp; 6×8½; †xerox. Simultaneous submissions accepted: no. Pub's reviews: 3 in 1998. §comics, subculture magazines. Ads: $20/$14/ 1/4 pg $7.50.

Doral Publishing, Luana Luther, Editor-in chief; Beverly Black, Editor; Jill Regez, Design, Layout, Production; Tim Baake, Design, Layout, Production; Alvin Grossman, Publisher; Mark Anderson, Associate Publisher; Lynn Grey, Marketing Manager; Doug Hewitt, Graphic Artist, 8560 SW Salish Lane, #300, Wilsonville, OR 97070-9625, 503-683-3307; Fax 503-682-2648. 1986. Non-fiction. "Doral publishes books for the purebred dog market. We specialize in breed books and those pertaining to purebred dogs in general. Hardback books average some 300 pages in length." avg. press run 3M-5M. Pub'd 4 titles 1998; expects 4 titles 1999, 5 titles 2000. 28 titles listed in the *Small Press Record of Books in Print* (28th Edition, 1999-00). avg. price, cloth: $26.95; paper: $17.95. 285pp; 6×9; of. Reporting time: 3-4 weeks. Simultaneous submissions accepted: yes. Publishes 10% of manuscripts submitted. Payment: 10% 1st book - paid January & July. Copyrights for author. Publishers Marketing Association, Dog Writer's Assoc. of America, Northwest Assoc. of Book Publishers.

●**Dorchester Press (see also METASEX)**, Michelle Clifford, PO Box 620, Old Chelsea Station, New York, NY 10011, e-mail metasex@hotmail.com. 1997. Photos, interviews, criticism, reviews, parts-of-novels, non-fiction. "Recent contributors: William Landis and Howard Ziehm." avg. press run 5M. Pub'd 1 title 1998; expects 1 title 1999, 2 titles 2000. avg. price, other: $10. 70pp; 8½×11; †of. Reporting time: immediate. Simultaneous submissions accepted: no. Publishes 1% of manuscripts submitted. Payment: negotiable. Copyrights for author. 504/700/7/38/58.

DorPete Press, PO Box 238, Briarcliff Manor, NY 10510, 914-941-7029. 1984. Non-fiction. avg. press run 1.4M. Pub'd 3 titles 1998. 9 titles listed in the *Small Press Record of Books in Print* (28th Edition, 1999-00). avg. price, cloth: $14.95; paper: $6.95. Discounts: 1 10%, 2-4 20%, 5-24 40%, 25+ 50%. 200pp; 6×9; of. Reporting time: 3 months. Payment: 10% on invoice price. Copyrights for author.

DOUBLE BILL, Jena Von Brucker, G.B. Jones, PO Box 55, Station 'E', Toronto, Ontario M6H 4E1, Canada. 1991. Articles, photos, cartoons, interviews, satire, criticism, reviews, music, letters, non-fiction. "Published by Bitch Nation. Pertaining to William Conrad, his movies, the TV shows 'Cannon,' 'Nero Wolfe,' 'Jake and the Fatman,' and/or William Burroughs (music, movies, books, etc.) and the Beat Generation. Also: William Conrad—radio recordings." circ. 1M. 1/yr. Pub'd 1 issue 1998; expects 2 issues 1999, 1 issue 2000. price per copy: $3; sample: $3. Back issues: $3. 40pp; 7×8½; †photocopies. Reporting time: 6 weeks. Simultaneous submissions accepted: no. Publishes 80% of manuscripts submitted. Payment: 1 free copy. Copyrighted, reverts to author. Ads: $50 1/2 page/$25 1/4 page/$10 1/8 page.

158

Dovehaven Press, Joseph R. Brockett, PO Box 6659, East Brunswick, NJ 08816-6659, 718-442-1325; fax 718-442-6225; e-mail wossumi@admin.con2.com. 1986. "At this time, we are not accepting submissions." avg. press run 5-10M. Expects 9 titles 1999. 9 titles listed in the *Small Press Record of Books in Print* (28th Edition, 1999-00). avg. price, paper: $20. Discounts: 1-2 books 20%, 3-4 books 40%, 5-199 books 40%, 200-499 books 50%, 500+ books 55%. 150pp; 8½×5½. SPAN.

DOVETAIL: A Journal by and for Jewish/Christian Families, Mary Helene Rosenbaum, 775 Simon Greenwell Lane, Boston, KY 40107, 502-549-5499; Fax 502-549-3543; di-ifr@bardstown.com. 1992. Articles, photos, cartoons, interviews, reviews, letters, news items, non-fiction. "Articles are 800-1,000 words, run with 2- or 3-sentence bio. We look for a wide variety of ideas and opinions on interfaith marriage." circ. 1M. 6/yr. Pub'd 6 issues 1998; expects 6 issues 1999, 6 issues 2000. sub. price: $25 US, $35 Intl.; per copy: $4.50; sample: $4.50. Back issues: $4.50. Discounts: call for quote. 16pp; 8½×11; lp. Reporting time: 2-4 months. We accept simultaneous submissions if notified. Publishes 25% of manuscripts submitted. Payment: $20/article. Copyrighted, does not revert to author. Pub's reviews: 6 in 1998. §Interfaith marriage, life cycle ceremonies, family rituals. Ads: $200/$125.

Dovetail Publishing, Joan C. Hawxhurst, PO Box 19945, Kalamazoo, MI 49019, 616-342-2900; FAX 616-342-1012; dovetail@mich.com. 1992. Fiction, articles, non-fiction. avg. press run 5M. Pub'd 2 titles 1998; expects 2 titles 2000. 3 titles listed in the *Small Press Record of Books in Print* (28th Edition, 1999-00). avg. price, paper: $14.95. Discounts: call for quote. 50pp; 8½×11; lp. Reporting time: 2-4 months. Simultaneous submissions accepted: yes. Publishes 50% of manuscripts submitted. Payment: to be determined. Does not copyright for author.

●**Down The Shore Publishing**, Ray Fisk, Box 3100, Harvey Cedars, NJ 08008, 609-978-1233; fax 609-597-0422. 1984. Fiction, non-fiction. "We are primarily a regional publisher, producing trade and gift books for the NJ shore and mid-atlantic." avg. press run varies. Pub'd 3 titles 1998; expects 5 titles 1999, 5 titles 2000. 8 titles listed in the *Small Press Record of Books in Print* (28th Edition, 1999-00). avg. price, cloth: $29; paper: $24. Discounts: 1-2 books 0%, 3-5 20%, 6-11 40%, 12+ 42%. Pages vary; size varies. Reporting time: 1-3 months. Simultaneous submissions accepted: yes. Publishes 1% of manuscripts submitted. Payment: varies. We sometimes copyright for author.

Down There Press, Joani Blank, Publisher, 938 Howard Street, Suite 101, San Francisco, CA 94103, 415-974-8985 x105; FAX 415-974-8989; e-Mail goodvibe@well.com. 1975. Fiction, non-fiction. "The only small press in the country publishing exclusively sex education & sexual enhancement books. New titles in 1983 were *A Kid's First Book About Sex*, and *Let's Talk About Sex & Loving*. New imprint in 1983, Yes Press. In 1986, revised edition of *Anal Pleasure and Health*. In 1988, *Herotica: A Collection of Women's Erotic Fiction*; 1989 revised edition of *Good Vibrations: The Complete Guide to Vibrators*; 1991, *Erotic by Nature*; 1992 reprint of *Aural Sex*, under title of *Sex Information, May I Help You?*; 1993, *Femalia*; 1995, *Exhibitionism for the Shy* 1996, *First Person Sexual*, 1997, *I Am My Lover* and *Sex Spoken Here*" avg. press run 5M. Pub'd 6 titles 1998; expects 2 titles 1999, 2 titles 2000. 18 titles listed in the *Small Press Record of Books in Print* (28th Edition, 1999-00). avg. price, cloth: $45; paper: $6, $13. Discounts: booksellers—1 copy 20%, 2-9 35%, 10+ 40%; by arrangement to therapists and educators. 48-200pp; 8½×11, 5½×8½, 6×9; of. Reporting time: 2 months. Simultaneous submissions accepted: yes. Publishes 1% of manuscripts submitted. Payment: varies, 8-10% cover price. Copyrights for author. Northern California Book Publicity & Marketing Assn. (NCBPMA), Bay Area Publishers Network (BAPN), Publishers Marketing Assn. (PMA), Women's Presses Library Project.

DOWN UNDER MANHATTAN BRIDGE, Elizabeth Morse, Dan Freeman, 224 E. 11th Street #5, New York, NY 10003-7329, 212-388-7051, lizard.evny@msn.com. 1979. Poetry, fiction, art, cartoons, satire, music, parts-of-novels, plays. "We'll be publishing on the Web exclusively for the time being. Address is [www.tiac.net/users/dumbzine] New themes: *perfect fit* reading mss Sept 199 to Jan 2000; *stubborn* reading mss Feb 2000; *twisted* reading mss May 2000; *naked/fishing* or *sport/sex* August 2000." circ. 1M+. 2/yr. Expects 2 issues 1999, 2 issues 2000. sub. price: $8; per copy: $4.89; sample: $4.89. Back issues: $50 for first edition. 32pp; 6×9; of. Reporting time: 6 months. Simultaneous submissions accepted: yes. Publishes 5% of manuscripts submitted. Payment: copies. Copyrighted, reverts to author. Ads: $200/$100/$50 1/4 page. The Unbearables, MWV, AIGA.

DOWNSTATE STORY, Elaine Hopkins, 1825 Maple Ridge, Peoria, IL 61614, 309-688-1409; email ehopkins@prairienet.org; http://www.wiu.bgu.edu/users/mfgeh/dss. 1992. Fiction, art. "2000 word maximum, mainstream fiction" 1/yr. Pub'd 1 issue 1998; expects 1 issue 1999, 1 issue 2000. price per copy: $8; sample: $8. Back issues: $5. Discounts: yes. 65pp; 5×8; of. Reporting time: varies. Simultaneous submissions accepted: yes. Publishes 10% of manuscripts submitted. Payment: $50. Copyrighted, reverts to author. Ads: negotiable.

THE DRAGON CHRONICLE, Ade Dimmick, PO Box 3369, London SW66JN, England, dragnet@stalkev-lab.ch. 1993. Poetry, fiction, articles, art, photos, cartoons, long-poems, non-fiction. "A journal of special-interest devoted entirely to dragon's and related themes" circ. 1M. 3/yr. Pub'd 3 issues 1998; expects 3 issues 1999, 3 issues 2000. sub. price: $12 bills only; per copy: $4 bills only; sample: $4. 40pp; 8×12. Reporting time: by return mail. Simultaneous submissions accepted: yes. Publishes 70% of manuscripts submitted. Payment: free subscription. Copyrighted, reverts to author. Pub's reviews: 47 in 1998. §Mythology, magic, paganism, zoomythlogy, occult/ecolh mystery. Ads: $90/$60/$45 1/4 page/$30 smaller. Association of Little Presses.

The Dragon Press, Richard Wills, Maureen Twyman, 4230 Del Rey Avenue, Suite 445, Marina del Rey, CA 90292, 818-568-9111; FAX 818-568-1119. 1986. Articles, photos, news items, non-fiction. avg. press run 250-500. Pub'd 2 titles 1998; expects 2-3 titles 1999, 2-3 titles 2000. 2 titles listed in the *Small Press Record of Books in Print* (28th Edition, 1999-00). avg. price, cloth: $29.95; paper: $19.95. Discounts: trade 2-49 books 20%, 50-99 45%, 100+ 50%. 140pp; 8½×11; of. Reporting time: 30 days or less. Simultaneous submissions accepted: yes. Publishes 10% of manuscripts submitted. Payment: varies according to project. Copyrights for author. PMA.

Drama Publishers, Ralph Pine, 260 Fifth Avenue, New York, NY 10001, 212-725-5377; fax 212-725-8506, e-mail dramapub@interport.net. 1967. "Mostly we are a nuts & bolts publishing house and have recently dropped over 150 titles from our backlist. We do quite a lot of co-publishing in the UK with houses like Macmillan, Batsford, etc." avg. press run 3M. Pub'd 8 titles 1998; expects 6 titles 1999, 10 titles 2000. avg. price, cloth: $25; paper: $12.95. Discounts: varies; make inquiry for schedule. 200pp. Reporting time: depends on how busy we are. Payment: usually 10% with advance. Copyrights for author. ABA.

Dramaline Publications, Courtney Marsh, 36851 Palm View Road, Rancho Mirage, CA 92270-2417, 760-770-6076, FAX 760-770-4507; dramaline@aol.com. 1983. Plays. "We publish scene-study books for actors. Monologues and scenes. The original monologues and scenes must be of no longer than a three minute duration, must embrace contemporary points of view, be written in modern language." avg. press run 2M. Pub'd 3 titles 1998; expects 4 titles 1999, 4 titles 2000. 42 titles listed in the *Small Press Record of Books in Print* (28th Edition, 1999-00). avg. price, paper: $8.95. Discounts: 1-99 books 40%, 100-199 43%, 200+ 45%. 64pp; 5½×8½; of. Reporting time: 1 month. Simultaneous submissions accepted: no. Publishes 5% of manuscripts submitted. Payment: 10% of cover price paid yearly. Does not copyright for author.

DRAMATIKA, John A. Pyros, Andrea Pyros, Associate Editor, 429 Hope Street, Tarpon Springs, FL 34689, 727-937-0109. 1968. Art, plays, concrete art. *"Performable pieces only*—must be easily photocopied. No submissions accepted; all works commissioned. Queries accepted." Irregular. price per copy: $5; sample: $5. Back issues: $5. Discounts: none. 25pp; 8×11; †photocopy. Payment: negotiated. Copyrights are negotiated. Ads: none.

DRAMATISTS GUILD NEWSLETTER, Gregory Bossler, 1501 Broadway Suite 701, New York, NY 10036. Articles, photos, interviews, news items. circ. 6.5M. 6/yr. Pub'd 8 issues 1998; expects 6 issues 1999, 6 issues 2000. 16pp; 8½×11; of. Reporting time: 2 months. Payment: none. Copyrighted, reverts to author. Ads: $40 for 40 words 75¢ each addional words. Professional Playwrights, Composers and Lyricists.

DRASTIC LIVES, Timothy Buie, 3721 Baugh Street, Raleigh, NC 27604, 919-981-0380. 1994. Art, photos, cartoons, reviews. circ. 1M. 6/yr. Expects 6 issues 1999, 6 issues 2000. sub. price: $20; per copy: $4; sample: $4. Discounts: 30% off for retailers, 40%+ off for distributors. 30pp; 8½×11; of. Payment: 4 copies. Copyrighted, reverts to author. Pub's reviews: 7 per issue in 1998. §Comics, sex, film, zines (culture), art. Ads: $200/$110/$60 1/4 page, $35 1/8 page.

DREAM INTERNATIONAL QUARTERLY, Chuck Jones, Editor-in-Chief & Publisher, 411 14th Street #H1, Ramona, CA 92065-2769. 1980. Poetry, fiction, articles, art, cartoons, satire, non-fiction. "All prose to above address. All poetry submissions to Senior Poetry Editor Carmen M. Pursifull, 809 W. Maple, Champaign, IL 61820-2810. Length of prose material accepted: 1,000-2,000 words. *Not commonly accepted*: sexually explicit material or use of vulgar or 'four-letter' words. Basic type of subject accepted: anything relating to dreams; dream fragments, fiction, poetry, non-fiction, haiku, etc. Articles on precognition, astral projection, etc. Mss will not be returned unless so requested at time of submission. Also fantasy pieces, fiction, prose and poetry. Checks/money orders and overseas drafts must be made payable to Charles Jones rather than DIQ. Send prose to Editor-in-Chief, Chuck Jones" circ. 65-80. 2-3/yr. Pub'd 2 issues 1998. sub. price: US $50 (domestic rate); per copy: $13 ppd. (Domestic), guidelines $2 for LSASE with 2 1st class stamps; sample: Outside US: $10. Consult US Editor for postage and handling costs. Back issues: $15 each. 140-180pp; 8½×11; †prof. xerox reproductions. Reporting time: 8-10 weeks. Simultaneous submissions accepted: yes. Publishes 40% of manuscripts submitted. Payment: in the form of complimentary copie(s) upon receipt of $3 for s/h. Copyrighted, reverts to author. Ads: $57/$35/$10. Society of Ethical and Professional Publishers of Literature.

DREAM NETWORK JOURNAL, Helen Roberta Ossana, Editor & Publisher, PO Box 1026, Moab, UT 84532-3031, 435-259-5936; dreamkey@lasal.net; http:dreamnetwork.net. 1982. Poetry, articles, art, photos, interviews, reviews, letters. "Articles: 1500-2000 words. Reproducible black and white original art and photos are preferred. We receive articles from some of the finest Dreamworkers in the country, both lay and professional, such as Arnold Mindell, Stanley Krippner, Gayle Delaney, Montague Ullman, Kelly Bulkley, Deborah Jay Hillman, David Feinstein, etc. Contributing artists include Deborah Koff-Chapin, Susan Boulet, Susan St. Thomas, etc. Spiritual, psychology, New Age. Exploration of the meaning of dreams and the evolution of relevant mythologies in our time." circ. 4M. 4/yr. Pub'd 4 issues 1998; expects 4 issues 1999, 4 issues 2000. sub. price: $22 USA; $30 Canada, Mexico, libraries; $38 foreign airmail; per copy: $5.95; sample: $5.95. Back issues: $5.95. Discounts: 50% jobbers, agents, distributors, etc. 52pp; 8½×11. Reporting time: maximum 1-2 months. We accept simultaneous submissions occassionally. Publishes 50-75% of manuscripts submitted. Payment: 10 copies of issue in which their work is published and 1-year subscription. Copyrighted, rights revert to author if requested. Pub's reviews: 20 in 1998. §Books on dreams, mythology, dream education—anything dream or myth related, vidoes, CD's, Cassette tapes. Ads: $700/$400/classified $10/20 words or $35 per year.

DREAM SCENE MAGAZINE, Dan Holzner, 3902 Folsom Street, San Francisco, CA 94110-6138, 415-221-0210. 1993. Art, photos, collages, non-fiction. "Transcriptions/narrations and images of dreams in all their surreal glory." circ. 750. 4/yr. Pub'd 1 issue 1998; expects 4 issues 1999, 4 issues 2000. sub. price: $11; per copy: $3; sample: $3. Back issues: $3. 24pp; 8½×11; †of. Reporting time: coupla weeks. Payment: none, free copy of issue contributors are included in. Not copyrighted. Ads: none.

●**Dream Street Publishing,** Del Kyger, PO Box 19028, Tucson, AZ 85731, 520-733-9695; Fax 520-529-3911. 1998. "Metaphysically oriented material that help us better understand and accept our relationship with God. Childrens stories (fables) that contain insights on living a full, rich, joyful and loving life." avg. press run 5M. Pub'd 1 title 1998; expects 1 title 1999, 3 titles 2000. 1 title listed in the *Small Press Record of Books in Print* (28th Edition, 1999-00). Discounts: 40-55%. of. Simultaneous submissions accepted: no. Payment: varies. Copyrights for author. PMA, RMBPA.

DREAM WHIP, Bill D. Whip, PO Box 53832, Lubbock, TX 79453, 806-794-9263. 1992. Fiction, articles, art, photos, cartoons, music, parts-of-novels, collages, news items, non-fiction. "It's a moody zine. Moody moody moody. It's what late-night clerks at 7-11 read when no one's in the store." circ. 44. 4/yr. Pub'd 1 issue 1998; expects 2 issues 1999, 4 issues 2000. sub. price: $4; per copy: $1. Back issues: $1. Discounts: Will trade, will discount for distributors/wholesalers (@ $.50). 30pp; 5½×4¼; †mi. Reporting time: whenever. Simultaneous submissions accepted: no. Publishes 1% of manuscripts submitted. Payment: the satisfaction of a job well-done. Not copyrighted. Ads: $10/$5.

Dreamboy Books, Richard Weaver, Andrew Gatheridge, PO Box 910133, 12413 Berlin, Germany, 030-2472-5060. 1995. Fiction. avg. press run 500. Pub'd 3 titles 1998; expects 4 titles 1999, 4 titles 2000. 6 titles listed in the *Small Press Record of Books in Print* (28th Edition, 1999-00). avg. price, paper: $12. Discounts: Write for details. 150pp; size A5 (uk); †Computer printed. Reporting time: 3 months. Simultaneous submissions accepted: yes. Publishes 10% of manuscripts submitted. Payment: yes. Copyrights for author.

DREAMS AND NIGHTMARES, David C. Kopaska-Merkel, 1300 Kicker Road, Tuscaloosa, AL 35404, 205-553-2284; e-Mail dragontea@earthlink.net. 1986. Poetry, art, cartoons. "Contributors: Charlee Jacob, Bruce Boston, Robert Frazier, Ann K. Schwader, Keith Daniels, Cathy Buburuz. Generally poems should fit, single-spaced, on 8½ X 11 paper. I print some longer ones. Don't like gory or trite poems, but gore and sex ok if not gratuitous. *Any* format is fine. I also publish prose poems and a small amount of short-short fiction" circ. 250. 3/yr. Pub'd 2 issues 1998; expects 3 issues 1999, 3 issues 2000. 7 titles listed in the *Small Press Record of Books in Print* (28th Edition, 1999-00). sub. price: $12/6 issues inside N. America and $15/6 issues elsewhere.; per copy: $3; sample: $3. Discounts: on a case-by-case basis. 24pp; 5½×8½; photocopied. Reporting time: 2-8 weeks, average 3 weeks. Simultaneous submissions accepted: no. Publishes less than 5% of manuscripts submitted. Payment: $5 per contribution on acceptance plus 2 contributor's copies. Copyrighted, reverts to author. Ads: $10 for 8½ X 11 insert. Science Fiction Poetry Assn.

DREAMS OF DECADENCE: Vampire Poetry and Fiction, DNA Publications, Inc., Angela G. Kessler, PO Box 2988, Radford, VA 24143-2988. 1994. Poetry, fiction. "1,000-5,000 words for fiction; I publish *only* vampire poetry and fiction; I want fresh ideas not rehashes of the same tired old cliches, and 3-dimensional characters not cardboard cutouts!" circ. 1M. 4/yr. Pub'd 1 issue 1998; expects 2 issues 1999, 4 issues 2000. sub. price: $15/4 issues; per copy: $5; sample: $5. 80pp; 5½×8½; of. Reporting time: 2 months. Simultaneous submissions accepted: yes. Publishes 1% of manuscripts submitted. Payment: 1-5¢/per word for original fiction; contributors copy. Copyrighted, reverts to author. Pub's reviews. §Vampires. Ads: $100/$55/$30 1/4 page.

THE DRIFTWOOD REVIEW, Jeff Vande Zande, David Larsen, PO Box 700, Linden, MI 48451, E-mail midrift@aol.com. 1996. Poetry, fiction, art, photos, long-poems. "Publishes current Michigan residents only. Recent contributors: Stephen Dunning, Anne Ohman Youngs, Jack Zucker." circ. 100. 1/yr. Pub'd 1 issue 1998; expects 1 issue 1999, 1 issue 2000. sub. price: $6; per copy: $6; sample: $6. Back issues: $5. 100pp; 6×9. Reporting time: 2-3 months. Simultaneous submissions accepted: no. Publishes 5% of manuscripts submitted. Payment: 1 copy at present. Copyrighted, reverts to author. Pub's reviews: 1 in 1998. §Recent chapbooks by

Michigan poets.

THE DROOD REVIEW OF MYSTERY, J. Huang, Editor & Publisher; B. Thoenen, Managing Editor; J. Jacobson, Managing Editor; H. Francini, Managing Editor, PO Box 50267, Kalamazoo, MI 49005. 1982. Articles, art, cartoons, interviews, criticism, reviews, news items, non-fiction. "Short reviews 50-500 words. Articles 1,500-5,000 words." circ. 1.5M. 6/yr. Pub'd 6 issues 1998; expects 6 issues 1999, 6 issues 2000. sub. price: $14; per copy: $2.50; sample: same. 20pp; 8½×11; of. Reporting time: 2-6 weeks. Simultaneous submissions accepted: no. Payment: none. Copyrighted, reverts to author. Pub's reviews: 150 in 1998. §Mystery & detective fiction. Ads: $225/$112.50.

DROP FORGE, Jade Moon Publications, Sean Winchester, Keil Winchester, 221 S. 3rd Street, Livingston, MT 59047-3003. 1991. Poetry, fiction, articles, cartoons, satire, music, plays, news items, non-fiction. "*DF* is a forum of quality verbal and visual expression still teething. Submissions: I want your trenchant visceral experiments as well as closer knit side-road stuff. I want works you had no choice but to create. I want evidence of humanity. I need proof of expressive compulsion from beyond this well-lit necropolis! How do you deal with your media? Prose and poetry, of course, can be overcome as barriers. Explore! Also print xeroxable art, sometimes color on the cover. If color, please submit color photocopies or photo prints. *Send no originals.* All submissions considered on aesthetic, not appelative basis. Flashy credentials get you nowhere, senor, but please do send bios of interest for the curious: previous/future projects and how they may be obtained. Discouraged: cliche, anal, unicorns, rainbows, comfy fireside cheese and wine MFA drivel, haiku, white boy fluff. Interested in trade ads and other forms of cheap mutual publicity. Everyone please send appropriate SASE! Also: issues of *6 Hz*, printed quite often for two postage stamps—chaos lit. Free w/DF." circ. pretty small right now, but growing. 4-6/yr. Pub'd 2 issues 1998; expects 3-4 issues 1999, 4 issues 2000. sub. price: $10/4 issues; per copy: $2.50/trade (within reason); sample: $2.50. Back issues: cover price (upon availability). Discounts: inquire. 32-40pp; 5½×8½; †of. Reporting time: ASAP—due to nomadic nature, sometimes up to a month or two. Payment: copy; may make token payments or gifts—hope someday to be able to pay. Copyrighted, reverts to author. Pub's reviews: 1-3 per issue in 1998. Ads: $60 1/2 page/$40 1/4 page/$10 2x1"/trade; send sample with ad.

‡**THE DROPLET JOURNAL**, Matthew Lopez, 29 Iron Mine Road, West Stockbridge, MA 01266-9223, 413-232-0052; E-mail droplet@bcn.net. 1995. Poetry, fiction, articles, art, photos, satire, criticism, parts-of-novels, long-poems, collages, concrete art, news items, non-fiction. "Norma West Linder, Michael Hoalihan, Jo J. Adamson, George Carmen. We want poetry that is fresh, new, and exciting. We will consider all topics and style, although we only accept work that has not been previously published. Make us smile, sad, shocked, wonder, dream, laugh, fall in love." circ. 300. 12/yr. Pub'd 2 issues 1998; expects 12 issues 1999, 12 issues 2000. sub. price: $10; per copy: $1; sample: $1. Back issues: $1. Discounts: will trade, and consign issues to retail/distributors. 16pp; 8½×11; †laser printer, xerox. Reporting time: 1 month. We accept simultaneous submissions with notice. Publishes 25% of manuscripts submitted. Payment: copies, fame. Copyrighted, reverts to author. Ads: $120/$60/$30 1/4 page.

Druid Press, Anne George, Jerri Beck, 2724 Shades Crest Road, Birmingham, AL 35216, 205-967-6580. 1982. Poetry, non-fiction. "Our first 2 books are a book of poetry and a linguistic study of Southern Indian tribes" avg. press run 1M. Expects 2 titles 1999. 14 titles listed in the *Small Press Record of Books in Print* (28th Edition, 1999-00). avg. price, paper: $8-$10. Discounts: 20%. 50-100pp; of. Reporting time: 3 weeks. Payment: negotiable. Copyrights for author. Southern Publishers' Group.

Drum, Craig Ellis, 40 Potter Street, Concord, MA 01742. 1995. Poetry, cartoons, music, concrete art. "No unsolicited mss. Queries/proposals welcome with SASE. Read listing carefully before spending time and postage. Available summer 1998: Herschel Silverman's little masterpiece from 1969, *Krishna Poems*, out of print for a quarter century, now in a new edition." avg. press run 1-1M. Expects 2 titles 1999, 6 titles 2000. 5 titles listed in the *Small Press Record of Books in Print* (28th Edition, 1999-00). Discounts: Standard. of,lp, hand, rubberstamped. Reporting time: 2 months. Payment: negotiable. Copyrights for author.

DRUMVOICES REVUE, Eugene B. Redmond, Southern Illinois University, English Dept., Box 1431, Edwardsville, IL 62026-1431, 618-650-2060; Fax 618-650-3509. 1990. Poetry, fiction, articles, art, photos, interviews, criticism, reviews, letters, non-fiction. "Prefer poems of no more than 3 pages. Multicultural-gender inclusive. Recent contributors: Maya Angelou, Gwendolyn Brooks, John Knoepfle, Carlos Cumpian, Rohan B. Preston, Derek Walcott, Amiri Baraka, Allison Funk, and Janice Mirikitani." circ. 1.5M. 1-2/yr. Pub'd 1-2 issues 1998; expects 2 issues 1999, 2 issues 2000. sub. price: $10; per copy: $10; sample: $5. Discounts: 40%. 132pp; 6×9; of. Reporting time: seasonal. Simultaneous submissions accepted: yes. Publishes 50% of manuscripts submitted. Payment: 2 copies. Copyrighted, reverts to author. Pub's reviews. §Anthologies, clusters of chapbooks or volumes of poetry, novels. Ads: $200/$100/others negotiable. AAAP.

Dry Bones Press (see also THE COMPLEAT NURSE), J. Rankin, PO Box 640345, San Francisco, CA 94164, 415-292-7371; FAX 415-252-7371; website http://www.drybones.com/. 1992. Poetry, fiction, non-fiction. "Nursing and health care, e.g., Literature of Patient and Response Series, a nursing series studying texts written by patients" Pub'd 5 titles 1998; expects 6 titles 1999. 27 titles listed in the *Small Press Record of Books in Print* (28th Edition, 1999-00). avg. price, paper: $14.95; other: $29.95. Discounts: Universal schedule, as of 1-1-94. 100+pp; 8½×5½; of. Reporting time: ASAP, especially with SASE. Simultaneous submissions accepted: yes. Publishes a significant % of manuscripts submitted. Payment: individual arrangement. Copyrights for author. PMA.

DRY CRIK REVIEW, John C. Dofflemyer, PO Box 44320, Lemon Cove, CA 93244, 209-597-2512; fax 209-597-2103. 1990. Poetry, art, cartoons, reviews, parts-of-novels. "Less than 4,000 words. Recent contributors include Charles Potts, Paul Zarzyski, Rod McQueary, Sue Wallis, Kell Robertson. Biases: range livestock culture; prefer shorter works, 44 lines." circ. 400. 4/yr. Pub'd 1 issue 1998. sub. price: $20; per copy: $7 + $1.25 postage; sample: $7 - some more. Back issues: limited 4/$40. Discounts: none. 72pp; 5½×8½; of. Reporting time: 30-60 days. Simultaneous submissions accepted: yes. Publishes 10% of manuscripts submitted. Payment: 2 copies. Copyrighted, reverts to author. Pub's reviews: 10 in 1998. §Must relate to rural culture. Ads: none.

THE DUCKBURG TIMES, Dana Gabbard, Editor, 3010 Wilshire Blvd., #362, Los Angeles, CA 90010-1146, 213-388-2364. 1977. Articles, art, photos, cartoons, interviews, criticism, reviews, letters, news items, non-fiction. "Our sole criterion for the acceptance of material is that it in some way relate to the works of Walt Disney and associates. We run quite a lot on famed comic book artist Carl Barks, but are also interested in material on other Disney artists, the studio, Disney animation, the theme parks, etc. If in doubt, contact us first. Especially on the lookout for material from overseas fans. We have special guidelines to follow when running Disney copyrighted art available upon request. Always open to the unusual and critical." circ. 1.4M. 1/yr. Pub'd 1 issue 1998; expects 1 issue 2000. sub. price: $12; per copy: inquire; sample: $3. Back issues: inquire. 28pp; 8½×11; of. Reporting time: ASAP. Payment: copy of issue material appears in. Copyrighted, rights revert to author upon written request. Pub's reviews: 0 in 1998. §Walt Disney, animation, Carl Barks, comics, theme parks, and related. classified free to subscriber if under 50 words, Disney-related.

Duckworth Press, Ann Phillips, Senior Editor; Larry K. Thompson, Publisher, 3005 66th Street, Lubbock, TX 79413-5707, 806-799-3706. 1995. Fiction, non-fiction. "Currently we accept only material from Texas authors who reside in Texas, New Mexico, and Oklahoma. We like stories about family legends, regional-county histories, novels-regionally oriented, romances and historical fiction. No poetry. Authors should first submit a letter of inquiry. ALL correspondance MUST contain SASE. Recent authors published are Catherine Troxell Gonzalez and John Wesley Curry. Prefer less than 500 ms. pages." avg. press run 200-500. Pub'd 1 title 1998; expects 4 titles 1999, 12 titles 2000. avg. price, cloth: $15-24; paper: $6-18. Discounts: 1 STOP copy 20%, 2-4 30%, 5-24 40%, 25 and up 50%. We pay postage and handling on prepaid orders. All orders must be prepaid. All unblemished books may be returned up to 6 months. Shipments must be returned prepaid. 200pp; 5½×8½; †of. Reporting time: 2 weeks. We accept simultaneous submissions if we are told in query letter. Publishes 20% of manuscripts submitted. Payment: 30% initially - 10% later. $50.00 advance and 5 copies. Copyrights for author.

Duende Press, Larry Goodell, Box 571, Placitas, NM 87043, 505-867-5877. 1964. Poetry. avg. press run 500. 4 titles listed in the *Small Press Record of Books in Print* (28th Edition, 1999-00). avg. price, paper: $5 up. Discounts: 40% plus mailing. of.

Dufour Editions Inc., Christopher May, President & Publisher; Thomas Lavoie, Associate Publisher & Marketing Director, PO Box 7, Chester Springs, PA 19425-0007, 610-458-5005; FAX 610-458-7103. 1949. Poetry, fiction, articles, criticism, reviews, long-poems, plays, non-fiction. "Dufour Editions publishes, co-publishes, and exclusively distributes selected titles of British or Irish origin. We also publish some works of American origin." avg. press run 500-5M. Pub'd 10 titles 1998; expects 15 titles 1999. 14 titles listed in the *Small Press Record of Books in Print* (28th Edition, 1999-00). avg. price, cloth: $35; paper: $14.95. Discounts: trade 1-4 20%, 5-14 40%, 15-24 41%, 25-49 42%, 50-99 43%, 100+ 44%; short discounted titles: 20% any quantity. SCOP & STOP 30%; libraries 10%. Pages vary; size varies; of. Reporting time: 1-6 months. Publishes 1% of manuscripts submitted. Payment: negotiated. Copyrights for author.

DUKE MATHEMATICAL JOURNAL, Duke University Press, Morris Weisfeld, Editor, Box 90660, Duke University, Durham, NC 27708-0660. 1935. "Published by Duke University Press since its inception in 1935, the *Duke Mathematical Journal* is one of the world's leading mathematical journals. Each year the journal presents original research in all areas of mathematics and its applications, with particular emphasis on papers significantly advancing the state of the science." circ. 1.4M. 15/yr. Pub'd 15 issues 1998; expects 15 issues 1999, 15 issues 2000. sub. price: $885 institutions, $442 individuals or $221 if institution already subscribes, additional $45 foreign. Ads: $165 full page, $135 for nonprofit publisher.

Duke University Press (see also AMERICAN LITERATURE; AMERICAN LITERATURE SECTION; BOUNDARY 2: An International Journal of Literature and Culture; DUKE MATHEMATICAL

163

JOURNAL; ENVIRONMENTAL HISTORY; ETHNOHISTORY: The Official Journal of the American Society for Ethnohistory; FRENCH HISTORICAL STUDIES; HISPANIC AMERICAN HISTORICAL REVIEW; HISTORY OF POLITICAL ECONOMY; INTERNATIONAL MATHEMATICS RESEARCH NOTICES; JOURNAL OF HEALTH POLITICS, POLICY AND LAW; JOURNAL OF MEDIEVAL AND EARLY MODERN STUDIES; JOURNAL OF PERSONALITY; LESBIAN AND GAY STUDIES NEWSLETTER; MEDITERRANEAN QUARTERLY: A Journal of Global Issues; MODERN LANGUAGE QUARTERLY: A Journal of Literary History; THE OPERA QUARTERLY; POETICS TODAY: International Journal for Theory and Analysis of Literature and Communication; POSITIONS: East Asia Cultures Critique; THE SOUTH ATLANTIC QUARTERLY; SOCIAL SCIENCE HISTORY; SOCIAL TEXT; SOCIALIST REVIEW; TRANSITION), Box 90660, Durham, NC 27708-0660, 919-687-3600; Fax 919-688-4574. "Street address: 905 W. Main Street, Durham, NC 27701."

Dumont Press, Jefferson P. Selth, 8710 Belford Avenue #B109, Los Angeles, CA 90045-4568. 1989. avg. press run 750. Pub'd 1 title 1998. 8 titles listed in the *Small Press Record of Books in Print* (28th Edition, 1999-00). avg. price, paper: $19. Discounts: 1-4 copies 20%, 5+ copies 40% (bookstores). 250pp; 8½×5½. Publishes 0% of manuscripts submitted. Copyrights for author.

Dunamis House, Bette Filley, 19801 SE 123rd Street, Issaquah, WA 98027, 206-255-5274; FAX 206-277-8780. 1991. Non-fiction. "Additional address: PO Box 321, Issaquah, WA 98027. Current specialty: Mountaineering (specifically Mount Rainier) books, Northwest guide books." avg. press run 3.5M. Pub'd 1 title 1998; expects 1 title 1999, 1-2 titles 2000. 2 titles listed in the *Small Press Record of Books in Print* (28th Edition, 1999-00). avg. price, cloth: $26.95; paper: $17.95. Discounts: 40% trade, 55% distributors. 216pp; 5½×8½; of, lp. Reporting time: 6 weeks. We accept simultaneous submissions if they're Mt. Rainier books. Payment: varies. Copyrights for author. Book Publishers Northwest, PMA, Northwest Outdoor Writers Association.

THE DUPLEX PLANET, David B. Greenberger, PO Box 1230, Saratoga Springs, NY 12866, 518-587-5356. 1979. Interviews. "ISSN# 0882-2549" circ. 600+. 10/yr. Pub'd 10 issues 1998; expects 10 issues 1999, 10 issues 2000. 25 titles listed in the *Small Press Record of Books in Print* (28th Edition, 1999-00). sub. price: $12/6 issues, $25/15 issues; per copy: $2.50; sample: $3. Back issues: 10 or more issues - $2.00 each; less than 10 - $2.50 each. Discounts: on request. 16pp; 5½×8½; of. Copyrighted.

‡**THE DURHAM UNIVERSITY JOURNAL,** Peter Lewis, School of English/University of Durham, Elvet Riverside, New Elvet, Durham, DH1 3JT, England, 091-374 2000 Ext. 2744. 1876. Articles, criticism, reviews. "Mss. and books for review should be sent to the editor. All correspondence on other matters relating to the journal should be sent to the Secretary, Durham University Journal, School of English, Elvet Riverside, New Elvet, Durham DH1 3JT, England. Subscriptions should be made payable to University of Durham. Articles are about 6,000 words long on average. Slightly longer or shorter articles are acceptable. The articles are of the usual academic standard for a learned journal. Recent contributors: J.W. Blench, Isobel Murray, Brocard Sewell." circ. 500. 2/yr. Pub'd 2 issues 1998; expects 2 issues 1999, 2 issues 2000. sub. price: U.K. £22, overseas £25, £18, (£16 by post) to members of staff and students of the Univ of Durham and Newcastle-upon-Tyne; per copy: £9; sample: £9. Back issues: variable, according to price on cover plus postage. Discounts: none. 150pp; 17×24.5cm; of. Reporting time: 6 weeks. Payment: none. Copyrighted, rights revert to author according to current British Law. Pub's reviews: 66 in 1998. §Art, literature, history, philosophy, classical studies, theology, archaeology, economics, film and television. Ads: £45/£28 (15% discount if ad appears in both numbers of a volume).

DUST (From the Ego Trip), Camel Press, James Hedges, Editor, Box 212, Needmore, PA 17238, 717-573-4526. 1984. Poetry, fiction, articles, non-fiction. "Contributions of good literary quality are welcome; manuscripts should be between 1M and 2.5M words in length." circ. 700. Irregular. Expects 2 issues 1999, 2 issues 2000. sub. price: $1-3 per issue on standing order; per copy: $1-3; sample: $1. Discounts: on request. 20pp; 4¼×5¾; †lp. Reporting time: 2 weeks. Simultaneous submissions accepted: yes. Publishes 5% of manuscripts submitted. Payment: 50 free copies. Copyrighted, rights revert to author if requested. No ads. Amalgamated Printers Assn. (APA), National Amateur Press Assn. (NAPA).

Dustbooks (see also THE SMALL PRESS REVIEW/SMALL MAGAZINE REVIEW), Len Fulton, PO Box 100, Paradise, CA 95967-0100, 530-877-6110, 1-800-477-6110, fax: 530-877-0222, email(s): dustbooks@telis.org; len@dustbooks.com; web address:http://www.dustbooks.com. 1963. "We have a small general trade list: poetry, novels, anthologies, non-fiction prose, how-to, etc. But it should be remembered that our real expertise & commitment is small press-mag info. On January 1st of every year we face a full year of publishing without looking at one new manuscript. Several years ago we partnered with the Associated Writing Programs (AWP), now at George Mason University in Fairfax, Virginia, to publish the *Official AWP Guide To Writing Programs*. The latest edition is the ninth. A new edition is published approximately every two years (the 9th Edition was published in January 1999). Otherwise, we do four annuals: this Directory you're holding (now in its Thirty-fifth annual edition) which takes 5 months from start to finish; its companion volume, the *Directory of Small Magazine/Press Editors and Publishers*, and the *Small Press Record of Books in Print* (in CD-ROM format only). In 1999 we published the Fifteenth edition of *Directory of Poetry Publishers* as a supplement to these information volumes. This directoy, by the way, contains our annual Sweepstakes — a listing of the dozen or so poets most popular with editors. We do a monthly, the *Small Press Review/Small Magazine Review* (see separate listing). We've done a nice string of general trade books, but our capacity is severely modified by our mainstay titles above. NOTES: The *International Directory* is distributed to bookstores by Pushcart Press/W.W. Norton (NYC), and in Europe by Gazelle Distribution (London)." avg. press run 1M-2M. Pub'd 5 titles 1998; expects 5 titles 1999, 5 titles 2000. 25 titles listed in the *Small Press Record of Books in Print* (28th Edition, 1999-00). avg. price, cloth: $55.00; paper: $22.95, $23.95, $34.95; other: $55 (CD-ROM). Discounts: 2-10 25%, 11-25 40%, 26+ 50% (bookstores), distributors by arrangement, jobbers 20-25%. Returns only after six months but before one year; returns are for credit ONLY. 300-1000pp; 6x9, 8½x11; of. Reporting time: 3-6 months. Simultaneous submissions accepted: yes. Publishes 1% of manuscripts submitted. Payment: royalty (15%). Copyrights for author. Small Press Center, PMA.

Duval-Bibb Publishing Company, Reese Coppage, President, PO Box 24168, Tampa, FL 33623-4168, 813-281-0091. 2 titles listed in the *Small Press Record of Books in Print* (28th Edition, 1999-00). Discounts: 1-2 copies 20% and $2.00 postage, 3+ copies 40% no postage.

DWAN, Donny Smith, Box 411, Swarthmore, PA 19081, e-mail dsmith3@swarthmore.edu. 1993. Poetry, interviews, reviews, parts-of-novels, long-poems, non-fiction. "We want queer writing, accept material in Spanish or English. Recent contributors: Janell Moon, Alicia Gallegos, Fabian Iriarte." circ. 1M. irregular. Pub'd 4 issues 1998; expects 3 issues 1999, 3 issues 2000. price per copy: $2; sample: $2. Discounts: free to prisoners. 38pp; 5½x8½; †photocopy. Reporting time: 1-12 weeks. Simultaneous submissions accepted: no. Publishes 10% of manuscripts submitted. Payment: copies. Copyrighted, reverts to author. Pub's reviews: 100 in 1998. §Queer history, feminism, sex.

DWELLING PORTABLY, Light Living Library, Po Box 190—DB, Philomath, OR 97370. 1980. Articles, reviews, letters. "Helpful suggestions about portable dwelling, long comfortable camping, low-cost light-weight living. How to save money, energy, weight, space, land, live and travel more imaginatively. Simultaneous, photocopy submission recommended." circ. 2M. 2/yr. Pub'd 2 issues 1998; expects 2 issues 1999, 2 issues 2000. 1 title listed in the *Small Press Record of Books in Print* (28th Edition, 1999-00). sub. price: $2; per copy: $1. 12pp; 5½x8½; of. Publishes 75% of manuscripts submitted. Payment: subscriptions or ads. Pub's reviews: 4 in 1998. Ads: 25¢ per word.

Dynamic Publishing, 148 San Remo Road, Carmel, CA 93923, 408-624-5534. 1 title listed in the *Small Press Record of Books in Print* (28th Edition, 1999-00).

E

E.M. Press, Inc., Beth Milier, PO Box 4057, Manassas, VA 22110-0706, 703-439-0304. 1991. Fiction, non-fiction. "We are currently focusing on children's books and non-fiction works by local authors (Virgina, Maryland, D.C.). We offer traditional contracts." avg. press run 1M. Pub'd 8 titles 1998; expects 10 titles 1999, 15 titles 2000. 4 titles listed in the *Small Press Record of Books in Print* (28th Edition, 1999-00). avg. price, cloth: $20; paper: $20. Discounts: handled on an individual basis. 200pp; 5½x8½; lp. Reporting time: 12 weeks. Simultaneous submissions accepted: yes. Payment: handled on an individual basis. Copyrights for author. PMA, PAS.

Eagle Publishing, PO Box 403, Red Bluff, CA 96080, 530-527-3640. 1989. Fiction, non-fiction. "Eagle Publishing began operation in August, 1989. Shortly thereafter released its first book regarding assault weapons permits. Its first major work, *Dead Man Walking*, made a January, 1991 release. In July 1993 Eagle Publishing became a subsidiary of Complete Office & Secretarial Service" avg. press run 1-5M. Pub'd 2 titles 1998; expects 3 titles 1999, 3 titles 2000. 3 titles listed in the *Small Press Record of Books in Print* (28th Edition, 1999-00). avg. price, cloth: $25; paper: $9.95. Discounts: wholesalers 2-4 20%, 5-10 30%, 11+ 40%. 200-300pp; 5½x8½. Reporting time: 30-60 days. Payment: varies. Copyrights for author. MSPA, PMA.

Eagle Publishing Company, James Gray, 7283 Kolb Place, Dublin, CA 94568, 415-828-1350. 1980. Non-fiction. avg. press run 1.1M. Pub'd 1 title 1998; expects 1 title 2000. 1 title listed in the *Small Press Record of Books in Print* (28th Edition, 1999-00). avg. price, cloth: $20. Discounts: 50%. 350pp; of. Reporting time: 6 months. Payment: 5% of list price. Copyrights for author.

Eagle's View Publishing, Monte Smith, Publisher-Editor; Denise Knight, Editor, 6756 North Fork Road, Liberty, UT 84310, 801-393-4555 (orders); editorial phone 801-745-0903. 1982. Non-fiction. avg. press run 10M. Pub'd 4 titles 1998; expects 6 titles 1999, 6 titles 2000. 41 titles listed in the *Small Press Record of Books in Print* (28th Edition, 1999-00). avg. price, cloth: $15.95 All currently out of print; paper: $9.95. Discounts: standard for trade and jobber. 80pp; size varies; of. Reporting time: 12 months. Simultaneous submissions accepted: yes. Publishes 10% of manuscripts submitted. Payment: varies. Copyrights for author. RMBPA, ABA, PMA.

EAP DIGEST, George Watkins, Performance Resource Press, Inc., 1270 Rankin Drive, Suite F, Troy, MI 48083-2843, 810-588-7733; fax 810-588-6633. 1979. Articles, art, photos, cartoons, interviews, news items. circ. 10M. 6/yr. Pub'd 6 issues 1998; expects 6 issues 1999, 6 issues 2000. 13 titles listed in the *Small Press Record of Books in Print* (28th Edition, 1999-00). sub. price: $36; per copy: $6. Back issues: $6. 56pp; 8½×11; of, web. Reporting time: 10 days. Payment: one-year subscription. Copyrighted, does not revert to author. Pub's reviews: 67 in 1998. §Alcohol and drug—Employee Assistance Programs. Ads: $1200/$700/$2 per word.

THE EAR, Marie Conners, Managing Editor, Irvine Valley Coll., School of Humanities, 5500 Irvine Center Drive, Irvine, CA 92620, 714-541-5341. 1983. Poetry, fiction, articles, art, photos, interviews, criticism, reviews, parts-of-novels, non-fiction. *"The Ear* is primarily a journal of Orange County writers and artists. We have published work from writers outside the county, but our purpose is to provide a forum for local work. Work must be submitted in duplicate; the writer's name should not appear on the work, but should be attached on a cover letter with address, phone number, and brief bio" circ. 2.5M. 1/yr. Pub'd 1 issue 1998; expects 1 issue 1999, 1 issue 2000. 150pp; 6×9; of. Reporting time: 1-5 months. Publishes 5-15% of manuscripts submitted. Payment: copies only. Copyrighted, reverts to author. Pub's reviews: 0 in 1998. §Contemporary poetry and fiction, art, film.

Earth Magic Productions, Inc., Robin Bernardi, Marion Weinstein, PO Box 50668, Eugene, OR 97405, 541-344-6394; fax 541-485-8773; E-mail support@earthmagic. 1989. Non-fiction. "At this time, only publishing work by Marion Weinstein. Not accepting submissions." avg. press run 5M. Pub'd 1 title 1998; expects 5 titles 1999, 1 title 2000. 3 titles listed in the *Small Press Record of Books in Print* (28th Edition, 1999-00). avg. price, paper: $13. Discounts: 1 copy 20% plus $1.75 for shipping + 4.00 for priority or ups ground. 175pp; 5×8; of.

Earth Star Publications (see also THE STAR BEACON), Ann Ulrich, PO Box 117, Paonia, CO 81428, 970-527-3257. 1987. Fiction, non-fiction. "Open to any subject matter and length. Recent titles have included metaphysical and New Age subjects. In 1987 published *Thought* by Julian Joyce (collection of metaphysical essays dealing with every aspect of life); in 1988 published *Intimate Abduction,* a sci-fi/romance novel by Ann Carol Ulrich, covering aspects of true-to-life UFO abduction experiences." avg. press run 500. Pub'd 2 titles 1998; expects 5 titles 1999, 8 titles 2000. 17 titles listed in the *Small Press Record of Books in Print* (28th Edition, 1999-00). avg. price, paper: $11.95. 180pp; 5½×8½; of. Reporting time: 6 weeks. Payment: 100% to author; publisher collects one-time fee; open to other arrangements. Copyrights for author.

Earth-Love Publishing House LTD, R. R. Jackson, Laodeciae Augustine, Senior Editor, 3440 Youngfield Street, Suite 353, Wheatridge, CO 80033, 303-233-9660. 1990. Fiction, non-fiction. "Interested in minerals/mineralogical themes. Publishes book an average of 8 months after acceptance." avg. press run 15M. Pub'd 1 title 1998; expects 2 titles 1999, 1 title 2000. 5 titles listed in the *Small Press Record of Books in Print* (28th Edition, 1999-00). avg. price, paper: $18.95. Discounts: Available only through distributors. 500+pp; 6×9; of. Reporting time: 3-4 months. Simultaneous submissions accepted: yes. Payment: 10% royalty on wholesale sales. Does not copyright for author. NABE (North American Bookdealers Exchange).

EARTH'S DAUGHTERS: Feminist Arts Periodical, Kastle Brill, Co-Editor; Joan Ford, Co-Editor; Bonnie Johnson, Co-Editor; Robin Willoughby, Co-Editor, PO Box 41, Central Park Station, Buffalo, NY 14215-0041, 716-627-9825. 1971. Poetry, fiction, art, photos, satire, parts-of-novels, long-poems, collages, plays. "We are a feminist arts periodical." circ. 1M. 2-4/yr. Pub'd 3 issues 1998; expects 3 issues 1999, 3 issues 2000. sub. price: $18/3 issues, instit. $22/3 issues; per copy: varies; sample: $5. Back issues: available upon inquiry. Discounts: trade 30-35%; bulk 35%; jobber-straight rates. 50pp; size varies; of. Reporting time: 5-6 weeks except for special issues. Simultaneous submissions accepted if notified immediately when published elsewhere. Publishes 5% of manuscripts submitted. Payment: 2 issues complimentary and reduced prices on further copies. Copyrighted, reverts to author. §Work by women or in feminist themes. Not presently accepting ads. CLMP, NYSSPA, Arts Council, Inc.

Easel Publishing Corporation, Rob Medved, Frank Cannella, Ted Yeager, 488 North Pine Street, Burlington, WI 53105, 414-763-3690. "We publish mass market computer software training guides" avg. press run 20M. Pub'd 1 title 1998; expects 5 titles 1999, 10 titles 2000. 6 titles listed in the *Small Press Record of Books in Print* (28th Edition, 1999-00). avg. price, paper: $16.99. 235pp; 7×9; web.

EAST EUROPEAN POLITICS & SOCIETIES, University of California Press, Jan T. Gross, John Welch,

Editorial Assistant, University of California Press, 2120 Berkeley Way, Berkeley, CA 94720, 510-643-7154. 1987. Articles, reviews. "Editorial address: Center for European Studies, 53 Washington Square South, 4th Floor, New York, NY 10012." circ. 1.2M. 3/yr. Pub'd 3 issues 1998; expects 3 issues 1999, 3 issues 2000. sub. price: $36 indiv., $75 instit., $28 students ($5 foreign postage); per copy: $13 indiv., $28 instit., $13 students; sample: free. Back issues: same as single copy price. Discounts: foreign subs. agent 10%, one-time orders 10+ 30%, standing orders (bookstores): 1-99 40%, 100+ 50%. 140pp; 6×9; of. Copyrighted, does not revert to author. Pub's reviews. Ads: $275/$200.

EAST EUROPEAN QUARTERLY, Stephen Fischer-Galati, Box 29 Regent Hall, University of Colorado, Boulder, CO 80309, 303-492-6683. 1967. Articles. "Articles ranging from 8 to 48 printed pages; reviews. All articles dealing with Eastern European problems in historical perspective. Contributors from US and foreign academic institutions." circ. 1M. 4/yr. Pub'd 4 issues 1998; expects 4 issues 1999, 4 issues 2000. sub. price: $15, $20 institutions; per copy: $5; sample: free. Back issues: same as regular rates. Discounts: agencies 12.5%. 128pp; 5½×8½; of. Reporting time: 6-8 weeks. Simultaneous submissions accepted: no. Publishes 70% of manuscripts submitted. Payment: none. Not copyrighted. Pub's reviews: 32 in 1998. §East European history, civilization, economics, society, politics. Ads: $100/$60.

EASTGATE QUARTERLY REVIEW OF HYPERTEXT, Eastgate Systems Inc., Diane Greco, 134 Main Street, Watertown, MA 02172, 617-924-9044; Fax 617-924-9051; info@eastgate.com. Poetry, fiction, articles, art, photos, interviews, satire, criticism, parts-of-novels, long-poems, collages, non-fiction. "Electronic submissions only; send disks, not paper. Works should be in some way 'hypertextual' (loosely construed). Recent contributors include Kathryn Cramer, Robert Kendall, Edward Falco, and Judith Kerman." sub. price: $49.95; per copy: $19.95. Discounts: site licenses available, call for details. Reporting time: 1-3 months. Simultaneous submissions accepted: yes. Copyrighted, reverts to author.

Eastgate Systems Inc. (see also EASTGATE QUARTERLY REVIEW OF HYPERTEXT), Diane Greco, 134 Main Street, Watertown, MA 02172, 617-924-9044; Fax 617-924-9051; info@eastgate.com. Poetry, fiction, articles, art, photos, satire, criticism, long-poems, non-fiction. "Electronic submissions only. Send disks *not* paper. Works should be in some way 'hypertextual' (loosely construed). Please visit our website (www.eastgate.com) or view our catalogue before submitting; familiarity with our publications will give a good sense of what we're looking for." Pub'd 8 titles 1998; expects 8-10 titles 1999. avg. price, other: $19.95 fiction, $49.95 nonfiction. Discounts: call for details. Reporting time: 3-6 months, longer submissions require more time. Simultaneous submissions accepted: yes.

Eat Your Hair, Shannon D. Harle, Publisher, Shannon D. Harle, PO Box 2224, Asheville, NC 28802. 1997. Cartoons, satire. "Subscription includes all the other zines I do=Eat your Hair and T.V. Heads and also Rotten Pepper." circ. 100-150. 2 or 3. Pub'd 2 issues 1998; expects 2 issues 1999, 3 issues 2000. sub. price: $10; per copy: $2; sample: $2. Back issues: $1 + 2 stamps. 20pp; 5½×8½; †mi. Reporting time: 1 month. Simultaneous submissions accepted: no. Payment: no. Copyrighted, reverts to author. §no.

Eau Gallie Publishing, Inc., John Steinberg, Editor; Allandra Smith, Publisher, PO Box 360817, Melbourne, FL 32936, 888-310-1530; 407-259-1122; fax 407-255-7586; E-mail mtravcler@eaugallie.com. 1996. Fiction, non-fiction. "Fiction - 85,000-100,000 words. Serious non-fiction primarily concerned with human life and how it fits into the total scheme of things; i.e. the environment, the world, the universe, and, perhaps most importantly, how humans are able to develop themselves so as to realize their full potential." avg. press run 5M. Pub'd 1 title 1998; expects 2 titles 1999, 3 titles 2000. 1 title listed in the *Small Press Record of Books in Print* (28th Edition, 1999-00). avg. price, cloth: $22; paper: $12. Discounts: trade, etc. write for schedule. 275pp; 6×9; of. Reporting time: 4 months. Simultaneous submissions accepted: no. Publishes .01% of manuscripts submitted. Payment: varies, write before sending. Copyrights for author. PMA, SPAN.

EBB AND FLOW, Blue Rock Publishing, Pamela Sheffield, PO Box 5246, Niceville, FL 32578, 610-658-0744; e-mail bluerock@home.com. 1997. Articles, non-fiction, reviews, letters. "We look for thought-provoking and creative non-fiction articles." circ. 800. 4/yr. Expects 4 issues 1999, 4 issues 2000. sub. price: $8; per copy: $2; sample: free. Back issues: $2. Discounts: 50% to retailers. 22pp; 5×8. Reporting time: 90 days. Simultaneous submissions accepted: no. Publishes 50% of manuscripts submitted. Payment: 3 copies and a one year subscription. Copyrighted, reverts to author. Pub's reviews: 6 in 1998. §Consciousness studies, pre-historic people, alternative realities, animal rights. Ads: varies.

Eborn Books (see also THE DEFENDER - RUSH UTAH'S NEWSLETTER), Bret Eborn, Cynthia Eborn, Box 559, Roy, UT 84067. 1988. Pub'd 10 titles 1998; expects 10 titles 1999, 10 titles 2000. 8 titles listed in the *Small Press Record of Books in Print* (28th Edition, 1999-00). 20pp. LDS Booksellers Association.

The Ecco Press, Daniel Halpern, Editor-in-Chief; Heather Winterer, Assistant Editor; William Crager, Publicity; Vincent Janoski, Production Manager; Christina Thompson, Administrator, 100 West Broad Street, Hopewell, NJ 08525-1919, 212-645-2214. 1971. Poetry, fiction, criticism, non-fiction. avg. press run 4M. Pub'd 25 titles 1998; expects 25 titles 1999, 25 titles 2000. 204 titles listed in the *Small Press Record of Books in Print*

(28th Edition, 1999-00). avg. price, cloth: $14.95; paper: $9.95. Distributed by Norton - their discount schedule. Catalogue Sales—50-55% discount through Ecco Press. Pages vary; size varies; of. Reporting time: 8-12 weeks. Payment: advance and royalties. Copyrights for author.

ECHOS DU MONDE CLASSIQUE/CLASSICAL VIEWS, University of Calgary Press, M. Joyal, Editor; J. Butrica, Editor; N. Kennell, Editor, University of Calgary Press, Univ. of Calgary, 2500 University Dr. N.W., Calgary, Alberta T2N 1N4, Canada, 403-220-7578, fax 403-282-0085, e-mail 470533@ucdasvm1.admin.ucalgary.ca. 1957. Articles, photos, reviews. "Reports on activities of Canadian classical archaeologists and articles on archaeological subjects, as well as articles and book reviews on classical history and literature." circ. 750. 3/yr. Pub'd 3 issues 1998; expects 3 issues 1999, 3 issues 2000. sub. price: Instit. $35 + GST Canada, $35US outside Canada; indiv. $20 + GST Canada, $20 US outside Canada; per copy: $7 + GST. Back issues: Vol. 26-28 issues are $5 each and $15 per volume. Vol. 29 to present cost $7 each, $18/volume. 160pp; 6×9; of. Reporting time: 6 weeks. Copyrighted, does not revert to author. Pub's reviews: 27 in 1998. §Classical studies. write for information. BPAA, ACUP, CALJ.

Eckankar, Attn: John Kulick, PO Box 27300, Minneapolis, MN 55427-0300, 612-474-0700, fax 612-474-1127. 1965. Non-fiction. Pub'd 3-5 titles 1998; expects 3-5 titles 1999, 3-5 titles 2000. 36 titles listed in the *Small Press Record of Books in Print* (28th Edition, 1999-00). avg. price, paper: $11-$14. 6×9, 5½×8½.

ECLIPSE, Kiirenza Lockhorn, GENERAL DELIVERY, Brownsville, MD 21715-9999, E-mail Kiirenza@aol.com. 1992. Poetry, fiction, articles, art, photos, cartoons, reviews, letters, long-poems, non-fiction. "Up to 5,000 words accepted for stories and poems. Non-fiction and articles must have relevance to horror, fantasy or science fiction. Recent contributors: Wayne Edwards, David G. Rogers, Robert Collins, Nicole Blackwell, Donna T. Burgess, John Grey, Ryan G. Van Cleave, Charlee Jacob, John Barrick, Ricky Krzysztofik." circ. 200. 4/yr. Pub'd 4 issues 1998; expects 4 issues 1999, 4 issues 2000. sub. price: $15; per copy: $4; sample: $5. Back issues: $5 each (ppd). 52pp; 8½×11; of. Reporting time: 4 months. Simultaneous submissions accepted: no. Publishes 25% of manuscripts submitted. Payment: 1 copy. Not copyrighted. Pub's reviews: 7 in 1998. §Horror, science fiction, fantasy. Ads: $12/$9/ad trades accepted too.

ECOLOGY LAW QUARTERLY, University of California Press, Univ. of California at Berkeley Students of Boalt Hall School of Law, University of California Press, 2120 Berkeley Way, Berkeley, CA 94720, 510-643-7154. 1970. Articles, reviews, non-fiction. "Editorial address: 493 Simon Hall, Univ. of CA, Berkeley, CA 94703. Copyrighted by Ecology Law Quarterly." circ. 1.4M. 4/yr. Pub'd 4 issues 1998; expects 4 issues 1999, 4 issues 2000. sub. price: $30 indiv., $50 instit., $22 students (+ $6 foreign postage); per copy: $8 indiv., $14 instit., $6 students (+ $6 foreign postage); sample: free. Back issues: $8 indiv., $13.50 instit.; $5.50 students (+ $6 foreign postage). Discounts: foreign subs. agent 10%, one-time order 10+ 30%, standing orders (bookstores): 1-99 40%, 100+ 50%. 200pp; 6¾×10; of. Reporting time: 1-2 months. Payment: none. Copyrighted, does not revert to author. Pub's reviews: 6 in 1998. Ads: $275/$200.

ECONOMIC AFFAIRS, Professor Colin Robinson, Editor, 2 Lord North Street, London SW1P 3LB, United Kingdom. 1980. Non-fiction. "Articles examine role of markets and state, developments in economic theory and political science. Emphasis on market as disseminator of information among participants in market process; price; government failure. Most papers are commissioned." circ. 2.5M. 4/yr. Pub'd 4 issues 1998; expects 4 issues 1999, 4 issues 2000. sub. price: $37 individuals; per copy: $11 individuals; sample: free. Discounts: details from Blackwell Publishers, 108 Cowley Road, Oxford, OX4 1JF. 64pp; size A4; of. Reporting time: 3-4 weeks or less. Simultaneous submissions accepted: no. Publishes 40% of manuscripts submitted. Payment: none. Copyrighted, rights revert to author if so desired. Pub's reviews: 29 in 1998. §Economics, government policy, etc. Anything with an economic aspect. Ads: details from Blackwell Publishers.

Ecopress, Christopher Beatty, 1029 NE Kirsten Place, Corvallis, OR 97330-6823, 541-758-7545. 1993. Non-fiction, art. "Books and art that enhance environmental awareness." avg. press run varies. Pub'd 2 titles 1998; expects 2 titles 1999, 4 titles 2000. 6 titles listed in the *Small Press Record of Books in Print* (28th Edition, 1999-00). Discounts: variable. 6×9. Reporting time: 1-3 months. Simultaneous submissions accepted: yes. Publishes 5% of manuscripts submitted. Payment: negotiable. Copyrights for author. PMA.

Ecrivez!, Nancy McClary, Chief Operating Officer, P.O. Box 247491, Columbus, OH 43224, 614-253-0773; FAX 614-253-0774. 1996. Fiction, non-fiction. Expects 2 titles 1999, 2 titles 2000. 4 titles listed in the *Small Press Record of Books in Print* (28th Edition, 1999-00). Discounts: negotiable. 250pp; 5½×8½; 2-color process. Simultaneous submissions accepted: no. Does not copyright for author.

ECW Press (see also ESSAYS ON CANADIAN WRITING), Jack David, Robert Lecker, 2120 Queen Street East, Suite 200, Toronto, Ontario M4E 1E2, Canada, 416-694-3348; FAX 416-698-9906. 1979. Articles, interviews, criticism, reviews. "As a press, we specialize in books of literary criticism, especially of Canadian writers and issues. We also specialize biographies, pop culture, and sports books" avg. press run 2M. Pub'd 35 titles 1998; expects 35 titles 1999, 25 titles 2000. 34 titles listed in the *Small Press Record of Books in Print* (28th Edition, 1999-00). avg. price, cloth: $40; paper: $16. Discounts: varies. 240pp; 6×9; of. Reporting time: 1

168

month. Simultaneous submissions accepted: yes. Publishes 5% of manuscripts submitted. Payment: 10% paid yearly. Copyrights for author. ACP, CPPA, LPG.

EDDIE THE MAGAZINE, Eddie Greenaway, Editor; Angela Collins, Advertising and Promotions; Di Buckley, Art Director, PO Box 199, Newtown, N.S.W. 2042, Australia, phone 61-2-211-2339; fax 61-2-211-2331. 1991. Poetry, fiction, articles, art, photos, cartoons, interviews, reviews, music, letters, parts-of-novels, collages. "Eddie is an Australian theme based magazine. We go where most fear to tread. Issues covered so far have been 'Bad Luck', 'Love', 'Law and Order', 'Music', 'Sport', and 'Sleaze'. We are looking forward to the 'future'. We mix graphic excellence with hard hititng comment guaranteed to expose the scum beneath any surface" circ. 3M. 3/yr. Pub'd 4 issues 1998; expects 3 issues 1999, 3 issues 2000. sub. price: $US20; per copy: $5; sample: $6. Back issues: #3,4,8,6,7,8,9, and 10. 100pp; size A4 trimmed; †of. Reporting time: varies, usually within 3 months. Simultaneous submissions accepted: no. Publishes 35% of manuscripts submitted. Payment: none (unfunded nonprofit). Copyrighted, reverts to author. Pub's reviews: started reviews in #9 (1995) in 1998. §Sport, crime, horror, cartoons, fantasy, sex, violence, drugs and rock 'n' roll, future. Ads: US$150/100/50 1/4 page.

THE EDGE CITY REVIEW, T.L. Ponick, Editor-in-Chief, 10912 Harpers Square Court, Reston, VA 20191, E-mail terryp17@aol.com. 1994. Poetry, fiction, articles, cartoons, interviews, satire, criticism, reviews, music, letters, parts-of-novels, long-poems, non-fiction. circ. 500+. 3/yr. Pub'd 3 issues 1998; expects 3 issues 1999, 3 issues 2000. sub. price: $15; per copy: $5; sample: $5/ppd. Back issues: $5. Discounts: none currently. 48pp; 8½x11; docutech, electronic from disk. Reporting time: 5 months. Simultaneous submissions accepted: yes. Publishes 20% of manuscripts submitted. Payment: 2 contributor's copies. Copyrighted, reverts to author. Pub's reviews: 20 in 1998. §University Presses, non-vanity published poetry, ficiton, literary criticism. Ads: $50 1/4 page.

Edge Publishing, George Fencl, Publisher, 2175 N. Forsyth Road, Orlando, FL 32807-5262, 407-277-0900. 1988. "Trade publisher of hardcover and paperback nonfiction originals. Will act as a subsidy publisher and assist the author with editing, proofreading, promotion and distribution. Computer printout submissions acceptable. Recent nonfiction titles: *The Central Florida Career Guide* and *The Tampa Bay Career Guide.*" avg. press run 3M. Pub'd 1 title 1998; expects 1 title 1999, 2 titles 2000. 3 titles listed in the *Small Press Record of Books in Print* (28th Edition, 1999-00). avg. price, paper: $24.95 spiral. Discounts: 50% wholesale. 100+pp; 8½x11; spiral binding, perfect-bound. Reporting time: 60 days. Payment: 10%-15% royalty on retail price with generally no advance given. Copyrights for author.

Edgewise Press, Richard Milazzo, Howard B. Johnson, Jr., Joy L. Glass, 24 Fifth Avenue #224, New York, NY 10011, 212-982-4818; FAX 212-982-1364. 1995. Poetry, articles, art, photos, interviews, criticism, letters. "Edgewise Press is dedicated to publishing quality paperback books of verse, essays, and other forms of writing." avg. press run 1M-2M. Pub'd 1 title 1998; expects 3 titles 1999, 4 titles 2000. 9 titles listed in the *Small Press Record of Books in Print* (28th Edition, 1999-00). avg. price, paper: $10. Discounts: 60/40. 64pp; 4¼x7¼. Publishes 0% of manuscripts submitted. Payment: 7-10%. Does not copyright for author.

Edgewood Press, Steve Pasechnick, PO Box 380264, Cambridge, MA 02238. 1989. Fiction. "I primarily publish collections of science fiction and fantasy. No horror, thrillers, mainstream. I've published Carol Emshwiller, R.A. Lafferty, Gwyneth Jones and Michael Bishop" avg. press run 600. Pub'd 1 title 1998; expects 2 titles 2000. 4 titles listed in the *Small Press Record of Books in Print* (28th Edition, 1999-00). avg. price, paper: $10. 160pp; 5½x8½; lp. Reporting time: 4 weeks. Payment: negotiable.

Edgeworth & North Books, Valla Dana Fotiades, V.P. Sales, Marketing, PO Box 812 West Side Station, Worcester, MA 01602-0812. 1989. Pub'd 1 title 1998; expects 1 title 1999. 1 title listed in the *Small Press Record of Books in Print* (28th Edition, 1999-00). avg. price, cloth: $24.95; paper: $19.95. Discounts: 2-4 copies 20%, 5-9 30%, 10-49 40%, 50-99 45%, 100+ 50%. 467pp; 7x10.

Edin Books, Inc., Linda S. Nathanson, Publisher and Editor, 102 Sunrise Drive, Gillette, NJ 07933. 1994. Non-fiction. avg. press run 7.5M. Pub'd 1 title 1998; expects 1 title 1999. 4 titles listed in the *Small Press Record of Books in Print* (28th Edition, 1999-00). avg. price, cloth: $21.95; paper: $14.95. Discounts: Available on request varies with title. 277pp; 6x9. Simultaneous submissions accepted: no. Publishes 0% of manuscripts submitted. Copyrights for author. PMA, APA.

‡**EDINBURGH REVIEW**, Murdo MacDonald, 22 George Square, Edinburgh EH8 9LF, Scotland, 0315581117/8. 1969. Poetry, fiction, articles, art, photos, interviews, criticism, reviews, long-poems. "Contributors, recent & future include: Henry Miller, James Baldwin, Douglas Dunn, George MacKay Brown, James Kelman, Chomsky, Trocchi." circ. 5M. 2/yr. Pub'd 4 issues 1998; expects 2 issues 1999, 2 issues 2000. sub. price: UK £10, o/seas £12; per copy: £5.95; sample: £5.95. Back issues: £4.75. Discounts: 35% to trade. 160pp; size A5 paperback; of. Reporting time: 1 month. Payment: by negotiation. Copyrighted. Pub's reviews: 15 in 1998. §Arts, history, politics, general literary. Ads: £75/£45. SPA.

Edition Gemini, Gernot U. Gabel, Juelichstrasse 7, Huerth-Efferen D-50354, Germany, 02233/63550; Fax: 02233/65866. 1979. Criticism, letters, non-fiction. avg. press run 150-300. Pub'd 3 titles 1998; expects 3 titles 1999. 3 titles listed in the *Small Press Record of Books in Print* (28th Edition, 1999-00). avg. price, paper: DM20. Discounts: trade 30%. 70pp; 6×8½; of. Reporting time: 1 month. Payment: yes. Copyrights for author.

Edition Stencil (see also C.S.P. WORLD NEWS), Guy F. Claude Hamel, Editor, Publisher, c/o Guy F. Claude Hamel, 1307 Bethamy Lane, Gloucester, Ont. K1J 8P3, Canada, 741-8675. 1962. Fiction, criticism, long-poems, collages, plays, concrete art. "Monthly literary magazine" avg. press run varies. 37 titles listed in the *Small Press Record of Books in Print* (28th Edition, 1999-00). 8½×14; †mi, lp. Reporting time: by return mail, 1 month. Payment: negotiable. Copyrights for author.

Editions Ex Libris, Jacques Michon, Prof.-Sherbrooke University, B.P. 34033, Sherbrooke, Quebec J1K 3B1, Canada, 819-564-8483. 1987. Non-fiction. avg. press run 300-600. Pub'd 2 titles 1998; expects 1 title 1999, 1 title 2000. 7 titles listed in the *Small Press Record of Books in Print* (28th Edition, 1999-00). avg. price, paper: 19.95$CAN; other: $19.95 Can. thermo-binding. Discounts: bookseller 40%. 200pp; 5½×8½; of. Reporting time: 2 months. Simultaneous submissions accepted: no. Publishes 40% of manuscripts submitted. Payment: 10%. Copyrights for author. Society for Scholarly Publishing.

Editorial El Sol De Baja (see also BAJA SUN), T. Michael Bircumshaw, 858 3rd Avenue #456, Chula Vista, CA 91911-1305, 1-800-WIN BAJA. 1990. Poetry, fiction, articles, photos, cartoons, interviews, satire, criticism, reviews, parts-of-novels, news items, non-fiction. "Just published *La Guia Historica de Baja California*, 276 pages, 8x 11, softbound (Spanish). The company is a Mexican corporation located at Au Pedro Loyola, Ensenada BC Mexico." avg. press run 5M-10M. Pub'd 1 title 1998; expects 3 titles 1999, 8 titles 2000. avg. price, paper: $15.95. Discounts: 55% to distributors, 40% to retail. 250pp; 8×11. Payment: negotiable. Copyrights for author.

THE EDITORIAL EYE, EEI Press, Linda Jorgensen, 66 Canal Center Plaza, Suite 200, Alexandria, VA 22314, 703-683-0683. 1978. Articles, reviews. "*The Editorial Eye* focuses on editorial standards and practices. Its purpose is to help its readers produce high quality publications. Information on content, usage, style, language, software, and production tips." circ. 2.5M. 12/yr. Pub'd 12 issues 1998; expects 12 issues 1999, 12 issues 2000. sub. price: $99, Canadian subs add $10 per year, overseas $119 year prepaid, US funds; per copy: $12; sample: free. Back issues: $12. Discounts: 10% to subscription agencies. 12pp; 8½×11; of. Reporting time: 30 days, query. Payment: $25-$100. Copyrighted, does not revert to author. Pub's reviews: 25 in 1998. §Editorial matters, style guides, proofreading, editing, software, production info. Ads: no advertising. ASI, SSP, Washington Book Publishers, Publishers Marketing Assn., Washington Edpress, Council of Biology Editors, American Medical Writers Assn., Women's Nat'l Book Assn., Bookbuilders.

Editorial Research Service, Laird M. Wilcox, P.O.Box 2047, Olathe, KS 66061, 913-829-0609. 1978. Articles, interviews, reviews, letters, news items. "Publications include: *Guide to the American Right* 1999, 1,500 entries; *Guide to the American Left* 1999, 1,500 entries" avg. press run 410. Pub'd 3 titles 1998; expects 8 titles 1999. 2 titles listed in the *Small Press Record of Books in Print* (28th Edition, 1999-00). avg. price, paper: $24.95. Discounts: 10% single copies, 25% 5 or more copies; prepayment required. 108pp; 8½×11; of. Reporting time: 30 days. Payment: flat fee. Does not copyright for author.

Editorial Review, William R. Taylor, Robert T. Taylor, 1009 Placer Street, Butte, MT 59701, 406-782-2546. 1983. "Not printing any more books in the near future" avg. press run 1M. Expects 2 titles 1999, 2 titles 2000. 3 titles listed in the *Small Press Record of Books in Print* (28th Edition, 1999-00). avg. price, paper: $11.95. Discounts: bookstore 40%, flexible for distributors, etc. 100pp; 6×9; of. Reporting time: 1 month. Payment: profit-sharing plan. Copyrights for author.

EduCare Press, Megan Hass, PO Box 17222, Seattle, WA 98107. 1988. Poetry, fiction, music, letters, non-fiction. avg. press run 2M. Pub'd 2 titles 1998; expects 3 titles 1999, 2 titles 2000. 7 titles listed in the *Small Press Record of Books in Print* (28th Edition, 1999-00). avg. price, cloth: $19.95; paper: $9.95. Discounts: usual. 200pp; 6×9; of. Copyrights for author.

THE EDUCATION DIGEST, Prakken Publications, Kenneth Schroeder, Managing Editor, PO Box 8623, Ann Arbor, MI 48107, 734-975-2800 ext. 207, fax 734-975-2787. 1935. Articles, cartoons, reviews, news items. "*Education Digest* does not accept original manuscripts, prior publication required. Selected by editorial staff. 'Outstanding Articles condensed for quick review'" circ. 22M. 9/yr. Pub'd 9 issues 1998; expects 9 issues 1999, 9 issues 2000. sub. price: $48; per copy: $6; sample: free on request. Back issues: $6. Discounts: agent 10%, individual multi-year rates: 2 yr $86, 3 yr $124. 80pp; 5½×8; of. Payment: honorarium possible for rights. Copyrighted, does not revert to author. Pub's reviews: 40 in 1998. §Education. Ads: $666/$433/$50 per col. inch. Ed Press.

EDUCATION IN FOCUS, Books for All Times, Inc., Joe David, Editor, PO Box 2, Alexandria, VA 22313, 703-548-0457. "A semi-annual newsletter which provides an *in focus* look at education from a rational and humane viewpoint." 2/yr. Pub'd 2 issues 1998; expects 2 issues 1999, 2 issues 2000. sub. price: $18 US and Canada; $28 elsewhere for 6 issues; per copy: $3. 6pp; 8½×11. Reporting time: 4 weeks. Payment: varies. Copyrighted, we buy rights to use in newsletter, book, and on Internet. Pub's reviews: 0 in 1998. §Education. Ads: $75 for 2¼ X 4½/$25 for 2¼ X 1½.

EDUCATIONAL FOUNDATIONS, Caddo Gap Press, William T. Pink, Editor, 3145 Geary Boulevard, Suite 275, San Francisco, CA 94118, 415-922-1911. 1986. Articles. *"Educational Foundations* seeks manuscripts of 20-25 double-spaced typewritten pages on issues, themes, research, and practice in the social foundations of education. Most contributors are scholars in the various social foundations disciplines." circ. 700. 4/yr. Pub'd 4 issues 1998; expects 4 issues 1999, 4 issues 2000. sub. price: $40 individuals, $60 institutions; per copy: $15. Discounts: agency 15%. 96pp; 6×9; of. Reporting time: 1-2 months. Publishes 25% of manuscripts submitted. Payment: none. Copyrighted, rights revert to author if desired. Ads: $200 full page. EDPRESS.

EDUCATIONAL LEADERSHIP & ADMINISTRATION, Caddo Gap Press, Marilyn Konostoff, Editor, 3145 Geary Boulevard #275, San Francisco, CA 94118, 415-922-1911. 1988. Articles. "Annual journal of the California Association of Professors of Educational Administration" circ. 200. 1/yr. Pub'd 1 issue 1998; expects 1 issue 1999, 1 issue 2000. sub. price: $20 individuals, $30 institutions; per copy: $20. 96pp; 6×9; of. Reporting time: 2 months. Publishes 25% of manuscripts submitted. Payment: none. Copyrighted, reverts to author. Ads: $200 per page. MPA, EDPRESS.

The Edwin Mellen Press (see also Mellen Poetry Press), Herbert Richardson, PO Box 450, Lewiston, NY 14092, 716-754-2266. 1974. "United Kingdom Division: The Edwin Mellen Press, Ltd., Lampeter, Dyfed, Wales SA48 7DY. Canadian Division: The Edwin Mellen Press-Canada, PO Box 67, Queenston, Ontario L0S 1L0. We now have a poetry series (Mellen Poetry Press Series). These are small softcover/paper books including works by first published poets. The price range is $15-$30. By the way, we pay NO royalties at all on ANY books, but also require NO subsidies. We also require camera-ready copy to our specifications." avg. press run 300. Pub'd 300 titles 1998; expects 300 titles 1999, 350 titles 2000. 192 titles listed in the *Small Press Record of Books in Print* (28th Edition, 1999-00). avg. price, cloth: $69.95; paper: $39.95. Discounts: 20% to resellers, special discounts for quantity orders, text prices for all books. 300pp; 6×9; †of. Reporting time: 2 months. Simultaneous submissions accepted: no. Payment: 5 free copies to the author/editor. We deposit 2 copies of the published book, copyrighted in the author's name, with the Copyright Office, and 1 copy with the Cataloging Division.

EEI Press (see also THE EDITORIAL EYE), Linda Jorgensen, 66 Canal Center Plaza #200, Alexandria, VA 22314, 703-683-0683. 1972. Articles, reviews. "We publish *The Editorial Eye* and 7 titles for professional publications people." avg. press run 5M. Expects 1 title 1999, 1 title 2000. 11 titles listed in the *Small Press Record of Books in Print* (28th Edition, 1999-00). avg. price, paper: $12-$35. Discounts: inquire. 100-482pp; size varies; of. Reporting time: 2 months. Payment: inquire. Does not copyright for author. Soc. Schol. Pub., Women's Nat'l Book Club, Amer Soc. Indexers, Washington Book Pub., Pub Marketing Assn., Edpress, Council of Biology Editors, American Medical Writers Assn., Bookbuilders.

Wm.B. Eerdmans Publishing Co., Jon Pott, Editor-in-Chief, 255 Jefferson Avenue, S.E., Grand Rapids, MI 49503, 616-459-4591. 1911. Non-fiction, photos. avg. press run 3M. Pub'd 106 titles 1998; expects 120 titles 1999, 130 titles 2000. avg. price, cloth: $34.99; paper: $18.00. Discounts: 40% trade. 250pp; †of. Reporting time: 4-6 weeks. Simultaneous submissions accepted if so noted. Publishes 5% of manuscripts submitted. Payment: 7-10% of retail. Copyrights for author.

EFRYDIAU ATHRONYDDOL, University Of Wales Press, J.I. Daniel, W.L. Gealey, 6 Gwennyth St., Cathays, Cardiff CF2 4YD, Wales, 44-1222-231919; Fax 44-1222-230908; press@press.wales.ac.uk. Articles. "Philosophical material." circ. 350. 1/yr. Pub'd 1 issue 1998; expects 1 issue 1999, 1 issue 2000. sub. price: £5; per copy: £5; sample: £5. Back issues: £5. Discounts: trade 10%. 80pp; 9½×6; of. Payment: none. Copyrighted, does not revert to author. Pub's reviews: 0 in 1998. §Philosophical. UWP.

EGW Publishing Company (see also WEEKEND WOODCRAFTS; TOLE WORLD; VEGGIE LIFE; WOOD STROKES & WOODCRAFTS), 1041 Shary Circle, Concord, CA 94518-2407. 1979. 8×10½.

Ehrman Entertainment Press, Dave Ehrman, PO Box 2951, Orange, CA 92859-0951, 714-997-7006; FAX 637-3341; Toll Free 888-997-7006; e-mail ehrmanent@Juno.com. 1 title listed in the *Small Press Record of Books in Print* (28th Edition, 1999-00).

Eidos (see also EIDOS: Sexual Freedom & Erotic Entertainment for Consenting Adults), Brenda Loew, PO Box 96, Boston, MA 02137, 617-262-0096. 1982. Poetry, fiction, articles, art, photos, cartoons, interviews, satire, criticism, reviews, letters, parts-of-novels, long-poems, plays, non-fiction. "In addition to our quarterly journal for consenting adults, *Eidos,* we have published three poetry chapbooks/collections. Our *Boston Collection of Women's Poetry, Volume 1* is comprised of material submitted to our poetry contest of 1983. We are constantly looking for material to publish. We read everything. Our editorial bias is to present work on the subject of erotica for women, men and couples of all erotic and sexual orientations, preferences and lifestyles. Material submitted to us is automatically considered for publication in *Eidos: Sexual Freedom & Erotic Entertainment For Consenting Adults.''* avg. press run 10M. Pub'd 1 title 1998; expects 1 title 1999, 1 title 2000. 3 titles listed in the *Small Press Record of Books in Print* (28th Edition, 1999-00). avg. price, paper: $5. Discounts: 5+ 50%. 44pp; 8¼×10¾; †of. Reporting time: 4-6 weeks. Simultaneous submissions accepted: no. Publishes 10% of manuscripts submitted. Payment: contributor's copies. Copyrights for author.

EIDOS: Sexual Freedom & Erotic Entertainment for Consenting Adults, Eidos, Brenda Loew, PO Box 96, Boston, MA 02137, 617-262-0096. 1982. Poetry, fiction, articles, art, photos, cartoons, interviews, satire, criticism, reviews, letters, parts-of-novels, long-poems, plays, non-fiction. *"Eidos* is a quarterly journal for women, men, and couples regardless of sexual orientation, preference or lifestyle. *Eidos* is a forum for the discussion and examination of two highly personalized dimensions on human sexuality: desire and satisfaction. Both new and established poets, writers, and visual artists are invited to submit. Artwork/photography may or may not be used with accompanying mss. Computer printout, submissions OK. Phone queries OK or submit complete ms. 100% of material is freelance written. We especially look for explicit erotic fiction. Submit short bio.'' circ. 10M. 4/yr. Pub'd 4 issues 1998; expects 4 issues 1999, 4 issues 2000. sub. price: $25; per copy: $5; sample: $7. Back issues: $5. Discounts: 5+ 50%. 44pp; 8¼×10¾; †of. Reporting time: 4-6 weeks. Simultaneous submissions accepted: no. Publishes 10% of manuscripts submitted. Payment: contributor copies. Copyrighted, reverts to author. Pub's reviews: approx. 450 in 1998. §All dimensions of human sexual self-expression, especially women and sexuality/eroticism, women and erotica, women's images (erotosexual), etc. Ads: $125/$100/$20 50 words.

1812, Rick Lupert, Richard Lynch, Box 1812, Amherst, NY 14226-7812, http://1812.simplenet.com. Poetry, fiction, articles, art, photos, cartoons, interviews, satire, criticism, reviews, music, letters, parts-of-novels, long-poems, collages, plays, concrete art, non-fiction. "Material with a BANG!'' 2/yr. Expects 1 issue 1999, 1 issue 2000. sub. price: free; per copy: free; sample: free. Back issues: free. HTML. Reporting time: 2 months. Payment: copies and arranged cash award. Copyrighted, reverts to author. Pub's reviews. §Various—inquire. Arranged.

The Eighth Mountain Press, Ruth Gundle, 624 Southeast 29th Avenue, Portland, OR 97214, 503-233-3936; fax 503-233-0774; e-mail Soapston@teleport.com. 1985. Poetry, fiction, non-fiction. "We publish only women writers.'' avg. press run 5M. Pub'd 2 titles 1998; expects 2 titles 1999, 2 titles 2000. avg. price, cloth: $20; paper: $12. Discounts: books are distributed to the trade by Consortium of St. Paul & subject to their discount schedule. 200pp; 6×9; of. Reporting time: 3 months. Simultaneous submissions not usually accepted; please notify if so. Publishes .05% of manuscripts submitted. Payment: 8% paper, 10% cloth usually. Copyrights for author.

EKPHRASIS, Frith Press, Laverne Frith, Editor; Carol Frith, Editor, PO Box 161236, Sacramento, CA 95816-1236, 916-451-3038. 1997. Poetry. "A poetry journal focusing on the growing body of verse based on individual works from any artistic genre. Recent contributors: William Doreski, Simon Perchik, Rhina Espaillat, William Greenway, Joseph Stanton, Susan Spilecki, Stephanie Strickland, and Ida Fasel.'' circ. 100+. 2/yr. Pub'd 2 issues 1998; expects 2 issues 1999, 2 issues 2000. sub. price: $12; per copy: $6; sample: $6. Discounts: none. 50pp; 5½×8½; photocopy. Reporting time: 2 weeks-6 months. Simultaneous submissions accepted: no. Publishes 5%-7% of manuscripts submitted. Payment: 1 copy. Copyrighted, reverts to author. Ads: none.

EL PALACIO, Cheryle Mitchell, Editor, PO Box 2087, Santa Fe, NM 87504-2087, 505-827-6451. 1913. Articles, art, photos, reviews. "Issues planned yr in advance; several articles per year by commission. Enquiries required in advance on freelance. College-level semi-popular style; 2.5M-5 words, art supplied by author. Museum of New Mexico related topics, Southwestern slant; archaeology, folk art, anthropology, history, the arts, geography. Recent contributors: Marc Simmons, John Nichols, Douglas Preston, and Richard Bradford.'' circ. 10M. 2/yr. Pub'd 2 issues 1998; expects 2 issues 1999, 2 issues 2000. sub. price: $12; per copy: $4.50; sample: $4.50. Back issues: to be determined under review-query. 60pp; 9½×12; of. Reporting time: 2 weeks-2 months. Publishes 25% of manuscripts submitted. Payment: $500. Copyrighted, reverts to author. Pub's reviews: 5 in 1998. §Arts, anthropology, social trends, history of the SW. Ads: inquire; no classified; full, 1/2 page, 1/4 page, 4-color/bw. Museum of New Mexico Foundation.

Elder Books, Susan Sullivan, PO Box 490, Forest Knolls, CA 94933. 1986. Non-fiction. "Health, coping, first-person accounts of coping with illness, aging, Alzheimer's Disease, inspirational books.'' avg. press run 3M. Pub'd 2 titles 1998; expects 5 titles 1999, 5 titles 2000. 1 title listed in the *Small Press Record of Books in Print* (28th Edition, 1999-00). avg. price, paper: $10.95. Discounts: 5-10 20%, 11-20 30%, 21-40 40%. 140pp; of. Reporting time: 3 months. Payment: royalty report once a year. Copyrights for author.

ELDERCARE FORUM, Laura Beller, 170 Elaine Drive, Roswell, GA 30075, 770-518-2767. 1993. News items, non-fiction. "Do not ordinarily use unsolicited manuscripts. Will review short items (200-300 words) of interest to readers" circ. 15M. 4/yr. Pub'd 4 issues 1998; expects 4 issues 1999, 4 issues 2000. sub. price: $14; per copy: $3; sample: $1. Discounts: Bulk discounts, annual subscriptions, minimum 50 copies/issue. 6pp; 8½×11; mi. Reporting time: 3 months. Payment: based on submission. Copyrighted. Pub's reviews: 1-2 in 1998. §Areas of interest to adult children of aging parents.

ELECTRIC VEHICLE NEWS, Lewis Gulick, Mary Ann Chapman, Associate Editor, PO Box 148, Arlington, VA 22210-0148. 1990. News items. "Non-technical updates on products and public policy related to electric vehicles (including boats and other on-road wheeled transportation). Also commentaries and book reviews." circ. 3M. 11/yr. Pub'd 12 issues 1998; expects 12 issues 1999, 12 issues 2000. sub. price: $40 in US and Canada, $65 elsewhere; per copy: $3.50; sample: $3.50. Back issues: $5. Discounts: none. 24pp; 8½×11; laser. Reporting time: 60 days. Simultaneous submissions accepted: yes. Payment: varies. Not copyrighted. Pub's reviews: 4 in 1998. Ads: $320/$200/1/3 page $160.

ELECTRONIC GREEN JOURNAL, Maria Anna Jankowska, Editor; Mike Pollastro, Managing Editor, University of Idaho Library, Moscow, ID 83844-2360, 208-885-6631; e-mail majanko@uidaho.edu; www.lib.uidaho.edu/70/docs/egj.html. 1994. Articles, reviews, non-fiction. "Contribution from authors on topics related to sources of information on environmental protection, conservation, management of natural resources, and ecologically balanced regional development. The international journal also seeks articles dealing with environmental issues specific to libraries, publishing industries, and information sciences. Our goal is to provide information in articles, essays, reports, annotated bibliographies and reviews that will be of interest to librarians, environmental educators, information consultants, publishers, booksellers, environmentalists, researchers, regional planners and students all over the world." circ. varies. 2/yr. Pub'd 2 issues 1998; expects 2 issues 1999, 2 issues 2000. sub. price: free; per copy: free; sample: free. Back issues: free. 84pp; **There is no 'printing' the journal in electronic; available only through the internet. Reporting time: 6-8 weeks.** Simultaneous submissions accepted: no. Publishes 60% of manuscripts submitted. Payment: none. Copyrighted, reverts to author. Pub's reviews: 25 in 1998. §Environmental protection, policy, science, nature/wildlife, global environment, conservation, environment information sources. Ads: $75/$50/$25 1/4 page. ALA.

THE ELECTRONIC PUBLISHING FORUM, Serendipity Systems, John Galuszka, PO Box 140, San Simeon, CA 93452, www.thegrid.net/bookware/epf.htm. 1990. Articles, criticism, reviews, news items. "Available on the Internet at above address." 4/yr. Pub'd 2 issues 1998; expects 4 issues 1999, 4 issues 2000. sub. price: free on Internet. Back issues: available at www.thegrid.net/bookware/bookware.htm. Discounts: to 45%. †online. Reporting time: 4 weeks. Payment: 25% royalty, pro-rated. Copyrighted, reverts to author. Pub's reviews. §Related to writing, electronic publishing, or similar topics. Digital Publishing Association.

THE ELEVENTH MUSE; a publication by Poetry West, J.R. Thelin, Editor, PO Box 2413, Colorado Springs, CO 80901. 1982. Poetry. circ. 300. 2/yr. Pub'd 2 issues 1998; expects 2 issues 1999, 2 issues 2000. sub. price: $8 for 2 issues; per copy: $4 in bookstores; sample: $4.50. Back issues: $3.50. 48-56pp; 8½×5½; of. Reporting time: 4 days to 4 months. Simultaneous submissions accepted: no. Publishes 7-10% of manuscripts submitted. Payment: 1 copy per poem accepted. Copyrighted, reverts to author. Ads: $75/$50/$35/must be camera ready.

ELF: ECLECTIC LITERARY FORUM (ELF MAGAZINE), Cynthia K. Erbes, PO Box 392, Tonawanda, NY 14150, 716-693-7006. 1990. Poetry, fiction, articles, non-fiction. "Fiction (maximum 3500 words); poetry (not to exceed 30 lines, but *ELF* will consider longer poems); essays (maximum 2500 words), subject matter limited to literary concerns, e.g.: creative process, various genres, critiques, etc. Premier issue Spring 1991. Published Gwendolyn Brooks, Judson Jerome, John Tagliabue, Nikki Giovanni, John Dickson, William Stafford, Daniel Berrigan, John Haines, Gail White, Allen GinsBerg, X.J. Kennedy, Joyce Carol Oates, featuring Native American folklore." circ. 4M. 3/4. Expects 3 issues 2000. sub. price: $16 (foreign rate: add $8); per copy: $6; sample: $5.50. Back issues: $5 + 50¢ s&h (if available). Discounts: 25% negotiable. 56-64pp; 8½×11; of. Reporting time: 6-8 weeks. Simultaneous submissions accepted with notification. Publishes 5-10% of manuscripts submitted. Payment: 1 sample copy. Copyrighted, reverts to author. Pub's reviews: 12-14 in 1998. §Literary, poetry, short stories, essays. Ads: $125/$70.

Elliott & Clark Publishing, Ashley Gordon, Jeff Slaton, PO Box 551, Montgomery, AL 36101-0551, 334-265-6753. 1991. Art, photos, non-fiction. avg. press run 10M. Expects 4 titles 1999, 4 titles 2000. 13 titles listed in the *Small Press Record of Books in Print* (28th Edition, 1999-00). avg. price, cloth: $29.95; paper: $12.95. 144pp; 10×10. Reporting time: 3-4 weeks. Payment: advance against royalties. Copyrights for author. ABA, PAS, WBG, PMA, MSA.

ELLIPSE, Charly Bouchara, Monique Gransmangin, Univ. de Sherbrooke, Box 10, Faculte des Lettres et Sciences Humaines, Sherbrooke, Quebec J1K 2R1, Canada, 819-821-7238. 1969. Poetry. "Poetry in translation." circ. 750. 2/yr. Pub'd 2 issues 1998; expects 2 issues 1999, 2 issues 2000. sub. price: $12; per copy: $7; sample: $7. Back issues: $4-$5. 120pp; 5½×8½. Simultaneous submissions accepted: no.

Copyrighted. Ads: no ads. CMPA.

ELT Press (see also ENGLISH LITERATURE IN TRANSITION, 1880-1920), Robert Langenfeld, English Department/U of North Carolina, P.O. Box 26170, Greensboro, NC 27402-6170, 910-334-5446; fax 910-334-5446; e-Mail langen.fagan.uncg.edu. 1988. Criticism. "ELT Press publishes the 1880-1920 British Author Series. We print books which make available new critical, biographical, bibliographical and primary works on 1880-1920 British authors. Cloth-bound books on acid-free paper, dust jackets, end sheets." avg. press run 500. Pub'd 2 titles 1998; expects 2 titles 1999, 2 titles 2000. 12 titles listed in the *Small Press Record of Books in Print* (28th Edition, 1999-00). avg. price, cloth: $30; paper: $18.95. Discounts: 20% to jobbers, agents. 300pp; 6×9; Electronic pre-press. Reporting time: 3-5 months. Simultaneous submissions accepted: no. Publishes 10% of manuscripts submitted. Payment: none. Copyrights for author.

Elysian Hills Publishing Company, Inc., Ed Dziczek, PO Box 40693, Albuquerque, NM 87196, 505-265-9041. 1992. Photos, non-fiction. "We publish only AIDS awareness, AIDS care, bereavement with a spiritual accent. All others will be returned unread." avg. press run 5M. Pub'd 1 title 1998; expects 1 title 1999, 1 title 2000. 2 titles listed in the *Small Press Record of Books in Print* (28th Edition, 1999-00). avg. price, paper: $13.95. Discounts: 40%-55%. 300pp; 5⅜×8¼. Reporting time: 3 months. Payment: negotiable. Copyrights for author. ABA.

Embassy Hall Editions (see also THE GALLEY SAIL REVIEW), Stanley McNail, PO Box 665, Centralia, IL 62801-0665. 1985. Poetry. "For the present unsolicited mss. are not being accepted. If interested in having work published under this imprint, poets should query first. Paperbacks are principal if not entire output. Some chapbooks in future" avg. press run 500. Pub'd 2 titles 1998; expects 2 titles 1999, 2 titles 2000. 6 titles listed in the *Small Press Record of Books in Print* (28th Edition, 1999-00). avg. price, paper: $6 ($3 chapbooks). Discounts: 40% to retail book dealers on consignment orders. 24-50pp; 5½×8½; of. Reporting time: 3 weeks to 30 days. Payment: subject to negotiation with individual author. Copyrights for author. CLMP.

Emerald Ink Publishing, Chris Carson, 7141 Office City Drive, Suite 220, Houston, TX 77087, 713-643-9945, fax 713-643-1986. 1994. Non-fiction. avg. press run 1-5M. Pub'd 2 titles 1998; expects 4 titles 1999, 5 titles 2000. 12 titles listed in the *Small Press Record of Books in Print* (28th Edition, 1999-00). avg. price, cloth: $25; paper: $20. Discounts: Distributed through Access Publishers Network. 144pp; 6×9. Reporting time: 1-2 weeks. Simultaneous submissions accepted: yes. Payment: 5-15%. Copyrights for author. ABA, Book Publishers of Texas, PMA, Houston Publishers Association.

Emerald Wave, PO Box 969, Fayetteville, AR 72702, Fax 501-575-0807; Tel 501-575-0019; sagebooks@aol.com. 1985. Non-fiction. "Emerald Wave began as a self-publisher and is now actively working with other New Age oriented books." avg. press run 5M. Expects 4 titles 1999, 1 title 2000. 4 titles listed in the *Small Press Record of Books in Print* (28th Edition, 1999-00). avg. price, paper: $11-$15. Discounts: 1-3 copies 20%, 4-9 30%, 10+ 40%, wholesalers 55%+/-. 200pp; 5½×8½. Reporting time: 4 months average. Simultaneous submissions accepted: yes. Publishes .02% of manuscripts submitted. Payment: 7-10% gross, no advance. Does not copyright for author. Publishers Marketing Assn.

EMERGING, LP Publications (Teleos Institute), Diane K. Pike, PO Box 12009-418, Scottsdale, AZ 85267, 480-948-1800; FAX 480-948-1870; E-mail teleosinst@aol.com. 1972. Articles, photos, letters. circ. 250. 3/yr. Pub'd 2 issues 1998; expects 3 issues 1999, 3 issues 2000. sub. price: $35; sample: free. Discounts: none. 24pp; 8½×11; of. Payment: none. Not copyrighted. No ads. Teleos Institute (aka The Love Project).

EMERGING VOICES, Lucille Tamm, 1722 N. 58th Street, Milwaukee, WI 53208-1618, 414-453-4678. 1995. Poetry, fiction, articles, art, photos, cartoons, interviews, satire, reviews, music, long-poems, collages, plays, non-fiction. "We are a vanity press/magazine for young authors. No rejections except for hate, graphic sex, violence. Additional guidelines, send SASE or SAE with IRC." Irregular. Pub'd 1 issue 1998; expects 6 issues 1999, 12 issues 2000. price per copy: $10; sample: $10. Discounts: none. 20pp; 8½×11; †xerox. Simultaneous submissions accepted: yes. Publishes 100% of manuscripts submitted. Copyrighted, reverts to author. Pub's reviews. §Children's writing. Ads: Sponsorship of economically disadvantaged kids acknowledged.

EMORY EDGE, Dyshaun Muhammed, Editor-in-Cheif; Alaina Browne, Managing Editor, PO Drawer BBB, Emory University, Atlanta, GA 30322, 404-727-6183. 1993. Articles, art, photos, interviews, news items, non-fiction. "Published once a semester, the *Emory EDGE* is here not only to serve as a window to the outside world, but as a mirror of reflection. The stories inside capture an aspect of Emory and where it stands in meeting the challenge of change, providing us with a new insight into this institution, its people, and its surrounding communities. The *Emory EDGE* can take you to new places, new sights, or just new views you might have overlooked. The *Emory EDGE* stands here, on the line of change." circ. 8M. 2/yr. Pub'd 2 issues 1998; expects 2 issues 1999, 2 issues 2000. sub. price: $10; per copy: $6; sample: $6. Back issues: $6. Discounts: contact us for details. 32+pp; 8½×11; of. Reporting time: 2 weeks. Payment: 3 copies. Copyrighted, does not revert to author. Ads: $600/$350/color available. CSPA, Georgia Press Association, ACP,

Southeastern Journalism Conference.

Empire Publishing Service, PO Box 1344, Studio City, CA 91614-0344. Fiction, plays, non-fiction. avg. press run 10M-50M. Pub'd 30 titles 1998; expects 20 titles 1999, 40 titles 2000. 170 titles listed in the *Small Press Record of Books in Print* (28th Edition, 1999-00). avg. price, cloth: $25; paper: $15. Discounts: 20%-45%. 150pp; 6×9. Reporting time: 3-12 months. Simultaneous submissions accepted: no. Payment: varies. ABA.

EMPLOI PLUS, Daniel Reid, 1256 Principale N. Street, Ste. #203, L'Annonciation, Quebec, Canada J0T 1T0, Canada, 819-275-3293 phone/Fax. 1990. Poetry, fiction, interviews, parts-of-novels, non-fiction. "ISSN 1180-4092. No unsolicited manuscripts." circ. 500. Occasional. Expects 1 issue 2000. price per copy: $10; sample: $5. 12pp; 7×8½; †of. Payment: free samples. Copyrighted. Ads: none.

Empty Closet Enterprises, Inc., Jr. Armstrong, Toni, 5210 N. Wayne, Chicago, IL 60640-2223, 312-769-9009, FAX 312-728-7002. 1977. *"Women's Music Plus* is the annual directory of the feminist women's music and culture industry. Names/addresses/phone #s/descriptions—performers, writers, producers, distributors, festivals, publications, publishers, editors, organizations, coffeehouses, artisans, film/video, photographers, more; first directory published 1977" avg. press run 1.2M. Pub'd 1 title 1998. avg. price, paper: $18. Discounts: 40% for order of 5 or more. 72pp; 8½×11; of.

THE EMSHOCK LETTER, Steve Erickson, Randall Flat Road, PO Box 411, Troy, ID 83871, 208-835-4902. 1977. Poetry, fiction, art, satire, criticism, letters, non-fiction. *"The Emshock Letter* is a philosophical, metaphysical, sometimes poetic expression of ideas and events. It covers a wide range of subjects and represents a free-style form of expressive relation. It is a newsletter quite unlike any other. (We are taking steps to expand our circulation). 'The writings range from down-to-earth, poignant, wise observations about dreams, love, suffering, and the ups and downs of the spiritual path to far-flung adventure tales...a mind-expanding journey to places you haven't been and may not even have known existed...' (*The SUN* Issue #123). Submissions accepted from subscribers only" circ. 1M. 3-12/yr. Pub'd 12 issues 1998; expects 8-10 issues 1999, 8-10 issues 2000. sub. price: $25; sample: none, *one issue cannot adequately depict a publication of this nature.* Back issues: $3.75/issue, when available. Discounts: none. 5-7pp; 8½×11; high quality xerox on colored paper. Reporting time: variable. Payment: copies. Copyrighted, reverts to author. Pub's reviews: 1 in 1998. §Poetry, philosophy, metaphysics, spirituality. No ads.

EN PASSANT, Chess Enterprises, B.G. Dudley, Owner, 107 Crosstree Road, Coraopolis, PA 15108. 1977. Non-fiction. circ. 400. 6/yr. Pub'd 6 issues 1998; expects 6 issues 1999, 6 issues 2000. sub. price: $7. 16pp; 8½×11; of. Not copyrighted. Pub's reviews: 8 in 1998. §Chess only. Ads: none.

‡**En Passant Poetry Press (see also EN PASSANT/POETRY),** James A. Costello, 4612 Sylvanus Drive, Wilmington, DE 19803. 1981. "Not interested in dazzle or schlock or mean street ravings." 1 title listed in the *Small Press Record of Books in Print* (28th Edition, 1999-00). avg. price, paper: $4. 48pp; 5½×8½; of. Reporting time: immediate. Copyrights for author.

‡**EN PASSANT/POETRY, En Passant Poetry Press,** James A. Costello, 4612 Sylvanus Drive, Wilmington, DE 19803. 1975. Poetry, art, reviews. "We prefer stylistic chastity (not desperation) that sacrifices everything to the poem." circ. 300. Irregular. price per copy: $3; sample: $3. 40pp; 5½×8½; of. Reporting time: immediate. Payment: copies. Copyrighted, publisher takes first rights, shares remaining rights with author. Pub's reviews. §Books of poetry especially those published by small presses. Query first. No ads.

●**Encircle Publications (see also THE AUROREAN, A POETIC QUARTERLY),** Cynthia Brackett-Vincent, PO Box 219, Sagamore Beach, MA 02562, 508-833-0805 phone/fax, phone before faxing. 1992. Poetry. "New additional projects by invitation only; not soliciting material. Encircle's products have sold to the Betty Ford Clinics Bookstore and we have published chapbooks by Errol Miller ('97 & '98). Not soliciting now." avg. press run 500. Pub'd 2 titles 1998; expects 4 titles 1999, 2 titles 2000. 36pp; 5½×8½; of. Simultaneous submissions accepted: no. Payment: varies; usually $150 & 150 copies; sometimes cost split. Does not copyright for author.

Encounter Books, Peter Collier, 116 New Montgomery St., Suite 206, San Francisco, CA 94105, 415-538-1460; fax 415-538-1461; e-mail read@encounterbooks.com; website www.encounterbooks.com. 1997. Non-fiction. "Quality non-fiction, serious books about history, culture, politics, religion, social criticism, public policy. Authors include Ward Connerly, Wesley Smith, Steven Mosher, Ronald Radosh, Sol Stern, Steven Watts, Joshua Muravchik." avg. press run 5M cl; 10M pa. Expects 4 titles 1999, 10 titles 2000. avg. price, cloth: $22; paper: $14. Discounts: text 20%; trade 1-4 25%; 5-24 42%; 25-49 43%; 50-99 45%; 100+ 48%; STOP orders 25%. 240pp; 6×9; of. Reporting time: 2 months. Simultaneous submissions accepted: yes. Publishes 2% of manuscripts submitted. Payment: 7% of list, advances vary. Copyrights for author. ABA.

ENDING THE BEGIN, Headveins Graphics, Brad Angell, PO Box 4816, Seattle, WA 98104-0816, 206-726-0948. 1992. Poetry, art, cartoons, collages. "Contributors: Brad Angell, Blair Wilson, Tim Tate, Paul Weiman, Dennis Zanoni, Marcel Feldmar and others." circ. 100. Irregular. Pub'd 1 issue 1998; expects 3 issues

1999, 4-5 issues 2000. sub. price: $2/3 issues; per copy: $1 postpaid; sample: $1 postpaid. Back issues: .50. Discounts: 45% for retail, 10% for others. 17-24pp; 2¾×4; †laserprint/xerox. Reporting time: 1-6 months. Publishes 10% of manuscripts submitted. Payment: copies.

Energeia Publishing, Inc., Raymond Meliza, Irene Turk, PO Box 985, Salem, OR 97308, 503-588-2926. 1990. Non-fiction. "Paperback 150-250+pp. Personal and business self-help. Recent contributor: Norman C. Tognazzini" avg. press run 5M-10M. Pub'd 40 titles 1998. avg. price, cloth: $10; paper: $10; other: $3 booklets. Discounts: varies. 200pp, booklets 8-32pp; 5½×8½; full web/off. Reporting time: 1 months with SASE. Simultaneous submissions accepted: no. Payment: per agreement. Copyrights for author.

ENGLISH LITERATURE IN TRANSITION, 1880-1920, ELT Press, Robert Langenfeld, English Department/U of North Carolina, P.O. Box 26170, Greensboro, NC 27402-6170, 910-334-5446; fax 910-334-3281; e-Mail langen.fagan.uncg.edu. 1957. Articles, criticism, reviews. "*ELT* publishes essays on fiction, poetry, drama, or subjects of cultural interest in the 1880-1920 period of British literature. We do not print essays on Joyce, Lawrence, Yeats, Virginia Woolf, or Henry James unless these authors are linked with minor figures in the period. 7,000 words is usually the maximum length for an essay." circ. 900. 4/yr. Pub'd 4 issues 1998; expects 4 issues 1999, 4 issues 2000. sub. price: $24; per copy: $7; sample: free. Back issues: single-copy rate, discounts for run of 5 years or more. No discounts on regular issues. 128pp; 6×9; of. Reporting time: 3 months. Simultaneous submissions accepted: no. Publishes 10% of manuscripts submitted. Payment: none. Copyrighted, does not revert to author. Pub's reviews: 100 in 1998. §Those related to the 1880-1920 period of British literature. Ads: $100.

Enitharmon Press, Stephen Stuart-Smith, 36 St George's Avenue, London N7 OHD, England, 0171-607-7194; FAX 0171-607-8694. 1969. Poetry, criticism. avg. press run 800. Pub'd 12 titles 1998. 78 titles listed in the *Small Press Record of Books in Print* (28th Edition, 1999-00). avg. price, cloth: £20; paper: £7.95. Discounts: 35% on wrapped and hardbound issues, 25% on signed, numbered. size 8VO; lp, of. Reporting time: 2 months. Publishes 1% of manuscripts submitted. Payment: royalty.

ENLIGHTENMENTS, Carole Ohl, 5449 Marina Drive, Dayton, OH 45449, 937-865-0767. 1990. Articles, art, photos, interviews, reviews, music. circ. 50M. 12/yr. Pub'd 12 issues 1998; expects 12 issues 1999, 12 issues 2000. sub. price: $14.95; per copy: free. Back issues: none. 32pp; of. Reporting time: 8 weeks. Simultaneous submissions accepted: no. Copyrighted, reverts to author. Pub's reviews: 12 in 1998. §Metaphysical. Ads: $525/$275/$150. TransNet.

ENOUGH IS ENOUGH!, Dennis W. Breznia, PO Box 683, Chesapeake City, MD 21915, 410-885-2887. 1995. Articles, art, cartoons. circ. 400. 4/yr. Pub'd 2 issues 1998; expects 4 issues 1999, 4 issues 2000. sub. price: $20; per copy: $3; sample: $3. 10pp; 8½×11.

ENTELECHY MAGAZINE, Steven Horn, Founding Editor; Karin Beuerlein, Poetry Editor, P.O. Box 413, El Granada, CA 94018, e-mail shorn@entelechy.org; website www.entelechy.org. 1993. Poetry, fiction, photos, parts-of-novels, non-fiction. "Submit up to 12 poems. Fiction word limit: 5,000; if longer query first." circ. 1M. 2/yr. Expects 2 issues 1999, 2 issues 2000. sub. price: $15.90; per copy: $8; sample: $8. Discounts: 25+ 20%, 50+ 30%. 208pp; 6×9; of. Reporting time: 6-8 weeks. Simultaneous submissions accepted: yes. Publishes 5% of manuscripts submitted. Payment: complimentary issues (3). Copyrighted, reverts to author. Pub's reviews. Ads: none.

Enthea Press, Carl Japikse, 4255 Trotters Way, Suite 13A, Alpharetta, GA 30004-7869. 1990. Poetry, fiction, art, satire, non-fiction. Pub'd 6 titles 1998; expects 7 titles 1999, 8 titles 2000. 17 titles listed in the *Small Press Record of Books in Print* (28th Edition, 1999-00). avg. price, paper: $10.95. Discounts: 2-4 20%, 5-24 40%, 25-49 43%, 50-99 46%, 100+ 50%. 200pp; 5½×8½. Reporting time: 6 months.

ENTROPY NEGATIVE, Les Recherches Daniel Say Cie., Daniel Say, PO Box 3355, Vancouver, B.C. V6B 3Y3, Canada. 1970. "Articles related to SF or fantasy, 1000 to 10,000 words usually of a serious mean. We cannot use U.S. stamps. Use i reply coupons for return postage" circ. 500. 4/yr. Pub'd 4 issues 1998; expects 4 issues 1999, 4 issues 2000. sub. price: $2; per copy: 75¢; sample: 75¢. 40pp; 28×21cm; †mi, of. Reporting time: 1 month. Payment: copies. Copyrighted. Pub's reviews: 50 in 1998.

Envirographics, Julianne T. McIntyre, Editor-in-Chief; John A. Harant, Editor & Publisher, Box 334, Hiram, OH 44234, (330) 527-5207. 1986. Non-fiction. avg. press run 10M. Pub'd 1 title 1998; expects 1 title 1999, 1 title 2000. 1 title listed in the *Small Press Record of Books in Print* (28th Edition, 1999-00). avg. price, cloth: $21.95; paper: $16.95. Discounts: dealers 4-40%, 100-45%, 200-50%, 500+ 55%. 250pp; 8½×5½; of. Does not copyright for author. Publishers Marketing Association (PMA).

ENVIRONMENT AND ART LETTER, Liturgy Training Publications, David Philippart, 1800 North Hermitage Avenue, Chicago, IL 60622, 312-486-8970. 1988. Articles, photos. "Focuses on the art and architecture of Catholic parish church buildings." circ. 2.3M. 12/yr. Pub'd 12 issues 1998; expects 12 issues 1999, 12 issues 2000. sub. price: $20; per copy: $2. Back issues: $2. Discounts: bulk 5+ $15/year. 12pp;

8½×11; of. Reporting time: 4 weeks. Payment: yes. Copyrighted, does not revert to author. Catholic Book Publishers Assn.

ENVIRONMENTAL & ARCHITECTURAL PHENOMENOLOGY NEWSLETTER, David Seamon, 211 Seaton Hall, Architecture Dept., Kansas State University, Manhattan, KS 66506-2901, 913-532-1121. 1990. Poetry, articles, art, criticism, reviews, letters, news items, non-fiction. "Articles and other materials focusing on the nature of environmental and architectural experience. Also, the question of what places are and why they are important to peoples' lives." circ. 200. 3/yr. Pub'd 3 issues 1998. sub. price: $10 US; $12 non-US payable in dollars; sample: free. Back issues: $10/volume (1990-1997). 16pp; 8½×8½; †of. Reporting time: 2 months. Simultaneous submissions accepted: no. Publishes 25% of manuscripts submitted. Payment: none, we're entirely non-profit. Not copyrighted. Pub's reviews: 15 in 1998. §Architecture as place making, environmental ethics, phenomenology, nature of place.

ENVIRONMENTAL HISTORY, Duke University Press, Hal K. Rothman, Box 90660, Duke University, Durham, NC 27708-0660. *"Environmental History* is an international journal dedicated to exploring the history of human interaction with the natural world. *Environmental History* is copublished by the American Society for Environmental History and the Forest History Society, as the successor publication to the two organizations' highly respected journals, *Forest & Conservation History* and *Environmental History Review*. Poised to become the journal of record in the field, *Environmental History* features up to four major articles, 25 book reviews, and bibliographic and archival news in each issue. Send review copies to Book Review Editor, Forest History Society, 701 Vickers Avenue, Durham, NC 27701." circ. 1.9M. 4/yr. Pub'd 4 issues 1998; expects 4 issues 1999, 4 issues 2000. sub. price: $60 libraries, $35 individuals, $17.50 student, additional $6 foreign. Pub's reviews. Ads: $300/$200/$400 back cover.

ENVIRONMENTAL NEWS DIGEST, Sahabat Alam Malaysia (Friends of the Earth Malaysia), 19 Kelawei Road, 10250 Penang, Malaysia. 1983. "A collection of over 200 newsbriefs which is summarized from over 300 major magazines/periodicals on Third World development and environment. Very useful as reference and documentation source. Useful for people who like to know more on environment but do not have the time or money to read or subscribe to all the magazines available." circ. 500. 3/yr. Pub'd 3 issues 1998; expects 3 issues 1999, 3 issues 2000. sub. price: $40/airmail or $30/seamail for 2 years (6 issues); per copy: US$7; sample: same. Back issues: $3. Discounts: 20-25%. 60pp; 8¾×11¾; of. Reporting time: 3 months. Payment: none, as we are a non-profit voluntary group. Not copyrighted. Pub's reviews: 30 in 1998.

EPICA (see also CHALLENGE: A Journal of Faith and Action in the Americas), Ann Butwell, Scott Wright, 1470 Irving Street NW, Washington, DC 20010, 202-332-0292. 1968. Articles, interviews, reviews, news items, non-fiction. "EPICA is a small press which specializes in titles on Central America and the Caribbean, focusing on U.S. policy and movements for social justice within the region. We have published several books of political analysis on Central America and often combine theological reflection with political analysis. In addition, EPICA publishes periodic reports on issues of current interest in the region. Our authors are predominantly EPICA staff, though we will consider and occasionally publish outside authors' work." avg. press run 2M. Pub'd 2 titles 1998; expects 2 titles 1999, 2 titles 2000. 10 titles listed in the *Small Press Record of Books in Print* (28th Edition, 1999-00). avg. price, paper: $10.95. Discounts: 20% for bulk (10 or more) or course adoptions; commercial bookstores 2-4 copies 20%, 5-9 30%, 10+ 40% (any combination of titles). 250pp; of. Payment: to be arranged.

Epicenter Press Inc., Kent Sturgis, Lael Morgan, PO Box 82368, Kenmore, WA 98028, 206-485-6822; FAX 206-481-8253. 1988. Art, photos, non-fiction. "We also publish regional travel guides under the imprint "Umbrella Books"." avg. press run 6M. Pub'd 4 titles 1998; expects 6 titles 1999, 6 titles 2000. 12 titles listed in the *Small Press Record of Books in Print* (28th Edition, 1999-00). avg. price, cloth: $24; paper: $14. Discounts: 40% retail; 50% wholesale; 20% libraries; we are distributed to the trade by Graphic Arts Center Publishing Co. of Portland, OR. 176pp; 8½×5½; of. Reporting time: 3 months. Payment: 10% of receipts. Copyrights for author. ABA, PMA, BPNW.

EPM Publications, Inc., 1003 Turkey Run Road, McLean, VA 22101, 703-442-7810. 1973. Non-fiction. "Non-fiction books about Washington, D.C., and the Mid-Atlantic region, plus a high-quality line of quilt books—mostly paperback, 8½ X 11, with color. We do not encourage submissions, prefer query letters first." avg. press run 5M. Pub'd 11 titles 1998; expects 12 titles 1999, 12 titles 2000. 80 titles listed in the *Small Press Record of Books in Print* (28th Edition, 1999-00). 250pp. Payment: competitive with big NY houses. Copyrights for author.

EPOCH, Michael Koch, Editor, 251 Goldwin Smith Hall, Cornell Univ., Ithaca, NY 14853, 607-255-3385. 1947. Poetry, fiction, reviews. "We are interested in the work of both new and established writers. Recent contributors include: William Kennedy, Michael Ondaatje, Bobbie Ann Mason, Robert Kelly, Wanda Coleman, Austin Wright, Marie-Claire Blais, Clayton Eshleman, Colleen McElroy, Joseph Langland, Josephine Miles, many other fine writers, some of whom are not yet well known. Submissions received between April 15 and

Sept. will be returned unread'' circ. 1M+. 3/yr. Pub'd 3 issues 1998; expects 3 issues 1999, 3 issues 2000. sub. price: $11; per copy: $5; sample: $5. Back issues: varies. Discounts: 40% dealers, bookstores, etc. 128pp; 6×9; of. Reporting time: 2-6 months. Simultaneous submissions accepted: no. Payment: copies, $5-$10 magazine page for fiction and poetry. Copyrighted, reverts to author. Ads: $180 (full cover); $160 (full page); $90 (half-page). CLMP.

EquiLibrium Press, Inc., Susan D. Goland, 10736 Jefferson Blvd. #680, Culver City, CA 90230, 310-204-3290; Fax 310-204-3550; equipress@mediaone.net. 1998. Non-fiction. "'Books that inform and inspire.' Wide range of wellness and health issues for an upscale female audience, eg., physical, financial, spiritual and psychological well-being. No poetry, fiction, erotica." avg. press run 3M. Expects 1 title 1999, 1-2 titles 2000. 1 title listed in the *Small Press Record of Books in Print* (28th Edition, 1999-00). avg. price, paper: varies. Discounts: upon request 128-288pp; 6×9. Reporting time: 45 days. Simultaneous submissions accepted: yes. Payment: varies. Copyrights for author. PMA.

Erespin Press (see also TITIVILLITIA: Studies of Illiteracy in the Private Press), David L. Kent, Copy Editor, 6906 Colony Loop Drive, Austin, TX 78724. 1980. Poetry, satire, non-fiction. "Particularly interested in historical translations." avg. press run 200. Pub'd 1 title 1998; expects 4 titles 1999, 4 titles 2000. 16 titles listed in the *Small Press Record of Books in Print* (28th Edition, 1999-00). avg. price, cloth: $25; paper: $15. 50pp; 6×9; †1p. Reporting time: 1 week. Payment: by arrangement. Copyrights for author. APA (Amalgamated Printers' Association), MBS (Miniature Book Society).

Paul S. Eriksson, Publisher, Paul S. Eriksson, Peggy Eriksson, PO Box 125, 368 Indian Trail/Dunmore, Forest Dale, VT 05745, 802-247-4210; fax 802-247-4256. 1960. avg. press run 3.5M. Pub'd 5 titles 1998; expects 5 titles 1999, 5 titles 2000. 26 titles listed in the *Small Press Record of Books in Print* (28th Edition, 1999-00). avg. price, cloth: $17.95; paper: $14.95. Discounts: trade distributions through Independent Publishers Group. of. Reporting time: 3 weeks. Simultaneous submissions accepted: no. Publishes a miniscule % of manuscripts submitted. Payment: 10%, 12½%, 15%, standard contract. Copyrights for author. Oblivion Press.

Eros Publishing, Mary Nicholaou, 463 Barlow Avenue, Staten Island, NY 10308, 718-317-7484. 1997. Fiction, non-fiction. "Any length that has literary merit. Send SASE for reply." avg. press run 1-5M. Pub'd 2 titles 1998; expects 1 title 1999, 6 titles 2000. 5 titles listed in the *Small Press Record of Books in Print* (28th Edition, 1999-00). avg. price, paper: $12.95; other: $15. Discounts: 55%. 100pp; 6×9, 5½×8½; of. Reporting time: within 8 weeks. Simultaneous submissions accepted: yes. Publishes 50% of manuscripts submitted. Payment: 25% on net, negotiated. Copyrights for author. SPAN.

THE EROTIC TRAVELER, Pan, PO Box 278537, Sacramento, CA 95827-8537, Fax 916-361-2364; E-mail asiafile@earthlink.net. 1991. Articles, photos, interviews, criticism, reviews, letters, news items, non-fiction. circ. 1M. 4-6/yr. Pub'd 4 issues 1998; expects 5 issues 1999, 6 issues 2000. sub. price: $36/4 issues; sample: $10. Back issues: contact us. 12pp; 8½×11; of. Reporting time: 1 month. Simultaneous submissions accepted: no. Publishes 50% of manuscripts submitted. Payment: trade for subscription/back issues. Copyrighted, reverts to author. Pub's reviews: 3 in 1998. §Prostitution, nightlife, sex. Ads: not available.

ESPERANTIC STUDIES, David K. Jordan, 3900 Northampton Street NW, Washington, DC 20015, 202-362-3963; Fax 202-363-6899; ejl@gwu.edu. 1991. Articles, reviews, non-fiction. circ. 12M. 2/yr. Pub'd 2 issues 1998; expects 2 issues 1999, 2 issues 2000. sub. price: free. 4pp; 8½×11; †1p. Payment: none. Not copyrighted. Pub's reviews: 1 in 1998. §Language problems (international, cross-cultural). Ads: none.

ESSAYS ON CANADIAN WRITING, ECW Press, Jack David, Robert Lecker, Lorraine York, 2120 Queen Street East, Suite 200, Toronto, Ontario M4E 1E2, Canada, 416-694-3348; FAX 416-698-9906. 1974. Articles, interviews, criticism, reviews. "We prefer intelligent, well-written criticism of Canadian writing from any period or genre. We lean towards formalist criticism, and specialize in bibliographies, small press reviews, and French-Canadian literature." circ. 1M. 3/yr. Pub'd 3 issues 1998; expects 3 issues 1999, 3 issues 2000. sub. price: $20 individuals, $40 institutions; per copy: $7; sample: free. Back issues: $7. Discounts: 10%. 250pp; 5½×8½; of. Reporting time: 1 month. Simultaneous submissions accepted: yes. Publishes 5% of manuscripts submitted. Payment: yes. Copyrighted, reverts to author. Pub's reviews: 20 in 1998. §Canadian writing or criticism. Ads: query. CPPA.

Estes Book Company, 15821 Hyland Pointe Court, Apple Valley, MN 55124, 612-432-1269. 1994. 1 title listed in the *Small Press Record of Books in Print* (28th Edition, 1999-00). avg. price, cloth: $17; paper: $12.

Etaoin Shrdlu Press (see also PABLO LENNIS), John Thiel, Fandom House, 30 N. 19th Street, Lafayette, IN 47904. 1976. Poetry, fiction, articles, art, photos, criticism, reviews, letters, non-fiction. "Science fiction, fantasy and science only." avg. press run 100. Expects 1 title 1999. 1 title listed in the *Small Press Record of Books in Print* (28th Edition, 1999-00). avg. price, paper: $5. 90pp; 8½×11; of. Reporting time: 2 weeks or less. Simultaneous submissions accepted: no. Publishes 80% of manuscripts submitted. Payment: none. Does not copyright for author.

ETC Publications, Dr. Richard W. Hostrop, 700 East Vereda Sur, Palm Springs, CA 92262-4816, 760-325-5352; fax 760-325-8841. 1972. "Considers timely topics in all non-fiction areas." avg. press run 2.5M. Pub'd 10 titles 1998; expects 12 titles 1999. 26 titles listed in the *Small Press Record of Books in Print* (28th Edition, 1999-00). avg. price, cloth: $19.95; paper: $12.95. Discounts: usual trade. 256pp; 6×9; of. Reporting time: 4 weeks. Payment: standard book royalties. Copyrights for author.

ETCETERA, Mindi Englart, P O Box 8543, New Haven, CT 06531, e-mail iedit4you@aol.com. 1996. Poetry, fiction, articles, art, photos, cartoons, interviews, satire, long-poems, collages, plays, concrete art, non-fiction. "Up to 1,500 words for prose; bias toward conceptual, word-play, multi-layered and multi-media work; especially looking for short fiction and b/w art and photos; linguistics. Recent contributors include: Michael Estabrook, Albert Huffstickler, John M. Bennett, Richard Kostelanetz, and Sheila E. Murphy." circ. 500. 2/yr. Pub'd 2 issues 1998; expects 2 issues 1999, 2 issues 2000. price per copy: $3; sample: $3. Back issues: $3. 28pp; 5½×8½; †of. Reporting time: acceptance/rejections announced in late March and Sept. Simultaneous submissions accepted: yes. Publishes 2% of manuscripts submitted. Payment: 1 copy + one year subscription. Copyrighted, reverts to author. Pub's reviews. §Experimental, humor, conceptual art and writing, book arts, poetry, short fiction, fine art, young people's mags (literary and art). Free mentions for other magazines I feel Etcetera readers would enjoy. Send magazine sample for inclusion in list.

ETHNOHISTORY: The Official Journal of the American Society for Ethnohistory, Duke University Press, Ross Hassig, Box 90660, Duke University, Durham, NC 27708-0660. "*Ethnohistory* emphasizes the joint use of documentary materials and ethnographic data, as well as the combination of historical and anthropological approaches, in the study of social and cultural processes and history. The journal has established a strong reputation for its studies of the history of native peoples in the Americas and in recent years has expanded its focus to cultures and societies throughout the world. *Ethnohistory* publishes articles, review essays, and book reviews by scholars in anthropology, history, linguistics, art history, geography, and other disciplines and is read by historians and anthropologists alike. Send review copies to: Susan Kellogg, Dept. of History, University of Houston, Houston, TX 77204-3785." circ. 1.5M. 4/yr. Pub'd 4 issues 1998; expects 4 issues 1999, 4 issues 2000. sub. price: $45 institutions, $25 individuals, $15 students/retired. Pub's reviews. Ads: $225/$150.

ETICA & CIENCIA, Zagier & Urruty Publicaciones, Patricia Morales, PO Box 94 Suc. 19, Buenos Aires 1419, Argentina, 541-572-1050. 1987. Articles, reviews, non-fiction. "We receive articles about scientific ethics and moral questions of scientists. Maximum 20 letter pages. Spanish or English." circ. 1.5M. 2/yr. Pub'd 2 issues 1998; expects 2 issues 1999, 2 issues 2000. sub. price: $8; per copy: $4; sample: $4. Back issues: $4. Discounts: 50% distributors, 30% bookstores. 36pp; 8½×11; of. Reporting time: 3 months. Payment: none. Copyrighted, reverts to author. Pub's reviews: 16 in 1998. §Science, philosophy, history, biographies, ethics. Ads: $400/$200.

ETR Associates, Mary Nelson, Publisher, PO Box 1830, Santa Cruz, CA 95061-1830, 408-438-4060. 1981. Non-fiction. avg. press run 1M. Pub'd 62 titles 1998; expects 75 titles 1999, 75 titles 2000. 1 title listed in the *Small Press Record of Books in Print* (28th Edition, 1999-00). size varies. PMA, PGW.

THE EUGENE O'NEILL REVIEW, Frederick C. Wilkins, Department of English, Suffolk University, Boston, MA 02114, 617-573-8272. 1977. Articles, art, photos, cartoons, interviews, criticism, reviews, letters, plays, news items, non-fiction. "*The Review's* aim is to serve as a meeting ground for O'Neill enthusiasts of academe and those of the Theatre. So it tries to blend critical articles of a scholarly sort, with news and reviews of current productions and publications. Articles of all sizes—from pithy notes to lengthy analysis—are welcome. Over-long articles are serialized. ISSN 1040-9483." circ. 550. 2/yr. Pub'd 2 issues 1998; expects 2 issues 1999, 2 issues 2000. sub. price: $15 for individuals in US + Canada, all others $25; per copy: $10; sample: free. Back issues: $10 per copy. Discounts: none. 200pp; 6×9; of. Reporting time: 2-6 months, frequently sooner. Simultaneous submissions accepted: yes. Publishes 60% of manuscripts submitted. Payment: none. Copyrighted, permissions to reprint (with acknowledgement) are never refused. Pub's reviews: 8 in 1998. §Any books or articles devoted to Eugene O'Neill (in whole or in part) or to 20th century drama and any film or stage performance of O'Neill's work. Ads: $200/$100. Eugene O'Neill Society.

Eureka Publishing Group, John Kennedy, Dixe Marquis, 1077 Pacific Coast Highway, #144, Seal Beach, CA 90740, 310-431-9912. 1994. Non-fiction. avg. press run 5M. Expects 3 titles 1999, 6 titles 2000. 1 title listed in the *Small Press Record of Books in Print* (28th Edition, 1999-00). avg. price, paper: $21.95. Discounts: Short only. 200pp; 8½×11; lp. Reporting time: 3-4 months. Payment: some advance, 10-15%. Copyrights optional.

EUROPEAN JUDAISM, Rabbi Dr. Albert H. Friedlander, Rabbi Professor Jonathan Magonet, Leo Baeck College, 80 East End Rd., Sternberg Centre for Judaism, London N3 2SY, United Kingdom, 44-181-349-4525; Fax 44-181-343-2558; leo-baeck-college@mailbox.ulcc.ac.uk; www.lb-college.demon.co.uk. 1966. Poetry, fiction, articles, interviews, criticism, reviews, letters. "Recent contributors include Elie Wiesel, Crown Prince

Hassan of Jordan, Karen Armstrong, Marc H. Ellis, Simone Veil, Hyam Maccoby. The name of the magazine describes its orientation." circ. 400. 2/yr. Pub'd 2 issues 1998; expects 2 issues 1999, 2 issues 2000. sub. price: £18 ($27); per copy: £9 ($13.50); sample: gratis from Berghahn Books. Back issues: as single copies. Discounts: please contact Berghahn Books, 401-861-9330. 156pp; 9×6; lp. Reporting time: 6 weeks. Simultaneous submissions accepted: yes. Publishes 60% of manuscripts submitted. Payment: 1 free copy. Copyrighted, reverts to author. Pub's reviews: 11 in 1998. §Judaism plus religion, philosophy and history in general, literary expression by Jews (poems, short stories). Ads: contact us.

Eurotique Press, Janet L. Przirembel, Kevin P. Grieco, 3109 45th Street, Suite 300, West Palm Beach, FL 33407-1915, 561-687-0455; 800-547-4326. 1995. Fiction, art, cartoons, non-fiction. avg. press run 1.5M-2M. Pub'd 1 title 1998; expects 4 titles 1999, 7-8 titles 2000. 2 titles listed in the *Small Press Record of Books in Print* (28th Edition, 1999-00). avg. price, paper: $16.95. Discounts: bookstores 20%. Reporting time: 2-3 months. Payment: worked out individually. Copyrights for author.

Evanston Publishing, Inc., Dorothy Kavka, Senior Editor, 4848 Brownsboro Center, Louisville, KY 40207-2342, 502-899-1919; 800-594-5190; EvanstonPB@aol.com. 1987. avg. press run 2M. Pub'd 13 titles 1998; expects 6 titles 1999, 3 titles 2000. 13 titles listed in the *Small Press Record of Books in Print* (28th Edition, 1999-00). avg. price, cloth: $25; paper: $15. Discounts: 2-4 20%, 5-9 40%, 100+ 50%. 224pp; 6×9. Reporting time: 1 month. Simultaneous submissions accepted: no. Publishes 10% of manuscripts submitted. Payment: standard small press agreement. Copyrights for author. PMA, ABPA, Small Press Assoc.

EVANSVILLE REVIEW, Ingrid Jendrzejewski, Univ. of Evansville, English Dept., 1800 Lincoln Avenue, Evansville, IN 47714, 812-488-1042. 1991. Poetry, fiction, interviews, satire, parts-of-novels, non-fiction, plays. "Nothing longer than 20 pages, please. We publish many undiscovered writers along with established writers. Please query with nonfiction and interviews. Recent contributors include Marge Piercy, David Ignatow, Lucian Stryk, John Updike, Felix Stefanile, Willis Barnstone, Charles Wright, and Tess Gallagher. All manuscripts are recycled, not returned. Please include SASE for reply. A brief bio or list of previous publications is appreciated as we print contributors notes." circ. 3M. 1/yr. Pub'd 1 issue 1998; expects 1 issue 1999, 1 issue 2000. price per copy: $5; sample: $5. Back issues: $5. Discounts: negotiable. 200pp; 6×9; of. Reporting time: We notify in late February. Manuscripts are not read between January and May and must be received by December 5th. We accept simultaneous submissions with notification. Publishes 3% of manuscripts submitted. Payment: 2 copies. Not copyrighted. Ads: none.

EVENT, Calvin Wharton, Douglas College, PO Box 2503, New Westminster, B.C. V3L 5B2, Canada, 604-527-5293. 1971. Poetry, fiction, reviews, long-poems. "Although we are devoted to those who are writing high-quality work but are not yet established, we feature prominent authors as well. Previous contributors include Kenneth J. Harvey, Susan Musgrave, Patricia Young and Tim Bowling." circ. 1.1M. 3/yr. Pub'd 3 issues 1998; expects 3 issues 1999, 3 issues 2000. sub. price: $18, $28/2 years; per copy: $7.00; sample: current $7.00. Back issues: $5. Discounts: 20%. 136-160pp; 6×9; of. Reporting time: 3-4 months. Payment: honorarium. Copyrighted, reverts to author. Pub's reviews: 22 in 1998. §Poetry, short fiction, novels. Ads: $100/$50. CMPA.

Event Horizon Press, Joseph Cowles, Barbora Cowles, PO Box 2006, Palm Springs, CA 92263, 760-329-3950. 1990. Poetry, fiction, art, photos, long-poems, plays, non-fiction. "Not presently accepting submissions." avg. press run 250-5M. Pub'd 2 titles 1998; expects 2 titles 1999, 2 titles 2000. 15 titles listed in the *Small Press Record of Books in Print* (28th Edition, 1999-00). avg. price, cloth: $24.95; paper: $12.95. Discounts: offered to distributors, bulk purchases and libraries. 48-352pp; 5½×8½, 6×9, 11×8½; of, lp. Publishes less than .05% of manuscripts submitted. Payment: contracts set up with each author. Copyrights for author.

THE EVER DANCING MUSE, Who Who Who Publishing, John A. Chorazy, PO Box 7751, East Rutherford, NJ 07073. 1993. Poetry, art, parts-of-novels, long-poems. circ. 50-100. 2/yr. Expects 2 issues 1999, 2 issues 2000. sub. price: $8/3 issues; per copy: $3; sample: $3. 20pp; 8½×5½; of. Reporting time: 1-4 weeks. Simultaneous submissions accepted if specified as such. Payment: 2 copies. Copyrighted, reverts to author.

THE EVERGREEN CHRONICLES, Susan Raffo, Managing Editor; Louisa Castner, PO Box 8939, Minneapolis, MN 55408-8939, 612-823-6638; e-mail evgrnchron@aol.com. 1985. Poetry, fiction, art, photos, cartoons, satire, criticism, reviews, letters, parts-of-novels, long-poems, collages, plays, non-fiction. "*The Evergreen Chronicles* is a journal of gay, lesbian, bisexual, transgender arts and cultures. We publish a wide spectrum of poetry, creative fiction, critical essays, and visual artwork. We are open to every genre. Writers may submit up to 25 pages per prose work; up to 10 pages of poetry; and artwork that is 5 X 7 minimum and up to 8½ X 11 maximum. Please send 4 copies and SASE." circ. 1M. 3/yr. Pub'd 3 issues 1998; expects 3 issues 1999, 3 issues 2000. sub. price: $20 individual, $40 institution, $25 international; per copy: $7.95 + $1 postage; sample: $7.95 + $1 postage. Back issues: $7.95 + $1 postage. Discounts: 60% wholesale. 90pp; 5½×8½; offset full run. Reporting time: 2 months from deadline. Simultaneous submissions are accepted but we would like to know that from cover letter. Publishes 10-15% of manuscripts submitted. Payment: in copies and honorarium. Copyrighted, reverts to author. Pub's reviews: 4 in 1998. §Gay, lesbian, bisexual, and transgenders literature, both fiction and nonfiction. Ads: $125/$95/$50.

Ex Machina Publishing Company, Margaret R. Robinson, Owner; Ronald L. Robinson, Editor, Box 448, Sioux Falls, SD 57101. 1986. Fiction, non-fiction. avg. press run 2M. Pub'd 1 title 1998; expects 2 titles 1999. 12 titles listed in the *Small Press Record of Books in Print* (28th Edition, 1999-00). avg. price, cloth: $15-$25; paper: $10-$20. Discounts: 6-49 40%, 50+ 50%-55%. 150-250pp; 5½×8½; contract for printing. Reporting time: varies. Simultaneous submissions accepted: yes. Publishes 5% of manuscripts submitted. Payment: 10% of retail. Copyrights for author. PMA.

Excalibur Publishing Inc., 511 Avenue of the Americas, Suite 392, New York, NY 10011, 212-777-1790. 1990. Fiction, non-fiction. "Not currently publishing new titles. First book is a novel, *Bloomin* by Maria Ciaccia; second, a children's book, *Alpha Beta and Gamma*; third, *Auditioning for Opera* by Joan Dornemann of Metropolitan Opera; fourth, *By Actors For Actors*, a compilation of scenes and monologues, in 1991. We are interested in books targeting the performing artist as well as business books. Other titles include *Dreamboats: Hollywood Hunks of the '50s* by Maria Ciaccia; *By Actors/For Actors, Vol. II*; *Practical Parenting* by Julie Ross." avg. press run 2-3M. Expects 4 titles 2000. 14 titles listed in the *Small Press Record of Books in Print* (28th Edition, 1999-00). avg. price, cloth: $18.95. Discounts: 1-4 20%; 5-9 30%; 10-24 40%; 25-49 42%; 50-74 44%; 75-99 46%; 100-199 48%; 200+50%. 6×9. Payment: standard author contract 6% (trade p'back) on first 7500, 7% on next 7500, etc. Copyrights for author. PMA.

Excelsior Cee Publishing, J.C. Marshall, PO Box 5861, Norman, OK 73070, 405-329-3909; Fax 405-329-6886; ecp@oecadvantage.net; www.oecadvantage.net/ecp. 1989. "Nonfiction and how-to publishing." avg. press run 3M. 5 titles listed in the *Small Press Record of Books in Print* (28th Edition, 1999-00). avg. price, paper: $5-$10. Discounts: available on request. 200pp; 5½×8½. Reporting time: 6 weeks. Simultaneous submissions accepted: yes. Payment: negotiable. Copyrights for author.

Exceptional Books, Ltd., John C. Allred, President; Thomas E. Elliott, Vice-President & Treasurer, 798 47th Street, Los Alamos, NM 87544, 505-662-7700. 1987. Fiction, non-fiction. "Primary history, science." avg. press run 2M. Pub'd 1 title 1998; expects 1 title 1999, 1 title 2000. 4 titles listed in the *Small Press Record of Books in Print* (28th Edition, 1999-00). avg. price, cloth: $25; paper: $12. Discounts: 40% to the trade, write for schedule. 300pp; 6×9; of. Reporting time: 4 weeks. Payment: negotiable; 15% typical. Copyrights for author. Rocky Mtn. Book Publishers Assn. (RMBPA), New Mexico Book Association (NMBA).

EXCEPTIONALITY EDUCATION CANADA, V. Timmons, University of PEI, 550 University Avenue, Charlottetown, PEI C1A 4P3, Canada. 1991. Articles. "The journal is intended to provide a forum for scholarly exchange among Canadian professionals in education and related disciplines who work with students across the spectrum of exceptionality. The purpose is to present current research and theory and to identify emerging trends and visions for the education of students with exceptionalities." circ. 225. 4/yr. Pub'd 4 issues 1998; expects 4 issues 1999, 4 issues 2000. sub. price: Inst. $50, Indiv. $30, Student $20; in Canada add GST, outside Canada price is in US dollars $55/2 years (indiv.); per copy: $9 + GST in Canada; outside Canada in US dollars. 108pp; 6×9; of. Reporting time: 2 months. Copyrighted, does not revert to author. Pub's reviews: 1 in 1998. §Education of students with exceptionalities. Ads: write for information. BPAA, ACUP.

EXCLAIM!, Exclaim! Brand Comics, Ian Danzig, 7b Pleasant Boulevard #966, Toronto, ON M4T 1K2, Canada, 416-535-9735; Fax 416-535-0566; exclaim@shmooze.net. 1992. Articles, art, photos, cartoons, interviews, satire, criticism, reviews, music, letters, collages, news items, non-fiction. circ. 85M. 11/yr. Pub'd 11 issues 1998; expects 11 issues 1999, 11 issues 2000. sub. price: $25 US; per copy: $2.50 US; sample: same. Back issues: $3 US. Discounts: free in Canada. 56pp; 10¼×11¾. We will possibly accept simultaneous submissions. Publishes 10% of manuscripts submitted. Payment: varies. Copyrighted, reverts to author. Pub's reviews: lots of in 1998. §Fanzines, comic books. Ads: $995 US/$655 US.

Exclaim! Brand Comics (see also EXCLAIM!), Ian Danzig, Tony Walsh, 7b Pleasant Boulevard #966, Toronto, ON M4T 1K2, Canada, 416-535-9735; Fax 416-535-0566; exclaim@schmooze.net. 1995. Fiction, art, cartoons. "We publish comic books." avg. press run 2M. Pub'd 1 title 1998; expects 2 titles 1999, 2 titles 2000. avg. price, paper: $2.75 US. Discounts: varies. 44pp; 6¾×10. Publishes 1% of manuscripts submitted. Payment: varies. Copyrights for author.

EXERCISE IMMUNOLOGY REVIEW (EIR), Human Kinetics Pub. Inc., H. Northhoff, P.O. Box 5076, Champaign, IL 61825-5076, 217-351-5076, fax 217-351-2674. 1995. "*Exercise Immunology Review* is committed to developing and enriching knowledge in all aspects of immunology that relate to sport, exercise, and regular physical activity" circ. 200. 1/yr. sub. price: $20 indiv., $40 instit., $12 students; per copy: $20 indiv., $40 instit., $12 students. Back issues: $20 indiv., $40 instit., $12 students. 144pp; 6×9; of. Copyrighted, does not revert to author. Ads: $300/$200.

Exhorter Publications International, Clarence Ray Johnson, Editor, 323 W. High Street, Elizabethtown, PA 17022-2141. 1995. Poetry, non-fiction. Pub'd 1 title 1998; expects 1 title 1999. 1 title listed in the *Small Press Record of Books in Print* (28th Edition, 1999-00). avg. price, paper: $10.95. Discounts: 40% to book dealers.

Exile Press, Leslie Woolf Hedley, Editor-Publisher; Koky Hedley, Managing Editor, 112 Chadwick Way, Cotati, CA 94931. 1983. Fiction, articles, satire. "Not accepting any submissions until further notice. Innovative stories. Founded in 1949 as Inferno Press, we're the oldest independent small press in the USA. Anglo-Eurocentric." avg. press run 500-1.5M. Pub'd 5 titles 1998; expects 3 titles 1999, 2 titles 2000. 11 titles listed in the *Small Press Record of Books in Print* (28th Edition, 1999-00). avg. price, other: $12.95 and up. Discounts: 30-40%. 116-248pp; 5½×8; †of. Reporting time: under 6 weeks. Payment: in copies. Copyrights for author.

EXIT 13 MAGAZINE, Tom Plante, Editor, P O Box 423, Fanwood, NJ 07023. 1987. Poetry, photos. "Previously published *Berkeley Works Magazine* (1981-1985). I seek manuscripts of poetry with a view of the terrain familiar to the writer. *Exit 13* prefers a geographic bent and uses work from all over the U.S. and occasional contributions from outside these borders. Fresh faces and views are welcome. Back issues are available. Photos of Exit 13 road signs earn a free magazine. ISSN 1054-3937." circ. 500. 1/yr. Pub'd 1 issue 1998; expects 1 issue 1999, 1 issue 2000. sub. price: $7; per copy: $7; sample: $7. Discounts: 40% for 5 or more copies of any one issue, prepaid. 64pp; 5½×8½; of. Reporting time: 4 months. Simultaneous submissions accepted: yes. Publishes 5-10% of manuscripts submitted. Payment: copy of issue containing author's work. Copyrighted, rights revert to author but *Exit 13* keeps anthology rights. Pub's reviews: 20 in 1998. §Small press poetry books, magazines and anthologies. Ads: $45 camera ready/$25/$13 1/4 page camera ready.

Expanded Media Editions, Pociao, PO Box 190136, Prinz Albert Str. 65, 53AA3 Bonn 1, Germany, Germany, 0228/22 95 83; FAX 0228/21 95 07. 1969. Poetry, fiction, art, photos, interviews, criticism, music, collages. "Recent contributors: W. S. Burroughs, Jurgen Ploog, Claude Pelieu-Washburn, Allen Ginsberg, Gerard Malanga, Paul Bowles." avg. press run 2M. Pub'd 3 titles 1998; expects 2 titles 1999, 4 titles 2000. 13 titles listed in the *Small Press Record of Books in Print* (28th Edition, 1999-00). avg. price, paper: DM 15. Discounts: 1-5 copies 25%, 6-20 30%, 21-50 40%, 50+ 50%. 100pp; 21×14; lp. Payment: 10% per sold book. Copyrights for author.

EXPERIMENTAL MUSICAL INSTRUMENTS, Bart Hopkin, PO Box 784, Nicasio, CA 94946, 415-662-2182. 1985. "For the design, construction, and enjoyment of unusual sound sources." circ. 1200. 4/yr. Pub'd 4 issues 1998; expects 4 issues 1999, 4 issues 2000. sub. price: $24; per copy: $6; sample: gratis. Back issues: varies. Discounts: write for schedule. 48pp; 8½×11; offset. Reporting time: 2 weeks. Simultaneous submissions accepted: yes. Publishes 50% of manuscripts submitted. Payment: none. Copyrighted, reverts to author. Pub's reviews: 8 in 1998. §Musical instruments. Ads: $60 1/2 pare/$40 1/4 page/$25 1/8 page/40¢ word classifieds, 15 word minimum.

EXPLORATIONS, Art Petersen, Editor; Alice Tersteeg, English Dept., Alaska Univ. Southeast, 11120 Glacier Highway, Juneau, AK 99801. 1981. Poetry, fiction. "A literary publication. Subject matter less important than quality. Poetry, fiction, fine arts. Best for submitters to send for guidelines first, SASE required. A reading fee is required: $6 for 1-2 poems; $3 each up to 5 poems, 60 lines maximum and $6 for each short story (up to 2, 3000 words maximum); those who submit recieve a copy of the publications in July. Deadline for submissions: May 15 of each year." circ. 650. 1/yr. Pub'd 1 issue 1998; expects 1 issue 1999, 1 issue 2000. sub. price: $6/1 issue, $11/2 issues, $10/3 issues; per copy: $6; sample: $5. Back issues: $5. Discounts: 50% for 10 or more. 60pp; 5½×8½; of. Reporting time: 6 months, December through May 15; notification in July. Simultaneous submissions accepted: yes. Publishes 3% of manuscripts submitted. Payment: copies, $1700 in prizes: one $1000 first prize and second $500, two third $100, for poetry and prose. Copyrighted. No ads.

Explorer Press, Terry Collins, 1449 Edgewood Drive, Mount Airy, NC 27030-5215, 336-789-6005; Fax 336-789-6005; E-mail terrycollins@advi.net. 1993. avg. press run 10M. Pub'd 2 titles 1998; expects 1 title 1999, 1 title 2000. 1 title listed in the *Small Press Record of Books in Print* (28th Edition, 1999-00). avg. price, cloth: $23.95; paper: $12.95; other: $2.95. Discounts: inquire. 200pp; 6×9; of. Reporting time: 3 months. Simultaneous submissions accepted: no. Payment: inquire. Copyrights for author. PMA.

Explorer's Guide Publishing, 4843 Apperson Drive, Rhinelander, WI 54501, 715-362-6029 phone/Fax; 800-487-6029. 1984. Non-fiction. avg. press run 2M-3M. Pub'd 2 titles 1998; expects 6 titles 1999. 11 titles listed in the *Small Press Record of Books in Print* (28th Edition, 1999-00). avg. price, paper: $4.95-$12.95. Discounts: 20%, 42%, 44% bookstores, wholesale rates on request. 144pp; 8½×11, 6×9; of. Reporting time: 2 months. Simultaneous submissions accepted: yes. Publishes .5% of manuscripts submitted. Payment: negotiable contract. Copyrights for author. Mid-America Publishers (MAP), Upper Midwest Booksellers Association (UMBA), Publishers Marketing Association (PMA).

EyeDEA Books, Jeff Norman, Editor, 477 Rich Street, Oakland, CA 94609, 510-653-7190. 1990. Fiction, art, photos. "EyeDEA Books is dedicated to the publication of artists' books. We're specifically interested in books that explore the relationship between visual images and text, or that combine images and text in new, interesting ways. Only work that is appropriate for printing in black and white will be considered. SASE required for return of materials.'' avg. press run 1M. Expects 2 titles 1999, 2 titles 2000. 2 titles listed in the *Small Press Record of Books in Print* (28th Edition, 1999-00). avg. price, paper: $8.95. Discounts: trade 1-4 20%, 1-4 prepaid 40%, 5-24 40%, 25-49 42%, 50-99 45%, 100+ 47%; add 3% additional discount for prepaid order. 56pp; 5½×8½; of. Reporting time: 30 days. Payment: not established. Copyrights for author.

EZ Nature Books, Ed Zolkoski, Owner, PO Box 4206, San Luis Obispo, CA 93403. 1983. Photos, non-fiction. avg. press run 3M-5M. Pub'd 3 titles 1998; expects 3 titles 1999, 2 titles 2000. 12 titles listed in the *Small Press Record of Books in Print* (28th Edition, 1999-00). avg. price, cloth: $30-$35; paper: $8.95. Discounts: 40% to retailers, other by negotiation. 128pp; 5½×8½, 8½×11; of. Publishes 5-10% of manuscripts submitted. Payment: 10% paid quarterly. Does not copyright for author. PMA.

F

●**Faben, Inc.**, PO Box 3133, Sarasota, FL 34230, 941-955-0050; fax 941-365-5472; e-mail sales@faben-books.com. 1977. 1 title listed in the *Small Press Record of Books in Print* (28th Edition, 1999-00).

FACES: The Magazine About People, Cobblestone Publishing, Inc., Lynn Sloneker, Editor, 7 School Street, Peterborough, NH 03458. 1984. Articles, art, photos, reviews, non-fiction. "*Faces* is designed to expose young people to other peoples and cultures of the world; to help them realize that no country is any better than any other; to learn and understand how other people live and do things; to see the world in new ways and to help them reflect on how they assign importance to things, ideas and people in their own lives. Material must be written for children ages 8-14. Write for guidelines as we focus each issue on a particular theme." circ. 13.5M. 9/yr. Pub'd 9 issues 1998; expects 9 issues 1999, 9 issues 2000. sub. price: $26.95; add $8 for foreign mail, Canadian subs add 7% GST; per copy: $4.50; sample: $4.50. Back issues: $4.50. Discounts: 15% for sub. agencies, bulk rate 3 or more $15.95/year sub. each. 48pp; 7×9; of. Reporting time: queries sent well in advance of deadline may not be answered for several months. Go-aheads usually sent 5 months prior to publication date. Payment: on publication. Copyrighted, Cobblestone Publishing buys all rights. Pub's reviews: 81 in 1998. §Books for children, age 8-14, related to themes covered. No ads. Classroom Publishers Assoc./Ed Press.

Factor Press, Allen Erich, editor, PO Box 8888, Mobile, AL 36689, 334-380-0606. 1990. "We commission books; we're not a freelance market." avg. press run 1-6M. Pub'd 4 titles 1998; expects 3 titles 1999, 4 titles 2000. 12 titles listed in the *Small Press Record of Books in Print* (28th Edition, 1999-00). avg. price, cloth: $18.95; paper: $12.95; other: $12.95. Discounts: exclusive distributor—LPC Group. 215pp; 5½×8½. Payment: varies. Copyrights for author. ABA, SPAN.

Facts on Demand Press (see also BRB Publications, Inc.), PO Box 27869, Tempe, AZ 85285-7869, 800-929-3811; Fax 800-929-4981; brb@brbpub.com. 3 titles listed in the *Small Press Record of Books in Print* (28th Edition, 1999-00).

FACTSHEET FIVE, R. Seth Friedman, Publisher, PO Box 170099, San Francisco, CA 94117, 415-668-1781. 1983. Articles, photos, cartoons, reviews, collages. "We review most small-press, independent magazines and zines sent in." circ. 16M. 3-4/yr. Pub'd 2 issues 1998; expects 3 issues 1999, 4 issues 2000. sub. price: $20 for 1½ years, 6 issues $40 for insitutions/corporations; per copy: $6; sample: $6. Back issues: $5. Discounts: premium rate available for $40 provides expedited delivery to individuals and institutions. 144pp; 8¼×10¾; web. Reporting time: 2 months. Simultaneous submissions accepted: yes. Publishes 10% of manuscripts submitted. Payment: 2 copies + $25 for cartoon, $150 for cover photo, $100 for article. Copyrighted, reverts to author. Pub's reviews: 1,200 per issue; 5000 per year in 1998. §All areas; must be less than 5,000 circulation; all magazines, some books. Ads: $460/$240/50¢ per word.

Faded Banner Publications, Don Allison, PO Box 101, Bryan, OH 43506-0101, 419-636-3807; fax 419-636-3970. 1997. Non-fiction. "We specialize in the American Civil War." avg. press run 1.2M. Expects 1 title 1999, 1 title 2000. 1 title listed in the *Small Press Record of Books in Print* (28th Edition, 1999-00). avg. price, paper: $15.95. Discounts: bulk 3-5 10%, 6-99 40%, 100+ 50%, 10+ on no return basis 50%. 192pp; of. Reporting time: 1 month. Simultaneous submissions accepted: yes. Publishes 0% of manuscripts submitted. Payment: to be determined. Does not copyright for author.

FAG RAG, Fag Rag Books, Good Gay Poets Press, Fag Rag Collective, Box 15331, Kenmore Station, Boston, MA 02215, 617-426-4469. 1970. Poetry, fiction, articles, art, photos, cartoons, interviews, satire, criticism, reviews, music, letters, parts-of-novels, long-poems, collages, plays, concrete art, non-fiction. "Prefer short contributions; need new b&w art always." circ. 5M, readership 20M. 1/yr. Expects 1 issue 1999. sub. price: US $10 for 4 issues, international $15 for 2 issues; per copy: $10; sample: $5. Back issues: $2.50. Discounts: $4 retail; 40% to retailers, 50% to distributors. 32pp; 11×17; web. Reporting time: max. 3 months. Simultaneous submissions accepted: yes. Publishes 5% of manuscripts submitted. Payment: copies. Copyrighted, reverts to author. Pub's reviews: 10 in 1998. §Politics, gay lit., poetry, essays, culture. Ads: none. CLMP, NESPA.

Fag Rag Books (see also FAG RAG), PO Box 15331, Boston, MA 02215.

Falcon Press Publishing Company, Richard F. Newby, PO Box 1718, Helena, MT 59624, 406-942-6597; 800-582-2665. 1978. Poetry, photos, non-fiction. avg. press run 10M. Pub'd 60 titles 1998; expects 70 titles 1999, 85 titles 2000. 115 titles listed in the *Small Press Record of Books in Print* (28th Edition, 1999-00). avg. price, cloth: $23; paper: $12.95. Discounts: 45% retail accounts; 50% wholesale; 20% library. 200pp; 6×9, 8½×11, 10×13½. Reporting time: 3 months. Simultaneous submissions accepted: yes. Publishes 5% of manuscripts submitted. Payment: royalty, payable twice yearly. Copyrights negotiable. Rocky Mtn. Booksellers Assn., Mtns. and Plains, PMA, No. Cal Booksellers Assn., Pac. NW Booksellers Assn., UMBA, SEBA, NEBA.

Fall Creek Press, Helen Wirth, PO Box 1127, Fall Creek, OR 97438, 503-744-0938. 1991. Fiction. "Publishes only books on spontaneous theatre." avg. press run 3M. Expects 1 title 2000. 5 titles listed in the *Small Press Record of Books in Print* (28th Edition, 1999-00). avg. price, paper: $14.95. 192pp; 5½×8½. Does not copyright for author.

Fallen Leaf Press, Ann Basart, PO Box 10034, Berkeley, CA 94709, 510-848-7805 phone/Fax. 1984. Music, non-fiction. "We publish reference books on music, scores of contemporary American music, and monographs on contemporary composers. We do not accept unsolicited musical scores" avg. press run music 150, books 500-1000. Pub'd 3 titles 1998; expects 3 titles 1999, 3 titles 2000. 18 titles listed in the *Small Press Record of Books in Print* (28th Edition, 1999-00). avg. price, cloth: $37; paper: music $25, books $20. Discounts: 1 20%, 2 23%, 3 25%, 4 27%, 5 29%, 6 31%, 7 33%, 8 35%, 9 37%, 10+ 40%. Music varies, books 200-400pp; 6×9, 7×10; of. Reporting time: 1-2 months. Simultaneous submissions accepted: no. Publishes 20% of manuscripts submitted. Payment: varies. We sometimes copyright for author. SPAN.

Fallout Shelter Press, Andrew Wertheimer, 2450 Sycamore Lane #16A, West Lafayette, IN 47906-1974. 1990. Poetry, interviews, non-fiction. "Not currently taking submissions" avg. press run 20-200. Expects 1 title 1999, 1 title 2000. 3 titles listed in the *Small Press Record of Books in Print* (28th Edition, 1999-00). avg. price, other: $4. Discounts: contact us. 20-50pp; 4¼×5½; †photocopy. Reporting time: varies. Payment: varies. Copyrights for author.

FAMILY THERAPY, Libra Publishers, Inc., Martin Blinder, Editor, 3089C Clairemont Dr., Suite 383, San Diego, CA 92117, 619-571-1414. 1960. Articles. circ. 1.5M. 3/yr. Pub'd 3 issues 1998; expects 3 issues 1999, 3 issues 2000. sub. price: $75; per copy: $25; sample: free. Back issues: $25. Discounts: 10% to subscriber agents. 128pp; 6×9; of. Reporting time: 3 weeks. Payment: none. Copyrighted. Pub's reviews. §Behavioral sciences. Ads: $150/$85.

FAMILY TIMES: The Newspaper for Chippewa Valley Parents, Nancy S. Walter, Publisher, PO Box 932, Eau Claire, WI 54702, 715-836-9499; fax 715-839-7052; e-mail familyt@discover-net.net. 1990. Articles, art, photos, reviews. "Articles and columns about parenting issues. Focus on west central Wisconsin." circ. 15M. 6/yr. Pub'd 6 issues 1998; expects 6 issues 1999, 6 issues 2000. sub. price: $9; per copy: free; sample: $2. Back issues: $2. 24pp; 11×17; of. Reporting time: 6 months. Publishes 10% of manuscripts submitted. Payment: columns $25, articles $35-50, illustrations $35. Copyrighted, reverts to author. Pub's reviews: 24 in 1998. §Parenting issues, how-to, children's books, homeschool books. Ads: $750/525/395 1/4 page/$230 1/8 page/$118 1/16/$70.

Family Works Publications, PO Box 22509, Honolulu, HI 96823-2509, 1-800-526-1478, Fax 808-538-0423. 1992. Non-fiction. "Concentrating on parenting and child care techniques. Published *Parachutes for Parents* - June 1993, 528 pages. Second edition May 1995, 552 pages" avg. press run 7.5M. Pub'd 1 title 1998; expects 1 title 1999, 2 titles 2000. 1 title listed in the *Small Press Record of Books in Print* (28th Edition, 1999-00). avg. price, paper: $19.95. Discounts: 1-2 0%, 3-199 40%, 200-499 50%, 500+ 40%/-25%. 360pp; 6×9; of. Reporting time: 14 days. Simultaneous submissions accepted: no. Payment: negotiated. Copyrights for author. PMA.

Fantagraphics Books (see also THE COMICS JOURNAL), Gary Groth, (Comics Journal), 7563 Lake City Way, Seattle, WA 98115. 1976. Articles, art, cartoons, interviews, criticism, reviews, news items. "Fantagraphics publishes the widest variety of classic and contemporary comics and cartoons of any publisher, including the works of Robert Crumb, Jules Feiffer, E.C. Segar, Winsor McCay, Harold Gray, Hal Foster, Gilbert and Jaime Hernandez, Peter Bagge, Dan Clowes, Ralph Steadman, Spain Rodriguez, Kim Deitch, Rick Geary, Jose Munoz, and Carlos Sampayo" avg. press run 6M. Pub'd 30 titles 1998; expects 35 titles 1999, 35 titles 2000. 118 titles listed in the *Small Press Record of Books in Print* (28th Edition, 1999-00). avg. price,

184

other: $5.95. Comics 32pp, books 150pp; 8½×11; of. Reporting time: 1-2 months. Simultaneous submissions accepted: yes. Publishes 1% of manuscripts submitted. Payment: on publication, royalties vary. Copyrights for author.

Fantail, PO Box 462, Hollis, NH 03049-0462. 1996. Art, photos, non-fiction. avg. press run 2.5M. Pub'd 1 title 1998; expects 1 title 1999, 1 title 2000. 2 titles listed in the *Small Press Record of Books in Print* (28th Edition, 1999-00). avg. price, cloth: $39.95; paper: $18.95. Discounts: 2-3 20%, 4-9 30%, 10-199 40%, 200+ 50%. 175pp; 11×9; of. Simultaneous submissions accepted: yes. Copyrights for author. PMA.

Far Corner Books, Thomas S. Booth, Managing Editor, PO Box 82157, Portland, OR 97282. 1991. Poetry, fiction, non-fiction. "We are not accepting unsolicited manuscripts in 1995-96" avg. press run 2.5M-5M. Pub'd 1 title 1998; expects 1 title 1999, 1 title 2000. 19 titles listed in the *Small Press Record of Books in Print* (28th Edition, 1999-00). avg. price, cloth: $23; paper: $10. Discounts: standard to bookstores. 64-350pp; 6×9; of. Reporting time: 2 months, SASE only! Payment: varies, depending upon author. Copyrights for author. PNBA, ABA.

FAR GONE, Todd Brendan Fahey, PO Box 43745, Lafayette, LA 70504-3745. 1995. Poetry, interviews, satire, long-poems. "The inagural issue features interviews with Ken Kessey. 'This is the most striking journal around'—Timothy Leary" circ. 100. 1/yr. Expects 2 issues 1999, 1 issue 2000. price per copy: $7; sample: $7. Discounts: $7. 48pp; 11×8½; of. Reporting time: continuing, until issue is filled. Publishes 15% of manuscripts submitted. Payment: 1 copy. Copyrighted, reverts to author. Pub's reviews. §Small press fiction, novels and short story collections, no genre, and small press poetry (no chaps).

FARM PULP MAGAZINE, Gregory Hischak, PO Box 2151, Seattle, WA 98111-2151, 206-782-7418. 1990. Fiction, articles, art, photos, cartoons, satire, reviews, collages. circ. 400. 5/yr. Pub'd 5 issues 1998; expects 5 issues 1999, 5 issues 2000. sub. price: $10; per copy: $2; sample: $2. Back issues: $2. Discounts: subscriptions of six for $10, 1/2 price for bulk purchase (over 15). 24pp; 6¾×11; †photocopy. Reporting time: 1 week. Payment: in samples. Not copyrighted. Pub's reviews: 20-25 in 1998. §Zines only.

FARMER'S DIGEST, Lessiter Publications, Frank Lessiter, PO Box 624, Brookfield, WI 53008-0624, 414-782-4480. 1938. Reviews. circ. 15M. 10/yr. Pub'd 10 issues 1998; expects 10 issues 1999, 10 issues 2000. sub. price: $17.95; per copy: $3.50; sample: $3.50. Back issues: $3.50. 100pp; 6×9; of. Reporting time: none. Simultaneous submissions accepted: no. Payment: none. Copyrighted, does not revert to author. Pub's reviews: 10 in 1998. §Agriculture, Nostalgia.

FARMING UNCLE, Louis Toro, Editor, C/O Toro, P O Box 580118, Bronx, NY 10458-0711. 1977. Articles, reviews, non-fiction. circ. 1M. 4/yr. Pub'd 4 issues 1998; expects 4 issues 1999, 4 issues 2000. sub. price: $8; per copy: $2; sample: $2. Back issues: $2 each. 24pp; 5×8; of. Reporting time: immediate. Simultaneous submissions accepted: yes. Publishes 90% of manuscripts submitted. Payment: .05¢. Copyrighted, reverts to author. Pub's reviews: 4 in 1998. §Agriculture, small farms, gardening, animal husbandry, etc. Ads: $47.50/$27.50/$4.50 1 inch.

FASTENING, Mike McGuire, 293 Hopewell Drive, Powell, OH 43065, 614-848-3232; 800-848-0304; FAX 614-848-5045. 1995. Articles, interviews, letters, news items. "Length of material: 1200-1500 words with or without photo(s)." circ. 26.5M. 4/yr. Pub'd 4 issues 1998; expects 4 issues 1999, 4 issues 2000. sub. price: $30; per copy: $7.50; sample: $10. Back issues: $10. 60pp; 8½×11; sheetfeed. Reporting time: 3-4 weeks. Simultaneous submissions accepted: yes. Payment: after publication - 30 days net. Copyrighted, does not revert to author. Pub's reviews. §Manufacturing, quality, assembly. Ads: $1750/$1075/$725 1/4 page.

FAT TUESDAY, F.M. Cotolo, Editor-in-Chief; B. Lyle Tabor, Associate Editor; Thom Savion, Associate Editor; Lionel Stevroid, Associate Editor; Kristen Vonoehrke, Managing Editor, 560, Manada Gap Road, Grantville, PA 17028, 717-469-7159. 1981. Poetry, fiction, art, satire, parts-of-novels, collages. "As *Fat Tuesday* rolls through its second decade, we find that publishing small press editions is more difficult than ever. Money remains a problem, mostly because small press seems to play to the very people who wish to be published in it. In other words, the cast is the audience, and more people want to be in *Fat Tuesday* than want to buy it. Unfortunately, sales are important even for renegade presses. It is through sales that our magazine supports itself. This is why we emphasize buying a sample issue ($5) before submitting. Our 1998 edition is an audio theater, a 40-plus-minute stereo cassette called *Fat Tuesday's Cool Noise*. It features original music, poetry readings, sound collage and more by 20 artists. And next, Fat Tuesday releases "Seven Squared," a stereo-audio-cassette album of original music by Frank Cotolo. As far as what we want to publish—send us shorter works. *Crystals of thought and emotion which reflect your individual experiences. As long as you dig into your guts and pull out pieces of yourself. Your work is your signature...Like time itself, it should emerge from the penetralia of your being and recede into the infinite region of the cosmos,* to coin a phrase. Certainly, perusing any of the issues we have published in the last decade will let you know what we admire in an author's work, an artist's stroke. We often answer submissions with personal comments, opinions, howdayados and the like. So, write to us, send us pieces of yourself, buy sample issues (and keep this in mind for all other small presses, too), please use SASEs and remember *Fat Tuesday* is mardi gras—so fill up before you fast. Bon soir.'' circ. 350-500. 1+. Pub'd 1 issue 1998; expects 1 issue 1999, 1 issue 2000. price per copy: $5; sample: $5. Back issues: contact our agent in Vienna. Discounts: inquire. 45pp; 5½x8½, 8½x11; of. Reporting time: have patience, but we're usually quick! Simultaneous submissions accepted: no. Publishes 5% of manuscripts submitted. Payment: 1 complimentary copy in which work appears. Copyrighted, reverts to author. Ads: $100/$50/25¢ per classified word.

Fathom Publishing Co., Constance Taylor, PO Box 200448, Anchorage, AK 99520-0448, 907-272-3305. 1978. Photos, cartoons, interviews, news items, non-fiction. avg. press run 3M-5M. Pub'd 2 titles 1998; expects 1 title 1999. 9 titles listed in the *Small Press Record of Books in Print* (28th Edition, 1999-00). avg. price, paper: $3.50-$15, $75. Discounts: Legal text to book stores 25%: other books: libraries 25%, bookstores 40% over 10 copies, 25% 5-10 copies, 10% less than 5. 200pp; of. Reporting time: 1 month. Simultaneous submissions accepted: yes. Publishes 1% of manuscripts submitted. Payment: varies. Copyrights for author. EMA.

FATHOMS, Todd Pierce, Rex West, PO Box 62634, Tallahassee, FL 32313. 1991. Poetry, fiction. ''Come aboard *fathoms*, a competitive, mid-size journal based in the Florida Gulf. We aren't the *New Yorker*: we're something completely different. We support diversity—different styles and forms, different points of view. After you've looked us over, submit your best work: *fathoms* accepts poetry, fiction, and creative non-fiction. The editors prefer short manuscripts and appreciate writing that is rich in imagery, character, and the musicality of language. Limit poetry submissions to five poems (to 100 lines); fiction and creative nonfiction to 2,000 words. Identify simultaneous submissions as such. Submit previously published poems elsewhere. Computer process or type manuscripts. Put name and address at top of all manuscripts. Include SASE (or SAE and IRC). Cover letter and brief biography appreciated. Recent contributors: Sesshu Foster, Sheila Cudahy, Robert Parham, and Mark Spencer.'' circ. 800. 2/yr. Pub'd 2 issues 1998; expects 2 issues 1999, 2 issues 2000. sub. price: $8; per copy: $4.50; sample: $4.50. Back issues: none. Discounts: inquire. 40pp; 5½x8½; of. Reporting time: 1-5 months. Payment: 1 copy. Copyrighted, reverts to author. Ads: inquire.

FAULTLINE, Journal of Art and Literature, Cullen Gerst, PO Box 599-4960, Irvine, CA 92716, 714-824-6712. 1992. Poetry, fiction, art, photos, interviews, parts-of-novels, plays, non-fiction. ''Poetry: 1-5 poems; fiction: any-20pp. double-spaced (5000 words); art: 8 X 10 B&W prints; non-fiction: 1000-2000 words. Any subject. All submissions are selected through anonymous judging of ms. submitted between Sept. 30 and March 15 (one issue per year). If a multiple submission, please specify in cover letter. Killarney Clary, Heather McHugh, Allan Grossman, Garrett Hongo, Thomas Lux, Thomas Keneally, Molly Giles, James D. Houston, Susan Straight, Jervey Tervalon, Judith Grossman, Amy Gertsler, Killarney Clary'' circ. 475. 1/yr. Pub'd 1 issue 1998; expects 1 issue 1999, 1 issue 2000. sub. price: $7; per copy: $7; sample: $5. Back issues: Fall 1992 $4, spring 1993 $5, Fall 1993 $5. Discounts: 40% to retailers. 100pp; 5x8½; of. Reporting time: 90 days or 1 month after close of submission period. Simultaneous submissions accepted, but please specify that work has been submitted elsewhere. Publishes 5% of manuscripts submitted. Payment: 2 copies. Copyrighted, reverts to author. Ads: $160/$90/$60 1/4 page, $40 business card.

FC-Izdat Publishing, Victor Pavlenkov, 3 Cottage Avenue, Winchester, MA 01890, 617-776-2262; vvv@tiac.net. 1982. Poetry, fiction, articles, reviews, letters, non-fiction. avg. press run 400. Pub'd 2 titles 1998; expects 2 titles 1999, 3 titles 2000. 6 titles listed in the *Small Press Record of Books in Print* (28th Edition, 1999-00). avg. price, paper: $7. 200pp; 5½x8½; of. Reporting time: 6 weeks. Simultaneous submissions accepted: yes. Publishes 10% of manuscripts submitted. Payment: 50%/50%. Copyrights for author.

FC2/Black Ice Books, Curtis White, Co-Director; Ronald Sukenick, Co-Director, Illinois State University, Campus Box 4241, Normal, IL 61790-4241, 309-438-3582, Fax 309-438-3523. 1974. Fiction. ''Novels and collections of short stories. Members are authors we have published or are about to publish. Distribution through Northwestern University Press, Chicago Distribution Center, 11030 South Langley Avenue, Chicago, IL 60628.'' avg. press run 2.2M. Pub'd 11 titles 1998; expects 10 titles 1999, 10 titles 2000. 112 titles listed in the *Small Press Record of Books in Print* (28th Edition, 1999-00). avg. price, cloth: $19.95; paper: $11.95. Discounts: 1-4 books 20%, 5-24 40%, 25-49 41%, 50-74 42%, 75-124 43%, 125-199 44%, 200-299 45%, 300+ 46%. 200pp; 5½x8½. Reporting time: 6 months to 1 year. Simultaneous submissions accepted: yes. Payment: 10% royalties, 75% of subsidiary rights sales. Copyrights for author.

The Feathered Serpent, Susan Acker, Mary McDermott, 55 Galli Drive #C, Novato, CA 94949-5715, 415-499-8751. 1952. Poetry, art, cartoons, music, letters. ''The press has been commissioned by book collectors clubs and historical assoc. to print limited editions of Californiana. Press has published artists books under its own imprint and looks forward to doing more. A specialty is printmaking. Irish topics are especially welcome.'' avg. press run 300-1M. Pub'd 4 titles 1998; expects 6 titles 1999. 1 title listed in the *Small Press Record of Books in Print* (28th Edition, 1999-00). avg. price, cloth: $75; paper: $16; other: $45 miniature. Discounts: 30%. 75pp; †lp, of. Reporting time: 2 weeks. Payment: to be arranged. Book Club of California.

186

FEDERAL SENTENCING REPORTER, University of California Press, Daniel Freed, Alexis Agathocleous, Publication Manager, University of California Press, 2120 Berkeley Way, Berkeley, CA 94720, 510-643-7154. 1988. "Editorial address: 377 Broadway, New York, NY 10013." circ. 2.5M. 6/yr. Pub'd 6 issues 1998; expects 6 issues 1999, 6 issues 2000. sub. price: $158, add $6 foreign, $95 academics; per copy: $30; sample: free. Back issues: $21. 348pp; 8½×11. Ads: none.

FELICITER, Canadian Library Association, Elizabeth Morton, Editor, 200 Elgin Street, Suite 602, Ottawa, Ontario K2P 1L5, Canada, 613-232-9625, ext. 322. 1956. Articles, photos, cartoons, interviews, reviews, letters, news items. circ. 3M. 6/yr. Pub'd 10 issues 1998; expects 6 issues 1999, 6 issues 2000. sub. price: $95 Cdn.; per copy: $9.50 Cdn.; sample: free. 56pp; 8½×11; of. Reporting time: 3 months. Simultaneous submissions accepted: no. Publishes 75% of manuscripts submitted. Payment: none. Copyrighted, does not revert to author. Pub's reviews: 15 in 1998. §Library and information science, Canadian reference. Ads: $820 Cdn./$580 Cdn. IFLA.

FELICITY, Kay Weems, HCR-13, Box 21AA, Artemas, PA 17211-9405, 814-458-3102. 1988. Poetry, fiction, articles, art. "Poetry to 36 lines, short stories to 2,500 words. No erotica—work must be in good taste. Recent contributors: Angie Monnens, Andria Watson, John Grey." circ. 200-250. 6/yr. Pub'd 6 issues 1998; expects 6 issues 1999, 6 issues 2000. sub. price: $15; per copy: $2.50; sample: $2.50. Back issues: $2.50. 30-40pp; 8½×11; †Sharp copier. Reporting time: approximately 4 months with copy of publication which shows winners of contest entered. Payment: cash awards for 1st, 2nd & 3rd place contest winners, copies to contributors. Copyrighted, reverts to author. info furnished upon request. PA Poetry Society, Walt Whitman Guild, UAPAA, National Arts Society, National Federation of State Poetry Societies Inc., New Horizons Poetry Club, Southern Poetry Assoc.

FELL SWOOP, Acre Press, X.J. Dailey, 3003 Ponce de Leon Street, New Orleans, LA 70119. 1983. Poetry, fiction, articles, art, cartoons, interviews, satire, letters, collages, plays, news items. "Recent contribs: Richard Martin, John Miller, Greg Boyd, Anselm Hollo, Andrei Codrescu, James Haug, Randall Schroth, Ed Dorn, Flung Hy, Elizabeth Thomas, Gordon Anderson. Please remember *Fell Swoop* is a gorilla/guerilla venture. Our writers use language rather than ape suits or bullets..." circ. 300. 3/yr. Pub'd 3 issues 1998; expects 3 issues 1999, 3 issues 2000. sub. price: $8; per copy: $3; sample: $3. Back issues: all issues $3. Discounts: none. 20pp; 8½×11; †xerox. Reporting time: quick as can be. Payment: copies and immortality on demand. Not copyrighted.

FELL'S HEALTH FITNESS MAGAZINE, Lifetime Books, Inc., Brian Feinblum, Editor-in-Chief, 2131 Hollywood Boulevard, Hollywood, FL 33020, 305-925-5242. 1943. Non-fiction. "We are the leading publisher of one-shot magazines in the United States. We have four categories in which we publish. These are diet & health, health, cookbook series and financial planning series. We are looking for full manuscripts that would lend themselves to these areas." circ. 50M. 8/yr. Pub'd 8 issues 1998; expects 8 issues 1999, 8 issues 2000. price per copy: $2.95. Back issues: cover price. 128pp; 5-3/16×7⅝; of. Reporting time: 3 months. Payment: negotiated. Copyrighted, reverts to author. Ads: $2,000. PBAA, ACIDA.

FELL'S U.S. COINS INVESTMENT QUARTERLY, Lifetime Books, Inc., Donald L. Lessne, 2131 Hollywood Boulevard, Hollywood, FL 33020, 925-5242. 1943. Non-fiction. circ. 55M. 4/yr. Pub'd 4 issues 1998; expects 4 issues 1999, 4 issues 2000. sub. price: $19.80; per copy: $4.95; sample: $4.95. Back issues: $4.95. Discounts: 5-25 45%, 25+ 47%. 128pp; 5-3/16×7⅝; of. Reporting time: 2 months. Payment: $1,000. Copyrighted, does not revert to author. ACIDA, PACINWA.

Fels and Firn Press, John M. Montgomery, Editor and Publisher, Attn: Laura Petersen, 6934 Lassen Street, Pleasanton, CA 94588-4918, 510-846-0304. 1961. Criticism, letters. "Both books are compiled essays by friends of Kerouac." avg. press run 1.5M. Pub'd 1 title 1998; expects 1 title 1999, 1 title 2000. 2 titles listed in the *Small Press Record of Books in Print* (28th Edition, 1999-00). Discounts: bulk 50%, jobber various. 150pp; 5½×9½, 5½×8½; of, lp. Reporting time: 30 days. Payment: conventional. Copyrights for author.

THE FEMINIST BOOKSTORE NEWS, Carol Seajay, Editor & Publisher, PO Box 882554, San Francisco, CA 94188, 415-642-9993; fax 415-642-9995; e-mail fbn@fembknews.com. 1976. Articles, art, photos, cartoons, non-fiction, criticism, reviews, letters, news items. "*FBN* is the trade magazine for feminist bookstores and the Women-in-Print movement. It reviews over 300 books per issue. Articles focus on feminist book selling and the Women-in-Print movement." circ. 800. 6/yr. Pub'd 6 issues 1998; expects 6 issues 1999, 6 issues 2000. sub. price: $70; per copy: $6; sample: $6. Back issues: $6. Discounts: 10% jobber. 124pp; 7×8½; of. Reporting time: 3 weeks. Payment: copies. Copyrighted, reverts to author. Pub's reviews: 1,800+ in 1998. §Books by, for, and about women—of interest to feminist bookstores and libraries. Ads: $770/$490/$10 for 1st 50 words, 15¢ for each additional word.

FEMINIST COLLECTIONS: A QUARTERLY OF WOMEN'S STUDIES RESOURCES, Women's Studies Librarian, University of Wisconsin System, Phyllis Holman Weisbard, Linda Shult, 430 Memorial Library, 728 State Street, Madison, WI 53706, 608-263-5754. 1980. Articles, interviews, criticism, reviews, non-fiction. "Publishes on topics such as feminist publishing, bookselling and distribution; feminist issues in librarianship; and resources for feminist research. Contributors are drawn mostly from the University of Wisconsin System. Submissions are solicited only." circ. 1.1M. 4/yr. Pub'd 4 issues 1998; expects 4 issues 1999, 4 issues 2000. sub. price: $30 individuals and women's programs, $55 institutions (includes subscriptions to *Feminist Collections*, *Feminist Periodicals*, and *New Books On Women & Feminism*); per copy: $3.50; sample: $3.50. Back issues: $3.50. 40pp; 8½×11; desktop publishing; offset printing. Reporting time: 1-2 weeks. Simultaneous submissions accepted: no. Payment: we are unfortunately unable to pay contributors. Copyrighted. Pub's reviews: 84 in 1998. §Any feminist or women-related books or magazines are of interest and help us stay current; we particularly note feminist reference works.

FEMINIST LEGAL STUDIES, Deborah Charles Publications, Belinda Meteyard, 173 Mather Avenue, Liverpool L18 6JZ, United Kingdom. 1993. Non-fiction. "Gender and law, feminism and law." 2/yr. Expects 2 issues 1999, 2 issues 2000. sub. price: £16 individuals, £55 institutions + postage; per copy: £10 individuals, £25 institutions; sample: £10. Discounts: 5% subscription agents. 112pp; royal octavo; Mac DTP. Reporting time: 3 months. Payment: none. Copyrighted, does not revert to author. Pub's reviews: 5 in 1998. §Modern law. Ads: exchange.

FEMINIST PERIODICALS: A CURRENT LISTING OF CONTENTS, Women's Studies Librarian, University of Wisconsin System, Phyllis Holman Weisbard, Ingrid Markhardt, 430 Memorial Library, 728 State Street, Madison, WI 53706, 608-263-5754. 1981. "Designed to increase public awareness of feminist periodicals, this publication reproduces table of contents pages from over 100 periodicals on a quarterly basis. An introductory section provides bibliographic background on each periodical." circ. 1.1M. 4/yr. Pub'd 4 issues 1998; expects 4 issues 1999, 4 issues 2000. sub. price: $30 individuals and women's programs, $55 institutions (includes subscriptions to *Feminist Periodicals*, *Feminist Collections*, and *New Books On Women & Feminism*); per copy: $3.50; sample: $3.50. Back issues: $3.50. 152pp; 8½×11; of. Copyrighted.

The Feminist Press at the City College (see also WOMEN'S STUDIES QUARTERLY), Florence Howe, Publisher; Jean Casella, Senior Editor, Convent Ave. & 138th St., New York, NY 10031, 212-360-5790. 1970. Fiction, non-fiction. "The Feminist Press is a non-profit, tax-exempt publishing house, engaged in educational change. We publish reprints of neglected women's writing, biographies, & materials for nonsexist curriculum at every educational level." avg. press run 3M-5M. Pub'd 6 titles 1998; expects 11 titles 1999, 12 titles 2000. 131 titles listed in the *Small Press Record of Books in Print* (28th Edition, 1999-00). avg. price, cloth: $35; paper: $18.00. Discounts: inquire (retail, wholesale, institutional). 1p, of. Reporting time: minimum of 2 months. Publishes 10% of manuscripts submitted. Payment: 10% of net. Copyrights for author.

FEMINIST REVIEW, Collective, 52 Featherstone Street, Brecknock Road, London EC1Y 8RT, United Kingdom. 1979. Articles, criticism, reviews. "A socialist *feminist* journal aiming to develop both theory and political strategy of the women's liberation movement, and women's position worldwide. Exploring the intersection among 'race', garden, class, sexuality" circ. 4M. 3/yr. Pub'd 3 issues 1998; expects 3 issues 1999, 3 issues 2000. sub. price: (institutions) £68 UK, $110 U.S., £74 rest of world, (individuals) £24 U.K., £30 overseas, $42 U.S.; per copy: £9.99, North America $12.95. Back issues: apply to office. 128pp; 240×170mm. Reporting time: 12-14 weeks. Payment: none. Copyrighted, reverts to author. Pub's reviews: 4-8 per issue in 1998. §Women: theory, politics, fiction, research. Ads: £110/£70/£55 1/3 page/£45 1/4 page.

FEMINIST STUDIES, Claire G. Moses, Editor & Manager, c/o Women's Studies Program, University of Maryland, College Park, MD 20742, 301-405-7413. 1972. Poetry, fiction, articles, art, photos, cartoons, interviews, criticism, reviews, parts-of-novels. "1997 -Twenty-Five Year Anniversary" circ. 6M. 3/yr. Pub'd 3 issues 1998; expects 3 issues 1999, 3 issues 2000. sub. price: $85 institutions, $30 individuals; per copy: $30 inst., $12 indiv.; sample: $25 inst., $12 indiv. Back issues: $12 indiv., $30 instit. Discounts: none. 200-250pp; 6×9; of. Reporting time: 3-4 months. Simultaneous submissions accepted: no. Publishes 10% of manuscripts submitted. Payment: none. Copyrighted, does not revert to author. Pub's reviews: 13 in 1998. §In all fields of women's studies, on feminism, on sexuality, on family, on human relations, on psychology, significant works by women authors. Ads: $250.

FEMINIST VOICES NEWSJOURNAL, 1105 Macarthur Road, Apt 7, Madison, WI 53714-1050, 608-251-9268. 1987. Poetry, fiction, articles, art, photos, cartoons, interviews, satire, criticism, reviews, music, letters, parts-of-novels, long-poems, collages, news items, non-fiction. "Articles should usually not exceed 1200 words. Minimal editing, with cooperation of the writer. *Feminist Voices* is an open forum by and for women which reflects the diversity of women's lives and experiences and provides a space where women can share, dialogue, debate, question, and create. *FV* will not consider for publication any material that perpetuates stereotypes or other oppressive attitudes and beliefs. Some issues have themes, write us for information on upcoming themes" circ. 7M. 10/yr. Pub'd 10 issues 1998; expects 10 issues 1999, 10 issues 2000. sub. price: $15/yr. Free to females in prison, $25 institution; per copy: free; sample: $1. Back issues: $1. 12-16pp; 9¾×16. Reporting time: 2 weeks to 2 months, depends on the piece. Publishes 60% of manuscripts submitted. Payment: no cash, contributors receive free copies. Copyrighted, reverts to author. Pub's reviews: 12 in 1998. §Women,

188

feminism, lesbian lives, feminism, motherhood. Ads: $13 column inch (discount for prepaid contract and non-profit orgs.).

FENICE BROADSHEETS, New Broom Private Press, Toni Savage, Esq., Cynthia A. Savage, 78 Cambridge Street, Leicester LE3 0JP, England, 547419. 1994. Poetry, art, long-poems. "Sheets are free, from the above address S.A.E. New Broom Private Press has a series of poems-sheets-finely illustrated. S.A.E. for samples. Nos. 1-350 issues, some handcoloured. Poetry mainly, sometimes excerpts from plays. Poets include: Brian Patten, Spike Milligan, Sue Mackrell, Charles Causley, Arthur Caddick, Edward Murch. Artists: Rigby Graham, Hans Erni, Toni Savage, Robert Tilling. American Poets: Jane Lord Bradbury, Gina Bergamino, Paul Humphrey, C.J. Stevens, Alix Weisz. We publish 10-15 sheets a year." circ. 2-300. Pub'd 12 issues 1998; expects 12 issues 1999, 12-15 issues 2000. sub. price: free plus postage; per copy: free plus postage; sample: free plus postage (to America, $1) ICRs only please. 1 page; 9×5 approx.; †lp. Payment: copies only. Copyrighted.

Feral House, Adam Parfrey, PO Box 3466, Portland, OR 97208, 503-276-8375. 1988. Articles, art, photos, interviews, criticism, reviews, non-fiction. "Cutting edge material that unflinchingly travels or navigates realms that other publishers are afraid to tread." avg. press run 5M-10M. Pub'd 4 titles 1998; expects 10 titles 1999, 10 titles 2000. 20 titles listed in the *Small Press Record of Books in Print* (28th Edition, 1999-00). avg. price, cloth: $20; paper: $12.95. Discounts: Distributed by publishers group west to the wholesale and retail book trade. 300pp; of. Reporting time: 2 month. Payment: 6-7% of retail price.

FERRY TRAVEL GUIDE, Dan Youra Studios, Inc., Dan Youra, Editor, PO Box 1169, Port Hadlock, WA 98339-1169. 1984. Articles, photos, non-fiction. "We purchase interesting articles and photos on NW ferries." circ. 110M. 3/yr. Pub'd 2 issues 1998; expects 3 issues 1999, 3 issues 2000. sub. price: $6, including shipping; per copy: $1.95; sample: $1. Back issues: $1.50 plus shipping. Discounts: 3-12 40%, 13-50 45%, 51-150 50%, 151+ 55%. 48pp; 8×10; of. Reporting time: fast. Payment: yes. Copyrighted, reverts to author. Pub's reviews: 3 in 1998. §Northwest travel. Ads: $3,000/$1500/$10. Pacific NW Book Publishers; Northwest Magazine Publishers.

●FETISH BAZAAR, Robert Dante, David Busch, 901 W. Victoria, Unit G, Compton, CA 90220, 310-631-1600; www.bondage.org. 1979. Fiction, articles, art, cartoons, interviews, reviews, news items, non-fiction. "Alternative, sexuality, erotica, stories, photos, and art." circ. 5M. 4/yr. Pub'd 4 issues 1998; expects 4 issues 1999, 4 issues 2000. sub. price: $22; per copy: $6.95; sample: $10. 44pp; 7¾×10¾; web. Reporting time: 1 month. Simultaneous submissions accepted: no. Publishes 25% of manuscripts submitted. Payment: $25-$50. Copyrighted, does not revert to author. Pub's reviews. §Sexuality, BDSM. Ads: $230/$125/$75 1/4 page/$45 business card.

FIBERARTS, Altamont Press, Inc., Nancy Orban, 50 College Street, Asheville, NC 28801, 704-253-0468. 1973. Articles, art, interviews, criticism, reviews, news items, non-fiction. circ. 24M. 5/yr. Pub'd 5 issues 1998; expects 5 issues 1999, 5 issues 2000. sub. price: $22; per copy: $5.50; sample: $5.50. Back issues: $4.50. Discounts: shops 35% US, 35% Canadian + postage, 50% foreign + postage. 80pp; 8⅜×10⅞; of. Reporting time: 3 weeks. Simultaneous submissions accepted: no. Publishes 10% of manuscripts submitted. Payment: yes, depends on length, content, etc. Copyrighted, does not revert to author. Pub's reviews: 5 in 1998. §Arts, textiles, basketry. Ads: $800/$450/$1.10.

FICTION, Mark Jay Mirsky, Editor; Michael W. Pollock, Managing Editor, c/o Dept. of English, City College, 138th Street & Convent Ave., New York, NY 10031, 212-650-6319. 1972. Fiction, parts-of-novels. "We are a journal of new directions for the novel and short story. *Fiction* has brought the unknown and the famous together in handsome pages to an international and discriminating audience of readers for 20 years. We represent no particular school of fiction, except the innovative, and in that sense our pages have been a harbor for many writers often at odds with each other. As a result of our willingness to publish the difficult and experimental, to look at the unusual and obscure, while not excluding the well known, *Fiction* has won a unique reputation in the U.S. and abroad, including in recent years, O.Henry Award, Pushcart Prize, and Best of the South." circ. 3M. 2/yr. Pub'd 2 issues 1998; expects 2 issues 1999, 2 issues 2000. sub. price: $18/year; per copy: $7.95 single, $10.95 double; sample: $5. Back issues: $8. 200pp; 6×9; of. Reporting time: 3+ months. Publishes 1% of manuscripts submitted. Payment: $25 + copies. Copyrighted, reverts to author.

FICTION FORUM, John C. Brainerd, 18600 West 58 Avenue, Golden, CO 80403-1070, 303-279-2462. 1987. Fiction. circ. 580. 12/yr. Pub'd 12 issues 1998; expects 12 issues 1999, 12 issues 2000. sub. price: $50; per copy: $5; sample: $5. Back issues: $5. 40pp; 5½×8½; †photo offset. Reporting time: 30-90 days. Payment: 1/2 net. Copyrighted, reverts to author. Pub's reviews: 16 in 1998. §History, theology, philosophy, theory of fiction. Ads: $35/page, $5/inch. Int. Pub. Assn.

FICTION INTERNATIONAL, San Diego State University Press, Harold Jaffe, San Diego State University, San Diego, CA 92182, 619-594-5443, 594-6220. 1973. Fiction, articles, art, photos, interviews, satire, criticism, reviews, parts-of-novels, non-fiction. "Direct editorial correspondence to Harold Jaffe & Larry McCaffery at the Dept. of English at the above address. Business correspondence should be directed to Harry Polkinhorn, Managing Editor, San Diego State University Press, San Diego, CA 92182. Note: Manuscripts will be considered for publication only if they are received between September 1 and January 15. Our twin biases are politics and technical innovation—either integrated in a particular fiction, or apart. Interested in fiction & theory. *Fiction International* does not regularly publish poetry—only occasionally in special issues." circ. 1M. 2/yr. Pub'd 2 issues 1998; expects 2 issues 1999, 2 issues 2000. sub. price: $14/individual, $28/institution; per copy: $7/individual, $14/institution; sample: $6 + $3 shipping. Discounts: trade distributors 50%, trade 40%. No discount on single copy orders. 220pp; 6×9; of. Reporting time: 1-2 months. Payment: varies. Copyrighted, reverts to author. Pub's reviews: 5 in 1998. §Fiction, aesthetics, politics. Ads: $125/$80.

FICTION WRITER'S GUIDELINE, Blythe Camenson, PO Box 72300, Albuquerque, NM 87195-2300, 505-352-9490; bcamenson@aol.com; www.fictionwriters.com. 1993. Articles, cartoons, interviews, reviews, news items, non-fiction. "500-1000 word articles covering 'how-to' write fiction topics, interviews with agents, editors, and well-known authors. New markets for fiction. Recent contributors: Betty Wright, Stephanie Krulik, and Sara Goodman." circ. 1M. 6/yr. Pub'd 6 issues 1998; expects 6 issues 1999, 6 issues 2000. sub. price: $21 (free to members of Fiction Writer's Connection); per copy: $3.50; sample: SASE/55¢. Back issues: $3.50. 8pp; 8½×11; of. Reporting time: 1 month. Simultaneous submissions accepted: yes. Publishes 70% of manuscripts submitted. Payment: $1-$25. Copyrighted, reverts to author. Pub's reviews: 5 in 1998. §Books on the craft and business of writing. Ads: $18 business card and run mimimum 3 issues. FWC.

THE FIDDLEHEAD, Ross Leckie, Managing Editor; Julie Dennison, Poetry Editor; Norman Ravoin, Fiction Editor; Ted Colson, Fiction Editor, Campus House, PO Box 4400, University of New Brunswick, Fredericton, NB E3B 5A3, Canada, 506-453-3501. 1945. Poetry, fiction, art, reviews, parts-of-novels, long-poems, plays. circ. 1.1M. 4/yr. Pub'd 4 issues 1998; expects 4 issues 1999, 4 issues 2000. sub. price: $20 Canada, U.S. $20US + $6 postage; per copy: $8 Can.; sample: $8 + postage Can. and US. Back issues: $5-8. Discounts: 10% on purchases of 10 copies or more; bookstores 33⅓%. 128-200pp; 6×9; of. Reporting time: 10-30 weeks, include SASE with Canadian stamp, IRC, or cash. Simultaneous submissions accepted: no. Publishes 1% of manuscripts submitted. Payment: $10 printed page. Copyrighted. Pub's reviews: 30-40 in 1998. §Canadian literature. Ads: $100/$52. CMPA.

FIDDLER MAGAZINE, Mary E. Larsen, PO Box 125, Los Altos, CA 94023, 650-948-4383. 1994. Articles, interviews, reviews, music, non-fiction. "Recent Contributors: Jay Ungar, John Hartford, Lindajoy Fenley, Craig Mishler, Stacy Phillips." circ. 3M. 4/yr. Pub'd 4 issues 1998; expects 4 issues 1999, 4 issues 2000. sub. price: $20; per copy: $6; sample: $6. Back issues: varies. 60+pp; 8½×11; of. Reporting time: 2 weeks to 1 month. Publishes 50% of manuscripts submitted. Payment: $10-200, depending on length & whether or not feature article. Copyrighted. Pub's reviews: 5 in 1998. §Music, must be related to fiddling. Ads: $300/$200/$110 1/4/$60 1/8/$45/50¢ per word classified.

FIDEI DEFENSOR: JOURNAL OF CATHOLIC APOLOGETICS, St. Michael's Press, Bro. John-Paul Ignatius, PO Box 52, Pisgah, IA 51564-0052, 515-279-7804; E-mail st-mike@mail.commonlink.com. 1994. Poetry, fiction, articles, photos, interviews, criticism, reviews, letters, non-fiction. "*Fidei Defensor* is a magazine of Catholic apologetics. Articles include pieces on church history, official church teachings on contemporary issues, devotional material on Marian spirituality, defending the orthodox faith against Catholic liberalism and Protestantism. We are currently focusing on Internet publishing." 2/yr. Expects 2 issues 2000. sub. price: $15; per copy: $7.50; sample: $7.50. Back issues: none. 64pp; 5½×8½; †of. Reporting time: 3 weeks to 3 months. Copyrighted, reverts to author. Pub's reviews. §Catholic apologetics, Marian spirituality, Catholic issues.

FIDELIS ET VERUS, Children Of Mary, John R. Walsh, PO Box 350333, Ft. Lauderdale, FL 33335. 1985. News items. "Traditional/Orthodox Roman Catholic items that are news plus doctrine (Catholic)." circ. 6M. 6/yr. Pub'd 6 issues 1998; expects 6 issues 1999, 6 issues 2000. sub. price: $10 for 10 issues; per copy: $1; sample: $1. Back issues: $1. Discounts: 10¢ per copy in bulk. 10pp; 8½×11; computer, laser printer, web press, typesetter, photocopy. Reporting time: bi-monthly. Simultaneous submissions accepted: yes. Publishes 5% of manuscripts submitted. Payment: submit cost of article. Not copyrighted. Pub's reviews: 2 in 1998. §Only traditional Roman Catholic books/magazines. Ads: $100/$55/$10 per column inch (2 column page); columns 3⅜ wide.

FIELD, Oberlin College Press, David Young, Co-Editor; David Walker, Co-Editor, Rice Hall, Oberlin College, Oberlin, OH 44074, 440-775-8408; Fax 440-775-8124; oc.press@oberlin.edu. 1969. Poetry, long-poems. "Also essays on poetry and translations of poetry" circ. 2.5M. 2/yr. Pub'd 2 issues 1998; expects 2 issues 1999, 2 issues 2000. sub. price: $14, $24/2 years; per copy: $7 ppd.; sample: $7 ppd. Back issues: $12, all backs, except most recent year. Discounts: 40% bookstores (minimum order 5 copies), 15% subscription agencies. 100pp; 5¼×8½. Reporting time: 4-6 weeks. Simultaneous submissions accepted: no. Publishes .25%-.50% of manuscripts submitted. Payment: $15-25 a page. Copyrighted, reverts to author. Pub's reviews: 8 in 1998. §New books of poetry and poetry in translation. Ads: none. CLMP.

FIFTH ESTATE, Collective Staff, 4632 Second Avenue, Detroit, MI 48201, 313-831-6800. 1965. Articles, photos, criticism, reviews, letters, non-fiction. "We don't encourage unsolicited mss." circ. 5M. 4/yr. Pub'd 4 issues 1998; expects 4 issues 1999, 4 issues 2000. sub. price: $6, $8 foreign, $10 institutions; per copy: $1.50; sample: $1.50. Back issues: $2. Discounts: none. 32pp; 10×13½. Payment: none. Not copyrighted. Pub's reviews: 25 in 1998. §Ecology, politics, anarchism, feminism. Ads: not accepted.

FIGMENTS, Figments Publishing, James Watson, 14 William Street, Donaghadee, Co. Down NI BT21 0HP, United Kingdom, 01247-884267. 1995. Poetry, fiction, articles, art, photos, cartoons, interviews, satire, criticism, reviews. "Poetry: max 40 lines, general themes. Short stories: max 4,000 words (but exceptions made) and serial. Generally Irish bias but not exclusively." circ. 750. 12/yr. Pub'd 12 issues 1998; expects 12 issues 1999, 12 issues 2000. sub. price: £18 + p/h; per copy: £1.50; sample: £1.50 + p/h. Back issues: same. Discounts: 30%. 24pp; 9×11½; of. Reporting time: 2 months. Simultaneous submissions accepted: yes. Publishes 15% of manuscripts submitted. Payment: by competition/by arrangement. Copyrighted, reverts to author. Pub's reviews: 10 in 1998. §Literature, Irish, poetry, short stories. Ads: £100/£60/others pro-rated.

Figments Publishing (see also FIGMENTS), James Watson, 14 William Street, Donaghadee, Co. Down N.I. BT21 0HP, United Kingdom, 01247-884267. 1995. Poetry, fiction, parts-of-novels, non-fiction. "Length: 100,000 words/20,000 words. Irish bias but not exclusively." avg. press run 2M. Pub'd 3 titles 1998; expects 3 titles 1999, 4 titles 2000. 3 titles listed in the *Small Press Record of Books in Print* (28th Edition, 1999-00). avg. price, cloth: £15; paper: £8.99. Discounts: 30%. 200pp; size A5; of. Reporting time: 6 months. Simultaneous submissions accepted: yes. Publishes 10% of manuscripts submitted. Payment: by arrangement. Copyrights for author.

The Figures, Geoffrey Young, 5 Castle Hill Avenue, Great Barrington, MA 01230-1552, 413-528-2552. 1975. Poetry, fiction. avg. press run 1M. Pub'd 3 titles 1998; expects 1 title 1999. 59 titles listed in the *Small Press Record of Books in Print* (28th Edition, 1999-00). avg. price, cloth: $15; paper: $10. 75pp; 5½×8½; of. Reporting time: 1 month. Payment: 10% edition, 40% off on extra sales. Copyrights for author.

FIJACTIVIST, Lawrence Dodge, Kathy Harrer, PO Box 59, Helmville, MT 59843, 406-793-5550. 1989. Articles, art, photos, cartoons, interviews, reviews, letters, news items, non-fiction. "Mostly in-house, but we have arranged to publish relevant articles" circ. 5M. 4/yr. Pub'd 4 issues 1998; expects 4 issues 1999, 4 issues 2000. sub. price: $25; sample: free info. package; sample FIJActivist $3. Discounts: $15/$10; 20 + $1 each. 28pp; 11½×15; newsprint. Payment: none. Not copyrighted. Pub's reviews: 2 in 1998. §Law. Ads: none.

Filibuster Press, Kyle Hannon, 55836 Riverdale Drive, Elkhart, IN 46514, 219-522-5151; filibstr@skyenet.net; www.filibuster.com. 1994. Fiction. "We focus on self-reliant stories with libertarian themes and capitalist heros. Mid-western base." avg. press run 1M. Pub'd 1 title 1998; expects 1 title 1999, 1 title 2000. 3 titles listed in the *Small Press Record of Books in Print* (28th Edition, 1999-00). avg. price, paper: $10.95. Discounts: 2-4 copies 30%, 5-24 40%, 25+ 45% higher discounts if you forgo the option of returning unsold copies. 270pp; 5¼×8; of. Reporting time: 1-4 months. Simultaneous submissions accepted: yes. Publishes 10% of manuscripts submitted. Payment: varies. Copyrights for author. PMA, SPAN.

●**Fillmore Publishing Company,** PO Box 12432, St. Louis, MO 63132, 800-989-0478; 314-989-0558. 1998. Non-fiction. avg. press run 3M. Pub'd 1 title 1998; expects 1 title 1999, 2 titles 2000. 1 title listed in the *Small Press Record of Books in Print* (28th Edition, 1999-00). avg. price, paper: $19.95. Discounts: standard. 250pp; 5½×8½. Reporting time: 90 days. Simultaneous submissions accepted: yes. Payment: varies. PMA.

FILM, Tom Brownlie, Editor, PO Box 1Dr, London W1A 1DR, England, 0171-736-9300. 1954. Articles, photos, interviews, criticism, reviews, letters, news items. "Film and video news, film society news, book reviews, criticisms, courses, diary of events, etc. Advertising managers: address as above." circ. 1.5M. 4/yr. Pub'd 4 issues 1998; expects 4 issues 1999. sub. price: £22 sterling surface mail, incl. p+p; per copy: £2.50 (incl. p+p); sample: usually free. Back issues: £3 (incl. p+p). 32pp; size A4; of. Reporting time: 4 weeks. Simultaneous submissions accepted: no. Payment: by arrangement. Copyrighted, reverts to author. Pub's reviews: 25 in 1998. §Cinema, television, video, social and critical uses of film. Ads: £420/£250.

The Film Instruction Company of America, Henry C. Landa, 5928 W. Michigan Street, Wauwatosa, WI 53213-4248, 414-258-6492. 1960. Non-fiction. "We seek manuscripts and do not accept unsolicited works." avg. press run 800-3M. Pub'd 1 title 1998; expects 2 titles 1999, 2 titles 2000. 1 title listed in the *Small Press Record of Books in Print* (28th Edition, 1999-00). avg. price, paper: $9-$38.50. Discounts: 40% to retailers and brokers, 50% to true wholesalers. 150+pp; 8½×11; †mi, of, lp. Simultaneous submissions accepted: no. Payment: 15%-25%. Copyrights for author.

FILM QUARTERLY, University of California Press, Ann Martin, University of California Press, 2120 Berkeley Way, Berkeley, CA 94720, 510-643-7154. 1945. Interviews, criticism, reviews. circ. 6,450. 4/yr. Pub'd 4 issues 1998; expects 4 issues 1999, 4 issues 2000. sub. price: $25 indiv., $63 instit. (+ $6 for postage); per copy: $6.50 indiv., $18 instit., $6.50 student; sample: free. Back issues: same as single copy price.

Discounts: foreign subs. agents 10%, 10+ one-time orders 30%, standing orders (bookstores): 1-99 40%, 100+ 50%. 64pp; 8½x11; of. Reporting time: 2-3 weeks. Payment: 2¢ per word. Copyrighted, does not revert to author. Pub's reviews: about 100 in 1998. §Film. Ads: $390/$280.

FILM SCORE MONTHLY, Lukas Kendall, 5455 Wilshire Blvd., Ste. 1500, Los Angeles, CA 90036-4201, 323-937-9890; Fax 323-937-9277; E-mail lukas@filmscoremonthly.com. 1990. Articles, interviews, criticism, reviews, letters, news items, non-fiction. "As one of the only film music publications in the world, *Film Score Monthly* covers all aspects of movie soundtracks, from the music itself to the recordings." circ. 1M+. 10/yr. Pub'd 10 issues 1998; expects 10 issues 1999, 10 issues 2000. sub. price: $36.95 Us; $42.95 Canada; $50 rest of world; per copy: $4.95; sample: $4. Back issues: $3. 48pp; 8½x11; of. Reporting time: 30 days. Publishes 90% of manuscripts submitted. Payment: copies. Copyrighted, does not revert to author. Pub's reviews: 200 in 1998. §Film music composers, scores, recordings, etc. Ads: $600/$400/$180 1/6 page.

Film-Video Publications, Alan Gadney, Editor, 7944 Capistrano Avenue, West Hills, CA 91304. 1976. "Current books are *Gadney's Guide to 1,800 International Contests, Festivals, and Grants in Film and Video, Photography, TV-Radio Broadcasting, Writing, Poetry, Playwriting and Journalism, Updated Address Edition* awarded 'Outstanding Reference Book of the Year' by the American Library Association (5½ x 8½, 610 pages, $15.95 for softbound, $23.95 for hardbound, plus $1.75 each postage & handling)." avg. press run 5M. Pub'd 2 titles 1998; expects 4 titles 1999, 8 titles 2000. 1 title listed in the *Small Press Record of Books in Print* (28th Edition, 1999-00). avg. price, cloth: $24.95; paper: $15.95. Discounts: bookstores 1-5 assorted copies 20%, 6+ 40%; wholesale up to 55%. 300pp; 8½x11. Reporting time: 6 weeks. Payment: trade standard. Copyrights for author. PMA, BPSC.

FINANCIAL FOCUS, Jack W. Everett, 2140 Professional Drive Ste. 105, Roseville, CA 95661-3734, 916-791-1447; Fax 916-791-3444; evercfp@ix.netcom.com. 1980. Non-fiction. circ. 5M. 12/yr. Pub'd 12 issues 1998; expects 12 issues 1999, 12 issues 2000. sub. price: $39.97; sample: free. Discounts: call for info. 8pp; 8½x11; lp. Reporting time: 1 month. Simultaneous submissions accepted: yes. Copyrighted, reverts to author. Pub's reviews: 2 in 1998. §Financial. Ads: none. SPAN, PMA.

●**Finbar Press**, Radio City Station, PO Box 2176, New York, NY 10101-2176, 212-957-0849; fax 212-957-0340; toll free 800-960-9355; e-mail finbarpress@onepine.com. 1998. Fiction, non-fiction. avg. press run 5M. Pub'd 1 title 1998; expects 2 titles 1999. 1 title listed in the *Small Press Record of Books in Print* (28th Edition, 1999-00). Reporting time: 3 weeks. Simultaneous submissions accepted: yes. Copyrights for author.

Fine Arts Press, Lincoln B. Young, PO Box 3491, Knoxville, TN 37927, 615-637-9243. 1957. "Not a market. No longer publishing poetry" avg. press run 2M. Pub'd 2 titles 1998; expects 2 titles 1999, 2 titles 2000. 31 titles listed in the *Small Press Record of Books in Print* (28th Edition, 1999-00). avg. price, cloth: $14.95; paper: $10. Discounts: to booksellers only. 64pp; 5½x8½; †of. Simultaneous submissions accepted: no. Payment: none. Copyrights for author.

Fine Edge Productions, Reanne Douglass, 13589 Clayton Lane, Anacortes, WA 98221-8477, 619-387-2412, Fax 619-387-2286; E-mail fineedgepr@aol.com. 1987. "We publish outdoor guidebooks for bicycling, ski touring, boating (sail & small vessels); recreational topographical maps; some adventure/travel." avg. press run 5M. Pub'd 5 titles 1998; expects 5 titles 1999, 5 titles 2000. avg. price, paper: $17; other: topo maps $9.95. Discounts: 40% wholesalers. 98-320pp; of. Reporting time: 3 months. Publishes 3% of manuscripts submitted. Payment: varies according to title. Copyrights for author. PMA.

FINE MADNESS, Sean Bentley, John Malek, Anne Pitkin, Al Wald, PO Box 31138, Seattle, WA 98103-1138. 1982. Poetry, fiction, long-poems, non-fiction. "Writers we have recently published include Albert Goldbarth, Caroline Knox, Peter Wild, Pattiann Rogers, and Melinda Mueller. We want to see evidence of minds at work. As T.S. Eliot wrote, '*The poet must become more and more comprehensive, more allusive, more indirect, in order to force, to dislocate if necessary, language into its meaning.*'" circ. 800. Irregular. Pub'd 1 issue 1998; expects 1 issue 1999, 2 issues 2000. sub. price: $9/2 issues; per copy: $5; sample: $4. Back issues: Volume 1 Number 1 $10. Discounts: 40% trade. 62pp; 5½x8; of. Reporting time: 4 months. Simultaneous submissions accepted: no. Publishes 6% of manuscripts submitted. Payment: 1 copy of their issue plus a one-year subscription. Copyrighted, reverts to author. Ads: none.

The Fine Print Press, Ltd., Thane Messinger, David Ronin, Scott Benbow, 350 Ward Avenue, Suite 106, Honolulu, HI 96814-4091, 808-536-7262; Fax 808-946-8581; E-mail fpp@hits.net; or http://www.hits.net/ ~fpp/. 1995. Photos, non-fiction. "Please query first, e-mail ok." avg. press run 4-5M. Pub'd 2 titles 1998; expects 2 titles 1999, 2-3 titles 2000. 4 titles listed in the *Small Press Record of Books in Print* (28th Edition, 1999-00). avg. price, paper: $20-25. Discounts: Partners Book Distributors (800-336-3137). 200-400pp; 6x9. Reporting time: usually less than 30 days. Simultaneous submissions accepted: yes. Percentage of manuscripts published varies. Payment: negotiable. Copyrights for author. PMA.

Finesse Publishing Company, Linda Doran, PO Box 657, Broomfield, CO 80038, 303-466-4734. 1986.

Non-fiction. avg. press run 1M. Expects 3 titles 1999, 3 titles 2000. 3 titles listed in the *Small Press Record of Books in Print* (28th Edition, 1999-00). avg. price, paper: $25. 300pp; 8½×11. Reporting time: 6 weeks. Payment: 15% of all monies actually received, royalty payments every 6 months. Copyrights for author. Colorado Independent Publishers Association.

FIRE, Jeremy Hilton, 3 Hollywell Mews, Holywell Road, Malvern WR14 4LF, United Kingdom. 1994. Poetry, fiction, art, long-poems, collages, concrete art. "Long poems welcome, but prose, especially fiction, should be *short.* Some bias towards experimental, alternative writing but not exclusively. Only minimal space for art/collage etc." circ. 200+. 2/yr. Pub'd 2 issues 1998; expects 2 issues 1999, 2 issues 2000. sub. price: £5; per copy: £3. Back issues: #1 £2, #2 £1. 150pp; size A5. Reporting time: 6-8 weeks. Simultaneous submissions accepted: yes. Payment: none. Not copyrighted.

The Fire!! Press, Thomas H. Wirth, 241 Hillside Road, Elizabeth, NJ 07208, 908-964-8476. 1981. Poetry, fiction, art. "Not soliciting manuscripts at this time." avg. press run 2M. 2 titles listed in the *Small Press Record of Books in Print* (28th Edition, 1999-00). avg. price, paper: $14. Discounts: 40%. 5½×8½.

THE FIREFLY (A Tiny Glow In a Forest of Darkness), Jane Kirby, Jon Lurie, 300 Broadway #107, St. Paul, MN 55101. 1990. Poetry, fiction, articles, art, photos, cartoons, interviews, satire, criticism, reviews, music, letters, parts-of-novels, long-poems, collages, news items, non-fiction. "Submissions should be limited to 1500 words. We want to recieve letters, articles, poetry, B&W artwork, from people interested in revolutionary change. This revolutionary change focusing on children, families and communities. We seek information on obtaining and using technology for the good of humankind and the Earth. We seek stories of injustices done to Americans by other Americans and the government." circ. 500. 4/yr. Pub'd 6 issues 1998; expects 2 issues 1999, 4 issues 2000. sub. price: $10/6 issues; per copy: $1+stamp; sample: $1+stamp. Back issues: $1 if available, $5 if we must reprint. Discounts: Free to prisoners and AFDC families, trades encouraged. 8-12pp; 8½×11; of. Reporting time: 30-60 days. Simultaneous submissions accepted: yes. Publishes less than 50% of manuscripts submitted. Payment: free copies for family and friends. Not copyrighted. Pub's reviews: 1 in 1998. §Politics, history, children's history, Afro-American history, Native American history, women's issues, revolutionary parenting and community life. Ads: please inquire.

Fireweed Press, PO Box 75418, Fairbanks, AK 99707-2136, 907-452-5070 or 907-488-5079. 1976. "BOX CLOSED 3/6/93 (PROOFS). Publishes anthologies and prize-winning works by contemporary Alaskan authors. Submissions accepted only for projects in progress; no unsolicited manuscripts read. 1983: "Hunger and Dreams, The Alaskan Women's Anthology", 22 contributors including Sheila Nickerson, Mary TallMountain, Donna Mack, Jean Anderson; edited by Pat Monaghan. 1984: "A Good Crew" Anthology of men's writings about relationships in the north, edited by Larry Laraby and Roland Wulbert; "The Compass Inside Ourselves" by Nany Lord, winning short-story collection chosen by Stanley Elkin" avg. press run 1M. 4 titles listed in the *Small Press Record of Books in Print* (28th Edition, 1999-00). avg. price, cloth: $21.95; paper: $7.95. Discounts: 40% to bookstores, orders of 5 or more. 130pp; 6×9. Reporting time: 1 month. Payment: varies. Copyrights for author.

FIRM NONCOMMITTAL: An International Journal of Whimsy, Brian Pastoor, Editor; Vince Cicchine, Artistic Director, 5 Vonda Avenue, Toronto, ON M2N 5E6, Canada, e-mail firmnon@idirect.com; webhome.idirect.com/~firmnon. 1995. Poetry, fiction, articles, satire, non-fiction. "Humorous poetry all styles, from concrete to villanelle, under 40 lines. Fiction and non-fiction under 800 words. We seek writers who 'take the utmost trouble to find the right thing to say and then say in with the utmost levity' - G.B. Shaw. May/June submissions only. IRCS, no American stamps, please" circ. 200. 1/yr. Pub'd 1 issue 1998; expects 1 issue 1999, 1 issue 2000. sub. price: $7CAN; per copy: $7CAN; sample: $5CAN. Back issues: $5CAN. 48pp; 6×8; xerox. Reporting time: 2 months. Simultaneous submissions accepted if notified. Publishes 10% of manuscripts submitted. Payment: none yet. Copyrighted, reverts to author. Pub's reviews: 1 in 1998. §Michael Moore, left-slanted humour. Ads: 5¢ per classified word. League of Canadian Poets, Wordwrights Canada.

●**First Amendment Press International Company,** 38 East Ridgewood Avenue, Suite 217, Ridgewood, NJ 07450-3123, 201-612-0734; website www.fapic.com. 1998. Poetry. "Publishers of quality fiction." avg. press run 1M. Expects 2 titles 1999, 5 titles 2000. 1 title listed in the *Small Press Record of Books in Print* (28th Edition, 1999-00). avg. price, cloth: $40. Discounts: Baker and Taylor clients 55% discount on 100 or more books. 400pp; 7×8; †computer. Reporting time: 2 months. Simultaneous submissions accepted: no. Publishes 2% of manuscripts submitted. Copyrights for author.

FIRST CLASS, Four-Sep Publications, Christopher M., PO Box 12434, Milwaukee, WI 53212, E-mail chrifton@execpc.com; www.execpc.com/~chrifton. 1996. Poetry, fiction, photos, long-poems, plays. "Prefer short fiction. Cover letter preferred. Desires good, thought-provoking, graphic, uncommon pieces. Recent: John Bennett, Gerald Locklin, Errol Miller, Greg Fitzsimmons, Alan Catlin, B.Z. Niditch." circ. 200-400. 4/yr. Pub'd 4 issues 1998; expects 4 issues 1999, 4 issues 2000. sub. price: $13/3 issues; per copy: $5 ppd.; sample: $1 sampler, $5 issue. Back issues: inquire. Discounts: inquire, offer, selective trades, 60-40 for distributors.

44pp; 8½×11; of, xerox. Reporting time: 1 week initial response, 2 months accept./reject. Simultaneous submissions accepted: yes. Publishes 15-20% of manuscripts submitted. Payment: 1 copy. Copyrighted, reverts to author. Pub's reviews: 10+ in 1998. §Short fiction and non-traditional poetics. Ads: inquire.

FIRST DRAFT, Dorian Tenore-Bartilucci, 3636 Fieldston Road, Apt. 7A, Riverdale Bronx, NY 10463-2041, 718-543-5493. 1992. Poetry, fiction, articles, art, cartoons, satire, criticism, reviews, parts-of-novels, long-poems, plays, non-fiction. *"First Draft* is not so much a magazine as a writers' group that meets by mail. It really falls under the category of Amateur Press Association/Alliance. Only members of *First Draft* (and potential members who write and send money for spec copies) receive issues, hence the small circulation." circ. 20. 6/yr. Pub'd 6 issues 1998; expects 6 issues 1999, 6 issues 2000. sub. price: $18 for one year of spec copies; per copy: $3; sample: $3. 250pp; 8½×11; †photocopy. Reporting time: 2 months for members. Payment: copies. Copyrighted, reverts to author. Pub's reviews: 10 in 1998. §Books on writing; mysteries; humor/satire.

FIRST INTENSITY, First Intensity Press, Lee Chapman, PO Box 665, Lawrence, KS 66044-0713, e-mail leechapman@aol.com. 1993. Poetry, fiction, art, photos, parts-of-novels. "Short stories: no more than 15 mss. pages (double-spaced). Poetry: no book-length mss. Recent contributors: Robert Kelly, Lucia Berlin, Nathaniel Tarn, Theodore Enslin, Barry Gifford, Kenneth Irby, Diane diPrima, John Yau, Thomas Meyer, Duncan McNaughton, Rochelle Owens, Etel Adnan, Patrick Doud, Phillip Foss" circ. 300. 2/yr. Pub'd 2 issues 1998; expects 2 issues 1999, 2 issues 2000. sub. price: $17; per copy: $9; sample: $9. 180pp; 6×9; of. Reporting time: 2 months. Simultaneous submissions accepted: no. Payment: 2 copies. Copyrighted, reverts to author. Ads: full page $150. CLMP.

First Intensity Press (see also FIRST INTENSITY), Lee Chapman, PO Box 665, Lawrence, KS 66044, e-mail leechapman@aol.com. 1993. "Do not accept unsolicited book mss." avg. press run 300. Pub'd 2 titles 1998. 4 titles listed in the *Small Press Record of Books in Print* (28th Edition, 1999-00). avg. price, paper: $10-$12. 40-70pp; 6×9; of. CLMP.

FIRSTHAND, Bob Harris, Editor, PO Box 1314, Teaneck, NJ 07666, 201-836-9177. 1980. Fiction, articles, art, photos, cartoons, reviews, letters, parts-of-novels, news items, non-fiction. "Must appeal to a male homosexual audience." circ. 60M. 13/yr. Pub'd 13 issues 1998; expects 13 issues 1999, 13 issues 2000. sub. price: $47.97; per copy: $4.99; sample: $5. Back issues: $5. 132pp; 5×8; web-of. Reporting time: 4-6 weeks. Simultaneous submissions accepted: no. Publishes 10% of manuscripts submitted. Payment: $150 for 10-20 pages typed double-spaced. Copyrighted, rights reverting to author can be discussed. Pub's reviews: 39 in 1998. §Homosexual-related items. Ads: $600/$300/no classified. Gay And Lesbian Press Association.

FISH DRUM MAGAZINE, Suzi Winson, PO Box 966, Murray Hill Station, New York, NY 10156, www.fishdrum.com. 1988. Poetry, fiction, articles, art, cartoons, interviews, criticism, reviews, music, letters, parts-of-novels, long-poems, collages, plays, concrete art, news items, non-fiction. *"Fish Drum* prefers West Coast poetry, the exuberant 'continuous nerve movie' that follows the working of the mind and has a relationship to the world and the reader. Philip Whalen's work, for example, and much of *Calafia, The California Poetry*, edited by Ishmael Reed. Also magical-tribal-incantatory poems, exemplified by the future/primitive *Technicians of the Sacred*, ed. Rothenberg. *Fish Drum* has a soft spot for schmoozy, emotional, imagistic stuff. Literate, personal material that sings and surprises, OK? We've published poetry by Philip Whalen, Miriam Sagan, Leslie Scalapino, Arthur Sze, Nathaniel Tarn, Alice Notley, John Brandi, Steve Richmond, Jessica Hagedorn, and Leo Romero, all of whom have books around worth finding and reading. We're looking for New Mexico authors, also prose: fiction, essays, what-have-you, and artwork, scores, cartoons, etc. - just send it along, with SASE. *Fish Drum* is being produced in memory of and to honor Robert Winson (April 28, 1959 - October 20, 1995) the founder, editor and publisher." circ. 2M. 1-2/yr. Expects 2 issues 1999, 2 issues 2000. sub. price: $24/4 issues; sample: $6. Back issues: not available. Discounts: 40%. 80pp; 6×9; of. Reporting time: 2 months. Simultaneous submissions accepted: no. Publishes 2-5% of manuscripts submitted. Payment: 2 or more copies. Copyrighted, reverts to author. Pub's reviews. §Poetry and fiction, natural history of the Southwest, Zen. No ads.

FISH STORIES, Amy Davis, 3540 N. Southport Avenue #493, Chicago, IL 60657-1436, 773-334-6690. 1994. Poetry, fiction. circ. 1.2M. 1/yr. Pub'd 1 issue 1998; expects 1 issue 1999, 1 issue 2000. sub. price: $10.95; per copy: $10.95; sample: $10.95. Discounts: call for schedule. 224pp; 5½×8½; of. Reporting time: 6-9 months. Simultaneous submissions accepted: yes. Publishes 5-10% of manuscripts submitted. Payment: copies. Copyrighted, reverts to author. Ads: $110/$65. WorkShirts - member of A.W.P.

Fisher Books, Howard W. Fisher, Publisher, 5225 W. Massingale Road, Tucson, AZ 85743-8416, 520-744-6110; Fax 520-744-0944. 1987. Non-fiction. "Our focus is on adult trade titles, including cookbooks, automotive, family health, pregnancy and childcare, self-help, regional gardening, business, nature, and Spanish language titles. Books range from 144 pages for $9.95 cookbooks, to 600 pages for $17.95 family health titles. Please do *not* send manuscripts; send letter of inquiry plus an outline. We require releases before reviewing manuscript." avg. press run 10M first printing. Pub'd 12 titles 1998; expects 20 titles 1999, 30 titles 2000. 101

194

titles listed in the *Small Press Record of Books in Print* (28th Edition, 1999-00). avg. price, cloth: $39.95; paper: $24.95. Discounts: retail, wholesale, library, mail order - upon request. 160pp; 7×9, 6×9, 8½×11. Reporting time: 1-2 months. Payment: upon request. Copyrights for author. ABA, PMA.

FISICA, Zagier & Urruty Publicaciones, Sergio Zagier, PO Box 94 Sucursal 19, Buenos Aires 1419, Argentina, 541-572-1050. 1985. Articles, reviews, non-fiction. "Scientific contributions about physics, its philosophy and its teaching are welcomed, in Spanish or English. Maximum 25 letter pages." circ. 1.5M. 2/yr. Pub'd 2 issues 1998; expects 2 issues 1999, 2 issues 2000. sub. price: $8; per copy: $4; sample: $4. Back issues: $4. Discounts: 50% distributors, 30% bookstores. 64pp; 6½×8; of. Reporting time: 3 months. Payment: none. Copyrighted, reverts to author. Pub's reviews: 20 in 1998. §Physics, philosophy, mathematics, computation, history of science. Ads: $200/$100/$500 back cover.

Fithian Press, John Daniel, Editor, PO Box 1525, Santa Barbara, CA 93102, 805-962-1780; Fax 805-962-8835; e-mail dandd@danielpublishing.com. 1985. Poetry, fiction, non-fiction. "We are open to anything but we specialize in memoir, fiction, poetry, and social issures. In addition to our general catalogue we issue annual catalogs in California and World War II books" avg. press run 1M. Pub'd 40 titles 1998; expects 40 titles 1999, 40 titles 2000. 39 titles listed in the *Small Press Record of Books in Print* (28th Edition, 1999-00). avg. price, cloth: $22.95; paper: $10.95. Discounts: trade 1-4 20%, 5+ 47%; wholesale 1-9 20%, 10+ 50%; library 20%. 160pp; 5½×8½; of. Reporting time: 6-8 weeks. Simultaneous submissions accepted: yes. Publishes 5% of manuscripts submitted. Payment: author pays production costs and receives 60% net royalty. Copyrights for author. Publishers Marketing Assn. (PMA).

5 AM, Ed Ochester, Judith Vollmer, 1109 Milton Avenue, Pittsburgh, PA 15218. 1987. Poetry. "Open to poems in any style, but particularly interested in content ignored by many literary magazines: poems about work, political poems, poems by and about gays, poems by and about ethnic minorities, comic and satirical poems, poems dealing with rural experience. We want to avoid the sameness of many poetry magazines. Recent contributors: Robin Becker, Renee Ashley, Charles Webb, Jan Beatty, Edward Field, Denise Duhamel, Billy Collins, David Newman, Alicia Ostriker, and many others." circ. 1M+. 2/yr. Pub'd 2 issues 1998; expects 2 issues 1999. sub. price: $8, $12/2 yrs/4 issues; per copy: $4; sample: $4. Back issues: $5. Discounts: 40% negotiable. 28pp; 11½×16; of. Reporting time: 2 weeks-2 months. Simultaneous submissions accepted: no. Publishes 1% of manuscripts submitted. Payment: copies. Copyrighted, reverts to author. Pub's reviews: 2 in 1998. §Poetry. Ads: $125 1/2 page/$75 1/4 page.

Five Corners Publications, Ltd., Donald Kroitzsh, Old Bridgewater Mill, PO Box 66, Bridgewater, VT 05034-0066, 802-672-3868; Fax 802-672-3296; e-mail don@fivecorners.com. 1990. Poetry, fiction, art, photos, non-fiction. avg. press run 5M. Pub'd 4 titles 1998; expects 6 titles 1999, 8 titles 2000. 16 titles listed in the *Small Press Record of Books in Print* (28th Edition, 1999-00). avg. price, cloth: $24.95; paper: $12.95. Discounts: 2-4 20%, 5-19 30%, 20-49 40%, 100-199 48%, 200+ 50%, 5% additional discount for nonreturnables. 96pp; 8½×11, 6×9; of. Reporting time: 1 month. Simultaneous submissions accepted: yes. Publishes 5% of manuscripts submitted. Copyrights for author. PMA.

Five Fingers Press (see also FIVE FINGERS REVIEW), Jaime Robles, PO Box 12955, Berkeley, CA 94712-3955. 1984. Fiction, interviews, non-fiction. avg. press run 1M. Pub'd 1 title 1998; expects 1 title 1999, 1 title 2000. 10 titles listed in the *Small Press Record of Books in Print* (28th Edition, 1999-00). avg. price, paper: $9.50. Discounts: subs. $16/2 issues, 40% consignment; 50% outright sale. 200pp; 6×9; of. Reporting time: 3-5 months. Payment: 2 copies of magazine, cash payment depends upon funding. Does not copyright for author. CLMP.

FIVE FINGERS REVIEW, Five Fingers Press, Jaime Robles, PO Box 12955, Berkeley, CA 94712-3955. 1984. Poetry, fiction, interviews, non-fiction. "The *Five Fingers Review* seeks to publish fresh, innovative writing and artwork that is not necessarily defined by the currently 'correct' aesthetic or ideology. *Five Fingers Review* welcomes work that crosses or falls between genres. In addition to new fiction and poetry, *Five Fingers Review* presents essays, interviews, and translations. Each issue explores a theme; recent issues have focused on Spirituality and the Avant-Garde, Beginnings, Birth/Rebirth and the New World and The Neighborhood: Cadences of the Numerous. Writers include Francisco Alarcon, C.D. Wright, Fanny Howe, Norman Fischer, Mikhail Epshtein, Leslie Scalapino, Lyn Hejinian, David Levi-Strauss, Jaime Robles, Keith Waldrop, Rosmarie Waldrop, Peter Gizzi, Aleksei Parschikov, Thaisa Frank." circ. 1M. 1/yr. Pub'd 1 issue 1998; expects 1 issue 1999, 1 issue 2000. sub. price: $16/2 issues; per copy: $9.50; sample: $6 + $1 postage. Back issues: $6 + $1 postage. Discounts: 40% consignment, 50% outright sale; negotiable. 200pp; 6×9; of. Reporting time: 3-5 months. Simultaneous submissions accepted: yes. Payment: 2 copies, cash payment depends upon funding. Copyrighted, reverts to author. Ads: $125 (4½ X 7½)/$75 (4½ X 3½)/$50 1/4 page (2 X 3). CLMP.

FIVE POINTS, David Bottoms, Pam Durban, Georgia State University, University Plaza, Atlanta, GA 30303-3083, 404-651-0071; Fax 404-651-3167. 1996. Poetry, fiction, art, photos, interviews, parts-of-novels, long-poems, non-fiction. "Recent contributors: James Dickey, Anne Beattie, Elizabeth Spires, Naomi Shihab

Nye, Peter Davison, Phillip Booth, Rick Bass, and Tess Gallagher.'' circ. 6M. 3/yr. Pub'd 3 issues 1998; expects 3 issues 1999, 3 issues 2000. sub. price: $15; per copy: $6; sample: $5. Back issues: $5. Discounts: classroom. 170pp; 6½×9; of. Reporting time: 6-8 weeks. Simultaneous submissions accepted: no. Payment: $50 per poem, $15 per prose page. Copyrighted, reverts to author. Ads: $200/$100/$50 1/4 page. CLMP, CELJ.

Five Star Publications, Linda F. Radke, Publisher, 4696 West Tyson Street #D, Chandler, AZ 85226-2903. 1985. ''We are accepting manuscripts by previously published instructors. Query letter first and a SASE. Recent contributors: *Shakespeare for Children: The Story of Romeo & Juliet* by Cass Foster; *Nannies, Maids & More: The Complete Guide for Hiring Household Help* by Linda F. Radke; *The Sixty-Minute Shakespeare: Romeo and Juliet* by Cass Foster; *Shakespeare: To Teach or Not To Teach, Grades 3 & Up* by Cass Foster and Lynn G. Johnson. Household Careers: The Complete Guide For Finding Household Employment or *If the Dog Likes You, You're Hired* by Linda F. Radke. The economical guide to self-publishing: How to Produce and Market Your Book on a Budget by Linda F. Radke'' Pub'd 4 titles 1998; expects 1 title 1999. 10 titles listed in the *Small Press Record of Books in Print* (28th Edition, 1999-00). avg. price, paper: $9.95-$19.95. Discounts: write for schedule. 100pp; 5½×8½, 8½×11. Reporting time: 90 days. Payment: to be arranged - we normally buy all rights. Does not copyright for author. PMA, Arizona Authors' Association, Arizona Press Women, Arizona Book Publishing Assocation.

Fjord Press, Steven T. Murray, Editor-in-Chief, PO Box 16349, Seattle, WA 98116, 206-935-7376, fax 206-938-1991, e-mail fjord@halcyon.com; web site www.fjordpress.com/fjord. 1981. Satire, articles. ''No unsolicited submissions please. Query first with SASE'' avg. press run 1.5M-5M. Pub'd 4 titles 1998; expects 4 titles 1999, 4 titles 2000. 24 titles listed in the *Small Press Record of Books in Print* (28th Edition, 1999-00). avg. price, paper: $14. Discounts: bookstores Stop 40%; other, order from Publishers Services, PO Box 2510, Novato, CA 94948, 415-883-3530; Fax 415-883-4280. 156-320pp; 5½×8½; of. Reporting time: 2 months. Simultaneous submissions are accepted if notified. Publishes 1% of manuscripts submitted. Payment: industry standard. Copyrights for author. PEN American Center; American Literary Translators Assn.

FkB Press (see also OLD CROW), John Gibney, PO Box 403, Easthampton, MA 01027-0403. 1991. Poetry, fiction, long-poems. ''FkB Press publishes fiction, poetry and essays by emerging writers both local and international.'' avg. press run 200-500. Pub'd 3 titles 1998; expects 6 titles 1999, 12 titles 2000. avg. price, paper: $10. Discounts: none. 200pp; 5½×8½; of. Reporting time: 4-8 weeks. Payment: negotiable. Copyrights for author.

FLASHPOINT: Military Books Reviewed by Military Professionals, Cole Morris, 5820 W. Peoria, Suite 107-54, Glendale, AZ 85302, 602-842-1726. 1993. Reviews, non-fiction. ''*Flashpoint* specializes in military book reviews from America's leading professional military journals. Focusing on the world of military books, the newsletter also features news items on recently released military books and videos, retailers and authors.'' circ. 300. 6/yr. Pub'd 6 issues 1998; expects 7 issues 1999, 7 issues 2000. sub. price: $21.95; per copy: $5; sample: $2. Back issues: none. Discounts: none. 20pp; 8½×11; copy machine. Reporting time: 2 months. Simultaneous submissions accepted: yes. Publishes 75% of manuscripts submitted. Payment: copies. Copyrighted, reverts to author. Pub's reviews: 100 in 1998. §Military history, military affairs, weapons, tactics, modern military operations, military videos. Ads: none.

Flatland Tales Publishing, 2450 Greenwood Dr., Ottawa, KS 66067. 1993. Fiction. ''24 page childrens books that teach good values in a fun lighthearted way. I prefer stories with a sense of humor, ones that are fun for kids to read, and fun for parents to read to their children. My most recent title 'Mommi Watta Spirit of the River' ia an adaptation of a liberian folktale which teaches children about temptation'' avg. press run 2.6M. Expects 1 title 1999, 2 titles 2000. 2 titles listed in the *Small Press Record of Books in Print* (28th Edition, 1999-00). avg. price, cloth: $14.95; paper: $5.95. Discounts: bulk. 24pp; 8×8. Copyrights for author. PMA.

Flax Press, Inc., Linda L. Holup, PO Box 2395, Huntington, WV 25724, 304-525-1109. 1988. Poetry, fiction, photos, music, non-fiction. ''T.S. Innocenti's *Song of Meditation*, published 11/88.'' avg. press run 5M-7M. Expects 1 title 1999, 1 title 2000. 1 title listed in the *Small Press Record of Books in Print* (28th Edition, 1999-00). avg. price, paper: $10.95. Discounts: 40% bookstores. Payment: negotiated individually. Does not copyright for author.

FLIPSIDE, David Eltz, Editor; Joseph Szejk, Editor, Dixon Hall, California University of PA, California, PA 15419, 412-938-4586. 1987. Poetry, fiction, articles, art, photos, cartoons, interviews, satire, criticism, non-fiction. ''We prefer non-fiction articles written in New Journalism style—strong person voice, strong point of view, *subject not important*, just so the article is *well-written*. Photos or art helpful. Poetry must have narrative line.'' circ. 5M. 2/yr. Pub'd 2 issues 1998; expects 2 issues 1999, 2 issues 2000. sub. price: $10; per copy: 3; sample: free with SASE. Back issues: same—if we have them. 56pp; of. Reporting time: 3 months. Simultaneous submissions accepted: yes. Publishes 2% of manuscripts submitted. Payment: 2 copies. Not copyrighted. Ads: $155/$90.

Floating Bridge Press, Peter Pereira, T. Clear, Jeff Crandall, Linda Greenmun, PO Box 18814, Seattle, WA

98118, 206-860-0508. 1994. Poetry. "We publish 1 poetry chapbook and 1 poetry anthology per year, from manuscripts submitted to our annual contest series. We are committed to producing a high-quality book, printed on acid-free, archival-quality paper, with cardstock cover and engaging cover art. We also produce a local reading for the winning poet(s). Send SASE for guidelines; $6.00 ppd. for sample book. We have a variety of tastes, but tend to prefer manuscripts that hold together thematically as a collection. We sometimes publish broadsides." avg. press run 200-400 chapbook; 500-1000 anthology. Pub'd 2 titles 1998; expects 3 titles 1999, 2 titles 2000. 7 titles listed in the *Small Press Record of Books in Print* (28th Edition, 1999-00). avg. price, paper: $7. Discounts: bookstores and libraries 40%. Chapbooks 24-32pp, anthologies 80-100pp; 5½×8½, 6×9, varies; of, lp. Reporting time: 2-3 months or longer. Simultaneous submissions accepted: yes. Payment: honorarium plus copies. Copyrights for author.

FLOATING ISLAND, Floating Island Publications, Michael Sykes, PO Box 7, Stonington, ME 04681, 207-367-6309. 1976. Poetry, fiction, articles, art, photos, cartoons, parts-of-novels, long-poems, collages. "No unsolicited manuscripts currently being accepted. Floating Island pubs. 1 every 3-4 years approx. 8½ X 11, 160pp, perfectbound cover in color, text B/W, 24pp of photographs (full-page) on coated stock, approx. 50 percent of text is poetry, 25 percent fiction & prose, 25 percent graphics-poetry fiction & prose is frequently illustrated, engravings, woodblocks, pen & pencil etc.-some artwork halftoned to retain fidelity, most is line-shot. Contributors include well-known poets & writers as well as previous unpublished artists. Editorial policy is determined solely by whim and is akin to a celebration which various persons have been invited to attend in the belief they may enjoy one another's company and perhaps find a small and appreciative audience as well. *Floating Island IV* (1989) ends First Series. No date set for start of Second Series." circ. 1M. Publish 1 every 3-4 years. Standing orders only - full price; price per copy: $15; sample: full-price. Back issues: full-price - all issues. Discounts: 50% to dist.; 40% to retail outlets. 160pp; 8½×11; of. Reporting time: 2-4 weeks. Publishes 1% of manuscripts submitted. Payment: copies. Copyrighted, rights revert to author upon request. Ads: none.

Floating Island Publications (see also FLOATING ISLAND), Michael Sykes, PO Box 7, Stonington, ME 04681, 207-367-6309. 1976. Poetry, fiction, articles, art, photos, parts-of-novels, long-poems. "No unsolicited manuscripts currently being accepted. I'll do 1 or 2 books a year, more if possible. I'm interested as much in the design and production of a book as its content and choose to work with manuscripts that offer me an interesting possibility of balancing these two areas of concern. Consequently the work is slow and deliberate. Authors must be patient." avg. press run 1M. Expects 1 title 2000. 36 titles listed in the *Small Press Record of Books in Print* (28th Edition, 1999-00). avg. price, cloth: $25; paper: $8. Discounts: 50% jobbers, 40% bookstores. 64pp; 6×9, 5½×8½; of. Reporting time: 2-4 weeks. Simultaneous submissions accepted: no. Payment: 10% of the press run. Does not copyright for author.

J. Flores Publications, Eli Flores, PO Box 830131, Miami, FL 33283, 305-559-4652. 1981. Photos, non-fiction. "J. Flores Publications primarily publishes original non-fiction manuscripts on military science, weaponry, improvised weaponry, self-defense, survival, personal finance, and current events. How-to manuscripts are given priority. Query or submit outline/synopsis and sample chapters." avg. press run 3M. Pub'd 10 titles 1998; expects 10 titles 1999, 13 titles 2000. 24 titles listed in the *Small Press Record of Books in Print* (28th Edition, 1999-00). avg. price, paper: $12. Discounts: 50% of retail price (3-9 comes 40% off, 10-99 50% off, over 100 comes 55%). 150pp; 5½×8½; of. Reporting time: 30 days. Simultaneous submissions accepted: yes. Publishes 50% of manuscripts submitted. Payment: 10% (copies 1-4,999), 12% (copies 5,000-10,000), 15% (over) based on NET receipts. Copyrights for author. PMA.

Florida Academic Press, Samuel Decalo, PO Box 540, Gainesville, FL 32602-0540, 352-332-5104; fax 352-331-6003; email FAPress@worldnet.att.net. 1997. "Non-fiction: scholarly and how-to; Africa; Middle East; politics and history." avg. press run 2M. Expects 2 titles 1999, 4 titles 2000. 4 titles listed in the *Small Press Record of Books in Print* (28th Edition, 1999-00). avg. price, cloth: $47.50; paper: $23.95. Discounts: 20% to distributers; bookstores to 3 20% on STOPS, 4+ 40%. 300pp; 5½×8½. Reporting time: 2-3 months if submission meets specifications, 1 week if it doesn't. Simultaneous submissions accepted: no. Payment: end of year 8% paperback/hardcover. Copyrights for author. PMA.

FLORIDA PRISON LEGAL PERSPECTIVES, Bob Posey, PO Box 660-387, Chuluota, FL 32766, 407-306-6211; fplp@aol.com; members.aol.com/fplp/fplp. 1994. Articles, interviews, reviews, letters, news items. "*FPLP* is a non-profit publication focusing on the Florida prison and criminal justice systems with the goal of providing a vehicle for news, information and resources affecting prisoners, their families, friends, and loved ones, and the general public of Florida and the U.S." circ. 2.5M. 6/yr. Pub'd 6 issues 1998; expects 6 issues 1999, 6 issues 2000. sub. price: $5 prisoners, $10 non-prisoners, $25 institutions/businesses; per copy: $5; sample: $1. Back issues: $2 prisoners, $5 others. Discounts: contact publisher for discount rates. 16pp; 8×10¾; of. Reporting time: 6 weeks. Simultaneous submissions accepted: yes. Publishes 25% of manuscripts submitted. Payment: none. Not copyrighted. Pub's reviews: 10 in 1998. §Criminal justice, prisons, penology, juvenile justice, criminology, etc. Ads: $300/$160/$120 1/3 page/$75 1/6 page.

THE FLORIDA REVIEW, Russell Kesler, Editor, PO Box 25000, English Department, University of Central Florida, Orlando, FL 32816, 407-823-2038. 1972. Poetry, fiction, reviews. "We look for fiction (up to 7,500 words) and poetry (any length). We are especially interested in new writers. We publish fiction of high quality—stories that delight, instruct, and aren't afraid to take risks, and we welcome experimental fiction, so long as it doesn't make us feel lost or stupid. Also, we look for clear, strong poems—poems filled with real things, real people, real emotions, poems that might conceivably advance our knowledge of the human heart. Some of our recent contributors include Philip F. Deaver, Stephen Dixon, Gary Fincke, Karen Fish, Ruthann Robson, William Stafford, and Tom Whalen." circ. 1M. 2/yr. Pub'd 2 issues 1998; expects 2 issues 1999, 2 issues 2000. sub. price: $10; per copy: $6; sample: $6. Back issues: $4. Discounts: 20%. 140pp; 5½x8½; of. Reporting time: 12 weeks. Simultaneous submissions accepted: yes. Publishes 2% of manuscripts submitted. Payment: occasional honoraria; 3 copies. Copyrighted, reverts to author. Pub's reviews: 6 in 1998. EBSCO, CLMP.

Flower Press, Mary Appelhof, 10332 Shaver Road, Kalamazoo, MI 49002, 616-327-0108. 1976. "Flower Press celebrates the energizing power of self-sufficiency by publishing books, primarily written by Mary Appelhof, which help people regain control over their own lives. I am currently concentrating on studies about earthworms. *Worms Eat My Garbage*, with illustrations by Mary Frances Fenton (paper, 164pp, 5¼ X 8½, $15.45 postpaid) has sold over 100,000 copies to date. A children's activities book, *Worms Eat Our Garbage: Classroom Activities for a Better Environment* uses earthworms in a non-invasive manner to teach interested learners science, math, writing, vocabulary, scientific method and other disciplines." avg. press run 10M. Pub'd 2 titles 1998; expects 3 titles 1999, 3 titles 2000. 6 titles listed in the *Small Press Record of Books in Print* (28th Edition, 1999-00). avg. price, paper: $15; other: Video $30. Discounts: 1-9 copies 20%, 10+ 40%. 150pp; 5¼x8¼, 8½x11; of. Payment: author defrays publishing cost. Copyrights for author.

FLYFISHER, Keokee Co. Publishing, Inc., Chris Bessler, Editor; Dick Wentz, Managing Editor, PO Box 722, Sandpoint, ID 83864, 208-263-3573; flyfisher@keokee.com. 1968. Articles, art, photos, reviews, letters, news items, non-fiction. "Physical address: 111 Cedar Street, Sandpoint, ID 83864." circ. 12000. 4/yr. Pub'd 4 issues 1998; expects 4 issues 1999, 4 issues 2000. sub. price: membership publication, Individual FFF membership is $29. Discounts: negotiable. 48pp; 8½x11; of. Reporting time: 2 months. Simultaneous submissions accepted: yes. Publishes 25% of manuscripts submitted. Payment: negotiable. Copyrighted. Pub's reviews: 20 in 1998. §fly fishing books. Ads: $1580/$1025/$15 for 2 lines, $8/additional line $1359/510/$45 per column inch. PNBA.

FLYING HORSE, Dennis Must, Editor; David Wagner, Associate Editor, PO Box 445, Marblehead, MA 01945. 1996. Poetry, fiction, art, photos, satire, criticism, parts-of-novels, long-poems. "*Flying Horse*, an alternative literary journal, features short fiction, poetry, essays and visuals. Although *Flying Horse* welcomes contributions from all talented artists, we particularly hope to give voice to those often excluded from the dominant media. For example, we actively encourage submissions from inner city learning centers, community and public colleges, prisons, homeless shelters, social service agencies, unions, the military, hospitals, clinics or group homes, Indian reservations and minority studies programs. *Flying Horse* espouses no political agenda. Entries should be limited to 7,500 words or less." circ. 1M. 2/yr. Expects 2 issues 1999, 2 issues 2000. sub. price: $7; per copy: $4; sample: $4. Discounts: inquire. 100+pp; 6x9; of. Reporting time: 2-3 months. Simultaneous submissions accepted: yes. Publishes 3-5% of manuscripts submitted. Payment: $10 per poem, $25 short story or essay, $10-$25 art, photo. Copyrighted, reverts to author. §Literary fiction, poetry and sociology. Ads: $100/$50. CLMP.

Flying Pencil Publications, Madelynne Diness Sheehan, 33126 Callahan Road, Scappoose, OR 97056. 1983. Non-fiction. "Fishing is our subject-specialty." avg. press run 5M. Pub'd 1 title 1998; expects 1 title 1999, 1 title 2000. 8 titles listed in the *Small Press Record of Books in Print* (28th Edition, 1999-00). avg. price, paper: $14.95. Discounts: 40% to retailers, 55% to distributors. 188pp; 6x9; of. Reporting time: 30 days. Simultaneous submissions accepted: yes. Payment: variable. Copyrights for author. NW Book Publishers Assoc.

FLYWAY, Debra Marquart, 206 Ross Hall, Iowa State University, Ames, IA 50011, 515-294-8273, FAX 515-294-6814, flyway@iastate.edu. 1995. Poetry, fiction, non-fiction. "*Flyway* is open to a range of poetry, fiction, and nonfiction. Recent contributors include Jane Smiley, Madison Smartt Bell, Lola Haskins, Neal Bowers, William Trowbridge, Ray A. Young Bear, Mary Swander, and Michael Martone." circ. 600. 3/yr. Pub'd 3 issues 1998; expects 3 issues 1999, 3 issues 2000. sub. price: $24; per copy: $8; sample: $8. Back issues: $8. Discount price: $24. 100pp; 9x6. Reporting time: 4 weeks or less. Simultaneous submissions accepted: no. Publishes 1-2% of manuscripts submitted. Payment: 1 copy free, additional copies at cost. Copyrighted, reverts to author. Pub's reviews: 2 in 1998. §Poetry, fiction, literary, non-fiction. Ads: exchange. CLMP.

FOCUS: Library Service to Older Adults, People with Disabilities, Michael G. Gunde, 216 N. Frederick Avenue, Daytona Beach, FL 32114-3408, 904-257-4259; e-mail gundem@mail.firn.edu. 1983. Articles, reviews, news items. "This is a monthly newsletter for librarians and other persons concerned with library service to persons with disabilities and older adults." circ. 175. 12/yr. Pub'd 12 issues 1998; expects 12 issues 1999, 12 issues 2000. sub. price: $18; per copy: $2; sample: free. Back issues: $2. 2pp; 8½×11; of. Copyrighted, does not revert to author. Pub's reviews: 30 in 1998. §Aging, books by and about people with disabilities, library service to these groups. No ads.

Focus Publications, Inc., Jan Haley, Barbara Smith, PO Box 609, Bemidji, MN 56601, 218-751-2183; focus@paulbunyan.net. 1994. Fiction, non-fiction. "Publications are primarily Christian (religion) and children. *No unsolicited manuscripts; send proposal.*" avg. press run 1M-10M. Pub'd 1 title 1998; expects 3-4 titles 1999, 3 titles 2000. 6 titles listed in the *Small Press Record of Books in Print* (28th Edition, 1999-00). avg. price, paper: $9.95. Discounts: 40-50%. 150pp; 6×9; †of. Reporting time: 60 days. Simultaneous submissions accepted: no. Payment: 7.5%. Copyrights for author.

FODDERWING, Edward Allan Faine, PO Box 5346, Takoma Park, MD 20913-5346, 301-587-1202. 1995. Poetry, fiction, articles, non-fiction. "Open to all mid-Atlantic writers and poets on any subject. Each issue will present 1) a stylistic mix of prose, 2) an essay or two, 3) a poetry centerfold, 4) an article on the arts - art, dance, film, music, photography, TV or theatre, 5) a short humor piece, 6) and (possibly) something different." circ. 1M. 2/yr. Pub'd 2 issues 1998; expects 2 issues 1999, 2 issues 2000. sub. price: $6; per copy: $3; sample: $3. 24pp; 8½×11; of. Reporting time: 3 weeks. Simultaneous submissions accepted: yes. Payment: 1 copy. Copyrighted, reverts to author. PMA, SPAN.

Foghorn Press, Vicki K. Morgan, Publisher, PO BOX 2036, Santa Rosa, CA 95405-0036, 415-241-9550. 1985. Photos, non-fiction. avg. press run 7.5M-15M. Pub'd 12 titles 1998; expects 19 titles 1999, 24 titles 2000. 47 titles listed in the *Small Press Record of Books in Print* (28th Edition, 1999-00). avg. price, paper: $16.95. Discounts: trade. 600-700pp; 5¾×8⅜; lp. Reporting time: 2 months. Payment: 10% net. Copyrights for author. Publishers Marketing Association (PMA), San Francisco Bay Area Book Council, Northern California Booksellers Assn., American Booksellers Assn., Northern California Book Marketing Assn.

FOLIO: A LITERARY JOURNAL, Editors change yearly, Dept. of Literature, American University, Washington, DC 20016, 202-885-2971. 1984. Poetry, fiction, art, photos, interviews, parts-of-novels, non-fiction. "Recent contributors include: Robert Bausch, William Stafford, Sheila Cudahy, Linda Pastan, Jean Valentine, Chitra Divakaruni, Henry Taylor, as well as new writers. Quality fiction, poetry, translations, essays, and art. We like to comment on pieces when time permits. We sponsor a fiction/poetry contest for which all submissions are considered. Please limit poetry submissions to batches of five; fiction to 5,000 words. We read from September to March 15." circ. 400. 2/yr. Pub'd 2 issues 1998; expects 2 issues 1999, 2 issues 2000. sub. price: $10; per copy: $5 (includes postage); sample: $5. Back issues: $2. Discounts: 33%. 64pp; 6×9; of. Reporting time: 6-10 weeks. Payment: 2 contributors copies. Copyrighted, reverts to author.

FOLK ART MESSENGER, Ann Oppenhimer, PO Box 17041, Richmond, VA 23226, 804-285-4532; fax 804-285-4532. 1987. Articles, art, photos, interviews, criticism, reviews, news items. "2000 words or less. Subject: contemporary folk art. Rarely select unsolicited manuscripts. Contributors: Roger Cardinal, Roger Manley, John Turner, Norman Girardot, Chuck Rosenak, Robert Hobbs, Willem Volkersz, Didi Barrett" circ. 1000. 4/yr. Pub'd 4 issues 1998; expects 4 issues 1999, 4 issues 2000. sub. price: $25, $35 overseas; per copy: $7; sample: $7. Back issues: $7. Discounts: $5 for 10 copies of one issue. 24pp; 8½×11; lp. Reporting time: 30 days. Simultaneous submissions accepted: no. Publishes less than 2% of manuscripts submitted. Payment: none. Copyrighted, rights revert to author after one year. Pub's reviews: 4 in 1998. §Folk art, contemporary self-taught art, Appalachia, outsider art. Ads: none.

Food First Books, Peter Rosset, Executive Director, 398 60th Street, Oakland, CA 94618, 510-654-4400; FAX 510-654-4551; foodfirst@foodfirst.org. 1975. Non-fiction. "Publications are progressive. Recent books include *The Paradox of Plenty: Hunger in a Bountiful World, A Siamese Tragedy: Development and Disintegration in Modern Thailand, Breakfast of Biodiversity; The Truth about Rain Forest Destruction, Education for Action: Undergraduate and Graduate Programs that Focus on Social Change,* and *Basta! Land and the Zapatista Rebellion in Chiapas*" avg. press run 3M. Pub'd 2 titles 1998; expects 1 title 1999, 1 title 2000. avg. price, paper: $12. 150pp; 5½×8½; lp. Reporting time: 3-6 months. Simultaneous submissions accepted: yes. Publishes 5% of manuscripts submitted. Payment: yes. Copyrights for author.

FOOD WRITER, Page One, Lynn Kerrigan, 20 West Athens Avenue, Ardmore, PA 19003, 610-896-2879; E-mail foodwriter@aol.com; www.food-journalist.net. 1997. Non-fiction. circ. 650. 6/yr. Pub'd 6 issues 1998; expects 6 issues 1999, 6 issues 2000. sub. price: $59.95; per copy: $7.50; sample: $7.50. Back issues: $5. 12pp; 8×11; of. Reporting time: 1 month. Simultaneous submissions accepted: yes. Publishes 50% of manuscripts submitted. Payment: $25. Copyrighted, reverts to author. Pub's reviews: 6 in 1998. §Food writing, nutrition reporting, food writer resources. IACP.

Footprint Press, Rich Freeman, Sue Freeman, PO Box 645, Fishers, NY 14453, 716-321-3666 phone/Fax; email freeman1@frontiernet.net; www.footprintpress.com. 1997. Non-fiction. "As a small publisher, we give each title the attention it deserves. We look for authors who are willing and able to participate in the promotion of their book." avg. press run 6M. Pub'd 3 titles 1998; expects 3 titles 1999, 3 titles 2000. 6 titles listed in the *Small Press Record of Books in Print* (28th Edition, 1999-00). avg. price, paper: $16.95. Discounts: 2-4 20%, 5+ 40%. 232pp; 5½×8½; of. Reporting time: 20 business days. Simultaneous submissions accepted: yes. Publishes 10% of manuscripts submitted. Payment: by individual arrangement. Copyrights for author. PMA.

Forbes/Wittenburg & Brown, Patricia Wood, 250 West 57th Street, Suite 1527, New York, NY 10107, 212-969-0969. 1988. Non-fiction. avg. press run 5M. Pub'd 1 title 1998; expects 1 title 1999, 1 title 2000. 3 titles listed in the *Small Press Record of Books in Print* (28th Edition, 1999-00). avg. price, paper: $9.95-$14.95. Discounts: 40-50%. 300pp; 5½×8½; of. Does not copyright for author.

FORESIGHT MAGAZINE, John W.B. Barklam, Judy Barklam, 44 Brockhurst Road, Hodge Hill, Birmingham B36 8JB, England, 021-783-0587. 1970. Articles, reviews, letters, news items. "Articles of approx. 1000 words welcomed. A bias towards philosophy as related to life. Dealing also in mysticism, occultism, UFOs and allied subjects. Aims are to help create peace and encourage spiritual awareness and evolution in the world." circ. 1.1M. 4/yr. Pub'd 4 issues 1998; expects 4 issues 1999, 4 issues 2000. sub. price: £5.20 - $9.00; per copy: £1.25-2.25; sample: £1.25-2.25. Back issues: 50p - $1. Discounts: none. 20pp; 12×8¼; †photocopying. Reporting time: immediate. Payment: none. Copyrighted, rights revert to author if requested. Pub's reviews: 40 in 1998. §Health, philosophy, psychic phenomena, UFOs, prediction, occult, spiritualism, and allied fiction. Ads: £9 ($16.25)/£5 ($9)/4p (8¢).

FOREST: The Freedom Organization for the Right to Smoke Tobacco (see also FREE CHOICE), Chris Tame, Director, 2 Grosvenor Gardens, London, SW1W ODH, England, 0171-823-6550; FAX 0171-823-4534. 1981. "FOREST's goal is not to promote smoking but to defend adult freedom of choice against prohibitionists, social authoritarians, and medical paternalists. It is not the role of the state to restrict the non-violent life styles of the individual, even if they involve a degree of risk (as virtually everything in life does, anyway). FOREST campaigns by publishing both scholarly and popular pamphlets, a regular magazine, Free Choice, organizing meetings, conferences and demonstrations, addressing debates and meetings at universities and political, business and trade union groups, presenting the case for free choice to Government and Parliamentary inquiries, by press releases, and by regular appearances on television and radio, and supporting employees and others suffering discrimination as a result of being smokers" avg. press run 1M. avg. price, paper: £2.50 ($5). Discounts: 33% for trade order. 8×11¾. Reporting time: immediate. Simultaneous submissions accepted: yes. Payment: none.

FOREVER ALIVE, Herb Bowie, PO Box 12305, Scottsdale, AZ 85267-2305, 602-922-0300; fax 602-922-0800; e-Mail HERBBOWIE@AOL.COM. 1989. Poetry, fiction, articles, art, photos, cartoons, interviews, criticism, reviews, letters, news items, non-fiction. "We publish material on human aliveness and living forever." circ. 3M. 4/yr. Pub'd 4 issues 1998; expects 4 issues 1999, 4 issues 2000. sub. price: $24; per copy: $6; sample: $6. 52pp; 8½×11; of. Reporting time: 90 days. Simultaneous submissions accepted: yes. Publishes 2% of manuscripts submitted. Payment: varies. Copyrighted, rights can revert to author by special arrangement. Pub's reviews: 4 in 1998. §Health, longevity, immortality.

THE FORMALIST, William Baer, Editor, 320 Hunter Drive, Evansville, IN 47711-2218. 1990. Poetry. "*The Formalist: A Journal of Metrical Poetry* publishes contemporary, *metrical* verse written in the great tradition of English-language poetry. Recent issues contain poetry by Howard Nemerov, Richard Wilbur, Derek Walcott, Mona Van Duyn, Donald Justice, Maxine Kumin, James Merrill, John Updike, X.J. Kennedy, May Swenson, W.S. Merwin, Karl Shapiro, W.D. Snodgrass, Louis Simpson, and many other poets — both known and unknown. The Editors suggest submitting 3-5 poems at one time. We're looking for well-crafted poetry in a contemporary idiom which uses meter and the full range of traditional poetic conventions in vigorous and interesting ways. We're especially interested in sonnets, couplets, tercets, ballads, the French forms, etc. We also consider metrical translations of major formalist non-English poets — from the ancient Greeks to the present. We're not, however, interested in haiku (or syllabic verse of any kind) or sestinas. Only rarely do we accept a poem over 2 pages, and we do not publish any type of erotica, blasphemy, vulgarity, or racism. We suggest that those wishing to submit become familiar with the journal beforehand. Submissions are considered throughout the year; a brief cover letter is recommended, and an SASE is necessary for a reply and the return of the mss. No simultaneous submissions, previously published work, or disk submissions. *The Formalist* also sponsors the annual Howard Nemerov Sonnet Award of $1,000; deadline June 15th; entry fee $3/sonnet; past judges were Richard Wilbur, Mona Van Duyn, Anthony Hecht, and Donald Justice. Send SASE for rules." 2/yr. Pub'd 2 issues 1998; expects 2 issues 1999, 2 issues 2000. sub. price: $12, foreign $15; per copy: $6.50; sample: $6.50. 128pp; 6×9; of. Reporting time: 4-8 weeks. Simultaneous submissions accepted: no. Payment: 2 copies. Copyrighted, reverts to author. Pub's reviews: 0 in 1998. no advertising.

Fort Dearborn Press, Gale Ahrens, 245 Bluff Court (LBS), Barrington, IL 60010, 312-235-8500. 1993. Fiction, non-fiction. "Open on all issues, topics, materials, etc." avg. press run 100M. Expects 6 titles 1999, 10 titles 2000. 4 titles listed in the *Small Press Record of Books in Print* (28th Edition, 1999-00). avg. price, cloth: $24.95; paper: $19.95. Discounts: Open to the trade. 500pp; 6×9. Reporting time: flexible. Simultaneous submissions accepted: yes. Publishes .0001% of manuscripts submitted. Payment: standard. Copyrights for author. PMA.

FORUM, Polebridge Press, Philip Sellew, Editor, PO Box 6144, Santa Rosa, CA 95406, 707-532-1323, fax 707-523-1350. 1981. Articles, criticism, reviews. *"Forum* is published by Polebridege Press on behalf of the Westar Institute and its seminars. The Westar Institute conducts research on biblical and American traditions and is devoted to improving biblical and religious literacy. A journal of the foundations and facets of Western culture" circ. 805. 4/yr. sub. price: $30; per copy: $7.50; sample: $7.50. 160pp; 6×9. Copyrighted. Pub's reviews. §Religious studies, especially critical biblical scholarship, and American cultural studies.

THE FORUM, Al-Anon Family Group Headquarters, Inc., Pat Quiggle, Editor, 1600 Corporate Parkway, Virginia Beach, VA 23456-0862, 757-563-1600. Articles, letters. "Articles and stories of personal recovery in Al-Anon from the effects of alcoholism in a spouse, lover, friend, parent, child or other individual. We often require the services of freelance writers/editors, copy editors and proofers who are Al-Anon members." circ. 35M. 12/yr. Pub'd 12 issues 1998; expects 12 issues 1999, 12 issues 2000. sub. price: $10; per copy: $1. 32pp; 5⅜×8⅛. Payment: none. Copyrighted, does not revert to author. Ads: none. ASAE, PMA, PM.

Fotofolio, Inc., Martin Bondell, Juliette Galant, Ron Schick, 536 Broadway, 2nd Floor, New York, NY 10012, 212-226-0923. 1975. Poetry, art, photos. "Publishers of art and photographs in poster, postcard, notecard, and postcardbook formats, and folios. Recent contributors: Richard Avedon, Maira Kalman, Robert Mapplethorpe, Duane Michals, Man Ray, Brassa, Keith Haring, Cindy Sherman, Bruce Weber, Berenice Abbott, Herb Ritts, Henri Cartier-Bresson, Alexander Rodchenko, Georgia O'Keeffe, Helen Frankenthaler, Frank Lloyd Wright, William Wegman, Annie Leibovitz, Andres Serrano, Adam Fuss, Neil Winokur, Wolfgang Tillmans, David La Chapelle, Mark Rothko." avg. press run 7.5M. Pub'd 300 titles 1998; expects 400 titles 1999. 5 titles listed in the *Small Press Record of Books in Print* (28th Edition, 1999-00). Discounts: 50%. duotone process, & four-color offset. ABA.

FOTOTEQUE, PO Box 440735, Miami, FL 33144-0735, 305-461-2770. 1995. Articles, photos, criticism, reviews. "Prefer work by new and emerging photographers, particularly those using view cameras. Need exhibit reviews from all over the world, guidelines with SASE. Annual photo contest and free artist listings for directory." 4/yr. Pub'd 1 issue 1998; expects 2 issues 1999, 4 issues 2000. sub. price: $60; per copy: $15 + p/h; sample: same. Back issues: $20 + p/h. Discounts: request in writing on company letterhead, 40% off multiples of 10. 48pp; 8½×11; of. Reporting time: 12-18 weeks. Simultaneous submissions accepted: no. Payment: cash varies, normally 2 copies. Copyrighted, reverts to author. Pub's reviews: 2 in 1998. §Books and mags about photography only, fine art, commercial, anything. Ads: $1200/$700/$400 1/4 page/$300 1/6 page.

Foundation Books, Duane Hutchinson, Stephen K. Hutchinson, PO Box 22828, Lincoln, NE 68542-2828, 402-438-7080; Fax 402-438-7099. 1970. Poetry, non-fiction. "History, biography and storytelling are our main areas of interest. The format of the paperback books is 5½ X 8½. The binding is Smythe-sewn for added strength and alkaline-based paper stock is used which meets the requirements of the American National Standard for Information Sciences - Permanence of Paper for Printed Library Materials, ANSI Z39.48-1984. The books are copyrighted by Foundation Books and Library of Congress Cataloging-in-Publication Data is included. Expanded bar codes are used on the back covers." avg. press run 1M-3M. Pub'd 4 titles 1998; expects 3 titles 1999, 4 titles 2000. 20 titles listed in the *Small Press Record of Books in Print* (28th Edition, 1999-00). avg. price, cloth: $19.95; paper: $6.95. Discounts: booksellers: 1 20%, 2-4 33%, 5-49 40%, 50-99 41%, 100-249 42%, 250+ 43%. 125-200pp; 5½×8½. Reporting time: acknowledge receipt, 1 week; reading 2-6 months. Payment: to be arranged with individual author. Copyright for author by special arrangement.

The Foundation Center, Sara L. Engelhardt, President, 79 Fifth Avenue, New York, NY 10003-3076, 212-620-4230; 1-800-424-9836. 1956. "The Foundation Center publishes and disseminates through its national library network of over 190 locations materials on foundation and corporate philanthropy. Reference. Production method: Primarily computer photocomposition, some in-house design with additional freelance support." avg. press run 500-2M. Pub'd 35 titles 1998. 55 titles listed in the *Small Press Record of Books in Print* (28th Edition, 1999-00). avg. price, cloth: $29.95-$210; paper: $10-$225. Discounts: 5-24 copies 20%, 25-49 25%, 50-99 30%, 100+ 35%. 25-3Mpp; size varies. Reporting time: 3 months. Payment: 10% royalty. Copyrights for author.

The Foundation for Economic Education, Inc. (see also THE FREEMAN: Ideas On Liberty), Sheldon Richman, 30 South Broadway, Irvington, NY 10533, 914-591-7230; Fax 914-591-8910; E-mail freeman@fee.org. 1946. Articles, photos, criticism, reviews, non-fiction. "Publish single-author and anthologized works in political-economic philosophy and history. Titles must be written from consistent free-market, private-property, limited-government philosophical perspective. Ideas for books should be queried first, with outline" avg. press run 2M-3M. Pub'd 12 titles 1998; expects 5 titles 1999, 4 titles 2000. 12 titles listed in the *Small Press Record of Books in Print* (28th Edition, 1999-00). avg. price, cloth: $24.95; paper: $12.95. Discounts: Trade - normal distributor terms. Direct/mail order: 2-4 20%, 5-49 40%, 50-499 50%, 500+

60%. 250pp; 6×9; of. Reporting time: 2-4 weeks. Payment: negotiated. Copyrights negotiated. ABA.

Four Peaks Press, Richard Dillon, PO Box 27401, Tempe, AZ 85285, 602-838-8726. 1992. Non-fiction. avg. press run 2M. Expects 2 titles 1999, 2 titles 2000. 2 titles listed in the *Small Press Record of Books in Print* (28th Edition, 1999-00). avg. price, paper: $8.95. Discounts: 40% 5+ books, 50% 100+ books. 112pp; 6×9; of. AZ Book Publishers Assoc.

Four Seasons Publishers, Frank Hudak, PO Box 51, Titusville, FL 32781, E-mail fourseasons@gnc.net. 1996. Poetry, fiction, music, non-fiction. avg. press run 10M. Pub'd 3 titles 1998; expects 12 titles 1999, 18 titles 2000. 4 titles listed in the *Small Press Record of Books in Print* (28th Edition, 1999-00). avg. price, paper: $9.95. Discounts: 40-50%. 250pp; 5½×8½; †digital dup. Reporting time: 2-4 weeks. Publishes 10% of manuscripts submitted. Payment: 10-15%. Copyrights for author. SEBA.

Four Seasons Publishing (see also YOUNG VOICES), Steve Charak, Judy Fitzpatrick, PO Box 2321, Olympia, WA 98507, 206-357-4683. 1990. Non-fiction. "We have published one collection of stories and three chapbooks thus far. We are not soliciting material, though we will publish two books this year. In April, we published *South Sound Places* by Nancy Patterson." avg. press run 1.5M-3M. Pub'd 1 title 1998; expects 3 titles 1999, 5 titles 2000. avg. price, paper: $9.95. 80pp; 5½×8½; of. Copyrights for author.

Four Walls Eight Windows, John Oakes, 39 West 14th Street #503, New York, NY 10011, e-mail edit@fourwallseightwindows.com. 1987. Fiction, non-fiction. avg. press run 4M. Pub'd 22 titles 1998; expects 24 titles 1999, 22 titles 2000. 131 titles listed in the *Small Press Record of Books in Print* (28th Edition, 1999-00). avg. price, cloth: $21.95-$25.95; paper: $14.95. Discounts: write for details. 240pp; 6×9, 5½×8¼; of. Reporting time: 3 months. Simultaneous submissions accepted: yes. Publishes 1% of manuscripts submitted. Payment: varies. Copyrights for author.

Four Way Books, Martha Rhodes, Dzvinia Orlowsky, Carlen Arnett, Jane Brox, PO Box 607, Marshfield, MA 02050. 1992. Poetry, fiction. "We seek to publish highest quality poetry and short fiction collections. We sponsor yearly poetry competitions. Past judges: Robert Pinsky, Stephen Dobyns, Gregory Orr, Heather McHugh. As well, we read poetry and fiction manuscripts year round, but please query first." avg. press run 1500. Expects 5 titles 1999, 5 titles 2000. 3 titles listed in the *Small Press Record of Books in Print* (28th Edition, 1999-00). avg. price, paper: $10.95. Discounts: standard. Pages vary; size varies; of. Reporting time: ASAP. Payment: standard. Copyrights for author.

4*9*1: Neo-Immanentist/Sursymbolist-Imagination, Donald Ryburn, Benjamin Norris, 3rd Assistant Editor, PO Box 91212, Lakeland, FL 33804, 941-607-9100; stompdncr@aol.com; www.fournineone.com. 1997. Poetry, articles, art, photos, interviews, criticism, reviews, letters. "*4*9*1* is an annual journal of the Noe-Immanentist/Sursymbolist Movement founded by Duane Locke. Contributors include Alan Britt, Steven Barfield, Lind Call, Damniso Lopez, Stra Schrag, and Decilio Lago." circ. 2M. 1/yr. Expects 1 issue 1999, 1 issue 2000. sub. price: $10; per copy: $10; sample: $10. Discounts: standard. 134pp; 6×9; of. Reporting time: varies. Simultaneous submissions accepted: yes. Publishes less than 1% of manuscripts submitted. Payment: cash or copies (editor's discretion). Copyrighted, reverts to author. Pub's reviews: 1 in 1998. §Work of the imagination but not psycho-babble or academic proslytizations. Ads: none accepted.

Four-Sep Publications (see also FIRST CLASS), Christopher M., PO Box 12434, Milwaukee, WI 53212, E-mail chriftor@execpc.com; www.execpc.com/~chriftor. 1996. Poetry, fiction, photos, long-poems. "Prefer short fiction. Cover letter preferred. Desires good, thought-provoking, graphic, uncommon pieces." avg. press run 100-200. Pub'd 4 titles 1998; expects 3 titles 1999, 5 titles 2000. avg. price, paper: $8; other: $4 chapbook. Discounts: inquire. 32-70pp; 5½×8½; of, xerox. Reporting time: 1 week initial response. Simultaneous submissions accepted: yes. Publishes 10-15% of manuscripts submitted. Payment: varies, personal. Copyrights for author.

FOURTEEN HILLS: The SFSU Review, Creative Writing Dept., SFSU, 1600 Holloway Avenue, San Francisco, CA 94132, 415-338-3083, fax 415-338-0504; E-mail hills@sfsu.edu. 1994. Poetry, fiction, interviews, criticism, parts-of-novels, long-poems, plays, non-fiction. "*Fourteen Hills* is an entirely graduate-student run literary review dedicated to high-quality, innovative creative literary work. Submissions should include a separate sheet with writer's name, address, phone number and the name of the piece. Do *not* put your name on the manuscript. Maximum 5 poems or 1 story, drama or creative non-fiction submission per writer. Maximum word length: 5,000. Recent contributors: Dorthy Allison, Amy Gerstler, Amiri Baraka, Paul Hoover, Bernadette Mayer, C.D. Wright, Leslie Scalapino, and Terese Svoboda." circ. 500. 2/yr. Pub'd 2 issues 1998; expects 2 issues 1999, 2 issues 2000. sub. price: $12; per copy: $7; sample: $5. 160pp; 6×9. Reporting time: 2-4 months. Simultaneous submissions accepted: no. Publishes 5% of manuscripts submitted. Payment: 2 contributor copies. Copyrighted, reverts to author. Ads: trade.

●**FOURTH GENRE: EXPLORATIONS IN NONFICTION, Michigan State University Press,** Michael Steinberg, ATL Department, 229 Bessey Hall, Michigan State University, East Lansing, MI 48824,

517-432-2556; fax 517-353-5250; e-mail fourthgenre@cal.msu.edu. 1999. Non-fiction. "Seeking reflective personal essays, memoirs, literary journalism and personal critical essays up to 8000 words. Reading periods 3/15-6/30 and 9/15-12/31. Send SASE for submissions guidelines or e-mail at fourthgenre@cal.msu.edu. Some recent contributors: David Huddle, Dinty Moore, Phyllis Barber, Scott Russell Sanders, Steven Harvey." circ. 1M. 2/yr. Expects 2 issues 1999, 2 issues 2000. sub. price: $15; per copy: $8; sample: $7.50. Back issues: $8. Discounts: 5% agent discount. 150-200pp; 6×9; of. Reporting time: 3-4 months. Simultaneous submissions accepted: yes. Publishes 5-10% of manuscripts submitted. Payment: varies. Copyrighted, reverts to author. Pub's reviews: 20 in 1998. §All books of creative nonfiction. Ads: $200/$100. AAUP.

THE FOURTH R, Polebridge Press, Culver H. Nelson, Editor, PO Box 6144, Santa Rosa, CA 95406, 707-523-1325, fax 707-523-1350. 1981. Articles, interviews, criticism, reviews. *"The Fourth R* is published by Polebride Press on behalf of the Westar Institute and its seminars. The Westar Institute conducts research on biblical and American traditions and is devoted to improving biblical and religious literacy. An advocate for biblical and religious literacy, *The Fourth R* addresses a broad range of questions about religion, past and present" circ. 1.5M. 6/yr. sub. price: $18; per copy: $3; sample: $3. 24pp; 8½×11. Copyrighted. Pub's reviews. §Religious studies, especially critical biblical scholarship, and American cultural studies.

FOURTH WORLD REVIEW, John Papworth, 24 Abercorn Place, London, NW8 9XP, England, 071-286-4366; FAX 071-286-2186. 1966. Articles, interviews, criticism, reviews, letters, news items, non-fiction. "Any material bearing on human scale concepts—politics and economics." circ. 2M. 5/yr. Pub'd 5 issues 1998; expects 5 issues 1999, 5 issues 2000. sub. price: according to self-assessed income status; per copy: £1; sample: £1. Back issues: £2. Discounts: 50%. 32pp; size A5. Payment: none. Pub's reviews: 18 in 1998. §Economics, politics, ecology. Ads: on application.

FPMI Communications, Inc., Ralph R. Smith, President, 707 Fiber Street NW, Huntsville, AL 35801-5833, 256-539-1850. 1985. Articles, interviews, non-fiction. "Formerly WordSmith, Inc. We normally publish short books of interest to Federal Government Employees, Federal Management issues, and other books of interest to public sector Gov't. employees." avg. press run 5M. Pub'd 4 titles 1998; expects 6 titles 1999, 6 titles 2000. 20 titles listed in the *Small Press Record of Books in Print* (28th Edition, 1999-00). avg. price, paper: $10.95; other: $22.95. 75pp; 8½×11; of. Reporting time: 60 days. Payment: varies depending upon nature of submission and subject matter. Does not copyright for author.

THE FRACTAL, Sean Newborn, David Gardner, 4400 University Drive, MS 2D6, Fairfax, VA 22075, 703-993-2911. 1992. Poetry, fiction, articles, art, photos, interviews, criticism, reviews, long-poems, non-fiction. "Journal of science fiction, fantasy and horror; we print fiction, poetry, art & academic essays" circ. 2M. 2/yr. Pub'd 2 issues 1998; expects 2 issues 1999, 2 issues 2000. sub. price: $8; per copy: $5; sample: $5. Back issues: $4. Discounts: $3 each for classroom use; distributors should contact us. 64pp; 5½×8½; of. Reporting time: 1-2 months. Publishes 10% of manuscripts submitted. Payment: $25 fiction, $50 nonfiction, $5 poetry, $24 cover, $5 interior art. Copyrighted, reverts to author. Pub's reviews: 1 in 1998. §Sci-fi, fantasy, horror, academic.

Franciscan University Press, Dawn Harris, Editor, 1235 University Boulevard, Steubenville, OH 43952, 740-283-6357, fax 740-283-6442. 1985. Non-fiction. "Looking for Catholic apologetics and biblical studies" avg. press run 2M. Pub'd 3 titles 1998; expects 3-4 titles 1999, 3-4 titles 2000. 11 titles listed in the *Small Press Record of Books in Print* (28th Edition, 1999-00). avg. price, paper: $7.95. Discounts: bookstores 40%, parishes, schools, libraries, prayergoups 20% (prepaid). 150pp; size varies; of. Reporting time: 1-3 months. Simultaneous submissions accepted: yes. Publishes 1-5% of manuscripts submitted. Payment: 10%. Copyrights for author.

FRANK: AN INTERNATIONAL JOURNAL OF CONTEMPORARY WRITING AND ART, David Applefield, Editor-Publisher, 32 rue Edouard Vaillant, 93100 Montreuil Sous Bois, France, (33) 1 48596658; e-mail david@paris-anglo.com. 1983. Poetry, fiction, art, photos, interviews, parts-of-novels, collages, plays. "All texts should be under 20 double-spaced typed pages—absolutely open to all styles, techniques, visions, genres, languages. Recent contributors include: George Plimpton, Octavio, Jim Morrison, Vaclav Havel, W.S. Merwin, Gennadi Aigi, Maurice Girodias, Rita Dove, Frederick Barthelme, Samuel Beckett, Duo Duo, Stephen Dixon, A.I. Bezzerides, Dennis Hopper, John Sanford, Bukowski, Hubert Selby, Italo Calvino, Breyten Breytenbach, Paul Bowles, Derek Walcott, Tom Waits, John Berger, Edmond Jabes, E.M. Cioran, Robert Coover, Edmund White, Henry Miller, Nancy Huston, C.K. Williams, and special feature on English-language writing in Paris today! 40 Philippino protest poets, Congolese fiction, and plenty of lesser known talent." circ. 4M. 2/yr. Pub'd 2 issues 1998; expects 2 issues 1999, 2 issues 2000. sub. price: $38 (4 issues), $60 instit.; per copy: $10; sample: $9. Back issues: issues 1-5 pack for $70. Discounts: 40% for bookstores and orders over 6 copies. 224pp; 8×5; of. Reporting time: 12 weeks. Simultaneous submissions accepted: yes. Publishes 5% of manuscripts submitted. Payment: 2 copies plus $5/printed page. Copyrighted, reverts to author. Pub's reviews. §Literature, poetry, politics, art, translation, interviews. Ads: $1,000/$500/$3500 back cover. CLMP.

●**Franklin Multimedia, Inc.**, Carrie Beasley Jones, 418 Kingsley Avenue, Orange Park, FL 32073, 904-278-1177; Fax 904-278-1070; Website www.thecigarmaster.com. 1998. Non-fiction. avg. press run 10M+. Expects 2 titles 1999, 4 titles 2000. avg. price, paper: $19.95. 230pp; 5½×8½. Publishes less than 1% of manuscripts submitted.

Franklin-Sarrett Publishers, 3761 Vineyard Trace, Marietta, GA 30062, 770-578-9410; Fax 770-973-4243; e-mail info@franklin-sarrett.com; Website http://www.franklin-sarrett.com. 1992. Non-fiction. avg. press run 3M. Expects 1 title 1999, 1 title 2000. 3 titles listed in the *Small Press Record of Books in Print* (28th Edition, 1999-00). avg. price, paper: $16.95. Discounts: write for details. 200pp; size varies; OF. Reporting time: 30 days. Payment: write for details. Copyrights for author. Publishers Marketing Association (PMA).

FREDIAN SLIP: THE LEONARD ZELIG OF ZINES, Fred Donini-Lenhoff, Alessandra Donini-Lenhoff, 735 Park Avenue, River Forest, IL 60305-1705, 708-366-6309. 1994. circ. 200. Varies. Pub'd 2 issues 1998; expects 2 issues 1999. price per copy: $1; sample: $1. Back issues: $1. 4pp; 8½×11. Copyrighted.

FREE CHOICE, FOREST: The Freedom Organization for the Right to Smoke Tobacco, 2 Grosvenor Gardens, London SW1W 0DH, England, 0171-823-6550; FAX 0171-823-4534. 1981. circ. 1.5M. 6/yr. Pub'd 6 issues 1998. sub. price: £15 ($25); per copy: £2.50 ($4); sample: £1 ($1). Discounts: 33.3% trade discounts. 12pp; 8×11¾. Simultaneous submissions accepted: yes. Pub's reviews: 1 in 1998. §Health to medical policy: issues on risk.

FREE INQUIRY, Paul Kurtz, Council For Secular Humanism, PO Box 664, Buffalo, NY 14226, 716-636-7571. 1980. Articles, cartoons, interviews, criticism, reviews, letters, non-fiction. "Recent contributors: Francis Crick, Camille Paglia, Martin Gardner, Marilyn French, Albert Ellis, Steve Allen, E.O. Wilson, Peter Ustinov, Richard Rorty" circ. 20M. 4/yr. Pub'd 4 issues 1998; expects 4 issues 1999, 4 issues 2000. sub. price: $28.50; per copy: $6.95; sample: same. Back issues: 20% discount on 5 or more copies, 40% for 10 or more. Discounts: agency remits—40% 1st year, 20% 2nd year and after. 68pp; 8½×11; of. Reporting time: varies. Publishes 10% of manuscripts submitted. Payment: varies. Copyrighted. Pub's reviews: 40 in 1998. §Philosophy, religion, morality, humanism. no ads.

FREE LUNCH, Ron Offen, PO Box 7647, Laguna Niguel, CA 92607-7647. 1988. Poetry, news items. "Please limit to three poems per submission between 9/1 and 5/31 *only*. Do not want ponderous, abstract, philosophic work with pithy observations, nicey-nice religious poems with tacked-on morals, greeting card love, nature, or animal verse. Lately I've grown a bit weary of the rambling personal lyric, poem-as-therapy verse, and flat-footed prose chopped up into lines to look like a poem. I want figurative language: similes, metaphors, alliteration, images, etc. Sympathetic to new poets, experimental work. Not opposed to form per se. Want to give all 'serious' U.S. poets a free subscription (based on submissions). Recent contributors: Neal Bowers, Thomas Carper, Jared Carter, Russell Edson, F.D. Reeve, Martha Modena Vertreace, Thom Ward, and Charles H. Webb. Always try to comment on submissions. Must have SASE with *all* submissions, inquiries, etc." circ. 1.1M. Irregular. Pub'd 2 issues 1998; expects 2 issues 1999, 2 issues 2000. sub. price: 3issues/$12 US, $15 foreign; per copy: $5 US, $6 foreign; sample: $5 US, $6 foreign. Back issues: query. 32pp; 5½×8½; of. Reporting time: 1-3 months. Simultaneous submissions accepted: yes. Publishes 5-10% of manuscripts submitted. Payment: 1 copy of appearance issue and free subscription. Copyrighted, does not revert to author. query.

Free People Press (see also BOTH SIDES NOW), Elihu Edelson, 10547 State Highway 110 North, Tyler, TX 75704-9537. 1974. "The main function of Free People Press is to publish *Both Sides Now*." 1 title listed in the *Small Press Record of Books in Print* (28th Edition, 1999-00). 8½×11; †photocopy. Reporting time: varies. Payment: copies. Author retains copyright.

Free Spirit Publishing Inc., Judy Galbraith, Pamela Espeland, 400 First Avenue North, Suite 616, Minneapolis, MN 55401-1730, 612-338-2068. 1983. Non-fiction, fiction. "Specializes in *Self-Help for Kids*. Topics include: creativity, emotional health, social skills, self-esteem, school success, youth empowerment, gifted education, and learning disabilities. Some materials for parents, educators, and counselors. Please request catalog and guidelines before submitting proposals." avg. press run 5M. Pub'd 15 titles 1998; expects 18 titles 1999, 18 titles 2000. 93 titles listed in the *Small Press Record of Books in Print* (28th Edition, 1999-00). avg. price, cloth: $14.62; paper: $12.36; other: $12.99. Discounts: 1-9 books no discount, 10-24 10%, 25-49 15%, 50-99 20%, 100+ 25% (general consumers). 150pp; 6×9, 8½×11, 7¼×9¼, 4⅛×6⅞, 5⅛×7⅜, 5×7, 5⅛×7½; of. Reporting time: 1-3 months. Simultaneous submissions accepted: yes. Publishes 1-3% of manuscripts submitted. Payment: individually negotiated. Copyrights for author. PMA, MAP, Publisher's Roundtable.

FREEBIES MAGAZINE, Gail M. Zannon, Publisher, 1135 Eugenia Place, Carpinteria, CA 93014-5025, 805-566-1225, e-mail freebies@aol.com. 1977. "All materials produced by in-house staff. We do not solicit or accept freelance materials." circ. 450M. 6/yr. Pub'd 6 issues 1998; expects 6 issues 1999, 6 issues 2000. sub. price: $7.95/5 issues; per copy: $3; sample: $3. Back issues: not available. Discounts: 20% off on bulk/agency purchases. 24pp; 8¼×10¼; of. Copyrighted. Ads: classified $5.50/word ($15 minimum).

FREEDOM ISN'T FREE, Temporary Vandalism Recordings, Robert Roden, Barton M. Saunders, PO Box 6184, Orange, CA 92863-6184. 1994. Poetry. "Recent contributors: Mary Panza, Charles Ardinger, Gerald Locklin, S.A. Griffin" circ. 500. 2/yr. Pub'd 2 issues 1998; expects 2 issues 1999, 2 issues 2000. price per copy: $1; sample: $1. 32pp; 5½×4¼; mi. Reporting time: 3-6 months. Simultaneous submissions accepted: yes. Publishes 5% of manuscripts submitted. Payment: 2 copies. Copyrighted, reverts to author. Ads: $50 full page.

FREEDOM OF EXPRESSION (FOE), Frank Pearn Jr., PO Box 4, Bethlehem, PA 18016, 215-866-9326. 1984. Articles, art, photos, cartoons, interviews, reviews, music. circ. 5M. 6/yr. Pub'd 6 issues 1998; expects 6 issues 1999, 6 issues 2000. sub. price: $6; per copy: $1; sample: $1. 48pp; 8½×11; newsprint. Reporting time: flexible. Payment: none. Not copyrighted. §music. Ads: contact.

THE FREEDONIA GAZETTE, Paul G. Wesolowski, Editor-in-Chief; Raymond D. White, U.K. Editor, 335 Fieldstone Drive, New Hope, PA 18938, 215-862-9734. 1978. Articles, art, photos, cartoons, interviews, criticism, reviews, letters, news items, non-fiction. "Articles range from 1 typewritten page (double-spaced) to 15 pages. We deal mainly with articles on the Marx Brothers and people associated with them, reviews of books on these topics, reviews of stage shows impersonating them, interviews with people who worked with the Marxes and with impersonators. We're especially in need of artwork, either drawings or caricatures of the Marxes. We have a strong reputation for well-researched articles which turn up facts not known to most fans and fanatics. U.K. subscriptions/submissions: Dr. Raymond D. White, 137 Easterly Road, Leeds LS8 2RY England." circ. 400. 2/yr. Pub'd 2 issues 1998; expects 2 issues 1999, 2 issues 2000. sub. price: $10; per copy: $5; sample: $5. Back issues: $5 when available (#1-#4,#8 currently sold-out). Discounts: 10 or more of the same issue (current or back issues) $4.50 each; 50 or more (mix and match current and/or back issues) $4 each. 20pp; 8½×11; of. Reporting time: maximum 1 month. Simultaneous submissions accepted: yes. Publishes 80% of manuscripts submitted. Payment: sample copy. Copyrighted, rights generally don't revert to author, but open to negotiation. Pub's reviews: 2 in 1998. §Marx Brothers, humor, people associated with Marxes in any way. Ads: $60/$34.

●**FREEFALL,** S. Amsden, C. Fuller, Alexandra Writers Centre Society, 922 9th Avenue S.E., Calgary, AB T2G 0S4, Canada, fax 403-264-4730; e-mail awcs@writtenword.org; website www.writtenword.org/awcs. 1990. Poetry, fiction, art, photos, interviews, parts-of-novels, plays, non-fiction. "Interviews must be with writers, publishers or those in the business of writing. Prose: maximum 3,000 words. Poetry: 2-5 poems, 6 pages maximum. Photos: must be glossy and black and white. Art work: black ink drawings. Non fiction: writing related topics or creative non fiction. Postcard stories maximum of 3." circ. 300. 2/yr. Pub'd 2 issues 1998; expects 2 issues 1999, 2 issues 2000. sub. price: $12 Canada; $14 US; sample: $7.50 Canada; $8.50 US. Back issues: $5.50 Canada; $6.50 US. 40pp; 8×11½; digital. Reporting time: 2 months from deadline. Simultaneous submissions accepted: no. Publishes 30% of manuscripts submitted. Payment: $5 per printed page upon publication. Copyrighted, reverts to author. Ads: $100/$50/$25-$15.

Freelance Communications, Randy Cassingham, P.O. Box 91970, Pasadena, CA 91109, FAX 500-442-True; phone 500-448-true, e-mail THIS-IS-TRUE-OWNER@NETCOM.COM. 1985. Non-fiction. "Not accepting any submissions next year (full up!)" avg. press run 3M-5M. Pub'd 1 title 1998; expects 2 titles 1999, 2 titles 2000. 3 titles listed in the *Small Press Record of Books in Print* (28th Edition, 1999-00). avg. price, paper: $11. Discounts: 1-4 20%, 5-24 40%, 25-49 43%, 50-99 46%, 100+ 50%, 500+ 55%. 160pp; 5½×8½; of. Reporting time: 1-2 weeks on queries. Payment: negotiable. Copyrights for author.

FREELANCE MARKET NEWS, The Association of Freelance Writers, Angela Cox, Editor, Sevendale House, 7 Dale Street, Manchester, M1 1JB, England, 0161-228-2362; Fax 0161-228-3533. 1962. "Provides market information telling writers and photographers where to sell. World-wide circulation" circ. 3M. 11/yr. Pub'd 11 issues 1998; expects 11 issues 1999, 11 issues 2000. sub. price: overseas £29; per copy: £2.50; sample: £2.50. 16pp; size A4. Reporting time: 1 month. Simultaneous submissions accepted: no. Publishes 50% of manuscripts submitted. Payment: £35 per 1000 words. Ads: classified: 25p per word.

FREELANCE WRITER'S REPORT, CNW Publishing, Dana K. Cassell, PO Box A, North Stratford, NH 03590, 603-922-8338, Fax 603-922-8339, e-mail danakcnw@ncia.net; www.writers-editors.com. 1977. Articles, interviews, news items, non-fiction. circ. 800. 12/yr. Pub'd 12 issues 1998; expects 12 issues 1999, 12 issues 2000. sub. price: $39; per copy: $4 current issue; sample: free with 9X12 SASE with 55¢ p/h. Back issues: $2.50. 8pp; 8½×11; of and desktop publishing. Reporting time: 1 month. Simultaneous submissions accepted: yes. Publishes 25% of manuscripts submitted. Payment: 10¢/word. Copyrighted, reverts to author. Pub's reviews: 72 in 1998. §Freelance writing and freelance photography, home business. Ads: 50¢ per word with discount for multiple insertions.

THE FREEMAN: Ideas On Liberty, The Foundation for Economic Education, Inc., Sheldon Richman, Editor; Beth Hoffman, Managing Editor, 30 South Broadway, Irvington, NY 10533, 914-591-7230; Fax 914-591-8910; E-mail freeman@fee.org. 1946. Articles, criticism, reviews, letters. "Solicits articles and book reviews from standpoint of a free-market, private-property, limited government philosophy. Length typically between 1000-4000 words. Columnists include Doug Bandow, Lawrence W. Reed, Mark Skousen, Walter Williams, and Russ Roberts." circ. 20M+. 12/yr. Pub'd 12 issues 1998; expects 12 issues 1999, 12 issues 2000. sub. price: $30; per copy: $3.500; sample: free. Discounts: $10 per carton (100+ copies) of back issues for classroom use. 64pp; 6¾×10; web offset. Reporting time: 2-4 weeks. Simultaneous submissions accepted: no. Publishes 20% of manuscripts submitted. Payment: 10¢ per word. Copyrighted, reverts to author. Pub's reviews: 50 in 1998. §Political science, history, biography & economics, from free-market perspective. Ads: $800/$500. ABA.

FREETHOUGHT HISTORY, Fred Whitehead, Box 5224, Kansas City, KS 66119, 913-588-1996. 1992. Poetry, articles, reviews, non-fiction. "A newsletter providing a center for exchange of information on research in the history of agnosticism, atheism, philosophical and religious controversy, also with attention to topics of freethought culture including poetry, art, music, etc. Features description and listing of work in progress, short biographies of freethinkers, notes and queries, reports on conferences and historic sites, and essays on the interpretation of intellectual history." circ. 200. 4/yr. Expects 4 issues 1999, 4 issues 2000. sub. price: $10; per copy: $3; sample: $3. Discounts: none. 12pp; 8½×11; high quality photocopy. Reporting time: 1 week. Payment: in copies. Copyrighted, reverts to author. Pub's reviews. §Atheism, freethought, intellectual and philosophical history.

French Bread Publications (see also PACIFIC COAST JOURNAL), Stillson Graham, Editor; Stephanie Kylkis, Fiction Editor, PO Box 23868, San Jose, CA 95153, e-mail paccoastj@juno.com. 1992. Poetry, parts-of-novels, fiction, art, photos, reviews, parts-of-novels. "Small ms. - up to 40 ms. pages. Do not send unsolicited ms." avg. press run 200. Pub'd 2 titles 1998; expects 1 title 1999. avg. price, other: $4. Discounts: 10-20 copies 15%, 21-50 25%, 51+ 45%. 40pp; 5½×8½; varies. Reporting time: 6 months. Publishes 1% of manuscripts submitted. Payment: varies. Copyrights for author.

FRENCH HISTORICAL STUDIES, Duke University Press, James R. Farr, John J. Contreni, Box 90660, Duke University, Durham, NC 27708-0660. "The official journal of the Society for French Historical Studies. The leading journal on the history of France, publishes groundbreaking articles, commentaries, and research notes on all periods of French history from the Middle Ages to the present. The journal's diverse format includes forums, review essays, special issues, and articles in French, as well as bilingual abstracts of the articles in each issue. Also featured are bibliographies of recent dissertations, books, and articles and announcements of fellowships, prizes, and conferences of interest to French historians." circ. 1,750. 4/yr. Expects 4 issues 1999, 4 issues 2000. sub. price: $65 institutions, $30 individuals, $15 students with copy of current ID, additional $12 foreign. Ads: $200/$150.

FRESH GROUND, Paul Andrew E. Smith, PO Box 383, Fox River Grove, IL 60021, 708-639-9200. 1993. Poetry. circ. 300+. 1/yr. Expects 1 issue 1999, 1 issue 2000. sub. price: $5.95; per copy: $5.95; sample: $5.95. Discounts: $3 each in tens. 30pp; of. Reporting time: 6 weeks. Payment: 1 copy. Copyrighted, reverts to author.

Friendly Oaks Publications, James D. Sutton, 1216 Cheryl Drive, PO Box 662, Pleasanton, TX 78064, 830-569-3586; Fax 830-281-2617; E-mail friendly@docspeak.com. 1990. Non-fiction. avg. press run 3-5M. Pub'd 5 titles 1998; expects 4 titles 1999, 6 titles 2000. 2 titles listed in the *Small Press Record of Books in Print* (28th Edition, 1999-00). avg. price, cloth: $22-$24; paper: $14-$18. Discounts: bulk. 240pp; 6×9; Cameron. Reporting time: 6 weeks. Simultaneous submissions accepted: yes. Publishes 5-10% of manuscripts submitted. Payment: negotiable. Copyrights for author.

FRIENDS OF PEACE PILGRIM, John Rush, Ann Rush, 43480 Cedar Avenue, Hemet, CA 92544, 909-927-7678. 1987. Poetry, articles, interviews, letters, non-fiction. circ. 10.5M. 2/yr. Expects 2 issues 1999. sub. price: free; per copy: free; sample: free. Back issues: free. Discounts: our printing cost. 8pp; 8½×11; of. Reporting time: 2 weeks. Payment: none. Not copyrighted. Pub's reviews: 4 in 1998. §World peace, inner peace. Ads: none.

Friends United Press, Barbara Mays, 101 Quaker Hill Drive, Richmond, IN 47374, 765-962-7573. 1969. Non-fiction. "Non-fiction books (average length 100-180 pages) relating to Quaker (Society of Friends) history, biography, faith experience, and religious practice" avg. press run 1M. Expects 3 titles 1999, 3 titles 2000. 29 titles listed in the *Small Press Record of Books in Print* (28th Edition, 1999-00). avg. price, paper: $10.95. Discounts: 40% to bookstores on orders over 5 copies. 150-175pp; 5½×8½; of. Reporting time: 2 to 4 months. Simultaneous submissions accepted: no. Publishes 8% of manuscripts submitted. Payment: 7½% of our income on each title after production costs are met. Copyrights for author. PCPA (Protestant Church-Owned Publishing Association); QUIP (Quakers Uniting in Publishing).

Frith Press (see also EKPHRASIS), Laverne Frith, Editor; Carol Frith, Editor, PO Box 161236, Sacramento, CA 95816-1236, 916-451-3038. 1995. Poetry. "In addition to publishing *Ekphrasis*, a poetry journal focusing on the growing body of verse based on works from any artistic genre, Frith Press also sponsors an annual poetry chapbook competition for poetry on any subject matter." avg. press run 200. Pub'd 4 titles 1998; expects 4 titles 1999, 4 titles 2000. 4 titles listed in the *Small Press Record of Books in Print* (28th Edition, 1999-00). avg.

price, paper: $6. 50pp; 5½×8½; photo copy. Reporting time: manuscripts selected through annual competition; could take up to a year. Simultaneous submissions accepted: no. Publishes 2-7% of manuscripts submitted. Payment: variable on chapbooks. Copyrights for author.

THE FROGMORE PAPERS, The Frogmore Press, Jeremy Page, 42 Morehall Avenue, Folkestone, Kent CT19 4EF, United Kingdom. 1983. Poetry, fiction. "Short stories of more than 2,000 words are unlikely to be chosen. Recent contributors: Pauline Stainer, John Latham, Roger Elkin, Myra Schneider, R. Nikolas Macioci, George Gott, John Harvey, Linda France, Tobias Hill, Judi Benson, Tamar Yoseloff, Elizabeth Garrett." circ. 500. 2/yr. Pub'd 2 issues 1998; expects 2 issues 1999, 2 issues 2000. sub. price: $20; per copy: $10; sample: $5 (dollar bills only). Back issues: $10 for special 50th issue. Discounts: none. 40pp; 6×8; photocopy reduced typescript. Reporting time: 3 months. Simultaneous submissions accepted: no. Publishes 2-3% of manuscripts submitted. Payment: 1 copy. Not copyrighted. Pub's reviews: approx. 20 in 1998. §mostly poetry collections/anthologies. Ads: not available.

The Frogmore Press (see also THE FROGMORE PAPERS), Jeremy Page, 42 Morehall Avenue, Folkestone, Kent. CT19 4EF, United Kingdom. 1983. Poetry. "Collections published tend to be by writers previously published in *The Frogmore Papers.* Recent titles have been *New Pastorals* by Robert Etty and *Bush Klaxon Has a Body Like a Trio Sonata* by Bob Mitchell. *Mongoose on His Shoulder* by Geoffrey Holloway appeared in October. Please write for details. Do not send unsolicited manuscripts." avg. press run 250. Pub'd 2 titles 1998. 2 titles listed in the *Small Press Record of Books in Print* (28th Edition, 1999-00). avg. price, paper: $10 (dollar bills only). Discounts: none. 44pp; 6×8; photocopy reduced typescript. Reporting time: 3 months. Simultaneous submissions accepted: no. Publishes 5% of manuscripts submitted. Payment: 12 complimentary copies. Copyrights for author.

FROGPOND: Quarterly Haiku Journal, Red Moon Press, Jim Kacian, Editor, PO Box 2461, Winchester, VA 22604, 540-722-2156; redmoon@shentel.net. 1978. Poetry, articles, art, criticism, reviews. "Publish haiku, haiku sequences, haibun, some tanka and renga, some translations, brief essays and book reviews. Material should show familiarity with modern developments in North American haiku; not interested in 'pretty nature pictures' or philosophical constructs; poems should focus on the 'suchness' of the here-and-now moment, avoiding cliches, simile and overt metaphor. Traditional and experimental haiku in 1-4 lines. Recent contributors: Dimitar Anakiev, Yu Chang, Dee Evetts, M. Kettner, Matthew Louviere. Publish 3 regular issues and 1 supplement." circ. 800. 4/yr. Pub'd 4 issues 1998; expects 4 issues 1999, 4 issues 2000. sub. price: $25 USA, $28 Canada, $35 overseas; per copy: $6 USA, $7 Canada, $9 overseas; sample: $6 USA, $7 Canada, $9 overseas except double issues (1992-93), $10 USA & Canada, $12 overseas. Back issues: same. Discounts: none. 96pp; 5½×8½; of. Reporting time: 2 weeks. Simultaneous submissions accepted: no. Publishes 1% of manuscripts submitted. Payment: $1/item accepted. Copyrighted, reverts to author. Pub's reviews: 20 in 1998. §Books and chapbooks of contemporary haiku, senryu, new translations of Japanese and other haiku. Ads: none.

From Here Press (see also THE STARLIGHT PAPERS; XTRAS), William J. Higginson, Penny Harter, PO Box 2740, Santa Fe, NM 87504-2740, 505-438-3249. 1975. Poetry, criticism, long-poems, non-fiction. "Not reading unsolicited work. *XTRAS* is a series title; *The Starlight Papers* is an irregular series of reports on cross-cultural poetics" avg. press run 200-1M. Expects 1 title 1999, 2 titles 2000. 18 titles listed in the *Small Press Record of Books in Print* (28th Edition, 1999-00). avg. price, paper: $3-$12. Discounts: 40% to trade (5 mixed titles). 40-120pp; 5½×8½, 8½×11; of. Payment: varies. Copyrights for author.

FROM THE MARGIN, Gail Schilke, 50 E. 1st Street, Storefront West, New York, NY 10003-9311. 1997. Poetry, art. "This is a zine of illustrated poems and stories, all written and illustrated by Gail Schilke." circ. 150. 4/yr. Pub'd 4 issues 1998. sub. price: $12; per copy: $3; sample: $3. Back issues: $3. 16pp; 8½×11; †laser prints. Copyrighted, reverts to author. Ads: none.

Fromm International Publishing Corporation, Thomas Thornton, Executive Editor, 560 Lexington Avenue, New York, NY 10022, 212-308-4010. 1982. Fiction, art, music, letters, non-fiction. avg. press run 5M. Pub'd 18 titles 1998; expects 16 titles 1999, 16 titles 2000. 26 titles listed in the *Small Press Record of Books in Print* (28th Edition, 1999-00). avg. price, cloth: $21.95; paper: $11.95. Discounts: retail 1-4 copies 33%, 5-9 44%, 10-19 44% free freight, 20+ 46% free freight, 50+ 45%; libraries 35% any quantity; jobbers 1-5 25%, 6+ 50%. 300pp; 5½×8½; of. Reporting time: 2 months. Publishes .2% of manuscripts submitted. Payment: annually, 10-15%. Copyrights for author. AAP.

FRONT & CENTRE MAGAZINE, Jason Copple, Leona McCharles, Matthew Firth, 25 Avalon Place, Hamilton, ON L8M 1R2, Canada. "Checks payable to J. Copple. *Front & Centre Magazine* publishes short works of fiction. *Front & Centre* demands quality above anything else. We want the brightest and boldest new fiction. We want work that is fresh, vibrant, intelligent, and intriguing. We are open to innovation, but are generally looking for no-nonsense fiction. Stories should be between 50-3,000 words, with few exceptions. Please include the following with your submission: a hard copy of your submission, a brief writer's biography on a separate sheet of paper, that includes your mailing address, telephone number and E-mail address if applicable, a SASE with sufficient Canadian postage, or a SASE with IRCs for submissions from outside Canada. If there is no SASE, there will be no reply." 2/yr. Pub'd 2 issues 1998; expects 2 issues 1999, 2 issues 2000. sample price: $4. Reporting time: 3 months.

Front Row Experience, Frank Alexander, 540 Discovery Bay Boulevard, Byron, CA 94514, 510-634-5710. 1974. Art, cartoons, non-fiction. "One page letter of inquiry first, submit manuscript only when requested. Submitted manuscripts should include self-addressed-stamped-return envelopes and should be typed double space of about 200 8½ X 11 size pages. They should be lesson plans or guidebooks for *teachers* from preschool to 6th Grade. We are not interested in areas other than 'perceptual-motor development', 'movement education', 'special education.' Some recently published books are: *Funsical Fitness, School Based Home Developmental P.E. Program, Dimondball Games.*" avg. press run 500. Pub'd 2 titles 1998; expects 1 title 1999, 1 title 2000. 20 titles listed in the *Small Press Record of Books in Print* (28th Edition, 1999-00). avg. price, paper: $10. Discounts: 1+ 20%, 5+ 45%, 100+ 50%. 100pp; 8½x11; of. Reporting time: 1 week for letter of inquiry, 1 month for manuscript (include SASE), and only send manuscript when requested to do so. Simultaneous submissions accepted: yes. Publishes 10% of manuscripts submitted. Payment: all authors 10% royalty. Copyrights for author. Pacific Marketing Association.

THE FRONT STRIKER BULLETIN, Bill Retskin, The Retskin Report, PO Box 18481, Asheville, NC 28814-0481, 828-254-4487; FAX 828-254-1066. 1986. Non-fiction. "The American Matchcover Collecting Club. Articles relating to matchcover collecting in America, and the matchbook industry in America, only" circ. 700. 4/yr. Pub'd 4 issues 1998; expects 4 issues 1999, 4 issues 2000. sub. price: $23 bulk, $28 first class; sample: $4. Back issues: $4. 52pp; 8½x11; †of. Reporting time: 30 days. Simultaneous submissions accepted: no. Payment: varies. Copyrighted, reverts to author. §Matchcover collecting-hobbies. Ads: $85/$50/$27.50.

Frontier Publishing, Inc., William E. Belk, 4933 West Craig Road, Suite 155, Las Vegas, NV 89130, Phone/Fax 702-647-0990. 6 titles listed in the *Small Press Record of Books in Print* (28th Edition, 1999-00).

FRONTIERS: A Journal of Women Studies, Sue Armitage, Editor; Patricia Hart, Managing Editor, Women's Studies, PO Box 644007, Washington State University, Pullman, WA 99164-4007, 509-335-7268. 1975. Poetry, fiction, articles, art, photos, interviews, criticism, reviews, letters, plays, news items, non-fiction. "*Frontiers* bridges the gap between academic and community women by publishing a journal that is substantive and accessible to all people interested in feminist issues. We seek both traditional and innovative work, collaborative and interdisciplinary manuscripts. Most issues have a theme, and articles and personal essays are included that express different viewpoints; also in each issue are a variety of other articles on nontheme topics plus creative work. We have no 'political bias' except feminism — in all its manifestations. We prefer to publish manuscripts under 40 pages. We also consider poetry, short stories, photographs, graphics, and review essays." circ. 1M. 3/yr. Pub'd 3 issues 1998; expects 3 issues 1999, 3 issues 2000. sub. price: $24 indiv., $36 instit.; per copy: $9 indiv., $12 instit.; sample: $9. Back issues: same as single copy. Discounts: bookstores 40%, bulk rate 10% if 10 (ten) or more copies of the same issue are purchased/ordered together; no other discounts. 208pp; 6x9; of. Reporting time: 3-6 months for articles, 2-4 months for poetry. Simultaneous submissions accepted: no. Publishes 13% of manuscripts submitted. Payment: 2 copies of issue. Rights revert to author only for poetry, fiction, or art. §All areas of interest to women, on all subjects, especially feminist and women's topics. Ads: $150/$100/$60 1/4 page/no classified.

Frontline Publications, Ernie Hernandez, PO Box 1104, El Toro, CA 92630. 1982. Articles, non-fiction. "Books about management, science, and computers. Am seeking manuscripts on computer technology— particularly 'how-to' guidebooks geared toward unsophisticated (non-programmer oriented) end-users i.e. applications software, systems development, language examples" avg. press run 5M. Expects 1 title 1999, 2 titles 2000. 4 titles listed in the *Small Press Record of Books in Print* (28th Edition, 1999-00). avg. price, cloth: $26.95; paper: $19.95. Discounts: trade-none, wholesaler-50%, college classrooms-10% (on verified orders: instructor desk copies-free). 279pp; 5⅜x8½; †of. Payment: 10-15% of net. Copyrights for author.

Frozen Waffles Press/Shattered Sidewalks Press; 45th Century Chapbooks, David Wade, Bro. Dimitrios, Rick Fox, The Writer's Group, 329 West 1st Street #5, Bloomington, IN 47403, 812-333-6304 c/o Rocky or Dimitrios. 1980. Poetry, art, interviews, reviews, parts-of-novels, long-poems. "Address for packages: c/o Writer's Group, PO Box 1941, Bloomington, IN 47402. Poetry, prose poems; almost any kind of short work (plays, aphorisms, parables [modern], fantasy, Si Fi, futureworlds, etc.). Oral & visual qualities to be expressed in cassettes, post cards, poster poems, etc. Please NO more unsolicited material until notified in this directory! 'Poetry videos' in the future are a possibility! Would like *input* on this." avg. press run varies. 4 titles listed in the *Small Press Record of Books in Print* (28th Edition, 1999-00). avg. price, cloth: $25; paper: $12; other: $25-$35 deluxe. Discounts: hope to give breaks to people over 40; mental institutions, prisons, etc. 22-45pp, 85-125pp; size varies; of. Reporting time: 5 seconds to 5 days; if you don't hear from us, we probably never got your material. Percentage of manuscripts published depends on quality. Payment: at least one free copy of your work(s); money later, much money much later; inflation has bloated our poverty. Copyrights for author.

Frugal Marketer Publishing, Warren A. Shuman, PO Box 6750, Denver, CO 80206-0750, Fax 303-377-0421. 1994. avg. press run 5M. Pub'd 1 title 1998; expects 4 titles 1999. avg. price, cloth: $20; other: $20. 200pp; 6×9; of/litho. Reporting time: 4 weeks. Simultaneous submissions accepted: no. Payment: varies. Does not copyright for author. PMA.

FUCK DECENCY, Andrew Roller, 5960 S. Land Park Drive #253, Sacramento, CA 95822. 1986. Poetry, fiction, articles, art, photos, cartoons, interviews, satire, criticism, music, letters, parts-of-novels, news items, non-fiction. "Send only a few poems" circ. 50. 200/yr. Pub'd 50 issues 1998; expects 50 issues 1999, 50 issues 2000. sub. price: Free by e-mail; per copy: Free; sample: Free. Back issues: Free from www.eroticstories.com. Discounts: free. 8pp; 8½×11; †Internet. Reporting time: 2-4 weeks or longer. Simultaneous submissions accepted: yes. Publishes 50% of manuscripts submitted. Payment: free over the internet. Copyrighted, reverts to author. Pub's reviews: 50+ in 1998. §Comics, poetry, we'll look at anything (nothing can be returned), Girlie videos and magazines. Ads: sponsored by Ad:$100. Small Press League.

FUEL MAGAZINE, Andy Lowry, 2434 North Greenview Avenue, Chicago, IL 60614-2013, 312-395-1706. 1992. Poetry, fiction, art, photos, parts-of-novels, collages. circ. 1.5M. 4/yr. Pub'd 4 issues 1998; expects 4 issues 1999, 4 issues 2000. sub. price: $10; per copy: $3; sample: $3. Back issues: $3. 40pp; 5½×8½; †of. Reporting time: 2-3 weeks. Payment: contributors copies. Copyrighted, reverts to author. Ads: $50/$25.

FUGUE, Ryan Witt, Managing Editor, Brink Hall, Room 200, Engl. Dept., University of Idaho, Moscow, ID 83844-1102, 208-885-6156. 1989. Poetry, fiction, articles, art, photos, interviews, satire, criticism, long-poems, non-fiction. circ. 300. 2/yr. Pub'd 1 issue 1998; expects 2 issues 1999, 2 issues 2000. sub. price: $10; per copy: $6; sample: $5. Back issues: issue #13+ $3; others inquire. 100pp; 6×9; of. Reporting time: 12 weeks. Simultaneous submissions accepted: no. We publish 2% or less of manuscripts submitted. Payment: $10-$20 for prose, $10 for poetry. Copyrighted, reverts to author.

Fugue State Press, James Chapman, PO Box 80, Cooper Station, New York, NY 10276, 212-673-7922. 1990. Fiction. "No unsolicited submissions." avg. press run 1M. Pub'd 1 title 1998; expects 3 titles 1999, 4 titles 2000. 7 titles listed in the *Small Press Record of Books in Print* (28th Edition, 1999-00). avg. price, paper: $8. Discounts: 40%. 250pp; 5×8; of.

Fulcrum, Inc., Robert C. Baron, Publisher, 350 Indiana Street, Suite 350, Golden, CO 80401, 303-277-1623. 1985. Non-fiction. "Nature narratives, American history, climbing and hiking guidebooks, self-help, science, biography, travel, outdoor adventure, gardening, books for children, teacher resources" avg. press run 4-6M. Pub'd 40 titles 1998; expects 50 titles 1999, 50 titles 2000. avg. price, cloth: $25; paper: $17. Discounts: bookstore 42% for 5, 45% for 25; non returnable 50%, libraries 20%. 230pp; size varies; desktop. Reporting time: 6 weeks. Simultaneous submissions accepted: yes. Publishes 10% of manuscripts submitted. Payment: negotiable. Copyrights for author. Rocky Mountain Book Publisher's Association.

FULL DISCLOSURE, Marinelli Publishing, Glen Roberts, PO Box 1533, Oil City, PA 16301-5533. Articles, photos, cartoons, interviews, reviews, letters, non-fiction. "Focus on privacy, electronic surveillance, government wrong-doing." circ. 7M. 6/yr. sub. price: $24.95; per copy: $3.50. 20pp; 11×17; Webb press. Copyrighted. Pub's reviews. §privacy, electronic surveillance, government wrong-doing. Ads: $450/$285/20¢.

FULL MOON DIRECTORY, Full Moon Publications, Sharida Rizzuto, Harold Tollison, Ann Hoyt, 577 Central Avenue, Box 4, Jefferson, LA 70121-1400, E-mail publisher@mailexcite.com; zines@rsnmail.com; www2.cybercities.com/z/zines/. Articles, art, photos, cartoons, reviews, non-fiction. "Mostly classified and display ads - a directory for gothic-vampire horror, occult, new age, paranormal, mystery, other genres, etc." circ. 800-1.2M. 3/yr. Pub'd 3 issues 1998; expects 3 issues 1999, 3 issues 2000. sub. price: $30; per copy: $10; sample: $10. Back issues: $10. Discounts: trade with other like publications. 8½×11; †of. Reporting time: 2-6 weeks. Simultaneous submissions accepted: yes. Publishes 30-35% of manuscripts submitted. Payment: free copies, fees paid to all contributors negotiable. Pub's reviews: 45 in 1998. §Horror, occult, New Age, mystery, other genres.

Full Moon Publications (see also FULL MOON DIRECTORY; THE HAUNTED JOURNAL; HORIZONS BEYOND; NIGHTSHADE; REALM OF THE VAMPIRE; NOCTURNAL REPORTER; REALM OF DARKNESS; THE SALEM JOURNAL; HORIZONS; MIXED BAG; VAMPIRE NIGHTS; WESTERN SKIES; SOUTHWEST JOURNAL; POW-WOW; HOLLYWOOD NOSTALGIA; DAYS AND NIGHTS OF A SMALL PRESS PUBLISHER; JEWISH LIFE; IRISH JOURNAL), Sharida Rizzuto, Harold Tollison, Ann Hoyt, Rose Dalton, Elaine Wolfe, 577 Central Avenue, Box 4, Jefferson, LA 70121-1400, e-mail fullmoon@eudoramail.com or haunted@rocketmail.com; www.eclecticity.com/zines/, www.members.xoom.com/blackie, www.route23.com/fullmoon.asp, www.spaceports.com/~haunted/, www2.cybercities.com/z/zines. 1983. Poetry, fiction, articles, art, photos, cartoons, interviews, satire, criticism, reviews, letters, long-poems, collages, news items, non-fiction. "We are looking for gothic-vampire, horror, science fiction and fantasy, mystery, western, occult/paranormal, literary, multi-cultural, historical movie nostalgia, and films and filming. We publish books, chapbooks, journals, newsletters, and catalogues." avg.

press run 2M-10M. Pub'd 7 titles 1998; expects 7 titles 1999, 7 titles 2000. 12 titles listed in the *Small Press Record of Books in Print* (28th Edition, 1999-00). avg. price, paper: $4.90-$7.90. Discounts: trade with other publications. 80-100pp; 8½×11, 5½×8½; †of. Reporting time: 2-6 weeks. Simultaneous submissions accepted: yes. Publishes 40% of manuscripts submitted. Payment: fee + free copies for non-fiction and art; free copy for poetry and fiction. Copyrights for author.

FUNNY PAGES, J. Workman, PO Box 317025, Dayton, OH 45437, e-mail jworkman@erinet.com. 1989. Cartoons, satire. *"Funny Pages* is a monthly collection of tasteless humor. The vast majority of what we print is reader submitted. 'To Delight & Offend' is our motto. We print sick jokes, political humor, celebrity jokes and ethnic humor. We also print a smattering of office humor. Anything funny or disgusting is apt to show up in print. George Hayduke's 'Get Even' column provides some levity and cool revenge techniques." circ. 600+. 12/yr. Pub'd 12 issues 1998; expects 12 issues 1999, 12 issues 2000. sub. price: $15, $28/2 years; per copy: $2; sample: 2 loose stamps. Back issues: $10 for 12 issues, $5 for 5 issues. Discounts: 20% for 10 or more copies, 30% for 25+. 8pp; 8 1/2×11; offset. Reporting time: anywhere from 1 day to 1 month. Simultaneous submissions accepted: yes. Publishes 10% of manuscripts submitted. Payment: complemetary issue. Not copyrighted. Ads: Business card size $30.

The Funny Paper, F.H. Fellhauer, Jane Jennings, Po Box 22557, Kansas City, MO 64113-0557, e-mail; felix22557@aol.com. 1985. Poetry, fiction, articles, cartoons, non-fiction. "SHORT - 500 to 1000 words - 16 line poem. NO FEE, contests pay $25 to $100." circ. varies. 4/yr. Pub'd 4 issues 1998; expects 4 issues 1999, 4 issues 2000. price per copy: $2; sample: $2. 10pp; 8½×11; photocopy. Reporting time: most entries not returned. Simultaneous submissions accepted: Y. Payment: prizes and awards; $5/25/100. Copyrighted, reverts to author. §Humor. Ads: $300/col. in.

THE FUNNY TIMES, Ray Lesser, Susan Wolpert, PO Box 18530, Cleveland Heights, OH 44118, 216-371-8600. 1985. Fiction, cartoons, interviews, satire, reviews. "Prefer anything humorous, political (liberal), or satirical; mainly dealing with politics, relationships, animals, environment, and basic slice-of-life nonsense." circ. 50M. 12/yr. Pub'd 12 issues 1998; expects 12 issues 1999, 12 issues 2000. sub. price: $21; per copy: $2.95; sample: $3. Back issues: $3 per issue. Discounts: available for newsstand distributors. 28pp; 10×16; of. Reporting time: 6-8 weeks. Simultaneous submissions accepted: yes. Payment: $160 per tabloid size (10 X 16") page, divided accordingly. Copyrighted, reverts to author. §Humor books, compilations of humor and/or political cartoons. Ads: none.

FURTHER TOO, Jon Simmons, Craig Wilson, 168 Elm Grove, Brighton, East Sussex BN2 3DA, England. 1991. Fiction, articles, art, interviews, criticism, reviews, letters, collages, news items, non-fiction. "Usually short pieces up to 500-1000 words, of a liberal, anarchic, spontaneous situationist concerned sceptic post-modernist persuasion. Recently including contributionss from R. Seth Friedman (editor *Factsheet 5*), Stephen Pastel (of *The Pastels*), Serge Segay (Russian mail artist)." circ. 1M. 3/yr. Pub'd 2 issues 1998; expects 2 issues 1999, 2 issues 2000. sub. price: $6; per copy: $3; sample: $3 or £1.20. Back issues: £1 each or $2. Discounts: More than 6 copies: $1.50 each to trade. 32pp; 5½×8¼; †xerox. Payment: none. Not copyrighted. Pub's reviews: 75 in 1998. §Non-mainstream art or fiction and other creativities (i.e., music, film...etc.).

Future Horizons, Inc., 720 North Fielder Road, Arlington, TX 76012-4635, 817-277-0727; 1-800-4890727; Fax 817-277-2270; E-mail edfuture@onramp.net. 1990. "Future Horizons specializes in autism/PDD information for families, employers, child care providers, and children. Although most our projects are first selected by our editor, we will accept outside proposals and manuscripts." avg. press run 2M. Pub'd 10 titles 1998; expects 5 titles 1999, 5 titles 2000. 34 titles listed in the *Small Press Record of Books in Print* (28th Edition, 1999-00). avg. price, cloth: retail; paper: $24.95; other: $49.95—video, $9.95—audiotape. Discounts: 50-555. 256pp; 8 1/2×11. Reporting time: 2 months. Publishes 2-3% of manuscripts submitted. Payment: 5-8%. Does not copyright for author. Texas Publishing Association.

The Future Press (see also PRECISELY), Richard Kostelanetz, Literature Director, Box 444 Prince Street, New York, NY 10012-0008. 1976. Poetry, fiction, articles, art, music, parts-of-novels, long-poems, concrete art. "Committed exclusively to radically alternative materials for books and radically alternative forms of books. Have so far done a ladderbook, a cut-out book, a collection of cards containing numerals, a looseleaf book, a fold-out book, a book exclusively of numbers, another entirely of photographs, the same verbal text in two radically different book formats. What we can do depends, alas, largely on grants; and since U.S. funding agencies have been notoriously ungenerous toward experimental work and its practitioners, The Future Press is scarcely sanguine. The artists are there; the audience is there; the trouble still lies in the middle. We can't encourage submissions until the funding jam is busted." avg. press run 600-1M. Expects 1 title 1999, 2 titles 2000. 12 titles listed in the *Small Press Record of Books in Print* (28th Edition, 1999-00). avg. price, cloth: $10; paper: $3; other: $1 newsprint. Discounts: 40% to legitimate retailers paying in advance, and adding $1.50 for postage. 1-48pp; size varies; of. Payment: generous percentage of edition. Copyrights for author.

THE FUTURIST, Edward S. Cornish, World Future Society, 7910 Woodmont Avenue, Suite 450, Bethesda, MD 20814, 301-656-8274. 1966. Articles, art, photos, letters, news items, non-fiction. "A journal of forecasts, trends, and ideas about the future. *The Futurist* does not normally encourage freelance writers. Most of our articles are written by experts in their field who are not writers by profession. Similarly, we do not publish books from outside our staff." circ. 30M. 10/yr. Pub'd 9 issues 1998; expects 10 issues 1999, 10 issues 2000. 5 titles listed in the *Small Press Record of Books in Print* (28th Edition, 1999-00). sub. price: $39; per copy: $4.95; sample: $4.95 + $3 postage. 60pp; 8¼x10¾; webb of. Reporting time: 8 weeks. Payment: author's copies (10). Copyrighted, does not revert to author. Pub's reviews: 35 in 1998. §Future studies. Ads: $1250/$750/$2.

G

Gabriel's Horn Publishing Co., Inc., James H. Bissland, Box 141, Bowling Green, OH 43402, 419-352-1338; fax 419-352-1488. 1981. "We do not consider unsolicited submissions. We prefer to recruit authors according to our editorial plans" avg. press run 3M. Pub'd 1 title 1998. 7 titles listed in the *Small Press Record of Books in Print* (28th Edition, 1999-00). avg. price, cloth: $21; paper: $12. Discounts: Different schedules for retailers, wholesalers, schools, and libraries. 160pp; of. MAPA.

Gaff Press, John Paul Barrett, Publisher; Nancy Butterfield, Senior Editor; Mary Cvitanovitch, Editor, PO Box 1024, 114 SW Willow Lane, Astoria, OR 97103, 503-325-8288; e-mail gaffpres@pacifier.com. 1987. Art, photos, cartoons, interviews, non-fiction. "*Sea Stories—Of Dolphins and Dead Sailors* by John Paul Barrett. True, harrowing tales of mystery, death, hardship and humor from the North Pacific Fishing Grounds. 128 pages, silkscreened sailcloth hardback. Handbound. ISBN 0-9619629-0-9. 1987. *Sea Stories—Book II: Seagods and Sundogs*, ISBN 0-9619629-1-7. Interested in seeing true and extraordinary ocean-related adventure stories with a point. Published in 1990 *Nine Wednesday Nights*, an anthology of eleven Northwest writers' stories and poems, limited printing 250 copies; also published in Spring 1993, *How to Make a Book*, ISBN 0-9619629-3-3" avg. press run 5M-10M. Expects 1 title 1999. 2 titles 2000. 4 titles listed in the *Small Press Record of Books in Print* (28th Edition, 1999-00). avg. price, cloth: $15; paper: $12.50. Discounts: standard quantity to booksellers and distributors. 128-160pp; 4¼x5½; of. Reporting time: 1 month. Publishes 10% of manuscripts submitted. Payment: negotiable, usually 1/2 and 1/2 payment and sales bonus. Copyrights for author.

Gahmken Press, Range D. Bayer, PO Box 1467, Newport, OR 97365. 1986. Non-fiction. avg. press run 100. Expects 1 title 1999, 1 title 2000. 8 titles listed in the *Small Press Record of Books in Print* (28th Edition, 1999-00). avg. price, paper: $14. Discounts: prepaid STOP order for 1 book 30% + $2 shipping, 2-5 30% + shipping, 6+ 30% + shipping. Shipping charges: $2.50 for first book, $1.50 for each add'l book. 70pp; 8½x11; photocopying. Reporting time: 3 weeks. Payment: open to negotiation. Does not copyright for author.

Gain Publications, Al Sheahen, Editor, PO Box 2204, Van Nuys, CA 91404, 818-981-1996. 1982. Non-fiction. avg. press run 5M. 3 titles listed in the *Small Press Record of Books in Print* (28th Edition, 1999-00). avg. price, paper: $9.95. Discounts: 40%. 240pp; 5½x8½; of.

The P. Gaines Co., Publishers, Phillip Williams, PO Box 2253, Oak Park, IL 60303, 312-524-9033. 1979. Non-fiction. "We are now concentrating on self-help, business and legal guidebooks. Current publications: *How to Form Your Own Illinois Corporation Before the Inc. Dries!*, *The Living Will and the Durable Power of Attorney Book, With Forms*, and *Naming Your Business and Its Products and Services*." avg. press run 1M-5M. Expects 3 titles 1999. 13 titles listed in the *Small Press Record of Books in Print* (28th Edition, 1999-00). avg. price, paper: $19.95-26.95. Discounts: standard. 150-200pp; 8½x11; of. Reporting time: 4 weeks. Payment: advances negotiable. Copyrights for author. PMA.

Galaxy Press, Lance Banbury, 71 Recreation Street, Tweed Heads, N.S.W. 2485, Australia, 075-361997. 1979. Poetry, art, satire, criticism, long-poems, plays, non-fiction. "So far, only self-written (self aggrandizing? no) material, due to lack of real personal collaboration and ongoing contact in cases where material submitted was desirable." avg. press run 150. Pub'd 3 titles 1998; expects 1 title 1999. 21 titles listed in the *Small Press Record of Books in Print* (28th Edition, 1999-00). avg. price, paper: $10. Discounts: none. 12pp; 15x21cm; of. Reporting time: 1 month. Does not copyright for author.

Galde Press, Inc., Phyllis Galde, David Godwin, PO Box 460, Lakeville, MN 55044. 1991. Fiction, satire, non-fiction. avg. press run 1.5M. Pub'd 11 titles 1998; expects 8 titles 1999, 10 titles 2000. 25 titles listed in the *Small Press Record of Books in Print* (28th Edition, 1999-00). avg. price, cloth: $24.95; paper: $14.95. Discounts: 1-2 copies 20%, 3-4 30%, 5+ 43%. 200pp; 6x9; †of. Reporting time: 1-2 months. Payment: 10% on

211

collected monies. Copyrights for author. MIPA.

Galen Press, Ltd., M.L. Sherk, PO Box 64400, Tucson, AZ 85728-4400, 520-577-8363; fax 520-529-6459. 1993. Non-fiction. "We publish non-clinical, health related books directed towards both health professionals and the public. Current publication areas include biomedical ethics and guides for health profession students and educators. We concentrate on publishing books for which there is a defined need not currently being met" avg. press run 15M. Pub'd 3 titles 1998; expects 4 titles 1999, 4 titles 2000. 13 titles listed in the *Small Press Record of Books in Print* (28th Edition, 1999-00). avg. price, cloth: $41.95; paper: $26.45; other: $10. Discounts: call. 448pp; 6×9, 8½×11. Reporting time: 5 weeks. Simultaneous submissions accepted: no. Publishes 10% of manuscripts submitted. Payment: negotiable. Copyrights for author. PMA, Tucson Book Pub. Assn.

The Galileo Press Ltd., Julia Wendell, Editor-in-Chief, 3637 Black Rock Road, Upperco, MD 21155-9322. 1980. Poetry, fiction, long-poems, non-fiction. "Prints collections of poetry, short fiction, novellas, non-fiction and children's literature. It is best to query first before submitting." avg. press run 1M. Pub'd 3 titles 1998; expects 6 titles 1999, 5 titles 2000. 25 titles listed in the *Small Press Record of Books in Print* (28th Edition, 1999-00). avg. price, cloth: $15.95; paper: $9.95. Discounts: 40% to all bookstores; 40% to all classroom orders of 8 or more; 20%-55% wholesale; 10% courtesy library. 80pp; size varies; of. Reporting time: 3-6 months. Payment: 10% royalties plus author's copies. Copyrights for author. AWP, CLMP, PSA.

Gallaudet University Press, John V. Van Cleve, Director and Editor-in Chief, 800 Florida Avenue NE, Washington, DC 20002, 202-651-5488. 1980. Fiction, non-fiction. "Gallaudet University Press is a scholarly publisher specializing in work related to deafness, speech pathology, audiology, and related fields. The Press has a children's imprint called Kendall Green Publications that publishes children's texts and literature with a relation to hearing impairment, and an imprint called Clerc Books for instructional materials" avg. press run 3M-5M. Pub'd 15 titles 1998; expects 10 titles 1999, 15 titles 2000. 123 titles listed in the *Small Press Record of Books in Print* (28th Edition, 1999-00). avg. price, cloth: $24.95; paper: $9.95; other: $29.95, videotape. Discounts: trade 40%, text 25%. 250pp; 6×9, 7×10, 8½×11; of. Reporting time: 2 months. Payment: 7.5% of net. Copyrights for author. AAP, AAUP, Society of Scholarly Publishing, ABA.

Gallery West Associates, James Parsons, Philip Bareiss, PO Box 1272, El Prado, NM 87529, 505-751-0073. 1980. Articles, art, non-fiction. "Writers must query. We are a very small art gallery press. *The Art Fever* is our first book publication." avg. press run varies. Pub'd 1 title 1998; expects 1 title 1999, 1 title 2000. 1 title listed in the *Small Press Record of Books in Print* (28th Edition, 1999-00). avg. price, cloth: $29.95 *The Art Fever*. Discounts: regular trade. of. Payment: by agreement. Usually copyrights for author.

THE GALLEY SAIL REVIEW, Embassy Hall Editions, Stanley McNail, PO Box 665, Centralia, IL 62801-0665. 1958. Poetry, criticism, reviews, news items. "GSR was founded in 1958 and published in San Francisco from 1958 through 1971. It has been revived for a second series. It has always been rather eclectic, but leaning toward modern romantic styles. We occasionally publish longer poems, but prefer shorter work because of space limitations. We are hospitable to new poets as well as established writers. Among contributors to our first series: Robert Hillyer, William Carlos Williams, Irving Layton, William Pillin, John Stevens Wade. Among recent contributors: James Broughton, Diane Wakoski, Lewis Turco, James Schevill, Thom Gunn, Ursula LeGuin. No particular biases; we prize sincerity and value craftsmanship" circ. 500. 3/yr. Pub'd 3 issues 1998; expects 3 issues 1999, 3 issues 2000. sub. price: 2-year $15 (add $2 outside US & CAN); per copy: $3; sample: $3. Back issues: none available at present. Discounts: sub rates are discounted-i.e., 1 yr., $8.00; 2 yrs., $15.00. 40% to retail book dealers on consignments. 40-44pp; 5½×8½; of. Reporting time: 3 weeks to 1 month. Payment: contributors are usually furnished 2-3 copies. Copyrighted, reverts to author. Pub's reviews. §Poetry collections, poetry journals, lit. criticism, biographies of poets, books concerning the craft of poetry or on the arts in relation to poetry. Ads: not available at present. CLMP.

Gallopade International, Michele Yother, President, 200 Northlake Drive, Peachtree City, GA 30269-1437. 1979. "We are not seeking submissions; do welcome inquiries about our writing/publishing books and workshops; as we begin developing CD-ROM titles, we will be looking for one freelance photographer in each state (video experience helpful); may hire one freelance writer in each state with Macintosh & who's willing to do work-for-hire following our guidelines. We also provide 3 month internships (non-paid) which include all aspects of our publishing company. Send resume and SASE for consideration." avg. press run based on demand. Pub'd 1200 titles 1998; expects 1000 titles 1999, 1000 titles 2000. 74 titles listed in the *Small Press Record of Books in Print* (28th Edition, 1999-00). avg. price, cloth: $29.95; paper: $19.95; other: $39.95 interactive media. Discounts: 1-9 20%, 10+ 50% non-returnable, all pre-paid. 36+pp; 8½×11, 6×9; †xerox. Women's National Book Assn.

Galloway Press, Renee Gassin, 1520 Old Henderson Road, Suite 100, Columbus, OH 43220, 800-504-2273. 1991. 3 titles listed in the *Small Press Record of Books in Print* (28th Edition, 1999-00).

Galt Press, Mark Warda, PO Box 8, Clearwater, FL 34617. 1983. avg. press run 3M. Pub'd 1 title 1998;

212

expects 2 titles 1999, 4 titles 2000. 3 titles listed in the *Small Press Record of Books in Print* (28th Edition, 1999-00). avg. price, paper: $15. Discounts: 1-4 20%; 5+ 42%. 190pp; 6×9. Reporting time: 90 days. Simultaneous submissions accepted: yes. Copyrights for author.

Galt Publishing, Greg Compton, Lisa Hanks, PO Box 848, Newport Beach, CA 92661, 714-675-2835; FAX 714-675-3219. 1995. Non-fiction. "Considering only non-fiction. Must be well-written and fill a unique niche in the marketplace. Publishing only a limited number of manuscripts at this time; please query before sending any manuscripts." avg. press run 5M. Expects 2 titles 1999, 2 titles 2000. 1 title listed in the *Small Press Record of Books in Print* (28th Edition, 1999-00). avg. price, paper: $19.95. Discounts: varies depending on customer and amount purchased. 200pp; 7×10. Reporting time: 6 months. Simultaneous submissions accepted: no. Payment: varies with each project. Copyrights vary with each project. PMA.

Alicia Z. Galvan, 426 Castroville Road, San Antonio, TX 78207, 210-433-9991. 1994. 3 titles listed in the *Small Press Record of Books in Print* (28th Edition, 1999-00).

Gan Publishing, PO Box 33458, Riverside, CA 92519, 909-788-9676; FAX 909-788-9677. 1991. avg. press run 5M+. Pub'd 1 title 1998; expects 3 titles 1999, 3 titles 2000. 1 title listed in the *Small Press Record of Books in Print* (28th Edition, 1999-00). avg. price, paper: $9.95. Discounts: 1-4 10%, 5-9 20%, 10-49 30%, 50-99 40%, 100+ 45%; bulk—up to 60%. of, web. Reporting time: 8 weeks. Payment: varies; average 10-15% of net. Sometimes copyrights for author. PMA.

Garden St Press, Naomi Feigelson Chase, Co-Director; Jean Flanagan, Co-Director, PO Box 1231, Truro, MA 02666-1231, 508-349-1991. 1993. Poetry. "We are a new press, dedicated to publishing quality poetry and beautiful books. We have one contest each year. Deadline: June 31. Reading fee: $15. SASE for guidelines. We are not yet accepting unsolicited mss." avg. press run 1M. Expects 3 titles 1999, 3 titles 2000. 5 titles listed in the *Small Press Record of Books in Print* (28th Edition, 1999-00). avg. price, paper: $11. Discounts: 60-40; 55% to jobbers. 64pp; 5½×8½. Payment: varies.

GARGOYLE, Paycock Press, Richard Myers Peabody, Jr., Co-Editor; Lucinda Ebersole, Co-Editor; M. Maja Prausnitz, Co-Editor, 1508 U Street NW, Washington, DC 20009, 202-667-8148; e-mail atticus@radix.net. 1976. Poetry, fiction, articles, art, photos, interviews, satire, reviews, long-poems, parts-of-novels, collages. "Contributors: Kim Addonizio, Elizabeth Alexander, Nicole Blackman, Alison Bundy,Mary Caponegro, Nick Cave, Lynn Crosbie, Russell Edson, Jennifer Egan, Janice Eidus, Eurydice, Lauren Fairbanks, Jaimy Gordon, Karen Elizabeth Gordon, David Haynes, Joanna McClure, Jeffrey McDaniel,Gregory Maguire, Ben Marcus, Carole Maso, Laura Mullen, Lance Olsen, Kate Pullinger, Margaret Randall, Helen Schulman, Lewis Shiner, Maya Sonenberg, Eugene Stein, Laren Stover, Alexander Theroux, Lee Upton, Janine Pommy Vega, Curtis White, Diane Williams, Valerie Wohlfeld. Additional Address: 152 Harringay Road/Haringey/London N15 3HL/U.K; e-mail maja@ursarum.demon.co.uk; website www.atticusbooks.com" circ. 3M. 1-2/yr. Pub'd 1 issue 1998; expects 1 issue 1999, 1-2 issues 2000. sub. price: $25 universities (2 Issues); per copy: $10; sample: $10. Back issues: inquire/limited. 350pp; usually 8½×11, but format varies, sometimes cassette; of. Reporting time: 1-2 month. Simultaneous submissions accepted: no. Publishes 10% of manuscripts submitted. Payment: 1 copy and 50% off on additional copies. Copyrighted, reverts to author. Ads: $100/$60. Writer's Center.

Garrett County Press, Harvey Wallbanger, Editor; Alec Michod, Editor, 720 Barracks Street, New Orleans, LA 70116-2517, 608-251-3921; web: http://www.gcpress.com. 1997. Fiction, articles, art, photos, cartoons, satire, letters, non-fiction. "The GCPress is pre-anti-ist" avg. press run 5M. Expects 3 titles 1999, 3 titles 2000. 2 titles listed in the *Small Press Record of Books in Print* (28th Edition, 1999-00). avg. price, paper: $10; other: $6. 200pp; 6×9; of. Reporting time: 3 months. Simultaneous submissions accepted: no. Publishes 2% of manuscripts submitted. Payment: good. Does not copyright for author. SCH, GGP, III.

Garrett Publishing, Inc., Arnold S. Goldstein, 384 S. Military Trail, Deerfield Beach, FL 33442, 954-480-8543; Fax 954-698-0057. 1990. Non-fiction. "Garrett Publishing, Inc. publishes mostly financially-based books, i.e. on asset protection and offshore financing, with the exception of *Dr. Amarnick's Mind Over Matter Pain Relief Program* and *Don't Put Me In A Nursing Home!*" avg. press run 5M. Pub'd 3 titles 1998; expects 2 titles 1999. 2 titles listed in the *Small Press Record of Books in Print* (28th Edition, 1999-00). avg. price, cloth: $29.95; paper: $19.95. Discounts: U.S. book retailers, foreign accounts please inquire for schedule and terms. 200pp; size varies; of. Publishes 1% of manuscripts submitted. Payment: to be determined. Florida Publishers Association, SPAN, ABA, PMA.

GATEAVISA, Halstensen, Stalvik, Movik, Dueivgis, Hansen, Straume, Zaphod Beeble Brox, Grekenquist, Hjelmsgt 3, 0355 Oslo 3, Norway, +47 2 69 12 84. 1970. Fiction, articles, art, photos, cartoons, interviews, satire, criticism, reviews, music, letters, collages, news items, non-fiction. "Biases: Anarchistic + Sosialistic" circ. 8M. 6/yr. Pub'd 3 issues 1998; expects 6 issues 1999, 6 issues 2000. sub. price: NOK120, US$17.50; per copy: NOK 25, US$3.50; sample: NOK 25, , US$3.50 (surface); NOK 50, US$7 (air). Back issues: same. Discounts: for bookshops and street vendors. 56pp; size A4, 30×21cm; of. Reporting time: inquire. Simultaneous submissions accepted: yes. Publishes 70% of manuscripts submitted. Payment: rarely. Not copyrighted. Pub's reviews: 50 in 1998. §Political, counter-culture, arts, rock music, lifestyle, meaning of life, death. Ads: 3960 NOK/2400 NOK/12 NOK 50% discount/non-profit. APS, Norsk Tidsskriftforum.

Gateway Books, 2023 Clemens Road, Oakland, CA 94602, 510-530-0299; FAX 510-530-0497. 1985. avg. press run 5M. Pub'd 3 titles 1998; expects 4 titles 1999, 5 titles 2000. 15 titles listed in the *Small Press Record of Books in Print* (28th Edition, 1999-00). avg. price, paper: $12.95. 250pp; 6×9; of. Reporting time: 90 days. Publishes 5% of manuscripts submitted. Payment: negotiable. Copyrights for author. Northern California Book Publicists Assn.

Gateways Books And Tapes (see also INNER JOURNEYS), Iven Lourie, Senior Editor; Linda Corriveau, Associate Editor; Della Heywood, Associate Editor, Box 370, Nevada City, CA 95959, 916-272-0180; fax 916-272-0184. 1972. "Length-varied, spiritual, metaphysical bias. E.J. Gold. Labyrinth trilogy." avg. press run 1M-5M. Pub'd 5 titles 1998; expects 4 titles 1999, 4 titles 2000. 15 titles listed in the *Small Press Record of Books in Print* (28th Edition, 1999-00). avg. price, paper: $12.50; other: $15 music cassettes. Discounts: 25/40% trade, 50% wholesalers (negotiable). 200pp; 5½×8½, 8½×11; of. Reporting time: 3 months maximum. Payment: negotiable. ABA.

A GATHERING OF THE TRIBES, Amy Ouzoonian, Associate Editor; Sheila Alson, Associate Editor; David Hammons, Visual Editor; Ron English, Visual Editor; Steve Cannon, Editor-in-Chief; Renee McManus, Managing Editor, PO Box 20693, Tompkins Square, New York, NY 10009, fax 212-674-5576. 1991. Poetry, fiction, articles, art, photos, cartoons, interviews, criticism, reviews, parts-of-novels, long-poems, collages. "*Tribes* is a multicultural literary magazine of the arts. Recent contributors are Ishmael Reed, Jessica Hagedorn, Quincy Troupe, Victor Hernandez Cruz, Jayne Cortez, Paul Beatty, Karen Yamashita, and David Hammons. We are interested in non-traditional, non-academic work only, accept few unsolicited contributions and will only return work with SASE." circ. 3M. 2/yr. Pub'd 1 issue 1998; expects 2 issues 1999, 2 issues 2000. sub. price: $20; per copy: $10; sample: $10. Back issues: $10. 160pp; 8½×11; †of. Reporting time: 3 months. Simultaneous submissions accepted: yes. Publishes 20% of manuscripts submitted. Payment: copies. Copyrighted. Pub's reviews: 4 in 1998. §Art, literature, culture, politics. Ads: $500/$275/$150 1/4 page/$110.

GAUNTLET: Exploring the Limits of Free Expression, Barry Hoffmann, 309 Powell Road, Springfield, PA 19064, 610-328-5476. 1990. Fiction, articles, art, photos, cartoons, interviews, satire, reviews, letters, news items, non-fiction. "Looking for material dealing with censorship - prints both sides of the issue. Also looking for censored work (with history of censorship), and censored art. Length 1000-2500 words. *No taboos.* Contributors include Ray Bradbury, Isaac Asimov, George Carlin, artist Rubert Williams, Douglas Winter, William F. Nolan, Henry Slesar and Harlan Ellison. No unsolicited submissions. Query with SASE." circ. 8M. 2/yr. Expects 2 issues 1999, 2 issues 2000. sub. price: $22 postage included; per copy: $9.95 + $2 p & h; sample: $9.95 + p & h. Back issues: $9.95 + $2 p & h. Discounts: 40-50% bookstores, 20% libraries, 50-60% distributors, 20-30% for bulk purchases for classroom (10 or more). 112pp; 7×10½ magazine format; of. Reporting time: 3-5 weeks. Publishes 10% of manuscripts submitted. Payment: 1/4¢ a word for text (up to 1¢), $2-$5 for art. Copyrighted, reverts to author. Pub's reviews: 20 in 1998. §Censored or controversial material, horror, fantasy or mystery. Ads: $400/$250/$175 1/4 page. Horror Writers of America (HWA), Myster Writers of America (MWA).

Gay Sunshine Press, Inc., Winston Leyland, PO Box 410690, San Francisco, CA 94141, 415-626-1935; Fax 415-626-1802. 1970. Poetry, fiction, interviews, criticism, reviews, music, letters, non-fiction. "*Gay Sunshine* was founded in 1970 to publish cultural, literary, political material by gay people. During the first five years of its existence it published only the tabloid cultural journal, *Gay Sunshine*, which ceased publication in 1982. Since 1975 it has been publishing chapbooks and books." avg. press run 5M. Pub'd 2 titles 1998; expects 2 titles 1999, 2 titles 2000. 40 titles listed in the *Small Press Record of Books in Print* (28th Edition, 1999-00). avg. price, cloth: $25; paper: $14.95. Discounts: distributors to the Book Trade: Book People Distributors and Bookazine, Koen, (N.J.) Alamo Square San Francisco (at 40% discount). No discounts to individuals or libraries. Discounts to book jobbers & specialty shops. 192pp; 6×9, 5½×8½; sheet fed. Reporting time: 1 month. Payment: royalties. Copyrights for author.

GAYELLOW PAGES, Frances Green, Box 533 Village Station, New York, NY 10014, 212-674-0120, Fax: 212-420-1126. 1973. "Directory of organizations, businesses, publications, bars, AIDS resources, churches, etc., of interest to gay women and men in USA & Canada. No charge to be listed; self-addressed stamped #10 envelope for details." circ. 50M. 1/yr. Pub'd 1 issue 1998; expects 1 issue 1999, 1 issue 2000. sub. price: $16; per copy: $16; sample: $16 by mail. Discounts: 40% consigned, 50% prepaid. 448pp; 5×8; of. §Gay-related topics, gay-supportive feminist. Ads: $995/$640.

Gazelle Publications, T.E. Wade, Jr., 11560 Red Bud Trail, Berrien Springs, MI 49103. 1976. Non-fiction. "We consider juvenile material that is not fantasy, material suitable for classroom use, or how-to material. Brochure available showing current titles. Query first. We are not currently using unsolicited material." avg. press run 4M. Pub'd 1 title 1998; expects 1 title 1999, 2 titles 2000. 9 titles listed in the *Small Press Record of*

Books in Print (28th Edition, 1999-00). avg. price, paper: $18; other: $10. Discounts: trade and library 20% to 48%. 150pp; 5½×8½; of. Reporting time: 1 week. Payment: open, depends on market potential. Copyrights for author.

GCT Inc., Fay L. Gold, Editor-Publisher; Marvin Gold, Editor, PO Box 6448, Mobile, AL 36660, 334-478-4700. 1978. avg. press run 2M. Pub'd 4 titles 1998; expects 4 titles 1999, 4 titles 2000. 23 titles listed in the *Small Press Record of Books in Print* (28th Edition, 1999-00). avg. price, paper: $8.97. 48pp; 8½×11; sheetfed.

Gearhead Press, Bruce Rizzon, Co-Editor; Barbara Rizzon, Co-Editor, 565 Lincoln, Northwest, Grand Rapids, MI 49504, 459-7861 or 459-4577. 1975. Poetry, long-poems. "Our favorite poet right now is Bruce Rizzon. Write for free list of our titles. *A Walk in the Spring Rain, Vol. 2,* Fall 1981, $1.00. Also expect *A Desolate Angel. Blood on the Moon* $2.00 and *Ninth Street, Five Raindrops* in 82 or 83, *Diamonds And Rust Poems, For Sale Poems, Dean Lake Poems* $1.00, *Asphalt Shadows Poems* $1.50, *Osiris Rising Poems, I Am The Lonely Sea* $6.00, *Dago Red, The Road* $2.50, and *The Blues,* all by Bruce Rizzon. Make all checks/money orders payable to Bruce Rizzon." avg. press run 10M. Pub'd 3 titles 1998; expects 5 titles 1999, 5 titles 2000. 36 titles listed in the *Small Press Record of Books in Print* (28th Edition, 1999-00). avg. price, cloth: $6; paper: $2.50; other: $1. Discounts: none. 26-60pp; 5½×8½; of. Reporting time: 4 minutes to 4 years? maybe. SASE on all submissions. We will read all manuscripts sent to us. Give us time before we return any unused mss or unwanted mss. Copyrights for author. PRCM, PSM, NFSPS, Peninsulapoets.

Geekspeak Unique Press (see also PLOPLOP), John Clark, PO Box 11443, Indianapolis, IN 46201, 317-849-6227; www.ploplop.com. 1991. Poetry, fiction, art, concrete art. "Recent books by Fielding Dawson, John Clark, Deb Sellers, J.T. Whitehead and Kit Andis." avg. press run 100. Pub'd 2 titles 1998; expects 6 titles 1999, 6 titles 2000. 6 titles listed in the *Small Press Record of Books in Print* (28th Edition, 1999-00). avg. price, paper: $5. Discounts: 20%. 25-30pp; 4×5; Xerox. Reporting time: 6-8 weeks. Simultaneous submissions accepted: yes. Publishes 5% of manuscripts submitted. Payment: negotiable. Sometimes copyrights for author.

Gemini Marine Publications, William Carpenter, Brook Borer, PO Box 700255, San Antonio, TX 78270-0255, 210-494-0426, Fax 210-494-0766. 1992. Non-fiction. "Always seeking books, booklets, articles on 'how-to' marine subjects (recreational boating)" avg. press run 1.5M. Pub'd 1 title 1998; expects 3 titles 1999, 3 titles 2000. 2 titles listed in the *Small Press Record of Books in Print* (28th Edition, 1999-00). avg. price, paper: $19.95. Discounts: 1-2 books no discount, 3-199 40%, 200-49 50%, 500+ 55%. 200pp; 6×9. Payment: all rights purchased up front. Copyrights for author. PMA, Book Publishers of Texas, North American Book Exchange.

Gemini Publishing Company, Don Diebel, 14010 El Camino Real, Houston, TX 77062, 281-488-6866, E-mail: getgirls@getgirls.com; website: http://www.getgirls.com. 1978. Non-fiction. avg. press run 2M-3M. Expects 1 title 2000. 6 titles listed in the *Small Press Record of Books in Print* (28th Edition, 1999-00). avg. price, paper: $14.95. Discounts: 1-24 50%; 25-49 55%; 50-99 60%; 100-199 65%; 200 or more books 70%. 200pp; 8½×5½; †of. Reporting time: 1 month. Simultaneous submissions accepted: yes. Payment: 5-10%. Copyrights for author. American Booksellers Exchange, Mailorder Associates, Texas Publishers Association, Publishers Marketing Association, Houston Publishers and Authors Association.

Gemstone House Publishing, Suzanne P. Thomas, PO BOX 19948, Boulder, CO 80308, sthomas170@aol. 1998. Plays. "Current emphasis on real estate titles and personal finance. Recent title *Rental Houses for the Successful Small Investor.* Also interested in small business success stories particularly with unusual occupations, i.e. grower of organic herbs or sailboat chartering in the Caribbean. Prefer e-mail queries, mail queries okay. Unsolicited submissions will be recycled, not returned even if postage is included." avg. press run 3-6M. Pub'd 1 title 1998; expects 2 titles 1999, 2 titles 2000. 1 title listed in the *Small Press Record of Books in Print* (28th Edition, 1999-00). avg. price, cloth: $23.95; paper: $18.95. Discounts: orders for 5+ books 40% if returnable, 50% if non-returnable. 256pp; 6×9. Reporting time: 3 months max. Simultaneous submissions accepted: yes. Payment: varies-competitive. Copyrights for author. PMA, CIPA, RMBPA.

GemStone Press, Stuart M. Matlins, LongHill Partners, Inc., PO Box 237, Woodstock, VT 05091, 802-457-4000. 1987. Non-fiction. "Gemology, jewelry, fashion." avg. press run 10M. Pub'd 2 titles 1998; expects 4 titles 1999, 4 titles 2000. 4 titles listed in the *Small Press Record of Books in Print* (28th Edition, 1999-00). avg. price, cloth: $29.95; paper: $16.95. Discounts: 1-4 copies: 20%; 5-4: 40%; 15-24: 42%; 25-49: 44%; 50-99: 46%; 100+: 48%. 304pp; 6×9; web. Reporting time: 2 months. Simultaneous submissions accepted: yes. Publishes 5% of manuscripts submitted. Payment: depends on title and author. Copyrights for author. PMA.

Genealogical Publishing Co., Inc., Michael Tepper, Sr. Vice President & Editor-in-Chief, 1001 North Calvert Street, Baltimore, MD 21202, 410-837-8271; 410-752-8492 fax. 1933. "We publish reference books (source records and how-to books) in the field of geneology, family history, and immigration" avg. press run 1M. Pub'd 50 titles 1998; expects 50 titles 1999, 50 titles 2000. avg. price, cloth: $25; paper: $19.95. Discounts:

25-50%. 300pp; 5×8; of. Reporting time: 2 weeks. Payment: negotiable. Copyrights for author.

GENERAL MAGAZINE, Patrick Hartigan, Endi Hartigan, 929 SW Salmon, Portland, OR 97205, 503-355-2487. 1997. *"General Magazine* is the form of General Magazine realized. Imagine the blue sky's skeleton. We prefer correspondence to submission." circ. 200+. 9/yr. Pub'd 4 issues 1998; expects 9 issues 1999, 9 issues 2000. sub. price: $5; per copy: $1; sample: $1. 2pp; 8½×11. Copyrighted, reverts to author.

Genesis Publishing Company, Inc., Trudy Doucette, 1547 Great Pond Road, North Andover, MA 01845-1216, 508-688-6688, fax 508-688-8686. 1994. Non-fiction. "General trade books on science, philosophy, and religion" avg. press run 3M. Pub'd 4 titles 1998; expects 3 titles 1999, 4 titles 2000. 9 titles listed in the *Small Press Record of Books in Print* (28th Edition, 1999-00). avg. price, cloth: $30; paper: $15. Discounts: bookstores 30%, 10-24 40%, agents 11-50 40%, 51- 50%. 180pp; 5¼×8½; of. Reporting time: 3 weeks. Simultaneous submissions accepted: no. Publishes 5% of manuscripts submitted. Payment: 10%. Copyrights for author. PMA/SPAN.

THE GENRE WRITER'S NEWS, Dark Regions Press, Bobbi Sinha-Morey, 30 Canyon View Drive, Orinda, CA 94563, 510-254-7442. Poetry, fiction, articles, art, interviews, reviews, news items, non-fiction. "Recent contributers include Wayne Allen Sallee, Sean Doolittle, George Scithers, Nancy Bennett, Alfred Klosterman, and Cathy Buburuz. Includes free comentary/critique services." circ. 300. 2/yr. Pub'd 2 issues 1998; expects 2 issues 1999, 2 issues 2000. sub. price: $25; per copy: $3.95; sample: $3.95. Discounts: free with membership to Genre Writer's Association. 43pp; 7¾×10¾; †of. Reporting time: 1-2 weeks. Simultaneous submissions accepted: yes. Publishes 50-60% of manuscripts submitted. Payment: contributer copies. Copyrighted, reverts to author. Pub's reviews: 18 in 1998. §Horror, science fiction, fantasy, dark fantasy, mystery. Ads: will do ad trades. HWA, SFPA.

THE GENTLE SURVIVALIST, Laura Martin-Buhler, PO Box 4004, St. George, UT 84770. 1991. Poetry, articles, interviews, news items, non-fiction. "Laura Martin-Buhler has embraced a philosophy she has defined as harmonic ecology. Harmonic ecology is a wholistic, God-centered, balanced approach to responsible stewardship of the earth and as such emphasizes Native American and prophetic, eclectic approaches to walking softly, yet self-sufficiently on the earth. Positive contributions that resonate with a faith in God/time-tested wisdom are welcomed. Survivors of neardeath, environmental illness or life threatening experiences" circ. 250+. 11/yr. Pub'd 11 issues 1998; expects 11 issues 1999, 11 issues 2000. sub. price: $20; per copy: $2; sample: $2. Back issues: $3. Discounts: we have barter situations and trade. 8pp; 8½×11; of. Reporting time: 2 months. Publishes 20% of manuscripts submitted. Payment: copy. Copyrighted, reverts to author. Pub's reviews: 12 in 1998. §Native American, env. illness, indoor pollution, self-sufficiency, natural health. Ads: none. Society of Environmental Journalism.

GEORGE & MERTIE'S PLACE: Rooms With a View, George Thomas, Mertie Duncan, PO Box 10335, Spokane, WA 99209-1335, 509-325-3738. 1995. Poetry, fiction, articles, interviews, satire, criticism, reviews, music, news items, non-fiction. "Our microzine is interested in all things human, expressed in poetry and prose. Humor is as welcome as doom, surrealism as much as realism - anything in between. If you can honestly say, 'Help! I'm alive and it feels ambiguous as hell,' then you know what we want, but when you say it, please enclose a SASE if you want unused material returned. Our limited space demands brevity. 1500 words prose is best, give or take a smidgeon." 11/yr. Pub'd 11 issues 1998; expects 11 issues 1999, 11 issues 2000. sub. price: $15; per copy: $1.50; sample: $2. 4-8pp; 8½×11; desktop masters, then xerox on colored 11 X 17 and 8½ X11 paper. Reporting time: 1-2 months. Simultaneous submissions accepted: no. Publishes 5-10% of manuscripts submitted. Payment: 1¢/word; $2 min., we offer a $25 "Richard Diver best of issue" award each month. Pub's reviews: 2 in 1998. §Anything that snares our fancy.

GEORGETOWN REVIEW, Victoria Lancelotta, Fiction Editor; Marvyn Petrucci, Poetry Editor, PO Box 6309, Hattiesburg, MS 39406-6309, e-mail gr@georgetownreview.com. 1992. Poetry, fiction, articles, parts-of-novels, long-poems. "Our only bias is that we want good work." circ. 1M. 2/yr. Expects 1 issue 1999, 2 issues 2000. sub. price: $15; per copy: $8; sample: $8. Back issues: $5. Discounts: 40% to retailers. 200-250pp; 5¼×8¼. Reporting time: 1-2 months; we read manuscripts September 1 to May 1. Simultaneous submissions accepted: yes. Publishes 5-10% of manuscripts submitted. Payment: 2 copies. Copyrighted, reverts to author. Ads: $100/$50. CLMP.

THE GEORGIA REVIEW, Stanley W. Lindberg, Editor; Stephen Corey, Associate Editor; Janet Wondra, Assistant Editor, Univ. of Georgia, Athens, GA 30602-9009, 706-542-3481. 1947. Poetry, fiction, art, photos, criticism, reviews, letters, non-fiction. "An international journal of arts and letters, winner of the National Magazine Award in Fiction. Contributors range from previously unpublished to the already famous. Nonfiction preferences: thesis-oriented essays, *not* scholarly articles. Fiction and poetry selections are especially competitive. Translations and novel excerpts are *not* desired. During the months of June, July, and August unsolicited manuscripts are not considered (and will be returned unread)." circ. 6.5M. 4/yr. Pub'd 4 issues 1998; expects 4 issues 1999, 4 issues 2000. sub. price: $18 in US, $23 outside US; per copy: $7; sample: $6.

216

Back issues: $7. Discounts: agency sub. 10% ads 15%. 208pp; 7×10; 1p. Reporting time: 2-3 months. Simultaneous submissions accepted: no. Publishes .5% of manuscripts submitted. Payment: $35 minimum page prose; $3 line poetry; plus copies and one-year subscription. Copyrighted, reverts to author. Pub's reviews: 71 in 1998. §General humanities, poetry, fiction, essays, the South, interdisciplinary studies. Ads: $350/$225. CLMP, CELJ, ASME.

Geraventure (see also LIVING OFF THE LAND, Subtropic Newsletter), Marian Van Atta, PO Box 2131, Melbourne, FL 32902-2131, 305-723-5554. 1973. "Has published *Living Off the Land: Space Age Homesteading* by Marian Van Atta. 1st edition 1972, 2nd 1974, and 3rd 1977 and *Wild Edibles*. No plans at present for publishing other authors - but may be able to in the future." avg. press run 5M. Pub'd 1 title 1998; expects 1 title 1999, 2 titles 2000. 2 titles listed in the *Small Press Record of Books in Print* (28th Edition, 1999-00). avg. price, paper: $5.95. Discounts: 40%. 60pp; 8×5½; of. Reporting time: 4 weeks. Publishes 10% of manuscripts submitted. Payment: yes. Copyrights for author.

GERBIL: Queer Culture Zine, Tony Leuzzi, Brad Pease, PO Box 10692, Rochester, NY 14610, 716-262-3966, gerbil@rpa.net. 1995. Poetry, fiction, articles, art, photos, cartoons, interviews, reviews, parts-of-novels, collages, concrete art, news items, non-fiction. "Length of material can be anywhere from 50-2,500 words (usually) for prose. No more than 30 lines (usually) for poems. Recent contributors: Kevin Killian, David Trinidad, Rane Arroyo, Glenn Sheldon, Beth Bailey, and John Goldberg. Also we are open to a wide range of writing syles and issues" circ. 3M. 4/yr. Pub'd 4 issues 1998; expects 4 issues 1999, 4 issues 2000. sub. price: $10; per copy: $3; sample: $3. Back issues: $10 for issue 2, $5 for all other issues. Discounts: none. 32pp; 7½×9½; †of. Reporting time: 3-5 months. Simultaneous submissions accepted: no. Publishes 10% of manuscripts submitted. Payment: 3 publication copies. Copyrighted, reverts to author. Pub's reviews: 16 in 1998. §Queer fiction, poetry, literature, culture, also zine reviews and visual art. Ads: Contact Gerbil fo ad rates on our web page.

GERMAN LIFE, Heidi L. Whitesell, 1068 National Highway, LaVale, MD 21502, 301-729-6190; fax 301-729-1720; e-mail editor@germanlife.com. 1994. Articles, art, photos, cartoons, interviews, satire, reviews, letters, news items. "We publish articles from newsbriefs to feature length in size. For editorial guidelines and a sample of *German Life*, please send $4.95 to the attention of the Editor at above address." circ. 45M. 6/yr. Expects 6 issues 1999, 6 issues 2000. sub. price: $19.95; per copy: $4.95; sample: $4.95. Back issues: $4.95. Discounts: Bulk 50%. 64pp; 8⅛×10⅞; off set web. Reporting time: 8-10 weeks. Simultaneous submissions accepted: yes. Publishes 20% of manuscripts submitted. Payment: varies. Copyrighted. Pub's reviews: 15+ in 1998. §German culture, history, travel, German-Americana. Ads: $2575/$1675/$1110½ page.

GESAR-Buddhism in the West, Dharma Publishing, 2910 San Pablo Avenue, Berkeley, CA 94702, 415-548-5407. 1973. Poetry, art, photos, interviews, reviews, news items. circ. 3.5M. 4/yr. Expects 4 issues 1999, 4 issues 2000. sub. price: $12; per copy: $3.50; sample: $2. Back issues: $2/copy. No discount for subscription. 48pp; 7×9¼; †of. Reporting time: 2 months. Payment: none. Copyrighted, does not revert to author. Pub's reviews. §Currenty, in-house creation by Gesar staff and Nyingma students. No ads accepted. LPS.

Gesture Press, Nicholas Power, 68 Tyrrel Avenue, Toronto M6G 2G4, Canada. 1983. Poetry, art, photos, long-poems, collages, concrete art. "We are currently *not* accepting submissions. (We're interested in expansive poems with new formal concepts or unique lexicons. The content will determine the form of publication, completing the gesture)." avg. press run 100-250. 7 titles listed in the *Small Press Record of Books in Print* (28th Edition, 1999-00). avg. price, paper: $2-$6; other: $1 postcards, 1¢-$1.75 emphemera. Discounts: trade-40%, short-30%, agents-10%, libraries-full price. 1-40pp; size varies; of, hand-turned gestetner, xerox. Reporting time: 3 months. Publishes 5% of manuscripts submitted. Payment: percentage of print run (usually 10%). Copyrights for author. Meet the Presses, Toronto Small Press Book Fair.

Get In-Line! Publishing, Chris Stevens, Acquisitions editor, PO Box 170340, San Francisco, CA 94117-0340, 415-292-5809, Fax: 415-292-4111. 1993. Non-fiction. "Publishes trade paperback originals and reprints. 75% of books from first-time authors, 50% from unagented authors. Book catalog and manuscript guidelines for #10 SASE with 2 first class stamps. Nonfiction: How-to, reference, sports and recreation. Subjects: biography, business/career, money/finance, sports, recreation. We publish innovative how-to books. Query or submit outline and sample chapters. Recent title: *Complete Guide and Resource to In-Line Skating*." avg. press run 10M. Expects 4 titles 1999, 3 titles 2000. avg. price, paper: $16.95. Discounts: Trade: 40-55%, Special Sales: 20-65%, Classroom: 20%. 200pp; 6×9; of. Reporting time: 4-6 weeks. Payment: advance $1500 plus royalty, 10-16% of list. Copyrights for author. AAP, ABA.

THE GETTYSBURG REVIEW, Peter Stitt, Editor, Gettysburg College, Gettysburg, PA 17325, 717-337-6770. 1988. Poetry, fiction, articles, art, photos, satire, criticism, parts-of-novels, long-poems, collages, non-fiction. "Suggested length for essays and fiction: 3,000-7,000 words. Recent contributors include: Joyce Carol Oates, Charles Simic, Marilyn Nelson Wanick, Ann Packer, Judith Kitchen, Arvind Krishna Mehrotra,

X.J. Kennedy, Kathleen Norris, E.L. Doctorow. We publish essay-reviews that treat books in broader context. Reading period Sept-May. Include SASE for reply" circ. 4M. 4/yr. Pub'd 4 issues 1998; expects 4 issues 1999, 4 issues 2000. sub. price: $24, $32 foreign; per copy: $6 + $1 p/h; sample: $6 + $1 p/h. Back issues: $6 + $1 p/h. Discounts: bookstores 40% with option to return unsold copies. 184pp; 6×9½; lp. Reporting time: 1-3 months. Simultaneous submissions accepted: no. Publishes less than 1% of manuscripts submitted. Payment: $2 per line for poetry, $25 per page for prose. Copyrighted, reverts to author. Pub's reviews: 11 books reviewed, in 3 essay-reviews in 1998. §all. Ads: $225. MLA, CLMP, CELJ.

Ghost Pony Press, Ingrid Swanberg, Editor, P.O. Box 260113, Madison, WI 53726-0113, 608-238-0175; irmarkha@students.wisc.edu; www.litline.org/html/abraxas.html, www.geocities.com/Paris/4614, www.thing-net/~grist/lexd/dalevy/dalevy.html. 1980. Poetry, art, photos, interviews, long-poems, collages, concrete art. "We are interested in lyric poetry and prose-poems. Open to all forms. Considerable emphasis on the lyric mode. Books, chapbooks, pamphlets, broadsides. Recent & upcoming contributors: Jonathan Moore, Stephen M. Miller, Peter Wild, d.a.levy, Ivan Arguelles, Connie Fox, W.R. Rodriguez, Gerald Locklin, prospero saiz." avg. press run 500. Expects 2 titles 1999, 2 titles 2000. 14 titles listed in the *Small Press Record of Books in Print* (28th Edition, 1999-00). avg. price, paper: $20; other: $23 special editions; $1 broadsides. Discounts: 20% 1-4 copies; 40% 5-9; 50% on orders of 10 and more copies. 120pp; 6×9, 7×10, varies; of, sewn bindings. Reporting time: 3 months or longer, we currently have a very great backlog of submissions (please send inquiries, not mss!). Simultaneous submissions accepted: yes. Publishes 2% of manuscripts submitted. Payment: copies. Copyrights for author.

Gifted Education Press/The Reading Tutorium, Maurice D. Fisher, PO Box 1586, 10201 Yuma Court, Manassas, VA 20109-1586, 703-369-5017; mdfish@cais.com; www.cais.com/gep. 1981. Non-fiction. "Our books present clear and rigorous techniques for teaching gifted children in grades K-12 based upon using educational theory and practice. We are mainly interested in books on teaching the humanities, the sciences, and mathematics to the gifted. They are sold primarily by direct mail to school districts, libraries and universities across the nation. Some of our books are: (1) *Applying Multiple Intelligences to Gifted Education* by Holt & Holt; (2) *Technology Resource Guide* by O'Neill & Coe; (3) *The Philosophy of Ethics Applied to Everyday Life* by James Logiudice & Michael E. Walters; (4) *Humanities Education for Gifted Children* by M. Walters; (5) *How to Increase Gifted Students' Creative Thinking and Imagination* by W. Wenger; and (6) *Teaching Shakespeare to Gifted Children* by M. Walters. We are actively seeking manuscripts of 50 to 70 pages on educating gifted students and how to use computers with the gifted. We are also actively searching for field representatives to sell our books across the USA through workshops and inservice training. *Will not accept unsolicited manuscripts*—they will be returned to the author without being read! *Send 1 page letter of inquiry first*—this is all we need to determine if we're interested in your book." avg. press run 500. Pub'd 3 titles 1998; expects 5 titles 1999, 5 titles 2000. 23 titles listed in the *Small Press Record of Books in Print* (28th Edition, 1999-00). avg. price, paper: $16. Discounts: 20% to jobbers & bookstores. 65pp; 8½×11; xerography. Reporting time: 3-4 months. Simultaneous submissions accepted: yes. Payment: 10% of retail price. Copyrights for author.

Gild of Saint George (see also LIVERPOOL NEWSLETTER), Anthony Cooney, Rose Cottage, 17 Hadassah Grove, Lark Lane, Liverpool L17 8XH, England, 051-728-9176. 1982. Poetry, letters, non-fiction. "By 'letters' and 'non-fiction' is meant 'essays'. Essays of social credit/decentralist/Catholic interest." avg. press run 200. Pub'd 1 title 1998; expects 3 titles 1999, 3 titles 2000. avg. price, paper: $1; other: $2. 32pp; 5½×8, 8×12; †mi, photocopy. Reporting time: poetry 3 months, prose 1 month. Payment: none. Copyrights for author.

Gilgal Publications, Judy Osgood, Executive Editor, PO Box 3399, Sunriver, OR 97707, 541-593-8418. 1983. Non-fiction. "We are currently publishing a series of 12 books on coping with stress and resolving grief. This is our Gilgal Meditation series. The contributors to each book are individuals who have lived through the experience they are talking about. For example, our first book was *Meditations For Bereaved Parents*. Some of the contributors to it were Paula D'Arcy, Meg Woodson & Joyce Landorf. The meditations are all 1 to 2 pages long and are written in what we call a "sharing tone". The authors aren't claiming to have all the answers. They are saying, "this is what helped me; maybe it will help you too". Our latest book released in Dec 1993 was *Meditations for Alcoholics and Their Families*. We ask that all potential contributors get our guidelines before they write a word for us" avg. press run 3M+. 5 titles listed in the *Small Press Record of Books in Print* (28th Edition, 1999-00). avg. price, paper: $6.95. Discounts: for resale—40% off list. 72pp; 5¼×7½; of. Reporting time: 2 weeks - 2 months. Simultaneous submissions accepted: no. Publishes 5% of manuscripts submitted. Payment: on acceptance. Copyrights for author.

GINOSKO, Robert Cesaretti, PO Box 246, Fairfax, CA 94978, 415-460-8436. 1993. Poetry, fiction, parts-of-novels, collages. "Between literary vision and spiritual realities." circ. 1M. 1/yr. sub. price: free; per copy: free; sample: free. Back issues: free. Discounts: none. Page number undetermined; 4×5½; †computer. Reporting time: 3-6 weeks. Payment: copy. Not copyrighted.

GIRLFRIENDS MAGAZINE, Heather Findlay, Editor-in-Chief, 3415 Cesar Chavez Street, Ste. 101, San Francisco, CA 94110, 415-648-9464; fax 415-648-4705; e-mail staff@gfriends.com; website www.gfriends.com. 1994. Poetry, fiction, articles, art, photos, cartoons, interviews, satire, criticism, reviews, letters. "Submissions should have something to do with lesbian culture, politics, and entertainment. Recent contributors include Betty Dodson and Pat Califia; interviews: Camryn Manheim and Ani Difranco." circ. 75M. 12/yr. Pub'd 12 issues 1998; expects 12 issues 1999, 12 issues 2000. sub. price: $29.95; per copy: $4.95. Back issues: $9-15. 48pp; 8½x11; Web Press, off. Reporting time: 6-8 weeks. Simultaneous submissions accepted: yes. Publishes 5% of manuscripts submitted. Payment: 10¢ per word. Copyrighted, reverts to author. Pub's reviews: 50 in 1998. §Lesbian, lesbian icon, feminist, gay, transgender. Ads: $2000/$1000/ 1/3 pg $800.

GLASS ART, Shawn Waggoner, PO Box 260377, Highlands Ranch, CO 80163-0377, 303-791-8998. 1985. Articles, art, photos, letters. circ. 7M. 6/yr. Pub'd 6 issues 1998; expects 6 issues 1999, 6 issues 2000. sub. price: $30; per copy: $6; sample: $6. Back issues: $6. 64-80pp; of. Copyrighted. Pub's reviews.

GLASS AUDIO, Edward T. Jr. Dell, PO Box 876, Peterborough, NH 03458, 603-924-9464. 1988. Articles, photos, interviews, reviews, letters, news items. circ. 8.5M. 6/yr. Pub'd 6 issues 1998; expects 6 issues 1999, 6 issues 2000. sub. price: $28; per copy: $6; sample: free trial issue available. Discounts: 50% bulk, 20% agent off institutional rates. 64pp; 8x10½; of. Reporting time: 4 weeks. Simultaneous submissions accepted: no. Publishes 8% of manuscripts submitted. Payment: yes. Copyrighted, reverts to author. Pub's reviews: 6 in 1998. §Vacuum tubes, do-it-yourself audio equipment. Ads: $525/$340/$1 per word.

THE GLASS CHERRY, The Glass Cherry Press, Judith Hirschmiller, Editor in Chief; Hugh Fox, Review Editor; Bill Embly, Contributing Fiction Editor, 901 Europe Bay Road, Ellison Bay, WI 54210-9643, 414-854-9042. 1994. Poetry, fiction, articles, art, photos, interviews, reviews, letters, parts-of-novels, long-poems, plays. "A magazine of the arts with an unstated focus on contemporary poetry and poets. A featured poet with each issue including photo and short bio. First featured poet: Lyn Lifshin. Fiction should be under 1,000 words." circ. 500. 4/yr. Expects 3 issues 1999, 3 issues 2000. sub. price: $15; per copy: $5; sample: $6. Back issues: $10. Discounts: 40%. 50pp; 5½x8½; †computer printing. Reporting time: 30 days. Simultaneous submissions accepted: no. Publishes 10% of manuscripts submitted. Payment: copy of issue published in. Copyrighted, reverts to author. Pub's reviews: 3 in 1998. §Poetry. Ads: ad space free to approved magazines, contests, and upcoming events. none.

The Glass Cherry Press (see also THE GLASS CHERRY), Judith Hirschmiller, Editor, 901 Europe Bay Road, Ellison Bay, WI 54210, 414-854-9042. 1994. Poetry, fiction, articles, art, photos, interviews, reviews, letters, parts-of-novels, long-poems, plays. "Poetry collections by one author; poetry anthologies. Short story collections by one author, short story anthologies." avg. press run 500. Expects 3 titles 1999, 3 titles 2000. avg. price, cloth: $15; paper: $10; other: $20. Discounts: 80%. 50pp; size varies; †computer printing. Reporting time: 30 days. Simultaneous submissions accepted: no. Publishes 10% of manuscripts submitted. Payment: negotiated individually with each author. Copyrights for author. none.

GLB Publishers, W.L Warner, Editor & Publisher; John Hanley, Associate Editor, 1028 Howard Street #503, San Francisco, CA 94103, 415-621-8307. 1990. Poetry, fiction, long-poems. "A contributory (cooperative) press for books of fiction, nonfiction and poetry by gay, lesbian, and bisexual authors. Both explicit and non-explicit. Also PO Box 78212, San Francisco, CA 94107." avg. press run 3M. Pub'd 2 titles 1998; expects 4 titles 1999, 4 titles 2000. 24 titles listed in the *Small Press Record of Books in Print* (28th Edition, 1999-00). avg. price, cloth: $27; paper: $13. Discounts: 55%. 176pp; 5½x8½, 6x9; of. Reporting time: 2 months. Simultaneous submissions accepted: no. Publishes 30% of manuscripts submitted. Payment: variable. Copyrights for author. PMA.

GLEN BURNIELAND, Chuck Jones, 9195-H Hitching Post Lane, Laurel, MD 20723, 301-604-8236. 1989. Satire, letters, non-fiction. "*Glen Burnieland* is a family humor newsletter in which the lives of my family, friends, and co-workers are chronicled in an adult story-telling style. No submissions except letters to the editor." circ. 600. 4/yr. Pub'd 4 issues 1998; expects 4 issues 1999, 4 issues 2000. sub. price: $10; per copy: $3; sample: free. Back issues: $2 each while supplies last. Discounts: none. 16pp; 8½x11; photocopy. Copyrighted. Ads: sponsorship-1 page ad in exchange for underwriting production costs.

Glenbridge Publishing Ltd., James A. Keene, Editor-in-Chief & Vice-President, 6010 West Jewell Avenue, Lakewood, CO 80232-7106, 303-986-4135; FAX 303-987-9037. 1986. Non-fiction. "Currently have 7 additional titles in process, all of which are appropriate for all types of libraries (university, historical, college, community college, public, reference, etc.), the trade market and use as auxiliary text/text material for college, university, and community college as well as for business (management, sales, etc.)" avg. press run 2.5-7.5M. Pub'd 6 titles 1998; expects 7 titles 1999, 7 titles 2000. 43 titles listed in the *Small Press Record of Books in Print* (28th Edition, 1999-00). avg. price, cloth: $18.95-$27.95; paper: $9.95-18.95; other: $42 (special edition). Discounts: jobber 20%, trade: 1-2 books 20%, 3-9 30%, 10-49 40%, 50-99 42%, 100-299 44%, 300-499 46%, 500-999 48%, 1000 50%. 200-300pp; 6x9, 5½x8½, 7x10, 8½x11; professionally manufactured by major book company. Reporting time: 6-8 weeks. Payment: hard cover, 10%, pay once yearly. Copyrights for author.

The Glencannon Press, R.B. Rose, Publisher, PO Box 633, Benicia, CA 94510, 707-745-3933; fax 707-747-0311. 1993. Fiction, non-fiction. "All ms. must relate to maritime history or subjects." avg. press run 1.5M. Pub'd 4 titles 1998; expects 4 titles 1999, 4 titles 2000. 20 titles listed in the *Small Press Record of Books in Print* (28th Edition, 1999-00). avg. price, cloth: $29; paper: $16. Discounts: 40% to retailers. Cloth 500pp, paper 200+pp; 6×9; lp. Reporting time: 2 months. Simultaneous submissions accepted: yes. Publishes 10% of manuscripts submitted. Payment: negotiable. Copyrights for author. PMA, MSPA, NCIBA.

The Gleniffer Press, Ian Macdonald, 'Benvoir' Wigtown, NEWTON STEWART, Galloway, DG8 9EE, Scotland, 041-889-9579. 1968. Poetry, art, photos, letters, long-poems, plays, news items. "Specialist in miniature books, limited editions. Mailing list of private buyers now established. 1985 published '*Smallest Book In The World*'." avg. press run 250-1M. Pub'd 1 title 1998; expects 4 titles 1999, 4 titles 2000. 3 titles listed in the *Small Press Record of Books in Print* (28th Edition, 1999-00). avg. price, cloth: $30; other: price varies. Discounts: 33⅓%. 30pp; †of, lp. Payment: single fees. Copyrights for author. MBS, BPS.

GLOBAL MAIL, Ashley Parker Owens, PO Box 410837, San Francisco, CA 94141-0837, 417-642-3731, e-mail soapbox@well.com. 1991. "A listing of over 800 art related projects from over 45 countries" circ. 4M. 3/yr. sub. price: $9 US, $12 foreign; per copy: $3; sample: free for 2 $.75 stamps. Back issues: $1. 40pp; 8×10. Reporting time: All listings are included in the next issue, if they are relevant. Payment: none.

Global Options (see also SOCIAL JUSTICE: A JOURNAL OF CRIME, CONFLICT, & WORLD ORDER), Gregory Shank, PO Box 40601, San Francisco, CA 94140, 415-550-1703. 1974. Articles, interviews, reviews. "Send editorial material and ordering information: Social Justice, PO Box 40601, San Francisco, CA 94610." avg. press run 3M. Pub'd 4 titles 1998; expects 4 titles 1999, 4 titles 2000. 2 titles listed in the *Small Press Record of Books in Print* (28th Edition, 1999-00). avg. price, paper: $12. Discounts: Distribution handled through DeBoer, Ingram, Far East Periodicals, Ubiquity. 168pp; 6×9; of. Reporting time: 1-3 months. Simultaneous submissions accepted: no. Payment: varies. Copyrights for author.

Global Sports Productions, Ltd., Ed Kobak, 1223 Broadway, Suite 102, Santa Monica, CA 90404, 310-454-9480; fax 310-454-6590; e-mail sportsaddresses@hotmail.com. 1980. avg. press run 15M. Pub'd 5 titles 1998; expects 5 titles 1999, 6 titles 2000. 5 titles listed in the *Small Press Record of Books in Print* (28th Edition, 1999-00). avg. price, paper: $26.95 (foreign add $9 airmail, Canada + $3). Discounts: 20% to bookstores and distributors. 495pp; 5½×8½. Publishes 0% of manuscripts submitted. PMA.

‡GLOBAL TAPESTRY, BB Books, Dave Cunliffe, Spring Bank, Longsight Road, Copster Green, Blackburn, Lancs BB1 9EU, England, 0254 249128. 1971. Poetry, fiction, articles, art, interviews, reviews, letters, parts-of-novels, long-poems, collages, concrete art. "Mainly concerned with creative poetry & prose. Also those energy communications networks which liberate human animal beast mind. Be it psychedelics, mutant vampires or dead history memory recall. PM Newsletter is now incorporated, printing reviews, notices and listings." circ. 1.3M. 4/yr. Pub'd 4 issues 1998; expects 4 issues 1999, 4 issues 2000. sub. price: $20/4 issues; per copy: $5; sample: $3. Back issues: $2. Discounts: one third trade. 72pp; size A5; †of. Reporting time: soon. Payment: 1 copy. Pub's reviews: 150 in 1998. §Poetry, creative prose. Ads: £20/£10/10p per word. NWASP.

The Globe Pequot Press, Linda Kennedy, President and Publisher; Michael Urban, Vice-president and Associate Publisher; Kevin Lynch, Production Director; Laura Strom, Acquisitions Editor; Hugh Shiebler, Sales Manager, 6 Business Park Road, Box 833, Old Saybrook, CT 06475, 203-395-0440; FAX 203-395-0312. 1947. Art, photos, non-fiction. "We publish domestic and international travel guides, outdoor recreation, how-to, cooking, business and Americana. No poetry, fiction, or children's stories. Query letters are preferred. Standard submissions consist of one sample chapter, a table of contents, a one-page precis detailing the book and its saleability plus cover letter with some information about the author's credentials. We extend some advances. A catalogue of all Globe Pequot Press books is available." avg. press run 5M. Pub'd 80 titles 1998; expects 90 titles 1999, 100 titles 2000. 347 titles listed in the *Small Press Record of Books in Print* (28th Edition, 1999-00). avg. price, cloth: $18.95; paper: $11.95. Discounts: trade 20% and ascending, contingent upon quantity. 192pp; 5½×8½, 7×10, 8½×11, 5×7, 5¼×8, 8×8, 6×9, 7×7; desktop. Reporting time: 8-12 weeks. Simultaneous submissions accepted: yes. Publishes 1% of manuscripts submitted. Payment: 8-12% of net. Sometimes copyright for author. American Booksellers Association.

Gloger Family Books, Yehoshua Gloger, PO Box 6955, Portland, OR 97228. 1989. avg. press run 2M. Pub'd 1 title 1998; expects 1 title 1999, 1 title 2000. 4 titles listed in the *Small Press Record of Books in Print* (28th Edition, 1999-00). avg. price, paper: $20. Discounts: 40%. 250pp; 6×9. Reporting time: 1 month. Simultaneous submissions accepted: yes. Publishes 10% of manuscripts submitted. Payment: 50% net profit. Does not copyright for author. Northwest Association of Book Publishers.

GLYPH: The Tabloid That Redefines Visual Literature, Sarah Byam, Editor-in-Chief; David Lee Ingersoll,

Advertising; Kip Manley, Fiction Editor; Derek Fetters, Assistant Editor; Jeff Swenson, Art Director; Tim Lowrey, Production & Design, 117 East Louisa #253, Seattle, WA 98102, 206-343-5650; chaosunit@aol.com. "A new tabloid that will redefine visual literature. From inner city love to post modern westerns, science fiction adventure to civilized murder, a fresh look at ancient myth to domestic commedy—you'll find it in *Glyph*." 12/yr. Expects 12 issues 1999, 12 issues 2000. sub. price: free in Seattle area.

Goats & Compasses, Peter Mittenthal, PO Box 524, Brownsville, VT 05037, 802-484-5169. 1991. Poetry, long-poems, plays. avg. press run 500. Pub'd 2 titles 1998; expects 2 titles 1999. 4 titles listed in the *Small Press Record of Books in Print* (28th Edition, 1999-00). avg. price, paper: $10. Discounts: none. 26pp; †lp. Reporting time: 3 months. Simultaneous submissions accepted: no. Publishes 1% of manuscripts submitted. Payment: percentage of copies. Copyrights for author.

god is DEAD, publications, Tracey Lee Williams, 910 North Martel, Suite #207, Los Angeles, CA 90046, 213-850-0067. 1995. Poetry, cartoons, interviews, criticism, parts-of-novels, long-poems, non-fiction. "Branching out into publishing other writers & poets. Looking for new talent with an edge; unafraid, and original with their thoughts - funky; hip; gutsy." avg. press run 1M. Pub'd 2 titles 1998; expects 2 titles 1999, 2+ titles 2000. 50pp. Reporting time: ASAP - within a few weeks. Simultaneous submissions accepted: yes. Payment: 1 copy. Copyrights for author.

●**THE GODDESS OF THE BAY,** Sandra DeLuca, PO Box 8214, Warwick, RI 02888, E-mail Belindafox@aol.com. 1998. Poetry, fiction, art, parts-of-novels, long-poems. "I prefer short-short stories, no more than 1,500 words. Good gothic/horror pen and ink drawings. Vampire themes preferred over other subject matter. Erotica okay, with good story line." circ. 200. 4-6/yr. Expects 4-6 issues 1999, 4-6 issues 2000. sub. price: $15/4 issues; per copy: $4; sample: $4. Back issues: $3 after a year old. 40pp; 8½x11; †desktop. Reporting time: 1 month. Simultaneous submissions accepted: yes. Publishes 10% of manuscripts submitted. Payment: copies (that will change as subscriptions increase). Copyrighted, reverts to author. Ads: $15/$7.50.

GOLD COAST NEWS, Charles Hesser, PO Box 3637, Miami Beach, FL 33140, 674-9746. 1983. Articles, interviews, reviews, news items. "Describes events happening in the area from Palm Beach to Key West (Florida's Gold Coast), South East Florida." circ. 100M. 12/yr. Pub'd 12 issues 1998; expects 12 issues 1999, 12 issues 2000. sub. price: $20; per copy: $5; sample: $5. Back issues: $10. Discounts: none. 12pp; 8½x14; sheetfed. Reporting time: 1 month. Simultaneous submissions accepted: yes. Publishes 10% of manuscripts submitted. Payment: varies. Copyrighted, reverts to author. Ads: none.

Golden Aura Publishing, 440 West Sedgwick Street, 120D, Philadelphia, PA 19119. 12 titles listed in the *Small Press Record of Books in Print* (28th Edition, 1999-00).

Golden Eagle Press, Mary Lou Romagno, Janet Floyd, 1400 Easton Drive, Suite 149, Bakersfield, CA 93309, 805-327-4329; Fax 805-327-1053; E-mail Mary Lou mapp@lightspeed.net. 1998. Fiction, non-fiction. "Length: 100,000 words. No poetry. 50% 1st time, 100% unagented. Hardcover and paperback. Published: *Flight Plan for Success, The Astral Gift, The Deadly Omen* (Crabtree Mystery Series)." avg. press run 1-5M. Expects 5 titles 1999, 10 titles 2000. 4 titles listed in the *Small Press Record of Books in Print* (28th Edition, 1999-00). avg. price, cloth: $20; paper: $6. Discounts: 10-40%. 275pp; 6x9. Reporting time: 2-3 months. Simultaneous submissions accepted: yes. Publishes 10% of manuscripts submitted. Payment: negotiable. Copyrights for author. PMA, BPSC.

Golden Grove Books, Peter Cherici, 348 Hartford Tpk, Hampton, CT 06247, 860-455-0039; Fax 860-455-9198. 1996. Fiction. "Literary fiction" avg. press run 3M. Expects 2 titles 1999, 2 titles 2000. 1 title listed in the *Small Press Record of Books in Print* (28th Edition, 1999-00). avg. price, cloth: $19.95. Discounts: 45% trade, 55% distributor. 200pp; 6x9. Reporting time: 2 weeks. Simultaneous submissions accepted: yes. Publishes 2% of manuscripts submitted. Payment: 10% net. Copyrights for author. PMA.

Golden Isis Press (see also PAGAN PRIDE), Gerina Dunwich, PO Box 4263, Chatsworth, CA 91313. 1980. Poetry, fiction, art, satire, long-poems, non-fiction. "A one-time reading fee of $10 (refunded upon publication of the work) plus return postage is required with each chapbook submission. Maximum length for manuscripts (including artwork, diagrams, etc.) is 80 pages. Query first with SASE or send complete manuscript with brief cover letter and reading fee. Simultaneous, photocopied and reprint submissions O.K. We also accept computer printout submissions. Sample chapbooks are available for $9.95 (postpaid)." avg. press run 1M. Expects 1 title 1999. 1 title listed in the *Small Press Record of Books in Print* (28th Edition, 1999-00). avg. price, paper: $9.95. 52pp; 5x8; †of. Reporting time: 1-2 months. Simultaneous submissions accepted: yes. Publishes 10% of manuscripts submitted. Payment: 10% royalties on all copies sold for as long as the book remains in print; we also offer 10 free copies of the book. Copyrights for author. The Pagan Poets Society.

Golden Meteorite Press, A. Mardon, PO Box 1223 Main Post Office, Edmonton, Alberta T5J 2M4, Canada. 1990. Non-fiction. "Looking for fiction, nonfiction from all genres, specifically science fiction, romance, westerns. Need Canadian SASE or IRC. We want discs & manuscripts in Word Perfect 5.0, 5.1 or 5.5." avg.

221

press run 500. Pub'd 10 titles 1998; expects 6 titles 1999, 5 titles 2000. 4 titles listed in the *Small Press Record of Books in Print* (28th Edition, 1999-00). avg. price, cloth: $30Can. 200pp; 5×8½; †of. Reporting time: 6 months. Simultaneous submissions accepted: yes. Publishes 5% of manuscripts submitted. Payment: 5%. Does not copyright for author.

●**The Golden Sufi Center**, PO Box 428, Inverness, CA 94937, 415-663-8773; FAX 415-663-9128; E-mail GoldenSufi@aol.com. 1993. 10 titles listed in the *Small Press Record of Books in Print* (28th Edition, 1999-00).

Golden Umbrella Publishing, Lorie Maloney, Associate Editor, PO Box 95, Yorba Linda, CA 92885-0095, 714-996-4001 phone/fax; gupub@aol.com. 1 title listed in the *Small Press Record of Books in Print* (28th Edition, 1999-00).

Golden West Books, Donald Duke, PO Box 80250, San Marino, CA 91118-8250, 626-458-8148. 1961. Photos. avg. press run 4M-5M. Expects 2 titles 1999, 2 titles 2000. avg. price, cloth: $20-$59.95; paper: $9.95. Discounts: 40%. 265pp; 8½×11; of. Reporting time: 3 weeks. Payment: 10% royalties. Copyrights for author.

Golden West Historical Publications, Carol Tomas, Dir. of Publ.; Eric Rhinehart, PO Box 1906, Ventura, CA 93002. 1977. Articles. "Generally between 50-80 pages in length in monograph set - only real bias is for historical/politically scientific accurate analyses - revisionist historian Daniel Patrick Brown *The Protectorate and The Northumberland Conspiracy: Political Intrigue in the Reign of Edward VI (1547-1553)*; Daniel Patrick Brown's *The Tragedy of Libby & Andersonville Prison Camps*; & political analyst Bruce Jennings *The Brest-Litovsk Controversy* (an examination of the Russian surrender to Wilhelmine Germany in November-December, 1917), et al." avg. press run 3.5M-5M. Expects 2 titles 1999, 4 titles 2000. 4 titles listed in the *Small Press Record of Books in Print* (28th Edition, 1999-00). avg. price, paper: $7.65. Discounts: in multiples of ten, 10%, for classroom, college bookstore purchases (regardless of quantity) 30%. 65-90pp; 6×9; of. Reporting time: 2 months. Simultaneous submissions accepted: no. Publishes less than 10% of manuscripts submitted. Payment: due to the fact that this firm is principally an outgrowth of the Valley Historical Alliance, only 3% per book. Copyrights for author.

●**GoldenIsle Publishers, Inc.**, Tena Ryals, Laura Garrettson, RR 2, Box 560, Golden Isle Parkway, N., Eastman, GA 31023, 912-374-5806(9455). 1998. "Novels (hardcover) Writers: Don Johnson; Fern Smith-Brown; Jack P. Jones. Novels are 224 pages in length. Two nonfiction and three novels scheduled for publication in 1999." avg. press run 1M. Expects 5-8 titles 2000. 3 titles listed in the *Small Press Record of Books in Print* (28th Edition, 1999-00). avg. price, cloth: $21.95. Discounts: 10-55%. 224pp; 5½×8½. Reporting time: not accepting any at present, except by invitation. Payment: industry standard with profit sharing arrangement (not a vanity publisher). All publishing at publisher's expense. Copyrights for author. PMA.

Good Book Publishing Company, Dick B., PO Box 837, Kihei, HI 96753-0837, 808-874-4876; e-mail dickb@dickb.com. 1991. Non-fiction. "Publishing company formed to enable books to be written and published and sold to members of Alcoholics Anonymous, Twelve Step programs, recovery centers and workers, the religious community, historians, archivists, and scholars. Titles should relate to the Biblical and spiritual roots of A.A. and to the history of the basic ideas A.A. derived from the Bible and Christian sources. Exclusive distributor of Paradise Research Publications, Inc." avg. press run 3M. Pub'd 3 titles 1998; expects 5 titles 1999, 6 titles 2000. avg. price, paper: $18. Discounts: 20% individual, 40% volume. 400pp; 6×9; of. Reporting time: 1 week. Simultaneous submissions accepted: yes. Payment: 10%, no advance. Does not copyright for author. SPAN.

GOOD COOKING SERIES, Lifetime Books, Inc., Feinblum Brian, Editor-in-Chief, 2131 Hollywood Boulevard, Hollywood, FL 33020, 305-925-5242. 1943. Non-fiction. "We are the leading publisher of one-shot magazines in the United States. We have four categories in which we publish. These are diet and health, health, cookbook series and financial planning series. We are looking for full manuscripts that would lend themselves to these areas." circ. 50M. 8/yr. Pub'd 8 issues 1998; expects 8 issues 1999, 8 issues 2000. price per copy: $2.95. Back issues: cover price. 128pp; 5-3/16×7⅝; of. Reporting time: 3 months. Payment: negotiated. Copyrighted, reverts to author. Ads: $2,000. PBAA, ACIDA.

Good Gay Poets Press (see also FAG RAG), Good Gay Poets Collective, Box 277, Astor Station, Boston, MA 02123. 1973. Poetry. "Unsolicited ms. not requested." avg. press run 500. Pub'd 1 title 1998; expects 1 title 1999. 9 titles listed in the *Small Press Record of Books in Print* (28th Edition, 1999-00). avg. price, cloth: $15; paper: $3-$5; other: $3-$5. Discounts: 40% to retailers, 50% to distributors. 64pp; 5½×8½; of. Payment: 10% of run to author; payment only after costs have been returned. Copyrights for author. CLMP.

Good Hope Enterprises, Inc. (see also THE AFRICAN HERALD), Dr. Richard O. Nwachukwu, PO Box 2394, Dallas, TX 75221, 214-823-7666; fax 214-823-7373. 1987. Non-fiction. "The company recently published *The Dark and Bright Continent: Africa in the Changing World, The Agony: The Untold Story of the Nigerian Society*." avg. press run 5M. Pub'd 1 title 1998; expects 2 titles 1999, 2 titles 2000. 2 titles listed in the *Small Press Record of Books in Print* (28th Edition, 1999-00). avg. price, cloth: $17.95; paper: $9.25. Discounts: 35% to 55%. 200pp; 5½x8½; of. Reporting time: 3 months. Payment: based on sales. Copyrights for author. Texas Publishers Association (TPA).

Good Karma Publications, Villa Interamericana Calle 7, G-9, San German, PR 00683, 787-892-2346; email Devashish@igc.org. 1 title listed in the *Small Press Record of Books in Print* (28th Edition, 1999-00).

Good Life Products, Inc./DBA Beauty Ed, Maria V. Vila, PO Box 170070, Hialeah, FL 33017-0070, 305-362-6998; fax 305-557-6123. 1986. Non-fiction. "We specialize in the field of Cosmetology. We publish books on haircutting, coloring and permanent waving. Also produce videotapes. We also publish in Spanish. Not accepting submissions at this time." avg. press run 5M. Pub'd 2 titles 1998; expects 2 titles 1999, 4 titles 2000. 7 titles listed in the *Small Press Record of Books in Print* (28th Edition, 1999-00). avg. price, paper: $16.95; other: $27.95. Discounts: 4-9 20%, 10-19 30%, 20-39 40%, 40+ 50%. 200pp; 8½x11; of. Copyrights for author. PMA.

Good Life Publications, 580 Washington Street #306, San Francisco, CA 94111. 25 titles listed in the *Small Press Record of Books in Print* (28th Edition, 1999-00).

Good Life Publishing, Luther McIntyre, PO Box 6925, Louisville, KY 40206, 502-491-6565; email lutherjr@msn.com. 1996. Non-fiction. avg. press run 3M. Pub'd 1 title 1998; expects 3 titles 1999, 3 titles 2000. 1 title listed in the *Small Press Record of Books in Print* (28th Edition, 1999-00). avg. price, paper: $5.95. Discounts: 20%-40%. 5½x8½. Reporting time: 3-6 months. Simultaneous submissions accepted: no. Payment: varies. Copyrights for author.

THE GOOD RED ROAD, The Turquoise Butterfly Press, Terri Andrews, Editor, PO Box 750, Athens, OH 45701. 1997. "A Native American - inspired, informative newsletter that acts as a direct link to the work, history, peoples, and plight of the Native American community. Subject matter includes: news and updates, natural healing, interviews, book reviews, social reform, editorials, and spiritual pieces. Tips: The publication is primarily written by Native Americans and read by Native Americans." 6/yr. Pub'd 6 issues 1998; expects 6 issues 1999, 6 issues 2000. sub. price: $24; per copy: $4; sample: $4. 12pp. Simultaneous submissions accepted: yes. Payment: in copies. Copyrighted. Pub's reviews. Ads: available.

Good Times Publishing Co., Dorothy Miller, 2211 West 2nd Avenue #209, Vancouver, B.C. V6K 1H8, Canada, 604-736-1045. 1989. Non-fiction. "Most recent publication: *Food For Success,* by Dr. Barbarah Tinskamper. At present we limit ourselves to self-help books only. In particular, nutrition and psychology. The author should have a university education of a reputable institution and have several years of experience in the field that he/she is writing about. The book should be geared to the general public; the style and format should be easy and fun to read." avg. press run 5M. Pub'd 3 titles 1998; expects 1 title 1999, 2 titles 2000. avg. price, paper: $8.95. Discounts: 55% wholesale, 40% bookstores. 140pp; 5½x8½; of. Reporting time: 2 months. Payment: 2-4%. Copyrights for author. PMA.

Goodheart-Willcox Publisher, 18604 W. Creek Drive, Tinley Park, IL 60477-6243. 1921. Art, photos, interviews, reviews, non-fiction. Pub'd 30 titles 1998; expects 30 titles 1999, 30 titles 2000. 33 titles listed in the *Small Press Record of Books in Print* (28th Edition, 1999-00). avg. price, cloth: $35. Discounts: trade and school. 400pp; 8½x11; of. Reporting time: 1 month to 1 year. Simultaneous submissions accepted: yes. Payment: 10% net sales. Copyrights for author.

Teri Gordon, Publisher, Teri Gordon, 10901 Rustic Manor Lane, Austin, TX 78750-1133, 512-258-8309. 1987. Non-fiction. avg. press run 2M. 2 titles listed in the *Small Press Record of Books in Print* (28th Edition, 1999-00). avg. price, paper: $5.95. Discounts: 10-99 copies 40%, 100+ 50%. 128pp; 8½x11, 4½x6½; Word Processor and Printing Press. Reporting time: 1 month. Simultaneous submissions accepted: no. Payment: individually arranged. Does not copyright for author. Austin Writers' League.

GORHAM, Axios Newletter, Inc., David Gorham, 30-32 Macaw Avenue, PO Box 279, Belmopan, Belize, 501-8-23284. 1981. Poetry, articles, art, photos, interviews, reviews, letters, parts-of-novels, news items, non-fiction. "A continuing journal of genealogy and history of all the various branches of the Gorham family. Need historical articles, on places named after the Gorhams, obscure Gorham pioneers, how to trace your ancestors, interviews of well-known persons involved in genealogy; new products about innovations in capturing, storing, indexing and retrieving data-personal opinion (must be in-depth and scholarly dealing with the Gorham genealogy and history); *Profiles of Present Day Gorham's."* circ. 3M. 4/yr. Pub'd 4 issues 1998; expects 4 issues 1999. sub. price: $15; per copy: $2; sample: $2. Back issues: $2. Discounts: 40%, write for further information. 24pp; 8½x11; †of. Reporting time: 6-8 weeks. Payment: $10 to $100 depending on article (sometimes 2¢ a word). Copyrighted, reverts to author. Pub's reviews: 25 in 1998. §Genealogy and history. Ads: $320/$175/30¢.

Gothic Press, Gary William Crawford, Steve Eng, 4998 Perkins Road, Baton Rouge, LA 70808-3043, 504-766-2906. 1979. Poetry, fiction, art, criticism. "We publish mainly horror and dark fantasy fiction, criticism, and poetry.'' avg. press run 150. Pub'd 1 title 1998; expects 2 titles 1999, 2 titles 2000. 2 titles listed in the *Small Press Record of Books in Print* (28th Edition, 1999-00). avg. price, paper: $6. Discounts: 40%. 20pp; 5½x8½; of. Reporting time: 1 month. Simultaneous submissions accepted: no. Payment: 10%. Copyrights for author.

GOTHIX, Landwaster Books, Astor Gravelle, Ron Gravelle, PO Box 3223, Frederick, MD 21705-3223, 301-682-7604; fax 301-682-9737. 1999. Articles, photos, cartoons, interviews, criticism, news items, non-fiction. "A personal zine from goth-Asatro Griswold.'' circ. 1M. 2/yr. sub. price: $12; per copy: $3; sample: $3. Discounts: 50% off cover price. 24-30pp; 8½x11; †digital printing. Reporting time: 3 months. Simultaneous submissions accepted, for review. Publishes 1% of manuscripts submitted. Copyrighted, reverts to author. Pub's reviews: none, company is relocating, moved to Maryland in 1998. §music, asatro, gothic, zines, anarchy, destruction, humor. Ads: $25/$12.50.

GOTTA WRITE NETWORK LITMAG, Denise Fleischer, 515 East Thacker Street, Hoffman Estates, IL 60194-1957, FAX 847-296-7631; e-mail Netera@aol.com. 1988. Poetry, fiction, articles, art, photos, cartoons, interviews, reviews, letters. "Fiction up to 11 typeset pages. Poetry up to 1 page, 5 max per batch. Articles, up to 3 double spaced pages. Very interested in Science Fiction/Fantasy material, poetry and fiction'' circ. 200. 2/yr. Pub'd 2 issues 1998; expects 2 issues 1999, 2 issues 2000. sub. price: $12.75; per copy: $5; sample: same. Back issues: $3.75. Discounts: only for contributors. 48-72pp; 8½x11; of. Reporting time: 2 months minimum. Simultaneous submissions accepted: no. Publishes 25% of manuscripts submitted. Payment: $10 short stories, $5 by-mail interviews. Copyrighted, reverts to author. Pub's reviews: 2-5 per issue in 1998. §Prefer a news release and book jacket print with book. Ads: $25inner page, $50 back cover/$15/$15 per 150 inserted flyers.

Bruce Gould Publications, Bruce Gould, PO Box 16, Seattle, WA 98111. 1976. Non-fiction. "Publish books in the field of finance (business, stock and commodity markets).'' avg. press run 10M. Expects 2 titles 1999. 12 titles listed in the *Small Press Record of Books in Print* (28th Edition, 1999-00). avg. price, cloth: $10.95; paper: $7.95. Discounts: 40% to bookstores, 55% to wholesalers. 200pp; 6x8½; †lp. Reporting time: 30 days. Payment: 10-20%. Copyrights for author.

Grade School Press, J. Lastman, L. Cohen, 3266 Yonge Street #1829, Toronto, Ontario M4N 3P6, Canada, 416-784-2883; FAX 416-784-3580. 1989. Fiction, articles, reviews, non-fiction. "Focus: Education 'self-help' books for parents/teachers, directory & curriculum guides and training manuals, children/parenting.'' avg. press run 5M-7M. Expects 4-6 titles 1999, 6-8 titles 2000. 3 titles listed in the *Small Press Record of Books in Print* (28th Edition, 1999-00). avg. price, paper: $14.95-$19.95; other: $65 reference (looseleaf) updating publication. Discounts: 40% bookstores, bulk (10+ copies same book) to individuals. 120-150pp; 5½x8½, 8½x11; of, desktop & pasteup. Reporting time: 2-4 months. Payment: individual arrangements. Copyrights for author. Association of Canadian Publishers (ACP).

GRAFFITI OFF THE ASYLUM WALLS, BrYan Westbrook, 1002 Gunnison Street #A, Sealy, TX 77474-3725. 1991. Poetry, fiction, articles, art, photos, cartoons, interviews, satire, collages, plays. "Writers must submit a personal bio in a cover letter. I do not read submissions from any writers who spell my name wrong. I hate with a passin sonnets and all stuffy poetry. I want the stuff you are afraid to show your mother, priest, and/or shrink. Some recent contributors include Belinda Subraman, Scott Holstad, Cheryl Townsend, Robert Nagler, and Allen Renfro.'' circ. varies. Published whenever I have enough material. Pub'd 1 issue 1998; expects 2 issues 1999, 2-4 issues 2000. sub. price: $10/4 issues; per copy: $3; sample: $3. Back issues: none. Discounts: none. 20pp; 8½x5½; †of. Reporting time: whenever I have time. Simultaneous submissions accepted: yes. Publishes an unknown % of manuscripts submitted. Payment: none, contributors get $2/copy discount price. Copyrighted, reverts to author. Pub's reviews. §Anything unusual or out of the mainstream, especially idependent CD's and albums. Ads: we're willing to trade ads with other small presses.

GRAIN, Saskatchewan Writers Guild, Elizabeth Philips, Editor; Dianne Warren, Fiction; Sean Virgo, Box 1154, Regina, Sask. S4P 3B4, Canada, 306-244-2828, e-mail grain.mag@sk.sympatico.ca. 1973. Poetry, fiction, art, parts-of-novels, long-poems, plays. "No e-mail submissions; queries only. We publish only the best literary art. Length—flexible, though submissions preferably should not be more than 8 pages of poetry and 30 pages of prose or drama. Fiction and poetry are the main focus but we also consider creative non-fiction, songs, and produced one-act plays or excerpts from produced full-length plays.'' circ. 1M. 4/yr. Pub'd 4 issues 1998; expects 4 issues 1999, 4 issues 2000. sub. price: $26.95; USA $26.95 + $4 p/h; foreign $26.95 + $6 p/h; per copy: $7.95; sample: $7.95. Back issues: $5. Discounts: 25% for CPPA subscriptions. 6x9; of. Reporting time: 3 months. Simultaneous submissions accepted: no. Payment: $30-$100 poems, $30-$100 fiction, $30 visual art, $100 cover art. Copyrighted, reverts to author. Ads: $350/$200 ODN funds. CPPA.

Grand River Press, Michael Maran, PO Box 1342, East Lansing, MI 48826, (517) 332-8181. 1986. Non-fiction. "We specialize in legal self-help publications for use in Michigan.'' avg. press run 1.5M. Pub'd 2 titles 1998; expects 2 titles 1999, 2 titles 2000. 4 titles listed in the *Small Press Record of Books in Print* (28th Edition, 1999-00). avg. price, paper: $25. Discounts: 40% trade. 200pp; 8½x11; of. Reporting time: 3 months.

Simultaneous submissions accepted: yes. Publishes 10% of manuscripts submitted. Payment: negotiable. Copyrights for author.

Grand Slam Press, Inc., 2 Churchill Road, Englewood Cliffs, NJ 07632, 201-541-9181; FAX 201-894-8036. 1995. Non-fiction. "Not accepting manuscripts at this time." avg. press run 3M. Pub'd 1 title 1998; expects 3 titles 1999. 1 title listed in the *Small Press Record of Books in Print* (28th Edition, 1999-00). avg. price, paper: $12.95. Discounts: bookstores 2-4 books 20%, 5-99 40%, 100+ 50%; wholesalers 25-49 50%, 50-99 52%, 100-999 55%, 1000+ 57%; schools and libraries 20% on orders of 5 or more. 168pp; 6×9.

GRAND STREET, Jean Stein, Editor; Deborah Treisman, Managing Editor; Tam Miller, 214 Sullivan Street #6C, New York, NY 10012, 212-533-2944. 1981. Poetry, fiction, articles, art, photos, interviews, criticism, music, parts-of-novels, long-poems, plays, non-fiction. "No writers' guidelines. Our magazine does not accept unsolicited fiction or nonfiction material, only poetry" circ. 4M. 4/yr. Pub'd 4 issues 1998; expects 4 issues 1999, 4 issues 2000. sub. price: $40 individual, $50 institutions, $55 foreign; per copy: $12.95; sample: $15 all issues after grand sheet #52. Back issues: $12 (includes postage) issues #36-51 are $12. Discounts: on request. 256pp; 7×9; of. Reporting time: 6-10 weeks. Payment: yes. Copyrighted, reverts to author. Ads: $450. CLMP.

GRANTA, Granta Publications Ltd, Ian Jack, 2-3 Hanover Yard, Noel Rd, London N1 8BE, England, 0171 704 9776, FAX: 0171 704 0474. 1979 (New Series). Fiction, articles, photos, interviews, satire, letters, parts-of-novels, non-fiction. "Additional address: 250 West 57th Street, Suite 1203, New York, NY 10107, (212) 246-1313. *Granta* is a mass-marketed paperback magazine co-published with Penguin Books, devoted to contemporary literature and political discussion. *Granta* publishes fiction, cultural and political journalism, and photography. Recent contributors include John Berger, George Steiner, Gabriel Garcia Marquez, Salman Rushdie, Russell Hoban, Milan Kundera, Mario Vargas Llosa, Nadine Gordimer, Richard Ford, Paul Theroux, Jeanette Winterson, Kazuo Ishiguro, and many others. There are no restrictions of length. *Granta* does not publish poetry. In the United States, *Granta* is published by Granta USA, Ltd., a joint company with the New York Review of Books, and distributed by Viking Penguin, Inc." circ. 100M. 4/yr. Pub'd 4 issues 1998; expects 4 issues 1999, 4 issues 2000. sub. price: £21.95 ($29.95); per copy: £7.99 (or $9.99); sample: £7.99 (or $9.99). Discounts: trade: 35%; bulk or classroom orders by arrangement (10% to 50% depending on order); agent 10%. 256pp; 5¾×8; of. Reporting time: 8-12 weeks. Payment: £75-£5,000 depending on length, topicality, etc. Copyrighted, reverts to author. Ads: £900/£500/special US rates available, display advertising only.

Granta Publications Ltd (see also GRANTA), Jack Ian, 2-3 Hanover Yard, Noel Rd, London N1 8BE, England, (071) 704 9776.

GRANULATED TUPPERWARE, Darin Johnson, 1420 NW Gilman Blvd., Suite 2400, Issaquah, WA 98027-7001. 1992. Fiction, articles, art, photos, cartoons, letters, parts-of-novels, news items, non-fiction. circ. 200. 4/yr. Pub'd 3 issues 1998; expects 4 issues 1999, 4 issues 2000. price per copy: $2. Back issues: $2 or trade for self-published magazine. Discounts: trades always welcome. 20-30pp; 5½×8½; †copy machine. Reporting time: varies. Publishes 5% of manuscripts submitted. Payment: none. Not copyrighted. Pub's reviews: 50 in 1998. §Fiction, travel, politics, illicit activities, anarchy, drugs, macrame, romance, music. Ads: none.

Grapevine Publications, Inc., Christopher M. Coffin, Managing Editor, PO Box 2449, Corvallis, OR 97339-2449, 503-754-0583; fax 503-754-6508. 1983. Fiction, photos, plays, non-fiction. avg. press run 3M-10M. Pub'd 4 titles 1998; expects 6 titles 1999, 4 titles 2000. 21 titles listed in the *Small Press Record of Books in Print* (28th Edition, 1999-00). avg. price, paper: $15. Discounts: for resale: 20-40% off (volume based); distributor discounts negotiable upon request and qualifications. 250pp; 6⅜×9; of. Reporting time: due to volume, we cannot reply unless interested. Publishes less than 1% of manuscripts submitted. Payment: 9% of net. Copyrights for author. Publishers Marketing Association (PMA), 2401 Pacific Coast Hwy, Ste. 206, Hermosa Beach, CA 90254.

GrapeVinePress, J. Qevinsanders Oji, PO Box 56057, Los Angeles, CA 90056, 213-980-3167. 1994. Poetry, fiction, photos, interviews, satire, criticism, letters, collages, concrete art, non-fiction. "Our focus is on material of the culture and sensibility of African Americans and the intersection of other racial and cultural (e.g., African/Native Americans) influences. Interested in work not readily accepted by the so-called mainstream; not fringe or marginal, but progressive and challenging. Human spirit celebrated here. Urban/Rural." avg. press run 1M-7.5M. Pub'd 1 title 1998; expects 1 title 1999, 3 titles 2000. avg. price, cloth: $18.95; paper: $10.95. Discounts: short 20%, 50% max. Pages vary; size varies; of. Reporting time: 3 months. Simultaneous submissions accepted: no. Payment: negotiable. Does not copyright for author.

G'RAPH, Henry Roll, 2419 Greensburg Pike, Pittsburgh, PA 15221. 1980. Articles, art, photos, cartoons, reviews, letters. circ. 70. 4/yr. Pub'd 4 issues 1998; expects 4 issues 1999, 4 issues 2000. sub. price: $5; per copy: $1; sample: $1. Back issues: $1. 8pp; 8½×11; †Mita copier. Reporting time: 1 month. Payment: copies. Copyrighted, reverts to author. Pub's reviews: 4 in 1998. §Cartoons, graphics, arts, book arts, visual arts, media.

225

GRASS ROOTS, Megg Miller, Mary Horsfall, PO Box 242, Euroa, Victoria 3666, Australia. 1973. Poetry, articles, photos, letters, non-fiction. "Similar to *Mother Earth News.*" circ. 25M. 6/yr. Pub'd 6 issues 1998; expects 6 issues 1999, 6 issues 2000. sub. price: $29.50, overseas $36.50; per copy: $4.75; sample: $2. Back issues: $4. 84pp; quarto; of. Reporting time: 3 months. Not copyrighted. Pub's reviews: 50 in 1998. §Alternatives, gardening, technology, horticulture, agriculture, craft, food, community, health, natural lifestyles, organics. Ads: $A575/$A310/30-40¢ per word. ABPA.

GRASSLANDS REVIEW, Laura B. Kennelly, PO Box 626, Berea, OH 44017. 1989. Poetry, fiction, photos. "Shorter pieces of fiction fare better. Editors' Prize Contest annually. In *FF5* #43 we are described as 'a litmag which consistently publishes an interesting mix of work, some good old-fashioned stories plus stuff from the more experimental (but still solid) edge.' Authors published include Jane Stuart, Cynthia Roth, Yvonne Jackson, Brett Weaver, William Freedman, and Catherine Jervey. Only material postmarked in October or March will be considered." circ. 300. 2/yr. Pub'd 2 issues 1998; expects 2 issues 1999, 2 issues 2000. sub. price: $10 individual, $20 libraries; per copy: $6 (recent); sample: $4. Discounts: none. 80pp; 6×8; †pagemaker plus xerox. Reporting time: can be as long as 3 months, depends due to limited reading period. Simultaneous submissions accepted: no. Publishes 10% of manuscripts submitted. Payment: 1 copy with special rate for extra copies. Copyrighted, reverts to author.

GRASSROOTS FUNDRAISING JOURNAL, Chardon Press, Kim Klein, Publisher; Stephanie Roth, Publisher; Nancy Adess, Editor, 3781 Broadway, Oakland, CA 94611, 510-596-8160; Fax 510-596-8822; chardon@chardonpress.com; www.chardonpress.com. 1981. Articles, non-fiction. "Left wing, grassroots fundraising for social justice causes. Contributors: Kim Klein, Gary Delgado, Stephanie Roth." circ. 3M. 6/yr. Pub'd 6 issues 1998; expects 6 issues 1999, 6 issues 2000. sub. price: $32; per copy: $5; sample: free. Back issues: none. Discounts: 40% for 5+ subs ordered at one time, discounts for bulk back issues. 16pp; 8½×11; web. Reporting time: 2 months. Simultaneous submissions accepted: yes. Publishes 20% of manuscripts submitted. Payment: $75. Copyrighted, reverts to author. Pub's reviews: 5 in 1998. §Fundraising, economics, organizational development. Ads: $400/$200/varies.

●**Gravity Presses, Inc. (see also NOW HERE NOWHERE),** Michael J. Barney, Paul Kingston, 27030 Havelock, Dearborn Heights, MI 48127, 313-563-4683; e-mail mikeb5000@yahoo.com. 1998. Poetry. avg. press run 250. Expects 3 titles 1999, 4 titles 2000. avg. price, paper: $5. Discounts: negotiable. 48pp; †laser print. Reporting time: 3-6 months. Simultaneous submissions accepted: yes. Payment: of the 250 copies the author gets 200, we get 50 to sell. Does not copyright for author.

GRAY AREAS, Netta Gilboa, PO Box 808, Broomall, PA 19008. 1991. Articles, photos, cartoons, interviews, reviews, music, letters, news items, non-fiction. "*Gray Areas* is dedicated to examining the gray areas of life. We specialize in subject matter which is illegal, potentially illegal, immoral and/or controversial. Recent topics include: UFO's, adult films, drug testing, computer crimes, bootleg tapes, sampling, prank phone calls, etc. We also review books, movies, CDs, comics, concerts, magazines, catalogs, software, live video and audio tapes." circ. 10M. Irregular, 1-2/yr. Pub'd 1 issue 1998. sub. price: $23, $32 1st class for 4 issues when published; per copy: $6.95; sample: $8. Back issues: $8 while available. Discounts: wholesaler and retail store available. 164pp; 8⅛×10⅞; web. Reporting time: 1 month or less. Simultaneous submissions accepted if notified as such. Publishes 25% of manuscripts submitted. Payment: masthead listing, byline, copies. Copyrighted, rights reverting to author negotiable. Pub's reviews: 150+ per issue in 1998. §Virtually everything received—over 60 pages of reviews per issue. Ads: $600/$300/$150 1/4 page/$75 1/8 page $40.

Grayson Bernard Publishers, Inc., Carl B. Smith, PO Box 5247, Bloomington, IN 47407, 812-331-8182; 1-800-925-7853; FAX 812-331-2776. 1990. Non-fiction. "Additional address: PO Box 5247, Bloomington, IN, 47407. Materials to enhance learning in schools and in the home" avg. press run 5M. Pub'd 12 titles 1998; expects 8 titles 1999, 10 titles 2000. 29 titles listed in the *Small Press Record of Books in Print* (28th Edition, 1999-00). avg. price, paper: varies. 100-250pp; 6×9; of. Reporting time: 4-8 weeks. Payment: negotiable, usually royalty of 6-12% of money received. PMA.

Graywolf Press, Fiona McCrae, Publisher & Editorial Director, 2402 University Avenue #203, St. Paul, MN 55114, 651-641-0077; 651-641-0036. 1974. Poetry, fiction, criticism, long-poems, non-fiction. avg. press run 3.5M-15M. Pub'd 16 titles 1998; expects 16 titles 1999, 16 titles 2000. 121 titles listed in the *Small Press Record of Books in Print* (28th Edition, 1999-00). avg. price, cloth: $24.95; paper: $14. Discounts: 1-4, 20%, 5-24 42%, 25-50 42%, 25-99 43%, 100-249 44%, 250-499 45%, 500-749 46%, 750+ 47%. 100-300pp; size varies; of. Reporting time: 12 weeks. Simultaneous submissions accepted: yes. Publishes less than 1% of manuscripts submitted. Payment: negotiable. Copyrights for author.

●**THE GREAT BLUE BEACON,** Andy J. Byers, 1425 Patriot Drive, Melbourne, FL 32940, E-mail ajircc@juno.com. 1996. Poetry, fiction, articles, art, cartoons, reviews, news items, non-fiction. "Short — up to 500 words. Material is for assisting all writers of all genres and skill levels in improving their writing skills. Sal

Amica M. Buttaci, prize-winning poet and fiction author, is a frequent contributor.'' circ. 100+. 4/yr. Pub'd 4 issues 1998; expects 4 issues 1999, 4 issues 2000. sub. price: $10, $8 students; per copy: $4; sample: $1. 8pp; 8½×11. Reporting time: 2-3 weeks. Simultaneous submissions accepted: yes. Publishes 10% of manuscripts submitted. Payment: copies. Copyrighted, reverts to author. Pub's reviews: 6-8 in 1998. §Writing—all genres. Ads: none.

Great Elm Press, Walt Franklin, 1205 County Route 60, Rexville, NY 14877. 1984. avg. press run 300. Pub'd 5 titles 1998; expects 2 titles 1999, 2 titles 2000. 20 titles listed in the *Small Press Record of Books in Print* (28th Edition, 1999-00). avg. price, paper: $5. 40pp; 5½×8½. Reporting time: 1 week.

THE GREAT IDEA PATCH, S.P. Bragg, 110 Jeffery Street, Shelburne, ON L0N 1S4, Canada. 1990. Poetry, articles, reviews, non-fiction. ''How-to material of interest to women. Areas considered range from cooking tips to fixing your own lawn mower and everything in between. Article lengths up to 500 words. Please include IRC or SASE (Canadian postage, please) if you wish your material returned.'' circ. 500. 6/yr. Pub'd 6 issues 1998; expects 6 issues 1999, 6 issues 2000. sub. price: $15; per copy: $2.50; sample: $2.25. 10pp; 8½×11. Reporting time: 1-3 months. Simultaneous submissions accepted: yes. Payment: 1 copy. Copyrighted, reverts to author. Pub's reviews. §Anything that has moved you to any degree; if there is a good book out there, we want to know about it.

The Great Rift Press, Katherine Daly, 1135 East Bonneville, Pocatello, ID 83201, 208-232-6857, orders 800-585-6857, fax 208-233-0410. 1987. Non-fiction. avg. press run 3M. Pub'd 1 title 1998; expects 2 titles 1999, 2 titles 2000. 4 titles listed in the *Small Press Record of Books in Print* (28th Edition, 1999-00). avg. price, cloth: $29.95; paper: $17.75. Discounts: resalers 25%=1; 40%=2-10; 42%=11-20; additional 5% discount and FREE shipping on pre-paid orders of 2 or more. 288-352pp; size varies; of. Reporting time: 1 month. Simultaneous submissions accepted: yes. Payment: negotiable. Assn. of Outdoor Rrecreation & Education.

GREAT RIVER REVIEW, Robert Hedin, Richard Broderick, PO Box 406, Red Wing, MN 55066, Fax 612-388-2528; E-mail acis@pressenter.com. 1977. Poetry, fiction, articles. ''Poetry, fiction, essays, translations. Some authors recently published: C.L. Rawlins, Carolyn Servid, Philip Levine, Maggie Anderson, Linda Pastan, and Marvin Bell.'' circ. 500. 2/yr. Pub'd 2 issues 1998; expects 2 issues 1999, 2 issues 2000. sub. price: $14; per copy: $6; sample: $6. Back issues: $6. 120pp; 5½×7; of. Reporting time: 1-4 months. Publishes 5% of manuscripts submitted. Payment: copies. Copyrighted, reverts to author. Pub's reviews: 12 in 1998. §poetry, fiction, non-fiction, translations. No ads. CLMP.

Great Western Publishing Company, John M. Cali, Jr., John M. Cali III, PO Box 2355, Reston, VA 20195-0355. 1987. News items, non-fiction. avg. press run 2M+. Pub'd 3 titles 1998; expects 1-2 titles 1999, 4-5 titles 2000. 4 titles listed in the *Small Press Record of Books in Print* (28th Edition, 1999-00). avg. price, paper: $15. Discounts: 1-99 50%, 100+ 60%. 128-224pp; 5½×8½, 8½×11. PMA.

GREEN ANARCHIST, John Conner, BM 1715, London WC1N 3XX, United Kingdom. 1984. Articles, cartoons, interviews, reviews, music, letters, news items, non-fiction. ''No unsolicited poetry.'' circ. 3M. 4/yr. Pub'd 4 issues 1998; expects 4 issues 1999, 4 issues 2000. sub. price: £22; per copy: £1; sample: free. Back issues: 50p/issue. Discounts: 33% for s/r, streetsell is £5 for a bundle of 10, £20 four a 50-issue bulk order, no s/r. 24pp; 8×12 (A3); †printing. Reporting time: deadline approx. 1 month before publication. Publishes 75% of manuscripts submitted. Payment: none. Not copyrighted. Pub's reviews: 24 in 1998. §Green/anarchist, radical politics, animal liberation, environmental protest, parapolitics, conspiracy theories. Ads: £60/£30/6p per word for small ads.

Green Bean Press, Ian Griffin, PO Box 237, Canal Street Station, New York, NY 10013, phone/fax 718-302-1955; e-mail gbpress@earthlink.net. 1995. Poetry, fiction, articles, art, long-poems. ''Previously have published books by Joe R, A.D. Winans, Margaret Bazzell, R.L. Nichols.'' avg. press run Chapbooks 100-200, paperbacks 500-750. Pub'd 3 titles 1998; expects 4 titles 1999, 4 titles 2000. 10 titles listed in the *Small Press Record of Books in Print* (28th Edition, 1999-00). avg. price, paper: $12; other: $3. Discounts: 1 40%, 2-10 43%, 11-25 47%, 26+ 50%. 150pp; 6×9; of. Reporting time: 1 month. Simultaneous submissions accepted: no. Publishes 1% of manuscripts submitted. Payment: arrangements vary. Does not copyright for author.

Green Duck Press, 335 Pony Trail, Mount Shasta, CA 96067, 530-926-6261. 1995. Fiction. ''Not accepting manuscripts at this time'' Pub'd 1 title 1998; expects 2 titles 1999. 2 titles listed in the *Small Press Record of Books in Print* (28th Edition, 1999-00). avg. price, paper: $12.00. 224pp.

Green Eagle Press, Cyro Adler, Daniel Jewel, Nina Rapoport, Sales, Box 20329, Cathedral Station, New York, NY 10025, 212-663-2167; FAX 212-316-7650. 1973. Fiction, satire, non-fiction. ''Environment, history, stories. Not accepting submissions.'' avg. press run 7M. Pub'd 1 title 1998; expects 1 title 1999, 2 titles 2000. 13 titles listed in the *Small Press Record of Books in Print* (28th Edition, 1999-00). avg. price, cloth: $25; paper: $12.95. Discounts: yes. 250pp; 5×8½.

GREEN EGG, Oberon G'Zell, Publisher; Maerian Morris, Editor, 212 S. Main Street #22B, Willits, CA

95490-3535, 707-456-0332; Fax 707-456-0333; e-mail admin@greenegg.org. 1968. Poetry, fiction, articles, art, photos, cartoons, interviews, satire, criticism, reviews, letters, news items, non-fiction. *"Green Egg* is a magazine of Paganism (i.e. Nature worship) and Goddess religion. Eco-Feminism, Mythology, Folklore are continuing themes. Articles: 1,000-3,000 words; fiction 1,000-3,000 words; reviews to 300 words; others varied. Contributors include Merlin Stone, Marion Zimmer Bradley, Antero Alli, Robert Anton Wilson, Anodea Judith, Ralph Metzner, Nybor, Starhawk, Lone Wolf Circles, John Rowan, Jacques Vallee, and many others. Send SASE for contributor's guide.'' circ. 11M. 6/yr. Pub'd 6 issues 1998; expects 6 issues 1999, 6 issues 2000. sub. price: $28; per copy: $6.95; sample: $6 (includes p/h). Back issues: $5 each, incl. postage (#81-126). Discounts: 50% for distributors (over 100 copies); 40% for retailers (lots of 12). 76pp; 8½x11; Web of. Reporting time: 3 month. Publishes 10% of manuscripts submitted. Payment: copy, sometimes free ad space, cover art='About Artist' Copyrighted, reverts to author. Pub's reviews: 21 in 1998. §Fantasy, Paganism, science fiction, mythology, history, nature, goddesses, feminist, ecology, Wicca. Ads: $495/$250/$195 1/3 page/$110 1/4 page/$95 1/6 page/$55 bus.card $100/90¢ word classified. WPPA, IPA.

GREEN FUSE POETRY, Brian Boldt, 3365 Holland Drive, Santa Rosa, CA 95404, 707-544-8303. 1984. Poetry. ''Length: 70 lines or less. Biases: environmental, peace, and social justice concerns. Recent contributors: Donald Hall, Antler, John Brandi, Ruth Daigon, Elliot Richman, John Bradley'' circ. 700. 2/yr. Pub'd 2 issues 1998; expects 2 issues 1999, 2 issues 2000. sub. price: $11, $16/3 issues; per copy: $6; sample: $4. Back issues: $4. 64pp; 5½x8½; of. Reporting time: within 12 weeks. Simultaneous submissions accepted: no. Publishes 2% of manuscripts submitted. Payment: copies. Copyrighted, reverts to author. Ads: none.

THE GREEN HILLS LITERARY LANTERN, Jack Smith, Editor; Ken Reger, Editor, PO Box 375, Trenton, MO 64683, 660-359-3948 x324. 1990. Poetry, fiction. ''Short story: 5,000 words. Poems less than six lines and over two pages are unlikely to be published. Recent contributors: Fiction-Walter Cummins, Karl Harshbarger, Joan Connor, Mark SaFranko, Robert McBrearty; Poetry-Donald Levering, Anne-Marie Oomen, Yvette A. Schnoeker-Shorb, and Jim Thomas.'' circ. 500. 1/yr. Pub'd 1 issue 1998; expects 1 issue 1999, 1 issue 2000. sub. price: $7; per copy: $7; sample: $7. 200pp; 6x9; of. Reporting time: 3-4 months. Simultaneous submissions accepted: yes. Publishes 2% of manuscripts submitted. Payment: 2 complimentary copies. Copyrighted, reverts to author. Ads: $50/$25/.

The Green Hut Press, Janet Wullner Faiss, Publisher & Editor, 1015 Jardin Street East, Appleton, WI 54911, 414-734-9728. 1972. Poetry, fiction, art, interviews, non-fiction. ''We publish the writing and art work of the late German-American artist Fritz Faiss (1905-1981) *exclusively*. Limited editions. Mail order, except for a few selected bookstores. Inquiries welcome. SASE please. Prices range between $9 and, for a hand-colored-by-artist edition, $200.'' avg. press run 200. 6 titles listed in the *Small Press Record of Books in Print* (28th Edition, 1999-00). Discounts: libraries 10% postpaid when accompanied by cash payment. 75pp; size varies; †of.

GREEN MOUNTAINS REVIEW, Neil Shepard, General Editor & Poetry Editor; Tony Whedon, Fiction Editor, Johnson State College, Johnson, VT 05656, 802-635-1350. 1987. Poetry, fiction, articles, art, interviews, criticism, reviews, parts-of-novels, long-poems, non-fiction. circ. 1.7M. 2/yr. Pub'd 2 issues 1998; expects 2 issues 1999, 2 issues 2000. sub. price: $14; per copy: $8.50; sample: $5. Back issues: $5. Discounts: 40% off for store buyers. 192pp; 6x9; lp. Reporting time: 3 months (we read Sept. 1-March 1). Simultaneous submissions accepted: yes. Publishes 2% of manuscripts submitted. Payment: 1 copy + 1 year subscription. Copyrighted, reverts to author. Pub's reviews: 4 in 1998. §Poetry, fiction, creative non-fiction, literary essays, interviews, book reviews. Ads: $150/$75. CLMP.

GREEN PRINTS, ''The Weeder's Digest'', Pat Stone, PO Box 1355, Fairview, NC 28730, 704-628-1902. 1990. Poetry, fiction, articles, art, non-fiction. ''Shares the human, *not* the how-to, side of gardening through fine stories and art.'' circ. 10M. 4/yr. Pub'd 4 issues 1998; expects 4 issues 1999, 4 issues 2000. sub. price: $17.97; per copy: $4.50; sample: $4.50. Discounts: 1/2 price, min. order 6. 80pp; 6x9; of. Reporting time: 1-3 months. Simultaneous submissions accepted: yes. Publishes 10% of manuscripts submitted. Payment: $50-100. Copyrighted, reverts to author. Ads: $200/140/110 1/2 page.

Green River Writers, Inc./Grex Press, Mary E. O'Dell, 11906 Locust Road, Middletown, KY 40243, 502-245-4902. 1993. Poetry. ''Solicited manuscripts only.'' avg. press run 1M. Expects 2 titles 1999, 1 title 2000. 6 titles listed in the *Small Press Record of Books in Print* (28th Edition, 1999-00). avg. price, cloth: $18; paper: $11. Discounts: 40% to booksellers. 60pp. Payment: on individual basis.

Green Stone Publications, PO Box 15623, Seattle, WA 98115-0623, 206-524-4744. 1987. Fiction. avg. press run 2M. Pub'd 1 title 1998; expects 1 title 2000. 1 title listed in the *Small Press Record of Books in Print* (28th Edition, 1999-00). avg. price, paper: $11.95. Discounts: 2-4 20%, 5-9 30%, 10-24 40%, 25-49 42%, 50-74 44%, 75-99 46%, 100-199 48%, 200+ 50%. 280pp; 5½x8½; of. Northwest Assn. of Book Publishers, Book Publishers Northwest.

GREEN WORLD: News and Views For Gardening Who Care About The Earth, Cathy Czapla, 12 Dudley Street, Randolph, VT 05060-1202, E-mail: gx297@cleveland.freenet.edu. 1994. Poetry, articles, reviews,

228

letters, news items, non-fiction. "Positive personal essays preferred" circ. 200. 6/yr. Pub'd 5 issues 1998; expects 6 issues 1999, 6 issues 2000. sub. price: $15; per copy: $3; sample: $3. 40pp; 8½×11; off. Reporting time: immediate. Simultaneous submissions accepted: no. Publishes 10% of manuscripts submitted. Payment: 1 copy. Not copyrighted. Pub's reviews: 3 in 1998. §Gardening, natural history. GWAA (Garden Writers Assn).

Greencrest Press, Philippe R. Falkenberg, Box 7746, Winston-Salem, NC 27109, 919-722-6463. 1980. "We specialize in study skills." avg. press run 2M. Expects 1 title 1999. 1 title listed in the *Small Press Record of Books in Print* (28th Edition, 1999-00). avg. price, cloth: $19.50. Discounts: 1-5, 20%; 6-49, 40%; 50-99,41%; 100+ 42%, stop order-40%. of. Reporting time: 60 days. Payment: 10%.

The Greenfield Review Press/Ithaca House, Joseph Bruchac III, Editor; Carol Worthen Bruchac, Editor; James Bruchac, Assistant Director, PO Box 308, Greenfield Center, NY 12833-0308, 518-584-1728. 1970. Poetry. "Our main interests are Native American and Asian American poetry. *NO* unsolicited manuscripts." avg. press run 2M. Pub'd 2 titles 1998; expects 4 titles 1999, 4 titles 2000. 145 titles listed in the *Small Press Record of Books in Print* (28th Edition, 1999-00). avg. price, paper: $9.95 single author, $13.95 anthologies. Discounts: trade: 1-5 copies, 25%; 5 or more copies, 40%; distributed to the trade by Talman Co. 80pp single author, anthologies 300pp; 5½×8½; of. Payment: 2% of press run, $250 advance on royalties of 10% retail price on each copy sold. Copyrights for author. CLMP.

Greenhouse Review Press, Gary Young, 3965 Bonny Doon Road, Santa Cruz, CA 95060, 831-426-4355. 1975. Poetry, parts-of-novels, long-poems. "Greenhouse Review Press publishes a chapbook and broadside series. We are interested in manuscripts of up to 20 pages. Titles: *The Fugitive Vowels* by D.J. Waldie; *The Dreams of Mercurius* by John Hall; *House Fires* by Peter Wild; *Thirteen Ways of Deranging An Angel* by Stephen Kessler; *Looking Up* by Christopher Budkley; *Any Minute* by Laurel Blossom; *Yes* by Timothy Sheehan; *By Me, By Any, Can and Can't Be Done* by Killarney Clary; *Begin, Distance* by Sherod Santos; *Jack the Ripper* by John Hall, *Unselected Poems* by Philip Levine." avg. press run varies. Pub'd 3 titles 1998; expects 4 titles 1999. 56 titles listed in the *Small Press Record of Books in Print* (28th Edition, 1999-00). avg. price, cloth: $50; paper: $20; other: $75 broadside. Discounts: 30% to bookstores. Pages vary; size varies; †lp. Reporting time: 4 weeks. Payment: copies. Copyrights for author.

Greenlawn Press, Dan DeCelles, Publisher; Tom Noe, Editor, 107 S. Greenlawn Avenue, South Bend, IN 46617, 219-234-5088, fax 219-236-6633, e-Mail Greenlanw@aol.com. 1982. Non-fiction. "We are a Christian publisher. Our primary sales come from charismatic Catholics, Pentecostal/charismatic Christians from other churches. We carry devotional/inspirational books of a general Christian nature, others primarily for Catholics. Books have been in the range of 100-150 pages. Publishing began under the auspices of a distributor of religious books and goods (Charismatic Renewal Services) in 1982. We published our first title with the Greenlawn Press imprint in 1985. We may also carry books of Christian-oriented political commentary and analysis." avg. press run 3M-5M. Pub'd 3 titles 1998; expects 2 titles 1999, 3 titles 2000. 21 titles listed in the *Small Press Record of Books in Print* (28th Edition, 1999-00). avg. price, paper: $5.95-11.95; other: $2.50 pamphlets-saddle stitched. Discounts: trade 30% on orders of $25 or more; wholesalers 25%, $25-$149 40%, $150+ 42%. 100-150pp; 5½×8½; of. Reporting time: variable. Simultaneous submissions accepted: yes. Publishes 20% of manuscripts submitted. Payment: negotiable, variable. Only copyright by specific arrangement. Catholic Book Publishers Association.

GREEN'S MAGAZINE, David Green, Box 3236, Regina, Saskatchewan S4P 3H1, Canada. 1972. Poetry, fiction. "Non-Canadian mss. must be accompanied by International Reply Coupons. Stories to approx 3,500 words, poems to 40 lines. Want deep characterization in complex conflicts. Prefer to avoid profanity, explicit sexuality. Recents: Robert H. Redding, Norma West Linder, Ruth Wildes Schuler. Prefer originals. (ISSN 0824-2992)." circ. 300. 4/yr. Pub'd 4 issues 1998; expects 4 issues 1999. sub. price: $15; per copy: $5; sample: $5. Discounts: negotiable. 96pp; 5¼×8½; †of. Reporting time: 8 weeks. Simultaneous submissions accepted: no. Publishes 25-35% of manuscripts submitted. Payment: copies. Copyrighted, reverts to author. Pub's reviews: 4 in 1998. §General. Ads: $100/$60.

THE GREENSBORO REVIEW, Jim Clark, Editor, PO Box 26170, Dept. of English, Univ. of North Carolina-Greensboro, Greensboro, NC 27402-6170, 336-334-5459; fax 336-334-3281; e-mail jlclark@uncg.edu. 1966. Poetry, fiction. "We like to see the best being written regardless of subject, style or theme. We publish new talent beside established writers, depending on quality. No restrictions on length of poetry; short stories should be 7,500 words or less. Recent contributors include Manette Ansay, Peter Ho Davies, Judith Slater, Dale Ray Phillips, Robert Olmstead, Lane von Herzen, Jill McCorkle, Brendan Galvin, Jessee Lee Kercheval. Submissions accepted between August 15 and February 15 (deadlines for the two issues: September 15 and February 15 each year). Literary Awards guidelines for SASE. SASE with mss. Stories anthologized in editions of *The Best American Short Stories, Prize Stories: The O. Henry Awards*, *The Pushcart Prize*, *Best of the West*, and in *New Stories from the South*." circ. 800. 2/yr. Pub'd 2 issues 1998; expects 2 issues 1999, 2 issues 2000. sub. price: $10; per copy: $5; sample: $5. Back issues: $1.50-$4/according to price on cover. Discounts: none. 128pp; 6×9; desk-top. Reporting time: 2-4 months. Simultaneous submissions

229

accepted: no. Publishes 1.6% of manuscripts submitted. Payment: 3 copies. Copyrighted, rights revert to author upon request. CELJ, CLMP.

Greensleeve Editions (see also URBAN GRAFFITI), Mark McCawley, PO Box 41164, Edmonton, AB T6J 6M7, Canada. 1988. Poetry, fiction. "Chapbook length books. Recent contributors: Daniel Jones, Stephen Morrissey, Carolyn Zonailo, Beth Jankola." avg. press run 250. Pub'd 2 titles 1998; expects 1 title 1999, 2 titles 2000. avg. price, other: $4.95. Discounts: none. 24pp; 5½×8½; desktop publishing. Reporting time: 6-8 weeks. Simultaneous submissions accepted: no. Publishes 5% of manuscripts submitted. Payment: 15% of copy run paid in copies. Copyrights for author.

Greeson & Boyle, Inc. (see also YOUR LIFE MATTERS), Janet Greeson, Eugene Boyle, 8058 Pinnacle Peak Avenue, Las Vegas, NV 89113, 702-222-1988. 1993. Articles, photos, interviews, reviews, letters, news items, non-fiction. avg. press run 1M. Pub'd 3 titles 1998; expects 5 titles 1999, 10 titles 2000. 2 titles listed in the *Small Press Record of Books in Print* (28th Edition, 1999-00). avg. price, cloth: $19.95; paper: $5.95. mi. Reporting time: 3 months. Copyrights for author. ABA, Audio Publishers Association.

●**Griffon House Publications**, Anne Paocucci, Jack Ryan, 1401 Pennsylvania Avenue, Suite 105, Wilmington, DE 19806, 302-656-3230. 1974. Poetry, fiction, criticism, reviews, plays, non-fiction. avg. press run 1.5M-2M. Pub'd 3 titles 1998; expects 2 titles 1999, 3 titles 2000. avg. price, cloth: $27.95; paper: $16.95. Discounts: 1 copy 10%; 2-5 20%; 11-25 30%; 26+ 35%; student 30%. 6×9; of, letterpress. Payment: copies. Copyrights for author.

The Groundwater Press, Rosanne Wasserman, PO Box 704, Hudson, NY 12534, 516-767-8503. 1974. Poetry. "We're a nonprofit press, dependent upon grants. No unsolicited material returned without SASE. We contact our own authors 99% of the time. Last titles: *Common Preludes* by Edward Barrett; *Double Time* by Star Black; *Every Question But One* by Pierre Mantory, translation by John Ashbery; *Mecox Road* by Marc Cohen; *The History of Rain* by Tomoyuki Iino." avg. press run 500. Pub'd 2 titles 1998; expects 1-2 titles 1999, 1-2 titles 2000. 9 titles listed in the *Small Press Record of Books in Print* (28th Edition, 1999-00). avg. price, paper: $10. Discounts: 60/40, 50/50 wholesalers. 32-80pp; 5½×8½, 6×9; of, laser. Reporting time: 1 year. Simultaneous submissions accepted: no. Publishes 1% of manuscripts submitted. Payment: varies according to grants and donations. Copyrights for author.

THE GROVE, Naturist Foundation, Editorial Committee, Naturist Headquarters, Orpington, BR5 4ET, England, 01689-871200. 1950. Articles, photos, cartoons, letters, news items, non-fiction. "House Journal of Naturist Foundation & Sun Societies, circulating internationally to naturists. Contributions on subjects of interest to naturists welcome—with or without illustrations. But no payment offered!" circ. 800. 3/yr. Pub'd 3 issues 1998; expects 3 issues 1999, 3 issues 2000. sub. price: £10 ($20); per copy: £3-50 ($7); sample: £3-50 ($7). Back issues: $5. 24pp; 9½×7½; lp. Payment: none. Copyrighted. Pub's reviews: 3 in 1998. §Naturism, outdoor recreation. Ads: £80 ($160)/£40 ($80).

THE GROWING EDGE MAGAZINE, Tom Alexander, PO Box 1027, Corvallis, OR 97339, 541-757-0027; FAX 541-757-0028. 1980. "Indoor and outdoor gardening for today's high-tech grower. Covers hydroponics, controlled environments, drip irrigation, organic gardening, water conservation and more" circ. 20M. 6/yr. Pub'd 4 issues 1998; expects 6 issues 1999, 6 issues 2000. sub. price: $37.95 1st class mail; $26.95 3rd class mail; per copy: $4.95 + $1.50 p/h; sample: $4.95 + $1.50 p/h. Back issues: same. 96pp; 8½×11; prepress-electronic/offset web printing. Reporting time: 2 months. Simultaneous submissions accepted: yes. Publishes 50% of manuscripts submitted. Payment: 20¢ per word/photos negotiable. Copyrighted, rights revert to publisher (1st and reprint). Pub's reviews: 16-20 in 1998. §horticulture and gardening. PMA, Small Press.

GROWING FOR MARKET, Lynn Byczynski, PO Box 3747, Lawrence, KS 66046, 785-748-0605; 800-307-8949. 1992. Articles. "*Growing for Market* is a practical, hands-on journal for farmers who direct-market produce and flowers. Therefore, writers must be knowledeable about growing on a commercial scale" circ. 3M. 12/yr. Pub'd 12 issues 1998; expects 12 issues 1999, 12 issues 2000. sub. price: $27; per copy: $3; sample: $3. 20pp; 8½×11; of. Reporting time: 6 months. Simultaneous submissions accepted: no. Publishes 75% of manuscripts submitted. Payment: $75/printed page, $200 maximum. Copyrighted, reverts to author. Pub's reviews: 12 in 1998. §Small-scale farming, flower gardening, herbs, dried flowers. Ads: $400/$240/$68 1/3 page/$120 1/4 page/$90 1/6 page.

Growing Room Collective (see also ROOM OF ONE'S OWN), Box 46160, Station D, Vancouver BC V6J 5G5, Canada. 1975. Poetry, fiction, art, photos, cartoons, interviews, criticism, reviews, parts-of-novels, long-poems, plays. "Good quality literary material by & about women, written from a feminist perspective." avg. press run 1M. Expects 4 titles 1999. avg. price, paper: $7. Discounts: 30% retail, trade; bulk negotiable; agent 15% off institutional orders only. 128pp; 5½×8½; of. Reporting time: 6 months. Publishes 8% of manuscripts submitted. Payment: $25 upon publication. Copyrights for author. CMPA.

GROWING WITHOUT SCHOOLING, Susannah Sheffer, 2380 Massachusetts Ave., Suite #104,

Cambridge, MA 02140-1884, 617-864-3100. 1977. Articles, interviews, reviews, news items, non-fiction. "Articles and stories about home education and learning outside or without schools." circ. 15M. 6/yr. Pub'd 6 issues 1998; expects 6 issues 1999, 6 issues 2000. sub. price: $25; per copy: $6; sample: $3. Back issues: $150 set of all back issues (110 issues). Discounts: standard on quantities over 10. 32pp; 8½×11; of. Reporting time: 2 months (we generally don't report—just print when we can). Payment: none. Copyrighted, reverts to author. Pub's reviews: 40-60 in 1998. §Education, parenting, community. Ads: $700/$350/write for rates. SPAN, PMA.

GRUE MAGAZINE, Peggy Nadramia, Hell's Kitchen Productions, PO Box 370, Times Square Station, New York, NY 10108, e-mail nadramia@panix.com. 1985. Poetry, fiction, art, criticism, long-poems. "5000 word maximum for fiction; no minimum length. We're seeking something different in the way of horror, new, experimental, rude, disturbing. We have no taboos or restrictions; send us your hard-to-place stuff, what editors may have told you is too 'weird' or 'explicit', as long as it's horror. No sword and sorcery or SF. Recent contributors include Ramsey Campbell, Jessica Amanda Salmonson, Steve Rasnic Tem, Joseph Payne Brennan, Joe R. Lansdale, t. Winter-Damon, Don Webb, G. Sutton Breiding" circ. 3M. 1/yr. Pub'd 1 issue 1998; expects 1 issue 1999, 1 issue 2000. sub. price: $14; per copy: $5; sample: $5. Discounts: negotiable. 96pp; 5½×8½; of. Reporting time: 3-6 months from receiving mss. Simultaneous submissions accepted: yes. Publishes 2% of manuscripts submitted. Payment: 2 copies plus 1/2¢ per word for fiction, upon publication, $5 per poem. Copyrighted, reverts to author. Ads: $50/$35/$25 per 1/4 page. Horror Writers Association.

Gryphon House, Inc., Larry Rood, PO Box 207, Beltsville, MD 20704-0207, 301-595-9500. 1971. Non-fiction. "We publish books of activities for use by pre-school teachers and parents" avg. press run 7M. Pub'd 7 titles 1998; expects 8 titles 1999, 8 titles 2000. 66 titles listed in the *Small Press Record of Books in Print* (28th Edition, 1999-00). avg. price, paper: $19.95. Discounts: available upon request. 256pp; 8½×11; of. Reporting time: 3 weeks. Simultaneous submissions accepted: no. Publishes 5% of manuscripts submitted. Payment: 8-10-12.5% on net sales. Copyrights for author. PMA.

Gryphon Publications (see also HARDBOILED; PAPERBACK PARADE), Gary Lovisi, PO Box 209, Brooklyn, NY 11228. 1983. Fiction, articles, art, interviews, satire, criticism, reviews, parts-of-novels, non-fiction. "A small press publisher that (in addition to publishing the magazines *Hardboiled* and *Paperback Parade*) publish numerous books on a variety of subjects dealing with paperback collecting, pulp magazines, detective fiction, science fiction, and fantasy, Sherlock Holmes—in fiction and non-fiction. Please Note: *Do not send mss*, on anything over 3,000 words-*send only* query letter about the story/novel, *with SASE*. Material received without SASE will not be returned. Writers can send letter with SASE for guidelines" avg. press run 500-1M. Pub'd 5 titles 1998; expects 4 titles 1999, 5 titles 2000. 3 titles listed in the *Small Press Record of Books in Print* (28th Edition, 1999-00). avg. price, cloth: $29.95; paper: $15. Discounts: 40% on 5 or more of the same item/issue ordered. 50-200pp; 5×8; of. Reporting time: 3-6 weeks. Query first before sending simultaneous submissions. Publishes 5% of manuscripts submitted. Payment: varies. Copyrights for author.

GUARD THE NORTH, Les Recherches Daniel Say Cie., Daniel Say, PO Box 3355, Vancouver, B.C. V6B 3Y3, Canada. 1971. Letters. "500 to 3000 word light writing of science, writing, SF, fantasy etc." circ. 300. 8/yr. Pub'd 8 issues 1998; expects 8 issues 1999, 8 issues 2000. sub. price: $4; per copy: $.50; sample: $.25. 20pp; 21×28cm; †mi. Reporting time: 1 month. Payment: copies. Copyrighted. Pub's reviews: 100 in 1998. §Science or science fiction.

Guardian Press, Richard W. Eaves, 10924 Grant Road #225, Houston, TX 77070, 713-955-9855. 1991. Fiction, non-fiction. "Manuscripts from 100 to 200 pages. Need good fiction and non-fiction pertaining to crime prevention, personal safety, health and fitness and natural healing. We also are seeking high quality children's book manuscripts, both fiction and non-fiction." avg. press run 5M. Pub'd 2 titles 1998; expects 3 titles 1999, 3 titles 2000. 6 titles listed in the *Small Press Record of Books in Print* (28th Edition, 1999-00). avg. price, paper: $4.95. Discounts: 25% to 55%. 122pp; 4¼×6½; of. Reporting time: 90 days. Payment: 10%-15% of wholesale; no cash advances. Does not copyright for author.

Guarionex Press Ltd., William E. Zimmerman, Chief Editor & Publisher, 201 West 77th Street, New York, NY 10024, 212-724-5259. 1979. Non-fiction. "The goal of *Guarionex Press* is to publish books that help people articulate their thoughts and feelings. Our books affirm the power of the human spirit and imagination to overcome life's problems. Our first book is *How to Tape Instant Oral Biographies*. The book teaches youngsters and grownups how to interview family members and friends and use the tape or video recorder to capture their life stories, memories and traditions on tape. Great family, school and vacation activity. Its second book is a new form of diary/journal called *A Book of Questions to Keep Thoughts and Feelings*; it helps people keep a diary. The third book is *Make Beliefs*, a gift book to spark the imagination. A new activity both for youngsters and adults. Our fourth is *Lifelines*; a book of hope to get you through the tough times of life." avg. press run 5M. Expects 1-2 titles 1999, 1-2 titles 2000. 4 titles listed in the *Small Press Record of Books in Print* (28th Edition, 1999-00). avg. price, paper: $6.95. Discounts: 10-50% depending on volume. 112pp; 4⅛×7⅛; of, lp. Reporting time: 3 months. Payment: fair arrangement negotiable. Copyrights for author.

Guernica Editions, Inc., Antonio D'Alfonso, Editor & Publisher, PO Box 117, Station P, Toronto, Ontario M5S 2S6, Canada, 416-658-9888; FAX 416-657-8885; e-Mail 102026.1331@compuserve.com. 1978. Poetry, fiction, photos, criticism, long-poems, plays, non-fiction. "Guernica Editions publish works of literature, criticism or culture. We specialize in translations and we focus on writing dealing with pluricultural realities. USA distributors: Small Press Distribution, LPC Group (Login Trade)." avg. press run 1M. Pub'd 22 titles 1998; expects 15 titles 1999, 15 titles 2000. 220 titles listed in the *Small Press Record of Books in Print* (28th Edition, 1999-00). avg. price, paper: $12-$20. Discounts: 40% to bookstores, 40% to jobbers and wholesalers, 46% for 10+ to library wholesalers. 96-250pp; 4½×7½, 5×8; of. Reporting time: 3-6 months; if we're definitely not interested, the answer is faster—within 2-4 weeks. Payment: authors receive about 10 copies and 10% royalty; copyright is shared by author and publisher for the duration of the edition. Does not copyright for author.

Guildford Poets Press (see also WEYFARERS), Jeffery Wheatley, Margaret Pain, Martin Jones, 9 White Rose Lane, Woking, Surrey, GU22 7JA, England. 1972. Poetry. "Production of booklets temporarily suspended; concentrating on *Weyfarers* poetry magazine." avg. press run 200. 10 titles listed in the *Small Press Record of Books in Print* (28th Edition, 1999-00). avg. price, paper: £1.60 (overseas, £2 sterling or cash, or $5 cheque). 28pp; 8×6; of. Reporting time: 3 months. Payment: booklets co-operative arrangement. Required copyright copies of all publications are dispatched.

Guilford Publications, Inc. (see also CAPITALISM, NATURE, SOCIALISM; RETHINKING MARXISM; SCIENCE & SOCIETY), 72 Spring Street, New York, NY 10012.

GULF COAST, Derick Burleson, Managing Editor, Dept. of English, University of Houston, Houston, TX 77204-3012. 1987. Poetry, fiction, art, photos, interviews, parts-of-novels, long-poems, non-fiction. "Recent contributors: Dawn Raffei, Barry Hannah, John Yau, Amy Gerstler, Adam Zagajewski, and Heather McHugh." circ. 1M. 2/yr. Pub'd 2 issues 1998; expects 2 issues 1999, 2 issues 2000. sub. price: $12; per copy: $7; sample: $7. Back issues: Barthelme issue, $12; regular back issue, $5. 144pp; 9×6; of. Reporting time: 6 months. Simultaneous submissions accepted: yes. Publishes 10% of manuscripts submitted. Payment: copies, sometimes small monetary reimbursement. Copyrighted, reverts to author. Pub's reviews: 0 in 1998. §Poetry, fiction, nonfiction. SMP, CLMP.

Gumbs & Thomas Publishers, Inc., Bob Gumbs, President, PO Box 381, New York, NY 10039-0381, 212-694-6677; fax 212-694-0602. 1985. Art, photos, non-fiction. "Specializing in African American adult and children's multicultural books and Kwanzaa products" avg. press run 10M-25M. Expects 2 titles 1999, 2 titles 2000. 11 titles listed in the *Small Press Record of Books in Print* (28th Edition, 1999-00). avg. price, cloth: $15-$25; paper: $6-$15. Discounts: 1-10 books 30%, 11-24 35%, 25-49 40%. 96pp; of, lp. Reporting time: 2-4 weeks. Payment: 5% to 8% annual. Copyrights for author. Small Press Center, PMA.

Gurze Books, Lindsey Hall, Editor; Leigh Cohn, Publisher, Box 2238, Carlsbad, CA 92018, 760-434-7533. 1980. Non-fiction. "Self-help, health/psychology." avg. press run 7.5M-10M. Pub'd 2 titles 1998; expects 3 titles 1999, 2 titles 2000. 15 titles listed in the *Small Press Record of Books in Print* (28th Edition, 1999-00). avg. price, cloth: $29.95; paper: $13.95. Discounts: trade distribution through PGW, B&T, Ingram. 176pp; 6×9. Reporting time: 2 months. Publishes 1% of manuscripts submitted. Payment: varies. Copyrights for author. PMA.

Gut Punch Press, Derrick Hsu, PO Box 105, Cabin John, MD 20818. 1988. Poetry, fiction. "Looking for material to excite and interest" avg. press run 1M. Pub'd 1 title 1998; expects 1 title 1999, 1 title 2000. 8 titles listed in the *Small Press Record of Books in Print* (28th Edition, 1999-00). avg. price, paper: $7.95. Discounts: write for schedule. 64pp; 5½×8½; of. Reporting time: 2 months. Payment: 50 copies of first printing. Copyrights for author.

The Gutenberg Press, Fred Foldvary, Sandra Fulmer, c/o Fred Foldvary, 1920 Cedar Street, Berkeley, CA 94709, 510-843-0248; e-mail gutenbergpress@pobox.com. 1980. Non-fiction. "Recent authors: Tertius Chandler, Fred Foldvary, John Hospers. Mostly publish books on social issues, social philosophy, and ancient history. Titles include: *The Soul of Liberty*, by Fred Foldvary. *The Tax We Need*, by Tertius Chandler. *Remote Kingdoms* and *Godly Kings and Early Ethics* by Tertius Chandler, *Anarchy or Limited Government?* by John Hospers. One art book also published." avg. press run 600. Pub'd 1 title 1998; expects 1 title 1999, 1 title 2000. 1 title listed in the *Small Press Record of Books in Print* (28th Edition, 1999-00). avg. price, paper: $10. Discounts: 40% bookstores and 52% jobbers. 300pp; 6×9; lp. Reporting time: within 1 month. Payment: after costs are met, profits are split 50/50. Copyrights for author.

H

H & C NEWSLETTER, Richard E. Mezo, PO Box 24814 GMF, Barrigada, GU 96921-4814, 671-477-1961. 1996. Poetry, articles, cartoons, interviews, criticism, reviews, news items, non-fiction. "Notes, brief articles, reviews, news items, commentary, etc. *HCN* is an iconoclastic publication devoted to exposing and correcting current pseudo-social science approaches to writing instruction (mostly college level). We insist upon a 'humanistic approach' to teaching composition. Due to space limitations, all submissions must be brief." circ. 150. Irregular. Expects 1 issue 1999, 2 issues 2000. sub. price: $10 (includes full membership in AASHC). 8-10pp; 8½×11; †mi. Reporting time: 1-3 months. Simultaneous submissions accepted: yes. Payment: 3 copies of magazine. Not copyrighted. Pub's reviews. §Humanities, teaching, teaching of writing, education. Ads: none.

HABERSHAM REVIEW, Frank Gannon, PO Box 10, Demorest, GA 30535, 706-778-3000 Ex 132. 1991. Poetry, fiction, interviews, satire, reviews, parts-of-novels. "We are a general literary journal with a regional (Southeastern U.S.) focus." 2/yr. Pub'd 2 issues 1998; expects 2 issues 1999, 2 issues 2000. sub. price: $12; per copy: $6; sample: $6. 96pp; 6×9; of. Reporting time: 4 months. Simultaneous submissions accepted: no. Publishes 5% of manuscripts submitted. Payment: 5 copies of issue. Copyrighted, reverts to author. Pub's reviews: 0 in 1998. §Southeastern U.S. Ads: $350/$200.

HAIGHT ASHBURY LITERARY JOURNAL, Alice Rogoff, Indigo Hotchkiss, Conyus, 558 Joost Avenue, San Francisco, CA 94127. 1980. Poetry, fiction, art, photos, reviews. "Recent contributors: Julia Vinograd, Jay Griswold, Opal Palmer Adisa, Bill Shields, Edgar Silex. Biases: culture and multi-cultural themes; street life, prison; feminist issues; political issues; family, crime, children, love and other visions." circ. 3M. 1-3/yr. Pub'd 2 issues 1998; expects 2 issues 1999, 2 issues 2000. sub. price: $35, includes 3 back issues and 9 future issues, $6 for 2 issues, $12 for 4 issues; per copy: $2; sample: $3 (with postage). Back issues: *This Far Together* (anthology) $15 (with postage), journals $3 (with postage). Discounts: $13 for 10. 16pp; 11½×17½; of. Reporting time: 3-6 months. Simultaneous submissions accepted: yes. Publishes 5% of manuscripts submitted. Payment: 3 copies if mailed, more copies per writer if picked up in person, "center" writers paid. Copyrighted. Pub's reviews. §International authors. Ads: $40 large/$30+/$20. CLMP.

Haight-Ashbury Publications (see also JOURNAL OF PSYCHOACTIVE DRUGS), David E. Smith, MD, Executive Editor; Richard B. Seymour, Managing Editor, 612 Clayton Street, San Francisco, CA 94117, 415-565-1904; fax 415-864-6162. 1967. Articles, art, photos, reviews, non-fiction. avg. press run 1.5M. Pub'd 1 title 1998; expects 1 title 1999, 1 title 2000. avg. price, paper: $35. We provide quantity discounts for our books; price list available. 100pp; 8½×11; of. Reporting time: 60 days. Payment: none. Does not copyright for author.

HAIR TO STAY, ALTERNATIVE LIFESTYLES DIRECTORY, Pam Winter, PO Box 80667, Dartmouth, MA 02748, 508-999-0078, order line 508-994-2908, Fax 508-984-4040. 1994. Poetry, articles, art, photos, cartoons, interviews, criticism, reviews, letters, news items, non-fiction. "A reader-contributed magazine for people who love and appreciate female body hair" circ. 5M. 4/yr. Expects 4 issues 1999, 4 issues 2000. sub. price: $50 US; $70 Int; per copy: $10 + $3ph US; $6ph Int; sample: same. Back issues: $10 if available. Discounts: 50%. 76pp; 8½×11; of. Simultaneous submissions accepted: yes. Publishes 100% of manuscripts submitted. Payment: negotiable. Copyrighted, reverts to author. Pub's reviews: 4 in 1998. §Body hair. Ads: $200/$150.

Halbar Publishing (see also SHARING & CARING), Bill Halbert, Mary Barnes, 289 Taylor Street, Wills Point, TX 75169-9732. 1994. Poetry, fiction, articles, art, photos, cartoons, interviews, satire, criticism, reviews, music, letters, parts-of-novels, long-poems, collages, plays, concrete art, news items, non-fiction. "No libel, no porn, no limit to length. We publish comb bound or perfect bound in the full letter size or the half letter size and perfect bound paperbacks trimmed slightly smaller in either size. We publish books for Memo-It Books out of Elkhart, Illinois and personal chapbooks for writers, color available. Also have musical consultant. We furnish books as needed, 5 or more per order once we have the master, furnish proof copy." avg. press run varies. Pub'd 20 titles 1998; expects 30 titles 1999, 40 titles 2000. 1 title listed in the *Small Press Record of Books in Print* (28th Edition, 1999-00). avg. price, paper: $8. 100pp; 5¼×7½; †Canon high speed and H.P. color. Reporting time: 2 weeks. Simultaneous submissions accepted: yes. Publishes 90% of manuscripts submitted. Payment: commensurate. Copyright for author if wanted.

Haley's, Marcia Gagliardi, PO Box 248, Athol, MA 01331, haleyathol@aolcom. 1989. Poetry, fiction, photos, interviews, non-fiction. "Looking for material that will appeal to readers in our region." avg. press run 1M. Pub'd 9 titles 1998; expects 8 titles 1999, 8 titles 2000. 4 titles listed in the *Small Press Record of Books in*

Print (28th Edition, 1999-00). avg. price, cloth: $24.95; paper: $14.95. Discounts: 40% trade. 100pp; 8½×11, 6×9, 7×10; of. Reporting time: 6 weeks. Accepting simultaneous submissions depends on prior arrangement. Publishes 10% of manuscripts submitted. Payment: varies. Copyrights for author.

HALF TONES TO JUBILEE, Walter F. Spara, Senior Editor, English Dept., 1000 College Blvd., Pensacola Jr. College, Pensacola, FL 32504, 904-484-1000 ext. 1400. 1986. Poetry, fiction, long-poems. "3-5 poem entries, SASE must accompany all submissions. Typed pages, clear photo copies or dot matrix accepted. No biases, 1200 words short story length for fiction. Deadline: April 30/open. Recent contributors: Gayle Ellen Harvey, Larry Rubin, Peter Wild, R.T. Smith. Annual poetry contest $300 first, $200 second, $100 third. Entry fee 2 per poem. Deadline: May 15" circ. 500. 1/yr. Pub'd 1 issue 1998; expects 1 issue 1999, 1 issue 2000. sub. price: $4; per copy: $4; sample: $4. Back issues: $2. 100pp; 6×9; †of. Reporting time: 8-10 weeks. Simultaneous submissions accepted: no. Publishes 10% of manuscripts submitted. Payment: copies. Copyrighted, reverts to author. No ads.

Halle House Publishing, Nicholas E. Bade, 5966 Halle Farm Drive, Willoughby, OH 44094-3076, 216-585-8687. 1991. Non-fiction. avg. press run 5M. Pub'd 2 titles 1998; expects 1 title 1999, 2 titles 2000. 1 title listed in the *Small Press Record of Books in Print* (28th Edition, 1999-00). avg. price, paper: $12.95. Discounts: STOP—45% and free shipping, 60% and free shipping on prepaid, non-returnable orders of 5 or more books. 134pp; 5½×8; of. Reporting time: varies. Simultaneous submissions accepted: no. Payment: negotiable. Does not copyright for author.

Halo Books, Hal Larson, Samm Coombs, PO Box 2529, San Francisco, CA 94126, 415-468-4256. 1988. Non-fiction. "Halo Books publishes quality non-fiction in trade paper format. Our books cover a wide range of topics, with an emphasis on self-help/inspirational titles. Recent additions to the list include *Time Happens*, a book for those 102 million Americans who are new at being old and a Garden of Woman's Wisdom, a secret haven for renewal using the power of flowers both metaphysical and medicinal." avg. press run 3M-5M. Pub'd 2 titles 1998; expects 1 title 1999, 2 titles 2000. 14 titles listed in the *Small Press Record of Books in Print* (28th Edition, 1999-00). avg. price, paper: $14.95. Discounts: 2-5 books 20%, 6-24 40%, 25-49 41%, 50-99 42%, 100-299 43%, 300+ 45%. 200pp; 5½×8½; of. Reporting time: 60 days or less. Simultaneous submissions accepted: yes. Publishes 1% of manuscripts submitted. Payment: varies. Copyrights for author. PMA.

Halyard Press, Inc., Sandra Merritt, PO Box 410308, Melbourne, FL 32941, 407-634-5022; Fax 407-636-5370. 1994. avg. press run 5M. Pub'd 1 title 1998; expects 3 titles 1999, 5 titles 2000. 3 titles listed in the *Small Press Record of Books in Print* (28th Edition, 1999-00). avg. price, paper: $19.95.

HAMMERS, Nat David, 1718 Sherman #203, Evanston, IL 60201. 1990. Poetry, reviews. "*Hammers* is an end-of-the-millenium irregular poetry magazine. While featuring poets from many other geographical regions, we continue to stress Chicago-area poets. I am looking for clear, well-stated, vibrant, honest poetry." circ. 500. Irregular, but usually 2/yr. Pub'd 2 issues 1998; expects 2 issues 1999, 2 issues 2000. sub. price: $15/4 issues; per copy: $5; sample: $5 + $1 postage/handling. 50pp; 7×8½; of. Reporting time: asap. Publishes less than 5% of manuscripts submitted. Payment: 1 copy. Copyrighted, reverts to author. Pub's reviews: 0 in 1998. §Poetry.

HAND PAPERMAKING, Michael Durgin, PO Box 77027, Washington, DC 20013-7027, 800-821-6604; FAX 800-538-7549; e-mail handpapermaking@bookarts.com. 1986. Articles, interviews, criticism, reviews. "Dedicated to advancing traditional and contemporary ideas in the art of hand papermaking." circ. 1.5M. 2/yr. Pub'd 2 issues 1998; expects 2 issues 1999, 2 issues 2000. sub. price: $40; per copy: $15; sample: $15. Back issues: $15 each. Discounts: 10% to agents. 40pp; 9×12; of. Reporting time: 2 months. Simultaneous submissions accepted: no. Publishes 25% of manuscripts submitted. Payment: $50-$150. Copyrighted, does not revert to author. Pub's reviews: 4 in 1998. §Paper and book arts. Ads: $270/$200/75¢.

Hands & Heart Books (see also Toad Hall, Inc.), RR 2 Box 2090, Laceyville, PA 18623, 717-869-2942; Fax 717-869-1031. 1995. Non-fiction. avg. press run 4M. Pub'd 1 title 1998; expects 2 titles 1999, 1 title 2000. avg. price, paper: $14.95. 224pp; 6×9; of. Reporting time: 3 months. Payment: $1000 advance and 10% royalty. Copyrights for author. PMA, SPAN, MABA, ABA.

Handshake Editions, Jim Haynes, Atelier A2, 83 rue de la Tombe-Issoire, Paris 75014, France, 4327-1767. 1971. Poetry, fiction, articles, photos, cartoons, parts-of-novels. "Only personal face-to-face submissions solicited. Handshake mainly publishes Paris-based writers. Small print-runs, but we attempt to keep everything in print (i.e., frequent re-prints). Libertarian bias. Writers recently published include Ted Joans, Sarah Bean, Michael Zwerin, Jim Haynes, Elaine J. Cohen, Ken Timmerman, Judith Malina, Lynne Tillman, Samuel Brecher, Suzanne Brogger, Jayne Cortez, Amanda P. Hoover, Echnaton, Yianna Katsoulos, William Levy, and Barry Gifford." avg. press run 1M. Pub'd 3 titles 1998; expects 12 titles 1999. 11 titles listed in the *Small Press Record of Books in Print* (28th Edition, 1999-00). avg. price, paper: $10. Discounts: 1/3 prepaid; all cheques payable to Jim Haynes. Payment: copies of the book. Does not copyright for author.

HANG GLIDING, Gil Dodgen, U.S. Hang Gliding Assoc., Inc., PO Box 1330, Colorado Springs, CO

80901-1330, 719-632-8300; fax 719-632-6417. 1974. Articles, photos, cartoons, interviews, reviews, letters, news items. "Information pertaining to hang gliding and soaring flight." circ. 10M. 12/yr. Pub'd 12 issues 1998; expects 12 issues 1999, 12 issues 2000. sub. price: $35; per copy: $3.95; sample: same. Back issues: prior 1982 $1.50, 1982-1990 $2, 1991+ $2.50. Discounts: newsstand 50%. 64pp; 8½×11; of. Reporting time: 2 months. Simultaneous submissions accepted: yes. Publishes 70% of manuscripts submitted. Payment: limited, cover photo $50, feature story. Copyrighted. Pub's reviews: 2 in 1998. §Aviation, outdoor recreation. Ads: b/w: $615/$365/50¢ per word classified.

HANGING LOOSE, Hanging Loose Press, Robert Hershon, Dick Lourie, Mark Pawlak, Ron Schreiber, Emmett Jarrett, Contributing Editor, 231 Wyckoff Street, Brooklyn, NY 11217. 1966. Poetry, fiction. "Emphasis remains on the work of new writers—and when we find people we like, we stay with them. Among recent contributors: Kimiko Hahn, Paul Violi, Donna Brook, D. Nurkse, Sherman Alexie, Ron Overton, Gary Lenhart, Sharon Mesmer, Charles North. We welcome submissions to the magazine, but artwork & book mss. are by invitation only. We suggest strongly that people read the magazine before sending work." circ. 2M. 3/yr. Pub'd 3 issues 1998; expects 3 issues 1999. sub. price: $17.50/3 issues (individuals); per copy: $7; sample: $8.50 (incl. postage). Back issues: prices on request, including complete sets. Discounts: 40% to bookstores, 20% to jobbers. 128pp; 7×8½; of. Reporting time: 2-3 months. Simultaneous submissions accepted: no. Payment: 2 copies + small check. Copyrighted, does not revert to author. Pub's reviews. §Poetry. No ads. CLMP.

Hanging Loose Press (see also HANGING LOOSE), Robert Hershon, Dick Lourie, Mark Pawlak, Ron Schreiber, Emmett Jarrett, Contributing Editor, 231 Wyckoff Street, Brooklyn, NY 11217. 1966. Poetry, fiction. "Book mss by invitation only." avg. press run 2M. Pub'd 6 titles 1998; expects 6 titles 1999, 6 titles 2000. 95 titles listed in the *Small Press Record of Books in Print* (28th Edition, 1999-00). avg. price, cloth: $18-$20; paper: $10-13. Discounts: bookstores, 40% (more than 4 copies), 20%, 1-4 copies; STOP orders 30%. 96-120pp; 5½×8½, varies; of. Payment: yes. Copyrights for author. CLMP.

Hannacroix Creek Books, Inc, Jan Yager, 1127 High Ridge Road #110, Stamford, CT 06905, 203-321-8674; Fax 203-968-0193; E-mail hcbbooks@aol.com. 1996. Poetry, fiction, non-fiction. "Not open to unsolicited manuscripts at this time." avg. press run 1M-3M. Expects 4 titles 1999, 4-6 titles 2000. 3 titles listed in the *Small Press Record of Books in Print* (28th Edition, 1999-00). avg. price, cloth: $16.95-$22.95; paper: $12.95. Discounts: distributed by LPC Group, Chicago to the trade. Pages vary. Payment: negotiable. Copyrights for author. PMA, NEBA, SPAN, ABA.

Hans Zell Publishers (see also THE AFRICAN BOOK PUBLISHING RECORD), Hans M. Zell, PO Box 56, Oxford 0X1 2SJ, England, +44-(0)1865-511428; FAX +44-(0)1865-311534; e-mail hzell@dial.pipex.com. 1975. Articles, interviews, criticism, reviews, non-fiction. "We are an imprint of Bowker-Saur/Reed Business" avg. press run 600. Expects 5 titles 1999. avg. price, cloth: £48. Discounts: 10% to subs. agents. 180-800pp; size A4, A5 or 240×160mm; of. Reporting time: 2-3 months. Publishes 10% of manuscripts submitted. Payment: negotiable. Copyrights for author.

Happy Rock Press, Philip R. Nurenberg, Phil Nurenberg, 8033 W. Sunset Blvd. #988, Los Angeles, CA 90046-2427. 1980. Poetry, articles, art, photos, interviews, reviews, letters, collages, non-fiction. "Address all correspondence *directly* to Phil Nurenberg. We solicit *interviewees* for *collaborative* ongoing works. Devoted to self-published-photostat-books of a *photo/interview* nature. Also manuscript consulting and editing. Designed to fill *any* size order in 6 to 8 weeks *with* pre-payment; within 2 weeks to 1 month for small orders; one copy orders fine too. To reach Henry Miller and Anais Nin fans, with bottomline new interview and photo material in semi-manuscript/semi-newsletter; informal; inexpensive manner; at cost. Also to remain in touch with, and exchange information with like-minded writers and readers" avg. press run 10+. Pub'd 1 title 1998; expects 2 titles 1999. 3 titles listed in the *Small Press Record of Books in Print* (28th Edition, 1999-00). avg. price, paper: $5; other: $5 photostat. Discounts: contact Phil Nurenberg. 10-20pp; 8×10; †mi, photostat/xerox. Reporting time: 6-8 weeks or sooner. Payment: only if net profit—but always 2 free copies of work they appear in; basically a non-profit enterprise for author publicity and publication at cost including p/h. Does not copyright for author. Maine Writers & Publishers Alliance.

Harbor House, Anne Shelander Floyd, VP Marketing; E. Randall Floyd, Publisher, 3010 Stratford Drive, Augusta, GA 30909, 706-738-0354; rfloyd2@aol.com. 1997. Fiction, non-fiction. "Harbor House's primary focus is quality fiction (historical, horror, thrillers in the 300-400 page range) as well as nonfiction topics ranging from historical oddities, the paranormal and unusual biographies (200-275 pages). Recent titles include *Deep in the Heart*, a Civil War novel, and the upcoming titles *100 of the World's Greatest Mysteries*; *The Good, the Bad, and the Mad: Weird People in American History*; *Natural Born Killers: Terrifying True Encounters Between Man and Beast*." avg. press run 5M. Expects 6 titles 1999, 6 titles 2000. 2 titles listed in the *Small Press Record of Books in Print* (28th Edition, 1999-00). avg. price, cloth: $24.95; paper: $19.95. 300pp; 5½×8½; of. Reporting time: 2 months. Simultaneous submissions accepted: yes. Publishes 5% of manuscripts submitted. Payment: 7-10% retail. Copyrights for author. PMA, WGA, SPAN.

Hard Press (see also COVER MAGAZINE), Jeff Wright, 632 East 14th Street, #18, New York, NY 10009, 212-673-1152. 1976. Poetry, art, photos, cartoons, music, letters, collages. "To date Hard Press has published 80 different *post cards*, generally poetry of two to twenty lines, sometimes accompanied by art-work, but sometimes just original art work, cartoons, collages, photos, by themselves. Contributors include: Kathy Acker, Amiri Baraka, Ted Berrigan, Robert Creeley, Allen Ginsberg, Anselm Hollo, Phillip Lopate, Alice Notley, Maureen Owen, Pedro Pietri, Anne Waldman, Jeff Wright. Also three books to date" avg. press run 500. Pub'd 4 titles 1998; expects 4 titles 1999, 4 titles 2000. 1 title listed in the *Small Press Record of Books in Print* (28th Edition, 1999-00). avg. price, paper: 50¢; other: postage. Discounts: 40%. 1 page; 5½×4¼; of. Reporting time: 8 weeks. Payment: 10% of copy. Copyrights for author. CLMP.

Hard Press, Inc. (see also LINGO), Jon Gams, PO Box 184, West Stockbridge, MA 01266, 413-232-4690. 1993. Poetry, fiction, articles, art, photos, interviews, letters, non-fiction. "Submissions not solicited. Recent contributors: Bernadette Mayer, Clark Coolidge, Michael Gizzi, Albert Mobilio, Lynne Crawford" avg. press run 2M. Pub'd 4 titles 1998; expects 6 titles 1999, 12 titles 2000. avg. price, cloth: $30; paper: $12.50. Discounts: 15% library jobbers, 50% trade. 200pp; of. Payment: varies.

HARDBOILED, Gryphon Publications, Gary Lovisi, PO Box 209, Brooklyn, NY 11228. 1988. Fiction, articles, interviews, letters, non-fiction. "Previously *Detective Story Magazine* and *Hardboiled Detective*. Publish the hardest, cutting-edge crime fiction, stories full of impact, action, violence. Also reviews, articles, interviews on hardboiled topics. Please Note: The best way to write for *Hardboiled* is to *read Hardboiled* and see *exactly* what we're after!*" circ. 1M. 4/yr. Pub'd 4 issues 1998; expects 4 issues 1999, 4 issues 2000. sub. price: $35/5 issues; per copy: $8; sample: $8. Back issues: #1-9 $29, or $6 each, (only 9 early issues of *Detective Story Magazine*). Discounts: 40% on 5 or more of each issue. 100-110pp; 5×8; of. Reporting time: 2-6 weeks. Simultaneous submissions accepted: no. Publishes 3% of manuscripts submitted. Payment: $5-$50 depending on quality and length, + 2 free copies on publication. Copyrighted, reverts to author. Pub's reviews: 18 in 1998. §Hardboiled, crime-fiction, mystery, suspense. Ads: $50/$25. MWA, PWA, OWA.

●Shannon D. Harle, Publisher (see also Rotten Pepper; Eat Your Hair; T.V. HEADS), PO Box 2224, Asheville, NC 28802.

HarMona Press (see also THE RAINTOWN REVIEW: A Forum for the Essayist's Art; THE RAINTREE REVIEW: Poetry Edition; THE ROSWELL LITERARY REVIEW), Harvey Stanbrough, PO Box 370, Pittsboro, IN 46167-0370, 505-623-0180.

HARMONY: VOICES FOR A JUST FUTURE, Sea Fog Press, Inc., Rose Evans, Managing Editor, PO Box 210056, San Francisco, CA 94121-0056, 415-221-8527. 1987. Poetry, articles, cartoons, interviews, criticism, reviews. "*Harmony Magazine* publishes articles on reverence for life—for animal rights, disabled rights, gay rights, peace, justice, ecology—against war, capital punishment, abortion, euthanasia, covert action, etc." circ. 1.4M. 6/yr. Pub'd 6 issues 1998; expects 6 issues 1999, 6 issues 2000. sub. price: $12; per copy: $2; sample: $2. Back issues: $2. Discounts: 10+ copies 40%. 28pp; 8½×11; of. Reporting time: 3-8 weeks. Simultaneous submissions accepted: yes. Publishes .03% of manuscripts submitted. Payment: copies only. Copyrighted, reverts to author. Pub's reviews: 10 in 1998. §War & peace, social justice, hunger, abortion, death penalty. Ads: $100/$50/10¢ per word.

HARP-STRINGS, Madelyn Eastlund, Editor; Sybella Beyer Snyder, Associate Editor, PO Box 640387, Beverly Hills, FL 34464. 1989. Poetry. "Recent contributors: Lin Schlossman, Elsie Pankowski, Duane Locke, Sharon Kouros, Catherine N. Fieleke. No short poems (under 14 lines), maximum lines 80. Looking for 'poems to remember.' Looking for narratives 'good story poems' ballads, patterned poetry. Annual contest: The Edna St. Vincent Millay Harp-Weaver Poetry Contest. Read only January 1 through February 28; May 1 through June 30; October 1 through November 30. Each reading is to plan the following issue—no files are kept. Poems kept only for current issue." circ. 100. 2/yr. Pub'd 2 issues 1998; expects 2 issues 1999, 2 issues 2000. sub. price: $11; per copy: $6; sample: $6. Back issues: $5. 40-44pp; 5½×8½; of. Reporting time: 3 weeks. Simultaneous submissions accepted: no. Publishes 2% of manuscripts submitted. Payment: copy. Copyrighted, reverts to author. Pub's reviews: 0 in 1998.

THE HARVARD ADVOCATE, Saadi Soudavar, President; Franklin Leonard, Publisher, 21 South St., Cambridge, MA 02138, 617-495-0737. 1866. Poetry, fiction, articles, art, photos, cartoons, interviews, criticism, reviews, long-poems, collages, plays, non-fiction. "*The Harvard Advocate* publishes work from Harvard undergraduates, affiliates, and alumni. We regret that we cannot read manuscripts from other sources" circ. 4M. 4/yr. Pub'd 4 issues 1998; expects 5 issues 1999, 5 issues 2000. sub. price: $25 for 4 issues; per copy: $5; sample: $5. Back issues: price varies. Discounts: none. 40pp; 8½×11; lp. Reporting time: 4-6 weeks. Simultaneous submissions accepted: yes. Publishes 10% of manuscripts submitted. Payment: none. Copyrighted, does not revert to author. Pub's reviews: 12 in 1998. §Literature, art, film, and music. Ads: $350/$250.

Harvard Common Press, Bruce Shaw, 535 Albany Street, Boston, MA 02118, 617-423-5803; 888-657-3755.

1976. Photos, non-fiction. avg. press run 7.5-50M. Pub'd 8 titles 1998; expects 8 titles 1999, 8 titles 2000. 79 titles listed in the *Small Press Record of Books in Print* (28th Edition, 1999-00). avg. price, cloth: $21.00; paper: $11.95. Discounts: 10-49 40%, 50-99 45%, 100-299 50%. 220pp; 6×9; of. Reporting time: 2-4 months. Simultaneous submissions accepted: yes. Copyrights for author.

HARVARD WOMEN'S LAW JOURNAL, Lisa Westfall, Editor-in-Chief, Publications Center, Harvard Law School, Cambridge, MA 02138, 617-495-3726. 1978. Articles, reviews. "We are a law review; all submissions are generally law related; however, legal histories, literary and sociological perspectives on the law as it affects women and feminism are welcomed." circ. 900. 1/yr. Pub'd 1 issue 1998; expects 1 issue 1999, 1 issue 2000. sub. price: $17 US, $20 foreign; per copy: $17; sample: not available. 350pp. Reporting time: varies. Copyrighted, does not revert to author. Pub's reviews: 7 in 1998. §Law related, legal histories and sociological literary perspectives on the law as it affects women and feminism. Ads: none.

●**Harvest Hill Press,** Sherri Eldridge, PO Box 55, Salisbury Cove, ME 04672, 207-288-8900; fax 207-288-3611. 1994. Non-fiction. "Cookbooks only." avg. press run 7M. Pub'd 7 titles 1998; expects 4 titles 1999, 8 titles 2000. 2 titles listed in the *Small Press Record of Books in Print* (28th Edition, 1999-00). avg. price, cloth: $19.95; paper: $13.95. 160pp. Simultaneous submissions accepted: no. Publishes 0% of manuscripts submitted. PMA.

THE HAUNTED JOURNAL, Full Moon Publications, Sharida Rizzuto, Harold Tollison, Ann Hoyt, Rose Dalton, 577 Central Avenue, Box 4, Jefferson, LA 70121-1400, e-mail fullmoon@edoramail.com or haunted@rocketmail.com; www.spaceports.com/~haunted, www.eclecticity.com/zines/, www.members.xoom.com/blackie or http://www.angelfire.com/la/hauntings/index.htm, www2.cyberci-ties.com/z/zines. 1983. Poetry, fiction, articles, art, photos, cartoons, interviews, satire, criticism, reviews, letters, long-poems, collages, news items, non-fiction. "Ghosts, haunted houses and other paranormal topics and themes" circ. 1M-1.2M. 2/yr. Pub'd 2 issues 1998; expects 2 issues 1999, 2 issues 2000. sub. price: $15.80; per copy: $7.90; sample: $7.90. Back issues: $7.90. Discounts: trade with other like publications. 100pp; 8½×11; †of, excellent offset covers. Reporting time: 2-6 weeks. Simultaneous submissions accepted: yes. Publishes 35% of manuscripts submitted. Payment: free copies, fees paid for articles, reviews and artwork negotiable. Copyrighted, reverts to author. Pub's reviews: 40 in 1998. §Paranormal - zines, books, films, internet websites. Ads: free. NWC, HWA, Small Press Genre Association, Mystery Writers of America (MWA), Western Writers of America (WWA), Arizona Authors Associaiton (AAA).

HAUNTS, Joseph K Cherkes, Nightshade Publications, PO Box 8068, Cranston, RI 02920-0068, 401-781-9438, Fax 401-943-0980. 1984. Poetry, fiction, art, interviews, reviews. "*Haunts* is a publication for people who enjoy reading horror, science-fantasy, and supernatural tales in the same vein as the famous *Weird Tales* We are looking for those stories that will make people think twice before turning out the lights or going to the basement to change a blown fuse. Our market will be open to review of material from June 1st to December 1st, inclusively. Strong characters and strong fantasy/supernatural elements combined with plausibility and continuity of storyline will go a long way in the consideration of your work. We *do not want* explicit sexual scences, famous rewrites, blow by blow dismemberments, or pure adventure. Stories should be between 1,500 and 8,000 words. Manuscripts should be double-spaced and typed as clearly as possible. Photocopies that are clearly legible are preferred as this leaves the original in your care in the event of lost mail. Place your name and address in the upper left hand corner of the first page and your name and story title on each succeeding page. Send SASE if you wish the return of your manuscript. We cannot be held responsible for the return of manuscripts unless this policy is strictly adhered to. Past contributors: Mike Hurley, Colleen Drippe, Scott Edelman, Tom Elliott, Geoffery A Landis, and Richard Lassiter" circ. 2.5M. 3/yr. Pub'd 3 issues 1998; expects 3 issues 1999, 3 issues 2000. sub. price: $16; per copy: $4.95 + $1 p/h; sample: $4.95 + $1 p/h. Back issues: limited copies of #1 and #2 $9.95 each + $1.25 p/h; write for our complete list. Discounts: 35-40% trade, 45-55% bulk (orders of 90 or more). 100pp; 6×9; of. Reporting time: 6-8 weeks. Simultaneous submissions accepted: yes. Publishes less than 1% of manuscripts submitted. Payment: $5-$50, poems $3 each. Copyrighted, reverts to author. Pub's reviews: 15 reviews of books, periodicals, and related items in 1998. §Horror, fantasy, science fiction. Ads: $100 body copy ad/$200 inside covers/$250 back cover/$225 page 1, four color process available for back copy only.

Haverford Business Press, Dorothy R. Berger, Lance A. Berger, PO Box 507, Haverford, PA 19041, 610-525-5965; Fax 610-525-9785; lberger@voicenet.com. 1997. Non-fiction. "Handbooks on current management trends. New ideas in business/management. Other address: 17 Courtney Circle, Bryn Mawr, PA 19010." Expects 2 titles 1999, 2-4 titles 2000. 1 title listed in the *Small Press Record of Books in Print* (28th Edition, 1999-00). avg. price, cloth: $24.95-$80. PMA.

HAWAII PACIFIC REVIEW, Patrice Wilson, Poetry Editor; Catherine Sustana, Fiction Editor, 1060 Bishop Street, Honolulu, HI 96813, 808-544-1107. 1987. Poetry, fiction, articles, satire, parts-of-novels, long-poems. "The *Hawaii Pacific Review* is looking for poetry, short fiction, and personal essays that speak with a powerful and unique voice. We encourage experimental narrative techniques and poetic styles. While we occasionally accept work form novice writers, we publish only work of the hightest quality. We will read one submission per contributor consisting of one prose piece of up to 5000 words or 5 poems. Please include a cover letter with a 5-line bio and an SASE. Experimental works, translations and long poetry (up to 100 lines) are all welcome, but in English only. Our reading period is Sept. 1 to Dec. 31." circ. 500-750. 1/yr. Pub'd 1 issue 1998; expects 1 issue 1999, 2 issues 2000. sub. price: $7; per copy: $6; sample: $4. Back issues: $4. Discounts: bulk $4 per copy. 80-100pp; 6×9; †of. Reporting time: 12-15 weeks. Simultaneous submissions accepted, but they must be indicated in the cover letter. Publishes 5% of manuscripts submitted. Payment: 2 copies. Copyrighted, reverts to author. Pub's reviews. §Poetry, fiction, essays. Ads: none.

HAWAI'I REVIEW, Kyle Koza, Editor; Lisa Kanae, Poetry Editor; Michael Puleloa, Fiction Editor, c/o Dept. of English, 1733 Donaghho Road, Honolulu, HI 96822, 808-956-3030. 1973. Poetry, fiction, articles, art, photos, cartoons, interviews, satire, criticism, reviews, music, parts-of-novels, long-poems, plays, concrete art, non-fiction. "Accept works of visual art, poetry, fiction, and non-fiction, including plays, short-short stories, essays, humor, cartoons. Publish all forms of literature including, but not limited to, works which focus on Hawai'i and the Pacific. Submissions *must* include SASE w/sufficient postage for return of material with reply." circ. 1M. 2/yr. Pub'd 3 issues 1998; expects 3 issues 1999, 2 issues 2000. sub. price: $20, $30/2 years; per copy: $10; sample: $10. Back issues: $5. 150-250pp; 5½×8½; of. Reporting time: 3 months. Simultaneous submissions accepted: yes. Publishes 5% of manuscripts submitted. Payment: 4 copies. Copyrighted, reverts to author. Ads: call for prices. CLMP.

●**Hawk Publishing Group**, William Bernhardt, 6420 S. Richmond Avenue, Tulsa, OK 74136, 918-492-3854; fax 918-492-2120; e-mail willbern@mindspring.com; website www.hawkpub.com. 1999. Poetry, fiction, non-fiction. "Publish both new books and reprints of out-of-print books. Recent books: *Remnants of Glory*, by Teresa Miller. *Old Fears*, by John Wooley and Ron Wolfe." avg. press run 5M. Expects 4 titles 1999, 8 titles 2000. avg. price, cloth: $22; paper: $14.95. Discounts: varies. Simultaneous submissions accepted: yes. Copyrights for author.

HAYDEN'S FERRY REVIEW, Salima Keegan, Managing Editor, Box 871502, Arizona State University, Tempe, AZ 85287-1502, 602-965-1243. 1986. Poetry, fiction, art, photos, interviews. "Publishes approximately 25 poems, 5 short stories. Past contributors: Raymond Carver, Rick Bass, Joy Williams, John Updike, T.C. Boyle, Rita Dove, Maura Stanton and Joseph Heller." circ. 1M. 2/yr. Pub'd 2 issues 1998; expects 2 issues 1999, 2 issues 2000. sub. price: $10; per copy: $6; sample: $6. Back issues: $6. 128pp; 6×9. Reporting time: 8-10 weeks after deadline. Payment: in copies (2). Copyrighted, reverts to author. CLMP.

HAZEL GROVE MUSINGS, Shirly Dawson-Myers, 1225 E. Sunset #304, Bellingham, WA 98226. 1992. Fiction, articles, interviews, satire, criticism, reviews, letters, non-fiction. "Each issues approximately 20-30 pages. No minimum or maximum article length. All benevolent opinions welcome. Focus is women's pagan spirituality." circ. 200. 3/yr. Pub'd 2 issues 1998; expects 3 issues 1999, 3 issues 2000. sub. price: $9; per copy: $3; sample: $3. Back issues: $2. Discounts: none. 30pp; 5½×8; lp. Reporting time: 1-2 weeks. Simultaneous submissions accepted: yes. Publishes 50% of manuscripts submitted. Payment: free issue copy. Copyrighted, does not revert to author. Pub's reviews: 6 in 1998. §Paganism, women's spirituality, witchcraft. Ads: $15/$7.50/$5 business card/20¢ per word for classifieds.

Headveins Graphics (see also ENDING THE BEGIN), Brad Angell, PO Box 4816, Seattle, WA 98104-0816, 206-726-0948. 1984. Poetry, fiction, articles, art, cartoons, music, long-poems, collages. avg. press run 100-200. Pub'd 6 titles 1998; expects 6 titles 1999, 8 titles 2000. 2 titles listed in the *Small Press Record of Books in Print* (28th Edition, 1999-00). avg. price, other: $1-2. Discounts: 45% for retail, 10% for others. 17-24pp; †laserprint/xerox. Reporting time: 1-6 months. Publishes 10-20% of manuscripts submitted. Payment: copies. Copyrights for author.

HEALTH AND HAPPINESS, Dr. Maria Kuman, 1414 Barcelona Drive, Knoxville, TN 37923, 423-539-1601 phone/fax; e-mail maria-k@juno.com. 4/yr. sub. price: $24; per copy: $2.50. Back issues: $2. 1 page; 6×8. Copyrighted, reverts to author. Pub's reviews. §health, happiness, new age, alternative medicine, spiritual education, creativity. Ads: $1,200/$600.

HEALTH MASTER, Conscious Living, Dr. Tim Lowenstein, PO Box 9, Drain, OR 97435. 1976. Articles, music, non-fiction. circ. 320M. 4/yr. Pub'd 2 issues 1998; expects 2 issues 1999, 2 issues 2000. sub. price: $1; per copy: $1; sample: $1. Discounts: on request. 16pp; 6×11; web-offset. Pub's reviews. §Self-improvement, self-help, health, psychology.

Health Plus Publishers, Paula E. Clure, PO Box 1027, Sherwood, OR 97140, 503-625-0589; fax 503-625-1525. 1965. Non-fiction. "We publish books on health, particularly holistic health, nutrition, and fitness. We are publishers of Dr. Paavo Airola's books, including *How to Get Well, Everywoman's Book*, and *Are You Confused?* Other publications include: *Change Your Mind/Change Your Weight*, by Dr. James McClernan, and *Exercise For Life*, by Mark L. Hendrickson and Gary J. Greene. Query first." avg. press run 7.5M-10M. Pub'd 1 title 1998; expects 2 titles 1999, 1 title 2000. 14 titles listed in the *Small Press Record of*

Books in Print (28th Edition, 1999-00). avg. price, cloth: $15.95; paper: $7.95. Discounts: inquire. 250pp; 5½×8½; of. Reporting time: 3-6 months. Payment: no advance, royalties negotiable. Copyrights for author.

Health Press, K. Schwartz, Box 1388, Santa Fe, NM 87504, 505-982-9373, fax 505-983-1733, e-mail hlthprs@trail.com. 1988. Non-fiction. "Books related to cutting-edge health topics, well-researched, geared to general public. Require outline with 3 chapters for submission—prefer complete manuscript. Authors must be credentialed (MD, PhD) or have credentialed professional write intro/preface. Controversial topics desired." avg. press run 5M. Pub'd 4 titles 1998; expects 4 titles 1999, 4 titles 2000. 3 titles listed in the *Small Press Record of Books in Print* (28th Edition, 1999-00). avg. price, cloth: $25; paper: $14.95. Discounts: bookstore 40%+, library 10%, (depending on quantity). 250pp; 6×9; of. Reporting time: 8-10 weeks. Simultaneous submissions accepted: yes. Payment: standard royalty. Copyrights for author. Rocky Mountain Book Publishers Association, PMA.

HEALTHY WEIGHT JOURNAL, Frances M. Berg, Editor, 402 South 14th Street, Hettinger, ND 58639, 701-567-2646, Fax 701-567-2602, e-mail fmberg@healthyweight.net. 1986. "Publishing office: 4 Hughson Street South, Hamilton, ON Canada L8N 3K7, 800-568-7281, e-mail info@bcdecker.com" circ. 1.5M. 6/yr. Pub'd 12 issues 1998; expects 6 issues 1999. sub. price: US & Canada: $59 individuals, $89 institutions, $30 students; elsewhere: $83 individual, $115 institutions, $24 students (U.S. funds only); per copy: $18 US & Canada, $23 elsewhere; sample: free. Back issues: $18 US & Canada, $23 elsewhere. Discounts: agents 10%. 20pp; 8½×11; desktop & print shop. Payment: none. Copyrighted, does not revert to author. Pub's reviews: 12-16 in 1998. §Obesity, weight management, Nutrition, eating disorders. Ads: contact Bob Sutherland at Canadian address above.

HEARTLAND (Australia), Dene Albert Vilkins, PO Box 435, Annerley, Queensland 4103, Australia. 1991. Poetry, fiction, art, cartoons. circ. 100. 4/yr. Pub'd 3 issues 1998; expects 4 issues 1999, 4 issues 2000. sub. price: AUS$34 institution, $25; per copy: AUS$5.95. Back issues: AUS$5.95. 32pp; 8½×11½. Reporting time: 3 months. Payment: none. Copyrighted, reverts to author.

Heartsong Books, PO Box 370, Blue Hill, ME 04614-0370, publishers/authors phone: 207-374-5170; e-mail maggie@downeast.net; uri:http://heartsongbooks.com. 1993. Fiction, non-fiction. "We are not accepting submissions at this time. The Heartsong vision is one of kinship. We trust that our books will help young people - all people - understand and respect the interconnectedness of all life and inspire them to act on that understanding in compassionate, powerful, and celebratory ways - for the good of Earth and for the good of generations to come. We at Heartsong express our kinship vision not only in the books we publish, but through gifts of money, outreach and opportunity." avg. press run 2M-4M. Expects 1 title 1999, 1 title 2000. 4 titles listed in the *Small Press Record of Books in Print* (28th Edition, 1999-00). avg. price, paper: $10. Discounts: trade, bulk, classroom. Pages vary; size varies; of. Copyrights for author. MWPA, PMA.

HEARTSONG REVIEW, Jennifer Washburn, Editor, 1835 North 50th Street #20, Phoenix, AZ 85008-4242. 1986. Articles, art, photos, cartoons, interviews, reviews, music, letters, news items. "We are a consumer's resource guide for New Age music of the Spirit, reviewing vocal and instrumental music of all positive spiritual paths. We welcome contributions relating to consciousness expansion and music. We have *very* little room for unsolicited written material - don't send it. We accept musical recordings of a new age spiritual orientation for review. Reviews have a specific format - do not send unsolicited reviews. News items relating to new age music, etc., are welcome, as are cartoons and art. Sampler tapes and CDs accompany each of our issues as an advertising medium." circ. 10M. 2/yr. Pub'd 2 issues 1998; expects 2 issues 1999, 2 issues 2000. sub. price: $8; per copy: $4 includes postage; sample: same. Back issues: $2 each. Discounts: $2/copy for 5 or more, $1.80/copy for 10+, $1.50/copy for 50+. 56pp; 8×10½; of. Reporting time: 1 month. Payment: none. Copyrighted, rights revert to author on articles, not reviews. Pub's reviews: 10 in 1998. §New age music, music therapy. Ads: $350/$225/$125 1/4 page/classified: $20 for 1st 30 words, + 30¢ each add. word.

Heat Press, Christopher Natale Peditto, Publisher & General Editor; Barbara Romain, Associate Editor; Teresa D'Ovido, Art Director; Harold Abramowitz, Associate Editor, PO Box 26218, Los Angeles, CA 90026, 213-482-8902. 1993. Poetry, long-poems. "Heat Press's roots are in Philadelphia, PA. Current series of published poets, Open Mouth Poetry Series (originally the name of an open poetry series in Philly), features poets close to the Beat Generation in their coming out and oral word sensibilities. Allied interests include the culture of jazz, 'Black' and pan-African cultures, the 'road' and nomadic cross-cultural traditions (versewinds), street poets of the oral tradition, and miscegenated-polyglottal-mouth-music poetry texts. Currently not accepting unsolicited manuscripts, but inquires are welcomed. Recent authors include Eric Priestley (*Abracadabra*), Charles Bivins (*Music in Silence*), Elliott Levin (*does it swing?*) and Will Perkins (*!Scat*)." avg. press run 1.5M. Pub'd 1 title 1998; expects 1 title 1999, 1 title 2000. 4 titles listed in the *Small Press Record of Books in Print* (28th Edition, 1999-00). avg. price, paper: $9.95. 100pp; 5×8; of. Payment: negotiable. Copyrights for author. CLMP, Poets House.

The Heather Foundation, Spencer H. MacCallum, P.O. Box 180, Tonopah, NV 89049-0180, 775-482-2038;

FAX 775-482-5897, email sm@look.net. 1973. Non-fiction. "The Heather Foundation is dedicated to furthering understanding of society as an evolving natural phenomenon of spontaneously patterned cooperation among freely-acting individuals. Taxation and other institutionalized coercions are viewed as evidence of insufficient development of social organization, a condition to be outgrown. The Foundation sponsors research, lectures and publications. It also preserves and administers the intellectual estates of persons who contributed notably to the humane studies. Areas of focus include philosophy of science, the inspirational aspect of religion and the aesthetic arts, monetary theory and alternative money systems, and the institution of property-in-land relative to community organization. Interested persons are invited to request the Foundation's booklist, 'Creative Alternatives in Social Thought.'" avg. press run 2M. Pub'd 1 title 1998; expects 1 title 1999, 1 title 2000. 4 titles listed in the Small Press Record of Books in Print (28th Edition, 1999-00). avg. price, cloth: $15; paper: $11. Discounts: 50% to bookstores, ppd. provided they supply name and address of customer. 175pp; 6×9; of. Reporting time: 30 days. Simultaneous submissions accepted: yes. Copyrights for author.

HEAVEN BONE MAGAZINE, Heaven Bone Press, Steven Hirsch, Gordon Kirpal, Contributing Editor, PO Box 486, Chester, NY 10918, 914-469-9018. 1986. Poetry, fiction, articles, art, photos, cartoons, interviews, satire, criticism, reviews, music, long-poems, collages, plays, concrete art. "Recent contributors: Kirpal Gordon, Charles Bukowski, Marge Piercy, Stephen-Paul Martin, Fielding Dawson, Jack Collom, Cynthia Hogue, Joseph Donahue. We like work that is deeply rooted in nature and image yet inspired by cosmic visions and spiritual practice. Current issues tending toward the surreal and eidetic. Editor loves work of Rilke. "Where are his followers?" Nothing turns us off more than artificially forced end-line rhyming; however, rhymed verse will be considered if obviously excellent and showing careful work. We would like to see more short stories and essays on various literary and esoteric topics. Reviews also being considered, but query first. SASE please." circ. 2.5M. 1/yr. Pub'd 1 issue 1998; expects 1 issue 1999, 1 issue 2000. sub. price: $19.95/4 issues; per copy: $8; sample: $8. Discounts: 40% to bookstores, 50% to distributors. 96pp; 8½×11; desktop, offset, chromapress. Reporting time: 3-36 weeks. Publishes 5% of manuscripts submitted. Payment: 2 free copies, 30% off additional copies. Copyrighted, reverts to author. Pub's reviews: 20 in 1998. §Literary, spiritual, experimental, metaphysical, music, spoken audio, spoken literature. Ads: $175/$90/$55 1/4 page.

Heaven Bone Press (see also HEAVEN BONE MAGAZINE), Steven Hirsch, PO Box 486, Chester, NY 10918, 914-469-9018. 1986. Poetry, fiction, articles, art, photos, cartoons, interviews, satire, criticism, reviews, music, long-poems, collages, plays, concrete art. "We publish a bi-annual poetry chapbook contest winner and 2-4 poetry and/or fiction titles. Recently published: Things, visual writing by Stephen-Paul Martin; Walking the Dead, poems by Lori Anderson; Red Bracelets, poems by Janine Pommy-Vega; Down With the Move, by Kirpal Gordon; Bright Garden at World's End, by David Dahl; Terra Lucida, by Joseph Donahue; and Fountains of Gold by Wendy Vig and Jon Anderson." avg. press run 500. Pub'd 3 titles 1998; expects 2 titles 1999, 5 titles 2000. 6 titles listed in the Small Press Record of Books in Print (28th Edition, 1999-00). avg. price, paper: $5.95. Discounts: 40% bookstores, 50% distributors. 40pp; 5½×8½; of. Reporting time: 6-36 weeks. Payment: varies; set fee or individual percentage of sales. Copyrights for author.

HECATE, Hecate Press, Carole Ferrier, Editor, P.O. Box 99, St. Lucia, Queensland 4067, Australia. 1975. Poetry, fiction, articles, art, criticism, plays. "Articles on historical, sociological, literary, etc. topics. Aspects of women's oppression and resistance. Some interviews and reviews. Some creative writing. Please make all payments in equivalent in Australian currency if possible. We almost never run American poets." circ. 2M. 2/yr. Pub'd 2 issues 1998; expects 2 issues 1999, 2 issues 2000. sub. price: $25/yr (ind), $100 (inst), please pay in Australian $; per copy: $6 (Ind); $30 (Inst); sample: $6 (ind); $10 (inst). Back issues: $8 volume (Ind); $100 (Inst); concession price may be negotiated. Discounts: 33% for bookshops. 180pp; 4×6½. Reporting time: varies. Publishes 6% of manuscripts submitted. Payment: $40 poem; $90 article. Copyrighted. Pub's reviews: 30 in 1998. §Socialist, feminist. Ads: negotiable, exchange.

Hecate Press (see also HECATE), C. Ferrier, PO Box 99, St. Lucia, QLD 4067, Australia. 1975. avg. press run 2.5M. Pub'd 2 titles 1998; expects 2 titles 1999, 2 titles 2000. 3 titles listed in the Small Press Record of Books in Print (28th Edition, 1999-00). avg. price, paper: $8. Discounts: 33⅓% for bookshops. 160pp; 4×6½; of. Reporting time: varies. Payment: $40 poem; $90 article. Copyrights for author.

HECATE'S LOOM - A Journal of Magical Arts, Yvonne Owens, Editor, Box 5206, Stn. B, Victoria, BC V8R 6N4, Canada, 604-478-0401, fax 604-478-9287, e-Mail Loom@islandnet.com. 1986. Fiction, articles, art, photos, cartoons, interviews, criticism, reviews, music, letters, news items, non-fiction. "Hecate's Loom is an impartial and indespensable news source written for Pagans by Pagans. The Loom offers local, national and international news and features about Paganism, Witchcraft, Wicca and Goddess spirituality. More than just news, the Loom chronicles the modern Pagan revival via opinions, fiction, art, interviews, and reviews. Well written and researched submissions of 1000-3000 words considered; send SASE and IRC for response. Limited space for poetry" circ. 6M. 4/yr. Pub'd 4 issues 1998; expects 4 issues 1999, 4 issues 2000. sub. price: $25.70 (institutional subscriptions $40) - in Canada. $31/$47 USA; per copy: $6.25; sample: $8.50. Back issues: $3.95. Discounts: trade 40%; agent discount negotiable. 60+pp; 8½×11; of. Reporting time: 2-3 months. Simultaneous submissions accepted: no. Publishes 30% of manuscripts submitted. Payment: 1 free copy. Copyrighted, reverts to author. Pub's reviews: 20 in 1998. §Witchcraft, Paganism, the Goddess, ancient religions, shamanism. Ads: $300/$190/35¢ per word. Wiccan/Pagan Press Alliance (WPPA), Canadian Magazine Publishers Association, The Canadian Index.

HEELTAP/Pariah Press, Pariah Press, Richard D. Houff, C/O Richard D. Houff, 604 Hawthorne Ave. East, St. Paul, MN 55101-3531. 1996. Poetry. "I like short, up to 32 lines, blank, free, post-beat, narrative, hit the mark and have something to say poems. Tom Clark, Dave Etter, and Paul Dickinson are recent contributors. The magazine is made from government trash bins materials." circ. 200. 2/yr. Expects 2 issues 1999, 2 issues 2000. sub. price: $18/4 issue sub.; per copy: $5; sample: $4. Back issues: $4. Discounts: none as yet. 48pp; 5½x8½; of, desktop. Reporting time: 2 weeks to 1 month. Simultaneous submissions accepted: yes. Publishes 5% of manuscripts submitted. Payment: copies. Copyrighted, reverts to author. Ads: none as yet.

Heidelberg Graphics, Larry S. Jackson, 2 Stansbury Court, Chico, CA 95928-9410, 530-342-6582. 1972. "Heidelberg Graphics publishes manuscripts by invitation only. For all others we offer complete services for self-publishing. We seek manuscripts for nonfiction books. Recent titles include *Riding the Tiger's Back* (Phillip Hemenway), *The Outfielder* (H.R. Counsen), *Cricket Moon* (Elizabeth Revere), *Greyhounding This America* (Maurice Kenny), and *Missing! Stranger Abduction: Teaching Your Child About How to Escape* (Robert Stuber)" avg. press run 600-6M. Pub'd 2 titles 1998; expects 2 titles 1999, 2 titles 2000. 14 titles listed in the *Small Press Record of Books in Print* (28th Edition, 1999-00). avg. price, cloth: $16.95; paper: $8.50; other: $8. Discounts: Write for prices or see ABA Book Buyers Handbook. 200pp; 6x9; of, lp. Reporting time: 8-16 weeks. Simultaneous submissions accepted: no. Publishes .001% of manuscripts submitted. Payment: negotiable. Copyrights for author.

Helicon Nine Editions, Gloria Vando-Hickok, Editor-in-Chief, Box 22412, Kansas City, MO 64113, 816-753-1095. 1977. Poetry, fiction. "We are publishing high quality volumes of fiction, poetry and/or essays. Please query before sending ms." avg. press run 1M-2.5M. Pub'd 2 titles 1998; expects 4 titles 1999, 6 titles 2000. 20 titles listed in the *Small Press Record of Books in Print* (28th Edition, 1999-00). avg. price, paper: $9.95-$25. Discounts: 60/40 bookstores, distributors-negotiable. 55-512pp; 6x9; of. Reporting time: varies. Payment: varies with individual writers. Copyrights for author. CLMP.

Helikon Press, Robin Prising, William Leo Coakley, 120 West 71st Street, New York City, NY 10023. 1972. Poetry, art, long-poems. "We try to publish the most vital contemporary poetry in the tradition of English verse—using the work of the finest artists, designers, and printers and the best materials possible. We cannot now encourage submissions—we read a wide variety of magazines and ask poets to build a collection around particular poems we have selected. We hope to continue without government subsidy. Poets: Helen Adam, George Barker, Thom Gunn, John Heath-Stubbs, and Michael Miller." avg. press run 100 for limited editions, 500 for 1st printing of trade editions. Expects 1 title 1999. 4 titles listed in the *Small Press Record of Books in Print* (28th Edition, 1999-00). avg. price, cloth: $20-$25; paper: $10-$20; other: limited eds. $10-$20. Discount to the book trade: 30% for limited editions and 1-4 of trade edition; 40% for 5 or more of trade edition. 16pp limited editions, 60pp trade edition; no standard size (each book is designed to suit the particular poems & poet); of, lp. Reporting time: 2 weeks. Payment: yes. Copyrights for author.

HELIOCENTRIC NET/STIGMATA, BAST Media, Inc., Lisa Jean Bothell, Managing Editor, 17650 1st Avenue S. Box 291, Seattle, WA 98148-0817, E-mail LBothell@wolfenet.com. 1992. Poetry, fiction, articles, art, cartoons, interviews, reviews, letters, non-fiction. "Closed to submissions." circ. 400. 1/yr. Pub'd 1 issue 1998. sub. price: $8.95 + book rate for appropriate country; per copy: same; sample: $8.95 + book rate for appropriate country. Back issues: $2 + book rate per country. Discounts: distributes 10 copy minimum, 50% disc no returns. 88pp; 8½x11. Reporting time: 6-8 weeks. Simultaneous submissions accepted: no. Publishes .5% of manuscripts submitted. Copyrighted, reverts to author. Ads: none.

THE HELIOCENTRIC WRITER'S NETWORK, BAST Media, Inc., Lisa Jean Bothell, 17650 1st Avenue S. Box 291, Seattle, WA 98148-0817, E-mail LBothell@wolfenet.com. 1994. "*The Network* is full of info, tips, ideas, announcements about writers, editors, publishers, poets, artists, the craft and industry, distributors, marketing, polls, interviews, etc. for all writers, artists, editors, publishers of all genres, and of amateur, semi-pro, and pro ranks. Keep sending us your announcements about new or folding 'zines, new anthologies or other publishing opportunities (contests, grants, awards, agents, etc.), helpful experience, or tips on writing, submitting, editing, marketing, publishing, distributing, keeping costs down. Tell us about writer's groups, workshops, conventions. We look for short articles of 750 words max on the business/craft of writing, editing, publishing, art, self-promotion, etc. Pays 1¢ per word + copy. We review magazines books." circ. 450. 6/yr. Pub'd 6 issues 1998; expects 6 issues 1999, 6 issues 2000. sub. price: $18 US, $24 Canada, int'l; per copy: $3 US, $4 foreign; sample: $3 US, $4 foreign. Back issues: none. 16pp; 8½x11. Reporting time: 6-8 weeks. Simultaneous submissions accepted: no. Publishes 5% of manuscripts submitted. Payment: 1¢/word for 750 word max. Copyrighted. Pub's reviews: 200+ in 1998. Ads: $50 1/4 pg; $5 a line.

HELIOTROPE: A Writer's Summer Solstice, George Thomas, Jan Strever, Iris Gribble-Neal, Tom Gribble, PO Box 9517, Spokane, WA 99209-9517, 509-624-0418; www.ior.com/heliotrope. 1997. Poetry, fiction, art, interviews, satire, criticism, reviews, long-poems, non-fiction. circ. 200. 1/yr. Pub'd 1 issue 1998; expects 1 issue 1999, 1 issue 2000. sub. price: $6.50; per copy: $6.50; sample: $4. Back issues: $4. 75pp; 5½x8½. Reporting time: 30 days. Simultaneous submissions accepted: no. Publishes 25% of manuscripts submitted. Payment: copy. Not copyrighted. Pub's reviews. §Poetry/short stories. Ads: none.

HELLAS: A Journal of Poetry & the Humanities, The Aldine Press, Ltd., Gerald Harnett, 304 South Tyson Avenue, Glenside, PA 19038, 215-884-1086. 1988. Poetry, articles, art, interviews, criticism, reviews, music, letters. *"Hellas* is a lively and provocative assault on a century of modernist barbarism in the arts. A unique, Miltonic wedding of *paideia* and *poiesis*, engaging scholarship and original poetry, *Hellas* has become the forum for a remarkable new generation of poets, critics and theorists dedicated to a rationalist reform of the arts. We welcome: elegant verse, especially metrical, which avoids obscurantism and prosaism; essays on ancient, Renaissance and modern poetry, and on literatures of other eras and traditions, particularly relating to the role of classicism and Hellenism in literary history; short (1000-2000 words) essays for our 'ARS POETICA' section on such technical matters as meter and diction, particularly as they relate to the 'New Formalism'; and short, highly literate and entertaining essays on any subject for our 'Divertimenti' section." 2/yr. Expects 2-4 issues 2000. sub. price: $16; per copy: $9 postpaid; sample: $9 postpaid. 180pp; 6x9; of. Reporting time: 3-4 months. Payment: copies. Copyrighted, reverts to author. Ads: by exchange.

HELLP!, Hellp! Press, Joe Musso, Editor; Rick Silvani, Editor, PO Box 38, Farmingdale, NJ 07727. 1997. Poetry, fiction, articles, art, cartoons, interviews, satire, criticism, reviews, letters, long-poems, news items, non-fiction. "No taboos. Recent contributors: Ana Christy, Rich Quatrone, Dave Church, Thuy-Duong Nguyen, Melody Rose Robins, John Sweet" circ. 150. 6-12/yr. Pub'd 9 issues 1998; expects 6-12 issues 1999, 6-12 issues 2000. sub. price: $25; per copy: $3; sample: $3. Back issues: $3. 40+pp; 5½x8; †mi. Reporting time: 1-2 months. Accepts simultaneous submissions if notified. Publishes 25% of manuscripts submitted. Payment: copies. Copyrighted, reverts to author. Pub's reviews: 4 in 1998. §Poetry/fiction. Ads: $10/$6.

Hellp! Press (see also HELLP!), Rick Silvani, Editor; Joe Musso, Editor, PO Box 38, Farmingdale, NJ 07727. 1997. Poetry, fiction, art, cartoons, letters, parts-of-novels, long-poems, non-fiction. "Length varies according to material. We fit format to the work instead of making the work fit an established format. Have published chapbooks" avg. press run 50, varies. Expects 10 titles 1999, 20 titles 2000. avg. price, other: $3-$6. 20-48pp; size varies; †mi. Reporting time: 1-2 months. Simultaneous submissions accepted if notified. Publishes 10% of manuscripts submitted. Payment: copies. Copyrights for author.

HEMLOCK TIMELINES, C.J Downie, Scott Judd, PO Box 101810, Denver, CO 80250-1810, Fax 303-639-1224, e-mail Hemlock@Prevatist.com. 1980. Articles, photos, interviews, reviews, letters, news items. circ. 40M. 6/yr. Pub'd 6 issues 1998; expects 6 issues 1999, 6 issues 2000. sub. price: $35; per copy: $6; sample: free. Back issues: $3. Discounts: none. 16pp; 11x8½; web of. Reporting time: 3 weeks. Simultaneous submissions accepted: yes. Publishes 10% of manuscripts submitted. Payment: none. Copyrighted, does not revert to author. Pub's reviews: 6 in 1998. §Assisted suicide, euthanasia. Ads: $2500/$1800/$950 1/3 page/$500 1/6 page.

HENNEPIN COUNTY LIBRARY CATALOGING BULLETIN, ASD/Accounting, Hennepin County Library, 12601 Ridgedale Drive, Minnetonka, MN 55305-1909, 612-694-8539. 1973. "Purpose of publication: to announce changes in the Hennepin County Library Catalog (e.g., new or altered cross-references, notes, DDC-numbers, and subject descriptors, citing authorities, precedents, & applications)." circ. 200. 6/yr. Pub'd 6 issues 1998; expects 6 issues 1999, 6 issues 2000. sub. price: $15/institutions, $6/individuals; per copy: $1.50; sample: free. Back issues: $1.50 each. Discounts: none. 30+pp; 8½x11; †of. Copyrighted. No ads.

Herald Press, S. David Garber, Book Editor, 616 Walnut Avenue, Scottdale, PA 15683, 724-887-8500. 1908. Fiction, non-fiction. "Herald Press, a division of the Mennonite Publishing House, Inc. which is owned by the Mennonite Church, each year releases a wide variety of new books for adults, young people, and children (primarily for ages 9 and up). We invite book proposals from Christian authors in the areas of current issues, peace and justice, missions and evangelism, family life, personal experience, juvenile fiction, adult fiction, Bible study, inspiration, devotional, church history, and Christian ethics and theory." avg. press run 3.5M. Pub'd 31 titles 1998; expects 28 titles 1999, 22 titles 2000. 23 titles listed in the *Small Press Record of Books in Print* (28th Edition, 1999-00). avg. price, cloth: $14.99; paper: $9.99. Discounts: Trade, text, jobber. 160pp; 5½x8¼; †of. Reporting time: 3 months. Simultaneous submissions accepted: yes. Payment: 10% of retail price up to 25,000 copies, going to 11% for the next 25,000, and 12% thereafter. Copyrights for author. ABA, CBA, International Christian Booksellers Association, ECPA, PCPA.

HERBAL CHOICE, Uni M. Tiamat, 3457 N. University, Suite 120, Peoria, IL 61604-1322. 1994. Articles, art, photos, cartoons, interviews, criticism, reviews, letters, long-poems, news items, non-fiction. "Forthcoming magazine, anticipated first issue Summer 1995" 1/yr. Expects 1 issue 1999, 1 issue 2000. 6pp; 8½x11;

†photocopy. Pub's reviews. §Herbal abortion, menstrual extraction, self-help abortion alternatives.

Herbelin Publishing, Steve Herbelin, Jocelyn Herbelin, PO Box 74, Riverbank, CA 95367, 209-869-6389; herbelin@netfeed.com; www.netfeed.com/~herbelin/homepage.htm. 1998. Fiction, cartoons, non-fiction. "We specialize in collecting and publishing mini and short stories related to the workplace." avg. press run 5M. Expects 1 title 1999, 2 titles 2000. 1 title listed in the *Small Press Record of Books in Print* (28th Edition, 1999-00). avg. price, cloth: $12.95; paper: $7.95. Discounts: standard trade for volume purchases. 192pp; 6×9; of. Reporting time: 30 days. Simultaneous submissions accepted: yes. Publishes 10% of manuscripts submitted. Payment: on acceptance. Copyrights for author. PMA.

HerBooks, Irene Reti, PO Box 7467, Santa Cruz, CA 95061. 1984. Poetry, fiction, articles, art, photos, cartoons, interviews, satire, letters, parts-of-novels, long-poems, non-fiction. "Primarily lesbian press, will not consider work by men. Our purpose is to publish radical, unassimilated, strong lesbian and feminist books." avg. press run 1.5M. Pub'd 2 titles 1998; expects 2 titles 1999, 2 titles 2000. 8 titles listed in the *Small Press Record of Books in Print* (28th Edition, 1999-00). avg. price, paper: $9. Discounts: 40% to bookstores, no minimum order; 40% to contributors. 128pp; 5½×8½; of. Reporting time: 1 month. Payment: 10% of cover price in copies on anthologies. Copyrights for author.

Heresy Press, George Beahm, 713 Paul Street, Newport News, VA 23605, 804-380-6595. 1975. "Checklists on current fantasy artists. The first of these, *The Vaughn Bode Index*, appeared in 1975. The second, *Kirk's Works*, on the artist Tim Kirk, was published in Oct. 1980. These books are done in cooperation with, and annotated by, the artist involved; they are extensively illustrated, with an original color cover and photos of the artist besides examples of his work." avg. press run 2M. 1 title listed in the *Small Press Record of Books in Print* (28th Edition, 1999-00). avg. price, cloth: $20; paper: $9. Discounts: wholesale 40% for 10 or more, 50% for 100 or more. 90pp; 8½×11, 9×12. Copyrights for author.

Heritage Books, Inc., Karen Ackermann, 1540-E Pointer Ridge Place, Bowie, MD 20716, 301-390-7708; Fax 301-390-7153; heritagebooks@pipeline.com. 1978. Non-fiction. "Subject matter of interest includes local and regional histories pertaining to eastern U.S. and source records of interest to historians and genealogists." avg. press run 200-300. Pub'd 60 titles 1998; expects 100 titles 1999, 120 titles 2000. avg. price, cloth: $35; paper: $25; other: $30 CD-ROM. Discounts: 1-5 assorted titles 20%, 6+ 40%; free shipping on both. 250pp; 5½×8½. Reporting time: 1 month. Simultaneous submissions accepted: yes. Publishes 80% of manuscripts submitted. Payment: 10% of retail price, paid semi-annually. Does not copyright for author.

Heritage Concepts Publishing Inc, PO Box 6121, Laramie, WY 82070, 307-742-4377; fax 307-721-8130. 1991. Non-fiction. avg. press run 5M. Pub'd 1 title 1998; expects 3 titles 1999, 6 titles 2000. 3 titles listed in the *Small Press Record of Books in Print* (28th Edition, 1999-00). avg. price, cloth: $14.95; paper: $9.95. Discounts: 1-9 copies 20%; 10-74 copies 40%, 75-99 copies 42%, 100-149 copies 45%, 150+ 50%. 102pp; 6×9. Reporting time: 2 months. Publishes 10% of manuscripts submitted. Payment: 10-15% on retail price. Copyrights for author.

●**Heritage Global Publishing,** J.V. Goldbach, PMB 225, 813 E. Blommingdale Avenue, Brandon, FL 33511-8113, 813-643-6029. 1998. "Book to be released early 1999: Help Your Child Avoid Multiple Sclerosis: A Parenting Decision" avg. press run 3-5M. Expects 1 title 1999, 2-3 titles 2000. 1 title listed in the *Small Press Record of Books in Print* (28th Edition, 1999-00). avg. price, paper: $23. Discounts: standard trade. 250pp; 6×9. Simultaneous submissions accepted: yes. Copyrights for author. PMA, SPAN, Florida Publishers Assn.

Heritage House Publishers, PO Box 194242, San Francisco, CA 94119, 415-776-3156. 1990. Non-fiction. "Not currently accepting submissions. Heritage House Publishers specializes in regional/city guidebooks and in California history and biography. Our first title, published October 1991, is *Historic San Francisco: A Concise History and Guide* by Rand Richards. Heritage House Publishers is currently distributed to the trade by Great West Books, PO Box 1028, Lafayette, CA 94549." avg. press run 3M. Expects 1 title 1999, 1 title 2000. 1 title listed in the *Small Press Record of Books in Print* (28th Edition, 1999-00). avg. price, paper: $12.95. Discounts: 1-4 books 20% (prepaid), 5-24 42%, 25-49 44%, 50-99 46%, 100+ 48%. 300pp; 5½×8½.

Heritage West Books, Sylvia Sun Minnick, 306 Regent Court, Stockton, CA 95204-4435, 209-464-8818. 1989. Non-fiction. "History, ethnography, biography." avg. press run 1M-3M. Pub'd 2 titles 1998; expects 3 titles 1999, 3 titles 2000. 11 titles listed in the *Small Press Record of Books in Print* (28th Edition, 1999-00). avg. price, cloth: $25; paper: $15. Discounts: trade-jobber, classroom: 2-4 20%, 5-24 40%. 6×9 to 9×13; of. Reporting time: 3 weeks. Payment: yes. Copyrights for author. PMA.

Hermes House Press, Inc. (see also KAIROS, A Journal of Contemporary Thought and Criticism), Richard Mandell, Alan Mandell, 113 Summit Avenue, Brookline, MA 02446-2319, 617-566-2468. 1980. Poetry, fiction, parts-of-novels, long-poems, plays. "Unsolicited manuscripts currently not being read. Experimental works, translations and artwork are encouraged; copy price and number of pages vary. Recent work: *The Deadly Swarm*, short stories by LaVerne Harrell Clark; *The Bats*, a novel by Richard Mandell; *Three Stories*, by R.V. Cassill; *Going West*, poetry by Stanley Diamond; *Bella B.'s Fantasy*, short stories by Raymond Jean; *Crossings*, a novel by Marie Diamond; *O Loma! Constituting a Self* (1977-1984), writings by sociologist Kurt H. Wolff; *Thinking, Feeling, and Doing*, critical essays by Emil Oestereicher." avg. press run 1M. Pub'd 1 title 1998. 8 titles listed in the *Small Press Record of Books in Print* (28th Edition, 1999-00). avg. price, paper: $6. Discounts: available upon request. Pages vary; 5½×8½, 4¼×7; of. Reporting time: 4-8 weeks. Payment: copies plus an agreed percentage after cost. Copyrights for author.

Hermitage (Ermitazh), Igor Yefimov, Marina Yefimov, PO Box 410, Tenafly, NJ 07670-0410, 201-894-8247; fax 201-894-5591; e-mail yefimovim@aol.com; http://users.aol.com/yefimovim/; http://Lexiconbridge.com/hermitage/. 1981. Poetry, fiction, articles, art, criticism, non-fiction. "We publish mostly books in Russian language or books in English dealing with Russian topics: literary criticism, history, translations from Russian, Russian culture, travel into Russia." avg. press run 1M. Pub'd 15 titles 1998; expects 15 titles 1999, 16 titles 2000. 10 titles listed in the *Small Press Record of Books in Print* (28th Edition, 1999-00). avg. price, cloth: $15; paper: $8.50. Discounts: 40% with 10 copies or more; 30% for jobbers if less than 10; no returns; no discount for libraries. 200pp; 5½×8½; of. Reporting time: 2 months. Payment: negotiable.

Heron Press, 14 Roberts Drive, Mayflower, AR 72106, 501-470-3946; Fax 501-470-1998; E-mail heron@ipa.net. 1996. avg. press run 2.5M. Expects 1 title 2000. 2 titles listed in the *Small Press Record of Books in Print* (28th Edition, 1999-00). avg. price, paper: $16.95. Discounts: 20%,30%. 400pp; 6×9. Reporting time: 3-4 months. Simultaneous submissions accepted: no. Publishes 20% of manuscripts submitted. Payment: 10%. Copyrights for author.

Heyday Books (see also NEWS FROM NATIVE CALIFORNIA), Jeannine Gendar, Managing Editor; Malcolm Margolin, Publisher, PO Box 9145, Berkeley, CA 94709, 510-549-3564; FAX 510-549-1889. 1974. Poetry, art, photos, non-fiction. "Books on California history and literature, California Indians, women of California, natural history, and regional guidebooks, fiction and poetry." avg. press run 7.5M. Pub'd 12 titles 1998; expects 15 titles 1999, 15 titles 2000. 60 titles listed in the *Small Press Record of Books in Print* (28th Edition, 1999-00). avg. price, cloth: $17.95; paper: $14.95. Discounts: retail 1-4 copies 20%, 5-24 40%, 25-49 43%, 50-99 45%, 100+ 46%. 200pp; 6×9; of. Reporting time: 3 weeks. Simultaneous submissions accepted: yes. Payment: comparable to what's offered by major publishers, in fact modeled on their contracts. Copyrights for author. ABA, NCIBA, PMA, NCBPMA, SF Book Council.

The Heyeck Press, Robin R. Heyeck, 25 Patrol Court, Woodside, CA 94062, 650-851-7491; Fax 650-851-5039; heyeck@ix.netcom.com. 1976. Poetry, long-poems, non-fiction. "Books on paper marbling. All books are printed letterpress." avg. press run 500. Pub'd 1 title 1998; expects 2 titles 1999, 2 titles 2000. 14 titles listed in the *Small Press Record of Books in Print* (28th Edition, 1999-00). avg. price, cloth: $225-$295; paper: $15-$19. Discounts: fine editions, book dealers only 30%; letterpress paper wrappers (trade) 1-3 copies 20%, 4+ 40%. 80pp; size varies; †lp. Reporting time: 90 days. Simultaneous submissions accepted: no. Publishes 1-2% of manuscripts submitted. Payment: percentage of sales paid in cash. Copyrights for author.

Hi Jinx Press, Greg Boyd, 203 F Street, Suite A, PO Box 1814, Davis, CA 95616, 916-759-8514; Fax 916-759-8639; E-mail hijinx@mother.com. 1996. Fiction. "Off-beat, hip, literary novels and story collections, 100-300 pages, typically around 200 pages. Recent Hi Jinx authors and editors: Stephen Dixon, Geoffrey Clark, John Richards, Mark Wisniewski, Joe Martin, Gilbert Alter-Gilbert." avg. press run 1.5-2.5M. Pub'd 5 titles 1998; expects 8 titles 1999, 8 titles 2000. 4 titles listed in the *Small Press Record of Books in Print* (28th Edition, 1999-00). avg. price, paper: $14-$15. Discounts: trade 25%-50%, bulk/jobber 40%-55%, classroom 10%-25%. 208pp; 5×8; of. Reporting time: 1-2 months. Simultaneous submissions accepted: yes. Publishes 20% of manuscripts submitted. Payment: variable/negotiable; usually 10% of net on all printings after first printing. Copyrights for author.

THE HIGGINSVILLE READER, Frank Magalhaes, Kathe Palka, PO Box 141, Three Bridges, NJ 08887, 908-788-0514; hgvreader@yahoo.com. 1991. Poetry, fiction, art, photos, long-poems, non-fiction. "All prose to 3,500 words. We can easily publish poetry up to 200 lines. The editors welcome all styles and forms. We are very receptive to new voices. Among the writers we have published are Hugh Fox, Taylor Graham, D.E. Steward, Robert Murray Davis, Joan Payne Kincaid, David Chorlton, and Robert Klein Engler." circ. 150. 4/yr. Pub'd 4 issues 1998; expects 4 issues 1999, 4 issues 2000. sub. price: $5; per copy: $1.50; sample: $1.50. Back issues: $1.50. Discounts: per issue: 8 copies for $10, 20 copies for $20. 16pp; 7×8½; †laser printer. Reporting time: 8 weeks. Simultaneous submissions accepted if advised and notified. Publishes prose 10-20%, poetry 8-10% of manuscripts submitted. Payment: 1 copy upon publication. Not copyrighted.

HIGH COUNTRY NEWS, Ed Marston, Publisher; Betsy Marston, Editor, PO Box 1090, Paonia, CO 81428, 303-527-4898. 1970. Articles, art, photos, cartoons, interviews, criticism, reviews, letters, news items. "We're after hard-hitting, but fairly-reported environmental journalism with a regional slant. We cover Montana, Wyoming, Colorado, Utah, Idaho, the Dakotas, Nevada, Arizona, New Mexico, Oregon and Washington." circ.

20M. 24/yr. Pub'd 24 issues 1998; expects 24 issues 1999, 24 issues 2000. 1 title listed in the *Small Press Record of Books in Print* (28th Edition, 1999-00). sub. price: $28 indiv., $38 instit.; per copy: $1.50; sample: free. Back issues: $2.50 (incl. p/h) single copy; bulk rates available on request. Discounts: sell in bulk to schools, libraries, organizations. 16pp; 10×16; of. Reporting time: 4 weeks. Simultaneous submissions accepted: no. Payment: 20¢ per word, $50-$100 per published B & W photo. Copyrighted, reverts to author. Pub's reviews: 50 short blurbs in 1998. §Conservation, wildlife, energy, land use, growth, unions and the rural economy, and other western community issues. $20/inch camera ready under 4 column inches, $40/inch over 4 column inches.

HIGH PLAINS LITERARY REVIEW, Robert O. Greer, Jr., Editor-in-Chief, 180 Adams Street, Suite 250, Denver, CO 80206, (303) 320-6828. 1986. Poetry, fiction, articles, interviews, reviews, long-poems, non-fiction. "The *High Plains Literary Review* seeks to bridge the gap between academic quarterlies and commercial reviews. Prefer material 3,000-8,000 words in length." circ. 1150. 3/yr. Pub'd 3 issues 1998; expects 3 issues 1999, 3 issues 2000. sub. price: $20; per copy: $7; sample: $4. Back issues: $4. Discounts: 20% to agent. 140pp; 6×9; of. Reporting time: 12 weeks. Simultaneous submissions accepted: yes. Payment: $5/page for prose, $10/page for poetry. Copyrighted, reverts to author. Pub's reviews: 9 in 1998. §Short story collection, poetry collections, essay collections. Ads: $100/$60/$40 1/4 page. CLMP.

High Plains Press, Nancy Curtis, Box 123, Glendo, WY 82213, 307-735-4370; Fax 307-735-4590; 800-552-7819. 1984. Poetry, non-fiction. "Specializes in Wyoming and the West." avg. press run 2M. Expects 4 titles 1999, 4 titles 2000. 28 titles listed in the *Small Press Record of Books in Print* (28th Edition, 1999-00). avg. price, cloth: $24.95; paper: $12.95. Discounts: bookstores 1-4 20%, 5+ 40%, wholesales more. 200pp; 5½×8½, 6×9, etc.; of. Reporting time: 2 months. Simultaneous submissions accepted: yes. Publishes 3% of manuscripts submitted. Payment: based on material, usually 10% net sales. Copyrights for author. PMA, Rocky Mtn. Publishers Assoc.

Highsmith Press, Donald Sager, Publisher; Nancy Knies, Managing Editor, PO Box 800, Ft. Atkinson, WI 53538, 414-563-9571; fax 414-563-4801; e-mail hpress@highsmith.com; web site http://www.hpress.highsmith.com. 1991. "We publish library professional and reference books and instructional resources for teachers and librarians" avg. press run 2M-3M. Pub'd 20 titles 1998; expects 20 titles 1999, 20 titles 2000. 9 titles listed in the *Small Press Record of Books in Print* (28th Edition, 1999-00). avg. price, cloth: $42; paper: $29. Discounts: 10-45% jobber; booksellers (please contact). 100-400pp; size varies; lp. Reporting time: 30 days. Simultaneous submissions accepted: yes. Publishes 1% of manuscripts submitted. Payment: 10-12% of net. Copyrights for author. PMA, MAPA.

THE HIGHWAY POET, Colorado T. Sky, National Secretary, PO Box 1400, Brewster, MA 02631. 1990. Poetry, articles, art, photos, cartoons, interviews, satire, criticism, reviews, letters, news items. "Intermittent journal and in-house pub of the HPMC. Accepts non-fiction and poetry, BW photos and line art from outside sources. Sub for one-time and reprint rights. Prefer 200-500 words with biker or publishing slant." circ. 200. Intermittent frequency. Pub'd 5 issues 1998; expects 4 issues 1999, 4-6 issues 2000. sub. price: $10/6; per copy: $2; sample: $2. 12pp; 8½×11; †of. Reporting time: 2-4 weeks. Payment: $10 + subscription. Copyrighted, reverts to author. Pub's reviews: 3 in 1998. §Poetry/prose with biker or alternative publishing lit slant.

HILL AND HOLLER, Seven Buffaloes Press, Art Coelho, Box 249, Big Timber, MT 59011. price per copy: $8.75; sample: $7.75.

Hill Country Books, J.O. Walker, PO Box 791615, San Antonio, TX 78279, 830-885-4375. 1994. Non-fiction. "Prefer mss. under 400pp. Will consider any good non-fiction. Especially interested in Texas or Southwest material; also health and recovery subjects" avg. press run 5M. Pub'd 1 title 1998; expects 2 titles 1999, 3 titles 2000. 1 title listed in the *Small Press Record of Books in Print* (28th Edition, 1999-00). avg. price, cloth: $24.95; paper: $9.95. Discounts: Averages 40%. 200pp; 5½×8½; †of. Reporting time: 2 weeks. Simultaneous submissions accepted: yes. Publishes 20% of manuscripts submitted. Payment: co-publishing arrangements. Copyrights for author. Texas Publishers Association.

Himalayan Institute Press, Deborah Willoughby, Director; Lawrence Clark, Editor, RR 1, Box 405, Honesdale, PA 18431, 717-253-5551; 800-822-4547; fax 717-251-7812; e-mail hibooks@epix.net. 1971. Non-fiction. "*The Himalayan International Press* has long been regarded as "The Resource for Holistic Living" by providing bestselling perennials on yoga, meditation, psychology, diet, exercise, preventive medicine, holistic health, and self-develoment. We believe that every person has the power to improve his life. Self-awareness and self-directed change is the theme of our publications. We believe the complex problems of modern life can be solved in natural ways. Our books provide unique synthesis of Eastern and Western disciplines, offering practical methods of living that foster inner balance and outer harmony. Our approach addresses the whole person—body, mind, and spirit—integrating the latest scientific knowledge with ancient healing and self-development techniques. Thus our publications, in addition to making sound holistic health principles and practices available to the public, are designed to help build a bridge between the timeless truths

245

of the East and the modern discoveries of the West, and are meant to aid in the integration of science and spirituality" avg. press run 5M. Pub'd 1 title 1998; expects 8 titles 1999, 7 titles 2000. 55 titles listed in the *Small Press Record of Books in Print* (28th Edition, 1999-00). avg. price, paper: $12.95. Discounts: conventional trade. 225pp; 8½×5½; †of. Reporting time: 3 months. Payment: individual. Copyrights for author. PMA, Jenkins Group, NAPRA.

HIP MAMA, Ariel Gore, Attn: Ariel Gore, PO Box 9097, Oakland, CA 94613, 510-658-4508. 1993. Poetry, fiction, articles, art, photos, cartoons, interviews, satire, criticism, reviews, music, letters, parts-of-novels, long-poems, collages, plays, concrete art, news items, non-fiction. "All work should address some aspect of honest mothering, parenting, changing families or cool/radical childrearing. We are interested in quality and honesty over mainstream marketability and are especially looking for more literary non-fiction articles as well as news items. Columns include commentary, 'Beyond Whirled Peas' (cooking), and 'Loose Grip.' We prefer articles and stories to be less than 1,000 words and columns to be 500-750 words. Recent contributors include Opal Palmer Adisa, Devorah Major, and Susan Ito. See recent issues, know our style and scope." circ. 5M. 4/yr. Pub'd 1 issue 1998; expects 4 issues 1999, 4 issues 2000. sub. price: $12-$22 sliding scale; per copy: $3.95; sample: $3.95. Back issues: $4. Discounts: subscriber decides what price between $12 and $22 s/he can pay. 28pp; 8½×11; of. Reporting time: 3 months. Publishes 50% of manuscripts submitted. Payment: copies, subscription, 5¢/word for cover story. Copyrighted, reverts to author. Pub's reviews: 4-8 in 1998. §Parenting, motherhood. Ads: $400/$210/30¢/word.

Hippopotamus Press (see also OUTPOSTS POETRY QUARTERLY), Roland John, B.A. Martin, Business Manager; Mansell Pargitter, 22, Whitewell Road, Frome, Somerset BA11 4EL, England, 0373-466653. 1974. Poetry, long-poems. "Size, number of pages, cost will vary with the material. Against: concrete, typewriter, neo-surrealism and experimental work. For: competent poetry in recognisable English, a knowledge of syntax and construction, finished work and not glimpses into the workshop, also translations. Recent books include G.S. Sharat Chandra (U.S.A.), Edward Lowbury (Canada), Stan Trevor (S. Africa) Shaun McCarthy, Peter Dale, William Bedford, Humphrey Chucas, Debjani Chatterjee, Peter Dent." avg. press run 750 paper, 250 cloth. Pub'd 2 titles 1998; expects 5 titles 1999. 23 titles listed in the *Small Press Record of Books in Print* (28th Edition, 1999-00). avg. price, cloth: £12, $24; paper: £6, $12. Discounts: 35% off singles, 45% off bulk orders. 80pp; size varies; of, lp. Reporting time: 1 month. Payment: by arrangement/royalty. Standard UK copyright, remaining with author. ALP.

HIRAM POETRY REVIEW, Hale Chatfield, Box 162, Hiram, OH 44234, 330-569-5331; fax 330-569-5449. 1967. Poetry, articles, art, photos, interviews, satire, criticism, reviews, letters, long-poems, collages, plays, concrete art. "We seek to discover new poets. Except for special features, ALL poems in *HPR* are selected from manuscripts submitted without specific invitation. (Reviews, plays, fiction, and supplements are by invitation only. Carbon, ditto, mimeograph, and electrostastic copies will not be read)." circ. 500. 1/yr. Pub'd 1 issue 1998; expects 1 issue 1999, 1 issue 2000. sub. price: $15, $35 for 3 yrs; per copy: $15; sample: free. Back issues: No. 1 unavail.; others vary; send for info. Discounts: 60-40 to subscription agencies; 60-40 to retail bookstores. CD-Rom. Reporting time: 8-25 weeks. Simultaneous submissions accepted: no. Publishes 17% of manuscripts submitted. Payment: 2 copies plus 1 year subscription. Copyrighted, rights revert to author by request. Pub's reviews: 2 in 1998. §Poetry, books, some little magazines. No ads. CLMP.

HISPANIC AMERICAN HISTORICAL REVIEW, Duke University Press, Mark D. Szuchman, Box 90660, Duke University, Durham, NC 27708-0660. "Published in cooperation with the Conference on Latin American History of the American Historical Association. *HAHR* pioneered the study of Latin American history and culture in the United States and remains the most widely respected journal in the field. *HAHR*'s comprehensive book review section provides commentary, ranging from brief notices to review essays, on every facet of scholarship on Latin American history and culture. Regular notices of the activities of the Conference on Latin American History appear in the journal." circ. 2.4M. 4/yr. Pub'd 4 issues 1998; expects 4 issues 1999, 4 issues 2000. sub. price: $105 institutions, $40 individuals, $20 students with photocopy of current I.D., additional $12 foreign. Pub's reviews. Ads: $300/$200/$350 back cover.

Historical Dimensions Press, Sandra Brent, PO Box 12042, Washington, DC 20005, 202-387-8070. 1985. Art, photos, non-fiction. "Write for a free list of our titles. Titles include: *Comparative Nationalism: Definitions, Interpretations, and the Black American and British West African Experience to 1947,* 1985. Also, we distribute books of historical significance including books on World War II experiences; the Muckrakers; the press media and the state; Black English and the media; and the unions of American journalists. Make checks or money orders payable to Historical Dimensions Press." avg. press run varies. Expects 1 title 1999, 2 titles 2000. 1 title listed in the *Small Press Record of Books in Print* (28th Edition, 1999-00). avg. price, cloth: $50; paper: $14. Discounts: normal trade, jobbers usual. 285pp; 5½×8¼; of, lp. Reporting time: 1-2 months. Payment: depends on author and subject matter. Copyrights for author. AAWG.

Historical Society of Alberta (see also ALBERTA HISTORY), Hugh A. Dempsey, 95 Holmwood Ave. NW, Calgary, Alberta T2K 2G7, Canada. 1907. avg. press run 1.6M. Pub'd 1 title 1998; expects 1 title 1999, 1 title

2000. 11 titles listed in the *Small Press Record of Books in Print* (28th Edition, 1999-00). avg. price, paper: $5.50. Discounts: 33%. 28pp; 8½×11; of. Reporting time: 3 months. Payment: none. Does not copyright for author.

HISTORICAL STUDIES IN THE PHYSICAL & BIOLOGICAL SCIENCES, University of California Press, J.L. Heilbron, University of California Press, 2120 Berkeley Way, Berkeley, CA 94720, 5610-643-7154. 1970. Non-fiction. "Editorial address: Office for History of Science & Technology, 470 Stephens Hall, Univ. of CA, Berkeley, CA 94720." circ. 750. 2/yr. Pub'd 2 issues 1998; expects 2 issues 1999, 2 issues 2000. sub. price: $27 indiv., $63 instit. (+ $4 foreign postage); per copy: $15 indiv.; $33 instit. (+ $4 foreign postage), $15 student; sample: free. Back issues: same as single copy price. Discounts: foreign subs. agent 10%, one-time orders 10+ 30%, standing orders (bookstores): 1-99 40%, 100+ 50%. 200pp; 6×9; of. Reporting time: 1-2 months. Copyrighted, does not revert to author. Ads: $275/$200.

HISTORY NEWS, Deanna Kerrigan, Editor-in-Chief, 530 Church Street, Suite 600, Nashville, TN 37219-2325, 615-255-2971. 1941. Articles, reviews. "*History News* welcomes articles of interest to readers who work at historic sites, history museums, or educational agencies that advance knowledge, understanding, and appreciation of state, local, and regional history in the United States and Canada. We favor articles that tell how to better manage and administer such institutions and thus to serve the public. We cannot consider work that is primarily about historical events or persons." circ. 5.2M. 4/yr. Pub'd 4 issues 1998; expects 4 issues 1999, 4 issues 2000. sub. price: $50; per copy: $4. 36pp; 8½×11; of. Reporting time: 2 months. Payment: 3-5 copies. Copyrighted, does not revert to author. Pub's reviews: 16 in 1998. §"How-to" books telling history agency administrators how to do their jobs better, and general interest to state and local history fields. Ads: $770/$570/available in 1-time, 2-times, 4-times discount.

HISTORY OF POLITICAL ECONOMY, Duke University Press, Craufurd D. Goodwin, Box 90660, Duke University, Durham, NC 27708-0660. "Focusing on the history of economic thought and analysis, the *History of Political Economy* has made significant contributions to the history of economics and remains the field's foremost means of communication. In addition to book reviews, each issue contains original research on the development of economic thought, the historical background behind major figures in the history of economics, the interpretation of economic theories, and the methodologies available to historians of economic theory. All subscribers to the *History of Political Economy* receive a hardbound annual supplement as part of their subscription. Send review copies to the Book Review Editor, S. Todd Lowry, Dept. of Economics, Washington and Lee University, Lexington, VA 24450." circ. 1.5M. 4/yr. Pub'd 4 issues 1998; expects 4 issues 1999, 4 issues 2000. sub. price: $145 institutions, $65 individuals, $32 students with photocopy of current I.D., additional $15 foreign. Pub's reviews. Ads: $200/$125.

W.D. Hoard & Sons Company (see also HOARD'S DAIRYMAN), Elvira Kau, Book Editor, 28 Milwaukee Avenue West, Fort Atkinson, WI 53538, 920-563-5551. 1870. Articles, non-fiction. avg. press run 4M. Pub'd 2 titles 1998; expects 4 titles 1999, 3 titles 2000. 11 titles listed in the *Small Press Record of Books in Print* (28th Edition, 1999-00). avg. price, paper: $7; other: $20. Discounts: college bookstore 20%, other retail 40%. 100pp; 8¼×10⅞, 6×9; †of. Reporting time: 1 week. Publishes 10% of manuscripts submitted. Payment: varies. Does not copyright for author. PMA.

HOARD'S DAIRYMAN, W.D. Hoard & Sons Company, 28 Milwaukee Avenue West, Fort Atkinson, WI 53538, 920-563-5551. 1885. Articles, photos, cartoons, interviews, letters, news items, non-fiction. circ. 110M. 20/yr. Pub'd 20 issues 1998; expects 20 issues 1999, 20 issues 2000. 3 titles listed in the *Small Press Record of Books in Print* (28th Edition, 1999-00). sub. price: $14; sample: no charge. Back issues: $2. 50pp; 10¼×14¼; †of. Payment: varies. Copyrighted, does not revert to author. Ads: $13,017/$8,343/$1.85.

HOAX!, John C.S. Quel, 64 Beechgrove, Aberhonddu, Powys Cymru LD3 9ET, United Kingdom. 1989. Articles, art, photos, cartoons, interviews, satire, criticism, reviews, music, letters, collages, concrete art, news items, non-fiction. "*Hoax!* is the world's only regular periodical which is devoted to the research and documentation of pranks and hoaxes in all of their manifestations, from urban legends to yippie situationism political parody to scathing social satire to neo-nazi holocaust propaganda bullshit. We have been called "a sort of 'Fortean Times' for pranksters" and have gained spectacular reviews from Robert Anton Wilson, Peter Lamborn Wilson, Adam Parfrey and many other counter-culture contemporaries who have also espoused wildly concerning our exploits. Recent contributors include: Stewart Home, Karen Eliot, John Trubee, Lawrence Burton, Billboard Liberation Front and Negativland." circ. 5M. 4/yr. Pub'd 3 issues 1998; expects 4 issues 1999, 4 issues 2000. price per copy: £2.30; sample: £2.30. Back issues: same as usual. Discounts: depending on means of distribution. 32-64pp; size A4; †mi. Reporting time: depends on deadlines. Payment: depends on work contributed. Not copyrighted. Pub's reviews: 230+ in 1998. §Humor, occult, industrial/experimental music, mail art pranks, UFOs, rabbits, conspiracies, drugs, cyberpunk, forteana, cartoons, media manipulation, propaganda. Small Press Group of Great Britain.

Hobblebush Books, 17-A Old Milford Road, Brookline, NH 03033, voice/fax 603-672-4317; E-mail shall@jlc.net; website http:www.jlc.net/~hobblebush/. 1993. "Publishes literary and non-literary books of the highest quality that present a unique voice and make a difference." avg. press run 3M. Pub'd 2 titles 1998; expects 2 titles 1999, 2 titles 2000. 3 titles listed in the *Small Press Record of Books in Print* (28th Edition, 1999-00). avg. price, paper: $12.95. 150pp; of. Reporting time: 1 month. Simultaneous submissions accepted: yes. Copyrights for author.

HOBO POETRY & HAIKU MAGAZINE, Dane Thwaites, PO Box 166, Hazelbrook NSW 2779, Australia. 1993. Poetry. "Australia's leading specialist poetry quarterly." circ. 700. 4/yr. Pub'd 4 issues 1998; expects 4 issues 1999, 4 issues 2000. sub. price: $20; per copy: $5.50; sample: $5.50. Back issues: $5.50. Discounts: negotiable. 64pp; 160×200mm; †of. Reporting time: 6 weeks. Simultaneous submissions accepted: yes. Publishes 2% of manuscripts submitted. Payment: approx. $15 per page. Copyrighted, reverts to author. Pub's reviews: 20 in 1998. §Poetry on haiku. Ads: $200/$120/$25 business card. Society of Editors (N.S.W.).

HOBSON'S CHOICE, David F. Powell, PO Box 98, Ripley, OH 45167, 513-392-4549. 1974. Fiction, articles, art, cartoons, interviews, satire, criticism, reviews, news items. "We look for science fiction (hard and soft), fantasy and non-fiction of scientific and technological interest. Length of fiction: 2,000-10,000 words. Length of non-fiction: 2,000-5,000 words." circ. 2.5M. 6/yr. Pub'd 3 issues 1998; expects 6 issues 1999, 6 issues 2000. sub. price: $12; per copy: $2; sample: $2.25. Back issues: $2.50. Discounts: 20% on consignment minimum 10. 16-20pp; 8½×11; †of. Reporting time: 8-12 weeks. Simultaneous submissions accepted: no. Publishes 10% of manuscripts submitted. Payment: 1-4¢/word; copy of issue in which work appears. Copyrighted. Pub's reviews: 9 in 1998. §Science fiction, science, technology, computers. Ads: $100/$60/$4 column inch.

Hochelaga Press, Raymond Beauchemin, Denise Roig, 4982 Connaught Avenue, Montreal, BC H4V 1X3, Canada, 514-484-3186; Fax 514-484-8971; hochelaga@sympatico.ca. 1995. Poetry, fiction, non-fiction. avg. press run 500-1M. Pub'd 1 title 1998; expects 1 title 2000. 3 titles listed in the *Small Press Record of Books in Print* (28th Edition, 1999-00). avg. price, paper: $10.95. Discounts: bookstore 40%, wholesale 50%. Reporting time: 4-6 months. Simultaneous submissions accepted: yes. Payment: yes. Copyrights for author.

Hoffman Press, Robert P. Hoffman, Co-Editor; Virginia M. Hoffman, Co-Editor, PO Box 2996, Santa Rosa, CA 95405-0996, 707-538-5527; fax 707-538-7371. 1989. Articles, satire, criticism, non-fiction. "Cookbooks" avg. press run 5M. Pub'd 2 titles 1998; expects 4 titles 1999, 7 titles 2000. 3 titles listed in the *Small Press Record of Books in Print* (28th Edition, 1999-00). avg. price, cloth: $18.95; paper: $12.95. Discounts: less 55% retail price to distributor. 200pp; 7×10; of. Reporting time: 1-2 weeks. Simultaneous submissions accepted: yes. Publishes 1-5% of manuscripts submitted. Payment: royalty paid upon publication. Copyrights for author. MSPA, PMA.

●**HOGTOWN CREEK REVIEW,** Elisa Maranzana, Michael Martin, PO Box 1249, Gainesville, FL 32602-1249, e-mail hogtown@bigfoot.com. 1999. Poetry, fiction, articles, art, photos, cartoons, interviews, reviews, parts-of-novels, non-fiction. "*Hogtown Creek Review* is a new magazine weaving literary art and popular culture. Based in the south, we welcome submissions from all over the map. Publishing imaginative writing and artwork in an inventive, accessible format. Looking for inspired fiction, poetry, creative non-fiction, reviews and artwork. First issue includes fiction by Lyn Di Iorio. Please acknowledge simultaneous submissions. Limit one story and five poems; SASE." 2/yr. Expects 1 issue 1999, 2 issues 2000. sub. price: $10; per copy: $5; sample: $5. Back issues: $5. 85pp; 8½×11; of. Reporting time: 1-3 months. Simultaneous submissions accepted: yes. Payment: 2 copies. Copyrighted. Ads: $100/$50/ 1/4 page $25. CLMP.

Hohm Press, Regina Sara Ryan, PO Box 2501, Prescott, AZ 86302, 520-778-9189; Fax 520-717-1779; e-mail pinedr@goodnet.com; www.booknotes.com/hohm/. 1975. Poetry, satire, criticism, non-fiction. avg. press run 3M. Pub'd 6 titles 1998; expects 6 titles 1999, 8 titles 2000. 29 titles listed in the *Small Press Record of Books in Print* (28th Edition, 1999-00). avg. price, paper: $14.95. Discounts: standard, 40% trade; distributors inquiry welcomed. 200pp; 6×9. Reporting time: 1-2 months. Simultaneous submissions accepted: yes. Publishes 5% of manuscripts submitted. Payment: usually 10%. Copyrights for author. PMA, AZ Book Publishers Assoc.

●**Holbrook Street Press,** PO Box 399, Cortaro, AZ 85652-0399, 520-616-7643; fax 520-616-7519; holbrookstpress@theriver.com; www.copshock.com. 1998. Non-fiction. avg. press run 5M. Expects 2 titles 1999, 2 titles 2000. 1 title listed in the *Small Press Record of Books in Print* (28th Edition, 1999-00). avg. price, paper: $20. 400pp; 6×9; of. Reporting time: 4 weeks. Simultaneous submissions accepted: yes. Publishes 2% of manuscripts submitted. PMA, SPAN.

Holistic Education Press (see also HOLISTIC EDUCATION REVIEW), C.S. Jakiela, PO Box 328, Brandon, VT 05733-0328, 802-247-8312 (voice and fax) e-mail holistic@sover.net. 1988. Articles, photos, reviews. "Topics relating to holistic education." avg. press run 2M. Pub'd 1 title 1998; expects 3 titles 1999, 3 titles 2000. 5 titles listed in the *Small Press Record of Books in Print* (28th Edition, 1999-00). avg. price, paper: $21. Discounts: available from publisher. 300pp; 6×9; of. Reporting time: 4 months. Payment: variable.

HOLISTIC EDUCATION REVIEW, Holistic Education Press, Jeffrey Kane, PO Box 328, Brandon, VT

248

05733-0328, 802-247-8312 (voice and fax) e-mail holistic@sover.net. 1988. Articles, photos, interviews, reviews. "Interested in articles on holistic education, learning styles, global education, whole language, etc." circ. 2M. 4/yr. Pub'd 4 issues 1998; expects 4 issues 1999, 4 issues 2000. sub. price: $65 instit., $35 indiv.; per copy: $10. Back issues: $10. Discounts: 10% to subscription agents. 68pp; 8½×11; of. Reporting time: 3 months. Publishes less than 50% of manuscripts submitted. Payment: none. Copyrighted. Pub's reviews: 12 in 1998. §Holistic education, learning styles, global education, whole language, etc. Ads: $250/$150/45¢ word ($20 minimum).

THE HOLLINS CRITIC, R.H.W. Dillard, Editor; Amanda Cockrell, Managing Editor, PO Box 9538, Hollins University, VA 24020. 1964. Poetry, criticism, reviews. "Essay on particular work of one author; several poems. Essay approximately 5000 words, no footnotes. No unsolicited essay or review mss. Essays by prior commitment only. Short poems are published in every issue. Other features are a cover picture of the author under discussion, a checklist of author's writing and a brief sketch of career, plus book reviews. Recent essayists: David Slavitt, Earl Rovit, Kelly Cherry, Henry Taylor, Jeanne Larsen." circ. 350. 5/yr. Pub'd 5 issues 1998; expects 5 issues 1999, 5 issues 2000. sub. price: $6 U.S.; $7.50 elsewhere; per copy: $2 U.S.; sample: $1.50 U.S. Back issues: $2 U.S.; ($3 elsewhere). 24pp; 7½×10; lp. Reporting time: 2 months. Simultaneous submissions accepted with an SASE. Publishes 4% of manuscripts submitted. Payment: $25 for poems. Copyrighted, poetry rights revert to auther. Pub's reviews: 15 in 1998. §Mainly current fiction and poetry and critical works. CLMP.

Hollis Publishing Company, Fred Lyford, Rebecca Shannon, 95 Runnells Bridge Road, Hollis, NH 03049, 800-635-6302; 603-889-4500. Criticism, news items, non-fiction. "We focus on academic, scholarly titles dealing with history, politics, social science; also titles with a New England focus." avg. press run 1M. Pub'd 3 titles 1998; expects 5 titles 1999, 10 titles 2000. 3 titles listed in the *Small Press Record of Books in Print* (28th Edition, 1999-00). avg. price, cloth: $29.95; paper: $15.95. Discounts: please contact us. 300pp; 6×9; †of. Reporting time: 1-3 months. Simultaneous submissions accepted: yes. Publishes 50% of manuscripts submitted. Payment: vary from 8% and higher. Copyrights for author. AAP, PMA, Bookbuilders of Boston, Scholarly Publishing Today, NE Booksellers Association.

THE HOLLYWOOD ACTING COACHES AND TEACHERS DIRECTORY, Acting World Books, Lawrence Parke, PO Box 3044, Hollywood, CA 90078, 818-905-1345. 1981. "Occasional articles by and or about subject material people, orgns, currently recommended procedures, etc." circ. 1.2M. 4/yr. Pub'd 4 issues 1998; expects 4 issues 1999, 4 issues 2000. No subscriptions available; price per copy: $15. Back issues: not available. Discounts: none except to bookstores (40%). 55pp; 8½×11; †of. Copyrighted, reverts to author. Ads: $400 1/2 page/special 6 months in both pub's, rate $800.

Hollywood Film Archive, D. Richard Baer, Editor, 8391 Beverly Boulevard #321, Hollywood, CA 90048. 1972. "HFA compiles and publishes film reference information. In addition to our own books, we are interested in high-quality comprehensive reference information on film or television. Please inquire before submitting material. Those submitting unsolicited material must include a self-addressed stamped envelope in order to have it returned. Our Cinema Book Society book club considers books of other publishers for sale to members, libraries, the film and TV industries, and the general public. We distribute motion picture reference books for other publishers, including *American Film Institute Catalogs, Screen World*, and the complete reprint of *Variety Film Reviews 1907-1990*, and *Variety Obituaries 1905-1992*" avg. press run 5M. Pub'd 8 titles 1998; expects 5 titles 1999. 6 titles listed in the *Small Press Record of Books in Print* (28th Edition, 1999-00). avg. price, cloth: $95; paper: $19. Discounts: 1-4 copies, 20% to bona fide booksellers, wholesalers, jobbers, etc., 5 or more 40%; large quantities, inquire. 8½×11; of. Reporting time: 3-4 weeks.

HOLLYWOOD NOSTALGIA, Full Moon Publications, Sharida Rizzuto, Harold Tollison, Ann Hoyt, Rose Dalton, 577 Central Avenue, Box 4, Jefferson, LA 70121-1400, e-mail: publisher@mailexcite.com or blackie@talkcity.com; Websites www.home.talkcity.com/SunsetBlvd/blackie, www.wbs.net/homepages/b/l/a/ blackkie.htm/, www2.cybercities.com/z/zines/. 1983. Poetry, fiction, articles, art, photos, cartoons, interviews, satire, criticism, reviews, letters, long-poems, collages, news items, non-fiction. "Articles, reviews, interviews, poetry, fiction, lots of photographs." circ. 500. 2/yr. Pub'd 2 issues 1998; expects 2 issues 1999, 2 issues 2000. sub. price: $15.80; per copy: $7.90; sample: $7.90. Back issues: $7.90. Discounts: trade with other like publications. 100pp; 8½×11; †of; excellent quality offset covers. Reporting time: 2-6 weeks. Simultaneous submissions accepted: yes. Publishes 30-35% of manuscripts submitted. Payment: free copies, fees paid to all contributors negotiable. Copyrighted, reverts to author. Pub's reviews: 50 in 1998. §Anything to do with Hollywood nostalgia. Ads: free. NWC, HWA, MWA, Western Writers of America (WWA), Arizona Author Assn. (AAA), Small Press Genre Assn.

Holy Cow! Press, Jim Perlman, PO Box 3170, Mount Royal Station, Duluth, MN 55803. 1977. Poetry, fiction, articles, parts-of-novels, long-poems. "Holy Cow! Press is a Midwestern independent publisher that features new work by both well-known and younger writers. Besides single author collections, we try to tastefully assemble anthologies centered around important themes. We are supportive of first books by younger writers;

249

PLEASE query before submitting manuscripts." avg. press run 1.5M. Pub'd 5 titles 1998; expects 4 titles 1999, 5 titles 2000. 29 titles listed in the *Small Press Record of Books in Print* (28th Edition, 1999-00). avg. price, cloth: $18; paper: $13. Discounts: 40% off to classrooms, bulk, institutions, bookstores. 96pp; 6×9; of. Reporting time: 2-4 months. We accept simultaneous submissions if informed. Publishes 2% of manuscripts submitted. Payment: negotiable with each author. Copyrights for author. UMBA.

HOLY SMOKE, Sweetlight Books, Guy Mount, 16625 Heitman Road, Cottonwood, CA 96022, 916-529-5392, www.snowcrest.net/swtlight/holysmoke.html. 1993. "Exclusively online. Dedicated to the legalization of marijuana as a sacrament and medicine. I am seeking written testimonials, stories and illustrations from people who have experienced spiritual growth or physical healing with the use of marijuana, especially reports from the dispirited victims of AIDS, cancer, glaucoma and other debilitating diseases. Contributors will receive a free subscription to the magazine and byline credit as desired." sub. price: free online. Internet. Reporting time: 2 weeks. Simultaneous submissions accepted: yes. Publishes 10% of manuscripts submitted. Payment: free copy, ad or newsletter page. Copyrighted, reverts to author. Pub's reviews: 8 in 1998. §Medical marijuana, hemp, sacramental and respectful use. Ads: $100/$50, free to distributors and pro-marijuana advocates.

●**Homa & Sekey Books,** Shawn X. Ye, 11 Colonial Parkway, Dumont, NJ 07628, 201-384-6692; fax 201-384-6055; e-mail wenye@aol.com. 1997. Fiction, art, non-fiction. "We mostly publish books on Asian topics, with China as focus. Both original English and English in translation." avg. press run 3M. Pub'd 1 title 1998; expects 3 titles 1999, 4 titles 2000. 2 titles listed in the *Small Press Record of Books in Print* (28th Edition, 1999-00). avg. price, paper: $15. Discounts: from 20% to 55%. 256pp; 5½×8½. Reporting time: 2-6 weeks. Payment: yearly or by contract. Can copyright for author if necessary. PMA.

HOME EDUCATION MAGAZINE, Mark Hegener, Editor; Helen Hegener, Editor, PO Box 1083, Tonasket, WA 98855, 509-486-1351; e-Mail HomeEdmag@aol.com. 1984. Poetry, articles, art, photos, cartoons, interviews, satire, criticism, reviews, letters, news items. "*Home Education Magazine* is for families who choose to teach their children at home. Please write for editorial guidelines, include SASE." circ. 12.5M. 6/yr. Pub'd 6 issues 1998; expects 6 issues 1999, 6 issues 2000. sub. price: $24; per copy: $4.50; sample: $4.50. Back issues: $3.50. Discounts: write for info, include SASE. 68pp; 8½×11; web of. Reporting time: 6 weeks. Simultaneous submissions accepted: no. Publishes 25% of manuscripts submitted. Payment: $25-$50 per article. Copyrighted, reverts to author. §Homeschooling, education, child development, alternative education, family. Ads: $925/$450/40¢ classified per word (min. $10/issue). PMA, EdPress, NADTP.

HOME PLANET NEWS, Home Planet Publications, Enid Dame, Donald Lev, P.O. Box 415 Stuyvesant Station, New York, NY 10009, 718-769-2854. 1979. Poetry, fiction, articles, art, photos, cartoons, interviews, criticism, reviews, letters, parts-of-novels, long-poems, news items. "We like lively work of all types and schools. Poetry should run about a page. (Need shorter ones right now.) For articles, reviews, etc., please query first. Some recent contributors include: Richard Kostelanetz, Andrew Glaze, Toi Derricotte, William Packard, Will Inman, Tuli Kupferberg, Dorothy Friedman, Gerald Locklin, Steve Kowit, Lyn Lifshin, Alicia Ostriker, Robert Peters, Edmund Pennant, Frank Murphy, Hal Sirowitz, David Zeiger, Denise Duhamel, David Gershutor, and Layle Silbert." circ. 3M. 3-4/yr. Pub'd 2 issues 1998; expects 3 issues 1999, 3 issues 2000. sub. price: $10; per copy: $3; sample: $3. Back issues: $2. Discounts: 40% consignment, 50% cash, 25% agents. 24pp; 10×15; of. Reporting time: 3-4 months. Payment: copies & 1 year gift subscription. Copyrighted, reverts to author. Pub's reviews: 26 books, 10 magazines in 1998. §Poetry, fiction. Ads: $150/$75. CLMP.

Home Planet Publications (see also HOME PLANET NEWS), Donald Lev, Enid Dame, PO Box 415 Stuyvesant Station, New York, NY 10009, 718-769-2854. 1991. Poetry. "Home Planet Publications publishes occasional books of poetry, but does not consider unsolicited manuscripts. For our magazine, *Home Planet News*, see listing above." avg. press run 400. avg. price, paper: $1.50. Discounts: 50% cash to stores; 40% consignment; 25% agents. 60pp; 5×8; of. Payment: negotiable. Copyrights for author.

Home Power, Inc. (see also HOME POWER MAGAZINE), Richard Perez, PO Box 275, Ashland, OR 97520, 916-475-3179. 1987. Non-fiction. "Our first book went to press May 1991, *The Battery Book*. Compendium of Home Power Magazine - availible on CD ROM. CD ROM Solar 2- available issues 1-42, CD ROM Solar 3 issues 43-60 - available 6/98. The new electric Vehicles Cavailable 4/15/96 *2nd Revised edition Heavan's Flame available 6/98*" avg. press run 5M. Pub'd 2 titles 1998. 1 title listed in the *Small Press Record of Books in Print* (28th Edition, 1999-00). avg. price, paper: $10; other: $20. Discounts: 40%. 100-400pp; size varies; of. Reporting time: 3-4 months. Payment: small advance, 16% of net sales 0-10K, 20% of net sales 10K+ - contract. Copyrights for author if so desired.

HOME POWER MAGAZINE, Home Power, Inc., Richard Perez, PO Box 520, Ashland, OR 97520, 916-475-3179; e-Mail karen.perez@home power.org, Order line 800-707-6585, 916-475-0830, Fax 916-475-0941. 1987. Articles, photos, reviews, letters, news items, non-fiction. "Length of material 1,000 to 8,000 words. All articles must contain hard, hands-on information about the use of renewable energy in home settings.'' circ. 20M. 6/yr. Pub'd 6 issues 1998; expects 6 issues 1999, 6 issues 2000. sub. price: $22.50; per copy: $4.75; sample: free. Back issues: #1-20 $3.25, #21-45 $4.75 each, #46 on $5.75 each (out of print) 1-12, 14, 15, 36. On CD $29- 1-42 Solar 11 (43-60- $29- Solar 3). Discounts: bulk, agent 50% of cover. 116pp; 8½×11; of, heatset. Reporting time: 8 weeks. Simultaneous submissions accepted: no. Publishes 33% of manuscripts submitted. Payment: none. Copyrighted, rights revert if author so desires. Pub's reviews: 4 in 1998. §Renewable energy, ecology. Ads: $1200/$672/$377 1/4 page/multiple insertion discounts.

Homestead Publishing, Carl Schreier, Box 193, Moose, WY 83012. 1980. Art, photos, non-fiction. ''Our specialty is natural history of North America, either children or adult, pictorial or literature.'' avg. press run 10M-25M. Pub'd 23 titles 1998; expects 55 titles 1999, 100 titles 2000. 7 titles listed in the *Small Press Record of Books in Print* (28th Edition, 1999-00). avg. price, cloth: $12-$25; paper: $10-$25. Discounts: 40% bookstores, 33% libraries, 50% jobbers. 90-600pp; 7×9; of. Reporting time: 3-4 months. Publishes 1% of manuscripts submitted. Payment: depends on the work. Copyrights for author.

Homeward Press, John Curl, PO Box 2307, Berkeley, CA 94702, 412-526-3254. 1980. Poetry, non-fiction. ''No unsolicited manuscripts.'' avg. press run 500. Expects 6 titles 1999, 1 title 2000. 8 titles listed in the *Small Press Record of Books in Print* (28th Edition, 1999-00). avg. price, paper: $5. 56pp; 5½×8½; of. Copyrights for author.

Honors Group, Martin Wasserman, Adirondack Community College, SUNY, Queensbury, NY 12804. 1997. Poetry, articles, criticism, non-fiction. ''We are looking for research articles, essays, and even poetry on the life and work of Franz Kafka. Contributions should be no longer than 15 pages. Send submissions with SASE. At this time, our press is only publishing anthologies and we will not look at book-length manuscripts.'' avg. press run 500. Expects 1 title 1999, 2 titles 2000. avg. price, paper: $15. 150pp; 6×9; lp. Reporting time: 1 month. Simultaneous submissions accepted: yes. Publishes 50% of manuscripts submitted. Payment: authors receive free books. Copyrights for author.

HOOTENANNY, David Keith, Ken Weathersby, 62 North 7th Street 3-R, Brooklyn, NY 11211, 718-388-5736, 315-423-9119. 1994. Poetry, fiction, art, photos, music, parts-of-novels, plays, concrete art, non-fiction. ''Interested in mixed-media, welcome handmade multiple originals. Those interested in hand-made contributions should contact editors prior'' circ. 200. 2/yr. Pub'd 1 issue 1998; expects 2 issues 1999, 2 issues 2000. sub. price: $20; per copy: $10; sample: $10. 75pp; 8½×11; †photocopy. Publishes 10% of manuscripts submitted. Payment: 1 copy. Copyrighted, reverts to author.

Hoover Institution Press, Patricia A. Baker, Executive Editor, Stanford University, Stanford, CA 94305-6010, 650-723-3373; e-mail baker@hoover.stanford.edu. Non-fiction. ''Subjects usually published are: economics, political science, public policy, studies of nationalities in Central and Eastern Europe, Asian Studies, international studies, and reference books'' avg. press run 1M. Pub'd 8 titles 1998; expects 8 titles 1999, 6 titles 2000. 40 titles listed in the *Small Press Record of Books in Print* (28th Edition, 1999-00). avg. price, cloth: $33.95; paper: $19.95. Discounts: wholesale: 1-4 copies 20%, 5-24 42%, 25-49 45%, 50-99 48%, 100+ 50%; Retail 1-2 copies 20%, 3-24 40%, 25-49 42%, 50-249 44%, 250+ 46%. 200pp; 6×9; of. Reporting time: varies, 2-4 months. Payment: individually arranged. Copyrights for author. Bookbuilders West.

Hoover's, Inc., 1033 La Posada Drive, Suite 250, Austin, TX 78752-3824, 512-374-4500, Fax 512-374-4501, E-mail info@hoovers.com. 1990. ''Business reference books, software, online business reference information.'' avg. press run 3M. Pub'd 11 titles 1998; expects 8 titles 1999, 8 titles 2000. 14 titles listed in the *Small Press Record of Books in Print* (28th Edition, 1999-00). avg. price, cloth: $98. 900pp; 6×9; web. Simultaneous submissions accepted: no. Publishes 0% of manuscripts submitted. Payment: none.

Hope Publishing House, Faith Annette Sand, Publisher, PO Box 60008, Pasadena, CA 91116, 818-792-6123; fax 818-792-2121. 1983. Criticism, non-fiction. ''We deal with religious and educational topics and like to facilitate getting women and minorities into print, although we publish men, too. We are a nonprofit publishing venture, a program unit of the So. Calif. Ecumenical Council. We have published a Spanish/English side-by-side children's book, as well as the Spanish edition of Steve Biko's last book. We are currently interested in ecology, health and justice issues'' avg. press run 3M-5M. Pub'd 6 titles 1998; expects 6 titles 1999, 6 titles 2000. 36 titles listed in the *Small Press Record of Books in Print* (28th Edition, 1999-00). avg. price, cloth: $14.95; paper: $10.95. Discounts: as required to trade and bulk buyers. 228pp; 6×9, 5½×8½, 8½×11; lp. Reporting time: 2 months. Payment: royalties are arranged, payments are made biannually. Copyrights for author. PMA.

HORIZON, Johnny Haelterman, Stationsstraat 232A, 1770 Liedekerke, Belgium, 053-669465. 1985. Poetry, fiction, articles, art, photos. ''*Horizon* is a Flemish magazine. Since #72 (sold out) of June 1991, every issue contains also a few English pages. Fiction: Stories for 'The English Pages' should have between 300 and 1000 words. Anything accepted for translation into Dutch may be longer. A realistic treatment is preferred but a touch of fantasy is sometimes acceptable. The content should be suitable for a general public, therefore no extreme violence or sex. Payment - two copies of the issue containing the story. Non-Fiction: Articles should have a minimum length of 1000 words. They should deal with a genre, trend, or theme in fiction. Payment - two copies of the issue containing the article. Poetry: Poems are used only as a filler. Preference is given to poems with punctuation, metre, and rhyme but that is not a hard and fast rule. If a poem is not published after a year, it means that it couldn't be used. Payment - one copy of the issue containing the poem(s). Artwork: Drawings are used only in relation to the text. A copy of the story or article for which I need illustrations is sent to the selected artist. Payment - two copies of the appropriate issue. If requested by the artist, a small payment in Belgian money is possible but in that case only one copy of the issue will be sent'' circ. 110. 2/yr. Pub'd 2 issues 1998; expects 2 issues 1999, 1 issue 2000. sub. price: $20; per copy: $10 (incl. p&p); sample: $10 (incl. p&p). 44-56pp; 8.34×11.73; photocopy. Reporting time: a few weeks, perhaps a few months for overseas. Publishes 55% of manuscripts submitted. Payment: usually 1-2 copies; 1BEF per 10 words (& copy) for original stories or articles in Dutch. Payment in Belgian funds also possible for artwork and photos to order. Copyrighted, reverts to author. Pub's reviews: about 50 magazines, 20 books in 1998. §Fiction, literature and art; all the reviews are in Dutch.

HORIZONS, Full Moon Publications, Sharida Rizzuto, Harold Tollison, Ann Hoyt, 577 Central Avenue, Box 4, Jefferson, LA 70121-1400, e-mail: horizons@altavista.net or publisher@mailexcite.com; Website www2.cybercities.com/z/zines/. 1983. Poetry, fiction, articles, art, photos, cartoons, interviews, satire, criticism, reviews, letters, long-poems, news items, non-fiction. ''Multi-cultural articles, reviews, interviews, essays'' circ. 300-500. 2/yr. Pub'd 2 issues 1998; expects 2 issues 1999, 2 issues 2000. sub. price: $15.80; per copy: $7.90; sample: $7.90. Back issues: $7.90. Discounts: trade with other like publications. 100pp; 8½×11. Publishes 30-35% of manuscripts submitted. Pub's reviews: 50 in 1998. §Anything to do with multiculturalism, ethic poetry & fiction, travel experiences.

HORIZONS BEYOND, Full Moon Publications, Sharida Rizzuto, Harold Tollison, Ann Hoyt, 577 Central Avenue, Box 4, Jefferson, LA 70121-0517, e-mail fullmoon@eudoramail.com or haunted@rocketmail.com; Websites www.members.xoom.com/blackie, www2.cybercities.com/z/zines/, www.eclecticity.com/zines/, www.spaceports.com/~haunted/. 1983. Poetry, fiction, articles, art, photos, cartoons, interviews, satire, criticism, reviews, letters, long-poems, collages, news items, non-fiction. ''Sci-fi and fantasy articles, reviews, fiction'' circ. 300. 2/yr. Pub'd 2 issues 1998; expects 2 issues 1999, 2 issues 2000. sub. price: $15.80; per copy: $7.90; sample: $7.90. Back issues: $7.90. Discounts: trade with other like publication. 100pp; 8½×11; †of, excellent quality offset covers. Reporting time: 2-6 weeks. Simultaneous submissions accepted: yes. Publishes 30% of manuscripts submitted. Payment: free copies, fees paid for articles, reviews, and artwork negotiable. Copyrighted, reverts to author. Pub's reviews: 40 in 1998. §Science fiction and fantasy,(but no hardcure scifi sword & sorcery welcome). Ads: free. NWC, HWA, Small Press Genre Association, MWA, Western Writers of America (WWA), Arizona Authors Association (AAA).

Horned Owl Publishing, Rob Von Rudloff, J. Bryony Lake, 3906 Cadboro Bay Rd., Victoria, BC V8N 4G6, Canada, 250-477-8488; fax 250-721-1029; e-mail hornowl@islandnet.com. 1992. Fiction, criticism, reviews, non-fiction. ''We publish scholarly books in the field of Pagan Studies and Pagan Children's Literature. We prefer submissions of at least 25,000 words for the former'' avg. press run 4M. Pub'd 2 titles 1998; expects 3 titles 1999, 3 titles 2000. 5 titles listed in the *Small Press Record of Books in Print* (28th Edition, 1999-00). avg. price, paper: $12.95. Discounts: trade 40%, distributor 55%. 200pp, children's literature 40pp; size variable, mostly 6×9; of. Reporting time: 2 months. Simultaneous submissions accepted only when identified as such. Publishes 20% of manuscripts submitted. Payment: advance based on anticipated production run; royalty 10% (less for foreign sales, etc.). Copyrights for author. Publishers Marketing Association (PMA).

●**Horse & Buggy Press,** Dave Wofford, 303 Kinsey Street, Raleigh, NC 27603, 919-828-2514. 1996. Poetry, fiction, articles, art, photos, criticism, letters, non-fiction. ''All of our books are letterpress printing by hand, hand-bindings, hand papermaking, and limited editions.'' avg. press run 250. Pub'd 2 titles 1998; expects 2 titles 1999, 2 titles 2000. avg. price, paper: $75. Discounts: 30% off for bookstores, dealers. (Orders of 5 books minimum, can be mix and match). 48pp; 7×10; †letterpress. Copyrights for author. Fine Press Book Association, Friends of Dard Hunter, Small Press Center.

HOR-TASY, Daniel Betz, PO Box 158, Harris, IA 51345. 1980. Fiction. ''We are looking for psychological horror & pure fantasy (eg: faeries, trolls, sword & sorcery, myths, legends). The horror we want is based on or in the mind, so we don't really want the over-used haunted houses, monsters, hexes, ghosts, etc. We'd like to get one issue out each year. We are not interested in science fiction.'' circ. 400. Expects 1 issue 1999, 1 issue 2000. price per copy: $4. 72pp; 5½×8½; †mi, with offset covers. Reporting time: immediately to 3 weeks. Payment: copies. Copyrighted, reverts to author.

HORTIDEAS, Greg Williams, Pat Williams, 750 Black Lick Road, Gravel Switch, KY 40328, 606-332-7606. 1984. Articles, reviews, news items, non-fiction. ''Short articles on vegetable, flower, and fruit growing, directed to amateur gardeners; including abstracts from the technical horticultural literature, new product reviews, and book reviews.'' circ. 1.2M. 12/yr. Pub'd 12 issues 1998; expects 12 issues 1999, 12 issues 2000. sub. price: $20; per copy: $2; sample: same. Back issues: $2. Discounts: none, mailorder only. 12pp; 8½×11; of.

252

Reporting time: 1 month. Payment: free issue. Copyrighted, does not revert to author. Pub's reviews: 30 in 1998. §Gardening, horticulture, agriculture, botany, forestry. No ads.

Horus Publishing, Inc., Suite 39, PO Box 7530, Yelm, WA 98597, 360-894-0965; Fax 360-458-1440; horus@nwrain.com. 1995. Fiction, non-fiction. avg. press run 5M. Pub'd 3 titles 1998; expects 3 titles 1999, 5 titles 2000. 3 titles listed in the *Small Press Record of Books in Print* (28th Edition, 1999-00). avg. price, cloth: $25.95; paper: $18.95. Discounts: wholesaler/distributor 55%, bookstores 40%. 380pp; 6×9. Simultaneous submissions accepted: no. Payment: 10%-15%.

The Hosanna Press, Cathie Ruggie Saunders, 215 Gale, River Forest, IL 60305, 708-771-8259. 1974. Poetry, fiction, art, concrete art. "Limited edition fine printings from foundry type on rag & unique handmade papers, w/ original graphics. Innovative concepts of book, paper, and print pursued." avg. press run 25-100. Expects 1 title 1999, 1 title 2000. 15 titles listed in the *Small Press Record of Books in Print* (28th Edition, 1999-00). avg. price, cloth: varies; paper: varies; other: varies. Pages vary; size varies; †lp. Reporting time: 3-6 weeks. Payment: 10% of edition. Copyrights for author. APHA, American Center for Design.

Host Publications, Inc. (see also THE DIRTY GOAT), Elzbieta Szoka, Joe W. Bratcher III, 2717 Wooldridge, Austin, TX 78703-1953, 512-479-8069. 1988. Poetry, fiction, art, photos, interviews, criticism, parts-of-novels, long-poems, plays. "Poetry books average 100 pages with illustrations. Drama books average 300 pages. Recent authors: Anna Frajlich, Gerald Nicosia, Urszula Koziol, Layle Silbert. Prefer to publish books by authors with some reputation. Other material, by less established artists, considered for *The Dirty Goat*." avg. press run 1M-1.5M. Pub'd 3 titles 1998; expects 3 titles 1999, 4 titles 2000. 3 titles listed in the *Small Press Record of Books in Print* (28th Edition, 1999-00). avg. price, paper: $10. Discounts: 1 copy 20%, 2-9 30%. 10-24 40%, 25-49 43%. 150pp; 5½×8½; of. Reporting time: indeterminate. Payment: advance up front with no payments later. Does not copyright for author. Small Press Center, Book Publishers of Texas (BPT).

HOT CALALOO, Michael I. Phillips, PO Box 429, Riderwood, MD 21139, 410-997-1381, e-mail mip@welchlink.welch.jhu.edu - (web page) http://www.welch.jhu.edu/homepages/mip/html/hcal.html. 1992. Poetry, articles, satire, news items, non-fiction. "Additional address: 5328 Lightning View Road, Columbia, MD 21045." 6/yr. Expects 4 issues 1999, 6 issues 2000. sub. price: $8; per copy: $1.50; sample: $1.50. Back issues: $1.50. 8pp; 8½×11; †desktop. Reporting time: 2 months. Simultaneous submissions accepted: yes. Payment: none. Copyrighted, reverts to author. Ads: $16 column inch.

HOT FLASHES, Robert Trammell, 1910 Mecca Street, Dallas, TX 75206-7226, 821-1308. 1985. Poetry, fiction, articles, art, photos, cartoons, satire, criticism, reviews, music, letters, long-poems, collages, concrete art, news items. "There is an emphasis on poetry, xerox and other kinds of photo art. Recent contributors include: Gerald Burns, Blaster Al, Robert Bly, Robert Creeley, Terry Allen, Randy Twaddle, Queen Octoroon, John M. Bennett, Roxy Gordon, James Hillman, Barry Silesky, Norman Weinstein, David Searey, LeAnne Howe and Martha King" circ. 200. 10/yr. Pub'd 9 issues 1998; expects 10 issues 1999, 10 issues 2000. 1 title listed in the *Small Press Record of Books in Print* (28th Edition, 1999-00). sub. price: $15; per copy: $2; sample: $2. Discounts: 40% off. 16pp; 8½×11; †of, and other photo processes. Reporting time: 6 weeks. Payment: 2 copies. Copyrighted, reverts to author. Pub's reviews: 5 in 1998. §Poetry, criticism, music, art. Ads: $110/$60/$35 1/4 page/$20 1/8.

Hot Pepper Press (see also THE ACORN), Taylor Graham, Hatch Graham, PO Box 39, Somerset, CA 95684, 916-621-1833. 1991. Poetry. "Not currently reading for chapbooks" 5 titles listed in the *Small Press Record of Books in Print* (28th Edition, 1999-00).

HOTHEAD PAISAN, HOMICIDAL LESBIAN TERRORIST, PO Box 1242, Northampton, MA 01061-1242. 1991. Cartoons. "Do not take submissions." circ. 5M. 4/yr. Pub'd 4 issues 1998; expects 4 issues 1999, 4 issues 2000. sub. price: $15; per copy: $3.50; sample: $3.50. Back issues: $3.50. Discounts: 40%. 28pp; 5½×8½; of. Copyrighted, reverts to author.

House of Hits, Inc., Dan McKinnon, North American Airlines Bldg 75, Suite 250, JFK International Airport, Jamaica, NY 11430, 718-656-2650. 1973. "We're basically interested in aviation and current history involving the Middle East." avg. press run 2M-10M. Pub'd 2 titles 1998; expects 3 titles 1999, 4 titles 2000. 4 titles listed in the *Small Press Record of Books in Print* (28th Edition, 1999-00). avg. price, cloth: $16.95; paper: $9.95. Discounts: libraries 20%, retailers 40%, wholesalers 50%. 200pp; 6×9; lp. Reporting time: 12 months. Publishes 2% of manuscripts submitted. Payment: negotiated. Copyrights for author. BMI.

House of the 9 Muses, Inc., Jerry J. Rubenstein, Publisher-President; Ben Shulman, Managing Editor; George McCormick, Senior Editor; Dick Trump, Audio Editor, Box 2974, Palm Beach, FL 33480, 407-697-0990. 1990. Fiction, non-fiction. "We publish books (both soft and hardcover), audiotapes (cassettes) and videotapes (or 16mm film format). We have publishing projects committed for next the two years and cannot add others until then. Recent/new publishing releases: *Wild Jake Hiccup: The History of America's First Frontiersman,* humor;

Enjoying American History, 200 creative projects for parents and teachers; *The Ballad of Wild Jake Hiccup* (audiocassette), music-bluegrass. We have 'backlog' for 2 years.'' avg. press run 4M+. Pub'd 9 titles 1998; expects 7 titles 1999, 6-7 titles 2000. 3 titles listed in the *Small Press Record of Books in Print* (28th Edition, 1999-00). avg. price, cloth: $19.95; paper: $14.95; other: $9.95 audiocassette. Discounts: 3-5 copies 10%, 6-10 20%, 11-50 25%, 50+ 40%. 80-200+pp; 5½×8½, 6×9; various. Simultaneous submissions accepted: no. Publishes 0% of manuscripts submitted. Payment: each negotiated separately. Copyrights for author. National Association of Independent Publishers (NAIP).

Howling Dog Press/Stiletto (see also STILETTO), Michael Annis, 1016 Deborah Drive, Loveland, CO 80537-7087. 1980. Poetry, fiction, art, photos, satire, parts-of-novels, long-poems, collages, plays, concrete art, non-fiction. *"Stiletto* is a book series featuring 8 primary writers per issue (with secondary/shorter pieces by others) and 2 main artists. Average 200 pages. Howling Dog also publishes Boxer Books and the American Cantos Broadsides. High visual content—send *slides* of artwork only (artists & illustrators, or writers who produce visual art). All submissions and correspondence for every Howling Dog publication *needs to have* an accompanying SASE.'' avg. press run 1M. Pub'd 2 titles 1998; expects 3 titles 1999. 3 titles listed in the *Small Press Record of Books in Print* (28th Edition, 1999-00). avg. price, cloth: varies; paper: varies. Discounts: 30% trade, 20% classroom. 96pp; 5×11½, 4×5, 6×9; †of, lp. Reporting time: up to 1 year. Publishes less than 5% of manuscripts submitted. Payment: by publication, no standard. Copyrights for author. PMA.

●**Howling Wolf Publishing,** Kirby Jonas, PO Box 1045, Pocatello, ID 83204, phone/fax 208-233-2708; e-mail kirbyjonas@integrityonline.com. 1997. Fiction. avg. press run 5M. Pub'd 1 title 1998; expects 2 titles 1999, 2 titles 2000. 2 titles listed in the *Small Press Record of Books in Print* (28th Edition, 1999-00). avg. price, paper: $12.95. Discounts: 20% short, 40% , 57% maximum. 290pp; 5½×8½. Reporting time: 4 months. Simultaneous submissions accepted: yes. Payment: 10% royalty. Copyrights for author.

Howln Moon Press, Betty A. Mueller, PO Box 238, Eliot, ME 03903, 207-439-3508; E-mail bmueller@howlnmoonpress.com. 1993. Fiction, art, photos, cartoons, non-fiction. ''We publish books about dogs and dog training. Books with a 'new' point of view or fresh ideas get our attention. Query with outline or sample chapter first. No unsolicited manuscripts please'' Pub'd 2 titles 1998; expects 2 titles 1999, 3-4 titles 2000. 13 titles listed in the *Small Press Record of Books in Print* (28th Edition, 1999-00). avg. price, other: vary. Discounts: 20% prepaid STOP orders. Pages vary; size varies. Reporting time: 2-3 months. Simultaneous submissions accepted: no. Payment: to be arranged. Copyrights for author.

HQ POETRY MAGAZINE (The Haiku Quarterly), Kevin Bailey, 39 Exmouth Street, Swindon, Wilshire, SN1 3PU, England. 1990. Poetry, articles, criticism, reviews. circ. 1.2M. 3-4/yr. Pub'd 3 issues 1998; expects 3 issues 1999, 4 issues 2000. sub. price: £12 overseas; £9 UK; per copy: £2.60; sample: £2.60. 56pp; size A5; of. Reporting time: varies. Payment: complementary copies. Copyrighted, reverts to author. Pub's reviews: 50 in 1998. §Poetry, literature, critcism.

●**HSC Publications,** Alex Hammer, 360-A West Merrick Road, Ste. 40, Valley Stream, NY 11580, 516-256-0223. 1996. Poetry, non-fiction. ''We specialize in sports directories, poetry, spirituality, and general non-fiction. New and established authors welcome.'' Pub'd 2 titles 1998; expects 3 titles 1999, 4 titles 2000. avg. price, paper: $9.95. 80pp; 8½×11. Reporting time: 2-4 weeks. Simultaneous submissions accepted, must be noted. Payment: negotiated. We do not usually copyright for author.

H2SO4, Jill Stauffer, PO Box 423354, San Francisco, CA 94142, 415-431-2135; h2so4@socrates.berkeley.edu. 1992. Poetry, articles, art, photos, interviews, criticism, reviews, music, letters, non-fiction. ''Any length, but the format does not accommodate extremely lengthy pieces. *h2so4* hopes to situate itself in the space between idea that is not entertainment, and entertainment with no idea. In other words, space for lit, crit, philos, fict, reviews, and humor, with none them making excuses for the rest. Order a sample, submit. Humor and seriousness cohabit.'' circ. 600. 2/yr. Pub'd 2 issues 1998; expects 2 issues 1999, 2 issues 2000. sub. price: $10, $20 for 5 issues; per copy: $5; sample: $5. Back issues: $5. Discounts: call for rates. 48pp; 8½×11; †mi, handscreened cover. Reporting time: 3-6 months. Simultaneous submissions accepted: no. Publishes 20% of manuscripts submitted. Payment: issues. Copyrighted, reverts to author. Pub's reviews: 10 in 1998. §Literary crit, literature, feminism, small publishers, language, philosophy, popular culture, history, politics. Ads: $200/$125/$35 for 1/8 pg/$60 for 1/4 pg. Contact us for additional sizes.

HUBBUB, Lisa Steinman, Jim Shugrue, 5344 S.E. 38th Avenue, Portland, OR 97202, 503-775-0370. 1983. Poetry. *"Hubbub* publishes poetry reviews by invitation only, but accepts submissions of all kinds of poetry: excellence is our only criterion.'' circ. 350. 1/yr. Pub'd 1 issue 1998; expects 1 issue 1999, 1 issue 2000. sub. price: $5; per copy: $5; sample: $3.35. Back issues: $3.75. Discounts: 40%. 70pp; 5½×8½; †of. Reporting time: 1-3 months. Simultaneous submissions accepted: no. Publishes .05% of manuscripts submitted. Payment: 2 contributor copies plus a small honorarium when we have grant funding. Copyrighted, reverts to author. Pub's reviews: 1 in 1998. §Poetry. Ads: $50/$25/will swap with other literary magazines in some cases.

THE HUDSON REVIEW, Paula Deitz, Editor, 684 Park Avenue, New York, NY 10021, 212-650-0020; fax

212-774-1911. 1948. Poetry, fiction, articles, criticism, reviews, parts-of-novels, long-poems, non-fiction. "Although we have developed a recognizable group of contributors who are identified with the magazine, we are always open to new writers and publish them in every issue. We have no university affiliation and are not committed to any narrow academic aim, nor to any particular political perspective." circ. 4.5M. 4/yr. Pub'd 4 issues 1998; expects 4 issues 1999, 4 issues 2000. 6 titles listed in the *Small Press Record of Books in Print* (28th Edition, 1999-00). sub. price: $28 domestic, $32 foreign; per copy: $8; sample: $8. Back issues: varies. Bulk rates and discount schedules on request. 176pp; 4½x7½; of. Reporting time: 12 weeks maximum. Simultaneous submissions accepted: no. Payment: 2½¢ per word for prose, 50¢ per line for poetry. Copyrighted, rights revert to author under 1978 law on request. Pub's reviews: 80 in 1998. §Literature, fine and performing arts, sociology and cultural anthropology. Ads: $300/$200.

HUG THE EARTH, A Journal of Land and Life, Hug The Earth Publications, Kenneth Lumpkin, 42 Greenwood Avenue, Pequannock, NJ 07440. "Features Charles Olson, Gary Snyder, Flavia Alaya, Ken Lumpkin, E. Durling Merrill, et al. Poems and prose on environment and place in literature" 24pp; 8½x11; private printing. Simultaneous submissions accepted: yes. Publishes 50% of manuscripts submitted. Copyrighted. §Myth, land, Magick.

Hug The Earth Publications (see also HUG THE EARTH, A Journal of Land and Life), Kenneth Lumpkin, 42 Greenwood Ave., Pequannock, NJ 07440. 1980. Poetry, art, criticism, reviews, letters, long-poems. "We publish broadsides, and a one-time only journal on land & life" avg. press run 500-1M. Pub'd 2 titles 1998; expects 1 title 1999. 1 title listed in the *Small Press Record of Books in Print* (28th Edition, 1999-00). avg. price, paper: $5; other: $2.50. 40pp; 4¼x5½; MacIntosh Model SE, with pagemaker 3.0 software. Reporting time: 6-8 weeks. Copyrights for author.

HUMAN, Excercises in the Crucial Arts, Nonsilent Press, Charles T. Dreamer, Route 1 Box 133, La Farge, WI 54639. 1996. Poetry, articles, art, photos, cartoons, interviews, criticism, reviews, letters, collages, news items. "Large discourse section; challenging indoctrinations of all stripes; send SASE for explanation of 'crucial arts'; discussing 'Spanarchy.' member Unorganization of Unorganizers (U.U.U.) and the American Society of They. Contributors include prisoners, dreamers, self-made, activists" circ. 300+. 4/yr. Expects 4 issues 1999, 4 issues 2000. sub. price: $7; per copy: $2; sample: $2. 20-40pp; 8½x11; †mi, photocopy. Reporting time: 6 weeks to 3 months. Simultaneous submissions accepted: yes. Publishes 50% of manuscripts submitted. Payment: in copies/barter. Not copyrighted. Pub's reviews. §Subjects dealing with variety of views challenging prevailing conceptions of fashionable, ignored, and taboo issues on all people-related subjects. Ads: inquire. Unorganized Unorganization of Unorganizers (UUU).

Human Kinetics Pub. Inc. (see also ADAPTED PHYSICAL ACTIVITY QUARTERLY (APAQ); JOURNAL OF APPLIED BIOMECHANICS (JAB); JOURNAL OF THE PHILOSOPHY OF SPORT (JPS); JOURNAL OF SPORT MANAGEMENT (JSM); JOURNAL OF SPORT AND EXERCISE PSYCHOLOGY (JSEP); JOURNAL OF TEACHING IN PHYSICAL EDUCATION (JTPE); QUEST; SOCIOLOGY OF SPORT JOURNAL (SSJ); THE SPORT PSYCHOLOGIST (TSP); CANADIAN JOURNAL OF APPLIED PHYSIOLOGY (CJAP); INTERNATIONAL JOURNAL OF SPORT NUTRITION (IJSN); PEDIATRIC EXERCISE SCIENCE (PES); TEACHING ELEMENTARY PHYSICAL EDUCATION (TEPE); JOURNAL OF SPORT REHABILITATION (JSR); JOURNAL OF STRENGTH AND CONDITIONING RESEARCH (JSCR); EXERCISE IMMUNOLOGY REVIEW (EIR); JOURNAL OF AGING AND PHYSICAL ACTIVITY (JAPA); STRENGTH AND CONDI-TIONING; SPORT HISTORY REVIEW (SHR); MOTOR CONTROL; ATHLETIC THERAPY TODAY (ATT); MARATHON & BEYOND (M&B)), Rainer Martens, President, Box 5076, Champaign, IL 61825-5076, 217-351-5076; Fax 217-351-2674. 1974. Non-fiction. "Scholarly books and journals in sports medicine, science, physical education, and professional journals in coaching issues and techniques." avg. press run 3M. Pub'd 56 titles 1998; expects 56 titles 1999, 60 titles 2000. avg. price, cloth: $40; paper: $15.95. Discounts: text 1-4 10%, 5+ 20%. 286pp; 6x9, 8½x11; of. Reporting time: 1-2 months. Payment: negotiable (7-18%). Copyrights for author. Midwest Book Publishers Association, American Booksellers Association.

Human Sciences Press, Inc. (see also THE AMERICAN JOURNAL OF PSYCHOANALYSIS; CHILDREN'S LITERATURE IN EDUCATION; RESEARCH IN HIGHER EDUCATION; THE URBAN REVIEW), 233 Spring Street, New York, NY 10013, 212-620-8000.

Humana Press, Thomas Lanigan, 999 Riverview Drive, Suite 208, Totowa, NJ 07512, 201-256-1699, Fax 201-256-8349, e-mail humana@interramp.com. 1977. Poetry, fiction, articles, art, photos, long-poems, plays, non-fiction. "Material accepted as the spirit moves." avg. press run 1.5M. Pub'd 27 titles 1998; expects 30 titles 1999, 30 titles 2000. 53 titles listed in the *Small Press Record of Books in Print* (28th Edition, 1999-00). avg. price, cloth: $19.95; paper: $13.95. Discounts: varies with quantity. 300pp; 5¾x8½; of. Reporting time: 2-3 months. Payment: variable to no royalties; 10 copies of book to author, annual royalty report. PMA, ABA.

THE HUMANIST, Frederick Edwords, Editor and Managing Editor; Karen Ann Gajewski, Editorial Assistant

255

and Production Manager; Valerie White, Senior Editor; Marian Hetherly, Copy Editor, 7 Harwood Drive, PO Box 1188, Amherst, NY 14226-7188, 716-839-5080. 1941. Articles, art, photos, cartoons, interviews, criticism, reviews, letters, non-fiction. "Nonfiction articles addressing ethical, cultural, social, philosophical or political concerns from a humanist or politically progressive perspective are most likely to be published." circ. 16M. 6/yr. Pub'd 6 issues 1998; expects 6 issues 1999, 6 issues 2000. sub. price: $24.95; per copy: $4.75; sample: same. Back issues: $5.50. Discounts: 40% bulk. 48pp; 8½×11; of, lp. Reporting time: 2-3 months. Payment: 10 free copies. Copyrighted, reverts to author. Pub's reviews: 42 in 1998. §Church-state separation, feminism, ethics, science, humanism, education, politics, popular culture, literature. Ads: $700/$350.

HUMANS & OTHER SPECIES, David C. Anderson, 8732 Rock Springs Road, Penryn, CA 95663-9622, 916-663-3294. 1990. Articles, cartoons, reviews, news items, non-fiction. "*Humans & Other Species* is a quarterly resource journal on human-animal relationships. It cites journal articles, books, videos, and reviews on the human-animal relationship, often quoting the journal abstract or conclusions. It publishes book reviews (300-350 words), and news about information resources to promote bibliographic access to this multidisciplinary literature. The field of human-animal interactions includes: the human-companion animal bond, animal assisted therapy, the behavior and training of companion animals (cats, birds, dogs, etc.), the humane community's interests, the ethics of animal use, management of laboratory, wild and zoo animals, etc." circ. 100. 4/yr. Pub'd 4 issues 1998; expects 4 issues 1999, 4 issues 2000. sub. price: $60; $75 international; discounted to members of International Society for Anthrozoology; per copy: $12.50 (North America), $16 other; sample: free. Back issues: Vol. 1-2 & index: $50; Vol.3+ $50 each. Discounts: not established. 40pp; 8½×11. Payment: copy of issue. Copyrighted, rights revert to book reviewers. Pub's reviews: 20 in 1998. §companion animals (behavior, animals in literature, ethics, training, care), animal rights and welfare. Council of Editors of Learned Journals.

Hundman Publishing (see also MAINLINE MODELER), Robert L. Hundman, 13110 Beverly Park Road, Mukilteo, WA 98275, 206-743-2607. 1979. Articles, photos, reviews, letters, non-fiction. "Books are railroad history, modeling and photography in nature" avg. press run 3.5M-5M. Pub'd 2 titles 1998; expects 6 titles 1999, 8 titles 2000. 2 titles listed in the *Small Press Record of Books in Print* (28th Edition, 1999-00). Discounts: dealer terms—20% for 1 book, 30% 2-3, 40% 4+, 10+ and we pay s/h. 100-350pp; 8½×11; of. Reporting time: 6-9 months. Payment: individual. Does not copyright for author.

Hungry Tiger Press (see also OZ-STORY), David Maxine, Eric Shanower, 1516 Cypress Avenue, San Diego, CA 92103-4517. 1994. Poetry, fiction, cartoons, letters, art. avg. press run 1.8M. Pub'd 2 titles 1998; expects 2 titles 1999, 2 titles 2000. 6 titles listed in the *Small Press Record of Books in Print* (28th Edition, 1999-00). avg. price, paper: $14.95. Discounts: 20-50% depending on quantity ordered. 128pp; 8½×11; of. Reporting time: 1-2 months. Simultaneous submissions accepted: no. Publishes 20% of manuscripts submitted. Payment: one-time fee, plus free copies, discount on further copies. Does not copyright for author.

THE HUNTED NEWS, The Subourbon Press, Mike Wood, PO Box 9101, Warwick, RI 02889, 401-739-2279. 1991. Poetry, fiction, articles, art, photos, cartoons, criticism, reviews, music, letters, parts-of-novels, non-fiction. "Will accept any work based on true feeling and intent. No self-impressed academic or arty work, and no tired 'anarchy' or other dead themes. Basically be direct, honest, and if you want to shock, then shock with intent, not with gimmick." circ. 500+. 3-4/yr. Pub'd 2 issues 1998; expects 2 issues 1999, 2 issues 2000. sub. price: free; per copy: $3. Back issues: free (Issue 1 out of print). 30-50pp; 8½×11; mi. Reporting time: 1 month. Payment: copies. Copyrighted, reverts to author. Pub's reviews: 15 in 1998. §Small press, independent music, experimental fiction, poetry, minimalist, anything with soul. Ads: none at this time.

Hunter House Inc., Publishers, Kiran Rana, PO Box 2914, Alameda, CA 94501. 1978. Non-fiction. avg. press run 5M. Pub'd 10 titles 1998; expects 11 titles 1999, 12 titles 2000. 62 titles listed in the *Small Press Record of Books in Print* (28th Edition, 1999-00). avg. price, cloth: $24.95; paper: $14.95. Discounts: retailers/wholesalers: 1 10%, 2+ 20%, 6+ 40%, 100+ 45%; libraries: 2+ 10%, 6+ 20%. 288pp; 6×9, 5½×8½, 7¼×9¼, 8½×11; of. Reporting time: 3-6 months. Simultaneous submissions accepted: yes. Publishes 25% of manuscripts submitted. Payment: 12% of net up to 15% pa; 15% of net up to 18% on cl; report and pay twice a year. Copyrights for author. PMA (Publishers Marketing Association), San Francisco Bay Area Book Council.

Hunter Publishing, Co., Diane Thomas, P.O. Box 9533, Phoenix, AZ 85068, 602-944-1022. 1975. "We publish creative Ojo books—4 separate titles now. Interested in undertaking publishing venture for good craft-oriented ideas—resale to craft & hobby shops, book stores, museum gift stores, etc. Also one book pub. on Japanese silk flower making. *Southwestern Indian Detours*, hardcover, ISBN 0-918126-12-6, $8.95. The above book encompasses 332+ pages, together with some 300+ photographs of the original Fred Harvey Co. & The Atchison, Topeka, and Santa Fe R.R. files of the tourist trips run in the Southwest, mainly in New Mexico, Arizona, Colorado, and California." avg. press run 10M-20M+. Pub'd 2 titles 1998. 8 titles listed in the *Small Press Record of Books in Print* (28th Edition, 1999-00). avg. price, cloth: $8.95; paper: $2.95-$5.95. Discounts: 40-50% retail; higher discount to distributors. 24-52pp; 8½×11. Reporting time: 4 weeks. Payment: negotiable. Copyrights for author.

Huntington Library Press (see also HUNTINGTON LIBRARY QUARTERLY), Susan Green, 1151 Oxford Road, San Marino, CA 91108, 626-405-2172; fax 626-585-0794; e-mail booksales@huntington.org. 1920. Non-fiction. avg. press run 1M. Pub'd 6 titles 1998; expects 6 titles 1999, 6 titles 2000. 22 titles listed in the *Small Press Record of Books in Print* (28th Edition, 1999-00). avg. price, cloth: $30; paper: $15. Discounts: 20% average. 200pp; 6×9; of. Reporting time: varies. Simultaneous submissions accepted: no. Publishes 1% of manuscripts submitted. Payment: generally no royalties paid. Copyrights for author.

HUNTINGTON LIBRARY QUARTERLY, Huntington Library Press, Susan Green, 1151 Oxford Road, San Marino, CA 91108, 818-405-2172. 1931. *"The Huntington Library Quarterly* publishes articles that primarily relate to the Huntington Collections of 16th-18th century art, history and literature of Great Britain and America.'' circ. 900. 4/yr. Pub'd 4 issues 1998; expects 4 issues 1999, 4 issues 2000. sub. price: $40; per copy: $15; sample: free to libraries. Back issues: $10. Discounts: agents 20%. 150pp; 7×10; of. Reporting time: varies. Simultaneous submissions accepted: no. Payment: none. Copyrighted, does not revert to author. Pub's reviews: 6 in 1998. Ads: none.

Huntington Press, Anthony Curtis, Deke Castleman, 3687 S. Procyon Avenue, Las Vegas, NV 89103, 702-252-0655; Fax 702-252-0675; LVA@infi.net. 1983. Non-fiction. avg. press run 5M-10M. Pub'd 1 title 1998; expects 3 titles 1999, 5 titles 2000. 5 titles listed in the *Small Press Record of Books in Print* (28th Edition, 1999-00). avg. price, cloth: $40; paper: $12. Discounts: trade 20%-50%. 218pp; 5½×8; of. Reporting time: 60 days. Simultaneous submissions accepted: yes. Payment: negotiable. Copyrights for author. PMA, SPAN Connection.

Huntsville Literary Association (see also POEM), Nancy Frey Dillard, Editor, c/o English Department, University of Alabama, Huntsville, AL 35899. 1967. Poetry. "Poems copyrighted by *Poem*, reverts to author'' avg. press run 500. Pub'd 2 titles 1998; expects 2 titles 1999, 2 titles 2000. avg. price, paper: $5 a copy. 70pp; 4½×7½; lp. Reporting time: 30 days. Payment: copy. We copyright for publication, then rights revert to poet. CLMP.

HURRICANE ALICE, Meureen T. Reddy, Executive Editor; Meg Carroll, Book Review Editor; Joan Dagle, Submissions, Dept. of English, Rhode Island College, Providence, RI 02908. 1983. Poetry, fiction, articles, art, photos, cartoons, interviews, satire, criticism, reviews, letters, parts-of-novels, collages, non-fiction. "Emphasis on feminist re-view of 1)books 2)performance 3)visual art 4)everything. Recent contributors include Mary Sharratt, Susan Koppelman, and Judith Arcana.'' circ. 1M. 4/yr. Pub'd 4 issues 1998; expects 4 issues 1999, 4 issues 2000. sub. price: $12; per copy: $2.50; sample: $2.50. Back issues: $2. 16pp; 11×17; of. Reporting time: 6 months. Simultaneous submissions accepted if indicated on ms. Publishes poetry 10%, others 30% of manuscripts submitted. Payment: in issues (6). Copyrighted, reverts to author. Pub's reviews: 16 in 1998. §Any work viewed critically. Ads: /$235/$35 for business-card (camera-ready). CLMP.

Hutton Publications (see also MYSTERY TIME ANTHOLOGY; RHYME TIME POETRY NEWSLETTER), Linda Hutton, Po Box 2907, Decatur, IL 62524. 1983. Poetry, fiction, art. avg. press run 150. Pub'd 2 titles 1998; expects 2 titles 1999, 2 titles 2000. avg. price, paper: $5. Discounts: half price to authors. 44pp; 8½×11; of. Reporting time: 1 month. Payment: 1/4¢ to 1¢ per word for fiction, 5¢ to 25¢ per line for poetry. Copyrights for author.

HWD Publishing, V.G. Loper, PO Box 220D, Veneta, OR 97487, 1-800-935-7323. 1991. Non-fiction. avg. press run 5M. Expects 2 titles 1999. 2 titles listed in the *Small Press Record of Books in Print* (28th Edition, 1999-00). avg. price, paper: $15.95. 150pp; 8½×11. Reporting time: 1 month. Copyrights for author. PMA.

Hyacinth House Publications/Caligula Editions (see also BROWNBAG PRESS; PSYCHOTRAIN), Randal D. Seyler, Shannon Frach, PO Box 120, Fayetteville, AR 72702-0120. 1989. Poetry, fiction, art, cartoons, satire. "We have two primary publications, as well as a series of chapbooks and novellas released as separate small press books. We are not currently looking at unsolicited material for anything except two of our zines, *Brownbag Press* and *PsychoTrain.*'' avg. press run varies. Pub'd 15 titles 1998; expects 13 titles 1999, 13 titles 2000. 38 titles listed in the *Small Press Record of Books in Print* (28th Edition, 1999-00). avg. price, paper: $4. 35pp; standard size; †Xerox. Reporting time: 2 weeks to 8 months. Publishes 10% or less of manuscripts submitted. One-time rights.

HYPATIA: A Journal of Feminist Philosophy, Nancy Tuana, Laurie Shrage, University of Oregon, Center for Study of Women in Society, Eugene, OR 97403-1201. 1986. Articles, reviews, non-fiction. "Address business and subscription correspondence to: Journals Manager, Indiana University Press, 10th & Morton Streets, Bloomington, IN 47401.'' circ. 1M. 4/yr. Pub'd 4 issues 1998; expects 4 issues 1999, 4 issues 2000. sub. price: $35 individual, $60 institution; per copy: $10 indiv., $20 inst. Back issues: $10 Individual; $20 Institution. Discounts: bulk 40% for 5 or more. 200-250pp; 6×9. Reporting time: 6 months. Simultaneous submissions accepted: no. Publishes 30% of manuscripts submitted. Payment: none. Copyrighted, reverts to author. Pub's reviews: 20 in 1998. §Feminist philosophy. Ads: $200/$100/$50 1/4 page.

IAAS Publishers, Inc. (see also 21ST CENTURY AFRO REVIEW), Nikongo Ba'Nikongo, 7676 New Hampshire Ave., Suite 330, Langley Park, MD 20783, 301-499-6308. "200 pages minimum." avg. press run 5M. Pub'd 2 titles 1998; expects 3 titles 1999, 5 titles 2000. 7 titles listed in the *Small Press Record of Books in Print* (28th Edition, 1999-00). avg. price, cloth: $29; paper: $18. Discounts: trade 55%; college bookstore 20%. 200pp; 6¼x9½. Reporting time: 6 weeks. Payment: 15% paid annually in July.

IASP NEWSLETTER, Michael Huter, Association President; Fred C. Bohm, Secretary-General, WUV Universitatsverlag, Berggasse 5, A-1090 Vienna, Austria. 1980. Letters, news items. "Future correspondence regarding the *IASP Newsletter* (e.g. press releases, notices of coming events and publications, books for review, exchange copies of journals) should be addressed to the editor, i.e. to the association's president at the above address. Other correspondence, including membership applications, should be addressed to the Secretary-General: Fred C. Bohm, Michigan State University Press, 1405 S. Harrison Road, East Lansing, MI 48823." circ. 600. 6/yr. Pub'd 6 issues 1998; expects 6 issues 1999, 6 issues 2000. sub. price: $60; per copy: $10; sample: free. Discounts: 10%. 8pp; size ISO A4; DTP/of. Reporting time: 4-6 weeks. Simultaneous submissions accepted: yes. Publishes 50% of manuscripts submitted. Payment: none. Copyrighted. Pub's reviews: 20 in 1998. §Scholarly publishing, University presses—world-wide. no ads accepted. SSP, IPA.

●**Ibbetson St. Press,** Doug Holder, Dianne Robitaille, Dick Wilhelm, Dave Michaud, 33 Ibbetson Street, Somerville, MA 02143. 1999. Poetry. "We want to publish 1 to 2 small chapbooks by unpublished poets over the next year...all dependent on funding." avg. press run 100. Expects 1 title 1999, 2 titles 2000. 1 title listed in the *Small Press Record of Books in Print* (28th Edition, 1999-00). avg. price, paper: $14. Reporting time: 3 months-1 year. Simultaneous submissions accepted: yes. Payment: 50 copies. Mass. Poetry Society, New England Poetry Club.

IBEX Publishers, Farhad Shirzad, President, 8014 Old Georgetown Road, Bethesda, MD 20814, 301-718-8188; FAX 301-907-8707. 1979. Fiction, news items, non-fiction. "We publish books about Iran and in Persian." avg. press run 2M-3M. Pub'd 5 titles 1998; expects 5 titles 1999, 7 titles 2000. 10 titles listed in the *Small Press Record of Books in Print* (28th Edition, 1999-00). Discounts: 1 copy 20%, 2-4 30%, 5+ 40%. of. Copyrights for author.

IBIS REVIEW, Gale Courey, Algis Stankus-Saulaitis, PO Box 133, Falls Village, CT 06031, 203-824-0355. 1995. Poetry, art, parts-of-novels, fiction. "Recent contributors: James Laughlin, Simon Percjol, John Briggs" circ. 500. 1/yr. Pub'd 1 issue 1998; expects 1 issue 1999, 1 issue 2000. sub. price: $8.95; per copy: $8.95; sample: $8.95. Discounts: distributor 50%, retailers 40%. 116pp; 5½x8½; off. Reporting time: 1-6 months. Simultaneous submissions accepted: yes. Publishes 15% of manuscripts submitted. Payment: 2 copies. Copyrighted, reverts to author. Ads: inquire for rates.

ICA Publishing, Carlos Bonilla, M.D., Editor & Publisher; President ICA, Inc., 1020 N. Commerce, Stockton, CA 95202, 209-466-3883. 1988. avg. press run 1M. Pub'd 1 title 1998; expects 6 titles 1999, 4 titles 2000. 12 titles listed in the *Small Press Record of Books in Print* (28th Edition, 1999-00). avg. price, paper: $19.95. 200+pp; 6x9, 8½x11; varies. Reporting time: 2 months. Simultaneous submissions accepted: no. Publishes 1% of manuscripts submitted. Payment: varies. Copyrights for author. PMA.

Icarus Books, David Diorio, Non-fiction Editor, 1015 Kenilworth Drive, Baltimore, MD 21204, 410-821-7807. 1980. Poetry, non-fiction. avg. press run 1M. Pub'd 3 titles 1998; expects 3 titles 1999, 3 titles 2000. 11 titles listed in the *Small Press Record of Books in Print* (28th Edition, 1999-00). avg. price, paper: $8.95. Discounts: 20-40%. 80pp; 6x9. Payment: will vary depending on type. MidAtlantic Publishers Association.

ICARUS WAS RIGHT, Itidwitir Publishing, Scott Ogilvie, PO Box 13731, Salem, OR 97309-1731, 619-461-0497; icaruswas@pobox.com. 1995. Poetry, fiction, articles, art, photos, cartoons, interviews, satire, criticism, reviews, music, letters, collages, non-fiction. circ. 3M. 4/yr. Pub'd 3 issues 1998; expects 4 issues 1999, 4 issues 2000. sub. price: $8; per copy: $2; sample: $3. Back issues: $3. Discounts: classroom 50% over 5. 120pp; 8⅛x10¾; web offset. Reporting time: 1-3 months. Simultaneous submissions accepted: yes. Publishes 10-20% of manuscripts submitted. Copyrighted, reverts to author. Pub's reviews: 40+ in 1998. §All, especially fiction, nonfiction and art. Ads: $55/$25/$10 1/4 page.

Ice Cube Press (see also SYCAMORE ROOTS: New Native Americans), S.H. Semken, 205 North Front Street, North Liberty, IA 52317-9302, 319-626-2055; e-mail icecube@soli.inav.net; Websites: http://soli.inav.net/~icecube. 1994. Fiction, art, non-fiction. "We publish tiny, soft-bound chapbooks of fiction and nonfiction essays which can include drawings and photos. In 1997 we will do 1 perfect bound'' Pub'd 1 title 1998; expects 1 title 1999, 1 title 2000. 1 title listed in the *Small Press Record of Books in Print* (28th Edition, 1999-00). avg. price, paper: $14.95. Discounts: 2-10 - 40%. 150pp; 6×9; of. Reporting time: 1-2 months. Publishes 2% of manuscripts submitted. Payment: negotiable. Copyrights negotiable. PMA, MIPA.

ICEA, Penny Simkin, PO Box 20048, Minneapolis, MN 55420, 800-624-4934. 1977. Non-fiction. ''Publisher of books and pamphlets on childbirth and parenting.'' avg. press run 3M books, 10M pamphlets. Pub'd 1-2 titles 1998; expects 1-3 titles 1999, 1-3 titles 2000. 7 titles listed in the *Small Press Record of Books in Print* (28th Edition, 1999-00). avg. price, paper: $8.95; other: pamphlets 30¢. Discounts: 1-4 20%, 5 or more 40%. 4-100pp; 5×8, 6×9, 8½×11; of. Reporting time: 0-6 months. Payment: 10% of net paid quarterly. Does not copyright for author.

ICON, Rachel Mathis, Dr. Michael Lynch, Advisor, KSU-TC, 4314 Mahoning Avenue NW, Warren, OH 44483, 330-847-0571. 1966. Poetry, fiction, art, photos, non-fiction. ''1,500 word limit on prose. Six submissions limit per issue. Typed or word processed only. Short bio (prefer bios with a personal touch). Recent contributors: Yvonne Sapia, Robert Cooperman, George Held, and Carolyn Moore. Art and photos: Black and white. Will accept high quality reproductions. Press dates: Mid-May and Early December.'' circ. 1M. 2/yr. Pub'd 2 issues 1998; expects 2 issues 1999, 2 issues 2000. sub. price: $6; per copy: $4; sample: $3. Back issues: rarely any available. Discounts: none. 50pp; 5½×8½. Reporting time: 3-6 months. Simultaneous submissions are accepted with warning that we do not read through the summer and withdrawals have to be made 1 week prior to press date. Publishes 10% of manuscripts submitted. Payment: 1 copy. Not copyrighted. Ads: none.

ICON THOUGHTSTYLE MAGAZINE, Robin Dolch, New Projects Director; David Getson, Editor-in-Chief; Dana Shapiro, Senior Editor; Evan Wiener, Associate Editor, 440 Park Avenue South, 2nd Floor, New York, NY 10016, 212-219-2654; Fax 212-219-4045. 1996. Articles, art, photos, cartoons, interviews, reviews, music, plays, concrete art, news items, non-fiction. ''*ICON*'s mission is to confront the concept of success carefully and objectively, and to explore its many meanings and manifestations boundlessly, so that young men are better able to define the concept for themselves. *ICON* will aim to fulfill the following principles: To educate and civilize. To inspire and encourage. The centerpiece of the magazine will be 3 monthly 'Profiles' of men who have reached a certain level of achievement in any given field. Length starts at approx. 5,000 words. The 'Features' extend the focus of the profiles to organizations, places, people, ideas, etc. 5,000 words is the average length. 'Iconnoisseur' is a 'service section' within *ICON* that celebrates and examines the tools and rituals of a man's life. The section brings a micro-focus to chosen subjects and provides a concise, comprehensive report to the reader. Length will run about 1,500-2,000 words. The Editor is seeking writers who, whether experts or not, have an irrepressible fascination for any one topic or subject. Send SASE for more complete guidelines. Deadlines will be set with an editor. Queries should be no more than one page and should be accompanied by a cover letter, writing samples (published or unpublished), and a SASE. Writers are invited to submit articles on speculation (include SASE).'' circ. 150M. 6/yr. Pub'd 6 issues 1998; expects 6 issues 1999, 6 issues 2000. sub. price: $19.95; per copy: $3.95. Back issues: $7.95. 128pp; 9×10¾; of. Reporting time: 1 month. Payment: 50¢ to $1 per word. Copyrighted, reverts to author. Pub's reviews. §Must either be timeless or ahead of its time, premature or posthumous, but never trendy for the sake of being trendy. Ads: $7950/$5170.

THE ICONOCLAST, Phil Wagner, 1675 Amazon Road, Mohegan Lake, NY 10547-1804. 1992. Poetry, fiction, art, parts-of-novels, non-fiction. ''Up to 3,000 words. Please: no stories or poems about characters unable or unwilling to improve their conditions. Likes fiction to have a beginning, middle, and end, all in the service of a noteworthy event or realization'' circ. 600-3M. 8/yr. Pub'd 8 issues 1998; expects 8 issues 1999, 8 issues 2000. sub. price: $13/8 issues; per copy: $2; sample: $2. Back issues: $2. Discounts: 5+/10%, 10+/20%, 15+/30%, 20+/40%. 32-40pp; 5½×8; photocopy, photo of. Reporting time: 2 weeks - 2 months. Simultaneous publication is not acceptable. Publishes 2% of manuscripts submitted. Payment: 1-3 copies, 40% discount on additional copies. Copyrighted, reverts to author. Pub's reviews: 30 in 1998. §Works of intelligence and craft. Ads: $35/$20/$12.50 1/4 page.

IDIOM 23, Liz Huf, Central Queensland University, Rockhampton, Queensland, 4702, Australia, 0011-079-360655. 1988. Poetry, fiction, art, photos, cartoons, satire, criticism, reviews, plays, non-fiction. ''Length: ss to 2000 words; poetry: short; book reviews: 600 words.'' circ. 500. 2/yr. Pub'd 2 issues 1998. sub. price: Aus $10; per copy: Aus $10. Back issues: Aus $3/issue. Discounts: current Aus $4. 90pp; 8¾×11¾; †desktop publishing. Reporting time: 4 weeks (outside). Simultaneous submissions accepted: yes. Payment: $10 poetry, $20 reviews. Copyrighted. Pub's reviews: 20 in 1998. §Anything pertaining to, or on sale in Australia. Ads: $160/$85/$45 1/4 page.

IDIOT WIND, Douglas Carroll, Chief Editor, PO Box 87, Occoquan, VA 22125, 703-494-1897 evenings. 1984. Poetry, fiction, articles, satire. ''We frequently describe ourselves as National-Lampoon-esque. But only because people hate it when we turn a word or phrase into an adjective by tacking-esque on the end of it. We've even started doing theme issues, so write us for a schedule of upcoming issue themes. We also accept

259

Letterman-esque lists for our crawlspace section. We can be reachhed by email at idiotwind@radix.net'' circ. 100-200. 4/yr. Pub'd 3 issues 1998; expects 4 issues 1999, 4 issues 2000. sub. price: free; per copy: free; sample: free. Back issues: Free; unless I have to photocopy (then cost of copies). Discounts: Residents of UT, NJ, & VT: 25%; Everyone else: free. 16+pp; 5½×8½; †Laserjet of photocopy. Reporting time: we shoot for within 4 weeks. Payment: copies. Copyrighted, reverts to author. Ads: will consider trading ads with other small humor mags.

IGNIS FATUUS REVIEW, Nadine Kachur, Poetry; Burt Webster, Fiction, 18 Yuma Trail, Bisbee, AZ 85603. 1991. Poetry, fiction, articles, art, cartoons, satire, letters, non-fiction. "Fiction to 2500 words; unique, irreverent and humorous stories in all the major categories are welcome. Poetry 50 lines or less have greater chance of being accepted than epic'' circ. 150. 4/yr. Pub'd 4 issues 1998; expects 4 issues 1999, 4 issues 2000. sub. price: $16; per copy: $4; sample: $4. Back issues: $4. Discounts: negotiable. 24pp; 8½×11; of. Reporting time: 90 days. Simultaneous submissions accepted: yes. Publishes 10% of manuscripts submitted. Payment: 1 copy. Not copyrighted. Ads: $100/$60/$35. The Desktop Publishers Association.

Ignite! Entertainment, Jeff Krell, PO Box 2273, Grand Central Stn., New York, NY 10163, 718-784-8229 phone/Fax; JeffKrell@aol.com. 1996. Fiction, cartoons. "Just acquired the right to translate and republish 4 graphic novels by German cartoonist Ralf Konig. Current biases: Gay-positive entertainment, cartoons, comedy. Warehouse address: 41-15 44th Street #1C, Sunnyside, NY 11104." avg. press run 3M. Expects 3 titles 1999, 3 titles 2000. 2 titles listed in the *Small Press Record of Books in Print* (28th Edition, 1999-00). avg. price, paper: $16.95. Discounts: 40%. 176pp; 7×10; of. Reporting time: 2 months. Simultaneous submissions accepted: yes. Payment: 5-10% cover price. Copyrights for author.

III Publishing, Bill Meyers, PO Box 1581, Gualala, CA 95445-0363, 707-884-1818. 1989. Fiction, satire. "Interested in short to medium length novels, especially satire from unusual viewpoints." avg. press run 2M. Pub'd 2 titles 1998; expects 1 title 1999, 3 titles 2000. 9 titles listed in the *Small Press Record of Books in Print* (28th Edition, 1999-00). avg. price, paper: $10. 192pp; 5½×8½; of. Reporting time: 6-8 weeks. Simultaneous submissions accepted: no. Publishes 5% of manuscripts submitted. Payment: New authors must pay cost of publication. Reimbursed from sales, plus percentage of profit, if any. Copyrights for author.

ILLINOIS ARCHITECTURAL & HISTORICAL REVIEW, David Alan Badger, Editor; Gene Fehler, Poetry Editor, 202 South Plum, Havana, IL 62644, 309-543-4644. 1993. Poetry. "Poetry *must* be sent to: Gene Fehler, Poetry Editor, 106 Laurel Lane, Seneca, SC 29678. Maximum length of poems: 40 lines, any form or style. Poems must relate to Illinois, especially its history, architecture, and/or historical figures." circ. 12M. 4/yr. Expects 4 issues 1999, 4 issues 2000. sub. price: $20; per copy: $5; sample: free. Back issues: $5. Discounts: 40% off retail. 96-104pp; 8½×11; of, web press. Simultaneous submissions accepted: yes. Payment: copies. Copyrighted, reverts to author. §Illinois history. Ads: $325/$175/$100 1/4 page/$75 1/8 page.

Illinois Heritage Press, John E. Hallwas, PO Box 25, Macomb, IL 61455, 309-836-8916. 1983. Non-fiction. "The press publishes books of popular history relating to Illinois. The books have a broad focus—as opposed to community histories, biographies, and narrow studies." avg. press run 2M. Pub'd 1 title 1998; expects 1 title 1999. 3 titles listed in the *Small Press Record of Books in Print* (28th Edition, 1999-00). avg. price, paper: $9-$15. 200-300pp; 6×9, 8×10; of. Reporting time: 90 days. Copyrights for author.

Illumination Arts, Ruth Thompson, John Thompson, PO Box 1865, Bellevue, WA 98009, 425-644-7185; fax 425-644-9274. 1987. avg. press run 20M. Pub'd 2 titles 1998; expects 3 titles 1999, 2 titles 2000. 6 titles listed in the *Small Press Record of Books in Print* (28th Edition, 1999-00). avg. price, cloth: $15.95. Discounts: wholesalers 50-55%, gift stores—keystone, bookstores sliding scale, schools and libraries 35%. Reporting time: 1 month. Simultaneous submissions accepted: yes. Publishes 1 out of every 250 manuscripts received. We sometimes copyright for the author. SPAN, PMA, NAPRA.

ILLUMINATIONS, Simon Lewis, English Dept., 66 George Street, College of Charleston, Charleston, SC 29424-0001. 1982. Poetry, fiction, cartoons, interviews, letters, parts-of-novels, long-poems. "*Illuminations* is devoted to promoting the work of new writers by publishing their work within the context of the work of established figures. Bias: Serious writers; we mostly publish poetry—will consider short fiction or short extracts. Recent contributors: Stephen Spender, James Dickey, Susan Sontag, Joseph Brodsky, Tom Stoppard, W.H. Auden, Seamus Heaney, Flannery O'Connor, Christopher Isherwood, Thomas Kinsella, Ezra Pound letters. Issues 9 and 10 were anthologies of East and South African writing. Issue 13 dedicated to Stephen Spender, Issue 14 to Southern African writing." circ. 500. 1/yr. Expects 1 issue 2000. sub. price: $20/3 issues; per copy: $10; sample: $10. Back issues: negotiable. Discounts: 33⅓ commission. 60pp; 6½×9, 5×8; of. Reporting time: 2-3 months minimum. Simultaneous submissions accepted: no. Publishes 5% of manuscripts submitted. Payment: none. Copyrighted, reverts to author. Ads: $150/$75/$40¼ page.

IllumiNet Press, Nancy Kratzer, Co-Owner; Ron Bonds, Co-Owner, PO Box 2808, Lilburn, GA 30048, 770-279-2745; FAX 770-279-8007. 1990. Fiction, non-fiction. "Interested in paranormal, UFO, conspiracy theory, magick, occult" avg. press run 3M-5M. Pub'd 4 titles 1998; expects 6 titles 1999, 8 titles 2000. 18 titles listed in the *Small Press Record of Books in Print* (28th Edition, 1999-00). avg. price, cloth: $24.95; paper: $14.95; other: $9.95 cassette. Discounts: 50% 10 or more copies, 20% libraries. 220pp; 6×9; of. Reporting time: 60 days. Payment: 6-10%. Does not copyright for author. PMA.

THE ILLUSTRATOR COLLECTOR'S NEWS, Denis C. Jackson, PO Box 1958, Sequim, WA 98382, 360-452-3810; ticn@olypen.com. 1983. Art, cartoons, reviews, news items, non-fiction. "Our publication caters to collectors and dealers and antique people who buy and sell old magazines, calendars, prints, and illustrated paper of all kinds." circ. 1,000. 6/yr. Pub'd 6 issues 1998; expects 6 issues 1999, 6 issues 2000. sub. price: $18; per copy: $3.50; sample: $3.50. Back issues: $3.50. Discounts: 20%-50% on guide/books only - no discount on *the Illustrator Collector's News* The Bi-monthly Publication. 24pp; 8½×11; of. Reporting time: 30 days. We sometimes accept simultaneous submissions. Publishes 25-50% of manuscripts submitted. Payment: $25 per article and illustrations. Copyrighted, does not revert to author. Pub's reviews: 5 in 1998. §Collectibles and antiques, antiquarian books, paper, and illustrations. Ads: $64/$32/20¢. PCM, PAC, KRAUSE.

ILLYA'S HONEY, PO Box 225435, Dallas, TX 75222. 1994. Poetry, fiction, art, photos. "Poetry any length. Short fiction up to 1,000 words. B&w art and photos. No forced rhyme or overly religious verse. Recent contributors: Lyn Lifshin, Bob Zordani, Clebo Rainey, Lisa Yun." circ. 200. 4/yr. Pub'd 4 issues 1998; expects 4 issues 1999, 4 issues 2000. sub. price: $18; per copy: $5; sample: $5. Back issues: none. Discounts: none. 40pp; 5½×8½. Reporting time: 3-5 months. Simultaneous submissions accepted: yes. Publishes about 5% of manuscripts submitted. Payment: 1 copy. Copyrighted, reverts to author. Ads: none.

Image Industry Publications, Jacqueline Thompson, 34 High Street, Hastings On Hudson, NY 10706-4003, 718-273-3229. 1978. Satire. avg. press run 3M. Expects 1 title 2000. avg. price, paper: $25. Discounts: available on request; only for purchases of 5 or more copies. 288pp; 6×9; of.

The Image Maker Publishing Co., Beverly Hammond, 29417 Bluewater Road, Malibu, CA 90265, 310-457-4031. 1992. Fiction, photos, non-fiction. "Recently published *Malibu's Cooking Again*, a community cookbook containing recipes and stories of heroism and kindness shown during Malibu's firestorm. Also a publisher of photo calendars such as 'Firestorm' (showing the firefighting efforts) and 'Santa Monica-Malibu Images'" avg. press run 5M. Pub'd 2 titles 1998; expects 4 titles 1999, 5 titles 2000. 1 title listed in the *Small Press Record of Books in Print* (28th Edition, 1999-00). avg. price, paper: $15. Discounts: 40% discount to the trade. 128pp; 8¾×8; of. Reporting time: 2 months. Simultaneous submissions accepted: yes. Payment: 10% royalty on wholesale price or outright purchase. Copyrights for author.

Images For Media/Sesquin (see also YEFIEF), Ann Racuya-Robbins, PO Box 8505, Santa Fe, NM 87504, 505-753-3648; FAX 505-753-7049; arr@ifm.com. 1996. Poetry, fiction, articles, art, photos, cartoons, interviews, satire, criticism, reviews, music, letters, parts-of-novels, long-poems, collages, plays, concrete art, news items, non-fiction. avg. press run 1M. Expects 1 title 1999, 2 titles 2000. Discounts: to be negotiated. 200pp; 8½×10½. Reporting time: 8 weeks. Simultaneous submissions accepted: yes. Publishes very small % of manuscripts submitted. Payment: to be arranged. Copyrights for author. CLMP, New Mexico Book Association, New Mexico Center for the Book.

The Imaginary Press, Mercedes Pena, PO Box 509, East Setauket, NY 11733, 516-751-3810; E-mail imaginary-press@iname.com. 1994. Fiction. "We are just getting started, launching two books this year. We will see where it takes us." avg. press run 750-1M. Pub'd 2 titles 1998; expects 1 title 1999, 2 titles 2000. 1 title listed in the *Small Press Record of Books in Print* (28th Edition, 1999-00). avg. price, paper: $4.95-$8.95. Discounts: 40% (flatrate retail). 1-200pp; 4¾×7¼; of, electrostatic. Reporting time: 2 months, authors must query first. Simultaneous submissions accepted: no. Payment: subsidy. Copyrights for author.

IMAGO, Philip Neilsen, Queensland Univ Technology, School of Media and Journalism, PO Box 2434, Brisbane Q1D 4001, Australia, (07)864 2976, FAX (07)864 1810. 1988. "Short stories and articles under 3000 words; poems preferably short; reviews 500 words." circ. 500. 3/yr. Pub'd 3 issues 1998; expects 3 issues 1999, 3 issues 2000. sub. price: $A28 (includes airmail postage overseas); per copy: $A11 (includes airmail postage overseas). 100pp; 7×9¾; of. Reporting time: 3-6 months. Copyrighted, reverts to author. Pub's reviews: 22 in 1998. §Novels, poetry, non-fiction, but such books need to be relevant to the Australian literary scene.

IMPACC USA, PO Box 1247, Greenville, ME 04441-1247, 800-762-7720, 207-695-3354. 1986. 2 titles listed in the *Small Press Record of Books in Print* (28th Edition, 1999-00). Discounts: 50%.

Impact Publishers, Inc., Robert E. Alberti, Publisher, PO Box 6016, Atascadero, CA 93423-6016, 805-466-5917; fax 805-466-5919. 1970. Photos, cartoons, non-fiction. "Personal development, relationships, families, health, "Little Imp" books for children, caregiving (American Source Books)" avg. press run 5M-10M. Pub'd 4 titles 1998; expects 8 titles 1999, 8 titles 2000. 26 titles listed in the *Small Press Record of Books in Print* (28th Edition, 1999-00). avg. price, cloth: $24.95; paper: $12.95. Discounts: bookstores: up to 4 copies, 25% prepaid; 5-49 copies 40%; 50 plus copies, contact Impact re terms; libraries paper 10%; cloth 15%; wholesale distributors: contact Impact re terms. 200-300pp; 6×9; of. Reporting time: 6-8 weeks minimum.

261

Simultaneous submissions accepted: yes. Payment: standard royalty contract. Copyrights for author. PMA, ABA.

Impatiens Publications, Tom Secor, 4028 Pleasant Avenue South, Minneapolis, MN 55409, 612-822-17991 impub@isd.net. 1993. Fiction, non-fiction. "Impatiens Publications focuses in three areas. They are children's, computer, & alternative medicine" avg. press run demand. Pub'd 1 title 1998; expects 1 title 1999, 2 titles 2000. 4 titles listed in the *Small Press Record of Books in Print* (28th Edition, 1999-00). avg. price, paper: $19.95. 208pp; 5½×8; mi. Reporting time: 4 months. Payment: negotiated with individuals. Copyrights for author.

IMPERIAL RUSSIAN JOURNAL, Pavlovsk Press, Paul Gilbert, 103 Bristol Road East, Unit 202, Mississauga, Ontario L4Z 3P4, Canada, 905-568-3522. 1993. Articles, photos, interviews, reviews, letters, news items, non-fiction. "Length of material varies depending on subject. The *IRJ* focuses specifically on history of Imperial Russia (pre-1918); and Russian culture and the arts. A large section is devoted to the study of the Imperial House of Russia and the Russian Sovereigns. Regular features include the Romanov Diary, the Final Reign, Imperial Russian Review, Imperial Palaces, Haute Societe St. Petersburg, the Russian Empire, Impressions of St. Petersburg, Impressions of Moscow, the Russian Orthodox Church and many more. *Journal* is fully illustrated with many rare photos. Formerly published under the name *Imperial Quarterly Magazine* for 3 years. Writer's guidelines available on request." circ. 2M. 4/yr. Expects 4 issues 1999, 4 issues 2000. sub. price: $25; per copy: $6.25; sample: $7. Back issues: $7 each or $25 for 4. Discounts: nil. 40pp; 5½×8½; of. Reporting time: 2-4 weeks. Payment: $25 for 500-1000 words, $50 for over 1000 words. Copyrighted, reverts to author. Pub's reviews: 8 in 1998. §Imperial Russian history, the Romanov dynasty (bio's), Russian culture and travel. Ads: $200/$100.

IMPETUS, Implosion Press, Cheryl A. Townsend, Editor-in-Chief, 4975 Comanche Trail, Stow, OH 44224, telephone/fax: 216-688-5210; E-mail: impetus@aol.com. 1984. Poetry, articles, art, cartoons, interviews, reviews, letters, collages, news items. "Into social/political protest work. Recent contributors include Lyn Lifshin, Gerald Locklin, Ron Androla, Lonnie Sherman, Sherman Alexie." circ. 1M. 4/yr. Pub'd 4 issues 1998; expects 4 issues 1999, 4 issues 2000. sub. price: $15, $20; per copy: $5; sample: $5. Back issues: $5. Discounts: trade with other publications. 100pp; 7×8½; †mi and Risograph and Computer. Reporting time: within 4 months. Simultaneous submissions accepted: no. Publishes 5% of manuscripts submitted. Payment: copy of issue appearing in. Copyrighted, reverts to author. Pub's reviews: 200+ in 1998. §Poetry, artwork, interviews. free to magazines I exchange with, rate sheet available.

THE IMPLODING TIE-DYED TOUPEE, Burning Llama Press, Keith Higginbotham, Tracy R. Combs, 82 Ridge Lake Drive, Columbia, SC 29209-4213. 1993. Poetry, fiction, art, satire, collages, concrete art, news items, non-fiction. "Poetry: experimental, surreal, visual. Prose: *very* short fiction/non-fiction on popular culture, critiques. Art: black & white drawings, collages. We don't like explicit sex or "blood & guts" stuff. Contributors: John M. Bennett, Michael H. Brownstein, F.M. Cotolo, John Elsberg, Sheila E. Murphy. We are also inuerested in new writers. Always include SASE if you want your work returned. We like interesting cover letters with biographical information." circ. 100-300. 1-2/yr. Expects 1 issue 1999, 2 issues 2000. sub. price: $7; per copy: $4; sample: $4. Back issues: $4. Discounts: none. 40pp; 5½×8½; photocopy. Reporting time: 1 day to 2 months. Publishes 1% of manuscripts submitted. Payment: copy. Copyrighted, reverts to author. Pub's reviews: 0 in 1998. §Poetry, surrealism. will exchange ads with other mags.

Implosion Press (see also IMPETUS), Cheryl A. Townsend, Editor-in-Chief, 4975 Comanche Trail, Stow, OH 44224, telphone/fax: 216-688-5210; E-mail: impetus@aol.com. 1984. Poetry, art, cartoons, interviews, reviews, letters, collages, news items. "Quarterly magazine takes in above listed items. Annual All Female issues take above items pertaining only to the gender of issue. Chapbooks series (usually 4-6 per year) is by invitation only, but will look at material sent in. Broadsides are also printed. Have published chapbooks by Gerald Locklin, Lyn Lifshin, Lonnie Sherman, Ron Androla, Bill Shields, amongst others." avg. press run 1M. Pub'd 4 titles 1998; expects 4 titles 1999, 4 titles 2000. 5 titles listed in the *Small Press Record of Books in Print* (28th Edition, 1999-00). avg. price, paper: $5. Discounts: free for review. 100pp; 8½×7; †mi and Risograph and Computer. Reporting time: within 4 months. Simultaneous submissions accepted: no. Publishes 5% of manuscripts submitted. Payment: 1 copy upon publication. Copyrights for author.

IMPRINT, A LITERARY JOURNAL, Benjamin Tomkins, Publisher; Melanie Booth, Editor, 4053 Harlan Street, Loft 314, Emeryville, CA 94608-2702. 1999. Fiction, art, photos, cartoons, satire, non-fiction. "*Imprint* strives to promote creative individual talents that have not yet been discovered, silenced, or commercialized and speak with a contemporary and distinctly literate voice." circ. 500. 2/yr. Expects 2 issues 1999, 2 issues 2000. sub. price: $9; per copy: $5; sample: $5. Discounts: none. 90pp; 5½×8½; of. Reporting time: 8-12 weeks. Simultaneous submissions accepted: yes. Publishes 1% of manuscripts submitted. Payment: 3 copies. Copyrighted, reverts to author. Ads: $50/$25/$15 business card.

**In Between Books (see also THE BUTTERFLY CHRONICLES, A Literary Journal from the Butterfly

Tree), Karla Andersdatter, PO Box 790, Sausalito, CA 94966, 383-8447. 1972. Poetry. avg. press run 1.2M. Pub'd 1 title 1998. 4 titles listed in the *Small Press Record of Books in Print* (28th Edition, 1999-00). avg. price, cloth: $25; paper: $16; other: $5 magazine. Discounts: 40% to stores, 20% to libraries. 8×5; varies. Reporting time: 2-4 weeks. We prefer hot to accept simultaneous submissions. Publishes 40% of manuscripts submitted. Payment: none. Copyrights for author.

In One Ear Publications (see also BUENO), Dr. Elizabeth Reid, Bueno Books, 1700 Wagon Gap, Round Rock, TX 78681. 1989. Articles, non-fiction. "In addition to books, we publish greeting cards and a magazine." avg. press run 3M. Pub'd 1 title 1998; expects 2 titles 1999, 2 titles 2000. 8 titles listed in the *Small Press Record of Books in Print* (28th Edition, 1999-00). avg. price, paper: $12.95. Discounts: bulk 40%; 50% per case on non-returnable with minimum order. 224pp; 5×8½; of. Reporting time: 3 months. Simultaneous submissions accepted: yes. Publishes 15% of manuscripts submitted. Payment: negotiated. Copyrights for author. PMA, San Diego Book Publicists, Rocky Mtn Book Pub, SPAN.

IN PRINT, ClockWorks Press, Nancy Frank, PO Box 1699, Shingle Springs, CA 95682, 916-676-0701. 1992. Articles, interviews, reviews, news items. "Length of material: up to 1,500 words per item." circ. 1.25M. 4/yr. Pub'd 4 issues 1998; expects 4 issues 1999, 6 issues 2000. sub. price: free; sample: free. 6pp; 8×11; mi. Reporting time: 45 days. Payment: per negotiation. Copyrighted, rights revert to author by negotiation. Pub's reviews: 6 in 1998. §Clocks, watches, related materials. Ads: $150/$80/50¢.

In Print Publishing, Tomi Keitlen, Sindja, PO Box 20765, Sedona, AZ 86341, 520-284-5298; Fax 520-284-5283. 1991. Fiction, non-fiction. "We are an eclectic publisher" avg. press run 5M. Pub'd 2 titles 1998; expects 4 titles 1999, 4 titles 2000. 17 titles listed in the *Small Press Record of Books in Print* (28th Edition, 1999-00). avg. price, paper: $13.95; other: $10.95 cassette, $19.95 video. Discounts: inquire. 200-350pp; 5½×8½; camera-ready. Reporting time: 6-8 weeks. Simultaneous submissions accepted: yes. We publish 1 out of 50 books submitted. Payment: 6%-8% depending on book. Copyrights for author. NAPRA, TBPA, NAIP, PMA, AAP.

THE INCLUSION NOTEBOOK, Pennycorner Press, Gayle Kranz, Publisher; Kathleen Whitbvead, Editor, PO Box 8, Gilman, CT 06336, 860-873-3545; Fax 860-873-1311. 1996. Articles, photos, interviews, reviews, non-fiction. circ. 1000. 4/yr. Pub'd 4 issues 1998; expects 4 issues 1999, 4 issues 2000. sub. price: $14.95; per copy: $5. Back issues: Vol. I & II $35. 12-16pp; 8½×11; LP. Publishes 1% of manuscripts submitted. Payment: negotiated. Copyrighted, reverts to author. Pub's reviews: 6-8 in 1998. §School inclusion. PMA, SPAN, NEBA.

INCREDIBLE INQUIRY REPORTS, A. Fry, HC76, Box 2207, Garden Valley, ID 83622. 1987. Criticism, non-fiction. "Strange events, conspiracies, mental control methodology" circ. 5M. Spasmodic. Pub'd 1 issue 1998; expects 1 issue 2000. price per copy: $1; sample: same. Back issues: $1. Discounts: none. 4pp. Not copyrighted. No ads.

INDEFINITE SPACE, Marcia Arrieta, Kevin Joy, PO Box 40101, Pasadena, CA 91114. 1992. Poetry, art, photos. "Prefer poems not to exceed two pages. Does not accept previously published poems. Open to: modern, imagistic, abstract, philosophical, natural, surreal, and experimental creations." circ. 2M. 2/yr. sub. price: $7; per copy: $4; sample: $4. 40pp; 5½×8½; of. Reporting time: 1-2 months or sooner. Publishes 10% of manuscripts submitted. Payment: 1 copy.

Indelible Inc. (see also MASSACRE), Roberta McKeown, BCM 1698, London WC1N 3XX, England. 1988. Poetry, fiction, photos, cartoons, satire, criticism, collages. "Indelible Inc. was founded to publish children's books, but has now branched out. Although the first 2 titles were hardcover picture books, later children's books are small chapbooks, published in 'The Black & White & Read All Over' Series. Indelible Inc. publishes *massacre*, an annual anthology of anti-naturalistic fiction and reprints neglected or out of print books of general interest with notes (titles include a 16th century poem about the Gout). Suitable submissions welcome: Criticism, suggestions for reprints from editors, short stories. No long novels or poetry (unless suggestions for out of print—and copyright—reprints). Indelible Inc. publishes the whimsical, odd, neglected and unusual. It's best-selling children's book, for example, is called *Derek the Dust-Particle* and has probably never been bought for a child." avg. press run 300. Pub'd 1 title 1998; expects 1 title 1999, 2 titles 2000. 9 titles listed in the *Small Press Record of Books in Print* (28th Edition, 1999-00). avg. price, cloth: £6.25-£15; paper: £2-£7. Discounts: libraries 10%, trade 35%. 72-148pp; 5½×8½; of. Reporting time: 1-2 months. Simultaneous submissions accepted: no. Publishes 25% of manuscripts submitted. Payment: 7% per net price of each book sold, 5 comp. copies; royalties do not amount to much since runs are so small. Copyrights for author.

The Independent Institute (see also THE INDEPENDENT REVIEW: A Journal of Political Economy), Robert Higgs, 100 Swan Way, Oakland, CA 94621-1428, 510-632-1366; fax 510-568-6040; email info@independent.org; www.independent.org. 1986. Articles, reviews, non-fiction. "Critical analysis of government policy, past and present. Articles should not exceed 7,500 words and should be submitted in triplicate, typed doublespaced with author's name, address and phone number (abstract of no more than 150 words should be included). Authors should be prepared to submit article on 3.5 inch computer disk in a recent

Macintosh Word or WordPerfect for Macintosh or DOS/Windows. Book manuscripts should be similarly prepared. Recent authors: Thomas Szasz, Stanley Engerman, Anna Schwartz, William Niskanen, Irving Horowitz, Leland Yeager, E.G. West.'' avg. press run 5M. Pub'd 10 titles 1998; expects 10 titles 1999, 10 titles 2000. 26 titles listed in the *Small Press Record of Books in Print* (28th Edition, 1999-00). avg. price, cloth: $34.95; paper: $19.95. Discounts: Returnable: 1-4 20%, 5-9 40%, 10-24 41%, 25-49 42%, 50-99 43%; Non-returnable: 1-4 25%, 5-9 42%, 10-24 43%, 25-49 44%, 50+ 45%. 250pp; 6×9; †of. Reporting time: 1-2 months. Simultaneous submissions accepted: no. Payment: negotiated. Does not copyright for author.

INDEPENDENT PUBLISHER, Jenkins Group, Inc., Mardi Link, Executive Editor, 121 East Front Street, Suite 401, Traverse City, MI 49684, voice 616-933-0445; fax 616-933-0448; e-mail jenkins.group@small-press.com. 1993. Poetry, fiction, articles, interviews, satire, criticism, reviews, letters, news items. "*INDEPENDENT PUBLISHER* reviews approx. 600 books from small presses each year" circ. 10M. 6/yr. Pub'd 6 issues 1998; expects 6 issues 1999, 6 issues 2000. sub. price: $34; per copy: $5.95; $10 - includes s&h, fully applicable to subscription. Discounts: 15% for assoc. members. 80pp; 8½×11; of. Simultaneous submissions accepted: no. Publishes 1% of manuscripts submitted. Payment: varies. Copyrighted, reverts to author. Pub's reviews: 500+ in 1998. §Books only - all areas. Call about ad rates. PMA, IPN, SPAN.

Independent Publishing Co. (see also YESTERDAY'S MAGAZETTE), Ned Burke, PO Box 18566, Sarasota, FL 34276, 941-924-3201; Fax 941-925-4468; E-mail ymagazette@aol.com. 1971. Poetry, fiction, articles, photos, interviews, reviews, letters, news items, non-fiction. "We specialize in meeting the printing needs of the desktop publisher & writer. We do first class books on 60# paper with glossy covers. Size & amount of copies needed can be small or large." avg. press run 500. Pub'd 6 titles 1998; expects 12 titles 1999, 20 titles 2000. 2 titles listed in the *Small Press Record of Books in Print* (28th Edition, 1999-00). avg. price, paper: $15. 60pp; 5½×8½; †of. Reporting time: 2 weeks. Payment: none. Copyrights for author.

THE INDEPENDENT REVIEW: A Journal of Political Economy, The Independent Institute, Robert Higgs, 100 Swan Way, Oakland, CA 94621-1428, 510-632-1366; fax 510-568-6040; email review@independent.org; www.independent.org/review. 1996. Articles, reviews, non-fiction. "Critical analysis of government policy, past and present. Articles: should not exceed 7,500 words and should be submitted in triplicate, typed double spaced with author's name, address and phone number (abstract of no more than 150 words should be included). Authors should be prepared to submit articles on 3.5 inch computer disk in a recent Macintosh Word or WordPerfect for Macintosh or DOS/Windows." circ. 5M. 4/yr. Pub'd 4 issues 1998; expects 4 issues 1999, 4 issues 2000. sub. price: $27.95; per copy: $7.50; sample: $7.50. Back issues: $7.50. Discounts: agent 10%, classroom 20%, bulk 20%, jobber 20%, distributors negotiated. 160pp; 7×10; †of. Reporting time: 1 month. Simultaneous submissions accepted: no. Payment: none. Copyrighted, does not revert to author. Pub's reviews: 50 in 1998. §Economics, history, political science, philosohpy, law (inquiries first before submission). Ads: $775/$350 1/4 page.

THE INDEPENDENT SHAVIAN, Dr. Richard Nickson, Douglas Laurie, The Bernard Shaw Society, PO Box 1159 Madison Square Stn., New York, NY 10159-1159, 212-982-9885. 1962. Poetry, articles, cartoons, interviews, satire, criticism, reviews, letters, news items. "Publication deals with items concerning Bernard Shaw, his circle and his world: theatre, politics, music, etc." circ. 500 worldwide. 3/yr. Pub'd 3 issues 1998; expects 3 issues 1999, 3 issues 2000. sub. price: $20 USA, $20 outside USA (airmail included); per copy: $2; sample: $2. Back issues: $2. Discounts: 13% for subscription agencies. 25pp; 6×9½; of. Reporting time: none. Payment: none. Not copyrighted. Pub's reviews: 8 in 1998. §Anything pertaining to Bernard Shaw.

Index Publishing Group, Inc, Linton M. Vandiver, Publisher, 3368 Governor Drive, Suite 273-F, San Diego, CA 92122-2925, 619-455-6100; FAX 619-522-9050; orders 800-546-6707; e-Mail ipgbooks@indexbooks.com; Website www.indexbooks.comlipgbooks. 1992. Non-fiction. avg. press run 5M. Expects 20 titles 1999, 24 titles 2000. 21 titles listed in the *Small Press Record of Books in Print* (28th Edition, 1999-00). avg. price, cloth: $29.50; paper: $19.95. Discounts: 6-99 copies 40%; 100-499 45%; 500+ 50%. 300pp; 5½×8½, 7×10, 8½×11; perfect bound and Smythe Sewn. Reporting time: 2 weeks. Simultaneous submissions accepted: yes. Publishes 25% of manuscripts submitted. Payment: stepped royalties, usually beginning at 10% and extending to 20% at ascending sales increments. Copyrights for author. APA.

INDEX TO FOREIGN LEGAL PERIODICALS, University of California Press, Thomas H. Reynolds, Kevin Durkin, Managing Editor, University of California Press, 2120 Berkeley Way, Berkeley, CA 94720, 510-643-7154. 1960. Articles, reviews, non-fiction. "Editorial address: L250A Boalt Hall, Berkeley, CA 94720. Copyrighted by The American Association of Law Libraries." circ. 600. 3/yr. Pub'd 3 issues 1998; expects 3 issues 1999, 3 issues 2000. sub. price: $605 (+ $12 foreign postage); per copy: $605. Back issues: $540. 250pp; 6×9; of. Copyrighted, does not revert to author. Ads: none accepted.

INDIA CURRENTS, Arvind Kumar, Box 21285, San Jose, CA 95151, 408-274-6966; 408-274-2733; e-Mail EDITOR@INDIACUR.COM. 1987. Fiction, articles, art, photos, cartoons, interviews, satire, criticism, reviews, music, letters, parts-of-novels, collages, news items, non-fiction. "Between 300-1500 words. We look for insightful approach to India, its arts, culture, people. Recent contributors: Sandip Roy-Chowdhury, Chitra Divakaruni, Rajeev Srinivasan, Laxmi Hisemath, Prasenjit Ranjan Gupta'' circ. 24M. 12/yr. Pub'd 12 issues 1998; expects 12 issues 1999, 12 issues 2000. sub. price: $19.95; per copy: $1.95 + $1 s/h; sample: same. Back issues: $3. 104pp; 8½×11; of. Reporting time: 3 months. Publishes 20% of manuscripts submitted. Payment: up to 5 subscriptions ($99.75 value). Copyrighted, reverts to author. Pub's reviews: 24 in 1998. §India and Indians, colonialism, immigration, multiculturalism, assimilation, racism. Ads: $650/$360/60¢.

THE INDIAN WRITER, Dr. P.K. Joy, 1-A, 59 Ormes Road, Chennai 600010, India, 6261370, 6284421. 1986. Poetry, reviews, news items, non-fiction. "We publish short poems, book reviews, scholarly notes on mechanics of writings and news about national and international literary activities." circ. 750. 4/yr. Pub'd 4 issues 1998; expects 4 issues 1999, 4 issues 2000. sub. price: $20; per copy: free; sample: free. Back issues: free if available in stock. 16pp; size A4; †lp. Reporting time: 1 month. Simultaneous submissions accepted: yes. Publishes 10% of manuscripts submitted. Payment: copy. Not copyrighted. Pub's reviews: over 40 in 1998. §Poetry. Ads: $50/$30. Writers Club of India.

INDIANA REVIEW, Laura McCoid, Editor; Brian Leung, Associate Editor, Ballantine Hall 465, Indiana University, Bloomington, IN 47405, 812-855-3439. 1976. Poetry, fiction, art, photos, interviews, reviews, parts-of-novels, long-poems, plays, non-fiction. "*Indiana Review* is a magazine of poetry, fiction, and essays. We prefer writing that shows both an awareness of language and of the world. We publish 10-12 stories and about 40-60 pages of poetry per issue. We like writers who take risks. All submissions are read start to finish. Recent contributors have included Dean Young, Heather McHugh, Tess Gallagher, Belle Waring, Bob Hicok, Dan Choon." circ. 2.5M. 2/yr. Pub'd 2 issues 1998; expects 2 issues 1999, 2 issues 2000. sub. price: $12, institutions $15, please add $2 for overseas; per copy: $7; sample: $7. Back issues: $5. Discounts: trade 60/40% split; 50-50 to distributors. 200pp; 6×9; of. Reporting time: 2 weeks-4 months. Simultaneous submissions accepted: yes. Publishes less than 1% of manuscripts submitted. Payment: $5 per page poem, $5 per page story, $10 minimum. Copyrighted, reverts to author. Pub's reviews: 18 in 1998. §New collections of poetry or fiction; anthologies of fiction on multicultural or sociopolitical themes; novels by new and established writers, especially from small presses; books of criticism or literary theory especially concerning multiculturalsim or themes of social change. Ads: $300/$150. CLMP.

INDY MAGAZINE, Jeff Mason, Editor-in-Cheif; Chris Waldron, Senior Editor, 611 NW 34th Drive, Gainesville, FL 32607-2429, 352-373-6336; E-mail jrm@grove.ufl.edu; http://www.indyworld.com. 1993. Articles, photos, cartoons, interviews, criticism, reviews, letters, news items. "*Indy Magazine* covers the world of alternative comic books and independent film." circ. 8M-12M. 5/yr. Pub'd 5 issues 1998; expects 5 issues 1999, 5 issues 2000. sub. price: $15; per copy: $2.95; sample: $3. Back issues: $3. Discounts: 1-9 copies 50%, 10-24 55%, 25+ 60%. 72pp; 8⅜×10¾; of. Simultaneous submissions accepted: no. Publishes 75% of manuscripts submitted. Payment: 2¢/word. Copyrighted, reverts to author. Pub's reviews: 250 in 1998. §Comic books, comix, film, anime, cartoons, TV. Ads: $150/$75/$40 1/4 page.

Infinite Corridor Publishing, Joe Wolosz, Editor-in-Chief, PO Box 640051, San Francisco, CA 94164-0051, 415-292-5639; Fax 415-931-5639; E-mail corridor@slip.net. 1996. "Hotel and Hospitality related texts. All matter relates to the operations of the hospitality industry." avg. press run 3M. Expects 1 title 1999, 2 titles 2000. 1 title listed in the *Small Press Record of Books in Print* (28th Edition, 1999-00). avg. price, paper: $24.95. 176pp; 5½×8½. Reporting time: 1 month. Simultaneous submissions accepted: no. Payment: 10% of net, paid every month. Copyrights for author.

Infinite Passion Publishing, Carol Brady, Editor, PO Box 340815, Columbus, OH 43234, 614-792-0053; e-mail infipas@iwaynet.net. 1996. "We publish spiritual books" Pub'd 1 title 1998; expects 2 titles 1999, 2 titles 2000. 2 titles listed in the *Small Press Record of Books in Print* (28th Edition, 1999-00). avg. price, paper: $12.45. Discounts: 1 book 20%, 2-3 40%, 4+ 50%. 128pp; 5½×8½. Reporting time: 6 weeks. Simultaneous submissions accepted: yes. Publishes 5% of manuscripts submitted. Payment: various. Copyrights for author.

The Infinity Group, Genie Lester, PO Box 2713, Castro Valley, CA 94546, 510-581-8172; kenandgenie@yahoo.com. 1987. Poetry, fiction, art, photos. "We are publishing our first full-length novel this year, *The Hostage* by Mary R. DeMaine. If this venture goes well, we will publish 1 or 2 novels a year. We have 5 authors lined up at present. We are not interested in submissions until we see how it goes. We are still reorganizing to determine future projects." avg. press run 2M+. Expects 1 title 1999, 1-2 titles 2000. 200pp; 4¼×6¾; of. Simultaneous submissions accepted: no. Copyrights for author.

INFOCUS, Christie Holmgren, Communications Manager, 319 SW Washington Street, Suite 710, Portland, OR 97204-2618, 503-227-3393. Articles, art, photos, interviews, reviews, news items, non-fiction. "Articles should be a maximum of 1.5M words. Especially interested in new technology and software and its impact on business and paperwork. Enclose SASE. Simultaneous submissions ok. Query or send manuscript. Recent titles: *Laser Forms Make Mark at AAL*; *Knowing When to Automate Forms Inventory Management*; *Integrating Office Technologies*; *Promoting Forms Management In Smaller Federal Agencies*." circ. 1.5M. 10/yr. Pub'd 8 issues

1998; expects 10 issues 1999, 10 issues 2000. sub. price: $50 (US, US Possession, Canada, Mexico), all others $65, library rate $35; per copy: $10; sample: free. Back issues: $10 as available. Discounts: call publisher for quote. 8pp; 8½×11; of. Reporting time: 2 months. Simultaneous submissions accepted: yes. Payment: negotiable. Copyrighted, rights reverting to author negotiable. Pub's reviews: 10 in 1998. §Office automation, management techniques, paperwork simplification, forms and procedures. Ads: write for rate card.

INFORMATION ENTREPRENUER, Tom Bodus, 121 East Front Street, Ste. 401, Traverse City, MI 49684, 616-933-0445. 1994. Articles, art, photos, interviews, reviews. "500-2000 words for feature articles" circ. 11M. 12/yr. Expects 8 issues 1999, 12 issues 2000. sub. price: $28; per copy: $3.50; sample: $3.50 + s/h. Discounts: $2 for over 10. 40pp; 10¾×13; of. Reporting time: 60 days. Publishes 80% of manuscripts submitted. Payment: $100-300 per article. Copyrighted, does not revert to author. Pub's reviews. §Entreprenuerism, information technology. Ads: $1620/$984. PMA.

Information International, Trish Phillips, Box 579, Great Falls, VA 22066, 703-450-7049, fax 703-450-7394, bobs@isquare.com. 1985. Non-fiction. "Specialize in books for small business and the entrepreneur" avg. press run 5M. Pub'd 1 title 1998; expects 3 titles 1999, 6 titles 2000. 4 titles listed in the *Small Press Record of Books in Print* (28th Edition, 1999-00). avg. price, paper: $15.95. 350pp; 5½×8½. Simultaneous submissions accepted: yes. Publishes 50% of manuscripts submitted. Payment: varies. Copyrights vary. SPAN, PMA.

Information Research Lab, Park Plaza Suite 144, 9824 Western Avenue, Evergreen Park, IL 60805, 773-375-0280; e-mail aah-irl@writeme.com. 1990. Non-fiction. avg. press run 2.5M. Pub'd 7 titles 1998; expects 4 titles 1999, 8 titles 2000. 5 titles listed in the *Small Press Record of Books in Print* (28th Edition, 1999-00). avg. price, cloth: $24.95; paper: $19. Discounts: contact for more information. 59pp; 8½×11; of. Copyrights for author.

Infotrends Press, 11620 Wilshire Blvd., Ste. 750, Los Angeles, CA 90025, 310-445-3265. 1992. "Additional address: PO Box 25356, Los Angeles, CA 90026-0356." avg. press run 10M. Expects 3 titles 1999, 4 titles 2000. avg. price, paper: $15; other: $14. Discounts: 0%-40% on volumes ordered. 200+pp; 5⅜×8½. Reporting time: 3 weeks. Payment: 7-10%. Copyrights for author. PMA.

INFUSION, Sonya Huber, Center for Campus Organizing, 165 Friend Street, Suite 1, Boston, MA 02114-2025, 617-725-2886; e-mail cco@igc.apc.org. 1991. Articles, art, photos, cartoons, reviews, letters, plays, news items. "Organizing resources and updates preferred. Theory pieces discouraged." circ. 5000. 6/yr. Pub'd 4 issues 1998; expects 5 issues 1999, 6 issues 2000. sub. price: $25 ($10 low-income); per copy: $1; sample: $1. Back issues: $2.50. 20pp; 8½×11; †offset. Reporting time: 1 month. Simultaneous submissions accepted: yes. Publishes 50% of manuscripts submitted. Payment: copies. Copyrighted, reverts to author. Pub's reviews: 4 in 1998. §Student activism, social justice organizing. Ads: $300/$160/10¢/word. Independent Press Association.

Inheritance Press Inc., Surena Bissette, 101 Henderson Lane, Trenton, NC 28585, 919-448-1113 phone & fax. 1993. Non-fiction. "Send SASE for manuscript submissin guidelines. No unsolicited manuscripts to be submitted" avg. press run 1.5M. Expects 3 titles 2000. 1 title listed in the *Small Press Record of Books in Print* (28th Edition, 1999-00). avg. price, cloth: $19.95; paper: $9.95. Discounts: Quoted on demand. 200pp; 5⅜×8½; of. Payment: quoted on acceptance of manuscript for publication. Copyrights for author. PMA, PAS.

Inner City Books, Daryl Sharp, Victoria Cowan, Box 1271, Station Q, Toronto, ON M4T 2P4, Canada, 416-927-0355; FAX 416-924-1814; icb@inforamp.net. 1980. Non-fiction. "We publish *only* studies in Jungian psychology by Jungian analysts. Now 86 titles by 40 authors. Over a million books sold worldwide; over 200 other language editions. No unsolicited manuscripts." avg. press run 3M. Pub'd 4 titles 1998; expects 6 titles 1999, 4 titles 2000. avg. price, paper: $16. Discounts: trade 40%/60 days or 50% prepaid; postfree. 160pp; 6×9; dektop publishing. Copyrights for author.

INNER JOURNEYS, Gateways Books And Tapes, Iven Lourie, Nancy Christie, PO Box 370, Nevada City, CA 95959, 916-272-0180; fax 916-272-0184; e-Mail doug+@dnai.com. 1987. Reviews, news items. "This is a *newsletter* with capsule reviews in the *spiritual and consciousness* field only. We do not solicit authors, only review books in our own field." circ. 2.5M. 4/yr. Expects 3-4 issues 1999, 3-4 issues 2000. sub. price: $5; per copy: $1; sample: free. 20pp; 8½×11; of. Copyrighted, reverts to author. Pub's reviews: 4-6 per issue; new format: 20-30 reviews per issue in 1998. §Sprituality, consciousness research, esotericism, science fiction, some literature. No ads. American Booksellers Assn.

Inner Traditions International, Ehud C. Sperling, President & Publisher; Jon Graham, Acquisitions Editor, One Park Street, Rochester, VT 05767, 802-767-3174; fax 802-767-3726; orders 800-246-8648; E-mailorders@gotoit.com; Website: www.gotoit.com. 1975. Art, non-fiction. "Esoteric philosophy, occult and hermetic sciences, astrology, holistic health, mysticism, diet, nutrition, cookbooks. Book-length only." avg. press run 5M-10M. Pub'd 60 titles 1998; expects 60 titles 1999, 60 titles 2000. 417 titles listed in the *Small Press Record of Books in Print* (28th Edition, 1999-00). avg. price, cloth: $24.95-$39.95; paper: $12.95.

266

Discounts: trade discounts vary according to quantity from 20-50%. 250pp; size varies; of. Reporting time: 3 months on queries, 3-6 months on mss. Simultaneous submissions accepted: yes. Publishes 10% of manuscripts submitted. Payment: standard for industry. Copyrights for author. A.B.A.

INNER VOICES: A New Journal of Prison Literature, Nolan Williams, PO Box 4500 #219, Bloomington, IN 47402. 1993. Poetry, fiction, art, cartoons, satire, parts-of-novels, long-poems, plays. *"Inner Voices* invites submissions of prisoners' creative writing including (but not limited to) poetry, raps, short stories, and short plays. We welcome a variety of topics and writing styles, but keep in mind that many prisons restrict access to material they feel teaches readers how to commit crimes. We want this journal to be available to as many prisoners as possible and will give preference to work on the safe side of this limitation. Sorry. No restriction on language or attitude, though. Energy, sincerity and originality are at least as important as polish. We will also have some room for cartoons and graphics. Authors are encouraged to include a *short* personal or biographical statement. Pseudonyms OK.*" circ. 200. 2/yr. Expects 2 issues 1999, 2 issues 2000. sub. price: $10 institutions, $8 individuals, $5 prisoners, free to contributors; per copy: $5; sample: $5. Back issues: none. Discounts: 40%. 50pp; 5½x8½. Reporting time: 2 months. Payment: copies. Copyrighted, reverts to author. Pub's reviews. §We'll review closely related books, i.e. on prison poetry, education, or book programs. Ads: none.

●**Innerwisdom Publishing**, 2609 Colorado Boulvard, PO Box 70793, Pasadena, CA 91107, phone/fax 626-683-3316. 1 title listed in the *Small Press Record of Books in Print* (28th Edition, 1999-00).

Innerworks Publishing, PO Box 270865, Houston, TX 77277-0865, telephone/fax: 713-661-8284, 800-577-5040; orders; E-mail empower@netropolis.com. 1990. Non-fiction. avg. press run 3M. Expects 1 title 1999, 1 title 2000. 6 titles listed in the *Small Press Record of Books in Print* (28th Edition, 1999-00). avg. price, paper: $10.95; other: $16.95. Discounts: Distributors 40-55%. 150pp; 5½x8½. NAPRA.

Innisfree Press, Marcia Broucek, 136 Roumfort Road, Philadelphia, PA 19119-1632, 215-247-4085 fax 215 247-2343 email InnisfreeP@aol.com. 1982. Non-fiction. avg. press run 5M. Pub'd 5 titles 1998; expects 8 titles 1999, 5 titles 2000. 43 titles listed in the *Small Press Record of Books in Print* (28th Edition, 1999-00). avg. price, paper: $12.95. Discounts: 1-4 20%, 5-249 45%, 250-499 46%, 500+ 47%. 160pp; 6×9; of. Reporting time: 2 months. Simultaneous submissions accepted: yes. Publishes 1% of manuscripts submitted. Payment: 10% net receipts. Copyrights for author. PMA, ABA, SPAN.

Innovanna Publishing Co., Inc., Dawn Huxtable, 14019 Southwest Fwy., Suite 301-517, Sugar Land, TX 77478, 800-577-9810; 281-242-9835; Fax 281-242-6498. 1995. Art, photos, non-fiction. "Not accepting submissions at this time. Recent non-fiction: *Romantic Wedding Destinations* by Jackie Carrington." avg. press run 1M. Pub'd 1 title 1998; expects 3 titles 1999, 4 titles 2000. 3 titles listed in the *Small Press Record of Books in Print* (28th Edition, 1999-00). avg. price, paper: $19.95. Discounts: query for schedule. 150pp; 8½x11; of.

INNOVATING, Harold S. Williams, The Rensselaerville Institute, Rensselaerville, NY 12147, 518-797-3783. 1963. Articles, interviews, reviews, letters, non-fiction. "Publication is dedicated to enabling people to lead change by example. The quarterly includes innovation assumptions, paradigms, research and examples. While the focus is on the public and voluntary sector, the content is also relevant to business and other kinds of organizations." circ. 2M. 4/yr. Pub'd 4 issues 1998; expects 4 issues 1999, 4 issues 2000. sub. price: $30 prepay; per copy: $8; sample: free. Back issues: $8. Discounts: according to volume. 70pp; 5½x8½; of. Reporting time: 6 weeks prior to publication date. Simultaneous submissions accepted: yes. Percentage of manuscripts received that are published varies. Payment: yes if they have a track record. We will publish first time writers if it fits. Copyrighted, reverts to author. Pub's reviews: 4 in 1998. §Innovation/creativity, entrepreneur, management, education, outcome funding, outcome management, due diligence. Ads: none.

Innovation Press, Jane Byrden, 2920 Industrial Park Road, Iowa City, IA 52240, 319-337-6316; fax 319-337-9034; email icanwork@aol.com. 1994. Non-fiction. avg. press run 2M-20M. Pub'd 2 titles 1998; expects 3 titles 1999. 1 title listed in the *Small Press Record of Books in Print* (28th Edition, 1999-00). avg. price, paper: $9.95. 190pp; 5½x8½; of. Reporting time: 60 days. Simultaneous submissions accepted: yes. Publishes 10% of manuscripts submitted. Payment: negotiated with each submission. Copyrights for author.

INQ Publishing Co., JanaSue Fitting, PO Box 10, N. Aurora, IL 60542, 708-801-0607. 1988. Fiction, articles, cartoons, news items, non-fiction. "Shipping address: 122 Juniper Dr., North Aurora, IL 60542" avg. press run varies. Pub'd 2 titles 1998; expects 2 titles 1999, 2 titles 2000. 4 titles listed in the *Small Press Record of Books in Print* (28th Edition, 1999-00). avg. price, paper: $9.95; other: spirals $10.95. Discounts: 1 20%, 2-4 40%, 5+ 42%; non-returnable (5 + 50% if paid net 30). Pages vary; size varies; of. Reporting time: 6 weeks. MAPA.

THE INQUIRER, Keith Gilley, 1-6 Essex Street, London WC2R 3HY, England. 1842. Poetry, articles, photos, cartoons, reviews, letters. circ. 2000. 26/yr. Pub'd 26 issues 1998; expects 26 issues 1999, 26 issues 2000. sub. price: $38 airmail; per copy: 30p; sample: free. 11pp; size A4 (297×210mm); of. Reporting time: 1 month. Payment: none. Copyrighted. Pub's reviews: 30 in 1998. §Religion, social matters. Ads: £5 + VAT @ 17.5%.

Inquiry Press, 1880 North Eastman, Midland, MI 48640-8838, 517-631-0009. 1975. *"A division of Wysong Medical."* 4 titles listed in the *Small Press Record of Books in Print* (28th Edition, 1999-00). avg. price, cloth: $15.95; paper: $12.95. Discounts: 4-10 15%, 11-25 20%, 26-50 30%, 51-100 40%, 100+ request quote. 450pp; 6×9; of, lp. Reporting time: 30 days.

INSECTS ARE PEOPLE TWO, H.R. Felgenhauer, 3150 N Lake Shore Drive #5-E, Chicago, IL 60657-4803, 312-772-8686. 1989. *"Looking for insects doing people things and especially people doing insect things. Prospective contributors should send $5 for sample copy to get perspective."* circ. 1M+. Erratic. Pub'd 1 issue 1998; expects 1 issue 2000. sub. price: $5; per copy: $5; sample: $5. Back issues: $5. 60+pp; 8½×11; commercial printers. Reporting time: 1-3 weeks. Simultaneous submissions accepted: yes. Publishes 30-50% of manuscripts submitted. Payment: liberal contributor's copies and/or modest honorarium. Copyrighted, reverts to author. Pub's reviews: 0 in 1998. §Insects doing people things, people doing insect things. Ads: $25/$15/inquire.

Insider Publications, Katherine Poyma, 2124 Kittredge Street, 3rd Floor, Berkeley, CA 94704, 800-782-6657; Fax 415-552-1978; E-mail info@travelinsider.com. 1989. Non-fiction. *"We specialize in all aspects of budget travel, and encourage submissions. We also use researchers based in each of the following cities: Chicago, Los Angeles, Miami, New York, San Francisco, Amsterdam, Frankfurt, London, Athens, Johannesburg, Bangkok, Hong Kong, Singapore, Sydney, and Tokyo."* avg. press run 10M. Pub'd 1 title 1998; expects 1 title 1999, 2 titles 2000. 1 title listed in the *Small Press Record of Books in Print* (28th Edition, 1999-00). avg. price, paper: $14.95. Discounts: 2-4 copies 20%, 5-24 43%. 244pp; 6×9; of. Reporting time: varies. Simultaneous submissions accepted: yes. Payment: negotiable. Copyrights negotiable. PMA.

Insomniac Press, Mike O'Connor, 393 Shaw Street, Toronto, ON, M6J 2X4, Canada, 416-536-4308. 1992. Poetry, fiction, parts-of-novels. *"Graphic-design enhanced short fiction and poetry"* avg. press run 2M. Pub'd 2 titles 1998; expects 4 titles 1999, 4 titles 2000. 13 titles listed in the *Small Press Record of Books in Print* (28th Edition, 1999-00). avg. price, paper: $12.99. Discounts: trade 40%, classroom 20%, others negotiable. 164pp; 6×9; of. Reporting time: 8 weeks. Simultaneous submissions accepted: no. Payment: royalty. Does not copyright for author. TSPG, SPC, OBPO, CPA.

Institute for Contemporary Studies, Melissa Stein, 1611 Telegraph Avenue, Ste. 902, Oakland, CA 94612-3010. 1972. Articles, news items. *"Books on domestic and international public policy issues. Books on international economics focus on developing countries."* avg. press run 3M. Pub'd 8-10 titles 1998; expects 8-10 titles 1999, 12 titles 2000. 60 titles listed in the *Small Press Record of Books in Print* (28th Edition, 1999-00). avg. price, cloth: $25.95; paper: $19.95. Discounts: on request. 300pp; 6×9; of. Reporting time: 1-3 months. Payment: works for hire and royalty arrangements. Copyrights for author. PMA, NCBPMA.

Institute for Southern Studies (see also SOUTHERN EXPOSURE), Pat Arnow, Editor, PO Box 531, Durham, NC 27702. 1973. Poetry, fiction, articles, art, photos, cartoons, interviews, reviews, plays, news items, non-fiction. avg. press run 8M. Pub'd 4 titles 1998; expects 4 titles 1999, 4 titles 2000. 42 titles listed in the *Small Press Record of Books in Print* (28th Edition, 1999-00). avg. price, paper: $5. Discounts: 50 or more copies 40%. 64pp; 8½×11; of. Reporting time: 4-6 weeks. Payment: on publication, no royalties. Copyrights for author.

Institute of Archaeology Publications, Marilyn Beaudry-Corbett, Director of Publications; Brenda Johnson-Grau, Senior Editor, Univ. of California-Los Angeles, Box 951510, Los Angeles, CA 90095-1510, 310-825-7411. 1975. Non-fiction. avg. press run 500. Pub'd 4 titles 1998; expects 4 titles 1999, 4 titles 2000. 19 titles listed in the *Small Press Record of Books in Print* (28th Edition, 1999-00). avg. price, cloth: $50; paper: $25. Discounts: 20% to agencies. 200pp; 8½×11; of. Reporting time: 60 days. Simultaneous submissions accepted: no. Payment: none. Does not copyright for author.

The Institute of Mind and Behavior (see also THE JOURNAL OF MIND AND BEHAVIOR), Raymond Russ, Ph.D., PO Box 522, Village Station, New York, NY 10014, 212-595-4853. 1980. Criticism, reviews, non-fiction. *"Send manuscripts to Raymond Russ, Ph.D., Department of Psychology Room 301, 5742 Little Hall, University of Maine, Orono, ME 04469-5742. We are interested in scholarly manuscripts, with interdisciplinary thrust, in the areas of: the mind/body problem in the social sciences; the philosophy of experimentalism and theory construction; historical perspectives on the course and nature of scientific investigation; and mind/body interactions and medical implications."* avg. press run 2M. Pub'd 1 title 1998; expects 1 title 1999, 1 title 2000. 7 titles listed in the *Small Press Record of Books in Print* (28th Edition, 1999-00). avg. price, paper: $15. Discounts: 18% on orders of 10 copies or more. 350pp; 5½×8½; of. Reporting time: 8-15 weeks. Payment: no fees to authors. Does not copyright for author.

●**Integra Press,** 1702 W. Camelback Road, Suite 119, Phoenix, AZ 85015, 602-996-2106; Fax 602-953-1552; info@integra.com. 4 titles listed in the *Small Press Record of Books in Print* (28th Edition, 1999-00).

Integral Publishing, Georg Feuerstein, PO Box 1030, Lower Lake, CA 95457, 707-928-5751. 1986.

Non-fiction. "Ideal length: 160-180 book pages (c. 64-72,000 words). Materials must be well researched and sophisticated but not aridly academic. General orientation: alternative thought. Lee Sannella, *The Kundalini Experience*; Howard S. Levi and Akira Ishihara, *The Tao of Sex*." avg. press run 4M. Expects 2 titles 1999, 2 titles 2000. 2 titles listed in the *Small Press Record of Books in Print* (28th Edition, 1999-00). avg. price, cloth: $20; paper: $12. Discounts: 20% STOP orders; otherwise order through Great Tradition. 160pp; 6×9; of. Reporting time: 2 weeks, preliminary letter essential. Payment: by arrangement. Copyrights for author.

INTEGRAL YOGA MAGAZINE, Prakash Shakti Capen, Editor-in-Chief, Route 1, Box 1720, Buckingham, VA 23921, 804-969-3121. 1969. Poetry, fiction, articles, interviews, letters, non-fiction. circ. 800. 4/yr. Pub'd 4 issues 1998; expects 4 issues 1999, 4 issues 2000. sub. price: $15; per copy: $3.75; sample: $4. Back issues: $1-$1.50. 40pp; 6×9; desktop. Copyrighted, reverts to author. Pub's reviews: 0 in 1998. §Spiritual, health, ecumenical, holistic medicine, yoga.

●Intelligenesis Publications, Sue Hansen, Richard King, Karen Lushbaugh, Pat Wright, 6414 Cantel Street, Long Beach, CA 90815, 562-598-0034; website httm://www.bookmasters.com/marktplc/00337.htm. 1998. "Shipping address: PO Box 545, Seal Beach CA 90740" avg. press run 3-5M. Pub'd 1 title 1998; expects 3 titles 1999, 3 titles 2000. 1 title listed in the *Small Press Record of Books in Print* (28th Edition, 1999-00). price, paper: $19.95. Discounts: trade 1-2 full price; bulk, agent, jobber 40%; wholesaler 50%. 536pp; 5½×8½; of. Reporting time: 3-6 months. Simultaneous submissions accepted: no. Publishes 5% of manuscripts submitted. We copyright as requested.

Interalia/Design Books, G. Brown, S. Ewing, PO Box 404, Oxford, OH 45056-0404, 513-523-6880; FAX 513-523-1553. 1989. Art, non-fiction. "It is the goal of Interalia/Design Books to make meaningful contributions to the art of the book as a container of knowledge—the textual manifestation of a culture's evolution—and to the book as an object by promoting the dissemination of quality design through an editorial focus on architecture, design/crafts, art criticism, art of the book, facsimiles of out-of-print primary sources on architecture, design/crafts and art criticism. Also by promoting quality in the art of bookmaking by experimenting with alternative structures for the production of books as objects, including alternative printing and binding methods, encouraging limited editions of experimental books and of books for the bibliophile, encouraging artist/writer/printer/binder collaborations." avg. press run 1M. Pub'd 1 title 1998; expects 1 title 1999, 4 titles 2000. 4 titles listed in the *Small Press Record of Books in Print* (28th Edition, 1999-00). avg. price, paper: $19. Discounts: 40% for orders of 10+. 100pp; 5½×8½; of. Reporting time: 4-6 weeks. Payment: varies. Copyrights for author.

INTERBANG, Heather Hoffman, PO Box 1574, Venice, CA 90294, 310-450-6372. 1995. Poetry, fiction, articles, art, cartoons, interviews, satire, criticism, reviews, letters, parts-of-novels, long-poems, non-fiction. "Please send 10-15 poems, or 2-3 short stroies of any length. Interbang places no restrichtions on lenth or content." circ. 2M. 4/yr. Pub'd 2 issues 1998; expects 4 issues 1999, 4 issues 2000. sub. price: $8; per copy: $2; sample: $2. Back issues: $2. Discounts: Writers who submit their work can request a free issue. 28pp; 8½×7; †of. Reporting time: 2-3 months. Simultaneous submissions accepted: yes. Publishes 40% of manuscripts submitted. Payment: multiple copies of issue. Copyrighted, reverts to author. Pub's reviews: 2 in 1998. §Poetry, fiction, other small magazines. Ads: $50/$35/$25 1/4 page.

Intercontinental Publishing, Inc, H.G. Smittenaar, 6451 Steeple Chase Lane, Manassas, VA 22111, 703-369-4992. 1991. "Additional Address: PO Box 7242, Fairfax Station, VA 22039. Currently concentrating on translations of European best-sellers. Are publishing the works of Baantjer and Elsinck and are negotiating for other authors" avg. press run 3M-7.5M. Pub'd 3 titles 1998; expects 3 titles 1999. 23 titles listed in the *Small Press Record of Books in Print* (28th Edition, 1999-00). avg. price, cloth: $13.95; paper: $8.95. Discounts: Distribution through Independant Publisher Group (IPG) in Chicago. Supply libraries from publisher at same discount as stores. Info upon request. 240pp; 8¼×8½. Reporting time: varies. Simultaneous submissions accepted: yes. Publishes 2% of manuscripts submitted. Payment: percentage of books sold. Copyrights for author.

Intercultural Press, Inc., Toby S. Frank, President; David S. Hoopes, Editor-in-Chief; Judy Carl-Hendrick, Managing Editor, PO Box 700, Yarmouth, ME 04096, 207-846-5168; e-mail books@interculturalpress.com. 1980. Non-fiction. "Office of David S. Hoopes: 143 Casseekee Trail, Melbourne Beach, FL 32951. Books on intercultural communication, intercultural education and cross-cultural training, especially practical materials for use in teaching and training; other areas: diversity, multicultural education, orientation for living abroad. Shipping address: 374 U.S. Route One, Yarmouth, ME 04096." avg. press run 2M. Pub'd 10 titles 1998; expects 12 titles 1999, 12 titles 2000. 78 titles listed in the *Small Press Record of Books in Print* (28th Edition, 1999-00). avg. price, cloth: $25; paper: $16.95. 200pp; 6×9, 5½×8½, 7×10; desktop. Reporting time: 2-8 weeks. Simultaneous submissions accepted: yes. Publishes 2% of manuscripts submitted. Payment: royalty. Copyrights for author. Small Press Center.

INTERCULTURAL WRITERS REVIEW, Marjorie E. Navarro, Managing Editor; Richard Navarro,

Executive Editor & Art Director, PO Box 1107, Blythe, CA 92226-1107. 1994. Poetry, articles, art, cartoons, letters, long-poems, satire, reviews, parts-of-novels, news items, non-fiction. "Poetry up to 45 lines any style. All checks/money orders should be made payable to Navarro Publications" circ. 400+. 4/yr. Pub'd 4 issues 1998; expects 4 issues 1999, 4 issues 2000. sub. price: $29.95 USA 35.95 foreign; per copy: $9.50 USA $14.50 foreign; sample: $9.50. 35pp; 7×8½; photocopy. Reporting time: 12-14 weeks. Simultaneous submissions accepted: yes. Publishes 35% of manuscripts submitted. Payment: discounted copy. Copyrighted, reverts to author. Pub's reviews: 3 in 1998. §anything intercultural. Ads: from $5-$95. Intercultural Writers Association.

INTERCULTURE, Robert Vachon, Editor, Intercultural Institute of Montreal, 4917 St-Urbain, Montreal, Quebec H2T 2W1, Canada, 514-288-7229; FAX 514-844-6800. 1968. Articles, reviews, non-fiction. "Printed in two separate editions: *Interculture* (English edition ISSN 0828-797X); *Interculture* (French edition ISSN 0712-1571). Length of material: 28M words average (each issue devoted to a particular theme). Material: cross-cultural understanding - themes include education, medicine, spirituality, communication, politics and law in an intercultural perspective. Recent titles: *Ecosophy and Sivilization, The Religion of the Future, The Archaeology of Development A Life Through Art, Intercultralism Under the African Sun, Grass Root's Post-Modernism, Ecosophy and Sivilization*. Recent contributors: Robert Vachon, Scott Eastham, Raimon Panikkar, Gustavo Esteva, Edward Goldsmith, Eric Wesselow, Lomomba Emongo, Gary Sneider, and Madhu S. Prakash" circ. 1M. 2/yr. Pub'd 2 issues 1998; expects 2 issues 1999, 2 issues 2000. 1 title listed in the *Small Press Record of Books in Print* (28th Edition, 1999-00). sub. price: $19 individuals, $33 institutions in Canada; outside Canada $23 individuals, $37 institutions; per copy: $9, instit. $15 + GST 7% in Canada and TVQ (7.5%) in Quebec; sample: $9. Back issues: $4.50 older issues, $9 newer. Discounts: subscription agencies receive 15%. 60pp; 6¼x9½; of. Reporting time: 3 months. Copyrighted. §Cross-cultural issues. Canadian Magazine Publishers Association, SODEP (Societe de developpement des periodiques culturels quebecois).

Interface Press (see also BRAIN/MIND BULLETIN, Bulletin of Breakthroughs), Marilyn Ferguson, Publisher, Editor, PO Box 42211, Los Angeles, CA 90042, 213-223-2500; 800-553-MIND. 1975. Articles, interviews, reviews, news items, non-fiction. avg. press run 5M. Pub'd 12 titles 1998; expects 12 titles 1999, 12 titles 2000. 2 titles listed in the *Small Press Record of Books in Print* (28th Edition, 1999-00). avg. price, other: $4. 8pp; 8½×11; of. Payment: none.

INTERIM, James Hazen, Editor; Claudia Keelan, Associate Editor; Tim Erwin, Associate Editor; John Heath-Stubbs, English Editor, Department of English, University of Nevada, Las Vegas, Las Vegas, NV 89154-5011, 702-895-3172. 1944 (now revived 1986 with Vol. 5, No. 1). Poetry, fiction, reviews. "Poetry any form and some fiction up to 7,000 words. Early issues of *Interim* (1944-55) have been reprinted by Kraus and Co. Occasional short reviews of books.Primarily poetry, occasional fiction. We presently use one story per issue." circ. 700. 1/yr. Pub'd 2 issues 1998; expects 2 issues 1999, 1 issue 2000. sub. price: $7/yr; $12/2 yrs; $15/3 yrs; per copy: $7 by mail; $9 international; libraries $14/yr subscription; sample: $7. Back issues: Write editor; libraries should contact Kraus for complete original sets, 1944-55. Discounts: 40% to bookstores on consignment, 5+ copies. Bookstore request welcome. 100pp; 6×9; †of. Reporting time: 2 months. Simultaneous submissions accepted: no. Publishes 2-3% of manuscripts submitted. Payment: contributor copies plus 2-year subscription. Copyrighted, rights revert to author on request. Pub's reviews: 5 in 1998. §Poetry, criticism, fiction. Ads: please write editor. CLMP.

Interim Press, Peter Dent, 3 Thornton Close, Budleigh Salterton, Devon EX9 6PJ, England, (0395) 445231. 1975. Poetry, art, criticism, letters, long-poems, plays. "Books include *Candid Fields: Essays and Reflections on the Work of Thomas A. Clark*; *The Blue Wind: Poems in English from Pakistan*; *Not Comforts But Vision: Essays on the Poetry of George Oppen*; *A Remote Beginning* by Daud Kamal; *Royal Murdoch: Chills and Fevers: Poems and Letters*; *Journal* by Ian Robinson; *Scented Leaves from a Chinese Jar* by Allen Upward; and *The Wreck of the Deutschland: An Historical Note* by Sean Street. Also poetry in other editions by Peter Dent" avg. press run 250. Expects 1 title 1999. 14 titles listed in the *Small Press Record of Books in Print* (28th Edition, 1999-00). avg. price, paper: £3. Discounts: 33% to trade; 10% libraries. 24-40pp; 5¾x8¾; of. Reporting time: 2 weeks. Simultaneous submissions accepted: no. Publishes 10% of manuscripts submitted. Payment: copies only. Copyrights for author.

Interlink Publishing Group, Inc., Michel Moushabeck, Phyllis Bennis, 99 Seventh Avenue, Brooklyn, NY 11215, 718-797-4292. 1987. Art, photos, non-fiction. avg. press run 10M. Pub'd 28 titles 1998; expects 32 titles 1999, 30 titles 2000. avg. price, cloth: $35; paper: $14.95. Discounts: Trade 40% & up. 160pp; 5¼x8, 6×9; of. Reporting time: 2 months. Payment: semi-annually, royalty varies. Copyrights for author. AAP, ABA.

INTERLIT, Isaac Phiri, Cook Communications Ministries, 4050 Lee Vance View, Colorado Springs, CO 80918-7100, 719-536-0100; Fax 719-536-3266. 1964. "Trade journal for Christian publishers around the world." circ. 2.5M. 6/yr. Pub'd 6 issues 1998; expects 6 issues 1999, 6 issues 2000. sub. price: $15. Back issues: $1.50 each. 24pp; 8½x10¾; †of. Reporting time: 1 month. Payment: varies. Copyrighted, does not revert to author. Pub's reviews. §Books about publishing. Ads: $500/$250/$125 1/4 page. ACP (Assoc. Church Press), Evangelical Press Assoc.

InterMedia Publishing, Inc., 2120 Southwest 33 Avenue, Ft. Lauderdale, FL 33312-3750, E-mail intermediapub@juno.com. 1996. Fiction, art, cartoons, non-fiction. "Query first" Expects 5 titles 1999, 35 titles 2000. 1 title listed in the *Small Press Record of Books in Print* (28th Edition, 1999-00). Simultaneous submissions accepted: yes. Copyrights for author. Florida Publishers Assn., Nat'l Assn. of Independent Publishers.

Intermountain Publishing, Walter J. Polt, 1713 Harzman Road SW, Albuquerque, NM 87105, 505-242-3333. 1989. Non-fiction. 2 titles listed in the *Small Press Record of Books in Print* (28th Edition, 1999-00).

INTERNATIONAL ART POST, Banana Productions, Anna Banana, PO Box 2480, Sechelt, B.C. V0N 3A0, Canada. 1988. Art, photos. "ISSN 0843-6312. *IAP* is a cooperatively published periodical of stamps by artists (Artistamps), printed in an edition of 1000 copies in full color on gummed, glossy paper. Editions go to press as sufficient art and money accumulate to cover costs. After payment to participants, Banana Productions distributes the rest of the edition (approx. 400 sheets) through gallery and stationery shops, or uses them in promotional mailings." circ. 1M. 2/yr. Pub'd 2 issues 1998; expects 2 issues 1999, 2 issues 2000. sub. price: $30; per copy: $15; sample: $16. Back issues: write for order form, it varies from issues to issue. Discounts: 50% wholesale. 2-7pp; size varies; of, full color on gummed stock, then pinhole perforated. Reporting time: 3-6 months, depending on how quickly a space or press sheet is sold. Payment: 500 copies their own stamp(s), 3 copies of the sheet on which it is printed, and 1 copy of any other sheet(s) in the edition. Copyrighted. Ads: none. SPAN (Small Press Action Network, Vancouver).

THE INTERNATIONAL FICTION REVIEW, Christoph Lorey, Dept. of German & Russian, UNB, PO Box 4400, Fredericton, N.B. E3B 5A3, Canada, 506-453-4636; fax 506-453-4659; e-mail ifr@unb.ca. 1973. "The *IFR* is an annual periodical devoted to international fiction. Mss are accepted in English and should be prepared in conformity with the *MLA Handbook for Writers of Research Papers*; articles: 10-20 typewritten pages; reviews: 600-800 words; spelling, hyphenation, and capitalization according to *Webster.*" circ. 600. 1/yr. Pub'd 1 issue 1998; expects 1 issue 1999, 1 issue 2000. sub. price: $15 instit., $12 indiv.; per copy: $12; sample: $12. Back issues: same $8. Discounts: 20% for agents and jobbers. 120pp; 6×9; of. Reporting time: 6 weeks - 3 months. Payment: none. Copyrighted. Pub's reviews: 35 in 1998. §Fiction and scholarly works on fiction. IFA.

International Jewelry Publications, Patricia Esparza, Beverly Newton, PO Box 13384, Los Angeles, CA 90013, 626-282-3781. 1987. Photos, interviews, non-fiction. "*Gemstone Buying Guide, The Diamond Ring Buying Guide: How to Spot Value & Avoid Ripoffs*, 5th edition, *The Ruby & Sapphire Buying Guide: How to Spot Value & Avoid Ripoffs*, 2nd edition by Renee Newman; *Pearl Buying Guide*, 3rd edition, *The Gold Jewelry Buying Guide.*" avg. press run 6M. Pub'd 2 titles 1998; expects 2 titles 1999, 2 titles 2000. 6 titles listed in the *Small Press Record of Books in Print* (28th Edition, 1999-00). avg. price, paper: $19. Discounts: 2-4 copies 30%, 5-24 40%, 25-49 45%, 50+ 48%. 180pp; 7×9; of. Reporting time: 1 month, but call first before submitting manuscript. Copyrights for author. PMA.

INTERNATIONAL JOURNAL FOR THE SEMIOTICS OF LAW, Deborah Charles Publications, D. Milovanovic, 173 Mather Avenue, Liverpool L18 6JZ, United Kingdom. 1988. Non-fiction. "English and French articles on semiotics of law" circ. 300. 3/yr. Pub'd 3 issues 1998; expects 3 issues 1999, 3 issues 2000. sub. price: £75 + postage; individuals via membership of IJSL (£30); per copy: £20; sample: £10. Back issues: on application. Discounts: 5% subscription agents. 112pp; royal octavo; DTP Macintosh. Reporting time: 3 months. Payment: none. Copyrighted, does not revert to author. Pub's reviews: 1 in 1998. §Linguistics, philosophy, semiotics of law. exchange basis.

INTERNATIONAL JOURNAL OF SPORT NUTRITION (IJSN), Human Kinetics Pub. Inc., Priscilla Clarkson, Ph.D., PO Box 5076, Champaign, IL 61825-5076, 217-351-5076. 1991. Articles, reviews. "Advances the understanding of the nutritional aspects of human physical and athletic performance." circ. 1150. 4/yr. Pub'd 4 issues 1998; expects 4 issues 1999, 4 issues 2000. sub. price: $42 individual, $100 institution, $26 student; per copy: $12 indiv., $26 instit.; sample: free. Back issues: $12 indiv., $26 instit. Discounts: 5% agency. 96pp; 6×9; of. Reporting time: 2 months. Payment: none. Copyrighted, does not revert to author. Pub's reviews: 0 in 1998. §Sport-related information on clinical nutrition, nutrition research, current thought in nutrition, and nutrition for the layman. Ads: $300/$200. Midwest Book Publishers Association, American Booksellers Association.

INTERNATIONAL MATHEMATICS RESEARCH NOTICES, Duke University Press, Morris Weisfeld, Box 90660, Duke University, Durham, NC 27708-0660. "*IMRN* publishes short papers announcing new results, examples, counterexamples, and comments on research of current interest. Each issue of *IMRN* is published in two forms: a printed issue and an electronic version. *IMRN* is now available on the World Wide Web to site-licensed subscribers, produced in Adobe Acrobat and downloadable at the *IMRN* URL. Subscribers can now have Web access with the look and feel of the printed version." circ. 200. Frequency determined by submission flow (10-18 issues expected annually). sub. price: $660 institutions, $330 individuals, additional $60 foreign. Ads: $200 full page.

INTERNATIONAL OLYMPIC LIFTER, Bob Hise II, Publisher & Editor, PO Box 65855, Los Angeles, CA 90065, 213-257-8762. 1973. Poetry. circ. 3M. 6/yr. Pub'd 5 issues 1998; expects 6 issues 1999, 6 issues 2000. sub. price: $28 1st class, $40 foreign air; per copy: $6; sample: $4. 36pp; 8½×11. Payment: $25-$100. Copyrighted, we're flexible on reverting rights. Pub's reviews: 10 in 1998. §general. Ads: $300/$165/up to 3 lines $15.

INTERNATIONAL POETRY REVIEW, Mark Smith-Soto, Dept of Romance Languages, The University of North Carolina at Greensboro, Greensboro, NC 27412-5001, 336-334-5655. 1975. Poetry, art. "Alexis Levitin, Ana Istaru, Fred Chappell, Coleman Barks, Jorge Teillier, Mary Crow, Jascha Kessler" circ. 400. 2/yr. Pub'd 2 issues 1998; expects 2 issues 1999, 2 issues 2000. sub. price: $10 individuals; $15 libraries, institutions; per copy: $5; sample: $5. Back issues: varies. 100pp; 5½×8½; of. Reporting time: 3-6 months. Simultaneous submissions accepted, but must be indicated. Publishes 2% of manuscripts submitted. Payment: copies. Copyrighted, reverts to author. Pub's reviews: 2 in 1998. §Poetry translation, poetry. Ads: $100/$50. CLMP.

International Publishers Co. Inc., Betty Smith, PO Box 3042, New York, NY 10116, 212-366-9816; fax 212-366-9820. 1924. Non-fiction. avg. press run 3M-5M. Pub'd 5 titles 1998; expects 4 titles 1999, 5 titles 2000. 5 titles listed in the *Small Press Record of Books in Print* (28th Edition, 1999-00). avg. price, cloth: $19; paper: $7-$14. Discounts: trade and short discount. 200-400pp, some 96-150pp; 5×8, 5½×8½, 6×9. Reporting time: 1 week to 2 months. Simultaneous submissions accepted: yes. Publishes 5% of manuscripts submitted. Payment: royalties. Copyrights for author. NACS, ABA.

INTERNATIONAL QUARTERLY, Van K. Brock, PO Box 10521, Tallahassee, FL 32302-0521, 904-224-5078. 1993. Poetry, fiction, articles, art, photos, interviews, reviews, letters, parts-of-novels, non-fiction. "We are interested in translations and in works in English. Our past issues have included Edmund Keeley, Wayne Brown, and Laure-Anne Bosselaar, and translations of Anna Akhmatova by Judith Hemschemeyer, Agnes Gergely by Bruce Berlind, and more. We also have a 'books of interest' and 'journals of interest' section where we annotate about 35 books, etc." circ. 2M. 4/yr. Pub'd 4 issues 1998; expects 4 issues 1999, 4 issues 2000. sub. price: $30 worldwide; per copy: $10; sample: $6 postpaid. Back issues: inquire. Discounts: inquire. 160pp; 7½×10; of. Reporting time: varies, we shoot for 8-16 weeks. Simultaneous submissions accepted: yes. Publishes 5% of manuscripts submitted. Payment: copies. Copyrighted, reverts to author. Pub's reviews: two in 1998. §Contemporary poetry, fiction, non-fiction, art, and reviews in original English or in translation. Ads: $450 page.

International University Line (IUL), Igor Tsigelny, PO Box 2525, La Jolla, CA 92038, 619-457-0595. 1992. Non-fiction. avg. press run 3M. Expects 3 titles 1999, 6 titles 2000. 5 titles listed in the *Small Press Record of Books in Print* (28th Edition, 1999-00). avg. price, cloth: $39.95; paper: $29.95. Discounts: up to 55%. 250pp; 5½×8½. Reporting time: 6 months. Payment: 10% royalty. Copyrights for author.

●**THE INTERPRETER'S HOUSE,** Merryn Williams, 38 Verne Drive, Ampthill, MK45 2PS, United Kingdom, 01525-403018. 1996. Poetry, fiction. "Stories up to 2000 words." circ. 150. 3/yr. Pub'd 3 issues 1998; expects 3 issues 1999, 3 issues 2000. sub. price: £8.50; per copy: £2.95; sample: £2.95. Back issues: £2.95. 74pp; size A5. Reporting time: 1 month. Simultaneous submissions accepted: yes. Publishes 10% of manuscripts submitted. Payment: free copy. Not copyrighted.

Intertext, Sharon Ann Jaeger, Editor, 2633 East 17th Avenue, Anchorage, AK 99508-3207. 1982. Poetry, criticism. "Our most noted titles have been *17 Toutle River Haiku*, by James Hanlen, done in calligraphy with full-color illustrations, and Louis Hammer's *The Mirror Dances*. Writers please note: query first, sending three poems in a legal-size (#10) envelope by *first-class mail*. Please do not send an entire manuscript unless we ask to see it; do not send material by manuscript rate, either. We cannot return anything sent without SASE or IRC. We consider only strong full-length collections by writers of demonstrated achievement. As we have several projects in progress, we will not be considering unsolicited material until 2001." avg. press run 300-1M; electronic media, on-demand publishing. 4 titles listed in the *Small Press Record of Books in Print* (28th Edition, 1999-00). avg. price, cloth: $25; paper: $15; other: $10 diskettes; $25 CD-ROM. Discounts: 1-4, 20%; 5-24, 40%; 25-49, 43%; 50-99, 46%; over 100, 50%. 64-96pp; electronic media. Reporting time: 3-6 months on average. Simultaneous submissions accepted: no. Payment: 10% royalty after all costs of production, promotion, and distribution have been met; no advances. Does not copyright for author. Small Press Center, PEN USA West.

INTERVENTION IN SCHOOL AND CLINIC, Gerald Wallace, Editor, Gerald Wallace - Graduate School of Education, George Mason University, Fairfax, VA 22030-4444. 1965. Articles, cartoons, interviews, letters. "*Intervention in School and Clinic* (formerly *Academic Therapy*) deals with the day-to-day aspects of special and remedial education. It's articles and instructional ideas provide practical and useful information appropriate for immediate implementation. Topics include, but are not limited to, assessment, curriculum, instructional practices, and school and family management of students experiencing learning or behavior problems." circ.

3.5M. 5/yr. Pub'd 5 issues 1998; expects 5 issues 1999, 5 issues 2000. sub. price: North America: indiv. $35, instit. $95; foreign: $105; per copy: $10. Back issues: $10. 64pp; 8½×11; sheet fed. Reporting time: 4-6 weeks. Simultaneous submissions accepted: no. Publishes 60% of manuscripts submitted. Payment: none. Copyrighted, does not revert to author. Pub's reviews: 20 in 1998. §Any books appropriate for the above stated aims and scope of the journal. Ads: $400/$200/$20 for 25 words or less (each add'l word 65¢).

Intrigue Press, Lee Ellison, PO Box 456, Angel Fire, NM 87710, 505-377-3474; e-mail publish@intrigue-press.com. 1994. Fiction. "We publish only book-length fiction in the mystery, suspense and adventure genres. Lead titles in 1995 and 1996 are the Charlie Parker mysteries by Connie Shelton" avg. press run 3M. Pub'd 1 title 1998; expects 2 titles 1999, 2-3 titles 2000. 20 titles listed in the *Small Press Record of Books in Print* (28th Edition, 1999-00). avg. price, cloth: $21.95. Discounts: 40% to stores, 55% to wholesalers. 200+pp; 6×9; of. Reporting time: 4 weeks on query and sample chapters. Simultaneous submissions accepted: yes. Publishes less than 1% of manuscripts submitted. Payment: varies. Copyrights for author. PMA, SPAN.

INTUITIVE EXPLORATIONS, Gloria Reiser, PO Box 561, Quincy, IL 62306-0561, 217-222-9082. 1987. Poetry, fiction, articles, art, cartoons, interviews, reviews, music, letters, news items, non-fiction. "Metaphysical/new age publication. Prefer articles under 1500 words. Encourage submissions. Products/books for review welcome." circ. 1M+. 6/yr. Pub'd 6 issues 1998; expects 6 issues 1999, 6 issues 2000. sub. price: $15; per copy: $3; sample: $3. Back issues: $3. Discounts: distributor price 75¢ per copy on minimum of 10 copies. 12-24pp; 8½×11. Reporting time: 6 weeks or less. Publishes 50-75% of manuscripts submitted. Payment: copies or advertising. Copyrighted, reverts to author. Pub's reviews: 50+ in 1998. §New Age metaphysics, magic and esoteric systems, self-help, occult sciences such as Tarot, philosophy, psychology, personal growth, mind potential, Runes & Astrology. Ads: $50/$30/$20 1/4 page/line ads 25¢ per word.

INVESTMENT COLUMN QUARTERLY (newsletter), NAR Publications, Nicholas A. Roes, PO Box 233, Barryville, NY 12719, 914-557-8713. 1977. Articles, criticism, reviews, news items. 4/yr. Pub'd 10 issues 1998; expects 10 issues 1999, 4 issues 2000. sub. price: $75; per copy: $20; sample: $20. Back issues: $20. 2-4pp; 8½×11; †of. Copyrighted. Pub's reviews: 2 in 1998. §Investments.

INVISIBLE CITY, Red Hill Press, San Francisco + Los Angeles, John McBride, Paul Vangelisti, PO Box 2853, San Francisco, CA 94126. 1971. Poetry, criticism, concrete art. "An eclectic gathering of poetry, translations, essays & visuals, published whenever enough good material is available. A tabloid (1971-81, 28 numbers),*Invisible City* is now in book-format with set themes. Forthcoming in 1991: *Daybook* by Robert Crosson, with *Division*, notes on American poetry edited by Paul Cuneo et al. 'Perhaps *the* orchestra of the eighth day.' Obviously experimental, *Invisible City* cherishes Samuel Johnson's phrase, "the reek of the human", and still observes E.P.'s precept, "OK, send 'em along: subject verb object". But please sample our wares ($3 postpaid) before submitting bundles of poetry" circ. 1M. 1-2/yr. Pub'd 1-2 issues 1998; expects 2+ issues 1999. sub. price: $10 postpaid (indiv.) $10 (libraries). 64pp; 5½×9; of. Copyrighted, reverts to author. Pub's reviews: 2 in 1998. §Poetry, translations, visuals. No ads. CLMP.

Ione Press, Jill Carpenter, PO Box 3271, Sewanee, TN 37375, 931-598-0795; e-mail jillc@infoave.net. 1998. Poetry, fiction, non-fiction. avg. press run 2M. Pub'd 1 title 1998; expects 1 title 1999, 1-2 titles 2000. 1 title listed in the *Small Press Record of Books in Print* (28th Edition, 1999-00). avg. price, paper: $10.95. Discounts: distributors, bookstores. 131pp; 6×9; of. Reporting time: 3-6 months. Simultaneous submissions accepted: yes. Payment: individually decided. Does not copyright for author.

IOTA, David Holliday, 67 Hady Crescent, Chesterfield, Derbyshire S41 0EB, Great Britain, 01246-276532. 1988. Poetry, reviews. "Poetry: all subjects and styles, bar concrete (no facilities or expertise). Space being limited, shorter poems have the edge. Recent contributors include Virginia Romming, Michael Cunningham, Anne Clarke, Robert Lumsden, Lee Duke, Thomas Land, M.A.B. Jones, Brian Daldorph" circ. 400. 4/yr. Pub'd 4 issues 1998; expects 4 issues 1999, 4 issues 2000. sub. price: $15 (add $10 if by cheque); per copy: $4; sample: $2. Back issues: $2. Discounts: shops 33%. 48pp; 5¾×8¼ (A5); of. Reporting time: first assessment, usually a couple of weeks, but a firm decision on inclusion or rejection may take months. Simultaneous submissions accepted: yes. Publishes 5% of manuscripts submitted. Payment: 2 complimentary copies. Copyrighted, reverts to author. Pub's reviews: 43 in 1998. §poetry. No ads.

IOWA HERITAGE ILLUSTRATED (formerly The Palimpsest), Ginalie Swaim, State Historical Society of Iowa, 402 Iowa Avenue, Iowa City, IA 52240, 319-335-3916. 1920. Articles, art, photos, interviews, letters, non-fiction. "*Iowa Heritage Illustrated* is Iowa's popular history magazine. It publishes manuscripts and edited documents on the history of Iowa and the Midwest that may interest a general reading audience. Submissions that focus on visual materials (photographs, maps, drawings) or on material culture are also welcomed. Originality and significance of the topic, as well as quality of research and writing, will determine acceptance. Manuscripts should be double-spaced, footnoted, and roughly 10-25 pages. Photographs or illustrations (or suggestions) are encouraged." circ. 4M. 4/yr. Pub'd 4 issues 1998; expects 4 issues 1999, 4 issues 2000. sub. price: $19.95; per copy: $6; sample: free. Back issues: 1920-1972—50¢, 1973-June '84—$1, July '84-Dec.

'86—$2.50, 1987—Summer '89 $3.50, fall 89 - winner 95 $4.50. Discounts: retailers get 40% off single issue cover price. 48pp; 8½×11; of. Reporting time: 2 months. Publishes 20% of manuscripts submitted. Payment: none, except for 10 complimentary copies. Copyrighted, does not revert to author.

THE IOWA REVIEW, David Hamilton, Editor; Mary Hussmann, Editor, 308 EPB, Univ. Of Iowa, Iowa City, IA 52242, 319-335-0462. 1970. Poetry, fiction, articles, interviews, criticism, reviews, parts-of-novels, long-poems, non-fiction. "We publish quality contemporary fiction, poetry, criticism, and book reviews. Recent contributors include Marianne Boruch, Mark Doty, Curtis White and Frankie Paino." circ. 1.5M. 3/yr. Pub'd 2 issues 1998; expects 3 issues 1999, 3 issues 2000. sub. price: instit. $20 (+$3 outside US), indiv. $18 (+$3 outside US); per copy: $6.95; sample: $6 for most recent issue. Discounts: 10% agency, 30% trade. 192pp; 6×9; of. Reporting time: 2-4 months. Simultaneous submissions accepted: yes. Publishes 5% of manuscripts submitted. Payment: $10 per page fiction, $1 per line poetry. Copyrighted, reverts to author. Pub's reviews: 10 in 1998. §Poetry, fiction, literary culture. Ads: $200/$100. CLMP.

IPSISSIMA VERBA/THE VERY WORDS: Fiction & Poetry in the First Person, P.D. Jordan, 32 Forest Street, New Britain, CT 06052, fax 860-832-9566; e-mail: ipsiverba@aol.com. 1989. Poetry, fiction, art, photos, cartoons, letters, parts-of-novels. "This press and magazine are starting production again after 6 years. All material must be written in first person singular!" 2/yr, with occasional "special" issues. Expects 2 issues 1999, 3 issues 2000. sub. price: $15; per copy: $6; sample: $6. 60pp; 8½×11; †of, digital duplicater. Reporting time: 1 month. Simultaneous submissions accepted: no. Publishes 15-20% of manuscripts submitted. Payment: copies (for now, will become $ in future). Not copyrighted. Pub's reviews. §Fiction. Ads: $75/$45/$20 1/4 page/classifieds 10¢/word.

IRIS: A Journal About Women, Eileen Boris, Box 323, HSC, University of Virginia, Charlottesville, VA 22908, 804-924-4500; iris@virginia.edu. 1980. Poetry, fiction, articles, art, photos, interviews, criticism, reviews, collages, news items, non-fiction. "We welcome high-quality submissions of poetry, fiction, art, book reviews, news, personal essays, non-fiction, medical, and legal issues. Our aim is to publish material on subjects that are of concern to women. Please send for a sample copy of our journal before submitting nonfiction." circ. 4M. 2/yr. Pub'd 2 issues 1998; expects 2 issues 1999, 2 issues 2000. sub. price: $9; per copy: $5; sample: $5. Discounts: 20% for trade or bulk. 72pp; 8½×11. Reporting time: about 2 months. Simultaneous submissions accepted: yes. Publishes 5% of manuscripts submitted. Payment: 1 year subscription. Copyrighted, reverts to author. Pub's reviews: 5 in 1998. §Books about women or that are written by women and feminist theory. Ads: $190/$120/$85 1/4 page.

IRISH FAMILY JOURNAL, Irish Genealogical Foundation, Michael C. O'Laughlin, Box 7575, Kansas City, MO 64116, 816-454-2410. 1978. Articles, art, photos, interviews, letters, news items, non-fiction. "Short articles, highlights, Irish American personalities, informal, tradition/history oriented. Time period: A) 1800's, B) current time for genealogy. Photos of Irish family castles, immigrants, lifestyle—1800's. Family names." circ. 2.5M+. 6 or 12/yr (12 issues to gold members). Pub'd 12 issues 1998; expects 12 issues 1999, 12 issues 2000. 8 titles listed in the *Small Press Record of Books in Print* (28th Edition, 1999-00). sub. price: $54/$104; per copy: $9; sample: $5. Back issues: $25 per year (6 issues). Discounts: bulk purchases: 40%-60% discount. 16pp; 8½×11; of. Reporting time: 2 weeks. Payment: inquire. Copyrighted, reverts to author. Pub's reviews: 50 in 1998. §Irish genealogy, history, folklore, tradition. Ads: $500/$300.

Irish Genealogical Foundation (see also IRISH FAMILY JOURNAL), Michael C. O'Laughlin, Box 7575, Kansas City, MO 64116, 816-454-2410; e-mail mike@irishroots.com. 1969. Articles, art, photos, interviews, letters, non-fiction. avg. press run 2M. Pub'd 2 titles 1998; expects 2 titles 1999, 2 titles 2000. 12 titles listed in the *Small Press Record of Books in Print* (28th Edition, 1999-00). avg. price, cloth: $45. Discounts: bulk purchases 40%-60% discount. 300pp; 8½×11; of. Reporting time: 30 days. Payment: inquire. Does not copyright for author.

IRISH JOURNAL, Full Moon Publications, Sharida Rizzuto, Rose Dalton, 577 Central Avenue, Box 4, Jefferson, LA 70121-1400, e-mail irishrose@cmpnetmail.com, rose.dalton@edmail.com; websites www.fortunecity.com/bally/harp/189/, www2.cybercities.com/z/zines/. 1983. Poetry, fiction, articles, art, photos, cartoons, interviews, satire, criticism, reviews, letters, long-poems, collages, news items, non-fiction. circ. 300-500. 2/yr. Pub'd 2 issues 1998; expects 2 issues 1999, 2 issues 2000. sub. price: $11.80; per copy: $5.80; sample: $5.80. Back issues: $5.80. Discounts: trade with other like publciations. 60pp; 8½×11; †of. Reporting time: 2-6 weeks. Simultaneous submissions accepted: yes. Publishes 35% of manuscripts submitted. Payment: free copies, fees paid to all contributors negotiable. Copyrighted, reverts to author. Pub's reviews: 60 in 1998. §All areas of Irish culture, history, literature. Ads: free. NWC, HWA, MWA, WWA, AAA, Small Press Genre Assn.

IRISH LITERARY SUPPLEMENT, Irish Studies, Robert G. Lowery, Editor-Publisher; Maureen Murphy, Features Editor, 2592 N Wading River Road, Wading River, NY 11792-1404, 516-929-0224. 1982. Interviews, criticism, reviews, parts-of-novels, non-fiction. "Published in association with Boston College. All work assigned." circ. 4.5M. 2/yr. Pub'd 2 issues 1998; expects 2 issues 1999, 2 issues 2000. sub. price: $6 ($7.50

libraries and foreign); per copy: $3; sample: $3. Back issues: $4. Discounts: only with subscription agencies. 32pp; 11×16; web. Reporting time: varies. Payment: copies and book for review. Copyrighted, reverts to author. Pub's reviews: 140 in 1998. §Irish material. Ads: $500/$300.

Irish Studies (see also IRISH LITERARY SUPPLEMENT), 2592 N Wading River Road, Wading River, NY 11792-1404, 516-929-0224.

Ironweed Press, Jin Soo Kang, Rob Giannetto, PO Box 754208, Parkside Station, Forest Hills, NY 11375, 718-268-2394. 1996. Fiction. avg. press run 2M. Expects 2 titles 1999, 2-4 titles 2000. 1 title listed in the *Small Press Record of Books in Print* (28th Edition, 1999-00). Discounts: 1-25%; 4-4-40%; 5-9-42%; 10-100-46%; 100+50%. 6×9, 5×8; web. Reporting time: 2 months on queries, 4 months on manuscripts. Simultaneous submissions accepted: yes. Payment: advances vary. Copyrights for author.

Irvington St. Press, Inc., Ce Rosenour, Tami Parr, 3439 NE Sandy Boulevard #143, Portland, OR 97232, E-mail; pdxia@aol.com. 1992. Poetry, fiction, plays. "We carry haiku and haiku-related works (senryu, tanka, renga) in addition to poetry. Recent interviews: Ann Charters, and Sam Hamill" Reporting time: 1-2 months. Simultaneous submissions accepted: no. Payment: contributor copy. Does not copyright for author.

Island Press, Barbara Dean, Executive Editor; Dan Sayre, Editor-In-Cheif; Chuck Savitt, Publisher, 1718 Connecticut Avenue NW #300, Washington, DC 20009, 202-232-7933; FAX 202-234-1328; e-mail info@islandpress.org; Website www.islandpress.org. 1978. Non-fiction. "Additional address: Box 7, Covelo, CA 95428. Books from original manuscripts on the environment, ecology, and natural resource management." avg. press run 3M. Pub'd 44 titles 1998; expects 48 titles 1999, 50 titles 2000. avg. price, cloth: $29.95; paper: $16.95. Discounts: trade 1-9 40%, 10-49 43%, 50-99 44%, 100-249 45%, 250+ 46%. 275pp; 6×9; of. Reporting time: 3 weeks, sometimes less. Simultaneous submissions accepted: yes. Publishes 15% of manuscripts submitted. Payment: standard contracts, graduated royalties. Copyrights for author. ABA.

Island Publishers, Thelma Palmer, Co-Publisher; Delphine Haley, Co-Publisher, Box 201, Anacortes, WA 98221-0201, 206-293-3285/293-5398. 1985. Poetry, non-fiction. avg. press run 5M. Pub'd 2 titles 1998; expects 1 title 1999. 5 titles listed in the *Small Press Record of Books in Print* (28th Edition, 1999-00). avg. price, paper: $11.95. Discounts: 1-4 20%, 5-49 40%, 50+ 41%. 200pp; of. Reporting time: 1 month. Payment: inquire. Copyrights for author.

●**Island Style Press**, Michael Dougherty, PO Box 296, Waimanalo, HI 96795, 808-259-8666. 2 titles listed in the *Small Press Record of Books in Print* (28th Edition, 1999-00).

Islewest Publishing, Mary Jo Graham, Anne Graham, 4242 Chavenelle Drive, Dubuque, IA 52002, 319-557-1500; Fax: 319-557-1376. 1994. Non-fiction. avg. press run 1M-10M. Pub'd 2 titles 1998; expects 8 titles 1999, 15 titles 2000. 13 titles listed in the *Small Press Record of Books in Print* (28th Edition, 1999-00). avg. price, paper: $12-35. Discounts: market norm. size varies. Reporting time: 4 months. Simultaneous submissions accepted: yes. Publishes 15% of manuscripts submitted. Copyrights for author. Publishers Marketing Association.

ISRAEL HORIZONS, Don Goldstein, Editor; Ralph Seliger, Arieh Lebowitz, Consulting Editors, 114 W. 26th Street #1001, New York, NY 10001-6812, 212-868-0377; FAX 212-868-0364. 1952. Poetry, articles, art, photos, cartoons, interviews, reviews, letters, news items, non-fiction. "Most of our articles are about 1.5M-3M words in length. The magazine is a progressive/Socialist Zionist periodical, dealing with: progressive forces in Israel, especially *Mapam Meretz* and the Kibbutz Artzi Federation—but not *exclusively* these groups—and general articles about Israeli life and culture. We also deal with problems facing Jewish communities around the world, from a progressive perspective. Finally, we are also interested in bringing our readers general info that wouldn't make space in more conventional Jewish periodicals." circ. 3M-5M. 4/yr. Pub'd 4 issues 1998; expects 4 issues 1999, 4 issues 2000. sub. price: $15; per copy: $4; sample: $4. Back issues: $4, depending on availability. 36pp; 8½×11; of. Reporting time: 6 weeks. Simultaneous submissions accepted: no. Publishes 25% of manuscripts submitted. Payment: $35 for articles, $25 for reviews. Copyrighted, does not revert to author. Pub's reviews: 7 in 1998. §Israel, culture and politics, Holocaust history, Jewish history, fiction prose and poetry with Jewish or Israeli themes. Ads: $300/$150. Americans for Progressive Israel.

ISSUES, Sue Perlman, PO Box 424885, San Francisco, CA 94142-4885, 415-864-4800 X136. 1978. Poetry, fiction, articles, art, photos, interviews, satire, reviews, non-fiction. "Messianic." circ. 40M. 6/yr. Pub'd 6 issues 1998; expects 6 issues 1999, 6 issues 2000. sub. price: free; per copy: free; sample: 50¢. Back issues: 75¢ each. 8-12pp; 8½×11; †of. Reporting time: 3-5 weeks. Payment: 10¢/word, minimum $25. Copyrighted, rights reverting to author is decided by contract. Pub's reviews: 5 in 1998. §Religion, Judaica, philosophy, Christianity. Ads: none.

ISSUES QUARTERLY, National Council for Research on Women, Nina Sonenberg, Coordinating Editor; Kate Daly, Associate Editor, 530 Broadway, 10th floor, New York, NY 10012, 212-274-0730, fax 212-274-0821. 1994. "Synthesizes research, policy, and action affecting women and girls in clear, accessible language for a broad influence. Formats encourage exchange across professions and areas of expertise. Each issue focuses on a specific topic of relevance to women and girls - a lead article presents an overview of the featured topic, and other regular sections expand on the issue with brief interviews of key researchers, policy specialists, and practitioners; lists of talking points; related public policy and issues around policy development and implementation; a discussion of funding, fundraising strategies, and concerns of grantmakers; and a focus on related work and labor issues. Each issue contains a 'bookshelf' of relevant books, reports, articles, and organizations as well as complete citations of all sources and projects referenced in the issue'' circ. 3M. 4/yr. Pub'd 2 issues 1998; expects 3 issues 1999, 4 issues 2000. sub. price: $20 indiv., $100 organization; per copy: $5; sample: $5. Back issues: none. Discounts: none. 24pp; 7½×11; of. Not copyrighted.

IT GOES ON THE SHELF, Purple Mouth Press, Ned Brooks, 4817 Dean Lane, Lilburn, GA 30047, nedbrooks@sprynet.com. 1984. Art, reviews. "Art only, I write the text myself." circ. 350. 2-3/yr. Pub'd 1 issue 1998; expects 2 issues 1999. Discounts: trade, etc. 13pp; 8½×11; photocopy. Reporting time: 1 week. Payment: copy. Not copyrighted. Pub's reviews: 12+ in 1998. §Science fiction, fantasy, typewriters, oddities. SFPA, Slanapa.

ITALIAN AMERICANA, Carol Bonomo Albright, Editor; Bruno A. Arcudi, Associate Editor; John Paul Russo, Review Editor & Senior Editor; Dana Gioia, Poetry Editor, University of Rhode Island, 80 Washington Street, Providence, RI 02903-1803. 1974. Poetry, articles, reviews. "*Italian Americana*, a multi-disciplinary journal concerning itself with all aspects of the Italian experience in America, publishes articles, short stories, poetry, memoirs and book reviews. It is published in cooperation with the American Italian Historical Association. Submissions of 20 double-spaced pages maximum, following the latest MLA Style Sheet, are invited in the areas of Italian American history, sociology, political science, literature, art, folk art, anthropology, music, psychology, etc., and short stories. Book reviews of 1,000 words are assigned and poetry of no more than three pages is accepted. Submissions by historians, social scientists, literary critics, etc., of Italian are encouraged when related to Italian American studies. Comparative analysis is welcome when related to Italian American issues. Please submit materials in triplicate with an SASE. All submissions will be reviewed by the editor and two readers. Name should appear on the first page only with article title on subsequent pages. For poetry, one copy of each poem is acceptable'' circ. 2.5M. 2/yr. Pub'd 2 issues 1998; expects 2 issues 1999, 2 issues 2000. 1 title listed in the *Small Press Record of Books in Print* (28th Edition, 1999-00). sub. price: $20 indiv., $22.50 instit., $15 student, $35 foreign; per copy: $8.50; sample: $7. Back issues: $7 for issues starting Fall 1990; no copies available for Spring/Summer '93. 150pp; 6×9; professional printer. Reporting time: 1-2 months. Simultaneous submissions accepted: no. Publishes 15% of manuscripts submitted. Payment: $500 for best historical article published each year and $1000 poetry prize annually, $500 for best fiction or memoir published each year. Copyrighted, reverts to author. Pub's reviews: 28 in 1998. §Significant books, films, plays, and art about Italian-American experience. Ads: $190/$100.

Italica Press, Inc., Ronald G. Musto, Eileen Gardiner, 595 Main Street, #605, New York, NY 10044, 212-935-4230; fax 212-838-7812; inquiries@italicapress.com. 1985. Poetry, fiction, art, letters, long-poems, plays, non-fiction. "We specialize in English translations of Italian and Latin works from the Middle Ages to the present. Primary interests are in history, literature, travel, and art. Published titles include Petrarch's *The Revolution of Cola di Rienzo*, the poet's letters to the revolutionary; *The Marvels of Rome*, a medieval guidebook to the city; and Theodorich's *Guide to the Holy Land*, written c. 1172; *The Fat Woodworker* by Antonio Manetti, a comic Renaissance tale about Brunelleschi and his circle; and new translations from Italian of twentieth-century novels, *Cosima* by Grazia Deledda and *Family Chronicle* by Vasco Pratolini, *The Wooden Throne* by Carlo Sgorlon, *Dolcissimo* by Guiseppe Bonaviri, and *Woman at War* by Dacia Maraina. Our audience is the general reader interested in works of lasting merit." avg. press run 1.5M. Pub'd 6 titles 1998; expects 6 titles 1999, 6 titles 2000. 29 titles listed in the *Small Press Record of Books in Print* (28th Edition, 1999-00). avg. price, paper: $15. Discounts: trade single copy 20%, 25% 2 copies, 30% 3-4, 35% 5-9, 40% 10-25, 43% 26-50, 50% 100+; classroom 25% on adoptions of 5 or more; others are negotiable. 200pp; 5½×8½; of. Reporting time: 6 weeks. Simultaneous submissions accepted: yes. Publishes 10% of manuscripts submitted. Payment: approx. 10% of net sales. Copyrights for author.

Ithaca Press, Charles E. Jarvis, PO Box 853, Lowell, MA 01853. 1974. Fiction, criticism. "*Visions of Kerouac; The Life of Jack Kerouac,* by Charles E. Jarvis. *Zeus Has Two Urns,* by Charles E. Jarvis. *The Tyrants* by Charles E. Jarvis, 1977, fiction, 5¼ x 8, 161 pp, SQPA, $2.95, The book is a socio-political novel of the United States in the era of the Great Depression." avg. press run 5M. Pub'd 1 title 1998. 8 titles listed in the *Small Press Record of Books in Print* (28th Edition, 1999-00). avg. price, cloth: $7.95; paper: $3.45. Discounts: 40%. 220pp; 5½×8½; of. Copyrights for author. NESPA.

Itidwitir Publishing (see also ICARUS WAS RIGHT), Scott Ogilvie, PO Box 13731, Salem, OR 97309-1731, 619-461-0497; icaruswas@pobox.com. 1994. Poetry, fiction, articles, art, photos, cartoons, interviews, satire, criticism, reviews, music, letters, collages, non-fiction. avg. press run 2.5M. Pub'd 4 titles 1998; expects 7 titles 1999, 10 titles 2000. avg. price, paper: $4. Discounts: classroom 50% over 5. 80pp; of.

Reporting time: 1-3 months. Simultaneous submissions accepted: yes. Publishes 5% of manuscripts submitted. Payment: varies. Copyrights for author.

●IWAN: INMATE WRITERS OF AMERICA NEWSLETTER, Michael D. Navton, Robert E. Plant, Theresa L. Johnson, Box 1673, Glen Burnie, MD 21060, e-mail inwram@netscape.com. 1998. Poetry, fiction, articles, art, cartoons, interviews, satire, criticism, reviews, news items, non-fiction. "Material should not exceed 3000 words. All submissions will be read beginning to end." circ. 120. 6/yr. Pub'd 2 issues 1998; expects 6 issues 1999, 6 issues 2000. sub. price: $14; per copy: $3; sample: $3. Back issues: none. 16pp; 8½×11. Reporting time: 2 weeks. Simultaneous submissions accepted: no. Publishes 50% of manuscripts submitted. Payment: $5-10. Copyrighted, reverts to author. Pub's reviews: 3 in 1998. §Writings from inmates or former inmates, how-to, and good writings in general. Ads: $22/$15/ 1/4 page $7.

J

J & J Consultants, Inc. (see also NEW ALTERNATIVES), Walter Jones, Jr., 603 Olde Farm Road, Media, PA 19063, 610-565-9692; Fax 610-565-9694; wjones13@juno.com; www.members.tripod.com/walterjones/. 1997. Poetry, articles, reviews, non-fiction. "Writers needed for magazine New Alternatives." avg. press run 250. Pub'd 1 title 1998; expects 1 title 1999. 1 title listed in the Small Press Record of Books in Print (28th Edition, 1999-00). avg. price, paper: $8.98. Discounts: 20% trade, 40% wholesale, 50% regional wholesale, 50% jobbers. 112pp; 5½×8½. Reporting time: 2 months. Simultaneous submissions accepted: yes. Publishes 50% of manuscripts submitted. Payment: royalty 5% list price/flat fee. Copyrights for author. PMA.

J & L Publications, Jenny Luoma, PO Box 360, Trinity Center, CA 96091, 530-778-3456 phone/Fax. 1989. Non-fiction. "We are not accepting submissions; we have a full schedule for next 2½ years. We do not work a format; we work subjects. Our books center on spiritual awakening. Our authors have all studied with Neville Goddard" avg. press run 1M-2M. Pub'd 1 title 1998; expects 2 titles 1999, 3 titles 2000. 4 titles listed in the Small Press Record of Books in Print (28th Edition, 1999-00). avg. price, cloth: $15. Discounts: bookstores 40% on 5 or more books; maximum 55% large order distributors. Pages vary; whatever it takes. Payment: by arrangement. Copyrights for author. Rocky Mtn. Book Publishing Association.

THE J MAN TIMES, J. Rassoul, 2246 Saint Francis Drive #A-211, Ann Arbor, MI 48104-4828, E-mail TheJMan99@aol.com. 1994. Poetry, fiction, articles, art, photos, cartoons, interviews, satire, criticism, reviews, letters, non-fiction. "Recent contributors: Robert Phelps, Dan Buck, David Van Hyle, Anthony Alba, Holly Day." circ. 100. 3/yr. Pub'd 3 issues 1998; expects 3 issues 1999, 3 issues 2000. sub. price: $3; per copy: $1; sample: $1. Back issues: $1. Discounts: none. 20pp; 5½×8½; †xerox. Reporting time: 1 week. Simultaneous submissions accepted: yes. Publishes 25% of manuscripts submitted. Payment: free copy. Copyrighted, reverts to author. Pub's reviews: 3 in 1998. §Religion, politics, fiction, sex, UFOs, true crime, movies, race. Ads: $100/$50.

J P Publications, Chris Paffrath, James Paffrath, 1895 Berry Court, Dixon, CA 95620-2506, 916-678-9727. 1980. Art, photos, interviews, non-fiction. "We do not actively seek material." avg. press run 8M. Pub'd 1 title 1998; expects 6 titles 1999, 10 titles 2000. 3 titles listed in the Small Press Record of Books in Print (28th Edition, 1999-00). avg. price, cloth: $20; paper: $12.50. Discounts: 2-5 20%; 6-24 40%; 25-49 42%; 50-100 45%; 101-200 48%; 201+ 50%. 200pp; 8×11; of. Payment: on an individual basis. Copyrights for author.

●J. Mark Press (see also POETS' VOICE), Barbara Fischer, Box 500901, Malabar, FL 32950, website www.worldtv3.com/jmark.htm. 1963. Poetry. "3-16 lines, maximum 95 words. Stirring messages, picturesque phrases. No vulgarity. Prefer poets see prize-winning poems on our website. If you have no computer, ask your librarian to get it on the screen. Poems must be accompanied by a SASE or they won't be read and will be disposed of." avg. press run 500. Pub'd 3 titles 1998; expects 6 titles 1999, 6 titles 2000. avg. price, cloth: $44.95 retail, $29.95 for poets. Discounts: 40%. 82pp; 7×8½; †of. Reporting time: 1 week. Simultaneous submissions accepted: yes. Publishes 40% of manuscripts submitted. Payment: prizes. Copyrights for author.

JACARANDA, Cornel Bonca, Editor, English Department, California State Univ—Fullerton, Fullerton, CA 92634, 714-773-3163. 1984. Poetry, fiction, articles, photos, interviews, reviews, parts-of-novels, long-poems. "Recent contributors include Jorge Luis Borges, Carolyn Forche, Alfred Corn, Phyllis Janowitz, Billy Collins, Daniel Menaker, Jascha Kessler, Barry Spacks. Contributors should look at the magazines to get an idea of our (eclectic) interests." circ. 1.5M. 2/yr. Pub'd 2 issues 1998; expects 2 issues 1999, 2 issues 2000. sub. price: $10; per copy: $5; sample: $6. Back issues: $3 each. Discounts: 20% for extra contributor copies. 160pp; 5½×8; of. Reporting time: 3 months. Simultaneous submissions accepted: yes. Publishes 1-2% of manuscripts submitted. Payment: 3 copies plus 20% discount on additional copies. Copyrighted, reverts to author. Pub's reviews: 8 in 1998. §Contemporary fiction and poetry from small presses as well as large ones. Ads: $75/$37.50/$20 1/4 page. CLMP, Index of American Periodical Verse.

JACK MACKEREL MAGAZINE, Rowhouse Press, Greg Bachar, PO Box 23134, Seattle, WA 98102-0434. 1994. Poetry, fiction, articles, art, photos, interviews, criticism, reviews, music, letters, parts-of-novels, long-poems, collages, news items. "Recent contributors: Mike McCoy, Ann Miller, William D. Waltz, John Rose, David Berman, Carl Faucher, Katie J. Kurtz, and Heather Hayes." circ. 500-1M. 4/yr. Pub'd 4 issues 1998; expects 4 issues 1999, 4 issues 2000. sub. price: $12; per copy: $5; sample: $5. Back issues: $5. 40-60pp; 8½×11; †varies. Reporting time: 2-4 weeks. Payment: copies. Copyrighted, reverts to author. Pub's reviews: 8 in 1998. §Fiction, poetry, art, artists, photography, physics. Ads: $25/$15/$5 1/4 page.

JACK THE RIPPER GAZETTE, Baker Street Publications, Sharida Rizzuto, Harold Tollison, Ann Hoyt, Rose Dalton, 577 Central Avenue, Box 4, Jefferson, LA 70121-1400, sherlockian@england.com, sherlockian@mailcity.com, www2.cybercities.com/z/zines/. 1983. Poetry, fiction, articles, art, photos, cartoons, interviews, satire, criticism, reviews, letters, long-poems, news items, non-fiction. circ. 500. 2/yr. Pub'd 2 issues 1998; expects 2 issues 1999, 2 issues 2000. sub. price: $10; per copy: $5; sample: $5. Discounts: trade with like publishers. 40-45pp; 8½×11; †of. Reporting time: 2-6 weeks. Simultaneous submissions accepted: yes. Publishes 30-40% of manuscripts submitted. Payment: fee (negotiable) for non-fiction and artwork, plus free copy; free copy only for poetry and fiction. Copyrighted, reverts to author. Pub's reviews: 24 in 1998. §Jack the Ripper, crime in Victorian times, other Victorian criminals such as Lizzie Borden, Jack the Ripper type murders in contemporary times, zines, books, films, internet websites. Ads: free.

Jackson Harbor Press, William H. Olson, RR 1, Box 107AA, Washington Island, WI 54246. 1993. Poetry, fiction, non-fiction. "We intend to do primarily regional works (Door County, Wisconsin), but are unable to accept unsolicited manuscripts at this time" avg. press run 1M. Pub'd 3 titles 1998; expects 2 titles 1999, 2 titles 2000. 14 titles listed in the *Small Press Record of Books in Print* (28th Edition, 1999-00). avg. price, paper: $5. Discounts: 2-4 20%, 5-9 30%, 10+ 40%. 64pp; 5½×8½; of. Reporting time: 2 weeks. Payment: each arrangement will be individually negotiated. Copyrights for author.

Jade Moon Publications (see also DROP FORGE), Sean Winchester, Keil Winchester, PO Box 4600, Bozeman, MT 59772-4600. 1991. Poetry, fiction, photos, music, long-poems, plays. "Not currently reading unsolicited mss." avg. press run 500-1M. Expects 1 title 1999, 1 title 2000. avg. price, paper: $3-$10. Discounts: inquire. 30-100pp; size varies; of. Reporting time: 1-6 weeks. Payment: handled on individual basis. Copyrights for author.

Jaffe Publishing Management Service (see also WORLD BOOK INDUSTRY), Nicy Punnoose, Kunnuparambil Buildings, Kurichy, Kottayam 686549, India, phone/fax 91-481-430470. 1985. "Jaffe specializes in publishing reports, manuals, directories, group catalogs, etc. for the book and magazine publishing industry." avg. press run 1.1M. Pub'd 2 titles 1998; expects 2 titles 1999, 2 titles 2000. avg. price, cloth: $10; paper: $50. Discounts: 25%. 96pp; 8½×11; †lp. Reporting time: 3 months. Payment: 10% on the published price on copies sold, payment annually. Copyrights for author.

Jaguar Books, Joseph Posa, 30043 US Hwy 19 North, Ste. 136, Clearwater, FL 34621, 800-299-0790; Fax 727-724-1677; jaguar@flanet.com. 1996. Fiction. "Thoughtful fiction, new age, ancient history, believable science fiction." avg. press run 10M. Expects 1 title 1999, 3 titles 2000. 1 title listed in the *Small Press Record of Books in Print* (28th Edition, 1999-00). avg. price, cloth: $21.95; paper: $12.95. Discounts: trade 1-24 copies 40%, 25-49 45%, 50+ 50%. 300pp; 6×9. Reporting time: 2 months. Simultaneous submissions accepted: yes. PMA, NAPRA, FPA.

Jahbone Press, Martin Nakell, 1201 Larrabee Street #207, Los Angeles, CA 90069-2065. 1992. "Have published such poets as Leland Hickman, Dennis Phllips, Pasquale Verdicchio. Am interested in work which challenges the form of poetry." avg. press run 1M. Expects 3 titles 1999, 4 titles 2000. 4 titles listed in the *Small Press Record of Books in Print* (28th Edition, 1999-00). avg. price, paper: $7.95. Discounts: 40%; distribution through Small Press Distributors, 1814 San Pablo, Berkeley, CA 94702. 60-80pp; 6×8. Reporting time: 2 months. Simultaneous submissions accepted: yes. Publishes 2% of manuscripts submitted. Payment: currently none; 15 copies with 40% discount on subsequent purchases. Copyrights for author.

Jalmar Press, Bradley L. Winch, President, 24426 S. Main Street, Suite 702, Carson, CA 90745. 1973. Poetry, fiction, art, photos, cartoons, interviews, satire, non-fiction. "Affiliated with B.L. Winch & Associates. Primarily interested in works in the humanistic area of psychology and books of general how-to interest. Have four series: 1) *Transactional Analysis for Everybody*, Warm Fuzzy Series, 2) *Conflict Resolution Series*, 3) *Right-Brain/Whole-Brain Learning Series*, 4) *Positive Self-Esteem Series*. Titles in *TA for Everybody Series*: Freed, Alvyn M. *TA for Tots (and Other Prinzes)*; Freed, Alvyn & Margaret *TA for Kids (and Grown-ups, too)*, 3rd edition newly revised and illustrated. Freed, Alvyn M. *TA for Teens (and Other Important People)*; Freed, Alvyn M. *TA for Tots Coloring Book*. TA for Tots Vol. II - Alvyn M. Freed. Steiner, Claude *Original Warm Fuzzy Tale*; *Songs of the Warm Fuzzy* cassette (all about your feelings)." avg. press run 3M. Pub'd 4 titles

278

1998; expects 4 titles 1999, 4 titles 2000. 38 titles listed in the *Small Press Record of Books in Print* (28th Edition, 1999-00). avg. price, cloth: $16.95; paper: $12.95. Discounts: trade 25-45%; agent/jobber 25-50%. 200pp; 8½×11, 6×9; of. Reporting time: 4 weeks. Payment: 7.5%-12.5% of net receipts. Copyrights for author. ABA, CBA, PMA (PASCAL), EDSA.

JAM RAG, Tom Ness, Box 20076, Ferndale, MI 48220, 248-542-8090. 1985. Articles, photos, cartoons, interviews, satire, criticism, reviews, music, letters, news items. circ. 15M. 16/yr. Pub'd 22 issues 1998; expects 18 issues 1999, 16 issues 2000. sub. price: $23; sample: $1. Back issues: $1. Discounts: $5 per 100. 48pp; 7½×10½; web newsprint minitab. Simultaneous submissions accepted: yes. Publishes 20% of manuscripts submitted. Payment: varies. Not copyrighted. Pub's reviews: 10-15 in 1998. §Political, music, arts, philosophy. Ads: $339/$177/up to 30% disc./class $2/10 words.

Jamenair Ltd., Peter K. Studner, PO Box 241957, Los Angeles, CA 90024-9757, 310-470-6688. 1986. Non-fiction. "Books and software related to job search and career changing." avg. press run 10M. 3 titles listed in the *Small Press Record of Books in Print* (28th Edition, 1999-00). avg. price, paper: $22.95. Discounts: depends on quantity. 352pp; 8⅜×10⅞; of. Reporting time: 30 days. Payment: open, depends on material. Copyrights for author. PMA, IWOSC, Soc. des Gens de Lettres de France, Society of Authors (UK).

JAMES DICKEY NEWSLETTER, Joyce M. Pair, Editor, 1753 Dyson Drive, Atlanta, GA 30307, 404-373-2989 phone/FAX. 1984. Poetry, articles, interviews, reviews, long-poems. "Lengthy mss. considered but may be published in sequential issues. All material should concern James Dickey/his work and includes comparative studies. We publish a few poems of *very* high caliber. Recent: Jes Simmons, Linda Roth, Paula Goff" circ. 200. 2/yr. Pub'd 2 issues 1998; expects 2 issues 1999, 2 issues 2000. sub. price: $12 USA individuals, $14 institutions; per copy: $5 ($12 to individuals includes membership in James Dickey Society); sample: $5. Back issues: $5 (Discount if all issues). Discounts: 25% to jobbers. 30pp; 8½×11; †of. Reporting time: 2 weeks. Simultaneous submissions accepted: no. Publishes a variable % of manuscripts submitted. Payment: 3 copies. Copyrighted, reverts to author. Pub's reviews: 3 in 1998. §Modern American, work of or about James Dickey only. Ads: full page flyer inserted $100—one time.

JAMES JOYCE BROADSHEET, Pieter Bekker, Editor; Richard Brown, Editor-in-Chief; Alistair Stead, Editor; Sarah Graham, Editorial Assistant, School of English, University of Leeds, West Yorkshire LS2 9JT, England, 0113-233-4739. 1980. Poetry, articles, art, photos, cartoons, criticism, reviews, letters, news items. circ. 800. 3/yr. Expects 3 issues 1999. sub. price: £7.50 Europe (£6 for students)/$18 ($15 for students elsewhere); per copy: £2 plus 50p postage Europe ($6 including postage elsewhere); sample: £2/$4. Back issues: at current annual subscription rate. Discounts: 33⅓% to bookshops only. 4-6pp; 11.7×16.5; of. Reporting time: 6 months-1 year. Payment: none. Copyrighted. Pub's reviews: 15 in 1998. §Modern literature, James Joyce, contemporary criticism. Ads: Please inquire.

JAMES JOYCE QUARTERLY, University of Tulsa, Robert Spoo, Editor, University of Tulsa, 600 S. College, Tulsa, OK 74104. 1963. Articles, criticism, reviews. "Academic criticism of Joyce's works; book reviews, notes, bibliographies; material relating to Joyce and Irish Renaissance and Joyce's relationship to other writers of his time. Articles should not normally exceed 20 pp. Notes should not excceed 6 pp. Please consult MLA *Handbook* and 'Special Note to Contributors' which appears on inside back cover of each issue of the *JJQ* regarding style & preparation of manuscript." circ. 1.9M. 4/yr. Pub'd 4 issues 1998; expects 4 issues 1999, 4 issues 2000. sub. price: $22 U.S., $24 foreign; per copy: $10 U.S. and foreign; sample: $5. Back issues: check price with reprint house- Swets & Zeitlinger, PO Box 517, Berwyn, Pa 19312. 150pp; 6×9; of. Reporting time: 6-12 weeks. Payment: contributors' copies & offprints. Copyrighted, does not revert to author. Pub's reviews: 11 in 1998. §Joyce studies. Ads: $200 ($260 includes copy of *JJQ* subscription list on set of self-adhesive address labels)/$100. CELJ.

JAMES WHITE REVIEW; A Gay Men's Literary Quarterly, Philip Willkie, Fiction Editor; Clif Mayhood, Poetry Editor; Terry Carlson, Art Editor, PO Box 73910, Washington, DC 20056-3910, 612-339-8317. 1983. Poetry, fiction, art, photos, interviews, satire, long-poems, non-fiction. "Submissions deadlines Aug. 1, Nov. 1, Feb. 1, May 1." circ. 4.5M. 4/yr. Pub'd 4 issues 1998; expects 4 issues 1999, 4 issues 2000. sub. price: $14 (institutions $14, foreign $20); per copy: $4; sample: $4. Back issues: 10 or more copies $1 a copy. Discounts: retailers get 40%t. 24pp; 13×18; of, web. Reporting time: 1-2 months. Simultaneous submissions accepted: no. Payment: $50 short story, $25 poem and artwork. Copyrighted, reverts to author. Pub's reviews: 40 in 1998. §Poetry, fiction, creative nonfiction, biography. Ads: $400/$200/$120 1/4 page/$75 1/5 page. CLMP.

JAPANOPHILE, Japanophile Press, Earl R. Snodgrass, Vada L. Davis, 6602 14th Avenue W, Bradenton, FL 34209-4527. 1974. Poetry, fiction, articles, art, photos, cartoons, interviews, satire, criticism, reviews, music, letters, news items, non-fiction. "Articles 700-1,200 words. Haiku to 40-line poems. What's going on in Japan now, America-Japan relations, short stories that include Western and Japanese, information on anything not in Japan but related to Japanese culture, criticism, nostalgia." circ. 1M. 4/yr. Pub'd 3 issues 1998; expects 4 issues 1999, 4 issues 2000. sub. price: $14; per copy: $4; sample: $4. Back issues: $4. Discounts: 15%, more by arrangement. 56pp; 5¾×8½; of. Reporting time: 3 months. Simultaneous submissions accepted if stated so. Payment: yes. Copyrighted, reverts to author. Pub's reviews: 12 in 1998. §Japan, Japanese-U.S. relations, Japanese culture. Ads: $95/$50/$3 per word classifieds. Michigan Independent Publishers Assn. (MIPA).

Japanophile Press (see also **JAPANOPHILE**), Earl R. Snodgrass, Vada L. Davis, 6602 14th Avenue W, Bradenton, FL 34209-4527, 517-669-2109; E-mail japanlove@aol.com. 1974. Poetry, fiction, articles, art, photos, cartoons, interviews, satire, criticism, reviews, letters, non-fiction. "We have a hardbound book of short stories: *East-West Encounters, An Anthology of Short Stories*, $16.95 (200pp)." Pub'd 1 title 1998; expects 4 titles 1999, 4-5 titles 2000. 1 title listed in the *Small Press Record of Books in Print* (28th Edition, 1999-00). avg. price, cloth: $16.95. Discounts: 15%, will consider less for jobbers. 200pp; of. Reporting time: 6 months. Payment: cash on publication; usually buy 1st rights, accept re-runs. Copyrights for author. Michigan Independent Publishers Assn.

JARRETT'S JOURNAL, A. Heath Jarrett, PO Box 184, Bath Beach Station, Brooklyn, NY 11214, E-mail anndell@rdz.stjohns.edu. 1995. Articles, reviews. "Disability, chronic illness, health, wellness, medicine, nutrition, and alternative therapies." 12/yr. Pub'd 12 issues 1998; expects 12 issues 1999, 12 issues 2000. sub. price: free - electronic (Internet) only. 14-20pp; 8½×11. Reporting time: 2 months. Simultaneous submissions accepted: no. Payment: none, just byline. Copyrighted, reverts to author. Pub's reviews: 120+ in 1998. §Disabled, health, politics. BWC.

Javelina Books, Caitlin L. Gannon, PO Box 42131, Tucson, AZ 85733. 1995. Poetry, fiction, parts-of-novels, long-poems, non-fiction. "Javelina Press publishes writing by women including fiction and poetry of the Southwest, and nonfiction including women's studies, popular culture and spirituality." avg. press run 1M. Expects 1 title 1999, 2 titles 2000. 2 titles listed in the *Small Press Record of Books in Print* (28th Edition, 1999-00). avg. price, cloth: $25; paper: $14. Discounts: upon request. 200pp; 5½×8½; lp. Reporting time: up to 3 months after confirmation of receipt. Simultaneous submissions accepted: no. Publishes 5% of manuscripts submitted. Payment: varies. Copyrights depend on the nature of publication. RMBPA, TBPA, NMBA.

JB Press (see also **AMERICAN PHYSICIANS ART ASSOCIATION NEWSLETTER**), James S. Benedict, 1130 North Cabrillo, San Pedro, CA 90731, 310-832-7024. 1992. Poetry. "Publishers of news magazines, bulletins, small books of poetry, short stories, anthologies." avg. press run 500. Pub'd 1 title 1998; expects 1 title 1999, 2 titles 2000. 7 titles listed in the *Small Press Record of Books in Print* (28th Edition, 1999-00). avg. price, cloth: $15; paper: $10; other: $5 chapbooks. Discounts: 10-15%. 125pp; 5½×8½. Reporting time: 2-3 months. Payment: by negotiation. Does not copyright for author.

‡**J'ECRIS**, Jean Guenot, 85, rue des Tennerolles, Saint-Cloud 92210, France, (1) 47-71-79-63. 1987. "Specialized on technical data concerning creative writing for French writers." circ. 2M. 4/yr. Pub'd 4 issues 1998; expects 4 issues 1999, 4 issues 2000. sub. price: $47; per copy: $12; sample: free. Back issues: $10. 32pp; 19×28cm; †of. Payment: yes. Copyrighted, reverts to author. Pub's reviews: 15 in 1998. §Only books dealing with creative writing techniques. No ads.

JEJUNE: america Eats its Young, Gwendolyn Albert, PO Box 85, Prague 1, 110 01, Czech Republic, 42-2-96141082; Fax 42-2-24256243. 1994. Poetry, fiction, art, photos, interviews, reviews, letters, parts-of-novels. "*Jejune* publishes poetry, prose, interviews and artwork emphasizing the individual voice. Past issues have featured the authors Eileen Myles, Jonathan Lethem, Jules Mann, Lucia Berlin, Alva Svoboda...to name a few, as well as translations of emerging Czech writers." circ. 700. 2/yr. Pub'd 2 issues 1998; expects 2 issues 1999, 2 issues 2000. sub. price: $10; per copy: $5; sample: $5. Back issues: $4. Discounts: Distributed through Small Press Distribution and Bernard DeBoer. 70pp; 6½×10½; †mi, of. Reporting time: 1 month. Simultaneous submissions accepted: yes. Publishes 25% of manuscripts submitted. Payment: 2 copies. Not copyrighted. Pub's reviews: 2 in 1998. §Poetry, politics, philosophy. Ads: trade.

Jenkins Group, Inc. (see also **PUBLISHING ENTREPRENEUR; INDEPENDENT PUBLISHER**), 121 East Front Street, Suite 401, Traverse City, MI 49684, voice 616-933-0445; fax 616-933-0448; e-mail jenkins.group@smallpress.com. 1993.

Jessee Poet Publications (see also **POETS AT WORK**), Jessee Poet, Box 113, VAMC, 325 New Castle Road, Butler, PA 16001. 1985. Poetry, long-poems. "Chapbook publisher, send SASE for price. National contests (poetry) sponsor, send SASE for details." avg. press run 350. Pub'd 75 titles 1998. 2 titles listed in the *Small Press Record of Books in Print* (28th Edition, 1999-00). avg. price, paper: send SASE; other: SASE for details. Pages vary; 5½×8½, 7×8½; †copy machine. Reporting time: 2 weeks. Simultaneous submissions accepted: yes. Publishes 100% of manuscripts submitted. Payment: none. Does not copyright for author.

Jesus Pinata Press (see also **BURNING CAR**), Jerry Rummonds, PO Box 26692, San Francisco, CA 94126, E-mail elfool@aol.com. 1995. Poetry, fiction, articles, art, photos, cartoons, interviews, satire, criticism, reviews, parts-of-novels, long-poems, collages, plays, non-fiction. avg. press run 1M. Pub'd 1 title 1998; expects 2 titles 1999, 2 titles 2000. 1 title listed in the *Small Press Record of Books in Print* (28th Edition,

1999-00). avg. price, paper: $7.50. 100pp; 6×9; of. Reporting time: 60 days. Simultaneous submissions accepted: yes. Publishes 10-15% of manuscripts submitted. Payment: none yet. Does not copyright for author. NASE.

JEWISH CURRENTS, Morris U. Schappes, 22 E. 17th Street, Suite 601, New York, NY 10003, 212-924-5740. 1946. Poetry, fiction, articles, art, photos, interviews, satire, criticism, reviews, letters, news items, non-fiction. "Articles of Jewish interest, progressive politics, Black-Jewish relations, 2M-3M words; reviews of books, records, plays, films, events, 1.8M-2M words; lively style, hard facts, secular p.o.v., pro-Israel/non-Zionist." circ. 2.5M. 11/yr. Pub'd 11 issues 1998; expects 11 issues 1999, 11 issues 2000. 3 titles listed in the *Small Press Record of Books in Print* (28th Edition, 1999-00). sub. price: $30; per copy: $3; sample: $3. Back issues: $2. Discounts: 40% retail/25% subscription agency. 48pp—except Dec., 80pp (average); 5½×8½; of. Reporting time: 2 months. Simultaneous submissions accepted: no. Publishes 30% of manuscripts submitted. Payment: 6 copies + subscription. Copyrighted. Pub's reviews: 30 in 1998. §Jewish affairs, political & cultural, feminism, civil rights, labor history, Holocaust resistance, Black-Jewish relations, Yiddish culture. Ads: $125/$75/$50 - for 2 col. inch (greetings and memorials); $300/$175/$40 1 col. inch (commercial ads).

JEWISH LIFE, Full Moon Publications, Sharida Rizzuto, Elaine Wolfe, 577 Central Avenue, Box 4, Jefferson, LA 70121-1400, E-mail publisher@jewishmail.com, jewishlife@newyorkoffice.com; www.world.up.co.il/jewishlife, www2.cybercities.com/z/zines/. 1983. Poetry, fiction, articles, art, photos, cartoons, interviews, satire, criticism, reviews, letters, long-poems, collages, news items, non-fiction. "All subject matter must pertain to Jews." circ. 300-500. 2/yr. Pub'd 2 issues 1998; expects 2 issues 1999, 2 issues 2000. sub. price: $15.80; per copy: $7.90; sample: $7.90. Back issues: $7.90. Discounts: trade with other like publications. 100pp; 8½×11; †of. Reporting time: 2-6 weeks. Simultaneous submissions accepted: yes. Publishes 35% of manuscripts submitted. Payment: free copies, fees paid to all contributors negotiable. Copyrighted, reverts to author. Pub's reviews: 60 in 1998. §All areas of Jewish life plus poetry and fiction. Ads: free. NWC, HWA, MWA, Western Writers of America (WWA), Arizona Author Assn. (AAA), Small Press Genre Assn.

Jewish Publication Society, Dr. Ellen Frankel, 1930 Chestnut Street, Philadelphia, PA 19103, 215-564-5925; Fax 215-564-6640. 1888. Poetry, art, photos, cartoons, letters, plays, non-fiction. avg. press run 3M. Pub'd 18 titles 1998; expects 20 titles 1999, 20 titles 2000. avg. price, cloth: $29.95; paper: $14.95. Simultaneous submissions accepted: yes. Copyrights for author.

Jewish Radical Education Project (see also J-REP NEWS AND VIEWS), PO BOX 7377, New York, NY 10150-7377. 1993. Articles, non-fiction. avg. press run 1M. Expects 2 titles 1999. 3 titles listed in the *Small Press Record of Books in Print* (28th Edition, 1999-00). avg. price, paper: $12. 300pp; 6×9; of.

JEWISH VEGETARIAN NEWSLETTER, Eva Mossman, Editor; Ziona Swigart, Associate Editor; Israel Mossman, Associate Editor, Jewish Vegetarians, 6938 Reliance Road, Federalsburg, MD 21632, 410-754-5550, e-mail imossman@skipjack.bluecrab.org; www.orbyss.com. 1983. Poetry, fiction, articles, photos, cartoons, interviews, reviews, letters, news items, non-fiction. circ. 800. 4/yr. Pub'd 4 issues 1998; expects 4 issues 1999, 4 issues 2000. sub. price: $12; per copy: $3; sample: SASE two first-class stamps or 55¢ postage. Back issues: inquire. Discounts: inquire. 16pp; 8½×11; of. Reporting time: 1 month. Simultaneous submissions accepted: yes. Publishes 75% of manuscripts submitted. Payment: copies. Not copyrighted. Pub's reviews: 12 in 1998. §Vegetarianism, animal rights, Judaism, nutrition, environment, world hunger. Ads: none.

JLA Publications, A Division Of Jeffrey Lant Associates, Inc., Dr. Jeffrey Lant, President, 50 Follen Street #507, Suite 507, Cambridge, MA 02138, 617-547-6372; drjlant@worldprofit.com; www.trafficcenter.com. 1979. Non-fiction. "We are interested in publishing books of particular interest to small businesses, entrepreneurs and independent professionals. To get an idea of what we publish, simply write us at the above address and request a current catalog. Up until now our titles have been all more than 100,000 words in length and are widely regarded as the most detailed books on their subjects. Recent books include Lant's *Multi Level Money*, Jeffrey Lant's Revised Third Edition of *Money Talks: The Complete Guide to Creating a Profitable Workshop or Seminar in any Field* and Lant's book *Cash Copy: How to Offer Your Products and Services So Your Prospects Buy Them...Now!* We are now open, however, to shorter (though still very specific and useful) books in the 50,000-75,000 word length and titles in human development as well as business development. We are different because we pay royalties *monthly* and get our authors very involved in the publicity process. We do not pay advances for material but do promote strenuously through our quarterly catalog and Dr. Lant's Sure-Fire Business Success Column." avg. press run 4M-5M. Pub'd 7 titles 1998; expects 2 titles 1999, 5 titles 2000. 12 titles listed in the *Small Press Record of Books in Print* (28th Edition, 1999-00). avg. price, paper: $35. Discounts: 1-9 copies 20%, 10-99 40% (you pay shipping); thence negotiable up to 60% discount on major orders. 300+pp; 9×12; †lp. Reporting time: 30-60 days. Payment: 10%, monthly. Copyrights for author.

J-Mart Press, Art Heine, PO Box 8884, Virginia Beach, VA 23450, 757-498-4060 (phone/fax), e-mail jmartpress@aol.com. 1990. avg. press run 5M. 3 titles listed in the *Small Press Record of Books in Print* (28th Edition, 1999-00). avg. price, cloth: $22.95; paper: $12.95. Discounts: standard trade. Pages vary; size varies. Simultaneous submissions accepted: no. Payment: trade. We will copyright for author if desired. PMA, SPAN.

Job Search Publishers, Joyce Edelbrock, 1311 Lindbergh Plaza Center, St. Louis, MO 63132, 314-993-6508. 1992. "Only accepts books, audios, videos, computer programs and supplies that assist people with job search/employment/career needs." avg. press run 5M-500M. Pub'd 1 title 1998; expects 10 titles 1999, 15 titles 2000. 1 title listed in the *Small Press Record of Books in Print* (28th Edition, 1999-00). avg. price, paper: $9.95. Discounts: standard. 150pp. Reporting time: 1 month. Payment: varies. Copyrighting for author varies. ALA, ABA, PMA.

THE JOE BOB REPORT, Joe Bob Briggs, Managing Editor; Tanja Lindstrom, Assistant Editor, PO Box 2002, Dallas, TX 75221, FAX 214-368-2310. 1985. Poetry, fiction, art, photos, cartoons, satire, criticism, reviews, music, letters, news items, non-fiction. "Anything that makes us laugh will get our attention. We are most open to poems or short essays (500 words or less). They should be humorous or deal with popular culture, especially the fields of movies, music, and stand-up comedy." circ. 2.5M. 26/yr. sub. price: $35; per copy: $3; sample: 1 free. Back issues: $4. 8pp; 8½×11; IBM Pagemaker, L300. Reporting time: 1 month. Payment: $25 maximum upon publication. Copyrighted, does not revert to author. Pub's reviews: 20 in 1998. §Popular culture—movies, music, stand-up comedy. Ads: $75 per inch.

Joelle Publishing, Norman Russell, PO Box 91229, Santa Barbara, CA 93190, 805-962-9887. 1987. Non-fiction. avg. press run 5M. Expects 2 titles 1999, 3 titles 2000. 3 titles listed in the *Small Press Record of Books in Print* (28th Edition, 1999-00). avg. price, paper: $10.95. Discounts: trade 40%, jobber 55%, library 20%. 140pp; 6×9; of. Reporting time: 3 weeks. Simultaneous submissions accepted: yes. Payment: to be arranged. Copyrights for author. PMA.

Jolly Roger Press, Kristan Lawson, PO Box 295, Berkeley, CA 94701, 510-548-7123. 1992. Non-fiction. "We are a tiny press. Our latest release was *The Unabomber Manifesto,* the political treatise authored anonymously by the notorious terrorist and philosopher. *The Unabomber Manifesto* was on regional bestseller lists, and received worldwide publicity. We're not really looking for manuscripts, but if we come across a mesmerizing but short manuscript on a notably peculiar non-fiction topic, we might consider it." avg. press run 5M. 2 titles listed in the *Small Press Record of Books in Print* (28th Edition, 1999-00). avg. price, paper: $9.95. Discounts: 50% to distributors and wholesalers 40% to retail outlets. 96pp; 5½×8½; of. Reporting time: 1 month. Payment: standard, negotiated individually with each author. Copyrights for author.

JOTS (Journal of the Senses), Ed Lange, Arthur Kunkin, 814 Robinson Road, Topanga, CA 90290, 310-455-1000; FAX 310-455-2007. 1961. Interviews, reviews, letters, news items. circ. 15M. 4/yr. Pub'd 4 issues 1998; expects 4 issues 1999, 4 issues 2000. sub. price: $6; per copy: $2; sample: $2. 40pp; 8½×11; of. Reporting time: 3 weeks. Payment: limited. Copyrighted. Pub's reviews: 6 in 1998. §Massage, self-appreciation, holistic health, nudism and clothing optionality. Ads: $300/$160.

THE JOURNAL, Kathy Fagan, Michelle Herman, OSU Dept. of English, 164 W. 17th Avenue, 421 Denney Hall, Columbus, OH 43210-1370, 614-292-4076; fax 614-292-7816; e-mail thejournal05@pop.service.ohio-state.edu. 1973. Poetry, fiction, articles, interviews, criticism, reviews, parts-of-novels, long-poems. "We are looking for quality poetry, fiction and reviews." circ. 1.6M. 2/yr. Pub'd 2 issues 1998; expects 2 issues 1999, 2 issues 2000. sub. price: $12; per copy: $7; sample: $7. 140pp; 6×9; lp. Reporting time: 3 months. Simultaneous submissions are accepted if informed. Publishes 5% of manuscripts submitted. Payment: $25. Copyrighted, reverts to author. Pub's reviews: 4 in 1998. §Poetry, fiction. Ads: $100/$50. CLMP, AWP, CELJ.

JOURNAL OF AESTHETICS AND ART CRITICISM, Philip Alperson, Editor, Dept of Philosophy, Anderson Hall 7th Floor, Temple University, Philadelphia, PA 19122, 502-852-0458; FAX 502-852-0459; email: jaac@blue.temple.edu. 1940. "*JAAC* is the journal of The American Society for Aesthetics, an interdisciplinary society which promotes study, research, discussion and publication in aesthetics" circ. 2.7M. 4/yr. Pub'd 4 issues 1998; expects 4 issues 1999, 4 issues 2000. sub. price: $36. 130pp. Reporting time: less than 3 months. Publishes 15% of manuscripts submitted. Payment: none. Copyrighted, does not revert to author. Pub's reviews: 50 in 1998. §Aesthetics and the arts.

THE JOURNAL OF AFRICAN TRAVEL-WRITING, Amber Vogel, PO Box 346, Chapel Hill, NC 27514. 1996. Poetry, fiction, articles, art, photos, interviews, reviews, letters, non-fiction. circ. 600. 2/yr. Pub'd 2 issues 1998; expects 2 issues 1999, 2 issues 2000. sub. price: $10; per copy: $6; sample: $6. 96pp; 7×10; perfectbound. Reporting time: 4-6 weeks. Simultaneous submissions accepted: no. Publishes 5% of manuscripts submitted. Payment: copies. Copyrighted, reverts to author. Pub's reviews: 3 in 1998. §Africa, travel. Ads: $150/$85. CELJ.

JOURNAL OF AGING AND PHYSICAL ACTIVITY (JAPA), Human Kinetics Pub. Inc., Wojtek Chodzko-Zajko, PhD, P. O. Box 5076, Champaign, IL 61825-5076, 217-351-5076, fax 217-351-2674. 1993.

"Multidisciplinary journal focusing on the relationship between physical activity and the aging process" circ. 630. 4/yr. Pub'd 4 issues 1998; expects 4 issues 1999, 4 issues 2000. sub. price: $42 indiv., $100 instit., $26 students; per copy: $12 indiv., $26 instit. Back issues: $12 ind., $26 inst. 104pp; 6×9; of. Copyrighted, does not revert to author. Pub's reviews.

JOURNAL OF ALASKA WOMEN, Lory B. Leary, Editor-in-Chief, HCR 64 Box 453, Seward, AK 99664, 907-288-3168. 1990. Poetry, fiction, articles, art, photos, cartoons, interviews, satire, reviews, non-fiction. "We review all work on Alaskan Women only, written by or about. Feature articles limited to 1,500 words. Photos must be B/W" Irregular. Expects 4 issues 1999. sub. price: none; per copy: $6.95. Back issues: $10, when available. Discounts: 50% plus postage/shipping on 100 or more; lesser amounts 30% plus postage/shipping. 36-40pp; 8½×11; Webb Press. Reporting time: 2 weeks. Payment: $5 to $25. Copyrighted, reverts to author. Pub's reviews: several in 1998. §books written by or about Alaska Women; submissions must include copy of book and b/w photo. Ads: request rates.

JOURNAL OF APPLIED BIOMECHANICS (JAB), Human Kinetics Pub. Inc., Mark D. Gradiner, PhD, PO Box 5076, Champaign, IL 61825-5076, 217-351-5076. 1985. Articles, reviews. "Research articles on biomechanics applied to exercise, sport and rehabilitation." circ. 1M. 4/yr. Pub'd 4 issues 1998; expects 4 issues 1999, 4 issues 2000. sub. price: $42 individual, $100 institution, $26 student; per copy: $12 indiv., $26 instit.; sample: free. Back issues: $12 indiv., $26 instit. Discounts: 5% agency. 136pp; 6×9; of. Reporting time: 2 months. Payment: none. Copyrighted, does not revert to author. Pub's reviews: 0 in 1998. §Sport, Sport science, and physical education related to biomechanics. Ads: $300/$200. Midwest Publishers Association, American Booksellers Association.

●**JOURNAL OF ASIAN MARTIAL ARTS, Via Media Publishing Company**, Michael A. DeMarco, 821 West 24th Street, Erie, PA 16502, 814-455-9517; fax 814-526-5262; e-mail info@goviamedia.com; website www.goviamedia.com. 1991. Articles, art, photos, interviews, reviews, non-fiction. "Article length and topic is open to anything dealing with Asian martial arts. Author must be very familiar with the subject and the history and culture discussed." circ. 12M. 4/yr. Pub'd 4 issues 1998; expects 4 issues 1999, 4 issues 2000. sub. price: $32; per copy: $10; sample: $10. Discounts: regular discounts offered. 124pp; 8½×11; of. Reporting time: 1-2 months. Simultaneous submissions accepted: no. Publishes 10% of manuscripts submitted. Payment: $75 to $500 for feature articles. Copyrighted, reverts to author. Pub's reviews: 14 in 1998. §Asian martial arts and related topics. Ads: $1,950; $590; $395 1/4 page. PMA.

JOURNAL OF CANADIAN POETRY, Borealis Press Limited, Frank M. Tierney, Advertising Editor; W. Glenn Clever, Business Editor; David Staines, General Editor, 110 Bloomingdale Street, Ottawa, Ont. K2C 4A4, Canada, 613-797-9299; Fax 613-798-9747. 1976. Criticism, reviews. "Concerned solely with criticism and reviews of Canadian poetry. Does *not* publish poetry per se; we are a critical journal." circ. 500. 1/yr. Pub'd 1 issue 1998; expects 1 issue 1999, 1 issue 2000. sub. price: $22.20 Canada, $20.95 others; $41.30/2 years Cdn., $39 others, $56.97/3 years Cdn. $53 others; per copy: $12.95; sample: $5. Back issues: $5. Discounts: book wholesalers 20%. 150pp; 5½×8½; of. Reporting time: 4 months. Payment: none. Copyrighted, reverts to author. Pub's reviews: 40 in 1998. §Poetry only (Canadian). Ads: inquire.

JOURNAL OF CANADIAN STUDIES/Revue d'etudes canadiennes, Robert M. Campbell, Trent University, Peterborough, Ont. K9J 7B8, Canada, 705-748-1279; 705-748-1655; e-Mail jcs-rec@trentu.co. 1966. Articles, criticism, reviews. circ. 1.4M. 4/yr. Expects 4 issues 1999. sub. price: $35 indiv., $55 instit., $15 special student rate; per copy: $10. Discounts: 15% agency. 200pp; 5¾×9; of. Reporting time: 6 months approx. Publishes 30% of manuscripts submitted. Payment: none. Copyrighted, joint rights. Pub's reviews: 8 in 1998. §Canadian studies. Ads: $200/$125.

JOURNAL OF CELTIC LINGUISTICS, University Of Wales Press, Mames Fife, Editor, 6 Gwennyth Street, Cathays, Cardiff CF2 4YD, Wales, 44-1222-231919; Fax 44-1222-230908; press@press.wales.ac.uk. Articles, reviews. circ. 500. Pub'd 1 issue 1998. sub. price: £15. Discounts: 10%. 128pp; size A5; of. Payment: none. Copyrighted, reverts to author. Pub's reviews. §Linguistics. Ads: £75/£37.50.

JOURNAL OF CHILD AND YOUTH CARE, Gerry Fewster, Editor, Malaspina University College, Human Services, 900 5th Street, Nanaimo, BC V9R 5S5, Canada. 1981. Poetry, fiction, articles, art, photos, reviews, non-fiction. "This journal is primarily intended for child and youth care workers and all individuals who assume the responsibility for the well being of children." circ. 375. 4/yr. Pub'd 4 issues 1998; expects 4 issues 1999, 4 issues 2000. sub. price: $49.50 indiv., $71.50 instit., in Canada add GST, outside Canada, price in U.S. dollars; per copy: $10 + GST in Canada, outside Canada in US dollars. Back issues: Back volume=$28. 106pp; 6×9; of. Reporting time: 8 months. Copyrighted, does not revert to author. Pub's reviews: 1 in 1998. §Child and youth care theory and practice. Ads: write for information. BPAA, ACUP.

THE JOURNAL OF COMMONWEALTH LITERATURE, John Thieme, Alan Bower, Bowker-Saur, Maypole House, Maypole Road, East Grinstead, W. Sussex RH19 1HU, England, 0865-511428; FAX 0865-311584. 1965. Articles, interviews, non-fiction. "Maximum length for articles: 4M words. Oxford style."

Style guide available on request. Published by: Bowker-Saur part of Reed Business Information." 3/yr. Pub'd 3 issues 1998; expects 3 issues 1999, 3 issues 2000. sub. price: £85 ($149) instit., £42.50 ($75) indiv.; per copy: negotiable; sample: inquire, at publisher's discretion. Back issues: negotiable. 128-256pp; 5½x8½; of/li. Reporting time: 6 months. Simultaneous submissions accepted: no. Payment: £8 a page for bibliographers; no payment to other contributors. Copyrighted, does not revert to author.

●JOURNAL OF CONTEMPARARY ANGLO-SCANDINAVIAN POETRY, Original Plus, Sam Smith, 11 Heatherton Park, Bradford on Tone, Taunton, Somerset TA4 1EU, England, 01823-461725; e-mail smithsssj@aol.com. 1994. Poetry, reviews. "We publish all types and length of poetry, from a ten page narrative poem by Genista Lewes in #5 to occasional haiku." circ. 150. 2/yr. Pub'd 2 issues 1998; expects 2 issues 1999, 2 issues 2000. sub. price: $11 US, £7 UK; per copy: $6 US, £4 UK; sample: £3. Back issues: £2. Discounts: 25%. 72pp; 5¾x8. Reporting time: 2-4 weeks. Simultaneous submissions accepted: yes. Publishes 2% of manuscripts submitted. Payment: 1 copy. Copyrighted, reverts to author. Pub's reviews: 1 in 1998. §contemporary poetry.

JOURNAL OF COURT REPORTING, National Court Reporters Association Press, Peter Wacht, Editor, 8224 Old Courthouse Road, Vienna, VA 22182, 703-556-6272; fax 703-556-6291; email pwacht@ncrahq.org. 1899. Cartoons, interviews, reviews, letters, news items, non-fiction. "Focus should be on stenographic court reporting and its various aspects such as ethics, technology, business. 500-2,000 words. Recent contributers: Richard Lederer, Rita Henley Jensen." circ. 35M. 10/yr. Pub'd 10 issues 1998; expects 10 issues 1999, 10 issues 2000. sub. price: $49; per copy: $5. Back issues: $5. Discounts: none. 132pp; 8⅛x10⅞; †of. Reporting time: 1-2 months. Accepts simultaneous submissions depending on where other submissions are sent. Publishes 50%-75% of manuscripts submitted. Payment: varies. Copyrighted, reverts to author. Pub's reviews: 15-30 in 1998. §Business, reference, law or medical related. Ads: $1,300/$815/varies. PMA, SPAN, ASAE.

THE JOURNAL OF DESIGN AND TECHNOLOGY EDUCATION, Trentham Books, Richard Kimbell, Westview House, 734 London Road, Oakhill, Stoke-on-Trent, Staffordshire ST4 5NP, England, 01782-745567; Fax 01782-745553. 1966. Articles, photos, cartoons, interviews, criticism, reviews, letters, concrete art, news items. "Prints articles on new developments in the whole field of design and technology education ranging from art through to applied science and technology." circ. 5M. 3/yr. Pub'd 2 issues 1998; expects 2 issues 1999, 3 issues 2000. sub. price: £45; per copy: £18; sample: £18. Back issues: £18. Discounts: 10% series disc/w ads. 92pp; 30x21cm; of. Reporting time: max. 1 month, usually 2 weeks. Payment: none. Copyrighted, rights held by magazine. Pub's reviews: 66 in 1998. §Craft, art, design, education. Ads: £400 full page back cover/£350 full page inner cover/£110 1/2 page/£55 1/4 page/£30 1/8 page.

THE JOURNAL OF EXPERIMENTAL FICTION, Depth Charge, Eckhard Gerdes, Matthew Sonnenberg, Senior Editor, PO Box 7037, Evanston, IL 60201-7037, 800-639-0008, 708-733-1565, fax 708-733-0928. 1994. Fiction, criticism, reviews, parts-of-novels. "We publish only experimental fiction (whether 'innovative,' 'metafiction,' 'subterficial fiction,' or 'avant-garde'), or criticism on and reviews of such. All critical articles should adhere to either MLA or Chicago style." circ. 500. 4/yr. Expects 1 issue 1999, 4 issues 2000. sub. price: $32; per copy: $9; sample: $9. Back issues: none. Discounts: 1-3 0%, 4-10 20%, 15+ 30%, distributors by contract. 64-100pp; 5½x8½; of. Reporting time: 6-8 weeks, query first. Payment: 5 copies. Copyrighted, reverts to author. Pub's reviews. §Experimental fiction. Ads: $100/$55/$30 1/4 page.

JOURNAL OF HEALTH POLITICS, POLICY AND LAW, Duke University Press, Mark A. Peterson, Box 90660, Duke University, Durham, NC 27708-0660. "The leading journal in the field of health politics, the Journal of Health Politics, Policy and Law focuses on the initiation, formulation, and implementation of health policy and analyzes the relations between government and health—past, present, and future. Each issue includes both a 'News and Notes' section and an extensive 'Books' section, making JHPPL the primary source of communication across the many disciplines it serves." 6/yr. Expects 6 issues 1999, 6 issues 2000. sub. price: $120 institutions, $52 individuals, $26 students with photocopy of current I.D., additional $18 foreign. Pub's reviews. Ads: $300/$200.

THE JOURNAL OF HISTORICAL REVIEW, Mark Weber, PO Box 2739, Newport Beach, CA 92659, 949-631-1490; ihr@ihr.org. 1979. Articles, reviews, non-fiction. "We specialize in historical material, notably from the Second World War, with an emphasis on revisionist viewpoints, especially the 'Holocaust.'" circ. 4M. 6/yr. Pub'd 6 issues 1998; expects 6 issues 1999, 6 issues 2000. sub. price: $40; per copy: $7.50; sample: $7.50. Discounts: 20% on books we distribute, 40% on books we publish (for booksellers). 40pp; 8½x11; of. Reporting time: varies. Simultaneous submissions accepted: no. Publishes 5% of manuscripts submitted. Payment: varies. Copyrighted. Pub's reviews: 12+ in 1998. §19th & 20th century history. Ads: $500/$300.

JOURNAL OF HUMANITIES, Pascal Kishindo, Faculty of Humanities, Chancellor College, Box 280, Zomba, Malawi, 265-522-222; Fax 265-522-046. 1987. Articles, art, criticism, reviews, music. "The Journal of Humanities is a theoretical journal which aims to excite thinking in the areas of classics, fine and performing arts, literature and orature, linguistics, theology and philosophy.'' circ. 500. 1/yr. Pub'd 1 issue 1998; expects 1 issue 1999, 1 issue 2000. sub. price: US$8 individuals, US$15 institutions. Discounts: negotiable. 88pp; 149×210mm; of. Reporting time: 3-4 months. Simultaneous submissions accepted: no. Publishes 40% of manuscripts submitted. Payment: none. Copyrighted. Pub's reviews: 2 in 1998. §The humanities. Ads: negotiable.

JOURNAL OF MEDIEVAL AND EARLY MODERN STUDIES, Duke University Press, Annabel Wharton, David Aers, Box 90660, Duke University, Durham, NC 27708-0660. *"The Journal of Medieval and Early Modern Studies* publishes articles informed by historical inquiry and alert to issues raised by contemporary theoretical debate. The journal fosters rigorous investigation of historiographical representations of European and Western Asian cultural forms from late antiquity to the 17th century. Its topics include art, literature, theater, music, philosophy, theology, and history, and it embraces material objects as well as texts; women as well as men; merchants, workers, and audiences as well as patrons; Jews and Muslims as well as Christians. This interdisciplinary journal will appeal to scholars of the medieval and early modern periods of Europe and Western Asia.'' circ. 1.1M. 3/yr. Pub'd 3 issues 1998; expects 3 issues 1999, 3 issues 2000. sub. price: $85 institutions, $32 individuals, additional $9 foreign. Ads: $250/$150/$300 back cover.

JOURNAL OF MENTAL IMAGERY, Akhter Ahsen, Ph.D., c/o Brandon House, PO Box 240, Bronx, NY 10471. 1977. Articles, reviews. circ. 5.4M in USA, 7.1M in foreign countries. 4/yr. Pub'd 4 issues 1998. sub. price: $40; per copy: $25; sample: free. Back issues: same as current prices. Discounts: none. 92pp; 6×9; of. Reporting time: 2 months. Payment: none. Copyrighted, does not revert to author. Pub's reviews: 2 in 1998. §Mental imagery. International Imagery Association.

THE JOURNAL OF MIND AND BEHAVIOR, The Institute of Mind and Behavior, Raymond Russ, Editor, PO Box 522, Village Station, New York, NY 10014, 212-595-4853. 1980. Articles, criticism, reviews, letters, non-fiction. *"The Journal Of Mind And Behavior (JMB)* is an academic journal dedicated to the interdisciplinary approach within psychology and related fields — building upon the assumption of a unified science. The editors are particularly interested in scholarly work in the following areas: the psychology, philosophy, and sociology of experimentation and the scientific method; the relationship between methodology, operationism, and theory construction; the mind-body problem in the social sciences, literature, and art; issues pertaining to the ethical study of cognition, self-awareness, and higher functions of consciousness in animals; mind-body interactions and medical implications; philosophical impact of a mind-body epistemology upon psychology; historical perspectives on the course and nature of science. All manuscripts *must* follow style and preparation of the *Publication Manual of the American Psychological Association* (fourth edition, 1994) and be submitted in quadruplicate for review to: Dr. Raymond Russ, Department of Psychology, 5742 Little Hall, University of Maine, Orono, ME 04469-5742.'' circ. 1.1M. 4/yr. Pub'd 4 issues 1998; expects 4 issues 1999, 4 issues 2000. sub. price: individual $42/yr, $78/2 yrs, $108/3 yrs, institutional $91/yr, $170/2 yrs, $250/3 yrs; per copy: $15; sample: free. Back issues: $108/3 yrs. individual; $250/3 yrs. institution (special package available upon request). Discounts: 15% on order of 10 copies or more. 140pp; 5½×8½; of. Reporting time: 10-15 weeks. Publishes 16% of manuscripts submitted. Payment: none. Copyrighted, does not revert to author. Pub's reviews: 26 in 1998. §Psychology (both thoeretical and experimental), philosophy, history of science, medicine, art. Ads: $230/$130/discounts on multiple runs.

JOURNAL OF MODERN LITERATURE, Morton P. Levitt, Editor-in-Chief, Indiania University Press, 601 North Morton, Bloomington, IN 47404, 812-855-9449. 1970. Articles, interviews, criticism, reviews. circ. 2.2M. 3/yr. Pub'd 3 issues 1998; expects 3 issues 1999, 3 issues 2000. sub. price: U.S.: $30 individuals, institutions: $65, foreign: $42.50 and $77.50, Asian: $42-50.; per copy: $12.95 individuals; $14.95 institution; sample: free. Discounts: 4% agencies on foreign addresses. 160pp; 7×10; desktop publishing. Reporting time: 10-12 weeks. Payment: 1 copy issue and 10 off prints. Copyrighted, does not revert to author. Pub's reviews: 300 in 1998. §Critical and scholarly works only. Ads: $250/$175/. CELJ.

JOURNAL OF MUSICOLOGY, University of California Press, Marian Green, University of California Press, 2120 Berkeley Way, Berkeley, CA 94720, 510-643-7154. 1972. Articles, reviews, non-fiction. "Editorial address: PO Box 1405, Boston, MA 02205.'' circ. 1.3M. 4/yr. Pub'd 4 issues 1998; expects 4 issues 1999, 4 issues 2000. sub. price: $36 indiv., $89 instit., $25 students (+ $5 foreign postage); per copy: $10 indiv., $24 instit., $10 students (+ $5 foreign postage); sample: free. Back issues: same as single copy price. Discounts: foreign subs. agent 10%, one-time order 10+ 30%, standing orders (bookstores) 1-99 40%, 100+ 50%. 128pp; 6×9; of. Reporting time: 1-2 months. Payment: varies. Copyrighted, does not revert to author. Pub's reviews: 8-10 in 1998. Ads: $275/$200.

JOURNAL OF NARRATIVE THEORY, Craig Dionne, Co-Editor; Ian Wojcik-Andrews, Co-Editor, Eastern Michigan University, Ypsilanti, MI 48197, 313-487-3175; Fax 313-483-9744; website www.emich.edu/public/english/JNT. 1971. Criticism. *"JNT* is a scholarly magazine with international circulation. Essays run from 15 to 30 typed pages. Contributors should follow MLA style.'' circ. 1.1M. 3/yr. Pub'd 3 issues 1998; expects 3 issues 1999, 3 issues 2000. sub. price: $20, libraries and institutions outside the US have a $10 postal surcharge,

$15 individuals; per copy: $8; sample: free. Back issues: $8. Discounts: 20% to subscription agents. 110pp; 6×9; photo typesetting, offset printing. Reporting time: 1-4 months. Publishes 10-15% of manuscripts submitted. Payment: copies only. Copyrighted, reverts to author. Pub's reviews: 10 in 1998. §Same subject matter as for submission of articles (literary criticism, literary theory, film criticism, cultural studies). Ads: $100 per issue/$200 per volume. Council of Editors of Learned Journals.

JOURNAL OF NEW JERSEY POETS, Sander Zulauf, Editor; North Peterson, Assoc. Editor; Sara Pfaffenroth, Assoc. Editor; Wendy Jones, Associate Editor; Wilma Martin, Layout Editor, 214 Center Grove Road, County College of Morris, Randolph, NJ 07869, 201-328-5471; e-mail szulauf@ccm.edu. 1976. Poetry, photos, reviews. "Open to submission of poetry from present and past residents of New Jersey; no biases concerning style or subject. Reviews of books by New Jersey poets." circ. 1M. 2/yr. Pub'd 2 issues 1998; expects 2 issues 1999, 2 issues 2000. sub. price: $10/2 issues, $16/4 issues, $10/4 issues students and seniors (please specify); per copy: $5; sample: $5. Back issues: available on request, printed each issue. Discounts: 50% booksellers. 64-72pp; 8½x5½; †of. Reporting time: 6 months to 1 year. Publishes 5% of manuscripts submitted. Payment: 5 copies plus 2 issue subscription. Copyrighted, reverts to author. Pub's reviews: 2 in 1998. §Poetry, books about poetry. Ads: upon request. CLMP.

JOURNAL OF PERSONALITY, Duke University Press, Howard Tennen, Box 90660, Duke University, Durham, NC 27708-0660. "The *Journal of Personality* publishes studies in the fields of personality and behavior dynamics that focus on personality development and individual differences in the cognitive, affective, and interpersonal domains. The journal reflects and stimulates interest in the growth of new theoretical and methodological approaches in personality psychology. Studies of special populations and community samples are welcome." circ. 2M. 4/yr. Pub'd 4 issues 1998; expects 4 issues 1999, 4 issues 2000. sub. price: $120 institutions, $52 individuals, $26 students with photocopy of current I.D., additional $12 foreign. Ads: $250/$200.

JOURNAL OF POLYMORPHOUS PERVERSITY, Glenn C. Ellenbogen, PO Box 1454, Madison Square Station, New York, NY 10159-1454, 212-689-5473; info@psychhumor.com; website www.psychhumor.com. 1984. Satire. "The *Wall Street Journal* (12/20/84) called *JPP* "...a social scientist's answer to Mad Magazine." *JPP* is a humorous and satirical journal of psychology (and psychiatry and the closely allied disciplines). Materials submitted should relate to psychology, psychiatry, mental health, or mental health research. First and foremost, the article *must* be humorous and/or satirical. Manuscripts should be no longer than 8 double-spaced (4 typeset) pages. Articles are reviewed for consideration by one or more of 18 Associate Editors, each representing a specialty area. Recent contributions include "Psychotherapy of the Dead," "New Improved Delusions," "A Modern Day Psychoanalytical Fable," "Nicholas Claus: A Case Study in Psychometrics," and "The Etiology and Treatment of Childhood". We do not ever consider poems or cartoons. The best way to get a clear idea of what we are looking for is read a real psychology or psychiatry journal. Then write a spoof of it. Vist our website at www.psychhumor.com to see example excerpts." circ. 4.2M. 2/yr. Pub'd 2 issues 1998; expects 2 issues 1999, 2 issues 2000. sub. price: $14.95; per copy: $7; sample: $7 includes postage. Back issues: $7 per issue. 24pp; 6¾x10; of. Reporting time: 4-6 weeks. Simultaneous submissions accepted: no. Publishes 3% of manuscripts submitted. Payment: 2 free copies. Copyrighted, does not revert to author. §Psychology, psychiatry, and medicine. Ads: $525/$625 back cover.

JOURNAL OF PROCESS ORIENTED PSYCHOLOGY, Lao Tse Press, Ltd., Leslie Heizer, Kate Jobe, PO Box 8898, Portland, OR 97207-8898, 503-222-3395. 1992. Articles, art, photos. "Work on process-oriented psychology only" circ. 1M. 2/yr. Pub'd 2 issues 1998; expects 2 issues 1999, 2 issues 2000. sub. price: $20; per copy: $10; sample: $5. Back issues: $5. Discounts: classroom 35%, trade 1-4 20%, 5-9 40%, 10-24 42%, 25-49 43%. 90pp; 8½x11; of. Reporting time: 3-6 months. Simultaneous submissions accepted: yes. Publishes 50% of manuscripts submitted. Payment: copy. Copyrighted, reverts to author. Pub's reviews: 0 in 1998. §only about process work. Ads: NWAPB, NAPRA.

JOURNAL OF PSYCHOACTIVE DRUGS, Haight-Ashbury Publications, David E. Smith, MD, Executive Editor; Richard B. Seymour, Managing Editor, 612 Clayton Street, San Francisco, CA 94117, 415-565-1904; fax 415-864-6162. 1967. Articles, art, photos. "The *Journal of Psychoactive Drugs* is a multidisciplinary forum for the study of drugs, every issue features a variety of articles by noted researchers and theorists. ISSN 0279-1072." circ. 1.2M. 4/yr. Pub'd 4 issues 1998; expects 4 issues 1999, 4 issues 2000. sub. price: $90 (indiv.), $160 (instit.), + $15/yr surface postage outside U.S., + $35/yr airmail postage outside U.S.; per copy: $40; sample: $25. Back issues: $150 while supplies last of Vol.4-28. Discounts: 5% subscription agency. 100pp; 8½x11; of. Reporting time: 60-90 days on articles; 30 days on art for cover or book reviews. Simultaneous submissions accepted: no. Payment: $50 for cover photo/art. Copyrighted, does not revert to author. Pub's reviews: 0 in 1998. §Alcohol and other drug-related topics. Ads: $350/$275.

THE JOURNAL OF PSYCHOHISTORY, Psychohistory Press, Lloyd deMause, 140 Riverside Drive, New York, NY 10024, 212-799-2294. 1973. Articles, reviews. "Psychohistory of individuals and groups, history of childhood and family." circ. 4M. 4/yr. Pub'd 4 issues 1998; expects 4 issues 1999. sub. price: $54 individual,

$129 organization; per copy: $13; sample: $13. Back issues: $13. 110pp; 7×9; of. Reporting time: 2 weeks. Payment: none. Copyrighted, does not revert to author. Pub's reviews: 40 in 1998. §Psychology & history. Ads: $200/$100.

JOURNAL OF REGIONAL CRITICISM, Arjuna Library Press, Count Prof. Joseph A. Uphoff Jr., Director, 1025 Garner Street, Box 18, Colorado Springs, CO 80905-1774. 1979. Poetry, art, photos, criticism, parts-of-novels, long-poems, plays, news items, non-fiction. "This journal is an ongoing development of mathematical theories in the Fine Arts and Surrealism, with illustrative material, published as a xerox manuscript copy. We cannot, at this time, pay contributors except by enhancing their reputations, but we have plans for the future. Previous contributors considered on a priority basis. We present criticism by quotation or annotation. In the context of performance art and choreography, various experimental manifestations are being documented with illustrative contributions that advance the system used to graph poetic and dynamic action. The current focus is upon the Eshkol-Wachman System of Movement Notation. From documentation, a system of biography can be formulated. The context of recognition has developed as an irony associating appraisal in quantitative terms as approximately correlated to qualitative analysis. The ideals for skill and knowledgeability cannot be abstracted except in pure and modernist compositions which remain in the context of an honest biographical background. Most orchestrations combine a vast array of differing methods, and the business technique of bookkeeping for expenses is only approximate. We include values seldom considered such as uncompensated learning experiences and the relation between the audience and the performance. Winning a contest is not a quantitative prospect nor is interfering with other competitors; ethical and value considerations are more important. We are not teaching writers to compete but to compose. Thus it is not necessary to misrepresent technique in emulation of popularity. The creation of beautiful images and essays should be a sufficient accomplishment to stand on its own merits." circ. open. 6-12/yr. Pub'd 12 issues 1998; expects 12 issues 1999, 12 issues 2000. sample price: at cost. Back issues: at current cost. 4pp; 8½×11; †xerography. Reporting time: indefinite. Payment: none. Copyrighted, reverts to author.

JOURNAL OF SCIENTIFIC EXPLORATION, Dr. Bernhard Haisch, Editor-in-Chief; Marsha Sims, Executive Editor, PO Box 5848, Stanford, CA 94309-5848, 650-593-8581, fax 650-595-4466, e-mail sims@jse.com. 1987. "Publishes original multi-disciplinary research aimed at scientific advance and the expansion of human knowledge in areas falling outside the established scientific disciplines. It is a refereed journal, providing a neutral, professional forum for discussion and debate of anomalous phenomena." circ. 3M. 4/yr. Pub'd 4 issues 1998; expects 4 issues 1999, 4 issues 2000. sub. price: $50 individuals, $55 foreign; $100 institutions; sample: $13.74. Back issues: Complete back issues available. 140pp; 6×9. Simultaneous submissions accepted: no. Publishes 25-50% of manuscripts submitted. Payment: none. Copyrighted, does not revert to author. Pub's reviews: 24 in 1998. §Science. Ads: exchanges. Society for Scientific Exploration.

JOURNAL OF SOCIAL BEHAVIOR AND PERSONALITY, Select Press, Roderick P. Crandall, PO Box 37, Corte Madera, CA 94925, 415-924-1612. 1986. "Academic research, psychology, speech, business, sociology, etc." 4/yr + extras. Pub'd 7 issues 1998; expects 6 issues 1999, 6 issues 2000. sub. price: $62; per copy: $15; sample: free. 200pp; 8½×5½. Reporting time: 4 weeks. Copyrighted, does not revert to author.

JOURNAL OF SPORT AND EXERCISE PSYCHOLOGY (JSEP), Human Kinetics Pub. Inc., Robert J. Brustad, Ph.D., Box 5076, Champaign, IL 61825-5076, 217-351-5076. 1979. Articles, reviews. "Scholarly journal." circ. 1.9M. 4/yr. Pub'd 4 issues 1998; expects 4 issues 1999, 4 issues 2000. sub. price: $42 indiv., $100 instit., $26 student; per copy: $26 indiv; $26 instit.; sample: free. Back issues: $12 indiv; $26 instit. Discounts: 5%. 120pp; 6×9; of. Reporting time: 2 months. Payment: none. Copyrighted, does not revert to author. Pub's reviews: 3 in 1998. §Sport, sport science, physical education. Ads: $300/$200. Midwest Book Publishers Association, American Booksellers Association.

JOURNAL OF SPORT MANAGEMENT (JSM), Human Kinetics Pub. Inc., Trevor Slack, Ph.D., Wendy Frisby, PhD, Box 5076, Champaign, IL 61825-5076, 217-351-5076. 1987. Articles, reviews. "Applied journal." circ. 850. 3/yr. Pub'd 2 issues 1998; expects 3 issues 1999, 3 issues 2000. sub. price: $42 indiv., $100 instit., $26 student; per copy: $12 indiv., $26 instit.; sample: free. Back issues: $12 indiv., $26 instit. Discounts: 5%. 120pp; 6×9; of. Reporting time: 2 months. Payment: none. Copyrighted, does not revert to author. Pub's reviews: 9 in 1998. §sport, sport science, and physical education related to management. Ads: $300/$200. Midwest Book Publishers Association, American Booksellers Association.

JOURNAL OF SPORT REHABILITATION (JSR), Human Kinetics Pub. Inc., Scott M. Lephart, Ph.D, PO Box 5076, Champaign, IL 61825-5076, 217-351-5076. 1992. Articles, reviews. "Covers the field of sport rehabilitation from a multidisciplinary perspective." circ. 720. 4/yr. Pub'd 4 issues 1998; expects 4 issues 1999, 4 issues 2000. sub. price: $42 individual, $100 institution, $26 student; per copy: $12 individual, $26 institution; sample: free. Back issues: $12 indiv., $26 instit. Discounts: 5% agency. 96pp; 6×9; of. Reporting time: 2 months. Payment: none. Copyrighted, does not revert to author. Pub's reviews: 13 in 1998. §Athletic training, sport injuries, conditioning, sports medicine, sport science. Ads: $300/$200. Midwest Book Publishers Association, American Booksellers Association.

JOURNAL OF STRENGTH AND CONDITIONING RESEARCH (JSCR), Human Kinetics Pub. Inc., William J. Kraemer, Ph.D, CSCS, PO Box 5076, Champaign, IL 61825-5076, 217-351-5076. 1987. Articles, reviews. "Covers the gamut of sport science research into strength and conditioning." circ. 9.8M. 4/yr. Pub'd 4 issues 1998; expects 4 issues 1999, 4 issues 2000. sub. price: Only univ./college libraries $80 US; foreign $84; per copy: $10 indiv., $21 instit; sample: free. Back issues: $10 indiv., $21 instit. Discounts: 5% agency. 64pp; 8½×11; of. Reporting time: 2 months. Simultaneous submissions accepted: no. Payment: none. Copyrighted, does not revert to author. §Weight training, sport science, conditioning, sports medicine. Ads: $500/$325. Midwest Book Publishers Association, American Booksellers Association.

JOURNAL OF TEACHING IN PHYSICAL EDUCATION (JTPE), Human Kinetics Pub. Inc., Nell Faucette, EdD, Patt PhD Dodds, Box 5076, Champaign, IL 61825-5076, 217-351-5076. 1981. Articles, reviews. "The teaching process and teacher education in physical education." circ. 1.3M. 4/yr. Pub'd 4 issues 1998; expects 4 issues 1999, 4 issues 2000. sub. price: $40 individual, $100 institution, $26 student; per copy: $12 indiv., $26 instit.; sample: free. Back issues: $12 indiv., $26 instit. Discounts: 5%. 128pp; 6×9; of. Reporting time: 2 months. Payment: none. Copyrighted, does not revert to author. Pub's reviews: 3 in 1998. §sport, sport science, and physical education. Ads: $300/$200. Midwest Book Publishers Association, American Booksellers Association.

JOURNAL OF THE HELLENIC DIASPORA, Pella Publishing Co, A. Kitroeff, 337 West 36th Street, New York, NY 10018, 212-279-9586. 1974. Fiction, articles, art, photos, cartoons, interviews, satire, criticism, reviews, music, parts-of-novels, long-poems, collages, plays. "The magazine is concerned with the entire spectrum of scholarly, critical, and artistic work that is based on contemporary Greece." circ. 1M. 2/yr. Pub'd 2 issues 1998; expects 2 issues 1999, 2 issues 2000. sub. price: Individual: domestic $20, foreign $25; Institutions: domestic $30, foreign $35; per copy: $12; sample: free. Back issues: $15. Discounts: jobbers & bookstores-20%. 96-112pp; 5½×8½; †lp. Reporting time: 12 weeks. Payment: 30 offprints for articles. Copyrighted, reverts to author. Pub's reviews: 8 in 1998. §Modern Greek studies and affairs. Ads: $125/$75.

THE JOURNAL OF THE ORDER OF BUDDHIST CONTEMPLATIVES, Rev. Chushin Passmore, 3724 Summit Drive, Mt. Shasta, CA 96067-9102, 530-926-4208; E-mail www.obcon.org. 1970. Articles, art, photos, letters, news items. "The Journal of the Order of Buddhist Contemplatives contains articles on Buddhist meditation and training written by priests of the Order and lay members of the congregation." circ. 500. 4/yr. Pub'd 4 issues 1998; expects 4 issues 1999, 4 issues 2000. sub. price: $20; per copy: $5; sample: $1.50 to cover postage appreciated. Back issues: $3 for single issue; $4 for double. 88pp; 5½×8½; of. Payment: none. Copyrighted, reverts to author. Ads: none accepted.

JOURNAL OF THE PHILOSOPHY OF SPORT (JPS), Human Kinetics Pub. Inc., William Morgan, Ph.D., Box 5076, Champaign, IL 61825-5076, 217-351-5076. 1974. Articles, reviews. "Scholarly journal." circ. 554. 1/yr. Pub'd 1 issue 1998; expects 1 issue 1999, 1 issue 2000. sub. price: $20 individuals, $32 institutions, $12 students; per copy: same; sample: free. Back issues: $20 indiv., $32 instit., $12 student. Discounts: 5%. 120pp; 6×9; of. Reporting time: 2 months. Simultaneous submissions accepted: no. Publishes 50% of manuscripts submitted. Payment: none. Copyrighted, does not revert to author. Pub's reviews: 3 in 1998. §Sport, sport science, and physical education related to philosophy. Ads: none. Midwest Book Publishers Association, American Booksellers Association.

JOURNAL OF THE WEST, Sunflower University Press, Robin Higham, Editor & President; Carol A. Williams, Publisher & Director of Marketing, 1531 Yuma (PO Box 1009), Manhattan, KS 66502, 785-539-1888, fax 785-539-2233. 1962. Articles, reviews. "We solicit our own articles for theme issues and reviews, but will consider articles submitted from outside for the *About the West* section." circ. 4.5M. 4/yr. Pub'd 4 issues 1998; expects 4 issues 1999, 4 issues 2000. sub. price: $42 individuals, $54 institutions; per copy: $12 prepaid individuals, $15 institutions; sample: $3 (s+h). Back issues: $12 prepaid. 112pp; 8½×11; †of. Reporting time: 3 months. Payment: 15 copies of issue. Copyrighted, does not revert to author. Pub's reviews: 160 in 1998. §The West, all angles. Ads: $375/$275. SSP.

JOURNAL OF THOUGHT, Caddo Gap Press, Frances O'Neill, 3145 Geary Boulevard #275, San Francisco, CA 94118, 415-922-1911. 1965. Articles. "*Journal of Thought* is an interdisciplinary scholarly journal focusing on educational philosophy, featuring articles by scholars and researchers." circ. 500. 4/yr. Pub'd 4 issues 1998; expects 4 issues 1999, 4 issues 2000. sub. price: $40 individuals, $60 institutions; per copy: $15. 96pp; 6×9; of. Reporting time: 2 months. Publishes 25% of manuscripts submitted. Payment: none. Copyrighted, reverts to author. Ads: $200 per page. MPE, EDPRESS.

JOURNAL OF UNCONVENTIONAL HISTORY, Dr. Ann Elwood, Dr. Aline Hornaday, PO Box 459, Cardiff-by-the-Sea, CA 92007, 619-459-5748; fax 619-459-0936; e-mail ahornaday@ucsd.edu. 1989. Articles, photos, interviews, reviews, letters, non-fiction. "As an unconventional magazine we are open to all kinds of historical material. Reviews are usually done as review articles combining several books." circ. 400. 3/yr. Pub'd 3 issues 1998; expects 3 issues 1999, 3 issues 2000. sub. price: $20; per copy: $7.50; sample: $7.50.

Back issues: $3.50. Discounts: jobber and institution $22.50 per year, jobber discount $2.50. 75-80pp; 5¼x8¼; of. Reporting time: 1-2 months. Simultaneous submissions accepted: no. We work with authors to make their work publishable, perhaps 5-10% can't be rescued. Payment: 5 copies, plus 20 offprints. Copyrighted, rights reverting to author are negotiable. Pub's reviews: 5 in 1998. §Original unconventional historical work. Ads: $75/$45.

JOURNAL OF VISION REHABILITATION, Westport Publishers, Randy Jose, 1102 Grand, 23rd Floor, Kansas City, MO 64106. 1987. Non-fiction. "Professional journal for low vision theoreticians and practitioners" circ. 700. 4/yr. Pub'd 4 issues 1998; expects 4 issues 1999, 4 issues 2000. sub. price: $50; per copy: $15; sample: free. Back issues: $15. Discounts: AOA low vision members, $35.00; Sub Services Co's, 10%, AER member, $39. 36pp; 8½x11; of. Reporting time: 1-3 months. Payment: none. Not copyrighted. Pub's reviews: 3-4 in 1998. §Low vision treatment, diagnose, rehabilitation. Ads: $240/$160/$125 1/3 page. MAPA.

Journey Books Publishing, Edward Knight, 3205 Highway 431, Spring Hill, TN 37174, 615-791-8006. 1997. Poetry, fiction. "We are dedicated to producing quality books. We publish novels (50,000 words or more) and plan a series of 'short novels' (30-40,000 words). Our most recent work is *Greed* by Donnie Clemons." avg. press run 2M. Pub'd 1 title 1998; expects 3 titles 1999, 3 titles 2000. 2 titles listed in the *Small Press Record of Books in Print* (28th Edition, 1999-00). avg. price, paper: $12. Discounts: trade discounts are available. 256pp; 5½x8½; of. Reporting time: 3 months. Simultaneous submissions accepted: yes. Publishes less than 1% of manuscripts submitted. Payment: 10% royalty, no advance. Does not copyright for author. PMA.

Journey Publications, Kent Babcock, PO Box 423, Woodstock, NY 12498, 914-657-8434. 1976. "We publish books on philosophy and meditation which we feel are important responses to the problems of modern life." avg. press run 3M-5M. Pub'd 1 title 1998; expects 1 title 1999, 1 title 2000. 4 titles listed in the *Small Press Record of Books in Print* (28th Edition, 1999-00). avg. price, paper: $9.95. Discounts: 25% for 1-4 books; 40% 5+; 50% postpaid to distributors. 125pp; 5½x8½; †of. Payment: contract. Copyrights for author.

JPS Publishing Company, Janice Brown, Patsy Stagner, Norma Phears, PO Box 540272, Grand Prairie, TX 75054-0272, 972-291-3944. 1997. Non-fiction. "We are primarily a self-help, how-to book publisher. Not accepting new manuscripts until 2000." avg. press run 3M. Expects 3 titles 1999, 5 titles 2000. 1 title listed in the *Small Press Record of Books in Print* (28th Edition, 1999-00). avg. price, paper: $12.95. Discounts: trade. 200pp; 5½x8½; of. Publishes 0% of manuscripts submitted. Copyrights for author.

J-REP NEWS AND VIEWS, Jewish Radical Education Project, PO BOX 7377, New York, NY 10150-7377, 212-675-9788. 1993. Poetry, articles, criticism, non-fiction. "Newsletter of the Jewish Radical Education Project." circ. 600. 12/yr. Expects 12 issues 1999, 12 issues 2000. sub. price: $10; per copy: $1; sample: free. 4pp; 8½x11; of. Payment: none. Pub's reviews: 1 in 1998. §Jewish history, Jewish concerns.

Judah Magnes Museum Publications, Rebecca Fromer, Editor; Paula Friedman, Editor; Nelda Cassuto, Editor, 2911 Russell Street, Berkeley, CA 94705. 1966. Art, non-fiction. "Primarily art, Judaica, Western Americana, and related. Query first." avg. press run 1M. Pub'd 3 titles 1998; expects 2 titles 1999, 2 titles 2000. 14 titles listed in the *Small Press Record of Books in Print* (28th Edition, 1999-00). avg. price, cloth: $25-$50; paper: $12-$20. Discounts: upon request - contact order Department, c/o magnes museum, 2911 Russell St. Berkely, CA. 94705. 150-200pp; size varies; photo-offset. Reporting time: 3 months - 2 years. Query first before sending simultaneous submissions. Of those mss. submitted after querying, we publish about 15%. Payment: varies. We do not usually copyright for author. American Jewish Publish Ass.

Juggernaut, Daniel X. O'Neil, PO Box 3824, Chicago, IL 60654-0824, 773-583-9261. 1992. "We are interested only in receiving full-length book manuscripts from American Performance Poets. We are expanding rapidly but publish only one book a year, and we are not actually seeking manuscripts at this time; but we do not want to rule it out - try if you like. Send SASE for return." avg. press run 1M. Pub'd 3 titles 1998; expects 3 titles 1999, 2 titles 2000. 2 titles listed in the *Small Press Record of Books in Print* (28th Edition, 1999-00). avg. price, cloth: $12; paper: $10; other: $6. Discounts: 40-45% direct to retailers, industry standard of 50-55% wholesalers. Open to query from book buyers. 48pp; 6x9; of. Reporting time: 3 months. Simultaneous submissions accepted: no. Publishes 5% of manuscripts submitted. Payment: as negotiated. Copyrights for author. CLMP.

July Blue Press, R.L. Kenvin, PO Box 2006, Arcadia, CA 91077, 626-445-4420. 1997. Fiction. "Additional address: 126 Mt. Cardigan Rd., Alexandria, NH 03222. New publisher interested only in high quality literary short fiction written by writers who are also excellent performers and willing to share publishing expenses." avg. press run 500. Expects 1 title 1999, 2 titles 2000. 3 titles listed in the *Small Press Record of Books in Print* (28th Edition, 1999-00). avg. price, paper: $14.95. Discounts: retail 1 copy 0%, 2-5 30%, 6+ 40%. 125pp; 6x9; of. Reporting time: 3 months. Simultaneous submissions accepted: yes. Payment: negotiated. Does not copyright for author. Maine Writers & Publishers Alliance; New Hampshire Writers Project; Small Press Center.

JUMP CUT, A Review of Contemporary Media, John Hess, Chuck Kleinhans, Julia Lesage, P.O. Box 865, Berkeley, CA 94701. 1974. Articles, art, photos, cartoons, interviews, criticism, reviews, letters. "Interested in commercial and independent film since 1970. Length as needed to make points, but shorter preferred; we strive for clarity in style. Biased to radical criticism, esp. Marxist and feminist. No cute and superficial reviews. Strongly suggest reading an issue before submission. Send SASE for 'Notice to Writers'." circ. 5M-6M. Irregular. Pub'd 1 issue 1998; expects 1 issue 1999, 1 issue 2000. sub. price: $14, Canada & abroad $18, $20 & $24 instit.; per copy: $8; Canada & abroad $10. Back issues: Nos. 1-13, 18, 19, 27-32 sold out. $3; Canada & abroad $3.50 (33-39 4/$4.50, Also they are available from [Xerox International Microfilm]. Discounts: institutional rate is $20, Canada & abroad $24, agency 10%, bookstores 30%. 128pp; 8½×11; of. Reporting time: 3 weeks-3 months. Payment: copies. Contributor may retain copyright. Pub's reviews: 3 in 1998. §On the subjects of film and marxist culture and criticism. Ads: $250/$125.

Junction Press, Mark Weiss, PO Box 40537, San Diego, CA 92164-0537, 619-702-4607. 1991. Poetry. "Modernist or postmodernist poetry, non-academic. Long, even book length poems welcomed. Recent books by Mervyn Taylor, Richard Elman, Susie Mee, Stephen Vincent, Ira Beryl Brakner, Rochelle Owens, and Armand Schwerner." avg. press run 1M. Pub'd 3 titles 1998; expects 2 titles 1999, 3 titles 2000. 10 titles listed in the *Small Press Record of Books in Print* (28th Edition, 1999-00). avg. price, paper: $11. Discounts: bookstores 40%, standing orders 20%. 96pp; 5½×8½; of. Reporting time: 3 months. Simultaneous submissions accepted: no. Payment: 10% paid in copies of first print, 8% thereafter. Copyrights for author. CLMP.

Jungle Man Press, R. Monroe-Smith, 211 W. Mulberry Street, 3rd Floor, Baltimore, MD 21201. 1993. Poetry, long-poems, collages. "For writers devoted to poetry as a vocation; sees new standard of poetic craft: transcendent expression: memorializing grit and dirt. Jungle Man Press is a one-man operation and does accept unsolicited queries or submissions with SASE. I am doing this for love of poetry, not people." avg. press run 50-100. Pub'd 1 title 1998; expects 4 titles 1999, 2 titles 2000. 4 titles listed in the *Small Press Record of Books in Print* (28th Edition, 1999-00). avg. price, paper: $3.50. Discounts: 50% off for Author. 30pp; 5½×8½; xerox. Reporting time: immediate. Simultaneous submissions accepted: no. Publishes 5% of manuscripts submitted. Payment: in copies. Does not copyright for author.

Juniper Sun Publishing, 10519 SE Center Street, Portland, OR 97266, 503-760-2852. 1 title listed in the *Small Press Record of Books in Print* (28th Edition, 1999-00).

Jupiter Scientific Publishing, Gezhi Weng, Stewart Allen, Columbia University Post Office, PO Box 250586, New York, NY 10025, 212-650-8194; email jupiter@ajanta.sci.ccny.cuny.edu. 1996. Non-fiction. "Jupiter Scientific Publishing specializes in popular science books. For additional information check the website at http://ajanta.sci.ccny.cuny.edu/~jupiter/pub/com/index.html" avg. press run 2M. Expects 1 title 1999, 1 title 2000. 1 title listed in the *Small Press Record of Books in Print* (28th Edition, 1999-00). avg. price, cloth: $30; paper: $24. Discounts: 2-3 20%, 4-7 25%, 8-11 30%, 12-15 35%, 16-47 40%, 48+ 45%. 300pp; 6×9; of. Reporting time: 1 month. Simultaneous submissions accepted: yes. Publishes 5% of manuscripts submitted. Payment: 10%. Copyrights for author. Publishers Marketing Association.

K

K & B Products, Susan Stafford, PO Box 1502, Suite 214, Red Bluff, CA 96080, 800-700-5096. 3 titles listed in the *Small Press Record of Books in Print* (28th Edition, 1999-00).

K.T. Publications (see also THE THIRD HALF), Kevin Troop, 16, Fane Close, Stamford, Lincs., PE9 1HG, England, (07180) 754193. 1987. Poetry, fiction, art, plays. "Up to 40 lines for poets; up to 2,000 words for fiction. Separate books or volumes of poetry. Naturally vary in length and style—"each book is different"." avg. press run varies. Pub'd 6 titles 1998; expects 6 titles 1999, 6 titles 2000. 2 titles listed in the *Small Press Record of Books in Print* (28th Edition, 1999-00). avg. price, cloth: varies; paper: varies. Discounts: please contact with details, requests, numbers. 40-50pp; size A5; †of. Reporting time: as quickly as humanly possible. Simultaneous submissions accepted, but not keen, really. Publishes up to 10% of manuscripts submitted. Payment: none. Copyrights for author.

KAIROS, A Journal of Contemporary Thought and Criticism, Hermes House Press, Inc., Alan Mandell, Richard Mandell, 113 Summit Avenue, Brookline, MA 02446-2319. 1981. Poetry, fiction, articles, art, photos, interviews, criticism, reviews, long-poems, concrete art, non-fiction. "Not currently reading unsolicited material. Volume I, No. 3 focused on the meaning and experience of learning. Vol. I, No. 4 focused on German culture and society in America. Vol. II, No. 1 focused on the writings of Ernest Becker. Vol. II, No. 2 included materials on technology and poetry-in-translation. Poetry, fiction and artwork are encouraged. Please include

SASE." circ. 500. 2/yr. Pub'd 2 issues 1998; expects 2 issues 1999, 2 issues 2000. sub. price: $11 individual, $15 institutions; per copy: $6 + $1 p/h; sample: $6 + $1 p/h. Discounts: available upon request. 120pp; 5½x8½; of. Reporting time: 4-8 weeks. Payment: copies. Copyrighted, reverts to author. Pub's reviews: 2 in 1998. §See past issues for tone, scope and direction. Ads: on exchange basis only.

Kairos World Press, William G. Brueggemann, Publisher, 2037 West Bullard, Box #202, Fresno, CA 93711-1200. 1 title listed in the *Small Press Record of Books in Print* (28th Edition, 1999-00).

KALDRON, An International Journal Of Visual Poetry, Karl Kempton, Karl Young, Harry Polkinhorn, Klaus Peter Dencker, Thalia, PO Box 7164, Halcyon, CA 93421-7164, 805-489-2770; Website http://www.thing.net/~grist/l&d/kaldron.htm. 1976. Poetry. "*KALDRON* is North America's longest running visual poetry magazine. Its on-line version opened on Bastille Day, 1997. Sections include 1) Selections from the Kaldron Archive: Number 21/22 and First Visualog Show, 1979; 2) Volume Two Continuing on-line issue of the magazine: samples from Fall, 1997 for Kaldron Wall Archives; 3) A Kaldron Wall Ancestor: Chumash Rock Painting showing a solar eclipse. 4) SURVEYS: A - Individual Poets: Avelino de Araujo; Doris Cross; Klaus Peter Dencker; Scott Helms; d.a.levy (includes visual poetry, book art, paintings, lexical poetry: a - holistic approach to this major figure); Hassan Massoudy; bpNichol (includes a wide variety of poems, continuation of TTA project, and commentary); Kenneth Patchen; Marilyn R. Rosenberg; Alain Satie; Carol Stetser; thalia; Edgardo Antonio Vigo (first instalments of a joint memorial to this great and typically unrecognized) Argentine polymath, shown in conjunction with Postypographika; B - Group Surveys: Lettriste Pages; A Collective Effort of Australian Visual Poets; A Workshop with Hungarian Visual Poets; U.S. and Canadian Pages for Nucleo Post Arte's VI Biennial; Festival of Experimental Art and Literature, Mexico City, November, 1998; FREE GRAPHZ: Meeting place for graffiti art and visual poetry. Much more including numerous essays by Karl Young who is also the site Webmaster." circ. web-www. sub. price: donations accepted; per copy: $10; sample: all back issues are $10 each, limit of 4 per order. Back issues: limited number of sets available, contact publisher. electronic. Reporting time: 2 weeks to 1 month. Simultaneous submissions accepted: yes. Publishes 2% of manuscripts submitted. Payment: none. Copyrighted, reverts to author. Pub's reviews. §Visual poetry, language art publications, art and poetry. No ads.

KALEIDOSCOPE: INTERNATIONAL MAGAZINE OF LITERATURE, FINE ARTS, AND DISABILITY, Darshan C. Perusek, Editor-in-Chief, United Disability Services, 701 S. Main Street, Akron, OH 44311-1019, 330-762-9755; 330-379-3349 (TDD), Fax 330-762-0912. 1979. Poetry, fiction, articles, art, photos, interviews, satire, reviews, parts-of-novels, non-fiction. "We publish fiction, poetry, and visual arts that capture and reflect the experience of disability. Also critical essays and book reviews, photo essays, interviews, personal experience narratives. Established writers/artists featured along with new promising writers. *Kaleidoscope* presents works that challenge stereotypical perceptions of people with disabilities by offering balanced realistic images." circ. 2M. 2/yr. Pub'd 2 issues 1998; expects 2 issues 1999, 2 issues 2000. sub. price: $9 indiv., $14 instit., add $8 Int'l and $5 Canada; per copy: $5 ($7 International, payable in US currency); sample: $4 to cover p/h. Back issues: $4. Discounts: 20%. 64pp; 8½x11; of. Reporting time: acknowledgment of manuscripts within 2 weeks; status of manuscripts within 2 weeks of deadline dates, March 1 and August 1. Simultaneous submissions accepted: yes. Publishes 10% of manuscripts submitted. Payment: contributors receive 2 complimentary copies plus $10-$150. Copyrighted, reverts to author. Pub's reviews: 0 in 1998. §Disability-related short story, poetry, visual art, books. CLMP.

Kaleidoscope Road Publications, Margaret L. Wark, Elizabeth Koerber, 19331 Cherry Creek Road, Grass Valley, CA 95949-9072. 1993. Poetry, cartoons. "Currently publishing a quarterly magazine of poetry. Plan to expand into chapbooks of poetry and lyrics as well as cartoons." avg. press run 100. Expects 1 title 1999, 3 titles 2000. Discounts: negotiable. 40pp; 7x8½; xerox. Payment: negotiable. Does not copyright for author.

Kali Press, Susan Tinkle, Editor; Peter Marritt, Editor, PO Box 2169, Pagosa Springs, CO 81147, 970-264-5200; fax 970-264-5202; e-mail kalipres@rmi.net. 1990. Poetry, fiction, art, photos, interviews, non-fiction. avg. press run 20-25M. Pub'd 2 titles 1998; expects 3 titles 1999, 4 titles 2000. 4 titles listed in the *Small Press Record of Books in Print* (28th Edition, 1999-00). avg. price, paper: $8. Discounts: open for discussion. 100pp; 5½x8½, 6½x11. Reporting time: 45 days. Simultaneous submissions accepted: yes. Publishes 5% of manuscripts submitted. Payment: open for discussion. Copyrights for author. PMA, RMBPA, SPAN, NAPRA, Small Press Book Center, IPN.

KALLIOPE, A Journal of Women's Art, Mary Sue Koeppel, Editor, 3939 Roosevelt Blvd, Florida Community College at Jacksonville, Jacksonville, FL 32205, 904-381-3511. 1979. Poetry, fiction, articles, art, photos, interviews, criticism, reviews, plays. "*Kalliope* devotes itself to women in the arts by publishing their work and providing a forum for their ideas and opinions. Besides introducing the work of many new writers, *Kalliope* has published the work of established writers such as Marge Piercy, Denise Levertov, Susan Fromberg Schaffer, Kathleen Spivak, Enid Shomer, and Ruth Moon Kempher. Most issues include an interview with a prominent woman in the arts. Most recent interviewees with *Kalliope* are Joyce Tenneson, Joy Harjo, Rosemary Daniell, Connie May Fowler, and Eavan Boland. We have featured the photographs of Diane Farris, Joanne

Leonard, Layle Silbert, and Anna Tomczak; the sculpture of Margaret Koscielny and Ella Tulin; the ceramics of Marilyn Taylor and Patti Warashina; and paintings and drawings by a large number of artists including Renee Faure, Marcia Isaacson, Mary Nash, Susan Zukowsky, and Mary Joan Waid. Theme issues have been devoted to women over 60; women under 30; women with disabilities; translations; Florida writers and artists; humor; women portraying men; the spiritual quest; the South as it was, as it is; and women's body images, family and secrets, men speak to women" circ. 1.6M. 3/yr. Pub'd 3 issues 1998; expects 3 issues 1999. sub. price: $15; per copy: $7 recent issues; sample: $4 pre-1987 issues, $7 recent issues. Back issues: $7 recent, $4 pre-1987. Discounts: 40% to bookstores and distributors. 80pp; 8¼×7¼; of. Reporting time: 3-6 months. Simultaneous submissions accepted: no. Publishes 10% of manuscripts submitted. Payment: copies or subscription, when possible, a small payment. Copyrighted, rights revert to author if requested for purposes of republication. Pub's reviews: 10 in 1998. §Books of poetry, novels, short stories. No ads. CLMP.

KARAMU, Olga Abella, Lauren Smith, Department of English, Eastern Illinois Univ., Charleston, IL 61920, 217-581-6297. 1966. Poetry, fiction. "Poems should be no longer than 2 pages; short stories no more than 3500 words. Submit no more than 5 poems or 1 story at a time. We are looking for material that will interest a sophisticated, college-educated audience. We advise aspiring contributors to purchase and examine a sample issue ($7.50, $6) to see what kind of material we like. Specify on your order whether your interest is *poetry* or *fiction*. Some recent contributors, poetry: Virgil Suarez, Robert Manaster, Janet St. John, Barbara Crooker. Fiction: Lorraine Bodger, Gina Ochsner, Michael Michaud, and Meredith Hasemann Cortes." circ. 400. 1/yr. Pub'd 1 issue 1998; expects 1 issue 1999, 1 issue 2000. sub. price: $7.50, $7.50; per copy: $7.50; sample: $7.50. Back issues: $6. Discounts: $50 for 10 copies. 128pp; 5½×8; of. Reporting time: initial screening 6-8 weeks, promising material may be held up to 4 months for final decisions. We do get behind, so please be patient! Simultaneous submissions accepted grudgingly. Publishes 7% of manuscripts submitted. Payment: 1 contributor's copy, 50% discount on additional copies. Copyrighted, reverts to author.

KARAWANE, Laura Winton, 402 S. Cedar Lake Road, Minneapolis, MN 55405, 612-381-1229. 1996. Poetry, fiction, art, criticism, reviews, long-poems, plays, news items. "We serve the Spoken Word community. All contributors must perform their poetry in public. Slams, reading, open mics., etc." circ. 600. 2/yr. Pub'd 2 issues 1998; expects 2 issues 1999, 2 issues 2000. sub. price: $10/4 issues; per copy: $3; sample: $1. Back issues: $2. Discounts: 50% to distributors and stores; ask me about bulk orders. 16-20pp; 8½×11; of. Reporting time: 6 months. Simultaneous submissions accepted: yes. Publishes 50% of manuscripts submitted. Payment: 3 free copies, more upon request. Copyrighted, reverts to author. Pub's reviews: 1 in 1998. §Spoken Word related, performance art, reviews of CD's. Ads: $100/$60/$35 1/4 page/$20 business card.

Kar-Ben Copies, Inc., Judyth Groner, Madeline Wikler, 6800 Tildenwood Lane, Rockville, MD 20852, 301-984-8733; 800-4KARBEN (in USA). 1975. "Juveniles on Jewish themes—fiction, holiday stories and texts, preschool and primary level." avg. press run 10M. Pub'd 6 titles 1998; expects 6 titles 1999, 6 titles 2000. 64 titles listed in the *Small Press Record of Books in Print* (28th Edition, 1999-00). avg. price, cloth: $13.95; paper: $5.95; other: $4.95 board book. Discounts: 40% to trade; 25% on quantity orders to schools; up to 50% to major distributors. 32-48pp; 8×10; of. Reporting time: 4-6 weeks. Simultaneous submissions accepted: yes. Publishes 10% of manuscripts submitted. Payment: royalty based on net sales, split between author/illustrator; sometimes small advance. Copyrights for author. Washington Book Publishers, Association of Children's Booksellers, Association of Jewish Publishers, Women's National Book Association, Society of Children's Book Writers, Jewish Book Council.

KARMA LAPEL, Heath Row, PO Box 441915, Sumerville, MA 02144-0016, e-mail heathr@ais.net. 1992. Fiction, articles, art, cartoons, satire, criticism, reviews, music, letters, non-fiction. "Basically a review zine of fringe print media and the small press, Karma Lapel also offers slice-of-life nonfiction, columns and semi-autobiographical fiction. Analytical essays about various media are also welcome" circ. 1M. Irregular. Pub'd 1 issue 1998; expects 4 issues 1999, 3 issues 2000. sub. price: $10; per copy: $2; sample: $2 or zine trade. Back issues: write if interested. Discounts: write if interested. Pages vary; size varies. Reporting time: sometimes as long as 3 months, mark submission envelopes as such. Payment: copies. Not copyrighted. Pub's reviews: hundreds in 1998. §Absolutely anything, self-published better than not. Ads: $4 per column inch.

Karmichael Press, HC 3, Box 155D, Port St. Joe, FL 32456-9536, 850-648-4488 phone/Fax, KarmikePr@aol.com. 1996. Poetry, fiction, non-fiction. avg. press run 3M. Expects 2 titles 1999, 3 titles 2000. 4 titles listed in the *Small Press Record of Books in Print* (28th Edition, 1999-00). avg. price, paper: $14.95; other: $16.95, audio. Discounts: bookstores 40%. 250pp; 5½×8½. Reporting time: 2 months. Simultaneous submissions accepted: yes. Publishes 5% of manuscripts submitted. Payment: no advance, average 10%. Copyrights for author. PMA.

KASPAHRASTER, Jean Heriot, PO Box 7844, Olympia, WA 98507, e-mail jaheriot@subsitu.com; www.subsitu.com. 1991. Fiction, articles, satire, criticism, reviews, non-fiction. "*KR* ia an anarcho-situ zine of essays, Kulturkampf, and sf. Areas of interest: nomadism, anarchism, post-situationsism, neoism, science fiction, psychogeography, TAZs, etc. In November 1995 it was converted to an electronic publication, available

292

on the World Wide Web. It is no longer available in paper. If you do not have an internet account, ask your local libary or infoshop whether they provide public access to web publications. u'' Irregular. Pub'd 4 issues 1998; expects 4 issues 1999, 4 issues 2000. Discounts: none. Reporting time: 2-3 weeks. Payment: none. Copyrighted, reverts to author. Pub's reviews: 30 (4 books, 5 chapbooks, 21 zines) in 1998. §Anarchist, situationist, marginals milieu. Ads: none.

Katydid Books, Thomas Fitzsimmons, Karen Hargreaves Fitzsimmons, 1 Balsa Road, Santa Fe, NM 87505. 1973. Poetry, criticism, long-poems, non-fiction. "We do not want submissions." avg. press run 1.5M. Pub'd 3 titles 1998; expects 3 titles 1999, 3 titles 2000. 29 titles listed in the *Small Press Record of Books in Print* (28th Edition, 1999-00). avg. price, cloth: $20; paper: $15. Discounts: query distributors: U. Hawaii Press for Asian titles,. 200pp; 5×8, 6×9, 7×9; typeset; of. Payment: varies. Does not copyright for author. Rocky Mtn. Book Publishing Assn., New Mexico Book Assn.

Kauai Press, Lee Williams, 1170 Ozone Drive, Santa Rosa, CA 95407-6438. 1994. Non-fiction. "Kauai Press publishes materials which celebrate the new day dawning on Earth and express the renewal of Spirit being born in the hearts of the human family. We have a special focus of promoting the traditional values of indigenous peoples worldwide. We know that this is a time of global transformation and we intend that the works published by Kauai Press will assist in the recognition of the union of Heaven and Earth." avg. press run 2.5M. Expects 3 titles 1999, 3 titles 2000. 1 title listed in the *Small Press Record of Books in Print* (28th Edition, 1999-00). avg. price, paper: $12.95. Discounts: standard. 130pp; size varies, 7×7. Reporting time: none requested. NAPRA.

Kawabata Press (see also SEPIA), Colin David Webb, Editor, Knill Cross House, Higher Anderton Road, Millbrook, Nr Torpoint, Cornwall, England. 1977. Poetry, fiction, articles. "At present not producing booklets outside *Sepia Magazine*'' avg. press run 100. Pub'd 1 title 1998; expects 1 title 1999. 12 titles listed in the *Small Press Record of Books in Print* (28th Edition, 1999-00). avg. price, paper: 50p; other: $1. 35pp; 6×8½; of. Reporting time: 14 days. Publishes 10% of manuscripts submitted. Copyrights for author.

Keel Publications, PO Box 160155, Austin, TX 78716-0155, 512-327-1280; swimdoc@texas.net. 1980. avg. press run 5M. Pub'd 1 title 1998; expects 1 title 1999, 1 title 2000. 9 titles listed in the *Small Press Record of Books in Print* (28th Edition, 1999-00). avg. price, paper: $16. Discounts: 3-11 books 10%, 12-24 25%, 25-199 40%, 200-499 45%. 110pp; 5½×8½, 8½×11. Copyrights for author. Publishers Marketing Assoc. (PMA).

Kells Media Group, Joseph Eamon Cummins, Po Box 60-DB, Oceanville, NJ 08231, 609-652-0524; fax 609-652-7448. 1993. Non-fiction. "New press. Interested principally in authors who, first, have a special skill or knowledge that is in general and recurring demand, but isn't well understood by the average layperson. And second, authors who understand the learning process and can communicate clearly, interestingly and effectively. Kells Media Group is dedicated to promoting new and 'easy learning' methods and ideas and to de-mystifying topics that, typically, are shrouded in elitism, jargon and self-serving technicalese. We prefer topics that have broad general appeal or specialized topics in which there is broad interest." avg. press run 6M-20M. Pub'd 1 title 1998; expects 3-4 titles 1999, 4+ titles 2000. 4 titles listed in the *Small Press Record of Books in Print* (28th Edition, 1999-00). avg. price, paper: $15. Normal trade discount, special situations considered on individual basis. 125pp; 6×9; of. Reporting time: aim for no longer than 6 weeks. Payment: individually set for each project. Does not copyright for author. PMA.

THE KELSEY REVIEW, G. Robin Schore, Mercer County, Community College, PO Box B, Trenton, NJ 08690, 609-586-4800 ext. 3326; e-mail kelsey.review@mccc.edu. Poetry, fiction, articles, art, cartoons, interviews, satire, criticism, parts-of-novels, long-poems, plays, non-fiction. "2,000 words maximum. Annual contributors limited to people who live or work in Mercer County, New Jersey'' circ. 2M. 1/yr. Pub'd 1 issue 1998; expects 1 issue 1999, 1 issue 2000. sub. price: free. Back issues: free, if available. 84pp; 7×11; of. Reporting time: 30 days. Simultaneous submissions accepted: no. Publishes 10% of manuscripts submitted. Payment: 5 copies of journal. Copyrighted, reverts to author. Pub's reviews: 0 in 1998. §Open. No ads.

Kelsey St. Press, Rena Rosenwasser, Director; Denise Lawson, Patricia Dientsfrey, Marian Chapman, Erin Corrigan, Karen McKevitt, 50 Northgate Avenue, Berkeley, CA 94708-2008, 510-845-2260; FAX 510-548-9185, e-mail kelseyst.@sirius.com; www.kelseyst.com. 1974. Poetry, fiction, art, non-fiction. "Special guidelines for submission." avg. press run 1M. Pub'd 2 titles 1998; expects 3 titles 1999, 3 titles 2000. 30 titles listed in the *Small Press Record of Books in Print* (28th Edition, 1999-00). avg. price, paper: $10; other: signed limited editions, hand-colored by the artist $75. Discounts: 40% to the trade. 48pp; 5½×8½; of, lp. Reporting time: 4 months. Payment: in copies or 10% of the gross price. Copyright retained by author unless otherwise agreed.

KELTIC FRINGE, Maureen Williams, PO Box 270, Greentown, PA 18426-0270, 717-679-2745. 1986. Poetry, fiction, articles, art, interviews, satire, criticism, reviews, music, letters, news items, non-fiction. "*Keltic Fringe* welcomes submissions from Kelts of the six nations: Scotland, Man, Ireland, Wales, Cornwall, Brittany, and from anyone in the world involved in Keltic creativity. We are looking for essays on Keltic matters, memories, mythology, history, literature & the other arts, personalities; work from poets, musicians, storytellers; interviews with Kelts in all fields; features on Keltic happenings; news items from the Keltic community of North America; calligraphy, artwork & illustrations accompanying written pieces or as separate items. Length 100-2,000; 200-1,000 preferred. Recent contributors: Laurel Speer, Gage McKinney, Helen Hancock, Robert Copperman, Alex Keegan, Siannan McKay'' circ. 350. 4/yr. Pub'd 4 issues 1998; expects 4 issues 1999, 4 issues 2000. sub. price: $10; per copy: $3.50; sample: $3.50. Back issues: $2-$3. Discounts: none. 16pp; 8½x11; of. Reporting time: 1 month or sooner. Publishes 25% of manuscripts submitted. Payment: copies. Copyrighted, reverts to author. Pub's reviews: 4 in 1998. §Keltic subjects, work of Kelts. Ads: classified $10 for 25 words/display $15 for 1/4 column.

Kelton Press, Maria B. Orlowoski, PO Box 4236, Jackson, MI 49204, 517-788-8542; 888-453-5880. 1 title listed in the *Small Press Record of Books in Print* (28th Edition, 1999-00).

Ken and Scatter Publications, Sam Abraham, PO Box 434, Woodbridge, NJ 07095, 732-750-2574; fax 732-750-0290. 1993. Non-fiction. "It is a most interesting socio-political treatise about rule, democracy and societal systems" avg. press run 10M. Expects 5 titles 2000. 2 titles listed in the *Small Press Record of Books in Print* (28th Edition, 1999-00). avg. price, cloth: $25. Discounts: 33% bulk, 20% classroom, no returns. 320-352pp; 5½x8½. Reporting time: 3 months. Simultaneous submissions accepted: no. Payment: varies. Copyrights for author.

Kent Information Services, Inc., 155 N. Water Street, Suite 205, Kent, OH 44240, 330-673-1300; Fax 330-673-6310; email@kentis.com; http://www.kentis.com. Fiction, non-fiction. avg. press run 4M. Pub'd 3 titles 1998; expects 4 titles 1999, 5 titles 2000. 5 titles listed in the *Small Press Record of Books in Print* (28th Edition, 1999-00). avg. price, paper: $35. Discounts: trade 40%, textbooks, college bookstores 20%. 300pp; 5x8, 7x9, 7x10. Reporting time: varies. Simultaneous submissions accepted: yes. Publishes 50% of manuscripts submitted. Payment: varies. Copyrights for author. PMA.

Kenyette Productions, Kenyette Adrine-Robinson, 20131 Champ Drive, Euclid, OH 44117-2208, 216-486-0544. 1976. Poetry, art, photos. "Permanent address: 4209 E. 186th Street, Cleveland, OH 44122 (216) 752-4069. Past president, Urban Literary Arts Workshop (ULAW). Member: Verse Writers Guild of Ohio, Poetry Society of America. Board member: Poets' League of Greater Cleveland, Member of the International Black Writers and Artists, Atlanta, GA chapter; Treasurer of the Writers Center of Greater Cleveland 1999-2000.'' avg. press run 750. Expects 1 title 1999, 2 titles 2000. 4 titles listed in the *Small Press Record of Books in Print* (28th Edition, 1999-00). avg. price, cloth: $15; paper: $8; other: none. Discounts: non-profit organizations, bookstores, warehouses, vendors, public schools, artists, retail outlets. 48pp; 5½x8½; of and desktop. Reporting time: 2 months. Simultaneous submissions accepted: yes. Publishes 10% of manuscripts submitted. Payment: negotiable. Copyrights for author. International Black Writers & Artists Inc.

THE KENYON REVIEW, David Lynn, Editor; Sheila Jordan, Book Review Editor; David Baker, Poetry Editor; Nancy Zafris, Fiction Editor, Kenyon College, Gambier, OH 43022, 740-427-5208, Fax 740-427-5417, e-mail kenyonreview@kenyon.edu. 1939. Poetry, fiction, articles, satire, criticism, reviews, parts-of-novels, long-poems, interviews, plays, non-fiction. "Because of the backlog of accepted manuscripts, not accepting new submissions until October 2000. We *strongly* discourage 'blind' submissions from writers who have not read a recent issue of the magazine. Bookstore distributors are Bernard DeBoer, Ingram, Ubiquity. Issue dates are Dec. (Winter), April (Spring), September (Summer/Fall)'' circ. 4M-5M. 3/yr. Pub'd 3 issues 1998; expects 3 issues 1999, 3 issues 2000. sub. price: $25 individuals, $35 libraries; sample: $9 includes postage. Back issues: available on request. Discounts: agency 15%. 200pp; 7x10; of. Reporting time: 2 months. Simultaneous submissions accepted: no. Publishes 3% of manuscripts submitted. Payment: $10 prose, $15 poetry (per printed page), $15 minimum per poem. Copyrighted, reverts to author. Pub's reviews: 14 in 1998. §Literature, criticism. Ads: $330/$205/$530 inside or back cover, 15% discount on ads for agencies and university presses. CLMP.

Keokee Co. Publishing, Inc. (see also FLYFISHER; SANDPOINT MAGAZINE), Chris Bessler, PO Box 722, Sandpoint, ID 83864, 208-263-3573; e-Mail info@keokee.com. 1990. Non-fiction, fiction, articles, art, photos, cartoons, interviews, reviews, news items. "Accept manuscripts. Interested in non-fiction, history, regional, outdoors, recreation guides, fly fishing'' avg. press run 5M. Pub'd 2 titles 1998; expects 3 titles 1999, 4 titles 2000. 6 titles listed in the *Small Press Record of Books in Print* (28th Edition, 1999-00). avg. price, cloth: $24.95; paper: $14.95. Discounts: STOP orders 40% retail 40%, wholesale/jobbers 50%. 224pp; 5½x8½, 6x9; of. Reporting time: 2 months. Simultaneous submissions accepted: yes. Publishes 1% of manuscripts submitted. Payment: depends, negotiable. Copyrights for author. PNBA, PMA.

KEREM: Creative Explorations in Judaism, Gilah Langner, Sara R. Horowitz, 3035 Porter Street, NW, Washington, DC 20008, 202-364-3006; fax 202-364-3806; e-mail srh@udel.edu; www.kerem.com. 1992. Poetry, articles, art, photos, interviews, non-fiction. circ. 2M. 1/yr. Pub'd 1 issue 1998; expects 1 issue 1999, 1 issue 2000. sub. price: $8.50; per copy: $8.50; sample: $8.50. 128pp; 6x9; of. Reporting time: 3-5 months. Simultaneous submissions accepted: yes. Publishes 20% of manuscripts submitted. Payment: none.

294

Copyrighted, reverts to author. Ads: $100/$50.

THE KERF, Ken Letko, 883 W. Washington Boulevard, Crescent City, CA 95531, 707-464-6867. 1985. Poetry. "The editors especially encourage themes related to humanity and/or environmental consciousness, but are open to diverse subjects. Poems: 1-2 pages, no more than 7 pages accepted. Contributors: George Keithley, John Bradley, Philip Dacey, Susan Clayton-Goldner, Meg Files, Ray Gonzalez, and Susan Thomas." circ. 275. 1/yr. Pub'd 1 issue 1998; expects 1 issue 1999, 1 issue 2000. sub. price: $5; per copy: $5; sample: $5. Back issues: $5. Discounts: none. 49pp; 8½x5½; †docutech. Reporting time: 2 months. Simultaneous submissions accepted: no. Publishes 5% of manuscripts submitted. Payment: 1 copy. Copyrighted, rights revert to author after 3 months. Ads: none.

Michael Kesend Publishing, Ltd., Michael Kesend, Publisher, 1025 Fifth Avenue, New York, NY 10028-0134, 212-249-5150. 1979. Fiction, non-fiction. "Travel guidebooks, outdoor guidebooks, sports books" avg. press run 3M-7M. Pub'd 4 titles 1998; expects 6 titles 1999, 6 titles 2000. 23 titles listed in the *Small Press Record of Books in Print* (28th Edition, 1999-00). avg. price, cloth: $21.95; paper: $14.95. Discounts: 40% to retailers, 50% to wholesalers. 240pp; 6x9; of. Reporting time: 6 weeks to 2 months. Copyrights for author. PMA.

KESTREL: A Journal of Literature and Art, Mary Dillow Stewart, John King, John Huppenthaler, Fairmont State College, Fairmont, WV 26554, 304-367-4815; 304-3674860; e-mail kestrel@mail.fscwv.edu. 1993. Poetry, fiction, art, photos, interviews, parts-of-novels, long-poems, plays, non-fiction. "We are interested in presenting a substantial selection of a contributor's work—3-7 poems; 6-8 pages of artwork; a selection from a novel, so long as it has thematic and structural integrity. We also ask that contributors write a brief preface to their work. What we hope to establish is a forum in which contributors may address issues, experiences, and insights that may draw artist and audience closer together." circ. 600. 2/yr. Expects 2 issues 1999, 2 issues 2000. sub. price: $10; per copy: $6; sample: $6. Back issues: $4. 100pp; 6x9; of. Reporting time: 3-4 months. Simultaneous submissions accepted: no. Payment: 5 copies of issue. Copyrighted, reverts to author. Ads: none.

Kettering Foundation (see also KETTERING REVIEW), Robert Kingston, Editor; Noelle McAfee, Associate Editor, 200 Commons Road, Dayton, OH 45459-2799, 937-434-7300. 1983. Articles. avg. press run 8M. Pub'd 2 titles 1998; expects 2 titles 1999, 3 titles 2000. 3 titles listed in the *Small Press Record of Books in Print* (28th Edition, 1999-00). avg. price, paper: $5. 64pp; 7x10; of. Reporting time: 2 months. Copyrights for author.

KETTERING REVIEW, Kettering Foundation, Robert J. Kingston, Editor-in-Chief, 200 Commons Road, Dayton, OH 45459-2799, 937-434-7300. 1983. "Designed for the intelligent lay public with special interest in governing, educating, science, international affairs or interdisciplinary fields. Non-fiction only. Requirements: Manuscripts of 1.5-3M words from those working in the fields of governing, educating or science who can address ideas of national importance in an interdisciplinary and popular readable fashion. Read a sample before submitting. Articles must be exceptionally well-written; issues usually organized around a theme. Uses 5-6 articles per issue. No footnotes. Mss. must be accompanied by SASE. No responsibility is assumed for the return of unsolicited manuscripts." circ. 8M. 2/yr. Pub'd 2 issues 1998; expects 2 issues 1999, 3 issues 2000. price per copy: $5; sample: free. 64pp; 7x10; of. Payment: copies. Copyrighted, reverts to author.

Kettle of Fish Press, PO Box 364, Exeter, NH 03833. 2 titles listed in the *Small Press Record of Books in Print* (28th Edition, 1999-00).

Key Publications, PO Box 6375, Woodland Hills, CA 91365, 818-224-4344. 1990. Non-fiction. "First book: *Parenting Your Aging Parents - How to Garantee and Protect Their Quality of Life, and Yours!*." avg. press run as needed. Expects 1 title 1999, 1 title 2000. 2 titles listed in the *Small Press Record of Books in Print* (28th Edition, 1999-00). avg. price, cloth: $21.95; paper: none. Discounts: negotiable. 300pp; 6x9; †of, desktop. Reporting time: 4 weeks with SASE. Simultaneous submissions accepted: no. Publishes 1% of manuscripts submitted. Payment: negotiable. Copyrights for author. PMA, ABA.

KEY SATCH(EL), Quale Press, Gian Lombardo, PO Box 363, Haydenville, MA 01039, 413-268-3632; E-mail keysatch@quale.com. 1997. Poetry, art, photos, collages. "Editorial focus is primarily on prose poetry. In 2000 mag shifts to publishing chapbook collections of prose poetry on a solicited basis only." circ. 200. 4/yr. Pub'd 4 issues 1998; expects 4 issues 1999, 4 issues 2000. sub. price: $16; per copy: $5; sample: $5. Back issues: $5. Discounts: 20% subscription agency on more than 10 copies. 24pp; 5½x8½; photocopy. Reporting time: 1-4 weeks. Accepts simultaneous submissions, with note that it is such. Publishes unsolicited 25% of manuscripts submitted. Payment: author copies. Copyrighted, reverts to author.

Keyboard Workshop, Duane Shinn, PO Box 700, Medford, OR 97501, 664-2317. 1966. Music. "Most publications are house-produced. Very little free lance material accepted" avg. press run 5M-25M. Expects 12 titles 1999. avg. price, paper: $10. Discounts: 50% basic; single copy 25%-over gross 67%. 40pp; 8½x11; of. Reporting time: 4 weeks. Payment: flat rate. Copyrights for author.

KICK IT OVER, Kick It Over Collective, PO Box 5811, Station A, Toronto, Ontario M5W 1P2, Canada. 1981. Poetry, fiction, articles, art, photos, cartoons, interviews, reviews, letters, collages, news items, non-fiction. "Articles and news shorts dealing with social change, ecology, feminism and related issues from anarchist perspective. Submissions welcome; send SASE for return if desired (if in USA, send a few coins instead of stamping the envelope)." circ. 1.5M. 4/yr. Pub'd 2 issues 1998; expects 3 issues 1999, 4 issues 2000. sub. price: $14; per copy: $3.50; sample: $3.50. Back issues: $1/copy + postage ($1 first copy, 50¢ each additional). Discounts: we trade selectively, 40% off cover for orders of more than 5 copies or to bookstore. Very lenient to our distributors in various cities. 68pp; 8½×10½; web. Reporting time: depends how bad/good it is—decisions by concensus take time; say 2 months from receipt. Simultaneous submissions accepted, but please let us know. Payment: 3 copies. Not copyrighted. Pub's reviews: 6 in 1998. §Radical feminism, anarchism, peace, alternative institutions and 'counter-culture', anti-racism, and ecology.

KID'S WORLD, Morgan Kopaska-Merkel, Editor, 1300 Kicker Road, Tuscaloosa, AL 35404, 205-553-2284. 1993. Poetry, fiction, art, cartoons, non-fiction. "Limited to contributions by people under 18 years old." circ. 100. 4/yr. Pub'd 4 issues 1998; expects 4 issues 1999, 4 issues 2000. sub. price: $5; per copy: $2; sample: $2. Back issues: $2. 16pp; 5½×8½; photocopy. Reporting time: 1-3 months. Simultaneous submissions accepted: no. Publishes 60% of manuscripts submitted. Payment: 1 copy per accepted piece. Not copyrighted. Ads: none.

KIDSCIENCE, Linda Broderson, Dr. Sally Goldberg, 14930 130th Street North, Stillwater, MN 55082-8504. 1987. Non-fiction. "Our content is science activities for preschool and elementary schools. The magazine is for elementary teachers." circ. 400. 4/yr. Pub'd 3 issues 1998; expects 4 issues 1999, 4 issues 2000. sub. price: $10; per copy: $2; sample: $2. Back issues: $2. Discounts: institutional sub with copying privileges $50/yr. 12pp; 8½×11; of. Reporting time: varies. Payment: free 1 year subscription to selected contributors. Copyrighted, reverts to author. §Science, especially elementary science. none.

Kimm Publishing, Inc., Lora Polack Oberle, PO Box 32927, Fridley, MN 55432-0927. 1995. Non-fiction. avg. press run varies. Pub'd 1 title 1998. 1 title listed in the *Small Press Record of Books in Print* (28th Edition, 1999-00). Reporting time: 1-2 months. Simultaneous submissions accepted: yes. Payment: varies. Copyrights for author. PMA, Midwest Independent Publishers Assn., MidAmerica Publishers Assn., SPAN.

Kindness Publications, Inc., 1859 N. Pine Island Road, Ste. 135, Plantation, FL 33322, 305-423-9323. 1993. Non-fiction. avg. press run 10M. Expects 3 titles 1999, 3 titles 2000. 1 title listed in the *Small Press Record of Books in Print* (28th Edition, 1999-00). avg. price, cloth: $18.95. Discounts: yes. 32pp; 8½×11; of. Copyrights for author. PMA, NABE.

Kingfisher Books, Erica S. Olsen, PO Box 4628, Helena, MT 59604, 800-879-4576, 406-442-2168; davidmdelo@prodigy.net. 1998. "Will not be open to submissions until 2005." avg. press run 2.5M. Pub'd 2 titles 1998; expects 1 title 1999, 2 titles 2000. 2 titles listed in the *Small Press Record of Books in Print* (28th Edition, 1999-00). Discounts: 30% 1 book, 40% 2+. 8½×5½, 6×9. PNBA, Mountains and Plains Booksellers.

Kings Estate Press, Ruth Moon Kempher, 870 Kings Estate Road, St. Augustine, FL 32086, 800-249-7485. 1993. Poetry, fiction, art, long-poems. "Query first—we are fully scheduled for the next two years. Have published Wayne Hogan, Michael Hathaway, Joan Payne Kincaid, John Elsberg, among others; two anthologies. Most, but not all, of our books were solicited by the editor." avg. press run 200-300. Pub'd 3 titles 1998; expects 5 titles 1999, 4 titles 2000. 2 titles listed in the *Small Press Record of Books in Print* (28th Edition, 1999-00). avg. price, paper: $13. Discounts: negotiated. 50-80pp; 7×8½; of. Reporting time: immediately - 3 months. Simultaneous submissions accepted: yes. Publishes 1% of manuscripts submitted. Payment: negotiated. Copyrights for author.

●**Kingston Press**, PO Box 86, West Kingston, RI 02892-0086, 401-789-6199; Fax 401-789-5780. 1 title listed in the *Small Press Record of Books in Print* (28th Edition, 1999-00).

KITE LINES, Aeolus Press, Inc., Valerie Govig, Publisher & Editor, PO Box 466, Randallstown, MD 21133-0466, 410-922-1212; fax 410-922-4262. 1977. Articles, art, photos, interviews, reviews, letters, news items. "All material is about *kites*. Do rights revert: rights limited to reprint in magazine; all other rights revert to author." circ. 13M. 4/yr. Expects 4 issues 1999. sub. price: $16; per copy: $4.50 + $1 shipping; sample: $4.50 + $1 shipping. Back issues: $4.50 each, 4 or more copies free shipping. Discounts: to kite shops, 10 copies minimum, $2.55 + shipping each for resale. 72pp; 8⅜×10⅞; of, web. Reporting time: 2 weeks to 3 months (varies with workload). May consider simultaneous submissions, but must be informed. Publishes about 15% of manuscripts submitted. Payment: pay varies + copies. Copyrighted, reverts to author. Pub's reviews: 11 in 1998. §Kites. Ads: $870/$495/$1 ($10 minimum). PMA.

THE KITHARA, Roderick Saxey, M.D., PO Box 1941, Lake Oswego, OR 97035, 503-251-4809. 1993. Poetry, articles, satire, criticism, reviews, news items, non-fiction. "Conservative commentary on culture, politics, and the modern condition, with a classical slant" circ. 120. 4/yr. Pub'd 4 issues 1998; expects 4 issues 1999, 4 issues 2000. sub. price: $7; per copy: $2; sample: $2. 8pp; 8½×11; of. Reporting time: 6-8 weeks.

296

Publishes 50% of manuscripts submitted. Payment: copies and subscription. Copyrighted, does not revert to author. Pub's reviews: 2 in 1998. §Politics, philosophy, history. PMA.

Kiva Publishing, Inc., Stephen W. Hill, Editor, 21731 East Buckskin Drive, Walnut, CA 91789, 909-595-6833; fax 909-860-9595. 1992. Poetry, fiction, art, non-fiction. "Strong emphasis on Southwest Native American painting." avg. press run 7.5M. Pub'd 2 titles 1998; expects 7 titles 1999, 8 titles 2000. 12 titles listed in the *Small Press Record of Books in Print* (28th Edition, 1999-00). avg. price, cloth: $24.95; paper: $14.95. Discounts: 1-4 30%, 5-25 40-45%, 25+ call for rates. 125pp; size varies; webb press. Reporting time: 3 months max. Simultaneous submissions accepted: yes. Payment: to be arranged. Copyrights for author. Rocky Mountain Publishers Assn., New Mexico Publishers Assn., SPAN, Mountains and Plains Booksellers Association, PMA.

Kivaki Press, Fred A. Gray, PO Box 1053, Skyland, NC 28776-1053, 704-684-1988; E-mail kivaki@cheta.net; Website www.kivaki.com. 1992. Non-fiction. "Kivaki Press is devoted to publishing books that cover topics within three interwoven themes: restoring our damaged ecosystems and wilderness areas; renewing our communities' economic and cultural vitality; and healing our bodies naturally and sustainably. We seek compelling narratives, essays, and demonstrations of successes in these areas of ecosystem, community, and body revitalization. We are a small press, which means that our authors realize higher quality relationships with Kivaki and to their published works. Recent works include: *Look to the Mountain: An Ecology of Indigenous Education,* by Gregory Cajete; *Seasons of Change: Growing Through Pregnancy and Birth,* by Suzanne Arms; and *Restoration Forestry,* by Michael Pilarski." avg. press run 25M. Pub'd 1 title 1998; expects 2 titles 1999, 3 titles 2000. Discounts: distributors 45%; resellers, libraries 1-3 (or S.T.O.P.) 25%, 4-11 40%, 12-23 42%, 24+ 45%. of. Reporting time: 4-8 weeks. Payment: 8-12% of cover price on net copies sold, depending on author's willingness to help market titles, payable quarterly. Copyrights for author. Rocky Mountain Book Publishers Assoc.; Publisher's Marketing Assoc.

KLIATT, Claire Rosser, Paula Rohrlick, Jean Palmer, 33 Bay State Road, Wellesley, MA 02481, 781-237-7577 phone/fax; kliatt@aol.com. 1967. Articles, reviews. "*Kliatt* publishes reviews of paperback books and hardcover young adult fiction, audiobooks, and educational software recommended for libraries and classrooms serving young adults. Each issue includes an article on a topic relevant to young adult librarians and teachers, and the last issue of the year (November) includes an index." circ. 2.3M. 6/yr. Pub'd 6 issues 1998; expects 6 issues 1999, 6 issues 2000. sub. price: $39 (add $2 for Canada, in U.S. funds); per copy: $6; sample: free. Back issues: none. Discounts: $2.50 agency discount; 2 years $68. 64pp; 8½×11. Payment: none. Copyrighted, does not revert to author. Pub's reviews: 1200+ in 1998. §New paperbacks and hardcover fiction for young adults, audiobooks, educational software. Ads: $250/$190/other sizes available; discounts for 3- and 6-time advertisers.

KMJ Educational Programs, Mary Johnson, 25 Wildwood Avenue, Providence, RI 02907, 401-781-7964; email keithbooks@aol.com. 1996. Non-fiction. "We publish how-to books for variety artists: jugglers, clowns, magicians, etc. Our first three books and two videos were written in house, but we plan to begin publishing others' work in the next year or so." avg. press run 1M. Pub'd 3 titles 1998; expects 1 title 1999, 5 titles 2000. 3 titles listed in the *Small Press Record of Books in Print* (28th Edition, 1999-00). avg. price, paper: $20; other: $25 video. Discounts: 1-0%, 2-4-20%, 4-99-40%, 100+-50%. 200pp; 5½×8½; †of. Reporting time: 90 days. Simultaneous submissions accepted: yes. Copyrights for author.

KMT, A Modern Journal of Ancient Egypt, KMT Communications, Dennis Forbes, 1531 Golden Gate Avenue, San Francisco, CA 94115, 415-922-7263 (phone/fax). 1990. Articles, art, photos, interviews, reviews, collages. "Focus is *Ancient Egypt*: history, art, archaeology and culture" circ. 9M. 4/yr. Pub'd 4 issues 1998; expects 4 issues 1999, 4 issues 2000. sub. price: $32; per copy: $8; sample: $9.50 (incl. p/h). Back issues: same. Discounts: distributor 40%-50%. 88pp; 8⅛×10⅝; of. Reporting time: 60 days. Payment: $50-$400. Copyrighted, reverts to author. Pub's reviews: 16-20 in 1998. §History, culture, archaeology and art of Egypt. Ads: $800,full/$600 2/3 p./$470 1/4 p./$360 1/3 p./$200 1/6 p. BAPA.

KMT Communications (see also KMT, A Modern Journal of Ancient Egypt), Dennis Forbes, PO Box 1475, Sebastopol, CA 95473-1475, 415-922-7263. 1990. Non-fiction. "Subject: *Ancient Egypt*, history, art, archaeology and culture of" avg. press run 8M. Discounts: 40% to distributors. 120pp; 8½×11; of. Reporting time: 60 days. Payment: by agreement. Copyrights for author. BAPA.

Knightraven Books, Wayne A. Reinagel, PO Box 100, Collinsville, IL 62234, 314-725-1111, Fax 618-345-7436. 1980. Poetry, art, cartoons, long-poems. avg. press run 5M. Pub'd 1 title 1998; expects 2 titles 1999, 3 titles 2000. 2 titles listed in the *Small Press Record of Books in Print* (28th Edition, 1999-00). avg. price, paper: $12.95. Discounts: negotiable. 256pp; 5½×8½; of. Reporting time: 3 months. Payment: negotiable. Does not copyright for author.

Allen A. Knoll Publishers, Abby Schott, 200 W. Victoria Street, 2nd Floor, Santa Barbara, CA 93101-3627, 805-564-3377, Fax 805-966-6657, e-mail aaknoll@aol.com. 1990. Fiction, non-fiction, photos. "Not looking for new submissions at this time." avg. press run 3-10M. Pub'd 5 titles 1998; expects 6 titles 1999, 6 titles 2000. 22 titles listed in the *Small Press Record of Books in Print* (28th Edition, 1999-00). avg. price, cloth: $19.95. Discounts: standard. 300pp; 5½x8½; of. Payment: percentage different for each book. Copyrights for author. PMA, ABA.

Kodiak Media Group, Grabenhorst Rhonda, Contact Person, PO Box 1029-DB, Wilsonville, OR 97070, FAX 503-625-4087. 1989. Non-fiction. "Specializing in deafness, disability, deaf education, deaf culture, parents of deaf children, ASL and sign language" avg. press run varies. Pub'd 1 title 1998; expects 2 titles 1999. 3 titles listed in the *Small Press Record of Books in Print* (28th Edition, 1999-00). avg. price, paper: $18.95-21.95. Discounts: 1-3 0%, 4+ 30%, 10 + 40% (non returnable) FOB Wilsonville, OR. 112pp; 5½x8½; of. Reporting time: varies. Payment: negotiable. Copyrights are negotiable. SPAN.

Kodomo Press, Susan Mau Larson, Daniel L. Larson, 15239 63RD Street N, Oak Park Heights, MN 55082-6871, 612-439-6383. 1994. Fiction, art. "A children's publisher dedicated to bringing awareness and understanding of the world's cultures and envirnoment to children of elementary school age. All books are picture books. Prefer mss. with a folk-tale flavor from a variety of cultures. Also looking for freelance illustrators" avg. press run 5M. Expects 2 titles 2000. 1 title listed in the *Small Press Record of Books in Print* (28th Edition, 1999-00). avg. price, cloth: $16. 32pp; 9x11. Reporting time: 1-2 months. Payment: pay royalty, no advance. Copyrights for author. MIPA, SCBWI.

KOJA, Mikhail Magazinnik, Editor; Igor Satanovsky, Editor, 7314 21 Avenue #6E, Brooklyn, NY 11204, email mikekoja@aol.com. 1996. Poetry, fiction, art, collages, plays, concrete art. "This is the magazine of experimental writing/art exploring Russian/American avant crossroads. Some contributers are: R. Kostelanetz, Eileen Myles, William James Austin, Spencer Selby, Raymond Federman, Bruce Andrews. Unsolicited submissions should be accompanied by $7 for a sample copy." circ. 200. 1-2/yr. Pub'd 1 issue 1998; expects 1 issue 1999, 2 issues 2000. sub. price: not available; per copy: $7; sample: $7. 64pp; 5½x8½, 8½x11; of, Xerox. Reporting time: 1-3 months, sometimes faster. Simultaneous submissions accepted: no. Publishes a variable % of manuscripts submitted. Payment: single copy. Copyrighted, reverts to author. Ads: $60/$40.

●**KOMIC FANTASIES,** Robert Dante, David Busch, 901 W. Victoria, Unit G, Compton, CA 90220, 310-631-1600; www.bondage.org. 1979. Fiction, articles, art, cartoons, interviews, reviews, news items, non-fiction. "Full page illustrations, complete comic stories" circ. 5M. 4/yr. Pub'd 4 issues 1998; expects 4 issues 1999, 4 issues 2000. sub. price: $22; per copy: $6.95; sample: $10. 44pp; 7¾x10¾; web. Reporting time: 1 month. Simultaneous submissions accepted: no. Publishes 25% of manuscripts submitted. Payment: $25-$50. Copyrighted, does not revert to author. Pub's reviews. §Sexuality, BDSM. Ads: $230/$125/$75 1/4 page/$45 business card.

Konocti Books, Noel Peattie, 23311 County Road 88, Winters, CA 95694. 1973. Poetry. "We have done six poetry books and five broadsides. Broadsides now appear under the imprint of Cannonade Press, using a 6 X 10 Kelsey. Query before sending!" avg. press run 300. Pub'd 2 titles 1998; expects 1 title 1999. 6 titles listed in the *Small Press Record of Books in Print* (28th Edition, 1999-00). avg. price, paper: $6; other: broadsides are free. Discounts: 40% booksellers. 40pp; lp. Reporting time: 3 weeks. Payment: author's copies only. Copyrights for author. CLMP.

KOOMA, Ismo Raty, Huvilate 4A2, 96300 Rovaniemi, Finland. 1994. Fiction, cartoons. "*Kooma* is comix magazine, specializing in the 'dark side of man'" Pub'd 1 issue 1998; expects 2-3 issues 1999, 3-4 issues 2000. sample price: $4. of. Payment: cash. Not copyrighted.

THE KOSCIUSZKO PORTFOLIO, Paula Anne, Sharkey Lemire, 405 Madison Avenue, Albany, NY 12210. Poetry, fiction, articles, art, photos, reviews, letters, non-fiction. "I'm looking for anything on Thaddeus Kosciuszko - or related subjects - this can be essays, fiction, poetry, comments, quotes, and collectibles." circ. varies. 4/yr. Expects 4 issues 1999, 4 issues 2000. sub. price: $20; per copy: $5; sample: $5. Discounts: inquire. Pages vary; 8½x11. Reporting time: asap. Payment: copies for now. Not copyrighted. Pub's reviews. §The American Revolution, Poland, Kosciuszko. Ads: inquire.

Kosmos, Kosrof Chantikian, 20 Millard Road, Larkspur, CA 94939. 1974. Poetry. "We have established a *Modern Poets in Translation Series* to introduce poets of other parts of this planet to the reading public in the United States. We are interested in publishing translations of contemporary works by poets from outside of the United States, as well as new interpretations of significant poetic works of the past. A letter of inquiry (along with a SASE) giving an outline of your proposed project should be sent to the editor *before* submission of a manuscript." avg. press run 1M. 7 titles listed in the *Small Press Record of Books in Print* (28th Edition, 1999-00). avg. price, cloth: $23; paper: $15. Discounts: 20% (1-4 copies); 40% (5+). 88-256pp; 6x9; of. Reporting time: 7 weeks. Simultaneous submissions accepted: no. Payment: arranged with author. Copyrights for author.

Kozmik Press, David Stuart Ryan, 134 Elsenham Street, London SW18 5NP, United Kingdom,

44-81-874-8218. 1975. Poetry, fiction. "Would like synopsis of any work before consideration. U.S. book orders to: Seven Hills Distributors, 49 Central Avenue, Cincinnati, OH 45202." avg. press run 1M. Pub'd 2 titles 1998; expects 2 titles 1999, 3 titles 2000. 10 titles listed in the *Small Press Record of Books in Print* (28th Edition, 1999-00). avg. price, cloth: $14; paper: $8. Discounts: 40% retail, 50% wholesale. 232pp. Payment: only after sales. Copyrights for author. ALP, IPG.

H J Kramer, PO Box 1082, Tiburon, CA 94920. 1983. Fiction, non-fiction. "Not accepting unsolicited submissions" avg. press run 10M-50M. Pub'd 5 titles 1998; expects 5 titles 1999, 5 titles 2000. 53 titles listed in the *Small Press Record of Books in Print* (28th Edition, 1999-00). avg. price, cloth: $16; paper: $12.95. Pages vary; 5½×8½, 6×9, 7½×9½; of. Reporting time: 60 days. Publishes .01% of manuscripts submitted. Payment: usual. Copyrights for author.

KRAX, Andy Robson, 63 Dixon Lane, Leeds, Yorkshire LS12 4RR, England. 1971. Poetry, fiction, articles, art, photos, cartoons, interviews. "Prefer whimsical and amusing work by both writers and artists." 2/yr. Pub'd 1 issue 1998; expects 2 issues 1999, 2 issues 2000. 7 titles listed in the *Small Press Record of Books in Print* (28th Edition, 1999-00). sub. price: £7($14); per copy: £3.50 ($7) incl. postage; sample: $1. Back issues: on request. 64pp; size A5; of. Reporting time: 6-8 weeks. Publishes .8% of manuscripts submitted. Payment: cover design only £10 ($20). Copyrighted, reverts to author.

Kumarian Press, Inc., Sondhi Krishna, Publisher-President; Briana Rosen, Director, Marketing and Sales; Linda Beyus, Acquistions Editor, 14 Oakwood Avenue, West Hartford, CT 06119-2127, 860-233-5895; FAX 860-233-6072; ordering 1-800-289-2667; e-Mail KPBook@aol.com. 1977. Non-fiction. "Please do not send a complete manuscript. Call and ask for a free copy of our writer's guidelines. The guidelines show you how to submit your book proposal for possible publication" avg. press run 1.5M-3M. Pub'd 10 titles 1998; expects 12 titles 1999, 12 titles 2000. 44 titles listed in the *Small Press Record of Books in Print* (28th Edition, 1999-00). avg. price, cloth: $45; paper: $20. Discounts: short/bookstores 10% on 1-2 mixed titles STOP orders, 15% on 3-4, 20% on 5+; wholesale and jobber 11+-30%. 224pp; 6×9, 8½×11, 5½×8½; of. Reporting time: 30-60 days. Simultaneous submissions accepted: yes. Payment: based on net, biannual. Copyrights for author in some instances. PMA.

KUMQUAT MERINGUE, Christian Nelson, PO Box 736, Pine Island, MN 55963-0736, e-mail moodyriver@aol.com; Website Http://www.geostar.com/kumquatcastle. 1990. Poetry, fiction, art, photos, satire, reviews. "Recent contributors: Lynne Douglass, Mark Weber, Ianthe Brautigan and Lyn Lifshin. Mostly use short poetry, some short prose. Looking for writings that 'remind' us of the same feeling we get from reading Richard Brautigan. Also like to read things 'about' Richard Brautigan." circ. 600. 1-2/yr. Expects 2 issues 1999, 2 issues 2000. sub. price: $10; per copy: $5; sample: $5. Back issues: usually sold to collectors at high prices. 40pp; 5½×8½ (digest size); highest quality Xerox. Reporting time: 30-60 days. Simultaneous submissions accepted, but let us know. Publishes 1% of manuscripts submitted. Payment: 1 copy for each issue they appear in. Copyrighted, reverts to author.

KUUMBA, BLK Publishing Company, Mark Haile, PO Box 83912, Los Angeles, CA 90083, 310-410-0808, fax 310-410-9250, e-mail newsroom@blk.com. 1991. Poetry, long-poems. "Poetry journal for black lesbians and gay men." circ. 1M. 2/yr. Expects 2 issues 1999, 2 issues 2000. sub. price: $7.50; per copy: $4.50; sample: $5.50. Back issues: $5.50. 48pp; 8⅛×10⅞; of. Reporting time: 4 weeks. Simultaneous submissions accepted: yes. Publishes 30% of manuscripts submitted. Payment: none. Copyrighted, rights reverting to author varies. Pub's reviews: 2 in 1998. §Black lesbian and gay community. Ads: $260.

L

L D A Publishers, 42-36 209 Street, Bayside, NY 11361, 718-224-9484; Fax: 718-224-9487; 888-388-9887. 1974. Non-fiction. avg. press run 1M. Pub'd 5 titles 1998; expects 6 titles 1999, 9 titles 2000. 5 titles listed in the *Small Press Record of Books in Print* (28th Edition, 1999-00). avg. price, paper: $89.95. Discounts: 10% over 24 copies. 300pp; 8½×11; of. Copyrights for author. LDA.

La Alameda Press, J.B. Bryan, 9636 Guadalupe Trail NW, Albuquerque, NM 87114. 1991. Poetry, fiction, non-fiction. "We are a small press with an emphasis on literature: poetry, fiction, and creative non-fiction. Kate Horsley won the "1996 Western States Book Award for Fiction" for *A Killing in New Town,* which is now in its second printing. Several other titles are also in further editions. We are distributed by the University of New Mexico Press. We do not accept unsolicited manuscripts becuase of our committment to regional writers and kindred spirits we know and work with. This simply happens to be our mission." avg. press run 1M. Pub'd 6 titles 1998; expects 6 titles 1999. 26 titles listed in the *Small Press Record of Books in Print* (28th Edition,

1999-00). avg. price, paper: $11-$14. Discounts: 40% bookstores, 55% distributors, 10% libraries or schools. 100-300pp; size varies; of. Simultaneous submissions accepted: no. Publishes 0% of manuscripts submitted. Payment: in books (10% of print run). Copyrights for author. New Mexico Book Assoc., Mountains and Plains Booksellers Assn.

●**La Casa Press**, PO Box 3297-RB, Casa Grande, AZ 85222, 1-877-8LA-CASA; Fax 520-723-9002; lacasapress@hotmail.com. Expects 4 titles 1999, 4 titles 2000. 1 title listed in the *Small Press Record of Books in Print* (28th Edition, 1999-00). avg. price, paper: $15.95. 300pp; 6×9; of. Reporting time: 12 weeks. Simultaneous submissions accepted: yes. Publishes 5% of manuscripts submitted. Payment: variable. Copyrights for author.

La Jolla Poets Press, Kathleen Iddings, PO Box 8638, La Jolla, CA 92038, 619-457-1399. 1985. Poetry. "Carolyn Kizer, Pulitzer, 1985, says of Editor/Publisher Kathleen Iddings: '(She) is a person of exceptional talent...cares deeply about poetry and poets...has published a valuable anthology concerning contemporary social issues...and books by promising poets. She comes with my highest recommendation.' La Jolla Poet's Press and its affiliate San Diego Poet's Press have published 35 individual poet's collections and five poetry anthologies since 1981. Both are non-profit; donations are deductible. The American Book Series was founded in 1989 by San Diego Poet's Press and the National Poetry Book Series in 1994 by La Jolla Poet's Press. Contest winners' manuscripts are published and authors awarded $500. Samples of winning poet's books are available for $10 (postage paid by press). Recent winners include: Melissa Morphew's *The Garden Where All Loves End*, and Kevin Pilkington's *Spare Change*. Please watch *The Small Press Review* and other poetry magazines for future contest announcements." avg. press run 500. Pub'd 2 titles 1998. 10 titles listed in the *Small Press Record of Books in Print* (28th Edition, 1999-00). avg. price, cloth: $18; paper: $10. Discounts: 40% for 6 or more. 75-100pp; 5½×8½. Reporting time: 2 months. Simultaneous submissions accepted: yes. Payment: usually books; contest winners get $500. Copyrights for author.

●**LA PERIPHERIE**, Ken Schroeder, Apartado 240, Portalegre, 7300, Portugal. 1998. Poetry, fiction, art, cartoons, satire, parts-of-novels, long-poems, collages, plays. "A wretched little multi-lingual zine for semi-brilliant stray dog heroes wandering the Franco-Iberian plenitudes. 3000 word limit, more or less." circ. 50-100. 4/yr. Pub'd 1 issue 1998; expects 4 issues 1999, 4 issues 2000. sub. price: $8; per copy: $2. 30pp; †xerox. Reporting time: fast. Simultaneous submissions accepted: yes. Publishes 25% of manuscripts submitted. Payment: copies. Not copyrighted.

LA RAZA LAW JOURNAL, University of California Press, Boalt Hall Students of the Univ. of California, University of California Press, 2120 Berkeley Way, Berkeley, CA 94720, 510-643-7154. 1983. "Editorial address: 585 Simon Hall, University of California, Berkeley, CA 94720. Copyrighted by the *La Raza Law Journal*." circ. 250. 2/yr. Pub'd 1 issue 1998; expects 1 issue 1999, 1 issue 2000. sub. price: $32 (+ $4 foreign postage); per copy: $17; sample: free. Back issues: $17. Discounts: foreign subs. agent 10%, one-time orders 10+ 30%, standing orders (bookstores) 1-99 40%, 100+ 50%. of. Ads: $275/$200.

Labor Arts Books, Emanuel Fried, 1064 Amherst St., Buffalo, NY 14216, 716-873-4131. 1975. Fiction, plays. "For the moment not seeking submissions. Still working on distribution of present publications: *The Dodo Bird, Drop Hammer, Meshugah and Other Stories, Elegy for Stanley Gurski, Big Ben Hood, The Un-American*." avg. press run 5M. Expects 1 title 1999. 6 titles listed in the *Small Press Record of Books in Print* (28th Edition, 1999-00). avg. price, paper: $2.50-$14.95. Discounts: write for information. 32-520pp; size varies; lp. Payment: individual arrangement. Copyrights for author.

LABOUR & TRADE UNION REVIEW, Dick Barry, 2 Newington Green Mansions, Green Lanes London N16 9BT, England, 0171-354-4902. 1987. Articles, photos, interviews, reviews, letters, news items. "The magazine provides a regular commentary on current developments within the British Labour Party and Trade Union Movement; analysis of major issues and developments in contemporary politics in the United Kingdom and abroad; discussion of policy issues from the standpoint of democratic socialism, interviews with leading labour politicians and trade unionists, plus articles on labour and socialist history. Items vary in length; major features up to 4,000 words. Main contributors: Hugh Roberts, Brendan Clifford, George Joffe, Jack Jones. Recent interviews: John Prescott, MP; Jimmy Knapp (General Secretary, RMT); Barbara Castle; Jack Jones (ex-General Secretary, TGWU); Bill Morris (General Secretary-elect, TGWU)." circ. 2M. 6/yr. Pub'd 6 issues 1998; expects 6 issues 1999, 6 issues 2000. sub. price: £11 UK, £13 Europe, £15 rest of world; multi-user rates available on application; per copy: £1.50; sample: £1. Back issues: at current subscription rates. Discounts: bulk order rates by negotiation; 15% to subscription services; 33⅓% to retailers. 24pp; 8.2×11.7 (A5); of. Reporting time: 1 month. Payment: none. Copyrighted, reverts to author. Pub's reviews: 10 in 1998. §Politics, current affairs, political history, trade unions, industrial relations. Ads: £100/£60.

LABOUR/LE TRAVAIL, Canadian Committee on Labour History, Bryan D. Palmer, History/CCLH, FM 2005, Memorial University, St. John's, NF A1C 5S2, Canada, 709-737-2144. 1976. Articles, reviews, non-fiction. "Articles 20-60 pages, reviews 1000 words. Mark Leier, History, Simon Fraser University." circ.

1M. 2/yr. Pub'd 2 issues 1998; expects 2 issues 1999, 2 issues 2000. sub. price: $25CDN, $30 US; per copy: $20 CDN, $20 US; sample: free. Back issues: Complete set $780 (42 issues, new subscribers $510). Discounts: 5 or more-20% discount. 400pp; 6×9; of. Reporting time: 4 months. Simultaneous submissions accepted: no. Publishes 40% of manuscripts submitted. Payment: none. Copyrighted, does not revert to author. Pub's reviews: 100 in 1998. §Labour, history, especially social. Ads: $200/$150. CMPA, APA, ACP, CALJ, CHJ, CELJ, HWCSH, IALHI, ITHA.

LADIES' FETISH & TABOO SOCIETY COMPENDIUM OF URBAN ANTHROPOLOGY, Kathy Biehl, PO Box 313194, Jamaica, NY 11431-3194, e-mail fortuna@pipeline.com. 1988. Articles, cartoons, satire, letters, news items, non-fiction. "A sardonic chronicle of the weirdness of modern life, with a penchant for detail, footnotes and tongue-in-cheek formality. Most of the magazine is written by the editor. The articles are not usually assigned. Unsolicited submissions rarely fit the editorial tone. Letters, on the other hand, are encouraged, and most are printed." circ. 160+. 4/yr. Pub'd 2 issues 1998; expects 1 issue 1999, 4 issues 2000. sub. price: $10; per copy: $3; sample: $3. Back issues: Vol. I & II $1 each, III & IV $2, all others $3 each. Discounts: wholesale 40-55%. 16pp; 8½×11; †photocopy. Reporting time: 2 weeks if SASE, otherwise no response. Simultaneous submissions accepted: yes. Publishes 10% of manuscripts submitted. Payment: copy of 'zine. Copyrighted, reverts to author. Pub's reviews: 6 in 1998. §humor; social commentary. Ads: none.

LADYBUG, the Magazine for Young Children, Marianne Carus, Editor-in-Chief; Paula Morrow, Editor, 315 5th Street, PO Box 300, Peru, IL 61354, 815-224-6656. 1990. Poetry, fiction, art, music, non-fiction. "Fiction: 300-800 words. Poems: 20 lines maximum. Crafts/activities/games: 1-4 pages. Original finger plays (12 lines max.) and action rhymes (20 lines max.). Ladybug is for children ages 2-6 and their parents and caregivers. SASE is required for a response" circ. 132M. 12/yr. Pub'd 12 issues 1998; expects 12 issues 1999, 12 issues 2000. sub. price: $35.97; per copy: $5; sample: $5. Back issues: $5. 36pp; 8×10; of. Reporting time: 12 weeks, SASE required. Simultaneous submissions accepted: yes. Publishes 1% of manuscripts submitted. Payment: up to 25¢/word (fiction); up to $3/line (poetry). Copyrighted, reverts to author. Ads: none. MPA.

Lahontan Images, Tim I. Purdy, 210 South Pine Street, Susanville, CA 96130, 916-257-6747, fax 916-251-4801. 1986. Non-fiction. "Primarily interested in the history and related topics of eastern California and Nevada. First title is Eric N. Moody's *Flanigan: Anatomy of a Railroad Ghost Town.*" avg. press run 2M. Expects 2 titles 1999, 4 titles 2000. 8 titles listed in the *Small Press Record of Books in Print* (28th Edition, 1999-00). avg. price, paper: $10. Discounts: 5 or more 40%. 150pp; 6×9; of. Reporting time: 1 month. Payment: percentage of sales. Copyrights for author.

LAKE SUPERIOR MAGAZINE, Paul L. Hayden, Lake Superior Port Cities, Inc., PO Box 16417, Duluth, MN 55816-0417, 218-722-5002. 1979. Fiction, articles, photos, cartoons, letters, news items, non-fiction. "We are a high-quality, glossy consumer magazine. We prefer manuscripts, but well-researched queries are attended to. We actively seek queries from writers in Lake Superior communities. Provide enough information on why the subject is important to the region and our readers, or why and how something is unique. We want details. The writer must have a thorough knowledge of the subject and how it relates to our region. We prefer a fresh, unused approach to the subject which provides the reader with an emotional involvement. Average 800-1,500 words, graphics/photos important." circ. 20M. 7/yr. Pub'd 7 issues 1998; expects 7 issues 1999, 7 issues 2000. 9 titles listed in the *Small Press Record of Books in Print* (28th Edition, 1999-00). sub. price: $21; per copy: $3.95; sample: $4.95. Back issues: all issues $10, except current year—list available. 80pp; 8⅛×11; of/lo. Reporting time: 3-5 months. Accept simultaneous submissions, but must know it is the case. Publishes 5% of manuscripts submitted. Payment: up to $600, pix $20 (B&W), $40 (color), cover $125. Copyrighted, first rights for 90 days after publication. Pub's reviews: 12 in 1998. §Must be regional (Lake Superior) in topics covered. Ads: $1435/$1735 full color/Half page $871 B&W/$1171 color. IRMA, Minnesota Publishers Association.

Lake View Press, Paul Elitzik, Director, PO Box 578279, Chicago, IL 60657, 312-935-2694. 1982. Fiction, non-fiction. "Areas of interest: books on social and cultural issues." avg. press run 3M. Expects 3 titles 1999, 6 titles 2000. 12 titles listed in the *Small Press Record of Books in Print* (28th Edition, 1999-00). avg. price, cloth: $25; paper: $10. Discounts: 20% 2-4 copies, 40% 5+ for trade titles. 250pp; 5½×8½; of. Reporting time: 2 weeks-2 months, send queries first. Simultaneous submissions accepted: no. Publishes 5% of manuscripts submitted. Payment: varies; percentage of selling price. Copyrights for author. Illinois Book Publishers Association.

Lakes & Prairies Press, Ned Haggard, 15774 S. LaGrange Road #172, Orland Park, IL 60462-4766, website www.lakesprairies.com. 1998. Poetry, fiction, criticism, letters, parts-of-novels, long-poems, non-fiction. "At present, Lakes & Prairies Press is a commercial vehicle. Blue Spruce Press, a subdivision of Lakes & Prairies Enterprises, Inc. is a invitational press. It may be opened (hopefully will be) for submission in the future." avg. press run 1-1.5M. Expects 2 titles 1999, 3 titles 2000. Discounts: negotiated as per circumstance. Pages vary; size varies. Reporting time: query via website, times vary by particular project. Simultaneous submissions accepted: yes. Payment: negotiable. Does not copyright for author. Poetry Society of America, Academy of American Poets, Modern Poetry Association.

LAMBDA BOOK REPORT, Jim Marks, Publisher; Kanani Kauka, Senior Editor; Terrance Heath, Assistant Editor, PO Box 73910, Washington, DC 20056, 202-462-7294; fax 202-462-5264; e-Mail lbreditor@aol.com. 1987. Articles, art, photos, cartoons, interviews, criticism, reviews, letters, parts-of-novels, news items. "Review of contemporary gay & lesbian literature. ISSN 1048-9487" circ. 10M. 12/yr. Pub'd 12 issues 1998; expects 12 issues 1999, 12 issues 2000. sub. price: $34.95; per copy: $4.95; sample: $5. Discounts: wholesale 40% guaranteed sales. 52pp; 8½×11; of. Reporting time: 6 weeks. Simultaneous submissions accepted: no. Payment: negotiable. Copyrighted, reverts to author. Pub's reviews: 500 in 1998. §Any books of interest to gay men, lesbians, their families and friends. Ads: $650/$375/$1 per word. GLPA, Alternative Press Index, Independent Press Association.

Lamp Light Press, A.C. Doyle, Founder, Publishing Division, PO Box 416, Denver, CO 80201-0416, 303-575-5676. 1983. avg. press run 600. 7 titles listed in the *Small Press Record of Books in Print* (28th Edition, 1999-00). avg. price, cloth: $19.95; paper: $29.95. Discounts: distributed by Prosperity & Profits Unlimited, PO Box 416, Denver, CO 80201. 60pp; 8½×11, 5½×8½. Reporting time: 6 weeks.

Lancaster Press (see also THE AMERICAN SCHOLAR), Anne Fadiman, 1811 Q Street NW, Washington, DC 20009, 202-265-3808. 1932.

Lancer Militaria, Box 1188, Mt. Ida, AR 71957-1188, 870-867-2232; www.warbooks.com. 1978. "Specialize in reference type material for military collectors/historians." avg. press run 3M. Pub'd 2 titles 1998; expects 3 titles 1999. 8 titles listed in the *Small Press Record of Books in Print* (28th Edition, 1999-00). avg. price, cloth: $22; paper: $13. Discounts: 40-50% depending on quantity. 112pp; 8½×11. Copyrights for author. ABA, PMA.

LANDSCAPE, Blair Boyd, Publisher; Rebecca McKee, Editor, PO Box 7107, Berkeley, CA 94707, 415-549-3233. 1951. Articles, photos, reviews. "A scholarly journal addressed to cultural geography, architecture, planning, environmental design, landscape architecture." circ. 3M. 3/yr. Pub'd 3 issues 1998; expects 3 issues 1999, 3 issues 2000. sub. price: $22 indiv. US, $42 institutions; per copy: $3.50; sample: $6.95. Back issues: on request. Discounts: on request. 48pp; 8½×11; of. Reporting time: 8-10 weeks. Simultaneous submissions accepted: yes. Payment: 2 year subscription. Copyrighted, does not revert to author. Pub's reviews: 6 in 1998. §Geography, architecture, landscape architecture, planning. No ads.

Landwaster Books (see also GOTHIX), Astor Gravelle, Ron Gravelle, PO Box 3223, Frederick, MD 21705-3223, website www.landwaster.com. 1999. Articles. avg. press run 1M. Expects 10 titles 2000. 2 titles listed in the *Small Press Record of Books in Print* (28th Edition, 1999-00). avg. price, paper: $12.95. Discounts: 50% off. 120pp; 7×10; †desktop published, digital printing. Reporting time: 1 month. Simultaneous submissions accepted: yes. Publishes 2% of manuscripts submitted. Payment: royalties vary on contracts. Copyrights for author. PMA.

Langmarc Publishing, R.J. Roberts, Renee Hermanson, Christy McBride, PO Box 33817, San Antonio, TX 78265, 210-822-2521. 1991. Non-fiction. "Most of our works are Christian religious in nature. We must be very selective and don't ordinarily encourage submissions without prior communication. Length varies: one publication in 1991 was 310pp.; 2 were in the 140-165pp category. In 1992, a 300-page novel, a 100-page hardcover book of poetry; the rest 145-350pp." avg. press run 1.5M. Pub'd 7 titles 1998; expects 4-5 titles 1999, 5 titles 2000. 24 titles listed in the *Small Press Record of Books in Print* (28th Edition, 1999-00). avg. price, cloth: $12.95; paper: $12.95. Discounts: 1-2 net, 3-4 20%, 5+ 40% for bookstores; STOP 40%; 45% for prepaid. 225pp; 5½×8½. Reporting time: 8 weeks. Simultaneous submissions accepted: yes. Payment: 10% on cover price of book usual. Copyrights for author.

THE LANGSTON HUGHES REVIEW, Dolan Hubbard, Managing Editor; R. Baxter Miller, Executive Editor, Box 2006, Univ. of Georgia, Athens, GA 30612-0006, 401-863-1815. 1982. Articles, interviews, criticism, reviews, news items. "Re: events on Hughes' work." circ. 300-325. 2/yr. Pub'd 1 issue 1998; expects 2 issues 1999, 2 issues 2000. sub. price: $10 ($12 foreign); per copy: $7. Back issues: $9. Discounts: through subscription agency: $9.50 US, $12.00 foreign, 1 yr. subscription. 40-60pp; 6×9; of. Reporting time: 6-8 weeks. Simultaneous submissions accepted: no. Publishes 3% of manuscripts submitted. Payment: none. Copyrighted, rights do not revert to author, but on request of author rights are assigned. Pub's reviews: 0 in 1998. §Langston Hughes and his contemporaries (e.g. DuBois McKay/Callen Toomer/Fauset Larson.

LANGUAGE INTERNATIONAL: THE MAGAZINE FOR THE LANGUAGE PROFESSIONS, Geoffrey Kingscott, Praetorius Limited, 5 East Circus Street, Nottingham NG1 5AF, England, 44-115-914-1087. 1989. Articles, photos, interviews, reviews, non-fiction. "International topical news magazine for the translation and language teaching professions. Additional address: John Benjamins B.V., Publisher & Bookseller, Amsteldijk 44, PO Box 75577, 1070 AN Amsterdam, Holland." circ. 2M. 6/yr. Pub'd 6 issues 1998; expects 6 issues 1999, 6 issues 2000. sub. price: $109 (private $71); per copy: $18; sample: free. Back issues: $7.50. 48pp; 21×27.9cm; of. Reporting time: 4 weeks. Copyrighted, rights revert to author after 2 years with the publisher. Pub's reviews: 46 in 1998. §Bilingual & multilingual dictionaries, books on translation, linguistics. Ads: $835/$470/$15 for 40 characters. KNUB (Dutch Publ. Assn.).

Lao Tse Press, Ltd. (see also JOURNAL OF PROCESS ORIENTED PSYCHOLOGY), Kate Jobe, Leslie Heizer, PO Box 8898, Portland, OR 97207-8898, 503-222-3395; fax 503-222-3778. 1995. Non-fiction. avg. press run 3-5M. Pub'd 2 titles 1998; expects 2 titles 1999, 4 titles 2000. 5 titles listed in the *Small Press Record of Books in Print* (28th Edition, 1999-00). avg. price, paper: $16. Discounts: trade 1-4 20%, 5-9 40%, 10-24 42%, 25-49 43%. 300pp; 5½×8½. Reporting time: 1-3 months. Simultaneous submissions accepted: yes. Publishes 90% of manuscripts submitted. Payment: yes. Copyrights for author.

Laocoon Books, M. Kettner, Kathleen K., PO Box 20518, Seattle, WA 98102, 206-323-7268; erotica@laocoonbooks.com. 1980. Poetry, fiction, art, photos, collages. "We are not actively seeking manuscripts this year" avg. press run 300. Expects 4 titles 1999, 1 title 2000. 4 titles listed in the *Small Press Record of Books in Print* (28th Edition, 1999-00). avg. price, paper: $4. Discounts: 40% to retailers, 50% to distributors. 28-40pp; size varies; of, mi.

THE LAS VEGAS INSIDER, Donald Currier, Good 'n' Lucky, PO Box 1185, Chino Valley, AZ 86323-1185. 1974. Articles, criticism, reviews, news items. circ. 5.1M. 12/yr. Pub'd 12 issues 1998; expects 12 issues 1999. sub. price: $45; sample: $4. Back issues: $50 per 12 issues (any) 52. 8pp; 8×11; †of. Reporting time: 1 week. Payment: yes. Copyrighted, reverts to author. Pub's reviews: 10-15 in 1998. §Gaming, travel, finance. Ads: none.

LATEST JOKES NEWSLETTER, Robert Makinson, PO Box 23304, Brooklyn, NY 11202-0066, 718-855-5057. 1974. Satire. 6/yr. Pub'd 6 issues 1998; expects 12 issues 1999, 12 issues 2000. sub. price: $24/12 issues/2 years; per copy: $3; sample: $3. Back issues: $2. 2pp; 8½×11; of. Reporting time: 30 days. Payment: $1-$3 ($1 outright purchase, plus $2 extra if it reappears in publication that pays me). Copyrighted, buy all rights. Pub's reviews. Ads: Free advertising to subscribers.

Latham Foundation (see also THE LATHAM LETTER), Hugh H. Tebault III, Latham Plaza, 1826 Clement Avenue, Alameda, CA 94501-1397, 510-521-0920; www.latham.org. Pub'd 4 titles 1998; expects 4 titles 1999, 4 titles 2000. 1 title listed in the *Small Press Record of Books in Print* (28th Edition, 1999-00). 24pp. Reporting time: varies.

THE LATHAM LETTER, Latham Foundation, Latham Foundation, Latham Plaza, 1826 Clement Avenue, Alameda, CA 94501-1397, 415-521-0920; www.latham.org. 1918. Poetry, articles, cartoons, interviews, reviews, letters, non-fiction. circ. 4M. 4/yr. Pub'd 4 issues 1998; expects 4 issues 1999, 4 issues 2000. sub. price: $12; per copy: $2.50. Back issues: special rates. Discounts: contact Latham Foundation. 24pp; 8½×10; of. Reporting time: 30 days next issue, if appropriate as to time frame. Copyrighted, rights revert to author, but authorization to republish is rarely withheld. Pub's reviews: 14 in 1998. §Human/companion animal bond, pet-facilitated therapy, humane welfare, child protection, domestic violence, promotion of respect for all life through education.

LATIN AMERICAN LITERARY REVIEW, Latin American Literary Review Press, Yvette E. Miller, 121 Edgewood Avenue, 1st Floor, Pittsburgh, PA 15218-1513, 412-371-9023; fax 412-371-9025. 1972. Fiction, articles, photos, interviews, criticism, reviews, music, non-fiction. "Length of article varies from 10-40 pages in special issues. Some recent contributors: Roberto Gonzales Echevarria, Jose J. Arrom, Guillermo Cabrera Infante, John Updike, Alistair Reid, Robert Coles, Jorge de Sena, Harold de Campos, Joaquin de Sousa Andrade et al. Articles published in English, Spanish & Portuguese." circ. 1M. 2/yr. Pub'd 2 issues 1998; expects 2 issues 1999, 2 issues 2000. sub. price: $35; per copy: $16; sample: $16. Back issues: $16. Discounts: less than 10% for subscription agencies. 150pp; 6×9; of. Reporting time: within 12 weeks. Simultaneous submissions accepted: no. Payment: on special issues. Not copyrighted. Pub's reviews: 10 in 1998. §Recent Latin American Fiction, poetry, theatre, criticism. Ads: $220/$145/$100. CLMP.

Latin American Literary Review Press (see also LATIN AMERICAN LITERARY REVIEW), Yvette E. Miller, 121 Edgewood Avenue, 1st Floor, Pittsburgh, PA 15218-1513, 412-371-9023; FAX 412-371-9025. 1977. Fiction, photos, criticism, plays, non-fiction. "English translations of works by prominent L.A. writers" avg. press run 1.5M. Pub'd 8 titles 1998; expects 10 titles 1999, 10 titles 2000. 63 titles listed in the *Small Press Record of Books in Print* (28th Edition, 1999-00). avg. price, cloth: $25; paper: $12; other: $10. Discounts: negotiable. 160pp; 5½×8½. Reporting time: 4 months. Simultaneous submissions accepted: yes. Publishes 1% of manuscripts submitted. Payment: 10%. Copyrights for author. CLMP.

LATIN AMERICAN PERSPECTIVES, Ronald H. Chilcote, Managing Editor, PO Box 5703, Riverside, CA 92517-5703, 909-787-5037ext. 1571; fax 909-787-5685. 1974. Articles, art, photos, interviews, reviews. "Obtain subscriptions through: Sage Publications, 2455 Teller Road, Thousand Oaks, Ca 91320." circ. 2M. 6/yr. Pub'd 4 issues 1998; expects 6 issues 1999, 6 issues 2000. sub. price: $54; $25 student; per copy: $11; sample: free on request. Back issues: $11. Discounts: 25% (5-10 copies) 30% (11-20 copies) 40% (21-40 copies) classroom & university bookstores. 128pp; 5×8; of. Reporting time: 6-9 months. Publishes 25% of manuscripts submitted. Payment: none. Copyrighted. Pub's reviews: 10 in 1998. §Latin America, radical theory, political economy. Ads: $225/$150.

LATINO STUFF REVIEW, LS Press, Inc., Nilda Cepero, PO Box 440195, Miami, FL 33144, www.ejl@lspress.net. 1990. Poetry, fiction, articles, interviews, criticism, reviews, letters. "Bilingual publication owned by Latino Stuff Review, Inc., a non-profit organization. We accept poetry (up to 45 lines), short stories and essays on literature and social issues up to 3,000 words, on Latino topics. Use SASE. Distributes over 100 subscriptions to libraries. Available in many bilingual bookstores nationwide. Contributers include Catfish McDaris, Frank Varela, Margarita Engle, Evangeline Blanco, Clyde James Aragon, and Nilda Cepero." circ. 1M. 2/yr. Pub'd 2 issues 1998; expects 2 issues 1999, 2 issues 2000. sub. price: $4; per copy: $3; sample: $3. Back issues: $3. Discounts: Institutional subscriptions: $12 with 50% to jobbers/distrubuters. 24pp; 8½×11; of. Reporting time: 6 months. Simultaneous submissions accepted: yes. Publishes 25% of manuscripts submitted. Payment: contributor copies. Not copyrighted. Pub's reviews: 2 in 1998. §Latino topics and/or authors. Ads: $25 1/4 page/$15 1/8 page.

The Latona Press, Marion K. Stocking, 24 Berry Cove Road, Lamoine, ME 04605. 1978. Non-fiction. "We are not looking for further manuscripts at the present time." avg. press run 1.5M. 1 title listed in the *Small Press Record of Books in Print* (28th Edition, 1999-00). avg. price, cloth: $25; paper: $12.95. Discounts: To bookstores and wholesalers: 1-4 copies 20%, 5 or more 40%. Postage and shipping extra. No discount on orders not paid for in 30 days. 200pp; 6×9; of. Payment: royalties. Copyrights for author.

LAUGHING BEAR NEWSLETTER, Tom Person, Editor, PO Box 613322, Dallas, TX 75261-3322, 817-283-6303; e-mail editor@laughingbear.com. 1976. Articles, news items. "LBN has been serving the small press community with news, information, and inspiration since 1976. Uses short articles (200-300 words) on small press publishing; press releases and review copies. *LBN* is for small press writers and publishers. The emphasis is on limited budget publishing: design and strategies, alternative marketing techniques, and resources. Visit our website at http://www.laughingbear.com to browse the Directory of Organizations for Small Presses and Self-Publishers and to dowload a copy of our hand-picked library mailing list." circ. 150. 12/yr. Pub'd 12 issues 1998; expects 12 issues 1999, 12 issues 2000. sub. price: $15, $17 in Canada, $25 overseas; per copy: $1; sample: free with SASE. Back issues: $20. 3pp; 8½×11; photocopy. Reporting time: 1 month. Publishes 5% of manuscripts submitted. Payment: 1 year subscription for articles. Copyrighted, reverts to author. Pub's reviews: 30+ in 1998. §Small press publications of all kinds including audio and CD-ROM; publishing how-to especially. Ads: insert ads, $50.

Owen Laughlin Publishers, Owen Laughlin, PO Box 6313, Clearwater, FL 33758-6313, 813-797-0404 Voice; Fax 813-447-1659 24 hours; 800-258-3806. 1955. Art, cartoons, non-fiction. "Prefer books of not less than 32 pages, or maximum of 128 pages, 8¼ X 11¼. We are especially interested in cookbooks." avg. press run 10M. Expects 2 titles 1999, 2 titles 2000. 3 titles listed in the *Small Press Record of Books in Print* (28th Edition, 1999-00). avg. price, paper: $12-$20. Discounts: 40% bookstores, 60% distributors, 80% mail order houses. 64pp; 8×11; †web. Reporting time: 30 days. Simultaneous submissions accepted: yes. Publishes 10% of manuscripts submitted. Payment: per submission and acceptance, amount varies with title. Copyrights for author.

LAUREATE LETTER, Trouvere Company, Brenda Williamson, 899 Williamson Trail, Eclectic, AL 36024. 1981. Poetry. "Any style of poetry, 20 word length max." circ. 1M. 1/yr. Pub'd 3 issues 1998; expects 1 issue 1999, 1 issue 2000. sub. price: $3.95; per copy: $3.95; sample: 3.95. Discounts: 20% library or jobber. 24pp; 5½×8½; of. Reporting time: 1-6 weeks. Simultaneous submissions accepted: yes. Publishes 50% of manuscripts submitted. Payment: tearsheet. Copyrighted, reverts to author.

Laureate Press, Lance C. Lobo, Publisher & Editor, 2710 Ohio Street, Bangor, ME 04401-1056, 800-946-2727. 1992. Non-fiction. "Distributed by Login Trade/LPC Group" avg. press run 10M. Pub'd 3 titles 1998; expects 3 titles 1999, 3 titles 2000. 6 titles listed in the *Small Press Record of Books in Print* (28th Edition, 1999-00). avg. price, paper: $19.95. Discounts: 1-50 books less 40%, 51+ books less 50%. 336pp; 5½×8½; of/li. Reporting time: 4-6 weeks. Simultaneous submissions accepted: no. Publishes 4% of manuscripts submitted. Payment: 5-10%. Copyrights for author. PMA.

Laurel & Herbert, Inc., PO Box 266, Sugarloaf Shores, FL 33042, 305-745-3506; Fax 305-745-9070; herbert@conch.net.com. 1 title listed in the *Small Press Record of Books in Print* (28th Edition, 1999-00).

Laurel Publications, 85 Echo Avenue, Miller Place, NY 11764, 516-474-1023 phone/FAX. 4 titles listed in the *Small Press Record of Books in Print* (28th Edition, 1999-00).

THE LAUREL REVIEW, William Trowbridge, Editor; David Slater, Editor; Beth Richards, Editor; Rosemurgy Catie, Editor; Randall R. Freisinger, Associate Editor; Steve Heller, Associate Editor; Nancy Vieira Couto, Associate Editor; Jim Simmerman, Associate Editor, Department of English, Northwest Missouri State University, Maryville, MO 64468, 816-562-1265. 1960. Poetry, fiction, art, parts-of-novels, long-poems, non-fiction. "We read September through May. We have no regional, political, ethnic, or religious bias. We seek well-crafted poems, stories, and creative non-fiction accessible to a wide range of serious readers. Recent contributors: David Citino, Gary Finke, Albert Goldbarth, Paul Zimmer, Katherine Soniat, Jonis Agee, Charlie

Buck, William Kloefkorn, Jim Daniels, Karla J. Kuban, Heather Ross Miller, Ian McMillan, Jonathan Holden.'' circ. 900. 2/yr. Pub'd 2 issues 1998; expects 2 issues 1999, 2 issues 2000. sub. price: $8; per copy: $6; sample: $5. Back issues: $5. Discounts: 40%. 128pp; 6×9; of. Reporting time: 1 week to 4 months. Simultaneous submissions accepted: no. Publishes less than 1% of manuscripts submitted. Payment: 2 copies, plus free one-year subsciption. Copyrighted, reverts to author. Pub's reviews: 2 in 1998. Ads: $80/$40. CLMP.

LAW AND CRITIQUE, Deborah Charles Publications, Costas Douzinas, Managing Editor, 173 Mather Avenue, Liverpool L18 6JZ, United Kingdom. 1990. Non-fiction. 2/yr. Pub'd 2 issues 1998; expects 2 issues 1999, 2 issues 2000. sub. price: £16 individuals, £55 institutions + postage; per copy: £10 individuals, £25 institutions; sample: £10. Discounts: 5% subscription agents. 112pp; royal octavo; Mac DTP. Reporting time: 3 months. Payment: none. Copyrighted, does not revert to author. Pub's reviews. §Critical Law and Theory. exchange basis.

Law Mexico Publishing, Marcela Caballero, 539 Telegraph Canyon Road #787, Chula Vista, CA 91910-6497, 619-482-8244. 1994. News items. ''Subjects dealing with Mexico and its laws'' avg. press run 15M. Pub'd 2 titles 1998; expects 6 titles 1999, 2 titles 2000. avg. price, paper: $19.95. 400pp; 5½×8½; †of. Reporting time: varies. Payment: negotiable. Copyrights for author.

Lawco Ltd./Moneytree Publications/Que-House, James R. Lawson, Founder, PO Box 9758, Denver, CO 80209-0758, 209-239-6006. 1980. Non-fiction. ''Interested in material on business strategies for our Moneytree imprint. We are also interested in material for the small business/business at home market, for our business imprint. We are interested in books on pocket billiards and other sports under the Que House imprint.'' avg. press run varies. Pub'd 2 titles 1998; expects 5 titles 1999, 3 titles 2000. 6 titles listed in the *Small Press Record of Books in Print* (28th Edition, 1999-00). avg. price, paper: $20; other: $20-$200. Discounts: 2-4 40%, 5-9 45%, 1/2 case 48%, 1/2-2 cases 52%, 2+ cases 60%. 256pp; 5½×8½, 8½×11; of, lp. Reporting time: 90 days. Simultaneous submissions accepted: no. Payment: negotiable. Copyrights for author. MSPA, PMA, SPA.

Leadership Education and Development, Inc., Donna Harrison, Joy Rhodes, 1116 West 7th Street, Suite 175, Columbia, TN 38401, 931-682-3796; 800-659-6135. 1987. Non-fiction. ''Biases: ethical management. Recent contributor: Fred A. Manske, Jr., CEO of Purolator Courier.'' avg. press run 5-10M. Expects 1-2 titles 1999, 2-3 titles 2000. 2 titles listed in the *Small Press Record of Books in Print* (28th Edition, 1999-00). avg. price, cloth: $18.95. Discounts: distributors 50%, bookstores 40-45%, quantity retail discounts up to 35%. 200pp; size varies. Reporting time: 2-3 months. Payment: negotiable. Copyrights are negotiable. Small Publishers Association of North America.

Leapfrog Press, Ira Wood, PO Box 1495, Wellfleet, MA 02667, 508-349-1925; fax 508-349-1180; email leapfrog@capecod.net; www.leapfrogpress.com. 1996. Poetry, fiction, non-fiction. ''Our list is eclectic and represents quality fiction, poetry and non-fiction memoirs—books that are referred to by the large commercial publishers as mid-list, and which we regard to be the heart and soul of literature. Please submit a query letter telling us about your publishing experience and no more than 50 pages. Manuscript to be returned must be accompanied by a SASE. Authors to be published in 1999 include Ruthann Robson, Annette Williams Jaffee and Marge Piercy. We are distributed by Consortium Book Sales & Distribution.'' avg. press run 1.5M. Expects 4 titles 2000. avg. price, cloth: $24.95; paper: $14.95. 160pp; 6×9. Reporting time: 4-6 months. Simultaneous submissions accepted: yes. Publishes less than 2% of manuscripts submitted. Payment: varies according to book. Copyrights for author. PMA, NEPA, PEN.

The Leaping Frog Press, PO Box 440735, Miami, FL 33144, 305-461-2770; FAX 305-668-0636. 1996. Fiction, photos. ''Strictly limited to short (max. 2,500 words) fiction. Has 'Best Of' S.E., N.E. Midwest, S.W., N.W., regional anthologies competition for new and emerging writers held each year. All correspondence must have a SASE for return of anything sent or wanted. Currently seeking essays of up to 200 words regarding doorways to homes and on trailer homes, two separate topics and books.'' avg. press run 1M-5M. Pub'd 1 title 1998; expects 2 titles 1999, 5 titles 2000. avg. price, cloth: $29.95; paper: $12.95. Discounts: minimum 40% up to 50 + 20% with quantities and no returns. 128pp; of. Reporting time: 12 weeks minimum. Simultaneous submissions accepted: yes. Publishes 60% of manuscripts submitted. Payment: by prior arrangements. Does not copyright for author. National Alliance of Short Story Authors (NASSA).

LEAPINGS LITERARY MAGAZINE, S.A. Warner, 2455 Pinercrest Drive, Santa Rosa, CA 95403, E-mail 72144.3133@compuserve.com. 1998. Poetry, fiction, articles, art, interviews, satire, criticism, reviews, parts-of-novels. ''Less than 3,000 words and 1,500 words desired most.'' circ. ~200. 2/yr. Expects 2 issues 1999, 2 issues 2000. sub. price: $10; per copy: $6; sample: $5 (back issue). Back issues: $5. 60pp; 5½×8½; †laser/desktop. Reporting time: 1 month. We accept simultaneous submissions if identified as such. Publishes 5% of manuscripts submitted. Payment: 2 contributor's copies. Copyrighted, reverts to author. Pub's reviews: 2 in 1998. §Poetry, fine literature.

Ledero Press, Michael M. Warren, U. T. Box 35099, Galveston, TX 77555-5099, 409-772-2091. 1990. Poetry, fiction, non-fiction. ''No special requirements. Recent contributor: *Deer Dad* A Hunter's Guide by Michael M.

Warren." avg. press run 2-5M. Expects 1 title 1999, 1 title 2000. 5 titles listed in the *Small Press Record of Books in Print* (28th Edition, 1999-00). avg. price, cloth: $15-$25; paper: $8-$15. Discounts: 2-5 10%; 5-25 40%; 26-50 43%; 51-100 46%; 100+ 50%. 200pp; 6×9; of. Reporting time: 4-6 weeks. Payment: negotiable. Copyright if needed.

THE LEDGE, Timothy Monaghan, Editor-in-Chief and Publisher, 78-44 80th Street, Glendale, NY 11385. 1988. Poetry. "Our purpose is to publish oustanding poetry. Please limit submissions to 5 poems or fewer. We have no restrictions on form or content. Excellence is our main criterion. Reading period: September through May." circ. 1M. 2/yr. Pub'd 2 issues 1998; expects 2 issues 1999, 2 issues 2000. sub. price: $12 2 issues or $22/4 issues or $30/6 issues. For subscriptions outside North America, please add $3 per issue; per copy: $7; sample: $7. 160pp; 5½×8½; of. Reporting time: 4-6 months. Simultaneous submissions accepted: yes. Publishes 5% of manuscripts submitted. Payment: 2 contributor's copies. Copyrighted, reverts to author. CLMP, Small Press Center.

Leete's Island Books, Peter Neill, Box 3131, Branford, CT 06405-1731, 203-488-3424; e-mail PNeill@compuserve.com. 1977. "Fiction, essays, interesting reprints; for the moment, because of time, no unsolicited manuscripts accepted" avg. press run 2.5M. Pub'd 2 titles 1998; expects 3 titles 1999, 4 titles 2000. 13 titles listed in the *Small Press Record of Books in Print* (28th Edition, 1999-00). avg. price, cloth: $12.95; paper: $7.95. Discounts: 40%, distributed by: Independent Publishers Group, Chicago Review Press, 814 N. Franklin, 2nd FL., Chicago, Illinois 60610, 312-337-0747. 250pp; 5½×8½; of. Payment: varies with title. Copyrights for author.

●**Edward J. Lefkowicz, Inc.,** 500 Angell Street, Providence, RI 02906-4457, 800-201-7901; fax 401-277-1459; E-mail seabooks@saltbooks.com. 1983. Art, non-fiction. *"Edward J. Lefkowicz, Inc.* is a Fairhaven, MA independent publisher of fine maritime books, including the highly acclaimed limited edition book and portfolio *American Whalers in the Western Arctic,* illustrated by marine painter William Gilkerson, with text by John Bockstoce. The firm was founded in 1974 as antiquarian booksellers specializing in rare maritime and naval books, in which they are one of the few specialists in the world. Another recent publication undertaken jointly with the Kendall Whaling Museum of Sharon, MA titled *The South Sea Whaler: An Annotated Bibliography of Published Historical Literary and Art Material Relating to Whaling in the Pacific Ocean in the Nineteenth Century* by Honore Forster" 1 title listed in the *Small Press Record of Books in Print* (28th Edition, 1999-00). avg. price, cloth: $25; paper: $18.95; other: limited eds. various. Discounts: Trade: 1-2 copies 20%; 3-5 30%; 6-25 40%; 26-74 45%; 75+ 50%. Pages vary; of. Reporting time: 6 weeks. Payment: royalties individually negotiated. Copyrights for author. PMA (Publishers Marketing Association), COSMEP, SSP.

LEFT BUSINESS OBSERVER, Doug Henwood, 250 West 85 Street, New York, NY 10024. 1986. Articles, interviews, reviews, letters, news items, non-fiction. "Pieces range from 100-3,000 words. Most written by editor, but occasional outside contributions" circ. 3M. 11/yr. Pub'd 11 issues 1998; expects 11 issues 1999, 11 issues 2000. sub. price: $22 indiv., $55 instit.; per copy: $2.50; sample: $2.50. Back issues: 4/$7.50, complete set 181 issues $75. Discounts: classroom up to 50%, bookstores 40%. 8pp; 8½×11; of. Reporting time: 1 week. Payment: varies, up to 10¢/word. Copyrighted, does not revert to author. Pub's reviews: 2 in 1998. §Economics, politics, feminism, social sciences. Ads: none.

LEFT CURVE, Csaba Polony, Editor; Jack Hirschman, P.J. Laska, Susan Schwartzenberg, Georg Pinter, Richard Olsen, Elizam Escobar, John Hutnyk, PO Box 472, Oakland, CA 94604, E-mail: leftcurv@wco.com. 1974. Poetry, fiction, articles, art, photos, cartoons, interviews, criticism, reviews, music, letters, long-poems, collages, concrete art, non-fiction. "*Left Curve* is an artist produced journal addressing the crises of modernity from an integrative social-historical context by publishing original visual and verbal art, as well as critical articles." circ. 2M. Irregular. Pub'd 2 issues 1998. sub. price: $25 indiv, $35 instit (3 issues); per copy: $10; sample: $8. Back issues: $10. Discounts: 30% trade. 112-144pp; 8½×11; of. Reporting time: max. 6 months. Simultaneous submissions accepted: no. Publishes 5% of manuscripts submitted. Payment: 5 copies. Copyrighted. Pub's reviews: 3 in 1998. §Contemporary art, poetry, cultural politics, literature, cultural. Ads: $200/$125/$15 min; $1 per word.

Left Hand Books, Bryan McHugh, Station Hill Road, Barrytown, NY 12507, 914-758-6478; FAX 914-758-4416. 1990. Poetry, art, photos, long-poems, plays. "Left Hand publishes poetry and artists' books in stunningly designed editions." avg. press run 1M. Pub'd 3 titles 1998; expects 3 titles 1999, 2 titles 2000. 25 titles listed in the *Small Press Record of Books in Print* (28th Edition, 1999-00). avg. price, cloth: $40; paper: $10.45. Discounts: contact Small Press Distribution. 72pp; size varies; of. Payment: arrangements vary. Author holds copyright.

THE LEFT INDEX, Joan Nordquist, 511 Lincoln Street, Santa Cruz, CA 95060, 408-426-4479. 1982. *"The Left Index* is a quarterly author/subject index to the contents of articles in journals of a left perspective." 4/yr. Pub'd 4 issues 1998; expects 4 issues 1999, 4 issues 2000. sub. price: $75 institution, $35 individual; per copy:

$18 institution; $10 individual; sample: same. Back issues: $70/volume. 75pp; 7×8½; of. Copyrighted.

LEFTHANDER MAGAZINE, Kim Kipers, Managing Editor, Lefthanders International, PO Box 8249, Topeka, KS 66608, (913) 234-2177. 1975. Articles, cartoons, interviews, reviews, news items, non-fiction. circ. 26M. 6/yr. Pub'd 6 issues 1998; expects 6 issues 1999, 6 issues 2000. sub. price: $15; per copy: $2; sample: same. Back issues: $3.50. Discounts: none. 32pp; 8¼×10¾; of. Reporting time: 3 weeks to 2 months. Payment: varying, payment on publication. Copyrighted, does not revert to author. Pub's reviews: 6 in 1998. §Anything dealing with handedness, brain dominance, teaching to the right brain. Ads: $1,200/$775.

LEGAL INFORMATION MANAGEMENT INDEX, Elyse H. Fox, Legal Information Services, P.O. Box 67, Newton Highlands, MA 02161-0067, 508-443-4087. 1984. Articles, reviews. "Indexes articles, and reviews appearing in periodicals relating to legal information management and law librarianship. Payments must be made in U.S. funds" 7/yr. Pub'd 7 issues 1998; expects 7 issues 1999, 7 issues 2000. sub. price: $118 U.S., Canada & Mexico, $140 others (air mail); sample: free on request. Back issues: $75 annual cumulation. 32pp; 8½×11; of. Copyrighted.

Legal Information Publications, Philip J. Hermann, 18221 East Park Drive, Cleveland, OH 44119-2019. 1990. Non-fiction. avg. press run 3M. Pub'd 1 title 1998; expects 2 titles 1999, 4 titles 2000. 2 titles listed in the *Small Press Record of Books in Print* (28th Edition, 1999-00). avg. price, cloth: $24.95. Discounts: 50-55% to wholesalers and distributors. 244pp; 1×9¼; of. Payment: 10-12.5-15% royalty to authors. Copyrights for author. MAPA.

Legas (see also ARBA SICULA; SICILIA PARRA), Gaetano Cipolla, PO Box 040328, Brooklyn, NY 11204. 1987. Poetry, fiction, articles, art, photos, interviews, satire, criticism, reviews, music, letters, long-poems, collages, plays, concrete art, non-fiction. "We come out with various supplements. Sicilian—English Press Bilingual." avg. press run 2M. Pub'd 1 title 1998. 11 titles listed in the *Small Press Record of Books in Print* (28th Edition, 1999-00). avg. price, paper: $12. Discounts: ask for quote. About 100pp per single issue; 5½×8½; laser. Payment: none.

Legation Press, John Becker, 3188 Plyers Mill Road, Kensington, MD 20895-2717. 1 title listed in the *Small Press Record of Books in Print* (28th Edition, 1999-00).

Dean Lem Associates, Inc., Dean Phillip Lem, PO Box 959, Kihei, Maui, HI 96753-0959, 808-874-5461; FAX 808-875-1404; E-mail: deanlem@maui.net or deanlem@aol.com; Website: http://www.graphics-master.com. 1974. Non-fiction. "Dean Lem Assoc., Inc currently publishes only *Graphic Master 6*." avg. press run 6M-7M. Pub'd 1 title 1998; expects 1 title 1999, 1 title 2000. 1 title listed in the *Small Press Record of Books in Print* (28th Edition, 1999-00). avg. price, cloth: $74.50; other: Poly cover $54.50. Discounts: Bookseller 1 copy 20%, 2-5 copies 30%, 6-24 copies 40%, 25-49 copies 42%, 50-99 copies 44%, 100-149 copies 48%, 150+ copies 50%. 155pp; size varies. Copyrights for author. AIGA, PMA, NAIP, NADTP, IGEA, AGAT, Ed Council of Graphic Arts.

●**Lemieux International Ltd.,** William Lemieux, PO Box 17134, Milwaukee, WI 53217, 414-962-2844;1-800-950-7723. 1985. Fiction, non-fiction. avg. press run 1-3M. Expects 1 title 1999, 2 titles 2000. 1 title listed in the *Small Press Record of Books in Print* (28th Edition, 1999-00). avg. price, paper: $14.95. Discounts: trade. 200-300pp; 5½×8. Reporting time: 3 weeks. Simultaneous submissions accepted: yes. Publishes a variable % of manuscripts submitted. Payment: TBA. Copyrights for author. PMA, SPAN.

LEO Productions LLC., Linda E. Odenborg, PO Box 1333, Portland, OR 97207, 360-694-0595, fax 360-694-8808. 1992. Poetry, fiction, art, letters, long-poems, plays, non-fiction. avg. press run 5M-10M. Pub'd 2 titles 1998; expects 3 titles 1999, 3 titles 2000. 4 titles listed in the *Small Press Record of Books in Print* (28th Edition, 1999-00). avg. price, other: $10.95-$15.95 for books on tape. Discounts: yes. Reporting time: 3 months. Publishes 0% of manuscripts submitted. Payment: varies. NW Assoc. of Book Publishers, PMA, SPAN.

L'Epervier Press, Bob McNamara, Editor, 1326 NE 62nd Street, Seattle, WA 98115. 1977. Poetry. "We are not reading at this time. Full length books only. Books by: Paul Nelson, Lynn Strongin, Pamela Stewart, Jack Myers, Bob Herz, Michael Burkard, Christopher Howell, Carolyn Maisel, Robert Morgan, Bruce Renner, Sam Pereira, Robert Lietz, Paul Jenkins, David Lenson, Barry Seiler, Mary Burritt, Bill Nelson, James Crenner, Albert Goldbarth, Linda Orr, Floyce Alexander" avg. press run 500-1M. 35 titles listed in the *Small Press Record of Books in Print* (28th Edition, 1999-00). avg. price, cloth: $20; paper: $8. Distributed by Small Press Distribution/Book Slinger. 64pp; 5½×8½; of. Payment: copies (10% of press run). Copyrights for author.

Les Recherches Daniel Say Cie. (see also GUARD THE NORTH; ENTROPY NEGATIVE), PO Box 3355, Vancouver, B.C. V6B 3Y3, Canada.

LESBIAN AND GAY STUDIES NEWSLETTER, Duke University Press, Margaret Morrison, Box 90660, Duke University, Durham, NC 27708-0660. "*LGSN* is published by the Gay and Lesbian Caucus for the

Modern Languages. A means of distributing information nationally and internationally on lesbian/gay/bisexual/ transgender/queer studies, *LGSN* features book reviews edited by Jonathan Goldberg, publishing news, campus news, conference updates, course syllabi, special articles, and an annual bibliography of books on relation subjects. Send review copies to Book Review Editor Jonathan Goldberg, *LGSN*, Duke University, Box 90021, Durham, NC 27708-0021.'' circ. 500. 3/yr. Pub'd 3 issues 1998; expects 3 issues 1999, 3 issues 2000. sub. price: $40 institutions and sustaining members, $20 individuals, $10 students, additional $5 foreign. Pub's reviews. Ads: $300/$150/$75 1/4 page.

The Philip Lesly Company, Philip Lesly, 155 Harbor Drive, Suite 5311, Chicago, IL 60601. 1986. Non-fiction. ''Book length; no mysticism, no leftist views. Recent book: *Bonanzas and Fool's Gold*, by Philip Lesly'' avg. press run 4M. Expects 2 titles 1999, 2 titles 2000. 1 title listed in the *Small Press Record of Books in Print* (28th Edition, 1999-00). avg. price, paper: $9.95. Discounts: trade 45%; wholesaler 50%. 200pp; 6×9; of. Reporting time: 2 weeks. Payment: 10%, 12 1/2%, and 15% of net. Copyrights for author.

Lessiter Publications (see also FARMER'S DIGEST), Frank Lessiter, PO Box 624, Brookfield, WI 53008-0624, 414-782-4480; Fax 414-782-1252. 1938. Photos, cartoons, interviews. avg. press run 2.5M. Pub'd 2 titles 1998; expects 3 titles 1999, 5 titles 2000. 5 titles listed in the *Small Press Record of Books in Print* (28th Edition, 1999-00). avg. price, cloth: $20.95; paper: $13.95. Discounts: trade, bulk. 150pp; 6×9; of. Reporting time: 45 days. Simultaneous submissions accepted: no. Payment: yes. Copyrights for author.

Lester Street Publishing, William V. Zucker, PO Box 41484, Tucson, AZ 85717-1484, phone and fax 520-326-0104; e-mail wzucker@compuserve.com. 1992. Articles, interviews, criticism, non-fiction. ''Seeking mss. that look *objectively and critically* at health and fitness related subjects, including exercise, pain ameliotation, nutrition (diet) and healing. Authors *must* have credentials. Also interested in new ideas about how to *provoke* curiosity in children via novel forms of communication, story-telling, and story-listening. Will consider mss. that enhance our knowledge of the plant and animal world. Danish translations also accepted in all subjects'' avg. press run 1M-5M. Expects 2 titles 1999, 2 titles 2000. 2 titles listed in the *Small Press Record of Books in Print* (28th Edition, 1999-00). avg. price, paper: $15. Discounts: 55% to jobbers, bookstores 2-4 20%, 5-24 40%, 25-49 45%, 50-99 50%, 100+ 55%. 200pp; 5½×8½. Reporting time: 1-3 months. Payment: open for negotiation. Copyrights for author.

LETTER ARTS REVIEW, Karyn L. Gilman, PO Box 9986, Greensboro, NC 27429. 1982. Articles, art, reviews. circ. 5M. 4/yr. Pub'd 4 issues 1998; expects 4 issues 1999, 4 issues 2000. 3 titles listed in the *Small Press Record of Books in Print* (28th Edition, 1999-00). sub. price: $42; per copy: $12.50; sample: $12.50. Back issues: varied. Discounts: 60/40 for outlets, others negotiable. 64pp; 8½×11; of. Reporting time: 8 weeks or less. Publishes 60% of manuscripts submitted. Payment: on publication. Copyrighted, reverts to author. Pub's reviews: 10+ in 1998. §Calligraphy, graphic arts, typography, book arts, computer fonts. Ads: $550/$400/$25 classified/all one time/4x rate available.

THE LETTER EXCHANGE, Stephen Sikora, Editor, The Readers' League, PO Box 2930, Santa Rosa, CA 95405. 1982. Articles, cartoons, criticism, reviews, letters. ''Very short contributions of any material about letter-writing.'' circ. 2M. 3/yr. Pub'd 3 issues 1998; expects 3-4 issues 1999, 4 issues 2000. sub. price: $22; per copy: $9 postage included; sample: $9. Back issues: $3. Discounts: none. 32pp; 5¼×8¼; of. Reporting time: 1 week. Payment: none. Copyrighted, reverts to author. Pub's reviews: 2 in 1998. §Letter-writing only. Ads: listings for correspondence cost 50¢ per word, commercial ads 70¢ per word, display $15 per col. inch (2'' wide).

THE LETTER PARADE, Bonnie Jo, PO Box 52, Comstock, MI 49041. 1985. Poetry, fiction, articles, art, photos, cartoons, interviews, satire, criticism, letters, collages, news items, non-fiction. ''Humor!'' circ. 100 or so. 4/yr. Pub'd 12 issues 1998; expects 12 issues 1999, 12 issues 2000. sub. price: $6; per copy: $1; sample: $1. Back issues: $1. 6pp; 8½×14; †xerox. Reporting time: monthly. Payment: free subscriptions. Not copyrighted. Pub's reviews. §President Nixon, popular culture, mathematics, Eastern Europe. Ads: all negotiable.

Lexikon Services, 3241 Boulder Creek Way, Antelope, CA 95843-4592, e-mail historycd@aol.com. 2 titles listed in the *Small Press Record of Books in Print* (28th Edition, 1999-00).

Lexikos, Mike Witter, PO Box 1289, Nevada City, CA 95959. 1980. Non-fiction. ''In 1988 *Lexikos* combined with *Don't Call it Frisco Press*. We will continue to publish under both imprints and pursue much the same editorial policies as before.'' avg. press run 4M. Pub'd 1 title 1998; expects 2 titles 1999, 2 titles 2000. 23 titles listed in the *Small Press Record of Books in Print* (28th Edition, 1999-00). avg. price, cloth: $24.95; paper: $9.95. Discounts: 50-55% to wholesalers; retail 1-4 20%, 5-9 40%, 10-24 42%, 25-49, 43%; 50+, 45%. 200pp; size varies; WEB Press. Reporting time: 1 month or less. Payment: negotiable; innovative publishing programs are being developed. Copyrights for author. ABA.

Leyland Publications, Winston Leyland, PO Box 410690, San Francisco, CA 94141, 415-626-1935; fax 415-626-1802. 1984. Fiction, cartoons, interviews, non-fiction, letters. avg. press run 7M. Pub'd 10 titles 1998;

expects 6 titles 1999, 7 titles 2000. 76 titles listed in the *Small Press Record of Books in Print* (28th Edition, 1999-00). avg. price, paper: $14.95. Discounts: Distributed to the booktrade: Bookpeople (Oakland, CA) Bookazine, Koen (N.J.), Alamo Square (San Francisco), Ingram. 192pp; 5½×8½, 7×10; sheet fed. Reporting time: 1 month. Simultaneous submissions accepted: no. Payment: royalties or outright purchase. Copyrights for author.

LFW Enterprises, PO Box 370234, Denver, CO 80237-0234, 303-750-1040. 1995. Poetry, fiction, long-poems, plays, non-fiction. avg. press run 3M. Pub'd 1 title 1998; expects 1 title 1999, 1 title 2000. 1 title listed in the *Small Press Record of Books in Print* (28th Edition, 1999-00). avg. price, paper: $12.95; other: $5.95 audio. Discounts: 3-199, 40%; 200-499, 50%; 500+ 40%/25%. 88pp; 6×9; of. Reporting time: 3 months. Simultaneous submissions accepted: no. Publishes 1% of manuscripts submitted. Payment: negotiated. Copyrights for author. CIPA, PMA, NAIP.

THE LIBERATOR, R.F. Doyle, 17854 Lyons Street, Forest Lake, MN 55025, 612-464-7663; Fax: 612-464-7135; E-mail: rdoyle@mensdefense.org. 1968. Articles, photos, interviews, news items. "Gender issues material." circ. 2M. sub. price: $24; per copy: $3; sample: $3. Back issues: $3 (some $5). Discounts: 40%. 24pp; 11×17; web. Simultaneous submissions accepted: yes. Publishes 40% of manuscripts submitted. Payment: seldom. Copyrighted, rights reverting to author conditional. Pub's reviews: 50 in 1998. §Gender issues. Ads: Write for ad schedule.

THE (LIBERTARIAN) CONNECTION, Erwin S. Strauss, 10 Hill St., #22-L, Newark, NJ 07102, 973-242-5999. 1968. Poetry, fiction, articles, art, photos, cartoons, interviews, satire, criticism, reviews, music, letters, parts-of-novels, long-poems, collages, plays, concrete art, news items, non-fiction. "Each subscriber is entitled to submit up to two pages of material to be printed in each issue. Additional pages run (unedited) for the cost of printing and mailing. Contributors you may have heard of include Bob ('The Abolition of Work') Black, Ace ('Twisted Image') Backwords, Robert ('Illuminatus!') Shea, Gerry ('Neutron Gun') Reith, Mike ('Loompanics') Hoy, Mike ('Factsheet Five') Gunderloy, Pat ('Salon') Hartman, Lev ('Anarchy') Chernyi, R.W. ('Liberty Magazine') Bradford." circ. 50. 8/yr. Pub'd 8 issues 1998; expects 8 issues 1999, 8 issues 2000. sub. price: $20; per copy: $2.50; sample: $2.50. Back issues: $2.50. Discounts: none. 50pp; 8½×11; xerography. Reporting time: none. Simultaneous submissions accepted: yes. Publishes 100% of manuscripts submitted. Payment: none. Copyrighted, reverts to author. Pub's reviews: about 2 dozen in 1998. §Each contributor makes his/her own choices; works of psychology and of objectivist philosophy have been popular recently. Ads: ads may be submitted by subscribers as their own free pages, or as paid extra pages (current charge: $7 per extra page).

Libertarian Press, Inc./American Book Distributors, Robert F. Sennholz, Lyn M. Sennholz, PO Box 309, Grove City, PA 16127-0309, 724-458-5861. 1952. Non-fiction. "LP publishes books and booklets on free market economics and political science. ABD is more diversified." avg. press run 2.5M-5M. Pub'd 2 titles 1998; expects 2 titles 1999, 4 titles 2000. avg. price, cloth: $20; paper: $8; other: $3 booklets. Discounts: up to 60%, based on quantity, larger discounts available on booklets. 300pp; 5×8; †of. Reporting time: 30 days. Payment: negotiable. Copyrights depend on contract.

LIBERTY, R.W. Bradford, Publisher & Editor; Timothy Virkkala, Managing Editor, PO Box 1181, Port Townsend, WA 98368, 360-379-0242. 1987. Poetry, fiction, articles, cartoons, interviews, criticism, reviews, non-fiction. "Quality writing of interest to political libertarians (ie. people who believe that the role of government should be radically reduced or even eliminated altogether)." circ. 15M. 6/yr. Pub'd 6 issues 1998; expects 6 issues 1999, 12 issues 2000. sub. price: $19.50; per copy: $4; sample: $4. Back issues: $4 each, varies. Discounts: 40%, minimum draw 10, fully returnable. 72pp; 8½×11; of/lo. Reporting time: 2-4 weeks. Simultaneous submissions accepted: no. Publishes 30% of manuscripts submitted. Payment: negotiable; usually nominal. Copyrighted, reverts to author. Pub's reviews: 43 in 1998. §Current events, public policy, history, philosophy, economic theory, political theory, psychology, literature, etc. Ads: $452/$244/50¢ + $1 per insertion.

Liberty Bell Press & Publishing Co., Ron Jorgensen, 4700 South 900 East, Suite 3-183, Salt Lake City, UT 84117, 801-943-8573. 1988. Articles, interviews, criticism, non-fiction. "Published *Men In The Shadows* by Jason Roberts in September, 1988." avg. press run 2M. Expects 2 titles 1999, 10 titles 2000. 2 titles listed in the *Small Press Record of Books in Print* (28th Edition, 1999-00). avg. price, paper: $17.95. 155pp; 8½×11; of. Reporting time: 90 days. Payment: to be arranged. Copyrights for author.

Liberty Publishing Company, Inc., Jeffrey B. Little, Publisher, PO BOX 4248, Deerfield Beach, FL 33442-4248, 305-360-9000. 1977. Non-fiction. "Nonfiction, horse racing, travel, consumer books, computer software, video." avg. press run 5M-20M. Pub'd 6 titles 1998; expects 7 titles 1999, 6 titles 2000. 8 titles listed in the *Small Press Record of Books in Print* (28th Edition, 1999-00). avg. price, cloth: $16.95; paper: $9.95; other: software $59.95, video $39.95. Discounts: 40% - 5 or more assorted titles. 180pp; 5½×8¼. Reporting time: 4-6 weeks. Payment: 6-12% semi-annual. Copyrights for author. ABA.

LIBIDO: The Journal of Sex and Sensibility, Marianna Beck, Jack Hafferkamp, PO Box 146721, Chicago, IL 60614, 773-275-0842. 1988. Poetry, fiction, articles, art, photos, cartoons, interviews, satire, criticism, reviews, letters, parts-of-novels, long-poems, plays, news items, non-fiction. "To paraphrase Oscar Wilde, *Libido* is the literary answer to a horizontal urge. It is a journal of the erotic arts and uses fiction (1,000-4,000 words), wordplay, photography, essays and reviews dealing in sex and sensibility. Very little poetry. Four to five poems per issue." circ. 10M. 4/yr. Pub'd 4 issues 1998; expects 4 issues 1999, 4 issues 2000. sub. price: $30; per copy: $8; sample: $8. Back issues: #1-3 $25 each, Vol. 2: #1 $20, #2 $15, #3 & #4 $10, Vol. 3: #1-3 $10, Vol. 4 1-4 $10, Vol. 5 1-4 $10, Vol. 6 1-4 $10, Vol. 7 1-4 $8, Vol. 8 1-4 $8. Discounts: contact publisher for group discounts. 88pp; 6½x9½; of, sheetfed. Reporting time: 5 months. Simultaneous submissions accepted with notice. Publishes 5% of manuscripts submitted. Payment: $50; poetry $10-$25. Copyrighted, reverts to author. Pub's reviews: 30-40 in 1998. §Any area having to do with sexuality. Ads: $500/$250/$125 1/4 page. Independent Publishers Assn.

Libra Publishers, Inc. (see also ADOLESCENCE; FAMILY THERAPY), William Kroll, President, 3089C Clairemont Dr., Suite 383, San Diego, CA 92117, 619-571-1414. 1960. Poetry, fiction, articles, art, photos, cartoons, interviews, satire, criticism, reviews, music, letters, parts-of-novels, long-poems, collages, plays, concrete art, news items. "Most interested in books in the behavioral sciences." avg. press run 3M. Pub'd 15 titles 1998; expects 20 titles 1999, 22 titles 2000. 6 titles listed in the *Small Press Record of Books in Print* (28th Edition, 1999-00). avg. price, cloth: $18.95; paper: $10. Discounts: 1-4 copies, 33⅓%; 5 or more, 40%. 160pp; 5½x8½; of. Reporting time: 4 weeks. Simultaneous submissions accepted: yes. Payment: 10% of retail price. Copyrights for author.

Librairie Droz S.A. (see also BIBLIOTHEQUE D'HUMANISME ET RENAISSANCE), A. Dufour, 11r.Massot, 1211 Geneve 12, Switzerland. 1934. Articles, criticism, reviews. "History of the 16th century." Pub'd 3 titles 1998; expects 3 titles 1999. avg. price, paper: 90 SW.FR. ($73) yr. 16×24; typography.

LIBRARIANS AT LIBERTY, Charles Willett, 1716 SW Williston Road, Gainesville, FL 32608, 352-335-2200. 1993. Articles, criticism, reviews, letters, news items. "Short articles critical of mainstream publishing and librarianship. Focus on progressive or anarchist alternatives. Contributors: Jason McQuinn, Earl Lee, Chris Atton, Sanford Berman, James Danky, James Schmidt." circ. 100. 2/yr. Pub'd 2 issues 1998; expects 2 issues 1999, 2 issues 2000. sub. price: $10 indiv., $15 institution; per copy: $5 + $3; sample: free. Back issues: $5 + $3. 16pp; 8½×11. Payment: none. Not copyrighted.

LIBRARY HI TECH, MCB University Press, MCB University Press, 60/63 Toller Lane, Bradford, W. Yorkshire BD8 9BY, England, 01274-777700; Fax 01274-785200 or 785201; www.mcb.co.uk. 1983. Articles, reviews. "Library/reference, library technology and automation" circ. 2,600. 4/yr. Pub'd 4 issues 1998; expects 4 issues 1999, 4 issues 2000. sub. price: $84; per copy: $22; sample: free. 112pp; 8½×11; of. Reporting time: 4 weeks. Payment: none. Ads: inquire.

LIBRARY HIGH TECH NEWS, MCB University Press, MCB University Press, 60/63 Toller Lane, Bradford, W. Yorkshire BD8 9BY, England, 01274-777700; Fax 01274-785200 or 785201; www.mcb.co.uk. 1984. Articles, reviews, news items. "Library/reference, library news, technology and automation" circ. 2M. 10/yr. Pub'd 10 issues 1998; expects 10 issues 1999, 10 issues 2000. sub. price: $98; per copy: $13; sample: free. 32pp; 8½×11; of. Reporting time: 4 weeks. Payment: none. Pub's reviews. §Library technology and automation. Ads: inquire.

●**Library Research Associates,** Elma Van Fossen, PO Box 32234, San Jose, CA 95152-2234, 408-946-0777; fax 408-946-0779. 1999. Non-fiction. avg. press run 3M. Expects 1 title 1999, 2 titles 2000. 1 title listed in the *Small Press Record of Books in Print* (28th Edition, 1999-00). avg. price, paper: $15.95. Discounts: 20%/40%/55%. 187pp; 6×9; of. Reporting time: 1 month. Simultaneous submissions accepted: yes. Payment: 10-15%. Does not copyright for author.

Library Research Associates, Inc., Matilda A. Gocek, Dianne D. McKinstrie, 474 Dunderberg Road, Monroe, NY 10950, 914-783-1144. 1968. Non-fiction, fiction. avg. press run 3.5M. Pub'd 7 titles 1998; expects 4 titles 1999. 34 titles listed in the *Small Press Record of Books in Print* (28th Edition, 1999-00). avg. price, cloth: $20; paper: $9. Discounts: 40% to book sellers; 1-9 books 30%, 10-49 books 40%, 50-99 books 45%, 100+ books 50%. 250pp; 5½x8½; of, lp. Reporting time: 3 weeks. Simultaneous submissions accepted: no. Publishes 1% of manuscripts submitted. Payment: 10% royalties. Copyrights for author.

LIBRARY TALK: The Magazine for Elementary School Librarians, Linworth Publishing, Inc., Marlene Woo-Lun, Publisher; Cynthia Allen, Director of Marketing, 480 East Wilson Bridge Road #L, Worthington, OH 43085-2372, 614-436-7107; fax 614-436-9490. 1988. Articles, reviews. "We publish article manuscripts only *about* the management of the school library *by* authors who have been or are elementary school librarians" circ. 8.6M. 5/yr. Pub'd 5 issues 1998; expects 5 issues 1999, 5 issues 2000. sub. price: $49 US, $60 Canada; per copy: $11; sample: complimentary copies free. Back issues: $11. Discounts: 5% classroom and subscription agency. 64pp; 8½×11. Copyrighted, does not revert to author. Pub's reviews: 1200 in 1998. §Materials suitable for elementary school libraries, grades 1-6. Ads: $990/$640 (1x b/w)/$395 1/3p B/W; 1 time rate add $875 for color. EDPress.

THE LICKING RIVER REVIEW, P. Andrew Miller, Faculty Advisor, Department of Literature and Language, Northern Kentucky University, Highland Heights, KY 41099. 1989. Poetry, fiction. "We welcome crafted work that leaves a memorable impression. Recent contributors include Tony Whedon, Fredrick Zydek, Rhonda Pettit, Bill Garten, Diana Lee. Poems uner 70 lines, fiction under 5,000 words. No Simultaneous submissions." circ. 1-1.5M. 1/yr. Pub'd 1 issue 1998; expects 1 issue 1999, 1 issue 2000. sub. price: $5; per copy: $5; sample: $5. Back issues: $5. Discounts: please inquire. 96pp; 7×10; †of. Reporting time: 1-9 months. Simultaneous submissions accepted: no. Publishes 5% of manuscripts submitted. Payment: 2 contributor's copies. Copyrighted, reverts to author. Ads: $100/$50.

LIES MAGAZINE, Matt Worley, Editor; Aaron Worley, Editor, 1112 San Pedro NE #154, Albuquerque, NM 87110, 505-268-7316; email okeefine@aol.com; www.cent.com/abetting/. 1994. Poetry, fiction, articles, art, photos, cartoons, interviews, satire, criticism, reviews, music, letters, parts-of-novels, long-poems, non-fiction. "Up to 3,000 words, don't use much poetry or interviews. Reviews are done in house. Humor does well. Would like to see good short story fiction. Recent contributers: Stepan Chapman, Michael Wexler." circ. 2M+. 4/yr. Pub'd 4 issues 1998; expects 4 issues 1999, 4 issues 2000. sub. price: $12/6 issues; per copy: $3; sample: $3. Back issues: 5 for $10, 6 for $12. Discounts: call or e-mail. 44pp; 8¼×10¾; of. Reporting time: 2 months. Simultaneous submissions accepted: yes. Publishes 10% of manuscripts submitted. Payment: free copy. Copyrighted, reverts to author. Pub's reviews: 10+ in 1998. §Non-mainstream literary titles. Ads: $150/$90/$60 1/4 page/$40 1/8 page.

●**Life Adventures Publishing,** PO Box 260479, Plano, TX 75026, 888-893-2224; fax 972-964-1255; e-mail thomasbell@msw.com; website www.life-adventures.com. 1998. Non-fiction. "To create and distribute information in publications that will educate, inform, and encourage people to receive the great benefits derived by taking time off of their regular work schedules to take short adventures in, through and among Mother Nature regularly." avg. press run 10M. Expects 1 title 1999, 3 titles 2000. 1 title listed in the *Small Press Record of Books in Print* (28th Edition, 1999-00). avg. price, paper: $23.95. Discounts: 40%. 224pp; 6×9; of. Reporting time: 60 days. Simultaneous submissions accepted: no. Payment: 10% of retail. Copyrights negotiable.

Life Energy Media, 15030 Ventura Blvd, Suite 908, Sherman Oaks, CA 91403, 818-995-3263. 1975. "Publishes and produces print, audio, and video materials on life energy concepts in the areas of organizations, massage, therapy, movement and dance, expressive arts, yoga, martial arts, spiritual evolution and other related areas" avg. press run 500-5M. Pub'd 3 titles 1998; expects 3 titles 1999, 3 titles 2000. 2 titles listed in the *Small Press Record of Books in Print* (28th Edition, 1999-00). avg. price, cloth: $19.95; paper: $12.95; other: articles $3.00. Discounts: trade, quantity, conferences, classroom, jobbers. 20-350pp; 5½×8½. Reporting time: initial interest 1 month. Payment: negotiable. We can copyright for author. PMA.

●**Life Lessons,** Mark Frakes, PO Box 382346, Cambridge, MA 02238, 617-576-2546; fax 617-576-3234; e-mail walkingwm@aol.com; website www.mindwalks.com. 1997. Non-fiction. "Will consider authors interested in building a brand compatible with existing publications. Query first, no ms." avg. press run 3M-10M. Pub'd 1 title 1998; expects 2 titles 1999, 3 titles 2000. 1 title listed in the *Small Press Record of Books in Print* (28th Edition, 1999-00). avg. price, paper: $13. Discounts: bulk to trade. 256pp; 4×6; of. Reporting time: 1 month. Simultaneous submissions accepted: yes. Publishes 2% of manuscripts submitted. Payment: negotiable. Copyrights for author. PMA, SPAN.

LIFE ON PLANET EARTH, VOL III, J.C. Coleman, PO Box 3194, Bellingham, WA 98227. 1983. Fiction, articles, art, photos, cartoons, satire, criticism, reviews. "A variety of offbeat material in every issue. Does not accept submissions or advertising. All payments must be in *cash*. Trade of similar publications is welcome." circ. 50. 4/yr. Pub'd 4 issues 1998; expects 4 issues 1999, 4 issues 2000. sub. price: $1/3 issues; per copy: 40¢; sample: 40¢. Back issues: $1 each. Discounts: none. 2pp; 8½×11; photocopy. Copyrighted. Pub's reviews: 30 in 1998. §Sci-fi, death. Ads: none.

●**LifeQuest Publishing Group,** PO Box 1444, Issaquah, WA 98027, fax 425-392-1854; e-mail lifequest@usa.net. 1994. Music, non-fiction. avg. press run 30M. Expects 7 titles 1999, 12 titles 2000. avg. price, paper: $29.95. Discounts: available upon request. 240pp; 7×9; of. Reporting time: 60 days. Simultaneous submissions accepted: yes. Payment: yes. Copyrights for author.

LifeThread Publications, Susan M. Osborn, President, 793 Harvey Way, Sacramento, CA 95831-4728, 916-395-8549; E-mail sosborn@ix.netcom.com. 1996. Non-fiction. "Accept materials related to system theory; systems perspectives on business & psychological issues" avg. press run 3M. Expects 1 title 1999, 1 title 2000. 1 title listed in the *Small Press Record of Books in Print* (28th Edition, 1999-00). avg. price, paper: $15-20. negotiable. 200pp; 6×9; of. Reporting time: 2 months. Simultaneous submissions accepted: yes. Payment: negotiable. Copyrights for author. PMA, BAIPA, SPA.

Lifetime Books, Inc. (see also FELL'S U.S. COINS INVESTMENT QUARTERLY; MONEY LINES; SPECIALTY COOKING MAGAZINE; DIET & HEALTH MAGAZINE; FELL'S HEALTH FITNESS MAGAZINE; GOOD COOKING SERIES), Brian Feinblum, Editor-in-Chief, 2131 Hollywood Boulevard, Hollywood, FL 33020. 1943. Non-fiction. avg. press run 5M. Pub'd 20 titles 1998; expects 20 titles 1999, 20 titles 2000. 17 titles listed in the *Small Press Record of Books in Print* (28th Edition, 1999-00). avg. price, cloth: $18.95; paper: $12.95. 240pp; 5½x8½, 6x9; of. Reporting time: 2 months. Simultaneous submissions accepted: yes. Payment: 6-7% trade paperback, 10% cloth. Copyrights for author. ABA.

LIFTOUTS, Preludium Publishers, Barry Casselman, Frederic Will, 1414 S. 3rd Street-#102, Minneapolis, MN 55454, 612-321-9044, Fax 612-305-0655. 1983. Poetry, fiction, criticism, reviews, parts-of-novels. *"Liftouts* is devoted primarily to reviews of new books and critical essays. Some short fiction and poetry is published, with an emphasis on translated works by foreign authors who have not previously been published in English. *Unsolicited submissions are not considered at this time.* Any inquiries should be accompanied by SASE. Translations of stories by Clarice Lispector, Luiz Vilela, Hans Christoph Buch, Sergio Sant'Anna and others have appeared in previous issues.'' circ. 5M. 1/yr. Expects 1 issue 2000. sub. price: $5; per copy: $5; sample: $5. Back issues: $5. Discounts: negotiable. 40-75pp; 5x8½; of. Payment: varies. Copyrighted, reverts to author. Pub's reviews: 35 in 1998. §Poetry, fiction, plays, literary criticism, all literature in translation. Ads: $495/$275/$7.50 per column inch.

Light Beams Press, 3463 State Street, #193, Santa Barbara, CA 93105, 805-565-9424; Fax 805-565-9824. 1997. Fiction, non-fiction. avg. press run 3-5M. Expects 3 titles 1999, 3 titles 2000. 1 title listed in the *Small Press Record of Books in Print* (28th Edition, 1999-00). avg. price, paper: $14.95. Reporting time: varies. Simultaneous submissions accepted: yes. Payment: negotiate. Does not copyright for author.

LIGHT: The Quarterly of Light Verse, John Mella, Lisa Markwart, PO Box 7500, Chicago, IL 60680. 1992. Poetry, fiction, articles, art, cartoons, interviews, satire, criticism, reviews, letters, news items. "Light is the only magazine in the United States that publishes light verse exclusively. Write for guidelines. Contributors include John Updike, X.J. Kennedy, Donald Hall, Michael Benedikt, and Tom Disch. We also publish cartoons, satire, reviews, and humor'' circ. 1M. 4+. Pub'd 4 issues 1998; expects 2+ issues 1999, 2+ issues 2000. sub. price: $18/4 issues, $30/8 issues, $28/4 issues international; per copy: $5 + $2 1st class mail; sample: $4 + $2 1st class mail. Back issues: same. Discounts: jobber 10%. 64pp; 6x9; of. Reporting time: 1-4 months. Simultaneous submissions accepted: no. Publishes 8% of manuscripts submitted. Payment: copies. Copyrighted, reverts to author. Pub's reviews: 60 in 1998. §Light verse, satire, cartoons. Ads: Write for ad card. CLMP.

Light, Words & Music, Dan Polin, 16710 16th N.W., Seattle, WA 98177, 206-546-1498, Fax 206-546-2585; sisp@aol.com. 1995. "This press specializes in 'fusion of the arts' books'' avg. press run 5M. Pub'd 1 title 1998; expects 1 title 1999, 1 title 2000. 3 titles listed in the *Small Press Record of Books in Print* (28th Edition, 1999-00). avg. price, paper: $25. 150pp; 8½x11.

LIGHTHOUSE, Tim Clinton, Lorraine Clinton, Lighthouse Publications, PO Box 1377, Auburn, WA 98071-1377. 1986. Poetry, fiction. "Content must be of a family 'G-rated' nature. Stories up to 5,000 words. Poems up to 50 lines. Free writer's guidelines available with SASE with one first-class stamp, and submission should be accompanied by SASE with sufficient postage for return of ms. We also have a children's section.'' circ. 300+. 4/yr. Pub'd 3 issues 1998; expects 4 issues 1999, 4 issues 2000. sub. price: $7.95 for 6 issues; per copy: $3; sample: $3 (includes writers' guidelines, p/h). Discounts: $2 each for authors who order copies. 56pp; 5½x8½; †xerox. Reporting time: 1-3 months, longer indicates interest. Simultaneous submissions accepted: no. Payment: up to $50 for story, up to $5 for a poem, upon publication. Copyrighted, reverts to author. No ads.

LIGHTNING & ASH, Paul Kremsreiter, Michael Douglas Hettinger, 3010 Hennepin Avenue South #289, Minneapolis, MN 55408. 1996. Poetry, fiction, satire, criticism, letters. circ. 500. 2/yr. Pub'd 1 issue 1998; expects 2 issues 1999. sub. price: $10; per copy: $6. Back issues: $3. Discounts: call for details. 100pp; 8½x5½; of. Reporting time: 2 months. Simultaneous submissions accepted: yes. Publishes 10% of manuscripts submitted. Payment: 2 copies. Copyrighted, reverts to author.

LIGHTWORKS MAGAZINE, Charlton Burch, Designer and Editor; Andrea Martin, Managing Editor, PO Box 1202, Birmingham, MI 48012-1202, 248-626-8026; FAX 248-737-0046. 1975. Articles, art, photos, interviews, collages, concrete art. "Illuminating new and experimental art. A tribute issue devoted to the life and art of Ray Johnson will be released in 1999.'' circ. 2M. Irregular. Pub'd 1 issue 1998; expects 1 issue 1999, 1 issue 2000. sub. price: $20 (4 future issues) individuals, $25 institutions; per copy: price varies; sample: $5. Back issues: #10 $2, #14/15-#18 $4, #13 $3, #5 $1, all orders must add $1.50 to cover postage costs, #19-#20/21 $5, Ray Johnson issue $13 includes audio CD. Discounts: 40% on orders of 12 copies of one issue at least, 50% on orders of 50 or more. 56pp; 8½x11; of. Reporting time: usually quick. Publishes 50% of manuscripts submitted. Payment: none, other than a couple copies. Copyrighted. Pub's reviews: 60 in 1998. §Books, periodicals, and recordings which explore alternative & intermediate artforms, and artists' publications. No ads.

LILITH, Susan W. Schneider, Editor-in-Chief, 250 West 57th, #2432, New York, NY 10107, 212-757-0818. 1976. Poetry, fiction, articles, art, photos, interviews, criticism, reviews, letters, parts-of-novels, long-poems, plays, news items, non-fiction. "The 'Jewish Woman's Quarterly'." circ. 10M. 4/yr. Pub'd 4 issues 1998; expects 4 issues 1999, 4 issues 2000. sub. price: $18; per copy: $4.50; sample: $6, includes postage. Back issues: $6 for in-print back issues. Out-of-print $50. Discounts: through distributors: DeBoer's, Ingram, Koens, small changes, desert moon. 48pp; 8⅛×10⅞; of. Reporting time: 3 months. Simultaneous submissions accepted, as long as we are told when another publication accepts. Payment: negotiable. Copyrighted, rights reverting to author negotiable. Pub's reviews: 20 in 1998. §Pertaining to the Jewish, female experience, history, biography/autobio., feminist, fiction, poetry. Ads: on request. AJPA.

LILLIPUT REVIEW, Don Wentworth, Editor, 282 Main Street, Pittsburgh, PA 15201. 1989. Poetry. "All poems must be 10 lines or *less*. All styles and forms considered. SASE or in the trash, period. 3 poems maximum per submissions. Any submission beyond the maximum will be returned unread." circ. 225-300. Irregular. Pub'd 8 issues 1998; expects 8 issues 1999, 8 issues 2000. 7 titles listed in the *Small Press Record of Books in Print* (28th Edition, 1999-00). sub. price: $12; per copy: $1; sample: $1 or SASE. Back issues: $1. Discounts: Individuals only: 6 issues=$5; 15 issues=$10. 16pp; 4.25×3.6; †laser printed. Reporting time: 1-12 weeks. Simultaneous submissions accepted: no. Publishes 5% of manuscripts submitted. Payment: 2 copies. Copyrighted, reverts to author.

Limberlost Press, Rick Ardinger, 17 Canyon Trail, Boise, ID 83716. 1976. Poetry, fiction, interviews, reviews. "Although *The Limberlost Review* first appeared in 1976 as a literary magazine, issues for the past few years have been devoted to the works of individual writers as books and chapbooks, and we will continue that trend indefinitely. Limberlost Press has published books, particularly essays and fiction in offset, larger editions, such as John Rember's collection of stories, *Coyote in the Mountains* (1989), Nancy Stringfellow's essays, *Report from Grimes Creek After a Hard Winter* (1990), and Rick Ardinger's *What Thou Lovest Well Remains: 100 Years of Ezra Pound* (1986), a collection of essays by poets. Limberlost poetry chapbooks however, are letterpressed in finely printed, hand-sewn limited editions. Recent chapbooks include *The Street's Kiss* by Lawrence Ferlinghetti (1993), and *Mind Writing Slogans* by Allen Ginsberg (1994). We try to press 3-4 titles a year. Limberlost also publishes poetry postcards and broadsides. A limited edition portfolio of letterpressed broadsides, featuring poems by Lawrence Ferlinghetti, Gary Snyder, Ann Waldman, Robert Creeley, Ed Sanders, Charles Bukowski, Ed Dorn, and others is forthcoming in 1995. Writers interested in submitting work for consideration should be familiar with the quality of the books and chapbooks Limberlost is currently publishing." avg. press run 350-1M. Pub'd 2 titles 1998; expects 2 titles 1999, 2-3 titles 2000. 18 titles listed in the *Small Press Record of Books in Print* (28th Edition, 1999-00). avg. price, paper: $15. Discounts: 40% for 5 or more. 36pp; size varies; †of, lp. Reporting time: 1-2 months. Payment: in copies. Copyrights for author. CLMP.

LIME GREEN BULLDOZERS (AND OTHER RELATED SPECIES), Oyster Publications, Lainie Duro, PO Box 4333, Austin, TX 78765. 1986. Poetry, fiction, art, photos. "No longer than one double-spaced page. No contributions welcome without some communication." circ. 300. 2/yr. Pub'd 2 issues 1998; expects 2 issues 1999, 2 issues 2000. price per copy: $3; sample: $3. 50pp; 8½×11; †xerox. Payment: none. Not copyrighted. Ads: none.

Limelight Editions, Mel Zerman, 118 East 30th Street, New York, NY 10016, 212-532-5525, fax 212-532-5526. 1984. Non-fiction. "Almost all of our books are paperback reprints of previously published works on the performing arts. We do occasional original publishing." avg. press run 4M. Pub'd 14 titles 1998; expects 14 titles 1999, 14 titles 2000. 96 titles listed in the *Small Press Record of Books in Print* (28th Edition, 1999-00). avg. price, cloth: $27.50; paper: $14.95. Discounts: graduated schedule for retailers, 50% for wholesalers. 300pp; 6×9; of. Reporting time: 3-4 weeks. Payment: generally 7½% against a modest advance for paperback, 10% cloth. Copyrights for author. ABA.

LIMESTONE: A LITERARY JOURNAL, Fred M. IV McCormick, Editor in Chief, English Dept., Univ. of Kentucky, 1215 Patterson Office Tower, Lexington, KY 40506-0027. 1979. Poetry, fiction, art, photos, interviews, criticism, reviews, parts-of-novels, long-poems, collages, non-fiction. "*Limestone: A Literary Journal*, ISSN 0899-5966, has published work by Gurney Norman, James Baker Hall, Wendell Berry, and Guy Davenport. We accept manuscripts from any interested contributors, September through April only" circ. 1M. 1/yr. Expects 1 issue 1999, 1 issue 2000. sub. price: $5 individual/$10 institution; per copy: $5 individual/$10 institution; sample: $5 individual/$10 institution. Back issues: $5 individual/$10 institution. 120-140pp; 5½×8½; of. Reporting time: 2-3 months. Simultaneous submissions accepted: yes. Publishes 5-10% of manuscripts submitted. Payment: 2 copies. Copyrighted, reverts to author. Pub's reviews: 0 in 1998. §Contemporary aesthetics. Ads: $75/$40.

Lincoln Springs Press, 40 Post Avenue, Hawthorne, NJ 07506-1809. 1987. Poetry, fiction, photos. "Please send 5 sample poems & bio. or 5 pages of prose plus SASE." avg. press run 1M. Expects 4 titles 1999, 4 titles 2000. 9 titles listed in the *Small Press Record of Books in Print* (28th Edition, 1999-00). avg. price, paper: $8.95. Discounts: 1-5 20%, 5-10 30%, 10+ 40%. 80pp; 5½×8½; of. Reporting time: 6 months. Payment: 15% royalty. Copyrights for author.

LINGO, Hard Press, Inc., Jon Gams, PO Box 184, West Stockbridge, MA 01266, 413-232-4690. 1993. Poetry, fiction, art, photos, interviews, cartoons, reviews, music, collages. "Mark Swed, David Shapiro, Lyn Hejinian, Clark Coolidge, Hubert Selby, Jr., John Wesley, Gillian McCain, Wang Ping, Rosmary Waldrop" circ. 3.5M. 2/yr. Pub'd 2 issues 1998; expects 2 issues 1999, 2 issues 2000. sub. price: $20; per copy: $12.50; sample: $12.50. Discounts: 55% trade, 20% classroom. 172pp; 8½×11. Reporting time: 6 months. Payment: varies. Copyrighted, reverts to author. Pub's reviews: 3 in 1998. Ads: $1000/$550.

LININGTON LINEUP, Rinehart S. Potts, 1223 Glen Terrace, Glassboro, NJ 08028-1315, 609-589-1571. 1984. Poetry, fiction, articles, art, photos, cartoons, interviews, satire, criticism, reviews, letters, news items, non-fiction. "Being devoted to the study of the writings of one person (Elizabeth Linington), the publication accepts any material relating to her, her books, the characters, etc. Her pen-names: Anne Blaisdell, Lesley Egan, Egan O'Neill, Dell Shannon. Types of writings: historical fiction, detective mysteries, political commentary." circ. 400. 6/yr. Pub'd 6 issues 1998; expects 6 issues 1999, 6 issues 2000. sub. price: $12, foreign $15; per copy: $3, foreign $4; sample: free. Back issues: same as current. Discounts: half-price to bookstores, teachers, etc. 16pp; 8½×11; of. Reporting time: 1 month. Payment: quantity of copies of issue. Copyrighted, does not revert to author. Pub's reviews: 20 in 1998. §Reference books in mystery/detective field. Ads: $40/$20. Elizabeth Linington Society.

LINKS, Bill Headdon, 'Bude Haven' 18 Frankfield Rise, Tunbridge Wells TN2 5LF, United Kingdom, 01892-539800. 1997. Poetry, reviews. "Nothing over 100 lines." circ. 200. 2/yr. Pub'd 2 issues 1998; expects 2 issues 1999, 2 issues 2000. sub. price: £4 (£5 ex UK); per copy: £2 (£3 ex UK); sample: £2 (£3 ex UK). Discounts: £7.50 for 2 years (£9.50 ex UK). 28pp; 5.5×8.3; †DTP. Reporting time: 2 weeks max. Simultaneous submissions accepted: no. Publishes 8% of manuscripts submitted. Payment: contributor's copy. Copyrighted, reverts to author. Pub's reviews: 15 in 1998. §Poetry. PALPI.

LINQ, Dr. Greg Manning, Editor; Dr. Gina Mercer, Editor, School Languages, Literature and Communication, James Cook Univ.-North Queensland, Townsville 4811, Australia, e-mail jw.linq@jeu.edu.au. 1971. Poetry, fiction, articles, interviews, criticism, reviews, parts-of-novels, long-poems, plays. "Critical articles about 3M words. Reviews 1M words." circ. 350. 2/yr. Pub'd 2 issues 1998; expects 2 issues 1999, 2 issues 2000. sub. price: $20 indiv.; $25 instit. including postage, Australian, Overseas $35 Australian; per copy: $10, Australian (including postage). Back issues: $3 prior to 1980. 140pp; 5½×8½; of. Reporting time: 2 months. Simultaneous submissions accepted: yes. Payment: poetry $20 per poem, short fiction $50, reviews $30, articles $50 Australian dollars. Copyrighted, reverts to author. Pub's reviews: 8 in 1998. §Any area of contemporary interest, political, sociological, literary.

Lintel, Mary Hume, Co-Publisher; Naomi May Miller, Co-Publisher; Walter James Miller, Editorial Director, 24 Blake Lane, Middletown, NY 10940, 212-674-4901. 1978. Poetry, fiction, art, long-poems. "We have gotten some good back-cover blurbs from Kurt Vonnegut, David Ignatow, Anthony Burgess, Robert Bly, Menke Katz, Richard Eberhart, et al. We finance a book through advance subscriptions." avg. press run 1.5M. Pub'd 2 titles 1998; expects 1 title 1999, 1 title 2000. 21 titles listed in the *Small Press Record of Books in Print* (28th Edition, 1999-00). avg. price, cloth: $20; paper: $9.95. Discounts: 40% to bookstores; 45% on 25 copies or more; 55% to wholesalers. 100pp; 5¾×9, 5×8; photo of. Reporting time: 2 months. Simultaneous submissions are accepted if they are so indicated. Publishes 1% of manuscripts submitted. Payment: author gets 100 copies on publication, and shares in the profits, if any; each contract is worked out individually. Copyrights for author.

Linworth Publishing, Inc. (see also THE BOOK REPORT: Journal for Junior & Senior High School Librarians; LIBRARY TALK: The Magazine for Elementary School Librarians), Carol Simpson, Editor; Marlene Woo-Lun, Publisher; Cynthia Allen, Director of Marketing, 480 East Wilson Bridge Road #L, Worthington, OH 43085-2372, 614-436-7107; FAX 614-436-9490. 1982. Discounts: 5%. 8½×11. EdPress.

THE LION AND THE UNICORN: A Critical Journal of Children's Literature, Louisa Smith, Jack Zipes, Mankato State University, English Dept Box 53, Mankato, MN 56002-8400, 780-5195. 1977. Articles, interviews, reviews. "Articles are generally 10-30 pp. typed and focus on some aspect of a theme or genre in children's literature. Articles should be critical rather than appreciative or purely historical. MLA form required for manuscripts. Letters of inquiry are encouraged. Recent contributors: Peter Hunt, Peter Hollindale, Maria Nikolajeva, Mark West; interviews of Phillip Pullman, Martha Conlon-McKenna, Peter Sis. For subs. write to The Lion & Unicorn, Journal Division, Johns Hopkins Univ. Press, 701 West 40th Street, Suite 275, Baltimore, MD 21211." circ. 1.5M. 3/yr. Pub'd 3 issues 1998; expects 3 issues 1999, 3 issues 2000. sub. price: $26 indiv., $65 instit.; per copy: $10. Back issues: $10; $16 for double issues. 164pp; 6×9; standard typesetting. Reporting time: 6 months, receipt of articles acknowledged immediately. Payment: 2 copies of book. Copyrighted, rights do not revert, but author may reprint in a publication entirely composed of his/her own work w/o permission or charge. Pub's reviews: 12 in 1998. §Children's and young adult literature, critical works on children's & young adult literature including fiction, poetry, drama.

Lion Press & Video, Norma L. Leone, PO Box 92541, Rochester, NY 14692, 716-381-6410; fax 716-381-7439; for orders only 800-597-3068. 1985. Non-fiction. avg. press run 1M-5M. Pub'd 1 title 1998; expects 2-3 titles 1999, 1 title 2000. 5 titles listed in the *Small Press Record of Books in Print* (28th Edition, 1999-00). avg. price, paper: $8-$15. Discounts: 20-50%. 1-200pp; 5½x8½; of. Reporting time: 1 month. Simultaneous submissions accepted: no. Copyrights for author. NAIP.

Lion Press, Ltd., Leslie Diamond, President, 108-22 Queens Boulevard, #221, Forest Hills, NY 11375, 718-271-1394. 1994. Fiction, non-fiction. avg. press run 2M. Pub'd 1 title 1998; expects 2 titles 1999, 3 titles 2000. 1 title listed in the *Small Press Record of Books in Print* (28th Edition, 1999-00). avg. price, cloth: $15.95; other: $21.95 hardcover. Discounts: 50%, nonreturnable, any amount. 400pp; 6x9; lp. Reporting time: 3 months. Payment: varies. Copyrights for author. ABA, Small Press Assn.

Lionheart Publishing, Charles Mitchley, Private Bag X5, Constantia, Cape Town 7848, Republic of South Africa, 002721-794-4923; Fax 002721-794-1487; cajmi@iafrica.com; www.toltec-foundation.org. 1996. avg. press run 6M. Pub'd 1 title 1998; expects 1 title 1999, 4 titles 2000. 4 titles listed in the *Small Press Record of Books in Print* (28th Edition, 1999-00). avg. price, cloth: $24.95; paper: $16.95. Discounts: 1-25 40%, 26-60 45%, 61-100 50%. 300pp; 5½x8¾. Copyrights for author. PMA.

LIPS, Laura Boss, PO Box 1345, Montclair, NJ 07042. 1981. Poetry. *"Lips* publishes the best contemporary poetry submitted. No biases. Recent Contributors: Allen Ginsberg, Richard Kostelanetz, Marge Piercy, Warren Woessner, Maria Gillan, Alice Notley, E. Ethelbert Miller, Lyn Lifshin, Gregory Corso, Ishmael Reed, Michael Benedikt, Robert Phillips, Nicholas Christopher, David Ignatow, Stanley H. Barkan, Dennis Brutus, Molly Peacock." circ. 1M. 2/yr. Pub'd 2 issues 1998; expects 2 issues 1999, 2 issues 2000. sub. price: $10 indiv, $12 instit; per copy: $5; sample: $5 + $1 p/h. 80pp; 5½x8½; of. Reporting time: 2 months. Payment: 2 copies. Copyrighted, reverts to author. Ads: $100. CLMP.

Liquid Paper Press (see also NERVE COWBOY), Joseph Shields, Jerry Hagins, PO Box 4973, Austin, TX 78765, www.eden.com/~jwhagins/nervecowboy. 1995. Poetry. "Recent books published by Liquid Paper Press include *The Active Ingredient, and Other Poems* and *The Back East Poems* by Gerald Locklin, *Butchers and Brain Surgeons* by Fred Voss, *Born Not to Laugh at Tornadoes* by Joan Jobe Smith, *Notes of a Human Warehouse Engineer* by Belinda Subraman, *E Pluribus Aluminum* by Thomas Michael McDade, and *Grappling* by Susanne R. Bowers. We do not accept unsolicited manuscripts." avg. press run 150. Pub'd 4 titles 1998; expects 4 titles 1999, 4 titles 2000. 8 titles listed in the *Small Press Record of Books in Print* (28th Edition, 1999-00). avg. price, paper: $4. Discounts: 40% on purchase of 3 or more copies. 32pp; 5½x8½; mi. We currently only accept solicited chapbook manuscripts, with the exception of our annual chapbook. Payment: 30 complimentary copies. Copyrights for author.

LISTEN, Lincoln Steed, Editor, 55 West Oak Ridge Drive, Hagerstown, MD 21740. 1948. Articles, art, cartoons, interviews, non-fiction. circ. 40M. 12/yr. Pub'd 12 issues 1998; expects 12 issues 1999, 12 issues 2000. sub. price: $19.97/$25.07 foreign; per copy: $2; sample: $1. Back issues: 40¢. 32pp; 10½x8. Reporting time: 60 days. Simultaneous submissions accepted: yes. Publishes 50% of manuscripts submitted. Payment: $50-$250. Copyrighted, reverts to author. Ads: $500/$300.

Listen and Learn Home Education, Inc. (see also BOOMERANG! MAGAZINE), David Strohm, PO Box 261, La Honda, CA 94020-0261, 415-882-7875. 1990. Fiction, articles, interviews, reviews, letters, parts-of-novels, news items, non-fiction. avg. press run 20M. Pub'd 12 titles 1998; expects 12 titles 1999, 12 titles 2000. avg. price, other: $5.95 cassette tape. Discounts: variable, average 40%, call for information. duplication. Reporting time: 1 month. Payment: variable. Does not copyright for author.

THE LISTENING EYE, Grace Butcher, Editor; Joanne Speidel, Co-Ass't Editor; James Wohlken, Co-Ass't Editor, KSU Geauga Campus, 14111 Claridon-Troy Road, Burton, OH 44021, 440-286-3840; e-mail hy151@cleveland.freenet.edu. 1970. Poetry, fiction, art, photos, non-fiction. "Send four poems, limit four pages, any subject, any style. We are small but look for quality work. Have published Walter McDonald, William Stafford, Steven Dunning, Ann Menebroker, Dennis Trudell. Thirty dollar prize for best sports poem each year. Thirty dollar prize for cover, 5 X 7, black & white, based on title of magazine, SASE for all submisisons. Short stories, creative essays, 750 words max, limit 3. Photos, black and white. Read January 1-April 15 only." circ. 250. 1/yr. Pub'd 1 issue 1998; expects 1 issue 1999, 1 issue 2000. sub. price: $4; per copy: $4; sample: $4. Back issues: $4. Discounts: N/A. 60pp; 5½x8½; Professionally printed. Reporting time: 4 months max, sometimes sooner. Simultaneous submissions accepted: no. Publishes maybe 20% of manuscripts submitted. Payment: 2 free copies. Copyrighted, reverts to author.

LITERAL LATTE, Jenine Gordon Bockman, Editor and Publisher; Jeff Bockman, Assoc.Editor and

Executive Publisher, 61 East 8th Street, Suite 240, New York, NY 10003, 212-260-5532. 1994. Poetry, fiction, art, photos, cartoons, satire, reviews, parts-of-novels, long-poems, collages, plays, concrete art, non-fiction. "6M word max. Recent contributors include John Updike, Stephen Dixon, Carol Muske, Phillip Lopate, Daniel Harris, Michael Brodskey, Robert Olen Botler, Lynne Sharon Schwartz. All forms, classic to experimental. Quality literary material the only requirement" circ. 25M. 6/yr. Pub'd 6 issues 1998; expects 6 issues 1999, 6 issues 2000. sub. price: $15 institution; $11 individual, $25 intern; per copy: $3; sample: $3 incl. postage. Back issues: $10. 24pp; 11×17; web. Reporting time: 3 months. Simultaneous submissions accepted: yes. Publishes 1-2% of manuscripts submitted. Payment: copies + subscription + $25 minimum. Copyrighted, reverts to author. Pub's reviews: 1-2 per issue in 1998. §Literary books. Ads: $1425/$713/$50 business card classified. CLMP.

LITERARY MAGAZINE REVIEW, Grant Tracey, Editor; Karen Tracey, Associate Editor; Vince Gotera, Associate Editor; G.W. Clift, Contributing Editor, Department of English Language and Literature, University of Northern Iowa, Cedar Falls, IA 50614-0502, 319-273-3782; fax 319-273-5807; e-Mail grant.tracey@uni.edu. 1981. Articles, criticism, reviews. "*LMR* is devoted to providing critical appraisals of the specific contents of small, predominantly literary periodicals for the benefit of readers and writers. We print reviews of about 1.5M words which comment on the magazines' physical characteristics, on particular articles, stories, and poems featured, and on editorial preferences as evidenced in the selections. Recent contributors include Fred Chappell, Kenneth Rosen, Peter Lasalle, D.E. Steward, Phil Miller, Ben Nyberg, Ben Reynolds, and JoAnn Castagna. We would be happy to entertain queries offering disinterested reviews and omnibus notices and pieces describing, explaining, or dissecting the current literary magazine scene. Subscription exchange inquiries are welcome." circ. 600. 4/yr. Pub'd 4 issues 1998; expects 4 issues 1999, 4 issues 2000. sub. price: $12.50; per copy: $4; sample: $4. Back issues: $5 an issue. Discounts: 10% to subscription agencies. 48-52pp; 5½×8½; of. Payment: copies. Copyrighted, rights revert on author's request. Pub's reviews: 70 in 1998. §Literary magazines. We are interested in magazines which publish at least some fiction or poetry or both. Ads: none.

Literary Moments, Larnette Phillips, PO Box 15503, Pensacola, FL 32514, 850-857-0178. 1999. Poetry, fiction, satire. "Up to 1500 words for short stories (all genres); no length on poetry; KIDSPEAK section publishes children ages 10 and up; no graphic sex, graphic violence or profanity; seeks to publish the 'unpublished/minimally published' writer recent contributors: David Stemen, Ed Sullivan, Kathleen Wheeler, Kevin Sanders, Linda Olson." circ. 500. quarterly. sub. price: $65; per copy: $10/$15; sample: $10/$15. 20-50pp; 8½×11; †Ip. Reporting time: 1-2 months. Simultaneous submissions accepted: Y. Publishes 98% of manuscripts submitted. Copyrighted.

THE LITERARY QUARTERLY, Aleta Kiya Engola, Editor-in-Chief; Roxanne Payne, Managing Editor, Submissions, PO Box 1840, New York, NY 10013-0872. 1994. Fiction, cartoons, interviews, satire, criticism, music, letters, plays. "Material of all lengths accepted. Shorts, short stories, serialized longer fiction. No poetry at this time. No excessive violence or pornography. Guidelines are available for a SASE. Send mss. and publishing history for material up to 7,000 words, query plus two consecutive chapters and publishing history for longer works" circ. 5M. 4/yr. Expects 4 issues 1999, 5 issues 2000. sub. price: $26; per copy: $6.75. Discounts: Contact publisher for bulk and classroom rates. 40pp; 8½×11; of. Reporting time: 8-12 weeks. Simultaneous submissions accepted: no. Payment: $10-25 plus two copies for short fiction, payment for longer and serialized fiction (over 7,000 words) will be negotiated. Copyrighted, we request first world serial and anthology rights. Pub's reviews. §New novels, anthologies, literary criticism and review.

LITERARY RESEARCH, Prof. Calin-Andrei Mihailescu, Editor, Dept. of Modern Languages & Lit., University of Western Ontario, London, ON N6A 3K7, Canada, 519-661-3196; 519-661-2111 X5862; Fax 519-661-4093; cmihails@julian.uwo.ca; www.uwo.ca/modlang/index.html. 1983. "The review publishes articles, review-articles, and short reviews of recent publications in various fields of comparative literature; it reflects books and journals published throughout the world. Prints materials in English, French, and occasionally in German, Italian, Portuguese, and Spanish." circ. 500. 2/yr. Pub'd 2 issues 1998; expects 2 issues 1999, 2 issues 2000. sub. price: distributed to members of the ICLA at no cost; per copy: $15; sample: $5. Back issues: $3/issue. Discounts: none. 150pp; 5½×8½. Reporting time: 1 month. Simultaneous submissions accepted: yes. Publishes 60% of manuscripts submitted. Payment: none. Pub's reviews: 35 in 1998. §Comparative literature, literary and critical theory. Ads: none.

THE LITERARY REVIEW, Walter Cummins, Editor-in-Chief; Martin Green, Co-Editor; Harry Keyishian, Co-Editor; William Zander, Co-Editor; Astrid Dadourian, Managing Editor, Fairleigh Dickinson University, 285 Madison Avenue, Madison, NJ 07940, 973-443-8564. 1957. Poetry, fiction, articles, interviews, criticism, reviews, long-poems. "We consider fiction and poetry submissions of any type and of any length (within reason) from new and established writers. We welcome critical articles on contemporary American and international literature and are eager to have submissions of essays that are written for a general literary audience rather than the academic quarterly market. *TLR* has always had a special emphasis on contemporary writing abroad (in translation) and we welcome submissions from overseas, and new translations of contemporary foreign literature. We are particularly interested in receiving translations of and essays on ethnic writing abroad." circ. 2M-2.5M. 4/yr. Pub'd 4 issues 1998; expects 4 issues 1999, 4 issues 2000. sub. price: $18 U.S., $21 foreign; per copy: $5 U.S., $6 foreign; sample: $5 recent issues. Back issues: varies. Discounts: negotiable. 128-152pp; 6×9; of. Reporting time: 2-3 months. Simultaneous submissions accepted: yes. Publishes 3% of manuscripts submitted. Payment: 2 free copies, additional copies at discount. Copyrighted, reverts to author. Pub's reviews: 12 in 1998. §Contemporary fiction, poetry, literary theory, US and world literature (contemporary). No ads. CLMP.

LITERARY ROCKET, Darren Johnson, PO Box 672, Water Mill, NY 11976-0672, e-mail RocketUSA@delphi.com. 1993. Poetry, fiction, cartoons, long-poems. "Here's how you can tell if you're sending us too much - if it costs more than 32¢ (including SASE) to mail, you're wasting postage, paper and time. Contributors: Leslie Scalapino, Ana Christy, Cheryl Townsend, Lyn Lifshin and Brandon Freels" circ. 2M. 4/yr. Pub'd 4 issues 1998; expects 4 issues 1999, 4 issues 2000. sub. price: $5; per copy: $1.50; sample: as low as 55¢ for issue #6 - send 2 unlicked stamps. Discounts: 50% off. 20pp; 4¼×11, 11×8½; newsprint. Reporting time: 1-3 months. Simultaneous submissions accepted: no. Publishes 1% of manuscripts submitted. Payment: none. Copyrighted, reverts to author. Pub's reviews: 50 in 1998. §Experimental and literary fiction and poetry, chapbooks, new forms.. Ads: $95/$50/40¢ per word.

LITERARY SKETCHES, Olivia Murray Nichols, PO Box 810571, Dallas, TX 75381-0571, 214-243-8776. 1961. Articles, interviews, reviews, letters. "1M word maximum." circ. 500. 11/yr. Expects 11 issues 1999. sub. price: $7-year, $12.50-2 yrs or 2 subscriptions $10, $18 outside USA; per copy: 75¢; sample: SASE (#10). Back issues: 75¢. 6pp; 11×8½; of. Reporting time: 1 month. Simultaneous submissions accepted: no. Publishes 50% of manuscripts submitted. Payment: 1/2¢ per word. Copyrighted, reverts to author. Pub's reviews: 15-20 in 1998. §Literary biographies only, books on books. Ads: $10 per inch.

LITRAG, Derrick Hachey, A.J. Rathbun, Kerri Lemoie, PO Box 21066, Seattle, WA 98111-3066, www.litrag.com. 1997. Poetry, fiction, art, photos, cartoons, interviews, criticism, reviews, long-poems. "Recent contributors include Lois Marie Herrod, J. Robert Lennon, Edward Skoog, Derick Burleson and Carmen Hoover." circ. 1M. 3/yr. Pub'd 3 issues 1998; expects 3 issues 1999, 3 issues 2000. sub. price: $12; per copy: $3; sample: $3. Discounts: Available upon request. 40pp; 11×17; †mi. Reporting time: 6-8 weeks. Simultaneous submissions accepted: yes. Publishes 5% of manuscripts submitted. Payment: 2 copies, special gift, per diam when possible. Copyrighted, reverts to author. Pub's reviews: 4 in 1998. §Well crafted original works. Ads: upon request.

Little Bayou Press, 1735 First Avenue North, St. Petersburg, FL 33713-8903, 813-822-3278. 1982. Expects 1 title 1999, 1 title 2000. 1 title listed in the *Small Press Record of Books in Print* (28th Edition, 1999-00). avg. price, cloth: $25. Discounts: 1-10 copies - 40%; 11 or more 45%. 200pp; 7½×5½; of. Reporting time: 6 months. Payment: 15% of sale price, or 10% of list price. Copyrights for author.

Little Buckaroo Press, Cynthia V. Nasta, Pat S. Zilka, PO Box 3016, West Sedona, AZ 86340, 602-282-6278. 1989. Fiction. "Publishes only children's material with predominantly Arizona/Southwest themes heavily oriented to a tourist market. Payment & copyright depends on material, will provide details." avg. press run 10M. Pub'd 1 title 1998; expects 1 title 1999, 1 title 2000. 1 title listed in the *Small Press Record of Books in Print* (28th Edition, 1999-00). avg. price, paper: $6.95. Discounts: 40%. 32pp; 9½×8½; of. Reporting time: 6-8 weeks. Arizona Authors Association.

LITTLE FREE PRESS, 730 3rd Street NE, Little Falls, MN 56345-2412, 812-273-4672; fax 812-273-4672. 1969. Articles, reviews, letters, news items, non-fiction. "Articles, etc, to focus on a better economic system for the world and total freedom for each individual" circ. 200. 36-48/yr. Pub'd 30 issues 1998; expects 40 issues 1999, 48 issues 2000. 2 titles listed in the *Small Press Record of Books in Print* (28th Edition, 1999-00). sub. price: Free + postage of .32 each issue in U.S.; per copy: Free + Postage; sample: $.32 in U.S., $.52 Canada, $.46 Mexico; $1 other countries. Back issues: Free-plus postage. Discounts: none. 4pp; 8½×11; of. Reporting time: 1 month. Publishes 50% of manuscripts submitted. Payment: gratis only. Not copyrighted. Pub's reviews: 65 in 1998. §Solutions to world problems. How to live simply, how to retire early. No ads.

THE LITTLE MAGAZINE, Dimitri Anastasopoulos, Christina Milletti, English Department, State Univ. of New York at Albany, Albany, NY 12222, website www.albany.edu/~litmag. 1965. Poetry, fiction. "*The Little Magazine* is an old literary magazine that refuses to die, revived as an annual under the editorship of SUNY-Albany's facilty and graduate student writers. In its latest incarnation, *TLM* has become a multi-media based journal published on the web and on CD-ROM in order to exploit the creative opportunites that now exist between literature-both poetry and fiction-and new media. *We have no set guidelines.* We will read work conceived as hypermedia/hypertextual work initially written for print, but which lends itself to hypermedia/hypertext production. We like poetry and fiction that foregrounds language, is innovative in form, that pushes its own limits, and the limits of genre. We'd like to see more work from minority writers. We do not read from May through August. Some recent contributors: Charles Bernstein, Raymond Federman, Christy

Sheffield Sanford, Mark Amerika, Eduardo Kac, Juliana Spahr, Richard Kostelanetz. TLM can be found on line at www.albany.edu/~litmag." circ. 2M. 1/yr. Pub'd 1 issue 1998; expects 2 issues 1999, 2 issues 2000. sub. price: $15 (for the CD-Rom); per copy: $15 (for the CD-Rom); sample: $15 (for the CD-Rom). Back issues: $6. Discounts: please inquire. of. Reporting time: 3 months. Simultaneous submissions accepted: yes. Publishes 20% of manuscripts submitted. Payment: 1 copy. Copyrighted, reverts to author. please inquire.

Little River Press, Ronald Edwards, 10 Lowell Avenue, Westfield, MA 01085, 413-568-5598. 1976. Poetry. "Little River Press does not read or return unsolicited mss. We do limited editions of poetry. *Arrangements and Transformations in 18 pt.* Century Oldstyle Bold, concrete poetry by R. Edwards, $1.50. *Tenerife Haiku, Islas Canarias* by Cliff Edwards, $5.00; *Messages* concrete poetry by R. Edwards, $2.50." avg. press run 50-100. Pub'd 2 titles 1998; expects 2 titles 1999, 2 titles 2000. 9 titles listed in the *Small Press Record of Books in Print* (28th Edition, 1999-00). avg. price, paper: $5. 16-20pp; 7½×6¼; †1p. Copyrights for author.

LITURGY 90, Liturgy Training Publications, David Philippart, 1800 North Hermitage Avenue, Chicago, IL 60622, 312-486-8970. 1970. Articles, photos. "A magazine for professional pastoral liturgists focusing on art, music, environment, and practical questions concerning Roman Catholic worship." circ. 7M. 8/yr. Pub'd 8 issues 1998; expects 8 issues 1999, 8 issues 2000. sub. price: $18; per copy: $2. Back issues: $2. Discounts: bulk 5+ $9/year. 16pp; 8½×11; of. Reporting time: 4 weeks. Payment: yes. Copyrighted, does not revert to author. Catholic Book Publishers Assn.

Liturgy Training Publications (see also CATECHUMENATE: A Journal of Christian Initiation; ENVIRONMENT AND ART LETTER; LITURGY 90; PLENTY GOOD ROOM; CHICAGO STUDIES; ASSEMBLY), 1800 North Hermitage Avenue, Chicago, IL 60622, 312-486-8970.

LIVE AND LET LIVE, James N. Dawson, Publisher and Editor, PO Box 613, Redwood Valley, CA 95470. 1992. "*Live and Let Live* seeks to explore and develop a theory and strategy of fetal and animal rights from a libertarian/individualist framework. Letters and other reader contributions are welcome. Communication of thoughts and ideas, content, takes precedence over journalistic professionalism." circ. 75-100. Irregular. Pub'd 1 issue 1998; expects 1 issue 1999, 1 issue 2000. sub. price: $1; per copy: $1; sample: $1. Back issues: from 50¢-$1. Discounts: none. 20pp; 5½×8½; xerox. Payment: none. Not copyrighted. Pub's reviews: 0 in 1998. §Pro-life, animal-rights, libertarianism, anything to do with the ethics and politics of socially sanctioned killing. Ads: negotiable; classified=2¢ per word, $1 min.

The Live Oak Press, David Mike Hamilton, Editor-In-Chief, PO Box 60036, Palo Alto, CA 94306-0036, 415-853-0197; e-mail liveoakprs@aol.com; web address http://members.aol.com/liveoakprs. 1982. Fiction, non-fiction. "Only articles for the betterment of mankind. No restrictions on length, etc." avg. press run 1M. Pub'd 1 title 1998; expects 1 title 1999, 2 titles 2000. 11 titles listed in the *Small Press Record of Books in Print* (28th Edition, 1999-00). avg. price, cloth: $45; paper: $20. Discounts: 40% 3 or more. 96-250pp; 6×9; of. Reporting time: 3 months. Simultaneous submissions accepted: yes. Payment: free copies, 10% after expenses recovered. Copyrights for author. Bookbuilders West, Publishers Marketing Association.

LIVERPOOL LAW REVIEW, Deborah Charles Publications, D. Leggie, A. Harvey, 173 Mather Avenue, Liverpool L18 6JZ, United Kingdom. 1979. Non-fiction. 2/yr. Pub'd 2 issues 1998. sub. price: £16 individuals, £55 institutions + postage; per copy: £10 individuals, £22 institutions; sample: £10. Discounts: 5% subscription agents. 112pp; royal octavo; Mac DTP. Reporting time: 3 months. Payment: none. Copyrighted, does not revert to author. Pub's reviews: 4 in 1998. §Modern law. exchange.

LIVERPOOL NEWSLETTER, Gild of Saint George, Kevin Aspen, PO Box 1243, London, SW7 2PB, England, 0171-373-3432, e-mail 10071.746@compuserve.com. 1960. Articles, art, criticism, reviews, music, letters. "750-1M words of Social Credit/Decentralist/Catholic interest." circ. 200. 4/yr. Pub'd 4 issues 1998; expects 5 issues 1999, 5 issues 2000. sub. price: $4; per copy: $1; sample: $1. Back issues: all issues sold out. 20pp; 8×12; †mi. Reporting time: 3 months. Payment: none. Copyrighted, reverts to author. Pub's reviews: 10 in 1998. §Politics, etc. Ads: $1.

Liverpool University Press (see also BULLETIN OF HISPANIC STUDIES), Dorothy Sherman Severin, Professor; James Higgins, Professor, Dept. of Hispanic Studies, The University, PO Box 147, Liverpool L69 3BX, England, 051 794 2774/5. 1923. Articles, reviews. "Specialist articles on the languages and literatures of Spain, Portugal and Latin America, in English, Spanish, Portuguese, and Catalan." avg. press run 1.2M. Expects 4 titles 1999. 17 titles listed in the *Small Press Record of Books in Print* (28th Edition, 1999-00). avg. price, paper: £20. 112pp; metric crown quarto; of. Reporting time: 3 months. Payment: none. Does not copyright for author. CELJ.

LIVING CHEAP NEWS, Larry Roth, PO Box 8178, Kansas City, MO 64112, 816-523-3161; fax 816-523-0224; livcheap@aol.com; www.livingcheap.com. 1992. "Usually, this is written in house, but we consider contributions (free), product recommendations, etc., from readers." circ. 2M. 10/yr. Expects 10 issues 1999, 10 issues 2000. sub. price: $12; per copy: $1.20; sample: $1.20. 4pp; 8½×11. Reporting time: varies.

Payment: none. Copyrighted, does not revert to author. Pub's reviews: 30 in 1998. §Cheap and meaningful cooking, products, lifestyles, etc. Ads: none.

LIVING FREE, Jim Stumm, Box 29, Hiler Branch, Buffalo, NY 14223. 1979. Articles, cartoons, reviews, letters, news items, non-fiction. "We are pro-individual, pro-private property. Discuss ways for individuals, families, and small groups to live freer, more self-reliant lives. Not interested in politics, or mass movements for social change. By publishing mostly unedited letters, we provide a forum for freedom-seekers, survivalists, libertarians, homesteaders, anarchists, and other outlaws." circ. 200. 4-6/yr. Pub'd 7 issues 1998; expects 6 issues 1999, 8 issues 2000. sub. price: $12 for 6 issues; per copy: $2; sample: $2. Back issues: $2 each, discounts for 10 or more. Discounts: 40% for 5 or more copies of 1 issue to 1 address, no returns, also applies to subscriptions. 8pp; 8½×11; photocopying. Simultaneous submissions accepted: yes. Payment: none. Not copyrighted. Pub's reviews: 6 in 1998. §Non-fiction: self-reliance, enhancing freedom, living cheap, avoiding govt. restrictions. Ads: no classified advertising; 25¢/word, $5 minimum/display advertising $20 for 1/4 page.

LIVING OFF THE LAND, Subtropic Newsletter, Geraventure, Marian Van Atta, Editor; Irene Gast, Associate Editor, PO Box 2131, Melbourne, FL 32902-2131, 305-723-5554. 1975. Articles, letters. "Publishes short articles (500) words on edibles of the subtropics. *The Surinam Cherry* by Dr. George Webster. *Red Bay, the Southland's Edible Aristocrat* by Donald Ray Patterson. Has a seed exchange." circ. 500. 5/yr. Pub'd 6 issues 1998; expects 5 issues 1999, 5 issues 2000. sub. price: $14 U.S. ($15 overseas); per copy: $3; sample: $2. Back issues: $2. Discounts: none. 6pp; 8½×11; of. Reporting time: 60 days. Payment: yes. Copyrighted, does not revert to author. Pub's reviews: 8 in 1998. §Subtropic gardening, foraging. Ads: $10 per ad per subscriber; $25 others.

Livingston Press (see also Swallow's Tale Press), Joe Taylor, Station 22, University of West Alabama, Livingston, AL 35470. 1984. Poetry, fiction. "Literary works only" avg. press run 1.5M. Pub'd 5 titles 1998; expects 5 titles 1999. 18 titles listed in the *Small Press Record of Books in Print* (28th Edition, 1999-00). avg. price, cloth: $22.95; paper: $10.95. Discounts: 40% trade for 5 or more. 90pp; 5½×8½; of. Reporting time: 6 months. Simultaneous submissions accepted: yes. Publishes 5% of manuscripts submitted. Payment: 15% of press run. Copyrights for author. PAS, Publishers ASSN of the South.

LLAMAS MAGAZINE, Clay Press, Inc., Cheryl Dal Porto, PO Box 250, Jackson, CA 95642, 209-295-7800 voice; FAX 209-295-7878; claypres@volcano.net. 1979. Fiction, articles, art, photos, cartoons, interviews, satire, reviews, letters, news items, non-fiction. "Length of material, varied. Recent contributors: Dr. Murray E. Fowler, Marty McGee, Lora Crawford, Cheryl Germain, Francie Greth-Peto, Charlie Hackberth, John Mallon, Kathleen McLeod, Sandy Stillwell" circ. 5M. 5/yr. Pub'd 7 issues 1998; expects 5 issues 1999, 5 issues 2000. sub. price: $20; per copy: $5.75; sample: $5.75. Back issues: separate publication-Best of 3L. Discounts: negotiated. 128pp; 8½×11; of, sheet fed press. Reporting time: 30 days. Publishes 20% of manuscripts submitted. Payment: negotiated. Copyrighted, reverts to author. Pub's reviews: 10-12 in 1998. §Camelids, backpacking, camping equipment, wool, showing. Ads: full: color $1174, b/w $617/half: color $762, b/w $440/classified ads 50¢ word $25 minimum. SMPG (Small Magazine Publishers Group).

LLEN CYMRU, University Of Wales Press, Ceri Lewis, 6 Gwennyth St., Cathays, Cardiff CF2 4YD, Wales, 44-1222-231919; Fax 44-1222-230908; press@press.wales.ac.uk. 1950. Articles. "Journal of various aspects of Welsh literature, printed in the Welsh language." circ. 300. 1/yr. Pub'd 1 issue 1998; expects 1 issue 1999, 1 issue 2000. sub. price: £6.50; per copy: £6.50; sample: £6.50. Back issues: £6.50. Discounts: 10%. 143pp; of. Payment: none. Not copyrighted. Pub's reviews: 4 in 1998. §Welsh literature. UWP.

Llewellyn Publications (see also LLEWELLYN'S NEW WORLDS OF MIND AND SPIRIT), Nancy Mostad, Acquisitions Editor, PO Box 64383, St. Paul, MN 55164, 612-291-1970. 1901. Non-fiction. "Llewellyn Publications is the oldest publisher of New Age books in the Western Hemisphere. We have been bringing literature on spirituality, healing, astrology and religious philosophy to readers worldwide since 1901. Other subjects include: crystals, chakra therapy and yoga, psychic development, hypnosis, past life regression and astral projection. All Llewellyn authors are specialists in their fields—and most of them have a fairly broad background in New Age thought." avg. press run 5M. Pub'd 65 titles 1998; expects 68 titles 1999, 68 titles 2000. 225 titles listed in the *Small Press Record of Books in Print* (28th Edition, 1999-00). avg. price, paper: $12.95. Discounts: dealer discounts: 1-2 20%, 3-4 30%, 5-99 43%, 100-499 45%, 500+ 50%. 200pp; 6×9, 5¼×8, 7×10; varies with printer. Reporting time: 1 month. Simultaneous submissions accepted: yes. Publishes 10% of manuscripts submitted. Payment: inquire for details. Copyrights for author. Minnesota Publishers Roundtable.

LLEWELLYN'S NEW WORLDS OF MIND AND SPIRIT, Llewellyn Publications, Krista Trempe, Editor, PO Box 64383, St. Paul, MN 55164-0383, 612-291-1970. Articles, interviews, reviews, letters. "*Llewellyn New Worlds* is a unique mix of magazine and catalog of New Age products and services. It features articles on Llewellyn's latest titles, articles from three authors as well as a complete networking section to connect people with similar interests. *New Worlds* is not limited to any particular area in the New Age. It is the most complete publication of its kind." circ. 62M. 6/yr. Pub'd 6 issues 1998; expects 6 issues 1999, 6 issues 2000. sub. price: free to all mail order buyers; $7/yr US and Canada, $20 foreign; per copy: $2; sample: free. Discounts: call *New Worlds* ad reps 1-800-THE MOON. 128pp; 8¼×10¾; of. Reporting time: 1 month. Payment: inquire for details and submission guidelines. Copyrighted, reverts to author. §New Age spirituality, alternative lifestyle, religious philosophy. Ads: $750/$415/$1.70.

LO STRANIERO: The Stranger, Der Fremde, L'Etranger, Ignazio Corsaro, Via Chiaia 149, Napoli 80121, Italy, ITALY/81/426052. 1985. Poetry, articles, art, photos, interviews, satire, criticism, letters, collages, concrete art. circ. 10M. 2/yr. Pub'd 2 issues 1998; expects 2 issues 1999, 2 issues 2000. sub. price: $50; per copy: $25; sample: $20. Back issues: $30. Discounts: distributor = $1/copy (at the order). 32pp; 8½×13; of. Payment: none. Registered at the Tribunal of Naples, Italy. §Politics, culture, sociology, avant gard/art, Italy, visual art. Ads: $200/$100/$20 ("spot" in the *network*).

A LOAD OF BULL, David Worton, Rupert, Charles Ross, Jim Heath, Box 277, 52 Call Lane, Leeds, W. Yorkshire LS1 6DT, England. 1989. Poetry, fiction, articles, art, photos, cartoons, interviews, satire, criticism, reviews, music, letters, collages, news items, non-fiction. "Anything from one-line jokes to cartoons to pages-long articles accepted. We are a fanzine written by Wolverhampton Wanderers supporters." circ. 3M. 4/yr. Pub'd 4 issues 1998; expects 4 issues 1999, 4 issues 2000. sub. price: £4; per copy: 80p (+ 20p p/h), $4 US (postage paid); sample: same. Back issues: 50p + p/p 20p, £3 US (postpaid). Discounts: commission= 10p per copy. 52pp; 5⅞×8-3/10; of. Reporting time: 1 week. Payment: free copy of issue in which contribution appears. Not copyrighted. Pub's reviews: 3 in 1998. §Soccer, football, all things Wolverhampton. Ads: none.

The Lockhart Press, Russell A. Lockhart, Franklyn B. Lockhart, Box 1366, Lake Stevens, WA 98258, fax 206-335-4818; e-Mail RAL@HALCYON.COM. 1982. Poetry, fiction, long-poems, non-fiction. "Our aim is to publish books devoted to the direct expression of the psyche's restless search for place and value in our time. Our books will be crafted by hand in every particular: printing by handpress from handset type on handmade paper and handbound in limited editions. Inqiries invited. Inaugural Publication *Midnight's Daughter*, poems by Janet Dallett, winner of Letterpress Prize, Festival of the Arts, Seattle, 1983. New paperback editions begin in 1991." avg. press run 120-200. Pub'd 1 title 1998; expects 1 title 1999, 1 title 2000. 3 titles listed in the *Small Press Record of Books in Print* (28th Edition, 1999-00). avg. price, cloth: $75-$125; paper: $10-$12. Discounts: 20% to distributors & subscribers to the press on handmade; standard discounts on paperbacks. 80pp; 6×9, 9×12; †1p. Reporting time: 2 months. Payment: 15% after direct cost recovery. Does not copyright for author. BAG.

Locks Art Publications, 600 Washington Square South, Philadelphia, PA 19106, 215-629-1000. 1968. Art. avg. press run 600 copies. Pub'd 4 titles 1998; expects 7 titles 1999, 5-7 titles 2000. 49 titles listed in the *Small Press Record of Books in Print* (28th Edition, 1999-00). avg. price, paper: $20. Discounts: 1-4 copies 20%, 5+ 40%. 32pp; 8×10. Reporting time: 3-4 months. Payment: variable. Copyrights for author.

LOCUS: The Newspaper of the Science Fiction Field, Charles N. Brown, Editor & Publisher in Chief; Faren Miller, Associate Editor; Marianne Jablon, Managing Editor, Box 13305, Oakland, CA 94661, 510-339-9196, 9198; FAX 510-339-8144. 1968. Articles, photos, interviews, criticism, reviews, letters, news items. "News stories, reports on SF events." circ. 9M. 12/yr. Pub'd 12 issues 1998; expects 12 issues 1999, 12 issues 2000. sub. price: $43 individual, $46 institution; per copy: $4.50; sample: $4.50. Back issues: $4.50. Discounts: 40% plus postage on 10 or more. 80pp; 8½×11; of. Reporting time: 3 weeks. Payment: yes. Copyrighted. Pub's reviews: 400 in 1998. §S.F., fantasy, horror, related non-fiction. Ads: $600/$335/$1.75 per line.

Log Cabin Manuscripts, Mike Macon, PO Box 507, Jacksonville, OR 97530-9316, 800-995-3652. 1991. Letters, non-fiction. "Non-fiction only, autobiography, biography, family history. Pays 10% on author's first book. No advance. Books from unagented writers only. Send SASE with manuscript submission. Will make outright purchase" avg. press run 3M. Pub'd 1 title 1998; expects 1 title 1999, 2-3 titles 2000. avg. price, paper: $16. 300pp; 5½×8½; of. Reporting time: 2 months. Simultaneous submissions accepted: yes. Payment: 10% on retail price. Copyrights for author. PMA.

Log Cabin Publishers, Kitty Miller, Editor and Publisher; Kathy Miller Rindock, Assistant Editor, PO Box 1536, Allentown, PA 18105, 610-434-2448. 1978. Articles, non-fiction. avg. press run 1M. Pub'd 2 titles 1998. 26 titles listed in the *Small Press Record of Books in Print* (28th Edition, 1999-00). avg. price, paper: $1.75 + 75¢ postage; other: $2+ 75¢ postage. Discounts: 40% booksellers; 10% and upwards on 5 or more copies. 18-24pp; 3½×8½; of. Reporting time: 2 weeks. Payment: all rights. Copyrights for author.

●**LOGIC LETTER,** Tom Ross, Sigrid Young, 13957 Hall Road, #185, Shelby Twp., MI 48315. Articles, criticism, reviews, letters, news items. "Logic Letter is a publication of the "truth society." LL shows how society (and often the individual) is going wrong. For example, few follow the axiom: "The solution begins where the problem began." Support to axioms (themes) often are taken from current news, from history and general experience. Please keep submissions to about 100 words." circ. 50. 12/yr. Pub'd 12 issues 1998; expects 8 issues 1999, 12 issues 2000. sub. price: $6; sample: $1. Back issues: $1. 2pp; 8½×11; mimeo.

320

Reporting time: 2 weeks. Copyrighted, reverts to author. Pub's reviews: 1 in 1998. §how-to, cats.

Logodaedalus (see also LOGODAEDALUS), Paul Weidenhoff, W.B. Keckler, PO Box 14193, Harrisburg, PA 17104. 1993. Poetry, art, plays. "Ms. length negotiable. We have only recently decided to open a press. The first book has been selected. We published (in 1996) Celestine Frost's *i gathered my ear from the green field*. We would especially like to see more experimental poetry (i.e. Gertrude Stein) for future books" avg. press run .5M. Pub'd 2 titles 1998; expects 1 title 1999, 1 title 2000. 4 titles listed in the *Small Press Record of Books in Print* (28th Edition, 1999-00). avg. price, paper: inquire for price. Pages vary; size varies; †photocopy. Reporting time: 6 months or less. Simultaneous submissions accepted: no. 20% of poetry manuscripts published, less than 1% of book manuscripts published. Payment: in copies. Copyrights for author.

LOGODAEDALUS, Logodaedalus, Paul Weidenhoff, W.B. Keckler, PO Box 14193, Harrisburg, PA 17104. 1991. Poetry, art, music, concrete art. "Recent contributors include Marty Esworthy, Mark Owens, Lisa Cooper, Celestine Frost, Bruce Andrews, Bob Grumman, and Spencer Selby. We tend to favor the lyric over the narrative. We also tend to favor work which is not centered around the life of the poet. We publish experimental work, but that does not mean the work should not be well crafted. In the future we hope to do special issues on various forms of experimental poetry (including one on verbo-visual, or concrete poetry) and our video issue was released in 1995. Our last issue was collaborative poetry." circ. 100+. 1-2/yr. Pub'd 3 issues 1998; expects 1 issue 1999, 1 issue 2000. price per copy: $5; sample: $5. Discounts: 1-4 are sold out. Issues 5 and 8 available; 5 is $5 (paper) and 8 video issue of readings ($15/$20 institutional role); issue 9 is sold out. 32-40pp; 8½x11; †photocopy. Reporting time: 3-6 weeks. Publishes 20% of manuscripts submitted. Payment: copies. Not copyrighted. Pub's reviews.

Lollipop Power Books, Ruth Smullin, Editor, 120 Morris Street, Durham, NC 27701, 919-560-2738. 1970. Fiction. "We publish non-sexist, multi-racial books for children. Our books show both girls and boys as adventurous and independent, emotional and expressive. We hope to expose children to the variety of choices open to them." avg. press run 4M. Expects 1 title 1999, 1 title 2000. 10 titles listed in the *Small Press Record of Books in Print* (28th Edition, 1999-00). avg. price, paper: $5.95. Discounts: bookstores: 1-4 copies 20%, 5+ 40%. 32pp; size varies greatly; of. Reporting time: 2-4 months. Payment: 10% bookrun. Copyrights for author. USUFLP.

LONDON FOG, London Fog Publishing, Jacquelyn D. Scheneman, 924 James Street, London, MN 56036-1202, contact via U.S.P.O for guidelines #10 SASE. 1998. Fiction, art, photos. "Contact via U.S.P.O for guidelines #10 SASE. 1000-8000 words; standard ms format; #10 SASE required. Favor mystery, suspense and character studies, all tightly knit. Carol Cullar, Robert E. Rhodes. Earl D. Brodie, Jnana Hodson, Judith A. Schmand, LJ Robinson." 4/yr. Expects 2 issues 1999, 4 issues 2000. sub. price: $22/4 issues; $30/6 issues; per copy: $7; sample: $5. Back issues: $5. Discounts: 10% on 50 or more. 32-52pp; 8½x11; †of. Reporting time: 2-8 weeks. Simultaneous submissions accepted: no. Publishes 50% of manuscripts submitted. Payment: copies. Copyrighted, reverts to author. Ads: inserts only. MN Womens Press; Small Press Association of Southern MN.

●London Fog Publishing (see also LONDON FOG), Jacquelyn D. Scheneman, 924 James Street, London, MN 56036-1202, Contact via U.S.P.O for guidelines #10 SASE. 1998. Poetry, fiction, art, photos, parts-of-novels. "Contact via U.S.P.O for guidelines #10 SASE.*Quintessential*: Annual anthology of five novella from five different authors, accepts fiction of 10,000-25,000 words: first issue scheduled for publication 11/99. *Triple Bypass*: Annual anthology of poetry of approximately 50 writers. First issue 12/99." avg. press run 500-2M. Expects 2 titles 1999, 6 titles 2000. avg. price, paper: under $20. Discounts: 10% on 25 or more. 200pp; 5½x8½; †of. Reporting time: 6-10 weeks. Simultaneous submissions accepted: no. Publishes 3% of manuscripts submitted. Payment: varies; copies + % of sales. Copyrights for author. MN Womens Press; Small Press Association of Southern MN.

LONDON REVIEW OF BOOKS, Mary-Kay Wilmers, 28-30 Little Russell Street, London WC1A 2HN, England, 0171-404-3338; fax 404-3339. 1979. Poetry, fiction, articles, art, photos, criticism, reviews, letters, non-fiction. circ. 17.5M. 24/yr. Pub'd 24 issues 1998; expects 24 issues 1999, 24 issues 2000. sub. price: $48; per copy: $2.95; sample: $2.95 + postage. Back issues: $3 + postage. Discounts: 20% agency. 28pp; 374x257mm; †of. Payment: negotiable. Not copyrighted. Pub's reviews: 692 in 1998. Ads: £1375/£810/ classifeid £3.50/line (average 6 words).

Lone Eagle Publishing Co., Joan Vietor Singleton, Ralph S. Singleton, 2337 Roscomare Road #9, Los Angeles, CA 90077-1815, fax 213-471-4969; 800-FILMBKS. 1982. "Professionals in the motion picture industry who specialize in a certain field are encouraged to submit ideas for our "filmmakers library" series of books. Present titles are: *Film Scheduling, Funny Business: The Craft of Comedy Writing, Film Editing Room Handbook*. We also publish nine annual directories, including *Michael Singers Film Directors: A Complete Guide*, an annual directory of motion picture directors with a cross-reference by film title." avg. press run 2.5M-3M. Pub'd 9 titles 1998; expects 12 titles 1999, 16 titles 2000. 19 titles listed in the *Small Press Record of Books in Print* (28th Edition, 1999-00). avg. price, cloth: $46.06; paper: $16.95. Discounts: 1-4, 20%; 5-9, 30%;

10-24, 40%; 25-99, 42%; 100-199, 44%; 200-299, 46%; 300-499, 48%; 500+, 50%. Textbook adoptions, 20%. 250pp; 6×9, 8½×11; of. Reporting time: 8 weeks. Payment: 5-10% monthly payment. Copyrights for author. PMA.

LONE STAR SOCIALIST, Cleveland Maxwell, Earl Divoky, PO Box 2640, Austin, TX 78768-2640, 210-833-5315. 1979. Articles, satire, letters, news items, non-fiction. circ. 1M. 2/yr. Pub'd 2 issues 1998; expects 2 issues 1999, 2 issues 2000. sub. price: $8 donation; per copy: donation; sample: donation. Back issues: SASE. 16pp; 8½×11; of. Reporting time: 3 months. Simultaneous submissions accepted: yes. Publishes 30-40% of manuscripts submitted. Payment: copies. Copyrighted, reverts to author. Pub's reviews: 1 in 1998. §leftist, radical, social history and politics. Ads: $100/$60/.

LONE STARS MAGAZINE, Milo Rosebud, 4219 Flinthill, San Antonio, TX 78230-1619. 1992. Poetry, art. "Recent contributors: Terry Lee, Emily Moore, Ralph Martin, Violet Wilcox, Jan Brevet, Marian Ford Park, Joseph Verrilli, Steven Duplij, Jo Anne Trinkle" circ. 200. 3/yr. Pub'd 4 issues 1998; expects 3 issues 1999, 3 issues 2000. sub. price: $15; per copy: $5; sample: $5. Back issues: When available, in-print. Discounts: if possible. 24pp; 8½×11; †mi. Reporting time: 4-6 weeks. Simultaneous submissions accepted: yes. Publishes 60-80% of manuscripts submitted. Payment: none. Copyrighted, reverts to author. Ads: $20 per 1/4 page with 3 issues.

Lone Willow Press, Dale Champy, PO Box 31647, Omaha, NE 68131-0647. 1994. Poetry. "We publish chapbooks. Usually by invitation only. We will, however, give a fair reading to all typescripts that meet our guidelines. Poems must reflect a single theme." avg. press run 200 first edition, 300 second edition. Expects 3 titles 1999, 3 titles 2000. 7 titles listed in the *Small Press Record of Books in Print* (28th Edition, 1999-00). avg. price, paper: $7.95. Discounts: standard discounts to bookstores (40%). 25-35pp; 5½×8½; of/lp. Reporting time: 2 months. Simultaneous submissions accepted: no. Publishes 3% of manuscripts submitted. Payment: 25 copies + 25% royalty once expenses are met, poets get 50% off additional copies. Copyrights for author.

LONG SHOT, Daniel Shot, Lynn Breitfeller, Art Editor; Nancy Mercado, PO Box 6238, Hoboken, NJ 07030. 1982. Poetry, fiction, articles, art, photos, cartoons, non-fiction. circ. 2M. 2/yr. Pub'd 2 issues 1998; expects 2 issues 1999, 2 issues 2000. sub. price: $12; per copy: $8; sample: $8. Back issues: $6. 228pp; 5×8; †of. Reporting time: 10-12 weeks. Simultaneous submissions accepted: yes. Publishes 2% of manuscripts submitted. Payment: copies. Copyrighted, reverts to author. Ads: $150/$90. CLMP.

THE LONG STORY, R. Peter Burnham, Editor, 18 Eaton Street, Lawrence, MA 01843, 978-686-7638, e-mail rpbtls@aol.com. 1982. Fiction. "Stories of 8,000-20,000 words, for serious educated literary people. Web: http://www.litline.org/html/thelongstory.html We have very specific tastes and look for stories about common folk and committed fiction. Since we are the only journal devoted strictly to long stories, we do not close the door or anything completely (except detective fiction, sci-fi, romance and other forms of popular fiction). But the best way to save yourself time and postage is to be familiar with us. Sample copies are $6, and writers are strongly urged to buy a copy before submitting (orders are filled on the same day that they are received). No multiple submissions. No parts of novels; please note that we are a journal devoted to long stories, a literary form with a beginning, middle, and an end. Best length is 8,000-12,000 words since we are very unlikely to print a 20,000 word story unless it conforms exactly to our literary tastes. We are not particularly interested in the usual produce of the writing programs—stories that are merely about relationships without any reaching after higher significance, stories with a psychological core as opposed to a thematic, moral core, stories that are thinly disguised autobiography, stories about writers, etc." circ. 1200. 1/yr. Expects 1 issue 1999, 1 issue 2000. sub. price: $6; per copy: $6; sample: $6. Back issues: $5. Discounts: 40% to bookstores. 160pp; 5½×8½; of. Reporting time: 1-2 months, sometimes longer. Simultaneous submissions accepted if notified. Publishes 2-3% of manuscripts submitted. Payment: 2 copies and gift subscription. Copyrighted, reverts to author. No ads. CLMP.

THE LONG TERM VIEW: A Journal of Informed Opinion, Dean Lawrence R. Velvel, Nancy Bernhard, Massachusetts School of Law, 500 Federal Street, Andover, MA 01810, 978-681-0800. 1992. Articles, interviews. "Each issue is devoted to a balanced discussion of a single topic (usually one that has not received adequate/in-depth coverage in the mainstream press). Contributors range from academics to professionals, have included Eugene McCarthy, Alfred Malabre of the *Wall Street Journal*, Eliot Janeway, John Anderson." circ. 3-4M. 4/yr. Pub'd 4 issues 1998; expects 4 issues 1999, 4 issues 2000. sub. price: $10; per copy: $3.95; sample: free. Back issues: $3.95. Discounts: negotiable. 70pp; 8½×11; of. Reporting time: 3-5 weeks. Simultaneous submissions accepted: yes. Publishes 50-75% of manuscripts submitted. Payment: negotiable. Copyrighted, reverts to author.

Long Wind Publishing, Jon Ward, 2208 River Branch Drive, Ft. Pierce, FL 34981, E-mail hievolved@aol.com; www.longwind.com. 1997. Fiction, photos, cartoons. "Children's picture books. Long Wind's *Howard Wise and the Monster Hop* won American Book Readers' Assn. 'Best Children's Novel of 1997.' Written and illustrated by Jon Ward." avg. press run 3-5M. Pub'd 2 titles 1998; expects 7 titles 1999, 5 titles 2000. 8 titles listed in the *Small Press Record of Books in Print* (28th Edition, 1999-00). avg. price, cloth: $15.95. Discounts: trade 40%, bulk 50%. 32pp; 11×8½; of. Reporting time: 4-6 weeks. Simultaneous submissions accepted: no. Publishes 10% of manuscripts submitted. Payment: varies. Does not copyright for author. PMA, FPA, SCBWI.

LONGHOUSE, Longhouse, Bob Arnold, 1604 River Road, Guilford, VT 05301, e-mail poetry@sover.net; www.sover.net/~poetry. 1973. Poetry, long-poems. *"Longhouse* takes on no grants, funding or subscription - rather supports itself thru the good hearts of poets & readers of the journal. We're a homespun publication on the lookout for poems from the serious working poet. Any region/any style. Recent contributors: Hayden Carruth, Barbara Moraff, Keith Wilson, James Koller, Janine Pommy-Vega, Mike O'Connor, Bobby Byrd, Frank Samperi, David Budbill, Cid Corman, Clive Faust, Theodore Enslin, Jane Brakhage, Drummond Hadley, Bill Deemer, Doc Dachtler, Ian Hamilton Finlay, John Perlman, Andrew Schelling, Charlie Mehrhoff, Gael Turnbull, John Martone, Laurent Grisel, Sam Green, Antler, James Weil, Emma Short-Lee, Anne Waldman, Terry Harptman. One should be familiar with the magazine before submitting poems." circ. 200. 1/yr. Pub'd 1 issue 1998; expects 1 issue 1999. sub. price: $12 (includes bookshop catalog of new and used books); sample: $10. 35pp; 8½×14, 8½×11; †mi, of. Reporting time: 2 weeks. Payment: copies. Pub's reviews: 10 in 1998. §Poetry, literary history, rural essays, music, film.

Longhouse (see also LONGHOUSE), Bob Arnold, 1604 River Road, Guilford, VT 05301, e-mail poetry@sover.net; www.sover.net/~poetry. 1973. Poetry, long-poems, concrete art. "Under the Longhouse imprint we have published 35 books of poetry including: *3*: poems by Bob Arnold, David Giannini and John Levy. *Scout* imprint has published booklets and folders by Theodore Enslin, Gerald Hausman, George Evans, David Huddle, Cid Corman, Jean Pedrick, Lyle Glazier, James Koller, Barbara Moraff, Bill Bathurst, Ian Hamilton Finlay, Jane Brakhage, Lorine Niedecker, Marcel Cohen, Janine Pommy Vega, Catherine Walsh, David Miller, Billy Mills, Bill Deemer, Keith Wilson, Andrew Schelling, Tim McNulty, Mike O'Conner. Mss. solicited. All books from *Longhouse* are limited to 100-250 print run, offset with letterpress wraps. A complete listing of publications may be obtained from our bookshop and catalog services: *Longhouse:* publishers and bookseller; same address." avg. press run 150-300. Pub'd 4 titles 1998; expects 4 titles 1999, 4 titles 2000. 15 titles listed in the *Small Press Record of Books in Print* (28th Edition, 1999-00). avg. price, paper: $10. 8-75pp; size varies; †of, lp. Payment: copies.

Longleaf Press, Michael Colonnese, Managing Editor; Robin Greene, Editor, Methodist College, English Dept., 5400 Ramsey Street, Fayetteville, NC 28311, 910-822-5403. 1997. Poetry. "A non-profit college press dedicated to contemporary literature with a special interest in poetry and new writers. Annual chapbook contest, write for guidelines" avg. press run 500. Pub'd 1 title 1998; expects 2 titles 1999, 2 titles 2000. avg. price, paper: $6. Discounts: none. 30pp; 5½×8½; of. Reporting time: 4 months. Simultaneous submissions accepted: yes. Publishes 2% of manuscripts submitted. Payment: honorarium to author. Copyrights for author.

Longview Press, Charles Turnbull, PO Box 616, Old Lyme, CT 06371, 203-434-2902. 1994. "Begun as self-publisher" avg. press run 1M. Expects 2 titles 1999. 1 title listed in the *Small Press Record of Books in Print* (28th Edition, 1999-00). avg. price, paper: $12. 5½×8½; of.

THE LONSDALE - The International Quarterly of The Romantic Six, Michael Jabri-Pickett, Trash City 3rd Floor, 6-18-16 Nishi-Gotanda, Shinagawa-ku, Tokyo 141, Japan, 03(5434)0729. 1994. Poetry, fiction, articles, art, cartoons, interviews, satire, criticism, reviews, letters, news items, non-fiction. "*The Lonsdale* deals with six writers, exclusively - W. Blake, W. Wordsworth, S.T. Coleridge, Lord Byron, P.B. Shelley, and J. Keats. Unsolicited, scholarly essays, criticisms, and the like will be considered. Poetry and fiction may also be submitted, but must be relevant. Vignettes rather than short stories. An article of 1200-1500 words is ideal, but not essential. All artwork must be black on white (too large is preferable to too small). Iconography is to be similar to that of *The New Yorker* (but without cats and dogs). Cartoons may also be submitted and so too may PSAs. A classified section detailing antiquarian announcements and business and personal services is also offered. All funds quoted are in Canadian dollars, but any currency may be sent equivalent to the Canadian amount. *The Lonsdale* is published in January, April, July, and October. Work sent on Macintosh diskettes is appreciated." circ. 30M. 4/yr. Expects 4 issues 2000. sub. price: $12, $20/2 years; per copy: $3; sample: free. Back issues: $3. Discounts: ask for quote. 12pp; 8½×11; of. Reporting time: 2 months. Payment: copies only. Not copyrighted. Pub's reviews. §Work concerned with W. Blake, W. Wordsworth, S.T. Coleridge, Lord Byron, P.B. Shelley, and J. Keats. Ads: $185 2x3½.

Loom Press, Paul Marion, Box 1394, Lowell, MA 01853. 1978. Poetry. avg. press run 500-1M. Expects 1 title 1999, 1 title 2000. 4 titles listed in the *Small Press Record of Books in Print* (28th Edition, 1999-00). avg. price, paper: $10 book. Discounts: trade 40%, libraries 20%. Pages vary; 6×9; of, lp. Reporting time: 60-90 days. Payment: individual negotiations. Copyrights for author.

LOONFEATHER: A magazine of poetry, short prose, and graphics, Loonfeather Press, Betty Rossi, Editor; Marsh Muirhead, PO Box 1212, Bemidji, MN 56619, 218-751-4869. 1979. Poetry, fiction, photos, non-fiction. "Short poems and fiction (1.5M words), 80% Minnesota writers." circ. 300. 2/yr. Pub'd 2 issues 1998; expects 2 issues 1999, 2 issues 2000. sub. price: $7.50; per copy: $5 postpaid; sample: $5 postpaid. Back issues: $2.50 through Summer '87, $5 Fall '87 to present. Discounts: write for rates on multiple copies. 48pp; 5½×8½; of. Reporting time: 1 month following publication date. Publishes 20% of manuscripts submitted. Payment: 2 copies. Copyrighted, reverts to author. Ads: $450 2 issues/$225/2 X 5 for 2 issues $95.

Loonfeather Press (see also LOONFEATHER: A magazine of poetry, short prose, and graphics), Betty Rossi, PO Box 1212, Bemidji, MN 56619, 218-751-4869. 1979. Poetry, fiction, art, photos, parts-of-novels, non-fiction. "We are particularly interested in publishing the work of emerging regional writers (Minnesota, Wisconsin, North Dakota, Canada) and works with regional settings. We will consider journals, memoirs, biography. No science fiction." avg. press run 1.5M. Pub'd 2 titles 1998; expects 3 titles 1999, 3 titles 2000. 6 titles listed in the *Small Press Record of Books in Print* (28th Edition, 1999-00). avg. price, paper: $9.95. Discounts: 40% bookstores, 55% distributors. 32pp chapbooks and children, 110pp fiction and non-fiction, 60pp poetry collections; 5½×8½; of. Reporting time: within 3 months. Simultaneous submissions accepted: no. Publishes .05% of manuscripts submitted. Payment: 10% on first 1000, copies, discount. Copyrights for author.

Loose Threads Publishing, PO Box 187, Hudson, MA 01749, 508-562-1611. 1993. Non-fiction. "Our books are aimed at the business audience, typically manufacturer's, and deal with quality-related topics and management strategies" avg. press run 3M. Pub'd 6 titles 1998; expects 3 titles 1999, 3 titles 2000. 1 title listed in the *Small Press Record of Books in Print* (28th Edition, 1999-00). avg. price, paper: $24.95. Discounts: Minimum order 3 copies, 3-47 40%, 48-299 50%, 300+ 55%. 310pp; 5½×8½. Publishes 80% of manuscripts submitted. Copyrights for author. PMA.

Lord John Press, Herb Yellin, 19073 Los Alimos Street, Northridge, CA 91326, 818-363-6621. 1977. "Work only with established authors - our primary market is collectors and universities. Do not want unsolicited manuscripts. Published authors: John Updike, Norman Mailer, Robert B. Parker, Ray Bradbury, Ursula K. Le Guin, John Barth, Raymond Carver, Stephen King, Dan Simmons." avg. press run 300-500. Pub'd 3 titles 1998; expects 3 titles 1999. 10 titles listed in the *Small Press Record of Books in Print* (28th Edition, 1999-00). avg. price, cloth: $75. Discounts: trade 40%. 50pp; 6×9; of, lp.

LORE AND LANGUAGE, J.D.A. Widdowson, National Centre for Eng. Cultural Tradition, The University, Sheffield S10 2TN, England, Sheffield 0114-2226296. 1969. Poetry, articles, reviews, letters. "Articles and items for those interested in language, folklore, cultural tradition and oral history." circ. 300. 2/yr. Pub'd 2 issues 1998; expects 2 issues 1999, 2 issues 2000. sub. price: £12 indiv, £50 institutions; sample: free. Back issues: price dependent on issue required; apply to Hisarlik Press. Discounts: none. 128pp; 15×21cm (A5); of. Reporting time: 3 weeks. Payment: none. Not copyrighted. Pub's reviews: 140 in 1998. §Language, folklore, cultural tradition, oral history. Ads: £95/£70/£40 1/4 page. Hisarlik Press.

LOS, Virginia M. Geoffrey, Editor; I.B. Scrood, Editor; P.N. Bouts, Editor, 150 North Catalina Street #2, Los Angeles, CA 90004. 1991. Poetry. price per copy: $2. Ads: $100/$50.

LOST AND FOUND TIMES, Luna Bisonte Prods, John M. Bennett, 137 Leland Ave, Columbus, OH 43214. 1975. Poetry, fiction, articles, art, photos, cartoons, satire, reviews, letters, parts-of-novels, long-poems, collages, concrete art. "Format and content for each issue will vary considerably. I am interested in the experimental and the primitive, and in anything new or unusual. Would like to see collaborations. Spanish and/or English. See Luna Bisonte Prods for further information." circ. 300. Irregular. Pub'd 2 issues 1998; expects 2 issues 1999, 2 issues 2000. 4 titles listed in the *Small Press Record of Books in Print* (28th Edition, 1999-00). sub. price: $25/5 issues; per copy: $6; sample: $6 for sample. Back issues: #1-41, $179. Discounts: 40% for resale. 56pp; size varies; of. Reporting time: 2 weeks. Payment: copies. Copyrighted, reverts to author. Pub's reviews. §Literature, art, reviews.

Lost Coast Press, John Fremont, Senior Editor, 155 Cypress Street, Fort Bragg, CA 95437. 11 titles listed in the *Small Press Record of Books in Print* (28th Edition, 1999-00).

LOST GENERATION JOURNAL, Thomas W. Wood, Jr., Deloris Wood, Route 5 Box 134, Salem, MO 65560, 314-729-2545; 729-5669. 1973. Poetry, fiction, articles, art, photos, cartoons, interviews, criticism, reviews, letters, news items, non-fiction. "*LGJ* topics deal with Americans in Europe, chiefly Paris, between 1919 and 1939. Primary emphasis is placed on Americans who began making a name for themselves in literature, graphic and performing arts such as Pound, Stein and Hemingway. Article length can vary, but we prefer pieces between 800 and 2,500 words. Poetry should be 20 lines or less. Good photographs and art should relate to the theme in time and place as should the articles and poetry. Scholars must document their work with footnotes and bibliography. Lost Generation people (those who started in Paris) must state when they were abroad and supply evidence of their qualifications or cite references for confirmation. Authors should supply a passport-size photograph of themselves and a 200-word biographical blurb. Recent contributors: Mark Bassett, Robin Dormin, Mark Orwoll, John McCall, Jerry Rosco." circ. 400. 1/yr. Pub'd 1 issue 1998; expects 1 issue 1999, 1 issue 2000. 1 title listed in the *Small Press Record of Books in Print* (28th Edition, 1999-00). sub. price:

$10; per copy: $10; sample: $10. Back issues: $10. Discounts: $9.50 per year to subscription agency. 32pp; 8½x11; of. Reporting time: 6 weeks, SASE earlier. Payment: 1¢ per word or 3 copies of issue article appears in. Copyrighted. Pub's reviews: 4 in 1998. §Twentieth Century literature, bibliography, biography, Americans in Paris, Hemingway, Pound, Stein, Miller. Ads: $150/$125/$85/$5 an inch. Conferences of Editors of Learned Journals, Society to Scholarly Publishing, AEJNC, MLA.

Lost Horse Press, Christine Holbert, Scott Poole, Christopher Howell, 9327 South Cedar Rim Lane, Spokane, WA 99224, 509-448-4047; e-mail losthorse@ior.com. 1998. Poetry, art, photos, long-poems, non-fiction. avg. press run 500-2.5M. Expects 3 titles 1999, 12 titles 2000. 3 titles listed in the *Small Press Record of Books in Print* (28th Edition, 1999-00). avg. price, cloth: $25; paper: $15. Discounts: To the trade: 4 or more items-40%; 3 items-30%; 2 items-20%. 200pp; 8¼x5½; of. Reporting time: 5 months. Simultaneous submissions accepted: yes. Publishes 5% of manuscripts submitted. Payment: 10%. Copyrights for author. PNBA.

THE LOST PERUKE, P.M. Kellermann, PO Box 8125, State College, PA 16803-8125. 1988. Satire. "No unsolicited manuscripts accepted." circ. 200. 6/yr. Pub'd 4 issues 1998; expects 6 issues 1999, 6 issues 2000. sub. price: $15; per copy: $2; sample: $2. Back issues: package rates available. Discounts: specified upon request. 24pp; 5½x8½; †xerography. Copyrighted, does not revert to author. Ads: $45/$25/rates specified to advertiser's needs.

Lost Prophet Press (see also THIN COYOTE), Christopher Jones, 3300 3rd Ave. South, Mineapolis, MN 55408-3204. 1992. Poetry, fiction, art, photos, long-poems, collages, plays. "We mostly publish chapbooks of good, well-crafted poetry, but will also look at submissions of fiction, plays, photogaphy, and artwork especially if you take the time to bribe us." avg. press run 100. Pub'd 2 titles 1998; expects 3 titles 1999, 4 titles 2000. 1 title listed in the *Small Press Record of Books in Print* (28th Edition, 1999-00). avg. price, paper: $5. Discounts: on request. 30pp; 5½x8½. Reporting time: 1 month. Simultaneous submissions accepted: yes. Publishes 1% of manuscripts submitted. Payment: 1/4 run in contributor copies. Does not copyright for author.

Lost Roads Publishers, C. D. Wright, Editor; Forrest Gander, Editor, 351 Nayatt Road, Barrington, RI 02806-4336, 401-245-8069. 1977. Poetry, fiction, photos, long-poems. "We recently published J.L. Jacob's *The Leaves in Her Shoes* and Sam Truitt's *Anamorphosis Eisenhower*. Other notable titles include *Conditions Uncertain and Likely to Pass* tales by Frank Stanford, the selected poems of Keith Waldrop, *The Vineyard* by Fanny Howe, and *I'm Lying*, translations of Philippe Soupault" avg. press run 1M. Pub'd 4 titles 1998; expects 4 titles 1999, 4 titles 2000. 25 titles listed in the *Small Press Record of Books in Print* (28th Edition, 1999-00). avg. price, paper: $12. Discounts: 1 copy net, 2-4 30%, 5-24 40%, 25+ 50%; we pay postage and handling on prepaid orders. 88pp; 6x9; of, lp. Reporting time: 3 months. Simultaneous submissions accepted: yes. Publishes 4% of manuscripts submitted. Payment: $300, 20 copies. Editor sends copyright forms to author to copyright in their name.

Lotus Press, Inc., Naomi Madgett, Editor, PO Box 21607, Detroit, MI 48221, 313-861-1280; fax 313-861-4740. 1972. Poetry. avg. press run 500-2M. Pub'd 2 titles 1998; expects 2 titles 1999, 2 titles 2000. 58 titles listed in the *Small Press Record of Books in Print* (28th Edition, 1999-00). avg. price, cloth: $25; paper: $12; other: $21 set of 7 laminated broadsides. Discounts: usually 30-40% depending on size of order. 80pp; 5½x8½; of/lo. Reporting time: 6-8 weeks. Simultaneous submissions accepted: no. Publishes 1% of manuscripts submitted. Payment: copies which author may sell. Copyrights for author.

●**THE LOUISIANA REVIEW**, Dr. Maura Gage, Barbara Deger, Division of Liberal Arts, Louisiana State Univ., PO Box 1129, Eunice, LA 70535. 1999. Poetry, fiction, art, photos, parts-of-novels, plays. "*The Louisiana Review* seeks the best writing it can get by Louisiana writers and poets as well as by those associated with or connected to the state in some way. We like imagistic and metaphoric poetry as well as poetry with surprising language and excellent craft. Recent contributors include Sandra Meek, Catharine Savage Brosman, William Major, David Middleton, and Stella Nassonovich. Longer works should be submitted on disk (Microsoft Word). Please let us know your connection to Louisiana. Submit work between January 7 - March 31." circ. 300-600. 1/yr. Expects 1 issue 1999, 1 issue 2000. sub. price: $3; per copy: $3. 48-72pp; 8½x11; of. Reporting time: 4 months. Accept simultaneous submissions if noted. Publishes 25% of manuscripts submitted. Payment: 2-3 copies in which their work appears. Not copyrighted.

THE LOUISVILLE REVIEW, Sena Jeter Naslund, Co-Editor; David Garrison, Co-Editor; Karen Mann, Managing Editor; Kathleen Driskell, Poetry Editor, Spalding University, 851 S. 4th Street, Louisville, KY 40203, 502-852-6801. 1976. Poetry, fiction, parts-of-novels, long-poems, plays. "Some recent contributors: Maura Stanton, Laurence Goldsmith, Jeffrey Skinner, Ursula Hegi, Stuart Dybek, Maureen Morehead, David Michael Kapian" circ. 500. 2/yr. Pub'd 1 issue 1998; expects 1 issue 1999, 2 issues 2000. sub. price: $8; per copy: $8; sample: $4. Back issues: $4 each (postpaid). 96pp; 6x9; lp. Reporting time: 3 months. Publishes 10% of manuscripts submitted. Payment: 1 compl. copy. Copyrighted, reverts to author. swap ads.

L'OUVERTURE, Bill Campbell, Angela Wiens, PO Box 8565, Atlanta, GA 30306, 404-572-9141. 1996.

Poetry, fiction, articles, art, photos, cartoons, interviews, satire, criticism, letters, parts-of-novels, long-poems, plays, news items, non-fiction. "Looking for works with strong social and political commentary and content. Things that make people really think about the world in which we live." circ. 500. 6/yr. Pub'd 3 issues 1998; expects 6 issues 1999, 6 issues 2000. sub. price: $15; per copy: $3.50; sample: $3.50. Back issues: $2. 44pp; 8½×11. Reporting time: 6-8 weeks. Simultaneous submissions accepted: yes. Publishes 20% of manuscripts submitted. Payment: 2 contributors copies. Copyrighted, reverts to author. Pub's reviews: 0, we have just started with vol.2 #1 in 1998. §small press literature and political, sociological, history writings. Ads: $110/$75/$60.

The Love and Logic Press, Inc., Nancy M. Henry, Publisher, 2207 Jackson Street, Golden, CO 80401, 303-278-7552. 1993. Non-fiction. "The Love and Logic Press, Inc. is a subsidiary of Cline/Fay Institute, Inc. CFI was founded in 1983 as a mail order publisher of audio and video tapes and books by Jim Fay and Foster W. Cline, M.D., internationally-recognized authorities on parenting, education and child psychiatry. CFI currently carries over 65 titles, available exclusively through mail order and catalog, www.loveandlogic.com. The Love and Logic Press, Inc. was started to publish audio, video and book titles for the general trade beginning in Fall 1994. LLPI will concentrate on titles dealing with parenting, psychology and current social trends." avg. press run 10M. Expects 12 titles 1999, 18 titles 2000. 8 titles listed in the *Small Press Record of Books in Print* (28th Edition, 1999-00). avg. price, cloth: $19.95; paper: $7.95; other: $11.95 audio, $24.95 video. Discounts: 1 copy 20% prepaid, 2-4 20%, 5-24 40%, 25-99 42% free freight, 100-249 43%, 250-499 44%, 500+ 45%; 25 or more copies include free freight. 256pp; 6×9; of. Reporting time: 90 days. Simultaneous submissions accepted: yes. Publishes 4% of manuscripts submitted. Payment: advance against royalties; 5-7.5% on net sales; royalties paid twice yearly. Copyrights for author. PMA, ABA, ALA, NAIP, Audio Publishers Assoc., Educational Dealers and Suppliers Assoc.

LOVE AND RAGE, A Revolutionary Anarchist Newspaper, Publishing Collective of 15-20 People, Box 853, Stuyvesant Station, New York, NY 10009. 1989. Articles, art, photos, cartoons, interviews, criticism, reviews, music, letters, collages, news items, non-fiction. "All material submitted should have an anti-authoritarian focus." circ. 5M. 6/yr. Pub'd 10 issues 1998; expects 6 issues 1999. sub. price: $9 3rd class, $13 1st class, overseas; per copy: $1; sample: $1. Back issues: donation. Discounts: free for prisoners, GIs, and persons with AIDS. 20pp; 11×17; of. Payment: none. Not copyrighted. Pub's reviews: 7 in 1998. §Political music/books/movies. Ads: none.

LOVING ALTERNATIVES MAGAZINE, Ric Alderson, Cindy Alderson, PO Box 459, San Dimas, CA 91773, 909-592-5217, FAX 818-915-4715. 1990. Fiction, articles, art, photos, cartoons, interviews, satire, criticism, reviews, letters, news items, non-fiction. "Focus on loving relationships in non-monogamous communities. Secondary focus on anti-censorship, the environment and the adult enterainment industry" 5M printed, 20M readership. 6/yr. Pub'd 6 issues 1998; expects 6 issues 1999, 6 issues 2000. sub. price: $20/6 issues, $35/2 years; per copy: $5; sample: $5. Back issues: $5. Discounts: distributors 10-49 $2.50, 50-100 $2, 101-200 $1.75, 200+ $1.50; add'l discount for COD. 64pp; 8¼×10¾; rotary press. Reporting time: max. 2 months if published. Publishes 60-80% of manuscripts submitted. Payment: none at this time. Copyrighted, copyrights revert to author by permission only. Pub's reviews: 2-3 in 1998. §Alternative lifestyles, censorship topics, erotic art & videos. Ads: $140/$80/$300 back cover; add'l discount for multiple inserts.

LOVING MORE, Brett Hill, Ryan Nearing, PO Box 4358, Boulder, CO 80306, 303-543-7540; lmm@lovemore.com. 1995. Articles, art, photos, cartoons, interviews, reviews, letters, news items, non-fiction. "Under 1,000 words" circ. 2M. 4/yr. Pub'd 4 issues 1998; expects 4 issues 1999, 4 issues 2000. sub. price: $24; per copy: $6; sample: $6. Back issues: $6. Discounts: 50% off for 3 or more. 40pp; 8½×11; of. Reporting time: varies. Simultaneous submissions accepted: no. Publishes 50% of manuscripts submitted. Payment: copies. Copyrighted, reverts to author. Pub's reviews: 10 in 1998. §New paradigm relationships, community. Ads: $150/$75.

THE LOWELL REVIEW, Judith Dickerman-Nelson, Rita Rouvalis Chapman, 3075 Harness Drive, Florissant, MO 63033-3711, E-mail rita@etext.org; website http://www.etext.org/Zines/LowellReview. 1994. Poetry, fiction, non-fiction. "We are chiefly interested in work that reflects what it is like to live, labor, bleed, sweat, die, and everything in between. Recent contributors include Sam Cornish, Jim Daniels, Lola Haskins, William Greenway, and Jay Atkinson." circ. 200. 1/yr. Pub'd 1 issue 1998; expects 1 issue 1999, 1 issue 2000. sub. price: $7; per copy: $7; sample: $5. Back issues: $5. Discounts: none. 70pp; 5½×8½; of. Reporting time: 1 week-4 months. Simultaneous submissions accepted: yes. Publishes 1-2% of manuscripts submitted. Payment: 1 copy. Copyrighted, reverts to author. Ads: $100/$50.

LOWLANDS REVIEW, Tom Whalen, 6109 Magazine, New Orleans, LA 70118. 1974. Poetry, fiction, art, interviews, reviews, parts-of-novels, long-poems. "We like the experimental/surreal, but are not averse to good work in any vein. Recent contributors include George Garrett, Stuart Dybek, Brian Swann, Julia Randall, Christopher Middleton, Robert Walser, William Harrison, Dino Buzzati, Henri Michaux. After LR 10, special issues are planned. We will not be reading unsolicited material." circ. 400. 2/yr. sub. price: $6; per copy: $3;

326

sample: $3. Back issues: 1-10 $3 each. 48pp; 6×9; of. Reporting time: 2 weeks to 2 months. Payment: 2 copies. Copyrighted, reverts to author. Pub's reviews. §Fiction, poetry (contemporary).

Low-Tech Press, Ron Kolm, 30-73 47th Street, Long Island City, NY 11103, 718-721-0946. 1981. Poetry, fiction, art, cartoons, interviews, satire, parts-of-novels, long-poems. "Low-Tech Press is currently not set up to receive any unsolicited mss at present." avg. press run 500. Pub'd 1 title 1998; expects 1 title 1999, 1 title 2000. 8 titles listed in the *Small Press Record of Books in Print* (28th Edition, 1999-00). avg. price, paper: $5. Discounts: 60/40% to bookstores + postage. 75-150pp; 5½×8½; of. Reporting time: 2-4 weeks. Payment: each arrangement differs - all profits to authors so far. Copyrights for author.

Lowy Publishing, David C. Lowy, President, Janitor, Sergeant-at-Arms, 5047 Wigton, Houston, TX 77096-5327, 713-723-3209. 1979. Fiction, art, cartoons, satire, letters, plays, non-fiction. "Not reading mss. presently." avg. press run 600. Pub'd 1 title 1998. 5 titles listed in the *Small Press Record of Books in Print* (28th Edition, 1999-00). avg. price, paper: $8.25, varies. Discounts: 40% to bookstores, 25% to libraries-not all titles. 112pp, varies; size varies; of, photocopying. Payment: 10% of gross based on monthly sales. Copyrights for author.

LP Publications (Teleos Institute) (see also EMERGING), Diane K. Pike, PO Box 12009-418, Scottsdale, AZ 85267, 480-948-1800; FAX 480-948-1870. 1972. Poetry, non-fiction. avg. press run 1M. 8 titles listed in the *Small Press Record of Books in Print* (28th Edition, 1999-00). avg. price, paper: $10. Discounts: available upon request. 120pp; size varies; of. Reporting time: variable. Copyrights for author.

LPD Press (see also TRADICION REVISTA), Barbe Awalt, Paul Rhetts, 2400 Rio Grande Blvd NW #1-213, Albuquerque, NM 87104-3222, 505-344-9382; fax 505-345-5129. 1994. Art, non-fiction, photos. "Actively seeking material on Southwestern artists, especially Native American and Hispanic. Ideal length of finished product with illustrations is 64-128pp. Recent contributions by Diana Pardue, Heard Museum, Rey Montez, Paul Pletka, and Carmella Padilla" avg. press run 5M. Pub'd 5 titles 1998; expects 2 titles 1999, 2 titles 2000. 7 titles listed in the *Small Press Record of Books in Print* (28th Edition, 1999-00). avg. price, paper: $39.95. Discounts: Library/school 25%, 1-4 40% with STOP, 5-19 40%, 20-49 43%, 50+ 45%. 128pp; 8½×11; of. Reporting time: 2-3 months. Simultaneous submissions accepted: yes. Payment: negotiable. Copyrights for author. MPBA, NMBA, RMBPA.

LRF Law Enforcement Training Services, LTD., 1245 Baring Blvd. #190, Sparks, NV 89434, 702-334-8605; email users.intercomm.com/LRF. 1 title listed in the *Small Press Record of Books in Print* (28th Edition, 1999-00).

LS Press, Inc. (see also LATINO STUFF REVIEW), E. Jerry Llevada, PO Box 440195, Miami, FL 33144, 305-262-1777; fax 305-447-8586; www.ejl@lspress.net. 1993. Poetry, fiction, non-fiction. "Has traditionally published high school text in math and English. Entered the poetry/fiction market in 1997. Future: 'How-To' books and economics. Will consider all and anything, gives advice and is willing to get into a subsidy pub. offering editing, publishing and distribution, on a very limited basis." avg. press run 10M text, 1M poetry. Pub'd 3 titles 1998; expects 4 titles 1999, 4 titles 2000. 4 titles listed in the *Small Press Record of Books in Print* (28th Edition, 1999-00). avg. price, paper: varies. Discounts: sells directly to schools, 40% to jobber, distributor, bookstores. Poetry 60pp, text 200pp; size varies; of. Reporting time: 1 month. Simultaneous submissions accepted: no. Payment: 10% gross sales with contract. Copyrights for author.

LUCIDITY, Bearhouse Publishing, Ted O. Badger, 398 Mundell Rd., Eureka Springs, AR 72631-9505, 501-253-9351; E-mail tbadger@ipa.net. 1985. Poetry. "Any subject or style of poetry but must be comprehensible: subtle, yes; obscure, no. Line length: 75 characters; number of lines 38, including title and spacing. We seek lucid verse dealing with the wide spectrum of human experience. Do not submit without requesting guidelines first. Include SASE." circ. 300. 4/yr. Pub'd 4 issues 1998; expects 4 issues 1999, 4 issues 2000. sub. price: $11; per copy: $2.75; sample: $2.75. Back issues: $2. Discounts: negotiable. 76pp; 5½×8½; †photocopy. Reporting time: 120-150 days. Simultaneous submissions accepted: yes. Publishes 10-12% of manuscripts submitted. Payment: copies and cash. Copyrighted, reverts to author. No ads.

LUCKY HEART BOOKS, Salt Lick Press, James Haining, 1900 West Highway 6, Waco, TX 76712. 1939. Poetry, fiction, articles, art, photos, cartoons, interviews, satire, criticism, reviews, music, letters, parts-of-novels, long-poems, collages, plays, concrete art. "*Letters to Obscure Men*, verse by Gerald Burns. *Catch My Breath*, verse, prose, and fiction by Michael Lally. *George Washington Trammell*, verse by Robert Trammell. *Two Kids & the Three Bears*, prose narrative by John Dennis Brown. *A Quincy History*, verse, journal record by James Haining. Three titles in 1979: *Next Services*, poetry by Michalea Moore; *Book of Spells* (first third), poetry by Gerald Burns; *New Icons*, verse by Peggy Davis. *Next Services*, verse by Michalea Moore; *A Book of Spells* (first & third), verse by Gerald Burns; *Lovers/Killers*, verse by Robert Trammell; *Pose Poems*, verse by Julie Siegel; *A Child's Garden*, verse by James Haining." circ. 1M. Irregular. Pub'd 1 issue 1998; expects 4 issues 1999, 3 issues 2000. sub. price: $15, $1 samplers. Back issues: write for information. Discounts: 60%-40%. 68pp; 8×10½, 9×6; †of, lp. Reporting time: 10 days-2 weeks. Payment: copies and money if available. Copyrighted, rights are released. Ads: none.

LULLWATER REVIEW, Rotating editors, Box 22036, Emory University, Atlanta, GA 30322, 404-727-6184. 1990. Poetry, fiction, art, photos, interviews, parts-of-novels, long-poems, plays. *"The Lullwater Review* is a trade-size journal for the literary arts, dedicated to presenting its readers with a wide variety of forms, styles, and perspectives in fiction, drama, and poetry. Recent contributors include: James Cushing, Denise Duhamel, Colette Inez, Aurel Rau, Josephine Humphreys (interview), Greg Grummer, Cindy Goff, Eve Shelnutt, and Charles Edward Eaton." circ. 2M-3M. 2/yr. Pub'd 2 issues 1998; expects 2 issues 1999, 2 issues 2000. sub. price: $12; per copy: $5; sample: $5. Back issues: $5 per copy. Discounts: none. 110pp; 6×9; 1p. Reporting time: 6-8 weeks, on average (longer during the summer). Simultaneous submissions accepted if we are notified upon submission and the event that the work is published elsewhere. Payment: 3 copies of the issue in which author's work appears. Copyrighted, reverts to author. Ads: $75 full page/we trade ads with other literary magazines. CLMP.

LUMMOX JOURNAL, Steve (Raindog) Armstrong, PO Box 5301, San Pedro, CA 90733-5301, 562-439-9858; e-mail lumoxraindog@earthlink.net. 1995. Poetry, fiction, articles, art, photos, cartoons, interviews, criticism, reviews, music, letters, news items. "Commentaries on creativity and the process that makes it possible—Raindog. Contributors welcome." circ. 200. 12/yr. Pub'd 12 issues 1998; expects 12 issues 1999, 12 issues 2000. sub. price: $20; per copy: $2; sample: $2 or trade. Back issues: $1. Discounts: trade for subscription. 20-24pp; 5½×8½; †copier. Reporting time: 2-3 months. Simultaneous submissions accepted: yes. Publishes 60% of manuscripts submitted. Payment: none/free copy. Not copyrighted. Pub's reviews: 30 in 1998. §Poetry, music, fiction. Ads: $30/$20/$10 1/4 page.

Luna Bisonte Prods (see also LOST AND FOUND TIMES), John M. Bennett, 137 Leland Ave, Columbus, OH 43214, 614-846-4126. 1974. Poetry, art, cartoons, satire, letters, collages, concrete art. "Interested in exchanges. We print broadsides and labels, chapbooks, poetry products, and a magazine. Would like to see more material in Spanish. See *Lost & Found Times* for further info." avg. press run 250. Pub'd 4 titles 1998; expects 4 titles 1999, 4 titles 2000. 82 titles listed in the *Small Press Record of Books in Print* (28th Edition, 1999-00). avg. price, paper: $7. Discounts: 40% for resale. 56pp; size varies; of, rubber stamps. Reporting time: 2 weeks. Payment: copies. Copyrighted to author, but author must do own registering for copyright.

Lunar Offensive Publications (see also RAG SHOCK), Stephen Fried, 1910 Foster Avenue, Brooklyn, NY 11230-1902. 1994. Poetry, fiction, articles, art, photos, cartoons, reviews, parts-of-novels, long-poems, collages, non-fiction. "Chapbooks by invitation only. Magazine acceptances will enter author into consideration" avg. press run 200. Pub'd 5 titles 1998; expects 8 titles 1999, 12 titles 2000. 4 titles listed in the *Small Press Record of Books in Print* (28th Edition, 1999-00). avg. price, paper: $5; other: none. Discounts: 20% on orders of 12 or more (+ $5 shipping + 10 copies). 32pp; 5½×8½; of, cover; photocopy (li-tes) interior pages. Reporting time: 3 weeks with SASE. Simultaneous submissions accepted: yes. Publishes 5-10% of manuscripts submitted. Payment: 30 copies from first run, sales split 50/50 on agreed chap price. Does not copyright for author. Small Press Center NYC.

LUNO, Gene Lehman, 31960 SE Chin Street, Boring, OR 97009, 503-663-5153. 1984. circ. 200+ network. 9/yr. Pub'd 9 issues 1998; expects 9 issues 1999, 9 issues 2000. sub. price: $10; per copy: $1.50; sample: $1 + stamp. 10pp; 8½×11; †copier. Payment: copies. Not copyrighted. Pub's reviews: 50+ in 1998. §Education, family, language, word play/games. Ads: exchange.

Luthers, Gary Luther, Alan Luther, 1009 North Dixie Freeway, New Smyrna Beach, FL 32168-6221, Phone/Fax 904-423-1600; E-mail http://www.luthers@n-jcenter.com. 1988. "We are private publishers, specializing in limited-run books. Unless partnership arrangements hae been made, the author pays to publish his/her work. We offer expertise in design, editing, art, typography, and production of a quality paperback/hardcover book. Marketing support includes copyright, generally registered in author's name. ISBN and Library of Congress number/CIP secured. UPC bar code provided as appropriate. Title entered into numerous indexes and data bases, as well as the Internet. News release/book review media package developed." avg. press run 500-1M. Pub'd 5 titles 1998; expects 7 titles 1999, 10 titles 2000. 36 titles listed in the *Small Press Record of Books in Print* (28th Edition, 1999-00). avg. price, cloth: $50; paper: $8.95. Discounts: 40% trade. 100+pp; 5½×8½, 6×9, 8½×11; of, 1200 dpi imagesetter. Reporting time: 10 working days. Copyrights for author.

Lux Fiat Press, George Atkins, PO Box 14626, Berkeley, CA 94712, caerula@hotmail.com. 1 title listed in the *Small Press Record of Books in Print* (28th Edition, 1999-00).

Luz Bilingual Publishing, Inc. (see also LUZ EN ARTE Y LITERATURA), Veronica S. Miranda, Director, PO Box 571062, Tarzana, CA 91357, 818-907-1454; Fax 818-907-8925. 1991. Poetry. avg. press run 500. Pub'd 2 titles 1998; expects 3 titles 1999, 3 titles 2000. 3 titles listed in the *Small Press Record of Books in Print* (28th Edition, 1999-00). avg. price, paper: $12; other: $6. Discounts: 50% distributor. 40-80pp; 8½×6½, 9×7½; desktop. Reporting time: 3-9 months. Publishes 5% of manuscripts submitted. Payment: in copies.

Copyrights for author.

LUZ EN ARTE Y LITERATURA, Luz Bilingual Publishing, Inc., Veronica S. Miranda, PO Box 571062, Tarzana, CA 91357, 818-907-1454; Fax 818-907-8925. 1992. Poetry, fiction, articles, art, photos, interviews, reviews. "Bilingual Spanish/English magazine. Recent contributors, writers: Laureano Alban, Isaac Goldemberg, Magali Alabau; translators: Frederick Fornoff, Samuel Zimmerman; artist: Betty Decter. Published once a year. Poetry, fiction, translations. Art and literature." circ. 1M. 1/yr. Pub'd 2 issues 1998; expects 1 issue 1999, 1 issue 2000. sub. price: $25; per copy: $19; sample: $8. Back issues: $8. Discounts: 50%. 100-120pp; 6½x8½; desktop. Reporting time: 3 months to a year. Simultaneous submissions accepted: yes. Publishes 10% of manuscripts submitted. Payment: copy. Copyrighted, reverts to author. Pub's reviews: 30 in 1998. §Poetry, short stories, magazines (literary). Ads: $400/$200/$100 1/4 page. Council of Literary Magazines and Presses.

Lycanthrope Press, Rev. Victor C. Klein, Laurence Talbot, PO Box 9028, Metairie, LA 70005-9028, 504-866-9756. 1993. Poetry, fiction, news items, non-fiction. "We are the publishing arm of Ordo Templi Veritatis. As such, our interest is theology, occult, etc." avg. press run 15M+. Pub'd 2 titles 1998; expects 3 titles 2000. 5 titles listed in the *Small Press Record of Books in Print* (28th Edition, 1999-00). avg. price, paper: $9.95. Discounts: as per fair market. 150+pp. Reporting time: 1 year; solicited only; letter. Simultaneous submissions accepted: yes. Publishes 100% of manuscripts submitted. Payment: standard. Copyrights for author. Gulf South Booksellers Association.

Lyceum Books, Inc., David Follmer, President, 5758 S. Blackstone, Chicago, IL 60637, 773-643-1902, Fax 723-643-1903; e-mail lyceum3@ibm.net. 1989. Non-fiction. avg. press run 2M. Pub'd 2 titles 1998; expects 5 titles 1999, 5 titles 2000. 18 titles listed in the *Small Press Record of Books in Print* (28th Edition, 1999-00). avg. price, cloth: $49.95; paper: $24.95. Discounts: bookstores, wholesalers 20%. 300pp; 5⅜x8¼, 6x9; of. Reporting time: 2 months. Simultaneous submissions accepted: yes. Payment: 10% net. Copyrights for author.

LYNX EYE, Pam McCully, Kathryn Morrison, 1880 Hill Drive, Los Angeles, CA 90041, 213-550-8522. 1994. Poetry, fiction, art, cartoons, satire, reviews, letters, parts-of-novels, plays, news items, non-fiction. "*Lynx Eye* is an eclectic magazine that publishes sharp, insightful work from all writers and artists. Tightly written, well crafted prose a must. We particularly encourage new and developing voices. At this time, the editors do not want to impose any subject or style restrictions. Our response to submissions will indicate whether the work is inappropriate to our readership. The *Lynx Eye* reader is a thoughtful adult who enjoys interesting reading and writing" circ. 500. 4/yr. Pub'd 4 issues 1998; expects 4 issues 1999, 4 issues 2000. sub. price: $25; per copy: $7.95; sample: $7.95. Discounts: negotiable. 120pp; 5½x8; offset. Reporting time: 12 weeks. Simultaneous submissions accepted if specified as such. Publishes 5-10% of manuscripts submitted. Payment: $10 per piece plus 3 complimentary copies. Copyrighted, reverts to author. Ads: $100/$50/$25 1/4 page. CLMP.

THE LYRIC, Commonwealth Press Virginia, Leslie Mellichamp, Editor; Elizabeth D. Mellichamp, Managing Editor, 307 Dunton Drive SW, Blacksburg, VA 24060-5127. 1921. Poetry. "Rhymed verse in traditional forms preferred, about 40 lines maximum. We print poetry only. No Contemporary political or social themes; we do not seek to shock, confound, or embitter. Poems must be original, unpublished, and not under consideration elsewhere. Send SASE for reply." circ. 650. 4/yr. Pub'd 4 issues 1998; expects 4 issues 1999, 4 issues 2000. sub. price: $12 a year, $22 for 2 years $30 for 3 years, Canada and other foreign add $2 per year postage; per copy: $3; sample: $3. Back issues: depends on availability. 36pp; 5⅜x7½; cold type. Reporting time: 2 months. Simultaneous submissions accepted: yes. Publishes 5% of manuscripts submitted. Payment: contributors receive complimentary copy of issue with their poem; quarterly and annual prizes for poetry published; $50 quarterly, $800 (total) annually. Copyrighted, reverts to author. No ads.

M

THE MAC GUFFIN, Arthur Lindenberg, Schoolcraft College, 18600 Haggerty Road, Livonia, MI 48152, 313-462-4400, ext. 5292 or 5327. 1983. Poetry, fiction, articles, art, photos, parts-of-novels, long-poems. "*The MacGuffin* is whatever everybody is after...*The MacGuffin* is where you find it... we are eclectic and holistic. We will print the best of everything with no biases. Contributors include Jim Daniels, Stuart Dybek, Lou Fisher, Diane Wakoski." circ. 600. 3/yr. Pub'd 3 issues 1998; expects 3 issues 1999, 3 issues 2000. sub. price: $15; per copy: $6; sample: $5. Back issues: varies. Discounts: varies. 160pp; 6x9; of. Reporting time: 10-12 weeks. Simultaneous submissions accepted: no. Payment: 2 contributor's copies. Copyrighted, reverts to author. Ads: not available. CLMP, CODA.

●**MacAdam/Cage Publishing Inc.**, Patrick Walsh, 465 California Street, Ste. 412, San Francisco, CA 94104,

415-986-7470; Fax 415-986-7414; ccom@earthlink.net. 1999. Fiction, non-fiction. "MacAdam/Cage publishes quality retail hardcover fiction and non-fiction with a West Coast emphasis." avg. press run 10M. Pub'd 1 title 1998; expects 2 titles 1999, 2-3 titles 2000. avg. price, paper: $15. Discounts: retail 40%, distributors/wholesalers 55%, book club 60%. 250pp; size varies; †of. Reporting time: 1 month. Simultaneous submissions accepted: yes. Publishes 5% of manuscripts submitted. Payment: equal to projected 1st year royalty. Copyrights for author. PMA, NICBA.

MacDonald/Sward Publishing Company, Catherine Snyder, Box 104A, RD 3, Greensburg, PA 15601, 724-832-7767. "Accepting no manuscripts at this time due to heavy schedule. We use historical material. Now focusing on American Indian subject matter and other minorities." avg. press run 500-1M. Expects 2 titles 2000. 23 titles listed in the *Small Press Record of Books in Print* (28th Edition, 1999-00). avg. price, paper: $17.95. Discounts: 1-5 books 20%; 6+ 40%. 250pp; 6×9, 8½×11. Publishes 19% of manuscripts submitted. Payment: varies. Does not copyright for author.

Mach 1, Inc., PO Box 7360, Chico, CA 95927, 916-893-4000. 1987. Photos, non-fiction. "Books, calendars and other publications are all aviation related. Mach 1 is famous for unique and high quality photography images that are used in its publications." avg. press run 10M. Pub'd 3 titles 1998; expects 3 titles 1999, 3 titles 2000. 6 titles listed in the *Small Press Record of Books in Print* (28th Edition, 1999-00). avg. price, cloth: $40. Discounts: 1-4 copies 20%, 5-49 40%, 50-99 41%, 100-249 42%, 250-499 43%, 500-999 44%, 1000-4999 50%, 5000+ 55%. 175pp; 10×12; of. Reporting time: 6 weeks. Payment: depends on subject matter. Copyrights depend on situation. ABA, CBA.

MACHINEGUN MAGAZINE: New Lit. Quarterly, Devin V. Hunter, Michael Wood, 601 S. Washington, Suite 281, Stillwater, OK 74074, E-mail chinaski00@aol.com. 1997. Poetry, fiction, articles, art, criticism, reviews, concrete art. "Submissions: Any readable length, cover letter w/bio required, SASE. Emphasis on image, truth, brave and/or risky thoughts. Nothing safe, overdone, and no self-engrossed crap." circ. 100. 4/yr. Expects 4 issues 1999, 4-6 issues 2000. sub. price: $12; per copy: $4; sample: $5. Back issues: $5. Discounts: negotiable. 46pp; 8½×11; †mi. Reporting time: 1-2 months. Simultaneous submissions accepted: yes. Publishes 10-25% of manuscripts submitted. Payment: 1 copy. Copyrighted, reverts to author. Pub's reviews. §Literary bios., art and lit. mags, literary criticism. Ads: negotiable.

MacMurray & Beck (see also Divina (A MacMurray & Beck imprint)), Frederick Ramey, Executive Director, 1490 Lafayette Street, Suite #108, Denver, CO 80218-2391. 1989. Fiction, non-fiction. avg. press run 9M. Pub'd 6 titles 1998; expects 6 titles 1999, 8 titles 2000. 25 titles listed in the *Small Press Record of Books in Print* (28th Edition, 1999-00). avg. price, cloth: $21.95; paper: $12.95. Discounts: 1-9 43% + freight, 10+ 47% + freight, or 50% no minimum, on a non-returnable basis. MB pays freight. 300pp; 6×9; of. Reporting time: 2-3 months. Simultaneous submissions accepted: yes. Payment: negotiated. Copyrights for author. Rocky Mt. Book Publishers Association (RMBPA).

MACROBIOTICS TODAY, George Ohsawa Macrobiotic Foundation, Bob Ligon, Editor; Carl Ferre, Managing Editor, PO Box 426, Oroville, CA 95965, 530-533-7702; fax 530-533-7908. 1970. Articles, interviews, reviews, non-fiction. "Length: 5-12 pages; double-spaced. Articles on macrobiotics, health, and nutrition accepted. Recent contributors include Dr. Benjamin Spock, Dr. Dean Ornish, Dr. Neal Barnard." circ. 5M. 6/yr. Pub'd 6 issues 1998; expects 6 issues 1999, 6 issues 2000. sub. price: $20; per copy: $4; sample: $1 ppd. Back issues: cover price. Discounts: 5-9 35%, 10-49 45%, 50+ 55%. 40pp; 8⅛×10¾; lp. Reporting time: 6 weeks. Payment: up to $75. Copyrighted, does not revert to author. Pub's reviews: 3 in 1998. §Macrobiotics, health, nutrition. Ads: $475/$270/$145 1/3 page/$90 1/6 pg/classifieds 50¢/frequency discounts. ABA.

Macrocosm USA, Inc., Sandi Brockway, Editor & President, PO Box 185, Cambria, CA 93428, 805-927-2515, e-Mail brockway@macronet.org Web http://www.macronet.org/macronet/. 1989. Non-fiction. "Reviews and articles focused on social changes and solutions. Supplemental update on the Web: http://www.macronet.org/macronet/" avg. press run 10M. Expects 1 title 1999, 1 title 2000. 3 titles listed in the *Small Press Record of Books in Print* (28th Edition, 1999-00). avg. price, cloth: $; paper: $6-$24.95. Discounts: very flexible, call. 400-500pp; 8½×11; webb. Reporting time: 60 days. Publishes 10% of manuscripts submitted. Payment: all works are loaned or contributed to Macrocosm USA, a nonprofit corporation. Does not copyright for author.

THE MAD FARMERS' JUBILEE ALMANACK, James Koehnline, Editor; Troy Skeels, Editor, PO Box 85777, Seattle, WA 98145, 206-633-2608. 1993. Poetry, fiction, articles, art, interviews, satire, criticism, reviews, letters, collages, news items, non-fiction, parts-of-novels. "Almanack is published quarterly, with Summer/Autumn produced as a double issue." circ. 250. 3/yr. Pub'd 3 issues 1998; expects 3 issues 1999, 3 issues 2000. sub. price: $16; per copy: $5; $6.50 with postage; sample: $5; $6.50. Back issues: none. Discounts: 40%. 42pp; 8½×11; †of. Reporting time: 60 days. Simultaneous submissions accepted: yes. Publishes 15% of manuscripts submitted. Payment: copy. Copyrighted, reverts to author. Pub's reviews: 0 in 1998. §calenders, time, agriculture, gardening, permaculture, anthropology, psychology, mythology, holidays. Ads: $40/$20; $10

1/4 page; $5 classifieds.

MAD POETS REVIEW, Eileen D'Angelo, Camelia Nocella, PO Box 1248, Media, PA 19063-8248. 1990. Poetry. "Anxious for work with 'joie de vivre' that startles and inspires, *MPR* places no restrictions on subject matter, form, or style, but assumes no responsibility for submissions received without adequate return postage. Submit original, unpublished work, limit 6 poems. We read submissions from Jan. 1 to June 1." 1/yr. Pub'd 2 issues 1998; expects 1 issue 1999, 1 issue 2000. sub. price: $8; per copy: $8; sample: $8. Discounts: negotiable. 70pp; 5½x8½. Reporting time: 6-8 weeks. Simultaneous submissions accepted: yes. Payment: copy of issue that work appears in. Copyrighted, reverts to author. Ads: none.

Mad River Press, Barry Sternlieb, Maureen Sternlieb, State Road, Richmond, MA 01254, 413-698-3184. 1986. Poetry, long-poems. "Manuscripts always solicited. Recent contributors: Gary Snyder, Linda Gregg, Cortney Davis, Richard Wilbur, W.S. Merwin, Hayden Carruth, Samuel Green, Tom Sexton, and John Daniel" avg. press run 125-500. Pub'd 3 titles 1998; expects 3 titles 1999, 3 titles 2000. 9 titles listed in the *Small Press Record of Books in Print* (28th Edition, 1999-00). avg. price, paper: $7-$25; sample $12; other: broadsides $15-$100. 20-28pp; 5½x8, 6x9; †lp, of. Payment: 10%-20% of press run. Copyrights for author.

●MAD SCIENTIST, Media Arts Publishing, Frank Dibari, PO Box 4765, Clearwater, FL 33758, e-mail frankie1@mindspring.com. 1990. Fiction, articles, art, photos, cartoons, satire, collages, non-fiction. "*Mad Scientist-The Journal of Science Gone Awry* is a blend of science, fiction and futurism. As an ongoing quarterly title, Mad Scientist dives headlong through the techno-quagmire of life. We present illustrated features about the impact of information overload, stories that are factual and fictional. To add an additional level of cohesion, an ongoing 16 chapter future-opera, "Mars 3000" was launched in issue one." circ. 1M. 4/yr. Pub'd 1 issue 1998; expects 4 issues 1999, 4 issues 2000. sub. price: $20; per copy: $8; sample: $5. 52pp; 7x8; of. Reporting time: 1 month. Simultaneous submissions accepted: no. Publishes 30%-50% of manuscripts submitted. Payment: copy or 1/2¢ per word. Copyrighted, reverts to author. Ads: call for rates.

THE MADISON REVIEW, Erin Hanusa, Poetry Editor; Jennifer Dobbins, Fiction Editor; Kristin Jensen, Fiction Editor, Dept of English, H.C. White Hall, 600 N. Park Street, Madison, WI 53706, 263-3303. 1978. Poetry, fiction, art, photos, parts-of-novels, long-poems. "Short, short stories welcome." circ. 500. 2/yr. Pub'd 2 issues 1998; expects 2 issues 1999, 2 issues 2000. sub. price: $8; per copy: $5; sample: $2.50. Back issues: $2.50. Discounts: $2/book for bulk orders be happy to trade copies. 80-150pp; 6x9; of. Reporting time: replies given by Dec. 15th for Fall issue and by April 15th for Spring issue. Simultaneous submissions accepted: yes. Payment: 2 copies. Copyrighted, reverts to author. Ads: $50/$35.

The Madson Group, Inc., Madeline Bright Ogle, Editor; Stephen A. Mart, Editor, 1329 Highway 395, Ste. 10-283, Gardnerville, NV 89410, 775-852-7743; fax 775-852-1253; email madsongroup@earthlink.net; http://www.petgroomer.com/madson.htm. 1987. Articles, non-fiction. "Business, career, vocation, education, pets, dog grooming, pet grooming." avg. press run 1M minimum. Expects 1 title 1999, 3 titles 2000. 1 title listed in the *Small Press Record of Books in Print* (28th Edition, 1999-00). avg. price, paper: $24.95-$39.95. 300pp; 8½x11. Reporting time: 30 days. Simultaneous submissions accepted: yes. Copyrights for author.

MAGIC CHANGES, Celestial Otter Press, John Sennett, Editor, 237 Park Trail Court, Schaumburg, IL 60173. 1978. Poetry, fiction, art, photos, cartoons, interviews, satire, criticism, reviews, music, long-poems, plays. "We invite you to submit poetry, short fiction, and drawings for our upcoming issue: 'Art: The Last Gasp of a Lost Grasp.' We are especially looking for cover art. *Magic Changes* is divided into sections such as 'The Order of the Celestial Otter,' 'State of the Arts,' 'Time,' 'Music,' and 'Skyscraper Rats.' A magical, musical theme pervades." circ. 500. 1 issue every 2 years. Expects 1 issue 2000. price per copy: $5; sample: $5. Back issues: $5. Discounts: inquire. 100pp; 8½x11; †desktop laser. Reporting time: 2 months. Payment: 1 or 2 issues, or cash. Copyrighted, reverts to author. Pub's reviews: 2 in 1998. §Poetry, rock n roll, short fiction, photography, all music. Ads: $60/$30/10¢.

Magic Circle Press, Valerie Harms, PO Box 1123, Bozeman, MT 59771. 1972. Fiction, art, photos, criticism, non-fiction. "Focus is now on book packaging for clients" avg. press run 2M. Expects 1 title 1999. 6 titles listed in the *Small Press Record of Books in Print* (28th Edition, 1999-00). avg. price, cloth: $12; paper: $10. Discounts: 40% trade, 15% library. 150pp; 6x9; of. Reporting time: 2 months. Payment: depends. Copyrights for author. NWU, Authors Guild.

MAGIC REALISM, Pyx Press, C. Darren Butler, Julie Thomas, PO Box 922648, Sylmar, CA 91392-2648. 1990. Poetry, fiction, articles, art, interviews, criticism, reviews, parts-of-novels, long-poems, non-fiction. "Prefer fiction under 8,000 words, but flexible. Query for more than 8,000 words. Uses exaggerated realism, magic realism, some genre fantasy and glib fantasy of the sort found in folktales and myths. Query on articles, interviews, criticism, reviews if unfamiliar with the mag." circ. 1M + Spanish version (200 projected). 4/yr. Pub'd 2 issues 1998; expects 4 issues 1999, 4 issues 2000. sub. price: $19.50; sample: $5.95. Back issues: $4.95 each, 3/$11, 4/$14. Discounts: query. 76pp; 5½x8½; of, B&W, xerox. Reporting time: 3 months, occasionally longer. Simultaneous submissions accepted: yes. Publishes .4% of manuscripts submitted. Payment: 1/4¢ per

331

word. Copyrighted, all rights revert to author but nonexclusive reprint rights. Pub's reviews: 60 in 1998. §Literary fantasy, magic realism, some literary, folktale, myth. query. AMP.

Magical Blend (see also MAGICAL BLEND MAGAZINE), Jerry Snyder, Editor; Michael Langevin, Publisher, PO Box 600, Chico, CA 95927. 1980. Fiction, articles, art, photos, interviews, reviews, letters, parts-of-novels, non-fiction. "We use work which brings a smile, invokes a sense of happiness, beauty, awe or reverence, or inspires one to create. Transpersonal psychology, new age thought, spiritual exploration, health, transformation of society." avg. press run 67M. Pub'd 6 titles 1998; expects 6 titles 1999. avg. price, paper: $4.99 US; $5.99 elsewhere. Discounts: 100+ copies 50% & shipping, 5+ copies 33% & shipping. 88pp; 8×10¾; of, web press. Reporting time: 3 months. Simultaneous submissions accepted: yes. Payment: copies and sometimes cash. Copyrights for author.

MAGICAL BLEND MAGAZINE, Magical Blend, Jerry Snider, Michael Peter Langevin, 133-1/2 Broadway, Chico, CA 95928, E-mail magical@crl.com. 1980. Articles, art, photos, interviews, reviews, letters, non-fiction. "Assess our style by looking at our magazine, or see our website at: www.magicalblend.com. Length approx 1,500 words average. Bias we print material which is of a positive, uplifting, cultural, psychic or spiritual nature. We hope to make our readers feel better about themselves & the world and help them get a better grasp of their destiny." circ. 65M. 6/yr. Pub'd 4 issues 1998; expects 6 issues 1999, 6 issues 2000. sub. price: $19.95; per copy: $4.99; sample: $4.99. Back issues: $250 for full set. Discounts: 100 or more, 50% retail. 88pp; 8×10¾; of, web press. Reporting time: 3 months. Simultaneous submissions accepted: yes. Payment: ranges from copies to $200. Copyrighted, reverts to author. Pub's reviews: 150 in 1998. §Psychic/spiritual, positive, music, health. Ads: $1500/$1250/$3.00 per word/$295 business cards/$150 column inch.

Magical Music Express, Greta Pedersen, Pam Donkin, 19363 Willamette Dr #252, West Linn, OR 97068, Voice 503-699-1814, e-mail accentm@teleport.com. 1983. Music. "Our product package are a music cassette and songbook for children. Material (original and folk music) reinforces important subject matter (assertiveness, peer pressure, environmental awareness), encourages creativity. For ages 4-10." avg. press run 2M. 2 titles listed in the *Small Press Record of Books in Print* (28th Edition, 1999-00). avg. price, cloth: $12; other: cassette/songbook $9.95. Discounts: depends on quantity and type of buyer. 5½×8½; of. Reporting time: 4 weeks. Payment: royalties paid semi-annualy; contract neg. Copyrights for author. BMI.

MAGNET MAGAZINE, Eric T. Miller, 1218 Chestnut Street, Suite 808, Philadelphia, PA 19107, 215-413-8570; fax 215-413-8569. 1993. circ. 25M. 6/yr. Pub'd 6 issues 1998; expects 6 issues 1999, 6 issues 2000. sub. price: $14.95; per copy: $3.50; sample: $4. Back issues: $4. 112pp; 8⅞×10⅞; of. Reporting time: varies. Simultaneous submissions accepted: no. Payment: varies. Copyrighted, does not revert to author. Pub's reviews: 10-12 in 1998. §music and music criticism. Ads: $3,000/$2,100.

Magnolia Publishing, Steve Keegan, PO Box 5537, Magnolia, MA 01930, 508-283-5283. 1993. avg. press run 10M. Pub'd 1 title 1998; expects 1 title 1999. 1 title listed in the *Small Press Record of Books in Print* (28th Edition, 1999-00). avg. price, paper: $8.95. Discounts: on request. 32pp; 10×8.

Magnus Press, Warren Angel, PO Box 2666, Carlsbad, CA 92018, 760-806-3743; Fax 760-806-3689; toll free 800-463-7818; e-mail magnuspres@aol.com. 1996. avg. press run 5M. Pub'd 2 titles 1998; expects 3-4 titles 1999, 6 titles 2000. 5 titles listed in the *Small Press Record of Books in Print* (28th Edition, 1999-00). avg. price, paper: $12. Discounts: 1-24 45%; 25-249 50%, 250+ 55%. 145pp; 5½×8½. Reporting time: 1-4 weeks. Simultaneous submissions accepted: yes. Publishes 3% of manuscripts submitted. Payment: graduating on retail price. Copyrights for author. CBA, SPAN.

MAIN STREET JOURNAL, John F. Moser, David A. Rose, 29 Princes Road, Ashford, Middlesex TW15 2LT, United Kingdom, 44-171-378-8809. 1992. Poetry, fiction, articles, photos, criticism, music, non-fiction. circ. 1.5M. 1/yr. Pub'd 1 issue 1998; expects 1 issue 1999, 1-2 issues 2000. sub. price: £6; per copy: £6; sample: educational institutions only. Back issues: none. Discounts: none. 96pp; 8×8; of. Reporting time: 1 month maximum. Simultaneous submissions accepted: yes. Publishes 20% of manuscripts submitted. Payment: flat fee £10 where possible. Copyrighted, reverts to author. Ads: £150/£90/£60 1/4 page.

MAIN STREET RAG POETRY JOURNAL, M. Scott Douglass, PO Box 25331, Charlotte, NC 28229-5331, 704-535-1918; E-mail mainstrag@mindspring.com. 1996. Poetry, art, photos, cartoons, letters. "Any style, any length. Emphasis on grittier material. Recent contributors: John Grey, Linda Lerner, Gerald Locklin, Chuck Sullivan, Susan Littlefield" circ. 500-700. 4/yr. Pub'd 2 issues 1998; expects 5 issues 1999, 4 issues 2000. sub. price: $16; per copy: $5; sample: $5. Back issues: varies by issue availability. 76pp; 5½×8½; of. Reporting time: 1-4 weeks. Simultaneous submissions accepted: no. Publishes 10-15% of manuscripts submitted. Payment: 1 contributor's copy. Copyrighted, reverts to author. Ads: $40/$20/$10 business card.

MAINE IN PRINT, 12 Pleasant Street, Brunswick, ME 04011, 207-729-6333, Fax 207-725-1014. 1975. Articles, interviews, reviews, letters, news items. "Published monthly, *Maine In Print* is the newsletter of Maine Writers & Publishers Alliance, a non-profit literary organization. Each issue contains feature articles about writers and their craft; a calendar of statewide literary events; submissions, contests and grant opportunities; profiles of Maine authors and publishers; reviews of new Maine books; and more." circ. 5M. 11/yr. Pub'd 11 issues 1998; expects 11 issues 1999, 11 issues 2000. sub. price: $30; sample: free. 16pp; 11×16; of. Reporting time: 6 weeks. Simultaneous submissions accepted: yes. Payment: $75 lead article. Copyrighted. §Writing craft, desktop and small press publishing, Maine literature. Ads: $450/$250/.20¢.

MAINLINE MODELER, Hundman Publishing, Robert L. Hundman, 13110 Beverly Park Road, Muklteo, WA 98275, 206-743-2607. 1979. Articles, photos, reviews, letters. circ. 14M. 12/yr. Pub'd 12 issues 1998; expects 12 issues 1999, 12 issues 2000. sub. price: $36; per copy: $3.50. Back issues: $3.50. Discounts: dealer price-$2.60 or 25.4% off. 96pp; 8½×11; of. Reporting time: 6-9 months. Payment: individual. Copyrighted, does not revert to author. Pub's reviews: 12-15 in 1998. §Railfan, railroad history or modeling. Ads: $450/$234/$162 1/3 pg/$128 1/4 pg/$96 1/6 pg/$62 1/12 pg.

Mainstream Press, Race Bannon, President, 584 Castro Street, Suite 518, San Francisco, CA 94114, 415-626-1867, fax 415-487-1137, e-mail MPBooks@aol.com. 1996. "Do not accept manuscripts, send letter first." avg. press run 3M-5M. Expects 2 titles 1999, 3 titles 2000. 1 title listed in the *Small Press Record of Books in Print* (28th Edition, 1999-00). avg. price, paper: $12.95. Discounts: 2-25 40%, 26-250 50%, 250+ 55%, stop 40% + $2. 128pp; 5½×8½. Payment: 10% quarterly. Copyrights for author. PMA.

Maisonneuve Press, Robert Merrill, Dennis Crow, Maria Hall, PO Box 2980, Washington, DC 20013-2980, 301-277-7505; FAX 301-277-2467. 1987. Criticism, non-fiction. "We seek compact and hard-hitting analyses of current cultural and theoretical developments—or articulations of how present conditions relate to earlier tendencies. Manuscripts should be freshly written and ideally have a published length of 200 pages. All manuscripts will be carefully and promptly reviewed by an editorial committee." avg. press run 1M-2M. Pub'd 3 titles 1998; expects 4 titles 1999, 4 titles 2000. 25 titles listed in the *Small Press Record of Books in Print* (28th Edition, 1999-00). avg. price, cloth: $26; paper: $14. Discounts: 1-4 copies 20%, 5-9 30%, 10+ 40% for paperbacks; 1-5 20%, 6+ 30% for cloth; distributors: Small Press Distribution (Berkeley), AK Distribution (San Francisco). 280pp; 6×9; offset, sewn binding. Reporting time: 4-5 months. Publishes 2-3% of manuscripts submitted. Payment: no advance, 5-10% of sales. Copyrights for author.

Majestic Books, Cindy MacDonald, PO Box 19097D, Johnston, RI 02919. 1991. Fiction. "We are currently searching for quality poetry and short stories under 2,000 words from writers under the age of 18 for an anthology. There are no restrictions in regards to genre. Our primary goal is to get writers published in a form they can treasure. No guidelines" avg. press run 300. Pub'd 3 titles 1998; expects 3 titles 1999, 3 titles 2000. 8 titles listed in the *Small Press Record of Books in Print* (28th Edition, 1999-00). avg. price, paper: $14.95. Discounts: quantity discounts available. 256pp; 5½×8½; of. Reporting time: 2 weeks. Simultaneous submissions accepted: yes. Payment: 10% royalty on sales directly relating to authors inclusion. Copyrights for author.

MAKING $$$ AT HOME, Darla Sims, PO Box 12280, Mill Creek, WA 98082, 209-485-7926. 1995. Fiction, cartoons, criticism, music, news items, non-fiction. "Articles to 1,000 words. Hints and tips, success profiles. Guidelines for SASE. How-to for how-to writers and designers." circ. 1M. 4/yr. Pub'd 2 issues 1998; expects 4 issues 1999, 4 issues 2000. sub. price: $29.95; sample: $4. 12pp; 8½×11; lp. Reporting time: 1 month. Publishes 75% of manuscripts submitted. Payment: .03¢/published word and copies. Copyrighted, reverts to author. Pub's reviews: 16-20 in 1998. §Writing, crafts, home business. Ads: $100/$50/$25 per 25 words.

MALACHITE AND AGATE, Marianne Milton, Founding Editor, 351 Pleasant Street, #317, Northampton, MA 01060, e-mail miltonmc@earthlink.net. 1995. Poetry, reviews. "This is an annual dedicated to lesbian poetry and fiction. Each issue contains selections of new poetry and fiction, rediscovered work, and related essays, reviews, letters, memoirs, etc. A long selection of a featured poet's work appears in each issue. Recent contributors include May Swenson, Adrian Oktenberg, Laurel Speer, Ellen Bass, and Meg Jochild." circ. 500. 1/yr. Expects 1 issue 1999, 1 issue 2000. sub. price: $9.95; per copy: $9.95; sample: $9.95. Back issues: $9.95. Discounts: 40% to bookstores. 104pp; 5½×8½; of. Reporting time: 3 months. Simultaneous submissions accepted: yes. Publishes 5% of manuscripts submitted. Payment: 1 copy, more at author's discount. Copyrighted, reverts to author. Pub's reviews: 21 in 1998. §Lesbian poetry and fiction. Ads: $30 per half page. CLMP.

Malafemmina Press, Rose Scrrentino, 4211 Fort Hamilton Parkway, Brooklyn, NY 11219. 1990. Poetry, plays. "Malafemmina Press is publishing a series of poetry chapbooks by Italian-American women on Italian-American themes. When ordering make checks payable to Rose Sorrentino." avg. press run 200. Pub'd 1 title 1998; expects 3 titles 1999. 2 titles listed in the *Small Press Record of Books in Print* (28th Edition, 1999-00). avg. price, paper: $2. 20pp; 5½×8½; of. Reporting time: 3 months. Simultaneous submissions accepted: no. Payment: 50 copies and 50% discount. Copyrights for author.

THE MALAHAT REVIEW, Marlene Cookshaw, Acting Editor, PO Box 1700, Stn. CSC, Victoria, British Columbia V8W 2Y2, Canada. 1967. Poetry, fiction, art, photos, interviews, criticism, parts-of-novels,

333

long-poems, plays. "Short works preferred. Index available 1967-1977, $3.95; $4.95 overseas." circ. 1.2M. 4/yr. Pub'd 4 issues 1998. sub. price: $25 in Canada, $35 other; per copy: $8, special issues $10; sample: $8. Back issues: $8. Discounts: 33⅓%, agents and bookstores only, no returns policy. 135pp; 9×6; of. Reporting time: 4-12 weeks. Simultaneous submissions accepted: no. Publishes approx. 3% of manuscripts submitted. Payment: $30 per magazine page, prose and poetry. Copyrighted. Pub's reviews: 20 in 1998. §Poetry, fiction. Ads: full page: $150 single issue, $500 four consecutive issues, half page: $100 single issue, $300 four consecutive issues, quarter page: $50 single issue, $160 four consecutive issues. CMPA.

Maledicta Press (see also MALEDICTA: The International Journal of Verbal Aggression), Reinhold A. Aman, Editor & Publisher, PO Box 14123, Santa Rosa, CA 95402-6123. 1975. Articles. "Material of 100 pp typed minimum for books, must deal with verbal aggression. Glossaries monolingual or bilingual, are preferred to other material. Backlog of 4 years. No cloth binding available." avg. press run 4M. Pub'd 1 title 1998; expects 1 title 2000. 18 titles listed in the *Small Press Record of Books in Print* (28th Edition, 1999-00). avg. price, paper: $15. Discounts: members 20%, booksellers 20-40%, jobbers 20-40%. 160pp; 5½×8½; of. Reporting time: 1 week. Simultaneous submissions accepted: no. Publishes 10% of manuscripts submitted. Payment: 10% paid annually, no advance. Copyrights for author.

MALEDICTA: The International Journal of Verbal Aggression, Maledicta Press, Reinhold A. Aman, Editor & Publisher, PO Box 14123, Santa Rosa, CA 95402-6123. 1975. Articles. "See any issue. 'Style Sheet' available. 25 pages maximum length of articles; must deal with verbal aggression. Glossaries in any languages preferred. Backlog 3 years" circ. 3M. 1/yr. Pub'd 1 issue 1998; expects 1 issue 1999, 1 issue 2000. sub. price: $15; per copy: $15; No sample copies available. Back issues: $20 per volume a year. Discounts: members 20%, booksellers 20-40%, jobbers 20-40%. 160pp; 5½×8½; of. Reporting time: 1 week. Simultaneous submissions accepted: no. Publishes 10% of manuscripts submitted. Payment: 10 free offprints. Copyrighted, reverts to author. Pub's reviews: 1 in 1998. §Verbal aggression (insults, curses, slang, etc.). No ads.

MAMA'S LITTLE HELPER, The Turquoise Butterfly Press, Terri Andrews, Editor, PO Box 1127, Athens, OH 45701. 1997. "A positive, informative newsletter for parents of children who have Attention Deficit Hyperactivity Disorder. Subject matter includes: news and updates, medication, natural and alternative treatment, tips, interviews, book reviews, editorials, medical information and behavior management. Tips: Study up on ADHD before you send us anything." 6/yr. Pub'd 6 issues 1998; expects 6 issues 1999, 6 issues 2000. sub. price: $24; per copy: $4; sample: $4. 12pp; 8½×11. Simultaneous submissions accepted: yes. Payment: in copies. Copyrighted. Ads: available.

Mandala Publishing Group, Vrindaranya Devidasi, 1585A Folsom Street, San Francisco, CA 94103-3728, 541-688-2258, 800-688-2218; Fax 541-461-3478; E-mail gvs@efn.org. 1995. Poetry, articles, art, photos, interviews, criticism, music, non-fiction. "We specialize in East Indian traditions and philosophy with an emphasis on Vedantic tradition. Vegetarian cookbooks would also be a priority." avg. press run 3M. Pub'd 5 titles 1998; expects 5 titles 1999, 7 titles 2000. 5 titles listed in the *Small Press Record of Books in Print* (28th Edition, 1999-00). avg. price, cloth: $19.95; paper: $7.95. Discounts: trade 60% (distributors) 45% (bookstores) 60% libraries. 200pp. Simultaneous submissions accepted: yes. Payment: none as of yet. Copyrights for author.

MANGAJIN, Vaughan P. Simmons, PO Box 77188, Atlanta, GA 30357-1188, 770-590-0092; FAX 770-590-0890. 1990. Articles, cartoons, reviews. "An inside, in-depth view of Japanese pop culture and language learning through comics. Also included are feature stories about various aspects of Japanese pop culture." circ. 28M. 10/yr. Pub'd 10 issues 1998; expects 10 issues 1999, 10 issues 2000. 5 titles listed in the *Small Press Record of Books in Print* (28th Edition, 1999-00). sub. price: $39.95; per copy: $5.50; sample: $6 include s/h. Back issues: $6 includes s/h. Discounts: write for schedule. 104pp; 8¼×10¾; of. Reporting time: 4 weeks. Simultaneous submissions accepted: yes. Payment: on acceptance. Copyrighted, does not revert to author. Pub's reviews: 15 in 1998. §Japanese language learning or Japanese pop culture. Ads: write for rates.

MANGROVE MAGAZINE, Send to Poetry or Fiction Editor, Dept. of English, Univ. of Miami, PO Box 248145, Coral Gables, FL 33124, 305-284-2182. 1994. Poetry, fiction, articles, art, interviews, parts-of-novels, long-poems. "The annual '98 issue contains poetry by Campbell McGrath and interviews with Dale Peck and Campbell McGrath. Authors should submit work August 1 through December 1. We report December through April, sometimes sooner" circ. 500. 1/yr. Pub'd 1 issue 1998; expects 1 issue 1999, 1 issue 2000. sub. price: $6; per copy: $6; sample: $6. Back issues: $6. Discounts: 10 for $40, 25 for $80. 125pp; 6×9; of. Reporting time: 1-6 months. Simultaneous submissions accepted: yes. Publishes 3% of manuscripts submitted. Payment: 2 free copies. Copyrighted, reverts to author. Pub's reviews. §Poetry books and fiction. Ads: none.

THE MANHATTAN REVIEW, Philip Fried, Founder and Editor, c/o Philip Fried, 440 Riverside Drive, #45, New York, NY 10027. 1980. Poetry, articles, interviews, criticism, long-poems. "'My only prejudice is against those who lack ambition, believing there is no more to writing than purveying superficial ironies, jokes, or shared sentiments; or those who dedicate themselves to the proposition that poetry of a word, by a word and for a word shall not perish from this earth. A poem is not purely a verbal artifact. It must speak to and for human concerns. I welcome experiments, but poetry must ultimately communicate to an audience. It is not an unobserved wave in the vast ocean of language.' (quoted from preface to 1st issue). ISSN 0275-6889. In recent issues: Christopher Bursk, Peter Redgrove, Penelope Shuttle, Baron Wormser, D. Nurkse, Bei Dao, Edmond Jabes, Patricia Goedicke, Louis Jenkins, Rose Auslander.'' circ. 500. 1/yr. Pub'd 1 issue 1998; expects 1 issue 1999, 1 issue 2000. sub. price: 1 volume (2 issues) $10 individuals (U.S. and Canada), $15 libraries (U.S. and Canada), $19 libraries elsewhere; per copy: $5 individuals, $7.50 libraries; sample: $5 individuals, $7.50 libraries. Back issues: same, with 6 X 9 envelope and $1.60 postage. 64pp; 5½x8½; of. Reporting time: 12-14 weeks. Simultaneous submissions accepted: no. Publishes .015% of manuscripts submitted. Payment: 2 copies. Copyrighted, reverts to author. Pub's reviews: 0 in 1998. §Poetry. Ads: $150/$75. CLMP.

●**Manifest Publications**, Virginia Cornell, Publisher, PO Box 429, Carpinteria, CA 93014, 805-684-4905; Fax 805-684-3100; vcornell@silcom.com. 5 titles listed in the *Small Press Record of Books in Print* (28th Edition, 1999-00).

MANKATO POETRY REVIEW, Roger Sheffer, Box 53, Mankato State University, Mankato, MN 56001, 507-389-5511. 1984. Poetry. "Up to 60 lines. Favor poems with strong sense of place—landscape or townscape. Have published Walter Griffin, Gary Fincke, Jane Varley, Judith Skillman.'' circ. 200. 2/yr. Pub'd 2 issues 1998; expects 2 issues 1999, 2 issues 2000. sub. price: $5; per copy: $2.50; sample: $2.50. Back issues: $2.50. 35pp; 7x8; of. Reporting time: 2 months. Payment: copies. Copyrighted, reverts to author. Pub's reviews: 0 in 1998. §Poetry books.

MANOA: A Pacific Journal of International Writing, Frank Stewart, Editor; Pat Matsueda, Managing Editor; Charlene Gilmore, Associate Editor, English Department, University of Hawaii, Honolulu, HI 96822, 956-3070; fax 956-3083; E-mail mjournal@hawaii.edu. 1988. Poetry, fiction, articles, art, photos, interviews, reviews, parts-of-novels, non-fiction. "Contributors include Janet Tan, Arthur Sze, Barry Lopez, Bei Ling, James D. Houston, Ursule Molinaro, Jack Marshall, Gene Frumkin, Alberto Rios, Robert Owen Butler, Ian MacMillan, Ai, Albert Wendt. Half or more of each issue will be American poetry, essays, and fiction; up to half of each issue will feature original translations of recent work from a Pacific or Asian country (Japan, the Philippines, Mexico, Pacific Islands, Russian Far East). Please note that in poetry, fiction, and essays we are *not* necessarily interested in Pacific or Asian subjects or topics, but are interested in high-quality writing on any subject. We want to bring outstanding work from Pacific and Asian countries to the general U.S. literary readership, and in turn present outstanding work from the U.S. at large to Pacific and readers, as well as to U.S. readers.'' circ. 2.5M. 2/yr. Pub'd 2 issues 1998; expects 2 issues 1999, 2 issues 2000. sub. price: $22 (beginning 1997); per copy: $15; sample: $15. Discounts: agency 10%, multiple orders: 10-19 20%, 20+ 30%. 220pp; 7x10; of. Reporting time: 4-6 weeks for poetry, reviews, essays; 3-6 months for fiction. Simultaneous submissions accepted, but we must be notified at time of submission. Publishes 2% of manuscripts submitted. Payment: competitive, depends on material and length. Copyrighted, reverts to author. Pub's reviews: 25 in 1998. §Anything of literary or cultural interest—poetry, fiction, arts, humanities, as long as related in some way to Pacific/Asia/Hawaii, which includes West Coast writers, presses. Ads: $200/$125. CLMP, CELJ.

●**Manta Press**, Carlene Reinhart, Bruce Reinhart, 2255 Hunter Mill Road, Vienna, VA 22181, 703-255-0659; fax 703-255-0566. 1999. News items, non-fiction. "Focus on organizational development and human resource development in the private and public sectors. This is often related to public policy, politics and current events.'' avg. press run 2-3M. Expects 2 titles 1999, 2 titles 2000. 2 titles listed in the *Small Press Record of Books in Print* (28th Edition, 1999-00). avg. price, cloth: $30; other: $25-150. 288pp; of. Reporting time: 3 months. Simultaneous submissions accepted: no. Payment: negotiable. Copyrights for author. Small Publishers Association of North America.

Manuscript Press (see also COMICS REVUE), Rick Norwood, PO Box 336, Mountain Home, TN 37684-0336, 423-926-7495. 1976. "Comic strips.'' avg. press run 2M-3M. Pub'd 1 title 1998; expects 1 title 1999, 1 title 2000. 3 titles listed in the *Small Press Record of Books in Print* (28th Edition, 1999-00). avg. price, cloth: $25; paper: $19.95; other: $150 folio. Discounts: 40% on 5 or more, 60% on 100 or more. 100-200pp; size varies, up to 16x22; various. Reporting time: slow. Simultaneous submissions accepted: no. Publishes 0% of manuscripts submitted. Payment: by arrangement. Copyrights for author.

MANUSHI - a journal about women & society, Madhu Kishwar, C-174 Lajpat Nagar - I, New Delhi, New Delhi 110024, India, 6833022 or 6839158. 1978. Poetry, fiction, articles, art, photos, cartoons, interviews, reviews, letters, parts-of-novels, news items, non-fiction. "South Asian women's issues and other movements for social justice: living/working conditions, reform struggles, education, government policies effecting women, minority rights, cultural/religious practices effecting women, poetry, fiction, book and film reviews.'' 6/yr. Pub'd 6 issues 1998; expects 6 issues 1999, 6 issues 2000. sub. price: $25 (USA), Rs 90 (India), $36 Rs 120 (instit); per copy: $4; sample: $4 (includes airmail postage). Back issues: $4 each. Discounts: 25% to agents on sales, 10% on subs. 44pp; 7x9; of. Reporting time: a month (approximate). Simultaneous submissions accepted: no. Payment: none. Copyrighted, copyright is author's (permission required to reprint). Pub's reviews: 6-8 in 1998. §Women, civil liberties, human rights, third world, art, literature, historical, sociological studies, ethnic relations, environment issues, issues related to economic and political reforms. Ads: Rs 4000/Rs 2000.

MANY MOUNTAINS MOVING, Naomi Horii, Marilyn Krysl, Luis Alberto Urrea, Contributing Editor; Beth Nugent, Fiction Editor; Alissa Reardon Norton, Poetry Editor, 420 22nd Street, Boulder, CO 80302, 303-545-9942, Fax 303-444-6510. 1994. Poetry, fiction, art, photos, cartoons, interviews, satire, letters, parts-of-novels, long-poems, non-fiction. "We invite fiction, poetry and essays from writers of all cultures. Contributors include Robert Bly, Lorna Dee Cervantes, Diane Glancy, Alicia Ostricker, Marge Piercy, Luis Urrea and many others. Poems have appeared in Best American Poetry." circ. 2.5M. 3/yr. Pub'd 3 issues 1998; expects 3 issues 1999, 3 issues 2000. sub. price: $18; per copy: $6.50; sample: $6.50. Back issues: $6.50. Discounts: Negotiable. 250pp; 6×8¾; web press. Reporting time: usually within 1 month, but sometimes longer if we are seriously considering a manuscript. Simultaneous submissions accepted: yes. Publishes 1% of manuscripts submitted. Payment: contributors' copies. Copyrighted, reverts to author. Ads: $200/$100/no classifieds. RMBPA, PMA.

MAP AFICIONADO, Mike McGuire, 293 Hopewell Drive, Powell, OH 43065, 614-848-3232; 800-848-0304; FAX 614-848-5045. 1996. Articles, interviews, letters, news items. "Length of material: 1200-1500 words with or without photo(s)." circ. 10M. 4/yr. Expects 4 issues 1999, 4 issues 2000. sub. price: $24; per copy: $6; sample: $10. Back issues: $10. Discounts: 40%. 60pp; 8½×11; sheet feed. Reporting time: 4 weeks. Simultaneous submissions accepted: yes. Publishes an unknown % of manuscripts submitted. Payment: after publication, 30 days net. Copyrighted, does not revert to author. Pub's reviews: 0 in 1998. §Maps, cartography. Ads: $995/$695/$495 1/4 page.

MARATHON & BEYOND (M&B), Human Kinetics Pub. Inc., Richard Benyo, PO Box 5076, Champaign, IL 61825-5076, 217-351-5076. 1996. "Trade journal, articles are solicited by editor, not submitted unsolicited. Interests are marathons, ultra marathons, training, physiology, and races." circ. 1.3M. 6/yr. Expects 6 issues 1999, 6 issues 2000. sub. price: $29.95 individuals, $44.95 institutions; per copy: $7.95 individuals, $12 institutions; sample: free. Back issues: $7.95 indiv., $12 instit. Discounts: 15%. 120pp; 6×9; of. Reporting time: 2 months. Simultaneous submissions accepted: no. Payment: none. Copyrighted, does not revert to author. Midwest Book Publishers Assn., ABA.

Marathon International Book Company, Jim Wortham, Publisher, Department SPR, PO Box 40, Madison, IN 47250-0040, ph/fax 812-273-4672; jwortham@seidata.com. 1969. "We are considering non-fiction and self help manuscripts. We are interested in considering other publishers' books for distribution. Please mail a sample copy of any title(s) you wish us to consider for distribution. We are also interested in purchasing small publishing companies. Contact us by mail or fax, please." avg. press run 3M. Pub'd 3 titles 1998; expects 3 titles 1999. 19 titles listed in the *Small Press Record of Books in Print* (28th Edition, 1999-00). avg. price, cloth: $19.95; paper: $9.95. Discounts: 40% to trade; write for discount schedule. 64-300pp; 5½×8½; of, lp. Reporting time: 2-3 weeks. Simultaneous submissions accepted: yes. Publishes 5% of manuscripts submitted. Payment: 10% royalty after book expenses are met. Copyright in author's name. PMA, SPAN, SPAWN.

Paul Maravelas, 15155 Co. Rd. 32, Mayer, MN 55360, 612-657-2237. 1981. avg. press run 100. Expects 1 title 2000. 1 title listed in the *Small Press Record of Books in Print* (28th Edition, 1999-00). †lp. Reporting time: 2 weeks. Payment: arranged. Copyrights for author.

Peter Marcan Publications, Peter Marcan, PO Box 3158, London SEI 4RA, England, UK, England, 0171-357-0368. 1978. Non-fiction. "I have five specialist directories: *Outlets for Specialist New Books in the UK,* (published previously under the title: Directory of Specialist Bookdealers in the UK Handling Mainly New Books); *The Marcan Handbook of arts organizations:* a compendium of information on the activities and publications of national (UK and Ireland), regional and international arts and cultural organizations; (published previously under the title: Arts Address Book); *Art Historians and Speicalists in the UK: A Directory of Expertise and Research; Greater London Local History Directory:* a borough by borough guide to local history organizations, thier activities and publications; in 1994 I published: *British Professional Violinist of Today:* a directory of achievement, current activity, and their related ensembles. In addition there are pictorial albums on London history and topography: *A London Docklands Album,* and *Visions of Southwork* are currently available. More specialist titles include: *Music For Solo Violin Unaccompanied:* a catalogue of published and unpublished works from the 17th century to 1989, compiled by Harry Edlund; and a reissue of *The Lord's Prayer in Black and White,* with drawings by Arthur Wragg (1903-1976), first published in 1946." avg. press run 350-1M. Pub'd 1 title 1998; expects 2 titles 1999, 2 titles 2000. 13 titles listed in the *Small Press Record of Books in Print* (28th Edition, 1999-00). avg. price, paper: £5.95-£20. Discounts: 35% discount to book trade for two or more copies. 62-120pp; size A5, A4; of.

March Street Press (see also PARTING GIFTS), Robert Bixby, 3413 Wilshire Drive, Greensboro, NC 27408-2923. 1988. Poetry, fiction. "Currently reading. I hope to publish at least 3 books of poetry and one book of short stories per year. Reading fee: $10." avg. press run 50. Pub'd 8 titles 1998; expects 6 titles 1999, 6 titles 2000. 50 titles listed in the *Small Press Record of Books in Print* (28th Edition, 1999-00). avg. price, paper: $6.

Discounts: write. 40pp; 5½x7½; †Xerox. Reporting time: 2-3 months. Payment: 10 free copies, 15% of sales. Does not copyright for author.

MARCH/Abrazo Press, Carlos Cumpian, c/o Movimiento Artistico Chicano, Inc., PO Box 2890, Chicago, IL 60690-2890, 312-539-9638. 1981. Poetry, photos, interviews, criticism, reviews, plays. "We publish poetry and art chapbooks and perfectbound poetry books." avg. press run 1M. Pub'd 4 titles 1998; expects 4 titles 1999, 4 titles 2000. 13 titles listed in the *Small Press Record of Books in Print* (28th Edition, 1999-00). avg. price, paper: $6.95, $3 chapbooks; other: $7. Discounts: libraries & individuals contact us for single copies; bookstores or any retail outfit contact our distributor Baker and Taylor Books, avg. 40% for six or more copies. 52pp; 8½x5; desktop. Reporting time: 6-9 weeks for submissions sent with SASE. Simultaneous submissions accepted, just let us know this is the case. Publishes 10% of manuscripts submitted. Payment: will provide a full contract with details. Copyrights for author.

MARGIN: EXPLORING MODERN MAGICAL REALISM, Tamara Kaye Sellman, 9407 Capstan Drive NE, Bainbridge Island, WA 98110-4624, e-mail msellma@ibm.net. 1999. Fiction, parts-of-novels. "E-mail submissions welcome if text is pasted into the body of the letter. No attachments, please. 4,000 words. Send SASE for writer's guidelines and criteria establishing "What is magical realism." Because Margin has a very specific literary goal, the editors suggest writers submit simultaneously. Our goal is to publish annually, but it may be more realistic to publish as we receive enough material. If you love magical realism, this is the place to publish/read!" Expects 1 issue 1999, 1 issue 2000. sub. price: free, on-line access; URL available fall 1999. electronic. Reporting time: 2 months. We encourage simultaneous submissions. Publishes 5% of manuscripts submitted. Payment: none right now, but will be looking for financial grants to cover the payment of authors in the near future. Copyrighted, reverts to author. Wild Dove Writers' Center.

Mariah Publications, Sheila Moak, PO Box 934, Waco, TX 76703, 817-753-3714 phone/Fax. 1 title listed in the *Small Press Record of Books in Print* (28th Edition, 1999-00).

Marinelli Publishing (see also FULL DISCLOSURE), Glen Roberts, Mag; Greg Hauser, Publishing, 8129 N 35th Avenue, #134, Phoenix, AZ 85051-5892, 800-NEED-A-PI. 1985. Articles, interviews, reviews, non-fiction. "12/92 released title *So Ya Wanna Be a Private Investigator, Huh Binky?*." avg. press run 5M-10M. Pub'd 7 titles 1998; expects 2 titles 1999. 5 titles listed in the *Small Press Record of Books in Print* (28th Edition, 1999-00). Discounts: 50% wholesale. 100+pp; †of. Reporting time: 6 weeks. Payment: varies, query first. Copyrights for author. PMA.

MARION ZIMMER BRADLEY'S FANTASY MAGAZINE, Mrs. Marion Z. Bradley, PO Box 249, Berkeley, CA 94701-0249, 510-644-9222. 1988. Fiction. "*Marion Zimmer Bradley's Fantasy Magazine* buys well-plotted short stories, up to 5,500 words. Our preferred length is 3,500 to 4,000 words, but we also buy short-shorts (under 1,000 words). We buy fantasy with no particular objection to modern settings, but we want action and adventure. Stories should stand alone. This is not a primary market for series and shared world stories. We are not a market for poetry, nor for hard science fiction or gruesome horror. No metaphysics, folklore, science fiction, rewritten fairy tales, 'hearth-witches,' and no radical feminism. Please read a few issues before submitting so that you can see the kind of thing we do buy. Manuscripts are returned only if accompanied by SASE. No simultaneous submissions. MZB cannot read dot-matrix. *Send SASE for guidelines before submitting.*" 4/yr. Pub'd 4 issues 1998; expects 4 issues 1999, 4 issues 2000. sub. price: $20/4 issues, $27 Canada, $44 foreign, in U.S. funds; per copy: $5.95; sample: $4. Back issues: $5.95 + $2.50 p/h per order. 64pp; 8½x11. Reporting time: 90% of submissions are returned in 4-6 weeks, but some stories may be held up to 6 months. Simultaneous submissions accepted: no. Publishes 1-2% of manuscripts submitted. Payment: on acceptance. Copyrighted, reverts to author. Ads: $350/$220.

MARK, Mike Donnelly, Student Union, Room 1501, University of Toledo, Toledo, OH 43606, 419-537-2373. 1967. Poetry, fiction, articles, art, photos, interviews, criticism, reviews, music, parts-of-novels, plays, non-fiction. "Please include a brief cover letter with name, address, date, and title(s) submitted. Send clean copies of your work - we get too many sloppy mss. We're open to all forms and types of poetry, although we're rather tired of the same old romance/love poetry. We prefer work with a social or political bent. Politically irresponsible work (racist, sexist, heterosexist, anti-choice) has no place with us" circ. 1M. 1/yr. Pub'd 1 issue 1998; expects 1 issue 1999, 1 issue 2000. sub. price: $3; per copy: $3; sample: $3. Back issues: limited number available at $2. 50pp; 6x9; of. Reporting time: 3-6 months. Simultaneous submissions accepted: yes. Payment: in copies. Copyrighted, reverts to author.

Marketing Department, 4516 Lovers Lane Suite 157, Dallas, TX 75225, 972-480-8669; Fax 972-480-8663; Toll-free 888-255-9139; E-mail dmwriter@aol.com. 1 title listed in the *Small Press Record of Books in Print* (28th Edition, 1999-00).

Markowski International Publishers, Marjorie L. Markowski, Editor; Michael A. Markowski, 1 Oakglade Circle, Hummelstown, PA 17036-9525, 717-566-0468; FAX 717-566-6423. 1981. Non-fiction. "Formerly Ultralight Publications, Inc. Publishes hardcover and trade paperback originals. Book catalog and ms guidelines for #10 SAE with two first class stamps. Publishes book on average of one year after acceptance. Simultaneous submissions OK. Primary focus is books on, human development, self-help, personal growth, sales and marketing, leadership training, network marketing, motivation and success. We are interested in how-to, motivational and instructional books of short to medium length that will serve recognized and emerging needs of society. Query or submit outline and three sample chapters. Reviews artwork/photos as part of ms package. Tips: 'We're very interested in publishing best sellers!'" avg. press run 5-50M. Pub'd 5 titles 1998; expects 25 titles 1999, 40 titles 2000. 12 titles listed in the *Small Press Record of Books in Print* (28th Edition, 1999-00). avg. price, paper: $9.95-$19.95. Discounts: 1-10, 2-4-20%, 5-9=30%, 10-24-40%, 25-49-42%, 50-74-45%, 75-99-47%, 100-499-50%, 500-999-55%, 1000 and up 60%. 144-352pp; 5¼×8¼; of. Reporting time: 2 months. Simultaneous submissions accepted: yes. Publishes 2% of manuscripts submitted. Payment: 10-15% royalty on wholesale price. Copyrights for author. PMA, Mid-Atlantic Publishers Association.

THE MARLBORO REVIEW, Ellen Dudley, Ruth Anderson Barnett, Poetry; Margaret Kaufman, Fiction; Helen Fremont, Fiction, PO Box 243, Marlboro, VT 05344. 1995. Poetry, fiction, interviews, criticism, reviews, parts-of-novels, long-poems, non-fiction. "Longpoems okay, translations and reviews welcome. Recent contributors: Brenda Hillman, William Matthews, Stephen Dobyns, D. Nurkse, Dionision Martinez. No deadlines." circ. 1M. 2/yr. Pub'd 2 issues 1998; expects 2 issues 1999, 2 issues 2000. sub. price: $16; per copy: $8 + 75¢ postage; sample: $8 + 75¢ postage. Back issues: none. Discounts: bookstores 40%. 100pp; 6×9; of. Reporting time: 2-3 months. Simultaneous submissions accepted if notified. Publishes 6% of manuscripts submitted. Payment: copies. Copyrighted. Pub's reviews: 8 in 1998. §Poetry, fiction, and nonfiction. Ads: $150/$75/none. CLMP.

Marlton Publishers, Inc., Bruce Rory Thomas, PO Box 223, Severn, MD 21144, 800-859-1073; fax 410-519-1439. 1997. Fiction. "Solicited manuscripts only." avg. press run 5M. Expects 1 title 1999, 2 titles 2000. avg. price, paper: $6.99. Discounts: 2-4 20%, 5-9 30%, 100+ 50%. 250pp; 4¼×6¾; †of. Simultaneous submissions accepted: no. Payment: outright purchase of manuscript. Copyrights for author. Independent Publishers Network, PMA, Small Publishers Association of North America.

Marmot Publishing, Steven Laurens, PO Box 725, Snoqualmie, WA 98065, 425-831-7022. 1993. Non-fiction. "Please send queries only. We do not have the staff to read unsolicited manuscripts. Almost any general adult non-fiction subjects are welcome and should support at least a 50-page book. We encourage, but by no means limit, queries on how-to, travel, self-sufficiency and the Pacific Northwest. We also accept controversial and counter-cultural material. Biased material must be of a conservative or libertarian viewpoint and challenge the dominant liberal ideas and viewpoints. We want the truth, supportable by facts, not the current dogma. We encourage individual rights and discourage a more powerful (i.e. intrusive) government. No pro-feminism, pro-multiculturalism or religion please." avg. press run 2M. Expects 1 title 2000. 1 title listed in the *Small Press Record of Books in Print* (28th Edition, 1999-00). avg. price, paper: $14.95. Discounts: bookstores-40%, distributor-55%. 300pp; 5½×8½; of. Reporting time: 2 months. Simultaneous submissions accepted: yes. Payment: no advances, royalty negotiable. Copyrights for author. BPNW, PMA.

MARQUEE, Steve Levin, York Theatre Building, 152 N. York Road, Suite 200, Elmhurst, IL 60126, 630-782-1800, Fax 630-782-1802; e-mail thrhistsoc@aol.com. 1969. Articles, photos, interviews, criticism. "Historical research on American Theatre buildings contributed by members. Recent article Metropolitan Opera House, Philadelphia and current article-history of Atlantic City theatres w/vintage pictures. Comprehensive study Chicago Theatre, Chicago, IL. Theatre Draperies Issue—1983 - Color issue - Fifth Avenue Th. Seattle, Washington. Special issue - 1984 - Preservation of OLD Theatres. 1985 Theatre Acoustics. 1976 Mastbaum Th. - Phila Pa; Earle Theatre, Philadelphia issue-1986; Al Ringling Th. Baraboo, WI - 1991. Michigan Thr, Detroit, 1995." circ. 1M. 5/yr. Pub'd 5 issues 1998; expects 5 issues 1999, 5 issues 2000. sub. price: $40; per copy: $6.50; sample: $6.50. Back issues: $6.50. Discounts: library rate $30. 30pp; 8½×11; lp. Reporting time: 3 months. Publishes 85% of manuscripts submitted. Copyrighted, reverts to author. Pub's reviews: 6 in 1998. §Theatre architecture. Ads: $200/$125/.

MARSHALL HOUSE JOURNAL, Jeanie Marshall, PO Box 918, Santa Monica, CA 90406, 310-458-1172. 1981. Non-fiction. "Empowerment and energetics for individuals, groups and organizations." circ. 1M. 10/yr. Pub'd 10 issues 1998; expects 10 issues 1999, 10 issues 2000. sub. price: $30; per copy: $3.50; sample: complimentary. Back issues: $3.50. 4pp; 8½×11; †of. Copyrighted, reverts to author. Pub's reviews: 2 in 1998. §Empowerment, organization development, healing, energetics. PMA, NAPRA.

MARTHA'S KIDLIT NEWSLETTER, Martha Rasmussesn, PO Box 1488, Ames, IA 50014, 515-292-9309; www.kidlitonline.com. 1989. Articles, interviews, reviews, news items. "Articles about children's book authors and illustrators. Discussion of particular titles i.e. "The Wizard of Oz" or types of books (poetry, reading primers, pop-up/movable books) needed. 250 words maximum, prefer around 150-200 words. Reviews of books which help collectors like biographies of writers or illustrators, information on publishers-like Saalfield or Altemus. Need humorous pieces; interviews with collectors." circ. 400. 6/yr. Pub'd 8 issues 1998; expects 6 issues 1999, 6 issues 2000. sub. price: $30, $31 Canada, $34 elsewhere (US funds only); per copy: $5; sample:

338

$5 each. Back issues: Sale prices Nov-Dec Holiday Special $3 each. Discounts: Packet of 10 copies per issue @$3 a copy ($30 for 10). 8pp; 8½×11; of. Reporting time: 2 weeks. Publishes 80% of manuscripts submitted. Payment: $10-20 per article or review (50-250 words). Not copyrighted. Pub's reviews: 8 in 1998. §Those that give information about Out of Print Children's books and authors; biographies, bibliographies of children's authors, illustration and illustrators. Ads: $80/$60.

MARTHA'S VINEYARD MAGAZINE, Laurence Michie, Editor, PO Box 66, Edgartown, MA 02539, 508-627-7444. 1985. Articles, art, photos, cartoons, interviews, non-fiction. *"All of our material focuses on the island of Martha's Vineyard. We feature many new writers as well as local talent such as Walter Cronkite, Mike Wallace, Art Buchwald, Marianne Wiggins. Martha's Vineyard Magazine is the Vineyard's only magazine. We place an emphasis on history, art, environment, lifestyles, poetry, culture and special island events."* circ. 10M. 4/yr. Pub'd 4 issues 1998; expects 4 issues 1999, 4 issues 2000. sub. price: $15; per copy: $3.95. Back issues: $3.95. Discounts: bulk purchase of any issue @ $2 each. 60pp; 8⅛×10⅞; of. Reporting time: 2 months. Payment: $50-$150. Copyrighted, reverts to author. Pub's reviews. §Related to Martha's Vineyard or Cape Cod areas. Ads: $1430/$830.

Maryland Historical Press, Vera F. Rollo, 9205 Tuckerman St, Lanham, MD 20706, 301-577-2436 and 557-5308; fax 301-577-8711; e-mail mhpress@erols.com. 1965. Non-fiction. *"We publish material for Maryland schools; and for colleges with Aviation courses on free-lance basis. U.S. Aviation Law; Aviation Insurance; Maryland. History, Govt., Geog., Biography, and Black History; Americana. Our books are mostly set in type, printed via off-set process, illustrated, and about 80 percent are casebound, 20 percent paperback. We buy almost nothing, sorry."* avg. press run 2M on paperbacks, 5M on casebound. Pub'd 1 title 1998; expects 1 title 1999, 1 title 2000. 21 titles listed in the *Small Press Record of Books in Print* (28th Edition, 1999-00). avg. price, cloth: $19.75; paper: $9.95. Discounts: 33% to jobbers/dealers. 100-400pp; 8½×11, 7×9; of. Payment: 10%. Copyrights for author.

Masefield Books, M. Bloomfield, Publisher, 7210 Jordan Avenue, Suite B54, Canoga Park, CA 91303. 1991. Non-fiction. avg. press run 500-1M. Expects 1 title 2000. 5 titles listed in the *Small Press Record of Books in Print* (28th Edition, 1999-00). avg. price, cloth: $27; paper: $20. Discounts: dealers 20%. 200pp; 6×9; of. Reporting time: within 1 month. Simultaneous submissions accepted: yes. Payment: 10% of gross price. Copyrights for author.

THE MASONIA ROUNDUP, Ardis Mason, Dan Mason, 200 Coolwell Road, Madison Heights, VA 24572-2719. 1991. Poetry, fiction, articles, cartoons, interviews, satire, criticism, reviews, letters, news items, non-fiction. *"The Masonia Roundup is a general interest, family-oriented quarterly magazine. Our primary interest is in short (500 word) non-fiction articles describing real events happening to real people. We do accept some short fiction and poetry, book, movie, and zine reviews also. We welcome puzzles. Eric Albert, who has written puzzles for Games magazine, has contributed several. Humor always welcome."* circ. 150. 4/yr. Pub'd 4 issues 1998; expects 4 issues 1999, 4 issues 2000. sub. price: $5; per copy: $1.50; sample: $1.50. Back issues: $1.50 if available. Discounts: special rates are available if enough advance notice is given; they are usually sent for postage amount. 16pp; 7×8½; †laser print and xerox. Reporting time: 6-8 weeks. Simultaneous submissions accepted: yes. Publishes 75% of manuscripts submitted. Payment: 2 complimentary copies. Copyrighted, reverts to author. Pub's reviews: 8 in 1998. §Almost anything except obscene or porn; humor, how-to, cartoons, family, etc. Ads: $25/$15/classifieds 10¢/word, minimum 15 words.

THE MASSACHUSETTS REVIEW, Mary Heath, Editor; Jules Chametzky, Editor; Paul Jenkins, Editor, South College, Univ. of Mass/Box 37140, Amherst, MA 01003-7140, 413-545-2689. 1959. Poetry, fiction, articles, art, photos, interviews, satire, criticism, letters, long-poems, plays, non-fiction. *"A SASE must accompany each manuscript + query. No fiction mss considered June 1 - Oct 1."* circ. 2M+. 4/yr. Pub'd 4 issues 1998; expects 4 issues 1999. sub. price: $18; per copy: $7; sample: $7. Back issues: $7-$14. Discounts: 15% on ads for adv. agencies; 40% bookstores; $50 full page ad for univ. and small presses. 172pp; 6×9; lp. Reporting time: 6-12 weeks. Payment: $50 prose, $10 min. poetry, 35¢ per line. Copyrighted, rights revert to author on request. Ads: $125 full page. CLMP.

MASSACRE, Indelible Inc., Roberta McKeown, BCM 1698, London WC1N 3XX, England. 1990. Fiction, art, photos, cartoons, satire, criticism, collages. *"massacre is an annual magazine of 'improbable' or 'anti-naturalistic' fiction. It does not publish genre sci-fi or, in general, stories that are futuristic or technology based. massacre is about juxtaposition, plundering, originality, the outre, weird and unexpected. It takes its precedents from dream literature, surrealism, satire and dada—writers like Beckett, Edward Gorey, Flann O'Brien. Stories can be up to 3,000 words in length. Poetry is seldom appropriate. Critical essays are also welcome if relevant; in the past these have featured French anti-naturalist playwrights, The Third Policeman, and the Theatre of the Absurd."* circ. 300. 1/yr. Pub'd 1 issue 1998; expects 1 issue 1999, 1 issue 2000. sub. price: £6.30; per copy: £6.30; sample: £6.30 ($13). Back issues: #1 £2; #1 + #2 £5; #3 £6; #1 +#2 + #3 £10; #1 + #2 + #3 + #4 (£16), please mention this directory when ordering. Discounts: libraries 10%, trade 35%. 128pp; 5½×8½; of. Reporting time: 1 month. Simultaneous submissions accepted: no. Publishes 25-30% of manuscripts submitted. Payment: copy of magazine; 50% discount on further copies. Copyrighted, reverts to author. Ads: none. Small Press Group of Britain (SPG), BM Bozo, London WC1N 3XX, UK; Women in Publishing (WIP).

MASSEY COLLECTORS NEWS—WILD HARVEST, Keith Oltrogge, Box 529, Denver, IA 50622, 319-984-5292. 1981. Articles. "Newsletter for collectors of Wallis, Ferguson, Massey Harris and Massey Ferguson tractors and farm equipment." circ. 2M. 6/yr. Pub'd 6 issues 1998; expects 6 issues 1999, 6 issues 2000. sub. price: $24; per copy: $4; sample: same. Back issues: $3. 32pp; 8½×11; of. Reporting time: 30 days. Publishes 90% of manuscripts submitted. Payment: subscription extensions. Not copyrighted. Ads: $75/$40/$20 1/4 page/classifieds are free.

●**Massey-Reyner Publishing,** Sandy Tayler, PO Box 323, Wallace, CA 95254, phone/fax 209-763-2590; e-mail learning@goldrush.com. 1996. Non-fiction. avg. press run 5M. Pub'd 1 title 1998; expects 1 title 1999, 1 title 2000. 1 title listed in the *Small Press Record of Books in Print* (28th Edition, 1999-00). avg. price, paper: $12.95. Discounts: 2-5 books 25%; 6-15 30%; 16-300 40%; 301-499 45%; 500 + up 50%. 150pp; 6×9. Reporting time: 2 months. Simultaneous submissions accepted: no. Payment: bi-annual payment. Copyrights for author. PMA, Sacramento Publishers Assn.

Master Key Inc., PO Box 17474, Boulder, CO 80308, 303-776-6103; Fax 303-682-2384; www.selfhealing.com. 1997. avg. press run 2.7M. Pub'd 1 title 1998; expects 3 titles 1999, 5 titles 2000. 9 titles listed in the *Small Press Record of Books in Print* (28th Edition, 1999-00). avg. price, paper: $14.95. 175pp; 1p. Simultaneous submissions accepted: yes. Payment: yes. Copyrights for author.

MASTER THOUGHTS, Friend Stuart, Editor, PO Box 4608, Salem, OR 97302-8608, 503-362-9634. 1972. Articles. "Advanced Christian metaphysics. Not recommended for beginners. Weekly, but published quarterly for 13 weeks ahead. Mailed 4 times per year. No mss. accepted." circ. 100. 52/yr. Pub'd 52 issues 1998; expects 52 issues 1999, 52 issues 2000. sub. price: $15. Back issues: 1972-76 complete, bound $19.95; 1977-80 complete, bound $19.95; 1981-86 complete, bound $19.95; 1987-92 complete, bound $19.95; 1993 and on, $19.95 (includes current year's subscription); full set $69.95. Discounts: 30% dealers and agencies only; 40% on bound volumes. 2pp; 5½×8½; of. No ads.

THE MATCH, Fred Woodworth, PO Box 3488, Tucson, AZ 85722. 1969. Fiction, articles, cartoons, interviews, criticism, reviews, letters, parts-of-novels, news items. "Recent articles include an expose of American atheists; part of novel, 'The Two Sisters'; serialization of 'Landmarks in the Desert.' Not seeking contributions." circ. 2M. 4/yr. Pub'd 1 issue 1998; expects 3 issues 1999, 4 issues 2000. sub. price: $12/4 issues; per copy: $2.50; sample: $2. Discounts: 50%, payable on receipt of copies. 60pp; 6½×9½; †of, lp. Pub's reviews: 17 in 1998. §Anarchism, government. No ads.

MATCHBOOK, Debrie Stevens, 242 North Broad Street, Doylestown, PA 18901, 215-489-7755; Fax 215-340-3965. 1995. Poetry, reviews, long-poems. "Eclectic. Suggest reviewing sample copy before submitting" circ. 300-500. 2/yr. Pub'd 2 issues 1998; expects 2 issues 1999, 2 issues 2000. sub. price: $10; copy: $6; sample: $6. Discounts: inquire. 64pp; 6×9; of. Reporting time: 2-4 weeks. Simultaneous submissions accepted if noted. Publishes 5% of manuscripts submitted. Payment: 2 copies. Copyrighted, reverts to author. Pub's reviews: 10-12 reviews in 1998. §Chapbooks, small press magazines featuring poetry. Ads: $50/$25.

MATHEMATICAL SPECTRUM, Applied Probability Trust, D.W. Sharpe, School of Mathmatics and Statistics, The University, Sheffield S3 7RH, England. 1968. Articles, reviews, letters. circ. 2M. 3/yr. Pub'd 3 issues 1998; expects 3 issues 1999, 3 issues 2000. sub. price: £8.50 ($14 U.S.). Back issues: on request. 24pp; 29.4×21cm; of. Simultaneous submissions accepted: no. Payment: none. Copyrighted, does not revert to author. Pub's reviews: 12 in 1998. §Books on mathematics suitable for senior students in schools and beginning undergraduates in colleges and universities. Ads: on request.

MATI, Ommation Press, Effie Mihopoulos, 5548 N. Sawyer, Chicago, IL 60625. 1975. Poetry, articles, art, photos, interviews, reviews, letters, long-poems. "Very open to experimental poetry and especially poems by women. The magazine was established to provide another source where new poets can see their work in print. The work doesn't have to be perfect, but show potential. *Mati* wants to encourage young poets to see as much of their work in print as possible. Open to exchange (magazines and ads) with other magazines. *Mati* will also be doing a series of poem postcards as special issues (both letterpress and offset, $2.00 a set) for which short poems (3-4 lines) are welcome to be submitted for consideration. The magazine will be changing this year from quarterly to once-annually. Recent contributors: Lyn Lifshin, Rochelle Ratner." circ. 500. Irregular. Expects 1 issue 1999. sub. price: $2; per copy: $1.50 + $1.05 bookrate postage; sample: $1.50 + $1.05 bookrate postage. Back issues: No. 1, $15; No. 2, $20; No. 3, $15; No. 6, $2. Discounts: 20% on 5 copies or more. 40pp; 8½×11; of. Reporting time: 2 weeks-1 month. Payment: 1 copy. Copyrighted, reverts to author. Ads: $80/$40/$15.

MATRIARCH'S WAY: The Journal of Female Supremacy, Shirley Oliveira, 3395 Nostrand Avenue #2-J, Brooklyn, NY 11229-4053, 718-648-8215. 1995. Fiction, articles, art, photos, cartoons, interviews, satire,

340

criticism, reviews, letters. "New journal soliciting mss. No minimum length" 4/yr. Pub'd 1 issue 1998; expects 1 issue 1999. sub. price: $30 US; $36 foreign/UK; per copy: $8.50; sample: $8.50. Back issues: $6. 150-200pp; 5½x8½; of. Reporting time: 7 days. Simultaneous submissions accepted: yes. Publishes (if appropriate) 80% of manuscripts submitted. Payment: free copies. Copyrighted. Pub's reviews: 20 in 1998. §Feminist-spiritual, sociopolitical, general, erotica. PMA, WNBA.

MATRIX, Steven M. Kappes, Editor & Director, c/o Channing-Murray Foundation, 1209 W Oregon, Urbana, IL 61801, 217-344-1176. 1975. Poetry. "We publish an anthology and high quality chapbooks by present members only. Not soliciting manuscripts at this time." circ. 200. 1/yr. Pub'd 1 issue 1998; expects 1 issue 1999, 1 issue 2000. sub. price: $5; per copy: $5; sample: $5. Back issues: $3.50-$8. Discounts: 40%. 60pp; 5½x8½; of. Payment: none. Copyrighted.

THE MATURE TRAVELER, Adele Malott, PO Box 50400, Reno, NV 89513-0400, 702-786-7419. 1984. Articles, photos, news items, non-fiction. "Uses senior-specific travel articles, senior discounts/trips for seniors 1M-1.2M words, B&W prints. Examples: seniors-only trips like snowmobiling, rafting, retirement areas and why." circ. 2.5M. 12/yr. Pub'd 12 issues 1998; expects 12 issues 1999, 12 issues 2000. sub. price: $29.95; per copy: $5; sample: $1 + SASE, 2 first class stamps (for potential contributors only). Back issues: $5. 12pp; 8½x11; of. Reporting time: 4-6 weeks. Simultaneous submissions are accepted when stated by author. Publishes 5% of manuscripts submitted. Payment: $100-$125. Copyrighted, reverts to author. Pub's reviews: 3 in 1998. §Senior-interest travel topics. Ads: $250/$175/$40 business card.

Maupin House, PO Box 90148, Gainesville, FL 32607, 1-800-524-0634. 1988. avg. press run 3M. Pub'd 4 titles 1998; expects 4 titles 1999, 5 titles 2000. 11 titles listed in the *Small Press Record of Books in Print* (28th Edition, 1999-00). avg. price, paper: $14.95. Discounts: industry standard. Pages vary. Reporting time: 2 months. Simultaneous submissions accepted: yes. Publishes 5-10% of manuscripts submitted. Payment: negotiable. Copyrights for author. ABA, PAS, PMA.

THE MAVERICK PRESS, Carol Cullar, Route 2, Box 4915, Eagle Pass, TX 78852-9605, 210-773-1836 phone/fax 8 am to 4 pm. 1991. Poetry, fiction, art. "In the interest of writers in general, TMP is changing its policy on multiple submissions; we will be happy to consider such, if notice is given at time of submission and if a timely notice arrives upon withdrawal. TMP will not accept previously published material, stories about children or teenagers, fiction over five pages, gothic, political or religious diatribes, shaped poetry. We are looking for uncluttered, figurative literature. Nov 1996 theme: taboos. In additon to the journal TMP also sponsors Southwest Poets' series Annual Chapbook Search for residents of AZ, CO, CA(s), OK, NV, UT, TX, NM acknowledgements, bio. Deadline Oct 31. for Feb 97' pub. SASE for guidelines" circ. 250. 2/yr. Pub'd 3 issues 1998; expects 5 issues 1999, 5 issues 2000. 6 titles listed in the *Small Press Record of Books in Print* (28th Edition, 1999-00). sub. price: $15; per copy: $8.50; sample: $8.50. Back issues: $7.50. 120pp; 6x9; of. Reporting time: 1½ months. Simultaneous submissions accepted: yes. Publishes 10-15% of manuscripts submitted. Payment: 1 copy. Copyrighted, reverts to author.

Maxima New Media, Simcha Shtull, Aron Trauring, 2472 Broadway #195, New York, NY 10025, 212-439-4177, Fax 212-439-4178, e-mail aronst@ibm.net. 1995. Poetry, art, photos, cartoons, music, letters, non-fiction. "Multimedia audio" avg. press run 10M. Pub'd 2 titles 1998; expects 8 titles 1999. 2 titles listed in the *Small Press Record of Books in Print* (28th Edition, 1999-00). avg. price, other: $24.95. Discounts: up to 50%. Simultaneous submissions accepted: yes. Copyrights for author. PMA.

MAYFLY, Brooks Books, Randy Brooks, Shirley Brooks, 4634 Hale Drive, Decatur, IL 62526-1117. 1985. Poetry. "*Mayfly* is a haiku magazine from High/Coo Press. In our opinion, haiku is best savored in small servings. Too often they are crowded together on a page, and the reader is overwhelmed by hundreds of haiku in a single issue. The result is that the reader is forced to become a critic and editor wading through the heaps of haiku in search of a few gems. We feel it is the duty of the editors and writers to make careful selection of only the very best, the most evocative, the truly effective haiku. We now use laser printing production and offer Macintosh haiku software." circ. 350. 2/yr. Pub'd 3 issues 1998; expects 2 issues 1999, 2 issues 2000. sub. price: $8/2 copies; per copy: $4; sample: $3.50. Back issues: none. Discounts: none. 16pp; 3½x5; of. Reporting time: 3 months. Payment: $5 per haiku published. Copyrighted, reverts to author.

Mayhaven Publishing, Doris R. Wenzel, PO Box 557, Mahomet, IL 61853-0557, 217-586-4493; fax 217-586-6330. 1990. Fiction, art, photos, cartoons, interviews, letters, non-fiction. "Additional address: PO Box 557, Mahomet, IL 61853. Our books (we presently have 50, are directed toward the general audience. New titles will include books on science fiction, mystery, humor, animals, biography, art, history, and cooking." avg. press run 2M-5M. Pub'd 7 titles 1998; expects 9 titles 1999, 9 titles 2000. 36 titles listed in the *Small Press Record of Books in Print* (28th Edition, 1999-00). avg. price, cloth: $24.95; paper: $14.95; other: Booklets—$5. Discounts: Provided. 100-300pp; 5½x8¼, 8½x11, 6x9; of. Reporting time: as soon as possible - many new submissions. Simultaneous submissions accepted: yes. Publishes 1% of manuscripts submitted. Payment: very small advance, royalties or co-op option with royalties. Copyrights for author.

Mayhill Press, Hilmur L. Saffell, PO Box 681804, Franklin, TN 37068-1804, 615-794-8542. 1982. Non-fiction. "Do not submit manuscript until told to do so. No longer taking submissions" avg. press run 1M. Pub'd 4 titles 1998; expects 4 titles 1999, 5 titles 2000. 1 title listed in the *Small Press Record of Books in Print* (28th Edition, 1999-00). avg. price, paper: $30; other: $18 map folios. 8½×11; of. Simultaneous submissions accepted: no.

●**MCB University Press (see also LIBRARY HI TECH; LIBRARY HIGH TECH NEWS; REFERENCE SERVICES REVIEW)**, 60/63 Toller Lane, Bradford, W. Yorkshire BD8 9BY, England.

McBooks Press, Alexander G. Skutt, Owner, Publisher; S.K. List, Editorial Director; Patricia Zafiriadis, Marketing Director, 120 West State Street, Ithaca, NY 14850, 607-272-2114; FAX 607-273-6068, e-mail alex908@aol.com http://www.mcbooks.com. 1979. Non-fiction. "We can accept *no* unsolicited manuscripts. Letters of inquiry are welcome. We publish a very few books and we make the decision to publish on the basis of both commercial potential and literary merit. Although we would consider other purposeful, well-written non-fiction, we are mostly interested in seeing inquiries about books on vegetarianism and regional books on upstate New York. A new interest is sports reference and sport history books. We are also now publishing parenting and nautical fiction books" avg. press run 4M. Pub'd 7 titles 1998; expects 12 titles 1999, 16 titles 2000. 23 titles listed in the *Small Press Record of Books in Print* (28th Edition, 1999-00). avg. price, cloth: $23.95; paper: $13.95; other: $23.95. Discounts: standard terms are available to bookstores, wholesalers, etc. 200pp; usually 5½×8½ or 8½×11; of. Reporting time: 2 months on query letters. Simultaneous submissions accepted: yes. Publishes 5% of manuscripts submitted. Payment: usual royalty basis with an advance. Copyrights for author. PMA.

McDonald & Woodward Publishing Company, Jerry N. McDonald, PO Box GG, Saltville, VA 24370-1161. 1986. Non-fiction. "Interested in book-length material (75 or more printed pages) for adults primarily. Main interests are natural & cultural history topics. Interested in socially-responsible controversial subjects, environmental issues, history of science, and travel-related subjects. Publish 'Guides to the American Landscape', a series of specialty guides to the natural and cultural history of the Americas." avg. press run 3M. Pub'd 5 titles 1998; expects 12 titles 1999, 12 titles 2000. 32 titles listed in the *Small Press Record of Books in Print* (28th Edition, 1999-00). avg. price, cloth: $40; paper: $16. Discounts: 20-43%. 200pp; 6×9; of. Reporting time: 1 week initial response. Simultaneous submissions accepted: no. Publishes 1% of inquiries; invited submissions 75% of manuscripts submitted. Payment: 10% on net receipts, payment semiannually. Copyrights for author.

McGregor Publishing, Lonnie Herman, David Rosenbaum, 4532 W. Kennedy Blvd., Tampa, FL 33609-2042, 813-681-0092; FAX 813-254-2665; Toll-free 888-405-2665. 1994. Poetry, non-fiction. "Interested in biographical non-fiction, business, sports, how-to books." avg. press run 5M. Pub'd 2 titles 1998; expects 5 titles 1999, 10 titles 2000. 1 title listed in the *Small Press Record of Books in Print* (28th Edition, 1999-00). avg. price, cloth: $24.95; paper: $17.95. Discounts: 2 books 20%, 3-9 25%, 10+ 50%. 240pp; 6×9. Reporting time: 4-6 weeks. Simultaneous submissions accepted: yes. Publishes 5%-15% of manuscripts submitted. Payment: to be arranged. Copyrights for author. Publishers Association of the South.

●**MCM Entertainment, Inc. Publishing Division**, PO Box 3051, Newport Beach, CA 92659-0597, 800-901-7979; newportmcm@aol.com. 1 title listed in the *Small Press Record of Books in Print* (28th Edition, 1999-00).

McNally & Loftin, Publishers, W.J. McNally, 5390 Overpass Road, Santa Barbara, CA 93111, 805-964-5117; fax 805-967-2818. 1956. "Specialize in Santa Barbara Channel Islands; Southern California and environmental history. Other address: 5390 Overpass Road, Santa Barbara, CA 93111." avg. press run 2.5M. Pub'd 4 titles 1998; expects 4 titles 1999, 4 titles 2000. 11 titles listed in the *Small Press Record of Books in Print* (28th Edition, 1999-00). avg. price, cloth: $18.50; paper: $12. Discounts: trade 40%. 172pp; 6×9, 5½×8½, 7×10; †of. Reporting time: 4 weeks. Payment: 10% cover price. Does not copyright for author. Bookbuilders West.

McPherson & Company Publishers, Bruce R. McPherson, PO Box 1126, Kingston, NY 12402, 914-331-5807, toll free order #800-613-8219. 1973. Fiction, art, photos, criticism, non-fiction. "Other imprints: Documentext, Treacle Press. Distributor of Saroff Editions. No unsolicited mss. Query." avg. press run 2M. Pub'd 3 titles 1998; expects 5 titles 1999, 6 titles 2000. 70 titles listed in the *Small Press Record of Books in Print* (28th Edition, 1999-00). avg. price, cloth: $20; paper: $10. Discounts: 1 copy 20%, 2-4 30%, 5-24 40%, 25-99 42%, 100+ 43%; prepaid STOP, 30%. 200pp; size varies; of. Reporting time: 2 weeks-2 months. Payment: royalties and copies. Copyrights for author.

MCS Publishing, Mia Sillanpoa, President, 5212 Chicago SW #2, Tacoma, WA 98499, 253-984-1345. 1994. Poetry, articles, letters, long-poems, news items. avg. press run 1-2.5M. Expects 2 titles 1999, 4 titles 2000. 2 titles listed in the *Small Press Record of Books in Print* (28th Edition, 1999-00). avg. price, paper: $9.95+. Discounts: 10% volume orders, 33⅓-40% gift stores, standard distributor 40-67%. 64pp; 5×7; of. Reporting time: 2 weeks to 1 month. Simultaneous submissions accepted: yes. Payment: 8% wholesale. Copyrights for author. National Federation of Press Women, Washington Press Assn., ABA, PNBA.

MCT - MULTICULTURAL TEACHING, Trentham Books, Gillian Klein, Editor, Westview House, 734 London Road, Oakhill, Stoke-on-Trent, Staffordshire ST4 5NP, England, 01782-745567; Fax 01782-745553. 1982. "For professionals in schools and community. It is concerned with all aspects of teaching and learning in a multicultural society. It is equally concerned with the wide range of social work serving young people, their families, and communities. It is, therefore, an inter-professional journal that focuses on practices of teachers and social and community workers in their day to day work with young people of all ethnic groups. Each issue consists of case studies of professional practice, discussion of its aims and purposes and examples of its achievements. There are also reviews of important new books and resources and information about courses, conferences, and events of professional interest to readers." 3/yr. Pub'd 3 issues 1998; expects 3 issues 1999, 3 issues 2000. sub. price: £27; per copy: £10; sample: £10. Back issues: £10. Discounts: 10% series disc. w/ ads. 64pp; 30×21cm; of. Reporting time: max 1 month, usually 2 weeks. Copyrighted. Pub's reviews: 47 in 1998. §Multi ethnic education, anti racist education. Ads: £200/£100/£.50.

ME MAGAZINE, Pittore Euforico, Carlo Pittore, PO Box 182, Bowdoinham, ME 04008, 207-666-8453. 1980. Poetry, art, criticism, reviews, collages, concrete art. "Important article on Maine's mighty artist, Bern Porter. Also, artwork-profusely illustrated. *An Artburst From Maine* by Carlo Pittore. ISSN 0272-5657." circ. 2M. Published at editor's discretion. Expects 5 issues 1999. sub. price: $20; per copy: $5; sample: $5. Back issues: $5, $7.50 for ME IV (Audio Cassette). Discounts: 40%. 8pp; 8½×11; of. Reporting time: 2 months. Payment: copies. Not copyrighted. §Art movements, art, mail art. Ads: $140/$75. MPWA.

Meadow Mountain Press, David Wiesenberg, 1375 Coney Island Ave., Ste. 136, Brooklyn, NY 11230, 718-338-1559. 1995. Non-fiction. "Length: 150-350 pages (5½ x 8½)". Biases: practical, layman-friendly, consumer guides." avg. press run varies, 5M-100M. Expects 3 titles 1999, 3 titles 2000. 1 title listed in the *Small Press Record of Books in Print* (28th Edition, 1999-00). avg. price, paper: $14.95. Discounts: for information contact BookWorld Services, Inc. at 800-444-2524. 272pp; 5½×8½. Reporting time: approx. 1 month. Publishes 5% of manuscripts submitted. Payment: standard terms. Copyrights for author. PMA, Small Press Center.

Meager Ink Press (see also COZY DETECTIVE MYSTERY MAGAZINE), David Workman, 686 Jakes Court, McMinnville, OR 97128, 503-435-1212; detectivemag@onlinemac.com. Poetry, fiction, non-fiction. "65,000 words or less in novella form (romance, mystery, thrillers, westerns, sci-fi, fantasy)." avg. press run 1M. Expects 6-8 titles 1999. avg. price, paper: $5.95. 155pp; 5½×8½; †of. Reporting time: 4-8 months. Simultaneous submissions accepted: no. Payment: yes. Copyrights for author.

MEANDER QUARTERLY, rotates annually Brendan Conley, 156 Rivington Street #1, New York, NY 10002-2481. 1988. Articles, cartoons, letters, news items. "Very limited for space. Really a newsletter. Subtitle reads "Newsletter of Evolutionary Anarchists". Discussion bulletin for of anarchist movement" circ. 100. 4/yr. Pub'd 4 issues 1998; expects 4 issues 1999, 4 issues 2000. sub. price: funded by donations; sample: $1. Back issues: not sold. Discounts: none. 24pp; 5½×8½; photocopy. Reporting time: don't report. Simultaneous submissions accepted: yes. Payment: none. Not copyrighted. Ads: no longer take ads (may change).

MEANJIN, Meanjin, Christina Thompson, Laurie Duggan, Poetry, 99 Barry Street, Carlton, Victoria 3053, Australia, 613-344-6950. 1940. Poetry, fiction, articles, art, photos, cartoons, interviews, criticism, reviews, non-fiction. "Prose range is 1500-8M words; poetry accepted. Emphasis on Australian and Pacific themes" circ. 2.5M. 4/yr. Pub'd 4 issues 1998; expects 4 issues 1999, 4 issues 2000. sub. price: $A40 surface; $A50 air mail; per copy: $A9.95 + postage; sample: $A9.95 + postage. Back issues: $A6-$A8.50. Discounts: Agent 10%; distributor 40%. 200pp; 5½×8¼; of. Reporting time: 12 weeks. Simultaneous submissions accepted: yes. Payment: $A100/1000 words prose avg.; $A100/poem minimum. Copyrighted, reverts to author. Pub's reviews: 20 in 1998. §Fiction, cultural studies, poetry, Pacific issues, history. Ads: $A500/$A250/$A125 quarter page.

Meanjin (see also MEANJIN), Jerry Lee, Philip Mead, Poetry, 99 Barry Street, Carlton, Victoria 3053, Australia, 613-344-6950. Poetry, fiction. "We're not exactly a self-publisher, but we don't have the resources to deal with unsolicited book-length manuscripts. Our one solo title so far is *Tandava*, published in 1993. Another is forthcoming" avg. press run 1M. Pub'd 1 title 1998; expects 1 title 1999. avg. price, paper: $12.95. Discounts: 33⅓% across the board for bulk distributors; 10% agents. 100pp; 5½×8¼; of. Payment: 5%. Copyrights for author.

●Media Arts Publishing (see also MAD SCIENTIST; TIME TRAVELER), Frank Dibari, PO Box 4765, Clearwater, FL 33758, e-mail frankie1@mindspring.com. 1990. Fiction, articles, art, photos, cartoons, satire, collages, non-fiction. "Media Arts Publishing creates and distributes SF-genre based periodicals such as *Mad Scientist-Journal of Science Gone Awry* and beginning in 1999, *Time Traveler* a practical guidebook of temporal existence. Our emphasis is on graphical presentation with stories and features. An occasional series of comic book pages is common. In past years, titles released by Media Arts include: *The AND, HYPER Agents, Time Slips,* and *Optic.*" avg. press run 500-3M. Pub'd 2 titles 1998; expects 6 titles 1999, 8 titles 2000.

50-100pp; of. Reporting time: 1 month. Simultaneous submissions accepted: no. Publishes 50% of manuscripts submitted. Payment: varies. Copyrights for author.

The Media Institute, Richard T. Kaplar, Vice President, 1000 Potomac Street NW, Ste. 301, Washington, DC 20007, 202-298-7512. 1975. Non-fiction. avg. press run 1M+. Pub'd 3 titles 1998; expects 3 titles 1999, 3 titles 2000. 12 titles listed in the *Small Press Record of Books in Print* (28th Edition, 1999-00). avg. price, paper: $12.95. Discounts: bulk rates begin at 10 copies or more. 100pp; 6×9; of. Payment: contract only. Does not copyright for author.

Media Periodicals (see also Westport Publishers), Paul Temme, Publisher, 1102 Grand, 23rd Floor, Kansas City, MO 64106, 816-842-8111; FAX 816-842-8188. "A division of Westport Publishers, Inc."

MEDIA SPOTLIGHT, Albert James Dager, Editor & Publisher, Po Box 290, Redmond, WA 98073. 1977. Articles, art, photos, cartoons, interviews, criticism, reviews, music, letters, news items, non-fiction. "Any unsolicited submissions might not be returned!" circ. 3M. 4/yr. Expects 4 issues 1999, 4 issues 2000. sub. price: any tax-deductible donation, preferably at least $25; per copy: any tax-deductible donation; sample: any tax-deductible donation. Back issues: for those available (some only by photocopy), any tax-deductible donation. 20pp; 8½×11; of. Reporting time: 4 weeks to 4 months. Simultaneous submissions accepted: no. Payment: copies. Copyrighted, reverts to author. Pub's reviews: 5 in 1998. §Media, Culture, Christian Lifestyle, Biblical analysis of media.

MEDICAL HISTORY, Wellcome Institute for the History of Medicine, W.F. Bynum, Professor; V. Nutton, Professor, 183 Euston Road, London NW1 2BE, England, 0171-611-8888/8563; fax 0171-611-8562. 1957. Articles, reviews, news items. circ. 900. 4/yr. Pub'd 4 issues 1998; expects 4 issues 1999. sub. price: individuals worldwide £28/$32 USA, institutions (worldwide) £69, $107 USA; per copy: £12. Back issues: £9 if available. 120pp; 5×8; of. Reporting time: 3 months. Simultaneous submissions accepted: no. Publishes 35% of manuscripts submitted. Payment: none. Copyright The Trustee, The Wellcome Trust. Pub's reviews: 114 in 1998. §All aspects of history of medicine and allied sciences. Ads: £540/£370/£240.

Medical Physics Publishing Corp., 4513 Vernon Boulevard, Madison, WI 53705-4964, 608-262-4021. 1985. Non-fiction. "We publish non-technical science and medical books for the general public, including two series called Focus on Health and Focus on Science. We also publish technical books for medical physicists and the medical community." avg. press run 2M. Pub'd 9 titles 1998; expects 12 titles 1999, 18 titles 2000. 29 titles listed in the *Small Press Record of Books in Print* (28th Edition, 1999-00). avg. price, cloth: $32; paper: $15. Discounts: 20% on all titles to bookstores. 200pp; 8½×11, 6×9, 7×10; of/lo. Reporting time: 2 weeks to 1 month. Payment: 10-20%. Copyrights for author. WAPA, UMBA, APA, ABA.

MEDICAL REFORM, Medical Reform Group, Janet Maher, 517 College Street, Suite 303, Toronto, Ontario M6G 4A2, Canada, 416-323-9903; Fax 416-323-0311; mrg@web.net. 1979. Articles, cartoons, reviews, news items. "The Medical Reform Group is an organization dedicated to the reform of the health care system, according to the following principles: 1. Health care is a right. The universal access of every person to high quality, appropriate health care must be guaranteed. The health care system must be administered in a manner which precludes any monetary or other deterrent to equal care. 2. Health is political and social in nature. Health care workers, including physicians, should seek out and recognize the social, economic, occupational, and environmental causes of disease. 3. The institutions of the health care system must be democratized. *Medical Reform* carries articles advancing these views" circ. 500. 4/yr. Pub'd 4 issues 1998; expects 4 issues 1999, 4 issues 2000. sub. price: $25; per copy: $4.25; sample: $1. Back issues: $60 for complete set of all back issues. Discounts: can be arranged. 24pp; 8½×11; of. Reporting time: 2 months. Payment: none. Copyrighted. Pub's reviews: 4 in 1998. §Health & medicine, especially social, environmental, economic, political aspects. Ads: $200/$120/25¢ per word.

Medical Reform Group (see also MEDICAL REFORM), Janet Maher, 517 College Street, Suite 303, Toronto, Ontario M6G 4A2, Canada, 416-323-9903; Fax 416-323-0311; mrg@web.net. 1979. Articles. "The MRG publishes booklets and research materials dealing with the social, political, and economic aspects of health, and with possible changes to the health care system" Pub'd 3 titles 1998; expects 3 titles 1999. avg. price, other: $10. 96pp; 8½×11; of.

MEDIPHORS, Eugene D. Radice, M.D., PO Box 327, Bloomsburg, PA 17815, e-mail mediphor@ptd.net; website www.mediphors.org. 1992. Poetry, fiction, art, photos, cartoons, satire, criticism, non-fiction. "*Mediphors* is a literary magazine publishing broad work in medicine and health. Types of work include short story, poetry and humor. Nonfiction works include essay, commentary and opinion. Artwork in the form of photography, cartoons and drawing is also published. *Mediphors* is not a technical journal of science. We do not publish research or review articles, except of a historical nature. Manuscripts should be typed and double spaced. Please enclose two copies that we can keep and a SSAE, particularly if return is desired for photographs or artwork. Of course, authors should always keep a copy of any materials sent through the mail. We are not responsible for the well-being of your work. If accepted, the author will be required to sign an authenticity of

344

authorship statement and copyright agreement. There are no reading or other fees." circ. 1M. 2/yr. Pub'd 2 issues 1998; expects 2 issues 1999, 2 issues 2000. sub. price: $15; per copy: $6.95; sample: $6. Back issues: $6. Discounts: negotiable. 72pp; 8×11; of. Reporting time: average 3 months. Simultaneous submissions accepted: no. Publishes 10% of manuscripts submitted. Payment: 2 copies. Copyrighted, reverts to author.

MEDITERRANEAN QUARTERLY: A Journal of Global Issues, Duke University Press, Nikolaos A. Stavrou, Box 90660, Duke University, Durham, NC 27708-0660. "Published under the editorial direction of Mediterranean Affairs, Inc. The Mediterranean Basin reaches across southern Europe from Spain to the former Soviet Union and includes both the Middle East and North Africa. As the only journal that specifically addresses the problems of this region, the *Mediterranean Quarterly* is in a unique position to account for many of the changes that are redefining the world order. In the *Mediterranean Quarterly*, important voices from around the world speak with clarity and depth about the effects of history, culture, politics, and economics on the Mediterranean and the world. The journal's distinguished contributors include leading academics, journalists, and political figures. Send review copies to the editorial office, Mediterranean Affairs, Inc., Suite 984 National Press Building, 14th and F Streets NW, Washington, DC 20045." circ. 850. 4/yr. Pub'd 4 issues 1998; expects 4 issues 1999, 4 issues 2000. sub. price: $44 institutions, $24 individuals, $12 students with photocopy of current I.D., additional $12 foreign. Pub's reviews. Ads: $500/$300, nonprofit $250/$150.

MedStudy Corporation, Robert A. Hannaman, PO Box 6008, Woodland Park, CO 80866, 800-844-0547, fax 719-687-2900, hannaman@medstudy.com. 1990. Photos, non-fiction. "Medical publishing" avg. press run 3M. Pub'd 1 title 1998; expects 1 title 1999, 1-2 titles 2000. 1 title listed in the *Small Press Record of Books in Print* (28th Edition, 1999-00). avg. price, other: $395. 520pp; 9×11½.

MEDUSA'S HAIRDO, Beverly Moore, Jason Chapman, PO Box 358, Catlettsburg, KY 41129, 606-928-4631; medusashairdo@yahoo.com. 1995. Poetry, fiction, art. "'The magazine of modern mythology.' 4000 word limit." circ. 50. 2/yr. Pub'd 2 issues 1998; expects 2 issues 1999, 2 issues 2000. sub. price: $8.70; per copy: $4.50; sample: $4.50. Back issues: none. Discounts: 2-5 copies $4.35 each, 6-9 $4.15 each, 10+ $4 each. 16-24pp; 8½×11; †mi. Reporting time: 2-4 weeks. Accepts simultaneous submissions if so noted. Publishes 2% of manuscripts submitted. Payment: 1 copy. Copyrighted, reverts to author. Ads: by arrangement.

Mehring Books, Inc., PO Box 48377, Oak Park, MI 48237-5977, 248-967-2924; 248-967-3023; e-mail sales@mehring.com. News items, non-fiction. "Mehring Books, Inc. publishes 2-5 books and 5-10 pamphlets a year" Pub'd 5 titles 1998; expects 3 titles 1999, 3 titles 2000. 11 titles listed in the *Small Press Record of Books in Print* (28th Edition, 1999-00). avg. price, paper: $25. Discounts: trade 40%, library 20%, minimum order for discounts 5 titles/copies. 5¼×8¼; of. ABA, PMA.

Mellen Poetry Press (see also The Edwin Mellen Press), Herbert Richardson, Director, PO Box 450, 415 Ridge Street, Lewiston, NY 14092-0450, 716-754-2266; Fax 716-754-4056; E-mail mellen@ag.net. 1974. Poetry, long-poems. avg. press run 200. Pub'd 34 titles 1998; expects 40 titles 1999, 45 titles 2000. avg. price, paper: $14.95. Discounts: bookstore 40% pre-publication on 10+ copies, 20% post-publication. 64-72pp; 6×9; †of. Reporting time: 2-4 months. We prefer not to accept simultaneous submissions. Publishes 50-70% of manuscripts submitted. Payment: 5 free copies to the author, no royalties. We deposit 2 copies of published book with copyright office; book is listed in C.P. with Library of Congress. Small Press Center, Poets House.

MEMO, Marco MccLean, Editor; W.J. Kovanda, Poetry Editor, PO Box 1497, Mendocino, CA 95460. "I print everything I get until the layout sheets are full, then I thrown away what's left." circ. 4.5M. 20/yr. Pub'd 19 issues 1998; expects 20 issues 1999, 20 issues 2000. sub. price: $25. 16pp; 11×17; wax. Simultaneous submissions accepted: yes. Publishes 100% of manuscripts submitted. Payment: none. The author keeps all rights. Pub's reviews: 5-10 in 1998. Ads: $260/$140/$75 1/4 page/$40 1/8 page.

The Menard Press, Anthony Rudolf, 8 The Oaks, Woodside Avenue, London N12 8AR, England. 1969. Poetry. "No new manuscripts can be considered for time being. Nuclear politics poetry, poetics, translated poetry. The press's poetry books are distributed in the USA by Small Press Distribution Inc., Berkely CA." avg. press run 1.5M. Expects 5 titles 2000. 22 titles listed in the *Small Press Record of Books in Print* (28th Edition, 1999-00). avg. price, paper: $12. Discounts: usual. Poetry 56pp, politics 24pp; demi octavo; of, lp. ALP.

Menasha Ridge Press, Bud Zehmer, Acquisitions Editor, 700 S. 28th Street, Suite 206, Birmingham, AL 35233, 800-247-9437; e-mail bzehmer@menasharidge.com. 1982. Non-fiction. avg. press run 5M. Pub'd 15 titles 1998; expects 18 titles 1999, 18 titles 2000. 2 titles listed in the *Small Press Record of Books in Print* (28th Edition, 1999-00). avg. price, paper: $14.95. Discounts: per catalogue. 200+pp; 6×9; of. Reporting time: 60 days. Simultaneous submissions accepted: yes. Publishes 2-5% of manuscripts submitted. Payment: 10-12% royalty based on net. Copyrights for author. PAS, AAP, SEBA.

MENTOR MAGAZINE, Alan Winter, Dick Gilkeson, 5707 NE 15TH Avenue, Portland, OR 97211-4974, 503-282-2108. Poetry, fiction, articles, art, photos, cartoons, interviews, satire, criticism, reviews, letters, news items, non-fiction. circ. 5M. 4/yr. Pub'd 4 issues 1998; expects 4 issues 1999, 4 issues 2000. sub. price: $15; per copy: $4.95; sample: $4.95. Back issues: $5. 32pp; 8½×11. Reporting time: 3-6 months. Publishes 75% of manuscripts submitted. Payment: up to $24 or copies. Not copyrighted. Pub's reviews: 10 in 1998. §Books on men. Ads: $190/$115.

Mercury House, Tom Christensen, 785 Market Street, Suite 1500, San Francisco, CA 94103-2003, 415-974-0729; Fax 415-974-0832 (Editorial). 1984. Fiction, non-fiction. "Mercury House is a nonprofit general trade publishing house of quality works from all over the world." avg. press run 5M. Pub'd 12 titles 1998; expects 12 titles 1999, 10 titles 2000. 131 titles listed in the *Small Press Record of Books in Print* (28th Edition, 1999-00). avg. price, cloth: $19.95; paper: $12.95. Discounts: 1-4 20%, 25-99 43%, 100-249 44%. 256pp; 5½×8½, 6×9, varies; of. Reporting time: 2-3 months. Simultaneous submissions accepted: no. Publishes less than 1% of manuscripts submitted. Payment: industry standard. Copyrights for author. ABA (American Booksellers Association), Northern California Book Publicists Association.

Merging Worlds Publishers, Inc., Michelle A. Gordon, 1655 Peachtree St. NE, Suite 1200, Atlanta, GA 30309, 404-892-8202; Fax 404-892-9757. 1995. avg. press run varies. Pub'd 1 title 1998; expects 2 titles 1999, 5 titles 2000. 5 titles listed in the *Small Press Record of Books in Print* (28th Edition, 1999-00). avg. price, paper: $12.95. Discounts: 20-40%. 220pp; 5½×8½. Reporting time: 1½ months. Simultaneous submissions accepted: yes. Publishes 20% of manuscripts submitted. Payment: 6-10%. Copyrights for author.

Meridional Publications, Robert Reckenbeil, Publisher, 7101 Winding Way, Wake Forest, NC 27587, 919-556-2940. 1977. "In the early years Meridional Publications started by publishing educational multi-media programs which are still in print today, but the company now has 8 books of regional interest, fiction and geneology." avg. press run 1M–6M. Pub'd 1 title 1998; expects 2 titles 1999, 2 titles 2000. 4 titles listed in the *Small Press Record of Books in Print* (28th Edition, 1999-00). avg. price, cloth: $26; paper: $16; other: multi-media $16 to $20. Discounts: 20%-40% to trade (bookstores), 50 to 55% to jobbers and distributors. Pages vary; size varies; of. Reporting time: less than 1 month. Publishes 10% of manuscripts submitted. Payment: 10% to 15% of gross price. Copyrights negotiable.

MERLYN'S PEN: Fiction, Essays, and Poems By America's Teens, R. Jim Stahl, Publisher, Editor, Merlyn's Pen, Inc., PO Box 910, East Greenwich, RI 02818-0964, 401-885-5175; www.merlynspen.com. 1985. Poetry, fiction, articles, art, photos, cartoons, reviews, letters, plays, non-fiction. "Authors must be students in grades 6-12, or age 11-18 if not in school." circ. 5M. 1/yr. Pub'd 1 issue 1998; expects 1 issue 1999, 1 issue 2000. sub. price: $29 + $9 for foreign orders; per copy: $29; sample: catalog=free. 100pp; 8½×10⅞; sheet fed. Reporting time: 10 weeks. Simultaneous submissions accepted: no. Publishes 1% of manuscripts submitted. Payment: 1 copy of mag and $20-$200. Copyrighted, does not revert to author. Pub's reviews: 5 in 1998. §Kids (grades 6-12) send unsolicited reviews of *current* books, magazines, movies or of material previously published in *Merlyn's Pen.* Ads: b/w $1,150/$585/$490 1/3 page. Edpress, P.M.A.

Merrimack Books, Wayne Edwards, PO Box 80702, Lincoln, NE 68501-0702, e-mail wedwards@info-com.com. 1989. avg. press run 1M+. Pub'd 2 titles 1998; expects 3 titles 1999, 2 titles 2000. 2 titles listed in the *Small Press Record of Books in Print* (28th Edition, 1999-00). avg. price, paper: $16.95. Discounts: 1-9 30%, 10-49 40%, 50 + 50%. 200-300pp; 5½×8½; of. Reporting time: 4 weeks. Simultaneous submissions accepted: no. Publishes .1% of manuscripts submitted. Payment: varies. Does not copyright for author. HWA.

Merwood Books, Heather Dunne, 237 Merwood Lane, Ardmore, PA 19003, 215-947-3934; fax 610-896-5853. 1997. Poetry, fiction, music. "Contemporary fiction and poetry with literary bent." avg. press run 1M. Pub'd 1 title 1998; expects 2 titles 1999, 2 titles 2000. 2 titles listed in the *Small Press Record of Books in Print* (28th Edition, 1999-00). avg. price, cloth: $22; paper: $12. Discounts: negotiable. 250-375pp; 5½×8½. Reporting time: 3-6 months. Simultaneous submissions accepted: yes. Publishes 10% of manuscripts submitted. Payment: negotiable. Does not copyright for author.

Mesa House Publishing, Karee Galloway, Managing Editor, 1701 River Run, Suite 800, Fort Worth, TX 76107, 817-339-8889; Fax 817-339-8818. 1995. Non-fiction. avg. press run 3M. Pub'd 1 title 1998; expects 3 titles 1999, 6 titles 2000. 6 titles listed in the *Small Press Record of Books in Print* (28th Edition, 1999-00). avg. price, cloth: $24; paper: $20. Discounts: Classroom 20%, STOP 40%, retail 1-4 30%, 5-24 40%, 25-49 43%, 50-99 45%, 100+ 50%. 200pp; 6×9, 7×10; of. Reporting time: 3 months. Simultaneous submissions accepted: yes. Publishes 5% of manuscripts submitted. Payment: royalties based on work and market. Publisher holds copyright. Book Publishers of Texas, Small Press Center, PMA.

MESECHABE: The Journal of Surre(gion)alism, Dennis Formento, 1539 Crete Street, New Orleans, LA 70119, 504-944-4823. 1988. Poetry, fiction, articles, art, photos, cartoons, interviews, satire, criticism, reviews, music, letters, long-poems, collages, non-fiction. "Poems usually limited to 300 lines, prose to 4,000 words. Exceptions made for the exceptional. Reviews 250-700 words. B&W art, collages, photos. Focus on the ecology of the imagination. Bioregionalism and surreality." circ. 500. 2/yr. Pub'd 1 issue 1998; expects 2 issues 1999, 2 issues 2000. sub. price: $25/5 issues, $35 institutions; per copy: $5; sample: $5. Back issues:

none. Discounts: 40%. 40pp; 8 1/2×11; web press. Reporting time: 2-6 weeks. Simultaneous submissions accepted: yes. Publishes 10% of manuscripts submitted. Payment: currently none, but 2 contributor's copies, more for major works. Copyrighted, reverts to author. Pub's reviews: 2 in 1998. §Poetry, ecology, anarchism, refusenik culture.

MESHUGGAH, Simeon Stylites, 200 East Tenth Street, #603, New York, NY 10003-7702. 1991. Fiction, articles, art, cartoons, interviews, satire, reviews, letters, collages, non-fiction. "Length: under 5000 words; often 500-2000. Recent contributors: Crad Kilodney, Al Ackerman" circ. 300. 2/yr. Pub'd 2 issues 1998; expects 2 issues 1999, 2 issues 2000. sub. price: $7; per copy: $2; sample: $2. Back issues: $2. Discounts: 10 copies or more @ $1. 56pp; 8½×11; of. Reporting time: 12 weeks. Simultaneous submissions accepted: yes. Publishes 3% of manuscripts submitted. Payment: 2 copies. Copyrighted, reverts to author. §Non-fiction, humor, alternatives, underground, society, fringe. Ads: $18/$9/5¢ per word, minimum 40.

The Message Company (see also BUSINESPIRIT JOURNAL), James Berry, 4 Camino Azul, Santa Fe, NM 87505, 505-474-0998; FAX 505-471-2584. 1994. Non-fiction. "We publish full length perfect bound books, and videos" avg. press run 3M. Pub'd 4 titles 1998; expects 8 titles 1999, 16 titles 2000. 7 titles listed in the *Small Press Record of Books in Print* (28th Edition, 1999-00). avg. price, paper: $14.95. Discounts: Stop 20% + free shipping, bookstores/resellers 50% + free shipping, distributors 55% + free shipping. 200pp; 8½×11, 6×9; of. Reporting time: 30-60 days. Simultaneous submissions accepted: yes. Publishes 50% of manuscripts submitted. Payment: 5-8%. Copyrights for author. PMA, SPAN.

MESSAGES FROM THE HEART, Lauren B. Smith, PO Box 64840, Tucson, AZ 85728, 520-577-0588; Fax 520-529-9657; e-mail lbsmith@theriver.com. 1993. Poetry, fiction, articles, art, photos, reviews, letters, news items, non-fiction. "A quarterly journal of writings, specifically letters, which nurture understanding between people. Writings from both famous and non-professional writers who share their thoughts and feelings about life's challenges and achievements, joys and sorrows. A celebration of the positive power of letter writing." circ. 600. 4/yr. Pub'd 4 issues 1998; expects 4 issues 1999, 4 issues 2000. sub. price: $15; per copy: $4; sample: $4. Back issues: $4. 21pp; 4¼×10½; of. Reporting time: 3 weeks. Simultaneous submissions accepted: yes. Publishes 5% of manuscripts submitted. Payment: 3 issues plus discounted additional copies. Copyrighted, reverts to author. Pub's reviews: 3 in 1998. §The art of letter writing, journaling, collections of letters, diaries. Ads: none. IWWG, TBBA.

Metacom Press, William Ferguson, Nancy Ferguson, 1 Tahanto Road, Worcester, MA 01602-2523, 617-757-1683. 1980. Poetry, fiction. "Booklets have ranged from 16 to 28 pages. Titles so far are by John Updike, William Heyen, Ann Beattie, James Tate, James Wright, Diane Wakoski, Raymond Carver, James Merrill, John McPhee, Edward Gorey. All titles to date have been published in a limited-edition format, using imported papers and hand-binding. Our intention is to establish ourselves financially with the limited editions and then to move to a more democratic, less exclusive type of publication. No unsolicited manuscripts." avg. press run 150-300. Pub'd 1 title 1998; expects 2 titles 1999, 3 titles 2000. 6 titles listed in the *Small Press Record of Books in Print* (28th Edition, 1999-00). avg. price, cloth: $75; paper: $25. Discounts: 30% to dealers, 10% to libraries. 20pp; 6×9; †lp. Payment: 10% of list value of the edition. Copyrights for author.

META4: Journal of Object Oriented Poetics (OOPS), Jurado, c/o Jurado, 1793 Riverside Drive #3F, New York, NY 10034. 1994. Poetry, art, photos, collages, concrete art. "Looking for new, talented voices with style. Be creative, yet accessible. Write haiku-like phrases. Articulate a structure around a character or story, manifesting a sense of closure. Make the poem focus: relish on the details of objects, develop metaphors, have a cinematic quality of show and tell, get to the subject with poignancy, reveal a deeper subtext. Be vivid, precise and intense with writing." circ. 250. 2/yr. Expects 2 issues 1999, 2 issues 2000. sub. price: $6; per copy: $3; sample: $5. 40pp. Reporting time: 4-6 months. Payment: 2 issue copies. Copyrighted, reverts to author. Ads: $35/$10.

MetaGnosis, Jane L. Robertson, Publisher, Po Box 1055, Boulder, CO 80306-1055, 303-938-9201. 1990. "Do not accept outside manuscripts." avg. press run 2M-3M. Pub'd 2 titles 1998; expects 2 titles 1999, 3 titles 2000. 1 title listed in the *Small Press Record of Books in Print* (28th Edition, 1999-00). avg. price, paper: $12.95. Discounts: retail only 1-4 20%, 5-99 40%; 100+ 50%. 150pp; 8½×5. Does not copyright for author.

METAL CURSE, Ray Miller, PO Box 302, Elkhart, IN 46515-0302, 219-294-6610; e-mail cursed@inter-serv.com. 1989. Poetry, fiction, articles, art, photos, cartoons, interviews, reviews, music, letters, news items. "Mostly reviews of Underground bands (all types), and interviews. Plus anti-censorship news, and other free-thought stuff. Biases, none that I know of, except for mainstream life" circ. 2M. 2/yr. Pub'd 2 issues 1998; expects 2 issues 1999, 2 issues 2000. 1 title listed in the *Small Press Record of Books in Print* (28th Edition, 1999-00). price per copy: $14.95; sample: $5. Back issues: #5, #6 $2 each. Sold out of 1-4. Others $3 each. Discounts: Trades possible. Write first. Wholesale: 10-25 copies - $3 each, 26-50 copies - $2.75, 51-100 copies - $2.50, 100+ copies - $2 each. 40pp; 8½×11; of. Reporting time: 1 month. Simultaneous submissions accepted: yes. Payment: copy of issue with contribution. Not copyrighted. Pub's reviews: 60 in 1998. §Music, poetry, anti-censorship movements, almost anything out of the ordinary. Ads: $80/$50/$30 1/4 page.

Metamorphous Press, David Balding, Publisher; Nancy Wyatt-Kelsey, Acquisitions Editor, PO Box 10616, Portland, OR 97296, 503-228-4972; fax 503-223-9117. 1982. Fiction, art, photos, cartoons, satire, non-fiction, concrete art. "We prefer submissions that give a brief outline of the book, table of contents, sample of the writing style, and potential market. We then decide whether to request a complete manuscript. We can return manuscripts that are submitted with return envelope and sufficient return postage. For acknowledgement of receipt of initial info, please include SASE." avg. press run 2M-5M. Pub'd 5 titles 1998; expects 10 titles 1999, 5 titles 2000. 37 titles listed in the *Small Press Record of Books in Print* (28th Edition, 1999-00). avg. price, paper: $14; other: $10 cassettes. Discounts: trade 40%; bulk depends on quantity—write for rates; classroom 20% on prepaid orders. 200pp; 5½×8½; of. Reporting time: 8-12 months. Simultaneous submissions accepted: yes. Publishes 1% of manuscripts submitted. Payment: negotiable. Copyrights for author. PNWBPA, ABA, PMA.

THE METAPHYSICAL REVIEW, Bruce Gillespie, 59 Keele Street, Collingwood, Victoria 3066, Australia, (03) 4194797. 1984. Articles, art, photos, cartoons, interviews, criticism, reviews, letters, non-fiction. "Personal journalism: witty, observant humane nonfiction of matters that interest readers *except* science fiction and fantasy. Recent contributors: Tom Disch, Yvonne Rousseau, Lucy Sussex, and George Turner." circ. 250-300. Infrequent. Pub'd 1 issue 1998; expects 3 issues 1999, 3 issues 2000. sub. price: $US25/5 issues; per copy: $6; sample: $6. Back issues: $6. Discounts: none. 40pp; 8¼×11¾; of. Reporting time: 4 weeks. Payment: none. Copyrighted, reverts to author. Pub's reviews: 10 in 1998. Ads: $US200/$100/$6 per column inch.

●**METASEX, Dorchester Press**, Michelle Clifford, Editor-in-Chief & Publisher; Bill Landis, Associate Editor, PO Box 620, Old Chelsea Station, New York, NY 10011, e-mail metasex@hotmail.com. 1997. Interviews, criticism, reviews, non-fiction. "Recent contributors: William Landis and Howard Ziehm. Special stories: the best of the roughies, history of Avon films, history of Deep Throat." circ. 2M. 1/yr. Pub'd 1 issue 1998; expects 1 issue 1999, 2 issues 2000. sub. price: $10, add $5 for overseas per issue; per copy: $10; sample: $10. Back issues: $15 #1 (premier). Discounts: none. 65pp; 8½×11; †of. Reporting time: immediate. Simultaneous submissions accepted: no. Publishes a very small % of manuscripts submitted. Payment: none. Copyrighted, reverts to author. Pub's reviews: over 100 in 1998. §Sex, music, erotica, film, exploitation, entertainment, literary. Ads: $250/$175/$85 1/4 page.

THE METROPOLITAN REVIEW, Mary Claire Ray, Editor; William Beverly, Associate Editor; Deborah Ager, Associate Editor, PO Box 32128, Washington, DC 20007. "Fiction, poetry, plays, photography, prints, other art, nonfiction, etc." 2/yr. sub. price: $10, $20 institution; per copy: $6.

MEXICAN STUDIES/ESTUDIOS MEXICANOS, University of California Press, Jaime E. Rodriguez, Carla Duke, Editorial Assistant, University of California Press, 2120 Berkeley Way, Berkeley, CA 94720, 510-643-7154. 1985. Non-fiction. "Editorial address: 340 Humanities Office Bldg., Univ. of CA, Irvine, CA 92717." circ. 1.3M. 2/yr. Pub'd 2 issues 1998; expects 2 issues 1999, 2 issues 2000. sub. price: $25 indiv., $63 instit., $18 students (+ $4 foreign postage); per copy: $15 indiv. $33 instit., $15 students (+ $4 foreign postage); sample: free. Back issues: $12 indiv.; $25 instit. (+ $4 foreign postage). Discounts: foreign subs. agent 10%, one-time orders 10+ 30%, standing orders (bookstores): 1-99 40%, 100+ 50%. 200pp; 6×9; of. Copyrighted, does not revert to author. Ads: $275/$200.

Meyer Publishing, Steve Meyer, PO Box 247, Garrison, IA 52229, 319-477-5041, Fax 319-477-5042, 800-477-5046. 1991. avg. press run 6. Pub'd 1 title 1998; expects 5 titles 1999. 5 titles listed in the *Small Press Record of Books in Print* (28th Edition, 1999-00). avg. price, cloth: $37.50; paper: $12. Discounts: 40% Stores and Dealers, 55% Distributors, Jobbers. 200pp; 6×9. Reporting time: 30 days. Publishes 10% of manuscripts submitted. Payment: negotiated. Copyrights for author.

Mho & Mho Works, Roman Gadzo, Editor, Box 33135, San Diego, CA 92163, 619-488-4991. 1969. Non-fiction. "We do books on communications arts, on occult sexual practices, and family therapy. We are also interested in material having to do with the physically handicapped (one title was *The Cripple Liberation Front Marching Band Blues*) — not the usual miracle-cure , but real and honest essays and book-length reports on the affect and effect of being physically handicapped in a Pepsi Generation World. Most of our books are of normal length. We require that any submissions be accompanied by self addressed stamped envelope—otherwise, the manuscripts will go into our scratch paper file. We wouldn't discourage any submissions, but they must be honest and direct." avg. press run 5M-10M. Pub'd 3 titles 1998; expects 3 titles 1999, 3 titles 2000. 9 titles listed in the *Small Press Record of Books in Print* (28th Edition, 1999-00). avg. price, cloth: $18.95; paper: $12.95. Discounts: 40% to bookstores; 20% to libraries. 200-400pp; 6×9; cold type. Reporting time: 6 weeks. Payment: we pay ourselves back for cost of publication out of earliest proceeds; then, we split 50/50 with author. Copyrights for author.

Miami University Press, James Reiss, English Dept., Miami University, Oxford, OH 45056, 513-529-5110; Fax 513-529-1392; E-mail reissja@muohio.edu. Poetry. "Considers mid-career poets only, i.e., poets who have published at least one full-length collection by a reputable small, university, or commercial press." avg. press run 1M. Pub'd 2 titles 1998; expects 2 titles 1999, 2 titles 2000. avg. price, cloth: $19.95; paper: $11.95. Discounts: 20% short discount, 40% full discount. 64pp; 5½x8½; 1p. Reporting time: 3 months. Simultaneous submissions accepted: yes. Publishes 1% of manuscripts submitted. Payment: 10%. Copyrights for author. Academy of American Poets.

Mica Press, J. Grant, 113 Cambridge Road, Madison, WI 53704-5909, 608-246-0759; Fax 608-246-0756; E-mail jgrant@bookzen.com; website www.bookzen.com. 1990. Poetry, cartoons, reviews, non-fiction. "Do not submit manuscripts. Submit description only. We provide free space on our website (www.bookzen.com) for small & academic press publishers to display books." avg. press run 2M. Pub'd 1 title 1998. 3 titles listed in the *Small Press Record of Books in Print* (28th Edition, 1999-00). 250-640pp. Payment: yes. Copyrights for author.

Micah Publications Inc., Robert Kalechofsky, Roberta Kalechofsky, 255 Humphrey Street, Marblehead, MA 01945, 617-631-7601. 1975. Fiction, articles, criticism. "Micah Publications publishes prose: scholarly, fictional, lyrical; a prose that addresses itself to issues without offending esthetic sensibilities, a prose that is aware of the esthetics of language without succumbing to esthetic solipsism. Three books a year. No unsolicited mss." avg. press run 800. Pub'd 2 titles 1998; expects 4 titles 1999, 2-3 titles 2000. 27 titles listed in the *Small Press Record of Books in Print* (28th Edition, 1999-00). avg. price, cloth: $20; paper: $15. Discounts: 2-5 20%, 6-9 30%, 10-49 40%, 50+ 50%. 280pp; 5¼x8½; author must submit camera-ready copy of text—we'll do designs and illustrations. Reporting time: 3 months. Simultaneous submissions accepted: yes. Publishes 5% of manuscripts submitted. Payment: 10% to authors after primary expenses of printing and advertising is met from sale of books. Copyrights for author. AJP, PMA.

MICHIGAN: Around and About, George Wahr Publishing Company, George Wahr Sallade, 304-1/2 South State Street, Ann Arbor, MI 48104, 313-668-6097. "Local, national and international government and political issues." circ. 1.2M. 12/yr. sub. price: $10. 4pp; 8½x11; of. Copyrighted, reverts to author. Pub's reviews: 6 in 1998. §Current events, politics, history, government, international sports, states.

MICHIGAN FEMINIST STUDIES, 234 W. Engineering, Women's Studies, University of Michigan, Ann Arbor, MI 48109, e-mail mfseditors@umich.edu. 1978. "A journal produced in conjunction with the Women's Studies Program at the University of Michigan" circ. 250. 1/yr. Pub'd 2 issues 1998; expects 1 issue 1999, 1 issue 2000. sub. price: $12 institutions, $5 individuals; per copy: same; sample: same. Back issues: $35 for full print run (1986-present). 150pp; 6x9. Reporting time: 2 months. Simultaneous submissions accepted: yes. Publishes 10% of manuscripts submitted. Payment: none. Copyrighted. Pub's reviews: 1 in 1998. §1998-99 - technology and gender. Ads: $50/$25.

MICHIGAN QUARTERLY REVIEW, Laurence Goldstein, 3032 Rackham Bldg., University of Michigan, Ann Arbor, MI 48109, 734-764-9265. 1962. Poetry, fiction, articles, art, interviews, criticism, reviews, letters, parts-of-novels, long-poems. "We are not solely a literary magazine. In addition to poetry, fiction, and reviews, we include essays on a variety of topics in the humanities, arts & sciences. Writers are advised to refer to a sample back issue before submitting ($2.50)." circ. 1.8M. 4/yr. Pub'd 4 issues 1998; expects 4 issues 1999, 4 issues 2000. sub. price: $18; per copy: $5; sample: $2.50. Back issues: cover price. Discounts: agency rates - $20 for institution subscription; 15% for agent. 160pp; 6x9; of. Reporting time: 6 weeks. Simultaneous submissions accepted: no. Publishes 1-2% of manuscripts submitted. Payment: $8/page of poetry, $8/page essays. Copyrighted, reverts to author. Pub's reviews: 14 in 1998. §Humanities, sciences, arts, literature. Ads: $100/$50. CLMP.

Michigan State University Press (see also FOURTH GENRE: EXPLORATIONS IN NONFICTION), 1405 S. Harrison Road, #25, East Lansing, MI 48823-5202, 517-355-9543; fax 517-432-2611; E-mail msp07@msu.edu. 1 title listed in the *Small Press Record of Books in Print* (28th Edition, 1999-00).

Microdex Bookshelf, Chris Brozek, Christopher Fara, 1212 N. Sawtelle, Suite 120, Tucson, AZ 85716, 520-326-3502. 1989. Non-fiction. "Microdex Bookshelf specializes in creating common-sense manuals, tutorials and reference books for computer users. Absolutely no tech-jargon, but no condescending either; concise; don't belabor the obvious, yet include all details. Unsolicited manuscripts not accepted; inquire by letter, include SASE." avg. press run 500-5M. Expects 2 titles 1999, 2 titles 2000. 6 titles listed in the *Small Press Record of Books in Print* (28th Edition, 1999-00). avg. price, paper: $19.95. Discounts: retail 40%, bulk 50-55%, libraries, teachers and S.C.O.P. 25%. 150pp; 5½x8½; †of. Reporting time: 30 days, include SASE, no returns unless prepaid. Payment: negotiable but typical 10% of list price. Copyrights negotiable.

MICROPRESS YATES, Gloria B. Yates, 29 Brittainy Street, Petrie, Queensland 4502, Australia, 07-32851462; gloriabe@powerup.com.au. 1992. Poetry. "Now in its 6th year; 1½ years ago gave birth to Micropress NZ and Valley Micropress. We work in association with New Zealand. Our aim is to publish as wide a range of poetry as possible, free and rhymed." circ. 4-500. 10/yr. Pub'd 10 issues 1998; expects 10 issues 1999, 10 issues 2000. sub. price: $10 AUS; $20 overseas; $17 US; per copy: 50¢; sample: 50¢. Back issues: none available except previous month. Discounts: none. 12pp; size A4; mi. Reporting time: 1 month. Simultaneous submissions accepted: yes. Publish 20% or less of manuscripts submitted. Payment: none. Ads: none.

MICROWAVE NEWS, VDT NEWS, Louis Slesin, PO Box 1799, Grand Central Station, New York, NY 10163, 212-517-2800. 1981. Articles, reviews, letters, news items. "A bimonthly report on non-ionizing radiation (from such sources as power lines, radar microwave transmitters, radio transmitters, cellular phones, VDTs etc.). Including the latest research, legislation, litigation, regulations." circ. 1M. 6/yr. Pub'd 6 issues 1998; expects 6 issues 1999, 6 issues 2000. sub. price: $285; per copy: $50; sample: $10. Back issues: $95 a calendar year; bound volumes available. Discounts: by arrangement with publisher. 20pp; 8½×11; lp. Copyrighted, does not revert to author. Pub's reviews: 25-30 in 1998. §Non-ionizing radiation, epidemiology, medical application. Ads: $2000/$1450-1150/$700 1/4 page/$425 1/8/$275 1/16.

MID-AMERICAN REVIEW, George Looney, Editor-in-Chief; Michael Czyzniejewski, Fiction Editor; David Hawkins, Poetry Editor, Dept of English, Bowling Green State University, Bowling Green, OH 43403, 419-372-2725. 1980. Poetry, fiction, articles, criticism, reviews, parts-of-novels, long-poems. "Contributors: C.K. Williams, Susan Ludvigson, David Foster Wallace, Chase Twichell, Alberto Rios, Martin Espada, Naomi Shihab Nye, Greg Pape, Stephen Dunn, Andre Dubus, Michael Martone, Jonathan Holden, Dorothy Barresi, Albert Goldbarth." circ. 1M. 2/yr. Pub'd 2 issues 1998; expects 2 issues 1999, 2 issues 2000. sub. price: $12; per copy: $7; sample: $5. Back issues: $10 for rare issues. Discounts: 20%/40%. 160pp; 5½×8½; of. Reporting time: 1-4 months. Simultaneous submissions accepted: no. Publishes 2% of manuscripts submitted. Payment: $10 per page up to $50 (when funding permits). Copyrighted, reverts to author. Pub's reviews: 2 in 1998. §Fiction, poetry and criticism of contemporary literature. Ads: $70/$35/will exchange. AWP, CLMP, CELJ.

The Middle Atlantic Press, Rubt. Koen, Publisher, 10 Twosome Drive, Box 600, Moorestown, NJ 08057, 609-235-4444; orders 800-257-8481; fax 800-225-3840. 1968. "We are a trade book and educational materials publisher. Our material is oriented to the Middle Atlantic region, but all of our books are sold nation-wide. Will not be responsible for unsolicited submissions." avg. press run varies. Pub'd 2 titles 1998; expects 4 titles 1999, 4-6 titles 2000. 22 titles listed in the *Small Press Record of Books in Print* (28th Edition, 1999-00). avg. price, cloth: $18; paper: $12. Pages vary with title; size varies; of. Reporting time: 1-2 months. Simultaneous submissions accepted: yes. Payment: 8% royalty on hardcover books, 5% + 10% on paperbacks to author, paid annually. Copyrights for author. PPG, PA.

MIDDLE EAST REPORT, Jeff Hartman, 1500 Massachusetts Ave., NW, #119, Washington, DC 20005, 202-223-3677. 1975. Poetry, fiction, articles, art, photos, cartoons, interviews, reviews, letters, news items, non-fiction. circ. 7M. 4/yr. Pub'd 6 issues 1998; expects 4 issues 1999, 4 issues 2000. sub. price: $32 individual, $58 institutions; per copy: $8.25 individual; $7.95 institutions plus postage; sample: $9.75 individuals, $11.25 institutions plus postage. Back issues: all issues #197 and before are $5.25 each; $6.75 institutions. Discounts: 40% for dealers with standing orders, 30% for orders of 5 or more from dealers without standing orders; 30% for non-trade bulk orders of 25 or more. 48pp; 8½×11; of. Reporting time: 4-8 weeks. Simultaneous submissions accepted: yes. Publishes 10% of manuscripts submitted. Copyrighted, does not revert to author. Pub's reviews: 30 in 1998. §Middle East politics, economics, culture, society, international economics, oil, Middle East fiction. Ads: $325/$180. APS.

Middle Passage Press, Barbara Bramwell, 5517 Secrest Drive, Los Angeles, CA 90043, 213-298-0266. 1986. Non-fiction. avg. press run 5M. Pub'd 2 titles 1998; expects 2 titles 1999, 3 titles 2000. 5 titles listed in the *Small Press Record of Books in Print* (28th Edition, 1999-00). avg. price, cloth: $19.95; paper: $12.95. Discounts: 10-25%. 200pp; 5½×8½; of. Reporting time: 3 months. Simultaneous submissions accepted: yes. Publishes 1% of manuscripts submitted. Payment: 10% retail, yes advances. Copyrights for author. PMA, Black Caucus ALA, ABA.

The Middleburg Press, Carl Vandermeulen, Box 166, Orange City, IA 51041, 712-737-4198. 1978. Fiction, photos, letters. "We specialize in books and novels with a Reformed background and perspective; and in high school journalism/photography books." avg. press run 3M. Pub'd 1 title 1998; expects 1 title 2000. 5 titles listed in the *Small Press Record of Books in Print* (28th Edition, 1999-00). avg. price, cloth: $12.95; paper: $6.95. Discounts: jobbers & bookstores: 1 copy-20%; 2-3 copies 30%; 4-7 copies 35%; 8 or more 40%. 128pp; 6×9; of. Reporting time: 6 months. Payment: to be negotiated. Copyrights for author.

Middlebury College (see also NEW ENGLAND REVIEW), Stephen Donadio, Editor, Middlebury College, Middlebury, VT 05753, 802-443-5075; E-mail nereview@middlebury.edu. 1978. Poetry, fiction, articles, interviews, criticism, reviews, parts-of-novels, long-poems. "Fiction, poetry, essays and reviews of the highest quality." avg. press run 2M. Pub'd 4 titles 1998; expects 4 titles 1999, 4 titles 2000. 2 titles listed in the *Small Press Record of Books in Print* (28th Edition, 1999-00). avg. price, paper: $7. Discounts: 25% classroom. 184pp; 7×10; of. Reporting time: 12 weeks. Simultaneous submissions accepted, if indicated. Payment:

competitive. Does not copyright for author. CLMP.

Mid-List Press, Lane Stiles, 4324 12th Avenue South, Minneapolis, MN 55407-3218, 612-822-3733; Fax 612-823-8387; guide@midlist.org; www.midlist.org. 1989. Poetry, fiction, non-fiction. "Please write or visit our website for guidelines before submitting. Since 1990 we have sponsored the First Series Awards in Poetry, the Novel, Short Fiction, and Creative Nonfiction for writers who have yet to publish a book-length work in that category. Notable authors include Alfred Corn and Dr. William Nolen." avg. press run 500-2.5M. Pub'd 3 titles 1998; expects 5 titles 1999, 5 titles 2000. avg. price, cloth: $24; paper: $11-$14. Discounts: wholesale 3-4 books 20%, 5-9 30%, 10-50 40%, 50+ 50%. Poetry 80pp; others 200pp; 5½x8½; of. Reporting time: 1-4 months. Simultaneous submissions accepted: yes. Publishes less than 1% of manuscripts submitted. Payment: by contract. Copyrights for author.

Midmarch Arts Press (see also WOMEN ARTISTS NEWS BOOK REVIEW), Judy Seigel, Editor, 300 Riverside Drive, New York City, NY 10025, 212-666-6990. 1975. Articles, art, photos, interviews, news items, non-fiction. avg. press run 3M-5M. Expects 2 titles 1999, 4 titles 2000. 26 titles listed in the *Small Press Record of Books in Print* (28th Edition, 1999-00). avg. price, cloth: $15; paper: $15. Discounts: Institutional L.P, Jobber L.P. for single copies; appropriate disc. for quantity. 100-318pp; 5½x8½, 6x9, 8½x11; of. Reporting time: 4 weeks. Publishes 35% of manuscripts submitted. Payment to authors, payment to essayists for books. Copyrights for author. CLMP, Small Press, American Booksellers Assn., College Art Association.

MIDWEST ART FAIRS, James W. Schiller, Publisher, PO Box 72, Pepin, WI 54759, 715-442-2022. 1990. "Bi-annual listing of art fairs and craft festivals with listings for artists, artisans, writers, poets, playwrights, organizations, businesses, services, suppliers." circ. 7.5M. 2/yr. Pub'd 2 issues 1998. sub. price: $13.95; per copy: $7.95; sample: $7.95. Back issues: $7.95. 120pp; 8½x11; max. quark xpress. Reporting time: 4 weeks. Payment: none. Copyrighted, reverts to author. Ads: $450/$225. New North Publishing.

MIDWEST POETRY REVIEW, John Ottley, Editor, PO Box 20236, Atlanta, GA 30325-0236, 404-350-0714. 1980. Poetry. circ. 246. 4/yr. Expects 4 issues 1999. sub. price: $20; per copy: $5; sample: $5. Back issues: $5 (when available). 40pp; 5½x8½; of. Reporting time: 4-6 weeks. Simultaneous submissions accepted: no. Publishes 10%-15% of manuscripts submitted. Payment: $5 to $20; contests $25 to $500. Copyrighted. Ads: $100 full page.

THE MIDWEST QUARTERLY, James B.M. Schick, Editor; Stephen Meats, Poetry; Patricia Dr. Behlar, Book Reviews, Pittsburg State University, English Department, Pittsburg, KS 66762, 316-235-4369. 1959. Poetry, articles, interviews, criticism, reviews, non-fiction. "Scholarly articles on history, literature, the social sciences (especially political), art, music, the natural sciences (in non-technical language). Most articles run 4M to 5M words. Can use a brief note of 1M to 2M words once in a while. Chief bias is an aversion to jargon and pedantry. Instead of footnotes we use a minimum of parenthetical documentation. Reviews and interviews are assigned. Contributors: Walter McDonald, Jeanne Murray Walker, Lyn Lifshin, Charles Bukowski, William Kloefkorn, among others, have been represented in our pages. Will consider all poems submitted." circ. 1M. 4/yr. Pub'd 4 issues 1998; expects 4 issues 1999. sub. price: $12 within U.S., otherwise $17; per copy: $4; sample: $4. Back issues: $4. Discounts: 10% to agencies. 110pp; 6x9; of. Reporting time: 3-6 months. Simultaneous submissions accepted: no. Publishes 15% of manuscripts submitted. Payment: copies only, varies 3 usually. Copyrighted, reverts to author. Pub's reviews: 12 in 1998. §Poetry, non-fiction. No ads. CLMP.

Midwest Villages & Voices, Gayla Ellis, PO Box 40214, St. Paul, MN 55104, 612-822-5810. 1981. "We are a publishing group and cultural organization for Midwestern writers and visual artists. Submission by invitation only." avg. press run 1M-3M. Pub'd 1 title 1998; expects 1 title 1999, 1 title 2000. 8 titles listed in the *Small Press Record of Books in Print* (28th Edition, 1999-00). avg. price, paper: $6-8. Discounts: 30%. 64-96pp; 5½x8½. Payment: negotiated. Copyrights negotiated.

MIDWIFERY TODAY, Midwifery Today Books, Jan Tritten, Box 2672, Eugene, OR 97402, 503-344-7438. 1985. "Birth information for midwives, childbirth educators and interested consumers. Photos, experiences, technical and non-technical articles." circ. 6M. 4/yr. Pub'd 4 issues 1998; expects 4 issues 1999, 4 issues 2000. sub. price: $50; per copy: $12.50; sample: $12.50. Back issues: $6/$10. Discounts: $7 each for 10 of one issue for resale. 72pp; 8½x11; sheet fed. Reporting time: 6 weeks. Payment: subscription. Copyrighted, reverts to author. Pub's reviews: 25 in 1998. §Midwifery, pregnancy, birth, childbirth education, breastfeeding. Ads: $475/$286/75¢ word classified, $5 minimum.

Midwifery Today Books (see also MIDWIFERY TODAY), Jan Tritten, Editor-in-Chief, PO Box 2672, Eugene, OR 97402, 541-344-7438; Fax 541-344-1422; midwifery@aol.com; www.members.aol.com/midwifery/. 1986. Articles, non-fiction. "Two books per year on the subject of midwifery which include articles on specialized topics such as shoulder dystocia, hemorrhage, normal birth. We solicit our own material 99% of the time. Query us first." avg. press run 1.5M. Pub'd 2 titles 1998; expects 2 titles 1999, 2 titles 2000. avg. price, paper: $25. Discounts: send for information. 150pp; 8½x11; web. Reporting time: 1-6 months. Simultaneous submissions accepted: no. Publishes 1% of manuscripts submitted. Payment: send for information. We retain copyright.

Mile Marker 12 Publishing, 6355 Long Island Drive, Atlanta, GA 30328, 770-455-8606; 888-868-6612; fax 770-455-6893. 1 title listed in the *Small Press Record of Books in Print* (28th Edition, 1999-00).

Miles & Miles, Matthew Miles, Aida Gonzalez-Miles, PO Box 6730, Eureka, CA 95502. 1992. Non-fiction. "Returns to: 3420 M. St, Eureka, CA 95501." avg. press run 3.2M. Expects 1 title 1999, 1 title 2000. 5 titles listed in the *Small Press Record of Books in Print* (28th Edition, 1999-00). avg. price, cloth: $16.95; paper: $8.95. Discounts: normal trade. 168pp; of. Reporting time: 8 weeks. Payment: small advance against 10% royalty. Copyrights for author. PMA.

Miles River Press, Peg Paul, President, 400 Madison Street #S1309, Alexandria, VA 22314-1755, 703-683-1500. 1981. Non-fiction. "Interested in current management and leadership theory, materials for latchkey children" avg. press run 5M-10M. Pub'd 1 title 1998; expects 1 title 1999, 1 title 2000. 4 titles listed in the *Small Press Record of Books in Print* (28th Edition, 1999-00). avg. price, paper: $10.25; other: range $4.95-$25.95. Discounts: trade. 64-278pp; size varies; of, lp. Reporting time: 1 month. Payment: varies. Copyrights for author. AAP.

THE MILITANT, Steve Clark, 410 West Street, New York, NY 10014, 212-243-6392. 1928. Articles, photos, interviews, satire, criticism, reviews, letters, news items, non-fiction. circ. 12M. 47/yr. Pub'd 47 issues 1998; expects 47 issues 1999, 47 issues 2000. sub. price: $45; per copy: $1.50; sample: free. Back issues: $1.50. 16pp; 11½×18; †of. Payment: none. Not copyrighted. Pub's reviews: 10 in 1998. §Labor issues, war, politics, economics, black studies, women's studies. Ads: $400/$250/75¢.

Milkweed Editions, Emilie Buchwald, Publisher, 430 1st Avenue North, Ste. 400, Minneapolis, MN 55401, 612-332-3192. 1984. Poetry, fiction, articles, non-fiction. avg. press run 3M-5M. Pub'd 11 titles 1998; expects 11 titles 1999, 14 titles 2000. 113 titles listed in the *Small Press Record of Books in Print* (28th Edition, 1999-00). avg. price, cloth: $21.95; paper: $13.95. 250pp; 6×9; of. Reporting time: 6 months. Simultaneous submissions accepted: yes. Publishes 1% of manuscripts submitted. Payment: advance against royalties, royalties payment varies by author. Copyrights for author.

Mille Grazie Press, David Oliveira, PO Box 92023, Santa Barbara, CA 93190, 805-963-8408. 1992. Poetry. "The focus of Mille Grazie Press is to publish the fine poets who live and work along California's Central Coast. The press is interested in carefully crafted works of high quality. Poets selected for publication are invited by the editors to submit manuscripts. No unsolicited manuscripts will be considered. The editors have a broad range of taste in subject matter and form. The primary consideration for selection is the skillful use of language and strong vision of the poet. Mille Grazie Press publishes perfect bound chapbooks, from 24 to 40 pages. Current offerings include work by Glenna Luschei, Wilma Elizabeth McDaniel, and Will Inman," avg. press run 100. Pub'd 4 titles 1998; expects 6 titles 1999, 6 titles 2000. 20 titles listed in the *Small Press Record of Books in Print* (28th Edition, 1999-00). avg. price, other: Chapbooks $6. 40pp; 5½×8½; of. Payment: copies. Copyrights for author.

Millennium Press, Christopher O'Keefe, PO Box 502, Groton, MA 01450, 978-433-3162; Fax 978-433-3110; E-mail millpres@ultranet.com. 1996. Fiction. "Millennium publishes literary novels. We are interested in writers who have a unique voice, something to say, and a controlled imagination. We do not accept unsolicited manuscripts." avg. press run 700. Expects 1 title 1999, 2 titles 2000. 1 title listed in the *Small Press Record of Books in Print* (28th Edition, 1999-00). avg. price, cloth: $15.95; paper: $8.95. Discounts: universal-1-0%; 2-4-20%; 5-99-40%; 100-up-50%. 200pp; 5½×8½. Reporting time: 6 months. Simultaneous submissions accepted, excerpts and query only. Publishes an unknown % of manuscripts submitted. Payment: The author receives a few copies of the first edition. If reviewed, a second edition is printed, 15% of retail. Copyrights for author. PMA, NAIP.

Mills & Sanderson, Publishers, Jan H. Anthony, Publisher & Sr. Editor, PO Box 833, Bedford, MA 01730-0833, 617-275-1410. 1986. Non-fiction. "200+ page manuscripts; secular in nature. Currently signing family problem-solving/positive living titles only. Recent titles: 'Recovering From Sexual Abuse and Incest', Gust and Sweeting; 'Pulling Together', Jester; 'Give Back the Pain', Bleck." avg. press run 2M. avg. price, paper: $12.95; other: ref. $35 (non-niche). Discounts: Authors get "best trade discount". 5-9 40%, 10-14 42%, 15-19 44%, 20-24 46%, 25-29 48%, 30+ 50%. 20% for Ref. (non-niche), non-returnable add 3% to above. 200pp; 5¾×8½; printed as perfect bound paper. Reporting time: initial 2 months; final contracting 4 months. Publishes about 10% of manuscripts submitted. Payment: no advances. Copyrights for author. PMA, Small Press Center, ABA.

MIM NOTES: Offcial Newsletter of the Maoist Internationalist Movement, PO Box 3576, Ann Arbor, MI 48106. 1984. Poetry, articles, art, photos, cartoons, interviews, satire, criticism, reviews, music, collages, news items. "We have Marxist-Lennist-Maoist line. We sometimes print things we do not agree with along with a *MIM* response. At least two pages each month are by and about prisoners; these may or may not follow the

MIM line. Letters to the editor strongly encouraged'' circ. 10M. 12/yr. Pub'd 12 issues 1998; expects 12 issues 1999, 12 issues 2000. sub. price: $12; per copy: $1; sample: $1. Back issues: $1. Discounts: $25, 200 bundle. 12pp; 11½×15; newsprint. Reporting time: 1 month. Publishes 80% of manuscripts submitted. Payment: none. Not copyrighted. Pub's reviews: 6 in 1998. §Communism, feminism, Black nationalism, indigenous, 3rd world, prisons.

MINAS TIRITH EVENING-STAR, W.W. Publications, Philip W. Helms, PO BOX 7871, Flint, MI 48507-0871, 813-585-0985, phone and fax. 1967. Poetry, fiction, articles, art, cartoons, interviews, criticism, reviews, letters, long-poems, news items, non-fiction. "Only Tolkien related material accepted. Questions to: Paul S. Ritz, PO Box 901, Clearwater, FL 34617." circ. 350+. 4/yr. Pub'd 6 issues 1998; expects 6 issues 1999, 8 issues 2000. sub. price: $10 U.S., $15 foreign, $12.50 Canada; per copy: $2; sample: $2. Back issues: $1 each. Discounts: over 10 copies 75¢ each. 25pp; 8½×11; of. Reporting time: 2 months. Payment: free issues. Copyrighted, reverts to author. Pub's reviews: 15 in 1998. §Any Tolkien related or fantasy work. Ads: $15/$10/$5¼ page. ATS.

MIND MATTERS REVIEW, Carrie L. Drake, Bunny Williams, Assistant Editor, 2040 Polk Street, Box 234, San Francisco, CA 94109. 1988. Articles, non-fiction. "The trend for *MMR* is to publish criticism of psychological and sociological theories that give greater power to mental health establishment as an enforcer of the status quo in education and science. Our critical approach is to focus on obstacles to intellectual cooperation, such as academic elitism, political partisanship, etc." circ. 1M-2M. 4/yr. Pub'd 4 issues 1998; expects 4 issues 1999, 4 issues 2000. sub. price: $15 US, $20 foreign; per copy: $4; sample: $4. Back issues: $2. Discounts: half price for librarians and institutions. 35-60pp; 8½×11; desktop. Reporting time: 4 weeks. Payment: copies. Copyrighted. Pub's reviews: 6 in 1998. §U.S.-Russian relations, cultural exchanges, comparison, science and education in U.S./Russia/Third World, information management, linguistic theory.

Mindfield Publications, James Carter, Maria Ramirez, PO Box 14114, Berkeley, CA 94712-5114, 510-433-7945; mindfld@dnai.com; www.dnai.com/mindfld. 1995. Poetry, fiction, articles, cartoons, satire, criticism, letters, parts-of-novels. "First title is *Illegals*, a novel by J.P. Bone. We plan on publishing one title a year, our second in September of 1997. Our magazine is available online as of January 15, 1997." Pub'd 1 title 1998; expects 1 title 1999, 1 title 2000. 1 title listed in the *Small Press Record of Books in Print* (28th Edition, 1999-00). avg. price, paper: $12.95. Discounts: 40%. 230pp; of. Reporting time: 2 months. Simultaneous submissions accepted: yes. Payment: negotiable. Copyrights for author.

THE MINDFULNESS BELL, Leslie Rawls, Editor, 14200 Fountain Lane, Charlotte, NC 28278, 510-527-3751; e-mail parapress@aol.com. 1990. Poetry, articles. "Short poems and articles on the integration of mindful awareness, social responsibility, and daily practice of mindfulness in the Buddhist tradition." circ. 3M. 3/yr. Pub'd 3 issues 1998; expects 3 issues 1999, 3 issues 2000. sub. price: $18; per copy: $6; sample: $6. Back issues: $6. Discounts: not available at this time. 40pp; 8½×11; of. Reporting time: 3-4 months. Simultaneous submissions accepted: yes. Publishes 25% of manuscripts submitted. Payment: none. Not copyrighted. ABA, PMA.

MINERVA: Quarterly Report on Women and the Military, Linda Grant DePauw, 20 Granada Road, Pasadena, MD 21122-2708, 410-437-5379. 1983. Poetry, fiction, articles, art, cartoons, interviews, reviews, letters, parts-of-novels, news items, non-fiction. "Editorial policy emphasizes diversity." circ. 700. 4/yr. Pub'd 4 issues 1998; expects 4 issues 1999, 4 issues 2000. sub. price: $50; per copy: $12.95; sample: $12.95. Discounts: 20% on 10-25 books to same address. 94pp; 5½×8½; of. Reporting time: 2-3 weeks. Payment: none. Copyrighted, reverts to author. Pub's reviews: 12 in 1998. §Military women and veterans, military wives, non-traditional occupations. No ads.

MINIATURE DONKEY TALK INC, Bonnie Gross, 1338 Hughes Shop Road, Westminster, MD 21158, 410-875-0118; fax 410-857-9145; email minidonk@qis.net; www.qis.net/~minidonk/donktext.htm. 1987. Non-fiction. circ. 5.5M. 6/yr. Pub'd 6 issues 1998; expects 6 issues 1999, 6 issues 2000. sub. price: $25; per copy: $5; sample: $5. Back issues: $5. 70pp; 7¾×10½; web press. Simultaneous submissions accepted: yes. Publishes 80% of manuscripts submitted. Copyrighted, does not revert to author. Ads: $220/$125/$65 1/4 page.

MINIMUS, Terence M. Mulligan, 2245 N. Buchanan Street, Arlington, VA 22207. 1989. Poetry, fiction. "5 poems or fiction to 3,000 words. No polemics. No political or social commentary. No diary. Imagination, originality, and craftsmanship welcome. Reading period: January *only*." circ. 200. 1/yr. Pub'd 1 issue 1998; expects 1 issue 1999, 1 issue 2000. sub. price: $9.75; per copy: $9.75; sample: $9.75. 84pp; 5½×8½. Reporting time: 3-6 months. Simultaneous submissions accepted: yes. Publishes 5% of manuscripts submitted. Payment: 1 copy. Copyrighted, reverts to author. Ads: $60/$30.

MINISTRY & LITURGY, Resource Publications, Inc., William Burns, Publisher; Nick Wagner, Editor, 160 East Virginia Street, #290, San Jose, CA 95112-5876, 408-286-8505, Fax; 408-287-8748, E-mail; mdrulitgy@aol.com, Internet; http://ww.rpinet.com. 1973. Poetry, fiction, articles, art, photos, cartoons, criticism, reviews, music, letters, plays, concrete art, non-fiction. "In-house graphics and typography." circ.

16M. 10/yr. Pub'd 9 issues 1998; expects 10 issues 1999, 10 issues 2000. sub. price: $40; per copy: $4; sample: $4. Back issues: $6. Discounts: 40% trade & bulk, 10% for prepaid agency subscriptions. 48pp; 8⅜×10⅞; of. Reporting time: 6 weeks. Simultaneous submissions accepted: no. Publishes 5% of manuscripts submitted. Payment: $1 to $100. Copyrighted, does not revert to author. Pub's reviews: 187 in 1998. §Religious arts, music, religious education, worship resources, symbol, myth, ritual. Ads: $1197/$961/$1 per word. CPA, PMA.

Minnesota Historical Society Press, Ann Regan, Managing Editor; Nordis Heyerdahl-Fowler, Marketing Manager, 345 Kellogg Blvd. West, St. Paul, MN 55102-1906, 612-296-2264. 1849. avg. press run 2M-3M. Pub'd 10 titles 1998; expects 8 titles 1999, 8 titles 2000. 50 titles listed in the *Small Press Record of Books in Print* (28th Edition, 1999-00). avg. price, cloth: $30; paper: $15. Discounts: 40% 2-25 books. 300pp; 6×9. Reporting time: 4 months. Payment: negotiated. Copyrights for author.

MINNESOTA LITERATURE, Mary Bround Smith, 1 Nord Circle, St. Paul, MN 55127, 651-483-3904. 1973. Articles, news items. "All material is written by editor and staff—all is news-oriented (information about Minnesota literature—publications, events, opportunities, opinions, essays by other writers)." circ. 750. 10/yr. Pub'd 10 issues 1998; expects 10 issues 1999, 10 issues 2000. sub. price: $10; sample: $1. Back issues: $1 if available. Discounts: we will arrange special classroom and group rates. 8pp; 8½×11; of. Reporting time: 1-2 months. Payment: $50 for essays related to creative writing. Not copyrighted. Ads: $15 column inch (3½").

THE MINNESOTA REVIEW, Jeffrey Williams, Dept. of English, Univ. of Missouri, Columbia, MO 65211. 1960. Poetry, fiction, articles, art, photos, cartoons, interviews, satire, criticism, reviews, letters, parts-of-novels, long-poems, collages, non-fiction. "A journal of committed writing. We have a long tradition of publishing marxist and politically engaged work (from a range of people, including Fredric Jameson, Gayatri Spivak, Jean Franco, and many others). Our aim now is to publish the work of engaged younger critics and writers, such as Bruce Robbins, Amitava Kumar, Michael Berube, and Barbara Foley in criticism; Jim Daniels, Katherine Lederer, and Martin Espada in poetry; and Carolyn Parkhurst, Stephen Gutierrez and Mark Brett in fiction. Many of our future issues will be organized around a special topic, such as our Fall 1992 issue on 'PC Wars' and recent issues on 'The Academics of Publishing' and 'Activism and the Academy.' In each issue, our aim is to present new writing that is *daring* and encroaches bounds, whether they be stylistic or conceptual. Theory's a good word here." circ. 1.5M. 2/yr. Pub'd 2 issues 1998; expects 2 issues 1999. sub. price: $12 individual, $36 institutions and/or overseas; per copy: $7.50; sample: $7.50. Back issues: $7.50. Discounts: 10%. 180-260pp; 8½×5½; of. Reporting time: 1-3 months. Simultaneous submissions accepted: yes. Publishes 5% of manuscripts submitted. Payment: 2 copies. Copyrighted, reverts to author. Pub's reviews: 23 in 1998. §Poetry, fiction, very interested in Left literary & cultural criticism (feminist, marxist, poststructural, postcolonial), literary theory. Ads: $125/$75. CLMP, CELJ.

Minor Heron Press, Anne MacNaughton, 5275 NDCBU, Taos, NM 87571, 505-758-1800. 1982. Poetry, fiction, photos, criticism, long-poems, non-fiction. "Quality literature: focusing on fiction and poetry, regional Southwestern Hispanic, Native American, national and international, some non-fiction and art. Recent author: Peter Rabbit." avg. press run 500-1M. Pub'd 6 titles 1998; expects 6 titles 1999, 6 titles 2000. 1 title listed in the *Small Press Record of Books in Print* (28th Edition, 1999-00). avg. price, paper: $12; other: $29.00 video tape. Discounts: standard 40% for bookstores. 100pp; 5×8; of. Simultaneous submissions accepted: no. Payment: by contract. Copyrights for author.

MinRef Press, Rick Lawler, Alice Tang, 2324 Dinwiddie Way, Elk Grove, CA 95758-7424. 1989. Non-fiction. "We plan to publish small, targeted reference guides that fill empty spots on the shelves of libraries. Books should also have appeal outside of libraries. We don't want to see complete manuscripts, but are interested in considering proposals and ideas." avg. press run 2M. Expects 2 titles 1999, 3 titles 2000. 4 titles listed in the *Small Press Record of Books in Print* (28th Edition, 1999-00). avg. price, paper: $10.95. Discounts: industry standard. 150pp; 5¼×8½; of. Reporting time: 1-2 months. Simultaneous submissions accepted: no. Publishes a variable % of manuscripts submitted. Payment: by arrangement. Copyrights for author. Authors Guild, National Writers Association, Genre Writers Association.

MIP Company, PO Box 27484, Minneapolis, MN 55427, 612-546-7578; fax 612-544-6077; E-mail; mp@mipco.com; On-line; http://www.mipco.com. 1984. Poetry, fiction, non-fiction. Pub'd 3 titles 1998. 10 titles listed in the *Small Press Record of Books in Print* (28th Edition, 1999-00). Discounts: 40% when 10 or more copies purchased. Simultaneous submissions accepted: yes. Copyrights for author.

MiraCosta College Press, Amelia Painter, 1 Barnard Drive, M/S 5B, Oceanside, CA 92056. 1 title listed in the *Small Press Record of Books in Print* (28th Edition, 1999-00).

Missing Spoke Press (see also AMERICAN JONES BUILDING & MAINTENANCE), Von G. Binuia, PO Box 9569, Seattle, WA 98109, 206-443-4693; von@singspeak.com. 1997. Poetry, fiction, art, photos, interviews, satire, parts-of-novels, long-poems, non-fiction. "Working class words for middle-class consumption." avg. press run 250. Expects 9 titles 1999, 8 titles 2000. 2 titles listed in the *Small Press Record of Books in Print* (28th Edition, 1999-00). avg. price, paper: $12. 75pp; 5½×8½. Reporting time: 4 months.

Simultaneous submissions accepted: yes. Publishes 2% of manuscripts submitted. Payment: varies. Copyrights for author.

●**Mission Press,** Lynda Kennedy, Kathy Wittert, PO Box 9586, Rancho Santa Fe, CA 92067, 619-792-1841; e-mail: MissionPress@compuserve.com. 1998. Photos, news items, non-fiction. avg. press run 2M. Expects 3 titles 1999, 4 titles 2000. 2 titles listed in the *Small Press Record of Books in Print* (28th Edition, 1999-00). avg. price, paper: $30. Discounts: 20-60%. 150pp; 5½x8½; of. Reporting time: 60 days. Simultaneous submissions accepted: yes. Publishes 30% of manuscripts submitted. Payment: flat fee or graduated royalties. Copyrights for author. Publishers Directory, CBI, LMP, Directories in Print.

MISSISSIPPI MUD, Mud Press, Joel Weinstein, 7119 Santa Fe Avenue, Dallas, TX 75223, 214-321-8955. 1973. Poetry, fiction, art, photos, cartoons, satire, parts-of-novels, long-poems, collages, plays, letters, concrete art. "Elegant, lucid writing and art from the *ne plus ultra* of the American scene." circ. 1.5M. Irregular. Pub'd 1 issue 1998; expects 2 issues 1999, 3 issues 2000. sub. price: $12/2 issues; per copy: $6 ppd; sample: $6 ppd. Back issues: $5/copy plus $1 postage. 96pp; 7¾x10; of. Reporting time: 4-6 months. Simultaneous submissions accepted: yes. Publishes less than 10% of manuscripts submitted. Payment: small payments for both writing and art, paid on publication. Copyrighted, reverts to author. Ads: $300/$175.

MISSISSIPPI REVIEW, Frederick Barthelme, Editor; Rie Fortenberry, Managing Editor, USM, Box 5144, Southern Station, Hattiesburg, MS 39406-5144, 601-266-4321. 1971. Poetry, fiction, art, photos, interviews, satire, criticism, reviews, parts-of-novels, long-poems, plays. circ. 1.5M. 2/yr. Pub'd 3 issues 1998; expects 2 issues 1999, 3 issues 2000. sub. price: $15; per copy: $12; sample: $8. Back issues: $8 and as offered. Discounts: none. 125-200pp; 5½x8¾; †of. Reporting time: 2-3 months. Simultaneous submissions accepted: yes. Payment: copies and honoraria. Copyrighted, reverts to author. Ads: $100/$50/ Will consider trade-out. CLMP.

THE MISSOURI REVIEW, Speer Morgan, Editor; Greg Michalson, Managing Editor; Evelyn Somers, Associate Editor, 1507 Hillcrest Hall, University of Missouri-Columbia, Columbia, MO 65211, 573-882-4474; Fax 573-884-4671; e-mail umcastmr@missouri.edu. 1978. Poetry, fiction, articles, art, cartoons, interviews, reviews, parts-of-novels, non-fiction. circ. 6.5M. 3/yr. Pub'd 3 issues 1998; expects 3 issues 1999, 3 issues 2000. 1 title listed in the *Small Press Record of Books in Print* (28th Edition, 1999-00). sub. price: $19, $35/2 years, $45/3 years, $22 foreign yearly; per copy: $7; sample: $7. Back issues: call. Discounts: none. 224pp; 6x9; of. Reporting time: 10-12 weeks. We discourage simultaneous submissions. Publishes 5% of manuscripts submitted. Payment: $15-$20 per page minimum to $750. Copyrighted, author can reprint material without charge if author acknowledges mag. Pub's reviews: 50 in 1998. §Poetry, fiction, literary biography, history, memoir, general nonfiction. Ads: $400 or exchange. CLMP.

Mr. Cogito Press, Robert A. Davies, Co-Editor; John M. Gogol, Co-Editor, 2518 N.W. Savier, Portland, OR 97210, 503-233-8131, 226-4135. 1978. Poetry, art, photos. "Line graphics-poetry by invitation." avg. press run 500. 9 titles listed in the *Small Press Record of Books in Print* (28th Edition, 1999-00). avg. price, paper: $10. Discounts: 40% bookstores for 5 or more copies, 20% otherwise. 35pp; 5½x8½; of. Reporting time: 1-2 months, no unsolicited mss. Publishes by invitation, 90% of manuscripts submitted. Payment: copies or payment. Usually press holds copyright. CLMP.

MIXED BAG, Full Moon Publications, Sharida Rizzuto, Harold Tollison, Ann Hoyt, 577 Central Avenue, Box 4, Jefferson, LA 70121-1400, e-mail: publisher@mailexcite.com, zines@theglobe.com, zines@rsnmail.com; Websites www.members.tripod.com/~literary/index.htm/, www.members.the globe.com/ zines/default.htm/, www2.cybercities.com/z/zines/, www.zines.freeservers.com. 1992. Poetry, fiction, articles, art, photos, cartoons, interviews, satire, criticism, reviews, letters, long-poems, collages, news items, non-fiction. "A very eclectic lit zine - non-fiction, poetry and fiction" circ. 800-1M. 2/yr. Pub'd 2 issues 1998; expects 2 issues 1999, 2 issues 2000. sub. price: $15.80; per copy: $7.90; sample: $7.90. Back issues: $7.90. Discounts: trade with like publisher. 100pp; 8½x11; †of. Reporting time: 2-6 weeks. Publishes 35% of manuscripts submitted. Payment: fee for non-fiction plus free copies, free copies only for poetry and fiction. Copyrighted. Pub's reviews: 80-100 in 1998. §Practically everything, zines, books, internet websites—very eclectic. Ads: free.

MOBILE BEAT: The DJ Magazine, Robert Lindquist, Editor; Michael Buonaccorso, Publishing Director, PO Box 309, East Rochester, NY 14445, 716-385-9920; fax 716-385-3637; info@mobilebeat.com. 1991. Articles, photos, interviews, reviews, music, letters, news items. circ. 18M. 6/yr + 1 buyers guide. Pub'd 6 issues 1998; expects 6 issues 1999, 6 issues 2000. sub. price: $23; per copy: $3.95; sample: $5. Back issues: $5. Discounts: libraries 25%, wholesales/distributors. 116pp; 8⅛x10⅞; web. Publishes 80% assigned, unassigned 25% of manuscripts submitted. Payment: varies. Copyrighted, reverts to author. Pub's reviews: 4 in 1998. §Music, sound/lighting equipment, performing, broadcasting. Ads: b/w $1665/$1100/$45 per inch.

MOCCASIN TELEGRAPH, Lee Francis, 5813 E. Saint Charles Road, Columbia, MO 65202-3025, 573-817-3301. 1992. Poetry, fiction, articles, interviews, satire, criticism, reviews, letters, parts-of-novels, long-poems, news items, non-fiction. "Accept material from Wordcraft Circle of Native Writers & Storytellers members and other Native American Indian writers" circ. 500-1M. 6/yr. Pub'd 6 issues 1998; expects 6 issues 1999, 6 issues 2000. sub. price: $40; per copy: $8; sample: $8. Back issues: none available. Discounts: none. 30-32pp; 8×11. Payment: none. Not copyrighted. Ads: $100/$50/$25 1/4 page.

MOCKINGBIRD, C.G. Macdonald, Joe Aimone, PO Box 761, Davis, CA 95617. 1994. Poetry, art, photos, interviews, criticism, reviews, long-poems. "We would like to lessen the animosity between formal and free-verse poets, by publishing a promiscuous mix of both. Our first issue included poems by Alan Williamson, Taylor Graham, Charles Bukowski, Mary Moore, Rigoberto Gonzalez, Leonard Cirino, Richard Kostelanetz and Aleka Chase. As our totem is a songbird, we lean toward the lyrical, but feel a seemingly contradictory tug toward the vernacular, the proletarian, the profane." circ. 250. 2/yr. Expects 2 issues 1999, 2 issues 2000. sub. price: $7; per copy: $4; sample: $4. Back issues: none yet. Discounts: standard. 38pp; 8½×5½; xeroxed desk top originals. Reporting time: 2 months, 3-4 months for acceptances and near misses. Simultaneous submissions accepted: no. Publishes 2% of manuscripts submitted. Payment: 1 copy, 2 copies to those who attend pub. reading. Copyrighted, reverts to author. Pub's reviews: 5 in 1998. §We would like to receive poetry books, chapbooks, and magazines for review. Ads: $40/$25/$15 1/4 page.

MODERN HAIKU, Robert Spiess, PO Box 1752, Madison, WI 53701. 1969. Poetry, articles, reviews. ""Best haiku magazine in North America"—Museum of Haiku Literature, Tokyo. International circulation. Good university and public library subscription list. Publishes haiku only, plus related book reviews and articles. No restrictions on article length. Contributors should enclose self-addressed, stamped return envelope." circ. 675. 3/yr. Pub'd 3 issues 1998; expects 3 issues 1999, 3 issues 2000. 2 titles listed in the *Small Press Record of Books in Print* (28th Edition, 1999-00). sub. price: $17.75; per copy: $5.95; sample: $5.95. Back issues: $5.95. 94-104pp; 5½×8½; of. Reporting time: 2 weeks. Simultaneous submissions accepted: no. Publishes 5% of manuscripts submitted. Payment: $1 for each haiku; $5 page for articles. Copyrighted, reverts to author. Pub's reviews: 50 in 1998. §Haiku and senryu. No ads.

THE MODERN LANGUAGE JOURNAL, Sally S. Magnan, Editor, University of Wisconsin, Department of French and Italian, Madison, WI 53706-1558, 608-262-5010. 1916. Articles, reviews, news items. "Sally S. Magnan, Editor, *The Modern Language Journal* (1994-present)" circ. c. 5000. 4/yr. Pub'd 4 issues 1998; expects 4 issues 1999, 4 issues 2000. sub. price: $27 indiv, $59 instit; per copy: $7; sample: $7. Back issues: $7. 150pp; 7½×10; of. Reporting time: 1-3 months. Simultaneous submissions accepted: no. Publishes 10-13% of manuscripts submitted. Payment: 2 copies of issue in which article appears. Copyrighted, does not revert to author. Pub's reviews: 175 in 1998. §Subjects of interest to language teachers and researchers. Ads: $280/$180/quarter pg $100. National Federation of Modern Language Teachers Associations.

MODERN LANGUAGE QUARTERLY: A Journal of Literary History, Duke University Press, Marshall Brown, Box 90660, Duke University, Durham, NC 27708-0660, E-mail amylee@acpub.duke.edu. 1940. Criticism, reviews, non-fiction. "No unsolicited reviews. The new focus of *MLQ* is on change, both in literary practice and within the profession of literature itself. *MLQ* is open to papers on literary change from the Middle Ages to the present and welcomes theoretical reflections on the relationship of literary change or historicism to feminism, ethnic studies, cultural materialism, discourse analysis, and all other forms of representation and cultural critique. Seeing texts as the depictions, agents, and vehicles of change, *MLQ* targets literature as a commanding and vital force. Send review copies to Marshall Brown, *Modern Language Quarterly*, Dept. of English, GN-30 Padelford Hall, Univ. of Washington, Seattle, WA 98195." circ. 1.6M. 4/yr. Pub'd 4 issues 1998; expects 4 issues 1999, 4 issues 2000. sub. price: $28 individual, $64 institution, add $12 for foreign; per copy: $10 domestic, $16 institution, $13 foreign, $19 foreign institutions; sample: free. 150pp; 6×9¼; of. Reporting time: 1-3 months. Payment: none. Copyrighted, does not revert to author. Pub's reviews: 20 in 1998. §Only literary criticism. Ads: $250/$175.

Modern Learning Press/Programs for Education, Robert Low, Managing Editor, PO Box 167, Rosemont, NJ 08556. 1965. avg. press run 4M. Pub'd 10 titles 1998. 30 titles listed in the *Small Press Record of Books in Print* (28th Edition, 1999-00). avg. price, paper: $9.95. of. Payment: semi-annual. Copyright for author if required.

MODERN LOGIC: An International Journal for the History of Mathematical Logic, Set Theory, and Foundations of Mathematics, Modern Logic Publishing, Irving H. Anellis, 2408-1/2 Lincoln Way (Upper Level), Ames, IA 50014-7217, 515-292-1819; e-Mail FI.MLP@ISUMVS.IASTATE.EDU. 1990. Non-fiction. "Specializes in 19th and 20th century history of mathematical logic and expository surveys of current research in mathematical logic." circ. 110. 4/yr. Pub'd 4 issues 1998; expects 4 issues 1999, 4 issues 2000. 1 title listed in the *Small Press Record of Books in Print* (28th Edition, 1999-00). sub. price: $40 individuals, $110 libraries, institutions beginning 1996; per copy: $20 + s/h; sample: free for one copy, $20 each additional. Back issues: 10% discount after 2 years, 20% after 3. Discounts: 0-20% subscription service agencies on 2+ copies per order. 110pp; 8½×11, 6×9 (Jan. '95); of. Reporting time: 3-6 months. Simultaneous submissions accepted: no. Publishes 80% of manuscripts submitted. Payment: none. Copyrighted, does not revert to author. Pub's reviews:

15 in 1998. §Mathematics, philosophy, computers, calculators. Ads: $50/$35/25¢ per word.

Modern Logic Publishing (see also MODERN LOGIC: An International Journal for the History of Mathematical Logic, Set Theory, and Foundations of Mathematics), Irving H. Anellis, 2408-1/2 Lincoln Way (Upper Level), Ames, IA 50014-7217, 515-292-1819; e-Mail FI.MLP@ISUMVS.IASTATE.EDU. 1990. Non-fiction. "MLP Books - specializing in history and philosophy of mathematics, history and philosophy of logic." avg. press run 150. Expects 4 titles 1999, 4 titles 2000. avg. price, cloth: $59.95; paper: $39.95. Discounts: 5-10%. 250pp; 6×9; of. Reporting time: average 6 months. Simultaneous submissions accepted: no. Publishes 50% of manuscripts submitted. Payment: 10%. Copyrights for author.

MOKSHA JOURNAL, Vajra Printing an Publishing of Yoga Anand Ashram, Yogi Ananda Satyam, Editor; Rocco Lobosco, Editor, 49 Forrest Place, Amityville, NY 11701, 516-691-8475; fax 516-691-8475. 1984. Poetry, non-fiction. "The editorial committee welcomes articles, pertaining to the *concept* of Moksha, defined by Monier-Williams as 'liberation, release' (A Sanskrit-English Dictionary, 1899). The paths to moksha are myriad, and it is hoped that this journal will reflect a multiplicity of perspectives, including works pertaining to Yoga, various schools of Buddhism, Sufism, Mystical Christianity, etc." circ. 300-500. 2/yr. Pub'd 2 issues 1998; expects 2 issues 1999, 2 issues 2000. sub. price: $8; per copy: $4; sample: $4. 60-80pp; 5¼×8¼; †of. Reporting time: 10 weeks. Simultaneous submissions accepted: yes. Publishes 15% of manuscripts submitted. Payment: 2 issues for articles and essays. Copyrighted, does not revert to author. No ads.

Moksha Press (see also WHAT IS ENLIGHTENMENT?), Andrew Cohen, PO Box 2360, Lenox, MA 01240, 413-637-6000; FAX 415-637-6015; E-mail moksha@moksha.org. 1989. Photos, non-fiction. avg. press run 10M. Pub'd 1 title 1998; expects 3 titles 1999, 2 titles 2000. 10 titles listed in the *Small Press Record of Books in Print* (28th Edition, 1999-00). avg. price, paper: $10.95. Discounts: 40%. 130pp; 6×9. Payment: none. Copyrighting for author depends. PMA, Independent Press Association.

MOM GUESS WHAT NEWSPAPER, Linda D. Birner, 1725 L Street, Sacramento, CA 95814-4023, 916-441-6397. 1978. Articles, photos, interviews, satire, criticism, reviews, letters, news items. circ. 21M. 24/yr. Pub'd 24 issues 1998; expects 24 issues 1999, 24 issues 2000. sub. price: $30; per copy: $1; sample: $1. Back issues: $1. Discounts: 5-15%. 24pp; 10¼×16; of. Reporting time: 1 week. Simultaneous submissions accepted: no. Publishes 10% of manuscripts submitted. Payment: mostly volunteer, depends on article. Copyrighted. Pub's reviews: 26 in 1998. §Politics, gay & human rights. Ads: $700/$350/50¢ a word/$10 col. inch. SPC.

Momentum Books, Ltd., 6964 Crooks Road, Suite #1, Troy, MI 48098, 810-828-3666; fax 810-828-0142. 1985. Non-fiction. avg. press run 5M. Pub'd 3 titles 1998; expects 4 titles 1999, 4 titles 2000. 30 titles listed in the *Small Press Record of Books in Print* (28th Edition, 1999-00). avg. price, cloth: $22.50; paper: $10; other: $125 collector's editions. 220pp; 6×9; of. Reporting time: varies. Simultaneous submissions accepted: yes. Publishes 5% of manuscripts submitted. Payment: by contract. Copyrights for author. PMA, SPAN.

MOMMY AND I ARE ONE, Jessica Hundley, Dave Stacey, PO Box 643, Allston, MA 02134, 617-254-9577. 1994. Fiction, articles, art, photos, cartoons, interviews, satire, criticism, reviews, music, letters, non-fiction. "Outside of the mainstream" circ. 2.5M. 2/yr. Pub'd 3 issues 1998. sub. price: $12/4 issues plus postage; per copy: $3 plus postage; sample: $3. Back issues: $5/$10. 70pp; 8½×11. Reporting time: 2 months. Simultaneous submissions accepted: yes. Publishes 20% of manuscripts submitted. Payment: none yet. Copyrighted, reverts to author. Ads: $300/$150/$75 1/4 page.

MONADNOCK GAY MEN, Kenneth E. DeVoid, Jr., PO Box 1124, Keene, NH 03431, 603-357-5544. 1982. Articles, art, photos, cartoons, criticism, reviews, letters, news items, non-fiction. "A monthly newsletter format which carries news of the Gay Community in the tri-state area of NH, VT and MA." circ. 250. 12/yr. Pub'd 12 issues 1998; expects 12 issues 1999, 12 issues 2000. sub. price: $12; per copy: $1; sample: $1. Back issues: $1. 4pp; 8×11. Reporting time: 1 month. Payment: none. Not copyrighted. Pub's reviews: 4 in 1998. §Gay issues. Ads: $50/$25/$10 business card.

MONEY LINES, Lifetime Books, Inc., Donald L. Lessne, 2131 Hollywood Boulevard, Hollywood, FL 33020, 925-5242. 1943. Non-fiction. circ. 55M. 4/yr. Pub'd 4 issues 1998; expects 4 issues 1999, 4 issues 2000. sub. price: $19.80; per copy: $4.95; sample: $4.95. Back issues: $4.95. Discounts: 5-25 45%, 25+ 47%. 128pp; 5-3/16×7⅞; of. Reporting time: 2 months. Payment: $1,000. Copyrighted, does not revert to author. ACIDA, PACINWA.

MONEYMAKING NEWSLETTER, Reyes Investment Enterprise Ltd., A. Pencos Reyes, PO Box 3418, Maraval, Trinidad & Tobago, 809-657-3657; 809-638-3756. 1988. Non-fiction. "We are looking for material on moneymaking ideas." circ. 5M. 12/yr. Pub'd 6 issues 1998; expects 12 issues 1999, 12 issues 2000. sub. price: $60; sample: $6. 18pp; 8×11; †of. Reporting time: 1-3 months. Payment: $30-$50. Copyrighted, reverts to author. Pub's reviews: 3 in 1998. §Moneymaking and self-help. Ads: $100/$60.

Monitor Publications AR, Michael Brooks, Senior Editor, 3856 Highway 88 East, Mena, AR 71953,

501-394-7893; Internet: 74353.2767@compuserve.com. 1994. Cartoons, satire, non-fiction. "Imprints: Razorbooks U.S.A.; Monitor Publications; YFB Books; Dip Chip Press. Interests are timely topical humor (political, entertainment satire), popular reference (travel, entertaiment), hobbies, sports, transportation, futures & forecasts. Recent title: *The Reader's Guide to Unavailable Literature* (satire)" avg. press run 1.5M. Pub'd 1 title 1998; expects 1 title 1999, 1 title 2000. 2 titles listed in the *Small Press Record of Books in Print* (28th Edition, 1999-00). avg. price, cloth: $95; paper: $7.50; other: $50. Discounts: buyers write for latest terms and discounts (san 298-3125). 350pp; 8½×11; of. Reporting time: 4 months; SASE or no reply. Simultaneous submissions accepted if so advised with SASE. Publishes 5% of manuscripts submitted. Payment: variable. Does not copyright for author.

Monographics Press, Susan Carol Hauser, Route 1, Box 81, Puposky, MN 56667, 218-243-2402. 1984. Poetry, articles, art, satire, criticism, letters. "Formerly Rasberry Press; 1972-84. No unsolicited submissions-return of unsolicited mss. immediately. Focus of each issue determined by whim of editor. R.P. 3 is poetry by Rich Behm. Work by: Carol Heckman, Beth Copeland, Tina Matthews, Judith Dunaway. R.P. 4/5 - a double issue, anthology format. R.P. 6 Dec, 1980, 10pp. Raspberry #7, December 1981, 8pp. $2.00 #8, Fall 1982 'Chickadee Issue', $2.00 Back issues of RP #3, 3, & 7 still available...$2 each; Mimeo Magic, 68 pp. How-To Book, 1984, $3.95. 1990 *Pictures From A Visit*, 16 pp, poetry, $5. 1991, "A Kiss," poetry broadside, $2. 1995 Tower View; poetry broadside, $3" avg. press run 100. Pub'd 1 title 1998; expects 1 title 1999, 1 title 2000. avg. price, paper: $5. Discounts: none. 50pp; size varies; †mi. Reporting time: 1 week. Payment: copy. Copyrights for author.

MONOZINE, Todd L., PO Box 598, Reisterstown, MD 21136. 1994. Articles, art, photos, cartoons, letters, news items, non-fiction. "Looking for stories describing the worst illness or injury writer has ever experienced...written very openly and graphically. Stories no longer than 5 typed pages. The grosser and funnier, the better! Will consider *all* submissions, including artwork." circ. 1000. 2/yr. Pub'd 1 issue 1998; expects 2 issues 1999, 3 issues 2000. sub. price: no subs; per copy: $2 + $1 shipping; sample: same. Back issues: $1 + $1 shipping. Discounts: Selective trades and consign issues to retail/distributors. 40pp; 8½×11; photocopy issue $5-offset. Reporting time: exact deadlines given upon inquiry. Simultaneous submissions accepted: yes. Publishes 90% of manuscripts submitted. Payment: none except free copies of mag. Copyrighted, reverts to author. Ads: given free to those who distribute and contribute.

Monroe Press, Dorothy Towvim, 362 Maryville Avenue, Ventura, CA 93003-1912. 1985. Non-fiction. "Manuscripts relating to family issues, parenting, communication, relationships, adolescents and children. Recent contribution: *Why Do Kids Need Feelings? - A Guide to Healty Emotions*, by Dr. Monte Elchoness." avg. press run 5M. Expects 2 titles 2000. 6 titles listed in the *Small Press Record of Books in Print* (28th Edition, 1999-00). avg. price, paper: $10.95. Discounts: available upon request. 200pp; 5½×8½; of. Reporting time: 4 weeks. Payment: industry standard. Copyrights for author. Publishers Marketing Association (PMA).

Montfort Publications (see also QUEEN OF ALL HEARTS), Patrick J Gaffney, 26 South Saxon Avenue, Bay Shore, NY 11706, 516-665-0726; FAX 516-665-4349. 1947. avg. press run 5M. Pub'd 1 title 1998; expects 1 title 1999, 1 title 2000. 1 title listed in the *Small Press Record of Books in Print* (28th Edition, 1999-00). Does not copyright for author. Catholic Press Association.

THE MONTHLY (formerly THE BERKELEY MONTHLY), Karen Klaber, Publisher; Tim Devaney, Editor, 1301 59th Street, Emeryville, CA 94608, 415-848-7900. 1970. Fiction, articles, art, photos, cartoons, interviews, satire, criticism, reviews, music, letters, parts-of-novels, long-poems, non-fiction. "Since 1970, *The Monthly* has established a reputation for its outstanding graphics and design, and for the literary quality of its editorial content. We publish first-rate interviews, investigative journalism, and opinionated arts and cultural essays. We do not publish fiction or poetry." circ. 65M. 12/yr. Pub'd 12 issues 1998; expects 12 issues 1999, 12 issues 2000. sub. price: $10; per copy: $1; sample: $1 if available, with SASE (needs 50¢ postage for 2nd class). Back issues: query. Discounts: query. 40-52pp; 11½×15; desktop. Reporting time: as soon as possible. Payment: nonfiction $100-$400, photos and art work negotiated on sliding scale. Copyrighted, *The Monthly* buys only first publication rights, and option to anthologize. Pub's reviews: 8 in 1998. §We consider all subjects and prefer a Bay Area connection. Ads: query.

THE MONTHLY INDEPENDENT TRIBUNE TIMES JOURNAL POST GAZETTE NEWS CHRONICLE BULLETIN, T.S. Child, Editor; Denver Tucson, Assistant Editor, 80 Fairlawn Drive, Berkeley, CA 94708-2106. 1983. Fiction, art, cartoons, satire, collages, non-fiction. "Due to our small size, the absolute maximum for any written piece is 1,200 words; the shorter the better. What we want is humor. No limitations as to form or topic. Send us things that will make us call an ambulance. Cartoons and drawings also welcome, but please no smarmy poetry. We will respond within a month." circ. 500. 1/yr. Pub'd 1 issue 1998; expects 1 issue 1999, 1 issue 2000. sub. price: $6; per copy: 50¢ (or 2 first class stamps); sample: same. Back issues: same. Discounts: will trade issues with any magazine. 8pp; 5½×8; of. Reporting time: 1-4 weeks. Payment: 3 contributors copies. Not copyrighted. Ads: $60/$30.

MOODY STREET IRREGULARS: A Jack Kerouac Magazine, Moody Street Irregulars, Inc., Joy Walsh, Tim Madigan, Lisa Jarnat, 32 S. Forest Beach Drive #31, Hilton Head Island, SC 29928-7005. 1977. Poetry, articles, art, photos, cartoons, interviews, criticism, reviews, music, letters, plays, news items. *"Moody Street Irregulars* is a Kerouac newsletter. We are looking for material on Kerouac and other Beat writers. The magazine will always retain the spirit of Jack Kerouac. Recent contributors: George Dardess, Joy Walsh, Ted Joans, John Clellon Holmes, Tetsuo Nakagami, Gerld Nicosia, Dennis McNally, Janet Kerouac, Jack Kerouac, George Montgomery, Bill Gargan, Ben Walters.'' circ. 500-1M. 2-3/yr. Pub'd 2 issues 1998; expects 3 issues 1999. sub. price: $10; per copy: $5; sample: $5. Back issues: $5. Discounts: 40% to bookstores. 50pp; 8½x11; of. Reporting time: 1-3 months. Payment: copies. Copyrighted, reverts to author. Pub's reviews: 3-9 in 1998. §Books on Kerouac and the Beats. Will accept contributions. Inquire as to ads; we now accept them. NEW.

Moody Street Irregulars, Inc. (see also MOODY STREET IRREGULARS: A Jack Kerouac Magazine), Joy Walsh, Tim Madigan, Lisa Jarnat, 32 S. Forest Beach Drive #31, Hilton Head Island, SC 29928-7005. 1977. Poetry, articles, art, photos, cartoons, interviews, criticism, reviews, music, letters, plays, news items. "Moody Street Irregulars will print poetry, and material pertaining to Kerouac and the Beats." avg. press run 1M-2.5M. Pub'd 2 titles 1998; expects 3 titles 1999. 2 titles listed in the *Small Press Record of Books in Print* (28th Edition, 1999-00). avg. price, paper: $5; other: $10 per year, $15 libraries. Discounts: 40% to bookstores. 50pp; 8½x11; of. Reporting time: 1-3 months. Payment: copies. Copyrights for author. NEW, Hallwalk, Jack Kerouac Club in Quebec, Alpha Beat Press in Montreal.

Moon Lake Media, PO Box 251466, Los Angeles, CA 90025, 310-535-2453. 1994. Pub'd 2 titles 1998; expects 2 titles 1999, 2 titles 2000. 4 titles listed in the *Small Press Record of Books in Print* (28th Edition, 1999-00). 250pp. PMA, RMBPA.

Moon Publications, Inc., Karen Bleske, Editorial Director, 101 Salem Street, Suite 6, Chico, CA 95928, 530-345-0282; FAX 530-345-0284; e-mail travel@moon.com Web: www.moon.com. 1973. Art, photos, criticism, letters. "Moon is now part of Avalon Publishing. Query first. Moon Publications specializes in travel handbooks for independent travelers. Each guide contains an informative introduction to the history and culture of the region, up-to-date travel information, clear and concise maps, color and black and white photographs, and a comprehensive subject/place-name index. All Moon guides are tradepaper 5X7 inches with a smyth-sewn binding. The geographic regions we are interested in are: Asia and the Pacific, North, Central and South America, Mexico and the Caribbean'' avg. press run 12M-20M. Pub'd 24 titles 1998; expects 24 titles 1999, 24 titles 2000. 73 titles listed in the *Small Press Record of Books in Print* (28th Edition, 1999-00). avg. price, paper: $15.95. Discounts: trade 40%, wholesalers 50%, libraries 20%, bulk 55%. 500pp; 5⅛x7⅜; desktop. Payment: 10-12% of publishers net invoice. Copyrights for author. ABA, Association of Travel Marketing.

Moonbeam Publications, Inc., 836 Hastings Street, Traverse City, MI 49684-3441, 616-922-0533. 1986. Non-fiction. "Moonbeam Publications publishes and distributes reference books and videos to the library and educational markets." 4 titles listed in the *Small Press Record of Books in Print* (28th Edition, 1999-00). Discounts: jobber 10% on most titles.

MoonFall Press, Silvia Cinca, George Simon, 7845 Glenister Drive, Springfield, VA 22152, 703-912-9774, Fax 703-866-9207, email gcinca@bellatlontic.net; silviacinca@yahoo.com. 1985. Poetry, fiction, non-fiction. avg. press run 500-1000. Pub'd 2 titles 1998; expects 3 titles 1999, 3 titles 2000. 17 titles listed in the *Small Press Record of Books in Print* (28th Edition, 1999-00). avg. price, paper: $9.99; other: $12.99-$14.99. Discounts: 20-50%. 200-300pp; 5½x8½; of. Reporting time: 1 year. Simultaneous submissions accepted: yes. Payment: very variate. Copyrights for author. PMA.

MOONRABBIT REVIEW, Jackie Lee, 2525 Arapahoe Avenue, Ste. E4-230, Boulder, CO 80302, 303-439-8860; Fax 439-8362; JHLee@ucsub.Colorado.edu. 1994. Poetry, fiction, art, photos, reviews, non-fiction. "*MoonRabbit Review* is a quality literary journal of Asian Pacific American voices." circ. 2M. 2/yr. Pub'd 1 issue 1998; expects 2 issues 1999, 2 issues 2000. sub. price: $17; per copy: $10; sample: $7. Back issues: $10. Discounts: 40% distributors and wholesalers. 144pp; 6x9; of. Reporting time: 2 months. Simultaneous submissions accepted: yes. Publishes 7% of manuscripts submitted. Payment: 3 copies of journal. Copyrighted, reverts to author. Pub's reviews: 2 in 1998. §Asian American fiction, nonfiction, poetry. Ads: $100/$50/$25 1/4 page. CLMP.

MOOSE BOUND PRESS JOURNAL/NEWSLETTER, Sonia Walker, Editor; Robert L. Walker, Publisher, PO Box 111781, Anchorage, AK 99511-1781, 907-333-1465 phone/FAX e-mail mbpress@alaska.net; Website http://www.alaska.net/~mbpress. 1995. Poetry, fiction, articles, art, photos, cartoons, parts-of-novels, non-fiction. "Short stories up to 2,000 words, poems up to 30 lines, essays up to 500 words. Recent contributors: Lyn Lifshin, Marian Ford Park, Michael Lizza. We accept wholesome, uplifting and energetic writing—something the entire family can enjoy." circ. 350. 4/yr. Pub'd 4 issues 1998; expects 4 issues 1999, 4 issues 2000. sub. price: $24; per copy: $8; sample: $3. 100pp; 8½x11; †high speed printing. Reporting time: 3-6 months. Simultaneous submissions accepted: yes. Publishes 80% of manuscripts submitted. Payment: none, "publication is payment" Copyrighted, reverts to author. Ads: none.

More To Life Publishing, Kim Michaels, Lorraine Michaels, 358 N. 600 E, Hyrum, UT 84319-1142. 1992. Fiction, non-fiction. avg. press run 1.5M. Expects 1 title 2000. 2 titles listed in the *Small Press Record of Books in Print* (28th Edition, 1999-00). avg. price, paper: $11. 200pp; 5½×8½; of.

Morgan-Rand Publishing, S. Phillips, Taia Butterworth, Maritza Dunn, 1 Sentry Parkway #1000, Blue Bell, PA 19422, 215-938-5511, Fax; 215-938-5549. 1982. Non-fiction. "We are interested in reviewing manuscripts on subjects dealing with directory publishing. We are also directory publishers." avg. press run 2.5M. Pub'd 3 titles 1998; expects 5 titles 1999, 5+ titles 2000. 3 titles listed in the *Small Press Record of Books in Print* (28th Edition, 1999-00). avg. price, paper: $50+. Discounts: 40%. 350pp; 6×9, 8½×11; of. Reporting time: varies, every effort made to be prompt. Payment: negotiable. Copyrights for author. IIA, NDPA, DMA.

Morning Glory Press (see also **PPT EXPRESS**), Jeanne Lindsay, Editor, 6595 San Haroldo Way, Buena Park, CA 90620. 1977. avg. press run 10M. Pub'd 4 titles 1998; expects 5 titles 1999, 4 titles 2000. 24 titles listed in the *Small Press Record of Books in Print* (28th Edition, 1999-00). avg. price, cloth: $15.95; paper: $9.95. Discounts: 1-5 books 20%, 6-25 40%, 26-100 45%, 101-200 48%, 201+ 50%. 192pp; 5½×8½; Camera-ready with Macintosh and lazer printer. Reporting time: 2 months. Simultaneous submissions accepted: yes. Publishes 3% of manuscripts submitted. Payment: 10% royalty; $500-$1000 advance. Copyrights for author. PMA.

MORNINGSTAR, Don Phillips, 225 West Wacker Drive, Chicago, IL 60606-1224, 312-696-6000. 1986. Non-fiction. 26/yr. Pub'd 26 issues 1998; expects 26 issues 1999, 26 issues 2000. sub. price: $395; per copy: $55/3 month trial. Discounts: 2 yr subscription $745, 3 yrs $985. 144pp + summary section (40pp); 8½×11; of. Copyrighted. Ads: none.

Morris Publishing, 3212 E. Hwy 30, Kearney, NE 68847, 800-650-7888. 1 title listed in the *Small Press Record of Books in Print* (28th Edition, 1999-00). 5½×8½ or 8½×11; †of. Simultaneous submissions accepted: yes. Copyrights for author.

Mortal Press, Terry James Mohaupt, 2315 North Alpine Road, Rockford, IL 61107-1422, 815-399-8432. 1975. Poetry, fiction, art, parts-of-novels, long-poems. avg. press run 250. Expects 1 title 2000. 2 titles listed in the *Small Press Record of Books in Print* (28th Edition, 1999-00). avg. price, cloth: $15; paper: $10. Discounts: 10/20/40. 80pp; 5½×8½; photo offset. Reporting time: 3-6 months, sometimes up to 1 year. Simultaneous submissions accepted: yes. Payment: negotiable. Copyrights for author.

Mosaic Press, Miriam Owen Irwin, 358 Oliver Road, Dept. 45, Cincinnati, OH 45215, 513-761-5977. 1977. Fiction, satire. "We publish fine, hard-bound miniature books on any subject we find fascinating. We also publish a $3.00 miniature book catalog." avg. press run 2M. Pub'd 2 titles 1998; expects 1 title 1999. 53 titles listed in the *Small Press Record of Books in Print* (28th Edition, 1999-00). avg. price, cloth: $28. 48pp; 3/4×1; of, traditional bindings. Reporting time: 2 weeks. Simultaneous submissions accepted: yes. Publishes less than 1% of manuscripts submitted. Payment: $50 and 5 copies of book. Copyrights for author. Miniature Book Society.

Mother Courage Press, Barbara Lindquist, Jeanne Arnold, 1533 Illinois St., Racine, WI 53405-3115, 414-634-1047; FAX: 414-637-8242. 1981. Non-fiction. "Books that are therapeutic, life preserving or enhancing from a feminist perspective. Two of our books, *Something Happened to Me* and *Why Me* are for victims of child sexual abuse. Interested in non-fiction books for adults on difficult subjects such as women's spirituality. Not accepting ms. at present." avg. press run 2M-5M. Pub'd 4 titles 1998; expects 2 titles 1999, 2 titles 2000. 20 titles listed in the *Small Press Record of Books in Print* (28th Edition, 1999-00). avg. price, cloth: $19.95; paper: $9.95. Discounts: bookstores 1-4 copies 20%, 5+ 40%; distributors 50% 10 or more. 189pp; 8½×11, 5½×8½; of. Simultaneous submissions accepted: yes.

MOTHER EARTH JOURNAL: An International Quarterly, Uniting the World Press, Inc., Herman Berlandt, Editor, Publisher; Maureen Hurley, Co-Editor, c/o National Poetry Association, 934 Brannan Street, 2nd Floor, San Francisco, CA 94103, 415-552-9261; fax 415-552-9271. 1990. Poetry. "*Mother Earth* is an international journal presenting the poet's perspective on the current political and ecological global crisis. Here poetry from six continents is represented in fine English translations. 'Let the voice of the poet be heard throughout the world' is our slogan. Among our contributors are Robert Bly, Gary Snyder, Anabel Torres, Marianne Larsen, Seamus Heaney, Miroslav Holub, Kofi Awoonor, Wole Soyinka, Bei Dao, Mahmoud Darwish, Lawrence Ferlinghetti, etc." circ. 1450. 4/yr. Pub'd 4 issues 1998; expects 3 issues 1999, 4 issues 2000. sub. price: $18; per copy: $5; sample: $3. Back issues: $3.50 each. Discounts: 50%. 40pp; 11×15; of. Reporting time: 3 months. Simultaneous submissions accepted: yes. Publishes 15% of manuscripts submitted. Payment: 2 copies. Not copyrighted. Ads: $300/$175/$100 1/4 page. Uniting the World Press.

THE MOTHER IS ME: Profiling the Cultural Aspects of Motherhood, Amy Condra-Peters, 3010 Woodlawn Avenue, Falls Church, VA 22042, 603-743-6828; E-mail zoey455@aol.com. 1996. Poetry, fiction, articles, art, photos, cartoons, interviews, satire, reviews, letters, news items, non-fiction. "Not just another parenting magazine, *The Mother Is Me* is filled with the real-life joys and frustrations of motherhood, told with honesty and affection in a no-holds barred style. Progressive, feminist slant." circ. 3M. 4/yr. Pub'd 3 issues 1998; expects 4 issues 1999, 4 issues 2000. sub. price: $15.95; per copy: $4.95; sample: $4. Back issues: $4. Discounts: bulk - 5 or more, $2.95/issue. 36pp; 8½x11; of. Reporting time: 2 months approx. Simultaneous submissions accepted: yes. Publishes 40% of manuscripts submitted. Payment: $10-15/essay, as well as one-year subscription. Copyrighted, reverts to author. Pub's reviews: 10 in 1998. §Parenting, feminism, children's literature. Ads: $495/$250. IPA.

Mother Lode Books, 7378 W. Atlantic Blvd. Box 228, Margate, FL 33063, 954-722-0624; books@aircadiz.net. 1 title listed in the *Small Press Record of Books in Print* (28th Edition, 1999-00).

MOTHERTONGUE, Sherry Roane Ellis, PO Box 640, Candler, NC 28715, 704-665-4572. 1993. Poetry, articles, art, photos, cartoons, interviews, reviews, letters, non-fiction. "Length: up to 2,000 words, will possible consider longer. Biases: progressive, 'natural' parenting ideas—gentle, peace-loving ways of interacting. Essays on family living; humor." circ. 7M-8M. 4/yr. Pub'd 4 issues 1998; expects 4 issues 1999, 4 issues 2000. sub. price: $8.48; per copy: $2; sample: $2. Back issues: $2 each. 36pp; of. Reporting time: 3 months. Simultaneous submissions accepted: yes. Publishes 75% of manuscripts submitted. Payment: copies and often $5-$10 depending on finances; do not pay cash usually for poetry. Copyrighted, reverts to author. Pub's reviews: 8 in 1998. §Progressive parenting, natural childbirth, breastfeeding, family-related, progressive education. Ads: $650/$330/$165 1/4 page/$85 1/8 page/$40 business cards/classifieds available.

MOTOR CONTROL, Human Kinetics Pub. Inc., Mark Latash, P. O. Box 5076, Champaign, IL 61825-5076, 217-351-5076. 1997. Articles, reviews. "Study of motor control and motor disorders." 4/yr. Expects 4 issues 1999, 4 issues 2000. sub. price: $40 individual, $90 institution, $24 student; per copy: $11 ind., $24 inst.; sample: free. Back issues: $11 ind., $24 inst. Discounts: 5% agency. 104pp; 6x9; of. Reporting time: 2 months. Payment: none. Copyrighted, does not revert to author. Pub's reviews. Ads: $300/$200. Midwest Publishers Assn., American Booksellers Assn.

MOTORBOOTY MAGAZINE, Mark Dancey, PO Box 02007, Detroit, MI 48202. 1987. Fiction, articles, art, photos, cartoons, interviews, satire, criticism, reviews, music, parts-of-novels, non-fiction. "This magazine promises 'attitude with an attitude'." circ. 15M. Sporadic. Pub'd 1 issue 1998; expects 2 issues 1999, 3 issues 2000. sub. price: $16; per copy: $6; sample: $6. Back issues: $4. Discounts: trade with other publishers. 100pp; 8½x11. Copyrighted, reverts to author. Pub's reviews. §Satire, comics, music. Ads: $400/$200.

Mount Ida Press, Diana S. Waite, 152 Washington Avenue, Albany, NY 12210-2203, 518-426-5935. 1984. Non-fiction. avg. press run 1.5M-2M. Pub'd 1 title 1998; expects 2 titles 1999, 2 titles 2000. avg. price, paper: $25. Discounts: 40% trade. 144pp; 8½x11; of. Reporting time: 2 months. Payment: royalty. Copyrights for author.

Mount Olive College Press (see also MOUNT OLIVE REVIEW), Pepper Worthington, Editor, Mount Olive College, 634 Henderson Street, Mount Olive, NC 28365. 1990. "The Mount Olive College Press accepts letters of inquiry year-round. If the Press is interested, the editor will request a complete manuscript." avg. press run 500-800. Pub'd 5-7 titles 1998; expects 5-7 titles 1999, 5-7 titles 2000. avg. price, paper: $10-14.95. Poetry 70-110pp, others 30-210pp. Reporting time: 6 months to 1 year. Simultaneous submissions accepted: no. Publishes 5% of manuscripts submitted. Payment: negotiated. Copyrights for author. NCLMP, CELJ, CLMP.

MOUNT OLIVE REVIEW, Mount Olive College Press, Pepper Worthington, Editor, Department of Language and Literature, 634 Henderson Street, Mount Olive, NC 28365, 919-658-2502. 1987. Poetry, art, reviews, non-fiction. "Future themes include topics of travel, film, and metaphor in literature as well as a focus on North Carolina writers and major American writers. Recent contributors: Janet Lembke, Joseph Bathanti, Gladys Owings Hughes, James L. Abrahamson. Length of literary criticism as it relates to theme 1M-6M words. MLA style appropriate. Length of creative genres flexible." 1/yr. sub. price: $25; per copy: $25; sample: $25. 394pp; 8x11. Reporting time: varies, 6-10 months. Simultaneous submissions accepted: no. Publishes 20% of manuscripts submitted. Payment: none. Copyrighted, reverts to author. Pub's reviews. §Interviews, essays. MLA International Biography, NCLMP, CELJ.

THE MOUNTAIN ASTROLOGER, Tem Tarriktar, PO Box 970, Cedar Ridge, CA 95924-0970, 530-477-8839. 1988. Poetry, articles, art, photos, cartoons, interviews, satire, reviews, letters, news items. "Any length; must be related to astrology. Send SASE for return of materials" circ. print run 19M. 6/yr. Pub'd 6 issues 1998; expects 6 issues 1999, 6 issues 2000. sub. price: $32.95 bulk rate, $40.95 1st class/Canada, $56 Europe Air Mail; per copy: $6 postpaid in U.S./Canada; sample: $6 postpaid in U.S./Canada. Back issues: $6 postpaid in U.S./Canada. Discounts: available through distributors; write for a list of distributors. 132pp; 8½x11; webb press. Reporting time: varies. Simultaneous submissions accepted: no. Publishes 30% of manuscripts submitted. Copyrighted, reverts to author. Pub's reviews: 30 in 1998. Ads: $650/$345/subject to change.

Mountain Automation Corporation, Claude Wiatrowski, PO Box 6020, Woodland Park, CO 80866, 719-687-6647, FAX: 719-687-2448. 1976. Art, photos, music, plays, non-fiction. "We currently publish promotional books and videos, especially tourist souvenirs for specific attractions. Orders to: PO Box 2324, Fort Collins, CO 80522. 800-487-3793, FAX 970-493-8781. Mostly videos." avg. press run 10M. Pub'd 2 titles 1998; expects 9 titles 1999, 1 title 2000. 19 titles listed in the *Small Press Record of Books in Print* (28th Edition, 1999-00). avg. price, paper: $4; other: $20 video. Discounts: 50%. 24pp; 8½×5½; of. Reporting time: 1 month. Payment: determined individually. Copyrights for author.

Mountain Meadow Press, Karen Laughy, PO Box 447, Kooskia, ID 83539. 1987. Non-fiction. "Adult nonfiction, NW history and travel; education, including home schooling." avg. press run 4M. Pub'd 2 titles 1998; expects 5 titles 1999, 3 titles 2000. 10 titles listed in the *Small Press Record of Books in Print* (28th Edition, 1999-00). avg. price, paper: $12.95. Discounts: STOP 40%, 5+ copies 42%, 50+ copies 44%, 100+ copies 46%, 400+ copies 47% freight free, saleable returns accepted with permission; nonreturnable 25+ copies 48%. 235pp; size varies.

Mountain Press Publishing Co., Rob Williams, Business Manager; John Rimel, General Manager; Jeannie Nuckolls, Production Coordinator; Dave Alt, Roadside Geology Series Editor; Don Hyndman, Roadside Geology Series Editor; Gwen McKenna, History Editor; Kathleen Ort, Editor-in-Chief; Jennifer Carey, Submissions Editor, PO Box 2399, Missoula, MT 59806, 406-728-1900. 1948 (became full time publisher in mid-70's - printing company prior to that). Non-fiction. "We publish primarily non-fiction. Besides our successful *Roadside Geology* series, we are publishing regional nature/outdoor guides such as *Birds of the Northern Rockies*. We also publish quality western history and western Americana. In addition, we have recently begun to reprint the works of Will James, a popular western writer and illustrator in the 1920s and 1930s best known for *Smokey the Cowhorse*, which won a Newberry Award in 1927." avg. press run 5M. Pub'd 12 titles 1998; expects 12 titles 1999, 12 titles 2000. 105 titles listed in the *Small Press Record of Books in Print* (28th Edition, 1999-00). avg. price, cloth: $30; paper: $15. Discounts: bookstores 2-14 copies 40%, $3 shipping, 15+ 45% free freight. 150-360pp; 6×9, 5×7, 8½×11; of. Reporting time: 2-6 months. Payment: twice a year; royalty of 10-12% based on the amount the publisher receives from sales of the book. Copyrights for author. Rocky Mountain Book Publishers Association, Publishers Marketing Association.

Mountain Publishing, PO Box 1747, Hillsboro, OR 97123, 503-628-3995; fax 503-628-0203; toll free 800-879-8719. 1989. Non-fiction. "Street address: 16175 S.W. Holly Hill Road. Manuscripts: book-length dealing with business." avg. press run 5M. Pub'd 1 title 1998; expects 2 titles 1999, 1 title 2000. 1 title listed in the *Small Press Record of Books in Print* (28th Edition, 1999-00). avg. price, paper: $29.95. Discounts: 2-5 copies 20%, 6-10 30%, 11-25 40%, 26-74 45%, 75+ 55%. 304pp; 6×9; of. Reporting time: 60 days. Publishes 2% of manuscripts submitted. Payment: negotiable. Copyrights for author.

MOUNTAIN RESEARCH & DEVELOPMENT, University of California Press, Jack D. Ives, University of California Press, 2120 Berkeley Way, Berkeley, CA 94720, 510-643-7154. "Editorial address: Jack D. Ives, 412 Thessaly Circle, Ottawa, K1H 5W5 Canada. Copyrighted by International Mountain Society." circ. 900. 4/yr. Pub'd 4 issues 1998; expects 4 issues 1999, 4 issues 2000. sub. price: $42 indiv., $112 instit., $24 students (+ $7 foreign postage); per copy: $12 indiv., $28 instit., $12 students (+ $7 foreign postage); sample: free. Discounts: foreign subs. agent 10%, one-time orders 10+ 30%, standing orders (bookstores) 1-99 40%, 100+ 50%. 88pp; 8½×11; of. Ads: $275/$200.

Mountain State Press, c/o University of Charleston, 2300 MacCorkle Avenue SE, Charleston, WV 25304-1099, 304-357-4767. 1978. Poetry, fiction, satire, criticism, plays. "We specialize in regional materials: Appalachian subjects and authors, primarily. We publish book-length mss. of fiction, nonfiction, and poetry." avg. press run 1.5M. Pub'd 3 titles 1998; expects 4 titles 1999, 8 titles 2000. 20 titles listed in the *Small Press Record of Books in Print* (28th Edition, 1999-00). avg. price, cloth: $20; paper: $10. Discounts: 40% to bookstores, 25% gift shops, 10% libraries, schools and churches. 250pp; 5½×8½; photo-offset. Reporting time: 2 months or more. Publishes 50% of manuscripts submitted. Payment: negotiable. Copyrights for author.

The Mountaineers Books, Art Freeman, Director; Margaret Foster, Editor in Chief, 1001 SW Klickitat Way, Suite 201, Seattle, WA 98134-1161, 206-223-6303. 1961. Non-fiction. "We have over 350 titles in print, all having to do with the outdoors - how to, where to, history, climbing, hiking, skiing, snowshoeing, bicycling, mountaineering & expeditions. Must relate to mountaineering or self-propelled, non-commercial, non-competitive outdoor activities; mountain and/or NW history; conservation of natural resources." avg. press run 3M-5M. Pub'd 30 titles 1998; expects 40 titles 1999, 40 titles 2000. 158 titles listed in the *Small Press Record of Books in Print* (28th Edition, 1999-00). avg. price, cloth: $22.95; paper: $14.95. Standard book trade discounts. 240pp; 5½×8½; of. Reporting time: 1-2 months. Simultaneous submissions accepted: yes. Publishes 5-10% of manuscripts submitted. Payment: negotiated royalties on net sales paid twice yearly. Copyrights for author. ABA, Pacific NW Book Sellers, Book Publishers NW, Rocky Mountain Book Publishers Association, N. CA Book Publicists Assn.

Mountaintop Books, Milton Forbes, PO Box 385, Glenwood, IA 51534-0385. 1989. Criticism, non-fiction. "Humanism, free thought, Biblical studies. Query only, SASE. Length 30,000-60,000 words. No poetry." avg. press run 1M-5M. Expects 1 title 2000. 2 titles listed in the *Small Press Record of Books in Print* (28th Edition, 1999-00). avg. price, cloth: $30; paper: $20. Discounts: Cost to bookstores and wholesalers is 50% of retail price plus shipping. 250pp; 6×9; of. Reporting time: 3 months. Payment: royalty 10% of retail price. Copyrights for author.

MOUTH: Voice of the Disability Nation, Lucy Gwin, PO BOX 558, Topeka, KS 66601-0558, fax 716-442-2916. 1989. Articles, photos, cartoons, interviews, letters, news items, non-fiction. "(Send SASE for publishing schedule and guidelines) Mouth speaks for 55 million Americans who are crippled up in one way or another. Mouth is known for its flaming exposes of charity's high rollers and bureaucracy's log jammers, for its consumer testing of deadening drugs and behavior modifiers, for its pride, its anger, its humor. Mouth is a crash course for Americans on the disability rights movement" circ. 5.6M. 6/yr. Pub'd 6 issues 1998; expects 6 issues 1999, 6 issues 2000. sub. price: $16-32; per copy: $3.75; sample: $1. Back issues: $5 each. Discounts: bulk: bundles of 100 $165; distributors 55%. 56pp; 8×10½; web press, newsprint. Reporting time: 21 days. Simultaneous submissions accepted: yes. Publishes 10% of manuscripts submitted. Payment: editor is unpaid, occasionally we pay $50-75 for items. Copyrighted, reverts to author. Pub's reviews: 2 in 1998. §Health care crime, euthanasia programs, disability rights. Ads: none.

MOVIE CLUB, Don Dohler, 4504 Hershey Way, Nottingham, MD 21236-2122, 410-256-5013. 1993. Articles, photos, reviews. "Most material is assigned. Writers should send query before submitting mss." circ. 10M. 4/yr. Expects 4 issues 1999. sub. price: $14; per copy: $4.50; sample: $6. Discounts: 30%. 52pp; 8⅜×10⅞; of. Reporting time: 2 weeks. Simultaneous submissions accepted: yes. Payment: 50¢/column inch. Copyrighted, rights revert to author by special arrangement. Pub's reviews. §Must be about movies or filmmaking. Ads: $200/$100/$140 2/3 page/$40 1/4 page/$60 1/3 page. FP-$250/HP-$140/QP-$80/TT-$180/OT-$100. CPDA.

Moving Parts Press, Felicia Rice, 10699 Empire Grade, Santa Cruz, CA 95060-9474, 408-427-2271. 1977. Poetry, fiction, art, letters, parts-of-novels, long-poems, collages. "*For Earthly Survival*, poems by Ellen Bass, was winner of 1980 Elliston Book Award. 1981 publication: *In the World's Common Grasses Poems of a Son, Poems of a Father* by William Pitt Root. 1992 publication: *Of Dark Love* by F.X. Alarcon, winner of 1993 Stiftung Book Design Award, Leipzig Book Fair, Germany" avg. press run 250. Pub'd 1 title 1998; expects 3 titles 1999, 2 titles 2000. 18 titles listed in the *Small Press Record of Books in Print* (28th Edition, 1999-00). avg. price, cloth: $75; paper: $25; other: $15. Discounts: 30%. 45pp; 6×9; †lp, of. Reporting time: 1-2 months. Payment: 10% copies. Copyrights for author. PCBA, Center for Book Arts, Printers' Chappel of Santa Cruz.

MSRRT NEWSLETTER: LIBRARY ALTERNATIVES, Christopher Dodge, 4645 Columbus Avenue South, Minneapolis, MN 55407, 612-694-8572; fax 612-541-8600; e-Mail cdodge@sun.hennepin.lib.mn.us. 1988. Articles, art, cartoons, interviews, reviews, letters, news items, non-fiction. "Publication of the Social Responsibilities Round Table of the Minnesota Library Association. Focus cultural and political commentary for library community with special emphasis on annotations of alternative periodicals. Also includes book/audio visual reviews and networking information." circ. 300. Irregular. Pub'd 6 issues 1998; expects 4 issues 1999, 4 issues 2000. sub. price: $15 payable MLA/MSRRT; sample: $2. 12pp; 8½×11. Payment: copy. Not copyrighted. Pub's reviews: 180 in 1998. §Peace, politics, counter-culture, libraries, human rights, arts, Native American, civil rights, feminism, Third World, global education, environment, labor, anarchist, Chicano, Black, communism, gay/lesbian, animal rights, socialist, seniors, disabled, Asian American, communications.

Mud Press (see also MISSISSIPPI MUD), Joel Weinstein, Lynn Darroch, 7119 Santa Fe Avenue, Dallas, TX 75223. 1973. Fiction, art, photos, cartoons, satire, criticism, parts-of-novels, collages, plays. "*Mala Noche* by Walt Curtis, Joel Weinstein, Editor. *Between Fire and Love, Contempry Peruvian Writing*; Lynn Darroch, Editor." avg. press run 1.5M. Expects 1 title 1999. 2 titles listed in the *Small Press Record of Books in Print* (28th Edition, 1999-00). avg. price, paper: $5. 132pp; 7×9¾; of. Copyrights for author.

MUDFISH, Box Turtle Press, Jill Hoffman, Editor; Jennifer Belle, Associate Editor; Doug Dorph, Associate Editor; Stephanie Emily Dickenson, Associate Editor; Rob Cook, Associate Editor; David Lawrence, Associate Editor; Paul Wuensche, Associate Editor; Charlotte Rindvi, Associate Editor, 184 Franklin Street, New York, NY 10013, 212-219-9278. 1983. Poetry, art, photos. circ. 1.2M. 1/yr. Pub'd 1 issue 1998; expects 1 issue 1999, 1 issue 2000. sub. price: $20 for 2 year subscription; per copy: $10 + $2.50; sample: $10 + $2.50. 200pp; 6⅞×8¼; lp. Reporting time: immediately to 2 months. Simultaneous submissions accepted: no. Publishes 5% of manuscripts submitted. Payment: 1 copy of magazine. Copyrighted, reverts to author. Ads: $250 per page/$125 per half page.

MUDLARK, William Slaughter, English Department, University of N. Florida, Jacksonville, FL 32224, 904-620-2273; Fax 904-620-3940; E-mail mudlark@unf.edu; www.unf.edu/mudlark. 1995. Poetry, interviews, criticism, long-poems. "*Mudlark* is "never in and never out of print." As our full name, *Mudlark: An*

Electronic Journal of Poetry & Poetics, suggests, we will consider accomplished work that locates itself anywhere on the spectrum of contemporary practice. We want poems, of course, but we want essays, too, that make us read poems (and write them?) differently somehow. Although we are not innocent, we do imagine ourselves capable of suprise. *Mudlark* has an ISSN (1081-3500), is refereed, copyrighted, archived and distributed free on the World Wide Web. Some recent contributors: Henry Gould, Sheila E. Murphy, Mike O'Connor, Diane Wald, and Andrew Schelling.'' circ. 500/week. Irregular but frequent. Pub'd 9 issues 1998; expects 9 issues 1999, 9 issues 2000. sub. price: free (online); per copy: free; sample: free. Back issues: free. 16-100pp; electronic. Reporting time: we answer our mail, soon. We'd prefer not to accept simultaneous submissions. Payment: In *Mudlark* poetry is free. Our authors give us their work and we, in turn, give it to our readers. What is the coin of poetry's realm? Poetry is a gift economy. One of the things we can do at *Mudlark* to pay our authors for their work is point to it here and there, wherever else it is. We can tell our readers how to find it, how to subscribe to it, and how to buy it if it is for sale. Copyrighted, reverts to author.

John Muir Publications, Inc., Cassandra Conyers, Acquisitions Editor; Dianna Delling, Senior Editor; Peg Goldstein, Editor; Krista Lyons-Gould, Editor; Sara Baldwin, Assistant Editor; Marybeth Griffen, Assistant Editor, PO Box 613, Santa Fe, NM 87504, 505-982-4078. 1969. Non-fiction. "Non-fiction. Travel and alternative health'' avg. press run 5M-10M. Expects 50 titles 1999, 65 titles 2000. avg. price, paper: $14.95 (adult); $5.95 (children's). Discounts: 25-50%. Adult 300pp, children's 64pp; 8½x11, 4½x8½, 5½x8½, 7x10, 7x9, 10¼x9. Reporting time: 3-6 months. Simultaneous submissions accepted if noted. Publishes 10% of manuscripts submitted. Payment: by individual contract. Copyrights for author. ABA, Rocky Mountain Booksellers Association, ALA.

Multi Media Arts, Jackie Mallis, Editorial Director, PO Box 141127, Austin, TX 78714-1127, 512-836-2541. 1978. "Not in the market for submissions. Our instructional kits, tapes, and books are all painstakingly designed by professional educators with extensive, practical, classroom experience. We cover a wide range of subject areas and target markets that include traditional classrooms, independent study, home-schooling, in-service training for staff development, and university programs. But there are some unifying themes: materials that have been tested and have proved successful; well-organized formats constructed upon recognized instructional models; time-saving, self-directed, self-contained units that require minimal or no preparation by the teacher or student; relevant, activity-oriented structures that actually teach specific skills based on coherent objectives and stated goals. Terms for discount schedules—FOB Austin, plus UPS shipping: Net 30 days on approved credit. No returns without advance authorization or after 30 days from purchase. Refund for purchase price only for returns that arrive back in new, saleable condition.'' avg. press run 500-1M. Pub'd 4 titles 1998; expects 7 titles 1999, 12 titles 2000. 37 titles listed in the *Small Press Record of Books in Print* (28th Edition, 1999-00). avg. price, paper: $15-$30. Discounts: standard to qualified dealers and distributors; quantity to bookstores and wholesalers 1-9 20%, 10-49 30%, 50-99 40%, 100-249 42%, 250-499 44%, 500-999 46%, 1000-2499 48%, 2500+ 50%. 100-450pp; 8½x11, 5½x8½; of. Simultaneous submissions accepted: no. Payment: We sometimes use freelance writers with whom we have worked on other projects and offer one-time payment. Copyrights for author.

MULTICULTURAL EDUCATION, Caddo Gap Press, Alan H. Jones, Editor, 3145 Geary Boulevard, Ste. 275, San Francisco, CA 94118, 415-922-1911. 1993. Articles, art, photos, interviews, reviews, letters, news items, non-fiction. "*Multicultural Education* features articles, reviews, listings of resources, and a variety of other materials geared to assist with multicultural education programs in schools and with development and definition of the field.'' circ. 5M. 4/yr. Pub'd 3 issues 1998; expects 4 issues 1999, 4 issues 2000. sub. price: $40 individuals, $60 institutions; per copy: $15; sample: free. Back issues: $10. Discounts: can be arranged. 40pp; 8½x11; of. Reporting time: 2 months. Publishes 25% of manuscripts submitted. Payment: only for solicited materials. Copyrighted, reverts to author. Pub's reviews: 12 in 1998. §Anything involved with multicultural education. Ads: $500/$300/$400 2/3 page/$200 1/3 page/$150 1/6 page/$50 1 inch. Multicultural Publishers Exchange (MPE), Educational Press Association (EDPRESS).

MULTIMEDIA REVIEWS FOR EDUCATION, MULTIMEDIA REVIEWS FOR INDUSTRY, Access Multimedia, Carol Anderson, PO Box 5182, Bellingham, WA 98227, 360-733-2155. 1985. Art, photos, reviews, non-fiction. "This is a newsletter for anyone in computer education. From elementary school teachers to corporate trainers. Includes new product reviews, training tips, hardware information, and industry advancements'' circ. 5M-10M. 10/yr. Expects 12 issues 1999, 12 issues 2000. sub. price: $69; per copy: $6; sample: same. 8pp; 8½x11; of. Reporting time: 2 months. Payment: varies per submission. Copyrighted. Pub's reviews. §Computer books and programs. No ads. PMA.

Multnomah Publishers, Inc., Rod Morris, Dan Benson, Jennifer Brooks, Karen Ball, PO Box 1720, Sisters, OR 97759, 541-549-1144; Fax 541-549-0432; mtennesen@multnomahpubl.com. 1987. Fiction, non-fiction. "Imprints: Gold 'n' Honey Books, Palisades, Alabaster.'' avg. press run 15M. Pub'd 60 titles 1998; expects 100 titles 1999, 100 titles 2000. avg. price, cloth: $13.99; paper: $8.99; other: $21.99 gift. Discounts: 40%. 280pp; of. Reporting time: 6 weeks. Simultaneous submissions accepted: yes. Publishes 1% of manuscripts submitted. Payment: varies. Copyrights for author. Christian Booksellers Assoc., Evangelical Christian Publishers Assn.

Mundus Artium Press, University of Texas at Dallas, Box 688, Richardson, TX 75083-0688. 1968. Poetry. "Bilingual poetry." avg. press run 1M-1.5M. Expects 2 titles 1999. 4 titles listed in the *Small Press Record of Books in Print* (28th Edition, 1999-00). avg. price, paper: $10. Discounts: 20% libraries. 6×9. Reporting time: 6 months.

Munklinde Vestergaard, D. Sorensen, RT 1, Box 126, Nambe, NM 87501, 505-455-3165. 1994. "Our emphasis right now is on reprinting interesting books that have slipped from view, and on translation. In July we will bring out a shorter version of Gertrude Stein's *The Making of Americans.* We're not totally opposed to submissions, but not seeking them" avg. press run 3M. Expects 1 title 1999, 1 title 2000. 1 title listed in the *Small Press Record of Books in Print* (28th Edition, 1999-00). avg. price, cloth: $23.95. 224pp; 5¾×8½; of. Rocky Mountain Book Publishers Association.

Munsey Music, T. Munsey, Box 511, Richmond Hill, Ontario L4C 4Y8, Canada, 905-737-0208; www.pathcom.com/~munsey. 1970. "Include SASE if return of submission is required. Only accept fantasy/science fiction" avg. press run 5M. Pub'd 1 title 1998; expects 2 titles 1999, 4 titles 2000. 7 titles listed in the *Small Press Record of Books in Print* (28th Edition, 1999-00). avg. price, paper: $4.99. Discounts: 1-4 copies no discount, 5-10 20%, 11-20 30%, 21-40 35%, 41+ 40%. 250pp; 4¼×7. Reporting time: 6-12 months. Simultaneous submissions accepted: yes. Payment: industry. Copyrights for author. PMA.

MURDER CAN BE FUN, John Marr, PO Box 640111, San Francisco, CA 94164, 415-666-8956. 1986. Articles, art, photos, cartoons, non-fiction. circ. 4M. 2/yr. Pub'd 2 issues 1998; expects 3 issues 1999, 2 issues 2000. sub. price: $4; per copy: $1.50; sample: $2. Back issues: $2. Discounts: inquire. 48pp; 5½×8½; of. Reporting time: 4 weeks. Payment: copies. Copyrighted, does not revert to author. Pub's reviews: 20 in 1998. §Nonfiction, especially about crimes or disasters. Ads: none.

MurPubCo, 3335 Chisholm Trail #206, Boulder, CO 80301. 1985. Poetry, fiction, articles, cartoons. "MurPubCo published 2 titles in 1986. They can be ordered from the publisher at the above address." Expects 1 title 2000. 1 title listed in the *Small Press Record of Books in Print* (28th Edition, 1999-00). avg. price, paper: $5; other: $1. Reporting time: 3 months. Does not copyright for author. Stone Soup Poets.

MUSE NATURA, A Sensual Journey of the Arts, Alexandra Lloyd, Editor; C. Owen Johnson, Managing Editor & Publisher, PO Box 2210, Livermore, CA 94550, 510-447-2245; e-mail pleiadespress@netwizards.net. 1996. Poetry, fiction, articles, art, photos, reviews. "Fiction should be less than 8,000 words (5,000 words prefered). Articles should be less than 3,000 words. Guidelines for SASE." circ. 750. 4/yr. Expects 1 issue 1999, 4 issues 2000. sub. price: $20; per copy: $7; sample: $7. Discounts: to be determined. 32pp; 8×11½; of. Reporting time: less than 4 weeks. Simultaneous submissions accepted: yes. Publishes 20% of manuscripts submitted. Payment: 1¢/word, $5/photo or art piece, $50 max print. Copyrighted, reverts to author. Pub's reviews. §Art, photography, erotica (especially women's). Ads: to be determined.

●**MUSE OF FIRE,** Tim Scannell, 21 Kruse Road, Port Angeles, WA 98362-8900. 1994. Poetry. "No taboos...no political correctness...craftsmanship the permanent standard" circ. 50. 25/yr. Pub'd 25 issues 1998; expects 25 issues 1999, 25 issues 2000. price per copy: $1; sample: $1 + SASE. Back issues: $1 each #'s 1-112. 6pp; 8½×11; †computer inkjet copier. Reporting time: 1 week. Simultaneous submissions accepted: yes. Publishes 40% of manuscripts submitted. Payment: 1 copy. Not copyrighted.

Museon Publishing, PO Box 17095, Beverly Hills, CA 90209-2095, 310-788-0228. 1996. Non-fiction. "Travel material related to museums and art only. Accept proposals only" avg. press run 5M. Pub'd 1 title 1998; expects 2 titles 1999, 3 titles 2000. 1 title listed in the *Small Press Record of Books in Print* (28th Edition, 1999-00). avg. price, paper: $20. Discounts: 2-4 20%, 5-9 40%, 10-49 42%, 50-99 44%, 100+ 46%. 270pp; 5½×9; of. Reporting time: 1 month. Simultaneous submissions accepted: no. Payment: varies. Does not copyright for author.

Museum of New Mexico Press, Mary Wachs, Editor-In-Chief; Ronald E. Latimer, Publisher, PO Box 2087, Santa Fe, NM 87504, 505-827-6454; Fax; 505-827-5941. 1913. Articles, art, photos, reviews. "Publishes general non-fiction books and catalogs of museum exhibitions within Museum of New Mexico system and general books for the trade, particularly relating to the Southwest." avg. press run 4.5M-7.5M. Pub'd 6-10 titles 1998; expects 6-10 titles 1999, 6-10 titles 2000. 92 titles listed in the *Small Press Record of Books in Print* (28th Edition, 1999-00). Discounts: retail 1-4 30%, 5-24 40%, 25-49 42%, 50 + 45%. of. Reporting time: 4 weeks. Payment: royalties negotiated on per contract basis. Copyrights for author.

MUSHROOM DREAMS, Jim Reagan, 14537 Longworth Avenue, Norwalk, CA 90650-4724. 1997. Poetry, fiction, art, cartoons. "Fiction to 1,800 words max, poetry to 30 lines, comix." circ. 110. 2/yr. Expects 1 issue 1999, 2 issues 2000. sub. price: $2; per copy: $1; sample: $1. 32pp; 5½×8½; photocopy. Reporting time: 2 months. Simultaneous submissions accepted: yes. Publishes 20% of manuscripts submitted. Payment: 2 copies.

Copyrighted, reverts to author. Ads: $10/$7.50/$5 1/4 page.

MUSIC AND LETTERS, Oxford University Press, Nigel Fortune, Timothy Carter, Journals Subscription Department, Pinkhill House, Southfield Road, Eynsham, Oxford OX8 1JJ, England. 1920. Articles, reviews, music, letters. "Not specialized in scope, being open to the discussion of anything from primitive music to the latest experiments in the laboratory. But preference is given to contributors who can write, who have a respect for the English language and are willing to take the trouble to use it effectively. All fields of musical enquiry, from earliest times to present day. Includes wide range of reviews: books, scholarly editions of music of the past, new music." circ. 1850. 4/yr. Pub'd 4 issues 1998; expects 4 issues 1999, 4 issues 2000. sub. price: £40 UK and Europe; $82 US; per copy: $22; sample: free. 150pp; 6x9¾; †of. Reporting time: 4 months. Payment: £1 per printed page. Copyrighted, reverts to author. Pub's reviews: 79 books, 95 pieces of music in 1998. §Music, musical criticism, musical history, etc. Ads: £40.00 & pro rata/£23.00.

MUSIC NEWS, David Island, 5536 NE Hassalo, Portland, OR 97213, 503-281-1191. 1896. Articles, art, photos, cartoons, music, news items, non-fiction. "2 pages double spaced typed maximum" circ. 55M. 3/yr. Pub'd 3 issues 1998; expects 3 issues 1999, 3 issues 2000. sub. price: controlled circulation; per copy: SASE; sample: SASE. Back issues: none. 8pp; 11x17; †lp. Reporting time: 1 month. Publishes 10% of manuscripts submitted. Payment: varies. Copyrighted, reverts to author. Pub's reviews: 8 in 1998. §Music. Ads: none. Church Music Publishers Association; Catholic Press Association.

MUSIC PERCEPTION, University of California Press, Jamshed J. Bharucha, Univ of CA Press, 2120 Berkeley Way, Berkeley, CA 94720, 510-643-7154. 1983. Reviews, music, non-fiction. "Editorial address: Department of Psychology, 6207 Gerry Hall Room 201, Dartmouth College, Hanover, NH 03755" circ. 750. 4/yr. Pub'd 2 issues 1998; expects 4 issues 1999, 4 issues 2000. sub. price: $52, $135 instit. (+ $6 foreign postage); per copy: $14, $35 instit., $14 student; sample: free. Back issues: same as single copy price. Discounts: foreign subs. agents 10%, one-time orders 10+ 30%, standing orders (bookstores): 1-99 40%, 100+ 50%. 128pp; 7x10; of. Copyrighted, does not revert to author. Pub's reviews: 20 in 1998. §Music, physical psychology, psychology of perception. Ads: $275/$200.

MUSICAL OPINION, Denby Richards, 2 Princes Road, St. Leonards-on-Sea, East Sussex TN37 6EL, England, 0424-715167; fax 0424-712214. 1877. Articles. "500-2M words of general musical interest, organ. No verse." circ. 5.5M. 4/yr. sub. price: £23 UK, £35/US $70 overseas; per copy: £3.50 + postage; sample: free. Back issues: from £5 + postage. Discounts: 10% for trade. 60pp; 8¼x11½; †of. Reporting time: by arrangement. Payment: on publication. Copyrighted. Pub's reviews: 30 in 1998. §General music, opera, organ, church music, musical instruments trade—festivals, CDs, books, music, dance. Ads: £550 color, £300/£180/£100/40p per classified word. British Soc. of Magazine Editors.

MUSICWORKS: The Journal of Sound Explorations (Audio-Visual), Gayle Young, Editor-in-Chief, 179 Richmond Street West, Toronto, Ontario M5V 1V3, Canada, 416-977-3546. 1978. Articles, art, photos, cartoons, interviews, criticism, reviews, music, letters, collages, news items. "Please send proposals, not finished materials." circ. 3M. 3/yr. Pub'd 3 issues 1998; expects 3 issues 1999, 3 issues 2000. sub. price: paper only $14 Canada, $20 U.S., $26 elsewhere, $30 institution, paper with cassette or CD $33 Canada, $39 U.S., $42 elsewhere, $55 institution; per copy: $5 mag only, $15 mag and cassette/CD; sample: $15/issue with cassette or CD. Back issues: $5/magazine, $8/cassette, $11 CD. Discounts: retail outlets 60%. 72pp; 8½x11; web-offset. Reporting time: varies. Payment: varies. Copyrighted, reverts to author. Pub's reviews: 19 in 1998. §Contemporary music—lp's, cd's, cassettes (non commercial). Ads: $300/$200/$180 1/3 page/$120 1/4 page/$75 1/8/$15 for 40 words classified. CMPA.

THE MUSING PLACE, Linda Krinsky, Laurie Peters, 2700 Lakeview, Chicago, IL 60614, 312-281-3800. 1983. Poetry, fiction, art, cartoons, interviews, satire. "Thresholds is a psychosocial rehablitaion social service agency serving severely mentally ill individuals. Thresholds attempts to reintegrate people into society through work programs, groups, and this magazine. We publish serious and satirical pieces, and poetry dealing with many subjects including, but not limited to, the rigors of living with mental illness. Hospital experiences, isolation, connection, and general life experiences are some subjects of recent work. Our schedule of printing is once yearly. Mark Gonciarz, Ken Hartfield, and Allen McNair are some recnt contributors" circ. 500. 1/yr. Pub'd 1 issue 1998; expects 1 issue 1999, 1 issue 2000. sub. price: $4; per copy: $3; sample: free. Back issues: $3. Discounts: 40%. 32pp; 8½x11; of. Reporting time: 6 months. Simultaneous submissions accepted: yes. Publishes 5% of manuscripts submitted. Payment: copies. Copyrighted, reverts to author. Ads: inquire to editors.

Mustang Publishing Co., Rollin Riggs, Editor-in-chief, PO Box 3004, Memphis, TN 38173, 901-521-1406; fax 901-521-1412; e-Mail MUSTANGPUB@AOL.COM. 1983. Non-fiction. "We're especially interested in books for the 18-40 year old crowd—travel, humor, how-to, etc. We want proposals! Please enclose an SASE with proposals. No phone calls or faxes please." avg. press run 7.5M. Pub'd 5 titles 1998; expects 5 titles 1999, 5 titles 2000. 22 titles listed in the *Small Press Record of Books in Print* (28th Edition, 1999-00). avg. price, cloth: $16.95; paper: $10.95. Discounts: contact our distributor, National Book Network, Lanham, MD (800-462-6420). 160pp; 5½×8¼; of. Reporting time: 2-3 weeks. Simultaneous submissions accepted: yes. Publishes 1% of manuscripts submitted. Payment: around 6-8%. Copyrights for author. PMA.

MUTUAL FUND SOURCEBOOK, Joe Mansueto, 225 West Wacker Drive, Chicago, IL 60606-1224, 312-696-6000. 1984. Non-fiction. 1/yr. Pub'd 1 issue 1998; expects 1 issue 1999, 1 issue 2000. sub. price: $225; per copy: $225. Back issues: none. Discounts: 2 yrs $405. 3000pp; 8×11½; of, lp. Reporting time: varies. Copyrighted. §Investments.

Mutual Publishing, Bernett Hymer, 1215 Center Street #210, Honolulu, HI 96816-3226. 1974. Fiction, photos, non-fiction. avg. press run 10M. Pub'd 30 titles 1998; expects 30 titles 1999, 30 titles 2000. 73 titles listed in the *Small Press Record of Books in Print* (28th Edition, 1999-00). avg. price, cloth: $29.95; paper: $7.95-$12.95. Discounts: 40% dealer, 55% distributor, 30% library. 200pp; 6×9 to 11×14. Reporting time: 1 year. Simultaneous submissions accepted: yes. Publishes 5% of manuscripts submitted. Payment: 10% of receipts. We sometimes copyright for author.

MY LEGACY, Kay Weems, HCR-13, Box 21AA, Artemas, PA 17211-9405, 814-458-3102. 1990. Poetry. "Any form or theme on poetry to 36 lines (sometimes longer). Short stories to 2,500 words, sometimes longer. Will try to use several poems in an issue by some poets—if I really like their work." circ. 150+. 4/yr. Pub'd 4 issues 1998; expects 4 issues 1999, 4 issues 2000. sub. price: $12; per copy: $3.50; sample: $3.50. Back issues: $3.50. 60-70pp; digest; †Sharp copier. Reporting time: 3 months. Payment: Editor's Choice Award to editor's favorite writer and poet in each issue. Copyrighted, reverts to author. I try not to use ads, not much room. PA Poetry Society, Walt Whitman Guild, UAPAA, National Arts Society, National Federation of State Poetry Societies Inc., New Horizons Poetry Club, Southern Poetry Assoc.

Myriad Press, Gloria Stern, 12535 Chandler Blvd. #3, N. Hollywood, CA 91607, 818-508-6296. 1993. Fiction, non-fiction. avg. press run 1M. Expects 1 title 1999, 2 titles 2000. 1 title listed in the *Small Press Record of Books in Print* (28th Edition, 1999-00). avg. price, paper: $18.95. 200pp; 5½×8½. Reporting time: 8-10 weeks. Simultaneous submissions accepted: yes. Payment: via contract. Copyrights for author.

MYSTERIOUS WYSTERIA, Eric E. Scott, 1136 Prospect Avenue #2, Ann Arbor, MI 48104-3968. 1993. Poetry, fiction, art. circ. 100. 4/yr. Expects 4 issues 1999, 4 issues 2000. sub. price: $5; per copy: $1; sample: $1. Back issues: none. Discounts: none. 27pp; 5½×8½; xerox. Reporting time: anytime. Payment: free magazine. Copyrighted, does not revert to author. Ads: will advertise for trade ad.

Mystery Notebook Editions, Stephen Wright, Attn: Stephen Wright, PO Box 1341, FDR Station, New York, NY 10150-1341. 1986. Fiction, non-fiction. "First Title: *The Adventures of Sandy West, Private Eye* (novel) by Stephen Wright." avg. press run 1M. Pub'd 1 title 1998. 1 title listed in the *Small Press Record of Books in Print* (28th Edition, 1999-00). avg. price, paper: varies. Pages vary; size varies; varies. Reporting time: 1-3 months, *query first*. Payment: individually arranged. Copyrights for author.

MYSTERY READERS JOURNAL, Janet A. Rudolph, PO Box 8116, Berkeley, CA 94707-8116, 510-339-2800. 1985. Articles, art, interviews, criticism, reviews, news items. "Each issue deals primarily with specific themes in mystery. Fiction (reviews of) 1989: Theatrical mysteries, murder on the job, legal mysteries, and bibliomysteries. 1990: Musical mysteries, murder on holiday, political mysteries, and beastly murders. 1991: Food mysteries, murder in the plot, gardening mysteries, holiday mysteries, murder on screen. 1992: Environmental mysteries, journalistic mysteries, art mysteries, religious mysteries. 1993 Sports mysteries, historical mysteries, the literary world, the gay detective. 1994: Literary Mysteries; The Senior Sleuth, Detectives in Pairs, Old Crimes, 1995: Suburban Mysteries; San Francisco; Regional British 1996 Mysteries; Technological Mysteries; New Orleans; Sports Mysteries; Academic Mysteries 1998: NY,NY; The Ethnic Detective, Parts I & II; Animals in Mysteries. 1999: Cross-Genre Mysteries, Chicago, The Story Story, Florida." circ. 2M. 4/yr. Pub'd 4 issues 1998; expects 4 issues 1999, 4 issues 2000. sub. price: $24/everyone in US/Canada; per copy: $6; sample: $7. Back issues: $7/issue. 64pp; 7×8; †of. Reporting time: 2 months. Simultaneous submissions accepted: yes. Publishes 80% of manuscripts submitted. Payment: free issue. Copyrighted, does not revert to author. Pub's reviews: 600 in 1998. §Mystery fiction, literary review magazines. No ads. Mystery Readers International.

THE MYSTERY REVIEW, Barbara Davey, PO Box 233, Colborne, Ont. K0K 1S0, Canada, 613-475-4440; fax 613-475-3400. 1992. Poetry, articles, art, interviews, criticism, reviews, letters. "Magazine content is geared to the interests of mystery readers, reviews of mystery and suspense titles, interviews with mystery authors, word games and puzzles related to mystery." circ. 7M. 4/yr. Pub'd 4 issues 1998; expects 4 issues 1999, 4 issues 2000. sub. price: $20 US in the United States; per copy: $5.95; sample: $5.95. Back issues: $5. 76pp; 8½×11; of. Reporting time: 1 month. Simultaneous submissions accepted: no. Payment: honorarium only. Copyrighted, does not revert to author. Pub's reviews: 50 in 1998. §Mystery, suspense, thrillers, adult. Ads: contact magazine. CMPA.

MYSTERY TIME ANTHOLOGY, Hutton Publications, Linda Hutton, Editor, PO Box 2907, Decatur, IL 62524. 1983. Fiction. "We use only mystery/suspense stories up to 1.5M words, which must be well-plotted." circ. 150. 2/yr. Pub'd 2 issues 1998; expects 2 issues 1999. sub. price: $10; per copy: $5; sample: $4. Back issues: $4. 44pp; 8½×11; of. Reporting time: 1 month. Publishes 25% of manuscripts submitted. Payment: 1/4¢ to 1¢ per word for fiction, $5 per poem. Copyrighted, reverts to author. Pub's reviews. §Mysteries by SINC members.

MYSTIC VOICES, Reyes Investment Enterprise Ltd., A. Pencos Reyes, PO Box 3418, Maraval, Trinidad & Tobago. "We are looking for material on occult, new age, WICCA, spiritual, dreams, magic, crystals, metaphysics, tarot, yoga, psychology" circ. 12. 12/yr. Expects 6 issues 1999, 12 issues 2000. sub. price: $60; per copy: $5; sample: $6. Discounts: 20-30%. 36-48pp; 5×7½; †of. Reporting time: 1-3 months. Simultaneous submissions accepted: yes. Payment: $30-50. Copyrighted, reverts to author. Pub's reviews. Ads: $100/$60/$2.

Myth Breakers, Mitchell Levy, 19672 Steers Creek Blvd, Suite 200, Cupertino, CA 95014, 408-257-7257. 1992. Satire, criticism, news items, non-fiction. avg. press run 5M. Pub'd 1 title 1998; expects 2 titles 1999, 3 titles 2000. 1 title listed in the *Small Press Record of Books in Print* (28th Edition, 1999-00). avg. price, paper: $12. Discounts: 2-4 20%, 5-9 30%, 10-24 40%, 25-49 42%, 50-74 44%, 75-99 46%, 100+ 50%. 160pp; 6×9. Payment: 6%. Copyrights for author. Publishers Marketing Association (PMA).

N

N D, Daniel Plunkett, PO Box 4144, Austin, TX 78765, 512-440-7609; fax 512-416-8007; e-Mail PLUNKETT@ND.ORG. 1984. Articles, art, photos, interviews, reviews, music, non-fiction. "Our focus is on alternative, experimental, extreme, and independent musicians, composers, and artists. Depending on material submitted, the length is flexible. Most recent contributions include: Interview with Stuart Brisley (Andie Stitt), Composer Hal Rammel (Jeff Filla), Irish Composer Roger Doyle (Gary McPhelan), interview and article on organum (Kevin Spencer) and an interview with Susanne Lewis (Rob Forman)." circ. 3M. 2/yr. Pub'd 2 issues 1998; expects 2 issues 1999, 2 issues 2000. sub. price: $9; per copy: $5; sample: $5. Back issues: $5. Discounts: distributors. 70pp; 7×8; †of. Reporting time: within 90 days. Payment: copies. Copyrighted, reverts to author. Pub's reviews: 300 in 1998. §Music, art, alternative, poetry, chapbooks, handmade books, networking magazines. Ads: $100 1/2 page/$75 1/4 page/$40 1/8 page.

N: NUDE & NATURAL, Lee Baxandall, PO Box 132, Oshkosh, WI 54902, 414-231-9950. 1981. Poetry, fiction, articles, art, photos, cartoons, letters, news items. "Must relate to body acceptance and nude recreation." circ. 25M. 4/yr. Pub'd 4 issues 1998; expects 4 issues 1999, 4 issues 2000. sub. price: $40; per copy: $8; sample: $8. Back issues: $8. Discounts: 40%, inquire. 124pp; 8½×10⅞; of. Reporting time: 1 week. Simultaneous submissions accepted: no. Publishes 50% of manuscripts submitted. Payment: small. Copyrighted, reverts to author. Pub's reviews: 8 in 1998. Ads: $975 4CP/$490 4C 1/2 page/$625 BWP/$350 bw 1/2 page.

Nada Press (see also BIG SCREAM), David Cope, 2782 Dixie S.W., Grandville, MI 49418, 616-531-1442. 1974. Poetry, fiction, art. "Poets and writers *must* include SASE with their submissions and make sure there's enough postage on the envelope." avg. press run 100. Pub'd 2 titles 1998; expects 1 title 1999, 1 title 2000. 1 title listed in the *Small Press Record of Books in Print* (28th Edition, 1999-00). avg. price, paper: $5; other: $5. 35pp; 8½×11; photo offset. Reporting time: 1 month. Payment: copies.

The Naiad Press, Inc., Barbara Grier, Publisher, PO Box 10543, Tallahassee, FL 32302, 904-539-5965; fax 904-539-9731. 1973. Fiction, non-fiction. "Small press publishing lesbian feminist materials only, emphasizing genre fiction, romances, gothics, mysteries, spy novels, westerns, serious fiction...all with lesbian theme. Also publishes self-help, biography, autobiography, history, and bibliography" avg. press run 8M. Pub'd 32 titles 1998; expects 32 titles 1999, 32 titles 2000. 259 titles listed in the *Small Press Record of Books in Print* (28th Edition, 1999-00). avg. price, cloth: $19.95; paper: $11.95. Discounts: 50% dealers - 5 or more copies - mixed titles. 240pp; 5½×8½; of. Reporting time: 16 weeks. Simultaneous submissions accepted: no. Payment: 15%, varies. Copyrights for author. Women in Print, Book Expo (ABA).

NAMBLA BULLETIN, Chris Farrell, PO Box 174, Midtown Station, New York, NY 10018, 212-631-1194; E-mail arnoldschoen@juno.com. 1979. Poetry, fiction, articles, art, photos, cartoons, interviews, satire, criticism, reviews, letters, parts-of-novels, collages, news items, non-fiction. circ. 2.2M. 10/yr. Pub'd 4 issues 1998; expects 4 issues 1999, 8 issues 2000. sub. price: $35 US & Canada, $50 international; per copy: $5; sample: $5. Back issues: $5. Discounts: 50%. 24pp; 8½×11; of. Simultaneous submissions accepted: yes. Publishes 25% of manuscripts submitted. Payment: none. Not copyrighted. Pub's reviews: 5 in 1998. §Gay, youth liberation, man/boy love. GLPA.

NANCY'S MAGAZINE, Nancy Bonnell-Kangas, N's M Publications, PO Box 02108, Columbus, OH 43202, 614-298-0372. 1983. Articles, art, photos, cartoons, interviews, reviews, music, letters, long-poems, plays, non-fiction. "An exuberant variety magazine with an emphasis on literature and graphics. Issues are broadly thematic. Poetry, recipes, survey results, histories, scientific diagrams, and social advice included. ISSN 0895-7576." circ. 2M. 1 every 2 years. Expects 1 issue 1999. sub. price: $4; per copy: $4; sample: $4. Back issues: no special price. 36pp; 7×8½; †of. Reporting time: 1 month. Simultaneous submissions accepted: yes. Payment: 2 copies. Copyrighted, reverts to author. Pub's reviews: 0 in 1998. §Music, American studies, comics, architecture.

NANNY FANNY, Lou Hertz, 2524 Stockbridge Drive #15, Indianapolis, IN 46268-2670, 317-329-1436; nightpoet@prodigy.net. 1998. Poetry, art. "Prefer 30 lines or less, prefer poems about people or events based on external observations, not through introspection. Art: B&W only, for cover, possibly inside." circ. 100. 3/yr. Pub'd 2 issues 1998; expects 3 issues 1999, 3 issues 2000. sub. price: $9; per copy: $3.50; sample: $3.50. Discounts: none. 32pp; 5½×8½; †laserjet. Reporting time: 2 weeks to 2 months. We accept simultaneous submissions if they are labelled as such. Publishes 7-10% of manuscripts submitted. Payment: contributor's copy. Not copyrighted.

NAR Publications (see also INVESTMENT COLUMN QUARTERLY (newsletter)), Nicholas A. Roes, Ed Guild, PO Box 233, Barryville, NY 12719, 914-557-8713. 1977. Articles, criticism, reviews, news items. "We publish educational, consumer, and general interest books. Titles have been plugged on Nat'l (Network) TV, wire services, radio, etc. Only 5 titles chosen yearly but given well co-ordinated PR campaign." avg. press run 5M. Pub'd 2 titles 1998; expects 3 titles 1999, 5 titles 2000. 7 titles listed in the *Small Press Record of Books in Print* (28th Edition, 1999-00). avg. price, paper: $9.95. Discounts: 25% library, classroom; 40% bookstore; special requests considered. 125pp; 5×7; of. Reporting time: 3 months. Payment: by arrangement. Copyrights for author.

Nashville House, Steve Eng, Editor, PO Box 111864, Nashville, TN 37222, 615-834-5069. 1991. Poetry, articles, photos, non-fiction. "Must relate to the Old West, or Civil War, or within limits, or science fiction, fantasy and horror, all interested parties should query first." avg. press run 500. Pub'd 1 title 1998; expects 1 title 1999, 1 title 2000. 4 titles listed in the *Small Press Record of Books in Print* (28th Edition, 1999-00). avg. price, cloth: $10; paper: $5. Discounts: standard dealer. 25-50pp; 5×8; of. Reporting time: 3 weeks, and only if queried first. Payment: standard, but by arrangement. Generally copyrights for author. Country Music Association (CMA), BMI, Science Fiction Poetry Association.

NATIONAL BUS TRADER, Transportation Trails, Larry Plachno, Editor; Christopher Plachno, Special Articles Editor, 9698 West Judson Road, Polo, IL 61064, 815-946-2341. 1977. "This is an equipment magazine for intercity buses. Similar to *Road and Track* except we cover 'Greyhound' type buses." circ. 6M. 12/yr. Pub'd 12 issues 1998; expects 12 issues 1999, 12 issues 2000. sub. price: $20; per copy: $1.50; sample: n/c (additional for foreign). Back issues: $1.50. Discounts: none. 56pp; 8½×11; of. Reporting time: 30 days. Payment: as agreed. Not copyrighted. Pub's reviews: 1 in 1998. Ads: $690/$360.

National Council for Research on Women (see also WOMEN'S RESEARCH NETWORK NEWS; ISSUES QUARTERLY), Nina Sonenberg, Coordinating Editor; Kate Daly, Editor, 530 Broadway, New York, NY 10012-3920, 212-274-0730; fax 212-274-0821. 1981. "The National Council for Research on Women is a coalition of seventy-seven member centers and organizations that support and conduct feminist research, policy analysis, and educational programs. Formed in 1981 as a working alliance to bridge traditional distinctions among scholarship, policy, and action programs, the Council works to strengthen ties with other national and international organizations and coalitions. Through its member centers, affiliates, and sponsored projects, the Council links over 10,000 women and men scholars and practitioners in this country and abroad and serves constituencies that include the academic community, public policy makers, and the public." avg. press run 1M. 14 titles listed in the *Small Press Record of Books in Print* (28th Edition, 1999-00). avg. price, paper: $15. Discounts: affiliates receive discount on books 20%. 100pp; 8½×11; of. Copyrights for author.

National Court Reporters Association Press (see also JOURNAL OF COURT REPORTING), Peter Wacht, Editor, 8224 Old Courthouse Road, Vienna, VA 22182, 703-556-6272; fax 703-556-6291; email pwacht@ncrahq.org. 1899. Non-fiction. "Focus should be on stenographic court reporting or language. References, such as dictionaries or glossaries, are always of interest." avg. press run 3M. Pub'd 6 titles 1998; expects 7 titles 1999, 6 titles 2000. 2 titles listed in the *Small Press Record of Books in Print* (28th Edition, 1999-00). avg. price, paper: $14.95. Discounts: varies. 250pp; size varies; of, docutech. Reporting time: 1-2 months. Simultaneous submissions accepted: yes. Publishes 50% of manuscripts submitted. Payment: varies. Will copyright if requested. PMA, SPAN.

NATIONAL MASTERS NEWS, Al Sheahen, Editor; Jerry Wojcik, Senior Editor; Suzy Hess, Administrative Editor, PO Box 50098, Eugene, OR 97405, 541-343-7716; Fax 541-345-2436; natmanews@aol.com. 1977.

Articles, art, photos, interviews, satire, criticism, reviews, letters, news items, non-fiction. "The *National Masters News* is the bible of the Masters Athletics Program. It is the only national publication devoted exclusively to track & field, race walking and long distance running for men and women over age 30. An official publication of USA Track & Field, each month it delivers 32-48 pages of results, schedules, entry blanks, age records, rankings, photos, articles, training tips. Columns are about 1M words; anything of interest to over-age-30 performer/individual. Recent contributors: Mike Tymn, Hal Higdon, Dr. John Pagliano." circ. 8M. 12/yr. Pub'd 12 issues 1998; expects 12 issues 1999, 12 issues 2000. sub. price: $26; per copy: $2.50. Back issues: $2.50 plus 50¢ for each order. 37pp; 10×13. Reporting time: 15-30 days. Simultaneous submissions accepted: yes. Publishes 60% of manuscripts submitted. Payment: none. Copyrighted, reverts to author. Pub's reviews: 3 in 1998. §Athletics for over-age-30 performer. Ads: $545/$360/$1. TAFWA.

National Poetry Association Publishers (see also POETRY USA), Herman Berlandt, Editor, Fort Mason Center, Building D, Room 270, San Francisco, CA 94123, 415-776-6602. 1985. Poetry. "The National Poetry Association is primarily a literary presenting organization, with weekly programs and the annual National Poetry Week Festival and Poetry-Film Festival. We are, however, occasional book publishers. Our last title was *Peace or Perish: A Crisis Anthology* (1983) with over 80 poets represented, including Creeley, Bly, Everson, Levertov, Kaufman, McClure, Mueller, etc. The anthology was edited by Neeli Cherkovski and Herman Berlandt. A forthcoming new title will be *The Living Word: A Tribute Anthology* of poets, writers and artists who have died of AIDS, edited by Jeffrey Lilly." avg. press run 1M. Expects 1 title 1999, 4 titles 2000. 2 titles listed in the *Small Press Record of Books in Print* (28th Edition, 1999-00). avg. price, cloth: $10; paper: $5. Discounts: 50%. 124pp; 5½×8½; of, perfect bound. Payment: 2 copies. Does not copyright for author. PEN.

National Woodlands Publishing Company, John D. Schultz, Joanne C. Schultz, 8846 Green Briar Road, Lake Ann, MI 49650-9607, phone/fax 616-275-6735; e-mail nwpc@traverse.com. 1979. Fiction, interviews, reviews, letters, non-fiction, articles, photos. "Besides books on American Indians/Native Americans, we intend to publish books (also calendars, appointment books, etc.) with concentration in the natural resources fields. (Publisher has PhD in natural resources/forest ecology.)" avg. press run 10M. Expects 1 title 2000. 5 titles listed in the *Small Press Record of Books in Print* (28th Edition, 1999-00). avg. price, cloth: $21.95; paper: $14.95; other: $3.95. Discounts: 1 copy 0%, 2-4 20%, 5-99 40%, 100-499 50%, 500+ 55% (same for all wholesale buyers). Pages vary; 6×9; of. Reporting time: 1 month. Simultaneous submissions accepted: no. Publishes 10% of manuscripts submitted. Payment: negotiable. Copyrights for author.

Native Plant Publishing, Rick Vester, 150 South Glenoaks, Suite 9135R, Burbank, CA 91502, 818-558-9543; Fax 818-352-5567. 1993. Fiction, non-fiction. "Will only consider well-written and professional ms. from writers in the New Age/Fantasy genre. Query first with SASE. Our authors know how to work hard and are gifted writers. Is that you? Our fiction imprint is HeartStrings Press. Many of our titles are now printed in foreign languages." avg. press run 10M. Pub'd 9 titles 1998; expects 14 titles 1999. 5 titles listed in the *Small Press Record of Books in Print* (28th Edition, 1999-00). avg. price, cloth: $24.95; paper: $9-$14. Discounts: 55% wholesale, 45% bookstores. 250pp; 5×8; of. Reporting time: 2 months. Simultaneous submissions accepted: yes. Publishes 2% of manuscripts submitted. Payment: negotiable. Copyrights for author.

NATURAL BRIDGE, Steven Schreiner, Editor; Howard Schwartz, Senior Editor; David Carkeet, Senior Editor; Mary Troy, Senior Editor; Charles Wartts, Senior Editor, English Dept., Univ. of Missouri, 8001 Natural Bridge Road, St. Louis, MO 63121, E-mail natural@jinx.umsl.edu. 1999. Poetry, fiction, non-fiction. "*Natural Bridge*, a continuation of *Webster Review* (1974-1994) premiers in 1999 with poetry, fiction, essays, and translations. Submit only during these two periods: July 1-August 31, and Nov. 1-Dec. 31." 2/yr. Expects 2 issues 2000. sub. price: $15; per copy: $6. 200pp; 6×9; 1p. Reporting time: 4 months. We accept simultaneous submissions if indicated. Payment: copies only. Copyrighted, reverts to author. Ads: $100/$50/exchange.

NATURAL LIFE, The Alternate Press, Wendy Priesnitz, 272 Highway 5, RR 1, St. George, Ontario N0E 1N0, Canada, 519-449-4001; fax 519-448-4411; email natural@life.ca. 1976. "We no longer use freelancers. An alternative lifestyle newspaper that circulates in USA and Canada." circ. 50M. 12/yr. Pub'd 6 issues 1998; expects 10 issues 1999, 12 issues 2000. sub. price: $24 (+ GST in Candada); per copy: $2.50; sample: $3.50ppd. Back issues: not available. 16pp; tabloid; web. Reporting time: 1 month. Simultaneous submissions accepted: no. Publishes 0% of manuscripts submitted. Copyrighted, reverts to author. Pub's reviews: 30 in 1998. §Health, renewable energy, alternative education, home business, ecology, vegetarian cooking, economics. Ads: $500/page, no classifieds.

NATURALLY, Bernard J. Loibl, PO Box 317, Newfoundland, NJ 07435, 973-697-3552; fax 973-697-8813; e-mail naturally@nac.net. 1981. Fiction, articles, art, photos, cartoons, interviews, reviews, news items, non-fiction. "*Naturally* focuses on wholesome nude family recreation—it is a glossy color magazine that includes many informative articles and photos on travel and upscale nudist resorts around the world." circ. 35M. 4/yr. Pub'd 4 issues 1998; expects 4 issues 1999, 4 issues 2000. sub. price: $21.95; per copy: $9 ppd.; sample: $9 ppd. Back issues: $9 ppd. Discounts: 50% distributors, 40% retailers. 60pp; 8⅛×10⅞; of. Reporting time: 6 weeks. Simultaneous submissions accepted: yes. Publishes 30% of manuscripts submitted. Payment:

$70 per page. Copyrighted, reverts to author. Pub's reviews: 4 in 1998. §Nudity, wholistic health, travel, personal freedoms. Ads: $650/$420/$15 (25 words or less).

NATURE SOCIETY NEWS, Harry Wright, Purple Martin Junction, Griggsville, IL 62340, (217) 833-2323. 1966. 12/yr. Pub'd 12 issues 1998; expects 12 issues 1999, 12 issues 2000. sub. price: $12, $17 US funds in Canada; sample: no charge. Discounts: 40% to agencies and catalogs. 24pp; 61×15½. Payment: only to regular staff contributors. Copyrighted, reverts to author. Pub's reviews: 24 in 1998. §Birds, nature (special emphasis: home-related; easter North America). No ads.

Naturegraph Publishers, Inc., Barbara Brown, Editor, PO Box 1047, Happy Camp, CA 96039, 530-493-5353; fax 530-493-5240; e-mail nature@sisqtel.net; www.naturegraph.com. 1946. Non-fiction. "Our list includes natural history, Native American studies, crafts, and outdoors." avg. press run 4M. Pub'd 6 titles 1998; expects 5 titles 1999, 6 titles 2000. 106 titles listed in the *Small Press Record of Books in Print* (28th Edition, 1999-00). avg. price, paper: $8.95. Discounts: 1-4 20%, 5-24 40%, 25-49 42%, 50-99 43%, 100-249 44%, 250-499 45%, 500 & up 46%. 160pp; 5½×8½, 4¼×7¼, 8½×11; †of. Reporting time: 1-8 weeks. Simultaneous submissions accepted, and prefer to do so. Publishes 2% of manuscripts submitted. Payment: royalties. Copyrights for author. ABA.

Naturist Foundation (see also THE GROVE), Editorial Committee, Naturist Headquarters, Orpington, BR5 4ET, England. 1950. Articles, photos, cartoons, letters, news items, non-fiction. "House Journal of Naturist Foundation and Sun Societies; international circulation to naturists. News and reports of interest to naturists are welcome." avg. press run 800. 1 title listed in the *Small Press Record of Books in Print* (28th Edition, 1999-00). avg. price, paper: £3.50 ($7) for single copies. Discounts: none. 24pp; 9½×7½; 1p. Reporting time: 1 month. Payment: none. Copyrights for author.

The Nautical & Aviation Publishing Co. of America, Inc., Jan Snouck-Hurgronje, Publisher; Rebecca Irish, Production Editor, 8 West Madison Street, Baltimore, MD 21201, 410-659-0220; fax 410-539-8832. 1979. Fiction, photos, non-fiction. "N & A's publishing program makes available high quality books that are genuinely needed in the military market. The books must be significant contributions to the literature and have popular appeal to gain the widest possible audience, which consists of the military and other people professionally concerned with defense affairs as well as readers of aviation, nautical, and military books who possess no specialized knowledge." avg. press run 2M. Pub'd 9 titles 1998; expects 10 titles 1999, 12 titles 2000. 3 titles listed in the *Small Press Record of Books in Print* (28th Edition, 1999-00). avg. price, cloth: $27.95; paper: $19.95. Discounts: trade 1-2 20%, 2-10 40%, 11-20 41%, 21-30 42%, 31-40 43%, 41-50 44%, 51+ 45%. 250pp; 6×9; of. Reporting time: 1-2 months. Publishes 5-10% of manuscripts submitted. Payment: 8-15% of net receipts. Copyrights for author.

THE NAUTILUS, J.H. Leal, PO Box 1580, Sanibel, FL 33957. 1886. Articles, non-fiction. "Original scientific research in malacology (mollusks). Now in volume 102 (1988)" circ. 800. 4/yr. Pub'd 4 issues 1998; expects 4 issues 1999, 4 issues 2000. sub. price: $28 (individuals), $45 (institutions), foreign postage $5; per copy: $20; sample: $20. Back issues: at current issue prices. Discounts: $3 to agents on institutional rate ($45 per year). Cost to agent $42. 50pp; 8½×11; of. Reporting time: 9 months. Simultaneous submissions accepted: no. Publishes 50% of manuscripts submitted. Payment: charge page-charges, $60/page. Copyrighted, does not revert to author. Pub's reviews: 2 in 1998. §Only on mollusks.

NBM Publishing Company, Terry Nantier, 185 Madison Avenue #1504, New York, NY 10016, 212-545-1223; FAX 212-545-1227. 1976. Cartoons. "We publish *graphic novels* high-quality *comics* in book form." avg. press run 5M. Pub'd 20 titles 1998; expects 20 titles 1999, 20 titles 2000. 61 titles listed in the *Small Press Record of Books in Print* (28th Edition, 1999-00). avg. price, cloth: $35; paper: $11. Discounts: wholesale 50% returnable 1 year, 60% non-returnable; retail 40%-48% returnable 1 year, 50% non-returnable. 80pp; 8½×11; of. Reporting time: 2-4 weeks. Payment: 8-12% of sales (retail). Copyrights for author.

N-B-T-V, D.B. Pitt, Narrow Bandwidth Television Association, 1 Burnwood Dr., Wollaton, Nottingham, Notts NG8 2DJ, England, 0115-9282896. 1975. Articles, photos, cartoons, interviews, criticism, reviews, letters, news items, non-fiction. "Normal maximum length of article 1M words. Longer articles would be serialised. Bias is towards projects on a low budget which readers can carry out at home/school/college etc." circ. 200. 4/yr. Pub'd 4 issues 1998; expects 4 issues 1999, 4 issues 2000. sub. price: £5, $12 US; per copy: £1; sample: 75p (Annual sub - £3 to non-earners). Back issues: bound volumes II + III (one book) £3. Discounts: under review, please inquire. 13pp; size A4; xerography. Reporting time: 1 week. Simultaneous submissions accepted: yes. Publishes 75% of manuscripts submitted. Payment: none. Copyrighted, copyright normally held on behalf of author but negotiable. Pub's reviews: 3 in 1998. §Television, hobby electronics, history of television (in English, Dutch, German, or French). Ads: £10/£6/small ads free to subscribers, otherwise negotiable.

NEBO, B.C Hall, Fiction; Paul Lake, Poetry; M.K. Ritchie, Non-Fiction & Translations, Department of English, Arkansas Tech University, Russellville, AR 72801, 501-968-0256. 1982. Poetry, fiction, articles, art, criticism, reviews, long-poems, non-fiction. "We are interested in quality poetry and fiction by both new and established writers. In fiction we are open to a wide range of styles. We seek poems whose rhythms are as compelling and memorable as their diction and images, and as a result we print a large number of formal poems (poems using meter and rhyme). We have published poems by Howard Nemerov, Timothy Steele, Julia Randall, Dana Gioia, Brenda Hillman, Turner Cassity, R. L. Barth, and many other excellent poets, many previously unknown to us. In addition, we are interested in well-written reviews and criticism of English language poetry. We encourage poetic translations from contemporary writers and personal essays about travel in other parts of the world." circ. 300. 1-2/yr. Pub'd 1 issue 1998; expects 2 issues 1999, 2 issues 2000. sub. price: $10; per copy: $6; sample: $5. Back issues: $5. 48-60pp; 5×8; of. Reporting time: 2 weeks to 4 months; between Aug 1 and Feb 1, issue is put together. Reporting time is March for year's submissions. Payment: 1 copy. Copyrighted, reverts to author. Pub's reviews: 6 in 1998. §Poetry, fiction, literature in translation. Ads: $75/$45.

THE NEBRASKA REVIEW, James Reed, Fiction; Susan Aizenberg, Poetry, FA 212, University of Nebraska-Omaha, Omaha, NE 68182-0324, 402-554-3159. 1972. Poetry, fiction, reviews. "Dedicated to the best contemporary fiction, essays and poetry. Previous contributors include Kelly Cherry, Jack Myers, David Hopes, Mary Swander, Stewart O'Nan, Chris Mazza, Patricia Goedicke, Leslie Pietrzyk, Jonis Agee, DeWitt Henry, Richard Jackson. Prefer fiction and poetry which shows control of form and an ear for language, and which transcends mere competence in technique. Closed April 15 - August 30." circ. 1M. 2/yr. Pub'd 2 issues 1998; expects 2 issues 1999, 2 issues 2000. sub. price: $11; per copy: $6; sample: $3. Discounts: bookstores 60/40, distributors 55/45. 108pp; 6×9; of. Reporting time: 3-6 months. Payment: 2 copies and 1 yr. subscription. Copyrighted, reverts to author. Ads: $50/$30. CLMP.

NEDGE, Henry Gould, Editor; Janet Sullivan, Editor, PO Box 2321, Providence, RI 02906. 1994. Poetry, fiction, articles, interviews, criticism, reviews, letters, long-poems. "*Nedge* is open to any work of quality." circ. varies. Irregular. Pub'd 1 issue 1998; expects 1 issue 1999, 1 issue 2000. sub. price: $12/2 issues; per copy: $6; sample: $6 ppd. Discounts: 33% to bookstores. 100pp; 5½×8½; of. Reporting time: 1-3 months. Simultaneous submissions accepted: no. Publishes 2% of manuscripts submitted. Payment: contributors copy. Copyrighted, reverts to author. Pub's reviews: 2 in 1998. §Poetry, criticism. Ads: write for information.

NEGATIVE CAPABILITY, Negative Capability Press, Sue Walker, Editor; Ron Walker, Assistant Editor, 62 Ridgelawn Drive East, Mobile, AL 36608, 205-460-6146. 1981. Poetry, fiction, articles, art, photos, cartoons, interviews, satire, criticism, reviews, letters, long-poems, collages, news items, non-fiction. "Our only qualification is excellence. We publish poets who are established and hope to help establish those who are less well known but deserve to be known better. We welcome new talent, have no particular biases, but want poems which communicate, poems that remain in readers' minds when the poem is no longer before them." circ. 1M. 3/yr. Pub'd 3 issues 1998; expects 3 issues 1999, 3 issues 2000. sub. price: $18; per copy: $6; sample: $6. Discounts: 40% jobber. 184pp; 5½×8½; of. Reporting time: 6 weeks. Simultaneous submissions accepted: no. Payment: 1 copy of publication. Copyrighted, reverts to author. Pub's reviews: 8 in 1998. §Poetry, fiction, non-fiction. Ads: $50/$25/10¢ a word. CLMP.

Negative Capability Press (see also NEGATIVE CAPABILITY), Sue Walker, Chief Editor; Ron Walker, Associate Editor, 62 Ridgelawn Drive East, Mobile, AL 36608, 334-460-6146. 1981. Poetry, criticism. avg. press run 1M. Pub'd 3 titles 1998; expects 1 title 1999, 1 title 2000. 17 titles listed in the *Small Press Record of Books in Print* (28th Edition, 1999-00). avg. price, cloth: $20; paper: $6; other: $14 hardcover. Discounts: 40% jobber. 100pp; 6×9; of. Reporting time: 6 weeks. Payment: yes. Copyrights for author. CLMP.

The Neo Herramann Group, 2075 Buffalo Creek Road, Lake Lure, NC 28746, 704-625-9153. 1987. Non-fiction. "Our first title, *The Creative Brain*, is a book that is geared toward individuals who want to gain full access to his or her mental capabilities, and learn how this can be a very creative process. The author has been a trainer of trainers in a corporate setting for over 20 years. Basing his work on brain dominance theory, the author has developed a model of thinking styles which can be used in training or for an individual's quest to know more about him or herself." avg. press run 5M. Pub'd 1 title 1998; expects 1 title 2000. 1 title listed in the *Small Press Record of Books in Print* (28th Edition, 1999-00). avg. price, paper: $26.95. Discounts: trade 2-7 35%, 8-48 40%, 49-104 50%, 105+ 55%, STOP 25%. 480pp; 11×8½; of. Copyrights for author. ABA.

NEOLOGISMS, Jim Fay, Box 869, 1102 Pleasant Street, Worcester, MA 01602. 1996. Poetry, fiction, photos, criticism, plays. "No 'love' poetry or essays about your pets or children" circ. 80. 4/yr. Pub'd 2 issues 1998; expects 4 issues 1999, 4 issues 2000. sub. price: $20; per copy: $5; sample: $5. Back issues: n/a. Discounts: nothing standard; interested parties should contact publisher. 65pp; 8½×11; †mi. Reporting time: 1-2 months. Simultaneous submissions are accepted, but they are frowned upon. Publishes 65% of manuscripts submitted. Payment: 1 copy. Not copyrighted. Pub's reviews: 2 in 1998. §Critical theory, poetry.

●**NEOTROPE, Broken Boulder Press,** Adam Powell, Paul Silvia, PO Box 172, Lawrence, KS 66044, e-mail apowell10@hotmail.com; website www.brokenboulder.com. 1998. Fiction, art, parts-of-novels, plays. "We need progressive and highly innovative fiction and drama. No minimum or maximum length. Looking especially for stories/works that blur the boundaries between fiction and other genres." circ. 1M. 1/yr. Pub'd 1 issue 1998; expects 1 issue 1999, 2 issues 2000. sub. price: $8/2 issues; per copy: $5; sample: $5. Back issues: $5. Discounts: classrooms 10 copies $3 each. 100pp; 5½x8½; letterpress. Reporting time: 4 weeks. Simultaneous submissions accepted: yes. Publishes 10% of manuscripts submitted. Payment: 2 copies. Copyrighted, reverts to author. Ads: by exchange only with other small presses.

NERVE COWBOY, Liquid Paper Press, Joseph Shields, Jerry Hagins, PO Box 4973, Austin, TX 78765, www.onr.com/user/jwhagins/nervecowboy.html. 1995. Poetry, fiction, art. "Open to all forms, styles and subject matter preferring writing that speaks directly and minimizes literary devices. Fiction (up to 5 pages), poetry, and black & white artwork submissions are welcome year round. Recent contributers include Hayley R. Mitchell, Mark Weber, Gerald Locklin, Joan Jobe Smith, and Belinda Subraman." circ. 250. 2/yr. Pub'd 2 issues 1998; expects 2 issues 1999, 2 issues 2000. sub. price: $7; per copy: $4; sample: $4. Back issues: $3. Discounts: selected trades, 40% on 3 or more copies (bookstores). 64pp; 7x8½; mi. Reporting time: 6-8 weeks. Simultaneous submissions accepted: no. Publishes 5% of manuscripts submitted. Payment: 1 copy. Copyrighted, reverts to author. Ads: trade ads with other small magazines.

Neshui Publishing, Bradley Hodge, 1345 Bellevue, St. Louis, MO 63117, 314-725-5562; e-mail info@neshui.com; website www.neshui.com. Pub'd 3 titles 1998; expects 3 titles 1999, 3 titles 2000. 6 titles listed in the *Small Press Record of Books in Print* (28th Edition, 1999-00). Discounts: 55% wholesalers.

NETWORK, Tatiana Stoumen, Box 810, Gracie Station, New York, NY 10028, 212-737-7536; Fax; 212-737-9469; E-mail; iwwg@iwwg.com; Ourside; http://www.iwwg.com. 1976. Interviews, reviews, news items. "A network for women who write, great variety of listings on where to submit work. New information every 2 months. Successes and questions of members. Lots more." circ. 3M. 6/yr. Pub'd 6 issues 1998; expects 6 issues 1999, 6 issues 2000. sub. price: $35 with membership in IWWG, $45 outside the U.S.; sample: $1. 32pp; 8½x11; of. Pub's reviews. Ads: $400/$200/$100 1/4 page/$50 1/8 page.

Network 3000 Publishing, Ron Johnson, 3432 Denmark Avenue #108, St. Paul, MN 55123-1088, 612-452-4173. 1992. Fiction, non-fiction. "Recently printed *The Gift: A Discovery of Happiness, Love and Fulfillment* by Kevin L. Hogan." avg. press run will vary. Pub'd 1 title 1998; expects 3 titles 1999, 6 titles 2000. 2 titles listed in the *Small Press Record of Books in Print* (28th Edition, 1999-00). avg. price, paper: $9.95. Discounts: upon request. 200pp; 5½x8½; †of. Reporting time: 3 months. Simultaneous submissions accepted: yes. Publishes 10% of manuscripts submitted. Payment: up to $500 in advance, 10-15% wholesale. Copyrights for author.

Nevada Publications, Stanley W. Paher, 4135 Badger Circle, Reno, NV 89509, 702-747-0800; Fax 702-747-2916. 1970. Poetry, articles, art, photos, cartoons. "We seek out the author, and do not solicit manuscripts. We publish books on Nevada, California and Arizona, mostly historic guides to scenic areas and ghost towns. All are lavishly illustrated and are solidly based in original research and are substantially edited." avg. press run 3M. Pub'd 9 titles 1998; expects 13 titles 1999, 9 titles 2000. 21 titles listed in the *Small Press Record of Books in Print* (28th Edition, 1999-00). avg. price, cloth: $20; paper: $9. Discounts: please inquire. Cloth 196pp, paper 48pp; 7x10; of. Payment: 10% 1st edition; subsequent editions negotiable. Will possibly copyright for author.

NEW AGE PATRIOT, Bruce W. Cain, PO Box 419, Dearborn Heights, MI 48127, 313-563-3192. 1989. Articles, art, photos, cartoons, interviews, criticism, reviews, letters, news items. circ. 3.5M. 4/yr. Pub'd 4 issues 1998; expects 4 issues 1999, 4 issues 2000. sub. price: $10; per copy: $2.95; sample: $2.95. 28pp; 8½x11; †lp. Payment: not at this time. Copyrighted, reverts to author. Pub's reviews: 4 in 1998. §Drug policy, environmental policy, social policy. Ads: $100/$60/$250 double page.

●**NEW ALTERNATIVES, J & J Consultants, Inc.,** Walter Jones, 603 Ole Farm Road, Media, PA 19063, 610-565-9692; Fax 610-565-9694; wjones13@juno.com; www.members.tripod/walterjones. 1993. Poetry, fiction, articles, cartoons, music, non-fiction. "Short: 100-200 words." circ. 300. 6/yr. Expects 6 issues 1999, 6 issues 2000. sub. price: $12; per copy: $3. 8pp; 8½x11. Reporting time: 2 months. Simultaneous submissions accepted: yes. Publishes 5% of manuscripts submitted. Payment: none. Copyrighted, reverts to author. Pub's reviews. §Parenting, childcare. Independent Publishers, Publishers Marketing Association.

NEW AMERICAN WRITING, Paul Hoover, Maxine Chernoff, 369 Molino Avenue, Mill Valley, CA 94941, 415-389-1877 phone and fax. 1971. Poetry, fiction, art, criticism, reviews. "Work by Ann Lauterbach, Nathaniel Mackey, Robert Coover, John Ashbery, Charles Bernstein, Charles Simic, Lyn Hejinian, Clark Coolidge, Wanda Coleman, Joric Graham, Robert Creeley and others. Special issues: #4 Australian poetry; #5, Censorship and the arts, #9 New British poetry. Covers by prominent artists." circ. 6M. 1/yr. Pub'd 1 issue 1998; expects 1 issue 1999, 1 issue 2000. sub. price: $21 three issues individuals, $27/3 issues institutions, $7 postal surcharge foreign mail; per copy: $8 domestic, $10 Canada; sample: $8. Back issues: varies, please inquire. Discounts: 60/40 to bookstores. 150pp; 5½x8½; of. Reporting time: 1-3 months. Payment: 2 copies. Copyrighted, reverts to author. Pub's reviews: 1 in 1998. §Poetry. Ads: $250. CLMP.

NEW ANGLICAN REVIEW, John C. Brainerd, 18600 West 58 Avenue, Golden, CO 80403-1070, 303-279-2462. 1983. Poetry, fiction, articles, art, photos, cartoons, interviews, satire, criticism, reviews, music, letters, parts-of-novels, long-poems, collages, plays, concrete art, non-fiction. circ. 822. 12/yr. Pub'd 12 issues 1998; expects 12 issues 1999, 12 issues 2000. sub. price: $50; per copy: $5; sample: $5. Back issues: $5. 40pp; 5½x8½; †of. Reporting time: 30-90 days. Publishes 90% of manuscripts submitted. Payment: 1/2 net. Copyrighted, there are no rights purchased. Pub's reviews: 12 in 1998. §Theology, philosophy, history, education. Ads: $35/page, $5/inch. Int. Pub. Assn.

NEW ART EXAMINER, George Bucciero, Publisher; Ann Wiens, Editor, 314 West Institute Place, Chicago, IL 60610-3007, 312-786-0200. 1973. Articles, art, photos, interviews, criticism, reviews, letters, news items. "Commentary on and analysis of the exhibition and making of the visual arts." circ. 4M. 10/yr. Pub'd 10 issues 1998; expects 10 issues 1999, 10 issues 2000. sub. price: $35, $62/2 years; per copy: $4.75; sample: $4.75. Back issues: $4.75 each. Discounts: 3x, 6x, 11x rates. 56pp; 8¼x10⅞; web. Reporting time: 2 months. Publishes 5% of manuscripts submitted. Payment: $40 reviews, $150-$300 article. Copyrighted, reverts to author. Pub's reviews: 5 in 1998. §Visual arts and architecture. Ads: $990 b&w, $1715 4-color/$550 b&w, $1275 4-color/60¢ word classified.

NEW BOOKS ON WOMEN & FEMINISM, Women's Studies Librarian, University of Wisconsin System, Phyllis Holman Weisbard, Lynne Chase, 430 Memorial Library, 728 State Street, Madison, WI 53706, 608-263-5754. 1979. "A subject-arranged, indexed bibliography of new titles in women's studies, listing books and periodicals." circ. 1.1M. 2/yr. Pub'd 2 issues 1998; expects 2 issues 1999, 2 issues 2000. sub. price: $30 individuals and women's programs, $55 institutions (includes subscriptions to *New Books On Women & Feminism, Feminist Collections*, and *Feminist Periodicals*; per copy: $3.50; sample: $3.50. Back issues: $3.50. 75pp; 8½x11; desktop publishing; offset printing. Copyrighted.

New Broom Private Press (see also FENICE BROADSHEETS), 78 Cambridge Street, Leicester, England. 1994. avg. press run 100-120. Pub'd 1 title 1998; expects 3 titles 1999. 3 titles listed in the *Small Press Record of Books in Print* (28th Edition, 1999-00). avg. price, paper: £6. 20pp; 8x5; †lp. Payment: 6 copies. Copyrights for author.

New Canaan Publishing Company Inc., Kathy Mittelstadt, PO Box 752, New Canaan, CT 06840, 203-966-3408 phone/Fax. 1995. Poetry, fiction, non-fiction. "Publisher of children's books with strong educational and/or moral content." avg. press run 5M. Pub'd 2 titles 1998; expects 12 titles 1999, 10 titles 2000. 5 titles listed in the *Small Press Record of Books in Print* (28th Edition, 1999-00). avg. price, paper: $5. Discounts: please call for rates. Pages vary; size varies; of. Reporting time: 1-2 months. Simultaneous submissions accepted: no. Publishes approx. 3% of manuscripts submitted. Payment: percentage royalty (4-12% depending on material). Copyrights for author.

NEW CATHOLIC REVIEW, John C. Brainerd, 18600 West 58 Avenue, Golden, CO 80403-1070, 303-279-2462. 1983. Poetry, fiction, articles, art, photos, cartoons, interviews, satire, criticism, reviews, music, letters, parts-of-novels, long-poems, collages, plays, concrete art, non-fiction. circ. 1160. 12/yr. Pub'd 12 issues 1998; expects 12 issues 1999, 12 issues 2000. sub. price: $50; per copy: $5; sample: $5. Back issues: $5. 40pp; 5½x8½; †photo offset. Reporting time: 30-90 days. Publishes 90% of manuscripts submitted. Payment: 1/2 net. Copyrighted, reverts to author. Pub's reviews: 12 in 1998. §Theology, philosophy, history, education. Ads: $35/$5 per inch. Int. Pub. Assn.

NEW CIVILIZATION STAFF REPORT, Various Editors, PO Box 260433, Encino, CA 91316, 818-725-3775. 1983. Articles, letters, non-fiction. circ. 100 + web page. 6/yr. Pub'd 12 issues 1998; expects 6 issues 1999, 6 issues 2000. sub. price: $10; per copy: $2; sample: $1. Back issues: $5. 20pp; 8½x11; †xerox/world wide web. Reporting time: 4 months. Payment: none. Not copyrighted. Pub's reviews: 4 in 1998. §New civilization design + operation. Ads: none.

NEW COLLAGE MAGAZINE, New Collage Press, A. McA. Miller, General Editor, 5700 N. Tamiami Trail, Sarasota, FL 34243-2197, 813-359-4360. 1970. Poetry. "We want poetry with clear focus and strong imagery. Would like to see fresh free verse and contemporary slants on traditional prosodies." circ. 500. 3/yr. Pub'd 3 issues 1998; expects 3 issues 1999. sub. price: $9, $17/2 years; per copy: $3; sample: $3. Back issues: all available, $3/issue or $9 volume. Discounts: 60%/40% to dealers. 32pp; 5½x8½; of. Reporting time: 6 weeks. Payment: 2 copies. Copyrighted, reverts to author. Pub's reviews: 2 in 1998. §Poetry, some interviews. No ads. CLMP.

New Collage Press (see also NEW COLLAGE MAGAZINE), A. McA Miller, General Editor, 5700 North Trail, Sarasota, FL 34234, 813-359-4360. 1970. Poetry, reviews. "Must query." avg. press run 500. Pub'd 1 title 1998; expects 1 title 1999. 14 titles listed in the *Small Press Record of Books in Print* (28th Edition, 1999-00). avg. price, paper: $3. Discounts: 60%/40% to dealers. 32pp; 5½x8½; of. Reporting time: 6 weeks. Payment: by negotiation. First N.A. serial rights purchased. CLMP.

THE NEW CRITERION, Hilton Kramer, 850 Seventh Avenue, New York, NY 10019, 212-247-6980. 1982. Poetry, articles, criticism, reviews. circ. 7M. 10/yr. Pub'd 10 issues 1998; expects 10 issues 1999, 10 issues 2000. sub. price: $36; per copy: $4.75; sample: $5. Back issues: $6. 90pp; 7×10; of. Reporting time: 1 month. Simultaneous submissions accepted: no. Payment: 10¢ per word for articles, $2.50 per line for poetry. Copyrighted, reverts to author. Pub's reviews: approx. 40 in 1998. §Art, architecture, music, poetry, theater. Ads: $800/$500.

●**The New Dawn Press**, 10801 Greenlawn Avenue, Cleveland, OH 44103, 216-431-9600; fax 216-431-4614; e-mail victorsapk.net. 1998. 1 title listed in the *Small Press Record of Books in Print* (28th Edition, 1999-00).

●**New Dawn Unlimited** (see also ALTERNATIVE HARMONIES LITERARY & ARTS MAGAZINE), Jerri Hardesty, 1830 Marvel Road, Brierfield, AL 35035, 205-665-7904; fax 205-665-2500; e-mail wytrabbit1@aol.com. 1997. Poetry, fiction, art, photos, cartoons, long-poems, plays, non-fiction. "Annual chapbook competition-send approximately 20-50 pages/manuscript with a $10 entry fee. Pays 100-200 copies, services, advertising, and artistic input. Recent chaps: Errol Miller, Susan S. Hahn, and Jerri Hardesty." avg. press run 500. Pub'd 2 titles 1998; expects 2-3 titles 1999, 2-3 titles 2000. avg. price, paper: $5. Discounts: $2 each for 20 or more; will consider this price for any good cause. 40-50pp; 5½×8½; †of. Reporting time: 3 months after annual deadline. Simultaneous submissions not accepted on chapbooks. Publishes 5% of manuscripts submitted. Payment: 100-200 copies. Does not copyright for author. ASPS.

NEW DELTA REVIEW, c/o Dept. of English, Louisiana State University, Baton Rouge, LA 70803-5001, 504-388-4079. 1984. Poetry, fiction, art, photos, interviews, reviews, long-poems, non-fiction. "We at *New Delta Review* publish new and established writers of poetry and fiction. We also accept literary interviews, reviews, essays, and black & white artwork, and full-color art." circ. 500. 2/yr. Pub'd 2 issues 1998; expects 2 issues 1999, 2 issues 2000. sub. price: $10; per copy: $6; sample: $5. Back issues: $4 for any issue prior to the current one, $5 for libraries. 150pp; 6×9; of. Reporting time: 2-4 months. Simultaneous submissions accepted: no. Publishes 1% of manuscripts submitted. Payment: 2 contributors' copies. Copyrighted, reverts to author. Pub's reviews: 8 in 1998. §Contemporary poetry, fiction and literary essays, popular culture, works on contemporary authors. mostly ad trades. CLMP.

New Earth Publications, Clifton Ross, Dave Karoly, 1921 Ashby Ave, Berkeley, CA 94703, 510-549-0176. 1990. Poetry. "Publisher of Latin American poetry anthologies with progressive political slant in bilingual editions. Poets include Nicaraguan (Ernesto Cardenal, Daisy Zamora, etc.), also chapbooks of North American spiritual/political poets (Henry Noyes, William Emerson and others). Also some prose, such as the spiritual writings of A.C. Sandino Zapatistas, non-sexist *Gospel of Mark*; autobiographies y by Luisa Gonzalez, Maud Morgan" avg. press run varies. Expects 3 titles 1999. 8 titles listed in the *Small Press Record of Books in Print* (28th Edition, 1999-00). avg. price, paper: $9.95. Discounts: 60/40. 8½×5½; †of. Reporting time: up to 3 months. Publishes 30-40% of manuscripts submitted. Payment: negotiable. Copyrights for author.

NEW ENGLAND ANTIQUES JOURNAL, Jamie Mercier, Managing Editor, Turley Publications, 4 Church Street, Ware, MA 01082, 413-967-3505. 1982. Articles, photos, reviews, news items, non-fiction, interviews. "Feature articles, 2,000-5,000 words and 12 color photos, slides, or transparencies on antiques. Know the subject you are writing about." circ. 30M. 12/yr. Pub'd 12 issues 1998; expects 12 issues 1999, 12 issues 2000. sub. price: $19.95; per copy: $2.00; sample: free. Discounts: by individual arrangement. 100pp; 11×16; †of. Reporting time: 2-6 weeks. Simultaneous submissions accepted if author informs us upon submission. Publishes 50% of manuscripts submitted. Payment: by individual arrangement. Copyrighted, does not revert to author. Pub's reviews: 144 in 1998. §Antiques & Collectibles. Ads: $595/$340/30¢ per word ($6 min).

New England Cartographics, Inc., Christopher J. Ryan, President; Bruce Scofield, Vice President; Valerie Vaughan, Editor, PO Box 9369, North Amherst, MA 01059, 413-549-4124; FAX 413-549-3621. 1986. Non-fiction. "Specialize in outdoor recreation maps and guidebooks; hiking, backpacking, bicycling, mountain biking, principally of areas in North Eastern United States" avg. press run 3M-5M. Pub'd 2 titles 1998; expects 3 titles 1999, 4 titles 2000. 8 titles listed in the *Small Press Record of Books in Print* (28th Edition, 1999-00). avg. price, paper: $8.95-$16.95. Discounts: trade 40-45% retail, 45-55% wholesale/distributors. 178pp; 6×9; 5½×8½, 8⅜×5⅝, 7¼×4¾, 8×10; of. Reporting time: 1 month. Simultaneous submissions accepted: yes. Publishes 25% of manuscripts submitted. Payment: 7-10% of cover price. Copyrights for author. IMTA, NEBA.

THE NEW ENGLAND QUARTERLY, Linda Smith Rhoads, Editor; William M. Fowler, Jr., Editor, 239 Meserve Hall, Northeastern University, Boston, MA 02115, 617-373-2734. 1928. Articles, criticism, reviews. "*The New England Quarterly*, a Historical Review of New England Life and Letters, publishes articles in the fields of literature, history, art, and culture; short memoranda and documents; and book reviews." circ. 2.5M. 4/yr. Pub'd 4 issues 1998; expects 4 issues 1999, 4 issues 2000. sub. price: $20; per copy: $7. Back issues: $10. 176pp; 6×9; of. Reporting time: 6-8 weeks. Simultaneous submissions accepted: no. Publishes 20% of manuscripts submitted. Payment: 1-year free subscription. Copyrighted, does not revert to author. Pub's reviews: 50 in 1998. §American literature (with some connection to New England), New England history, art, culture, biography (all with some connection to New England). Ads: $200/$100/$125.

NEW ENGLAND REVIEW, Middlebury College, Stephen Donadio, Editor, Middlebury College, Middlebury, VT 05753, 802-443-5075; fax 802-443-2088; e-mail nereview@mail.middlebury.edu. 1978. Poetry, fiction, articles, photos, interviews, criticism, reviews, parts-of-novels, long-poems. "We publish 4 issues every year. Submissions accepted Sept.1- June 1 only" circ. 2M. 4/yr. Pub'd 4 issues 1998; expects 4 issues 1999, 4 issues 2000. sub. price: $23 individual, $40 institution; per copy: $7; sample: $7. Back issues: $7. Discounts: 2 years, $43; 3 years, $62; 20% classroom. 184pp; 7×10; of. Reporting time: 3-4 months. Simultaneous submissions accepted, if indicated as such. Publishes 2% of manuscripts submitted. Payment: $10 per page, $20 minimum, plus 2 copies. Copyrighted. Pub's reviews: 4 in 1998. §Contemporary fiction, poetry, biography, autobiography, non-fiction. Ads: $200/$125/discounts for featured authors and books reviewed. CLMP.

NEW ENVIRONMENT BULLETIN, Harry Schwarzlander, 270 Fenway Drive, Syracuse, NY 13224, 315-446-8009. 1974. Articles, interviews, reviews, letters, news items. "Contains reports of activities of The New Environment Association, as well as articles and news items relating to the concerns of the Association, which are personal and social changes needed to achieve a sustainable society, and the creation of new communities which are humanly and environmentally sound. Content is contributed primarily by members and other readers." circ. 160. 10-11/yr. Pub'd 10 issues 1998; expects 10-11 issues 1999, 10-11 issues 2000. sub. price: $10 (North America); per copy: $1; sample: free. Back issues: $5 for 2-year series (even-to-odd years). 4-6pp; 8½×11; of, photocopy. Reporting time: not specified. Payment: none. Not copyrighted. Pub's reviews: 5 in 1998. §See above. Ads: none.

New Falcon Publications, Frank Martin, 1739 E. Broadway Road, Suite 1-277, Tempe, AZ 85282. 1 title listed in the *Small Press Record of Books in Print* (28th Edition, 1999-00).

New Fantasy Publications, Thomas H. Traubitz, Publisher, 203 Lexington Drive, Silver Spring, MD 20901-2637. 1991. Fiction, art. "New Fantasy Publications is devoted to printing original works of imaginative literature. Both novels and multi-author short fiction collections are published." avg. press run 500-1M. Expects 1 title 2000. avg. price, cloth: $20; paper: $15. 200pp; 7½×9; of. Reporting time: novels 180 days, short stories 90 days. Simultaneous submissions accepted: no. Payment: individually negotiated. Copyrights for author.

NEW FRONTIER, Swami Virato, Executive Editor & Founder; Alan Cohen, Assoc. Editor, PO Box 17397, Asheville, NC 28816-7397. 1980. Art, photos, music, news items. "We print that which is transformative and positive in nature. Material should address itself to personal and social transformation, the new age, holistic health, etc. showing the interconnection or harmony of spirit, mind, and body. Articles on assignment 1.5M to 4M word length. Submissions welcome with SASE" circ. 60M. 11/yr. Pub'd 11 issues 1998; expects 11 issues 1999, 11 issues 2000. sub. price: $18; per copy: $1.95; sample: $2. Back issues: $2. Discounts: 50% for 100 copies ppd. 56pp; 8¼×10½; webb press. Reporting time: 60 days. Payment: 4-5¢ a word. Copyrighted, reverts to author. Pub's reviews: 35 in 1998. §New Age, spiritual, holistic health, psychology, ecology, alternative lifestyle, parapsychological, appropriate technology, vegeterianism. Ads: $1180/$675/75¢.

NEW GERMAN REVIEW: A Journal of Germanic Studies, Martina Eidecker, Erik Eisel, Dept of Germanic Languages, University of CA, Los Angeles, Los Angeles, CA 90024, (310) 825-3955. 1985. Articles, interviews, criticism, reviews. "Manuscripts should be prepared in accordance with the 1984 *MLA Handbook* (paranthetical documentation) and not exceed 20 typed pages including documentation. Unsolicited book reviews are not accepted." circ. 250. 1/yr. Pub'd 1 issue 1998; expects 1 issue 1999, 1 issue 2000. sub. price: $8 students; $11 individuals; $14 institutions; per copy: $8; sample: free. 100pp; 6×9; of. Reporting time: 3 months after submission deadline. Payment: none. Copyrighted, does not revert to author. Pub's reviews: 1 in 1998. Ads on exchange basis. Graduate Students Association (GSA), University of California, Los Angeles.

New Hope International (see also AABYE (formerly New Hope International Writing); NEW HOPE INTERNATIONAL REVIEW), Gerald England, 20 Werneth Avenue, Gee Cross, Hyde SK14 5NL, United Kingdom, 0161-351 1878; www.nhi.clara.net/online.htm. 1970. Poetry, long-poems, concrete art, art, photos. "Founded as Headland in 1970. Onetime UK distributor of Dustbooks Directory. Partner stole the name Headland (and all the money in the bank a/c) in 1980 so New Hope International started up. Potential authors should have a body of work published in magazines before approaching. Have published *Hope of Peace* by Iranian concert pianist Novin Afrouz, a tribute to the late Basil Bunting, a collection by B.Z. Niditch. *Editor's Dilemma,* which tells the story of 20 years of small press publishing and *The Art of Haiku,* useful to newcomers to the genre as well as more established writers." avg. press run 500-1M. Pub'd 6 titles 1998; expects 6 titles 1999, 6 titles 2000. 18 titles listed in the *Small Press Record of Books in Print* (28th Edition, 1999-00). avg. price, paper: $10 cash; non-sterling charges not acceptable. Discounts: on application. 36-60pp; size A5; offset/litho. Reporting time: 3-6 months. Simultaneous submissions not encouraged. Publishes 1-2% of manuscripts submitted. Payment: varies, usually authors have a very generous discount on copies. Does not copyright for author. Association of Little Presses.

NEW HOPE INTERNATIONAL REVIEW, New Hope International, Gerald England, 20 Werneth Avenue, Gee Cross, Hyde, Cheshire SK14 5NL, United Kingdom, 061-351 1878. 1986. Reviews, letters, music. "Short reviews of a wide range of publications including records, cassettes & computer software but main emphasis on poetry, art and music. Unsolicited reviews not required but U.K. subscribers who can write fluently are welcome to join the reviewing team." circ. 1M. 2-3/yr. Pub'd 2 issues 1998; expects 2 issues 1999, 2 issues 2000. sub. price: £13 for 3 issues; per copy: $10 (includes postage) cash only. Back issues: $5 cash. 60pp; size A5; offset/litho. Reporting time: up to 9 months. Simultaneous submissions accepted: no. Publishes (solicited only) 90% of manuscripts submitted. Payment: copies. Not copyrighted. Pub's reviews: 1000 in 1998. §Poetry, fiction (inc. childrens), literary criticism, art, music, cassettes, videos, computer software (PC), records, CDs; anything interesting or unusual, 90% of items received are reviewed. Ads: on application. Small Press Group of Great Britain, Association of Little Presses.

The New Humanity Press, PO Box 215, Berkeley, CA 94701. 1986. Fiction, articles, art, photos, cartoons, interviews, satire, criticism, reviews, music, letters, parts-of-novels, news items, non-fiction. "All material book-length. Our slant is looking for the 'truth,' however we find it, and looking to improve our uniquely human condition, with a view to universal justice and peace-seeking harmony for all life everywhere." avg. press run 3M-5M. Expects 1 title 1999, 3 titles 2000. 2 titles listed in the *Small Press Record of Books in Print* (28th Edition, 1999-00). avg. price, paper: $19.95. Discounts: bulk and trade. 350pp; 6×9; of. Reporting time: 2-4 weeks. Payment: under consideration. Copyrights for author.

New International, Mary-Alice Waters, 410 West Street, New York, NY 10014, 212-741-0690, fax 212-727-0150. 1983. "Distributed by Pathfinder Press" avg. press run 7.5M. Pub'd 2 titles 1998; expects 2 titles 1999. 22 titles listed in the *Small Press Record of Books in Print* (28th Edition, 1999-00). avg. price, paper: $10. 300pp; 5¼×8¼.

New Issues Press, Herbert Scott, Editor; Nancy Elmers, Advisory Editor; Mark Halliday, Advisory Editor; William Olsen, Advisory Editor; J. Allyn Rosser, Advisory Editor, Western Michigan University, 1201 Oliver Street, Kalamazoo, MI 49008, 616-387-2592 or 616-387-8185; Fax 616-387-2562; newissues-poetry@wmich.edu; www.wmich.edu/english/fac/nipps. 1996. Poetry. "New Issues Poetry Prize, $1,000 and publication for a first book of poems. Deadline: Nov. 30, 1999. Judge: C.K. Williams. The Green Rose Prize in Poetry, $1,000 and publication for a book of poems by an established poet. Deadline: Sept. 30. Send SASE for complete guidelines or visit our website." avg. press run 1,250. Pub'd 6 titles 1998; expects 6-7 titles 1999, 7 titles 2000. 16 titles listed in the *Small Press Record of Books in Print* (28th Edition, 1999-00). avg. price, cloth: $22; paper: $12. Discounts: subscription: 3 titles $30 postpaid; individuals order direct; individual credit card orders call toll free 877-885-BOOK; bookstores may order through distributor, Partners 800-336-3137 or through Ingram. 72pp; 6×8½; offset. Reporting time: 3 months. Simultaneous submissions accepted: yes. We publish 1 out of 250 manuscripts submitted for publication. Payment: poet receives 10% of press run in lieu of royalties. Copyrights for author. PMA.

THE NEW LAUREL REVIEW, Lee Meitzen Grue, Editor, 828 Lesseps Street, New Orleans, LA 70117, 504-947-6001. 1971. Poetry, fiction, articles, art, photos, reviews, non-fiction. "We want fresh work; shy away from dry academic articles with footnotes, and from poems with the guts cut out. Recently published: Julie Kane, P.B. Parris, James Nolan, Arthur Pfister III, Len Roberts, Marilyn Coffey, Billy Marshall-Stoneking, and Jared Carter." circ. 500. 1/yr. Pub'd 1 issue 1998. 3 titles listed in the *Small Press Record of Books in Print* (28th Edition, 1999-00). sub. price: $10 individuals, $12 institutions, $15 foreign; per copy: double issue $9; sample: $8. Back issues: $8. Discounts: 5 copies for $40. 125pp; 6×9; of. Reporting time: varies, longer time for interesting work; somewhat crowded with fiction & poetry—about 6 weeks; do not read in summer. We prefer to be informed of simultaneous submissions, but simultaneous submissions not good practice; must have immediate notification upon another acceptance. Publishes maybe 10% of manuscripts submitted. Payment: 1 copy of the magazine in which their work appears. Copyrighted. Pub's reviews: 5 in 1998. §Poetry and books about poets and related matter, collections of short fiction. Ads: none. CELJ.

NEW LETTERS, James McKinley, University of Missouri, Kansas City, MO 64110, 816-235-1168; Fax 816-235-2611; www.umkc.edu/newsletters/. 1971 (Predecessor, *University Review,* 1934). Poetry, fiction, articles, art, photos, satire, parts-of-novels, long-poems. "The best in contemporary fiction, poetry, personal essay, art, interviews, and photography. Regular essays on art and culture include Janet Burroway, Gerald Early, Alberto Rios. Contributors include Bly, Gallagher, Oates, Price, Harrison, Levertov, Kumin. Special issues on Jack Conroy, the writer in politics, New S. African Writing, the writer and religion, the new inferno." circ. 2.5M. 4/yr. Pub'd 4 issues 1998; expects 4 issues 1999, 4 issues 2000. 5 titles listed in the *Small Press Record of Books in Print* (28th Edition, 1999-00). sub. price: $17; per copy: $5; sample: $5. Back issues: $5-$7.50, rare issues $20. Discounts: 25% on contract of 4 ads. 140pp; 6×9; of. Reporting time: 2-4 months. Simultaneous submissions accepted: no. Publishes 2-5% of manuscripts submitted. Payment: small, upon publication. Copyrighted, reverts to author. Ads: $150/$90. CLMP.

New Liberty Press, Fanny Semiglia, 405 West 48th Street Rm 2R, New York, NY 10036, 212-459-2614. 1990. avg. press run 2M. Pub'd 2 titles 1998. 1 title listed in the *Small Press Record of Books in Print* (28th Edition, 1999-00). avg. price, paper: $12.95. 350pp; 6×9.

New Management Publishing Company, Inc., PO Box 0879, Winter Park, FL 32790, 407-647-5344. 1993. Non-fiction. "Management books, how-to." avg. press run 30M-50M. Expects 3 titles 1999, 3 titles 2000. 3 titles listed in the *Small Press Record of Books in Print* (28th Edition, 1999-00). avg. price, paper: $19.95. Discounts: wholesaler 55%. 250pp; 6×9. Payment: 10% net. Copyrights for author. PMA.

NEW METHODS JOURNAL (VETERINARY), AHT Lippert, Editor & Publisher, PO Box 22605, San Francisco, CA 94122-0605, 415-664-3469. 1976. Poetry, articles, art, photos, cartoons, interviews, criticism, reviews, letters, news items, non-fiction. "Double-spaced with one inch margins; material should be relevant to Veterinary field (prefer staff related - animal health technicians); most contributors are in the veterinary field with some experience. *New Methods* has a list of other animal publications in the animal field for $20. (Sample copies of other Pet-Vet Publications available at $2.50, each 20% discount for orders of 12 or more." circ. 5.6M. Irregular. Pub'd 12 issues 1998. sub. price: $29 (additional cost outside of U.S.A., all monies must be in U.S. funds); per copy: $2.90; sample: $2.90. Back issues: $2.90 with 20% discount 12 or more copies, same or different. Discounts: free copies to published person. 4pp; 9×11; sheetfed. Reporting time: 2-6 weeks. Simultaneous submissions accepted: yes. Publishes 5% of manuscripts submitted. Payment: if published, $0 first time with increase with each publication; generally no payment, possible in the future; perks & commission. Copyrighted, reverts to author. Pub's reviews: 144 in 1998. §Animal, veterinary, employee related, pet, wildlife. Ads: $290/$145/29¢/smaller ad space is available.

THE NEW MOON REVIEW, Jerry Oleaf, 148 Eighth Avenue #417, New York, NY 10011. 1991. Poetry. "We've published Yuki Hartman, Janine Pommy Vega, Daniela Gioseffi, others. We can use all types of poetry whether it's sonnets influenced by Keats, or Zen poetry influenced by Basho, provided it's good quality. Include SASE." circ. 250. 2-3/yr. Pub'd 3 issues 1998; expects 4 issues 1999, 4 issues 2000. 32pp; 5½×8½; of. Reporting time: 3 weeks. Simultaneous submissions accepted: yes. Publishes 25% of manuscripts submitted. Payment: in copies. Copyrighted, reverts to author.

NEW MUSE OF CONTEMPT, Broken Jaw Press, Joe Blades, Box 596 Stn A, Canada, E3B 5A6, Fredericton, Canada, 902-423-5223. 1987. Poetry, fiction, reviews, concrete art. circ. 200-500. 2/yr. Pub'd 2 issues 1998; expects 2 issues 1999, 2 issues 2000. sub. price: $12; per copy: $6; sample: $6. 52pp; 5½×8½; photocopy. Reporting time: 2-6 months. Simultaneous submissions accepted: no. Publishes 5% of manuscripts submitted. Payment: copies. Copyrighted, reverts to author. Pub's reviews: 4 in 1998. §73/7. Ads: $100/$50. APMA, ACP, LPG.

New Native Press, Thomas Rain Crowe, Publisher; Nan Watkins, Managing Editor, PO Box 661, Cullowhee, NC 28723, 828-293-9237. 1979. Poetry, art. "No unsolicited manuscripts considered." avg. press run 1M. Pub'd 2 titles 1998; expects 1 title 1999, 1 title 2000. 11 titles listed in the *Small Press Record of Books in Print* (28th Edition, 1999-00). avg. price, paper: $9.95. Discounts: $7.50 for 10 or more. 80pp; 5½×8; of. Payment: varies (usually 1/3 of run), 50% discount on additional copies. Copyrights for author.

NEW ORLEANS REVIEW, Ralph Adamo, Loyola University, Box 195, New Orleans, LA 70118, 504-865-2295. 1968. Poetry, fiction, articles, art, photos, interviews, criticism, long-poems, non-fiction. "Contributors: Walker Percy, Norman Mailer, James Wright, Alain Robbe-Grillet, Amiri Baraka, Susan Fromberg Schaeffer, Peter Wild, Christopher Isherwood, David Madden, Annie Dillard, Rosemary Daniell, Natalie Petesch, Doris Betts, Larry Rubin, John William Corrington, Maxine Cassin, Kay Murphy, Jimmy Carter, Rodney Jones, William Matthews, Ginny Stanford" circ. 1M. 4/yr. Pub'd 4 issues 1998; expects 4 issues 1999, 4 issues 2000. sub. price: 4 issues - domestic $18 indiv, $21 instit, foreign $32; per copy: $9 domestic, $15 foreign; sample: $9 domestic, $15 foreign. Back issues: inquire. Discounts: none. 120-190pp; 9×6; of. Reporting time: 3 months. Simultaneous submissions accepted: yes. Publishes less than 1% of manuscripts submitted. Payment: copies, negotiable. Reprint permission available on request. Pub's reviews: 10 in 1998. §all areas—especially fiction, poetry, literature, and film critics. Ads: $700/$350. CLMP.

New Paradigm Books, John Chambers, 22783 South State Road 7, Suite 97, Boca Raton, FL 33428, 561-482-5971; fax 561-852-8322; e-mail jdc@flinet.com; website http://www.newpara.com. 1997. Non-fiction. "In general, we translate "new age" books that have done well abroad. *The Chinese Roswell*, by Hartwig Hausdorf, previously published in Germany as *Die Weisse Pyramide*, is an example." avg. press run 10M. Pub'd 2 titles 1998; expects 2 titles 1999, 3 titles 2000. 2 titles listed in the *Small Press Record of Books in Print* (28th Edition, 1999-00). avg. price, paper: $13.95. Discounts: to be negotiated. 272pp; 6×9; of. Reporting time: 2 months. Simultaneous submissions accepted: no. Payment: negotiable. Copyrights negotiable. PMA.

THE NEW PRESS LITERARY QUARTERLY, Joseph P. Sullivan, Editor-in-Chief and Co-Publisher;

Evie-Ivy Biber, Poetry Editor and Co-Publisher; Victoria Figueredo, Co-Publisher, 6539 108th Street #E6, Forest Hills, NY 11375-2214, 718-459-6807; Fax; 718-275-1646. 1984. Poetry, fiction, articles, art, interviews, satire, criticism, music, parts-of-novels, long-poems, concrete art, non-fiction. "We run imaginative stories up to 22 pages double-spaced. We use illustrations. We run commentary and social and political criticism as well. About one-third of our magazine is poetry." circ. 2M. 4/yr. Pub'd 4 issues 1998; expects 4 issues 1999, 4 issues 2000. sub. price: $15; per copy: $5.50; sample: $5.50. Back issues: $4.50. Discounts: 1 year subscription $15, 2 year $29, 3 year $43. 40-48pp; 8½×11; of. Reporting time: 4 months. Simultaneous submissions accepted: no. Publishes 10% of manuscripts submitted. Payment: 2 copies; $15 for prose ($10 under 500 words); annual essay contest, $100 first prize, $5 entry; annual poetry contest, $100 first prize, $5 entry. Copyrighted, reverts to author. Ads: $100/$65/$20 business card.

New Regency Publishing, David Solomon, PO Box 1443, Sacramento, CA 95812, 800-266-5639. 1994. Non-fiction. "If you can imagine a New Age publishing house, New Regency is the antithesis. We are looking for manuscripts that explore the virtues of 'traditional' points of view, and engagingly elucidate these 'lost' values. If you can recognize ageless principles and can communicate how they relate to real people, go for it. We want material that can appeal to niche market readers - conservative thinkers, home schoolers, monogamous marriages, etc. - and we want authors willing to work those markets once published. Query with clips, outline, and sample chapter. No phone queries." avg. press run 5M. Expects 3 titles 1999, 5 titles 2000. avg. price, cloth: $18.95; paper: $10.95. Discounts: bulk. 208pp; 5½×8½; †of. Reporting time: 3 weeks. Payment: 6%-10% gross receipts; modest advance for proven authors. Copyrights for author. PMA.

THE NEW RENAISSANCE, An International Magazine of Ideas & Opinions, Emphasizing Literature & The Arts, Louise T. Reynolds, Editor-in-Chief; Michal Ann Kucharski, Associate Editor; Ruth Moose, Consulting Editor; Olivera Sajkovia, Art Editor, Consulting Editor; Frank Finale, Poetry Editor, 26 Heath Road #11, Arlington, MA 02474-3645. 1968. Poetry, fiction, articles, art, photos, cartoons, interviews, satire, criticism, reviews, music, letters, parts-of-novels, long-poems, collages, plays, non-fiction. "Since April 1, 1995, our submission policy for fiction and poetry has been tied to our award programs for fiction and poetry and requires an entry fee: $15 per submission for non-subscribers; $10 per submission for subscribers. Unless a fiction ms is 4 double-spaced, typewritten pp or less, only one fiction ms per submission. Ficton: mss from 2 to 36 pp. Poetry: 3-6 one-page poems; 2-4 two page poems; only one long poem per submission. Translations are welcome (ALWAYS include originals) Submit as often as you like — but each submission requires an entry fee. Any fiction or poetry submission without the accompanying fee will be returned *unread.* The 1st awards were announced in the Fall 1996; the third awards will be announced winter 2000/2001. Submitting periods: January 2 - June 30 & Sept. 1 - Oct. 31 for fiction only. Only fiction and poetry published in a *tnr* volume are legible. All writers published in *tnr* recieve our regular payments as well as a copy or copies of the issue containing their work. Independent judges. Louise E. Reynolds Memorial Fiction Awards: 1st place: $500; 2nd $250; 3rd $100; one honorable mention $35. *tnr* Poetry Awards: 1st place - $250; 2nd - $125; 3rd - $50; three honorable mentions - $20 each. Unless you are unfamiliar with *tnr*, send mss with entry fees. Current subscibers may extend their subscription by an issue or receive two back issues (their choice). Non-subscribers may recieve two back issues or a recent issue (their choice). For those submitting non-fiction, we ask that mss be accompanied by $10 for which you'll recieve a recent issue. Non-fiction may be on a variety of topics — literature, cinema, music, theatre, visual art, etc., and, if directed to a general, literate audience, science. Submitting periods nonfiction: January 2 - November 30th. We are looking for writing that has something to say, that says it with style or grace, & which speaks in a highly personalized voice. All mss submissions MUST be accompanied by a SASE or IRC of sufficient size for their return. All queries re guidelines, questions about submissions, etc., *must* be accompanied by a SASE, IRC or stamped postcard. Fiction submissions generally take 5-8 months; poetry generally take 4-7 months; non-fiction takes 2-5 mon. Writers recently published: Estelle Gilson (translator), Marian Wolfe Laughlin, Marcia Tager, Ruth Moore, Jim Quinn, Alan Amenta, Ralph Salisbury, Antony Oldknow, and Mark Taska." circ. 1.3M. 2/yr. Pub'd 1 issue 1998; expects 2 issues 1999, 2 issues 2000. sub. price: $24/3 issues USA, $26/3 issues Canada; all others $28/3 issues; per copy: $10 USA, $10.30 Canada; $10.45 all others; sample: $10 USA; $10.30 Canada; $10.75 all others. Back issues: $6.50 USA; $7 Canada; $7.50 all others. Discounts: subscription agents, etc. 20%; 20 or more copies or classroom use 25%, 30+ 35%; bookstores 33⅓%, advance payment. 144-184pp; 6×9; of. Reporting time: poetry 3-5 months, prose 5-8 months. We reluctantly accept simultaneous submissions. Publishes fiction, poetry 5-10%, nonfiction 6-12% of manuscripts submitted. Payment: $20-$50 poems, $48-$80 fiction, $60-$150 non-fiction, $20-$25 per drawing. Copyrighted, reverts to author. Pub's reviews: 2 in 1998. §Want to see Press Releases *only, not books* (literature, arts, biographies); we'll *then* decide if we'd like to see the book. Ads: $170/$95.

New Rivers Press, Inc., Robert Alexander, Publisher; Mary Byers, Managing Editor, 420 North 5th Street #938, Minneapolis, MN 55401, 612-339-7114. 1968. Poetry, fiction, art, photos, long-poems, concrete art. "We publish new writing of merit and distinction—poetry, combinations of poetry and prose, short fiction, memoirs, and translations (mostly poetry). We are also involved in publishing such regional programs as the Minnesota

379

Voices Project and the Many Minnesotas Project (a series of ethnic anthologies)." avg. press run 1M-2.5M. Pub'd 8 titles 1998; expects 9 titles 1999, 8 titles 2000. 37 titles listed in the *Small Press Record of Books in Print* (28th Edition, 1999-00). avg. price, cloth: $22.95; paper: $12 poetry, $14.95 prose, $19.95 anthologies. Discounts: 1-5 copies 20%, 6+ 40% trade; 50% for outright purchases 1-4 20%, 5-24 42%, 24-99 43%, 100-249 44%, 250-499 45%, 500-750 46%, 750+ 47%. Bookstores order through Consortium Book Sales and Distribution 1045 Westgate Dr, Suite 90 St.Paul, MN 55114-1065, phone 800-283-3572, fax 612-221-0124. 96-300pp; 6×9. Simultaneous submissions accepted: no. Copyrights for author.

New Seed Press, 1665 Euclid Avenue, Berkeley, CA 94709-1213. 1972. Fiction, art. "New Seed Press is commited to publishing multicultural books for children which actively confront issues of sexism, racism, classism. Do not send unsolicited manuscripts. Query first with return stamped envelope." avg. press run 4M. Pub'd 1 title 1998; expects 2 titles 1999, 1 title 2000. 13 titles listed in the *Small Press Record of Books in Print* (28th Edition, 1999-00). avg. price, paper: $7. Discounts: 40% to bookstores and 55% to distributors; 10% postage. Pages vary; size varies; of. Reporting time: 2 months. Simultaneous submissions accepted: yes. Payment: varies. Copyrights for author.

New Sins Press, Rane Arroyo, Co-Publisher; Glenn Sheldon, Co-Publisher, 5804 Summit Street, Sylvania, OH 43560-1272. 1985. Poetry, art, photos, collages, plays. "New Sins Press poetry chapbooks by invitation only. Recent contributors: Barbara Hamby, Amy Yanity, Mark Magiera, Julie Parson-Nesbitt, and Edgar Silex." avg. press run 200-300. Pub'd 6 titles 1998; expects 1 title 1999, 1 title 2000. 1 title listed in the *Small Press Record of Books in Print* (28th Edition, 1999-00). avg. price, paper: $3. 12pp; 5½×8½; of. Reporting time: 1 month. Payment: in copies. Does not copyright for author.

The New South Company & Boson Books, Nancy Cooke, 3905 Meadow Field Lane, Raleigh, NC 27606-4470. 1976. Fiction, art. "We are publishing about 12 titles a year on the www @ http://www.cmonline.com. Our electronic imprint is Boson Books. Not publishing at this time under the New South Company, but New South titles are still available." Pub'd 12 titles 1998; expects 12 titles 1999, 12 titles 2000. 11 titles listed in the *Small Press Record of Books in Print* (28th Edition, 1999-00). avg. price, cloth: $12; paper: $7; other: $7.50 online editions. Discounts: 20% all titles, all quantities. lp, of. Reporting time: 3-4 weeks. Simultaneous submissions accepted: no. Publishes 1% of manuscripts submitted. Payment: 10% of retail price New South, 20% Boson Books. Does not copyright for author.

THE NEW SOUTHERN SURREALIST REVIEW, Burning Llama Press, Keith Higginbotham, 82 Ridge Lake Drive, Columbia, SC 29209-4213. 1996. Poetry, articles, art, interviews, criticism, reviews, letters, collages, concrete art, news items, non-fiction. "Surrealist perspectives on popular culture, media, and politics. Our 'Reports From the Front' section will feature contributors' accounts of surrealism in their hometown, state, or country. Will publish reviews of magazines, books, recordings, films, and television from a surrealist viewpoint. Art and collages welcome. Poetry should be surreal, language, or experimental *only*. Include cover letter and SASE. Recent contributors: Cliff Dweller, Barrett John Erickson, Richard Kostelanetz, and Larry Tomoyasu." circ. 100-200. Irregular. Expects 1-2 issues 1999, 2 issues 2000. sub. price: $10/3 issues (make checks payable to Keith Higginbotham); per copy: $4; sample: $4. Pages vary; 8½×11; †photocopy. Reporting time: immediate to 3 months. Simultaneous submissions accepted: no. Payment: copy of issue in which they appear. Copyrighted, reverts to author. Pub's reviews. §Poetry, surrealism, politics, native American, popular culture. Ads: will exchange ads with other publications.

New Spirit Press/The Poet Tree (see also POEMS THAT THUMP IN THE DARK/SECOND GLANCE), Ignatius Graffeo, 82-34 138 Street #6F, Kew Gardens, NY 11435, 718-847-1482. 1991. Poetry. "New Spirit Press/Poet Tree publishes a literary magazine with poetry book and magazine reviews, and also chapbooks. As New Spirit Press, we publish on a payment by copy basis. Usually we pay the author 50 copies. Submission through quarterly contest. Recent authors we published are Dorothy Brooks, Michael Gill, Tom Williams, Robert Simola, Vivina Ciolli, Lois M. Harrod, Alan Elyshevitz. 2) As The Poet Tree, we self-publish other authors and advertise their work in our catalogue and flyers. Recent authors include Marie Asner, Pascale Gousseland, Leigh Harrison, Scott Holstad, Zane Bond. 3) We also publish a literary magazine, *Poems That Thump in the Dark/Second Glance*. Send SASE for guidelines." avg. press run 100-200. Pub'd 20 titles 1998; expects 30 titles 1999, 25 titles 2000. avg. price, paper: $6; other: $6 (magazine); $20 for new subscription price to both magazines (4 issues). Discounts: we distribute to local independent bookstores and through mail order. 20pp; 5½×8½; high quality xerox. Reporting time: 3 months. Simultaneous submissions accepted: yes. Publishes 5% of manuscripts submitted. Payment: copies only. Copyrights for author.

New Spring Publications, Jacalyn Hughes, Editor; Doug DeBias, Editor, 293 Franklin Avenue, Princeton, NJ 08540, 609-279-0014; email nwspring@bellatlantic.net. 1997. Non-fiction. "Clear, grounded, humane, out-of-the-box writing." avg. press run 5M. Expects 1 title 1999, 1+ titles 2000. 1 title listed in the *Small Press Record of Books in Print* (28th Edition, 1999-00). avg. price, paper: $12. Discounts: 45% trade, 65% bulk, 20% classroom. 170pp; 6×6; of. Reporting time: 2 weeks. Simultaneous submissions accepted: yes. Payment: 10% of retail price. Copyrights for author. PMA.

New Star Books Ltd., Rolf Maurer, Publisher, #107, 3477 Commercial Street, Vancouver, B.C. V5N 4E8, Canada, 604-738-9429; FAX 604-738-9332. 1970. Non-fiction. *"New Star* is an independant press specializing in history, politics, environment, social issues, and literary titles." avg. press run 2M-3M. Pub'd 8 titles 1998; expects 7 titles 1999, 10 titles 2000. 52 titles listed in the *Small Press Record of Books in Print* (28th Edition, 1999-00). avg. price, cloth: $24; paper: $16. Discounts: 50% non-returnable (booksellers). 200pp; 5½×8½; of. Reporting time: 6-8 weeks. Simultaneous submissions accepted: yes. Publishes 1-2% of manuscripts submitted. Payment: varies with contract. Copyrights for author. ACP, ABPBC.

●**NEW STONE CIRCLE**, Mary Hays, Karen Singer, 1185 E 1900 N Road, White Heath, IL 61884. 1994. Poetry, fiction, art, photos, interviews, satire, parts-of-novels, long-poems, non-fiction. circ. 100. 1-2/yr. Pub'd 1 issue 1998; expects 2 issues 1999, 2 issues 2000. sub. price: $8; per copy: $4.50; sample: $4.50. Back issues: $4.50. 50pp; 5½×8½; xerox. Reporting time: 3-6 months. We accept simultaneous submissions, but let us know. We don't for contests. Publishes 5% of manuscripts submitted. Payment: 1 copy. Copyrighted, reverts to author.

NEW THOUGHT, Leo Fishbeck, Editor-in-Chief, International New Thought Alliance, 5003 East Broadway Road, Mesa, AZ 85206, 602-830-2461. 1913. Articles, interviews, reviews, news items. *"New Thought* is a self-help, metaphysical publication with articles designed to increase the creative fulfilling, and healing energies in each one of us. Material written from a philosophical and religious point of view is used in the magazine. Emphasis is always upon the positive, constructive, and inspirational." circ. 4M. 4/yr. Pub'd 4 issues 1998; expects 4 issues 1999. sub. price: $12; per copy: $3.00; sample: $3.00. Back issues: not offered. 48pp; 8½×11; of. Reporting time: 3-4 weeks. Payment: contributors' copies only. Copyrighted, reverts to author. Pub's reviews: 20 in 1998. §Metaphysics, spiritual enlightenments, self help. Ads: $565.90/$282.85/$24 column inch.

NEW THOUGHT JOURNAL, Jeffrey M. Ohl, 2520 Evelyn Drive, Kettering, OH 45409, Ph/Fax 937-293-9717; E-mail; ntjmag@aol.com. 1994. Poetry, fiction, articles, art, photos, interviews, criticism, reviews, music, parts-of-novels, long-poems, concrete art, news items, non-fiction. "Seek 1-2 page articles, Poetry, reviews on philosophy, spirituality, the enviornment, humanities, creativity." circ. 5M. 4/yr. Expects 4 issues 1999. sub. price: $15 for 4 issues; per copy: $4.95 on newsstands; sample: $6 covers p/h. Back issues: $6. Discounts: wholesale available. 40pp; 8½×11; †offset printing. Reporting time: 2-3 months. Simultaneous submissions accepted: yes. Publishes 10% of manuscripts submitted. Payment: copies or negotiated payment. Copyrighted, reverts to author. Pub's reviews: 12-15 in 1998. §Religion, philosophy, psychology, New Age, spirituality, poetry books, ecology, transformation. Ads: send for current rates.

NEW UNIONIST, Jeff Miiler, 1821 University Avenue W. Ste. S-116, Saint Paul, MN 55104-2801, 651-646-5546, E-mail nup@minn.net. 1975. Articles, photos, cartoons, reviews, letters, news items. "No outside manuscripts" circ. 9M. 12/yr. Pub'd 12 issues 1998; expects 12 issues 1999, 12 issues 2000. sub. price: 12 issues $5; per copy: 30¢; sample: free. Discounts: 15¢ each. 4pp; 11×17; of. Payment: copies only. Not copyrighted. Pub's reviews: 2 in 1998. §Socialism, labor, politics, current affairs.

New Victoria Publishers, Claudia Lamperti, PO Box 27, Norwich, VT 05055, 802-649-5297. 1976. Fiction. "Non-profit" avg. press run 5M. Pub'd 8 titles 1998; expects 8 titles 1999, 9 titles 2000. 78 titles listed in the *Small Press Record of Books in Print* (28th Edition, 1999-00). avg. price, cloth: $19.95; paper: $10.95. Discounts: distributed by Inbook. 200pp; 5½×8½, 8½×11, 5¼×8¼; of. Reporting time: 1 month. We'll possibly accept simultaneous submissions. Publishes 2-3% of manuscripts submitted. Payment: 10% of net. Copyrights for author. VT Book Publishers Association, ABA, PMA.

New View Publications, PO Box 3021, Chapel Hill, NC 27515-3021. 1987. Non-fiction. avg. press run 5M. Pub'd 2 titles 1998; expects 4 titles 1999, 4 titles 2000. 17 titles listed in the *Small Press Record of Books in Print* (28th Edition, 1999-00). avg. price, paper: $12. Discounts: Trade: 1-4 copies - 20% (if prepaid, 40%); 5-199 - 40%; 200-499 - 50%; 500+ - 55%. 100-200pp; 6×9; desktop computer. Reporting time: 3-4 weeks. Simultaneous submissions accepted: yes. Publishes 1-2% of manuscripts submitted. Payment: varies. Copyrights for author.

New Vision Publishing, Nicolette V. Phillips, 252 Roadrunner Drive, Sedona, AZ 86336, 520-282-7400; fax 520-282-0054; E-mail nvp@sedona.net. 1996. "We're not a self-publisher, but do not accept unsolicited manuscripts" avg. press run 3M. Expects 3 titles 1999, 4 titles 2000. 2 titles listed in the *Small Press Record of Books in Print* (28th Edition, 1999-00). avg. price, paper: $18.95 (trade). Discounts: 1 copy 20%; 2-4 copies 30%; 6+ copies 40%. 300pp; 5½×8; of. Does not copyright for author. PMA, NAPRA.

New Voice Media (see also SMALL PRESS CREATIVE EXPLOSION), Timothy R. Corrigan, PO Box 25, Houghton, NY 14744. 1984. Art, cartoons. "We publish 20-page minicomics with color covers. Sample package of three comics $3 PPD." avg. press run 500-1M. Pub'd 4 titles 1998; expects 6 titles 1999, 10 titles 2000. avg. price, other: $1 comic. Discounts: 40% discount of wholesale packages (minimum 10 copies). 20pp; 4½×5½; †of. Reporting time: 60 days maximum. Simultaneous submissions accepted: no. Payment: 5% retail value of print run. Copyrights for author.

New World Library, Mark Allen, Publisher, 14 Pamaron Way, Novato, CA 94949-6215. 1978. Fiction, non-fiction. avg. press run 15M. Pub'd 29 titles 1998; expects 32 titles 1999, 32 titles 2000. 41 titles listed in the *Small Press Record of Books in Print* (28th Edition, 1999-00). avg. price, cloth: $17; paper: $12.95; other: $16.95 audio cassettes. Discounts: 50-55% to distributors, 10% to individual consumers ordering 5 or more titles. 260pp; 5½x8½, 6x9, 5x7; of. Reporting time: 12 weeks. Publishes less than 1% of manuscripts submitted. Payment: 12-16% of net royalty to authors, paid semi-annually. Copyrights for author. APA, NAPRA.

New World Press, PO Box 640432, San Francisco, CA 94164-0432, 415-292-7008. 1995. Non-fiction. "We are a new publication (founded 1995) with an exclusive focus on contemporary biographies and autobiographies. We do not accept unsolicited manuscripts." avg. press run 5M-10M. Expects 4 titles 1999, 6 titles 2000. 1 title listed in the *Small Press Record of Books in Print* (28th Edition, 1999-00). avg. price, cloth: $20; paper: $12. Discounts: trade and bulk. 208pp; 5½x8½; of. Payment: yes. Copyrights for author. Bay Area Publishers.

New World Press (see also BLOODJET LITERARY MAGAZINE), Noni Ph.D Howard, Publisher, 20 Driftwood Trail, Half Moon Bay, CA 94019-2349, 650-726-5939; Fax 415-921-3730. 1974. Poetry, fiction, art, photos, letters, parts-of-novels, long-poems, collages. "Length is 100 pages plus, prefer women writers, Jennifer Stone, Adrian Marcus and Evelyn Hickey are recent contributors. Persons able to write grants or obtain other funding especially considered." avg. press run 1.2M. Expects 2 titles 1999, 1-3 titles 2000. 1 title listed in the *Small Press Record of Books in Print* (28th Edition, 1999-00). avg. price, paper: $15. Discounts: 40% bulk or to educational institutions, schools, etc. 100-200pp; 9x6; computer, laser. Reporting time: 60 days. Simultaneous submissions accepted: yes. Publishes less than 10% of manuscripts submitted. Payment: 200 free copies. Copyrights for author. Poets & Writers, Media Alliance, CLMP, Association of American Publishers, INA Coolbrith Circle, National League of American PEN Women.

New World Publications, Inc., 1861 Cornell Road, Jacksonville, FL 32207, 904-737-6558; FAX 904-731-1188. 1989. avg. press run 20M. Pub'd 3 titles 1998; expects 2 titles 1999, 2 titles 2000. 9 titles listed in the *Small Press Record of Books in Print* (28th Edition, 1999-00). avg. price, paper: $30. Discounts: 1-4 30%, 5-9 40%, 9-24 43%, 25-49 44%, 50-100 45%. 300pp. Copyrights for author. PMA.

THE NEW WRITER, Suzanne Ruthven, PO Box 60, Cranbrook, Kent TN17 2ZR, England, 01580-212626. 1996. Poetry, fiction, articles, interviews, reviews, letters, news items. circ. 1.5M. 10/yr. Expects 10 issues 1999, 10 issues 2000. sub. price: £42-50; per copy: £4.25; sample: £3. Back issues: £2.50. Discounts: negotiable. 48pp; 8¼x11¾. Reporting time: 2-3 weeks. Simultaneous submissions accepted: yes. Payment: varies. Copyrighted, reverts to author. Pub's reviews: 50 in 1998. §Short stories and writing techniques (but only if available in England). Ads: £95/£60/£40 1/4 page.

NEW WRITING, Sam Meade, Mason Deitz, Richard Lynch, Rita Howard, PO Box 1812, Amherst, NY 14226-7812, http://members.aol.com/newwriting/magazine.html. 1991. Poetry, fiction, art, cartoons, satire, letters, parts-of-novels, collages. "Length must be warranted by content. Submission critique available for a fee. Looking for honest work in unusual forms or literary merit. Project is an agency spin-off: we look for clients in our own pages. Magazine available FREE at the internet address given." circ. varies. Irregular. Expects 1 issue 1999, 2 issues 2000. sub. price: free; per copy: free; sample: free. Back issues: free. mi. Reporting time: 2 month. Payment: for exceptional submissions and contest winners. Copyrighted, reverts to author. Ads: based on organization, need, ability, exchange.

NEW YORK STORIES, Mark F. Lindberg, 120 Denton Avenue, Garden City Park, NY 11040, 212-561-1526; nystories@aolcom. 1998. Fiction, art, photos, cartoons, interviews, satire, letters, plays, concrete art, non-fiction. "Looking for sophisticated, well-crafted, high-quality fiction, short stories, short-shorts. Subjects not important as long as the story pertains in some way to NYC: native New Yorkers, commuters, tourists, careers, lifestyles, true-life experiences. 5,000 word max. Both new and established writers welcome to submit. Query on interviews, reviews, and essays. SASE a must! Send short bio for contributors page. Short story competition, send SASE for rules and guidelines." circ. 1M. 2/yr. Expects 2 issues 1999, 2 issues 2000. sub. price: $11; per copy: $6.95; sample: $6.95. Discounts: 40% on orders of 15 or more. 160pp; 6x9. Reporting time: 3 months. Simultaneous submissions accepted: no. Publishes 20% of manuscripts submitted. Payment: 2 contributors copies. Copyrighted, reverts to author. Ads: negotiable.

Newjoy Press, Joy Nyquist, PO Box 3437, Ventura, CA 93006, 805-876-1373; FAX 805-984-0503; njpublish@aol.com. 1993. Non-fiction. "We publish softcover books, 200+ pages. Submissions requested in form of letter, no full manuscripts. Writer's guidelines are free on request. Recent book: *Trust the Process: How to Enhance Recovery and Prevent Relapse* by Linda Free-Gardiner." avg. press run 3M. Pub'd 6 titles 1998; expects 12 titles 1999, 12 titles 2000. 17 titles listed in the *Small Press Record of Books in Print* (28th Edition, 1999-00). avg. price, paper: $16. Discounts: 3-6 books 20%, 7-50 30%, 51-199 40%, 200+ 42%; Bookstores 1-2 books 25%, 3-49 50-74 50%, 75-199 53%, 200+ 55%. 250pp; 5½x8; of, lp. Reporting time: 2

months max. Simultaneous submissions accepted: yes. Publishes 1% of manuscripts submitted. Payment: 10% 1st 5,000, 12% next 5,000, 15% thereafter. Copyrights for author. PMA, SPAN.

Newmark Publishing Company, PO Box 603, South Windsor, CT 06074, 860-282-7265. 1986. Fiction, non-fiction. *"Breast Care Options* by Paul Kuehn, M.D, published Sept. 1986. *Night Flying Avenger* by Pete Grant, published June 1990. *Breast Care Options for the 1990s* by Paul Kuehn, M.D., published Sept. 1991. *Who is Robin?* by Jon Dijon, published Sept 1993. *The Surgical Arena* by Peter Grant, M.D., published March 1994.'' avg. press run 7.5M. Expects 3 titles 1999, 5 titles 2000. 5 titles listed in the *Small Press Record of Books in Print* (28th Edition, 1999-00). avg. price, cloth: $20.95. Discounts: on request. 200pp; 6×9; of, lp. Reporting time: 3 months. Payment: individual contracts, negotiable. Copyrights for author. American Booksellers Association, New England Booksellers Association, Publishers Marketing Association.

NEWS FROM NATIVE CALIFORNIA, Heyday Books, Malcolm Margolin, Publisher; Jeannine Gendar, Managing Editor, PO Box 9145, Berkeley, CA 94709, 510-549-3564; FAX 510-549-1889. 1987. Articles, art, photos, interviews, criticism, reviews, letters, news items, non-fiction. ''We are interested in material related to California Indians, past and present.'' circ. 10M. 4/yr. Pub'd 4 issues 1998; expects 4 issues 1999, 4 issues 2000. sub. price: $19; per copy: $4.95; sample: $1. Back issues: range from $4 to $20. Discounts: 40% trade, call for other schedules. 56pp; 8½×11; of. Reporting time: 3 weeks. Simultaneous submissions accepted: yes. Payment: up to about $50/article. Copyrighted, does not revert to author. Pub's reviews: 5-10 in 1998. §Native American: culture, history, art, politics, literature. Ads: $545/$280/send for rate card. ABA, NCIBA, SF Book Council.

NEWS FROM THE SMALL PRESS CENTRE, John Nicholson, BM BOZO, London W1N 3XX, United Kingdom. 1990. Fiction, articles, art, photos, cartoons, interviews, satire, criticism, reviews, music, plays, news items, non-fiction. ''Complete information on the activities and events concerning British self-publishers.'' 6 & 4. Pub'd 4 issues 1998; expects 4 issues 1999, 4 issues 2000. sub. price: £12; per copy: £3.00. Back issues: £1.50. size A5, A4. Simultaneous submissions accepted: no. Payment: none. Ads: £5 for 30 words.

NewSage Press, Maureen Michelson, Publisher; Cindy McKechnie, PO Box 607, Troutdale, OR 97060-0607. 1985. Art, photos, interviews, non-fiction. ''We are interested in publishing quality tradebooks—in content as well as production. Our specialty is nonfiction.'' avg. press run 7.5M. Pub'd 2 titles 1998; expects 2 titles 1999, 3 titles 2000. 17 titles listed in the *Small Press Record of Books in Print* (28th Edition, 1999-00). avg. price, cloth: $30; paper: $14; other: $60 limited edition (collectors' edition with limited runs of 100 or 200 books). Discounts: 1-2 books 20%, 3-24 40%, 25-49 42%, 50-99 44%, 100-299 46%, 300-499 48%, 500+ 50%. 190pp; size varies; of, duotone photographs, laser scanned, also color. Reporting time: 3 months. Simultaneous submissions accepted: yes. Publishes 10% of manuscripts submitted. Payment: royalties paid, usually standard. Copyrights for author. ABA, PMA.

NEWSLETTER INAGO, Del Reitz, Editor and Publisher, Inago Press, PO Box 26244, Tucson, AZ 85726-6244, 520-294-7031. 1979. Poetry. ''*NI* is circulated internationally. Each issue features the writing of only one poet (except for filler guests) with biosketch and commentary. Submissions by invitation; however, all others will be read. MS size 10-15 poems of no more than 50 lines each with SASE or International Postal coupons. Periodic Inago anthologies of poetry in print and/or audio tape of Inago Poets. All checks or money orders *must be made payable to Del Reitz.''* circ. 200. 12/yr. Pub'd 12 issues 1998; expects 12 issues 1999, 12 issues 2000. sub. price: $17.50 U.S., $22.50 Canada, £21 U.K.; per copy: $3.50 U.S. & Canada, U.K. £8; sample: $3.50 U.S. & Canada, U.K. £8. Discounts: 10 or more copies $3 each, US & Canada. 4pp; 8×10½; photo copy. Reporting time: immediate. Simultaneous submissions accepted: yes. Publishes 20% of manuscripts submitted. Payment: contributor's copies (4 or more). Copyrighted, rights retained by author. No ads.

NEWSLETTER (LEAGUE OF CANADIAN POETS), Marvyne Jenoff, Newsletter Editor; Jan Horner, Museletter, 54 Wolseley Street 3rd Floor, Toronto, Ontario M5T IA5, Canada, 416-504-1657, Fax; 416-504-0096. 1966. Poetry, articles, art, photos, cartoons, news items. ''Museletter is essentially an in-house review of the Canadian poetry scene. Some feature articles, mostly of interest to all poets. Also publish a big issue twice-yearly titled *Museletter*. Newsletter is an in-house review on Canadian poetry contests, awards, league business matters.'' circ. 600. 6/yr. Pub'd 8-10 issues 1998; expects 8-10 issues 1999, 8-10 issues 2000. sub. price: $30; per copy: $6 Museletter, $3 Newsletter ppd; sample: $2. Back issues: $2.50 issue as available (complete runs do not exist). 32pp Museletter, 12pp Newsletter; 8½×11; of. Payment: none. Copyrighted, reverts to author. Pub's reviews: 5 in 1998. §poetry. Write for ad rates.

NEWSLETTERNEWS, WORLDLINKS - FRIENDSHIP NEWS, 70 Macomb, Suite 226, Mt. Clemens, MI 48043, E-mail worldlinks@prodigy.com; Website http:.pages.prodigy.com/worldlinks. 1997. Fiction, articles, reviews, letters, news items. ''Reviews self-published newsletters, zines, etc.'' 6/yr. sample price: $1. 11×13. Pub's reviews. §Newsletters, magazines, co-ops.

NEWSLETTER/POETIMES, Pleasure Dome Press (Long Island Poetry Collective Inc.), Binnie Pasquier,

Editor, PO Box 773, Huntington, NY 11743. 1974. Articles, criticism, reviews, news items. "Features include: calendar of regional literary events (Long Island-NY City), 1-2 reviews per issue, small press markets column, and other informational materials of use to readers/writers of poetry." circ. 200. 6/yr. Pub'd 6 issues 1998; expects 6 issues 1999. sub. price: available only as part of Long Island Poetry Collective, Inc. dues, which are $18; sample: $1. 4pp; 8½×11; of. Reporting time: none. Payment: none. Copyrighted, reverts to author. Pub's reviews: 6 in 1998. §Poetry. No ads.

Next Decade, Inc. (formerly New Decade Inc.), Barbara Brooks Kimmel, 39 Old Farmstead Road, Chester, NJ 07930-2732, Telephone/Fax; 908-879-6625. 1990. "Publish/distribute books (reference, how-to) and sold to universities, corporations, libraries and bookstores." avg. press run 5M. Pub'd 1 title 1998; expects 2 titles 1999, 3 titles 2000. 3 titles listed in the *Small Press Record of Books in Print* (28th Edition, 1999-00). avg. price, paper: $16.95-$25. Discounts: 50% on distribution arrangements. 80-250pp; 8½×11, 7×10. Reporting time: 1 month. Simultaneous submissions accepted: yes. Payment: varies. Copyrights for author. SPAN.

●**Nextstep Books**, Peter Peterson, 1070 Carolan Avenue #116, Burlingame, CA 94010, e-mail nextstep@nub.ml.org. 1998. Poetry, fiction, plays. avg. press run 100-1M. Expects 3 titles 1999, 4 titles 2000. 1 title listed in the *Small Press Record of Books in Print* (28th Edition, 1999-00). avg. price, cloth: $10; paper: $4. Discounts: 10% bookstores. 50pp; 5½×8½; †mi. Reporting time: 2-4 weeks. Simultaneous submissions accepted: yes. Publishes 10% of manuscripts submitted. Payment: in copies. Copyrights for author. YU News Service.

Nguoi Dan (see also NGUOI DAN), ManhHung Hoang, PO Box 2674, Costa Mesa, CA 92628, 714-549-3443; 714-241-8505, E-mail nguoidan@aix.netcom.com; Web site http://www.nguoidan.com/nd. 1990. Poetry, fiction, non-fiction. avg. press run 1.5M. Pub'd 2 titles 1998; expects 2 titles 1999, 2 titles 2000. 1 title listed in the *Small Press Record of Books in Print* (28th Edition, 1999-00). avg. price, paper: $10. Discounts: 20% for 5 copies, 30% for 10, 40% for 15, 50% for 20 and up. 300pp; 5×8; †of. Reporting time: 1 month. Simultaneous submissions accepted: no. Publishes 50% of manuscripts submitted. Payment: yes. Copyrights for author.

NGUOI DAN, Nguoi Dan, Nhiem Tong, PO Box 2674, Costa Mesa, CA 92628, 714-549-3443; 714-241-8505; E-mail nguoidan@ix.netcom.com; Web site http://www.nguoidan.com/nd. 1990. Poetry, fiction, articles, cartoons, interviews, satire, criticism, reviews, non-fiction. circ. 1.5M. 12/yr. Pub'd 12 issues 1998; expects 12 issues 1999, 12 issues 2000. sub. price: $18; per copy: $2. Back issues: $1.50 if available. Discounts: 20% for 5 copies, 30% for 10, 40% for 15, 50% for 20 and up. 40pp; 8×11; †of. Reporting time: 2 weeks. Simultaneous submissions accepted: no. Publishes 90% of manuscripts submitted. Payment: none. Not copyrighted. Pub's reviews: 5 in 1998. §Asia-Indochina, Asian-American. Ads: none.

Nico Professional Services, Ltd., 1515 West 2nd Avenue, #543, Vancouver, BC V6J 5C5, Canada, 604-733-6530. 1992. Non-fiction. "Only interested in the field of environmental illness or multiple chemical sensitivity" avg. press run 5M. Expects 2 titles 1999. 2 titles listed in the *Small Press Record of Books in Print* (28th Edition, 1999-00). avg. price, paper: $14. Discounts: Distribution handled by Baker & Taylor. 300pp; 6×9. Reporting time: 4 months. Does not copyright for author. PMA.

Nicolas-Hays, Inc., B. Lundsted, Box 2039, York Beach, ME 03910, 207-363-4393. 1976. Music, non-fiction. "We publish philosophy, music, psychology, alternative healing. We have recently published *Modern Woman in Search of Soul*, by June Singer and *Sophia: Aspects of the Divine Feminine Past and Present* by Dr. Susanne Schaup. We look to publish the author's life work - the books that have great meaning." avg. press run 5M-7.5M. Pub'd 2 titles 1998; expects 3 titles 1999, 6 titles 2000. 28 titles listed in the *Small Press Record of Books in Print* (28th Edition, 1999-00). avg. price, cloth: $18.95; paper: $18.95. Discounts: Normal trade discounts apply; write for account information; distributed by Samuel Weiser, Inc. at Box 612, York Beach, ME 03910. 256pp; 6×9, 5⅜×8¼; of. Reporting time: 3 months. Simultaneous submissions accepted: yes. Publishes 10% of manuscripts submitted. Payment: royalties, information available on request. Copyrights for author.

Nicolin Fields Publishing, Inc., Linda Chestney, 2 Red Fox Road, North Hampton, NH 03862-3320, 603-964-1727; Fax 603-964-4221 email:nfp@nh.ultranet.com; website PublishingWorks.com. 1994. Non-fiction. avg. press run 1.5-6M. Expects 3 titles 1999, 3-4 titles 2000. 5 titles listed in the *Small Press Record of Books in Print* (28th Edition, 1999-00). avg. price, paper: $14.95. Discounts: 40% retail stores (bike shops) and specialty stores, distributors 50-67%. 200pp; 6×9. Reporting time: 1-2 months. Simultaneous submissions accepted: yes. Publishes 20% of manuscripts submitted. Payment: varies/standard. Copyrights for author. PMA, Book Marketing Update, SPAN.

Nierika Editions (see also AMERICAN WRITING: A Magazine), Alexandra Grilikhes, 4343 Manayunk Avenue, Philadelphia, PA 19128, 215-483-7051. 1990. Poetry, fiction, articles, interviews, criticism, letters, parts-of-novels, long-poems, collages, non-fiction. "We are new and haven't published any books yet." avg. press run 1.5M.

NIGHT ROSES, Allen T. Billy, Editor; Sandy Taylor, Graphics Editor, PO Box 393, Prospect Heights, IL

60070, 847-392-2435. 1986. Poetry, art. "Interested in poems about bells, dance, clocks, romance, fashions, ghost images of past or future, nature, arts. General poems 6-20 lines, some longer. Some recent contributors: M. Riesa Clark, James R. Lowery, Kate Stewart. All poets are treated equal at *Night Roses*. Hopefully, each issue of *Night Roses* will take its own direction and speak for itself." circ. 300. 2-3/yr. Pub'd 2 issues 1998; expects 2 issues 1999, 2 issues 2000. sub. price: $10; per copy: $5; sample: $4. Back issues: $3.50. 44pp; 8½×11; mi. Reporting time: 8-14 weeks. Payment: 1 contributor's copy. Not copyrighted. §Poetry, dance, and art publications.

NightinGale Resources, Lila Teich Gold, PO Box 322, Cold Spring, NY 10516, 212-753-5383. 1982. Non-fiction. "We publish facsimile editions of quality books. Cookbooks, directories, original children's books, travel, facsimiles of out of print books." avg. press run 10M. Expects 3 titles 1999. 8 titles listed in the *Small Press Record of Books in Print* (28th Edition, 1999-00). avg. price, cloth: $21.95; paper: $12.95; other: $6.95 pocket guide. Discounts: on request. Does not copyright for author. Small Press Center, New York City.

NIGHTLORE, Trevor Elmore, PO Box 81482, Mobile, AL 36689, Email trevorelm@aol.com. 1994. Fiction, articles, art, interviews, criticism, reviews, letters, parts-of-novels, news items. "We're looking for short-short fiction (5 pages or less is best). Any types of horror are acceptable, vampires are a specialty. We also accept reviews and non-fiction material of interest to horror fans." circ. 400. 4/yr. Pub'd 4 issues 1998; expects 4 issues 1999, 4 issues 2000. sub. price: $16; per copy: $4; sample: $4. Back issues: $4. Discounts: available on request. 36pp; †mi. Reporting time: 3 months. Simultaneous submissions accepted: yes. Publishes 40% of manuscripts submitted. Payment: 1 contributor's copy. Copyrighted, reverts to author. Pub's reviews: 4 in 1998. §Horror, movies, comics. Ads: $10/$5.

NIGHTSHADE, Full Moon Publications, Sharida Rizzuto, Harold Tollison, Ann Hoyt, 577 Central Avenue, Box 4, Jefferson, LA 70121-1400, e-mail fullmoon@eudoramail.com or haunted@rocketmail.com; Websites www.members.xoom.com/blackie, www.eclecticity.com/zines/, www.spaceports.com/~haunted/, www2.cyber-cities.com/z/zines/. 1983. Poetry, fiction, articles, art, photos, cartoons, interviews, satire, criticism, reviews, letters, long-poems, collages, news items, non-fiction. "Weird horror poetry & stories plus articles, reviews and interviews about the horror genre" circ. 800-1M. 2/yr. Pub'd 2 issues 1998; expects 2 issues 1999, 2 issues 2000. sub. price: $15.80; per copy: $7.90; sample: $7.90. Back issues: $7.90. Discounts: trade with other like publications. 100pp; 8½×11; †of, excellent quality. Reporting time: 2-6 weeks. Simultaneous submissions accepted: yes. Publishes 30-35% of manuscripts submitted. Payment: free copies, fees paid for articles, reviews and art. Copyrighted, reverts to author. Pub's reviews: 60 in 1998. §entire horror genre - zines, books, films, internet websites. Ads: free. NWC, HWA, Small Press Genre Association, MWA, Western Writers of America (WWA), Arizona Authors Association (AAA).

Nightshade Press (see also POTATO EYES), Carolyn Page, Roy Zarucchi, PO Box 76, Ward Hill, Troy, ME 04987, 207-948-3427. 1988. Poetry, fiction, art. "We run one poetry competition per year—guidelines are available. We conduct one short story competition each year. The clay Potato Fiction Award" avg. press run 300-500. Pub'd 16 titles 1998; expects 16 titles 1999, 5 titles 2000. 9 titles listed in the *Small Press Record of Books in Print* (28th Edition, 1999-00). avg. price, paper: $7. Discounts: 40% to bookstores. 36pp; 8½×5½; of. We accept simultaneous submissions, but like to be told. Publishes 2% of manuscripts submitted. Payment: copies in lieu of royalties. Does not copyright for author. CLMP, Maine Writers & Publishers Alliance, The New Hampshire Writers & Publishers Project, North Carolina Writers Network.

NIGHTSUN, Douglas DeMars, English Department, Frostburg S. University, Frostburg, MD 21532, 301-687-4221. 1981. Poetry, fiction, articles, art, photos, cartoons, interviews, satire, collages. "We want highest quality poetry. Subject matter open. Prefer poems not much longer than 40 lines. Not interested in the extremes of sentimental, obvious poetry on the one hand and subjectless "great gossamer-winged gnat" school on the other. Have recently published work by Marge Piercy, Diane Wakoski, Linda Paston, Philip Dacey and Walter McDonald—and interviews with Carolyn Forche, Grace Cavalier, Lucille Clifton, Sharon Olds, Galway Kinnell, Stephen Dobyns, Marvin Bell, Maxine Kumin, and Marge Piercy" circ. 500-1M. Pub'd 1 issue 1998; expects 1 issue 1999, 1 issue 2000. sub. price: $5 + $1.50 p/h; per copy: $5 + $1.50 p/h; sample: $5 + $1.50 p/h. Back issues: inquire. Discounts: inquire. 60pp; 5½×8½; of. Reporting time: 2-3 months. Simultaneous submissions accepted: no. Publishes 1% of manuscripts submitted. Payment: free copies. Copyrighted, reverts to author.

Nightsun Books, Ruth Wiley, 823 Braddock Road, Cumberland, MD 21502-2622, 301-722-4861. 1987. Poetry, fiction, cartoons, criticism, plays, non-fiction. "Please inquire before submitting manuscripts!" avg. press run 200-1M. Pub'd 5 titles 1998; expects 1 title 1999, 1 title 2000. 14 titles listed in the *Small Press Record of Books in Print* (28th Edition, 1999-00). avg. price, paper: $3-$10. Discounts: 1 0%, 2-4 20%, 5-24 40%, 25-49 43%, 50-99 46%, 100+ 50%. 30-200pp; 5½×8½; of. Reporting time: varies. Payment: varies—inquire.

NIMROD INTERNATIONAL, Francine Ringold, 600 South College Avenue, Tulsa, OK 74104-3126. 1956.

Poetry, fiction, articles, art, photos, interviews, parts-of-novels, long-poems, plays. "Recent contributors: Janette Turner Hospital, Amy Clampitt, Josephine Jacobsen, Michael McBride, Pattiann Rogers, James Allen McPherson, Tess Gallagher, Ishmael Reed, Denise Levertov, Francois Camoin, Beckian Goldberg, Gish Jen, Alvin Greenberg, Mary La Chapelle, Sharon Sakson. Annual *Nimrod/Hardman* Awards: in poetry (Pablo Neruda Prize), in fiction (Katherine Anne Porter Prize). 1st prize in each category $2000, 2nd prize $1000. Submissions are accepted between January 1 and April 1 each year. Past judges include Marvin Bell, Richard Howard, Charles Johnson, Paul West, Mark Strand, William Stafford, Stanley Kunitz, Rosellen Brown, Gordon Lish, Carolyn Kizer, Stephen Dunn, George Garrett, W.D. Snodgrass, John Leonard. Please send business-size SASE for awards and guidelines." circ. 4M. 2/yr. Pub'd 2 issues 1998; expects 2 issues 1999. 10 titles listed in the *Small Press Record of Books in Print* (28th Edition, 1999-00). sub. price: $17.50/yr; $30/2 yr.; Outside US - $19/$33; per copy: $10; sample: $6.00 (pre-1988 issues), $10 1989-present. Back issues: varies; list of back issues available from *Nimrod*. Discounts: 10% orders over 20. 160pp; 6×9; of. Reporting time: 3 months. Simultaneous submissions accepted: yes. Payment: 2 copies of issue in which work is published. Copyrighted, reverts to author. Ads: $200/$100. CLMP, AWP.

nine muses books, margareta waterman, Publisher, 3541 Kent Creek Road, Winston, OR 97496, 541-679-6674; E-mail mw9muses@teleport.com. 1987. Poetry, fiction, long-poems. "nine muses is an artists' collective for the author-owned production of books and tapes. At this time twelve serious writers, highly esteemed by their colleagues, make up the list. A prime feature of nine muses books, in addition to the advantage of author ownership, is the design, which is done, not to a standard format, but with particular attention to each book as a work of art, so that illustration, color of paper and ink, balance of composition on each page, and so on, are fitted to the content and meaning of the book. Submissions are by invitation." avg. press run 500. Expects 3 titles 1999, 2 titles 2000. 17 titles listed in the *Small Press Record of Books in Print* (28th Edition, 1999-00). avg. price, paper: $5-$10. Discounts: trade to bookstores, bulk to libraries, etc. Single orders no discount, prepay on first orders. 65pp; 5½×8½; of, lazer. Payment: nine muses is an author's collective; see comments above. Author owns books. Author owns copyrights and books.

9N-2N-8N-NAA NEWSLETTER, G.W. Rinaldi, Robert R. Rinaldi, Jr., PO Box 275, East Corinth, VT 05040-0275. 1985. Articles, art, photos, cartoons, interviews, criticism, reviews, letters, news items. "Magazine consists of 36-40 pages/3 columns, several photos, column pages, small print, equal to 50 in larger print." circ. 9M. 4/yr. Pub'd 4 issues 1998; expects 4 issues 1999, 4 issues 2000. sub. price: $16 US, $19 Canada, $22 foreign; per copy: $6.50; sample: $6.50. Back issues: send for order form. Discounts: none. 36-40pp; 8½×11; †of. Reporting time: 1 month. Publishes 80% of manuscripts submitted. Payment: none. Copyrighted, does not revert to author. Pub's reviews: 6-8 in 1998. §Agriculture, old tractors, farm memorabilia, farm equipment, farm lifestyle. Ads: free non-commercial classifieds for members; commercial: .90/word, display rates: POR.

NINETEENTH-CENTURY LITERATURE, University of California Press, Joseph Bristow, Thomas Wortham, University of California Press, 2120 Berkeley Way, Berkeley, CA 94720, 510-643-7154. 1946. Reviews, non-fiction. "Editorial address: Dept. of English, Box 951530, 405 Hilgard Rolfe Hall, Room 2225, University of California, Los Angeles, CA 90095-1530." circ. 2,250. 4/yr. Pub'd 4 issues 1998; expects 4 issues 1999, 4 issues 2000. sub. price: $32 indiv., $62 instit., $19 students (+ $5 foreign postage); per copy: $12 (+ $6 foreign postage), $20 instit., $12 students; sample: free. Back issues: $6 (+ $6 foreign postage). Discounts: foreign subs. agents 10%, one-time orders 10+, standing orders (bookstores): 1-99 40%, 100+ 50%. 144pp; 6×9; of. Reporting time: 1-2 months. Copyrighted, does not revert to author. Pub's reviews: 4 in 1998. §19th-century literature, American and English. Ads: $275/$200.

19TH-CENTURY MUSIC, University of California Press, Lawrence Kramer, James Hepokoski, Chris Acosta, Managing Editor, University of California Press, 2120 Berkeley Way, Berkeley, CA 94720, 540-643-7154. 1977. Criticism, reviews, non-fiction. "Editorial address: Dept. of Music, 112 Music Building, University of California, Davis, CA 95616." circ. 1.5M. 3/yr. Pub'd 3 issues 1998; expects 3 issues 1999, 3 issues 2000. sub. price: $35 indiv., $89 instit. (+ $5 foreign postage); per copy: $14 indiv.; $21 instit. (+ $5 foreign postage), $14 student; sample: free. Back issues: same as single copy price. Discounts: foreign subs. agents 10%, one-time orders 10+ 30%, standing orders (bookstores): 1-99 40%, 100+ 50%. 96pp; 8½×10; of. Reporting time: 1-3 months. Copyrighted, does not revert to author. Pub's reviews: 3 in 1998. §19th-century music. Ads: $275/$200.

96 INC, Vera Gold, Julie Anderson, Nancy Mehegan, PO Box 15559, Boston, MA 02215. 1992. Poetry, fiction, articles, photos, interviews, letters, parts-of-novels. "*96 Inc.* publishes short fiction, poetry, and interviews. *96 Inc.* accepts occasional reviews and stories relating to the craft of writing and publishing. Writers should query first. Not accepting submissions until 2000." circ. 3M. 1/yr. Pub'd 1 issue 1998; expects 1 issue 1999, 1 issue 2000. sub. price: $15 for all mailings, newsletters and announcements of readings and special events.; per copy: $5; sample: $7.50. Back issues: $7.50. 50pp; 8½×11; lp. Reporting time: 6 months to 1 year. Simultaneous submissions accepted: yes. Publishes 5% of manuscripts submitted. Payment: 4 copies; modest fee when funding is available. Copyrighted. Pub's reviews: 1 in 1998. §Books relating to the craft of writing and publishing. Ads: $100/$75/$250 inside cover.

Ninety-Six Press, Gilbert Allen, William Rogers, Furman University, Greenville, SC 29613, 864-294-3156. 1991. Poetry. "Ninety-Six Press publishes books of poetry by authors from its region. The press reviews manuscripts only by invitation. No unsolicited manuscripts." avg. press run 500. Pub'd 1 title 1998; expects 1 title 1999, 1-2 titles 2000. 8 titles listed in the *Small Press Record of Books in Print* (28th Edition, 1999-00). avg. price, paper: $10. Discounts: 40%. 50-70pp; 6×9; of. Payment: copies. Copyrights for author.

Nite-Owl Press (see also NITE-WRITER'S INTERNATIONAL LITERARY ARTS JOURNAL), Sr. Thompson, John A., Exec.Editor-Publisher; Bree Ann Orner, Assoc. Editor, 137 Pointview Avenue, Suite 100, Pittsburgh, PA 15227-3131, 412-882-2259. 1993. Poetry, art, concrete art, non-fiction. "Send complete manuscript for review-enclose SASE in case returned. Attach cover letter giving credits and brief bio" avg. press run 100. Expects 2 titles 1999, 2 titles 2000. avg. price, other: $4.50 + $1.50 p/h. 40pp; 8½×11; †laser. Reporting time: up to 4 weeks. Simultaneous submissions accepted: yes. Publishes 25% of manuscripts submitted. Payment: must purchase copy. Copyrights for author.

NITE-WRITER'S INTERNATIONAL LITERARY ARTS JOURNAL, Nite-Owl Press, John A. Thompson, Sr., Exec. Editor, Publisher; Bree Ann Orner, Assoc. Editor, 137 Pointview Avenue, Suite 100, Pittsburgh, PA 15227-3131, 412-381-6893. 1993. Poetry, fiction, art, concrete art, non-fiction. "1-5 poems, 20 lines or less (double-spaced). Haiku: 3 per page. Art: B+W only, reduced for publication. Short stories: 2 pages. Original material, published or unpublished. State where published first. Must purchase copy in which their work appears—$6 per copy or $20 per year." circ. 100+. 4/yr. Expects 3 issues 1999, 4 issues 2000. sub. price: $20; per copy: $6. Back issues: $4.00 if available. Discounts: $4 postpaid when available. 30-50pp; 8½×11; of. Reporting time: as time permits, usually within 2 weeks. Simultaneous submissions accepted: yes. Publishes 25% of manuscripts submitted. Payment: none, must purchase copy in which work appears. Copyrighted, reverts to author. Pub's reviews: 4 in 1998. §poetry. Ads: $95/$65/discuss other arrangements for smaller ads.

No Starch Press, William Pollock, 555 De Haro Street, Suite 250, San Francisco, CA 94107-2365, 415-863-9900. 1994. Non-fiction. "Computer books for non-computer people. Books generally about 300 pages in length, we try to avoid long tomes at all costs. We will not publish cookie-cutter, how-to use software type books. Prefer authors with writing experience, especially journalistic. Bias toward authors with nationally syndicated columns or who are regular contributors to major computer magazines. Interest in computer humor, non-traditional computer books for average people. Recent contributors: Owen Linzmayer (*Mac Addict*, columnist), and Wally Wang (author of *Visual Basic for Dummies*)." avg. press run 7.5M. Pub'd 4 titles 1998; expects 7 titles 1999. 3 titles listed in the *Small Press Record of Books in Print* (28th Edition, 1999-00). avg. price, paper: $30. Standard trade discount schedule through Publisher's Group West. 300pp; 7×9. Reporting time: 3-4 weeks. Simultaneous submissions accepted: yes. Publishes 10% of manuscripts submitted. Payment: 15% on all cash received from all sales. Copyrights for author.

Noble Porter Press, Roger Karshner, 36-851 Palm View Road, Rancho Mirage, CA 92270, 760-770-6076, fax 760-770-4507. 1995. Non-fiction. "Not soliciting manuscripts." avg. press run 5M. avg. price, paper: $12.95. Discounts: trade 40%. 200pp; 6×9; of. Payment: 10% cover. Does not copyright for author.

NOBODADDIES, Doug Rice, 2491 State Route 45 South, Salem, OH 44460, E-mail rice@salem.kent.edu. 1994. Fiction, articles, art, photos, cartoons, interviews, criticism, reviews, letters, parts-of-novels, collages, non-fiction. "Recent contributors: Ray Federman, Larry McCaffery, Takyuki Tassumi, Steven Shaviro, Cris Mazza, Lance Olsen, Mark Amerika, Derek Pell. Biases: Literary texts that explode genres, that put pressure on the boundaries of discipline, that engage in nomadic narratives" circ. 500. 1/yr. Expects 1 issue 1999, 1 issue 2000. sub. price: $10; per copy: $10; sample: $5. Back issues: $30 for issue #1, $5 all other issues. Discounts: 40%. 56pp; 8×11½; of. Reporting time: 2 weeks to 2 months. Simultaneous submissions accepted: no. Publishes 10% of manuscripts submitted. Payment: 1 copy. Copyrighted, reverts to author. Pub's reviews: 20 in 1998. §Alternative fiction, avant garde, photography, cultural theory. Ads: $150/$80/$45 1/4 page. CLMP.

THE NOCTURNAL LYRIC, Susan Moon, Editor; Dan Breitenfeldt, Story Illustrator, PO Box 115, San Pedro, CA 90733-0115. 1987. Poetry, fiction, articles, satire, reviews. "No stories longer than 2,000 words." circ. 500. 4/yr. Pub'd 4 issues 1998; expects 4 issues 1999, 4 issues 2000. sub. price: $10; per copy: $3; sample: $3. Back issues: $2. Discounts: bulk rates: $2.25 each for 5 copies or more, $2 each for 10 copies or more. 40pp; 5½×8½; †photocopy. Reporting time: rejections within 2 months, acceptances 9 months - 1 year. Simultaneous submissions accepted: yes. Publishes 15-20% of manuscripts submitted. Payment: discount coupons on subscriptions. Not copyrighted. Pub's reviews: 16 in 1998. §Bizarre, previously published fiction. Ads: none, will trade ads.

NOCTURNAL REPORTER, Full Moon Publications, Sharida Rizzuto, 577 Central Avenue, Box 4, Jefferson, LA 70121-1400, E-mail fullmoon@endoramail.com, haunted@rocketmail.com; Websites www.an-gelfire.com/la/hauntings/index.htm/, www.members.xoom.com/blackie. 1983. Articles, art, photos, cartoons, interviews, satire, criticism, reviews, letters, news items, non-fiction. "True crime about serial murderers, ritual murders, child abuse, human vampires, and other bizarre crime" circ. 500. 3/yr. Pub'd 3 issues 1998; expects 3 issues 1999, 3 issues 2000. sub. price: $15; per copy: $5; sample: $5. Back issues: $5. Discounts: trade to like publishers. 50pp; 8½×11; †of. Reporting time: 2-6 weeks. Simultaneous submissions accepted: yes. Publishes 35% of manuscripts submitted. Payment: fee (negotiable) for non-fiction and artwork plus free copy. Copyrighted, reverts to author. Pub's reviews: 60 in 1998. §True crime books, zines, internet websites. Ads: free.

THE NOISE, T Max, Pulisher and Editor; Francis Dimenno, Associate Editor; Dee Mikey, Associate Editor; Einstein, Associate Editor, 74 Jamaica Street, Jamaica Plain, MA 02130, 617-524-4735, E-mail; tmaxnoise@aol.com. 1981. Articles, photos, cartoons, interviews, reviews, music, news items. "Interviews and articles - 1500-2000 words. Live reviews (of bands) - 150 words per band. Reviews of LPs - 300 words. Reviews of singles - 150 words. Our bias is away from commercial rock and roll, focusing on underground music from New England." circ. 5M. 10/yr. Pub'd 10 issues 1998; expects 10 issues 1999, 10 issues 2000. sub. price: $16; per copy: $2; sample: $2. Back issues: $2-$30. Discounts: none. 56pp; 8×10⅜; of. Reporting time: 1 month. Simultaneous submissions accepted: no. Publishes 95% of manuscripts submitted. Payment: none. Copyrighted, reverts to author. Pub's reviews: 2 in 1998. §New England based rock and roll books. Ads: $227/$130/$82 1/4 page/$46 1/8 page, band rate $129/$79/$49/$29.

Nolo Press, Ralph Warner, Publisher; Stephen Elias, Associate Publisher, 950 Parker Street, Berkeley, CA 94710, 510-549-1976. 1971. Non-fiction. "Our books are of a special nature: they are how-to guides for laypeople, instructive in various legal procedures, and are frequently (at least every 12-14 months) revised/updated to keep current with law changes. This means that our backlist books are often among our bestsellers and are treated as new books, which is very different from the backlist of other publishers. It also makes our new-books-per-year a little harder to figure (#10). Anywhere from 10-150 pages might change during a revision and we often re-introduce a backlist title that has been significantly changed to the media, complete with a new press release." avg. press run 12M. Pub'd 15 titles 1998; expects 20 titles 1999, 25 titles 2000. 76 titles listed in the *Small Press Record of Books in Print* (28th Edition, 1999-00). avg. price, paper: $17.95. Discounts: 50% to distributors, 40-46% bookstores. 240pp; 8½×11; of. Reporting time: 4-8 weeks. Publishes 1% of manuscripts submitted. Payment: 7-10% of retail, quarterly payment. Copyrights for author. NCBPA, AALL, AAP, ALA, ABA.

Nolo Press - Occidental, Charles Sherman, Editor; Trudy H. Devine, Manager, PO Box 722, Occidental, CA 95465, 707-874-3105, fax 707-874-1323. 1971. Non-fiction. avg. press run 10M. Pub'd 1 title 1998; expects 1 title 1999, 2 titles 2000. 7 titles listed in the *Small Press Record of Books in Print* (28th Edition, 1999-00). avg. price, paper: $20.65. Discounts: 1-4 25%, 5-99 40%, 100+ 50%. 200pp; 8½×11; lp. Reporting time: 1 month. Publishes .1% of manuscripts submitted. Payment: 8% of retail paid quarterly. Copyrights for author. ABA, PMA.

Nonsilent Press (see also HUMAN, Excercises in the Crucial Arts), Charles Dodson, c/o The Guide, PO Box 593, Boston, MA 02199. 1990. Articles, art, cartoons. "Publish serious take-offs on existing publications. Interested in alternative political cartoons/text that deal with 'crucual arts' ideahhs; send 52¢ SASE for guidelines. Published serious take-off (on sex hysteria) of a Noam Chomsky speech; contributors include prisoners, dreamers, self-made activists. Publications of interest to independent, once-duped critical thinkers interested about broad-reaching issues and 'connecting dots.' All publications fall within the 'zine' category." avg. press run 300+. Pub'd 5 titles 1998; expects 5 titles 1999, 5 titles 2000. avg. price, other: $2.50-$15. 40pp; 4½×11, 8½×11; †mi. Reporting time: 6 weeks to 3 months. Simultaneous submissions accepted: yes. Publishes 50% of manuscripts submitted. Payment: copies/barter if possible. Does not copyright for author. The Unorganized Unorganization of Unorganizers (UUU).

THE NONVIOLENT ACTIVIST, Andy Mager, War Resisters League, 339 Lafayette Street, New York, NY 10012, 212-228-0450, fax 212-228-6193, e-Mail wrl@igc.apc.org. 1984. Articles, cartoons, interviews, reviews, news items. "News of interest to the nonviolence movement; special focus on activities of the War Resisters League." circ. 8M. 6/yr. Pub'd 6 issues 1998; expects 6 issues 1999, 6 issues 2000. sub. price: $25 institutions, $15 individuals; per copy: $1.50; sample: $1. 24pp; 8½×11; of. Simultaneous submissions accepted, but we want to know about it. Payment: none. Not copyrighted. Pub's reviews: 16 in 1998. §Nonviolence, organizing ideas/skills, war/peace. Ads: $400/$220.

Noontide Press, PO Box 2719, Newport Beach, CA 92659, 949-631-1490; e-mail editor@noontidepress.com. 1962. Non-fiction. "Noontide Press sells a wide variety of special-interest books, including many that are 'politically incorrect.'" avg. press run 5M. Pub'd 10 titles 1998; expects 10 titles 1999. avg. price, cloth: $15; paper: $10. Discounts: 40% for book sellers. Pages vary; of. Reporting time: 4 weeks. Simultaneous submissions accepted: yes. Publishes 1% of manuscripts submitted. Payment: standard. Copyrights for author.

North American Bookdealers Exchange (see also BOOK DEALERS WORLD), Al Galasso, Editorial Director; Russ von Hoelscher, Associate Editor, PO Box 606, Cottage Grove, OR 97424-0026. 1979. Articles, interviews, news items, non-fiction. "Manuscripts should be about making or saving money, self-publishing, mail order or book marketing. Will also accept titles relating to sexual communication, new diets, and health. Recent titles are *Book Dealers' Dropship Directory* and *Exporting Without Investment*" avg. press run 1M. Pub'd 2 titles 1998; expects 2 titles 1999, 2 titles 2000. avg. price, paper: $12- $15. Discounts: 50%-75% on larger wholesale orders. 40pp; 5½×8, 8½×11; of. Reporting time: 2 weeks. Payment: outright purchase. Does not copyright for author.

THE NORTH AMERICAN REVIEW, Robley Wilson, Univ. Of Northern Iowa, Cedar Falls, IA 50614, 319-273-6455. 1815. Poetry, fiction, articles, reviews, long-poems, non-fiction. "Environmental focus." circ. 4M. 6/yr. Pub'd 6 issues 1998; expects 6 issues 1999, 6 issues 2000. sub. price: $22; per copy: $4.95; sample: $5. Back issues: $5. Discounts: Agent 20%; bulk (10 or more) 30%. 48pp; 8⅛×10⅞ (ABP Standard); of. Reporting time: 10 weeks. Publishes 1% of manuscripts submitted. Payment: $20 per published page; 50¢ a line for poetry minimum. Copyrighted, reverts to author. Pub's reviews: 12 in 1998. §Poetry & short fiction. Ads: $500/$275. CLMP.

●**North Atlantic Books,** PO Box 12327, Berkeley, CA 94712, 510-559-8277; fax 510-559-8272; www.northatlantic.com. 1974. avg. press run 3M. Pub'd 35 titles 1998; expects 40 titles 1999. 2 titles listed in the *Small Press Record of Books in Print* (28th Edition, 1999-00). avg. price, cloth: $25; paper: $16.95. Discounts: trade 1-4 books 20%, 5+ 40%. Reporting time: 4-8 weeks. Simultaneous submissions accepted: yes. Publishes .5-1% of manuscripts submitted. Payment: by contract. Only automatic copyrighting by publication.

NORTH CAROLINA LITERARY REVIEW, Margaret Bauer, English Department, East Carolina University, Greenville, NC 27858, 252-328-1537; Fax 252-328-4889. 1991. Articles, art, photos, interviews, criticism, reviews, letters, collages, news items, non-fiction. "Recent contributors: Fred Chappell, Janet Lembke, Leon Rooke, Robin Hemley, Michael Parker, Fielding Dawson, Paul Metcalf, Elaine Gottlieb, Linda Flowers; interviews with A.R. Ammons, Linda Beatrice Brown, James Applewhite, Charles Wright, Margaret Maton. Length: 1,000-6,000 words. Biases: critical and historical essays and scholarly articles about NC writers; interviews with NC writers; occasional essays by NC writers, and contemporary creative work in thematic sections; comprehensive essay reviews of recent books by NC writers; essays and articles on bookselling and libraries in NC. MLA style when appropriate; please query before submitting articles." circ. 1.5M. 1/yr. Pub'd 1 issue 1998; expects 1 issue 1999, 1 issue 2000. sub. price: $20/2 years, $35/4 years; per copy: $15 retail/$17.50 ppd; sample: $10.50 ppd. Back issues: $10-$12. Discounts: 40% non-returnable; 20% with full credit for returns. 224pp; 6¾×10; lp. Reporting time: 4-6 weeks on queries only. Simultaneous submissions accepted: no. Publishes 25% of manuscripts submitted. Payment: $50-$500 for all articles; kill fee for solicited articles not published. Copyrighted, rights revert to author on request. Pub's reviews: 6 in 1998. §North Carolina and Southern writers, literature, culture, history. Ads: $200/$110/$75 1/4 page. CLMP, CELJ.

NORTH COAST REVIEW, Poetry Harbor, Pat McKinnon, Ellie Schoenfeld, Liz Minette, Guest Editor, PO Box 103, Duluth, MN 55801-0103, e-mail poharb@toofarnorth.com. 1992. Poetry, art, photos. "We currently publish poetry by poets residing in Minnesota, Wisconsin, North Dakota, the Upper Peninsula of Michigan. Include SASE, and publishing history" circ. 1M. 2/yr. Pub'd 3 issues 1998; expects 2 issues 1999, 2 issues 2000. sub. price: $21.95/6 issues, $59 lifetime; per copy: $4.95; sample: $4.95. Back issues: $3.50. Discounts: 40% to bookstores, minimum order 3 copies, 55% to distributors, no minimum. 56pp; 7×8½; of. Reporting time: 1-6 months. Simultaneous submissions accepted: yes. Publishes 20% of manuscripts submitted. Payment: $10 and contributor's copies. Copyrighted, reverts to author. Ads: $30 1/3 page/$45 1/2 page. MMPA.

North Country Books, Inc., M. Sheila Orlin, 311 Turner Street, Utica, NY 13501, 315-735-4877. 1965. Non-fiction, photos. "NY State, history, biography, nostalgia, heavy accent on Adirondacks and upstate." avg. press run 3M-5M. Pub'd 12 titles 1998; expects 12 titles 1999, 20 titles 2000. 81 titles listed in the *Small Press Record of Books in Print* (28th Edition, 1999-00). avg. price, cloth: $20; paper: $12.95. Discounts: 1-4 20%, 5 40%. 200pp; 6×9, 7×10; of. Reporting time: 3-6 months. Simultaneous submissions accepted: yes. Publishes 5% of manuscripts submitted. Payment: 8% retail price, 20% withheld against returns. Copyrights for author.

NORTH DAKOTA QUARTERLY, UND Press, Robert W. Lewis, Editor; William Borden, Fiction Editor; Jay Meek, Poetry Editor, University of North Dakota, PO Box 7209, Grand Forks, ND 58202, 701-777-3322. 1910. Poetry, fiction, articles, art, photos, interviews, satire, criticism, reviews, long-poems, non-fiction. "Recent contributors include Alistair Elliot, R.T. Smith, Sherman Paul, Stuart Freibert, Elton Glaser, Maura Stanton, Marieve Rugo, Vasko Popa, and Ivan V. Lalic" circ. 750. 4/yr. Pub'd 4 issues 1998; expects 4 issues 1999, 4 issues 2000. sub. price: $25 individual, $30 institutional; per copy: $8 and $12; sample: $8. Back issues: $8 and $12 for special. Discounts: 20%. 175pp; 6×9; †of. Reporting time: 1-4 months. We accept simultaneous submissions for fiction and essays if noted in cover letter, but not for poetry. Publishes 5% of manuscripts submitted. Payment: in copies. Copyrighted, reverts to author. Pub's reviews: 60 in 1998. §Native American studies, Canadian studies, women studies, northern plains literature. Ads: $150/$100. CODA, CELJ, MLA.

●**North Star Books,** PO Box 259, Lancaster, CA 93584, 661-945-7529; nstarbks@aol.com. 1992. Non-fiction.

"Authors must be willing to promote aggressively - you believe in your own product and will promote it in the marketplace." avg. press run 3M. Expects 1 title 1999, 2 titles 2000. 1 title listed in the *Small Press Record of Books in Print* (28th Edition, 1999-00). avg. price, cloth: $22; paper: $15. Discounts: 60-65% distributor, 50-55% wholesaler, 20-40% retail. 200pp; 6×9. Reporting time: 8 weeks. Payment: trade standard. Copyrights for author. PMA.

North Stone Press (see also THE NORTH STONE REVIEW), PO Box 14098, Minneapolis, MN 55414. 1971. Poetry, fiction, criticism, reviews, letters. "At this point, these are the genres we're working with. More genres later, perhaps." avg. press run 1M-2M. Pub'd 1 title 1998; expects 1 title 1999, 2 titles 2000. avg. price, cloth: $15; paper: $7.95. Discounts: query, please, with proposal. Poetry 100pp, fiction 30-40pp; 5½×8½; of. Reporting time: 1 month to 6 weeks. Simultaneous submissions accepted: no. Payment: after costs, yes. Copyrights for author. CLMP.

THE NORTH STONE REVIEW, North Stone Press, James Naiden, Editor; Allen Topper, Associate Editor; Anne Duggan, Associate Editor; Sigrid Bergie, Contributing Editor; Eugene McCarthy, Contributing Editor; Michael Tjepkes, Contributing Editor; Jack Jarpe, Assistant Editor, PO Box 14098, Minneapolis, MN 55414. 1971. Poetry, fiction, articles, art, photos, interviews, reviews, long-poems, non-fiction. "David Ignatow, Ralph Mills Jr., Robert Bly, John Rezmerski, Karyn Sproles, G.T. Wright, Sigrid Bergie, etc., are among recent contributors." circ. 1.5M. 2/yr. Expects 1 issue 1999, 2 issues 2000. sub. price: $20/2 issues; per copy: $10; sample: $10. Back issues: query first. Discounts: depends—query first. 200-300pp; 8½×5½; of. Reporting time: 2-6 weeks. Publishes 2-3% of manuscripts submitted. Payment: 2 copies. Copyrighted, reprint permission on written request. Pub's reviews: 15 in 1998. §Poetry, fiction, literary biography and theory. Ads: $60/$35/$25 1/4 page. CLMP.

NORTHEAST, John Judson, Editor, 1310 Shorewood Drive, La Crosse, WI 54601-7033. 1962. Poetry, fiction, articles, art, photos, interviews, criticism, reviews, parts-of-novels, long-poems. "We solicit any work of quality that has a human being behind it whose words help shape his and our awareness of being human. This has always come before fashion, reputation or ambition. A subscription includes 1 *NE* and 2 to 3 books per year" circ. 400-500. 1/yr. Pub'd 1 issue 1998; expects 1 issue 1999, 1 issue 2000. sub. price: $33 for complete sub., includes 1 *NE* and all Juniper Press works for that year; $38 for institutions; per copy: $6; sample: $3. Back issues: write for information; most are available but in very small quantities. Discounts: dealer and bookstore 20% for one book, 30% for 2-4 books (no returns), 40% for 5 or more (no returns). 48-60pp; size varies; of, lp. Reporting time: 8-12 weeks. Payment: copies. Copyrighted, reverts to author. Pub's reviews: 3 in 1998. §Poetry, crit., fiction. Ads: none.

NORTHEAST ARTS MAGAZINE, Leigh Donaldson, Editor & Publisher, PO Box 94, Kittery, ME 03904-0094. 1990. Poetry, fiction, articles, art, photos, interviews, criticism, reviews, parts-of-novels, non-fiction. "We accept manuscripts: poetry, fiction, and non-fiction features, when accompanied by a SASE. Poetry under 30 lines, fiction and non-fiction between 750-1,500 words is preferred. Black and white camera-ready art and screened photos at 5x8" (full-page) or 5x4½" (half-page) format are also considered. *NorthEastARTS* is interested in material of all types and varied perspectives, but strongly discourages the submission of any work that reflects a lack of moral, social and political consciousness. Checks and money orders should be made to North East Arts" circ. 750-1M. 2/yr. Pub'd 2 issues 1998; expects 4 issues 1999, 4 issues 2000. sub. price: $10 domestic, $15 foreign; per copy: $4; sample: $4.50. Back issues: $4.50. Discounts: none. 32-36pp; 5×8; of. Reporting time: 1-2 months. Payment: 2 copies. Copyrighted, reverts to author. Pub's reviews: a few in 1998. §All books, exhibits, activities of interest to writers. Ads: $75/$45 1/2 (horizontal)/$50 1/2 (vertical)/classifieds: 25¢ per word, 30 word limit, $1 add'l word. CLMP.

NORTHERN CONTOURS, Cindy Robinson, PO Box 618, Quincy, CA 95971, 916-283-3402. 1994. Poetry, Poetry, Poetry. "We are a regional publication, representing the work of Northern California and Northwestern Nevada poets, writers and artists" circ. 500. 1/yr. Expects 1 issue 1999, 1 issue 2000. sub. price: $14; per copy: $7; sample: $6. Back issues: $6. Discounts: wholesale 10+ copies $4.20 each, 4-10 copies $4.20 each, 1-3 copies $5.25 each. 96pp; 5½×8; of. Reporting time: 1-8 months. Simultaneous submissions accepted, but please let the editor know. Publishes 1% of manuscripts submitted. Payment: copies. Copyrighted, reverts to author. CLMP.

NORTHERN PILOT, Peter M. Diemer, Publisher, PO Box 220168, Anchorage, AK 99522, 907-258-6898; Fax 907-258-4354; info@northernpilot.com. 1998. "*Northern Pilot* is seeking first-person stories and photographs. We want text with an authentic, powerful, unique voice. Our features will cover Alaska, Oregon, Washington, California, and Canada. We publish only work of the highest quality. Technical features run 3,000-3,500 words; fiction or nonfiction 1,100-3,000 words. Please query with SASE and 5-line bio stressing personal aviation experience/expertise." circ. 35M. 6/yr. Pub'd 6 issues 1998; expects 6 issues 1999, 6 issues 2000. sub. price: $19; per copy: $3.99; sample: $4.50. Back issues: $4.50. 44pp; 8×10. Reporting time: 8-12 weeks. Simultaneous submissions accepted: yes. Payment: $200-$400 on acceptance. Copyrighted, reverts to author. Pub's reviews. §Aviation. Ads: call for rates.

Northern Rim Press, 333 South 5th Street East, Missoula, MT 59801, 406-549-0385. 1993. Photos, non-fiction. "We also intend to publish short monographs and discussion papers. Contributions are welcome. We focus on publishing material of relevance that pertains to sustainable development of the region that encompasses the earth's mid-latitudes (the Northern Rim). Materials seek to explore development that balances innovation with tradition, ecology with economy, and culture with technology." avg. press run 10M. Expects 1 title 1999, 1 title 2000. avg. price, cloth: $22.95; paper: $17.95. Discounts: 40% trade, 20% classroom and libraries, 55% wholesaler. 140pp; 8¼×9. Reporting time: 1 month. Payment: 8% royalty. Copyrights for author.

Northern Star Press, PO Box 28814, San Jose, CA 95159. 1988. Expects 1 title 1999. 1 title listed in the *Small Press Record of Books in Print* (28th Edition, 1999-00). avg. price, paper: $10. Discounts: booksellers: 40%. 175pp; 8½×5½. Copyrights for author.

NORTHRIDGE REVIEW, Luisa Villani, Julie Kornblum, Donna Marsh, c/o CSUN, 18111 Nordoff Street, Mail Stop 8248, Northridge, CA 91330-8261, E-mail 102504.1176@compuserve.com. 1980. Poetry, fiction, art, photos, cartoons, interviews, satire, criticism, long-poems. circ. 400. 2/yr. Pub'd 2 issues 1998; expects 2 issues 1999, 2 issues 2000. sub. price: $14; per copy: $7; sample: $4. Back issues: $4. 100pp; 8×5. Reporting time: 3-4 months. Simultaneous submissions accepted: no. Publishes 10% of manuscripts submitted. Payment: 1 copy. Not copyrighted. Ads: $80/$60.

NORTHWEST REVIEW, John Witte, Editor; Jan MacRae, Fiction Editor; David Stairs, Art Editor, 369 P.L.C., University of Oregon, Eugene, OR 97403, 503-346-3957. 1957. Poetry, fiction, art, photos, reviews, parts-of-novels, long-poems, plays. "Recent contributors: Raymond Carver, Hans Magnus Enzensberger, Olga Broumas, Barry Lopez, Morris Grave, Joyce Carol Oates, Richard Kostelanetz. Bias: Quality in whatever form. No other predisposition." circ. 1.2M. 3/yr. Pub'd 3 issues 1998; expects 3 issues 1999. 5 titles listed in the *Small Press Record of Books in Print* (28th Edition, 1999-00). sub. price: $20; per copy: $7; sample: $3.50. Back issues: $7 all except double issues or specially priced issues. Discounts: bookstore/agencies 40% wholesale. 130pp; 6×9; of. Reporting time: 8 weeks average. Simultaneous submissions accepted: no. Publishes 1.5% of manuscripts submitted. Payment: 3 copies. Copyrighted, rights reassigned upon request for inclusion in a book. Pub's reviews: 15 in 1998. §Literature, poetry, fiction, small press publications. Ads: $160 full page only. CLMP.

NORTHWOODS JOURNAL, A Magazine for Writers, Conservatory of American Letters, Dan River Press, Northwoods Press, Century Press, Robert Olmsted, PO Box 298, Thomaston, ME 04861-0298, 207-345-0998; Fax 207-354-8953; cal@americanletters.org; www.americanletters.org. 1986. Poetry, fiction, articles, art, interviews, satire, criticism, reviews, letters, news items. circ. 1M. 4/yr. Pub'd 2 issues 1998; expects 4 issues 1999, 4 issues 2000. sub. price: $12, free to members of Conservatory of American Letters; per copy: $7.95 ppd.; sample: $7.95 ppd. Back issues: if available $12.95 ppd. Discounts: 10+ copies, $3 each. 56pp; 5½×8½; †of. Reporting time: 48 hours to 2 weeks after deadline (90 days max.). Simultaneous submissions accepted: no. Publishes 5-20% fiction, poetry 85-90% of manuscripts submitted. Payment: cash for all acceptances, except letters, range from $4+ per page depending on length, quality, relevancy, etc. Copyrighted, reverts to author. Pub's reviews: 6-8 in 1998. §Small press and self-published only. Ads: $150/$90/$54 1/4 page.

Northwoods Press (see also NORTHWOODS JOURNAL, A Magazine for Writers), Robert W. Olmsted, Publisher, PO Box 298, Thomaston, ME 04861-0298, 207-354-0998; Fax 207-354-8953; cal@americanletters.org; www.americanletters.org. 1972. Poetry, fiction, news items. "Request 15 point program. SASE 2 stamps. No reading fee for Northwoods Press." avg. press run 500. Pub'd 1 title 1998; expects 3 titles 1999, 3 titles 2000. 15 titles listed in the *Small Press Record of Books in Print* (28th Edition, 1999-00). avg. price, cloth: $29.95; paper: $12.95; other: $100 collector's. Discounts: no. of paperback copies ordered X2% to a maximum 50% for 25 or more copies. No discount on hardcovers or collectors or single copies. 80pp; 5½×8½; †of. Reporting time: 1-4 weeks. Simultaneous submissions accepted: no. Publishes 5% of manuscripts submitted. Payment: minimum advance $250, payable on contracting; minimum royalty 10% from first sale. Copyrights for author.

NORTHWORDS, Angus Dunn, The Stable, Long Road, Avoch, Ross-shire IV9 8QR, Scotland, website www.cali.co.uk/highexp/nwords/. 1991. Poetry, fiction, articles, art, satire, criticism, reviews, music, long-poems. circ. 500. 3/yr. Pub'd 2 issues 1998; expects 3 issues 1999, 3 issues 2000. sub. price: £7.50 for 3 issues; per copy: £2.50; sample: £2.50. Back issues: £2.50. Discounts: 33½% discount. 56pp; size A4; of. Reporting time: 6 weeks. Payment: copies. Copyrighted, reverts to author. Pub's reviews: 20 in 1998. §Poetry, fiction, Scottish, Irish.

Norton Coker Press, Edward Mycue, PO Box 640543, San Francisco, CA 94164-0543, 415-922-0395. 1988. Poetry, fiction, art, satire, criticism, reviews, music, letters, plays, news items. avg. press run 150. Pub'd 22 titles 1998; expects 15 titles 1999, 10 titles 2000. 33 titles listed in the *Small Press Record of Books in Print* (28th Edition, 1999-00). avg. price, paper: $8. Discounts: 5+ copies 40%. 44pp; 5×7; †various. Reporting time:

1-4 weeks. Payment: in copies. Copyrights for author.

NOSTALGIA, A Sentimental State of Mind, Connie Lakey Martin, PO Box 2224, Orangeburg, SC 29116. 1986. Poetry, art, photos, cartoons, interviews, non-fiction. "90% of material is selected through contest entries: Short Story & Poetry Cash Awards offered Spring and Fall. Short Stories: 1000-15000 words, nostalgic, true story from personal experience, *unpublished*, previously published ok with credits and permission from previous publisher; Poetry: any style, nostalgic content, unpublished, previously published ok with credits and permission from previous publisher. Entry fee reserves copy of next season's edition. Previously published okay for regular submissions only. Submit *unpublished* only for contests!!" circ. 1M. 2/yr. Pub'd 2 issues 1998; expects 2 issues 1999, 2 issues 2000. sub. price: $8; per copy: $5; sample: $5. Discounts: 50% to bookstores. 24pp; 5½×8½; of. Reporting time: 4-6 weeks. Payment: cash awards for short stories and poetry (through contests Spring and Fall). Copyrighted, reverts to author. Pub's reviews: 4 in 1998. §Poetry and short stories (non-fiction). Ads: $50 1/3 page.

NOSTOC MAGAZINE, Arts End Books, Marshall Brooks, Editor, Box 162, Newton, MA 02468. 1973. Poetry, fiction, articles, criticism, reviews, parts-of-novels. "A copy of our catalogue - detailing our past publications and describing our subscription package program is available upon request (please enclose a SASE). Not currently reading unsolicited mss." circ. 300. 2/yr. Pub'd 2 issues 1998; expects 2 issues 1999, 2 issues 2000. sub. price: $10/4 issues; per copy: $3.50; sample: $3.50. Back issues: rates on request. Discounts: on request. 30pp; size varies; lp, of. Simultaneous submissions accepted: no. Publishes 5% of manuscripts submitted. Payment: modest payment upon acceptance. Copyrighted, reverts to author. §Small press history, poetry, fiction & politics, bibliography. Ads: rates on request.

Nosukumo, Javant Biarujia, GPO Box 994-H, Melbourne, Victoria 3001, Australia, 9527-3964. 1982. Criticism, letters, long-poems. "Length generally below 60pp. Recent publications: Anais Nin, *Letters to a Friend in Australia* (1992), letters; Charles Roberts, *Infected Queer: Notes of an Activist* (April 1994), journal" avg. press run 300-1M. Pub'd 1 title 1998; expects 1 title 2000. 11 titles listed in the *Small Press Record of Books in Print* (28th Edition, 1999-00). avg. price, other: $10-$20 limp parchment wrappers. Discounts: 40% (postage charged unless order is paid in advance). 48pp; size A5; of. Reporting time: 6-8 weeks. Simultaneous submissions accepted: no. Publishes 5% of manuscripts submitted. Payment: 10% royalty on copies sold. Copyrights for author.

NOT BORED!, PO Box 1115, New York, NY 10009-9998. 1983. Fiction, articles, criticism, collages, news items. "Situationist-inspired" circ. 50. 1-2/yr. Pub'd 1 issue 1998; expects 1 issue 1999, 2 issues 2000. price per copy: $5; sample: $5. Back issues: $5. Discounts: none. 80pp; 8½×11; †photocopy. Reporting time: 2 weeks. Simultaneous submissions accepted: no. Publishes 1% of manuscripts submitted. Payment: a free issue or two. Not copyrighted. Pub's reviews: 1 in 1998.

NOTES AND ABSTRACTS IN AMERICAN AND INTERNATIONAL EDUCATION, Caddo Gap Press, Alan H. Jones, Editor, 3145 Geary Boulevard #275, San Francisco, CA 94118, 415-922-1911. 1961. Articles. "A semi-annual bulletin featuring information, news, research, and abstracts in the social foundations of education." circ. 100. 2/yr. Pub'd 2 issues 1998; expects 2 issues 1999, 2 issues 2000. sub. price: $20 indiv., $30 instit.; per copy: $15. 24pp; 5½×8½; of. Reporting time: 2 months. Publishes 25% of manuscripts submitted. Payment: none. Copyrighted, reverts to author. Ads: none. MPE, EDPRESS.

NOTES & QUERIES, Oxford University Press, L.G. Black, D. Hewitt, E.G. Stanley, Journals Subscription Department, Pinkhill House, Southfield Road, Eynsham, Oxford OX8 1JJ, England. 1849. Articles, reviews. "English language and literature, lexicography, history and scholarly antiquarianism. In addition to notes, readers' queries and replies there are book reviews. Each issue gives emphasis to the works of a particular period." circ. 1.7M. 4/yr. Pub'd 4 issues 1998; expects 4 issues 1999, 4 issues 2000. sub. price: $83; per copy: $25; sample: free. 150pp; 185×130mm. Reporting time: 1 week to 6 months. Payment: none. Copyrighted. Pub's reviews: 191 in 1998. §English literature, criticism, poetry, language. Ads: £225($405)/£140($250)/ £95($170) 1/4 page.

Not-For-Sale-Press or NFS Press, Lew Thomas, 243 Grand View Ave., San Francisco, CA 94114, 415-282-5372. 1975. Articles, art, photos, interviews. "*Photography & Language 8 x 10,* 1975, compiled by Lew Thomas, 48 pgs. 21 photos. *Performances And Installations,* Kesa, 1976, 62 pages, 50 photos." avg. press run 1.5-2M. Pub'd 1 title 1998; expects 3 titles 1999, 3 titles 2000. 6 titles listed in the *Small Press Record of Books in Print* (28th Edition, 1999-00). avg. price, paper: $25. Discounts: 40% trade, 55% wholesale, 6 titles 40% proforma. 48-120pp; 8×10, 9×12; of.

NOTRE DAME REVIEW, William O'Rourke, John Matthias, English Dept., Creative Writing, University of Notre Dame, Notre Dame, IN 46556, 219-631-6952; Fax 219-631-4268. 1995. Poetry, fiction, interviews, reviews, parts-of-novels. "Recent contributors: Edward Falco, Seamus Heaney, Richard Elman, Denise Levertov, and Czeslaw Milosz." circ. 2M. 2/yr. Pub'd 2 issues 1998; expects 2 issues 1999, 2 issues 2000. sub. price: $15 individuals, $20 institutions; per copy: $8; sample: $6. Discounts: 20%. 115pp; 6×9. Reporting time:

3-4 months. Simultaneous submissions accepted: yes. Publishes 8% of manuscripts submitted. Payment: variable. Copyrighted, reverts to author. Pub's reviews: 7 in 1998. §Fiction, poetry, literary criticism/history. Ads: $165/$90/$75 1/3 page. CLMP.

NOTTINGHAM MEDIEVAL STUDIES, Michael Jones, Professor, Dept. of History, University Park, Nottingham NG7 2RD, England, +44 115-9-515932; fax +44 115-9-515948; e-mail michael.jones@nottingham.ac.uk. 1957. Articles. "Articles on medieval language, literature, history, etc., concerning the whole of Europe making up to some 200pp of print @ 550 words per page." circ. 400. 1/yr. Expects 1 issue 1999. sub. price: £20 sterling only; per copy: £20 or $24; sample: £20. Back issues: £10. Discounts: £17.50. 200pp; 7×9½; †of. Reporting time: 2 months. Simultaneous submissions accepted: yes. Publishes 30-50% of manuscripts submitted. Payment: none. Copyrighted. Pub's reviews: 3 in 1998. §Same as for articles. Ads: none.

Nouveau Press, 14592 Palmdale Road, #D6-199, Victorville, CA 92392, 760-961-6088; fax 760-951-8388; e-mail nouveau@earthlink.net. 1 title listed in the *Small Press Record of Books in Print* (28th Edition, 1999-00).

NOVA EXPRESS, Lawrence Person, PO Box 27231, Austin, TX 78755, E-mail lawrence@bga.com. 1987. Poetry, fiction, articles, art, interviews, satire, criticism, reviews, non-fiction. "We cover cutting edge science fiction, fantasy, horror, and slipstream literature, with an emphasis on post cyberpunk works." circ. 750. 2/yr. Pub'd 1 issue 1998; expects 2 issues 1999, 2 issues 2000. sub. price: $12/4 issues; per copy: $4; sample: $4. Back issues: $3 each. Discounts: starts at 40% for 25 issues, write for rates. 48pp; 8½×11; of. Reporting time: 1-3 months, sometimes less. Simultaneous submissions accepted: no. Publishes 10% of manuscripts submitted. Payment: 2 contributor copies and 4-issue subscription. Copyrighted, reverts to author. Pub's reviews: 40 in 1998. §Science fiction, fantasy, horror, slipstream. Ads: $100/$60/$35 1/4 page.

Nova Press, Jeff Kolby, 11659 Mayfield Ave, Suite 1, Los Angeles, CA 90049, 310-207-4078, E-mail novapress@aol.com. 1993. "We publish only test prep books for college entrance exams such as the GRE, LSAT, SAT, GMAT, and MCAT, or closely related books such as college guides and vocabulary improvement." avg. press run 3M. Pub'd 5 titles 1998; expects 5 titles 1999, 10 titles 2000. 4 titles listed in the *Small Press Record of Books in Print* (28th Edition, 1999-00). avg. price, paper: $19.95. Discounts: 40%. 550pp; 8½×11; of. Payment: 10%-22.5% royalty.

NOW AND THEN, Jane Harris Woodside, Editor-in-Chief; Nancy Fischman, Managing Editor; Linda Parsons, Poetry Editor; Sandra Ballard, Reviews Editor; Jo Carson, Poetry Editor, PO Box 70556, East Tennessee State University, Johnson City, TN 37614-0556, 423-439-5348; fax 423-439-6340; e-mail woodsidj@etsu.edu. 1984. Poetry, fiction, articles, art, photos, interviews, criticism, reviews, letters. "*Now and Then* is the publication of the Center for Appalachian Studies and Service of East Tennessee State University. Each issue is divided between expository and imaginative material: studies of Appalachian nature and culture on the one hand, and visual art, imaginative writing on the other. Issues always have a thematic focus; for example, recent issues focused on food in Appalachia and photography. Each issue features juxtaposed visuals of an Appalachian locale now (present) and then (past). Photos, graphics, critical studies of Appalachian nature and culture, personal essays, poetry, fiction are welcomed for consideration on a continuing basis. 'Appalachia' is considered to cover the mountain region from New Yord State to Georgia. We'd like people to send for a free listing of upcoming issues and writer's guidelines." circ. 1.5M. 3/yr. Pub'd 3 issues 1998; expects 3 issues 1999, 3 issues 2000. sub. price: $20; per copy: $7; sample: $5. Back issues: $4.50. 44pp; 8½×11; of. Reporting time: 4 months. We accept simultaneous submissions, but we must be notified where else it's been submitted. Payment: $15-$75 generally for articles and fiction; $10 per poem and per review + copies of the magazine. Copyrighted, does not revert to author. Pub's reviews: 12 in 1998. §Appalachian arts, history, culture, ecology.

●NOW HERE NOWHERE, Gravity Presses, Inc., Paul Kingston, L.A. Beach, Patt Trama, 27030 Havelock, Dearborn Heights, MI 48127, 313-563-4683; e-mail mikeb5000@yahoo.com. 1998. Poetry, fiction, art, photos. "We have no formal guidelines for either form or contest; we've published sonnets, sestinas, language poetry and other experiments. However, we have high standards, so don't submit junk." circ. 500. 4/yr. Pub'd 2 issues 1998; expects 4 issues 1999, 4 issues 2000. sub. price: $20; per copy: $5.50; sample: $5.50. Discounts: negotiable. 48pp; 7×8½; †laser copy. Reporting time: 6-8 weeks. Simultaneous submissions accepted: yes. Publishes 30% of manuscripts submitted. Payment: $1-5 per issue + one copy. Copyrighted, reverts to author. Ads: $40/$25/ 1/4 page $15.

Now It's Up To You Publications, Tom Parson, 157 S. Logan, Denver, CO 80209, 303-777-8951. 1980. Poetry. "Interested in the intersection between poetry/fiction/the arts, and political and social reality/unreality— all the openings, all possibilities. The writer, the publisher take it this far, now it's up to you. Publishing poetry postcards, broadsides, and books on letterpress since 1984. Using handset types, linoleum cuts and printer's blocks for multi-color graphics with poems." avg. press run 300-1M. Pub'd 7 titles 1998; expects 7 titles 1999, 7 titles 2000. 24 titles listed in the *Small Press Record of Books in Print* (28th Edition, 1999-00). avg. price, paper: 50¢ postcards, $2-5 broadsides, $2-$3 chapbooks. Discounts: 40% booksellers; returns accepted anytime. †lp. Reporting time: I love to get poetry mss, but I'm largely unable to respond—sorry. Payment: copies, arrangement will vary (approx. 10% of press run). Copyrights for author.

Noyce Publishing, John Noyce, G.P.O. Box 2222T, Melbourne, Vic. 3001, Australia, e-mail noycepublishing@hotmail.com. 1970. Pub'd 12 titles 1998; expects 12 titles 1999, 16 titles 2000. 3 titles listed in the *Small Press Record of Books in Print* (28th Edition, 1999-00). avg. price, paper: varies. Discounts: 10% agents. 20-100pp; size A4.

NP Press, Elliot A. Ryan, 4141 Orchard Drive, Fairfax, VA 22032, 703-273-2779. 1995. "For return of ms. send SASE." avg. press run 500-700. Expects 2 titles 2000. Reporting time: 30 days. Payment: royalties. Does not copyright for author.

‡**NUDE BEACH**, Dan Tapper, Steve Starger, Andy Nelson, Curtis Kopf, c/o Dan Tapper, 57 Brandywine Lane, Suffield, CT 06078-2141, 203-342-1298 (Steve Starger). 1993. Poetry, fiction, art, satire, criticism, parts-of-novels, non-fiction. "Short fiction to 5,000 words; novel-length excerpts to 10,000 words; max. of 5 poems. Literary, experimental, dark or light subject matter. Content and style unrestricted, but no obvious genre or blatantly commercial material. We're looking for stylistic grace and compelling themes, characters, and ideas. Even the most experimental work should show consistent integrity and honesty. SASE for ms. guidelines. SASE or $1 postage for guidelines and sample." circ. 350+. 4/yr. Expects 4 issues 1999, 4 issues 2000. 1 title listed in the *Small Press Record of Books in Print* (28th Edition, 1999-00). sub. price: $10; per copy: $3; sample: $1. 45-50pp; 5×8½; †of. Reporting time: 4-6 weeks. Payment: 2 copies, honorariums when available. Copyrighted, reverts to author. Ads: send SASE for rates.

Nunciata, A.C. Doyle, Publishing Division, PO Box 416, Denver, CO 80201-0416, 303-575-5676. 1989. "Formerly Assoc. Advertisers Services." avg. press run 1.5M. Pub'd 3 titles 1998; expects 10 titles 1999. 9 titles listed in the *Small Press Record of Books in Print* (28th Edition, 1999-00). avg. price, cloth: $19.95; paper: $19.95. Discounts: standard to libraries + bookstores. 60pp; 8½×11.

NUTHOUSE, Ludwig VonQuirk, Chief of Staff, PO Box 119, Ellenton, FL 34222. 1993. Poetry, fiction, articles, cartoons, interviews, satire, non-fiction. "Humor, essays, stories and other amusements, preferably of 700 words or less. Recent contributors include Ken Rand, Logan McNeil, Tim Libby, P. Andrew Miller, Gregory Smith." circ. 100+. 6-10/yr. Pub'd 7 issues 1998; expects 10 issues 1999, 10 issues 2000. sub. price: $10 for 11 issues, checks payable to Twin Rivers Press; per copy: $1; sample: $1. Back issues: $1. 12pp; 5½×8½; †xerox. Reporting time: 1 month. Simultaneous submissions accepted: yes. Publishes 25% of manuscripts submitted. Payment: contributor's copy. Not copyrighted. Ads: trade; classfieds free for subscibers.

NUTRITION ACTION HEALTHLETTER, Stephen B. Schmidt, Editor-in-Chief, 1875 Connecticut Avenue NW #300, Washington, DC 20009, 202-332-9110. 1974. Articles, art, photos, cartoons, interviews, criticism, reviews, letters, news items. "No submissions." circ. 800M. 10/yr. Pub'd 10 issues 1998; expects 10 issues 1999, 10 issues 2000. sub. price: $24; per copy: $2.50; sample: free. Back issues: $3. Discounts: quantity discounts available. 16pp; 8½×11; of. Payment: negotiable. Copyrighted, rights revert to author only if requested. Pub's reviews: 10 in 1998. §Food, health, nutrition, fitness, gardening, related areas. No advertising accepted.

NWI National Writers Institute, Maria Valentin, Publisher; Shawn Davis, Director of Operations; Sandy Keller, Editor, PO Box 6314, Lawrenceville, NJ 08648-0314, E-mail express518@aol.com. 1996. Fiction, art, plays, non-fiction. "We accept unsolicited mss. of 50 pages or more, specifically non-fiction, plays and fiction. All submitted work must be done entirely with SASE." avg. press run 3M. Pub'd 10 titles 1998; expects 25 titles 1999, 25+ titles 2000. 6 titles listed in the *Small Press Record of Books in Print* (28th Edition, 1999-00). avg. price, cloth: $24.95; paper: $14.95. Discounts: 45-55% bookstores, 40-45% libraries. 120-176pp; 5½×8½; of, electronic pre-press. Reporting time: 2 weeks, turnaround from inquiry to publication 6 weeks. Simultaneous submissions accepted: yes. Publishes 80% of manuscripts submitted. Payment: 50% royalty of list, net price. Copyrights for author. PMA, SPAN.

Nystrom Publishing Co., Alex Jones, Mardi Nystrom, PO Box 378, Issaquah, WA 98027, 425-392-0451. 1985. Articles, photos, reviews. avg. press run 30M. Pub'd 2 titles 1998; expects 2 titles 1999, 2 titles 2000. 1 title listed in the *Small Press Record of Books in Print* (28th Edition, 1999-00). avg. price, paper: $19.95. 192pp; 8½×11; of. Reporting time: 30 days. Payment: individually arranged. Copyrights for author.

NYX OBSCURA MAGAZINE, Diana McCrary, PO Box 5554, Atlanta, GA 30307-0554, 704-684-6629; nyxobscura@aol.com. 1990. Poetry, fiction, articles, art, photos, interviews, reviews, music. "Recent contributors: John Grey, Patricia Russo. Vignettes are good; material with a folkloric or fairy tale slant especially sought." circ. 1.5M. 2/yr. Pub'd 2 issues 1998; expects 2 issues 1999, 2 issues 2000. sub. price: $10; sample: $5 + p/h. Discounts: available upon request. 40pp; of. We do not usually accept simultaneous submissions. Publishes 2% of manuscripts submitted. Payment: copies. Copyrights revert to author on publication. Pub's reviews: 50+ in 1998. §Aesthetic nonfiction, Fin de siecle fantasy, dark archaic fiction, fantasy, folklore. Ads: upon request.

O

The O Press, Julie Batsford-White, 702 45th Street, Oakland, CA 94609-1803. 1993. Fiction, music. "Short fiction prefered, but smart pop crit. okay. Intense, visionary, user-friendly stuff is best. Stuff which is humorous like Dostoyevsky." avg. press run 500. Pub'd 1 title 1998; expects 2 titles 1999, 3 titles 2000. 1 title listed in the *Small Press Record of Books in Print* (28th Edition, 1999-00). avg. price, paper: $8.95. Discounts: negotiable. 52pp; 7×7; copy. Reporting time: 2 months. Payment: negotiable. Copyrights for author.

O.ARS, Inc., Don Wellman, Cola Franzen, Irene Turner, 21 Rockland Road, Weare, NH 03281, 603-529-1060. 1981. Poetry, fiction, articles, art, photos, interviews, criticism, letters, long-poems, collages, concrete art, non-fiction. avg. press run 1M. Pub'd 1 title 1998; expects 1 title 1999, 1 title 2000. 1 title listed in the *Small Press Record of Books in Print* (28th Edition, 1999-00). avg. price, paper: $5. Discounts: 50-55% on 10 or more, 40% on 5 or more. 96pp; 7×10; of. Reporting time: 4-6 weeks. Does not copyright for author.

Oak Knoll Press, 310 Delaware Street, New Castle, DE 19720-5038, 302-328-7232, fax 302-328-7274. 1976. avg. press run 500-1M. Pub'd 10 titles 1998; expects 15 titles 1999, 15-20 titles 2000. 16 titles listed in the *Small Press Record of Books in Print* (28th Edition, 1999-00). Discounts: 1 book 10%, 2-4 20%, 5-25 40%, 26-99 45%, 100+ 50%, can mix titles. Pages vary; of, lp. Reporting time: 1 month. Payment: 10% of income, quarterly payments. Copyrights for author. ABAA, ABA, Philadelphia Pub. Group, PMA.

OASIS, Oasis Books, Ian Robinson, 12 Stevenage Road, London SW6 6ES, United Kingdom. 1969. Poetry, fiction, reviews, non-fiction. "Each issue is usually 16 pages long. Poetry: No long poems (45-50 lines max.). Fiction: 1200 max. usually, but exceptions are made. No biases." circ. 500. 6/yr. Pub'd 6 issues 1998; expects 6 issues 1999, 6 issues 2000. sub. price: $20; per copy: $5; sample: $5. Back issues: $5. Discounts: goes to subscribers only. 16pp; 5½×8¼; †of. Reporting time: 1 month max. Publishes 2% of manuscripts submitted. Payment: copies only. Copyrighted, reverts to author. Pub's reviews: 3 in 1998. §Poetry and fiction. Ads: none. ALP.

Oasis Books (see also OASIS; Shearsman Books), Ian Robinson, 12 Stevenage Road, London, SW6 6ES, United Kingdom. 1969. Poetry, fiction, long-poems, non-fiction. "No biases as to length or contributors, though we prefer short fiction. Contributors: Roy Fisher, Gustaf Sobin, Christopher Middleton, John Ash, De Stewart, Peter Dent, Ken Edwards, Andrea Moorhead, Vladimir Holan, Tomas Transtromer, Robin Fulton, Anna Akhmatova, and Douglas Gunn." avg. press run 200-600. Pub'd 3 titles 1998; expects 3 titles 1999. 41 titles listed in the *Small Press Record of Books in Print* (28th Edition, 1999-00). avg. price, paper: $1. Discounts: 25% over 1 copy, 33⅓% 2+ (trade only). 30-50pp; 5½×8¼; †of. Reporting time: 1 month max. Publishes 5% of manuscripts submitted. Payment: copies only, usually. Copyrights for author. ALP.

Oasis In Print, Beverly C. Smith, PO Box 314, Clarkdale, GA 30111, 770-943-3377. 1996. Poetry, non-fiction. "Poetry: deals with abusive situations, mental anguish. Collection of essays: essays by writers on writing." avg. press run 1M. Pub'd 2 titles 1998. avg. price, paper: $7.95-$10.95. Poetry 26pp, essays 100pp; 5½×8½. Does not copyright for author.

Oberlin College Press (see also FIELD), David Young, Co-editor; David Walker, Co-editor, Rice Hall, Oberlin College, Oberlin, OH 44074, 440-775-8408; Fax 440-775-8124; E-mail oc.press@oberlin.edu. 1969. Poetry, long-poems. "Also essays on poetry and translations of poetry." 29 titles listed in the *Small Press Record of Books in Print* (28th Edition, 1999-00). Discounts: 1 copy 20%, 2+ 30%, bookstores and agencies. 5¼×8½. Reporting time: 4-6 weeks. Simultaneous submissions accepted: no. Publishes 0.25%- 0.50% of manuscripts submitted. Copyrights for author. CLMP.

OBJECT PERMANENCE, Peter Manson, Robin Purves, Flat 3/2, 16 Ancroft Street, Glasgow G20 7HU, Scotland, 0141-332-7571. 1994. Poetry, reviews, long-poems, concrete art. "We publish an international range of experimental poetry in English, accompanied by as much small-press information, listing and reviewing as we can fit in." circ. 250-270. Published every 4-5 months. Pub'd 2 issues 1998; expects 3 issues 1999, 3 issues 2000. sub. price: £9 surface mail; per copy: £3; sample: £3. Discounts: 33⅓% to trade. 68pp; 5.8×8.3; of. Reporting time: usually within 2 months. Simultaneous submissions accepted: no. Publishes c. 10% of manuscripts submitted. Payment: no cash; 2 copies of issue concerned. Copyrighted, reverts to author. Pub's reviews: 100+ in 1998. §Experimental poetry, soundtext and visual work. Ads: by exchange.

OBLATES, Christine Portell, Managing Editor, 9480 N. De Mazenod Drive, Belleville, IL 62223-1160, 618-398-4848. 1943. Poetry, articles, non-fiction. "*Oblates* sent to members of Missionary Assn. of Mary

Immaculate." circ. 500M. 6/yr. Pub'd 6 issues 1998; expects 6 issues 1999, 6 issues 2000. sample price: sample copy and writer's guidelines sent free with 2 first class stamps and SAE. 20pp; 8½×5¼; †of. Reporting time: 6-8 weeks. Payment: $30 for poems, $80 for articles on acceptance. Ads: none. Catholic Press Association, National Catholic Development Conference.

OBLIVION, Jestapher, 120 State Avenue NE #76, Olympia, WA 98501-8212, E-mail oblivion@oblivion.net. 1995. Articles, letters, news items, non-fiction. circ. 200. 4/yr. Pub'd 4 issues 1998; expects 4 issues 1999, 4 issues 2000. price per copy: $1. 20pp; 5½×8½; †xerox. Payment: Email account. Copyrighted, reverts to author.

Obsessive Compulsive Anonymous, PO Box 215, New Hyde Park, NY 11040, 516-741-4901; FAX 212-768-4679. 1988. Non-fiction. "12-step program for obsessive compulsive disorder." avg. press run 5M. Pub'd 1 title 1998; expects 1 title 1999, 1 title 2000. 2 titles listed in the *Small Press Record of Books in Print* (28th Edition, 1999-00). avg. price, cloth: $14.95; paper: $8.95. Discounts: distributor—Hazelden (800) 328-9000. 125pp; 5½×8½; of. PMA.

OBSIDIAN II: BLACK LITERATURE IN REVIEW, Gerald Barrax, Editor; Doris Laryea, Associate Editor; Susie R. Powell, Fiction Editor; Kelley Sassano, Production Manager, Dept. of English, Box 8105, NC State University, Raleigh, NC 27695-8105, 919-515-3870. 1975. Poetry, fiction, articles, interviews, criticism, reviews, letters, parts-of-novels, long-poems, plays, news items. "Founded in 1975 by Alvin Aubert as *Obsidian: Black Literature in Review*, the journal was transferred to North Carolina State University in 1986 as *Obsidian II*. The journal publishes creative works in English by Black writers worldwide, or writers addressing black issues. with scholarly critical studies by all writers on Black literature in English. Contributors to *Obsidian* and *Obsidian II* (both creative and scholarly) have included Michael S. Harper, Jay Wright, Gayl Jones, Houston A. Baker, Jr., Eugenia Collier, Lloyd W. Brown, Gerald Early, Wanda Coleman, Jerry W. Ward, Nikki Grimes, Raymond R. Patterson, Akua Lezli Hope, Gary Smith, Bu-Buakei Jabbi, Yusef Komunyakaa, Jane Davis, Philip Royster." circ. 400. 2/yr. Pub'd 1 double issues 1998. sub. price: $12; per copy: $6; sample: $6. Back issues: $10. Discounts: 40% bookstores, 10% subscription agencies. 130pp; 6×9; †desktop/Macintosh SE. Reporting time: 3 months. Simultaneous submissions accepted: yes. Publishes 15% of manuscripts submitted. Payment: 2 copies. Copyrighted, reverts to author. Pub's reviews: 0 in 1998. §Creative works by Black writers or writers who address black issues (poetry, fiction, drama); scholarship and criticism on same. Ads: $200/$100. CLMP.

Occam Publishers, 250 East 40th Street #14-B, New York, NY 10016-1733, 607-849-5136. 1988. Non-fiction. "Religious and moral issues for thoughtful people; liberal or 'neoliberal' outlook." 1 title listed in the *Small Press Record of Books in Print* (28th Edition, 1999-00). avg. price, cloth: $19.95. Discounts: standard. 6×9; of. Reporting time: variable. Payment: negotiable. Copyrights for author. PMA.

Ocean View Books, Lee Ballentine, Editor; Jennifer MacGregor, Editor, PO Box 102650, Denver, CO 80250, Fax, 303-756-5374 (order line), e-mail proboak@csm.met. 1981. Long-poems. "We publish a variety of surrealist and speculative/science fiction texts, poetry and fiction. Our new series includes books on art in Colorado. Original material only. Nothing confessional, personal, modern or traditional. No rhyme. No blank verse, free verse, or couplets. No unsolicited manuscripts, but feel free to query on your project; if we're interested we will respond within 60 days. Recent authors: Dan Simmons, Rudy Rucker, Janet Hamill, Anselm Hollo, Kathryn Rantala. A sample book is avaliable for $5 postpaid. Please specify fiction or poetry." avg. press run 800. Pub'd 3 titles 1998; expects 4 titles 1999, 4 titles 2000. 32 titles listed in the *Small Press Record of Books in Print* (28th Edition, 1999-00). avg. price, cloth: $50; paper: $15.95. Discounts: 1-4 copies 20%, 5+ copies 35%, inquire for complete terms. 300pp; size varies; of. Reporting time: 4 months. Simultaneous submissions accepted: yes. Publishes less than 1% of manuscripts submitted. Payment: negotiable. Copyrights for author. SFPA (Science Fiction Poetry Association), Bookbuilders West, American Booksellers Association, American Book Producers Association, Science Fiction Writers of America.

Odysseus Enterprises Ltd., Joseph H. Bain, E. Angelo, PO Box 1548, Port Washington, NY 11050-0306, 516-944-5330; FAX 516-944-7540. 1984. avg. press run 100M. Pub'd 1 title 1998; expects 1 title 1999. 1 title listed in the *Small Press Record of Books in Print* (28th Edition, 1999-00). avg. price, paper: $25. Discounts: trade 40%, jobbers 50%, distributors 55%. 600pp; 5½×8½. Copyrights for author. GLPA.

ODYSSEY: Science Adventures in Science, Cobblestone Publishing, Inc., Elizabeth E. Lindstrom, Editor, 30 Grove Street, Suite C, Peterborough, NH 03458, 603-924-7209. 1979. Fiction, articles, art, photos, interviews, reviews, letters, non-fiction. "The magazine will accept freelance articles related to themes covered; write editor for guidelines." circ. 23M. 9/yr. Pub'd 9 issues 1998; expects 9 issues 1999, 9 issues 2000. sub. price: $26.95 + $8 foreign, Canadian subs add 7% GST; per copy: $4.50; sample: $4.50. Back issues: $4.50. Discounts: 15% to agencies, bulk rate—3 subs $15.95 each/yr. 48pp; of. Reporting time: queries sent well in advance of deadline may not be answered for several months. Go-aheads usually sent 3 months prior to publication date. Payment: on publication. Copyrighted, *Odyssey* buys all rights. Pub's reviews: 213 in 1998. §Science, math, and technology. Ads: none. EdPress, Classroom Publishers Association.

OF A LIKE MIND, Lynnie Levy, PO Box 6677, Madison, WI 53716, 608-257-5858. 1983. Fiction, articles, photos, cartoons, satire, criticism, music, news items, non-fiction. "We publish materials of interest to Goddess women and by Goddess women, maximum length 1500 words, but with graphics. Please send SASE for contributors guidelines before submitting." circ. 35M. 4/yr. Pub'd 4 issues 1998; expects 4 issues 1999, 4 issues 2000. sub. price: $15-35 (self-selected sliding scale); per copy: $4; sample: $4. Back issues: $4. Discounts: 40% to bookstores and in bulk (5 or more), 55% distributors. 56pp; 8½×11; of. Reporting time: 1 month. Simultaneous submissions accepted with notification, possibly depending on circumstances. Publishes 75% of manuscripts submitted. Payment: copies. Copyrighted, reverts to author. Pub's reviews: 10 in 1998. §Goddess spirituality, Wicca, magic, feminism, lesbianism, paganism. Ads: $560/$280. WPPA.

OF UNICORNS AND SPACE STATIONS, Gene Davis, PO Box 97, Bountiful, UT 84011-0097. 1994. Poetry, fiction. circ. 200. 2/yr. Pub'd 2 issues 1998; expects 2 issues 1999, 2 issues 2000. sub. price: $16/2 years; per copy: $4; sample: $4. Discounts: inquire with Gene Davis. 60pp; 5½×8½; printed cover, photocopy interior. Reporting time: 2 months. Simultaneous submissions accepted: yes. Publishes 10% of manuscripts submitted. Payment: 1¢/word for stories, $5 for poetry, payment on publication. Copyrighted, reverts to author. Ads: inquire.

OFF OUR BACKS, Editorial Collective, 2337B 18th Street, NW, 2nd Floor, Washington, DC 20009-2003, 202-234-8072. 1970. Articles, art, photos, cartoons, interviews, criticism, reviews, letters, news items, non-fiction. "Consider ourselves a radical feminist news journal, with complete coverage of national and international news about women. Free to prisoners." circ. 22M. 11/yr. Pub'd 11 issues 1998; expects 11 issues 1999, 11 issues 2000. sub. price: $25 indiv., $50 institutions (inc. libraries); $26 Canadian, $33 foreign, contributing subscription $35; per copy: $2.50 newsstand price; sample: $3 domestic, $3 foreign,. Back issues: $5. Discounts: 40% for 5 or more copies monthly; billed/paid quarterly. 28pp; 10½×13½; of. Reporting time: 3 months. Simultaneous submissions accepted: no. Publishes 50% of manuscripts submitted. Payment: copies. Copyrighted, reverts to author. Pub's reviews: 50 in 1998. §Women. Ads: $400/$210/40¢ (prepaid). NESPA.

OFF OUR BACKS, Bayla Travis, 3600 20th Street, #201, San Francisco, CA 94110-2351, 415-546-0384. 1984. Poetry, fiction, articles, art, photos, cartoons, interviews, criticism, reviews, music, letters, collages, concrete art, news items, non-fiction. "Long feature 2500 words, short feature 1500 words. Reviews 500 words. Contributors: Cherri Smyth, Pat Calitia, Lucy Blesoe, Chloe Atkins, Della Grace, Gayle Rubin, Tristich Taormine, Carol Queen, Jewelle Gomez, Dorothy Allison." circ. 45M. 6/yr. Pub'd 6 issues 1998; expects 6 issues 1999, 6 issues 2000. sub. price: $34.95; per copy: $5.95. Back issues: 3 for $15. Discounts: retail store 25%. 48pp. Reporting time: 4-6 weeks. Publishes 40% of manuscripts submitted. Payment: varies. Copyrighted, reverts to author. Pub's reviews. §Gay books, sex books, queer culture, erotica.

Off the Cuff Books, Damon Sauve, 191 Sickles Avenue, San Francisco, CA 94112-4046, email suavd@sunsite.unc.edu. 1996. Poetry, fiction, interviews. "Chapbooks and paperbacks. Website: http:/ /sunsite.unc/ob/otc" avg. press run 300. Pub'd 2 titles 1998; expects 2 titles 1999, 2 titles 2000. avg. price, paper: $12; other: $6 chapbook. Discounts: 30% libraries and bookstores. 60pp; of. Reporting time: 3 months. Simultaneous submissions accepted: no. Publishes 1% of manuscripts submitted. Copyrights for author.

OFF THE ROCKS, Greg Anderson, 921 W. Argyle #1W, Chicago, IL 60640, E-mail offtherock@aol.com. 1980. Poetry, fiction, art, interviews, parts-of-novels. circ. 500+. 1/yr. Pub'd 1 issue 1998; expects 1 issue 1999, 1 issue 2000. price per copy: $5. 42pp; 8×12; †lp. Reporting time: 1-2 months. Simultaneous submissions accepted: yes. Publishes 33% of manuscripts submitted. Payment: 2 issues to contributors. Copyrighted, reverts to author. Newtown Writers of Chicago.

OFFICE NUMBER ONE, Carlos B. Dingus, 1708 South Congress Avenue, Austin, TX 78704, 512-445-4489. 1989. Poetry, fiction, articles, cartoons, satire, letters. "*Office Number One* is a zine of satire. I need short (100 - 300 words) satirical news items, strange essays, or fiction. Poetry is limericks or haiku. Get it right for limericks. Satire should have an upbeat point and make sense—any kind of sense. Once in a great while I print a few serious words—500 or less on philosophy or religion—but it's got to be good" circ. 2M. 3/yr. Pub'd 2 issues 1998; expects 3 issues 1999, 3 issues 2000. sub. price: $8.84/6 issues; per copy: $2; sample: $2. Discounts: 24 copies $12 postpaid (minimum order). 12pp; 8½×11; of. Reporting time: 6-12 weeks. Simultaneous submissions accepted: yes. Publishes less than 10% of manuscripts submitted. Payment: contributor's copies. Copyrighted, reverts to author. §Other dimensions of existence. Ads: $125/$75/10¢ classifieds. Austin Writers League.

THE OFFICIAL MCCALLUM OBSERVER, Lynda Mendoza, PO Box 313, Lansing, IL 60438-0313, 708-895-0736; 708-895-1184; E-mail lsmtmo@juno.com; www.members.tripod.com/lsmtmo/index.html. 1985. Fiction, articles, art, photos, interviews, reviews, news items, non-fiction. circ. 250. 4/yr. Pub'd 5 issues 1998; expects 4 issues 1999, 4 issues 2000. sub. price: $11 US/Canada, $13 all other countries; per copy: $2 US/Canada, $2.50 others; sample: same. Back issues: same. Discounts: trade 1 year subscription for 1 year subscription. 28pp; 5½×8; of. Reporting time: Feb. 5, May. 5, Aug. 5, Nov. 5. Payment: none. Copyrighted, reverts to author. Ads: $20/$10/$5 5x4''

THE OHIO REVIEW, Wayne Dodd, 344 Scott Quad, Ohio University, Athens, OH 45701, 740-593-1900. 1959. Poetry, fiction, articles, interviews, reviews. circ. 3.5M. 2/yr. Pub'd 2 issues 1998; expects 2 issues 1999, 2 issues 2000. 9 titles listed in the *Small Press Record of Books in Print* (28th Edition, 1999-00). sub. price: $16; per copy: $8.95; sample: $6 (current issue will be sent). Back issues: varies. Discounts: vary, sent on request. 208pp; 6x9; of. Reporting time: 30 days. Simultaneous submissions accepted: no. Publishes 1% of manuscripts submitted. Payment: rates vary, copies plus min. $5 per page prose; $25 per poem. Copyrighted. Pub's reviews: 2 in 1998. §Poetry, fiction, books, including all chapbooks. Ads: $200/$175. CLMP.

OHIO WRITER, Ron Antonucci, Editor, PO Box 91801, Cleveland, OH 44101-0528. 1987. Articles, interviews, reviews. "Only service pieces published: interviews of writers, focus on aspect of writing in Ohio, reviews of books, writer's conferences. Major piece 2,000 words; focus piece 1,500 words; column 800 words; book review 400-500 words." circ. 1M. 6/yr. Pub'd 6 issues 1998; expects 6 issues 1999, 6 issues 2000. sub. price: $15, $20 institutions; per copy: $2.50; sample: $3. Back issues: $3. 16-20pp; 8½x11; desktop pub, laser printer, offset printer. Reporting time: 3 months. Simultaneous submissions accepted: yes. Publishes 5% of manuscripts submitted. Payment: $5-$50 depending on what. Copyrighted, reverts to author. Pub's reviews: 30 in 1998. §Books or magazines published in Ohio or by Ohio writers. Ads: $25 1/2/$35 1/9 page.

OHIOANA QUARTERLY, Barbara Maslekoff, Editor, 65 S. Front Street, Suite 1105, Columbus, OH 43215, 614-466-3831, Fax 614-728-6974, e-mail ohioana@winslo.state.oh.us. 1958. Articles, art, photos, interviews, criticism, reviews, news items, non-fiction. "Published by the Ohioana Library Association. Reviews by staff and guest reviewers. Length of review varies from 40 to 800 words. Ohio authors or books on Ohio only. Articles on Ohio authors, music, other arts in Ohio, up to 2M words." circ. 1.2M. 4/yr. Pub'd 4 issues 1998; expects 4 issues 1999, 4 issues 2000. sub. price: $25 (membership); per copy: $6.50; sample: gratis. Back issues: $6.50. Discounts: $25 to libraries. 88pp; 5½x8½; of. Reporting time: 2 weeks. Publishes 40% of manuscripts submitted. Payment: copies only. Copyrighted, rights do not revert to author, but we grant permission for full use by author. Pub's reviews: 450-500 in 1998. §Books about Ohio or Ohioans, books by Ohioans or former Ohioans, new magazines published in Ohio. Ads: none.

George Ohsawa Macrobiotic Foundation (see also MACROBIOTICS TODAY), Carl Ferre, Managing Editor; Bob Ligon, Editor, PO Box 426, Oroville, CA 95965, 530-533-7702; FAX 530-533-7908; foundation@gomf.macrobiotic.net. 1970. Articles, non-fiction. "Articles about macrobiotics and health. Books of at least 90 pages on macrobiotics, health, diet and nutrition. Special interest in cookbooks. Recent contributors include Julia Ferre, Natalie Buckley Rowland, Margaret Lawson, Rachel Albert, and Pam Henkel." avg. press run 3M-5M. Pub'd 1 title 1998; expects 1 title 1999, 2 titles 2000. 17 titles listed in the *Small Press Record of Books in Print* (28th Edition, 1999-00). avg. price, paper: $9.95. Discounts: 1 20%, 2-4 30%, 5+ 40%; distributors discount available. 192pp; 5½x8½, 6x9; typeset, lp. Reporting time: 6 weeks. Publishes 10% of manuscripts submitted. Payment: 5% of gross retail sales, or 10% of net sales. Copyrights for author. ABA.

OLD ABE'S NEWS, David T. Erb, 400 Carriage Drive, Plain City, OH 43064-2101, 614-873-3896. 1985. Interviews. "Agricultural history—'Old Iron' collecting. J.I. Case equipment, people, and history" circ. 1M. 4/yr. Pub'd 4 issues 1998; expects 4 issues 1999, 4 issues 2000. sub. price: $20, includes 1 yr. membership to J.I Case Collectors Assn., Inc.; per copy: $5 ppd; sample: $5. Back issues: $4 each for 10 or more, ppd. 52pp; 8½x11; produce camera ready mechanicals with Macintosh—photo offset printing. Payment: $100 honorarium for collector of History Stories published. Copyrighted, does not revert to author. Pub's reviews: 1 in 1998. §Agricultural history, farm equipment, ag. people stories. Ads: $125/$75/$40.

OLD CROW, FkB Press, John Gibney, Publisher; Tawnya Kelley, Editor-in-Chief; Karen Malley, Fiction Editor; Lynda Sperry, Fiction Editor; Lesle Lewis, Poetry Editor; Ricia Gordon, Poetry Editor, PO Box 403, Easthampton, MA 01027-0403. 1991. Poetry, fiction, art, photos, interviews, criticism, reviews, parts-of-novels, long-poems, collages, plays. "Recent contributors: Owen Barfield, Elmar Schenkel, William Monahan, Michael Ventura, Richard Exner, John Rose, Lyn Lifshin, and Nancy Berg." circ. 500. 2/yr. Pub'd 2 issues 1998; expects 2 issues 1999, 2 issues 2000. sub. price: $10 + $2 p/h make check or money order payable to John Gibney; per copy: $5 + $1 p/h; sample: $5 + $1 p/h. Discounts: none. 100pp; 5⅜x8⅜; of. Reporting time: 4-6 weeks. Simultaneous submissions accepted: yes. Publishes 1% of manuscripts submitted. Payment: free copy. Copyrighted, reverts to author. Pub's reviews: §Poetry, fiction, philosophy. Ads: exchange.

THE OLD RED KIMONO, Jon Hershey, Jeffery Mack, Ed Sharp, Humanities, Floyd College, Box 1864, Rome, GA 30162, 404-295-6312. 1972. Poetry, fiction. "*ORK* is looking for submissions of 3-5 short poems or one very short story (2,500 words max). Both poems and stories should be very concise and imagistic. Nothing sentimental or didactic. Mss read September 1 - March 1." circ. 1.2M. 1/yr. Pub'd 1 issue 1998; expects 1 issue 1999. price per copy: $3; sample: $3. 72pp; 8½x11; of. Reporting time: 1 month. Payment: 2 copies. Copyrighted, reverts to author.

398

Old West Publishing Co., 1228 E. Colfax Avenue, Denver, CO 80218. 1940. "Not seeking new material." avg. press run 2M. Expects 1 title 2000. 10 titles listed in the *Small Press Record of Books in Print* (28th Edition, 1999-00). avg. price, cloth: $35. Discounts: 40% any quantity non-returnable. 300pp; 9×12.

Olde & Oppenheim Publishers, Mike Gratz, 3219 North Margate Place, Chandler, AZ 85224-1051, 480-839-2280. 1984. "No submissions accepted." avg. press run 5M. Pub'd 3 titles 1998; expects 3 titles 1999, 3 titles 2000. 1 title listed in the *Small Press Record of Books in Print* (28th Edition, 1999-00). avg. price, cloth: $14.95. Discounts: 2-4 books 40%, 5-41 43%, 42-83 46%, 84+50%. 128pp; 5⅜×8; sheet-fed.

OLD-HOUSE JOURNAL, Gordon Bock, 2 Main Street, Gloucester, MA 01930, 508-283-3200; fax 508-283-4629. 1973. Articles. "Restoration and maintenance techniques for the pre-1939 house. Practical how-to information for restoring older houses." circ. 140M. 6/yr. Pub'd 6 issues 1998; expects 6 issues 1999, 6 issues 2000. sub. price: $27; per copy: $4; sample: $4.95 back issue price. Back issues: $4.95 per issue—also available in yearbooks through 1989, $18.95 one year of back issues. 90pp; 8¼×10¾; web of. Reporting time: 4-6 weeks. Copyrighted, does not revert to author. Pub's reviews: 24 in 1998. §Victorian and early 20th century antiques, architecture and architectural styles 1750-1940, also technical/construction methods. Ads: 4 color/$5595/$3995/$150.

Oline Publishing, Maria Telesco, Toni Weymouth, 4732 East Michigan, Fresno, CA 93703, 209-251-0169; oline@earthlink.net. 1997. Non-fiction. "Prison reform, families of prisoners." Expects 2 titles 1999, 2 titles 2000. 1 title listed in the *Small Press Record of Books in Print* (28th Edition, 1999-00). avg. price, cloth: $19.95. Reporting time: will begin looking in '99. Simultaneous submissions accepted: yes. Bay Area Independent Publishers Assn.

The Olive Press Publications, Addis Lynne Norris, PO Box 99, Los Olivos, CA 93441, Tel/Fax 805-688-2445. 1978. Poetry, non-fiction. "Not accepting submissions at this time. Specialize in historical material." avg. press run 5M. Pub'd 3 titles 1998; expects 5 titles 1999, 5 titles 2000. 37 titles listed in the *Small Press Record of Books in Print* (28th Edition, 1999-00). avg. price, cloth: $25; paper: $5. Discounts: 40% over 5 copies. 250pp; 6×9, 5½×8½, 8½×11; of. Copyrights for author.

The Olivia and Hill Press, Inc., Jacqueline Morton, Brian N. Morton, PO Box 7396, Ann Arbor, MI 48107, 734-663-0235 (voice), Fax 734-663-6590; theOHPress@aol.com; www.oliviahill.com. 1979. Non-fiction. "We began with *English Grammar for Students of French* in 1979, and have added editions in Spanish, German, Italian, Latin, Russian and Japanese; the first two have now come out in fourth editions. German is presently in third edition. All $12.95. We distribute foreign language cassettes (novels, plays and poetry) imported from France. We also distribute cassette + book packages (fairy tales and stories) for children in French. We publish two anecdotal street guides: *Americans in Paris* and *Americans in London*. Both are paperback, 350 pages, 60 photos, $12.95 each. Our new product is *French Slang and Publicities* for the first and second year French student. We are interested in receiving unsolicited manuscripts in our area of interest. We also publish an ESL version, Gramatica espanola pana estudiantes de ingles $12.95. Visit our website." avg. press run 10M. Pub'd 2 titles 1998; expects 1 title 1999, 1 title 2000. 11 titles listed in the *Small Press Record of Books in Print* (28th Edition, 1999-00). avg. price, paper: $12.95. Discounts: 20% to bookstores. 200pp; 6×9; of. Payment: standard. Copyrights for author.

C. Olson & Company, C.L. Olson, PO Box 100, Santa Cruz, CA 95063-0100, 408-458-9004. 1979. Poetry, fiction, articles, art, photos, cartoons, interviews, reviews, letters, parts-of-novels, news items, non-fiction. "Material length is usually 10M-15M words. Seeking manuscripts and books to distribute on natural health, Earth's ecology improvement projects, stress reduction, natural hygiene. Manuscripts must be provided with SASE, but query first with SASE." avg. press run 2M-4M. Expects 1 title 1999, 1 title 2000. 5 titles listed in the *Small Press Record of Books in Print* (28th Edition, 1999-00). avg. price, cloth: none; paper: $5.95; other: none. Discounts: 40%+. 40pp; 5⅜×8½; of/web. Reporting time: 4-6 weeks. Simultaneous submissions accepted: yes. Publishes 1% of manuscripts submitted. Payment: each book negotiated separately. We copyright for author for $100.

OM, David Lasky, Box #181, 4505 University Way, NE, Seattle, WA 98105, 206-322-6387. 1993. Cartoons. ""OM" is an anthology of comics which are a personal nature. We are looking for heartfelt short stories in comics form. This zine is completely non-commercial." circ. 1M. 1/yr. Expects 1 issue 1999, 1 issue 2000. price per copy: $2.50; sample: $3. Back issues: #1 is $1. 20pp; 8½×5½; xerox. Reporting time: 2 years. Simultaneous submissions accepted: no. Publishes 20% of manuscripts submitted. Payment: 5 copies of issue with their work. Copyrighted, reverts to author.

Omega Publications, Inc., Abi'l-Khayr, Director, 256 Darrow Road, New Lebanon, NY 12125, 518-794-8181, Fax 518-794-8187, e-mail omegapub@taconic.net. 1977. Non-fiction. "We publish works related to Sufism, featuring the teachings of Hazrat Inayat Khan and Pir Vilayat Khan. Translations of Sufi texts or works about the Sufis are invited for possible publication." avg. press run 2.5M. Pub'd 1 title 1998; expects 4 titles 1999, 3 titles 2000. 18 titles listed in the *Small Press Record of Books in Print* (28th Edition, 1999-00). avg. price, paper: $14. Discounts: trade 1-4 20%, 5-24 40%, 25+ 43%. 160pp; 5½x8½; of. Reporting time: 3 months. Simultaneous submissions accepted: yes. Payment: negotiable. Copyrights for author. PMA.

Ommation Press (see also MATI; SALOME: A Journal for the Performing Arts), Effie Mihopoulos, 5548 North Sawyer, Chicago, IL 60625. 1975. Poetry, fiction, art, photos, long-poems, plays, non-fiction. "Ommation Press is no longer publishing *The Ditto Rations Chapbook Series* (the chapbooks already published are still available for purchase—send SASE for list of titles), which has completed its proposed 20 titles. *Offset Offshoots* now has titles by Lyn Lifshin, Christine Zawadiwsky, Rochelle Ratner, Douglas MacDonald. *Dialogues on Dance* has eight titles to date and more are planned." avg. press run 500-1M. Pub'd 1 title 1998; expects 1 title 1999. 158 titles listed in the *Small Press Record of Books in Print* (28th Edition, 1999-00). avg. price, cloth: $18; paper: $1-$6; other: $1.50-$6. Discounts: 20% on purchase of 10 or more copies. 25-50pp; 8½x11, 5x9; of. Reporting time: 1 month. Accept simultaneous submissions, but must state that it is. Payment: 50 copies of book. Copyrights for author.

OMNIFIC, Kay Weems, HCR-13, Box 21AA, Artemas, PA 17211-9405, 814-458-3102. 1989. Poetry. "In this publication, everyone writing in good taste will have 4 poems/year published. Readers then vote on their favorites and awards will be given to the 3 receiving most votes, the poem in the "Lucky 7" slot, and the Editor's Choice. Along with the standard awards mentioned above, some readers have set up awards in their name and will send "something" to the person(s) that touched them in a special way with their writing. In the past these gifts have been stamps, newsletters, small cash awards, chapbooks, small gifts, and letters showing appreciation for a certain poem—all of which are most welcomed by the poet." circ. 200+. 4/yr. Pub'd 4 issues 1998; expects 4 issues 1999, 4 issues 2000. sub. price: $12; per copy: $3.50; sample: $3.50. Back issues: $3.50. 100pp; digest; †Sharp copier. Reporting time: 3 months. Payment: Editor's Choice Award of $5 to one or two people + various other small awards from readers and editor to several people. Copyrighted. uses ads only as fillers. PA Poetry Society, Walt Whitman Guild, UAPAA, National Arts Society, National Federation of State Poetry Societies Inc., New Horizons Poetry Club, Southern Poetry Assoc.

ON COURSE, Jon Mundy, Diane Berke, Meribeth Seaman, 25 South Street, Washingtonville, NY 10992-0250. 1983. Poetry, articles, art, photos, cartoons, interviews, satire, reviews, letters, news items, non-fiction. "Short articles: 1 to 2 page preferred, inspirational, homespun American philosophy, self-help, transpersonal psychology, holistic health, body work, yoga, zen, etc. Most articles are in house. Emphasis on *A Course in Miracles*. Interfaith approach." circ. 4M. 6/yr. Pub'd 12 issues 1998; expects 6 issues 1999, 6 issues 2000. sub. price: 36; per copy: $6; sample: free. Back issues: $2 uncirculated or circulated. 80pp; 8½x11; Web press. Reporting time: 3 weeks. Simultaneous submissions accepted: yes. Payment: minimal, copies. Not copyrighted. Pub's reviews: 14 in 1998. §Inspirational, self-help, A course in miracles. Ads: $255/3/4 $170/1/2 $135/1/3 $105/1/4 116-$80 1/8-$60 1/10-45 1/12-35. Small Magazine Publishers Group.

●**ON OUR BACKS MAGAZINE**, Athena Douris, 3415 Cesar Chavez Ste. 101, San Francisco, CA 94110, 415-648-9464; fax 415-648-4705; e-mail staff@gfriends.com. Poetry, fiction, articles, art, photos, cartoons, interviews, satire, criticism, reviews, music, letters, parts-of-novels, long-poems, news items, non-fiction. "Please send us a SASE for guidelines or check out our magazine to get a better understanding of what we like." circ. 30M. 6/yr. Pub'd 3 issues 1998; expects 6 issues 1999, 6 issues 2000. sub. price: $34.95; per copy: $5.95. Back issues: $10-20. 48pp. Reporting time: 6-8 weeks. Simultaneous submissions accepted: yes. Publishes 5% of manuscripts submitted. Payment: varies. Pub's reviews. §Sexuality and lesbian erotica-must query. Ads: $1200/$700/ 1/3 pg $550.

ON PARAGUAY, Anteater Press, Lynn Van Houten, 1724 Burgundy Court, Petaluma, CA 94954, 707-763-6835; E-mail paraguay@wco.com. 1994. Non-fiction. "Short articles relating to the culture, art, plants, animals and environment of Praguay and South America." circ. 250. 4/yr. Pub'd 4 issues 1998; expects 4 issues 1999, 4 issues 2000. sub. price: $25; per copy: $6.25. Back issues: $6.25. 8pp; 8½x11. Simultaneous submissions accepted: yes. Pub's reviews: 3 in 1998. §South America, Paraguay, children's folktales.

ON SPEC: More Than Just Science Fiction, Barry Hammond, Susan Macgregor, Jena Snyder, Diana L. Walton, Hazel Sangster, PO Box 4727, Edmonton, AB T6E 5G6, Canada, 403-413-0215; email onspec@earthling.net. 1989. Poetry, fiction. "Canadian writers preferred" circ. 1.75M. 4/yr. Pub'd 4 issues 1998; expects 4 issues 1999, 4 issues 2000. sub. price: $20CDN, $18US; per copy: $4.95 CON, $4.50 US; sample: $6CDN, $6US. Back issues: same as sample copies. Discounts: bookstore 40%. 112pp; 5x8; of. Reporting time: 4-6 months. We accept simultaneous submissions, but please let us know. Publishes 5% of manuscripts submitted. Payment: 3¢ per word. Copyrighted, reverts to author. Ads: $175/$125. CMPA, AMPA.

ON THE LINE, Mary Clemens Meyer, Editor, 616 Walnut Avenue, Scottdale, PA 15683. 1971. Poetry, fiction, articles, photos, cartoons, interviews, non-fiction. circ. 6M. 12/yr. sub. price: $21.05; per copy: $1.75; sample: send SASE (2 first-class stamps). 28pp; 7x10; †of. Reporting time: 1 month. Payment: from 3-5¢/word on acceptance. Copyrighted, reverts to author. No ads.

On The Way Press, Marlene Adler Marks, 23852 Pacific Coast Highway #504, Malibu, CA 90265,

400

310-456-1546; Fax: 310-456-7686; e-mail: onthewaypress@aol.com; http://members.aol.com/onthewaypress. 1 title listed in the *Small Press Record of Books in Print* (28th Edition, 1999-00).

ONE EARTH, Betsy Van Derlee, Findhorn Foundation, The Park, Forres, Morayshire 1V36 OTZ, Scotland, 44-1309-691128. 1979. Articles, art, photos, cartoons, interviews, reviews, letters, non-fiction. "The purpose of *One Earth* magazine is to offer perspectives on the emerging planetary culture and the application of holistic values in a variety of fields. Each issue has a different theme. Includes articles by Findhorn community members, and features speakers and artists from conferences and arts festival hosted by the Findhorn Foundation." circ. 4.5M. 4/yr. Pub'd 4 issues 1998; expects 4 issues 1999, 4 issues 2000. sub. price: UK £10, US (surface) $20, (airmail) $25; per copy: £2.40, $4.50; sample: £2.40, $5. Back issues: £1.50, $2.50. Discounts: 10-49 35%, 50+ 45%. 44pp; 12¼×8¾; †of. Reporting time: 2 months. Payment: by arrangement, usually by free copies. Copyrighted. Pub's reviews: 20 in 1998. §Metaphysics, the spiritual life, communities, social and political issues. On request. IPG.

●**ONE TRICK PONY, Banshee Press,** Louis McKee, PO Box 11186, Philadelphia, PA 19136-6186. 1997. Poetry, art, photos, interviews, criticism, reviews, collages. "Some recent contributors: David Kirby, Philip Dacey, Denise Duhamel, Naomi Shihab Nye, W.D. Ehrhart" circ. 400. 2/yr. Pub'd 2 issues 1998; expects 2 issues 1999, 2 issues 2000. sub. price: $10/3 issues; per copy: $5; sample: $5. 60pp; 5½×8½; †of, perfectbound. Reporting time: 2-4. Simultaneous submissions accepted: no. Payment: copies. Copyrighted, reverts to author. Pub's reviews: 4-5 in 1998. §Poetry or poetry-related.

ONIONHEAD, Susan Crawford, Editor; Dot D. Davis, Editor; Brenda Patterson, Editor, 115 North Kentucky Avenue, Lakeland, FL 33801, 941-680-2787. 1988. Poetry, fiction, articles, satire, non-fiction. "Poems to 60 lines, short stories to 3,000 words, essays to 1500 words. Our focus is on provocative political, social and cultural observations and hypotheses; but literary values are of prime consideration. Recent contributors: Lyn Lifshin, B.Z. Niditch, Jessica Freeman, Nancy Nicodemus, Laurel Speer, Jill Jones, and Robert Nagler." circ. 250. 4/yr. Pub'd 4 issues 1998; expects 4 issues 1999, 4 issues 2000. sub. price: $8; per copy: $3; sample: $3. Back issues: $3. Discounts: 50%. 40pp; 5½×8¼; †xerography. Reporting time: 10 weeks to report, 12 months to publish. Simultaneous submissions accepted: no. Publishes 5% of manuscripts submitted. Payment: 1 copy. Copyrighted, reverts to author.

Online Training Solutions, Inc., 15442 Bel-Red Road, Redmond, WA 98052, 425-885-1441. 1987. Non-fiction. "Formerly Online Press Inc. Online Training Solutions publishes the Quick Course computer training books and online products. Quick Course books are for people with limited time to learn today's most popular software programs. Training oriented, Quick Course books teach the software while showing how to create documents people can use in their business. Quick Course books are used by schools, universities, business, training, companies, and corporations both for classroom instruction and for self-training." avg. press run 10M+. Pub'd 12 titles 1998; expects 15 titles 1999, 15 titles 2000. 3 titles listed in the *Small Press Record of Books in Print* (28th Edition, 1999-00). avg. price, paper: $12.95-$14.95-$24.95. Discounts: volume discounts are available. 160-256pp; 8×10.

THE ONSET REVIEW, Scott Withiam, Susan Pizzolato, Box 3157, Wareham, MA 02571, E-mail spizzolo@sailsinc.org. 1994. Fiction, art, photos, reviews, long-poems, non-fiction. "Recent contributors: Carole Oles, Ted Deppe, Mark Cox, and Marsha de la O, Beckian Fritz-Goldberg, Martha Collins, Nancy Eimers, and Dzuinia Orlowsky." circ. 1M+. 2/yr. Pub'd 1 issue 1998; expects 2 issues 1999, 2 issues 2000. sub. price: $18; per copy: $10; sample: $5. Back issues: $3 each. 100pp; 6×9; of. Reporting time: 1-5 months. We accept simultaneous submissions if noted as such. No previously published work. Publishes 5% of manuscripts submitted. Payment: 2 copies. Copyrighted, reverts to author. Pub's reviews. §Poetry. Ads: not yet.

ONTHEBUS, Bombshelter Press, Jack Grapes, Bombshelter Press, P.O. Box 481270, Bicentennial Station, Los Angeles, CA 90048. 1989. Poetry, fiction, art, reviews. "*OntheBus* is a literary journal that includes work from poets and writers throughout the U.S. Guidelines for submission on copyright page of each issue. Editor expects those submitting work to have read a copy of our magazine and to be familliar with our guidelines printed on copyright page." circ. 3M. 2/yr. Pub'd 2 issues 1998; expects 2 issues 1999, 2 issues 2000. sub. price: $28 for 3 issues; per copy: $11 (double issues $13.50); sample: $11. Back issues: $13.50 for double issue #6/7, #8/9, #10/11 $11 for others. Discounts: 40% bookstores. 275pp; 8½×5½; of. Reporting time: 1-12 months. Simultaneous submissions accepted: yes. Publishes 5% of manuscripts submitted. Payment: 1 copy, $ if available. Copyrighted, reverts to author. Pub's reviews: 50 in 1998. §Books of poetry. Ads: $300/$200/$125 1/4 page. CLMP.

Oolichan Books, Ursula Vaira, Managing Editor; Ron Smith, Publisher, Poetry Editor; Jay Connolly, Fiction Editor, PO Box 10, Lantzville, B.C., V0R 2H0, Canada, 604-390-4839. 1975. Poetry, fiction, plays, non-fiction. "Oolichan Books publishes *full-length* manuscripts of poetry and fiction primarily by Canadian writers. We prefer letters of enquiry with sample writing and SASE (with sufficient Canadian postage stamps or international reply coupons). We attempt to maintain a balance between established and newer authors.

Generally we are not interested in the mass market book, but rather in serious fiction and poetry which indicates how the writer sees through language. We produce books of excellent quality in content and design, and many of our authors have won prestigious awards. Recent contributors include: John O'Neill, Carol Windley, Ralph Gustafson, George McWhirter, Robert Kroetsch, Robert Allen, Joe Rosenblatt, Ven Begamudre, Florence McNeil, Greg Hollingshead. Apart from our main interest in poetry and fiction we are also interested in western Canadian history, children's books, autobiography, and statements on poetics or collections of letters which reveal something of the stance of the writer and his/her attitude to the language." avg. press run 750-2M. Pub'd 4 titles 1998; expects 7 titles 1999, 7 titles 2000. 79 titles listed in the *Small Press Record of Books in Print* (28th Edition, 1999-00). avg. price, cloth: $29.95; paper: $14.95; other: $25 special editions, signed and numbered. Discounts: trade: 40% on all orders over 3 copies, fewer than 3 copies 30%. 160pp; 5½x8½, 6x9; lp. Reporting time: 1-3 months. Simultaneous submissions accepted: yes. Publishes 2% of manuscripts submitted. Payment: 10%. Copyrights for author. ACP, LPG, ABPBC, CBA.

Open Court Publishing, David Ramsay Steele, 332 S. Michigan #1100, Chicago, IL 60604, 312-939-1500; Fax 419-281-6883. 1887. Non-fiction. "Our order dept. address: c/o Book Masters, PO Box 388, 1444 State Rt. 42, Ashland OH 44805 800-815-2280" avg. press run 3M. Pub'd 20 titles 1998; expects 13 titles 1999, 13 titles 2000. avg. price, cloth: $35; paper: $15. 300pp; 6x9. Reporting time: 2-6 months. We will look at simultaneous submissions, but we give preference to exclusive submissions. Payment: varies. Copyrights for author. ABA, MAPA.

OPEN EXCHANGE MAGAZINE, Community Resource Institute Press, Bart Brodsky, PO Box 7880, Berkeley, CA 94707, 510-526-7190. 1974. Articles, art, photos, interviews, reviews, letters, news items, non-fiction. "Length of material: 500-2500 words. Interviews with Tim Leary, Deepak Chopra, Paul Ehrlich, Frances Moore Lappe, Ram Dass, Stephen Levine, Martin Rossman." circ. 102M. 6/yr. Pub'd 6 issues 1998. sub. price: $15; per copy: $3; sample: $3. Back issues: $3. Discounts: none. 92pp; 10½x13; web press. Copyrighted, reverts to author. Pub's reviews: 10 in 1998. §Health, politics, business, art, personal development, psychology. Ads: $1095/$749/$79 minimum 115 words.

Open Hand Publishing Inc., P. Anna Johnson, PO Box 22048, Seattle, WA 98122, 206-323-2187. 1981. Non-fiction. "Open Hand is a literary/political press publishing multicultural books which will help to promote social change. We are not accepting unsolicited manuscripts at this time." avg. press run 2.5M. Pub'd 1 title 1998; expects 3 titles 1999, 4 titles 2000. 20 titles listed in the *Small Press Record of Books in Print* (28th Edition, 1999-00). avg. price, cloth: $22.35; paper: $11.45. Discounts: 40% to bookstores. 250pp; 5½x8½; of. Reporting time: 4 weeks. Simultaneous submissions accepted: yes. Publishes 1% of manuscripts submitted. Copyrights for author. ABA, Book Publishers NW (BPNW).

Open Horizons Publishing Company (see also BOOK MARKETING UPDATE), John Kremer, PO Box 205, Fairfield, IA 52556-0205, 515-472-6130, Fax 515-472-1560, e-mail johnkremer@bookmarket.com. 1983. Articles, art, photos, cartoons, interviews, reviews, letters, news items, non-fiction. "Books on marketing, publishing, publicity, and anything that strikes the publisher's fancy. Jay Frederick Editions is an imprint." avg. press run 3M-5M. Pub'd 3 titles 1998; expects 3 titles 1999, 4 titles 2000. 5 titles listed in the *Small Press Record of Books in Print* (28th Edition, 1999-00). avg. price, cloth: $19.95; paper: $14.95. Discounts: 40%. 288pp; 6x9; of. Reporting time: 2 weeks. Payment: 10% of list price. Copyrights for author. PMA, MAP, MSPA, MIPA, ABA, UMBA.

Open University of America Press, Mary Rodgers, Dan Rodgers, 3916 Commander Drive, Hyattsville, MD 20782-1027, 301-779-0220 phone/Fax; openuniv@aol.com. 1965. Poetry, articles. "We publish literary work in our interests: poetry, the Catholic Italian-American experience, and distance learning using the latest information technologies. We prefer short pieces which we publish as collections, generally buying the writer's ms outright for preservation in our Literary Trust after one-time dissemination. English only. SASE required with query and submission. Recent contributor: Lucille Columbro, *Aurora Farm Revisited*, 1997 (Italian-American experience)." avg. press run 250. Pub'd 4 titles 1998; expects 4 titles 1999, 4 titles 2000. 10 titles listed in the *Small Press Record of Books in Print* (28th Edition, 1999-00). avg. price, cloth: $15; paper: $10. Discounts: 40%. 150pp; 6x9, 8½x11; of, lp, laser printing. Reporting time: 3-4 weeks. Simultaneous submissions accepted: no. Publishes 1% of manuscripts submitted. Payment: by contract. We copyright for author if necessary.

THE OPERA QUARTERLY, Duke University Press, William Ashbrook, Box 90660, Duke University, Durham, NC 27708-0660. "With an enthusiastic and varied readership, *The Opera Quarterly* provides an informed, substantial medium between the esoteric and the oversimplified. *OQ* features original and accessible articles by well-known and respected authors, interviews with and remembrances of great vocalists, and an exhaustive and in-depth review section of books, recordings, and videos. In addition, each issue of *The Opera Quarterly* is abundantly illustrated with rare, personal, and archival photographs, as well as with musical examples. Send books for review to Christopher Hatch, RR 2 Box 1590, Dorset, VT 05251. Send recordings and videos for review to E. Thomas Glasow, 197 Oaklawn Drive, Rochester, NY 14617-1813." circ. 3.8M.

4/yr. Pub'd 4 issues 1998; expects 4 issues 1999, 4 issues 2000. sub. price: $88 institutions, $36 individuals, additional $12 foreign. Pub's reviews. Ads: $500/$300.

Ophelia Editions, Lawrence Stanley, PO Box 2377, New York, NY 10185, 212-580-4654. 1990. Poetry, fiction, art. "Publisher of art and photography books relating to the female nude; also publishing erotic literature and poetry." avg. press run 1.5M. Pub'd 6 titles 1998; expects 8 titles 1999, 4 titles 2000. 3 titles listed in the *Small Press Record of Books in Print* (28th Edition, 1999-00). avg. price, cloth: $50. Discounts: 40% to trade. Fiction 250pp, photograph 80pp; 24×30cm; of. Reporting time: 6-8 weeks. Payment: yes. Copyrights for author.

OPTIMA Books, Eric Goodman, Robert Graul, 2820 8th Street, Berkeley, CA 94710, 510-848-8708; Fax 510-848-8737; esl@optimabooks.com; www.optimabooks.com. 1988. Non-fiction. "We specialize in ESL books and audio tapes. Most recent publications are *Biz Talk-2, More American Buisness Slang & Jargon,* and *Robert Takes Over,* an intermediate reading and grammar text." avg. press run 5M-10M. Pub'd 2 titles 1998; expects 2 titles 1999, 4 titles 2000. 1 title listed in the *Small Press Record of Books in Print* (28th Edition, 1999-00). avg. price, paper: $16.95. Discounts: retail 2-5 books 20%, 6-10 30%, 11-25 40%, 26-74 45%, 75+ 50%. 272pp; 6×9; of. Reporting time: 3 months. Simultaneous submissions accepted: yes. Payment: 10% up to 2500 copies, 12.5% 2500-5M, 15% 5M+. Copyrights for author. PMA, TESOL.

OPTIONS IN LEARNING, Katharine Houk, Seth Rockmuller, PO Box 59, East Chatham, NY 12060, 518-392-6900. 1989. Poetry, articles, art, photos, cartoons, reviews, letters, news items. "Articles: 2000 word maximum. Book reviews: 100-250 words." circ. 1.5M. Frequency varies. Pub'd 1 issue 1998; expects 2 issues 1999, 2 issues 2000. sub. price: $20; per copy: $3-$6. Back issues: $3-$6. 16pp; 8½×11; of. Payment: none at this time. Copyrighted, reverts to author. Pub's reviews: 20 in 1998. §Parent involvement in education, educational options, educational enrichment, alterative education.

OPUS LITERARY REVIEW, Poetic Page, Denise Martinson, PO Box 71192, Madison Heights, MI 48071-0192, 313-548-0865. 1993. Poetry. "*Opus Literary Review* appears biannual and publishes poetry only. No specifications as to form, length, style, subject matter, or purpose. They have recently published poetry by Rudy Zenker, Leonard Cirino, Daniel Gallik, John Grey, and Patricia A. Lawrence. *Opus Literary Review* is digest size, saddle-stitched, desktop and postscript-laser printed with a matte cover. Acquires first rights. No previously published poems or simultaneous submissions. Send SASE for guidelines. All accepted poets are listed with bio. Editor often comments on rejections. the editor says: "We want poetry that will last the ages. Poetry that is intelligent, well thought out. Use strong verbs and nouns and let your reader feel your work by showing, not telling. If you want to write a poem about a flower, go ahead. But make that flower unique—surprise us. Give us your best work; we want to publish it. But beginners beware, no trite rhyme here. However, we will publish a well-written rhyme if the rhyme is the poem, not the word endings. Free verse is what we prefer."" sub. price: $10; sample: $5 postpaid. desktop, postscript-laser. Payment: 1 copy.

ORACLE POETRY, Rising Star Publishers, Obi Harrison Ekwonna, PO Box 7413, Langley Park, MD 20787. 1989. Poetry, fiction, criticism, reviews, long-poems. "Only well-made poems with meanings will be considered. No lesbian and gay materials accepted." circ. 500. 4/yr. Pub'd 1 issue 1998; expects 2 issues 1999, 4 issues 2000. sub. price: $25, $30 institutions; per copy: $5; sample: $5. Back issues: $7 plus $1.50 p/h. Discounts: 30%, but may consider 40% bulk orders. 50pp; 5½×8½; web press. Reporting time: 6 weeks. Simultaneous submissions accepted: no. Publishes 50% of manuscripts submitted. Payment: in copies. Copyrighted, does not revert to author. Pub's reviews: one in 1998. §Any kind or genre, especially poetry. Ads: $500/$300/others on request. Association of African Writers.

ORACLE STORY, Rising Star Publishers, Obi Harrison Ekwonna, PO Box 7413, Langley Park, MD 20787. 1989. Fiction, criticism, reviews, long-poems. "Only well-made short stories with meanings will be considered. No lesbian and gay materials accepted." circ. 500. 4/yr. Pub'd 1 issue 1998; expects 2 issues 1999, 4 issues 2000. sub. price: $25, $30 institutions; per copy: $5; sample: $5. Back issues: $7 + $1.50 p/h. Discounts: 30%, but may consider 40% bulk orders. 50pp; 5½×8½; web press. Reporting time: 6 weeks. Simultaneous submissions accepted: no. Publishes 50% of manuscripts submitted. Payment: in copies. Copyrighted, does not revert to author. Pub's reviews: one in 1998. §Any kind or genre, especially short stories or short novels. Ads: $500/$300/others on request. Association of African Writers.

ORANGE COAST MAGAZINE, Patrick Mott, 3701 Birch Street, Suite 100, Newport Beach, CA 92660-2618, 949-862-1133. 1974. Fiction, articles, interviews, reviews, music, letters, parts-of-novels, non-fiction. "*Orange Coast* provides its affluent, educated readers with local insight. Articles range from in-depth investigations (local politics, crimes, etc) to consumer guides, calendar of events and personality profiles. Articles must have relevance to Orange County." circ. 40M. 12/yr. Pub'd 13 issues 1998; expects 13 issues 1999, 13 issues 2000. sub. price: $19.95; per copy: $2.95; sample: same. Back issues: $5 if available. Discounts: contact circulation manager. 260pp; 8⅜×10⅞; web inside, sheet-fed cover. Reporting time: 3 months. Payment: $100-$300. Copyrighted, reverts to author. Pub's reviews: 24 in 1998. §Film, music, restaurants, books. Ads: B/W $3300/$1860; color $4230/$2850, singles classified—$5.50/word. WPA.

ORBIS, Mike Shields, Publisher, 27 Valley View, Primrose, Jarrow, Tyne & Wear NE32 5QT, England, +44 (0)191 489 7055; fax/modem +44 (0)191 430 1297; e-mail Mshields12@aol.com; mikeshields@compuserve.com. 1968. Poetry, art, reviews, letters, long-poems. "Keep it short: not over 1M words in most cases. All types of material considered, but wildly experimental or excessively traditional work not likely to be accepted. IRC must be included with submissions overseas. I have been amazed and frustrated at the number of submissions received from the USA with US-stamped addressed envelopes enclosed!" circ. 1M. 4/yr. Pub'd 4 issues 1998; expects 4 issues 1999, 4 issues 2000. sub. price: $28; per copy: variable, but usually $7.50; sample: $2. Discounts: 30% to trade. 80pp; 5¾×8¼; of. Reporting time: up to 2 months. Simultaneous submissions accepted: no. Publishes 1% of manuscripts submitted. Payment: $10 or choice of copies, etc., to greater volume, plus cash prizes totalling £50/$75 per issue. Copyrighted, reverts to author. Pub's reviews: 70 in 1998. §Mainly collections of poetry; also reference books of interest to writers. Ads: $100/$50.

THE ORCADIAN, J.E. Miller, The Orcadian Limited, PO Box 18, Kirkwall, Orkney, Scotland. 1854. Articles, photos, interviews, criticism, reviews, letters, news items. circ. 11M. 52/yr. Expects 52 issues 1999. sub. price: £30.60 (surface mail); per copy: 52p; sample: 52p. Back issues: depends on availability. 28pp; 400×270mm; †web offset. Copyrighted. Pub's reviews: 50-100 in 1998. §Local interest. Ads: £556.8 + 17.5% fax (VAT). NS/SPA.

Orchises Press, Roger Lathbury, PO Box 20602, Alexandria, VA 22320-1602, 703-683-1243. 1983. Poetry, fiction, articles, concrete art. avg. press run 1M. Pub'd 4 titles 1998; expects 8 titles 1999, 7 titles 2000. 70 titles listed in the *Small Press Record of Books in Print* (28th Edition, 1999-00). avg. price, cloth: $21.95; paper: $12.95. Discounts: 40% on no-return items to bookstores with some exceptions, distributors and jobbers; 20% if a return privilege is wanted; items under $20 shipped no return unless otherwise stipulated. 80pp; 5×8½; of. Reporting time: 1 month. Payment: 36% royalty after costs recouped, generous free copy policy. Copyrights for author.

Oregon State University Press, Jo Alexander, Managing Editor; Warren Slesinger, Acquisitions Editor, 101 Waldo Hall, Corvallis, OR 97331, 541-737-3166. 1961. "We publish only book-length scholarly work, particularly of regional importance and especially in the fields of history and biography, American and especially regional literature, and natural resource management. No fiction, no poetry." avg. press run 1.5M-3M. Pub'd 19 titles 1998; expects 20 titles 1999, 25 titles 2000. avg. price, cloth: $30; paper: $19.95. Discounts: 20-45% depending on quantity. 320pp; 6×9, 7×10; of. Reporting time: 1-3 months. Simultaneous submissions accepted: no. Payment: varies. Copyrights for author. AAUP.

Organization for Equal Education of the Sexes, Inc., Lucy Picco Simpson, PO Box 438, Dept. DB, Blue Hill, ME 04614, 207-374-2489. 1977. Articles, art, photos, interviews, non-fiction. "Classroom posters, biographies of women, teacher guidelines." avg. press run 2M. 2 titles listed in the *Small Press Record of Books in Print* (28th Edition, 1999-00). avg. price, paper: $4. Discounts: 20% 20 of same poster, 15% 50 or more assorted posters. Biographies 4pp; 11×17 poster size; commercial printers. Reporting time: varies. Payment: varies. Does not copyright for author.

Origin Press, Byron Belitsos, 1122 Grant Avenue, Suite C, Novato, CA 94945, 415-898-7400; fax 415-898-4890; e-mail info@originbooks.com. 1996. Non-fiction. "Ralph Metzner, recent contributor. Biases according to subject matter published: spiritual, psychology, comparative religion." avg. press run 10M. Expects 2-4 titles 1999, 2-4 titles 2000. 2 titles listed in the *Small Press Record of Books in Print* (28th Edition, 1999-00). avg. price, cloth: $24.95; paper: $15.95. Discounts: trade 20-40%, others negotiable. 300pp; 6×9; of. Reporting time: 4 weeks. Simultaneous submissions accepted: yes. Publishes 2% of manuscripts submitted. Payment: 8% of list paid biannually. Copyrights for author. PMA, NCBPMA, SPAN.

THE ORIGINAL ART REPORT (TOAR), Frank Salantrie, 3024 Sunnyside Drive, Rockford, IL 61114-6025. 1967. Criticism. "Exclusive interest in (visual) fine art condition as it affects artists, individuals, and society and as they affect it. Material must take advocacy position, any side. Prefer controversial subject matter and originality of prose treatment. Also, artist's views on non-art topics/issues." Irregular to dormant. Pub'd 2 issues 1998. sub. price: $31/12 numbers per volume; per copy: $2.75; sample: $2.75. Back issues: $7 each. 8½×11; of. Reporting time: 2-4 weeks. Simultaneous submissions accepted: no. Publishes 5% of manuscripts submitted. Payment: 1¢/word; max 1000 words on publication. Not copyrighted. Pub's reviews. §Visual fine art: histories, philosophies, criticism, and business, of (from right to left). No ads.

●Original Plus (see also JOURNAL OF CONTEMPARARY ANGLO-SCANDINAVIAN POETRY), Sam Smith, 11 Heatherton Park, Bradford on Tone, Taunton, Somerset TA4 1EU, England, 01823-461725; e-mail smithsssj@aol.com. 1998. Poetry, fiction, articles, art, reviews, parts-of-novels, long-poems, plays, non-fiction. "Two dual text poetry collections, English/Danish and English/German; and one dual text English/Welsh." avg. press run 110. Pub'd 3 titles 1998; expects 2 titles 1999. 3 titles listed in the *Small Press Record of Books in Print* (28th Edition, 1999-00). avg. price, paper: £6. Discounts: 25%. 72pp; 5¾×8. Payment: 10% and copies.

404

Copyrights for author.

Orloff Press, John Spencer, Editor, PO Box 80774, Athens, GA 30608-0774, 706-548-0701. 1994. Fiction, non-fiction. avg. press run 5M. Pub'd 3 titles 1998; expects 3 titles 1999, 5 titles 2000. 5 titles listed in the *Small Press Record of Books in Print* (28th Edition, 1999-00). avg. price, cloth: $23; paper: $12.95. Discounts: Trade: 40% net 30. 45% prepaid (minimum order: 5 titles); STOP single 20% prepaid. 300pp; 5½x8½; of. Reporting time: 1 month; 2 weeks on queries. Simultaneous submissions accepted: yes. Payment: normally 10% of net sales. Copyrights for author.

ORNAMENT, Robert K. Liu, Co-Editor; Carolyn L.E. Benesh, Co-Editor; Whelly E. Wiles, Assistant Editor, PO Box 2349, San Marcos, CA 92079, 619-599-0222; fax 619-599-0228. 1974. Art, interviews, satire, criticism, letters, parts-of-novels, collages, news items. "Formerly published under the name of *The Bead Journal* which terminated with volume 3, #4. As of Volume 4, #1 published under the name of *Ornament*." circ. 50M. 4/yr. Pub'd 4 issues 1998; expects 4 issues 1999, 4 issues 2000. sub. price: $23 domestic, $27 foreign; per copy: $5.75; sample: $5.75. Back issues: write for information. Discounts: 40% on wholesale orders. 100pp; 8x11; offset web. Reporting time: 8-12 weeks. Simultaneous submissions accepted: yes. Payment: copies of the magazine in which article appears, number depends on length of article; also per page payments. Copyrighted, reverts to author. Pub's reviews: 23 in 1998. §Jewelry, ancient, ethnic, contemporary, forms of personal adornment, costume, clothing, beads, textiles. Write for rates. IGCJAP, ACC.

Ortalda & Associates, Claire Ortalda, Director & Associate Editor; Floyd Salas, Senior Editor, 1208 Delaware Street, Berkeley, CA 94702, 510-524-2040. 1985. Poetry, fiction, articles, art, interviews, parts-of-novels, long-poems, non-fiction. "Not accepting submissions." avg. press run 1M. avg. price, paper: $9.95. Discounts: 40% to bookstores, libraries, wholesalers, distributors. 507pp; 5½x8½. Payment: in copies. Copyrights for author.

ORTHODOX MISSION, Axios Newletter, Inc., Father Daniel, 30-32 Macaw Avenue, Belmopan, Belize, 011-501-8-23284. 1973. Articles, art, interviews, reviews, parts-of-novels, news items, non-fiction. circ. 3.5M. 12/yr. Pub'd 12 issues 1998; expects 12 issues 1999, 12 issues 2000. sub. price: $10; per copy: $2; sample: $2. 6pp; 8½x11. Reporting time: 2 months. Payment: $25 plus copies. Copyrighted, reverts to author. Pub's reviews: 3 in 1998. §Moral issues, politics, philosophy.

Orthodox Mission in Belize (see also Axios Newletter, Inc.), Father Daniel, 30-32 Macaw Avenue, PO Box 279, Belmopan, Belize, 501-8-23284, fax 501-8-23633. 1973. Articles, art, interviews, criticism, reviews, letters, parts-of-novels, news items, non-fiction. Pub'd 1 title 1998; expects 1 title 1999. avg. price, cloth: $25; paper: $15. 175pp. Reporting time: 2 months. Payment: open. Copyrights for author.

OSIRIS, Andrea Moorhead, Box 297, Deerfield, MA 01342, e-mail moorhead@k12s.phast.umass.edu. 1972. Poetry, interviews, long-poems. "*Osiris* is an international multi-lingual literary journal publishing contemporary poetry in the original language. English and French appear without translation. Poetry from other languages such as Polish, Danish and Hungarian often appear with facing English translation. Recent contributors: Robert Marteau (France), Hans Raimund (Austria), D.G. Jones (Canada), Miriam Van hee (Belgium), Robert Dassanowsky (USA), and Irene Speiser (USA)." circ. 1M. 2/yr. Pub'd 2 issues 1998; expects 2 issues 1999, 2 issues 2000. sub. price: $12 individuals and institutions; per copy: $6; sample: $3. 40pp; 6x9; of. Reporting time: 4 weeks. Simultaneous submissions accepted: no. Publishes 15% of manuscripts submitted. Payment: 5 copies. Copyrighted, rights revert to author, with credit line to *Osiris*. Ads: query. CPLM.

Osmyrrah Publishing, Sherry Roberts, Tony Roberts, PO Box 10134, Greensboro, NC 27404, 336-292-4061. 1993. Non-fiction. "Query first with cover letter and 3 sample chapters." avg. press run 1M. 3 titles listed in the *Small Press Record of Books in Print* (28th Edition, 1999-00). avg. price, paper: $14.95. Discounts: trade. 160pp; 6x9; of. Reporting time: 6 weeks. Payment: negotiable. Copyrights for author. PMA.

Osric Publishing (see also THE WHITE CROW), Christopher Herdt, PO Box 4501, Ann Arbor, MI 48106. 1993. Poetry, fiction, art, photos, satire, letters, parts-of-novels, collages, plays, non-fiction. avg. press run 200. Pub'd 3 titles 1998; expects 2 titles 1999, 2 titles 2000. avg. price, other: $2 chapbooks. 32pp; 5½x8½; photocopy. Reporting time: 4 months. Simultaneous submissions accepted: yes. Publishes 10% of manuscripts submitted. Payment: negotiable, contributors copies. Copyright for author upon request.

THE OTHER ISRAEL, Adam Keller, PO Box 2542, Holon 58125, Israel, 972-3-5565804 (also fax). 1983. Articles, interviews, reviews, letters, news items, non-fiction. circ. 3M. 6/yr. Pub'd 6 issues 1998; expects 6 issues 1999, 6 issues 2000. sub. price: $30 individual, $50 institution; $15 students, unemployed; per copy: $5; sample: free on request. Discounts: 33%. 12pp; 7x9½. Reporting time: 3 weeks average. Payment: none. Not copyrighted. Pub's reviews: 1 in 1998. §Middle East politics, Econimics, society ,peace movement, conflict resolution. Ads: $100/$60.

OTHER VOICES, Gina Frangello, Assistant Editor; Lisa Stolley, Assistant Editor; Lois Hauselman, Exee.

Editor, English Dept., M/C 162, UIC, 601 South Morgan Street, Chicago, IL 60607, 312-413-2209. 1985. Fiction, interviews, letters, parts-of-novels, plays. "A prize-winning, independent market for quality fiction, we are dedicated to original, fresh, diverse stories and novel excerpts by new, as well as recognized, talent. No taboos, except ineptitude and murkiness. 5M word maximum preferred but not mandatory. SASE required. Winner of 15 Illinois Arts Council Literary Awards. Reading period is October 1 to April 1 *only.*" circ. 1.5M. 2/yr. Pub'd 2 issues 1998; expects 2 issues 1999, 2 issues 2000. sub. price: $20/4 issues, $30 foreign surface ($32 foreign air); per copy: $7; sample: $7 (inc. postage); institutions $24/4 issues, add $8 per sub. for foreign. Back issues: $7 (inc. postage) when available. Discounts: 20% classroom, 40% trade, 50% general distributor. 180-225pp; 6×9; typesetter, printer. Reporting time: 10-12 weeks. Simultaneous submissions accepted: yes. Payment: copies, small cash gratuity. Copyrighted, reverts to author. Ads: $100/$60/exchange with non-profit lit mags. CLMP, ILPA.

Otherwind, Pat Smith, Senior Editor; David C.D. Gansz, Editor; Drew Gardner, Editor, 541 Lakeview Avenue, Ann Arbor, MI 48103-9704, 313-665-0703. 1986. avg. press run 500. Expects 1 title 2000. 6 titles listed in the *Small Press Record of Books in Print* (28th Edition, 1999-00). avg. price, paper: $6. Discounts: bookstores 40%. 96pp; 6×9; of. Reporting time: 3-4 months. Copyrights for author. CLMP.

OTTER, C. Southgate, M. Beeson, R. Skinner, E. Pryor, Parford Cottage, Chagford, Newton Abbot TQ13 8JR, United Kingdom. 1988. Poetry, long-poems. "*Otter* exists to publish the poetry of those connected by birth, upbringing or 'adoption' with Devon, England. We seek to develop a heightened understanding of community through poetry as a medium. We believe the medium is often at its most effective when traditional elements of prosody such as rhyme and metre are employed." circ. 400. 3/yr. Pub'd 3 issues 1998; expects 3 issues 1999, 3 issues 2000. sub. price: £6.50; per copy: £2.25; sample: £2.25 (convert to dollars and add $2 for US). Back issues: $2 each. Discounts: standard 33⅓% to trade. 48pp; 5¾×8; of. Reporting time: 6-8 weeks. Simultaneous submissions are discouraged. Publishes 25% of manuscripts submitted. Payment: 1 complimentary copy, plus one extra copy per poem. Copyrighted, reverts to author. Ads: £20/£12.

●**Otter Creek Press, Inc.**, 3154 Nautilus Road, Middleburg, FL 32068. 5 titles listed in the *Small Press Record of Books in Print* (28th Edition, 1999-00).

Oughten House Publications, Tony Stubbs, PO Box 2008, Livermore, CA 94551, 510-447-2332; Fax 510-447-2376; E-mail oughtenhouse.com. 1992. avg. press run 5M. Pub'd 3 titles 1998; expects 8 titles 1999. 14 titles listed in the *Small Press Record of Books in Print* (28th Edition, 1999-00). avg. price, cloth: $23.95; paper: $14.95. 6×9. Copyrights for author. PMA, SPAN, ABA, NCBIA, NAPRA, Bookbuilders West.

Our Child Press, Carol Hallenbeck, PO Box 74, Wayne, PA 19087, 610-964-0606; Fax 610-964-0938; ocp98@aol.com; www.members.aol.com/ocp98/index.html. 1984. Fiction, non-fiction. avg. press run 1M-2M. Pub'd 2 titles 1998; expects 2 titles 1999, 2 titles 2000. 7 titles listed in the *Small Press Record of Books in Print* (28th Edition, 1999-00). avg. price, paper: $12.95. Reporting time: 2 months. PMA.

Our Schools/Our Selves (see also OUR SCHOOLS/OUR SELVES), Repo Satu, Executive Editor, 107 Earl Grey Road, Toronto, Ontario, Canada, 416-463-6978 (phone and fax). 1988. Non-fiction. "Books are paperback, 150-300 pages. All touch on education; analyses, anti-racist, labour, socialist, feminist. We bill ourselves as being "for Canadian education activists"" avg. press run 2M. Pub'd 6 titles 1998; expects 6 titles 1999, 6 titles 2000. avg. price, paper: $14.95 for 150 pages; $19.95 for 300 pages. Discounts: Standard discounts for university and trade bookstores. 150pp. Payment: as discussed.

OUR SCHOOLS/OUR SELVES, Our Schools/Our Selves, Repo Satu, Executive Editor, 107 Earl Grey Road, Toronto, Ontario, Canada, 416-463-6978 (phone and fax). "Subscripers to OS/OS get 3 magazines and 3 books a year. Topics: education and labour, social justice, anti-racism, feminism, socialism, "A magazine for Canadian education activists."" circ. 1M. 6/yr. Pub'd 6 issues 1998; expects 6 issues 1999, 6 issues 2000. sub. price: $38 (Canada); per copy: $9; sample: $9. Back issues: $9. 150pp. Payment: none. Pub's reviews: at least 2 per issue in 1998. §Education. Ads: $350/$190. Canadian Magazine Publishers' Association.

OUR TWO CENTS, Jacque Rowden, Robert Press, 39 2nd Avenue, Secaucus, NJ 07094-3510. 1993. Photos, cartoons, criticism, reviews, letters, parts-of-novels, non-fiction. "submissions welcome!" circ. 150. 4/yr. Pub'd 4 issues 1998; expects 4 issues 1999, 4 issues 2000. sub. price: $10; per copy: $1; sample: $1. Back issues: $2. 14pp; 5½×8, stapled in the middle; †laser. Publishes 50% of manuscripts submitted. Payment: none. Not copyrighted. Pub's reviews: 5 in 1998. §All kinds of movies; as for books and magazines, whatever is fascinating to a layman; common touchstones (newsweeklies, fast food, campgrounds). Ads: none.

OUT WEST, Chuck Woodbury, 9792 Edmonds Way, #265, Edmonds, WA 98020-5940, 425-776-1228; fax 425-776-3398; e-Mail outwest@seanet.com. 1988. Articles, art, photos, news items, non-fiction. "750 words maximum. Black and white photos only. We buy 1x rights and reprints. We like offbeat travel articles about rural American West." circ. 10M. 4/yr. Pub'd 4 issues 1998; expects 4 issues 1999, 4 issues 2000. sub. price: $12.95; per copy: $3.50; sample: same. Back issues: same. Discounts: check with publisher if interested. 32pp;

10×16; of, web press, tabloid on newsprint. Reporting time: 2 weeks to 1 month. Simultaneous submissions accepted: yes. Publishes 5% of manuscripts submitted. Payment: $2 - $100. Copyrighted, reverts to author. Pub's reviews: 30 in 1998. §Camping, western travel, western U.S. travel guides, Americana, offbeat travel guides. Ads: $600/$350/classified 50¢ per word.

OUT YOUR BACKDOOR: The Magazine of Informal Adventure and Cheap Culture, Jeff Potter, 4686 Meridian Road, Williamston, MI 48895, 517-347-1689; jp@glpbooks.com; www.glpbooks.com/oyb. 1989. Poetry, fiction, articles, art, photos, cartoons, interviews, satire, criticism, reviews, music, letters, parts-of-novels, long-poems, collages, concrete art, news items, non-fiction. *"OYB* is about thrifty culture and exploration,the interface of art, action and hobbies. OYB is like a holistic *Outside* for normal people-as a result it is very refreshing. We cover hard-to-find, secret, insider, interesting, affordable equipment and projects by all kinds of aficianados. We cover the human and cultural aspects of boats, bikes, cars, travel, sleeper movies, unbestseller books, owner operated restaurants and everything else same in alt. culture. It's stylish by the open-minded, do-it-yourself mag of everything. We fight against fragmentation, go for practical harmony and cross-train the grain. We use lots of reprints that won't see the mainstream to achieve our tasty blend." circ. 5M. 2/yr. Pub'd 2 issues 1998; expects 3 issues 1999, 3 issues 2000. sub. price: $8/4 issues; per copy: $3; sample: $4. Back issues: $4. Discounts: retail 1-10 40%, wholesalers 30+ 50%. 48-64pp; 8×10½; web. Reporting time: immediate with SASE. Simultaneous submissions accepted: yes. Publishes 10% of manuscripts submitted. Payment: usually nothing, but *OYB* is booming and in the black now so payment may not be far off. Copyrighted, reverts to author. Pub's reviews: 40 in 1998. §Alternative, subculture, unusual, bikes, boats, equipment, hunting, fishing, travel, culture, thrifty lifestyles, inside info on places/things. Ads: $150/$75/$40 1/4 page/$50 1/3 page.

●**Outdoor Enterprises, Inc.,** James S. Koricich, PO Box 531, Irwin, PA 15642, 724-863-3865. 1998. Non-fiction. Expects 1 title 1999, 1 title 2000. 1 title listed in the *Small Press Record of Books in Print* (28th Edition, 1999-00). avg. price, paper: $15.95. Discounts: 50%. 193pp; 6×9; of.

●**Outer Space Press,** Orlando N. Acosta, PO Box 9593, Daytona Beach, FL 32120, 904-253-8179 voice/Fax; osp9593@aol.com. 1986. Fiction, non-fiction. avg. press run 2m. Pub'd 2 titles 1998; expects 3 titles 1999, 10 titles 2000. avg. price, cloth: $20.95; paper: $14.95. Discounts: 40% bookstores; 55% wholesalers. 200pp; 6×9; of. Reporting time: 6 weeks. Simultaneous submissions accepted: no. Publishes 2% of manuscripts submitted. Payment: negotiable. Copyrights for author.

OUTERBRIDGE, Charlotte Alexander, College of Staten Island, 2800 Victory Boulevard, Staten Island, NY 10314, 212-390-7654, 7779. 1975. Poetry, fiction, interviews, satire, reviews, parts-of-novels, plays. "Slight bias toward form, craft & against clearly socio-political statements. Among contributors: Philip Dacey, Walter McDonald, Candida Lawrence, Ben Brooks, Henry Alley, Mary Elsie Robertson, Marilyn Throne, Will Keeney, Ronald Berube, Marilyn McComas, Kim Roberts, Naomi Rachel. 1993 & 94: nature, animals, science phenomena." circ. 500-1M. 1/yr. Expects 3-4 issues 1999. sub. price: $6; per copy: $6; sample: $6. Back issues: $6. Discounts: 20% for 10 or more. 100-120pp; 5½×8½; of. Reporting time: 6 weeks poetry; 8-10 weeks fiction; except July and August. Simultaneous submissions accepted: no. Publishes 10% of manuscripts submitted. Payment: 2 copies. Copyrighted, reverts to author. §Poetry, fiction, novels (excerpts, rarely). CLMP, SPR, NESPA, AWP.

OUTLANDER, Robert Seaver Gebelein, PO Box 1546, Provincetown, MA 02657. 1994. Articles, fiction, satire, letters, non-fiction. "My bias is new civilization" Irregular. Expects 1 issue 1999, 1 issue 2000. sub. price: $10 for 10 issues; per copy: $1; sample: $1. Back issues: $1. Discounts: make me an offer. 10pp; 8½×11; xerox. Reporting time: not set. Copyrighted, reverts to author.

OUTLET, Trev Faull, 33 Aintree Crescent, Barkingside, Ilford, Essex IG6 2HD, United Kingdom, 081-551-3346. 1978. Photos, cartoons, interviews, reviews, music, letters, collages. circ. 600. 2/yr. Pub'd 1 issue 1998; expects 2 issues 1999, 2 issues 2000. price per copy: $7; sample: $7. Back issues: $6. Discounts: 30%. 60pp; size A5; duplicated. Payment: none. Not copyrighted. Pub's reviews: 15-20 in 1998. §Music.

OUTPOSTS POETRY QUARTERLY, Hippopotamus Press, Howard Sergeant, Founder, Editor; Roland John, Editor, 22, Whitewell Road, Frome, Somerset BA11 4EL, United Kingdom. 1943. Poetry, articles, criticism, reviews. *"Outposts* is the longest-lived independent poetry magazine in the UK. It was founded to provide a satisfactory medium for those poets, recognised or unrecognised, who are concerned with the potentialities of the human spirit, and who are able to visualize the dangers and opportunites which confront the individual and the whole of humanity. Although recent contributors have included famous poets like Ted Hughes, Peter Porter, Roy Fuller, Vernon Scannell, Blake Morrison, Seamus Heaney, etc., the magazine makes a special point of introducing the work of new and unestablished poets to the public." circ. 2.5M. 4/yr. Pub'd 4 issues 1998; expects 4 issues 1999, 4 issues 2000. sub. price: £14 or $24 (postage paid) for 1 year, £26 or $50 (postage paid) for 2 years; per copy: £3.50, $7; sample: $7. Back issues: price varies from £2-£10. Discounts: 35%. 80pp; size A5; litho. Reporting time: 2 weeks, 4 weeks non-U.K. Payment: depends on length of poem.

Copyrighted, reverts to author. Pub's reviews: 30 in 1998. §Poetry, criticism of poetry. Ads: £90 $120/£45 $70. ALP.

Outrider Press, Phyllis I. Nelson, President, 937 Patricia Lane, Crete, IL 60417-1375, 708-672-6630 (voice); fax 708-672-5820; e-mail outriderPr@aol.com; www.outriderpress.com. 1988. Poetry, fiction, art. "Must include SASE with mss. and all correspondence for response" avg. press run 12M-13M. Pub'd 1 title 1998; expects 3 titles 1999, 4 titles 2000. 7 titles listed in the *Small Press Record of Books in Print* (28th Edition, 1999-00). avg. price, paper: $13-$16. Discounts: Book stores: 60/40; others: up to 50% off, depending upon # ordered. 250pp; 5½x8½; Desktop publishing/offset. Reporting time: 1-2 months. Simultaneous submissions accepted: yes. Publishes a variable % of manuscripts submitted. Payment: negotiable. Copyrights for author.

THE OVAL MAGAZINE, Henry Eckert, 22 Douglass Street, Brooklyn, NY 11231. 1995. Poetry, parts-of-novels, fiction. "Poems: up to 200 lines—Fiction: up to 10 pages, double-spaced." circ. 225. 2/yr. Expects 1 issue 1999, 2 issues 2000. sub. price: $5; per copy: $3; sample: $3. 72pp; 5½x8½; of. Reporting time: 2 months. Simultaneous submissions accepted: yes. Payment: 1 year subscription. Not copyrighted.

OVERLAND, John D. McLaren, PO Box 14146, Melbourne 3000, Australia. 1954. Poetry, fiction, articles, art, photos, cartoons, interviews, satire, criticism, reviews, letters, parts-of-novels, long-poems, plays, concrete art, non-fiction. "Motto: 'Temper democratic, bias Australian'. Liberal/left in politics, Australian in content." circ. 2.4M. 4/yr. Pub'd 4 issues 1998; expects 4 issues 1999, 4 issues 2000. sub. price: $Aust 32 (local), $Aust 50 (foreign), $Aust 80 (airmail); per copy: $Aust 8 plus postage; sample: by arrangement. Back issues: by arrangement. Discounts: by arrangement. 88pp; 7¼x9¾; of. Reporting time: 3 months. Publishes 3% of manuscripts submitted. Payment: by arrangement, minimum rates published. Copyrighted. Pub's reviews: 50 in 1998. §Material of Australian interest. Ads: $Aust 320/300/250/180.

OVERLAND JOURNAL, Marilyn Holt, Oregon-California Trails Association, PO Box 1019, Independence, MO 64051-0519, 816-252-2276. 1983. Articles, photos, reviews, non-fiction. "Articles concerning the covered wagon migration to the American West in the 19th century: Oregon Trail, gold rush (various routes)" circ. 2.5M. 4/yr. Pub'd 4 issues 1998; expects 4 issues 1999, 4 issues 2000. sub. price: $30; per copy: $6.25; sample: free to public libraries. Back issues: $6.25. Discounts: none. 36pp; 8½x11; of. Reporting time: 30 days. Simultaneous submissions accepted: no. Publishes 75% of manuscripts submitted. Payment: none. Copyrighted, reverts to author. Pub's reviews: 25 in 1998. §Covered wagon migration to the American West in the 19th century, gold rush. Ads: $200/$100/$90 1/3 page/$50 1/4 page/$30 1/6 page.

THE OVERLOOK CONNECTION, David Hinchberger, PO Box 526, Woodstock, GA 30188, 770-926-1762, Fax 770-516-1469, e-mail overlookcn@aol.com. 1987. Fiction, articles, art, photos, cartoons, interviews, reviews, parts-of-novels, news items, non-fiction. "Annual issue - listing all items in stock - $15" circ. 8M. 8/yr. Pub'd 3 issues 1998; expects 4 issues 1999, 4 issues 2000. sub. price: $20; per copy: $2; sample: $1. Back issues: $2. 16pp; 7x10; of. Reporting time: 8 weeks. Payment: none. Copyrighted, reverts to author. Pub's reviews: over 150 in 1998. §Fiction and non-fiction in horror, science fiction, and fantasy, mystery. Ads: $100/$60. HWA.

The Overlook Press, Tracy Carns, Publishing Director, 386 West Broadway, New York, NY 10012-4302, 914-679-8571. 1971. "We are distributed by Penguin USA, although special sales are based in Woodstock, NY. Fiction: Literary fiction, *some* fantasy and sci-fi, and foreign literature in translation. Non-fiction: Art, architecture, design, history, film, biography, homestyle, children's, martial arts and Hudson Valley regional." Pub'd 75 titles 1998; expects 75 titles 1999, 75 titles 2000. Reporting time: 6-8 weeks. Copyrights for author. AAP.

The Overmountain Press, Archer M. Blevins, Sherry Lewis, PO Box 1261, Johnson City, TN 37605, 615-926-2691. 1970. avg. press run 2M. Pub'd 4 titles 1998; expects 10 titles 1999. 117 titles listed in the *Small Press Record of Books in Print* (28th Edition, 1999-00). avg. price, cloth: $18; paper: $8. Discounts: 1 20%, 2-4 30%, 5 40%. Pages vary; 5½x8½, 8½x11; †of. Reporting time: 4-6 weeks. Payment: subject to negotiations. Copyrights for author.

OWEN WISTER REVIEW, PO Box 3625, Laramie, WY 82071-3625, 307-766-4027; owr@uwyo.edu. 1978. Poetry, fiction, art, photos, interviews, satire, parts-of-novels, non-fiction. "100% freelance written publication. Submissions are considered from Aug 1-Dec 15 All submissions must be accompanied by a short biographical statement and SASE. Photocopied and computer-printout submissions will be accepted, but dot-matrix is discouraged. Prose submission poets submit no more than 5 poems. Artists between 5-20 35 mm slides; black and white or color artworks and graphics in any media, any size will be considered." circ. 300-500. 1/yr. Pub'd 1 issue 1998; expects 1 issue 1999, 1 issue 2000. sub. price: $8.20; per copy: $6.95 + $1.25 postage; sample: $5. Back issues: $5. Discounts: none. 120pp; 6x9; of. Reporting time: 1-4 months. Simultaneous submissions accepted: yes. Publishes 10-20% of manuscripts submitted. Payment: 1 complimentary copy and 10% discount on any additional copies. Copyrighted, reverts to author.

Owl Creek Press, Rich Ives, 2693 S.W. Camano Drive, Camano Island, WA 98292, 308-387-6101. 1979. Poetry, fiction, articles, long-poems. "Owl Creek Press sponsors two poetry contests each year. A contest for Chapbooks has a deadline period of August 15 and requires an entry fee of $10. For manuscripts under 40 pages. A contest for full-length books has a submission deadline of Feb. 15 and requires an entry fee of $15. For manuscripts over 50 pages. Both contests require an SASE. Winners receive publication and a $1000 prize award or 10% of the first edition press run with additional payment for any reprinting." avg. press run 500-2M. Pub'd 4 titles 1998; expects 4 titles 1999, 4 titles 2000. 47 titles listed in the *Small Press Record of Books in Print* (28th Edition, 1999-00). avg. price, cloth: $20; paper: $12. Discounts: standard. 5½x8½; lp, photo-offset. Reporting time: 3-6 months. Simultaneous submissions accepted: yes. Payment: varies. NEA.

Owlswick Press, George H. Scithers, 123 Crooked Lane, King of Prussia, PA 19406-2570, 215-382-5415. 1975. Fiction, criticism, non-fiction. "*Owlswick Press* publishes mostly deluxe editions of fantasy classics (Lord Dunsany and L. Sprague de Camp are two of our principal authors) and a few non-fiction titles of interest to the science fiction readership. We do not publish one-author poetry collections, short story collections, or original novels. Query first before submitting anything. Before you even query, become familiar with the books *Owlswick* has published (send for our free catalogue)." avg. press run 1.5M-2.5M. Expects 2 titles 1999. 19 titles listed in the *Small Press Record of Books in Print* (28th Edition, 1999-00). avg. price, cloth: $15-$20; paper: $7.95. Discounts: available upon request for buyers-for-resale. 250pp; 6x9; of. Reporting time: 2-3 weeks. Simultaneous submissions accepted: no. Payment: by arrangement. Copyrights for author.

Oxford House Publishing, Thelma Jackson, Managing Editor, 2556 Van Patten #8, Las Vegas, NV 89109. 1994. Fiction, non-fiction. "Oxford House pulblishes strictkly hardcover historical fiction from Post-Reconstruction (1870s) to World War II. We are a prestigious house, for we publish only the best manuscripts available" avg. press run 3M-5M. Expects -10 titles 1999, -10 titles 2000. 1 title listed in the *Small Press Record of Books in Print* (28th Edition, 1999-00). avg. price, cloth: $22.50. 300pp; 6x9; of. Reporting time: varies, average 30 days. Simultaneous submissions accepted: yes. Payment: standard with industry. Copyrights for author.

Oxford University Press (see also BRITISH JOURNAL OF AESTHETICS; COMMUNITY DEVELOPMENT JOURNAL; MUSIC AND LETTERS; NOTES & QUERIES), Journal Subscriptions Department, Pinkhill House, Southfield Road, Eynsham, Oxford OX8 1JJ, United Kingdom.

OXYGEN, Richard Hack, 535 Geary Street #1010, San Francisco, CA 94102, 415-776-9681. 1991. Poetry, fiction, articles, art, cartoons, interviews, satire, reviews, parts-of-novels, long-poems, collages, plays, concrete art, news items, non-fiction. "Vivid, independent, non-academic writing at its finest. We try to present literature in aesthetic, religious, political, and other personal dimensions. Almost entirely fiction and poetry, from very short to very long, including fragments and sketches. Modes: realist, surreal, expressionist, beat, devotional, satirical, invective, and corrective. Occasional nonfiction. Also short quotations from your reading in any subject (under 300 words to qualify as fair use). Recent contributors include Hafiz, David Fisher, Claus Reichert. Some of our favorites are Claude McKay, Martin Buber, Nelson Algren, Henry Miller. Inspirations include John Brown, Dorothy Day, Baal Shem Tov, Eugene Debs." circ. 300. 1/yr. Pub'd 1 issue 1998; expects 1 issue 1999, 1 issue 2000. sub. price: $14; $25 institutions and foreign 4 issues; per copy: $2.50, $3 cover, $5 ppd; sample: $5. Back issues: $5. 64pp; 5½x8½; printing. Reporting time: 2 weeks to 2 months. Simultaneous submissions accepted: yes. Publishes 1 to 2% of manuscripts submitted. Payment: 2 contributors' copies. Copyrighted, reverts to author. Pub's reviews: 3; also 2 interviews in 1998. §Psychology, poetry, fiction, religion, politics, communal responsibility, and sharing. Ads: no ads.

Oyez, Robert Hawley, PO Box 5134, Berkeley, CA 94705. 1964. Poetry, criticism. "Books usually designed by Graham McIntosh. Usually report promptly but not reading at this time." avg. press run 500-1M. Pub'd 3 titles 1998; expects 3 titles 1999. avg. price, cloth: $8-$10; paper: $2-$6. 60-80pp; 5½x8½. Payment: 10% royalties and copies. Copyrights for author.

OYSTER BOY REVIEW, Damon Sauve, Fiction Editor; Jeffery Beam, Poetry Editor; Chad Driscoll, Editor, 191 Sickles Avenue, San Francisco, CA 94112-4046, Email oyster-boy@sunsite.unc.edu; www.sunsite.unc.edu/ob. 1994. Poetry, fiction, art, photos, reviews. "We're interested in the ignored, the misunderstood, and the varietal. We'll make some mistakes." circ. 250. 3/yr. Pub'd 3 issues 1998; expects 3 issues 1999, 3 issues 2000. sub. price: $12; per copy: $4; sample: $4. Back issues: $4. Discounts: 30% libraries and bookstores. 60pp; 6½x11; docutech. Reporting time: 1-2 months. Simultaneous submissions accepted: no. Publishes 1% of manuscripts submitted. Payment: 2 copies. Copyrighted, reverts to author. Pub's reviews: 10 in 1998. §First books, chapbooks, poetry collections, novels. Ads: $60/$30/$15 1/4 page/$20 1/3 page.

Oyster Publications (see also BANAL PROBE; LIME GREEN BULLDOZERS (AND OTHER RELATED SPECIES)), Lainie Duro, PO Box 4333, Austin, TX 78765. 1 title listed in the *Small Press Record of Books in Print* (28th Edition, 1999-00).

O!!ZONE, A LITERARY-ART ZINE, The O!!Zone Press, Harry Burrus, Editor & Publisher, 1266 Fountain

View Drive, Houston, TX 77057, 713-784-2802. 1993. Poetry, fiction, art, photos, collages. *"O!!ZONE* Not for prudes, the politically correct, ultra conservatives, the judgmental - those who believe they can decide what is right and proper for others. If easily offended by unusual lifestyles, nudity & provocative words...don't bother. $5 an issue! *O!!ZONE* is an international publication featuring poetry, visual poetry, reviews, interviews, manifestos, and art. We are particularly intrigued by poets who also do photography, college (or draw or paint or do line drawings). We welcome artists & visual poets. We do broadsides, publish small, modest saddle-stitched collections, and will consider full book collections (on a collaborative basis) as time and dinero permits. Send work that isn't taught in schools, words that lack in oral history, unspoken on any reading circuit. Time is a tyranny to be abolished. The writer expresses; the writer does not communicate - that's up to the reader. We are interested in D-I-S-C-O-V-E-R-Y and self-transcendence. GET NAKID! SUBMISSIONS. *DO A COVER LETTER.* Always include SASE or sufficient international coupons for return of work. No religious or when I was 12 poems or if you lack the energy of Isidore Ducasse. Poetry=2-4 poems; EXPOSE YOURSELF! HIT US! BLEED! Photographic Submissions= 5 X 7 or 8 X 10 black and white prints. Desire nudes, surrealism, collage, & nude self-portraits. Yes, art brut. Liberate yourself. Do the unusal. CAN YOU SHOCK? ENHANCE YOUR CHANCES! Send to *Harry Burrus* Editor/Publisher, *O!!ZONE* 1266 Fountian View Drive-Houston, Texas 77057-2204 USA. Create & don't look over your shoulder. Inform your curious friends about *O!!ZONE.* Share the word. Transform, mutate...SOAR! ...tempus edax rerum. ROCK US, DON'T BORE" circ. 500. 2-4/yr. Pub'd 10 issues 1998; expects 5 issues 1999, 4 issues 2000. price per copy: $5; sample: $5. Back issues: $6. Discounts: none. 75pp; 5½x8½; of, desktop. Reporting time: ASAP. Simultaneous submissions accepted: yes. Payment: copy. Copyrighted, reverts to author. Pub's reviews: 0 in 1998. §Poetry books, art, photography.

The O!!Zone Press (see also O!!ZONE, A LITERARY-ART ZINE), Harry Burrus, Editor & Publisher, 1266 Fountain View Drive, Houston, TX 77057, 713-784-2802. 1993. Poetry, fiction, articles, art, photos, interviews, criticism, reviews. "Book mss. submit 30-40 poems. Query first. Will not respond unless SASE included. Read sample copy of *O!!Zone.* Books by Guy R. Beining, Laura Ryder, Anna Leonessa, and David H. Stone, plus 3 anthologies of International Visual Poetry is a major interest" avg. press run 50-300. Expects 4 titles 1999, 4-8 titles 2000. 13 titles listed in the *Small Press Record of Books in Print* (28th Edition, 1999-00). avg. price, paper: $6.50-$10; special editions are more; other: numbered, limited editions cost more. Discounts: none. 40-80pp, visual poetry anthologies 180pp; 8½x11; of. Reporting time: ASAP. Simultaneous submissions accepted: yes. Payment: copies. Copyrights for author.

OZ-STORY, Hungry Tiger Press, David Maxine, 1516 Cypress Avenue, San Diego, CA 92103-4517. 1994. Poetry, fiction, art, cartoons, letters. "All submissions must be based on or related to the land of OZ as created by L. Frank Baum. No graphic sex or violence, nothing based on MGM movie Wizard of Oz. Stories: 2000-7000 words. Stories and poetry—send complete manuscript. Comics—send story outline (or full script) plus thumbnail sketches. Reprints okay if not widely known." circ. 1.2M. 1/yr. Pub'd 1 issue 1998; expects 1 issue 1999, 1 issue 2000. sub. price: $14.95; per copy: $14.95; sample: $14.95. Discounts: 20-50% to trade depending on quantity ordered. 128pp; 8½x11; of. Reporting time: 4-10 weeks. Simultaneous submissions accepted: no. Publishes 20% of manuscripts submitted. Payment: 3 free copies, stories 1/2¢ per word, verse 25¢ per line, comics $30 per page. We generally ask for first printing rights.

P

P & K Stark Productions, Inc. (see also STARK NAKED), Kin-Ming Yee, Mr. Xavier, 17125C W. Bluemound Road, Ste. 171, Brookfield, WI 53005, 414-543-9013. 1990. Poetry, fiction, art, non-fiction. avg. press run 1M-10M. Expects 1-2 titles 1999, 2-3 titles 2000. 1 title listed in the *Small Press Record of Books in Print* (28th Edition, 1999-00). avg. price, cloth: $24.95; paper: $14.95. Discounts: 1=0%,2-4=35%,5-25=40%, 26-60=45%, 61-up=50%. 6x9; of. Payment: worked out individually for both payment and royalties. ABA.

P E N American Center, John Morrone, 568 Broadway, New York, NY 10012. 1922. "We publish the *Grants and Awards available to American writers* (New ISBN for the 20th edition - 0-934638-15-2). The booklet is a directory of financial assistance for the writer. The 1998-99 edition is considerably updated, and includes 182 new awards, as well as lists of writers' residences, and websites and e-mail addresses for sponsoring organizations." avg. press run 7M. 1 title listed in the *Small Press Record of Books in Print* (28th Edition, 1999-00). avg. price, paper: $15 (postpaid) for individuals, $18 (postpaid) for libraries and educators. Discounts: 40% off on orders of 5 or more copies. 7x9.

●P.D.Q., Spears of Ink, Joyce Odam, Vicki Asp, 5836 North Haven Drive, North Highlands, CA 95660, e-mail poetdpth@aol.com. 1995. Poetry, art. circ. 182. 4/yr. Pub'd 4 issues 1998; expects 4 issues 1999, 4

410

issues 2000. sub. price: $16; per copy: $4; sample: $4. Back issues: $4. 40pp; 4¼×5½; †xerox. Reporting time: 1 week to 2 months. Simultaneous submissions accepted: no. Publishes 5-10% of manuscripts submitted. Payment: copy. Copyrighted, reverts to author.

PABLO LENNIS, Etaoin Shrdlu Press, John Thiel, Editor, Fandom House, 30 N. 19th Street, Lafayette, IN 47904. 1976. Poetry, fiction, articles, art, photos, criticism, reviews, letters, non-fiction. "Material should be very short, due to space. Open policy. Material is most apt to be rejected if it would look more in place in some other publication, and the addresses of these are given the author when known. Recent well-known contributors include many directory responders. The contents of *Pablo Lennis* are extraordinarily reportative of modern life. Don't be surprised if the world of our writers in some way turns out to be yours." circ. 100. 12/yr. Pub'd 12 issues 1998; expects 12 issues 1999, 12 issues 2000. sub. price: $20-$25 overseas; per copy: $2; sample: $2. Back issues: none available. 26pp; 8½×11; of. Reporting time: 2 weeks or less. Simultaneous submissions accepted: no. Publishes 80% of manuscripts submitted. Payment: 1 copy of the issue plus copies of any commentary on the work. Not copyrighted. Pub's reviews: 42 in 1998. §Science fiction, fantasy, science. Ads: micro-ads 10¢ a word.

PACIFIC COAST JOURNAL, French Bread Publications, Stillson Graham, Editor; Stephanie Kylkis, Fiction Editor, PO Box 23868, San Jose, CA 95153, e-mail paccoastj@juno.com. 1991. Poetry, fiction, articles, art, interviews, satire, criticism, reviews, parts-of-novels, plays, non-fiction. "Slight Pacific bias. I've discovered that I like pieces about writing and/or the creative process. I like aesthetic poetry, language poetry, and stuff that hasn't been invented yet. Fictitious languages ok. I like fiction with good characters, plot is secondary." circ. 200. 4/yr. Pub'd 4 issues 1998; expects 4 issues 1999, 4 issues 2000. sub. price: $10; per copy: $3; sample: $2.50. Back issues: $2.50. Discounts: none. 56pp; 5½×8; photocopy. Reporting time: 4 months or less. Simultaneous submissions accepted if they let us know. Publishes 8-10% of manuscripts submitted. Payment: 1 copy. Copyrighted, reverts to author. Pub's reviews: 8 in 1998. §Fiction, poetry, sciences, philosophy. Ads: $35/$20/$15 business card.

PACIFIC ENTERPRISE, Rudy Ledesma, PO Box 1907, Fond du Lac, WI 54936-1907, 920-922-9218; rudyled@vbe.com. 1998. Poetry, fiction, articles, cartoons, interviews, reviews, parts-of-novels, non-fiction. "Although our primary readers are Filipino Americans, we aim to publish, plainly and simply, high-quality work without regard to the national origin of the author. Poetry: any style and length but must resonate. Short stories: high-quality, no more than 5,000 words, with name, word count and short bio attached. No fantasy, juvenile, western or avant garde pieces with four-letter words. Make us remember your character long after we've read the piece. Recent contributors: Eileen Tabios, Jon Pineda, Frank Scotello, and Jojo Sayson." circ. 5M. 6/yr. Expects 3 issues 1999, 6 issues 2000. sub. price: $19.95; per copy: $2.95; sample: $3. Back issues: $3. Discounts: 20% for bulk (more than 10), 20% for classroom. 32pp; 8⅜×10⅞; of. Reporting time: 4-6 weeks. Simultaneous submissions accepted: yes. Publishes 25% of manuscripts submitted. Payment: 2 copies, unless commissioned. Copyrighted, reverts to author. Pub's reviews: §Fiction, nonfiction (novels, memoirs, self-help). Ads: $290/$150/$80 1/4 page.

PACIFIC HISTORICAL REVIEW, University of California Press, David Johnson, Carl Abbot, Univ of California Press, 2120 Berkeley Way, Berkeley, CA 94720, 510-643-7154. 1931. Reviews, non-fiction. "Editorial address: Dept. of Urban Studies and Planning, Portland State University, PO Box 751, Portland, OR 97207-0751." circ. 1.5M. 4/yr. Pub'd 4 issues 1998; expects 4 issues 1999, 4 issues 2000. sub. price: $28 indiv., $69 instit., $19 students (+ $5 foreign postage); per copy: $9 indiv., $19 instit., $9 students (+ $5 foreign postage); sample: free. Back issues: $8 indiv., $15 instit., $8 students (+ $5 foreign postage). Discounts: foreign subs. agents 10%, one-time orders 10+ 30%, standing orders (bookstores): 1-99 40%, 100+ 50%. 128pp; 6×9; of. Reporting time: 3 months. Payment: none. Copyrighted, does not revert to author. Pub's reviews: 100 in 1998. §Asia, American West, history, diplomatic history. Ads: $275/$200.

THE PACIFIC REVIEW, James Brown, Faculty Editor; Juan Delgado, Faculty Editor, Department of English, Calif State University, San Bernardino, CA 92407, 714-880-5824. 1982. Poetry, fiction, articles, art, photos, interviews, satire, criticism, reviews, letters, parts-of-novels, long-poems, plays, non-fiction. "While the *PR* attempts to reflect its unique geographic region—Southern California—material is not limited to the area; the *PR* invites excellence in poetry, fiction, drama and essay." circ. 1M. 1/yr. Pub'd 1 issue 1998; expects 1 issue 1999, 1 issue 2000. sub. price: $7; per copy: $5; sample: $5 (libraries $6.50). Back issues: $2. Discounts: 40%. 104pp; 6×9; of. Reporting time: 2 months (mss are not read Feb.-Aug.). Payment: in copies. Copyrighted, reverts to author. Pub's reviews: 0 in 1998. §Poetry, fiction. Ads: $150/$100. CLMP.

Pacific View Press, Pam Zumwalt, PO Box 2657, Berkeley, CA 94702, fax 510-843-5835, pvp@sirius.com. 1992. Non-fiction. avg. press run 3-5M. Pub'd 3 titles 1998; expects 3 titles 1999, 2-3 titles 2000. 18 titles listed in the *Small Press Record of Books in Print* (28th Edition, 1999-00). avg. price, cloth: $24.95; paper: $18.95. 250pp; 6×9. Simultaneous submissions accepted: yes. Payment: royalty. Copyrights for author. PMA, SPAN.

PACK-O-FUN, Clapper Publishing Co., Julie Stephani, 2400 Devon, Suite 375, Des Plaines, IL 60018,

847-635-5800. 1951. circ. 300M. 10/yr. Pub'd 10 issues 1998; expects 10 issues 1999, 10 issues 2000. price per copy: $3.95-$4.95. 106pp; 8½x11. Reporting time: 3 months. Simultaneous submissions accepted: yes. Payment: yes. Copyrighted, does not revert to author. Pub's reviews. §Craft books. MPA.

Paerdegat Park Publishing Co., PO Box 978, Darien, CT 06820, 203-655-5412 phone/fax; Pag-Park@aol.com; www.paerdegatpark.com. 1998. avg. press run 1.5M. Expects 1 title 1999, 2 titles 2000. 1 title listed in the *Small Press Record of Books in Print* (28th Edition, 1999-00). avg. price, paper: $16. Discounts: short 20%, max. 40%. 225pp; 6x9; photo offset. Reporting time: to be determined. Simultaneous submissions accepted: yes. Payment: to be determined. Copyrights for author.

PAGAN AMERICA, Crescent Moon, Jeremy Robinson, Cassidy Hughes, PO Box 393, Maidstone, Kent ME14 5XU, United Kingdom. 1992. Poetry. *"Pagan America* is a bi-annual collection of poetry from North America and Canada. Many poets are unknown, others are well-established. One book each year features women's love poetry" circ. 200. 2/yr. Pub'd 2 issues 1998; expects 2 issues 1999, 2 issues 2000. sub. price: $17; per copy: $8.50; sample: $6. Back issues: $6 for 1, $5 for 2+. Discounts: Trade: 20% single order, 35% 2+. 80pp; 5⅞x8¼; mi. Reporting time: 3 months. Publishes 5% of manuscripts submitted. Payment: to be negotiated. Copyrighted, reverts to author. Ads: $20/$10/$5 1/4 page. Small Press Group.

PAGAN PRIDE, Golden Isis Press, Gerina Dunwich, PO Box 4263, Chatsworth, CA 91313. 1996. Poetry, art, reviews, letters. "The official journal of the Pagan Poets Society, a distinguished literary circle for poets who identify themselves and their work as 'pagan.' Offers networking opportunities and contests. Send SASE for membership application. Contributors must be members of the Pagan Poets Society." 2/yr. Expects 2 issues 1999, 2 issues 2000. sub. price: free with membership in the Pagan Poetry Society; membership $13/1 year, $25/2 years, $100/lifetime; sample: $5 (checks payable to Gerina Dunwich). 20pp; 5½x8½; †inkjet printer. Reporting time: 2 weeks. Simultaneous submissions accepted: yes. Publishes 25% of manuscripts submitted. Payment: free subscription, free listing in the P.P.S. directory, discounts on books and services. Copyrighted, reverts to author. Pub's reviews. §Poetry, Wicca/Paganism, New Age books, mags and tapes. Ads: $49/$25/open to exchanging ads with other pagan journals. North Country Wicca.

Page One (see also SUBSCRIBE, Ideas and Marketing Tips for Newsletter Publishers; FOOD WRITER), Lynn Kerrigan, 20 W. Athens Avenue, Ardmore, PA 19003-1308, 610-896-2879; e-mail pageone1@aol.com. 1994. Articles, interviews, reviews, news items, non-fiction. avg. press run 5M. Pub'd 2 titles 1998; expects 2 titles 1999, 4 titles 2000. 1 title listed in the *Small Press Record of Books in Print* (28th Edition, 1999-00). avg. price, paper: $5-10. 40pp; 5½x8½; of. Reporting time: 4 weeks. Simultaneous submissions accepted: no. Publishes 10% of manuscripts submitted. Payment: negotiable. Copyrights for author. IACP, PMA.

Pahsimeroi Press, Richard Norman, PO Box 190442, Boise, ID 83709. 1994. Fiction, non-fiction. "Pahsimeroi Press publishes fiction and nonfiction that focuses on rivers and whitewater paddle sports. Nonfiction titles are often river guidebooks. Works of fiction can have a broader, outdoor-oriented focus. Query first" avg. press run 5M. Pub'd 2 titles 1998; expects 2 titles 1999, 4 titles 2000. 2 titles listed in the *Small Press Record of Books in Print* (28th Edition, 1999-00). avg. price, paper: $18.48. Discounts: inquire. 380pp; 6x9; of. Reporting time: query first. Payment: negotiable. Copyrights for author.

Paint Rock Publishing, Inc., D. Faye Wilson, Operations Manager, 118 Dupont Smith Lane, Kingston, TN 37763, 423-376-3892. 1995. Fiction, art, photos, non-fiction. avg. press run 1-5M. Expects 3 titles 1999, 3-4 titles 2000. 1 title listed in the *Small Press Record of Books in Print* (28th Edition, 1999-00). avg. price, paper: $12-14. 300pp; 6x9; of. Reporting time: 3 months. Simultaneous submissions accepted: yes. Payment: to be determined case by case. Copyrights for author.

PAINTING, Clapper Publishing Co., Julie Stephani, 2400 Devon, Suite 375, Des Plaines, IL 60018, 847-635-5800. 1951. circ. 300M. 10/yr. Pub'd 10 issues 1998; expects 10 issues 1999, 10 issues 2000. price per copy: $3.95-$4.95. 106pp; 8½x11. Reporting time: 3 months. Simultaneous submissions accepted: yes. Payment: yes. Copyrighted, does not revert to author. Pub's reviews. §Craft books. MPA.

Paladin Enterprises, Inc., Peder C. Lund, President and Publisher; Jon Ford, Editorial Director, PO Box 1307, Boulder, CO 80306, 303-443-7250. 1970. Non-fiction. "Non-fiction manuscripts on military related subjects are given first consideration. These include weaponry technology, police science, military tactics, martial arts, self-defense, espionage, survival, terrorism. When accompanied with photos, mss are reviewed and returned within six weeks." avg. press run 1M-2M. Pub'd 39 titles 1998; expects 36 titles 1999, 38 titles 2000. 409 titles listed in the *Small Press Record of Books in Print* (28th Edition, 1999-00). avg. price, cloth: $24; paper: $16; other: $12 (reprints of technical manuals). Discounts: $50-$100 retail value - 20% all titles except supplementary list; $100-$500 40% ; $500-$1000 45%; $1000-$5000, 50% both all titles except supplementary list. Over $5000 55% except supplementary list. 175pp; 5½x8½, 8½x11; of. Reporting time: 6 weeks. Simultaneous submissions accepted: yes. Publishes 2% of manuscripts submitted. Payment: standard 10%, 12% & 15%. Copyrights for author.

412

Palanquin Press, Phebe Davidson, English Department, University of South Carolina-Aiken, Aiken, SC 29801, 803-648-6851 x3208; fax 803-641-3461; email phebed@aiken.edu; email scpoet@scescape.net. 1988. Poetry. "Sponsers 2 chapbook contests annually, fall and spring. Recently published: Lois Marie Harrod, Stuart Bartow, Laura Lee Washburn, Gay Brewer. Palanquin began its life publishing six pamphlets annually, each featuring a single poet, and then expanded its operation to include a spring chapbook contest. Currently, the press publishes three or four chapbooks annually with occasional longer titles. There are no restrictions on form or content, although Palanquin generally avoids sentimental, religious, and consciously academic work. Honest, well-crafted, accessible poems serve writers and readers alike to good advantage. Annual spring and fall chapbook contests: 20-25 pages of poetry plus bio and acknowledgements, $10 reading fee (includes copy of winning chapbook—checks payable to Palanquin Press), postmark deadlines May 1 and October 15 annually. SASE results only. Winner recieves $100 and 50 copies. Non-contest queries: include 3-5 poems with query letter." avg. press run Chapbooks 300, Full length 1M. Pub'd 4 titles 1998; expects 4 titles 1999, 5 titles 2000. 1 title listed in the *Small Press Record of Books in Print* (28th Edition, 1999-00). avg. price, cloth: $18; paper: $12; other: $5 chapbooks. 30pp; 6×9; of. Reporting time: 2-3 months. Simultaneous submissions accepted: yes. Publishes 5% of manuscripts submitted. Payment: copies. Copyrights for author.

Palari Publishing, David Smitherman, PO Box 9288, Richmond, VA 23227-0288, palaripub@aol.com; www.palari.net. 1998. Fiction, non-fiction. Pub'd 2 titles 1998; expects 4 titles 1999, 6 titles 2000. 1 title listed in the *Small Press Record of Books in Print* (28th Edition, 1999-00). avg. price, cloth: $21.95; paper: $15.95. Discounts: 2-4 copies 20%, 5-99 40%, 100+ 50%. 200pp; 6×9; of. Reporting time: 1 month. Simultaneous submissions accepted with notification. Publishes 2% of manuscripts submitted. Payment: varies. Copyrights for author. PMA.

Palladium Communications, Carol Shepherd, Publisher, 320 South Main Street, PO Box 8403, Ann Arbor, MI 48107-8403, 734-668-4646; FAX 734-663-9361. 1991. Poetry, fiction, articles, interviews, satire, music, long-poems, plays, non-fiction. "We are a *special-interest-only* mixed media house for pan-American works which 'speak to the deep relationship of person to place, and communicate landscape and culture similarities and differences, to other people in other places on the planet.' Examples: plays, fiction, poetry on exile/diaspora/immigration/Nueva Onda experience; travel journals from unusual perspectives; bilingual editions; linguistic, jargon, and language accessibility and preservation works; involvement of Internet/ technology with the above. For music: South American and North American singer/songwriters with contemporary/pop/worldbeat original material. We fully finance one title per year at most, mostly we joint venture titles which meet our mission, editorial, and involvement requirements. Submissions: *'one page query letter only, with a paragraph on who will buy a copy of your work and your resume of previous publications or releases. No unsolicited manuscripts or tapes- we simply pitch them in the trash.'* SASP for confirmation of receipt. We request samples or demos if interested." avg. press run 1000 units print/CD, 500 units cassette. Expects 2 titles 1999, 2 titles 2000. 3 titles listed in the *Small Press Record of Books in Print* (28th Edition, 1999-00). avg. price, cloth: $35 USD; paper: $15.95; other: Music CD: $15.95 USD Cassette: $10.95 USD. Discounts: Quantity discounts are for resellers providing a sales tax license number and 501 (c) institutional buyers. Quantity: 2-4 units, 20%;5-10 units, 40%; 51+ units, 60%. Cash discount of 5% and shipping at no charge applicable to orders paid in full. No special discounts. Discounts are fortified for orders not paid in full within 90 days. No returns after 90 days. 100pp; 6×9; Offset for trade paperbound titles. Reporting time: 3 months. We accept simultaneous submissions only within our strict submission guidelines. Publishes less than 2% of manuscripts submitted. Payment: royalties quarterly. If we finance a publication, author royalties are approximately 10% of net revenue collected. On joint ventures, consultations and subsidy projects, we retain a royalty percentage of net ranging from 10 to 50%. Copyrights for author.

Palm Drive Publishing, Mark Hemry, Publisher, 2755 Blucher Valley Road, 2nd Floor Suite, Sebastopol, CA 95472, 707-829-1930; Fax 707-829-1568; correspond@palmdrivepublishing.com; www.palmdrivepublishing.com. 1984. Fiction, plays, non-fiction. "For details, see website. Material itself determines length. All final manuscripts must be available in electronic form (IBM compatible only). In hard-copy, submit a 'TV-Guide' 100-word summary, first page, and first chapter. SASE. Leave politically correct messages on the editing-room floor." avg. press run 5M. Pub'd 3 titles 1998; expects 2 titles 1999, 2 titles 2000. 4 titles listed in the *Small Press Record of Books in Print* (28th Edition, 1999-00). avg. price, paper: $14.95. Discounts: wholesale 55%. 150-200pp; 5½×8½; webpress. Reporting time: 60 days. Simultaneous submissions accepted: yes. Publishes 5% of manuscripts submitted. Payment: full purchase or royalty arrangement (annual payment). Copyrights for author. PMA, SPAN.

Palm Island Press, Michael Keith, 411 Truman Avenue, Key West, FL 33040, 305-294-7834. 1994. Non-fiction. avg. press run 5M. Pub'd 3 titles 1998; expects 3 titles 1999, 3 titles 2000. 3 titles listed in the *Small Press Record of Books in Print* (28th Edition, 1999-00). avg. price, paper: $19.95. Discounts: 1-199 40%, 200-499 50%; 500+ 40-25%. 300pp; 5½×8½; of. Simultaneous submissions accepted: no. Publishes 0% of manuscripts submitted. PMA, FPA.

PalmTree Publishers, 4071 Valley Street, Omaha, NE 68105-3837. 1988. "We publish only solicited psychology, philosophy and religion. We do not seek submissions of any kind at this time." avg. press run 150. Pub'd 2 titles 1998; expects 6 titles 1999, 12 titles 2000. 7 titles listed in the *Small Press Record of Books in Print* (28th Edition, 1999-00). avg. price, paper: $9.95. Discounts: 2-4 20%, 5-99 40%, 100+ 50%. 50pp; 5½x8½; of, Xerox. Reporting time: 2 weeks. Payment: half up front, half when finished. Copyrights for author.

PALO ALTO REVIEW, Ellen Shull, Bob Richmond, 1400 West Villaret, San Antonio, TX 78224, 210-828-2998. 1992. Poetry, fiction, articles, art, photos, interviews, satire, reviews, letters, news items. "Diane Glancy (Native American Poet), Victor Villasenor (author of *Rain of Gold*). Interview: Richard Rodriguez (author, scholar). Generally, not more than 15pp. in length, we are looking for good, clear writing that makes a point" circ. 700. 2/yr. Pub'd 2 issues 1998; expects 2 issues 1999, 2 issues 2000. sub. price: $10; per copy: $5; sample: $5. Back issues: $5. 60pp; 8½x11; of. Reporting time: maximum of 3 months. Simultaneous submissions accepted, if noted as such. Publishes articles/essays 25%, poems 2%, stories 2-3% of manuscripts submitted. Payment: 2 copies. Copyrighted. Pub's reviews: 4 in 1998. §Not interested in children's, gay & lesbian. Ads: $100/$50/$35 1/4 page.

Pamlico Press, William Stephenson, 730 Washington Street #304, Raleigh, NC 27605-1289, 919-821-0858. 1987. "North Carolina history, biography, travel" avg. press run 1M. Expects 1 title 1999, 2-3 titles 2000. 1 title listed in the *Small Press Record of Books in Print* (28th Edition, 1999-00). avg. price, cloth: $18.95; paper: $12.95. Discounts: inquire. 200pp; 6x9. Reporting time: 3 months. Payment: to be arranged. Copyrights for author.

The Pamphleeter's Press, Rabia Ali, PO Box 3374, Stony Creek, CT 06405, Tel/fax 203-483-1429; E-mail pamphpress@igc.apc.org. 1991. Articles, photos, interviews, non-fiction. "The Pamphleeter's Press publishes books and pamphlets on politics, history & culture that address some of the mosu urgent functions of our times - which the major publishing houses have no time for" avg. press run 4M. Pub'd 3 titles 1998; expects 3 titles 1999, 3-4 titles 2000. 4 titles listed in the *Small Press Record of Books in Print* (28th Edition, 1999-00). avg. price, cloth: $30; paper: $19.95. Discounts: various discounts offered. Trade book orders are handled by our distributor: Inbook at 800-243-0138. 350pp; 7x9; of. Reporting time: 4-6 weeks. Simultaneous submissions accepted: yes. Publishes 25% of manuscripts submitted. Payment: 6½% to 7½%. Copyrights for author. Small Press Center, Association Book Exhibit.

Pancake Press, Patrick Smith, 163 Galewood Circle, San Francisco, CA 94131, 415-648-3573. 1973. Poetry, long-poems. "Not presently accepting unsolicited mss." avg. press run 1M. 4 titles listed in the *Small Press Record of Books in Print* (28th Edition, 1999-00). avg. price, paper: $10. Discounts: 40%. 35-50pp; 5½x7, 7x8½; of. Reporting time: 1 month. Payment: arranged by mutual consent. Does not copyright for author.

PANDALOON, David L. White, PO Box 21973, Milwaukee, WI 53221, 414-476-6030; fax 414-476-6989; email pandaloon@azml.com. 1997. Poetry. "16 to 20 short lines for small size chapbook." circ. 1M. 12/yr. Expects 2 issues 1999, 12 issues 2000. sub. price: $15; per copy: $1 w/ SASE; sample: $1 w/ SASE. Discounts: later perhaps. 16pp; 4x7; †of. Reporting time: 2 months. Simultaneous submissions accepted: yes. Payment: 20 copies to authors in issue. Copyrighted, reverts to author.

Pangaea, 226 South Wheeler Street, Saint Paul, MN 55105-1927, 651-690-3320, 888-690-3320, Fax 651-690-1485, info@pangaea.org; web http://pangaea.org. 1990. "No unsolicited submissions accepted at this time." avg. press run 7.5M. Pub'd 3 titles 1998; expects 3 titles 1999, 3 titles 2000. 9 titles listed in the *Small Press Record of Books in Print* (28th Edition, 1999-00). avg. price, cloth: $32.95; paper: $24.95; other: $12 posters. Discounts: bookstores 20%, 2-4 35% 5+ 40%, libraries 40%, wholesalers: Ingram, Baker & Taylor, Quality. 200pp; 6.6x9.7; of. Copyrights for author. PMA, AAP.

PANGOLIN PAPERS, Pat Britt, PO Box 241, Nordland, WA 98358, 360-385-3626. 1994. Fiction, parts-of-novels. "We accept literary fiction from short short stories to 7500 words. No poetry. No genre such as science fiction and romance. We are looking for new voices." circ. 500. 3/yr. Pub'd 3 issues 1998; expects 3 issues 1999, 3 issues 2000. 2 titles listed in the *Small Press Record of Books in Print* (28th Edition, 1999-00). sub. price: $15; per copy: $5.95; sample: $5.95. Back issues: $4.95. Discounts: 40%. 150pp; 5½x8½; †of. Reporting time: 2 months. Simultaneous submissions accepted: no. Publishes 5% of manuscripts submitted. Payment: 2 copies plus $200 annual prize. Copyrighted, reverts to author.

THE PANHANDLER, Laurie O'Brien, Editor, The Panhandler Press, English Dept., Univ. Of West Florida, Pensacola, FL 32514-5751, 904-474-2923. 1976. Poetry, fiction. "*The Panhandler* is a magazine of contemporary poetry and fiction. We want poetry and stories rooted in real experience of real people in language with a strong colloquial flavor. Works that are engaging and readable stand a better chance with us than works that are self-consciously literary. Recent contributors: Walter McDonald, Malcolm Glass, Enid Shomer, David Kirby, Joan Colby, Victor Gischler" circ. 500. 2/yr plus chapbook. Pub'd 3 issues 1998; expects 3 issues 1999, 3 issues 2000. sub. price: $10 includes yearly chapbook; per copy: $5; sample: $5. Back issues: $4.50. Discounts: 10 or more 40%. 70pp; 6x9; of. Reporting time: 4-6 months. Please inform us of simultaneous submissions and acceptance elsewhere. Publishes 5% of manuscripts submitted. Payment: copies. Copyrighted, reverts to author. Ads: $50/$25. CLMP, AWP.

Panjandrum Books (see also PANJANDRUM POETRY JOURNAL), Dennis Koran, David Guss, 6156 Wilkinson Avenue, North Hollywood, CA 91606, 818-506-0202. 1971. "Panjandrum Books publishes quality paperbacks on selected non-fiction subjects. Recently centering in the fields of health, diet, cooking, music, and literature. Panjandrum Press Inc. publishes poetry and occasionally fiction. Reading fee: $5." avg. press run 3M-5M, 1M poetry. Pub'd 3 titles 1998; expects 2 titles 1999, 3 titles 2000. 42 titles listed in the *Small Press Record of Books in Print* (28th Edition, 1999-00). avg. price, cloth: $16.95-$22.50; paper: $6.95-$12.95. Discounts: standard to bookstores and other retailers; wholesalers 50% & up. Non-fiction 150pp; poetry 64pp; size varies; of. Reporting time: 2 months. Payment: varies. Copyrights for author. CLMP.

PANJANDRUM POETRY JOURNAL, Panjandrum Books, Dennis Koran, Editor-in-Chief; David Guss, Associate Editor, 6156 Wilkinson Avenue, North Hollywood, CA 91606. 1971. Poetry, fiction, art, photos, cartoons, reviews, collages. "Eclectic; Rothenberg, Einzig, de Angulo, Bly, Ferlinghetti, Norse, McClure, Doria, Beausoleil, Vose, Weiss, Fraser, Vinograd, etc." circ. 2M. Expects 1 issue 1999, 1 issue 2000. sub. price: $20 instit. (3 issues); per copy: $6.95-$10; sample: varies with issue ordered as sample, plus shipping. Back issues: PAN 1: $25; 2-3, cassette: $15; 4, $6.95; 6/7: $7.95. Discounts: Trade: 1, 20%; 2-3, 30%; 4-25, 40%; 25-up, 50%. Library disc. Jobbers: 1-3, 20%; 4-25, 40%; 26-up, 45%. 10% on orders of 5-up copies. 100-140pp; 5½x8½; of, lp. Reporting time: 1 month. Payment: as grants are available; 2 copies of issue. Copyrighted, rights revert to author with written permission. Pub's reviews. §some areas. no ads. CLMP.

THE PANNUS INDEX, BGB Press, Inc., Vincent Bator, Leonard Cirino, Poetry Editor; Kevin Mooney, Contributing Editor, 14545 N. Frank Lloyd Wright Blvd. #276, Scottsdale, AZ 85260-8805, 413-584-4776; Fax 413-584-5674; www.javanet.com/~stout/pannus. 1995. Poetry, fiction, articles, art, photos, interviews, satire, criticism, reviews, letters, parts-of-novels, plays, non-fiction. "*The Pannus Index* is a journal devoted to aesthetics, delving into thematic genres of literature. Publication of manuscripts is based upon the principle of 'art for art's sake.' Past contributors include J.P. Donleavy, Errol Miller, Mark Axelrod, Hugh Fox, Simon Perchik, Walt Curtis Bruce Curley, Paul Roth, Dvane Locke, Alan Brett" circ. 500+. 2/yr. Pub'd 2 issues 1998; expects 2 issues 1999, 4 issues 2000. sub. price: $12, $18 foreign; per copy: $8. sample: $8. Back issues: $5. Discounts: 1-5 40%, 5-15 50%. 120pp; 6¾x10¼; of. Reporting time: 1-2 months. We prefer not to accept simultaneous submissions. Publishes 10% of manuscripts submitted. Payment: complimentary copies and discounts for add'l copies. Copyrighted, reverts to author. Pub's reviews: 6 in 1998. §Classic literature, i.e. "Olympia Press, Evergreen Press, Grove Press, language poetry." Ads: $125/$75/$45 1/4 page.

PANOPTICON, J. Moser, R. Moser, PO BOX 142, York Harbor, ME 03911-0142, E-mail jmoser41@portland.maine.edu. 1995. Poetry, fiction, art, photos, cartoons, interviews, criticism, reviews, letters, collages, plays. "Recent contributors: Matt Jasper, Mike Conlon, and Olga St. Vincent." circ. 100-300. 4+. Pub'd 2 issues 1998; expects 5 issues 1999, 5 issues 2000. sub. price: $8; per copy: $2; sample: $1. Back issues: none. Discounts: trades free with postage, free for contributors. 20pp; 5x7. Reporting time: asap, 2-3 weeks. Simultaneous submissions accepted: yes. Payment: free issue(s). Copyrighted, reverts to author. Pub's reviews: 10 in 1998. §Cultural theory, poetry, conspiracy, literature, rants. Ads: $5/$2/donations.

PANURGE, John Murray, Founder Editor, Crooked Home Farm Cottage, Brampton, Cumbria CA8 2AT, United Kingdom, 016977 41087. 1984. Fiction, articles, art, photos, interviews, letters, parts-of-novels. "Must be of *publishable* standard as we are regularly anthologised by Heinemann/Minerva. Our motto: *All lengths, styles and attitudes given serious consideration.* We write an individual reply to every single person who submits. NO form replies on principle." circ. 2M. 2/yr. Pub'd 2 issues 1998; expects 2 issues 1999, 2 issues 2000. sub. price: £15/$18; per copy: £7/$10; sample: same. Back issues: £3/$6. Discounts: 40%. 200pp; size A5 portrait; lp. Reporting time: 1 month; swift turnaround, except in case of 2-week summer vacation. Publishes 1-2% of manuscripts submitted. Payment: £10/1,000 words. Copyrighted, reverts to author. Ads: £60/£35.

THE PAPER BAG, The Paper Bag Press, Michael H. Brownstein, PO Box 268805, Chicago, IL 60626-8805, 312-285-7972. 1988. Poetry, fiction, art, cartoons, satire, long-poems, plays. "We are accepting black and white drawings (send originals), poetry any style (including Japanese forms), and short, short fiction—under 500 words (anything longer than 500 words will be returned). We are interested in new poets, artists, and writers as well as individuals who are established. Our only bias is with poetry that would work better as short fiction. We would like to see strong images in poetry. We comment on all rejections and many times steer the poet to another publication." circ. 200. 4/yr. Pub'd 4 issues 1998; expects 4 issues 1999, 4 issues 2000. sub. price: $12; per copy: $3; sample: $3. Back issues: $3. 30pp; 8½x6; of. Reporting time: 2 minutes to 8 weeks. Payment: contributor's copy. Not copyrighted.

The Paper Bag Press (see also THE PAPER BAG), Michael H. Brownstein, PO Box 268805, Chicago, IL 60626-8805, 312-285-7972. 1988. Poetry, fiction, art, cartoons, parts-of-novels, long-poems, plays. "We accept black and white drawings (please send originals), poetry (any style—this includes Japanese forms), and short,

short fiction (under 500 words—anything longer than 250 words will be returned). We have no biases other than we seek good images and frown on poetry that would better as fiction. We definitely comment on all rejections and many times give other publications' addresses for work we reject. We are actively seeking both new and established poets, artists, and writers. We plan to publish four chapbooks each year and many broadsheets. We are also interested in publishing poetry in other forms to reach the widest possible audience." avg. press run 20-300. Pub'd 2 titles 1998; expects 4 titles 1999, 4 titles 2000. 20pp; 8½×6; mi, of, lp. Reporting time: 2 minutes to 8 weeks. Payment: free contributors copies, but we hope to be able to pay some token amount soon. Does not copyright for author.

Paper Chase Press, Werner Riefling, P. Friedmann, Jennifer Osborn, 5721 Magazine Street, Suite 152, New Orleans, LA 70115, 504-522-2025; paperchasp@aol.com (for orders only-no manuscripts or queries). 1987. Non-fiction. "Recent title: *The Quickening: Today's Trends, Tomorrow's World* by Art Bell." avg. press run 10M+. Pub'd 2 titles 1998; expects 7 titles 1999, 2+ titles 2000. 7 titles listed in the *Small Press Record of Books in Print* (28th Edition, 1999-00). avg. price, cloth: $24.95; paper: $13. Discounts: 3-199 40%, 200-499 50%. 150pp; 6×9; of. Reporting time: 2 months. Simultaneous submissions accepted: yes. Payment: $100-$500 advance, if any up to 10% royalties based on retail price. Copyrights depend on title. Publishers Marketing Assoc. (PMA), New Orleans Gulf South Booksellers Assoc.

PAPER WASP: A Journal of Haiku, Jacqui Murray, Ross Clark, John Knight, Jan Bostok, 7 Bellevue Terrace, St. Lucia, Queensland 4067, Australia, 61-7-33713509; Fax 61-7-33715527. 1994. Poetry. "Haiku, senryu, and tanka." circ. 100. 4/yr. Pub'd 4 issues 1998; expects 4 issues 1999, 4 issues 2000. sub. price: $US26 airmail; per copy: $US7 airmail; sample: $US5. Back issues: $US7 each (airmail). Discounts: on application. 20pp; 6×8½; †of. Simultaneous submissions accepted: no. Publishes approx. 25% of manuscripts submitted. Payment: nil. Copyrighted, reverts to author.

PAPERBACK PARADE, Gryphon Publications, Gary Lovisi, PO Box 209, Brooklyn, NY 11228-0209. 1986. Articles, photos, interviews, criticism, reviews, letters, news items, non-fiction. "A bi-monthly digest magazine devoted to collectible vintage, rare paperbacks with articles, interviews, lists, on famous paperback authors, artists, publishers, and dozens of cover reproductions of scarce/rare books. Now with *color* covers!" circ. 1M. 5/yr. Pub'd 6 issues 1998; expects 6 issues 1999, 5 issues 2000. sub. price: $35; per copy: $8; sample: $8. Back issues: $8 per issue. Discounts: 40% on 5 or more of each issue. 100-110pp; 5×8; of. Reporting time: 2-4 weeks. Simultaneous submissions accepted: no. Payment: copies and other arrangements. Copyrighted, reverts to author. Pub's reviews: dozens in 1998. §Non-fiction. Ads: $50/$25.

PAPERPLATES, Bernard Kelly, 19 Kenwood Avenue, Toronto, ON M6C 2R8, Canada. 1991. Poetry, fiction, articles, art, photos, cartoons, interviews, satire, criticism, reviews, letters, parts-of-novels, plays, non-fiction. "Average length for secondary pieces (reviews, opinions, etc.) is 2,500 words. Maximum length for feature articles is 15,000 words. Maximum length for poetry is 1,500 words" circ. 350. Irregular. Pub'd 2 issues 1998; expects 2-3 issues 1999, 2-3 issues 2000. sub. price: $14.95; per copy: $4.95; sample: $2.50 + postage. 32pp; 8½×11; of. Reporting time: 3-4 months. Simultaneous submissions accepted: no. Publishes 25% of manuscripts submitted. Payment: copies. Copyrighted, reverts to author. Pub's reviews: 6 in 1998. §Fiction, poetry, essays. Ads: $300/$150/$100 1/3 page/$75 1/4 page/$50 1/6 page. CMPA.

Paperweight Press, L. H. Selman, 123 Locust Street, Santa Cruz, CA 95060-3907, 408-427-1177. 1975. Art. avg. press run 3M. Pub'd 1 title 1998; expects 2 titles 1999, 3 titles 2000. 17 titles listed in the *Small Press Record of Books in Print* (28th Edition, 1999-00). avg. price, cloth: $30; paper: $15; other: $40. Discounts: 6 or more copies, 40%; Jobber 200 or more, 60%. 200pp; 8½×11; of. Reporting time: 4-6 weeks. Payment: 5% cover price. Copyrights for author.

Papier-Mache Press, Shirley Coe, Acquisitions Editor, 627 Walker Street, Watsonville, CA 95076-4119, 408-763-1420, Fax 408-763-1421. 1984. Poetry, fiction, photos. "We specialize in books about women's issues as well as books for both women and men about the art of growing older. We publish theme anthologies. At these times we accept individual short stories and poems exploring an announced aspect of women's experiences, e.g., aging, parental relationships, or work. We think of our anthologies as 'word tapestries' and welcome a variety of writing styles. Authors should. Recent contributors include Ruth Daigon, Margaret Randall, Amber Sumrall, Janice Eidus, and Jess Wells" avg. press run 6M-12M. Pub'd 9 titles 1998; expects 10 titles 1999, 6 titles 2000. 62 titles listed in the *Small Press Record of Books in Print* (28th Edition, 1999-00). avg. price, cloth: $18; paper: $11. 216pp; 7×9¼; of. Reporting time: 4-6 months on anthology submissions. Simultaneous submissions accepted with notification. Payment: royalty. Copyrights for author. Publishing Marketing Association (PMA), American Bookseller Association.

Papillon Publishing, Lawrence Ford, PO Box 28553, Dallas, TX 75228, 214-686-4388, papillonco@aol.com. 1995. Fiction, art, non-fiction. "Our goal is to enrich families with creative publications from around the world. The *Ava Lawrence Collection* of illustrated, international children's stories is the centerpiece of our work. Our emphasis is to strengthen the family." avg. press run 3M. Expects 2 titles 1999, 5 titles 2000. 1 title listed in the

Small Press Record of Books in Print (28th Edition, 1999-00). avg. price, cloth: $15; paper: $10. Discounts: quantity discounts available. 32pp; 8½×11. Reporting time: 30 days. Simultaneous submissions accepted: yes. Publishes 25% of manuscripts submitted. Payment: yes. Copyrights for author. PMA.

PAPYRUS, Papyrus Literary Enterprises, Inc., Ginger Whitaker, 102 LaSalle Road, PO Box 270797, West Hartford, CT 06127, e-mail gwhitaker@imagine.com. 1994. "Articles on the art of writing, featuring the African American experience. Features fiction, non-fiction and poetry; African American-centered" circ. 3M. 4/yr. Pub'd 14 issues 1998; expects 14 issues 1999. sub. price: $8; per copy: $2.20; sample: $1. Back issues: $1.75. Discounts: $5.95 per sub for bulk, clasroom. 20pp; 8½×11; printer. Reporting time: 2 weeks. Simultaneous submissions accepted: no. Publishes 40% of manuscripts submitted. Payment: 2 copies; sometimes will pay for craft article, very good fiction piece, working poet's poetry. Copyrighted, reverts to author. Pub's reviews. §African American fiction, nonfiction, poetry. Ads: $500/$300/$200 business card.

Papyrus Literary Enterprises, Inc. (see also PAPYRUS), Ginger Whitaker, Edwina Walker, 102 LaSalle Road, PO Box 270797, West Hartford, CT 06127, 203-233-7478; e-mail gwhitaker@imagine.com; http://www.readersndex.com/papyrus. 1994. Poetry, fiction, articles, parts-of-novels, non-fiction. "African American centered literature" avg. press run 3-5M. Expects 2 titles 1999, 2 titles 2000. 2 titles listed in the *Small Press Record of Books in Print* (28th Edition, 1999-00). avg. price, cloth: $20; paper: $9.95. Discounts: 20% for bulk, classroom. 250pp; 6×9; of. Reporting time: 2-4 weeks. Publishes 20% of manuscripts submitted. Payment: yes. Copyrights for author. CELJ.

Para Publishing (see also PUBLISHING POYNTERS), Dan Poynter, Publisher, PO Box 8206 - Q, Santa Barbara, CA 93118-8206, 805-968-7277; fax 805-968-1379; fax-on-demand 805-968-8947; e-Mail 75031.3534@parapublishing.com; web site http://www.parapublishing.com/books/para/q; e-mail parapublishing@aol.com. 1969. Photos, cartoons, news items, non-fiction. "Para Publishing specializes in non-fiction books on parachutes/skydiving and book publishing/marketing. The technical parachute books and popular skydiving books have always been sold through non-traditional outlets. Publisher Dan Poynter is the author of 70+ books, 45 monographs and over 500 magazine articles, most of them on publishing. He serves as a consultant to the mail order and publishing industries and conducts workshops in Santa Barbara on book marketing, promotion and distribution. Poynter is a past director of COSMEP and a part Vice-President of the Publishers Marketing Association. No manuscripts, query first. Query regarding parachute and publishing books only. When offering a parachute manuscript, we want to know how many jumps you have made." avg. press run 5M-10M. Pub'd 7 titles 1998; expects 8 titles 1999, 8 titles 2000. 32 titles listed in the *Small Press Record of Books in Print* (28th Edition, 1999-00). avg. price, cloth: $29.95; paper: $19.95; other: $19.95 monographs. Discounts: 6-199 40%, 200-499 50%, 500+ 55%. 300pp; 5½×8½, 8½×11; of. Reporting time: 1 week. Publishes 60% of manuscripts submitted. Payment: 8% of list price. Copyrights for author. PMA, ABA.

PARA TROOP, Doug Miers, 115-A E. Fremont Avenue, Sunnyvale, CA 94087, 408-245-6275; Fax 408-245-2139; info@comicsconspiracy.com; www.comicsconspiracy.com. 1998. Fiction, art, cartoons. "No submissions at this time, please." circ. 2M. 6/yr. Expects 4 issues 1999, 6 issues 2000. sub. price: $15; per copy: $3; sample: $3 (free to retailers & media). Back issues: none. Discounts: wholesale 50% (must have reseller #). 32pp; 6⅝×10¼; of. Simultaneous submissions accepted: no. Payment: variable (very low). Copyrighted, does not revert to author. Ads: none.

Parabola (see also PARABOLA MAGAZINE), Joseph Kulin, Executive Publisher; David Appelbaum, Editor, 656 Broadway, New York, NY 10012, 212-505-6200. 1975. Poetry, fiction, interviews, non-fiction, articles. avg. press run 3M. Expects 2 titles 1999, 4 titles 2000. 17 titles listed in the *Small Press Record of Books in Print* (28th Edition, 1999-00). avg. price, cloth: $19.95; paper: $10.50. Discounts: 2-5 books 25%, 6-10 30%, 11-25 40%, 26-74 45%, 75+ 50%. 190pp; 5½×8½; of. Reporting time: 1 month. Simultaneous submissions accepted: yes. Publishes 6% of manuscripts submitted. Payment: yes. Copyrights for author. Publishers Marketing Association, American Booksellers Association.

PARABOLA MAGAZINE, Parabola, Joseph Kulin, Executive Publisher; David Appelbaum, Editor, 656 Broadway, New York, NY 10012-2317, 212-505-6200; fax 212-979-7325; e-Mail parabola@panix.com. 1976. Fiction, articles, art, photos, interviews, criticism, reviews, letters, non-fiction. "*Parabola* publishes articles of 2M-4M words, reviews of 500 words on scholarly subjects but with a literate and lively style. Recent contributors are Robert Thurman, Kathleen Norris, Helen Luke, Seyyed Hossein Nasr, Robert Aitken, P.L. Travers, Joseph Campbell, Ursula K. LeGuin. Issues are organized by theme: Addiction, Creative Response, Sense of Humor, Repetition and Renewal, Money, etc." circ. 41M. 4/yr. Pub'd 4 issues 1998; expects 4 issues 1999, 4 issues 2000. sub. price: $21.95; per copy: $6.95; sample: $5. Back issues: $8.95. Discounts: 2-5 books 25%, 6-10 30%, 11-25 40%, 26-74 45%, 75+ 50%. 128pp; 6½×10; of, web. Reporting time: 3 weeks-3 months. Payment: yes. Copyrighted, reverts to author. Pub's reviews: 35 in 1998. §Mythology, comparative religion, anthropology, folklore, children's books,. Ads: $875/$590. Publishers Marketing Assn., Small Press Center.

PARACHUTIST, Jason Bell, Editor; Suzanne R. Popielec, Advertising, Production Manager, 1440 Duke

Street, Alexandria, VA 22314, 703-836-3495. 1958. Articles, photos, reviews, letters, news items, non-fiction. "Photographs" circ. 30M. 12/yr. Pub'd 12 issues 1998; expects 12 issues 1999, 12 issues 2000. sub. price: $21.50; per copy: $3; sample: $3. Back issues: $3. 80pp; 8½×11; of. Reporting time: 6 weeks. Payment: $50 front cover, centerfold. Copyrighted, does not revert to author. Pub's reviews: 6 in 1998. §Aviation sports. Ads: $640/$384/75¢ ($10 min.).

Paradigm Publications, Robert L. Felt, 44 Linden Street, Brookline, MA 02445, voice 617-738-1235; voice 617-738-4664; fax 617-738-4620; e-Mail info@redwingbooks.com. 1981. Non-fiction. "Hardcover scholarship in acupuncture and oriental medicine" avg. press run 2M. Pub'd 4 titles 1998; expects 4 titles 1999, 4 titles 2000. 36 titles listed in the *Small Press Record of Books in Print* (28th Edition, 1999-00). avg. price, cloth: $50; paper: $19. Discounts: 40% net 30, library 20%. 500pp; 7×10; of. Reporting time: 2-4 months. Simultaneous submissions accepted: yes. Publishes 1% of manuscripts submitted. Payment: 10%/15%/18% on net. Does not copyright for author. American Association of Scholarship Publishers (AASP).

Paradise Publications, Christie Stilson, 8110 SW Wareham, Portland, OR 97223, 503-246-1555. 1983. Non-fiction. avg. press run 10M. Pub'd 2 titles 1998; expects 3 titles 1999, 3 titles 2000. 3 titles listed in the *Small Press Record of Books in Print* (28th Edition, 1999-00). avg. price, paper: $15. 320pp; 5½×8½. Reporting time: 2 months. Payment: negotiable. Copyrights for author. PMA, NWABP, IFW, TWA.

Paradise Research Publications, Inc., Kenneth C. Burns, Box 837, Kihei, HI 96753-0837, 808-874-4876; e-mail dickb@dickb.com. 1994. avg. press run 3000. Pub'd 4 titles 1998; expects 4 titles 1999, 4 titles 2000. 13 titles listed in the *Small Press Record of Books in Print* (28th Edition, 1999-00). avg. price, paper: $17.95; other: $17. Discounts: 20% for one book; 40% for all over one. 250pp; 6×9. Reporting time: 1 week. Simultaneous submissions accepted: yes. Publishes 10% of manuscripts submitted. Does not copyright for author. SPAN, PHA.

PARADOX, Dan Bodah, PO Box 643, Saranac Lake, NY 12983. 1991. Poetry, fiction, art, photos, music, letters, long-poems, collages. "More than any 'niche,' I'm interested in seeing a variety, as wide as possible, of incredible writings...the difficult, and the immediate. I'm extremely interested in collaborations, and also audio cassettes. Don't send what you *think* will fit in; *make* me fit what's good in." circ. 300. 2-3/yr. Pub'd 1 issue 1998; expects 2-3 issues 1999, 2-3 issues 2000. sub. price: $15/4 issues; per copy: $4; sample: $4. Back issues: $2.50. Discounts: trade issues with other 'zines; 40% for orders of 5 or more. 20-25pp; size varies; †ditto, photocopy. Reporting time: 2-3 weeks. Payment: 1-2 copies. Copyrighted, reverts to author. Ads: $10 1/2 page/will trade ads.

Paragon House Publishers, Gordon L. Anderson, Publisher and Editor in Chief, 2700 University Avenue, W., Saint Paul, MN 55114-1016, 612-644-3087; FAX 612-644-0997; internet address http://www.pwpu.org/Paragon. 1983. Non-fiction. "Religion, philosophy, literary criticism" avg. press run 5M-10M. Expects 24 titles 1999, 24 titles 2000. avg. price, cloth: $19.95; paper: $12.95. Discounts: short discount; 20% bookseller; standard trade discount schedule. 256pp; 6×9; standard. Reporting time: 6-8 weeks on average. Simultaneous submissions are limited. Publishes 5% of manuscripts submitted. Payment: standard. Copyrights for author. Continuum Publishing Group.

Parallax Press, Arnold Kotler, President, PO Box 7355, Berkeley, CA 94707, 510-525-0101; e-Mail parapress@aol.com; web address http://www.parallax.org. 1986. "Buddhist and related books-especially how Buddhism might become more engaged in peace and social justice work. Primary author: Thich Nhat Hanh" avg. press run 4M. Pub'd 9 titles 1998; expects 8 titles 1999, 9 titles 2000. 24 titles listed in the *Small Press Record of Books in Print* (28th Edition, 1999-00). avg. price, cloth: $23; paper: $12. Discounts: standard. 200pp; 5¼×8; Macintosh. Reporting time: 2 months. Publishes small % of manuscripts submitted. Payment: no advance, royalty. Copyrights for author. PMA, ABA, NEBA.

PARAMASITIC PROPISTITUTE, Pen-Dec Press, 2526 Chatham Woods, Grand Rapids, MI 49546. 1997. Irregular. sample price: $2. 20pp; 8½×5½.

PARA*PHRASE, Cosmic Trend, Tedy Asponsen, Sheridan Mall, Box 47014, Mississauga, Ontario L5K 2R2, Canada. 1989. Poetry, articles, art, criticism, reviews, news items. "Short poems or 'quotes' on life with a twist. Also poems related to ongoing Cosmic Trend major anthologies. Recently published poems by Charles David Rice, Susan Benischek, Charles Tuck, and Joanna Nealon" circ. 200. 2-3/yr. Pub'd 2 issues 1998; expects 3 issues 1999, 3 issues 2000. sub. price: $6 (for 4 issues); per copy: $2; sample: $2. Back issues: none. Discounts: $1 per issue. 20pp; 7×8½; †photocopy. Reporting time: 1 month. Simultaneous submissions accepted: yes. Publishes 20% of manuscripts submitted. Payment: 1 free copy. Copyrighted, reverts to author. Pub's reviews: 5 in 1998. §New age, erotica. Ads: $100/$50/$30 1/4 page and less.

Parenting Press, Inc., Carolyn Threadgill, Publisher, PO Box 75267, Seattle, WA 98125, 206-364-2900, Fax 206-364-0702. 1979. Non-fiction. "Non-fiction; parent education." avg. press run 5M. Pub'd 5 titles 1998; expects 12 titles 1999, 5 titles 2000. 65 titles listed in the *Small Press Record of Books in Print* (28th Edition,

1999-00). avg. price, cloth: $16.95/library bound; paper: $10. Discounts: contact publisher. 32pp childrens, 198pp parenting; 8½×11, 5½×8½, 6×9, 7×8½; of. Reporting time: 1-6 months. Simultaneous submissions accepted: yes. Publishes 1% of manuscripts submitted. Payment: case-by-case. Copyrights for author. Publishers Marketing Association, Book Publishers Northwest.

Pariah Press (see also HEELTAP/Pariah Press), Richard David Houff, 604 Hawthorne Avenue East, St. Paul, MN 55101-3531. 1992. Poetry. "Pariah Press is a non-profit chapbook publisher. Our reading fee of $5 covers material costs, printing, etc. We have published Cheryl Townsend, Christopher Jones, etc. The only requirement is to keep the work thematic in scope from beginning to end, and not to exceed 24 pages." avg. press run 100. Pub'd 1 title 1998; expects 1 title 1999, 1 title 2000. 2 titles listed in the *Small Press Record of Books in Print* (28th Edition, 1999-00). avg. price, cloth: $14; paper: $4. Discounts: none as yet. 24pp; 5½×8½; †of, desktop. Reporting time: post in Jan., report Sept. Simultaneous submissions accepted: yes. Publishes 5% of manuscripts submitted. Payment: 50 copies. Copyrights for author.

Paris Press, Inc., Jan Freeman, 1117 West Road, Williamsburg, MA 01096, 413-628-0051. 1993. Poetry, long-poems. "We publish 1-3 trade paperbacks per year in all genres except mystery, sci fi, and the like; highest quality LITERARY, FEMINIST books only; we do poetry, but only one such per volume per year; we do selected reprints; we also have a small book series for special presentation of short works; Paris Press authors include Ruth Stone, Jan Freeman, Muriel Rukeyser, Lisa Alther, and Francoise Gilot" avg. press run 2-5M. Pub'd 1 title 1998; expects 2 titles 1999, 2 titles 2000. 1 title listed in the *Small Press Record of Books in Print* (28th Edition, 1999-00). avg. price, paper: $13.95. Discounts: standard discounts to trade. 200pp; 6×9; of. Reporting time: 1 week to 3 months. Publishes 2% of manuscripts submitted. Payment: standard royalties, some advance. Copyrights for author. Small Press Center, Academy of American Poets.

PARIS/ATLANTIC, Elise Manley, The American University of Paris, 31, avenue Bosquet, 75007 Paris, France, 33-1-01 40 62 05 89; fax 33-1-01 45 51 89 13. Poetry, fiction, photos, plays. "Writers must submit their work including a return address (phone and fax numbers are helpful) and a short biography. We accept and welcome submissions from writers in English and French. Written work should be no more than 1000 words. *Paris/Atlantic* includes poetry, prose, short stories, plays, photography, and other creative works." circ. 1.5M. 2/yr. sample price: sufficient postage. 80-100pp. Payment: 2 copies.

Park Place Publications, Joelle Steele, PO Box 829, Pacific Grove, CA 93950-0829, 831-649-6640; fax 831-655-4489; e-mail info@parkplace-publications.com; website www.parkplace-publications.com. 1991. Non-fiction. avg. press run 5M. Pub'd 8 titles 1998; expects 2 titles 1999, 4 titles 2000. 15 titles listed in the *Small Press Record of Books in Print* (28th Edition, 1999-00). avg. price, paper: $30. Discounts: 40% bookstores; 20% single title. 100pp; 5½×8½; mi, of, lp. Reporting time: 30 days. Simultaneous submissions accepted: yes. Publishes 1% of manuscripts submitted. Payment: varies. Copyrights for author.

Parkhurst Press, Lynne Thorpe, PO Box 143, Laguna Beach, CA 92652, 949-499-1032. 1981. Fiction. "First book: *Alida - An Erotic Novel,* 180 pages. The intent of our press is to deal with material that changes the mythology of women." avg. press run 2.5M. Expects 1 title 1999, 1 title 2000. 1 title listed in the *Small Press Record of Books in Print* (28th Edition, 1999-00). avg. price, paper: $9. Discounts: 50%. 180pp; 5½×8½; of. Reporting time: 3 weeks. Payment: open.

Parkway Publishers, Inc., Rao Aluri, Box 3678, Boone, NC 28607, 704-265-3993. 1992. Non-fiction. "Scholarly books in sciences and social sciences; 300-400 pages double spaced; emphasis on scholarly contributions." avg. press run 500-1M. Expects 3 titles 1999, 6 titles 2000. 13 titles listed in the *Small Press Record of Books in Print* (28th Edition, 1999-00). avg. price, cloth: $45; paper: $30. Discounts: 30%. 200pp; 6×9¾; of. Reporting time: 6 weeks. Simultaneous submissions accepted: no. Publishes 25% of manuscripts submitted. Payment: 10% on first 1,000 copies, 15% afterward. Copyrights for author. American Library Association (ALA).

PARNASSUS LITERARY JOURNAL, Denver Stull, Kudzu Press, PO Box 1384, Forest Park, GA 30298-1384. 1975. Poetry, articles, reviews. "We are open to all poets. Also open to any subject or style, but please keep it clean. Short poetry has a better chance. Will not accept over 24 lines. Recent contributors include: Jean Calkins, Naiwa Brax, Diana Rubin, Ruth Schuler, and Carol Hamilton. Make checks payable to Denver Stull." circ. 200+. 3/yr. Pub'd 3 issues 1998; expects 3 issues 1999, 3 issues 2000. sub. price: $18 for US and Canada, $25 overseas, make checks payable to Denver Stull; per copy: $6; sample: $3. Back issues: $3 (when available). Discounts: 20% to schools, libraries, and order of 5 or more. 64pp; 5½×8½; lp. Reporting time: 30 days. Simultaneous submissions accepted: yes. Publishes 10% of manuscripts submitted. Payment: copy. Copyrighted, reverts to author. National Writers Club, Academy of American Poets, American Haiku Soc.

PARNASSUS: POETRY IN REVIEW, Herbert Leibowitz, 205 West 89th Street, Apartment 8F, New York, NY 10024, 212-362-3492; fax 212-875-0148; e-mail parnew@aol.com. 1972. "Length varies from four pages to forty. Editorial policy is intentionally eclectic. Recent and forthcoming contributors: Adrienne Rich, Jonathan Williams, Guy Davenport, Judith Gleason, Ross Feld, Zbigniew Herbert, Marjorie Perloff, Rafael Campo, Carl

Phillips, Rikki Duconnet, Wayne Koestenbaum, Hayden Carruth, William Harmon, Seamus Heaney, Alice Fulton, Helen Vendler. Publish one or two unsolicited poems per year" circ. 1.75M. 2/yr. Pub'd 2 issues 1998; expects 2 issues 1999, 2 issues 2000. sub. price: $27 individuals, $46 institutions; per copy: $7-$15; sample: $10-$15. Back issues: $10 per issue (indiv.), $20/issue (libraries). Discounts: 10% to magazine subscription agencies, 30% to bookstores. 350pp; 6×9¼; of. Reporting time: 3 weeks to 2 months. Simultaneous submissions accepted: yes. Publishes 10% of manuscripts submitted. Payment: $150 average, more if essay is long. Copyrighted, rights revert to author on request. Pub's reviews: 60-80 in 1998. §Poetry, poetic fiction. Ads: $250/$150. CLMP.

PARTING GIFTS, March Street Press, Robert Bixby, 3413 Wilshire Drive, Greensboro, NC 27408-2923. 1988. Poetry, fiction. "Poems any length—prefer up to 20 lines. Fiction to 1,000 words, but stress is on highly imagistic language." circ. 100. 2/yr. Pub'd 2 issues 1998; expects 2 issues 1999, 2 issues 2000. sub. price: $12; per copy: $6; sample: $6. Back issues: $6. Discounts: write. 72pp; 5½×7½; †Xerox. Reporting time: usually within 24 hours. Payment: 1 copy. Copyrighted, reverts to author.

●Partisan Press (see also BLUE COLLAR REVIEW), Al Markowitz, PO Box 11417, Norfolk, VA 23517, e-mail redart@pilot.infi.net. 1993. Poetry, fiction, long-poems. "Looking for working class poetry or short stories-mostly poetry. Social/political focus but with a broad range. High quality writing, no polemics or screed." avg. press run 150. Pub'd 4 titles 1998; expects 3-4 titles 1999. avg. price, paper: $5. 40-60pp; 5½×8½; †of. Reporting time: 3-6 weeks. Simultaneous submissions accepted: yes. Publishes 10% of manuscripts submitted. Payment: 40 copies. Does not copyright for author.

PARTISAN REVIEW, William Phillips, Editor-in-Chief; Edith Kurzweil, Editor, 236 Bay State Road, Boston, MA 02215, 617-353-4260. 1934. Poetry, fiction, articles, interviews, criticism, reviews, letters, parts-of-novels, long-poems, plays, non-fiction. circ. 8M. 4/yr. Pub'd 4 issues 1998; expects 4 issues 1999, 4 issues 2000. sub. price: $22; per copy: $6; sample: $7.50 including postage. Back issues: $6. 160pp; 6×9; of. Reporting time: 2-3 months. Simultaneous submissions accepted: no. Payment: $50 per poem, prose payment varies. Copyrighted. Pub's reviews: 25 in 1998. §Books literature, politics, art, general culture, have backlog now. Ads: $250/$150. CLMP.

Partners In Publishing, P.M. Fielding, Box 50347, Tulsa, OK 74150, 918-584-5906. 1976. Articles, interviews, reviews, letters, news items. "We are only interested in material directed to persons who work with learning disabled youth or adults *or* material directed to the learning disabled young person or adult. Emphasis on college, vocational training or career information. Authors should have academic credentials or practical experience." avg. press run 2M. Pub'd 1 title 1998; expects 1 title 1999, 2 titles 2000. 2 titles listed in the *Small Press Record of Books in Print* (28th Edition, 1999-00). avg. price, paper: $33. Discounts: bulk rate (over 5 copies). 6pp; 11×12; of. Reporting time: 1 month. Payment: varies. We own copyright. OSP.

PASSAGER: A Journal of Remembrance and Discovery, Kendra Kopelke, Rebecca Childers, Mary Azrael, 1420 N. Charles Street, Baltimore, MD 21202-5779, 301-625-3041. 1989. Poetry, fiction, interviews, parts-of-novels, long-poems, non-fiction. "Fiction and essays: 4,000 words maximum. Poetry: 40 lines maximum. No reprints. *Passager* publishes fiction, poetry, essays, interviews that give voice to human experience. We provide exposure for older writers, with a special interest in those who have recently discovered their creative self. We also act as a literary community for writers of all ages who are not connected to academic institutions or other organized groups." circ. 500. 4/yr. Pub'd 4 issues 1998; expects 4 issues 1999, 4 issues 2000. sub. price: $15; overseas US $28; libraries/institutions $30; per copy: $5; sample: $4. Back issues: $5. 32pp; 8×8; of. Reporting time: 3 months. Payment: 1 year subscription + 2 copies of issue in which work appears. Copyrighted, reverts to author. No ads. CLMP.

PASSAGES NORTH, Anne Ohman Youngs, Editor, English Dept., N. Michigan Univ., 1401 Presque Isle Ave., Marquette, MI 49855, 616-337-7331; Fax 906-227-1096. 1979. Poetry, fiction, interviews, parts-of-novels, long-poems, non-fiction. "*Passages North's* primary interest is high quality poetry and short fiction, interviews and creative non-fiction. Contributors: Established and emerging writers; encourages students in writing programs. Recently published Stephen Berg, Tess Gallagher, Linda Gregerman, Mark Halliday, Tony Hoagland, Jorie Graham, Thomas Lux, Medbh McGuckian, Roger Brown, Jack Driscoll, Bill Meissner, Len Roberts, Jim Daniels, Frances Leftkowitz. Send SASE for submission guidelines. Submit all prose double-spaced with ample margins; use paper clips, not staples. Name and address on top right corner of top page; submissions returned if a SASE (w/adequate postage) is included." circ. 1.5M. 2/yr. Pub'd 2 issues 1998; expects 2 issues 1999, 2 issues 2000. sub. price: $13/yr, $25/2 yrs; per copy: $6; sample: $7. Back issues: $2 (Summer '95 and earlier). Discounts: contact us. 115pp; 5½×8½; of. Reporting time: 4-6 weeks. Simultaneous submissions accepted: no. Payment: 1 copy. Copyrighted, rights revert to author's request in writing (right to reprint). Ads: exchange ads only.

PASSAIC REVIEW (MILLENNIUM EDITIONS), Richard P. Quatrone, 442 Stuyvesant Avenue, Lyndhurst, NJ 07071. 1979. Poetry, fiction, articles, art, photos, interviews, satire, criticism, reviews, long-poems. "No 'soviet poetry' please. Send real writing" circ. 100. 2-6/yr. Pub'd 1 issue 1998; expects 2-6 issues 1999, 2-6 issues 2000. sub. price: $10; per copy: $2 + 75¢ postage; sample: $2 + 75¢ postage. Back issues: $2 + 75¢ postage. Discounts: inquire. Pages vary; 7×8½; †photocopy. Reporting time: immediate to indefinite. Simultaneous submissions accepted only if indicated. Payment: copies of magazine. Copyrighted, reverts to author. Ads: $80/$40/$20/$10. CLMP.

Passeggiata Press, Inc., Donald Herdeck, Editor and Publisher; Norman Ware, Int'l Editor; Tingley Maureen, Associate Publisher, PO Box 636, Pueblo, CO 81002, 719-544-1038, Fax 719-546-7889, e-mail Passeggia@aol.com. 1996. Poetry, fiction, criticism, long-poems, plays. "Publishers of Third World literature (Africa, Caribbean, Middle East, Pacific, Asia), and the scholarship thereof: recently bio-lingual poetry collections (one poet per vol.) English language, English-Russian, English-Bulgaria and some architecture books" avg. press run 1M-2M. Pub'd 15 titles 1998; expects 10-15 titles 1999. 46 titles listed in the *Small Press Record of Books in Print* (28th Edition, 1999-00). avg. price, cloth: $25; paper: $12. Discounts: 30% prepaid by retailers and wholesalers; 20% prepaid by libraries; 20% not prepaid, university bookstores. No discounts on single-copy orders 40% on prepaid 100 copies, 10 titles min. 175-250pp; 6×9, 5½×8½, 8½×11; of. Reporting time: 5-6 weeks, but often much longer or shorter. Simultaneous submissions accepted: yes. Publishes 3-5% of manuscripts submitted. Payment: usually 7.5% with small advance. Copyrights for author. Rocky Mountain Publishers Assn.

Passing Through Publications, Fiona Rock, PO Box 604, Naalehu, HI 96772, 808-929-8673. 1996. Poetry, fiction, art, photos. "Our business is dedicated to publishing the works of non-mainstream travel; of people who have more lint in their pockets than money. For example, our first publication, *Transient Ways* is about hopping freight trains and 'squatting' abandoned buildings. We seek the new, the nomadic, and the utterly despised." avg. press run 2M. Pub'd 1 title 1998; expects 2-3 titles 1999, 2-3 titles 2000. 1 title listed in the *Small Press Record of Books in Print* (28th Edition, 1999-00). avg. price, paper: $5.99. Discounts: 5+ copies 40%. 100pp; 4×5½; of. Reporting time: immediate. Simultaneous submissions accepted: no. Publishes less than 1% of manuscripts submitted. Payment: individual agreements. Copyrights for author.

PASSION, Crescent Moon, Jeremy Robinson, PO Box 393, Maidstone, Kent ME14 5XU, United Kingdom. 1994. Poetry, articles, art, photos, interviews, criticism, reviews, music, letters, parts-of-novels. "Shortish mss. prefered; literature, media, cultural studies, feminism, arts topics." circ. 200. 4/yr. Pub'd 4 issues 1998; expects 4 issues 1999, 4 issues 2000. sub. price: $17; per copy: $4; sample: $4. Back issues: $3 for 1, $2.50 for 2 or more. Discounts: Trade 20% on single order, 35% on 2+. 50pp; 5⅞×8¼; mi. Reporting time: 2 months. Simultaneous submissions accepted: yes. Publishes 3% of manuscripts submitted. Payment: to be negotiated. Copyrighted, reverts to author. Pub's reviews: 100 in 1998. §Arts, literature, media, cultural studies, poetry. Ads: $20/$10/$5 1/4 page. Small Press Group.

Passport Press, Jack Levesque, Miranda d'Hauteville, PO Box 1346, Champlain, NY 12919-1346, 514-937-3868; fax 514-931-0871, e-mail travelbook@bigfoot.com. 1976. "Travel and children's items." avg. press run 10M. Pub'd 4 titles 1998; expects 6 titles 1999, 4 titles 2000. 6 titles listed in the *Small Press Record of Books in Print* (28th Edition, 1999-00). avg. price, paper: $16.95. Discounts: 20% with payment (small orders); 6 copies, 40%. 400pp; 5½×8½; of. Payment: as negotiated. Does not copyright for author. PMA.

Past Times Publishing Co., Jordan R. Young, Editorial Director, PO Box 661, Anaheim, CA 92815, 714-997-1157; jyoung@fea.net. 1980. "Formerly Moonstone Press. Although we're not soliciting manuscripts, Past Time Publishing is not strictly a self-publishing operation. Have been in business 18 years and have titles by four authors, with books in the works" Pub'd 1 title 1998; expects 1 title 1999, 1 title 2000. 11 titles listed in the *Small Press Record of Books in Print* (28th Edition, 1999-00).

PAST TIMES: The Nostalgia Entertainment Newsletter, Randy Skretvedt, 7308 Fillmore Drive, Buena Park, CA 90620, 714-527-5845; skretved@ix.netcom.com. 1990. Articles, reviews, news items. "News and reviews regarding movies and music of the '20s, '30s and '40s; also old-time radio, early television and popular culture. Nothing contemporary. Nothing about history or events outside the entertainment field. Nothing on antiques. No poetry" circ. 5M. 4/yr. Pub'd 3 issues 1998; expects 4 issues 1999, 4 issues 2000. sub. price: $11; per copy: $2.75; sample: $3. Back issues: $3-5. 32pp; 8½×11; of. Reporting time: varies. Publishes 75% of manuscripts submitted. Payment: copies. Copyrighted, reverts to author. Pub's reviews: 60+ in 1998. §movies, music of '20s, '30s, '40s; old-time radio; early '50s TV; classic reissues strips/comic books. $100/$60 (class. no longer available; we do have small ads as low as $10).

THE PATERSON LITERARY REVIEW, Maria Mazziotti Gillan, Editor, Passaic County Community College, College Boulevard, Paterson, NJ 07505-1179, 201-684-6555. 1979. Poetry, fiction, art. "Stories should be short. Poems: under 60 lines preferred. Poetry, fiction, reviews. 6 x 9 size for art work. Clear photocopies acceptable. *No unsolicited reviews.*" circ. 1M. 1/yr. Pub'd 1 issue 1998; expects 1 issue 1999, 1 issue 2000. sub. price: $12; per copy: $12; sample: $12. Back issues: $12. Discounts: 40% for orders of 10 or more. 200pp; 6×9; of. Reporting time: 3 months. Simultaneous submissions accepted: yes. Publishes 5% of manuscripts submitted. Payment: contributor's copies. Copyrighted, reverts to author. Pub's reviews: 7 in 1998. §Poetry, short stories, novels (particularly African American, Latino, Asian American, Native American), critical books on literature. Ads: $200/$100/$50 1/4 page. CLMP.

Path Press, Inc., Bennett J. Johnson, President; Herman C. Gilbert, Executive Vice President, PO Box 2925, Chicago, IL 60690-2925, 312-663-0167. 1969. Poetry, fiction, non-fiction. "Our books are distributed by African-American Book Dist., Inc. 53 West Jackson Blvd., Chicago, IL 60604-3610." avg. press run 5M. Expects 1 title 1999, 6-10 titles 2000. 7 titles listed in the *Small Press Record of Books in Print* (28th Edition, 1999-00). avg. price, cloth: $16; paper: $10. Usual trade discounts. 300pp; 5½×8½, varies; varies. Reporting time: 90-120 days. Payment: no advance, 10% royalty for first 5M copies, staggered rate to 15% after that. Copyrights for author. ABA, ALA.

Pathfinder Press, Michael Baumann, Editorial Director, 410 West Street, New York, NY 10014, 212-741-0690; fax 212-727-0150; CompuServe: 73321,414; Internet pathfinder@igc.apc.org. 1928. "Publisher of books on current events, history, economics, marxism, Black studies, labor, women's liberation, Cuba, South Africa. Authors include Malcolm X, Nelson Mandela, Che Guevara, Fidel Castro, V.I. Lenin, Karl Marx, and Leon Trotsky." avg. press run 3M. Pub'd 8 titles 1998; expects 5 titles 1999. 30 titles listed in the *Small Press Record of Books in Print* (28th Edition, 1999-00). avg. price, cloth: $45; paper: $15.95; other: $2.50 booklets. Discounts: retail bookstores 40-45%, wholesalers 50%. 300pp; 5×8; †of.

Pathway Books, James R. Sherman, P.O. Box 27790, Golden Valley, MN 55427-0790, 612-377-1521. 1979. Fiction, non-fiction. "List of books: *Stop Procrastinating—Do It!*, *Rejection*, and *Middle Age is Not a Disease* Do it ! Success series, caregiver survival series." avg. press run 10M. Pub'd 1 title 1998; expects 3 titles 1999, 4 titles 2000. 12 titles listed in the *Small Press Record of Books in Print* (28th Edition, 1999-00). avg. price, paper: $2.95-$9.95. Discounts: 50%. 100pp; 5½×8½, 8×10; of. Does not copyright for author. Publishers Marketing Association, Minnesota Independent Publishers Association, Minnesota Book Publishers Roundtable, Upper Midwest Booksellers Association.

Pathways Press, Inc., Jude Berman, PO Box 60175, Palo Alto, CA 94306, 415-529-1910; pathways@best.com. 1990. Fiction, non-fiction. avg. press run 4M. Expects 1 title 1999, 1 title 2000. 2 titles listed in the *Small Press Record of Books in Print* (28th Edition, 1999-00). avg. price, paper: $11.95. Reporting time: 1 month. Payment: 10%. NAPRA.

Patria Press, Inc., 3842 Wolf Creek Circle, Carmel, IN 46033, 317-844-6070; fax 317-844-8935; e-mail info@patriapress.com; website www.patriapress.com. 1991. Non-fiction. "Accepting only biographies of famous Americans who are deceased-written for children ages 8-12." avg. press run 3.5M. Expects 3 titles 1999, 6 titles 2000. 1 title listed in the *Small Press Record of Books in Print* (28th Edition, 1999-00). avg. price, cloth: $14.95. Discounts: 1-2 copies 20%; 3-9 40%; 10-25 42%; 25+ 44%. 120pp; 5½×8½. Reporting time: 4-6 months. Simultaneous submissions accepted: yes. Publishes 20% of manuscripts submitted. Payment: 6% on first 5000 copies sold; 8% on next 5000 copies sold; 10% on all copies sold there after. Copyrights for author. PMA, Society of Childrens Book Writers and Illustraters.

The Patrice Press, Gregory M. Franzwa, PO Box 85639, Tucson, AZ 85754-5639, 602-882-0906; FAX 602-882-4161. 1967. Non-fiction. "Full-length books, usually on history, primary emphasis on emigration to the American West in the 19th century." avg. press run 2M. Pub'd 6 titles 1998; expects 8 titles 1999, 8 titles 2000. 4 titles listed in the *Small Press Record of Books in Print* (28th Edition, 1999-00). avg. price, cloth: $25.95; paper: $12.95. Discounts: 1-4 20%, 5-9 40%, 10-24 42%, 25+ 43%. 300pp; 6×9; of. Reporting time: 30 days. Publishes 1% of manuscripts submitted. Payment: 12.5% net. Does not copyright for author.

THE PATRIOT, Runaway Publications, James L. Berkman, PO Box 1172, Ashland, OR 97520, 503-482-2578. 1984. Poetry, long-poems. "*The Patriot* is dedicated to the preservation of the Heroic American spirit" circ. 100. 1/yr. Pub'd 1 issue 1998; expects 1 issue 1999, 1 issue 2000. sub. price: $10; per copy: $10; sample: $10. Back issues: same. Discounts: 50% to govt. agencies/federal employees. 8pp; 5½×8½; of. Payment: negotiable. Copyrighted, rights reverting to author negotiable. Ads: negotiable.

PAVEMENT SAW, Pavement Saw Press, David Baratier, Editor, PO Box 6291, Columbus, OH 43206, 614-263-7115; baratier@megsinet.net. 1994. Poetry, art, photos, interviews, reviews, concrete art. "Five poems, clean photocopy (prefer type quality). One page prose or 1-2 pages short fiction, acceptable also. *Pavement Saw* seeks poetry, prose, and short fiction which elevats the ordinary. The work should not merely startle, but rather employ academic structural techniques to indirectly encourage its readers to search for resolutions within their own experience and context of the work. Juxtaposition for tension, caesura's, colons, and the like permeate the issue. Peruse a copy for further indications of style and content. *Pavement Saw* rarely accepts previously published material, simultaneous submissions, and letterless mass submissions. Named emotion and greeting cards will be returned in flaming envelopes. There is one featured writer (10 pages or so) each issue. #2 Glan Lombardo, #3 Sean Killian, #4 Sandra Kohler. We are one of the few journals who focus on the prose poems, short, short fiction, letter boundaries." circ. 500. 1/yr. Pub'd 1 issue 1998; expects 1 issue

1999, 1 issue 2000. sub. price: $8; per copy: $4; sample: $3.50. Discounts: Send query for schedule with number of copies you're interested in. 64pp; 6×9¼; of. Reporting time: 1-4 months. Simultaneous submissions accepted, only from writers who have not published their first full length collection. Publishes less than 1% of manuscripts submitted. Payment: 2 copies. Copyrighted, reverts to author. Pub's reviews. §Books of poetry by contemporary authors, not anthologies. Small Press Distribution.

Pavement Saw Press (see also PAVEMENT SAW), David Baratier, Editor, PO Box 6291, Columbus, OH 43206, baratier@megsinet.net. 1994. Poetry. "Our first full length book was by Chris Stroffolino. Often, material for the full length books are chosen from authors previously published in Pavement Saw. Reading the journal and submitting pieces before sending material to the press would be more than necessary for full length titles. We have an annual chapbook competition. The 1999 winner was Shelley Stenhouse as chosen by Ruth Anderson Barnett. We also have a full-length book competition in July and August. The 1999 just is Bin Ramke. The winner receives $500 and 10% of press run. Deadline for the competition is in mid-December of each year. Query before sending for guidelines or contest rules. *Hands Collected: The Poems of Simon Perchik 1949-1999*, 372pp will be released fall of 1999. *Selected Poems* by Alan Catlin, 186pp, will be released fall of 1999.'' avg. press run 1M-3.5M. Pub'd 3 titles 1998; expects 3 titles 1999, 4 titles 2000. 8 titles listed in the *Small Press Record of Books in Print* (28th Edition, 1999-00). avg. price, cloth: $75; paper: $12; other: chapbooks are always $6 perfect bound. Discounts: 40% for 5 copies or more. 64-372pp, 40pp chapbooks; 9×10; of. Simultaneous submissions accepted: yes. Publishes less than 1% of manuscripts submitted. Payment: 10% royalty plus copies. Copyrights for author. Small Press Distribution.

Pavlovsk Press (see also IMPERIAL RUSSIAN JOURNAL), Paul Gilbert, 103 Bristol Road East, Unit 202, Mississuaga, Ontario L4Z 3P4, Canada, 905-568-3522. 1993. Non-fiction. "Pavlovsk Press is seeking authors who have book proposals or completed manuscripts for publication. We are particularly interested in historical biographies pertaining to family members of the Imperial House of Russia; members of the Imperial Russian Court; and/or life in Czarist Russia. No fiction please.'' avg. press run 500 pa, 1M-2M cl. Expects 2 titles 1999, 3 titles 2000. avg. price, cloth: $24.95; paper: $19.95. Discounts: trade only, this varies. 200pp; 6×9. Reporting time: 6-8 weeks. Payment: varies for finished manuscript and royalties paid monthly to author. Copyrights for author.

Paw Print Publishing Co., Conrad Brown, 439 South Doheny Drive, Beverly Hills, CA 90211-4411, 310-556-2728. 1993. Fiction, non-fiction. "Screenplays, short story collections, self help nonfiction'' avg. press run 4M. Pub'd 2 titles 1998; expects 2 titles 1999, 2 titles 2000. 1 title listed in the *Small Press Record of Books in Print* (28th Edition, 1999-00). avg. price, paper: $14.95. Discounts: 40$ + 15% jobber. 160pp; 7×9; lp. Reporting time: 3 months. Simultaneous submissions accepted: no. Payment: 5% pub net. Copyrights for author.

Paycock Press (see also GARGOYLE), Richard Myers Peabody, Editor, 3938 Colchester Road, Apt. 364, Baltimore, MD 21229-5010, Fax; 410-644-5195; e-mail atticus@radix.net. 1976. Poetry, fiction, art, photos, satire, reviews, long-poems. "Poetry titles: *Blank Like Me* by Harrison Fisher, *Jukebox* by Tina Fulker, *I'm in Love with the Morton Salt Girl/Echt & Ersatz* by Richard Peabody, *Fernparallelismus* by Carlo Parcelli. Fiction titles: *The Love Letter Hack* by Michael Brondoli, *Natural History* by George Myers Jr. Anthology: *D.C. Magazines: A Literary Retrospective* ed. by Richard Peabody. Nonfiction: *Mavericks: Nine Independent Publishers* ed. by Richard Peabody.'' avg. press run 1M. Pub'd 1 title 1998; expects 1 title 1999, 1 title 2000. 8 titles listed in the *Small Press Record of Books in Print* (28th Edition, 1999-00). avg. price, paper: $3-$7.95. Dealer discount available. 60-100pp; 5½×8½, varies; of. Reporting time: 1 month. Copyrights for author.

PEACE & DEMOCRACY, Joanne Landy, Jennifer Scarlott, Thomas Harrison, PO Box 1640, Cathedral Station, New York, NY 10025, 212-666-5924. 1984. Poetry, articles, art, photos, cartoons, interviews, reviews, letters. "Published by the Campaign for Peace and Democracy. Their aim is to promote peace and human rights from below based on grass-roots democratic movements around the world. To this end, *Peace And Democracy* carries articles on topics ranging from the implications of changes in Eastern Europe for the Third World to the state of reproductive rights in various countries around the world.'' circ. 5M. 2/yr. Pub'd 1 issue 1998; expects 2 issues 1999, 2 issues 2000. sub. price: $7 individual, $15 institutions/international; per copy: $3.50; sample: free. Back issues: $2.50. Discounts: 10 or more copies, $2 apiece. 48pp; 8½×10½; regular printer, of. Reporting time: 1 month - 6 weeks. Payment: none. Copyrighted, rights revert to writers only on request. Pub's reviews: 1 in 1998. §Political, social, and economic human rights, economic development, U.S. foreign policy, peace movement, international environmental problems and policies. we solicit ads, often as an exchange.

PEACE MAGAZINE, Metta Spencer, 736 Bathurst Street, Toronto, Ont. M5S 2R4, Canada, 416-533-7581; Fax 416-531-6214; e-mail mspencer@web.net; website www.peace magazine.org. 1984. "Newsworthy: 250 words; reviews 500 words, articles and interviews—subject to space restrictions and what is needed to maintain the integrity of the piece—usually 2,500 to 3,000 words. *Peace Magazine* is multipartisan and looks at all aspects of peace and non-violence, from the impact of militarism on the environment to the roots of the conflict in Somalia to violence in the media. Mohamed Urdoh, Metta Spencer, Hans Sinn, Ursula Franklin, Liz

Burnstein, plus profiles of Richard Falk and Noam Chomsky." circ. 3M. 6/yr. Pub'd 6 issues 1998; expects 6 issues 1999, 6 issues 2000. sub. price: $20; per copy: $3.50; sample: $2.50. Back issues: $1.50. Discounts: $1.25 per copy for orders of 20 or more, paid in advance. 30pp; 8½×11; web. Reporting time: 2-6 weeks. Publishes 40% of manuscripts submitted. Payment: 5 copies. Copyrighted, reverts to author. Pub's reviews: 12 in 1998. §Peace and non-violence, human rights, economic justice. Ads: $360/$195/$140 1/3 page/$110 1/4 page/$75 1/6 page/$40 business card. Canadian Magazine Publishers Association (CMPA).

‡PEACE, The Magazine of the Sixties, Linda James, 2753 E. Broadway, 5101-1969, Mesa, AZ 85204, 602-817-0124. 1994. Poetry, fiction, articles, cartoons, interviews, reviews, music, letters, news items, non-fiction. "Recent contributors: Louvinia Smith, Eric Lief Davin, Liz Gips, Jules Archer. Our magazine is of, by and for people of the 60s. We prefer non-fiction, true stories, of everyday 60s experiences." circ. 1M. 4/yr. Pub'd 4 issues 1998; expects 4 issues 1999, 12 issues 2000. sub. price: $14; per copy: $3.95; sample: $4.50. 50pp; 8½×11; †of. Reporting time: 3-6 months. Simultaneous submissions accepted: yes. Publishes 80% of manuscripts submitted. Payment: 5¢ per word to $100 maximum. Copyrighted, reverts to author. Pub's reviews: 1 in 1998. §60s issues, women's movement, civil rights movement, Vietnam.

PEACEWORK, Patricia Watson, Editor; Sara Burke, Assistant Editor, 2161 Massachusetts Avenue, Cambridge, MA 02140, 617-661-6130. 1972. Articles, photos, cartoons. "*Peacework* covers 'global thought and local action for nonviolent social change.'" circ. 2K. 11/yr. Pub'd 11 issues 1998; expects 11 issues 1999, 11 issues 2000. sub. price: $14 by third class mail, $20 by first class mail; $7 students/low-income; per copy: $2; sample: free. 24pp; 8½×11; desktop. Reporting time: 2 weeks - 1 month. Payment: free subscription. Not copyrighted. Pub's reviews: 14 in 1998. §Peace and social justice. Paid advertising not accepted.

Peachtree Publishers, Ltd., Sarah Helyar Smith, Aquisition & Development Editor, 494 Armour Circle NE, Atlanta, GA 30324, 404-876-8761. 1977. Non-fiction. "Peachtree Publishers, Ltd. is interested in quality childrens fiction and adult non-fiction. To submit a manuscript, send an outline and sample chapters, along with biographical information on the author and a SASE large enough to hold the material. Please mark to the attention of the Editorial Dept." avg. press run 5M-25M. Pub'd 10-12 titles 1998; expects 19 titles 1999, 24 titles 2000. 12 titles listed in the *Small Press Record of Books in Print* (28th Edition, 1999-00). avg. price, cloth: $15.95; paper: $7.95. Discounts: retail 12+ copies 50% non-returnable; 1-4 20%, 5-10 40%, 11-24 42%, 25-49 43%, 50-199 44%, 200-499 45%, 500+ 46% returnable; jobbers 50% on 50 or more assorted. Pages vary; size varies; of. Reporting time: 4-6 months. Simultaneous submissions accepted: yes. Payment: individual basis subject to contractual terms. Copyrights for author. Publishers Association of the South (PAS), Southeastern Booksellers Assn. (SEBA), American Booksellers Assn. (ABA), Publishers Publicity Assn. (PPA), Georgia Publishers Assn. (GPA).

PEAKY HIDE, Valory Banister, PO Box 1591, Upland, CA 91785. 1996. Poetry, art, photos, reviews, collages. "Prefers short poems. Send no more than 3-5 at a time. Particularly interested in experimental poetry. Recent contributers include: Damiena S. Carmichael, John M. Bennett, Marcia Arrieta, Jen Hofer, and Gerald Locklin." circ. less than 200. 4/yr. Pub'd 1 issue 1998; expects 3 issues 1999, 4 issues 2000. sub. price: $17; per copy: $5; sample: $5. Back issues: none. Discounts: none. 48pp; size varies; †desktop. Reporting time: 1-2 months. Simultaneous submissions accepted: no. Publishes 40% of manuscripts submitted. Payment: 1 copy. Copyrighted, reverts to author. Pub's reviews: 6 in 1998. §Chapbooks of poetry. Ads: available for trade with other magazines/organizations.

●Peanut Butter and Jelly Press, Alyza Harris, PO Box 239, Newton, MA 02459-0002, 617-630-0945 phone/fax. 1998. Non-fiction. "No unsolicited manuscripts" avg. press run 50M. Expects 5 titles 1999, 5 titles 2000. 1 title listed in the *Small Press Record of Books in Print* (28th Edition, 1999-00). avg. price, cloth: $34.95; paper: $24.95. Discounts: 2-10 copies 50%, 10+ 55%. 300pp; 5½×8½. ABA.

PEARL, Pearl Editions, Joan Jobe Smith, Marilyn Johnson, Barbara Hauk, 3030 E. Second Street, Long Beach, CA 90803, 562-434-4523 or 714-968-7530. 1987. Poetry, fiction, art, cartoons. "We are interested in accessible, humanistic poetry and short fiction that communicates and is related to real life. Humor and wit are welcome, along with the ironic and serious. No taboos stylistically or subject-wise. Prefer poems up to 35 lines and short stories up to 1200 words. Submissions accepted September through May *only*. Our purpose is to provide a forum for lively, readable poetry and prose that reflects a wide variety of contemporary voices, viewpoints, and experiences and that speaks to *real* people about *real* life in direct, living language, from the profane to the sublime. Have recently published poetry by Charles Bukowski, Edward Field, Gerald Locklin, Lisa Glatt, Catherine Lynn." circ. 600. 2/yr. Pub'd 2 issues 1998; expects 2 issues 1999, 2 issues 2000. sub. price: $18 (2 issues)+ 1 poetry book; per copy: $7; sample: $7. 128pp; 5½×8½; of. Reporting time: 6-8 weeks. Simultaneous submissions accepted: yes. Publishes 5% of manuscripts submitted. Payment: 1 copy. Copyrighted, reverts to author.

Pearl Editions (see also PEARL), Joan Jobe Smith, Marilyn Johnson, Barbara Hauk, 3030 E. Second Street, Long Beach, CA 90803, 562-434-4523 or 714-968-7530. 1989. "Currently only publish solicited authors and

424

winner of our annual poetry book contest." avg. press run 300. Pub'd 4 titles 1998; expects 3 titles 1999, 3 titles 2000. 19 titles listed in the *Small Press Record of Books in Print* (28th Edition, 1999-00). avg. price, paper: $8. Discounts: 2+ 40%. 40pp; 5½×8½; †laser. Reporting time: 4-5 months. Payment: $1,000 + 25 copies (contest winners), 25 copies (solicited authors). Copyrights for author.

Pearl River Press (see also PEARL RIVER REVIEW), Kimberly Kelly, 32 Cambridge Avenue, Gulfport, MS 39507-4213. 1996. Poetry, fiction, articles, art, interviews, long-poems, non-fiction. avg. press run 500-1M. Pub'd 1 title 1998; expects 2 titles 1999, 2 titles 2000. avg. price, paper: $7.50. 50pp; 6×9. Reporting time: 2-3 months. Simultaneous submissions accepted: yes. Publishes 10% of manuscripts submitted. Payment: copies. Copyrights for author.

PEARL RIVER REVIEW, Pearl River Press, Kimberly Kelly, 32 Cambridge Avenue, Gulfport, MS 39507-4213. 1996. Poetry, fiction, articles, art, interviews, long-poems, non-fiction. "Recent contributors: David Scott Milton, James White, James Schevill, and Mary Gray Hughes" circ. 500. 2/yr. Pub'd 1 issue 1998; expects 2 issues 1999, 2 issues 2000. sub. price: $15; per copy: $7.50; sample: $7.50. 50pp; 6×9. Reporting time: 2-3 months. Simultaneous submissions accepted: yes. Publishes 10% of manuscripts submitted. Payment: in copies. Copyrighted, reverts to author. Pub's reviews. §Literary fiction.

Pearl-Win Publishing Co., Barbara Fitz Vroman, N4721 9th Drive, Hancock, WI 54943-7617, 715-249-5407. 1980. Poetry, fiction, non-fiction. "We are not enouraging submissions at this time since we have a backlog of good material." avg. press run 3M. Pub'd 2 titles 1998; expects 2 titles 1999. 7 titles listed in the *Small Press Record of Books in Print* (28th Edition, 1999-00). avg. price, cloth: $13.95; paper: $9.95. Discounts: 40% trade; 20% libraries. Poetry 64pp, prose 250pp; 6×9; of. Reporting time: reasonable. Payment: 10% hard, 7.5% paper. Copyrights for author. WAPA, Authors and Publishers Assoc.

Peartree Books & Music, Barbara Birenbaum, PO Box 14533, Clearwater, FL 33766-4533, 727-531-4973. 1985. "No prek picture books. Accept manuscripts and queries for GRL-S that lend themselves to pen + ink drawings. Also subsidy works w/full color illustrations all levels Pre K-Gr. 8." avg. press run 1M-3M. Expects 5 titles 1999, 5+ titles 2000. 9 titles listed in the *Small Press Record of Books in Print* (28th Edition, 1999-00). avg. price, cloth: $12.95-$19.95; paper: $6.95; other: $17.95. Discounts: 20% libraries, retail 40% paper, 30% cloth, jobbers 50%+. 50pp; 5½×8½, 6×9, 7×10. Reporting time: 6 weeks. Simultaneous submissions accepted: yes. Payment: percent of sales of book based on profit margin. Copyrights for author. FAIM, FAME, FRA, SEBA, IRA.

Peavine Publications, William P. Lowry, Box 1264, McMinnville, OR 97128, 503-472-1933; e-mail peapub@pnn.com. 1987. Non-fiction. "Specialty: a) weather & climate from the ecological perspective— mostly textbooks; b) 'philosophical' works concerning atmospheric ecology." avg. press run 600. Expects 1 title 1999, 1 title 2000. 2 titles listed in the *Small Press Record of Books in Print* (28th Edition, 1999-00). avg. price, cloth: $50; paper: $32-$37. Discounts: 20% to academic bookstores and suppliers, additional for larger and/or prepaid orders. 300-400pp; 6×9. Reporting time: 2 months, please write/call first. Payment: each project negotiated. Copyrights for author.

Pebble Press, Inc., Robert Piepenburg, 24723 Westmoreland, Farmington, MI 48336-1963, 248-478-5820; fax 248-478-6984. 1957. Art, photos. avg. press run 4M. Expects 1 title 1999, 1 title 2000. 3 titles listed in the *Small Press Record of Books in Print* (28th Edition, 1999-00). avg. price, paper: $26.95. Discounts: 40%. 159pp; 8×11; †of. Reporting time: 2 months. Payment: to be arranged. Copyrights for author.

Pecan Grove Press, H. Palmer Hall, Karen Narvarte, Academic Library, Box AL, 1 Camino Santa Maria, San Antonio, TX 78228-8608, 210-436-3441. 1988. Poetry. "Books and chapbooks: short stories, creative nonfiction. Poetry: Recent work by Vince Gotera, Laura Kennelly, Beth Simon, Cynthia Harper. Creative non-fiction: recent work by W. Scott Olsen. Fiction/Poetry: Best of Writers at Work 1995." avg. press run 300-600. Pub'd 7 titles 1998; expects 6 titles 1999. 26 titles listed in the *Small Press Record of Books in Print* (28th Edition, 1999-00). avg. price, paper: $10. Discounts: 40% to bookstores, 50% distributors, 20% libraries. 90pp; 8½×5½, 9×6; off set. Reporting time: 2-9 weeks. We accept simultaneous submissions with notification. Publishes 4% of manuscripts submitted. Payment: 10 copies to author + 50% once book has earned back price of production. Copyrights for author.

Pedestal Press, Deborah Cardile, PO Box 6093, Yorkville Station, New York, NY 10128, 212-876-5119. 1991. Non-fiction. "Office address: 170 East 89th Street, New York, NY 10128." avg. press run 5M. Expects 2 titles 1999, 2-3 titles 2000. 1 title listed in the *Small Press Record of Books in Print* (28th Edition, 1999-00). avg. price, cloth: $19.95. Discounts: 2-4 20%, 5-99 40%, 100+ 50%. 250pp; 6×9; of. Reporting time: 60-90 days. Payment: 10% of retail price on first 5M copies sold, 12.5% on next 5M, 15% on copies sold over 10M. Copyrights for author. PMA.

PEDIATRIC EXERCISE SCIENCE (PES), Human Kinetics Pub. Inc., Thomas W. Rowland, M.D., PO Box 5076, Champaign, IL 61825-5076, 217-351-5076. 1989. Articles, reviews. "Devoted to enriching the scientific knowledge of exercise during childhood." circ. 607. 4/yr. Pub'd 4 issues 1998; expects 4 issues 1999, 4 issues 2000. sub. price: $45 individual, $100 institution, $26 student; per copy: $12 indiv., $27 instit.; sample: free. Back issues: $12 indiv, $27 instit. Discounts: 5% agency. 104pp; 6×9; of. Reporting time: 2 months. Payment: none. Copyrighted, does not revert to author. Pub's reviews: 2 in 1998. §Sport sciences, such as biomechanics, exercise physiology, motor learning, sport psychology, socio-cultural issues, and sports medicine as they relate to exercise during childhood. Ads: $300/$200. Midwest Book Publishers Association, American Booksellers Association.

PEDIATRICS FOR PARENTS, Richard J. Sagall, 747 South 3rd Street #3, Philadelphia, PA 19147-3324. 1982. Non-fiction. *"Pediatrics for Parents* is the newsletter for parents and others who care for children." circ. 1M. 12/yr. Pub'd 12 issues 1998; expects 12 issues 1999, 12 issues 2000. sub. price: $20; per copy: $3; sample: $3. Back issues: one year of back issues $15. Discounts: write for details. 12pp; 8½×11; of. Reporting time: 1-2 months. Simultaneous submissions accepted: yes. Publishes 25% of manuscripts submitted. Payment: $25 on publication. Copyrighted, reverts to author. Pub's reviews: 12 in 1998. §Pediatrics, children. Ads: none.

Peel Productions, Inc., Susan DuBosque, 2533 N. Carson Street #3970, Carson City, NV 89706-0147, 704-894-8838; FAX 704-894-8839. avg. press run 5M. Pub'd 2 titles 1998; expects 3 titles 1999, 4 titles 2000. 16 titles listed in the *Small Press Record of Books in Print* (28th Edition, 1999-00). avg. price, cloth: $13.95; paper: $8.95. Discounts: STOP 40%.

●Peerless Publishing, Stuart Gray, PO Box 20466, Ferndale, MI 48220, 248-542-1930. 1998. *"Accepting children's book submissions only!"* avg. press run 5M. Expects 2 titles 1999, 4 titles 2000. 1 title listed in the *Small Press Record of Books in Print* (28th Edition, 1999-00). avg. price, cloth: $9.99; paper: $5.99. Discounts: bulk 100+ 40%, classroom 25+ 50%. 24pp; of. Reporting time: 1 month. Simultaneous submissions accepted: yes. Does not copyright for author. SPAN.

PEGASUS, M.E. Hildebrand, Pegasus Publishing, 525 Avenue B, Boulder City, NV 89005. 1986. Poetry. circ. 200. 4/yr. Pub'd 4 issues 1998; expects 4 issues 1999, 4 issues 2000. sub. price: $15, int'l add $5 postage; per copy: $5 includes postage; sample: $5 includes postage. Back issues: $5 includes postage. 32pp; 5½×8½; †Desktop Publishing. Reporting time: 2 weeks. Simultaneous submissions accepted: no. Publishes 10-15% of manuscripts submitted. Payment: publication. Copyrighted, reverts to author. §Poetry publishing.

Pegasus Communications, Inc., Kellie T. Wardman O'Reilly, Publisher; Janice Molloy, Managing Editor, 1 Moody Street, Waltham, MA 02453-5339. 1989. Non-fiction. "Specific articles/books related to organizational learning and systems thinking (a management science). Not general management. Contributors include Daniel Kim, Peter Senge, Russell Ackoff, Jay Forrester, Margaret Wheatley, Chris Argyris. Work in team learning, shared vision, personal mastery, and action science" avg. press run 4M. Pub'd 4 titles 1998; expects 2 titles 1999, 3 titles 2000. 2 titles listed in the *Small Press Record of Books in Print* (28th Edition, 1999-00). avg. price, cloth: $29.95; paper: $16.95. Discounts: bulk, resale. 75pp; 8½×11, 6×9; of. Reporting time: 3 months. Simultaneous submissions accepted: yes. Publishes 5% of manuscripts submitted. Payment: usually sliding scale based on quantities sold, starts at 10%. Copyrights for author. PMA, SPAN.

THE PEGASUS REVIEW, Art Bounds, PO Box 88, Henderson, MD 21640-0088, 410-482-6736. 1980. Poetry, fiction, art, cartoons, satire. "Upon publication writer will receive two copies of *The Pegasus Review.* Occasional book awards throughout the year. Recommend purchasing a sample copy to better understand format ($2.50) for 1997 themes - request by SASE. Occasionally comments on returned manuscripts." circ. 130. 6/yr + special issues. Pub'd 6 issues 1998; expects 6 issues 1999, 6 issues 2000. sub. price: $10; per copy: $2.50; sample: $2.50. Back issues: $2.50. 10-12pp; 6½×8½; of. Reporting time: 4-10 weeks. Simultaneous submissions accepted: yes. Publishes 35% of manuscripts submitted. Payment: 2 copies and additional book awards (throughout year). Copyrighted, reverts to author.

Pella Publishing Co (see also THE CHARIOTEER; JOURNAL OF THE HELLENIC DIASPORA), Leandros Papathanasiou, Publisher, President, 337 West 36th Street, New York, NY 10018, 212-279-9586. 1976. Poetry, fiction, articles, art, criticism, reviews, letters, plays, non-fiction. "We are interested in Modern Greek studies and culture, but also have a general list composed of new fiction and poetry by young writers and books on contemporary society and politics. We also publish books on the work of young artists." avg. press run 3M. Pub'd 4 titles 1998; expects 10 titles 1999, 10 titles 2000. 52 titles listed in the *Small Press Record of Books in Print* (28th Edition, 1999-00). avg. price, cloth: $25; paper: $12; other: $12. Discounts: Jobbers-30%; Bookstores-20%. 176pp; 5½×8½; †lp. Reporting time: 4-6 weeks. Simultaneous submissions accepted: no. Publishes 1% of manuscripts submitted. Payment: standard royalty arrangements. Copyrights for author.

PEMBROKE MAGAZINE, Shelby Stephenson, Editor; Norman Macleod, Founding Editor, UNCP, Box 1510, Pembroke, NC 28372-1510, 919-521-4214 ext 433. 1969. Poetry, fiction, articles, art, photos, criticism, reviews. "Contributors: Felix Pollak, Fred Chappell, A.R. Ammons, Betty Adcock, Robert Morgan, Barbara Guest, Fleda Jackson, Judson Crews, Reinhold Grimm, Gerald Barrax, Ronald H. Bayes." circ. 500. 1/yr. Pub'd 2 issues 1998; expects 1 issue 1999. sub. price: $8; per copy: $8 (overseas $12.03); sample: $8.

426

Discounts: 40% bookstores. 275pp; 6×9; of. Reporting time: 1-4 months. Simultaneous submissions accepted: no. Payment: copy. Copyrighted, rights revert to author, except for right of editor to reprint the magazine and to issue a *PM* anthology. Pub's reviews: 6 in 1998. §Native American poetry and novels. Ads: $40/$25. CLMP.

PEMMICAN, Pemmican Press, Robert Edwards, PO Box 121, Redmond, WA 98073-7507. 1992. Poetry, long-poems. "No length restrictions. Biased toward political, feminist, experimental, playful. Recent contributors: Margaret Randall, Adrian Louis, Sherman Alexie, Floyce Alexander, and Olga Cabral" circ. 300. 1/yr. Pub'd 1 issue 1998; expects 1 issue 1999, 1 issue 2000. sub. price: $5; per copy: $5; sample: $4. Back issues: $3. 70pp; 7×8½; of. Reporting time: 1 week to 1 month. Simultaneous submissions accepted: yes. Publishes 5-10% of manuscripts submitted. Payment: copies. Copyrighted, reverts to author. Ads: none.

Pemmican Press (see also PEMMICAN), Robert Edwards, PO Box 121, Redmond, WA 98073-7507. 1992. Poetry, long-poems. avg. press run 300. Pub'd 2 titles 1998; expects 1 title 1999, 1 title 2000. 1 title listed in the *Small Press Record of Books in Print* (28th Edition, 1999-00). avg. price, paper: $5. Discounts: varies. Pages vary; 5½×8½; of. Reporting time: 1 month, approximately. Simultaneous submissions accepted: yes. Publishes less than 5% of manuscripts submitted. Payment: none. Copyrights for author.

PEN & INK WRITERS JOURNAL, Baker Street Publications, Sharida Rizzuto, Harold Tollison, Ann Hoyt, 577 Central Avenue, Box 4, Jefferson, LA 70121-1400, E-mail editor@inforspacemail.com, publisher@mailexcite.com, www.zines.freeservers.com, www.members.theglobe.com/zines/default.html, www2.cybercities.com/z/zines/. 1983. Poetry, fiction, articles, art, photos, cartoons, interviews, satire, criticism, reviews, letters, long-poems, non-fiction. circ. 1M. 3/yr. Pub'd 3 issues 1998; expects 3 issues 1999, 3 issues 2000. sub. price: $15/3 issues; per copy: $5; sample: $5. Back issues: $5. Discounts: trade with other like publications. 40-50pp; 5½×8½; of, excellent quality offset covers. Reporting time: 2-6 weeks. Simultaneous submissions accepted: yes. Publishes 50% of manuscripts submitted. Payment: free copies, fees paid for articles, reviews, art work. Copyrighted, reverts to author. Pub's reviews: 16 in 1998. §Writers' craft and writers' market, also artists. Ads: free. NWC, SPGA, HWA, MWA, Western Writers of America (WWA), Arizona Authors Association (AAA).

Pendaya Publications, Inc., Earl J. Mathes, Manager, 510 Woodvine Avenue, Metairie, LA 70005, 504-834-8151. 1987. Non-fiction. "Design, construction, criticism" avg. press run 2M-3M. Pub'd 1 title 1998; expects 2 titles 1999, 2 titles 2000. 2 titles listed in the *Small Press Record of Books in Print* (28th Edition, 1999-00). avg. price, cloth: $50. Discounts: upon individual request. 175pp; 8½×11; of. Reporting time: varies, 2-3 months. Publishes .005% of manuscripts submitted. Payment: varies. Does not copyright for author.

Pen-Dec Press (see also PURPLE PEEK PI; TOY RIOT JUICE; PARAMASITIC PROPISTITUTE), Jim DeWitt, Editor, 2526 Chatham Woods, Grand Rapids, MI 49546. 1978. "Unsolicited mss. & B&W art welcome. Poetry only: juiced, with zip. Must include letter of purpose, brief bio, SASE." Expects 1 title 1999, 1 title 2000. 19 titles listed in the *Small Press Record of Books in Print* (28th Edition, 1999-00). avg. price, paper: $6. 24pp; 5½×8½. Reporting time: 3 months. Simultaneous submissions accepted: yes. Publishes 1% of manuscripts submitted. Copyrights for author.

●Pendragonian Publications (see also PENNY DREADFUL: Tales and Poems of Fantastic Terror; SONGS OF INNOCENCE), M. Malefica Gredelwolf Pendragon LeFay, Michael Pendragon, PO Box 719, New York, NY 10101-0719. 1995. Poetry, fiction, art, parts-of-novels, long-poems, non-fiction. "Poetry up to 3 pages (rhymed, metered, lyrical preferred), stories set in the 19th century or earlier. *Penny Dreadful* publishes tales and poems which celebrate the darker aspects of Man, the World and their Creator (Gothic/Romantic Horror). *Songs of Innocence* publishes tales and poems which celebrate the nobler aspects of mankind and the human experience. Recent contributors to *Penny Dreadful* include: John B. Ford, Laurel Robertson, Scott Thomas, Paul Bradshaw, Nancy Bennett, G.W. Thomas, Genevieve Stephens, Karen R. Porter, James S. Dorr, Jennifer Tobkin, David Kablack, Tamera Latham, Dennis Saleh, Cathy Buburuz, and D.M. Yorton." avg. press run 500. Pub'd 1 title 1998; expects 3 titles 1999. 48pp; 5½×8½; †xerox. Reporting time: 3 months. Simultaneous submissions accepted: yes. Payment: 1 copy. Does not copyright for author.

Penfield Press, Joan Liffring-Zug, 215 Brown Street, Iowa City, IA 52245-1358, FAX 319-351-6846. 1979. Photos, non-fiction. avg. press run 2.5M-10M. Pub'd 5 titles 1998; expects 6 titles 1999, 4 titles 2000. 41 titles listed in the *Small Press Record of Books in Print* (28th Edition, 1999-00). avg. price, cloth: $18.50; paper: $6.50-$8.95. Discounts: trade 40%, jobbers 60%. 88-128pp; 6×9, 3½×5½; of. Payment: varies, usually 5%. Does not copyright for author.

Peninhand Press, Tom Janisse, 3665 Southeast Tolman, Portland, OR 97202. 1979. Poetry, fiction, art, interviews, parts-of-novels. "We publish poetry, fiction & art, both national & international. No unsolicited manuscripts at this time." avg. press run 500. Expects 1 title 1999, 1 title 2000. 2 titles listed in the *Small Press Record of Books in Print* (28th Edition, 1999-00). avg. price, paper: $3 single issue. Discounts: 1-4 25%, 5 and over 40%. 30-104pp; 5½×8½; of. Reporting time: 2 weeks to 2 months. Payment: copies. Does not copyright for author.

PENNINE PLATFORM, Dr. K.E. Smith, 7 Cockley Hill Lane, Kirkheaton, Huddersfield HD5 OHH, West Yorkshire, England, 0937-584674. 1966. Poetry, articles, art, criticism, reviews. "The magazine is supported by the Yorkshire and Humberside Arts. Tries to keep a high standard, both in poetry & art. Copyrighted for contributors who retain copyright." circ. 250. 2/yr. Pub'd 2 issues 1998; expects 2 issues 1999, 2 issues 2000. sub. price: £8 uk, £12 abroad...sterling, £17 abroad...curency, £25 if by check... not in steding; per copy: £4; sample: £4. Back issues: £2.50. Discounts: trade for books in bulk less 30%. 48pp; size A5; of. Reporting time: within 4 monts. Simultaneous submissions accepted: no. Publishes 10% of manuscripts submitted. Payment: none. Copyrighted. Pub's reviews: 10 in 1998. §Poetry. Ads: £.5.

Pennsylvania State University Press (see also SHAW: THE ANNUAL OF BERNARD SHAW STUDIES), Fred D. Crawford, Penn State Press, Suite C, 820 N. University Drive, University Park, PA 16802-1711, 814-865-1327. 1951. Articles. avg. press run 2M. Pub'd 1 title 1998; expects 1 title 1999, 1 title 2000. avg. price, cloth: $35; other: $35. Discounts: short-20%. 265pp; 6×9; of. Reporting time: 2 months. Payment: 1 copy of the volume. Copyrights for author in name of publisher. AAUP.

PENNY DREADFUL: Tales and Poems of Fantastic Terror, Pendragonian Publications, M. Malefica Grendelwolf Pendragon Le Fay, PO Box 719, New York, NY 10101-0719. 1996. Poetry, fiction, art, photos. "Art: black and white line art only. All must be in the Gothic/Horror genre." circ. 500. 3/yr. Pub'd 3 issues 1998; expects 3 issues 1999, 3 issues 2000. sub. price: $12; per copy: $5; sample: $5. Back issues: $5. 48pp; 5½×8½; †photocopy. Reporting time: 3 months maximum. Simultaneous submissions accepted: yes. Publishes 10% of manuscripts submitted. Payment: 1 free issue. Not copyrighted. Ads: Ad/swaps are arranged 2 very.

PENNY-A-LINER, Redrosebush Press, Ella M. Dillon, PO Box 2163, Wenatchee, WA 98807-2163, 509-662-7858. 1991. Poetry, fiction, articles, art, photos, cartoons, interviews, satire, criticism, reviews, letters, non-fiction. "Prefer poetry 30 lines or less, other writings 500-1,500 words. Short stories, anecdotes, articles, essays, some poetry, puzzles, word games, jokes, cartoons all being accepted now. No pornography. Original work only. Please put name and address on each page. Please type all submissions, double-spaced. Send SASE if you desire an answer." circ. 1M+. 3/yr. Pub'd 3 issues 1998; expects 3 issues 1999, 3 issues 2000. sub. price: $18; per copy: $6.50; sample: free. Back issues: $3.25. 44pp; 8½×11; of. Reporting time: when published. Simultaneous submissions accepted: yes. Payment: 1¢/word and copy. Copyrighted, reverts to author. Pub's reviews: 5 in 1998. §No pornography. Ads: $300/$200/$25 and up.

Pennycorner Press (see also THE INCLUSION NOTEBOOK), Gayle Kranz, Publisher, PO Box 8, Gilman, CT 06336, 860-873-3545, Fax 860-873-1311. 1994. Non-fiction, fiction, articles, photos, interviews, reviews. avg. press run 500-5M. Pub'd 2 titles 1998; expects 3 titles 1999, 3 titles 2000. 2 titles listed in the *Small Press Record of Books in Print* (28th Edition, 1999-00). avg. price, cloth: $20+; other: $10-15. Discounts: negotiated. 250pp; 6×9, 8×11; offset. Reporting time: 2 months. Publishes 1% of manuscripts submitted. Payment: negotiated. Copyrights for author. PMA/SPAN.

PenRose Publishing Company, Inc., Roger E. Egan, Editor-in-Chief, PO Box 620, Mystic Island, NJ 08087, 609-296-1401. 1992. "Primarily subsidy publishing. 80-120pp. or more, books—soft cover. We welcome divergent and provocative material. We will decline manuscripts that do not meet minimum literary standards or are patently offensive to any group among our multicultural readership, or include explicit sex." avg. press run 1M. Expects 3 titles 1999, 6 titles 2000. 6 titles listed in the *Small Press Record of Books in Print* (28th Edition, 1999-00). avg. price, paper: $10. Discounts: national distribution (negotiable); retail stores 40%; retail chains negotian. 80pp; 6×9; of. Reporting time: average 2 months. Payment: authors retain all rights of ownership and are offered distribution agreements. Copyrights for author. Small Press Assoc., Poetry Society of America.

Pens of Voltaire Press, 1550 Kingston Road, Unit #4, Suite 1079, Pickering, Ontario L1V 6W9, Canada, 905-509-4808; Fax 905-509-7821; Toll free 800-866-1463. 1 title listed in the *Small Press Record of Books in Print* (28th Edition, 1999-00).

Pentagram Press, Michael Tarachow, 4925 South Nicollet, Minneapolis, MN 55409, 612-824-4576. 1974. Fiction, art, long-poems. "No unsolicited manuscripts." avg. press run 100-175. Expects 1 title 1999, 1 title 2000. 5 titles listed in the *Small Press Record of Books in Print* (28th Edition, 1999-00). avg. price, cloth: $250; paper: $20-$85. 24-100pp; size varies; †lp. Payment: varies. Does not copyright for author. APHA, N.Y. Typophiles, Ampersand Club.

Pentland Press, Inc., Carol A. Mitchell, Publisher, 5122 Bur Oak Circle, Raleigh, NC 27612, 919-782-0281. 1993. Poetry, fiction, long-poems, non-fiction. avg. press run 1000. Pub'd 43 titles 1998; expects 50 titles 1999, 55 titles 2000. 45 titles listed in the *Small Press Record of Books in Print* (28th Edition, 1999-00). avg. price, cloth: $24.95; paper: $12.95. Discounts: 1-4 35%, 5-99 40%, 100+ 45%. 175pp; 6×9. Reporting time: 4-6 weeks. Simultaneous submissions accepted: no. Publishes 50% of manuscripts submitted. Payment: quarterly. Copyrights for author. Publishers Association of the South, SEBA, National Association of Independent Pubrs., Publishers Marketing Assn.

428

PEOPLE'S CULTURE, Fred Whitehead, Box 5224, Kansas City, KS 66119. 1991. "This is in newsletter format. A continuation of publication edited by John Crawford, same title, New Series, #1 (January-February 1991), etc. Recent contributors include Crawford, Meridel LeSueur, Lyle Daggett, Robert Day. Dedicated to excavating and developing progressive, radical, socialist and communist culture, in the U.S. and internationally. Each issue includes a feature on 'An American Place' usually a historic site, monument, mural painting, etc." circ. growing. 6/yr. Expects 6 issues 1999, 6 issues 2000. sub. price: $15; per copy: $3; sample: $3. Back issues: $3. 12pp; 8½×11; photocopy (good quality). Reporting time: 1 week. Payment: copies. Copyrighted, reverts to author. Pub's reviews. §Poetry, history (esp. documentation), cultural theory, art, music, etc.

●**The People's Press**, Shirley Richburg, 4810 Norwood Avenue, Baltimore, MD 21207-6839. 5 titles listed in the *Small Press Record of Books in Print* (28th Edition, 1999-00).

Peradam Press, Linda Birkholz, Patricia Hicks, PO Box 21326, Santa Barbara, CA 93121-1326. 1993. Non-fiction. "*Three Sisters of Mercy* (with the Issan culture of Thailand), 320 pages, by Annette Parkinson; *Traveling With Heart* (a handbook for the socially conscious tourist), 240 pages, by Lisa French; *Age Plus Wisdom* (the art of thriving in a retirement community), 276 pages, by Libby Rollin." avg. press run 5M. Expects 4 titles 1999, 6 titles 2000. 1 title listed in the *Small Press Record of Books in Print* (28th Edition, 1999-00). avg. price, cloth: $20; paper: $11. Discounts: 3-99 40%, 100-299 50%, 300+ 55%. 300pp; 5½×8½; of. Reporting time: 4 months. Payment: varies. Copyrights for author.

PERCEPTIONS, Temi Rose, 73 Eastcombe Avenue, London, England SE7 7LL, England. 1982. Poetry, art, cartoons. "We have international contributions. Primarily women's poetry: Jasmin Javid, Chocolate Waters, Lyn Lifshin" circ. 300. 3/yr. Pub'd 3 issues 1998; expects 3 issues 1999, 3 issues 2000. sub. price: $15; per copy: $5; sample: $5. Back issues: $7.50. Discounts: trade - 15% to seller. 40pp; 4¼×5½; of. Reporting time: 1-3 months. Payment: 1 copy. Copyrighted, reverts to author.

PEREGRINE, Amherst Writers & Artists Press, Inc., Pat Schneider, Editor; Nancy Rose, Managing Editor, PO Box 1076, Amherst, MA 01004, 413-253-7764 phone/fax; e-mail awapress@javanet.com; www.javanet.com/~awapress. 1981. Poetry, fiction, reviews. "*Peregrine* has provided a forum for national and international writers for more than 18 years and is committed to finding excellent work by new writers as well as established authors. We seek poetry and fiction that is fresh, imaginative, human, and memorable. Annual Contest: The Peregrine Prize, and The Best of the Nest. #10 SASE for guidelines." circ. 1M. 1/yr. Pub'd 1 issue 1998; expects 1 issue 1999, 1 issue 2000. sub. price: $20/3 years; per copy: $9 postpaid; sample: $8 postpaid. Back issues: varies. Discounts: call for info. 100pp; 6×9; of. Reporting time: we read Oct.-April and report on non-contest mss. within 4-6 months. Simultaneous submissions accepted: yes. Publishes 1% of manuscripts submitted. Payment: 2 copies. Copyrighted, reverts to author. Pub's reviews: 1 in 1998. §Poetry books and collections. Ads: contact for info. CLMP.

The Permanent Press/The Second Chance Press, Martin Shepard, Judith Shepard, 4170 Noyac Road, Sag Harbor, NY 11963, 516-725-1101. 1979. Fiction, satire, news items. "We publish original material and specialize in quality fiction." avg. press run 2M. Expects 12 titles 1999, 12 titles 2000. 136 titles listed in the *Small Press Record of Books in Print* (28th Edition, 1999-00). avg. price, cloth: $22; paper: $16. Discounts: 20-50%. 250pp; 5½×8½; lp. Reporting time: 8-12 weeks. Simultaneous submissions accepted: yes. Publishes .17% of manuscripts submitted. Payment: 10% net, small standard advances, for all writers. Copyrights for author. ABA.

Permeable Press (see also PUCK: The Unofficial Journal of the Irrepressible), Brian Clark, 433 S. Cleveland Street #3, Moscow, ID 83843-3793. 1984. Poetry, fiction. avg. press run 5M. Pub'd 4 titles 1998; expects 6 titles 1999, 6 titles 2000. 15 titles listed in the *Small Press Record of Books in Print* (28th Edition, 1999-00). avg. price, cloth: $19.95; paper: $11.95. Discounts: 40%-55%. 200pp; 6×9; †of. Reporting time: 2 months. Publishes 1% of manuscripts submitted. Payment: varies. Copyrights for author.

Perpetual Press, Kevin Hile, PO Box 30413, Lansing, MI 48909-7913, 800-807-3030. 1993. Photos, non-fiction. avg. press run 5-7M. Pub'd 2 titles 1998; expects 3 titles 1999. 10 titles listed in the *Small Press Record of Books in Print* (28th Edition, 1999-00). avg. price, paper: $14.95. 300pp; 5½×8½. Simultaneous submissions accepted: yes.

PERSEPHONE, John Cobb, Rodney Dennis, Andrew Lear, Ann Dane, John Harrington, c/o John Cobb, 40 Avon Hill Street, Cambridge, MA 02138. 1995. Poetry, fiction, articles, art, interviews. "*Persephone* is a Classics journal published at the Harvard Dept. of Classics. We publish *exclusively* material that has a connection to the cultures of ancient Greece and Rome. We accept unsolicited poetry, fiction, art and translations from ancient Greek and Latin (but *not* articles). Some poets from recent editions: Jean Valentine, David Ferry, William Alfred, and Paolo Valesio." circ. 500. 1/yr. Pub'd 1 issue 1998; expects 1 issue 1999, 1 issue 2000. sub. price: $15/2 years; per copy: $6; sample: $6. 96pp; 7×9; of. Reporting time: 6 months. Simultaneous submissions accepted: no. Publishes 10% of manuscripts submitted. Payment: none. Not copyrighted.

Persephone Press (see also Scots Plaid Press), Mary Belle Campbell, Editor-Publisher, 600 Kelly Road, Carthage, NC 28327, 910-947-2587; Fax 910-947-5112. 1987. Poetry, art, photos, long-poems. "Persephone Press is now an adjunct to Birch Brook Press, PO Box 81, Delhi, NY 13753 and is exclusively for poetry. Poetry Book Publication Award Endowment series is for up coming workshop leaders or career poets who have published but no more than 2 books or chapbooks. No entry fee, no application process; must be nominated 24pg. ms. recommended *by university instructors or editors*" avg. press run 250-500-1000. Pub'd 2 titles 1998; expects 5 titles 1999, 4 titles 2000. avg. price, cloth: $25; paper: $12; other: $10-$95 hardcover/folio collecters' item signed limited edition. Discounts: orders of 5 copies 30%; of 10 copies 40%. 32-64-320pp; 6×9; lp, of, digital on archival paper. Reporting time: 1-6 months. Simultaneous submissions accepted: yes. Publishes 10% of manuscripts submitted. Payment: Persephone Press Award Series now endowed; no entry fee; 80-90% of edition paid as royalties in advance. Copyrights for author. NC Writers Network, listed in P&W.

PERSIMMON, James Taylor, Mary Taylor, 19626 Damman, Harper Woods, MI 48225. 1997. Poetry. "We accept single haiku poetry, in English." circ. 100. 2/yr. Expects 2 issues 1999, 2 issues 2000. sub. price: $8; per copy: $4; sample: $4. 40pp; 3¼×9; of. Reporting time: 2-3 weeks, often sooner. Simultaneous submissions accepted: no. Publishes 30-40% of manuscripts submitted. Payment: $1 per published haiku. Copyrighted, reverts to author. Ads: none.

Personal Fitness Publishing, Cathy Brunasso, PO Box 6400, Altadena, CA 91003, 818-798-6598, fax 818-798-2254. 1995. Non-fiction. "Accept only exercise and fitness books" avg. press run 4M. Expects 2 titles 1999, 3 titles 2000. 2 titles listed in the *Small Press Record of Books in Print* (28th Edition, 1999-00). avg. price, paper: $9.95. 120pp; 5½×8½. Reporting time: 2 months. Simultaneous submissions accepted: yes. Publishes 75% of manuscripts submitted. Payment: arranged individually. Copyrights for author. ABA.

PERSPECTIVES, Transeuropa, Editorial Collective, BM 6682, London WC1N 3XX, United Kingdom. 1990. Articles, art, photos, cartoons, interviews, satire, criticism, reviews, music, letters, news items, non-fiction. "Subtitled 'European Identities, Autonomies and Initiatives,' though contributors with alternative views from outside Europe are welcome. Bias towards regionalism." circ. 10M. 2/yr. Pub'd 2 issues 1998; expects 2 issues 1999, 2 issues 2000. sub. price: $10, £5 Europe; per copy: $6, £2.50; sample: $5 (inc. post from USA), £1.50. Discounts: negotiable. 32pp; size A4. Reporting time: varies. Payment: none. Copyrighted, does not revert to author. Pub's reviews: 20 in 1998. §Radical political (green, anarchist, autonomist, etc.) folklore, avant-garde. Ads: negotiable.

Perspectives Press, Patricia Irwin Johnston, PO Box 90318, Indianapolis, IN 46290-0318, 317-872-3055. 1982. Fiction, articles, plays, non-fiction. "Established to create materials related to adoption, infertility, and foster care" avg. press run 2M-5M. Pub'd 3 titles 1998; expects 3 titles 1999, 4 titles 2000. 17 titles listed in the *Small Press Record of Books in Print* (28th Edition, 1999-00). avg. price, cloth: $21.95 adult books; $12-$14 childrens; paper: $14. Discounts: 0-50%, begins at 1 copies with 10%. Adult 144-428pp, children 32-160pp; 6×9, 5½×8½ adult, 7×10 children. Reporting time: query, 1 month. Payment: varies. Copyrights for author. PMA, ABA, MAPA.

Perugia Press, Susan Kan, PO Box 108, Shutesbury, MA 01072, E-mail skan@valinet.com. 1997. Poetry. "Publishes first or second books by women." avg. press run 500. Pub'd 1 title 1998; expects 1 title 1999, 1 title 2000. 2 titles listed in the *Small Press Record of Books in Print* (28th Edition, 1999-00). avg. price, paper: $10.95. Discounts: standard. 88pp; 6×9; of. Reporting time: 1 month. Simultaneous submissions accepted: yes. Payment: none available. Copyrights for author.

The Petrarch Press, Peter Bishop, PO Box 488, Oregon House, CA 95962, 916-692-0828. 1985. Poetry, non-fiction. "The Petrarch Press specializes in publishing fine press books, using handpresses and quality papers. Literature that is deemed appropriate for the medium is considered. Our interests are diverse; the first two books from the press are 1800 years apart in the time of their writing, (the apostle Thomas and R.M. Rilke). Thus far I have not been looking at submitted mss." avg. press run 175. Pub'd 1 title 1998; expects 3 titles 1999, 5 titles 2000. 4 titles listed in the *Small Press Record of Books in Print* (28th Edition, 1999-00). avg. price, cloth: $150. Discounts: varies. 65pp; 6¼×9½; †lp. Payment: varies. Does not copyright for author.

Petroglyph Press, Ltd., 160 Kamekameha Avenue, Hilo, HI 96720-2834, 808-935-6006; www.basicallybooks.com. 1962. Non-fiction. avg. press run 2M. Pub'd 1 title 1998; expects 2 titles 1999, 2 titles 2000. avg. price, paper: $7.95. Discounts: 40% trade, 50% jobber, 55% 500+ books. 90pp; 5½×8½; †of. Payment: 10% author, 5% illustrator; paid quarterly. Does not copyright for author.

Pfeifer-Hamilton, Donald A. Tubesing, Nancy Loving Tubesing, 210 West Michigan, Duluth, MN 55802-1908, 218-727-0500; FAX 218-727-0620. 1977. Non-fiction. "*Regional books*: 'How-to', geography, guide books, essays and stories, field guide in upper Midwest USA, children's books." avg. press run 10M. Pub'd 5 titles 1998; expects 8 titles 1999, 10 titles 2000. 55 titles listed in the *Small Press Record of Books in Print* (28th Edition, 1999-00). avg. price, cloth: $16.95; paper: $14.95. Discounts: normal book trade conventions. 192pp; 6×9; web. Reporting time: 2 weeks. Payment: varies. Copyrights for author. PMA, Mid

America Publishers, ABA, Minnesota Independent Publishers.

Phantom Press Publications (see also RENAISSANCE MAGAZINE), Kim Guarnaccia, Editor-in-Chief, 13 Appleton Road, Nantucket, MA 02554-4307. 1989. Fiction, non-fiction. "Will consider any length material - always include an SASE with submission." Expects 1 title 1999, 1 title 2000. 1 title listed in the *Small Press Record of Books in Print* (28th Edition, 1999-00). avg. price, paper: $9.95. Discounts: 40% thru distributor. 144pp; 8½x11; of. Reporting time: 3-6 weeks. Simultaneous submissions accepted: yes. Publishes 10% of manuscripts submitted. Payment: contributors copies only. Does not copyright for author.

Phelps Publishing Company, PO Box 22401, Cleveland, OH 44122, 216-433-2531, 216-295-2181. 1993. Art. avg. press run 5M. Expects 2 titles 1999, 3 titles 2000. 4 titles listed in the *Small Press Record of Books in Print* (28th Edition, 1999-00). avg. price, paper: $5.95. Discounts: jobber 55%, trade 40%, bulk 65-75%. 36pp; 6⅝x10¼. Reporting time: 6-8 weeks. ABA.

PHILATELIC LITERATURE NEWS INTERNATIONAL, Corn Nieuwland, Brandespad 14, NL-3067 EB Rotterdam, Holland. 1991. Reviews, news items. circ. 250. 4/yr. Pub'd 4 issues 1998; expects 4 issues 1999, 4 issues 2000. sub. price: $10 surface, $12 air; sample: $3 (airmail). Back issues: on request. 20-28pp; size A5; †photostat. Not copyrighted. Pub's reviews: 600 in 1998. §Exclusively philatelic publications, press releases, etc.

Phillips Publications, Inc., Jim Phillips, PO Box 168, Williamstown, NJ 08094, 609-567-0695. 1972. Photos, news items. "Information and items needed for forthcoming books on WW II U.S. Airborne uniforms and equipment book, and U.S. Special Forces book, espionage, spycraft, weapons and equipment." avg. press run 500-5M. Pub'd 1 title 1998; expects 3 titles 1999, 3 titles 2000. 5 titles listed in the *Small Press Record of Books in Print* (28th Edition, 1999-00). avg. price, cloth: $19.95-$49.95; paper: $9.95. Discounts: 40%, 3 or more 20% single title, 50% case rate. 35-400pp; 6x9, 8½x11; †of. Reporting time: 1 month. Payment: 20% after publication & ad costs. Copyrights for author.

Philomel Books, Patricia Lee Gauch, Editorial Director; Michael Green, Editor; Alison Keehn, Editorial Assistant, 345 Hudson Street, New York, NY 10014, 212-414-3610. 1980. Poetry, fiction, non-fiction. "We are a hardcover children's trade book list. Our primary emphasis is on picturebooks, with a small number of young adult novels and middle grade novels. We publish some poetry. We look for fresh and innovative books imbued with a child's spirit and crafted with fine writing and art. Recent selections include *Akiak* by Robert J. Blake and *The Lost Years of Merlin* by T.A. Barron" avg. press run 5M-10M. Expects 25 titles 1999. avg. price, cloth: $15.95. Novels 200pp, picturebooks 32pp; size varies. Reporting time: 2 months on queries, 3 months on manuscripts. Simultaneous submissions accepted: yes. Publishes 1% of manuscripts submitted. Payment: varies. Does not copyright for author. Children's Book Council.

Philopsychy Press, Stephen Palmquist, PO Box 1224, Shatin Central, N.T., Hong Kong, phone/fax 852-26044403; email ppp@hkbu.edu.hk; www.hkbu.edu.hk/~ppp/ppp/intro.html. 1993. Articles, non-fiction. avg. press run 1M. Pub'd 2 titles 1998; expects 1 title 1999, 2 titles 2000. 4 titles listed in the *Small Press Record of Books in Print* (28th Edition, 1999-00). avg. price, paper: $8 U.S., HK $65. Discounts: bookstores 25% on consignment sales; 40% on advance payment. 200pp; 6x9; of. Reporting time: 1 month. Simultaneous submissions accepted: yes. Payment: negotiable. Copyrights for author.

PHOEBE: A JOURNAL OF LITERARY ARTS, Kurt Olsson, Editor; Charles Fox, Editor, G.M.U. 4400 University Dr., Fairfax, VA 22030, 703-993-2915. 1970. Poetry, fiction, photos, plays. "We are interested in publishing a wide diversity of poetry and fiction. Additionally, we now accept non-fiction, preferably personal and/or experimental." circ. 3M. 2/yr. Pub'd 2 issues 1998; expects 2 issues 1999, 2 issues 2000. sub. price: $8; per copy: $4; sample: $4. Back issues: $4. 108pp; 6x9; of. Reporting time: 2-3 months. Publishes 5% of manuscripts submitted. Payment: copies only. Copyrighted, reverts to author.

PHOENIX MAGAZINE, Phoenix Press, R.C. Poynter, PO Box 17, Berkeley, CA 94701-0317. 1996. Poetry, criticism, reviews, long-poems. "*Phoenix Magazine* began as a saddle-stapled 64-page 5x7" format; it was published quarterly its first year but has now become an annual. Poetry and some poetry reviews; no stories, art at this time. Poetry is political, controversial, Beat, confessional - we do not censor language or subject other than that we will not publish hate material or material which is disparaging to any specific individual's beliefs." circ. 5-10M. 1/yr. Pub'd 4 issues 1998; expects 1 issue 1999, 1 issue 2000. price per copy: $16.95; sample: $10 old issues #1-4. Discounts: we send free to prisons, hospitals, shelters; we will send free of charge to individuals if they request hardship consideration, must write for information. 140pp; 8½x11. Reporting time: 1-2 weeks. Simultaneous submissions accepted: yes. Publishes 60% of manuscripts submitted. Payment: copies. Copyrighted, reverts to author. Pub's reviews: 8 in 1998. §Only poetry books, chapbooks, magazines, and some biographies of poets; we are most interested, however, in the former. Ads: $75/$45/$2 per word. Bay Area Poets Network, Small Business/Berkeley.

Phoenix Press (see also PHOENIX MAGAZINE), R.C. Poynter, G. Hall, PO Box 317, Berkeley, CA

94701-0317. 1996. Poetry, interviews, satire, reviews, letters. "Chapbooks, some full-length collections of poetry, anthologies of poets edited and compiled by both the editors of Phoenix Press and outside individuals. No hate material - we will not publish racist, homophobic or hurtful materials. We enjoy working with imprisoned, disabled, and those in emotional recovery/the homeless, politically motivated individuals." avg. press run chapbooks 30. Pub'd 16 titles 1998; expects 26 titles 1999, 50-60 titles 2000. 3 titles listed in the *Small Press Record of Books in Print* (28th Edition, 1999-00). avg. price, paper: $14-$17; other: $6-8 chapbooks. Discounts: we mail free to hospitals, prisons, shelters, etc. We will allow individuals to request hardship discounts, write for info. Chapbooks 30pp, paperbacks 60-100pp; 5×7; †of. Reporting time: 2 weeks to 1 month. Simultaneous submissions accepted: yes. Publishes 50% of manuscripts submitted. Payment: co-op subsidy re: chapbooks for 1st editions; straight royalties for second and beyond editions. Copyrights for author. Bay Area Poets Network, Small Businesses/Berkeley, Poet's Market.

●**Phony Lid Publications (see also VAGABOND),** K. Vaughn Dessaint, PO Box 2153, Rosemead, CA 91770, e-mail vagrag@mindspring.com. 1998. Poetry, fiction, articles, art, photos, cartoons, interviews, satire, music, letters, non-fiction. "We accept manuscripts of any length with a focus on post punk urban gore." avg. press run 300 poetry, 500 fiction. Pub'd 4 titles 1998; expects 10 titles 1999, 20 titles 2000. avg. price, paper: $5. Discounts: 25%. 48pp; 5½×8½; †of, laser, Docutech, inkjet. Reporting time: 2 months. Simultaneous submissions accepted: yes. Publishes 10-20% of manuscripts submitted. Payment: 25%. Copyrights for author.

Photo Data Research, Arthur Evans, 800 S. Pacific Coast Highway, Suite 8332, Redondo Beach, CA 90277, 310-543-1085. 1989. Photos. "Usually 150 pages. Books regarding cameras, how to buy and sell new and used camera equipment, reference on Nikon equipment, career possibilities in photography." avg. press run 5M. Pub'd 1 title 1998; expects 2 titles 1999, 5 titles 2000. 7 titles listed in the *Small Press Record of Books in Print* (28th Edition, 1999-00). avg. price, paper: $19.95. Discounts: see Login Publishers Consortium (800) 626-4330; 1-4 20%, 5-24 42%, 25-49 44%, 50-99 46%, 100+ 48%. 150pp; 8½×11; of. Reporting time: 1 month. Payment: contract. Does not copyright for author. PMA.

PHOTOBULLETIN, Rohn Engh, Publisher; Tracy Rutledge, Editor, PhotoSource International, Pine Lake Farm, Osceola, WI 54020, (715) 248-3800, Our Fax# 715-248-7394. 1985. Photos, reviews, news items. "*Photobulletin* lists major book publishers and magazines." circ. 172. 50/yr. Pub'd 50 issues 1998; expects 50 issues 1999, 50 issues 2000. sub. price: $540; per copy: $11 (facimile); sample: $3. 3pp; 8½×11; of. Reporting time: 1 week. Payment: 25¢ per word. Copyrighted. No ads.

PHOTOGRAPHY IN NEW YORK, INTERNATIONAL, Bill Mindlin, 64 West 89th Street, New York, NY 10024, 212-787-0401, Fax 212-799-3014. 1988. Articles, photos, interviews, reviews, news items. "*Photography in New York* is a bimonthly pocket guide to current gallery N.Y.C., national and international and museum exhibitions, private dealers, authors, events, and a directory of services." circ. 8M. 6/yr. Pub'd 6 issues 1998; expects 6 issues 1999, 6 issues 2000. sub. price: $18; per copy: $2.95; sample: $5. Discounts: returnable: 40% (min. 20), nonreturnable: (min 10) 49%. 100pp; 4×9; †of. Reporting time: 5 weeks. Publishes 0% of manuscripts submitted. Copyrighted, reverts to author. Pub's reviews: 10+ in 1998. §Photography. Ads: $795/$474; discounts for contracts.

THE PHOTOLETTER, Rohn Engh, Publisher; Kathy Kay, Photography Editor; Tracy Rutledge, Editor, PhotoSource International, Pine Lake Farm, Osceola, WI 54020, (715) 248-3800, Our Fax # 715-248-7394. 1976. Photos, reviews, news items. "*The Photoletter* is a photo marketing newsletter (monthly) which pairs picture buyers with photographers." circ. 1.4M. 12/yr. Pub'd 12 issues 1998; expects 12 issues 1999, 12 issues 2000. sub. price: $110; per copy: $9; sample: $9. Back issues: $3 each; 4 for $10. 4pp; 8½×11; of. Reporting time: 1 week. Payment: 15¢ word. Copyrighted. Pub's reviews: 2-3 in 1998. §Photography. Ads: inserts 10¢ each. Newsletter Association of America.

PHOTOSTOCKNOTES, Angel Dober, Pine Lake Farm, Osceola, WI 54020, 715-248-3800; FAX 715-248-7394; E-mail info@ohotosource.com. 1993. circ. 723. 12/yr. sub. price: $36; sample: $5. 8pp; 8½×11. Pub's reviews.

Phrygian Press (see also ZYX), Arnold Skemer, 58-09 205th Street, Bayside, NY 11364. 1984. Fiction. "Focus is on innovative fiction. In 1995, published Arnold Skemer's D, part of novella-continuum, i.e., a series of novellae constituting a unity. Approximate completion in 2015. This and other works published in micro editions of 100. Basic size, 5 1/2 X 8 1/2. Occasionally will do 8 1/2 X 11, such as Skemer's *The Occupation* (1996). Binding done in house. In 1997, published Skemer's *Momus*, a novella-in-a-box, a 'shufflebook,' of unbound text to be read in random order. Future projects by invitation only, from pool of editor's small press colleagues. Query if it is your desire. We are considering chapbook series and will announce future developments" avg. press run 100. Pub'd 1 title 1998; expects 1 title 1999, 1 title 2000. 7 titles listed in the *Small Press Record of Books in Print* (28th Edition, 1999-00). avg. price, paper: $6. Discounts: libraries and institutions 20%; wholesalers and bookstores 1-4 30%. 108pp; 5½×8½; xe. Reporting time: timely. Simultaneous submissions accepted: no. Payment: negotiable. Copyrights for author.

432

Picaro Press, Caroline Smith, 700 North Colorado Blvd. #124, Denver, CO 80206-1304, www.picaro.com. 1998. Poetry, fiction. "Accepts highest quality mainstream fiction and poetry-no genre or traditional poems. No simultaneous submissions. Query with S.A.S.E." avg. press run 3-5M. Pub'd 1 title 1998; expects 1 title 1999, 2 titles 2000. 1 title listed in the *Small Press Record of Books in Print* (28th Edition, 1999-00). avg. price, cloth: $19.95; paper: $12.95. Discounts: Complete discount schedule available by calling 1-800-247-6553. Pages vary; of. Reporting time: 2-6 weeks. Simultaneous submissions accepted: no. Publishes 1-2% of manuscripts submitted. Payment: negotiable. Copyrights for author.

Piccadilly Books, Bruce Fife, PO Box 25203, Colorado Springs, CO 80936, 719-550-9887. 1985. Photos, cartoons, reviews. avg. press run 3M. Pub'd 4 titles 1998; expects 3 titles 1999, 3 titles 2000. 27 titles listed in the *Small Press Record of Books in Print* (28th Edition, 1999-00). avg. price, paper: $15. Discounts: 2-5 20%, 6-49 40%, 50-99 45%, 100-99-50%, 200+ 55%. 150pp; 8½×5½, 8½×11; of. Reporting time: 6 weeks. Payment: negotiable. Copyrights for author. PMA.

Pickle Point Publishing, Bonnie Stewart Mickelson, PO Box 4107, Bellevue, WA 98009, 206-641-7424. 1988. "Cookbooks" avg. press run 15M. Expects 1 title 1999, 3 titles 2000. avg. price, cloth: $23.95; paper: $16.95. Discounts: retail 40%, schedule adjusted to quantity. 220pp. Reporting time: varies. Payment: negotiated. Copyrights for author. PMA—Hermosa Beach, CA; NWABP—Marylhurst, OR; BPNW—Seattle, WA.

Pictorial Histories Pub. Co., Stan Cohen, 713 S. 3rd Street, Missoula, MT 59801, 406-549-8488. 1976. Non-fiction. "Only do history books, mainly military." avg. press run 2-3M. Pub'd 8 titles 1998; expects 5 titles 1999, 5 titles 2000. 1 title listed in the *Small Press Record of Books in Print* (28th Edition, 1999-00). avg. price, cloth: $24.95; paper: $12.95. Discounts: trade 40%, distributor 55%. 180pp; 8½×11; of. Reporting time: 1 month. Publishes 10% of manuscripts submitted. Payment: 10%. Copyrights for author. Rocky Mtn. Book Publishers.

Picturesque Publications, BJ Wheeler, PO Box 6175, Newport News, VA 23606, 757-249-1538. 1997. Fiction. "Additional address: 315 Dominion Drive, Newport News, VA 23602" avg. press run 3M. Expects 1 title 1999, 3 titles 2000. 1 title listed in the *Small Press Record of Books in Print* (28th Edition, 1999-00). Simultaneous submissions accepted: yes.

PIEDMONT LITERARY REVIEW, Gail White, Poetry Editor; Olga Kronmeyer, Fiction Editor; Dorothy McLaughlin, Oriental Verse Editor; William R. Smith, Newsletter Editior-Publisher, 3750 Woodside Avenue, Lynchburg, VA 24503. 1976. Poetry, fiction, reviews, news items, non-fiction. "All poetry forms and some...short prose as short stories; s.s. to 2,500 words. Poetry editor enjoys rhyme, meter, free verse, and coherence. Additional address: 1017 Spanish Mass Lane, Breaux Bridge LA 70517. Send subscriptions and copy guideline requests to William Smith." circ. 400. 4/yr. Pub'd 4 issues 1998; expects 4 issues 1999, 4 issues 2000. sub. price: $15, includes Piedmont Literary Society Membership with quarterly Newsletter; Literary Review and $25 foreign; per copy: $4, $3 pre-publication, $6 foreign ex Canada; sample: $4, $6 foreign ex Canada. Back issues: $4. Discounts: 10 or more copies; 25% discount. 42pp (plus newsletter); 5×9; of. Reporting time: 8-12 weeks. Simultaneous submissions accepted if we are told. Publishes 15% of manuscripts submitted. Payment: copies. Copyrighted, reverts to author. Pub's reviews: 6 in 1998. §Haiku and other poetry publications, particularly by members. Piedmont Literary Society.

Pierian Press, Ilene F. Rockman, C. Edward Wall, PO Box 1808, Ann Arbor, MI 48106, 313-434-5530, Fax; 313-434-6409. 1968. 115 titles listed in the *Small Press Record of Books in Print* (28th Edition, 1999-00).

PIG IRON, Pig Iron Press, Jim Villani, Editor, 26 North Phelps Street, PO Box 237, Youngstown, OH 44501, 216-747-6932; fax 216-747-0599. 1974. Poetry, fiction, articles, art, photos, cartoons, letters, long-poems, collages, plays, concrete art. "The high-energy series of popular culture, thematic anthologies. The voice of the cutting edge. Length: open. Style/bias: open. Paper only. Recent contributors: Louis McKee, Maggie Jaffe, Jim Elledge, Lloyd Mills, John Druska, Jim Sanderson, Andrena Zawinski, Marian Steele, T. Lane Millet, Joan Kincaid, Frank Polite, Richard Kostelanetz" circ. 1M. 1/yr. Pub'd 1 issue 1998; expects 2 issues 1999, 3 issues 2000. sub. price: $12.95; per copy: $12.95; sample: $6. Back issues: write for backlist. Discounts: booksellers/3 or more copies 20%. 128pp; 8½×11; of. Reporting time: 6 months. Simultaneous submissions accepted: no. Publishes 2% of manuscripts submitted. Payment: 2 copies, $5 per page fiction, $5 per poem. Copyrighted, reverts to author. Pub's reviews: 1 in 1998. §Themes. No ads. CLMP.

Pig Iron Press (see also PIG IRON), Jim Villani, Editor, 26 North Phelps Street, PO Box 237, Youngstown, OH 44501, 216-747-6932; fax 216-747-0599. 1974. Poetry, fiction, art, photos, collages, non-fiction. "Sponsors the Kenneth Patchen Competition. Awards, annually, to the selected ms. paperback publication. Fiction in even years, poetry in odd years. Judged by a writer of literary stature. Reading fee: $10" avg. press run 1M. Pub'd 1 title 1998; expects 2 titles 1999, 2 titles 2000. 27 titles listed in the *Small Press Record of Books in Print* (28th Edition, 1999-00). avg. price, paper: $10.95. Discounts: bookstores 20% (1-3 copies), libraries 10%. Pages open; 5½×8½; of. Reporting time: 6 months. Simultaneous submissions accepted: no. Publishes 2% of manuscripts submitted. Payment: 10%, no advance. Copyrights for author. CLMP.

Piggy Bank Press, C. Mitch Gallon, 5277 Talbot's Landing, Ellicott City, MD 21043, Fax 410-744-7121; Telephone 410-455-9410. 1993. Articles, cartoons, non-fiction. "Unsolicited manuscripts to be sent to: PO Box 2789, Columbia, MD 21045-1789. All printed matter related to personal finance for young adults welcome." avg. press run 2.5M-5M. Pub'd 1 title 1998; expects 5 titles 1999, 20 titles 2000. 1 title listed in the *Small Press Record of Books in Print* (28th Edition, 1999-00). avg. price, cloth: $30; paper: $20. Discounts: trade 40%, bulk 505. 150-200pp; 8½×11; of. Reporting time: 6 months to 1 year. Payment: 6-10%, payment arrangement negotiable. Copyrights for author. PMA.

Pikes Peak Press, 321 W. Henrietta Ave., Suite A, PO Box 1801, Woodland Park, CO 80866-1801, 719-687-1499; FAX 719-687-4127. 1996. Non-fiction. "Offering educational/technical material for hardware computer technicians. No software! Recent contributor: Tony Jomaa with our first title, *Monitors Made Simple.*" avg. press run 5M. Expects 2 titles 1999, 3 titles 2000. 1 title listed in the *Small Press Record of Books in Print* (28th Edition, 1999-00). avg. price, paper: $15. Discounts: 2-9 20%, 10-99 30%, 100-249 35%, 250+ 40%, no return basis min. 10 copies 45%, educational 20+ copies 45%, no returns accepted. 150pp; 7×10; of. Reporting time: 2 months. Simultaneous submissions accepted: yes. Payment: negotiable. Copyrights for author. PMA.

PIKEVILLE REVIEW, Elgin M. Ward, Editor, Humanities Department, Pikeville College, Pikeville, KY 41501, 606-432-9612. 1987. Poetry, fiction, articles, interviews, reviews. "We publish contemporary fiction and poetry, interviews, creative essays and book reviews. We offer a $50 fiction award with each issue and a $50 essay award." circ. 500. 1/yr. Pub'd 1 issue 1998; expects 1 issue 1999, 1 issue 2000. sub. price: $4; per copy: $4; sample: $3. Back issues: $2. 112pp; 5½×8½; of. Reporting time: 4 months. Simultaneous submissions accepted: no. Payment: copies. Copyrighted, reverts to author. Pub's reviews: 2 in 1998. Ads: $100/$50.

Pinched Nerves Press, Steven Hartman, 1610 Avenue P, Apt. 6-B, Brooklyn, NY 11229. 1989. Poetry. "Publish local poets in NYC area. Magazine *Make Room for Dada* is published irregularly." avg. press run 150. Pub'd 4 titles 1998; expects 2 titles 1999, 2 titles 2000. 3 titles listed in the *Small Press Record of Books in Print* (28th Edition, 1999-00). avg. price, other: $1 xerox. 8pp; 4¼×11; xerox. Payment: none. Does not copyright for author.

Pinchgut Press, Marjorie Pizer, 6 Oaks Avenue, Cremorne, Sydney, N.S.W. 2090, Australia, 02-9908-2402. 1948. Poetry, fiction, non-fiction. "Australian poetry in particular, psychology (i.e., self help)." avg. press run 1.2M-3M. Pub'd 1 title 1998. 14 titles listed in the *Small Press Record of Books in Print* (28th Edition, 1999-00). avg. price, paper: $17. Discounts: usual trade discounts. of. Reporting time: quite quickly. Payment: 10% retail price.

Pine Grove Press, Gertrude S. Eiler, PO Box 85, Jamesville, NY 13078, 315-423-9268. 1989. Poetry, fiction. "We have recently switched from our journal, *Just a Moment*, to a new literary anthology, entitled *Reader's Break*. We specialize in publishing short stories and poetry by authors *whose works have been previously published or not.* The emphasis is on quality. Authors we have published include Edwidge Danticat (1995 Book Award nominee)." avg. press run 750. Pub'd 3 titles 1998; expects 4 titles 1999, 4 titles 2000. 7 titles listed in the *Small Press Record of Books in Print* (28th Edition, 1999-00). avg. price, paper: $15. Discounts: 40% bookstores, 20% libraries. 250pp; 5¼×8¼; lp. Reporting time: 6-8 weeks. Simultaneous submissions accepted reluctantly. Publishes 10% of manuscripts submitted. Payment: 1 copy of book. Copyrights revert to author on publication.

PINE ISLAND JOURNAL OF NEW ENGLAND POETRY, Linda Porter, PO Box 317, West Springfield, MA 01090. 1998. Poetry. "Submissions limited to poets currently residing in New England. Up to thirty lines, haiku and other forms welcome, no horror, or erotica. No previously published material, please incluse SASE." circ. 100. 3/yr. Pub'd 1 issue 1998; expects 3 issues 1999, 3 issues 2000. sub. price: $15; per copy: $5; sample: $5. 32pp; 5½×8. Reporting time: 2-4 weeks. Simultaneous submissions accepted: no. Publishes 20% of manuscripts submitted. Payment: $1 per poem, plus one copy. Copyrighted, reverts to author.

Pine Press, Janet Pellam, Kerry Shawn Keys, RR 1 Box 198B, Loysville, PA 17047-9726, 717-789-4466. 1977. Poetry. "Chapbooks and poetry books of approx. 64 pages. No biases. Some recent authors: Hailji (Rim, Jong-joo), Craig Czury, Janet Pellam, Brian Young, and Michael Jennings." avg. press run 500. Pub'd 5 titles 1998; expects 7 titles 1999, 7 titles 2000. 13 titles listed in the *Small Press Record of Books in Print* (28th Edition, 1999-00). avg. price, paper: $6. Discounts: 40% jobbers. 36pp; 5½×8; of. Reporting time: 6 months. Payment: cash on publication plus 100 copies. Copyrights for author.

Pine Publications, 2947 Jerusalem Avenue, Wantagh, NY 11793-2020, 516-781-0707. 1997. Non-fiction. avg. press run 2M. Expects 1 title 1999, 2 titles 2000. 1 title listed in the *Small Press Record of Books in Print* (28th Edition, 1999-00). avg. price, paper: $65. 400pp; 8½×10⅞; of. Simultaneous submissions accepted: no. Copyrights for author.

Pineapple Press, Inc., June Cussen, PO Box 3899, Sarasota, FL 34230-3899, 941-359-0886, Fax

941-351-9988. 1982. Fiction, non-fiction. "We publish hard and soft cover adult trade fiction and nonfiction." avg. press run 3M+. Pub'd 20 titles 1998; expects 20 titles 1999, 18 titles 2000. 137 titles listed in the *Small Press Record of Books in Print* (28th Edition, 1999-00). avg. price, cloth: $21.95; paper: $12.95. Discounts: trade: 1-3 copies 20%; 4-15 copies 40%; 16-49 42%; 50-99 43%; 100-199 44%; 200+ 46%. 300pp; 5½x8½, 6x9, 8½x11; of, lo. Reporting time: 3 months. Simultaneous submissions accepted: yes. Publishes less than 1% of manuscripts submitted. Payment: negotiable. Copyrights for author. BISAC, PAS.

PINYON POETRY, Randy Phillis, Al Learst, Dept. of Languages, Lit., & Comm., Mesa State College, Grand Junction, CO 81502-2647, 970-248-1740. Poetry, reviews, long-poems. "No bias other than quality, though we appreciate a strong voice" circ. 200. 2/yr. Pub'd 2 issues 1998; expects 2 issues 1999, 2 issues 2000. sub. price: $8; per copy: $4.50; sample: $3.50. Back issues: $3.50. Discounts: standard. 48pp; 5½x8½; of. Reporting time: 8-12 weeks. Simultaneous submissions accepted: no. Publishes 5% of manuscripts submitted. Payment: copies. Copyrighted, reverts to author. Pub's reviews: 8 in 1998. §Small press poetry books & poetry chapbooks.

THE PIPE SMOKER'S EPHEMERIS, Tom Dunn, 20-37 120th Street, College Point, NY 11356-2128. 1964. Poetry, fiction, articles, art, photos, cartoons, interviews, satire, criticism, reviews, letters, parts-of-novels, collages, news items. circ. 5M. 2/yr. Pub'd 2 issues 1998; expects 2 issues 1999, 2 issues 2000. 84-96pp; 8½x11; of. Reporting time: immediately. Simultaneous submissions accepted: yes. Publishes 70% of manuscripts submitted. Payment: copies of journal. Copyrighted. Pub's reviews: 12 in 1998. §Tobacco, pipe smoking, cigars, books about books, smoking tobacco collectibles. TUCOPS.

Pipeline Press, Pam Richardson, Managing Editor, PO Box 9255, Chapel Hill, NC 27515-9255, 919-933-6480 phone/fax; E-mail joelbush@mindspring.com. 1997. Non-fiction. avg. press run 5M-10M. Expects 6 titles 1999, 12 titles 2000. 2 titles listed in the *Small Press Record of Books in Print* (28th Edition, 1999-00). avg. price, paper: $24.95. 300pp; 7x9; web. Reporting time: 6 weeks. Simultaneous submissions accepted: yes. Payment: standard. Copyrights for author.

PIPERS MAGAZINE, Aircraft Owners Group, Jodi Lindquist, Editor, PO Box 5000, Iola, WI 54945, 715-445-5000; e-mail piper@aircraftownergroup.com. Articles, photos, interviews. "Aimed at owners and pilots of Piper aircraft." circ. 3,978. 12/yr. Pub'd 12 issues 1998; expects 12 issues 1999, 12 issues 2000. sub. price: $42, includes membership in Piper Owner Society; per copy: $4; sample: free on request. Back issues: $3. Discounts: subscription only. 48pp; 8½x11; desktop, litho. Reporting time: varies. Payment: 5¢/word and up, on publication. Copyrighted, rights revert to author after 30 days. Pub's reviews: 6 in 1998. §Aviation, pilot's skills and experiences. Ads: call for media kit.

PIRATE WRITINGS, DNA Publications, Inc., Edward J. McFadden, Editor, PO Box 329, Brightwaters, NY 11718-0329, E-mail pwpubl@aol.com. 1992. Poetry, fiction, art, reviews. "Business Address (Publisher): PO Box 2988 Radford, VA 24143. *Pirate Writings* is a collection of contemporary, energetic, socially relevant, imaginative short stories and poems by 'under' published and experienced writers. Our theme is anything from the down deep to...the way out. Fiction: Sci/Fi, fantasy, mystery/suspense. 8000 words. Short shorts: 750-2000 words. No crude language or excessive violence. No 'hard' horror, western or romance. Manuscripts should be typed, double spaced and word count, name address should appear on the first page. Please send a cover letter. Poetry: All forms, all lengths, all styles - within our genres. Art: Send photocopied samples of your work. If selected, a topic list will follow. My goal is to provide a diverse, entertaining and thought-provoking magazine featuring sci/fi, fantasy and mystery in every issue. Hints: I love a good ending. Send only your best." circ. 7M. 4/yr. Pub'd 4 issues 1998; expects 4 issues 1999. sub. price: $15; per copy: $5; sample: $5. Back issues: $5. Discounts: available on request. 80pp; 4x2; lp. Reporting time: 1-2 months. Payment: 1¢-5¢ per word. Copyrighted, reverts to author. Pub's reviews: 50 in 1998. §Sci-fi, fantasy, mystery. Ads: $275 back cover;$150 last page;$125 page. SPWAO.

Pittenbruach Press, Teddy Milne, 15 Walnut Street, PO Box 553, Northampton, MA 01061. 1986. Poetry, fiction, non-fiction. "Not seeking manuscripts just now. Please no submissions" avg. press run 200. Expects 3 titles 1999, 3-4 titles 2000. 26 titles listed in the *Small Press Record of Books in Print* (28th Edition, 1999-00). avg. price, paper: $9.95. Discounts: 1-5 20% prepaid, 6+ 40% prepaid. 200pp; 5½x8½; electrostatic. Payment: varies. QUIP.

Pittore Euforico (see also ME MAGAZINE), Carlo Pittore, PO Box 182, Bowdoinham, ME 04008, 207-666-8453. 1978. Poetry, fiction, art, photos, satire, music, letters, parts-of-novels, collages, concrete art. "Contributors include: Bern Porter, Charlie Morrow, Richard Kostelanez, Bill Jacobson, Bob Holman, Jeff Wright, Rainer Wiens, Laura Dean, Katherine Bradford. Titles include: *Colleagues* edited by Carlo Pittore; *Maine Moments in New York* edited by Carlo Pittore; *Yurtyet* edited by Carlo Pittore; *The Adventures of Carlo Pittore* by Carlo Pittore." avg. press run 750. Pub'd 4 titles 1998; expects 5 titles 1999. 18 titles listed in the *Small Press Record of Books in Print* (28th Edition, 1999-00). avg. price, paper: $6. Discounts: trade 40%. 100pp; 8½x11; of. Reporting time: 2 months. Payment: not yet. Copyrights for author. MWPA.

The Place In The Woods (see also READ, AMERICA!), Roger A. Hammer, Editor & Publisher, 3900

Glenwood Avenue, Golden Valley, MN 55422, 612-374-2120. 1980. Poetry, art, photos, interviews, criticism, reviews, letters, news items, non-fiction. "SAN 689-058X. Primarily interested in short biographies (and art) on significant achievements by American minorities—African-American, Women, Native People, Seniors, Handicapped/Disabled, Hispanic, War Vets, Gay/Lesbians, Young Achievers, Business Person, Asian/Pacific, other minority persons with significant but *little-known* contributions to the American culture. Well-documented personalities (such as African-Americans in sports or entertainment) are unacceptable. Interested in developing role models for minorities (adults and children). Need talented illustrators at whatever level, age who speak for their minority. Bios can run 50 to 500 words. Pays for completed work or leads. Queries recommended. Also looking for new material with themes appealing to elementary through seconday educational levels. Should be creative and original—subjects not found in general textbooks, yet of interest to mainstream Americans, young and adult." avg. press run 2M. Pub'd 1 title 1998; expects 2 titles 1999, 4 titles 2000. 9 titles listed in the *Small Press Record of Books in Print* (28th Edition, 1999-00). avg. price, paper: $9.95. Discounts: 40% wholesaler/distributor; 40% to RIF programs; quantity rates on request. 30-80pp; 8½×11; †of. Reporting time: 1 week. Publishes 50% of manuscripts submitted. Payment: royalties vary with material, buys all rights with liberal reprint permission. Does not copyright for author.

PLAIN BROWN WRAPPER (PBW), Richard Freeman, 130 West Limestone, Yellow Springs, OH 45387, 513-767-7416. 1988. Poetry, fiction, articles, art, criticism, reviews, parts-of-novels, long-poems, non-fiction. "*PBW* comes out on floppy disc for Macintosh computers, so the only limitation is what can go onto a floppy disc. However, I can put in computer art if sent to me via floppy disc, and can print very long pieces if sent on floppy. Some contributors: Lisa B. Herskovits, Jennifer Blowdryer, Marie Markoe, Art Snyder, Danielle Willis, Anni Roberts." circ. 80 + several computer bulletin boards. 4/yr. Pub'd 4 issues 1998; expects 4 issues 1999, 4 issues 2000. price per copy: $2. Back issues: $2. Discounts: none. 5-600pp. Reporting time: 1 week. Payment: 1 copy. Not copyrighted. Pub's reviews: 60 in 1998. §I will send material to my reviewers; prefer underground zines. will trade.

Plain View Press, Inc., Susan Bright, PO Box 33311, Austin, TX 78764, (512) 441-2452. 1976. Poetry, art, photos, cartoons, long-poems. "We publish feminist literature by women and men. 80 titles. A part of each edition is signed, numbered editions." avg. press run 2M. Pub'd 7 titles 1998; expects 4 titles 1999, 7 titles 2000. 40 titles listed in the *Small Press Record of Books in Print* (28th Edition, 1999-00). avg. price, paper: $15.95. Discounts: standard terms. Pages vary; size varies; of. Reporting time: varies. Payment: varies. Does not copyright for author.

Plains Press, David R. Pichaske, PO Box 6, Granote Falls, MN 56241, 507-537-6463. 1984. "We focus on material from the Minnesota/Iowa/South Dakota region—poetry, fiction and prose/critism/scholarship" avg. press run 1M. Pub'd 1 title 1998; expects 1 title 1999, 1 title 2000. 4 titles listed in the *Small Press Record of Books in Print* (28th Edition, 1999-00). avg. price, cloth: $19.95; paper: $9.95. Discounts: 2-5 20%, 6+ 40%, STOP 40% and add shipping. 176pp; 5¼×8¼.

PLAINSONG, Frank Steele, Peggy Steele, Elizabeth Oakes, Box 8245, Western Kentucky University, Bowling Green, KY 42101, 502-745-5708. 1979. Poetry, articles, art, photos, interviews, criticism, reviews, letters. "We want to affirm the awareness of place as a source for poetry, to print work in which written language comes within hearing of spoken language, to cherish and preserve what it means to be, in the best sense, human during the dangerous decade ahead. We are not academic, although we have an interest in poetic form and craft, especially when alive but invisible. We are bored by the obvious—by irony as a reflex, by hysteria as a motive, by formulaic poems that stop where the formula stops. We favor relatively short poems. Recent contributors: Ken Fontenot, Fran Quinn, Robert Bly, Sallie Bingham, Max Garland. We have a sense of humor" circ. 500. Occasional. Expects 1 issue 1999. sub. price: $7 for 2 issues; per copy: $3.50; sample: $3. Back issues: first issue out of print—other back issues $3 each. 48pp; 6×9; of. Reporting time: 6 weeks. Payment: copies. Copyrighted, reverts to author. Pub's reviews: 0 in 1998. §Contemporary poetry (books and magazines), poetry in translation, criticism of poetry. Advertising free to selected publishers and schools.

Planning/Communications, Daniel Lauber, 7215 Oak Avenue, River Forest, IL 60305-1935. 1976. Non-fiction. "Interested in books, particularly dealing with careers, personal finance, urban affairs, housing, planning, government in general. Particularly interested in manuscripts that cut through the B.S. and ideological biases to deal with causes and solutions to domestic policy problems. Interested in career books on subjects that have not already been exhausted by other authors. Length of material: no less than 192 pages final book." avg. press run 6M. Pub'd 3 titles 1998; expects 3 titles 1999, 4 titles 2000. 7 titles listed in the *Small Press Record of Books in Print* (28th Edition, 1999-00). avg. price, cloth: $34.95; paper: $17.95. Discounts: trade standards (40%; standard return policy); bulk 10-29 copies 20%, 30-50 25%, 51+ 30%; write for classroom, jobber discounts. 352pp; 6×9; of. Reporting time: 4 months. Simultaneous submissions accepted: yes. Publishes 5% of manuscripts submitted. Payment: contact us, varies with author, but better than industry standards. Does not copyright for author. PMA.

Plantagenet Productions (see also PLANTAGENET PRODUCTIONS, Libraries of Spoken Word

436

Recordings and of Stagescripts), Westridge (Open Centre), Highclere, Nr. Newbury, Berkshire RG20 9PJ, England. Pub'd 1 title 1998; expects 1 title 2000. 40 titles listed in the *Small Press Record of Books in Print* (28th Edition, 1999-00). avg. price, paper: £1.50 plus postage for direct sales; other: £15-£12.75 family papers for direct sales.

PLANTAGENET PRODUCTIONS, Libraries of Spoken Word Recordings and of Stagescripts, Plantagenet Productions, Dorothy Rose Gribble, Director of Productions, Westridge (Open Centre), Highclere, Nr. Newbury, Royal Berkshire RG20 9PJ, England. 1964. "Recordings of poetry, philosophy, narrative and light work on cassette, tape, LP. Family history: *Gribble Annals 1* by Charles Besly Gribble, Captain East India Company, Besly 1986, £2.25 plus postage; *Gribble Annals 2* by Henry Gribble, Captain, East India Company, 1988, £4.50. *Milton Traditions*, compiled by F.G.M. Milton and D.R. Gribble, £10.50 + p/p (direct sales), 1990. *Gribble Annals 3: Family Letters 1822-1940*, 1992, £12.75 + p/p (direct sales)." Erratic. Pub'd 1 issue 1998; expects 3 issues 1999. price per copy: LP-£2.25, £2, £1 cassette tape £2.25, £1.75 postage extra.

THE PLASTIC TOWER, Carol Dyer, Roger Kyle-Keith, PO Box 702, Bowie, MD 20718. 1989. Poetry, art, reviews. "Prefer poems of two pages or shorter. No style or subject biases; our only 'no-no' is fiction. We just don't have the space to print stories right now! We read throughout the year, but typically are slowest in December." circ. 200. 4/yr. Pub'd 4 issues 1998; expects 4 issues 1999, 4 issues 2000. sub. price: $8; per copy: $2.50; sample: $2.50. Back issues: free for large SASE with 3 stamps postage. Discounts: schools, libraries and bulk; write for details. 48pp; 5½x8½; †mi. Reporting time: 5 months. Simultaneous submissions accepted: yes. Publishes 5% of manuscripts submitted. Payment: in copies. Copyrighted, reverts to author. Pub's reviews: 20 in 1998. §Poetry chapbooks and literary magazines.

PLAY THE ODDS, Tom Raley, 11614 Ashwood, Little Rock, AR 72211, 501-224-9452. 1996. Fiction, articles, photos, reviews, news items. "Articles up to 700 words, reviews up to 200 words, fiction up to 800 words, fillers vary in length." 12/yr. Expects 12 issues 1999, 12 issues 2000. sub. price: $22.50; per copy: $2.50; sample: $2.50. Back issues: $2.50 each. Discounts: none. 12pp; 8½x11; †of. Reporting time: 4-5 weeks. Simultaneous submissions accepted: yes. Publishes 25% of manuscripts submitted. Payment: average article $1,000, fiction $2,000, review $200. Copyrighted, reverts to author. Pub's reviews. §Games, gambling, travel, entertainment. Ads: varies per ad.

Players Press, Inc., Robert W. Gordon, Vice President Editorial, PO Box 1132, Studio City, CA 91614, 818-789-4980. 1965. Plays, non-fiction. avg. press run 2M-15M. Pub'd 28 titles 1998; expects 35 titles 1999, 35-50 titles 2000. 408 titles listed in the *Small Press Record of Books in Print* (28th Edition, 1999-00). avg. price, cloth: $30; paper: $15. Discounts: 20%-45% trade. 200pp; 5½x8½, 8½x11; lp. Reporting time: 3-6 months. Simultaneous submissions accepted: no. Publishes performing arts 12%, general 3% of manuscripts submitted. Payment: varies, dependent on material. Copyrights for author. ABA, CBA, ABPA.

Playground Books, Ann B. Faccenda, 26 Fox Hunt Drive #190, Bear, DE 19701-2534. 1994. Poetry, fiction, art, photos, cartoons. "All publications are targeted to children's market. Many publications are education oriented. Ages range from pre-kindergarten through teen years" avg. press run 5M. Pub'd 1 title 1998; expects 10 titles 1999, 10 titles 2000. 4 titles listed in the *Small Press Record of Books in Print* (28th Edition, 1999-00). avg. price, cloth: $12; paper: $5. Discounts: Varies, mostly industry standard. Reporting time: 1-4 months. Publishes 50% of manuscripts submitted. Payment: industry standard. Copyrights for author. PMA.

PLEASANT LIVING, Brandylane Publishers, Robert H. Pruett, PO Box 261, White Stone, VA 22578, 804-435-6900. 1989. Poetry, fiction, articles, photos, reviews, letters, non-fiction. "Material must be regionally oriented. Read a copy of our publication before submitting. Our readers are a diverse group, from 30-80 years of age, educated, interested in the Bay and its preservation and interested in reading clear, readable prose." circ. 15M. 6/yr. Pub'd 6 issues 1998; expects 7 issues 1999, 8 issues 2000. sub. price: $15; per copy: $3; sample: free. Back issues: $1.25. Discounts: 50%. 40pp; 8½x11; of. Reporting time: 6 weeks. Simultaneous submissions accepted: yes. Publishes 25% of manuscripts submitted. Payment: varies. Copyrighted, reverts to author. Pub's reviews: 8 in 1998. §non-fiction, fiction, poetry. Ads: $700/$400.

Pleasure Boat Studio, Jack Estes, 802 East Sixth, Port Angeles, WA 98362, 360-452-8686 tel/fax; email pbstudio@pbstudio.com; http://www.pbstudio.com. 1996. Poetry, fiction, non-fiction. "Pleasure Boat Studio is a publisher, in trade paperback editions, of the best poetry, fiction, and non-fiction (in English language original and translation) that it can find. Our first two books were *The Politics of My Heart*, poems and essays having to do with China, by William Slaughter, and *The Rape Poems* by Frances Driscoll. Our third and fourth books are *When History Enters the House*, essays from Central Europe by Michael Blumenthal, and *Setting Out*, a novel by Tung Nien translated from Chinese by Mike O'Connor. Query with sample and cover letter. But read what we publish before doing so." avg. press run 1-5M. Pub'd 1 title 1998; expects 3 titles 1999, 3 titles 2000. 4 titles listed in the *Small Press Record of Books in Print* (28th Edition, 1999-00). avg. price, paper: $14. Discounts: 1 copy 0%, 2-4 20%, 5+ 40%. Poetry 64-96pp, fiction and non-fiction 150-225pp; 6x9; of, electronic pre-press. Reporting time: 2 months to query, 2 months to manuscript, if invited. Simultaneous submissions accepted: yes. We are a small press. Chances of publication with us are correspondingly small. Payment: standard royalty contract. Copyrights for author. CLMP, PMA, BPNW.

Pleasure Dome Press (Long Island Poetry Collective Inc.) (see also XANADU; NEWSLETTER/ POETIMES), Mildred Jeffrey, Editor; Lois V. Walker, Editor; Weslea Sidon, Editor; Sue Kain, Editor; Binnie Pasquier, Editor, Box 773, Huntington, NY 11743. 1976. Poetry. "We are not open to unsolicited mss. at this time. PDP has not been able to bring out any titles for a long time. We consider it dormant, rather than dead" avg. press run varies. Discounts: 10% on orders of $20 or more (includes *Xanadu* and Newsletter subs.). Pages vary; size varies; †lp, of. Payment: varies. We buy all rights.

PLEIADES MAGAZINE-Philae-Epic Journal-Thoughts Journal, John L. Moravec, Editor-in-Chief; Cyril Osmond, Assistant Editor; Frank Klicpery, Literary Editor, Box 357, 6677 W. Colfax Avenue, Suite D, Lakewood, CO 80214, 303-237-1019. 1983; Philae founded 1947; Thoughts Magazine 1996. Poetry, fiction, articles, music, plays, non-fiction. "Short-shorts from 500-800 words." circ. 1.2M. 2/yr. Pub'd 2 issues 1998. sub. price: $9; per copy: $3; sample: $3. Back issues: $2. 75pp; 8½x11; †of, lp. Reporting time: 2 weeks. Payment: copies or cash awards. Copyrighted, reverts to author. Pub's reviews: 2 in 1998. §General humanitarian and social. Ads: $1 per word/block ads 3 X 2½ $25 two issues/customer furnishes ad (illustrations) black + white.

PLENTY GOOD ROOM, Liturgy Training Publications, J-Glenn Murray, Martin Connel, 1800 North Hermitage Avenue, Chicago, IL 60622, 312-486-8970. 1993. Articles, photos, reviews. "Established to aid in the blending of African-American culture and Roman Catholic rites." circ. 1M. 6/yr. Pub'd 6 issues 1998; expects 6 issues 1999, 6 issues 2000. sub. price: $20; per copy: $3. Back issues: $3. Discounts: bulk 5+ $8/year. 16pp; 6⅛x11½; of. Reporting time: 4 weeks. Payment: yes. Copyrighted, does not revert to author. Catholic Book Publishers Assn.

Plexus, 815-A Brazos, Suite 445, Austin, TX 78701, 512-444-7104; Fax 512-441-4741; info@cyber-plexus.com. 1996. Non-fiction. "We currently publish only specific authors and are not looking for submissions." avg. press run 3-5M. Expects 2 titles 1999, 3 titles 2000. 2 titles listed in the *Small Press Record of Books in Print* (28th Edition, 1999-00). avg. price, cloth: $23.95. 300pp; 6x9; of. Simultaneous submissions accepted: no. PMA.

Plexus Publishing, Inc. (see also BIOLOGY DIGEST), Thomas H. Hogan, 143 Old Marlton Pike, Medford, NJ 08055, 609-654-6500. 1977. Non-fiction. "Publish a limited number of books on biology and natural history." avg. press run 2M. Expects 4 titles 1999, 4 titles 2000. 13 titles listed in the *Small Press Record of Books in Print* (28th Edition, 1999-00). avg. price, cloth: $19.95. Discounts: 40%. 200pp; 5½x8½; of. Reporting time: 60 days. Payment: $500 advance against royalty of 10-15%. Does not copyright for author.

Plinth Books, James Finnegan, Box 271118, W. Hartford, CT 06127-1118. 1995. Poetry, long-poems. "No unsolicited mss. Query with short sample of the book." avg. press run 500. Expects 2 titles 1999, 3 titles 2000. 3 titles listed in the *Small Press Record of Books in Print* (28th Edition, 1999-00). avg. price, cloth: $20; paper: $12. 64pp; 6x9; of. Reporting time: 2 months. Simultaneous submissions accepted: yes. Publishes 1% of manuscripts submitted. Payment: copies. Copyrights for author.

PLOPLOP, Geekspeak Unique Press, John Clark, Kit Andis, Contributing Editor, PO Box 11443, Indianapolis, IN 46201, 317-630-9216. 1991. Poetry, fiction, articles, art, cartoons, interviews, satire, reviews, music, letters, parts-of-novels, collages, plays, concrete art, non-fiction. "Bukowski, Vonnegut, Fielding, Dawson, Eileen Myles, Kit Andis, Gerald Locklin, Edward Field, Hal Sirowitz, Deborah Sellers, and Dan Grossman. Perfers poetry that is witty and brief, concise and with impact. Open to most forms except for the extremely conventional and academic" circ. 300-500. 2/yr. Pub'd 2 issues 1998; expects 2 issues 1999, 2 issues 2000. sub. price: $10; per copy: $5; sample: $4. Discounts: 20%. 50pp; 8½x11; Xerox-covers handpainted. Reporting time: 6-8 weeks. Simultaneous submissions accepted: yes. Publishes 5% of manuscripts submitted. Payment: 1 copy. Copyrighted. Pub's reviews. §Avant-garde, experimental, humor, music-pop/rock.

PLOT, Christina C. Russell, Managing Editor, PO Box 1351, Sugar Land, TX 77487-1351. 1994. Fiction. "We exist to encourage new and emerging writers in the genres of fantasy, science fiction, horror, and suspense" circ. 1500. 4/yr. Pub'd 4 issues 1998; expects 4 issues 1999, 4 issues 2000. sub. price: $14.00; per copy: $5.00; sample: $5.00. Back issues: $5.00. Discounts: extra contributors copies at $3.00. 48pp; 8½x11; of. Reporting time: 90 days. Simultaneous submissions accepted: yes. Publishes 5% of manuscripts submitted. Payment: $10 + contributors copy. Copyrighted, reverts to author. Ads: write for prices. SPGA.

THE PLOUGH, Chris Zimmerman, Derek Wardle, Questions, Spring Valley Bruderhof, R.D. 2, Box 446, Farmington, PA 15437-9506, 412-329-1100; fax 412-329-0942, 800-521-0011. 1983. Poetry, articles, art, photos, interviews, criticism, reviews, letters, long-poems, non-fiction. "700-1,500 words/article. Freelance material very *seldom* published owing to limited space." circ. 8M. 4+. Pub'd 6 issues 1998; expects 4+ issues

1999. sub. price: no subscription, donations accepted; per copy: free; sample: free. Back issues: free. 32pp; 6×9; desktop. Reporting time: 3 weeks or less. Publishes very small % of manuscripts submitted. Payment: none. Copyrighted, rights reverting to author negotiable. Pub's reviews: 8 in 1998. §Religion—current events, non-fiction. No ads. Evangelical Press Association (EPA).

PLOUGHSHARES, Don Lee, Editor; David Daniel, Poetry Editor, Emerson College, 100 Beacon Street, Boston, MA 02116, 617-824-8753. 1971. Poetry, fiction, parts-of-novels, long-poems. "Maximum length for prose 6M words. Read an issue or two before submitting. In the past, we announced specific themes for issues, but we no longer restrict submissions to thematic topics. Recent contributors: Joseph Brodsky, Rita Dove, Garrett Kaoru Hongo, Seamus Heaney, Carol Frost, Sharon Olds, Joyce Carol Oates, Michael S. Harper, Mary Oliver, Phillip Lopate, Sue Miller, Gerald Stern. Reading period: August 1 to March 31 (Postmark dates)." circ. 6M. 3/yr. Pub'd 3 issues 1998; expects 3 issues 1999, 3 issues 2000. 2 titles listed in the *Small Press Record of Books in Print* (28th Edition, 1999-00). sub. price: $21/3 issues (domestic), $26/3 issues (foreign); $24/3 issues (institutional) Add $5/yr for international.; per copy: $9.95; sample: $8. Back issues: prices vary; full file, Vols. I-XXIV, $600. Discounts: 40% trade (6 copies or more); 10% agent. 224pp; 5½×8½; of. Reporting time: 3-5 months. Simultaneous submissions accepted: yes. Publishes 1% of manuscripts submitted. Payment: $25/page prose; $50/title minimum, $250 max. per author. Copyrighted, rights released on publication. Pub's reviews: 15 in 1998. §Quality literary poetry, fiction, non-fiction. Ads: $350/$235. CLMP.

THE PLOWMAN, Tony Scavetta, Box 414, Whitby, Ontario L1N 5S4, Canada, 905-668-7803. 1988. Poetry, art, photos, cartoons, music, letters, collages. "We publish endless chapbooks. Seeks submissions of poems, plays, songs, art, photography, war stories, short stories, prose and fiction." circ. 15M. 2/yr. Pub'd 2 issues 1998; expects 2 issues 1999, 2 issues 2000. sub. price: $10; per copy: $5; sample: free. Discounts: 10%. 20pp; tabloid; †Web Press. Reporting time: 1 week. Simultaneous submissions accepted: yes. Publishes 80% of manuscripts submitted. Payment: 20% royalties. Copyrighted, reverts to author. Pub's reviews: 400 in 1998. §ACC. Ads: $80/$40/$20/$8.

Pluma Productions, 1977 Carmen Avenue, Los Angeles, CA 90068, email pluma@earthlink.net. 1992. Poetry. "Will only consider works by Southern Dominicans - a Roman Catholic Order of Religious priests and brothers" avg. press run 1.5M. Expects 1 title 1999, 1 title 2000. 1 title listed in the *Small Press Record of Books in Print* (28th Edition, 1999-00). avg. price, paper: $11.95. Discounts: 40%. 96pp; 5½×8½; sub contract with printer. Simultaneous submissions accepted: no. Copyrights for author.

PLUME, Jan Bentley, Jen Fostec, 15 Bolehill Park, Hove Edge, Brighouse, W. Yorks HX3 8AL, England, 01484-717808; email plumelit@aol.com. 1996. Poetry, fiction, articles, art, cartoons, interviews, satire, criticism, letters, news items, non-fiction. "Stories: usually around 2000 words, but not prescriptive; poems: 50 lines or fewer." circ. 200. 2/yr. Pub'd 2 issues 1998; expects 2 issues 1999, 2 issues 2000. sub. price: £6.50; per copy: £3.95; sample: £2.50. Back issues: £2. Discounts: by arrangement. 35pp; 5¾×8¼; of. Reporting time: 6 weeks. We accept simultaneous submissions, but prefer not to. Publishes 10% of manuscripts submitted. Payment: by arrangement. Copyrighted, reverts to author. Ads: £5/£2.50/£1 box.

PLUMTREES, Peter Blewett, Nicholas Grider, Kate Pope, PO Box 23403, Milwaukee, WI 53223. 1986. Poetry, fiction, articles, art, photos, cartoons, interviews, satire, criticism, reviews, letters, parts-of-novels, long-poems, collages, plays, non-fiction. "Recent contributors: Daniel Tobin, Maurice Kilwein Guevara, Kelly Cherry" circ. 300. 2-3/yr. Expects 3 issues 1999, 3 issues 2000. sub. price: $10; per copy: $4; sample: $4. Back issues: $4. Discounts: none. 32pp; 8½×7; laserjet. Reporting time: 2-10 weeks. Simultaneous submissions accepted: no. Payment: 2 copies, plus discount for extra copies. Copyrighted, reverts to author. Pub's reviews: 2 in 1998. §literature, nonfiction, fiction, poetry, drama, art. Ads: $50/$35.

Plus Publications, Maria Rhinesmith, Managing Editor, 208 Bass Road, PO Box 265, Scotland, CT 06264, 860-456-0646; 800-793-0666; fax 860-456-2803; e-mail haelix@neca.com; www.plusyoga.necaweb.com. 1988. Non-fiction. "No submissions accepted currently." 4 titles listed in the *Small Press Record of Books in Print* (28th Edition, 1999-00). avg. price, paper: $15.95; other: videos $29.95. Discounts: trade 40%, wholesale 50%-60%. 200pp; 6×9; web. Simultaneous submissions accepted: no. SPAN, NAPRA, PMA.

Plympton Press International, Dorothy Rile, PMB 206, 955 Massachusetts Avenue, Cambridge, MA 02139, 313-994-1086. 1993. Non-fiction. "Editorial office: 1225 Fair Oaks Parkway, Ann Arbor, MI 48104." avg. press run 10M. Expects 2 titles 1999, 2 titles 2000. 1 title listed in the *Small Press Record of Books in Print* (28th Edition, 1999-00). avg. price, cloth: $22.95; paper: $13.95. 315pp; 6×9; lp. Reporting time: 1 month. Payment: negotiated. Copyrights for author. MAPA, PMA.

Pocahontas Press, Inc., Mary C. Holliman, President & Publisher, PO Drawer F, Blacksburg, VA 24063-1020, 703-951-0467; 800-446-0467. 1984. Poetry, fiction, non-fiction. "Our first trade book was the true story of the Golden Hill Indians of Connecticut told in the words of Chief Big Eagle. We are publishing a series of books for middle-school age children and teen-agers, short story length, in both Spanish and English with black-and-white illustrations; these are historical and biographical topics and most will be in the series Tales of the Virginia Wilderness. We are also interested in memoirs, family histories, poetry collections, and scientific monographs. We do not publish fiction unless it is closely tied to historical events and real people are main characters." avg. press run poetry 500, other 1M-3M. Pub'd 6 titles 1998; expects 6 titles 1999. 40 titles listed in the *Small Press Record of Books in Print* (28th Edition, 1999-00). avg. price, cloth: $21.95; paper: $5.95 poetry, $12.95 other. Discounts: for prepayment 5%, wholesalers: 1 20%, 2-50 40%, 51+ 50%. 80-180pp; 5½×8½; of. Reporting time: 3 months or more. Simultaneous submissions accepted: yes. Publishes probally no more than 1% of manuscripts submitted. Payment: 10% royalty. Copyrights for author. (VPW) Virginia Press Women, (NFPW) National Federation of Press Women, Small Press Center, Poet's House.

●**Pocket of Sanity**, Marilyn Harper McDaniel, PO Box 5241, Fresno, CA 93755, 559-222-2845; fax 559-225-3670; e-mail posanity@aol.com. 1997. Fiction, music. "We are primarily interested in high quality literature for children that is good reading for adults too." avg. press run 2.5M. Pub'd 1 title 1998; expects 2 titles 1999, 2 titles 2000. 3 titles listed in the *Small Press Record of Books in Print* (28th Edition, 1999-00). avg. price, cloth: $14.95; paper: $9.95; other: $14.95 spiral. Discounts: retailers 20-45%; libraries 20%; classrooms inquire for special discounts. 64pp; 8½×8½; of. Reporting time: 3-6 months. Simultaneous submissions accepted: yes. Payment: varies. Copyrights for author. Win-Win, Valley Independent Publishers, PMA.

POCKETS (Devotional Magazine for Children), Janet R. Knight, 1908 Grand Avenue, PO Box 189, Nashville, TN 37202-0189, 615-340-7333. 1981. Poetry, fiction, articles, art. "I would strongly advise writers to ask for guidelines and themes before submitting mss. Include SASE (32¢)." circ. 96M. 11/yr. Pub'd 11 issues 1998; expects 11 issues 1999, 11 issues 2000. sub. price: $16.95; per copy: $2.50; sample: SASE (4 first-class stamps). Back issues: 4 first class stamps. 48pp; 7×9½; of. Reporting time: initially 1 month; may be notified that ms. will be held for consideration for a specific issue. Simultaneous submissions accepted: no. Publishes 4% of manuscripts submitted. Payment: on acceptance. Copyrighted, rights revert if author so requests. Ads: none. Associated Church Press, Educational Press Association of America.

POEM, Huntsville Literary Association, Nancy Frey Dillard, c/o English Department, University of Alabama, Huntsville, AL 35899. 1967. Poetry. circ. 500. 2/yr. Pub'd 2 issues 1998; expects 2 issues 1999, 2 issues 2000. sub. price: $15; per copy: $5; sample: $5. Back issues: $5. 70pp; 4½×7⅓; lp. Reporting time: 30 days. Payment: copy. Copyrighted, reverts to author. No advertisement. CLMP.

POEMS & PLAYS, Gaylord Brewer, Department of English, Middle Tennessee State University, Murfreesboro, TN 37132, 615-898-2712. 1993. Poetry, art, plays. "Recent contributors include Stephen Dobyns and Charles Bukowski. Short plays (10-15 pgs.) have a better chance of publication. We *read* for this spring annual from Oct. 1-Jan. 15, either open submissions or 20-24 page manuscripts for the Tennessee Chapbook Prize. Contest entries can be any combo of poetry and drama. Winner is published as interior chapbook in *Poems & Plays*. Recent winners are Steve Sater (Drama) and Angela Kelly (poetry). Author receives 50 copies of issue. For contest, SASE and $10 (for reading fee and one copy of issue) required." circ. 750. 1/yr. Pub'd 1 issue 1998; expects 1 issue 1999, 1 issue 2000. sub. price: $10/2 issues; per copy: $6; sample: $6. Back issues: please call or write for availability. Discounts: please call/write. 80+pp; 6×9; lp. Reporting time: 1-2 months. Publishes 2% of manuscripts submitted. Payment: 1 copy. Copyrighted, reverts to author. Pub's reviews: beginning in 1999 in 1998. §poetry, plays. Ads: no advertising.

POEMS THAT THUMP IN THE DARK/SECOND GLANCE, New Spirit Press/The Poet Tree, Ignatius Graffeo, 82-34 138 Street #6F, Kew Gardens, NY 11435, 718-847-1482. 1993. Poetry, articles, art, satire, long-poems, non-fiction. "*Poems That Thump In the Dark/Second Glance* is a magazine of the most unusual, unforgettable, unspeakable, undeniably extraordinary poems that will prick up your ears and skin and leave you wanting for more! Submissions must reflect paradoxical, or hard truths of human life, emotion of the experience, and knowledge, conclusions, questions, that may shed more light on man's place in the universe. Send up to 4 poems, SASE. Recent contributors: Grace Schulman, Richard Kostelanetz, Nina Cassian, Linda Ann Loschiavo, Robert Cooperman, Donna Masini, Rachel Hadas, Linda Bierds." circ. 500. 2/yr. Expects 2 issues 1999, 2 issues 2000. sub. price: $20; per copy: $6; sample: $6. Back issues: $6. Discounts: mail order: 1/2 price 10 copies or more. 72pp; 5½×8½; high-quality Xerox. Reporting time: 3 months. Payment: 1 copy. Copyrighted, reverts to author. Pub's reviews: 95 in 1998. Ads: $60/$40/$25 1/4 page/$15 business card.

POET LORE, The Writer's Center, Elizabeth Poliner, Executive Editor; Geraldine Connolly, Executive Editor, The Writer's Center, 4508 Walsh Street, Bethesda, MD 20815-6006, 301-654-8664. 1889. Poetry, reviews. "All material submitted for possible publication must include a stamped, self-addressed envelope. Translations of contemporary world poets." circ. 650. 4/yr. Pub'd 4 issues 1998; expects 4 issues 1999, 4 issues 2000. sub. price: $15 indiv., $24 instit.; per copy: $4.50, $5 foreign postage; sample: $4. Back issues: $4.50. Discounts: agency 5%. 80pp; 6×9; of. Reporting time: 2-4 months. Simultaneous submissions accepted: no. Publishes 5% of manuscripts submitted. Payment: 2 copies of issue. Copyrighted, reverts to author. Pub's reviews: 17 in 1998. §Small press poetry books, and poetry books published by major publishers & university presses. Ads: $100/$55. CLMP.

POETALK, Bay Area Poets Coalition, PO Box 11435, Berkeley, CA 94712-2435, 510-272-9176. 1974. Poetry. "54¢ SASE required." circ. 500. 6/yr. Pub'd 6 issues 1998; expects 6 issues 1999, 6 issues 2000. sub. price: $15 membership (includes yearly anthology); $6 subscription (write for foreign rates); per copy: $1.50; sample: free (SASE, business size) 54¢ postage required. Back issues: most issues available. 24pp; 7×8½ (folded, printed both sides); of. Reporting time: 2-4 months. Publishes 20-30% of manuscripts submitted. Payment: copy. Copyrighted, reverts to author. Ads: none.

Poetic License Press, Carol A. Belding, Owner, Editor; Steve Belding, Operations Manager, PO Box 85525, Westland, MI 48185-0525, 734-326-9368; FAX 734-326-3480; e-mail steveblo30@aol.com. 1996. Poetry, fiction, long-poems, criticism. avg. press run 750. Pub'd 3 titles 1998; expects 1 title 1999, 2 titles 2000. 2 titles listed in the *Small Press Record of Books in Print* (28th Edition, 1999-00). avg. price, paper: $8.45. Discounts: trade 40%; library 50%. 100pp; 5½×8½; of. Reporting time: 2-6 months. Simultaneous submissions accepted: yes. Publishes 20-30% of manuscripts submitted. Payment: some pre-press work, so authors have sole ownership; if we publish, royalty and payment arrangements are set on an individual basis. We copyright for author for $20 fee. Publishers Marketing Association.

Poetic Page (see also OPUS LITERARY REVIEW), Denise Martinson, PO Box 71192, Madison Heights, MI 48071-0192, 313-548-0865. 1989. Poetry, fiction. "We are doing four chapbooks (invitation only)." avg. press run unlimited (by orders). Expects 5 titles 1999, 5 titles 2000. avg. price, other: $6 chapbooks. Discounts: none. 40pp; †desktop. Payment: no longer give royalties. Copyrights for author.

POETIC SPACE: Poetry & Fiction, Don Hildenbrand, Editor; Thomas Strand, Fiction Editor, PO Box 11157, Eugene, OR 97440. 1983. Poetry, fiction, articles, art, photos, interviews, criticism, reviews, news items. "Short to medium length poems, short fiction, short essays, articles, reviews, contemporary, modern poetry, film, video, drama reviews and B&W photography. Artwork (line drawings, sketches), graphics. Open to beginners. Open to experimental. Recent contributors: Poetry: John M. Bennett, Chan Yong, Albert Huffstickler, Peter Kime, Pete Lee, Walt Phillips, Crawdad Nelson, Lyn Lifshin, Simon Perchik, Albert Huffsmichlin, Sherman Alexie, Paul Weineman. Fiction: Laten Carter, John Lipton, Seamus O'Bannion. Essays; Sesshu Foster, Maggie Jaffre. Chinese translations: Scott Francis. Art: Albert Huffsticklan. Shakespeare Reviews: Don Hildenbrand. Interview with Diane Ann-Jabar: Arabian Jazz author." circ. 500-600. 2/yr plus one chapbook (poetry and fiction). Pub'd 2 issues 1998; expects 2 issues 1999, 2 issues 2000. sub. price: $7/2 issues, $13.50/4 issues, $5 anthology, 1987-1991; per copy: $4; sample: $3. Back issues: $5 per issue. 30-40pp; 8½×11; of. Reporting time: 1-2 months. Payment: in copies depending on budget (as in number). Copyrighted, rights revert to author, but reserve right to include in anthology. Pub's reviews: 2 in 1998. §Poetry, novels, plays, film. Ads: $150/$80/$40 1/4 page/$30 3 X 4/$25 business card. Lane Arts Council.

Poetical Histories, Peter Riley, 27 Sturton Street, Cambridge CB1 2QG, United Kingdom, 0223-327455. 1986. Poetry. "We publish only new British poetry in craft-produced pamphlets of 4-8 pages. Anyone submitting is strongly advised to consult previously published texts with regard to style." avg. press run 150-200. Pub'd 6 titles 1998; expects 6 titles 1999, 6 titles 2000. 15 titles listed in the *Small Press Record of Books in Print* (28th Edition, 1999-00). avg. price, paper: £3.50. Discounts: 1/3 off—trade. 8pp; octavo; lp. Reporting time: 2 weeks. Payment: usually none. Copyrights for author.

POETICS TODAY: International Journal for Theory and Analysis of Literature and Communication, Duke University Press, Meir Sternberg, Box 90660, Duke University, Durham, NC 27708-0660. "*Poetics Today* brings scholars from throughout the world who are concerned with developing systematic approaches to the study of literature (e.g. semiotics, structuralism, narratology) and with applying such approaches to the interpretation of literary works. *Poetics Today* presents a remarkable diversity of methodologies and examines a wide range of literary and critical topics. Several thematic review sections or special issues are published with each volume, and each issue contains a book review section, with article-length review essays. Send review copies to the Book Review Editor, *Poetics Today*, Porter Institute for Poetics and Semiotics, Tel Aviv University, Tel Aviv 69978, Israel." circ. 950. 4/yr. Pub'd 4 issues 1998; expects 4 issues 1999, 4 issues 2000. sub. price: $92 institutions, $34 individuals, $17 students with photocopy of current I.D., additional $12 foreign. Pub's reviews: Ads: $225/$175.

POETRY, Joseph Parisi, Editor, 60 West Walton Street, Chicago, IL 60610, 312-255-3703. 1912. Poetry, reviews, long-poems. circ. 8M. 12/yr. Pub'd 12 issues 1998; expects 12 issues 1999, 12 issues 2000. 3 titles listed in the *Small Press Record of Books in Print* (28th Edition, 1999-00). sub. price: individuals $30, $38 outside USA, institutions $33, $41 outside USA; per copy: $3.50 plus $1.50 post; sample: $3.50 plus $1.50 postage. Back issues: $4 plus $1.50 post. 64pp; 5½×9; of. Reporting time: 12 weeks. Simultaneous submissions accepted: no. Publishes less than 1% of manuscripts submitted. Payment: $50/page prose, $2/line verse. Copyrighted, does not revert to author. Pub's reviews: 60 in 1998. §Poetry. Ads: $320/$196. CLMP.

POETRY AND AUDIENCE, M Tranter, A. Goody, School of English, Cavendish Road, University of Leeds, Leeds Yorkshire, LS2 9JT, England. 1953. Poetry, reviews. "A market for serious, well-crafted poems and creative writing in any genre. Has a reputation for publishing established poets alongside quality material from unknown writers.'' circ. 400+. 2/yr. Pub'd 1 issue 1998; expects 2 issues 1999, 2 issues 2000. 2 titles listed in the *Small Press Record of Books in Print* (28th Edition, 1999-00). sub. price: overseas £3 per issue, inland £1.50/issue; per copy: £1.50; sample: £2 + 25% p/p. Back issues: £1 + 25% p/p. 32-52pp; quarto; of/lo. Reporting time: 1 month. Simultaneous submissions accepted: no. Publishes 30% of manuscripts submitted. Payment: none. Not copyrighted. Pub's reviews. §Poetry. Ads: £20/£15/back page £20. Yorkshire Federation of Small Presses.

POETRY BONE, Kiel Stuart, Editor; Reed Coleman, Editor, 12 Skylark Lane, Stony Brook, NY 11790. 1997. Poetry. "We're looking for high-quality poems, no style or form restrictions (rhyming poetry must be exceptional). Maximum length is 29 lines.'' 2/yr. Pub'd 2 issues 1998; expects 1 issue 1999, 2 issues 2000. sub. price: $8; per copy: $4.50; sample: $4.50. 30pp; 5½×8½; †Desktop Pub (Laser printer). Reporting time: 2-4 weeks. Simultaneous submissions accepted: no. Publishes 10% of manuscripts submitted. Payment: 1 contributer copy. Copyrighted, reverts to author.

POETRY BREAK JOURNAL, Marjorie Navarro, Editor; Richard LeJose Navarro, Executive Editor, PO Box 1107, Blythe, CA 92226-1107. 1998. "All subjects, no taboos, no line length limit. Checks/mo to Navarro Publications. Refundable reading fee of $3 per 6 poems.'' circ. 300+. 6/yr. Pub'd 4 issues 1998; expects 6 issues 1999, 6 issues 2000. sub. price: $6.75. 35-55pp; 7×8½. Reporting time: 12-14 weeks.

The Poetry Center Press/Shoestring Press, P.M. Morrison, Bill Johnson, Associate Editor, 3 Monte Vista Road, Orinda, CA 94513, 925-254-1939. 1986. Poetry, fiction, non-fiction. "Have published fime limited letter-press editions as well as modest chapbooks and hardcover and perfect bound editions. Professional consultation and assistance to self-publishers'' avg. press run 250-5M. Pub'd 5 titles 1998; expects 6 titles 1999, 8 titles 2000. 6 titles listed in the *Small Press Record of Books in Print* (28th Edition, 1999-00). avg. price, cloth: $45; paper: $10. Discounts: trade, wholesale. †of/lp. Payment: negotiated. Copyrights for author. PCBA.

The Poetry Connection (see also THE POETRY CONNECTION), Sylvia Shichman, Editor & Publisher, 13455 SW 16 Court #F-405, Pembroke Pines, FL 33027, 954-431-3016. 1988. Poetry. *"The Poetry Connection is a monthly newsletter in flyer format and service...whereby poetry, songwriting, greeting card and performing artists publications/organizations listings and contests and poetry flyers are distributed to editors and publishers...helping poets to get published. Provides assistance in getting poetry published...plus info on writing for greeting card companies...plus info on how to win cash for your talent...plus info on a directory that lists poetry contests with cash awards! (Large SASE for info!) The Poetry Connection has a huge active mailing list of poets, writers and songwriters of about 10,000 names and more available for rental. The Magic Circle* is a publicity/distribution service...whereby a bio and one poem is sent directly ot editors and publishers...helping poets to get published! Please enclose a large SASE for information. Sample issue...$7/1 year membership is $20. A 1 year membership for *The Magic Circle* is $30 (50 copies) or $60 (100 copies). Please make all checks payable to: Sylvia Shichman, Editor!'' †of/copies. Southern Poetry Association.

THE POETRY CONNECTION, The Poetry Connection, Sylvia Shichman, Editor & Publisher, 13455 SW 16 Court #F-405, Pembroke Pines, FL 33027, 305-431-3016. 1988. Poetry. *"The Poetry Connection is a monthly newsletter in flyer format and service...whereby poetry, songwriting, greeting card and performing artists publications/organizations listings and contests and poetry flyers are distributed to editors and publishers...helping poets to get published. Provides assistance in getting poetry published... plus info on writing for greeting card companies...plus info on how to win cash for your talent...plus info on a directory that lists poetry contests with cash awards! (large SASE for info)! The Poetry Connection has a huge active mailing list of poets, writers, and songwriters of about 10,000 names and more...available for rental! The Magic Circle* is a publicity/distribution service...whereby a bio and one poem is sent directly to editors and publishers...helping poets to get published! Please enclose a large SASE for information. Sample issue...$7/1 year membership is $20. A 1 year membership for *The Magic Circle* is $30 (50 copies) or $60 (100 copies). Please make all checks payable to: Sylvia Shichman, Editor!'' 12/yr. sub. price: $20 Poetry Connection, $30 Magic Circle (50 copies), $60 combined service (100 copies); per copy: (Sample - $5) plus $2 for postage; sample: (Sample - $5) plus $2 for postage. Back issues: $7. 8½×11; †of-xerox copies. Ads: $10 per listing or $60 (1 year). Florida State Poets Assn., Poets & Writers, Southern Poetry Association.

POETRY EAST, Richard Jones, Dept. of English, DePaul Univ., 802 West Belden Avenue, Chicago, IL 60614, 312-325-7487. 1980. Poetry, fiction, articles, art, photos, interviews, criticism, reviews, letters, collages, concrete art, news items. *"Poetry East* in the year 2000 is celebrating its 20th anniversary with a series of retrospective anthologies honoring work from the pages of the journal: *The Last Believer in Words: A Collection of Poems in Translation* (1998); *They Say This: A Collection of Essays on Poetry and Poetics* (1999); and *Who Are The Rich and Where Do They Live? A Collection of Contemporary American Poetry* (2000). Over two decades our contributors have included Amiri Baraka, Robert Hass, Stanley Kunitz, Gloria Fuertes, Philip Levine, Sharon Olds, Robert Bly, Louis Simpson, Richard Shelton, Miklos Radnoti, W.H.

442

Auden, Larry Levis, Donald Hall, David Ignatow, William Stafford, Linda Gregg, Czeslaw Milosz, James Tate, Denise Levertov, Louis Jenkins, June Jordan, Simon Ortiz, and Galway Kinnell. *Poetry East* also publishes volumes dedicated to a particular topic or poet. Recent special issues have included 'Surrealism and Recent American Poetry,' 'Art and Guns: Political Poetry at Home and Abroad,' 'Poetry and the Visual Arts'; a special issue dedicated to Murial Rukeyser; 'Poetics: A Collection of Essays on Poetic Form,' 'The Poetry of Thomas McGrath.' *Poetry East* is interested in reading essays on poetics, the relationship betwen art and the world, etc. We are also interested in translations and ideas for feature/symposia." circ. 1.5M. 2/yr. Pub'd 2 issues 1998; expects 1 issue 1999, 1 issue 2000. sub. price: $20; per copy: $10, $15 for anthologies; sample: $8. Back issues: #9/10 *Art & Guns: Political Poetry* $20; #19 *The Inward Eye: the Photographs of Ed Roseberry* $10; #43 *Origins* $15. Discounts: bookstores 30%. 200pp for single issue, 300pp for double issue; 5½x8½; of. Reporting time: 3 months. Simultaneous submissions accepted: no. Publishes less than 5% of manuscripts submitted. Payment: copies, honorariums. Copyrighted, reverts to author. Pub's reviews: 4-5 in 1998. §Poetry, criticism, biography, literature, film, art, photography, etc. Ads: $100/$50. CLMP.

THE POETRY EXPLOSION NEWSLETTER (THE PEN), Arthur C. Ford, PO Box 4725, Pittsburgh, PA 15206. 1985. Poetry. "We use poetry of max. length 30 lines, and prose max. 200-300 words. Rhyme and non-rhyme. Submit a max. of 5 poems, SASE and $1 reading fee." circ. 850. 4/yr. Pub'd 4 issues 1998; expects 4 issues 1999, 4 issues 2000. sub. price: $20; sample: $4. 10-15pp; 8½x11; lp. Reporting time: 4-6 weeks. Simultaneous submissions accepted: yes. Publishes 10-15% of manuscripts submitted. Payment: copies. Copyrighted, reverts to author. Pub's reviews: 2 in 1998. §Poetry, prose. Ads: $100/$50/$25 1/4 page/$10 bus. card.

POETRY FLASH, Joyce Jenkins, Publisher & Editor; Richard Silberg, Associate Editor, 1450 Fourth Street #4, Berkeley, CA 94710, 510-525-5476, Fax; 510-525-6752. 1972. Poetry, articles, art, photos, cartoons, interviews, criticism, reviews, letters, collages, news items. "*Poetry Flash* is a poetry review and literary calendar for the West, publishes reviews, essays, interviews, photos, and poems. Our editorial perspective is western, but our ultimate allegiance is to high quality poems and news about poets and writing, not to a geographical area. Our Calendar is a general literary calendar, listing fiction and other literary events as well as poetry readings." circ. 22M. 6/yr. Pub'd 6 issues 1998. sub. price: $16 individuals, $16 institutions; per copy: free at bookstores, libraries, cafes, art centers or by subscription; sample: one copy (one time) free on request. Back issues: $2. 48pp; 11½x15, tabloid; of. Reporting time: 4 months. Simultaneous submissions accepted: yes. Publishes 10% of manuscripts submitted. Payment: 2-year subscription for poems, payment for articles. Copyrighted, reverts to author. Pub's reviews: 150 in 1998. §Poetry, exploratory fiction, criticism or literary biography, especially poetry related. Ads: $580/$290/$14.50 column inch. CLMP, AWP.

Poetry Harbor (see also NORTH COAST REVIEW), Patrick McKinnon, Ellie Schoenfeld, Liz Minette, Guest Editor, PO Box 103, Duluth, MN 55801-0103, e-mail poharb@toofarnorth.com. 1992. avg. press run 1M. Pub'd 3 titles 1998; expects 2 titles 1999, 2 titles 2000. 8 titles listed in the *Small Press Record of Books in Print* (28th Edition, 1999-00). avg. price, paper: $4.95. Discounts: 40% booksellers; 55% wholesalers. 56pp; 8½x7; of. Reporting time: 1-6 months. Simultaneous submissions accepted: yes. Publishes 20% of manuscripts submitted. Payment: $10 + copies. Copyrights for author. MMPA.

POETRY INTERNATIONAL, San Diego State University Press, Fred Moramarco, San Diego State Univ., Eng. Dept., 5500 Campanile Drive, San Diego, CA 92182-8140, 619-594-1523; fax 619-594-4998; email fmoramar@mail.sdsu.edu. 1997. Poetry, articles, interviews, criticism, reviews, letters, long-poems. "Recent contributers include Charles Simic, Diane Wakoski, Marge Piercy, Many Grow, Peter Cooley, E. Ethelbert Miller, Elaine Equm, Susan Wheeler, Gary Soto. Especially looking for new translations of international poets." circ. 1M. 1/yr. Pub'd 1 issue 1998; expects 1 issue 1999, 1 issue 2000. price per copy: $12. Discounts: by request. lp. Reporting time: 6 weeks. We accept simultaneous submissions if author indicates same. Publishes 5% of manuscripts submitted. Payment: copies. Copyrighted. Pub's reviews: 20 in 1998. §Contemporary poetry, criticism of contemporary poetry, biography of poets. Ads: exchange with other literary magazines.

Poetry Ireland (see also POETRY IRELAND REVIEW), Catherine Phil MacCarthy, Bermingham Tower, Upper Yard, Dublin Castle, Dublin 2, Ireland. 1981. Poetry, reviews. avg. press run 1,100. Pub'd 4 titles 1998; expects 4 titles 1999, 4 titles 2000. avg. price, paper: US$8; other: IR £5.99. Discounts: agencies 10%. 136pp; 6x8; photoset. Reporting time: 3 months max. Simultaneous submissions accepted: no. Publishes 5-10% of manuscripts submitted. Payment: poems in copies, articles/reviews by arrangement IR £10 per contributor of 1 year subscription. Copyrights for author.

POETRY IRELAND REVIEW, Poetry Ireland, Catherine Phil McCarthy, Bermingham Tower, Upper yard, Dublin Castle, Dublin 2, Ireland, 6714632 + 353-1; fax 6714634 + 353-1. 1981. Poetry, interviews, criticism. "*Poetry Ireland Review* accepts material from outside Ireland. The themes do not have to be necessarily Irish. We prefer if they are not Irish. We publish both established and lesser-known poets" circ. 1,100. 4/yr. Pub'd 4 issues 1998; expects 5 issues 1999, 5 issues 2000. 1 title listed in the *Small Press Record of Books in Print* (28th

Edition, 1999-00). sub. price: airmail IRT 44.00, US$70; surface IRT 24.00, US$50; per copy: IR £5.99; sample: IR £5.99. Back issues: IR £5.99. Discounts: agencies 10%; bulk discount by arrangement. 136pp; 6×8; Photoset. Reporting time: 3 months max. Simultaneous submissions accepted: no. Publishes 5-10% of manuscripts submitted. Payment: IR£10 per contribution or subscription. Copyrighted, reverts to author. Pub's reviews: 50 in 1998. §New major collections of international interest and Irish collections. Ads: by arrangement.

POETRY KANTO, William Elliott, Kazuo Kawamura, Makoto Ooka, Shuntaro Tanikawa, Nishihara Katsumasa, Kanto Gakuin University, Kamariya Minami 3-22-1, Kanazawa-Ku, Yokohama 236-8502, Japan. 1984. Poetry. "Poems normally 30 lines or less. Bias against bathos, pornography, and 'woe is me!' Some recent contributors include (among Westerners); Denise Levertov, William Stafford, Kenneth Hanson, Vi Gale, Vern Rutsala, William Pitt Root, Harry Guest, W.S. Merwin, William Elliott, Eleanor Wilner, Seamus Heaney. Solicit poems in English or Japanese. *Query before submitting, with SAE and reply coupons.*" circ. 700. 1/yr. Pub'd 1 issue 1998; expects 1 issue 1999, 1-2 issues 2000. 1 title listed in the *Small Press Record of Books in Print* (28th Edition, 1999-00). Back issues: send reply coupons to cover air mail or sea mail. 50-60pp; 7×10; lp. Reporting time: 2-4 weeks. Simultaneous submissions accepted: no. Publishes 10% of manuscripts submitted. Payment: 3 contributor's copies. Not copyrighted.

THE POETRY MISCELLANY, Richard Jackson, English Dept. Univ of Tennessee, Chattanooga, TN 37403, 615-755-4213; 624-7279. 1971. Poetry, interviews, criticism, reviews, long-poems. "David Wagoner, Denise Levertov, Tomaz Salamun, Mark Strand, Laura Jensen, Richard Wilbur, Donald Justice, James Tate, Dara Wier, Carol Muske, Maxine Kumin, Robert Penn Warren, Marvin Bell, Jean Valentine, David St. John, A.R. Ammons, Stanley Kunitz, Charles Simic, John Hollander, Linda Pastan, William Stafford, John Haines, Pamela Stewart, Galway Kinnell, W. S. Merwin, William Meredith, Laurence Raab, Cynthia MacDonald, Robert Pack, Carolyn Forche, Anthony Hecht, John Ashbery, Donald Finkel, Michael Harper, Robert Creeley, David Ignatow, Donald Hall, Heather McHugh, Sharon Olds, Stanley Plumly, William Matthews. Review essays 1M words must be assigned/approved in advance. We use translations too. Send translations with originals to John Duval, Translation Workshop, University of Arkansas, Fayetteville, AK 72701." circ. 650. 1-2/yr. Pub'd 2 issues 1998; expects 2 issues 1999. sub. price: $5; per copy: $5; sample: $2. Back issues: same price as current issues. Discounts: 30% for orders of ten or more to groups and individuals. 12pp; tabloid; of. Reporting time: 6 months. Simultaneous submissions accepted: no. Publishes 1% of manuscripts submitted. Payment: copies. Copyrighted, rights revert to author upon request as for re-publication. Pub's reviews: 1 in 1998. §Poetry, poetics. Ads: $50 1/2 page. CLMP.

POETRY MOTEL, Suburban Wilderness Press, PO Box 103, Duluth, MN 55801-0103. 1984. Poetry, fiction, art, photos, interviews, satire, criticism, long-poems, collages. "We tend toward work that brings an interesting story. We prefer characters other than 'you' & 'me' & 'I.' We consider rhythm the element lacking in most of the work we pass up. We have published Ron Androla, Deb Marguart, Hugh Fox, Todd Moore, Albert Huffstickler and Linda Wing recently" circ. 800. Published every 260 days. Pub'd 1 issue 1998; expects 2 issues 1999, 1 issue 2000. sub. price: $19.95/3 issues, $69 lifetime sub.; per copy: $6.95; sample: $6.95. Back issues: $18.95 each. Discounts: none. 52pp; 7×8½; of. Reporting time: 1 week to never. Simultaneous submissions accepted: yes. Publishes a variable % of manuscripts submitted. Payment: varies. Copyrighted, reverts to author. no ads.

POETRY NEW YORK: A Journal of Poetry and Translation, Burt Kimmelman, Editor; Tod Thilleman, Editor, PO Box 3184, Church Street Station, New York, NY 10008. 1985. Poetry. "Translations welcome." circ. 700. 1/yr. Pub'd 1 issue 1998; expects 1 issue 1999, 1 issue 2000. price per copy: $7; sample: $7. Back issues: $4. 65pp; 6×9; of. Reporting time: 4 months. Publishes 5% of manuscripts submitted. Payment: copy. Copyrighted, reverts to author. Ads: negotiable per issue.

POETRY NOTTINGHAM INTERNATIONAL, Poetry Nottingham Society Publications, Cathy Grindrod, 71 Saxton Avenue, Heanor, Derbyshire DE75 7PZ, England, 0602 461267. 1946. Poetry, articles, art, criticism, reviews, letters, concrete art, news items. "Poems in any form. Overseas contributions welcome. Rates on application." circ. 300. 4/yr. Pub'd 4 issues 1998; expects 4 issues 1999, 4 issues 2000. sub. price: £15 sterling; per copy: £3 sterling or $8 US; sample: £2 in sterling; or $5 U.S. Back issues: half price and p.p. Discounts: 33% to bookshops. 44pp; 8¼×6; of. Reporting time: 2 months max, often sooner. Simultaneous submissions accepted: no. Publishes 10% of manuscripts submitted. Payment: complimentary copy. Copyright remains with author. Pub's reviews: estimate a dozen in 1998. §Poetry. Ads: £10/£5.

Poetry Nottingham Society Publications (see also **POETRY NOTTINGHAM INTERNATIONAL**), Cathy Grindrod, 71 Saxton Avenue, Heanor, Derbys DE75 7PZ, England. 1945. Poetry, articles, interviews, criticism, letters. "Articles up to 500w welcome, especially on the foreign poetry scene" avg. press run 250. Expects 1 title 1999, 1 title 2000. 3 titles listed in the *Small Press Record of Books in Print* (28th Edition, 1999-00). avg. price, paper: £3 sterling. Discounts: 1/3 off to bookshops. 40pp; 8¼×6; of, lp. Reporting time: 1-2 months. Simultaneous submissions accepted: no. Publishes 10% of manuscripts submitted. Payment: complimentary copy. Copyrights for author.

Poetry Now, Sacramento's Literary Calendar and Review, Heather Hutcheson, 1631 K Street, Sacramento, CA 95814, 916-441-7395; e-mail: spc@tomatoweb.com; www.tomatoweb.com/spc. 1994. Poetry, articles, photos, interviews, criticism, reviews. circ. 1500 + website. 12/yr. Pub'd 12 issues 1998; expects 12 issues 1999, 12 issues 2000. sub. price: $25; per copy: $3; sample: $3. Back issues: n/a. Discounts: call for information. 8pp; 11×14. Reporting time: 1-2 months. Simultaneous submissions accepted: yes. Publishes 60% of manuscripts submitted. Payment: none. Not copyrighted. Pub's reviews: 4+ in 1998. §poetry. Ads: call for information/3 X 5=$20/month. n/a.

POETRY NZ, Brick Row Publishing Co. Ltd., Alistair Paterson, PO Box 100-057, North Shore Mail Centre, Auckland 1310, New Zealand, 64-9-410-6993. 1990. Poetry. circ. 1M. 2/yr. Pub'd 2 issues 1998; expects 2 issues 1999, 2 issues 2000. sub. price: $35; per copy: $16.95. Back issues: $16.95. Discounts: trade 35% on single copies, 10% sub. agency, net for sub. libraries. 80-90pp; 6×8; of, 1p. Reporting time: 4 weeks. Simultaneous submissions accepted: no. Publishes 15-20% of manuscripts submitted. Payment: $25 per issue. Copyrighted, reverts to author. Pub's reviews: 5+ in 1998. §Poetry. Ads: none.

The Poetry Project (see also THE POETRY PROJECT NEWSLETTER; THE WORLD), Editorial Staff, St. Mark's Church, 131 East 10th Street, New York, NY 10003, 212-674-0910; e-mail popro;@artomatic.com. 1966. Poetry, fiction, art, photos, long-poems, non-fiction. "We mainly publish solicited work." avg. press run 4,000' 800 respectivly. Pub'd 1 title 1998; expects 1 title 1999, 1 title 2000. avg. price, paper: $7. Discounts: none. 128pp; 6×9; perfect bound. Reporting time: 6 months. Simultaneous submissions accepted: yes. Publishes 5% of manuscripts submitted. Payment: copies. Does not copyright for author.

THE POETRY PROJECT NEWSLETTER, The Poetry Project, St. Mark's Church, 131 East 10th Street, New York, NY 10003, 212-674-0910. 1966. Poetry, fiction, articles, art, interviews, criticism, reviews, letters. "We also list events scheduled at the Poetry Project and publications received." circ. 5M. 5/yr. Pub'd 4 issues 1998; expects 4 issues 1999, 4 issues 2000. sub. price: $20; per copy: $5; sample: $5. Back issues: $5 if available. Discounts: none. 32pp; 8½×11. Reporting time: 2 months. Simultaneous submissions accepted: yes. Payment: copies. Not copyrighted. Pub's reviews: 40 in 1998. Ads: $200/$130/$40-200.

POETRY REVIEW, Peter Forbes, 22 Betterton Street, London WC2H 9BU, England. 1912. Poetry, articles, photos, interviews, criticism, reviews, letters, long-poems. circ. 5M. 4/yr. Pub'd 4 issues 1998; expects 4 issues 1999. sub. price: $38 individuals, $45 institutions, $55 airmail; per copy: $10 surface; $15 airmail; sample: $10 surface, $15 airmail. Back issues: $10 surface, $15 airmail. Discounts: 1/3 to trade. 72pp; 240×170mm, copy size 198×147mm; of/lo. Reporting time: 3 months. Payment: £15 per poet for first poem, £20 for 2 poems. Copyrighted, reverts to author. Pub's reviews: 120 in 1998. §Poetry, criticism, relevant novels, biographies/autobiographies, belle-lettres, etc. Ads: £250/£170/£300 back page/£85 1/4 page/£275 3,500 loose inserts. The Poetry Society.

POETRY USA, National Poetry Association Publishers, Jack Mueller, Editor-in-Chief; Adam Shames, Managing Editor, 934 Brannan Street, 2nd floor, San Francisco, CA 94103, 415-552-9261; FAX 415-552-9291; E-mail gamuse@slip.net, http://www.slip.net.gamuse. 1985. Poetry, reviews. "Submission: Send no more than three poems, SASE, and e-mail address. *Poetry USA,* published by the National Poetry Association based in San Francisco, is a quarterly journal that aims to provide a common space for the diversity of voices that make up the American experience. Each issue usually includes poems from all over the country, and often includes sections from young people, people without a home, and people in prison. Our preference tends to be for shorter poems (under 50 lines, please) accessible to the non-literary general public. Poets from the community are invited to serve as guest editors, choosing different themes for each issue. *Poetry USA* was reorganizing during 1994 and 1995, and the summer 1996 issue marks the beginning of full output once again. The National Poetry Association, an all-volunteer organization founded in 1975, is committed to promoting the written, spoken and visual use of language in new and traditional ways." circ. 3M. 3-4/yr. Pub'd 4 issues 1998; expects 4 issues 1999, 4 issues 2000. sub. price: $10, $15 outside U.S.; per copy: $3; sample: $4 ppd. Back issues: $4 ppd. Discounts: 50%. 24-36pp; 11×17; of. Reporting time: 2-6 months. Simultaneous submissions accepted: yes. Publishes 5% of manuscripts submitted. Payment: 2 copies. Copyrighted, reverts to author. Pub's reviews: 4 in 1998. §Poetry and poetry anthologies. Ads: $200/$125/$50 1/8 page/$25 card. P.E.N.

POETRY WALES, Poetry Wales Press, Ltd., Robert Minhinnick, First Floor, 2 Wyndham Street, Bridgend, CF31 1EF, Wales. 1965. Poetry, articles, criticism, reviews, letters, long-poems. "Articles of not less than 2M words. All types of poetry considered. Originally biased towards Welsh, Anglo-Welsh poetry, or poetry by persons living in Wales. Now wider approach encompassing all British and US poets, writers and translations of foreign poets and critiques of same." circ. 1M. 4/yr. Pub'd 4 issues 1998; expects 4 issues 1999, 4 issues 2000. sub. price: £18 (payment in sterling, or add $ equivalent of £s for bank charges); per copy: £3; sample: £3 + postage. Discounts: trade 35%. 72pp; 177×248mm; of. Reporting time: 1-2 months. Simultaneous submissions accepted: no. Payment: by arrangement. Copyrighted, reverts to author. Pub's reviews: 50 in 1998. §Poetry,

445

criticism, literary history. Ads: £100/£50/£25 quarter-page.

Poetry Wales Press, Ltd. (see also POETRY WALES), M.R. Felton, First Floor, 2 Wyndham Street, Bridgend CF31 1EF, Wales. 1981. "America distribution: Dufour Editions Inc., PO Box 449, Chester Springs, PA 19425." avg. press run varies greatly. Pub'd 25 titles 1998; expects 25 titles 1999, 25 titles 2000. 99 titles listed in the *Small Press Record of Books in Print* (28th Edition, 1999-00). avg. price, cloth: $25; paper: $14. Discounts: 35% UK, 35% export. 100pp; size varies; of. Reporting time: up to 6 weeks. Payment: by contract. Copyrights for author.

Poets & Writers, Inc. (see also POETS & WRITERS MAGAZINE), Thesese Eiben, Editor, 72 Spring Street, New York, NY 10012, 212-226-3586, Fax 212-226-3963; e-Mail pwsubs@pw.org, www.pw.org. 1970. Articles, photos, interviews, letters, concrete art, news items, non-fiction. "Poets & Writers publishes *A Directory of American Poets and Fiction Writers*, 1999-2000 Edition, a listing of contact names, addresses, phone numbers, e-mail and website addresses and publications for over 7,400 poets, fiction writers, and performance writers. Additional titles: *Literary Agents: The Essential Guide for Writers*, and *Into Print: Guides to the Writing Life.*" avg. press run 3M. Pub'd 1 title 1998; expects 1 title 1999, 1 title 2000. 3 titles listed in the *Small Press Record of Books in Print* (28th Edition, 1999-00). avg. price, paper: $12.95-$34.95. Discounts: distributed through Small Press Distribution, 1341 7th Street, Berkeley, CA 94710-1403, 510-524-1668. Pages vary; size varies; web offset. Payment: minimal. Does not copyright for author.

POETS & WRITERS MAGAZINE, Poets & Writers, Inc., Therese Eiben, Editor, 72 Spring Street, New York, NY 10012, 212-226-3586, e-Mail pwsubs@pw.org; www.pw.org. 1973. Articles, photos, letters, concrete art, news items. "*Poets & Writers Magazine* publishes factual articles of interest to writers, editors, publishers, and all others interested in contemporary American literature. It also publishes essays, interviews with writers, and news and comments on publishing, political issues, grants and awards, and requests for submissions. Most articles are written by freelance writers. Always send a letter of inquiry to the editor prior to submitting a manuscript. *Poets & Writers Magazine* has a Letters column and encourages comment from readers. We publish occasional reviews of reference books, but do not review poetry or fiction." circ. 64M. 6/yr. Pub'd 6 issues 1998; expects 6 issues 1999, 6 issues 2000. sub. price: $19.95, $38/2 yrs for individuals; per copy: $4.95; sample: $4.95. Back issues: $3.95 prior to 1999, after $4.95. Discounts: bookstores, min. 10 copies, 40%; to distributors, min. 10 copies, 50%; to teachers, for bulk subscriptions, min. 20, 20% to one address. 120pp; 8½×11; web/of. Reporting time: 2 months. Simultaneous submissions accepted: no. Publishes 10% of manuscripts submitted. Payment: $100-$300. Copyrighted, reverts to author. Ads: $1,925/$1035, less 20% at 6X rate; classifieds $100 up to 50 words, over 50 $2 per add'l word.

POETS AT WORK, Jessee Poet Publications, Jessee Poet, Box 113, VAMC, 325 New Castle Road, Butler, PA 16001. 1985. Poetry. "Length—about 20 lines and under. I publish everyone who writes in good taste. William Middleton, Ralph Hammond, Ann Gasser, and at least 300 other poets. I am a marvelous market for unpublished poets." circ. 300+. 6/yr. Pub'd 6 issues 1998; expects 6 issues 1999, 6 issues 2000. sub. price: $20; per copy: $3.50; sample: $3.50. Back issues: $3. 36-40pp; 8½×11; †Mita copying machine. Reporting time: 2 weeks. Simultaneous submissions accepted and I accept previously published material (poetry). Payment: none. Copyrighted, reverts to author. Ads: negotiable.

POET'S FANTASY, Gloria Stoeckel, 227 Hatten Avenue, Rice Lake, WI 54868, 715-234-2205. 1991. Poetry, fiction, articles, art, photos, cartoons, reviews. "Poems: upto 24 lines. Short stories on fantasy only up to 1500 words. Articles up to 500 words. Contributors: Najwa Salam, Diana K. Rubin." circ. 250. 4/yr. Pub'd 4 issues 1998; expects 4 issues 1999, 4 issues 2000. sub. price: $18- $24 overseas; sample: $5; $8 overseas. Back issues: free with three 32¢ stamps. 40-48pp; 8½×11; †laser printer, Xerox. Reporting time: within 2 weeks. Simultaneous submissions accepted: no. Publishes 90% of manuscripts submitted. Payment: $5 off coupon for order of greeting cards with author's own verse on it, on publication $3 off subscription with coupon. Copyrighted, reverts to author. Pub's reviews: 20 in 1998. §How-to books (in writing field), poetry books, fantasy, short stories, fiction. $12 per 40 words a year; exchange ads to editors.

POET'S FORUM, John C. Brainerd, 18600 West 58 Avenue, Golden, CO 80403-1070, 303-279-2462. 1987. Poetry. circ. 689. 12/yr. Pub'd 12 issues 1998; expects 12 issues 1999, 12 issues 2000. sub. price: $50; per copy: $5; sample: $5. Back issues: $5. 40pp; 5½×8½; †of. Reporting time: 30-90 days. Payment: 1/2 net. Copyrighted, reverts to author. Ads: $50/$12/$5 per inch. Int. Pub. Assn.

POETS ON THE LINE, Linda Lerner, PO Box 020292, Brooklyn, NY 11202-0007, 212-766-4109. 1995. Poetry, interviews, non-fiction. "*No unsolicited manuscripts.* I have 8 issues of this anthology on line, including a double one: Nos. 6 7-Vietnam Veterans/Fall 1997 issue received a Puffin Foundation Grant. Included are: W.D. Ehrhart, Tony Moffeit, Enid Dame, Donald Lev, Bill Shields, etc. Ludwig Vogelstein Foundation Grant" 2/yr. Pub'd 1-2 issues 1998; expects 1 issue 1999, 1 issue 2000. 31pp. Payment: none. Copyrighted, reverts to author. Poets & Writers.

POET'S PARK, Richard Soos, 2745 Monterey Highway #76, San Jose, CA 95111-3129, 408-578-3546;

http://www.soos.com/poetpark. 1992. Poetry, art, cartoons, interviews, reviews, music, letters. "Important: On-line magazine; for all computers. The editor is not looking at credits, but at the poems themselves. Above all else, honesty and openness in style will get your published here." circ. unlimited. †World Wide Web. Reporting time: 1 week. Simultaneous submissions accepted: yes. Publishes 5% of manuscripts submitted. Payment: 1 copy, which is copyable. Copyrighted, reverts to author. Pub's reviews: 15 in 1998. §Poetry. Ads: $45 page.

POETS' ROUNDTABLE, Esther Alman, 826 South Center Street, Terre Haute, IN 47807, 812-234-0819. 1939. Poetry, news items. *"Poets' Rountable* is a bulletin published bimonthly for members of Poets' Study Club. It is not an open market for poetry. Open contests: One annual open competition—The International Contest, with awards of $25 and $15 in three categories: serious poems, light verse, traditional haiku. No entry fees. Deadline is February 1st each year. Send entries to Annual International Contest, Esther Alman, 826 South Center Street, Terre Haute, IN 47807. We use *only* material by members for publication, but annual contest is open to everyone. We keep manuscripts in a file, but will return on request, for publication of poems *by members only."* circ. 2M. 6/yr. Pub'd 6 issues 1998; expects 6 issues 1999, 6 issues 2000. sub. price: $10-membership; sample: free. 10pp; 8½x11; †mi. Payment: none. Copyrighted, reverts to author. Pub's reviews: 25 in 1998. No ads.

●**POETS' VOICE,** Barbara Fischer, Box 500901, Malabar, FL 32950, website www.worldtv3.com/jmark.htm. 1965. Articles, reviews, news items, non-fiction. "Up to 300 words. Tips to help poets improve skill and promote their books. We review self-published books. We also publish some items on our website. Always enclose a SASE." circ. 1M. 4/yr. Pub'd 4 issues 1998; expects 4 issues 1999, 4 issues 2000. sub. price: $4; per copy: $1; sample: free with SASE. 12pp; 7x8½; †of. Reporting time: 1 week. Simultaneous submissions accepted: yes. Publishes 60% of manuscripts submitted. Payment: copies, prizes. Copyrighted, reverts to author. Pub's reviews: 12 in 1998. §poetry, self-help, juvenile, non-fiction, history. Ads: $100/ $25 per quarter page.

●**POETS'PAPER, TWO RIVERS REVIEW,** Carole J. Heffley, PO Box 85, Easton, PA 18044-0085, 610-559-3887; Irregular@enter.net. 1997. Poetry, art, photos. "Contemporary, well-crafted poetry from national and international poets. A wide range of human emotions in poetic expression. No shock-value, rants, abusive, or pornographic words. Additional annual women's poetry edition in softcover book." circ. 500. 2/yr. Pub'd 2 issues 1998; expects 1 issue 1999, 1 issue 2000. price per copy: $5; sample: $5. Back issues: $3. Discounts: none. 20pp; 11x17; †of. Reporting time: 4-8 weeks. Simultaneous submissions accepted: no. Publishes approx. 60% of manuscripts submitted. Payment: none. Copyrighted, reverts to author. Ads: $340/$175/$85 1/4 page.

●**POETSWEST LITERARY JOURNAL,** Barbara A. Evans, Editor; J. Glenn Evans, Poetry Editor, 1011 Boren Avenue #155, Seattle, WA 98104, 206-682-1268; bjevans@postalzone.com. 1988. Poetry. "General poetry. Submit 6 poems not to exceed 60 lines. $6 reading fee includes pass to perform once and copy of *PoetsWest Literary Journal,* ten poets selected to read. Those selected and published expected to come to Seattle to recite at performance." 4/yr. Pub'd 4 issues 1998; expects 4 issues 1999, 4 issues 2000. price per copy: $5. Discounts: 40% to retailers. 80pp; 5½x8½. Reporting time: 2 months. Simultaneous submissions accepted: yes. Publishes 25% of manuscripts submitted. Payment: copy only. Copyrighted, reverts to author.

Pogo Press, Incorporated, Moira F. Harris, 4 Cardinal Lane, St. Paul, MN 55127, 651-483-4692, fax 651-483-4692, E-mail pogopres@minn.net. 1986. Art, non-fiction. "Submission by prearrangement only." avg. press run 3M. Pub'd 3 titles 1998; expects 3 titles 1999, 3 titles 2000. 20 titles listed in the *Small Press Record of Books in Print* (28th Edition, 1999-00). avg. price, cloth: $39.95; paper: $16.95. Discounts: query. Pages vary; size varies; of. Reporting time: 60 days. Simultaneous submissions accepted: no. Payment: negotiable. Copyrights for author.

●**Point Bonita Books,** Mark Rudinsky, 5920 Dimm Way, Richmond, CA 94805, 510-232-1401. 1998. Poetry, non-fiction. avg. press run 2.5M. Pub'd 1 title 1998; expects 1 title 1999, 1 title 2000. 2 titles listed in the *Small Press Record of Books in Print* (28th Edition, 1999-00). avg. price, paper: $12.95. Discounts: varies between 40-70%. 96pp; 5½x8½; of. Reporting time: varies. Simultaneous submissions accepted: yes. Publishes 1% of manuscripts submitted. Payment: varies. Copyrights for author. PMA, Access Publishers Network.

POINT OF CONTACT, Pedro Cuperman, 215 H.B. Crouse Building, Syracuse University, Syracuse, NY 13244-1160, 315-443-5497; FAX 315-443-5376. 1975. Fiction, articles, cartoons, satire, news items, non-fiction. circ. 2M. 2/yr. Pub'd 2 issues 1998; expects 1 issue 1999, 2 issues 2000. sub. price: $15, $24 institutions; per copy: $8. Back issues: $12. Discounts: 20%. 110pp; 7x10. Reporting time: 2 months. Payment: $50 per article. Copyrighted, does not revert to author. Ads: $550/$275/$175.

Point Riders Press, Arn Henderson, Frank Parman, PO Box 2731, Norman, OK 73070. 1974. Poetry, art, photos, non-fiction. "Publisher of books of poetry and non-fiction relation to southern great plains, history and people. Over 30 books in print. No unsolicited mss. Not impressed by academic letterhead or address." avg. press run 500-1M. Expects 2 titles 1999, 2 titles 2000. 36 titles listed in the *Small Press Record of Books in*

Print (28th Edition, 1999-00). avg. price, paper: $7. Discounts: single copy 15%, 2 to 4 copies 25%, 5 or more 40%. 64pp; 6×9, 5½×8½; of. Reporting time: 6 months. Payment: in copies. Copyrights for author.

●**Polar Bear & Company**, Paul Houx, Brook Street, Solon, ME 04979, e-mail polarbear@skow.net. Poetry, fiction, art, photos, non-fiction. "We are now accepting manuscripts, artwork, and photography for evaluation and assistance. Submit with SASE, possible publication." avg. press run 1-5M. Pub'd 2 titles 1998; expects 3 titles 1999, 3 titles 2000. 190pp; 4½×7. Reporting time: 1 month. Simultaneous submissions accepted: yes. Publishes 5% of manuscripts submitted. Payment: worked out with author. Copyrights for author. Maine Writers and Publishers Alliance.

Polar Bear Productions & Company, Paul Du Houx, Ramona Du Houx, PO Box 311 Brook Street, Solon, ME 04979, 207-643-2795. 1991. Poetry, fiction, art, photos, cartoons, letters, parts-of-novels, news items, non-fiction. "The length can be negotiable. The truth of bettering the world by improving ourselves and our environment in areas of everyday life is the main theme. Everyone makes a difference to keep a natural democracy alive. Submissions with SASE only." avg. press run 2M. Expects 3 titles 1999, 4 titles 2000. 3 titles listed in the *Small Press Record of Books in Print* (28th Edition, 1999-00). avg. price, paper: $5.95; other: $4.95 cassette. 200pp; 4½×7; of, lp. Simultaneous submissions accepted: no. Payment: individual. Copyrights for author. MWPA.

Polebridge Press (see also FORUM; THE FOURTH R), PO Box 6144, Santa Rosa, CA 95406, 707-523-1323, fax 707-523-1350. 1981. Articles, interviews, criticism, reviews.

Poltroon Press, Alastair Johnston, PO Box 5476, Berkeley, CA 94705, 510-845-8097. 1974. Poetry, fiction, art, photos, interviews, satire, criticism, concrete art, non-fiction. "Do not read unsolicited work. Recent books: Lucia Berlin's *Safe & Sound*, short stories, 1988; Alastair Johnston's *Musings On The Vernacular*, illustrated essays, 1988; Robert Gregory's *Interferences*, poetry, 1987; Dawn Kolokithas' *A Week In The Life Of The Marines, America's Elite Fighting Team*, experimental fiction, 1988." avg. press run 200-500. Pub'd 4 titles 1998; expects 5 titles 1999, 4 titles 2000. 5 titles listed in the *Small Press Record of Books in Print* (28th Edition, 1999-00). avg. price, cloth: $30; paper: $12. Discounts: distributor: Anacapa, Berkeley; Small Press Distribution. 64pp; 6×9; †lp. Payment: 15%. Copyrights for author. PCBA.

Polygonal Publishing House, Michael Weinstein, PO Box 357, Washington, NJ 07882, 908-689-3894. 1976. Non-fiction. "We publish books on mathematics." avg. press run 1M. Pub'd 1 title 1998; expects 1 title 1999, 1 title 2000. 14 titles listed in the *Small Press Record of Books in Print* (28th Edition, 1999-00). avg. price, cloth: $20; paper: $7. Discounts: 20% trade & bulk. 200pp; of. Payment: 17%.

Pomegranate Communications, PO Box 6099, Rohnert Park, CA 94927, 707-586-5500; fax 707-586-5518; e-mail info@pomegranate.com. 1965. Art, photos. avg. press run 5M-15M. Pub'd 24 titles 1998; expects 20 titles 1999, 20 titles 2000. 91 titles listed in the *Small Press Record of Books in Print* (28th Edition, 1999-00). avg. price, cloth: $30; paper: $20. Discounts: 50% non-returnable. 110pp; size varies widely; of. Reporting time: 6 weeks. Simultaneous submissions accepted: yes. Publishes a small % of manuscripts submitted. Copyrights for author.

Ponderosa Publishers, Esther Vm Hamel, 1369 Blue Lake Circle, Punta Gorda, FL 33983-5951, 406-745-4455. 1966. Non-fiction. "Not soliciting at this time. Moving offices to Seattle: 37522 21st Avenue South, Federal Way, WA 98003." avg. press run 1M-5M. avg. price, cloth: $23; paper: $5. Discounts: trade 24%, check with order. 250-300pp; 6×9. Reporting time: 2-3 months.

Poor Souls Press/Scaramouche Books, Paul Fericano, Katherine Daly, Pamela Meuser, Kate Fericano, PO Box 236, Millbrae, CA 94030. 1974. Satire. "Sorry, but Poor Souls Press cannot accept unsolicited material. If you're a satirist, we encourage self-publishing and close contact with others involved in the genre. Poor Souls Press is the book publishing subsidiary of Yossarian Universal (YU) News Service, the world's only parody news and disinformation syndicate with bureaus in 37 cities worldwide. We publish broadsides, postcards, chapbooks, pamphlets, and dispatches." avg. press run 3. Pub'd 3 titles 1998; expects 3 titles 1999, 3 titles 2000. 101 titles listed in the *Small Press Record of Books in Print* (28th Edition, 1999-00). avg. price, other: 2¢, 5¢, 10¢ etc. 1 page; 8½×11, 5½×8½; †of. Payment: usually pay our authors with half the print run. Copyrights for author. (YU) Yossarian Universal News Service.

Popular Medicine Press, Jack Z. Yetiv, PO Box 1212, San Carlos, CA 94070, 415-594-1855. 1986. Non-fiction. "Current active title is *Popular Nutritional Practices: A Scientific Appraisal*, a hard-hitting, unbiased book written by a physician/scientist. This 320-page book dispassionately evaluates multiple popular nutritional practices, including megavitamins, weight-loss diets, herbal remedies, starch blockers, food allergy and cytotoxic testing, Life Extension ideas and regimens, fish oil and heart disease, hypoglycemia, diets for diabetics, high blood pressure, and many others. Similar book manuscripts will be considered, although we are currently devoting most of our attention to the above title. This book is $17.95 (ppb.), $23.95 (case), retail, pp." avg. press run 5M. Expects 1 title 1999, 1 title 2000. 1 title listed in the *Small Press Record of Books in Print*

(28th Edition, 1999-00). Discounts: trade, 20% on STOP orders. 350pp; 6×9; of. Reporting time: 8 weeks. Payment: to be arranged. Copyrights for author.

The Porcupine's Quill, Inc., John Metcalf, John Newlove, 68 Main Street, Erin, Ontario N0B 1T0, Canada, 519-833-9158. 1974. Poetry, fiction, art, criticism. avg. press run 500-1M. Pub'd 6 titles 1998; expects 7 titles 1999, 7 titles 2000. 82 titles listed in the *Small Press Record of Books in Print* (28th Edition, 1999-00). avg. price, cloth: $20; paper: $8.95; other: $40 limited editions. Discounts: 5 & over, 40%. 112pp; 6×9; †of. Reporting time: 2 months. Payment: per contract. Copyrights for author. LPG, LCP.

PORTALS, Redrosebush Press, Ella M. Dillon, PO Box 2163, Wenatchee, WA 98807-2163, 509-662-7858. 1991. Poetry, fiction, articles, art, photos, cartoons, interviews, satire, criticism, reviews, letters, non-fiction. "Prefer poetry 30 lines or less, other writings 500-1,500 words." circ. 1M+. 4/yr. Pub'd 4 issues 1998; expects 4 issues 1999, 4 issues 2000. sub. price: $15; per copy: $5; sample: free. Back issues: $2.50. Discounts: none. 44pp; 8½×11; of. Reporting time: when published. Simultaneous submissions accepted: yes. Payment: none. Copyrighted, reverts to author. Pub's reviews: 5 in 1998. §No pornography. Ads: $300/$200/$25 and up.

Portals Press, John P. Travis, 4411 Fountainebleau Drive, New Orleans, LA 70125, 504-821-7723; E-mal jptravis@worldnet.att.net. 1992. Poetry, fiction. "Richard Katrouas - *Prague, USA* (short stories). Tom Whalen -*Reithamer's Universe* (SF novel). William S. Maddox - *Scacciato* (novel)." avg. press run 500-1M. Pub'd 2 titles 1998; expects 3 titles 1999, 2-3 titles 2000. 5 titles listed in the *Small Press Record of Books in Print* (28th Edition, 1999-00). avg. price, paper: $11. Discounts: 40% single, 50% multiple. 128pp; 5½×8½; of. Reporting time: 1 month. Simultaneous submissions accepted: no. Payment: 10-20%. Copyrights for author. Small Press Association.

Bern Porter Books, Bern Porter, 50 Salmond Road, Belfast, ME 04915, 207-338-3763. 1911. "Type of material used: vanguard, experimental and classic contemporary. Arts, bibliography, short story, drama, poetry, contemporary classic literature." avg. press run 1.75M. Pub'd 467 titles 1998; expects 482 titles 1999, 493 titles 2000. 9 titles listed in the *Small Press Record of Books in Print* (28th Edition, 1999-00). avg. price, cloth: $8.50; paper: $2.10; other: $12.50. Discounts: normal or all current standard. 167pp; 5½×7, 8½×11; lp. Reporting time: 3 weeks. Payment: 10% royalty on all sales. Copyrights in author's name. NESPA, MPW, STWP.

BERN PORTER INTERNATIONAL, Sheila Holtz, Editor, PO Box 553, Royersford, PA 19468. 1997. 6/yr. sub. price: $10; sample: $2.50. 12pp; 8½×11. Reporting time: 30 days. Payment: per wordage. Copyrighted. Pub's reviews: 7 in 1998. §World literature experimental.

PORTLAND REVIEW, Amber Black, Editor, PO Box 347, Portland, OR 97207-0347, 503-725-4533. 1955. Poetry, fiction, art, photos, satire, criticism, parts-of-novels, long-poems, collages, plays. "*Portland Review* is an arts and literary publication that seeks the innovative. Send for rate sheet. ISSN #0360-3091." circ. 600. 3/yr. Pub'd 2 issues 1998; expects 3 issues 1999, 3 issues 2000. sub. price: $23; per copy: $6 ($1 p/h); sample: $3 ($1 p/h) back issues, $6 ($1 p/h) current issues. Back issues: $3 ($1 p/h). 150pp; 6×9; of. Reporting time: 2 months. Simultaneous submissions accepted: yes. Publishes 5% of manuscripts submitted. Payment: copies and exposure. Copyrighted, reverts to author. Pub's reviews: 1 in 1998. §Broad areas of interest. Ads: $100/$60/$30 1/4 page. CLMP.

Portmanteau Editions, Harry H. Barlow, Jennifer M. Thornton, PO Box 665, Somers, NY 10589. 1987. Poetry, fiction, satire, non-fiction. "Publishing schedule filled. The editors, in the depressive phase of their manic-depression, can't consider new manuscripts or proposals at present." Pub'd 2 titles 1998; expects 2 titles 1999, 3 titles 2000. 3 titles listed in the *Small Press Record of Books in Print* (28th Edition, 1999-00). Discounts: standard. of. Reporting time: 4 months. Payment: standard royalties. Copyrights for author.

●**Portunus Publishing Company**, Christina Carpenter, 316 Mid Valley Center #270, Carmel, CA 93923, E-mail service@portunus.net; website www.portunus.net. 1994. "We publish children's picture books with strong, uplifting social messages." avg. press run 6M. Pub'd 1 title 1998; expects 4 titles 1999, 6 titles 2000. 3 titles listed in the *Small Press Record of Books in Print* (28th Edition, 1999-00). avg. price, cloth: $14.95; paper: $6.95. 32pp; 8½×11; †of. Reporting time: 2 months. Simultaneous submissions accepted: no. Publishes 12% of manuscripts submitted. Payment: negotiated royalty, $500 advance. Copyrights for author. PMA, ABA, ABC.

POSITIONS: East Asia Cultures Critique, Duke University Press, Tani E. Barlow, Box 90660, Duke University, Durham, NC 27708-0660. "Crossing boundaries and rethinking the terms of theoretical analysis, *positions* is the first journal to examine critically the histories and cultures of East Asia and Asian America. Through scholarly articles, commentary, essays, and in-depth book reviews, *positions* focuses on the profound intellectual, political, and economic transformations that are rapidly reconfiguring East Asia. Built on the premise that criticism must always be self-critical, *positions* offers East Asia historians, literary scholars, anthropologists, and cultural theorists a forum for debate and encourages and cultivates fresh approaches to East

Asia. Send review copies to James Hevia, RR 11, Box 308, Carrboro, NC 27510.'' circ. 700. 3/yr. Pub'd 3 issues 1998; expects 3 issues 1999, 3 issues 2000. sub. price: $60 institutions, $26 individuals, $18 students with photocopy of current I.D., additional $9 foreign. Pub's reviews. Ads: $175/$100.

Positive Press - Star Bear Books, Richard Gilbar, PO Box 7626, Chico, CA 95927, 530-894-5068; FAX 530-894-3310. 1994. ''32pp picturebooks, must be funny, off-beat with ethics/environment/spiritual orientation.'' avg. press run 3-4M. Expects 5 titles 1999, 5 titles 2000. 4 titles listed in the *Small Press Record of Books in Print* (28th Edition, 1999-00). avg. price, cloth: $14.95; paper: $6.95. Discounts: trade 40%, bulk 10-40%. 32pp; 10×8. Reporting time: 1 month. Simultaneous submissions accepted with SASE. Payment: will package/promote for % and costs. Copyrights for author. USBBY, Bookbuilders, SPAH.

Positive Publishing, Steve Cooper, 123 E. Pinelake Drive, suite 200, Williamsville, NY 14221, 716-639-0225; fax 716-636-1894; email positive-way@mail.com. 1996. Articles, non-fiction. ''All material must be positive in nature and educational in some way. Focus on aspects of what makes love and relationships work. Absolutely no unsolicited manuscripts! Must query with SASE. Recent title—*Talk to Me: How to Create Positive Loving Communication.*'' avg. press run 3M. Expects 1 title 1999, 3 titles 2000. 1 title listed in the *Small Press Record of Books in Print* (28th Edition, 1999-00). avg. price, paper: $12.95. Discounts: call. 150pp; 5½×8½. Reporting time: 8 weeks. Simultaneous submissions accepted: no. Publishes 2% of manuscripts submitted. Payment: to be discussed. Does not copyright for author. PMA, SPAN.

THE POST, Publishers Syndication Int'l (PSI), A.P. Samuels, Publishers Syndication Int'l, PO Box 6218, Charlottesville, VA 22906-6218. 1987. Fiction. ''No explicit sex, gore, sadism or horror. Manuscripts must be for a general audience. Just good plain story telling with unique plot. Photocopies okay, no simultaneous submissions, please. Fiction: Mystery/suspense short stories 10,000 words, buy 12 a year. We also buy 30,000 word mystery/suspense, buy 12 a year. Romance: 10,000 word, buy 12 a year, 30,000 word, buy 12 a year. Will buy first time manuscripts if good enough. The type of mystery we are looking for is devoid of references which might offend. (Sherlock Holmes would be a good example of the type of stories we require). Show word count on your submission. If you use a computer, please specify kind, disk size, density and the name of the word processing program you are using. In some cases we may request disk copy of your story. Please be aware that PSI is opening new markets for stories of this length and exact publishing date is not always available. When the story is published, the author will be notified.'' 24/yr. Expects 12 issues 1999, 24 issues 2000. 32pp; 8½×11; of. Reporting time: 4-6 weeks. Simultaneous submissions accepted: no. Payment: 1-4¢ per word on acceptance plus royalty. Copyrighted, does not revert to author.

The Post-Apollo Press, Simone Fattal, 35 Marie Street, Sausalito, CA 94965, 415-332-1458, fax 415-332-8045. 1982. Poetry, fiction. avg. press run 1M. Pub'd 2 titles 1998; expects 4 titles 1999, 2 titles 2000. 12 titles listed in the *Small Press Record of Books in Print* (28th Edition, 1999-00). avg. price, paper: $10.95. Discounts: trade 40%; distributors 55%; jobber, classroom 20%. of. Reporting time: 6 months. Simultaneous submissions accepted: no. Payment: percentage after all expenses are met. Copyrights for author.

POSTCARD, Jenny Fowler, PO Box 444, Tivioli, NY 12583. 1995. Poetry, fiction, art, photos, non-fiction. ''*Postcard* considers: short fiction, poetry, paragraphs, b/w art (no larger than 8 x 5). Written works may be handwritten (legibly please) or typed. Due to microcosmic format shorter pieces are preferred. Translations also welcome. Please send SASE with sufficient postage for a response.'' circ. 200. 2/yr. Pub'd 1 issue 1998; expects 2 issues 1999, 2 issues 2000. sub. price: $3; sample: spare change. Back issues: none. Discounts: none. 7-12pp; 4¼×5½; lasercopy. Reporting time: about 2 months. Simultaneous submissions accepted: yes. Payment: copies. Copyrights revert to author on publication. Ads: none.

POSTCARD CLASSICS, Deltiologists of America, Dr. James Lewis Lowe, PO Box 8, Norwood, PA 19074, 215-485-8572. 1960. ''Focuses on pre-1920 picture postcards including views, comics, greetings—all publishers, all countries, all types.'' circ. 1.2M. 6/yr. Pub'd 6 issues 1998; expects 6 issues 1999, 6 issues 2000. sub. price: $12; per copy: $2.50; sample: $2.50. Back issues: 60 back issues of *Deltiology* for $30 plus shipping. 16pp; 8½×11. Reporting time: 30 days. Payment: usually in copies. Not copyrighted. Pub's reviews: 6 in 1998. §Books about picture postcards only. Ads: $50/$27.50.

Pot Shard Press, M.L. Harrison Mackie, PO Box 215, Comptche, CA 95427, 707-937-2058. 1997. Poetry. ''Pot Shard's mission is to publish new poets and bring known poets to a wider audience.'' avg. press run 1M. Pub'd 2 titles 1998. 4 titles listed in the *Small Press Record of Books in Print* (28th Edition, 1999-00). avg. price, paper: $12.95. Discounts: returnable 1-9 40%, 10+ 44%, non-returnable 1-9 45%, 10+ 48%. 100pp; 9×6. Payment: negotiated privately. Copyrights for author. PMA, SPAN.

POTATO EYES, Nightshade Press, Roy Zarucchi, Carolyn Page, PO Box 76, Troy, ME 04987, 207-948-3427; Fax 207-948-5088; E-mail potatoeyes@uninets.net; website www.maineguide.om/giftshop/potatoeyes. 1988. Poetry, fiction, art, interviews, reviews, long-poems. ''Recent contributors: Richard Abrons, Jennifer B. MacPherson, Robert Morgan, Tim Suermondt, Barbara Presnell. Short Fiction: to 3,000 words. Poetry: concrete visual imagery, blank verse, free verse, narrative. We like poetry and fiction that is rural,

450

rebellious or thought-provoking, or all of the above. Artwork: pen and ink preferred, but other black on white ok. No photography. General: no haiku, 'religious', Hallmarkian, light verse or navel study. Submit anytime. Send SASE." circ. 800. 2/yr. Pub'd 2 issues 1998; expects 2 issues 1999, 2 issues 2000. sub. price: $11; per copy: $7; sample: $5. Back issues: $5. Discounts: 40% to bookstores. 112pp; 5½x8½; of. Reporting time: 8-14 weeks. Publishes 5% of manuscripts submitted. Payment: copies. Copyrighted, reverts to author. Pub's reviews: 8 in 1998. §Chapbooks, poetry and short story collections. no ads. MWPA, CLMP, NCWN, NHWP.

Potentials Development, Inc., Cindy B. Seide, President, 779 Cayuga Street, Apt#1, Lewiston, NY 14092-1728. 1978. Non-fiction. "Resource for caregivers of the elderly" avg. press run 500. Pub'd 1 title 1998; expects 2 titles 1999, 3 titles 2000. 20 titles listed in the *Small Press Record of Books in Print* (28th Edition, 1999-00). avg. price, paper: $10.95; other: games, quizzes $3.95. Please write for discount schedule. 65pp; 5½x8; of. Reporting time: 6 weeks. Payment: royalty schedule presently being reviewed. Copyrights for author if desired.

Potes & Poets Press Inc., Peter Ganick, 181 Edgemont Avenue, Elmwood, CT 06110, 203-233-2023; e-mail potepoet@home.com. 1980. Poetry. avg. press run 160. Pub'd 8 titles 1998; expects 8 titles 1999. 50 titles listed in the *Small Press Record of Books in Print* (28th Edition, 1999-00). avg. price, paper: $5. Discounts: 1-2 no discount, 3-5 20%, 6+ 40%. 20pp; 8½x11; stapled newsletter. Reporting time: 3 months. Publishes 5% of manuscripts submitted. Payment: 10 copies. Does not copyright for author.

POTOMAC REVIEW, Eli Flam, Editor; Hilary Tham, Poetry Editor, PO Box 354, Port Tobacco, MD 20677. 1994. Poetry, fiction, articles, art, photos, interviews, satire, reviews, letters, parts-of-novels, plays, non-fiction. "Prose submissions should be no more than 3,000 words. We carry first-timers as well as the previous published. Regionally based, we seek up to three poems to total at five pages. A full range of poets, writers (fiction-nonfiction) and artwork. Our aim is to inform, entertain and provide ethical depth to get at 'the concealed' side of life." circ. 1.7M. 4/yr. Pub'd 4 issues 1998; expects 4 issues 1999, 4 issues 2000. sub. price: $15; per copy: $4; sample: $3. Back issues: $3. Discounts: on ads $20 for a year's worth. 132pp; 5½x8½; of. Reporting time: within 90 days. Simultaneous submissions accepted, but should be noted. Publishes approx. 5% of manuscripts submitted. Payment: 1 copy, modest sum for assigned nonfiction. Copyrighted, reverts to author. Pub's reviews: about 30 in 1998. §From regionally-relevant fiction, non-fiction, poetry outward. Ads: $250/$150/$190. CLMP.

POTPOURRI: A Magazine of the Literary Arts, Polly W. Swafford, Senior Editor, PO Box 8278, Prairie Village, KS 66208, 913-642-1503; Fax 913-642-3128; e-mail potpourrppub@aol.com. 1989. Poetry, fiction, articles, interviews, non-fiction. "Prose - 3,500 word max. Poetry - length to 75 lines; no more than 3 poems per submission. No religious, confessional, racial, political, abusive, or sexual preference materials unless fictional and necessary to plot or characterization. Recent contributors: Alan Britt, David Ray, Walter Cummins, Deborah Shouse, Carol Hamilton, Robert Parham, Robert Cooperman. *Potpourri* publishes a wide genre; hence its name. It welcomes fiction, nonfiction, poetry, travel, essays." circ. 3.5M. 4/yr. Pub'd 4 issues 1998; expects 4 issues 1999, 4 issues 2000. sub. price: $15; per copy: $4.95; sample: $4.95 with 9 X 12 envelope. Back issues: incl. post/handling $3.50. Discounts: 40% to retail outlets and distributors even exchange with trade; bulk rates negotiable. 80pp; 8x10¾; of lithograph. Reporting time: 8-12 weeks on fiction. We accept simultaneous submissions if notified with submission. Publishes 12% of manuscripts submitted. Payment: copies. Copyrighted, reverts to author. Pub's reviews: 4 in 1998. §Broad interest, general public, following guidelines for *Potpourri.* Ads: $150/$90/up to 20% discount for repeat ads; Minikin ad (approx. 3 X 3) $35. CMA.

THE POTTERSFIELD PORTFOLIO, Douglas Arthur Brown, Managing Editor, PO Box 40, Station A, Sydney, Nova Scotia B1P 6G9, Canada, www.auracom.com/saunde/potters.html. 1979. Poetry, fiction, art, photos, parts-of-novels, long-poems, plays, non-fiction. "We publish work by new and award-winning writers and artists. No sexist, racist, homophobic or classist material. No erotica. Include SASE and short bio note. No simultaneous submissions. Buys first Canadian serial rights. Pays $5 per page to a max of $25." circ. 1M. 3/yr. Pub'd 3 issues 1998; expects 3 issues 1999, 3 issues 2000. sub. price: $17 Canadian, $26 US and overseas (in U.S. dollars); per copy: $6; sample: $6. Back issues: $5. Discounts: trade 40% on 4 copies or more. 96pp; 8½x11; of. Reporting time: 3 months. Simultaneous submissions accepted: no. Publishes 5% of manuscripts submitted. Payment: contributors copy-$5 per page (Canadian) to a max of $25. Copyrighted, reverts to author. Pub's reviews: 15 in 1998. §Books by Atlantic Canadian Authors. Ads: none. CMPA (Canadian Magazine Publishers Association), APA (Atlantic Publishers Association).

Pottersfield Press, Lesley Choyce, 83 Leslie Road, East Lawrencetown, NS, B2Z 1P8, Canada, 1-800-Nimbus 9 (for orders). 1979. Fiction, photos, cartoons, satire, non-fiction. "Interest in Canadian, Nova Scotian material, especially non-fiction right now. U.S. orders to:" avg. press run 1M-2M. Pub'd 6 titles 1998; expects 6 titles 1999, 6 titles 2000. 46 titles listed in the *Small Press Record of Books in Print* (28th Edition, 1999-00). avg. price, paper: $9.95. Discounts: 20% 1-5 books, 40% 6+ mixed titles. 192pp; 6½x9½; of. Reporting time: 3 months. Payment: 10% list. Copyrights for author. ACP, APA.

Samuel Powell Publishing Company, 2201 I Street, Sacramento, CA 95816, 916-443-1161. 1978. Fiction. avg. press run 750. Expects 1-2 titles 1999, 1-2 titles 2000. 5 titles listed in the *Small Press Record of Books in Print* (28th Edition, 1999-00). avg. price, paper: $5. Discounts: 55% distributors, 40% bookstores. 105pp; 5½×8½; of. Copyrights for author.

Power Publications (see also REVOLUTION), Elizabeth Wallace, 56 McArthur Avenue, Staten Island, NY 10312, 800-331-6534; Fax 718-317-0858. 1990. Non-fiction. "We accept only manuscripts pertaining to the field of nursing, women's issues and the health care field. In addition, we are looking to expand our horizons and will examine other submissions." avg. press run 2M. Pub'd 4 titles 1998; expects 2 titles 1999, 4 titles 2000. 10 titles listed in the *Small Press Record of Books in Print* (28th Edition, 1999-00). avg. price, paper: $19.95. Discounts: 20%-50%. 100+pp; 6×9. Reporting time: 3 weeks. Simultaneous submissions accepted: yes. Publishes 50% of manuscripts submitted. Payment: 15-20%. Copyrights for author.

The Power Within Institute, Inc., PO Box 595, Matlacha, FL 33993-0595, 1-941-283-3852. 1987. 2 titles listed in the *Small Press Record of Books in Print* (28th Edition, 1999-00).

POW-WOW, Full Moon Publications, Sharida Rizzuto, Harold Tollison, Elaine Wolfe, 577 Central Avenue #4, Jefferson, LA 70121-1400, e-mail: horizons@altavista.net or blueskies@discoverymail.com; Websites www.freeyellow.com/members2/oldwest/index.htm/, www2.cybercities.com/z/zines/. 1983. Poetry, fiction, articles, art, photos, cartoons, interviews, satire, criticism, reviews, letters, long-poems, collages, news items, non-fiction. "Articles, reviews, interviews about Native Americans" circ. 300. 2/yr. Pub'd 2 issues 1998; expects 2 issues 1999, 2 issues 2000. sub. price: $13.80; per copy: $6.90; sample: $6.90. Back issues: $6.90. Discounts: trade with other like publications. 80pp; 8½×11; †of. Reporting time: 2-6 weeks. Simultaneous submissions accepted: yes. Publishes 30-35% of manuscripts submitted. §Native Americans past and present. NWC, HWA, MWA, WWA, AAA, Small Press Genre Association.

THE POWYS JOURNAL, The Powys Society, Dr. Peter Foss, Louise De Bruin, 82 Linden Road, Gloucester, Gloucestershire GL1 5HD, England. 1991. Articles, reviews. "*The Powys Journal* is a refereed journal published by the Powys Society to promote the understanding and appreciation of the lives and works of the members of the Powys family, principally John Cowper Powys, Theodore Francis Powys and Llewelyn Powys. Scholarly and critical articles, memoirs and unpublished works by the Powys family are welcomed." circ. 500. 1/yr. Pub'd 1 issue 1998; expects 1 issue 1999, 1 issue 2000. sub. price: £7.50; per copy: £7.50; sample: £7.50. Back issues: 1991 £6, 1992 £7. Discounts: by arrangement. 230pp; 6×8½; of. Reporting time: 1 month. Payment: 2 copies of journal on publication. Copyrighted, reverts to author. Pub's reviews: 5 in 1998. §All material related to Powys family and their circle. Ads: by arrangement.

The Powys Society (see also THE POWYS JOURNAL), Dr. Peter Foss, Louis De Bruin, Hamilton's, Kilmersdon, Bath, Somerset, U.K. BA3 5TE, Gloucester, Gloucestershire GL1 5HD, England, 0452-304539. avg. press run 500. Pub'd 3 titles 1998; expects 2 titles 1999, 2 titles 2000. 6 titles listed in the *Small Press Record of Books in Print* (28th Edition, 1999-00). Discounts: by arrangement. Pages vary; size varies; of.

PPT EXPRESS, Morning Glory Press, Jeanne Warren Lindsay, Editor, 6595 San Haroldo Way, Buena Park, CA 90620. 1991. "A newsletter for teachers and others working with pregnant/parenting teens." circ. 6M. 4/yr. Pub'd 4 issues 1998; expects 4 issues 1999, 4 issues 2000. sub. price: $15/year, $25/2 years; sample: free. Back issues: #4. 12pp; 8½×11. Reporting time: 2 months. Simultaneous submissions accepted: yes. Publishes 3% of manuscripts submitted. Payment: to date, no pay. Copyrighted. Pub's reviews: 15-20 in 1998. §Books dealing with adolescent pregnancy and parenting. Ads: none. PMA.

THE PRAGMATIST, Jorge E. Amador, Box 392, Forest Grove, PA 18922, FAX: 215-348-8006. 1983. Articles, cartoons, satire, reviews, letters, non-fiction. "*The Pragmatist* presents practical proposals for saving every person thousands in taxes by opening up government monopolies & services to competition. Examines beliefs and legislation that hinder individuals' lifestyle choices. Length of material 1,000-2,500 words; best to inquire about topic first. Purchases first or second serial rights; will run copyright notice for individual authors on request. Foreign subscription (one year): US $15." circ. 1.2M. 6/yr. Pub'd 6 issues 1998; expects 7 issues 1999, 5 issues 2000. sub. price: $12; per copy: $3; sample: $3. Back issues: $3 each, $10 for volume sets (6 issues). Discounts: 50% to bookstores or reselling agents (3+ copies of same issue). 16pp; 8½×11; of. Reporting time: 8 weeks. Payment: 1¢ per word + 5 copies of issue with article, and 4 issue subscription. Not copyrighted. Pub's reviews: 11 in 1998. §Economics, civil liberties issues. Ads: $60/$35/$20 quarter-page/$12 eighth-page.

PRAIRIE FIRE, Andris Taskans, Managing Editor; Louise Jonasson, Art Director, 423-100 Arthur Street, Winnipeg MB R3B 1H3, Canada, 204-943-9066, fax 942-1555. 1978. Poetry, fiction, articles, art, photos, interviews, criticism, reviews, letters, parts-of-novels, long-poems. "Length: up to 5M words prose, up to 6 poems. Biases: Prairie or Canadian literature. Contributors: David Berger, Di Brandt, Patrick Friesen, Robert Kroetsch, Patrick Lane, Carol Shields, Aritha van Herk." circ. 1.5M. 4/yr. Pub'd 4 issues 1998; expects 4 issues 1999, 4 issues 2000. sub. price: $25 Can. $30 US $35 Fgr, institutions add $10 per annum; per copy: $10.95; sample: $9.95. Back issues: send for price list. Discounts: negotiable. 160pp; 9×6; of. Reporting time:

4+ months. Simultaneous submissions accepted: no. Publishes 5% of manuscripts submitted. Payment: 1 copy and contributor's fee. Copyrighted, reverts to author. Pub's reviews: 116 in 1998. §Poetry, fiction, criticism, authors' biography/memoir. Ads: $350/$200. CMPA, AMBP.

THE PRAIRIE JOURNAL OF CANADIAN LITERATURE, Prairie Journal Press, A. Burke, PO Box 61203 Brentwood P.O., 217, 3630 Brentwood Road N.W., Calgary, Alberta T2L 2K6, Canada. 1983. Poetry, fiction, interviews, criticism, reviews, long-poems. "Recent contributors: Laurie Anne Whitt, Fred Cogswell, interviews with poet Lorna Crozier, playwright James Reaney. Literary biases for reviews of Canadian prairie literature; also one act plays." circ. 500+. 2/yr. Pub'd 2 issues 1998; expects 2 issues 1999, 2 issues 2000. sub. price: $6, $12 institutions; per copy: $6; sample: $3. Back issues: $5. Discounts: negotiable. 40-60pp; 7×8½; of. Reporting time: 2 weeks. Payment: copies and honoraria. Copyrighted. Pub's reviews: 6 in 1998. §Western, prairie, literary, Canadian. Ads: $50/$25/exchange. CMPA, Alberta Magazine Publishers Association.

Prairie Journal Press (see also THE PRAIRIE JOURNAL OF CANADIAN LITERATURE), A. Burke, PO Box 61203 Brentwood P.O., 217, 3630 Brentwood Road N.W., Calgary, Alberta T2L 2K6, Canada. 1983. Poetry, fiction, interviews, criticism, reviews, long-poems, plays. "Recent publication of an anthology of short fiction by six authors and a collection of poetry by one author. *Prairie Journal Fiction* $6 and for $6 *A Vision of Birds* by Ronald Kurt. Potential contributors please send samples of work with IRC and envelope for reply, covering letter." avg. press run 500+. Pub'd 1 title 1998; expects 2 titles 1999, 1 title 2000. 13 titles listed in the *Small Press Record of Books in Print* (28th Edition, 1999-00). avg. price, paper: $6. Discounts: negotiable. 40-60pp; 7×8½; of. Reporting time: 2 weeks - 6 months. Publishes 20% of manuscripts submitted. Payment: copies. Copyrights for author. CMPA, Celebration of Women and the Arts, Alberta Writers' Guild, Small Press Action Network, AMPA (Alberta Magazine Publishers Association).

Prairie Publishing Company, Ralph E. Watkins, PO Box 2997, Winnipeg, MB R3C 4B5, Canada, 204-885-6496. 1966. avg. press run 2M. Expects 4 titles 1999. 13 titles listed in the *Small Press Record of Books in Print* (28th Edition, 1999-00). avg. price, paper: $5. Discounts: 40% bookstores, 20% libraries & schools. 165pp; 6×9; of. Reporting time: 6-8 weeks. Payment: 10%. Copyrights for author. AMBP.

PRAIRIE SCHOONER, Hilda Raz, Editor-in-Chief; Randolph Ladette, Managing Editor, 201 Andrews Hall, Univ. of Nebraska, Lincoln, NE 68588-0334, 402-472-0911. 1926. Poetry, fiction, art, photos, interviews, reviews, parts-of-novels, long-poems, non-fiction. "Manuscripts are read from September through May only." circ. 3.1M. 4/yr. Pub'd 4 issues 1998; expects 4 issues 1999, 4 issues 2000. sub. price: $22; per copy: $7.95; sample: $5. Write for information on back issue prices. Write for information on discounts. 200pp; 6×9; of/lo. Reporting time: 3-4 months. Simultaneous submissions accepted: no. Publishes 3% of manuscripts submitted. Payment: copies of magazine, and annual prizes; payments depend on grants rec'd. Copyrighted, rights revert to author upon request. Pub's reviews: 20 in 1998. §Current literature. Ads: $150, $135 nonprofit. CLMP, CELJ.

PRAIRIE WINDS, James C. Editor-In-Chief Van Oort, Dakota Wesleyan University, DWU Box 536, Mitchell, SD 57301. 1946. Poetry, fiction, art, photos. "Annual literary review. All submissions must have SASE. Art and photos—black and white only." circ. 500. 1/yr. Pub'd 1 issue 1998; expects 1 issue 1999, 1 issue 2000. sub. price: $4; per copy: $4; sample: $4. Back issues: $10. 60-80pp; 7½×9¼; of. Reporting time: 1 month from deadline. We rarely accept simultaneous submissions. Publishes 8% of manuscripts submitted. Payment: 1 copy each. Copyrighted, reverts to author. Ads: none.

Prakalpana Literature (see also PRAKALPANA SAHITYA/PRAKALPANA LITERATURE), Vattacharja Chandan, Dilip Gupta, P-40 Nandana Park, Calcutta-700034, West Bengal, India, (91) (033) 478-2347. 1974. Poetry, articles. "Biases: we invite in English or in Bengali: 1) only avant garde experimental poem, story having definitely visual, sonorous & mathematical dimensions—which we call Sarbangin poetry/story; 2) Prakalpana (=P for prose, poetry + R for story + A for art, essay + K for kinema, kinetic + L for play + N for song, novel...)—which is a composition using the above forms appropriately; 3) also articles on Prakalpana literature. If selected, at first we publish the work (if possible with translation) in our mags, then we include it in our future anthology. Submissions not returnable. Length of material: in any case within 2,400 words." avg. press run 500. 7 titles listed in the *Small Press Record of Books in Print* (28th Edition, 1999-00). avg. price, other: rupees 3/-. Discounts: 20%. 48pp; 5½×8½. Simultaneous submissions accepted: no. Payment: none. Does not copyright for author.

PRAKALPANA SAHITYA/PRAKALPANA LITERATURE, Prakalpana Literature, Vattacharja Chandan, P-40 Nandana Park, Calcutta-700034, West Bengal, India, (91) (033) 478-2347. 1977. Poetry, articles, reviews, letters, news items. "Biases: we invite in English or in Bengali: 1) only avant garde experimental poem, story having definitely visual, sonorous & mathematical dimensions—which we call Sarbangin poetry/story; 2) Prakalpana (=P for prose, poetry + R for story + A for art, essay + K for kinema, kinetic + L for play + N for song, novel...)—which is a composition using the above forms appropriately; 3) also criticism, essay & letters on Prakalpana literature. Submissions not returnable. Length of material: in any case within 2,400 words. Some recent contributors: Dilip Gupta, Vattacharja Chandan, J. Olsen, Shyamali Mukhopadhyay

Bhattacharya, Susan Smith Nash, Narak Dar.'' circ. 1M. 1/yr. Pub'd 1 issue 1998; expects 1 issue 1999, 1 issue 2000. sub. price: 6 rupees; per copy: 20 rupees. Overseas: 6 IRCs or exhcnage of little mags; sample: 20 rupees. Overseas: 6 IRCs or exchange of little mags. Back issues: 20 rupees. Discounts: 20%. 120pp; 5×7. Simultaneous submissions accepted: no. Payment: none. Not copyrighted. §Experimental/avant garde/ alternative literary & art books and magazines. Ads: 500 rupees/300 rupees/800 rupees (2nd, 3rd, 4th cover pages).

Prakken Publications (see also THE EDUCATION DIGEST; TECH DIRECTIONS), George F. Kennedy, Publisher, PO Box 8623, Ann Arbor, MI 48107-8623, 374-975-2800, fax 734-975-2787. 1935. Articles, photos, cartoons, letters, news items, non-fiction. *''Prakken Publications* publishes reference books, textbooks, magazines, workbooks, software and video primarily in vocational-technical and technology education. Recently published works include: *High School to Employment Transistion: Contemporary Issues; Machinists Ready Reference, 8th Edition; Technology's Past: American's Industrial Revolution and the People Who Delivered the Goods; Winning Ways: Best Practices in Work-Based Learning; Workforce Education: Issues for the New Century; Outdoor Power Equipment; Shopform* (software for mackimists).'' avg. press run 3M. Pub'd 2 titles 1998; expects 3 titles 1999, 4 titles 2000. 26 titles listed in the *Small Press Record of Books in Print* (28th Edition, 1999-00). avg. price, cloth: $20; paper: $18. Discounts: 20% educational; bookstores, jobbers call for pricing. 225pp; 5½×8½, 7×10, some 8½×11; of. Reporting time: 2 months *if* reply requested and SASE furnished. Simultaneous submissions accepted: yes. Publishes 10% of manuscripts submitted. Payment: negotiable royalty; generally 10% of receipts, payable June 30, Dec. 30, for books. Copyrights for author. Edpress, BPA.

PRECISELY, The Future Press, Richard Kostelanetz, Paul Zelevansky, Box 444 Prince Street, New York, NY 10012-0008. ''Critical essays on experimental literature, expecially of the past thirty years in North America. $2.00 for one number, $10.00 for five numbers, $18.00 for nine numbers, $32 for all sixteen numbers.'' 2/yr. Expects 1 issue 2000. price per copy: $2; sample: $2. 64pp; 5½×8½; of. Reporting time: 1 month. Payment: depends upon growth. Copyrighted, reverts to author. Pub's reviews: 0 in 1998. §Experimental literature.

Preludium Publishers (see also LIFTOUTS), Barry Casselman, 1414 South 3rd Street, No. 102, Minneapolis, MN 55454-1172, 612-321-9044, Fax 612-305-0655. 1971. Poetry, fiction, criticism, plays. ''Preludium Publishers is interested in experimental work in poetry and fiction, and in the translation of new writing which has not previously been published in English. *Unsolicited manuscripts are not considered at this time.* Translators should make inquiry before sending any manuscript, and must include an SASE for a reply.'' avg. press run 1M. Expects 2 titles 2000. of. Payment: negotiable; some payment to all authors. Copyrights for author.

Premier Publishers, Inc. (see also BOOK NEWS & BOOK BUSINESS MART), Neal Michaels, Owen Bates, PO Box 330309, Fort Worth, TX 76163, 817-293-7030. 1971. Non-fiction. ''We reprint and publish books on success, self-help, how-to, business success and the mail order industry. Also carburetor vaporization theory and instructions as well as other energy titles'' avg. press run 5M. Pub'd 6 titles 1998; expects 10 titles 1999, 8 titles 2000. 12 titles listed in the *Small Press Record of Books in Print* (28th Edition, 1999-00). avg. price, paper: $15; other: variable. Discounts: sold primarily through mail order trade. 50% discount to mail order dealers with quantity discounts averaging 60% and 70%. 96pp; 8×11; of, web. Reporting time: 4-12 weeks. Payment: negotiable; small royalty advances possible; outright royalties generally percentage of retail; amount dependent upon author and subject matter. Copyrights for author.

Premium Press America, G.C. Schnitzer, Jr., PO Box 159015, Nashville, TN 37215, 615-256-8484, fax 615-256-8624. 1993. Non-fiction. ''Additional address: 2606 Eugenia Avenue, Suite C, Nashville, TN 37211'' avg. press run 10M. Pub'd 6 titles 1998; expects 10 titles 1999, 10 titles 2000. 23 titles listed in the *Small Press Record of Books in Print* (28th Edition, 1999-00). avg. price, cloth: $24.95 $15.95; paper: $6.95. Discounts: 40-60%. 128-416pp; 5½×5½, 6×9; of, lp. Reporting time: 1 month. Simultaneous submissions accepted: yes. Publishes 10% of manuscripts submitted. Copyrights for author.

PREP Publishing, Anne McKinney, Box 66, Fayetteville, NC 28302, 910-483-6611, fax 910-483-2439. 1994. Fiction, non-fiction. ''Street address: 1110½ Hay Street, Fayetteville, NC 28305.'' avg. press run 5M+. Pub'd 3 titles 1998; expects 3 titles 1999, 5 titles 2000. 4 titles listed in the *Small Press Record of Books in Print* (28th Edition, 1999-00). avg. price, cloth: $22; paper: $16. Discounts: 20%-50%. 250-350pp; 5½×8½; of. Reporting time: 12 weeks. Simultaneous submissions accepted: yes. Publishes 5% of manuscripts submitted. Payment: 6%. Copyrights for author. PMA, PAS, ABA, CLMP, SEBA, CBA.

PrePress Publishing of Michigan, Jackie Justice-Brown, Elizabeth Johnson, Bruce Brown, Valerie Roberts, 709 Sunbright Avenue, Portage, MI 49024-2759, 616-323-2659. 1992. Poetry, fiction. avg. press run 1.8M. Pub'd 1 title 1998; expects 1 title 1999, 1 title 2000. 2 titles listed in the *Small Press Record of Books in Print* (28th Edition, 1999-00). avg. price, paper: $11.95. Discounts: 40% discount for retailers and insitutions; 50%

454

discount for wholesalers and distributors. 248pp; 6×9. Reporting time: 2 weeks to 6 months. Simultaneous submissions accepted: yes. Publishes 5% of manuscripts submitted. Payment: 1 copy free, additional at half price. Copyrights for author.

The Preservation Press, Buckley C. Jeppson, Director, 1785 Massachusetts Avenue, NW, Washington, DC 20036, 202-673-4057. 1975. Art, photos, non-fiction. "The Preservation Press is the book publisher of the National Trust for Historic Preservation, a nonprofit organization chartered by Congress in 1949 to encourage interest and participation in historic preservation. The Preservation Press publishes books for the general public on topics of historic preservation, architecture and American culture." avg. press run 7.5M-10M. Pub'd 21 titles 1998; expects 17 titles 1999, 23 titles 2000. 52 titles listed in the *Small Press Record of Books in Print* (28th Edition, 1999-00). avg. price, cloth: $30; paper: $10. Discounts: average to the trade - 40% 5-24 copies, libraries 10%, 20% standing order plan. 200-300pp; 7×10; of. Reporting time: 2 months. Payment: negotiable. Copyrights for author. Washington Book Publishers.

THE PRESIDENTS' JOURNAL, Cottontail Publications, Ellyn R. Kern, 79 Drakes Ridge, Bennington, IN 47011, 812-427-3921. 1984. Articles, art, photos, reviews, letters, news items, non-fiction. "This newsletter provides a glimpse at the personal and not the political side of the presidents and their families. By doing so we can learn more about the times they represented and the roots of our past as individuals in this great United States of America. Looking for columnists interested in writing for future issues on related topics. Submit ideas and sample of writing and qualifications." circ. 100. 4/yr. Pub'd 4 issues 1998; expects 4 issues 1999, 4 issues 2000. sub. price: $14; per copy: $3.50; sample: free for stamp (32¢). Back issues: $2.50. 6pp; 8½×11; †copy. Reporting time: 6 weeks. Payment: $5 for articles accepted for publication that review a presidentially related tourist site (not a home). Describe details of location, theme, cost, authenticity, and impressions. Enclose SASE for return of manuscript. Pay in subscription copies for 750 word articles. (Query) Up to $10 for reprints. Copyrighted, copyright for author, keep reprint rights. Pub's reviews: 1 in 1998. §Related to presidents. Ads: none.

PRESS, Daniel Roberts, Sean Anthony, 2124 Broadway, Suite 323, New York, NY 10023, 212-579-0873. 1995. Poetry, fiction. circ. 10M. 4/yr. Pub'd 4 issues 1998; expects 4 issues 1999. sub. price: $24; per copy: $6.95. Back issues: $5. Discounts: none. 150pp; digest size; of. Reporting time: 4-6 weeks. Simultaneous submissions accepted: no. Publishes 5% of manuscripts submitted. Payment: $50 min./poem, $100 min./short story. Copyrighted, does not revert to author. Ads: $1200/$700/$400 1/4 page.

The Press at Foggy Bottom, Mik Rosenthal, RR 4 Box 859, Little Marsh, PA 16950, 717-376-2718. 1994. Fiction, cartoons, criticism, music, plays. "The Press at Foggy Bottom publishes, on an ongoing basis, short run, reprintable trade books of anthologies of interest to children, young adults and the young at heart. Selected materials are also expressed as examples of the Book Arts in limited editions. We are interested in the whole range of literary expression including but not necessarily limited to short stories, humor, folk tales, plays, music, poetry, picture books, cartoons and even literary criticism which can be enjoyed by everyone including adults who are concerned with what children and young adults read. Our efforts, produced in either trade book or Book Art form, are intended to contain offerings children, young adults and parents can share, if not together, than separately within each volume. Great emphasis is placed on non-violence, where characters think up clever ways of besting the tribulations of any and all types of injustice and unfairness using the mental agility of matching wits and the understanding of people coupled with a concomitant, unstated message of ethical conduct. Lightheartedness, humor and good, clean fun are certainly always welcome! As always, we are interested in good secular material, but we are also more focused now, in Judaism. To this purpose, The Havurah for Jewish Storypeople: Tellers, Writers, Illustrators, & Scholars is performing free outreach services. We seek to help those who would like to publish while enjoying the benefits of a supportive, social, scholary and religious extended community. Please write to the Editor for details" avg. press run 500. Pub'd 1 title 1998; expects 3 titles 1999, 3-4 titles 2000. avg. price, cloth: varies, by arrangement; paper: $18. Discounts: by agreement. 100pp; 8½×11; †lp/book arts and shortrun 'commercial'/trade. Reporting time: 1-2 months. Simultaneous submissions accepted: yes. Publishes 25% of manuscripts submitted. Payment: by agreement. We copyright for author by agreement. PMA.

Press Here, Michael Dylan Welch, Editor & Publisher, PO Box 4014, Foster City, CA 94404, 415-571-9428, e-Mail WelchM@aol.com. 1989. Poetry, articles, interviews, satire, criticism. "Press Here publishes books of poetry, primarily haiku and related forms. Queries appreciated before sending manuscripts. Authors include Vincent Tripi, Anita Virgil, William J. Higginson, Sono Uchida, Lee Gurga, Michael Dylan Welch and others. Books have won Merit Book Awards from the Haiku Society of America. Manuscripts preferred only by those published in the leading haiku magazines, but open to all possibilities—surprise the editor with quality and creativity. Especially interested in books of criticism on or about haiku, or small-book-length interviews with established haiku poets. Also interested in concrete poetry." avg. press run 200-500. Pub'd 2 titles 1998; expects 3 titles 1999, 3 titles 2000. 14 titles listed in the *Small Press Record of Books in Print* (28th Edition, 1999-00). avg. price, paper: $4-$8. Discounts: at least 10% for 5-9 books (all one title); discounts negotiable.

28-96pp; 5½×8½; of. Reporting time: usually 1-4 weeks for queries, 2-6 months for manuscripts (query first please). Simultaneous submissions accepted if indicated. Publishes 5% of manuscripts submitted. Payment: usually in copies. Copyrights for author.

The Press of Appletree Alley, Barnard Taylor, Box 608 138 South Third Street, Lewisburg, PA 17837. 1982. avg. press run 150. Pub'd 2 titles 1998; expects 1 title 1999, 2 titles 2000. 17 titles listed in the *Small Press Record of Books in Print* (28th Edition, 1999-00). avg. price, cloth: $150; paper: $40 chapbook. Discounts: 30% dealers, 10% standing orders. 48-60pp; 6¼×9½; †letterpress. Payment: 10 copies of the limited edition. Does not copyright for author.

The Press of the Nightowl, Dwight Agner, 145 Yorkshire Road, Bogart, GA 30622-1799, 706-353-7719; fax 706-353-7719; e-mail nightowl@typehigh.com. 1965. Fiction, satire, letters, parts-of-novels, non-fiction. "Special interest in material related to typography, fine printing, printing history." avg. press run 300. Expects 1 title 1999, 1 title 2000. 6 titles listed in the *Small Press Record of Books in Print* (28th Edition, 1999-00). avg. price, cloth: $40-50; paper: $15; other: $80-$120 special editions (signed/numbered). Discounts: 1-2 books 20%; 3+ pbk 40%, cloth 30%; special editions 20%. 60pp; 5½×9; †lp. Reporting time: 1 month. Simultaneous submissions accepted: no. Publishes 5% of manuscripts submitted. Payment: no royalties; free copies of book and discount on additional purchases. Does not copyright for author.

The Press of the Third Mind, Bradley Lastname, 1301 N. Dearborn Street, Loft 1007, Chicago, IL 60610-6068, 312-337-3122; www.nogoitering.com. 1985. Fiction, articles, letters. "So far we have published an absurdist modernization of Georg Buchner's *Woyzeck* entitled *The Cultivation of Peas in a No-Crop Economy*; an anthology edited by a Ubangi called *The Sound of 2 Lip Disks Clacking*; a diary; a novel where Malcolm X and Madame X are Siamese twins; and a photobook called *Eraserhead Visits Wittgenstein*. We are now accepting material for the forthcoming anthology, *3 Nipple Ring Circus* which will be published in 1997. Watch the "Free Sample Mart" feature in a forthcoming issue of *S.P.R.* to obtain a free copy of *Empty Calories*." avg. press run 2M. Pub'd 1 title 1998; expects 1 title 1999, 1 title 2000. 2 titles listed in the *Small Press Record of Books in Print* (28th Edition, 1999-00). avg. price, paper: $5. Discounts: 40%. 100pp; size varies; of. Reporting time: a fortnight. Simultaneous submissions accepted: yes. Publishes 66.6% of manuscripts submitted. Payment: varies. Copyrights for author. CLMP, AAP.

Press-Tige Publishing Company Inc. (see also WRITER'S MONTHLY GAZETTE), Kelly O'Donnell, Editor; Martha Ivery, Associate Editor; Pam Muzoleski, Associate Editor, 291 Main Street, Catskill, NY 12414, 518-943-1440. 1972. Poetry, fiction, articles, art, photos, cartoons, interviews, reviews, music, parts-of-novels, long-poems, news items, non-fiction. "Any length, children's specialty" avg. press run 5M-10M. Pub'd 100 titles 1998; expects 300 titles 1999, 500 titles 2000. 25 titles listed in the *Small Press Record of Books in Print* (28th Edition, 1999-00). avg. price, cloth: $19.95; paper: $9.95; other: $7.95. Discounts: 10-15%. 350-400pp; 5¼×6¼; of. Reporting time: 3 months. Simultaneous submissions accepted: yes. Publishes 45% of manuscripts submitted. Payment: 30% on 1st 3000 copies sold and 15% thereafter. Copyrights for author. International Publishers, Inc., ABA, PMA, SPANET.

●Prestige Publications, Sandy S. Smith, 2450 Severn Avenue, Ste. 528, Metairie, LA 70001, 504-831-4030. 1996. Fiction, parts-of-novels, non-fiction. Pub'd 1 title 1998. 3 titles listed in the *Small Press Record of Books in Print* (28th Edition, 1999-00). avg. price, paper: $14.95. 100-125pp; 6×9; of. Copyrights for author.

Prestige Publishing, Linda Peters, PO Box 2786, Grapevine, TX 76099, 972-495-4374. 1966. Photos, non-fiction. "Prefer automotive material 'specifically corvette'. Early mustang or other specialty or collector vehicles. Technically oriented 'How-to' type material" avg. press run 1M-1.5M. Pub'd 4 titles 1998; expects 4 titles 1999, 4 titles 2000. 1 title listed in the *Small Press Record of Books in Print* (28th Edition, 1999-00). avg. price, paper: $15.95. Discounts: short discount 20% or less. 96pp; 8½×11; of. Reporting time: 3-6 months. Simultaneous submissions accepted: yes. Publishes 10% of manuscripts submitted. Payment: negotiable. Copyrights for author.

Prickly Pear Press, Dave Oliphant, Jim Jacobs, 1402 Mimosa Pass, Cedar Park, TX 78613, 512-331-1557. 1973. Poetry. "No unsolicited mss considered. Joseph Colin Murphey, William Barney, Rebecca Gonzales, James Hoggard, Dwight Fullingim." avg. press run 500. 10 titles listed in the *Small Press Record of Books in Print* (28th Edition, 1999-00). avg. price, cloth: $13.95; paper: $5. Discounts: 20% to jobbers. 64pp; 6×9; of. Payment: copies. Copyrights for author.

Pride & Imprints, Cris Newport, 7419 Ebbert Drive SE, Port Orchard, WA 98367-9753, email queries@pride-imprints.com. 1989. Poetry, fiction, art, photos, cartoons, satire, long-poems, collages, plays, non-fiction. "We are not accepting submissions/queries for new work until Sept. 2000. Pride publishes work in many genres that might be considered revolutionary or cutting edge.Novels should not be less than 50,000 words and poetry collections should be at least 100 poems" avg. press run 5M. Pub'd 4 titles 1998; expects 8 titles 1999, 15 titles 2000. 13 titles listed in the *Small Press Record of Books in Print* (28th Edition, 1999-00). avg. price, paper: $10.95. Discounts: f0% off retail, free bookrate shipping, payment in 90 days for all

456

bookstores, returns accepted. 250pp; 5½x8½; of. Reporting time: 3 months. Simultaneous submissions accepted: yes. Publishes 10% of manuscripts submitted. Payment: 10-15%. Copyrights for author.

Pride-Frost Publishing, Barbara Rayfield, 3390 Herman Avenue, San Diego, CA 92104-4622. 1995. Non-fiction. avg. press run 10M. Pub'd 1 title 1998; expects 3 titles 1999. 1 title listed in the *Small Press Record of Books in Print* (28th Edition, 1999-00). avg. price, paper: $13. Discounts: 55%. 200pp; 5½x8½; of. Reporting time: 6 weeks. Payment: varies. Does not copyright for author. PMA.

Primal Publishing, Lauren Leja, PO Box 1179, Allston, MA 02134-0007, 617-787-3412, Fax 617-787-5406; e-mail primal@primalpub.com. 1986. Poetry, fiction, art, photos, satire, letters, parts-of-novels, non-fiction. "Modern literature for primitive people." avg. press run 1M-2M. Pub'd 1 title 1998; expects 3 titles 1999, 5 titles 2000. 6 titles listed in the *Small Press Record of Books in Print* (28th Edition, 1999-00). avg. price, paper: $4.95. Discounts: 2-9=25% 10 or more 40%. 80pp; 4x5¼; of. Reporting time: 1-3 months. Publishes 25% of manuscripts submitted. Payment: $300; $100 upon acceptance, $100 upon publication, $100 6 months after publication. Does not copyright for author.

PRIMAVERA, Editorial Board, PO Box 37-7547, Chicago, IL 60637-7547, 773-324-5920. 1974. Poetry, fiction, art, photos, satire. "*Primavera* publishes work expressing the perspectives and experiences of women. We are interested equally in established and in unknown writers and artists. We will be happy to comment on your work in a personal letter *if you ask us to.* Please do not ask unless you are genuinely receptive to constructive, candid criticism. All submissions must be typed (double-spaced) and accompanied by a SASE of sufficient size, bearing sufficient postage. No simultaneous submissons. Recent contributors: Janet Hardison, Carol Kopec, L. Hluchan Sintebs, Sucha Cardoza, Ginnie Goulet Gavin." circ. 1M. 1/yr. Pub'd 1 issue 1998; expects 1 issue 1999. 12 titles listed in the *Small Press Record of Books in Print* (28th Edition, 1999-00). sub. price: $10; per copy: $10; sample: $5. Back issues: #1-#10 $5. Discounts: 10% off for orders of 3 or more. 128pp; 8½x5½; of. Reporting time: up to 6 months, usually 2 weeks. Simultaneous submissions accepted: no. Publishes 2.5% of manuscripts submitted. Payment: 2 copies. Copyrighted, reverts to author. No ads. CLMP, ILPA.

PRIME, Larry Edgerton, 7116 Helen C. White Hall, Madison, WI 53706, 688-262-3262. 1992. Poetry, fiction, art, photos, reviews. "Prime is a magazine intended as a voice for college students of color; the material should thus be by and reflect their experience" circ. 500. 1/yr. Pub'd 1 issue 1998; expects 1 issue 1999, 1 issue 2000. sub. price: $10; per copy: $10; sample: $5. Back issues: $5. Discounts: 40%. 36pp; 4¼x5½; of. Reporting time: 1 month. Publishes 10% of manuscripts submitted. Payment: 2 copies. Copyrighted, reverts to author.

Primer Publishers, Diane M. Fessler, Bill Fessler, Amanda Fessler, 4738 N. Central, Phoenix, AZ 85012, 602-234-1574. 1979. Non-fiction. "Publish books about Southwest, nature, the outdoors, and Arizona" avg. press run 5M. Pub'd 3 titles 1998; expects 2 titles 1999, 4 titles 2000. 70 titles listed in the *Small Press Record of Books in Print* (28th Edition, 1999-00). avg. price, paper: $5. Discounts: 40%. 96pp. Reporting time: 90 days. Simultaneous submissions accepted: yes. Publishes 1% of manuscripts submitted. Payment: negotiable. Does not copyright for author. Arizona Book Publishers Association.

Princess Publishing, Cecile Hammill, Editor; Cheryl A. Matschek, Publisher, PO Box 25406, Portland, OR 97298, 503-297-1565. 1987. Non-fiction. avg. press run 5M. Pub'd 1 title 1998; expects 2 titles 1999, 2 titles 2000. 4 titles listed in the *Small Press Record of Books in Print* (28th Edition, 1999-00). avg. price, cloth: $24.95; paper: $12.95. 150-200pp; 5½x8; of, lp. Reporting time: 1 month. Publishes 1-5% of manuscripts submitted. Payment: variable. Copyrights for author. NWBPA.

PRINCETON ARTS REVIEW, Donald N.S. Unger, Editor, 102 Witherspoon Street, Princeton, NJ 08540, 609-924-8777. 1996. Poetry, fiction, parts-of-novels, long-poems, non-fiction. "Seeking work which - while maintaining aesthetics, and reader interest - deals with social and political realities and quandaries" circ. 400. 2/yr. Expects 2 issues 1999, 2 issues 2000. sub. price: $10; per copy: $6; sample: $6. Discounts: call. 80pp; 5½x8½; †mi. Reporting time: 3 months. Simultaneous submissions accepted with notice. Publishes 20% of manuscripts submitted. Payment: 2 copies. Copyrighted, reverts to author. Ads: call.

Princeton Book Company, Publishers, Charles H. Woodford, President, PO Box 831, Hightstown, NJ 08520-0831, 609-737-8177; FAX 609-737-1869. 1975. Music, non-fiction. "Princeton Book Company, Publishers is a publisher of books on dance. Most of our books have a text as well as a trade market." avg. press run 3M. Pub'd 5 titles 1998; expects 4 titles 1999, 4 titles 2000. 114 titles listed in the *Small Press Record of Books in Print* (28th Edition, 1999-00). avg. price, cloth: $20; paper: $14.95. Discounts: 40% trade, 20% text. 200pp; 6x9; of. Reporting time: 6-8 weeks. Payment: 10% on net receipts; usually no advance. Copyrights for author.

PRISM INTERNATIONAL, Laisha Rosnau, Executive Editor; Kiera Miller, Jennica Harper, E462-1866 Main Mall, University of British Columbia, Vancouver BC V6T 1Z1, Canada, 604-822-2514, fax 604-822-3616, e-mail prism@urixg.ubc.ca web site: http://www.arts.ubc.ca/prism. 1959. Poetry, fiction, parts-of-novels, long-poems, plays, non-fiction, art. "Publish translation of poetry and fiction from languages other than English. No reviews or scholarly essays." circ. 1.25M. 4/yr. Pub'd 4 issues 1998; expects 4 issues 1999, 4 issues 2000. sub. price: $20 indiv., $28 libraries, Canadians add G.S.T., outside Canada pay US funds.; per copy: $5; sample: $5.50. Back issues: varies. Discounts: differs with the issue. 96pp; 6×9; of. Reporting time: 12-16 weeks. Simultaneous submissions accepted: no. Publishes 3-5% of manuscripts submitted. Payment: $20 per printed page + 1-year subscription. Selected authors get an additional $10/printed page for publication on the World Wide Web; $40 poetry, $20 prose, $10 web. Copyrighted, reverts to author. Ads: $100. CMPA.

PRISON LEGAL NEWS, Paul Wright, Dan Pens, Co-editor, 2400 NW 80th Street, Suite 148, Seattle, WA 98117, 206-781-6524; pln@prisonlegalnews.org. 1990. Articles, interviews, satire, criticism, reviews, letters, news items, non-fiction. "*PLN* reports on court decisions affecting the rights of prisoners, we cover news and analysis of prisons from around the world. The majority of each issue is written by prisoners (including the editor) and is uncensored by prison officials. *PLN* has a progressive point of view and seeks to educate its readers concerning racism, homophobia and sexism within the prison community and organize its readers into a force for progressive change within the penal system." circ. 4M. 12/yr. Pub'd 12 issues 1998; expects 12 issues 1999, 12 issues 2000. sub. price: $25 individuals, $60 institutions; per copy: $5; sample: $1. Back issues: $60 per year for 12 issues. $5 single issues. Discounts: contact editors to make special arrangements. 28pp; 8½×11; of. Reporting time: 6-8 weeks depending on timeliness. Simultaneous submissions accepted: yes. Publishes 10% of manuscripts submitted. Payment: 1 year free subscription. Not copyrighted. Pub's reviews: 60 in 1998. §Prisons, criminal justice, revolutionary struggle/politics, law, etc. Ads: $450/$250.

PRIVACY JOURNAL, Robert Ellis Smith, PO Box 28577, Providence, RI 02908. 1974. Articles, cartoons, reviews, letters, news items. 12/yr. Pub'd 12 issues 1998; expects 12 issues 1999, 12 issues 2000. 7 titles listed in the *Small Press Record of Books in Print* (28th Edition, 1999-00). sub. price: $118/$145 overseas; per copy: $10; sample: free. Back issues: $70 per whole year. Discounts: $35 to individuals if paid in advance. 8pp; 8½×11; of. Reporting time: 1 month. Payment: negotiable. Copyrights negotiable. Pub's reviews. §Privacy, computers and society, surveillance. No ads. SPAN.

Pro Musica Press, Edward V. Foreman, 2501 Pleasant Ave S, Minneapolis, MN 55404, 612-872-8362, e-Mail Voyceking@visi.com. 1966. Music. "Interested only in vocal music, new books, or translations of valuable works. Have published anthologies of music with commentary." avg. press run 500. Pub'd 3 titles 1998; expects 2 titles 1999, 2 titles 2000. 10 titles listed in the *Small Press Record of Books in Print* (28th Edition, 1999-00). avg. price, cloth: $30; paper: $15. Discounts: 20% to retail trade. Volume discounts depending upon volume. 150-250pp; size varies; of. Reporting time: 2-4 weeks. Publishes 90% of manuscripts submitted. Payment: 10% paid quarterly after publication. Copyright for author if requested.

Pro/Am Music Resources, Inc., Thomas P. Lewis, Denis Stevens, 63 Prospect Street, White Plains, NY 10606, 914-948-7436. 1982. Music. "We publish and import adult books in the field of music exclusively" avg. press run 1-5M. Pub'd 10 titles 1998; expects 10 titles 1999, 10 titles 2000. 37 titles listed in the *Small Press Record of Books in Print* (28th Edition, 1999-00). avg. price, cloth: $35; paper: $16. Discounts: write for schedule. 300pp; of. Payment: 10%. Copyrights for author.

PROBABLE CAUSE: A LITERARY REVUE, David P. Gold, Editor; Kim Perkins, Submissions Editor, PO Box 398657, Miami Beach, FL 33239, 305-538-6451. 1994. Poetry, fiction, articles, art, interviews, satire, reviews, letters. "Special interest in 1st Ammendent issues" circ. 18M. 4/yr. Pub'd 4 issues 1998; expects 4 issues 1999, 4 issues 2000. sub. price: $10; per copy: $2.50; sample: $2.50. 32pp; 11½×13¾; of. Reporting time: 1 month. Simultaneous submissions accepted: yes. Publishes 2% of manuscripts submitted. Payment: $0-$50. Copyrighted, does not revert to author. Pub's reviews: 24 in 1998. §Literary fiction, contemporary culture, graphic novels, biography. Ads: $800/$450.

PROCEEDINGS OF THE SPANISH INQUISITION, Robert Trumble, 2419 Greensburg Pike, Pittsburgh, PA 15221. 1984. Art, interviews, satire, reviews, letters, news items. "Monty Python Fan Club" circ. 70. 6/yr. Pub'd 6 issues 1998; expects 6 issues 1999, 6 issues 2000. sub. price: $5; per copy: $1; sample: $1. Back issues: $1. 8pp; 5½×8½; †Mita copier. Reporting time: 1 month. Payment: copies. Copyrighted, reverts to author. Pub's reviews: 2 in 1998. §Monty Python, John Cleese, etc. Ads: $25/$15/$5 classified.

Professional Resource Exchange, Inc., Lawrence G. Ritt, Box 15560, Sarasota, FL 34277-1560, 941-343-9601; Fax 941-343-9201; orders@prpress.com. 1979. Non-fiction. "Books for mental health practitioners. Manuscripts only solicited from practicing mental health professionals on topics of professional interest (e.g., no 'self-help' books)." avg. press run 2M-3M. Pub'd 8 titles 1998; expects 10 titles 1999, 15 titles 2000. 86 titles listed in the *Small Press Record of Books in Print* (28th Edition, 1999-00). avg. price, cloth: $40; paper: $19.95; other: $65, binder. Discounts: variable depending on quantity and payment options (0-50%). 250pp; 6×9, 8½×11, 7×10; web/of. Reporting time: 6 months average. Simultaneous submissions accepted: yes. Publishes 10% of manuscripts submitted. Payment: variable - percentage or fixed dollar amounts.

Copyrights for author.

Professor Solar Press, RFD #3, Box 627, Putney, VT 05346, 802-387-2601. "Not presently accepting submissions." 1 title listed in the *Small Press Record of Books in Print* (28th Edition, 1999-00). Discounts: single copy 20%, 2-4 30%, 5+ 40%.

Profile Press, 3004 S. Grant Street, Arlington, VA 22202, 703-684-6208. 1988. Non-fiction. avg. press run 5M. Pub'd 1 title 1998. 1 title listed in the *Small Press Record of Books in Print* (28th Edition, 1999-00). avg. price, paper: $16. Discounts: 5-20 copies, 40% - all over 50%. 100pp; 5½×8½; of. Reporting time: 3 months. Simultaneous submissions accepted: no. Copyrights for author.

Progresiv Publishr, Kenneth H. Ives, 401 E. 32nd #1002, Chicago, IL 60616, 312-225-9181. 1977. Articles, reviews. "Pamphlet series *Studies in Quakerism. Bookkeeping for Small Organizations* ($4.00), Spelling reform book *Written Dialects N Spelling Reforms: History N Alternatives* ($5.00). *Emamipation Without War* ($4.00), lengths so far, 32 to 112 pages. *Recovering the Human Jesus*, 300 pages, 1990, $5" avg. press run 300. Pub'd 1 title 1998; expects 1 title 1999, 1 title 2000. 20 titles listed in the *Small Press Record of Books in Print* (28th Edition, 1999-00). avg. price, paper: $4. Discounts: 5 or more 20%; 10 or more 30%; bookstore discount on items over $10: 40%. 45-60pp; 5×8 (pamphlets); xerox or of. Reporting time: about a month. Payment: 10 copies. Quakers Uniting In Publications (QUIP).

Progressive Education (see also PROGRESSIVE PERIODICALS DIRECTORY/UPDATE), Craig T. Canan, PO Box 120574, Nashville, TN 37212. 1980. Art, cartoons, reviews, concrete art. avg. press run 1.5M. 1 title listed in the *Small Press Record of Books in Print* (28th Edition, 1999-00). avg. price, paper: $16. Discounts: over 5 $9 each. 36pp; 8½×11; of. Reporting time: 1 month. Payment: none. Copyrights for author.

PROGRESSIVE PERIODICALS DIRECTORY/UPDATE, Progressive Education, Craig T. Canan, PO Box 120574, Nashville, TN 37212. 1980. Art, cartoons, reviews, concrete art. circ. 1.5M. Expects 1 issue 1999. sub. price: $16; per copy: $16; sample: $16. Back issues: $16. Discounts: over 5, $9 each. 36pp; 8½×11; of. Reporting time: 4 weeks. Payment: none. Copyrighted, reverts to author. Pub's reviews: 600 in 1998. §Progressive periodicals on social concerns in U.S. Ads: $200/$100.

Pro-Guides, Professional Guides Publications, S. Robert Read, PO Box 2071, Davis, CA 95617-2071, 510-283-1831. 1990. "Specialize in 'how to' publications in real estate and related fields. Property management, particularly residential by professionals, residents, and owners (doing self-management). Manuals are ultra simple and designed specifically for self-study and application. Typical is the manual - *How to Become An Apartment Manager (Fast) and Live Rent Free* by R. Robert Stuart, 28 sections, 21 working forms, resume guides, 112 pages; and *How to Become A Maintenance and Repair Handy-Person (Fast) and Have Real Job Security*, 104 pages." avg. press run 5M. Pub'd 3 titles 1998; expects 4 titles 1999, 4 titles 2000. 2 titles listed in the *Small Press Record of Books in Print* (28th Edition, 1999-00). avg. price, paper: $16.95. Discounts: distributor. 112pp; 7×8½; †xerography. Reporting time: 30 days. Payment: negotiable. Copyrights for author.

Prometheus Enterprises, Inc., Terry J. Jr. Dunlap, 60 Bellus Road, Hinckley, OH 44233, 216-278-2798, fax 216-278-2615, orders 1-800-249-2498, 1-800-393-3415. 1994. Non-fiction. avg. press run 5M. Pub'd 3 titles 1998; expects 5 titles 1999. 2 titles listed in the *Small Press Record of Books in Print* (28th Edition, 1999-00). avg. price, paper: $19.95. Discounts: 20% on oreders 5 or less 40% orders greater than 5. 250pp; 7⅜×9¼. Reporting time: 2 months. Simultaneous submissions accepted: yes. Publishes 10% of manuscripts submitted. Payment: negotiated percent of profits. Copyrights for author.

Proof Press (see also RAW NERVZ HAIKU), D. Howard, 67 Court Street, Aylmer, QC J9H 4M1, Canada, E-mail: dhoward@aix1.uottawa.ca. 1994. Poetry. "Haiku, renya." avg. press run 200. Pub'd 7 titles 1998; expects 10 titles 1999, 10 titles 2000. avg. price, paper: 50¢-$4. 6-40pp; 5½×8½, 3½×4-1/9; photocopy. Reporting time: 6 weeks to 3 months. Simultaneous submissions accepted: no. Publishes 10% of manuscripts submitted. Payment: 10% of run. Copyrights for author.

PROOF ROCK, Don R. Conner, Editor; Serena Fusek, Poetry Editor, Proof Rock Press, PO Box 607, Halifax, VA 24558. 1982. Poetry, fiction, articles, art, interviews, reviews. "Poems: 32 lines or less. Fiction: 2M words or less. Few subjects considered taboo if they are well done." circ. 300. 2/yr. Expects 2 issues 1999, 2 issues 2000. 6 titles listed in the *Small Press Record of Books in Print* (28th Edition, 1999-00). sub. price: $5; per copy: $3; sample: $3. Back issues: $2.50. Discounts: none. 40pp; 5½×8½; of. Reporting time: 3 months. Payment: contributor's copy. Not copyrighted. Pub's reviews: 20 in 1998. §Poetry. Ads: $25/$15/not available.

Proper PH Publications (see also CONFLICT OF INTEREST), Pam Hartney, 4701 East National Road, Springfield, OH 45505-1847, 330-630-5646 phone/Fax; E-mail phartney@aol.com. 1994. Poetry, articles, art, cartoons, interviews, reviews, long-poems. "No limit on length of material. No taboos! No rules! Poetry and artwork should be radical, concise, deliberate, unabashed, deadly if ingested. No rhyming, nature, or kissy, kissy poetry. SASE a must for return of poems or response from editor. Recent contributors: Lyn Lifshin, Ron Androla, Cheryl A. Townsend. Previously published work is okay if it is noted when and where." avg. press run 250-500. Pub'd 4 titles 1998; expects 4 titles 1999, 4 titles 2000. avg. price, paper: $5. 100pp; 11×17; †mi. Reporting time: 4-6 months. Simultaneous submissions accepted: yes. Publishes 20% of manuscripts submitted. Payment: in copies. Copyrights for author.

THE PROSE POEM: An International Journal, Peter Johnson, Editor; Brian Johnson, Asst. Editor, English Department, Providence College, Providence, RI 02918, 401-865-2292. 1992. Poetry. *"The Prose Poem: An International Journal* publishes prose poetry, translations, and short reflections of the prose poem. We are also open to short book reviews (please query first). Recent contributors: Jack Anderson, Robert Bly, Russell Edson, David Ignatow, Charles Simic, Yannis Ritsos, and Naomi Shihab. Read submissions between December 1 to March 1. We will not be reading again until Dec. of 2001." circ. 1M. 1/yr. Pub'd 1 issue 1998; expects 1 issue 1999, 1 issue 2000. sub. price: $8; per copy: $8; sample: $8. Back issues: $4. Discounts: $6 a copy for classroom use. 100-150pp; 6×9; printed by McNaughton/Gunn. Reporting time: 1-3 months. Simultaneous submissions accepted: no. Publishes 3-5% of manuscripts submitted. Payment: 2 copies. Copyrighted, reverts to author. Pub's reviews: 5 in 1998. §Books of prose poetry. Ads: contact editor.

PROSODIA, Gloria Frym, Faculty Advisor, New College of California/Poetics, 766 Valencia Street, San Francisco, CA 94110, 415-437-3479; Fax 415-437-3702. 1990. Poetry, fiction, photos, plays, concrete art. "Each issue has a different staff and different theme. Invitations to submit are based on taste of particular staff. Issues contain 20-25% student work." circ. 500. 1/yr. Pub'd 1 issue 1998; expects 1 issue 1999, 1 issue 2000. sub. price: $8. Back issues: order through SPD-Berkeley. 120pp; of, 1p. Reporting time: 5 months or less. Simultaneous submissions accepted: yes. Publishes 50% of manuscripts submitted. Payment: copies. Copyrighted, reverts to author. Ads: $120 negotiable. CLMP, SPD.

Prospect Hill Press, Eleanor Heldrich, 8 Over Ridge Court, Apt#4021, Baltimore, MD 21210-1129, 410-889-0320. 1981. Fiction, non-fiction. "Do not accept manuscripts prior to query. No more juveniles." avg. press run 5M. Pub'd 1 title 1998; expects 2 titles 2000. 6 titles listed in the *Small Press Record of Books in Print* (28th Edition, 1999-00). avg. price, cloth: $16; paper: $12.95. Discounts: 1 book—no discount, 2-5 25%, 6-49 40%, 50+ 50%. 80pp; 8½×11; perfect bound, or smyth-sewn case bound. Reporting time: 2 weeks. Payment: to be negotiated. Copyrights for author. BP.

Prosperity Press, Lily Maestas, Lorelei Snyder, 1503 Mountain Avenue, Santa Barbara, CA 93101, 805-963-3028; FAX 805-963-9272, 1-800-464-2074. 1995. Non-fiction. avg. press run 3M. Expects 1 title 1999, 1 title 2000. 1 title listed in the *Small Press Record of Books in Print* (28th Edition, 1999-00). avg. price, paper: $14.97. Discounts: quantity discounts available, bookstores 40%. 256pp; 5½×8½; of. PMA.

Protean Press, Terry Horrigan, 287-28th Avenue, San Francisco, CA 94121, fax 415-386-4980. 1984. Poetry, articles, letters, non-fiction, art. avg. press run 60. Pub'd 1 title 1998; expects 1 title 1999, 1 title 2000. 10 titles listed in the *Small Press Record of Books in Print* (28th Edition, 1999-00). Discounts: 1-4 25%, 5-9 35%. Pages vary; size varies; †1p. Simultaneous submissions accepted: no. Payment: varies.

Protean Publications, Paul Lester, 34 Summerfield Crescent, Flat 4, Edgbaston, Birmingham B16 OER, England. 1980. Poetry, fiction, cartoons, satire, criticism, non-fiction. "Deals with poetry, graphics, short stories and cultural criticism." avg. press run 300. Pub'd 2 titles 1998; expects 3 titles 1999. 38 titles listed in the *Small Press Record of Books in Print* (28th Edition, 1999-00). avg. price, paper: 40p. Discounts: by arrangement. 16-24pp; 4×6; of. Reporting time: 6 weeks. Payment: by arrangement. Copyrights for author.

PROVINCETOWN ARTS, Provincetown Arts Press, Christopher Busa, 650 Commercial Street, Provincetown, MA 02657, 508-487-3167. 1985. Poetry, fiction, articles, art, photos, cartoons, interviews, criticism, reviews, collages, non-fiction. "Published annually in July, *Provincetown Arts* focuses broadly on the artists and writers, emerging and established, who inhabit or visit the tip of Cape Cod. Previous cover subjects have included Norman Mailer, Robert Motherwell, and Annie Dillard, Stanley Kunitz, Mark Doty, Mary Oliver, and Karen Finley. Placing contemporary creative activity in a context that draws upon a 75-year tradition of literature, visual art, and theatre, *Provincetown Arts* seeks to consolidate the voices and images of the nation's foremost summer art colony. Some recent contributors include Olga Broumas, Douglas Huebler, Michael Klein, Susan Mitchell, Martha Rhodes, and Anne-Marie Levine." circ. 8M. 1/yr. Pub'd 1 issue 1998; expects 1 issue 1999, 1 issue 2000. sub. price: $10; per copy: $6.50; sample: $10. Back issues: $10. Discounts: 40% for resale. 184pp; 9×12; of. Reporting time: 2 months. Simultaneous submissions discouraged. Publishes 2% of manuscripts submitted. Payment: prose $100-300, poetry $25-125, art $25-300. Copyrighted, reverts to author. Pub's reviews: 20 in 1998. §Biographies of artists, exhibition catalogues, poetry, fiction. Ads: $950/$550/color available. CLMP.

Provincetown Arts Press (see also PROVINCETOWN ARTS), Christopher Busa, Editorial Director, PO Box 35, 650 Commercial Street, Provincetown, MA 02657, 508-487-3167; FAX 508-487-8634. "A non-profit press for artists and poets." avg. press run artbooks-3M, poetry-1.5M. Pub'd 3 titles 1998; expects 4 titles 1999, 4 titles 2000. 11 titles listed in the *Small Press Record of Books in Print* (28th Edition, 1999-00). avg. price, cloth: $35; paper: $10. Discounts: 40%. Art books 150pp, poetry 70pp; 6×8; of. Reporting time: 4 months.

460

Simultaneous submissions accepted: no. Publishes 2% of manuscripts submitted. Payment: $500 advance, 10% royalties. CLMP.

Prudhomme Press, Harrison Leonard, PO Box 11, Tavares, FL 32778, 904-589-0100. 1989. Non-fiction. "Although we only publish complete books occasionally, we are not 'self publishers.' However, *we do not accept unsolicited manuscripts.*" avg. press run 5M. Expects 2 titles 1999, 2 titles 2000. 1 title listed in the *Small Press Record of Books in Print* (28th Edition, 1999-00). avg. price, cloth: $18.95; paper: $14.95. Discounts: trade and jobber. 300+pp; 6x9; of. Copyrights for author.

Pruett Publishing Company, Jim Pruett, Publisher, 7464 Arapahoe Road, Suite A-9, Boulder, CO 80303-1500, 303-443-9019, toll free: 1-800-247-8224. 1959. Art, photos, non-fiction. "Publisher of books pertaining to outdoor travel and recreation, fishing, and the West. Books include *A Climbing Guide to Colorado's Fourteeners: 20th Anniversry Edition, Colorado Nature Almanac,* and *The Earth is Enough*" avg. press run varies per book. Pub'd 6 titles 1998; expects 12 titles 1999, 7-10 titles 2000. 60 titles listed in the *Small Press Record of Books in Print* (28th Edition, 1999-00). avg. price, cloth: $16-$40; paper: $10-$30. Discounts: write for a copy of our complete schedule. Pages vary; size varies. Reporting time: 4-6 weeks. Publishes about 10% of manuscripts submitted. Payment: generally a royalty basis for authors. Copyrights for author. ABA, RMBPA.

PSI Research/The Oasis Press/Hellgate Press, Emmett Ramey, Editor, PO Box 3727, Central Point, OR 97502, 503-479-9464 (CA); 800-228-2275. 1975. "Small business-oriented. Successful Business Library is a series of how-to business guides designed for entrepreneurs and small businesspersons. Hellgate is military history and adventure travel." avg. press run based on demand. Pub'd 29 titles 1998; expects 32 titles 1999, 35 titles 2000. 110 titles listed in the *Small Press Record of Books in Print* (28th Edition, 1999-00). avg. price, paper: $19.95; other: $29.95. Discounts: 20%-40% bookstores, 15% libraries. 250pp; 8½x11; †Desktop publishing system, laser printer, xerox copier, offset. Reporting time: 2 months for expression of interest. Publishes 1-2% of manuscripts submitted. Payment: as per licensing agreement. Does not copyright for author.

PSYCHOANALYTIC BOOKS: A QUARTERLY JOURNAL OF REVIEWS, Joseph Reppen, Editor, 211 East 70th Street, New York, NY 10021, 212-628-8792; FAX 212-628-8453, e-Mail psabooks@datagram.com. 1990. Reviews. "Book reviews of books in the *broad* field of psychoanalysis including clinical and theoretical psychoanalysis, Freud studies, history of psychoanalysis, psychobiography, psychohistory, and the psychoanalytic study of literature and the arts. News and notes on books and journals in psychoanalysis. ISSN 1044-2103. By invitation only." circ. 1M. 4/yr. Pub'd 4 issues 1998; expects 4 issues 1999, 4 issues 2000. sub. price: $55, $105 institutions; per copy: $15. Back issues: $15. 160pp; 6x9; of. Payment: none. Copyrighted, does not revert to author. Pub's reviews: 150 in 1998. §Psychoanalysis, Freud studies, history of psychoanalysis, psychobiography, psychohistory, psychoanalytic study of literature and the arts. Ads: $200/$125. CELJ.

Psychohistory Press (see also THE JOURNAL OF PSYCHOHISTORY), Lloyd deMause, Editor, 140 Riverside Drive, New York, NY 10024, 212-799-2294. 1973. Articles. avg. press run 2M. Pub'd 2 titles 1998; expects 3 titles 1999. 1 title listed in the *Small Press Record of Books in Print* (28th Edition, 1999-00). avg. price, cloth: $25; paper: $12. Discounts: 20%. 300pp; 7x9; of. Reporting time: 4 weeks. Copyrights for author.

PSYCHOLOGY OF WOMEN QUARTERLY, Nancy Felipe Russo, Psychology Department, Box 871104, Arizona State University, Tempe, AZ 85287-1104. 1976. Articles, reviews. circ. 6.5M. 4/yr. Pub'd 4 issues 1998; expects 4 issues 1999, 4 issues 2000. sub. price: $40 individual. Discounts: included with membership in Division 35 of the American Psychological Association. 140pp; 6x9. Reporting time: 11.8 weeks. Simultaneous submissions accepted: no. Publishes 10% of manuscripts submitted. Payment: none. Copyrighted, does not revert to author. Pub's reviews: 11 in 1998. §Psychology of women and gender. contact Cambridge Univ. Press.

PSYCHOPOETICA, Geoff Lowe, Trevor Millum, Department of Psychology, University of Hull, Hull HU6 7RX, United Kingdom, website www.fernhse.demon.co.uk/eastword/psycho. 1980. Poetry, reviews. "Psychologically-based poetry. Recent contributors: Peter Bakowski, John Brander, Jenni Collins, Rod Farmer, John Mingay, Debra S. Lynn" circ. 350. 2/yr plus occasional special anthologies. Pub'd 4 issues 1998; expects 4 issues 1999, 2 issues 2000. sub. price: $16 (plus postage); per copy: $6 (plus postage); sample: $5. Back issues: $3 (plus postage). Discounts: 20% on 5 or more. 60+pp; 8¼x11½ (A4); †mi. Reporting time: 4-6 weeks. Simultaneous submissions accepted: yes. Publishes 8% of manuscripts submitted. Payment: none. Copyrighted. Pub's reviews: 24 brief in 1998. §Modern poetry, bizarre poetry, 'off-beat', psychology.

PSYCHOTRAIN, Hyacinth House Publications/Caligula Editions, Randal Seyler, Fiction Editor; Shannon Frach, Editor-in-Chief, PO Box 120, Fayetteville, AR 72702-0120. 1989. Poetry, fiction, art, satire, reviews, parts-of-novels. "We seek quality fiction of 1,500 words or less. We also use poetry. All of our publications are decidedly 'left of center'—we value edgy, hard-hitting writing for an audience which appreciates powerful, often 'disturbed' perspectives in literature. We like to see material reflecting a wide array of counter-cultural viewpoints—occult, Dadaist, gay, Beat, psychedelic, etc. Recent contributors include John Kistner, Barbara

Peck, Raymond Tod Smith, Alice Olds-Ellingson, Tom Caufield and Steve Fried. We do *not* take romance or inspirational material. No rhyming poetry.'' circ. 200+. 2/yr. Pub'd 2 issues 1998; expects 3 issues 1999, 3 issues 2000. sub. price: $12/4 issues; per copy: $4; sample: $4. 40pp; 8½×11; †mi. Reporting time: 1 week to 8 months; depends on backlog. Publishes 5-10% of manuscripts submitted. Payment: we do not pay. Copyrighted, reverts to author. Ads: negotiable; we occasionally trade ads.

PT Publications, Inc., Kevin P. Grieco, Janet L. Przirembel, 3109 45th Street #100, West Palm Beach, FL 33407-1915, 561-687-0455; 800-547-4326; fax 561-687-8010; e-mail PTPubFl@aol.com; website http://www.ptpub.com/. 1988. Fiction, art, cartoons, non-fiction. avg. press run 1500-3M. Pub'd 4 titles 1998; expects 10 titles 1999, 12 titles 2000. 30 titles listed in the *Small Press Record of Books in Print* (28th Edition, 1999-00). avg. price, cloth: $29.95; paper: $14.95. Discounts: 20% bookstore, 40% association w/ business (NAPM, APICS, ASQC). 256pp; 6×9, 7×10. Reporting time: 2-3 months. Payment: worked out individually. Copyrights for author. PMA, ABA, PAS.

PTOLEMY/BROWNS MILLS REVIEW, David C. Vajda, 484 Lewistown Road #252, Juliustown, NJ 08042, 609-893-0896. 1979. Poetry, fiction, articles, satire, criticism, parts-of-novels, long-poems, concrete art. ''Refer to the *Small Press Record of Books in Print* for book listings.'' circ. 100-250. 1-2/yr. Expects 3-4 issues 1999, 2 issues 2000. 9 titles listed in the *Small Press Record of Books in Print* (28th Edition, 1999-00). sub. price: $4; per copy: $2; sample: $1-$2. Back issues: $1-$2. No discounts per se. 16pp; 5½×8½; of. Reporting time: 1 week to 1 month. Payment: 5 copies per acceptance. Copyrighted, rights revert to author with permission. No ads.

THE PUBLIC HISTORIAN, University of California Press, Shelley Bookspan, Lindsey Reed, Managing Editor, University of California Press, 2120 Berkeley Way, Berkeley, CA 94720, 510-643-7154. 1978. Articles, interviews, reviews, news items, non-fiction. ''Editorial address: Dept. of History, Ellison Hall, University of California, Santa Barbara, CA 93106.'' circ. 1,550. 4/yr. Pub'd 4 issues 1998; expects 4 issues 1999, 4 issues 2000. sub. price: $47 indiv., $79 instit., $21 students (+ $5 foreign postage); per copy: $13 indiv.; $22 instit., $13 students; sample: free. Back issues: same as single copy price. Discounts: foreign subs. agents 10%, one-time orders 10+ 30%, standing orders (bookstores): 1-99 40%, 100+ 50%. 128pp; 6×9; of. Reporting time: 2-3 months. Copyrighted, does not revert to author. Pub's reviews: 50 in 1998. §History. Ads: $275/$200.

THE PUBLIC RELATIONS QUARTERLY, Howard Penn Hudson, Editor-in-Chief, PO Box 311, Rhinebeck, NY 12572, 914-876-2081, fax 914-876-2561. 1955. Articles, interviews, reviews. 4/yr. Pub'd 4 issues 1998; expects 4 issues 1999, 4 issues 2000. sub. price: $65; per copy: $17. 48pp; 9×11. Reporting time: 1 month. Payment: in copies. Copyrighted, reverts to author. Pub's reviews: 6-8 in 1998. §Public relations, writing, management. Ads: $800/$400/$35-inch.

PUBLISHER'S REPORT, Betsy Lampe, PO Box 430, Highland City, FL 33846, 941-648-4420; e-Mail naip@aol.com. 1984. News items, articles, reviews. ''No contributions of anything but publishing news (small/independent presses). This is the bi-monthly newsletter of the National Association of Independent Publishers.'' circ. 500+. 4/yr. Pub'd 4 issues 1998; expects 4 issues 1999, 4 issues 2000. sub. price: $75 with membership; $40 subscription only; per copy: $15; sample: free. Back issues: available only at Florida conferences. 32pp; 8½×11; dtp. Reporting time: 2 weeks. Simultaneous submissions accepted: yes. Publishes 90% of manuscripts submitted. Payment: none - trade for ad space or copies of publication. Copyrighted, reverts to author. Pub's reviews: 30+ in 1998. §Books about publishing, writing, marketing, production. Ads: one advertiser per issue, usually a book manufacturer, prints the newsletters for me.

Publishers Syndication Int'l (PSI) (see also THE POST), Mary Staub, A.P. Samuels, Po Box 6218, Charlottesville, VA 22806-6218. 1987. Fiction. ''30,000 word mysteries, 30,000 word romances.'' avg. press run varies. Expects 2 titles 1999, 7 titles 2000. avg. price, paper: $1.95. 96+pp; 4⅝×5⅞; of. Reporting time: 3 weeks. Payment: .5¢-3¢ per word.

PUBLISHING ENTREPRENEUR, Jenkins Group, Inc., Mardi Link, 121 East Front Street, Suite 401, Traverse City, MI 49684, voice 616-933-0445; fax 616-933-0448; e-mail jenkins.group@smallpress.com. 1993. Letters, non-fiction. ''Profit strategies for the information & publishing industry'' circ. 8M. 6/yr. Pub'd 6 issues 1998; expects 6 issues 1999, 6 issues 2000. sub. price: $28.80; per copy: $3.50; $10 includes s&h, fully applicable to subscription price. Discounts: $15 for assoc. members. 40pp; 8½×11; of. Simultaneous submissions accepted: no. Publishes 1% of manuscripts submitted. Payment: varies. Copyrighted, reverts to author. Ads: call about rates. IPN.

PUBLISHING POYNTERS, Para Publishing, Dan Poynter, PO Box 8206-Q, Santa Barbara, CA 93118-8206, 805-968-7277; fax 805-968-1379; fax-on-demand 805-968-8947; e-Mail 75031.3534@parapublishing.com; web site http://www.parapublishing.com/books/para/q; e-mail parapublishing@aol.com. 1986. News items. ''Book marketing news and ideas from Dan Poynter. *Publishing Poynters* is full of non-fiction book marketing, promotion and distribution leads.'' circ. 14M. 4/yr. Pub'd 4 issues 1998; expects 4 issues 1999, 4 issues 2000. sub. price: $9.95/2 years; sample: $2. Back issues: $2 each ppd. 2pp; 8½×11; of. Reporting time: 2

weeks. Payment: none. Copyrighted. Pub's reviews: 20 in 1998. §Non-fiction book marketing, promotion or distribution *only*. PMA, ABA.

Publitec Editions, Maggie Rowe, Owner, PO Box 4342, Laguna Beach, CA 92652, 949-497-6100 tel/fax. 1983. Non-fiction. avg. press run 3M. Expects 1 title 1999, 1 title 2000. 5 titles listed in the *Small Press Record of Books in Print* (28th Edition, 1999-00). avg. price, cloth: $16.95; paper: $9.95. Discounts: 1-9 books 35%, 10+ 40% retail; 1-9 books 45%, 10+ 50% wholesale. 200pp; 6×9, 5½×8½; of. Reporting time: 1 month. Simultaneous submissions accepted: yes. Publishes 5% of manuscripts submitted. Payment: varies according to amount of writing/editorial assistance required. Copyrights for author. PMA.

PUCK: The Unofficial Journal of the Irrepressible, Permeable Press, Brian Clark, Barbara del Rio, 433 S. Cleveland Street #3, Moscow, ID 83843-3793. 1984. Poetry, fiction, articles, art, photos, cartoons, interviews, satire, criticism, reviews, music, letters, parts-of-novels, collages, plays, news items, non-fiction. "Material should be doubl-spaced, typewritten, or submitted on high density Macintosh diskette. SASE for return. Extremely biased, but you'll never know until you try. Radical reinterpretations of the mundane and overlooked." circ. 5M. 3/yr. Pub'd 1 issue 1998; expects 3 issues 1999, 3 issues 2000. sub. price: $17; per copy: $6.50; sample: $6.50. Back issues: $3.50, when available. Discounts: 40% trade. 80pp; 8½×11; †of. Reporting time: 2 weeks to 2 months. Publishes 1-5% of manuscripts submitted. Payment: copies and honorarium. Copyrighted, reverts to author. Pub's reviews: 250 in 1998. §All fiction small or independent publishing/printing, apocalypse/conspiracy, commodity aesthetics. Ads: $125/$70/no classifieds.

Puckerbrush Press (see also THE PUCKERBRUSH REVIEW), Constance Hunting, 76 Main Street, Orono, ME 04473-1430, 207-866-4868. 1971. Poetry, fiction, criticism. avg. press run 250-1M. Pub'd 2 titles 1998; expects 3 titles 1999, 3 titles 2000. 36 titles listed in the *Small Press Record of Books in Print* (28th Edition, 1999-00). avg. price, paper: $8.95-$15.95. Discounts: 40%. 60-200pp; 6×9; of. Reporting time: 2 months. Simultaneous submissions accepted: yes. Payment: 10% of each retail copy. Copyright to author. MWPA.

THE PUCKERBRUSH REVIEW, Puckerbrush Press, Constance Hunting, 76 Main Street, Orono, ME 04473-1430. 1978. Poetry, fiction, reviews. "Maine-oriented." circ. 250-300. 1-2/yr. Pub'd 1 issue 1998; expects 1 issue 1999, 2 issues 2000. sub. price: $11; per copy: $4; sample: $2. Back issues: $1. Discounts: 40%. 100+pp; 8½×11; of, compuprint. Reporting time: 1 month. Payment: copies. Copyrighted, does not revert to author. Pub's reviews: 20 in 1998. §Maine small/larger press and authors. Ads: $40. MWPS, MWPA.

Pudding House Publications (see also PUDDING MAGAZINE: THE INTERNATIONAL JOURNAL OF APPLIED POETRY), Jennifer Welch Bosveld, Editor; Doug Swisher, Associate Editor; Steve Abbott, Associate Editor; Sandra J. Feen, Associate Editor; Jim Bosweld, Associate Editor, 60 North Main Street, Johnstown, OH 43031, 740-967-6060; pudding@johnstown.net; www.puddinghouse.com. 1979. Poetry, non-fiction. "Will not return manuscripts for which SASE is not enclosed. $10.00 reading fee for chapbooks, outside of competition 10-40 pages, $15 over 40 pages" avg. press run 400 except for anthologies. Pub'd 8 titles 1998; expects 8 titles 1999, 10 titles 2000. 75 titles listed in the *Small Press Record of Books in Print* (28th Edition, 1999-00). avg. price, paper: $8.95; other: varies. Discounts: 10% for single copies to classrooms, teachers, bookstores, non-profit or charity organizations; 35% on 10 or more copies 40% 25 or more. 24-36pp; 5½×8½; †Sharp SF8570 (commercial). Reporting time: 2 weeks except for competition submissions; sometimes overnight. Simultaneous submissions accepted: no. Publishes less than 1% of manuscripts submitted. Payment: 20 copies of the book; deep discount on additionals. Copyrights for author, but we don't register the copyright.

PUDDING MAGAZINE: THE INTERNATIONAL JOURNAL OF APPLIED POETRY, Pudding House Publications, Jennifer Bosveld, Editor; Steve Abbott, Associate Editor; Doug Swisher, Associate Editor; Jim Bosveld, Associate Editor, 60 North Main Street, Johnstown, OH 43031, 740-967-6060; pudding@johnstown.net; www.puddinghouse.com. 1979. Poetry, articles, art, photos, cartoons, interviews, criticism, reviews, letters, non-fiction. "All styles and forms of poetry considered. Looking for the wildly different and the subtly profound. We recommend: reflections of intense human situations, conflict, and closure poems on popular culture, politics, social concern, quirky character, and the contemporary scene; concrete images and specific detail; artful expressions of unique situations; or the shock of recognition in things perhaps felt before (or almost felt) but never spoken. No trite comparisons, please. No cliches. No religious verse or sentimentality. Mini-Articles: by poets who share their craft in the human services; about *applied poetry* experiences either from clients/patients or from psychiatrists, teachers, or other professionals and paraprofesionals who put the art of poetry to use in helping others. Reviews of poetry books and chapbooks, how-to-write-poetry books, methodology books, and other relevant publications that would be beneficial to groups or individual readers. Likes dense, rich short short stories, 1-2 pages." circ. 2M. Irregular. Pub'd 4 issues 1998; expects 3 issues 1999, 3 issues 2000. sub. price: $18.95/3 issues; per copy: $6.95; sample: $6.95. Back issues: $7-$75 depending on issue; they are almost all out of print, $350 for back set. Discounts: 20% on 5 or more copies to classrooms, teachers, bookstores, non-profit or charity organizations; 35% on 10 or more. 45-95pp; 5½×8½; †Sharp SF8570 (commercial). Reporting time: usually overnight; if held, it's being considered, or we're traveling.

Simultaneous submissions accepted: no. Publishes way less than 1% of manuscripts submitted. Payment: 1 copy, featured poets receive 4 copies and $10. Copyrighted, rights revert to author, with Pudding House retaining permission to reprint. Pub's reviews: 18 in 1998. §Poetry, 'applied poetry', popular culture and the arts, social justice. Ads: $200/$135 only in our priorties no classifieds.

PUERTO DEL SOL, Kevin McIlvoy, Kathleen West, Box 3E, New Mexico State University, Las Cruces, NM 88003, 505-646-2345. 1961. Poetry, fiction, art, photos, interviews, reviews, parts-of-novels, long-poems, plays. "Emphasis on Southwestern Chicano, Nat. Am. The primary emphasis, however, is on *top quality writing*, wherever it comes from. Some Latin American with trans." circ. 1M. 2/yr. Pub'd 2 issues 1998; expects 2 issues 1999, 2 issues 2000. sub. price: $10; per copy: $7; sample: $6. Back issues: complete set $200 (vol 1 no. 1-vol 27 no. 2). Discounts: 40% general, 50% jobber. 200pp; 6×9; of. Reporting time: 9 weeks. Payment: copies. Copyrighted. Pub's reviews: 8 in 1998. §Chicano, Nat. Am., poetry, fiction, Southwestern, anthologies. Ads: $120/$75. CLMP.

PULSAR, David Pike, 34 Lineacre, Grange Park, Swindon, Wiltshire SN5 6DA, United Kingdom, 01793-875941; e-mail david.pike@virgin.net. 1994. Poetry, articles, art, photos, cartoons, reviews, letters, long-poems, news items. "The U.S. subscription price covers and includes the cost of mailing. £ Sterling cheques - UK £10 only. Not keen on religious poetry. Will not advertise vanity press" circ. 300. 4/yr. Pub'd 4 issues 1998; expects 4 issues 1999, 4 issues 2000. sub. price: $30; per copy: $7.50; sample: free. Back issues: $7.50/copy. Discounts: Special subscription price to colleges/universities = $24. 28pp; 5¾×8¼; professionally printed. Reporting time: if accepted, may not appear for two issues. Simultaneous submissions accepted: no. Publishes 1 in 30?% of manuscripts submitted. Payment: none. Copyrighted, reverts to author. Pub's reviews: 7 in 1998. §Poetry only, also poetry audio tapes. Ads: $10/$5. Association of Little Presses (UK).

PUNCTURE, Katherine Spielmann, Editor; Steve Connell, Managing Editor, PO Box 14806, Portland, OR 97293, e-mail puncture@teleport.com. 1982. Articles, art, photos, cartoons, interviews, reviews, non-fiction. "A magazine of alternative rock and other independent music. Also covers fiction, non-fiction, photography. We will respond to queries with SASE & samples but not unsolicited submissions." circ. 10½M. 4/yr. Pub'd 4 issues 1998; expects 4 issues 1999, 4 issues 2000. sub. price: $9.95/4 issues; per copy: $3.50; sample: $3.50. Back issues: varies. Discounts: retail 35% (min. 10), wholesale 50% (min. 25). 76pp; 8¼×10¾; of. Reporting time: 4 weeks. Simultaneous submissions accepted: no. Publishes 2% of manuscripts submitted. Payment: variable. Copyrighted, reverts to author. Pub's reviews: 12-50 per issue, plus a round-up of new titles briefly described in 1998. §CDs, records, tapes, books on rock, alternative music, culture, politics, photography, and strong current fiction. Ads: $700/$450.

Pura Vida Publishing Company, Michele K. Rogalin, PO Box 379, Mountlake Terrace, WA 98043-0379, 425-670-1346; 888-670-1346; Fax 425-744-0563; puravidapub@earthlink.net; www.puravidapub.com. 1996. Fiction, non-fiction. "We're looking for new, fresh material with mind-body-spirit unification as a theme. Environmental twist a plus. No religious submissions." avg. press run 5M first run. Expects 4 titles 1999. 1 title listed in the *Small Press Record of Books in Print* (28th Edition, 1999-00). avg. price, cloth: $23; paper: $16. Discounts: upon request. 250pp; 5½×8½. Reporting time: 2 months. Simultaneous submissions accepted: yes. Payment: royalties start at 6%. Copyrights for author. PMA, NAPRA.

Royal Purcell, Publisher, Royal Purcell, 806 West Second Street, Bloomington, IN 47403, 812-336-4195. 1985. Non-fiction. "Submit query first, preferably with specific outline of nonfiction subject and SASE." avg. press run 1M. Expects 1 title 1999, 1 title 2000. 3 titles listed in the *Small Press Record of Books in Print* (28th Edition, 1999-00). avg. price, paper: $19.95. Discounts: 1-5 20%; 6-24 30%; 25-49 40%; 50-99 45%; 100 up 50%. 150pp; 8½×11; †word processor/photocopier. Reporting time: 2 weeks for query. Payment: 10-15%. Copyrights for author.

The Purchase Press, John Guenther, Editor & Publisher, PO Box 5, Harrison, NY 10528, 914-967-4499. 1980. Poetry. "Specializing in poetry, including translation into English language. Recent contributor: *Sonnets to Orpheus*, Rilke, trans. by Kenneth Pitchford, 3rd printing 1983. Recent publication: *Quai Malaquais*, a novel 1984. Selected shorter poems (title: The Seeming) 1996." avg. press run 300. Pub'd 1 title 1998; expects 1 title 1999. 4 titles listed in the *Small Press Record of Books in Print* (28th Edition, 1999-00). avg. price, paper: $10. Discounts: 40% on all orders at wholesale; full list price on retail mail-order sales. 50pp; 6×9; of. Reporting time: 30 days. Payment: negotiated on each title. Copyrights for author. PEN.

PURPLE, Daniel Crocker, PO Box 341, Park Hills, MO 63601. 1997. Poetry, fiction, criticism, reviews, long-poems, non-fiction. "Length, style and subject matter all open. Recent contributors include A.D. Winans, Ana Christy, Gerald Locklin, Antler and Matthew D. Bridges." circ. 300. 2/yr. Pub'd 2 issues 1998; expects 2 issues 1999, 2 issues 2000. price per copy: free for a large SASE w/at least 7 stamps. 40pp; mi. Reporting time: 1 month. Simultaneous submissions accepted: yes. Publishes 10% of manuscripts submitted. Payment: 1-2 copies. Not copyrighted. Pub's reviews: 4 in 1998. §Poetry and fiction. Ads: free if I like it.

Purple Finch Press, Nancy Benson, PO Box 758, Dewitt, NY 13214, 315-445-8087. 1992. Poetry, fiction, art, photos, interviews, reviews, non-fiction. "We are not considering unsolicited manuscripts at this time. Additional address: 109 Warwick Road, Dewitt, NY 13214. Length of material: 100-300 pages. Biases: sensitive, literary prose, poetry, cookbooks, mystery novels—adult and juvenile." avg. press run 500-2M. Pub'd 1 title 1998; expects 2 titles 1999, 3 titles 2000. 2 titles listed in the *Small Press Record of Books in Print* (28th Edition, 1999-00). avg. price, cloth: $20; paper: $11. Discounts: 1 book 10%, 2-10 20%, 11+ 25%. 101pp; 5½x8½; typeset. Reporting time: 2 months. Simultaneous submissions accepted: yes. Publishes 20% of manuscripts submitted. Payment: 4-7.5% of net price. Copyrights for author.

THE PURPLE MONKEY, W. Brian Ellis, Scott Gilbert, 200 East Redbud Road, Knoxville, TN 37920. 1993. Poetry, fiction, art, photos, interviews, reviews, non-fiction. "We don't want art without craft. Recent contributors: Fred Chappell, Jeff Daniel Marion, Donald Secreast, Susan O'Dell Underwood, Lyn Lifshin, Ted Koosar" circ. 100. 4/yr. Pub'd 4 issues 1998; expects 4 issues 1999, 4 issues 2000. sub. price: $10; per copy: $2; sample: $2.50. Back issues: $2.50. 30-40pp; 5½x8½; mi. Reporting time: within 2 months. Simultaneous submissions accepted: yes. Publishes 20% of manuscripts submitted. Payment: 1 copy. Copyrighted, reverts to author. Pub's reviews. §Poetry, short stories. Ads: none.

Purple Mouth Press (see also IT GOES ON THE SHELF), Ned Brooks, 4817 Dean Lane, Lilburn, GA 30047, nedbrooks@sprynet.com. 1975. Poetry, fiction, art, satire. avg. press run 500. Pub'd 2 titles 1998. 4 titles listed in the *Small Press Record of Books in Print* (28th Edition, 1999-00). avg. price, paper: $5-$10. Discounts: 40% for 5 or more. 20pp; 7x10, 8½x11; xerox. Reporting time: 1 week. Payment: yes. Copyrights for author.

PURPLE PATCH, Geoff Stevens, 8 Beaconview House, Charlemont Farm, West Bromwich, West Midlands, England. 1976. Poetry, fiction, articles, art, reviews, news items. "Mainly poetry. Fiction should be short." circ. varies. 6/yr. Pub'd 6 issues 1998; expects 6 issues 1999, 6 issues 2000. sub. price: £3-00 for 3 (i.e. £6/yr); per copy: £1; $5 bill or £2 sterling cheque (due to postage/exchange charges etc.); sample: £1, $5 bill. 14pp; 8¼x11¾; †mi. Reporting time: 1 month. Simultaneous items may be sent outside UK. Publishes 5% of manuscripts submitted. Payment: none. Copyrighted, reverts to author. Pub's reviews: 150 in 1998. §Poetry, short stories, biographies of writers, art. Ads: free on acceptance.

PURPLE PEEK PI, Pen-Dec Press, 2526 Chatham Woods, Grand Rapids, MI 49546. 1997. Irregular. sample price: $2. 20pp; 8½x5½.

Pushcart Press, Bill Henderson, PO Box 380, Wainscott, NY 11975, 516-324-9300. 1973. "Each year we will publish *The Pushcart Prize: Best of the Small Presses*, with the help of our distinguished contributing editors. We also sponsor the annual Editors' Book Award for manuscripts overlooked by commercial publishers. (All manuscripts must be nominated by an editor.)" avg. press run varies. Pub'd 8 titles 1998; expects 8 titles 1999, 9 titles 2000. 37 titles listed in the *Small Press Record of Books in Print* (28th Edition, 1999-00). avg. price, cloth: $20; paper varies. Discounts: 1-9, 20%; 10+, 40%. 200-600pp; 5½x8½; of. Reporting time: varies. Payment: 10%. Copyrights for author.

Push/Pull/Press, Joe Ajlouny, 29205 Greening Boulevard, Farmington Hills, MI 48334-2945, 810-932-0090. 1983. Non-fiction. "Push/Pull/Press publishes humor joke books, books, other areas of popular culture and popular reference and light non-fiction. Queries and proposals are requested and will be returned with SASE." avg. press run 12M-20M. Pub'd 6 titles 1998; expects 6-8 titles 1999, 6-8 titles 2000. 4 titles listed in the *Small Press Record of Books in Print* (28th Edition, 1999-00). avg. price, paper: $6.95-$9.95. Discounts: distributed by Publishers Distribution Service, 121 E. Front Street, Suite 203, Traverse City, MI 49684, 800-507-2665 for orders. 100-200pp; 5½x7½; of. Reporting time: 1 month. Simultaneous submissions accepted: no. Publishes 3-5% of manuscripts submitted. Payment: typically 7% of list price and stepped up for improved sales. Copyrights for author. Mid-America Publishers Association, Publishers Marketing Association.

Pussywillow Publishing House, Inc., 621 Leisure World, Mesa, AZ 85206-3133. "We publish for authors if the book is good." avg. press run 2.5M-5M. 5 titles listed in the *Small Press Record of Books in Print* (28th Edition, 1999-00). avg. price, cloth: $8.95. Discounts: 40% stores; 15-20% reps; distributors 60%. 36pp; 11x8½, 5½x8½, 6x9. Copyrights for author. AAA Assoc., Society of Children Book Writers in Calif., National League of American Pen Women, Inc.

Pygmy Forest Press, Leonard Cirino, PO Box 7097, Eureka, CA 95502-4111, 707-268-1274. 1987. Poetry, fiction, art, reviews, non-fiction. "Query with 10-15 pages." avg. press run 150-300. Pub'd 2 titles 1998; expects 3 titles 1999. 8 titles listed in the *Small Press Record of Books in Print* (28th Edition, 1999-00). avg. price, cloth: $25; paper: $4-$10. Discounts: 1/3 off to retail and institutional prisoners; libraries full price. 20-80pp; 5½x8½; of. Reporting time: immediate to 1 month. Simultaneous submissions accepted: yes. Publishes 3-5% of manuscripts submitted. Payment: new format is that author must subsidy 50-75% of printing costs and will receive like in copies. Copyrights for author.

Pyncheon House, David Rhodes, 6 University Drive, Suite 105, Amherst, MA 01002. 1991. Poetry, fiction, criticism. "Recent contributors: F.D. Reeve, Jonathan Edward, Rebecca Scott and James Cole." avg. press run 2M-3M. Pub'd 4 titles 1998; expects 6 titles 1999, 6 titles 2000. 3 titles listed in the *Small Press Record of Books in Print* (28th Edition, 1999-00). avg. price, cloth: $22; paper: $12. Discounts: 1-5 10%, 6-15 15%, 16-25 20%; direct to library 20%, 26-100 30% 101+ negotiable. 150pp; 5½×8½; of. Reporting time: 3-6 months. Publishes 5% of manuscripts submitted. Payment: 10% and/or free books. Copyrights for author. Library of Congress CIP Program.

Pyramid Publishing, Brian Lucas, 110-64 Queens Boulevard, Suite 227, Forest Hills, NY 11375-6347, 718-341-4575, Fax 718-341-1880, e-mail 10227.241@compuserve.com. 1994. Art, non-fiction. avg. press run 2.5M. Expects 3 titles 1999, 3 titles 2000. 1 title listed in the *Small Press Record of Books in Print* (28th Edition, 1999-00). avg. price, cloth: $39.95; paper: $29.95. Discounts: yes, will provide upon inquiry (wholesale, distributors, STOP, library, premium, etc.). 400pp; 8½×11; of. Reporting time: 4 months. Payment: 10%, quarterly. Copyrights for author. PMA, National Association of Independent Publishers, ABA, Midalantic Publishers Assn., Author's Guide.

Pyx Press (see also MAGIC REALISM; A THEATER OF BLOOD), C. Darren Butler, Box 922648, Sylmar, CA 91392-2648. 1990. Poetry, fiction, satire, long-poems, non-fiction. "Query with synopsis and sample chapter/poems. No unsolicated submissions accepted." avg. press run 100-1M. Pub'd 1 title 1998; expects 6 titles 1999, 4 titles 2000. avg. price, paper: $22; other: $7. †hand sewn, fine press, saddle and stapled. Reporting time: up to 6 months. Simultaneous submissions accepted: no. Payment: varies.

Q

Q ZINE, Quark Bosch, 2336 Market Street #14, San Francisco, CA 94114-1521, bcclark@igc.apc.org. 1996. Articles, art, photos, satire, criticism, reviews, collages, non-fiction. "Prefer essays of 7,000-12,000 words, and of a provocative nature. Pays $.005/word plus copies. Potential reviewers should submit a writing sample and indicate areas of interest. Always include SASE." circ. 500. 4/yr. Expects 5 issues 1999, 4 issues 2000. sub. price: $20; per copy: $4; sample: $4. Back issues: $4. Discounts: 40-55%. 60pp; 4×9; †of. Reporting time: average 2 weeks. Simultaneous submissions accepted: no. Publishes 2% of manuscripts submitted. Payment: copies and $.005/word. Copyrighted, reverts to author. Pub's reviews: 110 in 1998. §Fiction, sexuality, ecology, gay/lesbian/bisexual studies, all science. Ads: $100/$60.

QECE: QUESTION EVERYTHING. CHALLENGE EVERYTHING., Larry Nocella, 406 Main Street #3C, Collegeville, PA 19426, e-mail qece@aol.com. 1996. Fiction, articles, art, photos, cartoons, interviews, satire, criticism, collages, news items, non-fiction. "Avoid references to mainstream media topics whenever possible. If you must reference a current trend, tie it to a timeless observation. Empower and inspire the reader, either with tales of your successful actions, or lessons learned from your less successful ones. *QECE* works to encourage independent thought AND action. Graphics, art and photos a major plus. *QECE* is always interested in seeing and possibly reviewing any material that encourages questioning and active challenging. However, we are a bit backed up at this time." circ. 450. 2/yr. Pub'd 2 issues 1998; expects 2 issues 1999, 2 issues 2000. sub. price: $7; per copy: $3; sample: $3. Back issues: $3. 60pp; 5½×8½; photocopy. Reporting time: varies. We accept simultaneous submissions, but please note it in the cover letter. Publishes a variable % of manuscripts submitted. Payment: 2 contributor copies. Copyrighted, reverts to author. Pub's reviews. Ads: contact for possible ad trade and/or rates.

QED, John Bibby, 1 Straylands Grove, York Y03 0EB, England, 904-424-381. 1982. Non-fiction. "Educational publisher and book supplier, specializing in science and maths" avg. press run 2M. Pub'd 20 titles 1998; expects 20 titles 1999, 20 titles 2000. avg. price, paper: £5. Discounts: 40% over £40. 100pp; size A5; of. Reporting time: 1-3 months. Payment: 20% after breakeven point. Copyright subject to agreement. SPG.

QED Press, Cynthia Frank, President, Managing Editor, 155 Cypress Street, Fort Bragg, CA 95437, 707-964-9520, Fax; 707-964-7531, E-mail; qedpress@mcn.org. 1986. Fiction, art, non-fiction. "QED Press is a small, Mendocino-based publishing house whose vision is to publish fiction and non-fiction that inspires readers to transcend national, racial and ethnic boundaries through appreciation of world literature and art. Each year QED publishes selected titles of uncommon interest and quality." avg. press run 3M. Pub'd 1 title 1998; expects 5 titles 1999, 5 titles 2000. 23 titles listed in the *Small Press Record of Books in Print* (28th Edition, 1999-00). avg. price, cloth: $19.95; paper: $12.95. Discounts: 1-2 books list, 3-5 33%, 6+ 40%. 224pp; 5½×8½; of. Reporting time: 3 months. Simultaneous submissions accepted: yes. Publishes less than 3% of manuscripts submitted. Payment: varies. Copyrights for author. Marin Self-Publishers Assoc., Mendocino-Ft. Bragg Chamber of Commerce, Northern California Book Publicists Association, Pacific Northwest Booksellers

Association, Publishers Marketing Association (PMA), ABA.

QP Publishing (see also QUALITY QUIPS NEWSLETTER), Nancy Sue Swoger, PO Box 237, Finleyville, PA 15332-0237, 724-348-8949. 1990. Non-fiction. "Primary focus is quality/technical non-fiction. Will consider other works in the non-fiction field. Also interested in any business publications." avg. press run 1M. Pub'd 2 titles 1998; expects 3 titles 1999. 3 titles listed in the *Small Press Record of Books in Print* (28th Edition, 1999-00). avg. price, cloth: $39.95; paper: $55 (manuals); other: newsletter $30. Discounts: 1-4 books 20%, 5-9 30%, 10-24 40%, 25-49 45%, 50+ 50%. 184pp; 5½×8½, 8½×11. Reporting time: unknown, will try within 30-60 days. Publishes 50% of manuscripts submitted. Payment: negotiable. Copyrights for author. PMA, TOWERS Club, Ad-Lib.

QRL POETRY SERIES, Quarterly Review of Literature Press, Theodore Weiss, Renee Weiss, Princeton University, 26 Haslet Avenue, Princeton, NJ 08540, 921-6976. 1943. Poetry, long-poems. "4-6 books under one cover and listed by volume number" circ. 3-5M. 4-6/yr. Pub'd 6 issues 1998; expects 6 issues 1999, 6 issues 2000. sub. price: 2 volumes paper $20, single $12, $20 institutional & hardback per volume; per copy: $20/cl, $10/pa, anniversary double volume $20/pa, $25/cl; sample: $10. Back issues: roughly $20 per volume, cloth; $10 per volume paper; write for catalog for complete list. Discounts: non-returnable—bookstores 40% on 5+ copies, 10% on 1 copy; agency 10%; 20% for returnable arrangements. 250-350pp; 5½×8½; of, typeset. Reporting time: 6 weeks-2 months. Simultaneous submissions accepted: yes. Payment: $1,000 for each prize-winning manuscript + 100 copies. Copyrighted, does not revert to author. Ads: $350/$200. CLMP, Academy of American Poets, Poets & Writers.

QUADRANT MAGAZINE, Robert Manne, PO Box 1495, Collingwood, Vic. 3066, Australia, (03) 417-6855. 1956. Poetry, fiction, articles, art, photos, cartoons, interviews, criticism, reviews, music, letters, long-poems, plays, non-fiction. "Articles vary from 1,000 to 6,000 words. Stories 2,000 words." circ. 8M. 10/yr. Pub'd 10 issues 1998; expects 10 issues 1999, 10 issues 2000. sub. price: $A45; per copy: $A5. Discounts: subscription agencies. 88pp; size A4; of. Payment: articles $90+, stories $90, reviews $60, poetry $40. Copyrighted, reverts to author. Pub's reviews: 45 in 1998. §Politics, economics, philosophy, history, literature. Ads: $250b&w/$120b&w/colour $2,000.

Quale Press (see also KEY SATCH(EL)), Gian Lombardo, PO Box 363, Haydenville, MA 01039, 413-268-3632 tel/fax; e-mail central@quale.com. 1997. "In 2000 press will only publish prose poetry chapbook collections under The Key Satch(el) series on a solicited basis only. Interested mainly in scientific, engineering and computer-related books emphasizing the humanistic aspect and effects of technology. Query first. Occasionally will publish literary titles (mostly prose poetry collections) by invitation only" avg. press run 500. Pub'd 2 titles 1998; expects 2 titles 1999, 4 titles 2000. 6 titles listed in the *Small Press Record of Books in Print* (28th Edition, 1999-00). avg. price, paper: $5. Discounts: 20% agent/jobber on more than 10 copies. 80pp; 5½×8½; of. Reporting time: 4-8 weeks. We accept simultaneous submission with notice. Payment: case by case basis. Copyrights for author.

QUALITY QUIPS NEWSLETTER, QP Publishing, Nancy Sue Swoger, Box 237, Finleyville, PA 15332-0237, 724-348-8949. 1991. "This quarterly newsletter deals with quality, customer service and team issues (non-fiction business). Book reviews are a regular feature (6-8 reviews per issue). Distribution is to quality managers, customer service managers and representatives, and quality engineers, to companies of all sizes." circ. 5M. 4/yr. Pub'd 4 issues 1998; expects 4 issues 1999, 4 issues 2000. sub. price: $30; sample: free upon request. 10pp; 8½×11. Payment: free 1 year subscription. Pub's reviews: 24-32 in 1998.

Quantum Mind Publications, Julia Garvey, MSC 338, 6677 W. Colfax Avenue, Denver, CO 80214, 303-205-9106; fax 303-205-0299; E-mail 105055.3354@compuserve.com. 1996. Fiction, non-fiction. "High literary quality. Non-relious, spiritual growth, divine intelligence, and mysticism" avg. press run 10M. Expects 3 titles 1999, 3 titles 2000. 1 title listed in the *Small Press Record of Books in Print* (28th Edition, 1999-00). avg. price, paper: $12.95. Discounts: 20% libraries; 40% bookstores; 55% distributors. 260pp; 5½×8½. Reporting time: 3 months. Simultaneous submissions accepted: yes. Publishes 5% of manuscripts submitted. Payment: inquire. Does not copyright for author.

QUARTER AFTER EIGHT, Tom Noyes, Matthew Cooperman, Imad Rahman, Ellis Hall, Ohio University, Athens, OH 45701. 1993. Fiction, articles, interviews, satire, criticism, letters, parts-of-novels, plays, non-fiction. "*QAE* seeks dynamic prose works—short fiction, prose-poetry, letters, drama, essays, memoirs, translations—that eschew the merely prosaic across a range of genres. Although *QAE* does not publish traditional verse and/or lyric poetry, the editors do welcome work that provocatively explores—even challenges—the prose/poetry distinction." circ. 1M. 1/yr. Pub'd 1 issue 1998; expects 1 issue 1999, 1 issue 2000. sub. price: $10; per copy: $10; sample: $10. Back issues: sold out. Discounts: 25+ copies 30%, distributed by Bernhard DeBoer, Ingram. 300pp; 6×9; of. Reporting time: 6-10 weeks. We accept simultaneous submissions if stated in cover letter. Publishes 7% of manuscripts submitted. Payment: 2 copies of upcoming issue. Copyrighted, reverts to author. Pub's reviews: 0 in 1998. §cutting edge prose books.

THE QUARTERLY, Gordon Lish, Dana Spitta, Jodi Davis, 650 Madison Avenue, New York, NY 10022, 212-888-4769. 1987. Poetry, fiction, articles, art, cartoons, interviews, satire, criticism, letters, parts-of-novels, long-poems, plays, non-fiction. "We bring out intergiving literary prose and poetry, and publish without person to literary republication" circ. 10M. 4/yr. Pub'd 4 issues 1998; expects 4 issues 1999, 4 issues 2000. sub. price: $30; per copy: $10; sample: $10. Back issues: $5.95-$12. 260pp; 5×8; of. Reporting time: 2 days. Payment: contributor's copies. Copyrighted, reverts to author.

Quarterly Committee of Queen's University (see also QUEEN'S QUARTERLY: A Canadian Review), Boris Castel, Queen's University, Kingston, Ontario K7L 3N6, Canada, e-mail qquartly@post.queensu.ca; website http://info.queensu.ca/quarterly. 1893. Poetry, fiction, articles, interviews, satire, criticism, parts-of-novels, plays. "Articles: 20-25 double-spaced pages plus copy on disk in Wordperfect. Recent contributors: Marlene Brant Castellano, Jerry S. Grafstein, Sylvia Ostry, Janice Gross Stein, Michael Ignatieff, Conor Cruise O'Brien." avg. press run 3.5M. Expects 1 title 1999. avg. price, paper: $6.50. 224pp; 6×9; of. Reporting time: 2-3 months. Payment: yes. Copyrights for author. CPPA, CELJ.

Quarterly Review of Literature Press (see also QRL POETRY SERIES), Theodore Weiss, Renee Weiss, Princeton University, 26 Haslet Avenue, Princeton, NJ 08540, 609-921-6976; fax 609-258-2230; e-mail qrl@princeton.edu. 1943. Poetry. "Manuscripts should be sent for reading during the months of November and May only. The collection need not be a first book. It should be between 50 and 100 pages if it is a group of poems, a selection of miscellaneous poems, a poetic play, a work of poetry translation, or it can be a single long poem of more than 30 pages. Some of the poems may have had previous magazine publication. Manuscripts in English or translated into English are also invited from outside the U.S.A. Only one manuscript may be submitted per reading period and must include an SASE. $1000 and 100 copies are awarded to each winning manuscript. The editors are grateful for the enthusiasm of all of those who entered into the support of the Series. They continue to require that each manuscript submitted be accompanied by a $20 subscription to the series. Please send SASE to QRL for special details." avg. press run 3M-5M. Pub'd 4-6 titles 1998. 72 titles listed in the *Small Press Record of Books in Print* (28th Edition, 1999-00). avg. price, cloth: $20; paper: $12; other: Special double volume, $20 pa, $25 cl. Discounts: 10%. 350pp; 5½×8½; lp. Reporting time: 1-3 months. Simultaneous submissions accepted: yes. Payment: $1000 and 100 copies for each manuscript printed. Copyright by QRL.

QUARTERLY WEST, Margot Schilpp, Editor, 200 South Central Campus Drive, Room 317, University of Utah, Salt Lake City, UT 84112, 801-581-3938. 1976. Poetry, fiction, interviews, criticism, reviews, parts-of-novels, long-poems, non-fiction. "We publish quality fiction, poetry, nonfiction and reviews in experimental or traditional forms, by new or established writers. We solicit our reviews but do read unsolicited ones. Manuscripts accepted for publication should be submitted on computer disk, preferably in a Macintosh format. Since 1982 we have sponsored a biennial novella competition with cash prizes for the two finalists. We read MSS year-round and accept simultaneous submissions (make this clear in your cover letter). Contributors: Ron Carlson, Andre Dubus, Barry Hannah, Chuck Rosenthal, Gordon Weaver, W.D. Wetherell, Ai, Stephen Dunn, Tess Gallagher, Patricia Goedicke, Larry Levis, Dave Smith, Philip Levine, Francine Prose, Kate Braverman, Lucia Perillo, Albert Goldbarth, Allison Joseph." circ. 1.9M. 2/yr. Pub'd 2 issues 1998; expects 2 issues 1999, 2 issues 2000. sub. price: $12; per copy: $7.50; sample: $7.50. Back issues: $5. Discounts: agents 25%, bookstores 40%. 224pp; 6×9; of. Reporting time: 1-4 months. Simultaneous submissions accepted: yes. Publishes less than 1% of manuscripts submitted. Payment: 2 copies; $25-$100 fiction, $15-100 poetry, $500 novella competition. Copyrighted, does not revert to author. Pub's reviews: 8 in 1998. §Fiction, poetry, and non-fiction. Ads: $150/$85. CLMP.

QUARTZ HILL JOURNAL OF THEOLOGY, Quartz Hill Publishing House, R.P. Nettelhorst, 43543 51st Street West, Quartz Hill, CA 93536, 802-722-0891; 805-943-3484; E-mail robin@theology.edu. 1993. Poetry, articles, interviews, criticism, reviews, non-fiction. "*Quartz Hill Journal of Theology* is the official journal of Quartz Hill School of Theology, a ministry of Quartz Hill Community Church. Quartz Hill Community Church is associated with the Southern Baptist Convention. We accept as our doctrinal statement *The Baptist Faith and Message*, adopted by the SBC in 1963. Length: 25,000 words max.; prefer 5,000-10,000. Submit complete manuscript. Enclose SASE for response. Submissions without SASE will be disposed of unread." circ. 200. 4/yr. Pub'd 2 issues 1998; expects 3 issues 1999, 4 issues 2000. sub. price: $20; per copy: $7.50; sample: $5. Back issues: $10. Discounts: none. 100pp; 8½×11; of. Reporting time: 30 days. Payment: 1 contributor's copy. Copyrighted, does not revert to author. Pub's reviews. §Bible, theology. Ads: $50/$25/will trade ads with other publishers. Small Press Genre Association (SPGA).

Quartz Hill Publishing House (see also QUARTZ HILL JOURNAL OF THEOLOGY), R.P. Nettelhorst, 43543 51st Street West, Quartz Hill, CA 93536, 805-722-0291; 805-943-3484; E-mail robin@theology.edu. 1993. Non-fiction. "Quartz Hill Publishing House is the official publishing arm of Quartz Hill School of Theology, a ministry of Quartz Hill Community Church. Quartz Hill Community Church is associated with the Southern Baptist Convention. We accept as our doctrinal statement *The Baptist Faith and Message*, adopted by the SBC in 1963. Length: 500,000 words max. for books. Query first. Must enclose SASE for response. Submissions without SASE will be disposed of unread." avg. press run 200. Pub'd 5 titles 1998; expects 5 titles 1999, 5 titles 2000. avg. price, paper: $10. 200pp; 5×8½; of. Reporting time: 30 days. Publishes 1% of manuscripts submitted. Payment: no advance; 10% royalty. Copyrights for author. Small Press Genre Association (SPGA).

QUEEN OF ALL HEARTS, Montfort Publications, J. Patrick Gaffney, Editor; Roger M. Charest, Managing Editor, 26 South Saxon Avenue, Bay Shore, NY 11706, 516-665-0726. 1950. Poetry, fiction, articles, art, non-fiction. *"Queen of all Hearts* Magazine promotes knowledge of and devotion to the Mother of God, by explaining the Scriptural basis as well as the traditional teaching of the Church concerning the Mother of Jesus; her place in theology, the apostolate and spiritual life of the Roman Catholic Church; to make known her influence, over the centuries, in the fields of history, literature, art, music, poetry, etc., and to keep our readers informed of the happenings and recent developments in all fields of Marian endeavors around the world. Length of article: 1500 to 2500 words. Authors: Roman Ginn, o.c.s.o., Viola Ward, Joseph Tusiani, etc." circ. 4M. 6/yr. Pub'd 6 issues 1998; expects 6 issues 1999, 6 issues 2000. sub. price: $20; per copy: $3.50; sample: $3.50. Back issues: 50% discount. Discounts: schedules upon request. 48pp; 7¾×10¾; of. Reporting time: less than a month. Payment: yes, most of the time. Not·copyrighted. Pub's reviews: 6 in 1998. §Marian topics. Ads: none. CPA-Catholic Press Assn., 3555 Veteran's Memorial Highway, United, Ronkonkama, NY 11779.

Queen of Swords Press, Elizabeth Claman, 1328 Arch Street #B, Berkeley, CA 94708-1825, 541-344-0509. 1993. Poetry, fiction, articles, art, photos, interviews, long-poems, collages, non-fiction. "The subtitle of our press is Literary Acts of Bravery and that's what we're all about. Queen of Swords Press is literary press and the work we publish exhibits literary excellence, yet we also offer a forum for underrepresented voices on issues of social concern, especially, although not exclusively, to women. We are dedicated to opening historically taboo subjects in the hope that thhe books we publish will help people to understand their own and others' experiences more deeply. While most of our books are anthologies, we are also interested in other book-length projects. Please query with SASE for more detailed information. Tell us about your work and if it sounds gook to us, we'll ask to see more" avg. press run 1M. Pub'd 1 title 1998; expects 1 title 1999, 1 title 2000. 4 titles listed in the *Small Press Record of Books in Print* (28th Edition, 1999-00). avg. price, paper: $15.95. Discounts: Standard discounts apply. 200-300pp; 5½×8½; of. Reporting time: 1-3 months, depending on deadline. Payment: at present, 2 copies of the book, hopefully more in the future. Copyrights for author. CLMP, PMA.

QUEEN'S QUARTERLY: A Canadian Review, Quarterly Committee of Queen's University, Boris Castel, Queen's University, Kingston, Ontario K7L 3N6, Canada, 613-545-2667; e-mail qquartly@post.queensu.ca; website http://info.queensu.ca/quarterly. 1893. Poetry, fiction, articles, interviews, satire, criticism, parts-of-novels, plays. "Articles: 20-25 double-spaced pages plus copy on disk in Wordperfect. Recent contributors: Michael Ignatieff, Michael Ondaatje, Conor Cruise O'Brien, Mavis Gallant." circ. 3.5M. 4/yr. Pub'd 4 issues 1998; expects 4 issues 1999, 4 issues 2000. sub. price: $20 Canada, $25 U.S.; sub: $6.50; sample: $6.50. Back issues: depends on age, min. $4, max. $6. Discounts: none. 160pp; 6×9; of. Reporting time: 1 month. Simultaneous submissions accepted: no. Payment: up to $150 (short stories), $40 per poem, copies, subscriptions. Copyrighted, reverts to author. Pub's reviews: 60 in 1998. §Serious books only, history, science, politics, philosophy, social science, literary studies, music, art, etc. Not interested in unsolicited reviews. Ads: $150/$85/no classified. CPPA, CELJ.

QUEST, Human Kinetics Pub. Inc., Karen DePaulw, Ph.D, Box 5076, Champaign, IL 61825-5076, 217-351-5076. 1964. Articles, reviews. "Scholarly journal." circ. 1.5M. 4/yr. Pub'd 3 issues 1998; expects 4 issues 1999, 4 issues 2000. sub. price: $40 indiv., $100 instit., $26 student; per copy: $11 indiv; $26 instit.; sample: free. Back issues: $11 indiv; $26 instit. Discounts: 5%. 136pp; 6×9; of. Reporting time: 2 months. Payment: none. Copyrighted, does not revert to author. Ads: $300/$200. Midwest Book Publishers Association, American Booksellers Association.

THE QUEST, Theosophical Publishing House, John Algeo, PO Box 270, Wheaton, IL 60189, 312-668-1571. 1988. Articles, art, photos, interviews, reviews, non-fiction. *"The Quest* is a wholistic metaphysical magazine, with articles on philosophy, comparative religion, science, arts, and psychology." circ. 25M+. 6/yr. Pub'd 4 issues 1998; expects 6 issues 1999, 6 issues 2000. sub. price: $15.97; per copy: $3.95; sample: $4. Back issues: $5. Discounts: 40% non-returnable; 20% returns accepted. 40pp; 8¼×10¾; web offset. Reporting time: 3 months. Simultaneous submissions accepted: no. Payment: on publication. Copyrighted, rights revert to author by special request. Pub's reviews. §Wholistic perspective, comparative philosophy, science, religion, and the arts. Ads: none.

Quest Books: Theosophical Publishing House, 306 W. Geneva Road, PO Box 270, Wheaton, IL 60189-0270, 630-665-0130; Fax 630-665-8791. 29 titles listed in the *Small Press Record of Books in Print* (28th Edition, 1999-00).

Questex Consulting Ltd., K. Slater, 8 Karen Drive, Guelph, Ontario N1G 2N9, Canada, 519-824-7423. 1978. "Currently accepting only Canadian plays (i.e. plays written by a resident of Canada, or by a Canadian living abroad, or with significant recognisable Canadian setting, content, etc.) for the CAPCAT series. CAPCAT (Canadian Amateur Playwrights' Catalogue) is a collective arrangement in which all members pay a fee (up to $200 per play, depending on the length of play submitted) for guaranteed publication if literary, etc., standards are met. Arrangements can be made for payment to be waived for high-quality plays in selected cases, but royalties are then not given until the membership fee has been "earned" from sales." Pub'd 8 titles 1998; expects 4 titles 1999, 10 titles 2000. 20 titles listed in the Small Press Record of Books in Print (28th Edition, 1999-00). avg. price, paper: $8-12. Discounts: 20% for libraries and multiple orders. 70pp; 5½×8½. Reporting time: 1 month. Simultaneous submissions accepted: yes. Publishes members 90%, non-members 20% of manuscripts submitted. Payment: 10% sales, 50% performance. Copyrights for author.

QUESTION EVERYTHING CHALLENGE EVERYTHING (QECE), Larry Nocella, 406 Main Street #3C, Collegeville, PA 19426, e-mail qece@aol.com. 1996. Fiction, articles, art, photos, cartoons, interviews, satire, criticism, reviews, music, letters, parts-of-novels, collages, concrete art, news items, non-fiction. "Avoid references to mainstream media topics whenever possible. If you must reference a current trend, tie it to a timeless observation. Be as timeless as possible. Empower the reader, either with tales of your actions, or straightforward inspiration. QECE works to inspire readers to independent thought and action. Graphics, art and photos a major plus. Send SASE for guidelines." circ. 300. 3/yr. Pub'd 4 issues 1998; expects 2 issues 1999, 3 issues 2000. sub. price: $6/3 issues; per copy: $3; sample: $3 (to cover postage). Back issues: $3. 44pp; 5½×8½; photocopy. Reporting time: 1 month. Simultaneous submissions accepted: yes. Publishes 10% of manuscripts submitted. Payment: 2 contributor copies and some cash sometimes. Copyrighted, reverts to author. Ads: contact for possible ad trade.

Quicksilver Press, Jeffrey A. Chavez, 26741 Portola Parkway 1E-222, Foothill Ranch, CA 92610, fax 714-837-6291. 1996. Non-fiction. avg. press run 10M-50M. Pub'd 1 title 1998; expects 5 titles 1999, 15 titles 2000. 1 title listed in the Small Press Record of Books in Print (28th Edition, 1999-00). avg. price, cloth: $21; paper: $12. 200pp. Reporting time: 6-8 weeks. Simultaneous submissions accepted: yes. Publishes 10% of manuscripts submitted. Copyrights for author.

Quicksilver Productions, Jim Maynard, P.O.Box 340, Ashland, OR 97520, 541-482-5343, Fax; 541-482-0960. 1973. "Not accepting manuscripts at this time." avg. press run 30M. Pub'd 5 titles 1998; expects 6 titles 1999, 5 titles 2000. 8 titles listed in the Small Press Record of Books in Print (28th Edition, 1999-00). avg. price, paper: $8.95. Discounts: trade and jobbers, (trade from 40% at 5 copies to 50% at 1,000 mixed titles). Prepaid orders receive 5% extra discount plus free shipping. of. Copyrights for author.

Quiet Lion Press (see also RAIN CITY REVIEW), Brian Christopher Hamilton, 7215 SW LaView Drive, Portland, OR 97219, 503-771-1907. 1992. Fiction, interviews, criticism, reviews, non-fiction. "In the future we plan to expand our publishing to short story collections and novels. The press does not accept unsolicited mss. No queries" avg. press run 1M-2M. Pub'd 1 title 1998; expects 4 titles 1999, 8-10 titles 2000. 13 titles listed in the Small Press Record of Books in Print (28th Edition, 1999-00). avg. price, paper: $8.95. Discounts: query. 140pp; 5½×8½; of. Payment: varies. Copyrights for author.

Quiet Tymes, Inc., Roger J. Wannell, Founder, 1400 Downing Street, Denver, CO 80218, 303-839-8628; 800-552-7360; FAX 303-894-9240. 1979. 2 titles listed in the Small Press Record of Books in Print (28th Edition, 1999-00). avg. price, other: $9.95 cassette. 4½×7; audio-cassette duplication. We sometimes copyright for author.

Quill Driver Books, Stephen Blake Mettee, Publisher, 8386 N. Madsen Ave, Clovis, CA 93611, 559-322-5917, fax 559-322-5967, 800-497-4909. 1993. Non-fiction. "Additional imprint is Word Dancer Press. Quill Driver Books publishes hardcover and trade paperback originals and reprints with national appeal. Word Dancer Press imprint is used for regional and special market hardcover and trade paperback books. Unagented submissions welcome. Please query before submitting manuscripts. Send SASE." avg. press run 2.5M-5M. Pub'd 6 titles 1998; expects 6 titles 1999, 8 titles 2000. 9 titles listed in the Small Press Record of Books in Print (28th Edition, 1999-00). avg. price, cloth: $23.95; paper: $16.95. Discounts: retailers 1 book 20%, 2-24 40%, 25-49 42%, 50-99 43%; 100-249 44%; 250+ 45% libraries and schools 20%. Special discounts apply to refrence titles, please inquire. 200pp; 6×9, 5½×8½, 8½×11; of. Reporting time: 30 days. Simultaneous submissions accepted: yes. Publishes 1/4 of 1% of manuscripts submitted. Payment: royalties negotiated. Copyrights for author. PMA, ABA.

●THE QUILL MAGAZINE QUARTERLY, Charlotte Austin, 2900 Warden Avenue, PO Box 92207, Toronto, Ontario, MIW 3Y9, Canada, 416-410-0277; fax 416-497-6737; e-mail austin@thequill.com. 1998. Fiction, articles, interviews, reviews. "The Quill Magazine Quarterly is an electronic publication (e-zine) available by subscription. It features details on the craft of writing and is specifically formulated for beginning writers. Length of articles: 800-1200 words; query." circ. 2.7M. 4/yr. Pub'd 4 issues 1998; expects 4 issues

470

1999, 4 issues 2000. sub. price: $19.99; sample: free, on website. 16pp; e-zine. Reporting time: 2 weeks. Simultaneous submissions accepted: no. Publishes 60% of manuscripts submitted. Payment: on acceptance—articles $50-60, reviews $15 each, short fiction $25. Copyrighted, reverts to author. Pub's reviews: 26 in 1998. §fiction, short fiction, short stories, nonfiction on the craft of writing.

●Quilted Walls Micropress, 426 N. Main Street, Herkimer, NY 13350. 1994. Poetry, fiction, articles, art, photos, cartoons, interviews, satire, criticism, reviews, music, letters, parts-of-novels, long-poems, collages, plays, concrete art, news items, non-fiction. "We will seriously consider any and all submissions which are accompanied by verfiable documentation showing that at the time of writing official medical personnel considered the author to be mentally ill." avg. press run 10. Expects 1 title 1999, 1 title 2000. avg. price, paper: $10. Discounts: 5+ 1/3 off. 5×8. Reporting time: 1 month. Simultaneous submissions accepted: yes. Payment: 15%.

QUINTILE, Quintile, PO Box 89, Hales Corners, WI 53130, 414-534-4620. 1991. Articles, reviews, news items. circ. 5M. 4/yr. Pub'd 1 issue 1998; expects 4 issues 1999, 4 issues 2000. sub. price: free. 12pp; †of. Copyrighted, reverts to author. Pub's reviews: 2 in 1998. §New Age, astrology, numerology, holism.

Quintile (see also QUINTILE), PO Box 89, Hales Corners, WI 53130, 414-534-4620. 1991. avg. press run 500-3M. Expects 2 titles 1999, 4 titles 2000. avg. price, cloth: $12.95-$24.95. Discounts: 45% trade. 250pp; 8×11, 5×8, 3½×6½; †of. Reporting time: 1 month. Payment: 4-8%, workable (retail). Copyrights for author.

R

R & E Publishers, 2132 O'Tode Avenue, Suite A, San Jose, CA 95131, 408-432-3443; fax 408-432-9221. 1967. "Publishes non-fiction books only — submissions in letter with abstract of book and table of contents. With stamped, self-addressed envelope. Free to fly. Chiropractic first aid. Successful parenting, self-esteem." avg. press run 1M-10M. Pub'd 20 titles 1998; expects 5 titles 1999. 58 titles listed in the *Small Press Record of Books in Print* (28th Edition, 1999-00). avg. price, cloth: $13; paper: $10. Discounts: 1-5 20%, 6 or more 40%; wholesaler 55%. 135pp; 6×9, 5½×8½; of. Reporting time: 2 months. Simultaneous submissions accepted: yes. Payment: royalties paid. Does not copyright for author. Penninsula Publishers/Writers Connection.

R & M Publishing Company, Dillard Haley, Editor; Barbara G. Blackwell, Editor; Mack B. Morant, McGorine Cassell, Editor, PO Box 1276, Holly Hill, SC 29059, 803-279-2262. 1978. "We will look at any subject of quality work. However, we are most interested in historical documentations, educational and how-to materials." avg. press run 1M-2M. Expects 1-3 titles 1999. 9 titles listed in the *Small Press Record of Books in Print* (28th Edition, 1999-00). avg. price, paper: $6.95; other: $7.95. Discounts: 20-55%. 42-110pp; 5½×8⅛; lp. Reporting time: 6-12 weeks or less. Publishes less than 1% of manuscripts submitted. Payment: negotiable. Copyrights for author. Multicultural Publishers Exchange.

R.G.E. Publishing (see also BLACKJACK FORUM), Arnold Snyder, 414 Santa Clara, Oakland, CA 94610. 1980. "Relating to casino blackjack: strategies, math/computer analyses, gambling etc." avg. press run 2.5M. Pub'd 1 title 1998; expects 1 title 1999, 1 title 2000. 8 titles listed in the *Small Press Record of Books in Print* (28th Edition, 1999-00). avg. price, paper: $12.95. Discounts: 40% off for 6 or more copies. 84-124pp; 8½×11; of. Reporting time: 2-6 weeks. Simultaneous submissions accepted: yes. Payment: royalty only. Copyrights for author.

Rabeth Publishing Company, Raymond Quigley, Elizabeth Quigley, 201 S. Cottage Grove, Kirksville, MO 63501, 660-665-5143; e-mail qurabeth@kvmo.net. 1990. Poetry, fiction, non-fiction. avg. press run 400-2M. Pub'd 2 titles 1998; expects 3 titles 1999, 3-4 titles 2000. 8 titles listed in the *Small Press Record of Books in Print* (28th Edition, 1999-00). avg. price, cloth: $16.50; paper: $9.95; other: $4.95 saddle-stitched. Discounts: 40% to trade. 100-125pp; 5½×8½, 6×9; prepare camera ready - computer. Reporting time: 2 weeks. Simultaneous submissions accepted: yes. Publishes 30-50% of manuscripts submitted. Payment: negotiable. Copyrights for author.

RABID ANIMAL KOMIX, Mike Hersh, PO Box 9389, Berkeley, CA 94709-0389, 415-440-0967; email krankinkmx@aol.com. 1995. Fiction, art, cartoons, satire. circ. 3M. 2/yr. Pub'd 2 issues 1998; expects 2 issues 1999, 4 issues 2000. price per copy: $2.95; sample: $1. 24pp; 6⅝×10¼. Simultaneous submissions accepted: no. Copyrighted. Ads: $100/$50/$25 1/4 page.

Race Point Press, PO Box 770, Provincetown, MA 02657, 508-487-1626. 1986. Non-fiction. "Publishers of adult non-fiction subjects. 1) For the elderly and their adult children (e.g. medicare, eldercare, services for the elderly); 2) Architectural barrier removal for the disabled" avg. press run 20M. Expects 2 titles 1999, 2 titles

2000. avg. price, paper: $19.95. Discounts: trade 40%. 250pp; 6×9; of. Payment: negotiated on an individual basis. Copyrights for author. PMA, ABA, SPAN.

RADIANCE, The Magazine For Large Women, Alice Ansfield, PO Box 30246, Oakland, CA 94604, 510-482-0680, E-mail info@radiancemagazine.com; www.radiancemagazine.com. 1984. Poetry, fiction, articles, art, photos, cartoons, interviews, satire, reviews, letters, parts-of-novels, long-poems, collages, concrete art, news items, non-fiction. *"Radiance* is an upbeat, positive, colorful, empowering magazine for women all sizes of large. Our quarterly issues feature in-depth interviews with plus-size celebrities, along with articles on health, media, fashion, and politics. Our focus is body acceptance — now. We want articles, interviews, essays, poetry, book reviews, and photo features on topics for all areas of our lives. Our tone is personal, intimate, honest. We celebrate the diversity on our pages and in our readership. We feature women all sizes of large, all ages, lifestyles, and ethnicities." circ. 15M. 4/yr. Pub'd 4 issues 1998; expects 4 issues 1999, 4 issues 2000. sub. price: $20; per copy: $5 + $1 postage (US rate); sample: $3.50 for writers only. 60pp; 8½×11; web. Reporting time: 2-4 months. Simultaneous submissions accepted: yes. Publishes 15% of manuscripts submitted. Payment: $50-$100 per feature article. Copyrighted, reverts to author. Pub's reviews: 10 in 1998. §Women, health, self-care, women's tools (financial info., home, family), fashion, self esteem, media, politics, profiles, culture, art. Ads: $1200 b/w/$680 b/w/color $2300.

RADICAL AMERICA, Marla Erlien, Brian Flynn, 237A Holland Street, Somerville, MA 02144-2402, 617-628-6585. 1967. Articles. circ. 5M. 4/yr. Pub'd 4 issues 1998; expects 4 issues 1999, 4 issues 2000. sub. price: $22; per copy: $5.50; sample: $5.50. Back issues: apply. Discounts: 40%. 80pp; 7×10; of. Reporting time: 6 weeks. Payment: none. Copyrighted, reverts to author. Pub's reviews: 10 in 1998. §Politics, history, film, sociology, feminism. Ads: $350/$250/$150 1/4 page.

Radnor-Hill Publishing, Inc., David Kephart, Bette Simons, PO Box 41051, Philadelphia, PA 19127, 215-483-1126; FAX 215-483-4079. 1993. Fiction, art, photos, cartoons, non-fiction. "We prefer non-fiction and how-to on popular topics such as woodworking, gardening and leisuretime/home activities. We are producing CD-Roms and we are actively seeking titles which are candidates for an interactive format" avg. press run 10M. Pub'd 8 titles 1998; expects 10 titles 1999, 12 titles 2000. 2 titles listed in the *Small Press Record of Books in Print* (28th Edition, 1999-00). avg. price, paper: $16.00; other: $29.95 CD-Rom. Discounts: title available through Baker and Taylor Books. 150pp; 8½×11; of. Reporting time: 60 days. Publishes 50% of manuscripts submitted. Payment: negotiable. Copyrights for author.

RAFTERS, Matt Uhler, Calder Square PO Box 10929, State College, PA 16805-0929, 814-867-4073; mdu103@psu.edu. 1996. Poetry, fiction, art, long-poems, non-fiction. "Recent contributors: Bruce Weigl, Colette Inez, Barry Spacks, Kevin Bowen, Russell Edson, John Haag, Thomas F. Kennedy, and Lucien Stryk. Nominated for a Pushcart Prize." circ. 500. 4/yr. Pub'd 2 issues 1998; expects 2-4 issues 1999, 2-4 issues 2000. sub. price: $17; per copy: $4.95 + p/h; sample: $3.50 + p/h. Back issues: same. Discounts: call or write for schedule. 114pp; 6×9; †Docutech. Reporting time: 3-4 months. Simultaneous submissions accepted: no. Payment: contributors copies. Copyrighted, reverts to author.

RAG MAG, Black Hat Press, Beverly Voldseth, Box 12, Goodhue, MN 55027, 651-923-4590. 1982. Poetry, fiction, articles, art, photos, cartoons, interviews, satire, criticism, reviews, letters, long-poems, plays, non-fiction. "Our only bias is quality. We are looking for poetry, satire, fiction, plays, articles, book reviews, and art & photos from any point of view and in any style. Fiction under 3M words. Reviews, satire, articles, and fiction under 1M words. Our first issue featured work by Kathleen Patrick, Sharon Chmielarz, Larry Schug, Paul A. Hanson and many known and totally unknown writers and artists" circ. 300. 2/yr. Pub'd 2 issues 1998; expects 2 issues 1999, 2 issues 2000. sub. price: $10; per copy: $6; sample: $4. Back issues: $4 when available. Discounts: 40% to stores. 112pp; 6×9; of. Reporting time: 1 week to 2 months. Simultaneous submissions accepted: yes. Publishes 10% of manuscripts submitted. Payment: in copies. Copyrighted, reverts to author. Pub's reviews: 2 in 1998. §Poetry, short stories, novels, plays. Ads: $30/$15.

RAG SHOCK, Lunar Offensive Publications, Stephen Fried, Publisher; Gregg Williard, Art Editor; Thea Hillman, Associate Editor; Nancy Bengis Friedman, Associate Editor; Tom Hansen, Chief Reviewer, 1910 Foster Avenue, Brooklyn, NY 11230-1902. 1994. Poetry, fiction, articles, art, photos, cartoons, reviews, parts-of-novels, long-poems, collages, non-fiction. "The censor has a collection. *Rag Shock* seeks the unprintable. Poetry to 100 lines, prose to 2000 words, reviews to 450 words, art to 8X10 B/W. Limit 5 pieces absolute. Include SASE." circ. 1.5M. 1/yr. Pub'd 1 issue 1998; expects 1 issue 1999, 1 issue 2000. sub. price: $5; per copy: $5; sample: $5. Discounts: 20% on orders of 12 or more (+ $5 postage on 10 copies). 144pp; 8½×10; of. Reporting time: 3 weeks. Simultaneous submissions accepted: yes. Publishes 5-10% of manuscripts submitted. Payment: 2 copies with diskette (IBM/DOS/ASCII), 1 copy with paper manuscripts. Copyrighted, reverts to author. Pub's reviews: 12 in 1998. §We want reviews, not publications, of experimental or any good writing. Ads: $100/$50/$25, need camera ready copy, all ads subject to approval. Small Press Center NYC.

Ragged Edge Press, Harold E. Collier, Acquisitions Editor, PO Box 152, 63 West Burd Street, Shippensburg,

PA 17257, 717-532-2237; FAX 717-532-7704. 1994. Non-fiction. "Editorial office: 353 Ragged Edge Road, Chambersburg, PA 17201. A division of White Mane Publishing Company, Inc." avg. press run 2M-3M. Expects 4 titles 1999, 10 titles 2000. 13 titles listed in the *Small Press Record of Books in Print* (28th Edition, 1999-00). avg. price, cloth: $19.95; paper: $9.95. Discounts: available on request. 200pp; 6×9; †1p. Reporting time: 60 days, proposal guidelines upon request. Simultaneous submissions accepted: yes. Payment: twice yearly. Copyrights for author.

RAIN CITY REVIEW, Quiet Lion Press, Brian Christopher Hamilton, Editor; Douglas Spangle, Senior Editor; Kelly Leno Allan, Associate Editor; Tracy Burkholder, Associate Editor, 7215 SW LaView Drive, Portland, OR 97219, 503-771-1907. 1993. Poetry, fiction, interviews, criticism, reviews, parts-of-novels, non-fiction. "We publish both short and long poetry and fiction. We tend to prefer slightly darker, edgier work, but not exclusively. Recent contributors include: Sherman Alexie, Kate Braverman, August Kleinzahler, Tom Clark, Gary Miranda, Ursula K. LeGuin, Anne Waldman, Lyn Lifshin, Walter Pavlich, Flora Durham, and Naomi Shihab Nye. We feature 40-50 writers in each issue." circ. 400-800. 2/yr. Pub'd 2 issues 1998; expects 2 issues 1999. sub. price: $13 postpaid; per copy: $7; sample: $7 postpaid. Back issues: $7 postpaid. Discounts: query. 100pp; 5½×8½; of. Reporting time: 1-5 months. Simultaneous submissions accepted: yes. Publishes 20% of manuscripts submitted. Payment: 1-3 copies. Copyrighted, reverts to author. Pub's reviews: 3 in 1998. §Poetry, fiction, non-fiction. Ads: $75/$45/na.

Rain Crow Publishing, 2127 W. Pierce Ave. Apt. 2B, Chicago, IL 60622-1824. 2 titles listed in the *Small Press Record of Books in Print* (28th Edition, 1999-00).

RAIN MAGAZINE, Greg Bryant, Danielle Janes, PO Box 30097, Eugene, OR 97403. 1974. Articles, art, photos, cartoons, reviews, non-fiction. "Very important that potential contributors write first for writer's guidelines and include a self-addressed envelope. Sustainable community revitalization projects that are successful and can serve as examples for others to follow." circ. 8.5M. 4/yr. Pub'd 4 issues 1998; expects 4 issues 1999, 4 issues 2000. sub. price: $20; per copy: $5; sample: $5. Back issues: $2 (1975-1985), $5 (1991-present). Discounts: available. 62pp; 8½×11; of. Reporting time: varies. Payment: none. Copyrighted, rights reverting to author depends on arrangement. Pub's reviews: 100's in 1998. §Ecology, anthropology, history, bicycles, politics, agriculture, health. none.

RAIN TAXI REVIEW OF BOOKS, Carolyn Kuebler, Randall Heath, Eric Lorberer, PO Box 3840, Minneapolis, MN 55403, 612-825-1528 tel/fax; E-mail raintaxi@bitstream.net; website www.raintaxi.com. 1995. Articles, interviews, reviews. "Book review run from 400 words to 1500 words. Interview lengths vary widely. Feature articles from 850 to 3000 words. Manuscripts are usually solicited." circ. 20M. 4/yr. Pub'd 4 issues 1998; expects 4 issues 1999, 4 issues 2000. sub. price: $10; per copy: $3. Back issues: $3. Discounts: distributed free of charge in bookstores & literary centers. 56pp; 8¼×10¾; web. Reporting time: 30 days. Simultaneous submissions accepted: yes. Payment: review copies of books, copies of magazines, otherwise none. Copyrighted, does not revert to author. Pub's reviews: 200 in 1998. §Books and audio- literary fiction & nonfiction, poetry, cultural studies, art. Ads: $650/$340/ $245 1/3 page/$190 1/4 page/$110 1/8 page. CLMP.

Rainbow Books, Inc., Betsy A. Lampe, PO Box 430, Highland City, FL 33846, 941-648-4420; rbibooks@aol.com. 1979. Non-fiction. "Writers' guidelines for 33¢ SASE; No work under 64 pages. No religious material; no biographies/autobiographies unless a celebrity, no diet books or business books. Looking for mystery fiction and how-to books for adults; self-help books for kids" avg. press run 10M. Pub'd 12 titles 1998; expects 14 titles 1999, 16 titles 2000. 21 titles listed in the *Small Press Record of Books in Print* (28th Edition, 1999-00). avg. price, cloth: $30; paper: $15. Discounts: 50% prepaid, you pay freight; one-copy orders must be pre-paid, no minimum. 250pp; 5½×8½; Desktop publishing to camera-ready work or to disk. Reporting time: 4 weeks (only with SASE). Simultaneous submissions accepted: yes. Publishes 5% of manuscripts submitted. Payment: depends on material, usually $500 advance, 6% royalty. Copyrights for author. SEBA, NAIP, FPA, PAS, AAP.

Rainbow's End, Bettie Tucker, Director, 354 Golden Grove Road, Baden, PA 15005, 800-596-RBOW; Fax 415-266-4997; www.adpages.com/rbebooks; e-mail btucker833@aol.com. 1983. Poetry, fiction, plays, non-fiction. "Primarily Christian self-help and recovery." avg. press run 1.5M. Pub'd 8 titles 1998; expects 4-6 titles 1999. avg. price, paper: $10. Discounts: 55%, 40% to bookstores. 100pp; 5×8½; of. Reporting time: 3 months. Simultaneous submissions accepted: yes. Publishes 1% of manuscripts submitted. Payment: $250 advance, royalty 10-12%. Copyrights for author. PMA.

THE RAINTOWN REVIEW: A Forum for the Essayist's Art, HarMona Press, Harvey Stanbrough, PO Box 370, Pittsboro, IN 46167-0370, 505-623-0180. 1998. Non-fiction. "Submit no more than 3 satirical, nostalgic (not just a remembrance, but nostalgia with a twist that either teaches a lesson or makes a point), *very* humorous, or serious essays between 400 and 3,000 words on any topic. Recently published Christine Westcott, Barbara J. Petoskey, Doug Rennie, and Allan Amenta." circ. 1.5M. 4/yr. Expects 4 issues 1999, 4 issues 2000. sub. price: $16; per copy: $4.50 ppd.; sample: same. Back issues: same. Discounts: contributors may purchase

473

add'l copies for $3 each postpaid. 58pp; 8½×5½; †inkjet, laserjet. Reporting time: 2 weeks. Simultaneous submissions accepted: yes. Publishes 20% of manuscripts submitted. Payment: 1 contributor copy plus $5-$15 on acceptance. Copyrighted, reverts to author. Ads: exchange ads only on insert and only with magazines I've seen and can endorse.

THE RAINTREE REVIEW: Poetry Edition, HarMona Press, Harvey Stanbrough, PO Box 370, Pittsboro, IN 46167-0370, 505-623-0180. 1998. Poetry. "Submit no more than 6 well-crafted poems, metered, syllabic, or free verse. End rhyme is neither a crime nor a requirement. No line limits. If your poem is so obscure that only you can understand it, we're not your market. No lovesick hearts, no overtly religious themes. Recently published Dara McLaughlin, Wayne Hogan, Anne Marie Cusmano, and John Grey." circ. 1.5M. 4/yr. Expects 4 issues 1999, 4 issues 2000. sub. price: $16; per copy: $4.50 ppd.; sample: $4.50 ppd. Back issues: same. Discounts: contributors may purchase additional copies for $3 each ppd. 58pp; 8½×5½; †inkjet, laserjet. Reporting time: 2 weeks. Simultaneous submissions accepted: yes. Publishes 15% of manuscripts submitted. Payment: 1 contributor copy, token cash payment when available. Copyrighted, reverts to author. Ads: exchange ads only on insert and only with magazines I've seen and can endorse.

Rainy Day Press, Mike Helm, 1147 East 26th, Eugene, OR 97403, 503-484-4626. 1978. "History and culture of the Pacific Northwest is the prime concern of Rainy Day Press. The Oregon Country Library is indicative of our emphasis. The first four volumes were written by Fred Lockley in the 1920's. They are conversations with Oregon Country pioneers, previously published in the *Oregon Journal*, an oral history of life on the Oregon Trail and in the civilization building at its western end. The fifth, by Mike Helm, is a collection of ghost stories and other local legends taken from towns throughout Oregon. The sixth, in the framework of a contemporary journal, tells of a search for the mythical and historical soul of Oregon. Though I refer to Rainy Day Press as 'we', it is still a one-horse show, and I am the horse. As I have a million ideas of my own for writing and publishing projects, I am not yet seeking manuscript submissions. Instead, some money." avg. press run 4M. Expects 2 titles 1999, 1 title 2000. 5 titles listed in the *Small Press Record of Books in Print* (28th Edition, 1999-00). avg. price, paper: $10.15. Discounts: 1 book 0%; 2-5, 10%; 6-24, 40%; 25-49, 42%; 50-74, 44%; 75-99, 46%; 100-149, 48%; 150 or more, 50%. 300+pp; 5½×8½, 6×9; of.

RALPH'S REVIEW, Ralph Cornell, 129 Wellington Avenue, #A, Albany, NY 12203-2637, e-mail rcpub@juno.com. 1988. Poetry, fiction, art, cartoons, letters. "No heavy racial, political, rape stories. No slasher stories. Up to 2,000 words; poems to 2 pages. Recent contributors: M.M. Loppiccolo, R. Cornell, Dr. Ralph Pray, Derek Bullard, Celeste Plowden, and Mark Fewell." circ. 100. 4/yr. Pub'd 4 issues 1998; expects 4-6 issues 1999, 6 issues 2000. sub. price: $15; per copy: $2; sample: $2. Back issues: varies. 25pp; 8½×11; †of. Reporting time: 2-4 weeks. Simultaneous submissions accepted: yes. Publishes 50-60% of manuscripts submitted. Payment: 1 copy. Copyrighted, reverts to author. Pub's reviews: 1 in 1998. §Fiction (fantasy, horror), art, environmental. Ads: $18/$10/$3 1″/$7 3x5/$5 business card.

Ram Press (see also CATAMARAN SAILOR), Amelia Norlin, PO Box 2060, Key Largo, FL 33037, 305-451-3287; FAX 305-453-0255; Email ram5@icanect.net; http://www.catsailor.com/. 1991. Fiction, non-fiction. Expects 4 titles 1999, 6 titles 2000. 3 titles listed in the *Small Press Record of Books in Print* (28th Edition, 1999-00). avg. price, paper: $29.95. Discounts: 2-4 20%, 5-99 40%, 100+ 60%. 352pp; 6×9; of. Reporting time: 60 days. Payment: standard.

Rama Publishing Co., Richard Aschwanden, Charles Aschwanden, PO Box 793, Carthage, MO 64836-0793, 417-358-1093. 1983. Fiction, articles, non-fiction. "In 40 years of married life Richard and Maria Aschwanden of Carthage, MO, have reared 10 healthy children and never have had a doctor's or dentist's bill because of illness. They attribute this to a philosophy of healthy living which includes preventative family nutrition. Rama Publishing Co. is interested in editing and publishing booklets and books dealing with regeneration of mankind in the physical, mental, and spiritual aspects." avg. press run 500-2M. Expects 3 titles 1999, 5 titles 2000. 9 titles listed in the *Small Press Record of Books in Print* (28th Edition, 1999-00). avg. price, paper: $5. Discounts: 5-25, 25%; 26-50, 40%; 51+, 50%. 150pp; 5½×8¼; of. Reporting time: 5 weeks. Payment: 10-15% on net receipts; no advance. Copyrights for author.

RAMBUNCTIOUS REVIEW, Mary Alberts, Co-Editor; Richard Goldman, Co-Editor; Nancy Lennon, Co-Editor; Elizabeth Hausler, Co-Editor, Rambunctious Press, Inc., 1221 West Pratt Blvd., Chicago, IL 60626. 1984. Poetry, fiction, art, photos, satire, plays. "*Rambunctious Review* accepts submissions from September through May. Length of material: poems 100 lines, fiction 12 pages. No biases. Recent contributors: Pamela Miller, Achy Obejas, Richard Calisch, Sean Lawrence." circ. 600. 1/yr. Pub'd 1 issue 1998; expects 1 issue 1999, 1 issue 2000. sub. price: $12/3 issues; per copy: $4; sample: $4. Back issues: $4. Discounts: please inquire. 48pp; 7×10; of. Reporting time: 6-9 months. Payment: 2 free copies of the magazine. Copyrighted, reverts to author. CLMP.

Rarach Press, Ladislav R. Hanka, 1005 Oakland Drive, Kalamazoo, MI 49008, 616-388-5631. 1981. Poetry, art, long-poems. "This is essentially a vehicle for my art and rather personal and idiosyncratic notions of what I wish to print: i.e. occasional small books, poems set into an etching, wood engravings, handbills, posters for exhibitions, and one substantial book of 100 pp. containing 5 long poems in Czech. This is labor-intensive hand-done bibliophilia. My bread and butter is printing my own artwork often as suites of etchings or wood engravings sometimes with a bit of type-set commentary, titles or description. The bibliophilia is an amusement appearing irregularly. I am essentially uninterested in unsolicited manuscripts, unless someone wants me to illustrate something I like." avg. press run 20-30. Pub'd 1 title 1998; expects 1 title 1999, 1 title 2000. 7 titles listed in the *Small Press Record of Books in Print* (28th Edition, 1999-00). avg. price, cloth: $50; other: $200 and up handbound. Discounts: 40% off for dealers. 10-100pp; size highly variable; †lp, intaglio, wood engraving. Payment: done individually, generally in copies of print. Does not copyright for author.

RARITAN: A Quarterly Review, Richard Poirier, Editor-in-Chief; Stephanie Volmer, Managing Editor, 31 Mine Street, New Brunswick, NJ 08903, 732-932-7887, Fax 732-932-7855. 1981. Fiction, articles, interviews, criticism, reviews, non-fiction. *"Raritan* is a cultural quarterly concerned with politics, literature, the arts, and social sciences. In particular, we are interested in the workings of cultural power, in how certain political, social, and artistic movements have won popular attention and become a part of our artistic heritage. In addition to essays, *Raritan* prints a *small* quantity of poetry. Contributors include Adam Phillips, Richard Rorty, Vicki Hearne, Edward Said, Frank Kermode, Marina Warner, John Hollander, and Harold Bloom." circ. 3.5M. 4/yr. Pub'd 4 issues 1998; expects 4 issues 1999. sub. price: $16 individuals, $20 institutions; per copy: $7; sample: $7 where applicable. Back issues: $8 per copy. Discounts: available for bookstores, distributors, and subscription agencies. 160pp; 6x9; of. Reporting time: 6 weeks. Simultaneous submissions accepted: no. Payment: $100. Copyrighted. Pub's reviews: 10 in 1998. §Literary criticism, philosophy, pol. sci., arts, linguistics, sociology. Ads: $275/$180. CLMP.

●**Raspberry Press Ltd.,** Betty J. Schultz, PO Box 1, Dixon, IL 61021-0001, 815-288-4910; fax 815-288-4910; e-mail raspberrypress@essexl.com. "Additional address: 1989 Grand Detour Road, Dixon, IL 61021." 4 titles listed in the *Small Press Record of Books in Print* (28th Edition, 1999-00).

The Rateavers, Bargyla Rateaver, Gylver Rateaver, 9049 Covina Street, San Diego, CA 92126, 619-566-8994, Fax; 619-586-1104, E-mail; brateaver@aol.com. 1973. Non-fiction. "Organic gardening and farming, conservation methods, reprints or abstracts, mostly." avg. press run 2.5M-3M. Expects 4 titles 1999. 12 titles listed in the *Small Press Record of Books in Print* (28th Edition, 1999-00). avg. price, cloth: $125; paper: $20. Discounts: none. 300pp; 5½x8½, 9x6, 8x11; lithography. Payment: 10% to author. Copyrights for author.

THE RATIONAL FEMINIST, Molly Gill, Editor-Publisher, 10500 Ulmerton Road #726-202, Largo, FL 34641. 1984. Articles, art, cartoons, reviews, non-fiction. "We seek guest editorials, letters to editor; media reviews (print & audio); feminist continuum and dissent; political, such as anarchist, Maoist, white loyalists, etc., factions; design and cartoons, black and white, 1x3''; all volunteer at this time; books to review. Journals and magazines of the feminist continuum to review plus the counter-culture. All relating to feminist cause. About 400 words, double-spaced, typed. Letters, 200 words, same. Reviews, 400 words tops. Essays same. Top quality poetry: 30-60 lines tops." circ. 100. 6-10/yr. Pub'd 10 issues 1998; expects 10 issues 1999, 6 issues 2000. sub. price: suggested donation for mv ministry $25; per copy: $3 suggested donation, $5 outside USA; sample: $3 suggested donation, $5 outside USA. Back issues: $3 suggested donation. Discounts: can discuss. 16-27pp; 8½x14, 8½x11; duplicating machine. Reporting time: 3-4 weeks leeway, but often 1 week. Simultaneous submissions accepted: yes. Publish 6 out of 50 manuscripts submitted. Payment: none at this time, mostly staff written. Copyrighted, reverts to author. Pub's reviews: 12 in 1998. §Feminists, censorship, film comedies, humor, quality TV reviews, re conservative women, women's sex lives, families-children-youth, Euro-Amer. only. Ads: ad chart available on request to subscribers only.

RATTAPALLAX, George Dickerson, Judith Werner, 532 La Guardia Place, Suite 353, New York, NY 10012, 212-560-7459; e-mail rattapallax@hotmail.com. 1998. Poetry, fiction, art, photos, satire, criticism, long-poems, concrete art, non-fiction. "Some recent contributors: Lamont Steptoe, Kate Light, Ron Price, Karen Swenson, Richard Levine, Mary Nichols." circ. 2M. 2/yr. Expects 2 issues 1999, 2 issues 2000. sub. price: $14; per copy: $7.95; sample: $7.95. Back issues: $6.95. 128pp; 6x9; of. Reporting time: 2 weeks. Simultaneous submissions accepted: yes. Copyrighted, reverts to author. Ads: $300/$150.

RATTLE, Alan Fox, Editor; Stellasue Lee, Poetry Editor, 13440 Ventura Boulevard #200, Sherman Oaks, CA 91423, 818-788-3232; fax 818-788-2831. 1993. Poetry, interviews, criticism, reviews. "Essays on writing 2000 words or less." circ. 4M. 2/yr. Pub'd 2 issues 1998; expects 2 issues 1999, 2 issues 2000. sub. price: $16; per copy: $8; sample: $8. Back issues: $5. Discounts: negotiable. 176pp; 5x8½; lp. Reporting time: 2-4 months. Simultaneous submissions accepted: yes. Publishes 10% of manuscripts submitted. Payment: 2 copies. Copyrighted, reverts to author. Pub's reviews: 8 in 1998. §Poetry essays on craft, process.

RAVEN - A Journal of Vexillology, Scot M. Guenter, Editor; Jon T. Radel, Managing Editor, 1977 North Olden Ave. Ext., Ste. 225, Trenton, NJ 08618-2193. 1994. Articles, art, photos, news items, non-fiction. "The North American Vexillological Association (NAVA) is a nonprofit organization dedicated to the promotion of vexillology, which is the scientific and scholarly study of flags and their history and symbolism'' circ. 400. 1/yr. Pub'd 1 issue 1998; expects 1 issue 1999, 1 issue 2000. sub. price: $30; per copy: $15, $25 double issue; sample: $15. Back issues: $15. Discounts: available. 96pp; 6×9; of. Reporting time: 40-60 days. Simultaneous submissions accepted: no. Publishes 50% of manuscripts submitted. Payment: copies. Copyrighted, does not revert to author.

THE RAVEN CHRONICLES, Phoebe Bosche, Managing Editor & Publisher; Kathleen Alcala, Phil RedEagle, 1634 11th Avenue, Seattle, WA 98122, 206-323-4316; ravenchr@speakeasy.org; www.speakeasy.org/ravenchronicles. 1991. Poetry, fiction, articles, art, photos, cartoons, interviews, satire, criticism, reviews, music, letters, parts-of-novels, plays, concrete art, news items, non-fiction. *"The Raven Chronicles* is a magazine of multicultural art, literature and the spoken word, published in an attractive, easily accessible format. Our audience includes elders, ESL and youth, and we encourage use in the classroom. We are distributed in Western states and Canada, distributed free on Puget Sound reservations. Submissions should be under 10 pp., SASE required. Recent contributors include: Diane Glancy, Dina Ben-Lev, Carolyn Lei-lani Lau, Abe Blashko, Charles Johnson, Elizabeth Woody, Sherman Alexie, Rita Chavez, Stacey Levine. We seek distributors in other parts of the country'' circ. 1M. 3/yr. Pub'd 3 issues 1998; expects 3 issues 1999, 3 issues 2000. sub. price: $15, $20 foreign; per copy: $3-$5; sample: $4. Back issues: $10 per volume (3 issues) or 1/2 cover price. Discounts: 50% to distributors; 50% to educators ordering 15 or more. 48-72pp; 8½×11; web press. Reporting time: 3-6 months. Simultaneous submissions accepted: yes. Publishes 7-9% of manuscripts submitted. Payment: $5-$45. Copyrighted, reverts to author. Pub's reviews: 10-12 in 1998. §High quality literature by or about artists/writers of color and all writers for adult or youth. Ads: $300/$100/$25 business card. CLMP.

Raven Rocks Press, Warren Stetzel, John Morgan, 53650 Belmont Ridge Road, Beallsville, OH 43716, 614-926-1705. 1972. Non-fiction. "Raven Rocks Press has published Warren Stetzel's book, *School for the Young* (explores some of our assumptions about our human nature and the nature of our world), and reprinted *Hollingsworth's Vision,* a first-person account by a 19th-century Quaker. We expect to publish materials which touch on a variety of fields: education, economics and social organization, environmental issues, solar and underground construction. Those involved in Raven Rocks Press are members of Raven Rocks, Inc., an organization which is engaged in these and other fields, and much of what we publish will be out of our own experience. We will hope, too, to publish relevant material from elsewhere. No exact price is set for *School for the Young.* Rather, contributions are accepted from those able to make them. With this policy, it has been possible for some to secure the book at little or no cost. Others have been able to contribute enough to make up the difference.'' avg. press run 1.5M. Expects 1 title 1999, 1 title 2000. 3 titles listed in the *Small Press Record of Books in Print* (28th Edition, 1999-00). avg. price, cloth: $25; paper: $15. Discounts: bookstores & jobbers 1 copy 20%, 2-3 copies 30%, 4+ 40%. 269pp; 5½×8½, 6×9; †of. Copyrights for author.

●**Ravenhawk Books,** Hans Jr. Shepherd, Carl Lasky, 7739 E. Broadway Boulevard #95, Tucson, AZ 85710, 520-886-9885; fax 520-886-9885; e-mail 76673.3165@compuserve.com. 1999. Fiction, non-fiction. "No unsolicited materials are accepted at this time. (Our production schedule is full through 2002). Editorial offices: 1820 South Sunburst Drive, Tucson, AZ 85748'' avg. press run 2.5M. Expects 5 titles 1999, 6 titles 2000. 1 title listed in the *Small Press Record of Books in Print* (28th Edition, 1999-00). avg. price, cloth: $28.95. Discounts: 55% off cover retail. 65% off if title is ordered 60 days prior to publication date. 320pp; 5½×8½. Simultaneous submissions accepted: no. Publishes .005% of manuscripts submitted. Payment: graduated royalty schedule 25%-35%-45% calculated from gross profits. Copyrights for author. SSA, NWA, NACAA.

Raw Dog Press, R. Gerry Fabian, 151 S. West Street, Doylestown, PA 18901, 215-345-6838. 1977. Poetry, photos, long-poems, collages. "We are now doing only our Post Poem Series. We publish in the summer. Submit any time. The type of poetry that we are looking for is short (2-10) lines. We want 'people-oriented' work. We'll send samples for $1.00. You MUST enclose a short note and a SASE. Neatness and professionalism really count with us. See our web page http://www.freeyellow.co/members/rawdog/'' avg. press run 100. Pub'd 1 title 1998; expects 2 titles 1999, 2 titles 2000. 24 titles listed in the *Small Press Record of Books in Print* (28th Edition, 1999-00). avg. price, paper: $8; other: $8. Discounts: will negotiate and haggle with anyone; will exchange. 12-15pp; 4×6; †laser printer. Reporting time: 1 month. Simultaneous submissions accepted: no. Publishes 10% of manuscripts submitted. Payment: varies with the material but we will work something out (copies +). Copyright is agreed upon.

RAW NERVZ HAIKU, Proof Press, Dorothy Howard, 67 Court Street, Aylmer, QC J9H 4M1, Canada, E-mail: dhoward@aix1.uottawa.ca. 1994. Poetry, fiction, articles, art, reviews, letters, collages. "Haiku, senryu, tanfa, haibun, haiga.'' circ. 250. 4/yr. Pub'd 4 issues 1998; expects 4 issues 1999, 4 issues 2000. sub. price: $20; per copy: $6; sample: $6. Back issues: $5 to contributors. 52pp; 5½×8½; photocopy. Reporting time: 4-6 weeks. Simultaneous submissions accepted: yes. Payment: none. Copyrighted, reverts to author. Pub's reviews: 3 in 1998. §Haiku, etc.

THE RAW SEED REVIEW, Sam Taylor, 780 Merion Greene, Charlottesville, VA 22901. 1998. Poetry, fiction, art, photos, cartoons, interviews, reviews, parts-of-novels, non-fiction. "Mostly poetry. We want work that springs from deep within—the unique urgency of the inner soul amid the modern wilderness. Work that explores and creates reality, foraging in new directions and opening up into the unknown." circ. 500. 2/yr. Expects 1 issue 1999, 2 issues 2000. sub. price: $14; per copy: $7.50; sample: $7. Back issues: $5.50. 80pp; 6x9; of. Reporting time: 1-16 weeks. We accept simultaneous submissions with notification up front and immediately upon acceptance elsewhere. Publishes 5% of manuscripts submitted. Payment: 1-2 copies. Copyrighted, reverts to author. Ads: $100/$60/$35 1/4 page.

●**Rayve Productions Inc.**, Norm Ray, Barbara Ray, PO Box 726, Windsor, CA 95492, 707-838-6200, Fax; 707-838-2220, E-mail; rayvepro@aol.com. 18 titles listed in the *Small Press Record of Books in Print* (28th Edition, 1999-00).

RAZOR WIRE, Shaun T. Griffin, PO Box 8876, University Station, Reno, NV 89507, 702-847-9311; fax 702-847-9335; e-mail shaungrif@aol.com. 1989. Poetry, fiction, satire, reviews, letters, parts-of-novels, long-poems, plays, non-fiction. "Will consider poems and short prose pieces (complete or excerpts) that are well thought out and well written, on any subject. Would like to see more reviews." 1/yr. Pub'd 1 issue 1998; expects 1 issue 1999, 1 issue 2000. sub. price: $6; per copy: $6; sample: inquire. Back issues: inquire. 50pp; 5x8; of. Reporting time: 4-8 weeks. Simultaneous submissions accepted: yes. Percentage of manuscripts published varies, depending on quantity and quality of work submitted. Payment: copies. Not copyrighted. Pub's reviews: 1 in 1998. §Poetry and fiction. Ads: none.

READ, AMERICA!, The Place In The Woods, Roger A. Hammer, Editor & Publisher, 3900 Glenwood Avenue, Golden Valley, MN 55422, 612-374-2120. 1982. Reviews. "A quarterly newsletter to Libraries, Reading Is Fundamental, Head Start, and migrant education programs. ISSN-0891-4214. Looking for professional children's librarians to do regular reviews. Three feature sections: powtry for children and adults, short stories for children, trends and case histories in education, literacy" circ. 10M. 4/yr. Pub'd 4 issues 1998; expects 4 issues 1999, 4 issues 2000. sub. price: $25; per copy: $7.50; sample: $7.50. Back issues: $5. Discounts: 15% to qualified book suppliers & librarians. 16pp; 8½x11; †of. Reporting time: 1 week to 6 months. Simultaneous submissions accepted: no. Publishes 20% of manuscripts submitted. Payment: 50 per review or article. Copyrighted, does not revert to author. Pub's reviews: 8 in 1998. §Children's books, P/K - 12, stories on trends, ideas, problem solving. Ads: use flier inserts—rates on request.

THE READER'S REVIEW, Peter Phillps, Review Editor; Paul Nagy, Publisher, 2966 Diamond Street, Suite 290, San Francisco, CA 94131, 415-585-2639. 1991. Articles, criticism, reviews, news items, non-fiction. "A trade newsletter for independent booksellers and libraries in the USA and Canada, we publish review essays and brief marketing analyses of new titles from trade, university and small presses. We have specialty focus on Native and African American studies, religion, philosophy and cultural and historical studies. We encourage readers to submit reviews of books and titles we publish letters to editor and promote small press titles with distinction." circ. 6.2M. 35/yr. Expects 35 issues 1999, 35 issues 2000. sub. price: $200; per copy: $7.50; sample: $7.50. Back issues: none. Discounts: none. 8-12pp; 8½x11; †of. Reporting time: 2-4 months. Publishes 50% of manuscripts submitted. Payment: 5¢ per word, max. 500 words per title; negotiable w/editor. Copyrighted, rights revert to author after 1 year. Pub's reviews: 2,471 in 1998. §Native American, African American, religion, philosophy, metaphysical, New Age, cultural and historical studies.

READERS SPEAK OUT!, Ron Richardson, 4003 - 50th Avenue SW, Seattle, WA 98116. 1997. Non-fiction. "Runs responses (50-150 words) to pertinent and controversial questions. Query first. Many contributors are teen homeschoolers. Publishing procedures internships (by mail) offered to young adults. ISSN 1523-7451." circ. 150. 4/yr. Pub'd 2 issues 1998; expects 4 issues 1999, 4 issues 2000. sub. price: free; per copy: free; sample: free. Back issues: free. 2pp; 8½x11; of/desktop. Reporting time: 1 month. Publishes 65% of manuscripts submitted. Payment: 2 copies. Copyrighted, reverts to author. Ads: free classifieds for contributors who have their own zines.

REAL DEAL MAGAZINE, R.D. Bone, PO Box 19129, Los Angeles, CA 90019, E-mail rdbone@earthlink.net. 1990. Cartoons, reviews. circ. 6M. 4/yr. Pub'd 4 issues 1998; expects 4 issues 1999, 4 issues 2000. Back issues: $2 each. 32pp; 8x11; web. Reporting time: 3 weeks. Simultaneous submissions accepted: yes. Publishes 2% of manuscripts submitted. Payment: $15. Copyrighted, reverts to author. Pub's reviews: Ads: $150/$75.

Real Life Storybooks, Heather Elyse, Judith Kahn, 8370 Kentland Avenue, West Hills, CA 91304-3324, 818-887-6431; 1-800-999-5668; e-Mail illanarls@aol, Fax; 818-887-4541. 1992. Poetry, fiction, art, interviews. "Real Life Storybooks publishes storybooks for all children ages 4-12 years. These storybooks focus upon "special needs". The education of our youth is the key to change. Real Life Storybooks was created to foster that change. Each storybook focuses upon a different disability, illness or problem faced by a child and his or her family. Each contains an epilogue written by an expert in that field. These books are designed to be used as learning tools by teachers, parents, therapists and physicians, and read by children. Each is designed to help break down that barrier which pervades our society and isolates the different as lepers. Contributors include Dr. Edward Ritvo, Dr. Stanley Schwartz, Dr. Alan Rosenthal, Dr. Sheldon Lavin, Dr. B.J. Freeman, Dr. Rebecca Cox, Dr. Sue Schmidt-Lackner, Dr. Alan Phillips, Arthur Schalow (Nobel Laureate), etc." avg. press run 2M-5M. Expects 4 titles 1999, 4-6 titles 2000. 4 titles listed in the *Small Press Record of Books in Print* (28th Edition, 1999-00). avg. price, cloth: $16.95; paper: $9.95. Discounts: libraries 25%, booksellers 40%, organazations 25%. 48pp; 7¾×10¼; of. Reporting time: 2-3 weeks, SASE required for response. Publishes 1% of manuscripts submitted. Payment: each individually arranged. Does not copyright for author. PMA.

REAL PEOPLE, Alex Polner, 450 Fashion Avenue, Suite 1701, New York, NY 10123-1799, 212-244-2351. 1988. Articles, photos, interviews, non-fiction. "1000-1500 words, articles about *celebrities and very interesting people*; articles about issues (e.g., entertainment world, TV, people and their "interesting" occupations)." circ. 100M. 6/yr. Pub'd 6 issues 1998; expects 6 issues 1999, 6 issues 2000. sub. price: $24; per copy: $4; sample: $4. Back issues: $3. Discounts: negotiable. 64pp; 5⅛×7⅜; of. Reporting time: 4 weeks. Simultaneous submissions accepted: no. Publishes 10% of manuscripts submitted. Payment: $50-$300. Copyrighted, we buy all rights. Pub's reviews: 15 in 1998. §Celebrities/biographies, autobiographies, memoirs, showbusiness, TV, fiction. Ads: color $2400, b&w $2000/color $1440, b&w $1200/75¢ per word (25 word minimum).

Reality Street Editions, Ken Edwards, Wendy Mulford, 4 Howard Court, Peckham Rye, London SE15 3PH, United Kingdom, 0171-639-7297. 1993. Poetry, long-poems. "Contemporary poetry from Britain, Europe and America. Books can be ordered from Small Press Distribution." avg. press run 300-400. Pub'd 1 title 1998; expects 4 titles 1999, 4 titles 2000. 12 titles listed in the *Small Press Record of Books in Print* (28th Edition, 1999-00). avg. price, paper: $10-$15. Discounts: negotiable. 48-96pp; of. Payment: copies and/or flat fee. Copyright remains with author.

●**Really Great Books,** Mari Florence, Amy Inouye, Nina Wiener, PO Box 292000, Los Angeles, CA 90029, 323-660-0620; fax 323-660-2571; website www.reallygreatbooks.com. 1998. Fiction, photos, non-fiction. "*Really Great Books* is publishing an ecclectic list of books inspired by Los Angeles. Most titles have a popular culture leaning. RGB is also the publisher of *The Glovebox Guides*, your roadmap to the city's best places to ear, drink, unwind, and play." avg. press run 2M. Expects 6 titles 1999, 10 titles 2000. 6 titles listed in the *Small Press Record of Books in Print* (28th Edition, 1999-00). avg. price, cloth: $24.95; paper: $17.95. 200pp; 6×9; of. Reporting time: 6 weeks. Simultaneous submissions accepted: yes. Publishes 5% of manuscripts submitted. Payment: no advance, competetive royalities paid quarterly. Copyrights for author. L.A. People in Publishing.

REALM OF DARKNESS, Full Moon Publications, Sharida Rizzuto, Ann Hoyt, Harold Tollison, 577 Central Avenue, Box 4, Jefferson, LA 70121-1400, e-mail: fullmoon@eduoramail.com or haunted@rocket-mail.com; Websites www.members.xoom.com/blackie, www.spaceports.com/~haunted/, www.eclecticity.com/ zines/, www2.cybercities.com/z/zines/, www.dreamers.dynip.com/zines/. 1983. Poetry, fiction, articles, art, photos, cartoons, interviews, satire, criticism, reviews, letters, long-poems, collages, news items, non-fiction. circ. 300. 2/yr. Pub'd 2 issues 1998; expects 2 issues 1999, 2 issues 2000. sub. price: $13.80; per copy: $6.90; sample: $6.90. Back issues: $6.90. Discounts: trade with like publishers. 80pp; 8½×11; of. Reporting time: 2-6 weeks. Simultaneous submissions accepted: yes. Publishes 30-35% of manuscripts submitted. Payment: free copy only. Copyrighted, reverts to.author. Ads: free.

REALM OF THE VAMPIRE, Full Moon Publications, Sharida Rizzuto, Harold Tollison, Ann Hoyt, 577 Central Avenue, Box 4, Jefferson, LA 70121-1400, e-mail fullmoon@eudoramail.com, haunted@rocket-mail.com, gothic@imaginemail.com; Websites www.eclecticity.com/zines/, www.freez.com/vampires, www.members.xoom.com/blackie, www.spaceports.com/~haunted/, www2.cybercities.com/z/zines/. 1983. Poetry, fiction, articles, art, photos, cartoons, interviews, satire, criticism, reviews, letters, long-poems, collages, news items, non-fiction. "*Realm of the Vampire* is both a zine and a newsletter. Published 2 times a year and the newsletter is published 3 times" circ. 500. 2+3. Pub'd 2 issues 1998; expects 2 issues 1999, 2 issues 2000. sub. price: $15.80, newsletter - $9; per copy: $7.90, newsletter - $3; sample: $7.90 - $3. Back issues: $7.90 - $3. Discounts: trade with other like publications. 40pp for newsletter, 100pp for journal; 8×11; †of, excellent quality. Reporting time: 2-6 weeks. Simultaneous submissions accepted: yes. Publishes 35% of manuscripts submitted. Payment: free copies, fees paid for articles, reviews, artwork negotiable. Copyrighted, reverts to author. Pub's reviews: 100 in 1998. §anything about vampires, gothic subculture, zines, books, music, films, internet websites. Ads: free. NWC, HWA, Small Press Genre Association, MWA, Western Writers of America (WWA), Arizona Authors Association (AAA).

Recon Publications, Chris Robinson, Editor; Lewis Bellis, Business Manager, PO Box 14602, Philadelphia, PA 19134. 1973. avg. press run 2M. 5 titles listed in the *Small Press Record of Books in Print* (28th Edition, 1999-00). of.

RECONSTRUCTIONIST, Reconstructionist Press, Dr. Herb Levine, Federation of Reconstructionist

Congregations and Havurot, Church Road & Greenwood Avenue, Wyncote, PA 19095, 215-887-1988. 1935. Poetry, fiction, articles, art, photos, reviews, letters, non-fiction. circ. 10M. 2/yr. Pub'd 6 issues 1998; expects 4 issues 1999, 4 issues 2000. sub. price: $35; per copy: $9. Discounts: for members of FRCH a dicount of 20%. 64pp; 8½x11; lp. Reporting time: 1-3 months. Copyrighted, reverts to author. Pub's reviews: 20 in 1998. §Judaica, public policy, religious studies. Ads: no advertising. AJBP.

Reconstructionist Press (see also RECONSTRUCTIONIST), Church Road & Greenwood Avenue, Wyncote, PA 19095, 215-887-1988. 3 titles listed in the *Small Press Record of Books in Print* (28th Edition, 1999-00).

Red Alder Books, David Steinberg, Box 2992, Santa Cruz, CA 95063, 831-426-7082, Fax 831-425-8825, E-mail eronat@aol.com. 1974. Poetry, fiction, art, photos, letters, long-poems, non-fiction. "Our present emphasis is on books of quality, imaginative erotic writing and photography." avg. press run 3M. Expects 1 title 1999, 1 title 2000. 5 titles listed in the *Small Press Record of Books in Print* (28th Edition, 1999-00). avg. price, cloth: $45; paper: $13. Discounts: 2-4 books 20%, 5+ 40%. 150pp; 6x9, 8½x11; of. Reporting time: 2-6 weeks. Simultaneous submissions accepted: yes. Publishes a very small % of manuscripts submitted. Payment: varies. Copyrights for author.

RED AND BLACK, Jack Grancharoff, PO Box 12, Quaama, NSW 2550, Australia. 1964. Reviews, non-fiction. circ. 200. 1-2/yr. Pub'd 1 issue 1998; expects 2 issues 1999, 2 issues 2000. sub. price: £6; per copy: £3; sample: free. Back issues: not a set price; depends on buyer's circumstances. 35-40pp; standard A4; †of. Reporting time: variable. Simultaneous submissions accepted: yes. Publishes 75% of manuscripts submitted. Payment: none. Not copyrighted. Pub's reviews: 1 in 1998. §Anarchism, libertarianism, feminism, any other anti-statist positions. none.

Red Apple Publishing, Peggy J. Meyer, 15010 113th Street KPN, Gig Harbor, WA 98329, 206-884-1450; 800-245-6595; FAX 206-884-1451; E-mail redaple@aol.com. 1990. Poetry, non-fiction. avg. press run 500-1M. Pub'd 1 title 1998; expects 3 titles 1999, 3 titles 2000. 23 titles listed in the *Small Press Record of Books in Print* (28th Edition, 1999-00). avg. price, paper: $13. Discounts: 40% bookstores, 55% wholesalers. 100-350pp; 6x9, 5½x8½; lp. Reporting time: 1 month. Simultaneous submissions accepted: yes. Publishes 25% of manuscripts submitted. Payment: authors pay me to assist them in self-publishing. Copyrights for author. Pacific Northwest Writers' Conference (PNWC), Book Publishers Northwest, PNBA, PMA, Pen Women.

RED BRICK REVIEW, Sean Thomas Dougherty, PO Box 6527, Syracuse, NY 13217. 1991. Poetry. "Gary Soto, John Hodgen, Cornelius Eady, Sherman Alexie, Philip Levine, Tess Gallagher, Patricia Smith, Thylias Moss, Donald Hall. Biases change with each issue" circ. 1M. 1/yr. Pub'd 1 issue 1998; expects 1 issue 1999, 1 issue 2000. sub. price: $5; per copy: $5; sample: $3. Back issues: $3. Discounts: 60/40. 64pp; 6x9. Reporting time: 4 months max. Payment: copies. Copyrighted, reverts to author. Pub's reviews. §Poetry. Ads: $150.

Red Candle Press (see also CANDELABRUM POETRY MAGAZINE), M.L. Mr. McCarthy, 9 Milner Road, Wisbech, PE13 2LR, England, tel: 01945 581067. 1970. Poetry. "Poetry. The Red Candle Press provides a (free) service to poets and does not aim to make a profit. Contributors to *Candelabrum Poetry Magazine* receive one free copy but no cash payment at present." avg. press run 1M for magazine. Expects 1 title 1999. 7 titles listed in the *Small Press Record of Books in Print* (28th Edition, 1999-00). Discounts: 1/3 to booksellers. 5½x8; of, lp. Reporting time: 1-3 months. Simultaneous submissions accepted: no. Payment: free copy to magazine contributors. Copyrights for author.

Red Cedar Press (see also RED CEDAR REVIEW), Carrie J. Preston, Editor, 325 Morrill Hall, Michigan State University, E. Lansing, MI 48824. 1963. avg. press run 500. Pub'd 2 titles 1998; expects 2 titles 1999, 2 titles 2000. 3 titles listed in the *Small Press Record of Books in Print* (28th Edition, 1999-00). avg. price, paper: $5. 100pp. Reporting time: 3 months. Simultaneous submissions accepted: no. Payment: in copies.

RED CEDAR REVIEW, Red Cedar Press, Carrie Preston, Poetry Editor, 17C Morrill Hall, English Dept., Michigan State Univ., E. Lansing, MI 48824, 517-355-9656. 1963. Poetry, fiction, art, photos, interviews, criticism, reviews, parts-of-novels, long-poems. "We have no particular editorial bias—clarity is appreciated, sentimentality isn't. Some recent contributors: William Stafford, Diane Wakoski, Hugh Fox, Judith McCombs, Barbara Drake, Charles Edward Eaton, Dan Gerber, Herbert Scott, Lyn Lifshin. We're also open to new writers; we generally try to comment on promising work that we don't accept. In some cases, we ask for resubmissions-no guarantees, of course. Our two annual issues come out around March/April and Oct/Nov, but submissions are considered year-round. Reporting time longer in summer. No simultaneous submissions, please." circ. 300. 2/yr. Pub'd 2 issues 1998; expects 2 issues 1999, 2 issues 2000. sub. price: $10; per copy: $5; sample: $3. Back issues: $3. Discounts: library $4/$8. 80pp; 8½x5½; of. Reporting time: 8-12 weeks. Simultaneous submissions accepted: no. Payment: 2 copies. Copyrighted, reverts to author. Pub's reviews: 0 in 1998. §Poetry, fiction. Ads: $100/$50/$25. CLMP.

Red Crane Books, Inc., 2008 Rosina Street #B, Santa Fe, NM 87505-3271, 505-988-7070; fax 505-989-7476;

800-922-3392; E-mail publish@redcrane.com; www.redcrane.com. 1989. "Books that present the complex cultures of the Americans; general trade books." avg. press run 8M. Pub'd 5 titles 1998; expects 5 titles 1999. 47 titles listed in the *Small Press Record of Books in Print* (28th Edition, 1999-00). avg. price, cloth: $24.50; paper: $13.50. Discounts: libraries 20%, bookstores 1-4 20%, 5-9 40%, 10-49 42%, 50-100 44%, 100+ 46%. 210pp; size varies; of. Reporting time: 3 months. We accept simultaneous submissions with note. Publishes 1% of manuscripts submitted. Payment: negotiable. Copyrights for author. Rocky Mountain Book Publishers Association (RMBPA), NMBA.

Red Dragon Press, 433 Old Town Court, Alexandria, VA 22314, 703-683-5877. 1993. Poetry, fiction. "Red Dragon Press is undertaking to promote authors of innovative, progressive, and experimental works, who aspire to evoke the emotions of the reader by stressing the symbolic value of language, and in the creation of meaningful new ideas, forms, and methods. We are proponents of works that represent the nature of man as androgynous, as in the fusing of male and female symbolism, and we support works that deal with psychological and parapsychological topics." avg. press run 500. Pub'd 3 titles 1998; expects 5 titles 1999, 5 titles 2000. 13 titles listed in the *Small Press Record of Books in Print* (28th Edition, 1999-00). avg. price, paper: $10.95. Discounts: retail 40%. 64pp; 5⅜x8½; of. Reporting time: 6 months or less. Simultaneous submissions accepted: yes. Publishes 8% of manuscripts submitted. Payment: none. Does not copyright for author.

Red Dust, Joanna Gunderson, PO Box 630, Gracie Station, New York, NY 10028, 212-348-4388. 1963. Poetry, fiction. "Short works, once accepted, must be sent on disc. In general, authors get 30 copies. There is no advance." avg. press run 500 short works. Pub'd 6 titles 1998; expects 2 titles 1999, 4 titles 2000. 65 titles listed in the *Small Press Record of Books in Print* (28th Edition, 1999-00). avg. price, cloth: $12.95; paper: $6.95 for the short works. Discounts: libraries 20%; wholesalers & booksellers 1 copy-30%, 2 or more-40%, paperback 1-4 copies-20%, 5 or more-40%. 140pp, short works 16-32pp; 8½x5½; of. Reporting time: 2 months. Simultaneous submissions accepted: yes. Payment: $300 advance against royalty, for short works we pay nothing and claim no rights. Copyrights for author.

Red Eye Press, James Goodwin, Richard Kallan, 845 W. Avenue 37, Los Angeles, CA 90065-3201, 323-225-3805. 1988. Art, photos, non-fiction. avg. press run 10M-18M. Pub'd 2 titles 1998; expects 2 titles 1999, 2 titles 2000. 3 titles listed in the *Small Press Record of Books in Print* (28th Edition, 1999-00). avg. price, paper: $19.95-$29.95; other: wire-spiral $23.95. Discounts: 37%-65%. 360pp; 5½x8⅜, 8x11; of. Reporting time: 8 weeks. Simultaneous submissions accepted: yes. Publishes 10% of manuscripts submitted. Payment: 10%. Copyrights for author. PMA, NCBPA, ABA.

Red Hen Press, Mark Cull, PO Box 902582, Palmdale, CA 93590, Fax 818-831-6659; E-mail redhen@vpg.net. 1995. Poetry, fiction, non-fiction. avg. press run 1M. Pub'd 3 titles 1998; expects 3 titles 1999, 6 titles 2000. 15 titles listed in the *Small Press Record of Books in Print* (28th Edition, 1999-00). avg. price, paper: $12.95. Discounts: 40% bookstores; 20% classroom. 100pp; 5½x8½. Reporting time: 2 months. Simultaneous submissions accepted: yes. Publishes 5% of manuscripts submitted. Payment: 10%. Copyrights for author. Valentine Publishing Group, CLMP.

Red Hen Press, Joanne O'Roark, Hope Bryant, PO Box 3774, Santa Barbara, CA 93130, 805-682-1278. 1984. Fiction. "Red Hen is a children's press, producing two-three titles a year. We have published five picture books in the three-seven year old age range, three in full-color, and two in three-color. We are soon to launch RED HEN Pullet Books for beginning and middle grade readers. It is our aim to introduce promising new authors and illustrators, and we are enthusiastic about combining them in good children's books." avg. press run 2M. Pub'd 2 titles 1998; expects 4 titles 1999, 2-3 titles 2000. avg. price, cloth: $14.95; paper: $3.95. Discounts: 40-50%. 32pp picture book, 50pp older; size varies; of. Reporting time: 2 months. Payment: advance against royalties. Does not copyright for author. Publishers Marketing Group.

Red Hill Press, San Francisco + Los Angeles (see also INVISIBLE CITY), John McBride, Paul Vangelisti, PO Box 2853, San Francisco, CA 94126. 1969. Poetry, criticism, concrete art. "Primarily a poetry & translation press, with emphasis on Italian and California poetry. Immediately forthcoming, *Aphorisms* by Edouard Roditi (with a very brief note by Paul Goodman), and *alephs again* by Paul Vangelisti" avg. press run 1M. Expects 3 titles 1999. 62 titles listed in the *Small Press Record of Books in Print* (28th Edition, 1999-00). avg. price, cloth: $15; paper: $5. Discounts: consult Small Press Distribution (Berkeley). 48-80pp; size varies moving to 9x5½; of. Reporting time: extended. Payment: copies. Copyrights for author. CLMP.

RED HOT HOME INCOME REPORTER, Ed Durham, 15 Brunswick Lane, Willingboro, NJ 08046, 609-835-2347. 1986. News items, non-fiction. "Articles are 1000 words or less, about issues relevant to small home-based businesses." circ. 1.2M. 6/yr. Pub'd 6 issues 1998; expects 6 issues 1999, 6 issues 2000. sub. price: $39; sample: $3. Back issues: not sold, given to new subscribers. Discounts: 50% jobbers, agents. 12pp; 8½x11; of. Reporting time: 3 months. Small payment for features. Copyrighted, reverts to author. Pub's reviews: 30 in 1998. §Business, motivational, money-making. Ads: ads no longer accepted. Small Business

Press.

●RED LAMP, Brad Evans, Editor, 5 Kahana Court, Mountain Creek, Queensland 4557, Australia, evans-baj@hotmail.com. "Additional address: Brad Evans (Ed.), 61 Glenmere Close, Cherry Hinton, Cambs. CB1 8EF U.K. *Red Lamp* publishes realist, socialist, and humanitarian poetry. Subscriptions should be made out in cheque to Brad Evans (Editor). The deadlines for forthcoming issues are June 30 and Nov. 30." 2/yr. Pub'd 2 issues 1998; expects 2 issues 1999, 2 issues 2000. price per copy: $5 Aust.

Red Letter Press, Helen Gilbert, Managing Editor, 409 Maynard Avenue South #201, Seattle, WA 98104, 206-682-0990; Fax 206-682-8120; Email redletterpress@juno.com. 1990. Non-fiction. avg. press run 3M. Pub'd 1 title 1998; expects 1 title 1999, 1-2 titles 2000. 6 titles listed in the *Small Press Record of Books in Print* (28th Edition, 1999-00). avg. price, paper: $10. Discounts: bookstores 1-5 20%, 6+ 40%; wholesalers/distributors negotiable; classes 20%. 200pp; 5½x8½, 6x9; of. Northwest Association of Book Publishers.

Red Moon Press (see also FROGPOND: Quarterly Haiku Journal), Jim Kacian, Editor, PO Box 2461, Winchester, VA 22604-1661, 540-722-2156; redmoon@shentel.net. 15 titles listed in the *Small Press Record of Books in Print* (28th Edition, 1999-00).

RED OWL, Edward O. Knowlton, 35 Hampshire Road, Portsmouth, NH 03801-4815, 603-431-2691; redowlmag@aol.com. 1995. "No stories currently desired, yet more artwork is always welcome. (Also, now using black and white photography to a minor extent.) One point to bear in mind would be to keep subs. to *Red Owl* pragmatic. Poetry, short stories, and art don't have to be depressing in order to ring a bell here. Poems that avoid rambling too far and off course stand a better chance. Your best advice might be to look up! Deadlines: none, yet in the fall I need spring material—and vice versa. Interested in new and unpublished poets. Submission quantity: 2-4. Special interests: Nothing overly rough—more fun stuff. Find a harmony between nature and industry. International subs. appreciated." circ. 200. 2/yr. Expects 2 issues 1999, 2 issues 2000. sub. price: $20; per copy: $10; sample: $10. 70pp; 8½x11; above average paper weight and copying, spiral bound. Reporting time: 2 weeks - 2 months. Simultaneous submissions accepted: yes. Payment: sample copy. Not copyrighted. Ads: none.

RED POWER, Daryl A. Miller, Box 277, Battle Creek, IA 51006, 712-365-4873. 1986. Articles, letters, news items. "Magazine for people interested in International Harvester and its products." circ. 9M. 6/yr. Pub'd 6 issues 1998; expects 6 issues 1999, 6 issues 2000. sub. price: $16; per copy: $3.50; sample: $2.50. Back issues: $3. Discounts: none. 52pp; 8½x11; of. Not copyrighted. Pub's reviews: 1 in 1998. §Farm equipment, trucks. Ads: $140/$80/$50 1/4 page.

RED ROCK REVIEW, Richard Logsdon, Todd Moffet, English Dept J2A/Com. College S. NV, 3200 E. Cheyenne Avenue, N. Las Vegas, NV 89030, www.ccsn.nevada.edu/departments/english/redrock.htm. 1996. Poetry, fiction, articles, reviews, non-fiction. "Each issue is 100-125 pages in length. Short stories no more than 10,000 words. Poems should be one page max. Essays to be no more than 5,000. No biases. Recent contributors: Michael Ventura, Steve Liu, Steve Orlin, Ron Carlson, Alberto Rios, L.J. Davis." 2/yr. Pub'd 2 issues 1998; expects 2 issues 1999, 2 issues 2000. sub. price: $9.50; per copy: $5.50. Back issues: $2. Discounts: $2.50 per copy to distributor, bookstores, etc. 120pp; 6½x9½; †lp. Reporting time: 2 months. Simultaneous submissions accepted: yes. Publishes 10%-15% of manuscripts submitted. Payment: 2 copies of current issue. Copyrighted, reverts to author. Pub's reviews. §New small literary magazines, collections of poetry, short stories, etc. CLMP, Index of American Periodical Verse, AWP, New England Writers.

Redbird Press, Inc., PO Box 11441, Memphis, TN 38111, 901-323-2233. 1981. Art, photos, reviews, music, non-fiction. avg. press run 5M. Expects 3 titles 1999, 3 titles 2000. 3 titles listed in the *Small Press Record of Books in Print* (28th Edition, 1999-00). avg. price, cloth: $15.95; other: $21.95 passport kit, book and 30 minute audio-CD audio. Discounts: 40% returnable, 45% non-returnable. 36pp; of.

RedBrick Press, Jack Erickson, PO Box 1895, Sonoma, CA 95476-1895, 707-996-2774. 1987. avg. press run 5M. Pub'd 1 title 1998; expects 1 title 1999, 2 titles 2000. 5 titles listed in the *Small Press Record of Books in Print* (28th Edition, 1999-00). avg. price, cloth: $16.95; paper: $14.95. Discounts: 40% book stores. 160pp; 6x9; of. Reporting time: 4 weeks. Washington Independent Writers (WIW), Publishers Marketing Association.

REDEMPTION, Mistress Xandria, PO Box 54063, Vancouver, BC V7Y 1B0, Canada, 604-264-9109; Fax 604-264-8692; Redemption@pacificgroup.net. 1993. Poetry, fiction, articles, art, interviews, reviews, letters, news items, non-fiction. circ. 500+. 4/yr. Pub'd 4 issues 1998; expects 5 issues 1999, 5 issues 2000. sub. price: $15; per copy: $5; sample: $5. Back issues: as per cover price. 22pp; 8½x11; †photocopy. Reporting time: 0-90 days. Simultaneous submissions accepted: yes. Publishes 85% of manuscripts submitted. Payment: free issue. Copyrighted, rights revert to author if requested. Pub's reviews: 20 in 1998. §Sexulity, sm/bd/ds, fetish. Ads: contra.

481

REDISCOVER MUSIC CATALOG, Allen Shaw, 705 South Washington, Naperville, IL 60540-0665, 630-305-0770, fax 630-308-0782, e-Mail FolkEra@aol.com. 1990. Photos, interviews, reviews, music, news items. "Generally short" circ. 25M-50M. 6/yr. Pub'd 6 issues 1998; expects 6 issues 1999, 6 issues 2000. sub. price: free; per copy: free; sample: free. 48pp; of. Reporting time: varies. Publishes 1% of manuscripts submitted. Payment: none. Not copyrighted. Pub's reviews. §Popular Music, Especially folk music from the 50's & 60's.

REDOUBT, Ruth Sless, Managing Editor; Ron Miller, Chair, Faculty of Communication, PO Box 1, Belconnen, ACT 2616, Australia, 06-201-5270; fax 06-201-5300. 1988. Poetry, fiction, articles, art, photos, interviews, criticism, reviews, parts-of-novels. "Our aim is to combine new unpublished writers and established writers. One issue per year contains the winners and selected runners-up of the University of Canberra National Short Story Competition." circ. 300. 2/yr. Pub'd 2 issues 1998; expects 2 issues 1999, 2 issues 2000. sub. price: $16; per copy: $8.50; sample: free (depends on issue). Back issues: 3 for $15, $6 each. Discounts: according to rates of bookseller, etc. - anything from 10%-40%. 140pp; 6¾×9¾. Reporting time: average 3 months. Simultaneous submissions accepted: yes. Publishes 10% of manuscripts submitted. Payment: yes, varies according to funds. Copyrighted, reverts to author. Pub's reviews: 15 in 1998. §General literature, Australian culture. Ads: $50/$25.

Redrosebush Press (see also PENNY-A-LINER; PORTALS), Ella M. Dillon, PO Box 2163, Wenatchee, WA 98807-2163, 509-662-7858. 1991. Poetry, fiction, articles, art, photos, cartoons, interviews, satire, criticism, reviews, letters, non-fiction. avg. press run 500-3.1M. Pub'd 3 titles 1998; expects 3 titles 1999, 1-3 titles 2000. 3 titles listed in the *Small Press Record of Books in Print* (28th Edition, 1999-00). avg. price, paper: $6-$16. 60-260pp; 6×9; of. Reporting time: asap. Simultaneous submissions accepted: yes. Publishes 100% of manuscripts submitted. Payment: customer pays printing costs, retains all proceeds. Copyrights for author.

Reference Desk Books, 430 Quintana Road, Suite 146, Morro Bay, CA 93442, 805-772-8806. Photos, non-fiction. "We generally look for material that fills a need or a gap in library reference collections and also will have trade appeal. Contributors and editors tend to be professional librarians, although that is not a requirement" avg. press run 1M. Expects 1 title 1999, 2-3 titles 2000. 3 titles listed in the *Small Press Record of Books in Print* (28th Edition, 1999-00). avg. price, paper: $25. Discounts: 1 copy-no discount; 2-4 copies 20%; 5-99 copies 40%; 100+ copies 50%. 175-200pp; 8½×11; of, lp. Reporting time: varies. Payment: varies. Does not copyright for author.

Reference Service Press, Eric Schlachter, Sandra Hirsh, 5000 Windplay Drive, Suite 4, El Dorado Hills, CA 95762, 916-939-9620; fax 916-939-9626; e-mail findaid@aol.com; website www.rspfunding.com. 1975. Non-fiction. "Reference Service Press is a library-oriented reference publishing company. We specialize in the development of directories of financial aid for special needs groups (e.g. women, minorities, the disabled)." avg. press run 5M. Pub'd 10 titles 1998; expects 8 titles 1999, 12 titles 2000. 16 titles listed in the *Small Press Record of Books in Print* (28th Edition, 1999-00). avg. price, cloth: $42.50. Discounts: up to 20%. 350pp; 8½×11, 6×9; lp. Reporting time: 60 days or less. Payment: 10% and up, depending upon sales; royalties paid annually. Copyrights for author. Publishers Marketing Association.

REFERENCE SERVICES REVIEW, MCB University Press, MCB University Press, 60/63 Toller Lane, Bradford, W. Yorkshire BD8 9BY, England, 01274-777700; Fax 01274-785200 or 785201; www.mcb.co.uk. 1972. Articles, reviews. "Library/reference" circ. 2M. 4/yr. Pub'd 4 issues 1998; expects 4 issues 1999, 4 issues 2000. sub. price: $84; per copy: $22; sample: free. 96pp; 8½×11; of. Reporting time: 4 weeks. Payment: none. Pub's reviews. §All subjects in reference format. Ads: inquire.

REFERRALS, Tim Pacileo, 2219 Long Hill Road, Guilford, CT 06437, 203-457-9020. 1994. Poetry, articles, cartoons, satire, letters, news items, non-fiction. "Material useful for real estate and mortgage banking sales professional relations to sales and technology" circ. 1M. 4/yr. Pub'd 8 issues 1998; expects 4 issues 1999, 4 issues 2000. sub. price: $94; per copy: $35; sample: $10. Back issues: $35. Discounts: based on volume. 12pp; 8½×11; of. Reporting time: 2 weeks. Payment: none. Not copyrighted. Pub's reviews. Ads: $100/$50/$25 4"

REFLECT, William S. Kennedy, 1317 Eagles Trace Path #D, Chesapeake, VA 23320-9461, 757-547-4464. 1979. Poetry, fiction, articles, art, cartoons, reviews, letters. "We have become a vehicle for the presentation of poetry and prose representing the 1980's Spiral Back-to-Beauty Movement, the euphony-in-writing school showing 'an inner-directed concern with sound...' Spiral writing in the terminology of the movement's adherents. Beauty is the criterion here; all forms judged and accepted with that in mind. We use two or three short stories per issue, mostly short-shorts, but of the newly emerging Spiral Fiction genre. See a copy of the magazine for the four rules of Spiral Fiction. Make checks payable to W.S. Kennedy, not Reflect" 4/yr. Pub'd 4 issues 1998; expects 4 issues 1999, 4 issues 2000. 2 titles listed in the *Small Press Record of Books in Print* (28th Edition, 1999-00). sub. price: $8; per copy: $2; sample: $2. Back issues: $2 (if available). 48pp; 5½×8½; †zerox. Reporting time: 2 weeks to 2 months. Simultaneous submissions accepted: no. Payment: 1 contributor's copy. Not copyrighted. Ads: none.

●**REFLECTIONS**, Dean Furbish, PO Box 1197, Roxboro, NC 27573, 336-599-1181; e-mail furbisd@piedmont.cc.nc.us. 1999. Poetry, fiction. "Poetry, short fiction, personal essays up to 3,000 words by established and emerging writers and poets at all levels. Local, regional, international (in English). Submit up to 5 poems or 1 fictional piece. Send two copies of ms, one with name and address, and one without. Send bio information in brief cover letter. Will consider all accessible forms of poetry, including traditional forms. Recent contributors: Gail White, Maureen Sherbondy, Virginia Love Long, Len Krisak, Bruce Bennett, Errol Miller." circ. 500. 1/yr. Expects 1 issue 1999, 1 issue 2000. sub. price: $7; per copy: $7; sample: $6. 128pp; 5½x8½; of. Reporting time: 3 months. Simultaneous submissions accepted: no. Publishes 15% of manuscripts submitted. Payment: copy of publication with their work. Copyrighted, reverts to author.

●**Reflective Books**, Charles M. Long, Chief Editor; Kimberly Kwatkowski, Editor, PO Box 26128, Collegeville, PA 19426-0128, 800-489-7170; fax 610-489-1841; e-mail cdutchlong@aol.com; website www.dokkencorp.com/reflective books. 5 titles listed in the *Small Press Record of Books in Print* (28th Edition, 1999-00).

Regent Press, Mark B. Weiman, 6020-A Adeline, Oakland, CA 94608, 415-548-8459. 1978. Poetry, fiction, non-fiction. avg. press run 1M-1.5M. Pub'd 3 titles 1998; expects 3 titles 1999, 3 titles 2000. 15 titles listed in the *Small Press Record of Books in Print* (28th Edition, 1999-00). avg. price, paper: $9.95. Discounts: 1 copy 20%, 2-3 30%, 4+ 40%. 156pp; 5½x8½; †of. Reporting time: varies. Payment: varies, % of gross. Copyrights for author. BAPN, NCBPMA.

THE REJECTED QUARTERLY, Daniel Weiss, Jeff Ludecke, PO Box 1351, Cobb, CA 95426, E-mail bplankton@juno.com. 1998. Poetry, fiction, articles, art, cartoons, interviews, satire, criticism, reviews, non-fiction. "Fiction to 8,000 words; all fiction must be accompanied by at least 5 rejection slips to show writing doesn't belong anywhere else. Looking for stories that do not reflect everyday consensus reality." 4/yr. Expects 4 issues 1999, 4 issues 2000. sub. price: $20; per copy: $5; sample: $5. Discounts: 20%. 40pp; 8½x11; of. Reporting time: 1-2 months. Simultaneous submissions accepted: no. Publishes 5% of manuscripts submitted. Payment: $5 flat fee. Copyrighted, reverts to author. Pub's reviews. §Speculative fiction. Ads: $20/$10. GWA.

Relief Press, R.L. Smith, PO Box 4033, South Hackensack, NJ 07606, 201-641-3003. 1995. Poetry, non-fiction. "Solicited material only. Books may be ordered directly from publisher or Alamo Square Distributors, San Francisco, CA, and Koen Book Distributors, Inc—Moorestown, NJ" avg. press run 2-3M. Pub'd 1 title 1998; expects 1 title 1999, 1 title 2000. 1 title listed in the *Small Press Record of Books in Print* (28th Edition, 1999-00). avg. price, paper: $9.95. Discounts: 20-55%. 70+pp; 5½x8½; of. Copyrights for author.

RELIX, Toni Brown, Publisher & Managing Editor, PO Box 94, Brooklyn, NY 11229, 718-258-0009. 1974. Articles, art, photos, cartoons, interviews, satire, criticism, reviews, music, letters, news items. "*Relix* covers rock music from the late 1960's to present. With accent on San Francisco groups. Focus of magazine on top groups, i.e. Led Zeppelin, Eric Clapton, and Current Groups such as Phish and Blues Traveler. Highlights on Grateful Dead, etc." circ. 70M. 6/yr. Pub'd 6 issues 1998; expects 6 issues 1999. 1 title listed in the *Small Press Record of Books in Print* (28th Edition, 1999-00). sub. price: $37/8 issues; per copy: $4.50; sample: $5. Back issues: $3 and up. Discounts: stores: 75% of cover, min. order 20 (heads for returns) distributors: 50% + credit terms available. 100pp; 8½x11; of. Reporting time: 8 weeks before publication. Payment: photos min. of $20, up to $500 for cover photo, articles minimum of $2 per col. inch, more for cover stories or major articles. Copyrighted, does not revert to author. Pub's reviews: 204 in 1998. §Rock music. Ads: $3500 color, $2250 b&w/$1800 color, $1200 b&w/write for info.

REMOTE JOCKEY DIGEST, D.H. Coleman, 5823 Cedros Avenue, Van Nuys, CA 91411-3114, Email: dcoleman@ix.netcom.com. 1995. Articles, art, photos, cartoons, interviews, satire, criticism, reviews, letters, news items, non-fiction. "Please query via e-mail or snail mail with ideas before sending material as our needs are very specific. A recent article, for example, was about Dan Perri, title designer of such pictures as *Star Wars*, etc." circ. 300+. 4/yr. Pub'd 2 issues 1998; expects 4 issues 1999, 4 issues 2000. sub. price: $8; per copy: $2; sample: $2. Back issues: please inquire. Discounts: please inquire, we do sell on consignment. 32pp; digest; †desktop & xerox. Reporting time: 1 week. Simultaneous submissions accepted: yes. Publishes 50% of manuscripts submitted. Payment: copy, credit, infamy. Copyrighted, reverts to author. Pub's reviews: 2 in 1998. §Our focus is exclusively on film as culture. Ads: $50/$30/$20 1/4 page.

RENAISSANCE MAGAZINE, Phantom Press Publications, Kim Guarnaccia, 13 Appleton Road, Nantucket, MA 02554, 508-325-0411; renzine@aol.com. 1996. Articles, interviews, reviews, news items. "Average article 2-3000 words. Historical or Renaissance, Medieval re-enactment, faire articles only." circ. 25M. 4/yr. Pub'd 4 issues 1998; expects 4 issues 1999, 4 issues 2000. sub. price: $17; per copy: $4.95; sample: $6. Back issues: $6 for back issues # 4-8, $7 for #9 on. Discounts: none. 96+pp; 8½x10⅞; web. Reporting time: 6 weeks. Simultaneous submissions accepted: no. Publishes 50% of manuscripts submitted. Payment: 5¢ per published word. Copyrighted, does not revert to author. Pub's reviews: 20-25 in 1998. §Renaissance, medieval non-fiction. Ads: $1000/$350 1/4 page.

RENDITIONS, Research Centre for Translation, Chinese University of Hong Kong, Eva Hung, Editor, Chinese University of Hong Kong, Shatin, NT, Hong Kong, 26-097-400, 26-097-407; fax 26-035-149; e-Mail renditions@cuhk.hk. 1973. "A Chinese-English translation magazine. Publishes translations only of Chinese poetry, prose and fiction, classical and contemporary. Also welcomes articles on related topics dealing with Chinese language, literature and arts, or on translation. All submitted translations must be accompanied by Chinese text; require *pinyin* romanization. Special issues include: Contemporary Women Writers; Hong Kong Writing; Middlebrow Fiction; Drama; Classical Prose; Taiwan literature." circ. 900. 2/yr. Pub'd 2 issues 1998; expects 2 issues 1999, 2 issues 2000. sub. price: US $25; per copy: US $17. Back issues: same as current prices. Discounts: trade discount for agents and bookstores. 160pp; 10¼×7½; of. Reporting time: 3 months. Simultaneous submissions accepted: no. Publishes 15% of manuscripts submitted. Payment: honoraria and 2 free copies to contributors. Copyrighted, does not revert to author. Ads: full page $200 US/1/2 page $110 US/inside back cover (full page only) $300 US.

Nancy Renfro Studios, Inc., Nancy Renfro, 3312 Pecan Springs Road, Austin, TX 78723, 1-800-933-5512; 512-927-7090. 1978. Art. "Emphasis on puppet educational media books." avg. press run 1.5M. Pub'd 2 titles 1998; expects 1 title 1999. 10 titles listed in the *Small Press Record of Books in Print* (28th Edition, 1999-00). avg. price, cloth: $16.95; paper: $13.95. Discounts: 1-4 books 20%; 5+ 40%. 150pp; 8½×11; †of. Reporting time: 2 weeks. Payment: 10%. Copyrights for author.

Reniets, Inc., Helen Feinsod, 3200 Port Royale Drive N. #1205, Fort Lauderdale, FL 33308, 800-767-7566; Fax 954-267-0260. 1992. Non-fiction. "We specialize in 'law books' for the layperson." avg. press run 10M. Expects 3 titles 1999, 4 titles 2000. 1 title listed in the *Small Press Record of Books in Print* (28th Edition, 1999-00). avg. price, paper: $15. Discounts: up to 60%. 200pp; 7×9. Reporting time: 4 weeks. Payment: 10%. Copyrights for author.

REPORTS OF THE NATIONAL CENTER FOR SCIENCE EDUCATION, Andrew Petto, Editor, NCSE, Box 9477, Berkeley, CA 94709, 510-526-1674; FAX 510-526-1675. 1980. Articles, criticism, reviews, letters, news items. "Scientists review creationist arguments and also report on developments in evolutionary science." circ. 3.5M. 6/yr. Pub'd 2 issues 1998; expects 6 issues 1999, 6 issues 2000. sub. price: $30, foreign $37, foreign air $39; per copy: $3; sample: same. Back issues: $3 for each back issue. Discounts: complete set $225 (all pubs), $150 *Creation Evolution Journal* only. 44pp; 8½×11; †of. Reporting time: 1 month. Simultaneous submissions accepted: yes. Payment: none; free issues are provided. Copyrighted, reverts to author. Pub's reviews: 5 in 1998. §The creation/evolution controversy. Ads: contact editor.

REPRESENTATIONS, University of California Press, Stephen Greenblatt, Carla Hesse, Jean Day, Managing Editor, University of California Press, 2120 Berkeley Way, Berkeley, CA 94720, 510-643-7154. 1982. Art, photos, criticism, non-fiction. "Editorial address: *Representations*, 320 Wheeler Hall, University of California, Berkeley, CA 94720." circ. 2,050. 4/yr. Pub'd 4 issues 1998; expects 4 issues 1999, 4 issues 2000. sub. price: $38 individual, $102 institution, $25 students (+ $5 foreign postage); per copy: $9.75 indiv.; $28 instit., $9.75 students (+ $6 foreign postage); sample: free. Back issues: same as single copy price. Discounts: foreign subs. agent 10%, one-time orders 10+ 30%, standing orders (bookstores): 1-99 40%, 100+ 50%. 152pp; 7×10; of. Reporting time: 1 month. Copyrighted, does not revert to author. Ads: $325/$225.

RES PUBLICA, Deborah Charles Publications, Bob Breecher, 173 Mather aAvenue, Liverpool L18 6JZ, United Kingdom. 1995. 2/yr. Expects 2 issues 1999, 2 issues 2000. sub. price: £20 individuals, £55 institutions; per copy: £10 individuals, £25 institutions; sample: £10. Discounts: 5% subscription agents. 112pp; royal octavo; Mac DTP. Reporting time: 3 months. Payment: none. Copyrighted, does not revert to author. Pub's reviews: 8 in 1998. §Legal & social philosophy. Ads: exchange.

Research & Discovery Publications, John C. Davis, PO Box 5701, Huntington, WV 25703-0100. 1986. "We are interested only in manuscripts on treasure hunting, buried treasure, lost mines, shipwrecks, salvage, and sunken treasure." avg. press run 2.5M. Pub'd 4 titles 1998; expects 6 titles 1999, 8 titles 2000. 3 titles listed in the *Small Press Record of Books in Print* (28th Edition, 1999-00). avg. price, paper: $5.95. Discounts: send inquiry. 150pp; 8½×11. Reporting time: 30 days. Payment: 20% on accepted works. Copyrights for author.

Research Centre for Translation, Chinese University of Hong Kong (see also RENDITIONS), Eva Hung, General Editor, Research Centre for Translation, Chinese University of Hong Kong, Shatin, NT, Hong Kong, 852-26097700/7407; e-Mail renditions@cuhk.hk. 1986. Poetry, articles, long-poems, plays. "Telex: 50301 CUHK HX. Fax: 852-26035149. Telegram: SINOVERSITY." avg. press run 2M. Pub'd 2 titles 1998; expects 2 titles 1999, 2 titles 2000. 19 titles listed in the *Small Press Record of Books in Print* (28th Edition, 1999-00). avg. price, paper: US$14.95. Discounts: trade discount to distributors and bookstores. 150pp; 5½×8½; of. Reporting time: 3 months. Simultaneous submissions accepted: no. Payment: 5-10% on sales. Publisher owns copyright.

484

RESEARCH IN HIGHER EDUCATION, Human Sciences Press, Inc., John C. Smart, 233 Spring Street, New York, NY 10013, 212-620-8000. 1973. Articles, non-fiction. *"Research in Higher Education* is directed to those concerned with the functioning of post-secondary educational institutions, including two-year and four-year colleges, universities, and graduate and professional schools. It is of primary interest to institutional researchers and planners, faculty, college and university administrators, student personnel specialists and behavioral scientists. All correspondence concerning subscriptions should be addressed to: Human Sciences Press, PO Box 735 Canal St. Sta., New York, NY, 10013-1573. All editorial correspondence should be addressed to the Editor, Charles F. Elton, Dept. of Higher Education, 111 Dickey Hall, University of Kentucky, Lexington, KY 40506" circ. 1.1M. 6/yr. Pub'd 6 issues 1998; expects 6 issues 1999, 6 issues 2000. sub. price: indiv. $65, instit. $225; sample: free. Back issues: Contact J.S. Canner, Inc. 10 Charles St, Needham, MA 02194. Discounts: 5% to subscription agents. 112pp; 6½×9½; of. Reporting time: 3 months. Payment: none. Copyrighted, does not revert to author.

RESEARCH IN YORUBA LANGUAGE & LITERATURE, Technicians of the Sacred, Lawrence O. Adewole, 1317 North San Fernando Boulevard, Suite 310, Burbank, CA 91504. Articles, interviews, reviews, music, non-fiction. circ. 2M. 4/yr. price per copy: $30; sample: $30. 110pp. Pub's reviews. Ads: $300.

Resolution Business Press, Inc., Karen Strudwick, 1035 156th Avenue NE #12, Bellevue, WA 98007-4679, 425-649-1902. 1987. Articles, non-fiction. "Computer/Internet-related books" avg. press run 3M. Pub'd 2 titles 1998; expects 4 titles 1999, 2 titles 2000. 7 titles listed in the *Small Press Record of Books in Print* (28th Edition, 1999-00). avg. price, paper: $24.95; other: $149.95 disk package. Discounts: terms and conditions for booksellers/distributors available on request. 300pp; 6×9, 5½×8½; of. Reporting time: 2-3 months. Payment: varies. Copyrights for author. NW Booksellers, Book Publishers Northwest.

RESONANCE, Judy Wall, 684 County Road 535, Sumterville, FL 33585, (352) 793-8748. 1985. Articles, photos, cartoons, interviews, criticism, reviews, letters, news items, non-fiction. "The purpose of *Resonance* is to review the scientific literature in the field of bioelectromagnetics; that is, the interaction between electric and/or magnetic fields and living organisms. Camera-ready copy—1-12 pages, single spaced, *include references*. Topics may focus on medical applications; zoological adaptations; natural and artificial radiation; biological, physical and chemical structures involved; weapons applications; mind control experiments and technology. Original research or reviews of books or articles accepted. I publish a bibliography listing of 200 books and articles in the field of bioelectromagnetics. Abstracts in English, French, German, Georgian and Urdu for recent issues. 3) Lending library books AC and VCR tapes. 4) To begin AC tape of resonance for blind/industry handicapped. 5) Selected articles on vericomm BBS: 510.891.0303 MINDNET" circ. 100. 2/yr. Expects 2 issues 1999, 2 issues 2000. sub. price: $15; per copy: $8; sample: $8. Back issues: price list available, prices vary. Discounts: 10% discount if ordering entire set of back issues. 40-48pp; 5½×8½, 8½×11; †copy machine. Reporting time: 2 weeks to 2 months. Simultaneous submissions accepted: yes. Publishes (unsolicited) 50% of manuscripts submitted. Payment: 1-4 copies depending on length of article. Copyrighted, reverts to author. Pub's reviews. §Bioelectromagnetics—literature in the field any/all topics based on fact. Ads: write for prices.

THE RESOURCE, M.K. Gladchun, PO Box 973, Bloomfield Hills, MI 48303, 810-644-3440 phone/FAX; ResKate@aol.com. 1991. Articles, photos, reviews, letters, news items. "Newsletter format." circ. 1.5M. 4/yr. Pub'd 3 issues 1998; expects 4 issues 1999, 4 issues 2000. sub. price: $7.95; sample: free. Discounts: none. 4pp; 8½×11; †of. Reporting time: 2 months. Simultaneous submissions accepted: yes. Payment: none. Copyrighted, reverts to author. Pub's reviews: 6 in 1998. §Home design, furniture shopping, money saving. Ads: $400 1/2 page.

RESOURCE CENTER BULLETIN, BORDERLINES, Tom Barry, PO Box 4506, Albuquerque, NM 87196, 505-842-8288, Fax 505-246-1601; E-mail resourcectr@igc.apc.org. 1979. Non-fiction, articles. circ. 4M. 4/yr. Pub'd 4 issues 1998; expects 4 issues 1999, 4 issues 2000. sub. price: $5; per copy: $2; sample: free. Back issues: $2. 8pp; 8½×11; of. Ads: none.

Resource Publications, Inc. (see also MINISTRY & LITURGY), William Burns, Publisher; Nick Wagner, Editorial Director, 160 East Virginia Street #290, San Jose, CA 95112-5876, 408-286-8505, Fax 408-287-8745, E-mail info@rpinet.com, www.rpinet.com. 1973. Poetry, fiction, articles, art, photos, cartoons, interviews, criticism, reviews, music, letters, plays, concrete art, news items, non-fiction. "Interested primarily in imaginative resources for worship, counseling, ministry, and education. In-house graphics and typography." avg. press run 2M-5M. Pub'd 20 titles 1998; expects 20 titles 1999, 20 titles 2000. 142 titles listed in the *Small Press Record of Books in Print* (28th Edition, 1999-00). avg. price, cloth: $17.95; paper: $14.95. Discounts: standard trade. 120pp; 5½×8½ to 8½×11; of. Reporting time: 8 weeks. Simultaneous submissions accepted: no. Publishes (unsolicited) 5% of manuscripts submitted. Payment: editorial fee or royalty on sales. Copyrights for author. NPM, NCGA, CBA, IFRAA, CPCA, NPHA, CIVA, CBPA.

RESOURCES FOR FEMINIST RESEARCH/DOCUMENTATION SUR LA RECHERCHE FEMIN-

ISTE, Philinda Masters, Editor, 252 Bloor Street W., Toronto, Ontario M5S 1V6, Canada, 416-923-6641, ext. 2278; Fax 416-926-4725; E-mail rfrdrf@oise.on.ca. 1972. Articles, interviews, criticism, reviews. "Documentation sur la recherche feministe/abstracts, articles, bibliographies, resource guides. Thematic issues regularly. Bilingual (English and French)." circ. 2M. 4/yr. Pub'd 4 issues 1998; expects 4 issues 1999, 4 issues 2000. sub. price: $38 Canadian, $58 foreign, $77 institution (Canada), $94 institution (outside Canada); per copy: $15 individual; sample: free to institutions and libraries. Back issues: individuals: $7-10 each, $38 volume, $58 outside Canada/vol; institutions: $10 each, $77 vol./Canada, $94 outside Canada. Discounts: write for details. 250pp; 6×9; desktop layout, of. Reporting time: 8-16 weeks. Simultaneous submissions accepted: no. Publishes 50% of manuscripts submitted. Payment: none. Copyrighted, joint rights. Pub's reviews: 60 in 1998. §Women's studies, feminist research. Ads: $300/$100/$75 1/4 page.

RESPONSE: A Contemporary Jewish Review, David R. Adler, Clarita Baunhaft, Michael Steinberg, PO BOX 250892, New York, NY 10025-1506. 1966. Poetry, fiction, articles, art, photos, interviews, criticism, reviews, non-fiction. "Material: short stories up to 20 pages double-spaced. Most material has a Jewish theme." circ. 1.6M. 4/yr. Pub'd 1 issue 1998; expects 3 issues 1999, 4 issues 2000. sub. price: $20 indiv., $36 instit., $12 students; per copy: $6; sample: $6. Back issues: $3. Discounts: distributor (DeBoer) 425 issues $2/issue, Ingram Periodicals 600 issues $2/issue. 120pp; 6×9. Reporting time: 8 weeks. Simultaneous submissions accepted: no. Publishes 20% of manuscripts submitted. Payment: 3 complimentary issues. Copyrighted, reverts to author. Pub's reviews: 5 in 1998. §Judaic studies, Jewish/Israeli culture. Ads: $250/$175/also exchanges.

RETHINKING MARXISM, Guilford Publications, Inc., Jack Amariglio, 72 Spring Street, New York, NY 10012, 212-431-9800. 1988. Articles, art, photos, criticism, reviews, non-fiction. "The journal stresses Marxian approaches to social theory as important for developing strategies toward radical social change—in particular, for ending class exploitation and the various forms of political, cultural, and psychological oppression. Research that explores these and related issues—in a theoretical, philosophical, or empirical way—from a Marxian perspective are particularly welcome." circ. 2.3M. 4/yr. Pub'd 4 issues 1998; expects 4 issues 1999, 4 issues 2000. sub. price: $35 indiv., $105 instit.; per copy: $7.50; sample: free. Back issues: $10. Discounts: 5% subscription agent, 50% distributor. 144pp; 6×9; of. Reporting time: 3 months. Payment: none. Copyrighted, does not revert to author. Pub's reviews. §Marxian economic and/or social analysis. Ads: $300/$150/none.

Reveal (see also THE AFFILIATE), Peter Riden, 4322 Cleroux, Chomedey, Laval, Quebec H7T 2E3, Canada, 514-687-8966. 1976. "Contact us way in advance if interested to get anything being printed. We are making use of photocopiers for the present times." avg. press run as requested. avg. price, paper: depending of pages and size. Discounts: 5% to all our Affiliates Members ($75/year '94). 40+pp; standard size; †photocopy. Reporting time: 1 month prior to due date(s). Simultaneous submissions accepted: yes. Publishes at least 25% of manuscripts submitted. Payment: complimentary copy. Copyrights are usually a mutual agreement.

THE REVIEW OF CONTEMPORARY FICTION, Dalkey Archive Press, John O'Brien, 4241 Illinois State University, Normal, IL 61790-4241, 309-438-7555. 1981. Articles, interviews, criticism, reviews. "No unsolicited manuscripts. First twenty issues devoted to Gilbert Sorrentino, Paul Metcalf, Hubert Selby, Douglas Woolf, Wallace Markfield, William Gaddis, Coleman Dowell, Nicholas Mosley, Paul Bowles, William Eastlake, Aidan Higgins, Jack Kerouac, Robert Pinget, Julio Cortazar, John Hawkes, William S. Burroughs, Ishmael Reed, Juan Goytisolo, Camilo Jose Cela, Charles Bukowski. Recent contributors: Gilbert Sorrentino, Robert Creeley, William S. Burroughs, Carlos Fuentes, Paul Metcalf, Edward Dorn, Edmund White, Thom Gunn, Luisa Valenzuela, Juan Goytisolo, Samuel Beckett, Gabriel Garcia Marquez." circ. 3.5M. 3/yr. Pub'd 3 issues 1998; expects 3 issues 1999, 3 issues 2000. sub. price: $17 indiv., $26 instit.; per copy: $8; sample: $8. Back issues: $8. Discounts: 10% to agencies; 47% to bookstores with a minimum order of 5 units. 240pp; 6×9; of. Payment: copy. Copyrighted, reverts to author. Pub's reviews: 75 in 1998. §Fiction, criticism. Ads: $250/exchange. CLMP.

Revive Publishing, Marilyn Bader, 1790 Dudley Street, Lakewood, CO 80215, 800-541-0558; E-mail Bader-tandm@msn.com. 1996. Fiction. "Looking for 'cross-over' materials. Christian stories which will appeal to a non-Christian audience." avg. press run 5M. Expects 1 title 1999, 1 title 2000. 1 title listed in the Small Press Record of Books in Print (28th Edition, 1999-00). avg. price, cloth: $19.95; paper: $14.95. 286pp; 6×9. Reporting time: 6 weeks. Simultaneous submissions accepted: no. Payment: individual. Copyrights for author. Colorado Independent Publishers Association.

REVOLUTION, Power Publications, Joan Swirsky, 56 McArthur Avenue, Staten Island, NY 10312, 800-331-6534; Fax 718-317-0858. 1991. Letters, non-fiction. "Revolution deals with the issue of nurse empowerment in the health care field. Other articles and topics explored include innovations in the nursing profession, personal experiences of nurses, technological advances, etc." circ. 10M. 4/yr. Pub'd 4 issues 1998; expects 4 issues 1999, 4 issues 2000. sub. price: $24.95; per copy: $8. Discounts: none. 96pp; 7⅛×9⅞; of. Reporting time: 3 weeks. Simultaneous submissions accepted: yes. Publishes 50% of manuscripts submitted. Payment: $50-$500. Copyrighted, reverts to author. Pub's reviews: 4 in 1998. §Nursing. Ads: $4,000 color,

$2,500 b/w/$2,200 color, $1,500 b/w/$1,500 color, $1,000 b/w 1/4 page.

REVUE CELFAN REVIEW, CELFAN Editions Monographs, Eric Sellin, Editor, Department of French and Italian, Tulane University, New Orleans, LA 70118. 1981. Articles, interviews, criticism, reviews. "Publishes only material pertaining to French-language literature of Northern Africa" circ. 150. 3/yr. Pub'd 3 issues 1998; expects 3 issues 1999, 3 issues 2000. sub. price: $7.50 for US and Canada, $10 elsewhere; per copy: $4.00. Back issues: prices on request. Discounts: on request for agencies. 40pp; 4½×7½; of. Reporting time: 1 month. Payment: copies only. Copyrighted, rights remain with journal, permissions on request. Pub's reviews: 20 in 1998. §French-language literature of Northern Africa and criticism of same. Occasional exchange ad, please query. Council of Editors of Learned Journals (CELJ).

Reyes Investment Enterprise Ltd. (see also MONEYMAKING NEWSLETTER; MYSTIC VOICES), A. Pencos Reyes, PO Box 3418, Maraval, Trinidad & Tobago, 809-638-3756; 809-657-3657. 1988. "We are looking for subjects from writers worldwide for books and magazines, non-fiction manuscripts will be given first consideration. Please send $2 to cover postage. Recent publications: *Radio and Television Program Sources,* by A. Pencos Reyes, $20; *A World of Opportunity,* by A. Pencos Reyes, a mystical series which contains 52 booklets on how to get whatever you want in life, $5 each." avg. press run 10M-25M. Pub'd 36 titles 1998; expects 9+ titles 1999, 36+ titles 2000. 2 titles listed in the *Small Press Record of Books in Print* (28th Edition, 1999-00). avg. price, paper: $10-$20. Discounts: 30%-50%. 50-300pp; 5½×8½; †of. Reporting time: 2-3 months. Payment: 15%-25% negotiable. Copyrights for author.

RFD, Short Mountain Collective, PO Box 68, Liberty, TN 37095, 615-536-5176. 1974. Poetry, fiction, articles, art, photos, cartoons, interviews, reviews, letters, news items, non-fiction. "*RFD* is a country journal by gay men, for gay men. Any material relevant to building our community is considered." circ. 3.4M. 4/yr. Pub'd 4 issues 1998; expects 4 issues 1999, 4 issues 2000. sub. price: $20 2nd Class mailing, $32 1st Class, $25 foreign; per copy: $6.50; sample: $6.50. Back issues: $2 each when available over 1 year old. Discounts: bookstores 40%. 80pp; 8½×11; of. Reporting time: 3 months minimum. Payment: 1 copy of the issue in which their work appears. Copyrighted, reverts to author. Pub's reviews: 33 in 1998. §Country concerns, spiritual realities, gay men, poetry, alternatives (new age). Ads: $350/$175. CLMP, GLPA, IGLA.

RHETORICA: A Journal of the History of Rhetoric, University of California Press, Peter Mack, Univ of California Press, 2120 Berkeley Way, Berkeley, CA 94720, 510-643-7154. "Publication of and copyrighted by the International Society for the History of Rhetoric. Editorial address: Dept. of English & Comparative Literature, Univ. of Warwick, Coventry CV4 7AL England." circ. 900. 4/yr. Pub'd 1 issue 1998; expects 4 issues 1999, 4 issues 2000. sub. price: $44 indiv., $88 instit., $18 students; per copy: $12 indiv., $23 instit., $12 students; sample: free. Back issues: same as single copy price. Discounts: foreign subs. agents 10%, one-time orders 10+ 30%, standing orders (bookstores): 1-99 40%, 100+ 50%. 112pp; 6×9; of. Reporting time: 2 months. Payment: none. Copyrighted, does not revert to author. Ads: $275/$200.

Rhiannon Press, Peg Carlson Lauber, 1105 Bradley Avenue, Eau Claire, WI 54701, 715-835-0598. 1977. Poetry, long-poems. "Concentration on midwest women's poetry. Line up chapbook authors on my own." avg. press run 200-250. Pub'd 1 title 1998; expects 1 title 1999, 1 title 2000. 7 titles listed in the *Small Press Record of Books in Print* (28th Edition, 1999-00). avg. price, paper: $6. 25-35pp; 5½×8½; of. Payment: copies of work or percentage of copies. Copyrights for author. CLMP.

●**RHINO: THE POETRY FORUM,** Alice George, Deborah Rosen, PO Box 554, Winnetka, IL 60093, website www.artic.edu/~ageorge/rhino. 1976. Poetry, art, collages, non-fiction. "Rhino is looking for compelling poetry, short stories, occasional essays on poetry, and translations. We encourage regional talent while listening to voices from around the world. Submit 3-5 poems with SASE." circ. 1M. 1/yr. Pub'd 1 issue 1998; expects 1 issue 1999, 1 issue 2000. sub. price: $6; per copy: $7; sample: $5. Back issues: $3.50. 100pp; 5½×8½; of. Reporting time: 3 months. Simultaneous submissions accepted: yes. Publishes 10% of manuscripts submitted. Payment: 2 copies. Copyrighted, reverts to author.

Rhino Publishing, George Cave, PO Box 282, Newbury Park, CA 91319, 800-341-0914; 805-499-0051; fax 805-499-1571. 1997. Non-fiction. avg. press run 25M. Expects 2 titles 1999, 4 titles 2000. 1 title listed in the *Small Press Record of Books in Print* (28th Edition, 1999-00). avg. price, cloth: $24.95. Discounts: 40%-65%. 200pp; 6×9; of. Reporting time: 60 days. Simultaneous submissions accepted: yes. Publishes 50% of manuscripts submitted. Payment: 15% of retail. Copyrights for author.

Rhizome, PO Box 265, Greensboro, PA 15338. 1989. Poetry, fiction, criticism. "Formerly The Post-Industrial Press. Contributors: Georges Perec, Gilles Deleuze, Johannes Poethen. Send queries. No simultaneous submissions" avg. press run 1M-2M. Expects 2 titles 1999, 3-5 titles 2000. avg. price, paper: $5-$12. Discounts: standard trade and library. 50-200pp; 6×9; of, lp. Reporting time: immediately. Payment: negotiable. Copyrights for author.

Rhodes & Easton, Mark Dressler, 121 E. Front Street, 4th Floor, Traverse City, MI 49684, 616-933-0445; fax

616-933-0448; e-mail smallpress.com. 1995. avg. press run 5M. Pub'd 4 titles 1998; expects 15 titles 1999, 20 titles 2000. 2 titles listed in the *Small Press Record of Books in Print* (28th Edition, 1999-00). avg. price, cloth: $20; paper: $14. Discounts: 55%. 225pp; 6×9. Reporting time: 1 month. Payment: 8-10%. Copyrighting for author depends. PMA, IPN.

RhwymBooks, Pace Rhwym, Anne Rutherford, PO Box 1706, Cambridge, MA 02238-1706, 617-623-5894; fax 617-623-5894; email rhwymbooks@aol.com; www.hometown.aol.com/rhwymbooks. 1995. Fiction. "We are a small, independent publisher of historical paperback reprints, fiction and poetry relating to religion and women's issues in history. We absolutely *do not accept* any unsolicited MSS and discard (or return in SASE) without reading." avg. press run varies. Pub'd 3 titles 1998; expects 1 title 1999, 1 title 2000. 10 titles listed in the *Small Press Record of Books in Print* (28th Edition, 1999-00). avg. price, paper: varies. Discounts: booksellers/libraries net 60 days with P.O.; individuals prepayment required, 1-5 copies 25% (we pay shipping), 6-149 40% (purchaser pays shipping), 150+ 55% (purchaser pays shipping). 33-220pp; 5½×8½; †laser, high quality photocopying. Simultaneous submissions accepted: no. Publishes 0% of manuscripts submitted. Does not copyright for author.

RHYME TIME POETRY NEWSLETTER, Hutton Publications, Linda Hutton, PO Box 2907, Decatur, IL 62524. 1981. Poetry. "We publish only the work of subscribers, but subscribing does not guarantee publication. November 1 annually is the deadline for our no-fee poetry contest open to all poets EXCEPT subscribers. No restriction as to length or genre. Prize is $25. Submit with a #10 SASE for winner's list" circ. 100. 4/yr. Pub'd 4 issues 1998; expects 4 issues 1999, 4 issues 2000. sub. price: $24; per copy: $4; sample: $4. Back issues: $4. 44-50pp; 5½×8½; of. Reporting time: 1 month. Payment: $10 to 1 poem for Best of Issue; $10 to Poet of the Year. Copyrighted, reverts to author.

THE RIALTO, Michael Mackmin, PO Box 309 Aylsham, Norwich NR11 6LN, England. 1984. Poetry. circ. 1.5M. 3/yr. Pub'd 3 issues 1998; expects 3 issues 1999, 3 issues 2000. sub. price: £16 sterling; per copy: £6 sterling; sample: £6 sterling. Back issues: same. Discounts: U.K. trade at 1/3 off, other enquiries welcome. 48pp; size A4; of. Reporting time: 12+ weeks. Payment: £20 per poem. Copyrighted, reverts to author. no advertising carried.

Ridge Times Press, Guest Editors, Box 90, Mendocino, CA 95460, 707-964-8465. 1981. "We are not currently accepting new titles." avg. press run 3.5M. 5 titles listed in the *Small Press Record of Books in Print* (28th Edition, 1999-00). avg. price, paper: $3. Discounts: 40% off cover price. 160pp; size varies; †of, lp. Reporting time: 2 months. Payment: $15 + 2 copies. Copyrights negotiable.

Ridgeway Press of Michigan, M.L. Liebler, PO Box 120, Roseville, MI 48066, 313-577-7713; Fax to M.L. Liebler 313-577-8615; E-mail mlieble@cms.cc.wayne.edu. 1973. avg. press run 300-1M. Pub'd 6 titles 1998; expects 6 titles 1999, 4 titles 2000. 17 titles listed in the *Small Press Record of Books in Print* (28th Edition, 1999-00). avg. price, cloth: $20; paper: $10; other: $20. Discounts: 20% to college bookstores, 40% to others. 30-60pp; 5½×8½, 6×9; of. Reporting time: up to 6 months. Simultaneous submissions accepted: no. Publishes less than 5% of manuscripts submitted. Payment: authors get 50 copies of book. Does not copyright for author.

Rio Grande Press (see also SE LA VIE WRITER'S JOURNAL), Rosalie Avara, Editor, Publisher, 4320 Canyon Drive #A12, Amarillo, TX 79109-5624. 1987. Poetry, fiction, articles, art, cartoons, interviews, satire, criticism, reviews, letters, plays, news items, non-fiction. "We have published over 15 poetry anthologies." avg. press run 150. Pub'd 7 titles 1998; expects 7 titles 1999, 7 titles 2000. 26 titles listed in the *Small Press Record of Books in Print* (28th Edition, 1999-00). avg. price, paper: $4, $5 foreign (US funds); other: $4.95, $5.95 foreign (US funds) for anthologies. 50-70pp; 5½×8½; photocopied, saddle stapled. Reporting time: 6-8 weeks. Simultaneous submissions accepted: no. Publishes 85% of manuscripts submitted. Payment: expect to pay $5-$25 plus 1 copy HM's on contests; 1 copy on cartoons, artwork. Copyrights for author.

RISING STAR, Scott E. Green, Star/Sword Publications, 47 Byledge Road, Manchester, NH 03104, 603-623-9796. 1980. Articles, reviews. "Basically I do a newsletter on markets for writers and artists in sf/fantasy/horror markets. All checks to be made out to Scott E. Green." circ. 150. 6/yr. Pub'd 6 issues 1998; expects 6 issues 1999, 6 issues 2000. sub. price: $7.50; per copy: $1.50; sample: same. Discounts: none. 3pp; 8½×11; mi. Reporting time: 3 weeks. Payment: $3 per piece. Not copyrighted. Pub's reviews: 8 in 1998. §Science fiction, fantasy, horror. Ads: $20/$12/$8 1/4 page.

Rising Star Publishers (see also ORACLE POETRY; ORACLE STORY), Obi Harrison Ekwonna, PO Box 7413, Langley Park, MD 20787. 1 title listed in the *Small Press Record of Books in Print* (28th Edition, 1999-00).

Rising Tide Press New Mexico, Pamela Tree, Publisher; Eva Correlli, Assoc. Publisher, PO Box 6136, Santa Fe, NM 87502-6136, 505-983-8484; fax 505-983-8484. 1991. Poetry. "We publish prose poetry. A division of American-Canadian Publishers, Inc., a non-profit corporation. Our latest book title says it all: *Every Person's Little Book of P=L=U=T=O=N=I=U=M* by Stanley Berne with Arlene Zekowski. This popular book, written for just plain folks, is a study of the Department of Energy and the Nuclear Power Industry, which demonstrates a U.S. Government out of control. Why should our own government agency poison us all? We are going to be hammering away on environmental issues, before it's too late! Please do *not* send unsolicited materials.'' avg. press run 6M. Expects 2 titles 1999, 2 titles 2000. 3 titles listed in the *Small Press Record of Books in Print* (28th Edition, 1999-00). avg. price, paper: $10.95. Discounts: 40% to all bookstores, 50% on 10—not one bookstore has returned this book. 200pp; 5⅜×8½; lp. Payment: yes. Copyrights for author.

‡THE RIVER, Melissa Gish, Editor, PO Box 8400, Mankato State University Box 58, Mankato, MN 56002-8400. 1994. Poetry, fiction, satire, parts-of-novels, long-poems, non-fiction. "Serving the interests of the Upper Midwest region; however, material need not be regionally bound. Reading windows: Sept. 1, 1994-Nov. 1, 1994; Jan. 1, 1995-March 1, 1995. General guidelines: Fiction 500-2500 words, mainstream, mystery, environmental themes, light satire. Nonfiction and essays 500-2500 words, North American literature and culture, regional (Upper Midwest) folklore, essays on writers (anyone who is not only popular, but also culturally significant - from William Blake to Anne Rice), nature, ecology. Poetry to 60 lines, any form, prefer regional themes. Artwork, pen and ink drawings. Fiction contest pays $50 cash award for single piece to be selected by judging staff. One prize per issue. No entry fee.'' circ. 3M. 2-3/yr. Pub'd 2 issues 1998. sub. price: no subs; per copy: $3 to contributors only; sample: $3 to contributors only. 60pp; digest; of. Reporting time: 3-4 weeks. Publishes 20-30% of manuscripts submitted. Payment: copies only; fiction contest pays $50 per issue. Not copyrighted. Ads: none.

RIVER CITY, Thomas Russell, Editor, University of Memphis, Department of English, Memphis, TN 38152, 901-678-4591. 1980. Poetry, fiction, articles, interviews. "*River City* publishes fiction, poetry, interviews, and essays. Please do not send unsolicited manuscripts during the summer. Essays, interviews/profile, personal experience. Query. Length 1000-5000 words. Upcoming theme. Summer '99 - Poetics. Fiction: mainstream and literary. No genre fiction. Send complete mss. Length 1000-5000 words. Poetry: free verse, traditional, experimental. Submit maximum of 5 poems. Annual fiction contest: $2000 first place, $500 second $300 third. Send SASE for guidelines. It's a good idea to see an issue of *River City* before submitting'' circ. 1M. 2/yr. Expects 2 issues 1999, 2 issues 2000. sub. price: $12, $24/3 years; per copy: $7; sample: $7. Back issues: $7. 100pp; 7×10; of. Reporting time: 2 weeks to 3 months. Simultaneous submissions accepted: no. Publishes 20% of manuscripts submitted. Payment: 2 copies. Copyrighted, reverts to author. CLMP.

RIVER KING POETRY SUPPLEMENT, Wayne Lanter, Donna Biffar, PO Box 122, Freeburg, IL 62243. 1995. circ. 4.4M. 3/yr. Pub'd 3 issues 1998; expects 3 issues 1999, 3 issues 2000. sub. price: free; per copy: free; sample: free. Back issues: none. 8pp; 11×17½. Reporting time: 2 months. Simultaneous submissions accepted: no. Publishes 10% of manuscripts submitted. Payment: 10 copies. Copyrighted, reverts to author. Ads: none.

River Press, Paul Marks, 499 Islip Avenue, Islip, NY 11751-1826, 516-277-8618; fax 516-277-8660. 1995. Non-fiction. "We publish self-help and self-improvement books and a/c tapes'' avg. press run 5M. Expects 4 titles 1999, 6 titles 2000. avg. price, paper: $15.95. 200pp; 5½×8½. Reporting time: 60 days. Simultaneous submissions accepted: yes. Payment: to be determined. Copyrights for author.

RIVER STYX, Richard Newman, Editor; Quincy Troupe, Senior Editor; Castro Michael, Senior Editor, 634 North Grand Blvd., 12th Floor, St. Louis, MO 63103-1002, 314-533-4541. 1975. Poetry, fiction, art, photos, cartoons, interviews, long-poems. "*River Styx* is an award-winning multi-cultural publication of literature and art. Recent issues have featured Alan Shapiro, Yusef Komunyakaa, Julia Alvarez, Andrew Hudgins, R.S. Gwynn, Reginald Shepherd, Catherine Bowman, Marilyn Hacker, and Rodney Jones. Art/photography by Deborah Luster.'' circ. 3M. 3/yr. Pub'd 3 issues 1998; expects 3 issues 1999, 3 issues 2000. sub. price: $20 individuals, $28 institutions; per copy: $7; sample: $7. Back issues: complete set, issues 5-52: $7-30. Discounts: 33% to stores, 40% with orders of 10 or more. 108pp; 6×9; of. Reporting time: 3-5 months. We accept simultaneous submissions, but not enthusiastically. Publishes 1% of manuscripts submitted. Payment: 2 contributor's copies, 1 year subsciption, $8/page if funds available. Copyrighted, reverts to author. Ads: $250/$175. CLMP.

RIVERSIDE QUARTERLY, Leland Sapiro, Sheryl Smith, Poetry, 1101 Washington Street, Marion, AL 36756-3213. 1964. Poetry, fiction, articles, art, cartoons, interviews, satire, criticism, reviews, letters. "*RQ* prints reviews, essays on all aspects of science-fiction and fantasy, but emphasis is on current scenes rather than, e.g., gothic horror or fantasy in the Gilded Age. Some recent titles: Marilyn House, "Miller's Anti-Utopian Vision: *A Canticle for Leibowitz*''; Dennis Kratz, "Heroism in Science Fiction: Two Opposing Views''; Justin Leiber, "Fritz Leiber: Swordsman and Philosopher''. No maximum word length for essays or review, but fiction is restricted to 3.5M words. Contributors are urged to read several copies of the *RQ* (available at any major public or university library) before submitting MSS. Send poetry to: 515 Saratoga, Santa Clara, CA 95050; send everything else to the editor at the above address.'' circ. 1.1M. Irregular. Pub'd 1 issue 1998; expects 2 issues 1999, 3 issues 2000. sub. price: $8/4 issues; per copy: $2.50; sample: $2.50. Back issues: $2.50. Discounts: agency 20%. 68pp; 8½×5½; of. Reporting time: 10 days. Simultaneous submissions accepted:

yes. Publishes 10% of manuscripts submitted. Payment: copies. Copyrighted, reverts to author. Pub's reviews: 4 in 1998. §Science-fiction and fantasy. Ads: traded or donated. CLMP.

Riverstone, A Press for Poetry, 1184A MacPherson Drive, West Chester, PA 19380. 1992. Poetry. "Annual contest deadline June 1st; reading fee $8. Guidelines available for SASE" avg. press run 300. Pub'd 1 title 1998; expects 1 title 1999, 1 title 2000. 6 titles listed in the *Small Press Record of Books in Print* (28th Edition, 1999-00). avg. price, paper: $5; other: sample copy $5. 32-40pp; 5½x8½; of. Reporting time: 2 months from deadline. Simultaneous submissions accepted: yes. Publishes 1% of manuscripts submitted. Payment: copies (50) and award of $100. Copyrights for author.

RIVERWIND, Audrey Naffziger, Editor; J.A. Fuller, Poetry Editor; Robert Clark Young, Fiction Editor, General Studies, Hocking College, Nelsonville, OH 45764, 614-753-3591. 1975. Poetry, fiction, art, reviews. "Open to new and established writers. Story length: not to exceed 15 manuscript pages, double-spaced. On poetry: batches of 3-6, any subject, any length, but typed. We enjoy both imagistic and lyric poems. We do not read manuscripts during the summer. Recent contributors include Phillip Arnold, Larry Smith, Betsy Brown, Cynie Cory, Roy Bently" circ. 400. 1/yr. Pub'd 1 issue 1998; expects 1 issue 1999, 1 issue 2000. sub. price: $5; per copy: $5; sample: $2.50. Back issues: $2.50. 112-156pp; 7x7; of. Reporting time: 1-3 months. Simultaneous submissions accepted: no. Payment: 2 copies. Copyrighted, reverts to author. Pub's reviews: 0 in 1998. §Contemporary American poetry and fiction. Ads: open. OATYC.

Roam Publishing, Thomas Wilson, 2447 Santa Clara Avenue, Suite 304, Alameda, CA 94501, 510-769-7075; fax 510-769-7076; e-mail editor@roampublishing.com; website www.roampublishing.com. 1998. Fiction, non-fiction. "Seeking travel-related how-to non-fiction on relationships, sex, technology, nomadics, overseas living and business. Need book manuscripts and five to fifteen thousand word special reports on these topics. Also interested in travel adventures set in exotic locations." avg. press run 2.5M. Expects 2 titles 1999, 4 titles 2000. 1 title listed in the *Small Press Record of Books in Print* (28th Edition, 1999-00). avg. price, paper: $15. Discounts: 50-70%. 200pp; 5½x8½. Reporting time: 1 month. Simultaneous submissions accepted: yes. Publishes 5% of manuscripts submitted. Payment: cash advance and royalties. Copyrights for author. PMA.

THE ROANOKE REVIEW, Robert R. Walter, English Dept., Roanoke College, Salem, VA 24153, 540-375-2367. 1968. Poetry, fiction. "Poems to 100 lines, fiction to 2500 words. Recent contributors include Ken Pobo, Norman Russell, and Mary Balazs." circ. 200-300. 2/yr. Pub'd 2 issues 1998; expects 2 issues 1999, 2 issues 2000. sub. price: $9; per copy: $5; sample: $3. Back issues: $2. Discounts: $5 to libraries and agencies. 48-60pp; 6x9; †of. Reporting time: 10-12 weeks. Payment: 3 copies. Copyrighted, rights revert to author but acknowledgement of original publisher demanded.

Roblin Press, 405 Tarrytown Road, Suite 414, White Plains, NY 10607, 914-347-5934. 1979. Non-fiction. "Looking for non-fiction—primarily 'how-to' and self-help and money making type book manuscripts." avg. press run 25M. Pub'd 3 titles 1998; expects 6 titles 1999. 3 titles listed in the *Small Press Record of Books in Print* (28th Edition, 1999-00). avg. price, paper: $9.95. Discounts: 4-10 copies 25%, 10-499 copies 40%, 500+ 50%. 200pp; 6x9. Reporting time: 30 days. Payment: flexible, prefer outright purchase. Copyrights for author. SPAN.

Rockbridge Publishing Co., Katherine Tennery, PO Box 351, Berryville, VA 22611, 540-955-3980; FAX 540-955-4126; E-mail cwpub@visuallink.com. 1989. Letters, non-fiction. "Americana, Virginiana, Civil War. Special interest in letters, diaries, biographies of 'minor' historical figures who none-the-less shaped our heritage." avg. press run 2.5M. Pub'd 3 titles 1998; expects 5-7 titles 1999, 6 titles 2000. 20 titles listed in the *Small Press Record of Books in Print* (28th Edition, 1999-00). avg. price, cloth: $25; paper: $14. Discounts: 1-5 20%, 6-14 40%, 15+ 42%; full case 45%. 200pp; 6x9; of. Reporting time: 4-8 weeks. Simultaneous submissions accepted: yes. Publishes 15% of manuscripts submitted. Payment: negotiated individually. Copyrights for author. Women's National Book Assn. (WNBA).

THE ROCKFORD REVIEW, David Ross, PO Box 858, Rockford, IL 61105. 1971. Poetry, fiction, art, satire, plays. "*Rockford Review*, a literary arts magazine, is published by the Rockford Writers' Guild each winter, spring and fall. The spring issue is devoted to Guild members who are invited to publish any one piece of their choice. *Review* seeks experimental or traditional poetry of up to 50 lines (shorter works are preferred). Short fiction, essays, and satire are welcome—in the 250 to 1300-word range. We also publish one-acts and other dramatic forms under 10 pages (1300 words). *Review* prefers genuine or satirical human dilemmas with coping or non-coping outcomes that ring the reader's bell. We are always on the lookout for black and white illustrations and glossy photos in a vertical format." circ. 740. 3/yr. Pub'd 3 issues 1998; expects 3 issues 1999, 3 issues 2000. sub. price: $15; per copy: $5; sample: $5. Back issues: $2 if available. Discounts: none. 52pp; 5¼x8½; of. Reporting time: 6-8 weeks. Simultaneous submissions accepted: yes. Publishes 5-10% of manuscripts submitted. Payment: copies, Editor's Choice $25 prizes 1) prose, 2) poetry. Copyrighted, reverts to author. Ads: none.

ROCTOBER COMICS AND MUSIC, Jake Austen, 1507 East 53rd Street #617, Chicago, IL 60615,

312-288-5448. 1992. Fiction, articles, photos, cartoons, interviews, reviews, music, collages, news items, non-fiction. "*Roctober* is commited to a joyful exploration into the history of popular music and it's most colorful characters" circ. 1M. 3/yr. Pub'd 3 issues 1998; expects 3 issues 1999, 3 issues 2000. sub. price: $10; per copy: $3; sample: $3. Back issues: $3. 64pp; 8½×11; †of. Reporting time: 2 weeks from receipt. Publishes 10% of manuscripts submitted. Payment: lifetime subscription. Copyrighted, reverts to author. Pub's reviews: 51 in 1998. §Music, film, baseball related themes, monsters. Ads: $160/$80.

ROMANTIC HEARTS, Debra L. Krauss, Executive Editor, PO Box 450669, Westlake, OH 44145-0612, 216-979-9793; D.Krauss@genie.com. 1996. Poetry, fiction, articles, non-fiction. "Short romance stories (2,000-6,000 words), how-to short fiction articles (500-2,000 words), essays with a romantic theme (500-2,000 words), love poems 25 lines or less. All stories must be a romance with a happy ending or the promise of one." 6/yr. Expects 4 issues 1999, 6 issues 2000. sub. price: $22; per copy: $4; sample: $4. Back issues: none. 24pp; 8½×11; of. Reporting time: 3-6 weeks. Simultaneous submissions accepted: no. Payment: copies of magazine. Copyrighted, reverts to author. Ads: $150/$100/$55 1/4 page/$25 business card.

THE ROMANTIST, The F. Marion Crawford Memorial Society, John C. Moran, Editor; Steve Eng, Co-Editor; Jesse F. Knight, Co-Editor; Don Herron, Contributing Editor, Saracinesca House, 3610 Meadowbrook Avenue, Nashville, TN 37205. 1977. Poetry, articles, art, photos, interviews, criticism, reviews, letters, long-poems, collages. "H. Warner Munn, Donald Sidney-Fryer, Clark Ashton Smith, Robert E. Howard, George Sterling, and kindred authors. Purview is Modern Romanticism, Ca. 1850 - Ca. 1950 especially Imaginative Literature (emphasis upon Fantasy); contains a regular section on F. Marion Crawford (1854-1909). Publishes mostly traditional (rhymed) poetry, but some 'free verse.' No fiction." circ. 300 (limited and numbered). 1/yr. Pub'd 1 issue 1998; expects 1 issue 1999, 1 issue 2000. price per copy: $15.00 incl postage. Back issues: out of print. Discounts: 20%-40% depending upon quantity. 160pp; 8½×11; of, lp. Reporting time: within 1 month. Payment: 1 copy (at present). Copyrighted, rights do not revert to author, but we permit repub. elsewhere without charge on condition that acknowledgement of *The Romantist* be made. Pub's reviews: 9 in 1998. §Fantasy, horror, weird, supernatural fiction, Romanticism, bibliographies. Ads: $50/$25/$15.

Ronin Publishing, Inc., Beverly A. Potter, Publisher, Box 522, Berkeley, CA 94701, 510-540-6278. 1983. Non-fiction. "No unsolicited material." avg. press run 5M-10M. Pub'd 5 titles 1998; expects 5 titles 1999, 5 titles 2000. 48 titles listed in the *Small Press Record of Books in Print* (28th Edition, 1999-00). avg. price, cloth: $19.95; paper: $16.95. Discounts: less than 5 25%, up to 50 40%, 51+ 50%,. Pages vary; 5½×8½, 8½×11, 6×9; desktop publishing, repackaging. Payment: 10% net, some advances. Copyrights for author. NCBPA, ABA, PMA.

Ronsdale Press, R. Hatch, Director, 3350 West 21st Avenue, Vancouver, B.C. V6S 1G7, Canada, 604-738-4688, Fax 604-731-4548. 1988. Poetry, fiction, art, photos, satire, parts-of-novels, long-poems, collages, plays, concrete art, non-fiction. avg. press run 1.2M-2M. Pub'd 6 titles 1998; expects 6 titles 1999, 6 titles 2000. 56 titles listed in the *Small Press Record of Books in Print* (28th Edition, 1999-00). avg. price, cloth: $29.95 CDN; paper: $11 CDN. Discounts: trade 40%, libraries 20%, wholesale (bulk) 50%. 108pp; 6×9; of. Reporting time: 1 month. Simultaneous submissions accepted, but must be stated so. Publishes 10% of manuscripts submitted. Payment: 10% of retail, royalties negotiated at contract signing. Copyrights for author. APBC, ACP, LPG.

Roof Publishing Company, 1017 El Camino Real, Suite 316, Redwood City, CA 94063, 1-800-810-3754; email info@roofpublishing.com; website http://www.roofpublishing.com. 1997. avg. press run 3M. 1 title listed in the *Small Press Record of Books in Print* (28th Edition, 1999-00). avg. price, cloth: $14.95. 32pp; 8×10. Copyrights for author. PMA.

ROOM, John Perlman, 38 Ferris Place, Ossining, NY 10562-2818. 1987. Poetry. "Room will publish single author chapbooks when and if a ms. so impresses the editor that he would be remiss in returning the work. Requests for copies will be honored" circ. 150. Pub'd 2 issues 1998; expects 2 issues 1999, 2 issues 2000. sub. price: gratis. Pages vary; 5½×8; of. Reporting time: ASAP. Payment: copies. Not copyrighted.

ROOM OF ONE'S OWN, Growing Room Collective, PO Box 46160, Station D, Vancouver, British Columbia V6J 5G5, Canada. 1975. Poetry, fiction, art, photos, cartoons, interviews, reviews, parts-of-novels, long-poems, plays. "Good quality literary material by & about women, written from a feminist perspective. Payment in Canadian funds only." circ. 500. 4/yr. Pub'd 4 issues 1998. sub. price: $22.50 ($32 foreign) indiv, $25 ($38 foreign) instit; per copy: $7; sample: $7 Canadian ($7 US foreign). Back issues: depends on availablility — query issues wanted. Discounts: trade 30%, bulk-negotiable. 128pp; 5½×8½; of. Reporting time: 6 months. Publishes 8% of manuscripts submitted. Payment: $25-$50. Copyrighted, reverts to author. Pub's reviews: 4 in 1998. §Literature, women. Ads: $60/$30/$20 1/3 page. CMPA.

Rose Alley Press, David D. Horowitz, 4203 Brooklyn Avenue NE #103A, Seattle, WA 98105, 206-633-2725. 1995. Poetry, non-fiction. "Rose Alley Press produces fine books and book-related products. We publish poetry and prose of formal precision and intellectual courage, hoping to enrich readers' aesthetic appreciation and public discussion. We have published books by poets Victoria Ford, William Dunlop, Michael Spence, and David D. Horowitz. We do *not* accept or read unsolicited manuscripts." avg. press run 1M. Pub'd 1 title 1998; expects 1 title 1999, 1 title 2000. 6 titles listed in the *Small Press Record of Books in Print* (28th Edition, 1999-00). avg. price, paper: $5-$10. Discounts: bookstores 40%, libraries 10%, distributors 40%; possible discount for bulk purchase. 25-100pp; 5½×8½, though this may vary slightly. Payment: 10 copies, percentage of any profit from sales of book. Copyrights for author. SPAN, PMA.

Rose & Crown Publishing, PO Box 36427, Richmond, VA 23235, 804-231-6217. 1 title listed in the *Small Press Record of Books in Print* (28th Edition, 1999-00).

Rose Publishing Co., Walter Nunn, 2723 Foxcroft Road, #208, Little Rock, AR 72227-6513, 501-227-8104; Fax 501-227-8338. 1973. Art, photos, cartoons. "Primarily books of nonfiction about Arkansas. Typical titles are 150-250 pp, usually cloth or trade paperback." avg. press run 1M. Pub'd 7 titles 1998; expects 6 titles 1999, 6 titles 2000. 14 titles listed in the *Small Press Record of Books in Print* (28th Edition, 1999-00). avg. price, cloth: $14.95; paper: $9.95. Discounts: trade, 5-24 copies, 40%; classroom, 10% for college and public schools. 200pp; 5½×8½; of. Reporting time: 6 weeks. Publishes 1% of manuscripts submitted. Payment: 10% of gross. Copyrights for author. ABA.

Rose Shell Press, Rochelle L. Holt, Publisher & Editor, 15223 Coral Isle Court, Fort Meyers, FL 33919-8434, 941-454-6546. 1992. Poetry, fiction, articles, art, photos, cartoons, interviews, criticism, reviews, letters, news items. "SW branch - 5111 North 42nd Avenue, Phoenix, AZ 85019. Only consider people who have purchased one of our books. Send SASE for current flyer. Primarily by invitation but also accept author as producer (low rates) projects" avg. press run 100-300. Pub'd 5 titles 1998; expects 3 titles 1999, 2 titles 2000. 12 titles listed in the *Small Press Record of Books in Print* (28th Edition, 1999-00). avg. price, paper: $10.50 plus shipping and handling. Discounts: 40% bookstores & classrooms & bulk over 10. 60-80pp; 5×8; of. Reporting time: 2 weeks. Simultaneous submissions accepted: yes. Publishes 50% of manuscripts submitted. Payment: contributors copies, and arrangement with author/producer. Does not copyright for author. AWP, P&W, IWWG.

ROSEBUD, Roderick Clark, PO Box 459, Cambridge, WI 53523, 608-423-9690. 1993. Poetry, fiction, articles, art, interviews, satire, parts-of-novels, long-poems, plays, non-fiction. "*Rosebud* is a new magazine designed 'for people who enjoy writing.' Each issue features five rotating themes, such as 'Songs of Suburbia' and 'Mothers Daughters, Wives.' Stories, articles, profiles and poems of love, alienation, travel, humor, nostalgia, and unexpected revelation. Send a SASE for guidelines. *Rosebud* is looking for new voices and discerning readers." circ. 12M. 4/yr. Expects 3 issues 1999, 4 issues 2000. sub. price: $22/5 issues; per copy: $5.95; sample: $5.95. Back issues: $5.95. Discounts: upon request. 136pp; 7×10; lp. Reporting time: 14 weeks. Simultaneous submissions accepted: yes. Publishes 5% of manuscripts submitted. Payment: $45 per piece. Copyrighted, reverts to author. Ads: $500/$300. ABA, CLM.

Rossi, B. Simon, PO Box 2001, Beverly Hills, CA 90213, 310-556-0337. 1979. "Interested in material on self-help, non-fiction, super creative ideas for books. Useful informative manuscripts on the human behaviors, personal experiences and life are welcome. Interesting guides on how-to and useful information are also of interest. Titles relating to health, nutrition, sports, fitness, well being and the human mind and body are appreciated. Topics such as personal computing, real estate, publishing, and investing, etc., may also be submitted." 1 title listed in the *Small Press Record of Books in Print* (28th Edition, 1999-00). avg. price, paper: $5. Discounts: 40% to recognized dealers. Special larger rates for quantity orders. Write for more info. *Orders are FOB Beverly Hills, Ca.* 100pp; 8½×5½; of. Reporting time: 3-5 weeks (return postage paid envelope must be included for return of material & quick response). Payment: negotiable. Copyrights for author.

THE ROSWELL LITERARY REVIEW, HarMona Press, Harvey Stanbrough, PO Box 370, Pittsboro, IN 46167-0370, 505-623-0180. 1996. Fiction. "Submit no more than three short stories to 5,000 words or so; and/or three short-stories to 1500 words; and/or five flash fiction stories to 100 words. Any genre except romance, but no gratuitous sex, violence, or "bad" language. Recently published Doug Rennie, Marcia Preston, Helen Patterson, and S. Joan Popek." circ. 2.5M. 4/yr. Pub'd 4 issues 1998; expects 4 issues 1999, 4 issues 2000. sub. price: $22; per copy: $6.50; sample: $6.50 ppd. Back issues: Jan & Apr 1998 (full-sized), $8 each postpaid; all others $6.50 each ppd. Discounts: Contributors may purchase additional copies for $4.50 each postpaid. 78pp; 8½×5½; †inkjet & laserjet. Reporting time: 2 weeks. Simultaneous submissions accepted: yes. Publishes 15% of manuscripts submitted. Payment: 1 contributor copy plus $5-$15 for short stories and short-shorts, $1-$10 for flash fiction, on acceptance. Copyrighted, reverts to author. Ads: Exchange ads only on insert and only with magazines I've seen and can endorse.

Roth Publishing, Inc., Lester Manning, 175 Great Neck Road, Great Neck, NY 11021, 516-466-3676. 1976. Poetry. "Roth is the foremost indexer of poetry in the world. We are the publisher of *Poem Finder on Disc*, an electronic poetry index on compact disc (CD-ROM) and Poem finder on the internet www.poemfinder.com. Indexes poetry in anthologies, single-author collections, magazines and periodicals. Submissions of published poetry are encouraged.''

THE ROTKIN REVIEW, Charles E. Rotkin, Editor, Publisher, PFI Publications, 38 Rick Lane West, Peekskill, NY 10566, 914-736-7693, Fax 914-736-7694. 1985. Articles, interviews, reviews. ''Reviews & direct marketing of books related to photographic, art and communication books. No unsolicited ms!'' circ. 10M. 4/yr. Pub'd 4 issues 1998; expects 4 issues 1999, 4 issues 2000. sub. price: $25; per copy: $7.50; sample: free to libraries or photo, art & book buyers. Back issues: free, if available, with new subscription. Discounts: 10%. 36pp; 8½×11; computer typeset, offset print. Payment: yes, negotiable. Copyrighted, reverts to author. Pub's reviews: 150 in 1998. §Only photography, art, and communication, books. Ads: $1250/$850/$500 1/4 page/agency discount granted. ASPP, ASMP, NPPA, PAI, NPC, OPC, PACA.

Rotten Pepper, Shannon D. Harle, Publisher, Shannon D. Harle, PO Box 2224, Asheville, NC 28802. 1997. Cartoons, satire. ''Subscription includes all the other zines I do= Eat Upir Hair and T.V. Heads and also Rotten Pepper.'' circ. 100-150. 2-3/yr. Pub'd 2 issues 1998; expects 2 issues 1999, 3 issues 2000. sub. price: $10; per copy: $2; sample: $2. Back issues: $1 + 2 stamps. 20pp; 5½×8½; †mi. Reporting time: 1 month. Simultaneous submissions accepted: no. Payment: no. Copyrighted, reverts to author. §no.

THE ROUND TABLE: A Journal of Poetry and Fiction, Alan Lupack, Barbara Tepa Lupack, PO Box 18673, Rochester, NY 14618. 1984. Poetry, fiction. ''We look for quality and craftsmanship rather than any particular form. We read poetry and fiction year-round. In 1987 we adopted an annual format, combining poetry & fiction. In 1989, we did another issue of the theme of King Arthur & the Knights of the Round Table. In 1990 we returned to general poetry and fiction. Now we will publish Arthurian chapbooks almost exclusively (with only occasional issues on other themes). We will publish volumes of Arthurian poetry or fiction by one author instead of an issue of the journal, as we did in 1991.'' circ. 125. Irregular. Expects 1 issue 1999, 1 issue 2000. sub. price: varies; sample: $7.50. Back issues: $6-$10. Discounts: arranged on request. 64pp; 8½×5½; of. Reporting time: we try for 2 months, usually longer. Payment: 2 copies. Copyrighted, reverts to author.

Rowan Mountain Press (see also SISTERS IN CRIME BOOKS IN PRINT), PO Box 10111, Blacksburg, VA 24062-0111, 540-961-3315, Fax 540-961-4883, e-mail faulkner@bev.net. 1988. Poetry, non-fiction. ''Appalachian poetry and short stories. Manuscript submission by invitation. Recent authors: R. Franklin Pate, Jim Wayne Miller, Sharyn McCrumb, Bennie Lee Sinclair, Harry Dean, Earl S. Zehr, Norman M. Bowman.'' avg. press run 300. Pub'd 1 title 1998; expects 1 title 1999, 1 title 2000. 8 titles listed in the *Small Press Record of Books in Print* (28th Edition, 1999-00). avg. price, paper: $10. Discounts: 2-4 copies 20%, 5+ 40%; 40% any quantity and s/h if prepaid. 75pp; 5½×8½; of. Payment: 10% of press run. Copyrights for author.

Rowhouse Press (see also JACK MACKEREL MAGAZINE), Greg Bachar, PO Box 23134, Seattle, WA 98102-0434. 1992. Poetry, fiction, art, photos, criticism, music, parts-of-novels, long-poems, non-fiction. ''Send money orders (cash only) to Greg Bachar.'' avg. press run varies. Pub'd 1 title 1998; expects 3-4 titles 1999, 7-8 titles 2000. 7 titles listed in the *Small Press Record of Books in Print* (28th Edition, 1999-00). avg. price, paper: $5; other: $4 chapbooks. Pages vary; size varies; †varies. Reporting time: 2-4 weeks. Payment: copies. Copyrights for author.

Royal Print, Joseph Manes, PO Box 4665, Westlake Village, CA 91359-1665. 1993. Fiction, art, non-fiction. ''Unagented, first-time authors welcomed. Query with outline and sample art, if any.'' avg. press run 10M. Expects 5 titles 1999, 7 titles 2000. 3 titles listed in the *Small Press Record of Books in Print* (28th Edition, 1999-00). avg. price, cloth: $19; paper: $6.50. Discounts: trade, bulk. 350pp; 6×9; of, lp. Reporting time: 1 month. Payment: 10%; $500-$2,000 advance; outright purchases also. Copyrights for author.

R-Squared Press, Dan Romanchik, Brenda Romanchik, 2113 Arborview Boulevard, Ann Arbor, MI 48103, 313-930-6564 (voice and FAX). 1994. Non-fiction. ''We publish books in areas that interest us personally, including adoption, cooking, and bicycle touring. Our first book, *A Birthmother's Book of Memories* was published in spring of 1994. Our latest book, *How to Open An Adoption*, appeared in the Spring of 1998.'' Expects 3 titles 1999, 3 titles 2000. 5 titles listed in the *Small Press Record of Books in Print* (28th Edition, 1999-00). Discounts: write for information. of. Payment: standard. Copyrights for author. MAPA.

RUBBER DUCKY MAGAZINE, Jon Accarrino, PO Box 799, Upper Montclair, NJ 07043, 201-783-0029. 1992. Poetry, fiction, articles, photos, cartoons, interviews, satire, criticism, music, collages, plays, non-fiction. ''Past issues have included: Fart Boy Comics, OJ Simpson word find, How Horney are You?, David Koresh jokes'' circ. 500. 4/yr. Pub'd 4 issues 1998; expects 4 issues 1999, 4 issues 2000. sub. price: $8; per copy: $2; sample: $2. Back issues: $2. 20pp; 8×11; †photocopy. Reporting time: 30 days. Publishes 70% of manuscripts submitted. Payment: back issues. Copyrighted, reverts to author. Pub's reviews: 30 in 1998. §Sex, humor, satire, drugs. Ads: $20/$10/$5 1/4 page. Zines Online.

RUBBERSTAMPMADNESS, Roberta Sperling, 408 SW Monroe #210, Corvallis, OR 97333. 1980. Articles, art, photos, interviews, reviews, letters. circ. 24M. 6/yr. Pub'd 6 issues 1998; expects 6 issues 1999, 6 issues 2000. sub. price: $24 for 6 issues; per copy: $5.95; sample: $7. Back issues: $3. Discounts: $7. 170pp; 8½×11;

sheet-fed. Payment: $50-$150 depending on size of article. Copyrighted. Pub's reviews: 1 in 1998. §Mail art, paper art, creative process, book arts, rubberstamping. Ads: $1270/$780/$1.75 per word.

Runaway Publications (see also THE PATRIOT), James L. Berkman, PO Box 1172, Ashland, OR 97520, 503-482-2578. 1977. Poetry, long-poems. "No unsolicited submissions" avg. press run 100. Pub'd 1 title 1998; expects 1 title 1999, 1 title 2000. 10 titles listed in the *Small Press Record of Books in Print* (28th Edition, 1999-00). avg. price, paper: $10. Discounts: 50% for govt. agencies/federal employees. 12pp; 5½x8½; of. Payment: negotiable. Copyrights for author.

The Runaway Spoon Press, Bob Grumman, Box 3621, Port Charlotte, FL 33949-3621, 941-629-8045. 1987. Poetry, art, cartoons, satire, criticism, reviews, long-poems, collages, plays, non-fiction. "Additional address: 1708 Hayworth Road, Port Charlotte, FL 33952. First 3 contributors: Bob Grumman, G. Huth, Karl Kempton. Bias against overt political content; especially interested in visual poetry. I consider myself eclectic—in favor of avant garde work with roots in tradition & traditional literature that's technically adventurous." avg. press run 100. Pub'd 4 titles 1998; expects 4 titles 1999, 6 titles 2000. 134 titles listed in the *Small Press Record of Books in Print* (28th Edition, 1999-00). avg. price, paper: $5. Discounts: 40% off for purchase of 5 or more copies of a book, 40% retailers' discount. 48pp; 5½x4¼; †xerox. Reporting time: indefinite. Simultaneous submissions accepted: yes. Publishes 10% of manuscripts submitted. Payment: author gets 25% of each printing. Does not copyright for author.

Running Press, Stuart Teacher, President; Brian Perrin, Associate Publisher; Carlo DeVito, Associate Publisher; Jennifer Worick, Editorial Director; Nancy Steele, Director of Acquisitions, 125 South 22nd Street, Philadelphia, PA 19103, 215-567-5080. 1973. Non-fiction. "Some of our more recent titles are: *Women Together - Portraits of Love, Commitment, and Life; The Best Man's Handbook; Georges Perrier - Le Bec-Fin Recipes; Twins; Men Together - Portraits of Love, Commitment, and Life; Sisters* (N.Y. Times bestseller); *Free to Be...You and Me and Free to Be...A Family; The Joy of Ballooning; Diana - Queen of Style; Daughters and Mothers* (N.Y. Times bestseller); *Streisand - The Pictorial Biography*; and many other new and interesting titles." avg. press run 30M. Pub'd 66 titles 1998; expects 90 titles 1999, 100 titles 2000. 493 titles listed in the *Small Press Record of Books in Print* (28th Edition, 1999-00). avg. price, cloth: $19.95; paper: $12.95. Discounts: 1-4 20%, 5-24 40%, 25-49 42%, 50-99 43%, 100-249 44%, 250-599 45%, 600-1499 46%, 1500+ 47%, 50% wholesale. of. Reporting time: 1 month. Payment: negotiable. Copyrights for author. ABA, AAP.

RURAL HERITAGE, Gail Damerow, 281 Dean Ridge Lane, Gainesboro, TN 38562-5039, 931-268-0655; E-mail editor@ruralheritage.com; website www.ruralheritage.com. 1976. Articles, photos, cartoons. "900-1200 words re: draft horses, mules, and oxen including implements, vehicles, uses, hitching methods, auction prices, logging, farming, how-to, etc. (SASE for guidelines). Contributors: Drew Conroy, Sam Moore, Nigel Westacott. We do not pay for reviews, reviewer gets to keep the book." circ. 6M. 6/yr. Pub'd 6 issues 1998; expects 6 issues 1999, 6 issues 2000. sub. price: $22; per copy: $5.75; sample: $7 includes S/H. Discounts: agent 30%. 100pp; 8½x11; of. Reporting time: 1-3 months. Simultaneous submissions rarely accepted. Publishes 10% of manuscripts submitted. Payment: 5¢/published word and $10/published illustration. Copyrighted, reverts to author. Pub's reviews: 42 in 1998. §Draft animals, gardening, country topics (construction, crafts, etc.). Ads: $240/$130/($6/20 words) send for rate card.

RURAL NETWORK ADVOCATE, O'Brien K, Rt. 1, Box 129, Gays Mills, WI 54631. 1980. Poetry, articles, art, photos, cartoons, satire, criticism, reviews, letters, non-fiction. "All items published must come from members of Rural Network (a social support group for country-oriented adults) or from subscribers to the *Rural Network Advocate*. All items published are original works." circ. 300. 12/yr. Pub'd 12 issues 1998; expects 12 issues 1999, 12 issues 2000. sub. price: $12; per copy: $1; sample: $1. Back issues: not available. Discounts: none. 8pp; 8½x11; of. Reporting time: 7 days. Publishes 80% of manuscripts submitted. Payment: none. Copyrighted, does not revert to author. Pub's reviews: 4 in 1998. §Single life, homesteading, rural life, sustainable agriculture, cottage industry. Ads: none.

Russian Information Services (see also RUSSIAN INFORMATION SERVICES), Paul Richardson, Stephanie Ratmeyer, 89 Main Street #2, Montpelier, VT 05602, 802-223-4955. 1990. Non-fiction. "Publish business and travel information for persons investing in or interested in investing in Russia." avg. press run 5M. Pub'd 5 titles 1998; expects 5 titles 1999, 5+ titles 2000. 4 titles listed in the *Small Press Record of Books in Print* (28th Edition, 1999-00). avg. price, paper: $20. Discounts: case by case. 200pp; 5⅜x8⅜; of. Reporting time: 1 month. Payment: case by case. Copyrights for author. Vermont Book Publishers Assn.

RUSSIAN INFORMATION SERVICES, Russian Information Services, 89 Main Street #2, Montpelier, VT 05602. 1956. "Monthly magazine on Russian history, culture, travel" sub. price: $29 US, $53 foreign. 40pp; 8⅞x10⅞.

Ryrich Publications, Barbara Gladding, 825 S. Waukegan Road, Ste. A-8, Lake Forest, IL 60045, 847-234-7968; fax 847-234-7967; e-mail ryrichpub@aol.com. 1996. Fiction. "Children's fiction to 30,000 words. Prefer middle-grade, 8-12 years, and young adult." avg. press run 1-5M. Expects 1 title 1999, 3 titles

494

2000. 1 title listed in the *Small Press Record of Books in Print* (28th Edition, 1999-00). avg. price, paper: $4.99. Discounts: universal. 100-200pp; 5×7½; of. Reporting time: 6-8 weeks. Simultaneous submissions accepted: yes. Payment: policy varies. Copyrighting for author available. PMA, Small Publishers Ass'n of N.A.

S

S Press, 527 Hudson Street, PO Box 20095, New York, NY 10014. 1982. Poetry, fiction, long-poems. "Mostly letterpress, but can vary. S Press-Blur was created and funded by the above editors. Recent authors: Richard Kostelanetz, John Bennet" avg. press run 500. Pub'd 2 titles 1998; expects 2 titles 1999, 2 titles 2000. 2 titles listed in the *Small Press Record of Books in Print* (28th Edition, 1999-00). avg. price, paper: $10. Discounts: 30%, 40% over 5 copies. 70pp; 6×9; lp. Reporting time: 4 weeks. Simultaneous submissions accepted: yes. Publishes 5% of manuscripts submitted. Payment: copies. Does not copyright for author.

S., Gary Duehr, 85 Winthrop Street, Medford, MA 02155. 1995. Poetry. "Preference for work with a strong voice and that takes risks. No SASE, no work returned. Only accpeted poems acknowledged within 8 weeks" circ. 500. 1/yr. Expects 1 issue 1999, 1 issue 2000. 5½×8; of. Reporting time: 8 weeks. Payment: 2 copies. Copyrighted, reverts to author.

S.E.T. FREE: The Newsletter Against Television, Steve Wagner, Box 10491, Oakland, CA 94610, 510-763-8712. 1982. Articles, cartoons, letters, news items, non-fiction. "Short items about the electronic media and related items from an anti-television viewpoint. Marie Winn, Charles Frink and Mary Dixon are recent contributors." circ. 1.2M. 4/yr. Pub'd 4 issues 1998; expects 4 issues 1999, 4 issues 2000. sub. price: $5 for 10 issues; sample: free. Back issues: not available. 4pp; 8½×14; of. Reporting time: by return mail if SASE included. Payment: none. Not copyrighted. Pub's reviews: 3 in 1998. §Anything related to television, propaganda, and the media. none.

S.I.R.S. Caravan Publications, Saadi Neil Klotz, Editor; Danya Veltfont, Editor, 65 Norwich Street, San Francisco, CA 94110, 415-285-0562. 1972. Long-poems, non-fiction. "We publish primarily works of Eastern philosophy and Sufism, generated from several established authors and musicians. Books include *Sufi Vision & Initiation* and *The Jerusalem Trilogy* by Samuel L. Lewis (Sufi Ahmed Murad Chisti) and musical recordings of the Sufi Choir." avg. press run 2M. Pub'd 1 title 1998. 4 titles listed in the *Small Press Record of Books in Print* (28th Edition, 1999-00). avg. price, paper: $12.95; other: music tapes, $9-$11.95/CD $17. Discounts: 45% to trade for payment with order; 40% on account; 55% to jobbers for orders of 10 or more. 101pp; 5½×8½; of. Reporting time: 2 months. Payment: varies. Copyrights for author. PMA.

Sachem Press, Louis Hammer, Editor, PO Box 9, Old Chatham, NY 12136, 518-794-8327. 1980. Poetry, fiction, art, photos, long-poems, collages. "No new submissions until Jan. '00. Statements of projects will be read before then. Prefer books of 60-150 pp. Translations, anthologies of poetry, collections of short fiction. Published: Louis Hammer's *Birth Sores/Bands*, 1980; *Selected Poems of Cesar Vallejo*, translated by H.R. Hays, June 1981; *Selected Poems of Miltos Sahtouris*, translated by Kimon Friar, Spring, 1982; Yannis Ritsos, *Erotica*, translated by Kimon Friar; *Recent Poetry of Spain*, translated & edited by Louis Hammer & Sara Schyfter, Dec. 1983; *The Danger & The Enemy* by Jos Vandeloo, 1986; *Remains: Stories of Vietnam* by William Crapser, 1988; R.M. Rilke, *The Duino Elegies*, translated by Louis Hammer and Sharon Ann Jaeger, 1991; Louis Hammer, *Poetry at the End of the Mind (Poems 1984-1990) & Postmodern Poems*, 1992." avg. press run 1.2M-2M. Expects 1 title 1999, 1 title 2000. 9 titles listed in the *Small Press Record of Books in Print* (28th Edition, 1999-00). avg. price, cloth: $17; paper: $8.95. Discounts: 5-24 40%, 25-49 43%, 50-99 46%, over 100 50%. 150pp; 5½×8½; of. Reporting time: 3-6 months. Payment: varies, individually negotiated. Copyrights for author.

The Sacred Beverage Press (see also BLUE SATELLITE), Amelie Frank, Matthew Niblock, PO Box 10312, Burbank, CA 91510-0312, Fax 818-780-1912; E-mail sacredbev@aol.com. 1994. Poetry, art, long-poems. "Sole editorial bias: Quality. Contributors: The Carma Bums, The Valley Contemporary Poets, FrancEyE, Nelson Gary, Richard Osborn Hood, and Diane DiPrima." avg. press run 500-1M. Pub'd 3 titles 1998; expects 3 titles 1999, 4 titles 2000. 6 titles listed in the *Small Press Record of Books in Print* (28th Edition, 1999-00). avg. price, paper: $10. Discounts: 40% retail. 100pp; 5½×8½; of. Reporting time: 2-3 months. Simultaneous submissions accepted: no. Publishes 5% of manuscripts submitted. Payment: % of sales after costs are met; 40% of consignment sales; 25 free author's copies; author's expenses. Copyrights for author. CLMP, PSA.

Saddle Mountain Press, Darlene Dube, 425 SW Coast Highway, Newport, OR 97365, 541-574-6004; 800-668-6105; oregonbook@netbridge.net. 1997. Fiction, letters, non-fiction. "Not accepting submissions at this time." avg. press run 5M. Pub'd 2 titles 1998; expects 2 titles 1999. 4 titles listed in the *Small Press Record*

495

of Books in Print (28th Edition, 1999-00). avg. price, paper: $14.95; other: $24.95. Discounts: trade 40%, distributors 55%. Reporting time: 1 week. Copyrights for author.

Sagapress, Inc., Ngaere Macray, Box 21, 30 Sagaponack Road, Sagaponack, NY 11962, 516-537-3717; Fax 516-537-5415. 1982. Non-fiction. "Distributed by Timber Press, 9999 SW Wilshire, Portland, OR 97225, 1-800-327-5680." avg. press run 5M. Pub'd 4 titles 1998; expects 5 titles 1999, 5 titles 2000. 25 titles listed in the *Small Press Record of Books in Print* (28th Edition, 1999-00). avg. price, cloth: $35; paper: $24. Discounts: trade. 300pp.

SAGEWOMAN, Anne Newkirk Niven, PO Box 641, Point Arena, CA 95468. 1986. Articles, art, photos, interviews, reviews, music. circ. 15M. 4/yr. Pub'd 4 issues 1998; expects 4 issues 1999, 4 issues 2000. sub. price: $21; per copy: $6; sample: $6. Back issues: $6. Discounts: none. 96pp; 8½×11; of. Reporting time: 1-2 months. Simultaneous submissions accepted: no. Publishes 30% of manuscripts submitted. Payment: minimum 1¢ per word, sometimes higher. Copyrighted, reverts to author. Pub's reviews: 12 in 1998. §Women's spirituality, ecology, feminism. Ads: $525/$275/$1 per word.

Sahabat Alam Malaysia (Friends of the Earth Malaysia) (see also ENVIRONMENTAL NEWS DIGEST), 19 Kelawei Road, 10250 Penang, Malaysia. 1977. 13 titles listed in the *Small Press Record of Books in Print* (28th Edition, 1999-00).

St. Andrew Press, Ray Buchanan, PO Box 329, Big Island, VA 24526, 804-299-5956. 1986. Poetry, non-fiction. avg. press run 1.5M. Pub'd 1 title 1998; expects 1 title 1999, 2 titles 2000. 7 titles listed in the *Small Press Record of Books in Print* (28th Edition, 1999-00). avg. price, paper: $7.50; other: $9.95. Discounts: standard. 100pp; 5½×8½; of. Reporting time: 6 weeks. Payment: by individual arrangement. Copyrights for author.

St. Andrews Press, Dan Auman, Director & Managing Editor; Ron Bayes, Fouding Editor, c/o St. Andrews College, Laurinburg, NC 28352-5598, 919-277-5310. 1969-70. Poetry, fiction, criticism, reviews, long-poems, plays. "The St. Andrews Press accepts letters of inquiry in the Spring and Fall. A reply is made within 4-6 months and if the Press is interested, will request a full manuscript. Books average 70 to 80 pages for poetry and 80 to 120 for fiction. Recent books: *This Metal*, Joseph Bathanti, *New York, New York*, Layle Silbert, *A Skeptic's Notebook*, David Rigsbee." avg. press run 500. Pub'd 6 titles 1998; expects 7 titles 1999, 7 titles 2000. 27 titles listed in the *Small Press Record of Books in Print* (28th Edition, 1999-00). avg. price, cloth: $14.95; paper: $10; other: $5 chapbooks. Discounts: 40%. 80pp; 5½×8½; lp. Simultaneous submissions accepted: no. Publishes 2% of manuscripts submitted. Payment: 50 copies to the author in lieu of royalty. Copyrights for author. CLMP.

St. Augustine Society Press, Frances Breckenridge, 68 Kingsway Crescent, Etobicoke, ON M8X 2R6, Canada. 1994. Fiction, non-fiction. "Manuscripts which serve to expand that circle of light so meticulously detailed by St. Augustine. We wouldn't be doing anything this interesting if we were affiliated with the church" avg. press run 500. Pub'd 1 title 1998; expects 1 title 1999, 2 titles 2000. 2 titles listed in the *Small Press Record of Books in Print* (28th Edition, 1999-00). avg. price, paper: $6.95US. Discounts: 40%. 200pp; 4¼×7. Reporting time: 2 months. Simultaneous submissions accepted: yes. Payment: to be arranged. Toronto Small Press Group.

ST. CROIX REVIEW, Angus MacDonald, Publisher; Barry Myles MacDonald, Editor, Box 244, Stillwater, MN 55082, 612-439-7190. 1968. Articles, criticism, reviews, letters. "19th century liberalism." circ. 2M. 6/yr. Pub'd 6 issues 1998; expects 6 issues 1999, 6 issues 2000. sub. price: $25 1-year membership price; per copy: $5; sample: $5 postage & handling. Back issues: $5. Discounts: 50% for bulk orders, of. 10. 64pp; 6×9; of. Reporting time: 14 days. Simultaneous submissions accepted: yes. Publishes 10% of manuscripts submitted. Payment: none. Copyrighted, does not revert to author. Pub's reviews: 25 in 1998. §Social commentary. Ads: none.

St. Georges Press, Johanna Bishop, Larry Ph.D Feldman, 991 Colonial Village North, New Castle, DE 19720, 302-328-4150. 1993. Articles, art, photos, non-fiction. "We have enough material for 2 years." avg. press run 2M. Expects 2 titles 1999, 4 titles 2000. 4 titles listed in the *Small Press Record of Books in Print* (28th Edition, 1999-00). avg. price, paper: $9.95; other: $29 textbook. Discounts: 40%. 128pp; 6×9. Copyrights for author. The Small Press Center.

St. John's Publishing, Inc., Timothy Montgomery, Editor-in-Chief; Donna L. Montgomery, President, 6824 Oaklawn Avenue, Edina, MN 55435, 612-920-9044. 1986. Fiction, non-fiction. "Trade paperback publisher of quality nonfiction. No manuscripts accepted for review without prior approval based on query letter and synopsis with SASE." avg. press run 5M. Pub'd 1 title 1998; expects 3 titles 1999, 3 titles 2000. 12 titles listed in the *Small Press Record of Books in Print* (28th Edition, 1999-00). avg. price, cloth: $14.95; paper: $9.95. Discounts: per quantity for individuals, schools, libraries, government agencies; up to 42% for bookstores; 50% for wholesalers and jobbers. 200pp; 5½×8½; of. Reporting time: 3 weeks or less. Payment: standard royalty; minimal advance; payments semi-annual. Copyrights for author. Publishers Marketing Association (PMA),

Minnesota Independent Publishers Assoc. (MIPA), Upper Midwest Booksellers Assoc. (UMBA), Mid-America Publishers Assoc. (MAPA).

ST. JOSEPH MESSENGER, Sister Mary Kuiken, Editor, PO Box 288, Jersey City, NJ 07303, 201-798-4141. 1898. circ. 15M. 2/yr. sub. price: $5; sample: free. 16pp; 8½×11. Reporting time: 2 weeks.

St Kitts Press, Elizabeth Whitaker, PO Box 8173, Wichita, KS 67208, 888-705-4887; 316-685-3201; Fax 316-685-6650; ewhitaker@skpub.com. 1998. Fiction. "Imprint of SK Publications. 70,000-90,000 words of material length. Biases: mystery and suspend fiction. Recent contributors: Laurel Schunk and Sandy Dengler." avg. press run 3M hardbacks, 12M paperbacks. Expects 3 titles 1999, 4 titles 2000. 4 titles listed in the *Small Press Record of Books in Print* (28th Edition, 1999-00). avg. price, cloth: $24.99; paper: $6.99. Discounts: trade - distributors and booksellers. 300pp; 5½×8½; of. Reporting time: 3 months. Simultaneous submissions accepted: yes. Publishes 15% of manuscripts submitted. Payment: 500 advances, 12-15% royalty, paid quarterly. Copyrights for author. SPAN.

ST. LOUIS JOURNALISM REVIEW, Charles L. Klotzer, Editor-Publisher Emeritus; Ed Bishop, Editor, 8380 Olive Boulevard, St. Louis, MO 63132, 314-991-1699. 1970. Articles, photos, cartoons, interviews, satire, criticism, reviews, letters, news items. circ. 4M. 10/yr. Pub'd 10 issues 1998; expects 10 issues 1999, 10 issues 2000. sub. price: $30; per copy: $3; sample: $3. Back issues: $5. Discounts: 20% to sub agencies, 40% to stores & outlets. 20pp; 11×16½; of. Reporting time: 2-3 weeks. We accept simultaneous submissions if so indicated. Payment: $40-$200 (or more). Not copyrighted. Pub's reviews: 20 in 1998. §Critique of print and broadcast media, journalism, particularly St Louis area, media, communications, press, broadcasting, cable, and items not covered by media. write for rates. SDX, Press Club of St. Louis, I.R.E., N.N.A.

Saint Mary's Press, Carl Koch, 702 Terrace Heights, Winona, MN 55987, e-mail smp.org. 1943. Poetry, fiction, non-fiction. "We publish books on the following subjects: prayer, reflection, spiritual memoirs, family spirituality, healing, grieving, caregiving, understanding Christian faith and practice, spiritual poetry, fiction for young adults." avg. press run 7.5M. Pub'd 20 titles 1998; expects 20 titles 1999, 20 titles 2000. avg. price, paper: $7. 150pp; 6×9. Reporting time: 3 months. Simultaneous submissions accepted: yes. Copyrights for author.

St. Matthew's Press, Michael Lister, PO Box 1130, Wewahitchka, FL 32465, 904-639-3700. 1992. Art, photos, interviews, reviews, parts-of-novels. avg. press run 2M-5M. Pub'd 2 titles 1998; expects 4 titles 1999, 5 titles 2000. avg. price, paper: $8.95. Discounts: 10 copies 20%, 20 copies 40%, 50 copies 50%, 60 copies 55%. 125pp; 5½×8½. Reporting time: 6 months. Payment: yes. Copyrights for author.

St. Michael's Press (see also FIDEI DEFENSOR: JOURNAL OF CATHOLIC APOLOGETICS), Bro. John-Paulard Ignatius, PO Box 52, Pisgah, IA 51564-0052, 515-279-7804; e-mail st-mike@mail.common-link.com. 1994. Poetry, fiction, articles, photos, cartoons, interviews, satire, criticism, reviews, letters, news items, non-fiction. "St. Michael's Press is the publishing arm of the *Order of the Legion of St. Michael,* a Catholic prayer and faith community. *The Legion* incorporates Carmelite, Montfort, Ignatian, Franciscan, and Benedictine spiritualities. Our mission includes defending the historic and orthodox Catholic faith through Apologetics and education. Books and magazines we publish are along these lines - spirituality that leads to Christ, Marian devotion, spiritual warfare, and apologetics of the orthodox Catholic faith. We are currently focusing on Internet publishing." avg. press run 500. Expects 2 titles 2000. 1 title listed in the *Small Press Record of Books in Print* (28th Edition, 1999-00). avg. price, paper: $9.95. 100pp; 5½×8½; of. Reporting time: 3 weeks to 3 months. Payment: we are a cooperative-royalty press in the tradition of Writers House Press (see entry under Writers House Press). Copyrights for author.

SALAMANDER, Jennifer Barber, 48 Ackers Avenue, Brookline, MA 02146. 1992. Poetry, fiction, art, photos, parts-of-novels. "We publish new and established writers, and works in translation. Recent contributors: Phillis Levin, Goran Tomcic, Dzvinia Orlowsky, Michael Collins, Reetika Vazirani, Martha Rhodes, and Heather Reid." circ. 1M. 2/yr. Pub'd 2 issues 1998; expects 2 issues 1999, 2 issues 2000. sub. price: $12; per copy: $6; sample: $3. Back issues: $3 when available. Discounts: write for details. 80pp; 5½×8½. Reporting time: 4 months. Simultaneous submissions accepted: no. Publishes 5% of manuscripts submitted. Payment: 2 copies of magazine. Copyrighted, reverts to author. Ads: $150.

THE SALEM JOURNAL, Full Moon Publications, Sharida Rizzuto, Harold Tollison, Lucinda MacGregor, 577 Central Avenue, Box 4, Jefferson, LA 70121-1400, e-mail: fullmoon@eudoramail.com or haunted@rocket-mail.com; Websites www.eclecticity.com/zines/, www2.cybercities.com/z/zines/, www.members.xoom.com/blackie, www.spaceports.com/~haunted/, www.dreamers.dynip.com/zines/. 1983. Poetry, fiction, articles, art, photos, cartoons, interviews, satire, criticism, reviews, letters, long-poems, news items, non-fiction. "Articles, reviews, interviews, poetry, fiction - wicca, voodoo, left-hand path, Native American, other systems of magic" circ. 1.2M. 2/yr. Pub'd 2 issues 1998; expects 2 issues 1999, 2 issues 2000. sub. price: $13.80; per copy: $6.90; sample: $6.90. Discounts: trade with like publishers. 80pp; 8½×11; †of. Reporting time: 2-6 weeks. Simultaneous submissions accepted: yes. Publishes 30-35% of manuscripts submitted. Payment: fee (negotiable) for nonfiction and artwork plus free copy; free copy only for poetry and fiction. Copyrighted, reverts to author. Pub's reviews: 40-50 in 1998. §All systems of magic in zines, books, films, music, internet websites. Ads: free.

Salina Bookshelf, Louise Lockard, 10250 Palomino Road, Flagstaff, AZ 86004, 520-527-0070; Fax 520-526-0386. 1994. "Children's bilingual picture books" avg. press run 3M. Pub'd 1 title 1998; expects 4 titles 1999, 4 titles 2000. 1 title listed in the *Small Press Record of Books in Print* (28th Edition, 1999-00). avg. price, paper: $9. Discounts: 40% bookseller & library distributors. 64pp; 9⅛x6¼; of. Reporting time: 90 days. Payment: 25% of first 5000. Copyrights for author. PMA.

SALMAGUNDI, Robert Boyers, Editor; Peggy Boyers, Executive Editor, Skidmore College, Saratoga Springs, NY 12866, 518-584-5000. 1965. Poetry, fiction, articles, photos, interviews, satire, criticism, reviews, letters, parts-of-novels, non-fiction. "Recent contributors: George Steiner, Conor Cruise O'Brien, Leszek Kolakowski, Christopher Lasch, Jean Elshtain, Renata Adler, Cynthia Ozick, Susan Sontag, Terry Eagleton, Carlos Fuentes, G. Cabrera Infante, John Bayley, Elizabeth Fox Genovese, Mary Gordon, Ellen Willis, and Orlando Patterson. For and indefinite period of time we will not be considering unsolicited manuscripts in any genre" circ. 5M-8M. 4/yr. Pub'd 4 issues 1998; expects 4 issues 1999, 4 issues 2000. sub. price: $15; per copy: $8; sample: $5. Back issues: send SASE for the list. Discounts: 40% to stores. 200pp; 5½x8½; cold type. Reporting time: 6 months: Simultaneous submissions accepted: no. Payment: none. Copyrighted, reverts to author. Pub's reviews: 12 in 1998. §Politics, social sciences, literary crit, poetry, fiction, essays. Ads: $150/$100/$200 cover. CLMP, PEN.

Salmon Run Press, John E. Smelcer, Chief Editor, PO Box 672130, Chugiak, AK 99567-2130, 907-688-4268. 1991. Poetry, fiction, art, non-fiction. "Recently published work by X.J. Kennedy, Joy Harjo, Denise Duhamel, John Haines, Ursula K. LeGuin, Molly Peacock, R.L. Barth, Phillip Levine, Denise Levertov" avg. press run 500-1M. Pub'd 5 titles 1998; expects 3-5 titles 1999, 3-5 titles 2000. 6 titles listed in the *Small Press Record of Books in Print* (28th Edition, 1999-00). avg. price, paper: $10-$14. Discounts: 40% to retailers, 50-55% to distributors, 30% to libraries. 68-156pp; 6x9, 5½x8½; of. Reporting time: 1-3 months. Simultaneous submissions accepted: yes. Publishes 1-2% of manuscripts submitted. Payment: 5-10% royalties and copies. Copyrights for author. CNP, PBA, CLMP.

SALOME: A Journal for the Performing Arts, Ommation Press, Effie Mihopoulos, Editor, 5548 N. Sawyer, Chicago, IL 60625, 312-539-5745. 1975. Poetry, fiction, articles, art, photos, cartoons, interviews, satire, criticism, reviews, music, letters, long-poems, collages, plays, concrete art. "*Salome* is a journal that covers the performing arts in all aspects—theatre, dance, performance art, poetry, music, film. Poetry and fiction submitted should relate to these topics somehow." circ. 500. Irregular. Expects 1 issue 1999. sub. price: $12; per copy: $4 poem postcard issues and double issues, $6 triple issues, $8 annuals; sample: $4 postcards and older issues, $8 current sample. Back issues: $4 each. Discounts: 40% 10 copies or more. 60-120pp; 8½x11; of. Reporting time: 2 weeks to 1 month. Payment: contributor's copy. Copyrighted, reverts to author. Pub's reviews: 50 in 1998. §Everything concerning performing arts (books, magazines, performances, films, video, etc.). Ads: $100/$60/$40.

SALON: A Journal of Aesthetics, Pat Hartman, 305 W. Magnolia, Suite 386, Ft. Collins, CO 80521, 970-224-3116. 1988. Articles, art, photos, cartoons, interviews, satire, criticism, reviews, music, letters, collages, news items, non-fiction. "Aesthetics is the relation between the arts and other areas of human endeavor. *Salon* has a libertarian focus. Recent contributors: L. Neil Smith, Richard Kostelanetz." circ. 150. 4/yr. Pub'd 4 issues 1998; expects 4 issues 1999, 4 issues 2000. sub. price: $20; per copy: $5; sample: $5. 100pp; 8½x11; xerox. Reporting time: asap. Simultaneous submissions accepted: yes. Publishes 80% of manuscripts submitted. Payment: 1 complimentary copy. Copyrighted, reverts to author. Pub's reviews: 20 in 1998. §Arts. Ads: $40/$20/$3 business card.

SALT HILL, Caryn Koplik, English Department, Syracuse University, Syracuse, NY 13244-1170, 315-424-8141. 1994. Poetry, fiction, articles, art, interviews, criticism, reviews, parts-of-novels, long-poems, non-fiction. "Fiction: 4,500 word maximum; poems - send 3-5. Recent contributers include: Bei Dao, Heather McHugh, Lydia Daves, Michael Martone, Jean Valentine, and Christine Schutt." circ. 1M. 2/yr. Pub'd 2 issues 1998; expects 2 issues 1999, 2 issues 2000. sub. price: $15; per copy: $8; sample: $8. Back issues: $5. 120-150pp; 5½x8½; of. Reporting time: 2-6 months. Simultaneous submissions accepted: yes. Publishes 5% of manuscripts submitted. Payment: 2 copies. Copyrighted, reverts to author. Pub's reviews: 15 in 1998. §Poetry, short story, fiction, hypertext. Ads: $100/$50. CLMP.

SALT LICK, Salt Lick Press, James Haining, 1900 West Highway 6, Waco, TX 76712-0682. 1939. Poetry, fiction, articles, art, photos, interviews, satire, criticism, reviews, letters, parts-of-novels, long-poems, collages, concrete art, non-fiction. circ. 1M. Irregular. Pub'd 1 issue 1998; expects 1 issue 1999, 1 issue 2000. price per copy: $8; sample: $10 + postage. Back issues: write for prices. Discounts: 40%. 64+pp; 8½x11; †of. Reporting time: 2-4 weeks. Publishes 5% of manuscripts submitted. Payment: copies. Copyrighted, reverts to author.

Salt Lick Press (see also LUCKY HEART BOOKS; SALT LICK), James Haining, 1900 West Hwy 6, Waco, TX 76712-0682. 1969. Poetry, fiction, articles, art, photos, criticism, letters, parts-of-novels, long-poems, non-fiction. "Open. Published materials by Lally, Burns, Olson, Searcy, Trammell, Shuttleworth, Creeley, Slater, Dante, Hungry Coyote, Firer, Nelson, King, Hart, Ackerman, Murphy, Musicmaster, et al." avg. press run 1M. Pub'd 1 title 1998; expects 1 title 1999, 1 title 2000. 15 titles listed in the *Small Press Record of Books in Print* (28th Edition, 1999-00). avg. price, paper: $8; other: $13. Discounts: Stores/libraries 40%. 100pp; 8½×11; †of/hand work. Reporting time: 2-3 weeks. Simultaneous submissions accepted: yes. Publishes 1% of manuscripts submitted. Payment: copies and $ if available. Copyrights for author. CLMP.

San Diego Poet's Press, Kathleen Iddings, Editor, Publisher, c/o Kathleen Iddings, PO Box 8638, La Jolla, CA 92038, (619) 457-1399. 1981. Poetry. "Carolyn Kizer, Pulitzer, 1985, says of Editor/Publisher/Poet Kathleen Iddings: '(She) is a person of exceptional talent...cares deeply about poetry and poets...has published a valuable anthology concerning contemporary social issues...and books by promising poets. She comes with my highest recommendation.' San Diego Poet's Press and its affiliate, La Jolla Poet's Press, have published 35 individual poet's collections and five poetry anthologies since 1981. Both are non-profit; donations are deductible. The American Book Series was founded in 1989 by San Diego Poet's Press and the National Poetry Book Series in 1994 by La Jolla Poet's Press. Contest winner's manuscripts are published and authors awarded $500. Samples of winning poet's books are available for $8 (postage paid by press). Recent winners include: Joan LaBombard's *The Counting of Grains* and Kevin Griffith's *Someone Had to Live*. Please watch *The Small Press Review* and other poetry magazines for future contest announcements." avg. press run 500. Pub'd 2 titles 1998; expects 6 titles 1999. 13 titles listed in the *Small Press Record of Books in Print* (28th Edition, 1999-00). avg. price, cloth: $20; paper: $10. Discounts: negotiable. 75pp; 5½×8½; of. Reporting time: 1 month. Simultaneous submissions accepted: yes. Payment: negotiable. Copyrights for author.

San Diego Publishing Company, Thomas Thomson, Fairbanks Ranch, PO Box 9393, Rancho Santa Fe, CA 92067, 1-800-494-BOOK. 1980. "Subsidy only. Author fronts what he/she can afford. Publisher prints and markets title. Publisher/author split revenue 50/50 *after* author is fully compensated for total initial investment. Unlimited subjects. Prefer phone call first." 4 titles listed in the *Small Press Record of Books in Print* (28th Edition, 1999-00). size varies. Reporting time: immediately. Simultaneous submissions accepted: yes. Publishes 100% of manuscripts submitted. Copyrights for author.

San Diego State University Press (see also FICTION INTERNATIONAL; POETRY INTERNATIONAL), Harry Polkinhorn, Editor, San Diego State University, San Diego, CA 92182, 619-594-6220. "Focus on Southwest History and Border and Cultural Studies, translation theory, theory" avg. press run 1M. Pub'd 5 titles 1998; expects 6 titles 1999, 6 titles 2000. 5 titles listed in the *Small Press Record of Books in Print* (28th Edition, 1999-00). avg. price, cloth: $25; paper: $15. Discounts: 20% multiple copies. 220pp; 6×9; printed and bound out of house. Reporting time: 90 days. Payment: copies of book. Copyrights for author.

Sand River Press, Bruce W. Miller, 1319 14th Street, Los Osos, CA 93402, 805-543-3591. 1987. Non-fiction. avg. press run 3M. Pub'd 2 titles 1998; expects 3 titles 1999, 1 title 2000. 7 titles listed in the *Small Press Record of Books in Print* (28th Edition, 1999-00). avg. price, cloth: $18.95; paper: $9.95. Discounts: 3+ 40%, 100+ 42%, 200+ 43%. 132pp; 6×9; of. Reporting time: 8 weeks, must send return postage. Payment: standard. Copyrights for author.

Sandberry Press, Pamela Mordecai, Managing Editor; Martin Mordecai, Associate Editor; Sonia Chin, Consulting Editor; Rachel Mordecai, Editor, PO Box 507, Kingston 10, Jamaica, West Indies, fax 809-968-4067, phone 809-929-8089. 1986. Poetry, fiction, art, photos, parts-of-novels, long-poems, non-fiction. "Caribbean poetry series has six titles; includes poetry by Caribbean authors; focus is on first collections. Number four poet is Dennis Scott (He played Lester, the father-in-law, on The Cosby Show). 5 titles planned for publication each year. Also plans for anthologies of fiction, poetry; for simultaneous publication of poetry collections on audio cassette; for publication of books for children and for publication of textbooks" avg. press run 4M. Pub'd 2 titles 1998; expects 6 titles 1999, 6+ titles 2000. 10 titles listed in the *Small Press Record of Books in Print* (28th Edition, 1999-00). avg. price, cloth: $12; paper: $9. Discounts: graduated according to size of order; 1-4 10%, 5-10 20%, 10+, at least 25%, increasing with size of order. 56-64pp; 8½×5½, 6×9, 8½×11; of. Reporting time: 3 months. Simultaneous submissions accepted: no. Publishes 5% of manuscripts submitted. Payment: usually 10% of net receipts; payments once P.A. on 31st December. Copyrights for author. Univ. of the West Indies Publishers' Assoc. (UWIPA), Book Industry Assoc. of Jamaica (BIAJ).

SANDBOX MAGAZINE, Sylvie Myerson, PO Box 150098, Brooklyn, NY 11215-0098, 718-768-4814; sandbox@echonyc.com; www.echonyc.com/~sandbox. 1994. Fiction, articles, art, photos, interviews, satire, criticism, reviews, music, concrete art, non-fiction. "Sandbox Open Arts, Sandbox Magazine and webzine are projects of a not-for-profit organization, whose mission is to provide a forum for experimentation in the visual arts, performing arts, music and digital arts with particular emphasis on interactive and multi-media work. Recent interviews include cyber-punk writer William Gibson (author of *Neuromancer*) and Larry Harvey, founder of the Burning Man Festival." circ. 1.8M. 2/yr in print and 2/yr online. Pub'd 1 in print, 1 online issues

1998; expects 1 in print, 1 online issues 1999, 2 in print, 2 online issues 2000. sub. price: $8/2 issues; per copy: $5; sample: $5. Back issues: $5. 52pp; 8½×11; of. Payment: 2 copies of magazine. Copyrighted, reverts to author. Ads: Print $200/$140/$80 1/4 page; Web $35 per 1,000 impressions with a minimum buy of $105.

●**Sandcastle Publishing**, Renee Rolle-Whatley, 1723 Hill Drive, South Pasadena, CA 91030, 213-255-3616. "We currently focus on childrens' theatre and are interested in having authors contact us." 6 titles listed in the *Small Press Record of Books in Print* (28th Edition, 1999-00).

SANDHILLS REVIEW (formerly ST. ANDREWS REVIEW), Stephen E. Smith, 2200 Airport Road, Pinehurst, NC 28374, 910-695-2756; FAX 910-695-3875. 1970. "Recent contributors have included P.B. Newman, Tony Abbott, Shelby Stephenson, Debra Kaufman, and Yukio Mishima translated by Hiroaki Sato. Issues no. 42 and 44 featured poetry and prose from the Republic of Georgia. Issue no. 43 focused on the work of Glenn Rounds. Issue no. 46 features Centennial Essay on the plays of Paul Green. Send five poems or one short story. Query concerning plays and reviews" circ. 300-500. 2/yr. Pub'd 2 issues 1998; expects 2 issues 1999, 2 issues 2000. sub. price: $14; per copy: $8.50; sample: $8.50. Back issues: on request. Discounts: 40%. 120pp; 6×9; of. Reporting time: average 3 months during academic year. Payment: copy. Copyrighted, reverts to author. Pub's reviews: 4 in 1998. §Books of poetry, fiction, no mags. Ads: $50/$25. CLMP.

Sandpiper Press, Marilyn Reed Riddle, PO Box 286, Brookings, OR 97415-0028, 541-469-5588. 1979. Poetry, fiction, articles, art, photos, non-fiction. "Specialize in large print. Books about 64-84 pages. Contact editor for needs. Next project: unusual sayings/quotes, wise/witty, slant toward peace, brotherhood, environment" avg. press run 2M. Expects 1 title 1999, 1 title 2000. 9 titles listed in the *Small Press Record of Books in Print* (28th Edition, 1999-00). avg. price, paper: $7-$8. Discounts: libraries - 20% single copy, 10 or more per order 40% wholesale. 24-84pp; 5½×8½; of. Reporting time: 90 days. Simultaneous submissions accepted: yes. Publishes 1% of manuscripts submitted. Payment: buy for cash. Does not copyright for author.

SANDPOINT MAGAZINE, Keokee Co. Publishing, Inc., Chris Bessler, Editor, PO Box 722, Sandpoint, ID 83864, 208-263-3573, e-mail keokee Co @aol.com. 1990. Fiction, articles, art, photos, cartoons, interviews, criticism, reviews, parts-of-novels, long-poems, news items, non-fiction. "Physical Address: 111 Cedar Street, Sandpoint, ID 83864. *Sandpoint Magazine* is a regional magazine for North Idaho" circ. 20,000. 2/yr. Pub'd 2 issues 1998; expects 2 issues 1999, 2 issues 2000. 2 titles listed in the *Small Press Record of Books in Print* (28th Edition, 1999-00). sub. price: $7; per copy: $2; sample: $3. Back issues: $3. Discounts: negotiable. 48pp; 8½×11; of. Reporting time: 2 months. Simultaneous submissions accepted: yes. Publishes 25% of manuscripts submitted. Payment: negotiable. Copyrighted. Ads: 1720/110/$45 for 25 words. PNBA.

Sandwich Islands Publishing (see also BEST OF MAUI), Joe Harabin, PO Box 10669, Lahaina Maui, HI 96761, 808-661-5844. 1984. Reviews. "Tip and trick strategy guides for video game machines (Sega Genesis, Nintendo, Gameboy, etc.)." avg. press run 30M. Pub'd 1 title 1998; expects 6 titles 1999, 6 titles 2000. 5 titles listed in the *Small Press Record of Books in Print* (28th Edition, 1999-00). avg. price, paper: $14.95. Discounts: 40% to 50% off. 250pp; 5½×8½; of. Reporting time: 2 weeks. Payment: negotiable, 10%-15% net. Copyrights for author.

Sanguinaria Publishing, Selma Miriam, Betsey Beaven, Noel Furie, 85 Ferris Street, Bridgeport, CT 06605, 203-576-9168. 1980. "We will publish material of interest to feminists." avg. press run 5M. Pub'd 1 title 1998; expects 1 title 2000. 4 titles listed in the *Small Press Record of Books in Print* (28th Edition, 1999-00). avg. price, paper: $12.95. Discounts: 40% for 5 or more copies; single copies, net. 348pp; 6×9. Payment: 10% royalty fees. Copyrights for author.

SANTA BARBARA REVIEW, Patricia Stockton Leddy, PO Box 808, Summerland, CA 93067, 805-969-0861; E-mail jtaeby@West.net. 1993. Poetry, fiction, art, photos, interviews, reviews, letters, parts-of-novels, non-fiction. "SASE with all inquiries and submissions." circ. 1M. 1/yr. Pub'd 3 issues 1998; expects 1 issue 1999, 1 issue 2000. sub. price: $10; per copy: $10; sample: $10 + $2.50 p/h. Back issues: $7. Discounts: trade discounts. 240pp; 6×9; of. Reporting time: 2 months. Simultaneous submissions accepted: no. Publishes 25% of manuscripts submitted. Payment: 2 copies. Copyrighted, reverts to author. Ads: $90/$60.

Santa Monica Press/Offbeat Press, PO Box 1076, Santa Monica, CA 90406, 310-395-4658, Fax 310-395-6394. 1991. Non-fiction. "Santa Monica Press publishes two lines of books: General how-to books written in simple, easy-to-understand terms; and offbeat books, which explore the realms of sports and arts and entertainment from an offbeat perspective." avg. press run 25M. 7 titles listed in the *Small Press Record of Books in Print* (28th Edition, 1999-00). Discounts: 2-4 20%, 5-99 40%, 100+ 50%. Reporting time: 3 months. Simultaneous submissions accepted: yes. Payment: 6%-12% net royalty; $500-$2500 advance. Copyrights for author.

THE SANTA MONICA REVIEW, Andrew Tonkovich, 1900 Pico Boulevard, Santa Monica, CA 90405. 1988. Fiction, parts-of-novels, non-fiction. "Recent contributors: Amy Gerstler, Judith Grossman, Jim Krusoe, Bernard Cooper, Michelle Latiolais. Looking for literary fiction and creative nonfiction." circ. 1M. 2/yr. Pub'd

1 issue 1998; expects 2 issues 1999, 2 issues 2000. sub. price: $12; per copy: $7; sample: $7. Back issues: varies. 200pp; 5½×8½; †of. Reporting time: 2-3 months. Simultaneous submissions accepted: yes. Publishes 1% of manuscripts submitted. Payment: 2 copies plus subscription. Copyrighted, reverts to author. Ads: $300/$150.

Saqi Books Publisher, 26 Westbourne Grove, London W2 5RH, England, 071-221-9347; FAX 071-229-7692. 1983. "Main focus is on works dealing with the Middle East, Islam and the Third World. Saqi's authors include some of the major European experts on the Middle East, as well as writers from the region itself: Germaine Tillion, Jacques Berque, Maxime Rodinson." avg. press run 3.5M. Pub'd 8 titles 1998; expects 8 titles 1999, 10 titles 2000. 24 titles listed in the *Small Press Record of Books in Print* (28th Edition, 1999-00). avg. price, cloth: $40; paper: $14.95. Discounts: as arranged by U.S. distributors—Interlink Publishing Group, Inc., Crosby Street, Northampton, MA 01060, tel.# 413-582-7054, fax # 413-582-7057. 224pp; 5¼×8; of. Reporting time: 8 weeks. Payment: annually (March). Copyrights for author.

Sarabande Books, Inc., Sarah Gorham, Editor-in-Chief, 2234 Dundee Road, Suite 200, Louisville, KY 40205. 1994. Poetry, fiction, long-poems. "While Sarabande Books will be open to unsolicited mss., the majority of its titles will come through invitation and through two national competitions: *The Kathryn A. Morton Prize in Poetry* and *The Mary McCarthy Prize in Short Fiction*, both judged by paid, well-established writers. Winners of these contests will receive a $2000 cash award, publication, and a standard royalty contract. Regarding unsolicited material: Writers must query first with a ten-page sample of poetry or a single short story, postmarked during the month of September only. Include SASE." avg. press run 1.2M poetry, 2M fiction. Pub'd 4 titles 1998; expects 6 titles 1999, 7-8 titles 2000. 27 titles listed in the *Small Press Record of Books in Print* (28th Edition, 1999-00). avg. price, cloth: $21.95; paper: $13.95. Poetry 80pp, fiction 192pp; 6×9; of. Reporting time: 3-6 months. Simultaneous submissions accepted: yes. Publishes less than 1% of manuscripts submitted. Payment: 10%. Copyrights for author. ABA, AWP, CLMP.

SARAGAM: A Musical Quarterly Magazine, PO Box 3872, Kathmandu, Nepal, Fax 977-1-229983. 1995. Articles, criticism, reviews, music. "Music magazine on Nepali & Indian subjects only, English & Nepali (Hindi) languages" 4/yr. Expects 4 issues 1999, 4 issues 2000. sub. price: $14; per copy: $3.50. Back issues: $2.50. 30pp; 8×11; of. Reporting time: 30 days. Payment: cash. Not copyrighted. Ads: $50/$25.

Raymond Saroff, Publisher, 461 Acorn Hill Road, Olive Bridge, NY 12461. 1989. Fiction, non-fiction. "Raymond Saroff, Publisher was established initially to bring into print the complete works of the late Howard Rose. Our areas of interest are American art (including folk art), and fiction from, of, or about Chicago. No unsolicited manuscripts. Send query and 2-page sample." avg. press run 1.5M. Expects 5 titles 1999, 2 titles 2000. 5 titles listed in the *Small Press Record of Books in Print* (28th Edition, 1999-00). avg. price, cloth: $20; paper: $10. Discounts: Distributed by McPherson & Co. 300pp; 5½×8½. Reporting time: 1-3 months. Payment: standard royalties. Copyrights for author.

SARU Press International, Drew Stroud, 3 Pine Terrace, 559 Jordan Road, Sedona, AZ 86336-4143. 1980. Poetry. "I am primarily interested in accurate, imaginative translations of Japanese and Hispanic poetry and short fiction." avg. press run 500. Pub'd 3 titles 1998; expects 4 titles 1999, 2 titles 2000. 19 titles listed in the *Small Press Record of Books in Print* (28th Edition, 1999-00). avg. price, paper: $10. Discounts: depends on size of order—on large orders, can supply at 50%. 70pp; 6×8½; of. Reporting time: will read immediately upon receipt. Publishes 50% of manuscripts submitted. Payment: depends how much of production cost is shared by author. Copyrights for author.

Saskatchewan Writers Guild (see also GRAIN), Box 3986, Regina, Saskatchewan S4P 3R9, Canada, 306-757-6310. 1969. of.

Sasquatch Books, Chad Haight, Publisher, 615 2nd Ave., Suite 260, Seattle, WA 98104, 206-467-4300; 800-775-0817; Fax 206-467-4301; books@SasquatchBooks.com. 1986. Pub'd 34 titles 1998; expects 41 titles 1999, 45 titles 2000. 132 titles listed in the *Small Press Record of Books in Print* (28th Edition, 1999-00). Reporting time: 6-8 weeks. Simultaneous submissions accepted: yes.

SAT SANDESH: THE MESSAGE OF THE MASTERS, Arthur Stein, PhD, Vinod Sena, PhD, 680 Curtis Corner Road, Wakefield, RI 02879, (401) 783-0662. 1968. Articles, photos, interviews, reviews, letters, parts-of-novels, long-poems. "Subscription address: Route 1, Box 24, Bowling Green, VA 22427. *Sat Sandesh: The Message of Truthful Living* is published for the purpose of sharing the teachings of Sant Rajinder Singh (the living spiritual guide of the Science of Spirituality), Sant Darshan Singh Ji, Param Sant Kirpal Singh Ji, and Hazur Baba Sawan Singh Ji, and earlier teachers of Surat Shabd Yoga (meditation on inner light and celestial sound). Includes poetry, experiences with spiritual teachers, responses to questions, children's corner, and other features" circ. 938. 12/yr. Pub'd 12 issues 1998; expects 12 issues 1999, 12 issues 2000. sub. price: $23; per copy: $2.50; sample: free. Back issues: $2.50. Discounts: bookstores & libraries 40%; distributors, contact for information. 32pp; 6×9; of. Payment: none. Not copyrighted. Pub's reviews: 2 in 1998. §Books of Sawan Kirpal Publications. Ads: none.

SATIRE, Larry Logan, PO Box 340, Hancock, MD 21750, 301-678-6999; satire@intrepid.net; www.intrepid.net/satire. 1994. Fiction, articles, cartoons, satire, non-fiction. "Articles and stories up to 6000 words" circ. 500. 4/yr. Pub'd 4 issues 1998; expects 4 issues 1999, 4 issues 2000. sub. price: $16; per copy: $5; sample: $5. Back issues: $4. 60-70pp; 8½×11; of. Reporting time: 3 months. Simultaneous submissions accepted: yes. Publishes 5% of manuscripts submitted. Payment: issues & any correspondence. Copyrighted, reverts to author. Pub's reviews: 2 in 1998. §Satire only. Ads: very limited, usually ad exchanges.

Saturday Press, Inc., PO Box 43548, Upper Montclair, NJ 07043, 973-256-5053. 1975. Poetry. "Sponsor of Eileen W. Barnes Award for women poets over forty. Not reading new submissions at this time" avg. press run 1M. 12 titles listed in the *Small Press Record of Books in Print* (28th Edition, 1999-00). avg. price, paper: $5-$7; other: audiocassette $9. Discounts: 40% to bookstores and jobbers. 64-102pp; 5½×8½, 6×9; of. Reporting time: responds to queries in 2 weeks. Publishes less than 1% of manuscripts submitted. Payment: individual arrangement. Copyrights for author.

The Saunderstown Press, Allen A. Johnson, 54 Camp Avenue, North Kingstown, RI 02852, 401-295-8810; Fax 401-294-9939. 1985. Poetry, fiction, satire, non-fiction. "We publish from 2-4 titles per year. Always interested in new authors but no unsolicited manuscripts. Current books in production include medicine, careers, religion cooking, and philosophy" avg. press run 1M. Expects 1 title 1999, 2 titles 2000. avg. price, cloth: $12.95; paper: $9.95. Discounts: 50% trade, 20% educational and library. 50-100pp; 6×9. Reporting time: 2-3 weeks from receipt. Simultaneous submissions accepted: no. Publishes 2% of manuscripts submitted. Payment: 20% (25% for exceptional) on sales (or 50% of profit). Copyrights for author. American Assn. of Career Education.

Savant Garde Workshop, Vilna Jorgen II, Publisher & Editor-in-Chief; Artemis Smith, Artistic Director, PO Box 1650, Sag Harbor, NY 11963-0060, 516-725-1414; website www.savantgarde.org. 1964. Poetry, fiction, criticism, long-poems, plays, concrete art, non-fiction. "Please query with SASE. Do not send ms. until invited upon query. Focus on multinational intelligentsia. Looking for people who have eventual Nobel Prize potential. Publish limited signed editions and their overruns." avg. press run 1M. Expects 1 title 1999, 1 title 2000. 3 titles listed in the *Small Press Record of Books in Print* (28th Edition, 1999-00). avg. price, cloth: $1,000 (originals); paper: $200 (overruns); other: $100 on-demand perfectbound teacher and reviewers' editions. Discounts: 25% rare bookdealers, bookdealers, wholesalers, art galleries & print shops. 300pp; 6×9; †computer desktop, multicolor dot-matrix and/or laser printers, signed and numbered. Reporting time: 2 weeks to 3 months on accepted manuscripts; 2 years on rejected submissions worth reconsidering for future budgets. Simultaneous submissions accepted: no. Publishes 1+% of manuscripts submitted. Payment: varies. Copyrights for author.

SCANDINAVIAN REVIEW, Edward P. Gallagher, Publisher; Adrienne Gyongy, Editor, 15 East 65 Street, New York, NY 10021, 212-879-9779. 1913. Poetry, fiction, articles, art, photos, interviews, satire, criticism, reviews, letters, parts-of-novels, long-poems, plays, non-fiction. "Suggested length of articles: 1500-2000 words. Include return postage and SAE. Recent contributors: R. Jeffrey Smith, Leslie Eliason, Ulla Tarres-Wahlberg, Jan-Erik Lundstrom. Focus: Scandinavian culture and society." circ. 5M. 3/yr. Pub'd 3 issues 1998; expects 3 issues 1999, 3 issues 2000. sub. price: $15, $20 foreign; per copy: $4; sample: $4. Back issues: 4/1987 Finnish Independence issue, 1/88 Swedish issue, 2/1988 Norwegian issue, 2/92 Education issue, 1/91, 1/92, 1/93, travel issues. Discounts: negotiable. 96-104pp; 6×9¼; of. Reporting time: 3 months to publish. Payment: poetry $10 p.(a/t), articles $100-$200, fiction $75-$125 (a/t). Copyrighted, reverts to author. Pub's reviews: several in 1998. Ads: $400/$250/$150 1/4 page.

Scarecrow Press (see also VOYA (Voice of Youth Advocate)), Shirley Lambert, Associate Publisher, 4720 Boston Way, Lanham, MD 20706, 301-459-3366; Fax 301-459-2118. 1950. Criticism, non-fiction. "Very varied list. Emphasis on reference books, scholarly monographs, some professional textbooks. Dominant subject areas include: Cinema, women, minorities, music, literature, library science, parapsychology, religion." avg. press run 750. Expects 165 titles 1999. avg. price, cloth: $45; paper: $24.50. Discounts: net to libraries, etc; 22% to bookstores. 390pp; 5½×8½; of. Reporting time: 2 months. We accept simultaneous submissions if they are marked as such. Publishes 35% of manuscripts submitted. Payment: 10% first 1M copies; 15% thereafter; 15% on all copies for camera ready mss. Copyrights for author. ALA.

Scarf Press, Mark L. Levine, 1385 Baptist Church Rte., Yorktown Hts., NY 10598, 914-245-7811. 1979. "Books available from Bloch Publishing. Publisher of M.C.Gaines *Picture Stories from the Bible: ...in Full Color Comic Strip Form* (old and new testament editions). No unsolicited manuscripts." avg. press run 50M. 2 titles listed in the *Small Press Record of Books in Print* (28th Edition, 1999-00). avg. price, cloth: $12.95. Discounts: order from wholesalers or Bloch Publishing, 37 W. 26 St. (9th floor), NYC 10010. 224pp (o.t.), 144pp (n.t.); 7¼×10; of. Copyrights for author.

Scars Publications (see also CHILDREN, CHURCHES AND DADDIES, A Non Religious, Non Familial Literary Magazine), Janet Kuypers, 3625 W. Wrightwood Avenue #2F, Chicago, IL 60647, E-mail ccandd@aol.com; www.members.aol.com/scarspub/scars.html. 1993. Poetry, fiction, art, photos, letters, long-poems, collages, non-fiction. "Scars Publications was created originally for the magazine *Children, Churches and Daddies* but now extends itself to printing perfect bound paperback collection volumes from the magazine and also for publishing an occasional book or 24-page special highlighting one or two authors alone. If you submit work, please let me know whether you want a single piece published in the magazine or are looking for a collection of your own work being published. A cover letter is appreciated. If you're published in a book, please be prepared to try to sell copies to your friends and in stores in your area. That's how we succeed. Otherwise, look at the guidelines for *Children, Churches and Daddies*. We also run a calander contest and book/chapbook contest. Contact Sears for more infomation. Permanant adress: 8830 West 120th Place, Palos Park Illinois, 60464, attn: Janet Kuypers. Electronic submissions (e-mail or text format, Macintash preferred) appreciated. Issues are available in print (paid only), electronic format, and on the World Wide Web at above address." avg. press run determined individually. Pub'd 6 titles 1998; expects 12 titles 1999, 12 titles 2000. 7 titles listed in the *Small Press Record of Books in Print* (28th Edition, 1999-00). avg. price, cloth: $11.95; paper: $5. Books 200pp, chapbooks 24-32pp; 5½x8; †mimeo. Reporting time: I'll get back to you in a week if there is a SASE in it; if not, you'll never hear from me. Simultaneous submissions accepted: yes. Publishes 20% of manuscripts submitted. Payment: none for collection volumes; contact me about printing larger volumes of individual artist's works. Does not copyright for author.

SCAVENGER'S NEWSLETTER, Janet Fox, 519 Ellinwood, Osage City, KS 66523, 913-528-3538; E-mail foxcav1@jc.net. 1984. Poetry, articles, art, cartoons, interviews, letters, news items, fiction. "*Scavenger's* is a newsletter listing markets for the sf/fantasy/horror/mystery writer or artist. Besides market news I use short (700-1000 wd.) articles of interest to the readership, poems under 10 lines as filler on sf/fantasy/horror/mystery. Art, covers 8½ X 7" and small inside drawings no larger than 4 X 4, all art b & w. Recent contributors include Steven Sawicki, Tim Emswiler, Charles S. Fallis, S.F. Willems. Currently looking at submissions of flash fiction 500-1200 words in the genres of SF, fantasy, horror, mystery." circ. 1M. 12/yr. Pub'd 12 issues 1998; expects 12 issues 1999, 12 issues 2000. sub. price: $17; per copy: $2.50; sample: $2.50. Back issues: none. 28pp; 8½x7; quick print. Reporting time: 2 weeks to 1 month. Simultaneous submissions accepted: yes. Publishes 10% of manuscripts submitted. Payment: $2 for poems/inside art, $4 for articles/covers on acceptance + 1 contributor's copy; $4 for fiction on acceptance. Copyright not registered but copyright stated at time of publication, all rights revert to contributors. Pub's reviews: 12 in 1998. §Sf/fantasy/horror/mystery small press publications. Ads: none (flyer inserts sent w/bulk mailing).

Scentouri, Publishing Division, A.C. Doyle, c/o Prosperity + Profits Unlimited, PO Box 416, Denver, CO 80201-0416, 303-575-5676. 1982. avg. press run 1.5M. 10 titles listed in the *Small Press Record of Books in Print* (28th Edition, 1999-00). avg. price, cloth: $18.95; paper: $17.95; other: $17.95. Discounts: 25% to libraries, bookstores, etc. 60pp; 8½x11, 5½x8½. Reporting time: 6 weeks.

●Schafer's Publishing, Madelain Hope, Nicklaus Copeland, Jasmine Kingfisher, 6864 Stahelin, Detroit, MI 48228, 313-982-1806; fax 313-982-1925; e-mail schaed@idt.net. 1996. Poetry, art, photos, non-fiction. "Currently publishing a golf series of seven books." Expects 3 titles 1999, 4 titles 2000. 3 titles listed in the *Small Press Record of Books in Print* (28th Edition, 1999-00). avg. price, cloth: $24.95; paper: $16.95. 256pp; 6x9; of. PMA, SPAN.

Schenkman Books, Joseph Q. Schenkman, Tepin Thoenen, PO Box 119, Rochester, VT 05767, 802-767-3702; Fax 802-767-9528; E-mail schenkma@sover.net. 1961. Non-fiction. avg. press run 1M. Pub'd 2 titles 1998; expects 3 titles 1999, 6 titles 2000. 2 titles listed in the *Small Press Record of Books in Print* (28th Edition, 1999-00). avg. price, cloth: $24.95; paper: $15.95. Discounts: bookstores 20%, libraries 10%. 250pp; 5½x8. Reporting time: 6 months. Simultaneous submissions accepted: yes. Publishes 2% of manuscripts submitted. Payment: varies. Copyrights for author.

Scherf, Inc./Scherf Books, Dietmar Scherf, Executive Editor; Gail Kirby, Editor, PO Box 80180, Las Vegas, NV 89180-0180, 702-243-4895; Fax 702-243-7460; ds@scherf.com; www.scherf.com. 1990. Fiction, non-fiction. "All material has to be of sound moral character, based on a Judeo-Christian faith. Send the first 3 chapters with outline. First-time authors welcome. Solid and sound grammar is important. Also, we want fresh ideas and we are not interested in fiction or non-fiction that has already been done over and over again, unless a unique and fresh approach!" avg. press run 2.5M-10M. Expects 1-2 titles 1999, 1-2 titles 2000. 1 title listed in the *Small Press Record of Books in Print* (28th Edition, 1999-00). avg. price, cloth: $24. Discounts: 50% (free s/h within USA) if bought directly from Scherf, (single copy orders welcome-same discount); prepayment required. 224pp; 5½x8½. Reporting time: up to 6 months. Simultaneous submissions accepted: yes. Publishes 1% of manuscripts submitted. Payment: varies (approx. 5-8% of sold books). Does not copyright for author.

SCHOOL MATES, U.S. Chess Federation, Brian Buggee, 186 Route 9W, New Windsor, NY 12553, 914-562-8350. 1987. Poetry, fiction, articles, art, photos, cartoons, interviews, collages. "Length: 500-750 words; i.e., short articles for grades 3-6 about chess and chessplayers. Games, puzzles, artwork relating to chess also welcome." circ. 21M. 6/yr. Pub'd 4 issues 1998; expects 6 issues 1999, 6 issues 2000. sub. price: $7.50 ($7 to US Chess Federation 'Scholastic' members); per copy: $2.25; sample: free. Back issues: $2.25. 20pp;

8⅜×11; of. Reporting time: 2 months lead time. Payment: $40/1,000-word mss. Copyrighted. Ads: $2565/$1290/$90 per inch.

SCIENCE & SOCIETY, Guilford Publications, Inc., David Laibman, 72 Spring Street, New York, NY 10012, 212-431-9800. 1936. Articles, interviews, criticism, reviews, non-fiction. "The journal presents scholarship in political economy and the economic analysis of capitalist and socialist societies; in philosophy and methodology of the natural and social sciences; in history, labor, Black and women's studies; in aesthetics, literature and the arts." circ. 2M. 4/yr. Pub'd 4 issues 1998; expects 4 issues 1999, 4 issues 2000. sub. price: $27 indiv., $110 instit.; per copy: $7; sample: free. Back issues: $10. Discounts: 5% subscription agents, 50% distributors. 128pp; 6×9; of. Payment: none. Copyrighted, does not revert to author. Pub's reviews. §Economic analysis, socialism, social sciences, history, women's studies. Ads: $250/$125/$350 back cover/$300 3rd cover.

SCIENCE AND TECHNOLOGY, Univelt, Inc., R.H. Jacobs, Series Editor, PO Box 28130, San Diego, CA 92198, 760-746-4005; Fax 760-746-3139; 76121.1532@compuserve.com; www.univelt.staigerland.com. 1964. "Space and related fields. An irregular serial. Publishers for the American Astronautical Society. Standing orders accepted. Vols. 1-96 published." circ. 400. Irregular. Pub'd 5 issues 1998; expects 5 issues 1999, 5 issues 2000. sub. price: varies. Back issues: no. Discounts: 20%, or more by arrangement; special prices for classroom use. 200-700pp; 7×9½; of. Reporting time: 60 days. Payment: 10% (if the volume author). Copyrighted, authors may republish material with appropriate credits given and authorization from publishers. Ads: none.

SCIENCE BOOKS & FILMS, Tracy Gath, Editor, 1333 H Street, Northwest, Washington, DC 20005, 202-326-6463. 1965. Articles, interviews, reviews, news items. "Reviews books, films, videos, filmstrips and software in all the sciences for all ages." circ. 4.5M. 9/yr. Pub'd 9 issues 1998; expects 9 issues 1999, 9 issues 2000. sub. price: $40; per copy: $7 + $1.50 p/h; sample: free. Back issues: $7, plus $1.50 p/h. Discounts: agents 10%. 32pp; 8¼×11; of. Payment: none. Copyrighted, reverts to author. Pub's reviews: 1500 in 1998. §Sciences.

SCIENCE FICTION CHRONICLE, Algol Press, Andrew Porter, Editor, Publisher; Don D'Ammassa, Book Critic; Vincent DiFate, Contributing Editor; Frederik Pohl, Contributing Editor; Stephen Jones, Contributing Editor; Jo Fletcher, Contributing Editor; Jeff Rovin, Contributing Editor, PO Box 022730, Brooklyn, NY 11202-0056, 718-643-9011; Fax 718-522-3308. 1979. Articles, art, photos, reviews, letters, news items, non-fiction. "*SF Chronicle* is a bi-monthly newsmagazine serving the SF and fantasy fields through current news, market reports, letters, comprehensive coverage of events, conventions and awards, columns, and reviews." circ. 6M. 6/yr. Pub'd 6 issues 1998; expects 6 issues 1999, 6 issues 2000. sub. price: $35 US, $42 Canada & US First class, $49 Europe, Australia, Africa, Asia; per copy: $3.95; sample: $3.95. Back issues: all issues $3. Discounts: 60% trade, write publisher; also distributed by Ingram Periodicals, IPD, Ubiquity, etc. 44-72pp; 8×11; of. Reporting time: 2-3 weeks. Simultaneous submissions accepted: no. Publishes 3-5% of manuscripts submitted. Payment: 3.5¢-5¢/word. Copyrighted, does not revert to author. Pub's reviews: 400 (300 book, 100 mag.) in 1998. §SF, fantasy, reference, horror, children's fantasy. Ads: $600/$325/35¢.

Science of Mind Publishing, Elaine Sonne, PO Box 75127, Los Angeles, CA 90075-0127, 213-388-2181. 1927. avg. press run 90M. 1 title listed in the *Small Press Record of Books in Print* (28th Edition, 1999-00). avg. price, paper: $2.95. 112pp; 5¼×7¾. Simultaneous submissions accepted: no. Does not copyright for author.

SCIENCE/HEALTH ABSTRACTS, Phylis Austin, PO Box 553, Georgetown, GA 31754. 1980. News items, non-fiction. circ. 1M. 6/yr. Pub'd 6 issues 1998; expects 6 issues 1999, 6 issues 2000. sub. price: $6; per copy: $1; sample: $1. Back issues: $1/issue. 4pp; 8½×11; †of. Reporting time: none needed. Payment: none. Copyrighted, reverts to author. Pub's reviews: 50 in 1998. §Health, computers, science, gardening, alternative medicine. Ads: none.

‡Scopcraeft (see also BLACKWATER), Cheryll Hendershot, Cyndy Hendershot, Scott Hendershot, Antony Oldknow, PO Box 1091, Portales, NM 88130-1091, 505-359-0901. 1966. Poetry, fiction, art, photos, interviews, criticism, reviews, non-fiction. "Recent Contributors: Richard Lyons, Kirpal Gordon, Francis Jammes" avg. press run 200. Pub'd 6 titles 1998; expects 10 titles 1999, 10 titles 2000. avg. price, paper: $15. 100pp; 8½×11, 5½×8½; mi. Reporting time: 1 month. Payment: varies. Copyrights for author.

Score (see also SCORE), Crag Hill, Selby Spencer, 1015 NW Clifford Street, Pullman, WA 99163-3203. 1983. Poetry, fiction, art, photos, interviews, criticism, reviews, music, letters, parts-of-novels, long-poems, collages, plays, concrete art, non-fiction. "Presently, because of other publishing commitments (a magazine, a broadside series, we are only able to publish 2 books per year. Please query." avg. press run 200. Pub'd 2 titles 1998; expects 2 titles 1999, 2 titles 2000. 19 titles listed in the *Small Press Record of Books in Print* (28th Edition, 1999-00). avg. price, paper: $8. 24-30pp; size varies; of, xerox. Reporting time: 3 months. Publishes 15% of manuscripts submitted. Payment: 1/4 of first edition then copies at cost. Does not copyright for author.

SCORE, Score, Crag Hill, Selby Spencer, 1015 NW Clifford Street, Pullman, WA 99163-3203. 1983. Articles, art, photos, interviews, criticism, reviews, letters, concrete art. "Our primary focus is the visual poem—creative, historical, theoretical—but we're also interested in any work pushing back boundaries, verse or prose. Subscription price includes 2 issues of *SCORE* plus occasional publications such as broadsides and postcards." circ. 150-250. 1/yr. Pub'd 1 issue 1998; expects 1 issue 1999, 1 issue 2000. sub. price: $10; per copy: $10; sample: $10. Back issues: query. 50pp; 8½×11; xerox. Reporting time: 2 weeks to 3 months. Publishes 20-25% of manuscripts submitted. Payment: 1 copy. Not copyrighted. Pub's reviews: 1 in 1998. §We would be interested in books and magazines with a visual/literal basis. Ads: none.

Scots Plaid Press (see also Persephone Press), Jeff Farr, President, 600 Kelly Road, Carthage, NC 28327, 910-947-2587; Fax 910-947-5112. 1987. Poetry. "Archival handbound chapbook. *Query first*; describe MS & PC include bio/vita, SASE. *Do not submit ms.* no more than 3 page sample. Accept no unsolicited ms." avg. press run 500-1.5M. Pub'd 9 titles 1998; expects 12 titles 1999, 24 titles 2000. avg. price, paper: $12. Discounts: 30% on orders of 5 copies; 40% for 10 copies. 40pp; 6×9, 5½×8½; †lp. Reporting time: 1 day to 1 month. Simultaneous submissions accepted: yes. Publishes 1% of manuscripts submitted. Payment: 10%. Does not copyright for author.

Scottwall Associates, Publishers, James Heig, 95 Scott Street, San Francisco, CA 94117, 415-861-1956. 1982. Non-fiction. "We publish books on California history, biographies." avg. press run 5M-10M. Pub'd 2 titles 1998; expects 2 titles 1999, 2-3 titles 2000. 3 titles listed in the *Small Press Record of Books in Print* (28th Edition, 1999-00). avg. price, cloth: $29.95; paper: $15. Discounts: 40% to bookstores in quantity orders; 40% to prepaid STOP orders; 30% single copy orders. 200pp; 8½×11; of. Reporting time: indefinite. Payment: 10% royalty on all books sold and paid for. Copyrights for author.

SCP NEWSLETTER, Tal Brooke, President and Editor; Brooks Alexander, Director of Research, PO Box 4308, Berkeley, CA 94704. 1975. Articles, interviews, reviews, letters, news items, non-fiction. "*SCP* is a non-profit organization that researches and publishes information on new religious cult movements and spiritual trends. No unsolicited Mss." circ. 18M. 4 journals, 4 newsletters published per year. Pub'd 4 issues 1998; expects 4 issues 1999, 4 issues 2000. sub. price: $25/year; per copy: $5; sample: free. Back issues: $5. Discounts: 40% for retailers. 40pp single journals; 60pp for double journals; 8½×11; desktop publishing. Reporting time: 3-6 weeks, only after telephone approval, do not submit before phone inquiry. Payment: varies. Copyrighted, does not revert to author. Pub's reviews: 4 in 1998. §Religion, metaphysics, cults, sociology and psychology of religion. Evangelical Press Assocation (EPA), Box 4550, Overland Park, KS 66204, Evangelical Council on Financial Accountability.

Scratch & Scribble Press, Lenore Good, PO Box 490, Ridge, NY 11961. 1995. Non-fiction. "We have been in the personalized childrens market and just started publishing outside material." avg. press run 5K. Expects 1 title 1999, 2-5 titles 2000. avg. price, paper: $19.95. Discounts: 1-4 copies 20%, 5-9 30%, 10-99 40% or 45% prepaid nonreturnable, 100+ 45% or 50% prepaid nonreturnable. 150pp; 8½×11. Simultaneous submissions accepted: yes. Publishes 5% of manuscripts submitted. Payment: individual. Copyrights for author. PMA.

SCRAWL MAGAZINE, Sam Lahoz, PO Box 205, New York, NY 10012, e-mail: Scrawlmag@Aol.com. 1995. Reviews, music. circ. 15M. 4/yr. Expects 4 issues 1999, 4 issues 2000. sub. price: $10; per copy: $2.50; sample: $3 ppd. Back issues: $3. 64pp; 8×10½. Reporting time: 2 months. Payment: none. Copyrighted, does not revert to author. Pub's review: 12 in 1998. §Music, art, comics, photography, politics, feminism, films. Ads: $235/$150/$90 1/4 page.

●THE SCRIBIA, Don A. Hoyt, Uju Ifeanyi, PO Box 68, Grambling State University, Grambling, LA 71245, 318-644-2072; hoytda@alpha0.gram.edu. 1966. Poetry, fiction, articles, art, interviews, criticism, reviews, letters, parts-of-novels, long-poems, plays, concrete art, non-fiction. "Emphasis on GSU student and alumni work, multi-culturalism, southern culture. Recent contributors: X.J. Kennedy, Pinkie Gordon Lane, Errol Miller, Mary Winters, Christopher Pressfield, Maitaika Favorite." circ. 800. 1/yr. Pub'd 1 issue 1998; expects 1 issue 1999, 1 issue 2000. sub. price: cops; per copy: cops; sample: cops. Back issues: cops. Discounts: none. 72pp; 5½×8½; †photocopies. Reporting time: 3-6 months. Simultaneous submissions accepted with notices. Publishes 20% of manuscripts submitted. Payment: 2 copies. Copyrighted, reverts to author. Pub's reviews: 2 in 1998. §Contemparary literature, multi-cultural issues. Ads: trade.

Scripta Humanistica, Bruno Damiani, Editor, 1383 Kersey Lane, Potomac, MD 20854, 301-294-7949; 301-340-1095. avg. press run 500. Pub'd 15 titles 1998. 4 titles listed in the *Small Press Record of Books in Print* (28th Edition, 1999-00). avg. price, cloth: $45. Discounts: 20%. 200pp; 6½×8½. Reporting time: 4 weeks. Simultaneous submissions accepted: no. Publishes 35% of manuscripts submitted. Payment: 5% of gross sales. Does not copyright for author.

SCRIVENER, Claire Ezzeddin, Coordinating Editor; Noah Bowers, Coordinating Editor; Rachel Appelbaum, Fiction Editor; Sam Semper, Fiction Editor; Emily Barton, Poetry Editor; Daphne Brunelle, Poetry Editor; Meredith Linden, Layout Editor, McGill University, 853 Sherbrooke Street W., Montreal, P.Q. H3A 2T6, Canada, 514-398-6588. 1980. Poetry, fiction, art, photos, interviews, criticism, reviews, non-fiction. "Recent

505

book reviews only. Prose less than 30 pages typed; creative shorts. Poetry 5-10 pages. Black & white photos and graphics. Please send international reply coupon (not U.S. stamps) + self-addressed envelopes. New material only—no reprints. Does not report from May to August." circ. 500. 1/yr. Pub'd 1 issue 1998; expects 1 issue 1999, 1 issue 2000. sub. price: $7 + $2 p/h; per copy: same; sample: same. Back issues: same. Discounts: 40% commission for 10 or more copies. 100pp; 8×8½. Reporting time: 4-6 months. We accept simultaneous submissions, but submitters must list the other journals to which they have made submissions. Payment: 1 free copy, more upon request. Copyrighted, reverts to author. Pub's reviews: 2 in 1998. §Canadian and American prose, poetry, criticism. Ads: currently under review. CMPA.

●**Scrivenery Press,** Ed Williams, Leila Joiner, PO Box 740969-180, Houston, TX 77274-0969, 713-665-6760; fax 713-665-8838; e-mail editors@scrivenery.com; website www.scrivenery.com. 1998. Fiction, non-fiction. "We are a royalty publisher of book-length fiction and nonfiction. Complete guidelines for #10 SASE. Needs: fiction-literary, mainstream, historical (no romance or fantasy), and literate thriller/suspense/mystery; nonfiction-humanities, pre-WWII history and biography, some how-to subjects. Query first with sample chapters; no unsolicited manuscripts. Open to unagented or new writers." avg. press run 2-5M. Expects 6 titles 1999, 12 titles 2000. avg. price, paper: $16. Discounts: distribution through Ingram Books; write with inquiries about bulk purchases. 300pp; 6×9; hi-res postscript rip electrostatic. Reporting time: queries: 4-8 weeks; ms: 8-16 weeks. Simultaneous submissions accepted: yes. Publishes 10% of manuscripts submitted. Payment: 10% to 12½% of retail price. Copyrights for author. PMA.

SE LA VIE WRITER'S JOURNAL, Rio Grande Press, Rosalie Avara, Editor, 4320 Canyon Drive #A12, Amarillo, TX 79109-5624. 1987. Poetry, fiction, articles, art, cartoons, interviews, reviews, letters, plays, concrete art, news items, non-fiction. "'Life' theme (La Vie) through; poems to 30 lines; short stories, essays, limited to 800 words. Recently published poems by Alan Frame, Myriam Bevers, Ruth McDaniels and Najwa Salam Brax. Also accept b&w cartoons, cover designs, b/w illustrations. Contests held each quarter in poetry, essays, short stories, with special monthly contests included. Subscribers receive free $5 entry coupon plus seasonal promotions" circ. 300. 4/yr. Pub'd 4 issues 1998; expects 4 issues 1999, 4 issues 2000. sub. price: $20 US, $25 others; per copy: $5 US, $6 others; sample: $2 US, $3 others. 80pp; 5½×8½; photocopied, saddle stapled. Reporting time: 6-8 weeks after contest ends. Simultaneous submissions accepted: no. Publishes 90% of manuscripts submitted. Payment: contests pay from $2 to $15; 1 copy to HM's and artists. Copyrighted, reverts to author. Pub's reviews: 12 in 1998. §Chapbooks of poetry, short stories, or mixed. Ads: $20/$10/$5 1/4 page.

Sea Challengers, Inc., 4 Sommerset Rise, Monterey, CA 93940, 831-373-6306, Fax 831-373-4566. 1977. avg. press run 5M. Pub'd 1 title 1998; expects 2 titles 1999, 2 titles 2000. 10 titles listed in the *Small Press Record of Books in Print* (28th Edition, 1999-00). avg. price, cloth: $25; paper: $21.50. Discounts: STOP 20%; 2-9 40%; 10-20 42%; 21-99 45%; 100+ 50%. 112pp; 7×9, 8×10; lp. Reporting time: 30 days. Simultaneous submissions accepted: yes. Publishes 10% of manuscripts submitted. Payment: 8% of retail on each book sold up to 49% & 4% of retail of books sold at 50% discount or below. Copyrights for author.

Sea Fog Press, Inc. (see also HARMONY: VOICES FOR A JUST FUTURE), Rose Evans, 447 20th Avenue, San Francisco, CA 94121, 415-221-8527. 1982. Non-fiction. "2 children's books published, 1 bimonthly magazine." avg. press run 5M. Expects 1 title 1999. 2 titles listed in the *Small Press Record of Books in Print* (28th Edition, 1999-00). avg. price, cloth: $12.95; paper: $7.95. Discounts: bookstores 4+ copies, 40%. 200pp; 8½×11; of. Reporting time: 1 month. Simultaneous submissions accepted: yes. Publishes .03% of manuscripts submitted. Payment: standard. Copyrights for author.

SEA KAYAKER, Christopher Cunningham, Editor; Leslie Forsberg, Executive Editor, PO Box 17170, Seattle, WA 98107-0870, 206-789-1326; Fax 206-781-1141; mail@seakayakermag.com. 1984. Fiction, articles, art, photos, cartoons, interviews, reviews, letters, non-fiction. "1M-3M words; specializing in sea kayaking; bias towards education and environmental." circ. 24M+. 6/yr. Pub'd 6 issues 1998; expects 6 issues 1999, 6 issues 2000. sub. price: $20.95; per copy: $3.95; sample: $5.75. Back issues: 1-2 issues $5.75, 3+ $4.90 each. Discounts: 45% minimum 10, no returns. 82+pp; 8×11; web. Reporting time: 2 months. Simultaneous submissions rarely accepted. Publishes 15% of manuscripts submitted. Payment: approx. $120 per publ. page, on publication. Copyrighted, reverts to author. Pub's reviews: 6 in 1998. §Sea kayaking. Ads: call for current rates 206-789-6413.

Sea Sports Publications, Robert J. Bachand, Editor; Mike Gachek, Associate Editor, PO Box 1435, Estero, FL 33928-1435, 941-992-2287, fax 941-992-2287. 1979. Photos, non-fiction. avg. press run 2M-3M. Pub'd 1 title 1998; expects 1 title 1999, 1 title 2000. 1 title listed in the *Small Press Record of Books in Print* (28th Edition, 1999-00). avg. price, cloth: $19.95; paper: $11.95. Discounts: 1 30%, 2-49 40%, 50+ 50%. 110-400pp; 6×9; of, camera-ready from laser printer. Reporting time: 6 weeks. Payment: 7.5%-10% of retail. Copyrights for author.

Seacoast Information Services, John Hacunda, 135 Auburn Road, Charlestown, RI 02813-6103, 401-364-6419. 1990. Non-fiction. "*Computers and Visual Stress: Staying Healthy.*" avg. press run 5M. Pub'd

1 title 1998; expects 1 title 1999, 2 titles 2000. 1 title listed in the *Small Press Record of Books in Print* (28th Edition, 1999-00). avg. price, paper: $12.95. Discounts: 3 or more, 40%; 200 or more, 50%. 100-200pp; 5½×8½; of. Copyrights for author.

Seal Press, Faith Conlon, Jennie Goode, 3131 Western Avenue, Suite 410, Seattle, WA 98121-1028, 206-283-7844, 800-754-0271 orders; fax 206-285-9410; E-mail sealprss@scn.org. 1976. Fiction, non-fiction. "Feminist fiction and women's studies. New Leaf Series for women in abusive relationships. Women in outdoors, sports, and popular culture, health and parenting." avg. press run 4M-10M. Pub'd 18 titles 1998; expects 12 titles 1999, 16 titles 2000. 116 titles listed in the *Small Press Record of Books in Print* (28th Edition, 1999-00). avg. price, cloth: $23.95; paper: $14.95. Discounts: standard. 5½×8½; of. Reporting time: 3 months. Payment: 7% (trade paperback); standard payment. Copyrights for author. PMA, Pacific NW Book Publishers' Association, Rocky Mtn. Book Publishers.

SeaStar Publishing Company, PO Box 741413, Dallas, TX 75374-1413. "Health care realted topics. Not accepting submissions at this time." avg. press run 2.5M-4M. Expects 3 titles 2000. 1 title listed in the *Small Press Record of Books in Print* (28th Edition, 1999-00). avg. price, paper: $9.95. Discounts: 2-3 10%, 4-6 20%, 7-10 30%, 11-24 40%, 25-49 42%, 50-99 45%, 100-299 50%, 300+ 53%. 80-120pp; 5×7. Does not copyright for author.

Second Aeon Publications, Peter Finch, 19 Southminster Road, Roath, Cardiff, Wales CF2 5AT, Great Britain, 01222-493093; peter.finch@dial.pipex.com. 1967. Poetry, art, long-poems, collages, concrete art. avg. press run 300-1M. Pub'd 1 title 1998. 2 titles listed in the *Small Press Record of Books in Print* (28th Edition, 1999-00). avg. price, paper: £3. Discounts: by arrangement. 50pp; size A4; mi, of. Reporting time: 2 weeks. Payment: by arrangement. Does not copyright for author. ALP.

Second Coming Press, A.D. Winans, PO Box 31249, San Francisco, CA 94131. 1972. Poetry, fiction. avg. press run 1M-1.5M. Pub'd 1 title 1998; expects 1 title 2000. 20 titles listed in the *Small Press Record of Books in Print* (28th Edition, 1999-00). avg. price, cloth: $12.95; paper: $4.95. Discounts: 20% library only if this listed source is quoted; bookstores 5+ books 40%. 64-72pp, anthologies 200-240pp; 5½×8½, anthologies 6×9; of. Reporting time: 30 days. Payment: 10% of press run, 50% of any profit after expenses are met. Only copyrights for author upon arrangement.

SECOND GUESS, Bob Conrad, PO Box 9382, Reno, NV 89507. 1991. Articles, photos, interviews, satire, criticism, reviews, music, letters, news items, non-fiction. "Mostly a punk slant or revolving issues relevant to punk rock" circ. 1M-2M. Sporadic. Pub'd 1 issue 1998. price per copy: $3; sample: $3. Back issues: $2. Discounts: none. 80pp; 5½×8½; †of. Publishes 10% of manuscripts submitted. Payment: none. Copyrighted, reverts to author. Pub's reviews: 50 in 1998. §Alternative living, music, anarchist politics, libertarianism, non-mainstream. Ads: none.

SECOND STONE, Jim Bailey, 1113 3rd Street, New Orleans, LA 70130-5630, 504-899-4014, e-Mail secstone@aol.com. 1988. Articles, photos, cartoons, interviews, reviews, music, letters, news items, non-fiction. circ. 4M. 6/yr. Pub'd 6 issues 1998; expects 6 issues 1999, 6 issues 2000. sub. price: $19; per copy: $4; sample: $4. Back issues: $4. 24pp; 11×14; web. Reporting time: 4-6 weeks. Payment: per agreement prior to publication. Copyrighted, reverts to author. Pub's reviews: 12 in 1998. §Religious, spiritual issues for gay/lesbian Christians. Ads: $450/$275.

Sedna Press, Joanne Townsend, Co-Editor; Ann Chandonnet, Co-Editor, 5522 Cope Street, Anchorage, AK 99518, 907-562-7835. 1981. Poetry. "We publish women poets of Alaska and the Pacific Northwest; by invitation." avg. press run 900. Expects 1 title 2000. 1 title listed in the *Small Press Record of Books in Print* (28th Edition, 1999-00). avg. price, paper: $10. Discounts: 40% standard. 90pp; 5½×8½. Publishes 0% of manuscripts submitted. Payment: we are a cooperative women's press; we share in costs and profits. Copyrights for author.

See Sharp Press, Charles Bufe, Publisher, PO Box 1731, Tucson, AZ 85702-1731, 520-628-8720; Fax 520-628-8720; seesharp@earthlink.net; home.earthlink.net/~seesharp. 1984. Non-fiction. "Length is unimportant—quality is the deciding factor; our published works range from a 4,000 word pamphlet to a 100,000-plus word quotations book. Biases are towards works with anarchist and/or atheist views and toward works providing practical information, especially in the areas of music, sex, and non-12 step alcohol abuse treatment" avg. press run 2M-4M. Pub'd 13 titles 1998; expects 7 titles 1999, 4 titles 2000. 30 titles listed in the *Small Press Record of Books in Print* (28th Edition, 1999-00). avg. price, paper: $11.95; other: $2.50 pamphlets. Discounts: books exclusively distributed by LPC, pamphlets distributed by AK Distribution and Left Bank Distribution in U.S. Books 192pp, pamphlets 32pp; 6×9, 5½×8½; of. Reporting time: 1 month. Simultaneous submissions accepted: no. Publishes under 1% of manuscripts submitted. Payment: for books - normally 7% first run, 8.5% to 10% thereafter; quarterly payments; for pamphlets - 10% of press run in lieu of royalties. Sometimes copyright for author if author overseas, otherwise no.

Seed Center, Norton DeRay, Director, PO Box 1700, Redway, CA 95560-1700, 707-923-2524. 1972. Fiction, non-fiction. "Generally oriented but not limited to self-awareness, self-discovery & metaphysical topics." avg. press run 3M. Expects 1 title 1999, 1 title 2000. 2 titles listed in the *Small Press Record of Books in Print* (28th Edition, 1999-00). avg. price, paper: $16. Discounts: trade, jobber. 150-300pp; 4¼×7⅛, 6×9; of. Reporting time: varies, 1-4 months. Payment: 8%-15% paid semi-annually. Copyrights for author.

SEED SAVERS EXCHANGE, Kent Whealy, 3076 North Winn Road, Decorah, IA 52101, 319-382-5990, Fax 319-382-5872. 1975. Articles, photos, interviews, letters, non-fiction. "Seed Exchange of Heirloom Vegetable & Fruit Varieties." circ. 8M. 3/yr. Pub'd 3 issues 1998; expects 3 issues 1999, 3 issues 2000. 4 titles listed in the *Small Press Record of Books in Print* (28th Edition, 1999-00). sub. price: $25 US, $30 Canada and Mexico, $40 overseas. Back issues: not available. 200pp; 7½×10½; of. Payment: none. Copyrighted. Ads: none accepted.

Seekers Press, Steve Ladd, 11538 Fremont N., Seattle, WA 98133, 206-367-3468. 1997. Fiction, non-fiction. "Cooperative publisher of serious ('seeking') fiction and non-fiction. Myself and several other authors are getting together to cooperatively publish. Hard to say how far this will go." avg. press run 1M. Expects 1 title 1999, 1-2 titles 2000. avg. price, paper: $19.95. Discounts: 1-2 no discount, 3-199 40%, 200-499 50%, 500+ 55%. 400pp; 6×9; of. Reporting time: 1 month. Simultaneous submissions accepted: yes. Payment: no royalties—each author finances own title and reeps all proceeds. Does not copyright for author.

SEEMS, Karl Elder, Editor, c/o Lakeland College, Box 359, Sheboygan, WI 53082-0359. 1971. Poetry, fiction, articles, reviews, parts-of-novels, long-poems. "No. 14, *What Is the Future of Poetry?*, in its third printing, contains essays by Cutler, Dacey, Dunn, Evans, Elliott, Etter, Flaherty, Gildner, Hathaway, Heffernan, Hershon, Heyen, Hilton, Matthews, McKeown, Morgan, Oliphant, Rice, Scott, Sobin, Stryk, and Zimmer. ($5)" circ. 350. Irregular. Pub'd 1 issue 1998; expects 1 issue 1999, 1 issue 2000. 3 titles listed in the *Small Press Record of Books in Print* (28th Edition, 1999-00). sub. price: $16/4 issues; per copy: $4; sample: $4. Discounts: 25%. 40pp; 8½×7; of. Reporting time: 1-4 months. Simultaneous submissions accepted: no. Publishes less than .5% of manuscripts submitted. Payment: copies. Copyrighted, reverts to author.

Selah Publishing, Curtis Jenkins, Melinda Mercury, PO Box 721508, Berkley, MI 48072-1508, 810-293-3169. 1986. Articles, photos, interviews, satire, criticism, reviews, letters, parts-of-novels, news items, non-fiction. avg. press run 3-5M. Pub'd 1 title 1998; expects 2 titles 1999. 1 title listed in the *Small Press Record of Books in Print* (28th Edition, 1999-00). avg. price, cloth: $22.95; paper: $14.95; other: $17.95 spiral (cone). Discounts: 10 40%. 275pp; 5⅜×8½; of, lp. Reporting time: 2 weeks - 1 month. Payment: negotiable. Copyrights for author.

Selah Publishing Co. Inc., David P. Schaap, PO Box 3037, 58 Pearl Street, Kingston, NY 12401, 914-338-2816, 914-338-2991, e-mail selahpub@aol.com. 1988. Poetry, music. "Publish primarily in the field of Church Music and Hymnology. Books vary in length from small to large publications." avg. press run 5M. Pub'd 2 titles 1998; expects 2 titles 1999, 3-4 titles 2000. 14 titles listed in the *Small Press Record of Books in Print* (28th Edition, 1999-00). avg. price, cloth: $12; paper: $9. Discounts: trade 1-3 copies 20%, 4-up 40%. 200pp; 6×9; of. Reporting time: 1-2 months. Simultaneous submissions accepted: yes. Payment: generally 10% of retail sales price. Copyrights for author.

Select Press (see also JOURNAL OF SOCIAL BEHAVIOR AND PERSONALITY), Roderick P. Crandall, Ph.D., PO Box 37, Corte Madera, CA 94925, 415-924-1612. 1986. "Academic reserch, psychology, speech, business, sociology, etc." Pub'd 7 titles 1998; expects 6 titles 1999, 6 titles 2000. 6 titles listed in the *Small Press Record of Books in Print* (28th Edition, 1999-00).

Selective Books, Inc., Lee Howard, Box 984, Oldsmar, FL 34677. 1970. "Business opportunity and moneymaking books related to business." avg. press run 6M. Expects 2 titles 1999, 2 titles 2000. 5 titles listed in the *Small Press Record of Books in Print* (28th Edition, 1999-00). avg. price, paper: $15. Discounts: 40% to retail stores; 50% to wholesalers or mail order dealers. Quantity lot prices for 100 or more by quote. 100pp; web offset. Reporting time: immediate, query first. Payment: individual. Does not copyright for author.

SelectiveHouse Publishers, Inc., Gerilynne Seigneur, PO Box 10095, Gaithersburg, MD 20898, 301-990-2999; email sr@selectivehouse.com; www.selectivehouse.com. 1997. Fiction, non-fiction. "See our web page for the types of books published. Primarily mainstream fiction with science fiction and/or spiritual overtones." avg. press run 2M. Pub'd 2 titles 1998; expects 2 titles 1999, 3 titles 2000. 4 titles listed in the *Small Press Record of Books in Print* (28th Edition, 1999-00). avg. price, paper: $12.95. 300pp; 5½×8½. Reporting time: 6-8 weeks. Simultaneous submissions accepted: yes. Publishes less than 1% of manuscripts submitted. Copyrights for author.

Self Healing Press, PO Box 13837, Scottsdale, AZ 85267, 602-998-1041. 1987. Poetry, non-fiction. "Looking for as yet undiscovered books on medical treatment, products, and therapy." avg. press run 2-10M. Pub'd 4-6 titles 1998; expects 4 titles 1999, 6 titles 2000. 2 titles listed in the *Small Press Record of Books in Print* (28th Edition, 1999-00). avg. price, paper: $9-$20. 50-300pp; 8×10; †web. Reporting time: 30 days. Payment:

standard. Copyrights for author.

Selous Foundation Press, 325 Pennsylvania Avenue, SE, Washington, DC 20001. 1987. avg. press run 3M. Pub'd 2 titles 1998; expects 4 titles 1999, 6 titles 2000. 7 titles listed in the *Small Press Record of Books in Print* (28th Edition, 1999-00). avg. price, cloth: $17.95; paper: $5.95. Discounts: bookstores-prorated by # of copies, discounters/sales reps—60%/60 days, 55%/90 days. 250pp; 6×9. Reporting time: 90 days. Payment: negotiable. Copyrights for author. Publishers Marketing Assoc., American Booksellers Assoc.

‡SEMIGLOSS, R.D. Granados, Maria Valle, 1623 Lenox Avenue #2, Miami Beach, FL 33139-2434. 1995. Fiction, articles, art, cartoons, interviews, satire, criticism, reviews, non-fiction. circ. 1M-5M. 2/yr. Pub'd 2 issues 1998; expects 2 issues 1999, 2 issues 2000. sub. price: $6; per copy: $3; sample: $2. Back issues: $2. 32pp; 8×10; of. Reporting time: 4 months. Publishes 50% of manuscripts submitted. Payment: none as of yet. Copyrighted, reverts to author. Pub's reviews: 10 in 1998. §Music, culture, anything interesting. Ads: $250/$150/$75 1/4 page.

Semiotext Foreign Agents Books Series (see also SEMIOTEXT(E)), Jim Fleming, Sylvere Lotringer, PO Box 568, Brooklyn, NY 11211, 718-963-2603; E-mail semiotexte@aol.com. 1983. "Small books under 250 pages; politics, philosophy and culture" avg. press run 5M. Pub'd 3 titles 1998; expects 5 titles 1999, 7 titles 2000. avg. price, paper: $7. Discounts: trade, 40%, distributors 50%. 200pp; 4½×7; of. Reporting time: 6 weeks. Payment: arranged per title. Copyrights for author.

SEMIOTEXT(E), Autonomedia, Inc., Semiotext Foreign Agents Books Series, Sylvere Lotringer, Jim Fleming, PO Box 568, Brooklyn, NY 11211, 718-963-2603, e-Mail semiotexte@aol.com. 1974. "Do not solicit submissions" circ. 6M. 2/yr. Pub'd 2 issues 1998; expects 2 issues 1999, 2 issues 2000. sub. price: $16; per copy: varies; sample: $12. Discounts: trade 40%, distributors 50%. 350pp; 6×10; of. Publishes 2% of manuscripts submitted. Payment: varies. Copyrighted, reverts to author. Pub's reviews.

Senay Publishing Inc., James Senay, President, PO Box 397, Chesterland, OH 44026, 216-256-4435, fax 216-256-2237. 1979. avg. press run 20M. Expects 1 title 1999. 2 titles listed in the *Small Press Record of Books in Print* (28th Edition, 1999-00). avg. price, paper: $7.95. Discounts: on request. 200pp; 6×9; of. Copyrights for author.

SENECA REVIEW, Deborah Tall, Hobart & William Smith Colleges, Geneva, NY 14456, 315-781-3392; Fax 315-781-3348; senecareview@hws.edu. 1970. Poetry, articles, interviews, criticism, long-poems. circ. 1M. 2/yr. Pub'd 2 issues 1998; expects 2 issues 1999, 2 issues 2000. sub. price: $8, $15/2 years; per copy: $5; sample: $5. Back issues: $5. Discounts: 40% trade for stores. 100pp; 8½×5½; lp. Reporting time: 8-12 weeks. Simultaneous submissions accepted: no. Publishes 1% of manuscripts submitted. Payment: 2 copies and a 2-year subscription. Copyrighted, reverts to author. Ads: $75, special small press rates, exchange. CLMP, NYSSPA.

Senior Press, Miriam Bush, PO Box 21362, Hilton Island Head, SC 29925, 803-681-5970, Fax 803-681-3971. 1993. Fiction. avg. press run 1M-2M. Pub'd 2 titles 1998; expects 2 titles 1999, 1 title 2000. 4 titles listed in the *Small Press Record of Books in Print* (28th Edition, 1999-00). avg. price, cloth: $18-$22; paper: $10-$13. 250-400pp; 5×8, 5½×8½; of. Reporting time: 2 months. Simultaneous submissions accepted: yes. Payment: negotiable. Copyrights for author. PAS.

THE $ENSIBLE SOUND, Karl Nehring, 403 Darwin Drive, Snyder, NY 14226, 716-833-0930. 1976. Articles, art, photos, cartoons, interviews, satire, criticism, reviews, music, letters, news items, non-fiction. "We run mainly audio equipment reviews, musical recording reviews, audio semi-technical articles, and audio and music industry news." circ. 13M. 6/yr. Pub'd 4 issues 1998; expects 6 issues 1999, 6 issues 2000. sub. price: $29; per copy: $6; sample: $3. Back issues: 5 each $3 each after one year old. Discounts: 5 or more - 20% discount. 112pp; 5½×8½; of. Reporting time: 2 weeks. Simultaneous submissions accepted: no. Publishes 30% of manuscripts submitted. Payment: yes. Copyrighted, reverts to author. Pub's reviews: 14 in 1998. §Technical, music related, audio related, Hi Fi, Stereo, Home theater. Ads: $700/$420/$800/$500.

SEPIA, Kawabata Press, Colin David Webb, Editor, Knill Cross House, Higher Anderton Road, Millbrook, Nr Torpoint, Cornwall, England. 1977. Poetry, fiction, articles, art, reviews. "Shorter prose (under about 2.5M words preferred), shorter poems (under 40 lines preferred), short reviews (under 2.5M words preferred). Recent contributors: Tom Kretz, Jonathan Berkowitz, Arnold Stead, Asher Torren, Jesse Glass Jur." circ. 100. 3/yr. Pub'd 3 issues 1998; expects 3 issues 1999, 3 issues 2000. sub. price: $10; per copy: $5; sample: $2. 32pp; 6×8½; of. Reporting time: 14 days. Payment: free copy. Copyrighted, reverts to author. Pub's reviews: 19 in 1998. §Poetry, fiction.

Serena Bay Books, Celeste Ewers, Publisher, PO Box 1655, Cooper Station, New York, NY 10276, 212-260-5580. 1992. Fiction, art, photos, non-fiction. avg. press run 1M-3M. 12 titles listed in the *Small Press Record of Books in Print* (28th Edition, 1999-00). avg. price, paper: $9.95. Discounts: 2-4 20%, 5+ 40%. 100-200pp; 5½×8½; of. Reporting time: 2 months. Payment: varies. Copyrights for author. PMA.

Serendipity Systems (see also THE ELECTRONIC PUBLISHING FORUM), John Galuszka, PO Box 140, San Simeon, CA 93452. 1986. Fiction, non-fiction. "Serendipity Systems publishes Books-on-Disks editions (fiction) and distributes Bookware editions (any genre or type of book). All books are 'printed' on IBM-PC computer disks." avg. press run printed to order. Pub'd 19 titles 1998. 17 titles listed in the *Small Press Record of Books in Print* (28th Edition, 1999-00). avg. price, other: Books-on-Disks $6-$10; Bookware $4. Discounts: to 45%. †IBM-PC computer disks. Reporting time: 4 weeks. Payment: Books-on-Disks 33%, Bookware 25%. Copyrights for author. Digital Publishing Association.

SERIE D'ECRITURE, Burning Deck Press, Rosmarie Waldrop, 71 Elmgrove Avenue, Providence, RI 02906. 1986. Poetry, fiction, long-poems. "Translations of current French writing. No unsolicited submissions needed." circ. 500. 1/yr. Pub'd 1 issue 1998; expects 1 issue 1999, 1 issue 2000. sub. price: $16/2 years; per copy: $10; sample: $10. Back issues: $6. Discounts: 40-50% dependent upon contract. 64pp; 5½x8½; of. Payment: copies. Copyrighted, reverts to author. ALP.

Serpent & Eagle Press, Jo Mish, RD#1 Box 29B, Laurens, NY 13796, 607-432-2990. 1981. Poetry, fiction, art, photos, non-fiction. "I've shifted emphasis to short book-length work on historical & folk-lore oriented subjects. I'll put out an occasional book of poetry. Not accepting submissions during 1999-00." avg. press run 200. Expects 1 title 2000. avg. price, cloth: $40; paper: $10. Discounts: 40%. 30pp; 6x8; †1p. Simultaneous submissions accepted: no. Payment: varies. Does not copyright for author.

Seven Buffaloes Press (see also BLACK JACK & VALLEY GRAPEVINE; THE AZOREAN EXPRESS; THE BREAD AND BUTTER CHRONICLES; HILL AND HOLLER; THE BADGER STONE CHRONICLES), Art Coelho, Box 249, Big Timber, MT 59011. 1973. Poetry, fiction, art, photos, interviews, reviews, parts-of-novels, long-poems, collages. "Book-length manuscripts are not being accepted at this time. I do publish some books, even novels, but the authors are those that have had work in my magazines." avg. press run 750. Pub'd 8 titles 1998; expects 2 titles 1999. 55 titles listed in the *Small Press Record of Books in Print* (28th Edition, 1999-00). avg. price, paper: $7.75. Discounts: 1-4, 0%; 5 copies or over, 40%. 80pp; 5½x8½; †of. Reporting time: within a week; sometimes same day. Payment: negotiable. Copyrights for author. CLMP.

●7th Generation, 621-202 4th Avenue North, Saskatoon, SK S7K 3L7, Canada, 306-652-6554; www.7th-Generation.com. 1999. Fiction, articles, non-fiction. "Publisher particularly interested in biographies, true accounts and Christian works. Publisher offers marketing, PR and legal support. Proposals accepted by email; manuscripts are not accepted by email." avg. press run 10M. Expects 1 title 1999, 3-5 titles 2000. 1 title listed in the *Small Press Record of Books in Print* (28th Edition, 1999-00). Discounts: varies up to 65%. Reporting time: 8 weeks. Simultaneous submissions accepted if notice given. Publisher arranges copyright.

SEWANEE REVIEW, George Core, Editor, Univ. of the South, 735 University Avenue, Sewanee, TN 37383-1000, 931-598-1246. 1892. Poetry, fiction, articles, criticism, reviews, letters, parts-of-novels, non-fiction. "Publish book reviews, but books and reviewers are selected by editor." circ. 3,560. 4/yr. Pub'd 4 issues 1998; expects 4 issues 1999, 4 issues 2000. sub. price: $24 instit., $18 indiv.; per copy: $6.25; sample: $6.25. Back issues: $8 for 1964 onward; before 1964 send inquiry. Discounts: 15% to subscription agents. 192pp; 6x9; lp. Reporting time: 3-6 weeks after receipt. Simultaneous submissions accepted: no. Publishes less than .5% of manuscripts submitted. Payment: $10-$12/printed page for prose; 60¢/line for poetry. Copyrighted, we request partial rights. Pub's reviews: 126 in 1998. §New fiction & poetry; literary criticism; biography, memoirs, and general nonfiction. Ads: $210/$132. CLMP.

SF COMMENTARY, Bruce Gillespie, 59 Keele Street, Collingwood, Victoria 3066, Australia, (03) 419-4797. 1969. Articles, art, photos, cartoons, interviews, criticism, reviews, letters, non-fiction. "'Straight talk about science fiction': non-academic but rigorous reviews and criticism of science fiction and fantasy field. Recent contributors: George Turner, Dave Langford, Colin Steele." circ. 250-300. Infrequent. Pub'd 3 issues 1998; expects 3 issues 1999, 3 issues 2000. sub. price: $US25/5 issues; per copy: $US6; sample: $US6. Back issues: $US6. Discounts: none. 40pp; 8¼x11¾; of. Reporting time: 4 weeks. Payment: none. Copyrighted, reverts to author. Pub's reviews: 200 in 1998. §science fiction/criticism of SF/FANTASY cinema/general literature. Ads: $US200/$100/$6 per column inch.

SF EYE, Stephen P. Brown, PO Box 18539, Asheville, NC 28814, Fax 828-285-9400; eyebrown@interpath.com. 1987. Articles, art, interviews, satire, criticism, non-fiction, reviews, letters. "Size of mag allows some lengthy material up to 12M words. Mag is known for graphic innovation. The leading critical journal in the genre, has published original material by most of the fields well-known writers" circ. 5M. 2/yr. Pub'd 2 issues 1998; expects 2 issues 1999, 2 issues 2000. sub. price: $12.50 for 3 issues; per copy: $5; sample: $5. Back issues: write for details. Discounts: 40% to stores, 50% to wholesalers. 124pp; 8x10½; of. Reporting time: 1-2 months. Publishes 20% of manuscripts submitted. Payment: copies. Copyrighted, reverts to author. Pub's reviews: 35 in 1998. §Science fiction, contemporary culture, science. Ads: write for details.

SFEST, LTD., M.T. Nowak, S.J. Cucchiana, G. Carlson, S. Borowski, M. Tatlow, PO Box 1238, Simpsonville, SC 29681. 1990. Poetry, fiction, art, cartoons, interviews, satire, criticism, reviews, letters. "We look for humor, satire, wit and intelligence in all we publish." circ. 500. 4/yr. Pub'd 4 issues 1998; expects 4 issues 1999, 4 issues 2000. sub. price: $20; per copy: $5; sample: $5. Discounts: none. 50-100pp; 8½×11; of. Reporting time: 3-4 weeks (usually). Payment: complimentary copy. Not copyrighted. Pub's reviews: 5 in 1998. §Poetry, fiction. Ads: $500/$200/$100 1/4 page.

SF3**, Jeanne Gomoll, PO Box 1624, Madison, WI 53701-1624, 608-267-7483 (days); 608-255-9905 (evenings). 1988. 3 titles listed in the *Small Press Record of Books in Print* (28th Edition, 1999-00). 112pp; 7×8½.

SHADES OF DECEMBER, Alexander Danner, Brandy L. Straus, PO Box 244, Selden, NY 11784, E-mail eilonwy@innocent.com; www2.crosswinds.net/new-york/~shadesof12. 1998. Poetry, fiction, satire, letters, parts-of-novels, long-poems, plays, non-fiction. "Contributors: Joe Lucia, Judy Thompson, and Sharron Belson. Prose length: up to 1500 words. Poetry length: up to 150 lines. $1 reading fee for non-electronic submissions." circ. 200. 4/yr. Pub'd 4 issues 1998; expects 4 issues 1999, 4 issues 2000. sub. price: $10; per copy: $2.75; sample: $2.75. Back issues: $3. 52pp; 5½×8½; †mi. Reporting time: 4-6 weeks. Accept simultaneous submissions if noted as such. Payment: 2 copies. Not copyrighted. Ads: $50/$30.

SHADOW KNOWS MOVIEEYE, Greg LaLiberte, PO Box 223, Brighton, MI 48116, E-mail greg@videovamp.com; www.movieeye.com/video; www.tln.org/~greg; www.jamrag.com. 1995. News items, non-fiction. "Length of material: 500 words." circ. 1M. 6/yr. Pub'd 6 issues 1998; expects 6 issues 1999, 10 issues 2000. sub. price: $6; per copy: $1; sample: $1. Back issues: negotiable. Discounts: negotiable. 12pp; 8½×11; of. Simultaneous submissions accepted: yes. Publishes 50% of manuscripts submitted. Payment: none. Copyrighted, reverts to author. Pub's reviews: 6 in 1998. §Alternative journalism, generation X. Ads: none. Free Press Association.

Shadowlight Press, Robert Randolph Jr. Medcalf, PO Box 746, Biglerville, PA 17307. 1981. Poetry. "Short anthologies of poetry. For now I will be publishing a backlog inherited from our earlier incarnation as Quixsilver Press." avg. press run 50-100. Expects 1 title 1999, 1 title 2000. avg. price, paper: $3. 16pp; 6×9; †computer printer. Reporting time: 3 months. Simultaneous submissions accepted: yes. Publishes 10% of manuscripts submitted. Payment: contributor copy. Does not copyright for author.

THE SHAKESPEARE NEWSLETTER, John W. Mahon, Thomas A. Pendleton, English Department, Iona College, New Rochelle, NY 10801. 1951. Poetry, articles, criticism, reviews, letters, news items. circ. 2.5M. 4/yr. Pub'd 4 issues 1998; expects 4 issues 1999, 4 issues 2000. sub. price: indiv. $12, instit. $12, $14 foreign; per copy: $3; sample: $3 + 50¢ postage. Back issues: $3 each $12 per yr plus $1.50 postage. Discounts: none. 20pp; 8½×11; †of. Reporting time: 1-2 months. Payment: 3 copies. Not copyrighted. Pub's reviews: 30+ in 1998. §Scholarly and any interesting Shakespeareana and related material. Ads: $420/$230.

Shallowater Press, Todd Knowlton, PO Box 1151, Shallowater, TX 79363, 806-873-3617, e-mail swpress@aol.com. 1995. Non-fiction. avg. press run 3.5M. Pub'd 1 title 1998; expects 2 titles 1999, 3 titles 2000. 1 title listed in the *Small Press Record of Books in Print* (28th Edition, 1999-00). avg. price, cloth: $18.95. 256pp; 5½×8½; of. Reporting time: 6 weeks. Simultaneous submissions accepted: yes. Payment: 7-15% royalty. Copyrights for author.

SHAMAN'S DRUM: A Journal of Experiential Shamanism, Timothy White, PO Box 97, Ashland, OR 97520, 541-552-0839. 1985. Poetry, articles, art, photos, interviews, reviews, letters, news items, non-fiction. "We seek contributions directed to a general but well-informed audience. Past contributors have included Jeanne Achterberg, Paula Gunn Allen, Brooke Medicine Eagle, Richard Erdoes. We see *Shaman's Drum* as an ongoing effort to expand, challenge, and refine our readers' and our own understanding of shamanism in practice. In the process, we cover a wide range of related topics—from indigenous medicineway practices to contemporary shamanic psychotherapies, from transpersonal healing ceremonies to ecstatic spiritual practices. Our focus is on experiential shamanism. We prefer original material that is based on, or illustrated with, firsthand knowledge and personal experience. Articles should, however, be well documented with descriptive examples and pertinent background information. We are looking for examples of not only how shamanism has transformed individual lives but also practical ways it can help ensure the survival of life on this planet. We want material that captures the heart and feeling of shamanism and that can inspire people to direct action and participation." circ. 18M. 4/yr. Pub'd 4 issues 1998; expects 4 issues 1999, 4 issues 2000. sub. price: $16; per copy: $5.95; sample: $5. Back issues: $5 each or 4 for $12. Discounts: retail 30%, classroom 30%, wholesale 50%. 80+pp; 8½×11; of. Reporting time: 3 months. Simultaneous submissions accepted: no. Publishes 5% of manuscripts submitted. Payment: 5¢ per word. Copyrighted, rights reverting to author is optional. Pub's reviews: 24 in 1998. §Shamanism, Native American spirituality, Entheogens. Ads: $1100/$575/$400 1/3 page.

Shann Press, Yun-Pi Shann, PO Box 524, Wickenburg, AZ 85358, 520-684-9142; Fax 520-684-0202; E-mail jbarj@primenet.com. 1989. Fiction. "Vietnam fiction." Expects 1 title 1999, 3 titles 2000. 1 title listed in the *Small Press Record of Books in Print* (28th Edition, 1999-00). avg. price, paper: $4.95. 250-300pp; 4-3/16×6⅞; lp. Reporting time: 8-12 weeks. Copyrights for author.

Shaolin Communications, Richard O'Connor, PO Box 58547, Salt Lake City, UT 84158, 801-595-1123. 1993. Poetry, fiction, articles, art, photos, music, non-fiction. "We will be publishing a wide range of materials from Kung Fu and Tai Chi instruction books, to novels and photography/art books. Exercise videos are also in preproduction. One of our first releases is *Sid's Place*. This 357 page novel tells the story of a 1969 drug runner who is forced into the underground movement. A how-to book is also scheduled for spring release: *American Tenant Handbook* is a renter's guide that will also benefit landlords." avg. press run 5M. Pub'd 4 titles 1998; expects 4 titles 1999, 4 titles 2000. 1 title listed in the *Small Press Record of Books in Print* (28th Edition, 1999-00). avg. price, cloth: $24.95; paper: $18.88; other: Student Tai Chi and Kung Fu manuals = $10. 96-352pp; 8½×11. Reporting time: 6 weeks. Simultaneous submissions accepted: yes. Payment: varied. Copyrights for author.

SHARE INTERNATIONAL, Benjamin Creme, Peter Liefhebber, PO Box 971, North Hollywood, CA 91603, 818-785-6300, Fax 818-904-9132, share@shareintl.org, www.shareintl.org/. 1982. Articles, photos, interviews, reviews, letters, news items, non-fiction. "Combines socially-conscious and spiritual perspectives on world events and news about emergence of Maitreya, the World Teacher." circ. 5M. 10/yr. Pub'd 10 issues 1998; expects 10 issues 1999, 10 issues 2000. sub. price: $30; per copy: $3.50; sample: $3.50. Back issues: $3.50. Discounts: library $20, volume discount on back issues 20%. 24-40pp; 8½×11; of. Payment: none. Copyrighted, does not revert to author. Pub's reviews: 4 in 1998. §Subjects we cover. Ads: none. PMA, NAPRA.

SHARING & CARING, Halbar Publishing, Bill Halbert, Mary Barnes, 289 Taylor Street, Wills Point, TX 75169-9732. 1994. Poetry, fiction, articles, art, photos, cartoons, interviews, satire, criticism, reviews, music, letters, long-poems, news items, non-fiction. "Will publish long or continued material and furnish extra pages if paid for, our cost. Marian Ford Park, Linda Hutton, Uncle Mickey (Mickey H. Clarke), Terri Warden, Mary Kraft, Victoria Widry, Robert R. Hentz, Ni Nichi, Charles H. Thornton, Thomas Lynn, Joe Sharp, Jeff Klein, Betty Webster Bishop, Jani Johe Webster, Bruce Ellison (archives), many of the best too numorous to list." circ. 100+. 4/yr. Pub'd 4 issues 1998; expects 4 issues 1999, 4 issues 2000. sub. price: $55; per copy: $9; sample: $9. Discounts: commensurate with inquiry, ours run $2.16 to mail, multiples would cut this down. 80pp; 8½×11; †mi. Reporting time: with SASE, next day's mail usually. Simultaneous submissions accepted: yes. Publishes 90% of manuscripts submitted. Payment: lots of cash contests w/cash award for best voted poetry and prose each quarter. Not copyrighted. Pub's reviews: 8 in 1998. §All except porn, occult, excess sex and profanity. Ads: $22/$15/25¢ per word classifieds.

SHARING IDEAS FOR PROFESSIONAL SPEAKERS, Dorothy M. Walters, PO Box 398, Glendora, CA 91740, 626-335-8069; fax 626-335-6127. 1978. "Our newsmagazine is to the world of paid speaking what Variety is to show business. We feature stories, news, announcements about speakers, their books, cassette albums, meeting planners and all elements of the world of paid speaking. We restrict material: by and about speakers. Submissions by subscribers only." circ. 6M. 6/yr. Pub'd 6 issues 1998; expects 6 issues 1999, 6 issues 2000. sub. price: $95 2/yr, includes free *Directory of Agents & Bureaus* and *How to Be Booked by Speakers Bureaus* album; Canada and Mexico $124 2/yr (includes book in Mexico); all other foreign $179 2/yr, includes book; sample: $10 one time only. Back issues: varies as to availability, $10. 48+pp; 8½×11; web offset. Reporting time: 2 months. Payment: none. Copyrighted, reverts to author. Pub's reviews: 90 in 1998. §We are interested in anything on the subject of paid speaking. Must be advertiser or subscriber. Ads: $539/$350/$600 outside back cover/$570 inside cover. NSA, GVCNSA.

SHARK QUARTERLY, Wayne Ellwood, 129 Dunbarton Court, Ottawa, Ontario, K1K 4L6, Canada, 613-741-7407 tel/fax. 1995. Photos, interviews, criticism, news items, non-fiction. "500-2,000 words average. Multi-part serial articles" circ. 2M. 4/yr. Pub'd 4 issues 1998; expects 4 issues 1999, 4 issues 2000. sub. price: $20. Back issues: $10. 48pp; 8½×11; †of. Payment: negotiable/solicit many items free. Copyrighted, generally rights revert to author. Pub's reviews: 2 in 1998. Ads: $2400/yr; $1400/yr; $200 2 X 2.

Sharp Publishing, Margaret L. Mooney, Carroll Menges, Peter Libby, 2767 Highland Drive, Carlsbad, CA 92008, fax 619-729-3838; 619-729-2582. 1991. Non-fiction. "Health, self-help, etc. Lonely pain of cancer, home care, terminally ill, swingingin, in the wind, kids, survivors of a crisis, widows are special, first hours through recovery, home health, home nursing. No new age materials please." avg. press run 3M-5M. Pub'd 2 titles 1998; expects 2 titles 1999, 4 titles 2000. 4 titles listed in the *Small Press Record of Books in Print* (28th Edition, 1999-00). avg. price, paper: $15; other: $11-$16. Discounts: 55%. 150pp; 5½×8½. Reporting time: 3 weeks. Payment: we buy all rights. PMA, ABA.

SHATTERED WIG REVIEW, Sonny Bodkin, 425 E. 31st, Baltimore, MD 21218, 301-243-6888. 1988. Poetry, fiction, articles, art, photos, cartoons, interviews, satire, letters, parts-of-novels, collages, non-fiction. "Recent contributors include John Bennet, Al Ackerman, Cynthia Hendershot and Dan Raphael. Interested in the blurry areas between 'sanity' and 'madness' and how society shapes consciousness" circ. 500. 2/yr. Expects 4 issues 1999, 4 issues 2000. sub. price: $9; per copy: $5; sample: $4. 80pp; 8½×8½; of. Reporting time: 1-2 months. Simultaneous submissions accepted: yes. Publishes 30% of manuscripts submitted. Payment: 1 copy. Not copyrighted. Pub's reviews: 3 in 1998. §Prose poetry, social commentary, rants.

512

SHAW: THE ANNUAL OF BERNARD SHAW STUDIES, Pennsylvania State University Press, Fred D. Crawford, Penn State Press, Suite C, 820 N. University Drive, University Park, PA 16802-1711, 814-865-1327. 1951. Articles, interviews, criticism, reviews, letters. circ. 2M. 1/yr. Pub'd 1 issue 1998; expects 1 issue 1999, 1 issue 2000. sub. price: $35; per copy: $35. 265pp; 6×9; of. Reporting time: 2 months. Simultaneous submissions accepted: no. Publishes 25-30% of manuscripts submitted. Payment: 1 copy of the volume. Copyrighted, does not revert to author. Pub's reviews: 3 in 1998. §Shaw. Ads: none. AAUP.

Shearer Publishing, Katherine Shearer, President, 406 Post Oak Road, Fredericksburg, TX 78624, 830-997-6529. 1981. Fiction, non-fiction. avg. press run 2M-40M. Pub'd 2 titles 1998; expects 4 titles 1999, 4 titles 2000. 41 titles listed in the *Small Press Record of Books in Print* (28th Edition, 1999-00). avg. price, cloth: $15.95; paper: $14.95. 250pp. Reporting time: average is 3 months. Payment: depends on book. Copyrights for author. American Booksellers Assn., SPAN.

Shearsman Books (see also Oasis Books), Tony Frazer, c/o IPD (Independent Press Distribution), 12 Stevenage Road, London SW6 6ES, United Kingdom, 0752-779682. 1981. Poetry. "Main interests are postmodernist poetry and poetry in translation, particularly contemporary French poetry. This year's books are by George Evans (*Wrecking*) and David Wevill (*Figure of Eight*). Distribution address: Independent Press Distribution, 12 Stevenage Road, London SW6 6ES, England." avg. press run 400. Pub'd 1 title 1998; expects 3 titles 1999, 3 titles 2000. 9 titles listed in the *Small Press Record of Books in Print* (28th Edition, 1999-00). avg. price, paper: £3.95. Discounts: on application to distributor. 40pp; 4½×6½; of. Reporting time: 1 month. Payment: negotiable number of copies of the book. Copyrights for author in UK only. ALP.

Sheed & Ward, Robert Heyer, Editor-in-Chief, 7373 S. Lovers Lane Road, Franklin, WI 53132-1850, 800-444-8910. 1984. Non-fiction. "Parish Ministry, euthanasia, health care, spirituality, leadership, sacraments" avg. press run 3.5M-5M. Pub'd 30 titles 1998; expects 30 titles 1999, 30 titles 2000. avg. price, cloth: $20; paper: $8.95. Discounts: books-1 copy 20%, 2-4 30%, 5-49 40%, 50-259 42%, 250-849 44%, 850+ 46%. 150pp; 5⅜×8⅜; of. Reporting time: 3 months or sooner. Simultaneous submissions accepted: no. Payment: royalty 6/8/10% on retail, flex advance, some work for hire. Copyrights for author. Catholic Book Publishers Association.

The Sheep Meadow Press, Stanley Moss, Publisher, Editor-in-Chief, PO Box 1345, Riverdale-on-Hudson, NY 10471, 212-548-5547. 1976. Poetry, fiction. avg. press run 2.5M. Pub'd 4 titles 1998; expects 14 titles 1999, 8 titles 2000. 77 titles listed in the *Small Press Record of Books in Print* (28th Edition, 1999-00). avg. price, cloth: $14.95; paper: $10.95. Discounts: 40%. 100pp; 8½×5½, 6×9; of. Reporting time: 6 months. Payment: 6%. Copyrights for author.

Sheer Joy! Press, Patricia Adams, Editor, PO Box 608, Pink Hill, NC 28572, 919-568-6101. 1986. Fiction, non-fiction. avg. press run 1M. Expects 2 titles 1999, 2 titles 2000. 6 titles listed in the *Small Press Record of Books in Print* (28th Edition, 1999-00). avg. price, paper: $9.95. Discounts: 2-10=10%, 11-24=20%, 25-49=30%, 50-up=40%. 200pp; 5½×8½; of. Reporting time: 60 days. Simultaneous submissions accepted: yes. Copyrights for author.

SHEILA-NA-GIG, Hayley R. Mitchell, 23106 Kent Avenue, Torrance, CA 90505. 1990. Poetry, fiction, art. "We encourage new poets with a strong 'voice,' and look for poetry and fiction on the edge, especially that which is not afraid to speak out on sexuality, politics and society, and feminist issues. Send up to 5 poems, any length; up to 2 short stories, 1-4 pages max.; b&w art/photos, 5x7 (easy to reproduce). Please do not send religious, or ultra-traditional or conservative material. *SASE a must!* Recent contributors: Gerald Locklin, Charles Webb, Lyn Lifshin, Susan Terris. For 1996, I will produce *one* large edition of *Sheila-Na-Gig*. The new submissions deadline will be May 31, and these submissions will be read in June. Query first for poetry contest and chapbook contest rules. June 30th deadline" circ. 500. 1/yr. Pub'd 1 issue 1998; expects 1 issue 1999, 1 issue 2000. sub. price: $7, $12/2 years; per copy: $7 (recent copy); sample: $7. Back issues: none. Discounts: some trades. 100-150pp; 5½×8½; xerox. Reporting time: 2 months after submission deadlines. Simultaneous submissions accepted: yes. Publishes 10-15% of manuscripts submitted. Payment: 1 copy. Copyrighted, reverts to author. Ads: $60/$35/$18/$3 3 line classified.

SHEMP! The Lowlife Culture Magazine, Lawrence K. Yoshida, 593 Waikala Street, Kahului, HI 96732-1736, e-mail shempzine@yahoo.com. 1993. Articles, photos, criticism, reviews, letters. "Not for artsy types! No submissions. We are pro-choice carnivores. We are low-life scum, slackers, and shemps. We accept cash donations and money orders (made out to Lawrence Yoshida)" circ. 400. 6/yr. Expects 6 issues 1999, 6 issues 2000. price per copy: $1 + 2 stamps; sample: $1 + 2 stamps. Back issues: same (when available). 12pp; 4¼×6½; †photocopy. Publishes 0% of manuscripts submitted. Not copyrighted. Pub's reviews: 18 in 1998. §Punk rock, cocktail music, soundtracks, B-movies, Asian/Asian related films, true crime books.

SHENANDOAH, R.T. Smith, Editor; Lynn L. Leech, Managing Editor, Troubadour Theater, 2nd Floor, Washington and Lee University, Lexington, VA 24450-0303, 540-463-8765. 1950. Poetry, fiction, reviews, parts-of-novels. "Literary quarterly publishing award-winning fiction, poetry, essays." circ. 1.3M. 4/yr. Pub'd

513

4 issues 1998; expects 4 issues 1999, 4 issues 2000. sub. price: $15; per copy: $5; sample: $5. Back issues: $8. Discounts: 50% bulk rate to bookstores. 128pp; 6×9; of. Reporting time: 3 weeks. Simultaneous submissions accepted: no. Payment: $25/page prose, $2.50/line poetry + 1 year free subscription, 1 free copy of issue in which work appears, $300/cover art. Copyrighted, rights revert to author by request. Pub's reviews: 3 in 1998. §Short fiction/poetry—solicited reviews only. Ads: $200/$100. CLMP.

SHENANDOAH NEWSLETTER, Scan Doa, 736 West Oklahoma Street, Appleton, WI 54914. 1973. Poetry, articles, criticism, reviews, letters, news items, non-fiction. "All material must relate to American Indian by Indians. Editor holds strict rights on this." circ. 1M. 12/yr. Pub'd 12 issues 1998; expects 12 issues 1999, 12 issues 2000. sub. price: $17.50; per copy: $1.75; sample: $1.75. 21pp; 8½×11; †mi. Reporting time: material must be into office by 24th of previous month. Payment: none. Not copyrighted. Pub's reviews: 60 in 1998. §Material relating to Native Peoples and their struggles/history. Ads: none.

Shenango River Books, Don Feigert, Jack Smith, Jeanne Mahon, PO Box 631, Sharon, PA 16146, 412-342-3811. 1994. Poetry, fiction, non-fiction. "Currently publishing by invitation only. No unsolicited mss." avg. press run 500. Pub'd 1 title 1998; expects 3 titles 1999, 3 titles 2000. 6 titles listed in the *Small Press Record of Books in Print* (28th Edition, 1999-00). avg. price, paper: $8. 64pp; 5⅜×8½. Payment: co-op marketing. Copyrights for author.

SHERLOCKIAN TIDBITS, Arnold Korotkin, 42 Melrose Place, Montclair, NJ 07042. 1987. Photos, cartoons, news items. "Our publication contains article, graphics, reviews, etc., pertaining to the master detective, Sherlock Holmes." circ. 221. 4/yr. Pub'd 4 issues 1998; expects 4 issues 1999, 4 issues 2000. sub. price: $8; per copy: $2; sample: $2. 13pp; 8½×11; †of. Not copyrighted. Pub's reviews: 4 in 1998. §Mystery books, magazines, etc.

Sherman Asher Publishing, Judith Rafaela, PO Box 2853, Santa Fe, NM 87504, 505-984-2686; FAX 505-820-2744, e-mail 71277.2057@comperserve.com. 1995. Poetry. "Solicit poems for anthologies. Query first for project information" avg. press run 1M. Pub'd 3 titles 1998; expects 4 titles 1999, 3 titles 2000. avg. price, paper: $14. Discounts: 20% library, 40% trade, 50% bulk. Pages vary; size varies. Reporting time: 2 months. Publishes a variable % of manuscripts submitted. Payment: in copies. Copyrights for author. PEN, Poetry Center of New Mexico, American Booksellers Assoc., Rocky Mountain Book Publishers Assoc., Publishers Marketing Associates.

●Shimoda Publishing, PO Box 32, Atlanta, ID 83601, 1-800-218-6110. 1993. avg. press run 20M. Pub'd 1 title 1998. avg. price, paper: $16.95. Discounts: varies. 368pp; 5½×8½.

SHIRIM, Marc Steven Dworkin, 4611 Vesper Avenue, Sherman Oaks, CA 91403-5615. 1982. Poetry. "*Shirim* seeks poetry (original + translated) of Jewish reference. Such known poets as Yehuda Amichai, Robert Mezey, Deena Metzger, Karl Shapiro, Irving Layton, Jerome Rothenberg, and Howard Schwartz have had poetry appear in the magazine. All submissions are welcome." circ. 250. 2/yr. Expects 1 issue 1999, 2 issues 2000. sub. price: $7; per copy: $4; sample: $4. 36pp; 5¼×8½; †of. Reporting time: 2 months. Payment: copies. Copyrighted, reverts to author. Pub's reviews: 2 in 1998.

Shivam Publications, Route 1, Box 41, Houghton, MI 49931-9801, 906-482-0487. 1996. Expects 1 title 1999. 1 title listed in the *Small Press Record of Books in Print* (28th Edition, 1999-00). avg. price, paper: $12.95. Discounts: 2-10 10%, 11-50 20%. 20pp; 6×9.

SHOCKBOX, C.F. Roberts, PO Box 120, Fayetteville, AR 72702-0120. 1991. Poetry, fiction, art, cartoons, satire, collages. "Looking for short-short fiction (4 pages max.), b/w art. Poetry 1 page max. Please take contemporary standards of literature and art and turn them inside out." circ. varies. 4/yr. Pub'd 4 issues 1998; expects 4 issues 1999, 4 issues 2000. sub. price: $12; per copy: $3; sample: $3. Back issues: $3. Discounts: trades welcome, $1 discount to contributors for extra copies. 56pp; 5½×8½; xerox. Reporting time: 6 months maximum. Payment: 1 contributor copy. Copyrighted, reverts to author. Ads: $20/$10/$5 1/4 page/$3 business card.

SHORT FUSE, Holden, PO Box 90436, Santa Barbara, CA 93190. 1983. Poetry, fiction, articles, art, photos, cartoons, interviews, satire, criticism, music, letters, parts-of-novels, long-poems, collages, plays, concrete art, non-fiction. "Some recent contributors: Lyn Lifshin, Blair Wilson, Richard Kostelanetz, Bob Zorak, Hector, Kim Traub, John M. Bennett, Frank Moore. *Short Fuse* is open to anyone's participation and material from people from all walks of life is included. The physical form of the magazine is adaptable to the requirements of the pieces included. Its sociological and ideological context is antiauthoritarian-populist. Esthetically, there's an openness to the avant-garde and experimental but no single aesthetic theory is endorsed to the exclusion of others. However, some ideas derived from dada, surrealism, and punk are of lingering interest." circ. 500+. 6/yr. sub. price: $9, free to institutionalized persons; per copy: $1; sample: $1. Back issues: $1. 20pp; †xerox. Reporting time: 1 week. Payment: copies. Copyrighted, reverts to author.

SHRIKE, Jo Mariner, Editor; Paul Wright, Editor, 13 Primrose Way, Alperton, MDDX HA0 1DS, United

514

Kingdom, 44-081-998-5707. 1995. Poetry. circ. 100. 1/yr. Pub'd 1 issue 1998; expects 1 issue 1999, 1 issue 2000. sub. price: £4; per copy: £4; sample: £2. 36pp; 5×8. Reporting time: 1 month. Simultaneous submissions accepted: yes. Publishes 10% of manuscripts submitted. Payment: contributer copies. Copyrighted, reverts to author.

Sibyl Publications, Inc, Miriam Selby, 1007 SW Westwood Drive, Portland, OR 97201, 503-293-8391; 1-800-240-8566; fax 503-293-8941. 1993. Non-fiction. *"Not accepting mss. at this time. Small press of women's books. Nonfiction, positive themes. No poetry or fiction. Topics are: cooking, women and change, aging, women in midlife, mythology, spirituality, health, other women's issues. No manuscripts accepted. Inventing Ourselves Again: Woman Face Middle Age, Sacred Myths: Stories of World Religion, The Goddess Speaks,* revised edition and *Mythmaking: Heal Your Past, Claim Your Future, Spirited Threads, Oh Boy, Oh Boy, Oh Boy!, Love, Loss & Healing: A Woman's Guide to Transforming Grief, Food No Matter What! Stories & Recipes for Perfect Dining in an Imperfect World,* and *Classic Liqueurs."* avg. press run 7.5M. Pub'd 2 titles 1998; expects 5 titles 1999, 5 titles 2000. 6 titles listed in the *Small Press Record of Books in Print* (28th Edition, 1999-00). avg. price, cloth: $26.95; paper: $14.95; other: book & card set $29.95. Discounts: trade 40%, schools 25%. 200pp; 5½×8½. Payment: 10-12% of net (minus discounts and returns). Copyrights for author. PMA, NWABP, SPAN, PNBA.

SICILIA PARRA, Legas, Gaetano Cipolla, c/o Modern Foreign Languages, St. John's University, Jamaica, NY 11439-0002, 718-331-0613. 1979. Poetry, fiction, articles, art, photos, reviews, music, letters, long-poems, collages, plays, news items, non-fiction. *"This is the newsletter of Arba Sicula, primarily in English with one page in Sicilian"* circ. 2M. 2/yr. Pub'd 2 issues 1998; expects 2 issues 1999, 2 issues 2000. sub. price: $20; per copy: $10; sample: $10. Back issues: ask for quote. Discounts: ask for quote. 20pp; 8½×11; laser. Reporting time: flexible. Payment: none. Copyrighted, does not revert to author. Pub's reviews: several in 1998. §Sicilian ethnic worldwide. Ads: $150/$75/$6 column inch.

SIDEWALKS, Tom Heie, PO Box 321, Champlin, MN 55316. 1991. Poetry, fiction, art, photos, interviews. *"The editor has very eclectic tastes and likes a variety of voices and styles, prose poems, short memoir and fiction, preferably under 3,000 words. He prefers accessible over abstract, highly personal abstruse stuff. Likes innovation; poems don't need to fit traditional definitions. In the end he looks for well-crafted work. Some recent contributors are Michael Dennis Browne, Kenneth Pobo, Marilyn Boe, and Robert Cooperman."* circ. 300. 2/yr. Expects 2 issues 1999, 2 issues 2000. sub. price: $9; per copy: $6; sample: $6. Discounts: 40%. 60-70pp; 5½×8½; of. Reporting time: 3-5 weeks after deadlines (5/31 and 12/31). Simultaneous submissions accepted: no. Payment: single copy. Copyrighted, reverts to author.

Sidran Foundation and Press, 2328 W. Joppa Road, Suite 15, Lutherville, MD 21093, 410-825-8888; Fax 410-337-0747; E-mail sidran@access.digex.net; http://www.access.digex.net/sidran. 1991. Non-fiction. *"Our focus is on psychology and mental illness, primarily in the area of trauma (sexual abuse, child abuse, war, violent crime, etc.)."* avg. press run 1M. Pub'd 4 titles 1998; expects 2 titles 1999, 2 titles 2000. avg. price, paper: $18.95. Discounts: trade 1-2 copies 20%, 3-49 40%, 50-99 41%, 100+ 42%. 300pp; 6×9; of. Simultaneous submissions accepted: no. Payment: varies. PMA.

Sierra Club Books, Peter Beren, Publisher, 85 Second Street, San Francisco, CA 94105-3441, 415-977-5500; FAX 415-977-5793 and 415-977-5792. 1892. Fiction, non-fiction. *"Natural history, science, environmental issues, and photographic works, literature."* avg. press run 7.5M. Pub'd 25 titles 1998; expects 22 titles 1999, 25 titles 2000. avg. price, cloth: $25; paper: $15. Discounts: 40-50% trade/wholesalers. 200+pp; 6×9, 9×12; of. Reporting time: 4-6 weeks. Payment: customary advance against royalties. Copyrights for author.

Sierra Outdoor Products Co., Joseph F. Petralia, PO Box 2497, San Francisco, CA 94126-2497, 415-258-0777 phone/fax. 1979. Non-fiction. *"Publisher looking for additional manuscripts."* avg. press run 2M-5M. Pub'd 2 titles 1998; expects 1 title 1999, 2 titles 2000. 2 titles listed in the *Small Press Record of Books in Print* (28th Edition, 1999-00). avg. price, paper: $16.95; other: $12.95. Discounts: 40-55%. 250pp; 7×10; of. Reporting time: 90 days. Simultaneous submissions accepted: yes. Publishes 5-10% of manuscripts submitted. Payment: negotiable. Copyrights for author.

Signal Books, Gina Tkach, Publicity & Marketing, 7117 Tyndall Court, Raleigh, NC 27615, 919-870-8505 phone/fax; gtkach@worldnet.att.net. 1985. Poetry, fiction, non-fiction. avg. press run 3.5M. Pub'd 2 titles 1998; expects 4 titles 1999, 6 titles 2000. 4 titles listed in the *Small Press Record of Books in Print* (28th Edition, 1999-00). avg. price, cloth: $16; paper: $15. Discounts: standard industry. 250pp. Reporting time: 6 weeks. Payment: standard industry contracts. Copyrights for author.

‡THE SIGNAL - Network International, Joan Silva, David Chorlton, 1118 West Outer Drive, Oak Ridge, TN 37830-8611, 208-365-5812. 1987. Poetry, fiction, articles, art, interviews, criticism, reviews, letters. *"Signal will not be publishing in 1995 - future uncertain. Additional address: 1118 West Outer Dr., Oak Ridge, TN 37830. Length: no hard and fast rule, fiction under 3,000 words pref. Biases: no religious or tract material - we like translation(s), very broad range on style, subject matter."* circ. 500. 2/yr. sub. price: $12 when publication is resumed; per copy: $5; sample: $6. Back issues: $5. 50-60pp; 8½×11; of. Reporting time: from 2 weeks to 2-3 months, no reading during June, July, August. Payment: in copies. Copyrighted, reverts to author. Pub's reviews: 7 in 1998. §Art, lit. criticism, women's issues, social commentary.

Signature Books, Gary James Bergera, Attn: Boyd Payne, 564 West 400 North, Salt Lake City, UT 84116, 801-531-1483, fax 801-531-1488. 1981. Poetry, fiction, articles, art, photos, cartoons, interviews, criticism, non-fiction. "Not accepting *any* submissions until further notice. Western USA subjects—fiction/non-fiction." avg. press run 4M. Pub'd 12 titles 1998; expects 23 titles 1999, 24 titles 2000. 123 titles listed in the *Small Press Record of Books in Print* (28th Edition, 1999-00). avg. price, cloth: $34.95; paper: $19.95. Discounts: 43%. 250pp; 6×9. Reporting time: 6 months. Payment: 8% semi-annual. Copyrights for author. Association of Utah Publishers.

SIGNPOST FOR NORTHWEST TRAILS, Dan A. Nelson, Editor, 1305 Fourth Avenue #512, Seattle, WA 98101, 206-625-1367. 1966. Articles, art, photos, cartoons, interviews, reviews, letters, news items, non-fiction. "Editorial content is heavily weighted for *Pacific Northwest backpackers*, ski tourers, snow shoers, etc. We frequently purchase outside material, but pay no more than $25.00 per manuscript." circ. 3M. 12/yr. Pub'd 12 issues 1998; expects 12 issues 1999, 12 issues 2000. sub. price: $25; per copy: $2.50; sample: n/c. Back issues: $3.50. 40pp; 8×10¾; of. Reporting time: 2 months. Copyrighted, reverts to author. Pub's reviews: 6 in 1998. §Hiking, backpacking, cross-country skiing, snowshoeing, nature study and related activities—all with NW focus where applicable. Ads: $285/$143/50¢-wd. $12 min.

Signpost Press Inc. (see also THE BELLINGHAM REVIEW), Robin Hemley, Editor, Mail Stop 9055, WWU, Bellingham, WA 98225, 360-650-3209. 1975. Poetry, fiction, art, photos, reviews. "Not accepting book mss. at present." avg. press run 500. Pub'd 1 title 1998; expects 1 title 1999, 1 title 2000. 15 titles listed in the *Small Press Record of Books in Print* (28th Edition, 1999-00). avg. price, cloth: $12; paper: $3 for chapbooks, $8 for books. Discounts: 40% on 5 or more copies. 24-68pp; 5½×8½; of. Reporting time: 1-3 months. Payment: varies. Copyrights for author.

SIGNS: JOURNAL OF WOMEN IN CULTURE AND SOCIETY, Carolyn Allen, Editor; Judith Howard, Editor, C14 Padelford Hall, Box 354345, University of Washington, Seattle, WA 98195-4345, 206-616-4705, fax 206-616-4756, e-mail signs@u.washington.edu. 1975. Articles, criticism, reviews, letters, non-fiction, interviews. circ. 7M. 4/yr. Pub'd 4 issues 1998; expects 4 issues 1999, 4 issues 2000. sub. price: $38 indiv., $111 instit., $27 students; per copy: $8.50 indiv.; $27.75 instit. Back issues: contact business office, University of Chicago Press, Journals Division, PO Box 37005, Chicago IL 60637, for this information. Discounts: standard agencies. 265pp; 6×9; of. Reporting time: 3-6 months, contact editorial office for this information. Payment: 10 copies of journal issue or 1/yr subscription. Copyrighted, does not revert to author. Pub's reviews: 40 in 1998. §Women, feminist studies.

Sigo Press, Sisa M. Sternback, PO Box 8748, Boston, MA 02114-0037, 508-740-0113. 1981. "Imprint: Coventure, Ltd." avg. press run 5M. Pub'd 10 titles 1998; expects 10 titles 1999, 10 titles 2000. 21 titles listed in the *Small Press Record of Books in Print* (28th Edition, 1999-00). avg. price, cloth: $35; paper: $15.95. Discounts: trade 1-4 10%, 5-24 40%, 25-44 41%, 45-99 42%, 100-199 43%, 200-399 44%, 400-499 46%, 500+ 48%. 210pp; 6×9; sheet fed of. Reporting time: 3 months. Payment: negotiable. Does not copyright for author. ABA, International Publisher's Group of Boston, NEBA, CBA.

SILHOUETTE MAGAZINE, Candace J. Joseph, PO Box 53763, Baton Rouge, LA 70892, 504-358-0617. 1995. Poetry, fiction, art, cartoons, satire, reviews, letters, parts-of-novels, long-poems, plays, concrete art. circ. 250. 4/yr. Pub'd 2 issues 1998; expects 4 issues 1999, 4 issues 2000. sub. price: $15; per copy: $2.75; sample: $3. Back issues: $4.50. Discounts: negotiable. 8½×11; of. Reporting time: 6-8 weeks. Simultaneous submissions accepted: yes. Publishes 55% of manuscripts submitted. Payment: publication. Copyrighted, reverts to author. Pub's reviews. §Fiction, poetry, spirituality, politics. BWIP, NABJ, MWG.

Silver Dollar Press, Arthur W. Smith, 2301 Division #712, North Little Rock, AR 72114, 501-834-4099. 1984. "Uses illustrations. Fourth edition." avg. press run 1M. Pub'd 1 title 1998; expects 2 titles 1999, 1 title 2000. 2 titles listed in the *Small Press Record of Books in Print* (28th Edition, 1999-00). avg. price, paper: $9.95 Fourth edition. Discounts: 25% to dealers, 40% to distributors. 70pp; 8½×11; †of. Simultaneous submissions accepted: no. Payment: none. Does not copyright for author.

Silver Mountain Press, Scott Owens, Jon Owens, Casilla 6572 Torres Sofer, Cochabamba, Bolivia. 1993. Poetry, fiction. "We publish contemporary fiction that captures the point between the 'cerebral' literary novel and the pure action, genre-based 'bestseller.' We are interested in the novel that combines the best of these two literary poles. Send query letter and SASE only. Our production schedule for this year and the next is already filled." avg. press run 7M. Expects 2 titles 1999, 3 titles 2000. 5 titles listed in the *Small Press Record of Books in Print* (28th Edition, 1999-00). avg. price, cloth: $22; paper: $12. Discounts: available, please inquire for schedules. 240pp; 5½×8½; of. Reporting time: 4 weeks. Publishes 2% of manuscripts submitted. Payment: standard. Copyrights for author.

Silver Phoenix Press, Marc P. Schwarz, Managing Editor, PO Box 26554, Austin, TX 78755-0554, 512-343-8803; Fax 512-338-0224; E-mail silphoenix@aol.com. 1995. Fiction, non-fiction. "We are a literary agency making the transition into publishing our own imprint. Accordingly, we evaluate submissions for possible agent representation to other houses as well as the work's appropriateness for our list. We are always looking for innovative, well-written, purposeful novel-length fiction or non-fiction whose audiences can be clearly defined and targeted." avg. press run 1-2M. Expects 2 titles 1999, 3-4 titles 2000. 2 titles listed in the *Small Press Record of Books in Print* (28th Edition, 1999-00). avg. price, paper: $14.95. Discounts: short (2-4) 20%, 5-99 40%, 100 & up (in even case lots) 50%. 300pp; 5½x8½; 1p. Reporting time: 4 weeks. Simultaneous submissions accepted: yes. Publishes 5% of manuscripts submitted. Payment: variable. Copyrights for author. PMA, Book Publishers of Texas.

Silver Print Press, Peter Miller, RD 1, Box 1515, Waterbury, VT 05676, 802-244-5339; petermiller@ibm.net; www.silverprintpress.com. 1990. Non-fiction. "No submissions accepted. Formerly Vermont People Project. Publishers of *Vermont People, Yankee Weather Proverbs* and *People of the Great Plains.*" avg. press run 7M. Pub'd 1 title 1998; expects 1 title 2000. 1 title listed in the *Small Press Record of Books in Print* (28th Edition, 1999-00). avg. price, cloth: $30. Discounts: 55% wholesale, 40% bookstore, 20% library. 140pp; 12x9; 1p. Payment: by negotiation. Copyrights for author. PMA.

Silver Seahorse Press, Joan G. Downing, 2506 N. Clark Street, Suite 320, Chicago, IL 60614, 773-871-1772; Fax 773-327-8978. 1991. Fiction. "We publish juvenile fiction. Currently scheduled are picture books for PreK to 4th grade and softcover and board books for toddlers. We expect to gradually expand our list to include books for ages through young adult. Our emphasis is on fresh, beautiful books for today's child." avg. press run 10M. Pub'd 2 titles 1998; expects 1 title 1999, 2 titles 2000. 6 titles listed in the *Small Press Record of Books in Print* (28th Edition, 1999-00). avg. price, cloth: $14.95; paper: $5.95. Discounts: standard schedule. 24-32pp; 8x8, 9½x10½; of. Reporting time: 4 weeks. Payment: advance against royalties. Copyrights for author. PMA, SPAN.

THE SILVER WEB, Ann Kennedy, PO Box 38190, Tallahassee, FL 32315. 1989. Poetry, fiction, articles, art, photos, cartoons, interviews, satire, reviews. "*The Silver Web* is a semi-annual publication featuring new fiction, poetry and art. The Editor is looking for thought-provoking works ranging from speculative fiction to dark fantasy and all weirdness in between. FICTION: Short stories of 8000 words or less (don't send anything longer w/o a query first, or it will be returned unread). Looking for a twist of the bizarre. This could be classified as horror, dark fantasy, speculative fiction or science fiction. No S & S or fantasy/quest stories. Also, please, please, PLEASE no typical revenge stories. Give me strong believable characters and a solid imaginative story that surprises me, not merely shocks me. I'd like to see works that may possibly fall between the cracks of other magazines. Above all, the writing must be good. POETRY: Use above descriptions. The poetry must be well-written and provide good imagery. ART: Pen & Ink, Black & White photography, charcoals, pencils (if dark enough and clearly defined). Separate guidelines for artists available. NON-FICTION: Please query about specific articles. Interested in interviews with writers, poets, artists, publishers, editors and other people in the industry. Satire and humor also invited and I love Letters to the Editor. Reprints considered (include info on prior publication). Simultaneous submissions accepted, but please no multiple submissions. Give me time to respond to one manuscript before sending me another. Cover letters are enjoyed but not essential. Please don't explain your story in the cover letter. Let the work speak for itself. You must provide an SASE with proper postage to insure a response. If the postage is not enough to return the work, it will be considered disposable." circ. 2M. 2/yr. Pub'd 2 issues 1998; expects 2 issues 1999, 2 issues 2000. sub. price: $12; per copy: $5.95 + $1.25 p/h; sample: $5.95 + $1.25 p/h. Back issues: all sold out. Discounts: $3.57 @ wholesale, $4 to contributors. 80+pp; 8½x11. Reporting time: 4-6 weeks. Simultaneous submissions accepted: yes. Publishes less than 1% of manuscripts submitted. Payment: 2-3¢ a word. Copyrighted, reverts to author. Pub's reviews: 4 in 1998. §Horror, speculative fiction, science fiction, experimental, surreal, slipstream. Ads: $100/$50/$25 1/4 page/$35 digest.

SILVER WINGS/MAYFLOWER PULPIT, Jackson Wilcox, PO Box 1000, Pearblossom, CA 93553-1000, 805-264-3726. 1983. Poetry. "Poems with Christian foundation focusing on the realities of faith." circ. 250. 6/yr. Pub'd 4 issues 1998; expects 6 issues 1999, 6 issues 2000. sub. price: $10; per copy: $2; sample: $2. Back issues: $2 as available. Discounts: 20%. 12-32pp; 5½x8½; †copier. Reporting time: 4 weeks. We rarely accept simultaneous submissions. Publishes 10% of manuscripts submitted. Payment: 1 copy. Not copyrighted. Ads: none.

Silvercat Publications, Robert L. Outlaw, 4070 Goldfinch Street, Suite C, San Diego, CA 92103, 619-299-6774, fax 619-299-9119. 1988. Non-fiction. "We stress titles which discuss consumer and quality-of-life issues." avg. press run 5M. Pub'd 1 title 1998; expects 1 title 1999, 2 titles 2000. 5 titles listed in the *Small Press Record of Books in Print* (28th Edition, 1999-00). avg. price, paper: $14. Discounts: all sales to the trade are handled by Associated Publishers Group. 180pp; 6x9; of. Reporting time: 2 months. Simultaneous submissions accepted: yes. Publishes 1-2% of manuscripts submitted. Payment: percentage of net receipts,

517

payable quarterly. Copyrights for author. PMA.

SILVERFISH REVIEW, Rodger Moody, Editor, PO Box 3541, Eugene, OR 97403, 503-344-5060. 1979. Poetry, fiction, interviews, reviews, long-poems, collages. "Also publishes translations." circ. 300. 2/yr. Pub'd 2 issues 1998; expects 2 issues 1999, 2 issues 2000. 14 titles listed in the *Small Press Record of Books in Print* (28th Edition, 1999-00). sub. price: $8/2 issues individuals, $12/2 issues institutions; per copy: $4 regular issues, $6 poetry chapbooks; sample: $4 plus $1.50 for postage. Discounts: 20% consignment, 40% wholesale for bookstores. 32pp reg. issues, 32pp chapbooks; 5½×8½; of. Reporting time: 1-16 weeks. Simultaneous submissions accepted: no. Publishes 5% of manuscripts submitted. Payment: 2 copies regular issues plus 1-year subscription and small payment when funding permits, $1000 to winner of annual poetry book contest (for author who has yet to publish a book). Copyrighted, reverts to author. Pub's reviews: 2 in 1998. §Poetry, fiction. Ads: none. CLMP.

SIMPLY WORDS, Ruth Niehaus, 605 Collins Avenue #23, Centerville, GA 31028, E-mail simplywords@hotmail.com. 1991. Poetry, fiction, articles, letters, non-fiction. 4/yr. Pub'd 4 issues 1998; expects 4 issues 1999, 4 issues 2000. sub. price: $18.50; per copy: $5; sample: $5. Back issues: none. Discounts: none. 25pp; 8×11; computer printer. Reporting time: 4-8 weeks. Simultaneous submissions accepted: no. Publishes 80% of manuscripts submitted. Payment: none. Not copyrighted. Pub's reviews: 1-2 in 1998. Ads: must write for rates.

SINCERE SINGLES, Adrienne Schiff, 512 Glendale Circle, Ann Arbor, MI 48103-4177. 1982. Photos, non-fiction. "Once in a while a display advertisement." circ. 25M. 12/yr. Pub'd 12 issues 1998; expects 12 issues 1999, 12 issues 2000. sub. price: $16/year, $10/6 months; per copy: $2; sample: $2. 32pp; 8½×5½; of, webb. Ads: 450/225 3 words $32/50¢/add. SPA.

SING HEAVENLY MUSE! WOMEN'S POETRY AND PROSE, Sue Ann Martinson, Editor, PO Box 13320, Minneapolis, MN 55414. 1977. Poetry, fiction, art, photos. "We are interested in publishing a variety of fine writing by women. Contributors include: Meridel LeSueur, Patricia Hampl, Diane Glancy, Carol Bly, Celia Gilbert, and Linda Hogan. Please inquire about artwork." circ. 1M. 1/yr. Expects 1 issue 1999, 1 issue 2000. sub. price: $20/3 issues; per copy: $8 + $1.50 p/h; sample: $4. Back issues: $4. Discounts: 40% trade. 125pp; 6×9; of. Reporting time: 3-6 months; inquire for reading periods and themes. Payment: 2 copies, honorarium. Copyrighted, reverts to author. please inquire. CLMP.

SING OUT! The Folk Song Magazine, Mark Moss, Editor; Geoff Millar, Managing Editor, PO Box 5460, Bethlehem, PA 18015-0460, 610-865-5366; Fax 610-865-5129; info@singout.org. 1950. Articles, art, photos, interviews, reviews, music, letters, news items. "No unsolicited submissions. We print music and lyrics of folk songs." circ. 12.5M. 4/yr. Pub'd 4 issues 1998; expects 4 issues 1999, 4 issues 2000. sub. price: $22 indiv., $25 institution; per copy: $5.50; sample: $6. Back issues: $3 to $8 depending on the issue, write to Circulation Department for complete list. 216pp; 7¾×10; of. Reporting time: variable. Simultaneous submissions accepted: no. Payment: 7¢ per word. Copyrighted, does not revert to author. Pub's reviews: 100 in 1998. §Music, folklore, politics, arts, third world, ethnic materials, etc., women history labor, folk music records. Ads: $570/$350/60¢.

Singing Horse Press, Gil Ott, Editor & Publisher, PO Box 40034, Philadelphia, PA 19106. 1976. Poetry, long-poems. "New titles include: *S*PeRM**K*T* by Harryette Mullen, *Her Angel* by Karen Kelly, and *the cairo notebooks* by Ammiel Aloalay. Solicited material only." avg. press run 1M. Pub'd 2 titles 1998; expects 2 titles 1999, 2 titles 2000. 12 titles listed in the *Small Press Record of Books in Print* (28th Edition, 1999-00). avg. price, paper: $9.50. Discounts: 2-3 books 20%, 4+ 40%; no returns. 64pp; of. Payment: 10% of press run. CLMP.

Single Parent Press, Webster Watnik, PO Box 1298, Claremont, CA 91711, 909-624-6058, fax 909-624-2208. 1995. avg. press run 3M. Expects 2 titles 1999. 2 titles listed in the *Small Press Record of Books in Print* (28th Edition, 1999-00). avg. price, paper: $19.95. Discounts: 1-2 0%, 4-10 40%, 10+ 50%. 400pp; 6×9; of. Simultaneous submissions accepted: yes. Copyrights for author. PMA, SPAN.

SINGLE SCENE, Janet L. Jacobsen, Editor, 7432 East Diamond, Scottsdale, AZ 85257, 602-945-6746. 1972. Poetry, articles, interviews, reviews, letters, news items, non-fiction. "Positive, helpful information on how to live a happy single life and how to improve relationships. Article length 600-1200 words." circ. 8M. 12/yr. Pub'd 12 issues 1998; expects 12 issues 1999, 12 issues 2000. sub. price: $9.50; per copy: 75¢; sample: $1. Back issues: $2. Discounts: contact editor. 24pp; 10¼×16; web press. Reporting time: up to 2 months. Simultaneous submissions accepted: yes. Publishes 15% of manuscripts submitted. Payment: not currently paying for material. Copyrighted, reverts to author. Pub's reviews: 1 in 1998. §Single life, personal growth, self-improvement. Ads: $768/$394/$15 per column inch/40¢ word classified. Singles Press Association (SPA).

SINGLE TODAY, September Young, 5830 Mount Moriah Road, Suite 17, Memphis, TN 38115-1628, 901-365-3988. 1987. Articles, cartoons, interviews, reviews, news items. "500-1000 words of interest to single adults, singles coping with divorce, etc." circ. 35M. 6/yr. Pub'd 6 issues 1998; expects 6 issues 1999, 6 issues

2000. sub. price: $12; per copy: $4; sample: $4. Back issues: $4. Discounts: first class. 24pp; 8½×11; web press. Reporting time: 2 weeks. Publishes 1% of manuscripts submitted. Payment: copies. Copyrighted, reverts to author. Pub's reviews: 5 in 1998. §Communication/relationships, single living. Ads: $585/$315/$180 1/4 page/$25 typeset fee. SPA.

Singular Speech Press, Don D. Wilson, Editor & Publisher, Ten Hilltop Drive, Canton, CT 06019, 860-693-6059; Fax 860-693-6338; e-mail dondwilson@aol.com. 1976. Poetry. "No longer mostly self-publishing; published 2 books by 2 fine poets in 1989; one in 1990; 5 books of poetry in 1991 by 5 fine poets; 4 in 1992; 6 in 1993; 5 in 1994; 4 in 1996, 4 in 1997." avg. press run 400-500. Pub'd 4 titles 1998; expects 5 titles 1999, 6 titles 2000. 39 titles listed in the *Small Press Record of Books in Print* (28th Edition, 1999-00). avg. price, paper: $7-$9. Discounts: 40%, 25% to libraries. 48-72pp; 5½×8½; of. Reporting time: 2 weeks max. Simultaneous submissions accepted if so notified. Publishes 5% of manuscripts submitted. Payment: 75 copies. Copyrights for author.

SINISTER WISDOM, Margo Mercedes Rivera, PO Box 3252, Berkeley, CA 94703, 510-532-5222. 1976. Poetry, fiction, articles, art, photos, cartoons, interviews, satire, criticism, reviews, letters, parts-of-novels, long-poems, collages, plays, concrete art, non-fiction. "*Sinister Wisdom* is a magazine for the lesbian imagination in the arts and politics. Contributors range from 'famous' writers to first-time submitters—quality and original voice are what count. Subject matter may be anything that expresses depth of vision. Multi-cultural: writing by lesbians of color, Jewish, disabled, fat, ethnic, working class, older and younger lesbians encouraged." circ. 3M. 3/yr. Pub'd 3 issues 1998; expects 8 issues 1999, 3 issues 2000. sub. price: $20, $25 foreign; per copy: $7.50 (pp); sample: $6.50 (pp). Back issues: price as published, from $3-$5. Discounts: 40% to bookstores, 45-50% for bulk sales of 50 or more. 128-144pp; 5×8; of. Reporting time: 3-9 months. Payment: 2 copies. Copyrighted, reverts to author. Pub's reviews: 10 in 1998. §Lesbian and women's poetry, fiction, theatre, arts and non-fiction, especially with radical emphasis. Ads: $200/$100/$50 1/4/write for classified.

SISTERS IN CRIME BOOKS IN PRINT, Rowan Mountain Press, Vicki Cameron, Editor, PO Box 10111, Blacksburg, VA 24062-0111, 540-961-3315, Fax 540-951-7340, e-mail faulkner@bev.net. 1989. "Compendium of information on current mystery titles by women authors." circ. 10M. 2/yr. Pub'd 2 issues 1998; expects 1 issue 1999, 2 issues 2000. price per copy: $2.50 includes s/h, free to bookstores and libraries. Back issues: none available. Discounts: 2-4 20%, 5+ 40%; 40% if prepaid and s/h any quantity. 64pp; 8½×11; web of. Payment: none. Not copyrighted. Ads: none.

SISTERSONG: Women Across Cultures, Valerie Staats, PO Box 7405, Pittsburgh, PA 15213, E-mail sistersong@trfn.clpgh.org; www.sistersong.org. 1992. Poetry, fiction, art, photos, reviews, letters, non-fiction. "A theme journal; write for guidelines and deadlines. 1999 themes: The Kitchen; First Menses; Sports. Seeking original, unpublished work by new and emerging women writers and artists. We publish primarily in English but especially encourage non-Anglo contributors and works in translation (include original-language version). Printed on recycled paper." circ. 1M. 3/yr. Pub'd 3 issues 1998; expects 3 issues 1999, 3 issues 2000. sub. price: $28 institutions, $24 outside USA, $16 individuals; per copy: $6; sample: $6. Back issues: $5. Discounts: none. 80pp; 6×9; of. Reporting time: 3-6 months on the average. Publishes 10% of manuscripts submitted. Payment: 3 copies. Copyrighted, rights revert to author with conditions. Pub's reviews: 4 in 1998. §New titles only by independent presses: women in *all* areas (politics, art, culture, int'l affairs, history, literature, etc.). Ads: none. International Women's Media Foundation.

SITUATION, Wallace Mark, 10402 Ewell Avenue, Kensington, MD 20895-4025. 1992. Poetry. "24 pages, formally innovative poetry. Recent contributors include Bernstein, Weiner, Chadwick, Smith, Martin, Brannen, Spahr, Nash, Toscano, Retallack, Silliman" circ. 150. 3/yr. Pub'd 3 issues 1998; expects 3 issues 1999, 3 issues 2000. sub. price: $10; per copy: $3; sample: $3. Back issues: $3 per issue. 24pp; 7×8½; †mi. Reporting time: 3 months. Payment: none. Copyrighted, reverts to author.

SIVULLINEN, Jouni Waarakangas, Kaarelantie 86 B 28, 00420 Helsinki, Finland. 1986. Poetry, art, cartoons. "Recent contributors: Bob Z., Paul Weinman, John Borkowski, Fucci, Blair Wilson, Wayne Edwards, and Jeff Bien" circ. 300-500. 1-2/yr. Pub'd 2 issues 1998; expects 1 issue 1999, 1-2 issues 2000. price per copy: $3 surface, $4 airmail; sample: $3 surface, $4 airmail. Back issues: $3 #18, #20-#22. Discounts: trade okay. 28-32pp; 21×29.6cm; of. Reporting time: 4-8 weeks. Simultaneous submissions accepted: yes. Publishes 10% of manuscripts submitted. Payment: none, only contributors copy. Not copyrighted. none.

Six Strings Music Publishing, PO Box 7718-155, Torrance, CA 90504-9118, 800-784-0203; Fax 310-324-8544; contact@sixstringsmusicpub.com; www.sixstringsmusicpub.com. 1997. avg. press run 3-5M. Pub'd 1 title 1998; expects 7 titles 1999, 10 titles 2000. 2 titles listed in the *Small Press Record of Books in Print* (28th Edition, 1999-00). Discounts: contact us for details. Copyrights for author. Publishers Marketing Association.

69 FLAVORS OF PARANOIA, Rycke Foreman, Miranda Foreman, Connie Walters, 2816 Rio Vista Court,

519

Farmington, NM 87401-4557. 1996. Poetry, fiction, art, photos, cartoons, satire, parts-of-novels, long-poems. circ. 200. 6/yr. Pub'd 4 issues 1998; expects 6 issues 1999, 6 issues 2000. sub. price: $16; per copy: $3.50; sample: $3.50. Back issues: $4. Discounts: $2 each for 10-35, $1.50 each thereafter. 51pp; 5½×8½; †mi. Reporting time: 2-24 weeks. Simultaneous submissions accepted: yes. Publishes 90% of manuscripts submitted. Payment: 2 copies. Copyrighted, reverts to author. Pub's reviews. §Horror. Ads: $50/$20/$15 1/4 page/$10 1/8 page.

SJL Publishing Company, S.J. Cassady, PO Box 152, Hanna, IN 46340-0152, 219-324-9678. 1991. Fiction, articles, photos, cartoons, news items, non-fiction. *"SJL Publishing Company* has interests in publishing a wide range of general and specific topics. Length of material varies from short publications to complete short courses on very specific topics. Page length runs from 10 to 320 pages. We tend to prefer non-fiction writing. Recent contributions include *A Short Course in Permanent Magnet Materials* and *The World Before Man - In Search of the Circle."* avg. press run 5M. Pub'd 4 titles 1998; expects 6 titles 1999, 8 titles 2000. 2 titles listed in the *Small Press Record of Books in Print* (28th Edition, 1999-00). avg. price, paper: $25; other: short courses $49.99. Discounts: 1 bk 0%, 2-4 20%, 5-9 30%, 10-24 40%, 25-49 42%, 50-74 44%, 75-99 46%, 100-199 48%, 200+ 50%. 192pp; 8½×11; of. Reporting time: 90 days. Payment: negotiated. Copyrights for author. Publishers Marketing Association (PMA), Mid American Publishers Association (MAPA).

SKEPTICAL INQUIRER, Kendrick Frazier, PO Box 703, Amherst, NY 14226, 716-636-1425; Skeptinq@aol.com. 1976. Articles, art, photos, cartoons, criticism, reviews, letters, news items, non-fiction. "Articles 2,000-3,500 words, reviews 600-1,200 words, news and comments 250-1,000 words, letters and forum 250-1,000 words. Contributors: Martin Gardner, Stephen Jay Gould, James Randi and Richard Dawkins. We investigate science, paranormal, and pseudo science claims from a skeptical point of view" circ. 40M. 6/yr. Pub'd 6 issues 1998; expects 6 issues 1999, 6 issues 2000. sub. price: $35; per copy: $4.95; sample: free. Back issues: $4.95. Discounts: 50% off 10 or more copies. 68pp; 8½×11. Reporting time: 2 months. Simultaneous submissions accepted: no. Payment: issues. Copyrighted, does not revert to author. Pub's reviews: 25-30 in 1998. §Science, paranormal, psychology, popular culture, fringe science. Ads: none.

Skidmore-Roth Publishing, Inc., 400 Inverness Drive South #260, Englewood, CO 80112, 303-662-8793; Fax 303-662-8079; info@skidmore-roth.com. 1987. Non-fiction. "Publishes books on nursing, medicine, allied health. Does own distribution." avg. press run 2.5M-5M. Pub'd 24 titles 1998; expects 24 titles 1999, 24 titles 2000. 45 titles listed in the *Small Press Record of Books in Print* (28th Edition, 1999-00). avg. price, other: $39.88. Discounts: 0-50% depending on quantity. 341pp; 3×6, 5×7, 6×9, 8×11½, 5½×8½; 1p, web. Reporting time: 4 weeks. Simultaneous submissions accepted: yes. Publishes 1% of manuscripts submitted. Payment: varies. Copyrights for author.

Skinny Lamb Publishing Company, Route 3 Box 521-H, Wichita Falls, TX 76308, 940-696-5735; Fax 940-696-5830; skinylamb@aol.com. 1997. Poetry, fiction. Expects 2 titles 1999, 3 titles 2000. 1 title listed in the *Small Press Record of Books in Print* (28th Edition, 1999-00). avg. price, cloth: $14.95. 38pp; 8×11; of. Simultaneous submissions accepted: yes. Publishes 1% of manuscripts submitted. Payment: negotiable. Copyrights for author.

SKINNYDIPPING, Peter Kacalanos, Nakeditor, 51-04 39th Avenue, Woodside, NY 11377-3145, 718-651-4689; FAX 718-424-1883. 1990. Poetry, fiction, articles, art, photos, cartoons, interviews, satire, criticism, reviews, letters, plays, news items, non-fiction. *"Skinnydipping* is published by a large nudist social organization, The Skinnydippers, covering all the northeastern states. The club schedules many non-sexual clothing-optional activities every weekend. All submissions must be about nudism (health benefits, social opportunities, back-to-nature movement, loss of body shame, nudist resorts, nude beaches, legal hassles, etc.). Satire and parody are especially welcome. Length can range from 50 to 1,500 words. Illustrations can be anatomically correct; *Skinnydipping's* readers are nudes, not prudes. Write for free sample." circ. 3M-5M. 4/yr. Pub'd 4 issues 1998; expects 4 issues 1999, 4 issues 2000. sub. price: $20, including membership; sample: free. Back issues: free. Discounts: call for details. 12pp; 8½×11; of. Reporting time: 1 week or less. Simultaneous submissions accepted: yes. Publishes 25% of manuscripts submitted. Payment: no money; many free copies of magazine. Copyrighted, reverts to author. Pub's reviews: 6 in 1998. §All must be about social nudism or body acceptance, at least reviewed part must be. Ads: $130/$70/$90 2/3 page/$50 1/3/$30 1/6/$20 1/12.

SKYDIVING, Michael Truffer, 1725 North Lexington Avenue, DeLand, FL 32724, 904-736-9779; fax 904-736-9786. 1979. Articles, photos, cartoons, interviews, news items, non-fiction. "Contributors must be knowledgeable about sport parachuting." circ. 14,250. 12/yr. Pub'd 12 issues 1998; expects 12 issues 1999, 12 issues 2000. 2 titles listed in the *Small Press Record of Books in Print* (28th Edition, 1999-00). sub. price: $20; per copy: $4; sample: $5. Back issues: $5. Discounts: depends, inquire. 64pp; 11×14; of. Reporting time: 3 weeks. Copyrighted, rights revert to author, but depends. Pub's reviews: 10 in 1998. §Aviation, parachuting, skydiving. Ads: $817/$482/50¢ per word.

SKYLARK, Pamela Hunter, Editor-in-Chief, 2200 169th Street, Purdue University Calumet, Hammond, IN

46323, 219-989-2273; Fax 219-989-2165; skylark@nwi.calumet.purdue.edu. 1972. Poetry, fiction, articles, art, photos, interviews, satire, criticism, plays, non-fiction. *"Skylark* is the fine arts annual of Purdue University Calumet. We are equally interested in the works of known and unknown authors. All submissions must be accompanied by a S.A.S.E. with sufficient postage. Cover letter must state that submission is not simultaneous.'' circ. 800-1M. 1/yr. Pub'd 1 issue 1998; expects 1 issue 1999, 1 issue 2000. sub. price: $8; per copy: $8; sample: $6 back issues. Discounts: orders of 10+ at $5/copy. 100pp; 8½×11; lp. Reporting time: 3-6 months (do not read May 1 to November 1). Simultaneous submissions accepted: no. Publishes 15% of manuscripts submitted. Payment: copy of publication per poem, up to 3 copies for prose. Copyrighted, reverts to author. Ads: $100/$50/$25 1/4 page (rates subject to change).

Skyline Publications, Inc., Charles G. Gee, 680 NW 35th Ct, Oakland Park, FL 33309-5007, 954-772-1236. 1994. avg. press run 5K-10K. Pub'd 3 titles 1998; expects 5 titles 1999. avg. price, cloth: $25; paper: $13.95. 300+pp; 6×9; web. Reporting time: 3 months. Publishes 20% of manuscripts submitted. Payment: negotiated. Copyrights for author. Florida Publishers.

Skyline West Press/Wyoming Almanac, Philip J. Roberts, 1409 Thomes, Laramie, WY 82072, 307-745-8205. 1982. Non-fiction. ''Submitted manuscripts should deal with history, politics and culture of Wyoming or reference works on that geographic area.'' avg. press run 2M. Pub'd 1 title 1998; expects 2 titles 1999, 2 titles 2000. 5 titles listed in the *Small Press Record of Books in Print* (28th Edition, 1999-00). avg. price, paper: $12.95. Discounts: 40% to recognized dealers. 24-460pp; size varies with type of publication; of. Reporting time: 4-5 weeks. Simultaneous submissions accepted: no. Publishes 10% of manuscripts submitted. Payment: varies with author (negotiable). Copyrights vary.

Skytop Publishing, PO Box 134-M, Cathedral Station, New York, NY 10025, 212-932-0858 phone/Fax; E-mail skytop@mystic21.com. 1997. avg. press run 5M. Expects 2 titles 1999, 2 titles 2000. 1 title listed in the *Small Press Record of Books in Print* (28th Edition, 1999-00). avg. price, paper: $19.95. Discounts: bookstores 40%, wholesalers 50-60%, other 1-9 copies 20%, 10-99 45%, 100+ 50%, 500+ 65%. 300pp; 6×9. Simultaneous submissions accepted: no. PMA, NAPRA, SPAN.

●**Skyward Publishing**, Shirleen Sando, Paul Block, 17440 N. Dallas Parkway, Ste. 100, Dallas, TX 75287-1884, 1-800-537-6727; 972-735-7827. 6 titles listed in the *Small Press Record of Books in Print* (28th Edition, 1999-00).

SKYWRITERS, Stained Glass Press, Tara Allan, Editor; Jr. Farris, Lyman, Publisher, 245 Spring Street, SW, Concord, NC 28025. 1995. Poetry, fiction, interviews, satire, criticism, reviews, letters, long-poems, non-fiction. *"Skywriters* Literary Magazine is primarily read by people with disabilities, (not exclusively). Because of this, we are very liberal with deadlines and presentation'' circ. 100. 4/yr. Expects 4 issues 1999, 4 issues 2000. sub. price: $20; per copy: $5; sample: free or $5. Back issues: $5 when available. 40pp; 4×6; laser. Reporting time: 4-6 months. Payment: 1 copy. Copyrighted, reverts to author.

Slab-O-Concrete Publications, Peter Pavement, PO Box 148, Hove BN3 3DQ, United Kingdom, 011-44-1273-739634; Fax 011-44-1273-205502. 1992. Articles, art, photos, cartoons, interviews, satire, criticism, reviews, collages, non-fiction. ''We primarily publish cutting edge comics and graphics in large format square bound books as well as in miniature formats. We also produce anthologies with articles and graphics covering a wide range of subjects, usually based around a theme.'' avg. press run 1M. Pub'd 10 titles 1998; expects 20 titles 1999, 25 titles 2000. 2 titles listed in the *Small Press Record of Books in Print* (28th Edition, 1999-00). avg. price, paper: £5, $10; other: £1, $2. Discounts: retail 33-45%, distributors 50-60%, library 10%. 80pp; 8¼×11½; of. Reporting time: 2-3 months. Simultaneous submissions accepted: yes. Payment: 10% of cover price. Does not copyright for author. Comics Creators Guild (London).

SLAM!, Michael R. Brown, 24 Arlington Street, Medford, MA 02155, 781-488-3636; bosslam@cybercom.net. 1992. Articles, photos, news items. circ. 3.5M. 4/yr. Pub'd 3 issues 1998; expects 3 issues 1999, 4 issues 2000. sub. price: $6; per copy: free; sample: free. Back issues: free while they last. 4pp; 8½×11; of. Reporting time: 1 weeks. Payment: none. Not copyrighted. Ads: $300/$100/$25 per 1/8.

SLANT: A Journal of Poetry, James Fowler, University of Central Arkansas, PO Box 5063, Conway, AR 72035-5000, 501-450-5107. 1987. Poetry. ''We use traditional and 'modern' poetry, even experimental, moderate length, any subject on approval of Board of Readers. Our purpose is to publish a journal of fine poetry from all regions. No haiku, no translations. No previously published poems. No multiple submissions. Recent contributors include Jack Butler, Vivian Shipley, John McKernan and Mary Winters. Submission deadline is November 15 for annual spring publication.'' circ. 175. 1/yr. Pub'd 1 issue 1998; expects 1 issue 1999, 1 issue 2000. sub. price: $10; per copy: $10; sample: $10. Back issues: $6. Discounts: negotiable. 120pp; 6×9; of, lp. Reporting time: 3-4 months from deadline. Simultaneous submissions accepted: no. Publishes 5% of manuscripts submitted. Payment: 1 copy on publication. Copyrighted, reverts to author. Ads: none.

Slapering Hol Press, Stephanie Strickland, Margo Stever, 300 Riverside Drive, Sleepy Hollow, NY

10591-1414, 914-332-5953. 1988. Poetry. "We alternate between thematic anthologies and chapbooks by poets who have never published in book form. 1994, *What's Become of Eden: Poems of Family at Century's End*; 1998, *The Last Campaign*, Rachel Loden; *Weathering*, Pearl Karrer; 1992, *River Poems*; 1991, *Note for a Missing Friend*, Dina Ben-Lev. Contributors include Maxine Kumin, Floyd Skloot, Denise Duhamel'' avg. press run 1M. Pub'd 1 title 1998; expects 1 title 1999, 1 title 2000. 9 titles listed in the *Small Press Record of Books in Print* (28th Edition, 1999-00). avg. price, paper: $8. Discounts: standard. 40-80pp; 6×9; of. Reporting time: 3-4 months. Simultaneous submissions accepted: yes. Payment: chapbooks pay $500 plus 20 copies; anthology 1 copy. Copyrights for author. CLMP, Small Press Center.

Slate Press, David Ebony, Box 1421, Cooper Station, New York, NY 10276. 1986. Fiction, criticism, non-fiction. "Recent books published by Slate Press include *Loop, 50 Ideas for Pictures*, a collection of 50 short prose condensations of the rhetoric of film by Peter Zabelskis; and *The Age of Oil*, essays on selected topics in psychoanalysis and popular culture by Duncan Smith. Forthcoming titles include *Days in the Clouds*, essays by Duncan Smith on art, nature, philosophy, literature and AIDs'' avg. press run 1.5M. 2 titles listed in the *Small Press Record of Books in Print* (28th Edition, 1999-00). avg. price, paper: $4.95-$5.95. Discounts: 40%. 150pp; 5⅛×7¾; of, perfect binding, film lamination on covers. Reporting time: varies. Payment: varies. Copyrights for author, assist in obtaining author-held copyright.

SLEUTH JOURNAL, Baker Street Publications, Sharida Rizzuto, Harold Tollison, Ann Hoyt, 577 Central Avenue, Box 4, Jefferson, LA 70121-1400, E-mail sherlockian@mailcity.com, blackie@taskcity.com, www2.cybercities.com/z/zines, www.wbs.net/homepages/b/l/a/blackkie.html. 1983. Poetry, fiction, articles, art, photos, cartoons, interviews, satire, criticism, reviews, letters, long-poems, collages, news items, non-fiction. circ. 800. 2/yr. Pub'd 2 issues 1998; expects 2 issues 1999, 2 issues 2000. sub. price: $15.80; per copy: $7.90; sample: $7.90. Back issues: $7.90. Discounts: trade with other like publications. 100pp; 8½×11; †of, excellent quality offset covers. Reporting time: 2-6 weeks. Simultaneous submissions accepted: yes. Publishes 35% of manuscripts submitted. Payment: free copies, fees paid for articles, reviews, and artwork negotiable. Copyrighted, reverts to author. Pub's reviews: 28 in 1998. §Mystery in film and literature, true crime, zines, books films, internet websites. Ads: free. NWC, HWA, MWA, Arizona Authors Association (AAA), Western Writers of America (WWA), Small Press Genre Association.

SLIGHTLY WEST, Sarah Dougherty, Editor; Brian Nadal, Editor, The Evergreen State College, CAB 320, Olympia, WA 98505, 360-866-6000 x6879. 1985. Poetry, fiction, art, photos, cartoons, satire, criticism, collages. "*Slightly West* accepts all types of literal expulsion from new and previously published authors. Anyone is welcome to submit. To submit please remove your name from your work and include a cover letter with your name, telephone number, current address, and title(s) and/or description of visual material. Please limit submissions to three pieces per genre. Please include SASE if you wish your material returned'' circ. 1M. 2/yr. Pub'd 2 issues 1998; expects 2 issues 1999, 2 issues 2000. sub. price: $5; per copy: $2.50; sample: $2.50. Back issues: $2.50 issues printed in the last two years are available. Discounts: none. 50pp; 6×9. Reporting time: 3 months at the most. Simultaneous submissions accepted: yes. Publishes 10% of manuscripts submitted. Payment: 1 copy. Copyrighted, reverts to author. none.

SLIPSTREAM, Slipstream Productions, Dan Sicoli, Robert Borgatti, Livio Farallo, Box 2071, New Market Station, Niagara Falls, NY 14301, 716-282-2616 (after 5 p.m., E.S.T.). 1980. Poetry, art, photos, parts-of-novels, long-poems, collages, concrete art. "Submissions are completely open. Query for themes. Reading through 1998 for a general issue. Some recent contributors are Gerald Locklin, Kurt Nimmo, Charles Bukowski, Diana Pickney, Eric Gansworth, Leasa Burton, A.D. Winans, Normal, Belinda Subraman, and Al Masarik.'' circ. 500. 1/yr. Pub'd 1 issue 1998; expects 1 issue 1999, 1 issue 2000. sub. price: $15; per copy: $5; sample: $5. Back issues: available upon request. 80pp; 7×8½; of. Reporting time: 2-8 weeks. Payment: presently only in copies. Copyrighted, reverts to author.

Slipstream Productions (see also **SLIPSTREAM**), Dan Sicoli, Robert Borgatti, Livio Farallo, Box 2071, New Market Station, Niagara Falls, NY 14301. 1981. Poetry, fiction, art, photos, collages, long-poems. avg. press run 500. Pub'd 2 titles 1998; expects 3 titles 1999, 2 titles 2000. 12 titles listed in the *Small Press Record of Books in Print* (28th Edition, 1999-00). avg. price, paper: $6. 40pp; of. Simultaneous submissions accepted: yes.

Slough Press, Jim Cole, Box 1385, Austin, TX 78767. 1973. "Slough Press publishes essay, poetry, nonfiction, and short story books. Quality is our only criteria. We dont consider work from writerw who are unfamiiar with our line of books. Read before you send'' avg. press run 500. Pub'd 3 titles 1998; expects 4 titles 1999, 4 titles 2000. 5 titles listed in the *Small Press Record of Books in Print* (28th Edition, 1999-00). avg. price, cloth: $10.95; paper: $5.95. Discounts: vary. 80pp; 5½×8½; of. Reporting time: 2 weeks. Payment: varies. Copyrights for author.

A Slow Tempo Press, David McCleery, PO Box 83686, Lincoln, NE 68501-3686, 402-466-8689; slowtemp@aol.com. 1989. Poetry. "By invitation only. Recent books by William Kloefkorn, Nancy Peters

Hastings, Twyla Hansen, and Don Welch." avg. press run 500. Pub'd 2 titles 1998; expects 2 titles 1999. 7 titles listed in the *Small Press Record of Books in Print* (28th Edition, 1999-00). avg. price, paper: $11. Discounts: none. 72pp; 6×9; of. Reporting time: 3 months. Simultaneous submissions accepted: no. Payment: ask. Copyrights for author. MAPA.

SLUG & LETTUCE, Christine Boarts, PO Box 26632, Richmond, VA 23261-6632. 1986. Photos, reviews, music. "Networking newspaper for communication and contacts within the underground punk scene. Includes photographs and reviews of zines and music" circ. 8M. 6/yr. Pub'd 6 issues 1998; expects 6 issues 1999, 6 issues 2000. sub. price: 6 stamps-6 55¢; per copy: SASE-55¢; sample: SASE-55¢. Back issues: 55¢ Stamp per issue. 16pp; 10×15; of. Not copyrighted. Pub's reviews: tons in 1998. §Punk, alternative music, alternative culture, environmental, political left. Ads: 2½ X 5 $25, 5 X 5 $50, 5 X 7½ $75.

THE SMALL BUSINESS ADVISOR, Joseph Gelb, PO Box 436, Woodmere, NY 11598, 516-374-1387; Fax 516-374-1175; smalbusadu@aol.com. 1974. Poetry, articles, cartoons, reviews, letters. "Length of material 900-1500 words." circ. 1M. 12/yr. Pub'd 2 issues 1998; expects 12 issues 1999, 12 issues 2000. sub. price: $45; per copy: $7.25; sample: $3. Back issues: $8. Discounts: Bulk rate to be negotiated. 16pp; 8½×11; of. Reporting time: 2 months. Simultaneous submissions accepted: yes. Publishes 60% of manuscripts submitted. Payment: copies 2 times. Copyrighted. Pub's reviews: 1 in 1998. §Business management, marketing, human resources, cash management. PMA.

Small Helm Press, Pearl Evans, Cynthia Horkey, Contact Person, 622 Baker Street, Petaluma, CA 94952, 707-763-5757. 1986. Non-fiction. "Small Helm Press is able to receive unsolicited contributions at this time, but will not return without SASE" Expects 1 title 2000. 5 titles listed in the *Small Press Record of Books in Print* (28th Edition, 1999-00). avg. price, cloth: $17.95; paper: $10. Discounts: 3 up 40%, 25 up 50% for bookstores. 180pp; 5½×8½; of. Payment: individual basis. Copyrights for author. Society for Scholarly Publishing (SSP).

THE SMALL POND MAGAZINE OF LITERATURE aka SMALL POND, Napoleon St. Cyr, PO Box 664, Stratford, CT 06615, 203-378-4066. 1964. Poetry, fiction, articles, art, satire, reviews, concrete art, non-fiction. "Max: Fiction 2.5M words, poetry approx 100 lines, other prose 2.5M words. Recent contributors: some nobodies—some somebodies." circ. 300. 3/yr. Pub'd 3 issues 1998; expects 3 issues 1999. sub. price: $10; per copy: $4; sample: $4, $2.50 random back issue. Back issues: inquire. Discounts: inquire. 42pp; 5½×8½; of. Reporting time: 15-45 days. Simultaneous submissions accepted: no. Publishes 1-3% of manuscripts submitted. Payment: 2 copies. Copyrighted, does not revert to author. Ads: $40/$20/$10 1/4 page. CLMP.

THE SMALL PRESS BOOK REVIEW, Henry Berry, Editor, PO Box 176, Southport, CT 06490, 203-332-7629. 1985. Articles, reviews, news items. "Reviews: 150-200 words, plus annotation books also received. Electronically published for libraries and on-line computer networks, including the Internet and America Online" 4/yr. Pub'd 4 issues 1998; expects 4 issues 1999, 4 issues 2000. electronic. Reporting time: 2 months. Not copyrighted. Pub's reviews: 800 in 1998. §Interested in all areas.

SMALL PRESS CREATIVE EXPLOSION, New Voice Media, Timothy R. Corrigan, PO Box 25, Houghton, NY 14744. 1984. Art, cartoons, reviews, music. "Interviews with small press comics publishers to 3000 words. Profiles of small press characters to 2000 words, opinions 500 words." circ. 500-1M. 12/yr. Pub'd 12 issues 1998; expects 12 issues 1999, 12 issues 2000. sub. price: $12; per copy: $1; sample: $1. Back issues: $1. Discounts: 40% off bulk orders, $6 PPD for wholesale package of 10 copies. 20pp; 4¼×7; †of. Reporting time: 60 days. Simultaneous submissions accepted: yes. Publishes a variable % of manuscripts submitted. Payment: copies. Copyrighted, reverts to author. Pub's reviews. §Home-grown, self-published comics, music, and videos. Ads: $25/$13/$7 1/4 page.

THE SMALL PRESS REVIEW/SMALL MAGAZINE REVIEW, Dustbooks, Len Fulton, Editor-Publisher; Laurel Speer, Contributing Editor ('Speer'); Bob Grumman, Contributing Editor ('Experioddica'); Bob Peters, Contributing Editor ('Black & Blue Guide'); Michael Andre, Contributing Editor ('New York Letter'), PO Box 100, Paradise, CA 95967-9999, 530-877-6110, 800-477-6110, fax: 530-877-0222, email(s): dustbooks@telis.org; len@dustbooks.com; web page address: http:www.dustbooks.com. 1966. Articles, cartoons, interviews, reviews, letters, news items. "The *Small Press Review* seeks to study and promulgate the small press and little magazine (i.e. the *independent* publisher) worldwide. It was started in 1966 as part of an effort by its publisher to get a grip on small press/mag information since no one at the time (or for some years thereafter) seemed interested in doing it. It was also designed to promote the small press in a variety of ways. In June of 1993 we started a new magazine called the *Small Magazine Review*, which ran eight separate issues before being merged with *SPR*. So now *SPR/SMR* publishes reviews, guest editorials and other material related to BOTH books and magazines published by small publishers. We are always on the lookout for competently written reviews (yes, we have a 'style sheet'), as long as they hold to a page in length and review a title published by a small press or magazine. *SPR/SMR* has regular 'News Notes' sections which give info about small press activities, manuscript needs (*and there are many!*), contests, prizes and so on. We print full-info listings bi-monthly on twenty or so new small presses and twenty or so new magazines. In the case of these latter listings, we generally utilize data from *Int'l Directory* report forms which come in to us throughout the year (if your magazine or press is not listed in either the *Int'l Directory* or *Small Press Record of Books in Print* please write to us for a form. If you fill out a form for the *Directory* you will automatically receive a form for the *Record* later.) A particularly popular feature of the magazine section is the 'Free Sample Mart' which lists about two dozen free samples of small magazines and books available each issue. NOTE: Canadian and foreign please remit in US funds only when ordering." circ. 3.5M. 6/yr. Pub'd 11 issues 1998; expects 6 issues 1999, 6 issues 2000. sub. price: individuals $25/yr, $33/2 yrs, $36/3 yrs, $39/4 yrs; institutions $29/yr, $39/2 yrs, $47/3 yrs, $52/4 yrs; per copy: $2.50; sample: free. Back issues: inquire. Discounts: schedule available for agents. 32pp; 8½×11; of. Reporting time: 3-6 weeks. Publishes 75% of manuscripts submitted. Not copyrighted. Pub's reviews: 200 in 1998. §Anything published by a small press. Ads: $150/$90/$75/$50/(display).

SMALL PUBLISHER, Nigel Maxey, PO Box 1620, Pineville, WV 24874, 304-732-8195. 1993. Articles, photos, cartoons, reviews, letters, news items. "Small Publisher features profiles of successful small publishers. These are normally produced by the Editor. Photos are a must. We are interested in purchasing advise or "how-to" articles dealing with most aspects of self-publishing. These should normally run 1M-2500 words. However, if a topic only warrants 500 words or requires 5M words, that's ok. All material must be genuinely useful" circ. 5800. 12/yr. Expects 10 issues 1999, 12 issues 2000. sub. price: $18; per copy: $2.95; sample: $2.95. 32pp; 11½×14½; of. Reporting time: varies. Payment: varies, approx. 3¢ per word. Copyrighted, reverts to author. Pub's reviews: 35 in 1998. §Primarily publishing, writing. Miscellaneous small press titles are noted as space is available. Ads: $200/$140/$12 column inch, 30¢ per word classified.

The Smallest County Press, S. Linden, 37 Northgate, Oakham, Rutland LE15 6QR, England, 01572-770011. 1993. Fiction. "High quality, collectible, beautifully designed little books for people who care what they read, published in England's smallest traditional county." Pub'd 1 title 1998; expects 2 titles 1999. 1 title listed in the *Small Press Record of Books in Print* (28th Edition, 1999-00). avg. price, cloth: £8.95. Discounts: standard trade rates. of.

SMARANDACHE NOTIONS, C. Dumitrescu, V. Seleacu, Department of Mathematics, University of Craiova, Craiova 1100, Romania, research37@aol.com. 1990. Articles. "From one to ten pages. Recent contributors: Charles Ashbacker, L. Seagull, L. Tutescu, St. Zanfir, N. Virlan" circ. 1M. 2-3/yr. Pub'd 2 issues 1998; expects 2 issues 1999, 2 issues 2000. 1 title listed in the *Small Press Record of Books in Print* (28th Edition, 1999-00). sub. price: $19.95; per copy: $19.95. Discounts: 10-50%, depending on quantity. 70pp; 8½×11. Reporting time: 1-2 months. Simultaneous submissions accepted: yes. Publishes 60% of manuscripts submitted. Payment: copies. Copyrighted, reverts to author. Pub's reviews. §Smarandache type sequences, Smarandache pradotes, Smarandache geometrics, Smarandache experiments.

SMARANDACHE NOTIONS JOURNAL, Dr. R. Muller, M. Perez, Box 141, Rehoboth, NM 87322, E-Mail: arp@cia-g.com; http://www.gallup.unm.edu/~smarandache/. 1990. Articles. "Research papers on Smarandache Notions such as: Smarandache type functions, Smarandache type sequences, Smarandache class of paradoxes, Smarandache geometries, Smarandache logic, Smarandache algebraic structures, etc." circ. 5M. 1-2/yr. Pub'd 1 issue 1998; expects 1 issue 1999, 1-2 issues 2000. 5 titles listed in the *Small Press Record of Books in Print* (28th Edition, 1999-00). sub. price: $39.95; per copy: $39.95; sample: $39.95. Back issues: none available. 150-200pp; 8½×11; of. Reporting time: 1 month. Simultaneous submissions accepted: yes. Publishes 80-90% of manuscripts submitted. Payment: free copies of the magazine. Copyrighted, reverts to author. Pub's reviews: 4 in 1998. §Papers, books, etc. about Smarandache Notions. Ads: $20/page. Number Theory Association.

SMART DRUG NEWS, Steven William Fowkes, Editor; Ward Dean, MD, Medical Editor; Anne Fowkes, Assistant Editor, PO Box 4029, Menlo Park, CA 94026, 415-321-2374. 1991. Articles, interviews, reviews, letters, news items. circ. 3M. 10/yr. Pub'd 10 issues 1998; expects 10 issues 1999, 10 issues 2000. sub. price: $44, $46 (Canada, Mexico), $55 overseas; per copy: $6; sample: $6. Back issues: $30/10 issues, $50/20 issues, $67.50/30 issues, $80/40 issues. 12pp; 8½×11; of. Reporting time: variable. Payment: to be arranged. Copyrighted, does not revert to author. Pub's reviews: 2 in 1998. Ads: none.

Smart Publications, PO Box 4667, Petaluma, CA 94955. 1990. 8 titles listed in the *Small Press Record of Books in Print* (28th Edition, 1999-00).

SMELT MONEY (A Poetics Newsletter from the KAW River Bottoms), Jim McCrary, Editor, PO Box 591, Lawrence, KS 66044. 1995. Poetry, reviews. "Length of material: Short (1 page). Recent contributors: Stephen Ellis, Susan Smith Nash, Sheila Murphy, Crag Hill, Steve Tills, Spencer Shelby." circ. 500. 8-10/yr. Pub'd 6 issues 1998; expects 4 issues 1999. sub. price: none. Back issues: $5. Discounts: none. 1 page; 17×11; †lazer. Reporting time: 3-6 months. Simultaneous submissions accepted: yes. Publishes 75% of manuscripts submitted. Payment: none. Not copyrighted. Pub's reviews: 10 in 1998. Ads: none.

Smiling Dog Press, Dean Creighton, 9875 Fritz, Maple City, MI 49664, 616-334-3695. 1989. Poetry, fiction.

"Recent contributors: Ron Androla, Scarecrow, Judson Crews, Mark Hartenbach." avg. press run 300. Pub'd 2 titles 1998; expects 1 title 1999. 2 titles listed in the *Small Press Record of Books in Print* (28th Edition, 1999-00). avg. price, paper: $4. 12pp; †1p. Reporting time: 2 months. Payment: in copies. All rights revert to author.

The Smith (subsidiary of The Generalist Assn., Inc.), Harry Smith, Editor; Michael McGrinder, Associate Editor, 69 Joralemon Street, Brooklyn, NY 11201-4003. 1964. Poetry, fiction. "Current emphasis is on poetry. Recent contributors: Menke Katz, Matthew Paris, Lloyd Van Brunt, Karen Swenson, Glenna Luschei, and David Rigsbee." avg. press run 1.5M. Expects 3 titles 1999, 3 titles 2000. 68 titles listed in the *Small Press Record of Books in Print* (28th Edition, 1999-00). avg. price, cloth: $22.95; paper: $14.95. Discounts: varies to bookstores and wholesalers. 80pp; 6×9; of, lp. Reporting time: 3 months. Simultaneous submissions accepted: yes. Publishes 1% of manuscripts submitted. Payment: $500 outright against royalties. Copyrights for author. CLMP, PMA.

Genny Smith Books, Genny Smith, Editor, Publisher, 23100 Via Esplendor, Villa 44, Cupertino, CA 95014, 650-964-4071. 1976. Articles, photos, non-fiction. "I specialize in publications on the Eastern Sierra region of California — to date, guidebooks, natural history, regional history and sets of historic postcards. My guidebooks (I edit and coauthor them) to this mountain-and-desert vacation area include chapters on roads, trails, natural history and history. Best known localities in this region are Owens Valley and Mammoth Lakes. These guidebooks are for sightseers, campers, hikers, fishermen, nature lovers and history buffs. Alternate address: PO Box 1060, Mammoth Lakes, CA 93546 (summer only). All my books are now distributed by Live Oak Press, PO Box 60036, Palo Alto, CA 94306, (650) 853-0197." avg. press run 7M. Pub'd 1 title 1998; expects 1 title 1999, 1 title 2000. 5 titles listed in the *Small Press Record of Books in Print* (28th Edition, 1999-00). avg. price, cloth: $17.50; paper: $13.95. 224pp; 6×9, 7½×10; of. Payment: varies from sharing of royalties to flat payment for material. Copyrights for author. Bookbuilders West, Writers Connection.

Gibbs Smith, Publisher, Madge Baird, Editorial Director; Gail Yngve, Editor; Theresa Desmond, Children's Book Editor; Paul VanDenBerghe, Editor, 1877 East Gentile Street, PO Box 667, Layton, UT 84041, 801-544-9800; Fax 801-544-5582; E-mail info@GibbsSmith.com. 1969. Poetry, fiction, art, criticism, non-fiction. "Trade imprint: Peregrine Smith Books. Books on architecture, arts, reprints, short stories, novels, guide books, natural environment, poetry, photography." avg. press run 5M-7M. Pub'd 45 titles 1998; expects 36 titles 1999. avg. price, cloth: $18.95-$49; paper: $6.95-$21.95. Discounts: 49.5% average. 144-160pp; 4¼×6¾ to 11×11; of. Reporting time: 12 weeks. Publishes 1% of manuscripts submitted. Payment: 10% on net. Copyrights for author. AAP, ABA, Rocky Mountain Book Publishers.

Richard W. Smith Military Books, PO Box 2118, Hendersonville, TN 37077. avg. press run 1.5M. Pub'd 1 title 1998; expects 1 title 1999. 3 titles listed in the *Small Press Record of Books in Print* (28th Edition, 1999-00). avg. price, cloth: $25; paper: $20. 200pp; 8½×11. Payment: yes. Copyrights for author.

SMOKE, Windows Project, Dave Ward, 40 Canning Street, Liverpool L8 7NP, England. 1974. Poetry, fiction, art, photos, cartoons, long-poems, collages, concrete art. "Tom Pickard, Jim Burns, Dave Calder, Roger McGough, Frances Horovitz." circ. 1,500. 2/yr. Pub'd 3 issues 1998; expects 3 issues 1999. sub. price: £2/3 issues incl. postage; per copy: 50p plus post; sample: 50p plus post. 24pp; size A5; of. Reporting time: as quickly as possible. Payment: none. Not copyrighted. No ads.

Smyrna Press, Dan Georgakas, Jim Malick, Barbara Saltz, Box 1151, Union City, NJ 07087. 1964. Poetry, fiction, art, parts-of-novels, collages, plays, non-fiction. "We try to publish 1-3 books a year which combine the latest technical breakthroughs with a concern for social change that is essentially Marxist but undogmatic. Our current projects combine art and politics as well as themes of sexual liberation. We can use good line drawings or woodcuts. We also distribute books of publishers in Denmark and Australia. Query before sending any material. Sample copies of literary books, $2; sample copies of art books, $3." avg. press run 2M. Pub'd 2 titles 1998; expects 2 titles 1999, 2 titles 2000. 21 titles listed in the *Small Press Record of Books in Print* (28th Edition, 1999-00). avg. price, cloth: $25; paper: $10; other: $2. Discounts: 40% bookstores, 10% education, bulk by arrangement, 30% prepaid bookstores. 60-250pp; 6×9; lp. Reporting time: 2-3 weeks, query before submitting. Simultaneous submissions accepted: no. Publishes 1% of manuscripts submitted. Payment: copies and 10% net. Copyrights for author.

Smyth & Helwys Publishing, Inc., Jackie Riley, Editor, 6316 Peake Road, Macon, GA 31210-3960, 912-752-2117; Fax 912-752-2264. 1990. Fiction, non-fiction. "Publisher of Christian books and educational resources." avg. press run 2M. Pub'd 30 titles 1998; expects 23 titles 1999, 22 titles 2000. avg. price, cloth: $25; paper: $11.95. 100-150pp; 6×9; of, electronic. Reporting time: 2 weeks queries, 3-4 months proposals and mss. Simultaneous submissions accepted: yes. Publishes 20% of manuscripts submitted. Payment: on paperback, we pay 10% of net sales. Copyrights for author.

The Snail's Pace Press, Inc., Darby Penney, Ken Denberg, 85 Darwin Road, Cambridge, NY 12816, 518-677-5208. 1990. Poetry. Pub'd 3 titles 1998; expects 3 titles 1999, 3 titles 2000. avg. price, paper: $6.

Discounts: 40% trade. 36pp; 5½×8½; of. Reporting time: 4 months. Simultaneous submissions accepted: no. Publishes 10% of manuscripts submitted. Payment: $50 and 50 copies. Copyrights for author. CLMP.

SNAKE NATION REVIEW, Roberta George, Founding Editor; Nancy Phillips, Associate Editor, 110 #2 West Force, Valdosta, GA 31601, 912-249-8334. 1989. Poetry, fiction, art, photos. circ. 1M. 4/yr. Pub'd 2 issues 1998; expects 4 issues 1999, 4 issues 2000. sub. price: $20; per copy: $6; sample: $6 (includes mailing). Back issues: $6 (includes mailing). Discounts: 40% to bookstores, jobbers. 110pp; 6×9; lp. Reporting time: 3-6 months. Simultaneous submissions accepted: yes. Publishes 10% of manuscripts submitted. Payment: 2 copies or prize money. Copyrighted, reverts to author. Ads: $100/$50/$25.

SNAKE RIVER REFLECTIONS, William White, 1863 Bitterroot Drive, Twin Falls, ID 83301, 208-734-0746, e-mail wjan@aol.com. 1990. Poetry, fiction, articles, cartoons, satire, criticism, reviews, letters, news items, non-fiction. "Short stories: 1,500 words max. Poetry: 30 lines max." circ. 250+. 10/yr (monthly, except Oct. & Dec.). Pub'd 10 issues 1998; expects 10 issues 1999, 10 issues 2000. sub. price: $7.50; per copy: 75¢; sample: 75¢. Back issues: 75¢. Discounts: Libraries $6/10 issues. 12pp; 5½×8½; †laser printer. Reporting time: 3 weeks. Simultaneous submissions accepted: no. Publishes 5% of manuscripts submitted. Payment: 1 copy. Copyrighted, reverts to author. Pub's reviews: 4 in 1998. §Anything of interest to writers. none.

SNOW LION NEWSLETTER & CATALOG, Snow Lion Publications, Inc., PO Box 6483, Ithaca, NY 14851. 1985. "News, announcements and products on Tibetan culture." circ. 30M. 4/yr. Pub'd 4 issues 1998; expects 4 issues 1999, 4 issues 2000. price per copy: free. 60pp; 11×17; newsprint.

Snow Lion Publications, Inc. (see also SNOW LION NEWSLETTER & CATALOG), PO Box 6483, Ithaca, NY 14851, 607-273-8506; 607-273-8519; fax 607-273-8508. 1980. Non-fiction. "130 titles in print." avg. press run 10M. Pub'd 12 titles 1998; expects 16 titles 1999, 18 titles 2000. 14 titles listed in the *Small Press Record of Books in Print* (28th Edition, 1999-00). avg. price, cloth: $45; paper: $15. Discounts: 40% average. 250pp; 5½×8½; of. Payment: 8% average. Copyrights for author.

SNOWY EGRET, Philip Repp, Editor; Karl Barnebey, Publisher, PO Box 9, Bowling Green, IN 47833. 1922. Poetry, fiction, articles, art, interviews, satire, criticism, reviews, letters, parts-of-novels, long-poems, non-fiction. "Emphasis on natural history and human beings in relation to nature from literary, artistic, philosophical, and historical points of view. Prose generally not môre than 3M words but will consider up to 10M; poetry generally less than page although long poems will be considered. Interested in works that celebrate the abundance and beauty of nature and examine the variety of ways, both positive and negative, through which human beings connect psychologically and spiritually with the natural world and living things. Looking for nature-oriented original graphics (offset prints, lithographs, woodcuts, etc) that can be editioned as part of an issue. Review copies of books desired. Originality of material or originality of treatment and literary quality and readability important. Payment on publication plus 2 contributor's copies. Recent contributors: Conrad Hilberry, David Abrams, James Armstrong, Justin D'Ath, Patricia Hooper. Send #10 SASE for writer's guidelines." circ. 500. 2/yr. Pub'd 2 issues 1998; expects 2 issues 1999, 2 issues 2000. sub. price: $12/1 year, $20/2 years; per copy: $8; sample: $8. Back issues: available on request. 52pp; 8½×11; †of. Reporting time: 2 months. Publishes less than 5% of manuscripts submitted. Payment: prose, $2 mag page; poetry, $4/poem, $4 mag page. Copyrighted, reverts to author. Pub's reviews: 2 in 1998. §People in relation to natural surroundings, fresh nature poetry, fiction, essays, criticism, philosophy, biography. Ads: none.

SO TO SPEAK, Hope Smith, SUB 1, Room 254 A, George Mason University, Fairfax, VA 22030, 703-993-3625. 1991. Poetry, fiction, art, photos, interviews, reviews, long-poems, plays, non-fiction. "Looking for positive, empowering feminist voice" circ. 1.3M. 2/yr. Pub'd 2 issues 1998; expects 2 issues 1999, 2 issues 2000. sub. price: $10; per copy: $5; sample: $5. Back issues: $2. 120pp; 5×8; lp. Reporting time: 6-8 months. Simultaneous submissions accepted: yes. Publishes 10% of manuscripts submitted. Payment: 2 copies, small payment for artwork. Copyrighted, reverts to author. Pub's reviews: 6 in 1998. §New poetry, fiction, and non-fiction. Ads: $50/$25-negotiable.

SO YOUNG!, Anti-Aging Press, Julia M. Busch, PO Box 141489, Coral Gables, FL 33114, 305-662-3928; FAX 305-661-4123. 1996. Poetry, articles, cartoons, reviews, letters, news items, non-fiction. "Positive, very up-paced. 200-500 words. Aromatherapy, cosmetics, acupressure, short subjects also, short *up* poetry. Recent contributors: Nancy Dahlberg, Joe Polansky, astrologers, experts in fields, Phil Breman investigative reporter. Milton Feher, Relaxation/Dance, therapist, Lisa Curtis, president Sophrological Society." circ. 1M. 6/yr. Expects 6 issues 1999, 6 issues 2000. sub. price: $35 USA, $42 Canada; per copy: $6 USA, Canada; sample: same. Back issues: same. Discounts: 25-49 20%, 50-100 30%, 100-499 40%, 500-999 50%, 1000+ 55%. 12pp; 8½×11; †photocopy. Reporting time: 1 month. Simultaneous submissions accepted: yes. Payment: newsletter copies. Copyrighted, reverts to author. Pub's reviews: 30+ in 1998. §Anti-aging, positive thought, holistic health, spiritual, cutting-edge medical breakthrough. Ads: $150/$75/$15 1/8 page. PMA, PAS, NAPRA, SPAN, NAIP, FPA, ABA, NPA.

SOCIAL ANARCHISM: A Journal of Practice and Theory, Howard J. Ehrlich, 2743 Maryland Avenue,

Baltimore, MD 21218, 410-243-6987; sociala@nothingness.org. 1980. Poetry, fiction, articles, art, photos, cartoons, interviews, satire, criticism, reviews, letters, non-fiction. "Essays should be between 1,000 and 15,000 words. Book reviews: 500-2,000 words. Recent contributors: Neala Schleuning, Kingsley Widmer, Brian Martin, Colin Ward, Elaine Leeder, Gaetano Piluso, David Bouchier, Murray Bookchin, Jane Myerding" circ. 1.2M. 2/yr. Pub'd 2 issues 1998; expects 2 issues 1999, 2 issues 2000. sub. price: $16 for 4 issues; per copy: $4; sample: $5. Back issues: $5. Discounts: 40%. 112pp; 6×9; of. Reporting time: 6 weeks. Payment: 3 copies. Not copyrighted. Pub's reviews: 40 in 1998. §Anarchism, feminism, ecology, radical arts and culture.

SOCIAL JUSTICE: A JOURNAL OF CRIME, CONFLICT, & WORLD ORDER, Global Options, Gregory Shank, PO Box 40601, San Francisco, CA 94140, 415-550-1703. 1974. Poetry, articles, interviews, satire, reviews, letters, news items, non-fiction. "Maximum length: 30 double-spaced ms pages, including footnotes. Recent authors: Edward Herman, Tony Platt, Samir Amin, Elaine Kim, Nancy Sheper-Hughes. A journal of progressive criminology and international law." circ. 3M. 4/yr. Pub'd 4 issues 1998; expects 4 issues 1999, 4 issues 2000. sub. price: $35 individual, $75 institution; per copy: $10 individual, $20 institutions; sample: $10. Back issues: same as single copy price or available from University Microfilms, Ann Arbor, MI. Discounts: agency 15%, trade discount to stores, distribution handled through De Boer, Ingram, Far East Periodicals, Ubiquity. 150-175pp; 6×9; of. Reporting time: 90 days. Simultaneous submissions accepted: no. Payment: none. Copyrighted, does not revert to author. Pub's reviews: 6 in 1998. §Criminology, international law, civil liberties, minority issues, pedagogy, women, human rights. Ads: $125/$75.

SOCIAL POLICY, Audrey Gartner, Managing Editor; Frank Riessman, Founding Editor; Andy Humm, Editor, 25 West 43rd Street, Room 620, New York, NY 10036, 212-642-2929. 1970. Articles, art, photos, interviews, criticism, reviews, letters, non-fiction. "Articles run 2M-5M words, on contemporary social thought and policy analysis (environmental, economics, community development, education). Recent special issues dealt with self-help, campaign finance reform, national service, women's movement, school reform. *Social Policy* is the magazine about movements" circ. 3M. 4/yr. Pub'd 4 issues 1998; expects 4 issues 1999. sub. price: $20 individuals, $50 institutions; per copy: $5; sample: $3. Back issues: $4. Discounts: 10% agent. 64pp; 7×11; lp. Reporting time: 2-4 weeks. Publishes 25% of manuscripts submitted. Payment: none. Copyrighted, rights do not revert to author unless requested. Pub's reviews: 4 in 1998. §Nonfiction, social policy materials, esp. in area of economics and human services, sociology. Ads: $300/$180.

SOCIAL PROBLEMS, University of California Press, Joel Best, Carolyn Palmer-Johnson, Managing Editor, University of California Press, 2120 Berkeley Way, Berkeley, CA 94720, 510-643-7154. 1953. Articles, reviews, non-fiction. "Editorial address: Sociology Dept., Southern Illinois Univ., Carbondale, IL 62901. Copyrighted by Society for the Study of Social Problems." circ. 3.7M. 5/yr. Pub'd 5 issues 1998; expects 5 issues 1999, 5 issues 2000. sub. price: $97 (+ $6 foreign postage); per copy: $26; sample: free. Back issues: same as single copy price. Discounts: foreign subs. agent 10%, one-time order 10+ 30%, standing orders (bookstores): 1-99 40%, 100+ 50%. 160pp; 7×10; of. Copyrighted, does not revert to author. Ads: $275/$200.

SOCIAL SCIENCE HISTORY, Duke University Press, Paula Baker, Joseph Alter, Werner Troksen, Katherine Lynch, Elizabeth Faue, Box 90660, Duke University, Durham, NC 27708-0660. "The official journal of the Social Science History Association. *Social Science History* is a forum for social scientists interested in the study of change over time and for historians interested in the development of consciously theoretical approaches to historical explication. It presents both innovative research that applies rigorous methodologies to the study of the past and essays that reflect upon the nature of the theories and methods used by scholars as they attempt to make sense of past events or trends." circ. 1.6M. 4/yr. Pub'd 4 issues 1998; expects 4 issues 1999, 4 issues 2000. sub. price: $80 institutions, $50 individuals, $15 students with photocopy of current I.D., additional $12 foreign. Ads: $225/$175.

SOCIAL TEXT, Duke University Press, Bruce Robbins, Andrew Ross, Box 90660, Duke University, Durham, NC 27708-0660. "*Social Text* covers a broad spectrum of social and cultural phenomena, applying the latest interpretive methods to the world at large. A leader in the field of cultural studies, the journal consistently focuses attention on questions of gender, sexuality, race, and the environment, publishing key works by the most influential social and cultural theorists. Daring and innovative, *Social Text* invites provocative interviews and challenging articles from emerging critical voices. Each issue breaks new ground in the debates about postcolonialism, postmodernism, and popular culture. Send review copies to Monica Marciczkiewicz, Center for the Critical Analysis of Contemporary Culture, 8 Bishop Place, New Brunswick, NJ 08903." circ. 850. 4/yr. Pub'd 4 issues 1998; expects 4 issues 1999, 4 issues 2000. sub. price: $75 institutions, $28 individuals, additional $12 foreign. Pub's reviews. Ads: $200/$150.

SOCIALIST REVIEW, Duke University Press, Greg Smith, Box 90660, Duke University, Durham, NC 27708-0660. "Sponsored by the Center for Social Research and Education. For more than two decades, the *Socialist Review* has occupied a distinctive position within the intellectual left in the United States, standing out among intellectual journals by virtue of its highly accessible language, inviting design, and compelling combination of activist politics and theoretical analysis. The *Socialist Review* is a widely respected forum for debates on a variety of topics, including the politics of identity, new approaches to radical political economy, and the relevance of postmodern theory to grassroots activist work. Send review copies to the Book Review Committee, *Socialist Review*, 1095 Market Street, Suite 618, San Francisco, CA 94103." circ. 1.3M. 4/yr. Pub'd 4 issues 1998; expects 4 issues 1999, 4 issues 2000. sub. price: $65 institutions, $28 individuals, additional $12 foreign. Pub's reviews. Ads: $325/$200.

SOCIETE, Technicians of the Sacred, Courtney Willis, 1317 N. San Fernando Blvd, Suite 310, Burbank, CA 91504. 1983. Poetry, fiction, articles, art, photos, interviews, reviews, music, non-fiction. "Related to African, neo-African systems, religion, magic, hermetic, etc." circ. 500. 3/yr. Pub'd 3 issues 1998; expects 3 issues 1999, 3 issues 2000. sub. price: $15; per copy: $10; sample: $10. Back issues: $10. 130pp; 8½×11; †perfect binding. Reporting time: 4 weeks. Payment: copy of issue. Copyrighted. Pub's reviews: 1 in 1998. §Voodoo-neo African, African religions, magic, occult, religion, gnosticism, hermetics.

SOCIETY, Irving Louis Horowitz, Editor-in-Chief, Transaction, Rutgers University, New Brunswick, NJ 08903, 908-932-2280. 1963. Articles, photos, interviews, reviews, non-fiction. "Most articles submitted are not more than 6000 words long. Subject matter is diversified, but confined to social science and public policy. Most authors are social scientists; most readers are generally informed about social science, but are not specialists." circ. 10M. 6/yr. Pub'd 6 issues 1998; expects 6 issues 1999, 6 issues 2000. sub. price: $48 individual, $24 students; per copy: $8. Back issues: $20. Discounts: agents 10%. 96pp; 8½×11; DTP. Reporting time: varies, often within 1 month. Payment: none. Copyrighted, does not revert to author. Pub's reviews: 30+ in 1998. §Books about social science, public policy. Ads: $850/$530. AAP.

SOCIOLOGY OF SPORT JOURNAL (SSJ), Human Kinetics Pub. Inc., Cynthia Hasbrook, Ph.D., Box 5076, Champaign, IL 61825-5076, 217-351-5076. 1984. Articles, reviews. "Human behavior in the context of sport and physical activity." circ. 1060. 4/yr. Pub'd 4 issues 1998; expects 4 issues 1999, 4 issues 2000. sub. price: $40 individual, $100 institution, $26 student; per copy: $11 indiv., $26 instit.; sample: free. Back issues: $11 indiv., $26 instit. Discounts: 5%. 120pp; 6×9; of. Reporting time: 2 months. Payment: none. Copyrighted, does not revert to author. Pub's reviews: 7 in 1998. §Sport, sport science, and physical education related to sociology. Ads: $300/$200 (4X rate). Midwest Book Publishers Association, American Booksellers Association.

SOCKS, DREGS AND ROCKING CHAIRS, Ge(of Huth), editor, 875 Central Parkway, Schenectady, NY 12309. 1982. Poetry, cartoons, collages, concrete art. "*Socks, Dregs & Rocking Chairs (SD&RC)* is an irregular comicbook (xeroxed), publishing all formats of underground/experimental comic art. Subscriptions can be of any dollar amount—cost (which varies) per issue will be subtracted when mailed." circ. 100. 1/yr. Pub'd 1 issue 1998; expects 1 issue 1999, 1 issue 2000. sub. price: varies; per copy: 75¢; sample: 75¢. Back issues: 75¢. Discounts: none. 8pp; size varies; †photocopy. Reporting time: 2 weeks. Payment: at least 2 copies; 1/4 of press run is divided among contributors. Copyrighted, reverts to author.

SOJOURNER, THE WOMEN'S FORUM, Stephanie Poggi, Editor, 42 Seaverns Avenue, Jamaica Plain, MA 02130-1109, 617-524-0415. 1975. Poetry, fiction, articles, photos, cartoons, interviews, criticism, reviews, letters, news items, non-fiction. "*Sojourner* has an open editorial policy—we attempt to present a forum for women, and we will consider anything for publication which is not racist, sexist, or homophobic." circ. 45M. 12/yr. Pub'd 12 issues 1998; expects 12 issues 1999, 12 issues 2000. sub. price: $21; per copy: $2.50; sample: $3. Back issues: $5. Discounts: 50% agent, 40% bookstore. 52pp; 11×17; of, web press. Reporting time: 2 months. We accept simultaneous submissions for fiction and poetry, not for features. Publishes 10% of manuscripts submitted. Payment: 2 free copies, one-year subscription, $15. Copyrighted, reverts to author. Pub's reviews: 100 in 1998. §Feminism, women's issues, any book, film, etc., by a woman or about women. Ads: $1350/$675/$20 for 4 lines, 40 characters/line.

SOLO, Glenna Luschei, Founding Editor; David Oliveira, Co-Editor; Jackson Wheeler, Co-Editor, 5146 Foothill, Carpinteria, CA 93013, E-mail swharton@ohm.elee.calpoly.edu; berrypress@aol.com. 1996. Poetry, criticism, reviews, long-poems. "Recent contributors include: Fred Chappell, Jane Hirshfield, Carolyn Kizer, Linda Pastan, Carol Muske, Ronald Bayes, Forest Gander, Ron Koertge, Robert Creeley, Robert Bly, and Sherman Alexie." circ. 1M. 2/yr. Pub'd 1 issue 1998; expects 2 issues 1999, 2 issues 2000. sub. price: $16; per copy: $9; sample: $9. Back issues: $5 for old *Cafe Solo*. Discounts: tradition. 130pp; 6×9; of. Reporting time: 2 weeks. Simultaneous submissions accepted: no. Publishes 75% of manuscripts submitted. Payment: copies. Copyrighted, rights reverting negotiable. Pub's reviews: 1 book of poetry review, 4 small book review(s) notes in 1998. §Poetry, criticism.

SOLO FLYER, David B. McCoy, 2115 Clearview NW, Massillon, OH 44646. 1979. Poetry, long-poems. "Three or more 4-page flyers will be published a year, each by an individual author. All styles of poetry using capitalization and punctuation will be considered" circ. 100. 3/yr. Pub'd 3 issues 1998; expects 3 issues 1999, 3 issues 2000. sample price: free with SASE. 4pp; 5¼×8½; †photocopy. Reporting time: 1-3 months. Simultaneous submissions accepted: yes. Publishes 5-10% of manuscripts submitted. Payment: 20-25 copies.

Copyrighted, reverts to author.

Solution Publishing, Jean Hicks, President, 1647 Willow Pass Road #101, Concord, CA 94520. 1994. News items, non-fiction. avg. press run 1M-5M. Expects 1 title 1999, 3 titles 2000. 3 titles listed in the *Small Press Record of Books in Print* (28th Edition, 1999-00). avg. price, cloth: $25. Discounts: 45-55%. 250-300pp; 5½×8½; of. Reporting time: 60 days. Payment: 6-8%. Copyrights for author. PMA, NABE.

SOM Publishing, division of School of Metaphysics (see also THRESHOLDS JOURNAL), Dr. Barbara Condron, CEO & Editor-in-Chief, HCR 1, Box 15, Windyville, MO 65783, 417-345-8411. 1973. "Educational, inspirational, uplifting books designed to raise the consciousness of humanity" avg. press run 5M. Pub'd 1 title 1998; expects 4 titles 1999, 4 titles 2000. 21 titles listed in the *Small Press Record of Books in Print* (28th Edition, 1999-00). avg. price, paper: $13 (range: $4.95-$15). Discounts: 40% trade, 50% jobbers, 20% organizations, churches, groups without sales tax number. 180pp; 5½×8½, 4½×7; web press. Payment: none. SOM holds copyright. School of Metaphysics Associates.

Somesuch Press, Stanley Marcus, 300 Crescent Court, Suite 875, Dallas, TX 75201, 214-871-8080. 1974. Fiction, articles, art, non-fiction. avg. press run 200. Expects 2 titles 1999, 1 title 2000. 22 titles listed in the *Small Press Record of Books in Print* (28th Edition, 1999-00). avg. price, cloth: $40. Discounts: 40%, 10 or more copies, 33⅓%, 1-10 copies; 10% libraries. 40pp; 2⅞×3; lp. Reporting time: 1 month. Payment: by negotiation. Copyrights for author.

SOMNIAL TIMES, Gloria Reiser, Michael Banys, Box 561, Quincy, IL 62306-0561, 217-222-9082. 1989. Poetry, articles, interviews, reviews, letters, news items, non-fiction. "Anything relating to dreams and dreaming." circ. 85-100. 6/yr. Pub'd 6 issues 1998; expects 6 issues 1999, 6 issues 2000. sub. price: $12; per copy: $3; sample: $3. Back issues: $2. Discounts: $1 each for resale, $1 each for classroom or group use. 10pp; 8½×11; †photocopy. Reporting time: 4-8 weeks. Simultaneous submissions accepted: yes. Publishes 80% of manuscripts submitted. Payment: none, advertising if desired. Not copyrighted. Pub's reviews: 3-4 in 1998. §Anything related to dreams and dreaming, reveries, daydreams, fantasy, etc. Ads: $5 per issue for 3½ X 3½ space.

SONAR MAP, Shawn Mediaclast, Kelly Newcomer, Co-Editor, PO Box 25243, Eugene, OR 97402, Voice/fax: 541-688-1523; eleg-sci@efn.org. 1996. Poetry, articles, art, photos, reviews, music, letters, collages. "*Sonar Map* supports/recognizes experimental music, art, and communication" circ. 2M. 4/yr. Expects 4 issues 1999, 4 issues 2000. sub. price: $10; per copy: $2.50; sample: trade for reviews. 24pp; 8¼×10¾; of. Payment: zero at this time. Copyrighted, reverts to author. Pub's reviews: 8 in 1998. §D.I.Y., music, art, culture. Ads: $95/$40/$26 1/3 page/$17 1/4 page/$9 1/8 page.

SONGS OF INNOCENCE, Pendragonian Publications, Michael Pendragon, PO Box 719, New York, NY 10101-0719. 1999. Poetry, fiction, art. "Poetry, short stories (2,500 word maximum), essays and b/w artwork which celebrate the nobler aspects of mankind and the human experience. Rhymed, metered, lyrical verse preferred. Publishes literary poetry and prose in the tradition of Blake, Shelley, Keats, Whitman, Emerson, Wordsworth, Thoreau and Twain." circ. 500. 3/yr. Expects 2 issues 1999, 3 issues 2000. sub. price: $12; per copy: $5. 48pp; 5½×8½; †xerox. Reporting time: up to 3 months. Simultaneous submissions accepted: yes. Payment: 1 copy. Not copyrighted.

SONORA REVIEW, Dept. of English, University of Arizona, Tucson, AZ 85721, 520-626-8383. 1980. Poetry, fiction, articles, interviews, satire, criticism, reviews, letters, parts-of-novels, non-fiction. "We publish poetry, fiction, and creative non-fiction, as well as interviews and annual special features. Annual contests in poetry, fiction and creative nonfiction. Submissions should be accompanied by *SASE!*. Editors change every year. Please address work to the appropriate genre editor: Fiction, Poetry, etc. Address business/subscription matters and any questions or forms to Managing Editor. Revisions only upon editorial request. Simultaneous submissions accepted" circ. 800. 2/yr. Pub'd 2 issues 1998; expects 2 issues 1999, 2 issues 2000. sub. price: $12; per copy: $6; sample: $6. Discounts: 40% to bookstores. 120pp; 6×9; of. Reporting time: 6 months-1 year. Simultaneous submissions accepted: yes. Publishes 1% of manuscripts submitted. Payment: 2 contributor's copies. Copyrighted, reverts to author. Pub's reviews: 2 in 1998. Ads: $90/$45. CLMP.

Sonoran Publishing, George A. Fathauer, 116 North Roosevelt, Suite 121, Chandler, AZ 85226, 602-961-5176. 1994. Art, non-fiction. "Books on history of radio and electronics, for historians and collectors of radios. Purchased existing inventory and publishing rights to several titles from another publisher" avg. press run 3M. Pub'd 1 title 1998; expects 2 titles 1999, 1 title 2000. 5 titles listed in the *Small Press Record of Books in Print* (28th Edition, 1999-00). avg. price, paper: $26.95. Discounts: 6-24 copies 40%, 25-49 copies 42%, 50-99 44%, 100+ 46%. 250pp; 8½×11; of. Reporting time: 60 days. Simultaneous submissions accepted: yes. Publishes 20% of manuscripts submitted. Payment: usually 10% royalty. Does not copyright for author. PMA.

Sorenson Books, A.E. Nelson, 1093 Beacon Street, Suite 1-B, Brookline, MA 02146, 617-264-8800; FAX

617-969-6369. 1995. Fiction, non-fiction. "We are interested in literary fiction; cultural, political and intellectual history; psychodynamic psychology. Most recent title: *Solace and Romance* by Kenneth Levin. We are not accepting unsolicited manuscripts at this time." Expects 3 titles 1999, 3 titles 2000. 1 title listed in the *Small Press Record of Books in Print* (28th Edition, 1999-00). avg. price, cloth: $24.95. Discounts: 1 copy 33%, 5 40%, 25 42%, 50 44%, 100 46%, 250 50%, 1000 55%. 300pp; 6×9. Copyrights for author.

SOS JAZZ, Mark Corroto, PO Box 1382, Youngstown, OH 44501. 1994. Poetry, articles, art, photos, interviews, criticism, reviews, letters, collages, news items, non-fiction. circ. 4M. 6/yr. Pub'd 6 issues 1998; expects 6 issues 1999, 6 issues 2000. sub. price: $5; per copy: 2 stamps; sample: same. Back issues: none. Discounts: 20%. 8pp; 5½×8½, 8½×14; †photocopy/print. Reporting time: 6 months. Simultaneous submissions accepted: yes. Publishes 25% of manuscripts submitted. Payment: 1 copy. Not copyrighted. Pub's reviews: 5-10 in 1998. §Jazz, Avant, rap - musics. Ads: $25/$15. NYCS, ASCA.

SOUND PRACTICES, Joe Roberts, PO Box 180562, Austin, TX 78718, e-mail sp@tpoint.com. 1992. Articles, interviews, reviews. "Interested in audio experimentation, history of sound technology" circ. 1M. 4/yr. Pub'd 4 issues 1998; expects 4 issues 1999, 4 issues 2000. sub. price: $20; per copy: $5; sample: $5. Discounts: negotiable. 60pp; 8½×11; of. Payment: varies. Not copyrighted. Pub's reviews: 5 in 1998. §Electronics, music, hi-fi, sound. Ads: $300/$175.

Sound View Press, Peter Hastings Falk, 859 Boston Post Road, PO Box 833, Madison, CT 06443, 203-245-2246, Fax; 203-245-5116, E-mail; soundviewpress@att.net. 1985. "Publisher of the biographical dictionary, *Who Was Who In American Art*, and monographs on American artists in conjunction with museum or gallery exhibitions." avg. press run 2M. Pub'd 3 titles 1998; expects 3 titles 1999, 3 titles 2000. avg. price, cloth: $39-$300. Discounts: varies by title. 250-1,750pp; 8½×11, 6×9; we subcontract printing, binding, fulfillment, etc. Reporting time: 2 weeks. Payment: negotiable. Copyrights for author.

Soundboard Books, 1030 E. El Camino Real, Suite 124, Sunnyvale, CA 94087, 408-738-1705. 1990. Non-fiction. avg. press run 2M. Pub'd 1 title 1998; expects 2 titles 1999, 2 titles 2000. 3 titles listed in the *Small Press Record of Books in Print* (28th Edition, 1999-00). avg. price, paper: $6.95. Discounts: 2-15 20%, 16+ 40%. 48pp; 6×9; of. Copyrights for author.

SOUNDINGS EAST, Kathleen Boudreau, Editor, English Dept., Salem State College, Salem, MA 01970, 508-741-6000. 1973. Poetry, fiction, art, photos. "Our primary interest is poetry and short fiction. We print several stories in each issue. Since 1980 we have presented a 'Feature Poet' section, usually a New England poet who has not yet published a book. These have included: Christopher Jane Corkery, Michelle Gillet, Don Johnson, Susan Donnelly, Jackie Crews, Guri Andermann, Carole Borges, Debra Allbery, Robert Cooperman, and Martha Ramsey." circ. 2M. 2/yr. Pub'd 2 issues 1998; expects 2 issues 1999, 2 issues 2000. sub. price: $10; per copy: $5; sample: $3. Back issues: usually $3 per copy. Discounts: we charge $18 for 2 years, $26 for 3 years. 64pp; 5½×8½. Reporting time: 7 months, we do *not* read from April 21 to Sept 21. Payment: 2 free copies. Copyrighted, reverts to author.

THE SOUNDS OF POETRY, The Sounds of Poetry Press, Jacquiline Sanchez, Publisher & Editor, 2076 Vinewood, Detroit, MI 48216-5506. 1983. Poetry, articles, reviews. "Recent contributors: John Binns, Denice Childers, Bernard Hewitt, Rod Farmer, Ruben de la Vega, Trinidad Sanchez Jr., Gil Saenz. We are open to poetry submissions from truckers, Harley Davidson motorcyclists, Vietnam veterans as well as from the general poetry writers. *The Sounds of Poetry Magazine* is an international magazine with international poetry contributors. We accept birth, wedding and other special occasion announcements. Once a writer submits material, it's the writer's responsibility to keep us informed of address changes." circ. 200. 3/yr. Pub'd 3 issues 1998; expects 3 issues 1999, 3 issues 2000. sub. price: $10; per copy: $4.50; sample: $4.50. Back issues: not available. Discounts: libraries, free copy. 20-32pp; 5½×8½; desktop. Reporting time: 2 weeks to 1 year. We prefer not to receive simultaneous submissions. Publishes 50% of manuscripts submitted. Payment: 1 copy in which work appears. Copyrighted, reverts to author. Pub's reviews: 1 in 1998. §Poetry. Ads: $50/$25/$15 1/4 page/$10 1/8.

The Sounds of Poetry Press (see also THE SOUNDS OF POETRY), Jacqueline Sanchez, Publishser, 2076 Vinewood, Detroit, MI 48216-5506. 1983. Poetry, articles, reviews, news items. avg. press run 200. Pub'd 1 title 1998; expects 1 title 1999, 1 title 2000. 1 title listed in the *Small Press Record of Books in Print* (28th Edition, 1999-00). avg. price, paper: $4.50. Discounts: none. 24-32pp; 5½×8½; desktop publishing. Reporting time: 1 month to 1 year. Simultaneous submissions accepted: no. Payment: negotiable. Copyrights for author.

Sourcebooks, Inc., Mark Warda; Todd Stocke, 121 N. Washington Street, Naperville, IL 60540, 630-961-3900; Fax 630-961-2168. 1987. Non-fiction. "Shipping Address: 1725 Clearwater/Largo Rd. S., Clearwater, FL 33756. Also publish under the imprint of Sphinx Publishing." Pub'd 15 titles 1998; expects 65 titles 1999, 65 titles 2000. 106 titles listed in the *Small Press Record of Books in Print* (28th Edition, 1999-00). avg. price, paper: $19. 130pp; 8½×11, 6×9. Reporting time: 3 months. Copyrights for author. PMA, MAPA.

SOUTH AMERICAN EXPLORER, Don Montague, 126 Indian Creek Road, Ithaca, NY 14850, 607-277-0488; Fax 607-277-6122; explorer@samexplo.org. 1977. Articles, photos, interviews, reviews, letters, news items, non-fiction. circ. 7M. 4/yr. Pub'd 4 issues 1998; expects 4 issues 1999, 4 issues 2000. sub. price: $22/4 issues; subs included in $40 Club membership; per copy: $4; sample: $3. Back issues: $4. Discounts: $1 per issue. 65pp; 8½×11; of, sheet fed. Reporting time: 8 weeks. Simultaneous submissions accepted: yes. Publishes 80% of manuscripts submitted. Payment: negotiable. Copyrighted, reverts to author. Pub's reviews: 16 in 1998. §Latin America, natural history, field sciences, adventure, folk art, outdoor sports, travel, South American history. Ads: $775/$395/25, also color $975/$495.

THE SOUTH ATLANTIC QUARTERLY, Duke University Press, Fredric Jameson, Box 90660, Duke University, Durham, NC 27708-0660. "*SAQ* targets the intellectual reader with special issues on current, diverse, and often controversial cultural topics. Past issues have included Ireland and Irish Cultural Studies, Mathematics, Science, and Postclassical Theory, Materialist Feminism, and Readin' Country Music. Future collections will cover Cubans on Cuba, Derek Walcott, Trauma: Writing, Therapy, Testimony." circ. 1.4M. 4/yr. Pub'd 4 issues 1998; expects 4 issues 1999, 4 issues 2000. sub. price: $75 institutions, $28 individuals, additional $12 foreign. Ads: $300/$200.

SOUTH CAROLINA REVIEW, Wayne Chapman, Editor; Donna Haisty Winchell, Editor, English Dept, Clemson Univ, Clemson, SC 29634-1503, 803-656-3151. 1968. Poetry, fiction, articles, interviews, satire, criticism, reviews, non-fiction. "Recent contributors: Joyce Carol Oates, Leslie Fiedler, Cleanth Brooks, George Garrett" circ. 600. 2/yr. Pub'd 2 issues 1998. sub. price: $10 + $1.50 s/h; per copy: $10; sample: $10. Back issues: $10. 200-208pp; 9×6; †desktop, pagemaker. Reporting time: 6-9 weeks. Simultaneous submissions accepted: no. Payment: copies. Copyrighted. Pub's reviews: 35 in 1998. §Poetry, literary history, criticism. CLMP, CELJ.

SOUTH DAKOTA REVIEW, Brian Bedard, Editor; Geraldine Sanford, Editorial Assistant, University of South Dakota, 414 East Clark, Vermillion, SD 57069, 605-677-5229/5966. 1963. Poetry, fiction, articles, art, interviews, criticism, parts-of-novels. "Issues vary in content; not every type of material will be in each issue. Still committed to Western subjects and focuses as primary interest. Occasional annotated listing of selected 'Books Received'." circ. 500. 4/yr. Pub'd 4 issues 1998; expects 4 issues 1999, 4 issues 2000. sub. price: $18, $30/2 years; per copy: $6; sample: $4. Back issues: most are available, send for price list. Discounts: 40% to bookstores. 150-180pp; 6×9; of. Reporting time: 6-10 weeks, except during summer. Simultaneous submissions accepted: no. Publishes 5%-10% of manuscripts submitted. Payment: 1 or more copies plus 1 year subscription. We reserve our own reprint rights. Ads: none. CLMP.

South End Press, Loie Hayes, Sonia Shah, Lynn Lu, Anthony Arnove, 7 Brookline Street #1, Cambridge, MA 02139-4146. 1977. Criticism, non-fiction. "At South End Press—a collectively managed, non-profit publisher of non-fiction—our goal is to provide books that encourage critical thinking and constructive action, thereby helping to create fundamental social change. Since 1977, we have released over 200 titles addressing the key issues of the day, focusing on political, economic, cultural, gender, race, and ecological dimensions of life in the United States and the world." avg. press run 3M. Pub'd 6 titles 1998; expects 10 titles 1999, 11 titles 2000. 67 titles listed in the *Small Press Record of Books in Print* (28th Edition, 1999-00). avg. price, cloth: $40; paper: $16. Discounts: bookstores 20-50%. 250pp; 5½×8½; in-house desktop publishing. Reporting time: 6-8 weeks. Simultaneous submissions accepted: yes. Publishes 1-5% of manuscripts submitted. Payment: 11% of discount price. Copyrights for author.

THE SOUTHERN CALIFORNIA ANTHOLOGY, James Ragan, Editor-in-Chief, Master of Professional Writing Program, WPH 404/Univ. of Southern Calif., Los Angeles, CA 90089-4034, 213-740-5775. 1983. Poetry, fiction. "Fiction submissions - 25 pp. maximum. Poetry submissions - limited to 5 poems. Please enclose SASE. Recent contributors include John Updike, James Merrill, Robert Bly, Joyce Carol Oates, James Ragan, Marge Piercy, Doris Grumbach, Amiri Baraka, Czeslaw Milosz, Andrei Voznesensky, Yevgeny Yevtushenko, Donald Hall, Denise Levertov, X.J. Kennedy, and W.S. Merwin." circ. 1M. 1/yr. Pub'd 1 issue 1998; expects 1 issue 1999, 1 issue 2000. sub. price: $9.95; per copy: $9.95; sample: $5. Back issues: $5. Discounts: Bookstores 40%. 140pp; 5½×8½; †lp. Reporting time: 3 months. Simultaneous submissions accepted: no. Publishes 10% of manuscripts submitted. Payment: 3 copies. Copyrighted, reverts to author.

SOUTHERN EXPOSURE, Institute for Southern Studies, Pat Arnow, Managing Editor, PO Box 531, Durham, NC 27702, 919-419-8311. 1973. Fiction, articles, art, photos, interviews, reviews, parts-of-novels, long-poems, collages, plays. "All material must be related to social change, cultural features, oral history, economic and political aspects of the South. A query letter can be helpful, but is not necessary. Very little fiction or poetry published. We publish four regular issues each year." circ. 10M. 4/yr. Pub'd 4 issues 1998; expects 4 issues 1999, 4 issues 2000. sub. price: $24; per copy: $6; sample: $4. Back issues: $2.50-$8.95. Discounts: 40% 50 or more. 64pp; 8½×11; of. Reporting time: 8 weeks. Payment: $75-$200. Copyrighted, does not revert to author. Pub's reviews: 4 in 1998. §Southern, related to the South. Ads: $600/$300.

SOUTHERN HUMANITIES REVIEW, Dan R. Latimer, Co-Editor; Virginia M. Kouidis, 9088 Haley Center, Auburn Univ., Auburn, AL 36849, 334-844-9088. 1967. Poetry, fiction, articles, interviews, satire, criticism, reviews, parts-of-novels, non-fiction. "Peter Green, Christopher Norris, Lars Gustafsson, Donald Hall, Ann Deagon." circ. 700. 4/yr. Pub'd 4 issues 1998; expects 4 issues 1999, 4 issues 2000. sub. price: $15 U.S., $20 foreign; per copy: $5 U.S.; $7 foreign; sample: $5 U.S.; $7 foreign. Back issues: same as single copy price/or complete volumes, $15 US $20 foreign. Discounts: none. 100pp; 6×9; 1p. Reporting time: 1-3 months. Simultaneous submissions accepted: no. Publishes poetry 2%, fiction 1%, essays 12% of manuscripts submitted. Payment: $100 best essay, $100 best story, $50 best poem *published* each volume. Copyrighted, reverts to author. Pub's reviews: 53 in 1998. §Criticism, fiction, poetry. Ads: $100 inside back cover, full page only, arranged well in advance. CELJ, CLMP.

SOUTHERN INDIANA REVIEW, T. Kramer, Editor; T. Wilhelmus, Editor; K. Waters, Editor; M. Graham, Editor, Liberal Arts Department, Univ. of Southern Indiana, Evansville, IN 47712, 812-464-1735. fax 812-465-7152. email tkramer@evansville.net. 1994. Poetry, fiction, articles, art, photos, interviews, criticism, reviews, letters, parts-of-novels, long-poems, plays, non-fiction. circ. 350. 1/yr. Pub'd 1 issue 1998; expects 1 issue 1999, 1 issue 2000. sub. price: $10; per copy: $10; sample: $10. Back issues: $6. 150pp; 6×9. Reporting time: 2 months. Simultaneous submissions accepted: yes. Publishes 10% of manuscripts submitted. Payment: copy of magazine. Copyrighted, reverts to author. Pub's reviews. §Midwestern themes. CLMP.

THE SOUTHERN JOURNAL, Appalachian Log Publishing Company, Ron Gregory, PO Box 20297, Charleston, WV 25362, 304-722-6866. 1991. Poetry, fiction, articles, photos, cartoons, interviews, satire, non-fiction. "Use only writing by or about Southeastern US, includes West Virginia. Keep it short, to be run in one issue, usually 300 words. No profanity. Accept personal profiles, historic articles, family history and genealogy, poetry, travel, short stories, fiction, non-fiction. No religion" circ. 5M. 12/yr. Pub'd 12 issues 1998; expects 11 issues 1999, 11 issues 2000. sub. price: $15; per copy: $1.50; sample: $1.50. Back issues: $2.50 each. Discounts: 2 years $25.00. 33pp; 8½×11; †of. Reporting time: 30-60 days. Payment: 50¢ per column inch. Not copyrighted. Pub's reviews: 20 in 1998. §Civil war-confederate, genealogy, local history. Ads: $200/$115/$3.00 per 20 words classified.

SOUTHERN POETRY REVIEW, Ken McLaurin, Editor, Advancement Studies Dept., Central Piedmont Community College, Charlotte, NC 28235, 704-330-6002. 1958. Poetry. "*SPR* is not a regional mag, though we function naturally as an outlet for new Southern talent. We emphasize variety and intensity. No restrictions on style, content or length. (We do not consider poems during the summer months.)" circ. 1M-1.2M. 2/yr. Pub'd 2 issues 1998; expects 2 issues 1999, 2 issues 2000. sub. price: $8; per copy: $5; sample: $3. Back issues: $3. Discounts: 25%. 80pp; 6×9; of. Reporting time: 4-6 months. Simultaneous submissions accepted: no. Publishes 2% of manuscripts submitted. Payment: contributor copy. Copyrighted, reverts to author. Pub's reviews: 6 in 1998. §Eclectic. Ads: none. CLMP.

SOUTHERN QUARTERLY: A Journal of the Arts in the South, Stephen Flinn Young, Editor; Noel Polk, Advisory Editor; Thomas J. Richardson, Advisory Editor; Lola Norris, Editorial Assistant, Box 5078, Southern Station, USM, Hattiesburg, MS 39406-5078, 601-261-1301; Fax 601-266-5800; Robert.Young@usm.edu. 1962. Articles, photos, interviews, criticism, reviews, music, letters. "The editor invites essays, articles and book reviews on both contemporary and earlier literature, music, art, architecture, popular and folk arts, theatre and dance in the South. Particularly sought are survey papers on the arts and arts criticism — achievements, trends, movements, colonies. Special issues are available on southern women playwrights, contemporary southern theatre, and on southern art and artists, on Erskine Caldwell, in the art South, Caroline Gordon. Inquiries and manuscripts should be addressed to *The Southern Quarterly* at the above address." circ. 950. 4/yr. Pub'd 4 issues 1998; expects 4 issues 1999, 4 issues 2000. sub. price: $18/yr, $32/2 yr individual; $35/yr institutions, add $5 for international mailing; per copy: $7; sample: $7. Back issues: vary, price list available. Discounts: subscription agency $15/individual subscriptions; $30 institutional subscriptions, add $5 for int'l mailing. 156pp; 7×10; of. Reporting time: 3-5 months. Simultaneous submissions accepted: no. Payment: 2 copies of journal and 1 yr. subscription. Copyrighted, reverts to author. Pub's reviews: 30 books, 3 films in 1998. §Studies of the arts in the South: literature, music, art, architecture, popular and folk arts, theatre and dance. Ads: 100/$75. CELJ.

THE SOUTHERN REVIEW, James Olney, Editor; Dave Smith, Editor, 43 Allen Hall, Louisiana State University, Baton Rouge, LA 70803, 225-388-5108. 1965 new series (1935 original series). Poetry, fiction, articles, interviews, criticism, reviews, letters, parts-of-novels. "We emphasize craftsmanship and intellectual content. We favor articles on contemporary literature and on the history and culture of the South. Recent contributors: Lewis P. Simpson, W.D. Snodgrass, Seamus Heaney, Reynolds Price, Lee Smith, Mary Oliver, Medbh McGuckian, Eavan Boland" circ. 3.1M. 4/yr. Pub'd 4 issues 1998; expects 4 issues 1999, 4 issues 2000. sub. price: $25 ind., $50 inst.; per copy: $8 ind., $16 inst.; sample: $8 ind., $16 inst. Back issues: same. 250pp; 6¾×10; 1p. Reporting time: 6-8 weeks. Simultaneous submissions accepted: no. Publishes 1% or less of manuscripts submitted. Payment: poetry $20/page, prose $12/page. Copyrighted, reverts to author. Pub's reviews: 12 in 1998. §Contemporary literature, fiction, poetry, culture of the South. Ads: $250/$150. CLMP.

Southern Star Publishing, 123 Brentwood Point, Brentwood, TN 37027. 1994. "Artwork, design book covers and illus. and typeset text." avg. press run 500. Pub'd 1 title 1998; expects 2 titles 1999, 2-3 titles 2000. 4 titles listed in the *Small Press Record of Books in Print* (28th Edition, 1999-00). avg. price, paper: $10.95; other: $4.95 (diskbook). Discounts: 20% single copy, 50% volume to booksellers. 150pp; 4.3×7, 4×8. Reporting time: 2 weeks. Simultaneous submissions accepted: yes. Publishes 50% of manuscripts submitted. Copyrights for author. SPAN, RWA, BookStar Reviews, Conservatory of American Letters, ABA Exhibit.

●**Southpaw Press,** 1653 S. Mountain Springs Blvd., New Harmony, UT 84757, 435-865-1785; Fax 435-865-1786; mp@southpawpress.com. 1996. 1 title listed in the *Small Press Record of Books in Print* (28th Edition, 1999-00).

SOUTHWEST JOURNAL, Full Moon Publications, Sharida Rizzuto, Harold Tollison, Ann Hoyt, Elaine Wolfe, 577 Central Avenue, Box 4, Jefferson, LA 70121-0517, e-mail: horizons@altavista.net or blueskies@discoverymail.com; Websites www.freeyellow.com/members2/oldwest/index.htm/ or www2.cyber-cities.com/z/zines/. 1988. "*The Southwest Journal* is the Old Southwest, history, bios, autobiographies, stories, and legends." circ. 300-500. 2/yr. Pub'd 2 issues 1998; expects 2 issues 1999, 2 issues 2000. sub. price: $13.80; per copy: $7.90; sample: $7.90. Back issues: $7.90. Discounts: trade with other like publications. 80pp; 8½×11; †of, excellent quality offset covers. Reporting time: 2-6 weeks. Simultaneous submissions accepted: yes. Publishes 40% of manuscripts submitted. Payment: free copies, fees paid to all contributors negotiable. Copyrighted, reverts to author. Pub's reviews: 14 in 1998. §The Old West, bios, history, autobios, stories, legends. Ads: free. NWC, SPGA, HWA, MWA, Western Writers of America (WWA), Arizona Authors Association (AAA).

Southwest Research and Information Center (see also THE WORKBOOK), Kathy Cone, Editor; Cynthia Taylor, Managing Editor, PO Box 4524, Albuquerque, NM 87106, 505-346-1455; Fax 505-346-1459. 1974. Articles, reviews, news items. "Resource information for citizen action of all kinds. Review of small and 'alternative' press publications in more than 30 categories of environmental justice and social change issues." avg. press run 2.5M. Pub'd 4 titles 1998; expects 4 titles 1999, 4 titles 2000. 5 titles listed in the *Small Press Record of Books in Print* (28th Edition, 1999-00). avg. price, paper: $3.50. Discounts: 40% to distributors. 48pp; 8½×11; of. Reporting time: 1 month. Payment: occasional funding secured. Does not copyright for author. Independent Press Association.

SOUTHWEST REVIEW, Willard Spiegelman, Editor; Elizabeth Mills, Senior Editor and Director of Development, Southern Methodist University, 307 Fondren Library W., Box 750374, Dallas, TX 75275-0374, 214-768-1037. 1915. Poetry, fiction, articles, interviews, criticism, parts-of-novels, long-poems, non-fiction. "Poetry, fiction, essays, interviews. A quarterly that serves the interests of its region but is not bound by them. The *Southwest Review* has always striven to present the work of writers and scholars from the surrounding states and to offer analyses of problems and themes that are distinctly southwestern, and at the same time publish the works of good writers regardless of their locales." circ. 1.5M. 4/yr. Pub'd 4 issues 1998; expects 4 issues 1999, 4 issues 2000. sub. price: $24; per copy: $6; sample: $6. Back issues: available on request. Discounts: 15% to agencies. 144pp; 6×9; of. Reporting time: 3 months. Simultaneous submissions accepted: yes. Publishes 3% of manuscripts submitted. Payment: yes. Copyrighted, reverts to author. Ads: $250 (1X), $700 (4X)/$150 (1X), $469 (4X). CLMP, CELJ.

SOU'WESTER, Fred W. Robbins, Editor, Southern Illinois University, Edwardsville, IL 62026-1438. 1960. Poetry, fiction, satire, long-poems. "We have no particular editorial biases or taboos. We publish the best poetry and fiction we can find. However, we do not publish science fiction or fantasy." circ. 300. 2/yr. Pub'd 3 issues 1998; expects 2 issues 1999, 2 issues 2000. sub. price: $10, $18 2 years; per copy: $5; sample: $5. Back issues: price varies. 120pp; 6×9; of. Reporting time: 3-4 months. Simultaneous submissions accepted: yes. Publishes 2% of manuscripts submitted. Payment: copies; 1 year subscription. Copyrighted, reverts to author. Ads: $90/$50. CLMP.

Sovereignty Press, Zardoya Eagles, 1241 Johnson Avenue, #353, San Luis Obispo, CA 93401, 805-543-6100; fax 805-543-1085; sovtypress@aol.com. 1996. Fiction, parts-of-novels, non-fiction. "Sovereignty Press specializes in professional nonfiction. We seek contributions that address past and current trends, personal and professional evolution, and growth of professional stature and esteem." avg. press run 5M. Pub'd 2 titles 1998; expects 2 titles 1999, 2 titles 2000. 3 titles listed in the *Small Press Record of Books in Print* (28th Edition, 1999-00). avg. price, paper: $19.95. Discounts: 2-5 copies 20%, 6-25 40%, 26-74 45%, 75+ 50%. 250pp; 6×9. Reporting time: 30 days. Simultaneous submissions are sometimes accepted. Payment: to be arranged. Copyrights for author. PMA.

THE SOW'S EAR POETRY REVIEW, The Sow's Ear Press, Larry Richman, 19535 Pleasant View Drive, Abingdon, VA 24211-6827, 540-628-2651; richman@preferred.com. 1989. Poetry, art, photos, interviews, reviews. "No length limits on poems. We try to be eclectic. We look for work which 'makes the familiar strange, or the strange familiar,' which shines the light of understanding on the particular, and which uses sound and rhythms to develop meaning. Recent contributors: Penelopy Scambly Schott, Virgil Suarez, Susan Terris, Madeline Tiger, and Charles H. Webb.'' circ. 500. 4/yr. Pub'd 4 issues 1998; expects 4 issues 1999, 4 issues 2000. sub. price: $10; per copy: $5; sample: $5. Discounts: trade 30%. 32pp; 8½×11; of. Reporting time: 3-4 months. Simultaneous submissions accepted: yes. Publishes 5% of manuscripts submitted. Payment: 2 copies. Copyrighted, reverts to author. Pub's reviews: 3 in 1998. §Any poetry. Ads: none. CLMP.

•The Sow's Ear Press (see also THE SOW'S EAR POETRY REVIEW), Larry K. Richman, 19535 Pleasant View Drive, Abingdon, VA 24211-6827, e-mail richman@preferred.com. 1989. Poetry. ''We publish chapbooks and trade paperbacks of poetry from the upper South/Southern Appalachia. We do only 2-3 books a year. Most but not all of our books are first books. Recent books by Dabney Stuart, Ruth Moose, Dana Wildsmith, Bill Brown, Linda Parsons.'' avg. press run 600. Pub'd 3 titles 1998; expects 3 titles 1999, 3 titles 2000. avg. price, paper: $12. Discounts: trade 30%. 64pp; 6×9; of. Reporting time: 1 month. Simultaneous submissions accepted: yes. Payment: 5% on net, then 35% on net after expenses are met. Copyrights for author.

SPACE AND TIME, Space and Time Press, Gordon Linzner, Editor-in-Chief; Gerard Houarner, Fiction Editor; Linda D. Addison, Poetry Editor, 138 West 70th Street 4-B, New York, NY 10023-4432. 1966. Poetry, fiction, art, cartoons. ''*Space and Time* is a fantasy and science fiction magazine, we have a very broad definition of fantasy (which includes SF) and we aren't fussy about sub-genre barriers, but we want nothing that obviously falls outside of fantasy (i.e. straight mystery, mainstream, etc.). Prefer under 10M words.'' circ. 2M. 2/yr. Pub'd 1 issue 1998; expects 2 issues 1999, 2 issues 2000. sub. price: $10; per copy: $5 + 1.50 p/h; sample: $5 + 1.50 p/h. Discounts: 40% off on orders of 5 or more copies of an issue. 48pp; 8½×11; of. Reporting time: 6-8 weeks. Simultaneous submissions accepted: no. Publishes 1% of manuscripts submitted. Payment: 1¢ per word on acceptance. Copyrighted, reverts to author. Ads: $150/$75/50¢ per word ($10 min.). SPWAO.

Space and Time Press (see also SPACE AND TIME), Gordon Linzner, Publisher & Editor, 138 West 70th Street 4-B, New York, NY 10023-4468. 1984. Fiction. ''Not actively soliciting at this time. Fantasy and science fiction novels—preferably ones that don't fit neatly into a sub-genre. Interested in seeing borderline fantasy-mysteries, along lines of George Chesbro's *Mongo* series. We are still overstock and not considering new book proposals for the indefinite future. We *are* looking for short stories for the magazine.'' avg. press run 1M. Pub'd 1 title 1998; expects 1 title 1999, 1 title 2000. 10 titles listed in the *Small Press Record of Books in Print* (28th Edition, 1999-00). avg. price, cloth: $15.95; paper: $7.95. Discounts: 1 30%, 2-4 35%, 5-24 40%. 160pp; 5½×8½; of. Payment: 10% of cover price, based on print run, within 3 months of publication. Copyrights for author. Small Press Writers and Artists Organization.

SPARE RIB, Editorial Collective, 27 Clerkenwell Close, London EC1 0AT, England. 1972. Articles, news items. ''We print articles by women only on a wide range of subjects. For features, brief proposals (rather than finished article) should be submitted to Marcel Farry. We welcome unsolicited short items of news or for our regular columns. Contributors are usually also readers (but not always).'' circ. 25M. 12/yr. Pub'd 12 issues 1998; expects 12 issues 1999, 12 issues 2000. sub. price: £27; per copy: £1.50; sample: £2.20 incl. postage airmail. Back issues: £2.20 incl. postage airmail. Discounts: trade discount by negotiation with distributor, Central Books, 14 Leathermarket, London SE1, Britain. 60pp; size A4; of. Reporting time: 3 weeks minimum. Payment: low! Joint copyright, does not revert to author. Pub's reviews: 6 per month in 1998. §Books by women, about women, feminist writing. Ads: £675 + VAT/£345 + VAT/70p per word.

Sparkling Diamond Paperbacks, Eric Tobin, Eugene Tuohey, 66 St. Joseph's Place, Off Blessington Street, Dublin 7, Ireland. 1972. Non-fiction. ''Non-fiction, dramatic, personal experience. Sent post-free, world-wide.'' avg. press run 5M. Pub'd 1 title 1998; expects 1 title 2000. 1 title listed in the *Small Press Record of Books in Print* (28th Edition, 1999-00). avg. price, paper: £5.50. Discounts: 50%. 136pp; 5½×8. Reporting time: no particular length of time. Payment: the usual. Copyrights for author.

SPARROW, Felix Stefanile, Selma Stefanile, 103 Waldron Street, West Lafayette, IN 47906. 1954. Poetry. ''Sparrow Press announces the revival of *Sparrow* as a poetry miscellany, and the retirement of the 'poverty pamphlets.' We publish only in the field of the contemporary sonnet, based upon the great English and Italian traditions, and shall consider no other type of writing for publication. The editors believe the time is ripe for such a departure in our activities. We invite the submission of four or five pieces at a time. We offer a small payment, on publication, for each sonnet accepted. Usual rules for submission apply—typed copy, SASE for return, no simultaneous submission. We are a 100-page (9 X 12) yearbook. We do not read MSS. From october through December'' circ. 500-1.5M. 1/yr. Pub'd 1 issue 1998. sub. price: $6; per copy: $6 indiv., $10 instit.; sample: $5. Back issues: $5. Discounts: 25% to agents, etc., 20% on single orders, (short discount). 100pp; 8½×11; of. Reporting time: within 6 weeks. Simultaneous submissions accepted: no. Publishes 5-10% of manuscripts submitted. Payment: $3 a poem, plus copy (1). Copyrighted, rights revert to author on request, we reserve the right to reprint. §Reveiws are assigned. Ads: by invitation only.

Sparrow Hawk Press, Charles C. Harra, 22 Summit Ridge Drive, Tahlequah, OK 74464, 918-456-3421. 1987.

Art, photos, non-fiction. "Sparrow Hawk Press is also available to do book design and production on a contract basis for other publishers. Full editorial, graphic design, and production services are available. We primarily publish our own manuscripts." avg. press run 4M. Pub'd 1 title 1998; expects 3 titles 1999, 3 titles 2000. 11 titles listed in the *Small Press Record of Books in Print* (28th Edition, 1999-00). avg. price, paper: $9.95. Discounts: industry standard. 250pp; size varies; of. Reporting time: 3 weeks. Publishes 1% of manuscripts submitted. Payment: negotiated for each project. Copyrights for author. NAPRA.

●**SPEAK UP, Speak Up Press**, Bryant. G.J., PO Box 100506, Denver, CO 80250, 303-715-0837; Fax 303-715-0793; speakupres@aol.com; www.speakuppress.org. 1999. Poetry, fiction, art, photos, plays, non-fiction. "Non-profit teen literary journal - original work of young people 13-19 years old. Written work: 5000 words max. Currently seeking submissions - a creative voice for teens." circ. 500. 1/yr. Expects 1 issue 1999, 1 issue 2000. sub. price: $10; per copy: $10; sample: $8. Discounts: classroom 25% on 10 or more. 64pp; 5½×8½. Reporting time: 2-3 months. Simultaneous submissions accepted: yes. Publishes 10% of manuscripts submitted. Payment: 2 copies. Copyrighted, reverts to author. Ads: none.

●**Speak Up Press (see also SPEAK UP)**, G.J. Bryant, PO Box 100506, Denver, CO 80250, 303-715-0837; Fax 303-715-0793; speakupres@aol.com; www.speakuppress.org. 1999. Poetry, fiction, non-fiction. "Young adult novels, non-fiction and poetry of interest to young adults. Not currently accepting submissions." avg. press run 1M. avg. price, cloth: $19.95. Reporting time: 2 months. Simultaneous submissions accepted: yes. Payment: negotiable. Copyrights for author.

●**Spears of Ink (see also P.D.Q.)**, G. Elton Warrick, 5836 North Haven Drive, North Highlands, CA 95660, e-mail p1toall@aol.com. 1990. Poetry. "Currently not taking submissions" avg. press run 300. Pub'd 2 titles 1998; expects 2 titles 1999, 2 titles 2000. avg. price, paper: $8. 60pp; 4½×5½; †xerox. Reporting time: 1 month. Simultaneous submissions accepted: no. Publishes .5% of manuscripts submitted. Payment: profit after cost divided 50/50. Does not copyright for author.

SPECIALTY COOKING MAGAZINE, Lifetime Books, Inc., Feinblum Brian, Editor-in-Chief, 2131 Hollywood Boulevard, Hollywood, FL 33020, 305-925-5242. 1943. Non-fiction. "We are the leading publisher of one-shot magazines in the United States. We have four categories in which we publish. These are diet & health, health, cookbook series and financial planning series. We are looking for full manuscripts that would lend themselves to these areas." circ. 50M. 8/yr. Pub'd 8 issues 1998; expects 8 issues 1999, 8 issues 2000. price per copy: $2.95. Back issues: cover price. Discounts: I.D. Distribution, Kable News Company-national distributor. 128pp; 5-3/16×7⅝; of. Reporting time: 3 months. Payment: negotiated. Copyrighted, reverts to author. Ads: $2,000. PBAA, ACIDA.

SPECIALTY TRAVEL INDEX, R. Weinreb, 305 San Anselmo Avenue #313, San Anselmo, CA 94960-2660, 415-459-4900. 1980. Non-fiction. "Directory of special interest travel." circ. 46K. 2/yr. Pub'd 2 issues 1998; expects 2 issues 1999, 2 issues 2000. sub. price: $10; per copy: $6; sample: $6. Back issues: $10. Discounts: 1-10 copies 40%; 10+ 50%. 198pp; 8⅜×10⅞; of. Simultaneous submissions accepted: yes. Payment: 20¢ per word. Copyrighted. Ads: $1,580 b&w, $1,975 4-c/100 words $350, extra words $25 for 25 word increment.

‡**Spectacular Diseases (see also SPECTACULAR DISEASES)**, Paul Green, 83(b) London Road, Peterborough, Cambs, England. 1975. Poetry, art, long-poems. "Bias toward the long poem, or material taken from work in progress. Eight issues of magazine produced so far. 24 books produced so far. Material usually solicited." avg. press run 150-350. Expects 2 titles 1999. 24 titles listed in the *Small Press Record of Books in Print* (28th Edition, 1999-00). avg. price, paper: 75p (ascending up to £5). Discounts: trade 33⅓%. 5-25pp; 5¾×8; of. Reporting time: 3-4 weeks. Payment: copies only. Copyrights for author. ALP.

‡**SPECTACULAR DISEASES, Spectacular Diseases**, Paul Green, Paul Buck, Robert Vas Dias, 83(b) London Road, Peterborough, Cambs, England. 1975. Poetry, art, long-poems. "Bias to the long poem or work in progress. Work usually solicited. Enquire before submitting." circ. 350-500. 1/yr. Pub'd 1 issue 1998; expects 1 issue 1999, 1 issue 2000. sub. price: £4.00/2 issues; per copy: £1.00; sample: as issued. Back issues: #1 £1, #2 & #3 50p, #4 75p, #5 & #7 £1.50, #6 £1, $8 £1.80. Discounts: 33%. 40-60pp; 5¾×8; of. Reporting time: 3-4 weeks. Payment: copies. Copyrighted, reverts to author. Ads: inquire first. ALP.

Spectrum Press, Daniel Vian, Editor-in-Chief; Kristi Sprinkle, Senior Editor, 3023 N Clark Street, #109, Chicago, IL 60657. 1991. Poetry, fiction, criticism, plays, non-fiction. "We publish electronic books only, text-file format" Pub'd 50 titles 1998; expects 50 titles 1999, 50 titles 2000. avg. price, other: $3. Reporting time: 2 weeks. Simultaneous submissions accepted: yes. Publishes 1% of manuscripts submitted. Payment: 30%, author retains print media rights. Does not copyright for author.

Spectrum Productions, Nick Starbuck, 979 Casiano Rd., Los Angeles, CA 90049. 1974. Plays. "We are interested in receiving inquiries (not mss.) in the field of translations of European drama before the twentieth century." 7 titles listed in the *Small Press Record of Books in Print* (28th Edition, 1999-00). lp. Copyrights for author.

SPECTRUM—The Wholistic News Magazine, Roger G. Windsor, 3519 Hamstead Ct, Durham, NC 27707-5136, 603-528-4710. 1988. Articles, cartoons, interviews, news items. "We do not accept articles from outside our staff." circ. 5M+. 6/yr. Pub'd 6 issues 1998; expects 6 issues 1999, 6 issues 2000. sub. price: $20; per copy: $3; sample: $4.00 (includes postage). Back issues: $3.50, $45 - 9 years of back issues on disk. Discounts: 40% retailers, 50% distributors. 36pp; 8¼×10⅞; web and sheet fed press, four color cover. Copyrighted, reverts to author. Pub's reviews: 1 in 1998. §Health, diet, spiritual, environmental, lifestyle. Ads: $295/$155/$115 1/3 page/$58 1/6 page/$205 2/3 page.

The Speech Bin, Inc., Jan J. Binney, Senior Editor, 1965 25th Avenue, Vero Beach, FL 32960, 561-770-0007, FAX 561-770-0006. 1984. "The Speech Bin publishes educational materials and books in speech-language pathology, audiology, occupational and physical therapy, special education, and treatment of communication disorders in children and adults. One publication is *Getting Through: Communicating When Someone You Care For Has Alzheimer's Disease*, a unique book written for caregivers (both family members and professionals) of Alzheimer's victims. Most Speech Bin authors are specialists in communication disorders, rehabilitation, or education although we are eager to receive queries for new books and materials from all authors who write for our specialized market. Please study our market before submitting fiction. The Speech Bin also publishes educational card sets and games plus novelties. We do not accept faxed submissions or telephone inquiries." avg. press run varies. Pub'd 8-10 titles 1998; expects 10-12 titles 1999, 10-12 titles 2000. 59 titles listed in the *Small Press Record of Books in Print* (28th Edition, 1999-00). avg. price, paper: $10-$25; other: $4-$50. Discounts: 20%. 40-400pp; 8½×11; of. Reporting time: 2-3 months. Simultaneous submissions accepted: no. Publishes 2-5% of manuscripts submitted. Payment: varies. Copyrights for author.

Spelman Publishing, Inc., Philip O. Spelman, President, 582 Windrift Lane, Spring Lake, MI 49456-2168. 1984. Photos, non-fiction. "HealthProInk & 33 Publishing are imprints. We publish books only. Automotive, sexual improvement and self-help, celebrity biography and autobiography." avg. press run 5M-10M. Pub'd 1 title 1998; expects 3 titles 1999, 3-4 titles 2000. 3 titles listed in the *Small Press Record of Books in Print* (28th Edition, 1999-00). avg. price, cloth: $19.95; paper: $12.95. Discounts: 3 copies 20%, 9 copies 40%, 200 copies 50%. 200pp; 6×9; of, laser typeset from Mac. Reporting time: varies, write first before ms. Payment: varies. Copyrights for author. PMA, Book Exchange.

SPELUNKER FLOPHOUSE, Chris Kubica, Wendy Morgan, PO Box 617742, Chicago, IL 60661, e-mail Spelunkerf@aol.com and sflophouse@aol.com; www.members.aol.com/spelunkerf. 1996. Poetry, fiction, art, photos, cartoons, satire, letters, collages, plays. "We offer the best poetry, fiction, and artwork we can in an inventive, original format. We cooperate regularly with other literary magazines. Support this necessary forum for the arts by purchasing copies of literary magazines, reading them, and increasing local awareness of magazines/forums such as ours whenever possible. Study the market; then submit. And keep in touch. We love to hear from members/supporters of the literary community. Check out our website...you could win free magazines!" circ. 1.5M. 1/yr. Pub'd 4 issues 1998; expects 1 issue 1999, 1 issue 2000. sub. price: $9.95; per copy: $9.95; sample: $9.95. Discounts: 50% for contributors. 96pp; 8½×7; of. Reporting time: 6 months. We accept simultaneous submissions if notified as such. Publishes 5% of manuscripts submitted. Payment: copies and occasional small sums ($), also awards given in annual contest. Copyrighted, reverts to author. Pub's reviews. §Literary magazines and books of fiction/poetry similar to what we publish. Ads: $512 full page. CLMP.

SPEX (SMALL PRESS EXCHANGE), Margaret Sneaker Yucan, PO Box E, Corte Madera, CA 94957, 415-924-1612, 415-257-8275. 1979. Articles, reviews, letters, news items. "This is the newsletter of the Bay Area Independent Publishers Association, a non-profit public benefit organization." circ. 300. 12/yr. Pub'd 12 issues 1998; expects 12 issues 1999, 12 issues 2000. sub. price: $20; or included in membership in MSPA, $40; sample: SASE. 8pp; 8½×11; lp. Payment: none. Copyrighted, reverts to author. Pub's reviews: 50 in 1998. §Self-publishing, book marketing, book production and new books published by members of BAIDA (Bay Area Independent Publishers Association). Ads: no ads at present.

SPIDER, Marianne Carus, Editor-in-Chief; Laura Tillotson, Senior Editor, PO Box 300, Peru, IL 61354, 815-224-6656. 1994. "Word limit for fiction - 1000 words, nonfiction - 800 words. Include bibliography with nonfiction. SASE required for response." circ. 92M. 12/yr. Pub'd 12 issues 1998; expects 12 issues 1999, 12 issues 2000. sub. price: $35.97; per copy: $4.95; sample: $5. Back issues: $5. 34pp; 8×10. Reporting time: approx. 3 months. We accept simultaneous submissions, but please indicate as such. Publishes 1% of manuscripts submitted. Payment: stories and articles up to 25¢ per word, poems up to $3 per line. Copyrighted, reverts to author. Pub's reviews: 8 in 1998. §Chapter books, middle grade fiction, poetry, younger nonfiction, joke, craft, or puzzle collections. Ads: none. MPA.

●**SPILLWAY, Tebot Bach,** Mifanwy Kaiser, Mark Bergendahl, 20592 Minerva Lane, Huntington Beach, CA 92646, 714-968-0905. 1993. Poetry, photos, criticism, reviews, long-poems. "Recent contributors: John

Balaban, Eleanor Wilner, Richard Jones, David St. John, M.L. Liebler, Allison Joseph, Sam Homill, Jody Azzouni, Jan Wesley, Jeanette Clough, and Amy Uyematsu.'' 2/yr. Pub'd 2 issues 1998; expects 2 issues 1999, 2 issues 2000. sub. price: $14; per copy: $8 + postage; sample: $8 + postage. Back issues: $6. Discounts: by arrangement. 176pp; 6×9. Reporting time: 2 weeks to 6 months. Simultaneous submissions accepted, must be stated in cover letter. Publishes 10% of manuscripts submitted. Payment: 1 copy. Copyrighted, reverts to author. Pub's reviews: 5 in 1998. §Poetry related material.

Spillway Publications, K. Wieder, Managing Editor, 48 Pershing Drive, Rochester, NY 14609. 1992. Poetry, fiction, satire, plays, non-fiction. "We are a Writers' Cooperative specializing in Erie Canal-related subjects and authors. No unsolicited MSS please.'' avg. press run 500-1M. Pub'd 1 title 1998; expects 1 title 1999, 1 title 2000. 2 titles listed in the *Small Press Record of Books in Print* (28th Edition, 1999-00). avg. price, paper: $9. Discounts: Standard 40% discount to booksellers. 100pp; 5½×8½; of. Payment: varies. Copyrights for author.

SPIN, P.N.W. Donnelly, 7 Megan Avenue, Pakuranga, Auckland 1706, New Zealand, 006495768577. 1986. Poetry. "*Spin* accepts contributions from subscribers only.'' circ. 100. 3/yr. Pub'd 3 issues 1998; expects 3 issues 1999, 3 issues 2000. sub. price: $US12, includes airmail p/h outside New Zealand; per copy: $US5; sample: $US3. Back issues: back issues as samples. Discounts: refer EBSCO. 60pp; 5¾×8¼; †photocopy. Reporting time: 4 months max. - usually less. Simultaneous submissions accepted: no. Publishes 50% of manuscripts submitted. Payment: nil. Copyrighted, reverts to author. Pub's reviews: 3 in 1998. §Poetry and criticism. Ads: gratis to subscribers.

SPINNING JENNY, Black Dress Press, C.E. Harrison, PO Box 213, Village Station, New York, NY 10014, website www.blackdresspress.com. 1994. Poetry, fiction, plays. circ. 1M. 1/yr. Pub'd 1 issue 1998; expects 1 issue 1999, 1 issue 2000. sub. price: $12; per copy: $6; sample: $6. Discounts: Please write for discounts. 96pp; 5½×9¼; of. Reporting time: 8 weeks. Simultaneous submissions accepted: no. Publishes 5% of manuscripts submitted. Payment: contributors copies. Copyrighted, reverts to author.

The Spinning Star Press, Carl Tate, Bob Starr, 1065 E. Fairview Blvd., Inglewood, CA 90302, 213-464-3024. 1986. Music. "We may slow down on some submitted materials, but will be more active soon. Length of material: 108 pages. Biases: cataloging and chronicle of recording artists from the South and West. Recent contributors: Bob Starr, Carl Tate, The All-Star Band, etc. We are inactive as of now on #18, 19, 20, 25., science fiction, biography, music.'' avg. press run 1M. Pub'd 1 title 1998; expects 1 title 1999, 2 titles 2000. 1 title listed in the *Small Press Record of Books in Print* (28th Edition, 1999-00). avg. price, paper: $15; other: $20 abroad. Discounts: bulk, classroom, agents, jobbers, libraries, cultural events. 108pp; 5½×8½; †mi. Reporting time: indefinite.

Spinsters Ink, Joan Drury, 32 East First Street, #330, Duluth, MN 55802-2002, 218-727-3222, fax 218-727-3119. 1978. Fiction, non-fiction. "We publish books by women for women. Recent authors: Mariana Romo-Carmona, Sandra Butler, Ellyn Bache, Val McDermid, Theresa Park, Helen Campbell, and Joni Rodgers.'' avg. press run 3M-5M. Pub'd 5 titles 1998; expects 6 titles 1999, 6 titles 2000. 50 titles listed in the *Small Press Record of Books in Print* (28th Edition, 1999-00). avg. price, cloth: $24.95; paper: $12. Discounts: 40% on STOP orders, distributed by Words. 185pp; 5½×8½; of. Reporting time: 3 months. We accept simultaneous submissions, but send a query letter before doing anything else. Publishes 1.5% of manuscripts submitted. Payment: 7% on first 10M; increased thereafter. Copyrights for author. Minnesota Book Publishers Roundtable, Midwest Independent Publishers Association, Publishers Marketing Assn., ABA.

THE SPIRIT GARDEN, Bro. Johannes Zinzendorf, RD 1, Box 149, Pitman, PA 17964. 1993. Poetry, fiction, articles, art, interviews, music, non-fiction. "Pantheist, gay religious publication printing our own work. No submissions accepted'' circ. 300. 4/yr. Expects 4 issues 1999, 4 issues 2000. sub. price: $15; per copy: $3; sample: free. Back issues: $3. Discounts: none. 16pp; 8×11; †xerox. Not copyrighted. Ads: none.

SPIRIT MAGAZINE, Carol Woodruff Youssef, PO Box 27244, Minneapolis, MN 55427. 1993. Poetry, fiction, articles, art, photos, cartoons, interviews, reviews, music, long-poems, collages, non-fiction. "250-1000 words. Copy due by 15th of month. Interested in articles on alternative living; New Age, spirituality, psychology, healing arts, creative arts, humanitarian issues (especially women's), dreams, alternative living styles (intentional communities), environmental issues; new philosophers'' circ. 4.5M. 6/yr. Pub'd 6 issues 1998; expects 6 issues 1999, 6 issues 2000. sub. price: $22; per copy: $3; sample: $3 by mail. Back issues: $3. 40pp; 8½×11; of. Reporting time: 1 month. Simultaneous submissions accepted: no. Publishes 75% of manuscripts submitted. Payment: author's copies and/or advertisement. Pub's reviews: 4 in 1998. §New Age, spirituality, healing and creative arts. Ads: $150/$880/back cover $200.

Spirit of Arts Press, Tom Arbino, Editor, 7871 Ravencrest Court, Cincinnati, OH 45255-2426. 1992. "We like to form a co-op with some authors who will work with us and do some of the promotional work him or herself to save costs. We are not a vanity press. Publishes book an average 3 months after acceptance. Simultaneous submissions OK. Computer printed OK, no dot-matrix. Prefers letter quality. SASE cover letter, proposal/synopsis and 3 sample chapters. Accepts unsolicited manuscripts. Nonfiction: spirituality and mysticism. Though primarily Christian, will consider other religions. Psychology, religion, health, herbs, alternative medicine, philosophy, theology, self-help. No new age unless based on Buddhist etc. teachings/scripture. No reincarnation, past lives, UFO, or other stuff. All submissions must be original and from fresh angles. Fiction: literary/artistic type works. No genre criterion but no romance, western, or mysteries. No slush or works that preach. We want to see books that are creative/artistic and show that the writer is an artist. Get in touch with your inner creative before you sit down to write and write what only you can, not rehashes of someone else's thought. We want writers who are willing to learn the publishing business and work independently, doing some of the marketing. Take the time to learn the business you're going into.'' avg. press run 250-1M. Pub'd 1 title 1998; expects 2 titles 1999. avg. price, cloth: $9.95; paper: $6.95. Discounts: 20% bookstores. 175pp; 4×7; subcontract. Reporting time: 1 month (average). Payment: no advance, 10% royalty, some subsidy publishing. Copyrights for author.

SPIRIT TALK, Spirit Talk Press, Bear Chief, PO Box 390, Browning, MT 59417, 406-338-2882; E-mail blkfoot4@3rivers.net. 1993. Poetry, fiction, articles, art, photos, cartoons, interviews, satire, criticism, reviews, music, letters, parts-of-novels, long-poems, collages, plays, concrete art, news items, non-fiction. ''This is a specialty periodic book which focuses on Native American cultures, especially the Plains Indian.'' circ. 10M. 4/yr. Pub'd 4 issues 1998; expects 4 issues 1999, 4 issues 2000. sub. price: $25; per copy: $7.95; sample: $4.95. Back issues: $25 - 4 issues. Discounts: 40% to bookstores, 50% to distributors. 64pp; 8½×11; of. Reporting time: 1 month. Simultaneous submissions accepted: yes. Publishes 80% of manuscripts submitted. Payment: negotiable. Copyrighted, does not revert to author. Pub's reviews: 4 in 1998. §All materials pertaining to American Indians, including video and audio cassettes.

Spirit Talk Press (see also SPIRIT TALK), Bear Chief, PO Box 390, Browning, MT 59417, 406-338-2882; E-mail blkfoot4@3rivers.net. 1992. Poetry, fiction, articles, art, photos, cartoons, interviews, satire, criticism, reviews, music, letters, parts-of-novels, long-poems, collages, plays, concrete art, news items, non-fiction. ''We publish only books and other media by and about Native American culture.'' avg. press run 6M. Pub'd 1 title 1998; expects 2 titles 1999, 6 titles 2000. 1 title listed in the *Small Press Record of Books in Print* (28th Edition, 1999-00). avg. price, paper: $10. Discounts: 40% stores, 50% book distributor. 8½×11; of. Reporting time: 4 weeks. Simultaneous submissions accepted: yes. Publishes 20% of manuscripts submitted. Payment: negotiable. Copyrights for author.

THE SPIRIT THAT MOVES US, The Spirit That Moves Us Press, Inc., Morty Sklar, Editor & Publisher; Marcela Bruno, Technical Consultant, PO Box 720820-DB, Jackson Heights, Queens, NY 11372-0820, 718-426-8788; msklar@mindspring.com. 1975. Poetry, fiction, art, photos, parts-of-novels, long-poems, collages, concrete art, non-fiction. ''We are in limbo at present. Please query for theme with SASE before sending work. My only prejudices are those of personal taste. Will publish anything that grabs me; prefer work that comes from feeling. I like translations from all languages.'' circ. 1.5M. Irregular. Pub'd 1 issue 1998; expects 2 issues 1999, 1 issue 2000. sub. price: $12 per volume. A volume could be in one year or two years. Our anthologies are part of the subscriptions; per copy: varies with issue; sample: $6 ppd for *The Spirit That Moves Us Reader* (reg. $9), or *Free Parking: 15th Anniversary Collection*. Back issues: 12-volume set, 1) with photocopies of Vol 1, #3 & Vol 2, #1: $141; 2) with clothbounds where published: $206. Includes eleven special issues. Discounts: 40% for 5 or more, 20% for 2-4; 10% for 1, (may mix issues or combine with books). Distributors query; bulk rates available, for classes, etc. 202pp; 5½×8½; of. Reporting time: 3 months after deadline date. We accept simultaneous submissions if the author lets us know ahead of time. Publishes 1.5-2% of manuscripts submitted. Payment: clothbound or two paperbacks, money when possible, + 40% off paperback copies and 25% off extra clothbounds. Copyrighted, reverts to author. Small Press Center, PEN (Poets, Essayists, Novelists).

The Spirit That Moves Us Press, Inc. (see also THE SPIRIT THAT MOVES US), Morty Sklar, Editor, Publisher; Marcela Bruno, Technical Consultant, PO Box 720820-DB, Jackson Heights, Queens, NY 11372-0820, 718-426-8788; msklar@mindspring.com. 1974. Poetry, fiction, art, photos, parts-of-novels, long-poems, collages, concrete art, non-fiction. ''We are in limbo at present. Please query with a SASE or call before sending work, for our needs and time-frames. Catalog available for the asking. We have two series going: the *Editor's Choice* series, which contains selections from other small press books and magazines, and the Ethnic Diversity Series, the latest of which is *Patchwork of Dreams: Voices from the Heart of the New America*. Sample copies: *Editor's Choice III* $10 (reg $15); Fifteenth Anniversary Issue $6 (reg. $9).'' avg. press run 1M-4.2M. Pub'd 1 title 1998; expects 1 title 1999, 1 title 2000. 20 titles listed in the *Small Press Record of Books in Print* (28th Edition, 1999-00). avg. price, cloth: $12-$17.50; paper: $2-$11.50. Discounts: 10% for 1; 20% for 2-4; 40% for 5 or more (may mix titles); Distributors query. Classroom orders (10 or more): 30% plus free desk copy. 16-504pp; 5½×8½ pa, 6×9 cl; of. Reporting time: 3 months after deadline date. Publishes 1.5% poetry, fiction 2% of manuscripts submitted. Payment: cash for single author book; cash and clothbound copy for anthologies, 40% off paperback copies and 25% off extra clothbounds. Copyrights for author. Small Press Center, PEN (Poets, Essayists, Novelists).

538

SPIRIT TO SPIRIT, Marlana Navarro, Editor; Richard Navarro, Executive Editor & Art Director, PO Box 1107, Blythe, CA 92226-1107. 1994. Poetry, fiction, articles, art, interviews, reviews, letters, non-fiction. "Poetry up to 45 lines, articles up to 3,500 words pertaining to astrology, spells, metaphysical, Wicca, Shamanism, soul inspired, god/goddesses, magickal mystical. Short stories same subject matter up to 7,500 words. Recently published works by C. Weaver, C. Mulrooney, John Thomas Romano, Don Clarkson, Paris Flammonde, Hugh Fox, and Steven Rossi. All checks/money orders should be made out to Navarro Publications" circ. 500+. 4/yr. Pub'd 4 issues 1998; expects 4 issues 1999, 4 issues 2000. sub. price: $20 USA, $25 Foreign; per copy: $6.50; sample: $6.50. 50-70pp; 7×8½; photocopied with card stock cover. Reporting time: 12-14 weeks. Simultaneous submissions accepted: yes. Publishes about 40% of manuscripts submitted. Payment: discounted copies (refundable). Copyrighted, reverts to author. Pub's reviews: 4 in 1998. §metaphysical, spirtitual. Ads: $80/$40/others range $4-$20.

SPIRITCHASER, Elizabeth Hundley, 3183 Sharon-Copley Road, Medina, OH 44256, 330-722-1561. 1994. Articles. "After my sister and her husband died of cancer 23 days apart, I began my spiritual search. I interview people I am drawn to, of different faiths. Naomi Judd was my first subscriber. I've interviewed Deepak Chopra, Bernie Siegel, Cece Winans, Dave Dravecky, Dr. Joyce Brothers, Sonya Friedman." circ. 100. 4/yr. Pub'd 1 issue 1998; expects 3 issues 1999, 4 issues 2000. sub. price: $15; per copy: $3; sample: $3. Back issues: $3. Discounts: none. 12-16pp; 8½×11; of. Publishes 0% of manuscripts submitted. Copyrighted, reverts to author.

SPITBALL: The Literary Baseball Magazine, Mike Shannon, Editor-in-Chief & Publisher; Virgil Smith, Contributing Editor; Larry Dickson, Contributing Editor; Kevin Grace, Contributing Editor; Greg Rhodes, Contributing Editor; Tom Chase, Contributing Editor; Dick Miller, Contributing Editor; Mark Schraf, Fiction Editor; William J. McGill, Poetry Editor; Tom Eckel, Book Review Editor, 5560 Fox Road, Cincinnati, OH 45239-7271, 513-541-4296. 1981. Poetry, fiction, articles, art, cartoons, interviews, satire, criticism, reviews, parts-of-novels, long-poems, collages, plays, concrete art, non-fiction. "*Spitball* is a unique litarary magazine devoted to baseball. We publish primarily poetry & fiction, with no biases concerning style or technique or genre. We strive to publish only what we consider to be good work, however, and using baseball as subject matter does not guarantee acceptance. We have no big backlog of accepted material, nevertheless, and good baseball poetry and fiction submitted to us can be published reasonably quickly. If one has never written about baseball, it would probably help a great deal to read the magazine or our book, *The Best of Spitball*, an anthology, published by Pocket Books, March 1988. We try to give considerate fair treatment to everything we receive. We occasionally publish special issues. First issue of 1989 was devoted entirely to David Martin's sequence of poems connecting one-time Milwaukee Brewers outfielder Gorman Thomas to Wisconsin lorre and mythology. A $6 payment must accompany submissions from writers submitting to *Spitball* for the first time. We will send a sample copy in return. The $6 is a one-time charge. Once you have paid it, you may submit additional material as often as you like at no charge." circ. 1M. 2/yr. Pub'd 2 issues 1998; expects 2 issues 1999, 2 issues 2000. sub. price: $12; per copy: $6; sample: $6. Back issues: many sold out, write for prices and availability. Discounts: can be negotiated. 96pp; 5½×8½; of. Reporting time: from 1 week to 3 months. Simultaneous submissions accepted: no. Payment: copies. Not copyrighted. Pub's reviews: 60 in 1998. §We would love to receive review copies of any small press publications dealing with baseball, especially baseball poetry and fiction. Ads: $100/$60.

THE SPITTING IMAGE, Julia Solis, PO Box 20400 Tompkins Square Stn., New York, NY 10009. 1994. Poetry, fiction, art, photos, criticism, collages. "*The Spitting Image* seeks material that is imaginative, disturbing, explosive, absurd. Guidelines are available at www.seatopia.com; Recently published: John Shirley, Bob Flanagan, Unica Zurn, and Todd Grimson." circ. 500. 1-2/yr. Pub'd 1 issue 1998; expects 1 issue 1999, 1 issue 2000. price per copy: inquire; sample: $6.50. Discounts: 40%. 80pp; 7×8½. Simultaneous submissions accepted: yes. Publishes less than 1% of manuscripts submitted. Payment: contributor's copy. Not copyrighted. Ads: none.

SPLIT SHIFT, Split Shift, Roger Taus, 2461 Santa Monica Blvd. #C-122, Santa Monica, CA 90404. 1996. Poetry, art. "Recent contributors: Antler, Jack Hirschman, Terry Kennedy, Vincent Ferrini, Vagabond poet Tony Seldin, Maggie Jaffe, Tom Wayman, and Peter Kidd." circ. 750. Expects 1 issue 1999. price per copy: $15. 150pp; 5×8; of. Simultaneous submissions accepted: no.

Split Shift (see also SPLIT SHIFT), Roger Taus, 2461 Santa Monica Blvd. #C-122, Santa Monica, CA 90404. Poetry. "Buffalo, Rome-Eric Johnson" avg. press run 500. 80pp; 5×8; of.

Spoon River Poetry Press, David R. Pichaske, PO Box 6, Granite Falls, MN 56241. 1976. Poetry. "We do not, as a rule, solicit book-length manuscripts. Mostly we favor Midwest writers working with Midwest subjects and themes" avg. press run 1.5M. Pub'd 6 titles 1998; expects 3 titles 1999, 3 titles 2000. avg. price, cloth: $15; paper: $9.95. Discounts: 2-5 20%, 6+ 40% to bookstores; textbook orders 20%; 20% if payment accompanies order to individuals and libraries. 32-400+pp; 5½×8½, 6×9; of. Payment: 50% of receipts over set, print, bind costs. Copyrights for author.

SPOON RIVER POETRY REVIEW, Lucia Getsi, Editor, Department of English 4240, Illinois State University, Normal, IL 61790-4241, 309-438-7906; 309-438-3025. 1976. Poetry. circ. 1200. 2/yr. Pub'd 2 issues 1998; expects 2 issues 1999, 2 issues 2000. sub. price: $14 ($18 institutions); per copy: $8; sample: $8. Back issues: $5-$8. Discounts: 30%. 128pp; 5½x8½; laserset. Reporting time: 2 months. We reluctantly accept simultaneous submissions. Publishes 1-2% of manuscripts submitted. Payment: year's subscription. Copyrighted, reverts to author. Pub's reviews: 8 in 1998. §Books of poems; poetry translations; anthologies of poems; criticism and poetics. Ads: $150/$75. CCM.

SPORT HISTORY REVIEW (SHR), Human Kinetics Pub. Inc., Don Morrow, PhD, Box 5076, Champaign, IL 61825-5076, 217-351-5076. 1996. Articles, reviews. "Published as the *Canadian Journal of the History of Sport* 1970-1995. Study of sport history." circ. 250. 2/yr. Expects 2 issues 1999, 2 issues 2000. sub. price: $28 individual, $60 institution, $18 students; per copy: $15 indiv., $31 instit.; sample: free. Back issues: Vol. 1-26 $8 ind., $10 inst.; Vol. 27+ $15 ind., $31 inst. Discounts: 5% agency. 96pp; 6x9; of. Reporting time: 2 months. Simultaneous submissions accepted: no. Publishes 55% of manuscripts submitted. Payment: none. Copyrighted, does not revert to author. Pub's reviews: 12 in 1998. Ads: $300/$200. Midwest Book Publishers Association, American Booksellers Association.

SPORT LITERATE, Honest Reflections on Life's Leisurely Diversions, William Meiners, Jotham Burrello, PO Box 577166, Chicago, IL 60657, 765-496-6524; sportlit@aol.com; www.avalon.net/~librarian/sportliterate. 1995. Poetry, photos, cartoons, interviews, non-fiction. "Guidelines available on web site. Strongly encourage to check out." circ. 1.5M. 4/yr. Pub'd 3 issues 1998; expects 3 issues 1999, 4 issues 2000. sub. price: $15; per copy: $4; sample: $5.75. Back issues: $4. 156pp; 5½x8½; lp. Reporting time: 6-8 weeks. We accept simultaneous submissions if you let us know. Publishes 8-10% of manuscripts submitted. Payment: 3 copies. Copyrighted, reverts to author. Ads: $225/$155. CLMP.

THE SPORT PSYCHOLOGIST (TSP), Human Kinetics Pub. Inc., Peter Crocker, Box 5076, Champaign, IL 61825, 217-351-5076. 1987. Articles, reviews. "Applied journal." circ. 1.2M. 4/yr. Pub'd 4 issues 1998; expects 4 issues 1999, 4 issues 2000. sub. price: $40 indiv., $100 instit., $26 student; per copy: $11 indiv., $26 instit.; sample: free. Back issues: $11 indiv., $26 instit. Discounts: 5%. 120pp; 6x9; of. Reporting time: 2 months. Payment: none. Copyrighted, does not revert to author. Pub's reviews: 10 in 1998. §Sport, sport science, and physical education related to psychology. Ads: $300/$200. Midwest Book Publishers Association, American Booksellers Association.

Sports Barn Publishing Company, Richard L. Barnes, 5335 Wisconsin Avenue NW #440, Washington, DC 20015, 202-895-1513; fax 301-320-5218; email dbarnes@erols.com; web http//www.sportsbarn.com. 1996. Fiction, non-fiction. "Only material related to sports, especially soccer. Two current books are *The Soccer Mom Handbook* and *What? Me Manage the Soccer Team?*" avg. press run 5M. Pub'd 1 title 1998; expects 1-2 titles 1999. avg. price, paper: $9.95. Discounts: trade sales through distributer IPG, library through IPG or Quality Books, 50% in bulk for fundraisers. Pages vary; 5½x8½. Reporting time: 2-3 weeks for first reaction. Payment: varies. Copyrights for author. PMA.

Sports Services of America Publishing, KT "Jaquan" Myers, 333 Washington Blvd., Suite 360, Marina del Rey, CA 90292, 310-821-4490; Fax 821-0522. 1987. Articles, photos, interviews, news items, non-fiction. avg. press run 3M. Expects 1 title 1999, 1 title 2000. avg. price, paper: $22. 330pp; 6x9; †web press. Payment: none. Copyrights for author.

SPOUT, Spout Press, John Colburn, Chris Watercott, Michelle Filkins, 28 West Robie Street, Saint Paul, MN 55107-2819. 1989. Poetry, fiction, articles, art, cartoons, interviews, letters, collages, non-fiction. "Accepts poetry, prose, and fiction for publication. Submission should include SASE. Looking for the unique voice, for someone with something to say in an offbeat way" circ. 200+. 2-3/yr. Pub'd 3 issues 1998; expects 2 issues 1999, 3 issues 2000. sub. price: $12; per copy: $4; sample: $4. Back issues: $3. 40pp; 8½x11; mi. Reporting time: 2-4 months. Simultaneous submissions accepted: yes. Publishes 10% of manuscripts submitted. Payment: copy. Copyrighted, reverts to author.

Spout Press (see also SPOUT), John Colburn, Michelle Filkins, Chris Watercott, 28 W. Robie Street, St. Paul, MN 55107. 1996. Poetry, fiction, non-fiction. "Recent anthology includes Carol Bly, Margaret Hasse, John Engman, Jeffrey Little. Tend to put out calls for anthologies or theme-related books rather than publish single-author manuscripts." avg. press run 500. Expects 2 titles 1999, 2 titles 2000. 1 title listed in the *Small Press Record of Books in Print* (28th Edition, 1999-00). avg. price, paper: $7.95. 110pp; 5½x8½. Reporting time: 2-3 months. Simultaneous submissions accepted: yes. Publishes 5% of manuscripts submitted. Payment: varies. Copyrights for author.

SPRING: A Journal of Archetype and Culture, Charles Boer, Editor; James Hillman, Senior Editor; Jay Livernois, Managing Editor, Box 583, Putnam, CT 06260, 203-974-3229. 1941. Articles, interviews, criticism. "Approx. 176 pages, 20 page articles in magazine." circ. 3M. 2/yr. Pub'd 2 issues 1998; expects 2 issues 1999, 2 issues 2000. sub. price: $24 + shipping if billed, no shipping charge if prepaid; per copy: $17.50. Discounts:

classroom 40%, jobbers & trade 40% 1-4 copies, 40% 5-99. 176pp; 6×9; of. Reporting time: 3 months. Publishes .01% of manuscripts submitted. Payment: none. Copyrighted, does not revert to author. Pub's reviews: 22 in 1998. §Depth psychology, mythology, art, architecture, Renaissance, philosophy, the occult, classical studies, religion. Ads: $200/$135. CELJ, ABA.

Spring Publications Inc., James Hillman, Publisher; Jay Livernois, Managing Editor, 299 East Quassett Road, Woodstock, CT 06281, 203-974-3428, fax 203-974-3195. 1941. Non-fiction. "Jungian background but critical reflection on Jungian tradition; intellectual but neither academic nor new age. Psychology, mythology, religion, eco-psychology" avg. press run 3M. Pub'd 11 titles 1998; expects 11 titles 1999, 12 titles 2000. 72 titles listed in the *Small Press Record of Books in Print* (28th Edition, 1999-00). avg. price, paper: $18. Discounts: Continuum is our distributor. 196pp; 5½×8½, 6×9; of. Reporting time: 3-6 months. Simultaneous submissions accepted: no. Publishes 5% of manuscripts submitted. Payment: varies. Copyrights for author. CELJ.

SPROUTLETTER, Michael Linden, Box 62, Ashland, OR 97520, 800-746-7413. 1980. Articles, interviews, reviews, letters, news items, non-fiction. "*Sproutletter* publishes articles, book reviews, recipes and news items relating to sprouting, algae (blue-green), indoor live food growing, live foods, vegetarianism, holistic health and nutrition. Query requested before submitting works. Articles should be no more than 1M words." circ. 3.1M. 4/yr. Pub'd 4 issues 1998; expects 4 issues 1999, 4 issues 2000. sub. price: $12 USA, $14 Canada and Mexico, $14 foreign surface, $25 foreign airmail; per copy: $3, $4.50 Can/Mex, $4.50 surf, $5.50 air; sample: same. Back issues: 20% pff 1-45. Discounts: 10-50 40%, 51-100 45%, 101-200 50%. 12pp; 8½×11; of. Reporting time: 4 weeks. Payment: $25-$100. Copyrighted, reverts to author. Pub's reviews: 20 in 1998. §Sprouting, algae, raw foods, indoor gardening, holistic health, nutrition. Ads: $160/$90/25¢.

SPSM&H, Amelia Press, Frederick A. Raborg, Jr., Editor, 329 'E' Street, Bakersfield, CA 93304, 805-323-4064. 1986. Poetry, fiction, articles, art, cartoons, criticism, reviews. "Sonnets, sonnet sequences, traditional or experimental, fiction to 3,000 words pertaining somehow to the sonnet; essays to 2,000 words about the form, history and/or technique; pen & ink sketches, line drawings and cartoons with romantic or Gothic themes. We welcome newcomers. Sponsors the annual Eugene Smith Sonnet Awards. Reviews collections of sonnets and books about the form. Contributors include: Margaret Ryan, Robert Wolfkill, Michael J. Bugeja, William John Watkins, Ruth M. Parks, Gail White and many others." circ. 600. 4/yr. Pub'd 4 issues 1998; expects 4 issues 1999, 4 issues 2000. sub. price: $14; per copy: $4.95; sample: $4.95. Back issues: $4.50 when available. Discounts: contributor's discount, 20% on five or more copies. 20pp; 5½×8½; of. Reporting time: 2 weeks. We reluctantly accept simultaneous submissions. Publishes 5% of manuscripts submitted. Payment: none, except two *best of issue* poets each receive $14 on publication, plus copy and 20% discount on subscriptions. Copyrighted. Pub's reviews: 5 in 1998. §Collections of sonnets, books which contain a substantial number of sonnets and books about the form. Ads: will consider ads based on $60/$40/$25.

SQUARE, Michael Jacob Rochlin, PO Box 33671, Los Angeles, CA 90033. 1996. Articles, satire. "Free bilingual downtown newspaper. English/Spanish. No submissions at present." circ. 1M-5M. 4/yr. Pub'd 6 issues 1998; expects 4 issues 1999, 4 issues 2000. Back issues: $2 each and p/h. 12pp; 5½×8½; of. Simultaneous submissions accepted: no. Publishes 0% of manuscripts submitted. Payment: none. Copyrighted, reverts to author. Ads: $30 per 2 inches/square.

SQUARE ONE - A Magazine of Disturbing Fiction, William D. Gagliani, Editor & Publisher, PO Box 11921, Milwaukee, WI 53211-0921. 1984. Fiction, art. "500-7,500 words (3,000-5,000 words preferred). *Query for longer.* No biases—only taboo is boredom. Currently seeking dark fantasy, steampunk, cyberpunk, magic realism, mystery and genre blends. Actively exploring dark themes in all genres" circ. 250. 1/yr. Pub'd 1 issue 1998; expects 1 issue 1999, 1-2 issues 2000. sub. price: currently $6.50 postpaid; 2-issue subscription $14 postpaid, may change soon, so send SASE to inquire; sample: make checks payable to William D. Gagliani. Back issues: All back issues sold out. 75-90pp; 8½×5½; DTP/commercial printer. Reporting time: currently 1-14 months, 75% receive critique (time permitting), do not read mss May-September unless clearly marked *"keep on file"* We accept simultaneous submissions if clearly marked. Payment: 2 copies. Copyrighted, reverts to author. Ads: $50/$30/$20 1/4 page/$10 1/8.

Square Peg Press, PO Box 2194, Gilbert, AZ 85299, Fax 602-813-2621; E-mail reunion@primenet.com. 1 title listed in the *Small Press Record of Books in Print* (28th Edition, 1999-00). Discounts: 1 copy 20%, 2-48 40%, 49-96 45%, 97+ 50%.

The Square-Rigger Press, Daniel Talbot von Koschembahr, 1201 North 46th Street, Seattle, WA 98103-6610, 206-548-9385. 1973. Poetry, fiction, articles, art, non-fiction. "There have been two miniatures published by the Square-Rigger Press. The first, *Moving With the Wind* (32 pp, 8 illustrations) oriental binding/blind embossed sup case and *An Italic Alphabet* (30 pp, bound in a similar manner)." avg. press run 150-200. Expects 1 title 1999, 2+ titles 2000. 1 title listed in the *Small Press Record of Books in Print* (28th Edition, 1999-00). avg. price, other: bound in boards: 1st miniature $15.00, 2nd miniature $35. 30pp; 1¾×1-3/16, 1¼×2⅜; †1p.

George Sroda, Publisher, George Sroda, PO Box 97, Amherst Jct., WI 54407, 715-824-3868. Articles. "Has published two books, *Facts About Nightcrawlers*, and *The 'Life Story' of TV Star and Celebrity Herman the Worm.*" avg. press run 30M. Pub'd 1 title 1998; expects 1 title 1999. 2 titles listed in the *Small Press Record of Books in Print* (28th Edition, 1999-00). avg. price, paper: $13.95. 157-199pp; 8¼×5½.

STAGNANCY IS REVOLTING, F. Mitchell, PO Box 55138, Atlanta, GA 30308-0138, 404-876-7183. 1996. "Focus on underground music, art" circ. 1M. 6/yr. Pub'd 1 issue 1998; expects 6 issues 1999, 6 issues 2000. price per copy: $1; sample: $1. Back issues: none. Discounts: no. 20pp; 8½×11. Simultaneous submissions accepted: yes. Publishes 20% of manuscripts submitted. Payment: sample copy. Not copyrighted. Pub's reviews: 10 in 1998. §Occult, underground/dangerous music, bizarre, obscure, taboo art.

Stained Glass Press (see also SKYWRITERS), Tara Allan, 245 Spring Street, SW, Concord, NC 28025. 1994. Poetry, articles, interviews, satire, criticism, reviews, long-poems, non-fiction. "I work from bedside - multiple disability. My husband, Lyman Farris, Jr., is publisher. Profits go to the CFIDS association for research into a cure. Recent contributors include Floyd Skloot and Stacy E. Tuthell." avg. press run 50-100. Pub'd 1 title 1998; expects 5 titles 1999, 5 titles 2000. Reporting time: up to 6 months. Publishes 50% of manuscripts submitted. Payment: 25 copies. Copyrights for author.

STAND MAGAZINE, Lorna Tracy, Rodney Pybus, 179 Wingrove Road, Newcastle-on-Tyne NE49DA, England, +44 011-273-3280. 1952. Poetry, fiction, art, interviews, criticism, reviews, letters. circ. 4.5M. 4/yr. Pub'd 4 issues 1998; expects 4 issues 1999. sub. price: $25; per copy: $8; sample: $5. Back issues: $10. 84pp; 6-1/10×8; of. Reporting time: 1-2 months. Simultaneous submissions accepted: no. Publishes 5% of manuscripts submitted. Payment: $45/poem, $45/1,000 words prose. Copyrighted, reverts to author. Pub's reviews: 30 in 1998. §Literature. Ads: $225/$112/$56 1/4 page. CLMP.

‡**STANDARD DEVIATIONS,** Brad Kohler, B.B. Billings, 127 Greenlea Drive, Moon Twp., PA 15108-2609, 412-269-4167. 1994. Poetry, fiction. "We are new, still trying to find our voice and direction. All submissions will be considered, emphasis on dark, seedy aspects of life. Submissions should be able to be read to old men in a fernless bar where hard-boiled eggs are regularly eaten, while yellowed newspaper clippings are being discussed. Authors should subsist mainly on beer and pretzels and regularly complain about things like baseball players wearing earrings." circ. 100. 3/yr. Expects 2 issues 1999, 3 issues 2000. sub. price: $10; per copy: $3.50; sample: $3.50. Back issues: no back issues. 50pp; 5½×8½. Reporting time: 3-4 months. Simultaneous submissions accepted: yes. Publishes 25-50% of manuscripts submitted. Payment: none. Not copyrighted.

STAPLE, Donald Measham, Bob Windsor, Tor Cottage, 81 Cavendish Road, Matlock, Derbyshire DE4 3HD, United Kingdom. 1982. Poetry, fiction, interviews, parts-of-novels. "One of the few magazines where the new writer can be first published side by side with the established, and the very well known: we have published Silkin, Fanthorpe, Hilbert, Brockaway, Bartlett, Adcock. *Staple* open poetry competition runs *annually* (deadline 31 December). *Staple First Editions* chapbook project is rested. Also *Staple* poetry cards. In 15 years we have published 3,000 pieces by nearly 1,000 writers" circ. 600. 4/yr. Pub'd 4 issues 1998; expects 4 issues 1999, 4 issues 2000. sub. price: £14 overseas (sterling only surface mail; £17.50 airmail); per copy: £4/£5 (sterling only, surface/air); sample: £2 (sterling only surface mail, £3 airmail). Back issues: as sample. Discounts: 20%. 96pp; size A5; of. Reporting time: 3 months maximum. Payment: Europe £5-£10; overseas, complimentaries; but competition £500 in prizes; chapbooks: £10 royalty (advance) or share of £200 (one-off payment). Not copyrighted. Ads: none.

THE STAR BEACON, Earth Star Publications, Ann Ulrich, PO Box 117, Paonia, CO 81428, 970-527-3257; e-mail starbeacon@galaxycorp.com; website www.galaxycorp.com/starbeacon. 1987. Poetry, articles, art, photos, cartoons, interviews, reviews, letters, long-poems, news items, non-fiction. "*Star Beacon* readers are looking for the latest information on UFOs and related phenomena, as most of them are UFO percipients of various degrees, searching for answers. Because science, for the most part, has rejected them, *Star Beacon* readers are turning to metaphysics (the science of higher mind) for such answers as why are we here, where are we going, how can we make our world and the universe better." circ. 500+. 12/yr. Pub'd 8 issues 1998; expects 12 issues 1999, 12 issues 2000. sub. price: $20; per copy: $1.50; sample: $1.50. Back issues: $1.50. 12pp; 8½×11; of. Reporting time: 2 weeks. Simultaneous submissions accepted: yes. Publishes 80% of manuscripts submitted. Payment: copies/subscription. Not copyrighted. Pub's reviews: 3 in 1998. §UFOs, metaphysics, psychic phenomena, New Age living. Ads: $80/$40/$20 1/4 page/$10 1/8 page/$3 per column inch/$20 word classifieds.

THE BOBBY STAR NEWSLETTER, X-it Press, Bobby Star, PO Box 3756, Erie, PA 16508. 1996. Poetry, fiction, articles, art, photos, cartoons, criticism, reviews, letters, collages. "We want beat/streetwise, working class poetry. Gay. Real life. Open to haiku, sonnets, free verse, etc. Prefer 3-40 lines. No academic, bombastic, or 'third person' work. Recent contributors: Ana Christy, Kevin Hibshman, Alice Olds-Ellingson and Mr. Paul Weinman." circ. 300. 3/yr. Pub'd 3 issues 1998; expects 3 issues 1999, 3 issues 2000. price per copy: free; sample: $1. Back issues: they go pretty fast. 6-8pp; 8½×11; †of. Reporting time: 1-17 weeks. Simultaneous submissions accepted: yes. Publishes 10% of manuscripts submitted. Payment: 1-2 copies. Not copyrighted. Pub's reviews: 4 in 1998. §Basic interest is poetry chapbooks. Ads: $12/$5/others free.

Star Publications, Dave Damon, Editor, PO Box 2144, Eureka Springs, AR 72632, 816-523-8228. 1977. Pub'd 1 title 1998; expects 2 titles 1999. 6 titles listed in the *Small Press Record of Books in Print* (28th Edition, 1999-00). avg. price, cloth: $12.95. Discounts: 40% w/approved credit.

Starbooks Press/FLF Press, P.J. Powers, Founder, 2516 Ridge Avenue, Sarasota, FL 34235, 941-957-1281; Fax 941-955-3829; starxxx@gte.net. 1980. Poetry, fiction, art, photos, long-poems, collages, plays, non-fiction. avg. press run 5M. Pub'd 10 titles 1998; expects 12 titles 1999. 7 titles listed in the *Small Press Record of Books in Print* (28th Edition, 1999-00). avg. price, paper: $14.95. Discounts: 55% distributors, 40% booksellers. 512pp; 5½x8½. Reporting time: 2-3 months. Payment: negotiable. Copyrights for author. ABA, FPA.

STARBURST, Creative Arts & Science Enterprises, Charles J. Palmer, Jacqueline Palmer, 341 Miller Street, Abilene, TX 79605-1903. 1989. Poetry, articles, art. "Poetry: 32 lines or less. Prose: 400 words or less. Any subject suitable for a general reading audience. $5.00 gift certificate if used. Articles: 500-1500 words, on the writing world, i.e. the who, what, why, when or how of writing. $10.00 cash if used. Art work: any reasonable size to be reduced or enlarged to 6x6" for magazine cover (black/grey/white). $10.00 if used. Art for inside magazine: no larger than 8½x11" (black/grey/white). $5.00 if used." circ. 2M. 3/yr. Pub'd 4 issues 1998; expects 3 issues 1999, 3 issues 2000. sub. price: $21; per copy: $7; sample: $7. Back issues: $6. Discounts: 20%. 46pp; 8½x11; †of. Reporting time: 90 days to be used within 1 year; no regrets. Payment: cash or gift certificate to our products upon acceptance. Copyrighted, reverts to author. Pub's reviews: 5 in 1998. §Poetry, short story books. Ads: $95/$48/$32 1/3 page/$24 1/4 page/$16 1/6 page/$12 1/8 page.

Starfish Press, David J.A. Shears, Publisher, 6525-32nd Street NW, PO Box 42467, Washington, DC 20015, 202-244-STAR (7827) phone/Fax. 1989. Non-fiction. avg. press run 3M. Expects 1 title 1999. 2 titles listed in the *Small Press Record of Books in Print* (28th Edition, 1999-00). avg. price, paper: $14.45. Discounts: 40% retail, 50% wholesale & orders over 100 copies. 300pp; 5⅜x8½; of. Reporting time: 2 months. Simultaneous submissions accepted: yes. Publishes 0% of manuscripts submitted. Payment: royalties only. Copyrights for author. PMA, SPAN.

STARGREEN, Patrick Smith, PO Box 380406, Cambridge, MA 02238, 617-868-3981. 1993. Poetry, fiction, photos, criticism, music, letters, non-fiction. "'The magazine for the modern sentimentalist', unpretentious writing in a gritty, no-nonsense format. Looking for submissions that are terse, biting, and sardonic, but which remain humane at heart." circ. 500-1M. Irregular. Pub'd 3 issues 1998; expects 3 issues 1999, 3+ issues 2000. sub. price: $10; per copy: $2; sample: $2. 30pp; 5½x8½; †seat-of-the-pants. Reporting time: quick. Simultaneous submissions accepted: yes. Publishes a small % of manuscripts submitted. Payment: copies. Copyrighted, reverts to author. Ads: $50/$25.

STARK NAKED, P & K Stark Productions, Inc., 17125C W. Bluemound Road, Ste. 171, Brookfield, WI 53005, 414-543-9013. 1997. "Newsletter covering entertainment industry: films, TV, books, magazines, comics, etc." price per copy: free. 2-4pp; 8½x11.

StarLance Publications, James B. King, 5104 Cooperstown Lane, Pasco, WA 99301-8984. 1987. Fiction, art, cartoons. "All currently planned books are collections of cartoons, science fiction and fantasy illustration, illustrated science fiction and fantasy short fiction, and graphic novels. Desired art is black line and all mediums that reproduce well in b/w halftone. Books aimed at mainstream market, including young adults. Profanity, nudity, and sexually explicit material are not desired." avg. press run 5M. Pub'd 1 title 1998; expects 1 title 1999, 1 title 2000. 8 titles listed in the *Small Press Record of Books in Print* (28th Edition, 1999-00). avg. price, paper: $9.95. Discounts: 20-55% based on quantity. 128pp; 5½x8½, 8½x11; of. Reporting time: 2-6 weeks. Simultaneous submissions accepted: no. Publishes 5% of manuscripts submitted. Payment: per word, upon publication, sometimes royalties. Does not copyright for author.

THE STARLIGHT PAPERS, From Here Press, William J. Higginson, PO Box 2740, Santa Fe, NM 87504-2740, 505-438-3249. 1993. Criticism. "Each issue is a single essay of criticism and/or literary history relating to cross-cultural poetics; for example, the world-wide spread of poetical genres originating in single cultures, such as the sonnet and haiku. Especially interested in the tension between adoption of the original culture's modes and adaptation to the foreign ground. First issues: 'North America and the Democracy of Haiku' by William J. Higginson, 'The Uses of Nature in Japanese Poetry' by Jane Hirshfield, 'The Haiku World in the Year 2058' by George Swede. While these all deal with the Japanese-originated haiku or tanka, I am also especially interested in interactions between oral tradition and tribal poetics and international 'modernist' and 'post-modernist' poetics. Prefer MLA (parenthetical doc.) style. Submitted work should include hard copy and DOS disk (either size, DD or HD formats) with files in ASCII or a common word-processor format (WordPerfect preferred, but can convert). If you use a different computer format query with hard copy only and describe format (many conversions possible)." circ. 50-100. Irregular, 1-2/yr. Expects 2 issues 1999, 2 issues

2000. price per copy: $3 + $1 p/h. 16pp; 8½×11; xerography. Reporting time: 3 months. Payment: 10 copies plus set of repro masters. Copyrighted, rights are in author's name. Ads: none.

Starlight Press, Ira Rosenstein, Box 3102, Long Island City, NY 11103. 1980. Poetry. "Anthology published in 1992. No immediate publishing plans." avg. press run 300. 6 titles listed in the *Small Press Record of Books in Print* (28th Edition, 1999-00). avg. price, paper: $4. Discounts: normal trade. 35pp; 8½×7; of. Reporting time: 2 months. Payment: 2 free copies & 50% discount on further Starlight copies (any title). Copyrights for author.

StarMist Books, Beth Boyd, President, Box 12640, Rochester, NY 14612. 1986. Poetry, fiction. "StarMist Books publishes poetry with depth, sensitivity and power. Award-winning poet Jani Johe Webster is one of our authors, as is Virginia Johe." avg. press run 500. Expects 2 titles 1999, 2-4 titles 2000. 2 titles listed in the *Small Press Record of Books in Print* (28th Edition, 1999-00). avg. price, paper: $6. 75pp; 5½×8½; of. Reporting time: 2 weeks. Payment: negotiable. Copyrights for author. UAPAA, WWA, Writers & Books, Nat'l Assoc. of Independent Publishers, The Academy of American Poets.

STATE AND LOCAL GOVERNMENT REVIEW, Richard W. Campbell, Ann Allen, Contact Person, Carl Vinson Institute of Government, 201 N. Milledge Ave., Univ. of GA, Athens, GA 30602, 706-542-2736. 1968. "A journal of research and viewpoints on state, local, and intergovernmental issues" circ. 1.4M. 3/yr. Pub'd 3 issues 1998; expects 3 issues 1999, 3 issues 2000. sub. price: $16 individual, $24 library; per copy: $5. Back issues: volumes 1-7 $1/copy, all other $5/copy. 72pp; 7×10. Reporting time: 10 weeks. Publishes 25% of manuscripts submitted. Copyrighted. Pub's reviews.

State Street Press, Judith Kitchen, Stan Sanvel Rubin, Bruce Bennett, Linda Allardt, PO Box 278, Brockport, NY 14420, 716-637-0023. 1981. Poetry. "20-24 pages of poetry that works *as a collection*. We are looking for variety and excellence in many styles. We choose 3-5 chapbooks from an anonymous competition. Cost: $10 handling fee. Chapbook sent to each contestant. Authors include: Stephanie Strickland, Marcia Falk, Nancy Simpson, Michael Cadnum, Judson Mitcham, Hilda Raz, Cornelius Eady, Naomi Shihab Nye, Pamela Gross, Stuart Dybek, Dennis Nurkse, Jonathan Holden, Jane Mead, Dionisio Martinez, Jan Beatty, Joe Survant, and William Greenaway." avg. press run 400. Pub'd 4 titles 1998; expects 4 titles 1999, 4 titles 2000. 41 titles listed in the *Small Press Record of Books in Print* (28th Edition, 1999-00). avg. price, paper: $6. Discounts: 40% to bookstores. 32pp; of. Reporting time: 4-5 months after contest deadline (May 15). Payment: 25 copies to the author, 25 review copies, author can buy at cost. Copyrights for author.

Station Hill Press, George Quasha, Publisher & Director; Susan Quasha, Associate Publisher & Co-Director, Station Hill Road, Barrytown, NY 12507, 914-758-5840. 1978. Poetry, fiction, art, photos, satire, criticism, music, letters, long-poems, collages, plays, concrete art, non-fiction. "Publisher of international literature & visual and performing arts, emphasizing the contemporary & innovative, yet excluding neither the ancient nor the traditional, presented with a commitment to excellence in book design and production. Prose fiction by Maurice Blanchot, Rosemarie Waldrop, Franz Kamin, Lydia Davis, Spencer Holst; poetry by John Cage, Jackson Mac Low, Kenneth Irby, Robert Kelly, Paul Auster, Armand Schwerner, Charles Bernstein, Norman Weinstein, etc.; discourse by James Hillman, Ed Sanders, Blanchot, Porphyry, etc; visual arts by Russian avant-garde, Wolf Kahn, Thomas Dugan, etc. Other imprints and series include: *Artext, Contemporary Artist Series, Open Book,* and *P-U-L-S-E Books.*" avg. press run 1.5M-3M. Pub'd 12 titles 1998; expects 20 titles 1999, 20 titles 2000. 75 titles listed in the *Small Press Record of Books in Print* (28th Edition, 1999-00). avg. price, cloth: $29.95; paper: $9.95; other: $12-$100 special editions. Discounts: 50% distributor, 20% on single orders, escalating with qty. 64-200pp; 5¾×8¾, 5½×8½, 6×9, 7×10. Reporting time: no guarantee except by written arrangement. Payment: usually 10% of edition in copies or 10% of gross. Copyrights for author.

Steam Press/LAD Publishing, Stan Cohen, 5455 Meridian Mark, Suite 100, Atlanta, GA 30342, 404-257-1577; FAX 256-5475. 1990. Poetry, fiction, art. "No submissions currently accepted. Our initial efforts are to establish a series based on the collaborations of authors and artists in synergistic, beautiful volumes. Our participants include: David Bottoms, Stan Cohen, Glenn Goldberg, Gary Stephan, and Ed Ruscha. The books are issued in limited signed editions and trade paperback." Expects 1 title 1999, 1 title 2000. 3 titles listed in the *Small Press Record of Books in Print* (28th Edition, 1999-00). avg. price, cloth: $750.00; paper: $14-$18. 40-80pp; 8×10; of, lp. Publishes 0% of manuscripts submitted. Copyrights for author.

Steamshovel Press (see also STEAMSHOVEL PRESS), Kenn Thomas, PO Box 23715, St. Louis, MO 63121. 1988. Articles, interviews, reviews, letters, news items, non-fiction. "Manuscripts for future book projects to be considered by Steamshovel Press should be of a documentary nature on topics related to the Beat movement, the counter-culture, or conspiracy theories. In 1995, an anthology of Steamshovel Press back issues entitled *Popular Alienation* was published by Illuminet Press. In 1997, two other Steamshovel Press books were published: *NASA, Nazis & JFK* (Adventures Unlimited Press) and *The Octopus: Secret Government and the Death of Danny Casolaro* (Feral House)." avg. press run 4M. Pub'd 3 titles 1998; expects 3 titles 1999, 3 titles 2000. 3 titles listed in the *Small Press Record of Books in Print* (28th Edition, 1999-00). avg. price, other: $5.50

544

saddle stapled. Discounts: 50% to bookstores & magazine outlets, 55% to distributors. 65pp; 8×11. Reporting time: 30 days. Payment: 3 contributor copies. Does not copyright for author.

STEAMSHOVEL PRESS, Steamshovel Press, Kenn Thomas, PO Box 23715, St. Louis, MO 63121. 1988. Articles, interviews, criticism, reviews, letters, news items, non-fiction. *"Steamshovel Press* continues its challenge to consensus reality with on-going looks at current conspiracy activity. Each issue studies hidden history and exposes the parapolitical undercurrents of contemporary life. Recent articles have looked at connections between the Nation of Islam and the American Nazi Party; 'paranoia' as a media buzz word; Danny Casolaro's Octopus theory and its link with UFO lore; anti-conspiracy activist John Judge; Timothy Leary's post-mortem; flying saucers and Flight 800; and the conspiratorial dimension of the Oklahoma City bomb. 'Research the mainstream press doesn't have the *cajones* to publish.' says *Cult Rapture* author Adam Parfey. A definitive source of conspiracy currents in the country: the White House used *Steamshovel* material in its report on the 'conspiracy commerce stream'; and the Higher Source death cult published its UFO rants in *Steamshovel* three years prior to its infamous suicides." circ. 3M. 4/yr. Pub'd 3 issues 1998; expects 4 issues 1999, 4 issues 2000. sub. price: $22/4 issues; per copy: $5; sample: $5. Back issues: only issues 5, 7-15 available ($5). Discounts: 50% consignment rate available to bookstores, 55% available to distributors. 64pp; 8½×11. Reporting time: 30 days. Payment: 3 contributor copies. Copyrighted, reverts to author. Pub's reviews: 25 in 1998. §Conspiracy theories, UFOs, revisionist history, the Kennedy and King assassinations, writings of the Beat poets and novelists. Ads: $100/$80/$60 1/4 page/$300 back cover/$200 inside back cover.

Steel Balls Press, John J. White, E.F. Bellevue, PO Box 1532, Kona, HI 96745, E-mail donsteel@gte.net. 1986. Non-fiction. "No unsolicited m/s! 1 page. Query letters only. Specialize in controversial how-to/self help. *Absolutely* no New Age, poetry, fiction." avg. press run 20M. Expects 2 titles 1999, 2 titles 2000. 3 titles listed in the *Small Press Record of Books in Print* (28th Edition, 1999-00). avg. price, cloth: $23.95; paper: $18.95. Discounts: normal trade; STOP 25%. 224pp; 8½×5½; web of. Reporting time: 6 weeks. Simultaneous submissions accepted: yes. Publishes 2% of manuscripts submitted. Payment: 10% retail cover price after 500 copies. Does not copyright for author. ABA, PMA, SCBP, SDBP, SCBA, SDBA.

Steerforth Press, L.C., Thomas Powers, Michael Moore, Alan Lelchuk, Robin Butcher-Bayer, 105-106 Chelsea Street, PO Box 70, South Royalton, VT 05068, 802-763-2808. 1993. Fiction, non-fiction. "No unsolicited manuscripts accepted." avg. press run 5M. Pub'd 15 titles 1998; expects 15 titles 1999, 20 titles 2000. 18 titles listed in the *Small Press Record of Books in Print* (28th Edition, 1999-00). avg. price, cloth: $26; paper: $13. 275pp; 5½×8½; of. Reporting time: query first. Payment: standard cuts for clothbound and paperbacks. Copyrights for author. ABA, NEBA, VBPA (VT Book Publishers Assoc.).

Stemmer House Publishers, Inc., Barbara Holdridge, 2627 Caves Road, Owings Mills, MD 21117. 1975. Fiction, non-fiction. avg. press run 5M. Pub'd 20 titles 1998; expects 15 titles 1999, 15 titles 2000. 19 titles listed in the *Small Press Record of Books in Print* (28th Edition, 1999-00). avg. price, cloth: $10.95-$35; paper: $5.95-$14.95. Discounts: 42% for 5 assorted titles or more to retailers. 170pp; 6×9, 7×10, 8½×11; of. Reporting time: 4 weeks. Simultaneous submissions accepted: yes. Publishes .1% of manuscripts submitted. Payment: royalty and advance. Copyrights for author. CBC.

THE WALLACE STEVENS JOURNAL, The Wallace Stevens Society Press, John N. Serio, Editor; Joseph Duemer, Poetry Editor, Clarkson University, Box 5750, Potsdam, NY 13699-5750, 315-268-3987. 1977. Poetry, articles, criticism, reviews, letters, news items. *"The Wallace Stevens Journal* publishes criticism on the poetry of Wallace Stevens. It also publishes archival material, Stevensesque poems, a current bibliography, and book reviews. Recent contributors have been: Eleanor Cook, Alan Filreis, Diane Wakoski, B.J. Leggett, Margaret Dickie, Helen Vendler" circ. 600. 2/yr. Pub'd 2 issues 1998; expects 2 issues 1999, 2 issues 2000. sub. price: $25 for individuals ($45 2-years), $32 for institutions, $37 for foreign; per copy: $10; sample: $3 (postage. Back issues: $5 per number. 120pp; 6×9; desktop, typeset. Reporting time: 6 weeks. Simultaneous submissions accepted: no. Publishes 25% of manuscripts submitted. Payment: copies. Copyrighted, reverts to author. Pub's reviews: 5 in 1998. §Wallace Stevens. Ads: $150/$100. Wallace Stevens Society, Inc.

The Wallace Stevens Society Press (see also THE WALLACE STEVENS JOURNAL), John N. Serio, Series Editor, Box 5750 Clarkson University, Potsdam, NY 13699-5750, 315-268-3987; FAX 268-3983; serio@clarkson.edu; http://www.clarkson.edu/~wsj. 1992. Poetry. "We initiated a poetry series with the publication of *Inhabited World: New & Selected Poems 1970-1995* by John Allman (166pp). We hope to publish a book of poetry each year." avg. press run 900. Pub'd 1 title 1998; expects 1 title 1999, 1 title 2000. 1 title listed in the *Small Press Record of Books in Print* (28th Edition, 1999-00). avg. price, paper: $14.95. Discounts: 20-30% depending on quantity. 80pp; 6×9; of. Reporting time: 6-8 weeks. Simultaneous submissions accepted: no. Publishes 5% of manuscripts submitted. Payment: 10%. Copyrights for author.

Stewart Publishing & Printing, Robert Stewart, 17 Sir Constantine Drive, Markham, ON L3P 2X3, Canada, 905-294-4389; FAX 905-294-8718; rstewart@pathcom.com. 1992. Non-fiction. avg. press run 1.2M. Pub'd 5 titles 1998; expects 12 titles 1999, 20 titles 2000. 6 titles listed in the *Small Press Record of Books in Print*

545

(28th Edition, 1999-00). avg. price, paper: $15. Discounts: 3 or more 25%. 200pp; 6×8½; †of. Copyrights for author.

STILETTO, Howling Dog Press/Stiletto, Michael Annis, 1016 Deborah Drive, Loveland, CO 80537-7087. 1989. Poetry, fiction, art, photos, satire, parts-of-novels, long-poems, collages, plays, non-fiction. "Recent contributors: Burroughs, Waldman, Codrescu, Leary, DiPrima, DeCormier-Shekerjian, Tavel, Ray, Vando, Bergt, Annis, Jaffe, Antler, Wakoski, DeClue, Heyen, Tarn, Low, Goldbarth. 'If you have a statement to make, make it here...' Forthcoming: Bukowski, Gregory Greyhawk." circ. 1M. 1/yr. Expects 1 issue 1999, 1 issue 2000. sub. price: no subscriptions, standing orders only; per copy: $21.50 pa; sample: $21.50. Back issues: *Stiletto One* $100 - out of print/collections given priority; no discount. Discounts: 30% trade, 20% classroom. 200-300pp; 5×11¼; †of. Reporting time: up to 1 year. Simultaneous submissions accepted: yes. Publishes less than 5% of manuscripts submitted. Payment: 20 copies major contribs., 1-4 copies additional contribs. Copyrighted, reverts to author. no ads. PMA.

Still Waters Poetry Press, Shirley Lake, Editor, 459 S. Willow Avenue, Absecon, NJ 08201-4633. 1989. Poetry, non-fiction. "Chapbooks of poetry, the essay. Dedicated to the discovery and cultivation of significant works by or about women. Some books on poetic craft, especially as practiced by women, are planned." avg. press run 300. Pub'd 5 titles 1998; expects 5 titles 1999, 5 titles 2000. 31 titles listed in the *Small Press Record of Books in Print* (28th Edition, 1999-00). avg. price, paper: $5. Discounts: 40%—dealers only. 24-48pp; 5½×8½; of. Reporting time: 1 month, no report if SASE is not included with submission/correspondence. Simultaneous submissions accepted: yes. Payment: 10% of press run, discounts to author on additional copies, 10% of sales, if any, on 2nd and subsequent press runs. Copyrights for author. Small Press Center.

Stillpoint Publishing, Errol G. Sowers, Chairman & Co-Publisher, Box 640, Walpole, NH 03608, 603-756-9281, Fax 603-756-9282, e-mail stillpoint@monad.net. 1983. "Best selling Authors: Meredith L. Young-Sowers, Carolyn M. Myss, with C. Norman Shealy MD Ph.D, Dan Millman, John Robbins, Naomi Stephan Ph.D. Book format, nonfiction publishing in the field of personal growth, holistic health and healing, divination tools, and spirituality." avg. press run 5M-15M. Pub'd 5 titles 1998; expects 5 titles 1999, 8-10 titles 2000. 35 titles listed in the *Small Press Record of Books in Print* (28th Edition, 1999-00). avg. price, cloth: $18.95; paper: $14.95. Discounts: per Publishers' Group West, California. Adult 256pp; 5½×8¼, 6×9. Reporting time: 6-8 weeks. Simultaneous submissions accepted: yes. Payment: varies. Copyrights for author.

Stone and Scott, Publishers, Les Boston, PO Box 56419, Sherman Oaks, CA 91413-1419, 818-904-9088. 1990. Poetry, non-fiction. "We are over-committed for foreseeable future and are not seeking submissions." avg. press run 1M. Pub'd 1 title 1998; expects 3 titles 1999. 4 titles listed in the *Small Press Record of Books in Print* (28th Edition, 1999-00). avg. price, cloth: $20; paper: $10. 100pp; 6×9. PMA.

Stone Bridge Press, Peter Goodman, Publisher, PO Box 8208, Berkeley, CA 94707, 510-524-8732. 1989. Fiction, non-fiction. "Interested in material on Japan and Japanese culture: 1) Language—classroom texts and self-study, especially intermediate level. 2) Japanese fiction in translation—novels and short story collections, fine literature primarily, but will consider mysteries and science fiction. 3) Design—especially gardens and architecture. 4) Current affairs and business. Do *not* want cliched treatments of Japan, *haiku* diaries, or books based entirely on second sources and outdated studies/translations. Wish to present contemporary portrait of Japan of use to people who need to interact or deal with Japan. Also distributes software for learning Japanese." avg. press run 3M. Pub'd 9 titles 1998; expects 5 titles 1999, 5 titles 2000. 34 titles listed in the *Small Press Record of Books in Print* (28th Edition, 1999-00). avg. price, cloth: $24; paper: $15. Discounts: available through distributor (Weatherhill, Inc.). 160pp; 5½×8½; of. Reporting time: 2-3 months, 3 weeks if proposal only. Simultaneous submissions accepted: yes. Publishes less than 5% of manuscripts submitted. Payment: advance vs. royalties. Copyrights for author. Marin Small-Publishers (Box 309, Mill Valley, CA 94942), PMA.

Graham Stone, Graham Stone, GPO Box 4440, Sydney 1044, Australia, 043-926540. 1989. Fiction, criticism, non-fiction. "Reprints of old Australian science fiction works. Present plans will take several years. No submissions wanted. Production is by good quality photocopier, bound by hand in traditional cloth hard covers. I am compiling a comprehensive bibliography of Australian science fiction for eventual publication, and collecting my numerous book reviews and historical notes on this field. But most books will be reprints of old books and magazine items by Australian authors. These are not limited editions, intend to keep in print." avg. press run 100. Pub'd 1 title 1998; expects 1 title 1999, 2 titles 2000. 5 titles listed in the *Small Press Record of Books in Print* (28th Edition, 1999-00). avg. price, cloth: $24. Discounts: 50%. 150pp; size A5; †photocopy. Payment: half share of proceeds. Copyrights for author.

STONE SOUP, The Magazine By Young Writers and Artists, Gerry Mandel, William Rubel, Box 83, Santa Cruz, CA 95063, 831-426-5557, Fax 831-426-1161, e-mail editor@stonesoup.com; www.stonesoup.com. 1973. Poetry, fiction, art, photos, reviews, letters, parts-of-novels, long-poems, plays. "All material written & drawn by children 3-13." circ. 20M. 6/yr. Pub'd 5 issues 1998; expects 6 issues 1999, 6 issues 2000. sub. price: $32;

per copy: $5.50; sample: $5.50. Back issues: prices upon request. Discounts: schedule available upon request. 48pp; 7×10; of. Reporting time: 4 weeks. Simultaneous submissions accepted: no. Publishes .5% of manuscripts submitted. Payment: 2 copies, $10 plus certificate. Copyrighted, does not revert to author. Pub's reviews: 10 in 1998. §Children's books. Ads: $800 inside front or back cover, full page, b/w; $1200 back cover, 2/3 page, color.

Stone Wall Press, Inc, Henry C. Wheelwright, Publisher, 1241 30th Street NW, Washington, DC 20007, 202-333-1860. 1972. Non-fiction. "Non-fiction—Frontier or second tier national outdoor recreational material with photos or illustrations. Optimally combining pragmatic material with adventure, humor, and overriding sense of ecology. Natural history; environmental issues; endangered plants, animals, etc. Also, modern culture." avg. press run 3M-4M. Expects 1 title 2000. 8 titles listed in the *Small Press Record of Books in Print* (28th Edition, 1999-00). avg. price, cloth: $24.95; paper: $14.95. Discounts: standard. 240pp; 6×9; of. Reporting time: 2 weeks. Simultaneous submissions accepted: yes. Payment: to be arranged. Copyrights for author. Washington Book Publishers Assoc.

StoneBrook Publishing, Jim McCulloch, PO Box 30696, Charlotte, NC 28230, 704-849-6878; FAX 704-841-8557. 1996. Fiction, photos, non-fiction. "Just released a stock car racing humor book; currently working on a children's book series and a golf how-to release." avg. press run 10M-20M. Expects 2 titles 1999, 4 titles 2000. avg. price, cloth: $24.95; paper: $11.95. Discounts: varies. 100pp. Reporting time: 1 month. Simultaneous submissions accepted: yes. Payment: varies. Copyrights for author. PMA.

STONEFLOWER LITERARY JOURNAL, Brenda Davidson-Shaddox, 1824 Nacogdoches, Suite 191, San Antonio, TX 78209. 1995. Poetry, fiction, art, photos, interviews. "We also accept works by children. 2500 words short fiction; 30 lines poetry preferred (not required); B&W photos & line drawings - no color. Recent contributors: Russell Lewis, Jaclyn Rivers, Pat Mondy, Quynh Cao" circ. 1M. 1/yr. Pub'd 1 issue 1998; expects 1 issue 1999, 1 issue 2000. price per copy: $8 + $2 s&h; sample: $6 includes s&h. Back issues: $6 includes s&h. Discounts: 40%. 100pp; 5½×8½; lp. Reporting time: up to 90 days. Simultaneous submissions accepted: yes. Publishes approx. 10% of manuscripts submitted. Payment: Poetry - $5; fiction - $8; art, photo - $8. Copyrighted, reverts to author. Ads: $100/$55/$25 1/3 page.

Stonehouse Publications, Lewis Watson, Sharon Watson, Timber Butte Road, Box 390, Sweet, ID 83670, 208-584-3344. 1974. Photos. avg. press run 10M. Expects 1 title 2000. 1 title listed in the *Small Press Record of Books in Print* (28th Edition, 1999-00). avg. price, paper: $11.95. Discounts: trade 40% any quantity, fully refundable; mail order 46%, jobber & bulk 50%; library 40%. 100pp; 8½×11; of.

STONES IN MY POCKET, Mark Abouzeid, 11863 Wimbeldon Circle, #402, Wellington, FL 33414. 1996. Poetry, fiction, articles, art, photos, reviews, music, letters, long-poems, news items, non-fiction. "Spiritual - Holistic-Recovery, inspirational small pieces" circ. 30M. 4/yr. Pub'd 1 issue 1998; expects 4 issues 1999, 4 issues 2000. sub. price: $22; per copy: none; sample: free. Back issues: postage and handling. Discounts: Have not yet been established. 18-22pp; 8½×11; 4/color slick paper. Reporting time: 3 months. Simultaneous submissions accepted: yes. Copyrighted, reverts to author. Pub's reviews: 40 in 1998. §Spiritual, holistic health, recovery, inspirational, self help, alternative medicine. Ads: none. ABA, FPA.

Stones Point Press, Barbara Feller-Roth, Ramon de Rosas, PO Box 384, Belfast, ME 04915, 207-338-1921. 1992. Fiction, articles, reviews, letters, non-fiction. avg. press run 5M. Pub'd 1 title 1998; expects 2 titles 1999, 1 title 2000. 8 titles listed in the *Small Press Record of Books in Print* (28th Edition, 1999-00). avg. price, paper: $15. Discounts: STOP 40%. Pages vary; 5½×8½. Copyrights for author.

Storm Peak Press, Floyd Loomis, 2629 Nob Hill Avenue North, Seattle, WA 98109-1861. 1993. Non-fiction. avg. press run 4M. Pub'd 3 titles 1998; expects 3 titles 1999, 3 titles 2000. 6 titles listed in the *Small Press Record of Books in Print* (28th Edition, 1999-00). avg. price, paper: $12.00. 200pp. Reporting time: 2-3 months.

Stormline Press, Inc., Raymond Bial, Linda LaPuma Bial, PO Box 593, Urbana, IL 61801, 217-328-2665. 1985. Fiction, art, photos. "Stormline Press publishes works of literary and artistic distinction with preference for work which deals sensitively with rural and small town life. All publications are professionally designed and printed to critical standards. *First Frost*, the debut publication of the press, was a "Writer's Choice" selection. Other noteworthy titles are *Dim Tales* by John Knoepfle, *A Turning* by Greg Kuzma and *Silent Friends* by Margaret Lacey, as well as *Living With Lincoln* and *The Alligator Inventions*, both by Dan Guillory. No unsolicited manuscripts. Publishes by invitation only." avg. press run 1.5M. Pub'd 3 titles 1998; expects 3 titles 1999, 3 titles 2000. 13 titles listed in the *Small Press Record of Books in Print* (28th Edition, 1999-00). avg. price, cloth: $17.95; paper: $8.95; other: $14.95 *First Frost* which includes 18 duotones. Discounts: 40% bookstores; 55% jobbers; Bulk discounts to be negotiated. Poetry 40-80pp, fiction 80-200pp; 6×9. Payment: 15% on sale of first 1000 copies after production costs have been recouped. Copyrights for author.

STORY, Lois Rosenthal, Editor, 1507 Dana Avenue, Cincinnati, OH 45207, 513-531-2222. 1989. Fiction, parts-of-novels. "We want short stories and self-contained novel excerpts that are extremely well written. Our audience is sophisticated and accustomed to the finest imaginative writing by new and established authors. *Story* won the National Magazine Award for Fiction in 1992 and 1995, and was nominated in 1994, 1996, and 1997. The magazine sponsors two annual contests, the Story Short Short Competition and the Carson McCullers Prize for the Short Story. Fiction guidelines and contest rules for #10 SASE. 8,000 word maximum. No fax submissions. We publish 50-60 stories a year." circ. 40M. 4/yr. Pub'd 4 issues 1998; expects 4 issues 1999, 4 issues 2000. sub. price: $19.96; per copy: $6.95; sample: $6.95 + $2.40 postage. Back issues: $4 each or 3 for $10. Discounts: 40% off cover, retailers only (contact Eastern News Distributors, Inc., One Media Way, 12406 Rt. 250, Milan, OH 44846-9705). 128pp; 6¼x9½; of. Reporting time: 4-6 weeks. We accept simultaneous submissions if identified as such. Publishes .3% of manuscripts submitted. Payment: $750-$1,000. Copyrighted, reverts to author. Ads: nonprofit rates: full page 1X $865, 2X $835, 4X $780; 1/2 page: 1X $500, 2X $490, 4X $450. General rates: full 1X $1,085, 2X $1035, 4X $980; 1/2 page: 1X $630, 2X $605, 4X $570. Classified: $2.20/word 1X, $1.95/word 4X $1.70, 15 word minimum. MPA.

Story County Books, Theresa Pappas, Co-Editor; Michael Martone, Co-Editor, PO Box 21179, Tuscaloosa, AL 35402-1179. 1984. Fiction. "Story County Books was published in Story County, Iowa. We publish one story chapbooks in formats that vary with each story. We publish cheap chapbooks, and we try to keep the price under $1. Our first book was Michael Wilkerson's *Can This Story Be Saved?* a take-off of the *Ladies Home Journal* piece. We chose a Dell Purse Book format to complement the 'self-improvement' parody of the piece. We are interested in clever stories, regional stories, stories with a voice" avg. press run 100. Pub'd 1 title 1998; expects 1 title 1999, 1 title 2000. 5 titles listed in the *Small Press Record of Books in Print* (28th Edition, 1999-00). avg. price, paper: $1. Discounts: 50%. Pages vary; size varies; †desktop, xerography. Reporting time: 14 months. Simultaneous submissions accepted: no. Publishes 1% of manuscripts submitted. Payment: by arrangement. Copyrights for author.

STORYBOARD, Jeannine E. Talley, Robert Alan Burns, Christopher S. Lobban, James E. Martin, Division of English, University of Guam, Mangilao, GU 96923, E-mail jtalley@uog9.uog.edu. 1991. Poetry, fiction, art, photos, interviews, parts-of-novels, long-poems, non-fiction. "Material should have Pacific regional focus or be written by a resident of this region" circ. 200. 1/yr. Pub'd 1 issue 1998; expects 1 issue 1999, 1 issue 2000. sub. price: $7.50; per copy: $7.50; sample: $4. Back issues: $5. Discounts: 30% retail; 50% distributor. 100pp; 5½x8½; of. Reporting time: 4-6 months, SASE required. Simultaneous submissions accepted: no. Publishes 45% of manuscripts submitted. Payment: 2 copies. Copyrighted, reverts to author. Ads: $150/$100/$50 1/3 page. CLMP.

STORYQUARTERLY, Anne Brashler, Co-Editor; M.M.M. Hayes, Co-Editor, PO Box 1416, Northbrook, IL 60065. 1974. Poetry, interviews, parts-of-novels. "*StoryQuarterly* wishes to see great fiction. We publish many writers for the first time." circ. 2M. 1/yr. Pub'd 1 issue 1998; expects 1 issue 1999, 1 issue 2000. sub. price: $12/4 issues, $32 library & institution, $34 Canada, $36 foreign, $40 air; per copy: $5; sample: $5. Back issues: $5 (SQ). Discounts: 40% bookstores; 20% distributors. 250pp; 5¾x8¾; of. Reporting time: up to 4 months. Simultaneous submissions accepted: yes. Publishes 1% of manuscripts submitted. Payment: 5 copies. Copyrighted. Ads: $150/$100 or lit mag exchange. CLMP, IAC (Illinois Arts Council).

Storytime Ink International, Christine Petrell Kallevig, PO Box 470505, Broadview Heights, OH 44147, 440-838-4881; e-mail storytimeink@worldnet.att.net. 1991. "Looking for material that combines storytelling with a tangible art form, i.e. cutting stories, drawing stories, folding stories. Should be less than 1,000 words with an ironic twist at the end. No violence. Should be appropriate for children, but entertaining for adults." avg. press run 5M. Expects 2 titles 1999, 2 titles 2000. 5 titles listed in the *Small Press Record of Books in Print* (28th Edition, 1999-00). avg. price, paper: $11.50. Discounts: usual trade. 100pp; 8½x11; of. Reporting time: 1 month. Payment: negotiable. Copyrights for author.

STOVEPIPE: A Journal of Little Literary Value, Sweet Lady Moon Press, Troy Teegarden, PO Box 1076, Georgetown, KY 40324, troyteegarden@worldradio.org. 1995. Poetry, fiction, art, cartoons, interviews, criticism, parts-of-novels. "We're looking for your best work. Don't send anything less." circ. 250. 4/yr. Pub'd 4 issues 1998; expects 4 issues 1999, 4 issues 2000. sub. price: $10; per copy: $2; sample: $2 or trade. Back issues: $5, but usually hard to find. 28pp; 8½x5½; †of. Reporting time: 1 month (usually less). We accept simultaneous submissions, but very reluctantly, and must be stated somewhere. Publishes 10% of manuscripts submitted. Payment: varies, at least 1 copy. Copyrighted, reverts to author. Ads: will occasionally trade ads with other publications.

STRANGE GROWTHS, Jenny Zervakis, 909 Lancaster, Durham, NC 27701. 1991. Cartoons. "This is a autobiographical/personal comic book. It is a 12-16 page photocopy that consists of work written and drawn by Jenny Zervakis with generally no outside contributors. Also available, 32 page Strange Growth compilations I, 1-6; Strange Growths II, 32pp, 7-12" circ. 100. 3/yr. Pub'd 3 issues 1998; expects 3 issues 1999, 3 issues 2000. price per copy: $1.50; sample: $1.50. Discounts: if ordering more than 1, $1 each after the 1st one. 16pp; †photocopy. Copyrighted.

STRANGE MAGAZINE, Mark E. Chorvinsky, PO Box 2246, Rockville, MD 20847, 301-460-4789. 1987. Articles, interviews, reviews, letters, non-fiction. "Web site http://www.cais.com/strangemag/home.html" circ. 10M. 2/yr. Pub'd 2 issues 1998; expects 2 issues 1999, 2 issues 2000. sub. price: $19.75/2 years; per copy: $4.95; sample: $5.95. Back issues: prices based on availability. 64pp; 8½×11; of. Reporting time: varies. Simultaneous submissions accepted: no. Publishes less than 5% of manuscripts submitted. Payment: complimentary issues. Copyrighted, reverts to author. Pub's reviews: 16 in 1998. §Occult, folklore, supernatural, focus on unexplained phenomena and folkore (less so occult, supernatural) We have no occult/supernatural. Only strange phenomena.

STRANGER THAN MADNESS, Jay L. Findlay, Publisher-Editor, Zieglerstrasse 8, 01217 Dresden, Germany. 1998. "I am interested in all types of poetry, especially hard-nosed, avant garde, humour and general madness. I prefer almost anything that's 'off the wall,' but racism, nazism or overdone porno will not be accepted. Short stories of up to 2,000 words on any subject, as long as they are not overdone with flowery language. I also have a distinct dislike for plagiarism; when it's discovered the poet submitting will receive a not-so-kind response. I will give no response to mss. without SAE and 2 IRCs. *No exceptions unless work is better than excellent.*" circ. 250-400. 4/yr. sub. price: DM30, $20US; per copy: $3 and 2 IRCs. 40-60pp; size A5. Reporting time: 2-4 weeks. Simultaneous submissions accepted: yes. Payment: 3 copies.

Strata Publishing, Inc., Kathleen Domenig, PO Box 1303, State College, PA 16804, 814-234-8545, fax 814-238-7222, www.stratapub.com. 1990. Non-fiction. "We publish mid-and upper-level textbooks for college courses, as well as scholarly and professional books that might be used extensively in such courses" avg. press run 1M-2M. Pub'd 3 titles 1998; expects 2 titles 1999, 1 title 2000. 5 titles listed in the *Small Press Record of Books in Print* (28th Edition, 1999-00). Discounts: net pricing. 7×10, 6×9; of. Reporting time: 1-3 months. Simultaneous submissions accepted: yes. Payment: varies. Copyrights for author.

●**Strategic Press,** 774 Morwood Road, Teiford, PA 18969, 215-723-8422; 800-974-4393; strategic4@aol.com. 1 title listed in the *Small Press Record of Books in Print* (28th Edition, 1999-00).

Stratton Press, Stephen S. Ashley, PO Box 22391, San Francisco, CA 94122, 415-759-5270. 1985. Non-fiction. Expects 1 title 1999, 1 title 2000. 1 title listed in the *Small Press Record of Books in Print* (28th Edition, 1999-00). avg. price, paper: $16. 200pp; 5×8; lp.

Strawberry Hill Press, Joseph Lubow, Anne Ingram, 3848 SE Division St, Portland, OR 97202-1641, 503-235-5989. 1973. Non-fiction. "*NO* poetry or religion. No manuscripts under 300 pages. Primary interests: self-help, biography/autobiography, third world, health & nutrition, cookbooks, inspiration, history. Some fiction—mostly mysteries. We look at nothing, and return nothing, that is not accompanied by SASE with *proper* postage. We prefer receiving query letters first." avg. press run 5M. Pub'd 8 titles 1998; expects 12 titles 1999, 12 titles 2000. 6 titles listed in the *Small Press Record of Books in Print* (28th Edition, 1999-00). avg. price, cloth: $16.95; paper: $14.95. 240pp; 6×9. Reporting time: roughly 7 weeks. Simultaneous submissions accepted: no. Publishes .01% of manuscripts submitted. Payment: 10% of gross; no advances, ever; every 12 months. Copyrights for author.

Strawberry Patchworks, Susan A. McCreary, 11597 Southington Lane, Herndon, VA 20170-2417, 703-709-0751, e-mail berrybooks@aol.com. 1982. Non-fiction. "We specialize in one subject cookbooks, softcover using 4 color process on cover. Emphasis on originality of subject and exploring every aspect of the subject. Poetry, art and history are incorporated throughout books." avg. press run 2M-4M. Pub'd 1 title 1998; expects 1 title 1999, 1 title 2000. 6 titles listed in the *Small Press Record of Books in Print* (28th Edition, 1999-00). avg. price, paper: $9-$15. Discounts: trade 40%, wholesaler 50%. 100-200pp; 6×9; of. Reporting time: 1 month or less. Payment: negotiable, no advances. Copyrights for author.

STREET VOICE, Curtis Price, PO Box 22962, Baltimore, MD 21203-4962, 410-837-0643. 1991. Poetry, articles, interviews, news items. "1 page broadsheet distributed directly to street people every month. Focus on resource information, point of view articles and observations/anecdotes from street corner community, politics of everyday life. Outside submissions not encouraged, will consider on a case-by-case basis." circ. 5M. 12/yr. Expects 12 issues 1999, 12-24 issues 2000. sub. price: $6; per copy: SASE; sample: SASE. Back issues: write for information. Discounts: write for information. 1 page; 8½×11; of. Payment: none. Not copyrighted. Ads: none at present.

STRENGTH AND CONDITIONING, Human Kinetics Pub. Inc., Harvey Newton, 1607 N. Market Street, Champaign, IL 61820, 217-351-5076, fax 217-351-2674. 1994. "Professional journal devoted to the practical applications of both research findings and experimental knowledge in strength and conditioning" circ. 11.5M. 6/yr. Pub'd 4 issues 1998; expects 4 issues 1999, 4 issues 2000. sub. price: $80 instit.; per copy: $8 indiv., $14 instit. Back issues: $8 indiv., $14 instit. 80pp; 8½×11; of. Simultaneous submissions accepted: no. Copyrighted, does not revert to author.

STROKER, Irving Stettner, Editor; Thomas Birchard, Publisher, c/o Trantino, RR 2 Box 280, Harveys Lake,

PA 18618-9503. 1974. Poetry, fiction, articles, art, photos, interviews, collages. "An 'unliterary' literary review looking for beauty, Zen, humor, sincerity, and/or good writing. Print stories, essays, ink drawings, few poems. Unsolicited manuscripts accepted. Already published: Henry Miller, Tommy Trantino, Seymour Krim, Mohammed Mrabet (translated by Paul Bowles) and others known and unknown. Pay in contributor copies; lacking distribution, relatively unknown, we're still the best mag in America!" circ. 600. 3-4/yr. Pub'd 3 issues 1998; expects 3 issues 1999, 3 issues 2000. 2 titles listed in the *Small Press Record of Books in Print* (28th Edition, 1999-00). sub. price: $15 for 3 issues, $29 for 6 issues, $48 for 12 issues; per copy: $5.25; sample: $5.25. Back issues: $7 + 75¢ postage. 48pp; 5½×8½; of. Reporting time: 4-6 weeks. Payment: contributor copies. Not copyrighted. §Fiction, art. Ads: $100/$50/$25.

STRUGGLE: A Magazine of Proletarian Revolutionary Literature, Tim Hall, PO Box 13261, Detroit, MI 48213-0261. 1985. Poetry, fiction, articles, art, cartoons, satire, criticism, reviews, music, letters, collages, plays. "We want literature and art of rebellion against the ruling class." 4/yr. Pub'd 3 issues 1998; expects 4 issues 1999, 4 issues 2000. sub. price: $10, $12 to institutions, $15 overseas, free to prisoners, trades ok; per copy: $2; sample: $2.50 via mail. Back issues: by arrangement (vol. 1 available, photocopied at extra charge), $210 for full set (12 years). Discounts: by arrangement. 36pp; 5½×8½; xerox. Reporting time: 3 months. Simultaneous submissions accepted: yes. Publishes 10% of manuscripts submitted. Payment: 2 copies. Not copyrighted. Ads: none.

●**STS Publishing,** Andrew Duggan, David Muriott, 5580 La Jolla Boulevard #376, La Jolla, CA 92037, www.futurelessons.com. 1 title listed in the *Small Press Record of Books in Print* (28th Edition, 1999-00).

STUDENT LAWYER, Ira Pilchen, Editor, ABA Publishing, Ira Pilchen, 750 N. Lake Shore Drive, Chicago, IL 60611. 1972. Articles. "*Student Lawyer* is a monthly legal affairs magazine circulated to members of the American Bar Association's Law Student Division. It is a features magazine, not a legal journal, competing for a share of law students' limited spare time, so the articles we publish must be informative, lively 'good reads.' We have no interest whatsoever in footnoted, academic articles. *Student Lawyer* has 4 feature articles in each issue, ranging from 2,500 to 4,000 words apiece. We also have 5 to 6 departments , 1,200-1,800 word articles covering innovative legal programs, commentary, and brief law school and legal world news items. Writers should write according to the amount of their material and not beyond. We are interested in professional and legal education issues, sociolegal phenomena, legal career features, profiles of lawyers who are making an impact on the profession. We do not accept poetry." circ. 30M. 9/yr. Pub'd 9 issues 1998; expects 9 issues 1999, 9 issues 2000. sub. price: $22; per copy: $8; sample: same. Discounts: included in membership to ABA's Law Student Division. 48pp; 8⅜×10⅞; of, web. Reporting time: 4 weeks. Payment: varies, $100-$700. Copyrighted, reverts to author. Ads: $1,970/$1,280/$22.50 first 20 words, $1/word thereafter. BPA.

STUDENT LEADERSHIP JOURNAL, Jeff Yourison, Editor, PO Box 7895, Madison, WI 53707-7895, 608-274-4823 X425, 413. 1988. Poetry, articles, photos, cartoons, reviews. "For college students: A Christian approach to the needs and issues leaders face. Articles should be aimed at evangelical student leaders of college age." circ. 8M. 4/yr. Pub'd 4 issues 1998; expects 4 issues 1999, 4 issues 2000. sub. price: $16; per copy: $4; sample: $4. Discounts: none. 32pp; 8×11. Reporting time: 3-6 months. Payment: $35-$100. Copyrighted, reverts to author. Pub's reviews: 1 in 1998. §Books on spiritual growth or other areas of interest to college students. none.

STUDIA CELTICA, University Of Wales Press, J. Beverley Smith, University of Wales Press, 6 Gwennyth St., Cathays, Cardiff CF2 4YD, Wales, 44-1222-231919; Fax 44-1222-230908; press@press.wales.ac.uk. 1966. Articles. "Devoted mainly to philological and linguistic studies of the Celtic languages." circ. 300. 1/yr. sub. price: £25 individuals, £40 institutions; per copy: £25 individuals, £40 institutions; sample: same. Back issues: £20 per double issue. Discounts: 10%. 350pp; 9½×6; of. Payment: none. Pub's reviews: 9 in 1998. §Celtic. Ads: none. UWP.

Studia Hispanica Editors, Luis A. Ramos-Garcia, Dave Oliphant, Carol E. Klee, Luis Fernando Vidal, Attn: Luis Ramos-Garcia, 5626 W. Bavarian Pass, Fridley, MN 55432, 612-574-9460. 1978. Poetry, fiction, art, photos, criticism, letters. "Studia Hispanica Editors, along with Prickly Pear Press, has just published *From The Threshold/Desde el umbral,* Contemporary Peruvian fiction in translation. It is a bilingual edition featuring writers who wrote their works during the 1978-1985 period. The second edition of *Studia Hispanica I: Latin American & Spanish Literary Articles* (with an introduction of the Spanish poet Jorge Guillen and Juan Goytisolo) in honour of Rodolfo Cardona is available now. Forthcoming: *Bilingual Anthology of Contemporary Spanish Poetry: Circa 1970-1988,* edited and translated by Luis A. Ramos-Garcia and Dave Oliphant, and *Embers of Meaning/Pavesas de Sentido,* contemporary bilingual poetry from Spain by Jenaro Talens, edited by Luis Ramos-Garcia and Giulia Colaizzi, translated by G. Colaizzi." avg. press run 1M. Pub'd 1 title 1998; expects 1 title 1999, 2 titles 2000. 10 titles listed in the *Small Press Record of Books in Print* (28th Edition, 1999-00). avg. price, cloth: $25; paper: $9.95. Discounts: 20%-40%. 200pp; 8×5½; of, lp. Reporting time: 3 months. Payment: none. Does not copyright for author.

STUDIO - A Journal of Christians Writing, Paul Grover, Managing Editor; Robert Leighton-Jones, Kate Lumley, 727 Peel Street, Albury, N.S.W. 2640, Australia. 1980. Poetry, fiction, articles, reviews, letters. "Published poets by reputable Australian publishing houses have been represented. Material varies from short poems to short stories of 2M to 5M words." circ. 300. 4/yr. Pub'd 4 issues 1998; expects 4 issues 1999, 4 issues 2000. sub. price: $AUD40; per copy: $AUD8; sample: $AUD8 (air mail). Discounts: order of 20 or more in advance of printing receives 10%. 36pp; 14.5×21cm; lp. Reporting time: 3 months. Simultaneous submissions accepted: yes. Publishes 5% of manuscripts submitted. Payment: for contests $AUD75, no payment for ordinary submissions but free copy posted for submissions. Copyrighted, reverts to author. Pub's reviews: 30 in 1998. §Poetry, fiction, books for children. Ads: $AUD100/$AUD50/no classified.

STUDIO ART MAGAZINE, Sarah Breitberg-Semel, Studio, PO Box 23570, Tel Aviv, 61231, Israel, 03-5255701; fax 03-5255702; e-mail studio1@netvision.net.il. 1989. *"Studio* publishes articles up to 5,000 words. Subjects: art, art criticism, Israeli and international. Texts are often accompanied by photos of art work. The writers are artists, critiques, philosophers, and historians, etc. Names of few: Villem Fluser, Donald Kuspit, Carol Naggar, Fred Richen, and David Shapiro, Avital Ronell, Dave Hickey, T.J. Clark" circ. 4M. 11/yr. Pub'd 11 issues 1998; expects 11 issues 1999, 11 issues 2000. sub. price: $115; per copy: $11.50. Back issues: $14. 92pp; 9¼×13¼. Reporting time: 1 month. Payment: $100. Copyrighted, joint rights. Pub's reviews: 15 in 1998. §Art criticism, philosophy of art, contemporary art. Ads: $1000/$600.

Studio Editions, Beverly Jones, Managing Agent; Martha Keltz, Managing Editor, 250 S. President Street, Ste. 300, Baltimore, MD 21202, 410-539-1161; Fax 410-783-4697; studioedtn@aol.com; www.members.aol.com/beverb/studio.htm. 1990. Plays. "Additional address: 1502 E. Osborne Road #452, Phoenix, AZ 85014. Short, verse, one-act, two-act and ten-minute plays with spiritual or metaphysical dimensions. Recent playwright published: Michael H. Burton. Books are published in limited editions; if they do well, they're done as offset." avg. press run 50-100, sometimes more. Pub'd 5 titles 1998; expects 2 titles 1999, 3 titles 2000. 1 title listed in the *Small Press Record of Books in Print* (28th Edition, 1999-00). avg. price, paper: $12. Discounts: phone, fax or write for bulk rates. 60pp; 7×9; of, xerox. Reporting time: 2-3 weeks. Simultaneous submissions accepted: yes. Publishes 33% of manuscripts submitted. Payment: 10% on each book after 50% of cost is met; royalty with production negotiable. Copyrights for author.

Studio 4 Productions, Karen Ervin-Pershing, PO Box 280400, Northridge, CA 91328-0400, 818-700-2522. 1972. "Length: +/-200 pages. Most recent publication: *Seeing Beyond the Wrinkles."* avg. press run 3M-6M. Pub'd 6 titles 1998; expects 6 titles 1999, 6 titles 2000. 7 titles listed in the *Small Press Record of Books in Print* (28th Edition, 1999-00). avg. price, paper: $11.95. Discounts: bulk average 30%, maximum 50%. 190pp; 5½×8½. Reporting time: 30 days. Simultaneous submissions accepted: yes. Publishes 5% of manuscripts submitted. Payment: 10% list paid annually. We hold copyrights on most books.

STUDIO ONE, College of St. Benedict, St. Joseph, MN 56374. 1976. Poetry, fiction, art, photos, satire, long-poems. "Short fiction should generally be fewer than 5,000 words. *Studio One* accepts submissions of literary and visual art from across the nation, but contributors from the Midwest are especially encouraged to submit. Art should reproduce well in black and white. Now accept color visual art." circ. 900. 1/yr. Pub'd 1 issue 1998; expects 1 issue 1999, 1 issue 2000. sub. price: free, availability is extremely limited; all contributors receive one complimentary copy, all others are asked to send enough postage. 70-100pp; 7½×10; of. Reporting time: we try to send out acceptance/rejection letters within 1 month of the deadline. Simultaneous submissions accepted: yes. Publishes 10% of manuscripts submitted. Payment: 1 copy. Copyrighted, reverts to author.

THE STYLUS, Roger Reus, 9412 Huron Avenue, Richmond, VA 23294. 1993. Articles, interviews, criticism, letters, parts-of-novels. "Recent contributors: Mark Rich, Don Herron, Joyce Fante, Geoffrey Dunn. Readable articles on writers (i.e. no scholarly/heavily foot-noted/dull literary theses). Also original fiction & author intervies. Some of the zine's favorites: John Fante, Charles Bukowski, Poe, Bierce, Charles Willeford, William Eastlake" circ. 300. 1/yr. Pub'd 1 issue 1998; expects 1 issue 1999, 1 issue 2000. sub. price: $3; per copy: $3; sample: $3. Back issues: $3/issue. 48pp; 5½×8½; of/li. Reporting time: 1-4 weeks. Simultaneous submissions accepted: yes. Publishes 1% of manuscripts submitted. Payment: copies. Copyrighted, reverts to author. Pub's reviews: 9 in 1998. §Literary, little.

The Subourbon Press (see also THE HUNTED NEWS), Mike Wood, PO Box 9101, Warwick, RI 02889, 401-739-2279. 1991. Poetry, fiction, non-fiction. "No longer publish chapbooks at this point; maybe in 1999." avg. press run 500-1M. Pub'd 1 title 1998; expects 2 titles 1999. 2 titles listed in the *Small Press Record of Books in Print* (28th Edition, 1999-00). avg. price, paper: $3. 30pp; mi. Reporting time: 1-2 months. Payment: will work with author. Does not copyright for author.

SUBSCRIBE, Ideas and Marketing Tips for Newsletter Publishers, Page One, Lynn Kerrigan, 20 W. Athens Avenue, Ardmore, PA 19003-1308, 610-896-2879; E-mail pageone1@aol.com. 1997. Articles, interviews, reviews, news items. circ. 500. 6/yr. Pub'd 6 issues 1998. sub. price: $40; per copy: $10; sample: $10. Back issues: $10. 20pp; 8½×11; of. Reporting time: 4 weeks. Simultaneous submissions accepted: no.

Publishes 10% of manuscripts submitted. Payment: $25 + year's subscription. Copyrighted, reverts to author. Pub's reviews. §Newsletter production, design, publication, and marketing. IACP, PMA.

SUB-TERRAIN, Anvil Press, Brian Kaufman, Managing Editor; Paul Pitre, Poetry Editor; Dennis E. Bolen, Associate Editor, PO Box 1575, Bentall Centre, Vancouver, B.C. V6C 2P7, Canada, 604-876-8710. 1988. Poetry, fiction, photos, satire, criticism, long-poems, plays. "We sponsor three annual contests: Last Poems Poetry Contest and the Sub-Terrain Short Story Contest, and the Creative Non-fiction Contest." circ. 3M. 3/yr. Pub'd 3 issues 1998; expects 3 issues 1999, 3 issues 2000. sub. price: $15; per copy: $4.95; sample: $5 to cover post. Back issues: $5. 48pp; 8½×11; computer typeset, of. Reporting time: 2-3 months. We accept simultaneous submissions if author informs us upon publication elsewhere. Publishes 10% of manuscripts submitted. Payment: in copies, 2-5 depending on article/story/poem length used. Copyrighted, reverts to author. Pub's reviews: 12 in 1998. §Poetry, fiction, social issues (primarily releases from small to med. size publishers not receiving attention they deserve). Send review copies Attn: Review Column. Ads: $210/$120/$65 1/4 page. Publishing industry, bookstores, literary related *only*. Small Press Action Network (SPAN), Can. Magazine Publishers Assoc., BC Association of Magazine Publishers.

THE SUBTLE JOURNAL OF RAW COINAGE, Ge(of Huth), editor, 875 Central Parkway, Schenectady, NY 12309. 1987. Poetry, cartoons, collages, concrete art. *"The Subtle Journal of Raw Coinage (SJRC)* is a monthly magazine publishing undefined neologisms in poetic/expressive contexts and formats. Some poetry written *exclusively* with neologisms will be considered for publication. Pwoermds (one-word poems such as Aram Saroyan's 'eyeye') are especially welcome." circ. 50-500. 12/yr. Pub'd 12 issues 1998; expects 12 issues 1999, 12 issues 2000. sub. price: can be any dollar amount—cost (which varies) per issue will be subtracted when mailed; per copy: 1¢-$3; sample: $1. Discounts: none. 5pp; size varies; †photocopy, rubberstamp, mimeograph, handtyping, hectography, handwriting, spirit duplicating, dot-matrix, laser printing, linoleum block printing, GOCCO printing. Reporting time: 2 weeks. Payment: at least 2 copies; 1/4 of press run is divided among contributors. Not copyrighted.

Suburban Wilderness Press (see also POETRY MOTEL), PO Box 103, Duluth, MN 55801-0103. 1984. Poetry, fiction, art, photos, collages. "Broadsides." avg. press run 150. Pub'd 40 titles 1998; expects 40 titles 1999, 40 titles 2000. avg. price, paper: 25 for $9.95. Discounts: none. 1 page broadsides; 8½×11; of. Reporting time: 1 week to never. Publishes a variable % of manuscripts submitted. Payment: varies. Copyrights for author.

Success Publishing, Allan H. Smith, 3419 Dunham Drive, Box 263, Warsaw, NY 14569. 1978. Non-fiction. "How to make money. How to start in business. How to market your product. How to publish. Sewing, craft, business." avg. press run 2M-5M. Pub'd 6 titles 1998; expects 4 titles 1999, 6 titles 2000. 14 titles listed in the *Small Press Record of Books in Print* (28th Edition, 1999-00). avg. price, paper: $15. Discounts: 1 10%, 2-6 25%, 7-15 40%, 16-50 50%, 50-100 53%; library 25%. 150pp; 8½×11; lp. Reporting time: 90-120 days. Payment: varies. Copyrights for author. NAIP, FPG.

Sherwood Sugden & Company, Publishers, Sherwood Sugden, 315 Fifth Street, Peru, IL 61354, 815-223-2520, Fax 815-223-4486. 1975. Non-fiction. avg. press run 3M. Pub'd 3 titles 1998; expects 3 titles 1999, 3 titles 2000. 28 titles listed in the *Small Press Record of Books in Print* (28th Edition, 1999-00). avg. price, cloth: $24.95; paper: $10. Discounts: 40% STOP; otherwise 20%-1 copy, 25% 2-3 copies, 40%-5+ copies. 300pp; 5½×8½, 6×9; of, typeset. Reporting time: 2-3 months. Payment: 8%-12%. Copyrights for author.

SUITCASE: A Journal of Transcultural Traffic, Babak Nahid, UCLA, PO Box 951536, Los Angeles, CA 90095, 310-836-8855; E-mail suitcase@humnet.ucla.edu; www.humnet.ucla.edu/suitcase. 1995. "Literary journal with a focus on cultural production under siege and across boundaries." circ. 1M. 2/yr. Pub'd 2 issues 1998; expects 2 issues 1999, 2 issues 2000. sub. price: $20 individual, $35 institution. Discounts: none. 350pp; 9×13. Reporting time: 6 months. Simultaneous submissions accepted: yes. Publishes 50% of manuscripts submitted. Copyrighted, copyrights revert to author after 6 months. Ads: $500 1/2 page.

SULFUR, Clayton Eshleman, 210 Washtenaw, Ypsilanti, MI 48197-2526, 313-483-9787. 1981. Poetry, art, photos, interviews, criticism, reviews, long-poems. *"Sulfur* primarily made up of regular contributors; concerned with explorative poetry & poetics, translations, reviews & essays; also archival materials." circ. 2M. 2/yr. Pub'd 2 issues 1998; expects 2 issues 1999, 2 issues 2000. sub. price: $14 indiv., $20 inst. (add $4 for out of US mailing); per copy: $9; sample: $8. Back issues: $8 each; Nos. 1, 15, 17, 19 & 22 only available with purchase of complete sets (1-38 $336). Discounts: institution $20 a year; jobber or agent $16; double & triple for 2 & 3 year sub. 256pp; 6×9; of, lazer type. Reporting time: 2 weeks. Simultaneous submissions accepted: no. Publishes 10% of manuscripts submitted. Payment: $35-$45. Copyrighted, reverts to author. Pub's reviews: 50 in 1998. §Current poetry, criticism, & translations. Ads: $300/$160. CLMP.

The Sulgrave Press, John S. Moremen, President; John R. Moremen, Secretary-Treasurer, 2005 Longest Avenue], Louisville, KY 40204, 502-459-9713, Fax 502-459-9715. 1988. Poetry, fiction, non-fiction. "Kentucky authors or subjects only. First: *Bo McMillin: Man & Legend,* C. Akers and J. Carter—biography. Second: *In a Yellow Room,* Maureen Morehead—poetry. Third: *The Jack Daniels Old Time Barbecue*

Cookbook, V. Staten—cookbook. Fourth: co-publisher of *The Royal Military Academy at Sandhurst*." avg. press run 5M first book, second book 500, third book 35M, fourth 10M. Pub'd 2 titles 1998; expects 2 titles 1999. 2 titles listed in the *Small Press Record of Books in Print* (28th Edition, 1999-00). avg. price, cloth: $18.50; other: varies. Discounts: 40% to trade, 50% to jobbers. 175pp; contract printers & binders. Reporting time: 2 weeks. Publishes a very small % of manuscripts submitted. Payment: varies. Copyrights for author.

●**Sulisa Publishing**, 625 SW 10th Avenue, PMB 388C, Portland, OR 97205-2788, 503-233-5232; e-mail sulisa@teleport.com. 1998. Fiction, art, photos. "We publish an annual anthology of short fiction by undergraduate writers. Send SASE for information." avg. press run 3M. Expects 1 title 1999, 2 titles 2000. 1 title listed in the *Small Press Record of Books in Print* (28th Edition, 1999-00). avg. price, paper: $12.95. Discounts: 3-5 books 20%; 6-10 40%; 11-50 42%; 51-100 43%; 101-250 44%; 251-500 45%; 501+ 50%. 256pp; 5½x8½; of. Reporting time: 1 month. Simultaneous submissions accepted: yes. Publishes 10% of manuscripts submitted. Payment: variable. Does not copyright for author.

Sullivan Press (see also CHRYSALIS: The Journal of Transgressive Gender Identities), Dallas Denny, PO Box 33724, Decatur, GA 30033, 770-939-2128; Fax 770-939-1770; E-mail aegis@gerder.org. 1995. Fiction, non-fiction. Pub'd 1 title 1998; expects 2 titles 1999, 2 titles 2000. avg. price, paper: $17.95. Discounts: 40% wholesale. 125pp; of. Reporting time: 1 month. Simultaneous submissions accepted: no. Publishes 20% of manuscripts submitted. Payment: yes. We copyright for author on request.

SULPHUR RIVER LITERARY REVIEW, James Michael Robbins, PO Box 19228, Austin, TX 78760-9228, 512-292-9456. 1978. Poetry, fiction, articles, art, photos, interviews, satire, criticism, non-fiction. circ. 200. 2/yr. Pub'd 2 issues 1998; expects 2 issues 1999, 2 issues 2000. sub. price: $12; per copy: $7; sample: $7. Back issues: $7. 130pp; 5½x8½; camera-ready copy. Reporting time: 1 month. Simultaneous submissions accepted: yes. Publishes 1% of manuscripts submitted. Payment: 2 contributor's copies. Copyrighted, reverts to author.

SUMMER ACADEME: A Journal of Higher Education, Caddo Gap Press, David Schejbal, Editor, 3145 Geary Boulevard #275, San Francisco, CA 94118, 415-922-1911. 1997. Articles. "An annual journal of college and university summer session administrators." circ. 1M. 1/yr. Pub'd 1 issue 1998; expects 1 issue 1999, 1 issue 2000. sub. price: $20 indiv., $30 instit.; per copy: $20. 96pp; 6x9; of. Reporting time: 2 months. Publishes 25% of manuscripts submitted. Payment: none. Copyrighted, reverts to author. Ads: none. MPE, EDPRESS.

Summer Stream Press, David Duane Frost, Editor, PO Box 6056, Santa Barbara, CA 93160-6056, 805-962-6540. 1978. Poetry, non-fiction. "This press is now producing and marketing a series of cassette tapes under the general title: Poetic Heritage. #102180 Elinor Wylie/Amy Lowell; #103010 Sara Teadsale/Margaret Widdemer; #103150 Edna St. Vincent Millay; #103290 Emily Dickinson/Lizette Woodworth Reese." avg. press run 5M. Expects 1 title 2000. 3 titles listed in the *Small Press Record of Books in Print* (28th Edition, 1999-00). avg. price, cloth: $34.95; paper: $19.95; other: $10 (tapes). Discounts: 50% no returns. 450pp; 5½x8½; of. Reporting time: 6 months to 1 year. Publishes 2% of manuscripts submitted. Payment: 15% - paid annually January 1st. Copyrights for author.

Summerset Press, Brooks Robards, Jim Kaplan, 20 Langworthy Road, Northampton, MA 01060, 413-586-3394 phone/FAX; JKaplan105@aol.com. 3 titles listed in the *Small Press Record of Books in Print* (28th Edition, 1999-00).

Summerthought Ltd., Peter Steiner, PO Box 1420, Banff, Alberta T0L0C0, Canada, 762-3919; fax 403-762-4126. 1969. Poetry, photos. avg. press run 10M. Pub'd 2 titles 1998; expects 1 title 1999, 1 title 2000. 7 titles listed in the *Small Press Record of Books in Print* (28th Edition, 1999-00). avg. price, cloth: $14.95; paper: $6.95. Discounts: 40% trade, 20% classroom. 160pp; 6x9; lp. Payment: 10%-12½% reprint. Copyrights for author. CBA.

Summit Crossroads Press, Eileen Haavik, 126 Camp Harmison Drive, Berkeley Springs, WV 25411-4009, 304-258-8653, 1-800-362-0985, Fax 304-258-9282; e-mail SumCross@aol.com; www.parentsuccess.com. 1993. Non-fiction. "Publishes books relating to family and school." avg. press run 5M. Pub'd 2 titles 1998; expects 1 title 1999, 3 titles 2000. 4 titles listed in the *Small Press Record of Books in Print* (28th Edition, 1999-00). avg. price, paper: $14.95. Discounts: wholesaler/distributor 55%, bookstores 40%. 250pp; 6x9; of. Reporting time: 2 weeks. Simultaneous submissions accepted: yes. Payment: 10% of net receipts. Copyrights for author. PMA, Mid-Atlantic Publishers Assn.

THE SUN, A MAGAZINE OF IDEAS, Sy Safransky, 107 North Roberson Street, Chapel Hill, NC 27516, 919-942-5282. 1974. Poetry, fiction, articles, art, photos, cartoons, interviews, satire, letters, parts-of-novels, long-poems, collages, non-fiction. "A monthly magazine of ideas in its twenty-fifth year of publication, *The Sun* celebrates good writing—and the warmth of shared intimacies—in essays, fiction, interviews, and poetry. People write in the magazine of their struggle to understand their lives, often baring themselves with remarkable candor. Recent contributors: Poe Ballantine, Anwar Accawi, Alison Luterman, Gillian Kendall, and

Sybil Smith.'' circ. 40M. 12/yr. Pub'd 12 issues 1998; expects 12 issues 1999, 12 issues 2000. sub. price: $34; per copy: $3.95; sample: $5. Back issues: complete set of all available back issues for $300. Discounts: 50% for distributors. 48pp; 8½×11; of. Reporting time: 3 months. Simultaneous submissions accepted: no. Publishes 1% of manuscripts submitted. Payment: essays and interviews $300-$1,000; short stories $300-$500; poetry and photos $50-$200. Copyrighted, reverts to author. Ads: none.

Sun Books (see also THE TOWNSHIPS SUN), Patricia Ball, Box 28, Lennoxville, Quebec J1M 1Z3, Canada. "Books published only for clients to their specs. They hold all rights, etc." 6 titles listed in the *Small Press Record of Books in Print* (28th Edition, 1999-00).

Sun Designs, PO Box 6, Oconomowoc, WI 53066, 414-567-4255. 1979. Photos. "These are books of designs, with some plans, some books have a short history, toy book has children's story" avg. press run 20M. Pub'd 2 titles 1998; expects 1 title 1999, 1 title 2000. 1 title listed in the *Small Press Record of Books in Print* (28th Edition, 1999-00). 96pp; 8½×11; †of. Copyrights for author.

Sun Dog Press, Al Berlinski, 22058 Cumberland Drive, Northville, MI 48167, 248-449-7448; Fax 248-449-4070; sundogpr@voyager.net. 1987. Poetry, fiction, letters. "Hard-edged and innovative fiction, poetry, letters. Book length manuscripts considered." avg. press run 500-1M. Pub'd 2 titles 1998; expects 2 titles 1999, 2 titles 2000. 11 titles listed in the *Small Press Record of Books in Print* (28th Edition, 1999-00). avg. price, cloth: $35; paper: $13. Discounts: 20%-48%. 200pp; 6×9; of. Reporting time: 8 weeks. Simultaneous submissions accepted: yes. Payment: royalty on sales. Copyrights for author.

THE SUNDAY SUITOR POETRY REVIEW, Elizabeth Fuller, 506 Stevenson Street, Salinas, CA 93907-2017, 209-858-1453. 1996. Poetry, art, photos, reviews, letters. "Length restricted to 40 lines, love/life affirming poetry; no erotica; recent contributors - Barbara Ann Porte, A.D. Winans, Louise Jaffe, John Grey, Douglas Johnson'' circ. 350. 6/yr. Pub'd 1 issue 1998; expects 6 issues 1999, 6 issues 2000. sub. price: $17 US, $20 international; per copy: $4 U.S., $7 international; sample: $4 U.S., $7 international. Back issues: same. Discounts: none. 50pp; 5½×8½; †of. Reporting time: 1-3 weeks. Simultaneous submissions accepted: yes. Publishes 50% of manuscripts submitted. Payment: 1 copy. Copyrighted, reverts to author. Pub's reviews: 5-10 in 1998. §Poetry; articles or books on writing. Ads: none.

Sunflower University Press (see also JOURNAL OF THE WEST), Robin Higham, President; Carol A. Williams, Publisher & Director of Marketing, 1531 Yuma, (Box 1009), Manhattan, KS 66502, 785-539-1888, fax 785-539-2233. 1977. Satire, reviews. "Aviation, military and Western American history; paper and hardback books." avg. press run 2M. Pub'd 2 titles 1998; expects 4-8 titles 1999, 10-15 titles 2000. 186 titles listed in the *Small Press Record of Books in Print* (28th Edition, 1999-00). avg. price, cloth: $29-$44; paper: $14-$24. Discounts: on a no-returns basis for wholesalers, paperbacks, 1-4 25%, 5+ 40%. 200pp; 8½×11, 5½×8½, 6×9; †of. Reporting time: 3 months. Copyrights for author.

Sunlight Publishers, Joseph Kent, Poetry Editor, PO Box 640545, San Francisco, CA 94109, 415-776-6249. 1989. Poetry. "Some bias toward poetic consciousness of an evolutionary nature and organic poetry in the modernist vein based on experience of the perceiver." avg. press run 700. Expects 2 titles 1999. 3 titles listed in the *Small Press Record of Books in Print* (28th Edition, 1999-00). avg. price, paper: $6.95. Discounts: 2-4 30%, 5-100 40%. 64pp; 6×9; of. Reporting time: 1 month. Payment: 10% royalty on all sales, paid twice yearly. Copyrights for author.

Sun-Scape Publications, a division of Sun-Scape Enterprises Ltd., Megan MaQueen, Mary Joy Leaper, 65 High Ridge Road, Suite 103, Stamford, CT 06905, 203-838-3775; FAX 203-838-3775; orders 1-800-437-1454; info@sun-scape.com; www.sun-scape.com. 1975. Poetry, art, photos, interviews, reviews, music, long-poems, non-fiction. "Home office: PO Box 793, Station F, Toronto, Ontario M4Y 2N7, Canada, Tel: 416-665-7623; Fax 416-665-8376. Philosophical, educational. Primarily the works of Canadian philosopher, poet, composer and conductor, artist Kenneth George Mills. Prose, poetry, and spoken-word cassettes. Not currently accepting submissions." avg. press run 2M. Pub'd 2 titles 1998; expects 2 titles 1999, 2 titles 2000. 14 titles listed in the *Small Press Record of Books in Print* (28th Edition, 1999-00). avg. price, cloth: $29.95; paper: $21.95; other: $10.95 cassette and booklet. Discounts: 40% to trade. 260pp; 7×8½. New Age Publishing & Retailing Alliance (NAPRA), Quill & Quire, PMA.

SunShine Press Publications, Inc., Jack Hofer, PO Box 333, Hygiene, CO 80533, 303-772-3556; sunshinepress@sunshinepress.com; www.sunshinepress.com. 1986. Fiction, non-fiction. "Subjects: health, wellness, psychology, self-help, fiction, alternative healing, spiritual, inspirational." avg. press run 2M. Pub'd 4 titles 1998; expects 4 titles 1999, 4 titles 2000. 16 titles listed in the *Small Press Record of Books in Print* (28th Edition, 1999-00). avg. price, cloth: $20; paper: $14. Discounts: 40% trade, STOP 20%. 176pp; 5½×8½, 6×9; lp. Reporting time: 3 months SASE. Simultaneous submissions accepted: yes. Publishes 10% of manuscripts submitted. Payment: author assisted publishing and standard royalty. Copyrights for author.

Sunstar Publishing, Rodney Charles, Managing Editor, 204 S. 20th Street, Fairfield, IA 52556-4221. 1990.

Fiction. "We are also looking for material on business, cookbooks, new age, reference, inspirational, and childrens" avg. press run 5M-10M. Pub'd 6 titles 1998; expects 20 titles 1999, 40 titles 2000. avg. price, cloth: $21.95; paper: $14.95. Discounts: 40% Ingram etc. 200-400pp. New Author Enterprises (NAE).

Sunstone Press, James Clois Smith, Jr., President, PO Box 2321, Santa Fe, NM 87504-2321, 505-988-4418; fax 505-988-1025. 1971. Fiction, non-fiction. "Primarily southwestern US subjects" avg. press run 3M. Pub'd 24 titles 1998; expects 24 titles 1999, 30 titles 2000. 128 titles listed in the *Small Press Record of Books in Print* (28th Edition, 1999-00). avg. price, cloth: $24.95; paper: $12.95; other: $14.95. Discounts: standard. 160pp; 5½×8½, 8½×11; of. Reporting time: 90 days or less. Simultaneous submissions accepted: no. Payment: royalty only. Copyrights for author. RMPG.

SUPER TROUPER, Andrew Savage, 35 Kearsley Road, Sheffield, S2 4TE, United Kingdom. 1985. Poetry, reviews, music, news items. "The magazine is produced on cassette." circ. 100. Pub'd 4 issues 1998; expects 3 issues 1999, 3 issues 2000. audio cassette. Reporting time: 3 months. Simultaneous submissions accepted: yes. Publishes 15% of manuscripts submitted. Payment: 1 copy of it that hasn't already been eaten.

Survival News Service, Christopher Nyerges, Box 41834, Los Angeles, CA 90041, 213-255-9502. 1980. "Topics: Wild foods, recycling, urban survival, plants, thinking, American Indians, practical applications of spiritual principles." avg. press run 4M. Expects 6 titles 1999, 6 titles 2000. 1 title listed in the *Small Press Record of Books in Print* (28th Edition, 1999-00). avg. price, paper: $1. Discounts: 40% to dealers, 50% to jobbers (minimum order is set). 30-240pp; 5×8; of. Reporting time: 1 month; however, we do *most* of our own material. Payment: to be arranged. Copyrights for author if applicable.

The Survival Series Publishing Co., Jeff Adachi, Kathy Asada, PO Box 77313, San Francisco, CA 94107, 415-979-6785. 1990. Non-fiction. "Publish bar exam review materials and law reference books" avg. press run 3M. Expects 1 title 1999, 2 titles 2000. 10 titles listed in the *Small Press Record of Books in Print* (28th Edition, 1999-00). Pages vary. Reporting time: depends. Simultaneous submissions accepted: yes. Publishes 20% of manuscripts submitted. Payment: negotiated. Copyrights for author.

Swallow's Tale Press (see also Livingston Press), Joe Taylor, Editor, c/o LU Press, Station 22, University of West Alabama, Livingston, AL 35470. 1983. Poetry, fiction. avg. press run 1M. Expects 1 title 2000. 8 titles listed in the *Small Press Record of Books in Print* (28th Edition, 1999-00). avg. price, cloth: $25; paper: $10. Discounts: 20-50%. 88pp; 5½×8½; of. Reporting time: 6 months. Publishes 1% of manuscripts submitted. Payment: percentage of books. Copyrights for author.

Swamp Press (see also TIGHTROPE), Ed Rayher, 323 Pelham Road, Amherst, MA 01002. 1975. Poetry, art, long-poems. "We make limited edition books which live up to the standards of the fine-crafted poem. We're open to almost anything, as long as it's the best...to last 1,000 years. Recent contributors: Bonnie Gordon, Phil Cox, Robert Bensen." avg. press run 300. Pub'd 2 titles 1998; expects 2 titles 1999, 2 titles 2000. 10 titles listed in the *Small Press Record of Books in Print* (28th Edition, 1999-00). avg. price, cloth: $25; paper: $5. Discounts: dealers and booksellers 40%, continuing collectors 40%, libraries 20%. 36pp; size varies; †lp. Reporting time: 8 weeks. Simultaneous submissions accepted: no. Publishes 1% of manuscripts submitted. Payment: 10% press run. Does not copyright for author. LGNE, MBS.

Swan Publishing Company, Sharon Davis, Hal Davidson, Pete Billac, Melinda Wallace, Kimberly Morrison, 126 Live Oak, Alvin, TX 77511, 281-388-2547; swanbooks@ghg.net; www.swan-pub.com. 1987. Fiction, non-fiction. "Our first two books have been successful; *How Not To Be Lonely* is approaching 400,000 copies in print in 13 months. Our authors work with us to promote their books and we work under an unusual arrangement. We are not a vanity publisher but we sought investors for the authors and worked the arrangements to mutual satisfaction." avg. press run 10M. Pub'd 12 titles 1998; expects 15 titles 1999, 20 titles 2000. 25 titles listed in the *Small Press Record of Books in Print* (28th Edition, 1999-00). avg. price, paper: $9.95. Discounts: call for rates. 128pp; 5½×8½, 6×9; of. Reporting time: 1 month maximum. Payment: 10%, more with volume sales. Copyrights for author.

Swan Raven & Company, Amy Owen, Managing Editor, PO Box 190, Mill Spring, NC 28756-0190. 1992. "We do books in the areas of shamanisn/indigevous; alternative healthy positive speculations for the future, and men/women issues" avg. press run 5M. Pub'd 2 titles 1998; expects 2 titles 1999, 3 titles 2000. 6 titles listed in the *Small Press Record of Books in Print* (28th Edition, 1999-00). avg. price, paper: $14.95. Discounts: 40% wholesale. 220pp; 6×9; of. Reporting time: 1 month-45 days. Simultaneous submissions accepted: no. Publishes 1% of manuscripts submitted. Payment: 8%-15% at 7,500 increments. Copyrights for author. PMA, AMWBP, NAPRA.

SWEET ANNIE & SWEET PEA REVIEW, Sweet Annie Press, Beverly A. Clark, 7750 Highway F-24 West, Baxter, IA 50028, 515-792-3578; FAX 515-792-1310. 1995. Poetry, fiction, photos, reviews. "Short stories, poems of short to medium length. No violence." circ. 100+. 4/yr. Pub'd 4 issues 1998; expects 4 issues 1999, 4 issues 2000. sub. price: $24; per copy: $6; sample: $6. 40pp; 5×8. Reporting time: 4-6 months or shorter. Simultaneous submissions accepted: yes. Publishes 25% of manuscripts submitted. Payment: 1 copy. Copyrighted, reverts to author. Pub's reviews. §Environmental (land, sea), women's issues, natural living, health, food, stress reduction, simplified living, solitude, meditation.

Sweet Annie Press (see also SWEET ANNIE & SWEET PEA REVIEW), Beverly A. Clark, 7750 Highway F-24 West, Baxter, IA 50028, 515-792-3578; FAX 515-792-1310. 1995. Poetry, fiction, photos, reviews, letters, long-poems, non-fiction. avg. press run 100. Expects 4 titles 1999, 4 titles 2000. avg. price, paper: $6. Discounts: none. 5×8. Reporting time: 4-6 months, will be shorter in future. Simultaneous submissions accepted: yes. Publishes 25% of manuscripts submitted. Payment: 1 copy. Does not copyright for author. ABA.

Sweet Lady Moon Press (see also STOVEPIPE: A Journal of Little Literary Value), Troy Teegarden, PO Box 1076, Georgetown, KY 40324, troyteegarden@worldradio.org. 1995. Poetry, fiction, art, cartoons, interviews, parts-of-novels. "We usually contact authors we'd like to publish in a chapbook, but are open to submissions of 5 poems for consideration." avg. press run 1st edition 100 copies, goes from there. Pub'd 3 titles 1998; expects 4 titles 1999, 4 titles 2000. 4 titles listed in the *Small Press Record of Books in Print* (28th Edition, 1999-00). avg. price, paper: $3. 40pp; 8½×5½, 4¼×11; †of. Reporting time: 1 month (usually less). We accept simultaneous submissions, but very reluctantly, and must be stated somewhere. Publishes 10% of manuscripts submitted. Payment: varies. Copyrights for author.

Sweetlight Books (see also HOLY SMOKE), Guy Mount, 16625 Heitman Road, Cottonwood, CA 96022, 916-529-5392, holysmoke.htme, www.snowcrest.net/swtlight. 1980. Fiction, art, photos, non-fiction. "We publish quality paperback books (length 128-160 pages) for people who love the earth, specializing in Native American studies, ecology and herbal medicine." avg. press run 2M. Pub'd 1 title 1998; expects 2 titles 1999, 1 title 2000. 5 titles listed in the *Small Press Record of Books in Print* (28th Edition, 1999-00). avg. price, paper: $9.95. Discounts: books - 40% 3-9 copies to bookstores, 50% 10+; 55% distributors; booklets - 3 copies $10, 40% 5+. 80-144pp; 5½×8½; of. Reporting time: 3 weeks. Simultaneous submissions accepted: yes. Payment: 5% on retail price, will subsidy publish. Copyrights for author.

SYCAMORE REVIEW, Numsiri C. Kunakemakorn, Department of English, Purdue University, West Lafayette, IN 47907, 765-494-3783. 1988. Poetry, fiction, art, photos, interviews, reviews, parts-of-novels, plays, non-fiction. "*Sycamore Review* accepts personal essays, short fiction, translations, drama (one act or standalone pieces) and quality poetry in any form. We are a journal devoted to contemporary literature, publishing both traditional and experimental forms. There are no official restrictions as to subject matter. Both American and international authors will be represented. Submissions read between Sept. and March 31 (the academic year)" circ. 1M. 2/yr. Pub'd 2 issues 1998; expects 2 issues 1999, 2 issues 2000. sub. price: $12, $14 foreign; per copy: $7; sample: $7. Back issues: 20% off cover. Discounts: call for info. 160pp; 6×9; of. Reporting time: 4 months maximum. Simultaneous submissions accepted: yes. Publishes 5% of manuscripts submitted. Payment: 2 copies. Copyrighted, reverts to author. Pub's reviews: 6 in 1998. §Poetry collections, short story and essay collections, novels, nonfiction that would appeal to readers of literature. Ads: ad swap only. CELJ, CLMP.

SYCAMORE ROOTS: New Native Americans, Ice Cube Press, S.H. Semken, 205 North Front Street, North Lib., IA 52317-9302, 319-626-2055; e-mail icecube@inav.net. 1994. Fiction, photos, interviews, reviews, parts-of-novels, news items, non-fiction, poetry. "Emphasis on developing home and land. ISSN 1079-5308 accept photos and nature poetry" circ. 500. 4/yr. Pub'd 2 issues 1998; expects 2 issues 1999, 2 issues 2000. 2 titles listed in the *Small Press Record of Books in Print* (28th Edition, 1999-00). sub. price: $8; per copy: $2; sample: $2. Back issues: $2. Discounts: negotiable. 8pp; 8½×11, on-line newsletter; of. Reporting time: 2-3 weeks. Simultaneous submissions accepted: yes. Publishes 20% of manuscripts submitted. Payment: 5 copies with contribution. Not copyrighted. Pub's reviews: 12 in 1998. §Natural history, creative essays, sense of place issues/most essays and fiction done serialzation. Ads: 1/6 page $10/issue $35/year. PMA, MIPA.

Sylvan Books, Thomas Duncan, PO Box 772876, Steamboat Springs, CO 80477-2876, 970-870-6071. 1984. 1 title listed in the *Small Press Record of Books in Print* (28th Edition, 1999-00).

SYMBIOTIC OATMEAL, Xu Juan, PO Box 14938, Philadelphia, PA 19149. 1997. Poetry, art, cartoons. "Encourage submissions from Asians and Asian-Americans." circ. 50-100. Irregular. Pub'd 3 issues 1998; expects 2 issues 1999, 2 issues 2000. 16pp; 8½×11. Reporting time: varies. Simultaneous submissions accepted: yes. Publishes 10% of manuscripts submitted. Payment: 1 copy. Not copyrighted.

SYMPLOKE: A Journal for the Intermingling of Literary, Cultural and Theoretical Scholarship, Jeffrey R. Di Leo, Univ. of IL, English Dept. MC 162, 601 S. Morgan Street, Chicago, IL 60607-7120, 773-506-7516; dileo@uci.edu. 1993. Articles, interviews, criticism, non-fiction. "*Symploke* has no theoretical bias, and supports scholarship on any aspect of the intermingling of discourses and/or disciplines" circ. 650. 2/yr. Pub'd 2 issues 1998; expects 2 issues 1999, 2 issues 2000. sub. price: $30; per copy: $15; sample: $10. Back issues: $40 per volume (2 issues). 130pp; 6½×9¼; of. Reporting time: 3 months. Simultaneous submissions accepted: yes. Publishes 10% of manuscripts submitted. Payment: none. Copyrighted, does not revert to author. Pub's reviews. Ads: $25/$15/exchanges.

SYNAESTHETIC, Alex Cigale, Editor, PO Box 91, New York, NY 10013. 1994. Poetry, fiction, art, photos, cartoons. "Should send inquiries before submitting—accept submissions April-November." circ. 1M. 1/yr. Pub'd 1 issue 1998; expects 1 issue 1999, 1 issue 2000. sub. price: $10; per copy: $10; sample: $7. Back issues: $15 double issue #4/5 "History" 100+pp; 8½×11; of. Reporting time: 3 months. Payment: 1 copy. Not copyrighted. Ads: $200/$100.

Synapse-Centurion, Jeff Curry, 1211 Berkeley St., Suite 3, Santa Monica, CA 90404, 310-829-2752. 1992. "High quality fiction and non-fiction. Mostly Green thinking. No unsolicited submissions." avg. press run 3M. Pub'd 1 title 1998; expects 2 titles 1999, 2 titles 2000. 4 titles listed in the *Small Press Record of Books in Print* (28th Edition, 1999-00). avg. price, cloth: $20; paper: $10. Discounts: normal trade. 250pp; 5×8; of. Payment: 8-10% paid bi-yearly. Copyrights for author.

SYNCOPATED CITY, Liti Kitiyakara, Jerry Fogel, PO Box 2382, Providence, RI 02906, litik@aol.com. 1996. Poetry, fiction, art, long-poems, collages. "Poetry by John Grey, fiction by Kathryn Kulpa. We look for original, artistic more than academic work. We encourage expression and consider ourselves an outlet for those who write 'for themselves.' We are open to beginners as well as established writers. Here's the place the latter can 'experiment' with different styles" circ. 200. 4/yr. Pub'd 5 issues 1998; expects 4+ issues 1999, 4+ issues 2000. sub. price: $12; per copy: $3; sample: $3. Back issues: $3. 60pp; 5½×8½; copy center. Reporting time: 1-3 months. Simultaneous submissions accepted: yes. Publishes 20% of manuscripts submitted. Payment: 1 copy. Copyrighted, reverts to author. Ads: $45/$25/$15 business card.

Synergistic Press, Bud Johns, 3965 Sacramento St., San Francisco, CA 94118, 415-EV7-8180; Fax 415-751-8505. 1968. Articles, art, letters, non-fiction. "Our non-fiction interests are wide ranging, which is best shown by several titles in print: *My ABC Book of Cancer*, written and illustrated by a 10-year-old cancer patient with supplemental text about her and childhood cancer; *What Is This Madness?*, the story of a new sport's invention and its early years; *Last Look At The Old Met*, a personal portrait in drawings and text of the old Metropolitan Opera House, *Not a Station But a Place*, an art and text portrait of the Gare de Lyon in Paris and *Bastard In The Ragged Suit*, the published work of a leading protetarian writer of the '20s and '30s, with selections from manuscript fragments and drawings during the last two decades of his life when he didn't submit his work for publication, plus a biographical introduction. To date most of our titles have been developed internally and that will probably be true of a majority of our titles in the immediate future. Average $7.50 (high $12.50, low $2.50)." avg. press run 3M-5M. Expects 2 titles 1999, 2 titles 2000. 12 titles listed in the *Small Press Record of Books in Print* (28th Edition, 1999-00). avg. price, cloth: $8.50; paper: $5. Discounts: trade: single copies, 20%; 2-5, 35%, 6-11, 37%; 12-49, 40%, 50 or more, 44%; wholesaler/jobber discounts upon request. Pages vary, have published from 52-240pp; of. Reporting time: 1 month. Payment: varies with title. Copyrights for author.

SYNERJY: A Directory of Renewable Energy, Jeff Twine, Box 1854/Cathedral Station, New York, NY 10025, 212-865-9595; twine@synerjy.com. 1974. "Bibliographic directory of renewable energy: solar, biomass, hydrogen, wind, water, geothermal; heat transfer & energy storage. Thousands of publications, products, facilities and conferences. Summer/Fall issues are yearly cumulations." circ. 200. 2/yr. Pub'd 2 issues 1998; expects 2 issues 1999, 2 issues 2000. sub. price: $62 institution, $30 individual; per copy: $30 winter issue; $40 summer cumulation. Back issues: $150 for any 10 cumulative back issues. Discounts: $56/yr for standing order. 70pp; 8½×11; of. Copyrighted, reverts to author.

Syracuse Cultural Workers/Tools for Change, Dik Cool, Director, Publisher, PO Box 6367, Syracuse, NY 13217, 315-474-1132, fax 315-475-1277. 1982. Art, photos, cartoons, collages. "SCW publishes and distributes the annual Peace Calendar, the Women Artists Datebook, posters, notecards, postcards, T-shirts, and selected books. We are a multicultural, visual arts publisher and distributor. Our images, in general, relate to peace and social justice, personal or social liberation and feminism. We sell wholesale and by direct mail and are a nonprofit corporation founded in 1982" avg. press run 5-17M. Pub'd 20 titles 1998; expects 25 titles 1999, 25 titles 2000. avg. price, paper: $11.95-13.95; other: $6-$40. Discounts: 40% returnable, 50% nonreturnable calendars; posters and cards 50%; books 40%, t-shirts 40%. 28pp; 14×11; of, silkscreen. Reporting time: 3-6 months. Simultaneous submissions accepted: yes. Payment: 6%, one time calendar payment $100-200, cover $400. Does not copyright for author.

T

T.V. HEADS, Shannon D. Harle, Publisher, Shannon D. Harle, PO Box 2224, Asheville, NC 28802. 1997. Cartoons, satire. "Subscription includes all the other zines I do= Eat Your Hair and T.V. Heads and also Rotten Pepper." circ. 100-150. 2-3/yr. Pub'd 2 issues 1998; expects 2 issues 1999, 3 issues 2000. sub. price: $10; per copy: $2; sample: $2. Back issues: $1 + 2 stamps. 20pp; 5½×8½; †mi. Reporting time: 1 month. Simultaneous submissions accepted: no. Payment: no. Copyrighted, reverts to author. §no.

Tafford Publishing, Philip Jr. Gurlik, PO Box 4474, Annapolis, MD 21403-6474, 410-267-9608 phone/Fax. 1984. Fiction. "Most of the books we publish are by established science fiction and fantasy writers, not necessarily in these genres however. Not looking at new submissions." avg. press run 3M-4M. Pub'd 4 titles 1998; expects 4 titles 1999, 3 titles 2000. 7 titles listed in the *Small Press Record of Books in Print* (28th Edition, 1999-00). avg. price, cloth: $19.95; paper: $12.95. Discounts: retail 1 copy 20%, 2-4 30%, 5+ 40%; 10 or more, 20% library, free shipping; 50% wholesale. 250pp; 5½×8½; of. Payment: varies. Copyrights for author. Small Press Center.

TAG Publications, Don & Joyce Brandon, PO Box 294, Hanover, VA 23069. 1995. avg. press run 2M. Expects 3 titles 2000. 1 title listed in the *Small Press Record of Books in Print* (28th Edition, 1999-00). avg. price, cloth: $24.95. Discounts: 55%. 320pp; 6×9. Reporting time: 6 weeks. Simultaneous submissions accepted: yes. Payment: percentage. Copyrights for author.

TAI CHI, Wayfarer Publications, Marvin Smalheiser, Editor, PO Box 26156, Los Angeles, CA 90026, 213-665-7773. 1977. Articles, interviews, reviews, letters, news items. "Articles about T'ai Chi Ch'uan, acupuncture, Chi kung, meditation, health about 700-4M words each." circ. 40M. 6/yr. Pub'd 6 issues 1998; expects 6 issues 1999, 6 issues 2000. sub. price: $20; per copy: $3.50; sample: $3.50. 72pp; 8½×11; of. Reporting time: 3 weeks. Simultaneous submissions accepted: no. Publishes 80% of manuscripts submitted. Payment: up to $500. Copyrighted. Ads: $800/$390.

TAIL SPINS, Brent Ritzel, Editor; Jenn Solheim, Associate Editor, PO Box 1860, Evanston, IL 60204, 847-424-9910; Fax 847-424-9978; tailspin@interaccess.com. 1991. Fiction, articles, art, photos, cartoons, interviews, criticism, reviews, music, letters, news items. circ. 10M. 3/yr. Pub'd 3 issues 1998; expects 3 issues 1999, 3 issues 2000. sub. price: $8; per copy: $3; sample: $3. Back issues: $3 each. 96pp; 8½×11; of. Simultaneous submissions accepted: no. Publishes 60% of manuscripts submitted. Payment: none. Copyrighted, reverts to author. Pub's reviews: 200 in 1998. §Music, independently published zines. Ads: $350/$190.

Tailored Tours Publications, Inc., Jenny Caneen, PO Box 22861, Lake Buena Vista, FL 32830. 1991. Fiction, non-fiction. "Particularly interested in Southern regional travel, fiction, biographies." avg. press run 10M. Pub'd 2 titles 1998; expects 4 titles 1999, 8 titles 2000. avg. price, paper: $14.95. Discounts: standard. 224pp; 7×9; lp, web press. Reporting time: 1 month. Payment: yes. Copyrights vary with each title. PAS, SEBA.

TAKAHE, Cassandra Fusco, Sarah Quigley, Bernadette Hall, Isa Moynihan, Mark Johnstone, James Norcliffe, Tony Scanlan, PO Box 13-335, Christchurch 1, New Zealand, 03-5198133. 1989. Poetry, fiction, art, cartoons, long-poems. "*Takahe* is a literary magazinewhich has no preconceived biases as to length or form. It aims to introduce young writers to a larger readership than they might otherwise enjoy by publishing them along side established figures (e.g. Kapka Kassabova, David Eggleton, David Hill, Mike Johnson). *Takahe* is interested in translation in addition to original fiction/poetry." circ. 320. 3/yr. Pub'd 4 issues 1998; expects 3 issues 1999, 3 issues 2000. sub. price: $24NZ; per copy: $6NZ; sample: $7.50NZ. 60pp; 8×11¾; copy, laser, disk. Reporting time: 1-4 months. Simultaneous submissions accepted if advised. Publishes 15% of manuscripts submitted. Payment: complimentary copy, plus small increment at editor's discretion. Copyrighted, reverts to author. Pub's reviews: 7 in 1998. Ads: $80NZ/$40NZ.

Tal San Publishing/Distributors, Sandi J. Lloyd, 7614 W. Bluefield Avenue, Glendale, AZ 85308, 602-843-1119; fax 602-843-3080. 1995. Fiction, non-fiction. "Mysteries, sci-fi, fantasy, history, romance, etc. All categories, all genres no poetry" avg. press run 5M. Expects 10 titles 1999, 20 titles 2000. avg. price, cloth: $20-25; paper: $6.95. Discounts: returnable: 1-4 20%, 5-24 40%, 25-49 42%, 50-99 43%, 100-999 45%, 1000+ 57%. Libraries: 1-9 10%, 10+ 15%. 5½×8½. Reporting time: 2-3 weeks. Payment: standard 7-10%. Copyrights for author.

Talent House Press, Paul Hadella, 1306 Talent Avenue, Talent, OR 97540, 541-535-9041. 1992. Poetry, fiction, art, photos, cartoons, satire, non-fiction. "We sponsor a chapbook contest every spring with guidelines announced in small press pubs. like *Poets & Writers* and *Small Press Review*. Other projects vary but never stem from unsolicited mss." avg. press run 150-300. Pub'd 2 titles 1998; expects 2 titles 1999, 2 titles 2000. avg. price, paper: $4. 40pp; 5½×8½; †of. Reporting time: 6 weeks. Payment: varies. Does not copyright for author.

TALISMAN: A Journal of Contemporary Poetry and Poetics, Talisman House, Publishers, Edward Foster, PO Box 3157, Jersey City, NJ 07303-3157, 201-938-0698. 1988. Poetry, articles, interviews, criticism, reviews. "Each issue of *Talisman* is centered on the work of a major contemporary poet. We publish poetry, interviews with poets, reviews of poetry, articles on poetics, articles on poetry." circ. 1M. 2/yr. Pub'd 2 issues 1998; expects 2 issues 1999, 2 issues 2000. sub. price: $11/2 issues individual, $15/2 issues institutions; per copy: $6; sample: $6. Discounts: negotiable. 268pp; 5½×8½; of. Reporting time: 1 month. Payment: copy. Copyrighted, reverts to author. Pub's reviews: 6 in 1998. §The best current poetry, poetic theory. Ads: $100/$50. CLMP.

Talisman House, Publishers (see also TALISMAN: A Journal of Contemporary Poetry and Poetics), Edward Foster, PO Box 3157, Jersey City, NJ 07303-3157, 201-938-0698. 1993. Poetry, fiction, interviews, criticism. avg. press run 1M-2M. Pub'd 2 titles 1998; expects 7 titles 1999, 7 titles 2000. 14 titles listed in the *Small Press Record of Books in Print* (28th Edition, 1999-00). avg. price, paper: $12; other: library binding $32. Discounts: negotiated individually. 60-250pp; 5½×8½, 6×9. Reporting time: 3 months. Payment: negotiated individually. Copyrights for author. CLMP.

TALKING RIVER REVIEW, Lewis-Clark State College, 500 8th Avenue, Lewiston, ID 83501, 208-799-2307; triver@lcsc.edu. 1994. Poetry, fiction, art, photos, parts-of-novels, long-poems, non-fiction. "Maximum length of prose is 7,500 words. Up to 5 poems may be submitted, any length or style. Recent contributers include: William Kittredge, Pattiann Rogers, Stephen Dunn, and Dorianne Laux." circ. 500. 2/yr. Pub'd 2 issues 1998; expects 2 issues 1999, 2 issues 2000. sub. price: $10; per copy: $5; sample: $5. Back issues: $5. Discounts: 40% to bookstores. 140pp; 6×9; of. Reporting time: 3 months. We accept simultaneous submissions with notification. Publishes 2% of manuscripts submitted. Payment: 2 copies and a year's subscription. Copyrighted, reverts to author. Ads: none.

Tamal Vista Publications, Katherine deFremery, 222 Madrone Ave, Larkspur, CA 94939, 924-7289. 1976. Non-fiction. *"The Stripper's Guide to Canoe-Building."* 3 titles listed in the *Small Press Record of Books in Print* (28th Edition, 1999-00). Discounts: 1-4 copies 20%, must have CWO; 5+ 40%. 96pp; 9×12; of. Reporting time: 1 month. Copyrights for author.

Tamarack Books, Inc., Kathy Gaudry, Publisher; Maggie Chenore, General Editor, PO Box 190313, Boise, ID 83719, 800-962-6657, 208-387-2656, fax 208-387-2650. 1992. Non-fiction. "We do not accept hard copy which is printed on dot matrix. Author involvement with promotion is very important to us" avg. press run 3M-5M. Pub'd 5 titles 1998; expects 5 titles 1999, 5 titles 2000. 1 title listed in the *Small Press Record of Books in Print* (28th Edition, 1999-00). avg. price, paper: $15.95. Discounts: trade 1-2 copies 20%, 3-25 42%, 26-50 43%, 51-99 44%, 100+ 45%. 250pp; 6×9. Reporting time: 3-4 months. Simultaneous submissions accepted: no. Publishes 5% of manuscripts submitted. Payment: negotiated. Copyrights for author. PMA, SPAN.

●**Tamarind,** PO Box 75442, Honolulu, HI 96836, 808-942-1794; dcasey7@concentric.net. 1 title listed in the *Small Press Record of Books in Print* (28th Edition, 1999-00).

TAMPA REVIEW, Richard B. Mathews, Editor; Paul Linnehan, Nonfiction Editor; Don Morrill, Poetry Editor; Lisa Birnbaum, Fiction Editor; Kathryn Van Spanckeren, Poetry Editor, 401 W. Kennedy Boulevard, University of Tampa-19F, Tampa, FL 33606-1490. 1988. Poetry, fiction, art, photos, interviews, non-fiction. *"Tampa Review* is the faculty-edited literary journal of the University of Tampa. It publishes new works of poetry, fiction, non-fiction and art. Each issue includes works from other countries in order to reflect the international flavor of the city of Tampa and its ties to the international cultural community. We would like to increase the amount of creative non-fiction in our contents and we are now publishing two issues per year. Recent contributors: Tom Disch, W.S. Merwin, Naomi Nye, Elizabeth Jolley, Denise Levertov, Louis Simpson." circ. 750. 2/yr. Pub'd 2 issues 1998; expects 2 issues 1999, 2 issues 2000. sub. price: $10; per copy: $5.95; sample: $5. Back issues: $5.95. Discounts: retail booksellers: cash, 1-4 copies 20% off cover price, 5 or more 40%; consignment up to 3 copies, 15% off cover price. 72-96pp; 7½×10½; of. Reporting time: we read from September to December; reports by end of January, mid-February. Simultaneous submissions accepted: no. Publishes 4% of manuscripts submitted. Payment: $10 per printed page. Copyrighted, reverts to author. exchange ads. CLMP, CELJ.

TANDEM, Michael J. Woods, 13 Stephenson Road Barbourne, Worchester, WR1 3EB, England, 01705-28002. 1993. Poetry, fiction, articles, reviews, letters. circ. 300. Published when funds allow. Pub'd 2 issues 1998; expects 2 issues 1999, 2 issues 2000. sub. price: £12, £15 overseas; per copy: £4.95 + pp; sample: No. 3 (£3.00 + pp). Discounts: 10% for 10 or more. 100pp; size A5. Reporting time: 2 weeks - try to be quick. Simultaneous submissions accepted: no. Publishes Percentage of manuscripts published depends entirely on quality - varies accordingly% of manuscripts submitted. Payment: None - free copy of magazine if included.

Copyrighted, reverts to author. Pub's reviews: 2 in 1998. §Poetry. Ads: $50/$30.

‡TANTRA PRESS, David B. Prather, David W. Carvell, 2111 Florida Street, Parkersburg, WV 26101-9032, 304-422-3112. 1993. Poetry. "We accept all lengths, styles, forms, and topics of poetry. Our only bias is quality (but this is entirely subjective, so we are open to all experience). Some contributors for our premier issue of April 1994 are: Jane Somerville, Susan Sheppard, Kenneth Pobo, Debra Conner, and Sherrell Wigal - most of whom are local authors whose voices have been shaped by the Mid-Ohio Valley lifestyle." circ. 200. 4/yr. Expects 3 issues 1999, 4 issues 2000. sub. price: $14; per copy: $4; sample: $4. Back issues: $4. Discounts: bulk $3/issue starting at 50 copies; classroom $2.50/issue. 60pp; 5½x8½; †laser printer. Reporting time: immediate to 2 months. Payment: 1 contributor copy and 50¢ discount on extra copies. Copyrighted, reverts to author. Ads: $50/$25/$12 1/4 page.

TAPROOT, a journal of older writers, Philip W. Quigg, Editor; Enid Graf, Associate Editor, Fine Arts Center 4290, University at Stony Brook, Stony Brook, NY 11794-5410, 516-632-6635. 1974. Poetry, articles, art, photos, non-fiction. "Poetry, prose and art by elder writers. Publication limited to Taproot Workshop members." circ. 1M. 2/yr. Pub'd 2 issues 1998; expects 2 issues 1999, 2 issues 2000. sub. price: $18; per copy: $8; sample: $8. Back issues: variable $3-$6. Discounts: please inquire. 100pp; 8½x11; Xerox. Reporting time: 2 months. Payment: 1 copy. Copyrighted, reverts to author. Ads: $1,000/$500/negotiable.

TAPROOT LITERARY REVIEW, Tikvah Feinstein, Amy Dobsch, Marc Rosenberg, Box 204, Ambridge, PA 15003, 412-266-8476; E-mail taproot10@aol.com. 1987. Poetry, fiction, art, photos, long-poems, non-fiction. "Taproot Literary Review, a locally published anthology with growing national and international participation and audience, will offer money prizes, publication, promotion and public readings for winners and authors in its annual poetry and fiction writing contest. Poetry and short fiction will be accepted. First-place winners in fiction and poetry will win $25 prizes. A university appointed panel will judge the entries. Deadline for entry is Dec. 31. For guidelines, send a self-addressed, stamped envelope to above address. Submissions accepted between September and December only." circ. 500. 1-2/yr. Pub'd 3 issues 1998. sub. price: $7.50; per copy: $5.50 + $2 p/h (contributor copies); sample: $4 + $1.50 stamps. Back issues: same. Discounts: classroom, libraries or retailers $4. 84-100pp; 6x9; of. Reporting time: 3 months or less. Simultaneous submissions accepted: no. Publishes 20-30% of manuscripts submitted. Payment: copies or cash prizes on contest. Copyrighted, reverts to author. Ads: ask for rates.

TAR RIVER POETRY, Peter Makuck, Department of English, East Carolina University, Greenville, NC 27858-4353, 919-328-6041. 1978. Poetry, reviews. "Among recent featured contributors have been Laurence Lieberman, Tom Reiter, Leslie Norris, Brendan Galvin, Jonathan Holden, Michael Bugeja, Betty Adcock, Emily Grosholz, Louis Simpson, Julie Suk, Susan Ludvieson, Mark Jarman, Deborah Cummins, Elizabeth Dodd, Henry Carlile." circ. 700. 2/yr. Expects 2 issues 2000. sub. price: $10, $18/2 yrs; per copy: $6.50; sample: $5.50. Back issues: $4. Discounts: 40% to bookstores. 64pp; 6x8¾; desktop. Reporting time: 4-6 weeks. Simultaneous submissions accepted: no. Publishes 15-20% of manuscripts submitted. Payment: contributor's copies. Rights reassigned to author upon request. Pub's reviews: 10 in 1998. §Poetry. Ads: we swap ads.

Taurean Horn Press, Bill Vartnaw, PO Box 641097, San Francisco, CA 94164. 1974. Poetry. "Publications in print: *In Concern: for Angels* by Bill Vartnaw, *From Spirit to Matter* by Carol Lee Sanchez, *Spectacles* by Tom Sharp. No submissions accepted." avg. press run 500. Expects 2 titles 1999, 1 title 2000. 3 titles listed in the *Small Press Record of Books in Print* (28th Edition, 1999-00). avg. price, paper: $7.95-$14.95. Discounts: 40% to book trade. 100pp; 6x9; of. Publishes 0% of manuscripts submitted. Payment: copies and/or other arrangements agreed upon prior to publication. Copyrights for author.

Tax Property Investor, Inc., F. Marea, PO Box 4602, Winter Park, FL 32793, 407-671-0004. 1989. Non-fiction. "Publishing for real estate investors." avg. press run 5M. Expects 1 title 1999, 3 titles 2000. 1 title listed in the *Small Press Record of Books in Print* (28th Edition, 1999-00). avg. price, paper: $29.95. Discounts: trade 3-99 40%; 100-199 45%; 200499 50%, 500+ 55%. 160pp; 8½x11; of. Reporting time: 30 days. Payment: to be negotiated.

TEACHER EDUCATION QUARTERLY, Caddo Gap Press, Alan H. Jones, Editor, 3147 Geary Boulevard #275, San Francisco, CA 94118, 415-392-1911. 1971. Articles. "The quarterly journal of the California Council on the Education of Teachers." circ. 900. 4/yr. Pub'd 4 issues 1998; expects 4 issues 1999, 4 issues 2000. sub. price: $40 indiv., $60 instit.; per copy: $15. 96pp; 6x9; of. Reporting time: 2 months. Publishes 25% of manuscripts submitted. Payment: none. Copyrighted, reverts to author. Ads: $200 full page. MPE, EdPress.

TEACHER LIBRARIAN: The Journal for School Library Professionals, Ken Haycock, Dept. 284, PO Box 34069, Seattle, WA 98124-1069, 604-925-0266. 1973. Articles, art, criticism, reviews, letters, news items. "Emphasis on library service to children and young adults." circ. 7.5M. 5/yr. Pub'd 5 issues 1998; expects 5 issues 1999, 5 issues 2000. sub. price: $49 billed, $44 prepaid; per copy: $9.80; sample: free on request. Back issues: on request. Discounts: on request. 72pp; 8½x11; Web offset. Reporting time: 2 months. Payment:

$100/article. Not copyrighted. Pub's reviews: 250 in 1998. §Professional materials for librarians, magazines for young people, new paperbacks for children, new paperbacks for young adults. Ads: $720/$400. Edpress, CMPA.

Teachers & Writers Collaborative (see also TEACHERS & WRITERS MAGAZINE), Ron Padgett, Christopher Edgar, 5 Union Square West, New York, NY 10003, 212-691-6590, 212-675-0171. 1967. Articles, interviews, reviews. "No poetry." avg. press run 3M. Pub'd 3 titles 1998; expects 3 titles 1999, 4 titles 2000. 37 titles listed in the *Small Press Record of Books in Print* (28th Edition, 1999-00). avg. price, cloth: $20.95; paper: $12.95. Discounts: varies. 160pp; 6×9; of. Reporting time: varies. Simultaneous submissions accepted: no. Publishes 2% of manuscripts submitted. Payment: varies. Copyrights for author. EPAA.

TEACHERS & WRITERS MAGAZINE, Teachers & Writers Collaborative, Ron Padgett, Senior Editor; Christopher Edgar, Editor, 5 Union Square West, New York, NY 10003, 212-691-6590. 1967. Articles, interviews, reviews, letters. "No poetry" circ. 2M. 5/yr. Pub'd 5 issues 1998; expects 5 issues 1999. sub. price: $16; per copy: $3 plus $1 shipping; sample: same. Back issues: $3-$5 plus $1 p+h. Discounts: none. 12pp; 8½×11; of. Reporting time: varies. Simultaneous submissions accepted: no. Publishes 5% of manuscripts submitted. Payment: varies. Copyrighted, reverts to author. Pub's reviews: 5 in 1998. §Education and writing. Ads: none. EPAA.

TEACHING ELEMENTARY PHYSICAL EDUCATION (TEPE), Human Kinetics Pub. Inc., Linda Morford, Box 5076, Champaign, IL 61825-5076, 217-351-5076; Fax 212-351-2674. 1990. Articles, interviews, reviews, letters, news items, non-fiction. "Bridges the gap between theory and the real world of children's physical education." circ. 3.6M. 6/yr. Pub'd 6 issues 1998; expects 6 issues 1999, 6 issues 2000. sub. price: $24 indiv, $60 instit., $16 student; per copy: $5 indiv, $11 instit.; sample: free. Back issues: volumes 7-8: $5 indiv., $11 instit., vol. 1-6: $4 indiv., $7 instit. Discounts: 5% agency. 32pp; 8½×11; of. Reporting time: 2 weeks. Payment: none. Copyrighted, does not revert to author. Pub's reviews: 12 in 1998. §Resources, events, programs of interest to elementary physical educators. Ads: $600/$400 (discounts available for multiple ads). Midwest Book Publishers Association, American Booksellers Association.

TEAK ROUNDUP, Robert Anstey, #5-9060 Tronson Road, Vernon, BC V1H 1E7, Canada, 250-545-4186, Fax 250-545-4194. 1994. Poetry, fiction, articles, art, photos, cartoons, interviews, satire, criticism, reviews, letters, parts-of-novels, news items, non-fiction. "Write for guidelines. Subscribers only eligible for publication." circ. 500. 4/yr. Pub'd 1200 issues 1998; expects 1400 issues 1999, 1400 issues 2000. sub. price: $17 Can, $13 U.S., $24 overseas; per copy: $5 Can, $3 U.S., $8 overseas; sample: $5 Can, $3 U.S., $8 overseas. Back issues: $5 or any 4 for $17 Can. 56pp; 5½×8½; †quality photocopy. Reporting time: 1 week. Simultaneous submissions accepted: yes. Publishes 90% of manuscripts submitted. Payment: none. Copyrighted, reverts to author. Pub's reviews: 16 in 1998. §general. Ads: $40/$20/$5 classified.

Tears in the Fence (see also TEARS IN THE FENCE), David Caddy, 38 Hod View Stourpaine, Blandford Forum, Dorset DT11 8TN, United Kingdom. 1995. Poetry, fiction. "Recent contributors include: Damian Furniss, Gerald Locklin, Gregory Warren Wilson, K.V. Skene, Joan-Jobe Smith" avg. press run 300. Pub'd 8 titles 1998; expects 6 titles 1999, 10 titles 2000. 3 titles listed in the *Small Press Record of Books in Print* (28th Edition, 1999-00). avg. price, cloth: $4; paper: $5. 48pp; 4×8; Docu-tech. Reporting time: no unsolicited submissions. Payment: yes. Copyrights for author.

TEARS IN THE FENCE, Tears in the Fence, David Caddy, Sarah Hopkins, 38 Hod View, Stourpaine, Blandford Forum, Dorset DT11 8TN, England. 1985. Poetry, fiction, art, interviews, criticism, reviews. circ. 1.5M. 2-3/yr. Pub'd 2 issues 1998; expects 3 issues 1999, 3 issues 2000. sub. price: £10, $6.50 including postage; per copy: £4, $1.75 including postage; sample: same. Back issues: sold out. 96pp; 4×8; docutech. Reporting time: 2-3 weeks. Simultaneous submissions accepted: no. Publishes 1-2% of manuscripts submitted. Payment: 1 copy. Copyrighted, reverts to author. Pub's reviews: 42 in 1998.

●Tebot Bach (see also SPILLWAY), Mifanwy Kaiser, Mark Bergendahl, 20592 Minerva Lane, Huntington Beach, CA 92646, 714-968-0905. 1998. Poetry, photos, criticism, reviews, long-poems. avg. press run 800-1M. Pub'd 3 titles 1998; expects 3 titles 1999, 3 titles 2000. 1 title listed in the *Small Press Record of Books in Print* (28th Edition, 1999-00). avg. price, paper: $10. Discounts: by arrangement. 96pp; 6×9. Reporting time: 2 weeks-6 months. Payment: contract.

TEC Publications, Timothy Edward Curley, 4511 Del Rio Road #5, Sacramento, CA 95822, 916-362-0402. 1980. avg. press run 60M. Expects 2 titles 1999, 3 titles 2000. 4 titles listed in the *Small Press Record of Books in Print* (28th Edition, 1999-00). avg. price, paper: $11.95. Discounts: 50%. 198pp; 8½×11; of. Reporting time: varies. Payment: 10% for first run. Does not copyright for author.

TECH DIRECTIONS, Prakken Publications, Tom Bowden, Managing Editor, PO Box 8623, Ann Arbor, MI 48107, 734-975-2800 ext. 212 fax 734-975-2787. 1941. Articles, cartoons, collages, news items, non-fiction. "*Tech Directions* serves the fields of industrial education, technology education and vocational-technical education, which includes automotive, drafting, general shop, graphic arts, electronics, machine shop, welding, woodworking, computer technology and other subjects of interest to teachers in junior highs, senior highs, vocational-technical schools, and community colleges." circ. 42M. 10/yr. Pub'd 10 issues 1998; expects 10 issues 1999, 10 issues 2000. sub. price: $30; per copy: $5; sample: free (note: qualified individuals receive the mag free on request). Back issues: $5. Discounts: agent= 10%, individual multi-year rates= 2 yr, $55, 3 yr $80 (US). 50pp; 8½×11; of. Reporting time: 2 months. Accept simultaneous submissions only in exceptional cases. Publishes 20% of manuscripts submitted. Payment: honorarium $25-$250, depends on length, illustrations. Copyrighted, does not revert to author. Pub's reviews: 40 in 1998. §Industrial/technical/vocational education, technology, crafts. Ads: $4185/$2535/$215 col. inch. Edpress, Educational Exhibitors Assn./SHIP.

TECHNICALITIES, Westport Publishers, Brian Alley, Editor, 1102 Grand, 23rd Floor, Kansas City, MO 64106. 1980. Interviews, news items, non-fiction. "Professional newsletter for libraries and librarians working at or towards automation. Articles should be typed and double-spaced; no more than 8 pages in length." circ. 650. 12/yr. Pub'd 12 issues 1998; expects 12 issues 1999, 12 issues 2000. sub. price: $50; per copy: $5; sample: no charge. Back issues: $4.50. 16pp; 8½×11; of. Payment: varies. Not copyrighted. Pub's reviews: 4 in 1998. §Librarianship and microcomputers for library use. Ads: write for rate card information. MAPA.

Technicians of the Sacred (see also RESEARCH IN YORUBA LANGUAGE & LITERATURE; SOCIETE), Courtney Willis, 1317 N. San Fernando Boulevard, Suite 310, Burbank, CA 91504. 1983. Non-fiction. avg. press run 500. Pub'd 3 titles 1998; expects 4 titles 1999. 4 titles listed in the *Small Press Record of Books in Print* (28th Edition, 1999-00). avg. price, paper: $25. 130pp; 8½×11; of. Reporting time: 4 weeks. Copyrights for author.

Tecolote Publications, Carol Bowers, 4918 Del Monte Avenue, San Diego, CA 92107. 1986. Poetry, fiction, non-fiction. "Main publications are local history books (San Diego County) and nature poster/brochures (12" X 24"); author - subsidize" avg. press run 1-5M. Pub'd 11 titles 1998; expects 10 titles 1999, 10 titles 2000. 25 titles listed in the *Small Press Record of Books in Print* (28th Edition, 1999-00). avg. price, cloth: $35; paper: $10. Discounts: trade - 40%; wholesalers - 50%; distributors - 55%. 150pp; 5½×8½.

TEEN VOICES MAGAZINE, Alison Amoroso, Editor-in-Chief; Shannon Berning, Managing Editor, 515 Washington Street, 6th floor, Boston, MA 02111-1759, 617-426-5505; fax 617-426-5577; e-mail womenexp@teenvoices.com; website www.teenvoices.com. 1988. Poetry, fiction, articles, art, photos, cartoons, interviews, satire, criticism, reviews, music, letters, news items, non-fiction. "Additional address: PO Box 120-027, Boston, MA 02112-0027. We publish the writing of teenage girls *only*." circ. 75M. 4/yr. Pub'd 4 issues 1998; expects 4 issues 1999, 4 issues 2000. sub. price: $20; per copy: $3; sample: $5. Back issues: $5-$10 depending on issue. Discounts: bulk, human service agencies, classrooms. 60pp; 8½×11. Simultaneous submissions accepted: yes. Publishes 20% of manuscripts submitted. Payment: 3 copies of magazine. Copyrighted, does not revert to author. Pub's reviews: 6 in 1998. §books teenage girls or teenagers in general might want to know about. Ads: $1,200/$750/$2.50 word. IPA.

TEENAGE GANG DEBS, Erin Smith, Don Smith, PO Box 1754, Bethesda, MD 20827-1754. 1989. Articles, photos, interviews, satire, criticism, reviews, music, letters, collages, non-fiction. circ. 2M. 1/yr. Pub'd 1 issue 1998; expects 1 issue 1999, 1 issue 2000. price per copy: $3; sample: same. Discounts: $1.25. 24pp; 8½×11; †xerox. Copyrighted, does not revert to author. Pub's reviews: 9 in 1998. §Television, film, entertainment, music, teens.

TEENS IN MOTION NEWS, Pamela Costa, PO Box 1264, Santa Clara, CA 95052, 408-244-3718. 1995. Poetry, fiction, articles, art, photos, cartoons, reviews, music, letters, long-poems, concrete art, news items, non-fiction. "Length of articles, short stories, poetry: 300 words or less, but all looked at. We publish material from teens, one talented teen appears each month, plus at least two other talented teens. We accept real-life experiences from teens, questions, and advice" circ. 2.5M. 11/yr. Pub'd 4 issues 1998; expects 11 issues 1999, 11 issues 2000. sub. price: $8.50; per copy: $1; sample: free. Back issues: $1. Discounts: free ad with subscription. 20pp; 8½×5½. Reporting time: 2 weeks. Simultaneous submissions accepted: yes. Publishes 99% of manuscripts submitted. Payment: copy, subscriptions. Copyrighted, reverts to author. Pub's reviews: 1 in 1998. §Mystery, poetry, anything related to youth, careers, education. Ads: $40/$30/classified & calendar free to subscribers. PMA.

The Teitan Press, Inc., Martin P. Starr, Vice-President; Franklin C. Winston, President, PO Box 10258, Chicago, IL 60610, 773-929-7892; FAX 773-871-3315, e-mail teitanpr@aol.com Web Site: http://users.aol.com/teitanpr. 1985. Fiction, non-fiction. "We only use in-house material." avg. press run 1M. Pub'd 1 title 1998; expects 1 title 1999, 1 title 2000. 6 titles listed in the *Small Press Record of Books in Print* (28th Edition, 1999-00). avg. price, cloth: $29.95. Discounts: 50% to wholesalers, 20%-40% to retail outlets depending on quantity; 10% to libraries postpaid. 200pp; 6×9; of. Copyrights for author.

Telephone Books, Maureen Owen, 109 Dunk Rock Rd., Guilford, CT 06437, 203-453-1921. 1971. Poetry, fiction, plays. "Press will do 2 books in 1999, but titles remain available. Books: *The Amerindian Coastline*

Poem by Fanny Howe; *Hot Footsteps* by Yuki Hartman; *Ciao Manhattan* by Rebecca Wright; *Delayed: Not Postponed* by Fielding Dawson; *The Secret History of the Dividing Line* by Susan Howe; *The Temple* by Janet Hamill; *No More Mr. Nice Guy* by Sam Kashner; *Audrey Hepburn's Symphonic Salad and the Coming of Autumn* by Tom Weigel; *The Telephone Book* by Ed Friedman; *3-Way Split* by Rebecca Brown; *Hot* by Joe Johnson; *The Celestial Splendor Shining Forth From Geometric Thought* and *On the Motion of the Apparently Fixed Stars* by Britt Wilkie. No unsolicited ms." avg. press run 750-1M. Pub'd 2 titles 1998. 17 titles listed in the *Small Press Record of Books in Print* (28th Edition, 1999-00). avg. price, cloth: $7.95; paper: $4 (all checks made out to Maureen Owen). 40pp; size varies; of. Payment: in copies. Copyrights for author. CLMP, NESPA, BC.

Tell Publishing, N. Heyd, 5679 South Transit Road, Ste. 181, Lockport, NY 14094, 800-726-8932, 416-693-4302. 1992. Fiction, long-poems, non-fiction. "Focus is more on fiction and non-fiction topics of current interest than on poetry" avg. press run 10M. Expects 3 titles 1999, 2 titles 2000. 3 titles listed in the *Small Press Record of Books in Print* (28th Edition, 1999-00). avg. price, paper: $11.50. 220pp; 5¼×8; of. Reporting time: 4 weeks. Simultaneous submissions accepted: yes. Payment: 10%. Copyrights for author. Canadian Booksellers Assn.

TELOS, Telos Press, Paul Piccone, Jen Paul, Managing Editor, 431 East 12th Street, New York, NY 10009, 212-228-6479. 1968. Articles, criticism, reviews. circ. 3.5M. 4/yr. Pub'd 4 issues 1998; expects 4 issues 1999, 4 issues 2000. sub. price: indiv. $35, instit. $90; per copy: indiv. $11; instit. $30; sample: same. Back issues: $14. Discounts: 30% bulk orders; 10% agent, 30% bookstores. 240pp; 6×9; of. Reporting time: 6 months. Payment: none. Copyrighted. Pub's reviews: 40 books, 40 journals in 1998. §Left-wing philosophy, lit. criticism, politics. Ads: $500/$300/$150 1/4 page.

Telos Press (see also TELOS), Paul Piccone, Jen Paul, Managing Editor, 431 East 12th Street, New York, NY 10009, 212-228-6479. 1968. Articles, criticism, reviews. avg. press run 4.5M. Expects 2 titles 1999, 2 titles 2000. 14 titles listed in the *Small Press Record of Books in Print* (28th Edition, 1999-00). avg. price, cloth: $26; paper: $16. Discounts: usual is 30%, other can be arranged. 200pp; size varies; of. Reporting time: 6 months. Publishes a variable % of manuscripts submitted. Payment: no set policy. Copyrights for author.

THE TEMPLE, Tsunami Inc., Charles Potts, PO Box 100, Walla Walla, WA 99362-0033, E-mail tsunami@wwics.com. 1995. Poetry, articles, criticism, reviews, long-poems. "We publish Spanish and Chinese contemporary poets with translations. John Oliver Simon, Denis Mair, Barbara LaMorticella, Susana Villalba, Michael Finley, Stephen Thomas, Linda Hasselstrom" circ. 5M. 4/yr. Expects 4 issues 1999, 4 issues 2000. sub. price: $20; per copy: $5; sample: $5. Back issues: inquire. Discounts: 40%. 80pp; 6×9; web press. Reporting time: varies, usually quick. Simultaneous submissions accepted: yes. Publishes 1% of manuscripts submitted. Payment: copies. Copyrighted, reverts to author. Pub's reviews: 15 in 1998. §Poetry, criticism. Ads: $150/$100/1/4 page $60. PNBA, WWPP.

Temporary Vandalism Recordings (see also FREEDOM ISN'T FREE), Robert Roden, Barton M. Saunders, PO Box 6184, Orange, CA 92863-6184, e-mail tvrec@yahoo.com. 1991. Poetry. "Have never published unsolicited manuscripts for our chapbooks. Suggest a ten poem sample with SASE for reply. We only publish 2 to 3 chapbooks per year so far" 100 first run, optional reprinting if needed. Pub'd 2 titles 1998; expects 2 titles 1999, 3 titles 2000. 9 titles listed in the *Small Press Record of Books in Print* (28th Edition, 1999-00). avg. price, paper: $5; other: $8. Discounts: 40%. 40pp; 5½×8½; mi. Reporting time: 3-6 months. Simultaneous submissions accepted: yes. Publishes 1% of manuscripts submitted. Payment: 5 copies, 50% of net sales. Does not copyright for author.

Ten Penny Players, Inc. (see also WATERWAYS: Poetry in the Mainstream), Barbara Fisher, Co-Editor; Richard Spiegel, Co-Editor, 393 St. Paul's Avenue, Staten Island, NY 10304-2127, 718-442-7429. 1975. Poetry, fiction, plays. "Books: Age range is child to adult. Varying lengths: 8pp-150pp. We stress an integration of language and picture so that the material can be used either as a book to read or a book to perform. Also child + adult poets published monthly in magazine and 40 literary magazines from NYC high schools. No unsolicited manuscripts, please." avg. press run 200. Pub'd 2 titles 1998; expects 2 titles 1999, 3 titles 2000. 34 titles listed in the *Small Press Record of Books in Print* (28th Edition, 1999-00). avg. price, paper: $5; other: *Waterways*: $2.25 copy/$25 subscription. Discounts: standard 60/40. 60pp; 8½×5½; †of, lp, xerox. Simultaneous submissions accepted: no. Payment: negotiable. Copyrights for author. WP.

Ten Star Press, D. Millhouse, 2860 Plaza Verde, Santa Fe, NM 87505, 505-473-4813 phone/Fax; E-mail dorbil@rt66.com. 1988. Poetry, fiction, criticism, reviews, parts-of-novels, plays, non-fiction. "Primarily fiction (novels and novellas), non-fiction and collections of various types of material. Radical left and socialist oriented. All orders go to Ten Star." avg. press run 2M-3M. Pub'd 2 titles 1998; expects 1 title 1999. 3 titles listed in the *Small Press Record of Books in Print* (28th Edition, 1999-00). avg. price, cloth: $15; paper: $10. Discounts: can be arranged. 250-350pp; 5½×8½; of. Reporting time: 1 month. Simultaneous submissions accepted: yes. Payment: to be arranged. Does not copyright for author.

TERMINAL FRIGHT, Kenneth E. Abner, Jr., PO Box 100, Black River, NY 13612. 1993. Fiction. "1,500 to 10K traditional/Gothic horror. *Terminal Fright* has two intentions, to take readers back to the roots of horror and to bring traditional and Gothic horror back to the mainstream. *TF* is not a market for splatter-punk, slasher stories, tales purely psychological, anything with excessive vulgarity, explicit sex, gratuitous, graphic gore or anything which can be seen on the nightly news. *TF* tales take readers away from the frights of the real world and sets them down in a world where the monsters are very real. I'm particularly fond of ghosts, monsters (any type but human) and the occult. This is not a hard rule, but I prefer stories with likable people in bizarre situations. For the most part, I don't go for tales where shock value or an oddity is the main selling point. I want tales which truly intrigue me; tales with imagery and atmosphere." 4/yr. Pub'd 1 issue 1998; expects 5 issues 1999, 4 issues 2000. sub. price: $18; per copy: $5; sample: $5. 76pp; 8½×11. Reporting time: 6-8 weeks. We accept simultaneous submissions if noted. Payment: 1/2¢-2¢/word and contributor's copy. Copyrighted, reverts to author. HWA.

Terra Nova Press, Susan Curry, 1309 Redwood Lane, Davis, CA 95616, 916-753-1519. 1984. Non-fiction. "Not accepting manuscripts at present." avg. press run 5M. Expects 1 title 1999, 2 titles 2000. 1 title listed in the *Small Press Record of Books in Print* (28th Edition, 1999-00). avg. price, cloth: $14.95; paper: $8.95. Discounts: trade 1-4 20%, 5-24 40%, 25-49 43% and up; wholesalers and jobbers 1-4 20%, 5-49 45%, 50-99 50% and up; bulk on request. 250pp; 5½×8½; of. Payment: reporting twice/year, accompanied by check. Copyrights for author. SPAN.

Tesseract Publications, Janet Leih, PO Box 164, Canton, SD 57013-0164, 605-987-5071. 1981. Poetry, fiction, non-fiction. "Prefer feminist, non-fiction, poetry." avg. press run 300-500. Pub'd 1 title 1998; expects 2 titles 1999, 2 titles 2000. 27 titles listed in the *Small Press Record of Books in Print* (28th Edition, 1999-00). avg. price, cloth: $12; paper: $5. Discounts: available on request. 60pp; 5½×8½, or author's request; †of/ laser printer. Reporting time: 3 months. Simultaneous submissions accepted: yes. Payment: subsidized publications only. Copyrights for author if asked.

THE TEXAS REVIEW, Texas Review Press, Paul Ruffin, English Department, Sam Houston State University, Huntsville, TX 77341-2146. 1976. Poetry, fiction, articles, photos, interviews, reviews. "Because of the size of our magazine, we do not encourage the submission of long poems or exceptionally long short stories. Now accept photography, critical essays on literature and culture, etc. Each year we publish the *The Texas Review* Poetry Award Chapbook. We will no longer read during May through August." circ. 750-1M. 2/yr. Pub'd 2 issues 1998; expects 2 issues 1999. sub. price: $20; 2 years $35; 3 years $50; per copy: $10. Back issues: $5. Discounts: 40% to libraries. 148pp; 6×9; of. Reporting time: 8 weeks. Payment: copies, subscription (1 year). Copyrighted, rights revert to author on request. Pub's reviews: 24 in 1998. §Poetry, fiction, history, art, literary criticism, informal essays. Exchange ads only. CLMP.

Texas Review Press (see also THE TEXAS REVIEW), Paul Ruffin, English Department, Sam Houston State University, Huntsville, TX 77341-2146. 1979. "We do not read May-August" avg. press run 500. 19 titles listed in the *Small Press Record of Books in Print* (28th Edition, 1999-00). avg. price, paper: $10. 160pp; 6×9; of. Copyrights for author.

TEXAS YOUNG WRITERS' NEWSLETTER, Susan Currie, PO Box 942, Adkins, TX 78101. 1994. Poetry, fiction, news items, non-fiction. "Poetry - no more than 30 lines. Stories and articles - 400-900 words. SASE must be included. Poetry and stories may only be submitted by writers ages 12-19" circ. 300. 9/yr. Pub'd 9 issues 1998; expects 9 issues 1999, 9 issues 2000. sub. price: $10; per copy: $1; sample: $1. Back issues: none. Discounts: none. 7pp; 8½×11; mi. Reporting time: 3 weeks. Simultaneous submissions accepted: no. Publishes 40% of manuscripts submitted. Payment: 5 copies. Not copyrighted. Pub's reviews: 1-2 in 1998. §Writers' books. Ads: $50/$25.

TEXTSHOP, Andrew Stubbs, Andrew Stubbs, English Dept., University of Regina, Regina, Sask. S4S 0A2, Canada. 1992. Poetry, fiction, articles, interviews, satire, reviews, letters, parts-of-novels, non-fiction. "Poetry/poem sequences (up to 4 pages); story, fictions, personal narrative (creative non-fiction), 'popular' essays ('experience' writing) 3-5 pages. Recent contributors: Bruce Bond, Gerald Noonan, wide range of new writers (including young and child writers). Each submission is printed with a critical (editorial) comment." circ. up to 250. 1/yr. Pub'd 1 issue 1998; expects 1 issue 1999, 1 issue 2000. sub. price: $6; per copy: $6; sample: $6. Back issues: $2 per issue. 80pp; 8½×11; of. Reporting time: 3 months. Simultaneous submissions accepted: no. Payment: 1 free copy. Copyrighted, reverts to author. Pub's reviews: Ads: none.

TEXTURE, Texture Press, Susan Smith Nash, 3760 Cedar Ridge Drive, Norman, OK 73072, 405-366-7730. 1989. Poetry, fiction, articles, art, photos, cartoons, interviews, criticism, reviews, collages, concrete art. "Prefer experimental, avant-garde, dada, surrealism" circ. 2M. 1/yr. Pub'd 1 issue 1998; expects 1 issue 1999, 1 issue 2000. price per copy: $8; sample: $6. Back issues: $6. Discounts: 40% discount to trade. 100pp; 8½×11; of. Reporting time: 6 months. Payment: contributor's copy. Copyrighted, reverts to author. Pub's reviews: 100 in 1998. §Literary criticism, experimental art.

Texture Press (see also **TEXTURE**), Susan Smith Nash, 3760 Cedar Ridge Drive, Norman, OK 73072, 405-366-7730. 1989. Poetry, fiction, articles, photos, cartoons, interviews, criticism, reviews, long-poems, collages, concrete art. "Prefer experimental poetry and essays on issues in contemporary poetics" avg. press run 750. Pub'd 6 titles 1998; expects 6 titles 1999, 10 titles 2000. 2 titles listed in the *Small Press Record of Books in Print* (28th Edition, 1999-00). avg. price, paper: $6. Discounts: 40% discount to trade. 40pp; 8½×11; of. Reporting time: 6 months. Copyrights for author.

THALIA: Studies in Literary Humor, Jacqueline Tavernier-Courbin, Dept of English, Univ of Ottawa, Ottawa K1N 6N5, Canada, 613-230-9505; Fax 613-565-5786. 1978. Articles, art, cartoons, interviews, satire, criticism, reviews, letters, collages, non-fiction. circ. 500. 2/yr or 1 double issue. Pub'd 1 issue 1998; expects 2 issues 1999, 2 issues 2000. sub. price: $23 individuals, $25 libraries, discounts for 2 or 3 year subs.; per copy: $8-$10 except for double issues; sample: $8-$10 except for double issues. Back issues: $12-$15 for most volumes. Discounts: by direct query only. 75-125pp; 7×8½; lp. Reporting time: varies with ms. content. We accept simultaneous submissions, but we must know about it and get first copyrights. Publishes 25-30% of manuscripts submitted. Payment: none. Copyrighted, copyrights contract signed prior to publication. Pub's reviews: 2 in 1998. §Any area connected to humor. Ads: $150/$75. Association for the Study of Literary Humor.

:THAT:, Stephen Dignazio, Stephen Ellis, 1070 Easton Valley Road, Easton, NH 03580. 1992. Non-fiction. "Directions seem pertinent upon arrival, not much chance of :that:. Suffice to say this series continues under the rubric 'descriptions of practice.' We're looking for 15+ pages on the figure and ground of poetic experience. Thus far, this series has presented Robert Grenier on the texts and contexts of his recent work, and Robert Podgurski and Jeff Gburek on 'poetry and magic.' We strongly suggest you see a copy before submitting." circ. 250. 2/yr. Pub'd 2 issues 1998; expects 2 issues 1999, 2 issues 2000. sub. price: $5 per issue; per copy: $5; sample: $5. Back issues: $2 each, as available. Discounts: less 40%. 15pp; size varies; xerox. Reporting time: 1 week-6 months. Payment: 5 copies. Copyrighted, reverts to author.

THEATER, Erika Munk, 222 York Street, New Haven, CT 06520, 203-432-1568, Fax 203-432-8336, e-mail theater.magazine@quick.yale.edu. 1968. Articles, interviews, satire, criticism, reviews, letters, plays. "*Theater* a critical journal of contemporary theatre, publishes the most noted American and international critics, playwrights, and scholars. Each issue contains a group of essays, a major new playscript, reports from abroad, interviews with renowned theater professionals, fine performance photographys, and theater and book reviews. Recent topics include Theatrical Utopias, New Scripts, Money & Power, Afro-American Theater." circ. 3M. 3/yr. Pub'd 3 issues 1998; expects 3 issues 1999, 3 issues 2000. sub. price: $22 individuals, $45 libraries; per copy: $8; sample: $8. Back issues: $5/$8. Discounts: agents 8%; bookstores 20%-25%; bulk 10-15% (back issues only). 121pp; 7½×10; of. Reporting time: 8 weeks. Simultaneous submissions accepted: yes. Payment: $50-$150. Copyrighted, playwrights retain copyright. Pub's reviews: 2 per issue in 1998. §New books on theater, new plays, production. Ads: $250/$150. CLMP, CELJ.

A THEATER OF BLOOD, Pyx Press, C. Darren Butler, Editor; Lisa S. Laurencot, Associate Editor, PO Box 922648, Sylmar, CA 91392-2648. 1990. Fiction, interviews, non-fiction. "Literary horror and dark fantasy. Reads only Sept 1 - Nov 30." circ. 500. 1/yr. Pub'd 1 issue 1998; expects 1 issue 1999, 1 issue 2000. sub. price: query; per copy: query. Back issues: 3/$6.50. Discounts: query. 5½×8½; xerox or of. Reporting time: 3 months, occasionally longer. Simultaneous submissions accepted: yes. Publishes .5% of manuscripts submitted. Payment: $2-$30 and a copy. Copyrighted. Ads: query. AMP.

THEATRE DESIGN AND TECHNOLOGY, United States Institute for Theatre Technology, Inc., David Rodger, Editor; Deborah Hazlett, Art Editor, 6443 Ridings Road, Syracuse, NY 13206-1111. 1965. Articles, photos, interviews, reviews, letters, news items. "The magazine covers the art and technology of producing live performing arts and entertainment. Articles discuss historical scene design as well as contemporary design. Pieces on lighting and sound focus on both the artistic effects of these elements and the newest, most effective ways to use these elements. Costume design and designers are often highlighted. Reports on newly created standards in the industry, health and safety issues, new facilities, and new products appear regularly. Interpretative articles as well as technical research findings all combine to make *TD&T* an important and one-of-a-kind source for practitioners of theatre design, theatre building, and theatre technology." circ. 4M. 5/yr. Pub'd 5 issues 1998; expects 5 issues 1999, 5 issues 2000. sub. price: $48 domestic, $58 foreign (libraries only). Back issues: $6 members; $9 non-members. Discounts: none. 76pp; 8¼×11; web offset. Reporting time: 6 weeks. Payment: none. Copyrighted, rights held by magazine after publication unless author wishes separate copyright. Pub's reviews: 13 in 1998. §Books only, scenography, scene design, engineering, architecture, costume. Ads: $890/$535 for black/white; color available at additional cost.

●**THEECLECTICS, Creative With Words Publications (CWW),** Brigitta Geltrich, Editor & Publisher; Bert Hower, Editor, PO Box 223226, Carmel, CA 93922, fax 831-655-8627; e-mail cwwpub@usa.net; website http://members.tripod.com/~CreativeWithWords. 1998. Poetry, fiction, cartoons, satire. "On any topic, written by adults only (20 and older), poetry preferred." 2/yr. Pub'd 2 issues 1998; expects 2 issues 1999, 2 issues

2000. price per copy: $6. Discounts: authors 20%; offices, schools, libraries, clubs 10%; legitimate shutins get a one time only free copy. 16+pp; 8½×11. Reporting time: 2-4 weeks after set deadline. Simultaneous submissions accepted: no. Publishes 90% of manuscripts submitted. Payment: 20% discount. Copyrighted, reverts to author. Ads: $125/$70/$35/$16.

THEMA, Virginia Howard, PO BOX 8747, Metairie, LA 70011-8747. 1988. Poetry, fiction, art, cartoons. "Each issue related to a unique central premise. Upcoming themes: (pub. date), Jan. 2000 On the road to the villa, May 2000 The Wrong Cart, Sept. 2000 Toby Came Today, Jan. 2001 Addie Hasn't Been the Same Since..." circ. 300. 3/yr. Pub'd 3 issues 1998; expects 3 issues 1999, 3 issues 2000. sub. price: $16; per copy: $8; sample: $8. Back issues: $8. Discounts: 10%. 180pp; 5½×8½; of. Reporting time: 5-6 months after manuscript submission deadline of specific issue. Simultaneous submissions accepted: yes. Publishes 5% of manuscripts submitted. Payment: $25 short stories, $10 poetry, $10 b/w artwork, $25 b/w cover art, $10 short-short pieces. Copyrighted, reverts to author. §Fiction. Ads: $150/$100/$50 1/4 page. CLMP.

THEOLOGIA 21, A. Stuart Otto, Editor, PO Box 4608, Salem, OR 97302-8608, 503-362-9634. 1970. Articles, reviews, letters. "No mss accepted." circ. 100. 4/yr. Pub'd 4 issues 1998; expects 4 issues 1999, 4 issues 2000. sub. price: $15; per copy: not available; sample: not available. Back issues: 1976-80 complete, bound $24.95; 1981-86 complete, bound $24.95; 1987-90 complete, bound $24.95; full set $69.95. Discounts: 30% to dealers, agencies; 40% on bound volumes. 4pp; 8½×11; of. Pub's reviews: 1 in 1998. §Theology (Christian). No ads.

Theosophical Publishing House (see also THE QUEST), Brenda Rosen, Executive Editor, 306 West Geneva Road, Wheaton, IL 60187, 708-665-0130, fax 708-665-8791. 1968. Art, non-fiction. "Esoteric, comparative religion, psychology, philosophy, health, holistic healing, astrology, meditation, holistic living." avg. press run 5M. Pub'd 12 titles 1998; expects 12 titles 1999, 12 titles 2000. 56 titles listed in the *Small Press Record of Books in Print* (28th Edition, 1999-00). avg. price, cloth: $24.95; paper: $14.00; other: $8 miniatures. 200pp; 6×9; sheetfed & web offset. Reporting time: 1-6 months. Simultaneous submissions accepted: yes. Payment: paid once a year. Copyrights for author. American Booksellers Association.

THEY WON'T STAY DEAD!, Brian Johnson, 11 Werner Road, Greenville, PA 16125, 412-588-3471. 1989. Articles, art, photos, cartoons, interviews, satire, criticism, reviews, music, letters, news items. "8 pages of 'Psychotronic' film and culture, including horror and 'trash' film reviews and commentary. Also comments on anything oddball or shocking. Recent contributors include Greg Goodsell, Dave Szurek, D.Ho Grover and Webster Colcord, Angus E. Crane, Joseph A. Wawrzyniak, Gene Suicide. Biases include all the above." circ. 500+. 3/yr. Pub'd 3 issues 1998; expects 3 issues 1999, 3 issues 2000. price per copy: Send SASE; sample: SASE. Back issues: $2-$3. 4pp; 8½×11; †xerox. Simultaneous submissions accepted: yes. Publishes 20% of manuscripts submitted. Payment: 1 copy of issue. Not copyrighted. Pub's reviews: 12 in 1998. §Horror, controversial or true crime. Ads: negotiable.

Theytus Books Ltd., Greg Young-Ing, Manager, PO Box 20040, Penticton, B.C. V2A 8K3, Canada, 250-493-7181. 1980. Poetry, fiction, photos, non-fiction. "Recent contributors: Jeannette Armstrong, Beth Cuthand, Douglas Cardinal, Ellen White." avg. press run 4M. Pub'd 4 titles 1998; expects 4 titles 1999, 4 titles 2000. 23 titles listed in the *Small Press Record of Books in Print* (28th Edition, 1999-00). avg. price, paper: $13.95; other: $49.95. Discounts: applicable to retail and wholesale dealers, cloth or paper, single or assorted titles: 1 copy 20%, 2-4 30%, 5-99 40%, 100-199 41%, 200-299 42%, 300-399 43%, 400-499 45%, 500+ 50%, wholesalers 55%. 150pp; 5½×8½; of. Reporting time: 6 months to 1 year. Payment: 8-10% 2 times a year. Copyrights for author. ACP, 260 King Street East, Toronto, Ont., CBIC (same), ABPBC 1622 W. 7th Ave., Vancouver, B.C. Canada V6J 1S5.

THIN AIR, Lance Laurier, Editor-in-Chief, PO Box 23549, Flagstaff, AZ 86002, www.nau.edu/~english/thinair/taframes.html. 1995. Poetry, fiction, articles, art, photos, cartoons, interviews, satire, criticism, reviews, music, letters, parts-of-novels, long-poems, collages, plays, concrete art, news items, non-fiction. circ. 400-600. 2/yr. Pub'd 1 issue 1998; expects 2 issues 1999, 2 issues 2000. sub. price: $9; per copy: $4.95; sample: $4. 80-100pp; 5½×8½. Reporting time: 2-3 months. We accept simultaneous submissions but we must be notified if the piece is accepted elsewhere. Publishes 5-10% of manuscripts submitted. Payment: publication and 2 copies. Copyrighted, rights revert to the author upon acknowledgement of *Thin Air* as an original publisher. Pub's reviews: 4 in 1998. §We are open to reviews of all types, but please query first.

THIN COYOTE, Lost Prophet Press, Christopher Jones, Maggie McKnight, 3300 3rd Avenue South, Minneapolis, MN 55408-3204. 1992. Poetry, fiction, art, photos, interviews, satire, collages, plays. "When we are able to stop guzzling whiskey long enough to read submissions, we tend to favor the work of scofflaws, muleskinners, seers, witchdoctors, maniacs, alchemists, giant-slayers, and their ilk." circ. 200-300. 3/yr. Pub'd 2 issues 1998; expects 3 issues 1999, 3 issues 2000. sub. price: $15; per copy: $5; sample: $5. Back issues: available on request. Discounts: on request. 45pp; 8½×11. Reporting time: 1 month. Simultaneous submissions accepted: yes. Publishes 2-3% of manuscripts submitted. Payment: 1 copy of issue in which they appear.

Copyrighted, reverts to author. Pub's reviews. §Poetry, fiction, artwork. Ads: $100/$50/$25. Table of Sin.

THIRD COAST, Kathleen McGookey, Managing Editor; Darrin Doyle, Fiction Editor, Department of English, Western Michigan University, Kalamazoo, MI 49008-5092, 616-387-2675; Fax 616-387-2562; www.wmich.edu/thirdcoast. 1995. Poetry, fiction, art, interviews, parts-of-novels, long-poems, non-fiction. "For fiction, we're interested in both short-shorts & novel excerpts, as well as stories of traditional length. Recent contributors include Reginald Shepherd, Robin Behn, Gian Lombardo, Sara McAulay, Richard Lyons, and Beth Lee Simon." circ. 500. 2/yr. Pub'd 2 issues 1998; expects 2 issues 1999, 2 issues 2000. sub. price: $11; per copy: $6; sample: $6. Back issues: $5. Discounts: classroom - $5/issue. 150pp; 6×9; typeset. Reporting time: 12 weeks. Simultaneous submissions accepted: yes. Publishes 2-5% of manuscripts submitted. Payment: 2 copies, year subscription, discounted copies. Not copyrighted. Pub's reviews. §Poetry and fiction. Ads: negotiable - will consider ad swaps. MLA, AWP.

THE THIRD HALF, K.T. Publications, Kevin Troop, "Amikeco", 16, Fane Close, Stamford, Lincs., PE9 1HG, England, (01780) 754193. 1987. Poetry, fiction. "Length of stories: up to 2,000 words. Poems: up to 40 lines. Recent contributors: Michael Newman, Lee Bridges, David Lightfoot, Vladimir Orlov, Pauline Kirk, John C. Desmond, Joan Board, Kenneth C. Steven, Isabel Cortan, Kat Ricker. Well-written stories or poems in good English is the aim!" circ. varies. 1-2/yr. Pub'd 3 issues 1998; expects 3 issues 1999, 3 issues 2000. sub. price: £5.50 by post in Britain, £8 overseas; per copy: £5.50, £8 overseas; sample: £5.50, £8 overseas. Back issues: same. Discounts: available on request. 100+pp; size A5; of. Reporting time: as quickly as humanly possible. Simultaneous submissions accepted: no. Publishes about 10% of manuscripts submitted. Payment: free copy of the relevant issue/issues. Copyrighted, reverts to author.

Third Side Press, Inc., Midge Stocker, Publisher, 2250 West Farragut, Chicago, IL 60625, 773-271-3029; FAX 773-271-0459; E-mail ThirdSide@aol.com. 1991. Fiction, non-fiction. "Third Side Press publishes books with a feminist perspective, focusing on women's health (broadly defined, to include not only disease and psychology but also economics and spirituality) and lesbian fiction (which we define as written by a lesbian and having at least one central character who is lesbian). We have published nonfiction anthologies, as well as books with a single author. We are not currently seeking new projects. Representative fiction: *Not So Much the Fall* by Kerry Hart, and *The Mayor of Heaven* by Lynn Kanter. Representative nonfiction: *Beyond Bedlam*, and *SomeBody to Love: A Guide to Loving the Body You Have* by Leslea Newman" avg. press run 3M. Pub'd 2 titles 1998. 11 titles listed in the *Small Press Record of Books in Print* (28th Edition, 1999-00). avg. price, cloth: $29; paper: $12. Discounts: set by Consortium, our distributor 1-800-283-3572. 224pp; 5½×8½; of. Reporting time: variable, generally within 6 months. Simultaneous submissions accepted: yes. Publishes 1% of manuscripts submitted. Payment: by contract. Copyrights for author.

THIRST (CYBERTHIRST), Carpe Diem Publishing, William A. Conner, Jessica E. Griffin, 1705 E. 17th Street, #400, The Dalles, OR 97058, 503-296-1552; waconner@aol.com. 1996. Poetry, fiction, articles, cartoons, interviews, satire, criticism, reviews, music, letters, parts-of-novels, long-poems, news items, non-fiction. "Pencillers, inkers and comic based proffesionals always welcome" circ. 800-1M. 6/yr. Pub'd 1 issue 1998; expects 6 issues 1999. price per copy: $2.95; sample: $2.50. 32pp; 8×7. Reporting time: 3-12 months. Simultaneous submissions accepted: yes. Publishes 40-55% of manuscripts submitted. Payment: varies, depending on subject and format. Copyrighted. Pub's reviews: 2 in 1998. §Music, youth culture (15+), sci-fiction, political and non-fiction in general. Ads: $200 b/w, $250 f/c/$100 b/w, $150 f/c. PMA.

Thirteen Colonies Press, John F. Millar, 710 South Henry Street, Williamsburg, VA 23185, 804-229-1775. 1986. Art, music, non-fiction. "We specialize in popular history (non-fiction) from the period of the Renaissance up to 1800." avg. press run 3M. Pub'd 2 titles 1998; expects 3 titles 1999, 3 titles 2000. 4 titles listed in the *Small Press Record of Books in Print* (28th Edition, 1999-00). avg. price, cloth: $30; paper: $20. Discounts: retailer 40% up to 24 copies, 45% 24+ copies; wholesaler 20% up to 6 copies, 50% up to 24 copies, 60% 24+ copies; libraries 10% 1 book, 2+ books 30%. 200pp; 6×9 to 12×12; of. Payment: 10% gross sales, paid quarterly on previous quarter's sales. Copyrights for author. PMA.

13TH MOON, Judith E. Johnson, Editor, 1400 Washington Avenue, SUNY, English Department, Albany, NY 12222-0001, 518-442-4181. 1973. Poetry, fiction, articles, art, photos, interviews, criticism, reviews, parts-of-novels, long-poems, plays, news items, non-fiction. "Current issues include work by Josephine Jacobsen, Lyn Lifshin, Lori Anderson, Kim Vaseth, Carolyn Beard Whitlow, Nell Altizer, Toi Derricotte, Judith Barrington, Ethel Schwabacher, Sallie Bingham, Lavonne Mueller, Star Olderman, Cassandra Medley, Courtland Jessup, Alicia Ostriker, Laurel Speer, Kathleene West, Ursula K. LeGuin, Chitra Divakaruni, E.M. Broner, Susan Montez and Frances Sherwood. Volume XI, Nos. 1 & 2, features translations of the work of Italian women writers and a special sectin on Feminist Fiction(s). Future issues will feature work by Eastern European and Caribbean women writers and feminist politics." circ. 1.5M. 1 double-issue per year. Pub'd 1 issue 1998; expects 1 issue 1999. sub. price: $10 for 1 double issue; per copy: $10; sample: $10. Back issues: $10. Discounts: varies. 275pp; 6×9; of. Reporting time: 2 weeks to 4 months. Payment: copies. Copyrighted, reverts to author. Pub's reviews: 3 in 1998. §Poetry by women small press books by women/literature by women/women's literary history by women. Ads: $200/$125. CLMP.

32 PAGES, Michael S. Manley, 2127 W. Pierce Avenue #2B, Chicago, IL 60622-1824, 773-276-9005; 32pp@rain-crow-publishing.com; www.rain-crow-publishing.com/32pp/. 1997. Poetry, fiction, letters, plays, non-fiction. "Personal essay and new journalism only for nonfiction." circ. 1M. 6/yr. Pub'd 4 issues 1998; expects 6 issues 1999, 6 issues 2000. sub. price: $10; per copy: $2.50; sample: $2.50. 32pp; 8½x11; of. Reporting time: 3 months. Simultaneous submissions accepted: yes. Publishes 10% of manuscripts submitted. Payment: $5/page, copies and subscription. Copyrighted, reverts to author. Ads: $100 1/2 page/$50 1/4 page. CLMP, Small Publisher's Co-op.

THIS IS IMPORTANT, F.A. Nettelbeck, Editor, PO Box 336, Sprague River, OR 97639, 503-533-2486. 1980. Poetry. "Patterned after a religious tract and features one poem from six different poets each issue. The pamphlets are distributed on buses, subways, toilet floors, in laundromats, bars, theaters, etc., with the aim being to get poetry out to non-literary types and others. Some of the featured poets have included: William S. Burroughs, Richard Kostelanetz, Wanda Coleman, Todd Moore, Tom Clark, John Giorno, Lyn Lifshin, David Fisher, James Bertolino, John M. Bennett, Jack Micheline, Ann Menebroker, Judson Crews, Anselm Hollo, Flora Durham, Charles Bernstein, Robin Holcomb, Michael McClure, Douglas Blazek, James Grauerholz, Nila Northsun, Allen Ginsberg...as well as many others. Send poems. We want it *all* as long as it's *small...but, make me cry*. Make checks payable to F.A. Nettelbeck." circ. 1M. 4/yr. Pub'd 2 issues 1998; expects 2 issues 1999, 2 issues 2000. sub. price: $10; per copy: SASE; sample: $1. Back issues: individual issues vary in price, when available. Limited complete sets of Issues #1-#16 are available for $100 per set. Discounts: none. 8pp; 2¾x4¼; of. Reporting time: immediate. Payment: 50 copies. Copyrighted, reverts to author.

Thistledown Press Ltd., Allan Forrie, Production Manager; Glen Sorestad, President; Sonia Sorestad, Treasurer; Patrick O'Rourke, Editor-in-Chief, 633 Main Street, Saskatoon, Saskatchewan S7H 0J8, Canada, 306-244-1722. 1975. Poetry, fiction. "Canadian authors only." avg. press run 1M. Pub'd 8 titles 1998; expects 8 titles 1999. 107 titles listed in the *Small Press Record of Books in Print* (28th Edition, 1999-00). avg. price, paper: $13 poetry, $18 fiction. Discounts: bookstores 1-4 20%, 5+ 40% (with return privilege), 50% (non-returnable); jobbers 40%. Poetry 80pp, prose 176pp; 5½x8½; of. Reporting time: 8-12 weeks. Simultaneous submissions accepted: no. Publishes 3-5% of manuscripts submitted. Payment: 10% of list. Copyrights for author. ACP, LPG, SPG.

Thomas Jefferson University Press, Paula Presley, Director-Editor in Chief; Nancy Reschley, Marketing-Poetry Editor, Truman State University, 100 East Normal Street, Kirksville, MO 63501, 816-785-4665; FAX 816-785-4181. 1986. Poetry, art, photos, criticism, non-fiction. "Recent contributors: Betty Alt, Harold Pagliaro, and William Baer." avg. press run 750. Pub'd 9 titles 1998; expects 10 titles 1999, 10 titles 2000. 8 titles listed in the *Small Press Record of Books in Print* (28th Edition, 1999-00). avg. price, cloth: $40; paper: $20. Discounts: 20%; 2 to 10 copies= 30%; 11 and more= 40%; 100+= 50%. 350pp; 6x9; camera ready copy. Reporting time: 3 months. Simultaneous submissions accepted: no. Publishes 10% of manuscripts submitted. Payment: 15%-20% of gross sales after production cost regained. Does not copyright for author.

Thorntree Press, Eloise Bradley Fink, John Dickson, 547 Hawthorn Lane, Winnetka, IL 60093, 708-446-8099. 1985. Poetry. "Sorry, our Troika Competition is temporarily discontinued." avg. press run 1M. 18 titles listed in the *Small Press Record of Books in Print* (28th Edition, 1999-00). avg. price, paper: $5.95. Discounts: to be arranged. 96pp; 6x9; mi. Payment: no editor or poet is paid. Copyrights for author.

THORNY LOCUST, Silvia Kofler, Editor; Celeste Kuechler, Assistant Editor, PO Box 32631, Kansas City, MO 64171-5631, 816-756-5096. 1993. "Looking for material with some bite, no sweetness unless its the sugar-coating on a strychnine pill" circ. 150. 4/yr. Expects 1 issue 1999, 4 issues 2000. sub. price: $15; sample: $3. 28-32pp; 7x8½; †photocopy. Reporting time: 4-12 weeks. We accept simultaneous submissions, but previously unpublished material only. Publishes 20% of manuscripts submitted. Payment: copy. Copyrighted, reverts to author. Ads: none.

THOUGHTS FOR ALL SEASONS: The Magazine of Epigrams, Michel Paul Richard, Editor-in-Chief; Roger Wescott, Ray Mizer, 478 NE 56th Street, Miami, FL 33137-2621, 305-756-8800. 1976. Articles, art, satire. "Form: One sentence or one paragraph original thoughts. Art work: Pen and ink." circ. 1M. Irregular, special issues. Expects 1 issue 1999. sub. price: $4.75 + $1.25 p/h; per copy: $4.75 + $1.25 p/h; sample: $4.75 + $1.25 p/h. Back issues: Vol. 2&3 available $3.75 + $1.25 p/h. Discounts: none. 84pp; 5½x8½; of. Reporting time: 30 days. Simultaneous submissions accepted: yes. Publishes 20% of manuscripts submitted. Payment: 1 free copy of magazine. Copyrighted, reverts to author. §Epigrams and aphorisms, as well as essays on the epigram as a literary form. Ads: $125/$80.

A Thousand Autumns Press, Chiaki Takeuchi, Publisher; Yagu Jube, General Manager, Chiaki International, Inc., 7564 Placid Street, Las Vegas, NV 89123, 702-361-0676. 1988. Fiction, non-fiction. avg. press run 2M. Pub'd 1 title 1998; expects 1 title 1999, 1 title 2000. 3 titles listed in the *Small Press Record of Books in Print*

(28th Edition, 1999-00). avg. price, cloth: $19.95; other: $19.95. Discounts: 20%-40%. 300pp; 5½×8½. Reporting time: 30 days (really not looking now). Payment: 10%, no advance. Copyrights for author. PMA, American Booksellers Association.

Three Pyramids Publishing, 201 Kenwood Meadows Drive, Raleigh, NC 27603-8314, 919-773-2080; Fax 919-779-9508; E-mail JFS999@mindspring.com. 1989. Non-fiction. "Trade paperbacks on New Age, occult, metaphysics, tarot, spiritual and associated topics. Practical advice, how-to information. 64-200 pages average. Manuscripts must be on IBM-compatible disks. Will read submissions, prefer query letter & sample chapter first" avg. press run 500-3M. Pub'd 1 title 1998; expects 3 titles 1999, 3 titles 2000. 3 titles listed in the *Small Press Record of Books in Print* (28th Edition, 1999-00). avg. price, paper: $15.95. Discounts: trade 3-299 40%, 300-499 50%, 500+ 55%. 200pp; 5½×8½, 8½×11. Reporting time: 2 weeks to 1 month. We accept simultaneous submissions if noted when submitting. Payment: 10% net; no advance. Copyrights for author. PMA, Small Press Center, SPAN.

THE THREEPENNY REVIEW, Wendy Lesser, Editor; Paul Bowles, Consulting Editor; John Berger, Consulting Editor; Frank Bidart, Consulting Editor; Anne Carson, Consulting Editor; Elizabeth Hardwick, Consulting Editor; Robert Hass, Consulting Editor; Grace Paley, Consulting Editor; Gore Vidal, Consulting Editor, PO Box 9131, Berkeley, CA 94709, 510-849-4545. 1979. Poetry, fiction, art, interviews, criticism, reviews. "Length of material: Reviews should be 1M-3M words, covering several books or an author in depth, or dealing with a whole topic (e.g., the current theater season in one city, or the state of jazz clubs in another). Fiction should be under 5M words; poems should be under 100 lines. Special features: Though primarily a literary and performing arts review, *The Threepenny Review* will contain at least one essay on a topic of current social or political concern in each issue. Interested essayists should first submit a letter of inquiry. Recent Contributors: John Berger, Thom Gunn, Amy Tan. *SASE must accompany all manuscripts.*" circ. 10M. 4/yr. Pub'd 4 issues 1998; expects 4 issues 1999, 4 issues 2000. sub. price: $20, $35/2 years; per copy: $5; sample: $7. Back issues: variable (price list available). 40pp; 11×17; of. Reporting time: 2 weeks to 2 months. Payment: $100-$200. Copyrighted, reverts to author. Pub's reviews: 20 in 1998. §Fiction, poetry, essays, philosophy, social theory, visual arts and architecture, history, criticism. Ads: $900/$500. CLMP.

Threshold Books, Edmund Helminski, 3108 Tater Lane, Guilford, VT 05301, 802-254-8300; Fax 802-257-2779. 1981. Poetry, fiction, music, non-fiction. "Additional address: RR 4 Box 600, Putney, VT 05346. Most recent publications include translations of Rumi. Interested in World literature of high quality, spiritual and philosophical works from Eastern and Western traditions; books of cultural importance." avg. press run 4M. Pub'd 2 titles 1998; expects 3 titles 1999, 2 titles 2000. 18 titles listed in the *Small Press Record of Books in Print* (28th Edition, 1999-00). avg. price, cloth: $18; paper: $12. Discounts: 40% trade. 160pp; 5½×8½; of, lp. Reporting time: 60 days. Publishes 5% of manuscripts submitted. Payment: 10-15%. Copyrights for author. SSP.

THRESHOLDS JOURNAL, SOM Publishing, division of School of Metaphysics, Dr. Barbara Condron, Editor-in-Chief; Dr. Laurel Fuller Clark, Managing Editor, HCR 1, Box 15, Windyville, MO 65783, 417-345-8411. 1975. "Quarterly Themes: Dreams, Visions, Creative Imagery; Wholeness and Healing; Intuitive Arts; Spirituality and Global Issues. Submissions in eight categories considered: Arts and Sciences, Business, Health, Creative Writing, Humor, Personal Insight, Education (Most Influential Teacher), Scholar's Report. Double-spaced, typed manuscripts 5-10 pages in length. Interview with well-known people who are successful in their fields. Recent interviews with Bernie Siegel, Diane Stein, Fred Pryor, Raymond Moody, Deena Metzger, Barbara Max Hubbard, Swami Beyondananda, Dalai Lama." circ. 5M+. 4/yr. Pub'd 4 issues 1998; expects 4 issues 1999, 4 issues 2000. sub. price: by membership in School of Metaphysics Association (SOMA) only; per copy: subscription only; sample: on request. Back issues: $5 for available issues. Discounts: available only through SOMA. 32pp; 7×10; †of. Reporting time: 5 weeks-3 months. Payment: if accepted, international exposure, up to 5 complimentary issues, membership to SOMA ($60 value). Copyrighted, does not revert to author. Pub's reviews: 20 in 1998. §Self-development, personal insight, metaphysics, health, fiction, astrology. classified only, by donation to School of Metaphysics.

Thunder & Ink, Tim Burke, Publisher; Ann Burke, Illustrator, PO Box 7014, Evanston, IL 60201. 1988. Fiction. "Children's fiction." avg. press run 1-2M. Expects 2 titles 2000. 1 title listed in the *Small Press Record of Books in Print* (28th Edition, 1999-00). avg. price, paper: $5. Discounts: trade 30-40%, jobber 40-60%. 32pp; size varies; of. Payment: to be arranged. Copyrights for author.

Thunder Rain Publishing Corp., Katherine (Rhi) Christoffel, Russell A. Louden, PO Box 1407, Denham Springs, LA 70727-1407, 504-686-2002; Fax 686-2285; E-mail rhi@earthlink.net. 1996. Poetry, fiction, art, photos, letters, long-poems, non-fiction. "*Beyond Magnolias* ISBN 0-9654569 by Katherine Christoffel & Thurman Mizzell, Jr. A poetry book based on life, dreams, and fantasies - Published October 1996. Presently accepting submissions for Louisiana Poetry book, send SASE for guidelines or web pages at *http://home.earthlink.net/rhi/thrain/index.htm.* Upcoming publications: book of Short Stories, Novel, Louisiana Poetry Book. Works with a network of freelance artists to bring recognition to new and unpublished writers."

avg. press run 2M. Pub'd 1 title 1998; expects 2-3 titles 1999, 3-4 titles 2000. avg. price, paper: $14.95. Discounts: trade @ 40-60%. 20pp; 5½x8½. Reporting time: 30-60 days. Simultaneous submissions accepted: yes. Payment: 5-20% on net/outright purchase. Copyrights for author. ABA.

Tia Chucha Press, Luis J. Rodriguez, PO Box 476969, Chicago, IL 60647, 773-377-2496. 1989. Poetry, fiction. "A project of The Guild Complex, a not-for-profit corporation. Distributed by: Northwestern University Press, 625 Colfax, Evanston, IL 60208; 800-621-2736; FAX 800-621-8476." avg. press run 1M. Pub'd 3 titles 1998; expects 3 titles 1999, 4 titles 2000. 28 titles listed in the *Small Press Record of Books in Print* (28th Edition, 1999-00). avg. price, paper: $10.95. 64pp; 6×9. Reporting time: 6 weeks to 6 months. We accept simultaneous submissions, but we must be informed if another publisher is interested. Publishes .05% of manuscripts submitted. Payment: 10% royalties, discount on books. Copyrights for author. CLMP.

Tiare Publications, Gerry L. Dexter, President, PO Box 493, Lake Geneva, WI 53147, 414-248-4845. 1986. Non-fiction. "Publish radio communications and radio communications monitoring books. General non-fiction (Limelight Books); Jazz bands (Balboa Books)" avg. press run 2M. Pub'd 14 titles 1998; expects 2 titles 1999, 2 titles 2000. avg. price, paper: $16.95. Discounts: standard. 100pp; 5½x8½, 8½x11; of. Reporting time: 1 month. Simultaneous submissions accepted: no. Payment: 15% royalty. Publisher holds copyright.

Tickerwick Publications, Gayle Bachicha, PO Box 100695, Denver, CO 80250, 303-761-9940. 1994. Fiction, non-fiction. "Our primary focus is publishing spiritual/metaphysical fiction and non-fiction, including some astrology. Lesbian fiction is an area we will do a few titles. We intend to publish books of talent and quality and will be very choosy about the quality and depth of any manuscript we accept. We are wanting new authors more than established authors, but will accept both" avg. press run 2-3M. Expects 4 titles 1999, 4-6 titles 2000. 5 titles listed in the *Small Press Record of Books in Print* (28th Edition, 1999-00). avg. price, cloth: $14.95; paper: $9.95; other: $24.95 textbooks. Discounts: inquire by mail. 64-250pp; 4x5½, 6x9; of. Reporting time: 60 days. Payment: submit inquiry by mail. Does not copyright for author. NAPRA, CIPA.

Ticket to Adventure, Inc., Anne Wright, Administrative V.P.; Mary Miller, Director, PO Box 41005, St. Petersburg, FL 33743, 813-822-1515. 1986. Non-fiction. "Minimum length: 124 pages. Target market: job seekers, college students, career changers, females age 17-42. Specific, how to gain employment, tips and advice from experts. No general overview. We desire bibliography, index, glossary, charts, photos. Travel, fun and unusual occupations. Include brief outline of marketing plan" avg. press run 5M-10M. Pub'd 1 title 1998; expects 2 titles 1999, 3 titles 2000. 1 title listed in the *Small Press Record of Books in Print* (28th Edition, 1999-00). avg. price, paper: $12.95. 160-224pp; 6×9; of, direct disk to film. Reporting time: query 1 month, proposal 2 months, manuscript 3 months; query first, no unsolicited manuscripts. Payment: % wholesale, buy outright/rights. Copyrights for author. PMA.

Tide Book Publishing Company, Rose Safran, Box 101, York Harbor, ME 03911-0101, 207-363-4534. 1979. Articles, art, interviews, news items, non-fiction. "Currently specializing in popular sociological issues. Most recent title is *Don't Go Dancing Mother* by Rose Safran; subject matter is social gerontology. All titles will be brief. Line drawings are used. Will produce only quality trade paperbacks." avg. press run 2M-5M. Expects 1 title 1999. 1 title listed in the *Small Press Record of Books in Print* (28th Edition, 1999-00). avg. price, paper: $9.95. Discounts: 20% single copy trade, 40% 5+ copies trade, jobber 50-55%, salesman 10% of the net sale, inquire about bulk. 100pp; 6×9; lp. Reporting time: ASAP. Payment: no fixed arrangements. Copyrights for author. NESPA.

TIERRA DEL FUEGO MAGAZINE, Zagier & Urruty Publicaciones, Sergio Zagier, Dario Urruty, PO Box 94 Sucursal 19, Buenos Aires 1419, Argentina, 541-572-1050. 1989. Articles, photos, reviews, non-fiction. "We need manuscripts about travel subjects concerning southern South America and Antarctica. Also photos and drawings. Any language. Maximum 3 letter pages." circ. 7M. 1/yr. Pub'd 1 issue 1998; expects 1 issue 1999, 2 issues 2000. sub. price: $8; per copy: $8; sample: $8. Back issues: $8. Discounts: 50% distributors, 30% bookstores, 20% travel companies and institutions. 84pp; 8x11½; of. Reporting time: 6 weeks. Payment: depends on the kind of work. Copyrighted, reverts to author. Pub's reviews: 3 in 1998. §Travel, South America, Antarctica, cruises, fishing, natural history, adventour. Ads: $1,150/$600/$2,500 back cover.

TIGER MOON, Tiger Moon, Terry Kennedy, Publisher, 3/677 Coconut Grove, Prasanthi Nilayam A.P. 515134, India. 1991. Poetry, fiction, articles, interviews, non-fiction. "We are looking for work that big houses simply can't risk running. We are not a vanity or subsidy press but we help the author self publish. We consider ourselves service oriented—serving *real* needs of writers as well as readers" Pub'd 5 issues 1998. sub. price: $100; per copy: $25; sample: $10. Back issues: $12. Discounts: our books are available free to prisons and we give discounts to people who will write to us directly. Reporting time: within 2 months. Publishes 90% of manuscripts submitted. Payment: copies; but you can collect the cover price at readings or direct selling. Copyrighted, reverts to author. Pub's reviews: 1 in 1998. §Native American, spiritual, poetry, fiction, Asian, Indian. Ads: $2000 full page.

Tiger Moon (see also TIGER MOON), Terry Kennedy, 3/677 Coconut Grove, Prasanthi Nilayam A.P., India.

1991. Poetry, fiction, non-fiction. "We are looking for work that big houses simply can't risk running. We are not a vanity or subsidy press but we help the author self publish. We consider ourselves service-oriented—serving *real* needs of writers as well as readers." avg. press run 1M. Pub'd 4 titles 1998; expects 5 titles 1999. 2 titles listed in the *Small Press Record of Books in Print* (28th Edition, 1999-00). avg. price, cloth: $19.99; paper: $24. 100-200pp; size varies. Reporting time: 2 months. Simultaneous submissions accepted: yes. Publishes 90% of manuscripts submitted. Payment: copies. Copyrights for author.

Tiger Press, Harry Monteith, 803 Sherwick Terrace, Suite 101, Manchester, MO 63021, 314-394-4191. 1995. Non-fiction. avg. press run 2M. Pub'd 1 title 1998; expects 1 title 1999, 2 titles 2000. 2 titles listed in the *Small Press Record of Books in Print* (28th Edition, 1999-00). avg. price, cloth: $25; paper: $13. Discounts: 40% wholesale. 176-256pp; 6×9, 8½×11. Reporting time: 1 month. Simultaneous submissions accepted: yes. Payment: varies. Copyrights for author.

TIGHTROPE, Swamp Press, Ed Rayher, 323 Pelham Road, Amherst, MA 01002. 1975. Poetry, art, long-poems. "Fine poetry and graphic art printed by letterpress in artistic and sometimes unconventional formats. Recent contributors: Julie Juarez, Alan Catlin." circ. 350. 2/yr. Pub'd 1 issue 1998; expects 2 issues 1999, 2 issues 2000. sub. price: $10; per copy: $6; sample: $6. Back issues: $6. Discounts: bookstores and dealers 40%. 36pp; size varies; †lp. Reporting time: 8 weeks. Publishes 1% of manuscripts submitted. Payment: copies. Copyrighted, reverts to author. Pub's reviews: 0 in 1998. §Poetry.

Tilbury House, Publishers, Jennifer Elliott, 132 Water Street, Gardiner, ME 04345, 207-582-1899. 1990. Non-fiction. "Tilbury House, Publishers publishes adult non-fiction books about Maine and the Northeast, and nonfiction children's picture books that deal with issues of cultural diversity and the environment." avg. press run 2.5M-10M. Pub'd 3 titles 1998; expects 10 titles 1999, 8 titles 2000. 49 titles listed in the *Small Press Record of Books in Print* (28th Edition, 1999-00). avg. price, cloth: $26.95; paper: $16.95. Discounts: returnable, non-returnable, text orders, STOP orders, libraries. 200pp; size varies; of, lp. Reporting time: 2 months. Simultaneous submissions accepted: yes. Publishes 1.5% of manuscripts submitted. Payment: 7.5-15%. Copyrights for author. MWPA, ABC, NEBA, ABA.

TIMBER CREEK REVIEW, J.M. Freiermuth, Editor; Celestine Woo, Associate Editor, c/o J.M. Freiermuth, 3283 UNCG Station, Greensboro, NC 27413, 336-334-6970. 1994. Poetry, fiction, articles, photos, cartoons, interviews, satire, letters, non-fiction. "*Timber Creek Review* is a quarterly collection of short stories with a few poems. Contributors in the fourth year include Geoffrey Clark, D.L. Nelson, Paul B.Price, Lisa Madsen de Rubilar, Bruce Tucker, Karl Nilsson, Catherine Uroff, Roslyn Willett. Send all correspondence and make all checks payable to: J.M. Freiermuth. Published 43 stories in 1998-99." circ. 150-180. 4/yr. Pub'd 4 issues 1998; expects 4 issues 1999, 4 issues 2000. sub. price: $15 individuals, $16 institutions and Canada, $22 international; per copy: $4.25; sample: $4.25. Discounts: 50% for creative writing classes and groups. 76-84pp; 5½×8½; †xerographic, laserprinter. Reporting time: from the next mail to 4 months. Simultaneous submissions accepted: yes. Publishes 8-12% of manuscripts submitted. Payment: 1 year subscription for first story, 1 copy for poems, additional short stories and short-short stories to 2 pages. Pays $25 to $50 for stories, including annual subscription. Not copyrighted. Pub's reviews: 0 in 1998. §Books of short stories. Ads: none.

Timber Press, Dale Johnson, Acquisitions Editor; Neal Maillet, Aquisitions Editor, 133 SW Second Avenue, Suite 450, Portland, OR 97204-3527. 1976. Art, photos, non-fiction. "Other imprints: Dioscorides Press, Amadeus Press. Main emphasis is Northwestern subject matter, horticulture, forestry, botany, classical music." avg. press run 5M. Pub'd 60 titles 1998; expects 60 titles 1999, 60 titles 2000. avg. price, cloth: $32.95; paper: $22.95. Discounts: 1 20%, 5 40%, 25 42%, 100 43%, 250 44%, 500 46%. 275pp; 8×5, 8½×11; of. Reporting time: 2 months. Simultaneous submissions accepted: yes. Payment: by arrangement. Copyrights for author. Pacific Northwestern Publications Assn. (PNWPA), RMPA, PNBA.

TIMBER TIMES, Steven R. Gatke, PO Box 219, Hillsboro, OR 97123. 1992. Articles, photos, cartoons, interviews, reviews, news items, non-fiction. circ. 2.7M. 4/yr. Pub'd 4 issues 1998; expects 4 issues 1999, 4 issues 2000. sub. price: $19; per copy: $4.75; sample: $6. Back issues: $6. Discounts: 40% on minimum quantity of 5 to all retailers. 52pp; 8½×11; of. Simultaneous submissions accepted: yes. Publishes 90+% of manuscripts submitted. Payment: 1 yr. subscription. Copyrighted, reverts to author. Pub's reviews: 20 in 1998. §Railroad, logging, lumbering, forestry. Ads: $125/$65/$35 1/4 page/$20 1/8 page.

Timberline Press, Clarence Wolfshohl, 6281 Red Bud, Fulton, MO 65251, 573-642-5035. 1975. Poetry, non-fiction. "Print chapbooks of 20-50 pages (prefer shorter 20-30 pp). We look at all poetry sent, but lean toward nature poetry with a sense of place or good lyrical, imagistic poetry. Actually, our taste is eclectic with quality being our primary criterion. We also publish short essays of natural history (under 20 pages) which will be printed in a reduced size format (not miniature). No set preference, but possible contributors should be familiar with better contemporary writers of natural history." avg. press run 200. Pub'd 2 titles 1998; expects 2 titles 1999, 2 titles 2000. 12 titles listed in the *Small Press Record of Books in Print* (28th Edition, 1999-00). avg. price, paper: $7.50-$10. Discounts: 1-4 books 25%, 5+ 40%. 25-45pp; 5½×7, 6×9; †lp. Reporting time: 30

days. Payment: 50-50 split after expenses. Does not copyright for author.

TIME FOR RHYME, Richard W. Unger, Editor, c/o Richard Unger, PO Box 1055, Battleford SK S0M 0E0, Canada, 306-445-5172. 1995. Poetry. "This is a handcrafted, pocket-sized quarterly magazine that publishes *only* rhyming poetry. Writer's guidelines or advertisers guidelines available with SASE (IRC or $1US acceptable from non-Canadians without Canadian postage)." circ. 80. 4/yr. Pub'd 4 issues 1998; expects 4 issues 1999, 4 issues 2000. sub. price: $12 Cdn. for Canadians, $12US for Americans, $17.50 Cdn. for overseas; per copy: $3.25 with SASE, Americans use either Canadian postage or IRCs; sample: same. Back issues: same. 32pp; 4×5½; †lp, photocopy. Reporting time: as quickly as possible. Simultaneous submissions accepted: no. Publishes 25% of manuscripts submitted. Payment: 1 copy (when financially viable, will consider cash payment). Copyrighted, reverts to author. Pub's reviews: 5 in 1998. §Those mostly or entirely containing rhyming poetry (either new or old with artwork). Ads: classifieds 15¢/word.

TIME HAIKU, Dr. Erica Facey, 105, Kings Head Hill, London E4 7JG, England, 0181-529-6478. 1994. Poetry, articles, reviews. "Aimed at the experts. Some recent contributors: Gavin Ewart, Dan Pugh, Chris Sykes, Douglas Johnson, M. Kettner, John Light." 2/yr. Pub'd 2 issues 1998; expects 2 issues 1999, 2 issues 2000. sub. price: £10 USA; per copy: £5. Back issues: £5 per copy. Discounts: none. 36pp; 5.8×8.3; †computing. Reporting time: 6 months. Simultaneous submissions accepted: yes. Publishes 80% of manuscripts submitted. Payment: none. Copyrighted, reverts to author. Pub's reviews: 2 in 1998. §Haiku poem books. Ads: £50/£25.

TIME PILOT, Gary Bryant, 1050 Larrabee Avenue #104-354, Bellingham, WA 98225-7367. 1992. Fiction, articles, satire, reviews, letters, news items. "Science fiction newspaper with publication date 500 years from now" circ. 3.5M. 10/yr. Pub'd 3 issues 1998; expects 12 issues 1999, 12 issues 2000. sub. price: $10; per copy: $1; sample: $1. Back issues: $2. Discounts: 35% quantities of 50+. 8-12pp; 8½×11; 1p. Reporting time: 6-8 weeks. Publishes 50% of manuscripts submitted. Payment: 1 year subscription - entry into award competition. Copyrighted, does not revert to author. Pub's reviews: 3 in 1998. §All areas of science, politics, education. Ads: $250/$150/$1.

●**TIME TRAVELER, Media Arts Publishing,** Frank Dibari, PO Box 4765, Clearwater, FL 33758, e-mail frankie1@mindspring.com. 1990.

Timeless Books, Rita Foran, Editor; Julie McKay, Editor; Karin Lenman, Editor, PO Box 3543, Spokane, WA 99220-3543, 509-838-6652; info@timeless.org. 1977. Non-fiction. "Timeless publications are for those who seek a deeper meaning and purpose to their lives. Our focus is on the ancient teachings of yoga and Buddhism. Inspiration is combined with practical tools for living a life of quality to bring out the best in ourselves and others." avg. press run 5M books, 1M booklets. Pub'd 6 titles 1998; expects 2 titles 2000. 15 titles listed in the *Small Press Record of Books in Print* (28th Edition, 1999-00). avg. price, cloth: $22.95; paper: $14.95; other: $5 booklets. Discounts: books and booklets, 45% over nine copies. 250pp; 6×9; of. Copyrights for author. PMA, NAPRA.

TIMELINES, Newsletter of the Hemlock Society U.S.A., Kris Larson, PO Box 11830, Eugene, OR 97440. 1980. Non-fiction. "Only articles on death with dignity are used. Will consider thoughtful submissions." circ. 40M. 6/yr. Pub'd 4 issues 1998; expects 4 issues 1999, 4 issues 2000. sub. price: $35; per copy: $3; sample: free. Back issues: $3. Discounts: none. 16pp; 8½×11; web offset. Reporting time: 3 weeks. Publishes 10% of manuscripts submitted. Payment: none, a non-profit educational group. Not copyrighted. Pub's reviews: 6 in 1998. §Voluntary euthanasia, assisted suicide. Ads: $2,500 full page.

Times Change Press, Michael J. Sherick, Editor & Publisher, 8453 Blackney Road, Sebastopol, CA 95472-4608. 1970. Criticism, non-fiction. "Times Change Press produces books on politics (leftist, sexual and ecological), culture, philosophy, history, music, and literature." avg. press run 3.5M. Expects 3 titles 1999, 6 titles 2000. 29 titles listed in the *Small Press Record of Books in Print* (28th Edition, 1999-00). avg. price, cloth: $13; paper: $6. Discounts: 1-4 copies 20%, 5+ 40%. 96pp; 5½×7, 5½×8½; of. Reporting time: 3 months. Payment: negotiable. Copyrights for author. PMA, Small Press Center.

The Times Journal Publishing Co., Darlene Melville, Managing Editor, PO Box 1286, Puyallup, WA 98371, 206-848-2779. 1946. Fiction, photos, non-fiction. "We are a subsidy publisher only and prefer a query letter. We will work closely with the author on editing, page layouts, cover design and promoting distribution." avg. press run 1200. Pub'd 1 title 1998; expects 2 titles 1999, 4 titles 2000. avg. price, paper: $13.95. Discounts: standard. 290pp; size denoted by author and contents. Reporting time: 3 months. Payment: individually negotiated. Copyrights for author.

TIMESHARE AND VACATION OWNERSHIP REVIEW, Keith Trowbridge, 11595 Kelly Road, Fort Myers, FL 33908, 941-454-1100; 941-466-3299; email orders@prefpress.com; web www.prefpress.com. 1997. Articles, reviews, non-fiction. circ. 5M. 2/yr. Expects 1 issue 1999, 2 issues 2000. sub. price: $29.95; per copy: $14.95; sample: $10. Back issues: $20. Discounts: available upon request. 150pp; 7×10. Reporting time: 2

months. Simultaneous submissions accepted: yes. Publishes 50% of manuscripts submitted. Payment: none. Copyrighted, reverts to author. Pub's reviews. §Vacations. Ads: $1,700/$975/$1250 2/3 page/$750 2/3 page/$3200 inside cover (full page only). American Resort and Development Association.

Tiptoe Literary Service, Anne Grimm-richardson, 434-6th Street #206, Raymond, WA 98577-1804, 360-942-4596; anne@willapabay.org; www.willapabay.org/~anne. 1985. "We publish how-to pamphlets. Please query with SASE. We can provide a link—free—to your Home Page or E-mail address. We also accept barter advertising. We list manuscripts and books available for reprint on our web site, with synopsis and links." avg. press run 1M. Pub'd 10 titles 1998; expects 6 titles 1999, 4 titles 2000. 60 titles listed in the *Small Press Record of Books in Print* (28th Edition, 1999-00). avg. price, paper: $7. Discounts: 20% for 2 or more. 12pp; 5½x3½; †computer typeset, photocopied. Reporting time: 30 days. Simultaneous submissions accepted: yes. Publishes 50% of manuscripts submitted. Payment: 5¢ per copy royalty, paid following year. Does not copyright for author. WAHPACWA - CWI (Wahkiakum Pacific Writers Association - Crossroads Writers International), Cascade Sydicate Associates.

TITIVILLITIA: Studies of Illiteracy in the Private Press, Erespin Press, David L. Kent, 6906 Colony Loop Drive, Austin, TX 78724. 1993. Articles, reviews, letters. "'The truest index to a printer's motive and artistic integrity is the extent to which he attends to the pedestrian details of his work.'" 4/yr. Pub'd 4 issues 1998; expects 4 issues 1999, 4 issues 2000. sub. price: $5. Discount schedule available on request. 3-6pp; 8½x11; †lp, photocopy. Not copyrighted. Pub's reviews: 46 in 1998. §Private press only. Amalgamated Printers' Association (APA).

TitleWaves Publishing, Rob Sanford, R. Stephen Sanford, PO Box 288, Lihue, HI 96766-0288, orders 800-867-7323. 1989. Poetry, fiction, photos, cartoons, news items, non-fiction. avg. press run 50M. Pub'd 1 title 1998; expects 3 titles 1999, 4 titles 2000. 2 titles listed in the *Small Press Record of Books in Print* (28th Edition, 1999-00). avg. price, paper: $18. Discounts: 3-299 40%, 300-499 50%, 500+ 55%, STOP orders 40% + $1.75/order. 235pp; 5½x8½, 8½x11; of. Reporting time: 30 days. Simultaneous submissions accepted: yes. Publishes 50% of manuscripts submitted. Payment: varies; better than standard. Copyrights for author. PMA, ABA.

Toad Hall, Inc. (see also Belfry Books; The Bradford Press; Hands & Heart Books; Toad Hall Press), Sharon Jarvis, RR 2 Box 2090, Laceyville, PA 18623, 717-869-2942; Fax 717-869-1031. 1995. Non-fiction. "Book-length only. Manuscripts by invitation only." avg. press run 3-5M. Pub'd 2 titles 1998; expects 4 titles 1999, 4 titles 2000. 8 titles listed in the *Small Press Record of Books in Print* (28th Edition, 1999-00). avg. price, paper: $14.95. Discounts: Books sold through Access Publishers Network; other discounts for bulk vary. 224pp; 6x9; of. Reporting time: 3 months. Simultaneous submissions accepted: no. Payment: $1000 advance and up, 10% royalty. Copyrights for author. PMA, SPAN, MABA, ABA.

Toad Hall Press (see also Toad Hall, Inc.), RR 2 Box 2090, Laceyville, PA 18623, 717-869-1031. 1995. Non-fiction. avg. press run 4M. Pub'd 1 title 1998; expects 2 titles 1999, 2 titles 2000. avg. price, paper: $14.95. 224pp; 6x9; of. Reporting time: 3 months. Payment: $1000 advance and 10% royalty. Copyrights for author. PMA, SPAN, MABA, ABA.

TODAY'S $85,000 FREELANCE WRITER, Brian S. Konradt, PO Box 554, Oradell, NJ 07649, 201-262-3277; bskcom@tiac.net. 1992. Non-fiction. *"Today's $85,000 Freelance Writer* is for the professional self-employed commercial copywriter (or anyone thinking about freelancing) who wants to boost sales, secure high-paying clients, cut competition, and operate a profitable writing/consulting business." circ. 5M. 6/yr. Pub'd 6 issues 1998; expects 6 issues 1999, 6 issues 2000. sub. price: $72; per copy: $12; sample: $12. Back issues: $12. 30pp; 8½x11; of. Reporting time: 1 month. Simultaneous submissions accepted: no. Payment: 5¢/word, 10¢/word for columnists. Copyrighted, reverts to author. Pub's reviews. §Business, consulting, writing, advertising, marketing. Ads: call for rates.

TOLE WORLD, EGW Publishing Company, Judy Swager, 1041 Shary Circle, Concord, CA 94518-2407, 510-671-9852. 1977. Poetry, art, photos, interviews, reviews, letters, non-fiction. "Creative designs for decorative paintings." circ. 90M. 6/yr. Pub'd 6 issues 1998; expects 6 issues 1999, 6 issues 2000. sub. price: $29.70; per copy: $4.95. 86pp; 8x10½; of, web. Reporting time: 2-6 weeks. Payment: upon publication, first serial rights. Copyrighted, reverts to author. Pub's reviews: 80 in 1998. Ads: $2595/$1661/$2.50 word.

Tomar House Publishers, M.J. Cushwa, Thomas Houle, 1034 Main Street North, Box 630, Southbury, CT 06488-0630, 203-262-6106. 1972. "Short practically written scientifically based psychological self-help, books and programs" avg. press run 1.5M. Pub'd 1 title 1998; expects 1 title 1999, 2 titles 2000. 8 titles listed in the *Small Press Record of Books in Print* (28th Edition, 1999-00). avg. price, paper: $10.95. 112pp; 6x9. Reporting time: varies. Payment: 15%. Does not copyright for author.

Tomart Publications, Tom Tumbusch, Jack Wade, Customer Service; Rebecca Trissel, Assistant to Publisher, 3300 Encrete Lane, Dayton, OH 45439-1944, 937-294-2250; Fax 937-294-1024. 1977. Non-fiction. "We are publishers of antique & collectible photo price guides for Disneyana (any Disney product), radio premiums, character glasses, space adventure collectibles, etc. Other non-fiction on related subjects. Books on musical theatre." avg. press run 6M-10M. Pub'd 3 titles 1998; expects 6 titles 1999, 5 titles 2000. 10 titles listed in the *Small Press Record of Books in Print* (28th Edition, 1999-00). avg. price, cloth: $39.95; paper: $27.95. Discounts: booksellers 40%, distributors up to 60%. 220pp; 8½×11; of. Reporting time: 30 days. Payment: 10% advance. Copyrights for author.

Tombouctou Books, Michael Wolfe, 1472 Creekview Lane, Santa Cruz, CA 95062, 408-476-4144. 1975. Poetry, fiction, interviews, long-poems. "No unsolicited mss. Distributed to the trade by Inland Book Co., POB 261, East Haven, CT 06512." avg. press run 500-2M. Pub'd 4 titles 1998; expects 4 titles 1999, 4 titles 2000. 17 titles listed in the *Small Press Record of Books in Print* (28th Edition, 1999-00). avg. price, cloth: $10; paper: $7; other: signed hardback, limited edition, $35. Discounts: inquire publisher. 48-200pp; 5½×8½; †of. Publishes 1% of manuscripts submitted. Payment: varies. Copyrights for author.

The Tonal Company, Donald G. Lindsay, Publisher, 5300 Cliffside Circle, PO Box 3233, Ventura, CA 93003, 805-644-1364. 1970. "Current book is: *Medical Cost Crisis! A Solution Before It's Too Late* which is a detailed, intelligent, and logical plan for solving the current American medical cost crisis, including providing medical care for everyone, preserving the patient's right to choose, decreasing the cost of medical care and insurance, and still maintaining a quality medical profession. The Tonal Company publishes books, audio tapes, CD-ROM, and computer programs in medical and related fields, including computer software for decision support systems" avg. press run 10M. Expects 1 title 1999, 3 titles 2000. 1 title listed in the *Small Press Record of Books in Print* (28th Edition, 1999-00). avg. price, cloth: $25; paper: $15. Discounts: 1-4 copies 20%, 5 or more copies 40%; wholesalers 50%. 288pp; 6×9. Reporting time: 6 weeks. Publishes 1% of manuscripts submitted. Payment: trade standard. Copyrights for author. PMA.

Top Of The Mountain Publishing, Dr. Tag Powell, Dr. Judith L. Powell, 11337 Starkey Road, Suite G2, Largo, FL 34643-4735, 813-391-3843, fax 813-391-4598. 1979. Non-fiction. avg. press run 5M. Pub'd 6 titles 1998; expects 20 titles 1999, 20 titles 2000. 21 titles listed in the *Small Press Record of Books in Print* (28th Edition, 1999-00). avg. price, cloth: $22.95; paper: $12.95. Discounts: standard. 250pp; 5½×8½; of. Reporting time: up to 6 months. Publishes 2% of manuscripts submitted. Payment: 8%-10% of net. Copyrights for author. PMA, ABA, PAS, International Publishers Alliance, Florida Publishers Group.

TOPICAL TIME, George Griffenhagen, Editor, 2501 Drexel Street, Vienna, VA 22180, 703-560-2413. 1949. Articles, photos, cartoons. "A magazine for stamp collectors who are interested in the subjects shown on stamps." circ. 8M. 6/yr. Pub'd 6 issues 1998; expects 6 issues 1999, 6 issues 2000. sub. price: $20, $25 overseas; per copy: $4; sample: $4. Back issues: $4. Discounts: inquire. 96pp; 5×8; of, lp. Reporting time: 2 weeks. Publishes 50% of manuscripts submitted. Payment: tearsheets of articles, no money. Copyrighted. Pub's reviews: 100 in 1998. §Stamp collecting books + periodicals. Ads: $190/$105/1/4 $60/classifieds 30¢/word. American Topical Association.

Topping International Institute, Inc., Wayne W. Topping, 2622 Birchwood Ave, #7, Bellingham, WA 98225, 360-647-2703. 1984. Non-fiction. "Wholistic health area only. Alternative health care. Stress management." avg. press run 2M+. Pub'd 1 title 1998; expects 1 title 1999, 1 title 2000. 7 titles listed in the *Small Press Record of Books in Print* (28th Edition, 1999-00). avg. price, paper: $16. Discounts: 3+ 40%, 200+ 50%, 500+ 40%-25%. 150pp; 5½×8½, 8½×11; of. Reporting time: 3 months. Payment: 8-10% royalty. Copyrights for author.

Torchlight Publishing, PO Box 52, Badger, CA 93603. 1989. Art, photos, interviews, news items, non-fiction. avg. press run 5M. Pub'd 1 title 1998; expects 6 titles 1999, 6 titles 2000. 7 titles listed in the *Small Press Record of Books in Print* (28th Edition, 1999-00). avg. price, cloth: $30; paper: $12; other: $20 videos. 200pp; 6×9. Copyrights for author. PMA.

TORRE DE PAPEL, Arcea Zapata de Aston, 111 Phillips Hall, The University of Iowa, Iowa City, IA 52242, 319-335-2245. 1991. Poetry, fiction, articles, art, interviews, criticism, reviews. circ. 400. 3/yr. Pub'd 2 issues 1998; expects 3 issues 1999, 3 issues 2000. sub. price: $30; per copy: $10; sample: $10. Back issues: $15. 110pp; 8¾×11½; of. Reporting time: 2 months (may vary). Payment: none. Copyrighted, rights revert to author and publisher. Pub's reviews. §Latin American literature (Hispanic and Brazilian), Caribbean literature, Spanish literature, Portuguese literature, Chicano/Puerto Rican/Cuban American/Afro-American literature, transtlations and linguistics.

Tortilla Press, David L. Eppele, 8 S. Cactus Lane, Bisbee, AZ 85603, 602-432-7040. 1988. Fiction, articles, art, photos, cartoons, interviews, satire, criticism, reviews, letters, parts-of-novels, plays, news items, non-fiction. "We specialize in publishing books on cactus and succulents, arid land plants, deserts and southwestern essays on nature. IBM compatible disks accepted." avg. press run 8M-10M. Pub'd 3 titles 1998; expects 6 titles 1999, 8 titles 2000. 4 titles listed in the *Small Press Record of Books in Print* (28th Edition, 1999-00). avg. price, cloth: $30; paper: $17.95. Discounts: 20% classroom, 40% wholesale (trade, bulk, agents).

574

250pp; size varies; of. Reporting time: 1 month. Payment: varies. Copyrights for author. AAP.

●**Tortuga Books,** Carolyn Glocckner, PO Box 420564, Summerland Key, FL 33042, 305-745-8709; fax 305-745-2704; website www.tortugabooks.com. 1998. Non-fiction. avg. press run 5M. Expects 6 titles 1999, 8 titles 2000. 2 titles listed in the *Small Press Record of Books in Print* (28th Edition, 1999-00). avg. price, cloth: $15; paper: $25. Discounts: 2-3 10%; 4-10 20%; 11-20 30%; 21-100 40%; 100+ 50%. 200pp; 6×9; of. Reporting time: 2 months. Simultaneous submissions accepted: no. Payment: cash. Does not copyright for author. PMA, SPAN, FPA.

Tory Corner Editions, Alan Quincannon, Editor-in-Chief; Loretta Bolger, Jeanne Wilcox, Holly Benedict, Patricia Drury, PO Box 8100, Glen Ridge, NJ 07028, 973-669-8367; torycorner@webtv.net; website www.inc.com/users/ToryCorner.html. 1990. avg. press run 2.5M. Pub'd 5 titles 1998; expects 5 titles 1999, 5 titles 2000. 10 titles listed in the *Small Press Record of Books in Print* (28th Edition, 1999-00). Copyrights for author.

Totally Bogus, PO Box 4560, Laguna Beach, CA 92652, 714-479-5039. 1 title listed in the *Small Press Record of Books in Print* (28th Edition, 1999-00).

TOUCHSTONE LITERARY JOURNAL, William Laufer, Publisher; Guida Jackson, Managing Editor; Chris Woods, Contributing Editor; Julia Mercedes Castilla, Fiction Editor; T.E. Walthen, Asst. Poetry Editor, PO Box 8308, Spring, TX 77387-8308. 1976. Poetry, fiction, interviews, criticism, reviews, non-fiction. "No line limit for good poetry, prose." circ. 1M. 1/yr, plus chapbook supplements. Pub'd 2 issues 1998; expects 2 issues 1999, 2 issues 2000. 7 titles listed in the *Small Press Record of Books in Print* (28th Edition, 1999-00). sub. price: contribution: 1 book postage stamps; per copy: same; sample: same. Back issues: same. 80pp; 5½×8½; †of, typeset, perfect bound. Reporting time: 6 weeks. Payment: 1 copy. Copyrighted, reverts to author. Pub's reviews: 6 in 1998. §Poetry, short story collections. CLMP, The American Humanities Index.

TOWARD FREEDOM, Greg Guma, Editor, PO Box 468, Burlington, VT 05402-0468, 802-658-2523; Fax 802-658-3738; tfmag@aol.com; www.towardfreedom.com. 1952. Articles, photos, cartoons, interviews, criticism, reviews, letters, news items. "International politics, arts and cultures" circ. 2M. 8/yr. Pub'd 8 issues 1998; expects 8 issues 1999, 8 issues 2000. sub. price: $25; per copy: $2.95; sample: $3. Back issues: $3, Xerox $4. Discounts: 1-5 10%, 5-10 20%, 10+ 40%. 24pp; 8½×11; of. Reporting time: 30 days. Publishes 10% of manuscripts submitted. Payment: $80-$250. Copyrighted, reverts to author. Pub's reviews: 8 in 1998. §Global solutions, human rights, nonviolence, racism, third World, politics, culture, non-alignment, eastern Europe. Ads: $300/$150/70¢ per word.

TOWER, Tower Poetry Society, Joanna Lawson, c/o McMaster University, 1280 Main Street W Box 1021, Hamilton, Ontario, L8S ICO, Canada. 1950. Poetry. "Length of material should be up to 40 lines." circ. 250. 2/yr. Pub'd 2 issues 1998; expects 2 issues 1999, 2 issues 2000. sub. price: $8 Canada and US, $9.50 abroad plus $2 p/h (Can. funds); per copy: $3 + $1p/h (Can. Funds); sample: $2+ $1p/h (Can. funds). Back issues: $3. Discounts: 40%. 44pp; 5½×8½; of. Reporting time: 2 months if submitted in February or August. Simultaneous submissions accepted: no. Publishes 15-20% of manuscripts submitted. Payment: 1 copy. Copyrighted, reverts to author.

Tower Poetry Society (see also TOWER), Joanna Lawson, c/o McMaster University, 1280 Main Street W. Box 1021, Hamilton, Ontario, L8S 1CO, Canada. 1950. Poetry. avg. press run 250. Pub'd 100 titles 1998; expects 100 titles 1999. avg. price, paper: $3 (Can.). 44pp; 5½×8½. Reporting time: 2 months for submissions in Feb. + Aug. Simultaneous submissions accepted: no. Publishes 20% of manuscripts submitted. Payment: none. Does not copyright for author.

TOWERS CLUB, USA INFO MARKETING REPORT, Jerry Buchanan, Sole Editor-Publisher, PO Box 2038, Vancouver, WA 98668, 360-574-3084. 1974. "Mostly staff created copy. Publish bios of successful self-publisher/mail order entrepreneurs, other news of SP industry." circ. 1.5M. 12/yr. Pub'd 12 issues 1998; expects 12 issues 1999, 12 issues 2000. sub. price: $95 ($69.95 to first-time subscribers); per copy: $9; sample: $9. Back issues: yearbooks each 80-pages $44.95 each. Discounts: libraries 1/2 price per year ($30). 10pp; 8¼×11; lp. Reporting time: 1 month. Payment: free 1 yr. subscription or $25 per page. Copyrighted, reverts to author. Pub's reviews: 5 in 1998. §Successful self-publishing/marketing, mail order entrepreneurship.

THE TOWNSHIPS SUN, Sun Books, Patricia Ball, Editor; Marion Greenlay, Business Manager; Patricia Ball, Advertising Manager, Box 28, Lennoxville, Quebec J1M 1Z3, Canada. 1972. Articles, photos, interviews, letters, news items, non-fiction. "*The Townships Sun* is Quebec's only rural English-language alternative newspaper. We cover agriculture, ecology, farts & crafts, how-to, and anything else of importance or interest to the people of Quebec's Eastern Townships. Because the English speaking popluation of Quebec is declining, we are broadening our circulation to reach adjacent parts of New England, the Maritimes, and Ontario; thus articles pertaining to these regions may also be welcome. We do use reprints from other periodicals, providing that they do not have substantial circulation in the Eastern Townships." circ. 1M. 12/yr.

Pub'd 12 issues 1998; expects 12 issues 1999, 12 issues 2000. sub. price: $16, $21 outside Canada; per copy: $1.50; sample: $1.50. Back issues: $2. 16pp; 10¼×13¾; of. Reporting time: 1 month. Payment: $1 per inch. Copyrighted, reverts to author. Pub's reviews: 12 in 1998. §Agriculture, back-to-earth alternative philosophy, folklore, Canadiana, ecology, regional history, topics current interest - drugs, travel, etc. Ads: 55¢ MAL or $15 CNU. QCNA (Quebec Community Newspaper Association), CCNA (Canadian Community Newspaper Association).

TOWPATHS, W.B. Bond, 101 Hillside Way, Marietta, OH 45750-2746, 740-374-6715. 1963. Articles, photos. "The Canal Society of Ohio, business address: 111 Richards Road, Columbus, OH 43214-3749." circ. 350. 4/yr. Pub'd 4 issues 1998; expects 4 issues 1999, 4 issues 2000. sub. price: $18; per copy: $2.50; sample: same. Back issues: varies. Discounts: none. 16-20pp; 6×9; of. Reporting time: varies. Payment: none. Not copyrighted. No ads.

TOY RIOT JUICE, Pen-Dec Press, 2526 Chatham Woods, Grand Rapids, MI 49546. 1997. Irregular. sample price: $2. 20pp; 8½×5½.

Trace Publications, Anthony N. Cabot, 325 S. 3rd Street, #1305, Las Vegas, NV 89101, 702-383-8840; fax 702-383-8845; e-mail acabot@lvcm.com. 1991. "Casino industry related books only. Industry-oriented including law, management and marketing" avg. press run 2M. Pub'd 2 titles 1998; expects 3 titles 1999, 3 titles 2000. 1 title listed in the *Small Press Record of Books in Print* (28th Edition, 1999-00). avg. price, cloth: $100. Discounts: 1-19 40%; 20 units 45%; 40 units 50%. 500pp; 6×9. Reporting time: 2 months. Simultaneous submissions accepted: yes. Publishes 10% of manuscripts submitted. Payment: varies. Copyrights for author.

TRADICION REVISTA, LPD Press, Paul Rhetts, Barbe Awalt, 2400 Rio Grande Blvd. NW #1-213, Albuquerque, NM 87104-3222, 505-344-9382; FAX 505-345-5129. 1995. Articles, art, photos, non-fiction. "A journal on contemporary and traditional Spanish Colonial art and culture." circ. 3-5M per issue. 4/yr. Pub'd 4 issues 1998; expects 4 issues 1999, 4 issues 2000. sub. price: $30; per copy: $10; sample: $10. Back issues: $10. 60-80pp; 8×10½. Copyrighted. Pub's reviews: 20 in 1998. §Southwest art and culture; Hispanic topics. Ads: b/w: $250/$150/$90, 4-color: $750/$375/$200. NMBA.

TRADITION, Bob Everhart, Editor, PO Box 492, Anita, IA 50020. 1976. *"Must* deal with traditional country bluegrass and folk music." circ. 2.5M. 6/yr. Pub'd 6 issues 1998; expects 6 issues 1999, 6 issues 2000. sub. price: $20; per copy: $3.50; sample: $3.50. Back issues: $4. 56pp; 8½×11; newspaper. Reporting time: 6 weeks. Simultaneous submissions accepted: yes. Payment: yes, determined. Copyrighted, reverts to author. Pub's reviews: 20 in 1998. §Traditional country-bluegrass-faith music, old-time music. Ads: $100/$75/$50.

TRAFIK - Internationales Journal zur Libertaren Kultur & Politik, Peter Peterson, EduardstraBe 40, Mulheim/Ruhr 45468, Germany. 1981. Articles, art, photos, cartoons, interviews, satire, criticism. "All free." circ. 1M. 2/yr. Pub'd 2 issues 1998; expects 2 issues 1999, 2 issues 2000. sub. price: 20DM; per copy: 10DM. Back issues: 7DM. Discounts: 30%. 100pp; 6.6×9.5; of. Reporting time: 2 months. Payment: 30%. Copyrighted, reverts to author. Pub's reviews: 6 in 1998. §Anarchist theory and practices. Ads: 180DM/100DM.

Trafton Publising, Rick Singer, 109 Barcliff Terrace, Cary, NC 27511-8900. 1993. Cartoons, satire, music. "We look for well conceived how to manuals/books/cassettes or videos for music lovers. Also, we need clean and original humor of any length, from a joke to a complete book" avg. press run 10M. Pub'd 3 titles 1998; expects 3-5 titles 1999, 3-5 titles 2000. avg. price, paper: $6.95-29.95. Discounts: 30%-65%, depending on book and quantity. 150pp; 6×9, 8½×11; of. Reporting time: 1-3 months. Publishes 5% of manuscripts submitted. Payment: varies. Does not copyright for author. PMA.

Training Systems, Inc., G. Michael Durst, Ph.D., Box 788, Evanston, IL 60204, 847-864-8664. 1974. Non-fiction. "Book length mss, philosophical, psychological topics" avg. press run 5M. Expects 2 titles 1999. 2 titles listed in the *Small Press Record of Books in Print* (28th Edition, 1999-00). avg. price, cloth: $15; paper: $10, $15. Discounts: 30% trade, 40% wholesalers. 230pp; 5¼×8½, 8½×11. Payment: no arrangement yet made. Copyrights for author.

TRANET, William N. Ellis, Editor, Box 567, Rangeley, ME 04970, 207-864-2252. 1976. Reviews, news items. "Newsletter-directory." circ. 2M. 6/yr. Pub'd 6 issues 1998; expects 6 issues 1999, 6 issues 2000. sub. price: $150 organizations, $30 subsidizing, $15 for third world workers, $50 libraries; per copy: $5; sample: $5. Back issues: $5. Discounts: to organizational members for bulk copies. 20pp; 8×11; of. Reporting time: 30 days. Payment: none. Not copyrighted. Pub's reviews: 150 in 1998. §The New Social Paradigm, and social activism including ecology, peace, human rights, feminism, holistic education and humanist economics. no ads. NPC.

TRANSCAUCASUS: A Chronology, Christopher M. Hekimian, 888 17th Street NW, Suite 904, Washington, DC 20006, 202-775-1918; FAX 202-775-5648; anca-dc@ix.netcom.com. 1992. News items, non-fiction. "Chronological summary of the significant social, economic, and political events in the lower caucasus as reported by local and international media and selected sources in the region." circ. 2M. 12/yr. Pub'd 12 issues 1998; expects 12 issues 1999, 12 issues 2000. sub. price: free to restricted circulation. 12pp; 8½×11.

TRANSCENDENT VISIONS, David Kime, Beth Greenspan, 251 South Olds Boulevard, 84-E, Fairless Hills, PA 19030-3426, 215-547-7159. 1992. Poetry, fiction, art, photos, cartoons. "We publish fiction under ten pages. Typed, double spaced. All material published is by psychiatric survivors (ex-mental patients). Past contributors include Beth Greenspan, Dean Patrick Carvin and Warren F. Stewart." circ. 200. 3/yr. Pub'd 3 issues 1998; expects 3 issues 1999, 3 issues 2000. sub. price: $6; per copy: $2; sample: $2. Back issues: $2. Discounts: will trade for zine with 20-30 pages. 26pp; 8½×11; photocopy. Reporting time: 1 month. Simultaneous submissions accepted: yes. Publishes 50% of manuscripts submitted. Payment: 1 issue. Not copyrighted. Pub's reviews: 10 in 1998. §Psychiatric survivor magazines primarily.

Transcending Mundane, Tommy Kirchhoff, Kat Kirchhoff, Andy Baillargeon, 5026 E. Weaver Avenue, Littleton, CO 80121, 303-796-0631; Fax: 303-741-1521;e-mail: transmun@paracreative.com/www.paracreative.com. 1998. Poetry, fiction, articles, art, photos, cartoons, satire, reviews, letters, plays, concrete art, non-fiction. "Currently, we are publishing work by Tommy Kirchhoff, but we look forward to fostering talented artists of all kinds to their own successes." avg. press run 15-3M. Pub'd 1 title 1998; expects 1-3 titles 1999, 3-5 titles 2000. 1 title listed in the *Small Press Record of Books in Print* (28th Edition, 1999-00). avg. price, paper: $16. Discounts: commercial-40% off all orders over five books. 123pp; 5½×8½; †High-speed copy when applicable. Reporting time: not set yet. Simultaneous submissions accepted: yes. Payment: not set yet. Copyrights for author. MPBA.

Transeuropa (see also PERSPECTIVES), Collective, BM 6682, London WC1N 3XX, United Kingdom. 1990. Articles, art, photos, cartoons, interviews, satire, criticism, reviews, music, letters, news items, non-fiction. "Cultural and metapolitical collective, involved in promoting European regionalism, ideas of radical political synthesis, avant-garde and folklore cultural manifestations. International news sections." avg. press run 10M. Pub'd 1 title 1998; expects 1 title 1999, 1 title 2000. avg. price, other: £2.50. Discounts: on application. 32pp; size A4. Reporting time: varies. Payment: none. Does not copyright for author.

TRANSITION, Duke University Press, Kwame Anthony Appiah, Henry Louis Gates, Jr., Box 90660, Duke University, Durham, NC 27708-0660. "*Transition* is a unique publication, written in sharp, sensible, accessible prose, profusely and sassily illustrated with contemporary art and photography. Each issue of *Transition* features book reviews and essays on topics such as Mike Tyson, Theodor Adorno, the Zapatista rebellion, visual anthropology, bisexuality, British history, African art, and Haitian film. Issues also contain award-winning interviews with personalities from Angela Davis and Ice Cube to Maxine Hong Kingston, Tony Kushner, Spike Lee, and Louis Farrakhan." circ. 2.3M. 4/yr. Pub'd 4 issues 1998; expects 4 issues 1999, 4 issues 2000. sub. price: $60 institutions, $24 individuals, additional $12 foreign. Pub's reviews. Ads: $300/$200/$325 inside back cover/$500 2-page spread.

TRANSITIONS ABROAD: The Guide to Living, Learning, and Working Overseas, Clayton A. Hubbs, Editor & Publisher, 18 Hulst Road, PO Box 1300, Amherst, MA 01004, 413-256-3414; 413-256-0373; e-mail info@transitionsabroad.com; website www.transitionsabroad.com. 1977. Articles, art, photos, letters, news items, non-fiction. "We like material with detailed practical information on long-stay educational, low-budget, and socially responsible travel abroad." circ. 20M. 6/yr. Pub'd 6 issues 1998; expects 6 issues 1999, 6 issues 2000. sub. price: $24.95; per copy: $4.75; sample: $6.25 postpaid. Discounts: 50%. 96pp; 8⅛×10⅞; sheet fed. Reporting time: 1 month. Simultaneous submissions accepted: yes. Publishes 25% of manuscripts submitted. Payment: at publication. Copyrighted, reverts to author. Pub's reviews: 50 in 1998. §Literary travel material, travel books, language study, resource material on work, study and travel abroad. Ads: $1,056/$799/$2 per word. Small Magazine Publishers, SPAN.

TRANSLATION REVIEW, Rainer Schulte, Editor; Dennis Kratz, Editor, Univ. of Texas-Dallas, Box 830688, Richardson, TX 75083-0688, 214-690-2093. 1978. Articles, interviews, criticism, reviews, news items, non-fiction. "The *Translation Review* is a publication of the American Literary Translators Association and is distributed to members and subscribing libraries. The *Review* deals exclusively with the theory, application and evaluation of literary works in translation." circ. 1M. 3/yr. Pub'd 3 issues 1998; expects 3 issues 1999, 3 issues 2000. sub. price: subscription by membership to ALTA only; $35 for libraries, $30 for individuals; per copy: $10; sample: $10. Back issues: $7.50 each. Discounts: for classroom use 40%. 44pp; 8½×11; of. Reporting time: 8-12 weeks. Payment: copies. Copyrighted. Pub's reviews: 40 in 1998. §Any literary work in recent translation. Ads: $200/$125. Society for Scholarly Publishing.

TRANSMOG, Forrest Richey, Route 6, Box 138, Charleston, WV 25311, E-Mail: far@medin-ah.atc.ucarb.com. 1991. Poetry, art, cartoons, collages. "Short poetry, prose, graphic art. Unconventional, experimental, dislocational, "edge". Not blood and guts. Recent contributors: John Bennett, Harry Polkinhorn, MALOK, Miekal And, Bob Grumman, Wharton Hood, Michael Basinski, Blair Wilson, Paul Weinman. We print contributors name and address unless requested otherwise" circ. 200. 2-6/yr. Pub'd 3 issues 1998; expects

3 issues 1999, 3 issues 2000. sub. price: no subscriptions; per copy: $1; sample: $1. Back issues: 1-6 $1.50 ppd, 7-10 $2 ppd, limited supply. 30pp; 8½×11; †xerox. Reporting time: 2-8 weeks. Simultaneous submissions accepted: yes. Publishes 50% of manuscripts submitted. Payment: 1 copy of issue containing work. Copyrighted, reverts to author. Pub's reviews: 10 in 1998. §Experimental prose and poetry.

TRANSNATIONAL PERSPECTIVES, Rene Wadlow, CP 161, CH-1211 Geneva 16, Switzerland. 1974. Poetry, articles, art, reviews. "Basically a journal of world politics with an emphasis on conflict resolution, human rights, arms control. Poems on a wide range of topics. Book reviews on culture as well as politics." circ. 5M. 3/yr. Pub'd 3 issues 1998; expects 3 issues 1999, 3 issues 2000. sub. price: $20; per copy: $7; sample: free. Back issues: $3. 48pp; 29×20cm; of. Reporting time: 2 months. Simultaneous submissions accepted: yes. Publishes 5% of manuscripts submitted. Payment: 5 or more copies of issue with poem. Not copyrighted. Pub's reviews: 14 in 1998. §World politics, culture, poetry. no ads.

Transportation Trails (see also BUS TOURS MAGAZINE; NATIONAL BUS TRADER), Larry Plachno, Senior Editor; Joe Plachno, Book Editor, 9698 West Judson Road, Polo, IL 61064, 815-946-2341. 1985. "Transportation Trails specializes in titles that are definitive historical reviews on a transportation subject. Primary emphasis is on electric interurban railways, steam railroads, maritime subjects, horsecars, fire apparatus, streetcars and aviation. Binding has been saddle stitching, perfect bound and hardbound." avg. press run 1.5M-3M. Pub'd 6 titles 1998; expects 7 titles 1999, 5 titles 2000. 7 titles listed in the *Small Press Record of Books in Print* (28th Edition, 1999-00). avg. price, cloth: $50; paper: $30. Discounts: 15% to libraries, 40% to dealers, 50% to distributors. 100-400pp; 8½×11, 5½×8½; of. Reporting time: 30 days. Simultaneous submissions accepted: yes. Publishes 15-20% of manuscripts submitted. Payment: 10% on first 10,000, 12% on additional. Copyrights for author.

TRANSVERSIONS, Dale L. Sproule, Sally McBride, Phyllis Gotlieb, Poetry Editor, 1019 Colville Road, Victoria, BC V9A 4P5, Canada, 604-380-7150; FAX 604-383-4413. 1994. Poetry, fiction, articles, art. "Poetry should be sent to: 706-19 Lower Village Gate, Toronto, ON M5P 3L9 Canada. Literature of the fantastic (sf/fantasy/horror/magic realism, etc.). Recent contributors: Sean Stewart, Robert J. Sawyer, Michael Coney, Heather Spears, Charles de Lint." circ. 450. 2-3/yr. Pub'd 3 issues 1998; expects 3 issues 1999, 2 issues 2000. sub. price: $18; per copy: $4.95; sample: $4.95. Back issues: $4. 72pp; 5¼×8¼. Reporting time: 4-8 weeks. Simultaneous submissions accepted: no. Publishes 4% of manuscripts submitted. Payment: 1¢ (Canadian) per word, $5 or 25¢ per line for poems. Copyrighted, reverts to author. Ads: $45/$25/$75 back cover/$50 inside front or back.

TRANVIA - Revue der Iberischen Halbinsel, Walter Frey, Brunhilde Wehinger, PO Box 303626, D-0727 Berlin 19, Germany, 883-2561; tranvia@aol.com. 1986. Fiction, articles, interviews, reviews. circ. 2M. 4/yr. Pub'd 4 issues 1998; expects 4 issues 1999, 4 issues 2000. sub. price: 36,-DM; per copy: 9,-DM. Discounts: 35%. 68pp; 210×305mm. Payment: none. Copyrighted, reverts to author. Pub's reviews: ca. 50 in 1998. §Cultures and politics of Portugal and Spain, Latin America. Ads: 600,-DM/300,-DM.

TRAVEL BOOKS WORLDWIDE, Travel Keys, Peter Manston, Publisher; Robert Bynum, Editor, PO Box 160691, Sacramento, CA 95816-0691, 916-452-5200. 1991. "A review of travel books and related maps, etc. No submissions please; 100% staff written." circ. 1.2M. 10/yr. Pub'd 10 issues 1998; expects 10 issues 1999, 10 issues 2000. sub. price: $36 US, $48 Canada, US$72 or £42 elsewhere; per copy: $4; sample: $4. 16pp; 8½×11; †of. Simultaneous submissions accepted: no. Copyrighted, does not revert to author. Pub's reviews: 263 in 1998. §Travel, cooking, maps & globes. Ads: none. ABA.

Travel Keys (see also TRAVEL BOOKS WORLDWIDE), Peter B. Manston, Publisher; Robert Bynum, Associate Editor, PO Box 160691, Sacramento, CA 95816-0691, 916-452-5200. 1984. Reviews, non-fiction. "Practical, succinct travel and antique guides. Staff-written or sometimes work for hire." avg. press run 5M-12M. Expects 4 titles 1999, 3 titles 2000. 5 titles listed in the *Small Press Record of Books in Print* (28th Edition, 1999-00). avg. price, paper: $6.95-$15.95. Discounts: bookstores 40% less than 30 books, 46% 31+ books. 320pp; 3¾×7½, 5½×8½; of. Reporting time: 1 month. We accept simultaneous submissions if mentioned as such in cover letter. Publishes 4% of manuscripts submitted. Payment: variable. Copyrights for author, but copyright fee charged against author's royalty account. ABA.

Treasure Chest Books LLC, W. Ross Humphreys, PO Box 5250, Tucson, AZ 85703, 520-623-9558. 1975. avg. press run 10M. Pub'd 2 titles 1998; expects 5 titles 1999, 7 titles 2000. avg. price, cloth: $24.95; paper: $9.95. Pages vary; size varies. Reporting time: 90 days. Payment: semi-annual. Copyrights for author. Rocky Mountain Book Publisher's Assoc.

TREASURE HOUSE, J.G. Wolfensberger, Editor; Anzy L. Wells, Contributing Editor, 20351 Kings Crest Blvd, Hagerstown, MD 21742-8146. 1994. Fiction. "*Treasure House* is working hard to bring readers the finest literary magazine of its kind—unpretentious, independent, and committed to emerging talent. No university affiliations. No inside clique. Submit original, unpublished works. Submit fiction (6,000 words max.) to our publishing address in Hagerstown, MD. Adhere to standard manuscript mechanics. We seek contemporary works which engage and surprise us. Always include SASE. Query first for guidelines" circ. 350. 3/yr. Pub'd 3 issues 1998; expects 3 issues 1999, 3 issues 2000. sub. price: $11/one year; per copy: $4; sample: $4. Back issues: none. Discounts: please inquire. 28-32pp; 8½×11; of. Reporting time: within 3 months. Simultaneous submissions accepted: yes. Publishes 3% of manuscripts submitted. Payment: minimum of 2 copies. Copyrighted, reverts to author. Ads: please inquire.

Treehouse Micropress, 435 N. Main St., Herkimer, NY 13350. 1994. Poetry, fiction, art, cartoons, letters, parts-of-novels, long-poems, collages, plays. "We publish the work of preteen children. Due to the impossibility of verifying authenticity, we never accept unsolicited manuscripts." avg. press run 10. Expects 1 title 1999, 1 title 2000. avg. price, paper: $10.00. Discounts: 5+ -1/3. 20pp; 5×8. Simultaneous submissions accepted: no. Payment: 15%.

Trellis Publishing, Inc., Mary Koski, PO Box 16141-D, Duluth, MN 55816. 1997. "We will be taking on a few, high-quality children's picture books; however, we need to wait a year before taking submissions." avg. press run 10M. Pub'd 1 title 1998; expects 2 titles 1999, 2 titles 2000. 3 titles listed in the *Small Press Record of Books in Print* (28th Edition, 1999-00). avg. price, cloth: $15.95; other: workbooks $4.95. Discounts: yes. Cloth 32pp, workbooks 16pp; 8×10. Reporting time: 8 weeks. Simultaneous submissions accepted: yes. Payment: 10% paid to author/illustrator on retail price. Copyrights for author. PMA, UMBA.

Trentham Books (see also THE JOURNAL OF DESIGN AND TECHNOLOGY EDUCATION; MCT - MULTICULTURAL TEACHING), Westview House, 734 London Road, Oakhill, Stoke-on-Trent, Staffordshire ST4 5NP, England, 01782-745567; Fax 01782-745553. 1982. Articles. avg. press run 2M. Pub'd 27 titles 1998. 23 titles listed in the *Small Press Record of Books in Print* (28th Edition, 1999-00). Discounts: usual trade. 56-280pp; size A4; of. Reporting time: 1 month. Simultaneous submissions accepted: no. Publishes 25% of manuscripts submitted. Payment: 7½% on price. Copyrights for author. Publishers Association, U.K.

Triad Press, Clifford C. Segerstrom, 8983 Briar Forest Drive, Houston, TX 77024-7219, 713-789-0424. 1980. Art, photos, non-fiction. avg. press run 5M-10M. Expects 1 title 2000. 3 titles listed in the *Small Press Record of Books in Print* (28th Edition, 1999-00). avg. price, paper: $14.95. Discounts: 1-10 40%, 11-99 40%pp, 100+ 50%. 168pp; 8½×11; of. Reporting time: 4 weeks. Payment: standard royalties, advance-on-completion. Copyrights for author.

THE TRIBUNE, Anne S. Walker, Executive Director + Editor, 777 United Nations Plaza, 3rd floor, New York, NY 10017, 212-687-8633. 1976. "Attached copy of a typical newsletter. International Women's Tribune Centre. We do not accept submissions." circ. 20M. Eng. & Span. 4/yr, French 3/yr. 2 titles listed in the *Small Press Record of Books in Print* (28th Edition, 1999-00). sub. price: free in developing countries, $12 U.S. & Canada, $16 Europe, Aust/New Zealand/Japan; per copy: $3; sample: same. 48pp; 8½×11; camera-ready copy prepared by IWTC. offset printing. Desk top publishing using macintosh computer, laser printer. Payment: none. Not copyrighted. no ads.

TRICYCLE: The Buddhist Review, Helen Tworkov, Carole Tonkinson, 92 Vandam Street, New York, NY 10013-1007. 1991. Poetry, fiction, articles, art, photos, cartoons, interviews, reviews, letters, parts-of-novels, news items, non-fiction. circ. 50M. 4/yr. Pub'd 4 issues 1998; expects 4 issues 1999, 4 issues 2000. sub. price: $24; per copy: $7.50; sample: $7.50. Back issues: $10. 104pp; 8½×11. Reporting time: 3 months. Simultaneous submissions accepted: no. Publishes 10% of manuscripts submitted. Payment: varies. Copyrighted, reverts to author. Pub's reviews: 32 in 1998. §Buddhism, religion, philosophy, Asian studies. Ads: $1190/$695/$520 1/3 page/$410 1/4 page. The Tricycle Exchange.

Trigon Press, Roger Sheppard, Judith Sheppard, 117 Kent House Road, Beckenham, Kent BR3 1JJ, England, 081-778-0534; FAX 081-776-7525; trigon@easynet.co.uk. 1975. Non-fiction. "No subs required at present. Publish books for the new and antiquarian book trade. Mostly edit our own material: hope to be able to publish more bibliographies and co-editions of book trade and library reference material. Our 6th edition of the *International Directory of Book Collectors* now available." avg. press run 1.5M. Pub'd 2 titles 1998; expects 2 titles 1999, 2 titles 2000. 3 titles listed in the *Small Press Record of Books in Print* (28th Edition, 1999-00). avg. price, cloth: $40; paper: $20. Discounts: singles 25%, multiples 35%; export postage extra. 280pp; 5×9; of. Payment: 10%. Copyrights for author. IPG (UK).

Trilogy Books, Marge Wood, 3579 E. Foothill Blvd. #236, Pasadena, CA 91107-3119, 818-440-0669. 1990. Non-fiction. avg. press run 5M. Expects 2 titles 1999, 3 titles 2000. avg. price, paper: $14.95. 6×9; of. Reporting time: 2 months. Payment: negotiable. Copyrights for author. PMA, 2401 Pacific Coast Hwy, Suite 206, Hermosa Beach, CA 90254.

Trimarket, Tony Svensson, 2264 Bowdoin Street, Palo Alto, CA 94306, 650-494-1406; 70470.527@compuserve.com. 1985. Non-fiction. "Triathlon/duathlon, swimming, cycling, running are topics of interest. Recent contributors are Mark Allen, Paula Newby-Fraser, Dave Scott, Scott Tinley, and Thomas Hellriegel." avg. press run 15M. Pub'd 2 titles 1998; expects 4 titles 1999, 5 titles 2000. 9 titles listed in the *Small Press Record* *of Books in Print* (28th Edition, 1999-00). avg. price, paper: $12.95. Discounts: trade normal. 160pp; 7×9, 6×8, 8×5; web. Reporting time: 4-8 weeks. Publishes 5% of manuscripts submitted. Payment: negotiable. Copyrights for author. PMA.

TRIQUARTERLY, Kim Maselli, Publisher; Susan Hahn, Editor; Kirstie Felland, Managing Editor; Ian Morris, Associate Editor, Northwestern University Press, 2020 Ridge, Evanston, IL 60208-4302, 847-491-7614. 1964. Poetry, fiction, art, photos, criticism, reviews, parts-of-novels. "Write for contributor's guidelines." circ. 5M. 3/yr. Pub'd 3 issues 1998; expects 3 issues 1999, 3 issues 2000. sub. price: $24; per copy: $11.95; sample: $5. Back issues: price list on request. Discounts: available on request. 256pp; 6×9¼; of. Reporting time: 8-12 weeks. Simultaneous submissions accepted: no. Publishes .2% of manuscripts submitted. Payment: varies. Copyrighted, rights revert to author upon request. Pub's reviews: 2 in 1998. §Literature, the arts, general culture. Ads: $250/$125 (quantity discount of 20% for three insertions). CLMP.

Triumph Books, Mitch Rogatz, Publisher; Siobhan Drummond, Managing Editor; John Delehanty, Vice President, 644 S. Clark Street, Chicago, IL 60605, 939-3330. 1990. avg. press run 8M. Pub'd 30 titles 1998; expects 30 titles 1999, 30 titles 2000. 48 titles listed in the *Small Press Record of Books in Print* (28th Edition, 1999-00). avg. price, cloth: $25; paper: $15. Discounts: sliding. 300pp; 6×9; of. Payment: 7%-12%. Does not copyright for author. ABA.

TRIVIUM, Colin Clifford Eldridge, Dept. Of History, St. David's University College, Lampeter, Dyfed SA48 7ED, Great Britain, 0570-422351 ext 244. 1966. Articles, criticism, reviews. "Articles: av. length - 5M-7M words. Bias: towards the humanities." circ. 300. 1/yr. Pub'd 1 issue 1998; expects 1 issue 1999, 1 issue 2000. 2 titles listed in the *Small Press Record of Books in Print* (28th Edition, 1999-00). sub. price: £8 sterling; per copy: £8 sterling. Back issues: contact business editor. 180pp; size A5; †of. Reporting time: 6-8 weeks. Simultaneous submissions accepted: yes. Payment: none. Copyright vested in editor of *Trivium*. Pub's reviews: 0 in 1998. §Humanities. Ads: £25/£12.50.

Trojan Homes Publishing Co., 4 Miller Hill Drive, LaGrangeville, NY 12540-5605, 914-223-7514; e-mail wbuild28@juno.com. 1995. Non-fiction. avg. press run 1M. Pub'd 1 title 1998; expects 1 title 1999. 1 title listed in the *Small Press Record of Books in Print* (28th Edition, 1999-00). avg. price, paper: $39.95. Discounts: 25-55%. 280pp. Simultaneous submissions accepted: no. Copyrights for author.

Trout Creek Press, Laurence F. Hawkins, Editor, 5976 Billings Road, Parkdale, OR 97041, 503-352-6494; e-Mail Lfh42@AOL.COM. 1981. Poetry. avg. press run 300. Pub'd 2 titles 1998; expects 2 titles 1999, 2 titles 2000. 33 titles listed in the *Small Press Record of Books in Print* (28th Edition, 1999-00). avg. price, paper: $4. Discounts: 40% (order of 5 or more). Variespp; size varies; †of. Reporting time: 3 months. Simultaneous submissions accepted: yes. Publishes 4% of manuscripts submitted. Payment: negotiable. Copyrights for author.

Trouvere Company (see also **WRITERS GAZETTE**; **LAUREATE LETTER**), Brenda Williamson, 899 Williamson Trail, Eclectic, AL 36024-6131. 1980. avg. press run 500. Pub'd 1 title 1998; expects 1-2 titles 1999, 2-4 titles 2000. avg. price, paper: $5; other: $3-$10. Discounts: wholesale 25%-40%, library-institution 20% per copy. 20-200pp; 5½×8, 8½×11; custom printer. Reporting time: 4-6 weeks. Payment: 5% on retail or flat fee; no advance. Copyrights for author.

Truly Fine Press, Jerry Madson, PO Box 891, Bemidji, MN 56601. 1973. "Truly Fine Press has in the past published a pamphlet series, and also published Minnesota's first tabloid novel. Must query first. Only publish ulra limited edition visual poetry that gravitates toward art" avg. press run varies. 16 titles listed in the *Small Press Record of Books in Print* (28th Edition, 1999-00). Pages vary; size varies; †of, mi. Reporting time: 2 weeks to 6 months. Copyrights for author.

Truman Press, Samantha Nichols, 15445 Ventura Blvd., Ste. 905, Sherman Oaks, CA 91403, 818-907-1889; FAX 818-907-8046. 1993. avg. press run 10M. Pub'd 1 title 1998; expects 1 title 1999. 1 title listed in the *Small Press Record of Books in Print* (28th Edition, 1999-00). avg. price, cloth: $19.95; paper: $5.95. Discounts: standard. 250-750pp; 6×9. Reporting time: varies. We sometimes accept simultaneous submissions. Publishes less than 10% of manuscripts submitted. Payment: advances against standard rates. We copyright for author if necessary.

THE TRUTH SEEKER, Bonnie Lange, Tim C. Leedon, 16935 W. Bernardo Drive #103, San Diego, CA 92127, 619-676-0430; Fax 619-676-0433; tsmelton@aol.com; www.truthseeker.com. 1873. Articles, interviews, criticism, news items. "Length of material: 400-1,600 words. Recent contributors: Steve Allen, Gerald LaRue, Howard Blume, Arthur Melville." circ. 3M. 2/yr. Pub'd 4 issues 1998; expects 2 issues 1999, 2 issues 2000. sub. price: $20; per copy: $10; sample: $10. Back issues: $20. Discounts: 40% brokers. 88pp; 8½×11; web press. Simultaneous submissions accepted: yes. Publishes 20% of manuscripts submitted. Payment: $75 per article plus 1 year subscription. Copyrighted, reverts to author. Pub's reviews: 12 in 1998. §Free thought, religion, government. Ads: none.

Tryckeriforlaget (see also **ALLA TIDERS BODER**), Leif Lindberg, Tumstocksvagen 19, Taby S-18366,

Sweden, 08-7567445. 1993. Pub'd 1 title 1998; expects 1 title 1999, 1 title 2000. avg. price, cloth: SEK 170; paper: SEK 90. 200pp; of. Swedish Association of Publishers.

Tsunami Inc. (see also THE TEMPLE), Charles Potts, PO Box 100, Walla Walla, WA 99362-0033, E-mail tsunami@wwics.com. 1995. Poetry, non-fiction. "Recent contributors include: Stephen Thomas, Teri Zipf, Jim Bodeen. Query with SASE before submitting." avg. press run 500-1.2M. Pub'd 2 titles 1998; expects 3 titles 1999, 4 titles 2000. 6 titles listed in the *Small Press Record of Books in Print* (28th Edition, 1999-00). avg. price, cloth: $30; paper: $15. Discounts: 40% trade. 120pp; 5½x8½; of. Reporting time: varies. Simultaneous submissions accepted: yes. Publishes 1% of manuscripts submitted. Payment: 10%. Copyrights for author. PNBA.

TUCUMCARI LITERARY REVIEW, Troxey Kemper, Editor, 3108 W. Bellevue Avenue, Los Angeles, CA 90026. 1988. Poetry, fiction, articles, cartoons, satire, criticism, reviews, letters, non-fiction. "We prefer familiar, rhyming poems in the standard forms, not rambling, disjointed fragments and words that are not tied together to *mean* anything." circ. 200. 6-8/yr. Pub'd 7 issues 1998; expects 6 issues 1999, 8 issues 2000. sub. price: $12; per copy: $2; sample: $2 (includes postage). Back issues: $2 postpaid. 40pp; 5½x8½; †xerox. Reporting time: 2 weeks, sooner if rejected, later if accepted and SASE is returned with copy of magazine. Simultaneous submissions accepted: yes. Publishes 35% of manuscripts submitted. Payment: 1 copy. Not copyrighted. CLMP.

Tudor Publishers, Inc., Eugene Pfaff, Jr., Attn: Eugene E. Pfaff Jr., PO Box 38366, Greensboro, NC 27408, 910-282-5907. 1985. Fiction, non-fiction. "Tudor is interested in the following types of material: commercial books of wide general interest, either fiction or non-fiction, which we will consider for a straight royalty contract; and quality manuscripts of almost any type which we occasionally offer to publish. We would prefer to see material from writers with at least some record of publication in mags and journals, but we will consider a well-done proposal or query from anyone. We try to be open and to respond promptly." avg. press run 3M-5M. Pub'd 3 titles 1998; expects 3 titles 1999, 4 titles 2000. 2 titles listed in the *Small Press Record of Books in Print* (28th Edition, 1999-00). avg. price, cloth: $18.95; paper: $9.95. Discounts: write for schedules. 200pp; 5½x8½, 6x9; of. Reporting time: 2-4 weeks. Payment: standard, royalty. Copyrights for author.

Tug Press, Timothy Allen Board, PO Box 15188, Newport Beach, CA 92659, 714-551-9591; FAX 714-551-9591. 1992. Fiction, non-fiction. "Tug Press publishes books with nautical themes. We publish both fiction and non-fiction. We are looking for books with environmental messages, especially for the young adult audience." avg. press run 5M. Pub'd 1 title 1998; expects 1 title 1999, 1 title 2000. 2 titles listed in the *Small Press Record of Books in Print* (28th Edition, 1999-00). avg. price, paper: $12.95. of. Reporting time: 30 days. Copyrights for author. Publishers Marketing Association.

TULSA STUDIES IN WOMEN'S LITERATURE, Holly Laird, Editor; Linda Frazier, Managing Editor, 600 S. College, Tulsa, OK 74104-3189, 918-631-2503, Fax 918-584-0623; linda-frazier@utulsa.edu. 1982. Articles, criticism, reviews, letters. circ. 1M. 2/yr. Pub'd 2 issues 1998; expects 2 issues 1999, 2 issues 2000. sub. price: U.S. individuals $12/1 yr, $23/2 yrs, $34/3 yrs, institutions $14/$27/$40, other individuals $15/$29/$43, institutions $16/$31/$46, U.S. students $10/$19/$28, elsewhere students $12/$23/$34, airmail surcharge $10; per copy: $7 US/$8 elsewhere; sample: $7US/$8 elsewhere. Back issues: $10. 150pp; 6x9; of. Reporting time: 6 months. Simultaneous submissions accepted: no. Payment: none. Copyrighted, does not revert to author. Pub's reviews: 25 in 1998. §Women's literature—critical studies. Ads: $150/$75. CELJ.

Tuns Press, Faculty of Architecture, Dalhousie University, Box 1000, Halifax, Nova Scotia B3J 2X4, Canada, 902-420-7641, Fax 902-423-6672, tuns.press@dal.ca; www.dal.ca/tunspress. 1989. Non-fiction. "Faculty press. Publishes books on architecture and related fields." avg. press run 1M-2M. Pub'd 3 titles 1998. 5 titles listed in the *Small Press Record of Books in Print* (28th Edition, 1999-00). Discounts: trade. 8½x8½; of.

TURNING THE TIDE: A Journal of Anti-Racist Activism, Research & Education, Michael Novick, PO Box 1055, Culver City, CA 90232-1055, e-mail part2001@usa.net. 1987. Poetry, articles, photos, cartoons, interviews, satire, criticism, reviews, news items, non-fiction. "Prefer short pieces." circ. 7.5M-10M. 4/yr. Pub'd 4 issues 1998; expects 4 issues 1999, 4 issues 2000. sub. price: $15 individuals, $25 institutions; per copy: $3.95; sample: $4. 24pp; 11x14; webb press. Reporting time: 1-2 months. Simultaneous submissions accepted: yes. Publishes 10-12% of manuscripts submitted. Payment: 5 free copies. Not copyrighted. Pub's reviews: 2-3 in 1998. §Racism, sexism, homophobia, liberation movements. Ads: $100/$65/$35 1/4 page.

TURNING WHEEL, Susan Moon, PO Box 4650, Berkeley, CA 94704. 1980. Poetry, articles, art, photos, cartoons, interviews, criticism, reviews, letters, news items, non-fiction. "*Turning Wheel* is about 'engaged' buddhism, or buddhism and social activism. We print articles, art, poetry, etc. about nonviolent protest, about issues of activism, sexism, human rights, etc. in American buddhist communities and Asian Buddhist countries. We print Gary Snyder, Thich Nhat Hanh, grassroots activists." circ. 5M. 4/yr. Pub'd 4 issues 1998; expects 4 issues 1999, 4 issues 2000. sub. price: $35 membership, $20 low-income; per copy: $4 newstand; sample: $6 by mail. 48pp; 8½x11. Reporting time: about 1 month. Simultaneous submissions accepted: yes. Publishes 20% of manuscripts submitted. Payment: 2 copies of magazine, one year subscription. Copyrighted, reverts to author. Pub's reviews: about 20 in 1998. §Buddhism and social activism, engaged spirituality, deep ecology, social ecology. Ads: $250/$135/25¢.

TURNSTILE, 175 5th Avenue, Suite 2348, New York, NY 10010. 1988. Poetry, fiction, articles, art, photos, interviews, satire, criticism, parts-of-novels, long-poems, non-fiction. "Quality material in all categories listed above. Our average piece is about 10-15 typewritten pages. We have published stories by Fenton Johnson, David Shields, Ann Copeland and Ron Tanner. Please query for submission guidelines." circ. 1.5M-2M. 1/yr. Pub'd 1 issue 1998; expects 1 issue 1999, 1 issue 2000. sub. price: $7; per copy: $7; sample: $7. Discounts: query for library rates. Contributors have reduced subscription rates. 128pp; 6×9; lp. Reporting time: 3 months. Simultaneous submissions accepted: yes. Publishes 1% of manuscripts submitted. Payment: in issues. Copyrighted, reverts to author. Ads: one-time: $150/$100/$75; 2 time: $125/$80/$65. CLMP.

Turnstone Press, Manuela Dias, Managing Editor; Patrick Gunter, Marketing Director, 607-100 Arthur Street, Winnipeg R3B 1H3, Canada, 204-947-1555, E-mail; acquisitions@turnstonepress.mb.ca. 1976. Poetry, fiction, criticism, long-poems. "Contemporary Canadian writing." avg. press run 1M. Pub'd 10 titles 1998; expects 8 titles 1999, 8 titles 2000. 137 titles listed in the *Small Press Record of Books in Print* (28th Edition, 1999-00). avg. price, cloth: $25.95; paper: $12.95. Discounts: bookstores 1-9 copies 20%, 10+ 40%; schools & libraries 40%; wholesalers 45%. Poetry 80pp, fiction & criticism 220pp; 5½×8½; of. Reporting time: 2-3 months. Query first before sending simultaneous submissions. Publishes .8% of manuscripts submitted. Payment: 10% paid annually. Copyrights for author. LPG, ACP, AMBP, CBIC, CBA.

The Turquoise Butterfly Press (see also **THE GOOD RED ROAD; MAMA'S LITTLE HELPER**), Terri Andrews, PO Box 750, Athens, OH 45701.

Turtle Island Press, Inc., Tara Sues, Vice President Operations; Kyle Porter, Marketing-Distribution, 3104 E. Camelback Road, Suite 614, Phoenix, AZ 85016, 602-468-1141; orders 888-432-5362; fax 602-954-8560; info@turtleislandpress.com; www.turtleislandpress.com. 1996. Fiction, non-fiction. "Dr. H Books; trademark of Turtle Island Press, Inc. (TIPI) for children's book series." avg. press run 5M-10M. Pub'd 2 titles 1998; expects 2 titles 1999, 2 titles 2000. 4 titles listed in the *Small Press Record of Books in Print* (28th Edition, 1999-00). avg. price, cloth: $16.95-$20; paper: $13; other: $20-$30 audio. Discounts: standard, thru distributor. Children 32pp, adult 180pp; 9×10, 8½×5½; of. Reporting time: 6-8 weeks. Simultaneous submissions accepted: yes. Publishes 3% of manuscripts submitted. Payment: per project arrangements; usually doesn't exceed 10%. Does not copyright for author.

Turtle Press, division of S.K. Productions Inc., Cynthia Kim, PO Box 290206, Wethersfield, CT 06129-0206, 860-529-7770. 1990. Non-fiction. "We publish primarily non-fiction titles of interest to martial artists and those readers interested in self-protection. We are especially interested in new, unique or previously unpublished facets of the arts. Will also consider topics related to Asian culture, such as Zen, philosophy, etc." avg. press run 3M-4M. Pub'd 4 titles 1998; expects 5 titles 1999, 5 titles 2000. 11 titles listed in the *Small Press Record of Books in Print* (28th Edition, 1999-00). avg. price, paper: $12.95. 150pp; 6×9; of. Reporting time: 1 month. Simultaneous submissions accepted: yes. Publishes 2-4% of manuscripts submitted. Payment: 5-10% on retail (royalties), advance of $500-$1000. Copyrights for author. PMA.

Twelve Star Publishing, Nancy McCarthy, PO Box 123, Jefferson, MD 21755, 301-473-9035. 1994. Fiction, non-fiction. avg. press run varies. Expects 2-3 titles 1999, 2-3 titles 2000. 2 titles listed in the *Small Press Record of Books in Print* (28th Edition, 1999-00). avg. price, paper: $12.95. of, lp. Reporting time: 3-4 weeks. Simultaneous submissions accepted: yes. Payment: variable. Copyrights for author. NAPRA.

Twelvetrees Press, Jack Woody, PO Box 10229, Santa Fe, NM 87504-1022. 1980. Poetry, art, photos. "Books include work by: Herb Ritts, Herbert List, Joel-Peter Witkin, Duane Michals. Previous work by Robert Mapplethorpe, Dennis Hopper, Gus Van Sant, George Platt Lynes, among others. Total number published: 50." avg. press run 5M. Pub'd 1 title 1998; expects 1 title 1999, 1 title 2000. 1 title listed in the *Small Press Record of Books in Print* (28th Edition, 1999-00). avg. price, cloth: $50. Discounts: bookstores 20% 1 title, 30% 2-4, 40% + free freight for 5+ titles; individuals receive 10% if order is over $100. 125pp; oversized; roto-grauvre, of, duotone. Reporting time: indefinite. Payment: dependent on individual agreement. Copyrights for author.

21ST CENTURY AFRO REVIEW, IAAS Publishers, Inc., Nikongo Ba'Nikongo, Editor; L. Wright, Review Editor, 7676 New Hampshire Ave., Suite 330, Langley Park, MD 20783. 1992. "25 pages, double spaced maximum." 3/yr. Pub'd 1 issue 1998; expects 2 issues 1999, 3 issues 2000. sub. price: $32; per copy: $18; sample: $3. Back issues: $8. Discounts: trade 40%. 150pp; 7×10. Reporting time: 6 weeks. Copyrighted. Pub's reviews: 3 in 1998. §Black/Africana studies, social sciences, humanities, international affairs, policy studies. Ads: $200/$125/double page $350. International Association of Africanist Scholars.

21st Century Publishing, Inc., Steven Perry, PO Box 1314, Clearwater, FL 34617-1314, 813-274-4974; Fax 813-581-0038. 1994. Art. "Publishing 3D art books called *Another Dimension, Another Dimension: The Little*

Book and *Another Dimension: The Big Book*. Published a calendar with Day Dream Publishing and *Henry's Gift* with Andrews and McNeel.'' avg. press run 10M. Pub'd 2 titles 1998. avg. price, paper: $6.95-$16.95. Discounts: standard. 10-87pp; 8½×11, 4×6, 17×15; of. Reporting time: 8 weeks. Payment: standard royalties. Does not copyright for author. Publishers Marketing Assoc.

The Twickenham Press, Arnold Greissle-Schoenberg, 31 Jane Street, New York, NY 10014, 212-741-2417. 1980. Fiction. "Our orientation has been and will remain literary and feminist. As of 1993, we will be issuing one to two novels per year. Queries should include a literary profile, a brief description of the work intended for submission, and a SASE. Agents and other strictly commercial types need *not* apply.'' avg. press run 1M. Expects 1 title 1999, 1-2 titles 2000. 4 titles listed in the *Small Press Record of Books in Print* (28th Edition, 1999-00). avg. price, cloth: $22; paper: $14. Discounts: 20% to libraries; 40-50% to dealers; returns to 99 years. 250pp; 6×9; lp. Reporting time: long. Simultaneous submissions accepted: yes. Payment: 10-15% of list. Copyrights for author. CLMP.

Twin Palms Publishers, Jack Woody, PO Box 10229, Santa Fe, NM 87504-1022. 1986. avg. press run 4M. Pub'd 4 titles 1998; expects 4 titles 1999, 5 titles 2000. 6 titles listed in the *Small Press Record of Books in Print* (28th Edition, 1999-00). avg. price, cloth: $60. Discounts: 40% (free freight) to bookstores. 124pp; oversized.

Twin Peaks Press, Helen Hecker, PO Box 129, Vancouver, WA 98666, 360-694-2462, Fax 360-696-3210. 1984. "Query first, publish books.'' avg. press run 10M. Pub'd 6 titles 1998; expects 6 titles 1999, 6 titles 2000. 6 titles listed in the *Small Press Record of Books in Print* (28th Edition, 1999-00). avg. price, paper: $19.95. Discounts: retail 1 book 0%, 2-6 20%, 6+ 40%, distributors write. 192pp; 5½×8½. Reporting time: varies. Payment: negotiable. Copyrights for author. Northwest Assn. of Book Publishers.

Twin Sisters Productions, 1340 Home Avenue, Suite D, Akron, OH 44310-1302, 800-248-TWIN; 330-633-8900; FAX 330-633-8988. 1987. avg. press run 10M. Pub'd 4 titles 1998; expects 4 titles 1999, 4 titles 2000. 32 titles listed in the *Small Press Record of Books in Print* (28th Edition, 1999-00). avg. price, paper: $6.99-$9.98. 24-64pp; 7×10, 8½×11. Reporting time: 4-6 weeks. Simultaneous submissions accepted: yes. Copyrights for author. ABA, PMA.

‡**TWISTED IMAGE NEWSLETTER,** Ace Backwords, 1630 University Avenue #26, Berkeley, CA 94703, 415-644-8035. 1982. Articles, cartoons, interviews, satire, reviews, music. "95% of the material is created by me, so I'm not particularly interested in unsolicited material.'' circ. 400. 12/yr. Pub'd 12 issues 1998; expects 12 issues 1999, 12 issues 2000. sub. price: $20; per copy: $2; sample: $2. Back issues: set of 7 back issues $10. 10pp; 8½×11; †xerox. Reporting time: within a week if accompanied by SASE. Payment: absolutely zero. Copyrighted, reverts to author. Pub's reviews: 4 in 1998. §I like comics, Bukowski, hate poetry, like humor and sex. Ads: none. United Coalition of Fuckups & Studs, Inc.

TWISTED TIMES, Stuart Mangrum, PO Box 271222, Concord, CA 94527. 1991. Articles, photos, cartoons, satire, criticism, reviews, letters, news items, non-fiction. "No poetry or fiction. Real-world weirdness only. Always looking for good 1-panel cartoons and misc. bizarre graphics. Also use short (under 1,000 wd.) essays on current events, culture jamming, advertising, arts, etc. Nothing mainstream.'' circ. 1M. 4/yr. Pub'd 4 issues 1998; expects 4 issues 1999, 4 issues 2000. sub. price: $10 (cash only); per copy: $3; sample: $3. Back issues: none. 42pp; 8½×7; mi. Reporting time: 1-3 months. Simultaneous submissions accepted: yes. Publishes 20% of manuscripts submitted. Payment: copy. Not copyrighted. Pub's reviews: 10 in 1998. §Fringe, dada, non-fiction only. Ads: none.

2AM MAGAZINE, 2AM Publications, Gretta M. Anderson, PO Box 6754, Rockford, IL 61125-1754. 1986. Poetry, fiction, articles, art, cartoons, interviews, reviews, letters. "Recent contributors: J.N. Williamson, Leonard Carpenter, William Relling Jr., Wayne Allen Sallee, Jessica Amanda Salmonson, Avram Davidson, John Coyne.'' circ. 2M. 4/yr. Pub'd 4 issues 1998; expects 4 issues 1999, 4 issues 2000. sub. price: $19; per copy: $4.95; sample: $5.95. Back issues: $5.95. Discounts: 40% trade. 68pp; 8½×11; of. Reporting time: 8-12 weeks. Payment: 1/2¢ per word minimum. Copyrighted, reverts to author. Pub's reviews: 100+ in 1998. §Horror fiction, science fiction, how to write. Ads: $200/$75/$50 1/4 page.

2AM Publications (see also 2AM MAGAZINE), Gretta McCombs Anderson, PO Box 6754, Rockford, IL 61125-1754. 1986. Fiction. avg. press run 2M. Pub'd 1 title 1998; expects 1 title 1999. avg. price, cloth: $19.95; paper: $9.95. Discounts: 40% trade. 150pp; 6×9; of. Reporting time: 2-4 months. We accept simultaneous submissions, but please inform us that others are reviewing. Payment: negotiable, offer individual contract. Copyrights for author.

Two Bytes Publishing, Elizabeth F. Clark, PO Box 1043, Darien, CT 06820-1043, 203-656-0581; 888-588-7171; Fax 203-655-3910; E-mail efctbp@aol.com. 1985. Poetry, fiction, non-fiction. avg. press run 3M-7500. Pub'd 5 titles 1998; expects 5 titles 1999, 5 titles 2000. 5 titles listed in the *Small Press Record of Books in Print* (28th Edition, 1999-00). avg. price, cloth: $24.95-$30; paper: $16-$18; other: children's—$6.50.

Discounts: trade, library. 16-200pp; 5½×8½, 6×9; †of. Reporting time: 6 weeks. Simultaneous submissions accepted: no. Copyrights for author. NEBA, Small Press.

Two Dog Press, Karen Kaiser, PO Box 307, Deer Isle, ME 04627, 207-348-6819; fax 207-348-6016; email human@twodogpress.com. 1997. Poetry, fiction, art, photos, non-fiction. "We publish books about dogs. Our preference is for material that features dogs without getting sentimental. We're looking for fresh, innovative prose and poetry, art and interesting non-fiction about dogs." avg. press run 8M. Pub'd 1 title 1998; expects 1 title 1999, 1 title 2000. 3 titles listed in the *Small Press Record of Books in Print* (28th Edition, 1999-00). avg. price, cloth: $19.95; paper: $9.95. Discounts: jobber 55%, bookstores: 1 10%, 2-4 20%, 5 or more 40%. 100pp; size varies; of. Reporting time: 3 months. Simultaneous submissions accepted: no. Publishes 2% of manuscripts submitted. Payment: varies. Copyrights for author. Maine Alliance of Publishers and Writers, SPAN, PMA, Academy of American Poetry, Poets House.

Two Eagles Press International, Dr. Paul E. Huntsberger, PO Box 208, Las Cruces, NM 88004, 505-523-7911; Fax 523-1953; pjhuntsber@aol.com. 1991. Non-fiction. "Additional address: 1029 Hickory Drive, Las Cruces, NM 88005. Crosscultural/international oriented materials only; book length 50-200 pages; will consider bilingual English/Spanish submissions." avg. press run 1.5M. Expects 1 title 1999, 1 title 2000. 2 titles listed in the *Small Press Record of Books in Print* (28th Edition, 1999-00). avg. price, paper: $14.95-19.95. Discounts: booksellers regular 1-5 books 20%, 6-25 40%, 26-74 45%, 75+ 50%; individuals 1 0%, 2-5 10%, 6+ 20%. 240pp; 6×9; of. Reporting time: 6 weeks. Simultaneous submissions accepted: yes. Publishes 25% of manuscripts submitted. Payment: 8%, negotiable. Copyrights for author. New Mexico Book Association, SPAN.

TWO LINES, Olivia E. Sears, PO Box 641978, San Francisco, CA 94164-1978, 415-863-8586 phone/Fax; editors@twolines.com; www.twolines.com. 1995. Poetry, fiction, articles, art, photos, cartoons, interviews, satire, criticism, reviews, music, letters, parts-of-novels, long-poems, plays, news items, non-fiction. "*Two Lines* is a forum for translation. We seek the best of international literature in translations from any language into English. Each submission must be accompanied by a translator's introduction regarding the original author and work and comments on the translation process. All genres of literature in translation will be considered. Each issue is thematic; themes are announced each August. Published annually in the spring." circ. 500. 1/yr. Pub'd 1 issue 1998; expects 1 issue 1999, 1 issue 2000. sub. price: $11 + $2 s/h domestic, $4 s/h int'l; per copy: same; sample: same. Back issues: same; buy set of 5 ('95-99) for $45. Discounts: 20% libraries, 40% bookstores/agent. 225pp; 8½×5½. Reporting time: 2 months after submission deadline. Simultaneous submissions accepted: no. Publishes 5% of manuscripts submitted. Payment: none. Copyrighted, reverts to author. Ads: space provided, we hope to advertise in the future. CLMP.

●**TWO RIVERS REVIEW, POETS'PAPER**, Phillip Memmer, 215 McCartney Street, Easton, PA 18042, 610-559-3887; tworiversreview@juno.com; www.members.tripod.com/~tworiversreview/index.html. 1997. Poetry, art, photos. "Recent contributors include: Billy Collins, Naomi Shihab Nye, and Mark Jarman." circ. 500. 2/yr. Pub'd 2 issues 1998; expects 2 issues 1999, 2 issues 2000. sub. price: $15; per copy: $7.50; sample: $5. Discounts: 30%. 50pp; 5½×8½; †of. Reporting time: 6 weeks maximum. We accept simultaneous submissions if specified by author. Publishes 1% of manuscripts submitted. Payment: 1 copy. Copyrighted, reverts to author. Ads: $360/$205/$125 1/4 page.

2.13.61 Publications, PO Box 1910, Los Angeles, CA 90078, 213-969-8791. 1984. avg. press run 2M. Pub'd 10 titles 1998; expects 10 titles 1999, 10 titles 2000. 34 titles listed in the *Small Press Record of Books in Print* (28th Edition, 1999-00). avg. price, paper: $11. Discounts: PGW discount schedule. 150pp; 5½×8½. Copyrights for author.

Two Thousand Three Associates, 4180 Saxon Drive, New Smyrna Beach, FL 32169-3851, 904-427-7876; Fax 904-423-7523; ttta@worldnet.att.net. 1994. Non-fiction. "No unsolicited manuscripts. *Proposals only.*" avg. press run 4M. Pub'd 2 titles 1998; expects 4 titles 1999, 4 titles 2000. 6 titles listed in the *Small Press Record of Books in Print* (28th Edition, 1999-00). avg. price, paper: $13.95. Discounts: IPG (Independent Publishers Group) distributes our books and sets discount rate. 144pp; 6×9. Reporting time: 1 month. Simultaneous submissions accepted: yes. Payment: per author/individual basis. Copyrights for author. PMA, Florida Publishers Association (FPA), National Association of Independent Publishers (NAIP).

Tyro Publishing, Stan Gordon, 194 Carlbert Street, Sault St. Marie, Ontario P6A 5E1, Canada, 705-253-6402, Fax 705-942-3625; tyro@sympatico.ca. 1984. Poetry, fiction, articles, art, cartoons, satire, reviews, parts-of-novels, long-poems, non-fiction. "We seriously consider work from previously unpublished authors." Pub'd 2 titles 1998; expects 2 titles 1999, 2 titles 2000. 7 titles listed in the *Small Press Record of Books in Print* (28th Edition, 1999-00). avg. price, paper: $10. Discounts: 25%-40%. 150pp; 5½×8½; depends on size and press run. Reporting time: 2 weeks to 1 month. Payment: varies. Does not copyright for author.

U

U.S. Chess Federation (see also CHESS LIFE; SCHOOL MATES), Glenn Petersen, (CL); Brain Bughee, (SM), 186 Route 9W, New Windsor, NY 12553, 914-562-8350. 1939. Articles, photos, cartoons, news items, non-fiction.

UC Books, Franette Armstrong, Box 1036, Danville, CA 94526, 510-820-3710; Fax 510-820-3711; E-mail ucbooks@aol.com. 1996. Non-fiction. "Very small list of selected health books. Primary interest: technology and medicine. Send query letter. No unsolicited manuscripts" avg. press run varies. Expects 2 titles 1999, 2-4 titles 2000. 1 title listed in the *Small Press Record of Books in Print* (28th Edition, 1999-00). avg. price, paper: $19.95. Contact publisher for discount information. 350pp; 6×9; of. Copyrights for author. PMA.

ULITARRA, Michael Sharkey, Coordinating Editor; Winifred Belmont, Stephen Harris, Prose Editor, PO Box 195, Armidale, New South Wales 2350, Australia, +612 6772 9135. 1992. Poetry, fiction, articles, photos, interviews, satire, criticism, parts-of-novels. circ. 600. 2/yr. Pub'd 2 issues 1998; expects 2 issues 1999, 2 issues 2000. sub. price: $19AUS (oversea airmail rate $30AUS); per copy: $10AUS (Oversea airmail rate $15AUS); sample: $10AUS (Oversea $15AUS). Back issues: $10AUS (Oversea $15AUS). Discounts: 20% for bulk orders. 150pp; 5⅞×8¼. Reporting time: 2 weeks. Simultaneous submissions accepted: no. Publishes .2% of manuscripts submitted. Payment: poems $60, short stories & essays/articles $120. Copyrighted, reverts to author. Pub's reviews: 35 in 1998. §Poetry, fiction, history, biography, magazines. Ads: $120 per 1/2 page.

UMBRELLA, Judith A. Hoffberg, PO Box 3640, Santa Monica, CA 90403, 310-399-1146. 1978. Articles, art, photos, cartoons, interviews, criticism, reviews, news items, non-fiction. "News and of artists' books & artists' periodicals." circ. 1M. 2-3/yr. Pub'd 3 issues 1998; expects 3 issues 1999, 3 issues 2000. sub. price: $18; per copy: $6; sample: $5. Back issues: $8 and above. Discounts: none. 36pp; 8½×11; of. Reporting time: 4 weeks. Payment: none. Copyrighted, reverts to author. Pub's reviews: 200 in 1998. §Contemporary art, photography, bookworks by artists, new artists' publications like periodicals, pamphlets, audioworks by artists, records by artists, copy art. Ads: /$100/25¢ - no full pages.

Umbrella Books, Kent Sturgis, Box 82368, Kenmore, WA 98028. 1988. "Twelve books available. Additional titles in preparation. Umbrella Books specializes in travel guides to the Pacific Northwest. We are seeking manuscripts for regional travel guides" avg. press run 5M. Pub'd 2 titles 1998; expects 2 titles 1999, 2 titles 2000. 17 titles listed in the *Small Press Record of Books in Print* (28th Edition, 1999-00). avg. price, paper: $12.95. Discounts: In process. 150pp; 5½×8½. Copyrights for author. ABA, PMA, BPNW.

THE U*N*A*B*A*S*H*E*D LIBRARIAN, THE "HOW I RUN MY LIBRARY GOOD" LETTER, Mary P. Ph.D Scilken, Editor, G.P.O. Box 2631, New York, NY 10116. 1971. Poetry, fiction, articles, photos, cartoons, interviews, satire, criticism, reviews, letters, non-fiction. "*U*L* seeks long (and especially short) articles on innovative library procedures; forms and book lists. Articles should be complete to enable the reader to 'do it' with little or no research. Single paragraph 'articles' are ok with *U*L*. We ask for non-exclusive rights. Also humorous library situations, library poetry, library fiction, library cartoons." 4/yr. Pub'd 4 issues 1998; expects 4 issues 1999. sub. price: $48 foreign & Canadian postage add $8, payable in US funds on US bank; per copy: $12 foreign + Canadian postage add $2, airmail $5; sample: free to libraries and librarians (send address label). Back issues: (most are in print) are $12 each, add $2 foreign + Canadian p/h. 32pp; 8½×11; of. Payment: none. Copyrighted. Pub's reviews. §Library subjects only.

UNARIUS LIGHT JOURNAL, Barbara Rogers, Editor, 145 S. Magnolia Avenue, El Cajon, CA 92020, 619-444-7062, 1-800-475-7062, fax 1-619-444-9637, E-mail; uriel@unarius.org, Web; http://www.unarius.org. 1974. Poetry, articles, art, photos, interviews, reviews, long-poems, non-fiction. "A specialized publication of the Unarius Academy of Science featuring articles on Past Life Therapy, Extraterrestrial Intelligence, and current topics of global interest. Focus is on elements of positive, progressive change, and the growth and development of the mental-spiritual faculties of humankind on Earth. Includes book, video, and film reviews, personal experiences, and consciousness reincornation" circ. 1.5M. 4/yr. Pub'd 2 issues 1998; expects 4 issues 1999, 4 issues 2000. sub. price: $30, $40 foreign; per copy: $7 + postage; sample: $7 + postage. Back issues: $7 + postage if available. Discounts: 40%. 52-66pp; 6×9; †of. Copyrighted. Pub's reviews.

UND Press (see also NORTH DAKOTA QUARTERLY), Robert W. Lewis, Editor; William Borden, Fiction Editor; Jay Meek, Poetry Editor, University of North Dakota, PO Box 7209, Grand Forks, ND 58202, 701-777-3321. 1910. 4 titles listed in the *Small Press Record of Books in Print* (28th Edition, 1999-00). †of.

UNDER THE SUN, Michael O'Rourke, Editor, Department of Eng., Tennessee Tech Univ., Box 5053,

Cookeville, TN 38505. 1995. Non-fiction. "'An essay,' it has been said, 'is a short piece of prose in which the author reveals himself in relation to any subject under the sun.' Hence, the name of our magazine. It is devoted exclusively to the publication of a form that began with Montaigne and that continues, despite neglect, to thrive today. No academic articles, reviews, feature stories, or excerpts. An essay from our inauguual issue was chosen for inclusion in the 1997 volume of Best American Essays." circ. 500. 1/yr. Pub'd 1 issue 1998; expects 1 issue 1999, 1 issue 2000. sub. price: $8; per copy: $8; sample: $8. 100-150pp; 5½×8½; †of. Reporting time: 1-4 months. Payment: 1 copy. Copyrighted, reverts to author. Ads: $100/$50.

UNDER THE VOLCANO, Richard Black, PO Box 236, Nesconset, NY 11767, 516-585-7471. 1991. Articles, reviews, music. circ. 7M. 6/yr. Pub'd 6 issues 1998; expects 6 issues 1999, 6 issues 2000. sub. price: $15; per copy: $3; sample: $3. Back issues: $3. Discounts: bulk 80¢ per copy over 50 copies. 60pp; 8¼×10¾; of. Reporting time: 120 days. Simultaneous submissions accepted: no. Payment: none. Not copyrighted. Pub's reviews: 15 in 1998. §Politics, sex, the occult, music. Ads: $325/$175/$110 1/4 page.

THE UNDERGROUND, PO Box 14311, Milwaukee, WI 53214. 1995. Poetry, fiction, articles, art, photos, interviews, satire, criticism, reviews, letters, parts-of-novels, long-poems, non-fiction. "We want writers who take risks, challenge assumptions, and subvert authority, including their own. New or unestablished writers welcome" 3/yr. Pub'd 1 issue 1998; expects 3 issues 1999, 3 issues 2000. sub. price: $5; per copy: $2; sample: $2. 12pp; 8½×11. Reporting time: 4 weeks. Payment: 2 copies. Not copyrighted. Pub's reviews.

THE UNDERGROUND FOREST - LA SELVA SUBTERRANEA, Joseph Richey, Anne Becher, 2737 Kalmia Avenue, Boulder, CO 80304, 303-413-9649. 1986. Poetry, fiction, articles, cartoons, interviews, criticism, reviews, letters, long-poems, concrete art, news items, non-fiction. "Half of *TUF* material is reprinted with permission from other small press publications from North, South and Central Americas. Our emphasis is on creative non-fiction, be it poetry, song, investigative journalism. We are a bilingual hemispheric journal. We especially welcome translations to or from Spanish. Some recent contributors: Eduardo Galeano, Glenn Gant, Daisy Zamora, Diana Bellessi, Jack Collom, Tom Clark, Diane diPrima, William Burroughs, Anne Waldman, Allen Ginsberg, Barry Commoner, Ed Sanders, Ernesto Cardenal, Daniel Sheehan, Andre Gregory, Jose Arguelles, Margaret Randall..." circ. 5M. 2/yr. Pub'd 1 issue 1998; expects 1 issue 1999. 6 titles listed in the *Small Press Record of Books in Print* (28th Edition, 1999-00). sub. price: $12/4 issues; per copy: $10; sample: $10. Back issues: $5. Discounts: 40% to bookstores. 5½×17; †of. Reporting time: 180 days. Simultaneous submissions accepted: yes. Publishes 5% of manuscripts submitted. Payment: in copies. Not copyrighted. Pub's reviews: 4 in 1998. §Art, Latin America, translations, non-fiction, poetry, creative journalist productions, ecology, sustainable development. Ads: $100/$50. A.H.A.B., Book Arts League.

UNDERGROUND SURREALIST MAGAZINE, Mick Cusimano, Underground Surrealist Studio, PO Box 2565, Cambridge, MA 02238, 617-628-4101. 1987. Poetry, cartoons, satire. "Comic strips and cartoons on any subject. Pointless and pornographic material discouraged." circ. 300. 1/yr. Pub'd 1 issue 1998. sub. price: $3; per copy: $3; sample: same. Back issues: $3. Discounts: inquire. 28pp; 8½×11; of. Reporting time: 1 month. Payment: contributor's copy. Copyrighted, reverts to author. Ads: $150/$75. Small Press Alliance.

Underwhich Editions, Paul Dutton, Steven Smith, PO Box 262, Adelaide Street Station, Toronto, Ontario M5C 2J4, Canada, 536-9316. 1978. Poetry, fiction, art, interviews, music, long-poems, collages, plays, concrete art, non-fiction. "Dedicated to presenting, in diverse and appealing physical formats, new works by contemporary creators, focusing on formal invention and encompassing the expanded frontiers of literary and musical endeavor. Recent contributors include: Paul Dutton, Gerry Gilbert, Gerry Shikatani, Mary Maxwell" avg. press run 200-500. Expects 2 titles 1999, 3 titles 2000. 45 titles listed in the *Small Press Record of Books in Print* (28th Edition, 1999-00). avg. price, paper: $10; other: $4. Discounts: 40% to retailers, 20% to educational institutions and libraries, 20% to radio stations on audiocassettes only. 30-50pp; of, lp. Payment: 10% (copies or sales). Copyright remains with author.

Unfinished Monument Press, James Deahl, 237 Prospect Street South, Hamilton, Ontario L8M 2Z6, Canada. 1978. Poetry, long-poems. "At the moment we have a large backlog and are not looking for new material. UnMon has published Milton Acorn, Raymond Souster, Robert Priest, Linda Rogers, and Tanis MacDonald. We like People's Poetry." avg. press run 300-1M. Pub'd 1 title 1998; expects 3 titles 1999, 4 titles 2000. 94 titles listed in the *Small Press Record of Books in Print* (28th Edition, 1999-00). avg. price, paper: $7-15. Discounts: 40% trade and libraries. 126pp; 5½×8½; of. Reporting time: 6 months. Simultaneous submissions accepted: yes. Payment: 10% in cash or copies. Copyrights for author. PMA.

Unfoldment Publications, Richard Barrett, Vicki Worthington, 1200 Huntly Place, Alexandria, VA 22307-2001. 1994. Non-fiction. "Spriual, psychology" avg. press run 3M-10M. Expects 1 title 1999, 2 titles 2000. 1 title listed in the *Small Press Record of Books in Print* (28th Edition, 1999-00). avg. price, cloth: $24.95. 160pp; 6×9; lp. Reporting time: 5 weeks. Payment: negotiable. Copyrights for author. PMA.

THE UNFORGETTABLE FIRE, Jordan O'Neill, Editor, 206 North 6th Street, Prospect Park, NJ 07508-2025. 1991. Poetry, reviews, long-poems. "Short stories pertaining to women's issues." circ. 5M. 2/yr.

Expects 4 issues 1999, 4 issues 2000. sub. price: $10; per copy: $5; sample: $5. Back issues: $5. 25-30pp; 8½×11. Reporting time: 4-6 weeks. Publishes 50% of manuscripts submitted. Payment: free subscriptions. Not copyrighted. Pub's reviews: 3 in 1998. §Women's issues, feminist ideas, non-violence, poetry, racial harmony. Ads: $25/$10.

Unified Publications, 5214-F Diamond Heights #218, San Fransisco, CA 94131, 415-642-0364. 1990. Non-fiction. "Do not submit." avg. press run 5M. Pub'd 1 title 1998; expects 1 title 1999, 1 title 2000. avg. price, paper: $9.95. Discounts: 40% for wholesale to bookstore. 150pp; 5¾×8⅜; of.

Union Park Press, William A. Koelsch, PO Box 2737, Boston, MA 02208. 1978. Non-fiction. "At present the press confines itself to material on gay life and liberation. It has so far published two books, A. Nolder Gay's *The View from the Closet: Essays on Gay Life and Liberation,* (1978); and *Some of My Best Friends: Essays in Gay History and Biography,* (1990)." avg. press run 2M. 2 titles listed in the *Small Press Record of Books in Print* (28th Edition, 1999-00). avg. price, paper: $7. 140pp; 5¼×8¼; of. Reporting time: 1 month. Payment: none. Copyrights for author.

UNION RECORDER, University of Sydney Union, Jason Harty, Level One, Manning House, University of Sydney, NSW 2006, Australia. 1921. Poetry, fiction, articles, art, photos, cartoons, interviews, satire, criticism, reviews, music, letters, parts-of-novels, long-poems, collages, plays, concrete art, news items, non-fiction. circ. 6M. 13/yr. Pub'd 13 issues 1998; expects 13 issues 1999, 13 issues 2000. sub. price: $36A; per copy: $3A; sample: free. Back issues: $3 per copy when available. 36pp; of. Reporting time: 7-10 days. Payment: $10 per page when published. Copyrighted, reverts to author. Pub's reviews: 40-50 in 1998. §All areas from technical to sci-fi. Ads: $A460/$A290/$A160 1/4 page, $A80 1/8 page.

THE UNIT CIRCLE, Kevin Goldsmith, Derek Chung, Nita Daniel, PO Box 20352, Seattle, WA 98102, 206-322-1702, E-mail; zine@unitcircle.org. 1992. Poetry, fiction, articles, art, photos, cartoons, interviews, satire, criticism, reviews, music, parts-of-novels, long-poems, collages, concrete art, non-fiction. "Started as a 32-40pp. magazine, last 2 issues have been 16pp. to reduce cover price and increase frequency. Now accepting ads so size will increase in the near future" circ. 500. 3/yr. Pub'd 3 issues 1998; expects 3 issues 1999, 4 issues 2000. sub. price: $4; per copy: $1; sample: $1. Back issues: $2 for issues 1-3, $1 for issue 4. Discounts: Free to libraries, trade with other small mags., bulk negotiable. 20pp; 5½×8½; †xerox. Reporting time: 2 weeks. Simultaneous submissions accepted: yes. Publishes 15% of manuscripts submitted. Payment: copies. Copyrighted, reverts to author. Pub's reviews: 12 in 1998. §Literature, art, design, commentary, politics, music. Ads: $20/$10/$5.

United Lumbee Nation (see also UNITED LUMBEE NATION TIMES), Silver Star Reed, P.O. Box 512, Fall River Mills, CA 96028, 916-336-6701. 1977. Art. "We have two copyrighted books out: *United Lumbee Indian Ceremonies*; and an Indian cookbook, *Over The Cooking Fires,* both edited and compiled by Princess Silver Star Reed." avg. press run 100. Pub'd 1 title 1998; expects 1 title 2000. 1 title listed in the *Small Press Record of Books in Print* (28th Edition, 1999-00). avg. price, paper: $3.75-$7.50. Discounts: $2.50 per copy. 20-25pp; 5½×8½. Payment: none. Does not copyright for author.

UNITED LUMBEE NATION TIMES, United Lumbee Nation, Silver Star Reed, P.O. Box 512, Fall River Mills, CA 96028, 530-336-6701. 1979. circ. 2M. 3-4/yr. Pub'd 3 issues 1998; expects 3 issues 1999, 4 issues 2000. sub. price: $7/4 issues; per copy: $1.75; sample: $1.75. 8-12pp; 11½×15. Reporting time: no set time, write for press time of next issue. Payment: none. Not copyrighted. Pub's reviews: 1-3 in 1998. §Native American Indian Heritage and Native American Indians today. Ads: $120/$60/Business card size $12/10% discount if put in four issues.

United States Institute for Theatre Technology, Inc. (see also THEATRE DESIGN AND TECHNOLOGY), David Rodger, Editor; Deborah Hazlett, Art Director, 6443 Ridings Road, Syracuse, NY 13206-1111. 1965. Articles, interviews, criticism, reviews. avg. press run 5M. 76pp; 8¼×11; electronic. Reporting time: 6-10 weeks. Payment: none.

Uniting the World Press, Inc. (see also MOTHER EARTH JOURNAL: An International Quarterly), Herman Berlandt, Maureen Hurley, c/o National Poetry Association, 934 Brannan Street, #2ND-FL, San Francisco, CA 94103, 415-552-9261; fax 415-552-9271. 1990. Poetry. "We invite poems from colleagues beyond our borders in good English translations." avg. press run 2M. Pub'd 1 title 1998; expects 2 titles 1999, 2 titles 2000. 1 title listed in the *Small Press Record of Books in Print* (28th Edition, 1999-00). avg. price, other: $5 per copy tabloid. Discounts: 50%. 40pp; 11×15; of. Reporting time: no special deadlines. Simultaneous submissions accepted: yes. Publishes 15% of manuscripts submitted. Payment: 2 free copies. Does not copyright for author. PEN - Oakland.

Unity Books (see also UNITY MAGAZINE; DAILY WORD), Michael Maday, Editor, 1901 NW Blue Parkway, Unity Village, MO 64065, 816-524-3550, fax 816-251-3550. 1889. Poetry, non-fiction. "Types of books sought: spiritual, metaphysical, Christian, self-help, motivational, healing, mysticism." avg. press run

10M. Pub'd 16 titles 1998; expects 18 titles 1999, 20 titles 2000. 80 titles listed in the *Small Press Record of Books in Print* (28th Edition, 1999-00). avg. price, cloth: $11.95; paper: $10.95. Discounts: wholesalers 52%, retailers 40%. 200pp; 5½×8½. Reporting time: 2 months. Simultaneous submissions accepted: no. Payment: upon acceptance. Copyrights for author. MAPA, PMA, NAPRA.

UNITY MAGAZINE, Unity Books, Philip White, Unity Village, MO 64065, 816-524-3550. 1889. Poetry, articles, photos, non-fiction. "Types of materials sought: spiritual, metaphysical, Christian, self-help, motivational, healing, mysticism." circ. 115M. 12/yr. Pub'd 12 issues 1998; expects 12 issues 1999, 12 issues 2000. sub. price: $10.95; per copy: $1.35; sample: free. 80pp; 5.5×8.37; web. Reporting time: 3 months. Simultaneous submissions accepted: no. Payment: upon acceptance. Copyrighted, reverts to author. Pub's reviews: 4 in 1998. Ads: none.

Univelt, Inc. (see also AAS HISTORY SERIES; ADVANCES IN THE ASTRONAUTICAL SCIENCES; SCIENCE AND TECHNOLOGY), R.H. Jacobs, Series Editor, PO Box 28130, San Diego, CA 92198-0130, 760-746-4005; Fax 760-746-3139; 76121.1532@compuserve.com; www.univelt.staigerland.com. 1970. "We are publishing books on space, astronomy, veterinary medicine (esp. first aid for animals). *To Catch a Flying Star: A Scientific Theory of UFOs*; *Realm of the Long Eyes* (astronomy); *General First Aid for Dogs* (veterinary medicine); *The Case for Mars*; *Spacecraft Tables 1957-1990*; *The Human Quest in Space* (space). Publishers for the American Astronautical Society." avg. press run 500-2M. Pub'd 10 titles 1998; expects 10 titles 1999, 10 titles 2000. 50 titles listed in the *Small Press Record of Books in Print* (28th Edition, 1999-00). avg. price, cloth: $25-$120; paper: $20-$90; other: some books at $7 to $15. Discounts: 20%; special discounts for classroom use; larger discounts by arrangement. 100-700pp; 7×9½ and others; of. Reporting time: 60 days. Payment: 10% for a volume author. Copyright held by Society or Univelt but obtained by Univelt.

Universal Unity, S. Dr. Karipineni, 1860 Mowry Ave. #400, Fremont, CA 94538-2167. 1992. avg. press run 20M. Pub'd 3 titles 1998; expects 2 titles 1999. 4 titles listed in the *Small Press Record of Books in Print* (28th Edition, 1999-00). avg. price, paper: $7-$10; other: $19-25. Discounts: 40% 1-4, 50% 5 or more. 300pp; 6×9. Reporting time: varies. Publishes 1-10% of manuscripts submitted. Payment: varies. Copyrights for author.

University Editions, Inc., Ira Herman, Managing Editor, 59 Oak Lane, Spring Valley, Huntington, WV 25704, 304-429-7204. 1984. Poetry, fiction, non-fiction. "Open to new writers. Publishes book-length (45-400 page mss) fiction, poetry, and non-fiction works. Will read first novels. Open to Academic and creative writing. Recent authors include Patricia Guinan, Geriard Flynn and Shirley Ovw. Publishes paperback originals and reprints. Presently reading unsolicited manuscripts in all categories. Enclose SASE for return of material. Simultaneous and photocopied submissions are acceptable. Will consider mss in areas not mentioned if quality is high. A brief synopsis (one or two pages) is helpful. During the next year, at least, we will be doing primarily subsidized publication, although we may be open to doing an occasional non-subsidized title. On subsidized books, author receives all sales proceeds until breakeven point, and royalty thereafter. Attempts to encourage and establish new writers. Occasionally publishes hardcover editions" avg. press run 500-1M. Pub'd 50 titles 1998; expects 50 titles 1999, 50 titles 2000. 6 titles listed in the *Small Press Record of Books in Print* (28th Edition, 1999-00). avg. price, cloth: $16.95; paper: $5-$9. Discounts: 40% bulk order; free examination copies to potential adopters and jobbers. 64-300pp; 5½×8½; of. Reporting time: 1 month. Payment: depends on author and subject matter; 15% royalty on nonsubsidized titles. Copyrights for author.

University of Calgary Press (see also CANADIAN JOURNAL OF PHILOSOPHY; CANADIAN JOURNAL OF PROGRAM EVALUATION/LA REVUE CANADIENNE D'EVALUATION DE PROGRAMME; CANADIAN REVIEW OF AMERICAN STUDIES; ECHOS DU MONDE CLASSI-QUE/CLASSICAL VIEWS), Shirley Onn, Director; John King, Production Editor; Judy Powell, Journals Editor, 2500 University Drive NW, Calgary, Alberta T2N 1N4, Canada, 403-220-7578, fax 403-282-0085. 1981. Non-fiction. "The University of Calgary Press (UCP) was established in 1981 and since then has developed an active publishing program that includes up to 15 new scholarly titles each year and 4 journals. UCP publishes in a wide variety of subject areas and is willing to consider any innovative scholarly publication. The intention is not to restrict the publication list to specific areas. All prices and specifications are subject to change without notice. Prices are in US dollars outside of Canada. Postage & Handling In Canada and the U.S., $5 per corporate or individual order. International orders, $9 per corporate or individual order. Orders go to Univ. of Calgary Press, c/o UBC Press, 6344 Memorial Road, Vancouver, BC V6T 1Z2. 604-822-5959 (toll free fax for orders (Canada/US) 800-668-0821). Fax 604-822-6083. Canadians please add 7% GST to total amount" avg. press run 1M. Pub'd 12 titles 1998; expects 13 titles 1999, 10 titles 2000. 170 titles listed in the *Small Press Record of Books in Print* (28th Edition, 1999-00). avg. price, cloth: $24.95; paper: $22.95. Discounts: booksellers. 287pp; 6×9; desktop. Reporting time: 2-6 weeks; acknowledge receipt 2 weeks, review process 8-12 weeks. Simultaneous submissions accepted: no. Publishes 8% of manuscripts submitted. Payment: after all costs are covered, %. Copyrights for author. BPAA, ACUP, ACP.

University of California Press (see also AGRICULTURAL HISTORY; ASIAN SURVEY; BERKELEY WOMEN'S LAW JOURNAL; CALIFORNIA LAW REVIEW; CLASSICAL ANTIQUITY; EAST

EUROPEAN POLITICS & SOCIETIES; ECOLOGY LAW QUARTERLY; FEDERAL SENTENCING REPORTER; FILM QUARTERLY; BERKELEY TECHNOLOGY LAW JOURNAL; HISTORICAL STUDIES IN THE PHYSICAL & BIOLOGICAL SCIENCES; INDEX TO FOREIGN LEGAL PERIODICALS; BERKELEY JOURNAL OF EMPLOYMENT AND LABOR LAW; BERKELEY JOURNAL OF INTERNATIONAL LAW; JOURNAL OF MUSICOLOGY; LA RAZA LAW JOURNAL; MEXICAN STUDIES/ESTUDIOS MEXICANOS; MOUNTAIN RESEARCH & DEVELOPMENT; MUSIC PERCEPTION; NINETEENTH-CENTURY LITERATURE; 19TH-CENTURY MUSIC; PACIFIC HISTORICAL REVIEW; THE PUBLIC HISTORIAN; REPRESENTATIONS; RHETORICA: A Journal of the History of Rhetoric; SOCIAL PROBLEMS), Rebecca Simon, Journals Manager, 2120 Berkeley Way, Berkeley, CA 94720, 510-642-6263, e-mail journal@ucop.edu. 1893. Articles, photos, interviews, criticism, reviews. "The Journal is an interdisciplinary law journal focusing on the legal concerns of underrepresented women, such as women of color, lesbians, disabled women, and poor women." avg. press run varies. Pub'd 28 titles 1998; expects 30 titles 1999, 32 titles 2000. avg. price, cloth: varies; paper: varies. Pages vary; 6×9, 7×10; of. Reporting time: varies widely. Payment: none. Copyrights in the name of Regents of the University of California (see individual listings). AAUP.

University of Massachusetts Press, Bruce Wilcox, Director; Clark Dougan, Senior Editor, Box 429, Amherst, MA 01004-0429, 413-545-2217. 1964. Poetry, fiction, non-fiction, criticism, letters. "Scholarly publications in the humanities and social sciences" avg. press run 1.25M-1.5M. Pub'd 42 titles 1998; expects 50 titles 1999. 33 titles listed in the *Small Press Record of Books in Print* (28th Edition, 1999-00). avg. price, cloth: $35; paper: $13.95. Discounts: short 20-25%, trade 40-50%. 244pp; 5½×8½. Reporting time: 2-3 months. Simultaneous submissions accepted: yes. Publishes 7% of manuscripts submitted. Payment: varies. Copyrights for author. AAUP.

University of Sydney Union (see also UNION RECORDER), Jason Harty, Level One, Manning House, University of Sydney, NSW 2006, Australia. 1884. Poetry, fiction, articles, art, photos, interviews, criticism, parts-of-novels, long-poems, plays, concrete art. "An annual collection of work contributed from writers across Australia. Recent contributors include John Tranter, Robert Adamson, J.S. Harry and Fiona Machregor" avg. price, other: $8A RRP. 120pp; of. Reporting time: selection in July.

University of Tulsa (see also JAMES JOYCE QUARTERLY), Robert Spoo, Editor, 600 South College, Tulsa, OK 74104. 1963. Articles, criticism, reviews. avg. press run 1.9M. Expects 4 titles 2000. 3 titles listed in the *Small Press Record of Books in Print* (28th Edition, 1999-00). avg. price, paper: $22. 150pp; 6×9; of. Reporting time: 5-6 months. Payment: contributor's copies and offprints. Copyrights for author. CELJ.

University Of Wales Press (see also CONTEMPORARY WALES; EFRYDIAU ATHRONYDDOL; LLEN CYMRU; STUDIA CELTICA; WELSH HISTORY REVIEW; WELSH JOURNAL OF EDUCATION; JOURNAL OF CELTIC LINGUISTICS; ALT-J: Association for Learning Technology Journal), 6 Gwennyth Street, Cathays, Cardiff CF2 4YD, Wales, +44-1222-231919; Fax +44-1222-230908; press@press.wales.ac.uk. 1922. Articles, criticism, non-fiction. "Available in North America from Paul & Company Publishers Consortium" avg. press run 500. Pub'd 8 titles 1998; expects 8 titles 1999, 8 titles 2000. avg. price, paper: £20. Discounts: 10%. 100pp; of. Payment: none. Does not copyright for author. UWP.

UNIVERSITY OF WINDSOR REVIEW, Alistair MacLeod, Fiction Editor; John Ditsky, Poetry Editor; Susan Gold Smith, Art Editor; Simon Watson, Editorial Assistant, Department of English, University of Windsor, Windsor, Ontario N9B3P4, Canada, 519-293-4232 X2332; Fax 519-973-7050; uwrevu@uwindsor.ca. 1965. Poetry, fiction, articles, art, photos, cartoons, interviews, satire, criticism, parts-of-novels, long-poems, collages, plays, concrete art, non-fiction. "We try to offer a balance of fiction and poetry distinguished by excellence—among those who have appeared are: W.D. Valgardson, Joyce Carol Oates, Tom Wayman, etc." circ. 250. 2/yr. Pub'd 2 issues 1998; expects 2 issues 1999, 2 issues 2000. 1 title listed in the *Small Press Record of Books in Print* (28th Edition, 1999-00). sub. price: $19.95 CDN. (+ 7% GST) and $19.95 U.S. per year; per copy: $10 Cdn. and $7 U.S. per year; sample: $8 Cdn. and $7 U.S. per year. Back issues: please write. Discounts: n/a at present. 100pp; 6×9; lp. Reporting time: 6 weeks. Simultaneous submissions accepted: no. Payment: $50 for story or essay, $15 for poem. Copyrighted, reverts to author. Ads: no paid ads at present, though possibly in near future; same for exchange ads—please write.

THE UNKNOWN WRITER, D.S. Davis, Robert Sidor, 5 Pothat Street, Sloatsburg, NY 10974, 914-753-8363; Fax 914-753-6562; E-mail rsidor@worldnet.att.net. 1995. Poetry, fiction, articles, art, photos, interviews, satire, criticism, reviews, letters, news items, non-fiction. "Nothing longer than 5,000 words. Excellent market for new and unpublished writers. Recent contributors: Satig Mesropian, Joshua J. Mark, and David Castleman." circ. 500. 3/yr. Pub'd 3 issues 1998; expects 3 issues 1999, 3 issues 2000. sub. price: $7; per copy: $2.50; sample: $2.50. Back issues: $2. Discounts: 40% to distributors. 48pp; 5½×8½; xerox docutech. Reporting time: 3 months. Simultaneous submissions accepted: yes. Publishes 15% of manuscripts submitted. Payment: 2 sample copies. Not copyrighted. Pub's reviews: 20 in 1998. §Literary bios., environment/nature. Ads: $20/$10/$30 back cover.

UNMUZZLED OX, ZerOX Books, Michael Andre, 43B Clark Lane, Staten Island, NY 10304, 781-448-3395; 212-226-7170; MAndreOX@aol.com. 1971. Poetry, fiction, articles, art, photos, interviews, criticism, reviews, music, letters, parts-of-novels. "It's helpful if contributors already understand pre-anti-post-modernism. Tabloid. Additional address: Box 550, Kingston, K7L 4W5 Ontario, Canada. We do not publish reviews, but we review books elsewhere and love to get them." circ. 20M. 2/yr. sub. price: $20; per copy: $5; sample: $7. Back issues: 1-6: $12 each 7-21 cover price. Discounts: 40%. 140pp; 8½x5½; of. Reporting time: 2 weeks. Payment: none. Copyrighted. §Art, literature, music, politics. Ads: $65/$35. CLMP.

UNO MAS MAGAZINE, Jim Saah, PO Box 1832, Silver Spring, MD 20915, Fax; 301-770-3250, E-mail; unomasmag@aol.com; website http://www.unomas.com/. Poetry, fiction, articles, art, photos, cartoons, interviews, satire, criticism, reviews, music, Poetry, articles, long-poems, non-fiction. "Recent features: T.C. Boyle, Harvey Pekar, Larry Brown, Suzie Bright. Bands: Sugar, Lucinda Williams, Sebadoh, Fugazi, Uncle Tufelo, John Zorn" circ. 3.5M. 4/yr. Pub'd 3 issues 1998; expects 4 issues 1999, 4 issues 2000. sub. price: $11; per copy: $3.50 ppd; sample: $3.50. Back issues: $3.50. 50pp; 8½x11; of. Reporting time: varies. Payment: in copies (will pay for art or photo supplies). Copyrighted, reverts to author. Pub's reviews: 3 in 1998. §Fiction, poetry, music, art, photography. Ads: $200/150/100-new ad rates.

UNWOUND, Lindsay Wilson, PO Box 10205, Bakersfield, CA 93389-0205, 509-687-8046. 1998. "I want writing on contemporary human life. I like writing that is clear, honest, identifiable...written in real life language. Looking for poetry based on poet's life, or people they see, but is tied to universal meaning and themes. Every issue has a featured poet that is given 3 to 5 pages, last two have been C.C. Russell and Dan Crocker. Must send SASE for reply and only send copies of art...it won't be coming back." circ. 100-150. 2/yr. Expects 5 issues 1999, 2 issues 2000. sub. price: $4; per copy: $2; sample: $2. Back issues: $2. Discounts: varies, write for info. 32-36pp; 5½x8½; †copied, printed. Reporting time: 3 weeks-3 months. Simultaneous submissions accepted if so noted. Publishes 25% of manuscripts submitted. Payment: 1 copy. Copyrighted, reverts to author. Pub's reviews: 5 in 1998. §poetry, chapbooks, music, raves. Ads: $15/$7.50/trade with like magazines.

‡UP CLOSE, A Quarterly Review of New Age & Alternative Publication Newsletter, Darla Sims, PO Box 12280, Mill Creek, WA 98082, FAX 206-485-7926. 1996. Poetry, fiction, photos, cartoons, criticism, music, news items, non-fiction. "Articles to 1,000 words pertaining to content (New Age and alternative publications and topics)." circ. 1M. 4/yr. Expects 2 issues 1999, 4 issues 2000. sub. price: $20; per copy: $10; sample: $10. 16-20pp; 8½x11; lp. Reporting time: 1 month. Publishes 50% of manuscripts submitted. Payment: 3¢ per published word and copies. Copyrighted, reverts to author. Pub's reviews: 100+ in 1998. §New Age and alternative.

Upney Editions, 19 Appalachian Crescent, Kitchener, Ontario N2E 1A3, Canada. 1996. Pub'd 2 titles 1998; expects 3 titles 1999, 3 titles 2000. 5 titles listed in the *Small Press Record of Books in Print* (28th Edition, 1999-00). Discounts: 1-2 books 15%; 3-5 books 30%; 6+ 40%. Simultaneous submissions accepted: no. Payment: 10% royalty; no advance; 20 complimentary copies. Copyrights for author.

Upper Access Inc., Steve Carlson, Lisa Carlson, PO Box 457, 1 Upper Access Road, Hinesburg, VT 05461, 800-356-9315 (orders only); 802-482-2988; fax 802-482-3125; books@upperaccess.com. 1987. Non-fiction. "*No* genre focus. We are looking for unique non-fiction to improve the quality of life. (We also have a mail order bookstore to market books of other small publishers. Wide range of topics considered. Annual circ. 100,000.) We offer 800 fulfillment sevice (Visa, American Express, Discover and MC) for retail sales for other small publishers. Marketing a low-cost software program that we developed for small presses, PIIGS: Publishers Invoice and Information Generating System, V.2.2. for Dos, Windows 95 edition expected soon." avg. press run 8M. Pub'd 1 title 1998; expects 3 titles 1999, 2 titles 2000. 7 titles listed in the *Small Press Record of Books in Print* (28th Edition, 1999-00). avg. price, paper: $14.95. Discounts: library 15%; up to $60 retail 20%, $60+ retail 40%; we pay postage on prepaid orders. 195-603pp; 6x9; of. Reporting time: 2 weeks, usually. We accept simultaneous submissions, but inquire first. Publishes a very small % of manuscripts submitted. Payment: 10% of net sales to 5,000 books, 15% thereafter, modest advance for finished mss. Copyrights for author. PMA, Vermont Pub. Group, Nat'l Assoc. of Independent Publishers, SPAN.

Upstart Publishing Company, Inc., Cynthia A. Zigmud, Executive Editor; Danielle Egan-Miller, Acquisitions Editor, 155 North Wacker Drive, Chicago, IL 60606-1719, 1-800-621-9621 ex. 4310. 1976. Articles, non-fiction. "Small business management books with an emphasis on practical, jargon-free how-to information for the owner/manager/student. We prefer information that is based on experience. We also like lots of examples, checklists and devices that involve the reader." avg. press run 7M. Pub'd 10 titles 1998; expects 10 titles 1999, 10 titles 2000. 7 titles listed in the *Small Press Record of Books in Print* (28th Edition, 1999-00). avg. price, paper: $19.95. Discounts: distributed by Dearborn Trade, Chicago, IL. 200pp; 8½x11, 6x9; desktop. Reporting time: 6-8 weeks. Simultaneous submissions accepted: yes. Publishes 5% of manuscripts submitted. Payment: negotiable. Copyrights negotiable. ABA.

590

URBAN GRAFFITI, Greensleeve Editions, Mark McCawley, PO Box 41164, Edmonton, AB T6J 6M7, Canada. 1993. Poetry, fiction, articles, art, photos, cartoons, interviews, satire, criticism, reviews, parts-of-novels, long-poems, collages, plays, concrete art, non-fiction. *"Urban Graffiti* is a litzine of transgressive, discursive, post-realist writing concerned with the struggles of hard-edged urban living, alternative lifestyles, deviance, and presented in their most raw and unpretentious form." circ. 250. 2/yr. Pub'd 2 issues 1998; expects 2 issues 1999, 2 issues 2000. sub. price: $10; per copy: $5; sample: $4. Back issues: none. Discounts: none. 24pp; 7×11; †desktop published. Reporting time: 6-8 weeks. Simultaneous submissions accepted: yes. Publishes 20% of manuscripts submitted. Payment: copies. Copyrighted, buys First N. American Serial Rights and First Anthology Rights. Pub's reviews: 2 in 1998. §Alternative magazines and small press books. Ads: on individual basis.

Urban Legend Press (see also THE URBANITE), Mark McLaughlin, Editor & Publisher, PO Box 4737, Davenport, IA 52808. 1991. Poetry, fiction, reviews, parts-of-novels, long-poems, non-fiction. "Writers must request our guidelines (w/SASE) if interested in submitting to *The Urbanite,* and must query (again, w/SASE) before submitting book projects." avg. press run 500-1M. Pub'd 4 titles 1998; expects 5 titles 1999, 5 titles 2000. avg. price, paper: $5. Discounts: interested companies should inquire. 60-92pp; 8½×11; of. Reporting time: 2-3 months. Simultaneous submissions accepted: no. Publishes less than 5% of manuscripts submitted. Payment: for anthologies, we pay 'per word,' varies for chapbooks (negotiable). Does not copyright for author.

THE URBAN REVIEW, Human Sciences Press, Inc., George W. Noblit, William T. Pink, 233 Spring Street, New York, NY 10013, 212-620-8000. 1966. Articles, non-fiction. *"The Urban Review* provides a forum for communication among urban educators, scholars, administrators, and all others concerned with improving public education in urban communities. The journal publishes original reports on important empirical studies and theoretical essays that examine the basic issues confronting urban schools. All correspondence concerning subscriptions should be addressed to: Subscription Dept., Human Sciences Press, Inc., PO Box 735 Canal St. Sta., New York, NY 10013. All editorial correspondence should be addressed to: David E. Kapel, Editor, College of Education, University of New Orleans, New Orleans, LA 70148" 4/yr. Pub'd 4 issues 1998; expects 4 issues 1999, 4 issues 2000. sub. price: indiv. $33, instit. $140. Back issues: Contact: J.S. Canner, Inc., 10 Charles St, Needham, MA 02194. Discounts: 5% to subscription agents. 64pp; 6½×9½; of. Reporting time: 3 months. Payment: none. Copyrighted, does not revert to author.

The Urbana Free Library, Frederick A. Schlipf, 201 South Race Street, Urbana, IL 61801, 217-367-4057. 1874. Articles, photos, non-fiction. "Currently, all the library's publications are on the history and people of east central Illinois." avg. press run 500-1.5M. 7 titles listed in the *Small Press Record of Books in Print* (28th Edition, 1999-00). avg. price, cloth: $12-$50; other: $6-$100 maps. Discounts: retail and wholesale schedules are available on request. Items 1, 2, 3, and 8 are short-discounted. Pages vary; size varies; of. Payment: usually 15% of net.

THE URBANITE, Urban Legend Press, Mark McLaughlin, Editor & Publisher, PO Box 4737, Davenport, IA 52808. 1991. Poetry, fiction, reviews, parts-of-novels, non-fiction. "Stories to 3,000 words; poetry up to 2 typed pages. Submitters must write for guidelines (and include a SASE) prior to sending us material. Fiction and poetry must concern the surreal; plus, we have theme issues. Recent contributors: Pamela Briggs, M.R. Scofidio, Thomas Ligotti, Hugh B. Cave, Joel Lane, Basil Copper, Thomas Wiloch, and W.H. Pugmire." circ. 500-1M. 3/yr. Pub'd 2 issues 1998; expects 3 issues 1999, 3 issues 2000. sub. price: $13.50/3 issues; per copy: $5; sample: $5. Back issues: #2,#5 $5 ea. Discounts: interested companies should inquire. 60-92pp; 8½×11; of. Reporting time: 2-3 months. Simultaneous submissions accepted: no. Publishes less than 5% of manuscripts submitted. Payment: 2¢ to 3¢/word for fiction and nonfiction, $10 per poem; for first N. American serial rights and non-exclusive rights for public readings (we give public readings on a local/regional level). Copyrighted, reverts to author. Pub's reviews: 0 in 1998. §Publications (books=story collections and novels) with surreal content. Ads: inquire.

URBANUS/RAIZIRR, Peter Drizhal, PO Box 192921, San Francisco, CA 94119-2921. 1987. Poetry, fiction, art, interviews, reviews. "We seek fiction and poetry with an eye on being anti-mainstream, though sometimes it becomes necessary to cross over...All styles. Recently published: Ursula K. LeGuin, Pat Murphy, James Sallis, Yusef Komunyakaa, Susan Moon, Louise Rafkin" circ. 1M. 2/yr. Pub'd 1 issue 1998; expects 2 issues 1999, 2 issues 2000. sub. price: $12/3 issues, $15/3 issues institutions; per copy: $5; sample: $5 (postpaid). Back issues: $10 for 3 most recent issues. 64pp; 5½×8½; of. Reporting time: 4-12 weeks. Simultaneous submissions accepted: no. Publishes 1% or less of manuscripts submitted. Payment: $10-$25 for fiction and nonfiction (1000-5000 words) plus 5 copies; ($10-$75 max) 1-2¢/word, $10/poem + 5 copies. Copyrighted, rights revert to author, but reserve the right to use material in a future "best of" anthology. Ads: $100/$50/$25 quarter-page. CLMP.

Urion Press, Alan Rosenus, PO Box 10085, San Jose, CA 95157, 408-867-7695 Fax/phone. 1972. Fiction. "Reprints, fiction, history. Please send letter of inquiry first." avg. press run 2.5M. Expects 1 title 1999. 6 titles listed in the *Small Press Record of Books in Print* (28th Edition, 1999-00). avg. price, cloth: $21.95; paper:

$14.95. Discounts: bookstores 40% on orders over 3, jobbers 50% on orders over 10. 250pp; of. Reporting time: 1 month. Copyrights for author.

Urthona Press, David Hopes, Lightman Lily, 62 LakeShore Drive, Asheville, NC 28804-2436. 1995. Poetry, fiction, art, photos, plays, non-fiction. "Book length only." avg. press run 750-1M. Expects 4 titles 1999, 4 titles 2000. 3 titles listed in the *Small Press Record of Books in Print* (28th Edition, 1999-00). avg. price, cloth: $20; paper: $8. Pages vary; lp. Reporting time: 5 months or less. Simultaneous submissions accepted: yes. Publishes 10% of manuscripts submitted. Payment: case by case. Copyrights for author.

US1 Poets' Cooperative (see also US1 WORKSHEETS), Rotating board, PO Box 127, Kingston, NJ 08528-0127, 609-921-1489; fax 609-279-1513. 1973. Poetry, fiction. avg. press run 500. Pub'd 1 title 1998; expects 1 title 1999, 1 title 2000. 2 titles listed in the *Small Press Record of Books in Print* (28th Edition, 1999-00). avg. price, paper: $7. Discounts: inquire. 70pp; 5½x8½; of. Reporting time: 2-3 months if reading, query first; 1 week if not reading. Simultaneous submissions accepted: no. Publishes 10% of manuscripts submitted. Payment: 1 copy. Copyrights for author. CLMP.

US1 WORKSHEETS, US1 Poets' Cooperative, Rotating panel, PO Box 127, Kingston, NJ 08528-0127, 609-921-1489; fax 609-279-1513. 1973. Poetry, fiction, satire, parts-of-novels, long-poems. "Fiction should not be over 2500 words, double-spaced. Five poems, single or double-spaced. A wide range of tastes represented in the rotating panel of editors. No restriction on subject or point of view. We read unsolicited mss, but accept very few. Send SAS-postcard for notification of reading periods, which vary. All inquiries and mss should be sent to the secretary, c/o Jane Rawlings, PO Box 401, Bernardsville, NJ 07924; 908-221-0076." circ. 500. 1/yr. Pub'd 1 issue 1998; expects 1 issue 1999, 1 issue 2000. sub. price: $10 (2 double issues); per copy: $7 (double issue); sample: $5; (old format) $4). Back issues: inquire. No. 1 and No. 2 have become quite rare, several issues sold out. Discounts: inquire. 70pp; 5½x8½; of. Reporting time: best to query first if we are reading at that time—send SAS-postcard as per above. Simultaneous submissions accepted: no. Publishes 10% of manuscripts submitted. Payment: 1 copy. Copyrighted, reverts to author. Ads: none. CLMP.

Utah Geographic Series, R. Reese, Box 8325, Salt Lake City, UT 84108. 1985. Non-fiction. "Full color books about Utah. 50% text (about 30,000-70,000 words each volume) and 50% color photos, maps, charts." avg. press run 10M. 3 titles listed in the *Small Press Record of Books in Print* (28th Edition, 1999-00). avg. price, cloth: $28.95; paper: $17.95. Discounts: 40% to retailers. 120pp; 11½x8¾. Payment: negotiated. Does not copyright for author. Utah Assn. of Publishers.

UTNE READER, Eric Utne, Chairman; Hugh Delehanty, Editor; Craig Cox, Managing Editor, 1624 Harmon Place #330, Minneapolis, MN 55403, 612-338-5040. 1984. Articles, art, photos, cartoons, interviews, satire, criticism, reviews, letters, news items, non-fiction. "*Utne Reader* is a digest of alternative ideas and material reprinted from alternative and independent media. We don't accept unsolicited reviews, but we do accept unsolicited cartoons." circ. 260M. 6/yr. Pub'd 6 issues 1998; expects 6 issues 1999, 6 issues 2000. sub. price: $19.97; per copy: $4.99; sample: $7 (includes p/h). Back issues: $7, some older issues are $25. Discounts: inquire. 120pp; 7⅜x10; web of. Reporting time: 2 months. Payment: varies. Copyrighted, reverts to author. Pub's reviews: 60-100 in 1998. §All small circulation, independently-published periodicals welcome. Ads: $16,025/$9,620/$4.75 classified word.

V

VACUITY, 1512 Canyon Run Road, Naperville, IL 60565. 1994. Poetry, fiction, art, photos, music, non-fiction. "*Vacuity* is the logical extention of *Fragmented*, a musical project of mine. The two can go together or separate, the each have enough for their own bizzare worlds. Philosophy, fiction, photography. All about darkness and living alone in it." circ. 500. Erratic. Pub'd 1 issue 1998; expects 2 issues 1999, 2-3 issues 2000. price per copy: $1. Back issues: $1 for any previous issue. Discounts: $7 for 10, $10 for 20, $35 for 100. 25-30pp; 8½x10; †mi. Reporting time: ASAP. Ads: No Ads.

●**VAGABOND, Phony Lid Publications**, K. Vaughn Dessaint, PO Box 2153, Rosemead, CA 91770, e-mail vagrag@mindspring.com. 1998. Poetry, fiction, articles, art, photos, cartoons, satire, reviews, music, letters, non-fiction. "We accept manuscripts of any length with a focus on post punk, urban gore." circ. 200. 6/yr. Pub'd 4 issues 1998; expects 10 issues 1999, 20 issues 2000. sub. price: $20; per copy: $5; sample: $3. Back issues: $3. Discounts: 25% over 20. 64pp; 5½x8½; †docutech, laser and inkjet. Reporting time: 2 months. Simultaneous submissions accepted: yes. Publishes 10-20% of manuscripts submitted. Payment: copies and subscription. Copyrighted, reverts to author. Ads: $50/$35/$20 1/4 page.

Vagabond Press, John Bennett, 605 East 5th Avenue, Ellensburg, WA 98926-3201, 509-962-8471; bangsj@eburg.com. 1966. Poetry, fiction, articles, art, photos, interviews, reviews, letters, parts-of-novels, plays. "Query before submitting." avg. press run 1M. Pub'd 1 title 1998; expects 1 title 1999, 1 title 2000. 9 titles listed in the *Small Press Record of Books in Print* (28th Edition, 1999-00). avg. price, cloth: $10; paper: $5.95. Discounts: 20% trade; orders over $30, 40%; 20% book jobbers. 200pp; 6×9; of. Reporting time: 3-4 weeks. Simultaneous submissions accepted: yes. Payment: by agreement. Copyrights for author.

Vajra Printing an Publishing of Yoga Anand Ashram (see also MOKSHA JOURNAL), Yogi Ananda Satyam, Rocco LoBosco, 49 Forrest Place, Amityville, NY 11701, 516-691-8475; fax 516-691-8475. 1989. Non-fiction. "Primarily interested in books pertaining to Samkhya and Yoga, although we will consider other manuscripts relating to liberation schools such as various forms of Buddhism, Sufism, Mystical Christianity, etc. We are not interested in 'self help' books of any kind. Our 'slant' is philosophical and the writing that interests us pertains to the concept of Moksha defined by Monier-Williams as 'liberation, release' (A Sanskrit-English Dictionary, 1899). Query before sending manuscript." avg. press run 500-1M. Pub'd 1 title 1998; expects 2 titles 1999, 2 titles 2000. 3 titles listed in the *Small Press Record of Books in Print* (28th Edition, 1999-00). avg. price, paper: $9.95. 150pp; 3½×5½; †of. Reporting time: 5-10 weeks. Simultaneous submissions accepted: yes. Payment: after costs are met, profits split 50/50. Does not copyright for author.

Valentine Publishing & Drama Co., James L. Rodgers, Executive Director, PO Box 1378, Ashland, OR 97520-0046, 503-773-7035. 1981. "We are only interested in mss. on Shakespearean and pre-Twentieth Century world drama for now; full length mss.; monographs acceptable." avg. press run 3M-5M. Pub'd 1 title 1998; expects 3 titles 1999, 5 titles 2000. 2 titles listed in the *Small Press Record of Books in Print* (28th Edition, 1999-00). avg. price, cloth: $21.95; paper: $11.95. Discounts: universal discount schedule. 425pp; 5½×8½; of. Reporting time: 30 days. Payment: Author's Guild Contract. Copyrights for author if desired. PMA, Northwest Publishers Assoc.

Valiant Press, Inc., Charity Johnson, PO Box 330568, Miami, FL 33233, 305-665-1889. 1991. Articles, art, photos, non-fiction. "*Senior Pursuits, Making the Golden Years Worth the Wait*, by Roberta Sandler; *Tropical Tastes, and Tantalizing Tales*, by Carol Garvin; *Sarasota Times Past*, by Bernice Brooks Bergen. Only interested in Florida non-fiction subject matter." avg. press run 3M. Pub'd 1 title 1998; expects 1 title 1999, 2 titles 2000. 7 titles listed in the *Small Press Record of Books in Print* (28th Edition, 1999-00). avg. price, cloth: $20; paper: $15. Discounts: trade, wholesale. 200pp; 6×9, 8×10, 5½×8½; of. Reporting time: 30-60 days. Simultaneous submissions accepted: yes. Payment: varies, payment twice a year. Copyrights for author.

VAMPIRE NIGHTS, Full Moon Publications, Sharida Rizzuto, 577 Central Avenue, Box 4, Jefferson, LA 70121-1400, e-mail: smallpress@theglobe.com or fullmoon@eudoramail.com; Website www.members.theg-lobe.com/smallpress/default.htm/, www2.cybercities.com/z/zines/. 1983. Fiction, art. circ. 500-800. 2/yr. Pub'd 2 issues 1998; expects 2 issues 1999, 2 issues 2000. sub. price: $15.80; per copy: $7.90; sample: $7.90. Back issues: $7.90. Discounts: trade with other like publications. 100pp; 8½×11; †of. Reporting time: 2-6 weeks. Simultaneous submissions accepted: yes. Publishes 30-35% of manuscripts submitted. Payment: free copies, fee paid to all contributors negotiable. Copyrighted, reverts to author. Ads: free. NWC, HWA, MWA, WWA, AAA, Small Press Genre Association.

VanderWyk & Burnham, PO Box 2789, 411 Massachusetts Avenue, Acton, MA 01720, 978-263-5906. 1994. Non-fiction. avg. press run 5M. Pub'd 3 titles 1998; expects 2 titles 1999, 2 titles 2000. 9 titles listed in the *Small Press Record of Books in Print* (28th Edition, 1999-00). avg. price, cloth: $21.95; paper: $17.95. 182pp; size varies; of. Reporting time: 1-3 months. Simultaneous submissions accepted: yes. Publishes 2% of manuscripts submitted. Payment: advances $500-3000; royalty 3-10%. Copyrights for author. ABA, PMA, Small Press Center.

Vanessapress, Janet Baird, Vice President, PO Box 82761, Fairbanks, AK 99708, 907-488-5079; jrb@mosquitonet.com. 1984. Poetry, fiction, art, long-poems, non-fiction. "Vanessapress offers publication opportunity to Alaskan women authors for their stories and dreams of life in the Great Land. Publications include poetry, short stories, adventure, cancer journal, pioneer and homestead family experiences. All titles are in stock. Manuscripts or sample chapters are to be typed, double spaced, four copies with SASE if manuscript is to be returned." avg. press run 1.25M. Pub'd 1 title 1998; expects 1 title 1999, 1 title 2000. 7 titles listed in the *Small Press Record of Books in Print* (28th Edition, 1999-00). avg. price, paper: $12.95. Discounts: 40% to retail bookstores, (order through Vanessapress); special orders prepay required on single copy. 125pp; 6×9; of. Reporting time: 3 months. Simultaneous submissions accepted: no. Payment: arranged by contract. Does not copyright for author. Consortium of Northern Publishers, PO Box 60529, Fairbanks, AK 99706.

Vanitas Press, March Laumer, Publisher, Platslagarevagen 4E1, 22730 Lund, Sweden. 1978. Fiction, art, non-fiction. "From 1965 to 1969 books were published under the name of *Opium Books*. Most recent releases pertain to "Oziana" themes. To contact the publisher directly, send to March Laumer, Plaatslagarevagen 4 E 1, 22730 Lund, Sweden." avg. press run 30. Pub'd 2 titles 1998; expects 3 titles 1999, 3 titles 2000. 7 titles listed in the *Small Press Record of Books in Print* (28th Edition, 1999-00). avg. price, cloth: $30 US; paper: $20 US. Discounts: all publications sold at production cost; no discounts. 200pp; 6×8; mi, of. Reporting time: 3-5 weeks. Simultaneous submissions accepted: yes. Payment: each case treated individually. Copyrights for author.

Vanity Press/Strolling Dog Press, Tuli Kupferberg, 160 6th Avenue, New York, NY 10013, 212-925-3823. 1980. Cartoons, satire, music. "Will accept little (if any) unsolicited work. Interested in aphoristic forms, cartoons, 'funny' advertisements, documents, ephemera (found materials)." avg. press run 5M. Pub'd 1 title 1998; expects 1 title 1999, 1 title 2000. 8 titles listed in the *Small Press Record of Books in Print* (28th Edition, 1999-00). avg. price, paper: $1. Discounts: 40%. 32pp; 4¼×5½, 8½×11½; of. Reporting time: short. Does not copyright for author.

VARIOUS ARTISTS, Tony Lewis-Jones, 65, Springfield Avenue, Horfield, Bristol BS7 9QS, England. 1992. Fiction, cartoons, interviews, satire, music, letters, parts-of-novels, collages, plays, concrete art, non-fiction. "Length varies, but longer work must be sustained. Recent contributors include: Dylan Pugh, Jessica Freeman, Helen Kelly, Evangeline Paterson." circ. 250. Pub'd 2 issues 1998. sub. price: £3 ($4.50); per copy: £1 ($1.50); sample: same. Back issues: 75p ($1). 25pp; size A4; photocopied. Reporting time: 2 weeks - 1 month. Payment: 2 complimentary copies. Copyrighted, reverts to author. Pub's reviews: 30 in 1998. §Any poetry which meets the criteria above. Ads: none.

Varro Press, Michael Nossaman, PO Box 8413, Shawnee Mission, KS 66208, 913-385-2034; FAX 913-385-2039; varropress@aol.com. 1992. Non-fiction. "Publisher of law enforcement, security, executive protection training manuals, handbooks, etc." avg. press run 2M. Pub'd 1 title 1998; expects 5 titles 1999, 5 titles 2000. 6 titles listed in the *Small Press Record of Books in Print* (28th Edition, 1999-00). avg. price, paper: $25. Discounts: 1-9 20%, 10-19 30%, 20+ 40%. Pages vary; size varies; of. Reporting time: 60 days. Simultaneous submissions accepted: yes. Publishes 50% of manuscripts submitted. Payment: yes. Copyrights for author. PMA.

VDT NEWS, MICROWAVE NEWS, Louis Slesin, PO Box 1799, Grand Central Station, New York, NY 10163, 212-517-2802. 1984. Articles, reviews, letters, news items. "A newsletter on the health effects of working with computers. We cover legislation, litigation, new research, labor agreements, etc...concerning possible radiation risks, repetition strain injuries and vision problems." circ. 1M approx. 6/yr. Pub'd 6 issues 1998; expects 6 issues 1999, 6 issues 2000. sub. price: $147; per copy: $25; sample: $5. Back issues: $50 for a calendar year, $225 for a bound volume of 1984-1988 or 1989-1993. Discounts: $50.00/year for students. 16pp; 8½×11; lp. Payment: none. Copyrighted, does not revert to author. Pub's reviews: 20 in 1998. §Computers, worker health and safety, epidemiology, non-ionizing radiation, RSIS. Ads: $1,200/$750/$450 1/4 page/$275 1/8 page/$150 1/16 page.

Vedanta Press, R. Adjemian, 1946 Vedanta Place, Hollywood, CA 90068, 213-465-7114. 1947. Non-fiction. "Although I am open to 'that special title', we generally do not print from outside our organization. As a matter of fact, we are mainly keeping our previous titles in print. Rarely is a 'new' title published" avg. press run 3M. Pub'd 2 titles 1998; expects 1 title 1999, 3 titles 2000. 18 titles listed in the *Small Press Record of Books in Print* (28th Edition, 1999-00). avg. price, cloth: $7.95; paper: $7.95. Discounts: 5+ 40%. 150pp; 5×7; of. Payment: no royalty to authors - no payments.

VEGETARIAN JOURNAL, The Vegetarian Resource Group, Mike Vogel, PO Box 1463, Baltimore, MD 21203, 410-366-VEGE (8343). 1982. Articles, art, cartoons, interviews, reviews, letters, news items, non-fiction. circ. 25M. 6/yr. Pub'd 6 issues 1998; expects 6 issues 1999, 6 issues 2000. sub. price: $20; per copy: $3.50; sample: $3. Back issues: inquire. Discounts: inquire. 36pp; 8½×11; of. Reporting time: 1 month. Simultaneous submissions accepted: no. Payment: inquire. Copyrighted, we retain reprint rights. Pub's reviews: 40 in 1998. §Vegetarianism, animal rights, scientific nutrition, recipes. Ads: none.

The Vegetarian Resource Group (see also **VEGETARIAN JOURNAL**), Debra Wasserman, Charles Stahler, PO Box 1463, Baltimore, MD 21203, 410-366-8343. 1982. avg. press run 8M. Pub'd 1 title 1998; expects 2 titles 1999, 2 titles 2000. 10 titles listed in the *Small Press Record of Books in Print* (28th Edition, 1999-00). avg. price, paper: $15. Discounts: 40% bookstores. 224pp; 5×8½, 6×9; of.

VEGGIE LIFE, EGW Publishing Company, Sharon Barela, 1041 Shary Circle, Concord, CA 94518-2407, 510-671-9852. 1993. Art, photos, interviews, reviews, letters, non-fiction. "Growing green, cooking lean, feeling good" circ. 250M. 6/yr. Pub'd 6 issues 1998; expects 6 issues 1999, 6 issues 2000. sub. price: $23.70; per copy: $3.95. 100pp; 8×10½; of, web. Reporting time: 2-6 weeks. Payment: upon publication, first serial rights. Copyrighted, reverts to author. Pub's reviews. Ads: $6435/$4118/$4.75 word.

Vehicule Press, Simon Dardick, General Editor; Michael Harris, Poetry Editor, PO Box 125, Place du Parc Station, Montreal, Quebec H2W 2M9, Canada, 514-844-6073; FAX 514-844-7543, E-mail: vpress@com.org. 1973. Poetry, fiction, non-fiction. "Publishers of Canadian literary works with occasional titles in the area of urban social history and feminism. Actively publish fiction in translation (French(Quebec)-English). Recent publications: *A Private Performance* by Kenneth Radu, *WSW (West South West)* by Erin Moure.'' avg. press run 1M-1.5M. Pub'd 11 titles 1998; expects 12 titles 1999, 12 titles 2000. 148 titles listed in the *Small Press Record of Books in Print* (28th Edition, 1999-00). avg. price, cloth: $30; paper: $16. Discounts: jobbers 20%; bookstores 40%; occasional short-discounted title 20%; please inquire. Poetry 76pp, other 300pp; 6×9; of. Reporting time: 3 months. Payment: generally 10-12%. Copyrights for author. Association of Canadian Publishers (ACP), 260 King St. E., 3rd Floor, Toronto, Canada M6K 1K3, Literary Press Group.

VELONEWS, John Wilcockson, Editor; John Rezell, Senior Editor, 1830 North 55th Street, Boulder, CO 80301. 1972. Articles, photos, cartoons, interviews, reviews, letters, news items, non-fiction. "We now do color editorial." circ. 50M. 20/yr. Pub'd 18 issues 1998; expects 18 issues 1999, 18 issues 2000. sub. price: $39.97; per copy: $3.95; sample: free (followed by subscription). Back issues: $6 each. Discounts: none. 120pp; 14½×11; of. Reporting time: several weeks. Simultaneous submissions accepted: no. Publishes 30% of manuscripts submitted. Payment: flat fee with penalty if story not modemed or sent on disk; $19.80-$120 for photos, $100-$300 for color cover. Copyrighted, reverts to author. Pub's reviews: 15 in 1998. §Competitive cycling. Ads: $2845/$1730/$1 (4-color rates). ABC.

Venom Press (see also CURARE), Jan Schmidt, J.D. Rage, c/o Whalen, 20 Clinton Street #1G, New York, NY 10002. 1991. Poetry, fiction, art, photos. "Length of material: 2pp single-spaced. Biases in favor of women and minority writers. Recent contributors: Susan Sherman, Diane Spodarek, David Huberman, Mike Halchin, Will Inman, and Jan Schmidt" avg. press run 200. Pub'd 5 titles 1998; expects 5 titles 1999, 5 titles 2000. 3 titles listed in the *Small Press Record of Books in Print* (28th Edition, 1999-00). avg. price, paper: $5. Discounts: none. 50pp; 5×7; †laser. Reporting time: at least 3 months. Publishes 30% of manuscripts submitted. Payment: 1 copy. Does not copyright for author.

Venus Communications, PO Box 48822, Athens, GA 30604, 706-369-1547; fax 706-369-8598; email venus@venuscomm.com; www.venuscomm.com. 1996. Art, photos, non-fiction. avg. press run 2M-10M. Pub'd 1 title 1998; expects 2 titles 1999. 1 title listed in the *Small Press Record of Books in Print* (28th Edition, 1999-00). avg. price, cloth: $39.95. †of. Simultaneous submissions accepted: yes. Payment: to be negotiated. Copyrights negotiable.

Veracity Press, Leon Barber, 3765 Motor, Box 702, Los Angeles, CA 90034, 310-820-8269; Veracity96@aol.com. 1995. Poetry, music. "*Markhum Who? Struggling 2B Free*, a collection of 43 poems, 80 pages." avg. press run 5M. Pub'd 1 title 1998; expects 2-3 titles 1999, 5-7 titles 2000. avg. price, paper: $10.95-$19.95. Wholesale, education discount schedules available on request. 80pp; 5½×8½. Reporting time: 8-10 weeks. Simultaneous submissions accepted: yes. Publishes 5% of manuscripts submitted. Payment: negotiated individually. Copyrights for author. PMA.

VERANDAH, Faculty of Arts, Deakin University, 221 Burwood Highway, Burwood, Victoria 3125, Australia, 03-9244-6742. 1986. Poetry, fiction, art, photos, cartoons, music, long-poems. circ. 1M. 1/yr. Pub'd 1 issue 1998; expects 1 issue 1999, 1 issue 2000. sub. price: $10 (Aus); per copy: $10 (Aus). 96pp. Reporting time: 6 months. Copyrighted, reverts to author.

Verbatim, Laurence Urdang, 4 Laurel Heights, Old Lyme, CT 06371-1462, 860-434-2104. 1974. Non-fiction. "Language (English) mainly." avg. press run 3M. avg. price, cloth: $25. Discounts: 50% ppd for +4 copies; 55% ppd for +4 payment with order. 360pp; 6×9, 7×10, varies; of. Reporting time: 6 weeks. Payment: 10% of list price on trade sales; 5% on mail order; 50% of subsidiary rights sales. Copyrights for author.

Verity Press Publishing, Carolyn Porter, Nancy Henderson, PO Box 31, Covina, CA 91723, 818-332-0794. 1995. avg. press run 10M. Expects 1 title 1999, 3 titles 2000. 1 title listed in the *Small Press Record of Books in Print* (28th Edition, 1999-00). avg. price, cloth: $16.95. Discounts: Trade: 1-4 20%, 5+ 40%, wholesale 55%. 144pp; 5½×8½. Reporting time: 6 weeks. Payment: trade standard. Copyrights for author. NAPRA, PMA.

●**Verona Publishing,** 3300 Edinborough Way, Suite 209, Edina, MN 55435, 612-830-0709. 1998. Fiction, art, photos, letters, non-fiction. avg. press run 25m. Expects 5 titles 1999, 7 titles 2000. 2 titles listed in the *Small Press Record of Books in Print* (28th Edition, 1999-00). avg. price, cloth: $10; paper: $6. 160pp; 8½×8½. Reporting time: 1-2 months. Simultaneous submissions accepted: yes. Payment: 5% to 15%.

Veronica Lane Books, 513 Wilshire Boulevard #282, Santa Monica, CA 90401, 800-651-1001, Fax; 310-315-9182. 1992. "Publishes children's picture books primarily presented in unusual and interesting manner. No submissions please." Pub'd 2 titles 1998; expects 6 titles 1999. 1 title listed in the *Small Press Record of Books in Print* (28th Edition, 1999-00). avg. price, cloth: $14.95; paper: $5.95. Discounts: 1-5 books 40%, 6-10 42%, 11-20 44%, 21-30 46%, 31-40 48%, 41+ 50%. 32pp; 8¼×14. APA.

VERSE, Nancy Schoenberger, Brian Henry, English Dept., PO Box 8795, College of William & Mary, Williamsburg, VA 23187-8795. 1984. Poetry, articles, interviews, criticism, reviews. "Articles on contemporary, 10 to 20 pages long, most suitable. We publish a large number of translations of poetry, and poetry by British and American writers. Recent conributors: A.R. Ammons, Seamus Heaney, Galway Kinnell,

Mary Jo Salter, Rovanna Warren, Lavinia Greenlaw, Eavan Boland, Medbh McGuckian, Robert Pinsky, Charles Wright, Richard Kenney. Translations of Michel Deguy, Miroslav Holub, Pier Pasolini, Tomas Trastromer" circ. 1M. 3/yr. Pub'd 3 issues 1998; expects 3 issues 1999, 3 issues 2000. sub. price: $15 individual, $24 institution; per copy: $6; sample: $6. Back issues: $6. 160pp; 6×9; of. Reporting time: 3 months. Simultaneous submissions accepted: yes. Publishes less than 1% of manuscripts submitted. Payment: 2 copies. Copyrighted, reverts to author. Pub's reviews: 16 in 1998. §Poetry, poetry criticism, interviews with poets. Ads: $200/$100.

VERSE: A Journal of Poetry & Poetics, Tim Gavin, Editor, 33 Lowry's Lane, Rosemont, PA 19010. 1991. Poetry, reviews. "Poetry up to 60 we have no restrictions on content or style. No pornography! Recent contributors are Bruce Bennett, Louis McKee, ave jeanne, Ray Greenblatt, Lili Bita, Robert Zeller, Ken Fifer, Harry Humes, Len Roberts, and others. *Verse* is a bi-monthly literary journal interested in publishing excellence in form and content. All manuscripts must include SASE and cover letter." circ. 200 and growing. 6/yr. Pub'd 6 issues 1998; expects 6 issues 1999, 6 issues 2000. sub. price: $6; per copy: $1; sample: available upon request with a 6 X 9 SASE. Back issues: available upon request with a 6 X 9 SASE. 12pp; 8½×5½; †lazer. Reporting time: 3-4 months. Publishes less than 1% of manuscripts submitted. Payment: copies. Copyrighted, reverts to author. Pub's reviews: 1 in 1998. §Poetry. Ads: none.

VERTICAL IMAGES, Mike Diss, Brian Docherty, A.W. Kindness, 10A Dickenson Road, Crouch End, London N8 9ET, England, 0181-340-5974. 1986. Poetry. "*V.I.* is London's leading live-action poetry cabaret circus. We present workshops, readings, guerilla cabaret and public outrages. Our guest readers and contributors include Ken Edwards, Miles Champion, Gavin Selerie, Birdyak, chris cheek, Ulli Freer, Frances Presley, and Chris Putnam. We like sharp, witty, political, post-modernist, post-Frank O'Hara texts." circ. 200. 1/yr. Pub'd 1 issue 1998; expects 1 issue 1999, 1 issue 2000. sub. price: £2.50 UK, $4 US; per copy: same; sample: same. Back issues: varies, #1-5 sold out, #7-9 £1.50 UK, $3 US. Discounts: 33% for 3 or more, larger for bulk, N.B. U.S. sales are post-plus. 64pp; 6×8; mi. Simultaneous submissions accepted: no. Percentage of manuscripts published of those submitted varies. Payment: 3 copies. Copyrighted, reverts to author.

VERVE, Ron Reichick, PO Box 630305, Simi Valley, CA 93063-0305. 1989. Poetry, fiction, photos, reviews, non-fiction. "Poetry max length 2 pages, fiction and non-fiction to 1000 words. Each issue has a theme, listed in guidelines." circ. 700. 2/yr. Pub'd 4 issues 1998; expects 2 issues 1999, 2 issues 2000. sub. price: $12/4 issues; per copy: $3.50; sample: $3.50. Back issues: $4. Discounts: none. 40pp; 5½×8½; of. Reporting time: 4-6 weeks after deadline. Simultaneous submissions accepted: no. Publishes 5% of manuscripts submitted. Payment: copy. Copyrighted, reverts to author. Pub's reviews: 0 in 1998. §Poetry. Ads: none.

Verve Press, Glyn Goldfisher, Assistant Editor, PO Box 1997, Huntington Beach, CA 92647. 1986. avg. press run 4M. Pub'd 1 title 1998; expects 1 title 1999, 1 title 2000. 2 titles listed in the *Small Press Record of Books in Print* (28th Edition, 1999-00). avg. price, paper: $16.95. Discounts: bookstores less than 4 20%, more 50% non-returnable; 40% returnable, 20% college textbook stores. 216pp; 5½×8½. Does not copyright for author. PMA.

verygraphics (see also YELLOW SILK: Journal Of Erotic Arts), Lily Pond, PO Box 6374, Albany, CA 94706, 510-644-4188. 1981. Pub'd 1 title 1998; expects 1 title 1999, 1 title 2000. avg. price, paper: $14. Discounts: varies. 300pp; 6×9. Reporting time: 3 months. Simultaneous submissions accepted: no. Publishes 1-2% of manuscripts submitted. Payment: upon publication. Copyrights for author.

Vesta Publications Limited (see also WRITER'S LIFELINE), Stephen Gill, Editor-in-Chief, PO Box 1641, Cornwall, Ont. K6H 5V6, Canada, 613-932-2135; FAX 613-932-7735. 1974. Poetry, fiction, criticism, plays. avg. press run 1M. Pub'd 11 titles 1998; expects 10 titles 1999, 20 titles 2000. 110 titles listed in the *Small Press Record of Books in Print* (28th Edition, 1999-00). avg. price, cloth: $15; paper: $5; other: $3.50. Discounts: wholesalers 50%, libraries 10%, no shipping charges to American customers or other customers outside Canada. 120pp; 5×8; †of. Reporting time: 4-6 weeks. Payment: 10% paid annually. Copyrights for author. CPA.

Vestal Press Ltd, Vito Mannina, Publisher; Elaine Stuart, Director of Marketing and Publicity, 4720 Boston Way, Lanham, MD 20706-4310, 607-797-4872, fax 607-797-4872. 1961. Non-fiction. "Vestal is recognized world-wide as the leading publisher of books on antique mechanical musical instruments. Also publish in theatre, early film history, and woodcarving. In addition, we distribute books for Emprise Publications, Al-Mar Press and Thistle Ridge Press" avg. press run 2.5M. Pub'd 2 titles 1998; expects 10 titles 1999, 10 titles 2000. 33 titles listed in the *Small Press Record of Books in Print* (28th Edition, 1999-00). avg. price, cloth: $29.95; paper: $19.95. Discounts: 1-5 25%, 6-24 40%, 25-49 42%, 50-99 44%, 100 or more 50%. 200pp; 8½×11, some smaller; of, lo. Reporting time: 3-4 months. Simultaneous submissions accepted: yes. Publishes 20% of manuscripts submitted. Payment: special arrangements made with each, most often 10% of net on each title. Copyrights for author. PMA, ABA.

Vestibular Disorders Association, Jerry L. Underwood, PO Box 4467, Portland, OR 97208-4467,

503-229-7705; fax 503-229-8064; toll-free 1-800-837-8428; e-mail veda@vestibular.org; website http://www.vestibular.org. 1983. Non-fiction. ''Please do not send unsolicited manuscripts.'' avg. press run 2.5M. Pub'd 1 title 1998; expects 1 title 2000. 1 title listed in the *Small Press Record of Books in Print* (28th Edition, 1999-00). avg. price, cloth: $35; paper: $25. Discounts: none. 325pp; 6×9. Simultaneous submissions accepted: no. Payment: negotiated. Copyrights for author.

Via God Publishing, PO BOx 996, Beverly Hills, CA 90213, 310-390-0843. 1989. Poetry, fiction, photos, cartoons, music, non-fiction. avg. press run 5M. Pub'd 4 titles 1998; expects 6 titles 1999, 10 titles 2000. 1 title listed in the *Small Press Record of Books in Print* (28th Edition, 1999-00). avg. price, cloth: $16; paper: $9. Discounts: to be discussed with appropriate persons. 208pp; 5⅜×8⅜; of, lp. Reporting time: 1 month. Payment: varies (8-10%). Copyrights for author. ABA, PMA, ALA.

●**Via Media Publishing Company (see also JOURNAL OF ASIAN MARTIAL ARTS),** Michael A. DeMarco, 821 W. 24th Street, Erie, PA 16502, 814-455-9517; fax 814-526-5262; e-mail info@goviamedia.com; website www.goviamedia.com. 1991. Fiction, art, photos, non-fiction. ''Asian martial arts, European martial arts, Asia-related topics. Length is open. First publication, ''Martial Musings: A Portrayal of Martial Arts in the 20th Century'' by Robert W. Smith.'' avg. press run 6M. Expects 2 titles 1999, 5 titles 2000. avg. price, cloth: $40. Discounts: regular discounts offered. of. Reporting time: 1-2 months. Simultaneous submissions accepted: no. Publishes 10% of manuscripts submitted. Payment: standard. Copyrights for author. PMA.

●**VICTORY PARK: THE JOURNAL OF THE NEW HAMPSHIRE INSTITUTE OF ART,** Linda Butler, 148 Concord Street, Manchester, NH 03104-4858, 603-623-0313 ext 20. 1996. Poetry, fiction, photos, parts-of-novels, long-poems, concrete art. ''Accepts previously unpublished fiction and poetry. Fiction must be under 5,000 words; no more than 5 poems per submission, please. Recent contributors include Wes McNair, James Patrick Kelly, Ellen Dudley, Rebecca Rule, Alice Fogel.'' circ. 400. 2/yr. Pub'd 2 issues 1998; expects 2 issues 1999, 2 issues 2000. sub. price: $16; per copy: $10; sample: $5. Back issues: $5. Discounts: 50% discount 10+. 120pp; 5½×8½; of. Reporting time: 30-40 days after submissions close. Simultaneous submissions accepted, notification required. Publishes 12% of manuscripts submitted. Payment: 2 copies. Copyrighted, reverts to author. Ads: $500/$250/$125. AWP, CLMP.

Victory Press, 543 Lighthouse Avenue, Monterey, CA 93940-1422, 408-883-1725, Fax 408-883-8710. 1988. ''We do not accept freelance submissions.'' avg. press run 2.5-5M. Pub'd 2 titles 1998; expects 6 titles 1999, 6 titles 2000. 12 titles listed in the *Small Press Record of Books in Print* (28th Edition, 1999-00). avg. price, cloth: $14.95; paper: $7.95. Discounts: 40% for 5 or more, 50% 50 or more. 100+pp. Simultaneous submissions accepted: no. Publishes 1% of manuscripts submitted. Payment: 10%. Copyrights for author. PMA, MPE, BAIBA.

VIETNAM GENERATION: A Journal of Recent History and Contemporary Issues, Burning Cities Press, Kali Tal, Dan Duffy, PO Box 13746, Tucson, AZ 85732-3746. 1988. Poetry, fiction, articles, art, photos, cartoons, interviews, criticism, reviews, letters, non-fiction. ''*Vietnam Generation* provides a forum for interdisciplinary scholarship on all subjects of importance to the Vietnam Generation—those born between 1945 and 1960. Each issue is devoted to a single topic, contains no advertising or ephemera in the text, and can, therefore, be used as a teaching resource in college and university courses. Articles should run no more than 10,000 words, and can deal with any aspect of the Vietnam war, 1960s, counterculture, antiwar movement, veteran's issues, political trends, etc. We have a strong focus on gender, class, and race. Contributors have included: Ruth Rosen, David Cortright, John A. Williams, Holly Near, Peter Davies, and many others.'' circ. 400. 2/yr. Pub'd 4 issues 1998; expects 4 issues 1999, 2 issues 2000. sub. price: $40 individual, $75 institutions; per copy: $15 for single issues; $20 for double issues; sample: $15. Back issues: $15 each, $20 double issues, $40 whole volume-year sets. Discounts: 20% for over 10 issues. 220pp; 8½×11; †of. Reporting time: 6-8 weeks. Publishes 25% of manuscripts submitted. Payment: 2 copies of journal. Copyrighted, reverts to author. Pub's reviews: 50 in 1998. §Vietnam war, 1960s, veteran's issues, feminist criticism, popular culture, CIA, military, Asian Americans, Indochina, Afro-Americans. Ads: $75/$40/$25 1/4 page. SSP.

VIGIL, John Howard-Greaves, 12 Priory Mead, Bruton, Somerset BA10 0DZ, United Kingdom, Bruton 813349. 1986. Poetry, fiction, articles, art, criticism. ''As of May 1988 *Period Piece & Paperback* was absorbed by the title *Vigil*. Recent contributors include Sheila Jacob, Teresinka Pereira, Geoff Stevens, Alice Willen and Angela Peluso'' circ. 200. 2/yr. Pub'd 2 issues 1998; expects 2 issues 1999, 2 issues 2000. 1 title listed in the *Small Press Record of Books in Print* (28th Edition, 1999-00). sub. price: £8, $10; per copy: £3, $4; sample: £3. Back issues: £1.50. 44pp; size A5; of/li. Reporting time: 8 weeks USA. Simultaneous submissions accepted: no. Publishes 20% of manuscripts submitted. Payment: 2 copies. Copyrighted, reverts to author. Pub's reviews: 35 in 1998. §Poetry, fiction, writing. ALP.

THE VINCENT BROTHERS REVIEW, Kimberly Willardson, Editor; Michelle Whitley Turner, Associate Editor; Roger Willardson, Associate Editor; Yalkut, Jud, Art Editor, Illustrator, 4566 Northern Circle,

Riverside, OH 45424-5733. 1988. Poetry, fiction, articles, art, photos, cartoons, interviews, satire, criticism, reviews, letters, parts-of-novels, collages, plays, non-fiction. "Our format has changed. Send SASE for updated submission guidelines. Also, send $6.50 for a sample copy and read it before submitting material to *TVBR*. Recent contributors include Gordon Wilson, Florin Firimita, Todd Fry, Janet Paszkowski, Michael E. Waldecki, Robert Miltner, Virginia Van Druten." circ. 350. 3/yr. Pub'd 1 issue 1998; expects 3 issues 1999, 3 issues 2000. sub. price: $12; per copy: $6.50; sample: $6.50. Back issues: $6.50 for recent, $6 for perfect-bound back issue, $4.50 for saddle-stitched back issue. Discounts: $5 per copy for contributors (above 2 payment copies). 96pp; 5×8; docutech, perfect binding. Reporting time: 2-3 months. We accept simultaneous submissions of fiction only, if notified. Publishes 5% of manuscripts submitted. Payment: $10 minimum on publication plus 2 copies for fiction and articles; 2 copies of mag for all other textual contributors; $5 per poem used on 'Page Left' (back page); artwork payment is negotiable have paid up to $50 per piece. Copyrighted, reverts to author. Pub's reviews: 0 in 1998. §Lit mags; small press novels; poetry chapbooks; essay chapbooks; short story collections. Ads: We no longer accept advertising. Council of Literary Magazines and Presses (CLMP).

Vincent Laspina (see also BATH AVENUE NEWSLETTER (BATH)), Rhett Moran, 1980 65th Street #3D, Brooklyn, NY 11204, 718-331-5960; Fax 718-331-4997; Laspina@msn.con, VLaspina@wow.con. 1986. Poetry, art, non-fiction. "We publish limited editions of art portfolios and poetry. Our most recent: Joseph Pavone (artist). We will begin a trade list in 1997 with 12 books per year in the areas of history, political science, biography, lit. crit., reprints of Gold Rush and westward expansion books." avg. press run 50. Pub'd 2 titles 1998; expects 6 titles 1999, 12 titles 2000. avg. price, cloth: $50-$1000 wraps. Discounts: 10%-20% selected art and rare book dealers. Pages vary; †of. Reporting time: 1 month. Payment: 15%-50%. Copyrights for author.

VINEGAR CONNOISSEURS INTERNATIONAL NEWSLETTER, Lawrence Diggs, PO Box 41, Roslyn, SD 57261, 605-486-4536; vinegar@itctec.com. 1996. Non-fiction. "All articles related to vinegar." circ. 20M. 4/yr. Expects 4 issues 1999, 4 issues 2000. sub. price: $10; per copy: $3; sample: $3. Back issues: $3. Discounts: 50% over 10 copies. 8pp; 8½×11; of. Reporting time: 3 months. Simultaneous submissions accepted: yes. Publishes 10% of manuscripts submitted. Payment: none. Copyrighted, reverts to author. Pub's reviews: 4 in 1998. §Vinegar. Vinegar Connoisseurs International.

VINTAGE NORTHWEST, Jane Boren Kaake, Co-Editor; Sylvia Tacker, Co-Editor, PO Box 193, Bothell, WA 98041, 206-821-2411. 1980. Poetry, fiction, articles, satire, non-fiction. "A non-profit, and unfunded, literary magazine, *Vintage Northwest* is sponsored by the Northshore Senior Center of Bothell, WA, and produced by volunteers - illustrators, readers, typists, typesetters, and editors. A showcase for senior talents, *Vintage NW* caters to authors over fifty years old. Submissions and subscribers come from all over the North American continent and from across both oceans. Submissions should be typed, double-spaced, and should be less than 1,000 words in length. We are looking for up-beat stories and essays. We do not use political or religious material. We prefer poetry of less than 32 lines. If you wish your manuscript returned, include an SASE with enough postage to cover cost of mailing. Manuscripts of less than six pages may be sent in a #10 envelope. Only one submission per issue is accepted. Deadlines are February for our summer issue and August for our winter issue." circ. 550. 2/yr. Pub'd 2 issues 1998; expects 2 issues 1999, 2 issues 2000. sub. price: we are unable to take subscriptions as we are only volunteers. We do have a mailing list if people desire to be on it. Mailed copies are $3.25 (includes postage); per copy: $2; sample: $3.25 (includes postage). 72-80pp; 7×8½; †typesetting. Reporting time: 3 months. Simultaneous submissions accepted: yes. Payment: copy of magazine. Not copyrighted. Ads: $80/$40/$20 business card.

Vipassana Publications, Richard R. Crutcher, PO Box 15926, Seattle, WA 98115, 206-522-8175; Fax 206-522-8295; info@vrpa.com; http://www.vrpa.com. 15 titles listed in the *Small Press Record of Books in Print* (28th Edition, 1999-00).

VIRGIN MEAT E-ZINE, Steve Blum, 2325 West Avenue K-15, Lancaster, CA 93536, E-mail virginmeat@aol.com; www.members.aol.com/virginmeat/magazine/gothic.html. 1986. Poetry, fiction, art, cartoons, reviews. "Fiction: under 2,000 words; non-violent, horror. Vampires, ghosts, suspense and depression. Mildly erotic is fine. Poetry: free verse, dark and depressing. No references to modern objects. Not reading anything by anybody who has not e-mailed for recent guidelines" circ. 5M. 3/yr. Pub'd 3 issues 1998; expects 3 issues 1999, 3 issues 2000. price per copy: $5; sample: $5. Back issues: $2. One 3.5 floppy disk; Macintosh. Reporting time: 6 months poetry, 6 weeks fiction and art. Publishes 10% of manuscripts submitted. Payment: 1 copy for each poem, 1 for fiction; art varies. Not copyrighted. Pub's reviews: 5000 in 1998. §Fiction, poetry, software. Ads: $15/$10/$5/$2 classifieds—40 words. Ad trades are available.

VIRGINIA LIBERTY, Stew Engel, PO Box 28263, Richmond, VA 23228-0263. 1985. Articles, news items. "Typical submission length: 3/4 page (typed, double-spaced)." circ. 1200. 6/yr. Pub'd 6 issues 1998; expects 6 issues 1999, 6 issues 2000. sub. price: $15; per copy: $1; sample: $1. Back issues: $1 each. Discounts: bulk $10/100 for classrooms or local affiliates for events. 4pp; web offset. Payment: none. Not copyrighted. Pub's reviews: 3 in 1998. §Libertarian. Ads: $75/$40/$25 1/4 page/$15 1/8 page/$10, classified ads free up to 60 words for individuals; classified for businesses, 10¢ word; classifieds for government agencies, $30 word.

VIRGINIA LITERARY REVIEW, Dan Kennedy, Box 413 Newcomb Hall Station, Charlottesville, VA 22904, Email dpk2c@virginia.edu. 1979. Poetry, fiction, art, photos, cartoons, parts-of-novels, long-poems, collages, plays. "We're looking for innovative, inspired artistic work, genre bending pieces, experiments with language and image, as well as solid, traditional literary work." circ. 3M. 2/yr. Pub'd 2 issues 1998; expects 2 issues 1999, 2 issues 2000. sub. price: $12; per copy: $5; sample: $2. Back issues: $4 while supplies last. 36pp; 6½×10½. Reporting time: 2 months. Simultaneous submissions accepted: no. Publishes 5-10% of manuscripts submitted. Payment: none. Copyrighted, reverts to author. Ads: $120/$70/$40 1/4 page.

THE VIRGINIA QUARTERLY REVIEW, Staige D. Blackford, Editor, One West Range, Charlottesville, VA 22903, 804-924-3124. 1925. Poetry, fiction, articles, satire, criticism, reviews. "Recent contributors: Louis Rubin, George Garrett, Russell Fraser, Edwin M. Yoder, Robert Coles, Mary Lee Settle, Rita Dove, Robert Olin Butler" circ. 4.5M. 4/yr. Pub'd 4 issues 1998; expects 4 issues 1999, 4 issues 2000. sub. price: $18 individual, $22 institution; per copy: $5; sample: $5. Back issues: $5. Discounts: agent's commission: $3. 224pp; 5½×8; of. Reporting time: 6 weeks. Publishes less than 10% of manuscripts submitted. Payment: essays & short stories, $10 per printed page; poetry $1 per line. Copyrighted, rights revert to author upon request. Pub's reviews. §All. Ads: $150/$75.

VIRTUTE ET MORTE MAGAZINE, Lynnea Ranalli, PO Box 63113, Philadelphia, PA 19114-0813, 215-671-6419 pager, 215-338-8234. 1992. Poetry, fiction, articles, art, photos, cartoons, interviews, satire, criticism, reviews, music, long-poems, collages, news items, non-fiction. "Recently gone from covering the Local Philadelphia art and music underground culture to obtaining international acts and renowned poets" circ. 250-500. 1/yr. Pub'd 1 issue 1998; expects 1 issue 1999, 1 issue 2000. sub. price: $16 4 issues; per copy: $5; sample: $5. Back issues: 1st issue $3, 2nd issue $4, 3rd issue $5. Discounts: Exchange policy-with other zines of same or similar value, $4 off subscriptions. 100pp; 8½×11; xerox, laser copy. Reporting time: depends on size of mail pile, approx. 1 month. Simultaneous submissions accepted: yes. Publishes 99% of manuscripts submitted. Payment: discount subscription, all we can currently afford, pull out sheet of contribution. Copyrighted, reverts to author. Pub's reviews: 3 in 1998. §Music, shows. Ads: $40/$30/$20 1/4 page, $10 1/8 page, $60 back cover, $50 inside back.

Visa Books (Division of South Continent Corporation Pty Ltd), Louise N. Gold, PO Box 1024, Richmond North, Victoria 3121, Australia, 03-429-5599. 1975. Non-fiction. avg. press run 3M. Pub'd 5 titles 1998; expects 3 titles 1999, 5 titles 2000. avg. price, cloth: $30; paper: $20; other: $12. Discounts: trade 40%, jobber up to 55%. 240pp; 6×8½; of. Reporting time: 8 weeks. Copyrights for author. AIPA, RVHS.

Visions Communications, 205 E. 10th Street, Suite 2D, New York, NY 10003, 212-529-4029. 1995. Non-fiction. avg. press run 3M. Pub'd 4 titles 1998; expects 4 titles 1999, 5 titles 2000. 5 titles listed in the *Small Press Record of Books in Print* (28th Edition, 1999-00). avg. price, paper: $50. Discounts: 20% w/flexibility. 150pp. Reporting time: 2 months. Simultaneous submissions accepted: yes. Publishes 30% of manuscripts submitted. Payment: 10-25%. Copyrights for author. AMA, SNAP, DMA.

VISIONS-INTERNATIONAL, The World Journal of Illustrated Poetry, Black Buzzard Press, Bradley R. Strahan, Publisher, Poetry Editor; Shirley G. Sullivan, Associate Editor; Melissa Bell, Review Editor; Jeff Minor, Art Editor; Lane Jennings, Circulation, 1007 Ficklen Road, Fredericksburg, VA 22405. 1979. Poetry, art, photos, reviews. "We are looking for poetry that excites the imagination, that says things in fascinating new ways (even if they are the same old things), that hits people 'where they live.' We are open minded about poetry styles but send us *only your best*. You may include matching pen and ink illustrations. We don't care if you're a big name but we do expect poetry that is well worked (no poetasters please). We are always looking for good translations, particularly of work not previously rendered into English and from unusual languages such as Catalan, Celtic languages, Malayan (please include original language version when submitting). Prefer poems under 60 lines (but will consider longer). Recent contributors: Ted Hughes, Louis Simpson, Naomi Shihab-Nye, Lawrence Ferlinghetti, Marilyn Hacker, Michael Mott, Ai, Sharon Olds, Philip Appleman, Miller Williams, Lee Upton, Medbh McGuckian, Andrei Codrescu and Marilyn Krysl. Please don't submit more than 6, or less than 3 poems at a time (not more than once a year unless requested). Strongly recommend getting a sample copy (cost $4.50) before submitting material. *Submissions without SASE will be trashed!* We are indexed in The *Index of American Periodical Verse*, the *Roths Periodical Index*, the *American Humanities Index*, and *Roths Index of Poetry Periodicals*. We are also in *Ulrich's* periodicals listings." circ. 750. 3/yr. Pub'd 3 issues 1998; expects 3 issues 1999, 3 issues 2000. sub. price: $15/1 yr, $28/2 yrs., special rate for libraries only—3 yrs. $45; per copy: $5.50 add $3 per copy for Europe Airmail, $4 for airmail to Asia, Africa and the South Pacific or $2 for Airmail to Latin America and the Carribean; sample: $4.50 plus same postage as single copy. Back issues: quoted on request (a full backrun is still available). Discounts: bulk 30+ copies 30%. 48pp; 5½×8½; of. Reporting time: 3 days to 3 weeks, unless we are out of the country. Payment: 1 contributor's copy, we hope to get money to pay contributors at least $5 per poem in future. Copyrighted, reverts to author. Pub's reviews: 30 in 1998. §Poetry. Ads: none.

Vista Mark Publications, Gene Hines, 4528 S. Sheridan, Suite 114, Tulsa, OK 74145, 918-665-6030; Fax 918-665-6039. 1989. Articles, interviews. avg. press run 2.5M-5M. Pub'd 1 title 1998; expects 3 titles 1999, 5 titles 2000. 1 title listed in the *Small Press Record of Books in Print* (28th Edition, 1999-00). avg. price, paper: $5.95. Discounts: prepay 2-4 20%; 5-9 30%; 10-24 40%; 25-49 42%; 50-74 44%; 75-99 46%; 100-199 48%; 200+ 50%. 78pp; 5½×8½; of. Copyrights for author.

Vista Publishing, Inc., Carolyn S. Zagury, 422 Morris Avenue, Suite 1, Long Branch, NJ 07740, 732-229-6500; Fax 732-229-9647; czagury@vistapubl.com. 1991. Poetry, fiction, non-fiction. "We focus on nurse authors." avg. press run 1M. Pub'd 12 titles 1998; expects 12 titles 1999, 15 titles 2000. 54 titles listed in the *Small Press Record of Books in Print* (28th Edition, 1999-00). avg. price, paper: $14.95. Discounts: offered. Pages vary; 6×9. Reporting time: 90 days. Simultaneous submissions accepted: yes. Payment: based on project. Copyrights for author.

VISUAL ASSAULT OMNIBUS, Rhyan Scorpio-Rhys, Murray Hill Station, Po Box 1122, NY, NY 10156. 1993. Fiction, art. "We specialize in showcasing new and amateur talent. Our current story lines feature science fiction, fiction, action/adventure and horror. Anyone interested should write us for guidelines before submitting. We do not publish 'creator-owned' material." circ. 2M-3M. 4/yr. Pub'd 1 issue 1998; expects 2¾ issues 1999. price per copy: $3; sample: free for review purposes with a $2 postage stamp. Back issues: inquire. Discounts: offered to retail outlets or bulk sales. 64pp; standard comic size; of. Reporting time: all submissions are answered, as long as accompanied by a SASE. Include proper postage for return of submission. Simultaneous submissions accepted: no. Payment: flat rate. Copyrighted, does not revert to author. Ads: $200/$100/25¢ per word.

Visual Studies Workshop (see also AFTERIMAGE), Joan Lyons, Cordinator, USW Press, Research Center, 31 Prince Street, Rochester, NY 14607, 716-442-8676. 1972. Art, photos, interviews, criticism, reviews, concrete art, news items. avg. press run 1M. Pub'd 12 titles 1998; expects 12 titles 1999, 12 titles 2000. 36 titles listed in the *Small Press Record of Books in Print* (28th Edition, 1999-00). avg. price, cloth: $18; paper: $10. Discounts: 10% VSW members - standard to bookstores. Pages vary; size varies; †of. Payment: varies. Copyrights for author.

VITAE SCHOLASTICAE: The Journal of Educational Biography, Caddo Gap Press, Lucy Townsend, Co-Editor; Harvey Neufeldt, Co-Editor, 3145 Geary Boulevard #275, San Francisco, CA 94118, 415-922-1911. 1980. Articles. "The semi-annual journal of the International Society of Educational Biography." circ. 200. 2/yr. Pub'd 2 issues 1998; expects 2 issues 1999, 2 issues 2000. sub. price: $40 indiv., $60 instit.; per copy: $20. 96pp; 6×9; of. Reporting time: 2 months. Publishes 25% of manuscripts submitted. Payment: none. Copyrighted, reverts to author. Ads: $200 per page. MPE, EDPRESS.

Vitreous Group/Camp Colton, Kathleen Lundstrom, Camp Colton, Colton, OR 97017, 503-824-3150. 1983. Art, concrete art, non-fiction. "So far only in house, will consider outside material; glass art subjects." avg. press run 15M. 3 titles listed in the *Small Press Record of Books in Print* (28th Edition, 1999-00). avg. price, paper: $30. Discounts: 35% booksellers, 50% distributors. 140pp; 8½×11; of. Reporting time: 1-2 months. Payment: negotiable. Copyrights for author.

VIVA PETITES, Ann Lauren, Stephen Douglas, 537 Newport Center Drive #119, Newport Beach, CA 92660, FAX 714-643-5367. 1996. Fiction, articles, interviews, criticism, reviews, music, letters, non-fiction. "Focused towards petite women for fashion and other women's issues." circ. 30M. 4/yr. Expects 2 issues 1999, 4 issues 2000. sub. price: $15; per copy: $4; sample: $4. Back issues: $5. Discounts: none. 48pp; 8½×11. Reporting time: 30-45 days. Simultaneous submissions accepted: yes. Payment: 10¢ a word. Copyrighted, does not revert to author. Pub's reviews. §Fashion, talen industry. PMA.

A VOICE WITHOUT SIDES, Ge(of Huth), po.ed.t, 875 Central Parkway, Schenectady, NY 12309. 1987. Poetry, cartoons, collages, concrete art. "*A Voice Without Sides (VWOS)* is an irregular magazine publishing short avant-garde poetry and visual art in strange formats (in jars, on large self-adhesive labels as earrings, on erasers, etc.). *VWOS* is a limited edition magazine, printing no more than 50 copies per issue." circ. 24-50. 1/yr. Pub'd 1 issue 1998; expects 1 issue 1999, 1 issue 2000. sub. price: can be any dollar amount—cost (which varies) will be subtracted when issue is mailed; per copy: $1-$4; sample: $1-$4. Discounts: none. 5pp; size varies; †rubberstamp, photocopying, handwriting, handtyping. Reporting time: 2 weeks. Payment: at least 2 copies; 1/4 of press run is divided among contributors. Copyrighted, reverts to author.

Voices From My Retreat, Cora T. Schwartz, Marian Butler, Asst. Editor, Box 1077, S. Fallsburg, NY 12779, 914-436-7455; 1-800-484-1255 ex. 2485. 1996. Poetry, fiction, art, photos, interviews, satire, parts-of-novels. avg. press run 500. Expects 2 titles 1999, 2-3 titles 2000. avg. price, paper: $7. 100pp; 4×5; lp. Reporting time: 2 months. Simultaneous submissions accepted: yes. Publishes 10% of manuscripts submitted. Payment: copies. Does not copyright for author.

VOICES INTERNATIONAL, Clovita Rice, 1115 Gillette Drive, Little Rock, AR 72227, 501-225-0166.

1966. Poetry. "We look for poetry with haunting imagery and significant statement." circ. 350. 4/yr. Pub'd 4 issues 1998; expects 4 issues 1999, 4 issues 2000. sub. price: $10 ($18 for 2 yrs); per copy: $2.50; sample: $2. Back issues: $2. 32pp; 6×9. Reporting time: 6 weeks. Payment: 1 free copy. Not copyrighted, rights revert to author.

VOICES - ISRAEL, Mark Levinson, Editor-in-Chief; Gretti Izak, Associate Editor; Luiza Carol, Associate Editor, c/o Mark Levinson, PO Box 5780, Herzliya 46157, Israel, 09-9552411. 1972. Poetry. *"Voices Israel* is the only magazine in Israel devoted entirely to poetry in English. It calls for the submission of intelligible and feeling poetry concerned with the potentialities of the human spirit, and the dangers confronting it. It also seeks the peace of all mankind. Copyright to all poems is vested in the poets themselves; the only request of the Editorial Board is that if a poem is first printed in *Voices Israel*, that fact should be made known in any subsequent publications of it. No more than four poems to be submitted to each issue (one a year), preferably 40 lines or less in seven copies, to reach the Editor by the end of February each year." circ. 350. 1/yr. Expects 1 issue 1999, 1 issue 2000. sub. price: $15 postpaid; per copy: $15 postpaid; sample: $10 postpaid. Back issues: $10 as available. Discounts: 33⅓% off to recognized booksellers only. No library discounts. 125pp; 6½x9¼; †of. Reporting time: report in fall/winter each year. Simultaneous submissions accepted: no. Payment: none. Copyrighted, reverts to author. Ads: $150/$100.

VOL. NO. MAGAZINE, Richard Weekley, Jerry Danielsen, Don McLeod, Los Angeles Poets' Press, 24721 Newhall Avenue, Newhall, CA 91321, 805-254-0851. 1983. Poetry, art, photos. "Limit of 4-6 submissions at a time. 80 lines or less preferably. Must relate to specified themes; 'Epicenter' (August '96). Solid, concise, adventuresome work wanted. All In A Days Work (Aug 97), Overload (Aug 98)" circ. 300. 1/yr. Pub'd 1 issues 1998; expects 1 issue 1999, 1 issue 2000. 4 titles listed in the *Small Press Record of Books in Print* (28th Edition, 1999-00). sub. price: $10; per copy: $5; sample: $5. Back issues: $5. Discounts: 20%. 36pp; 5½x8½; of. Reporting time: 1-5 months. Simultaneous submissions accepted: yes. Publishes 2% of manuscripts submitted. Payment: 2 copies. Copyrighted, reverts to author. Ads: $30/$15.

Volcano Press, Inc, Ruth Gottstein, PO Box 270, Volcano, CA 95689, 209-296-3445; fax 209-296-4515; Credit card orders only: 1-800-VPWYMEN; e-mail ruth@volcanopress.com; website http://volcanopress.com. 1976. Poetry, art, non-fiction. "All materials published in book form only. We have just released an audio-cassette, "Learning to Live Without Violence," to accompany book of same name." avg. press run 5M-10M. Pub'd 2 titles 1998; expects 2 titles 1999, 4 titles 2000. 13 titles listed in the *Small Press Record of Books in Print* (28th Edition, 1999-00). avg. price, paper: $14.95. Discounts: 1 copy 20% (prepaid 35%), 2-9 copies 35%, 10+ copies 40%. 200pp; size usually 6×9; of. Reporting time: 3 months. Payment: outright fee, or royalties. Copyrights for author.

VOLITION, Vortex Editions, Bonnie Lateiner, Editor, PO Box 314, Tenants Harbor, ME 04860. 1982. Poetry, fiction, parts-of-novels. "A magazine of prose and poetry edited by B. Lateiner. The dramatic presentation of each issue highlights the work of writers such as: Bobbie Louise-Hawkins, Stephen Emerson, Maureen Owen, Barrett Watten, Bill Berkson, Duncan McNaughton, Fielding Dawson, Lucia Berlin, and others. The covers of each issue are color-xeroxed to produce a vital textured magnetic appearance." circ. 400. 1/yr. Pub'd 2 issues 1998; expects 2 issues 1999, 5 issues 2000. sub. price: $12; per copy: $4; sample: $4. Discounts: trade available. 50pp; 7×8; mi, of, color xeroxed covers, offset text. Payment: 3 copies of issue. Copyrighted, reverts to author. CLMP.

THE VOLUNTARYIST, Carl Watner, Box 1275, Gramling, SC 29348, 864-472-2750. 1982. Articles, cartoons, interviews, criticism, letters. circ. 300. 6/yr. Pub'd 6 issues 1998; expects 6 issues 1999, 6 issues 2000. sub. price: $18, $23 overseas; per copy: $4; sample: $1. Back issues: 10 different issues $25. 8pp; 8½x11. Reporting time: 2 weeks. Payment: free subscription. Not copyrighted. Pub's reviews: 4 in 1998. Ads: $25 business card.

Vonpalisaden Publications Inc., 60 Saddlewood Drive, Hillsdale, NJ 07642-1336, 201-664-4919. 1986. Non-fiction. "Currently pet/hobby (dogs) animal book publisher (so far non-fiction only). *The Rottweiler: An International Study of the Breed*, by Dr. Dagmar Hodinar." avg. press run 5M. Pub'd 1 title 1998. 1 title listed in the *Small Press Record of Books in Print* (28th Edition, 1999-00). avg. price, paper: $25.95. Discounts: for resale: 1-9 copies 20%, 10-25 30%, 26-50 40%, 51-99 45%, 100+ 50% plus addit. 10% on net if displayed in catalogue. 350+pp; 6×9; lp.

THE VORTEX, Axios Newletter, Inc., David Gorham, 30-32 Macaw Avenue, PO Box 279, Belmopan, Belize, 501-8-23284. 1981. Fiction, articles, art, photos, cartoons, interviews, satire, criticism, reviews, letters, parts-of-novels, collages, concrete art, news items, non-fiction. "A historical + wargamers journal. Articles needed on politics and battles and wars, in the period between 1812 and 1930—especially Europe and America. Also articles on wargames, the people into wargames, and photos, art and cartoons on the same. Write for an intelligent lay reader rather than a professional historian, length 400-2.5M words. By-line given. Emphasis on articles that would interest wargamers!! Some poetry (on our subject matter)." circ. 2.33M. 13/yr. Pub'd 13 issues 1998; expects 13 issues 1999, 13 issues 2000. sub. price: $15, $25/2 years; per copy: $2; sample: $2. Back issues: $2. Discounts: write for information (about 40% discount). 12pp; 8½×11; †of, li. Reporting time: 6-8 weeks. Payment: $20-$100 depending on article. Copyrighted, reverts to author. Pub's reviews: 16 in 1998. §Wargames, military history. Ads: $160/$87.50/5¢. I.D.A., S.C.V., Belize Publishers.

Vortex Editions (see also VOLITION), Bonnie Lateiner, PO Box 314, Tenants Harbor, ME 04860. 1979. Parts-of-novels. "Vortex publishes post-modern progressive poetry and prose with emphasis on large range in styles. Contributing authors: Maureen Owen, Ed Friedman, Bill Berkson, Johanna Drucker, Michael Amnasan, Bobbie Louise Hawkins, Stephen Emerson, Alan Bernheimer, Barrett Watten, Carla Harryman, Simone O., Fielding Dawson, and Duncan McNaughton. NO unsolicited manuscripts." avg. press run 500-1M. Pub'd 2 titles 1998; expects 3 titles 1999, 3 titles 2000. 4 titles listed in the *Small Press Record of Books in Print* (28th Edition, 1999-00). avg. price, paper: $5. Discounts: trade available. 100pp; 6×9, 5×8, 7×8; of. Payment: arranged with respective authors according to needs of both author & publisher. Copyrights for author. CLMP.

VOYA (Voice of Youth Advocate), Scarecrow Press, Cathi Dunn MacRae, Editor, 4720 Boston Way, Lanham, MD 20706, 301-459-3366. 1978. circ. 4M. 6/yr. Pub'd 6 issues 1998; expects 6 issues 1999, 6 issues 2000. sub. price: $38.50; per copy: $6.42; sample: write for info. Back issues: $10. Discounts: write for info. 70pp; 8½×11. Payment: yes, varies. Copyrighted. Pub's reviews: 2500 in 1998. §Young adult. Ads: write for info.

W

W.E.C. Plant Publishing, Al Plant, Julie Umbenhower, PO Box 61751, Honolulu, HI 96839, 808-622-0043; FAX 808-622-1345; e-mail alandjulie.plant@worldnet.att.net; website http://homepage.usr.com/a/alandtulie. 1978. Cartoons, non-fiction. "Artists collections-cartoons, Hawaii history, Great Lakes history, archaeology, cooking and travel. Publish family, club or company history books upon request. No unsolicited material accepted. Query with SASE for information." avg. press run 500. Pub'd 2 titles 1998; expects 2 titles 1999, 2 titles 2000. 7 titles listed in the *Small Press Record of Books in Print* (28th Edition, 1999-00). avg. price, cloth: $16.95; paper: $12.95. Discounts: 55% distributor, 40% bookseller; we pay shipping to bookseller on prepaid order of 5 or 6 books, depends on package. 120pp; 5¼×8¼; †of. Reporting time: query for information. Simultaneous submissions accepted: no. Payment: co-venture with authors. Does not copyright for author.

W.W. Publications (see also MINAS TIRITH EVENING-STAR), Philip W. Helms, PO Box 373, Highland, MI 48357-0373, 813-585-0985, phone and fax. 1967. Poetry, fiction, articles, art, photos, cartoons, interviews, satire, criticism, reviews, music, letters, long-poems, news items, non-fiction. "Send questions to: Paul S. Ritz, PO Box 901, Clearwater, FL 34617." avg. press run 200-500. Pub'd 2 titles 1998; expects 1 title 1999, 3 titles 2000. 13 titles listed in the *Small Press Record of Books in Print* (28th Edition, 1999-00). avg. price, paper: $3.50. 200pp; 8½×11; †of. Reporting time: 2 months. Payment: 5 free copies. Copyrights for author. ATS.

George Wahr Publishing Company (see also MICHIGAN: Around and About), Elizabeth K. Davenport, Editor, 304-1/2 South State Street, Ann Arbor, MI 48104, 313-668-6097. 1883. Non-fiction. "We are a *book* publishing company, not a magazine. We do publish a newsletter, *Michigan: Around and About*; circulation 1200; editor: George Wahr Sallade; 4pp.; $10 per year, 12 issues. Local, national and international government and political issues." avg. press run 1200. Pub'd 2 titles 1998; expects 3-4 titles 1999, 3-4 titles 2000. avg. price, cloth: $22.50; paper: $16.95; other: $17.50. Discounts: 40% to trade bookstores, 20-50% text bookstores, some bulk negotiable. 200-400pp; 6×9, 8½×11; of. Reporting time: 4-6 months. Simultaneous submissions accepted: yes. Publishes 50% of manuscripts submitted. Payment: negotiable, generally 10%. Copyrights for author.

Walnut Publishing Co., Inc., Jeff Mackler, Nat Weinstein, 3425 Army Street, San Francisco, CA 94110, 415-821-0511. 1987. Non-fiction. avg. press run 3M. Pub'd 2 titles 1998; expects 2 titles 1999, 2 titles 2000. 7 titles listed in the *Small Press Record of Books in Print* (28th Edition, 1999-00). avg. price, cloth: $19.95; paper: $8.95. Discounts: 40% for bookstores, distributors, schools, libraries, etc. 155pp; 6×9, varies; of, desktop layout. Reporting time: 1 month. Payment: varies. Copyrights for author.

WALT WHITMAN QUARTERLY REVIEW, Ed Folsom, 308 EPB The University of Iowa, Iowa City, IA 52242-1492, 319-335-0454; 335-0592; fax 319-335-2535; e-mail wwqr@uiowa.edu. 1983. Articles, criticism, letters, non-fiction. "The *Walt Whitman Quarterly Review* is a literary quarterly begun in the summer of 1983. *WWQR* features previously unpublished letters and documents written by Whitman, critical essays dealing with Whitman's work and its place in American literature, thorough reviews of Whitman-related books, and an ongoing Whitman bibliography—one of the standard reference sources for Whitman studies. The journal is edited by Ed Folsom and published at The University of Iowa and the editorial board is made up of some of the most distinguished Whitman scholars including Betsy Erkkila, Harold Aspiz, Arthur Golden, Jerome Loving, James E. Miller Jr., Roger Asselineau, and M. Wynn Thomas. We also offer for sale selected back issues of the *Walt Whitman Review* (1955-1982). Please write for details." circ. 1M. 4/yr. Pub'd 4 issues 1998; expects 4 issues 1999, 4 issues 2000. sub. price: $12 individuals, $15 institutions ($3 postage charge on foreign subs); per copy: $3; sample: $3. Back issues: $3 each. Discounts: 10% to agencies for subscriptions, 40% to bookstores, 25% to classroom. 56pp; 6×9; of. Reporting time: 1-3 months. Payment: contributor copies. Copyrighted, reverts to author. Pub's reviews: 8 in 1998. §Whitman scholarship, 19th and 20th American and World literature that discusses Whitman, poetry collections that reveal Whitman influences. Ads: $100/$50.

Ward Hill Press, E. Davis, PO Box 04-0424, Staten Island, NY 10304, 718-816-4056. 1989. Fiction, art, non-fiction. "Fiction and nonfiction for children 10 and up, with an emphasis on American history and multiculturalism" avg. press run 2M-5M. Pub'd 2 titles 1998; expects 4 titles 1999, 4 titles 2000. 7 titles listed in the *Small Press Record of Books in Print* (28th Edition, 1999-00). avg. price, cloth: $14.95; paper: $10.95. Discounts: 1-4 copies 20%, 5-24 40%, 25-49 42%, 50-99 43%, 100+ 45%. 120pp; 6×9; of. Reporting time: 4-8 weeks. Simultaneous submissions accepted: yes. Publishes 10% or less of manuscripts submitted. Payment: a small advance and a royalty based on retail. Copyrights for author. PMA, ABA.

Warthog Press, Patricia Fillingham, 29 South Valley Road, West Orange, NJ 07052, 201-731-9269. 1979. Poetry, art, photos, music. "Warthog Press is interested in poetry that will bring poetry back to people, rather than using it as an academic exercise. We are interested in poetry that says something, and says it well." avg. press run 1M. Pub'd 2 titles 1998. 13 titles listed in the *Small Press Record of Books in Print* (28th Edition, 1999-00). avg. price, paper: $10. 64pp; 5½×8½; of. Reporting time: 1 month. Simultaneous submissions accepted: yes. Does not copyright for author.

WASCANA REVIEW OF CONTEMPORARY POETRY AND SHORT FICTION, Kathleen Wall, Editor; Jeanne Shami, Fiction Editor; Troni Grande, Poetry Editor, Department of English, University of Regina, Regina, Sask S4S 0A2, Canada, 584-4302. 1966. Poetry, fiction, articles, reviews. circ. 300-500. 2/yr. Pub'd 2 issues 1998; expects 2 issues 1999, 2 issues 2000. sub. price: $12 ($10 Canadian); per copy: $5; sample: $5. Discounts: 20% for subscription agencies. 90pp; 9×5½. Reporting time: 2-3 months. Simultaneous submissions accepted: no. Publishes 10% of manuscripts submitted. Payment: poetry $10 per page; fiction, reviews, critical articles $3 per page. Copyrighted, reverts to author. Pub's reviews: 2 in 1998. §Canadian literature, modern literature,contemporary world literature in English.

WASHINGTON INTERNATIONAL ARTS LETTER, Nancy A. Fandel, 317 Fairchild Street, Iowa City, IA 52245-2115, 515-255-5577. 1962. "We publish financial information for the arts and artists. Federal actions and grants; private foundation and business corporation arts program information. And we have the following titles in books: *National Directory of Grants and Aid to Individuals*, 280pp, paper, 8th ed., $30; *National Directory of Arts and Education Support By Business Corporations*, 160 pp, paper, $75, 3rd edition." circ. 15M. 10/yr. Pub'd 6 issues 1998; expects 10 issues 1999, 10 issues 2000. 2 titles listed in the *Small Press Record of Books in Print* (28th Edition, 1999-00). sub. price: individuals (personal address & check) $55, institutions $82; per copy: $12 (by mail only); sample: free. Back issues: $12. Discounts: departments & non-profits: 20% (off of $124 price). 6-8pp; 8½×11; of. Payment: none. Copyrighted. Pub's reviews: 350 in 1998. §All arts, and grants to them. Ads: classified word only - $5 per word, 5 line minimum, approx. 5 wds per line.

THE WASHINGTON MONTHLY, Charles Peters, 1611 Connecticut Avenue NW, Washington, DC 20009, 202-462-0128. 1969. Articles, art, photos, satire, reviews, letters, non-fiction. "Art & photos commissioned to accompany articles." circ. 35M. 10/yr. Pub'd 10 issues 1998; expects 10 issues 1999, 10 issues 2000. sub. price: $29.50; per copy: $3.95; sample: $5. Back issues: $5. 64pp; 7½×9¾; heatset, web offset. Reporting time: 2 months. Payment: 10¢/word. Copyrighted, does not revert to author. Pub's reviews: 60 in 1998. §Government, bureaucracy, politics, education, media, society. Ads: $4000/$2500/rates are lower for publishers.

THE WASHINGTON REPORT, Wm. A. Leavell, Editor, 3610 38th Avenue South #88, St. Petersburg, FL 33711-4392, 813-866-1598. 1979. News items. "We are a political newsletter. We receive information from 'Sources' which we consider 'Confidential'. We do not pay for information and welcome all information regarding national politics." circ. 17.5M. 12/yr. Pub'd 12 issues 1998; expects 12 issues 1999, 12 issues 2000. sub. price: $25; per copy: $2.25; sample: free. Back issues: available upon request. Discounts: none. 4pp; 8½×11; of. Reporting time: timely. Payment: none. Not copyrighted. no ads.

WASHINGTON REVIEW, Clarissa Wittenberg, Editor; Mary Swift, Managing Editor; Pat Kolmer, Art Editor & Film Reviews; Heather Fuller, Literary Editor; Jeff Richards, Associate Literary Editor; Ross Taylor, Associate Literary Editor; Anne Pierce, Dance Editor, PO Box 50132, Washington, DC 20091-0132, 202-638-0515. 1975. Poetry, fiction, articles, art, photos, interviews, criticism, reviews, parts-of-novels, non-fiction. "Articles: 2,000 words at most. Review: 500-1,000 words. Interested in in-depth articles on all arts, with particular emphasis on DC. Recent contributors: E. Ethelbert Miller, Lee Fleming, Terence Winch, Carmen Delzell." circ. 10M. 6/yr. Pub'd 6 issues 1998; expects 6 issues 1999, 6 issues 2000. sub. price: $12/yr, $20/2 years; per copy: $2; sample: $2.50. Back issues: $3.50. Discounts: 15% bulk, 15% classroom, 10% agencies, 40% to bookstores for resale. 32pp; 11¼×16; of. Reporting time: 2 months. Simultaneous submissions accepted: no. Publishes 2% of manuscripts submitted. Payment: in issues. Copyrighted, reverts to author. Pub's reviews: 25 in 1998. §Arts, poetry, fiction, theater. Ads: $250/$175/$15 col. inch. CLMP.

Washington Writers' Publishing House, Laura B. Miller, Co-President; Dan Johnson, Co-President; Paul Haenel, Treasurer, PO Box 15271, Washington, DC 20003, 202-543-1905, 703-527-5890. 1975. Poetry. "Open to poets in the Greater Washington and Baltimore area only. A *cooperative* press." avg. press run 750. Pub'd 2 titles 1998; expects 2 titles 1999, 2 titles 2000. 42 titles listed in the *Small Press Record of Books in Print* (28th Edition, 1999-00). avg. price, paper: $10. Discounts: bulk orders-5 or more titles 40%; bookstores 20%. 64-72pp; 5½×8½; of. Reporting time: about 2 months, submissions are accepted only once a year, June 1 to September 30, decisions made by the end of October. Simultaneous submissions accepted: yes. Publishes 3% of manuscripts submitted. Payment: authors receive 50 copies. Does not copyright for author.

Water Mark Press, Coco Gordon, 138 Duane Street, New York, NY 10013, 212-285-1609. 1978. Poetry, art. "We are in the process of changing format to artist books. 1983 publications: *Loose Pages*, Alison Knowles (pages of flax paper to sound & wear on the body), deluxe limited edition of 10 copies, $3,600; *The Opaque Glass*, Barbara Roux (an artist's bookwork both hand & machine made/xerox hand-colored, longpoem with visuals), edition 50 copies, $50. I focused in '83-'84 on new current literature (6 chapbooks) written in crossover genres. I produced three full-length traditional poetry books 1980-84 and feel that need has been filled by other presses. I use handmade papers designed specifically for parts, covers, or all of our publications, and sell to other presses—our papers from flax, linen and many plant fibers. No more unsolicited submissions please." avg. press run 50-600. Pub'd 2 titles 1998; expects 1 title 1999. 14 titles listed in the *Small Press Record of Books in Print* (28th Edition, 1999-00). avg. price, cloth: $40; paper: $20; other: $100-$3,000 deluxe editions. Discounts: 1 copies 25%, 2+ 40%. 20-96pp; size varies; of, lp. Payment: contributor's copies. Does not copyright for author.

Water Row Press (see also WATER ROW REVIEW), Cisco Harland, PO Box 438, Sudbury, MA 01776. 1985. Poetry, fiction, interviews, criticism, plays. "Our main focus are books and broadsides relative to the understanding and appreciation of the writings and times of 'Beat' writers. We are also seeking poetry and fiction from second generation 'Beats' and 'Outsiders'. Editions include signed limitations. Some recent contributors include Tom Clark, Arthur Knight, R. Crumb, Joy Walsh, William Burroughs. Any manuscripts which add to the understanding of Kerouac, Ginsberg, Bukowski are welcome. Tributes, poetry, dissertations, artwork. New poets' submissions always welcome." avg. press run 500-1M. Pub'd 5 titles 1998; expects 10 titles 1999, 10 titles 2000. 11 titles listed in the *Small Press Record of Books in Print* (28th Edition, 1999-00). avg. price, paper: $8. Discounts: 2-5 copies 25%, 6 or more 40%, distributors inquire. lp, of. Reporting time: 4-8 weeks. Payment: copies of work and additional payment on publication to be arranged. Copyrights for author.

WATER ROW REVIEW, Water Row Press, Cisco Harland, PO Box 438, Sudbury, MA 01776. 1986. Poetry, fiction, articles, interviews, criticism, reviews, parts-of-novels. "Recent contributors: William Burroughs, Charles Bukowski, Jeffrey Weinberg." circ. 2.5M. 4/yr. Pub'd 4 issues 1998; expects 4 issues 1999, 4 issues 2000. sub. price: $24; per copy: $6; sample: $6. Discounts: 2-10 20%, 11 or more 40%. 100pp; 6×9; of. Copyrighted. Pub's reviews: 12 in 1998. §Literature, fiction, poetry.

Waterfront Books, Sherrill N. Musty, 85 Crescent Road, Burlington, VT 05401-4126, 802-658-7477. 1983. Non-fiction. avg. press run 2.5M-5M. Pub'd 2 titles 1998; expects 2 titles 1999, 2 titles 2000. 10 titles listed in the *Small Press Record of Books in Print* (28th Edition, 1999-00). avg. price, cloth: $15.95; paper: $12.95. Discounts: 50% to jobbers; 40% trade; 20% classroom and libraries. of. Reporting time: 2 months. Payment: standard 10%, 15% net, sometimes higher. Copyrights for author. Publishers Marketing Association (PMA), American Booksellers Association (ABA), Association of Booksellers for Children.

WATERFRONT WORLD SPOTLIGHT, Beverly Bandler, Editor, 1622 Wisconsin Ave. N.W., Washington, DC 20007, 202-337-0356. 1981. Photos, news items. "ISSN: 0733-0677" circ. 1M-1.2M. 4/yr. Pub'd 4 issues 1998; expects 4 issues 1999, 4 issues 2000. sub. price: US $60, Canada/Mexico $70, foreign $80; per copy: $10; sample: free. Back issues: $36/set for *Waterfront World* 1981-1992, $30/1 yr set of *Waterfront World Spotlight* 1993 on. 16pp; 8½×11; of. Copyrighted. Pub's reviews: 20 in 1998. §Urban design, architecture, city planning, economic development, real estate, boating. Ads: none.

Waters Edge Press, 98 Main Street #527, Tiburon, CA 94920, 415-435-2837; Fax 415-435-2404; E-mail books@watersedgepress.com; website www.watersedgepress.com. 1996. Art, photos, non-fiction. avg. press run 7.5M-10M. Expects 1 title 1999, 2 titles 2000. 1 title listed in the *Small Press Record of Books in Print*

(28th Edition, 1999-00). avg. price, cloth: $21.95. Discounts: 50% gift stories, bookstores through distributors Midpoint Trade Books, Ingram, Baker and Taylor, Bookazine, Quality, Unique Common Ground, Brodart, Amazon.com, Barnes and Noble.com, Borders.com. 64pp; 7½x8¼. Simultaneous submissions accepted: yes. Copyrights for author. PMA, Bay Area Independent Publishers Assn., SPAN.

Watershed Books, Joy Riley, Publisher, 130 Warner Street, Marietta, OH 45750-3453, 800-484-1624 +(MCI code #)7036, Fax; 614-373-0253; e-mail 103043.1017@compuserve.com. 1995. Fiction, non-fiction. "Query first, please" avg. press run 2-3M. Expects 1 title 1999, 3 titles 2000. 1 title listed in the *Small Press Record of Books in Print* (28th Edition, 1999-00). avg. price, paper: $14.95. Discounts: wholesalers 55%, dealers 40%, 45% for unopened box of 48. Pages vary; size varies. Reporting time: 1 month on query. We accept simultaneous submissions, but query first.

Waterview Press, Inc., Stephen M. Combs, Publisher, 169 West Broadway, Oviedo, FL 32765, 407-365-8500; oviedo@bellsouth.net. 1996. Criticism, non-fiction. "Query first with SASE." avg. press run 5M. Pub'd 2 titles 1998; expects 3 titles 1999, 4 titles 2000. 5 titles listed in the *Small Press Record of Books in Print* (28th Edition, 1999-00). avg. price, cloth: varies; paper: varies. Discounts: bulk, agent, jobber up to 50%, 55% to distributors. 216pp; 6x9; of. Reporting time: 3 weeks. Simultaneous submissions accepted: yes. Publishes less than 1% of manuscripts submitted. Payment: negotiable. Copyrights for author. PMA, FPA.

WATERWAYS: Poetry in the Mainstream, Ten Penny Players, Inc., Bard Press, Barbara Fisher, Co-Editor; Richard Spiegel, Co-Editor, 393 St. Paul's Avenue, Staten Island, NY 10304-2127, 718-442-7429. 1978. Poetry. circ. 100-200. 11/yr. Pub'd 11 issues 1998; expects 11 issues 1999, 11 issues 2000. sub. price: $25; per copy: $2.25; sample: $2.25. Back issues: $2.80 (includes postage). 40pp; 7x4¼; †xerography. Reporting time: 1 month. Simultaneous submissions accepted: yes. Publishes 50% of manuscripts submitted. Payment: copies. Copyrighted, reverts to author.

Wave Publishing, Carol Doumani, PO Box 688, Venice, CA 90294, 310-306-0699. 1994. Fiction, non-fiction. "Our goal is to create the highest quality hardcover books." avg. press run 4M. Pub'd 2 titles 1998; expects 3 titles 2000. 3 titles listed in the *Small Press Record of Books in Print* (28th Edition, 1999-00). avg. price, cloth: $25. Discounts: 1-2 books no discount, 3-9 books 40%, 10-19 books 45%, 20+ books 50%. 360pp; 6x9; of. Simultaneous submissions accepted: no. Publishes 0% of manuscripts submitted. PMA, SPAN.

Waverly House Publishing, Nora Wright, PO Box 1053, Glenside, PA 19038, 215-884-5873; 1-800-858-2253; e-mail info@natsel.com; website www.natsel.com. 1996. Fiction, criticism, non-fiction. "African-American authors only." avg. press run 2M. Expects 1 title 1999, 2 titles 2000. 3 titles listed in the *Small Press Record of Books in Print* (28th Edition, 1999-00). avg. price, cloth: $22.95; paper: $14.95. Discounts: 40% retail, 50-55% wholesale. 325pp; 5½x8½; of. Reporting time: 30 days. Simultaneous submissions accepted: no. Payment: flexible. Does not copyright for author. PMA, SPAN.

WAY STATION MAGAZINE, Randy Glumm, Managing Editor; Francisco Gonzalez, Spanish Editor, 1319 South Logan-MLK, Lansing, MI 48910-1340. 1989. Poetry, fiction, articles, art, photos, cartoons, interviews, satire, criticism, reviews, letters, parts-of-novels, news items, non-fiction. "Poetry: submit up to 3 poems, each no longer than one page. Fiction/non-fiction: Submit up to 3000 words, typed. May include art or photos with submissions. Avoid pornography and religion unless an integral part of the work. Recent contributors: E.G. Burrows, Diane Wakoski, Doug Lawder, Stuart Dybek, D. Bock, Robert VanderMolen, Marcus Cafagna, T. Kilgore Splake, Denver Sasser, Judith Minty, Etheridge Knight, Willie D. Williams, Trinidad Sanchez Jr., Fred Barton, D.M. Rosenberg, Robert McDonald, Leah Weed, Bruce Curtis, Terri Jewell, Francisco Gonzalez, Dan Gerber, Lawrence Thomas, Charles Bukowski, Kurt Eisenlohr, Libby Brahms, David Castleman. Always include SASE. $5 processing fee promptly returned if work is not accepted or is withdrawn prior to being set for print. We also need cartoon submissions." circ. 1M+. 4/yr. Pub'd 1 issue 1998; expects 2 issues 1999, 4 issues 2000. sub. price: $18 for 4 issues; per copy: $5 newstands; sample: $6 mail-includes postage. Back issues: undecided but probably $8. Discounts: undecided. 56pp; 8½x11; of. Reporting time: 30-90 days, or sooner. Simultaneous submissions accepted: yes. Publishes 20% of manuscripts submitted. Payment: 2 copies but with plans to pay by the page or arbitrary amount in future. Copyrighted, reverts to author. Pub's reviews: 3 in 1998. §Poetry chaps, poetry collections, fiction, essay, emerging cultures, Americana. Possible novel excerpts or entire novel, query first. Ads: $275/$155/$115 1/3 page/$80 1/4 page/$50 1/8 page/$70 1/6 page/35¢ per word classifieds. MPCA (Midwest Popular Culture Association), ACA (American Culture Association).

Wayfarer Publications (see also TAI CHI), Marvin Smalheiser, PO Box 26156, Los Angeles, CA 90026, 213-665-7773. 1981. Articles, interviews, reviews, letters, news items, non-fiction. avg. press run 15M. Pub'd 1 title 1998; expects 2 titles 1999, 3 titles 2000. 1 title listed in the *Small Press Record of Books in Print* (28th Edition, 1999-00). of. Simultaneous submissions accepted: no.

Wayfinder Press, Marcus E. Wilson, PO Box 217, Ridgway, CO 81432, 970-626-5452. 1980. Non-fiction. "We specialize in history and guide books about the Southwest." avg. press run 3M. Pub'd 2 titles 1998; expects 2 titles 1999, 2 titles 2000. 12 titles listed in the *Small Press Record of Books in Print* (28th Edition,

1999-00). avg. price, paper: $11.50. Discounts: bookstores 40%, jobbers 50%. 150pp; 5½x8½; †of. Reporting time: 10 days. Simultaneous submissions accepted: yes. Publishes 1% of manuscripts submitted. Payment: quarterly. Does not copyright for author. RMBPA (Rocky Mountain Book Publishers Association).

WE INTERNATIONAL (formerly WOMEN AND ENVIRONMENTS), Weed Foundation Board Member—rotating editors, 736 Bathurst Street, Toronto, Ontario M5S 2R4, Canada, 416-516-2600; FAX 416-531-6214. 1976. Articles, photos, interviews, reviews, letters, news items, non-fiction. "Women and Built, Social, Natural and Political Environments; Women as Urban Planners and Developers; Rural and Urban Business and Agriculture; The Politics of Athletics and Leisure; a Networking Directory; Gender and the Politics of Health; Spirituality; Environmental Law and Policy." circ. 1M. 4/yr. Pub'd 1 issue 1998; expects 4 issues 1999, 4 issues 2000. sub. price: $22 individual, $32 institutional (add $8 foreign overseas); per copy: $8; sample: $8. Back issues: $8. Discounts: sub. agents 5%, bookstores 20%. 28pp; 8½x11; of. Reporting time: 2-3 months. We accept simultaneous submissions if notified. Payment: none. Copyrighted, reverts to author. Pub's reviews: 10 in 1998. §Gender issues, housing, planning, work, natural, built or social environments. Ads: $360/$200/$150 1/3 page/$125 1/4 page/$75 bus. card. CMPA.

WEBER STUDIES: Voices and Viewpoints of the Contemporary West, Sherwin W. Howard, Editor; Michael Wutz, Associate Editor; Brad L. Roghaar, Associate Editor, Weber State University, 1214 University Circle, Ogden, UT 84408-1214, 801-626-6473 or 6657. 1984. Poetry, fiction, articles, art, photos, interviews, parts-of-novels, long-poems, plays, non-fiction. "Recent Contributors: Maxine Hong Kingston, Melissa Pritchard, Nancy Takacs, Amy Ling, Donald Anderson, Dipti Ranjan Pattanaik, N.W.O. Royle, Fred Marchant, G.S. Sharat Chandra, Max Oelschlaeger, James Welch, William Bevis, Janice Gould, Louis Owens, Dell Hymes, Jami Huntsinger Hacker, Robin Cohen, David Lee, Katharine Coles, Aden Ross, Robert Hodgson Wagoner, Linda Sillito, A.J. Simmonds, Barre Toelken, Wayne C. Booth, Thomas G. Alexander, Robert Olmstead, Jadwiga Lukanty-Nkosi, Nancy Kline, Lyn Lifshin, K. Narayana Chandran, Peggy Shumaker, Gregory Ulmer, Pattiann Rogers, Linda Dalrmple Henderson, Joseph M. Ditta, Lance Olsen, Joseph Tabbi, Vil em Flusser, Bruce Clarke, Cynthia Hogue, Daniel R. Schwarz, Anca Vlasopolos, Nicole Cooley. Length of articles: 2,000 to 5,000 words. We are known for our fiction/interview series in which we feature original work by an author followed by an interview with her/him in the same issue. We like to publish 2-3 pages of poetry per poet in order to give a genuine flavor of the poet to our readers. Generally we ask for about 3-5 poems for submission. We like manuscripts that inform the culture and environment (both broadly defined) of the contemporary Western United States." circ. 800-1,000. 3/yr. Pub'd 3 issues 1998; expects 3 issues 1999, 3 issues 2000. sub. price: $30 institutions, $20 individuals; per copy: $7; sample: $7. Back issues: $7-8. Discounts: 15%. 120pp; 7½x10; of. Reporting time: 3-4 months. Simultaneous submissions accepted: no. Publishes 30% of manuscripts submitted. Payment: $25-$50 or more depending on our grant monies and length of mss. Copyrighted, reverts to author. Ads: $150/$100. CELJ.

WEEKEND WOODCRAFTS, EGW Publishing Company, Rob Joseph, Editor, 1041 Shary Circle, Concord, CA 94518-2407, 510-671-6852. 1981. Articles, photos, cartoons, interviews, reviews, letters, news items, non-fiction. "Easy and fun wood projects to build and finish." circ. 90M. 6/yr. Pub'd 6 issues 1998; expects 6 issues 1999, 6 issues 2000. sub. price: $29.70; per copy: $4.95; sample: $4.95. Back issues: $4.95. 68pp; 8⅛x10⅞; web of. Reporting time: within 6 weeks. Payment: upon publication; First serial rights. Copyrighted, rights revert to author unless otherwise stated. Pub's reviews: 50 in 1998. Ads: $3718/$2380/$3 word.

Weidner & Sons, Publishing, James H. Weidner, Box 2178, Riverton, NJ 08077, 609-486-1755; fax 609-486-7583; e-mail weidner@waterw.com. 1980. Poetry, fiction, parts-of-novels, non-fiction. "Weidner & Sons Publishing and its publishing divisions (Pulse Publications, Hazlaw Books, MedLaw Books, Bird-Sci Books, and Tycooly Publishing USA) is also the official distributor for publications of books in ornithology and conchology for the Delaware Museum of Natural History. Books published in the USA under the Bird-Sci Books imprint carry the ISBN 0-938198. Bird-Sci Books publishes in the arts and sciences; Tycooly Publishing USA a wholly owned subsidiary of Weidner & Sons Publishing (see *Literary Market Place*). We publish scientific and medical books only-no fiction or poetry. All submissions must have SASE for response or return of materials. We try to respond in 2-3 months. See our web site at http://www.waterw.com/~weidner for author guidelines, as well as a catalog of our over 100 publications." avg. press run 1M-5M. Expects 6 titles 1999, 6 titles 2000. 10 titles listed in the *Small Press Record of Books in Print* (28th Edition, 1999-00). avg. price, cloth: $90 U.S.; paper: $40 U.S. Discounts: 5-30%. Pages vary considerably; size varies; †of. Reporting time: 2 months. Simultaneous submissions accepted: yes. Publishes 5% of manuscripts submitted. Payment: negotiable. Copyrights negotiable. AMWA, SSP.

THE WEIRD NEWS, Donald F. Busky, 7393 Rugby Street, Philadelphia, PA 19138-1236. 1989. Cartoons, satire. "Subtitled The Word About An Absurd World, *The Weird News* is a free zine of satirical mock news stories. Submissions wanted." circ. 100. 4/yr. Pub'd 4 issues 1998; expects 4 issues 1999, 4 issues 2000. sub. price: free; per copy: free; sample: free. Back issues: free. Discounts: free trades. 4pp; 8½x11; †computer printed. Reporting time: 1 week. Simultaneous submissions accepted: yes. Payment: weirdness. Not copyrighted. Pub's reviews: goose egg in 1998. §Politics, humor, anti-racism. Ads: 1 animal skin per page.

WEIRD POETRY, American Living Press, Michael Shores, Angela Mark, PO Box 901, Allston, MA 02134, 617-522-6196. 1993. Poetry, art. "Currently not accepting submissions" circ. 500. 1/yr. Pub'd 1 issue 1998; expects 2 issues 1999, 2 issues 2000. price per copy: $5; sample: $5. 50+pp; 5½x8½; †xerox. Reporting time: 2-6 weeks. Payment: copy. Copyrighted, reverts to author.

Samuel Weiser, Inc., B. Lundsted, PO Box 612, York Beach, ME 03910, 207-363-4393; fax 207-363-5799; e-mail email@weiserbooks.com. 1955. Non-fiction. "Publishes Eastern philosophy, alternative health, alternative religion-such as mystical Kabbalah, or the mystical side of Christianity, Astrology, tarot, magic, psychology, etc. *Zen O'clock* by Scott Shaw and *The Tower of Alchemy* by David Goddard are two recent titles that illustrate spirituality from our perspective." avg. press run 7.5M. Pub'd 29 titles 1998; expects 30 titles 1999, 25 titles 2000. 398 titles listed in the *Small Press Record of Books in Print* (28th Edition, 1999-00). avg. price, cloth: $25; paper: $14.95. Discounts: 1-4 25%, 5-24 40%, 25-49 42%, 50-199 43%, 200+ 44%. 240pp; 5⅜x8¼; of. Reporting time: 10-12 weeks. Simultaneous submissions accepted: yes. Publishes 10% of manuscripts submitted. Payment: twice a year. Copyrights for author. B OF B, ABA, PMA, SPAN.

Wellcome Institute for the History of Medicine (see also MEDICAL HISTORY), 183 Euston Road, London NW1 2BE, England. 17 titles listed in the *Small Press Record of Books in Print* (28th Edition, 1999-00).

WELLSPRING, Meg Miller, Editor-in-Chief, Publisher; Sandra Swanson, Managing Editor, 4080 83rd Ave. N, St. A, Brooklyn Park, MN 55443-0527, 612-566-6663; fax 612-566-9754. 1989. Fiction. "Short story contest, 2,000 words max. $10 entry fee per story/adults. $5 entry fee per story/teens." circ. 300. 2/yr. Pub'd 2 issues 1998; expects 2 issues 1999, 2 issues 2000. sub. price: $10; per copy: $6; sample: $6. 40pp; 8½x11; mi. Reporting time: 6 months from contest deadline. Simultaneous submissions accepted: yes. Payment: prize money $25-100 contributor copies/adults, $20-50 contributor copies/teens. Copyrighted, reverts to author. Ads: $200/$300 back cover.

The Wellsweep Press, John Cayley, Harold Wells, 1 Grove End Ho., 150 Highgate Road, London HW5 1PD, England, (0171)267-3525, e-mail ws@shadoof.demon.co.uk. 1988. Poetry, fiction, non-fiction. "Specializes in literary translation from Chinese literature." avg. press run 750-1M. Pub'd 4 titles 1998; expects 5 titles 1999, 5-6 titles 2000. avg. price, paper: $12. Discounts: trade 35%. 96pp; 13cm x 20cm; of. Reporting time: can be 2 months. Payment: by arrangement, up to 6%. Association of Little Presses (ALP).

WELSH HISTORY REVIEW, University Of Wales Press, Kenneth O. Morgan, 6 Gwennyth Street, Cathays, Cardiff CF2 4YD, Wales, 44-1222-231919; Fax 44-1222-230908; press@press.wales.ac.uk. 1960. Articles. "Articles in English on various aspects of Welsh history." circ. 500. 2/yr. Pub'd 2 issues 1998; expects 2 issues 1999, 2 issues 2000. sub. price: £13; per copy: £6.50; sample: £6.50. Back issues: £6.50. Discounts: 10%. 120pp; size A5; of. Payment: none. Copyrighted, does not revert to author. Pub's reviews: 20 in 1998. §History, esp. Welsh history. Ads: £75/£37.50.

WELSH JOURNAL OF EDUCATION, University Of Wales Press, Gareth Elwyn Jones, Anthony Packer, 6 Gwennyth Street, Cathays, Cardiff CF2 4YD, Wales, 44-1222-231919; Fax 44-1222-230908; press@press.wales.ac.uk. Articles, reviews. circ. 500. Pub'd 2 issues 1998. sub. price: £30; per copy: £15. Discounts: 10%. 64pp; size A5; of. Payment: none. Copyrighted, reverts to author. Pub's reviews. §Education. Ads: £75/£37.50.

Wescott Cove Publishing Co., Julius M. Wilensky, Box 130, Stamford, CT 06904, 203-322-0998. 1968. Non-fiction. "We publish cruising guides and nautical books. Areas covered by cruising guides are Caribbean, New England, Mediterranean, South Pacific. Some subjects covered by nautical books are how-to, history, humor, crafts. Contributors (authors) are all experts in their fields. All have been previously published." avg. press run 5.5M. Pub'd 4 titles 1998; expects 2 titles 1999, 4 titles 2000. 18 titles listed in the *Small Press Record of Books in Print* (28th Edition, 1999-00). avg. price, paper: $19.95. Discounts: trade 40%, bulk (includes anyone who advertises or catalogs our books) 46%. 220pp; 8½x11, 6x9; of. Reporting time: 1 week. Simultaneous submissions accepted: yes. Payment: varies. Copyrights for author. SPAN.

West Anglia Publications, Helynn Hoffa, Editor; Wilama Lusk, Publisher, PO Box 2683, La Jolla, CA 92038, 619-457-1399. 1978. Poetry, fiction, art, photos, satire, long-poems, non-fiction. "We are a publishing company that assumes the cost of the book and pays the author in royalties or books. Our press and Baker and Taylor distribute our books. 'We look for excellence. We have recently printed poets John Theobald, Kathleen Iddings, and Gary Morgan. These are award winning poets whose books received excellent reviews. Kathleen Iddings was our Decade of Excellence Award winner, 1989-1999. We published her 5th book, *Rings of Saturn: Selected and New Poems, 1999.* Query with 5 poems, SASE. Cover letter should include previous publication credits and awards." avg. press run 500. Pub'd 2 titles 1998; expects 3 titles 1999, 3 titles 2000. 5 titles listed in the *Small*

Press Record of Books in Print (28th Edition, 1999-00). avg. price, cloth: $18; paper: $10. Discounts: negotiable. 75-100pp; 5½×8½; †of. Reporting time: 1 month. Simultaneous submissions accepted: yes. Payment: negotiable/usually in books. Copyrights for author.

WEST BRANCH, Karl Patten, Robert Taylor, Bucknell Hall, Bucknell University, Lewisburg, PA 17837, 570-577-1440 or 577-1554. 1977. Poetry, fiction, reviews. *"West Branch* continues to seek the best work being written today, both poetry and fiction. We believe that the most effective poems and stories make their way on terms established in the work itself; therefore we strive to read without prejudice all the prose and poetry sent to *West Branch*, trying to keep our own ideologies separate from our judgments of what constitutes 'the best work being written today.' Contributors to past issues include David Citino, Betsy Sholl, Harry Humes, Sally Jo Sorensen, Gary Fincke, Martha Collins, Victor Depta, Brigit Pegeen Kelly, Ken Poyner, Deborah Burnham, Julia Kasdorf, D. Nurkse, Anneliese Wagner, Barbara Crooker, Len Roberts, Layle Silbert, William F. Van Wert, Paul Shuttleworth, Molly Best Tinsley, Melissa Pritchard, Colette Inez, Timothy Russell, Earl Keener, William Kloefkorn, Emily Otis, David Ray, Doris Panoff, David Brooks, Jane Coleman, Steven Allaback, and others." circ. 500. 2/yr. Pub'd 2 issues 1998; expects 2 issues 1999, 2 issues 2000. sub. price: $7; per copy: $4; sample: $3. Discounts: 20-40% to bookstores. 96-118pp; 5½×8½; of. Reporting time: 4-6 weeks, but not reading ms. between April 1, 99 and May 1, 2000. Simultaneous submissions accepted: no. Payment: 2 copies and a year's subscription. Copyrighted, reverts to author. Pub's reviews: 3 in 1998. §Small press fiction & poetry, primarily by writers who publish in West Branch. Ads: exchange ads only. CLMP.

WEST COAST LINE: A Journal of Contemporary Writing and Criticism, Roy Miki, 2027 EAA, Simon Fraser University, Burnaby, B.C. V5A 1S6, Canada. 1990. Interviews, criticism. "Criticism, bibliography, reviews, and interviews concerned with contemporary Canadian and American writing poetry and short fiction." circ. 500. 3/yr. Pub'd 3 issues 1998; expects 3 issues 1999, 3 issues 2000. sub. price: $25 individuals, $40 libraries; per copy: $10; sample: $10. Back issues: $8. Discounts: $7 agents & jobbers. 128-144pp; 6×9; of. Reporting time: 3-4 months. Simultaneous submissions accepted: no. Publishes 20% of manuscripts submitted. Payment: 2 contributor's copies & modest royalty fee. Copyrighted, reverts to author. Pub's reviews: 3 in 1998. §Postmodern poetry, prose, criticism, cultural studies. Canadian Periodical Publishers Association.

West End Press, PO Box 27334, Albuquerque, NM 87125. 1976. Poetry, fiction, art, photos. "Politically progressive material favored." avg. press run 1.5M-3M. Pub'd 4 titles 1998; expects 4 titles 1999, 4 titles 2000. 41 titles listed in the *Small Press Record of Books in Print* (28th Edition, 1999-00). avg. price, paper: $8.95-$12.95. Discounts: write for info. 48-200pp; 5½×8½, 6×9; of. Reporting time: up to 6 months. Payment: in copies, at least 10% of run; or 6% cash payment. Copyrights for author.

WESTART, Martha Garcia, PO Box 6868, Auburn, CA 95604, 530-885-0969. 1962. Articles, art, photos, interviews, criticism, reviews, letters. circ. 4M. 24/yr. Pub'd 24 issues 1998; expects 24 issues 1999. sub. price: $16; per copy: 75¢; sample: free. Back issues: available thru xerox University Microfilms. Discounts: on request. 12pp; 10×15; web, of. Reporting time: 2 weeks. Payment: 50¢ per column inch. Copyrighted, reverts to author. Pub's reviews: 10 in 1998. §Arts, art techniques, crafts, craft techniques. Ads: $420/$210/25¢ per word.

Westchester House, Erin Wence, Editor, 218 South 95 Street, Omaha, NE 68114. 1986. Non-fiction. avg. press run 2M. Pub'd 1 title 1998; expects 1 title 1999. 2 titles listed in the *Small Press Record of Books in Print* (28th Edition, 1999-00). avg. price, paper: $15. Discounts: 40% 5 or more. 320pp; 7×9½; of.

WESTERN AMERICAN LITERATURE, Melody Graulich, Editor; Evelyn Funda, Book Review Editor, English Dept., Utah State Univ., Logan, UT 84322-3200, 435-797-1603; Fax 435-797-4099; wal@cc.usu.edu. 1966. Articles, art, photos, cartoons, interviews, criticism, reviews. "Send books for review to Book Review Editor. No unsolicited reviews" circ. 1M+. 4/yr. Pub'd 4 issues 1998; expects 4 issues 1999, 4 issues 2000. sub. price: $22 individuals, $45 institutions, $30 for individuals who want to be members of the Western Literature Association, $25 students; per copy: $7.50; sample: $7.50. Back issues: $7.50. Discounts: 20% agency. 112pp; 6×9; of. Reporting time: 2 months. Simultaneous submissions accepted: no. Publishes 10% of manuscripts submitted. Payment: 1-3 copies, tear sheets (for articles); tear sheets only for reviewers. Copyrighted, does not revert to author. Pub's reviews: 100-120 in 1998. §Books by western authors, about western authors or western literature, or books that focus on the West. Ads: $150/$90/no classifieds. Western Literature Association.

WESTERN HUMANITIES REVIEW, Barry Weller, Editor; David Kranes, Fiction Editor; Richard Howard, Poetry Editor; Amanda Pecor, Managing Editor, University of Utah, Salt Lake City, UT 84112, 801-581-6070. 1947. Poetry, fiction, articles, art, interviews, satire, criticism, reviews, music, letters, parts-of-novels, long-poems, plays, concrete art, non-fiction. "We prefer 2-3M words; We print articles in the humanities, fiction, poetry, and film and book reviews. Recent contributors: Joseph Brodsky, Jeanette Haien, Deborah Eisenberg, Tom Disch, Allen Grossman, Debora Greger, Bin Ramke, Nicholas Christopher, Lucie Brock-Broido, James McManus, Richard Pairier, Helen Vendler" circ. 1.5M. 4/yr. Pub'd 4 issues 1998; expects 4 issues 1999. sub. price: $26 (institutions) $20 (individuals); per copy: $6; sample: $6. Back issues: $6 for issues pub'd in 70s and 80s; $10 for earlier issues. Discounts: 25% to agents. 96pp; 6×9; photoset.

Reporting time: 3-6 months. Simultaneous submissions accepted: yes. Publishes *1% of manuscripts submitted.* Payment: $150 for stories and articles, $50 for poems. Copyrighted, rights revert to author on request. We don't use ads.

WESTERN SKIES, Full Moon Publications, Sharida Rizzuto, Harold Tollison, Elaine Wolfe, Rose Dalton, 577 Central Avenue, Box 4, Jefferson, LA 70121-1400, e-mail: horizons@altavista.net or blueskies@discover-ymail.com; Websites www.freeyellow.com/members2/oldwest/index.htm/, www2.cybercities.com/z/zines/. 1992. Poetry, fiction, articles, art, photos, cartoons, interviews, satire, criticism, reviews, letters, long-poems, collages, news items, non-fiction. "Articles, reviews, interviews, poetry, fiction, about the old west" circ. 500-800. 2/yr. Pub'd 2 issues 1998; expects 2 issues 1999, 2 issues 2000. sub. price: $15.80; per copy: $7.90; sample: $7.90. Back issues: $7.90. Discounts: trade with other like publications. 100pp; 8½×11; †of, excellent quality offset covers. Reporting time: 2-6 weeks. Simultaneous submissions accepted: yes. Publishes 30-35% of manuscripts submitted. Payment: free copies, fees paid to all contributors negotiable. Copyrighted, reverts to author. Pub's reviews: 40-50 in 1998. §Anything to do with the Old West. Ads: free.

WESTERN WATER, Rita Schmidt Sudman, 717 K Street, Suite 517, Sacramento, CA 95814, www.water-ed.org. 1977. Articles. circ. 40M. 6/yr. Pub'd 6 issues 1998; expects 6 issues 1999, 6 issues 2000. sub. price: $35; per copy: $3. Back issues: $2.50. Discounts: classroom in bulk. 18pp; 8×11; of. Simultaneous submissions accepted: no. Publishes 0% of manuscripts submitted. Copyrighted, does not revert to author. Ads: none.

Westgate Press, Lorraine Chandler, Editor, 5219 Magazine Street, New Orleans, LA 70115-1858. 1979. Art, photos, collages, non-fiction. "Metaphysical material, occult science and philosophy, esoteric mss. in related areas. Presently we are publishing *The Book Of Azrael* by Leilah Wendell, 'an intimate and first person encounter with the True Personification of Death! This dark and melancholy Angel is revealed through the writings of His Earthbound 'Bride' as well as direct communications with the Angel of Death Himself! Never before and never again will a book of this nature be offered. *This is not fiction.* But rather an account of the journey of an ancient spirit from the beginning of time to the present and beyond!...A Divine Dance Macabre!' That should give you an idea of what we are interested in. We request that *only* queries be sent at this time with appropriate SASE." avg. press run 500-5M. Pub'd 3 titles 1998; expects 3 titles 1999, 5 titles 2000. 3 titles listed in the *Small Press Record of Books in Print* (28th Edition, 1999-00). avg. price, cloth: $24.95; paper: $6.50 to $40; other: series folios @ $5 each. Discounts: 1-5 books 20%, 6-25 40%, 26-50 43%, 51-100 46%, 100+ 50%, discount applies to booksellers and others. 200+pp; 5×8, 7×10; of. Reporting time: 1 month on ms., 2 weeks on query. Simultaneous submissions accepted: yes. Publishes 20% of manuscripts submitted. Payment: negotiable on a project to project basis; no advance at present. Copyrights for author. AG/ALA, P&W Inc., NWC, PMA, NAPRA, ABE.

Westgate Publishing & Entertainment, Inc., 260 Crandon Blvd, Suite 32-109, Miami, FL 33149, 305-361-6862. 1990. Fiction, non-fiction. avg. press run 5M. Pub'd 1 title 1998; expects 2 titles 1999. 2 titles listed in the *Small Press Record of Books in Print* (28th Edition, 1999-00). avg. price, paper: $10.95. Discounts: 40% to bookstores, 50% to distributors/wholesalers. 192pp; 6×9. PMA.

Westhaven Publishing, Neil Pinter, 205 Sarasota Street, Borger, TX 79007. 1990. Non-fiction. avg. press run 3M. Pub'd 1 title 1998; expects 3 titles 1999, 8 titles 2000. 1 title listed in the *Small Press Record of Books in Print* (28th Edition, 1999-00). avg. price, paper: $12.95. Discounts: single title 0%, 3-5 20%, 6-9 30%, 10+ 40%. 240pp; lp. Reporting time: 1 month. Payment: open. Copyrights for author. AMA.

Westport Publishers (see also Media Periodicals; JOURNAL OF VISION REHABILITATION; TECHNICALITIES), Paul C. Temme, Publisher, 1102 Grand Boulevard, Suite 2300, Kansas City, MO 64106-2305, 816-842-8111. 1984. "Trade paperbacks in parenting, nutrition, wellness. Recent contributors include Dr. Edward Christophersen, Dr. James McClernan, Celeste Stuhring R.N." avg. press run 3M. Pub'd 5 titles 1998; expects 8 titles 1999, 12 titles 2000. 9 titles listed in the *Small Press Record of Books in Print* (28th Edition, 1999-00). avg. price, paper: $9.95-11.95. Discounts: 1-3 20%, 4-24 40%, 25-49 42%, 50+ 44%. 200pp; 6×9, 8½×11. Reporting time: 2 months. Payment: negotiable. Sometimes copyrights for author.

WEYFARERS, Guildford Poets Press, Jeffery Wheatley, Margaret Pain, Martin Jones, 9 White Rose Lane, Woking, Surrey GU22 7JA, England. 1972. Poetry. "All kinds of poetry: free verse and rhymed/metred, serious and humorous; mostly 'mainstream modern.'" circ. 300. 3/yr. Pub'd 3 issues 1998; expects 3 issues 1999, 3 issues 2000. sub. price: £4.50 (overseas £5.50 sterling or cash, or $15 cheque); per copy: £1.60 (overseas, £2 sterling or cash, or $5 cheque); sample: £1.60 (overseas, £2 sterling or cash, or $5 cheque). Back issues: £1 (overseas, £1.50 sterling or cash, or $4 cheque). 32pp; 8×6; of. Reporting time: 3-4 months maximum. Simultaneous submissions accepted: no. Payment: free copy of issue sent. Copyrighted, reverts to author. Pub's reviews: approx. 53 brief reviews (inc mags) in Newsletter in 1998. §Poetry only. No ads.

Whalesback Books, W.D. Howells, Box 9546, Washington, DC 20016, 202-333-2182. 1988. Art, photos, non-fiction. "Books of interest to museums: art, architecture and graphic presentations." avg. press run

2M-5M. Pub'd 1 title 1998; expects 1-2 titles 1999, 2 titles 2000. 2 titles listed in the *Small Press Record of Books in Print* (28th Edition, 1999-00). avg. price, cloth: $45; paper: $28. Discounts: standard. 200-300pp; 9×12; of. Payment: negotiable. Copyrights for author. SSP, PMA, Washington Book Publishers.

●**Wharton Publishing, Inc.,** T. Losasso, 3790 Via de la Valle Suite 204, Del Mar, CA 92014, 619-756-4922; Fax 619-759-7097; e-mail wharton@gte.net. 1991. Non-fiction. "Effective and easy to apply information that impacts people's wealth, health, relationships, time or attitude. Books with commercial tie-ins to products or services." Pub'd 1 title 1998; expects 2 titles 1999, 4 titles 2000. 3 titles listed in the *Small Press Record of Books in Print* (28th Edition, 1999-00). avg. price, paper: $16.95. 140pp; 6×9; of. Reporting time: 30 days or less. Simultaneous submissions accepted: no. Payment: varies. Copyrights for author. PMA.

●**WHAT IF...THE MAGAZINE OF THE MODERN PHILOSOPHER,** Austin Hodgens, PO Box 4193, San Dimas, CA 91773, mdrnphil@aol.com; http://members.tripod.com/~mdrnphil/whatifmag.html. 1997. Fiction, articles, cartoons, interviews, satire, letters. "Prefer pieces to be between 750-1500 words. Must have humorous slant." circ. ~250. 6/yr. Expects 2 issues 1999, 6 issues 2000. sub. price: $20/6 issues; per copy: $5; sample: $5. Back issues: same. Discounts: willing to trade and discount on larger orders. 32pp; 8½×11; †lp. Reporting time: 2 weeks, e-mail replies faster. Simultaneous submissions accepted: yes. Publishes 50% of manuscripts submitted. Payment: copies. Not copyrighted. Ads: $125/$70/$40 1/4 page.

WHAT IS ENLIGHTENMENT?, Moksha Press, Andrew Cohen, PO Box 2360, Lenox, MA 01240, 413-637-6000; FAX 413-637-6015; wie@moksha.org. 1991. Articles, photos, cartoons, interviews, criticism, reviews, letters, non-fiction. "Recent contributor: Ken Wilbur, Dalai Lama, Georg Feurstein" circ. 30M. 2/yr. Pub'd 2 issues 1998; expects 2 issues 1999, 3 issues 2000. sub. price: $12; per copy: $6.95; sample: $6.95. Back issues: recent issues $7.50, early issues $3. Discounts: 40%. 100+pp; 8½×11. Simultaneous submissions accepted: yes. Payment: none. Copyrighted, rights possibly revert to author on publication. Pub's reviews: 2 in 1998. §Spirituality. Ads: $450/$275. PMA.

What The Heck Press, Jenny Stein, PO Box 149, Ithaca, NY 14851-0149, 607-275-0806; Fax 607-275-0702. 1992. Poetry, fiction, non-fiction. "Childrens audio. Currently not accepting submissions." avg. press run 5M. 3 titles listed in the *Small Press Record of Books in Print* (28th Edition, 1999-00). avg. price, paper: $9; other: $12 book and audiotape set. Discounts: trade 40%, call or write for discounts on large or special orders. 100pp; 3⅜×4. Payment: confidential. Copyrights for author.

Wheat Forders/Trabuco Books, E.S. Lawrence, Christopher Whiteford Boyle, Chief Editor; Renee K. Boyle, Box 6317, Washington, DC 20015-0317, 202-362-1588. 1974. Poetry, long-poems, non-fiction. "Interested in book-length analyses of the significance of discoveries in such sciences as quantum physics, evolutionary biology, analytical psychology, brain functions analysis as they relate to the modern metaphysical outlook, Metahistory and interpretations of modern times in light of one or other of its theories is also of interest as is the extension of A. Huxley's interpretations of the parallels in the Great Religions and the discovery of a common Mysticism below them all. Work must be interdisciplinary and show how all these sciences support a single world view. We print a series: Primers for the Age of Inner Space to which anyone having anything to contribute has equal access. We have been approached by the Accademy of Independent Scholars to print/publish certain books. We publish cooperatively with the author required to arrange for the sale of 200 books @ cover price. (for paperbacks this is in the range of $10-$20)." avg. press run 2M. Pub'd 2-4 titles 1998. 1 title listed in the *Small Press Record of Books in Print* (28th Edition, 1999-00). avg. price, cloth: $15-$20; paper: $10-$15. Discounts: wholesalers 45%; libraries 25%; university classroom 45%; poor student, but interested, free on showing of need. 100-250pp; 5½×8½; of. Reporting time: 6-7 weeks. Payment: cooperative with author purchasing 200 copies via his connections. Copyrights for author. SP, AAP, AIS.

Whelks Walk Press (see also WHELKS WALK REVIEW), Marianne Mitchell, Publisher; Joan Peternel, Editor-in-Chief, 37 Harvest Lane, Southampton, NY 11968, 516-283-5122; Fax 516-283-1902; whelks-walk@aol.com. 1995. Poetry, fiction, art. "We published one book in 1997, Joan Peternel's book of poems, *Howl and Hosanna*. In 1998 and 1999 we have been busy putting out, the *Whelks Walk Review*. Authors, please wait for our calls for manuscripts, or send for guidelines, available in 1999. In 1999 we are publishing Joan Petenel's collection of short stories, *Nintotem: Indiana Stories*." avg. press run 500-1M. Pub'd 1 title 1998; expects 1 title 1999, 2 titles 2000. 2 titles listed in the *Small Press Record of Books in Print* (28th Edition, 1999-00). avg. price, paper: $10. Discounts: usual bookstore, library discounts. 120pp; 5½×8½; of. Reporting time: several weeks to several months. Simultaneous submissions accepted: no. Payment: yes. Copyrights for author.

WHELKS WALK REVIEW, Whelks Walk Press, Marianne Mitchell, Publisher; Joan Peternel, Editor-in-Chief, 37 Harvest Lane, Southampton, NY 11968, 516-283-5122; Fax 516-283-1902; whelks-walk@aol.com. 1998. Poetry, fiction, articles, art, photos, interviews, criticism, reviews, plays, non-fiction. "Poems 1-2 pages. Stories, essays, articles 5-12 pages. Reviews by invitation at present. Recent contributors: Dana Gioia, Harvey Shapiro, Joseph Bruchac, Mark Terrill, Tom Whalen, John Ditsky, Felix Stefanile." 2/yr.

Expects 2 issues 1999, 2 issues 2000. sub. price: $15; per copy: $8; sample: $5. Back issues: vol. 1 $25. Discounts: usual bookstore and library discounts. 125pp; 5½×8½; of. Reporting time: several weeks to several months. Simultaneous submissions accepted: no. Payment: contributor's copy. Copyrighted, reverts to author. Pub's reviews: 4 in 1998. §At present, we are inviting reviews, but this may change. Try us; we're open to suggestions. Interested in all the arts. Ads: $100/$50.

WHETSTONE, Sandra Berris, Marsha Portnoy, Jean Tolle, Barrington Area Arts Council, PO Box 1266, Barrington, IL 60011, 847-382-5626. 1983. Poetry, fiction, interviews, parts-of-novels, non-fiction. "Prefer to see 3-5 poems or up to 25 pages of fiction or non-fiction. Include SASE. Recent contributors include: poetry—Helen Reed, John Dickson, Ted May, Shulanaith Wechter Caine; fiction or non-fiction—Leslie Pietryzk, Barbara Croft, Ann Joslin Williams." circ. 800. 1/yr. Pub'd 1 issue 1998; expects 1 issue 1999, 1 issue 2000. sub. price: $8.50 ppd; per copy: $8.50 ppd; sample: $5 ppd., includes guidelines. Back issues: same as sample. Discounts: 50% to bookstores. 120pp; 5⅞×9; of. Reporting time: 3-5 months. Simultaneous submissions accepted: yes. Publishes 2% of manuscripts submitted. Payment: variable plus eligible for *The Whetstone Prize*, annual cash awards, in 1998 totaled $750. Copyrighted, reverts to author. CLMP.

WHISPERING WIND MAGAZINE, Jack B. Heriard, PO Box 1390, Folsom, LA 70437-1390, 504-796-5433; e-mail whiswind@i-55.com; website www.whisperingwind.com. 1967. Articles, art, photos, cartoons, interviews, reviews, letters, news items. "Magazine for those interested in the American Indian; the traditions and crafts, past and present." circ. 24M. 6/yr. Pub'd 6 issues 1998; expects 6 issues 1999, 6 issues 2000. sub. price: $20; per copy: $4; sample: $6. Back issues: included in each issue. Discounts: 5-20 $2.10 ea. 52pp; 8½×11; of. Reporting time: 4-8 weeks. Simultaneous submissions accepted: yes. Publishes 80% of manuscripts submitted. Payment: copies and subscription. Copyrighted, does not revert to author. Pub's reviews: 25 in 1998. §American Indian. Ads: $362/$186/60¢. AMA.

White Buck Publishing, David J. Thomas, Rebekka K. Nielson, 5187 Colorado Avenue, Sheffield Village, OH 44054-2338, 440-934-4454 phone/fax. 1996. Poetry, art, photos, interviews, criticism, long-poems, non-fiction. "Accept only material which reflect Christian theology, ethics, and morals. Work with book length manuscripts only. Poetry, non-fiction, apologetics, etc. are solicited." avg. press run 10-25M. Expects 2 titles 1999, 4 titles 2000. 1 title listed in the *Small Press Record of Books in Print* (28th Edition, 1999-00). avg. price, cloth: $29.95; paper: 9.95. Discounts: retail base 40%, wholesale 50-55%, distribution 60-65%; sliding scale on basis of single order quantity. 175pp; 5½×8½; of. Reporting time: 2-4 months. Simultaneous submissions accepted: yes. Publishes 5-10% of manuscripts submitted. Payment: as circumstances dictate. Copyrights for author if requested. PMA, SPAN.

White Cliffs Media, Inc., Lawrence Aynesmith, 400 Del Verde Circle, Unit 2, Sacramento, CA 95833-3051. 1985. Poetry, art, photos, music. "Current emphasis is on innovative publications in world and popular music. Compact Discs, cassettes often included. General trade titles also considered. Current title: *The New Folk Music* by Craig Harris." avg. press run varies. Pub'd 12 titles 1998; expects 3 titles 1999, 10 titles 2000. 13 titles listed in the *Small Press Record of Books in Print* (28th Edition, 1999-00). avg. price, cloth: $40; paper: $18; other: cassette $10.95; CD $15. Discounts: follow industry standards. 180pp; 6×9; of. Reporting time: 1-3 months. Payment: varies. Copyrights for author.

The White Cross Press, Claude W. Horton, Sr., 4401 Spicewood Springs Road #232, Austin, TX 78759-8589. 1974. Poetry, fiction, non-fiction. "Manuscripts by invitation only." avg. press run 500. Expects 1 title 1999. 3 titles listed in the *Small Press Record of Books in Print* (28th Edition, 1999-00). avg. price, cloth: $15.95; paper: $7.95. Discounts: bookstores (on consignment) 40%, 2 or more copies, returns permitted. 200pp; 6×9; lp. Payment: varies. Copyrights for author.

THE WHITE CROW, Osric Publishing, Christopher Herdt, PO Box 4501, Ann Arbor, MI 48106. 1994. Poetry, fiction, art, photos, satire, plays. circ. 200. 4/yr. Pub'd 4 issues 1998; expects 4 issues 1999, 4 issues 2000. sub. price: $6; per copy: $2; sample: $2. Discounts: 50% to libraries and teachers. 32pp; 5½×8; photocopy. Reporting time: 4 months. Simultaneous submissions accepted: yes. Publishes 10% of manuscripts submitted. Payment: negotiable, copies. Not copyrighted. Pub's reviews: 4 in 1998. §Literature, zines. Ads: $20/$10.

THE WHITE DOT - Survival Guide for the TV-Free, Jean L. Lotus, PO Box 577257, Chicago, IL 60657, www3.mistral.co.uk/white. 1996. Articles, art, photos, cartoons, interviews, criticism, letters, news items, non-fiction. "Articles about television's impact on humanity are welcome. We run comics making fun of television. Practical articles for the TV-free include: following sports, starting a book group, parenting tips." circ. 700. 4/yr. Expects 4 issues 1999, 4 issues 2000. sub. price: $8; per copy: $2; sample: $2. Discounts: none. 12pp; 8½×11; mi. Reporting time: 1 month. Simultaneous submissions accepted: yes. Payment: copies. Copyrighted, reverts to author. Pub's reviews. §Media criticism.

White Knight Press, Xavier DeWeer, 95 Fern Street, Naugutack, CT 06770-2642, 203-723-6872 tel/fax; E-mail nwfg@erols.com. 1996. Non-fiction. avg. press run 3M. Expects 2-4 titles 1999. 1 title listed in the

Small Press Record of Books in Print (28th Edition, 1999-00). avg. price, cloth: $24.95; paper: $13.95. Discounts: 20-50% depending on volume. 240pp; 5½×8½; of. Reporting time: 2-4 weeks. Simultaneous submissions accepted: yes. Payment: varies. Copyrights for author.

White Mane Publishing Company, Inc., Martin K. Gordon, Executive Editor; Diane R. Gordon, Associate Editor, 63 West Burd Street, PO Box 152, Shippensburg, PA 17257, 717-532-2237; fax 717-532-7704. 1987. Non-fiction. "White Mane specializes in military history (esp. the American Civil War period). Also, regional topics. Our authors are the top historians in their fields. No proposal will be considered unless presented in conformity with our guidelines." avg. press run 3M-5M. Pub'd 15 titles 1998; expects 18 titles 1999, 20 titles 2000. 82 titles listed in the *Small Press Record of Books in Print* (28th Edition, 1999-00). avg. price, cloth: $24.95; paper: $9.95. Discounts: available on request. 200-300pp; 6×9; †lp. Reporting time: 120 days with guideline and manuscript, proposal guidelines available on request. Simultaneous submissions accepted: yes. Payment: twice yearly statements. Copyrights for author.

White Oak Press, Robert McGill, PO Box 188, Reeds Spring, MO 65737, 417-538-4220. 1986. "Recent contributors: Mary Hartmann, Jory Sherman, Leanne Potts, Kathleen van Buskirk." avg. press run 2.5M. Pub'd 2 titles 1998; expects 4 titles 1999. avg. price, paper: $10.95. 180pp; 5½×8½, 8½×11. Reporting time: 90 days. Payment: standard, although no advances. Copyrights for author. MAP.

White Phoenix Publishing, Cheryl Long Riffle, PO Box 2157, Lake Oswego, OR 97035, 503-639-4549; Fax 503-620-4933; wphoenixp@aol.com. 1997. Non-fiction. avg. press run 4M. Pub'd 1 title 1998; expects 1-2 titles 1999, 2-3 titles 2000. 1 title listed in the *Small Press Record of Books in Print* (28th Edition, 1999-00). avg. price, paper: $12.95. Discounts: standard (ask for discount sheet). 176pp; 5½×8½. Reporting time: 90 days (query first). Simultaneous submissions accepted: no. Payment: quarterly royalties. Copyrights for author. PMA, NWABP.

White Pine Press, Dennis Maloney, Editor; Douglas Carlson, Associate Editor; Elaine LaMattina, Fiction Editor, PO Box 236, Buffalo, NY 14201-0236, 716-672-5743. 1973. Poetry, fiction, long-poems, non-fiction. "White Pine Press continues to publish a variety of translations, poetry, fiction, and non-fiction. Do not send unsolicited ms without querying first. White Pine Press has published fine works of poetry, fiction, essays, non-fiction, and literature in translation from many languages." avg. press run 1M-2M. Pub'd 10 titles 1998; expects 10 titles 1999, 10 titles 2000. 95 titles listed in the *Small Press Record of Books in Print* (28th Edition, 1999-00). avg. price, cloth: $20; paper: $12-$14. Discounts: 2-4, 20%; 5 & over, 40%. 200-300pp; 5½×8½; of. Reporting time: 1-3 months. Simultaneous submissions accepted: yes. Publishes 1% of manuscripts submitted. Payment: copies, honorarium, royalties. Copyrights for author. PMA, CLMP.

White Plume Press, Gene Nelson, 2442 NW Market Street #370, Seattle, WA 98107-4137, 206-525-1812, Fax; 206-525-1925, E-mail; bd72@scn.org. 1988. Poetry, non-fiction. "We are interested in seeing quality material on the pacific Northwest, The Puget Sound Area, and/or Seattle." avg. press run 2M. Expects 3 titles 1999, 3 titles 2000. avg. price, paper: $9. 64pp; 6×9; of. Reporting time: 30 days with SASE. Simultaneous submissions accepted: yes. Payment: open. Copyrights for author. BPNW.

White Urp Press (see also ABBEY), 5360 Fallriver Row Court, Columbia, MD 21044. avg. press run 200. 6 titles listed in the *Small Press Record of Books in Print* (28th Edition, 1999-00). 15-20pp; 8½×11. Simultaneous submissions accepted: no. Does not copyright for author.

White Wolf Publishing, Staley Krause, Editor-in-Chief; Erin Kelly, Executive Editor; Robert Hatch, Executive Editor, 780 Park North Blvd., Ste. 100, Clarkson, GA 30021, 404-292-1819. 1986. Poetry, fiction, art, photos. "We are interested in dark fantasy, horror and sci-fi. We are a venue for mature themes and content but are not interested in eroticism or porm. We are receptive to heretofore unpublished writers and will give special attention to speculative, cutting edge fiction." avg. press run varies. Pub'd 40 titles 1998; expects 65 titles 1999, 84 titles 2000. avg. price, cloth: $21.99; paper: $5.99; other: $15.99. Reporting time: 6 months. Publishes 5% of manuscripts submitted. Payment: varies. Copyrights for author.

White-Boucke Publishing, PO Box 400, Lafayette, CO 80026-1526, 303-604-0661, Fax 303-604-0662, e-mail cwhite@white-boucke.com. 1989. Photos, cartoons, interviews, satire, music, non-fiction. Expects 3 titles 1999. 14 titles listed in the *Small Press Record of Books in Print* (28th Edition, 1999-00). avg. price, paper: $16.50. Discounts: Discount per volume. 300pp; 5½×8½; of. Reporting time: 4 weeks. Simultaneous submissions accepted: yes. Publishes 5% of manuscripts submitted. Payment: royalties paid in April annually. Copyrights for author.

WHITECHAPEL JOURNAL, Stephen Wright, Attn: Stephen Wright, PO Box 1341, FDR Station, New York, NY 10150-1341. 1996. Articles, criticism, reviews, letters, news items, non-fiction. "*Whitechapel Journal* is a newsletter mainly concerned with the notorious Jack the Ripper, who in 1888 murdered prostitutes in Whitechapel and other districts in the East End of London. Articles: 400-1200 words (400-800 words preferred). Reviews: 400-800 words (400 words preferred). Recent contributors: John Kennedy Melling,

Stephen Wright, Dr. Frederick Walker." 2/yr. Pub'd 1 issue 1998; expects 2 issues 1999, 2 issues 2000. sub. price: $15 US, £10; per copy: $8.50 US, £6; sample: same. Back issues: same. Discounts: none. 16pp; 8½x11; photocopy/xerox. Reporting time: 2-4 weeks. We will accept simultaneous submissions, if notified first. Publishes 50% of manuscripts submitted. Payment: copy of issue. Copyrighted, reverts to author. Pub's reviews: 3 in 1998. §Jack the Ripper is *the* subject. (The general topic of serial killers, or a contemporary, individual serial murderer is also of interest.) Some aspect of the Ripper case: victims, witnesses, suspects, police or politicians, theories and solutions, and so forth. Ads: none. Mystery Writers of America.

WHITEWALLS: A Journal of Language and Art, Anthony E. Elms, Managing Editor, PO Box 8204, Chicago, IL 60680, 312-409-4344; email aeelms@aol.com. 1978. Articles, art, photos, concrete art. "Recent contributers: Louis Camanitzer, Lucy Lippard, Robert Blancheor, Lynne Tillman, Scott Rankin, Lavne Palmer." circ. 1.5-2M. 2/yr. Pub'd 1 issue 1998; expects 2 issues 1999, 2 issues 2000. sub. price: $15, overseas $25, institutions $18, $35 overseas air; per copy: $8; sample: $8 except museums and libraries. Back issues: $8 for most issues, some are $10. Negotiable price for complete set. 120-150pp; 8x9½; †of. Reporting time: 6-12 months. We accept simultaneous submissions on occasion. Payment: none. Copyrighted, does not revert to author. Pub's reviews: 0 in 1998. §Art, critical theory. Ads: $250 1x, $400 per year/$150 1x, $250 per year.

Whitford Press, Ellen Taylor, Editor, 4880 Lower Valley Road, Atglen, PA 19310, 610-593-1777; Fax 610-593-2002. 1987. Non-fiction. "Whitford Press distributes for the Donning Company." avg. press run 5M. Pub'd 2 titles 1998; expects 3 titles 1999, 3 titles 2000. 50 titles listed in the *Small Press Record of Books in Print* (28th Edition, 1999-00). avg. price, paper: $19.95. Discounts: 1 10%, 2-4 20%, 5-24 40%, 25-49 42%, 50-99 43%, 100-249 44%, 250-499 45%, 500+ 46%. 200pp; 6½x9¼. Reporting time: usually 1 month. Simultaneous submissions accepted: no. Payment: royalties paid twice yearly. Copyrights for author. ABA, NEBA.

Whitmore Publishing Company, Roy Sandstrom, Managing Editor, 35 Cricket Terrace, Ardmore, PA 19003, 215-896-6116. 1961. Non-fiction. "*Whitmore* focuses on books that will provide the reader insight and techniques to manage his or her life more effectively. *Whitmore* book subjects are as follows: community life, education, family planning, career planning, nutrition, philosophy, and self improvement" avg. press run 3M. Expects 2 titles 1999. 6 titles listed in the *Small Press Record of Books in Print* (28th Edition, 1999-00). avg. price, cloth: $15.95; paper: $8.95. Discounts: 20% educational/library, 40% (5 or more copies), 30% (1-4) to bookstores. 128pp; 6x9; †of. Reporting time: 4 weeks. Payment: 10% of retail price. Copyrights for author.

Who Who Who Publishing (see also THE EVER DANCING MUSE), John A. Chorazy, PO Box 7751, East Rutherford, NJ 07073. 1993. Poetry, art, parts-of-novels, long-poems. avg. press run 150. Pub'd 2 titles 1998; expects 2 titles 1999, 2 titles 2000. avg. price, paper: $3. 20pp; 8½x5½; of. Reporting time: 1-4 weeks. We accept simultaneous submissions if specified. Payment: 2 copies. Does not copyright for author.

WHOLE EARTH, Peter Warshall, Editor, 1408 Mission Avenue, San Rafael, CA 94901-1971. 1974. Fiction, articles, cartoons, interviews, satire, reviews, letters, non-fiction, art, photos, criticism, music. "Subscription address: PO Box 3000, Denville, NJ 07834. Credit card orders: 800-783-4903" circ. 30M. 4/yr. Pub'd 4 issues 1998; expects 4 issues 1999, 4 issues 2000. 1 title listed in the *Small Press Record of Books in Print* (28th Edition, 1999-00). sub. price: $24; per copy: $6.95; sample: $6.95. Back issues: write for information. 120pp; 7¾x10½. Reporting time: 3-6 months. Payment: ranges from $40 for book reviews to $500 for a major article. Copyrighted, reverts to author. Pub's reviews: 300-400 in 1998. §Soft tech., craft, architecture, sports & travel, educational mat'ls, agriculture, small business, music, parenting, environment, politics, economics. Ads: $2/word classified. ABA, SMPG (Small Magazine Publishers Group).

WHOLE NOTES, Whole Notes Press, Nancy Peters Hastings, PO Box 1374, Las Cruces, NM 88004, 505-541-5744. 1984. Poetry. "*Whole Notes* seeks original poetry from beginning and established writers. All forms are considered. Recent contributors include Ted Kooser, Carol Oles, Bill Kloefkorn, Roy Scheele, Keith Wilson, Don Welch." circ. 400. 2/yr. Pub'd 2 issues 1998; expects 2 issues 1999, 2 issues 2000. sub. price: $6; per copy: $3; sample: $3. Back issues: $3. Discounts: available upon request. 28pp; 5½x8½; of. Reporting time: 1 month. Simultaneous submissions accepted: no. Publishes 5% of manuscripts submitted. Payment: 2 copies. Copyrighted, does not revert to author. Ads: $50/$25. CLMP.

Whole Notes Press (see also WHOLE NOTES), Nancy Peters Hastings, PO Box 1374, Las Cruces, NM 88004, 505-382-7446. 1988. Poetry. "Each year Whole Notes Press features the work of a single poet in a chapbook. Submissions to the Whole Notes Chapbook Series are welcomed. Send a sampler of 3-8 poems along with a stamped, self-addressed envelope. Recent chapbooks by Roy Scheele and Dan Stryk." avg. press run 400. Pub'd 1 title 1998; expects 1 title 1999, 1 title 2000. 6 titles listed in the *Small Press Record of Books in Print* (28th Edition, 1999-00). avg. price, paper: $3; other: $3 chapbook. Discounts: available upon request. 20pp; 5½x8½; of. Reporting time: 1 month. Simultaneous submissions accepted: no. Publishes 1% of manuscripts submitted. Payment: author will receive 25 copies of the chapbook. Copyrights for author. CLMP.

Whole Person Associates Inc., Susan Gustafson, 210 West Michigan Street, Duluth, MN 55802-1908,

218-727-0500; FAX 218-727-0505. 1977. avg. press run 5M-10M. Pub'd 5 titles 1998. 41 titles listed in the *Small Press Record of Books in Print* (28th Edition, 1999-00). avg. price, paper: $15.95; other: $24.95. Discounts: normal trade for some books/professional discounts. 192pp; 6×9. Simultaneous submissions accepted: yes. Copyrights for author. PMA, Mid Ameno Publisher, ABA, Minnesota Independent Publisher.

WHOLE TERRAIN - REFLECTIVE ENVIRONMENTAL PRACTICE, 40 Avon Street, Antioch New England, Keene, NH 03431-3516, 603-357-3122 ex. 272. 1992. Poetry, interviews, reviews, non-fiction. "1000-5000 words non-fictional essays on specific yearly themes; as well as book reviews and poetry. Recent contributors: Stefanie Kaza, author of *The Attentive Heart: Conversations with Trees*, Paul Shepard, author of *Nature and Madness*; Bell Hooks, author of *Sisters of the Yam*, David Rothenberg, Professor and author of *Hand's End*; David Abram, author of *The Spell of the Sensuous*; Rick Bass, author of *Where the Sea Used to Be*." circ. 3M. 1/yr. Pub'd 1 issue 1998; expects 1 issue 1999, 1 issue 2000. sub. price: $7; per copy: $5; sample: $5. Back issues: $5. 72pp; 7½×10½; of. Reporting time: 6-8 weeks. Simultaneous submissions accepted: yes. Publishes 30% of manuscripts submitted. Payment: none. Copyrighted, reverts to author. Pub's reviews: 1 in 1998. §Environmental topics, nature related fiction and non-fiction.

WICKED MYSTIC, Andre Scheluchin, 532 LaGuardia Place #371, New York, NY 10012, 718-638-1533. 1990. Poetry, fiction, articles, art, photos, cartoons, interviews, satire, criticism, reviews, music, letters, long-poems, non-fiction. "Fiction: double-spaced, 3,000 words max., previously unpublished. Poetry: 35 lines max., submit no more than 5 at once, previously unpublished. Artwork: black and white line art, no larger than 8½ by 11. Please include SASE with all submissions and inquiries. Include bio and interests. We are looking for explicit, gut-wrenching, brutally twisted, warped, sadistic, deathly, provocative, nasty, blatant horror, horror, horror. Recent contributors include Buzz Lovko, Wayne Edwards, Richard Levesque, Allen Koszowski, Harold Cupec, and Maria A. Vega. Send cash or make check/money order payable to Andre Scheluchin." circ. 10M. 4/yr. Pub'd 4 issues 1998; expects 4 issues 1999, 4 issues 2000. sub. price: $24; per copy: $6 (mention Dustbooks $5); sample: $6 (mention Dustbooks $5). Back issues: same. Discounts: trade. 80pp; 8½×11; lp. Reporting time: average 1-2 months. Simultaneous submissions accepted: no. Publishes 5% of manuscripts submitted. Payment: for each story accepted is 1.25¢/word; copies of the issue and a free 1/4 page ad ($50 value) for a product or service you are promoting. Copyrighted, reverts to author. Pub's reviews: 30 in 1998. §Anything horror related. Ads: $125/$85/$50.

Wide World Publishing/TETRA, Elvira Monroe, PO Box 476, San Carlos, CA 94070, 650-593-2839, Fax 650-595-0802. 1976. Articles, photos, non-fiction. "Imprint—Math Products Plus." avg. press run varies. Pub'd 10 titles 1998; expects 8 titles 1999, 8 titles 2000. 42 titles listed in the *Small Press Record of Books in Print* (28th Edition, 1999-00). avg. price, paper: $9.95-$15.95. Discounts: 2-4 books 20%, 5-24 40%, 25-49 42%, 50-99 44%, 100+ 48%. 200pp; size varies; lp. Reporting time: 30 days. Payment: 10%. Copyrights for author. American Booksellers Association, Museum Store Association.

WIDENER REVIEW, Humanities Division, Widener Univ., Chester, PA 19013, 610-499-4341. 1984. Poetry, fiction, interviews, reviews, parts-of-novels. circ. 250. 1/yr. Pub'd 1 issue 1998; expects 1 issue 1999, 1 issue 2000. sub. price: $5; per copy: $5; sample: $4. Back issues: $4. Discounts: 40% on 10 copies or more. 100-120pp; 5½×8½; of. Reporting time: 1-6 months. Simultaneous submissions accepted: no. Publishes 6% of manuscripts submitted. Payment: 1 copy of the magazine. Copyrighted, reverts to author. Ads: $40/$25.

Wild Dove Studio and Press, Inc., Glenda Bailey-Mershon, PO Box 789, Palatine, IL 60078-0789, 847-991-5615. 1993. Poetry, fiction, articles, art, photos, cartoons, interviews, satire, parts-of-novels, long-poems, non-fiction. "This is an eco-feminist press with primary interest in feminist fiction and commentary and in environmental information and art; especially interested in fiction and poetry exhibiting a strong sense of place. Graphic illustrations or photos along these lines for books, stationary and other gift items are also especially welcome. *Until further notice we will not be accepting unsolicited manuscripts.* We also operate the Wild Dove Writer's Center, which offers workshops and other events, and publish the Wild Dove Review, a newsletter for writers. Send $2 for newsletter sample and $7 for chapbook or anthology sample." avg. press run 5M. Expects 2 titles 1999, 4-5 titles 2000. 9 titles listed in the *Small Press Record of Books in Print* (28th Edition, 1999-00). avg. price, paper: $9.95. Discounts: write for schedules. 125pp; 5½×8½; of. Reporting time: We are inundated, but we try for 60 days, in response to calls for manuscripts only. We accept simultaneous submissions for announced publications.

WILD DUCK REVIEW, Casey Walker, PO BOX 388, Nevada City, CA 95959-0388, 530-478-0134; Fax 530-265-2304; casey@wildduckreview.com. 1994. Poetry, fiction, articles, art, photos, interviews, satire, criticism, reviews, letters, news items, non-fiction. "Recent contributors include: Gary Snyder, Dave Foreman, Arne Naess, Joanne Macy, Galway Kinnell, Pattiann Rogers, Elizabeth Herron, Anne Ehrlich, Jim Harrison, Wendell Berry, Jane Hirshfield, Terry Tempest Williams, Jerry Mander. Biases: Literature that promotes an ecological worldview, literature that is news. Does not read unsolicited manuscripts." circ. 3M. 4/yr. Pub'd 3 issues 1998; expects 4 issues 1999, 4 issues 2000. sub. price: $24; per copy: $4; sample: $4. Back issues: complete set of back issues $3 each. Discounts: 50% for orders of 10+ for educational purposes. 40pp; 11×14;

offset web. Payment: copies. Copyrighted, reverts to author. Pub's reviews: 3 in 1998. §Not accepting reviews at this time.

WILD EARTH, Tom Butler, PO Box 455, Richmond, VT 05477, 802-434-4077; fax 802-434-5980; e-mail info@wild-earth.org. 1991. Poetry, articles, art, cartoons, interviews, criticism, reviews, letters, news items, non-fiction. circ. 9M. 4/yr. Pub'd 4 issues 1998; expects 4 issues 1999, 4 issues 2000. sub. price: $25; per copy: $5; sample: $2. Back issues: $8 subscribers/$10 non-subscribers. 108pp; 8½×11; of. Reporting time: varies. Simultaneous submissions accepted: no. Payment: yes. Pub's reviews: 25 in 1998. §conservation/wilderness issues. Ads: full $500/ half $275. Independent Press Assoc.

THE WILD FOODS FORUM, Vickie Shufer, PO Box 61413, Virginia Beach, VA 23462, 804-421-3929, E-mail; wildfood@infi.net. 1989. Articles, art, photos, reviews, letters, news items, non-fiction. ''Our bias is upbeat, outdoorsy, and environmentally-friendly. *The Wild Foods Forum* is a newsletter for people who are interested in foraging, that is, eating dandelions and other wild things. Articles range in length from a few paragraphs to 1,000 words. Most contributors are avid foragers or herbalists. I am especially interested in hearing from contributors who actually *teach* wild foods.'' circ. 1M. 6/yr. Pub'd 6 issues 1998; expects 6 issues 1999, 6 issues 2000. sub. price: $15; per copy: $3; sample: $3. Back issues: $2. Discounts: negotiable. 16pp; 8½×11; of. Reporting time: 2 months. Simultaneous submissions accepted: yes. Publishes 60% of manuscripts submitted. Payment: 0-$25. Copyrighted, reverts to author. Pub's reviews: 16 in 1998. §Foraging, wild foods, survival skills, medicinal plants, ethnobotany, anthropology, gardening with unusual plants, herbs, nature travel. Ads: $85/$45/$50 2/3 page/$45 1/3 page/$35 1/4 page/$25 1/6 page/$17 1/8 page/$15 1/9 page/$10 1/12 page/discounts for multiple runs.

Wilderness Adventure Books, Erin Sims Howorth, Po Box 576, Chelsea, MI 48118-0576, fax 734-433-1595; e-mail wildernessbooks.org. 1983. Photos, non-fiction. ''We publish mostly how to guides of the Great Lakes outdoors. Recent books include: *Edible Medicinal Plants of the Great Lakes Region*'' avg. press run 3M. Pub'd 4 titles 1998; expects 4 titles 1999, 4 titles 2000. 3 titles listed in the *Small Press Record of Books in Print* (28th Edition, 1999-00). avg. price, paper: $15.95. Discounts: 30-50%. 300pp; 5½×8½. Reporting time: 6 weeks. Simultaneous submissions accepted: yes. Publishes 5% of manuscripts submitted. Payment: 5-10% of retail/every 6 months. Copyrights for author.

Wilderness Press, Caroline Winnett, Publisher, 2440 Bancroft Way, Berkeley, CA 94704, 510-843-8080; fax 510-548-1355; e-mail mail@wildernesspress.com. 1966. Non-fiction. ''Conservation, environmental bias. Bias for accuracy. Bias against sloppy writing.'' avg. press run 5M. Pub'd 10 titles 1998; expects 15 titles 1999, 15 titles 2000. 35 titles listed in the *Small Press Record of Books in Print* (28th Edition, 1999-00). avg. price, cloth: $25; paper: $13. 180pp; 6×9; of. Reporting time: 2 weeks. Simultaneous submissions accepted: yes. Publishes 5% of manuscripts submitted. Payment: competitive royalty paid quarterly or semi-annually. Copyrights for author.

Wildstone Media, PO Box 270570, St. Louis, MO 63127, 314-487-0402; FAX 314-487-1910; 800-296-1918; website www.wildstonemedia.com. 1992. Fiction, non-fiction. ''We also produce, manufacture and distribute audio books'' avg. press run 5M. Pub'd 4 titles 1998; expects 4 titles 1999, 4 titles 2000. 3 titles listed in the *Small Press Record of Books in Print* (28th Edition, 1999-00). avg. price, paper: $12; other: $18 audio. 150pp; 6×9; lp. Payment: varies. Copyrights for author. SPAN, APA.

Willendorf Press, Miriam Berg, Nancy Summer, PO Box 407, Bearsville, NY 12409, 914-679-1209; fax 914-679-1206. 1991. Non-fiction. avg. press run 3M. Expects 1 title 1999, 1 title 2000. avg. price, paper: $14.95. Discounts: negotiable. 200pp; 5×8½. Reporting time: 30 days. Payment: negotiable. Copyrights for author.

WILLIAM AND MARY REVIEW, Brian Hatlebery, Campus Center, PO Box 8795, Williamsburg, VA 23187-8795, 757-221-3290, fax 757-221-3451. 1962. Poetry, fiction, art, photos, interviews, criticism, reviews, parts-of-novels, long-poems, non-fiction. ''The *Review* is a national literary magazine published without faculty supervision, but with college funding, by the students of William and Mary. In our most recent issues, we have published works by Cornelius Eady, Dana Gioia, David Ignatow, Phyllis Janowitz, Michael Mott, W.S. Penn, Valerie Smith, and Debbie Lee Wesselmann, Amy Clampitt, Richard Kostelanetz, Robert Bly, Elizabeth Spires, among others.'' circ. 5M. 1/yr. Pub'd 1 issue 1998; expects 1 issue 1999, 1 issue 2000. sub. price: $5.50; per copy: $6; sample: $5.50. Back issues: $5.50 per issue. Discounts: 40% off list for trade. 115pp; 6×9; of. Reporting time: 2-3 months. We accept simultaneous submissions, but not preferred. Publishes 5% of manuscripts submitted. Payment: 5 copies of issue. Copyrighted, reverts to author. Pub's reviews. §Current literature, fiction, poetry or non-fiction. CLMP.

Williamson Publishing Company, Inc., Susan Williamson, Editorial Director; Jennifer Ingersoll, Editor; Emily Stetson, Editor, Box 185, Church Hill Road, Charlotte, VT 05445, 802-425-2102. 1983. Non-fiction. ''Childrens' how-to non-fiction; Kids Can, Little Hands, Tales Alive!, Kaleidoscope Kids, and Good Times! Series.'' avg. press run 15M. Pub'd 10 titles 1998; expects 10 titles 1999. 60 titles listed in the *Small Press*

Record of Books in Print (28th Edition, 1999-00). avg. price, paper: $12.95. Discounts: 5 copies, 40%; 15, 42%; 25, 43%; 50, 44%; 100, 45%; 250, 46%; wholesalers-straight 50%; libraries 5+ 20%. 96-220pp; 6×9, 8¼×7¼, 11×8½, 10×8, 10×10, 8×10; of. Reporting time: 3 months. Simultaneous submissions accepted, but we prefer 3 months exclusivity. Payment: standard industry terms, 10% of net price, modest advances, pay twice a year. Copyrights for author. ABA, NEBA, VBPA (Vermont Book Publishers Association).

WILLOW SPRINGS, Christopher Howell, Editor, Eastern Washington Univ., MS-1, 526 5th Street, Cheney, WA 99004-2431, 509-623-4349. 1977. Poetry, fiction, art, photos, interviews, criticism, reviews, parts-of-novels, long-poems, plays, non-fiction. "Michael Burkard, Russell Edson, Alison Baker, Thomas Lux, Alberto Rios, Carolyn Kizer, Madeline DeFrees, Peter Cooley, Yusef Komunyakaa, Donald Revell, William Stafford, Lee Upton, David Russell Young, William Van Wert. We encourage the submissions of translations from all languages and periods, as well as essays and essay-reviews." circ. 1,700. 2/yr. Pub'd 2 issues 1998; expects 2 issues 1999, 2 issues 2000. sub. price: $10.50; per copy: $5.50; sample: $5.50. Back issues: $5.50 each. Discounts: 40%. 128pp; 6×9; of. Reporting time: 1-3 months. Simultaneous submissions accepted: no. Publishes 2% of manuscripts submitted. Payment: 2 contributor copies, 1-yr subscription. Copyrighted, reverts to author. Pub's reviews: 3 in 1998. §Poetry, fiction, nonfiction. Ads: $100/$50. CLMP.

Willow Tree Press, Inc. (see also CRIMINAL JUSTICE ABSTRACTS), Richard S. Allinson, PO Box 249, Monsey, NY 10952, 914-354-9139. 1983. Non-fiction. avg. press run 750. Pub'd 2 titles 1998; expects 3 titles 1999, 3 titles 2000. 4 titles listed in the *Small Press Record of Books in Print* (28th Edition, 1999-00). avg. price, cloth: $47.50; paper: $25. Discounts: 1-9 books 30%, 10-99 40%. 300pp; 6×9; of. Reporting time: 2 months. Simultaneous submissions accepted: yes. Payment: 10%. SSP.

WillowBrook Publishing, Laura L. Moleski, PO Box 2606, Chandler, AZ 85224, 602-821-5222. 1994. Non-fiction. "Publish books and workbooks. Focus on psychology/self-improvement. Also publish shorter (20-30 pages) workbooks on various topics including depression, fear and anxiety and anger" avg. press run 5M. Pub'd 6 titles 1998; expects 1 title 1999, 3 titles 2000. avg. price, cloth: $23.95; paper: $4; other: $7 for workbooks. Discounts: Standard trade discounts. 250pp; 6×9; of. Reporting time: 1 month. Payment: industry standards, varies with each project. Does not copyright for author. PMA, ABPA.

Willowood Press, Larry Greenwood, Judy Greenwood, PO Box 1846, Minot, ND 58702, 701-838-0579. 1980. Non-fiction. "Guides to library research for undergraduate and graduate university students specialized by subject and level of difficulty. University reference-bibliography; art." avg. press run 1M+. 180pp; 5½×8½, 8½×11; of.

Wilton Place Publishing, Michele C. Osterhout, PO Box 291, La Canada, CA 91012, 818-790-5601. 1982. Fiction. avg. press run 5M. Expects 2 titles 1999, 3 titles 2000. 1 title listed in the *Small Press Record of Books in Print* (28th Edition, 1999-00). avg. price, paper: $9.75. Discounts: 3-199 40%, 200-499 50%. 301pp; 6×9. Reporting time: 6 months. Payment: case by case. Copyrights for author.

WIN NEWS, Fran P. Hosken, Editor & Publisher, 187 Grant Street, Lexington, MA 02173, 781-862-9431; Fax 781-862-1734. 1975. "*WIN News* (*Women's International Network*) has ongoing columns on women and health, women and development, women and media, environment, violence, united nations and more. International career opportunities are listed; an investigation on genital/sexual mutilations regularly reports; news from Africa, the Middle East, Asia & Pacific, Europe and the Americas are featured in every issue. You are invited to send news and participate! *WIN* is a non-profit organization. Contributions tax-deductible. We hope to hear from you soon. Deadline (next issue): July." circ. 1M-1.1M. 4/yr. Pub'd 4 issues 1998; expects 4 issues 1999, 4 issues 2000. 7 titles listed in the *Small Press Record of Books in Print* (28th Edition, 1999-00). sub. price: $48 institution, $35 individual, add $4/yr postage abroad, add $10/yr air abroad; per copy: $5; sample: $5. Back issues: $15/year. Discounts: available on request. 80pp; 7×11; of. Simultaneous submissions accepted, but must be 1-2 pages of facts, documented reports, and no fiction. Payment: none. Copyrighted. Pub's reviews: 18-20+ in 1998. §Women and international development, women's right world-wide. Ads: $300/$150/$75 1/4 page.

B. L. Winch & Associates, Bradley L. Winch, President, 24426 Main Street, Suite 702, Carson, CA 90745-6329, 310-816-3085. 1971. Non-fiction. "Affiliated with Jalmar Press. Educationally oriented books on self-concept/values; self-esteem; parent involvement; parent-oriented self-help materials (infant to teen); affective curriculum guidebooks." avg. press run 5M. Pub'd 4 titles 1998; expects 4 titles 1999, 4 titles 2000. 14 titles listed in the *Small Press Record of Books in Print* (28th Edition, 1999-00). avg. price, cloth: $16.95; paper: $9.95. Discounts: trade 40%-45%; agent/jobber 40-50%. 150pp; 8½×11, 6×9; of. Reporting time: 12 weeks if interested, 3 weeks if no interest. Simultaneous submissions accepted: yes. Payment: royalty (5-12.5%) paid on semi-annual basis on net receipts, minimum advances as a general rule. Copyrights for author. PMA, NSSEA, EDSA, ABA, CBA.

Winchester/G. Ander Books, Jeff Holinday, President; Michael Tanners, Editor; Lucas O'Connell, Acquisitions, PO Box 11662, Philadelphia, PA 19116, www.dynamicmarches.com. 1980. Fiction, non-fiction.

avg. press run 10M. Pub'd 11 titles 1998; expects 10 titles 1999, 12 titles 2000. 1 title listed in the *Small Press Record of Books in Print* (28th Edition, 1999-00). avg. price, paper: $12.95. size varies. Simultaneous submissions accepted: no. Payment: "we make our authors happy" Copyrights for author.

WIND, Charlie G. Hughes, Fiction Editor; Leatha Kendrick, Poetry Editor, PO Box 24548, Lexington, KY 40524, 606-885-5342. 1971. Poetry, fiction, articles, reviews, interviews, criticism, news items, non-fiction. "No set length on poetry. 5000 words on fiction. No biases." circ. 425. 2/yr. Pub'd 2 issues 1998. sub. price: $10 individual, $12 institutional, $15 foreign; per copy: $6; sample: $4.50. Back issues: $4.50. Discounts: extra copies available to contributors at cost. 100pp; 8½×5½; of. Reporting time: 2-8 weeks. Simultaneous submissions accepted reluctantly. Publishes 1% of manuscripts submitted. Payment: 1 contributor's copy. Copyrighted, reverts to author. Pub's reviews: 10 in 1998. §Small presses only. CLMP, SSSL, Academy of American Poets.

Wind River Institute Press/Wind River Broadcasting, Jim McDonald, 117 East 11th, Loveland, CO 80537, 970-669-3442, fax 970-663-6081, 800-669-3993. 1985. Non-fiction. "Convert to technical regulatory in broadcast industry." avg. press run 5M. Pub'd 1 title 1998; expects 2 titles 1999, 3-4 titles 2000. 1 title listed in the *Small Press Record of Books in Print* (28th Edition, 1999-00). avg. price, other: looseleaf workbook $129. Discounts: 2 20%. 200pp; 8½×11.

WINDHOVER: A Journal of Christian Literature, Donna Walker-Nixon, PO Box 8008, UMHB, Belton, TX 76513, 817-939-4564. 1995. Poetry, interviews, reviews, parts-of-novels, long-poems, plays, non-fiction. circ. 500. 1/yr. Pub'd 1 issue 1998; expects 1 issue 1999, 1 issue 2000. sub. price: $8; per copy: $8; sample: $5. Back issues: $5. 148pp; 6×9. Reporting time: 3 months, sometimes longer. Simultaneous submissions accepted: yes. Publishes 10% of manuscripts submitted. Payment: 2 copies. Copyrighted, reverts to author. Pub's reviews: 4 in 1998. §Collections of stories or poetry by Christian writers. CLMP.

‡**WINDOW PANES**, Daniel & Margaret Crocker, PO Box 1565, Rolla, MO 65402, 314-368-4464. 1994. Poetry, fiction, articles, art, interviews, satire, criticism, reviews, letters, long-poems, plays, non-fiction. "We will publish anything that moves us, despite length, or subject matter. Recently published: Antler, A.D. Winans, Kavira, George Dowden, & Matthew Bridges" circ. 200. 4/yr. Pub'd 10 issues 1998; expects 4 issues 1999, 4 issues 2000. sub. price: $35; per copy: $10; sample: $10. Back issues: $4-10. 80pp; 8½×11; photo copy. Reporting time: 1 month. Publishes 10% of manuscripts submitted. Payment: 1 copy. Pub's reviews: 20 in 1998. §Poetry, prose, novels. Ads: $50/$20.

Windows Project (see also SMOKE), Dave Ward, 40 Canning Street, Liverpool L8 7NP, England. 1974. Poetry, fiction, art, photos, cartoons, long-poems, collages, concrete art. avg. press run 500. Pub'd 1 title 1998; expects 1 title 1999. 30 titles listed in the *Small Press Record of Books in Print* (28th Edition, 1999-00). avg. price, paper: 50p. Discounts: 33%. 24pp; size A4, A5; of. Reporting time: as quickly as possible.

Windsong Press, Sharon Haney, PO Box 644, Delta Jct., AK 99737, 907-895-4179. 1981. Poetry, fiction, articles, art, photos, letters, news items, non-fiction. "*By personal solicitation only*. FYI editor/publisher Sharon Haney was named 'Best Regional Poet' in a contest conducted by Alaska's public radio stations in October 1995." avg. press run 500. Expects 2 titles 1999, 1 title 2000. 2 titles listed in the *Small Press Record of Books in Print* (28th Edition, 1999-00). avg. price, paper: $7.95. Discounts: 40%. Pages vary; 5½×8½, 8½×11; of. Reporting time: 1 month. Payment: individual contracts. Copyrights for author.

Wind-Up Publications, 2828 University Avenue #103-121, San Diego, CA 92104, 619-497-5081; fax 619-297-6701; email antinuous@home.net. 1 title listed in the *Small Press Record of Books in Print* (28th Edition, 1999-00).

Wineberry Press, Elisavietta Ritchie, 3207 Macomb Street, NW, Washington, DC 20008-3327, 202-363-8036; e-mail chfarnsworth@compuserve.com. 1983. Poetry. "To order books: Wineberry Press, PO Box 298, Broomes Island, MD 20615, 410-586-3086. Send check or money order. Press formed as collaborative to publish anthology *Finding The Name*, 1983. Published *20/20 Visionary Eclipse*, a chapbook of conceptual art by Judith McCombs in 1985; *No One Is Listening*, a pamphlet of poems by Elizabeth Follin-Jones in 1987; *Swimming Out of the Collective Unconscious*, a chapbook of poems by Maxine Combs in 1989; *Get With It, Lord*, chapbook by Beatrice Murphy, 1990; *Horse and Cart: Stories from the Country*, fiction by Elisabeth Stevens, 1990. Can't handle unsolicited manuscripts—already have plenty I'd like to publish." avg. press run 500-2M. Pub'd 2 titles 1998; expects 1 title 1999. 3 titles listed in the *Small Press Record of Books in Print* (28th Edition, 1999-00). avg. price, paper: $3-$7.95 chapbooks. Discounts: 40% to booksellers. 32-200pp; 5½×8½. Reporting time: ASAP. Simultaneous submissions accepted: no. Publishes 1% of manuscripts submitted. Payment: copies (as many as they need). Does not copyright for author.

Wings of Fire Press, James L. Gardner, PO Box 520725, Salt Lake City, UT 84105-0725. 1990. Poetry, non-fiction. "We are a coop. press limited by money and energy. Our interests are Buddhism, Zen Buddhism, art, bibliography, social issues and Asia. Eventually we will be bringing out a journal on issues and poetry. We are interested in images in poetry that function as symbol as well as picture. We read Trakl, Celan, Char, Jack Spicer, Lorca, Vellejo, Pound, and like writers. Give us a year or two and we will be better defined, and more firmly set up." avg. press run 1M. Pub'd 1 title 1998; expects 1 title 1999, 1 title 2000. 2 titles listed in the *Small Press Record of Books in Print* (28th Edition, 1999-00). Discounts: 1 copy 25%, 2-3 30%, 4+ 40%, p/h add $1.50 per copy. of. Reporting time: 1 month. Payment: 12% of gross per copy; for contributors pro rate to the number of pages. Copyrights for author.

Winslow Publishing, Carolyn Winslow, Box 38012, 550 Eglinton Avenue West, Toronto, Ontario M5N 3A8, Canada, 416-789-4733. 1981. Non-fiction. "After publishing for mail order only since 1981, we moved into book stores in 1986. Title range from *The Complete Guide To Companion Advertising* to *The No-Bull Guide To Getting Published And Making It As A Writer*. At present, most business is still in mail order, and we are always looking for new reps to drop ship for. Please send *Queries only* (no mss)—non-fiction only, which can be marketed through the mail. Books do *not* have to have Canadian content - we are well represented in the U.S., and will be expanding greatly in the next couple of years. (Someday we'll be a *Big* Press!) We are completely computerized, and would appreciate mss on disk." avg. press run 1M-5M (mail order), 5M (bookstore). Pub'd 4 titles 1998; expects 4 titles 1999, 4 titles 2000. 7 titles listed in the *Small Press Record of Books in Print* (28th Edition, 1999-00). avg. price, paper: $9.95; other: cheaper mail-order paperback $5.95. Discounts: 40% on 5 or more copies of a title. 160pp; 5½×8½; of, lp. Reporting time: 1-2 weeks. Payment: usual royalties, or purchase ms. outright. Copyrights for author.

Winwin Publications, Phillip Lebel, 1315 Madison Street #456, Seattle, WA 98104, 250-658-4211 phone/fax; winwin@vanisle.net. "Canadian address: 3297 Douglas Street #23, Victoria BC Canada V8Z 3K9." 1 title listed in the *Small Press Record of Books in Print* (28th Edition, 1999-00).

WISCONSIN ACADEMY REVIEW, Faith B. Miracle, Editor, 1922 University Ave., Madison, WI 53705, 608-263-1692. 1954. Poetry, fiction, articles, art, photos, interviews, criticism, reviews. "We use poetry, short fiction, art and literary history, and book reviews that have Wisconsin connected author or subject, as well as scientific articles or political essays which have Wisconsin tie-in. Quarterly journal of the Wisconsin Academy of Sciences, Arts and Letters. If not Wisconsin return address, include Wisconsin connection with submission or query. Include SASE" circ. 1.5M. 4/yr. Expects 4 issues 1999. sub. price: $16; per copy: $4.25; sample: $2. Back issues: $3.75. Discounts: none. 48-52pp; 8½×11; of. Reporting time: 8-10 weeks. Simultaneous submissions accepted: no. Publishes 12% of manuscripts submitted. Payment: 5 copies (articles), 3 copies (poetry), 2 copies (reviews). Copyrighted. Pub's reviews: 24 in 1998. §Wisconsin connected books by author or subject. No ads.

WISCONSIN REVIEW, Greg Anderson, Josh Stokdyk, Box 158, Radford Hall, Univ. of Wisconsin-Oshkosh, Oshkosh, WI 54901, 920-424-2267. 1966. Poetry, fiction, art, photos, cartoons, interviews, satire, reviews, collages, plays, non-fiction. "Poetry in all forms, fiction to 3,000 words, reviews, essays, interviews and artwork (black and white or color) suitable for offset printing. Artwork may be full-page (6 X 9''), half-page, or proportioned to run alongside poems. Photographs considered also. In poetry, we publish mostly free verse with strong images and fresh approaches. We want new turns of phrase. Poems should be single-spaced. In fiction, we look for strong characterization, fresh situations and clipped, hammering dialogue. Fiction should be typed and double-spaced. SASEs mandatory; we accept no responsibility for unsolicited manuscripts. Recent contributors include William Stafford, Antler, Kelly Cherry, Martin Rosenblum, Ronald Wallace, William Silver, G.E. Murray, Richard Kostelanetz." circ. 2M. 3/yr. Pub'd 3 issues 1998; expects 3 issues 1999, 3 issues 2000. sub. price: $10 (3 issues); per copy: $4; sample: $4. Back issues: varies. 80pp; 6×9; of. Reporting time: 6 months, never w/out SASE (mss. held during summer months till fall); do not read mss. during summer. Simultaneous submissions accepted: no. Publishes 10% of manuscripts submitted. Payment: 2 copies. Copyrighted, reverts to author. Pub's reviews: 0 in 1998. §Poetry, fiction, art. Ads: none.

WISCONSIN TRAILS, Wisconsin Trails, Scott Klug, Editor; Kate Bast, Managing Editor; Tom Davis, Senior Editor, PO Box 5650, Madison, WI 53705, 608-231-2444; fax 608-231-1557; e-mail editor@wis-trails.com. 1960. Articles, photos. "*Wisconsin Trails* at present is interested in articles about Wisconsin: nature and the environment, heritage, and folklore, and guides to city and countryside as well as outdoor sports. Magazine submissions should contain detailed outline. No phone calls please." circ. 50-51M. 6/yr. Pub'd 6 issues 1998; expects 6 issues 1999, 6 issues 2000. sub. price: $22.95; per copy: $3.95; sample: $3.95 + $2 p/h. Back issues: reg. issues $3.95, rare issues $4.50. Discounts: subscription agency, all other universal schedule. 84+pp; trim 7⅛×9¾, bleed 8¼×11⅛; of. Reporting time: 3 months. Simultaneous submissions accepted: yes. Publishes 5% of manuscripts submitted. Payment: on publication. Copyrighted, rights revert to author after 60 days. Pub's reviews: less than 10 in 1998. §Outdoor sports, activities, anything dealing w/Wisconsin, photography. Ads: frequency discounts available, full page: $2,560 b/w, $3,200 4c. IRMA.

Wisconsin Trails (see also WISCONSIN TRAILS), Scott Klug, Editor; Patty Mayers, Books & Products Manager; Stanley Stoga, Acquisitions Editor, P.O.Box 5650, Madison, WI 53705, 608-231-2444; fax 608-231-1557; e-mail pam@wistrails.com. 1960. Fiction, articles, art, photos, cartoons, interviews, non-fiction.

"We conduct no major business by phone. Wisconsin Trails is interested in books about travel/environment/ heritage/recreation: Wisconsin theme. Other states in our region will be considered." avg. press run 5M. Pub'd 4 titles 1998; expects 5 titles 1999, 4 titles 2000. avg. price, cloth: $27.95; paper: $16.95. Discounts: universal schedule. 200pp; 8½×11, 6×9; of. Reporting time: queries, outline & sample chapters 2 months. Simultaneous submissions accepted: yes. Publishes 50% of manuscripts submitted. Payment: varies. Copyrights for author. AAP, IRMA, PMA.

THE WISDOM CONSERVANCY NEWSLETTER, Steven McFadden, 148 Merriam Hill Road, Greenville, NH 03048, 603-878-1818. 1993. Interviews, news items. "Mostly in-house written - interviews and feature articles on learned, compassionate and wise elders from the diverse cultures of the world." circ. 300. 4/yr. Pub'd 2 issues 1998; expects 4 issues 1999, 4 issues 2000. sub. price: $30 US, $45 foreign. 8pp; 8½×11; of. Reporting time: 3 weeks. Payment: 10 free copies. Pub's reviews: 2 in 1998. §Aging, wisdom, spiritual development. Ads: none.

Wisdom Publications, Inc., Timothy McNeill, Publisher; David Strom, Managing Editor; E. Gene Smith, Acquisitions Editor, 199 Elm Street, Somerville, MA 02144-3129, 617-776-7416; Fax 617-776-7841. 1975. Non-fiction. avg. press run 5M. Pub'd 12 titles 1998; expects 12 titles 1999, 14 titles 2000. 16 titles listed in the *Small Press Record of Books in Print* (28th Edition, 1999-00). avg. price, cloth: $35; paper: $16; other: $6 transcript. Discounts: Trade sales thru National Book Network (NBN) Maryland. 224pp; 6×9; of. Reporting time: 3 months. Simultaneous submissions accepted: yes. Publishes 5% of manuscripts submitted. Payment: once a year based on net sales. We sometimes copyright for author. ABA, BIP, NEBA.

Wise Owl Press, Mary J. Mooney-Getoff, Editor & Publisher, PO Box 377 (1475 Waterview Dr.), Southold, NY 11971, 516-765-3356. 1980. Non-fiction. "At present we are interested only in the following subjects: Laura Ingalls Wilder, Foods, Nutrition, Cooking, Travel, Long Island (New York), and it must fit into our standard length of about 40 pages, 5½ X 8½ inches. We also distribute books and booklets on the above subjects for other small presses. Our SAN is 217-5754." avg. press run 2.5M. Expects 2 titles 1999, 2 titles 2000. avg. price, paper: $5. Discounts: 40% over 10 copies; 10% to libraries and schools if prepaid. 40pp; 5½×8½; of. Reporting time: 2 months or shorter. Simultaneous submissions accepted: no. Copyrights for author.

THE WISE WOMAN, Ann Forfreedom, 2441 Cordova Street, Oakland, CA 94602, 510-536-3174. 1980. Poetry, articles, art, photos, cartoons, interviews, reviews, music, news items, non-fiction. "No longer accepting unsolicited submissions. Focus of *The Wise Woman*: feminist spirituality, feminist witchcraft, feminist issues. Includes articles, columns (such as *The War Against Women* and *The Rising of Women*). Annotated songs appropriate to subject, interviews, poems, art, wise sayings, cartoons by Bulbul, photos. Also available on microfilm through University Microfilms International" circ. small but influential. 4/yr. Pub'd 2 issues 1998; expects 2 issues 1999, 4 issues 2000. sub. price: $15; per copy: $4; sample: $4. Back issues: $4. 20pp; 8½×11; of, photocopy. Reporting time: varies, try to reply promptly when SASE is included. Simultaneous submissions accepted: no. Payment: copy of the issue. Copyrighted, rights revert to author, but TWW reserves the right to reprint.

WISEBLOOD, Robert Westermeyer, Maria Montgomery, 315 S. Coast Hwy. 101, Ste. U226, Encinitas, CA 92024, E-mail wstrmyr@cts.com; www.wiseblood-zine.com. 1998. Poetry, fiction, articles, art, photos, cartoons, criticism, parts-of-novels, long-poems. "We're interested in normalizing the abnormal, and pathologizing everything else. We're an E-zine anticipating first printed issue this year." 4/yr. Expects 4 issues 1999, 4 issues 2000. sub. price: free; per copy: free. 30pp; 8½×5½; †mi. Reporting time: 2 weeks. Simultaneous submissions accepted: yes. Publishes 10% of manuscripts submitted. Payment: 3 copies. Copyrighted, reverts to author.

THE WISHING WELL, Laddie Hosler, Editor and Publisher, PO Box 178440, San Diego, CA 92177-8440, 619-270-2779. 1974. Poetry, articles, art, photos, criticism, reviews, letters, news items, non-fiction. "*The Wishing Well* is the largest national/international magazine featuring hundreds of current self-descriptions, some with photos, (by code number) of loving women wishing to safely write/meet one another. Offers many original features not found elsewhere for women. Is a highly supportive, dignified, award winning publication serving women in 50 states and the world. We publish work by members, only. *Free info.*" circ. 3M. 6/yr. Pub'd 6 issues 1998; expects 6 issues 1999, 6 issues 2000. 5-7 mo. membership: $60; 3-5 mo $35; $120 U.S.; $150 foreign (except Canada/Mexico); photo published $10 extra (optional); price per copy: $5; sample: $5. Back issues: $5. Discounts: renewal $55 (membership) by next deadline date following current membership. 40pp; 7×8½; of. Payment: none. Copyrighted. Pub's reviews: 60 in 1998. §Women, book reviews (relating to readership), human rights, relating to women, bi-sexual women, human relationships, growth, lesbian. Ads: query, $10 per inch one time (3¼" wide) $8 per inch 3 insertions or more. $1 word one time; 80¢ word 3 times in one year.

WITNESS, Peter Stine, Oakland Community College, 27055 Orchard Lake Road, Farmington Hills, MI 48334,

313-471-7740. 1987. Poetry, fiction, articles, art, photos, parts-of-novels, long-poems, non-fiction. "Highlights role of writer as witness, fiction, non-fiction essays, poetry. Special issues (sixties, holocaust, writings from prison, nature writings, autobiographies). Contributors: Joyce Carol Oates, Donald Hall, Madison Smartt Bell, Lynn Sharon Schwartz, Gordon Lish." circ. 2.8M. 2/yr. Pub'd 2 issues 1998; expects 2 issues 1999, 2 issues 2000. sub. price: $12; per copy: $7; sample: $6. Back issues: $5. Discounts: 40% to distributor/retailer. 192pp; 6×9; of. Reporting time: 2 months. Payment: $6/page for prose, $10/page for poetry. Copyrighted, reverts to author. Ads: $100/$50.

‡**Witwatersrand University Press (see also AFRICAN STUDIES)**, Professor W.D. Hammond-Tooke, African Studies; Professor G.I. Hughes, English Studies in Africa, WITS, 2050 Johannesburg, Republic of South Africa, 011-716-2029. 1923. Poetry, articles, criticism, reviews, non-fiction. avg. press run 1M. Pub'd 5 titles 1998; expects 4 titles 1999, 5 titles 2000. 42 titles listed in the *Small Press Record of Books in Print* (28th Edition, 1999-00). avg. price, paper: R30. Discounts: 25% to libraries, 30% to booksellers. 200pp; 15×21cm; of. Reporting time: up to 1 year. Payment: individual arrangement. Copyrights for author, press holds copyright.

Wizard Works, Jan O'Meara, PO Box 1125, Homer, AK 99603, 907-235-8157; Fax 907-399-1834. 1988. Poetry, fiction, art, photos, cartoons, reviews, non-fiction. "Alaska subjects only. No unsolicited manuscripts without query first." avg. press run 1M. Pub'd 2 titles 1998; expects 2 titles 1999, 2 titles 2000. 9 titles listed in the *Small Press Record of Books in Print* (28th Edition, 1999-00). avg. price, paper: $12. Discounts: library 20%, wholesale 1-5 20%, 6-99 40%, 100+ 50%. 130pp; 5½×8½; of. Payment: negotiable. Copyrights for author. Northern Publishers Consortium.

Wolf Angel Press, Doug Flaherty, Editor-in-Chief; Kimberly Newport, Assistant Editor; James Stevens, Managing Editor, 1011 Babcock Street, Neenah, WI 54956, 920-722-5826; e-mails flaherty@uwosh.edu, newpok32@uwosh.edu, stevens@tcccom.net; www.english.uwosh.edu/wolfangel/. 1996. Poetry. "Wolf Angel is a cooperative press. The poet is expected to edit and print his/her own chapbook. How can we truly love books unless we have actually gone through the process of creating a book? Our press affords editorial assistance, printing consultation, plus some advertising and distribution. The poet keeps all profits realized from sales of the chapbook. Interested poets who have well-crafted poems are encouraged to send 15-20 poems, some of which should have previously appeared in literary magazines. Published *An Opening of Bright Wings* by Jim Last (1997), and *A Halo of Watchful Eyes* by Karla Huston (1998). Wolf Angel also offers *Pigs 'n Poets* E-zine, 'Best Picks of the Poetry Web Pages,' a poetry-writing manual, *There Is A Cricket In My Blood* by Doug Flaherty, plus other services on its web site." avg. press run 500. Expects 1 title 1999, 4 titles 2000. avg. price, paper: $5. 24-32pp; 5½×8½; †of. Reporting time: 1 month. Simultaneous submissions accepted: yes. Publishes 5% of manuscripts submitted. Payment: author subsidized. Does not copyright for author.

THE THOMAS WOLFE REVIEW, Terry Roberts, Editor; Aldo P. Magi, Associate Editor Emeritus; John Idol, Articles Editor, 305 Spruce Street, Chapel Hill, NC 27514, 336-334-3831. 1977. Poetry, fiction, articles, criticism. "Our chief interest is articles about Thomas Wolfe, either scholarly or at least of interest to an educated reader of Wolfe. Maximum length of articles, double-spaced, 25 pages, but we prefer shorter pieces. Articles longer than 25 pages, typed double-spaced, are divided in two and run in separate issues." circ. 800. 2/yr. Pub'd 2 issues 1998; expects 2 issues 1999, 2 issues 2000. sub. price: $10; per copy: $5; sample: free. Back issues: $5. Discounts: 20% to agencies. 100pp; 5½×8½; lp. Reporting time: 6 weeks. Simultaneous submissions accepted: no. Publishes 80% of manuscripts submitted. Payment: in copies. Copyrighted, does not revert to author. Pub's reviews. §Books having to do with Wolfe on the American Literary/cultural scene of the 1920s & 1930s. Ads: $200/$150/20% discount to university presses.

Wolfhound Press, 68 Mountjoy Square, Dublin 1, Ireland, 740354. 1974. Fiction, art. avg. press run 3M. Pub'd 30 titles 1998. 177 titles listed in the *Small Press Record of Books in Print* (28th Edition, 1999-00). avg. price, cloth: £12.99(IR); paper: £5.95 (IR). Pages vary; size varies; of. Reporting time: 12+ weeks. Payment: yes, vary with type of title. CLE - Irish Book Publishers Association.

Wolfsong Publications, Gary C. Busha, Editor & Publisher, 3123 South Kennedy, Sturtevant, WI 53177, Fax 414-886-5809; E-mail wolfsong@wi.net. 1974. Poetry, fiction. "Queries ok, unsolicited not accepted." avg. press run 200. Pub'd 2 titles 1998; expects 2 titles 1999, 2 titles 2000. 8 titles listed in the *Small Press Record of Books in Print* (28th Edition, 1999-00). avg. price, paper: $5; other: $12 signed. Discounts: none. 26-36pp; 5½×8½; of, photocopy. Reporting time: immediate to 2 weeks. Simultaneous submissions accepted: no. Payment: 5 copies. Does not copyright for author. WFOP (Wisconsin Fellowship of Poets), Racine Root River Poets, Council of Wisconsin Writers (CWW).

Wolf-Wise Press, Roy Lee, 12235 N. Cave Creek, Suite 6, Phoenix, AZ 85022, 602-493-9383; FAX 602-482-0668. 1994. Poetry, fiction. "Looking for exquisitely written fiction that is politically incorrect or otherwise controversial. Could be ecoanarchist like Edward Abbey's *The Monkey Wrench Gang*, or right-of-center fictional exploration of race conflict ala *Illiberal Education* by Dinesh D'Souza." avg. press run 500-1.5M. Expects 3 titles 1999, 3 titles 2000. 1 title listed in the *Small Press Record of Books in Print* (28th

Edition, 1999-00). avg. price, cloth: $25; paper: $7-$17. Discounts: short discount. Pages vary; 5½x8½. Reporting time: 2-8 weeks. Simultaneous submissions accepted: no. Publishes very small % of manuscripts submitted. Payment: in copies. Copyrights for author. PMA.

Woman in the Moon Publications (W.I.M. Publications), Diane Adamz-Bogus, Editor-in-Chief, PO Box 2087, Cupertino, CA 95015-2087, E-mail womaninmoon@earthlink.net. 1979. Poetry, long-poems. "We offer four prize money poetry contests: T. Nelson Gilbert Poetry Prize Jan. 1-April 30. May 1-July 1 (Pat Parker Memorial Award), (Audre Lorde Prose Prize, Sept. 1-Dec 30. Write for details. We are now accepting 'new age' manuscripts during Spring, from Jan. 1-April 30 (48-200 pages).Book reviews cover letter required. We do reviews of small press poetry books. We offer our 3M name mailing list $65. Write for catalog, $5.01 We request ms. fees (includes sub. to our quarterly *The Spirit*) reading fee for all manuscripts book length. Interested in new age, spiritual phenomanon and experience, auto biography/novels, cartoons, book reviews, essays." avg. press run 1M. Pub'd 4 titles 1998; expects 6 titles 1999. 32 titles listed in the *Small Press Record of Books in Print* (28th Edition, 1999-00). avg. price, cloth: $25; paper: $15; other: $3 or less. Discounts: 40% with agency letterhead with order of 5 minimum (for individuals also). 300pp; 5½x8½, 6x9, 8½x11; of. Reporting time: acknowledgement upon receipt, report by personal letter during or at end of reading season (6 weeks maximum). Simultaneous submissions accepted: yes. Publishes 25% of manuscripts submitted. Payment: 8-15% after costs and returns. Copyrights for author. Women's Presses Library Project, Ebsco Distribution.

WOMAN POET, Women-in-Literature, Inc., Elaine Dallman, Editor-in-Chief, PO Box 60550, Reno, NV 89506, 702-972-1671. 1978. Poetry, photos. "Unpublished fine poems of any length are included in our series of regional book/journals—*The West*, *The East*, *The Midwest*. Interviews and critical reviews of featured poets. We have an international readership interested in fine women's poetry. Well-written articles will let readers have deeper insights into—How is good literature written? What kind of women write it? What is their education? What does it take to write and to write well? Other material of human interest about writers will be presented. Well-known contributors: Josephine Miles, Ann Stanford, Madeline DeFrees, Marilyn Hacker, June Jordan, Marie Ponsot, Audre Lorde, Lisel Mueller, Judith Minty. We urge writers to read our poetry before submitting. We are a non-profit corporation (literary-educational)—we welcome tax-deductible donations. We plan to publish individual poetry books. Watch for notices in *Poets & Writers* and *American Poetry Review*" circ. 4M. Irregular. Expects 1 issue 2000. sub. price: $12.95 plus $1.75 shipping and insurance per copy; per copy: $12.95 indiv. + $1.75 shipping and insurance; sample: $12.95 + $1.75 shipping and insurance. Discounts: 1, list; 2-4, 20%; 5-24, 40%; write for classroom rates; on approval copy on request to libraries, professors; prepaid only to individuals. 100-130pp; 8x9½; of. Reporting time: 3 weeks to 3 months. Payment: copies. Copyrighted, does not revert to author.

WOMAN'S ART JOURNAL, Elsa Honig Fine, 1711 Harris Road, Laverock, PA 19038-7208, 215-233-0639. 1980. Articles, art, reviews. "*WAJ* is a semiannual publication devoted to women and issues related to women in all areas of the visual arts. It is concerned with recovering a lost heritage and with documenting the lives and work of contemporary women in the arts, many of whom have been neglected previously because of their sex. *WAJ* represents sound scholarship presented with clarity, and it is open to all ideas and encourages research from all people." circ. 2M. 2/yr. Pub'd 2 issues 1998; expects 2 issues 1999, 2 issues 2000. sub. price: $16 indiv., $25 instit.; per copy: $13; sample: $13. Back issues: $13. Discounts: trade $4.75 per issue plus mailing. 64pp; 8½x11; of. Reporting time: 1 month. Simultaneous submissions accepted: no. Publishes 50% of manuscripts submitted. Payment: none. Copyrighted. Pub's reviews: 50 in 1998. §Women in all areas of visual arts-Images of women. Ads: $475/$325/$625 full back color cover/$550 inside front cover/$500 inside back cover.

WOMEN AND LANGUAGE, Anita Taylor, Executive Editor, Communication Dept, George Mason University, Fairfax, VA 22030. 1975. Articles, cartoons, interviews, criticism, reviews, news items, non-fiction. "*Women and Language* is an interdisciplinary research periodical. WL attends to communication, language, gender and women's issues. It reports books, journals, articles and research in progress; publishes short articles and speeches." circ. 500+. 2/yr. Pub'd 2 issues 1998; expects 2 issues 1999, 2 issues 2000. sub. price: $20 all US institutions, $15 US individuals; $15 Canada and $20 other foreign individuals (US funds only); $25 all international institutions; per copy: $8 special issues; $6 individual issues. Back issues: $130 for Vols 1-18, plus postage. 70pp; 8½x11; of. Reporting time: 2-3 months. Publishes 50% of manuscripts submitted. Payment: none. Copyrighted, does not revert to author. Pub's reviews: 12 in 1998. §Women's studies, language, gender, linguistics, writing, communication, speech, public address. No ads. Organization for Study of Communication, Language & Gender.

WOMEN & THERAPY, Esther D. Rothblum, Ph.D., Marcia Hill, Ed.D., Dr. Esther Rothblum, Dept. of Psychology, University of Vermont, Burlington, VT 05405, (802) 656-2680. 1982. Articles, reviews, non-fiction. "*Women & Therapy* is the only professional journal that focuses entirely on the complex interrelationship between women and the therapeutic experience. The journal is devoted to descriptive, theoretical, clinical, and empirical perspectives on the topic of women and therapy. Women comprise the overwhelming majority of clients in therapy, yet there has been little emphasis on this area in the training of therapists or in the professional literature. *Women & Therapy* is designed to fill this void of information. The Journal will only consider articles not published elsewhere or submitted for publication consideration elsewhere. Your manuscript may be no longer than 10-20 pages double-spaced (including references and abstract). Lengthier manuscripts may be considered, but only at the discretion of the Editor.'' circ. 1M. 4/yr. Pub'd 4 issues 1998; expects 4 issues 1999, 4 issues 2000. sub. price: $40; sample: free. Back issues: ranges from $10 to $29. 120pp; 5½x8½. Reporting time: 3 months. Simultaneous submissions accepted: no. Publishes 30% of manuscripts submitted. Payment: none. Copyrighted, does not revert to author. Pub's reviews: 6 in 1998. §Psychology of women, women's mental health.

WOMEN ARTISTS NEWS BOOK REVIEW, Midmarch Arts Press, Cynthia Navaretta, Executive Editor; Judy Seigel, Editor, 300 Riverside Drive, New York City, NY 10025, 212-666-6990. 1975. Art, photos, interviews, criticism, reviews. ''300-1000 word articles; emphasis on books on visual arts; coverage of books on dance, film, music, arts events, etc.'' circ. 5M. 1/yr. Pub'd 1 issue 1998. price per copy: $5 (including back issues), plus $1 postage; sample: $5. Back issues: on application. Discounts: jobber & agent 40%; bookstores, galleries 40%; classroom 40%. 64-72pp; 8½x11; of. Reporting time: 2-3 months. Simultaneous submissions accepted: no. Publishes 30% of manuscripts submitted. Payment: only in years when funded for payment to writers. Copyrighted, reverts to author. Pub's reviews: 75 in 1998. §Art, (visual arts, film, dance) women, arts legislation, literature, poetry. Ads: $300/$250/$35 classified 6-8 lines. CLMP, Small Press.

WOMEN IN THE ARTS BULLETIN/NEWSLETTER, Women In The Arts Foundation, Inc., Erin Butler, c/o R. Crown, 1175 York Avenue #2G, New York, NY 10021, 212-751-1915. 1971. Articles, photos, interviews, letters, news items. ''Length: 200 to 1,000 words—must be on women's art movement or topics relevant to women artists.'' circ. 1M. 4/yr. Pub'd 6 issues 1998; expects 4 issues 1999, 4 issues 2000. sub. price: $9, $15 institution, $19 foreign; per copy: $1; sample: free. 6pp; 8½x11; of. Reporting time: 2-3 months. Payment: none. Copyrighted, reverts to author. Pub's reviews: 1 in 1998. §Women's visual art & writing. Ads: $110/$60.

Women In The Arts Foundation, Inc. (see also WOMEN IN THE ARTS BULLETIN/NEWSLETTER), Erin Butler, Editor, 1175 York Avenue, New York, NY 10021. 1971. 1 title listed in the *Small Press Record of Books in Print* (28th Edition, 1999-00).

Women of Diversity Productions, Inc., 5790 Park Street, Las Vegas, NV 89129-2304, 702-341-9807; fax 702-341-9828; E-mail dvrsty@aol.com. 1995. Art, photos, cartoons, non-fiction. avg. press run 3.5M. Pub'd 1 title 1998; expects 1 title 1999, 2 titles 2000. 3 titles listed in the *Small Press Record of Books in Print* (28th Edition, 1999-00). avg. price, cloth: $20; paper: $14. Discounts: 40% trade; 50% for 100 or more bulk, agent, author; 20% classroom. 150pp; 6x9, 7x9, 5½x8½; lp. Reporting time: 1-2 months. Simultaneous submissions accepted: yes. Publishes *50% of manuscripts submitted.* Payment: 8% first 1000, increasing increments. Copyrights for author. PMA.

Women-in-Literature, Inc. (see also WOMAN POET), Elaine Dallman, Editor-in-Chief, PO Box 60550, Reno, NV 89506. 1978. Poetry, photos. ''Unpublished fine poems of any length, by women, are included in our series of regional book/journals—the West, the Midwest, the East. Interviews and critical reviews of featured poets. We have an international readership interested in fine women's poetry. Well-written articles will let readers have deeper insights into: How is good literature written? What kind of women write it? What is their education? What does it take to write and to write well? Other material of human interest about writers will be presented. Well-known contributors: Madeline DeFrees, June Jordan, Judith Minty, Marilyn Hacker, Marie Ponsot, Andre Lorde, Lisel Mueller and Mona Van Duyn. We urge writers to inspect our poetry before submitting. We are a non-profit corporation (literary-educational) and all donations to us are needed and are tax-deductible. We plan to publish individual poetry books. Watch for notices in *Poets & Writers* and *American Poetry Review.''* avg. press run 4M. Expects 1 title 2000. 4 titles listed in the *Small Press Record of Books in Print* (28th Edition, 1999-00). avg. price, cloth: $19.95 + $1.75 shipping and insurance; paper: $12.95 + $1.75 shipping and insurance. Discounts: 1, list; 2-4, 20%; 5-24, 40%; write for classroom rates; on approval copy on request to libraries, professors; prepaid only to individuals. 100-130pp; 8x9½; of. Reporting time: 3 weeks to 3 months. Payment: copies. Does not copyright for author.

Women's Press, Martha Ayim, Managing Editor, 517 College Street, Ste. 302, Toronto, Ontario M6G 4A2, Canada. 1972. Fiction, non-fiction. avg. press run 2M. Pub'd 4-6 titles 1998. 90 titles listed in the *Small Press Record of Books in Print* (28th Edition, 1999-00). avg. price, paper: $12.00. Discounts: regular. 200pp; 5½x8½. Reporting time: 6 months to 1 year. Simultaneous submissions accepted: yes. Payment: varies. Copyrights for author. ACP, Canadian Book Information Center (CBIC).

WOMEN'S RESEARCH NETWORK NEWS, National Council for Research on Women, Nina Sonenberg, Coordinating Editor; Kate Daly, Associate Editor, 530 Broadway, New York, NY 10012-3920, 212-274-0760; fax 212-274-0821. 1988. ''Includes News from the Council; News from Member Centers; News from International Centers; News from the Caucuses; News from Funders; Publications and Resources; Upcoming Events; Job Opportunities; Opportunities for Research, Study, and Affiliation as well as other news of interest to the women's research, action, policy, and funding communities." 4/yr. Pub'd 4 issues 1998; expects 3 issues 1999, 4 issues 2000. sub. price: $35 indiv., $100 organizations; per copy: $5; sample: $5. 36pp; 8½×11; of. Not copyrighted. Ads: none.

THE WOMEN'S REVIEW OF BOOKS, Linda Gardiner, Wellesley College, Center For Research On Women, Wellesley, MA 02481, 781-283-2555. 1983. Reviews. "Book reviews only; average length 1.5M words; only recent books by and about women. Some contributors: Barbara Kingsolver, Nancy Mairs, Patricia Williams, Marge Piercy; Michele Wallace; Ann Snitow; Heidi Hartmann. Unsolicited material is not normally accepted." circ. 14M. 11/yr. Pub'd 11 issues 1998; expects 11 issues 1999, 11 issues 2000. sub. price: $25 individuals, $40 institutions; per copy: $4; sample: free. Back issues: $4. Discounts: 10 or more 60%. 28pp; 10×15; of. Publishes 0% of manuscripts submitted. Payment: varies, $75 minimum. Copyrighted, reverts to author. Pub's reviews: 250 in 1998. §Feminism, women's studies. Ads: $1900/$1030/$45 (c.i.)/$1.10 per word.

Women's Studies Librarian, University of Wisconsin System (see also FEMINIST COLLECTIONS: A QUARTERLY OF WOMEN'S STUDIES RESOURCES; FEMINIST PERIODICALS: A CURRENT LISTING OF CONTENTS; NEW BOOKS ON WOMEN & FEMINISM), Phyllis Holman Weisbard, Linda Shult, Lynne Chase, 430 Memorial Library, 728 State Street, Madison, WI 53706, 608-263-5754. 1977. Articles, interviews, criticism, reviews, non-fiction. "In addition to the three periodicals listed above, we publish a series *Wisconsin Bibliographies in Women's Studies*" avg. press run 1.1M. 3 titles listed in the *Small Press Record of Books in Print* (28th Edition, 1999-00). 8½×11; offset. Reporting time: 1-2 weeks. Simultaneous submissions accepted: no. Payment: none. Does not copyright for author.

WOMEN'S STUDIES QUARTERLY, The Feminist Press at the City College, Florence Howe, Publisher; Sara Cahill, Managing Edition, The Feminist Press c/o City College, Convent Ave. & 138th St., New York, NY 10031, 212-360-5790. 1971. Poetry, articles, art, photos, cartoons, interviews, satire, criticism, reviews, letters, news items, non-fiction. "News, issues, events in women's studies; articles are from 1M to 3M words usually" circ. 1.5M. 2/yr. Pub'd 2 issues 1998; expects 2 issues 1999, 2 issues 2000. 10 titles listed in the *Small Press Record of Books in Print* (28th Edition, 1999-00). sub. price: $30 individuals, $40 institutions, foreign $40 individual, $50 institution; per copy: $18 (double issue); sample: $13. Back issues: $3.50 per copy; 15 years for $170. 200-250pp; 5½×8½; of. Reporting time: 2-3 months. Publishes 5% of manuscripts submitted. Payment: 2 copies of the issue. Copyrighted, does not revert to author. Pub's reviews: 4 in 1998. §Women's studies, nonsexist education at all levels and in all settings. Ads: $300/$150/$100 1/3 page.

WOMEN'S WORK, Editorial Collective, 606 Avenue A, Snohomish, WA 98290-2416, 360-568-5914; e-Mail dammit@eskimo.com; Fax available. 1991. Poetry, fiction, articles, art, photos, cartoons, interviews, satire, criticism, reviews, music, letters, news items, non-fiction. "We're a women's journal whose purpose is to explore traditional and modern 'women's work' in all its guises, from the perspectives of women from diverse cultural, generational, and economic backgrounds. Recent contributors include Sibyl James, Sue Pace, and Mary Lou Sanelli. Maximum length on all material (excluding poetry) is 4,000 words" circ. 10M. 4/yr. Pub'd 3 issues 1998; expects 4 issues 1999, 4 issues 2000. sub. price: $12; per copy: $4; sample: $4. Back issues: $1 each + $1 p/h for 1st copy, add 50¢ each additional copy. Discounts: varies, call or send for specific info. 32-48pp; 8×10½; web. Reporting time: 4-6 weeks, queries and non-fiction (incl. articles, artwork, etc.); 12-16 weeks literary depts. (poetry, fiction, etc.). Simultaneous submissions accepted: yes. Publishes 20-30% of manuscripts submitted. Payment: copies and subscription and/or advertising. Copyrighted, reverts to author. Pub's reviews: 30 in 1998. §Women, feminist, lesbian. Ads: $300/$150/$75 1/4 page/$30 business card (2 x 3½")/classified $1 per line (35 char. per line).

WOMENWISE, Susanne Hendrick, Editor; Luita Spangler, Editor, 38 South Main Street, Concord, NH 03301, 603-225-2739. 1977. Poetry, articles, art, photos, cartoons, interviews, letters, news items, non-fiction. "*WomenWise* is the quarterly of the Concord, NH Feminist Health Center. Its purpose is to share women's health resources and information. Articles should be 4-12 pages, double spaced, 1 inch margins. Recent contributors: Luita Spangler, Meredith Tenney, Carol Leonard." circ. 2.5M. 4/yr. Pub'd 4 issues 1998; expects 4 issues 1999, 4 issues 2000. sub. price: $10; per copy: $2.95; sample: $3.50. Back issues: $3.50. Discounts: bulk arrangements made. 12pp; 11×19; of. Reporting time: 1-3 months. Simultaneous submissions accepted: no. Publishes 15-20% of manuscripts submitted. Payment: 1 year subscription and 5 free copies. Copyrighted, reverts to author. Pub's reviews: 4 in 1998. §Health, reproductive freedom and rights, lesbian liberation articles.

WONDER TIME, Donna Fillmore, Editor; Patty Craft, Associate Editor, 6401 The Paseo, Kansas City, MO 64131, 816-333-7000. 1969. Fiction, photos. "Inspirational and character building for 6 to 8-year-old children in corralation with Sunday school Bible Story." circ. 42M. 52/yr. Pub'd 52 issues 1998. sub. price: $6.75; sample: free with SASE. 4pp; 8¼×11. Reporting time: 8-12 weeks. Payment: $25 per story (250-350 words). Copyrighted, rights sometimes revert to author, we retain reprint rights.

Wood River Publishing, Gary H. Schwartz, 1099 D Street, Suite A, San Rafael, CA 94901-2843, 415-256-9300; Fax 415-256-9400; info@picturenet.com. 1989. avg. press run 10M. 5 titles listed in the *Small Press Record of Books in Print* (28th Edition, 1999-00). Discounts: standard.

WOOD STROKES & WOODCRAFTS, EGW Publishing Company, Sandra Wagner, 1041 Shary Circle, Concord, CA 94518-2407, 510-671-9852. 1992. Art, photos, interviews, reviews, letters, non-fiction. "Easy projects to build and finish." circ. 120M. 6/yr. Pub'd 6 issues 1998; expects 6 issues 1999, 6 issues 2000. sub. price: $29.70; per copy: $4.95. 48pp; 8⅛×10⅞; of, web. Reporting time: 2-6 weeks. Payment: upon publication, first serial rights. Copyrighted, reverts to author. Pub's reviews: 80 in 1998. Ads: $3718/$2380/$3 per word.

Wood Thrush Books, Walt McLaughlin, Publisher, Editor; Judy Ashley, Associate Editor, 96 Intervale Avenue, Burlington, VT 05401, 802-863-9767. 1985. Non-fiction. "Currently looking at collections of essays on outdoor/nature themes." avg. press run 100-500. Expects 1 title 1999, 2 titles 2000. 8 titles listed in the *Small Press Record of Books in Print* (28th Edition, 1999-00). avg. price, paper: $12; other: $4 chapbooks. Discounts: 40%. Pages vary; 8×5¼; of. Reporting time: 3 months. Publishes 2% of manuscripts submitted. Payment: copies. Copyrights for author.

Woodbine House, Susan Stokes, Editor, 6510 Bells Mill Road, Bethesda, MD 20817-1636, 301-468-8800. 1985. Non-fiction. "Full length mss - only non-fiction" avg. press run 5M-10M. Pub'd 9 titles 1998; expects 10 titles 1999, 12 titles 2000. 17 titles listed in the *Small Press Record of Books in Print* (28th Edition, 1999-00). avg. price, cloth: $16.95. Discounts: available on request. 300pp; 5½×8½, 8½×11, 6×9, 7×10; of. Reporting time: 6 weeks. Publishes less than 1% of manuscripts submitted. Payment: on an individual basis. Does not copyright for author. ABA.

The Woodbridge Group, Stan Ulkowski, PO Box 849, Eugene, OR 97440, 541-683-6731. 1997. Non-fiction. "Our focus is on books that reflect the metaphysical concept that beliefs, attitudes and emotions are the catalysts that create what we experience in life. We strongly support the idea that metaphysical philosophy can be converted into practical application. Manuscripts that parallel the ideas in the Seth material are especially interesting to us." Pub'd 4 titles 1998; expects 3 titles 2000. 5 titles listed in the *Small Press Record of Books in Print* (28th Edition, 1999-00). avg. price, paper: $14. of. Reporting time: 4 weeks.

Woodbridge Press, Howard Weeks, PO Box 209, Santa Barbara, CA 93102-0209, 805-965-7039. 1971. Non-fiction. avg. press run 5M. Pub'd 3 titles 1998; expects 2 titles 1999, 2 titles 2000. avg. price, cloth: $24.95; paper: $12.95. Discounts: 5-14 42%, 15-99 44%, 100-499 46%, 500 48%; wholesale 52%. 200pp; 6×9; of. Reporting time: 30-60 days. Simultaneous submissions accepted: yes. Publishes 2% of manuscripts submitted. Payment: 10-12% net receipt. Copyrights for author. ABA.

WOODNOTES, Michael Dylan Welch, 248 Beach Park Boulevard, Foster City, CA 94404, 415-571-9428, e-mail WelchM@aol.com. 1989. Poetry, articles, interviews, reviews. "*Woodnotes* is published quarterly by the Haiku Poets of Northern California. We accept haiku, senryu and tanka from members (no more than 2 per issue), short articles, reviews if requested. Recent contributors include Garry Gay, Paul O. Williams, William Higginson, Yvonne Hardenbrook, and Alexis Rotella" circ. 220. 4/yr. Pub'd 4 issues 1998; expects 4 issues 1999, 4 issues 2000. sub. price: $12; per copy: $4; sample: $4. Back issues: $4 if available. Discounts: none. 44pp; 5½×8½; †of. Reporting time: usually 2 weeks or less. Simultaneous submissions accepted: no. Publishes 10% of manuscripts submitted. Payment: none, but we give a $10 best-of-issue award. Copyrighted, reverts to author. Pub's reviews: 47 in 1998. §Books on or containing haiku and related forms, including senryu, tanka, haibun, renku, and sequences. Ads: none.

Woods Hole Press, D. Shephard, PO Box 44, Woods Hole, MA 02543, 508-548-9600. 1973. Poetry, non-fiction. "Poetry of local interest only." avg. press run 500. Pub'd 1 title 1998; expects 2 titles 1999, 2 titles 2000. 4 titles listed in the *Small Press Record of Books in Print* (28th Edition, 1999-00). avg. price, paper: $5.50. Discounts: 1-5 copies 25%, 6+ 40%. 100pp; 5½×8½; †of. Payment: variable. Copyrights for author.

WOODWORKER'S JOURNAL, Larry Stoaiken, Editor; Rob Johnstone, Executive Editor, 4365 Willow Drive, Medina, MN 55340, 612-478-8232; FAX 612-478-8396. 1989. Articles. "Woodworking articles." circ. 200M. 6/yr. Pub'd 6 issues 1998; expects 6 issues 1999, 6 issues 2000. sub. price: $19.95; per copy: $4.95. Back issues: $4.95. 86pp; 7⅞×10½; web offset. Payment: 25¢/word. Copyrighted, reverts to author. Pub's reviews. §Woodworking. Ads: $6,610 4-color/$3,890 4-color/$3.50 per word. MN Magazines Publishers Association.

THE WORCESTER REVIEW, Rodger Martin, 6 Chatham Street, Worcester, MA 01609, 603-924-7342; 978-797-4770. 1973. Poetry, fiction, art, photos, satire, criticism. "Submit up to five poems. Fiction to 4,000 words maximum. Literary articles and criticism should have a central New England connection. Photography: black and white glossy, minimum 5"x 7". Graphic art: black and white, minimum 5"x 7". Author's name should appear in upper left of each page. We permit simultaneous submissions." circ. 1M. 1/yr. Pub'd 1 issue 1998; expects 1 issue 1999, 1 issue 2000. sub. price: $20; per copy: $8; sample: $5. Discounts: 20% on orders of 10 or more of current issues. 150pp; 6×9. Reporting time: 6+ months. Simultaneous submissions accepted: yes. Payment: 2 contributor's copies + 2 year subscription. Copyrighted, reverts to author. Pub's reviews: 1 in 1998. §Central-New England writers. Ads: $150 benefactors/$75 patrons; Full page per issue $250/1/2 pg. $150. CLMP.

The Word Works, Inc., Karren L. Alenier, President & Director of the Board; Hilary Tham, Editor-in-Chief & Director of the Board; Jim Beall, Grants Manager & Director of the Board; Robert Sargent, Director of the Board; Miles David Moore, Program Director, The Washington Prize, PO Box 42164, Washington, DC 20015. 1974. Poetry. "We welcome inquiries including SASE." avg. press run 500. Pub'd 3 titles 1998; expects 4 titles 1999, 3 titles 2000. 37 titles listed in the *Small Press Record of Books in Print* (28th Edition, 1999-00). avg. price, paper: $10; other: $15 anthologies. Discounts: 40% for bookstores, 30% institutions (5+ copies). 54pp; 5½×8½; of. Reporting time: 3 months. Payment: 15% of run. Does not copyright for author.

Wordcraft of Oregon, David Memmott, Editor & Publisher, PO Box 3235, La Grande, OR 97850, 503-963-0723; E-mail wordcraft@oregontrail.net. 1984. Poetry, fiction, art. "In 1997 Wordcraft of Oregon will be publishing two novels (*The Book of Angels* by Thomas E. Kennedy and *The Winter Dance Party Murders* by Greg Herriges), two books of short fiction (*The Din of Celestial Birds* by Brian Evenson and *The Explanation and Other Sound Advice* by Don Webb). We have published over twenty books to date including books by Conger Beasley, Jr., Misha, Jessica Amanda Salmonson, Don Webb, Thomas Wiloch, among others. Our objective is to develop a broader audience for literary work of more speculative nature, i.e. magic realism, modern fantasy, surrealism, literary science fiction and a literature of the fantastic. The press will be taking a one year sabbatical in 1998 and will not be reading until the summer of 1998. Do not send queries until then." avg. press run 250 for signed, limited editions, 500-1,000 for trade editions. Pub'd 2 titles 1998; expects 4 titles 1999, 6 titles 2000. 20 titles listed in the *Small Press Record of Books in Print* (28th Edition, 1999-00). avg. price, paper: $7.95-$12.95; other: $6 chapbooks. Discounts: standard schedule to bookstores and distributors. 40-250pp; 7×8½, 5½×8½; of. Reporting time: 60 days. Simultaneous submissions accepted: no. Payment: copies or percentage by arrangement. Copyrights for author.

Words & Pictures Press, Alan Graham, 1921 Sherry Lane, Apt. #87, Santa Ana, CA 92705-7621, 714-544-7282; Fax 714-544-7430; E-mail publisher@earthlink.net. 1994. Poetry, fiction, cartoons, satire, long-poems, non-fiction. "Not soliciting" avg. press run 1M. Pub'd 2 titles 1998; expects 2 titles 1999, 3 titles 2000. 5 titles listed in the *Small Press Record of Books in Print* (28th Edition, 1999-00). avg. price, paper: $12.95. Discounts: trade 40%. 150pp; 5½×8½. Reporting time: 6 weeks. Payment: none at present. Copyrights for author.

WORDS OF WISDOM, Mikhammad Abdel-Ishara, Editor; Celestine Woo, Associate Editor, 3283 UNCG Station, Greensboro, NC 27413, 336-334-6970; e-mail wowmail@hoopsmail.com. 1981. Poetry, fiction, articles, photos, cartoons, interviews, satire, letters, non-fiction. "*Words of Wisdom* is a quarterly collection of short stories with a few poems. We published 48 stories by 45 authors in 1998. Contributors in the last three years include Wright Walcott Salisbury, Jim Sullivan, Delray K. Dvoracek, J. Michael Blue, Toby Tucker Hecht, Charles F. Ricklin, Carolyn West, Mark Wisniewski, Dan May, and J.D. Wade." circ. 150-180. 4/yr. Pub'd 4 issues 1998; expects 4 issues 1999, 4 issues 2000. sub. price: $15 individuals, $16 institutions and Canada, $24 international; per copy: $4; sample: $4. Back issues: $4. Discounts: 50% for creative writing classes and groups. 76-88pp; 5½×8½; †xerographic, laser printer. Reporting time: usually 2 weeks to 4 months. Simultaneous submissions accepted, but no reprints please. Publishes 8-12% of manuscripts submitted. Payment: 1 year subscription for first story, 1 copy for poems, additional stories, and short-shorts. Not copyrighted. Pub's reviews: 0 in 1998. §Books of short stories. none.

The Wordtree, Dr. Henry G. Burger, Publisher, 10876 Bradshaw, Overland Park, KS 66210-1148, 913-469-1010; burger@cctr.umkc.ed; www.wordtree.com. 1984. Non-fiction. "This word-pinpointing reverse dictionary, called The Wordtree, analyzes each transitive verb. For example: To enlarge & develop = to grow; to grow & complete = to mature, etc. Since all parts are cross-referenced, you can look up any goal, and "ripple" your way backward to all its causes and forward to its effects." avg. press run 1M. Pub'd 1 title 1998. 1 title listed in the *Small Press Record of Books in Print* (28th Edition, 1999-00). avg. price, cloth: $149; paper: not available. Discounts: sold directly 10% for 2-3 copies; also via any distributor 20%. 380pp; 8½×11; of, photo-offset. Reporting time: 1 month. Simultaneous submissions accepted: yes. Publishes 5% of manuscripts submitted. Payment: not standardized. Copyrights for author. DSNA, EURALEX (European Assn. for Lexicography), Academie Europeenne des Sciences.

WordWorkers Press, Linda Bishop, 115 Arch Street, Philadelphia, PA 19106-2003, 215-925-2838; 800-357-6016; e-mail eye@independenteye.org. 1989. Plays. "Devoted to publication of plays of high literary merit in progressive forms, both in anthologies and acting editions." avg. press run 2M. Pub'd 1 title 1998; expects 1 title 1999, 2 titles 2000. 5 titles listed in the *Small Press Record of Books in Print* (28th Edition, 1999-00). avg. price, paper: $9.95; other: $5, acting edition. Discounts: text 35%, bookstores 40%, wholesalers 55%. 50-208pp; 6×9, 5½×8½; of. Reporting time: 4 months. Payment: negotiable. Copyrights for author.

Wordwrights Canada, Susan Ioannou, PO Box 456, Station O, Toronto, Ontario M4A 2P1, Canada. 1985. avg. press run 100-300. Pub'd 1 title 1998; expects 1 title 2000. 4 titles listed in the *Small Press Record of Books in Print* (28th Edition, 1999-00). avg. price, paper: $7. Discounts: only on orders of 10 or more—20%. 24-72pp; 5½×8½; of. Reporting time: 1 month. Simultaneous submissions accepted: no. Publishes less than 1% of manuscripts submitted. Payment/honorarium on publication plus copies. Author owns copyright.

THE WORKBOOK, Southwest Research and Information Center, Kathy Cone, Editor; Cynthia Taylor, Managing Editor, PO Box 4524, Albuquerque, NM 87106, 505-346-1455; Fax 505-346-1459. 1974. Articles, reviews, news items. "Activist oriented. Political position is progressive. Reviews small press publications in more than 30 categories of environmental justice and social change issues" circ. 2.5M. 4/yr. Pub'd 4 issues 1998; expects 4 issues 1999, 4 issues 2000. sub. price: $8.50 students and senior citizens, $12 individuals, $25 institutions; per copy: $3.50; sample: $2. Back issues: $2.50. Discounts: 40% to distributors. 48pp; 8½×11; of. Reporting time: 1 month. Payment: occasional. Copyrighted by Southwest Research & Information Center. Pub's reviews: 100 in 1998. §Environmental, consumer & social problems. Ads: $250/$150/$80/$45/no classified. Independent Press Association.

Working Press, Karen Eliot, 54 Sharsled Street, London SE17 4TN, England, 071-735-6221; FAX 071-582-7021. 1987. Art, criticism, reviews, collages, concrete art. "Working Press is an umbrella under which books by and about working class artists can be published and promoted. Write for full catalogue. US distribution by AK Books, Box 40682, San Francisco, CA 94140-0682, Fax 415-923-0607" avg. press run 1M. Pub'd 1 title 1998; expects 1 title 1999, 1 title 2000. 13 titles listed in the *Small Press Record of Books in Print* (28th Edition, 1999-00). avg. price, cloth: £10 + postage; paper: £6 + postage, $20 US institutions (air mail); other: £3 pamphlets, chapbooks, comix, etc. Discounts: 1/3 off to general trade shops ideally minimum of 5 books, 50% to major distributor in a country. 30-150pp; size A5; of. Reporting time: 30 days. Payment: authors pay all production and printing cost; pay w.p. 10% cover price towards promotion, etc. Copyrights for author. Federation of Worker Writers and Community Publishers (FWWCP).

WorkLife Publishing, 4532 E Grandview Road, Phoenix, AZ 85032, 602-992-0144. 1996. Non-fiction. avg. press run 3M. Pub'd 1 title 1998; expects 2 titles 1999, 2 titles 2000. avg. price, paper: $12.95. 200pp; 6×9; †of. PMA, ABPA.

THE WORLD, The Poetry Project, Staff of the Poetry Project, St. Marks Church/The Poetry Project, 131 East 10th Street, New York, NY 10003. 1966. Poetry, fiction, interviews, long-poems. "Recent contributors: Alice Notley, John Ashbery, Amiri Baraka, Diane de Prima, Wang Ping, Ron Padgett, Paul Beatty, Eric Bogosian, Wanda Coleman, Harryette Mullen, Brenda Coultas, Tracie Morris, Jamie Manrique." circ. 500. 3/yr. Pub'd 3 issues 1998; expects 3 issues 1999, 3 issues 2000. sub. price: $25/4 issues; per copy: $7; sample: $7. Back issues: on request. Discounts: none. 128pp; 6×9; perfectbound. Reporting time: 6 months. Simultaneous submissions accepted: yes. Publishes 5% of manuscripts submitted. Payment: copies. Copyrighted, reverts to author. Ads: $125/$75.

WORLD BOOK INDUSTRY, Jaffe Publishing Management Service, Kunnuparambil P. Punnoose, Kunnuparambil Buildings, Kurichy, Kottayam 686549, India, 91-481-430470; FAX 91-481-561190. 1975. Interviews, criticism, reviews. "*World Book Industry* is a book promotion journal specialising in promoting American small press books and magazines in India and other Asian countries." circ. 3M. 4/yr. Pub'd 4 issues 1998; expects 4 issues 1999, 4 issues 2000. sub. price: $10; per copy: $2.50; sample: same. Back issues: not available. Discounts: 15% on the annual subscription price. 48pp; 8½×11; †lp. Reporting time: 3 months. Payment: in copies. Copyrighted, reverts to author. Pub's reviews: 200 in 1998. §All subjects of human interest. Ads: $200/$125.

World Changing Books, Jason Wolf, Justin Pahio, PO Box 5491, Hilo, HI 96720, 808-934-7942. 1993. Non-fiction. "Second address: 489 Ocean View Dr., Hilo, HI 96720. Our primary concern this year is with the book *Never 'Old': The Ultimate Success Story* by Jesse Anson Dawn. This book is the product of 24 years of study and research, and presents unprecedented breakthroughs in health and anti-aging - all presented in a lively and delightful style" avg. press run 5M. Pub'd 1 title 1998; expects 3-4 titles 1999, 1 title 2000. 2 titles listed in the *Small Press Record of Books in Print* (28th Edition, 1999-00). avg. price, paper: $9.95. Discounts: 40-50% for wholesale and bookstores. 250pp; 4×7. Reporting time: 1-2 weeks. Payment: negotiable. Copyrights for author. NAW National Association of Independent Publishers.

WORLD DOMINATION REVIEW, Larry M. Taylor, Po Box 823, Madison, WI 53701-0823, 608-273-8701. 1991. Fiction, cartoons, satire, criticism, reviews, collages. "Journal of amateur paranoia, humor, social satire, political parody, editorial cartoons, laugh at the powers that be" circ. 100. 4/yr. Pub'd 4 issues 1998; expects 4 issues 1999, 4 issues 2000. sub. price: $4; per copy: $1; sample: $1. Back issues: #2,3,4 all available, $2 each (all other back issues available at $1 each). Discounts: none. 8pp; 8½×11; †photocopy. Reporting time: 1 month. Publishes 10% of manuscripts submitted. Payment: none, may run ad for contributor. Not copyrighted. Pub's reviews: 4 in 1998. §Humor, social satire, science fiction, dystopia.

WORLD LETTER, Jon Cone, 729 Kimball Road, Iowa City, IA 52245, 319-337-6022. 1991. Poetry, fiction, art, letters, parts-of-novels, long-poems. "Material primarily solicited. Include SASE. Letter of introduction appreciated. Contributors: Amiri Baraka, Charles Bukowski, Cesar Vallejo, Clayton Eshleman, James Laughlin, Cid Corman, Saul Yurkievich, Edouard Roditi, Mario Benedetti, Irving Stettner, Chandler Brossard, Carol Adderley, and etc. My advice: before submitting to any publication, become familiar with it." circ. 200-300. 1+. Pub'd 1 issue 1998; expects 1 issue 1999, 1 issue 2000. sub. price: $7/single issue ($5 + $2 shipping); per copy: $7; sample: $7. Back issues: $10. 48pp; 5½×8½ to 6½×10; of. Reporting time: 2-4 weeks or as soon as possible; will comment on solicited material only. Payment: none. Copyrighted, reverts to author. Ads: $100/$50.

World Music Press, Judith Cook Tucker, Editor & Publisher, PO Box 2565, Danbury, CT 06813, 203-748-1131; fax 203-748-3432; e-mail wmpress@aol.com; website www.worldmusicpress.com. 1985. Photos, music, non-fiction. "We are looking for manuscripts of traditional music from non-Western cultures with in-depth annotation, prepared with the participation and knowledge of the indigenous musicians from whose repertoires the material is drawn. Slant is definitely for use by educators, and should be accurate and authentic but not dry or scholarly in tone. Range: grades 3-12 in particular. Current authors include Ghanaian master musician Abraham Kobena Adzinyah, Dumisani Maraire (ethnomusicologist/musician from Zimbabwe). *Vocal Traditions* choral series (choral pieces for school use inspired by or drawn from traditional music of many cultures, including Africa, Latin America, the rural south (US), Israel, Native America). Composers/arrangers include Lorre Wyatt, Pete Seeger, Dumisani Maraire, and Alejandro Jimenez." avg. press run 1.5M books, 3M-10M choral pieces. Pub'd 2 titles 1998; expects 3 titles 1999, 3 titles 2000. 16 titles listed in the *Small Press Record of Books in Print* (28th Edition, 1999-00). avg. price, paper: $14.95 books/$24.95 book & tape sets; other: indiv. choral pcs. $.80-$2.00; cassette companion tapes $6-$10.95, CDs $12.95. Discounts: 40% 1-50; 45% 51-100, 50% 101+ mixed titles ok; mixed books/tapes ok; S.T.O.P. orders ok; non-returnable 10+ copies 50%. 135pp; 8½×11, 6×9; of. Reporting time: 1 month. Payment: 10% net (nego.) royalty; small advance; annual payments. Copyrights for author. PMA.

WORLD OF FANDOM MAGAZINE, Allen Shevy, Chris Mygrant, PO Box 9421, Tampa, FL 33604, 813-933-7424. 1987. Fiction, articles, art, photos, cartoons, interviews, criticism, reviews, music, non-fiction. "Physical address: 2525 W. Knollwood Street, Tampa, FL 33614-4334. We will run most anything as long as it has to do with comic books, movies, music, or TV. Art is also acceptable." circ. 70M+. 4/yr. Pub'd 4 issues 1998; expects 4 issues 1999, 4 issues 2000. sub. price: $14, $35 foreign; per copy: $4.25, $7.50 foreign; sample: same. Back issues: upon request, based on copies in stock. Discounts: will trade with mags; wholesale 60% non-returnable, 40% returnable. 108pp; 8½×11; of. Payment: depends on content but usually complimentary copies. Copyrighted, reverts to author. Pub's reviews. §SciFi, horror, movie, music, TV, review comic books. Ads: $400/$225/$125 1/4 page/discounts for more than 1 issue.

●**WORLD OF ROMANCE,** Regina Miller, PO Box 1220, South Bend, WA 98586, 360-875-6551; e-mail rkmiller@willapabay.org. 1999. Fiction, letters, parts-of-novels. "Looking for romantic fiction, from 1000 to 6000 words. The story line must be focused on the romance, with an upbeat ending. Please go easy on any explicit sex scenes." 4/yr. Expects 2 issues 1999, 4 issues 2000. sub. price: $18; per copy: $4.95; sample: $4.95. 100pp; 5½×11; of. Reporting time: 3-6 months. Simultaneous submissions accepted: yes. Payment: varies. Copyrighted, reverts to author. Ads: $100/$50/$25 1/4 page/$25 business card.

World Peace University Publications, PO Box 20728, Portland, OR 97294-0728, 503-252-3639, fax 503-255-5216. 1986. avg. press run 3M. Pub'd 1 title 1998; expects 4 titles 1999, 4 titles 2000. 4 titles listed in the *Small Press Record of Books in Print* (28th Edition, 1999-00). avg. price, paper: $10.95. Discounts: 30% on 5+ copies, 40% to wholesalers. 120pp; 5⅜×8½. Copyrights for author.

WORLD RAINFOREST REPORT, Randy Hayes, President, Rainforest Action Network, 221 Pine Street, Suite 500, San Francisco, CA 94104-2715, 415-398-4404, fax 415-398-2732, e-mail rainforest@ran.org. 1985. News items, photos. "The *World Rainforest Report* is an international newsletter dealing with all aspects of tropical and temperate rainforest protection, reporting current threats to the world's rainforests and their indigenous people with suggestions on what members can do to help" circ. 25M. 3/yr. Pub'd 2 issues 1998; expects 3 issues 1999, 3 issues 2000. sub. price: $25 (membership); sample: free. 8pp; 8½×11. Reporting time: 10 days prior to publication. Simultaneous submissions accepted: yes. Publishes 5% of manuscripts submitted. Payment: none. Copyrighted, reverts to author. Pub's reviews: 4 in 1998. §Environmental, human rights, animal rights, globalization. No ads.

World Travel Institute, Inc., Gladson I. Nwanna, Ph.D, 8268 Streamwood Drive, PO Box 32674, Baltimore, MD 21208, 410-922-4903; website www.worldtravelinstitute.com. 1992. Articles, news items, non-fiction. avg. press run 10M. Expects 2 titles 1999, 4 titles 2000. 11 titles listed in the *Small Press Record of Books in Print* (28th Edition, 1999-00). avg. price, paper: $39.99. Discounts: available (standard trade). 400pp; 8½×11; of. Reporting time: 4 weeks. Simultaneous submissions accepted: no. Copyrights for author. Publishers Marketing Association (PMA).

World Wide Publishing Corp., Hans J. Schneider, PO Box 105, Ashland, OR 97520. 5 titles listed in the *Small Press Record of Books in Print* (28th Edition, 1999-00).

World Wisdom Books, Inc., PO Box 2682, Bloomington, IN 47402, 812-332-1663; e-mail wwbooks@world-wisdom.com. 1981. Non-fiction. avg. press run 3M. Pub'd 2 titles 1998; expects 1 title 1999, 2 titles 2000. 21 titles listed in the *Small Press Record of Books in Print* (28th Edition, 1999-00). avg. price, cloth: $37.50; paper: $10.95. Discounts: trade 40% no minimum; libraries 50%. 195pp; 5½×8¼; photo offset. Reporting time: 3-6 months. Publishes 2% of manuscripts submitted. Copyrights for author.

WORLDLINKS - FRIENDSHIP NEWS, NEWSLETTERNEWS, Wendy Fisher, 70 Macomb Place, #226, Mt. Clemens, MI 48043, e-mail worldlinks@prodigy.com. 1995. Poetry, fiction, articles, art, photos, letters, news items. "Newspaper dedicated to friendship, penpals, newsletter news, etc." circ. 1M. 6/yr. Pub'd 6 issues 1998; expects 6 issues 1999, 6-12 issues 2000. sub. price: $15; per copy: $3; sample: $3. Discounts: please write and inquire. 20pp; 11×13; newsprint/tabloid. Simultaneous submissions accepted: yes. Publishes 80% of manuscripts submitted. Payment: copies only. Copyrighted, reverts to author. Pub's reviews. §Women, correspondence, culture/foreign countries, publishing/editors, newsletters, psychology, crafts, how-to. Ads: 5¢/word classifieds.

WORLDVIEWS: A Quarterly Review of Resources for Education and Action, Tom Fenton, Mary Heffron, 1515 Webster Street, #305, Oakland, CA 94612, 510-451-1742; fax 510-835-9631; e-mail worldviews@igc.org. 1985. Reviews. "*WorldViews* (formerly *Third World Resources*) contains notices and descriptive listings of organizations and newly released print, audiovisual, CD-ROM, on-line, and other educational resources on Third World regions and issues. Each issue contains a focus-page listing of resources on a topic of current interest (e.g., human rights in Burma, international debt, landmines)." circ. 2M. 4/yr. Pub'd 4 issues 1998; expects 4 issues 1999, 4 issues 2000. sub. price: $50 U.S. & Canada organizational; $25 individual; foreign $65 organizational; $45 individual; per copy: $5; sample: $10. Back issues: $40 per volume (organizations); $20 per volume (individuals). 28pp; 8½×11; of. Payment: none. Pub's reviews: 200 in 1998. §Third world - economy, women, environment, minorities, human rights. Ads: $600/$300/$200 1/3 page/$400 2/3 page/$20 column inch.

WORMWOOD REVIEW, Laura Winton, Editor; Scott Adam, Publisher, PO Box 50003, Loring Station, Minneapolis, MN 55405-0003, 612-381-1229. 1995. Poetry, fiction, art, interviews, satire, criticism, reviews, parts-of-novels, long-poems, plays. "We are a gay/lesbian/bi/trans literary journal. While work doesn't have to be on-theme and you don't have to prove your 'queerness,' *don't* send us stories with heterosexual relationships, unless they explore some bisexual ambivalences, ok? Read the *full* guidelines, please!! Right now is poetry/fiction/art. Open to expansion. Fiction should be up to 2,000-2,500 words. Plays must be short - 10pp or less." circ. 100. 2-3/yr. Pub'd 2 issues 1998; expects 3 issues 1999, 2 issues 2000. sub. price: $15/4 issues; per copy: $5; sample: $3. Back issues: $3 issues 1-4. Discounts: bookstore/distributor 40% + credit for returns; will negotiate bulk orders. 20pp; 8½×11; †mi. Reporting time: rejects—right away; if we hold more than 2 months, you are being considered. Simultaneous submissions accepted: yes. Publishes 20% of manuscripts submitted. Payment: 1 copy + 1/2 price on additional copies. Copyrighted, reverts to author. Pub's reviews. §Queer literary artists, Beat-related mags. Ads: $100/$60/$35 1/4 page/$20 business card.

WRESTLING - THEN & NOW, Evan Ginzburg, PO Box 640471, Oakland Gdns. Station, Flushing, NY 11364. 1990. Articles, interviews, satire, reviews, letters, news items, non-fiction. "Explores history of professional wrestling. Features warm reminisces, where are they now type features, interviews, clippings, etc." circ. 275. 12/yr + annual. Pub'd 11 issues 1998; expects 12 issues 1999, 12 issues 2000. sub. price: $20; per copy: $2; sample: free with SASE. Back issues: $1.25. 16pp; 8½×11; xerox. Reporting time: varies. Simultaneous submissions accepted: yes. Publishes 75% of manuscripts submitted. Payment: copies. Copyrighted, does not revert to author. Pub's reviews: 6 in 1998. §Book, video, fanzine reviews. Ads: $40/$25/15¢ per word to subscribers, 75¢ non-subscribers.

Wright-Armstead Associates, Sara Ellen Messmer, Editor; Madrue Chavers-Wright, Publisher, 2410 Barker Avenue, Suite 14-G, Bronx, NY 10467, 212-654-9445. 1985. Art, photos, letters, non-fiction. "Special interests: history, social science, ethnic studies. Interested in image-building among people of color. Recent title: *The Guarantee* is a biography of P.W. Chavers, Ohio journalist and industrialist, his move to Chicago torn with bank failures and race riots after WW1, his establishing a national bank, campaigning for economic freedom in the Black Belt midst power struggles. The impact on his health and well-being of his family, revealing the triumphs and tragedies of the 'Black Experience' in the urban midwest of the 'Roaring Twenties'. Considerable history of bank legislation to protect depositors accounts in national banks: P.W. Chavers' work with the *Federal Reserve Board*, his writing the earliest federal legislation to guarantee depositors' bank accounts in national banks, urban politics and economics, *The Crash*; *The Great Depression*; *The Bank Holiday*; the emergence of the *Federal Depositors Insurance Corporation*. Also *The Great Migration*; *Federal Douglass*; *Booker T. Washington*; *WEB DuBois*; *The Marcus Garvey & Jean Baptiste Point DeSaible Movements*; and ethnic diversity and multiculturalism in the early 20th century." 1 title listed in the *Small Press Record of*

Books in Print (28th Edition, 1999-00). avg. price, cloth: $25 first edition, $27.95 second edition; paper: $14.95 first edition, $16.95 second edition. Discounts: 20% on multiple orders only, prepayment preferred, 40% on 10+ copies. 450pp; 5½×8½; Braun-Brumfield. Small Press Center, General Society of Mechanics and Tradesmen.

THE WRITE WAY, Anne Larberg, 810 Overhill Road, Deland, FL 32720, 904-734-1955. 1988. Poetry, articles, art, cartoons, reviews, letters, non-fiction. "Newsletter format. Articles not to exceed 750 words. Poetry to 15 lines" circ. 2M. 4/yr. Pub'd 4 issues 1998; expects 4 issues 1999, 4 issues 2000. sub. price: $6; per copy: $3; sample: $2. Back issues: $1 + SASE. Discounts: Bulk rates to creative writing instructors. 6-8pp; 8½×11; of. Reporting time: 6 weeks. Payment: 2 copies, cash awards for contests. Copyrighted, reverts to author. Pub's reviews: 8 in 1998. §Writing, poetry, journalism, English grammar, etc. Ads: $25/$12.50/$5 inch, 25¢ word classified.

Write Way Publishing, Dorrie O'Brien, 10555 E. Dartmouth, Ste. 210, Aurora, CO 80014, 800-680-1493, fax 303-368-8004. 1993. Fiction, non-fiction. "WWP prints hardback fiction (excluding children's books and contemporary/mainstrian) for the national trade. WWP is only interested in works of American or British history, or biographies, in its non-fiction categories." avg. press run 2.5M. Pub'd 11 titles 1998; expects 13 titles 1999. 43 titles listed in the *Small Press Record of Books in Print* (28th Edition, 1999-00). avg. price, cloth: $20. Discounts: ask for catalog. 300pp; 5×8. Reporting time: 1 month on queries, 6-9 months on mss. Simultaneous submissions accepted: yes. Publishes 2% of manuscripts submitted. Payment: 8-10% of net receipts on books sold. Copyrights for author.

●**WRITER TO WRITER**, Barbara L. Croft, Norman R. Hane, PO Box 2336, Oak Park, IL 60303. 1997. Poetry, fiction, articles, interviews, reviews, non-fiction. "Publishes sophisticated articles on poetry and fiction writing technique, essays, reviews, poetry and fiction. We look for articles that expand upon what experienced writers know and adopt the voice of a colleague, not a teacher. Under 3,000 words for prose." circ. 125. 2/yr. Pub'd 2 issues 1998; expects 2 issues 1999, 2 issues 2000. sub. price: $10; per copy: $5; sample: $5. Discounts: 40% discount for bookstores. 32pp; 8½×11; xerox. Reporting time: 2 weeks. Simultaneous submissions accepted: yes. Publishes 5% of manuscripts submitted. Payment: 2 copies and 1 year subscription. Copyrighted, reverts to author. Pub's reviews: 6 in 1998. §how-to books on writing, bios. Ads: $75/$50/$30 1/4 page.

Writers & Scholars International Ltd., Andrew Graham-Yooll, 33 Islington High Street, London N1 9LH, England, 171-278-2313, Fax 171-278-1878. 34 titles listed in the *Small Press Record of Books in Print* (28th Edition, 1999-00).

The Writers Block, Inc., Sandra Thomas Wales, President, Laurel Run Route One, Box 254, Bruceton Mills, WV 26525-9748, 304-379-8162; fax 304-379-8161; writersbl@aol.com; www.spannet.org/writersblock. 1994. Fiction. "Historical novels run about 450 pages. That is our main interest, but we do publish good mystery novels, very little romance, and some mainstream is in the works. We are operating slowly to remain debt free. Note: No unsolicited or unagented materials." avg. press run 5-10M. Pub'd 1 title 1998; expects 2 titles 1999, 3 titles 2000. 2 titles listed in the *Small Press Record of Books in Print* (28th Edition, 1999-00). avg. price, paper: $18-$20. Discounts: 2-4 20%, 5-99 40%, 100+ in even case lots 55%. 450pp; 5¼×8½. Reporting time: 3 months. Simultaneous submissions accepted: yes. Publishes 1% of manuscripts submitted. Payment: 10%, no advance. Copyrights for author. SPAN, National Writers Union, PMA.

WRITER'S CAROUSEL, The Writer's Center, Allan Lefcowitz, Editor; Jean-Marc Faureau, Editor, 4508 Walsh Street, Bethesda, MD 20815-6006, 301-654-8664. 1976. Articles, art, cartoons, interviews, reviews, letters, news items. "We are a writer's journal, featuring articles on the writing trade, interviews with writers, book reviews, calls for submissions, and a calendar of literary events for the Washington DC/Baltimore metro area" circ. 6M. 6/yr. Pub'd 6 issues 1998; expects 6 issues 1999, 6 issues 2000. sub. price: $30. Back issues: out of print almost immediately. 24pp; 8½×11; of. Reporting time: 30 days. Simultaneous submissions accepted: no. Payment: copies. Copyrighted. Pub's reviews: 24 in 1998. §Books about writing, new poetry, fiction and drama, litmags. Ads: write for rate sheet.

The Writer's Center (see also POET LORE; WRITER'S CAROUSEL), 4508 Walsh Street, Bethesda, MD 20815-6006, 301-654-8664. 1977. 4 titles listed in the *Small Press Record of Books in Print* (28th Edition, 1999-00).

WRITER'S CHRONICLE, Associated Writing Programs, D.W. Fenza, Tallwood House, Mail Stop 1E3, Fairfax, VA 22030-0079, 703-993-4301. Articles, interviews, criticism, news items. "Articles pertaining to contemporary literature, writing, and the teaching of writing welcome. Book reviews, news items, grants & awards, magazine submission notices. Occasional interviews." circ. 17M. 6/yr. Pub'd 6 issues 1998; expects 6 issues 1999, 6 issues 2000. sub. price: $20/6 editions, $25 in Canada; $32/12 issues; $40 overseas; per copy: $3.95; sample: $3.95. Back issues: $5. 36pp; 10×15. Reporting time: 3 months. Publishes 5% of manuscripts submitted. Payment: honorarium and copies, $5/100 words. Copyrighted, reverts to author. Pub's reviews: 10 in 1998. §Nonfiction books on contemporary authors, 20th Century authors, anthologies, pedagogy of creative writing, and lit. crit. Ads: $795 (full); $465 (6¼ x 8⅛); $195 (3 x 4⅛).

●**WRITERS CORNER**, T.L. Dorn, PO Box 456, Glenoma, WA 98336-0456. 1998. Fiction, non-fiction. "Stories 1-7 pages mostly excepted. Exceptional stories up to 23 pages have been published." circ. 300. 6/yr. sub. price: $17; per copy: $5; sample: $5. Back issues: $6. 80pp; 5½×8½; xerox. Reporting time: 2 months. Simultaneous submissions accepted: yes. Publishes 85% of manuscripts submitted. Payment: free copy. Copyrighted, reverts to author. Pub's reviews. Ads: $30/$17/bus card $7.

WRITER'S EXCHANGE, Gene Boone, 100 Upper Glen Drive, Blythewood, SC 29016-7806, E-mail eboone@aol.com; www.users.aol.com/writernet. 1986. Poetry, articles, art, cartoons, interviews, letters. "Poetry, to 24 lines, various subjects/forms. Articles on writing-related topics, to 1200 words. Interviews, to 1200 words with writers/poets or publishers. Art-small drawings (ink), any subject: nature, etc. Cartoons-writing-related cartoons" circ. 250-300. 4/yr. Pub'd 4 issues 1998; expects 4 issues 1999, 4 issues 2000. sub. price: $12; per copy: $2; sample: $2. Back issues: $1 and SASE. 40pp; 5⅓×8; of. Reporting time: 2-4 weeks. Publishes 80% of manuscripts submitted. Payment: contributors copy. Copyrighted, reverts to author. Pub's reviews: 250-300 in 1998. §Literary and commercial fiction, poetry, nonfiction, art, books on writing. Ads: $50/$25/$5 small display ad.

WRITERS' FORUM, C. Kenneth Pellow, Editor-in-Chief; Bret Lott, Corresponding Editor; Victoria McCabe, Poetry Editor; Paul Scott Malone, Corresponding Editor, University of Colorado, PO Box 7150, Colorado Springs, CO 80933-7150, 719-262-4006. 1974. Poetry, fiction, parts-of-novels, long-poems. "We publish a book representing some of the best new American literature by authors both established and unrecognized, especially but not necessarily resident in or associated with states west of the Mississippi. We will publish up to 5 poems, including long ones, by one author and fiction, including excerpts from novels, up to 8M words. Ranked third in nation for non-paying fiction market (Writer's Digest)." circ. 1M. 1/yr. Pub'd 1 issue 1998; expects 1 issue 1999, 1 issue 2000. sub. price: $10 includes postage; per copy: $10 includes postage; sample: $7 (includes postage) for readers of *International Directory of Little Magazines & Small Presses*. Back issues: Vols. 1-7 lowcost microfiche. Discounts: 20% libraries, 20% bookstores. 200pp; 5½×8½; of. Reporting time: 3-5 weeks. Simultaneous submissions accepted: yes. Publishes (fiction) 4%-6% of manuscripts submitted. Payment: free copies. Copyrighted, reverts to author. Ads: $175/$100. AWP, CLMP.

Writers Forum, Bob Cobbing, 89A Petherton Road, London N5 2QT, England, 0171-226-2657. 1963. Poetry, fiction, art, photos, criticism, music, long-poems, concrete art. "Mainly members' work." avg. press run 200 but often reprinted. Pub'd 33 titles 1998; expects 70 titles 1999, 30 titles 2000. 108 titles listed in the *Small Press Record of Books in Print* (28th Edition, 1999-00). avg. price, paper: £1.50. Discounts: 1/3 off. 20pp; size varies; †photo-copy. Reporting time: 3 weeks. Simultaneous submissions accepted: no. Publishes 33% of manuscripts submitted. Payment: copies. Copyrights for author on request. ALP, COLP.

WRITERS GAZETTE, Trouvere Company, Brenda Williamson, 899 Williamson Trail, Eclectic, AL 36024-6131. 1980. Poetry, fiction, articles, art, photos, cartoons, interviews, satire, criticism, reviews, long-poems, news items, non-fiction. "Short story to 2,000 words, non-fiction to 2,000 words, poetry to 100 lines. Sometimes we go over these limits, but mostly we prefer under these limits. Except for poetry, fiction, satire, art and photos, material should be writer related" circ. 2M. 4/yr. Pub'd 4 issues 1998; expects 4 issues 1999, 4 issues 2000. sub. price: $18; per copy: $5; sample: $5. Discounts: 20% library, 10% all others. 28pp; 8½×11; of. Reporting time: 2-8 weeks. Simultaneous submissions accepted: yes. Publishes 50% of manuscripts submitted. Payment: tearsheet, $5-$30, copies. Copyrighted, reverts to author. Pub's reviews: 10 in 1998. §Mostly writer related, except we do include novels, chapbooks, etc. especially from self-publishers. Reviews are staffwritten, send book. Ads: 15¢ per word. Discounts for multi. insertion on displays, display $1.25 per sq. inch.

WRITER'S GUIDELINES: A Roundtable for Writers and Editors, Susan Salaki, Box 608, Pittsburg, MO 65724. 1988. Poetry, fiction, articles, art, cartoons, interviews, satire, criticism, reviews, letters, news items, non-fiction. "We have decided to change our reader focus at *Writer's Guidelines*. Previously, we published beginning-writer material. Starting in 1992, we will publish material for active, experienced writers only—and because of this change, we have an immediate need for material in all our departments, especially our Roundtable Discussion section. We also need feature material (900-1200 words). At *Writer's Guidelines*, we do not publish reprinted material (except on rare occasions) nor do we publish material written with generic male pronouns. We yearn for material on unique and original subjects, ideas, and topics. We look for intensity in the work. The writer must strongly believe in the importance of the material. We are shy of all written material that upon reading seems to create a distance between the article and the reader. We go for intimacy, emotional power, and conviction of beliefs on the part of all our writers. Intelligent satire and humorous pieces are always welcome with open checkbooks. The basic premise all writers should hold in their minds while writing for *WG* is that our readers are their peers; they are experienced writers." circ. 1M. 6/yr. Pub'd 6 issues 1998; expects 6 issues 1999, 6 issues 2000. sub. price: $18; per copy: $4; sample: $4. Back issues: $4. 32pp; 8½×11; †mi. Reporting time: 1-4 weeks. Payment: depends upon the quality of the work, but on the average 1¢/word on publication. Copyrighted, reverts to author. Pub's reviews: 30 in 1998. §Open to all areas. Ads: $45/$26/$89 back cover.

WRITER'S GUIDELINES & NEWS, E.P. "Ned" Burke, PO Box 18566, Sarasota, FL 34276, 941-924-3201; Fax 941-925-4468; e-mail writersgn@aol.com. 1988. Poetry, fiction, articles, art, photos, cartoons, interviews, reviews, letters, news items, non-fiction. circ. 2.5M. 4/yr. Pub'd 4 issues 1998; expects 4 issues 1999, 4 issues 2000. sub. price: $19.95; per copy: $5; sample: $5. Back issues: $4. Discounts: 25% off. 48pp; 8½×11; of. Reporting time: 2 months. Simultaneous submissions accepted: no. Publishes 20% of manuscripts submitted. Payment: yes. Copyrighted, reverts to author. Pub's reviews: 10+ in 1998. §Writing slant, mainstream. Ads: $600/$360/$2 per word.

Writers House Press (see also THE BAREFOOT POET: Journal of Poetry, Fiction, Essays, & Art), John-Paul Ignatus, L.S.M, Editor, PO Box 52, Pisgah, IA 51564-0052, 515-279-7804; Internet: smichael@commanlink.com. 1982. Poetry, fiction, articles, art, photos, interviews, satire, letters, parts-of-novels, long-poems, plays, news items, non-fiction. "Not accepting manuscripts at this time. We publish high quality manuscripts only. We currently have the following series: 1) Political & Social Affairs Series (books concerning politics & social problems); 2) Contemporary Studies in the Humanities (books concerning psychology, philosophy, history, religion, theology, etc. 3) Contemporary literature for children; 4) Contemporary Poets Series; 5) Poetry in Translation; 6) Fiction in Translation; and 7) Works in translation (other than poetry or fiction). Writers House Press is a Cooperative Press. We believe, as established authors published by major Houses have found, that when one has participated in the entire publishing process (writing, publishing, distributing) a greater sense of satisfaction is felt when seeing the final result on the bookstore shelves. In a Cooperative Royalty publishing venture the author shares in the investment and the profits. Traditional publishing houses keep the majority of the proceeds and leave the author with as little as 6% for paperbacks and 10% for hardbacks. As a participant in the publishing process, the author maintains more artistic control, assists in promotion and distribution plans, and shares equally in the financial success of the book. See specifics of financial arrangements under the Royalty and Payment Arrangement with Authors section below. Authors should first send a proposal with a sample chapter (or ten pages of poetry). The proposal should include information about the purpose of the book (if non-fiction), table of contents (if applicable), full text of any introduction or Foreword, story/plot outline, theme, potential audience, distribution ideas, copies of any reviews, personal background (including qualifications to write on a non-fiction subject), and any other information that may aid us in our decision. We are NOT a vanity press publishing any manuscript that comes with a check. All proposals must be submitted to a committee who will vote on whether to invite the submission of the entire manuscript. Expect one-two months for response to the proposal. Within three months of receiving the entire manuscript, we will notify the author if the work has been accepted for publication, at which time a contract will be negotiated. All material and correspondence must include an SASE. We also publish a magazine entitled *The Barefoot Poet: Journal of Poetry, Fiction, Essays, & Art*. Writers House Press has been acquired by St. Michael's Press" avg. press run 100-1.5M. Expects 1 title 2000. 8 titles listed in the *Small Press Record of Books in Print* (28th Edition, 1999-00). avg. price, paper: $9.95-$19.95; other: $6.95-$9.95. Discounts: 2-5 copies 20%, 6-10 25%, 11-25 30%, 26-50 35%, 51-100 40%; jobbers 20%; bookstores 40%. Pages vary; 4¼×5½; of. Reporting time: 3 minutes to 3 months. Publishes 15% of manuscripts submitted. As a cooperative venture the cost of publishing is shared as are the profits. We pay about 70% of the costs; the author pays about 30%. As a royalty house, the author receives a royalty of 10%-16%. In addition, the author may participate as his or her own distributor and receive up to 50% of the cover price in profits in addition to royalty payments. Specific contract items may vary, depending on the needs of the particular book project. Copyrights for author.

WRITERS IN PARADISE, David Sinclair, 4615 Gulf Boulevard, Ste. 104, St. Pete Beach, FL 33706, E-mail writers.in.paradise@worldnet.att.net. 1998. Poetry, fiction, criticism, reviews, parts-of-novels, plays, non-fiction. "We accept electronic submissions only. Send either on computer disk (3.5" pc format) or e-mail us at above address." circ. 250. 12/yr. Expects 12 issues 1999, 12 issues 2000. sub. price: $20, $12/6 month sub.; per copy: $3; sample: $3. Back issues: $3. 16-32pp; 8×11; of. Reporting time: 2 months. Simultaneous submissions accepted: yes. Publishes 50% of manuscripts submitted. Payment: contributor's copy. Copyrighted, does not revert to author. Pub's reviews. §Literature, literary biography. Ads: none.

WRITERS INK, Writers Unlimited Agency, Inc, Writers Ink Press, David B. Axelrod, PO Box 2344, Seldon, NY 11784, 516-451-0478 phone/fax. 1975. Articles, art, photos, cartoons, interviews, satire, criticism, reviews, collages. "Maximum article or story length 500 w. Though longer material might be serialized. Filler, humor for writers used. Limited to L.I. authors or items/ads of interest to L.I. literary scene. *No unsolicited manuscripts at present.*" circ. 2M. 0-4/yr. Pub'd 1 issue 1998; expects 2 issues 1999, 1 issue 2000. sub. price: $6; per copy: $1; No samples. Back issues: specific issues by request, free if available. Discounts: none-but free to worthy folks or groups—sold, $6 yearly rate direct by 1st class mail from WI. 4-12pp; 5×7; †desktop, photocopy. Reporting time: immediate (maximum 2 weeks) only if we are interested; no reply means "no thanks" Payment: 50¢/col. inch or $2/photo. Copyrighted, reverts to author. Pub's reviews: 1 in 1998. §All aids to writers, general interest and of course, L.I. works, mags, books. Ads: $15/$8/25¢. LIPS, EEAC.

Writers Ink Press (see also WRITERS INK), David B. Axelrod, 233 Mooney Pond, PO Box 2344, Seldon, Long Island, NY 11784-2344, 516-451-0478 phone/Fax. 1975. Poetry. "No unsolicited mss. at this time." avg. press run 800. Pub'd 2 titles 1998; expects 3 titles 1999, 3 titles 2000. 16 titles listed in the *Small Press Record of Books in Print* (28th Edition, 1999-00). avg. price, cloth: $18; paper: $12; other: $8 chapbook. Discounts: 30% bookstores & distributors. Chapbooks 24-48pp, perfectbound 72-128pp; 5×7, 6×9; of, desktop. Payment: 50% profit over cost, varies. Copyrights for author.

WRITERS' JOURNAL, Leon Ogroske, Editor; John Ogroske, Publisher-Managing Editor, PO Box 394, Perham, MN 56573-0394, 218-346-7921; fax 218-346-7924; e-mail writersjournal@wadena.net. 1980. "Articles on the art of writing - inspirational and informative - 500-2000 words. News, Book Reviews, Markets Report. *Writers' Journal* is a bi-monthly journal for writers and poets. Short story and fiction contests twice a year...poetry contest 3 times a year. Cash prizes. We also have an annual romance, travel writing, horror/ghost, and photo contests. We have a "write to win" contest where a starter phrase is given. All contests under 2000 words." circ. 26M. 6/yr. Pub'd 6 issues 1998; expects 6 issues 1999, 6 issues 2000. sub. price: $19.97; per copy: $3.99; sample: $5. Back issues: $5. Discounts: varies. 64pp; 6¾×8½, trim 8⅜×10⅞; of. Reporting time: 3-4 weeks. Simultaneous submissions accepted: yes. Publishes 20% of manuscripts submitted. Payment: $10-$50. Copyrighted, reverts to author. Pub's reviews: about 36 in 1998. §On writing, poetry, communications. Ads: $750-900/$420-500/ $1.35 per word.

WRITER'S LIFELINE, Vesta Publications Limited, Stephen Gill, Editor, PO Box 1641, Cornwall, Ont. K6H 5V6, Canada. 1974. circ. 2M. 3/yr. Pub'd 3 issues 1998; expects 3 issues 1999, 3 issues 2000. sub. price: $18; per copy: $3; sample: $8 for 3 issues. Back issues: $1.50. Discounts: 30%. 36pp; 5¼×8¼; †of. Reporting time: 4-6 weeks. Payment: in copies at present. Copyrighted. Pub's reviews: 80 in 1998. §All, but particularly about writing and publishing. Ads: $150/$100/$15. CPPA.

WRITER'S MONTHLY GAZETTE, Press-Tige Publishing Company Inc., Kelly O'Donnell, Editor; Martha Ivery, Associate Editor, HCR 1 Box 309, Leeds, NY 12451, 518-622-8806; 800-707-2752. 1972. Poetry, fiction, articles, photos, cartoons, interviews, criticism, reviews, letters, non-fiction. circ. 160M. 12/yr. Pub'd 12 issues 1998; expects 12 issues 1999, 12 issues 2000. sub. price: $48; per copy: $4; sample: $2. Back issues: $1. Discounts: 20% agent. 10pp; 8½×11; †1p. Reporting time: 2 months. Publishes 50% of manuscripts submitted. Payment: $25 + up, depends on length of article. Copyrighted, reverts to author. Pub's reviews: 6 in 1998. §Non-fiction, first-person accounts, senior lifestyles, baby boomers. Ads: $450/$200/$4 per word classified. Hudson Valley Writers Group, International Publishers, Inc., PMA, ABA.

WRITERS NEWS, Richard Bell, PO Box 4, Nairn IV12 4HU, Scotland, 01667-454441. 1989. Poetry, fiction, articles, interviews, criticism, reviews, letters, parts-of-novels, news items, non-fiction. "News magazine full of details of market opportunities, competitions, events and in-depth 'know-how' articles, interviews with famous writers, columns, the magazine's own extensive range of competitions with nearly £10,000 worth of prizes annually and stories are published with critiques." circ. 19.5M. 12/yr. Pub'd 12 issues 1998; expects 12 issues 1999, 12 issues 2000. sub. price: £38.90 by DD or CC, £43.90 by cash; Europe £43.90 by DD, £48.90 by cash; overseas £48.90 by DD, £53.90 by cash; per copy: £3; sample: £3. Back issues: 5 for price of 6. Discounts: only available by mail. 28-52pp; 8½×11¾; of. Reporting time: 1 month. Payment: £40 per 1,000 minimum. Copyrighted, reverts to author. Pub's reviews: 100+ in 1998. §Anything to do with writing and publishing. Ads: £295/£165/£85 1/4 page/£48 1/8 page.

WRITER'S NEWS, Elizabeth J. Klungness, 2130 Sunset Drive #47, Vista, CA 92083, 760-941-9293; Fax 760-941-5719; lizklung@earthlink.net. 1993. Articles, interviews, news items. "The latest information for writers seeking markets, plus craft tips and interviews" circ. 300. 12/yr. Pub'd 12 issues 1998; expects 12 issues 1999, 12 issues 2000. sub. price: $22; per copy: $2; sample: free with 55¢ stamp. 10pp; 8½×11. Reporting time: turn around. Simultaneous submissions accepted: yes. We only accept subscribers' short work. Payment: copy. Not copyrighted. Pub's reviews: 15 in 1998. §Writing. Ads: none.

Writers Unlimited Agency, Inc (see also WRITERS INK), David B. Axelrod, PO Box 2344, Seldon, NY 11784, 516-451-0478 phone/Fax. 1975. "We keep an active file of poets' work and can sometimes provide referals for publication and/or readings. No unsolicited mss." avg. press run 800. Pub'd 2 titles 1998; expects 3 titles 1999, 3 titles 2000. avg. price, cloth: $16; paper: $12; other: $10 chapbook. Discounts: 30% distributor/bookseller. 40pp; 5½×8½, 5×8; IBM/pagemaker to format. Payment: varies. Copyrights for author.

WRITER'S WORKSHOP REVIEW, Rhia R. Drouillard, 511 West 24th Street, Vancouver, WA 98660, 360-693-6509. 1993. Poetry, articles, art, cartoons, interviews, satire, criticism, reviews, letters, long-poems, plays, news items, non-fiction. circ. 500. 12/yr. Pub'd 12 issues 1998; expects 12 issues 1999, 12 issues 2000. sub. price: $20; per copy: $3; sample: $3. Back issues: $3 if available $5 special order. 20pp; 8½×11; mi,lp. Reporting time: 2 days to 2 months. Payment: 1 contributor's copy. Copyrighted, reverts to author. Pub's reviews: 3 in 1998. §Computer, internet, writing, marketing, fiction. Ads: $50/$25/1/3 page $18. Southwest Washington Writers, New England Writers.

632

WRITER'S WORLD, Gainelle Murray, 204 East 19th Street, Big Stone Gap, VA 24219, 703-523-0830, fax 703-523-5757. 1990. Poetry, fiction, articles, art, photos, cartoons, interviews, letters, non-fiction. "Nonfiction: General interest, how-tos, humor, inspirational, personal experience, historical/nostalgia, opinion, interview/ profile (Pro writers), all related to writing. Length, 700-900 words. Fiction: Romance, mystery, fantasy, humorous, suspense, historical. No violence or explicit sex. Length, 800-1000 words. Poetry: Free verse, light verse, traditional, humorous. Length, 12-16 lines. Fillers: Anecdotes, short humor, (about the writing life), writing tips. Length, 50-200 words. Columns are assigned to contributing editors. Photos: Submit photos with manuscript. Offers no additional payment for photos submitted with manuscript. Captions, model releases and identification of subjects required. Rights: We assume First North American Serial Rights which revert to the author upon publication. Previously published material must state publication history. Payment on publication. Each contributor receives two copies of the issue in which their work appears. Manuscripts should be typed double-spaced on 8½ x 11 bond paper. Please keep a copy of your manuscript, as we cannot be held responsible for lost or damaged manuscripts. Material submitted without a SASE will not be read, returned, or accepted. We have an annual fiction contest offering cash awards" circ. 2.6M. 6/yr. Pub'd 6 issues 1998; expects 6 issues 1999, 6 issues 2000. sub. price: $15; per copy: $3.25; sample: $4.50. Discounts: none. 24pp; 8½×11. Reporting time: 1 month. Simultaneous submissions accepted: no. Publishes 15% of manuscripts submitted. Payment: 2 copies of the issue in which their work appears. Copyrighted, reverts to author. Ads: $200/$100/$50 1/4 page/$25 1/8 page/classified: $10 minimum, 20 words maximum, 25¢ each additional word.

Writer's World Press, Lavern Hall, Publisher, 35 N. Chillicothe Road, Unit D, Aurora, OH 44202-8741, 330-562-6667; Fax 330-562-1216; WritersWorld@juno.com. 1991. Non-fiction. "Books about how to write, books for writers and publishers." avg. press run 1.5M. Expects 3 titles 2000. 4 titles listed in the *Small Press Record of Books in Print* (28th Edition, 1999-00). avg. price, paper: varies. Discounts: standard trade. 184pp; size varies. Reporting time: 1 month. Simultaneous submissions accepted: yes. Publishes a very selective % of manuscripts submitted. Payment: negotiable. Copyrights for author. PMA, SPAN.

WRITES OF PASSAGE, Laura Hoffman, Wendy Mass, 817 Broadway, 6th Floor, New York, NY 10003, 212-473-7564; wpusa@aol.com; http://www.writes.org. 1994. Poetry, fiction. "Contains poems and short stories written by teenagers as well as special features on writing, interviews with authors and tips and advice for young authors. Also contains Teacher's Guide as supplement to journal. We do not publish any reviews in the journal, but we will on the website." circ. 3M. 2/yr. Pub'd 2 issues 1998; expects 2 issues 1999, 2 issues 2000. sub. price: $12; per copy: $6; sample: $6. Back issues: $6. Discounts: 10 subscriptions at $95, 20 at $180, 50 at $400. 96pp; 5½×8½; †of. Reporting time: 2 months. Simultaneous submissions accepted: yes. Publishes 5% of manuscripts submitted. Payment: 2 free copies of journal. Copyrighted, reverts to author. Pub's reviews. §Bestsellers, anything of interest to teenagers. Ads: $850/$500/$300 1/4 page.

WRITING FOR OUR LIVES, Janet M. McEwan, 647 N. Santa Cruz Ave., The Annex, Los Gatos, CA 95030, 408-354-8604. 1991. Poetry, fiction, letters, parts-of-novels, non-fiction. "This periodical serves as a vessel for poems, short fiction, stories, letters, autobiographies, and journal excerpts from the life-stories, experiences, and spiritual journeys of women. Maximum length, approx. 2100 words. Women writers only, please." circ. 600. 1/yr. Pub'd 2 issues 1998; expects 1 issue 1999, 1 issue 2000. sub. price: 2 issues $15.50 U.S., $21 overseas; per copy: $8, $11 overseas; sample: $6-$8, $9-$11 overseas. Back issues: $4-$6, $6-$9 overseas. Discounts: trade 40%. 80pp; 5¼×8¼; of. Reporting time: first report immediate, second varies. Simultaneous submissions accepted: yes. Publishes less than 5% of manuscripts submitted. Payment: 2 copies, plus discount on copies and subscription. Copyrighted, reverts to author.

WRITING MAGAZINE, Richard Bell, PO Box 4, Nairn IV12 4HU, Scotland, 01667-454441. 1992. circ. 46M. 11/yr. Pub'd 6 issues 1998; expects 6 issues 1999, 6 issues 2000. sub. price: subscription is to *Writers New* (a sister publication) which is £48.90 and is for 12 issues + 6 issues of *Writing Magazine*; per copy: £2.50; sample: £3.50 inc. postage. 64pp. Pub's reviews: 36 in 1998. §New authors, writing books. Ads: £1000 full page colour/£500 1/2 page colour.

THE WRITING SELF, Julia Nourok, Publisher; Scot Nourok, Helen Gorenstein, PO Box 245, Lenox Hill Station, New York, NY 10021. 1992. Poetry, fiction, articles, interviews, reviews, parts-of-novels, non-fiction. "Broad range of subjects that share with our readers the writing life and stimulate them to keep writing. Pieces with a personal tone. Recent essays by Michael Steinberg, Lev Raphael. Ms. length: 500-1,200 words. Some poetry. Interview with writers in each issue: Wendy Wasserstein, Calvin Trillin, Stephen Dixon, Lorrie Moore" circ. 800. 4/yr. Pub'd 4 issues 1998; expects 4 issues 1999, 4 issues 2000. sub. price: $10; per copy: $3; sample: $3. Back issues: $4. Discounts: 35% minimum of 10 copies. 16pp; 8½×11; of. Reporting time: 3-6 months. Payment: $5-$20. Copyrighted, reverts to author. Pub's reviews: 10 in 1998. §First novels, first collections, writer's journals, letters, memoirs, and essays about the writing life. Ads: $70/$50/$30.

WRITING ULSTER, Bill Lazenbatt, U. of Ulster-Jordanstown, Shore Rd, Newtownabbey Co. Antrim, BT 370QB, Northern Ireland, 011-44-232-365131; fax 232-366824. 1990. Poetry, articles, art, photos, interviews, criticism, reviews, parts-of-novels. "Focus on Irish or Irish/American material with bias towards Ulster/Scots

Irish/Northern writers, commentators, etc. Recent contributors include Brendan Kennelly, M. McGuckian, Demot Bolger" 1/yr. Expects 1 issue 1999, 1 issue 2000. sub. price: £5; per copy: £5. Back issues: £2.50 for Nos. 1-3. Discounts: phone/fax for details. 192pp; 6×9. Reporting time: 6 weeks. Simultaneous submissions accepted: no. Publishes approx. 70% of manuscripts submitted. Payment: £50-£100 depending on reputation etc. Copyrighted, reverts to author. Pub's reviews: 1 in 1998. §Irish or Irish/American literature, creative arts. Ads: £100/£50.

WWW.TOMORROWSF.COM, Algis Budrys, Editor, PO Box 6038, Evanston, IL 60204, 708-864-3668. 1992. Poetry, fiction. "Poems, articles, cartoons." circ. 5M. 6/yr. Pub'd 1 issue 1998; expects 6 issues 1999, 6 issues 2000. sub. price: $10; per copy: $2; sample: $5. Back issues: $4 up to #14, $4.50 thereafter, $5 from #20-24, electronic thereafter. Internet pages. Reporting time: 2 weeks. Simultaneous submissions accepted: no. Publishes .5% of manuscripts submitted. Payment: 50¢/7¢/$25. Copyrighted, reverts to author. Pub's reviews: 20 in 1998. §Speculative literature. Ads: $150/$80/$50/$40/25¢ per word min 20 words.

Wynn Publishing, Edward Wincentsen, PO Box 1491, Pickens, SC 29671, 803-878-6469. 1994. Articles, photos, interviews, criticism, reviews, music. avg. press run 5M. Pub'd 1 title 1998; expects 2 titles 1999, 4 titles 2000. 1 title listed in the *Small Press Record of Books in Print* (28th Edition, 1999-00). avg. price, paper: $14.95. Discounts: 20-55%. 122pp; 6×9; of. Reporting time: 2-4 weeks. Simultaneous submissions accepted: yes. Payment: varies. Copyrights for author.

X

XANADU, Pleasure Dome Press (Long Island Poetry Collective Inc.), Weslea Sidon, Editor; Mildred Jeffrey, Editor; Lois V. Walker, Editor; Sue Kain, Editor, Box 773, Huntington, NY 11743, 516-248-7716. 1975. Poetry, art, photos, long-poems. "Poetry, including prose poems. Poems to 60 lines are most welcome, though longer work will be considered. We like to see 3-5 poems by an individual at one time" circ. 300. 1/yr. Pub'd 1 issue 1998; expects 1 issue 1999, 1 issue 2000. sub. price: $7 (includes p/h); per copy: $7 (include p/h); sample: $5. Discounts: 10% on orders of $20 or more, in any combination of titles (Pleasure Dome Press also included.). 64pp; 5½×8½; of. Reporting time: 3-12 weeks. Payment: 1 copy per contributor. Copyrighted, reverts to author.

XAVIER REVIEW, Thomas Bonner, Jr., Editor; Robert E. Skinner, Managing Editor, Box 110C, Xavier University, New Orleans, LA 70125, 504-486-7411 X481; 483-7304; FAX 504-488-3320. 1980. Poetry, fiction, photos, criticism, reviews, parts-of-novels. circ. 300. 2/yr. Pub'd 2 issues 1998; expects 3 issues 1999, 2 issues 2000. sub. price: $10 individuals, $15 institutions; per copy: $5; sample: $5. Back issues: inquire. Discounts: inquire. 75pp; 6×9; of. Reporting time: 1 month. Payment: 2 issues. Copyrighted, rights reassigned to author upon request. Pub's reviews: 4 in 1998. §Southern ethnic, and Latin-American culture. Ads: $40/$20. Council of Editors of Learned Journals.

XCP: CROSS-CULTURAL POETICS, Mark Nowak, College of St. Catherine, 601 25th Avenue South, Minneapolis, MN 55454. 1997. "Seeks to address the increasingly untenable boundaries between poetic and enthnographic practices. Recent contributors: Amiri Baraka, Edwin Torres, Diane Glancy, Forrest Gander, Juan Felipe Herrera" circ. 750. 2/yr. sub. price: $25 indivduals (4 issues), $40 institutions (4 issues), foreign add $5; checks payable to College of St. Catherine.; per copy: $9; sample: $9. 150pp; 6×9. Reporting time: 1 month or less. Simultaneous submissions accepted: no. Payment: 2 copies. Copyrighted, reverts to author. Pub's reviews: 15 in 1998. §ethnographies (anthropology, folklore), poetry and poetics, ethnic, cultural and performance studies. Ads: $125. CLMP.

Xenos Books, Karl Kvitko, Box 52152, Riverside, CA 92517, 909-370-2229; E-mail info@xenosbooks.com; http://www.xenosbooks.com. 1986. Poetry, fiction, art, satire, long-poems, plays, non-fiction. avg. press run 300-500. Pub'd 5 titles 1998; expects 5 titles 1999, 5 titles 2000. 13 titles listed in the *Small Press Record of Books in Print* (28th Edition, 1999-00). avg. price, cloth: $25; paper: $13. 120-200pp; 5½×8¼, 8½×11; of. Reporting time: 1-3 months. Simultaneous submissions accepted: yes. Publishes 1% of manuscripts submitted. Payment: individual agreements. Copyrights for author if requested. R.R. Bowker.

‡XIB, Xib Publications, Tolek, 930 24th Street, San Diego, CA 92102-2006. 1991. Poetry, fiction, art, photos, satire, long-poems, collages. "Open to all forms, styles. Not partial to rhyme/meter, romanticism, nature. Recent contributors: Lyn Stefanhagens, Robert Nagler, Lisa Glatt" circ. 500. 1-2/yr. Pub'd 2 issues 1998; expects 1 issue 1999, 2 issues 2000. sub. price: $10; per copy: $5; sample: $5. Back issues: $4. Discounts: trade for similar, bulk varies. 60pp; 6¾×8½; photocopy and/or mi. Reporting time: 2-3 weeks. Payment: 1 or 2 copies. Copyrighted, reverts to author. Ads: $9/$4.

‡**Xib Publications (see also XIB),** Tolek, 930 24th Street, San Diego, CA 92102-2006. 1991. Poetry, fiction, art, photos, satire, long-poems, collages. *"All styles, forms."* avg. press run 50. Pub'd 1 title 1998; expects 2 titles 1999, 2 titles 2000. 2 titles listed in the *Small Press Record of Books in Print* (28th Edition, 1999-00). avg. price, other: $2 saddle, card stock. Discounts: trades for similar. 20pp; 5½×8½; photocopy. Reporting time: 1-2 weeks. Payment: 40 copies initially; more to suit market demand. Copyrights for author.

X-it Press (see also THE BOBBY STAR NEWSLETTER), Bobby Star, PO Box 3756, Erie, PA 16508. 1993. Poetry, fiction, articles, art, photos, cartoons, collages. *"Recent chapbook contributor published: Kevin Hibshman"* avg. press run 100. Expects 6 titles 1999. Pages vary; 8×5; †photocopy. Reporting time: 1-17 weeks. Payment: 10-50% of press run. We usually copyright for author.

XIZQUIL, Uncle River, Blue Route, Box 90, Blue, AZ 85922. 1989. Poetry, fiction, articles, art, cartoons, interviews, satire, parts-of-novels, long-poems, plays, non-fiction. *"Xizquil* publishes 'Speculative' fiction, poetry and nonfiction, what I might call Cultural Science Fiction. Especially looking for work that addresses question of *how* culture changes, has, or might, from one view or *functioning* way of life to some other. *Do not* want works in which the *only* significant thing to happen is that someone kills someone else. *Xizquil* uses a variety of lengths in every issue if possible, to 15,000 words, occasionally to 25,000 words. Receive too many bad short submissions, not enough good long ones." circ. 200. 1-2/yr. Expects 1 issue 1999. sub. price: $11/3 issues; per copy: $4; sample: $4. Back issues: $3 1 issue #2-12, $2 each additional. Discounts: 40% to retailers and contributors, plus postage; distributors and others inquire. 64pp; 5½×8½; of. Reporting time: 1 week to 2 months. Simultaneous submissions accepted: no. Publishes 8% of manuscripts submitted. Payment: copies. Copyrighted, reverts to author. Ads: none.

X-RAY, Johnny Brewton, PO Box 170011, San Francisco, CA 94117, e-mail johnny@xraybookco.com. 1989. Poetry, fiction, art, interviews. *"X-Ray* is a literary and art magazine. Recent contributors include Ruth Weiss, Wanda Gleman, Dan Fante, Bern Porter, A.D. Winans, Allen Ginsberg, Jaime Hernandez, Charles Bukowski, August Kleinzahler, Neeli Cherkovski, Jack Micheline and Hunter S. Thompson. Correspondence artists are encouraged to contribute. Accepting short fiction, poetry, erotica, prose, found poems, experimental poetry, found objects, assemblage, original art, comics, interviews, photography, etc. Materials range from Chinese telephone directory, sheet music from the early 1900's to hemp and colored craft paper. Every page a different paper. Chapbooks can be found within the pages stuffed into envelopes and fold-out broadsides also grace the pages. When sending original art keep layout to the right of the binding edge at least 1½ inch. Use permanent adhesives and pigments. Size is 8½ X 7 exactly. Send one completed piece for approval. After approval send at least 226 pieces as the edition is limited to 226. Send SASE for guideline information" circ. 226. 2/yr. Pub'd 1 issue 1998; expects 3 issues 1999, 4 issues 2000. sub. price: none; per copy: $35. Back issues: none. Discounts: 20% to dealers. 80pp; 7×8½; †mi, of, lp. Reporting time: 2 weeks. Simultaneous submissions accepted: no. Publishes 25% of manuscripts submitted. Payment: 1 copy. Copyrighted, reverts to author. Pub's reviews. §novels, poetry, music. Ads: none.

XTRAS, From Here Press, William J. Higginson, Penny Harter, PO Box 2740, Santa Fe, NM 87504-2740, 505-438-3249. 1975. Poetry, fiction, criticism, parts-of-novels, long-poems, plays, non-fiction. *"Xtras,* a cooperative periodical/chapbook series, features writing in both verse and prose. Issues of *Xtras* are devoted to the work of one or a related group of writers who cooperate in publishing their own chapbooks, and receive a substantial number of copies in payment. Individual issues of *Xtras* feature poems by Penny Harter, W.J. Higginson, and Ruth Stone, haiku and sequences by Alan Pizzarelli, W.J. Higginson, Adele Kenny, and Elizabeth Searle Lamb, workshop writings by teens and elderly, haiku and short poems by Allen Ginsberg, diary in haiku-prose by Rod Tulloss, essays and long poems by WJH. Not reading unsolicited mss now" circ. 200-500. 0-1/yr. Expects 1 issue 2000. price per copy: $3-$4.95. Discounts: 40% to trade (5 mixed titles; titles can be mixed with From Here Press books). 28-72pp; 5½×8½; of. Reporting time: 1 month. Payment: a substantial number of copies. Copyrighted, reverts to author. No ads.

‡**XY: Men, Sex, Politics,** Michael Flood, Coordinating Editor, PO Box 26, Ainslie, Canberra, Act. 2602, Australia, phone/fax 06-248-5215. 1990. Poetry, fiction, articles, art, photos, cartoons, interviews, reviews, letters. circ. 800. 4/yr. Pub'd 4 issues 1998; expects 4 issues 1999, 4 issues 2000. sub. price: $19; per copy: $4.95; sample: $7.50. Back issues: $5 each + $2.50 p/h per request. 36pp; size A4. Reporting time: 3 months maximum. Publishes 50% of manuscripts submitted. Payment: none. Not copyrighted. Pub's reviews: 8 in 1998. §Men, masculinity, gender, sexuality, feminism, gay. Ads: $110/$60/$40 1/3 page/$35 1/4 page/$25 1/6 page/$15 1/12 page/$85 inserts.

Y

THE YALE REVIEW, J.D. McClatchy, Editor; Susan Bianconi, Managing Editor, Yale University, PO Box 208243, New Haven, CT 06520-8243. 1911. Poetry, fiction, articles, criticism, reviews, non-fiction, long-poems, letters, plays. "Advertising, subscription office: Blackwell Publishers, 350 Main Street, Malden, MA 02148." circ. 6M. 4/yr. Pub'd 4 issues 1998; expects 4 issues 1999. sub. price: $65 institutions, $27 individuals; per copy: $10 (includes postage and handling); sample: $10 (includes postage and handling). Back issues: on request. Discounts: distributor, 50%, agent 20% bookstores 10%. 160pp plus 16-24pp front matter; 6⅛×9⅛; of, lp. Reporting time: 1-2 months. Simultaneous submissions accepted: no. Publishes 5% *of manuscripts submitted.* Payment: on publication. Copyright Yale University, remaining so on publication by agreement with author or transfer of copyright to author. Pub's reviews: 12 in 1998. §Literature, history, fiction, poetry, economics, biography, arts & architecture, politics, foreign affairs. Ads: on request. CLMP.

YARROW, A JOURNAL OF POETRY, Harry Humes, Editor, English Dept., Lytle Hall, Kutztown State University, Kutztown, PA 19530, 683-4353. 1981. Poetry, interviews. "Recent contributors: Bruce Weigl, Fleda Jackson, Jared Carter, Gibbons Ruark, Jonathan Holden." circ. 350. 2/yr. Expects 2 issues 1999, 2 issues 2000. 5 titles listed in the *Small Press Record of Books in Print* (28th Edition, 1999-00). sub. price: $7/2 years; per copy: $3; sample: $1. 40pp; 6×9; of. Reporting time: 1-2 months. Payment: 2 copies of mag. Not copyrighted.

Yatra Publications/11:11 Studio, Kelli Bickman, Connie Bickman, PO Box 208, Old Chelsea Station, New York, NY 10113-0208, 212-260-9306; e-mail 1111@the-web-lab.com. 1996. "Arts, photography, obscure materials focusing on underground culture. Looking for unique, un-conventional ideas and images for 1997 high quality designed publication." avg. press run 2M-3M. Pub'd 2 titles 1998; expects 2 titles 1999, 3 titles 2000. avg. price, paper: $23.95. Discounts: 1-3 books 0%, 4-5 25%, 5-10 30%, 10-25 40%, 25+ 50%. 96pp; 8½×8½; of. Reporting time: 6 months. Simultaneous submissions accepted: yes. Publishes 2% of manuscripts submitted. Payment: copies. Copyrights for author.

Ye Galleon Press, Glen Adams, Owner; Susan Cardwell-Paulson, Manager-Editor; Teresa Ruggles, PO Box 287, Fairfield, WA 99012, 509-283-2422; E-mail galleon@mt.arias.net. 1937. Non-fiction. "Ye Galleon Press publishes rare re-prints, Oregon and California trail material; Northwest history, maritime, rare Americana, Native American titles, fur trade, and some poetry. We print quality non-fiction material and accept manuscripts although the quality must be high. We look for unpublished CA/OR trail accounts and all historic material. We have printed over 632 titles to date and prefer items of historic nature. Recent publications include *Boyden, Warrior of the Mist, Journal/Paul DeRue."* avg. press run 500-1M. Pub'd 37 titles 1998. 8 titles listed in the *Small Press Record of Books in Print* (28th Edition, 1999-00). avg. price, cloth: $10-$32; paper: $3.95-$15. Discounts: 10% libraries; trade 1 copy 25% or 2 or more of the same title 40%; 40% on 10 or more assorted singles. We accept returns with *no* time limit and no restocking charge. 5½×7½, 6×9, 7×10, 8½×11, 9×12; †of. Reporting time: 30 days. Publishes 10% of manuscripts submitted. Payment: few royalty deals. We can copyright for author. Pacific Northwest Book Publishers Association.

●**Ye Olde Font Shoppe,** Victoria Rivas, PO Box 8328, New Haven, CT 06530, e-mail yeolde@webcom.com; website www.webcom.com/yeolde. 1995. Poetry. "Chapbooks and perfect bound poetry books. Recent authors: Linda Lerner, A.D. Winana, Lynne Savitt, Tony Moffeit." avg. press run 500. Pub'd 8 titles 1998; expects 15 titles 1999, 30 titles 2000. avg. price, paper: $11; other: $5 Godiva books. Discounts: 40% off author and reseller. 40 and 80pp; 5½×8½; laser. Reporting time: 6-8 weeks. Simultaneous submissions accepted: no. Publishes 25% of manuscripts submitted. Payment: 10% of retail, once a year. Copyrights for author.

YE OLDE NEWES, Cy & Libby Stapleton, Po Box 151107, Lufkin, TX 75915-1107, 409-637-7475. 1981. "Magazine about the Scarborough Faire." circ. 30M. 1/yr. Pub'd 2 issues 1998; expects 1 issue 1999, 1 issue 2000. sub. price: $5; per copy: $4; sample: $5. Back issues: not available. 156pp; 8½×11; of. Reporting time: done in March each year. Simultaneous submissions accepted: yes. Publishes less than 5% of manuscripts submitted. Payment: none. Copyrighted, reverts to author. Ads: none accepted.

Years Press, F. Richard Thomas, Editor, Publisher; Leonora H. Smith, Associate Editor, Dept. of ATL, EBH, Michigan State Univ, E. Lansing, MI 48824-1033. 1973. Poetry. "Occasional publisher of chapbooks, usually solicited after hearing a reading. *Centering Magazine* has become a series of one-author chapbooks." avg. press run 300-400. Pub'd 1 title 1998; expects 1 title 1999, 1 title 2000. 8 titles listed in the *Small Press Record of Books in Print* (28th Edition, 1999-00). avg. price, paper: $5. 12-24pp; 7×8½; of. Reporting time: 1 month. Payment: 5 copies.

636

YEFIEF, Images For Media/Sesquin, Ann Racuya-Robbins, PO Box 8505, Santa Fe, NM 87504. 1992. Poetry, fiction, articles, art, photos, interviews, criticism, reviews, music, parts-of-novels, long-poems, collages, plays, concrete art, non-fiction. "Innovative, visionary work of all kinds. All submissions with SASE. Also publishes limited edition each year with original fine art print on cover" circ. 1.5M. 2/yr. Pub'd 1 issue 1998; expects 2 issues 1999, 2 issues 2000. sub. price: $24.95. Back issues: YEF 1 $19.95; YEF 2 $15.95; YEF 3 $19.95. Discounts: on request. 175pp; 8¼×10½. Reporting time: 8 weeks. Payment: 2 copies. Copyrighted, reverts to author. Pub's reviews: 0 in 1998. Ads: $250/$150/$75 1/4 page.

Yellow Moon Press, Robert B. Smyth, PO Box 381316, Cambridge, MA 02238-0001, 617-776-2230; Fax 617-776-8246; E-mail ymp@tiac.net; web site www.yellowmoon.com. 1978. Poetry, music, non-fiction. "Authors/Storytellers include: Coleman Barks, Robert Bly, Rafe Martin, Michael Meade, Elizabeth McKim, Lorraine Lee Hammond, Doug Lipman, Robert Smyth and Maggi Peirce. *Yellow Moon* is committed to publishing material related to the oral tradition. It is our goal to make available material that explores the history of the oral tradition while breathing new life into it." avg. press run varies with title. Pub'd 3 titles 1998; expects 3 titles 1999, 3-4 titles 2000. 42 titles listed in the *Small Press Record of Books in Print* (28th Edition, 1999-00). avg. price, cloth: $12.95; paper: $10.95; other: $9.95. Discounts: 1-4 copies 30%; 5+ 40%. 32-56pp; 6×9, 8½×11; of. Reporting time: 6-8 weeks. Simultaneous submissions accepted: no. Publishes 1% of manuscripts submitted. Payment: varies according to book. Copyrights for author.

YELLOW SILK: Journal Of Erotic Arts, verygraphics, Lily Pond, PO Box 6374, Albany, CA 94706, 510-644-4188. 1981. Poetry, fiction, art, photos, cartoons, satire, criticism, reviews, letters, parts-of-novels, long-poems, collages, non-fiction. "*Yellow Silk: Journal of Erotic Arts* is a international, prize-winning annual featuring fiction and poetry. Editorial policy: all persuasions; no brutality. 'Perhaps the most sensual magazine of literary erotica currently published,' The *Millennium Whole Earth Catalog* Readers write, 'What a gift your magazine is to married couples whose responsibilities make them forget each other.' Literary quality is equal in importance to erotic content. *Yellow Silk* has featured writing by Louise Erdrich, Galway Kinnell, Mary Oliver, Marge Piercy, Jane Hirshfield, Angela Carter, David Mamet, Robert Silverburg as well as many others. SASE. Name, address, phone on each page. Currently prefer work by established authors" 1/yr. Pub'd 4 issues 1998; expects 1 issue 1999, 1 issue 2000. sub. price: bookstores only; per copy: $14; sample: $7.50. Back issues: $7.50 (or more for rare ones). 300pp; 6×9; of. Reporting time: 3 months. Simultaneous submissions accepted: no. Publishes 1-2% of manuscripts submitted. Copyrighted, rights revert to author after 1 year except in case of anthology. CLMP.

Yes You Can Press, Mary Wilder, PO Box 337, Desert Hot Springs, CA 92240, 760-251-1103, fax 760-251-5064. 1989. Non-fiction. "We publish adult self-help books and specialize in belief systems. We are a highly specialized publishing company. We are not equipped to deal with unsolicited manuscripts." avg. press run 3M. Pub'd 2 titles 1998; expects 1 title 1999, 1 title 2000. 2 titles listed in the *Small Press Record of Books in Print* (28th Edition, 1999-00). avg. price, paper: $7.50. Discounts: 55% distributors; 40% trade; 40% on any order of 10 books. 100pp; 5½×8½; of. Payment: 7%.

YESTERDAY'S MAGAZETTE, Independent Publishing Co., Ned Burke, PO Box 18566, Sarasota, FL 34276, 914-924-3201; Fax 941-925-4468; E-mail ymagazette@aol.com. 1973. Poetry, fiction, articles, photos, interviews, letters, non-fiction. "Must be nostalgia-related—publish memories & believe that everyone has a yesterday. 1,000 word (max) usually. Departments include opinion, small talk, I Remember When..., comments from readers, quips & quotes, memories." circ. 6.5M. 6/yr. Pub'd 6 issues 1998; expects 6 issues 1999, 12 issues 2000. sub. price: $18; per copy: $3; sample: $3. Back issues: $2. Discounts: 50-100 $1/copy, 100-500 75¢/copy, 500+ 55¢/copy. 28pp; 8½×11; †of. Reporting time: 2-6 weeks. Payment: 1st choice story receives $10-$25, others contributors copies. Copyrighted, reverts to author. Pub's reviews: 2 in 1998. §nostalgia, biography, history, writing, writers' humor. Ads: $400/$200/$1 per word.

Yggdrasil Books, Alex Selkirk, Box 1098, Waldron Island, WA 98297, 206-738-6072. 1998. Fiction. "Our initial focus will be on short stories (though there is no size limitation). We are interested in work of enduring quality and relevance-work that will still be interesting in 100 years." avg. press run 5M. Expects 2-3 titles 2000. 1 title listed in the *Small Press Record of Books in Print* (28th Edition, 1999-00). avg. price, cloth: $45; paper: $15. Discounts: 35%; 55%; plus 5% cash discount. 150pp; 5×7½; of. Reporting time: 60 days. Simultaneous submissions accepted if notified. Payment: negotiable.

YOUNG VOICES, Four Seasons Publishing, Mark Shetterly, Gwen Anderson, PO Box 2321, Olympia, WA 98507, 360-357-4683, E-mail; patcha@holcyar.com. 1988. Poetry, fiction, articles, art, photos, cartoons, reviews, non-fiction. "Everything in *Young Voices* is written and drawn by children for people of all ages. Only those elementary through high school may submit work." circ. 3M. 6/yr. Pub'd 6 issues 1998; expects 6 issues 1999, 6 issues 2000. sub. price: $20; per copy: $4; sample: $4. Back issues: $2. Discounts: 50% wholesale. 32pp; 8½×11½. Reporting time: 6 weeks. Simultaneous submissions accepted: yes. Publishes 10% of manuscripts submitted. Payment: $3-$5. Copyrighted, reverts to author. Pub's reviews: 6-8 in 1998. §Books for children. Ads: $300/$160.

YOUR LIFE MATTERS, Greeson & Boyle, Inc., Janet Greeson, Eugene Boyle, 8058 Pinnacle Peak Avenue, Las Vegas, NV 89113, 702-222-1988. 1993. Articles, photos, interviews, letters, long-poems, news items, non-fiction. circ. 100M. 2/yr. Pub'd 2 issues 1998; expects 2 issues 1999, 2 issues 2000. 8½×11. Reporting time: 3 months. Ads: $2,100/$950. ABA, Audio Publishers Association.

Dan Youra Studios, Inc. (see also FERRY TRAVEL GUIDE), Dan Youra, PO Box 1169, Port Hadlock, WA 98339-1169. 1980. Articles, photos, non-fiction. "We are generally self-publishers. We do publish on a co-operative basis with others." avg. press run 50M. Pub'd 3 titles 1998; expects 3 titles 1999, 3 titles 2000. 1 title listed in the *Small Press Record of Books in Print* (28th Edition, 1999-00). avg. price, paper: $4.95; other: $1.95 magazines. Discounts: 3-12 40%, 13-50 45%, 51-150 50%, 151+ 55%. 128pp; 5½×8½; of. Reporting time: fast. Payment: varies, co-operative. Pacific NW Book Publishers, Northwest Magazine Publishers.

Youth Sports Press, Inc., 3433 Highway 190 #285, Mandeville, LA 70471, 888-444-4345; fax 504-727-2322. 1 title listed in the *Small Press Record of Books in Print* (28th Edition, 1999-00).

Yucca Tree Press, Janie Matson, 2130 Hixon Drive, Las Cruces, NM 88005-3305, 505-524-2357. 1987. Non-fiction. "Publishers of southwestern and military history, full-length books." avg. press run 1M-5M. Pub'd 4 titles 1998; expects 4 titles 1999, 3 titles 2000. 19 titles listed in the *Small Press Record of Books in Print* (28th Edition, 1999-00). avg. price, cloth: $18.95-$28.95; paper: $9.95-$19.95. Discounts: 20% libraries, 40% bookstores, 45%-55% distributors. 175-448pp; 6×9; commercial printers. Reporting time: 2-4 months. Simultaneous submissions accepted: yes. Publishes 20% of manuscripts submitted. Payment: on an individual basis, depending upon how much responsibility they take for promotion. Copyrights for author. Rocky Mountain Book Publishers Assoc. (RMBPA), Mountains & Plains Booksellers Assoc., New Mexico Book Assoc., SPAN.

YUMTZILOB: Tijdschrift over de Americas, Kees Nieuwland, General Editor, PO Box 32077, 2303 DB Leiden, The Netherlands, 31-10-4131960; FAX 31-10-4045357; E-mail yumtzilob@freemail.nl. 1988. Articles, photos, reviews. "Indigenous cultures and nations of North, Middle, and South America, including the Caribbean area, past and present; anthropology, archaeology, (art) history, linguistics. Written in English and Dutch; articles in other languages are translated in English." circ. 150. 4/yr. Pub'd 4 issues 1998; expects 4 issues 1999, 4 issues 2000. sub. price: $30 (including postal expenses); per copy: $8.50 (including postal expenses); sample: same. Back issues: same. 100pp; size A5; laser printer, xerox copy. Reporting time: receipt 2 weeks, acceptance 4 weeks. Simultaneous submissions accepted: yes. Publishes 90% of manuscripts submitted. Payment: 1 copy, 5 offprints (except reviews). Copyrighted, reverts to author. Pub's reviews: 4 in 1998. §Books, journals, exhibitions, films. Ads: $10/$5.

YUWITAYA LAKOTA, David Seals, 114 Hillcrest Drive, Rapid City, SD 57701-3656. 1991. Poetry, articles, art, photos, cartoons, interviews, reviews, news items, non-fiction. "Short informative journalism and well-written essays (1500 words maximum) about indigenous political and religious rights, based on the ancient Black Hills bioregionalism, buffalo economy, and the anti-American revolution into the next century." circ. 2M. 4/yr. Pub'd 4 issues 1998; expects 4 issues 1999, 4 issues 2000. sub. price: $4; per copy: $1. Back issues: free. 24pp; 8½×11; lp. Reporting time: 2 months. Payment: none. Copyrighted, reverts to author. Pub's reviews: 3 in 1998. §Indians, bioregionalism, revolutionary. No ads.

Z

Z MAGAZINE, Lydia Sargent, Editor; Eric Sargent, Editor, 18 Millfield Street, Woods Hole, MA 02543, 508-548-9063; Fax 508-457-0626; Lydia.sargent@lbbs.org. 1988. Articles, art, photos, cartoons, interviews, satire, criticism, reviews, music, letters, news items, non-fiction. "Length of material: 700-4,000 words." circ. 22M. 11/yr. Pub'd 11 issues 1998; expects 11 issues 1999, 11 issues 2000. sub. price: $26; per copy: $5; sample: $4. Back issues: $5. Discounts: jobber 50%. 64pp; 8×10¾; lp. Reporting time: 6-8 weeks. We accept simultaneous submissions, but we don't like it. Publishes 33% of manuscripts submitted. Payment: yes, month following issue it appears in. Copyrighted, reverts to author. Pub's reviews: 12+ in 1998. Ads: free at our discretion.

Z W L Publishing, Inc., Bettye Pierce Zoller, Founder, Principal Owner & CEO; Hugh Lampman, Marketing, Promotion, Principal & President; Scott Blackman, Marketing Director, PO Box 7991, Dallas, TX 75209, 214-638-TALK (8255), fax 214-631-1476, e-Mail ZWLPUB@AOL.COM, 800-206-5384; for on-line magazine http://www.zwlpub.com. 1994. "We are *audiobook* publishers, consultants, authors, readers. We produce audiobooks, audio projects of all kinds including radio/t.v. commercials." avg. press run 5M-7.5M. Pub'd 2 titles 1998; expects 2 titles 1999, 3 titles 2000. 11 titles listed in the *Small Press Record of Books in*

Print (28th Edition, 1999-00). avg. price, paper: $24.95; other: $16.95. Discounts: 40% book retailers, discounts on quantities. 180pp; 8½×5¾; of/audiobooks. Reporting time: 3 months. We accept simultaneous submissions for non-fiction only. Publishes a variable % of manuscripts submitted. Payment: varies. Copyrights for author. APA, ABA, Broadcast Education Assoc.

Zagier & Urruty Publicaciones (see also ETICA & CIENCIA; FISICA; TIERRA DEL FUEGO MAGAZINE), Sergio Zagier, Dario Urruty, PO Box 94 Sucursal 19, Buenos Aires 1419, Argentina, 541-572-1050. 1985. Articles, photos, reviews, letters, news items, non-fiction. "We publish basically about travel and tourism (books, maps, guides, magazines) and about science. Manuscripts about traveling through South America and Antarctica are welcome. Spanish, English, German and French. We also are interested in photographies travel and adventour-oriented. Any length of manuscripts are considered." avg. press run 5M. Pub'd 6 titles 1998; expects 6 titles 1999, 12 titles 2000. 9 titles listed in the *Small Press Record of Books in Print* (28th Edition, 1999-00). avg. price, cloth: $20; paper: $15; other: $5 magazines. Discounts: 50% distributor, 30% bookstores, 20% travel companies. 128pp; 6×8; of. Reporting time: 6 weeks. Payment: on an individual basis depending on the kind of work. Copyrights for author.

Paul Zelevansky, Lynn Zelevansky, Paul Zelevansky, 1455 Clairidge Drive, Beverly Hills, CA 90210-2214. 1975. "Material used: work that mixes visual and verbal forms." avg. press run 500-1M. Pub'd 1 title 1998; expects 1 title 1999, 1 title 2000. 8 titles listed in the *Small Press Record of Books in Print* (28th Edition, 1999-00). avg. price, cloth: $20; paper: $9. Discounts: bookstores 40%. 80pp; 8½×11; of. Author has copyright of work; we have copyright of book.

Zephyr Press, J. Kates, Leora Zeitlin, 50 Kenwood Street, Brookline, MA 02446, 617-713-2813. 1980. Poetry, fiction, non-fiction. "We publish literary fiction, non-fiction and poetry, with an emphasis on contemporary Russian and Slavic literature in translation. We do not read unsolicited manuscripts, but will consider a query (must include a brief summary of publications and professional credits, and a sample of the proposed work no longer than 10 pages)." avg. press run 2-3M. Expects 2 titles 1999, 2 titles 2000. 12 titles listed in the *Small Press Record of Books in Print* (28th Edition, 1999-00). avg. price, cloth: $25; paper: $15.95. Discounts: trade 30%; libaries and individuals 20% if pre-paid; distributed by LPC, 800-626-4330. 300pp; 6×9; of. Reporting time: 2-12 weeks. Simultaneous submissions accepted: yes. Payment: 10-12% of publisher's net. Copyrights for author. CLMP, SPAN, American Assoc. for Advancement of Slavic Studies.

ZERO HOUR, Zero Hour Publishing, Jim Jones, PO Box 766, Seattle, WA 98111, 206-323-3648. 1988. Poetry, fiction, articles, art, photos, cartoons, interviews, satire, reviews, music, letters, news items, non-fiction. "*ZH* is a magazine devoted to popular culture: religion, literature, sex, music; in tabloid form. Contributions should be 1,500 words or less." circ. 3M. 3/yr. Expects 3 issues 1999, 3 issues 2000. price per copy: $4; sample: $4. Discounts: $1.50 per issue for distributors who take over 25 copies; $2 per copy for orders less than 25. 48pp; 10×16; web press. Payment: 5 copies of magazine or free 1/4 page ad. Copyrighted, reverts to author. Pub's reviews. §The occult, subculture, music, literature, sociology. Ads: $200/$120/$80 1/4 page/$40 1/8. Small Press Alliance.

Zero Hour Publishing (see also ZERO HOUR), Jim Jones, Alice Wheeler, PO Box 766, Seattle, WA 98111, 206-282-5712. 1987. Fiction, photos. "We're looking for short fiction and novels which deal with American subcultures - our motto is 'where culture meets crime.' Authors published: Steven Jesse Bernstein, Rebecca Brown, Denise Ohio" avg. press run 5M. Pub'd 1 title 1998; expects 2 titles 1999, 3 titles 2000. 3 titles listed in the *Small Press Record of Books in Print* (28th Edition, 1999-00). avg. price, paper: $12.95. Discounts: 40% for orders of 10 or more. 225pp. Reporting time: 2 months. Publishes 4% of manuscripts submitted. Payment: $25 for short fiction, $650 for novels. Does not copyright for author.

ZerOX Books (see also UNMUZZLED OX), Michael Andre, 105 Hudson Street, #311, New York, NY 10013. 1971. "ZerOx Books is an occasional imprint of Unmuzzled Ox Books." avg. press run 105. 6 titles listed in the *Small Press Record of Books in Print* (28th Edition, 1999-00). avg. price, other: $25. 8½×11; xerox.

Zerx Press, Mark Weber, 725 Van Buren Place SE, Albuquerque, NM 87108. 1983. Poetry, fiction, art, photos. "46 chapbooks since 1983. Contributors: Gerald Locklin, Judson Crews, Todd Moore, Ann Menebroker, Ron Androla, Hugh Fox, Kurt Nimmo, Kell Robertson, Cheryl Townsend, and Brent Leake. Am not really in the market financially for unsolicited mss." avg. press run 200-500. Pub'd 5 titles 1998; expects 6 titles 1999, 2+ titles 2000. 11 titles listed in the *Small Press Record of Books in Print* (28th Edition, 1999-00). avg. price, other: $3 chapbook. 44pp; 5½×8½; of, photocopy. Reporting time: less than a week. Payment: we've never made back initial printing costs but think it'd be like 10% or 15% after 1000 sold; author usually gets 25-35 copies and is able to buy extra at Zerx cost. Copyrights for author.

Zino Press Children's Books, Liza DiPrima, PO Box 52, Madison, WI 53701, 608-836-6660; Fax 608-831-1570; zinoguy@ku.com. 1994. Art, long-poems. "We publish rhyming children's books and multicultural books for children." avg. press run 5M. Pub'd 3 titles 1998; expects 2 titles 1999, 2 titles 2000.

avg. price, cloth: $15; paper: $12. Discounts: 50% to booksellers, 40% to libraries, 20% to schools. 32pp; 8×10; of. Reporting time: 3 months or more. Simultaneous submissions accepted: yes. Publishes less than 1% of manuscripts submitted. Payment: varies. Copyrights for author. ABA, ALA, UMBA, WLA, CCBC.

ZOETROPE: All-Story, Adrienne Brodeur, Editor-in-Chief; Samantha Schnee, Managing Editor, 260 Fifth Avenue, Suite 1200, New York, NY 10001, 212-696-5720; www.zoetrope-stories.com. 1997. Fiction, plays. "Short stories and one-act plays under 7,000 words. We no not accept manuscripts from June 1 to August 31. Submissions must be accompanied by an SASE. Recent contributors: Gabriel Gancia Marquez, David Mamet, Melissa Bank, Dale Peck." circ. 40M. 4/yr. Pub'd 3 issues 1998; expects 4 issues 1999, 4 issues 2000. sub. price: $20; per copy: $5; sample: $5 with SASE with $1.50 p/h. 56pp; 10½×14. Reporting time: 5 months. Simultaneous submissions accepted: yes. Publishes .05% of manuscripts submitted. Payment: $1,200 and 5 copies of magazine. Copyrighted, we buy 1st serial rights. Ads: $5,000 full page with discount of 10% with annual program.

Zoland Books, Roland F. Pease, Jr., Publisher & Editor, 384 Huron Avenue, Cambridge, MA 02138, 617-864-6252; FAX 617-661-4998. 1987. Poetry, fiction, art, photos, criticism, non-fiction. avg. press run 3M. Pub'd 10 titles 1998; expects 12 titles 1999, 15 titles 2000. 54 titles listed in the *Small Press Record of Books in Print* (28th Edition, 1999-00). avg. price, cloth: $20; paper: $14.95. Discounts: trade 5/40%. 168pp; size varies; acid-free paper, of. Reporting time: 3-6 months. Payment: varies. Copyrights for author.

Zombie Logic Press (see also ZOMBIE LOGIC REVIEW), Thomas L. Vaultonburg, 420 E. 3rd Street Box 319, Byron, IL 61010, email Dobe 1969@aol.com. 1997. Poetry. "I want to discover and publish the great poets of the 21st century. Blow me away and I'll publish your book. I'm especially interested in doing the first work of a great poet." avg. press run 1M. Pub'd 1 title 1998; expects 1 title 1999, 1 title 2000. 1 title listed in the *Small Press Record of Books in Print* (28th Edition, 1999-00). avg. price, paper: $6. Discounts: 40%. 70pp; 5½×8; of. Reporting time: 2 weeks. Simultaneous submissions accepted: yes. Publishes 1% of manuscripts submitted. Payment: 10% of press run. Copyrights for author.

●**ZOMBIE LOGIC REVIEW, Zombie Logic Press,** Thomas L. Vaultonburg, 420 E. Third Street, Box 319, Byron, IL 61010, website http://members.aol.com/dobe1968/page/index.htm. 1997. Poetry, fiction, reviews. "I'm especially interested in publishing younger, emerging poets." circ. 500. 1/yr. Expects 1 issue 1999, 1 issue 2000. price per copy: $6; sample: $6. Discounts: 50% off cover. 100pp; of. Reporting time: 2 weeks. Simultaneous submissions accepted: yes. Publishes 5% of manuscripts submitted. Payment: contributors copy. Copyrighted, reverts to author. Pub's reviews. §Poets may send their books for review consideration.

Zon International Publishing Co., William Manns, PO Box 6459, Santa Fe, NM 87502, 505-995-0102, Fax 505-995-0103; e-mail zon@nets.com. 1985. Art. avg. press run 15M. Pub'd 1 title 1998; expects 3 titles 1999, 6 titles 2000. 3 titles listed in the *Small Press Record of Books in Print* (28th Edition, 1999-00). avg. price, cloth: $45. Discounts: 1 copy 33%, 4-9 40%, 10-49 45%, 50+ 50%. 250pp; 9×12; of. Publishes almost 0% of manuscripts submitted. Payment: flat fee and royalty. Does not copyright for author. ABA, RMBA.

ZONE, Zone Books, Sanford Kwinter, Michel Feher, Hal Foster, Jonathan Crary, 611 Broadway, Suite 608, New York, NY 10012, 212-529-5674, fax 212-260-4572, e-mail urzone@aol.com. 1985. Articles, art, photos, non-fiction. "*Zone* explores critical developments in modern culture. Each issue examines a single theme from a transdisciplinary perspective, with texts on art, literature, economics, history and philosophy, as well as photographic essays, historical and technical dossiers, artists projects and formal questionnaires. The theme of the first issue was the contemporary city. Future issues will explore the human body and technology, pragmatics, the global West, politics and time." circ. 7M. 0/yr. sub. price: varies; per copy: varies; sample: varies. Back issues: vary. Discounts: sold to trade through The MIT Press. 450pp; 7¼×9¼. Copyrighted, rights reverting to author varies.

Zone Books (see also ZONE), Jonathan Crary, Michel Feher, Sanford Kwinter, Ramona Naddaff, 611 Broadway, Suite 608, New York, NY 10012, 212-529-5674, fax 212-260-4572, e-mail urzone@aol.com. 1985. Articles, art, photos, non-fiction. avg. press run 4M. Pub'd 6 titles 1998; expects 8 titles 1999, 8 titles 2000. 47 titles listed in the *Small Press Record of Books in Print* (28th Edition, 1999-00). avg. price, cloth: $45; paper: $25. Discounts: distributed by The MIT Press, contact MIT sales department, 1-800-356-0343. Pages vary; 6×9. Payment: negotiated. Copyrights for author.

ZONE 3, Malcolm Glass, David Till, Barry Kitterman, PO Box 4565, Austin Peay State University, Clarksville, TN 37044, 931-221-7031/7891. 1986. Poetry. "*Zone 3* is a poetry and fiction journal published in Tennessee but seeking submissions and readership nationwide and beyond. For title, see the planting zone map on back of seed package. Editors want poems that are deeply rooted in place, mind, heart, experience, rage, imagination, laughter, etc. Published fall/winter and spring/summer. Submissions deadlines: Jan. 1 and July 1. First 17 issues include work by Bruchac, Etter, Speer, Struthers, Orr, Fincke, Burkard, deCourcy, Kloefkorn, Stafford, Budy, Nameroff, Bowers, and Hey." circ. 1M. 2/yr. Pub'd 2 issues 1998; expects 2 issues 1999, 2 issues 2000. sub. price: $8/yr, $10 to libraries & institutions; per copy: $4; sample: $4. Back issues: $5.

Discounts: 33%. 70pp; 6×9; of. Reporting time: 1-5 months after deadline date. Payment: copies. Copyrighted, reverts to author. Pub's reviews. §Poetry and fiction.

Zookeeper Publications, Allan Falk, Jacqueline DeRouin, 2010 Cimarron Drive, Okemos, MI 48864-3908, 517-347-4697. 1991. Non-fiction. avg. press run 1.5M. Pub'd 3 titles 1998; expects 2 titles 1999. 7 titles listed in the *Small Press Record of Books in Print* (28th Edition, 1999-00). avg. price, paper: $10-14. Discounts: 50% wholesale, 40% consignment. 165-240pp; 5½×8½, 8½×11; of. Reporting time: 1 month. Payment: negotiable; principally self-funded. Copyrights for author.

ZUZU'S PETALS: QUARTERLY ONLINE, T. Dunn, Poetry Editor; Douglas Du Cap, Fiction Editor, PO Box 4853, Ithaca, NY 14852-4853, e-mail zuzu@zuzu.com Web Site http://www.zuzu.com. 1992. Poetry, fiction, articles, art, cartoons, satire, criticism, reviews, parts-of-novels, collages, concrete art, non-fiction. "High quality non-pretentious art. We provide a showcase for some of America's finest writing and publish talented and relatively undiscovered writers. No sing song verse or amateur stuff please. We also run a poetry contest which helps fund the publication of our magazine. Write for guidelines. We are proudly ad-free. *Library Journal* calls us 'An exciting new little.'" circ. unlimited. 4/yr. Pub'd 4 issues 1998; expects 4 issues 1999, 4 issues 2000. price per copy: Availible on the World Wide Web; sample: $5 for our print poetry sample. 200pp; HTML. Reporting time: 2 weeks - 2 months. Simultaneous submissions accepted: yes. Publishes 5% of manuscripts submitted. Payment: none, the magazine is free through the net. Copyrighted, reverts to author. Pub's reviews: 40+ in 1998. §Poetry, literary fiction, sociology, biography.

ZYX, Phrygian Press, Arnold Skemer, 58-09 205th Street, Bayside, NY 11364. 1990. Criticism, reviews. "Essays and commentary on innovative/experimental fiction. We are interested in tendencies in avant-garde fiction, useful techniques and stratagems that a fictioneer can avail himself of, author resources (self-publishing, technological changes and publishing empowerment). Some reviews. Accepting original fiction, but make it compact, ideally 1-2 pages. Poetry accepted. Recent contributors: Richard Kostelanetz, Andy diMichele, Spencer Shelby, Sheila Murphy, Jacques Debrot, Greg Bachar, Gregory Vincent St. Thomasino, Alan Catlin, Bob Grumman, Guy Beining, Ficus Strangulensis, John Grey, John M. Bennett, Mark Sonnenfeld, Arnold Falleder, B.Z. Niditch, Jonathan Brannen, Stanley Berne." circ. 333. 2/yr. Pub'd 3 issues 1998; expects 2 issues 1999, 2 issues 2000. price per copy: gratis; send return postage appropriate for 33¢, 55¢, etc; sample: gratis; send return postage appropriate 33¢, 55¢, etc. Back issues: gratis; send return postage appropriate 33¢, 55¢, etc. 9pp; 8½×11; †Xerography. Reporting time: 4-5 months. Simultaneous submissions accepted: no. Payment: copies. Copyrighted, reverts to author. Pub's reviews: 0 in 1998. §Innovative fiction and criticism.

ZYZZYVA, Howard Junker, Editor; Will Rose, Managing Editor, 41 Sutter Street, Suite 1400, San Francisco, CA 94104. 1985. Poetry, fiction, art, photos, satire, letters, concrete art. "West Coast writers only. SASE. ISSN 8756-5633." circ. 4M. 3/yr. Pub'd 3 issues 1998; expects 3 issues 1999, 3 issues 2000. sub. price: $27; per copy: $9; sample: $10. 192pp; 6×9; of. Reporting time: prompt. Simultaneous submissions accepted: no. Publishes 1% of manuscripts submitted. Payment: $50. Copyrighted, reverts to author. Ads: $500/$300/$200 1/4 page. CLMP.

Regional Index

ALABAMA

ALTERNATIVE HARMONIES LITERARY & ARTS MAGAZINE, 1830 Marvel Road, Brierfield, AL 35035, 205-665-7904; fax 205-665-2500; e-mail wytrabbit1@aol.com
New Dawn Unlimited, 1830 Marvel Road, Brierfield, AL 35035, 205-665-7904; fax 205-665-2500; e-mail wytrabbit1@aol.com
Doctor Jazz Press, 119 Pintail Drive, Pelham, AL 35124, 205-663-3403
Druid Press, 2724 Shades Crest Road, Birmingham, AL 35216, 205-967-6580
Menasha Ridge Press, 700 S. 28th Street, Suite 206, Birmingham, AL 35233, 800-247-9437; e-mail bzehmer@menasharidge.com
AURA LITERARY/ARTS REVIEW, Box 76, University Center, Birmingham, AL 35294, 205-934-3216
BIRMINGHAM POETRY REVIEW, English Department, University of Alabama-Birmingham, Birmingham, AL 35294, 205-934-8573
Story County Books, PO Box 21179, Tuscaloosa, AL 35402-1179
DREAMS AND NIGHTMARES, 1300 Kicker Road, Tuscaloosa, AL 35404, 205-553-2284; e-Mail dragontea@earthlink.net
KID'S WORLD, 1300 Kicker Road, Tuscaloosa, AL 35404, 205-553-2284
ALABAMA REVIEW, 1306 Overlook Road, N, Tuscaloosa, AL 35406-2176
Livingston Press, Station 22, University of West Alabama, Livingston, AL 35470
Swallow's Tale Press, c/o LU Press, Station 22, University of West Alabama, Livingston, AL 35470
THE BLACK WARRIOR REVIEW, PO Box 862936, University of Alabama, Tuscaloosa, AL 35486-0027, 205-348-4518
Doone Publications, 7950 Hwy 72 W. #G106, Madison, AL 35758
FPMI Communications, Inc., 707 Fiber Street NW, Huntsville, AL 35801-5833, 256-539-1850
Catamount Press, 2519 Roland Road SW, Huntsville, AL 35805, 205-536-9801
COTYLEDON, 2519 Roland Road SW, Huntsville, AL 35805, 205-536-9801
Huntsville Literary Association, c/o English Department, University of Alabama, Huntsville, AL 35899
POEM, c/o English Department, University of Alabama, Huntsville, AL 35899
LAUREATE LETTER, 899 Williamson Trail, Eclectic, AL 36024
Trouvere Company, 899 Williamson Trail, Eclectic, AL 36024-6131
WRITERS GAZETTE, 899 Williamson Trail, Eclectic, AL 36024-6131
ALABAMA LITERARY REVIEW, Smith 253, Troy State University, Troy, AL 36082, 334-670-3307;FAX 334-670-3519
Elliott & Clark Publishing, PO Box 551, Montgomery, AL 36101-0551, 334-265-6753
NEGATIVE CAPABILITY, 62 Ridgelawn Drive East, Mobile, AL 36608, 205-460-6146
Negative Capability Press, 62 Ridgelawn Drive East, Mobile, AL 36608, 334-460-6146
GCT Inc., PO Box 6448, Mobile, AL 36660, 334-478-4700
Factor Press, PO Box 8888, Mobile, AL 36689, 334-380-0606
NIGHTLORE, PO Box 81482, Mobile, AL 36689, Email trevorelm@aol.com
RIVERSIDE QUARTERLY, 1101 Washington Street, Marion, AL 36756-3213
BEYOND DOGGEREL, 1141 Knollwood Court, Auburn, AL 36830-6126, e-mail feild@mindspring.com
SOUTHERN HUMANITIES REVIEW, 9088 Haley Center, Auburn Univ., Auburn, AL 36849, 334-844-9088

ALASKA

Alaska Northwest Books, 203 West 15th Avenue, Ste. 108, Anchorage, AK 99501-5128, 907-278-8838
ALASKA QUARTERLY REVIEW, University of Alaska-Anchorage, 3211 Providence Drive, Anchorage, AK 99508, 907-786-6916
Intertext, 2633 East 17th Avenue, Anchorage, AK 99508-3207
Alaska Geographic Society, PO Box 93370, Anchorage, AK 99509, 907-562-0164, Fax 907-562-0479, e-mail akgeo@aol.com
MOOSE BOUND PRESS JOURNAL/NEWSLETTER, PO Box 111781, Anchorage, AK 99511-1781, 907-333-1465 phone/FAX e-mail mbpress@alaska.net; Website http://www.alaska.net/~mbpress
Sedna Press, 5522 Cope Street, Anchorage, AK 99518, 907-562-7835
Fathom Publishing Co., PO Box 200448, Anchorage, AK 99520-0448, 907-272-3305
Circumpolar Press, Box 221955, Anchorage, AK 99522, 907-248-7323
NORTHERN PILOT, PO Box 220168, Anchorage, AK 99522, 907-258-6898; Fax 907-258-4354; info@northernpilot.com
Salmon Run Press, PO Box 672130, Chugiak, AK 99567-2130, 907-688-4268
Wizard Works, PO Box 1125, Homer, AK 99603, 907-235-8157; Fax 907-399-1834
JOURNAL OF ALASKA WOMEN, HCR 64 Box 453, Seward, AK 99664, 907-288-3168
Fireweed Press, PO Box 75418, Fairbanks, AK 99707-2136, 907-452-5070 or 907-488-5079
Vanessapress, PO Box 82761, Fairbanks, AK 99708, 907-488-5079; jrb@mosquitonet.com
Windsong Press, PO Box 644, Delta Jct., AK 99737, 907-895-4179
Alaska Native Language Center, University of Alaska, PO Box 757680, Fairbanks, AK 99775-7680, 907-474-7874, fax 907-474-6586
EXPLORATIONS, English Dept., Alaska Univ. Southeast, 11120 Glacier Highway, Juneau, AK 99801
The Denali Press, PO Box 021535, Juneau, AK 99802, 907-586-6014; FAX 907-463-6780; e-mail denalipr@alaska.net

ARIZONA

HEARTSONG REVIEW, 1835 North 50th Street #20, Phoenix, AZ 85008-4242
Primer Publishers, 4738 N. Central, Phoenix, AZ 85012, 602-234-1574
Integra Press, 1702 W. Camelback Road, Suite 119, Phoenix, AZ 85015, 602-996-2106; Fax 602-953-1552; info@integra.com
Turtle Island Press, Inc., 3104 E. Camelback Road, Suite 614, Phoenix, AZ 85016, 602-468-1141; orders 888-432-5362; fax 602-954-8560; info@turtleislandpress.com; www.turtleislandpress.com
Wolf-Wise Press, 12235 N. Cave Creek, Suite 6, Phoenix, AZ 85022, 602-493-9383; FAX 602-482-0668

WorkLife Publishing, 4532 E Grandview Road, Phoenix, AZ 85032, 602-992-0144
Arizona Master Gardener Press, 4341 E. Broadway Road, Phoenix, AZ 85040-8807, 602-470-8086 ext. 312, FAX 602-470-8092
Marinelli Publishing, 8129 N 35th Avenue, #134, Phoenix, AZ 85051-5892, 800-NEED-A-PI
Hunter Publishing, Co., P.O. Bcx 9533, Phoenix, AZ 85068, 602-944-1022
CPG Publishing Company, PO Box 50062, Phoenix, AZ 85076, 800-578-5549
Blue Bird Publishing, 2266 S. Dobson #275, Mesa, AZ 85202, 602-831-6063
PEACE, The Magazine of the Sixties, 2753 E. Broadway, 5101-1969, Mesa, AZ 85204, 602-817-0124
NEW THOUGHT, International New Thought Alliance, 5003 East Broadway Road, Mesa, AZ 85206, 602-830-2461
Pussywillow Publishing House, Inc., 621 Leisure World, Mesa, AZ 85206-3133
CHASQUI, Dept of Languages and Literature, Arizona State University, Tempe, AZ 85207-0202
La Casa Press, PO Box 3297-RB, Casa Grande, AZ 85222, 1-877-8LA-CASA; Fax 520-723-9002; lacasapress@hotmail.com
Olde & Oppenheim Publishers, 3219 North Margate Place, Chandler, AZ 85224-1051, 480-839-2280
WillowBrook Publishing, PO Box 2606, Chandler, AZ 85224, 602-821-5222
Five Star Publications, 4696 West Tyson Street #D, Chandler, AZ 85226-2903
Sonoran Publishing, 116 North Roosevelt, Suite 121, Chandler, AZ 85226, 602-961-5176
SINGLE SCENE, 7432 East Diamond, Scottsdale, AZ 85257, 602-945-6746
BGB Press, Inc., 14545 N. Frank Lloyd Wright Blvd., Suite 276, Scottsdale, AZ 85260, www.home.earthlink.net/~bgbpress
THE PANNUS INDEX, 14545 N. Frank Lloyd Wright Blvd. #276, Scottsdale, AZ 85260-8805, 413-584-4776; Fax 413-584-5674; www.javanet.com/~stout/pannus
EMERGING, PO Box 12009-418, Scottsdale, AZ 85267, 480-948-1800; FAX 480-948-1870; E-mail teleosinst@aol.com
FOREVER ALIVE, PO Box 12305, Scottsdale, AZ 85267-2305, 602-922-0300; fax 602-922-0800; e-Mail HERBBOWIE@AOL.COM
LP Publications (Teleos Institute), PO Box 12009-418, Scottsdale, AZ 85267, 480-948-1800; FAX 480-948-1870
Self Healing Press, PO Box 13837, Scottsdale, AZ 85267, 602-998-1041
AMERICAN AMATEUR JOURNALIST, P.O.Box 18117, Fountain Hills, AZ 85269
BEHIND BARS, PO Box 2975, Tempe, AZ 85280-2975
New Falcon Publications, 1739 E. Broadway Road, Suite 1-277, Tempe, AZ 85282
Aspire Publishing Company, 1008 E. Baseline Road #878, Tempe, AZ 85283, 602-225-1447
BRB Publications, Inc., PO Box 27869, Tempe, AZ 85285-7869, 800-929-3811; Fax 800-929-4981; brb@brbpub.com
Facts on Demand Press, PO Box 27869, Tempe, AZ 85285-7869, 800-929-3811; Fax 800-929-4981; brb@brbpub.com
Four Peaks Press, PO Box 27401, Tempe, AZ 85285, 602-838-8726
Bilingual Review/Press, Hispanic Research Center, Arizona State Univ., Box 872702, Tempe, AZ 85287-2702, 602-965-3867
BILINGUAL REVIEW/Revista Bilingue, Hispanic Research Center, Arizona State Univ., Box 872702, Tempe, AZ 85287-2702, 602-965-3867
HAYDEN'S FERRY REVIEW, Box 871502, Arizona State University, Tempe, AZ 85287-1502, 602-965-1243
PSYCHOLOGY OF WOMEN QUARTERLY, Psychology Department, Box 871104, Arizona State University, Tempe, AZ 85287-1104
Square Peg Press, PO Box 2194, Gilbert, AZ 85299, Fax 602-813-2621; E-mail reunion@primenet.com
FLASHPOINT: Military Books Reviewed by Military Professionals, 5820 W. Peoria, Suite 107-54, Glendale, AZ 85302, 602-842-1726
Tal San Publishing/Distributors, 7614 W. Bluefield Avenue, Glendale, AZ 85308, 602-843-1119; fax 602-843-3080
Shann Press, PO Box 524, Wickenburg, AZ 85358, 520-684-9142; Fax 520-684-0202; E-mail jbarj@primenet.com
THE CARETAKER GAZETTE, P.O. Box 5887, Carefree, AZ 85377-5887, 480-488-1970
IGNIS FATUUS REVIEW, 18 Yuma Trail, Bisbee, AZ 85603
Tortilla Press, 8 S. Cactus Lane, Bisbee, AZ 85603, 602-432-7040
Holbrook Street Press, PO Box 399, Cortaro, AZ 85652-0399, 520-616-7643; fax 520-616-7519; holbrookstpress@theriver.com; www.copshock.com
See Sharp Press, PO Box 1731, Tucson, AZ 85702-1731, 520-628-8720; Fax 520-628-8720; seesharp@earthlink.net; home.earthlink.net/~seesharp
Treasure Chest Books LLC, PO Box 5250, Tucson, AZ 85703, 520-623-9558
Ravenhawk Books, 7739 E. Broadway Boulevard #95, Tucson, AZ 85710, 520-886-9885; fax 520-886-9885; e-mail 76673.3165@compuserve.com
CONTACT!, 2900 East Weymouth, Tucson, AZ 85716-1249, 602-881-2232
Microdex Bookshelf, 1212 N. Sawtelle, Suite 120, Tucson, AZ 85716, 520-326-3502
Lester Street Publishing, PO Box 41484, Tucson, AZ 85717-1484, phone and fax 520-326-0104; e-mail wzucker@compuserve.com
SONORA REVIEW, Dept. of English, University of Arizona, Tucson, AZ 85721, 520-626-8383
THE MATCH, PO Box 3488, Tucson, AZ 85722
NEWSLETTER INAGO, Inago Press, PO Box 26244, Tucson, AZ 85726-6244, 520-294-7031
Galen Press, Ltd., PO Box 64400, Tucson, AZ 85728-4400, 520-577-8363; fax 520-529-6459
MESSAGES FROM THE HEART, PO Box 64840, Tucson, AZ 85728, 520-577-0588; Fax 520-529-9657; e-mail lbsmith@theriver.com
Dream Street Publishing, PO Box 19028, Tucson, AZ 85731, 520-733-9695; Fax 520-529-3911
Burning Cities Press, PO Box 13746, Tucson, AZ 85732-3746
VIETNAM GENERATION: A Journal of Recent History and Contemporary Issues, PO Box 13746, Tucson, AZ 85732-3746
Javelina Books, PO Box 42131, Tucson, AZ 85733
Fisher Books, 5225 W. Massingale Road, Tucson, AZ 85743-8416, 520-744-6110; Fax 520-744-0944
The Patrice Press, PO Box 85639, Tucson, AZ 85754-5639, 602-882-0906; FAX 602-882-4161
XIZQUIL, Blue Route, Box 90, Blue, AZ 85922
THIN AIR, PO Box 23549, Flagstaff, AZ 86002, www.nau.edu/~english/thinair/taframes.html
Salina Bookshelf, 10250 Palomino Road, Flagstaff, AZ 86004, 520-527-0070; Fax 520-526-0386
Hohm Press, PO Box 2501, Prescott, AZ 86302, 520-778-9189; Fax 520-717-1779; e-mail pinedr@goodnet.com; www.booknotes.com/hohm/
Cosmoenergetics Publications, PO Box 12011, Prescott, AZ 86304-2011, 520-778-0867

Blacksmith Corporation, PO Box 1752, Chino Valley, AZ 86323, 520-636-4456; Fax 520-636-4457
THE LAS VEGAS INSIDER, Good 'n' Lucky, PO Box 1185, Chino Valley, AZ 86323-1185
New Vision Publishing, 252 Roadrunner Drive, Sedona, AZ 86336, 520-282-7400; fax 520-282-0054; E-mail nvp@sedona.net
SARU Press International, 3 Pine Terrace, 559 Jordan Road, Sedona, AZ 86336-4143
Little Buckaroo Press, PO Box 3016, West Sedona, AZ 86340, 602-282-6278
In Print Publishing, PO Box 20765, Sedona, AZ 86341, 520-284-5298; Fax 520-284-5283

ARKANSAS

Cedar Hill Publications, 3722 Highway 8 West, Mena, AR 71953, 501-394-7029
CEDAR HILL REVIEW, 3722 Highway 8 West, Mena, AR 71953, 501-394-7029
Monitor Publications AR, 3856 Highway 88 East, Mena, AR 71953, 501-394-7893; Internet: 74353.2767@compu-serve.com
Lancer Militaria, Box 1188, Mt. Ida, AR 71957-1188, 870-867-2232; www.warbooks.com
SLANT: A Journal of Poetry, University of Central Arkansas, PO Box 5063, Conway, AR 72035-5000, 501-450-5107
Heron Press, 14 Roberts Drive, Mayflower, AR 72106, 501-470-3946; Fax 501-470-1998; E-mail heron@ipa.net
Silver Dollar Press, 2301 Division #712, North Little Rock, AR 72114, 501-834-4099
CRAZYHORSE, 2801 S. University, Dept. of English, Univ. of Arkansas-Little Rock, Little Rock, AR 72204, 501-569-3161
PLAY THE ODDS, 11614 Ashwood, Little Rock, AR 72211, 501-224-9452
Bradley Publishing, 15 Butterfield Lane, Little Rock, AR 72212, 501-224-0692; FAX 501-224-0762; 76503.1622@compu-serve.com
Rose Publishing Co., 2723 Foxcroft Road, #208, Little Rock, AR 72227-6513, 501-227-8104; Fax 501-227-8338
VOICES INTERNATIONAL, 1115 Gillette Drive, Little Rock, AR 72227, 501-225-0166
AQUATERRA, METAECOLOGY & CULTURE, 5473 Highway 23N, Eureka Springs, AR 72631
Bearhouse Publishing, 398 Mundell Rd., Eureka Springs, AR 72631-9505, 501-253-9351, E-mail tbadger@ipa.net
LUCIDITY, 398 Mundell Rd., Eureka Springs, AR 72631-9505, 501-253-9351; E-mail tbadger@ipa.net
Star Publications, PO Box 2144, Eureka Springs, AR 72632, 816-523-8228
BROWNBAG PRESS, PO Box 120, Fayetteville, AR 72702-0120
Emerald Wave, PO Box 969, Fayetteville, AR 72702, Fax 501-575-0807; Tel 501-575-0019; sagebooks@aol.com
Hyacinth House Publications/Caligula Editions, PO Box 120, Fayetteville, AR 72702-0120
PSYCHOTRAIN, PO Box 120, Fayetteville, AR 72702-0120
SHOCKBOX, PO Box 120, Fayetteville, AR 72702-0120
NEBO, Department of English, Arkansas Tech University, Russellville, AR 72801, 501-968-0256

CALIFORNIA

LOS, 150 North Catalina Street #2, Los Angeles, CA 90004
THE DUCKBURG TIMES, 3010 Wilshire Blvd., #362, Los Angeles, CA 90010-1146, 213-388-2364
International Jewelry Publications, PO Box 13384, Los Angeles, CA 90013, 626-282-3781
Big Sky Press, 3647 Kalsman Drive, Suite 4, Los Angeles, CA 90016-4447, 310-838-0807
REAL DEAL MAGAZINE, PO Box 19129, Los Angeles, CA 90019, E-mail rdbone@earthlink.net
AAIMS Publishers, 11000 Wilshire Boulevard, PO Box 241777, Los Angeles, CA 90024-9577, 213-968-1195; 888-490-2276; fax 213-931-7217; email aaims1@aol.com
Jamenair Ltd., PO Box 241957, Los Angeles, CA 90024-9757, 310-470-6688
NEW GERMAN REVIEW: A Journal of Germanic Studies, Dept of Germanic Languages, University of CA, Los Angeles, Los Angeles, CA 90024, (310) 825-3955
Ariko Publications, 12335 Santa Monica Blvd., Suite 155, Los Angeles, CA 90025
Infotrends Press, 11620 Wilshire Blvd., Ste. 750, Los Angeles, CA 90025, 310-445-3265
Moon Lake Media, PO Box 251466, Los Angeles, CA 90025, 310-535-2453
Heat Press, PO Box 26218, Los Angeles, CA 90026, 213-482-8902
TAI CHI, PO Box 26156, Los Angeles, CA 90026, 213-665-7773
TUCUMCARI LITERARY REVIEW, 3108 W. Bellevue Avenue, Los Angeles, CA 90026
Wayfarer Publications, PO Box 26156, Los Angeles, CA 90026, 213-665-7773
Really Great Books, PO Box 292000, Los Angeles, CA 90029, 323-660-0620; fax 323-660-2571; website www.reallygreatbooks.com
SQUARE, PO Box 33671, Los Angeles, CA 90033
Veracity Press, 3765 Motor, Box 702, Los Angeles, CA 90034, 310-820-8269; Veracity96@aol.com
FILM SCORE MONTHLY, 5455 Wilshire Blvd., Ste. 1500, Los Angeles, CA 90036-4201, 323-937-9890; Fax 323-937-9277; E-mail lukas@filmscoremonthly.com
LYNX EYE, 1880 Hill Drive, Los Angeles, CA 90041, 213-550-8522
Survival News Service, Box 41834, Los Angeles, CA 90041, 213-255-9502
BRAIN/MIND BULLETIN, Bulletin of Breakthroughs, P O Box 42211, Los Angeles, CA 90042, 213-223-2500; 800-553-MIND
Interface Press, PO Box 42211, Los Angeles, CA 90042, 213-223-2500; 800-553-MIND
Middle Passage Press, 5517 Secrest Drive, Los Angeles, CA 90043, 213-298-0266
BOOTSTRAPPIN' ENTREPRENEUR: The Newsletter For Individuals With Great Ideas and a Little Bit of Cash, 6308 West 89th St, Suite 306-SPD, Los Angeles, CA 90045, 310-568-9861 emailibootstrap@aol.com
Dumont Press, 8710 Belford Avenue #B109, Los Angeles, CA 90045-4568
god is DEAD, publications, 910 North Martel, Suite #207, Los Angeles, CA 90046, 213-850-0067
Happy Rock Press, Phil Nurenberg, 8033 W. Sunset Blvd. #988, Los Angeles, CA 90046-2427
Hollywood Film Archive, 8391 Beverly Boulevard #321, Hollywood, CA 90048
Ages Publications, 8391 Beverly Blvd., Suite 323-DS, Los Angeles, CA 90048, 800-652-8574
BLITZ, PO Box 48124, Los Angeles, CA 90048-0124, 818-985-8618; e-mail blitzmed@aol.com
Bombshelter Press, P.O. Box 481266, Bicentennial Station, Los Angeles, CA 90048, 213-651-5488
ONTHEBUS, Bombshelter Press, P.O. Box 481270, Bicentennial Station, Los Angeles, CA 90048
Adams-Hall Publishing, PO Box 491002, Los Angeles, CA 90049, 310-826-1851; 800-888-4452
Black Diamond Book Publishing, PO Box 492299, Los Angeles, CA 90049-8299, 800-962-7622; fax 310-472-9833; E-mail 103615.1070@compuserve.com or nancy-shaffron@compuserve.com

Cygnet Trumpeter, 11661 San Vicente Blvd., Ste. 615, Los Angeles, CA 90049, 310-442-0102/Fax 310-442-9011
Nova Press, 11659 Mayfield Ave, Suite 1, Los Angeles, CA 90049, 310-207-4078, E-mail novapress@aol.com
Spectrum Productions, 979 Casiano Rd., Los Angeles, CA 90049
GrapeVinePress, PO Box 56057, Los Angeles, CA 90056, 213-980-3167
Alef Design Group, 4423 Fruitland Avenue, Los Angeles, CA 90058, 800-845-0662; Fax 213-585-0327; misrad@alefdesign.com; www.alefdesign.com
Borden Publishing Co., 2623 San Fernando Road, Los Angeles, CA 90065, 213-223-4267
INTERNATIONAL OLYMPIC LIFTER, PO Box 65855, Los Angeles, CA 90065, 213-257-8762
Red Eye Press, 845 W. Avenue 37, Los Angeles, CA 90065-3201, 323-225-3805
AMNESIA, PO Box 661441, Los Angeles, CA 90066
Courtyard Publishing Company, 3725 May Street, Los Angeles, CA 90066
Vedanta Press, 1946 Vedanta Place, Hollywood, CA 90068, 213-465-7114
Pluma Productions, 1977 Carmen Avenue, Los Angeles, CA 90068, email pluma@earthlink.net
Jahbone Press, 1201 Larrabee Street #207, Los Angeles, CA 90069-2065
Science of Mind Publishing, PO Box 75127, Los Angeles, CA 90075-0127, 213-388-2181
By-The-Book Publishing, 2337 Roscomare Road, #2-218, Bel Air, CA 90077, 310-440-4809
Lone Eagle Publishing Co., 2337 Roscomare Road #9, Los Angeles, CA 90077-1815, fax 213-471-4969; 800-FILMBKS
Acting World Books, PO Box 3044, Hollywood, CA 90078, 818-905-1345/Fax 800-210-1197
THE AGENCIES-WHAT THE ACTOR NEEDS TO KNOW, PO Box 3044, Hollywood, CA 90078, 818-905-1345
THE ANGRY THOREAUAN, PO Box 3478, Hollywood, CA 90078-3478
THE HOLLYWOOD ACTING COACHES AND TEACHERS DIRECTORY, PO Box 3044, Hollywood, CA 90078, 818-905-1345
Alyson Publications, Inc., PO Box 4371, Los Angeles, CA 90078-4371, 213-860-6065, Fax 213-467-0173
Alyson Wonderland, PO Box 4371, Los Angeles, CA 90078-4371, 213-871-1225; Fax 213-467-6805
2.13.61 Publications, PO Box 1910, Los Angeles, CA 90078, 213-969-8791
BLACK LACE, PO Box 83912, Los Angeles, CA 90083, 310-410-0808, fax 310-410-9250, e-mail newsroom@blk.com
BLACKFIRE, PO Box 83912, Los Angeles, CA 90083, 310-410-0808, fax 310-410-9250, e-mail newsroom@blk.com
BLK, PO Box 83912, Los Angeles, CA 90083, 310-410-0808, fax 310-410-9250, e-mail newsroom@blk.com
BLK Publishing Company, PO Box 83912, Los Angeles, CA 90083, 213-410-0808
KUUMBA, PO Box 83912, Los Angeles, CA 90083, 310-410-0808, fax 310-410-9250, e-mail newsroom@blk.com
THE SOUTHERN CALIFORNIA ANTHOLOGY, Master of Professional Writing Program, WPH 404/Univ. of Southern Calif., Los Angeles, CA 90089-4034, 213-740-5775
AMERICAN INDIAN CULTURE AND RESEARCH JOURNAL, 3220 Campbell Hall, Box 951548, Los Angeles, CA 90095-1548, 310-825-7315; Fax 310-206-7060; www.sscnet.ucla.edu/esp/aisc/index.html
American Indian Studies Center, 3220 Campbell Hall, Box 951548, UCLA, Los Angeles, CA 90095-1548, 310-825-7315; Fax 310-206-7060; www.sscnet.ucla.edu/esp/aisc/index.html
AZTLAN: A Journal of Chicano Studies, University of California-Los Angeles, PO Box 951544, Los Angeles, CA 90095, 310-825-2642
Chicano Studies Research Center Publications, University of California-Los Angeles, PO Box 951544, Los Angeles, CA 90095, 310-825-2642
Institute of Archaeology Publications, Univ. of California-Los Angeles, Box 951510, Los Angeles, CA 90095-1510, 310-825-7411
SUITCASE: A Journal of Transcultural Traffic, UCLA, PO Box 951536, Los Angeles, CA 90095, 310-836-8855; E-mail suitcase@humnet.ucla.edu; www.humnet.ucla.edu/suitcase
Bleeding Heart Press, PO Box 15902, Beverly Hills, CA 90209-1902
THE BLIND HORSE REVIEW, PO Box 15902, Beverly Hills, CA 90209-1902
Museon Publishing, PO Box 17095, Beverly Hills, CA 90209-2095, 310-788-0228
Chelsey Press, 441 N. Oakhurst Drive #205, Beverly Hills, CA 90210, 310-275-0803; fax 310-271-6634; e-mail chelseyink@aol.com
Paul Zelevansky, 1455 Clairidge Drive, Beverly Hills, CA 90210-2214
Paw Print Publishing Co., 439 South Doheny Drive, Beverly Hills, CA 90211-4411, 310-556-2728
Rossi, PO Box 2001, Beverly Hills, CA 90213, 310-556-0337
Via God Publishing, PO BOx 996, Beverly Hills, CA 90213, 310-390-0843
BONDAGE FANTASIES, 901 W. Victoria, Unit G, Compton, CA 90220, 310-631-1600; www.bondage.org
BOUDOIR NOIR, 901 W. Victoria, Unit G, Compton, CA 90220, 310-631-1600; www.bondage.org
FETISH BAZAAR, 901 W. Victoria, Unit G, Compton, CA 90220, 310-631-1600; www.bondage.org
KOMIC FANTASIES, 901 W. Victoria, Unit G, Compton, CA 90220, 310-631-1600; www.bondage.org
EquiLibrium Press, Inc., 10736 Jefferson Blvd. #680, Culver City, CA 90230, 310-204-3290; Fax 310-204-3550; equipress@mediaone.net
TURNING THE TIDE: A Journal of Anti-Racist Activism, Research & Education, PO Box 1055, Culver City, CA 90232-1055, e-mail part2001@usa.net
AlphaBooks, Inc., 30765 Pacific Coast Hwy #355, Malibu, CA 90265, 310-317-4855, Fax 310-589-9523, e-Mail: alphabooks@aol.com
The Image Maker Publishing Co., 29417 Bluewater Road, Malibu, CA 90265, 310-457-4031
On The Way Press, 23852 Pacific Coast Highway #504, Malibu, CA 90265, 310-456-1546; Fax: 310-456-7686; e-mail: onthewaypress@aol.com; http://members.aol.com/onthewaypress
Blue Arrow Books, PO Box 1669, Pacific Palisades, CA 90272, 310-216-1160 phone/Fax; goodbooks@compuserve.com
Photo Data Research, 800 S. Pacific Coast Highway, Suite 8332, Redondo Beach, CA 90277, 310-543-1085
JOTS (Journal of the Senses), 814 Robinson Road, Topanga, CA 90290, 310-455-1000; FAX 310-455-2007
The Bieler Press, 4216-1/4 Glencoe Avenue, Marina del Rey, CA 90292
The Dragon Press, 4230 Del Rey Avenue, Suite 445, Marina del Rey, CA 90292, 818-568-9111; FAX 818-568-1119
Sports Services of America Publishing, 333 Washington Blvd., Suite 360, Marina del Rey, CA 90292, 310-821-4490; Fax 821-0522
Acrobat Books, PO Box 870, Venice, CA 90294, 310-578-1055, Fax 310-823-8447
INTERBANG, PO Box 1574, Venice, CA 90294, 310-450-6372
Wave Publishing, PO Box 688, Venice, CA 90294, 310-306-0699
BLACK TALENT NEWS (The Entertainment Industry Publication for African Americans), 1620 Centinela Avenue, Ste. 204, Inglewood, CA 90302-1045

The Spinning Star Press, 1065 E. Fairview Blvd., Inglewood, CA 90302, 213-464-3024
Veronica Lane Books, 513 Wilshire Boulevard #282, Santa Monica, CA 90401, 800-651-1001, Fax; 310-315-9182
Angel City Press, 2118 Wilshire Blvd., Suite 880, Santa Monica, CA 90403, 310-395-9982; fax 310-395-3353; angelcitypress@aol.com
UMBRELLA, PO Box 3640, Santa Monica, CA 90403, 310-399-1146
Global Sports Productions, Ltd., 1223 Broadway, Suite 102, Santa Monica, CA 90404, 310-454-9480; fax 310-454-6590; e-mail sportsaddresses@hotmail.com
SPLIT SHIFT, 2461 Santa Monica Blvd. #C-122, Santa Monica, CA 90404
Split Shift, 2461 Santa Monica Blvd. #C-122, Santa Monica, CA 90404
Synapse-Centurion, 1211 Berkeley St., Suite 3, Santa Monica, CA 90404, 310-829-2752
THE SANTA MONICA REVIEW, 1900 Pico Boulevard, Santa Monica, CA 90405
MARSHALL HOUSE JOURNAL, PO Box 918, Santa Monica, CA 90406, 310-458-1172
Santa Monica Press/Offbeat Press, PO Box 1076, Santa Monica, CA 90406, 310-395-4658, Fax 310-395-6394
Clover Park Press, PO Box 5067, Santa Monica, CA 90409-5067, 310-452-7657; cloverparkpr@loop.com
DIRECT RESPONSE, 1815 West 213th Street, Ste. 210, Torrance, CA 90501, 310-212-5727; cdms@earthlink.net
Six Strings Music Publishing, PO Box 7718-155, Torrance, CA 90504-9118, 800-784-0203; Fax 310-324-8544; contact@sixstringsmusicpub.com; www.sixstringsmusicpub.com
SHEILA-NA-GIG, 23106 Kent Avenue, Torrance, CA 90505
Morning Glory Press, 6595 San Haroldo Way, Buena Park, CA 90620
PAST TIMES: The Nostalgia Entertainment Newsletter, 7308 Fillmore Drive, Buena Park, CA 90620, 714-527-5845; skretved@ix.netcom.com
PPT EXPRESS, 6595 San Haroldo Way, Buena Park, CA 90620
MUSHROOM DREAMS, 14537 Longworth Avenue, Norwalk, CA 90650-4724
Afcom Publishing, PO Box H, Harbor City, CA 90710-0330, 213-326-7589
AMERICAN PHYSICIANS ART ASSOCIATION NEWSLETTER, 1130 North Cabrillo, San Pedro, CA 90731, 310-832-7024
JB Press, 1130 North Cabrillo, San Pedro, CA 90731, 310-832-7024
LUMMOX JOURNAL, PO Box 5301, San Pedro, CA 90733-5301, 562-439-9858; e-mail lumoxraindog@earthlink.net
THE NOCTURNAL LYRIC, PO Box 115, San Pedro, CA 90733-0115
Eureka Publishing Group, 1077 Pacific Coast Highway, #144, Seal Beach, CA 90740, 310-431-9912
Jalmar Press, 24426 S. Main Street, Suite 702, Carson, CA 90745
B. L. Winch & Associates, 24426 Main Street, Suite 702, Carson, CA 90745-6329, 310-816-3085
BLACK CROSS, 3121 Corto Place #2, Long Beach, CA 90803, 562-987-4305; wstien@csulb.edu
PEARL, 3030 E. Second Street, Long Beach, CA 90803, 562-434-4523 or 714-968-7530
Pearl Editions, 3030 E. Second Street, Long Beach, CA 90803, 562-434-4523 or 714-968-7530
Intelligenesis Publications, 6414 Cantel Street, Long Beach, CA 90815, 562-598-0034; website httm://www.bookmasters.com/marktplc/00337.htm
Personal Fitness Publishing, PO Box 6400, Altadena, CA 91003, 818-798-6598, fax 818-798-2254
Wilton Place Publishing, PO Box 291, La Canada, CA 91012, 818-790-5601
Sandcastle Publishing, 1723 Hill Drive, South Pasadena, CA 91030, 213-255-3616
July Blue Press, PO Box 2006, Arcadia, CA 91077, 626-445-4420
BOVINE GAZETTE, PO Box 2263, Pasadena, CA 91102, e-Mail GREENHEART.COM
Innerwisdom Publishing, 2609 Colorado Boulvard, PO Box 70793, Pasadena, CA 91107, phone/fax 626-683-3316
Trilogy Books, 3579 E. Foothill Blvd. #236, Pasadena, CA 91107-3119, 818-440-0669
Huntington Library Press, 1151 Oxford Road, San Marino, CA 91108, 626-405-2172; fax 626-585-0794; e-mail booksales@huntington.org
HUNTINGTON LIBRARY QUARTERLY, 1151 Oxford Road, San Marino, CA 91108, 818-405-2172
Freelance Communications, P.O. Box 91970, Pasadena, CA 91109, FAX 500-442-True; phone 500-448-true, e-mail THIS-IS-TRUE-OWNER@NETCOM.COM
INDEFINITE SPACE, PO Box 40101, Pasadena, CA 91114
AMBASSADOR REPORT, PO Box 60068, Pasadena, CA 91116, 626-799-3754, E-mail mejhlp@aol.com
Hope Publishing House, PO Box 60008, Pasadena, CA 91116, 818-792-6123; fax 818-792-2121
Golden West Books, PO Box 80250, San Marino, CA 91118-8250, 626-458-8148
Balcony Press, 512 E. Wilson, #306, Glendale, CA 91206
Masefield Books, 7210 Jordan Avenue, Suite B54, Canoga Park, CA 91303
Film-Video Publications, 7944 Capistrano Avenue, West Hills, CA 91304
Real Life Storybooks, 8370 Kentland Avenue, West Hills, CA 91304-3324, 818-887-6431; 1-800-999-5668; e-Mail illanarls@aol, Fax; 818-887-4541
Golden Isis Press, PO Box 4263, Chatsworth, CA 91313
PAGAN PRIDE, PO Box 4263, Chatsworth, CA 91313
NEW CIVILIZATION STAFF REPORT, PO Box 260433, Encino, CA 91316, 818-725-3775
Rhino Publishing, PO Box 282, Newbury Park, CA 91319, 800-341-0914; 805-499-0051; fax 805-499-1571
VOL. NO. MAGAZINE, Los Angeles Poets' Press, 24721 Newhall Avenue, Newhall, CA 91321, 805-254-0851
Brooke-Richards Press, 9420 Reseda Blvd., Suite 511, Northridge, CA 91324, 818-893-8126
Lord John Press, 19073 Los Alimos Street, Northridge, CA 91326, 818-363-6621
Studio 4 Productions, PO Box 280400, Northridge, CA 91328-0400, 818-700-2522
NORTHRIDGE REVIEW, c/o CSUN, 18111 Nordoff Street, Mail Stop 8248, Northridge, CA 91330-8261, E-mail 102504.1176@compuserve.com
Brason-Sargar Publications, PO Box 872, Reseda, CA 91337, 818-994-0089; e-mail sonbar@bigfoot.com
Luz Bilingual Publishing, Inc., PO Box 571062, Tarzana, CA 91357, 818-907-1454; Fax 818-907-8925
LUZ EN ARTE Y LITERATURA, PO Box 571062, Tarzana, CA 91357, 818-907-1454; Fax 818-907-8925
Royal Print, PO Box 4665, West!ake Village, CA 91359-1665
The Center Press, 30961 W. Agoura Road #223-B, Westlake Village, CA 91361, 818-889-7071; FAX 818-879-0806;
CROSSCURRENTS, A QUARTERLY, 2200 Glastonbury Road, Westlake Village, CA 91361, 818-991-1694
Key Publications, PO Box 6375, Woodland Hills, CA 91365, 818-224-4344
MAGIC REALISM, PO Box 922648, Sylmar, CA 91392-2648
Pyx Press, Box 922648, Sylmar, CA 91392-2648
A THEATER OF BLOOD, PO Box 922648, Sylmar, CA 91392-2648

Life Energy Media, 15030 Ventura Blvd, Suite 908, Sherman Oaks, CA 91403, 818-995-3263
SHIRIM, 4611 Vesper Avenue, Sherman Oaks, CA 91403-5615
Truman Press, 15445 Ventura Blvd., Ste. 905, Sherman Oaks, CA 91403, 818-907-1889; FAX 818-907-8046
Gain Publications, PO Box 2204, Van Nuys, CA 91404, 818-981-1996
REMOTE JOCKEY DIGEST, 5823 Cedros Avenue, Van Nuys, CA 91411-3114, Email: dcoleman@ix.netcom.com
Stone and Scott, Publishers, PO Box 56419, Sherman Oaks, CA 91413-1419, 818-904-9088
Center Press, PO Box 16452, Encino, CA 91416-6425
RATTLE, 13440 Ventura Boulevard #200, Sherman Oaks, CA 91423, 818-788-3232; fax 818-788-2831
Native Plant Publishing, 150 South Glenoaks, Suite 9135R, Burbank, CA 91502, 818-558-9543; Fax 818-352-5567
RESEARCH IN YORUBA LANGUAGE & LITERATURE, 1317 North San Fernando Boulevard, Suite 310, Burbank, CA 91504
SOCIETE, 1317 N. San Fernando Blvd, Suite 310, Burbank, CA 91504
Technicians of the Sacred, 1317 N. San Fernando Boulevard, Suite 310, Burbank, CA 91504
Ascension Publishing, Box 3001-323, Burbank, CA 91508, 818-848-8145
BLUE SATELLITE, PO Box 10312, Burbank, CA 91510-0312, Fax 818-780-1912; E-mail sacredbev@aol.com
The Sacred Beverage Press, PO Box 10312, Burbank, CA 91510-0312, Fax 818-780-1912; E-mail sacredbev@aol.com
SHARE INTERNATIONAL, PO Box 971, North Hollywood, CA 91603, 818-785-6300, Fax 818-904-9132, share@shareintl.org, www.shareintl.org/
Panjandrum Books, 6156 Wilkinson Avenue, North Hollywood, CA 91606, 818-506-0202
PANJANDRUM POETRY JOURNAL, 6156 Wilkinson Avenue, North Hollywood, CA 91606
Myriad Press, 12535 Chandler Blvd. #3, N. Hollywood, CA 91607, 818-508-6296
Empire Publishing Service, PO Box 1344, Studio City, CA 91614-0344
Players Press, Inc., PO Box 1132, Studio City, CA 91614, 818-789-4980
ABE Press, PO Box 521, Alta Loma, CA 91701
Single Parent Press, PO Box 1298, Claremont, CA 91711, 909-624-6058, fax 909-624-2208
Verity Press Publishing, PO Box 31, Covina, CA 91723, 818-332-0794
SHARING IDEAS FOR PROFESSIONAL SPEAKERS, PO Box 398, Glendora, CA 91740, 626-335-8069; fax 626-335-6127
Bookworm Publishing Company, PO Box 3037, Ontario, CA 91761
Phony Lid Publications, PO Box 2153, Rosemead, CA 91770, e-mail vagrag@mindspring.com
VAGABOND, PO Box 2153, Rosemead, CA 91770, e-mail vagrag@mindspring.com
LOVING ALTERNATIVES MAGAZINE, PO Box 459, San Dimas, CA 91773, 909-592-5217, FAX 818-915-4715
WHAT IF...THE MAGAZINE OF THE MODERN PHILOSOPHER, PO Box 4193, San Dimas, CA 91773, mdrnphil@aol.com; http://members.tripod.com/~mdrnphil/whatifmag.html
PEAKY HIDE, PO Box 1591, Upland, CA 91785
Kiva Publishing, Inc., 21731 East Buckskin Drive, Walnut, CA 91789, 909-595-6833; fax 909-860-9595
Black Forest Press, 539 Telegraph Canyon Road #521, Chula Vista, CA 91910, 619-656-8048; FAX 619-482-8704; E-mail BFP@flash.net/~dbk
Law Mexico Publishing, 539 Telegraph Canyon Road #787, Chula Vista, CA 91910-6497, 619-482-8244
BAJA SUN, 858 3rd Avenue #456, Chula Vista, CA 91911-1305, 1-800-WIN BAJA
Editorial El Sol De Baja, 858 3rd Avenue #456, Chula Vista, CA 91911-1305, 1-800-WIN BAJA
JOURNAL OF UNCONVENTIONAL HISTORY, PO Box 459, Cardiff-by-the-Sea, CA 92007, 619-459-5748; fax 619-459-0936; e-mail ahornaday@ucsd.edu
Sharp Publishing, 2767 Highland Drive, Carlsbad, CA 92008, fax 619-729-3838; 619-729-2582
Craftsman Book Company, 6058 Corte Del Cedro, Carlsbad, CA 92009, 619-438-7828
Andrew Scott Publishers, 15023 Tierra Alta, Del Mar, CA 92014, 619-755-0715; e-mail andrewscottpublishers@juno.com
Wharton Publishing, Inc., 3790 Via de la Valle Suite 204, Del Mar, CA 92014, 619-756-4922; Fax 619-759-7097; e-mail wharton@gte.net
Gurze Books, Box 2238, Carlsbad, CA 92018, 760-434-7533
Magnus Press, PO Box 2666, Carlsbad, CA 92018, 760-806-3743; Fax 760-806-3689; toll free 800-463-7818; e-mail magnuspres@aol.com
UNARIUS LIGHT JOURNAL, 145 S. Magnolia Avenue, El Cajon, CA 92020, 619-444-7062, 1-800-475-7062, fax 1-619-444-9637, E-mail; uriel@unarius.org, Web; http://www.unarius.org
WISEBLOOD, 315 S. Coast Hwy. 101, Ste. U226, Encinitas, CA 92024, E-mail wstrmyr@cts.com; www.wiseblood-zine.com
STS Publishing, 5580 La Jolla Boulevard #376, La Jolla, CA 92037, www.futurelessons.com
International University Line (IUL), PO Box 2525, La Jolla, CA 92038, 619-457-0595
La Jolla Poets Press, PO Box 8638, La Jolla, CA 92038, 619-457-1399
San Diego Poet's Press, c/o Kathleen Iddings, PO Box 8638, La Jolla, CA 92038, (619) 457-1399
West Anglia Publications, PO Box 2683, La Jolla, CA 92038, 619-457-1399
MiraCosta College Press, 1 Barnard Drive, M/S 5B, Oceanside, CA 92056
DREAM INTERNATIONAL QUARTERLY, 411 14th Street #H1, Ramona, CA 92065-2769
Mission Press, PO Box 9586, Rancho Santa Fe, CA 92067, 619-792-1841; e-mail: MissionPress@compuserve.com
San Diego Publishing Company, Fairbanks Ranch, PO Box 9393, Rancho Santa Fe, CA 92067, 1-800-494-BOOK
Alpine Publishing Inc., 991 Lomas Santa Fe, Ste. C-195, Solana Beach, CA 92075, 619-591-8001, 619-794-7302
ORNAMENT, PO Box 2349, San Marcos, CA 92079, 619-599-0222; fax 619-599-0228
Apples & Oranges, Inc., PO Box 2296, Valley Center, CA 92082, 619-751-8868
WRITER'S NEWS, 2130 Sunset Drive #47, Vista, CA 92083, 760-941-9293; Fax 760-941-5719; lizklung@earthlink.net
XIB, 930 24th Street, San Diego, CA 92102-2006
Xib Publications, 930 24th Street, San Diego, CA 92102-2006
Hungry Tiger Press, 1516 Cypress Avenue, San Diego, CA 92103-4517
OZ-STORY, 1516 Cypress Avenue, San Diego, CA 92103-4517
Silvercat Publications, 4070 Goldfinch Street, Suite C, San Diego, CA 92103, 619-299-6774, fax 619-299-9119
Anaphase II, 2739 Wightman Street, San Diego, CA 92104-3526, 619-688-1959
Pride-Frost Publishing, 3390 Herman Avenue, San Diego, CA 92104-4622
Wind-Up Publications, 2828 University Avenue #103-121, San Diego, CA 92104, 619-497-5081; fax 619-297-6701; email antinuous@home.net
Tecolote Publications, 4918 Del Monte Avenue, San Diego, CA 92107

ADOLESCENCE, 3089C Clairemont Dr., Suite 383, San Diego, CA 92117, 619-571-1414
FAMILY THERAPY, 3089C Clairemont Dr., Suite 383, San Diego, CA 92117, 619-571-1414
Libra Publishers, Inc., 3089C Clairemont Dr., Suite 383, San Diego, CA 92117, 619-571-1414
Blue Dove Press, 4204 Sorrento Valley Blvd, Ste. K, San Diego, CA 92121, 619-623-3330; orders 800-691-1008; FAX 619-623-3325; bdp@bluedove.com; www.bluedove.com
Dawn Sign Press, 6130 Nancy Ridge Drive, San Diego, CA 92121-3223
ASTERISM: The Journal of Science Fiction, Fantasy, and Space Music, 3525 Lebon Drive #201, San Diego, CA 92122-4547, 847-568-3957; FAX 847-568-3999; asterismsf@aol.com
Index Publishing Group, Inc, 3368 Governor Drive, Suite 273-F, San Diego, CA 92122-2925, 619-455-6100; FAX 619-522-9050; orders 800-546-6707; e-Mail ipgbooks@indexbooks.com; Website www.indexbooks.comlipgbooks
The Rateavers, 9049 Covina Street, San Diego, CA 92126, 619-566-8994, Fax; 619-586-1104, E-mail; brateaver@aol.com
THE TRUTH SEEKER, 16935 W. Bernardo Drive #103, San Diego, CA 92127, 619-676-0430; Fax 619-676-0433; tsmelton@aol.com; www.truthseeker.com
ACS Publications, PO Box 34487, San Diego, CA 92163, 619-492-9919
ASTROFLASH, PO Box 34487, San Diego, CA 92163, 619-297-9203
Mho & Mho Works, Box 33135, San Diego, CA 92163, 619-488-4991
Junction Press, PO Box 40537, San Diego, CA 92164-0537, 619-702-4607
Birth Day Publishing Company, PO Box 7722, San Diego, CA 92167, 619-296-3194
Brenner Information Group, PO Box 721000, San Diego, CA 92172-1000, 619-538-0093
THE WISHING WELL, PO Box 178440, San Diego, CA 92177-8440, 619-270-2779
FICTION INTERNATIONAL, San Diego State University, San Diego, CA 92182, 619-594-5443, 594-6220
POETRY INTERNATIONAL, San Diego State Univ., Eng. Dept., 5500 Campanile Drive, San Diego, CA 92182-8140, 619-594-1523; fax 619-594-4998; email fmoramar@mail.sdsu.edu
San Diego State University Press, San Diego State University, San Diego, CA 92182, 619-594-6220
Altair Publications, PO Box 221000, San Diego, CA 92192-1000, e-mail altair@astroconsalting.com
AAS HISTORY SERIES, PO Box 28130, San Diego, CA 92198, 760-746-4005; Fax 760-746-3139; 76121.1532@compu-serve.com; www.univelt.staigerland.com
ADVANCES IN THE ASTRONAUTICAL SCIENCES, PO Box 28130, San Diego, CA 92198, 760-746-4005; Fax 760-746-3139; 76121.1532@compuserve.com; www.univelt.staigerland.com
SCIENCE AND TECHNOLOGY, PO Box 28130, San Diego, CA 92198, 760-746-4005; Fax 760-746-3139; 76121.1532@compuserve.com; www.univelt.staigerland.com
Univelt, Inc., PO Box 28130, San Diego, CA 92198-0130, 760-746-4005; Fax 760-746-3139; 76121.1532@compu-serve.com; www.univelt.staigerland.com
DARK STARR, PO Box 1107, Blythe, CA 92226-1107
INTERCULTURAL WRITERS REVIEW, PO Box 1107, Blythe, CA 92226-1107
POETRY BREAK JOURNAL, PO Box 1107, Blythe, CA 92226-1107
SPIRIT TO SPIRIT, PO Box 1107, Blythe, CA 92226-1107
Yes You Can Press, PO Box 337, Desert Hot Springs, CA 92240, 760-251-1103, fax 760-251-5064
ETC Publications, 700 East Vereda Sur, Palm Springs, CA 92262-4816, 760-325-5352; fax 760-325-8841
Event Horizon Press, PO Box 2006, Palm Springs, CA 92263, 760-329-3950
Dramaline Publications, 36851 Palm View Road, Rancho Mirage, CA 92270-2417, 760-770-6076, FAX 760-770-4507; dramaline@aol.com
Noble Porter Press, 36-851 Palm View Road, Rancho Mirage, CA 92270, 760-770-6076, fax 760-770-4507
Nouveau Press, 14592 Palmdale Road, #D6-199, Victorville, CA 92392, 760-961-6088; fax 760-951-8388; e-mail nouveau@earthlink.net
The Borgo Press, Box 2845, San Bernardino, CA 92406, 714-884-5813; 714-885-1161; Fax 714-888-4942
THE PACIFIC REVIEW, Department of English, Calif State University, San Bernardino, CA 92407, 714-880-5824
LATIN AMERICAN PERSPECTIVES, PO Box 5703, Riverside, CA 92517-5703, 909-787-5037ext. 1571; fax 909-787-5685
Xenos Books, Box 52152, Riverside, CA 92517, 909-370-2229; E-mail info@xenosbooks.com; http://www.xenos-books.com
Gan Publishing, PO Box 33458, Riverside, CA 92519, 909-788-9676; FAX 909-788-9677
FRIENDS OF PEACE PILGRIM, 43480 Cedar Avenue, Hemet, CA 92544, 909-927-7678
FREE LUNCH, PO Box 7647, Laguna Niguel, CA 92607-7647
Quicksilver Press, 26741 Portola Parkway 1E-222, Foothill Ranch, CA 92610, fax 714-837-6291
Career Publishing, Inc., PO Box 5486, Orange, CA 92613-5486, 714-771-5155; 800-854-4014; fax 714-532-0180
THE EAR, Irvine Valley Coll., School of Humanities, 5500 Irvine Center Drive, Irvine, CA 92620, 714-541-5341
Nguoi Dan, PO Box 2674, Costa Mesa, CA 92628, 714-549-3443; 714-241-8505, E-mail nguoidan@aix.netcom.com; Web site http://www.nguoidan.com/nd
NGUOI DAN, PO Box 2674, Costa Mesa, CA 92628, 714-549-3443; 714-241-8505; E-mail nguoidan@ix.netcom.com; Web site http://www.nguoidan.com/nd
Frontline Publications, PO Box 1104, El Toro, CA 92630
JACARANDA, English Department, California State Univ—Fullerton, Fullerton, CA 92634, 714-773-3163
SPILLWAY, 20592 Minerva Lane, Huntington Beach, CA 92646, 714-968-0905
Tebot Bach, 20592 Minerva Lane, Huntington Beach, CA 92646, 714-968-0905
Verve Press, PO Box 1997, Huntington Beach, CA 92647
Parkhurst Press, PO Box 143, Laguna Beach, CA 92652, 949-499-1032
Publitec Editions, PO Box 4342, Laguna Beach, CA 92652, 949-497-6100 tel/fax
Totally Bogus, PO Box 4560, Laguna Beach, CA 92652, 714-479-5039
Companion Press, PO Box 2575, Laguna Hills, CA 92654, 949-362-9726
THE JOURNAL OF HISTORICAL REVIEW, PO Box 2739, Newport Beach, CA 92659, 949-631-1490; ihr@ihr.org
MCM Entertainment, Inc. Publishing Division, PO Box 3051, Newport Beach, CA 92659-0597, 800-901-7979; newportmcm@aol.com
Noontide Press, PO Box 2719, Newport Beach, CA 92659, 949-631-1490; e-mail editor@noontidepress.com
Tug Press, PO Box 15188, Newport Beach, CA 92659, 714-551-9591; FAX 714-551-9591
ORANGE COAST MAGAZINE, 3701 Birch Street, Suite 100, Newport Beach, CA 92660-2618, 949-862-1133
VIVA PETITES, 537 Newport Center Drive #119, Newport Beach, CA 92660, FAX 714-643-5367
Balboa Books, PO Box 658, Newport Beach, CA 92661, 714-720-8464

Galt Publishing, PO Box 848, Newport Beach, CA 92661, 714-675-2835; FAX 714-675-3219
Words & Pictures Press, 1921 Sherry Lane, Apt. #87, Santa Ana, CA 92705-7621, 714-544-7282; Fax 714-544-7430; E-mail publisher@earthlink.net
FAULTLINE, Journal of Art and Literature, PO Box 599-4960, Irvine, CA 92716, 714-824-6712
Canterbury Press, 5540 Vista Del Amigo, Anaheim, CA 92807, Fax 714-998-1929
Past Times Publishing Co., PO Box 661, Anaheim, CA 92815, 714-997-1157; jyoung@fea.net
Ehrman Entertainment Press, PO Box 2951, Orange, CA 92859-0951, 714-997-7006; FAX 637-3341; Toll Free 888-997-7006; e-mail ehrmanent@Juno.com
CALIFORNIA STATE POETRY QUARTERLY (CQ), CSPS/CQ, PO Box 7126, Orange, CA 92863, 805-543-8255
FREEDOM ISN'T FREE, PO Box 6184, Orange, CA 92863-6184
Temporary Vandalism Recordings, PO Box 6184, Orange, CA 92863-6184, e-mail tvrec@yahoo.com
Golden Umbrella Publishing, PO Box 95, Yorba Linda, CA 92885-0095, 714-996-4001 phone/fax; gupub@aol.com
ART/LIFE, PO Box 23020, Ventura, CA 93002, 805-648-4331
Art/Life Limited Editions, PO Box 23020, Ventura, CA 93002, 805-648-4331
Golden West Historical Publications, PO Box 1906, Ventura, CA 93002
Monroe Press, 362 Maryville Avenue, Ventura, CA 93003-1912
The Tonal Company, 5300 Cliffside Circle, PO Box 3233, Ventura, CA 93003, 805-644-1364
Newjoy Press, PO Box 3437, Ventura, CA 93006, 805-876-1373; FAX 805-984-0503; njpublish@aol.com
SOLO, 5146 Foothill, Carpinteria, CA 93013, E-mail swharton@ohm.elee.calpoly.edu; berrypress@aol.com
FREEBIES MAGAZINE, 1135 Eugenia Place, Carpinteria, CA 93014-5025, 805-566-1225, e-mail freebies@aol.com
Manifest Publications, PO Box 429, Carpinteria, CA 93014, 805-684-4905; Fax 805-684-3100; vcornell@silcom.com
Dimension Engineering Press, 1620 Beacon Place, Oxnard, CA 93033, 805-487-2248; FAX 805-486-2491
VERVE, PO Box 630305, Simi Valley, CA 93063-0305
SANTA BARBARA REVIEW, PO Box 808, Summerland, CA 93067, 805-969-0861; E-mail jtaeby@West.net
Bandanna Books, 319 Anacapa Street #B, Santa Barbara, CA 93101, 805-564-3559; FAX 805-564-3278
COLLEGIUM NEWSLETTER, 319-B Anacapa Street, Santa Barbara, CA 93101, fax 805-564-3278; website bandannabooks.com
Allen A. Knoll Publishers, 200 W. Victoria Street, 2nd Floor, Santa Barbara, CA 93101-3627, 805-564-3377, Fax 805-966-6657, e-mail aaknoll@aol.com
Prosperity Press, 1503 Mountain Avenue, Santa Barbara, CA 93101, 805-963-3028; FAX 805-963-9272, 1-800-464-2074
Fithian Press, PO Box 1525, Santa Barbara, CA 93102, 805-962-1780; Fax 805-962-8835; e-mail dandd@danielpublishing.com
Woodbridge Press, PO Box 209, Santa Barbara, CA 93102-0209, 805-965-7039
Light Beams Press, 3463 State Street, #193, Santa Barbara, CA 93105, 805-565-9424; Fax 805-565-9824
CAMERA OBSCURA: Feminism, Culture, and Media Studies, c/o Film Studies Program, University of California, Santa Barbara, CA 93106, 805-893-7069; fax 805-893-8630; e-mail cameraob@humanitas.ucsb.edu
McNally & Loftin, Publishers, 5390 Overpass Road, Santa Barbara, CA 93111, 805-964-5117; fax 805-967-2818
Butterfield Press, 283 Carlo Drive, Goleta, CA 93117-2046, 805-964-8627
Para Publishing, PO Box 8206 - Q, Santa Barbara, CA 93118-8206, 805-968-7277; fax 805-968-1379; fax-on-demand 805-968-8947; e-Mail 75031.3534@parapublishing.com; web site http://www.parapublishing.com/books/para/q; e-mail parapublishing@aol.com
PUBLISHING POYNTERS, PO Box 8206-Q, Santa Barbara, CA 93118-8206, 805-968-7277; fax 805-968-1379; fax-on-demand 805-968-8947; e-Mail 75031.3534@parapublising.com; web site http://www.parapublishing.com/books/para/q; e-mail parapublishing@aol.com
Capra Press, PO Box 2068, Santa Barbara, CA 93120, 805-966-4590; FAX 805-965-8020
John Daniel and Company, Publishers, PO Box 21922, Santa Barbara, CA 93121, 805-962-1780; fax 805-962-8835; email dand@danielpublishing.com
Peradam Press, PO Box 21326, Santa Barbara, CA 93121-1326
Red Hen Press, PO Box 3774, Santa Barbara, CA 93130, 805-682-1278
Aegean Publishing Company, PO Box 6790, Santa Barbara, CA 93160, 805-964-6669
Summer Stream Press, PO Box 6056, Santa Barbara, CA 93160-6056, 805-962-6540
AMUSING YOURSELF TO DEATH, PO Box 91934, Santa Barbara, CA 93190-1934, E-mail rgaviola@aol.com
Joelle Publishing, PO Box 91229, Santa Barbara, CA 93190, 805-962-9887
Mille Grazie Press, PO Box 92023, Santa Barbara, CA 93190, 805-963-8408
SHORT FUSE, PO Box 90436, Santa Barbara, CA 93190
DRY CRIK REVIEW, PO Box 44320, Lemon Cove, CA 93244, 209-597-2512; fax 209-597-2103
AMELIA, 329 'E' Street, Bakersfield, CA 93304, 805-323-4064
Amelia Press, 329 'E' Street, Bakersfield, CA 93304, 805-323-4064
CICADA, 329 'E' Street, Bakersfield, CA 93304, 805-323-4064
SPSM&H, 329 'E' Street, Bakersfield, CA 93304, 805-323-4064
Barney Press, 3807 Noel Place, Bakersfield, CA 93306, 805-871-9118
Golden Eagle Press, 1400 Easton Drive, Suite 149, Bakersfield, CA 93309, 805-327-4329; Fax 805-327-1053; E-mail Mary Lou mapp@lightspeed.net
BitterSweet Publishing Company, PO Box 30407, Bakersfield, CA 93385, 805-665-0326
UNWOUND, PO Box 10205, Bakersfield, CA 93389-0205, 509-687-8046
Sovereignty Press, 1241 Johnson Avenue, #353, San Luis Obispo, CA 93401, 805-543-6100; fax 805-543-1085; sovtypress@aol.com
Sand River Press, 1319 14th Street, Los Osos, CA 93402, 805-543-3591
EZ Nature Books, PO Box 4206, San Luis Obispo, CA 93403
KALDRON, An International Journal Of Visual Poetry, PO Box 7164, Halcyon, CA 93421-7164, 805-489-2770; Website http://www.thing.net/~grist/l&d/kaldron.htm
American Source Books, a division of Impact Publishers, PO Box 6016, Atascadero, CA 93423-6016, 805-466-5917; Fax 805-466-5919
Impact Publishers, Inc., PO Box 6016, Atascadero, CA 93423-6016, 805-466-5917; fax 805-466-5919
Macrocosm USA, Inc., PO Box 185, Cambria, CA 93428, 805-927-2515, e-Mail brockway@macronet.org Web http://www.macronet.org/macronet/
The Olive Press Publications, PO Box 99, Los Olivos, CA 93441, Tel/Fax 805-688-2445
Reference Desk Books, 430 Quintana Road, Suite 146, Morro Bay, CA 93442, 805-772-8806

649

Cyclone Books, 420 Pablo Lane, Nipomo, CA 93444, 805-929-4430 phone/Fax; cyclone@utech.net

THE ELECTRONIC PUBLISHING FORUM, PO Box 140, San Simeon, CA 93452, www.thegrid.net/bookware/epf.htm

Serendipity Systems, PO Box 140, San Simeon, CA 93452

VIRGIN MEAT E-ZINE, 2325 West Avenue K-15, Lancaster, CA 93536, E-mail virginmeat@aol.com; www.members.aol.com/virginmeat/magazine/gothic.html

QUARTZ HILL JOURNAL OF THEOLOGY, 43543 51st Street West, Quartz Hill, CA 93536, 802-722-0891; 805-943-3484; E-mail robin@theology.edu

Quartz Hill Publishing House, 43543 51st Street West, Quartz Hill, CA 93536, 805-722-0291; 805-943-3484; E-mail robin@theology.edu

SILVER WINGS/MAYFLOWER PULPIT, PO Box 1000, Pearblossom, CA 93553-1000, 805-264-3726

North Star Books, PO Box 259, Lancaster, CA 93584, 661-945-7529; nstarbks@aol.com

Red Hen Press, PO Box 902582, Palmdale, CA 93590, Fax 818-831-6659; E-mail redhen@vpg.net

Torchlight Publishing, PO Box 52, Badger, CA 93603

Quill Driver Books, 8386 N. Madsen Ave, Clovis, CA 93611, 559-322-5917, fax 559-322-5967, 800-497-4909

Oline Publishing, 4732 East Michigan, Fresno, CA 93703, 209-251-0169; oline@earthlink.net

Kairos World Press, 2037 West Bullard, Box #202, Fresno, CA 93711-1200

Pocket of Sanity, PO Box 5241, Fresno, CA 93755, 559-222-2845; fax 559-225-3670; e-mail posanity@aol.com

THE SUNDAY SUITOR POETRY REVIEW, 506 Stevenson Street, Salinas, CA 93907-2017, 209-858-1453

Creative With Words Publications (CWW), PO Box 223226, Carmel, CA 93922-3226, Fax: 831-655-8627; e-mail: cwwpub@usa.net; http://members.tripod.com/~creativewithwords

THEECLECTICS, PO Box 223226, Carmel, CA 93922, fax 831-655-8627; e-mail cwwpub@usa.net; website http://members.tripod.com/~CreativeWithWords

Dynamic Publishing, 148 San Remo Road, Carmel, CA 93923, 408-624-5534

Portunus Publishing Company, 316 Mid Valley Center #270, Carmel, CA 93923, E-mail service@portunus.net; website www.portunus.net

Sea Challengers, Inc., 4 Sommerset Rise, Monterey, CA 93940, 831-373-6306, Fax 831-373-4566

Victory Press, 543 Lighthouse Avenue, Monterey, CA 93940-1422, 408-883-1725, Fax 408-883-8710

The Boxwood Press, 183 Ocean View Blvd, Pacific Grove, CA 93950, 408-375-9110; FAX 408-375-0430

Park Place Publications, PO Box 829, Pacific Grove, CA 93950-0829, 831-649-6640; fax 831-655-4489; e-mail info@parkplace-publications.com; website www.parkplace-publications.com

Alchemist/Light Publishing, P.O. Box 1275, Belmont, CA 94002-6275, 650-345-6812; email bbp@alchemist-light.com; http://www.alchemist-light.com

Cove View Press, 2165 Carlmont #205, Belmont, CA 94002

Buddhist Text Translation Society, 1777 Murchison Drive, Burlingame, CA 94010-4504, phone/fax 415-692-9286, e-mail drbabtts@jps.net

Nextstep Books, 1070 Carolan Avenue #116, Burlingame, CA 94010, e-mail nextstep@nub.ml.org

ENTELECHY MAGAZINE, P.O. Box 413, El Granada, CA 94018, e-mail shorn@entelechy.org; website www.entelechy.org

BLOODJET LITERARY MAGAZINE, 20 Driftwood Trail, Half Moon Bay, CA 94019-2349, 650-726-5939; Fax 415-921-3730

New World Press, 20 Driftwood Trail, Half Moon Bay, CA 94019-2349, 650-726-5939; Fax 415-921-3730

BOOMERANG! MAGAZINE, PO Box 261, La Honda, CA 94020-0261, 415-747-0978

Listen and Learn Home Education, Inc., PO Box 261, La Honda, CA 94020-0261, 415-882-7875

FIDDLER MAGAZINE, PO Box 125, Los Altos, CA 94023, 650-948-4383

Allergy Publications, 1259 El Camino #254, Menlo Park, CA 94025, 415-322-1663, e-mail: alergyaid@aol.com

Ballena Press, 823 Valparaiso Avenue, Menlo Park, CA 94025, 650-323-9261; orders: 415-883-3530; fax 415-883-4280

SMART DRUG NEWS, PO Box 4029, Menlo Park, CA 94026, 415-321-2374

Poor Souls Press/Scaramouche Books, PO Box 236, Millbrae, CA 94030

BACKBOARD, 561 Paloma Avenue, Pacifica, CA 94044-2438, 650-355-4640; FAX 650-355-3630; joski@ix.netcom.com

Backspace Ink, 561 Paloma Avenue, Pacifica, CA 94044-2438, 650-355-4640; FAX 650-355-3630; joski@ix.netcom.com

Creatures At Large Press, PO Box 687, 1082 Grand Teton Drive, Pacifica, CA 94044, 415-355-READ; fax 415-355-4863

The Heyeck Press, 25 Patrol Court, Woodside, CA 94062, 650-851-7491; Fax 650-851-5039; heyeck@ix.netcom.com

Roof Publishing Company, 1017 El Camino Real, Suite 316, Redwood City, CA 94063, 1-800-810-3754; email info@roofpublishing.com; website http://www.roofpublishing.com

Popular Medicine Press, PO Box 1212, San Carlos, CA 94070, 415-594-1855

Wide World Publishing/TETRA, PO Box 476, San Carlos, CA 94070, 650-593-2839, Fax 650-595-0802

PARA TROOP, 115-A E. Fremont Avenue, Sunnyvale, CA 94087, 408-245-6275; Fax 408-245-2139; info@comicscons-piracy.com; www.comicsconspiracy.com

Soundboard Books, 1030 E. El Camino Real, Suite 124, Sunnyvale, CA 94087, 408-738-1705

OXYGEN, 535 Geary Street #1010, San Francisco, CA 94102, 415-776-9681

Down There Press, 938 Howard Street, Suite 101, San Francisco, CA 94103, 415-974-8985 x105; FAX 415-974-8989; e-Mail goodvibe@well.com

GLB Publishers, 1028 Howard Street #503, San Francisco, CA 94103, 415-621-8307

Mandala Publishing Group, 1585A Folsom Street, San Francisco, CA 94103-3728, 541-688-2258, 800-688-2218; Fax 541-461-3478; E-mail gvs@efn.org

Mercury House, 785 Market Street, Suite 1500, San Francisco, CA 94103-2003, 415-974-0729; Fax 415-974-0832 (Editorial)

MOTHER EARTH JOURNAL: An International Quarterly, c/o National Poetry Association, 934 Brannan Street, 2nd Floor, San Francisco, CA 94103, 415-552-9261; fax 415-552-9271

POETRY USA, 934 Brannan Street, 2nd floor, San Francisco, CA 94103, 415-552-9261; FAX 415-552-9291; E-mail gamuse@slip.net, http://www.slip.net.gamuse

Uniting the World Press, Inc., c/o National Poetry Association, 934 Brannan Street, #2ND-FL, San Francisco, CA 94103, 415-552-9261; fax 415-552-9271

MacAdam/Cage Publishing Inc., 465 California Street, Ste. 412, San Francisco, CA 94104, 415-986-7470; Fax 415-986-7414; ccom@earthlink.net

WORLD RAINFOREST REPORT, Rainforest Action Network, 221 Pine Street, Suite 500, San Francisco, CA 94104-2715, 415-398-4404, fax 415-398-2732, e-mail rainforest@ran.org

ZYZZYVA, 41 Sutter Street, Suite 1400, San Francisco, CA 94104

650

CALLBOARD, 657 Mission Street #402, San Francisco, CA 94105, 415-957-1557
Children's Book Press, 246 First Street, Suite 101, San Francisco, CA 94105-1028, 415-995-2200, FAX: 415-995-2222; cbookpress@cbookpress.org
Encounter Books, 116 New Montgomery St., Suite 206, San Francisco, CA 94105, 415-538-1460; fax 415-538-1461; e-mail read@encounterbooks.com; website www.encounterbooks.com
Sierra Club Books, 85 Second Street, San Francisco, CA 94105-3441, 415-977-5500; FAX 415-977-5793 and 415-977-5792
No Starch Press, 555 De Haro Street, Suite 250, San Francisco, CA 94107-2365, 415-863-9900
The Survival Series Publishing Co., PO Box 77313, San Francisco, CA 94107, 415-979-6785
CAVEAT LECTOR, 400 Hyde Street, Apt. 606, San Francisco, CA 94109, 415-928-7431
MIND MATTERS REVIEW, 2040 Polk Street, Box 234, San Francisco, CA 94109
Sunlight Publishers, PO Box 640545, San Francisco, CA 94109, 415-776-6249
BLUEBOOK, 766 Valencia Street, San Francisco, CA 94110, 415-437-3450; Fax 415-626-5541
China Books & Periodicals, Inc., 2929 24th Street, San Francisco, CA 94110, 415-282-2994; info@chinabooks.com
CLUTCH, 147 Coleridge Street, San Francisco, CA 94110
DREAM SCENE MAGAZINE, 3902 Folsom Street, San Francisco, CA 94110-6138, 415-221-0210
GIRLFRIENDS MAGAZINE, 3415 Cesar Chavez Street, Ste. 101, San Francisco, CA 94110, 415-648-9464; fax 415-648-4705; e-mail staff@gfriends.com; website www.gfriends.com
OFF OUR BACKS, 3600 20th Street, #201, San Francisco, CA 94110-2351, 415-546-0384
ON OUR BACKS MAGAZINE, 3415 Cesar Chavez Ste. 101, San Francisco, CA 94110, 415-648-9464; fax 415-648-4705; e-mail staff@gfriends.com
PROSODIA, New College of California/Poetics, 766 Valencia Street, San Francisco, CA 94110, 415-437-3479; Fax 415-437-3702
S.I.R.S. Caravan Publications, 65 Norwich Street, San Francisco, CA 94110, 415-285-0562
Walnut Publishing Co., Inc., 3425 Army Street, San Francisco, CA 94110, 415-821-0511
Good Life Publications, 580 Washington Street #306, San Francisco, CA 94111
Off the Cuff Books, 191 Sickles Avenue, San Francisco, CA 94112-4046, email suavd@sunsite.unc.edu
OYSTER BOY REVIEW, 191 Sickles Avenue, San Francisco, CA 94112-4046, Email oyster-boy@sunsite.unc.edu; www.sunsite.unc.edu/ob
ASSPANTS, 2232 15th Street, San Francisco, CA 94114-1238, E-mail asspants@sirius.com
THE BLOWFISH CATALOG, 2261 Market Street #284, San Francisco, CA 94114, 415-864-0880; fax 1-415-864-1858; e-Mail blowfish@blowfish. rom
Blowfish Press, 2261 Market Street #284, San Francisco, CA 94114, 415-864-0880; fax 1-415-864-1858; e-Mail blowfish@blowfish. com
BOTH COASTS BOOK REVIEW, 882 14th Street, San Francisco, CA 94114, 415-252-7276 (phone & fax)
Bright Moon Press, 584 Castro Street, Ste. 232, San Francisco, CA 94114
Cleis Press, PO Box 14684, San Francisco, CA 94114-0684, cleis@aol.com; www.cleispress.com
Daedalus Publishing Company, 584 Castro Street, Suite 518, San Francisco, CA 94114, office 415-626-1867; fax 415-487-1137; e-Mail DPCBooks@aol.com
Mainstream Press, 584 Castro Street, Suite 518, San Francisco, CA 94114, 415-626-1867, fax 415-487-1137, e-mail MPBooks@aol.com
Not-For-Sale-Press or NFS Press, 243 Grand View Ave., San Francisco, CA 94114, 415-282-5372
Q ZINE, 2336 Market Street #14, San Francisco, CA 94114-1521, bcclark@igc.apc.org
KMT, A Modern Journal of Ancient Egypt, 1531 Golden Gate Avenue, San Francisco, CA 94115, 415-922-7263 (phone/fax)
ClearPoint Press, PO Box 170658, San Francisco, CA 94117, 415-386-5377 phone/Fax
FACTSHEET FIVE, PO Box 170099, San Francisco, CA 94117, 415-668-1781
Get In-Line! Publishing, PO Box 170340, San Francisco, CA 94117-0340, 415-292-5809, Fax: 415-292-4111
Haight-Ashbury Publications, 612 Clayton Street, San Francisco, CA 94117, 415-565-1904; fax 415-864-6162
JOURNAL OF PSYCHOACTIVE DRUGS, 612 Clayton Street, San Francisco, CA 94117, 415-565-1904; fax 415-864-6162
Scottwall Associates, Publishers, 95 Scott Street, San Francisco, CA 94117, 415-861-1956
X-RAY, PO Box 170011, San Francisco, CA 94117, e-mail johnny@xraybookco.com
Caddo Gap Press, 3145 Geary Boulevard, Suite 275, San Francisco, CA 94118, 415-922-1911
EDUCATIONAL FOUNDATIONS, 3145 Geary Boulevard, Suite 275, San Francisco, CA 94118, 415-922-1911
EDUCATIONAL LEADERSHIP & ADMINISTRATION, 3145 Geary Boulevard #275, San Francisco, CA 94118, 415-922-1911
JOURNAL OF THOUGHT, 3145 Geary Boulevard #275, San Francisco, CA 94118, 415-922-1911
MULTICULTURAL EDUCATION, 3145 Geary Boulevard, Ste. 275, San Francisco, CA 94118, 415-922-1911
NOTES AND ABSTRACTS IN AMERICAN AND INTERNATIONAL EDUCATION, 3145 Geary Boulevard #275, San Francisco, CA 94118, 415-922-1911
SUMMER ACADEME: A Journal of Higher Education, 3145 Geary Boulevard #275, San Francisco, CA 94118, 415-922-1911
Synergistic Press, 3965 Sacramento St., San Francisco, CA 94118, 415-EV7-8180; Fax 415-751-8505
TEACHER EDUCATION QUARTERLY, 3147 Geary Boulevard #275, San Francisco, CA 94118, 415-392-1911
VITAE SCHOLASTICAE: The Journal of Educational Biography, 3145 Geary Boulevard #275, San Francisco, CA 94118, 415-922-1911
Heritage House Publishers, PO Box 194242, San Francisco, CA 94119, 415-776-3156
URBANUS/RAIZIRR, PO Box 192921, San Francisco, CA 94119-2921
HARMONY: VOICES FOR A JUST FUTURE, PO Box 210056, San Francisco, CA 94121-0056, 415-221-8527
Protean Press, 287-28th Avenue, San Francisco, CA 94121, fax 415-386-4980
Sea Fog Press, Inc., 447 20th Avenue, San Francisco, CA 94121, 415-221-8527
Bicycle Books (Publishing) Inc., 1282 7th Avenue, San Francisco, CA 94122, 415-665-8214
The Communication Press, PO Box 22541, San Francisco, CA 94122, 415-386-0178
NEW METHODS JOURNAL (VETERINARY), PO Box 22605, San Francisco, CA 94122-0605, 415-664-3469
Stratton Press, PO Box 22391, San Francisco, CA 94122, 415-759-5270
Acada Books, 1850 Union Street, Suite 1236, San Francisco, CA 94123, 415-776-2325
National Poetry Association Publishers, Fort Mason Center, Building D, Room 270, San Francisco, CA 94123,

415-776-6602
Alan Wofsy Fine Arts, PO Box 2210, San Francisco, CA 94126, 415-986-3030
BURNING CAR, PO Box 26692, San Francisco, CA 94126, E-mail elfool@aol.com
Halo Books, PO Box 2529, San Francisco, CA 94126, 415-468-4256
INVISIBLE CITY, PO Box 2853, San Francisco, CA 94126
Jesus Pinata Press, PO Box 26692, San Francisco, CA 94126, E-mail elfool@aol.com
Red Hill Press, San Francisco + Los Angeles, PO Box 2853, San Francisco, CA 94126
Sierra Outdoor Products Co., PO Box 2497, San Francisco, CA 94126-2497, 415-258-0777 phone/fax
HAIGHT ASHBURY LITERARY JOURNAL, 558 Joost Avenue, San Francisco, CA 94127
BLACK SHEETS MAGAZINE, PO Box 31155, San Francisco, CA 94131-0155, 415-431-0173; Fax 415-431-0172; blacksheets@blackbooks.com
Bottom Line Pre$$, PO Box 31420, San Francisco, CA 94131-0420
Pancake Press, 163 Galewood Circle, San Francisco, CA 94131, 415-648-3573
THE READER'S REVIEW, 2966 Diamond Street, Suite 290, San Francisco, CA 94131, 415-585-2639
Second Coming Press, PO Box 31249, San Francisco, CA 94131
Unified Publications, 5214-F Diamond Heights #218, San Fransisco, CA 94131, 415-642-0364
Androgyne Books, 930 Shields, San Francisco, CA 94132, 415-586-2697
FOURTEEN HILLS: The SFSU Review, Creative Writing Dept., SFSU, 1600 Holloway Avenue, San Francisco, CA 94132, 415-338-3083, fax 415-338-0504; E-mail hills@sfsu.edu
City Lights Books, Attn: Bob Sharrard, Editor, 261 Columbus Avenue, San Francisco, CA 94133, 415-362-8193
CITY LIGHTS JOURNAL, 261 Columbus Avenue, San Francisco, CA 94133, 415-362-8193
AK Press, PO Box 40682, San Francisco, CA 94140, 415-864-0892; FAX 415-864-0893; akpress@org.org
CREEPY MIKE'S OMNIBUS OF FUN, PO Box 401026, San Francisco, CA 94140-1026, aueplayer@aol.com
Global Options, PO Box 40601, San Francisco, CA 94140, 415-550-1703
SOCIAL JUSTICE: A JOURNAL OF CRIME, CONFLICT, & WORLD ORDER, PO Box 40601, San Francisco, CA 94140, 415-550-1703
Aunt Lute Books, PO Box 410687, San Francisco, CA 94141, 415-826-1300; FAX 415-826-8300
Gay Sunshine Press, Inc., PO Box 410690, San Francisco, CA 94141, 415-626-1935; Fax 415-626-1802
GLOBAL MAIL, PO Box 410837, San Francisco, CA 94141-0837, 417-642-3731, e-mail soapbox@well.com
Leyland Publications, PO Box 410690, San Francisco, CA 94141, 415-626-1935; fax 415-626-1802
H2SO4, PO Box 423354, San Francisco, CA 94142, 415-431-2135; h2so4@socrates.berkeley.edu
ISSUES, PO Box 424885, San Francisco, CA 94142-4885, 415-864-4800 X136
ABERRATIONS, PO Box 460430, San Francisco, CA 94146, 415-648-3908
Carrier Pigeon Press, PO Box 460141, San Francisco, CA 94146-0141, 415-821-2090
BALLOT ACCESS NEWS, PO Box 470296, San Francisco, CA 94147, 415-922-9779; fax 415-441-4268; e-Mail ban@igc.apc.org
Creighton-Morgan Publishing Group, Po Box 470862, San Francisco, CA 94147-0862
THE COMPLEAT NURSE, PO Box 640345, San Francisco, CA 94164, 415-252-7371; fax 415-292-7314
Dry Bones Press, PO Box 640345, San Francisco, CA 94164, 415-292-7371; FAX 415-252-7371; website http://www.drybones.com/
Infinite Corridor Publishing, PO Box 640051, San Francisco, CA 94164-0051, 415-292-5639; Fax 415-931-5639; E-mail corridor@slip.net
MURDER CAN BE FUN, PO Box 640111, San Francisco, CA 94164, 415-666-8956
New World Press, PO Box 640432, San Francisco, CA 94164-0432, 415-292-7008
Norton Coker Press, PO Box 640543, San Francisco, CA 94164-0543, 415-922-0395
Taurean Horn Press, PO Box 641097, San Francisco, CA 94164
TWO LINES, PO Box 641978, San Francisco, CA 94164-1978, 415-863-8586 phone/Fax; editors@twolines.com; www.twolines.com
THE FEMINIST BOOKSTORE NEWS, PO Box 882554, San Francisco, CA 94188, 415-642-9993; fax 415-642-9995; e-mail fbn@fembknews.com
Bull Publishing Co., P O Box 208, Palo Alto, CA 94302, 415-322-2855
Anamnesis Press, PO Box 51115, Palo Alto, CA 94303-0688, 415-244-8366; fax 415-255-3190; web site ourworld.compuserve.com/homepages/anamnesis/ E-mail:anamnesis@compuserve.com
Hoover Institution Press, Stanford University, Stanford, CA 94305-6010, 650-723-3373; e-mail baker@hoover.stanford.edu
The Live Oak Press, PO Box 69036, Palo Alto, CA 94306-0036, 415-853-0197; e-mail liveoakprs@aol.com; web address http://members.aol.com/liveoakprs
Pathways Press, Inc., PO Box 60175, Palo Alto, CA 94306, 415-529-1910; pathways@best.com
Trimarket, 2264 Bowdoin Street, Palo Alto, CA 94306, 650-494-1406; 70470.527@compuserve.com
JOURNAL OF SCIENTIFIC EXPLORATION, PO Box 5848, Stanford, CA 94309-5848, 650-593-8581, fax 650-595-4466, e-mail sims@jse.com
Press Here, PO Box 4014, Foster City, CA 94404, 415-571-9428, e-Mail WelchM@aol.com
WOODNOTES, 248 Beach Park Boulevard, Foster City, CA 94404, 415-571-9428, e-mail WelchM@aol.com
Hunter House Inc., Publishers, PO Box 2914, Alameda, CA 94501
Latham Foundation, Latham Plaza, 1826 Clement Avenue, Alameda, CA 94501-1397, 510-521-0920; www.latham.org
THE LATHAM LETTER, Latham Foundation, Latham Plaza, 1826 Clement Avenue, Alameda, CA 94501-1397, 415-521-0920; www.latham.org
Roam Publishing, 2447 Santa Clara Avenue, Suite 304, Alameda, CA 94501, 510-769-7075; fax 510-769-7076; e-mail editor@roampublishing.com; website www.roampublishing.com
The Glencannon Press, PO Box 633, Benicia, CA 94510, 707-745-3933; fax 707-747-0311
The Poetry Center Press/Shoestring Press, 3 Monte Vista Road, Orinda, CA 94513, 925-254-1939
Front Row Experience, 540 Discovery Bay Boulevard, Byron, CA 94514, 510-634-5710
EGW Publishing Company, 1041 Shary Circle, Concord, CA 94518-2407
TOLE WORLD, 1041 Shary Circle, Concord, CA 94518-2407, 510-671-9852
VEGGIE LIFE, 1041 Shary Circle, Concord, CA 94518-2407, 510-671-9852
WEEKEND WOODCRAFTS, 1041 Shary Circle, Concord, CA 94518-2407, 510-671-6852
WOOD STROKES & WOODCRAFTS, 1041 Shary Circle, Concord, CA 94518-2407, 510-671-9852
C & T Publishing, 1651 Challenge Drive, Concord, CA 94520-5206, 925-677-0377
Solution Publishing, 1647 Willow Pass Road #101, Concord, CA 94520

Dark Regions Press, PO Box 6301, Concord, CA 94524
DARK REGIONS: The Years Best Fantastic Fiction, PO Box 6301, Concord, CA 94524
UC Books, Box 1036, Danville, CA 94526, 510-820-3710; Fax 510-820-3711; E-mail ucbooks@aol.com
TWISTED TIMES, PO Box 271222, Concord, CA 94527
Universal Unity, 1860 Mowry Ave. #400, Fremont, CA 94538-2167
THE COMPANY NORTH AMERICA, PO Box 20766, Castro Valley, CA 94546, 510-888-1485
The Infinity Group, PO Box 2713, Castro Valley, CA 94546, 510-581-8172; kenandgenie@yahoo.com
MUSE NATURA, A Sensual Journey of the Arts, PO Box 2210, Livermore, CA 94550, 510-447-2245; e-mail pleiadespress@netwizards.net
Oughten House Publications, PO Box 2008, Livermore, CA 94551, 510-447-2332; Fax 510-447-2376; E-mail oughtenhouse.com
African Ways Publishing, 33 Hansen Court, Moraga, CA 94556-1580, 925-631-0630; Fax 925-376-1926
THE GENRE WRITER'S NEWS, 30 Canyon View Drive, Orinda, CA 94563, 510-254-7442
Eagle Publishing Company, 7283 Kolb Place, Dublin, CA 94568, 415-828-1350
Fels and Firn Press, Attn: Laura Petersen, 6934 Lassen Street, Pleasanton, CA 94588-4918, 510-846-0304
AltaMira Press, 1630 N. Main Street, Suite 367, Walnut Creek, CA 94596, 510-938-7243; FAX 510-933-9720
Devil Mountain Books, PO Box 4115, Walnut Creek, CA 94596, 925-939-3415; Fax 925-937-4883; devlmtn@aol.com
Gateway Books, 2023 Clemens Road, Oakland, CA 94602, 510-530-0299; FAX 510-530-0497
THE WISE WOMAN, 2441 Cordova Street, Oakland, CA 94602, 510-536-3174
LEFT CURVE, PO Box 472, Oakland, CA 94604, E-mail: leftcurv@wco.com
RADIANCE, The Magazine For Large Women, PO Box 30246, Oakland, CA 94604, 510-482-0680, E-mail info@radiancemagazine.com; www.radiancemagazine.com
IMPRINT, A LITERARY JOURNAL, 4053 Harlan Street, Loft 314, Emeryville, CA 94608-2702
THE MONTHLY (formerly THE BERKELEY MONTHLY), 1301 59th Street, Emeryville, CA 94608, 415-848-7900
Regent Press, 6020-A Adeline, Oakland, CA 94608, 415-548-8459
THE BLACK SCHOLAR: Journal of Black Studies and Research, PO Box 2869, Oakland, CA 94609, 510-547-6633
Broken Shadow Publications, 472 44th Street, Oakland, CA 94609-2136, 510-450-0640
CROSS ROADS, PO Box 2809, Oakland, CA 94609, 510-843-7495
EyeDEA Books, 477 Rich Street, Oakland, CA 94609, 510-653-7190
The O Press, 702 45th Street, Oakland, CA 94609-1803
ANT ANT ANT ANT ANT, PO Box 16177, Oakland, CA 94610
BLACKJACK FORUM, 414 Santa Clara Avenue, Oakland, CA 94610, 510-465-6452; FAX 510-652-4330
R.G.E. Publishing, 414 Santa Clara, Oakland, CA 94610
S.E.T. FREE: The Newsletter Against Television, Box 10491, Oakland, CA 94610, 510-763-8712
Chardon Press, 3781 Broadway, Oakland, CA 94611, 510-596-8160; Fax 510-596-8822; chardon@chardonpress.com; www.chardonpress.com
COLORLINES, 4096 Piedmont Avenue, PMB 319, Oakland, CA 94611, 510-653-3415; Fax 510-653-3427; colorlines@arc.org; www.colorlines.com
GRASSROOTS FUNDRAISING JOURNAL, 3781 Broadway, Oakland, CA 94611, 510-596-8160; Fax 510-596-8822; chardon@chardonpress.com; www.chardonpress.com
Institute for Contemporary Studies, 1611 Telegraph Avenue, Ste. 902, Oakland, CA 94612-3010
WORLDVIEWS: A Quarterly Review of Resources for Education and Action, 1515 Webster Street, #305, Oakland, CA 94612, 510-451-1742; fax 510-835-9631; e-mail worldviews@igc.org
Burning Bush Publications, PO Box 9636, Oakland, CA 94613-0636, 510-482-9996; www.home.earthlink.net/~abbyb
HIP MAMA, Attn: Ariel Gore, PO Box 9097, Oakland, CA 94613, 510-658-4508
Food First Books, 398 60th Street, Oakland, CA 94618, 510-654-4400; FAX 510-654-4551; foodfirst@foodfirst.org
The Independent Institute, 100 Swan Way, Oakland, CA 94621-1428, 510-632-1366; fax 510-568-6040; email info@independent.org; www.independent.org
THE INDEPENDENT REVIEW: A Journal of Political Economy, 100 Swan Way, Oakland, CA 94621-1428, 510-632-1366; fax 510-568-6040; email review@independent.org; www.independent.org/review
LOCUS: The Newspaper of the Science Fiction Field, Box 13305, Oakland, CA 94661, 510-339-9196, 9198; FAX 510-339-8144
CC. Marimbo Communications, PO Box 933, Berkeley, CA 94701-0933
Jolly Roger Press, PO Box 295, Berkeley, CA 94701, 510-548-7123
JUMP CUT, A Review of Contemporary Media, P.O. Box 865, Berkeley, CA 94701
MARION ZIMMER BRADLEY'S FANTASY MAGAZINE, PO Box 249, Berkeley, CA 94701-0249, 510-644-9222
The New Humanity Press, PO Box 215, Berkeley, CA 94701
PHOENIX MAGAZINE, PO Box 17, Berkeley, CA 94701-0317
Phoenix Press, PO Box 317, Berkeley, CA 94701-0317
Ronin Publishing, Inc., Box 522, Berkeley, CA 94701, 510-540-6278
Dharma Publishing, 2910 San Pablo Avenue, Berkeley, CA 94702
GESAR-Buddhism in the West, 2910 San Pablo Avenue, Berkeley, CA 94702, 415-548-5407
Homeward Press, PO Box 2307, Berkeley, CA 94702, 412-526-3254
Ortalda & Associates, 1208 Delaware Street, Berkeley, CA 94702, 510-524-2040
Pacific View Press, PO Box 2657, Berkeley, CA 94702, fax 510-843-5835, pvp@sirius.com
AGADA, 2020 Essex Street, Berkeley, CA 94703, 510-848-0965
New Earth Publications, 1921 Ashby Ave, Berkeley, CA 94703, 510-549-0176
SINISTER WISDOM, PO Box 3252, Berkeley, CA 94703, 510-532-5222
TWISTED IMAGE NEWSLETTER, 1630 University Avenue #26, Berkeley, CA 94703, 415-644-8035
Insider Publications, 2124 Kittredge Street, 3rd Floor, Berkeley, CA 94704, 800-782-6657; Fax 415-552-1978; E-mail info@travelinsider.com
SCP NEWSLETTER, PO Box 4308, Berkeley, CA 94704
TURNING WHEEL, PO Box 4650, Berkeley, CA 94704
Wilderness Press, 2440 Bancroft Way, Berkeley, CA 94704, 510-843-8080; fax 510-548-1355; e-mail mail@wilderness-press.com
Judah Magnes Museum Publications, 2911 Russell Street, Berkeley, CA 94705
Oyez, PO Box 5134, Berkeley, CA 94705
Poltroon Press, PO Box 5476, Berkeley, CA 94705, 510-845-8097

verygraphics, PO Box 6374, Albany, CA 94706, 510-644-4188

YELLOW SILK: Journal Of Erotic Arts, PO Box 6374, Albany, CA 94706, 510-644-4188

Carousel Press, PO Box 6038, Berkeley, CA 94706-0038, 510-527-5849; info@carousel-press.com; www.carousel-press.com

Banyan Tree Books, 1963 El Dorado Avenue, Berkeley, CA 94707, 510-524-2690

The Dibble Fund for Marriage Education, PO Box 7881, Berkeley, CA 94707-0881, 800-695-7975; Fax: 510-528-1956; e-mail: dibblefund@aol.com

LANDSCAPE, PO Box 7107, Berkeley, CA 94707, 415-549-3233

MYSTERY READERS JOURNAL, PO Box 8116, Berkeley, CA 94707-8116, 510-339-2800

OPEN EXCHANGE MAGAZINE, PO Box 7880, Berkeley, CA 94707, 510-526-7190

Parallax Press, PO Box 7355, Berkeley, CA 94707, 510-525-0101; e-Mail parapress@aol.com; web address http://www.parallax.org

Stone Bridge Press, PO Box 8208, Berkeley, CA 94707, 510-524-8732

BLUE UNICORN, 22 Avon Road, Kensington, CA 94707, 510-526-8439

Kelsey St. Press, 50 Northgate Avenue, Berkeley, CA 94708-2008, 510-845-2260; FAX 510-548-9185, e-mail kelseyst.@sirius.com; www.kelseyst.com

THE MONTHLY INDEPENDENT TRIBUNE TIMES JOURNAL POST GAZETTE NEWS CHRONICLE BULLETIN, 80 Fairlawn Drive, Berkeley, CA 94708-2106

Queen of Swords Press, 1328 Arch Street #B, Berkeley, CA 94708-1825, 541-344-0509

Berkeley Hills Books, PO Box 9877, Berkeley, CA 94709, 510-848-7303 phone/Fax; E-mail bhbsales@berkeleyhills.com

Community Resource Institute Press, 1442-A Walnut #51, Berkeley, CA 94709, 415-526-7190

Fallen Leaf Press, PO Box 10034, Berkeley, CA 94709, 510-848-7805 phone/Fax

The Gutenberg Press, c/o Fred Foldvary, 1920 Cedar Street, Berkeley, CA 94709, 510-843-0248; e-mail gutenbergpress@pobox.com

Heyday Books, PO Box 9145, Berkeley, CA 94709, 510-549-3564; FAX 510-549-1889

New Seed Press, 1665 Euclid Avenue, Berkeley, CA 94709-1213

NEWS FROM NATIVE CALIFORNIA, PO Box 9145, Berkeley, CA 94709, 510-549-3564; FAX 510-549-1889

RABID ANIMAL KOMIX, PO Box 9389, Berkeley, CA 94709-0389, 415-440-0967; email krankinkmx@aol.com

REPORTS OF THE NATIONAL CENTER FOR SCIENCE EDUCATION, NCSE, Box 9477, Berkeley, CA 94709, 510-526-1674; FAX 510-526-1675

THE THREEPENNY REVIEW, PO Box 9131, Berkeley, CA 94709, 510-849-4545

THE BERKELEY REVIEW OF BOOKS, 1731 10th Street, Apt. A, Berkeley, CA 94710, 415-528-8713

Conari Press, 2550 Ninth Street, Suite 101, Berkeley, CA 94710, 501-649-7175, 1-800-685-9595

DESIGN BOOK REVIEW, 720 Channing Way, Berkeley, CA 94710, 415-486-1956; fax 415-644-3930; e-mail DBReview@ix.netcom.com

Nolo Press, 950 Parker Street, Berkeley, CA 94710, 510-549-1976

OPTIMA Books, 2820 8th Street, Berkeley, CA 94710, 510-848-8708; Fax 510-848-8737; esl@optimabooks.com; www.optimabooks.com

POETRY FLASH, 1450 Fourth Street #4, Berkeley, CA 94710, 510-525-5476, Fax; 510-525-6752

Bay Area Poets Coalition, POETALK, PO Box 11435, Berkeley, CA 94712-2435, 510-272-9176

THE CHEROTIC (r)EVOLUTIONARY, PO Box 11445, Berkeley, CA 94712, 510-526-7858; FAX 510-524-2053

Five Fingers Press, PO Box 12955, Berkeley, CA 94712-3955

FIVE FINGERS REVIEW, PO Box 12955, Berkeley, CA 94712-3955

Lux Fiat Press, PO Box 14626, Berkeley, CA 94712, caerula@hotmail.com

Mindfield Publications, PO Box 14114, Berkeley, CA 94712-5114, 510-433-7945; mindfld@dnai.com; www.dnai.com/mindfld

North Atlantic Books, PO Box 12327, Berkeley, CA 94712, 510-559-8277; fax 510-559-8272; www.northatlantic.com

POETALK, PO Box 11435, Berkeley, CA 94712-2435, 510-272-9176

AGRICULTURAL HISTORY, University of California Press, 2120 Berkeley Way, Berkeley, CA 94720, 510-643-7154

ASIAN SURVEY, University of California Press, 2120 Berkeley Way, Berkeley, CA 94720, 510-643-7154

BERKELEY JOURNAL OF EMPLOYMENT AND LABOR LAW, University of California Press, 2120 Berkeley Way, Berkeley, CA 94720, 510-643-7154

BERKELEY JOURNAL OF INTERNATIONAL LAW, University of California Press, 2120 Berkeley Way, Berkeley, CA 94720, 410-643-7154

BERKELEY POETRY REVIEW, 201 MLK Student Union, University of California, Berkeley, CA 94720

BERKELEY TECHNOLOGY LAW JOURNAL, University of California Press, 2120 Berkeley Way, Berkeley, CA 94720, 510-643-7154

BERKELEY WOMEN'S LAW JOURNAL, 2 Boalt Hall, Univ. of Ca., School of Law, Berkeley, CA 94720, 510-642-6263

CALIFORNIA LAW REVIEW, University of California Press, 2120 Berkeley Way, Berkeley, CA 94720, 510-643-7154

CLASSICAL ANTIQUITY, Univ of California Press, 2120 Berkeley Way, Berkeley, CA 94720, 510-643-7154

EAST EUROPEAN POLITICS & SOCIETIES, University of California Press, 2120 Berkeley Way, Berkeley, CA 94720, 510-643-7154

ECOLOGY LAW QUARTERLY, University of California Press, 2120 Berkeley Way, Berkeley, CA 94720, 510-643-7154

FEDERAL SENTENCING REPORTER, University of California Press, 2120 Berkeley Way, Berkeley, CA 94720, 510-643-7154

FILM QUARTERLY, University of California Press, 2120 Berkeley Way, Berkeley, CA 94720, 510-643-7154

HISTORICAL STUDIES IN THE PHYSICAL & BIOLOGICAL SCIENCES, University of California Press, 2120 Berkeley Way, Berkeley, CA 94720, 510-643-7154

INDEX TO FOREIGN LEGAL PERIODICALS, University of California Press, 2120 Berkeley Way, Berkeley, CA 94720, 510-643-7154

JOURNAL OF MUSICOLOGY, University of California Press, 2120 Berkeley Way, Berkeley, CA 94720, 510-643-7154

LA RAZA LAW JOURNAL, University of California Press, 2120 Berkeley Way, Berkeley, CA 94720, 510-643-7154

MEXICAN STUDIES/ESTUDIOS MEXICANOS, University of California Press, 2120 Berkeley Way, Berkeley, CA 94720, 510-643-7154

MOUNTAIN RESEARCH & DEVELOPMENT, University of California Press, 2120 Berkeley Way, Berkeley, CA 94720, 510-643-7154

MUSIC PERCEPTION, Univ of CA Press, 2120 Berkeley Way, Berkeley, CA 94720, 510-643-7154

NINETEENTH-CENTURY LITERATURE, University of California Press, 2120 Berkeley Way, Berkeley, CA 94720,

510-643-7154
19TH-CENTURY MUSIC, University of California Press, 2120 Berkeley Way, Berkeley, CA 94720, 540-643-7154
PACIFIC HISTORICAL REVIEW, Univ of California Press, 2120 Berkeley Way, Berkeley, CA 94720, 510-643-7154
THE PUBLIC HISTORIAN, University of California Press, 2120 Berkeley Way, Berkeley, CA 94720, 510-643-7154
REPRESENTATIONS, University of California Press, 2120 Berkeley Way, Berkeley, CA 94720, 510-643-7154
RHETORICA: A Journal of the History of Rhetoric, Univ of California Press, 2120 Berkeley Way, Berkeley, CA 94720, 510-643-7154
SOCIAL PROBLEMS, University of California Press, 2120 Berkeley Way, Berkeley, CA 94720, 510-643-7154
University of California Press, 2120 Berkeley Way, Berkeley, CA 94720, 510-642-6263, e-mail journal@ucop.edu
Point Bonita Books, 5920 Dimm Way, Richmond, CA 94805, 510-232-1401
WHOLE EARTH, 1408 Mission Avenue, San Rafael, CA 94901-1971
Wood River Publishing, 1099 D Street, Suite A, San Rafael, CA 94901-2843, 415-256-9300; Fax 415-256-9400; info@picturenet.com
Axiom Press, Publishers, PO Box L, San Rafael, CA 94913, 415-956-4859
Cassandra Press, Inc., PO Box 150868, San Rafael, CA 94915, 415-382-8507
Cadmus Editions, PO Box 126, Belvedere Tiburon, CA 94920-0126
H J Kramer, PO Box 1082, Tiburon, CA 94920
Waters Edge Press, 98 Main Street #527, Tiburon, CA 94920, 415-435-2837; Fax 415-435-2404; E-mail books@watersedgepress.com; website www.watersedgepress.com
JOURNAL OF SOCIAL BEHAVIOR AND PERSONALITY, PO Box 37, Corte Madera, CA 94925, 415-924-1612
Select Press, PO Box 37, Corte Madera, CA 94925, 415-924-1612
Context Publications, PO Box 2909, Rohnert Park, CA 94927, 707-576-1700
Pomegranate Communications, PO Box 6099, Rohnert Park, CA 94927, 707-586-5500; fax 707-586-5518; e-mail info@pomegranate.com
Exile Press, 112 Chadwick Way, Cotati, CA 94931
Elder Books, PO Box 490, Forest Knolls, CA 94933
The Golden Sufi Center, PO Box 428, Inverness, CA 94937, 415-663-8773; FAX 415-663-9128; E-mail GoldenSufi@aol.com
BARNABE MOUNTAIN REVIEW, PO Box 529, Lagunitas, CA 94938
Kosmos, 20 Millard Road, Larkspur, CA 94939
Tamal Vista Publications, 222 Madrone Ave, Larkspur, CA 94939, 924-7289
NEW AMERICAN WRITING, 369 Molino Avenue, Mill Valley, CA 94941, 415-389-1877 phone and fax
Origin Press, 1122 Grant Avenue, Suite C, Novato, CA 94945, 415-898-7400; fax 415-898-4890; e-mail info@originbooks.com
EXPERIMENTAL MUSICAL INSTRUMENTS, PO Box 784, Nicasio, CA 94946, 415-662-2182
Chandler & Sharp Publishers, Inc., 11A Commercial Blvd., Novato, CA 94949, 415-883-2353, FAX: 415-883-4280
The Feathered Serpent, 55 Galli Drive #C, Novato, CA 94949-5715, 415-499-8751
New World Library, 14 Pamaron Way, Novato, CA 94949-6215
THE BOOKWATCH, 12424 Mill Street, Petaluma, CA 94952, 415-437-5731
Small Helm Press, 622 Baker Street, Petaluma, CA 94952, 707-763-5757
ON PARAGUAY, 1724 Burgundy Court, Petaluma, CA 94954, 707-763-6835; E-mail paraguay@wco.com
Smart Publications, PO Box 4667, Petaluma, CA 94955
SPEX (SMALL PRESS EXCHANGE), PO Box E, Corte Madera, CA 94957, 415-924-1612, 415-257-8275
SPECIALTY TRAVEL INDEX, 305 San Anselmo Avenue #313, San Anselmo, CA 94960-2660, 415-459-4900
The Post-Apollo Press, 35 Marie Street, Sausalito, CA 94965, 415-332-1458, fax 415-332-8045
Arctos Press, PO Box 401, Sausalito, CA 94966, E-mail Runes@aol.com
THE BUTTERFLY CHRONICLES, A Literary Journal from the Butterfly Tree, PO Box 790, Sausalito, CA 94966, 415-383-8447
In Between Books, PO Box 790, Sausalito, CA 94966, 383-8447
Anteater Press, PO Box 750745, Petaluma, CA 94975-0745, 707-763-6835; E-mail paraguay@wco.com
GINOSKO, PO Box 246, Fairfax, CA 94978, 415-460-8436
Big Star Press, 1770 48th Avenue, #2-D, Capitola, CA 95010, 408-464-3625 ph/fax
BOTTOMFISH, 21250 Stevens Creek Blvd., De Anza College, Cupertino, CA 95014, Fax 408-864-5533; splitter@cruzio.com
Myth Breakers, 19672 Steers Creek Blvd, Suite 200, Cupertino, CA 95014, 408-257-7257
Genny Smith Books, 23100 Via Esplendor, Villa 44, Cupertino, CA 95014, 650-964-4071
Woman in the Moon Publications (W.I.M. Publications), PO Box 2087, Cupertino, CA 95015-2087, E-mail womaninmoon@earthlink.net
The Crossing Press, PO Box 1048, Freedom, CA 95019-1048, 408-722-0711 e-mail crossing@aol.com
WRITING FOR OUR LIVES, 647 N. Santa Cruz Ave., The Annex, Los Gatos, CA 95030, 408-354-8604
Amethyst & Emerald, 1556 Halford Avenue, Suite 124, Santa Clara, CA 95051-2661, 408-296-5483; fax 408-249-7646
TEENS IN MOTION NEWS, PO Box 1264, Santa Clara, CA 95052, 408-244-3718
ALCATRAZ, 133 Towne Terrace, Santa Cruz, CA 95060
Alcatraz Editions, 325 Kramaur Lane, Santa Cruz, CA 95060
Greenhouse Review Press, 3965 Bonny Doon Road, Santa Cruz, CA 95060, 831-426-4355
THE LEFT INDEX, 511 Lincoln Street, Santa Cruz, CA 95060, 408-426-4479
Moving Parts Press, 10699 Empire Grade, Santa Cruz, CA 95060-9474, 408-427-2271
Paperweight Press, 123 Locust Street, Santa Cruz, CA 95060-3907, 408-427-1177
Dakota Books, PO Box 1551, Santa Cruz, CA 95061, 408-464-9636
ETR Associates, PO Box 1830, Santa Cruz, CA 95061-1830, 408-438-4060
HerBooks, PO Box 7467, Santa Cruz, CA 95061
Tombouctou Books, 1472 Creekview Lane, Santa Cruz, CA 95062, 408-476-4144
C. Olson & Company, PO Box 100, Santa Cruz, CA 95063-0100, 408-458-9004
Red Alder Books, Box 2992, Santa Cruz, CA 95063, 831-426-7082, Fax 831-425-8825, E-mail eronat@aol.com
STONE SOUP, The Magazine By Young Writers and Artists, Box 83, Santa Cruz, CA 95063, 831-426-5557, Fax 831-426-1161, e-mail editor@stonesoup.com; www.stonesoup.com
Papier-Mache Press, 627 Walker Street, Watsonville, CA 95076-4119, 408-763-1420, Fax 408-763-1421
POET'S PARK, 2745 Monterey Highway #76, San Jose, CA 95111-3129, 408-578-3546; http://www.soos.com/poetpark

MINISTRY & LITURGY, 160 East Virginia Street, #290, San Jose, CA 95112-5876, 408-286-8505, Fax; 408-287-8748, E-mail; mdrulitgy@aol.com, Internet; http://www.rpinet.com
Resource Publications, Inc., 160 East Virginia Street #290, San Jose, CA 95112-5876, 408-286-8505, Fax 408-287-8745, E-mail info@rpinet.com, www.rpinet.com
CAESURA, San Jose Museum of Art, 110 S. Market, San Jose, CA 95113, FAX 408-624-7432
R & E Publishers, 2132 O'Tode Avenue, Suite A, San Jose, CA 95131, 408-432-3443; fax 408-432-9221
INDIA CURRENTS, Box 21285, San Jose, CA 95151, 408-274-6966; 408-274-2733; e-Mail EDITOR@INDIACUR.COM
Library Research Associates, PO Box 32234, San Jose, CA 95152-2234, 408-946-0777; fax 408-946-0779
R.J. Bender Publishing, PO Box 23456, San Jose, CA 95153, 408-225-5777; Fax 408-225-4739; order@bender-publishing.com
French Bread Publications, PO Box 23868, San Jose, CA 95153, e-mail paccoastj@juno.com
PACIFIC COAST JOURNAL, PO Box 23868, San Jose, CA 95153, e-mail paccoastj@juno.com
Urion Press, PO Box 10085, San Jose, CA 95157, 408-867-7695 Fax/phone
Northern Star Press, PO Box 28814, San Jose, CA 95159
ICA Publishing, 1020 N. Commerce, Stockton, CA 95202, 209-466-3883
Heritage West Books, 306 Regent Court, Stockton, CA 95204-4435, 209-464-8818
Auromere Books and Imports, 2621 W. US Highway 12, Lodi, CA 95242-9200, 800-735-4691; 209-339-3710; FAX 209-339-3715; sasp@aol.com
Massey-Reyner Publishing, PO Box 323, Wallace, CA 95254, phone/fax 209-763-2590; e-mail learning@goldrush.com
Herbelin Publishing, PO Box 74, Riverbank, CA 95367, 209-869-6389; herbelin@netfeed.com; www.netfeed.com/~herbelin/homepage.htm
Black Sparrow Press, 24 Tenth Street, Santa Rosa, CA 95401
Cole Publishing Group, Inc., PO Box 4089, Santa Rosa, CA 95402-4089, 707-526-2682
Maledicta Press, PO Box 14123, Santa Rosa, CA 95402-6123
MALEDICTA: The International Journal of Verbal Aggression, PO Box 14123, Santa Rosa, CA 95402-6123
LEAPINGS LITERARY MAGAZINE, 2455 Pinercrest Drive, Santa Rosa, CA 95403, E-mail 72144.3133@compu-serve.com
GREEN FUSE POETRY, 3365 Holland Drive, Santa Rosa, CA 95404, 707-544-8303
Clamshell Press, 160 California Avenue, Santa Rosa, CA 95405
Foghorn Press, PO BOX 2036, Santa Rosa, CA 95405-0036, 415-241-9550
Hoffman Press, PO Box 2996, Santa Rosa, CA 95405-0996, 707-538-5527; fax 707-538-7371
THE LETTER EXCHANGE, The Readers' League, PO Box 2930, Santa Rosa, CA 95405
FORUM, PO Box 6144, Santa Rosa, CA 95406, 707-532-1323, fax 707-523-1350
THE FOURTH R, PO Box 6144, Santa Rosa, CA 95406, 707-523-1325, fax 707-523-1350
Polebridge Press, PO Box 6144, Santa Rosa, CA 95406, 707-523-1323, fax 707-523-1350
Kauai Press, 1170 Ozone Drive, Santa Rosa, CA 95407-6438
THE REJECTED QUARTERLY, PO Box 1351, Cobb, CA 95426, E-mail bplankton@juno.com
Pot Shard Press, PO Box 215, Comptche, CA 95427, 707-937-2058
Cypress House, 155 Cypress Street, Fort Bragg, CA 95437, 707-964-9520, Fax 707-964-7531; E-mail publishing@cypres-shouse.com
Lost Coast Press, 155 Cypress Street, Fort Bragg, CA 95437
QED Press, 155 Cypress Street, Fort Bragg, CA 95437, 707-964-9520, Fax; 707-964-7531, E-mail; qedpress@mcn.org
AHA Books, PO Box 767, Gualala, CA 95445, 707-882-2226
III Publishing, PO Box 1581, Gualala, CA 95445-0363, 707-884-1818
Integral Publishing, PO Box 1030, Lower Lake, CA 95457, 707-928-5751
MEMO, PO Box 1497, Mendocino, CA 95460
Ridge Times Press, Box 90, Mendocino, CA 95460, 707-964-8465
Nolo Press - Occidental, PO Box 722, Occidental, CA 95465, 707-874-3105, fax 707-874-1323
SAGEWOMAN, PO Box 641, Point Arena, CA 95468
LIVE AND LET LIVE, PO Box 613, Redwood Valley, CA 95470
Palm Drive Publishing, 2755 Blucher Valley Road, 2nd Floor Suite, Sebastopol, CA 95472, 707-829-1930; Fax 707-829-1568; correspond@palmdrivepublishing.com; www.palmdrivepublishing.com
Times Change Press, 8453 Blackney Road, Sebastopol, CA 95472-4608
CRCS Publications, PO Box 1460, Sebastopol, CA 95473-1460
KMT Communications, PO Box 1475, Sebastopol, CA 95473-1475, 415-922-7263
Big Mouth Publications, 284 Clay Street, Sonoma, CA 95476-7551
RedBrick Press, PO Box 1895, Sonoma, CA 95476-1895, 707-996-2774
Acton Circle Publishing Company, PO Box 1564, Ukiah, CA 95482, 707-463-3921, 707-462-2103, Fax 707-462-4942; actoncircle@pacific.net
Bell Springs Publishing, P.O. Box 1240, Willits, CA 95490, 707-459-6372, Fax 707-459-8614
GREEN EGG, 212 S. Main Street #22B, Willits, CA 95490-3535, 707-456-0332; Fax 707-456-0333; e-mail admin@greenegg.org
Rayve Productions Inc., PO Box 726, Windsor, CA 95492, 707-838-6200, Fax; 707-838-2220, E-mail; rayvepro@aol.com
Miles & Miles, PO Box 6730, Eureka, CA 95502
Pygmy Forest Press, PO Box 7097, Eureka, CA 95502-4111, 707-268-1274
AUTO-FREE TIMES, PO Box 4347, Arcata, CA 95518, 707-826-7775
Borderland Sciences Research Foundation, PO Box 220, Bayside, CA 95524-0220
BORDERLANDS: A Quarterly Journal Of Borderland Research, PO Box 220, Bayside, CA 95524-0220
THE KERF, 883 W. Washington Boulevard, Crescent City, CA 95531, 707-464-6867
Seed Center, PO Box 1700, Redway, CA 95560-1700, 707-923-2524
WESTART, PO Box 6868, Auburn, CA 95604, 530-885-0969
A.R.A. JOURNAL, Dr. Ion Manea-Manoliu, 3328 Monte Vista Avenue, Davis, CA 95616, 916-758-7720
American Romanian Academy, University of California, Dept. of French & Italian, Davis, CA 95616, 916-758-7720
Hi Jinx Press, 203 F Street, Suite A, PO Box 1814, Davis, CA 95616, 916-759-8514; Fax 916-759-8639; E-mail hijinx@mother.com
Terra Nova Press, 1309 Redwood Lane, Davis, CA 95616, 916-753-1519
AMERICAS REVIEW, PO Box 72466, Davis, CA 95617
MOCKINGBIRD, PO Box 761, Davis, CA 95617

Pro-Guides, Professional Guides Publications, PO Box 2071, Davis, CA 95617-2071, 510-283-1831
J P Publications, 1895 Berry Court, Dixon, CA 95620-2506, 916-678-9727
THE ACORN, PO Box 1266, El Dorado, CA 95623, 916-621-1833
Adams-Blake Publishing, 8041 Sierra Street, Fair Oaks, CA 95628, 916-962-9296
Clay Press, Inc., PO Box 250, Jackson, CA 95642
LLAMAS MAGAZINE, PO Box 250, Jackson, CA 95642, 209-295-7800 voice; FAX 209-295-7878; claypres@volcano.net
P.D.Q., 5836 North Haven Drive, North Highlands, CA 95660, e-mail poetdpth@aol.com
Spears of Ink, 5836 North Haven Drive, North Highlands, CA 95660, e-mail p1toall@aol.com
FINANCIAL FOCUS, 2140 Professional Drive Ste. 105, Roseville, CA 95661-3734, 916-791-1447; Fax 916-791-3444; evercfp@ix.netcom.com
HUMANS & OTHER SPECIES, 8732 Rock Springs Road, Penryn, CA 95663-9622, 916-663-3294
Bluestocking Press, PO Box 1014, Dept. D, Placerville, CA 95667-1014, 530-621-1123, Fax 530-642-9222, 1-800-959-8586 (orders only)
ClockWorks Press, PO Box 1699, Shingle Springs, CA 95682, 916-676-0701
IN PRINT, PO Box 1699, Shingle Springs, CA 95682, 916-676-0701
Hot Pepper Press, PO Box 39, Somerset, CA 95684, 916-621-1833
Volcano Press, Inc, PO Box 270, Volcano, CA 95689, 209-296-3445; fax 209-296-4515; Credit card orders only: 1-800-VPWYMEN; e-mail ruth@volcanopress.com; website http://volcanopress.com
Konocti Books, 23311 County Road 88, Winters, CA 95694
MinRef Press, 2324 Dinwiddie Way, Elk Grove, CA 95758-7424
Reference Service Press, 5000 Windplay Drive, Suite 4, El Dorado Hills, CA 95762, 916-939-9620; fax 916-939-9626; e-mail findaid@aol.com; website www.rspfunding.com
New Regency Publishing, PO Box 1443, Sacramento, CA 95812, 800-266-5639
Cougar Books, 1228 N Street, Suite 10, Sacramento, CA 95814, 916-442-1434
MOM GUESS WHAT NEWSPAPER, 1725 L Street, Sacramento, CA 95814-4023, 916-441-6397
Poetry Now, Sacramento's Literary Calendar and Review, 1631 K Street, Sacramento, CA 95814, 916-441-7395; e-mail: spc@tomatoweb.com; www.tomatoweb.com/spc
WESTERN WATER, 717 K Street, Suite 517, Sacramento, CA 95814, www.water-ed.org
EKPHRASIS, PO Box 161236, Sacramento, CA 95816-1236, 916-451-3038
Frith Press, PO Box 161236, Sacramento, CA 95816-1236, 916-451-3038
Samuel Powell Publishing Company, 2201 I Street, Sacramento, CA 95816, 916-443-1161
TRAVEL BOOKS WORLDWIDE, PO Box 160691, Sacramento, CA 95816-0691, 916-452-5200
Travel Keys, PO Box 160691, Sacramento, CA 95816-0691, 916-452-5200
Athanor Books (a division of ETX Seminars), P.O.Box 22201, Sacramento, CA 95820, 916-424-4355
FUCK DECENCY, 5960 S. Land Park Drive #253, Sacramento, CA 95822
TEC Publications, 4511 Del Rio Road #5, Sacramento, CA 95822, 916-362-0402
THE EROTIC TRAVELER, PO Box 278537, Sacramento, CA 95827-8537, Fax 916-361-2364; E-mail asiafile@earthlink.net
LifeThread Publications, 793 Harvey Way, Sacramento, CA 95831-4728, 916-395-8549; E-mail sosborn@ix.netcom.com
White Cliffs Media, Inc., 400 Del Verde Circle, Unit 2, Sacramento, CA 95833-3051
Lexikon Services, 3241 Boulder Creek Way, Antelope, CA 95843-4592, e-mail historycd@aol.com
THE MOUNTAIN ASTROLOGER, PO Box 970, Cedar Ridge, CA 95924-0970, 530-477-8839
Mach 1, Inc., PO Box 7360, Chico, CA 95927, 916-893-4000
Magical Blend, PO Box 600, Chico, CA 95927
Positive Press - Star Bear Books, PO Box 7626, Chico, CA 95927, 530-894-5068; FAX 530-894-3310
Heidelberg Graphics, 2 Stansbury Court, Chico, CA 95928-9410, 530-342-6582
MAGICAL BLEND MAGAZINE, 133-1/2 Broadway, Chico, CA 95928, E-mail magical@crl.com
Moon Publications, Inc., 101 Salem Street, Suite 6, Chico, CA 95928, 530-345-0282; FAX 530-345-0284; e-mail travel@moon.com Web: www.moon.com
Comstock Bonanza Press, 18919 William Quirk Drive, Grass Valley, CA 95945-8611, 530-273-6220
Kaleidoscope Road Publications, 19331 Cherry Creek Road, Grass Valley, CA 95949-9072
Blue Dolphin Publishing, Inc., PO Box 8, Nevada City, CA 95959, 916-265-6925
Crystal Clarity, Publishers, 14618 Tyler Foote Road, Nevada City, CA 95959, 1-800-424-1055; 530-478-7600; fax 530-478-7610
Dawn Publications, 14618 Tyler Foote Road, Nevada City, CA 95959, 530-292-7540; toll free 800-545-7475; fax 530-478-7541; email dawnpub@oro.net
Gateways Books And Tapes, Box 370, Nevada City, CA 95959, 916-272-0180; fax 916-272-0184
INNER JOURNEYS, PO Box 370, Nevada City, CA 95959, 916-272-0180; fax 916-272-0184; e-Mail doug+@dnai.com
Lexikos, PO Box 1289, Nevada City, CA 95959
WILD DUCK REVIEW, PO BOX 388, Nevada City, CA 95959-0388, 530-478-0134; Fax 530-265-2304; casey@wildduckreview.com
The Petrarch Press, PO Box 488, Oregon House, CA 95962, 916-692-0828
MACROBIOTICS TODAY, PO Box 426, Oroville, CA 95965, 530-533-7702; fax 530-533-7908
George Ohsawa Macrobiotic Foundation, PO Box 426, Oroville, CA 95965, 530-533-7702; FAX 530-533-7908; foundation@gomf.macrobiotic.net
Dustbooks, PO Box 100, Paradise, CA 95967-0100, 530-877-6110, 1-800-477-6110, fax: 530-877-0222, email(s): dustbooks@telis.org; len@dustbooks.com; web address:http://www.dustbooks.com
THE SMALL PRESS REVIEW/SMALL MAGAZINE REVIEW, PO Box 100, Paradise, CA 95967-9999, 530-877-6110, 800-477-6110, fax: 530-877-0222, email(s): dustbooks@telis.org; len@dustbooks.com; web page address: http:www.dustbooks.com
Asylum Arts, 5847 Sawmill Rd., Paradise, CA 95969, 530-876-1454; asyarts@sunset.net
NORTHERN CONTOURS, PO Box 618, Quincy, CA 95971, 916-283-3402
Bear Star Press, 185 Hollow Oak Drive, Cohasset, CA 95973, 530-891-0360
HOLY SMOKE, 16625 Heitman Road, Cottonwood, CA 96022, 916-529-5392, www.snowcrest.net/swtlight/holysmoke.html
Sweetlight Books, 16625 Heitman Road, Cottonwood, CA 96022, 916-529-5392, holysmoke.htme, www.snowcrest.net/swtlight

United Lumbee Nation, P.O. Box 512, Fall River Mills, CA 96028, 916-336-6701
UNITED LUMBEE NATION TIMES, P.O. Box 512, Fall River Mills, CA 96028, 530-336-6701
Naturegraph Publishers, Inc., PO Box 1047, Happy Camp, CA 96039, 530-493-5353; fax 530-493-5240; e-mail nature@sisqtel.net; www.naturegraph.com
Green Duck Press, 335 Pony Trail, Mount Shasta, CA 96067, 530-926-6261
THE JOURNAL OF THE ORDER OF BUDDHIST CONTEMPLATIVES, 3724 Summit Drive, Mt. Shasta, CA 96067-9102, 530-926-4208; E-mail www.obcon.org
Eagle Publishing, PO Box 403, Red Bluff, CA 96080, 530-527-3640
K & B Products, PO Box 1502, Suite 214, Red Bluff, CA 96080, 800-700-5096
ALADDIN'S WINDOW, Box 399, Shingletown, CA 96088, 916-474-1385
J & L Publications, PO Box 360, Trinity Center, CA 96091, 530-778-3456 phone/Fax
Coyote Publishing, PO Box 1854, Yreka, CA 96097, 916-842-5788
Lahontan Images, 210 South Pine Street, Susanville, CA 96130, 916-257-6747, fax 916-251-4801

COLORADO

Write Way Publishing, 10555 E. Dartmouth, Ste. 210, Aurora, CO 80014, 800-680-1493, fax 303-368-8004
White-Boucke Publishing, PO Box 400, Lafayette, CO 80026-1526, 303-604-0661, Fax 303-604-0662, e-mail cwhite@white-boucke.com
Earth-Love Publishing House LTD, 3440 Youngfield Street, Suite 353, Wheatridge, CO 80033, 303-233-9660
CAK Publishing, PO Box 953, Broomfield, CO 80038, 303-469-3133; glen-hanket@stortek.com
Clearwater Publishing Co., PO Box 778, Broomfield, CO 80038-0778, 303-436-1982; fax 303-465-2741; e-mail wordguise@aol.com
Finesse Publishing Company, PO Box 657, Broomfield, CO 80038, 303-466-4734
Cage Consulting, Inc., 13275 E. Fremont Place, Ste. 315, Englewood, CO 80112, 888-899-CAGE; Fax 303-799-1998; www.cageconsulting.com
Skidmore-Roth Publishing, Inc., 400 Inverness Drive South #260, Englewood, CO 80112, 303-662-8793; Fax 303-662-8079; info@skidmore-roth.com
Transcending Mundane, 5026 E. Weaver Avenue, Littleton, CO 80121, 303-796-0631; Fax: 303-741-1521;e-mail: transmun@paracreative.com/www.paracreative.com
GLASS ART, PO Box 260377, Highlands Ranch, CO 80163-0377, 303-791-8998
Affinity Publishers Services, c/o Continuous, PO Box 416, Denver, CO 80201-0416, 303-575-5676
Arden Press, Inc., PO Box 418, Denver, CO 80201, 303-697-6766
Center For Self-Sufficiency, PO Box 416, Denver, CO 80201-0416, 305-575-5676
Lamp Light Press, Publishing Division, PO Box 416, Denver, CO 80201-0416, 303-575-5676
Nunciata, Publishing Division, PO Box 416, Denver, CO 80201-0416, 303-575-5676
Scentouri, Publishing Division, c/o Prosperity + Profits Unlimited, PO Box 416, Denver, CO 80201-0416, 303-575-5676
THE BLOOMSBURY REVIEW, 1553 Platte Street, Suite 206, Denver, CO 80202, 303-455-3123, Fax 303-455-7039
Frugal Marketer Publishing, PO Box 6750, Denver, CO 80206-0750, Fax 303-377-0421
HIGH PLAINS LITERARY REVIEW, 180 Adams Street, Suite 250, Denver, CO 80206, (303) 320-6828
Picaro Press, 700 North Colorado Blvd. #124, Denver, CO 80206-1304, www.picaro.com
DENVER QUARTERLY, University of Denver, Denver, CO 80208, 303-871-2892
Lawco Ltd./Moneytree Publications/Que-House, PO Box 9758, Denver, CO 80209-0758, 209-239-6006
Now It's Up To You Publications, 157 S. Logan, Denver, CO 80209, 303-777-8951
Arrowstar Publishing, 100134 University Park Station, Denver, CO 80210-0134, 303-231-6599
Quantum Mind Publications, MSC 338, 6677 W. Colfax Avenue, Denver, CO 80214, 303-205-9106; fax 303-205-0299; E-mail 105055.3354@compuserve.com
PLEIADES MAGAZINE-Philae-Epic Journal-Thoughts Journal, Box 357, 6677 W. Colfax Avenue, Suite D, Lakewood, CO 80214, 303-237-1019
Revive Publishing, 1790 Dudley Street, Lakewood, CO 80215, 800-541-0558; E-mail Bader-tandm@msn.com
Divina (A MacMurray & Beck imprint), 1490 Lafayette Street, Suite #108, Denver, CO 80218-2391
MacMurray & Beck, 1490 Lafayette Street, Suite #108, Denver, CO 80218-2391
Old West Publishing Co., 1228 E. Colfax Avenue, Denver, CO 80218
Quiet Tymes, Inc., 1400 Downing Street, Denver, CO 80218, 303-839-8628; 800-552-7360; FAX 303-894-9240
THE CLIMBING ART, 6390 E. Floyd Dr., Denver, CO 80222-7638
Glenbridge Publishing Ltd., 6010 West Jewell Avenue, Lakewood, CO 80232-7106, 303-986-4135; FAX 303-987-9037
LFW Enterprises, PO Box 370234, Denver, CO 80237-0234, 303-750-1040
HEMLOCK TIMELINES, PO Box 101810, Denver, CO 80250-1810, Fax 303-639-1224, e-mail Hemlock@Prevatist.com
Ocean View Books, PO Box 102650, Denver, CO 80250, Fax, 303-756-5374 (order line), e-mail proboak@csm.met
SPEAK UP, PO Box 100506, Denver, CO 80250, 303-715-0837; Fax 303-715-0793; speakupres@aol.com; www.speakuppress.org
Speak Up Press, PO Box 100506, Denver, CO 80250, 303-715-0837; Fax 303-715-0793; speakupres@aol.com; www.speakuppress.org
Tickerwick Publications, PO Box 100695, Denver, CO 80250, 303-761-9940
Blue Poppy Press Inc., 3450 Penrose Place, Suite 110, Boulder, CO 80301, 303-442-0796
MurPubCo, 3335 Chisholm Trail #206, Boulder, CO 80301
VELONEWS, 1830 North 55th Street, Boulder, CO 80301
MANY MOUNTAINS MOVING, 420 22nd Street, Boulder, CO 80302, 303-545-9942, Fax 303-444-6510
MOONRABBIT REVIEW, 2525 Arapahoe Avenue, Ste. E4-230, Boulder, CO 80302, 303-439-8860; Fax 439-8362; JHLee@ucsub.Colorado.edu
Pruett Publishing Company, 7464 Arapahoe Road, Suite A-9, Boulder, CO 80303-1500, 303-443-9019, toll free: 1-800-247-8224
THE UNDERGROUND FOREST - LA SELVA SUBTERRANEA, 2737 Kalmia Avenue, Boulder, CO 80304, 303-413-9649
Dead Metaphor Press, PO Box 2076, Boulder, CO 80306, 303-417-9398
LOVING MORE, PO Box 4358, Boulder, CO 80306, 303-543-7540; lmm@lovemore.com
MetaGnosis, Po Box 1055, Boulder, CO 80306-1055, 303-938-9201
Paladin Enterprises, Inc., PO Box 1307, Boulder, CO 80306, 303-443-7250
THE BOOMERPHILE, PO Box 17446, Boulder, CO 80308-0446, 303-444-3363

Gemstone House Publishing, PO BOX 19948, Boulder, CO 80308, sthomas170@aol
Master Key Inc., PO Box 17474, Boulder, CO 80308, 303-776-6103; Fax 303-682-2384; www.selfhealing.com
BLACK ICE, English Dept., Publications Center, Box 494, University of Colorado, Boulder, CO 80309-0494, 303-492-8938
EAST EUROPEAN QUARTERLY, Box 29 Regent Hall, University of Colorado, Boulder, CO 80309, 303-492-6683
Fulcrum, Inc., 350 Indiana Street, Suite 350, Golden, CO 80401, 303-277-1623
The Love and Logic Press, Inc., 2207 Jackson Street, Golden, CO 80401, 303-278-7552
DAYSPRING, 18600 West 58 Avenue, Golden, CO 80403-1070, 303-279-2462
FICTION FORUM, 18600 West 58 Avenue, Golden, CO 80403-1070, 303-279-2462
NEW ANGLICAN REVIEW, 18600 West 58 Avenue, Golden, CO 80403-1070, 303-279-2462
NEW CATHOLIC REVIEW, 18600 West 58 Avenue, Golden, CO 80403-1070, 303-279-2462
POET'S FORUM, 18600 West 58 Avenue, Golden, CO 80403-1070, 303-279-2462
Alpine Guild, Inc., PO Box 4846, Dillon, CO 80435, fax 970-262-9378, e-Mail ALPINEGLD@aol.com
Bardsong Press, PO Box 775396, Steamboat Springs, CO 80477, 970-870-1401; fax 970-879-2657
Sylvan Books, PO Box 772876, Steamboat Springs, CO 80477-2876, 970-870-6071
Cottonwood Press, Inc., 305 West Magnolia, Suite 398, Fort Collins, CO 80521, 970-204-0715
SALON: A Journal of Aesthetics, 305 W. Magnolia, Suite 386, Ft. Collins, CO 80521, 970-224-3116
COLORADO REVIEW: A Journal of Contemporary Literature, 359 Eddy, English Dept., Colorado State University, Fort Collins, CO 80523, 303-491-5449
SunShine Press Publications, Inc., PO Box 333, Hygiene, CO 80533, 303-772-3556; sunshinepress@sunshinepress.com; www.sunshinepress.com
Alpine Publications, Inc., 225 S. Madison Avenue, Loveland, CO 80537, 970-667-9317; Fax 970-667-9157; alpinepubl@aol.com; www.alpinepub.com
Howling Dog Press/Stiletto, 1016 Deborah Drive, Loveland, CO 80537-7087
STILETTO, 1016 Deborah Drive, Loveland, CO 80537-7087
Wind River Institute Press/Wind River Broadcasting, 117 East 11th, Loveland, CO 80537, 970-669-3442, fax 970-663-6081, 800-669-3993
S. Deal & Assoc., 5128 Neeper Valley Road, Manitou Springs, CO 80829-3862
MedStudy Corporation, PO Box 6008, Woodland Park, CO 80866, 800-844-0547, fax 719-687-2900, hannaman@med-study.com
Mountain Automation Corporation, PO Box 6020, Woodland Park, CO 80866, 719-687-6647, FAX: 719-687-2448
Pikes Peak Press, 321 W. Henrietta Ave., Suite A, PO Box 1801, Woodland Park, CO 80866-1801, 719-687-1499; FAX 719-687-4127
THE ELEVENTH MUSE, a publication by Poetry West, PO Box 2413, Colorado Springs, CO 80901
HANG GLIDING, U.S. Hang Gliding Assoc., Inc., PO Box 1330, Colorado Springs, CO 80901-1330, 719-632-8300; fax 719-632-6417
Arjuna Library Press, 1025 Garner Street, D, Space 18, Colorado Springs, CO 80905-1774
JOURNAL OF REGIONAL CRITICISM, 1025 Garner Street, Box 18, Colorado Springs, CO 80905-1774
CURRENTS, National Organization for Rivers, 212 W. Cheyenne Mountain Blvd., Colorado Springs, CO 80906, 719-579-5759
INTERLIT, Cook Communications Ministries, 4050 Lee Vance View, Colorado Springs, CO 80918-7100, 719-536-0100; Fax 719-536-3266
WRITERS' FORUM, University of Colorado, PO Box 7150, Colorado Springs, CO 80933-7150, 719-262-4006
Blue River Publishing Inc., PO Box 6786A, Colorado Springs, CO 80934-6786, 719-634-3918; FAX 719-634-7559
Piccadilly Books, PO Box 25203, Colorado Springs, CO 80936, 719-550-9887
Paul Dilsaver, Publisher, PO Box 1621, Pueblo, CO 81002
Passeggiata Press, Inc., PO Box 636, Pueblo, CO 81002, 719-544-1038, Fax 719-546-7889, e-mail Passeggia@aol.com
Kali Press, PO Box 2169, Pagosa Springs, CO 81147, 970-264-5200; fax 970-264-5202; e-mail kalipres@rmi.net
Communication Creativity, 425 Cedar, PO Box 909, Buena Vista, CO 81211, 719-395-8659; span@spannet.org; www.spannet.org/cc
Custom Services, PO Box 3311, Montrose, CO 81402
Earth Star Publications, PO Box 117, Paonia, CO 81428, 970-527-3257
HIGH COUNTRY NEWS, PO Box 1090, Paonia, CO 81428, 303-527-4898
THE STAR BEACON, PO Box 117, Paonia, CO 81428, 970-527-3257; e-mail starbeacon@galaxycorp.com; website www.galaxycorp.com/starbeacon
Wayfinder Press, PO Box 217, Ridgway, CO 81432, 970-626-5452
Acclaim Publishing Co. Inc., PO Box 3918, Grand Junction, CO 81502-3918, 719-784-3712
PINYON POETRY, Dept. of Languages, Lit., & Comm., Mesa State College, Grand Junction, CO 81502-2647, 970-248-1740

CONNECTICUT

Singular Speech Press, Ten Hilltop Drive, Canton, CT 06019, 860-693-6059; Fax 860-693-6338; e-mail dondwilson@aol.com
IBIS REVIEW, PO Box 133, Falls Village, CT 06031, 203-824-0355
IPSISSIMA VERBA/THE VERY WORDS: Fiction & Poetry in the First Person, 32 Forest Street, New Britain, CT 06052, fax 860-832-9566; e-mail: ipsiverba@aol.com
Newmark Publishing Company, PO Box 603, South Windsor, CT 06074, 860-282-7265
NUDE BEACH, c/o Dan Tapper, 57 Brandywine Lane, Suffield, CT 06078-2141, 203-342-1298 (Steve Starger)
THE CATBIRD SEAT, PO Box 506, Tolland, CT 06084-0506
The Book Department, 107 White Rock Drive, Windsor, CT 06095-4348
Potes & Poets Press Inc., 181 Edgemont Avenue, Elmwood, CT 06110, 203-233-2023; e-mail potepoet@home.com
Kumarian Press, Inc., 14 Oakwood Avenue, West Hartford, CT 06119-2127, 860-233-5895; FAX 860-233-6072; ordering 1-800-289-2667; e-Mail KPBook@aol.com
Plinth Books, Box 271118, W. Hartford, CT 06127-1118
PAPYRUS, 102 LaSalle Road, PO Box 270797, West Hartford, CT 06127, e-mail gwhitaker@imagine.com
Papyrus Literary Enterprises, Inc., 102 LaSalle Road, PO Box 270797, West Hartford, CT 06127, 203-233-7478; e-mail gwhitaker@imagine.com; http://www.readersndex.com/papyrus
Turtle Press, division of S.K. Productions Inc., PO Box 290206, Wethersfield, CT 06129-0206, 860-529-7770

Curbstone Press, 321 Jackson Street, Willimantic, CT 06226, 203-423-5110; fax 203-423-9242; e-Mail TAYLORAL@EC-SUC.CTSTATEV.EDU
Derrynane Press, PO Box 93, Hampton, CT 06247, 860-455-0039; Fax 860-455-9198
Golden Grove Books, 348 Hartford Tpk, Hampton, CT 06247, 860-455-0039; Fax 860-455-9198
SPRING: A Journal of Archetype and Culture, Box 583, Putnam, CT 06260, 203-974-3229
Plus Publications, 208 Bass Road, PO Box 265, Scotland, CT 06264, 860-456-0646; 800-793-0666; fax 860-456-2803; e-mail haelix@neca.com; www.plusyoga.necaweb.com
Spring Publications Inc., 299 East Quassett Road, Woodstock, CT 06281, 203-974-3428, fax 203-974-3195
THE INCLUSION NOTEBOOK, PO Box 8, Gilman, CT 06336, 860-873-3545; Fax 860-873-1311
Pennycorner Press, PO Box 8, Gilman, CT 06336, 860-873-3545, Fax 860-873-1311
Longview Press, PO Box 616, Old Lyme, CT 06371, 203-434-2902
Verbatim, 4 Laurel Heights, Old Lyme, CT 06371-1462, 860-434-2104
THE CONNECTICUT POETRY REVIEW, PO Box 818, Stonington, CT 06378
Leete's Island Books, Box 3131, Branford, CT 06405-1731, 203-488-3424; e-mail PNeill@compuserve.com
The Pamphleeter's Press, PO Box 3374, Stony Creek, CT 06405, Tel/fax 203-483-1429; E-mail pamphpress@igc.apc.org
The Benefactory, Inc., 1 Post Road, Fairfield, CT 06430, 203-255-7744
REFERRALS, 2219 Long Hill Road, Guilford, CT 06437, 203-457-9020
Telephone Books, 109 Dunk Rock Rd., Guilford, CT 06437, 203-453-1921
Sound View Press, 859 Boston Post Road, PO Box 833, Madison, CT 06443, 203-245-2246, Fax; 203-245-5116, E-mail; soundviewpress@att.net
CRITICAL REVIEW, PO Box 10, Newtown, CT 06470-0010, 203-270-8103; fax 203-270-8105; e-mail info@criticalreview.com
Catbird Press, 16 Windsor Road, North Haven, CT 06473-3015, 203-230-2391; FAX 203-230-8029; e-Mail catbird@pipeline.com
The Globe Pequot Press, 6 Business Park Road, Box 833, Old Saybrook, CT 06475, 203-395-0440; FAX 203-395-0312
Tomar House Publishers, 1034 Main Street North, Box 630, Southbury, CT 06488-0630, 203-262-6106
THE SMALL PRESS BOOK REVIEW, PO Box 176, Southport, CT 06490, 203-332-7629
Cider Mill Press, P O Box 211, Stratford, CT 06497
DIRIGIBLE, 101 Cottage Street, New Haven, CT 06511, email dirigibl@javanet.com
CONNECTICUT REVIEW, SCSU, 501 Crescent Street, New Haven, CT 06515, 203-392-6737; FAX 203-392-5355
THEATER, 222 York Street, New Haven, CT 06520, 203-432-1568, Fax 203-432-8336, e-mail theater.magazine@quick.yale.edu
THE YALE REVIEW, Yale University, PO Box 208243, New Haven, CT 06520-8243
Ye Olde Font Shoppe, PO Box 8328, New Haven, CT 06530, e-mail yeolde@webcom.com; website www.webcom.com/yeolde
ETCETERA, P O Box 8543, New Haven, CT 06531, e-mail iedit4you@aol.com
Sanguinaria Publishing, 85 Ferris Street, Bridgeport, CT 06605, 203-576-9168
AMARANTH, PO Box 184, Trumbull, CT 06611, 203-452-9652
THE SMALL POND MAGAZINE OF LITERATURE aka SMALL POND, PO Box 664, Stratford, CT 06615, 203-378-4066
CONNECTICUT RIVER REVIEW: A National Poetry Journal, PO Box 4053, Waterbury, CT 06704-0053
Chicory Blue Press, Inc., 795 East Street North, Goshen, CT 06756, 860-491-2271; FAX 860-491-8619
White Knight Press, 95 Fern Street, Naugutack, CT 06770-2642, 203-723-6872 tel/fax; E-mail nwfg@erols.com
World Music Press, PO Box 2565, Danbury, CT 06813, 203-748-1131; fax 203-748-3432; e-mail wmpress@aol.com; website www.worldmusicpress.com
Paerdegat Park Publishing Co., PO Box 978, Darien, CT 06820, 203-655-5412 phone/fax; PagPark@aol.com; www.paerdegatpark.com
Two Bytes Publishing, PO Box 1043, Darien, CT 06820-1043, 203-656-0581; 888-588-7171; Fax 203-655-3910; E-mail efctbp@aol.com
Benchmark Publications Inc., 65 Locust Avenue, New Canaan, CT 06840-5328, 203-966-6653; FAX 203-972-7129; Benchpress@gnn.com
New Canaan Publishing Company Inc., PO Box 752, New Canaan, CT 06840, 203-966-3408 phone/Fax
Devin-Adair Publishers, Inc., PO Box A, Old Greenwich, CT 06870
The Bold Strummer Ltd., PO Box 2037, Westport, CT 06880-0037, 203-259-3021; Fax 203-259-7369; bstrummer@aol.com
Wescott Cove Publishing Co., Box 130, Stamford, CT 06904, 203-322-0998
Hannacroix Creek Books, Inc, 1127 High Ridge Road #110, Stamford, CT 06905, 203-321-8674; Fax 203-968-0193; E-mail hcbbooks@aol.com
Sun-Scape Publications, a division of Sun-Scape Enterprises Ltd., 65 High Ridge Road, Suite 103, Stamford, CT 06905, 203-838-3775; FAX 203-838-3775; orders 1-800-437-1454; info@sun-scape.com; www.sun-scape.com

DELAWARE

Playground Books, 26 Fox Hunt Drive #190, Bear, DE 19701-2534
BLADES, Poporo Press, 335 Paper Mill Road, Newark, DE 19711-2254
Oak Knoll Press, 310 Delaware Street, New Castle, DE 19720-5038, 302-328-7232, fax 302-328-7274
St. Georges Press, 991 Colonial Village North, New Castle, DE 19720, 302-328-4150
En Passant Poetry Press, 4612 Sylvanus Drive, Wilmington, DE 19803
EN PASSANT/POETRY, 4612 Sylvanus Drive, Wilmington, DE 19803
Griffon House Publications, 1401 Pennsylvania Avenue, Suite 105, Wilmington, DE 19806, 302-656-3230
A & M Books, PO Box 283, Rehoboth Beach, DE 19971, 302-227-2893; 800-489-7662

DISTRICT OF COLUMBIA

Selous Foundation Press, 325 Pennsylvania Avenue, SE, Washington, DC 20001
Gallaudet University Press, 800 Florida Avenue NE, Washington, DC 20002, 202-651-5488
Washington Writers' Publishing House, PO Box 15271, Washington, DC 20003, 202-543-1905, 703-527-5890
ARTSLINK, 1000 Vermont Avenue NW, 12th Floor, Washington, DC 20005, 212-223-2787
Historical Dimensions Press, PO Box 12042, Washington, DC 20005, 202-387-8070
MIDDLE EAST REPORT, 1500 Massachusetts Ave., NW, #119, Washington, DC 20005, 202-223-3677

660

SCIENCE BOOKS & FILMS, 1333 H Street, Northwest, Washington, DC 20005, 202-326-6463
ASC NEWSLETTER, 1725 K Street NW, Suite 601, Washington, DC 20006-1401, 202-347-2850
TRANSCAUCASUS: A Chronology, 888 17th Street NW, Suite 904, Washington, DC 20006, 202-775-1918; FAX 202-775-5648; anca-dc@ix.netcom.com
AERIAL, P.O. Box 25642, Washington, DC 20007, 202-362-6418; aerialedge@aol.com
The Media Institute, 1000 Potomac Street NW, Ste. 301, Washington, DC 20007, 202-298-7512
THE METROPOLITAN REVIEW, PO Box 32128, Washington, DC 20007
Stone Wall Press, Inc, 1241 30th Street NW, Washington, DC 20007, 202-333-1860
WATERFRONT WORLD SPOTLIGHT, 1622 Wisconsin Ave. N.W., Washington, DC 20007, 202-337-0356
KEREM: Creative Explorations in Judaism, 3035 Porter Street, NW, Washington, DC 20008, 202-364-3006; fax 202-364-3806; e-mail srh@udel.edu; www.kerem.com
Wineberry Press, 3207 Macomb Street, NW, Washington, DC 20008-3327, 202-363-8036; e-mail chfarnsworth@compuserve.com
THE AMERICAN SCHOLAR, 1811 Q Street NW, Washington, DC 20009, 202-265-3808
CONSCIENCE, 1436 U Street NW, Washington, DC 20009
GARGOYLE, 1508 U Street NW, Washington, DC 20009, 202-667-8148; e-mail atticus@radix.net
Island Press, 1718 Connecticut Avenue NW #300, Washington, DC 20009, 202-232-7933; FAX 202-234-1328; e-mail info@islandpress.org; Website www.islandpress.org
Lancaster Press, 1811 Q Street NW, Washington, DC 20009, 202-265-3808
NUTRITION ACTION HEALTHLETTER, 1875 Connecticut Avenue NW #300, Washington, DC 20009, 202-332-9110
OFF OUR BACKS, 2337B 18th Street, NW, 2nd Floor, Washington, DC 20009-2003, 202-234-8072
THE WASHINGTON MONTHLY, 1611 Connecticut Avenue NW, Washington, DC 20009, 202-462-0128
CHALLENGE: A Journal of Faith and Action in the Americas, 1470 Irving Street NW, Washington, DC 20010, 202-332-0292
EPICA, 1470 Irving Street NW, Washington, DC 20010, 202-332-0292
AMERICAN FORESTS, PO Box 2000, Washington, DC 20013, 202-955-4500
THE BOOK ARTS CLASSIFIED, PO Box 77167, Washington, DC 20013-7167, 800-821-6604; fax 800-538-7549; e-mail pagetwo@bookarts.com
HAND PAPERMAKING, PO Box 77027, Washington, DC 20013-7027, 800-821-6604; FAX 800-538-7549; e-mail handpapermaking@bookarts.com
Maisonneuve Press, PO Box 2980, Washington, DC 20013-2980, 301-277-7505; FAX 301-277-2467
ESPERANTIC STUDIES, 3900 Northampton Street NW, Washington, DC 20015, 202-362-3963; Fax 202-363-6899; ejl@gwu.edu
Sports Barn Publishing Company, 5335 Wisconsin Avenue NW #440, Washington, DC 20015, 202-895-1513; fax 301-320-5218; email dbarnes@erols.com; web http//www.sportsbarn.com
Starfish Press, 6525-32nd Street NW, PO Box 42467, Washington, DC 20015, 202-244-STAR (7827) phone/Fax
Wheat Forders/Trabuco Books, Box 6317, Washington, DC 20015-0317, 202-362-1588
The Word Works, Inc., PO Box 42164, Washington, DC 20015
The Compass Press, Box 9546, Washington, DC 20016, 202-333-2182; orders 212-564-3730
FOLIO: A LITERARY JOURNAL, Dept. of Literature, American University, Washington, DC 20016, 202-885-2971
Whalesback Books, Box 9546, Washington, DC 20016, 202-333-2182
ANQ: A Quarterly Journal of Short Articles, Notes, and Reviews, Heldref Publications, 1319 18th Street, NW, Washington, DC 20036-1802, 202-296-5149
The Preservation Press, 1785 Massachusetts Avenue, NW, Washington, DC 20036, 202-673-4057
JAMES WHITE REVIEW; A Gay Men's Literary Quarterly, PO Box 73910, Washington, DC 20056-3910, 612-339-8317
LAMBDA BOOK REPORT, PO Box 73910, Washington, DC 20056, 202-462-7294; fax 202-462-5264; e-Mail lbreditor@aol.com
THE DESK, PO Box 50376, Washington, DC 20091
WASHINGTON REVIEW, PO Box 50132, Washington, DC 20091-0132, 202-638-0515

FLORIDA

Otter Creek Press, Inc., 3154 Nautilus Road, Middleburg, FL 32068
Franklin Multimedia, Inc., 418 Kingsley Avenue, Orange Park, FL 32073, 904-278-1177; Fax 904-278-1070; Website www.thecigarmaster.com
Kings Estate Press, 870 Kings Estate Road, St. Augustine, FL 32086, 800-249-7485
CIN-DAV, Inc., Route 1, Box 778, Starke, FL 32091, 904-964-5370; Fax: 904-964-4917
FOCUS: Library Service to Older Adults, People with Disabilities, 216 N. Frederick Avenue, Daytona Beach, FL 32114-3408, 904-257-4259; e-mail gundem@mail.firn.edu
Outer Space Press, PO Box 9593, Daytona Beach, FL 32120, 904-253-8179 voice/Fax; osp9593@aol.com
African American Audio Press, 138 Palm Coast Parkway NE #217, Palm Coast, FL 32137-8241
AFRICAN AMERICAN AUDIOBOOK REVIEW, 138 Palm Coast Parkway NE #217, Palm Coast, FL 32137-8241
Luthers, 1009 North Dixie Freeway, New Smyrna Beach, FL 32168-6221, Phone/Fax 904-423-1600; E-mail http://www.luthers@n-jcenter.com
Two Thousand Three Associates, 4180 Saxon Drive, New Smyrna Beach, FL 32169-3851, 904-427-7876; Fax 904-423-7523; ttta@worldnet.att.net
KALLIOPE, A Journal of Women's Art, 3939 Roosevelt Blvd, Florida Community College at Jacksonville, Jacksonville, FL 32205, 904-381-3511
New World Publications, Inc., 1861 Cornell Road, Jacksonville, FL 32207, 904-737-6558; FAX 904-731-1188
MUDLARK, English Department, University of N. Florida, Jacksonville, FL 32224, 904-620-2273; Fax 904-620-3940; E-mail mudlark@unf.edu; www.unf.edu/mudlark
Anhinga Press, PO Box 10595, Tallahassee, FL 32302, 850-521-9920; Fax 850-442-6323; info@anhinga.org; www.anhinga.org
INTERNATIONAL QUARTERLY, PO Box 10521, Tallahassee, FL 32302-0521, 904-224-5078
The Naiad Press, Inc., PO Box 10543, Tallahassee, FL 32302, 904-539-5965; fax 904-539-9731
FATHOMS, PO Box 62634, Tallahassee, FL 32313
THE SILVER WEB, PO Box 38190, Tallahassee, FL 32315
Anubian Press, PO Box 12694, Centerville Station, Tallahassee, FL 32317-2694, 904-668-7414; anubis@polaris.net
Boulevard Books, Inc. Florida, PO Box 16267, Panama City, FL 32406, 904-785-1922

Karmichael Press, HC 3, Box 155D, Port St. Joe, FL 32456-9536, 850-648-4488 phone/Fax, KarmikePr@aol.com
St. Matthew's Press, PO Box 1130, Wewahitchka, FL 32465, 904-639-3700
HALF TONES TO JUBILEE, English Dept., 1000 College Blvd., Pensacola Jr. College, Pensacola, FL 32504, 904-484-1000 ext. 1400
Literary Moments, PO Box 15503, Pensacola, FL 32514, 850-857-0178
THE PANHANDLER, The Panhandler Press, English Dept., Univ. Of West Florida, Pensacola, FL 32514-5751, 904-474-2923
Bookhome Publishing/Panda Publishing, PO Box 5900, Navarre, FL 32566, E-mail bookhome@gte.net; www.bookhome.com
Blue Rock Publishing, PO Box 5246, Niceville, FL 32578, 850-897-7267; e-mail bluerock@home.com
EBB AND FLOW, PO Box 5246, Niceville, FL 32578, 610-658-0744; e-mail bluerock@home.com
Florida Academic Press, PO Box 540, Gainesville, FL 32602-0540, 352-332-5104; fax 352-331-6003; email FAPress@worldnet.att.net
HOGTOWN CREEK REVIEW, PO Box 1249, Gainesville, FL 32602-1249, e-mail hogtown@bigfoot.com
INDY MAGAZINE, 611 NW 34th Drive, Gainesville, FL 32607-2429, 352-373-6336; E-mail jrm@grove.ufl.edu; http://www.indyworld.com
Maupin House, PO Box 90148, Gainesville, FL 32607, 1-800-524-0634
COUNTERPOISE: For Social Responsibilities, Liberty and Dissent, 1716 SW Williston Road, Gainesville, FL 32608-4049, 352-335-2200
LIBRARIANS AT LIBERTY, 1716 SW Williston Road, Gainesville, FL 32608, 352-335-2200
Desktop, Ink., PO Box 548, Archer, FL 32618-0548, 352-486-6570 phone/Fax; E-mail dktop@aol.com
THE WRITE WAY, 810 Overhill Road, Deland, FL 32720, 904-734-1955
SKYDIVING, 1725 North Lexington Avenue, DeLand, FL 32724, 904-736-9779; fax 904-736-9786
Waterview Press, Inc., 169 West Broadway, Oviedo, FL 32765, 407-365-8500; oviedo@bellsouth.net
FLORIDA PRISON LEGAL PERSPECTIVES, PO Box 660-387, Chuluota, FL 32766, 407-306-6211; fplp@aol.com; members.aol.com/fplp/fplp
Prudhomme Press, PO Box 11, Tavares, FL 32778, 904-589-0100
Four Seasons Publishers, PO Box 51, Titusville, FL 32781, E-mail fourseasons@gnc.net
New Management Publishing Company, Inc., PO Box 0879, Winter Park, FL 32790, 407-647-5344
Tax Property Investor, Inc., PO Box 4602, Winter Park, FL 32793, 407-671-0004
Edge Publishing, 2175 N. Forsyth Road, Orlando, FL 32807-5262, 407-277-0900
THE FLORIDA REVIEW, PO Box 25000, English Department, University of Central Florida, Orlando, FL 32816, 407-823-2038
Tailored Tours Publications, Inc., PO Box 22861, Lake Buena Vista, FL 32830
Bio-Probe, Inc., PO Box 608010, Orlando, FL 32860-8010, Phone 407-290-9670; fax 407-299-4149
American Malacologists, Inc., 2208 Colonial Drive, Melbourne, FL 32901-5315, 407-725-2260
Geraventure, PO Box 2131, Melbourne, FL 32902-2131, 305-723-5554
LIVING OFF THE LAND, Subtropic Newsletter, PO Box 2131, Melbourne, FL 32902-2131, 305-723-5554
THE BLAB, 3073 Rio Bonita Street, Indialantic, FL 32903
Eau Gallie Publishing, Inc., PO Box 360817, Melbourne, FL 32936, 888-310-1530; 407-259-1122; fax 407-255-7586; E-mail mtravcler@eaugallie.com
THE GREAT BLUE BEACON, 1425 Patriot Drive, Melbourne, FL 32940, E-mail ajircc@juno.com
Halyard Press, Inc., PO Box 410308, Melbourne, FL 32941, 407-634-5022; Fax 407-636-5370
J. Mark Press, Box 500901, Malabar, FL 32950, website www.worldtv3.com/jmark.htm
POETS' VOICE, Box 500901, Malabar, FL 32950, website www.worldtv3.com/jmark.htm
The Speech Bin, Inc., 1965 25th Avenue, Vero Beach, FL 32960, 561-770-0007, FAX 561-770-0006
Good Life Products, Inc./DBA Beauty Ed, PO Box 170070, Hialeah, FL 33017-0070, 305-362-6998; fax 305-557-6123
DIET & HEALTH MAGAZINE, 2131 Hollywood Boulevard, Hollywood, FL 33020, 305-925-5242
FELL'S HEALTH FITNESS MAGAZINE, 2131 Hollywood Boulevard, Hollywood, FL 33020, 305-925-5242
FELL'S U.S. COINS INVESTMENT QUARTERLY, 2131 Hollywood Boulevard, Hollywood, FL 33020, 925-5242
GOOD COOKING SERIES, 2131 Hollywood Boulevard, Hollywood, FL 33020, 305-925-5242
Lifetime Books, Inc., 2131 Hollywood Boulevard, Hollywood, FL 33020
MONEY LINES, 2131 Hollywood Boulevard, Hollywood, FL 33020, 925-5242
SPECIALTY COOKING MAGAZINE, 2131 Hollywood Boulevard, Hollywood, FL 33020, 305-925-5242
The Poetry Connection, 13455 SW 16 Court #F-405, Pembroke Pines, FL 33027, 954-431-3016
THE POETRY CONNECTION, 13455 SW 16 Court #F-405, Pembroke Pines, FL 33027, 305-431-3016
CATAMARAN SAILOR, PO Box 2060, Key Largo, FL 33037, 05-451-3287; FAX 305-453-0255; E-mail ram5@icanect.net; Website http://www.catsailor.com
Ram Press, PO Box 2060, Key Largo, FL 33037, 305-451-3287; FAX 305-453-0255; Email ram5@icanect.net; http://www.catsailor.com/
CAYO, A MAGAZINE OF LIFE IN THE KEYS, P.O. Box 4516, Key West, FL 33040, 305-296-4286
Palm Island Press, 411 Truman Avenue, Key West, FL 33040, 305-294-7834
Laurel & Herbert, Inc., PO Box 266, Sugarloaf Shores, FL 33042, 305-745-3506; Fax 305-745-9070; herbert@conch.net.com
Tortuga Books, PO Box 420564, Summerland Key, FL 33042, 305-745-8709; fax 305-745-2704; website www.tortugabooks.com
Mother Lode Books, 7378 W. Atlantic Blvd. Box 228, Margate, FL 33063, 954-722-0624; books@aircadiz.net
Anti-Aging Press, Box 141489A, Coral Gables, FL 33114, 305-661-2802; 305-662-3928; Fax 305-661-4123; julia2@gate.net
SO YOUNG!, PO Box 141489, Coral Gables, FL 33114, 305-662-3928; FAX 305-661-4123
MANGROVE MAGAZINE, Dept. of English, Univ. of Miami, PO Box 248145, Coral Gables, FL 33124, 305-284-2182
THOUGHTS FOR ALL SEASONS: The Magazine of Epigrams, 478 NE 56th Street, Miami, FL 33137-2621, 305-756-8800
SEMIGLOSS, 1623 Lenox Avenue #2, Miami Beach, FL 33139-2434
GOLD COAST NEWS, PO Box 3637, Miami Beach, FL 33140, 674-9746
FOTOTEQUE, PO Box 440735, Miami, FL 33144-0735, 305-461-2770
LATINO STUFF REVIEW, PO Box 440195, Miami, FL 33144, www.ejl@lspress.net
The Leaping Frog Press, PO Box 440735, Miami, FL 33144, 305-461-2770; FAX 305-668-0636

LS Press, Inc., PO Box 440195, Miami, FL 33144, 305-262-1777; fax 305-447-8586; www.ejl@lspress.net
Comparative Sedimentology Lab., University of Miami, RSMAS/MGG, 4600 Rickenbacker Cswy., Miami, FL 33149
Westgate Publishing & Entertainment, Inc., 260 Crandon Blvd, Suite 32-109, Miami, FL 33149, 305-361-6862
Valiant Press, Inc., PO Box 330568, Miami, FL 33233, 305-665-1889
PROBABLE CAUSE: A LITERARY REVUE, PO Box 398657, Miami Beach, FL 33239, 305-538-6451
J. Flores Publications, PO Box 830131, Miami, FL 33283, 305-559-4652
Reniets, Inc., 3200 Port Royale Drive N. #1205, Fort Lauderdale, FL 33308, 800-767-7566; Fax 954-267-0260
Skyline Publications, Inc., 680 NW 35th Ct, Oakland Park, FL 33309-5007, 954-772-1236
InterMedia Publishing, Inc., 2120 Southwest 33 Avenue, Ft. Lauderdale, FL 33312-3750, E-mail intermediapub@juno.com
Kindness Publications, Inc., 1859 N. Pine Island Road, Ste. 135, Plantation, FL 33322, 305-423-9323
Consumer Press, 13326 SW 28th Street, Ste. 102, Fort Lauderdale, FL 33330, 954-370-9153, Fax 954-370-5722; e-mail
    bookguest@aol.com
Children Of Mary, PO Box 350333, Ft. Lauderdale, FL 33335
FIDELIS ET VERUS, PO Box 350333, Ft. Lauderdale, FL 33335
Eurotique Press, 3109 45th Street, Suite 300, West Palm Beach, FL 33407-1915, 561-687-0455; 800-547-4326
PT Publications, Inc., 3109 45th Street #100, West Palm Beach, FL 33407-1915, 561-687-0455; 800-547-4326; fax
    561-687-8010; e-mail PTPubFl@aol.com; website http://www.ptpub.com/
STONES IN MY POCKET, 11863 Wimbeldon Circle, #402, Wellington, FL 33414
Creative Concern Publications, 12066 Suellen Circle, West Palm Beach, FL 33414, 407-793-5854
American Cooking Guild, 3600-K South Congress Avenue, Boyton Beach, FL 33426, 561-732-8111; Fax 561-732-8183
New Paradigm Books, 22783 South State Road 7, Suite 97, Boca Raton, FL 33428, 561-482-5971; fax 561-852-8322;
    e-mail jdc@flinet.com; website http://www.newpara.com
Blue Horizon Press, 397 NW 35th Place, Boca Raton, FL 33431-5847
Garrett Publishing, Inc., 384 S. Military Trail, Deerfield Beach, FL 33442, 954-480-8543; Fax 954-698-0057
Liberty Publishing Company, Inc., PO BOX 4248, Deerfield Beach, FL 33442-4248, 305-360-9000
House of the 9 Muses, Inc., Box 2974, Palm Beach, FL 33480, 407-697-0990
Heritage Global Publishing, PMB 225, 813 E. Blommingdale Avenue, Brandon, FL 33511-8113, 813-643-6029
RESONANCE, 684 County Road 535, Sumterville, FL 33585, (352) 793-8748
WORLD OF FANDOM MAGAZINE, PO Box 9421, Tampa, FL 33604, 813-933-7424
TAMPA REVIEW, 401 W. Kennedy Boulevard, University of Tampa-19F, Tampa, FL 33606-1490
McGregor Publishing, 4532 W. Kennedy Blvd., Tampa, FL 33609-2042, 813-681-0092; FAX 813-254-2665; Toll-free
    888-405-2665
Duval-Bibb Publishing Company, PO Box 24168, Tampa, FL 33623-4168, 813-281-0091
Axelrod Publishing of Tampa Bay, 1304 De Soto Avenue, PO Box 14248, Tampa, FL 33690, 813-251-5269
WRITERS IN PARADISE, 4615 Gulf Boulevard, Ste. 104, St. Pete Beach, FL 33706, E-mail writers.in.paradise@world-
    net.att.net
THE WASHINGTON REPORT, 3610 38th Avenue South #88, St. Petersburg, FL 33711-4392, 813-866-1598
Little Bayou Press, 1735 First Avenue North, St. Petersburg, FL 33713-8903, 813-822-3278
Ticket to Adventure, Inc., PO Box 41005, St. Petersburg, FL 33743, 813-822-1515
Owen Laughlin Publishers, PO Box 6313, Clearwater, FL 33758-6313, 813-797-0404 Voice; Fax 813-447-1659 24 hours;
    800-258-3806
MAD SCIENTIST, PO Box 4765, Clearwater, FL 33758, e-mail frankie1@mindspring.com
Media Arts Publishing, PO Box 4765, Clearwater, FL 33758, e-mail frankie1@mindspring.com
TIME TRAVELER, PO Box 4765, Clearwater, FL 33758, e-mail frankie1@mindspring.com
Peartree Books & Music, PO Box 14533, Clearwater, FL 33766-4533, 727-531-4973
Byte Masters International, PO Box 3805, Clearwater, FL 33767, 727-593-3717; FAX 727-593-3605; Email
    BernieByte@aol.com
Bolton Press, 7671 121st Avenue, Largo, FL 33773, 813-535-4668
ONIONHEAD, 115 North Kentucky Avenue, Lakeland, FL 33801, 941-680-2787
4*9*1: Neo-Immanentist/Sursymbolist-Imagination, PO Box 91212, Lakeland, FL 33804, 941-607-9100;
    stompdncr@aol.com; www.fournineone.com
PUBLISHER'S REPORT, PO Box 430, Highland City, FL 33846, 941-648-4420; e-Mail naip@aol.com
Rainbow Books, Inc., PO Box 430, Highland City, FL 33846, 941-648-4420; rbibooks@aol.com
TIMESHARE AND VACATION OWNERSHIP REVIEW, 11595 Kelly Road, Fort Myers, FL 33908, 941-454-1100;
    941-466-3299; email orders@prefpress.com; web www.prefpress.com
Rose Shell Press, 15223 Coral Isle Court, Fort Meyers, FL 33919-8434, 941-454-6546
Sea Sports Publications, PO Box 1435, Estero, FL 33928-1435, 941-992-2287, fax 941-992-2287
The Runaway Spoon Press, Box 3621, Port Charlotte, FL 33949-3621, 941-629-8045
THE NAUTILUS, PO Box 1580, Sanibel, FL 33957
Ponderosa Publishers, 1369 Blue Lake Circle, Punta Gorda, FL 33983-5951, 406-745-4455
The Power Within Institute, Inc., PO Box 595, Matlacha, FL 33993-0595, 1-941-283-3852
Admiral House Publishing, PO Box 8176, Naples, FL 34101, email AdmHouse@aol.com
JAPANOPHILE, 6602 14th Avenue W, Bradenton, FL 34209-4527
Japanophile Press, 6602 14th Avenue W, Bradenton, FL 34209-4527, 517-669-2109; E-mail japanlove@aol.com
NUTHOUSE, PO Box 119, Ellenton, FL 34222
A Cappela Publishing, PO Box 3691, Sarasota, FL 34230, 941-351-2050; fax 941-362-3481
The Cresset Press, Inc., PO Box 2578, Sarasota, FL 34230, 813-371-8544
Faben, Inc., PO Box 3133, Sarasota, FL 34230, 941-955-0050; fax 941-365-5472; e-mail sales@fabenbooks.com
Pineapple Press, Inc., PO Box 3899, Sarasota, FL 34230-3899, 941-359-0886, Fax 941-351-9988
New Collage Press, 5700 North Trail, Sarasota, FL 34234, 813-359-4360
Starbooks Press/FLF Press, 2516 Ridge Avenue, Sarasota, FL 34235, 941-957-1281; Fax 941-955-3829; starxxx@gte.net
Computer Press, 4101 Winners Circle, #126, Sarasota, FL 34238-5554
Capital Communications, 10611 Fruitville Road, Sarasota, FL 34240, 941-342-9088; capital@investors.org
NEW COLLAGE MAGAZINE, 5700 N. Tamiami Trail, Sarasota, FL 34243-2197, 813-359-4360
Independent Publishing Co., PO Box 18566, Sarasota, FL 34276, 941-924-3201; Fax 941-925-4468; E-mail
    ymagazette@aol.com
WRITER'S GUIDELINES & NEWS, PO Box 18566, Sarasota, FL 34276, 941-924-3201; Fax 941-925-4468; e-mail
    writersgn@aol.com

YESTERDAY'S MAGAZETTE, PO Box 18566, Sarasota, FL 34276, 914-924-3201; Fax 941-925-4468; E-mail ymagazette@aol.com
Ageless Press, PO Box 5915, Sarasota, FL 34277-5915, 941-952-0576, e-Mail irishope@home.com
Professional Resource Exchange, Inc., Box 15560, Sarasota, FL 34277-1560, 941-343-9601; Fax 941-343-9201; orders@prpress.com
ALBATROSS, PO Box 7787, North Port, FL 34287-0787
Anabiosis Press, PO Box 7787, North Port, FL 34287-0787
HARP-STRINGS, PO Box 640387, Beverly Hills, FL 34464
Galt Press, PO Box 8, Clearwater, FL 34617
21st Century Publishing, Inc., PO Box 1314, Clearwater, FL 34617-1314, 813-274-4974; Fax 813-581-0038
Jaguar Books, 30043 US Hwy 19 North, Ste. 136, Clearwater, FL 34621, 800-299-0790; Fax 727-724-1677; jaguar@flanet.com
THE RATIONAL FEMINIST, 10500 Ulmerton Road #726-202, Largo, FL 34641
Top Of The Mountain Publishing, 11337 Starkey Road, Suite G2, Largo, FL 34643-4735, 813-391-3843, fax 813-391-4598
Selective Books, Inc., Box 984, Oldsmar, FL 34677
DRAMATIKA, 429 Hope Street, Tarpon Springs, FL 34689, 727-937-0109
Company of Words Publishing, 2082 Shannon Lakes Blvd., Kissimmee, FL 34743-3648, 617-492-7930; FAX 617-354-3392; e-mail wordspub@aol.com; web page www.wordspublishing.com
Long Wind Publishing, 2208 River Branch Drive, Ft. Pierce, FL 34981, E-mail hievolved@aol.com; www.longwind.com
Adaptive Living, 4922 SE Pompano Terrace, Stuart, FL 34997, 561-781-6153; Fax 561-781-9179

GEORGIA

Enthea Press, 4255 Trotters Way, Suite 13A, Alpharetta, GA 30004-7869
White Wolf Publishing, 780 Park North Blvd., Ste. 100, Clarkson, GA 30021, 404-292-1819
CHRYSALIS: The Journal of Transgressive Gender Identities, PO Box 33724, Decatur, GA 30033, 770-939-2128; Fax 770-939-1770; aegis@gender.org
Sullivan Press, PO Box 33724, Decatur, GA 30033, 770-939-2128; Fax 770-939-1770; E-mail aegis@gerder.org
IT GOES ON THE SHELF, 4817 Dean Lane, Lilburn, GA 30047, nedbrooks@sprynet.com
Purple Mouth Press, 4817 Dean Lane, Lilburn, GA 30047, nedbrooks@sprynet.com
IllumiNet Press, PO Box 2808, Lilburn, GA 30048, 770-279-2745; FAX 770-279-8007
Cherokee Publishing Company, PO Box 1730, Marietta, GA 30061, 404-467-4189
Franklin-Sarrett Publishers, 3761 Vineyard Trace, Marietta, GA 30062, 770-578-9410; Fax 770-973-4243; e-mail info@franklin-sarrett.com; Website http://www.franklin-sarrett.com
Bayhampton Publications, PMB 264, 2900 Delk Road, Suite 700, Marietta, GA 30067-5320, 905-455-7331; FAX 905-455-0207
ELDERCARE FORUM, 170 Elaine Drive, Roswell, GA 30075, 770-518-2767
Oasis In Print, PO Box 314, Clarkdale, GA 30111, 770-943-3377
Dava Books, 513 Bankhead Avenue, Suite 194, Carrollton, GA 30117, 770-214-1764
THE OLD RED KIMONO, Humanities, Floyd College, Box 1864, Rome, GA 30162, 404-295-6312
THE OVERLOOK CONNECTION, PO Box 526, Woodstock, GA 30188, 770-926-1762, Fax 770-516-1469, e-mail overlookcn@aol.com
Coreopsis Books, 1384 Township Drive, Lawrenceville, GA 30243, 404-995-9475
Gallopade International, 200 Northlake Drive, Peachtree City, GA 30269-1437
PARNASSUS LITERARY JOURNAL, Kudzu Press, PO Box 1384, Forest Park, GA 30298-1384
FIVE POINTS, Georgia State University, University Plaza, Atlanta, GA 30303-3083, 404-651-0071; Fax 404-651-3167
Clarity Press, Inc., 3277 Roswell Road NE, Suite 469, Atlanta, GA 30305, 404-231-0649; FAX 404-231-3899; 1-800-533-0301; clarity@islandnet.com; www.bookmaster.com/clarity
L'OUVERTURE, PO Box 8565, Atlanta, GA 30306, 404-572-9141
JAMES DICKEY NEWSLETTER, PO Box 2 Dyson Drive, Atlanta, GA 30307, 404-373-2989 phone/FAX
NYX OBSCURA MAGAZINE, PO Box 5554, Atlanta, GA 30307-0554, 704-684-6629; nyxobscura@aol.com
STAGNANCY IS REVOLTING, PO Box 55138, Atlanta, GA 30308-0138, 404-876-7183
Merging Worlds Publishers, Inc., 1655 Peachtree St. NE, Suite 1200, Atlanta, GA 30309, 404-892-8202; Fax 404-892-9757
Bosck Publishing House, PO Box 42487, Atlanta, GA 30311-3246, 404-755-8170
Buckhead Press, 3777 Peachtree Road, Suite 1401, Atlanta, GA 30319, 404-949-0527; fax 404-949-0528; e-mail buckheadpress@worldnet.att.net
EMORY EDGE, PO Drawer BBB, Emory University, Atlanta, GA 30322, 404-727-6183
LULLWATER REVIEW, Box 22036, Emory University, Atlanta, GA 30322, 404-727-6184
Peachtree Publishers, Ltd., 494 Armour Circle NE, Atlanta, GA 30324, 404-876-8761
MIDWEST POETRY REVIEW, PO Box 30236, Atlanta, GA 30325-0236, 404-350-0714
Mile Marker 12 Publishing, 6355 Long Island Drive, Atlanta, GA 30328, 770-455-8606; 888-868-6612; fax 770-455-6893
Bayley & Musgrave, 4949 Trailridge Pass, Suite 230, Atlanta, GA 30338, 404-668-9738
THE CHATTAHOOCHEE REVIEW, Georgia Perimeter College, 2101 Womack Road, Dunwoody, GA 30338-4497, 404-551-3019
A G M Enterprises, Inc., 3232 Cobb Parkway, Suite 203, Atlanta, GA 30339, 404-951-1603; 800-645-1323
Advisory Press, Inc., 5600 Roswell Road, Suite 210N, Atlanta, GA 30342, 404-250-1991; FAX 404-705-8249
Steam Press/LAD Publishing, 5455 Meridian Mark, Suite 100, Atlanta, GA 30342, 404-257-1577; FAX 256-5475
The Chicot Press, Box 53198, Atlanta, GA 30355, 770-640-9918; fax 770-640-9819
MANGAJIN, PO Box 77188, Atlanta, GA 30357-1188, 770-590-0092; FAX 770-590-0890
HABERSHAM REVIEW, PO Box 10, Demorest, GA 30535, 706-778-3000 Ex 132
THE CLASSICAL OUTLOOK, Department of Classics, The University of Georgia, Athens, GA 30602, 706-542-9257, fax 706-542-8503; mricks@arches.uga.edu
THE GEORGIA REVIEW, Univ. of Georgia, Athens, GA 30602-9009, 706-542-3481
STATE AND LOCAL GOVERNMENT REVIEW, Carl Vinson Institute of Government, 201 N. Milledge Ave., Univ. of GA, Athens, GA 30602, 706-542-2736
Venus Communications, PO Box 48822, Athens, GA 30604, 706-369-1547; fax 706-369-8598; email venus@venus-comm.com; www.venuscomm.com
Orloff Press, PO Box 80774, Athens, GA 30608-0774, 706-548-0701
THE LANGSTON HUGHES REVIEW, Box 2006, Univ. of Georgia, Athens, GA 30612-0006, 401-863-1815

The Press of the Nightowl, 145 Yorkshire Road, Bogart, GA 30622-1799, 706-353-7719; fax 706-353-7719; e-mail nightowl@typehigh.com
BLUE HORSE, P.O. Box 6061, Augusta, GA 30906, 706-798-5628
Blue Horse Publications, PO Box 6061, Augusta, GA 30906, 706-798-5628
Harbor House, 3010 Stratford Drive, Augusta, GA 30909, 706-738-0354; rfloyd2@aol.com
GoldenIsle Publishers, Inc., RR 2, Box 560, Golden Isle Parkway, N., Eastman, GA 31023, 912-374-5806(9455)
SIMPLY WORDS, 605 Collins Avenue #23, Centerville, GA 31028, E-mail simplywords@hotmail.com
ATLANTA REVIEW, PO Box 8248, Atlanta, GA 31106
BABYSUE, PO Box 8989, Atlanta, GA 31106, 404-320-1178
BABYSUE MUSIC REVIEW, PO Box 8989, Atlanta, GA 31106, 404-320-1178
ART PAPERS, PO Box 5748, Atlanta, GA 31107-5748, 404-588-1837; FAX 404-588-1836
Smyth & Helwys Publishing, Inc., 6316 Peake Road, Macon, GA 31210-3960, 912-752-2117; Fax 912-752-2264
SNAKE NATION REVIEW, 110 #2 West Force, Valdosta, GA 31601, 912-249-8334
SCIENCE/HEALTH ABSTRACTS, PO Box 553, Georgetown, GA 31754

GUAM

H & C NEWSLETTER, PO Box 24814 GMF, Barrigada, GU 96921-4814, 671-477-1961
STORYBOARD, Division of English, University of Guam, Mangilao, GU 96923, E-mail jtalley@uog9.uog.edu

HAWAII

Petroglyph Press, Ltd., 160 Kamekameka Avenue, Hilo, HI 96720-2834, 808-935-6006; www.basicallybooks.com
World Changing Books, PO Box 5491, Hilo, HI 96720, 808-934-7942
SHEMP! The Lowlife Culture Magazine, 593 Waikala Street, Kahului, HI 96732-1736, e-mail shempzine@yahoo.com
Steel Balls Press, PO Box 1532, Kona, HI 96745, E-mail donsteel@gte.net
Good Book Publishing Company, PO Box 837, Kihei, HI 96753-0837, 808-874-4876; e-mail dickb@dickb.com
Paradise Research Publications, Inc., Box 837, Kihei, HI 96753-0837, 808-874-4876; e-mail dickb@dickb.com
Dean Lem Associates, Inc., PO Box 959, Kihei, Maui, HI 96753-0959, 808-874-5461; FAX 808-875-1404; E-mail: deanlem@maui.net or deanlem@aol.com; Website: http://www.graphics-master.com
BEST OF MAUI, PO Box 10669, Lahaina, HI 96761, 808-661-5844
Sandwich Islands Publishing, PO Box 10669, Lahaina Maui, HI 96761, 808-661-5844
TitleWaves Publishing, PO Box 288, Lihue, HI 96766-0288, orders 800-867-7323
Passing Through Publications, PO Box 604, Naalehu, HI 96772, 808-929-8673
Island Style Press, PO Box 296, Waimanalo, HI 96795, 808-259-8666
Buddhist Study Center Press, 876 Curtis Street #3905, Honolulu, HI 96813, 808-597-8967
HAWAII PACIFIC REVIEW, 1060 Bishop Street, Honolulu, HI 96813, 808-544-1107
The Fine Print Press, Ltd., 350 Ward Avenue, Suite 106, Honolulu, HI 96814-4091, 808-536-7262; Fax 808-946-8581; E-mail fpp@hits.net; or http://www.hits.net/~fpp/
The Bess Press, 3565 Harding Avenue, Honolulu, HI 96816, 808-734-7159
Mutual Publishing, 1215 Center Street #210, Honolulu, HI 96816-3226
CBR, 735 Ekekela Place, Honolulu, HI 96817, 808-595-7089
COMPUTER BOOK REVIEW, 735 Ekekela Place, Honolulu, HI 96817, 808-595-7089
CHINA REVIEW INTERNATIONAL, 1890 East-West Road, Rm. 417, Honolulu, HI 96822-2318, 808-956-8891; fax 808-956-2682
HAWAI'I REVIEW, c/o Dept. of English, 1733 Donaghho Road, Honolulu, HI 96822, 808-956-3030
MANOA: A Pacific Journal of International Writing, English Department, University of Hawaii, Honolulu, HI 96822, 956-3070; fax 956-3083; E-mail mjournal@hawaii.edu
Family Works Publications, PO Box 22509, Honolulu, HI 96823-2509, 1-800-526-1478, Fax 808-538-0423
Tamarind, PO Box 75442, Honolulu, HI 96836, 808-942-1794; dcasey7@concentric.net
BAMBOO RIDGE, A HAWAI'I WRITERS JOURNAL, PO Box 61781, Honolulu, HI 96839-1781
Bamboo Ridge Press, PO Box 61781, Honolulu, HI 96839-1781
W.E.C. Plant Publishing, PO Box 61751, Honolulu, HI 96839, 808-622-0043; FAX 808-622-1345; e-mail alandjulie.plant@worldnet.att.net; website http://homepage.usr.com/a/alandtulie

IDAHO

Christian Martyrs' Press, 1050 E. Center Street, Pocatello, ID 83201
The Great Rift Press, 1135 East Bonneville, Pocatello, ID 83201, 208-232-6857, orders 800-585-6857, fax 208-233-0410
Howling Wolf Publishing, PO Box 1045, Pocatello, ID 83204, phone/fax 208-233-2708; e-mail kirbyjonas@integrityon-line.com
SNAKE RIVER REFLECTIONS, 1863 Bitterroot Drive, Twin Falls, ID 83301, 208-734-0746, e-mail wjan@aol.com
DIVINATION FOR DECISION-MAKERS, PO Box 80, Bellevue, ID 83313, phone/fax 208-788-8585; e-mail visionpb@micron.net
Confluence Press, Inc., Lewis-Clark State College, 500 8th Avenue, Lewiston, ID 83501-2698, 208-799-2336
TALKING RIVER REVIEW, Lewis-Clark State College, 500 8th Avenue, Lewiston, ID 83501, 208-799-2307; triver@lcsc.edu
Mountain Meadow Press, PO Box 447, Kooskia, ID 83539
Shimoda Publishing, PO Box 32, Atlanta, ID 83601, 1-800-218-6110
The Caxton Press, 312 Main Street, Caldwell, ID 83605, 208-459-7421
INCREDIBLE INQUIRY REPORTS, HC76, Box 2207, Garden Valley, ID 83622
Stonehouse Publications, Timber Butte Road, Box 390, Sweet, ID 83670, 208-584-3344
Pahsimeroi Press, PO Box 190442, Boise, ID 83709
Limberlost Press, 17 Canyon Trail, Boise, ID 83716
Dalrymple Publishing Company, P.O. Box 170133, Boise, ID 83717-0133, 208-333-0488
Tamarack Books, Inc., PO Box 190313, Boise, ID 83719, 800-962-6657, 208-387-2656, fax 208-387-2650
Ahsahta, Boise State University, Department of English, Boise, ID 83725, 208-426-1999; orders 1-800-526-6522; www.bsubkst.idbsu.edu/
COLD-DRILL, 1910 University Drive, Boise, ID 83725, 208-426-3862
Cold-Drill Books, Dept. of English, Boise State University, Boise, ID 83725
Permeable Press, 433 S. Cleveland Street #3, Moscow, ID 83843-3793

PUCK: The Unofficial Journal of the Irrepressible, 433 S. Cleveland Street #3, Moscow, ID 83843-3793
ELECTRONIC GREEN JOURNAL, University of Idaho Library, Moscow, ID 83844-2360, 208-885-6631; e-mail majanko@uidaho.edu; www.lib.uidaho.edu/70/docs/egj.html
FUGUE, Brink Hall, Room 200, Engl. Dept., University of Idaho, Moscow, ID 83844-1102, 208-885-6156
FLYFISHER, PO Box 722, Sandpoint, ID 83864, 208-263-3573; flyfisher@keokee.com
Keokee Co. Publishing, Inc., PO Box 722, Sandpoint, ID 83864, 208-263-3573; e-Mail info@keokee.com
SANDPOINT MAGAZINE, PO Box 722, Sandpoint, ID 83864, 208-263-3573, e-mail keokee Co @aol.com
THE EMSHOCK LETTER, Randall Flat Road, PO Box 411, Troy, ID 83871, 208-835-4902

ILLINOIS

THE CREATIVE WOMAN, 126 East Wing Street #288, Arlington Heights, IL 60004, 708-255-1232; FAX 708-255-1243
Fort Dearborn Press, 245 Bluff Court (LBS), Barrington, IL 60010, 312-235-8500
WHETSTONE, Barrington Area Arts Council, PO Box 1266, Barrington, IL 60011, 847-382-5626
BRIDAL CRAFTS, 2400 Devon, Suite 375, Des Plaines, IL 60018, 847-635-5800
Clapper Publishing Co., 2400 Devon, Suite 375, Des Plaines, IL 60018, 847-635-5800
CRAFTS 'N THINGS, 2400 Devon, Suite 375, Des Plaines, IL 60018, 847-635-5800
THE CROSS STITCHER, 2400 Devon, Suite 375, Des Plaines, IL 60018, 847-635-5800
PACK-O-FUN, 2400 Devon, Suite 375, Des Plaines, IL 60018, 847-635-5800
PAINTING, 2400 Devon, Suite 375, Des Plaines, IL 60018, 847-635-5800
FRESH GROUND, PO Box 383, Fox River Grove, IL 60021, 708-639-9200
Airplane Books, PO Box 111, Glenview, IL 60025
DeerTrail Books, 637 Williams Court, PO Box 171, Gurnee, IL 60031, 312-367-0014
December Press, Box 302, Highland Park, IL 60035
BAYBURY REVIEW, 40 High Street, Highwood, IL 60040, email baybury@flash.net
Ryrich Publications, 825 S. Waukegan Road, Ste. A-8, Lake Forest, IL 60045, 847-234-7968; fax 847-234-7967; e-mail ryrichpub@aol.com
Calibre Press, Inc., 666 Dundee Road, Suite 1607, Northbrook, IL 60062-2760, 708-498-5680, fax 708-498-6869, e-mail calivrepr@aol.com
STORYQUARTERLY, PO Box 1416, Northbrook, IL 60065
NIGHT ROSES, PO Box 393, Prospect Heights, IL 60070, 847-392-2435
Wild Dove Studio and Press, Inc., PO Box 789, Palatine, IL 60078-0789, 847-991-5615
Bolchazy-Carducci Publishers, Inc., 1000 Brown Street, Wauconda, IL 60084, 847-526-4344; fax 847-526-2867
RHINO: THE POETRY FORUM, PO Box 554, Winnetka, IL 60093, website www.artic.edu/~ageorge/rhino
Thorntree Press, 547 Hawthorn Lane, Winnetka, IL 60093, 708-446-8099
Crossroads Communications, PO Box 7, Carpentersville, IL 60110
BLACK DIRT, ECC 1700 Spartan Drive, Elgin, IL 60123-7193
Black Dirt Press, ECC 1700 Spartan Drive, Elgin, IL 60123-7193
MARQUEE, York Theatre Building, 152 N. York Road, Suite 200, Elmhurst, IL 60126, 630-782-1800, Fax 630-782-1802; e-mail thrhistsoc@aol.com
AIM MAGAZINE, PO Box 1174, Maywood, IL 60153-8174
Amnos Publications, 2501 South Wolf Road, Westchester, IL 60154, 312-562-2744
Celestial Otter Press, 237 Park Trail Court, Schaumburg, IL 60173
MAGIC CHANGES, 237 Park Trail Court, Schaumburg, IL 60173
Crossway Books, 1300 Crescent Street, Wheaton, IL 60187, 630-682-4300
Theosophical Publishing House, 306 West Geneva Road, Wheaton, IL 60187, 708-665-0130, fax 708-665-8791
THE QUEST, PO Box 270, Wheaton, IL 60189, 312-668-1571
Quest Books: Theosophical Publishing House, 306 W. Geneva Road, PO Box 270, Wheaton, IL 60189-0270, 630-665-0130; Fax 630-665-8791
GOTTA WRITE NETWORK LITMAG, 515 East Thacker Street, Hoffman Estates, IL 60194-1957, FAX 847-296-7631; e-mail Netera@aol.com
BRILLIANT STAR, Baha'i National Center, 1233 Central Street, Evanston, IL 60201
DAUGHTERS OF SARAH, 2121 Sheridan Road, Evanston, IL 60201
Depth Charge, PO Box 7037, Evanston, IL 60201-7037, 708-733-9554;800-639-0008; fax 708-733-0928
HAMMERS, 1718 Sherman #203, Evanston, IL 60201
THE JOURNAL OF EXPERIMENTAL FICTION, PO Box 7037, Evanston, IL 60201-7037, 800-639-0008, 708-733-1565, fax 708-733-0928
Thunder & Ink, PO Box 7014, Evanston, IL 60201
TAIL SPINS, PO Box 1860, Evanston, IL 60204, 847-424-9910; Fax 847-424-9978; tailspin@interaccess.com
Training Systems, Inc., Box 788, Evanston, IL 60204, 847-864-8664
WWW.TOMORROWSF.COM, PO Box 6038, Evanston, IL 60204, 708-864-3668
TRIQUARTERLY, Northwestern University Press, 2020 Ridge, Evanston, IL 60208-4302, 847-491-7614
The P. Gaines Co., Publishers, PO Box 2253, Oak Park, IL 60303, 312-524-9033
WRITER TO WRITER, PO Box 2336, Oak Park, IL 60303
FREDIAN SLIP: THE LEONARD ZELIG OF ZINES, 735 Park Avenue, River Forest, IL 60305-1705, 708-366-6309
The Hosanna Press, 215 Gale, River Forest, IL 60305, 708-771-8259
Planning/Communications, 7215 Oak Avenue, River Forest, IL 60305-1935
Outrider Press, 937 Patricia Lane, Crete, IL 60417-1375, 708-672-6630 (voice); fax 708-672-5820; e-mail outriderPr@aol.com; www.outriderpress.com
THE OFFICIAL MCCALLUM OBSERVER, PO Box 313, Lansing, IL 60438-0313, 708-895-0736; 708-895-1184; E-mail lsmtmo@juno.com; www.members.tripod.com/lsmtmo/index.html
Beaudoin Publishing Co., 14222 Clearview Drive, Orland Park, IL 60462, 708-349-7140
Lakes & Prairies Press, 15774 S. LaGrange Road #172, Orland Park, IL 60462-4766, website www.lakesprairies.com
CHILDREN, CHURCHES AND DADDIES, A Non Religious, Non Familial Literary Magazine, 8830 W. 120th Place, Palos Park, IL 60464-1203, E-ail ccandd96@aol.com; www.members.aol.com/scarspub/scras.html
CHAOS FOR THE CREATIVE MIND, PO Box 633, Tinley Park, IL 60477
Goodheart-Willcox Publisher, 18604 W. Creek Drive, Tinley Park, IL 60477-6243
The Design Image Group Inc., 231 S. Frontage Road, Suite 17, Burr Ridge, IL 60521, 630-789-8991; Fax 630-789-9013
REDISCOVER MUSIC CATALOG, 705 South Washington, Naperville, IL 60540-0665, 630-305-0770, fax 630-308-0782,

e-Mail FolkEra@aol.com
Sourcebooks, Inc., 121 N. Washington Street, Naperville, IL 60540, 630-961-3900; Fax 630-961-2168
INQ Publishing Co., PO Box 10, N. Aurora, IL 60542, 708-801-0607
VACUITY, 1512 Canyon Run Road, Naperville, IL 60565
The Philip Lesly Company, 155 Harbor Drive, Suite 5311, Chicago, IL 60601
Open Court Publishing, 332 S. Michigan #1100, Chicago, IL 60604, 312-939-1500; Fax 419-281-6883
Triumph Books, 644 S. Clark Street, Chicago, IL 60605, 939-3330
MORNINGSTAR, 225 West Wacker Drive, Chicago, IL 60606-1224, 312-696-6000
MUTUAL FUND SOURCEBOOK, 225 West Wacker Drive, Chicago, IL 60606-1224, 312-696-6000
Upstart Publishing Company, Inc., 155 North Wacker Drive, Chicago, IL 60606-1719, 1-800-621-9621 ex. 4310
OTHER VOICES, English Dept., M/C 162, UIC, 601 South Morgan Street, Chicago, IL 60607, 312-413-2209
SYMPLOKE: A Journal for the Intermingling of Literary, Cultural and Theoretical Scholarship, Univ. of IL, English Dept.
   MC 162, 601 S. Morgan Street, Chicago, IL 60607-7120, 773-506-7516; dileo@uci.edu
A Cappella Books, 814 N. Franklin Avenue, Chicago, IL 60610, 312-337-0747; FAX 312-337-5985
Chicago Review Press, 814 North Franklin Street, Chicago, IL 60610, 312-337-0747
NEW ART EXAMINER, 314 West Institute Place, Chicago, IL 60610-3007, 312-786-0200
POETRY, 60 West Walton Street, Chicago, IL 60610, 312-255-3703
The Press of the Third Mind, 1301 N. Dearborn Street, Loft 1007, Chicago, IL 60610-6068, 312-337-3122;
   www.nogoitering.com
The Teitan Press, Inc., PO Box 10258, Chicago, IL 60610, 773-929-7892; FAX 773-871-3315, e-mail teitanpr@aol.com
   Web Site: http://users.aol.com/teitanpr
Bonus Books, Inc., 160 East Illinois Street, Chicago, IL 60611, 312-467-0580
CHRISTIANITY & THE ARTS, PO Box 118088, Chicago, IL 60611, 312-642-8606
STUDENT LAWYER, ABA Publishing, Ira Pilchen, 750 N. Lake Shore Drive, Chicago, IL 60611
ACM (ANOTHER CHICAGO MAGAZINE), 3709 N. Kenmore, Chicago, IL 60613, 312-248-7665
FUEL MAGAZINE, 2434 North Greenview Avenue, Chicago, IL 60614-2013, 312-395-1706
LIBIDO: The Journal of Sex and Sensibility, PO Box 146721, Chicago, IL 60614, 773-275-0842
THE MUSING PLACE, 2700 Lakeview, Chicago, IL 60614, 312-281-3800
POETRY EAST, Dept. of English, DePaul Univ., 802 West Belden Avenue, Chicago, IL 60614, 312-325-7487
Silver Seahorse Press, 2506 N. Clark Street, Suite 320, Chicago, IL 60614, 773-871-1772; Fax 773-327-8978
ROCTOBER COMICS AND MUSIC, 1507 East 53rd Street #617, Chicago, IL 60615, 312-288-5448
Progresiv Publishr, 401 E. 32nd #1002, Chicago, IL 60616, 312-225-9181
ASSEMBLY, 1800 N. Hermitage Avenue, Chicago, IL 60622-1101, 773-486-8970
CATECHUMENATE: A Journal of Christian Initiation, 1800 North Hermitage Avenue, Chicago, IL 60622, 312-486-8970
CHICAGO STUDIES, 1800 North Hermitage Avenue, Chicago, IL 60622, 312-486-8970
DANGER!, 1573 N. Milwaukee Avenue, #481, Chicago, IL 60622-2029
ENVIRONMENT AND ART LETTER, 1800 North Hermitage Avenue, Chicago, IL 60622, 312-486-8970
LITURGY 90, 1800 North Hermitage Avenue, Chicago, IL 60622, 312-486-8970
Liturgy Training Publications, 1800 North Hermitage Avenue, Chicago, IL 60622, 312-486-8970
PLENTY GOOD ROOM, 1800 North Hermitage Avenue, Chicago, IL 60622, 312-486-8970
Rain Crow Publishing, 2127 W. Pierce Ave. Apt. 2B, Chicago, IL 60622-1824
32 PAGES, 2127 W. Pierce Avenue #2B, Chicago, IL 60622-1824, 773-276-9005; 32pp@rain-crow-publishing.com;
   www.rain-crow-publishing.com/32pp/
MATI, 5548 N. Sawyer, Chicago, IL 60625
Ommation Press, 5548 North Sawyer, Chicago, IL 60625
SALOME: A Journal for the Performing Arts, 5548 N. Sawyer, Chicago, IL 60625, 312-539-5745
Third Side Press, Inc., 2250 West Farragut, Chicago, IL 60625, 773-271-3029; FAX 773-271-0459; E-mail
   ThirdSide@aol.com
THE PAPER BAG, PO Box 268805, Chicago, IL 60626-8805, 312-285-7972
The Paper Bag Press, PO Box 268805, Chicago, IL 60626-8805, 312-285-7972
RAMBUNCTIOUS REVIEW, Rambunctious Press, Inc., 1221 West Pratt Blvd., Chicago, IL 60626
THE BAFFLER, PO Box 378293, Chicago, IL 60637
CHICAGO REVIEW, 5801 South Kenwood, Chicago, IL 60637, 773-702-0887
Lyceum Books, Inc., 5758 S. Blackstone, Chicago, IL 60637, 773-643-1902, Fax 723-643-1903; e-mail lyceum3@ibm.net
PRIMAVERA, PO Box 37-7547, Chicago, IL 60637-7547, 773-324-5920
CORNERSTONE, 939 W. Wilson Avenue, Chicago, IL 60640, 773-561-2450 ext. 2080; fax 773-989-2076
Empty Closet Enterprises, Inc., 5210 N. Wayne, Chicago, IL 60640-2223, 312-769-9009, FAX 312-728-7002
OFF THE ROCKS, 921 W. Argyle #1W, Chicago, IL 60640, E-mail offtherock@aol.com
African American Images, 1909 West 95th Street, Chicago, IL 60643-1105, 312-445-0322; FAX 312-445-9844
Alicubi Publications, 1658 N. Milwaukee Avenue, Box 380, Chicago, IL 60647, e-mail alicubi@earthlink.net
Scars Publications, 3625 W. Wrightwood Avenue #2F, Chicago, IL 60647, E-mail ccandd@aol.com;
   www.members.aol.com/scarspub/scars.html
Tia Chucha Press, PO Box 476969, Chicago, IL 60647, 773-377-2496
Juggernaut, PO Box 3824, Chicago, IL 60654-0824, 773-583-9261
FISH STORIES, 3540 N. Southport Avenue #493, Chicago, IL 60657-1436, 773-334-6690
INSECTS ARE PEOPLE TWO, 3150 N Lake Shore Drive #5-E, Chicago, IL 60657-4803, 312-772-8686
Lake View Press, PO Box 578279, Chicago, IL 60657, 312-935-2694
Spectrum Press, 3023 N Clark Street, #109, Chicago, IL 60657
SPORT LITERATE, Honest Reflections on Life's Leisurely Diversions, PO Box 577166, Chicago, IL 60657,
   765-496-6524; sportlit@aol.com; www.avalon.net/~librarian/sportliterate
THE WHITE DOT - Survival Guide for the TV-Free, PO Box 577257, Chicago, IL 60657, www3.mistral.co.uk/white
SPELUNKER FLOPHOUSE, PO Box 617742, Chicago, IL 60661, e-mail Spelunkerf@aol.com and sflophouse@aol.com;
   www.members.aol.com/spelunkerf
Black Light Fellowship, PO Box 5369, Chicago, IL 60680, 312-563-0081; fax 312-563-0086
LIGHT: The Quarterly of Light Verse, PO Box 7500, Chicago, IL 60680
WHITEWALLS: A Journal of Language and Art, PO Box 8204, Chicago, IL 60680, 312-409-4344; email aeelms@aol.com
Coker Publishing House, PO BOX 81017, Chicago, IL 60681-0017
MARCH/Abrazo Press, c/o Movimiento Artistico Chicano, Inc., PO Box 2890, Chicago, IL 60690-2890, 312-539-9638

667

Path Press, Inc., PO Box 2925, Chicago, IL 60690-2925, 312-663-0167
Information Research Lab, Park Plaza Suite 144, 9824 Western Avenue, Evergreen Park, IL 60805, 773-375-0280; e-mail aah-irl@writeme.com
Zombie Logic Press, 420 E. 3rd Street Box 319, Byron, IL 61010, email Dobe 1969@aol.com
ZOMBIE LOGIC REVIEW, 420 E. Third Street, Box 319, Byron, IL 61010, website http://members.aol.com/dobe1968/page/index.htm
Raspberry Press Ltd., PO Box 1, Dixon, IL 61021-0001, 815-288-4910; fax 815-288-4910; e-mail raspberrypress@es-sexl.com
BUS TOURS MAGAZINE, 9698 West Judson Road, Polo, IL 61064, 815-946-2341
NATIONAL BUS TRADER, 9698 West Judson Road, Polo, IL 61064, 815-946-2341
Transportation Trails, 9698 West Judson Road, Polo, IL 61064, 815-946-2341
THE ROCKFORD REVIEW, PO Box 858, Rockford, IL 61105
Mortal Press, 2315 North Alpine Road, Rockford, IL 61107-1422, 815-399-8432
THE ORIGINAL ART REPORT (TOAR), 3024 Sunnyside Drive, Rockford, IL 61114-6025
2AM MAGAZINE, PO Box 6754, Rockford, IL 61125-1754
2AM Publications, PO Box 6754, Rockford, IL 61125-1754
CRICKET, PO Box 300, Peru, IL 61354, 815-224-6656
LADYBUG, the Magazine for Young Children, 315 5th Street, PO Box 300, Peru, IL 61354, 815-224-6656
SPIDER, PO Box 300, Peru, IL 61354, 815-224-6656
Sherwood Sugden & Company, Publishers, 315 Fifth Street, Peru, IL 61354, 815-223-2520, Fax 815-223-4486
Illinois Heritage Press, PO Box 25, Macomb, IL 61455, 309-836-8916
AFTERTOUCH: New Music Discoveries, 1024 West Willcox Avenue, Peoria, IL 61604, 309-685-4843
HERBAL CHOICE, 3457 N. University, Suite 120, Peoria, IL 61604-1322
DOWNSTATE STORY, 1825 Maple Ridge, Peoria, IL 61614, 309-688-1409; email ehopkins@prairienet.org; http://www.wiu.bgu.edu/users/mfgeh/dss
CLOCKWATCH REVIEW, James Plath, English Department, Illinois Wesleyan University, Bloomington, IL 61702, 309-556-3352; http://titan.iwu.edu/~jplath/clockwatch.html
THE AMERICAN BOOK REVIEW, Unit for Contemporary Literature, IL State Univ., Campus Box 4241, Normal, IL 61790-4241, 309-438-3026, Fax 309-438-3523
Dalkey Archive Press, 4241 Illinois State University, Normal, IL 61790-4241, 309-438-7555
FC2/Black Ice Books, Illinois State University, Campus Box 4241, Normal, IL 61790-4241, 309-438-3582, Fax 309-438-3523
THE REVIEW OF CONTEMPORARY FICTION, 4241 Illinois State University, Normal, IL 61790-4241, 309-438-7555
SPOON RIVER POETRY REVIEW, Department of English 4240, Illinois State University, Normal, IL 61790-4241, 309-438-7906; 309-438-3025
MATRIX, c/o Channing-Murray Foundation, 1209 W Oregon, Urbana, IL 61801, 217-344-1176
Stormline Press, Inc., PO Box 593, Urbana, IL 61801, 217-328-2665
The Urbana Free Library, 201 South Race Street, Urbana, IL 61801, 217-367-4057
STRENGTH AND CONDITIONING, 1607 N. Market Street, Champaign, IL 61820, 217-351-5076, fax 217-351-2674
ADAPTED PHYSICAL ACTIVITY QUARTERLY (APAQ), Box 5076, Champaign, IL 61825-5076, 217-351-5076
ATHLETIC THERAPY TODAY (ATT), Box 5076, Champaign, IL 61825-5076, 217-351-5076
CANADIAN JOURNAL OF APPLIED PHYSIOLOGY (CJAP), PO Box 5076, Champaign, IL 61825-5076, 217-351-5076
EXERCISE IMMUNOLOGY REVIEW (EIR), P.O. Box 5076, Champaign, IL 61825-5076, 217-351-5076, fax 217-351-2674
Human Kinetics Pub. Inc., Box 5076, Champaign, IL 61825-5076, 217-351-5076; Fax 217-351-2674
INTERNATIONAL JOURNAL OF SPORT NUTRITION (IJSN), PO Box 5076, Champaign, IL 61825-5076, 217-351-5076
JOURNAL OF AGING AND PHYSICAL ACTIVITY (JAPA), P. O. Box 5076, Champaign, IL 61825-5076, 217-351-5076, fax 217-351-2674
JOURNAL OF APPLIED BIOMECHANICS (JAB), PO Box 5076, Champaign, IL 61825-5076, 217-351-5076
JOURNAL OF SPORT AND EXERCISE PSYCHOLOGY (JSEP), Box 5076, Champaign, IL 61825-5076, 217-351-5076
JOURNAL OF SPORT MANAGEMENT (JSM), Box 5076, Champaign, IL 61825-5076, 217-351-5076
JOURNAL OF SPORT REHABILITATION (JSR), PO Box 5076, Champaign, IL 61825-5076, 217-351-5076
JOURNAL OF STRENGTH AND CONDITIONING RESEARCH (JSCR), PO Box 5076, Champaign, IL 61825-5076, 217-351-5076
JOURNAL OF TEACHING IN PHYSICAL EDUCATION (JTPE), Box 5076, Champaign, IL 61825-5076, 217-351-5076
JOURNAL OF THE PHILOSOPHY OF SPORT (JPS), Box 5076, Champaign, IL 61825-5076, 217-351-5076
MARATHON & BEYOND (M&B), PO Box 5076, Champaign, IL 61825-5076, 217-351-5076
MOTOR CONTROL, P. O. Box 5076, Champaign, IL 61825-5076, 217-351-5076
PEDIATRIC EXERCISE SCIENCE (PES), PO Box 5076, Champaign, IL 61825-5076, 217-351-5076
QUEST, Box 5076, Champaign, IL 61825-5076, 217-351-5076
SOCIOLOGY OF SPORT JOURNAL (SSJ), Box 5076, Champaign, IL 61825-5076, 217-351-5076
SPORT HISTORY REVIEW (SHR), Box 5076, Champaign, IL 61825-5076, 217-351-5076
THE SPORT PSYCHOLOGIST (TSP), Box 5076, Champaign, IL 61825, 217-351-5076
TEACHING ELEMENTARY PHYSICAL EDUCATION (TEPE), Box 5076, Champaign, IL 61825-5076, 217-351-5076; Fax 212-351-2674
DISC GOLF JOURNAL, PO Box 3577, Champaign, IL 61826-3577, 217-398-7880;fax 217-398-7881; e-mail kathyig@aol.com
Mayhaven Publishing, PO Box 557, Mahomet, IL 61853-0557, 217-586-4493; fax 217-586-6330
NEW STONE CIRCLE, 1185 E 1900 N Road, White Heath, IL 61884
KARAMU, Department of English, Eastern Illinois Univ., Charleston, IL 61920, 217-581-6297
DRUMVOICES REVUE, Southern Illinois University, English Dept., Box 1431, Edwardsville, IL 62026-1431, 618-650-2060; Fax 618-650-3509
SOU'WESTER, Southern Illinois University, Edwardsville, IL 62026-1438
OBLATES, 9480 N. De Mazenod Drive, Belleville, IL 62223-1160, 618-398-4848
Knightraven Books, PO Box 100, Collinsville, IL 62234, 314-725-1111, Fax 618-345-7436
RIVER KING POETRY SUPPLEMENT, PO Box 122, Freeburg, IL 62243
INTUITIVE EXPLORATIONS, PO Box 561, Quincy, IL 62306-0561, 217-222-9082

668

SOMNIAL TIMES, Box 561, Quincy, IL 62306-0561, 217-222-9082
NATURE SOCIETY NEWS, Purple Martin Junction, Griggsville, IL 62340, (217) 833-2323
Dolphin Books, Inc., PO Box 2877, Decatur, IL 62524, 217-876-1232, fax 217-876-9210
Hutton Publications, Po Box 2907, Decatur, IL 62524
MYSTERY TIME ANTHOLOGY, PO Box 2907, Decatur, IL 62524
RHYME TIME POETRY NEWSLETTER, PO Box 2907, Decatur, IL 62524
Brooks Books, 4634 Hale Dr, Decatur, IL 62526-1117, 217-877-2966
MAYFLY, 4634 Hale Drive, Decatur, IL 62526-1117
ILLINOIS ARCHITECTURAL & HISTORICAL REVIEW, 202 South Plum, Havana, IL 62644, 309-543-4644
Embassy Hall Editions, PO Box 665, Centralia, IL 62801-0665
THE GALLEY SAIL REVIEW, PO Box 665, Centralia, IL 62801-0665
CRAB ORCHARD REVIEW, Dept. of English, Southern Illinois University, Carbondale, IL 62901, 618-453-6833

INDIANA

Patria Press, Inc., 3842 Wolf Creek Circle, Carmel, IN 46033, 317-844-6070; fax 317-844-8935; e-mail info@patriapress.com; website www.patriapress.com
HarMona Press, PO Box 370, Pittsboro, IN 46167-0370, 505-623-0180
THE RAINTOWN REVIEW: A Forum for the Essayist's Art, PO Box 370, Pittsboro, IN 46167-0370, 505-623-0180
THE RAINTREE REVIEW: Poetry Edition, PO Box 370, Pittsboro, IN 46167-0370, 505-623-0180
THE ROSWELL LITERARY REVIEW, PO Box 370, Pittsboro, IN 46167-0370, 505-623-0180
Geekspeak Unique Press, PO Box 11443, Indianapolis, IN 46201, 317-849-6227; www.ploplop.com
PLOPLOP, PO Box 11443, Indianapolis, IN 46201, 317-630-9216
NANNY FANNY, 2524 Stockbridge Drive #15, Indianapolis, IN 46268-2670, 317-329-1436; nightpoet@prodigy.net
Perspectives Press, PO Box 90318, Indianapolis, IN 46290-0318, 317-872-3055
SKYLARK, 2200 169th Street, Purdue University Calumet, Hammond, IN 46323, 219-989-2273; Fax 219-989-2165; skylark@nwi.calumet.purdue.edu
SJL Publishing Company, PO Box 152, Hanna, IN 46340-0152, 219-324-9678
COOKING CONTEST CHRONICLE, PO Box 10792, Merrillville, IN 46411-0792
Filibuster Press, 55836 Riverdale Drive, Elkhart, IN 46514, 219-522-5151; filibstr@skyenet.net; www.filibuster.com
METAL CURSE, PO Box 302, Elkhart, IN 46515-0302, 219-294-6610; e-mail cursed@interserv.com
Cottage Publications, Inc., 24396 Pleasant View Drive, Elkhart, IN 46517, 219-293-7553
NOTRE DAME REVIEW, English Dept., Creative Writing, University of Notre Dame, Notre Dame, IN 46556, 219-631-6952; Fax 219-631-4268
and books, 702 South Michigan, Suite 836, South Bend, IN 46601
Greenlawn Press, 107 S. Greenlawn Avenue, South Bend, IN 46617, 219-234-5088, fax 219-236-6633, e-Mail Greenlanw@aol.com
Americana Books, PO Box 14, Decatur, IN 46733, 219-728-2810; Fax 219-724-9755; E-mail maclean@amerbook.com
Cottontail Publications, 79 Drakes Ridge, Bennington, IN 47011, 812-427-3921
THE PRESIDENTS' JOURNAL, 79 Drakes Ridge, Bennington, IN 47011, 812-427-3921
Marathon International Book Company, Department SPR, PO Box 40, Madison, IN 47250-0040, ph/fax 812-273-4672; jwortham@seidata.com
THE BENT, 719 E. Main Street, Muncie, IN 47305, tomwhon@hotmail.com
Friends United Press, 101 Quaker Hill Drive, Richmond, IN 47374, 765-962-7573
BARNWOOD, PO Box 146, Selma, IN 47383
The Barnwood Press, PO Box 146, Selma, IN 47383
Birdalone Books, 9245 E. Woodview Drive, Bloomington, IN 47401-9101, 812-337-0118
BATHTUB GIN, PO Box 2392, Bloomington, IN 47402, 812-323-2985
INNER VOICES: A New Journal of Prison Literature, PO Box 4500 #219, Bloomington, IN 47402
World Wisdom Books, Inc., PO Box 2682, Bloomington, IN 47402, 812-332-1663; e-mail wwbooks@worldwisdom.com
Frozen Waffles Press/Shattered Sidewalks Press; 45th Century Chapbooks, The Writer's Group, 329 West 1st Street #5, Bloomington, IN 47403, 812-333-6304 c/o Rocky or Dimitrios
Royal Purcell, Publisher, 806 West Second Street, Bloomington, IN 47403, 812-336-4195
JOURNAL OF MODERN LITERATURE, Indiania University Press, 601 North Morton, Bloomington, IN 47404, 812-855-9449
INDIANA REVIEW, Ballantine Hall 465, Indiana University, Bloomington, IN 47405, 812-855-3439
Deep In Lingo, Inc., PO Box 6491, Bloomington, IN 47407, 812-339-2072
Grayson Bernard Publishers, Inc., PO Box 5247, Bloomington, IN 47407, 812-331-8182; 1-800-925-7853; FAX 812-331-2776
THE FORMALIST, 320 Hunter Drive, Evansville, IN 47711-2218
SOUTHERN INDIANA REVIEW, Liberal Arts Department, Univ. of Southern Indiana, Evansville, IN 47712, 812-464-1735. fax 812-465-7152. email tkramer@evansville.net
EVANSVILLE REVIEW, Univ. of Evansville, English Dept., 1800 Lincoln Avenue, Evansville, IN 47714, 812-488-1042
POETS' ROUNDTABLE, 826 South Center Street, Terre Haute, IN 47807, 812-234-0819
AFRICAN AMERICAN REVIEW, Indiana State University, Dept. of English, Terre Haute, IN 47809, 812-237-2968
SNOWY EGRET, PO Box 9, Bowling Green, IN 47833
Etaoin Shrdlu Press, Fandom House, 30 N. 19th Street, Lafayette, IN 47904
PABLO LENNIS, Fandom House, 30 N. 19th Street, Lafayette, IN 47904
Dearborn Business Press, 2878 Bridgeway Drive, Ste. 200, West Lafayette, IN 47906, 765-583-2422
Fallout Shelter Press, 2450 Sycamore Lane #16A, West Lafayette, IN 47906-1974
SPARROW, 103 Waldron Street, West Lafayette, IN 47906
SYCAMORE REVIEW, Department of English, Purdue University, West Lafayette, IN 47907, 765-494-3783

IOWA

FLYWAY, 206 Ross Hall, Iowa State University, Ames, IA 50011, 515-294-8273, FAX 515-294-6814, flyway@iastate.edu
MARTHA'S KIDLIT NEWSLETTER, PO Box 1488, Ames, IA 50014, 515-292-9309; www.kidlitonline.com
MODERN LOGIC: An International Journal for the History of Mathematical Logic, Set Theory, and Foundations of Mathematics, 2408-1/2 Lincoln Way (Upper Level), Ames, IA 50014-7217, 515-292-1819; e-Mail FI.MLP@ISUMVS.IASTATE.EDU

Modern Logic Publishing, 2408-1/2 Lincoln Way (Upper Level), Ames, IA 50014-7217, 515-292-1819; e-Mail FI.MLP@ISUMVS.IASTATE.EDU
TRADITION, PO Box 492, Anita, IA 50020
SWEET ANNIE & SWEET PEA REVIEW, 7750 Highway F-24 West, Baxter, IA 50028, 515-792-3578; FAX 515-792-1310
Sweet Annie Press, 7750 Highway F-24 West, Baxter, IA 50028, 515-792-3578; FAX 515-792-1310
LITERARY MAGAZINE REVIEW, Department of English Language and Literature, University of Northern Iowa, Cedar Falls, IA 50614-0502, 319-273-3782; fax 319-273-5807; e-Mail grant.tracey@uni.edu
THE NORTH AMERICAN REVIEW, Univ. Of Northern Iowa, Cedar Falls, IA 50614, 319-273-6455
MASSEY COLLECTORS NEWS—WILD HARVEST, Box 529, Denver, IA 50622, 319-984-5292
RED POWER, Box 277, Battle Creek, IA 51006, 712-365-4873
The Middleburg Press, Box 166, Orange City, IA 51041, 712-737-4198
HOR-TASY, PO Box 158, Harris, IA 51345
Mountaintop Books, PO Box 385, Glenwood, IA 51534-0385
THE BAREFOOT POET: Journal of Poetry, Fiction, Essays, & Art, PO Box 52, Pisgah, IA 51564-0052, 515-279-7804; Compuserve 76330,3325; Internet stmichael@commonlink.com
FIDEI DEFENSOR: JOURNAL OF CATHOLIC APOLOGETICS, PO Box 52, Pisgah, IA 51564-0052, 515-279-7804; E-mail st-mike@mail.commonlink.com
St. Michael's Press, PO Box 52, Pisgah, IA 51564-0052, 515-279-7804; e-mail st-mike@mail.commonlink.com
Writers House Press, PO Box 52, Pisgah, IA 51564-0052, 515-279-7804; Internet: smichael@commanlink.com
Islewest Publishing, 4242 Chavenelle Drive, Dubuque, IA 52002, 319-557-1500; Fax: 319-557-1376
SEED SAVERS EXCHANGE, 3076 North Winn Road, Decorah, IA 52101, 319-382-5990, Fax 319-382-5872
Meyer Publishing, PO Box 247, Garrison, IA 52229, 319-477-5041, Fax 319-477-5042, 800-477-5046
THE ANNALS OF IOWA, 402 Iowa Avenue, Iowa City, IA 52240, 319-335-3931; fax 319-335-3935; e-mail mbergman@blue.weeg.uiowa.edu
COMMON LIVES / LESBIAN LIVES, 1802 7th Ave. Ct., Iowa City, IA 52240-6436
Innovation Press, 2920 Industrial Park Road, Iowa City, IA 52240, 319-337-6316; fax 319-337-9034; email icanwork@aol.com
IOWA HERITAGE ILLUSTRATED (formerly The Palimpsest), State Historical Society of Iowa, 402 Iowa Avenue, Iowa City, IA 52240, 319-335-3916
THE IOWA REVIEW, 308 EPB, Univ. Of Iowa, Iowa City, IA 52242, 319-335-0462
TORRE DE PAPEL, 111 Phillips Hall, The University of Iowa, Iowa City, IA 52242, 319-335-2245
WALT WHITMAN QUARTERLY REVIEW, 308 EPB The University of Iowa, Iowa City, IA 52242-1492, 319-335-0454; 335-0592; fax 319-335-2535; e-mail wwqr@uiowa.edu
Penfield Press, 215 Brown Street, Iowa City, IA 52245-1358, FAX 319-351-6846
WASHINGTON INTERNATIONAL ARTS LETTER, 317 Fairchild Street, Iowa City, IA 52245-2115, 515-255-5577
WORLD LETTER, 729 Kimball Road, Iowa City, IA 52245, 319-337-6022
SYCAMORE ROOTS: New Native Americans, 205 North Front Street, North Lib., IA 52317-9302, 319-626-2055; e-mail icecube@inav.net
Ice Cube Press, 205 North Front Street, North Liberty, IA 52317-9302, 319-626-2055; e-mail icecube@soli.inav.net; Websites: http://soli.inav.net/~icecube
Ad-Lib Publications, 51-1/2 West Adams, Fairfield, IA 52556, 515-472-6617
BOOK MARKETING UPDATE, PO Box 205, Fairfield, IA 52556-0205, 515-472-6130, Fax 515-472-1560, e-mail johnkremer@bookmarket.com
Open Horizons Publishing Company, PO Box 205, Fairfield, IA 52556-0205, 515-472-6130, Fax 515-472-1560, e-mail johnkremer@bookmarket.com
Sunstar Publishing, 204 S. 20th Street, Fairfield, IA 52556-4221
Urban Legend Press, PO Box 4737, Davenport, IA 52808
THE URBANITE, PO Box 4737, Davenport, IA 52808

KANSAS

Broken Boulder Press, PO Box 172, Lawrence, KS 66044-0172, E-mail paulsilvia@hotmail.com; website www.brokenboulder.com
FIRST INTENSITY, PO Box 665, Lawrence, KS 66044-0713, e-mail leechapman@aol.com
First Intensity Press, PO Box 665, Lawrence, KS 66044, e-mail leechapman@aol.com
NEOTROPE, PO Box 172, Lawrence, KS 66044, e-mail apowell10@hotmail.com; website www.brokenboulder.com
SMELT MONEY (A Poetics Newsletter from the KAW River Bottoms), PO Box 591, Lawrence, KS 66044
COTTONWOOD, 400 Kansas Union, Box J, University of Kansas, Lawrence, KS 66045, 785-864-2528
Cottonwood Press, 400 Kansas Union, Box J, Univ. of Kansas, Lawrence, KS 66045, 785-864-2528
GROWING FOR MARKET, PO Box 3747, Lawrence, KS 66046, 785-748-0605; 800-307-8949
Editorial Research Service, P.O.Box 2047, Olathe, KS 66061, 913-829-0609
Flatland Tales Publishing, 2450 Greenwood Dr., Ottawa, KS 66067
FREETHOUGHT HISTORY, Box 5224, Kansas City, KS 66119, 913-588-1996
PEOPLE'S CULTURE, Box 5224, Kansas City, KS 66119
POTPOURRI: A Magazine of the Literary Arts, PO Box 8278, Prairie Village, KS 66208, 913-642-1503; Fax 913-642-3128; e-mail potpourrpub@aol.com
Varro Press, PO Box 8413, Shawnee Mission, KS 66208, 913-385-2034; FAX 913-385-2039; varropress@aol.com
The Wordtree, 10876 Bradshaw, Overland Park, KS 66210-1148, 913-469-1010; burger@cctr.umkc.ed; www.word-tree.com
Cypress Publishing Group, Inc., 11835 Roe #187, Leawood, KS 66211, 913-681-9875
JOURNAL OF THE WEST, 1531 Yuma (PO Box 1009), Manhattan, KS 66502, 785-539-1888, fax 785-539-2233
Sunflower University Press, 1531 Yuma, (Box 1009), Manhattan, KS 66502, 785-539-1888, fax 785-539-2233
ENVIRONMENTAL & ARCHITECTURAL PHENOMENOLOGY NEWSLETTER, 211 Seaton Hall, Architecture Dept., Kansas State University, Manhattan, KS 66506-2901, 913-532-1121
SCAVENGER'S NEWSLETTER, 519 Ellinwood, Osage City, KS 66523, 913-528-3538; E-mail foxscav1@jc.net
MOUTH: Voice of the Disability Nation, PO BOX 558, Topeka, KS 66601-0558, fax 716-442-2916
Content Communications, PO Box 4763, Topeka, KS 66604, 913-233-9066
LEFTHANDER MAGAZINE, Lefthanders International, PO Box 8249, Topeka, KS 66608, (913) 234-2177

670

THE MIDWEST QUARTERLY, Pittsburg State University, English Department, Pittsburg, KS 66762, 316-235-4369
Al-Galaxy Publishing Company, PO Box 2591, Wichita, KS 67201, 316-651-0072; Fax 316-651-2790
St Kitts Press, PO Box 8173, Wichita, KS 67208, 888-705-4887; 316-685-3201; Fax 316-685-6650; ewhitaker@skpub.com
Chiron Press, 702 North Prairie, St. John, KS 67576-1516, 316-549-6156; chironreview@hotmail.com; www.geocities.com/soho/nook/1748
CHIRON REVIEW, 702 North Prairie, St. John, KS 67576-1516, 316-549-6156; 316-786-4955; chironreview@hotmail.com; www.geocities.com/soho/nook/1748

KENTUCKY

DOVETAIL: A Journal by and for Jewish/Christian Families, 775 Simon Greenwell Lane, Boston, KY 40107, 502-549-5499; Fax 502-549-3543; di-ifr@bardstown.com
The Advocado Press, PO Box 145, Louisville, KY 40201, 502-459-5343
THE DISABILITY RAG & RESOURCE, PO Box 145, Louisville, KY 40201, 502-459-5343
THE AMERICAN VOICE, 332 West Broadway, #1215, Louisville, KY 40202, 502-562-0045
THE LOUISVILLE REVIEW, Spalding University, 851 S. 4th Street, Louisville, KY 40203, 502-852-6801
The Sulgrave Press, 2005 Longest Avenue], Louisville, KY 40204, 502-459-9713, Fax 502-459-9715
Sarabande Books, Inc., 2234 Dundee Road, Suite 200, Louisville, KY 40205 .
Good Life Publishing, PO Box 6925, Louisville, KY 40206, 502-491-6565; email lutherjr@msn.com
Chicago Spectrum Press, 4848 Brownsboro Center, Louisville, KY 40207-2342, 502-899-1919; Fax 502-896-0246; evanstonpb@aol.com
Evanston Publishing, Inc., 4848 Brownsboro Center, Louisville, KY 40207-2342, 502-899-1919; 800-594-5190; EvanstonPB@aol.com
CHANCE MAGAZINE, 3929 South Fifth Street, Louisville, KY 40214
Green River Writers, Inc./Grex Press, 11906 Locust Road, Middletown, KY 40243, 502-245-4902
STOVEPIPE: A Journal of Little Literary Value, PO Box 1076, Georgetown, KY 40324, troyteegarden@worldradio.org
Sweet Lady Moon Press, PO Box 1076, Georgetown, KY 40324, troyteegarden@worldradio.org
HORTIDEAS, 750 Black Lick Road, Gravel Switch, KY 40328, 606-332-7606
APPALACHIAN HERITAGE, Appalachian Center, Berea College, Berea, KY 40404, 606-986-9341 ext. 5260; e-mail sidney-farr@berea.edu
CHAFFIN JOURNAL, Department of English, 467 Case Annex, Eastern Kentucky University, Richmond, KY 40475-3140
LIMESTONE: A LITERARY JOURNAL, English Dept., Univ. of Kentucky, 1215 Patterson Office Tower, Lexington, KY 40506-0027
WIND, PO Box 24548, Lexington, KY 40524, 606-885-5342
DIARIST'S JOURNAL, 209 E. 38th Street, Covington, KY 41015, 717-645-4692
THE LICKING RIVER REVIEW, Department of Literature and Language, Northern Kentucky University, Highland Heights, KY 41099
MEDUSA'S HAIRDO, PO Box 358, Catlettsburg, KY 41129, 606-928-4631; medusashairdo@yahoo.com
PIKEVILLE REVIEW, Humanities Department, Pikeville College, Pikeville, KY 41501, 606-432-9612
PLAINSONG, Box 8245, Western Kentucky University, Bowling Green, KY 42101, 502-745-5708
CLASS ACT, PO Box 802, Henderson, KY 42419

LOUISANA

Prestige Publications, 2450 Severn Avenue, Ste. 528, Metairie, LA 70001, 504-831-4030
DESIRE STREET, 257 Bonnabel Boulevard, Metairie, LA 70005-3738, 504-833-0641; Fax 504-834-2005; ager80@worldnet.att.net
Lycanthrope Press, PO Box 9028, Metairie, LA 70005-9028, 504-866-9756
Pendaya Publications, Inc., 510 Woodvine Avenue, Metairie, LA 70005, 504-834-8151
THEMA, PO BOX 8747, Metairie, LA 70011-8747
Paper Chase Press, 5721 Magazine Street, Suite 152, New Orleans, LA 70115, 504-522-2025; paperchasp@aol.com (for orders only-no manuscripts or queries)
Westgate Press, 5219 Magazine Street, New Orleans, LA 70115-1858
Manya DeLeon Booksmith, 940 Royal Street, Suite 201, New Orleans, LA 70116, 504-895-2357
Garrett County Press, 720 Barracks Street, New Orleans, LA 70116-2517, 608-251-3921; web: http://www.gcpress.com
THE NEW LAUREL REVIEW, 828 Lesseps Street, New Orleans, LA 70117, 504-947-6001
CELFAN Editions Monographs, Dept. of French & Italian, Tulane University, New Orleans, LA 70118
LOWLANDS REVIEW, 6109 Magazine, New Orleans, LA 70118
NEW ORLEANS REVIEW, Loyola University, New Orleans, LA 70118, 504-865-2295
REVUE CELFAN REVIEW, Department of French and Italian, Tulane University, New Orleans, LA 70118
Acre Press, 3003 Ponce De Leon Street, New Orleans, LA 70119
FELL SWOOP, 3003 Ponce de Leon Street, New Orleans, LA 70119
MESECHABE: The Journal of Surre(gion)alism, 1539 Crete Street, New Orleans, LA 70119, 504-944-4823
BAKER STREET GAZETTE, 577 Central Avenue, Box 4, Jefferson, LA 70121-1400, E-mail sherlockian@mailcity.com, sherlockian@england.com, www2.cybercities.com/z/zines/
Baker Street Publications, 577 Central Avenue, Box 4, Jefferson, LA 70121-1400, E-mail sherlockian@mailcity.com, sherlockian@england.com, www2.cybercities.com/z/zines/
DAYS AND NIGHTS OF A SMALL PRESS PUBLISHER, 577 Central Avenue, Box 4, Jefferson, LA 70121-1400, e-mail popculture@popmail.com, publisher@mailexcite.com; www2.cybercities.com/z/zines/
FULL MOON DIRECTORY, 577 Central Avenue, Box 4, Jefferson, LA 70121-1400, E-mail publisher@mailexcite.com; zines@rsnmail.com; www2.cybercities.com/z/zines/
Full Moon Publications, 577 Central Avenue, Box 4, Jefferson, LA 70121-1400, e-mail fullmoon@eudoramail.com or haunted@rocketmail.com; www.eclecticity.com/zines/, www.members.xoom.com/blackie, www.route23.com/fullmoon.asp, www.spaceports.com/~haunted/, www2.cybercities.com/z/zines
THE HAUNTED JOURNAL, 577 Central Avenue, Box 4, Jefferson, LA 70121-1400, e-mail fullmoon@edoramail.com or haunted@rocketmail.com; www.spaceports.com/~haunted, www.eclecticity.com/zines/, www.members.xoom.com/blackie or http://www.angelfire.com/la/hauntings/index.htm/, www2.cybercities.com/z/zines
HOLLYWOOD NOSTALGIA, 577 Central Avenue, Box 4, Jefferson, LA 70121-1400, e-mail: publisher@mailexcite.com or blackie@talkcity.com; Websites www.home.talkcity.com/SunsetBlvd/blackie, www.wbs.net/homepages/b/l/a/blackie.htm/, www2.cybercities.com/z/zines/

HORIZONS, 577 Central Avenue, Box 4, Jefferson, LA 70121-1400, e-mail: horizons@altavista.net or publisher@mailex-cite.com; Website www2.cybercities.com/z/zines/
HORIZONS BEYOND, 577 Central Avenue, Box 4, Jefferson, LA 70121-0517, e-mail fullmoon@eudoramail.com or haunted@rocketmail.com; Websites www.members.xoom.com/blackie, www2.cybercities.com/z/zines/, www.eclecti-city.com/zines/, www.spaceports.com/~haunted/
IRISH JOURNAL, 577 Central Avenue, Box 4, Jefferson, LA 70121-1400, e-mail irishrose@cmpnetmail.com, rose.dalton@edmail.com; websites www.fortunecity.com/bally/harp/189/, www2.cybercities.com/z/zines/
JACK THE RIPPER GAZETTE, 577 Central Avenue, Box 4, Jefferson, LA 70121-1400, sherlockian@england.com, sherlockian@mailcity.com, www2.cybercities.com/z/zines/
JEWISH LIFE, 577 Central Avenue, Box 4, Jefferson, LA 70121-1400, E-mail publisher@jewishmail.com, jewishlife@newyorkoffice.com; www.world.up.co.il/jewishlife, www2.cybercities.com/z/zines/
MIXED BAG, 577 Central Avenue, Box 4, Jefferson, LA 70121-1400, e-mail: publisher@mailexcite.com, zines@theglobe.com, zines@rsnmail.com; Websites www.members.tripod.com/~literary/index.htm/, www.members.the globe.com/zines/default.htm/, www2.cybercities.com/z/zines/, www.zines.freeservers.com
NIGHTSHADE, 577 Central Avenue, Box 4, Jefferson, LA 70121-1400, e-mail fullmoon@eudoramail.com or haunted@rocketmail.com; Websites www.members.xoom.com/blackie, www.eclecticity.com/zines/, www.space-ports.com/~haunted/, www2.cybercities.com/z/zines/
NOCTURNAL REPORTER, 577 Central Avenue, Box 4, Jefferson, LA 70121-1400, E-mail fullmoon@endoramail.com, haunted@rocketmail.com; Websites www.angelfire.com/la/hauntings/index.htm/, www.members.xoom.com/blackie
PEN & INK WRITERS JOURNAL, 577 Central Avenue, Box 4, Jefferson, LA 70121-1400, E-mail editor@inforspace-mail.com, publisher@mailexcite.com, www.zines.freeservers.com, www.members.theglobe.com/zines/default.html, www2.cybercities.com/z/zines/
POW-WOW, 577 Central Avenue #4, Jefferson, LA 70121-1400, e-mail: horizons@altavista.net or blueskies@discovery-mail.com; Websites www.freeyellow.com/members2/oldwest/index.htm/, www2.cybercities.com/z/zines/
REALM OF DARKNESS, 577 Central Avenue, Box 4, Jefferson, LA 70121-1400, e-mail fullmoon@eduoramail.com or haunted@rocketmail.com; Websites www.members.xoom.com/blackie, www.spaceports.com/~haunted/, www.eclecti-city.com/zines/, www2.cybercities.com/z/zines/, www.dreamers.dynip.com/zines/
REALM OF THE VAMPIRE, 577 Central Avenue, Box 4, Jefferson, LA 70121-1400, e-mail fullmoon@eudoramail.com, haunted@rocketmail.com, gothic@imaginemail.com; Websites www.eclecticity.com/zines/, www.freez.com/vampires, www.members.xoom.com/blackie, www.spaceports.com/~haunted/, www2.cybercities.com/z/zines/
THE SALEM JOURNAL, 577 Central Avenue, Box 4, Jefferson, LA 70121-1400, e-mail: fullmoon@eudoramail.com or haunted@rocketmail.com; Websites www.eclecticity.com/zines/, www2.cybercities.com/z/zines/, www.members.xoom.com/blackie, www.spaceports.com/~haunted/, www.dreamers.dynip.com/zines/
SLEUTH JOURNAL, 577 Central Avenue, Box 4, Jefferson, LA 70121-1400, E-mail sherlockian@mailcity.com, blackie@taskcity.com, www2.cybercities.com/z/zines, www.wbs.net/homepages/b/l/a/blackkie.html
SOUTHWEST JOURNAL, 577 Central Avenue, Box 4, Jefferson, LA 70121-0517, e-mail: horizons@altavista.net or blueskies@discoverymail.com; Websites www.freeyellow.com/members2/oldwest/index.htm/ or www2.cybercities.com/z/zines/
VAMPIRE NIGHTS, 577 Central Avenue, Box 4, Jefferson, LA 70121-1400, e-mail: smallpress@theglobe.com or fullmoon@eudoramail.com; Website www.members.theglobe.com/smallpress/default.htm/, www2.cybercities.com/z/zines/
WESTERN SKIES, 577 Central Avenue, Box 4, Jefferson, LA 70121-1400, e-mail: horizons@altavista.net or blueskies@discoverymail.com; Websites www.freeyellow.com/members2/oldwest/index.htm/, www2.cybercities.com/z/zines/
Portals Press, 4411 Fountainebleau Drive, New Orleans, LA 70125, 504-821-7723; E-mal jptravis@worldnet.att.net
XAVIER REVIEW, Box 110C, Xavier University, New Orleans, LA 70125, 504-486-7411 X481; 483-7304; FAX 504-488-3320
SECOND STONE, 1113 3rd Street, New Orleans, LA 70130-5630, 504-899-4014, e-Mail secstone@aol.com
WHISPERING WIND MAGAZINE, PO Box 1390, Folsom, LA 70437-1390, 504-796-5433; e-mail whiswind@i-55.com; website www.whisperingwind.com
Youth Sports Press, Inc., 3433 Highway 190 #285, Mandeville, LA 70471, 888-444-4345; fax 504-727-2322
DIE YOUNG, English Department, Univ of Southwestern Louisiana, Lafayette, LA 70504-4691
FAR GONE, PO Box 43745, Lafayette, LA 70504-3745
THE LOUISIANA REVIEW, Division of Liberal Arts, Louisiana State Univ., PO Box 1129, Eunice, LA 70535
Thunder Rain Publishing Corp., PO Box 1407, Denham Springs, LA 70727-1407, 504-686-2002; Fax 686-2285; E-mail rhi@earthlink.net
CPHC Press and Products, 861 Main Street, Baton Rouge, LA 70802-5529, 504-383-3013; 800-445-8026; FAX 504-383-0030; email ssd720@aol.com; itoldson@premier.net
NEW DELTA REVIEW, c/o Dept. of English, Louisiana State University, Baton Rouge, LA 70803-5001, 504-388-4079
THE SOUTHERN REVIEW, 43 Allen Hall, Louisiana State University, Baton Rouge, LA 70803, 225-388-5108
Gothic Press, 4998 Perkins Road, Baton Rouge, LA 70808-3043, 504-766-2906
Claitor's Law Books & Publishing Division, Inc., PO Box 261333, Baton Rouge, LA 70826-1333, 504-344-0476; FAX 504-344-0480; claitors@claitors.com, www.claitors.com
SILHOUETTE MAGAZINE, PO Box 53763, Baton Rouge, LA 70892, 504-358-0617
THE SCRIBIA, PO Box 68, Grambling State University, Grambling, LA 71245, 318-644-2072; hoytda@alpha0.gram.edu

MAINE

Howln Moon Press, PO Box 238, Eliot, ME 03903, 207-439-3508; E-mail bmueller@howlnmoonpress.com
NORTHEAST ARTS MAGAZINE, PO Box 94, Kittery, ME 03904-0094
Nicolas-Hays, Inc., Box 2039, York Beach, ME 03910, 207-363-4393
Samuel Weiser, Inc., PO Box 612, York Beach, ME 03910, 207-363-4393; fax 207-363-5799; e-mail email@weiser-books.com
PANOPTICON, PO BOX 142, York Harbor, ME 03911-0142, E-mail jmoser41@portland.maine.edu
Tide Book Publishing Company, Box 101, York Harbor, ME 03911-0101, 207-363-4534
ME MAGAZINE, PO Box 182, Bowdoinham, ME 04008, 207-666-8453
Pittore Euforico, PO Box 182, Bowdoinham, ME 04008, 207-666-8453
Coyote Books, PO Box 629, Brunswick, ME 04011
MAINE IN PRINT, 12 Pleasant Street, Brunswick, ME 04011, 207-729-6333, Fax 207-725-1014

Clamp Down Press, PO Box 727'), Cape Porpoise, ME 04014, 207-967-2605
Intercultural Press, Inc., PO Box 700, Yarmouth, ME 04096, 207-846-5168; e-mail books@interculturalpress.com
THE CAFE REVIEW, c/o Yes Books, 20 Danforth Street, Portland, ME 04101, e-mail seegerlab@aol.com, www.thecapereview.com
Booksplus of Maine, RR 2 Box 2568, Sabattus, ME 04280, 207-375-6251
Tilbury House, Publishers, 132 Water Street, Gardiner, ME 04345, 207-582-1899
Laureate Press, 2710 Ohio Street, Bangor, ME 04401-1056, 800-946-2727
IMPACC USA, PO Box 1247, Greenville, ME 04441-1247, 800-762-7720, 207-695-3354
Puckerbrush Press, 76 Main Street, Orono, ME 04473-1430, 207-866-4868
THE PUCKERBRUSH REVIEW, 76 Main Street, Orono, ME 04473-1430
Astarte Shell Press, HC 63 Box 89, Bath, ME 04530-9503, 207-828-1992
BELOIT POETRY JOURNAL, 24 Berry Cove Road, Lamoine, ME 04605, 207-667-5598
The Latona Press, 24 Berry Cove Road, Lamoine, ME 04605
Heartsong Books, PO Box 370, Blue Hill, ME 04614-0370, publishers/authors phone: 207-374-5170; e-mail maggie@downeast.net; uri:http://heartsongbooks.com
Organization for Equal Education of the Sexes, Inc., PO Box 438, Dept. DB, Blue Hill, ME 04614, 207-374-2489
Two Dog Press, PO Box 307, Deer Isle, ME 04627, 207-348-6819; fax 207-348-6016; email human@twodogpress.com
Harvest Hill Press, PO Box 55, Salisbury Cove, ME 04672, 207-288-8900; fax 207-288-3611
FLOATING ISLAND, PO Box 7, Stonington, ME 04681, 207-367-6309
Floating Island Publications, PO Box 7, Stonington, ME 04681, 207-367-6309
Brook Farm Books, PO Box 246, Bridgewater, ME 04735
VOLITION, PO Box 314, Tenants Harbor, ME 04860
Vortex Editions, PO Box 314, Tenants Harbor, ME 04860
Century Press, PO Box 298, Thomaston, ME 04861, 207-354-0998; Fax 207-354-8953; cal@americanletters.org; www.americanletters.org
Conservatory of American Letters, PO Box 298, Thomaston, ME 04861-0298, 207-354-0998; Fax 207-354-8953; cal@americanletters.org; www.americanletters.org
Dan River Press, PO Box 298, Thomaston, ME 04861-0298, 207-354-0998; Fax 207-354-8953; cal@americanletters.org; www.americanletters.org
NORTHWOODS JOURNAL, A Magazine for Writers, PO Box 298, Thomaston, ME 04861-0298, 207-345-0998; Fax 207-354-8953; cal@americanletters.org; www.americanletters.org
Northwoods Press, PO Box 298, Thomaston, ME 04861-0298, 207-354-0998; Fax 207-354-8953; cal@americanletters.org; www.americanletters.org
Bern Porter Books, 50 Salmond Road, Belfast, ME 04915, 207-338-3763
Stones Point Press, PO Box 384, Belfast, ME 04915, 207-338-1921
Alice James Books, University of Maine at Farmington, 98 Main Street, Farmington, ME 04938-1911
Common Courage Press, Box 702, Monroe, ME 04951, 207-525-0900
TRANET, Box 567, Rangeley, ME 04970, 207-864-2252
Polar Bear & Company, Brook Street, Solon, ME 04979, e-mail polarbear@skow.net
Polar Bear Productions & Company, PO Box 311 Brook Street, Solon, ME 04979, 207-643-2795
Nightshade Press, PO Box 76, Ward Hill, Troy, ME 04987, 207-948-3427
POTATO EYES, PO Box 76, Troy, ME 04987, 207-948-3427; Fax 207-948-5088; E-mail potatoeyes@uninets.net; website www.maineguide.om/giftshop/potatoeyes

MARYLAND

POTOMAC REVIEW, PO Box 354, Port Tobacco, MD 20677
Gryphon House, Inc., PO Box 207, Beltsville, MD 20704-0207, 301-595-9500
CORRECTIONS TODAY, American Correctional Association, 4380 Forbes Boulevard, Lanham, MD 20706-4322, 301-918-1800
Maryland Historical Press, 9205 Tuckerman St, Lanham, MD 20706, 301-577-2436 and 557-5308; fax 301-577-8711; e-mail mhpress@erols.com
Scarecrow Press, 4720 Boston Way, Lanham, MD 20706, 301-459-3366; Fax 301-459-2118
Vestal Press Ltd, 4720 Boston Way, Lanham, MD 20706-4310, 607-797-4872, fax 607-797-4872
VOYA (Voice of Youth Advocate), 4720 Boston Way, Lanham, MD 20706, 301-459-3366
Heritage Books, Inc., 1540-E Pointer Ridge Place, Bowie, MD 20716, 301-390-7708; Fax 301-390-7153; heritagebooks@pipeline.com
THE PLASTIC TOWER, PO Box 702, Bowie, MD 20718
GLEN BURNIELAND, 9195-H Hitching Post Lane, Laurel, MD 20723, 301-604-8236
Acorn Publishing, 4431 Lehigh Road #288, College Park, MD 20740-3127
FEMINIST STUDIES, c/o Women's Studies Program, University of Maryland, College Park, MD 20742, 301-405-7413
Open University of America Press, 3916 Commander Drive, Hyattsville, MD 20782-1027, 301-779-0220 phone/Fax; openuniv@aol.com
AMERICAN JOURNALISM REVIEW, 8701 Adelphi Road, Adelphi, MD 20783-1716
IAAS Publishers, Inc., 7676 New Hampshire Ave., Suite 330, Langley Park, MD 20783, 301-499-6308
21ST CENTURY AFRO REVIEW, 7676 New Hampshire Ave., Suite 330, Langley Park, MD 20783
ORACLE POETRY, PO Box 7413, Langley Park, MD 20787
ORACLE STORY, PO Box 7413, Langley Park, MD 20787
Rising Star Publishers, PO Box 7413, Langley Park, MD 20787
THE FUTURIST, World Future Society, 7910 Woodmont Avenue, Suite 450, Bethesda, MD 20814, 301-656-8274
IBEX Publishers, 8014 Old Georgetown Road, Bethesda, MD 20814, 301-718-8188; FAX 301-907-8707
POET LORE, The Writer's Center, 4508 Walsh Street, Bethesda, MD 20815-6006, 301-654-8664
WRITER'S CAROUSEL, 4508 Walsh Street, Bethesda, MD 20815-6006, 301-654-8664
The Writer's Center, 4508 Walsh Street, Bethesda, MD 20815-6006, 301-654-8664
COMMON BOUNDARY MAGAZINE, 7005 Florida Street, Chevy Chase, MD 20815, 301-652-9495; FAX 301-652-0579; e-mail connect@commonboundary.org; website www.commonboundary.org
Woodbine House, 6510 Bells Mill Road, Bethesda, MD 20817-1636, 301-468-8800
Gut Punch Press, PO Box 105, Cabin John, MD 20818
THE CRESCENT REVIEW, PO Box 15069, Chevy Chase, MD 20825

TEENAGE GANG DEBS, PO Box 1754, Bethesda, MD 20827-1754
STRANGE MAGAZINE, PO Box 2246, Rockville, MD 20847, 301-460-4789
Kar-Ben Copies, Inc., 6800 Tildenwood Lane, Rockville, MD 20852, 301-984-8733; 800-4KARBEN (in USA)
Ariadne Press, 4817 Tallahassee Avenue, Rockville, MD 20853, 301-949-2514
Scripta Humanistica, 1383 Kersey Lane, Potomac, MD 20854, 301-294-7949; 301-340-1095
Legation Press, 3188 Plyers Mill Road, Kensington, MD 20895-2717
SITUATION, 10402 Ewell Avenue, Kensington, MD 20895-4025
Bob & Bob Publishing, PO Box 10246, Gaithersburg, MD 20898-0246, 301-977-3442; FAX 301-990-2393; Bobowo@aol.com; www.members.aol.com/bobowo
SelectiveHouse Publishers, Inc., PO Box 10095, Gaithersburg, MD 20898, 301-990-2999; email sr@selectivehouse.com; www.selectivehouse.com
New Fantasy Publications, 203 Lexington Drive, Silver Spring, MD 20901-2637
AMERICAN HIKER, 1422 Fenwick Lane, Silver Spring, MD 20910-2160, 301-565-6704
American Hiking Society, 1422 Fenwick Lane, Silver Spring, MD 20910-2160, 301-565-6704
FODDERWING, PO Box 5346, Takoma Park, MD 20913-5346, 301-587-1202
UNO MAS MAGAZINE, PO Box 1832, Silver Spring, MD 20915, Fax; 301-770-3250, E-mail; unomasmag@aol.com; website http://www.unomas.com/
Piggy Bank Press, 5277 Talbot's Landing, Ellicott City, MD 21043, Fax 410-744-7121; Telephone 410-455-9410
ABBEY, 5360 Fallriver Row Court, Columbia, MD 21044
White Urp Press, 5360 Fallriver Row Court, Columbia, MD 21044
Daedal Press, 2315 Belair Road, Fallston, MD 21047
IWAN: INMATE WRITERS OF AMERICA NEWSLETTER, Box 1673, Glen Burnie, MD 21060, e-mail inwram@netscape.com
Sidran Foundation and Press, 2328 W. Joppa Road, Suite 15, Lutherville, MD 21093, 410-825-8888; Fax 410-337-0747; E-mail sidran@access.digex.net; http://www.access.digex.net/sidran
BRIDGES: An Interdisciplinary Journal of Theology, Philosophy, History, and Science, PO Box 186, Monkton, MD 21111-0186, 410-329-3055; Fax 410-472-3152; E-mail Bridges23@aol.com
Stemmer House Publishers, Inc., 2627 Caves Road, Owings Mills, MD 21117
MINERVA: Quarterly Report on Women and the Military, 20 Granada Road, Pasadena, MD 21122-2708, 410-437-5379
Aeolus Press, Inc., PO Box 466, Randallstown, MD 21133-0466, 410-922-1212; fax 410-922-4262
KITE LINES, PO Box 466, Randallstown, MD 21133-0466, 410-922-1212; fax 410-922-4262
BLACK MOON, 233 Northway Road, Reisterstown, MD 21136, 410-833-9424
MONOZINE, PO Box 598, Reisterstown, MD 21136
THE BALTIMORE REVIEW, PO Box 410, Riderwood, MD 21139, 410-377-5265; Fax 410-377-4325; E-mail hdiehl@bcpl.net
HOT CALALOO, PO Box 429, Riderwood, MD 21139, 410-997-1381, e-mail mip@welchlink.welch.jhu.edu - (web page) http://www.welch.jhu.edu/homepages/mip/html/hcal.html
Marlton Publishers, Inc., PO Box 223, Severn, MD 21144, 800-859-1073; fax 410-519-1439
The Galileo Press Ltd., 3637 Black Rock Road, Upperco, MD 21155-9322
ACME Press, PO Box 1702, Westminster, MD 21158, 410-848-7577
MINIATURE DONKEY TALK INC, 1338 Hughes Shop Road, Westminster, MD 21158, 410-875-0118; fax 410-857-9145; email minidonk@qis.net; www.qis.net/~minidonk/donktext.htm
Jungle Man Press, 211 W. Mulberry Street, 3rd Floor, Baltimore, MD 21201
The Nautical & Aviation Publishing Co. of America, Inc., 8 West Madison Street, Baltimore, MD 21201, 410-659-0220; fax 410-539-8832
Genealogical Publishing Co., Inc., 1001 North Calvert Street, Baltimore, MD 21202, 410-837-8271; 410-752-8492 fax
PASSAGER: A Journal of Remembrance and Discovery, 1420 N. Charles Street, Baltimore, MD 21202-5779, 301-625-3041
Studio Editions, 250 S. President Street, Ste. 300, Baltimore, MD 21202, 410-539-1161; Fax 410-783-4697; studioedtn@aol.com; www.members.aol.com/beverb/studio.htm
Dolphin-Moon Press, PO Box 22262, Baltimore, MD 21203
STREET VOICE, PO Box 22962, Baltimore, MD 21203-4962, 410-837-0643
VEGETARIAN JOURNAL, PO Box 1463, Baltimore, MD 21203, 410-366-VEGE (8343)
The Vegetarian Resource Group, PO Box 1463, Baltimore, MD 21203, 410-366-8343
Bacchus Press Ltd., 1751 Circle Road, Baltimore, MD 21204, 301-576-0762
BrickHouse Books, Inc., 541 Piccadilly Road, Baltimore, MD 21204, 410-828-0724; 830-2938
Icarus Books, 1015 Kenilworth Drive, Baltimore, MD 21204, 410-821-7807
The People's Press, 4810 Norwood Avenue, Baltimore, MD 21207-6839
World Travel Institute, Inc., 8268 Streamwood Drive, PO Box 32674, Baltimore, MD 21208, 410-922-4903; website www.worldtravelinstitute.com
Bancroft Press, PO Box 65360, Baltimore, MD 21209-9945, 410-358-0658; Fax 410-764-1967
Prospect Hill Press, 8 Over Ridge Court, Apt#4021, Baltimore, MD 21210-1129, 410-889-0320
CELEBRATION, 2707 Lawina Road, Baltimore, MD 21216-1608, 410-542-8785
ALTERNATIVE PRESS INDEX, Alternative Press Center, Inc., PO Box 33109, Baltimore, MD 21218, 410-243-2471
CALLALOO, 2715 North Charles Street, Baltimore, MD 21218-4319, 301-338-6901
SHATTERED WIG REVIEW, 425 E. 31st, Baltimore, MD 21218, 301-243-6888
SOCIAL ANARCHISM: A Journal of Practice and Theory, 2743 Maryland Avenue, Baltimore, MD 21218, 410-243-6987; sociala@nothingness.org
THE ANIMALS' AGENDA, PO Box 25881, Baltimore, MD 21224-0581, 410-675-4566; FAX 410-675-0066
Paycock Press, 3938 Colchester Road, Apt. 364, Baltimore, MD 21229-5010, Fax; 410-644-5195; e-mail atticus@radix.net
American Literary Press Inc./Noble House, 8019 Belair Road #10, Baltimore, MD 21236, 410-882-7700; fax 410-882-7703; e-mail amerlit@erols.com; www.erols.com/amerlit
MOVIE CLUB, 4504 Hershey Way, Nottingham, MD 21236-2122, 410-256-5013
DIRTY LINEN, PO Box 66600, Baltimore, MD 21239-6600, 410-583-7973; fax 410-337-6735
Barefoot Press, 1856 Cherry Road, Annapolis, MD 21401
THE DIPLOMAT, 111 Conduit Street, Annapolis, MD 21401-2603
Tafford Publishing, PO Box 4474, Annapolis, MD 21403-6474, 410-267-9608 phone/Fax
Nightsun Books, 823 Braddock Road, Cumberland, MD 21502-2622, 301-722-4861

674

GERMAN LIFE, 1068 National Highway, LaVale, MD 21502, 301-729-6190; fax 301-729-1720; e-mail editor@german-life.com
THE COOL TRAVELER, 196 Bowery Street, Frostburg, MD 21532-2255, 215-440-0592
NIGHTSUN, English Department, Frostburg S. University, Frostburg, MD 21532, 301-687-4221
Cornell Maritime Press, Inc., FO Box 456, Centreville, MD 21617, 301-758-1075
JEWISH VEGETARIAN NEWSLETTER, Jewish Vegetarians, 6938 Reliance Road, Federalsburg, MD 21632, 410-754-5550, e-mail imossman@skipjack.bluecrab.org; www.orbyss.com
THE PEGASUS REVIEW, PO Box 88, Henderson, MD 21640-0088, 410-482-6736
GOTHIX, PO Box 3223, Frederick, MD 21705-3223, 301-682-7604; fax 301-682-9737
Landwaster Books, PO Box 3223, Frederick, MD 21705-3223, website www.landwaster.com
ECLIPSE, GENERAL DELIVERY, Brownsville, MD 21715-9999, E-mail Kiirenza@aol.com
ANTIETAM REVIEW, 41 S. Potomac Street, Hagerstown, MD 21740-5512, 301-791-3132
LISTEN, 55 West Oak Ridge Drive, Hagerstown, MD 21740
TREASURE HOUSE, 20351 Kings Crest Blvd, Hagerstown, MD 21742-8146
SATIRE, PO Box 340, Hancock, MD 21750, 301-678-6999; satire@intrepid.net; www.intrepid.net/satire
Twelve Star Publishing, PO Box 123, Jefferson, MD 21755, 301-473-9035
ART CALENDAR, PO Box 199, Upper Fairmount, MD 21867, 410-651-9150
ENOUGH IS ENOUGH!, PO Box 683, Chesapeake City, MD 21915, 410-885-2887

MASSACHUSETTS

Pyncheon House, 6 University Drive, Suite 105, Amherst, MA 01002
Swamp Press, 323 Pelham Road, Amherst, MA 01002
TIGHTROPE, 323 Pelham Road, Amherst, MA 01002
THE MASSACHUSETTS REVIEW, South College, Univ. of Mass/Box 37140, Amherst, MA 01003-7140, 413-545-2689
Amherst Writers & Artists Press, Inc., PO Box 1076, Amherst, MA 01004, 413-253-7764 phone/fax; e-mail awapress@javanet.com
PEREGRINE, PO Box 1076, Amherst, MA 01004, 413-253-7764 phone/fax; e-mail awapress@javanet.com; www.javanet.com/~awapress
TRANSITIONS ABROAD: The Guide to Living, Learning, and Working Overseas, 18 Hulst Road, PO Box 1300, Amherst, MA 01004, 413-256-3414; 413-256-0373; e-mail info@transitionsabroad.com; website www.transitionsabroad.com.
University of Massachusetts Press, Box 429, Amherst, MA 01004-0429, 413-545-2217
Adastra Press, 16 Reservation Road, Easthampton, MA 01027-1227
FkB Press, PO Box 403, Easthampton, MA 01027-0403
OLD CROW, PO Box 403, Easthampton, MA 01027-0403
KEY SATCH(EL), PO Box 363, Haydenville, MA 01039, 413-268-3632; E-mail keysatch@quale.com
Quale Press, PO Box 363, Haydenville, MA 01039, 413-268-3632 tel/fax; e-mail central@quale.com
New England Cartographics, Inc., PO Box 9369, North Amherst, MA 01059, 413-549-4124; FAX 413-549-3621
MALACHITE AND AGATE, 351 Pleasant Street, #317, Northampton, MA 01060, e-mail miltonmc@earthlink.net
Summerset Press, 20 Langworthy Road, Northampton, MA 01060, 413-586-3394 phone/FAX; JKaplan105@aol.com
BALL MAGAZINE, PO Box 775, Northampton, MA 01061, 413-584-3076
HOTHEAD PAISAN, HOMICIDAL LESBIAN TERRORIST, PO Box 1242, Northampton, MA 01061-1242
Pittenbruach Press, 15 Walnut Street, PO Box 553, Northampton, MA 01061
Perugia Press, PO Box 108, Shutesbury, MA 01072, E-mail skan@valinet.com
NEW ENGLAND ANTIQUES JOURNAL, Turley Publications, 4 Church Street, Ware, MA 01082, 413-967-3505
Little River Press, 10 Lowell Avenue, Westfield, MA 01085, 413-568-5598
PINE ISLAND JOURNAL OF NEW ENGLAND POETRY, PO Box 317, West Springfield, MA 01090
Paris Press, Inc., 1117 West Road, Williamsburg, MA 01096, 413-628-0051
Deerbridge Books, PO Box 2266, Pittsfield, MA 01201, 413-499-2255; Fax 413-442-5025; riverd@vgernet.net
ANAIS: An International Journal, PO Box 276, Becket, MA 01223, 413-623-5170
The Figures, 5 Castle Hill Avenue, Great Barrington, MA 01230-1552, 413-528-2552
Moksha Press, PO Box 2360, Lenox, MA 01240, 413-637-6000; FAX 415-637-6015; E-mail moksha@moksha.org
WHAT IS ENLIGHTENMENT?, PO Box 2360, Lenox, MA 01240, 413-637-6000; FAX 413-637-6015; wie@moksha.org
Mad River Press, State Road, Richmond, MA 01254, 413-698-3184
THE DROPLET JOURNAL, 29 Iron Mine Road, West Stockbridge, MA 01266-9223, 413-232-0052; E-mail droplet@bcn.net
Hard Press, Inc., PO Box 184, West Stockbridge, MA 01266, 413-232-4690
LINGO, PO Box 184, West Stockbridge, MA 01266, 413-232-4690
Haley's, PO Box 248, Athol, MA 01331, haleyathol@aolcom
OSIRIS, Box 297, Deerfield, MA 01342, e-mail moorhead@k12s.phast.umass.edu
Ash Grove Press, PO Box 365, Sunderland, MA 01375-0365, 413-665-1200
Millennium Press, PO Box 502, Groton, MA 01450, 978-433-3162; Fax 978-433-3110; E-mail millpres@ultranet.com
BUTTON, PO Box 26, Lunenburg, MA 01462, E-mail buttonx26@aol.com
ATL Press, Inc., PO Box 4563 T Station, Shrewsbury, MA 01545, 508-898-2290; FAX 508-898-2063; E-mail 104362.2523@compuserve.com; atlpress@compuserve.com
(THE) BRAVE NEW TICK, PO Box 24, S. Grafton, MA 01560, 508-799-3769
Edgeworth & North Books, PO Box 812 West Side Station, Worcester, MA 01602-0812
Metacom Press, 1 Tahanto Road, Worcester, MA 01602-2523, 617-757-1683
NEOLOGISMS, Box 869, 1102 Pleasant Street, Worcester, MA 01602
THE WORCESTER REVIEW, 6 Chatham Street, Worcester, MA 01609, 603-924-7342; 978-797-4770
VanderWyk & Burnham, PO Box 2789, 411 Massachusetts Avenue, Acton, MA 01720, 978-263-5906
Mills & Sanderson, Publishers, PO Box 833, Bedford, MA 01730-0833, 617-275-1410
Discovery Enterprises, Ltd., 31 Laurelwood Drive, Carlisle, MA 01741-1205
The American Dissident, 1837 Main Street, Concord, MA 01742, e-mail; members. theglobe.com/enmarge@hotmail.com
Artifact Press, Ltd., 900 Tanglewood Drive, Concord, MA 01742, 978-287-5296; Fax 978-287-5299; hershey@tiac.net
Drum, 40 Potter Street, Concord, MA 01742
BUZZARD, PO Box 576, Hudson, MA 01749, 508-568-0793
Loose Threads Publishing, PO Box 187, Hudson, MA 01749, 508-562-1611

Bliss Publishing Company, Inc., PO Box 920, Marlboro, MA 01752, 508-779-2827

Water Row Press, PO Box 438, Sudbury, MA 01776

WATER ROW REVIEW, PO Box 438, Sudbury, MA 01776

THE LONG TERM VIEW: A Journal of Informed Opinion, Massachusetts School of Law, 500 Federal Street, Andover, MA 01810, 978-681-0800

THE LONG STORY, 18 Eaton Street, Lawrence, MA 01843, 978-686-7638, e-mail rpbtls@aol.com

AT-HOME DAD, 61 Brightwood Avenue, North Andover, MA 01845, E-mail: athomedad@aol.com; www.athome-dad.com

Genesis Publishing Company, Inc., 1547 Great Pond Road, North Andover, MA 01845-1216, 508-688-6688, fax 508-688-8686

DHARMA BEAT, Box 1753, Lowell, MA 01853-1753

Ithaca Press, PO Box 853, Lowell, MA 01853

Loom Press, Box 1394, Lowell, MA 01853

FC-Izdat Publishing, 3 Cottage Avenue, Winchester, MA 01890, 617-776-2262; vvv@tiac.net

CC600, 7-9 Rantoul Street, Suite 206, Beverly, MA 01915, 978-927-5556; Fax 978-927-5558

BACKSPACE: A QUEER POETS JOURNAL, 25 Riverside Avenue, Gloucester, MA 01930-2552, e-mail bkspqpj@aol.com

OLD-HOUSE JOURNAL, 2 Main Street, Gloucester, MA 01930, 508-283-3200; fax 508-283-4629

Magnolia Publishing, PO Box 5537, Magnolia, MA 01930, 508-283-5283

FLYING HORSE, PO Box 445, Marblehead, MA 01945

Micah Publications Inc., 255 Humphrey Street, Marblehead, MA 01945, 617-631-7601

SOUNDINGS EAST, English Dept., Salem State College, Salem, MA 01970, 508-741-6000

Four Way Books, PO Box 607, Marshfield, MA 02050

APPALACHIA JOURNAL, 5 Joy Street, Boston, MA 02108, 617-523-0636

Appalachian Mountain Club Books, 5 Joy Street, Boston, MA 02108, 617-523-0636

Beacon Press, 25 Beacon Street, Boston, MA 02108, 617-742-2110

Walter H. Baker Company (Baker's Plays), 100 Chauncy St., Boston, MA 02111, 617-482-1280; Fax 617-982-7613; E-mail http://www.ziplink.net/bakers.plays.html

TEEN VOICES MAGAZINE, 515 Washington Street, 6th floor, Boston, MA 02111-1759, 617-426-5505; fax 617-426-5577; e-mail womenexp@teenvoices.com; website www.teenvoices.com

THE EUGENE O'NEILL REVIEW, Department of English, Suffolk University, Boston, MA 02114, 617-573-8272

INFUSION, Center for Campus Organizing, 165 Friend Street, Suite 1, Boston, MA 02114-2025, 617-725-2886; e-mail cco@igc.apc.org

Sigo Press, PO Box 8748, Boston, MA 02114-0037, 508-740-0113

THE NEW ENGLAND QUARTERLY, 239 Meserve Hall, Northeastern University, Boston, MA 02115, 617-373-2734

D.B.A. Books, 291 Beacon Street #8, Boston, MA 02116, 617-262-0411

PLOUGHSHARES, Emerson College, 100 Beacon Street, Boston, MA 02116, 617-824-8753

ASSEMBLAGE: A Critical Journal of Architecture and Design Culture, PO Box 180299, Boston, MA 02118, email assmblag@gsd.harvard.edu

BAY WINDOWS, 631 Tremont Street, Boston, MA 02118, 617-266-6670, X211

Harvard Common Press, 535 Albany Street, Boston, MA 02118, 617-423-5803; 888-657-3755

Good Gay Poets Press, Box 277, Astor Station, Boston, MA 02123

COLLEGE ENGLISH, Dept. of English, U Mass/Boston, 100 Morrissey Boulevard, Boston, MA 02125-3393

The Ark, 115 Montebello Road, Jamaica Plain, MA 02130, 617-522-1922

THE NOISE, 74 Jamaica Street, Jamaica Plain, MA 02130, 617-524-4735, E-mail: tmaxnoise@aol.com

SOJOURNER, THE WOMEN'S FORUM, 42 Seaverns Avenue, Jamaica Plain, MA 02130-1109, 617-524-0415

The B & R Samizdat Express, PO Box 161, West Roxbury, MA 02132, 617-469-2269; E-mail seltzer@samizdat.com; www.samizdat.com

American Living Press, PO Box 901, Allston, MA 02134, 617-522-6196

ATELIER, 8 Holton Street, Allston, MA 02134-1337

MOMMY AND I ARE ONE, PO Box 643, Allston, MA 02134, 617-254-9577

Primal Publishing, PO Box 1179, Allston, MA 02134-0007, 617-787-3412, Fax 617-787-5406; e-mail primal@primal-pub.com

WEIRD POETRY, PO Box 901, Allston, MA 02134, 617-522-6196

Eidos, PO Box 96, Boston, MA 02137, 617-262-0096

EIDOS: Sexual Freedom & Erotic Entertainment for Consenting Adults, PO Box 96, Boston, MA 02137, 617-262-0096

THE BOSTON BOOK REVIEW, 30 Brattle Street, 4th floor, Cambridge, MA 02138, 617-497-0344, BBR-info@BostonBookReview.org, www.BostonBookReview.org

DAEDALUS, Journal of the American Academy of Arts and Sciences, American Academy of Arts and Sciences, 136 Irving Street, Cambridge, MA 02138, 617-491-2600; fax 617-576-5088; e-mail daedalus@amacad.org

THE HARVARD ADVOCATE, 21 South St., Cambridge, MA 02138, 617-495-0737

HARVARD WOMEN'S LAW JOURNAL, Publications Center, Harvard Law School, Cambridge, MA 02138, 617-495-3726

JLA Publications, A Division Of Jeffrey Lant Associates, Inc., 50 Follen Street #507, Suite 507, Cambridge, MA 02138, 617-547-6372; drjlant@worldprofit.com; www.trafficcenter.com

PERSEPHONE, c/o John Cobb, 40 Avon Hill Street, Cambridge, MA 02138

Zoland Books, 384 Huron Avenue, Cambridge, MA 02138, 617-864-6252; FAX 617-661-4998

BOSTON REVIEW, 30 Wadsworth Street, MIT, Cambridge, MA 02139, 617-253-3642, fax 617-252-1549

Plympton Press International, PMB 206, 955 Massachusetts Avenue, Cambridge, MA 02139, 313-994-1086

South End Press, 7 Brookline Street #1, Cambridge, MA 02139-4146

Circlet Press, Inc., 1770 Mass Avenue #278, Cambridge, MA 02140, 617-864-0492; Fax 617-864-0663; circlet-info@circlet.com

GROWING WITHOUT SCHOOLING, 2380 Massachusetts Ave., Suite #104, Cambridge, MA 02140-1884, 617-864-3100

PEACEWORK, 2161 Massachusetts Avenue, Cambridge, MA 02140, 617-661-6130

Ibbetson St. Press, 33 Ibbetson Street, Somerville, MA 02143

RADICAL AMERICA, 237A Holland Street, Somerville, MA 02144-2402, 617-628-6585

Wisdom Publications, Inc., 199 Elm Street, Somerville, MA 02144-3129, 617-776-7416; Fax 617-776-7841

KARMA LAPEL, PO Box 441915, Sumerville, MA 02144-0016, e-mail heathr@ais.net

SALAMANDER, 48 Ackers Avenue, Brookline, MA 02146
Sorenson Books, 1093 Beacon Street, Suite 1-B, Brookline, MA 02146, 617-264-8800; FAX 617-969-6369
Branden Publishing Company, 17 Station Street, Box 843, Brookline Village, MA 02147, 617-734-2045; FAX 617-734-2046, E-mail: branden@usa1.com, Web page: http://www1.usa1.com/nbranden/
S., 85 Winthrop Street, Medford, MA 02155
SLAM!, 24 Arlington Street, Medford, MA 02155, 781-488-3636; bosslam@cybercom.net
Blue Reef Publications, Inc., PO Box 42, Newton Centre, MA 02159, 617-332-7965, fax 617-332-7967, e-mail Info@bluereef.com
LEGAL INFORMATION MANAGEMENT INDEX, Legal Information Services, P.O. Box 67, Newton Highlands, MA 02161-0067, 508-443-4087
BUSINESS CONSUMER GUIDE, 125 Walnut Street, Watertown, MA 02172, Subscriptions 800-938-0088, editorial 617-924-0044; brg@buyrszone.com
EASTGATE QUARTERLY REVIEW OF HYPERTEXT, 134 Main Street, Watertown, MA 02172, 617-924-9044; Fax 617-924-9051; info@eastgate.com
Eastgate Systems Inc., 134 Main Street, Watertown, MA 02172, 617-924-9044; Fax 617-924-9051; info@eastgate.com
WIN NEWS, 187 Grant Street, Lexington, MA 02173, 781-862-9431; Fax 781-862-1734
Nonsilent Press, c/o The Guide, PO Box 593, Boston, MA 02199
Union Park Press, PO Box 2737, Boston, MA 02208
AGNI, Boston University, 236 Bay State Road, Boston, MA 02215, 617-353-7135
FAG RAG, Box 15331, Kenmore Station, Boston, MA 02215, 617-426-4469
Fag Rag Books, PO Box 15331, Boston, MA 02215
96 INC, PO Box 15559, Boston, MA 02215
PARTISAN REVIEW, 236 Bay State Road, Boston, MA 02215, 617-353-4260
BANANAFISH, PO Box 381332, Cambridge, MA 02238-1332, 617-868-0662 phone/Fax; bananafi@aol.com
Blue Crane Books, PO Box 0291, Cambridge, MA 02238, 617-926-8989
Edgewood Press, PO Box 380264, Cambridge, MA 02238
Life Lessons, PO Box 382346, Cambridge, MA 02238, 617-576-2546; fax 617-576-3234; e-mail walkingwm@aol.com; website www.mindwalks.com
RhwymBooks, PO Box 1706, Cambridge, MA 02238-1706, 617-623-5894; fax 617-623-5894; email rhwym-books@aol.com; www.hometown.aol.com/rhwymbooks
STARGREEN, PO Box 380406, Cambridge, MA 02238, 617-868-3981
UNDERGROUND SURREALIST MAGAZINE, Underground Surrealist Studio, PO Box 2565, Cambridge, MA 02238, 617-628-4101
Yellow Moon Press, PO Box 381316, Cambridge, MA 02238-0001, 617-776-2230; Fax 617-776-8246; E-mail ymp@tiac.net; web site www.yellowmoon.com
Paradigm Publications, 44 Linden Street, Brookline, MA 02445, voice 617-738-1235; voice 617-738-4664; fax 617-738-4620; e-Mail info@redwingbooks.com
Hermes House Press, Inc., 113 Summit Avenue, Brookline, MA 02446-2319, 617-566-2468
KAIROS, A Journal of Contemporary Thought and Criticism, 113 Summit Avenue, Brookline, MA 02446-2319
Zephyr Press, 50 Kenwood Street, Brookline, MA 02446, 617-713-2813
Pegasus Communications, Inc., 1 Moody Street, Waltham, MA 02453-5339
Peanut Butter and Jelly Press, PO Box 239, Newton, MA 02459-0002, 617-630-0945 phone/fax
Arts End Books, Box 162, Newton, MA 02468
NOSTOC MAGAZINE, Box 162, Newton, MA 02468
THE NEW RENAISSANCE, An International Magazine of Ideas & Opinions, Emphasizing Literature & The Arts, 26 Heath Road #11, Arlington, MA 02474-3645
KLIATT, 33 Bay State Road, Wellesley, MA 02481, 781-237-7577 phone/fax; kliatt@aol.com
THE WOMEN'S REVIEW OF BOOKS, Wellesley College, Center For Research On Women, Wellesley, MA 02481, 781-283-2555
MARTHA'S VINEYARD MAGAZINE, PO Box 66, Edgartown, MA 02539, 508-627-7444
Woods Hole Press, PO Box 44, Woods Hole, MA 02543, 508-548-9600
Z MAGAZINE, 18 Millfield Street, Woods Hole, MA 02543, 508-548-9063; Fax 508-457-0626; Lydia.sargent@lbbs.org
Phantom Press Publications, 13 Appleton Road, Nantucket, MA 02554-4307
RENAISSANCE MAGAZINE, 13 Appleton Road, Nantucket, MA 02554, 508-325-0411; renzine@aol.com
THE AUROREAN, A POETIC QUARTERLY, PO Box 219, Sagamore Beach, MA 02562-0219, 508-833-0805 phone/fax, phone before faxing
Encircle Publications, PO Box 219, Sagamore Beach, MA 02562, 508-833-0805 phone/fax, phone before faxing
THE ONSET REVIEW, Box 3157, Wareham, MA 02571, E-mail spizzolo@sailsinc.org
THE HIGHWAY POET, PO Box 1400, Brewster, MA 02631
Ash Lad Press, PO Box 294, East Orleans, MA 02643, phone/fax 508-255-2301
OUTLANDER, PO Box 1546, Provincetown, MA 02657
PROVINCETOWN ARTS, 650 Commercial Street, Provincetown, MA 02657, 508-487-3167
Provincetown Arts Press, PO Box 35, 650 Commercial Street, Provincetown, MA 02657, 508-487-3167; FAX 508-487-8634
Race Point Press, PO Box 770, Provincetown, MA 02657, 508-487-1626
Garden St Press, PO Box 1231, Truro, MA 02666-1231, 508-349-1991
Leapfrog Press, PO Box 1495, Wellfleet, MA 02667, 508-349-1925; fax 508-349-1180; email leapfrog@capecod.net; www.leapfrogpress.com
ALTERNATIVE LIFESTYLES DIRECTORY, PO Box 80667, Dartmouth, MA 02748, 508-999-0078
HAIR TO STAY, PO Box 80667, Dartmouth, MA 02748, 508-999-0078, order line 508-994-2908, Fax 508-984-4040
Annedawn Publishing, PO Box 247, Norton, MA 02766, 508-222-9069

MICHIGAN

LIGHTWORKS MAGAZINE, PO Box 1202, Birmingham, MI 48012-1202, 248-626-8026; FAX 248-737-0046
NEWSLETTERNEWS, 70 Macomb, Suite 226, Mt. Clemens, MI 48043, E-mail worldlinks@prodigy.com; Website http:..pages.prodigy.com/worldlinks
WORLDLINKS - FRIENDSHIP NEWS, 70 Macomb Place, #226, Mt. Clemens, MI 48043, e-mail worldlinks@prodigy.com

Christian Traditions Publishing Co., 7728 Springborn Road, Casco, MI 48064-3910, 810-765-4805; searcher@in-gen.net
Ridgeway Press of Michigan, PO Box 120, Roseville, MI 48066, 313-577-7713; Fax to M.L. Liebler 313-577-8615; E-mail mlieble@cms.wayne.edu
ALARM CLOCK, PO Box 1551, Royal Oak, MI 48068, 313-593-9677
DEAD FUN, PO Box 752, Royal Oak, MI 48068-0752
Autumn Publishing Group, LLC., PO Box 71604, Madison Heights, MI 48071, 810-589-5249; fax 810-585-5715; email TSMPublish@aol.com
OPUS LITERARY REVIEW, PO Box 71192, Madison Heights, MI 48071-0192, 313-548-0865
Poetic Page, PO Box 71192, Madison Heights, MI 48071-0192, 313-548-0865
Selah Publishing, PO Box 721508, Berkley, MI 48072-1508, 810-293-3169
EAP DIGEST, Performance Resource Press, Inc., 1270 Rankin Drive, Suite F, Troy, MI 48083-2843, 810-588-7733; fax 810-588-6633
Momentum Books, Ltd., 6964 Crooks Road, Suite #1, Troy, MI 48098, 810-828-3666; fax 810-828-0142
Anderson Press, 706 West Davis, Ann Arbor, MI 48103, 734-995-0125; 734-994-6182; fax 734-994-5207
Otherwind, 541 Lakeview Avenue, Ann Arbor, MI 48103-9704, 313-665-0703
R-Squared Press, 2113 Arborview Boulevard, Ann Arbor, MI 48103, 313-930-6564 (voice and FAX)
SINCERE SINGLES, 512 Glendale Circle, Ann Arbor, MI 48103-4177
Center for Japanese Studies, 202 S. Thayer Street, University of Michigan, Ann Arbor, MI 48104-1608, 734-998-7265; FAX 734-998-7982
THE J MAN TIMES, 2246 Saint Francis Drive #A-211, Ann Arbor, MI 48104-4828, E-mail TheJMan99@aol.com
MICHIGAN: Around and About, 304-1/2 South State Street, Ann Arbor, MI 48104, 313-668-6097
MYSTERIOUS WYSTERIA, 1136 Broadway Avenue #2, Ann Arbor, MI 48104-3968
George Wahr Publishing Company, 304-1/2 South State Street, Ann Arbor, MI 48104, 313-668-6097
AFFABLE NEIGHBOR, PO Box 3635, Ann Arbor, MI 48106
Affable Neighbor Press, PO Box 3635, Ann Arbor, MI 48106
MIM NOTES: Offcial Newsletter of the Maoist Internationalist Movement, PO Box 3576, Ann Arbor, MI 48106
Osric Publishing, PO Box 4501, Ann Arbor, MI 48106
Pierian Press, PO Box 1808, Ann Arbor, MI 48106, 313-434-5530, Fax; 313-434-6409
THE WHITE CROW, PO Box 4501, Ann Arbor, MI 48106
aatec publications, PO Box 7119, Ann Arbor, MI 48107, 800-995-1470 (phone & fax), e-mail aatecpub@aol.com
Axiom Information Resources, PO Box 8015, Ann Arbor, MI 48107, 313-761-4842
THE EDUCATION DIGEST, PO Box 8623, Ann Arbor, MI 48107, 734-975-2800 ext. 207, fax 734-975-2787
The Olivia and Hill Press, Inc., PO Box 7396, Ann Arbor, MI 48107, 734-663-0235 (voice), Fax 734-663-6590; theOHPress@aol.com; www.oliviahill.com
Palladium Communications, 320 South Main Street, PO Box 8403, Ann Arbor, MI 48107-8403, 734-668-4646; FAX 734-663-9361
Prakken Publications, PO Box 8623, Ann Arbor, MI 48107-8623, 374-975-2800, fax 734-975-2787
TECH DIRECTIONS, PO Box 8623, Ann Arbor, MI 48107, 734-975-2800 ext. 212 fax 734-975-2787
Center for South and Southeast Asian Studies Publications, 130 Lane Hall, University of Michigan, Ann Arbor, MI 48109-1290, Editorial: 313-763-5790; distribution: 313-763-5408
Department of Romance Languages, University of Michigan, 4108 MLB, Ann Arbor, MI 48109-1275, 734-764-5344; fax 734-764-8163; e-mail kojo@umich.edu
MICHIGAN FEMINIST STUDIES, 234 W. Engineering, Women's Studies, University of Michigan, Ann Arbor, MI 48109, e-mail mfseditors@umich.edu
MICHIGAN QUARTERLY REVIEW, 3032 Rackham Bldg., University of Michigan, Ann Arbor, MI 48109, 734-764-9265
SHADOW KNOWS MOVIEEYE, PO Box 223, Brighton, MI 48116, E-mail greg@videovamp.com; www.movieeye.com/video; www.tln.org/~greg; www.jamrag.com
Wilderness Adventure Books, Fo Box 576, Chelsea, MI 48118-0576, fax 734-433-1595; e-mail wildernessbooks.org
Gravity Presses, Inc., 27030 Havelock, Dearborn Heights, MI 48127, 313-563-4683; e-mail mikeb5000@yahoo.com
NEW AGE PATRIOT, PO Box 419, Dearborn Heights, MI 48127, 313-563-3192
NOW HERE NOWHERE, 27030 Havelock, Dearborn Heights, MI 48127, 313-563-4683; e-mail mikeb5000@yahoo.com
THE MAC GUFFIN, Schoolcraft College, 18600 Haggerty Road, Livonia, MI 48152, 313-462-4400, ext. 5292 or 5327
Sun Dog Press, 22058 Cumberland Drive, Northville, MI 48167, 248-449-7448; fax 248-449-4070; sundogpr@voyager.net
Poetic License Press, PO Box 85525, Westland, MI 48185-0525, 734-326-9368; FAX 734-326-3480; e-mail steveblo30@aol.com
JOURNAL OF NARRATIVE THEORY, Eastern Michigan University, Ypsilanti, MI 48197, 313-487-3175; Fax 313-483-9744; website www.emich.edu/public/english/JNT
SULFUR, 210 Washtenaw, Ypsilanti, MI 48197-2526, 313-483-9787
FIFTH ESTATE, 4632 Second Avenue, Detroit, MI 48201, 313-831-6800
MOTORBOOTY MAGAZINE, PO Box 02007, Detroit, MI 48202
STRUGGLE: A Magazine of Proletarian Revolutionary Literature, PO Box 13261, Detroit, MI 48213-0261
THE SOUNDS OF POETRY, 2076 Vinewood, Detroit, MI 48216-5506
The Sounds of Poetry Press, 2076 Vinewood, Detroit, MI 48216-5506
JAM RAG, Box 20076, Ferndale, MI 48220, 248-542-8090
Peerless Publishing, PO Box 20466, Ferndale, MI 48220, 248-542-1930
Lotus Press, Inc., PO Box 21607, Detroit, MI 48221, 313-861-1280; fax 313-861-4740
PERSIMMON, 19626 Damman, Harper Woods, MI 48225
Schafer's Publishing, 6864 Stahelin, Detroit, MI 48228, 313-982-1806; fax 313-982-1925; e-mail schaed@idt.net
THE BRIDGE: A Journal of Fiction and Poetry, 14050 Vernon Street, Oak Park, MI 48237, 313-547-6823
Mehring Books, Inc., PO Box 48377, Oak Park, MI 48237-5977, 248-967-2924; 248-967-3023; e-mail sales@mehring.com
THE RESOURCE, PO Box 97, Bloomfield Hills, MI 48303, 810-644-3440 phone/FAX; ResKate@aol.com
BLACK LITERARY PLAYERS, 829 Langdon Court, Rochester Hills, MI 48307, 810-556-7335
LOGIC LETTER, 13957 Hall Road, #185, Shelby Twp., MI 48315
Alpha Omega Press, 3198 Brookshear Circle, Auburn Hills, MI 48326-2208, 910-245-3560
Push/Pull/Press, 29205 Greening Boulevard, Farmington Hills, MI 48334-932-0090
WITNESS, Oakland Community College, 27055 Orchard Lake Road, Farmington Hills, MI 48334, 313-471-7740
Pebble Press, Inc., 24723 Westmoreland, Farmington, MI 48336-1963, 248-478-5820; fax 248-478-6984

W.W. Publications, PO Box 373, Highland, MI 48357-0373, 813-585-0985, phone and fax
THE DRIFTWOOD REVIEW, PO Box 700, Linden, MI 48451, E-mail midrift@aol.com
MINAS TIRITH EVENING-STAR, PO BOX 7871, Flint, MI 48507-0871, 813-585-0985, phone and fax
Inquiry Press, 1880 North Eastman, Midland, MI 48640-8838, 517-631-0009
Michigan State University Press, 1405 S. Harrison Road, #25, East Lansing, MI 48823-5202, 517-355-9543; fax 517-432-2611; E-mail msp07@msu.edu
THE CENTENNIAL REVIEW, 312 Linton Hall, Mich. State Univ., E. Lansing, MI 48824-1044, 517-355-1905
Red Cedar Press, 325 Morrill Hall, Michigan State University, E. Lansing, MI 48824
RED CEDAR REVIEW, 17C Morrill Hall, English Dept., Michigan State Univ., E. Lansing, MI 48824, 517-355-9656
Years Press, Dept. of ATL, EBH, Michigan State Univ, E. Lansing, MI 48824-1033
FOURTH GENRE: EXPLORATIONS IN NONFICTION, ATL Department, 229 Bessey Hall, Michigan State University, East Lansing, MI 48824, 517-432-2556; fax 517-353-5250; e-mail fourthgenre@cal.msu.edu
Bennett & Kitchel, PO Box 4422, East Lansing, MI 48826
Grand River Press, PO Box 1342, East Lansing, MI 48826, (517) 332-8181
Zookeeper Publications, 2010 Cimarron Drive, Okemos, MI 48864-3908, 517-347-4697
OUT YOUR BACKDOOR: The Magazine of Informal Adventure and Cheap Culture, 4686 Meridian Road, Williamston, MI 48895, 517-347-1689; jp@glpbooks.com; www.glpbooks.com/oyb
Perpetual Press, PO Box 30413, Lansing, MI 48909-7913, 800-807-3030
WAY STATION MAGAZINE, 1319 South Logan-MLK, Lansing, MI 48910-1340
Flower Press, 10332 Shaver Road, Kalamazoo, MI 49002, 616-327-0108
THE DROOD REVIEW OF MYSTERY, PO Box 50267, Kalamazoo, MI 49005
New Issues Press, Western Michigan University, 1201 Oliver Street, Kalamazoo, MI 49008, 616-387-2592 or 616-387-8185; Fax 616-387-2562; newissues-poetry@wmich.edu; www.wmich.edu/english/fac/nipps
Rarach Press, 1005 Oakland Drive, Kalamazoo, MI 49008, 616-388-5631
THIRD COAST, Department of English, Western Michigan University, Kalamazoo, MI 49008-5092, 616-387-2675; Fax 616-387-2562; www.wmich.edu/thirdcoast
Dovetail Publishing, PO Box 19945, Kalamazoo, MI 49019, 616-342-2900; FAX 616-342-1012; dovetail@mich.com
PrePress Publishing of Michigan, 709 Sunbright Avenue, Portage, MI 49024-2759, 616-323-2659
THE LETTER PARADE, PO Box 52, Comstock, MI 49041
Blue Mouse Studio, 26829 37th Street, Gobles, MI 49055, 616-628-5160; fax 616-628-4970
Cosmic Concepts, 2531 Dover Lane, St. Joseph, MI 49085, 616-428-2792
CLUBHOUSE, Your Story Hour, PO Box 15, Berrien Springs, MI 49103, (616) 471-9009
Gazelle Publications, 11560 Red Bud Trail, Berrien Springs, MI 49103
Kelton Press, PO Box 4236, Jackson, MI 49204, 517-788-8542; 888-453-5880
Bigwater Publishing, PO Box 170, Caledonia, MI 49316, 616-891-1113; Fax 616-891-8015
BIG SCREAM, 2782 Dixie S.W., Grandville, MI 49418, 616-531-1442
Nada Press, 2782 Dixie S.W., Grandville, MI 49418, 616-531-1442
Spelman Publishing, Inc., 582 Windrift Lane, Spring Lake, MI 49456-2168
Wm.B. Eerdmans Publishing Co., 255 Jefferson Avenue, S.E., Grand Rapids, MI 49503, 616-459-4591
Gearhead Press, 565 Lincoln, Northwest, Grand Rapids, MI 49504, 459-7861 or 459-4577
ANGELFLESH, PO Box 141123, Grand Rapids, MI 49514
Angelflesh Press, PO Box 141123, Grand Rapids, MI 49514
PARAMASITIC PROPISTITUTE, 2526 Chatham Woods, Grand Rapids, MI 49546
Pen-Dec Press, 2526 Chatham Woods, Grand Rapids, MI 49546
PURPLE PEEK PI, 2526 Chatham Woods, Grand Rapids, MI 49546
TOY RIOT JUICE, 2526 Chatham Woods, Grand Rapids, MI 49546
THE BANNER, 2850 Kalamazoo SE, Grand Rapids, MI 49560, 616-246-0819
CRC Publications, 2850 Kalamazoo SE, Grand Rapids, MI 49560
National Woodlands Publishing Company, 8846 Green Briar Road, Lake Ann, MI 49650-9607, phone/fax 616-275-6735; e-mail nwpc@traverse.com
Smiling Dog Press, 9875 Fritz, Maple City, MI 49664, 616-334-3695
INDEPENDENT PUBLISHER, 121 East Front Street, Suite 401, Traverse City, MI 49684, voice 616-933-0445; fax 616-933-0448; e-mail jenkins.group@smallpress.com
INFORMATION ENTREPRENUER, 121 East Front Street, Ste. 401, Traverse City, MI 49684, 616-933-0445
Jenkins Group, Inc., 121 East Front Street, Suite 401, Traverse City, MI 49684, voice 616-933-0445; fax 616-933-0448; e-mail jenkins.group@smallpress.com
Moonbeam Publications, Inc., 836 Hastings Street, Traverse City, MI 49684-3441, 616-922-0533
PUBLISHING ENTREPRENEUR, 121 East Front Street, Suite 401, Traverse City, MI 49684, voice 616-933-0445; fax 616-933-0448; e-mail jenkins.group@smallpress.com
Rhodes & Easton, 121 E. Front Street, 4th Floor, Traverse City, MI 49684, 616-933-0445; fax 616-933-0448; e-mail smallpress.com
Avery Color Studios, 511 D Avenue, Gwinn, MI 49841, 800-722-9925
PASSAGES NORTH, English Dept., N. Michigan Univ., 1401 Presque Isle Ave., Marquette, MI 49855, 616-337-7331; Fax 906-227-1096
Shivam Publications, Route 1, Box 41, Houghton, MI 49931-9801, 906-482-0487

MINNESOTA

THE LIBERATOR, 17854 Lyons Street, Forest Lake, MN 55025, 612-464-7663; Fax: 612-464-7135; E-mail: rdoyle@mensdefense.org
Black Hat Press, Box 12, Goodhue, MN 55027, 651-923-4590
RAG MAG, Box 12, Goodhue, MN 55027, 651-923-4590
Galde Press, Inc., PO Box 460, Lakeville, MN 55044
GREAT RIVER REVIEW, PO Box 406, Red Wing, MN 55066, Fax 612-388-2528; E-mail acis@pressenter.com
Kodomo Press, 15239 63RD Street N, Oak Park Heights, MN 55082-6871, 612-439-6383
KIDSCIENCE, 14930 130th Street North, Stillwater, MN 55082-8504
ST. CROIX REVIEW, Box 244, Stillwater, MN 55082, 612-439-7190
THE FIREFLY (A Tiny Glow In a Forest of Darkness), 300 Broadway #107, St. Paul, MN 55101
HEELTAP/Pariah Press, C/O Richard D. Houff, 604 Hawthorne Ave. East, St. Paul, MN 55101-3531

Pariah Press, 604 Hawthorne Avenue East, St. Paul, MN 55101-3531
Minnesota Historical Society Press, 345 Kellogg Blvd. West, St. Paul, MN 55102-1906, 612-296-2264
NEW UNIONIST, 1821 University Avenue W. Ste. S-116, Saint Paul, MN 55104-2801, 651-646-5546, E-mail nup@minn.net
Midwest Villages & Voices, PO Box 40214, St. Paul, MN 55104, 612-822-6878
Pangaea, 226 South Wheeler Street, Saint Paul, MN 55105-1927, 651-690-3320, 888-690-3320, Fax 651-690-1485, info@pangaea.org; web http://pangaea.org
SPOUT, 28 West Robie Street, Saint Paul, MN 55107-2819
Ally Press, 524 Orleans St., St. Paul, MN 55107, 651-291-2652; pferoc@pclink.com; www.catalog.com/ally
Spout Press, 28 W. Robie Street, St. Paul, MN 55107
ARTWORD QUARTERLY, 5273 Portland Avenue, White Bear Lake, MN 55110-2411, 612-426-7059; email artword@wavefront.com
Brighton Publications, Inc., PO Box 120706, St. Paul, MN 55112-0706, 651-636-2220
Paragon House Publishers, 2700 University Avenue, W., Saint Paul, MN 55114-1016, 612-644-3087; FAX 612-644-0997; internet address http://www.pwpu.org/Paragon
Graywolf Press, 2402 University Avenue #203, St. Paul, MN 55114, 651-641-0077; 651-641-0036
Blue Sky Marketing, Inc., PO Box 21583, Saint Paul, MN 55121-0583, 651-456-5602
Network 3000 Publishing, 3432 Denmark Avenue #108, St. Paul, MN 55123-1088, 612-452-4173
Estes Book Company, 15821 Hyland Pointe Court, Apple Valley, MN 55124, 612-432-1269
MINNESOTA LITERATURE, 1 Nord Circle, St. Paul, MN 55127, 651-483-3904
Pogo Press, Incorporated, 4 Cardinal Lane, St. Paul, MN 55127, 651-483-4692, fax 651-483-4692, E-mail pogopres@minn.net
Llewellyn Publications, PO Box 64383, St. Paul, MN 55164, 612-291-1970
LLEWELLYN'S NEW WORLDS OF MIND AND SPIRIT, PO Box 64383, St. Paul, MN 55164-0383, 612-291-1970
HENNEPIN COUNTY LIBRARY CATALOGING BULLETIN, ASD/Accounting, Hennepin County Library, 12601 Ridgedale Drive, Minnetonka, MN 55305-1909, 612-694-8539
SIDEWALKS, PO Box 321, Champlin, MN 55316
WOODWORKER'S JOURNAL, 4365 Willow Drive, Medina, MN 55340, 612-478-8232; FAX 612-478-8396
Book Peddlers, 15245 Minnetonka Boulevard, Minnetonka, MN 55345, 612-912-0036; fax 612-912-0105; e-Mail VickileeAol.com.
Paul Maravelas, 15155 Co. Rd. 32, Mayer, MN 55360, 612-657-2237
Coffee House Press, 27 N. 4th Street, Minneapolis, MN 55401, 612-338-0125; Fax 612-338-4004
Free Spirit Publishing Inc., 400 First Avenue North, Suite 616, Minneapolis, MN 55401-1730, 612-338-2068
Milkweed Editions, 430 1st Avenue North, Ste. 400, Minneapolis, MN 55401, 612-332-3192
New Rivers Press, Inc., 420 North 5th Street #938, Minneapolis, MN 55401, 612-339-7114
RAIN TAXI REVIEW OF BOOKS, PO Box 3840, Minneapolis, MN 55403, 612-825-1528 tel/fax; E-mail raintaxi@bitstream.net; website www.raintaxi.com
UTNE READER, 1624 Harmon Place #330, Minneapolis, MN 55403, 612-338-5040
Pro Musica Press, 2501 Pleasant Ave S, Minneapolis, MN 55404, 612-872-8362, e-Mail Voyceking@visi.com
Crossgar Press, 2116 W. Lake Isles Parkway, Minneapolis, MN 55405, 612-867-5837
KARAWANE, 402 S. Cedar Lake Road, Minneapolis, MN 55405, 612-381-1229
WORMWOOD REVIEW, PO Box 50003, Loring Station, Minneapolis, MN 55405-0003, 612-381-1229
Mid-List Press, 4324 12th Avenue South, Minneapolis, MN 55407-3218, 612-822-3733; Fax 612-823-8387; guide@midlist.org; www.midlist.org
MSRRT NEWSLETTER: LIBRARY ALTERNATIVES, 4645 Columbus Avenue South, Minneapolis, MN 55407, 612-694-8572; fax 612-541-8600; e-Mail cdodge@sun.hennepin.lib.mn.us
Lost Prophet Press, 3300 3rd Ave. South, Mineapolis, MN 55408-3204
THE EVERGREEN CHRONICLES, PO Box 8939, Minneapolis, MN 55408-8939, 612-823-6638; e-mail evgrnchron@aol.com
LIGHTNING & ASH, 3010 Hennepin Avenue South #289, Minneapolis, MN 55408
THIN COYOTE, 3300 3rd Avenue South, Minneapolis, MN 55408-3204
Impatiens Publications, 4028 Pleasant Avenue South, Minneapolis, MN 55409, 612-822-1799l impub@isd.net
Pentagram Press, 4925 South Nicollet, Minneapolis, MN 55409, 612-824-4576
Chaos Warrior Productions, PO Box 14407, University Station, Minneapolis, MN 55414, 612-788-4491
DISTURBED GUILLOTINE, PO Box 14871, University Station, Minneapolis, MN 55414-0871
North Stone Press, PO Box 14098, Minneapolis, MN 55414
THE NORTH STONE REVIEW, PO Box 14098, Minneapolis, MN 55414
SING HEAVENLY MUSE! WOMEN'S POETRY AND PROSE, PO Box 13320, Minneapolis, MN 55414
Best Sellers Publishing, 9201 E. Bloomington Fwy, Minneapolis, MN 55420, 612-888-7672; FAX 612-884-8901; E-mail booker@bestsellerspub.com; www.bestsellerspub.com
ICEA, PO Box 20048, Minneapolis, MN 55420, 800-624-4934
The Place In The Woods, 3900 Glenwood Avenue, Golden Valley, MN 55422, 612-374-2120
READ, AMERICA!, 3900 Glenwood Avenue, Golden Valley, MN 55422, 612-374-2120
Pathway Books, P.O. Box 27790, Golden Valley, MN 55427-0790, 612-377-1521
Eckankar, Attn: John Kulick, PO Box 27300, Minneapolis, MN 55427-0300, 612-474-0700, fax 612-474-1127
MIP Company, PO Box 27484, Minneapolis, MN 55427, 612-546-7578; fax 612-544-6077; E-mail; mp@mipco.com; On-line; http://www.mipco.com
SPIRIT MAGAZINE, PO Box 27244, Minneapolis, MN 55427
Kimm Publishing, Inc., PO Box 32927, Fridley, MN 55432-0927
Studia Hispanica Editors, Attn: Luis Ramos-Garcia, 5626 W. Bavarian Pass, Fridley, MN 55432, 612-574-9460
St. John's Publishing, Inc., 6824 Oaklawn Avenue, Edina, MN 55435, 612-920-9044
Verona Publishing, 3300 Edinborough Way, Suite 209, Edina, MN 55435, 612-830-0709
WELLSPRING, 4080 83rd Ave. N, St. A, Brooklyn Park, MN 55443-0527, 612-566-6663; fax 612-566-9754
Contemax Publishers, 17815 24th Ave N. Suite 100, Minneapolis, MN 55447, phone/fax 612-473-6436
LIFTOUTS, 1414 S. 3rd Street #102, Minneapolis, MN 55454, 612-321-9044, Fax 612-305-0655
Preludium Publishers, 1414 South 3rd Street, No. 102, Minneapolis, MN 55454-1172, 612-321-9044, Fax 612-305-0655
XCP: CROSS-CULTURAL POETICS, College of St. Catherine, 601 25th Avenue South, Minneapolis, MN 55454
NORTH COAST REVIEW, PO Box 103, Duluth, MN 55801-0103, e-mail poharb@toofarnorth.com

Poetry Harbor, PO Box 103, Duluth, MN 55801-0103, e-mail poharb@toofarnorth.com
POETRY MOTEL, PO Box 103, Duluth, MN 55801-0103
Suburban Wilderness Press, PO Box 103, Duluth, MN 55801-0103
Pfeifer-Hamilton, 210 West Michigan, Duluth, MN 55802-1908, 218-727-0500; FAX 218-727-0620
Spinsters Ink, 32 East First Street, #330, Duluth, MN 55802-2002, 218-727-3222, fax 218-727-3119
Whole Person Associates Inc., 210 West Michigan Street, Duluth, MN 55802-1908, 218-727-0500; FAX 218-727-0505
Holy Cow! Press, PO Box 3170, Mount Royal Station, Duluth, MN 55803
LAKE SUPERIOR MAGAZINE, Lake Superior Port Cities, Inc., PO Box 16417, Duluth, MN 55816-0417, 218-722-5002
Trellis Publishing, Inc., PO Box 16141-D, Duluth, MN 55816
KUMQUAT MERINGUE, PO Box 736, Pine Island, MN 55963-0736, e-mail moodyriver@aol.com; Website Http://www.geostar.com/kumquatcastle
Saint Mary's Press, 702 Terrace Heights, Winona, MN 55987, e-mail smp.org
MANKATO POETRY REVIEW, Box 53, Mankato State University, Mankato, MN 56001, 507-389-5511
THE LION AND THE UNICORN: A Critical Journal of Children's Literature, Mankato State University, English Dept Box 53, Mankato, MN 56002-8400, 780-5195
THE RIVER, PO Box 8400, Mankato State University Box 58, Mankato, MN 56002-8400
LONDON FOG, 924 James Street, London, MN 56036-1202, contact via U.S.P.O for guidelines #10 SASE
London Fog Publishing, 924 James Street, London, MN 56036-1202, Contact via U.S.P.O for guidelines #10 SASE
Spoon River Poetry Press, PO Box 6, Granite Falls, MN 56241
Plains Press, PO Box 6, Granote Falls, MN 56241, 507-537-6463
THE BURNING CLOUD REVIEW, 225 15th Avenue N, St. Cloud, MN 56303-4531, E-mail ERhinerson@aol.com
LITTLE FREE PRESS, 730 3rd Street NE, Little Falls, MN 56345-2412, 812-273-4672; fax 812-273-4672
STUDIO ONE, College of St. Benedict, St. Joseph, MN 56374
ASCENT, Department of English, Concordia College, Moorhead, MN 56562, E-mail Ascent@cord.edu
WRITERS' JOURNAL, PO Box 394, Perham, MN 56573-0394, 218-346-7921; fax 218-346-7924; e-mail writersjournal@wadena.net
Focus Publications, Inc., PO Box 609, Bemidji, MN 56601, 218-751-2183; focus@paulbunyan.net
Truly Fine Press, PO Box 891, Bemidji, MN 56601
LOONFEATHER: A magazine of poetry, short prose, and graphics, PO Box 1212, Bemidji, MN 56619, 218-751-4869
Loonfeather Press, PO Box 1212, Bemidji, MN 56619, 218-751-4869
Monographics Press, Route 1, Box 81, Puposky, MN 56667, 218-243-2402

MISSISSIPPI

GEORGETOWN REVIEW, PO Box 6309, Hattiesburg, MS 39406-6309, e-mail gr@georgetownreview.com
MISSISSIPPI REVIEW, USM, Box 5144, Southern Station, Hattiesburg, MS 39406-5144, 601-266-4321
SOUTHERN QUARTERLY: A Journal of the Arts in the South, Box 5078, Southern Station, USM, Hattiesburg, MS 39406-5078, 601-261-1301; Fax 601-266-5800; Robert.Young@usm.edu
Pearl River Press, 32 Cambridge Avenue, Gulfport, MS 39507-4213
PEARL RIVER REVIEW, 32 Cambridge Avenue, Gulfport, MS 39507-4213

MISSOURI

Tiger Press, 803 Sherwick Terrace, Suite 101, Manchester, MO 63021, 314-394-4191
THE LOWELL REVIEW, 3075 Harness Drive, Florissant, MO 63033-3711, E-mail rita@etext.org; website http://www.etext.org/Zines/LowellReview
Beverly Cracom Publications, 12685 Dorsett Road, #179, Maryland Heights, MO 63043-2100, 314-291-0880; fax 314-291-3829
RIVER STYX, 634 North Grand Blvd., 12th Floor, St. Louis, MO 63103-1002, 314-533-4541
BOULEVARD, 4579 Laclede Avenue, #332, St. Louis, MO 63108-2103, 215-568-7062
Neshui Publishing, 1345 Bellevue, St. Louis, MO 63117, 314-725-5562; e-mail info@neshui.com; website www.neshui.com
NATURAL BRIDGE, English Dept., Univ. of Missouri, 8001 Natural Bridge Road, St. Louis, MO 63121, E-mail natural@jinx.umsl.edu
Steamshovel Press, PO Box 23715, St. Louis, MO 63121
STEAMSHOVEL PRESS, PO Box 23715, St. Louis, MO 63121
Albion Press, 9701 Twincrest Drive, St. Louis, MO 63126, 888-787-4477; fax 314-962-7808; e-mail albionpr@stlnet.com
Wildstone Media, PO Box 270570, St. Louis, MO 63127, 314-487-0402; FAX 314-487-1910; 800-296-1918; website www.wildstonemedia.com
Cave Books, 756 Harvard Avenue, Saint Louis, MO 63130-3134, 314-862-7646
Fillmore Publishing Company, PO Box 12432, St. Louis, MO 63132, 800-989-0478; 314-989-0558
Job Search Publishers, 1311 Lindbergh Plaza Center, St. Louis, MO 63132, 314-993-6508
ST. LOUIS JOURNALISM REVIEW, 8380 Olive Boulevard, St. Louis, MO 63132, 314-991-1699
Afrimax, Inc., PO Box 946, Kirksville, MO 63501-0946, 660-665-0757; Fax 660-665-8778; email afrimax@afrimax.com; www.afrimax.com
CHARITON REVIEW, Truman University, Kirksville, MO 63501, 660-785-4499
Rabeth Publishing Company, 201 S. Cottage Grove, Kirksville, MO 63501, 660-665-5143; e-mail qurabeth@kvmo.net
Thomas Jefferson University Press, Truman State University, 100 East Normal Street, Kirksville, MO 63501, 816-785-4665; FAX 816-785-4181
PURPLE, PO Box 341, Park Hills, MO 63601
THE CAPE ROCK, English Dept, Southeast Missouri State, Cape Girardeau, MO 63701, 314-651-2500
Abiding Mystery Press, PO Box 138, Independence, MO 64051
OVERLAND JOURNAL, Oregon-California Trails Association, PO Box 1019, Independence, MO 64051-0519, 816-252-2276
DAILY WORD, Unity Village, MO 64065, 816-524-3550, fax 816-251-3553
Unity Books, 1901 NW Blue Parkway, Unity Village, MO 64065, 816-524-3550, fax 816-251-3550
UNITY MAGAZINE, Unity Village, MO 64065, 816-524-3550
DISC GOLF WORLD NEWS, Disc Golf World, PO Box 025678, Kansas City, MO 64102-5678, 816-471-3472; fax 816-471-4653, email RickdGwn@aol.com
JOURNAL OF VISION REHABILITATION, 1102 Grand, 23rd Floor, Kansas City, MO 64106

Media Periodicals, 1102 Grand, 23rd Floor, Kansas City, MO 64106, 816-842-8111; FAX 816-842-8188
TECHNICALITIES, 1102 Grand, 23rd Floor, Kansas City, MO 64106
Westport Publishers, 1102 Grand Boulevard, Suite 2300, Kansas City, MO 64106-2305, 816-842-8111
BkMk Press, University of Missouri-Kansas City, 5100 Rockhill, University House, Kansas City, MO 64110, 816-235-2558; FAX 816-235-2611; freemank@smtpgate.ssb.umkc.edu
NEW LETTERS, University of Missouri, Kansas City, MO 64110, 816-235-1168; Fax 816-235-2611; www.umkc.edu/newsletters/
LIVING CHEAP NEWS, PO Box 8178, Kansas City, MO 64112, 816-523-3161; fax 816-523-0224; livcheap@aol.com; www.livingcheap.com
The Funny Paper, Po Box 22557, Kansas City, MO 64113-0557, e-mail; felix22557@aol.com
Helicon Nine Editions, Box 22412, Kansas City, MO 64113, 816-753-1095
Acorn Books, 7337 Terrace, Suite 200, Kansas City, MO 64114-1256, 816-523-8321; fax 816-333-3843; e-mail jami.parkison@micro.com
IRISH FAMILY JOURNAL, Box 7575, Kansas City, MO 64116, 816-454-2410
Irish Genealogical Foundation, Box 7575, Kansas City, MO 64116, 816-454-2410; e-mail mike@irishroots.com
WONDER TIME, 6401 The Paseo, Kansas City, MO 64131, 816-333-7000
Compact Clinicals, 7205 NW Waukomis Drive, Kansas City, MO 64151, 816-587-0044 or 800-408-8830; Fax 816-587-7198
THORNY LOCUST, PO Box 32631, Kansas City, MO 64171-5631, 816-756-5096
THE LAUREL REVIEW, Department of English, Northwest Missouri State University, Maryville, MO 64468, 816-562-1265
THE GREEN HILLS LITERARY LANTERN, PO Box 375, Trenton, MO 64683, 660-359-3948 x324
Rama Publishing Co., PO Box 793, Carthage, MO 64836-0793, 417-358-1093
MOCCASIN TELEGRAPH, 5813 E. Saint Charles Road, Columbia, MO 65202-3025, 573-817-3301
ALTERNATIVE PRESS REVIEW, PO Box 1446, Columbia, MO 65205, 573-442-4352
American Audio Prose Library (non-print), PO Box 842, Columbia, MO 65205, 573-443-0361; 800-447-2275; FAX 573-499-0579
Columbia Alternative Library, PO Box 1446, Columbia, MO 65205-1446, 573-442-4352
AFRO-HISPANIC REVIEW, Romance Languages, Univ. of Missouri, 143 Arts & Science Building, Columbia, MO 65211, 573-882-5040 or 573-882-5041
THE MINNESOTA REVIEW, Dept. of English, Univ. of Missouri, Columbia, MO 65211
THE MISSOURI REVIEW, 1507 Hillcrest Hall, University of Missouri-Columbia, Columbia, MO 65211, 573-882-4474; Fax 573-884-4671; e-mail umcastmr@missouri.edu
Timberline Press, 6281 Red Bud, Fulton, MO 65251, 573-642-5035
WINDOW PANES, PO Box 1565, Rolla, MO 65402, 314-368-4464
LOST GENERATION JOURNAL, Route 5 Box 134, Salem, MO 65560, 314-729-2545; 729-5669
WRITER'S GUIDELINES: A Roundtable for Writers and Editors, Box 608, Pittsburg, MO 65724
White Oak Press, PO Box 188, Reeds Spring, MO 65737, 417-538-4220
SOM Publishing, division of School of Metaphysics, HCR 1, Box 15, Windyville, MO 65783, 417-345-8411
THRESHOLDS JOURNAL, HCR 1, Box 15, Windyville, MO 65783, 417-345-8411
Armchair Publishing, 1121 South John, Springfield, MO 65804

MONTANA

THE AZOREAN EXPRESS, PO Box 249, Big Timber, MT 59011
THE BADGER STONE CHRONICLES, PO Box 249, Big Timber, MT 59011
BLACK JACK & VALLEY GRAPEVINE, Box 249, Big Timber, MT 59011
THE BREAD AND BUTTER CHRONICLES, PO Box 249, Big Timber, MT 59011
HILL AND HOLLER, Box 249, Big Timber, MT 59011
Seven Buffaloes Press, Box 249, Big Timber, MT 59011
DROP FORGE, 221 S. 3rd Street, Livingston, MT 59047-3003
Council For Indian Education, 2032 Woody Drive, Billings, MT 59102-2852, 406-252-7451
Cattpigg Press, PO Box 565, Billings, MT 59103, 406-248-4875; e-mail starbase@mcn.net; website www.mcn.net/~starbase/dawn
SPIRIT TALK, PO Box 390, Browning, MT 59417, 406-338-2882; E-mail blkfoot4@3rivers.net
Spirit Talk Press, PO Box 390, Browning, MT 59417, 406-338-2882; E-mail blkfoot4@3rivers.net
American & World Geographic Fublishing, PO Box 5630, Helena, MT 59601, 406-443-2842
Kingfisher Books, PO Box 4628, Helena, MT 59604, 800-879-4576, 406-442-2168; davidmdelo@prodigy.net
Falcon Press Publishing Company, PO Box 1718, Helena, MT 59624, 406-942-6597; 800-582-2665
Editorial Review, 1009 Placer Street, Butte, MT 59701, 406-782-2546
CORONA, Dept. of Hist. & Phil., Montana State University, Bozeman, MT 59717, 406-994-5200
Magic Circle Press, PO Box 1123, Bozeman, MT 59771
Jade Moon Publications, PO Box 4600, Bozeman, MT 59772-4600
Northern Rim Press, 333 South 5th Street East, Missoula, MT 59801, 406-549-0385
Pictorial Histories Pub. Co., 713 S. 3rd Street, Missoula, MT 59801, 406-549-8488
Mountain Press Publishing Co., PO Box 2399, Missoula, MT 59806, 406-728-1900
ADVENTURE CYCLIST, PO Box 8308, Missoula, MT 59807, 406-721-1776
CHRONICLE OF COMMUNITY, PO Box 8291, Missoula, MT 59807-8291, 406-721-7415; Fax 406-721-7416; chronicle@bigsky.net; www.batesinfo.com/chronicle
CUTBANK, English Dept., University of Montana, Missoula, MT 59812
FIJACTIVIST, PO Box 59, Helmville, MT 59843, 406-793-5550
Backcountry Publishing, PO Box 343, Rexford, MT 59930, 541-955-5650

NEBRASKA

The Backwaters Press, 3502 North 52nd Street, Omaha, NE 68104-3506, 402-451-4052
PalmTree Publishers, 4071 Valley Street, Omaha, NE 68105-3837
Westchester House, 218 South 95 Street, Omaha, NE 68114
Lone Willow Press, PO Box 31647, Omaha, NE 68131-0647
Business By Phone, Inc., 13254 Stevens Street, Omaha, NE 68137, 402-895-9399, fax 402-896-3353

Addicus Books, Inc., PO Box 45327, Omaha, NE 68145, 402-330-7493
THE NEBRASKA REVIEW, FA 212, University of Nebraska-Omaha, Omaha, NE 68182-0324, 402-554-3159
Merrimack Books, PO Box 80702, Lincoln, NE 68501-0702, e-mail wedwards@infocom.com
A Slow Tempo Press, PO Box 83686, Lincoln, NE 68501-3686, 402-466-8689; slowtemp@aol.com
Foundation Books, PO Box 22828, Lincoln, NE 68542-2828, 402-438-7080; Fax 402-438-7099
PRAIRIE SCHOONER, 201 Andrews Hall, Univ. of Nebraska, Lincoln, NE 68588-0334, 402-472-0911
Morris Publishing, 3212 E. Hwy 30, Kearney, NE 68847, 800-650-7888

NEVADA

PEGASUS, Pegasus Publishing, 525 Avenue B, Boulder City, NV 89005
RED ROCK REVIEW, English Dept J2A/Com. College S. NV, 3200 E. Cheyenne Avenue, N. Las Vegas, NV 89030, www.ccsn.nevada.edu/departments/english/redrock.htm
The Heather Foundation, P.O. Box 180, Tonopah, NV 89049-0180, 775-482-2038; FAX 775-482-5897, email sm@look.net
Trace Publications, 325 S. 3rd Street, #1305, Las Vegas, NV 89101, 702-383-8840; fax 702-383-8845; e-mail acabot@lvcm.com
Huntington Press, 3687 S. Procyon Avenue, Las Vegas, NV 89103, 702-252-0655; Fax 702-252-0675; LVA@infi.net
Oxford House Publishing, 2556 Van Patten #8, Las Vegas, NV 89109
Greeson & Boyle, Inc., 8058 Pinnacle Peak Avenue, Las Vegas, NV 89113, 702-222-1988
YOUR LIFE MATTERS, 8058 Pinnacle Peak Avenue, Las Vegas, NV 89113, 702-222-1988
Crystal Publishers, Inc., 4947 Orinda Court, Las Vegas, NV 89120, 702-434-3037 phone/Fax
A Thousand Autumns Press, Chiaki International, Inc., 7564 Placid Street, Las Vegas, NV 89123, 702-361-0676
Women of Diversity Productions, Inc., 5790 Park Street, Las Vegas, NV 89129-2304, 702-341-9807; fax 702-341-9828; E-mail dvrsty@aol.com
Frontier Publishing, Inc., 4933 West Craig Road, Suite 155, Las Vegas, NV 89130, Phone/Fax 702-647-0990
INTERIM, Department of English, University of Nevada, Las Vegas, Las Vegas, NV 89154-5011, 702-895-3172
ART:MAG, PO Box 70896, Las Vegas, NV 89170, 702-734-8121
Scherf, Inc./Scherf Books, PO Box 80180, Las Vegas, NV 89180-0180, 702-243-4895; Fax 702-243-7460; ds@scherf.com; www.scherf.com
The Madson Group, Inc., 1329 Highway 395, Ste. 10-283, Gardnerville, NV 89410, 775-852-7743; fax 775-852-1253; email madsongroup@earthlink.net; http://www.petgroomer.com/madson.htm
LRF Law Enforcement Training Services, LTD., 1245 Baring Blvd. #190, Sparks, NV 89434, 702-334-8605; email users.intercomm.com/LRF
CALIFORNIA EXPLORER, 1135 Terminal Way, Suite 209, Reno, NV 89502, E-mail 2xp1@metro.net
Delta-West Publishing, Inc., 2720 Wrondel Way, Reno, NV 89502, 775-828-9398; 888-921-6788 (outside of NV); fax 775-828-9163; info@deltawest.com
WOMAN POET, PO Box 60550, Reno, NV 89506, 702-972-1671
Women-in-Literature, Inc., PO Box 60550, Reno, NV 89506
RAZOR WIRE, PO Box 8876, University Station, Reno, NV 89507, 702-847-9311; fax 702-847-9335; e-mail shaungrif@aol.com
SECOND GUESS, PO Box 9382, Reno, NV 89507
Nevada Publications, 4135 Badger Circle, Reno, NV 89509, 702-747-0800; Fax 702-747-2916
THE MATURE TRAVELER, PO Box 50400, Reno, NV 89513-0400, 702-786-7419
Carson Street Publishing Inc., 205 East John Street, Carson City, NV 89701, 702-882-1528
America West Publishers, PO Box 2208, Carson City, NV 89702, 800-729-4131
Peel Productions, Inc., 2533 N. Carson Street #3970, Carson City, NV 89706-0147, 704-894-8838; FAX 704-894-8839

NEW HAMPSHIRE

Hobblebush Books, 17-A Old Milford Road, Brookline, NH 03033, voice/fax 603-672-4317; E-mail shall@jlc.net; website http:www.jlc.net/~hobblebush/
THE WISDOM CONSERVANCY NEWSLETTER, 148 Merriam Hill Road, Greenville, NH 03048, 603-878-1818
Fantail, PO Box 462, Hollis, NH 03049-0462
Hollis Publishing Company, 95 Runnells Bridge Road, Hollis, NH 03049, 800-635-6302; 603-889-4500
ACCCA Press, 149 Cannongate III, Nashua, NH 03063-1953
RISING STAR, Star/Sword Publications, 47 Byledge Road, Manchester, NH 03104, 603-623-9796
VICTORY PARK: THE JOURNAL OF THE NEW HAMPSHIRE INSTITUTE OF ART, 148 Concord Street, Manchester, NH 03104-4858, 603-623-0313 ext 20
O.ARS, Inc., 21 Rockland Road, Weare, NH 03281, 603-529-1060
WOMENWISE, 38 South Main Street, Concord, NH 03301, 603-225-2739
BONE & FLESH, PO Box 349, Concord, NH 03302-0349
MONADNOCK GAY MEN, PO Box 1124, Keene, NH 03431, 603-357-5544
WHOLE TERRAIN - REFLECTIVE ENVIRONMENTAL PRACTICE, 40 Avon Street, Antioch New England, Keene, NH 03431-3516, 603-357-3122 ex. 272
William L. Bauhan, Publisher, PO Box 443, Dublin, NH 03444-0443, 603-563-8020
CALLIOPE: World History for Young People, 7 School Street, Peterborough, NH 03458, 603-924-7209
Cobblestone Publishing, Inc., 7 School Street, Peterborough, NH 03458, 603-924-7209
COBBLESTONE: The History Magazine for Young People, 7 School Street, Peterborough, NH 03458, 603-924-7209
FACES: The Magazine About People, 7 School Street, Peterborough, NH 03458
GLASS AUDIO, PO Box 876, Peterborough, NH 03458, 603-924-9464
ODYSSEY: Science Adventures in Science, 30 Grove Street, Suite C, Peterborough, NH 03458, 603-924-7209
:THAT:, 1070 Easton Valley Road, Easton, NH 03580
CNW Publishing, PO Box A, North Stratford, NH 03590-0167, 603-922-8338, fax 603-922-8339; danakcnw@ncia.net; www.writers-editors.com
FREELANCE WRITER'S REPORT, PO Box A, North Stratford, NH 03590, 603-922-8338, Fax 603-922-8339, e-mail danakcnw@ncia.net; www.writers-editors.com
Stillpoint Publishing, Box 640, Walpole, NH 03608, 603-756-9281, Fax 603-756-9282, e-mail stillpoint@monad.net
RED OWL, 35 Hampshire Road, Portsmouth, NH 03801-4815, 603-431-2691; redowlmag@aol.com
Kettle of Fish Press, PO Box 364, Exeter, NH 03833
Nicolin Fields Publishing, Inc., 2 Red Fox Road, North Hampton, NH 03862-3320, 603-964-1727; Fax 603-964-4221

683

email:nfp@nh.ultranet.com; website PublishingWorks.com

NEW JERSEY

CHRISTIAN*NEW AGE QUARTERLY, PO Box 276, Clifton, NJ 07011
EXIT 13 MAGAZINE, P O Box 423, Fanwood, NJ 07023
Tory Corner Editions, PO Box 8100, Glen Ridge, NJ 07028, 973-669-8367; torycorner@webtv.net; website www.inc.com/users/ToryCorner.html
LONG SHOT, PO Box 6238, Hoboken, NJ 07030
Consumer Education Research Center, 1980 Springfield Ave, Maplewood, NJ 07040, 201-275-3955, Fax 201-275-3980
LIPS, PO Box 1345, Montclair, NJ 07042
SHERLOCKIAN TIDBITS, 42 Melrose Place, Montclair, NJ 07042
RUBBER DUCKY MAGAZINE, PO Box 799, Upper Montclair, NJ 07043, 201-783-0029
Saturday Press, Inc., PO Box 43548, Upper Montclair, NJ 07043, 973-256-5053
Child's Play, 64 Wellington Avenue, West Orange, NJ 07052, 201-731-3777
Warthog Press, 29 South Valley Road, West Orange, NJ 07052, 201-731-9269
Anacus Press, Inc., PO Box 4544, Warren, NJ 07059-0544, 908-748-0400; email anacus@worldnet.att.net
PASSAIC REVIEW (MILLENNIUM EDITIONS), 442 Stuyvesant Avenue, Lyndhurst, NJ 07071
THE EVER DANCING MUSE, PO Box 7751, East Rutherford, NJ 07073
Who Who Who Publishing, PO Box 7751, East Rutherford, NJ 07073
Smyrna Press, Box 1151, Union City, NJ 07087
OUR TWO CENTS, 39 2nd Avenue, Secaucus, NJ 07094-3510
Ken and Scatter Publications, PO Box 434, Woodbridge, NJ 07095, 732-750-2574; fax 732-750-0290
THE (LIBERTARIAN) CONNECTION, 10 Hill St., #22-L, Newark, NJ 07102, 973-242-5999
The Fire!! Press, 241 Hillside Road, Elizabeth, NJ 07208, 908-964-8476
ST. JOSEPH MESSENGER, PO Box 288, Jersey City, NJ 07303, 201-798-4141
TALISMAN: A Journal of Contemporary Poetry and Poetics, PO Box 3157, Jersey City, NJ 07303-3157, 201-938-0698
Talisman House, Publishers, PO Box 3157, Jersey City, NJ 07303-3157, 201-938-0698
NATURALLY, PO Box 317, Newfoundland, NJ 07435, 973-697-3552; fax 973-697-8813; e-mail naturally@nac.net
HUG THE EARTH, A Journal of Land and Life, 42 Greenwood Avenue, Pequannock, NJ 07440
Hug The Earth Publications, 42 Greenwood Ave., Pequannock, NJ 07440
First Amendment Press International Company, 38 East Ridgewood Avenue, Suite 217, Ridgewood, NJ 07450-3123, 201-612-0734; website www.fapic.com
THE PATERSON LITERARY REVIEW, Passaic County Community College, College Boulevard, Paterson, NJ 07505-1179, 201-684-6555
Lincoln Springs Press, 40 Post Avenue, Hawthorne, NJ 07506-1809
THE UNFORGETTABLE FIRE, 206 North 6th Street, Prospect Park, NJ 07508-2025
Humana Press, 999 Riverview Drive, Suite 208, Totowa, NJ 07512, 201-256-1699, Fax 201-256-8349, e-mail humana@interramp.com
Relief Press, PO Box 4033, South Hackensack, NJ 07606, 201-641-3003
Homa & Sekey Books, 11 Colonial Parkway, Dumont, NJ 07628, 201-384-6692; fax 201-384-6055; e-mail wenye@aol.com
Grand Slam Press, Inc., 2 Churchill Road, Englewood Cliffs, NJ 07632, 201-541-9181; FAX 201-894-8036
Vonpalisaden Publications Inc., 60 Saddlewood Drive, Hillsdale, NJ 07642-1336, 201-664-4919
CYBERCOPYWRITER, PO Box 554, Oradell, NJ 07649, 201-262-3277; Fax 201-599-2635; bskcom@tiac.net; www.tiac.net/users/bskcom
TODAY'S $85,000 FREELANCE WRITER, PO Box 554, Oradell, NJ 07649, 201-262-3277; bskcom@tiac.net
BRAVO, THE POET'S MAGAZINE, 1081 Trafalgar Street, Teaneck, NJ 07666, 201-836-5922
John Edwin Cowen/Bravo Editions, 1081 Trafalgar Street, Teaneck, NJ 07666
FIRSTHAND, PO Box 1314, Teaneck, NJ 07666, 201-836-9177
Hermitage (Ermitazh), PO Box 410, Tenafly, NJ 07670-0410, 201-894-8247; fax 201-894-5591; e-mail yefimovim@aol.com; http://users.aol.com/yefimovim/; http://Lexiconbridge.com/hermitage/
HELLP!, PO Box 38, Farmingdale, NJ 07727
Hellp! Press, PO Box 38, Farmingdale, NJ 07727
Vista Publishing, Inc., 422 Morris Avenue, Suite 1, Long Branch, NJ 07740, 732-229-6500; Fax 732-229-9647; czagury@vistapubl.com
BLACK MOON MAGAZINE, 1385 Route 35, Suite 169, Middletown, NJ 07748, 908-787-2445
Black Moon Publishing, 1385 Route 35, Suite 169, Middletown, NJ 07748, 908-787-2445
JOURNAL OF NEW JERSEY POETS, 214 Center Grove Road, County College of Morris, Randolph, NJ 07869, 201-328-5471; e-mail szulauf@ccm.edu
Polygonal Publishing House, PO Box 357, Washington, NJ 07882, 908-689-3894
The Bradford Book Company, Inc., PO Box 818, Chester, NJ 07930, 908-879-1284; fax 908-879-1263
Next Decade, Inc. (formerly New Decade Inc.), 39 Old Farmstead Road, Chester, NJ 07930-2732, Telephone/Fax; 908-879-6625
Edin Books, Inc., 102 Sunrise Drive, Gillette, NJ 07933
THE LITERARY REVIEW, Fairleigh Dickinson University, 285 Madison Avenue, Madison, NJ 07940, 973-443-8564
Down The Shore Publishing, Box 3100, Harvey Cedars, NJ 08008, 609-978-1233; fax 609-597-0422
Barnegat Light Press/Pine Barrens Press, PO Box 607, 3959 Route 563, Chatsworth, NJ 08019-0607, 609-894-4415; Fax 609-894-2350
LININGTON LINEUP, 1223 Glen Terrace, Glassboro, NJ 08028-1315, 609-589-1571
PTOLEMY/BROWNS MILLS REVIEW, 484 Lewistown Road #252, Juliustown, NJ 08042, 609-893-0896
RED HOT HOME INCOME REPORTER, 15 Brunswick Lane, Willingboro, NJ 08046, 609-835-2347
PTOLEMY, PO Box 252, Juliustown, NJ 08052
THE BROWNS MILLS REVIEW, PO Box 252, Juliustown, NJ 08052
BIOLOGY DIGEST, 143 Old Marlton Pike, Medford, NJ 08055, 609-654-6500
Plexus Publishing, Inc., 143 Old Marlton Pike, Medford, NJ 08055, 609-654-6500
The Middle Atlantic Press, 10 Twosome Drive, Box 600, Moorestown, NJ 08057, 609-235-4444; orders 800-257-8481; fax 800-225-3840
Weidner & Sons, Publishing, Box 2178, Riverton, NJ 08077, 609-486-1755; fax 609-486-7583; e-mail weidner@wa-

684

terw.com
PenRose Publishing Company, Inc., PO Box 620, Mystic Island, NJ 08087, 609-296-1401
Phillips Publications, Inc., PO Box 168, Williamstown, NJ 08094, 609-567-0695
Still Waters Poetry Press, 459 S. Willow Avenue, Absecon, NJ 08201-4633
Kells Media Group, Po Box 60-DB, Oceanville, NJ 08231, 609-652-0524; fax 609-652-7448
A COMPANION IN ZEOR, 307 Ashland Ave., Egg Harbor Township, NJ 08234-5568, 609-645-6938; fax 609-645-8084;
    E-mail Klitman323@aol.com; website http://www.geocities.com/~rmgiroux/cz; http://www.simegen-com/index.html
DEVIL BLOSSOMS, PO Box 5122, Seabrook, NJ 08302
Branch Redd Books, 9300 Atlantic Avenue, Apt. 218, Margate City, NJ 08402-2340
BRANCH REDD REVIEW, 9300 Atlantic Ave, Apt 218, Margate City, NJ 08402-2340
Princeton Book Company, Publishers, PO Box 831, Hightstown, NJ 08520-0831, 609-737-8177; FAX 609-737-1869
The Ecco Press, 100 West Broad Street, Hopewell, NJ 08525-1919, 212-645-2214
US1 Poets' Cooperative, PO Box 127, Kingston, NJ 08528-0127, 609-921-1489; fax 609-279-1513
US1 WORKSHEETS, PO Box 127, Kingston, NJ 08528-0127, 609-921-1489; fax 609-279-1513
New Spring Publications, 293 Franklin Avenue, Princeton, NJ 08540, 609-279-0014; email nwspring@bellatlantic.net
PRINCETON ARTS REVIEW, 102 Witherspoon Street, Princeton, NJ 08540, 609-924-8777
QRL POETRY SERIES, Princeton University, 26 Haslet Avenue, Princeton, NJ 08540, 921-6976
Quarterly Review of Literature Press, Princeton University, 26 Haslet Avenue, Princeton, NJ 08540, 609-921-6976; fax
    609-258-2230; e-mail qrl@princeton.edu
Modern Learning Press/Programs for Education, PO Box 167, Rosemont, NJ 08556
RAVEN - A Journal of Vexillology, 1977 North Olden Ave. Ext., Ste. 225, Trenton, NJ 08618-2193
NWI National Writers Institute, PO Box 6314, Lawrenceville, NJ 08648-0314, E-mail express518@aol.com
THE KELSEY REVIEW, Mercer County, Community College, PO Box B, Trenton, NJ 08690, 609-586-4800 ext. 3326;
    e-mail kelsey.review@mccc.edu
Bell Publishing, 15 Surrey Lane, East Brunswick, NJ 08816, 201-257-7793
Dovehaven Press, PO Box 6659, East Brunswick, NJ 08816-6659, 718-442-1325; fax 718-442-6225; e-mail
    wossumi@admin.con2.com
Broken Rifle Press, 2 Rowland Place, Metuchen, NJ 08840-2534, 732-549-0631 e-mail: jerrkate@erols.com
BLACK BOUGH, 188 Grove Street #1, Somerville, NJ 08876
THE HIGGINSVILLE READER, PO Box 141, Three Bridges, NJ 08887, 908-788-0514; hgvreader@yahoo.com
RARITAN: A Quarterly Review, 31 Mine Street, New Brunswick, NJ 08903, 732-932-7887, Fax 732-932-7855
SOCIETY, Transaction, Rutgers University, New Brunswick, NJ 08903, 908-932-2280

NEW MEXICO

Duende Press, Box 571, Placitas, NM 87043, 505-867-5877
Alamo Square Press, 103 FR 321, Tajique, NM 87057, 503-384-9766; alamosquare@earthlink.net
LPD Press, 2400 Rio Grande Blvd NW #1-213, Albuquerque, NM 87104-3222, 505-344-9382; fax 505-345-5129
TRADICION REVISTA, 2400 Rio Grande Blvd. NW #1-213, Albuquerque, NM 87104-3222, 505-344-9382; FAX
    505-345-5129
Intermountain Publishing, 1713 Harzman Road SW, Albuquerque, NM 87105, 505-242-3333
Southwest Research and Information Center, PO Box 4524, Albuquerque, NM 87106, 505-346-1455; Fax 505-346-1459
THE WORKBOOK, PO Box 4524, Albuquerque, NM 87106, 505-346-1455; Fax 505-346-1459
Zerx Press, 725 Van Buren Place SE, Albuquerque, NM 87108
LIES MAGAZINE, 1112 San Pedro NE #154, Albuquerque, NM 87110, 505-268-7316; email okeefine@aol.com;
    www.cent.com/abetting/
BOOK TALK, 8632 Horacio Pi NE, Albuquerque, NM 87111, 505-299-8940; fax 505-294-8032
La Alameda Press, 9636 Guadalupe Trail NW, Albuquerque, NM 87114
West End Press, PO Box 27334, Albuquerque, NM 87125
BLUE MESA REVIEW, Department of English, Humanities Building, Albuquerque, NM 87131, 505-277-6347; fax
    277-5573; e-Mail psprott@unm.edu
ATOM MIND, PO Box 22068, Albuquerque, NM 87154
Amador Publishers, PO Box 12335, Albuquerque, NM 87195, 505-877-4395, 800-730-4395, Fax 505-877-4395,
    harry@nmia.com, www.amadorbooks.com
FICTION WRITER'S GUIDELINE, PO Box 72300, Albuquerque, NM 87195-2300, 505-352-9490; bcamenson@aol.com;
    www.fictionwriters.com
Elysian Hills Publishing Company, Inc., PO Box 40693, Albuquerque, NM 87196, 505-265-9041
RESOURCE CENTER BULLETIN, PO Box 4506, Albuquerque, NM 87196, 505-842-8288, Fax 505-246-1601; E-mail
    resourcectr@igc.apc.org
American Research Press, Box 141, Rehoboth, NM 87322, e-mail arp@cia-g.com; website http://www.gallup.unm.edu/
    ~smarandache/
SMARANDACHE NOTIONS JOURNAL, Box 141, Rehoboth, NM 87322, E-Mail: arp@cia-g.com; http://
    /www.gallup.unm.edu/~smarandache/
69 FLAVORS OF PARANOIA, 2816 Rio Vista Court, Farmington, NM 87401-4557
Munklinde Vestergaard, RT 1, Box 126, Nambe, NM 87501, 505-455-3165
American Canadian Publishers, Inc., PO Box 4595, Santa Fe, NM 87502-4595, 505-983-8484, fax 505-983-8484
Ancient City Press, PO Box 5401, Santa Fe, NM 87502, 505-982-8195
Rising Tide Press New Mexico, PO Box 6136, Santa Fe, NM 87502-6136, 505-983-8484; fax 505-983-8484
Zon International Publishing Co., PO Box 6459, Santa Fe, NM 87502, 505-995-0102, Fax 505-995-0103; e-mail
    zon@nets.com
Adolfo Street Publications, PO Box 490, Santa Fe, NM 87504, 505-986-2010, Fax 505-986-1353, toll free order line
    800-526-2010; email adolfostr@aol.com
Bear & Company, Inc., Box 2860, Santa Fe, NM 87504, 505-983-5968; 1800-WE-BEARS
Bennett Books, PO Box 1553, Santa Fe, NM 87504, 505-989-8381
Burning Books, PO Box 2638, Santa Fe, NM 87504, Fax 505-820-6216; E-mail brnbx@nets.com
COALITION FOR PRISONERS' RIGHTS NEWSLETTER, PO Box 1911, Santa Fe, NM 87504, 505-982-9520
EL PALACIO, PO Box 2087, Santa Fe, NM 87504-2087, 505-827-6451
From Here Press, PO Box 2740, Santa Fe, NM 87504-2740, 505-438-3249
Health Press, Box 1388, Santa Fe, NM 87504, 505-982-9373, fax 505-983-1733, e-mail hlthprs@trail.com

Images For Media/Sesquin, PO Box 8505, Santa Fe, NM 87504, 505-753-3648; FAX 505-753-7049; arr@ifm.com
John Muir Publications, Inc., PO Box 613, Santa Fe, NM 87504, 505-982-4078
Museum of New Mexico Press, PO Box 2087, Santa Fe, NM 87504, 505-827-6454; Fax; 505-827-5941
Sherman Asher Publishing, PO Box 2853, Santa Fe, NM 87504, 505-984-2686; FAX 505-820-2744, e-mail 71277.2057@comperserve.com
THE STARLIGHT PAPERS, PO Box 2740, Santa Fe, NM 87504-2740, 505-438-3249
Sunstone Press, PO Box 2321, Santa Fe, NM 87504-2321, 505-988-4418; fax 505-988-1025
Twelvetrees Press, PO Box 10229, Santa Fe, NM 87504-1022
Twin Palms Publishers, PO Box 10229, Santa Fe, NM 87504-1022
XTRAS, PO Box 2740, Santa Fe, NM 87504-2740, 505-438-3249
YEFIEF, PO Box 8505, Santa Fe, NM 87504
BUSINESPIRIT JOURNAL, 4 Camino Azul, Santa Fe, NM 87505, 505-474-7604; Fax 505-471-2584; message@nets.com; www.bizspirit.com
COUNTERMEASURES, Creative Writing Program, College of Santa Fe, St. Michael's Drive, Santa Fe, NM 87505
Danrus Publishers, 1233 Siler Road, #A, Santa Fe, NM 87505-3132, 505-474-5858; FAX 505-474-6100
Katydid Books, 1 Balsa Road, Santa Fe, NM 87505
The Message Company, 4 Camino Azul, Santa Fe, NM 87505, 505-474-0998; FAX 505-471-2584
Red Crane Books, Inc., 2008 Rosina Street #B, Santa Fe, NM 87505-3271, 505-988-7070; fax 505-989-7476; 800-922-3392; E-mail publish@redcrane.com; www.redcrane.com
Ten Star Press, 2860 Plaza Verde, Santa Fe, NM 87505, 505-473-4813 phone/Fax; E-mail dorbil@rt66.com
Gallery West Associates, PO Box 1272, El Prado, NM 87529, 505-751-0073
Exceptional Books, Ltd., 798 47th Street, Los Alamos, NM 87544, 505-662-7700
Minor Heron Press, 5275 NDCBU, Taos, NM 87571, 505-758-1800
Columbine Publishing Group, PO Box 456, Angel Fire, NM 87710, 505-377-3474, 800-996-9783, FAX 505-377-3526, publish@intriguepress.com
Intrigue Press, PO Box 456, Angel Fire, NM 87710, 505-377-3474; e-mail publish@intriguepress.com
PUERTO DEL SOL, Box 3E, New Mexico State University, Las Cruces, NM 88003, 505-646-2345
Bilingue Publications & Productions, PO Box 1629, Las Cruces, NM 88004, 505-526-1557
Two Eagles Press International, PO Box 208, Las Cruces, NM 88004, 505-523-7911; Fax 523-1953; pjhuntsber@aol.com
WHOLE NOTES, PO Box 1374, Las Cruces, NM 88004, 505-541-5744
Whole Notes Press, PO Box 1374, Las Cruces, NM 88004, 505-382-7446
Yucca Tree Press, 2130 Hixon Drive, Las Cruces, NM 88005-3305, 505-524-2357
BORDERLINES, Box 2178, Silver City, NM 88062, 505-388-0208; fax 505-388-0619; e-Mail info@ire-online.org
BLACKWATER, PO Box 1091, Portales, NM 88130-1091, 505-359-0901
Scopcraeft, PO Box 1091, Portales, NM 88130-1091, 505-359-0901

NEW YORK

BLIND SPOT, 210 11th Avenue FL 10, New York, NY 10001-1210, 212-633-1317
Drama Publishers, 260 Fifth Avenue, New York, NY 10001, 212-725-5377; fax 212-725-8506, e-mail dramapub@inter-port.net
ISRAEL HORIZONS, 114 W. 26th Street #1001, New York, NY 10001-6812, 212-868-0377; FAX 212-868-0364
ZOETROPE: All-Story, 260 Fifth Avenue, Suite 1200, New York, NY 10001, 212-696-5720; www.zoetrope-stories.com
CURARE, c/o Whalen, 20 Clinton Street #1G, New York, NY 10002, 212-533-7167
MEANDER QUARTERLY, 156 Rivington Street #1, New York, NY 10002-2481
Venom Press, c/o Whalen, 20 Clinton Street #1G, New York, NY 10002
THE ASIAN PACIFIC AMERICAN JOURNAL, 37 Saint Marks Place, New York, NY 10003-7801, 212-228-6718
CINEASTE MAGAZINE, 200 Park Avenue South, New York, NY 10003, 212-982-1241; fax 212-982-1241
CONJUNCTIONS, 21 East 10th Street #3E, New York, NY 10003-5924
DOWN UNDER MANHATTAN BRIDGE, 224 E. 11th Street #5, New York, NY 10003-7329, 212-388-7051, lizard.evny@msn.com
The Foundation Center, 79 Fifth Avenue, New York, NY 10003-3076, 212-620-4230; 1-800-424-9836
FROM THE MARGIN, 50 E. 1st Street, Storefront West, New York, NY 10003-9311
JEWISH CURRENTS, 22 E. 17th Street, Suite 601, New York, NY 10003, 212-924-5740
LITERAL LATTE, 61 East 8th Street, Suite 240, New York, NY 10003, 212-260-5532
MESHUGGAH, 200 East Tenth Street, #603, New York, NY 10003-7702
The Poetry Project, St. Mark's Church, 131 East 10th Street, New York, NY 10003, 212-674-0910; e-mail popro;@artomatic.com
THE POETRY PROJECT NEWSLETTER, St. Mark's Church, 131 East 10th Street, New York, NY 10003, 212-674-0910
Teachers & Writers Collaborative, 5 Union Square West, New York, NY 10003, 212-691-6590, 212-675-0171
TEACHERS & WRITERS MAGAZINE, 5 Union Square West, New York, NY 10003, 212-691-6590
Visions Communications, 205 E. 10th Street, Suite 2D, New York, NY 10003, 212-529-4029
THE WORLD, St. Marks Church/The Poetry Project, 131 East 10th Street, New York, NY 10003
WRITES OF PASSAGE, 817 Broadway, 6th Floor, New York, NY 10003, 212-473-7564; wpusa@aol.com; http://www.writes.org
CLWN WR, PO Box 2165 Church Street Station, New York, NY 10008-2165
POETRY NEW YORK: A Journal of Poetry and Translation, PO Box 3184, Church Street Station, New York, NY 10008
COVER MAGAZINE, 632 East 14th Street, #18, New York, NY 10009, 212-673-1152; Fax 212-253-7614
A GATHERING OF THE TRIBES, PO Box 20693, Tompkins Square, New York, NY 10009, fax 212-674-5576
Hard Press, 632 East 14th Street, #18, New York, NY 10009, 212-673-1152
HOME PLANET NEWS, P.O. Box 415 Stuyvesant Station, New York, NY 10009, 718-769-2854
Home Planet Publications, PO Box 415 Stuyvesant Station, New York, NY 10009, 718-769-2854
LOVE AND RAGE, A Revolutionary Anarchist Newspaper, Box 853, Stuyvesant Station, New York, NY 10009
NOT BORED!, PO Box 1115, New York, NY 10009-9998
THE SPITTING IMAGE, PO Box 20400 Tompkins Square Stn., New York, NY 10009
TELOS, 431 East 12th Street, New York, NY 10009, 212-228-6479
Telos Press, 431 East 12th Street, New York, NY 10009, 212-228-6479
Allworth Press, 10 East 23rd Street, Suite 400, New York, NY 10010, 212-777-8395; FAX 212-777-8261; E-mail Pub@allworth.com

TURNSTILE, 175 5th Avenue, Suite 2348, New York, NY 10010
THE AMICUS JOURNAL, 40 West 20th Street, New York, NY 10011, 212-727-2700
BabelCom, Inc., 231 W. 16th Street #5WR, New York, NY 10011-6015, 212-627-2074
Barricade Books, 150 5th Avenue #700, New York, NY 10011
Biblio Press, PO Box 20195, London Terrace Station, New York, NY 10011-0008, 212-989-2755; E-mail bibook@aol.com
Boog Literature, PO Box 20531, New York, NY 10011, e-mail dak@cunytimessqr.gc.cuny.edu
Crime and Again Press, 245 Eighth Avenue, Ste. 283, New York, NY 10011, 212-727-0151; crimepress@aol.com
Dorchester Press, PO Box 620, Old Chelsea Station, New York, NY 10011, e-mail metasex@hotmail.com
Edgewise Press, 24 Fifth Avenue #224, New York, NY 10011, 212-982-4818; FAX 212-982-1364
Excalibur Publishing Inc., 511 Avenue of the Americas, Suite 392, New York, NY 10011, 212-777-1790
Four Walls Eight Windows, 39 West 14th Street #503, New York, NY 10011, e-mail edit@fourwallseightwindows.com
METASEX, PO Box 620, Old Chelsea Station, New York, NY 10011, e-mail metasex@hotmail.com
THE NEW MOON REVIEW, 148 Eighth Avenue #417, New York, NY 10011
ASSEMBLING, Box 444 Prince Street, New York, NY 10012-0008
Assembling Press, Box 444 Prince Street, New York, NY 10012-0008
Black Thistle Press, 491 Broadway, New York, NY 10012, 212-219-1898
BOMB MAGAZINE, 594 Broadway, Suite 905, New York, NY 10012, 212-431-3943, FAX 212-431-5880
CAPITALISM, NATURE, SOCIALISM, 72 Spring Street, New York, NY 10012, 212-431-9800
Fotofolio, Inc., 536 Broadway, 2nd Floor, New York, NY 10012, 212-226-0923
The Future Press, Box 444 Prince Street, New York, NY 10012-0008
GRAND STREET, 214 Sullivan Street #6C, New York, NY 10012, 212-533-2944
Guilford Publications, Inc., 72 Spring Street, New York, NY 10012
ISSUES QUARTERLY, 530 Broadway, 10th floor, New York, NY 10012, 212-274-0730, fax 212-274-0821
National Council for Research on Women, 530 Broadway, New York, NY 10012-3920, 212-274-0730; fax 212-274-0821
THE NONVIOLENT ACTIVIST, War Resisters League, 339 Lafayette Street, New York, NY 10012, 212-228-0450, fax
    212-228-6193, e-Mail wrl@igc.apc.org
The Overlook Press, 386 West Broadway, New York, NY 10012-4302, 914-679-8571
P E N American Center, 568 Broadway, New York, NY 10012
Parabola, 656 Broadway, New York, NY 10012, 212-505-6200
PARABOLA MAGAZINE, 656 Broadway, New York, NY 10012-2317, 212-505-6200; fax 212-979-7325; e-Mail
    parabola@panix.com
Poets & Writers, Inc., 72 Spring Street, New York, NY 10012, 212-226-3586, Fax 212-226-3963; e-Mail pwsubs@pw.org,
    www.pw.org
POETS & WRITERS MAGAZINE, 72 Spring Street, New York, NY 10012, 212-226-3586, e-Mail pwsubs@pw.org;
    www.pw.org
PRECISELY, Box 444 Prince Street, New York, NY 10012-0008
RATTAPALLAX, 532 La Guardia Place, Suite 353, New York, NY 10012, 212-560-7459; e-mail rattapallax@hot-
    mail.com
RETHINKING MARXISM, 72 Spring Street, New York, NY 10012, 212-431-9800
SCIENCE & SOCIETY, 72 Spring Street, New York, NY 10012, 212-431-9800
SCRAWL MAGAZINE, PO Box 205, New York, NY 10012, e-mail: Scrawlmag@Aol.com
WICKED MYSTIC, 532 LaGuardia Place #371, New York, NY 10012, 718-638-1533
WOMEN'S RESEARCH NETWORK NEWS, 530 Broadway, New York, NY 10012-3920, 212-274-0760; fax
    212-274-0821
ZONE, 611 Broadway, Suite 608, New York, NY 10012, 212-529-5674, fax 212-260-4572, e-mail urzone@aol.com
Zone Books, 611 Broadway, Suite 608, New York, NY 10012, 212-529-5674, fax 212-260-4572, e-mail urzone@aol.com
THE AMERICAN JOURNAL OF PSYCHOANALYSIS, 233 Spring Street, New York, NY 10013, 212-620-8000
Box Turtle Press, 184 Franklin Street, New York, NY 10013
CHILDREN'S LITERATURE IN EDUCATION, 233 Spring Street, New York, NY 10013, 212-620-8000
Green Bean Press, PO Box 237, Canal Street Station, New York, NY 10013, phone/fax 718-302-1955; e-mail
    gbpress@earthlink.net
Human Sciences Press, Inc., 233 Spring Street, New York, NY 10013, 212-620-8000
THE LITERARY QUARTERLY, PO Box 1840, New York, NY 10013-0872
MUDFISH, 184 Franklin Street, New York, NY 10013, 212-219-9278
RESEARCH IN HIGHER EDUCATION, 233 Spring Street, New York, NY 10013, 212-620-8000
SYNAESTHETIC, PO Box 91, New York, NY 10013
TRICYCLE: The Buddhist Review, 92 Vandam Street, New York, NY 10013-1007
THE URBAN REVIEW, 233 Spring Street, New York, NY 10013, 212-620-8000
Vanity Press/Strolling Dog Press, 160 6th Avenue, New York, NY 10013, 212-925-3823
Water Mark Press, 138 Duane Street, New York, NY 10013, 212-285-1609
ZerOX Books, 105 Hudson Street, #311, New York, NY 10013
Bank Street Press, 24 Bank Street, New York, NY 10014, 212-255-0692
Black Dress Press, PO Box 213, Village Station, New York, NY 10014, website www.blackdresspress.com
GAYELLOW PAGES, Box 533 Village Station, New York, NY 10014, 212-674-0120, Fax: 212-420-1126
The Institute of Mind and Behavior, PO Box 522, Village Station, New York, NY 10014, 212-595-4853
THE JOURNAL OF MIND AND BEHAVIOR, PO Box 522, Village Station, New York, NY 10014, 212-595-4853
THE MILITANT, 410 West Street, New York, NY 10014, 212-243-6392
New International, 410 West Street, New York, NY 10014, 212-741-0690, fax 212-727-0150
Pathfinder Press, 410 West Street, New York, NY 10014, 212-741-0690; fax 212-727-0150; CompuServe: 73321,414;
    Internet pathfinder@igc.apc.org
Philomel Books, 345 Hudson Street, New York, NY 10014, 212-414-3610
S Press, 527 Hudson Street, PO Box 20095, New York, NY 10014
SPINNING JENNY, PO Box 213, Village Station, New York, NY 10014, website www.blackdresspress.com
The Twickenham Press, 31 Jane Street, New York, NY 10014, 212-741-2417
COLLECTORS CLUB PHILATELIST, 22 East 35th Street, New York, NY 10016, 212-683-0559
Dawnwood Press, 387 Park Avenue South, 5th Floor, New York, NY 10016-8810, 212-532-7160; fax 212-213-2495;
    800-367-9692
ICON THOUGHTSTYLE MAGAZINE, 440 Park Avenue South, 2nd Floor, New York, NY 10016, 212-219-2654; Fax

212-219-4045
Limelight Editions, 118 East 30th Street, New York, NY 10016, 212-532-5525, fax 212-532-5526
NBM Publishing Company, 185 Madison Avenue #1504, New York, NY 10016, 212-545-1223; FAX 212-545-1227
Occam Publishers, 250 East 40th Street #14-B, New York, NY 10016-1733, 607-849-3186
THE COOPERATOR, 301 East 45th Street, New York, NY 10017, 212-697-1318
THE TRIBUNE, 777 United Nations Plaza, 3rd floor, New York, NY 10017, 212-687-8633
Blacfax, Midtown Station, PO Box 542, New York, NY 10018
THE CHARIOTEER, 337 West 36 Street, New York, NY 10018, 212-279-9586
JOURNAL OF THE HELLENIC DIASPORA, 337 West 36th Street, New York, NY 10018, 212-279-9586
NAMBLA BULLETIN, PO Box 174, Midtown Station, New York, NY 10018, 212-631-1194; E-mail arnolds-choen@juno.com
Pella Publishing Co, 337 West 36th Street, New York, NY 10018, 212-279-9586
AMERICA, 106 West 56th Street, New York, NY 10019, 212-581-4640
THE NEW CRITERION, 850 Seventh Avenue, New York, NY 10019, 212-247-6980
AMERICAN LETTERS & COMMENTARY, 850 Park Avenue, Suite 5B, New York, NY 10021, fax 212-327-0706; email rabanna@aol.com; amleters.org
DIAMOND INSIGHT, 790 Madison Avenue, New York, NY 10021, 212-570-4180; FAX 212-772-1286
THE HUDSON REVIEW, 684 Park Avenue, New York, NY 10021, 212-650-0020; fax 212-774-1911
PSYCHOANALYTIC BOOKS: A QUARTERLY JOURNAL OF REVIEWS, 211 East 70th Street, New York, NY 10021, 212-628-8792; FAX 212-628-8453, e-Mail psabooks@datagram.com
SCANDINAVIAN REVIEW, 15 East 65 Street, New York, NY 10021, 212-879-9779
WOMEN IN THE ARTS BULLETIN/NEWSLETTER, c/o R. Crown, 1175 York Avenue #2G, New York, NY 10021, 212-751-1915
Women In The Arts Foundation, Inc., 1175 York Avenue, New York, NY 10021
THE WRITING SELF, PO Box 245, Lenox Hill Station, New York, NY 10021
Americans for the Arts/ACA Books, One East 53rd Street, New York, NY 10022-4201, 212-223-2787; fax 212-753-1325
ARARAT, 55 E 59th Street, New York, NY 10022-1112
Avocet Press Inc., 635 Madison Avenue, Suite 400, New York, NY 10022, 212-754-6300; email oopc@interport.net; www.avocetpress.com
Fromm International Publishing Corporation, 560 Lexington Avenue, New York, NY 10022, 212-308-4010
THE QUARTERLY, 650 Madison Avenue, New York, NY 10022, 212-888-4769
AUFBAU, 2121 Broadway, New York, NY 10023, 212-873-7400, fax 212-496-5736
The Consultant Press, Ltd., 163 Amsterdam Avenue, New York, NY 10023, 212-838-8640
PRESS, 2124 Broadway, Suite 323, New York, NY 10023, 212-579-0873
SPACE AND TIME, 138 West 70th Street 4-B, New York, NY 10023-4432
Space and Time Press, 138 West 70th Street 4-B, New York, NY 10023-4468
Helikon Press, 120 West 71st Street, New York City, NY 10023
Creative Roots, Inc., 140 Riverside Drive, New York, NY 10024, 212-799-2294
Guarionex Press Ltd., 201 West 77th Street, New York, NY 10024, 212-724-5259
THE JOURNAL OF PSYCHOHISTORY, 140 Riverside Drive, New York, NY 10024, 212-799-2294
LEFT BUSINESS OBSERVER, 250 West 85 Street, New York, NY 10024
PARNASSUS: POETRY IN REVIEW, 205 West 89th Street, Apartment 8F, New York, NY 10024, 212-362-3492; fax 212-875-0148; e-mail parnew@aol.com
PHOTOGRAPHY IN NEW YORK, INTERNATIONAL, 64 West 89th Street, New York, NY 10024, 212-787-0401, Fax 212-799-3014
Psychohistory Press, 140 Riverside Drive, New York, NY 10024, 212-799-2294
CARIBBEAN NEWSLETTER, Box 20392, Park West Station, New York, NY 10025
Green Eagle Press, Box 20329, Cathedral Station, New York, NY 10025, 212-663-2167; FAX 212-316-7650
Jupiter Scientific Publishing, Columbia University Post Office, PO Box 250586, New York, NY 10025, 212-650-8194; email jupiter@ajanta.sci.ccny.cuny.edu
Maxima New Media, 2472 Broadway #195, New York, NY 10025, 212-439-4177, Fax 212-439-4178, e-mail aronst@ibm.net
PEACE & DEMOCRACY, PO Box 1640, Cathedral Station, New York, NY 10025, 212-666-5924
RESPONSE: A Contemporary Jewish Review, PO BOX 250892, New York, NY 10025-1506
Skytop Publishing, PO Box 134-M, Cathedral Station, New York, NY 10025, 212-932-0858 phone/Fax; E-mail skytop@mystic21.com
SYNERJY: A Directory of Renewable Energy, Box 1854/Cathedral Station, New York, NY 10025, 212-865-9595; twine@synerjy.com
Midmarch Arts Press, 300 Riverside Drive, New York City, NY 10025, 212-666-6990
WOMEN ARTISTS NEWS BOOK REVIEW, 300 Riverside Drive, New York City, NY 10025, 212-666-6990
THE MANHATTAN REVIEW, c/o Philip Fried, 440 Riverside Drive, #45, New York, NY 10027
Michael Kesend Publishing, Ltd., 1025 Fifth Avenue, New York, NY 10028-0134, 212-249-5150
NETWORK, Box 810, Gracie Station, New York, NY 10028, 212-737-7536; Fax; 212-737-9469; E-mail; iwwg@iwwg.com; Ourside; http://www.iwwg.com
Red Dust, PO Box 630, Gracie Station, New York, NY 10028, 212-348-4388
The Feminist Press at the City College, Convent Ave. & 138th St., New York, NY 10031, 212-360-5790
FICTION, c/o Dept. of English, City College, 138th Street & Convent Ave., New York, NY 10031, 212-650-6319
WOMEN'S STUDIES QUARTERLY, The Feminist Press c/o City College, Convent Ave. & 138th St., New York, NY 10031, 212-360-5790
META4: Journal of Object Oriented Poetics (OOPS), c/o Jurado, 1793 Riverside Drive #3F, New York, NY 10034
DRAMATISTS GUILD NEWSLETTER, 1501 Broadway Suite 701, New York, NY 10036
New Liberty Press, 405 West 48th Street Rm 2R, New York, NY 10036, 212-459-2614
SOCIAL POLICY, 25 West 43rd Street, Room 620, New York, NY 10036, 212-642-2929
CULTUREFRONT, 150 Broadway, Room #1700, New York, NY 10038-4401, 212-233-1131; fax 212-233-4607; e-mail hum@echonyc.com
Gumbs & Thomas Publishers, Inc., PO Box 381, New York, NY 10039-0381, 212-694-6677; fax 212-694-0602
Italica Press, Inc., 595 Main Street, #605, New York, NY 10044, 212-935-4230; fax 212-838-7812; inquiries@italica-press.com

ARISTOS, PO Box 1105, Radio City Station, New York, NY 10101, aristos@aristos.org; www.aristos.org
Finbar Press, Radio City Station, PO Box 2176, New York, NY 10101-2176, 212-957-0849; fax 212-957-0340; toll free 800-960-9355; e-mail finbarpress@onepine.com
Pendragonian Publications, PO Box 719, New York, NY 10101-0719
PENNY DREADFUL: Tales and Poems of Fantastic Terror, PO Box 719, New York, NY 10101-0719
SONGS OF INNOCENCE, PO Box 719, New York, NY 10101-0719
Forbes/Wittenburg & Brown, 250 West 57th Street, Suite 1527, New York, NY 10107, 212-969-0969
LILITH, 250 West 57th, #2432, New York, NY 10107, 212-757-0818
Calliope Press, PO Box 2408, New York, NY 10108-2408, 212-564-5068
GRUE MAGAZINE, Hell's Kitchen Productions, PO Box 370, Times Square Station, New York, NY 10108, e-mail nadramia@panix.com
Yatra Publications/11:11 Studio, PO Box 208, Old Chelsea Station, New York, NY 10113-0208, 212-260-9306; e-mail 1111@the-web-lab.com
International Publishers Co. Inc., PO Box 3042, New York, NY 10116, 212-366-9816; fax 212-366-9820
THE U*N*A*B*A*S*H*E*D LIBRARIAN, THE "HOW I RUN MY LIBRARY GOOD" LETTER, G.P.O. Box 2631, New York, NY 10116
REAL PEOPLE, 450 Fashion Avenue, Suite 1701, New York, NY 10123-1799, 212-244-2351
Pedestal Press, PO Box 6093, Yorkville Station, New York, NY 10128, 212-876-5119
Jewish Radical Education Project, PO BOX 7377, New York, NY 10150-7377
J-REP NEWS AND VIEWS, PO BOX 7377, New York, NY 10150-7377, 212-675-9788
Mystery Notebook Editions, Attn: Stephen Wright, PO Box 1341, FDR Station, New York, NY 10150-1341
WHITECHAPEL JOURNAL, Attn: Stephen Wright, PO Box 1341, FDR Station, New York, NY 10150-1341
FISH DRUM MAGAZINE, PO Box 966, Murray Hill Station, New York, NY 10156, www.fishdrum.com
VISUAL ASSAULT OMNIBUS, Murray Hill Station, Po Box 1122, NY, NY 10156
Broken Mirrors Press, PO Box 1110, New York, NY 10159-1110
THE INDEPENDENT SHAVIAN, The Bernard Shaw Society, PO Box 1159 Madison Square Stn., New York, NY 10159-1159, 212-982-9885
JOURNAL OF POLYMORPHOUS PERVERSITY, PO Box 1454, Madison Square Station, New York, NY 10159-1454, 212-689-5473; info@psychhumor.com; website www.psychhumor.com
Ignite! Entertainment, PO Box 2273, Grand Central Stn., New York, NY 10163, 718-784-8229 phone/Fax; JeffKrell@aol.com
MICROWAVE NEWS, PO Box 1799, Grand Central Station, New York, NY 10163, 212-517-2800
VDT NEWS, PO Box 1799, Grand Central Station, New York, NY 10163, 212-517-2802
Ophelia Editions, PO Box 2377, New York, NY 10185, 212-580-4654
CHELSEA, PO Box 773, Cooper Station, New York, NY 10276-0773
Fugue State Press, PO Box 80, Cooper Station, New York, NY 10276, 212-673-7922
Serena Bay Books, PO Box 1655, Cooper Station, New York, NY 10276, 212-260-5580
Slate Press, Box 1421, Cooper Station, New York, NY 10276
Bard Press, 393 St. Paul's Avenue, Staten Island, NY 10304-2127, 718-442-7429
Ten Penny Players, Inc., 393 St. Paul's Avenue, Staten Island, NY 10304-2127, 718-442-7429
UNMUZZLED OX, 43B Clark Lane, Staten Island, NY 10304, 781-448-3395; 212-226-7170; MAndreOX@aol.com
Ward Hill Press, PO Box 04-0424, Staten Island, NY 10304, 718-816-4056
WATERWAYS: Poetry in the Mainstream, 393 St. Paul's Avenue, Staten Island, NY 10304-2127, 718-442-7429
APHRODITE GONE BERSERK, 233 Guyon Avenue, Staten Island, NY 10306
Eros Publishing, 463 Barlow Avenue, Staten Island, NY 10308, 718-317-7484
CRIPES!, 110 Bemont Avenue, Staten Island, NY 10310, 718-273-9447
AMERICAN TANKA, PO Box 120-024, Staten Island, NY 10312-0024, email editor@americantanka.com; web site www.americantanka.com
Power Publications, 56 McArthur Avenue, Staten Island, NY 10312, 800-331-6534; Fax 718-317-0858
REVOLUTION, 56 McArthur Avenue, Staten Island, NY 10312, 800-331-6534; Fax 718-317-0858
OUTERBRIDGE, College of Staten Island, 2800 Victory Boulevard, Staten Island, NY 10314, 212-390-7654, 7779
FARMING UNCLE, C/O Toro, P O Box 580118, Bronx, NY 10458-0711
FIRST DRAFT, 3636 Fieldston Road, Apt. 7A, Riverdale Bronx, NY 10463-2041, 718-543-5493
Blind Beggar Press, Box 437 Wiliamsbridge Station, Bronx, NY 10467, 914-683-6792
Wright-Armstead Associates, 2410 Barker Avenue, Suite 14-G, Bronx, NY 10467, 212-654-9445
JOURNAL OF MENTAL IMAGERY, c/o Brandon House, PO Box 240, Bronx, NY 10471
The Sheep Meadow Press, PO Box 1345, Riverdale-on-Hudson, NY 10471, 212-548-5547
DorPete Press, PO Box 238, Briarcliff Manor, NY 10510, 914-941-7029
NightinGale Resources, PO Box 322, Cold Spring, NY 10516, 212-753-5383
The Purchase Press, PO Box 5, Harrison, NY 10528, 914-967-4499
The Foundation for Economic Education, Inc., 30 South Broadway, Irvington, NY 10533, 914-591-7230; Fax 914-591-8910; E-mail freeman@fee.org
THE FREEMAN: Ideas On Liberty, 30 South Broadway, Irvington, NY 10533, 914-591-7230; Fax 914-591-8910; E-mail freeman@fee.org
THE ICONOCLAST, 1675 Amazon Road, Mohegan Lake, NY 10547-1804
Curtis/Strongmen Publishing, 70 Barker Street #603, Mount Kisco, NY 10549-1703
ROOM, 38 Ferris Place, Ossining, NY 10562-2818
THE ROTKIN REVIEW, PFI Publications, 38 Rick Lane West, Peekskill, NY 10566, 914-736-7693, Fax 914-736-7694
Aletheia Publications, Inc., 46 Bell Hollow Road, Putnam Valley, NY 10579-1426, 914-526-2873, Fax 914-526-2905
Portmanteau Editions, PO Box 665, Somers, NY 10589
Slapering Hol Press, 300 Riverside Drive, Sleepy Hollow, NY 10591-1414, 914-332-5953
Scarf Press, 1385 Baptist Church Rte., Yorktown Hts., NY 10598, 914-245-7811
Pro/Am Music Resources, Inc., 63 Prospect Street, White Plains, NY 10606, 914-948-7436
Roblin Press, 405 Tarrytown Road, Suite 414, White Plains, NY 10607, 914-347-5934
Image Industry Publications, 34 High Street, Hastings On Hudson, NY 10706-4003, 718-273-3229
THE SHAKESPEARE NEWSLETTER, English Department, Iona College, New Rochelle, NY 10801
CROSS CURRENTS, College of New Rochelle, New Rochelle, NY 10805-2339, 914-235-1439; fax: 914-235-1584; aril@ecunet.org

HEAVEN BONE MAGAZINE, PO Box 486, Chester, NY 10918, 914-469-9018
Heaven Bone Press, PO Box 486, Chester, NY 10918, 914-469-9018
Chicken Soup Press, Inc., PO Box 164, Circleville, NY 10919, 914-692-6320; fax 914-692-7574; e-mail poet@warwick.net
Lintel, 24 Blake Lane, Middletown, NY 10940, 212-674-4901
Library Research Associates, Inc., 474 Dunderberg Road, Monroe, NY 10950, 914-783-1144
CRIMINAL JUSTICE ABSTRACTS, PO Box 249, Monsey, NY 10952, 914-354-9139
Criminal Justice Press, PO Box 249, Monsey, NY 10952, 914-362-8376 fax
Willow Tree Press, Inc., PO Box 249, Monsey, NY 10952, 914-354-9139
Alms House Press, PO Box 217, Pearl River, NY 10965-0217
THE UNKNOWN WRITER, 5 Pothat Street, Sloatsburg, NY 10974, 914-753-8363; Fax 914-753-6562; E-mail rsidor@worldnet.att.net
ON COURSE, 25 South Street, Washingtonville, NY 10992-0250
Roth Publishing, Inc., 175 Great Neck Road, Great Neck, NY 11021, 516-466-3676
Application Publishing, Inc., PO Box 4124, Great Neck, NY 11023, 516-482-5796; Fax 516-773-4743
Avery Publishing Group, Inc., 120 Old Broadway, Garden City Park, NY 11040, 516-741-2155
NEW YORK STORIES, 120 Denton Avenue, Garden City Park, NY 11040, 212-561-1526; nystories@aolcom
Obsessive Compulsive Anonymous, PO Box 215, New Hyde Park, NY 11040, 516-741-4901; FAX 212-768-4679
Bain-Dror International Travel, Inc. (BDIT), PO Box 1405, Port Washington, NY 11050, 513-944-5508; fax 516-944-7540
Odysseus Enterprises Ltd., PO Box 1548, Port Washington, NY 11050-0306, 516-944-5330; FAX 516-944-7540
APKL Publications, 42-07 34th Ave., Apt. 4-D, Long Island City, NY 11101-1115
Low-Tech Press, 30-73 47th Street, Long Island City, NY 11103, 718-721-0946
Starlight Press, Box 3102, Long Island City, NY 11103
The Smith (subsidiary of The Generalist Assn., Inc.), 69 Joralemon Street, Brooklyn, NY 11201-4003
Algol Press, PO Box 022730, Brooklyn, NY 11202-0056, 718-643-9011; fax 718-522-3308; sf-chronicle@compuserve.com
LATEST JOKES NEWSLETTER, PO Box 23304, Brooklyn, NY 11202-0066, 718-855-5057
POETS ON THE LINE, PO Box 020292, Brooklyn, NY 11202-0007, 212-766-4109
SCIENCE FICTION CHRONICLE, PO Box 022730, Brooklyn, NY 11202-0056, 718-643-9011; Fax 718-522-3308
BATH AVENUE NEWSLETTER (BATH), 1980 65th Street #3D, Brooklyn, NY 11204, 718-331-5960; Fax 718-331-4997; E-mail Laspina@msn.con, VLaspina@wow.con
KOJA, 7314 21 Avenue #6E, Brooklyn, NY 11204, email mikekoja@aol.com
Legas, PO Box 040328, Brooklyn, NY 11204
Vincent Laspina, 1980 65th Street #3D, Brooklyn, NY 11204, 718-331-5960; Fax 718-331-4997; Laspina@msn.con, VLaspina@wow.con
Autonomedia, Inc., PO Box 568, Brooklyn, NY 11211, 718-936-2603, e-Mail autonobook@aol.com
HOOTENANNY, 62 North 7th Street 3-R, Brooklyn, NY 11211, 718-388-5736, 315-423-9119
Semiotext Foreign Agents Books Series, PO Box 568, Brooklyn, NY 11211, 718-963-2603; E-mail semiotexte@aol.com
SEMIOTEXT(E), PO Box 568, Brooklyn, NY 11211, 718-963-2603, e-Mail semiotexte@aol.com
JARRETT'S JOURNAL, PO Box 184, Bath Beach Station, Brooklyn, NY 11214, E-mail anndell@rdz.stjohns.edu
BOOGLIT, PO Box 150570, Brooklyn, NY 11215-0570
Interlink Publishing Group, Inc., 99 Seventh Avenue, Brooklyn, NY 11215, 718-797-4292
SANDBOX MAGAZINE, PO Box 150098, Brooklyn, NY 11215-0098, 718-768-4814; sandbox@echonyc.com; www.echonyc.com/~sandbox
HANGING LOOSE, 231 Wyckoff Street, Brooklyn, NY 11217
Hanging Loose Press, 231 Wyckoff Street, Brooklyn, NY 11217
Malafemmina Press, 4211 Fort Hamilton Parkway, Brooklyn, NY 11219
ANGLE, PO BOX 220027, Brooklyn, NY 11222-0027, 415-864-3228
Gryphon Publications, PO Box 209, Brooklyn, NY 11228
HARDBOILED, PO Box 209, Brooklyn, NY 11228
PAPERBACK PARADE, PO Box 209, Brooklyn, NY 11228-0209
MATRIARCH'S WAY: The Journal of Female Supremacy, 3395 Nostrand Avenue #2-J, Brooklyn, NY 11229-4053, 718-648-8215
Pinched Nerves Press, 1610 Avenue P, Apt. 6-B, Brooklyn, NY 11229
RELIX, PO Box 94, Brooklyn, NY 11229, 718-258-0009
Actium Publishing, Inc., 1375 Coney Island Ave., Ste. 122, Brooklyn, NY 11230, 718-382-2129; fax 718-621-0402; email home@actium1.com
Lunar Offensive Publications, 1910 Foster Avenue, Brooklyn, NY 11230-1902
Meadow Mountain Press, 1375 Coney Island Ave., Ste. 136, Brooklyn, NY 11230, 718-338-1559
RAG SHOCK, 1910 Foster Avenue, Brooklyn, NY 11230-1902
THE BROWNSTONE REVIEW, 335 Court St. #114, Brooklyn, NY 11231-4335
THE OVAL MAGAZINE, 22 Douglass Street, Brooklyn, NY 11231
Cardoza Publishing, 132 Hastings Street, Brooklyn, NY 11235, 718-743-5229; FAX 718-743-8284
THE PIPE SMOKER'S EPHEMERIS, 20-37 120th Street, College Point, NY 11356-2128
L D A Publishers, 42-36 209 Street, Bayside, NY 11361, 718-224-9484; Fax: 718-224-9487; 888-388-9887
Phrygian Press, 58-09 205th Street, Bayside, NY 11364
ZYX, 58-09 205th Street, Bayside, NY 11364
WRESTLING - THEN & NOW, PO Box 640471, Oakland Gdns. Station, Flushing, NY 11364
THE SPIRIT THAT MOVES US, PO Box 720820-DB, Jackson Heights, Queens, NY 11372-0820, 718-426-8788; msklar@mindspring.com
The Spirit That Moves Us Press, Inc., PO Box 720820-DB, Jackson Heights, Queens, NY 11372-0820, 718-426-8788; msklar@mindspring.com
BlackBox, 77-44 Austin Street #3F, Forest Hills, NY 11375
Ironweed Press, PO Box 754208, Parkside Station, Forest Hills, NY 11375, 718-268-2394
Lion Press, Ltd., 108-22 Queens Boulevard, #221, Forest Hills, NY 11375, 718-271-1394
THE NEW PRESS LITERARY QUARTERLY, 6539 108th Street #E6, Forest Hills, NY 11375-2214, 718-459-6807; Fax; 718-275-1646
Pyramid Publishing, 110-64 Queens Boulevard, Suite 227, Forest Hills, NY 11375-6347, 718-341-4575, Fax 718-341-1880, e-mail 10227.241@compuserve.com
Celtic Heritage Books, PO Box 770637, Woodside, NY 11377-0637, 718-478-8162; 1-800-273-5281

SKINNYDIPPING, 51-04 39th Avenue, Woodside, NY 11377-3145, 718-651-4689; FAX 718-424-1883
THE LEDGE, 78-44 80th Street, Glendale, NY 11385
House of Hits, Inc., North American Airlines Bldg 75, Suite 250, JFK International Airport, Jamaica, NY 11430, 718-656-2650
LADIES' FETISH & TABOO SOCIETY COMPENDIUM OF URBAN ANTHROPOLOGY, PO Box 313194, Jamaica, NY 11431-3194, e-mail fortuna@pipeline.com
New Spirit Press/The Poet Tree, 82-34 138 Street #6F, Kew Gardens, NY 11435, 718-847-1482
POEMS THAT THUMP IN THE DARK/SECOND GLANCE, 82-34 138 Street #6F, Kew Gardens, NY 11435, 718-847-1482
ARBA SICULA, c/o Modern Foreign Languages, St. John's University, Jamaica, NY 11439-0002
SICILIA PARRA, c/o Modern Foreign Languages, St. John's University, Jamaica, NY 11439-0002, 718-331-0613
CONFRONTATION, English Department, C.W. Post of Long Island Univ., Greenvale, NY 11548, 516-299-2391
Callawind Publications Inc., 2083 Hempstead Turnpike, Suite 355, East Meadow, NY 11554-1730, 514-685-9109, Fax: 514-685-7055, E-mail info@callawind.com
AERO-GRAMME, 417 Roslyn Road, Roslyn Heights, NY 11577, 516-621-2195
HSC Publications, 360-A West Merrick Road, Ste. 40, Valley Stream, NY 11580, 516-256-0223
Career Advancement Center, Inc., PO Box 436, Woodmere, NY 11598, 516-374-1387, Fax: 516-374-1175, E-mail: caradvctr@aol.com
THE SMALL BUSINESS ADVISOR, PO Box 436, Woodmere, NY 11598, 516-374-1387; Fax 516-374-1175; smalbusadu@aol.com
MOKSHA JOURNAL, 49 Forrest Place, Amityville, NY 11701, 516-691-8475; fax 516-691-8475
Vajra Printing an Publishing of Yoga Anand Ashram, 49 Forrest Place, Amityville, NY 11701, 516-691-8475; fax 516-691-8475
Montfort Publications, 26 South Saxon Avenue, Bay Shore, NY 11706, 516-665-0726; FAX 516-665-4349
QUEEN OF ALL HEARTS, 26 South Saxon Avenue, Bay Shore, NY 11706, 516-665-0726
PIRATE WRITINGS, PO Box 329, Brightwaters, NY 11718-0329, E-mail pwpubl@aol.com
AFFAIR OF THE MIND: A Literary Quarterly, 8 Mare Lane, Commack, NY 11725, 516-864-5135
The Imaginary Press, PO Box 509, East Setauket, NY 11733, 516-751-3810; E-mail imaginary-press@iname.com
NEWSLETTER/POETIMES, PO Box 773, Huntington, NY 11743
Pleasure Dome Press (Long Island Poetry Collective Inc.), Box 773, Huntington, NY 11743
XANADU, Box 773, Huntington, NY 11743, 516-248-7716
River Press, 499 Islip Avenue, Islip, NY 11751-1826, 516-277-8618; fax 516-277-8660
BOOK/MARK SMALL PRESS QUARTERLY REVIEW, 9 Garden Avenue, Miller Place, NY 11764, 516-331-4118
Laurel Publications, 85 Echo Avenue, Miller Place, NY 11764, 516-474-1023 phone/FAX
UNDER THE VOLCANO, PO Box 236, Nesconset, NY 11767, 516-585-7471
Belle Terre Press, Inc., 655-74 Belle Terre Road, Port Jefferson, NY 11777, 516-473-7630; RWunder100@aol.com
SHADES OF DECEMBER, PO Box 244, Selden, NY 11784, E-mail eilonwy@innocent.com; www2.crosswinds.net/new-york/~shadesof12
WRITERS INK, PO Box 2344, Seldon, NY 11784, 516-451-0478 phone/fax
Writers Unlimited Agency, Inc, PO Box 2344, Seldon, NY 11784, 516-451-0478 phone/Fax
Writers Ink Press, 233 Mooney Pond, PO Box 2344, Seldon, Long Island, NY 11784-2344, 516-451-0478 phone/Fax
POETRY BONE, 12 Skylark Lane, Stony Brook, NY 11790
Celebrity Profiles Publishing, PO Box 344, Stonybrook, NY 11790, 516-862-8555; FAX 862-0139
IRISH LITERARY SUPPLEMENT, 2592 N Wading River Road, Wading River, NY 11792-1404, 516-929-0224
Irish Studies, 2592 N Wading River Road, Wading River, NY 11792-1404, 516-929-0224
Pine Publications, 2947 Jerusalem Avenue, Wantagh, NY 11793-2020, 516-781-0707
TAPROOT, a journal of older writers, Fine Arts Center 4290, University at Stony Brook, Stony Brook, NY 11794-5410, 516-632-6635
Scratch & Scribble Press, PO Box 490, Ridge, NY 11961
Sagapress, Inc., Box 21, 30 Sagaponack Road, Sagaponack, NY 11962, 516-537-3717; Fax 516-537-5415
The Bookman Press, PO Box 1892, Sag Harbor, NY 11963, 516-725-1115
The Permanent Press/The Second Chance Press, 4170 Noyac Road, Sag Harbor, NY 11963, 516-725-1101
Savant Garde Workshop, PO Box 1650, Sag Harbor, NY 11963-0060, 516-725-1414; website www.savantgarde.org
BEGINNINGS - A Magazine for the Novice Writer, PO Box 92-R, Shirley, NY 11967, 516-924-7826; scbeginnings@juno.com; www.v.scbeginnings.com
Whelks Walk Press, 37 Harvest Lane, Southampton, NY 11968, 516-283-5122; Fax 516-283-1902; whelkswalk@aol.com
WHELKS WALK REVIEW, 37 Harvest Lane, Southampton, NY 11968, 516-283-5122; Fax 516-283-1902; whelkswalk@aol.com
Wise Owl Press, PO Box 377 (1475 Waterview Dr.), Southold, NY 11971, 516-765-3356
Pushcart Press, PO Box 380, Wainscott, NY 11975, 516-324-9300
LITERARY ROCKET, PO Box 672, Water Mill, NY 11976-0672, e-mail RocketUSA@delphi.com
OPTIONS IN LEARNING, PO Box 59, East Chatham, NY 12060, 518-392-6900
Omega Publications, Inc., 256 Darrow Road, New Lebanon, NY 12125, 518-794-8181, Fax 518-794-8187, e-mail omegapub@taconic.net
Sachem Press, PO Box 9, Old Chatham, NY 12136, 518-794-8327
INNOVATING, The Rensselaerville Institute, Rensselaerville, NY 12147, 518-797-3783
RALPH'S REVIEW, 129 Wellington Avenue, #A, Albany, NY 12203-2637, e-mail rcpub@juno.com
A & U AMERICA'S AIDS MAGAZINE, 25 Monroe Street, Suite 205, Albany, NY 12210, 518-426-9010, fax 518-436-5354, mailbox@aumag.org
THE KOSCIUSZKO PORTFOLIO, 405 Madison Avenue, Albany, NY 12210
Mount Ida Press, 152 Washington Avenue, Albany, NY 12210-2203, 518-426-5935
THE LITTLE MAGAZINE, English Department, State Univ. of New York at Albany, Albany, NY 12222, website www.albany.edu/~litmag.
13TH MOON, 1400 Washington Avenue, SUNY, English Department, Albany, NY 12222-0001, 518-442-4181
ALABAMA DOGSHOE MOUSTACHE, 875 Central Parkway, Schenectady, NY 12309
SOCKS, DREGS AND ROCKING CHAIRS, 875 Central Parkway, Schenectady, NY 12309
THE SUBTLE JOURNAL OF RAW COINAGE, 875 Central Parkway, Schenectady, NY 12309
A VOICE WITHOUT SIDES, 875 Central Parkway, Schenectady, NY 12309

Selah Publishing Co. Inc., PO Box 3037, 58 Pearl Street, Kingston, NY 12401, 914-338-2816, 914-338-2991, e-mail selahpub@aol.com
McPherson & Company Publishers, PO Box 1126, Kingston, NY 12402, 914-331-5807, toll free order #800-613-8219
Willendorf Press, PO Box 407, Bearsville, NY 12409, 914-679-1209; fax 914-679-1206
Press-Tige Publishing Company Inc., 291 Main Street, Catskill, NY 12414, 518-943-1440
Black Dome Press Corp., Route 296, Box 422, Hensonville, NY 12439, 518-734-6357
WRITER'S MONTHLY GAZETTE, HCR 1 Box 309, Leeds, NY 12451, 518-622-8806; 800-707-2752
ART TIMES, PO Box 730, Mount Marion, NY 12456-0730, 914-246-6944; email arttimes@alster.net
Raymond Saroff, Publisher, 461 Acorn Hill Road, Olive Bridge, NY 12461
Ash Tree Publishing, PO Box 64, Woodstock, NY 12498, 914-246-8081
Beekman Publishers, Inc., Po Box 888, Woodstock, NY 12498, 914-679-2300
Ceres Press, PO Box 87, Woodstock, NY 12498
Journey Publications, PO Box 423, Woodstock, NY 12498, 914-657-8434
Left Hand Books, Station Hill Road, Barrytown, NY 12507, 914-758-6478; FAX 914-758-4416
Station Hill Press, Station Hill Road, Barrytown, NY 12507, 914-758-5840
The Groundwater Press, PO Box 704, Hudson, NY 12534, 516-767-8503
Trojan Homes Publishing Co., 4 Miller Hill Drive, LaGrangeville, NY 12540-5605, 914-223-7514; e-mail wbuild28@juno.com
CHESS LIFE, United States Chess Federation, 186 Route 9W, New Windsor, NY 12553, (914) 562-8350
SCHOOL MATES, 186 Route 9W, New Windsor, NY 12553, 914-562-8350
U.S. Chess Federation, 186 Route 9W, New Windsor, NY 12553, 914-562-8350
BLU, PO Box 517, New Paltz, NY 12561, 1-800-778-8461; e-mail revcenter@hotmail.com; website www.revolution-center.org
THE PUBLIC RELATIONS QUARTERLY, PO Box 311, Rhinebeck, NY 12572, 914-876-2081, fax 914-876-2561
POSTCARD, PO Box 444, Tivioli, NY 12583
INVESTMENT COLUMN QUARTERLY (newsletter), PO Box 233, Barryville, NY 12719, 914-557-8713
NAR Publications, PO Box 233, Barryville, NY 12719, 914-557-8713
Voices From My Retreat, Box 1077, S. Fallsburg, NY 12779, 914-436-7455; 1-800-484-1255 ex. 2485
Honors Group, Adirondack Community College, SUNY, Queensbury, NY 12804
The Snail's Pace Press, Inc., 85 Darwin Road, Cambridge, NY 12816, 518-677-5208
The Greenfield Review Press/Ithaca House, PO Box 308, Greenfield Center, NY 12833-0308, 518-584-1728
ADIRONDAC, 814 Goggins Road, Lake George, NY 12845-4117, 518-668-4447; e-mail ADKinfo@adk.org
Adirondack Mountain Club, Inc., 814 Goggins Road, Lake George, NY 12845-4117, 518-668-4447; FAX 518-668-3746, e-mail pubs@adk.org
CHRONICLES OF DISORDER, 20 Edie Road, Saratoga Springs, NY 12866-5425
THE DUPLEX PLANET, PO Box 1230, Saratoga Springs, NY 12866, 518-587-5356
SALMAGUNDI, Skidmore College, Saratoga Springs, NY 12866, 518-584-5000
Astrion Publishing, PO Box 783, Champlain, NY 12919, 514-935-4097
Passport Press, PO Box 1346, Champlain, NY 12919-1346, 514-937-3868; fax 514-931-0871, e-mail travelbook@bigfoot.com
PARADOX, PO Box 643, Saranac Lake, NY 12983
BITTER OLEANDER, 4983 Tall Oaks Drive, Fayetteville, NY 13066-9776, FAX 315-637-5056; E-mail bones44@ix.netcom.com
Pine Grove Press, PO Box 85, Jamesville, NY 13078, 315-423-9268
THEATRE DESIGN AND TECHNOLOGY, 6443 Ridings Road, Syracuse, NY 13206-1111
United States Institute for Theatre Technology, Inc., 6443 Ridings Road, Syracuse, NY 13206-1111
THE COMSTOCK REVIEW, Comstock Writers' Group, Inc., 907 Comstock Avenue, Syracuse, NY 13210
Purple Finch Press, PO Box 758, Dewitt, NY 13214, 315-445-8087
RED BRICK REVIEW, PO Box 6527, Syracuse, NY 13217
Syracuse Cultural Workers/Tools for Change, PO Box 6367, Syracuse, NY 13217, 315-474-1132, fax 315-475-1277
NEW ENVIRONMENT BULLETIN, 270 Fenway Drive, Syracuse, NY 13224, 315-446-8009
POINT OF CONTACT, 215 H.B. Crouse Building, Syracuse University, Syracuse, NY 13244-1160, 315-443-5497; FAX 315-443-5376
SALT HILL, English Department, Syracuse University, Syracuse, NY 13244-1170, 315-424-8141
Berry Hill Press, 2349 State Route 12-B, Deansboro, NY 13328, 315-821-6188 phone/fax
Baba Yoga Micropress, 430 N. Main Street, Herkimer, NY 13350
Quilted Walls Micropress, 426 N. Main Street, Herkimer, NY 13350
Treehouse Micropress, 435 N. Main St., Herkimer, NY 13350
Brownout Laboratories, RD 2, Box 5, Little Falls, NY 13365
North Country Books, Inc., 311 Turner Street, Utica, NY 13501, 315-735-4877
TERMINAL FRIGHT, PO Box 100, Black River, NY 13612
Caliban Press, 14 Jay Steet, Canton, NY 13617-1414, 315-386-4923
BLUELINE, State University College, English Dept., Potsdam, NY 13676, 315-267-2043
Danzon Press, 14 Hamilton Street, Potsdam, NY 13676, 315-265-3466
CADENCE: THE REVIEW OF JAZZ & BLUES: CREATIVE IMPROVISED MUSIC, Cadence Building, Redwood, NY 13679, 315-287-2852; Fax 315-287-2860
THE WALLACE STEVENS JOURNAL, Clarkson University, Box 5750, Potsdam, NY 13699-5750, 315-268-3987
The Wallace Stevens Society Press, Box 5750 Clarkson University, Potsdam, NY 13699-5750, 315-268-3987; FAX 268-3983; serio@clarkson.edu; http://www.clarkson.edu/~wsj
Birch Brook Press, PO Box 81, Delhi, NY 13753, 212-353-3326 messages; Phone & Fax orders & inquiries 607-746-7453
Serpent & Eagle Press, RD#1 Box 29B, Laurens, NY 13796, 607-432-2990
Bright Hill Press, PO Box 193, Treadwell, NY 13846, Fax 607-746-7274; E-mail wordthurs@aol.com
The Edwin Mellen Press, PO Box 450, Lewiston, NY 14092, 716-754-2266
Mellen Poetry Press, PO Box 450, 415 Ridge Street, Lewiston, NY 14092-0450, 716-754-2266; Fax 716-754-4056; E-mail mellen@ag.net
Potentials Development, Inc., 779 Cayuga Street, Apt#1, Lewiston, NY 14092-1728
Tell Publishing, 5679 South Transit Road, Ste. 181, Lockport, NY 14094, 800-726-8932, 416-693-4302
ELF: ECLECTIC LITERARY FORUM (ELF MAGAZINE), PO Box 392, Tonawanda, NY 14150, 716-693-7006

692

White Pine Press, PO Box 236, Buffalo, NY 14201-0236, 716-672-5743
EARTH'S DAUGHTERS: Feminist Arts Periodical, PO Box 41, Central Park Station, Buffalo, NY 14215-0041, 716-627-9825
Labor Arts Books, 1064 Amherst St., Buffalo, NY 14216, 716-873-4131
BUFFALO SPREE, 5678 Main Street, Buffalo, NY 14221-5563, 716-634-0820; fax 716-634-4659
Positive Publishing, 123 E. Pinelake Drive, suite 200, Williamsville, NY 14221, 716-639-0225; fax 716-636-1894; email positive-way@mail.com
LIVING FREE, Box 29, Hiler Branch, Buffalo, NY 14223
Amherst Media, Inc., P.O. Box 586, Amherst, NY 14226, 716-874-4450
Amherst Press, 3380 Sheridan Drive, Suite 365, Amherst, NY 14226, 716-633-5434 phone/fax
1812, Box 1812, Amherst, NY 14226-7812, http://1812.simplenet.com
THE HUMANIST, 7 Harwood Drive, PO Box 1188, Amherst, NY 14226-7188, 716-839-5080
NEW WRITING, PO Box 1812, Amherst, NY 14226-7812, http://members.aol.com/newwriting/magazine.html
SKEPTICAL INQUIRER, PO Box 703, Amherst, NY 14226, 716-636-1425; Skeptinq@aol.com
FREE INQUIRY, Council For Secular Humanism, PO Box 664, Buffalo, NY 14226, 716-636-7571
THE $ENSIBLE SOUND, 403 Darwin Drive, Snyder, NY 14226, 716-833-0930
SLIPSTREAM, Box 2071, New Market Station, Niagara Falls, NY 14301, 716-282-2616 (after 5 p.m., E.S.T.)
Slipstream Productions, Box 2071, New Market Station, Niagara Falls, NY 14301
State Street Press, PO Box 278, Brockport, NY 14420, 716-637-0023
MOBILE BEAT: The DJ Magazine, PO Box 309, East Rochester, NY 14445, 716-385-9920; fax 716-385-3637; info@mobilebeat.com
Footprint Press, PO Box 645, Fishers, NY 14453, 716-321-3666 phone/Fax; email freeman1@frontiernet.net; www.footprintpress.com
SENECA REVIEW, Hobart & William Smith Colleges, Geneva, NY 14456, 315-781-3392; Fax 315-781-3348; senecareview@hws.edu
Success Publishing, 3419 Dunham Drive, Box 263, Warsaw, NY 14569
BOA Editions, Ltd., 260 East Avenue, Rochester, NY 14604, 716-546-3410
AFTERIMAGE, 31 Prince Street, Rochester, NY 14607, 716-442-8676
Austen Press, 620 Park Avenue #119, Rochester, NY 14607, 716-271-8520
Visual Studies Workshop, Research Center, 31 Prince Street, Rochester, NY 14607, 716-442-8676
Spillway Publications, 48 Pershing Drive, Rochester, NY 14609
GERBIL: Queer Culture Zine, PO Box 10692, Rochester, NY 14610, 716-262-3966, gerbil@rpa.net
StarMist Books, Box 12640, Rochester, NY 14612
THE ROUND TABLE: A Journal of Poetry and Fiction, PO Box 18673, Rochester, NY 14618
Lion Press & Video, PO Box 92541, Rochester, NY 14692, 716-381-6410; fax 716-381-7439; for orders only 800-597-3068
New Voice Media, PO Box 25, Houghton, NY 14744
SMALL PRESS CREATIVE EXPLOSION, PO Box 25, Houghton, NY 14744
McBooks Press, 120 West State Street, Ithaca, NY 14850, 607-272-2114; FAX 607-273-6068, e-mail alex908@aol.com http://www.mcbooks.com
SOUTH AMERICAN EXPLORER, 126 Indian Creek Road, Ithaca, NY 14850, 607-277-0488; Fax 607-277-6122; explorer@samexplo.org
SNOW LION NEWSLETTER & CATALOG, PO Box 6483, Ithaca, NY 14851
Snow Lion Publications, Inc., PO Box 6483, Ithaca, NY 14851, 607-273-8506; 607-273-8519; fax 607-273-8508
What The Heck Press, PO Box 149, Ithaca, NY 14851-0149, 607-275-0806; Fax 607-275-0702
ZUZU'S PETALS: QUARTERLY ONLINE, PO Box 4853, Ithaca, NY 14852-4853, e-mail zuzu@zuzu.com Web Site http://www.zuzu.com
EPOCH, 251 Goldwin Smith Hall, Cornell Univ., Ithaca, NY 14853, 607-255-3385
Great Elm Press, 1205 County Route 60, Rexville, NY 14877
THE CIVIL ABOLITIONIST, Box 26, Swain, NY 14884, 607-545-6213
Civitas, Box 26, Swain, NY 14884, 607-545-6213

NORTH CAROLINA

Explorer Press, 1449 Edgewood Drive, Mount Airy, NC 27030-5215, 336-789-6005; Fax 336-789-6005; E-mail terrycollins@advi.net
John F. Blair, Publisher, 1406 Plaza Drive, Winston-Salem, NC 27103, 336-768-1374
Greencrest Press, Box 7746, Winston-Salem, NC 27109, 919-722-6463
AMERICAN MODELER, The Newspaper of Scale Modeling, PO Box 273, Whitsett, NC 27377-0273, 336-449-0809; Fax 336-222-6294; fotodroid@aol.com
ELT Press, English Department/U of North Carolina, P.O. Box 26170, Greensboro, NC 27402-6170, 910-334-5446; fax 910-334-5446; e-Mail langen.fagan.uncg.edu
ENGLISH LITERATURE IN TRANSITION, 1880-1920, English Department/U of North Carolina, P.O. Box 26170, Greensboro, NC 27402-6170, 910-334-5446; fax 910-334-3281; e-Mail langen.fagan.uncg.edu
THE GREENSBORO REVIEW, PO Box 26170, Dept. of English, Univ. of North Carolina-Greensboro, Greensboro, NC 27402-6170, 336-334-5459; fax 336-334-3281; e-mail jlclark@uncg.edu
CITIES AND ROADS: A Collection of Short Stories for North Carolina Readers and Writers., PO Box 10886, Greensboro, NC 27404, E-mail cities@nr.infi.net
Osmyrrah Publishing, PO Box 10134, Greensboro, NC 27404, 336-292-4061
Avisson Press, Inc., 3007 Taliaferro Road, Greensboro, NC 27408, 336-288-6989 phone/FAX
March Street Press, 3413 Wilshire Drive, Greensboro, NC 27408-2923
PARTING GIFTS, 3413 Wilshire Drive, Greensboro, NC 27408-2923
Tudor Publishers, Inc., Attn: Eugene E. Pfaff Jr., PO Box 38366, Greensboro, NC 27408, 910-282-5907
INTERNATIONAL POETRY REVIEW, Dept of Romance Languages, The University of North Carolina at Greensboro, Greensboro, NC 27412-5001, 336-334-5655
TIMBER CREEK REVIEW, c/o J.M. Freiermuth, 3283 UNCG Station, Greensboro, NC 27413, 336-334-6970
WORDS OF WISDOM, 3283 UNCG Station, Greensboro, NC 27413, 336-334-6970; e-mail wowmail@hoopsmail.com
LETTER ARTS REVIEW, PO Box 9986, Greensboro, NC 27429
Trafton Publising, 109 Barcliff Terrace, Cary, NC 27511-8900

THE JOURNAL OF AFRICAN TRAVEL-WRITING, PO Box 346, Chapel Hill, NC 27514
THE THOMAS WOLFE REVIEW, 305 Spruce Street, Chapel Hill, NC 27514, 336-334-3831
New View Publications, PO Box 3021, Chapel Hill, NC 27515-3021
Pipeline Press, PO Box 9255, Chapel Hill, NC 27515-9255, 919-933-6480 phone/Fax; E-mail joelbush@mindspring.com
THE SUN, A MAGAZINE OF IDEAS, 107 North Roberson Street, Chapel Hill, NC 27516, 919-942-5282
APDG, Publishing, 4736 Shady Greens Drive, Suite D, Fuguay-Varina, NC 27526, 919-557-2260; fax 919-557-2261; toll
    free 800-277-9681; toll free fax 800-390-5507; email success@APDG-Inc.com; www.apdg-inc.com
REFLECTIONS, PO Box 1197, Roxboro, NC 27573, 336-599-1181; e-mail furbisd@piedmont.cc.nc.us
Meridional Publications, 7101 Winding Way, Wake Forest, NC 27587, 919-556-2940
THE CAROLINA QUARTERLY, CB# 3520 Greenlaw Hall, Univ of N. Carolina, Chapel Hill, NC 27599-3520,
    919-962-0244; fax 919-962-3520
AC, 306 Parham Street, Suite 200, Raleigh, NC 27601, 919-834-5433; Fax 919-834-2449; E-mail
    gstudios@mindspring.com
Alternating Crimes Publishing, 306 Parham St. Ste 200, Raleigh, NC 27601, 919-834-5433; fax 919-834-2449; e-mail
    6studios@mindspring.com
Horse & Buggy Press, 303 Kinsey Street, Raleigh, NC 27603, 919-828-2514
Three Pyramids Publishing, 201 Kenwood Meadows Drive, Raleigh, NC 27603-8314, 919-773-2080; Fax 919-779-9508;
    E-mail JFS999@mindspring.com
DRASTIC LIVES, 3721 Baugh Street, Raleigh, NC 27604, 919-981-0380
Pamlico Press, 730 Washington Street #304, Raleigh, NC 27605-1289, 919-821-0858
The New South Company & Boson Books, 3905 Meadow Field Lane, Raleigh, NC 27606-4470
Pentland Press, Inc., 5122 Bur Oak Circle, Raleigh, NC 27612, 919-782-0281
DeeMar Communications, 6325-9 Falls of Neuse Road, #320, Raleigh, NC 27615, 919-870-6423; deemar@aol.com;
    www.deemarcommunications.com; www.deemar.com
Signal Books, 7117 Tyndall Court, Raleigh, NC 27615, 919-870-8505 phone/fax; gtkach@worldnet.att.net
OBSIDIAN II: BLACK LITERATURE IN REVIEW, Dept. of English, Box 8105, NC State University, Raleigh, NC
    27695-8105, 919-515-3870
Carolina Academic Press, 700 Kent Street, Durham, NC 27701
Carolina Wren Press/Lollipop Power Books, 120 Morris Street, Durham, NC 27701, 919-560-2738
Lollipop Power Books, 120 Morris Street, Durham, NC 27701, 919-560-2738
STRANGE GROWTHS, 909 Lancaster, Durham, NC 27701
Institute for Southern Studies, PO Box 531, Durham, NC 27702
SOUTHERN EXPOSURE, PO Box 531, Durham, NC 27702, 919-419-8311
SPECTRUM—The Wholistic News Magazine, 3519 Hamstead Ct, Durham, NC 27707-5136, 603-528-4710
AMERICAN LITERATURE, Box 90660, Duke University, Durham, NC 27708-0660, 919-684-3948
AMERICAN LITERATURE SECTION, Box 90660, Duke University, Durham, NC 27708-0660
BOUNDARY 2: An International Journal of Literature and Culture, Box 90660, Duke University, Durham, NC 27708-0660
DUKE MATHEMATICAL JOURNAL, Box 90660, Duke University, Durham, NC 27708-0660
Duke University Press, Box 90660, Durham, NC 27708-0660, 919-687-3600; Fax 919-688-4574
ENVIRONMENTAL HISTORY, Box 90660, Duke University, Durham, NC 27708-0660
ETHNOHISTORY: The Official Journal of the American Society for Ethnohistory, Box 90660, Duke University, Durham,
    NC 27708-0660
FRENCH HISTORICAL STUDIES, Box 90660, Duke University, Durham, NC 27708-0660
HISPANIC AMERICAN HISTORICAL REVIEW, Box 90660, Duke University, Durham, NC 27708-0660
HISTORY OF POLITICAL ECONOMY, Box 90660, Duke University, Durham, NC 27708-0660
INTERNATIONAL MATHEMATICS RESEARCH NOTICES, Box 90660, Duke University, Durham, NC 27708-0660
JOURNAL OF HEALTH POLITICS, POLICY AND LAW, Box 90660, Duke University, Durham, NC 27708-0660
JOURNAL OF MEDIEVAL AND EARLY MODERN STUDIES, Box 90660, Duke University, Durham, NC 27708-0660
JOURNAL OF PERSONALITY, Box 90660, Duke University, Durham, NC 27708-0660
LESBIAN AND GAY STUDIES NEWSLETTER, Box 90660, Duke University, Durham, NC 27708-0660
MEDITERRANEAN QUARTERLY: A Journal of Global Issues, Box 90660, Duke University, Durham, NC 27708-0660
MODERN LANGUAGE QUARTERLY: A Journal of Literary History, Box 90660, Duke University, Durham, NC
    27708-0660, E-mail amylee@acpub.duke.edu
THE OPERA QUARTERLY, Box 90660, Duke University, Durham, NC 27708-0660
POETICS TODAY: International Journal for Theory and Analysis of Literature and Communication, Box 90660, Duke
    University, Durham, NC 27708-0660
POSITIONS: East Asia Cultures Critique, Box 90660, Duke University, Durham, NC 27708-0660
SOCIAL SCIENCE HISTORY, Box 90660, Duke University, Durham, NC 27708-0660
SOCIAL TEXT, Box 90660, Duke University, Durham, NC 27708-0660
SOCIALIST REVIEW, Box 90660, Duke University, Durham, NC 27708-0660
THE SOUTH ATLANTIC QUARTERLY, Box 90660, Duke University, Durham, NC 27708-0660
TRANSITION, Box 90660, Duke University, Durham, NC 27708-0660
NORTH CAROLINA LITERARY REVIEW, English Department, East Carolina University, Greenville, NC 27858,
    252-328-1537; Fax 252-328-4889
TAR RIVER POETRY, Department of English, East Carolina University, Greenville, NC 27858-4353, 919-328-6041
CRUCIBLE, English Department, Barton College, Wilson, NC 27893, 919-399-6456
SKYWRITERS, 245 Spring Street, SW, Concord, NC 28025
Stained Glass Press, 245 Spring Street, SW, Concord, NC 28025
A. Borough Books, PO Box 15391, Charlotte, NC 28211, 704-364-1788; 800-843-8490 (orders only)
MAIN STREET RAG POETRY JOURNAL, PO Box 25331, Charlotte, NC 28229-5331, 704-535-1918; E-mail
    mainstrag@mindspring.com
StoneBrook Publishing, PO Box 30696, Charlotte, NC 28230, 704-849-6878; FAX 704-841-8557
SOUTHERN POETRY REVIEW, Advancement Studies Dept., Central Piedmont Community College, Charlotte, NC
    28235, 704-330-6002
THE CHRISTIAN LIBRARIAN, Southern Evangelical Seminary, 4298 McKee Road, Charlotte, NC 28270
THE MINDFULNESS BELL, 14200 Fountain Lane, Charlotte, NC 28278, 510-527-3751; e-mail parapress@aol.com
PREP Publishing, Box 66, Fayetteville, NC 28302, 910-483-6611, fax 910-483-2439
Longleaf Press, Methodist College, English Dept., 5400 Ramsey Street, Fayetteville, NC 28311, 910-822-5403

Persephone Press, 600 Kelly Road, Carthage, NC 28327, 910-947-2587; Fax 910-947-5112
Scots Plaid Press, 600 Kelly Road, Carthage, NC 28327, 910-947-2587; Fax 910-947-5112
Construction Trades Press, PO Box 953, Clinton, NC 28328, 919-592-1310
Averasboro Press, PO Box 482, Erwin, NC 28339, E-mail jpowell@nceye.net
CAPE FEAR JOURNAL, PO Box 482, Erwin, NC 28339, E-mail jpowell@nceye.net
St. Andrews Press, c/o St. Andrews College, Laurinburg, NC 28352-5598, 919-277-5310
Mount Olive College Press, Mount Olive College, 634 Henderson Street, Mount Olive, NC 28365
MOUNT OLIVE REVIEW, Department of Language and Literature, 634 Henderson Street, Mount Olive, NC 28365, 919-658-2502
PEMBROKE MAGAZINE, UNCP, Box 1510, Pembroke, NC 28372-1510, 919-521-4214 ext 433
SANDHILLS REVIEW (formerly ST. ANDREWS REVIEW), 2200 Airport Road, Pinehurst, NC 28374, 910-695-2756; FAX 910-695-3875
Arnold & Johnson, Publishers, 5024 College Acres Drive, Willington, NC 28403-1741
Banks Channel Books, PO Box 4446, Wilmington, NC 28406, phone/fax 910-762-4677; E-mail bankschan@aol.com
Sheer Joy! Press, PO Box 608, Pink Hill, NC 28572, 919-568-6101
Inheritance Press Inc., 101 Henderson Lane, Trenton, NC 28585, 919-448-1113 phone & fax
Parkway Publishers, Inc., Box 3678, Boone, NC 28607, 704-265-3993
Appalachian Consortium Press, University Hall, Appalachian State University, Boone, NC 28608, 704-262-2064, fax 704-262-6564
BurnhillWolf, 321 Prospect Street, SW, Lenoir, NC 28645, 704-754-0287; FAX 707-754-8392
Celo Valley Books, 346 Seven Mile Ridge Road, Burnsville, NC 28714, 828-675-5918
MOTHERTONGUE, PO Box 640, Candler, NC 28715, 704-665-4572
New Native Press, PO Box 661, Cullowhee, NC 28723, 828-293-9237
GREEN PRINTS, "The Weeder's Digest", PO Box 1355, Fairview, NC 28730, 704-628-1902
The Neo Herramann Group, 2075 Buffalo Creek Road, Lake Lure, NC 28746, 704-625-9153
Swan Raven & Company, PO Box 190, Mill Spring, NC 28756-0190
Kivaki Press, PO Box 1053, Skyland, NC 28776-1053, 704-684-1988; E-mail kivaki@cheta.net; Website www.kivaki.com
Ammons Communications, Ltd., 55 Woody Hampton Road, Sylva, NC 28779, 704-631-0414 phone/FAX
COMMUNITIES, 290 McEntire Road, Tryon, NC 28782-9764, 828-863-4425; e-mail communities@ic.org
Altamont Press, Inc., 50 College Street, Asheville, NC 28801, 704-253-0468
FIBERARTS, 50 College Street, Asheville, NC 28801, 704-253-0468
Eat Your Hair, PO Box 2224, Asheville, NC 28802
Shannon D. Harle, Publisher, PO Box 2224, Asheville, NC 28802
Rotten Pepper, PO Box 2224, Asheville, NC 28802
T.V. HEADS, PO Box 2224, Asheville, NC 28802
Bright Mountain Books, Inc., 138 Springside Road, Asheville, NC 28803, fax/phone 828-681-1790
Urthona Press, 62 LakeShore Drive, Asheville, NC 28804-2436
THE FRONT STRIKER BULLETIN, The Retskin Report, PO Box 18481, Asheville, NC 28814-0481, 828-254-4487; FAX 828-254-1066
SF EYE, PO Box 18539, Asheville, NC 28814, Fax 828-285-9400; eyebrown@interpath.com
NEW FRONTIER, PO Box 17397, Asheville, NC 28816-7397

NORTH DAKOTA

NORTH DAKOTA QUARTERLY, University of North Dakota, PO Box 7209, Grand Forks, ND 58202, 701-777-3322
UND Press, University of North Dakota, PO Box 7209, Grand Forks, ND 58202, 701-777-3321
HEALTHY WEIGHT JOURNAL, 402 South 14th Street, Hettinger, ND 58639, 701-567-2646, Fax 701-567-2602, e-mail fmberg@healthyweight.net
Willowood Press, PO Box 1846, Minot, ND 58702, 701-838-0579

OHIO

Cumberland, 7652 Sawmill Road, Suite 194, Dublin, OH 43017
THE KENYON REVIEW, Kenyon College, Gambier, OH 43022, 740-427-5208, Fax 740-427-5417, e-mail kenyonreview@kenyon.edu
Pudding House Publications, 60 North Main Street, Johnstown, OH 43031, 740-967-6060; pudding@johnstown.net; www.puddinghouse.com
PUDDING MAGAZINE: THE INTERNATIONAL JOURNAL OF APPLIED POETRY, 60 North Main Street, Johnstown, OH 43031, 740-967-6060; pudding@johnstown.net; www.puddinghouse.com
OLD ABE'S NEWS, 400 Carriage Drive, Plain City, OH 43064-2101, 614-873-3896
FASTENING, 293 Hopewell Drive, Powell, OH 43065, 614-848-3232; 800-848-0304; FAX 614-848-5045
MAP AFICIONADO, 293 Hopewell Drive, Powell, OH 43065, 614-848-3232; 800-848-0304; FAX 614-848-5045
The Daniels Publishing Company, 10443 Shelley Road, Thornville, OH 43076
THE BOOK REPORT: Journal for Junior & Senior High School Librarians, 480 East Wilson Bridge Road #L, Worthington, OH 43085-2372
LIBRARY TALK: The Magazine for Elementary School Librarians, 480 East Wilson Bridge Road #L, Worthington, OH 43085-2372, 614-436-7107; fax 614-436-9490
Linworth Publishing, Inc., 480 East Wilson Bridge Road #L, Worthington, OH 43085-2372, 614-436-7107; FAX 614-436-9490
NANCY'S MAGAZINE, N's M Publications, PO Box 02108, Columbus, OH 43202, 614-298-0372
PAVEMENT SAW, PO Box 6291, Columbus, OH 43206, 614-263-7115; baratier@megsinet.net
Pavement Saw Press, PO Box 6291, Columbus, OH 43206, baratier@megsinet.net
DIONYSIA, Box 1500, Capital University, Columbus, OH 43209, 614-236-6563
THE JOURNAL, OSU Dept. of English, 164 W. 17th Avenue, 421 Denney Hall, Columbus, OH 43210-1370, 614-292-4076; fax 614-292-7816; e-mail thejournal05@pop.service.ohio-state.edu
Carpenter Press, PO Box 14387, Columbus, OH 43214
LOST AND FOUND TIMES, 137 Leland Ave, Columbus, OH 43214
Luna Bisonte Prods, 137 Leland Ave, Columbus, OH 43214, 614-846-4126
OHIOANA QUARTERLY, 65 S. Front Street, Suite 1105, Columbus, OH 43215, 614-466-3831, Fax 614-728-6974, e-mail ohioana@winslo.state.oh.us

Cartoon Books, PO Box 16973, Columbus, OH 43216, 614-224-4487, fax 614-224-4488
Galloway Press, 1520 Old Henderson Road, Suite 100, Columbus, OH 43220, 800-504-2273
Ecrivez!, P.O. Box 247491, Columbus, OH 43224, 614-253-0773; FAX 614-253-0774
Infinite Passion Publishing, PO Box 340815, Columbus, OH 43234, 614-792-0053; e-mail infipas@iwaynet.net
Gabriel's Horn Publishing Co., Inc., Box 141, Bowling Green, OH 43402, 419-352-1338; fax 419-352-1488
MID-AMERICAN REVIEW, Dept of English, Bowling Green State University, Bowling Green, OH 43403, 419-372-2725
Faded Banner Publications, PO Box 101, Bryan, OH 43506-0101, 419-636-3807; fax 419-636-3970
New Sins Press, 5804 Summit Street, Sylvania, OH 43560-1272
MARK, Student Union, Room 1501, University of Toledo, Toledo, OH 43606, 419-537-2373
Raven Rocks Press, 53650 Belmont Ridge Road, Beallsville, OH 43716, 614-926-1705
Franciscan University Press, 1235 University Boulevard, Steubenville, OH 43952, 740-283-6357, fax 740-283-6442
GRASSLANDS REVIEW, PO Box 626, Berea, OH 44017
THE LISTENING EYE, KSU Geauga Campus, 14111 Claridon-Troy Road, Burton, OH 44021, 440-286-3840; e-mail
    hy151@cleveland.freenet.edu
Senay Publishing Inc., PO Box 397, Chesterland, OH 44026, 216-256-4435, fax 216-256-2237
White Buck Publishing, 5187 Colorado Avenue, Sheffield Village, OH 44054-2338, 440-934-4454 phone/fax
FIELD, Rice Hall, Oberlin College, Oberlin, OH 44074, 440-775-8408; Fax 440-775-8124; oc.press@oberlin.edu
Oberlin College Press, Rice Hall, Oberlin College, Oberlin, OH 44074, 440-775-8408; Fax 440-775-8124; E-mail
    oc.press@oberlin.edu
Halle House Publishing, 5966 Halle Farm Drive, Willoughby, OH 44094-3076, 216-585-8687
BLOOD & FEATHERS: Poems of Survival, PO Box 55, Willoughby, OH 44096-0055, 440-951-1875
OHIO WRITER, PO Box 91801, Cleveland, OH 44101-0528
The New Dawn Press, 10801 Greenlawn Avenue, Cleveland, OH 44103, 216-431-9600; fax 216-431-4614; e-mail
    victorsapk.net
Cleveland State Univ. Poetry Center, 1983 East 24th Street, Cleveland, OH 44115-2400, 216-687-3986; Fax 216-687-6943;
    poetrycenter@popmail.csuohio.edu
Kenyette Productions, 20131 Champ Drive, Euclid, OH 44117-2208, 216-486-0544
THE FUNNY TIMES, PO Box 18530, Cleveland Heights, OH 44118, 216-371-8600
Legal Information Publications, 18221 East Park Drive, Cleveland, OH 44119-2019
Phelps Publishing Company, PO Box 22401, Cleveland, OH 44122, 216-433-2531, 216-295-2181
ROMANTIC HEARTS, PO Box 450669, Westlake, OH 44145-0612, 216-979-9793; D.Krauss@genie.com
Business Smarts, Inc., 3505 E. Royalton Road, #150, Broadview Heights, OH 44147, 808-639-4656, fax 216-526-1203,
    102563134@compuserve.com
Storytime Ink International, PO Box 470505, Broadview Heights, OH 44147, 440-838-4881; e-mail storytimeink@world-
    net.att.net
Writer's World Press, 35 N. Chillicothe Road, Unit D, Aurora, OH 44202-8741, 330-562-6667; Fax 330-562-1216;
    WritersWorld@juno.com
Briarwood Publishing, 1587 10th Street, Cuyahoga Falls, OH 44221-4635
IMPETUS, 4975 Comanche Trail, Stow, OH 44224, telephone/fax: 216-688-5210; E-mail: impetus@aol.com
Implosion Press, 4975 Comanche Trail, Stow, OH 44224, telphone/fax: 216-688-5210; E-mail: impetus@aol.com
Prometheus Enterprises, Inc., 60 Bellus Road, Hinckley, OH 44233, 216-278-2798, fax 216-278-2615, orders
    1-800-249-2498, 1-800-393-3415
Envirographics, Box 334, Hiram, OH 44234, (330) 527-5207
HIRAM POETRY REVIEW, Box 162, Hiram, OH 44234, 330-569-5331; fax 330-569-5449
Kent Information Services, Inc., 155 N. Water Street, Suite 205, Kent, OH 44240, 330-673-1300; Fax 330-673-6310;
    email@kentis.com; http://www.kentis.com
SPIRITCHASER, 3183 Sharon-Copley Road, Medina, OH 44256, 330-722-1561
Timothy A. Dimoff/SACS Consulting, 143 Northwest Avenue, Bldg. B-102, Tallmadge, OH 44278, 330-633-9551; Fax
    330-633-5862
Twin Sisters Productions, 1340 Home Avenue, Suite D, Akron, OH 44310-1302, 800-248-TWIN; 330-633-8900; FAX
    330-633-8988
KALEIDOSCOPE: INTERNATIONAL MAGAZINE OF LITERATURE, FINE ARTS, AND DISABILITY, United
    Disability Services, 701 S. Main Street, Akron, OH 44311-1019, 330-762-9755; 330-379-3349 (TDD), Fax 330-762-0912
NOBODADDIES, 2491 State Route 45 South, Salem, OH 44460, E-mail rice@salem.kent.edu
Alegra House Publishers, PO Box 1443-D, Warren, OH 44482, 216-372-2951
ICON, KSU-TC, 4314 Mahoning Avenue NW, Warren, OH 44483, 330-847-0571
PIG IRON, 26 North Phelps Street, PO Box 237, Youngstown, OH 44501, 216-747-6932; fax 216-747-0599
Pig Iron Press, 26 North Phelps Street, PO Box 237, Youngstown, OH 44501, 216-747-6932; fax 216-747-0599
SOS JAZZ, PO Box 1382, Youngstown, OH 44501
SOLO FLYER, 2115 Clearview NW, Massillon, OH 44646
ARTFUL DODGE, Department of English, College of Wooster, Wooster, OH 44691
Brittain Communications, PO Box 2567, North Canton, OH 44720, phone/fax 330-497-2304; email brittainak@aol.com
The Ashland Poetry Press, Ashland University, Ashland, OH 44805, 419-289-5110; FAX 419-289-5329
Bottom Dog Press, c/o Firelands College of BGSU, Huron, OH 44839, 419-433-5560
Cambric Press dba Emerald House, 208 Ohio Street, Huron, OH 44839-1514, 419-433-5660; 419-929-4203
Interalia/Design Books, PO Box 404, Oxford, OH 45056-0404, 513-523-6880; FAX 513-523-1553
Miami University Press, English Dept., Miami University, Oxford, OH 45056, 513-529-5110; Fax 513-529-1392; E-mail
    reissja@muohio.edu
HOBSON'S CHOICE, PO Box 98, Ripley, OH 45167, 513-392-4549
STORY, 1507 Dana Avenue, Cincinnati, OH 45207, 513-531-2222
Mosaic Press, 358 Oliver Road, Dept. 45, Cincinnati, OH 45215, 513-761-5977
Creative Consortium, Inc., 4850 Marieview Court, Ste. 101, Cincinnati, OH 45236-2012, 513-984-0614, 800-320-8631;
    Fax 513-984-0635; creatcon@fuse.net
SPITBALL: The Literary Baseball Magazine, 5560 Fox Road, Cincinnati, OH 45239-7271, 513-541-4296
Spirit of Arts Press, 7871 Ravencrest Court, Cincinnati, OH 45255-2426
THE ANTIOCH REVIEW, PO Box 148, Yellow Springs, OH 45387, 937-767-6389
Community Service, Inc., P.O. Box 243, Yellow Springs, OH 45387, 513-797-2161
COMMUNITY SERVICE NEWSLETTER, P.O. Box 243, Yellow Springs, OH 45387, 513-767-2161

PLAIN BROWN WRAPPER (PBW), 130 West Limestone, Yellow Springs, OH 45387, 513-767-7416
NEW THOUGHT JOURNAL, 2520 Evelyn Drive, Kettering, OH 45409, Ph/Fax 937-293-9717; E-mail; ntjmag@aol.com
THE VINCENT BROTHERS REVIEW, 4566 Northern Circle, Riverside, OH 45424-5733
FUNNY PAGES, PO Box 317025, Dayton, OH 45437, e-mail jworkman@erinet.com
Tomart Publications, 3300 Encrete Lane, Dayton, OH 45439-1944, 937-294-2250; Fax 937-294-1024
ENLIGHTENMENTS, 5449 Marina Drive, Dayton, OH 45449, 937-865-0767
Kettering Foundation, 200 Commons Road, Dayton, OH 45459-2799, 937-434-7300
KETTERING REVIEW, 200 Commons Road, Dayton, OH 45459-2799, 937-434-7300
CONFLICT OF INTEREST, 4701 East National Road, Springfield, OH 45505-1847, 330-630-5646 phone/Fax; E-mail
    PHartney@aol.com
Proper PH Publications, 4701 East National Road, Springfield, OH 45505-1847, 330-630-5646 phone/Fax; E-mail
    phartney@aol.com
THE GOOD RED ROAD, PO Box 750, Athens, OH 45701
MAMA'S LITTLE HELPER, PO Box 1127, Athens, OH 45701
THE OHIO REVIEW, 344 Scott Quad, Ohio University, Athens, OH 45701, 740-593-1900
QUARTER AFTER EIGHT, Ellis Hall, Ohio University, Athens, OH 45701
The Turquoise Butterfly Press, PO Box 750, Athens, OH 45701
CONFLUENCE, PO Box 336, Belpre, OH 45714, 304-422-3112; e-mail dbprather@prodigy.net
TOWPATHS, 101 Hillside Way, Marietta, OH 45750-2746, 740-374-6715
Watershed Books, 130 Warner Street, Marietta, OH 45750-3453, 800-484-1624 +(MCI code #)7036, Fax; 614-373-0253;
    e-mail 103043.1017@compuserve.com
RIVERWIND, General Studies, Hocking College, Nelsonville, OH 45764, 614-753-3591

OKLAHOMA

BYLINE, PO Box 130596, Edmond, OK 73013, 405-348-5591
Excelsior Cee Publishing, PO Box 5861, Norman, OK 73070, 405-329-3909; Fax 405-329-6886; ecp@oecadvantage.net;
    www.oecadvantage.net/ecp
Point Riders Press, PO Box 2731, Norman, OK 73070
TEXTURE, 3760 Cedar Ridge Drive, Norman, OK 73072, 405-366-7730
Texture Press, 3760 Cedar Ridge Drive, Norman, OK 73072, 405-366-7730
AMERICAN POETRY MONTHLY, PO Box 187, Sapulpa, OK 74067
MACHINEGUN MAGAZINE: New Lit. Quarterly, 601 S. Washington, Suite 281, Stillwater, OK 74074, E-mail
    chinaski00@aol.com
CIMARRON REVIEW, 205 Morrill Hall, Oklahoma State University, Stillwater, OK 74078-0135, 405-744-9476
JAMES JOYCE QUARTERLY, University of Tulsa, 600 S. College, Tulsa, OK 74104
NIMROD INTERNATIONAL, 600 South College Avenue, Tulsa, OK 74104-3126
TULSA STUDIES IN WOMEN'S LITERATURE, 600 S. College, Tulsa, OK 74104-3189, 918-631-2503, Fax
    918-584-0623; linda-frazier@utulsa.edu
University of Tulsa, 600 South College, Tulsa, OK 74104
Cardinal Press, Inc., 76 N Yorktown, Tulsa, OK 74110, 918-583-3651
Council Oak Books, 1350 East 15th Street, Tulsa, OK 74120, 918-587-6454; Fax 918-583-4995; oakie@ionet.net
Hawk Publishing Group, 6420 S. Richmond Avenue, Tulsa, OK 74136, 918-492-3854; fax 918-492-2120; e-mail
    willbern@mindspring.com; website www.hawkpub.com
Vista Mark Publications, 4528 S. Sheridan, Suite 114, Tulsa, OK 74145, 918-665-6030; Fax 918-665-6039
Partners In Publishing, Box 50347, Tulsa, OK 74150, 918-584-5906
Sparrow Hawk Press, 22 Summit Ridge Drive, Tahlequah, OK 74464, 918-456-3421

OREGON

Cobra Publishing, PO Box 217, Antelope, OR 97001, 503-244-0805; e-mail bbeas10010@aol.com
DISSONANCE MAGAZINE, 1315 NW 185TH Ave. #220, Beaverton, OR 97006-1947, 802-860-6285
LUNO, 31960 SE Chin Street, Boring, OR 97009, 503-663-5153
Vitreous Group/Camp Colton, Camp Colton, Colton, OR 97017, 503-824-3150
Arch Grove Press, PO Box 2387, Lake Oswego, OR 97035, 503-624-7811 phone/fax
Culinary Arts Ltd., PO Box 2157, Lake Oswego, OR 97035, 503-639-4549; FAX 503-620-4933
THE KITHARA, PO Box 1941, Lake Oswego, OR 97035, 503-251-4809
White Phoenix Publishing, PO Box 2157, Lake Oswego, OR 97035, 503-639-4549; Fax 503-620-4933; wphoen-
    ixp@aol.com
Trout Creek Press, 5976 Billings Road, Parkdale, OR 97041, 503-352-6494; e-Mail Lfh42@AOL.COM
CLACKAMAS LITERARY REVIEW, 19600 South Molalla Avenue, Oregon City, OR 97045
Flying Pencil Publications, 33126 Callahan Road, Scappoose, OR 97056
Carpe Diem Publishing, 1705 E. 17th Street, #400, The Dalles, OR 97058, 503-296-1552, waconner@aol.com
THIRST (CYBERTHIRST), 1705 E. 17th Street, #400, The Dalles, OR 97058, 503-296-1552; waconner@aol.com
NewSage Press, PO Box 607, Troutdale, OR 97060-0607
Accent on Music, 19363 Willamette Drive #252, West Linn, OR 97068, 503-699-1814; FAX 503-699-1813; e-mail
    accentm@teleport.com
Magical Music Express, 19363 Willamette Dr #252, West Linn, OR 97068, Voice 503-699-1814, e-mail
    accentm@teleport.com
BookPartners, Inc., PO Box 922, Wilsonville, OR 97070, 503-682-9821; FAX 503-682-8684; bpbooks@teleport.com
Doral Publishing, 8560 SW Salish Lane, #300, Wilsonville, OR 97070-9625, 503-683-3307; Fax 503-682-2648
Kodiak Media Group, PO Box 1029-DB, Wilsonville, OR 97070, FAX 503-625-4087
Alioth Press, PO Box 1554, Beaverton, OR 97075, 503-644-2927
The Bacchae Press, c/o The Brown Financial Group, 10 Sixth Street, Astoria, OR 97103-5315, 503-325-7972; FAX
    503-325-7959; 800-207-4358; E-mail brown@pacifier.com
Gaff Press, PO Box 1024, 114 SW Willow Lane, Astoria, OR 97103, 503-325-8288; e-mail gaffpres@pacifier.com
Mountain Publishing, PO Box 1747, Hillsboro, OR 97123, 503-628-3995; fax 503-628-0203; toll free 800-879-8719
TIMBER TIMES, PO Box 219, Hillsboro, OR 97123
Beyond Words Publishing, Inc., 20827 NW Cornell Road, Ste. 500, Hillsboro, OR 97124-9808, 503-693-8700, fax
    503-693-6888, e-mail BeyondWord@aol.com

COZY DETECTIVE MYSTERY MAGAZINE, 686 Jakes Court, McMinnville, OR 97128, 503-435-1212; Fax 503-472-4896; e-mail papercapers@yahoo.com
Meager Ink Press, 686 Jakes Court, McMinnville, OR 97128, 503-435-1212; detectivemag@onlinemac.com
Peavine Publications, Box 1264, McMinnville, OR 97128, 503-472-1933; e-mail peapub@pnn.com
Health Plus Publishers, PO Box 1027, Sherwood, OR 97140, 503-625-0589; fax 503-625-1525
Sibyl Publications, Inc, 1007 SW Westwood Drive, Portland, OR 97201, 503-293-8391; 1-800-240-8566; fax 503-293-8941
HUBBUB, 5344 S.E. 38th Avenue, Portland, OR 97202, 503-775-0370
Peninhand Press, 3665 Southeast Tolman, Portland, OR 97202
Strawberry Hill Press, 3848 SE Division St, Portland, OR 97202-1641, 503-235-5989
INFOCUS, 319 SW Washington Street, Suite 710, Portland, OR 97204-2618, 503-227-3393
Timber Press, 133 SW Second Avenue, Suite 450, Portland, OR 97204-3527
Blue Heron Publishing, Inc., 1234 SW Stark Street, Portland, OR 97205, 503-221-6841; Fax 503-221-6843; bhp@teleport.com; www.teleport.com/~bhp
GENERAL MAGAZINE, 929 SW Salmon, Portland, OR 97205, 503-355-2487
Sulisa Publishing, 625 SW 10th Avenue, PMB 388C, Portland, OR 97205-2788, 503-233-5232; e-mail sulisa@teleport.com
Continuing Education Press, Portland State University, PO Box 1394, Portland, OR 97207
JOURNAL OF PROCESS ORIENTED PSYCHOLOGY, PO Box 8898, Portland, OR 97207-8898, 503-222-3395
Lao Tse Press, Ltd., PO Box 8898, Portland, OR 97207-8898, 503-222-3395; fax 503-222-3778
LEO Productions LLC., PO Box 1333, Portland, OR 97207, 360-694-0595, fax 360-694-8808
PORTLAND REVIEW, PO Box 347, Portland, OR 97207-0347, 503-725-4533
Feral House, PO Box 3466, Portland, OR 97208, 503-276-8375
Vestibular Disorders Association, PO Box 4467, Portland, OR 97208-4467, 503-229-7705; fax 503-229-8064; toll-free 1-800-837-8428; e-mail veda@vestibular.org; website http://www.vestibular.org
Mr. Cogito Press, 2518 N.W. Savier, Portland, OR 97210, 503-233-8131, 226-4135
MENTOR MAGAZINE, 5707 NE 15TH Avenue, Portland, OR 97211-4974, 503-282-2108
MUSIC NEWS, 5536 NE Hassalo, Portland, OR 97213, 503-281-1191
Beynch Press Publishing Company, 1928 S.E. Ladd Avenue, Portland, OR 97214, 503-232-0433
The Eighth Mountain Press, 624 Southeast 29th Avenue, Portland, OR 97214, 503-233-3936; fax 503-233-0774; e-mail Soapston@teleport.com
Quiet Lion Press, 7215 SW LaView Drive, Portland, OR 97219, 503-771-1907
RAIN CITY REVIEW, 7215 SW LaView Drive, Portland, OR 97219, 503-771-1907
Paradise Publications, 8110 SW Wareham, Portland, OR 97223, 503-246-1555
Gloger Family Books, PO Box 6955, Portland, OR 97228
Communicom Publishing Company, 19300 NW Sauvie Island Road, Portland, OR 97231, 503-621-3049
Irvington St. Press, Inc., 3439 NE Sandy Boulevard #143, Portland, OR 97232, E-mail; pdxia@aol.com
Blue Unicorn Press, Inc., PO Box 40300, Portland, OR 97240-3826, 503-775-9322
Juniper Sun Publishing, 10519 SE Center Street, Portland, OR 97266, 503-760-2852
Collectors Press, Inc., PO Box 230986, Portland, OR 97281, 503-684-3030, fax 503-684-3777
Far Corner Books, PO Box 82157, Portland, OR 97282
PUNCTURE, PO Box 14806, Portland, OR 97293, e-mail puncture@teleport.com
World Peace University Publications, PO Box 20728, Portland, OR 97294-0728, 503-252-3639, fax 503-255-5216
THE BEAR DELUXE, PO Box 10342, Portland, OR 97296, 503-242-1047; Fax 503-243-2645; bear@teleport.com
Metamorphous Press, PO Box 10616, Portland, OR 97296, 503-228-4972; fax 503-223-9117
Princess Publishing, PO Box 25406, Portland, OR 97298, 503-297-1565
Dimi Press, 3820 Oak Hollow Lane, SE, Salem, OR 97302, 503-364-7698; fax 503-364-9727
MASTER THOUGHTS, PO Box 4608, Salem, OR 97302-8608, 503-362-9634
THEOLOGIA 21, PO Box 4608, Salem, OR 97302-8608, 503-362-9634
Doggerel Press, PO Box 985, Salem, OR 97308, 503-588-2926
Energeia Publishing, Inc., PO Box 985, Salem, OR 97308, 503-588-2926
ICARUS WAS RIGHT, PO Box 13731, Salem, OR 97309-1731, 619-461-0497; icaruswas@pobox.com
Itidwitir Publishing, PO Box 13731, Salem, OR 97309-1731, 619-461-0497; icaruswas@pobox.com
Alta Research, 131 NW 4th Street #290, Corvallis, OR 97330-4702, 500-288-ALTA; 541-929-5738; alta@alta-research.com
Ecopress, 1029 NE Kirsten Place, Corvallis, OR 97330-6823, 541-758-7545
Oregon State University Press, 101 Waldo Hall, Corvallis, OR 97331, 541-737-3166
RUBBERSTAMPMADNESS, 408 SW Monroe #210, Corvallis, OR 97333
CALYX: A Journal of Art and Literature by Women, PO Box B, Corvallis, OR 97339, 541-753-9384
Calyx Books, PO Box B, Corvallis, OR 97339
Grapevine Publications, Inc., PO Box 2449, Corvallis, OR 97339-2449, 503-754-0583; fax 503-754-6508
THE GROWING EDGE MAGAZINE, PO Box 1027, Corvallis, OR 97339, 541-757-0027; FAX 541-757-0028
The Apostolic Press, 547 NW Coast Street, Newport, OR 97365, 503-265-4641
Gahmken Press, PO Box 1467, Newport, OR 97365
Saddle Mountain Press, 425 SW Coast Highway, Newport, OR 97365, 541-574-6004; 800-668-6105; oregonbook@net-bridge.net
DWELLING PORTABLY, Light Living Library, Po Box 190—DB, Philomath, OR 97370
BIRTHKIT NEWSLETTER, PO Box 2672, Eugene, OR 97402, 503-344-7438
BRIDGES: A Journal for Jewish Feminists and Our Friends, PO Box 24839, Eugene, OR 97402, 541-935-5720, E-mail: ckinberg@pond.net
MIDWIFERY TODAY, Box 2672, Eugene, OR 97402, 503-344-7438
Midwifery Today Books, PO Box 2672, Eugene, OR 97402, 541-344-7438; Fax 541-344-1422; midwifery@aol.com; www.members.aol.com/midwifery/
SONAR MAP, PO Box 25243, Eugene, OR 97402, Voice/fax: 541-688-1523; eleg-sci@efn.org
HYPATIA: A Journal of Feminist Philosophy, University of Oregon, Center for Study of Women in Society, Eugene, OR 97403-1201
NORTHWEST REVIEW, 369 P.L.C., University of Oregon, Eugene, OR 97403, 503-346-3957
RAIN MAGAZINE, PO Box 30097, Eugene, OR 97403
Rainy Day Press, 1147 East 26th, Eugene, OR 97403, 503-484-4626
SILVERFISH REVIEW, PO Box 2541, Eugene, OR 97403, 503-344-5060

Circa Press, PO Box 5856, Eugene, OR 97405, 541-465-9111
Earth Magic Productions, Inc., PO Box 50668, Eugene, OR 97405, 541-344-6394; fax 541-485-8773; E-mail support@earthmagic
NATIONAL MASTERS NEWS, PO Box 50098, Eugene, OR 97405, 541-343-7716; Fax 541-345-2436; natmanews@aol.com
Sandpiper Press, PO Box 286, Brookings, OR 97415-0028, 541-469-5588
BOOK DEALERS WORLD, PO Box 606, Cottage Grove, OR 97424-0026
North American Bookdealers Exchange, PO Box 606, Cottage Grove, OR 97424-0026
Conscious Living, PO Box 9, Drain, OR 97435
HEALTH MASTER, PO Box 9, Drain, OR 97435
Fall Creek Press, PO Box 1127, Fall Creek, OR 97438, 503-744-0938
POETIC SPACE: Poetry & Fiction, PO Box 11157, Eugene, OR 97440
TIMELINES, Newsletter of the Hemlock Society U.S.A., PO Box 11830, Eugene, OR 97440
The Woodbridge Group, PO Box 849, Eugene, OR 97448, 541-683-6731
Beacon Point Press, PO Box 460, Junction City, OR 97448
Brannon Enterprises, Inc., 1224 NE Walnut Street, #337, Roseburg, OR 97470-5106
HWD Publishing, PO Box 220D, Veneta, OR 97487, 1-800-935-7323
nine muses books, 3541 Kent Creek Road, Winston, OR 97496, 541-679-6674; E-mail mw9muses@teleport.com
Keyboard Workshop, PO Box 700, Medford, OR 97501, 664-2317
PSI Research/The Oasis Press/Hellgate Press, PO Box 3727, Central Point, OR 97502, 503-479-9464 (CA); 800-228-2275
Home Power, Inc., PO Box 275, Ashland, OR 97520, 916-475-3179
HOME POWER MAGAZINE, PO Box 520, Ashland, OR 97520, 916-475-3179; e-Mail karen.perez@home power.org, Order line 800-707-6585, 916-475-0830, Fax 916-475-0941
THE PATRIOT, PO Box 1172, Ashland, OR 97520, 503-482-2578
Quicksilver Productions, P.O.Box 340, Ashland, OR 97520, 541-482-5343, Fax; 541-482-0960
Runaway Publications, PO Box 1172, Ashland, OR 97520, 503-482-2578
SHAMAN'S DRUM: A Journal of Experiential Shamanism, PO Box 97, Ashland, OR 97520, 541-552-0839
SPROUTLETTER, Box 62, Ashland, OR 97520, 800-746-7413
Valentine Publishing & Drama Co., PO Box 1378, Ashland, OR 97520-0046, 503-773-7035
World Wide Publishing Corp., PO Box 105, Ashland, OR 97520
Log Cabin Manuscripts, PO Box 507, Jacksonville, OR 97530-9316, 800-995-3652
Castle Peak Editions, PO Box 277, Murphy, OR 97533, 503-846-6152
Angst World Library, PO Box 593, Selma, OR 97538-0593
Talent House Press, 1306 Talent Avenue, Talent, OR 97540, 541-535-9041
The Blue Oak Press, HC10 Box 621, Lakeview, OR 97630-9704, 916-994-3397
THIS IS IMPORTANT, PO Box 336, Sprague River, OR 97639, 503-533-2486
Gilgal Publications, PO Box 3399, Sunriver, OR 97707, 541-593-8418
Multnomah Publishers, Inc., PO Box 1720, Sisters, OR 97759, 541-549-1144; Fax 541-549-0432; mtennesen@multnomah-publ.com
The Bear Wallow Publishing Company, 809 South 12th Street, La Grande, OR 97850, 541-962-7864
CALAPOOYA, School of Arts and Sciences, Eastern Oregon University, La Grande, OR 97850, 541-962-3633
Wordcraft of Oregon, PO Box 3235, La Grande, OR 97850, 503-963-0723; E-mail wordcraft@oregontrail.net

PENNSYLVANIA

TAPROOT LITERARY REVIEW, Box 204, Ambridge, PA 15003, 412-266-8476; E-mail taproot10@aol.com
Rainbow's End, 354 Golden Grove Road, Baden, PA 15005, 800-596-RBOW; Fax 415-266-4997; www.adpages.com/rbebooks; e-mail btucker833@aol.com
THE AGUILAR EXPRESSION, 1329 Gilmore Avenue, Donora, PA 15033, 412-379-8019
ABELexpress, PO Box 668, Carnegie, PA 15106-0668, 412-279-0672; fax 412-279-5012; email ken@abelexpress.com
Chess Enterprises, 107 Crosstree Road, Coraopolis, PA 15108, 412-262-2138; fax 412-262-2138
EN PASSANT, 107 Crosstree Road, Coraopolis, PA 15108
Bookhaven Press, LLC, PO Box 1243, Moon Township, PA 15108, 412-262-5578; Fax 412-262-5417; e-Mail bookhaven@aol.com; website http://federaljobs.net
STANDARD DEVIATIONS, 127 Greenlea Drive, Moon Twp., PA 15108-2609, 412-269-4167
LILLIPUT REVIEW, 282 Main Street, Pittsburgh, PA 15201
THE POETRY EXPLOSION NEWSLETTER (THE PEN), PO Box 4725, Pittsburgh, PA 15206
SISTERSONG: Women Across Cultures, PO Box 7405, Pittsburgh, PA 15213, E-mail sistersong@trfn.clpgh.org; www.sistersong.org
5 AM, 1109 Milton Avenue, Pittsburgh, PA 15218
LATIN AMERICAN LITERARY REVIEW, 121 Edgewood Avenue, 1st Floor, Pittsburgh, PA 15218-1513, 412-371-9023; fax 412-371-9025
Latin American Literary Review Press, 121 Edgewood Avenue, 1st Floor, Pittsburgh, PA 15218-1513, 412-371-9023; FAX 412-371-9025
ATROCITY, 2419 Greensburg Pike, Pittsburgh, PA 15221
G'RAPH, 2419 Greensburg Pike, Pittsburgh, PA 15221
PROCEEDINGS OF THE SPANISH INQUISITION, 2419 Greensburg Pike, Pittsburgh, PA 15221
Nite-Owl Press, 137 Pointview Avenue, Suite 100, Pittsburgh, PA 15227-3131, 412-882-2259
NITE-WRITER'S INTERNATIONAL LITERARY ARTS JOURNAL, 137 Pointview Avenue, Suite 100, Pittsburgh, PA 15227-3131, 412-381-6893
CREATIVE NONFICTION, 5501 Walnut St., #202, Pittsburgh, PA 15232-2329, 412-688-0304; fax 412-683-9173
THE CONSTANTIAN, The Constantian Society, 840 Old Washington Rd, McMurray, PA 15317-3228, 724-942-5374
QP Publishing, PO Box 237, Finleyville, PA 15332-0237, 724-348-8949
QUALITY QUIPS NEWSLETTER, Box 237, Finleyville, PA 15332-0237, 724-348-8949
Rhizome, PO Box 265, Greensboro, PA 15338
FLIPSIDE, Dixon Hall, California University of PA, California, PA 15419, 412-938-4586
THE PLOUGH, Spring Valley Bruderhof, R.D. 2, Box 446, Farmington, PA 15437-9506, 412-329-1100; fax 412-329-0942, 800-521-0011
MacDonald/Sward Publishing Company, Box 104A, RD 3, Greensburg, PA 15601, 724-832-7767

699

Outdoor Enterprises, Inc., PO Box 531, Irwin, PA 15642, 724-863-3865
Herald Press, 616 Walnut Avenue, Scottdale, PA 15683, 724-887-8500
ON THE LINE, 616 Walnut Avenue, Scottdale, PA 15683
Cherubic Press, PO Box 5036, Johnstown, PA 15904-5036, 814-535-4300, Fax: 814-535-4580
Jessee Poet Publications, Box 113, VAMC, 325 New Castle Road, Butler, PA 16001
POETS AT WORK, Box 113, VAMC, 325 New Castle Road, Butler, PA 16001
THEY WON'T STAY DEAD!, 11 Werner Road, Greenville, PA 16125, 412-588-3471
Libertarian Press, Inc./American Book Distributors, PO Box 309, Grove City, PA 16127-0309, 724-458-5861
Shenango River Books, PO Box 631, Sharon, PA 16146, 412-342-3811
FULL DISCLOSURE, PO Box 1533, Oil City, PA 16301-5533
ALLEGHENY REVIEW, Box 32, Allegheny College, Meadville, PA 16335, 814-332-6553
JOURNAL OF ASIAN MARTIAL ARTS, 821 West 24th Street, Erie, PA 16502, 814-455-9517; fax 814-526-5262; e-mail
info@goviamedia.com; website www.goviamedia.com
Via Media Publishing Company, 821 W. 24th Street, Erie, PA 16502, 814-455-9517; fax 814-526-5262; e-mail
info@goviamedia.com; website www.goviamedia.com
THE BOBBY STAR NEWSLETTER, PO Box 3756, Erie, PA 16508
X-it Press, PO Box 3756, Erie, PA 16508
Pennsylvania State University Press, Penn State Press, Suite C, 820 N. University Drive, University Park, PA 16802-1711,
814-865-1327
SHAW: THE ANNUAL OF BERNARD SHAW STUDIES, Penn State Press, Suite C, 820 N. University Drive, University
Park, PA 16802-1711, 814-865-1327
THE LOST PERUKE, PO Box 8125, State College, PA 16803-8125
The Carnation Press, PO Box 101, State College, PA 16804, 814-238-3577
Strata Publishing, Inc., PO Box 1303, State College, PA 16804, 814-234-8545, fax 814-238-7222, www.stratapub.com
RAFTERS, Calder Square PO Box 10929, State College, PA 16805-0929, 814-867-4073; mdu103@psu.edu
The Press at Foggy Bottom, RR 4 Box 859, Little Marsh, PA 16950, 717-376-2718
Exhorter Publications International, 323 W. High Street, Elizabethtown, PA 17022-2141
FAT TUESDAY, 560, Manada Gap Road, Grantville, PA 17028, 717-469-7159
Markowski International Publishers, 1 Oakglade Circle, Hummelstown, PA 17036-9525, 717-566-0468; FAX
717-566-6423
Pine Press, RR 1 Box 198B, Loysville, PA 17047-9726, 717-789-4466
Logodaedalus, PO Box 14193, Harrisburg, PA 17104
LOGODAEDALUS, PO Box 14193, Harrisburg, PA 17104
THE BOTTOM LINE PUBLICATIONS, HCR-13, Box 21AA, Artemas, PA 17211-9405, 814-458-3102
FELICITY, HCR-13, Box 21AA, Artemas, PA 17211-9405, 814-458-3102
MY LEGACY, HCR-13, Box 21AA, Artemas, PA 17211-9405, 814-458-3102
OMNIFIC, HCR-13, Box 21AA, Artemas, PA 17211-9405, 814-458-3102
Camel Press, Box 212, Needmore, PA 17238, 717-573-4526
DUST (From the Ego Trip), Box 212, Needmore, PA 17238, 717-573-4526
Burd Street Press, PO Box 152, 63 W. Burd Street, Shippensburg, PA 17257, 717-532-2237; FAX 717-532-7704
Ragged Edge Press, PO Box 152, 63 West Burd Street, Shippensburg, PA 17257, 717-532-2237; FAX 717-532-7704
White Mane Publishing Company, Inc., 63 West Burd Street, PO Box 152, Shippensburg, PA 17257, 717-532-2237; fax
717-532-7704
Shadowlight Press, PO Box 746, Biglerville, PA 17307
THE GETTYSBURG REVIEW, Gettysburg College, Gettysburg, PA 17325, 717-337-6770
BIG WORLD, PO Box 8743-DB, Lancaster, PA 17601, 717-569-0217; E-mail bigworld@bigworld.com
MEDIPHORS, PO Box 327, Bloomsburg, PA 17815, e-mail mediphor@ptd.net; website www.mediphors.org
The Press of Appletree Alley, Box 608 138 South Third Street, Lewisburg, PA 17837
WEST BRANCH, Bucknell Hall, Bucknell University, Lewisburg, PA 17837, 570-577-1440 or 577-1554
THE SPIRIT GARDEN, RD 1, Box 149, Pitman, PA 17964
SING OUT! The Folk Song Magazine, PO Box 5460, Bethlehem, PA 18015-0460, 610-865-5366; Fax 610-865-5129;
info@singout.org
FREEDOM OF EXPRESSION (FOE), PO Box 4, Bethlehem, PA 18016, 215-866-9326
TWO RIVERS REVIEW, 215 McCartney Street, Easton, PA 18042, 610-559-3887; tworiversreview@juno.com;
www.members.tripod.com/~tworiversreview/index.html
POETS' PAPER, PO Box 85, Easton, PA 18044-0085, 610-559-3887; Irregular@enter.net
Log Cabin Publishers, PO Box 1536, Allentown, PA 18105, 610-434-2448
Desk-Drawer Micropress, 209 W. Ann Street, Milford, PA 18337
KELTIC FRINGE, PO Box 270, Greentown, PA 18426-0270, 717-679-2745
Himalayan Institute Press, RR 1, Box 405, Honesdale, PA 18431, 717-253-5551; 800-822-4547; fax 717-251-7812; e-mail
hibooks@epix.net
STROKER, c/o Trantino, RR 2 Box 280, Harveys Lake, PA 18618-9503
Belfry Books, RR 2 Box 2090, Laceyville, PA 18623, 717-869-2942; Fax 717-869-1031
The Bradford Press, RR 2 Box 2090, Laceyville, PA 18623, 717-869-2942; Fax 717-869-1031
Hands & Heart Books, RR 2 Box 2090, Laceyville, PA 18623, 717-869-2942; Fax 717-869-1031
Toad Hall, Inc., RR 2 Box 2090, Laceyville, PA 18623, 717-869-2942; Fax 717-869-1031
Toad Hall Press, RR 2 Box 2090, Laceyville, PA 18623, 717-869-1031
MATCHBOOK, 242 North Broad Street, Doylestown, PA 18901, 215-489-7755; Fax 215-340-3965
Raw Dog Press, 151 S. West Street, Doylestown, PA 18901, 215-345-6838
THE PRAGMATIST, Box 392, Forest Grove, PA 18922, FAX: 215-348-8006
Alpha Beat Press, 31 Waterloo Street, New Hope, PA 18938, 215-862-0299
ALPHA BEAT SOUP, Alpha Beat Press, 31 Waterloo Street, New Hope, PA 18938
BOUILLABAISSE, 31 Waterloo Street, New Hope, PA 18938, 215-862-0299
COKEFISH, 31 Waterloo Street, New Hope, PA 18938
Cokefish Press, 31 Waterloo Street, New Hope, PA 18938
THE FREEDONIA GAZETTE, 335 Fieldstone Drive, New Hope, PA 18938, 215-862-9734
Strategic Press, 774 Morwood Road, Teiford, PA 18969, 215-723-8422; 800-974-4393; strategic4@aol.com
FOOD WRITER, 20 West Athens Avenue, Ardmore, PA 19003, 610-896-2879; E-mail foodwriter@aol.com;

www.food-journalist.net
Merwood Books, 237 Merwood Lane, Ardmore, PA 19003, 215-947-3934; fax 610-896-5853
Page One, 20 W. Athens Avenue, Ardmore, PA 19003-1308, 610-896-2879; e-mail pageone1@aol.com
SUBSCRIBE, Ideas and Marketing Tips for Newsletter Publishers, 20 W. Athens Avenue, Ardmore, PA 19003-1308, 610-896-2879; E-mail pageone1@aol.com
Whitmore Publishing Company, 35 Cricket Terrace, Ardmore, PA 19003, 215-896-6116
GRAY AREAS, PO Box 808, Broomall, PA 19008
VERSE: A Journal of Poetry & Poetics, 33 Lowry's Lane, Rosemont, PA 19010
WIDENER REVIEW, Humanities Division, Widener Univ., Chester, PA 19013, 610-499-4341
Black Bear Publications, 1916 Lincoln Street, Croydon, PA 19021-8026
BLACK BEAR REVIEW, Black Bear Publications, 1916 Lincoln Street, Croydon, PA 19021, E-mail bbreview@aol.com; Website http://members.aol.com//bbreview/index.htm
TRANSCENDENT VISIONS, 251 South Olds Boulevard, 84-E, Fairless Hills, PA 19030-3426, 215-547-7159
The Aldine Press, Ltd., 304 South Tyson Avenue, Glenside, PA 19038
HELLAS: A Journal of Poetry & the Humanities, 304 South Tyson Avenue, Glenside, PA 19038, 215-884-1086
Waverly House Publishing, PO Box 1053, Glenside, PA 19038, 215-884-5873; 1-800-858-2253; e-mail info@natsel.com; website www.natsel.com
WOMAN'S ART JOURNAL, 1711 Harris Road, Laverock, PA 19038-7208, 215-233-0639
Haverford Business Press, PO Box 507, Haverford, PA 19041, 610-525-5965; Fax 610-525-9785; lberger@voicenet.com
J & J Consultants, Inc., 603 Olde Farm Road, Media, PA 19063, 610-565-9692; Fax 610-565-9694; wjones13@juno.com; www.members.tripod.com/walterjones/
MAD POETS REVIEW, PO Box 1248, Media, PA 19063-8248
NEW ALTERNATIVES, 603 Ole Farm Road, Media, PA 19063, 610-565-9692; Fax 610-565-9694; wjones13@juno.com; www.members.tripod/walterjones
GAUNTLET: Exploring the Limits of Free Expression, 309 Powell Road, Springfield, PA 19064, 610-328-5476
Deltiologists of America, PO Box 8, Norwood, PA 19074, 610-485-8572
POSTCARD CLASSICS, PO Box 8, Norwood, PA 19074, 215-485-8572
DWAN, Box 411, Swarthmore, PA 19081, e-mail dsmith3@swarthmore.edu
ATS Publishing, 996 Old Eagle School Road, Suite 1105, Wayne, PA 19087, 610-688-6000
Our Child Press, PO Box 74, Wayne, PA 19087, 610-964-0606; Fax 610-964-0938; ocp98@aol.com; www.members.aol.com/ocp98/index.html
RECONSTRUCTIONIST, Federation of Reconstructionist Congregations and Havurot, Church Road & Greenwood Avenue, Wyncote, PA 19095, 215-887-1988
Reconstructionist Press, Church Road & Greenwood Avenue, Wyncote, PA 19095, 215-887-1988
AMERICAN POETRY REVIEW, 1721 Walnut St., Philadelphia, PA 19103, 215-496-0439
Jewish Publication Society, 1930 Chestnut Street, Philadelphia, PA 19103, 215-564-5925; Fax 215-564-6640
Running Press, 125 South 22nd Street, Philadelphia, PA 19103, 215-567-5080
CASTAWAYS, c/o Derek Davis, 3311 Baring Street, Philadelphia, PA 19104
Locks Art Publications, 600 Washington Square South, Philadelphia, PA 19106, 215-629-1000
Singing Horse Press, PO Box 40034, Philadelphia, PA 19106
WordWorkers Press, 115 Arch Street, Philadelphia, PA 19106-2003, 215-925-2838; 800-357-6016; e-mail eye@independenteye.org
AXE FACTORY REVIEW, PO Box 40691, Philadelphia, PA 19107
Cynic Press, PO Box 40691, Philadelphia, PA 19107
MAGNET MAGAZINE, 1218 Chestnut Street, Suite 808, Philadelphia, PA 19107, 215-413-8570; fax 215-413-8569
VIRTUTE ET MORTE MAGAZINE, PO Box 63113, Philadelphia, PA 19114-0813, 215-671-6419 pager, 215-338-8234
Winchester/G. Ander Books, PO Box 11662, Philadelphia, PA 19116, www.dynamicmarches.com
Golden Aura Publishing, 440 West Sedgwick Street, 120D, Philadelphia, PA 19119
Innisfree Press, 136 Roumfort Road, Philadelphia, PA 19119-1632, 215-247-4085 fax 215 247-2343 email InnisfreeP@aol.com
JOURNAL OF AESTHETICS AND ART CRITICISM, Dept of Philosophy, Anderson Hall 7th Floor, Temple University, Philadelphia, PA 19122, 502-852-0458; FAX 502-852-0459; email: jaac@blue.temple.edu
Radnor-Hill Publishing, Inc., PO Box 41051, Philadelphia, PA 19127, 215-483-1126; FAX 215-483-4079
AMERICAN WRITING: A Magazine, 4343 Manayunk Avenue, Philadelphia, PA 19128
Nierika Editions, 4343 Manayunk Avenue, Philadelphia, PA 19128, 215-483-7051
Bloody Someday Press, 3721 Midvale Avenue, Philadelphia, PA 19129, 610-667-6687; FAX 215-951-0342; E-mail poettes@erols.com; website http://www.libertynet.org/bsomeday
Recon Publications, PO Box 14602, Philadelphia, PA 19134
Banshee Press, PO Box 11186, Philadelphia, PA 19136-6186
ONE TRICK PONY, PO Box 11186, Philadelphia, PA 19136-6186
THE WEIRD NEWS, 7393 Rugby Street, Philadelphia, PA 19138-1236
PEDIATRICS FOR PARENTS, 747 South 3rd Street #3, Philadelphia, PA 19147-3324
SYMBIOTIC OATMEAL, PO Box 14938, Philadelphia, PA 19149
Whitford Press, 4880 Lower Valley Road, Atglen, PA 19310, 610-593-1777; Fax 610-593-2002
Riverstone, A Press for Poetry, 1184A MacPherson Drive, West Chester, PA 19380
Owlswick Press, 123 Crooked Lane, King of Prussia, PA 19406-2570, 215-382-5415
Morgan-Rand Publishing, 1 Sentry Parkway #1000, Blue Bell, PA 19422, 215-938-5511, Fax; 215-938-5549
Dufour Editions Inc., PO Box 7, Chester Springs, PA 19425-0007, 610-458-5005; FAX 610-458-7103
QECE: QUESTION EVERYTHING. CHALLENGE EVERYTHING., 406 Main Street #3C, Collegeville, PA 19426, e-mail qece@aol.com
QUESTION EVERYTHING CHALLENGE EVERYTHING (QECE), 406 Main Street #3C, Collegeville, PA 19426, e-mail qece@aol.com
Reflective Books, PO Box 26128, Collegeville, PA 19426-0128, 800-489-7170; fax 610-489-1841; e-mail cdutchlong@aol.com; website www.dokkencorp.com/reflective books
BERN PORTER INTERNATIONAL, PO Box 553, Royersford, PA 19468
YARROW, A JOURNAL OF POETRY, English Dept., Lytle Hall, Kutztown State University, Kutztown, PA 19530, 683-4353

701

PUERTO RICO

Good Karma Publications, Villa Interamericana Calle 7, G-9, San German, PR 00683, 787-892-2346; email Devashish@igc.org

RHODE ISLAND

Lost Roads Publishers, 351 Nayatt Road, Barrington, RI 02806-4336, 401-245-8069
Seacoast Information Services, 135 Auburn Road, Charlestown, RI 02813-6103, 401-364-6419
MERLYN'S PEN: Fiction, Essays, and Poems By America's Teens, Merlyn's Pen, Inc., PO Box 910, East Greenwich, RI 02818-0964, 401-885-5175; www.merlynspen.com
The Brookdale Press, 566 E. Shore Rd., Jamestown, RI 02835, 203-322-2474
Aegis Publishing Group, Ltd., 796 Aquidneck Avenue, Newport, RI 02842, 401-849-4200; FAX 401-849-4231
The Saunderstown Press, 54 Camp Avenue, North Kingstown, RI 02852, 401-295-8810; Fax 401-294-9939
SAT SANDESH: THE MESSAGE OF THE MASTERS, 680 Curtis Corner Road, Wakefield, RI 02879, (401) 783-0662
THE GODDESS OF THE BAY, PO Box 8214, Warwick, RI 02888, E-mail Belindafox@aol.com
THE HUNTED NEWS, PO Box 9101, Warwick, RI 02889, 401-739-2279
The Subourbon Press, PO Box 9101, Warwick, RI 02889, 401-739-2279
Kingston Press, PO Box 86, West Kingston, RI 02892-0086, 401-789-6199; Fax 401-789-5780
ITALIAN AMERICANA, University of Rhode Island, 80 Washington Street, Providence, RI 02903-1803
Burning Deck Press, 71 Elmgrove Avenue, Providence, RI 02906
Copper Beech Press, P O Box 2578, English Department, Providence, RI 02906, 401-351-1253
Edward J. Lefkowicz, Inc., 500 Angell Street, Providence, RI 02906-4457, 800-201-7901; fax 401-277-1459; E-mail seabooks@saltbooks.com
NEDGE, PO Box 2321, Providence, RI 02906
SERIE D'ECRITURE, 71 Elmgrove Avenue, Providence, RI 02906
SYNCOPATED CITY, PO Box 2382, Providence, RI 02906, litik@aol.com
KMJ Educational Programs, 25 Wildwood Avenue, Providence, RI 02907, 401-781-7964; email keithbooks@aol.com
HURRICANE ALICE, Dept. of English, Rhode Island College, Providence, RI 02908
PRIVACY JOURNAL, PO Box 28577, Providence, RI 02908
THE ALEMBIC, Department of English, Providence College, Providence, RI 02918-0001
THE PROSE POEM: An International Journal, English Department, Providence College, Providence, RI 02918, 401-865-2292
Majestic Books, PO Box 19097D, Johnston, RI 02919
HAUNTS, Nightshade Publications, PO Box 8068, Cranston, RI 02920-0068, 401-781-9438, Fax 401-943-0980

SOUTH CAROLINA

WRITER'S EXCHANGE, 100 Upper Glen Drive, Blythewood, SC 29016-7806, E-mail eboone@aol.com; www.users.aol.com/writernet
R & M Publishing Company, PO Box 1276, Holly Hill, SC 29059, 803-279-2262
NOSTALGIA, A Sentimental State of Mind, PO Box 2224, Orangeburg, SC 29116
CURMUDGEON, 3420 Earlwood Drive, Columbia, SC 29201-1422, 803-736-1449
Burning Llama Press, 82 Ridge Lake Drive, Columbia, SC 29209-4213
THE IMPLODING TIE-DYED TOUPEE, 82 Ridge Lake Drive, Columbia, SC 29209-4213
THE NEW SOUTHERN SURREALIST REVIEW, 82 Ridge Lake Drive, Columbia, SC 29209-4213
THE VOLUNTARYIST, Box 1275, Gramling, SC 29348, 864-472-2750
ILLUMINATIONS, English Dept., 66 George Street, College of Charleston, Charleston, SC 29424-0001
Ninety-Six Press, Furman University, Greenville, SC 29613, 864-294-3156
SOUTH CAROLINA REVIEW, English Dept, Clemson Univ, Clemson, SC 29634-1503, 803-656-3151
Wynn Publishing, PO Box 1491, Pickens, SC 29671, 803-878-6469
SFEST, LTD., PO Box 1238, Simpsonville, SC 29681
THE DEVIL'S MILLHOPPER, USC - Aiken, 471 University Parkway, Aiken, SC 29801-6399, Fax/Phone 803-641-3239 e-mail Gardner@vm.sc.edu
The Devil's Millhopper Press (TDM Press), USC - Aiken, 471 University Parkway, Aiken, SC 29801-6399, phone/fax 803-641-3239; e-Mail gardner@vm.sc.edu
Palanquin Press, English Department, University of South Carolina-Aiken, Aiken, SC 29801, 803-648-6851 x3208; fax 803-641-3461; email phebed@aiken.edu; email scpoet@scescape.net
APOSTROPHE: USCB Journal of the Arts, 801 Carteret Street, Beaufort, SC 29902, 803-521-4158; FAX 803-522-9733; E-Mail ibfrt56@vm.sc.edu
Senior Press, PO Box 21362, Hilton Island Head, SC 29925, 803-681-5970, Fax 803-681-3971
MOODY STREET IRREGULARS: A Jack Kerouac Magazine, 32 S. Forest Beach Drive #31, Hilton Head Island, SC 29928-7005
Moody Street Irregulars, Inc., 32 S. Forest Beach Drive #31, Hilton Head Island, SC 29928-7005

SOUTH DAKOTA

Tesseract Publications, PO Box 164, Canton, SD 57013-0164, 605-987-5071
SOUTH DAKOTA REVIEW, University of South Dakota, 414 East Clark, Vermillion, SD 57069, 605-677-5229/5966
Astro Black Books, P O Box 46, Sioux Falls, SD 57101, 605-338-0277
Ex Machina Publishing Company, Box 448, Sioux Falls, SD 57101
VINEGAR CONNOISSEURS INTERNATIONAL NEWSLETTER, PO Box 41, Roslyn, SD 57261, 605-486-4536; vinegar@itctec.com
PRAIRIE WINDS, Dakota Wesleyan University, DWU Box 536, Mitchell, SD 57301
YUWITAYA LAKOTA, 114 Hillcrest Drive, Rapid City, SD 57701-3656

TENNESSEE

Southern Star Publishing, 123 Brentwood Point, Brentwood, TN 37027
ZONE 3, PO Box 4565, Austin Peay State University, Clarksville, TN 37044, 931-221-7031/7891
AC Projects, Inc., 7111 Sweetgum Drive SW #B, Fairview, TN 37062-9384, 615-646-3757
The Arthritis Trust of America/The Rheumatoid Disease Foundation, 7111 Sweetgum Drive SW, Suite A, Fairview, TN

37062-9384, 615-799-1002
Mayhill Press, PO Box 681804, ?ranklin, TN 37068-1804, 615-794-8542
Richard W. Smith Military Books, PO Box 2118, Hendersonville, TN 37077
RFD, PO Box 68, Liberty, TN 37095, 615-536-5176
POEMS & PLAYS, Department of English, Middle Tennessee State University, Murfreesboro, TN 37132, 615-898-2712
Journey Books Publishing, 3205 Highway 431, Spring Hill, TN 37174, 615-791-8006
POCKETS (Devotional Magazine for Children), 1908 Grand Avenue, PO Box 189, Nashville, TN 37202-0189, 615-340-7333
The F. Marion Crawford Memorial Society, Saracinesca House, 3610 Meadowbrook Avenue, Nashville, TN 37205
THE ROMANTIST, Saracinesca House, 3610 Meadowbrook Avenue, Nashville, TN 37205
CUMBERLAND POETRY REVIEW, Poetics, Inc., PO Box 120128 Acklen Station, Nashville, TN 37212, 615-373-8948
Progressive Education, PO Box 120574, Nashville, TN 37212
PROGRESSIVE PERIODICALS DIRECTORY/UPDATE, PO Box 120574, Nashville, TN 37212
Cucumber Island Storytellers, PO Box 158544, Nashville, TN 37215-8544, 800-730-3030
Premium Press America, PO Box 159015, Nashville, TN 37215, 615-256-8484, fax 615-256-8624
The Battery Press, Inc., PO Box 198885, Nashville, TN 37219, 615-298-1401; E-mail battery@aol.com
HISTORY NEWS, 530 Church Street, Suite 600, Nashville, TN 37219-2325, 615-255-2971
Nashville House, PO Box 111864, Nashville, TN 37222, 615-834-5069
Ione Press, PO Box 3271, Sewanee, TN 37375, 931-598-0795; e-mail jillc@infoave.net
SEWANEE REVIEW, Univ. of the South, 735 University Avenue, Sewanee, TN 37383-1000, 931-598-1246
THE POETRY MISCELLANY, English Dept. Univ of Tennessee, Chattanooga, TN 37403, 615-755-4213; 624-7279
The Overmountain Press, PO Box 1261, Johnson City, TN 37605, 615-926-2691
NOW AND THEN, PO Box 70556, East Tennessee State University, Johnson City, TN 37614-0556, 423-439-5348; fax 423-439-6340; e-mail woodsidj@etsu.edu
COMICS REVUE, PO Box 336 -Manuscript Press, Mountain Home, TN 37684-0336, 432-926-7495
Manuscript Press, PO Box 336, Mountain Home, TN 37684-0336, 423-926-7495
Paint Rock Publishing, Inc., 118 Dupont Smith Lane, Kingston, TN 37763, 423-376-3892
THE SIGNAL - Network International, 1118 West Outer Drive, Oak Ridge, TN 37830-8611, 208-365-5812
Ashton Productions, Inc., 1014 Gay Street, Sevierville, TN 37862-4213, 423-774-0174; api@ssmagnolia.com
THE PURPLE MONKEY, 200 East Redbud Road, Knoxville, TN 37920
HEALTH AND HAPPINESS, 1414 Barcelona Drive, Knoxville, TN 37923, 423-539-1601 phone/fax; e-mail: maria-k@juno.com
Fine Arts Press, PO Box 3491, Knoxville, TN 37927, 615-637-9243
Redbird Press, Inc., PO Box 11441, Memphis, TN 38111, 901-323-2233
SINGLE.TODAY, 5830 Mount Moriah Road, Suite 17, Memphis, TN 38115-1628, 901-365-3988
RIVER CITY, University of Memphis, Department of English, Memphis, TN 38152, 901-678-4591
Mustang Publishing Co., PO Box 3004, Memphis, TN 38173, 901-521-1406; fax 901-521-1412; e-Mail MUSTANGPUB@AOL.COM
Leadership Education and Development, Inc., 1116 West 7th Street, Suite 175, Columbia, TN 38401, 931-682-3796; 800-659-6135
UNDER THE SUN, Department of Eng., Tennessee Tech Univ., Box 5053, Cookeville, TN 38505
RURAL HERITAGE, 281 Dean Ridge Lane, Gainesboro, TN 38562-5039, 931-268-0655; E-mail editor@ruralheritage.com; website www.ruralheritage.com

TEXAS

Life Adventures Publishing, PO Box 260479, Plano, TX 75026, 888-893-2224; fax 972-964-1255; e-mail thomasbell@msw.com; website www.life-adventures.com
JPS Publishing Company, PO Box 540272, Grand Prairie, TX 75054-0272, 972-291-3944
Mundus Artium Press, University of Texas at Dallas, Box 688, Richardson, TX 75083-0688
TRANSLATION REVIEW, Univ. of Texas-Dallas, Box 830688, Richardson, TX 75083-0688, 214-690-2093
Halbar Publishing, 289 Taylor Street, Wills Point, TX 75169-9732
SHARING & CARING, 289 Taylor Street, Wills Point, TX 75169-9732
Arjay Associates, PO Box 850251, Mesquite, TX 75185-0251, 972-226-0336 tel/fax; E-mail jake4@airmail.net
Somesuch Press, 300 Crescent Court, Suite 875, Dallas, TX 75201, 214-871-8080
HOT FLASHES, 1910 Mecca Street, Dallas, TX 75206-7226, 821-1308
Z W L Publishing, Inc., PO Box 7991, Dallas, TX 75209, 214-638-TALK (8255), fax 214-631-1476, e-Mail ZWLPUB@AOL.COM, 800-206-5384; for on-line magazine http://www.zwlpub.com
Cerberus Books, 381 Casa Linda Plaza, Suite 179, Dallas, TX 75218, 214-324-0894
THE AFRICAN HERALD, PO Box 2394, Dallas, TX 75221
Good Hope Enterprises, Inc., PO Box 2394, Dallas, TX 75221, 214-823-7666; fax 214-823-7373
THE JOE BOB REPORT, PO Box 2002, Dallas, TX 75221, FAX 214-368-2310
ILLYA'S HONEY, PO Box 225435, Dallas, TX 75222
MISSISSIPPI MUD, 7119 Santa Fe Avenue, Dallas, TX 75223, 214-321-8955
Mud Press, 7119 Santa Fe Avenue, Dallas, TX 75223
Marketing Department, 4516 Lovers Lane Suite 157, Dallas, TX 75225, 972-480-8669; Fax 972-480-8663; Toll-free 888-255-9139; E-mail dmwriter@aol.com
Coldwater Press, 9806 Coldwater Circle, Dallas, TX 75228, 214-328-7612
Papillon Publishing, PO Box 28553, Dallas, TX 75228, 214-686-4388, papillonco@aol.com
Behavioral Sciences Research Press, Inc., 12803 Demetra Drive, Ste. 100, Dallas, TX 75234, 214-243-8543, fax 214-243-6349
LAUGHING BEAR NEWSLETTER, PO Box 613322, Dallas, TX 75261-3322, 817-283-6303; e-mail editor@laughingbear.com
SOUTHWEST REVIEW, Southern Methodist University, 307 Fondren Library W., Box 750374, Dallas, TX 75275-0374, 214-768-1037
Skyward Publishing, 17440 N. Dallas Parkway, Ste. 100, Dallas, TX 75287-1884, 1-800-537-6727; 972-735-7827
SeaStar Publishing Company, PO Box 741413, Dallas, TX 75374-1413
LITERARY SKETCHES, PO Box 810571, Dallas, TX 75381-0571, 214-243-8776
Browder Springs, PO Box 823521, Dallas, TX 75382, 214-368-4360

BOTH SIDES NOW, 10547 State Highway 110 North, Tyler, TX 75704-9537, 903-592-4263
Free People Press, 10547 State Highway 110 North, Tyler, TX 75704-9537
YE OLDE NEWES, Po Box 151107, Lufkin, TX 75915-1107, 409-637-7475
COPING WITH TURBULENT TIMES, PO Box 4630, Nacogdoches, TX 75962, e-mail iii2k@yahoo.com
Future Horizons, Inc., 720 North Fielder Road, Arlington, TX 76012-4635, 817-277-0727; 1-800-4890727; Fax 817-277-2270; E-mail edfuture@onramp.net
Bold Productions, PO Box 152281, Arlington, TX 76015, 817-468-9924; info@boldproductions.com
CON-TEMPORAL, 5202 Tacoma Drive, Arlington, TX 76017-1866, 817-467-0681; Fax 817-467-5346
Camino Bay Books, PO Box 2487, Glen Rose, TX 76043-2487, 254-897-3016
Prestige Publishing, PO Box 2786, Grapevine, TX 76099, 972-495-4374
Mesa House Publishing, 1701 River Run, Suite 800, Fort Worth, TX 76107, 817-339-8889; Fax 817-339-8818
DESCANT, English Department, TCU, Box 297270, Fort Worth, TX 76129
BOOK NEWS & BOOK BUSINESS MART, PO Box 330309, Fort Worth, TX 76163, 817-293-7030
Premier Publishers, Inc., PO Box 330309, Fort Worth, TX 76163, 817-293-7030
AMERICAN LITERARY REVIEW, Dept of English, University of North Texas, Denton, TX 76203-6827, 817-565-2127
Skinny Lamb Publishing Company, Route 3 Box 521-H, Wichita Falls, TX 76308, 940-696-5735; Fax 940-696-5830; skinylamb@aol.com
WINDHOVER: A Journal of Christian Literature, PO Box 8008, UMHB, Belton, TX 76513, 817-939-4564
Mariah Publications, PO Box 934, Waco, TX 76703, 817-753-3714 phone/Fax
LUCKY HEART BOOKS, 1900 West Highway 6, Waco, TX 76712
SALT LICK, 1900 West Highway 6, Waco, TX 76712-0682
Salt Lick Press, 1900 West Hwy 6, Waco, TX 76712-0682
CONCHO RIVER REVIEW, English Department, Angelo State University, San Angelo, TX 76909, 915-942-2273; james.moore@angelo.edu
Triad Press, 8983 Briar Forest Drive, Houston, TX 77024-7219, 713-789-0424
O!!ZONE, A LITERARY-ART ZINE, 1266 Fountain View Drive, Houston, TX 77057, 713-784-2802
The O!!Zone Press, 1266 Fountain View Drive, Houston, TX 77057, 713-784-2802
Gemini Publishing Company, 14010 El Camino Real, Houston, TX 77062, 281-488-6866, E-mail: getgirls@getgirls.com; website: http://www.getgirls.com
Guardian Press, 10924 Grant Road #225, Houston, TX 77070, 713-955-9855
Emerald Ink Publishing, 7141 Office City Drive, Suite 220, Houston, TX 77087, 713-643-9945, fax 713-643-1986
Colophon House, 17522 Brushy River Court, Houston, TX 77095, 218-304-9502; Fax 281-256-3442
Lowy Publishing, 5047 Wigton, Houston, TX 77096-5327, 713-723-3209
Arte Publico Press, University of Houston, Houston, TX 77204-2090, 713-743-2841
GULF COAST, Dept. of English, University of Houston, Houston, TX 77204-3012
THE AUCTION MAGAZINE, PO Box 62101-411, Houston, TX 77205, 713-359-1200
Black Tie Press, PO Box 440004, Houston, TX 77244-0004, 713-789-5119 fax
Scrivenery Press, PO Box 740969-180, Houston, TX 77274-0969, 713-665-6760; fax 713-665-8838; e-mail editors@scrivenery.com; website www.scrivenery.com
Innerworks Publishing, Po Box 270865, Houston, TX 77277-0865, telephone/fax: 713-661-8284, 800-577-5040; orders; E-mail empower@netropolis.com
THE TEXAS REVIEW, English Department, Sam Houston State University, Huntsville, TX 77341-2146
Texas Review Press, English Department, Sam Houston State University, Huntsville, TX 77341-2146
BLUE VIOLIN, PO Box 1175, Humble, TX 77347-1175
TOUCHSTONE LITERARY JOURNAL, PO Box 8308, Spring, TX 77387-8308
GRAFFITI OFF THE ASYLUM WALLS, 1002 Gunnison Street #A, Sealy, TX 77474-3725
Innovanna Publishing Co., Inc., 14019 Southwest Fwy., Suite 301-517, Sugar Land, TX 77478, 800-577-9810; 281-242-9835; Fax 281-242-6498
PLOT, PO Box 1351, Sugar Land, TX 77487-1351
Swan Publishing Company, 126 Live Oak, Alvin, TX 77511, 281-388-2547; swanbooks@ghg.net; www.swan-pub.com
Doctors Press, Inc., PO Box 2200, Angleton, TX 77516, 409-848-2704
Ledero Press, U. T. Box 35099, Galveston, TX 77555-5099, 409-772-2091
CONTEXT SOUTH, Box 4504, Schreiner College, Kerrville, TX 78028, 512-896-7945
Friendly Oaks Publications, 1216 Cheryl Drive, PO Box 662, Pleasanton, TX 78064, 830-569-3586; Fax 830-281-2617; E-mail friendly@docspeak.com
TEXAS YOUNG WRITERS' NEWSLETTER, PO Box 942, Adkins, TX 78101
Alicia Z. Galvan, 426 Castroville Road, San Antonio, TX 78207, 210-433-9991
STONEFLOWER LITERARY JOURNAL, 1824 Nacogdoches, Suite 191, San Antonio, TX 78209
Chili Verde, 736 E. Guenther Street, San Antonio, TX 78210, 210-532-8384
Corona Publishing Co., PO Drawer 12407, San Antonio, TX 78212, 210-341-7525
Candlestick Publishing, PO Box 39241, San Antonio, TX 78218-1241
PALO ALTO REVIEW, 1400 West Villaret, San Antonio, TX 78224, 210-828-2998
Pecan Grove Press, Academic Library, Box AL, 1 Camino Santa Maria, San Antonio, TX 78228-8608, 210-436-3441
LONE STARS MAGAZINE, 4219 Flinthill, San Antonio, TX 78230-1619
Langmarc Publishing, PO Box 33872, San Antonio, TX 78265, 210-822-2521
Gemini Marine Publications, PO Box 700255, San Antonio, TX 78270-0255, 210-494-0426, Fax 210-494-0766
Hill Country Books, PO Box 791615, San Antonio, TX 78279, 830-885-4375
CHACHALACA POETRY REVIEW, English Department, Univ. of Texas - Brownsville, Brownsville, TX 78520, 956-544-8239; Fax 956-544-8988; E-Mail mlewis@b1.utb.edu
Prickly Pear Press, 1402 Mimosa Pass, Cedar Park, TX 78613, 512-331-1557
Shearer Publishing, 406 Post Oak Road, Fredericksburg, TX 78624, 830-997-6529
Armadillo Books, PO Box 2052, Georgetown, TX 78627-2052, 512-863-8660
BUENO, 1700 Wagon Gap, Round Rock, TX 78681
In One Ear Publications, Bueno Books, 1700 Wagon Gap, Round Rock, TX 78681
Plexus, 815-A Brazos, Suite 445, Austin, TX 78701, 512-444-7104; Fax 512-441-4741; info@cyberplexus.com
THE DIRTY GOAT, 2717 Wooldridge, Austin, TX 78703, 512-482-8229; E-mail jbhost@cerf.net
Host Publications, Inc., 2717 Wooldridge, Austin, TX 78703-1953, 512-479-8069
OFFICE NUMBER ONE, 1708 South Congress Avenue, Austin, TX 78704, 512-445-4489

AMERICAN SHORT FICTION, Parlin 108 English Department, University of Texas-Austin, Austin, TX 78712-1164, 512-471-1772
Multi Media Arts, PO Box 141127, Austin, TX 78714-1127, 512-836-2541
Keel Publications, PO Box 160155, Austin, TX 78716-0155, 512-327-1280; swimdoc@texas.net
SOUND PRACTICES, PO Box 180562, Austin, TX 78718, e-mail sp@tpoint.com
Nancy Renfro Studios, Inc., 3312 Pecan Springs Road, Austin, TX 78723, 1-800-933-5512; 512-927-7090
Erespin Press, 6906 Colony Loop Drive, Austin, TX 78724
TITIVILLITIA: Studies of Illiteracy in the Private Press, 6906 Colony Loop Drive, Austin, TX 78724
ARTHUR'S COUSIN, 6811 Greycloud, Austin, TX 78745, 512-445-7065
Teri Gordon, Publisher, 10901 Rustic Manor Lane, Austin, TX 78750-1133, 512-258-8309
Hoover's, Inc., 1033 La Posada Drive, Suite 250, Austin, TX 78752-3824, 512-374-4500, Fax 512-374-4501, E-mail info@hoovers.com
NOVA EXPRESS, PO Box 27231, Austin, TX 78755, E-mail lawrence@bga.com
Silver Phoenix Press, PO Box 26554, Austin, TX 78755-0554, 512-343-8803; Fax 512-338-0224; E-mail silphoenix@aol.com
The White Cross Press, 4401 Spicewood Springs Road #232, Austin, TX 78759-8589
SULPHUR RIVER LITERARY REVIEW, PO Box 19228, Austin, TX 78760-9228, 512-292-9456
BORDERLANDS: Texas Poetry Review, PO BOX 33096, Austin, TX 78764, fax 512-499-0441; e-mail cemgilbert@earthlink.net; website http://www.fastair.com/borderlands
Plain View Press, Inc., PO Box 33311, Austin, TX 78764, (512) 441-2452
Argo Press, PO Box 4201, Austin, TX 78765-4201
ART-CORE, PO Box 49324, Austin, TX 78765
BANAL PROBE, PO Box 4333, Austin, TX 78765
LIME GREEN BULLDOZERS (AND OTHER RELATED SPECIES), PO Box 4333, Austin, TX 78765
Liquid Paper Press, PO Box 4973, Austin, TX 78765, www.eden.com/~jwhagins/nervecowboy
N D, PO Box 4144, Austin, TX 78765, 512-440-7609; fax 512-416-8007; e-Mail PLUNKETT@ND.ORG
NERVE COWBOY, PO Box 4973, Austin, TX 78765, www.onr.com/user/jwhagins/nervecowboy.html
Oyster Publications, PO Box 4333, Austin, TX 78765
Slough Press, Box 1385, Austin, TX 78767
LONE STAR SOCIALIST, PO Box 2640, Austin, TX 78768-2640, 210-833-5315
THE MAVERICK PRESS, Route 2, Box 4915, Eagle Pass, TX 78852-9605, 210-773-1836 phone/fax 8 am to 4 pm
BOOKS OF THE SOUTHWEST, PO Box 398, Sabinal, TX 78881, e-mail books@peppersnet.com
Westhaven Publishing, 205 Sarasota Street, Borger, TX 79007
THE ADVOCATE, HCR 2, Box 25, Panhandle, TX 79068, 806-335-1715
Rio Grande Press, 4320 Canyon Drive #A12, Amarillo, TX 79109-5624
SE LA VIE WRITER'S JOURNAL, 4320 Canyon Drive #A12, Amarillo, TX 79109-5624
Shallowater Press, PO Box 1151, Shallowater, TX 79363, 806-873-3617, e-mail swpress@aol.com
Duckworth Press, 3005 66th Street, Lubbock, TX 79413-5707, 806-799-3706
DREAM WHIP, PO Box 53832, Lubbock, TX 79453, 806-794-9263
Creative Arts & Science Enterprises, 341 Miller Street, Abilene, TX 79605-1903
STARBURST, 341 Miller Street, Abilene, TX 79605-1903

UTAH

OF UNICORNS AND SPACE STATIONS, PO Box 97, Bountiful, UT 84011-0097
Gibbs Smith, Publisher, 1877 East Gentile Street, PO Box 667, Layton, UT 84041, 801-544-9800; Fax 801-544-5582; E-mail info@GibbsSmith.com
THE DEFENDER - RUSH UTAH'S NEWSLETTER, PO Box 559, Dept. RU, Roy, UT 84067, 801-393-6699
Eborn Books, Box 559, Roy, UT 84067
Wings of Fire Press, PO Box 520725, Salt Lake City, UT 84105-0725
Utah Geographic Series, Box 8325, Salt Lake City, UT 84108
QUARTERLY WEST, 200 South Central Campus Drive, Room 317, University of Utah, Salt Lake City, UT 84112, 801-581-3938
WESTERN HUMANITIES REVIEW, University of Utah, Salt Lake City, UT 84112, 801-581-6070
Signature Books, Attn: Boyd Payne, 564 West 400 North, Salt Lake City, UT 84116, 801-531-1483, fax 801-531-1488
Liberty Bell Press & Publishing Co., 4700 South 900 East, Suite 3-183, Salt Lake City, UT 84117, 801-943-8573
Business Resource Publishing, PO Box 526193-DS, Salt Lake City, UT 84152, Fax 801-273-0167
Commune-A-Key Publishing, Inc., PO Box 58637, Salt Lake City, UT 84158, 801-581-9191, Fax 801-581-9196, 800-983-0600
Shaolin Communications, PO Box 58547, Salt Lake City, UT 84158, 801-595-1123
Eagle's View Publishing, 6756 North Fork Road, Liberty, UT 84310, 801-393-4555 (orders); editorial phone 801-745-0903
More To Life Publishing, 358 N. 600 E, Hyrum, UT 84319-1142
WESTERN AMERICAN LITERATURE, English Dept., Utah State Univ., Logan, UT 84322-3200, 435-797-1603; Fax 435-797-4099; wal@cc.usu.edu
WEBER STUDIES: Voices and Viewpoints of the Contemporary West, Weber State University, 1214 University Circle, Ogden, UT 84408-1214, 801-626-6473 or 6657
DREAM NETWORK JOURNAL, PO Box 1026, Moab, UT 84532-3031, 435-259-5936; dreamkey@lasal.net; http:dreamnetwork.net
Southpaw Press, 1653 S. Mountain Springs Blvd., New Harmony, UT 84757, 435-865-1785; Fax 435-865-1786; mp@southpawpress.com
THE GENTLE SURVIVALIST, PO Box 4004, St. George, UT 84770

VERMONT

Chelsea Green Publishing Company, PO Box 428, White River Junction, VT 05001-0428, 802-295-6300
Five Corners Publications, Ltd., Old Bridgewater Mill, PO Box 66, Bridgewater, VT 05034-0066, 802-672-3868; Fax 802-672-3296; e-mail don@fivecorners.com
Goats & Compasses, PO Box 524, Brownsville, VT 05037, 802-484-5169
9N-2N-8N-NAA NEWSLETTER, PO Box 275, East Corinth, VT 05040-0275
New Victoria Publishers, PO Box 27, Norwich, VT 05055, 802-649-5297

GREEN WORLD: News and Views For Gardening Who Care About The Earth, 12 Dudley Street, Randolph, VT 05060-1202, E-mail: gx297@cleveland.freenet.edu
Steerforth Press, L.C., 105-106 Chelsea Street, PO Box 70, South Royalton, VT 05068, 802-763-2808
THE CIVIL WAR NEWS, RR 1 Box 36, Tunbridge, VT 05077, 802-889-3500
THE ANTHOLOGY OF NEW ENGLAND WRITERS, PO Box 483, Windsor, VT 05089, 802-674-2315; newvtpoet@aol.com
GemStone Press, LongHill Partners, Inc., PO Box 237, Woodstock, VT 05091, 802-457-4000
LONGHOUSE, 1604 River Road, Guilford, VT 05301, e-mail poetry@sover.net; www.sover.net/~poetry
Longhouse, 1604 River Road, Guilford, VT 05301, e-mail poetry@sover.net; www.sover.net/~poetry
Threshold Books, 3108 Tater Lane, Guilford, VT 05301, 802-254-8300; Fax 802-257-2779
THE MARLBORO REVIEW, PO Box 243, Marlboro, VT 05344
Professor Solar Press, RFD #3, Box 627, Putney, VT 05346, 802-387-2601
Waterfront Books, 85 Crescent Road, Burlington, VT 05401-4126, 802-658-7477
Wood Thrush Books, 96 Intervale Avenue, Burlington, VT 05401, 802-863-9767
TOWARD FREEDOM, PO Box 468, Burlington, VT 05402-0468, 802-658-2523; Fax 802-658-3738; tfmag@aol.com; www.towardfreedom.com
WOMEN & THERAPY, Dr. Esther Rothblum, Dept. of Psychology, University of Vermont, Burlington, VT 05405, (802) 656-2680
Williamson Publishing Company, Inc., Box 185, Church Hill Road, Charlotte, VT 05445, 802-425-2102
Upper Access Inc., PO Box 457, 1 Upper Access Road, Hinesburg, VT 05461, 800-356-9315 (orders only); 802-482-2988; fax 802-482-3125; books@upperaccess.com
WILD EARTH, PO Box 455, Richmond, VT 05477, 802-434-4077; fax 802-434-5980; e-mail info@wild-earth.org
Russian Information Services, 89 Main Street #2, Montpelier, VT 05602, 802-223-4955
RUSSIAN INFORMATION SERVICES, 89 Main Street #2, Montpelier, VT 05602
GREEN MOUNTAINS REVIEW, Johnson State College, Johnson, VT 05656, 802-635-1350
Silver Print Press, RD 1, Box 1515, Waterbury, VT 05676, 802-244-5339; petermiller@ibm.net; www.silverprintpress.com
Holistic Education Press, PO Box 328, Brandon, VT 05733-0328, 802-247-8312 (voice and fax) e-mail holistic@sover.net
HOLISTIC EDUCATION REVIEW, PO Box 328, Brandon, VT 05733-0328, 802-247-8312 (voice and fax) e-mail holistic@sover.net
Paul S. Eriksson, Publisher, PO Box 125, 368 Indian Trail/Dunmore, Forest Dale, VT 05745, 802-247-4210; fax 802-247-4256
Atrium Society Publications/DBA Education For Peace Publications, PO Box 816, Middlebury, VT 05753, 802-388-0922; fax 802-388-1027; e-mail atrium@sover.net; www.atriumsoc.org
Middlebury College, Middlebury College, Middlebury, VT 05753, 802-443-5075; E-mail nereview@middlebury.edu
NEW ENGLAND REVIEW, Middlebury College, Middlebury, VT 05753, 802-443-5075; fax 802-443-2088; e-mail nereview@mail.middlebury.edu
Inner Traditions International, One Park Street, Rochester, VT 05767, 802-767-3174; fax 802-767-3726; orders 800-246-8648; E-mailorders@gotoit.com; Website: www.gotoit.com
Schenkman Books, PO Box 119, Rochester, VT 05767, 802-767-3702; Fax 802-767-9528; E-mail schenkma@sover.net

VIRGIN ISLANDS

THE CARIBBEAN WRITER,'RR 2, Box 10,000, Univ of Virgin Islands, Kingshill, St. Croix, VI 00850, 340-692-4152; fax 340-692-4026; e-mail ewaters@uvi.edu or qmars@uvi.edu

VIRGINIA

Gifted Education Press/The Reading Tutorium, PO Box 1586, 10201 Yuma Court, Manassas, VA 20109-1586, 703-369-5017; mdfish@cais.com; www.cais.com/gep
Bereshith Publishing, PO Box 2366, Centreville, VA 20122-2366, 703-222-9387; e-mail tempus@bereshith.com; website www.bereshith
The Brookfield Reader, 137 Peyton Road, Sterling, VA 20165-5605, email info@brookfieldreader.com; prodir@erols.com
Strawberry Patchworks, 11597 Southington Lane, Herndon, VA 20170-2417, 703-709-0751, e-mail berrybooks@aol.com
THE EDGE CITY REVIEW, 10912 Harpers Square Court, Reston, VA 20191, E-mail terryp17@aol.com
DEANOTATIONS, 11919 Moss Point Lane, Reston, VA 20194, 703-471-7907; fax 703-471-6446; e-mail blehert@aol.com; website www.blehert.com
Great Western Publishing Company, PO Box 2355, Reston, VA 20195-0355
Associated Writing Programs, Tallwood House, Mail Stop 1E3, George Mason Umiversity, Fairfax, VA 22030-0079, 703-993-4301
INTERVENTION IN SCHOOL AND CLINIC, Gerald Wallace - Graduate School of Education, George Mason University, Fairfax, VA 22030-4444
PHOEBE: A JOURNAL OF LITERARY ARTS, G.M.U. 4400 University Dr., Fairfax, VA 22030, 703-993-2915
SO TO SPEAK, SUB 1, Room 254 A, George Mason University, Fairfax, VA 22030, 703-993-3625
WOMEN AND LANGUAGE, Communication Dept, George Mason University, Fairfax, VA 22030
WRITER'S CHRONICLE, Tallwood House, Mail Stop 1E3, Fairfax, VA 22030-0079, 703-993-4301
NP Press, 4141 Orchard Drive, Fairfax, VA 22032, 703-273-2779
THE MOTHER IS ME: Profiling the Cultural Aspects of Motherhood, 3010 Woodlawn Avenue, Falls Church, VA 22042, 603-743-6828; E-mail zoey455@aol.com
BLACK BUZZARD REVIEW, 1007 Ficklen Road, Fredericksburg, VA 22045
CHANTEH, the Iranian Cross Cultural Qu'ly, PO Box 703, Falls Church, VA 22046, 703-533-1727
Information International, Box 579, Great Falls, VA 22066, 703-450-7049, fax 703-450-7394, bobs@isquare.com
THE FRACTAL, 4400 University Drive, MS 2D6, Fairfax, VA 22075, 703-993-2911
EPM Publications, Inc., 1003 Turkey Run Road, McLean, VA 22101, 703-442-7810
E.M. Press, Inc., PO Box 4057, Manassas, VA 22110-0706, 703-439-0304
Intercontinental Publishing, Inc, 6451 Steeple Chase Lane, Manassas, VA 22111, 703-369-4992
IDIOT WIND, PO Box 87, Occoquan, VA 22125, 703-494-1897 evenings
MoonFall Press, 7845 Glenister Drive, Springfield, VA 22152, 703-912-9774, Fax 703-866-9207, email gcinca@bellatlontic.net; silviacinca@yahoo.com
Beachway Press, 9201 Beachway Lane, Springfield, VA 22153, 703-644-8544, e-mail smadate@beachway.com
TOPICAL TIME, 2501 Drexel Street, Vienna, VA 22180, 703-560-2413

Manta Press, 2255 Hunter Mill Road, Vienna, VA 22181, 703-255-0659; fax 703-255-0566
JOURNAL OF COURT REPORTING, 8224 Old Courthouse Road, Vienna, VA 22182, 703-556-6272; fax 703-556-6291; email pwacht@ncrahq.org
National Court Reporters Association Press, 8224 Old Courthouse Road, Vienna, VA 22182, 703-556-6272; fax 703-556-6291; email pwacht@ncrahq.org
BOGG, 422 N Cleveland Street, Arlington, VA 22201
Bogg Publications, 422 North Cleveland Street, Arlington, VA 22201
BRUTARIAN, PO Box 25222, Arlington, VA 22202-9222, 703-360-2514
Profile Press, 3004 S. Grant Street, Arlington, VA 22202, 703-684-6208
MINIMUS, 2245 N. Buchanan Street, Arlington, VA 22207
AD/VANCE, 1581 Colonial Terrace, Suite 101, Arlington, VA 22209-1428
ELECTRIC VEHICLE NEWS, PO Box 148, Arlington, VA 22210-0148
American Homeowners Foundation Press, 6776 Little Falls Road, Arlington, VA 22213, 703-536-7776
Unfoldment Publications, 1200 Huntly Place, Alexandria, VA 22307-2001
Books for All Times, Inc., PO Box 2, Alexandria, VA 22313, 703-548-0457; e-mail staff@bfat.com
EDUCATION IN FOCUS, PO Box 2, Alexandria, VA 22313, 703-548-0457
THE EDITORIAL EYE, 66 Canal Center Plaza, Suite 200, Alexandria, VA 22314, 703-683-0683
EEI Press, 66 Canal Center Plaza #200, Alexandria, VA 22314, 703-683-0683
Miles River Press, 400 Madison Street #S1309, Alexandria, VA 22314-1755, 703-683-1500
PARACHUTIST, 1440 Duke Street, Alexandria, VA 22314, 703-836-3495
Red Dragon Press, 433 Old Town Court, Alexandria, VA 22314, 703-683-5877
Orchises Press, PO Box 20602, Alexandria, VA 22320-1602, 703-683-1243
Black Buzzard Press, 1007 Ficklen Road, Fredericksburg, VA 22405
VISIONS-INTERNATIONAL, The World Journal of Illustrated Poetry, 1007 Ficklen Road, Fredericksburg, VA 22405
Brandylane Publishers, PO Box 261, White Stone, VA 22578, 804-435-6900; Fax 804-435-9812
PLEASANT LIVING, PO Box 261, White Stone, VA 22578, 804-435-6900
FROGPOND: Quarterly Haiku Journal, PO Box 2461, Winchester, VA 22604, 540-722-2156; redmoon@shentel.net
Red Moon Press, PO Box 2461, Winchester, VA 22604-1661, 540-722-2156; redmoon@shentel.net
Rockbridge Publishing Co., PO Box 351, Berryville, VA 22611, 540-955-3980; FAX 540-955-4126; E-mail cwpub@visuallink.com
Publishers Syndication Int'l (PSI), Po Box 6218, Charlottesville, VA 22806-6218
THE RAW SEED REVIEW, 780 Merion Greene, Charlottesville, VA 22901
ARCHIPELAGO, PO Box 2485, Charlottesville, VA 22902-2485, 804-979-5292; editor@archipelago.org
BELLES LETTRES, 1243 Maple View Drive, Charlottesville, VA 22902-6779, 301-294-0278
dbS Productions, PO Box 1894, University Station, Charlottesville, VA 22903, 800-745-1581; 804-296-6172; Fax 804-293-5502
THE VIRGINIA QUARTERLY REVIEW, One West Range, Charlottesville, VA 22903, 804-924-3124
VIRGINIA LITERARY REVIEW, Box 413 Newcomb Hall Station, Charlottesville, VA 22904, Email dpk2c@virginia.edu
THE POST, Publishers Syndication Int'l, PO Box 6218, Charlottesville, VA 22906-6218
IRIS: A Journal About Women, Box 323, HSC, University of Virginia, Charlottesville, VA 22908, 804-924-4500; iris@virginia.edu
TAG Publications, PO Box 294, Hanover, VA 23069
Thirteen Colonies Press, 710 South Henry Street, Williamsburg, VA 23185, 804-229-1775
VERSE, English Dept., PO Box 8795, College of William & Mary, Williamsburg, VA 23187-8795
WILLIAM AND MARY REVIEW, Campus Center, PO Box 8795, Williamsburg, VA 23187-8795, 757-221-3290, fax 757-221-3451
FOLK ART MESSENGER, PO Box 17041, Richmond, VA 23226, 804-285-4532; fax 804-285-4532
Palari Publishing, PO Box 9288, Richmond, VA 23227-0288, palaripub@aol.com; www.palari.net
VIRGINIA LIBERTY, PO Box 28263, Richmond, VA 23228-0263
Rose & Crown Publishing, PO Box 36427, Richmond, VA 23235, 804-231-6217
SLUG & LETTUCE, PO Box 26632, Richmond, VA 23261-6632
THE STYLUS, 9412 Huron Avenue, Richmond, VA 23294
REFLECT, 1317 Eagles Trace Path #D, Chesapeake, VA 23320-9461, 757-547-4464
J-Mart Press, PO Box 8884, Virginia Beach, VA 23450, 757-498-4060 (phone/fax), e-mail jmartpress@aol.com
A.R.E. Press, PO Box 656, Virginia Beach, VA 23451, 804-428-3588
Al-Anon Family Group Headquarters, Inc., 1600 Corporate Parkway, Virginia Beach, VA 23454-0862, 757-563-1600
THE FORUM, 1600 Corporate Parkway, Virginia Beach, VA 23456-0862, 757-563-1600
THE WILD FOODS FORUM, PO Box 61413, Virginia Beach, VA 23462, 804-421-3929, E-mail; wildfood@infi.net
Achievement Publications, 1920-125 Centerville Tnpk, PMB 140, Virginia Beach, VA 23464-6800, 757-474-7955; fax 757-474-9154; achievepubs@mindspring.com
BLUE COLLAR REVIEW, PO Box 11417, Norfolk, VA 23517, 757-627-0952; e-mail redart@pilot.infi.net
Partisan Press, PO Box 11417, Norfolk, VA 23517, e-mail redart@pilot.infi.net
Heresy Press, 713 Paul Street, Newport News, VA 23605, 804-380-6595
Picturesque Publications, PO Box 6175, Newport News, VA 23606, 757-249-1538
Brunswick Publishing Corporation, 1386 Lawrenceville Plank Road, Lawrenceville, VA 23868, 804-848-3865; Fax 804-848-0607; brunspub@jnent.com
INTEGRAL YOGA MAGAZINE, Route 1, Box 1720, Buckingham, VA 23921, 804-969-3121
THE HOLLINS CRITIC, PO Box 9538, Hollins University, VA 24020
CCM Publishing, PO Box 12624, Roanoke, VA 24027
CE CONNECTION COMMUNIQUE, PO Box 12624, Roanoke, VA 24027
THE LYRIC, 307 Dunton Drive SW, Blacksburg, VA 24060-5127
Rowan Mountain Press, PO Box 10111, Blacksburg, VA 24062-0111, 540-961-3315, Fax 540-961-4883, e-mail faulkner@bev.net
SISTERS IN CRIME BOOKS IN PRINT, PO Box 10111, Blacksburg, VA 24062-0111, 540-961-3315, Fax 540-951-7340, e-mail faulkner@bev.net
Pocahontas Press, Inc., PO Drawer F, Blacksburg, VA 24063-1020, 703-951-0467; 800-446-0467
Commonwealth Press Virginia, 415 First Street, Box 3547, Radford, VA 24141
ABSOLUTE MAGNITUDE, PO Box 2988, Radford, VA 24143-2988, 413-772-0725; Wilder@shaysnet.com

DNA Publications, Inc., PO Box 2988, Radford, VA 24143-2988, 413-772-0725; wilder@shaysnet.com
DREAMS OF DECADENCE: Vampire Poetry and Fiction, PO Box 2988, Radford, VA 24143-2988
Briarwood Publications, Inc., 150 West College Street, Rocky Mount, VA 24151, 540-483-3606; website www.briarwoodva.com
THE ROANOKE REVIEW, English Dept., Roanoke College, Salem, VA 24153, 540-375-2367
CJE NEWS (Newsletter of the Coalition for Jobs & the Environment), PO Box 645, Abingdon, VA 24210-0645, 703-628-8996
THE SOW'S EAR POETRY REVIEW, 19535 Pleasant View Drive, Abingdon, VA 24211-6827, 540-628-2651; richman@preferred.com
The Sow's Ear Press, 19535 Pleasant View Drive, Abingdon, VA 24211-6827, e-mail richman@preferred.com
WRITER'S WORLD, 204 East 19th Street, Big Stone Gap, VA 24219, 703-523-0830, fax 703-523-5757
McDonald & Woodward Publishing Company, PO Box GG, Saltville, VA 24370-1161
SHENANDOAH, Troubadour Theater, 2nd Floor, Washington and Lee University, Lexington, VA 24450-0303, 540-463-8765
PIEDMONT LITERARY REVIEW, 3750 Woodside Avenue, Lynchburg, VA 24503
St. Andrew Press, PO Box 329, Big Island, VA 24526, 804-299-5956
PROOF ROCK, Proof Rock Press, PO Box 607, Halifax, VA 24558
THE MASONIA ROUNDUP, 200 Coolwell Road, Madison Heights, VA 24572-2719

WASHINGTON

ARNAZELLA, 3000 Landerhoim Circle SE, Bellevue, WA 98007, 206-641-2373
Resolution Business Press, Inc., 1035 156th Avenue NE #12, Bellevue, WA 98007-4679, 425-649-1902
Illumination Arts, PO Box 1865, Bellevue, WA 98009, 425-644-7185; fax 425-644-9274
Pickle Point Publishing, PO Box 4107, Bellevue, WA 98009, 206-641-7424
OUT WEST, 9792 Edmonds Way, #265, Edmonds, WA 98020-5940, 425-776-1228; fax 425-776-3398; e-Mail outwest@seanet.com
Dunamis House, 19801 SE 123rd Street, Issaquah, WA 98027, 206-255-5274; FAX 206-277-8780
GRANULATED TUPPERWARE, 1420 NW Gilman Blvd., Suite 2400, Issaquah, WA 98027-7001
LifeQuest Publishing Group, PO Box 1444, Issaquah, WA 98027, fax 425-392-1854; e-mail lifequest@usa.net
Nystrom Publishing Co., PO Box 378, Issaquah, WA 98027, 425-392-0451
Epicenter Press Inc., PO Box 82368, Kenmore, WA 98028, 206-485-6822; FAX 206-481-8253
Umbrella Books, Box 82368, Kenmore, WA 98028
VINTAGE NORTHWEST, PO Box 193, Bothell, WA 98041, 206-821-2411
Pura Vida Publishing Company, PO Box 379, Mountlake Terrace, WA 98043-0379, 425-670-1346; 888-670-1346; Fax 425-744-0563; puravidapub@earthlink.net; www.puravidapub.com
Online Training Solutions, Inc., 15442 Bel-Red Road, Redmond, WA 98052, 425-885-1441
Marmot Publishing, PO Box 725, Snoqualmie, WA 98065, 425-831-7022
LIGHTHOUSE, Lighthouse Publications, PO Box 1377, Auburn, WA 98071-1377
MEDIA SPOTLIGHT, Po Box 290, Redmond, WA 98073
PEMMICAN, PO Box 121, Redmond, WA 98073-7507
Pemmican Press, PO Box 121, Redmond, WA 98073-7507
MAKING $$$ AT HOME, PO Box 12280, Mill Creek, WA 98082, 209-485-7926
UP CLOSE, A Quarterly Review of New Age & Alternative Publication Newsletter, PO Box 12280, Mill Creek, WA 98082, FAX 206-485-7926
SIGNPOST FOR NORTHWEST TRAILS, 1305 Fourth Avenue #512, Seattle, WA 98101, 206-625-1367
Bear Creek Publications, 2507 Minor Avenue East, Seattle, WA 98102, 206-322-7604
GLYPH: The Tabloid That Redefines Visual Literature, 117 East Louisa #253, Seattle, WA 98102, 206-343-5650; chaosunit@aol.com
JACK MACKEREL MAGAZINE, PO Box 23134, Seattle, WA 98102-0434
Laocoon Books, PO Box 20518, Seattle, WA 98102, 206-323-7268; erotica@laocoonbooks.com
Rowhouse Press, PO Box 23134, Seattle, WA 98102-0434
THE UNIT CIRCLE, PO Box 20352, Seattle, WA 98102, 206-322-1702, E-mail; zine@unitcircle.org
BUTTERFLY GARDENERS' QUARTERLY, PO Box 30931, Seattle, WA 98103, 206-783-3924
CITY PRIMEVAL, PO Box 30064, Seattle, WA 98103, 206-440-0791
Cune Press, PO Box 31024, 911-N 67th Street, Seattle, WA 98103, 206-782-1433
FINE MADNESS, PO Box 31138, Seattle, WA 98103-1138
The Square-Rigger Press, 1201 North 46th Street, Seattle, WA 98103-6610, 206-548-9385
ENDING THE BEGIN, PO Box 4816, Seattle, WA 98104-0816, 206-726-0948
Headveins Graphics, PO Box 4816, Seattle, WA 98104-0816, 206-726-0948
POETSWEST LITERARY JOURNAL, 1011 Boren Avenue #155, Seattle, WA 98104, 206-682-1268; bjevans@postal-zone.com
Red Letter Press, 409 Maynard Avenue South #201, Seattle, WA 98104, 206-682-0990; Fax 206-682-8120; Email redletterpress@juno.com
Sasquatch Books, 615 2nd Ave., Suite 260, Seattle, WA 98104, 206-467-4300; 800-775-0817; Fax 206-467-4301; books@SasquatchBooks.com
Winwin Publications, 1315 Madison Street #456, Seattle, WA 98104, 250-658-4211 phone/fax; winwin@vanisle.net
OM, Box #181, 4505 University Way, NE, Seattle, WA 98105, 206-322-6387
Rose Alley Press, 4203 Brooklyn Avenue NE #103A, Seattle, WA 98105, 206-633-2725
EduCare Press, PO Box 17222, Seattle, WA 98107
SEA KAYAKER, PO Box 17170, Seattle, WA 98107-0870, 206-789-1326; Fax 206-781-1141; mail@seakayakermag.com
White Plume Press, 2442 NW Market Street #370, Seattle, WA 98107-4137, 206-525-1812, Fax; 206-525-1925, E-mail; bd72@scn.org
Aviation Book Company, 7201 Perimeter Road South, Seattle, WA 98108-2999
AMERICAN JONES BUILDING & MAINTENANCE, PO Box 9569, Seattle, WA 98109, 206-443-4693; von@singspeak.com
Missing Spoke Press, PO Box 9569, Seattle, WA 98109, 206-443-4693; von@singspeak.com
Storm Peak Press, 2629 Nob Hill Avenue North, Seattle, WA 98109-1861
MARGIN: EXPLORING MODERN MAGICAL REALISM, 9407 Capstan Drive NE, Bainbridge Island, WA 98110-4624,

e-mail msellma@ibm.net
FARM PULP MAGAZINE, PO Box 2151, Seattle, WA 98111-2151, 206-782-7418
Bruce Gould Publications, PO Box 16, Seattle, WA 98111
LITRAG, PO Box 21066, Seattle, WA 98111-3066, www.litrag.com
ZERO HOUR, PO Box 766, Seattle, WA 98111, 206-323-3648
Zero Hour Publishing, PO Box 766, Seattle, WA 98111, 206-282-5712
THE COMICS JOURNAL, 7563 Lake City Way, Seattle, WA 98115
D.D.B. Press, 401 N.E. Ravenna Blvd., Ste. 152, Seattle, WA 98115, 904-224-0478
Fantagraphics Books, 7563 Lake City Way, Seattle, WA 98115
Green Stone Publications, PO Eox 15623, Seattle, WA 98115-0623, 206-524-4744
L'Epervier Press, 1326 NE 62nd Street, Seattle, WA 98115
Vipassana Publications, PO Box 15926, Seattle, WA 98115, 206-522-8175; Fax 206-522-8295; info@vrpa.com; http://www.vrpa.com
Fjord Press, PO Box 16349, Seattle, WA 98116, 206-935-7376, fax 206-938-1991, e-mail fjord@halcyon.com; web site www.fjordpress.com/fjord
READERS SPEAK OUT!, 4003 - 50th Avenue SW, Seattle, WA 98116
PRISON LEGAL NEWS, 2400 NW 80th Street, Suite 148, Seattle, WA 98117, 206-781-6524; pln@prisonlegalnews.org
Floating Bridge Press, PO Box 18814, Seattle, WA 98118, 206-860-0508
The Ballard Locks Publishing Co., PO Box.C79005, Seattle, WA 98119-3185, 206-720-8337
Bay Press, 115 West Denny Way, Seattle, WA 98119, 206-284-5913
Seal Press, 3131 Western Avenue, Suite 410, Seattle, WA 98121-1028, 206-283-7844, 800-754-0271 orders; fax 206-285-9410; E-mail sealprss@scn.org
Ananse Press, PO Box 22565, Seattle, WA 98122, 206-325-8205
Open Hand Publishing Inc., PO Box 22048, Seattle, WA 98122, 206-323-2187
THE RAVEN CHRONICLES, 1634 11th Avenue, Seattle, WA 98122, 206-323-4316; ravenchr@speakeasy.org; www.speakeasy.org/ravenchronicles
TEACHER LIBRARIAN: The Journal for School Library Professionals, Dept. 284, PO Box 34069, Seattle, WA 98124-1069, 604-925-0266
Parenting Press, Inc., PO Box 75267, Seattle, WA 98125, 206-364-2900, Fax 206-364-0702
Seekers Press, 11538 Fremont N., Seattle, WA 98133, 206-367-3468
ALWAYS JUKIN', 1952 1st Avenue S #6, Seattle, WA 98134-1406
Always Jukin', 1952 1st Avenue S #6, Seattle, WA 98134-1406
The Mountaineers Books, 1001 SW Klickitat Way, Suite 201, Seattle, WA 98134-1161, 206-223-6303
Bellowing Ark Press, PO Box 45637, Seattle, WA 98145, 206-545-8302
Black Heron Press, PO Box 95676, Seattle, WA 98145
THE MAD FARMERS' JUBILEE ALMANACK, PO Box 85777, Seattle, WA 98145, 206-633-2608
BAST Media, Inc., 17650 1st Avenue South, Box 291, Seattle, WA 98148
HELIOCENTRIC NET/STIGMATA, 17650 1st Avenue S. Box 291, Seattle, WA 98148-0817, E-mail LBothell@wolfen-et.com
THE HELIOCENTRIC WRITER'S NETWORK, 17650 1st Avenue S. Box 291, Seattle, WA 98148-0817, E-mail LBothell@wolfenet.com
BELLOWING ARK, PO Box 55564, Shoreline, WA 98155, 206-440-0791
Light, Words & Music, 16710 16th N.W., Seattle, WA 98177, 206-546-1498, Fax 206-546-2585; sisp@aol.com
CRAB CREEK REVIEW, 7265 S. 128th St., Seattle, WA 98178, 206-772-8489; http://www.drizzle.net/nccr
SIGNS: JOURNAL OF WOMEN IN CULTURE AND SOCIETY, C14 Padelford Hall, Box 354345, University of Washington, Seattle, WA 98195-4345, 206-616-4705, fax 206-616-4756, e-mail signs@u.washington.edu
Fine Edge Productions, 13589 Clayton Lane, Anacortes, WA 98221-8477, 619-387-2412, Fax 619-387-2286; E-mail fineedgepr@aol.com
Island Publishers, Box 201, Anacortes, WA 98221-0201, 206-293-3285/293-5398
THE BELLINGHAM REVIEW, Mail Stop 9053, WWU, Bellingham, WA 98225, 360-650-3209
Signpost Press Inc., Mail Stop 9055, WWU, Bellingham, WA 98225, 360-650-3209
TIME PILOT, 1050 Larrabee Avenue #104-354, Bellingham, WA 98225-7367
Topping International Institute, Inc., 2622 Birchwood Ave, #7, Bellingham, WA 98225, 360-647-2703
HAZEL GROVE MUSINGS, 1225 E. Sunset #304, Bellingham, WA 98226
Access Multimedia, PO Box 5182, Bellingham, WA 98227, 360-733-2155
Ana Libri Press, PO Box 5961, Bellingham, WA 98227-5961, 360-715-1836; Fax 360-715-1869; ana-libri@themystery-box.com; web themysterybox.com
LIFE ON PLANET EARTH, VOL III, PO Box 3194, Bellingham, WA 98227
MULTIMEDIA REVIEWS FOR EDUCATION, MULTIMEDIA REVIEWS FOR INDUSTRY, PO Box 5182, Bellingham, WA 98227, 360-733-2155
Bright Ring Publishing, Inc., PO Box 31338, Bellingham, WA 98228-3338, 360-734-1601, 800-480-4278
ANIMAL PEOPLE, PO Box 960, Clinton, WA 98236-0960
Archipelago Publishing, PO Box 1249, Friday Harbor, WA 98250, 800-360-6166; Fax 360-378-7097; info@gmex.com
The Lockhart Press, Box 1366, Lake Stevens, WA 98258, fax 206-335-4818; e-Mail RAL@HALCYON.COM
Buckhorn Books, 9330 B State Suite 257, Marysville, WA 98270, 360-658-0373
Hundman Publishing, 13110 Beverly Park Road, Mukilteo, WA 98275, 206-743-2607
MAINLINE MODELER, 13110 Beverly Park Road, Mukilteo, WA 98275, 206-743-2607
WOMEN'S WORK, 606 Avenue A, Snohomish, WA 98290-2416, 360-568-5914; e-Mail dammit@eskimo.com; Fax available
Owl Creek Press, 2693 S.W. Camano Drive, Camano Island, WA 98292, 308-387-6101
Brooding Heron Press, Bookmonger Road, Waldron Island, WA 98297
Yggdrasil Books, Box 1098, Waldron Island, WA 98297, 206-738-6072
Red Apple Publishing, 15010 113th Street KPN, Gig Harbor, WA 98329, 206-884-1450; 800-245-6595; FAX 206-884-1451; E-mail redaple@aol.com
WRITERS CORNER, PO Box 456, Glenoma, WA 98336-0456
FERRY TRAVEL GUIDE, PO Box 1169, Port Hadlock, WA 98339-1169
Dan Youra Studios, Inc., PO Box 1169, Port Hadlock, WA 98339-1169
PANGOLIN PAPERS, PO Box 241, Nordland, WA 98358, 360-385-3626

MUSE OF FIRE, 21 Kruse Road, Port Angeles, WA 98362-8900
Pleasure Boat Studio, 802 East Sixth, Port Angeles, WA 98362, 360-452-8686 tel/fax; email pbstudio@pbstudio.com; http://www.pbstudio.com
Pride & Imprints, 7419 Ebbert Drive SE, Port Orchard, WA 98367-9753, email queries@pride-imprints.com
Breakout Productions, PO Box 1643, Port Townsend, WA 98368
Copper Canyon Press, P.O. Box 271, Port Townsend, WA 98368
LIBERTY, PO Box 1181, Port Townsend, WA 98368, 360-379-0242
The Times Journal Publishing Co., PO Box 1286, Puyallup, WA 98371, 206-848-2779
THE ILLUSTRATOR COLLECTOR'S NEWS, PO Box 1958, Sequim, WA 98382, 360-452-3810; ticn@olypen.com
Cultivated Underground Press, PO Box 7610, Tacoma, WA 98407-0610
THE CUP, PO Box 7610, Tacoma, WA 98407-0610
MCS Publishing, 5212 Chicago SW #2, Tacoma, WA 98499, 253-984-1345
OBLIVION, 120 State Avenue NE #76, Olympia, WA 98501-8212, E-mail oblivion@oblivion.net
SLIGHTLY WEST, The Evergreen State College, CAB 320, Olympia, WA 98505, 360-866-6000 x6879
Four Seasons Publishing, PO Box 2321, Olympia, WA 98507, 206-357-4683
KASPAHRASTER, PO Box 7844, Olympia, WA 98507, e-mail jaheriot@subsitu.com; www.subsitu.com
YOUNG VOICES, PO Box 2321, Olympia, WA 98507, 360-357-4683, E-mail; patcha@holcyar.com
Blue Star Press, PO Box 645, Oakville, WA 98568, 360-273-7656
Tiptoe Literary Service, 434-6th Street #206, Raymond, WA 98577-1804, 360-942-4596; anne@willapabay.org; www.willapabay.org/~anne
WORLD OF ROMANCE, PO Box 1220, South Bend, WA 98586, 360-875-6551; e-mail rkmiller@willapabay.org
Horus Publishing, Inc., Suite 39, PO Box 7530, Yelm, WA 98597, 360-894-0965; Fax 360-458-1440; horus@nwrain.com
WRITER'S WORKSHOP REVIEW, 511 West 24th Street, Vancouver, WA 98660, 360-693-6509
Twin Peaks Press, PO Box 129, Vancouver, WA 98666, 360-694-2462, Fax 360-696-3210
TOWERS CLUB, USA INFO MARKETING REPORT, PO Box 2038, Vancouver, WA 98668, 360-574-3084
Blue Raven Publishing, 9 South Wenatchee Avenue, Wenatchee, WA 98801-2210, 509-665-8353
PENNY-A-LINER, PO Box 2163, Wenatchee, WA 98807-2163, 509-662-7858
PORTALS, PO Box 2163, Wenatchee, WA 98807-2163, 509-662-7858
Redrosebush Press, PO Box 2163, Wenatchee, WA 98807-2163, 509-662-7858
Desert Oasis Publishing Co., PO Box 1805, Moses Lake, WA 98837, 509-766-0477
HOME EDUCATION MAGAZINE, PO Box 1083, Tonasket, WA 98855, 509-486-1351; e-Mail HomeEdmag@aol.com
Vagabond Press, 605 East 5th Avenue, Ellensburg, WA 98926-3201, 509-962-8471; bangsj@eburg.com
WILLOW SPRINGS, Eastern Washington Univ., MS-1, 526 5th Street, Cheney, WA 99004-2431, 509-623-4349
Ye Galleon Press, PO Box 287, Fairfield, WA 99012, 509-283-2422; E-mail galleon@mt.arias.net
Score, 1015 NW Clifford Street, Pullman, WA 99163-3203
SCORE, 1015 NW Clifford Street, Pullman, WA 99163-3203
FRONTIERS: A Journal of Women Studies, Women's Studies, PO Box 644007, Washington State University, Pullman, WA 99164-4007, 509-335-7268
GEORGE & MERTIE'S PLACE: Rooms With a View, PO Box 10335, Spokane, WA 99209-1335, 509-325-3738
HELIOTROPE: A Writer's Summer Solstice, PO Box 9517, Spokane, WA 99209-9517, 509-624-0418; www.ior.com/heliotrope
Arthur H. Clark Co., PO Box 14707, Spokane, WA 99214, 509-928-9540
Timeless Books, PO Box 3543, Spokane, WA 99220-3543, 509-838-6652; info@timeless.org
Lost Horse Press, 9327 South Cedar Rim Lane, Spokane, WA 99224, 509-448-4047; e-mail losthorse@ior.com
StarLance Publications, 5104 Cooperstown Lane, Pasco, WA 99301-8984
THE TEMPLE, PO Box 100, Walla Walla, WA 99362-0033, E-mail tsunami@wwics.com
Tsunami Inc., PO Box 100, Walla Walla, WA 99362-0033, E-mail tsunami@wwics.com

WEST VIRGINIA

SMALL PUBLISHER, PO Box 1620, Pineville, WV 24874, 304-732-8195
Mountain State Press, c/o University of Charleston, 2300 MacCorkle Avenue SE, Charleston, WV 25304-1099, 304-357-4767
TRANSMOG, Route 6, Box 138, Charleston, WV 25311, E-Mail: far@medinah.atc.ucarb.com
Appalachian Log Publishing Company, PO Box 20297, Charleston, WV 25362, 304-342-5789
THE SOUTHERN JOURNAL, PO Box 20297, Charleston, WV 25362, 304-722-6866
Summit Crossroads Press, 126 Camp Harmison Drive, Berkeley Springs, WV 25411-4009, 304-258-8653, 1-800-362-0985, Fax 304-258-9282; e-mail SumCross@aol.com; www.parentsuccess.com
The Bunny & The Crocodile Press/Forest Woods Media Productions, Inc, PO Box 416, Hedgesville, WV 25427-0416, 304-754-8847
Research & Discovery Publications, PO Box 5701, Huntington, WV 25703-0100
Aegina Press, Inc., 1905 Madison Avenue, Huntington, WV 25704, 304-429-7204; fax 304-429-7234
University Editions, Inc., 59 Oak Lane, Spring Valley, Huntington, WV 25704, 304-429-7204
Flax Press, Inc., PO Box 2395, Huntington, WV 25724, 304-525-1109
TANTRA PRESS, 2111 Florida Street, Parkersburg, WV 26101-9032, 304-422-3112
The Writers Block, Inc., Laurel Run Route One, Box 254, Bruceton Mills, WV 26525-9748, 304-379-8162; fax 304-379-8161; writersbl@aol.com; www.spannet.org/writersblock
KESTREL: A Journal of Literature and Art, Fairmont State College, Fairmont, WV 26554, 304-367-4815; 304-3674860; e-mail kestrel@mail.fscwv.edu

WISCONSIN

P & K Stark Productions, Inc., 17125C W. Bluemound Road, Ste. 171, Brookfield, WI 53005, 414-543-9013
STARK NAKED, 17125C W. Bluemound Road, Ste. 171, Brookfield, WI 53005, 414-543-9013
FARMER'S DIGEST, PO Box 624, Brookfield, WI 53008-0624, 414-782-4480
Lessiter Publications, PO Box 624, Brookfield, WI 53008-0624, 414-782-4480; Fax 414-782-1252
Sun Designs, PO Box 6, Oconomowoc, WI 53066, 414-567-4255
SEEMS, c/o Lakeland College, Box 359, Sheboygan, WI 53082-0359
Easel Publishing Corporation, 488 North Pine Street, Burlington, WI 53105, 414-763-3690
QUINTILE, PO Box 89, Hales Corners, WI 53130, 414-534-4620

710

Quintile, PO Box 89, Hales Corners, WI 53130, 414-534-4620
Sheed & Ward, 7373 S. Lovers Lane Road, Franklin, WI 53132-1850, 800-444-8910
Tiare Publications, PO Box 493, Lake Geneva, WI 53147, 414-248-4845
Wolfsong Publications, 3123 South Kennedy, Sturtevant, WI 53177, Fax 414-886-5809; E-mail wolfsong@wi.net
AT THE LAKE MAGAZINE, PO Box 96, Walworth, WI 53184, 414-275-9474; Fax 414-275-9530; at-the-lake@idcnet.com
B & B Publishing, Inc., PO Box 96, 820 Wisconsin Street, Walworth, WI 53184, 414-275-9474
THE CREAM CITY REVIEW, PO Box 413, English Dept, Curtin Hall, Univ. of Wisconsin, Milwaukee, WI 53201, 414-229-4708
EMERGING VOICES, 1722 N. 58th Street, Milwaukee, WI 53208-1618, 414-453-4678
SQUARE ONE - A Magazine of Disturbing Fiction, PO Box 11921, Milwaukee, WI 53211-0921
FIRST CLASS, PO Box 12434, Milwaukee, WI 53212, E-mail chriftor@execpc.com; www.execpc.com/~chriftor
Four-Sep Publications, PO Box 12434, Milwaukee, WI 53212, E-mail chriftor@execpc.com; www.execpc.com/~chriftor
The Film Instruction Company of America, 5928 W. Michigan Street, Wauwatosa, WI 53213-4248, 414-258-6492
THE UNDERGROUND, PO Box 14311, Milwaukee, WI 53214
Lemieux International Ltd., PO Box 17134, Milwaukee, WI 53217, 414-962-2844;1-800-950-7723
PANDALOON, PO Box 21973, Milwaukee, WI 53221, 414-476-6030; fax 414-476-6989; email pandaloon@azml.com
PLUMTREES, PO Box 23403, Milwaukee, WI 53223
BGS Press, 1240 William Street, Racine, WI 53402, 414-639-2406
Mother Courage Press, 1533 Illinois St., Racine, WI 53405-3115, 414-634-1047; FAX: 414-637-8242
ACORN WHISTLE, 907 Brewster Avenue, Beloit, WI 53511
BELOIT FICTION JOURNAL, Box 11, Beloit College, Beloit, WI 53511, 608-363-2308
BLOCK'S MAGAZINE, 1419 Chapin Street, Beloit, WI 53511, 608-364-4893
ROSEBUD, PO Box 459, Cambridge, WI 53523, 608-423-9690
W.D. Hoard & Sons Company, 28 Milwaukee Avenue West, Fort Atkinson, WI 53538, 920-563-5551
HOARD'S DAIRYMAN, 28 Milwaukee Avenue West, Fort Atkinson, WI 53538, 920-563-5551
Highsmith Press, PO Box 800, Ft. Atkinson, WI 53538, 414-563-9571; fax 414-563-4801; e-mail hpress@highsmith.com; web site http://www.hpress.highsmith.com
Dog-Eared Publications, PO Box 620863, Middleton, WI 53562-0863, 608-831-1410
MODERN HAIKU, PO Box 1752, Madison, WI 53701
SF**3, PO Box 1624, Madison, WI 53701-1624, 608-267-7483 (days); 608-255-9905 (evenings)
WORLD DOMINATION REVIEW, Po Box 823, Madison, WI 53701-0823, 608-273-8701
Zino Press Children's Books, PO Box 52, Madison, WI 53701, 608-836-6660; Fax 608-831-1570; zinoguy@ku.com
CREATIVITY CONNECTION, Room 622 Lowell Hall, 610 Langdon Street, Madison, WI 53703, 608-262-4911
ART'S GARBAGE GAZZETTE, 1938 East Mifflin Street, Madison, WI 53704-4729, 608-249-0715
Mica Press, 113 Cambridge Road, Madison, WI 53704-5909, 608-246-0759; Fax 608-246-0756; E-mail jgrant@book-zen.com; website www.bookzen.com
Medical Physics Publishing Corp., 4513 Vernon Boulevard, Madison, WI 53705-4964, 608-262-4021
WISCONSIN ACADEMY REVIEW, 1922 University Ave., Madison, WI 53705, 608-263-1692
WISCONSIN TRAILS, PO Box 5650, Madison, WI 53705, 608-231-2444; fax 608-231-1557; e-mail editor@wistrails.com
Wisconsin Trails, P.O.Box 5650, Madison, WI 53705, 608-231-2444; fax 608-231-1557; e-mail pam@wistrails.com
CONTEMPORARY LITERATURE, 7141 Helen C. White Hall, University of Wisconsin, 600 N. Park St. Madison, WI 53706
FEMINIST COLLECTIONS: A QUARTERLY OF WOMEN'S STUDIES RESOURCES, 430 Memorial Library, 728 State Street, Madison, WI 53706, 608-263-5754
FEMINIST PERIODICALS: A CURRENT LISTING OF CONTENTS, 430 Memorial Library, 728 State Street, Madison, WI 53706, 608-263-5754
THE MADISON REVIEW, Dept of English, H.C. White Hall, 600 N. Park Street, Madison, WI 53706, 263-3303
THE MODERN LANGUAGE JOURNAL, University of Wisconsin, Department of French and Italian, Madison, WI 53706-1558, 608-262-5010
NEW BOOKS ON WOMEN & FEMINISM, 430 Memorial Library, 728 State Street, Madison, WI 53706, 608-263-5754
PRIME, 7116 Helen C. White Hall, Madison, WI 53706, 688-262-3262
Women's Studies Librarian, University of Wisconsin System, 430 Memorial Library, 728 State Street, Madison, WI 53706, 608-263-5754
STUDENT LEADERSHIP JOURNAL, PO Box 7895, Madison, WI 53707-7895, 608-274-4823 X425, 413
FEMINIST VOICES NEWSJOURNAL, 1105 Macarthur Road, Apt 7, Madison, WI 53714-1050, 608-251-9268
OF A LIKE MIND, PO Box 6677, Madison, WI 53716, 608-257-5858
ABRAXAS, PO Box 260113, Madison, WI 53726-0113, 608-238-0175; irmarkha@students.wisc.edu; www.litline.org/html/abraxas.html; www.geocities.com/paris/4614
Center for Public Representation, PO Box 260049, Madison, WI 53726-0049, 608-251-4008
Ghost Pony Press, P.O. Box 260113, Madison, WI 53726-0113, 608-238-0175; irmarkha@students.wisc.edu; www.litline.org/html/abraxas html, www.geocities.com/Paris/4614, www.thingnet/~grist/lexd/dalevy/dalevy.html
PHOTOBULLETIN, PhotoSource International, Pine Lake Farm, Osceola, WI 54020, (715) 248-3800, Our Fax# 715-248-7394
THE PHOTOLETTER, PhotoSource International, Pine Lake Farm, Osceola, WI 54020, (715) 248-3800, Our Fax # 715-248-7394
PHOTOSTOCKNOTES, Pine Lake Farm, Osceola, WI 54020, 715-248-3800; FAX 715-248-7394; E-mail info@ohoto-source.com
Wm Caxton Ltd, PO Box 220, Ellison Bay, WI 54210-0220, 414-854-2955
THE GLASS CHERRY, 901 Europe Bay Road, Ellison Bay, WI 54210-9643, 414-854-9042
The Glass Cherry Press, 901 Europe Bay Road, Ellison Bay, WI 54210, 414-854-9042
DOOR COUNTY ALMANAK, 10905 Bay Shore Drive, Sister Bay, WI 54234, 414-854-2742
Jackson Harbor Press, RR 1, Box 107AA, Washington Island, WI 54246
George Sroda, Publisher, PO Box 97, Amherst Jct., WI 54407, 715-824-3868
Explorer's Guide Publishing, 4843 Apperson Drive, Rhinelander, WI 54501, 715-362-6029 phone/Fax; 800-487-6029
NORTHEAST, 1310 Shorewood Drive, La Crosse, WI 54601-7033
RURAL NETWORK ADVOCATE, Rt. 1, Box 129, Gays Mills, WI 54631
HUMAN, Excercises in the Crucial Arts, Route 1 Box 133, La Farge, WI 54639

711

Rhiannon Press, 1105 Bradley Avenue, Eau Claire, WI 54701, 715-835-0598
FAMILY TIMES: The Newspaper for Chippewa Valley Parents, PO Box 932, Eau Claire, WI 54702, 715-836-9499; fax 715-839-7052; e-mail familyt@discover-net.net
MIDWEST ART FAIRS, PO Box 72, Pepin, WI 54759, 715-442-2022
Michael E. Coughlin, Publisher, PO Box 205, Cornucopia, WI 54827
THE DANDELION, Cornucopia, WI 54827
POET'S FANTASY, 227 Hatten Avenue, Rice Lake, WI 54868, 715-234-2205
WISCONSIN REVIEW, Box 158, Radford Hall, Univ. of Wisconsin-Oshkosh, Oshkosh, WI 54901, 920-424-2267
N: NUDE & NATURAL, PO Box 132, Oshkosh, WI 54902, 414-231-9950
The Green Hut Press, 1015 Jardin Street East, Appleton, WI 54911, 414-734-9728
SHENANDOAH NEWSLETTER, 736 West Oklahoma Street, Appleton, WI 54914
PACIFIC ENTERPRISE, PO Box 1907, Fond du Lac, WI 54936-1907, 920-922-9218; rudyled@vbe.com
Pearl-Win Publishing Co., N4721 9th Drive, Hancock, WI 54943-7617, 715-249-5407
Aircraft Owners Group, PO Box 5000, Iola, WI 54945, 800-331-0038; e-mail cessna@aircraftownergroup.com or piper@aircraftownergroup.com
CESSNA OWNER MAGAZINE, PO Box 5000, Iola, WI 54945, 715-445-5000; E-mail cessna@aircraftownergroup.com
PIPERS MAGAZINE, PO Box 5000, Iola, WI 54945, 715-445-5000; e-mail piper@aircraftownergroup.com
Wolf Angel Press, 1011 Babcock Street, Neenah, WI 54956, 920-722-5826; e-mails flaherty@uwosh.edu, newpok32@uwosh.edu, stevens@tcccom.net; www.english.uwosh.edu/wolfangel/.

WYOMING

Calypso Publications, 5810 Osage Avenue #205, Cheyenne, WY 82009
Heritage Concepts Publishing Inc, PO Box 6121, Laramie, WY 82070, 307-742-4377; fax 307-721-8130
OWEN WISTER REVIEW, PO Box 3625, Laramie, WY 82071-3625, 307-766-4027; owr@uwyo.edu
Skyline West Press/Wyoming Almanac, 1409 Thomes, Laramie, WY 82072, 307-745-8205
High Plains Press, Box 123, Glendo, WY 82213, 307-735-4370; Fax 307-735-4590; 800-552-7819
Cougar Imprints, PO Box .573, Rawlins, WY 82301-1573, 307-864-3328, fax 307-864-5279, e-mail Cougar-Book@AOL.com
Agathon Books, PO Box 630, Lander, WY 82520-0630, 307-332-5252; Fax 307-332-5888; agathon@rmisp.com; www.rmisp.com/agathon/
Alpine Press, PO Box 1930, Mills, WY 82644, 307-234-1990
Andmar Press, PO Box 217, Mills, WY 82644, e-mail fjozwik@csi.com; www.andmarpress.com
Avalon Writing Center, Inc., PO Box 183, Mills, WY 82644, 307-235-6177; E-mail fehanson@juno.com
CRONE CHRONICLES: A Journal of Conscious Aging, PO Box 81, Kelly, WY 83011, 307-733-5409
Homestead Publishing, Box 193, Moose, WY 83012

ARGENTINA

ETICA & CIENCIA, PO Box 94 Suc. 19, Buenos Aires 1419, Argentina, 541-572-1050
FISICA, PO Box 94 Sucursal 19, Buenos Aires 1419, Argentina, 541-572-1050
TIERRA DEL FUEGO MAGAZINE, PO Box 94 Sucursal 19, Buenos Aires 1419, Argentina, 541-572-1050
Zagier & Urruty Publicaciones, PO Box 94 Sucursal 19, Buenos Aires 1419, Argentina, 541-572-1050

AUSTRALIA

ANARCHIST AGE MONTHLY REVIEW, PO Box 20, Parkville, Melbourne, Victoria 3052, Australia, 03/8282856; FAX 03/4824371
ANARCHIST AGE WEEKLY REVIEW, PO Box 20, Parkville, Melbourne, Victoria 3052, Australia, 03/8282856; FAX 03/4844371
BLAST, PO Box 3514, Manuka, Act. 2603, Australia
EDDIE THE MAGAZINE, PO Box 199, Newtown, N.S.W. 2042, Australia, phone 61-2-211-2339; fax 61-2-211-2331
Galaxy Press, 71 Recreation Street, Tweed Heads, N.S.W. 2485, Australia, 075-361997
GRASS ROOTS, PO Box 242, Euroa, Victoria 3666, Australia
HEARTLAND (Australia), PO Box 435, Annerley, Queensland 4103, Australia
HECATE, P.O. Box 99, St. Lucia, Queensland 4067, Australia
Hecate Press, PO Box 99, St. Lucia, QLD 4067, Australia
HOBO POETRY & HAIKU MAGAZINE, PO Box 166, Hazelbrook NSW 2779, Australia
IDIOM 23, Central Queensland University, Rockhampton, Queensland, 4702, Australia, 0011-079-360655
IMAGO, Queensland Univ Technology, School of Media and Journalism, PO Box 2434, Brisbane Q1D 4001, Australia, (07)864 2976, FAX (07)864 1810
LINQ, School Languages, Literature and Communication, James Cook Univ.-North Queensland, Townsville 4811, Australia, e-mail jw.linq@jeu.edu.au
MEANJIN, 99 Barry Street, Carlton, Victoria 3053, Australia, 613-344-6950
Meanjin, 99 Barry Street, Carlton, Victoria 3053, Australia, 613-344-6950
THE METAPHYSICAL REVIEW, 59 Keele Street, Collingwood, Victoria 3066, Australia, (03) 4194797
MICROPRESS YATES, 29 Brittainy Street, Petrie, Queensland 4502, Australia, 07-32851462; gloriabe@powerup.com.au
Nosukumo, GPO Box 994-H, Melbourne, Victoria 3001, Australia, 9527-3964
Noyce Publishing, G.P.O. Box 2222T, Melbourne, Vic. 3001, Australia, e-mail noycepublishing@hotmail.com
OVERLAND, PO Box 14146, Melbourne 3000, Australia
PAPER WASP: A Journal of Haiku, 7 Bellevue Terrace, St. Lucia, Queensland 4067, Australia, 61-7-33713509; Fax 61-7-33715527
Pinchgut Press, 6 Oaks Avenue, Cremorne, Sydney, N.S.W. 2090, Australia, 02-9908-2402
QUADRANT MAGAZINE, PO Box 1495, Collingwood, Vic. 3066, Australia, (03) 417-6855
RED AND BLACK, PO Box 12, Quaama, NSW 2550, Australia
RED LAMP, 5 Kahana Court, Mountain Creek, Queensland 4557, Australia, evans-baj@hotmail.com
REDOUBT, Faculty of Communication, PO Box 1, Belconnen, ACT 2616, Australia, 06-201-5270; fax 06-201-5300
SF COMMENTARY, 59 Keele Street, Collingwood, Victoria 3066, Australia, (03) 419-4797
Graham Stone, GPO Box 4440, Sydney 1044, Australia, 043-926540
STUDIO - A Journal of Christians Writing, 727 Peel Street, Albury, N.S.W. 2640, Australia
ULITARRA, PO Box 195, Armidale, New South Wales 2350, Australia, +612 6772 9135

UNION RECORDER, Level One, Manning House, University of Sydney, NSW 2006, Australia
University of Sydney Union, Level One, Manning House, University of Sydney, NSW 2006, Australia
VERANDAH, Faculty of Arts, Deakin University, 221 Burwood Highway, Burwood, Victoria 3125, Australia, 03-9244-6742
Visa Books (Division of South Continent Corporation Pty Ltd), PO Box 1024, Richmond North, Victoria 3121, Australia, 03-429-5599
XY: Men, Sex, Politics, PO Box 26, Ainslie, Canberra, Act. 2602, Australia, phone/fax 06-248-5215

AUSTRIA

IASP NEWSLETTER, WUV Universitatsverlag, Berggasse 5, A-1090 Vienna, Austria

BELGIUM

HORIZON, Stationsstraat 232A, 1770 Liedekerke, Belgium, 053-669465

BELIZE

AXIOS, 30-32 Macaw Avenue, PO Box 279, Belmodan, Belize, 501-8-23284
Axios Newletter, Inc., 30-32 Macaw Avenue, PO Box 279, Belmopan, Belize, 501-8-23284
GORHAM, 30-32 Macaw Avenue, PO Box 279, Belmopan, Belize, 501-8-23284
ORTHODOX MISSION, 30-32 Macaw Avenue, Belmopan, Belize, 011-501-8-23284
Orthodox Mission in Belize, 30-32 Macaw Avenue, PO Box 279, Belmopan, Belize, 501-8-23284, fax 501-8-23633
THE VORTEX, 30-32 Macaw Avenue, PO Box 279, Belmopan, Belize, 501-8-23284

BOLIVIA

Silver Mountain Press, Casilla 6572 Torres Sofer, Cochabamba, Bolivia

CANADA

Aardvark Enterprises (A Division of Speers Investments Ltd.), 204 Millbank Drive S.W., Calgary, Alta T2Y 2H9, Canada, 403-256-4639
ABILITY NETWORK, PO Box 24045, Dartmouth, Nova Scotia B3A 4T4, Canada, 902-461-9009; FAX 902-461-9484; e-Mail: anet@fox.nstn.ca
THE AFFILIATE, 777 Barb Road, #257, Vankleek Hill, Ontario K0B 1R0, Canada, 613-678-3453
AFTERTHOUGHTS, 1100 Commissioners Rd. E, PO Box 41040, London, ON N5Z 4Z7, Canada
ALBERTA HISTORY, 95 Holmwood Ave NW, Calgary Alberta T2K 2G7, Canada, 403-289-8149
Alive Books, PO Box 80055, Burnaby, BC V5H 3X1, Canada, 604-435-1919; FAX 604-435-4888
ALIVE: Canadian Journal of Health and Nutrition, PO Box 80055, Burnaby, BC V5H 3X1, Canada, 604-435-1919; FAX 604-435-4888; editorial@ultranet.ca
The Alternate Press, 272 Highway 5, RR 1, St. George, Ont. N0E 1N0, Canada, 519-448-4001; fax 519-448-4411; e-mail natural@life.ca
THE AMETHYST REVIEW, 23 Riverside Avenue, Truro, N.S. B2N 4G2, Canada, 902-895-1345
Annick Press Ltd., 15 Patricia Avenue, Willowdale, Ontario M2M 1H9, Canada, 416-221-4802
THE ANTIGONISH REVIEW, St Francis Xavier University, PO Box 5000, Antigonish, Nova Scotia B2G 2W5, Canada
Anvil Press, PO Box 1575, Bentall Centre, Vancouver, B.C. V6C 2P7, Canada
ARIEL—A Review of International English Literature, The University of Calgary, 2500 University Drive NW, Calgary, Alberta T2N 1N4, Canada, 403-220-4657
ARTISTAMP NEWS, PO Box 3655, Vancouver, B.C. V6B 3Y8, Canada
AU NATUREL, 4545 Pierre-de-Coubertin, C.P. 1000 succ. M., Montreal, Quebec, H1V 3R2, Canada, 514-252-3014, 514-254-1363, legrand@generation.net
Author's Partner in Publishing, Suite 551-800-15355 24th Avenue, White Rock, B.C. V4A 2H9, Canada, 604-535-8558; 604-535-9653; dchivers@uniserve.com
B.A Cass Publishing, #1101-140 10th Avenue S.W., Calgary Alberta T2R 0A3, Canada, 403-264-9714; fax 403-261-3673; E-mail bacass@iul-ccs.com
Banana Productions, PO Box 2480, Sechelt, BC V0N 3A0, Canada, 604-885-7156; fax 604-885-7183
BARDIC RUNES, 424 Cambridge Street South, Ottawa, Ontario K1S 4H5, Canada, 613-231-4311
Betelgeuse Books, F24-122 St. Patrick St., Ste. 193, Toronto Ont. M5T 2X8, Canada
Between The Lines, 720 Bathurst Street, Suite 404, Toronto, Ontario M5S 2R4, Canada, 416-535-9914, fax 416-535-1484; btlbooks@web.net
Black Bile Press, 1315 Niagara Street #4, Windsor, Ont. N9A 3V8, Canada, 519-253-3237
Black Rose Books Ltd., C.P. 1258, Succ. Place du Parc, Montreal, Quebec H2W 2R3, Canada, 514-844-4076
BLACKFLASH, 2nd Floor, 12-23rd Street East, Saskatoon, Saskatchewan S7L 5E2, Canada, 306-244-8018; fax 306-665-6568; E-mail af248@sfn.saskatoon.sk.ca
BLOOD & APHORISMS: A Journal of Literary Fiction, PO Box 702, Station P, Toronto, ON M5S 2Y4, Canada
Borealis Press Limited, 110 Bloomingdale Street, Ottawa, Ont. K2C 4A4, Canada, 613-798-9299; Fax 613-798-9747
Broken Jaw Press, PO Box 596 Stn A, Canada, Fredericton, NB E3B 5A6, Canada, ph/fax 506-454-5127; e-mail jblades@nbnet.nb.ca; www.brokenjaw.com
BROKEN PENCIL, PO Box 203 Station P, Toronto, ON M5S 2S7, Canada, 416-538-2813; E-mail editor@brokenpencil.com
C.S.P. WORLD NEWS, c/o Guy F. Claude Hamel, 1307 Bethamy Lane, Gloucester, Ont. K1J 8P3, Canada, 613-741-8675
CANADIAN CHILDREN'S LITERATURE, SLAPSIE, University of Guelph, Guelph, Ontario N1G 2W1, Canada, 519-824-4120 ext. 3189; FAX 519-837-1315; E-mail ccl@uoguelph.ca; http://www.uoguelph.ca/englit/ccl/
Canadian Children's Press, SLAPSIE, University of Guelph, Guelph, Ontario N1G 2W1, Canada
Canadian Committee on Labour History, History/CCLH, FM 2005, Memorial University, St. John's, NF A1C 5S7, Canada, 709-737-2144
Canadian Educators' Press, 100 City Centre Drive, PO Box 2094, Mississauga, ON L5B 3C6, Canada, 905-826-0578
CANADIAN JOURNAL OF PHILOSOPHY, University of Calgary Press, Univ. of Calgary, 2500 University Dr. N.W., Calgary, Alberta T2N 1N4, Canada, 403-220-7578; FAX 403-282-0085, e-mail 75003@aoss.ucalgary.ca
CANADIAN JOURNAL OF PROGRAM EVALUATION/LA REVUE CANADIENNE D'EVALUATION DE PROGRAMME, University of Calgary Press, Univ. of Calgary, 2500 University Dr. N.W., Calgary, Alberta T2N 1N4, Canada, 403-220-7578; FAX 403-282-0085; powell@ucalgary.ca

713

Canadian Library Association, 200 Elgin Street, Suite 602, Ottawa, Ontario K2P 1L5, Canada, 613-232-9625 X322

CANADIAN LITERATURE, University of British Columbia, 2029 West Mall, Vancouver, B.C. V6T 1Z2, Canada, 604-822-2780

CANADIAN MONEYSAVER, Box 370, Bath, Ontario K0H 1G0, Canada

CANADIAN PUBLIC POLICY- Analyse de Politiques, School of Policy Studies, Queens University, Kingston, Ontario K7L 3N6, Canada, 613-533-6644; fax 613-533-6960

CANADIAN REVIEW OF AMERICAN STUDIES, University of Calgary Press, 2500 University Drive NW, Calgary, Alberta T2N 1N4, Canada, 403-220-7578, fax 403-282-0085, 75003@aoss.ucalgary.ca

CANADIAN WOMAN STUDIES/les cahiers de la femme, 212 Founders College, York Univ., 4700 Keele Street, New York, Ontario M3J 1P3, Canada, 416-736-5356; fax 416-736-5765; e-mail cwscf@yorku.ca

THE CAPILANO REVIEW, 2055 Purcell Way, North Vancouver, B.C. V7J 3H5, Canada, 604-984-1712

CODA: The Jazz Magazine, PO Box 1002, Station O, Toronto, Ont. M4A 2N4, Canada, 416-593-7230

CONNEXIONS DIGEST, PO Box 158, Station D, Toronto, Ontario M6P 3J8, Canada, 416-537-3949; connex@sources.com; www.connexions.org

Connexions Information Services, Inc., PO Box 158, Station D, Toronto, Ontario M6P 3J8, Canada, 416-537-3949

Cosmic Trend, Sheridan Mall, Box 47014, Mississauga, Ontario L5K 2R2, Canada

Coteau Books, 401-2206 Dewdney Avenue, Regina, Sask. S4R 1H3, Canada, 306-777-0170; e-Mail coteau@coteau.unibase.com

COUNTRY CHARM MAGAZINE, Box 696, Palmerston, ON N0G 2P0, Canada, 519-343-3059

CROSSCURRENTS, 516 Ave K South, Saskatoon, Saskatchewan, Canada, fax: 306-244-0795; e-mail: green@webster.sk.ca; http://www.webster.sk.ca/greenwich/xc.htm

THE DALHOUSIE REVIEW, Dalhousie University, Halifax, Nova Scotia B3H 3J5, Canada, 902-494-2541; fax 902-494-3561; email dalhousie.review@dal.ca

DESCANT, PO Box 314, Station P, Toronto, Ontario M5S 2S8, Canada

DOUBLE BILL, PO Box 55, Station 'E', Toronto, Ontario M6H 4E1, Canada

ECHOS DU MONDE CLASSIQUE/CLASSICAL VIEWS, University of Calgary Press, Univ. of Calgary, 2500 University Dr. N.W., Calgary, Alberta T2N 1N4, Canada, 403-220-7578, fax 403-282-0085, e-mail 470533@ucdasvm1.admin.ucal-gary.ca

ECW Press, 2120 Queen Street East, Suite 200, Toronto, Ontario M4E 1E2, Canada, 416-694-3348; FAX 416-698-9906

Edition Stencil, c/o Guy F. Claude Hamel, 1307 Bethamy Lane, Gloucester, Ont. K1J 8P3, Canada, 741-8675

Editions Ex Libris, B.P. 34033, Sherbrooke, Quebec J1K 3B1, Canada, 819-564-8483

ELLIPSE, Univ. de Sherbrooke, Box 10, Faculte des Lettres et Sciences Humaines, Sherbrooke, Quebec J1K 2R1, Canada, 819-821-7238

EMPLOI PLUS, 1256 Principale N. Street, Ste. #203, L'Annonciation, Quebec, Canada J0T 1T0, Canada, 819-275-3293 phone/Fax

ENTROPY NEGATIVE, PO Box 3355, Vancouver, B.C. V6B 3Y3, Canada

ESSAYS ON CANADIAN WRITING, 2120 Queen Street East, Suite 200, Toronto, Ontario M4E 1E2, Canada, 416-694-3348; FAX 416-698-9906

EVENT, Douglas College, PO Box 2503, New Westminster, B.C. V3L 5B2, Canada, 604-527-5293

EXCEPTIONALITY EDUCATION CANADA, University of PEI, 550 University Avenue, Charlottetown, PEI C1A 4P3, Canada

EXCLAIM!, 7b Pleasant Boulevard #966, Toronto, ON M4T 1K2, Canada, 416-535-9735; Fax 416-535-0566; exclaim@shmooze.net

Exclaim! Brand Comics, 7b Pleasant Boulevard #966, Toronto, ON M4T 1K2, Canada, 416-535-9735; Fax 416-535-0566; exclaim@schmooze.net

FELICITER, 200 Elgin Street, Suite 602, Ottawa, Ontario K2P 1L5, Canada, 613-232-9625, ext. 322

THE FIDDLEHEAD, Campus House, PO Box 4400, University of New Brunswick, Fredericton, NB E3B 5A3, Canada, 506-453-3501

FIRM NONCOMMITTAL: An International Journal of Whimsy, 5 Vonda Avenue, Toronto, ON M2N 5E6, Canada, e-mail firmnon@idirect.com; webhome.idirect.com/~firmnon

FREEFALL, Alexandra Writers Centre Society, 922 9th Avenue S.E., Calgary, AB T2G 0S4, Canada, fax 403-264-4730; e-mail awcs@writtenword.org; website www.writtenword.org/awcs

FRONT & CENTRE MAGAZINE, 25 Avalon Place, Hamilton, ON L8M 1R2, Canada

Gesture Press, 68 Tyrrel Avenue, Toronto M6G 2G4, Canada

Golden Meteorite Press, PO Box 1223 Main Post Office, Edmonton, Alberta T5J 2M4, Canada

Good Times Publishing Co., 2211 West 2nd Avenue #209, Vancouver, B.C. V6K 1H8, Canada, 604-736-1045

Grade School Press, 3266 Yonge Street #1829, Toronto, Ontario M4N 3P6, Canada, 416-784-2883; FAX 416-784-3580

GRAIN, Box 1154, Regina, Sask. S4P 3B4, Canada, 306-244-2828, e-mail grain.mag@sk.sympatico.ca

THE GREAT IDEA PATCH, 110 Jeffery Street, Shelburne, ON L0N 1S4, Canada

GREEN'S MAGAZINE, Box 3236, Regina, Saskatchewan S4P 3H1, Canada

Greensleeve Editions, PO Box 41164, Edmonton, AB T6J 6M7, Canada

Growing Room Collective, Box 46160, Station D, Vancouver BC V6J 5G5, Canada

GUARD THE NORTH, PO Box 3355, Vancouver, B.C. V6B 3Y3, Canada

Guernica Editions, Inc., PO Box 117, Station P, Toronto, Ontario M5S 2S6, Canada, 416-658-9888; FAX 416-657-8885; e-Mail 102026.1331@compuserve.com

HECATE'S LOOM - A Journal of Magical Arts, Box 5206, Stn. B, Victoria, BC V8R 6N4, Canada, 604-478-0401, fax 604-478-9287, e-Mail Loom@islandnet.com

Historical Society of Alberta, 95 Holmwood Ave. NW, Calgary, Alberta T2K 2G7, Canada

Hochelaga Press, 4982 Connaught Avenue, Montreal, BC H4V 1X3, Canada, 514-484-3186; Fax 514-484-8971; hochelaga@sympatico.ca

Horned Owl Publishing, 3906 Cadboro Bay Rd., Victoria, BC V8N 4G6, Canada, 250-477-8488; fax 250-721-1029; e-mail hornowl@islandnet.com

IMPERIAL RUSSIAN JOURNAL, 103 Bristol Road East, Unit 202, Mississauga, Ontario L4Z 3P4, Canada, 905-568-3522

Inner City Books, Box 1271, Station Q, Toronto, ON M4T 2P4, Canada, 416-927-0355; FAX 416-924-1814; icb@inforamp.net

Insomniac Press, 393 Shaw Street, Toronto, ON, M6J 2X4, Canada, 416-536-4308

INTERCULTURE, Intercultural Institute of Montreal, 4917 St-Urbain, Montreal, Quebec H2T 2W1, Canada, 514-288-7229; FAX 514-844-6800

714

INTERNATIONAL ART POST, PO Box 2480, Sechelt, B.C. V0N 3A0, Canada
THE INTERNATIONAL FICTION REVIEW, Dept. of German & Russian, UNB, PO Box 4400, Fredericton, N.B. E3B 5A3, Canada, 506-453-4636; fax 506-453-4659; e-mail ifr@unb.ca
JOURNAL OF CANADIAN POETRY, 110 Bloomingdale Street, Ottawa, Ont. K2C 4A4, Canada, 613-797-9299; Fax 613-798-9747
JOURNAL OF CANADIAN STUDIES/Revue d'etudes canadiennes, Trent University, Peterborough, Ont. K9J 7B8, Canada, 705-748-1279; 705-748-1655; e-Mail jcs-rec@trentu.co
JOURNAL OF CHILD AND YOUTH CARE, Malaspina University College, Human Services, 900 5th Street, Nanaimo, BC V9R 5S5, Canada
KICK IT OVER, Kick It Over Collective, PO Box 5811, Station A, Toronto, Ontario M5W 1P2, Canada
LABOUR/LE TRAVAIL, History/CCLH, FM 2005, Memorial University, St. John's, NF A1C 5S2, Canada, 709-737-2144
Les Recherches Daniel Say Cie., PO Box 3355, Vancouver, B.C. V6B 3Y3, Canada
LITERARY RESEARCH, Dept. of Modern Languages & Lit., University of Western Ontario, London, ON N6A 3K7, Canada, 519-661-3196; 519-661-2111 X5862; Fax 519-661-4093; cmihails@julian.uwo.ca; www.uwo.ca/modlang/index.html
THE MALAHAT REVIEW, PO Box 1700, Stn. CSC, Victoria, British Columbia V8W 2Y2, Canada
MEDICAL REFORM, 517 College Street, Suite 303, Toronto, Ontario M6G 4A2, Canada, 416-323-9903; Fax 416-323-0311; mrg@web.net
Medical Reform Group, 517 College Street, Suite 303, Toronto, Ontario M6G 4A2, Canada, 416-323-9903; Fax 416-323-0311; mrg@web.net
Munsey Music, Box 511, Richmond Hill, Ontario L4C 4Y8, Canada, 905-737-0208; www.pathcom.com/~munsey
MUSICWORKS: The Journal of Sound Explorations (Audio-Visual), 179 Richmond Street West, Toronto, Ontario M5V 1V3, Canada, 416-977-3546
THE MYSTERY REVIEW, PO Box 233, Colborne, Ont. K0K 1S0, Canada, 613-475-4440; fax 613-475-3400
NATURAL LIFE, 272 Highway 5, RR 1, St. George, Ontario N0E 1N0, Canada, 519-449-4001; fax 519-448-4411; email natural@life.ca
NEW MUSE OF CONTEMPT, Box 596 Stn A, Canada, E3B 5A6, Fredericton, Canada, 902-423-5223
New Star Books Ltd., #107, 3477 Commercial Street, Vancouver, B.C. V5N 4E8, Canada, 604-738-9429; FAX 604-738-9332
NEWSLETTER (LEAGUE OF CANADIAN POETS), 54 Wolseley Street 3rd Floor, Toronto, Ontario M5T IA5, Canada, 416-504-1657, Fax; 416-504-0096
Nico Professional Services, Ltd., 1515 West 2nd Avenue, #543, Vancouver, BC V6J 5C5, Canada, 604-733-6530
ON SPEC: More Than Just Science Fiction, PO Box 4727, Edmonton, AB T6E 5G6, Canada, 403-413-0215; email onspec@earthling.net
Oolichan Books, PO Box 10, Lantzville, B.C., V0R 2H0, Canada, 604-390-4839
Our Schools/Our Selves, 107 Earl Grey Road, Toronto, Ontario, Canada, 416-463-6978 (phone and fax)
OUR SCHOOLS/OUR SELVES, 107 Earl Grey Road, Toronto, Ontario, Canada, 416-463-6978 (phone and fax)
PAPERPLATES, 19 Kenwood Avenue, Toronto, ON M6C 2R8, Canada
PARA*PHRASE, Sheridan Mall, Box 47014, Mississauga, Ontario L5K 2R2, Canada
Pavlovsk Press, 103 Bristol Road East, Unit 202, Mississauga, Ontario L4Z 3P4, Canada, 905-568-3522
PEACE MAGAZINE, 736 Bathurst Street, Toronto, Ont. M5S 2R4, Canada, 416-533-7581; Fax 416-531-6214; e-mail mspencer@web.net; website www.peace magazine.org
Pens of Voltaire Press, 1550 Kingston Road, Unit #4, Suite 1079, Pickering, Ontario L1V 6W9, Canada, 905-509-4808; Fax 905-509-7821; Toll free 800-866-1463
THE PLOWMAN, Box 414, Whitby, Ontario L1N 5S4, Canada, 905-668-7803
The Porcupine's Quill, Inc., 68 Main Street, Erin, Ontario N0B 1T0, Canada, 519-833-9158
THE POTTERSFIELD PORTFOLIO, PO Box 40, Station A, Sydney, Nova Scotia B1P 6G9, Canada, www.auracom.com/saunde/potters.html
Pottersfield Press, 83 Leslie Road, East Lawrencetown, NS, B2Z 1P8, Canada, 1-800-Nimbus 9 (for orders)
PRAIRIE FIRE, 423-100 Arthur Street, Winnipeg MB R3B 1H3, Canada, 204-943-9066, fax 942-1555
THE PRAIRIE JOURNAL OF CANADIAN LITERATURE, PO Box 61203 Brentwood P.O., 217, 3630 Brentwood Road N.W., Calgary, Alberta T2L 2K6, Canada
Prairie Journal Press, PO Box 61203 Brentwood P.O., 217, 3630 Brentwood Road N.W., Calgary, Alberta T2L 2K6, Canada
Prairie Publishing Company, PO Box 2997, Winnipeg, MB R3C 4B5, Canada, 204-885-6496
PRISM INTERNATIONAL, E462-1866 Main Mall, University of British Columbia, Vancouver BC V6T 1Z1, Canada, 604-822-2514, fax 604-822-3616, e-mail prism@urixg.ubc.ca web site: http://www.arts.ubc.ca/prism
Proof Press, 67 Court Street, Aylmer, QC J9H 4M1, Canada, E-mail: dhoward@aix1.uottawa.ca
Quarterly Committee of Queen's University, Queen's University, Kingston, Ontario K7L 3N6, Canada, e-mail qquartly@post.queensu.ca; website http://info.queensu.ca/quarterly
QUEEN'S QUARTERLY: A Canadian Review, Queen's University, Kingston, Ontario K7L 3N6, Canada, 613-545-2667; e-mail qquartly@post.queensu.ca; website http://info.queensu.ca/quarterly
Questex Consulting Ltd., 8 Karen Drive, Guelph, Ontario N1G 2N9, Canada, 519-824-7423
THE QUILL MAGAZINE QUARTERLY, 2900 Warden Avenue, PO Box 92207, Toronto, Ontario, MIW 3Y9, Canada, 416-410-0277; fax 416-497-6737; e-mail austin@thequill.com
RAW NERVZ HAIKU, 67 Court Street, Aylmer, QC J9H 4M1, Canada, E-mail: dhoward@aix1.uottawa.ca
REDEMPTION, PO Box 54063, Vancouver, BC V7Y 1B0, Canada, 604-264-9109; Fax 604-264-8692; Redemption@pacificgroup.net
RESOURCES FOR FEMINIST RESEARCH/DOCUMENTATION SUR LA RECHERCHE FEMINISTE, 252 Bloor Street W., Toronto, Ontario M5S 1V6, Canada, 416-923-6641, ext. 2278; Fax 416-926-4725; E-mail rfrdrf@oise.on.ca
Reveal, 4322 Cleroux, Chomedey, Laval, Quebec H7T 2E3, Canada, 514-687-8966
Ronsdale Press, 3350 West 21st Avenue, Vancouver, B.C. V6S 1G7, Canada, 604-738-4688, Fax 604-731-4548
ROOM OF ONE'S OWN, PO Box 46160, Station D, Vancouver, British Columbia V6J 5G5, Canada
St. Augustine Society Press, 68 Kingsway Crescent, Etobicoke, ON M8X 2R6, Canada
Saskatchewan Writers Guild, Box 3986, Regina, Saskatchewan S4P 3R9, Canada, 306-757-6310
SCRIVENER, McGill University, 853 Sherbrooke Street W., Montreal, P.Q. H3A 2T6, Canada, 514-398-6588
7th Generation, 621-202 4th Avenue North, Saskatoon, SK S7K 3L7, Canada, 306-652-6554; www.7th-Generation.com
SHARK QUARTERLY, 129 Dunbarton Court, Ottawa, Ontario, K1K 4L6, Canada, 613-741-7407 tel/fax

Stewart Publishing & Printing, 17 Sir Constantine Drive, Markham, ON L3P 2X3, Canada, 905-294-4389; FAX 905-294-8718; rstewart@pathcom.com
SUB-TERRAIN, PO Box 1575, Bentall Centre, Vancouver, B.C. V6C 2P7, Canada, 604-876-8710
Summerthought Ltd., PO Box 1420, Banff, Alberta T0L0C0, Canada, 762-3919; fax 403-762-4126
Sun Books, Box 28, Lennoxville, Quebec J1M 1Z3, Canada
TEAK ROUNDUP, #5-9060 Tronson Road, Vernon, BC V1H 1E7, Canada, 250-545-4186, Fax 250-545-4194
TEXTSHOP, Andrew Stubbs, English Dept., University of Regina, Regina, Sask. S4S 0A2, Canada
THALIA: Studies in Literary Humor, Dept of English, Univ of Ottawa, Ottawa K1N 6N5, Canada, 613-230-9505; Fax 613-565-5786
Theytus Books Ltd., PO Box 20040, Penticton, B.C. V2A 8K3, Canada, 250-493-7181
Thistledown Press Ltd., 633 Main Street, Saskatoon, Saskatchewan S7H 0J8, Canada, 306-244-1722
TIME FOR RHYME, c/o Richard Unger, PO Box 1055, Battleford SK S0M 0E0, Canada, 306-445-5172
TOWER, c/o McMaster University, 1280 Main Street W Box 1021, Hamilton, Ontario, L8S ICO, Canada
Tower Poetry Society, c/o McMaster University, 1280 Main Street W. Box 1021, Hamilton, Ontario, L8S 1CO, Canada
THE TOWNSHIPS SUN, Box 28, Lennoxville, Quebec J1M 1Z3, Canada
TRANSVERSIONS, 1019 Colville Road, Victoria, BC V9A 4P5, Canada, 604-380-7150; FAX 604-383-4413
Tuns Press, Faculty of Architecture, Dalhousie University, Box 1000, Halifax, Nova Scotia B3J 2X4, Canada, 902-420-7641, Fax 902-423-6672, tuns.press@dal.ca; www.dal.ca/tunspress
Turnstone Press, 607-100 Arthur Street, Winnipeg R3B 1H3, Canada, 204-947-1555, E-mail: acquisitions@turnstone-press.mb.ca
Tyro Publishing, 194 Carlbert Street, Sault St. Marie, Ontario P6A 5E1, Canada, 705-253-6402, Fax 705-942-3625; tyro@sympatico.ca
Underwhich Editions, PO Box 262, Adelaide Street Station, Toronto, Ontario M5C 2J4, Canada, 536-9316
Unfinished Monument Press, 237 Prospect Street South, Hamilton, Ontario L8M 2Z6, Canada
University of Calgary Press, 2500 University Drive NW, Calgary, Alberta T2N 1N4, Canada, 403-220-7578, fax 403-282-0085
UNIVERSITY OF WINDSOR REVIEW, Department of English, University of Windsor, Windsor, Ontario N9B3P4, Canada, 519-293-4232 X2332; Fax 519-973-7050; uwrevu@uwindsor.ca
Upney Editions, 19 Appalachian Crescent, Kitchener, Ontario N2E 1A3, Canada
URBAN GRAFFITI, PO Box 41164, Edmonton, AB T6J 6M7, Canada
Vehicule Press, PO Box 125, Place du Parc Station, Montreal, Quebec H2W 2M9, Canada, 514-844-6073; FAX 514-844-7543, E-mail; vpress@com.org
Vesta Publications Limited, PO Box 1641, Cornwall, Ont. K6H 5V6, Canada, 613-932-2135; FAX 613-932-7735
WASCANA REVIEW OF CONTEMPORARY POETRY AND SHORT FICTION, Department of English, University of Regina, Regina, Sask S4S 0A2, Canada, 584-4302
WE INTERNATIONAL (formerly WOMEN AND ENVIRONMENTS), 736 Bathurst Street, Toronto, Ontario M5S 2R4, Canada, 416-516-2600; FAX 416-531-6214
WEST COAST LINE: A Journal of Contemporary Writing and Criticism, 2027 EAA, Simon Fraser University, Burnaby, B.C. V5A 1S6, Canada
Winslow Publishing, Box 38012, 550 Eglinton Avenue West, Toronto, Ontario M5N 3A8, Canada, 416-789-4733
Women's Press, 517 College Street, Ste. 302, Toronto, Ontario M6G 4A2, Canada
Wordwrights Canada, PO Box 456, Station O, Toronto, Ontario M4A 2P1, Canada
WRITER'S LIFELINE, PO Box 1641, Cornwall, Ont. K6H 5V6, Canada

CZECH REPUBLIC

JEJUNE: america Eats its Young, PO Box 85, Prague 1, 110 01, Czech Republic, 42-2-96141082; Fax 42-2-24256243

ENGLAND

A.L.I., 20 Byron Place, Bristol, B58 1JT, England, E-mail: DSR@maths.bath.ac.uk
THE AFRICAN BOOK PUBLISHING RECORD, PO Box 56, Oxford 0X13EL, England, +44-(0)1865-511428; fax +44-1865-311534
AMBIT, 17 Priory Gardens, London, N6 5QY, England, 0181-340-3566
ANIMAL ACTION, RSPCA, Causeway, Horsham, West Sussex RH12 1HG, England, 01403-64181
ANIMAL LIFE, RSPCA, Causeway, Horsham, West Sussex RH12 1HG, England, 0403-64181
Applied Probability Trust, School of Mathmathmatics and Statistics, The University, Sheffield S3 7RH, England
AQUARIUS, Flat 4, Room B, 116 Sutherland Avenue, London W9, England
The Association of Freelance Writers, Sevendale House, 7 Dale Street, Manchester, M1 1JB, England, 0161-228-2362; Fax 0161-228-3533
BB Books, 1 Spring Bank, Longsight Road, Copster Green, Blackburn, Lancs BB1 9EU, England, 0254 249128
BLITHE SPIRIT, Farneley Gate Farmhouse, Riding Mill, Northumberland NE 44 6AA, England, (UK) 0434-682-465
THE BOUND SPIRAL, 72 First Avenue, Bush Hill Park, Enfield, Middlesex, EN1 1BW, England
BULLETIN OF HISPANIC STUDIES, Dept. Of Hispanic Studies, The University, PO Box 147, Liverpool L69 3BX, England, 051 794 2774/5
CANDELABRUM POETRY MAGAZINE, 9 Milner Road, Wisbech PE13 2LR, England, tel: 01945 581067
Carrefour Press, Saddle Fold, Hawkins Lane, Rainow, Macclesfield, Cheshire, England
COMMUNITY DEVELOPMENT JOURNAL, Foldyard House, Naburn, York YO1 4RU, England, 0904-87329
CURRENT ACCOUNTS, 16 Mill Lane, Horwich, Bolton BL6 6AT, England, 01204 669858 tel/fax; e-mail 100417.37226@compuserve.com
DANDELION ARTS MAGAZINE, Casa Alba, 24 Frosty Hollow, E. Hunsbury, Northants NN4 0SY, England, 01604-701730
THE DRAGON CHRONICLE, PO Box 3369, London SW66JN, England, dragnet@stalkevlab.ch
THE DURHAM UNIVERSITY JOURNAL, School of English/University of Durham, Elvet Riverside, New Elvet, Durham, DH1 3JT, England, 091-374 2000 Ext. 2744
Enitharmon Press, 36 St George's Avenue, London N7 0HD, England, 0171-607-7194; FAX 0171-607-8694
FENICE BROADSHEETS, 78 Cambridge Street, Leicester LE3 0JP, England, 547419
FILM, PO Box 1Dr, London W1A 1DR, England, 0171-736-9300
FORESIGHT MAGAZINE, 44 Brockhurst Road, Hodge Hill, Birmingham B36 8JB, England, 021-783-0587
FOREST: The Freedom Organization for the Right to Smoke Tobacco, 2 Grosvenor Gardens, London, SW1W ODH,

England, 0171-823-6550; FAX 0171-823-4534

FOURTH WORLD REVIEW, 24 Abercorn Place, London, NW8 9XP, England, 071-286-4366; FAX 071-286-2186

FREE CHOICE, 2 Grosvenor Gardens, London SW1W 0DH, England, 0171-823-6550; FAX 0171-823-4534

FREELANCE MARKET NEWS, Sevendale House, 7 Dale Street, Manchester, M1 1JB, England, 0161-228-2362; Fax 0161-228-3533

FURTHER TOO, 168 Elm Grove, Brighton, East Sussex BN2 3DA, England

Gild of Saint George, Rose Cottage, 17 Hadassah Grove, Lark Lane, Liverpool L17 8XH, England, 051-728-9176

GLOBAL TAPESTRY, Spring Bank, Longsight Road, Copster Green, Blackburn, Lancs BB1 9EU, England, 0254 249128

GRANTA, 2-3 Hanover Yard, Noel Rd, London N1 8BE, England, 0171 704 9776, FAX: 0171 704 0474

Granta Publications Ltd, 2-3 Hanover Yard, Noel Rd, London N1 8BE, England, (071) 704 9776

THE GROVE, Naturist Headquarters, Orpington, BR5 4ET, England, 01689-871200

Guildford Poets Press, 9 White Rose Lane, Woking, Surrey, GU22 7JA, England

Hans Zell Publishers, PO Box 56, Oxford 0X1 2SJ, England, +44-(0)1865-511428; FAX +44-(0)1865-311534; e-mail hzell@dial.pipex.com

Hippopotamus Press, 22, Whitewell Road, Frome, Somerset BA11 4EL, England, 0373-466653

HQ POETRY MAGAZINE (The Haiku Quarterly), 39 Exmouth Street, Swindon, Wilshire, SN1 3PU, England

Indelible Inc., BCM 1698, London WC1N 3XX, England

THE INQUIRER, 1-6 Essex Street, London WC2R 3HY, England

Interim Press, 3 Thornton Close, Budleigh Salterton, Devon EX9 6PJ, England, (0395) 445231

JAMES JOYCE BROADSHEET, School of English, University of Leeds, West Yorkshire LS2 9JT, England, 0113-233-4739

THE JOURNAL OF COMMONWEALTH LITERATURE, Bowker-Saur, Maypole House, Maypole Road, East Grinstead, W. Sussex RH19 1HU, England, 0865-511428; FAX 0865-311584

JOURNAL OF CONTEMPARARY ANGLO-SCANDINAVIAN POETRY, 11 Heatherton Park, Bradford on Tone, Taunton, Somerset TA4 1EU, England, 01823-461725; e-mail smithsssj@aol.com

THE JOURNAL OF DESIGN AND TECHNOLOGY EDUCATION, Westview House, 734 London Road, Oakhill, Stoke-on-Trent, Staffordshire ST4 5NP, England, 01782-745567; Fax 01782-745553

K.T. Publications, 16, Fane Close, Stamford, Lincs., PE9 1HG, England, (07180) 754193

Kawabata Press, Knill Cross House, Higher Anderton Road, Millbrook, Nr Torpoint, Cornwall, England

KRAX, 63 Dixon Lane, Leeds, Yorkshire LS12 4RR, England

LABOUR & TRADE UNION REVIEW, 2 Newington Green Mansions, Green Lanes London N16 9BT, England, 0171-354-4902

LANGUAGE INTERNATIONAL: THE MAGAZINE FOR THE LANGUAGE PROFESSIONS, Praetorius Limited, 5 East Circus Street, Nottingham NG1 5AF, England, 44-115-914-1087

LIBRARY HI TECH, MCB University Press, 60/63 Toller Lane, Bradford, W. Yorkshire BD8 9BY, England, 01274-777700; Fax 01274-785200 or 785201; www.mcb.co.uk

LIBRARY HIGH TECH NEWS, MCB University Press, 60/63 Toller Lane, Bradford, W. Yorkshire BD8 9BY, England, 01274-777700; Fax 01274-785200 or 785201; www.mcb.co.uk

LIVERPOOL NEWSLETTER, PO Box 1243, London, SW7 2PB, England, 0171-373-3432, e-mail 10071.746@compuserve.com

Liverpool University Press, Dept. of Hispanic Studies, The University, PO Box 147, Liverpool L69 3BX, England, 051 794 2774/5

A LOAD OF BULL, Box 277, 52 Call Lane, Leeds, W. Yorkshire LS1 6DT, England

LONDON REVIEW OF BOOKS, 28-30 Little Russell Street, London WC1A 2HN, England, 0171-404-3338; fax 404-3339

LORE AND LANGUAGE, National Centre for Eng. Cultural Tradition, The University, Sheffield S10 2TN, England, Sheffield 0114-2226296

Peter Marcan Publications, PO Box 3158, London SEI 4RA, England, UK, England, 0171-357-0368

MASSACRE, BCM 1698, London WC1N 3XX, England

MATHEMATICAL SPECTRUM, School of Mathmatics and Statistics, The University, Sheffield S3 7RH, England

MCB University Press, 60/63 Toiler Lane, Bradford, W. Yorkshire BD8 9BY, England

MCT - MULTICULTURAL TEACHING, Westview House, 734 London Road, Oakhill, Stoke-on-Trent, Staffordshire ST4 5NP, England, 01782-745567; Fax 01782-745553

MEDICAL HISTORY, 183 Euston Road, London NW1 2BE, England, 0171-611-8888/8563; fax 0171-611-8562

The Menard Press, 8 The Oaks, Woodside Avenue, London N12 8AR, England

MUSIC AND LETTERS, Journals Subscription Department, Pinkhill House, Southfield Road, Eynsham, Oxford OX8 1JJ, England

MUSICAL OPINION, 2 Princes Road, St. Leonards-on-Sea, East Sussex TN37 6EL, England, 0424-715167; fax 0424-712214

Naturist Foundation, Naturist Headquarters, Orpington, BR5 4ET, England

N-B-T-V, Narrow Bandwidth Television Association, 1 Burnwood Dr., Wollaton, Nottingham, Notts NG8 2DJ, England, 0115-9282896

New Broom Private Press, 78 Cambridge Street, Leicester, England

THE NEW WRITER, PO Box 60, Cranbrook, Kent TN17 2ZR, England, 01580-212626

NOTES & QUERIES, Journals Subscription Department, Pinkhill House, Southfield Road, Eynsham, Oxford OX8 1JJ, England

NOTTINGHAM MEDIEVAL STUDIES, Dept. of History, University Park, Nottingham NG7 2RD, England, +44 115-9-515932; fax +44 115-9-515948; e-mail michael.jones@nottingham.ac.uk

ORBIS, 27 Valley View, Primrose, Jarrow, Tyne & Wear NE32 5QT, England, +44 (0)191 489 7055; fax/modem +44 (0)191 430 1297; e-mail Mshields12@aol.com; mikeshields@compuserve.com

Original Plus, 11 Heatherton Park, Bradford on Tone, Taunton, Somerset TA4 1EU, England, 01823-461725; e-mail smithsssj@aol.com

PENNINE PLATFORM, 7 Cockley Hill Lane, Kirkheaton, Huddersfield HD5 OHH, West Yorkshire, England, 0937-584674

PERCEPTIONS, 73 Eastcombe Avenue, London, England SE7 7LL, England

Plantagenet Productions, Westridge (Open Centre), Highclere, Nr. Newbury, Berkshire RG20 9PJ, England

PLANTAGENET PRODUCTIONS, Libraries of Spoken Word Recordings and of Stagescripts, Westridge (Open Centre), Highclere, Nr. Newbury, Royal Berkshire RG20 9PJ, England

PLUME, 15 Bolehill Park, Hove Edge, Brighouse, W. Yorks HX3 8AL, England, 01484-717808; email plumelit@aol.com

POETRY AND AUDIENCE, School of English, Cavendish Road, University of Leeds, Leeds Yorkshire, LS2 9JT, England
POETRY NOTTINGHAM INTERNATIONAL, 71 Saxton Avenue, Heanor, Derbyshire DE75 7PZ, England, 0602 461267
Poetry Nottingham Society Publications, 71 Saxton Avenue, Heanor, Derbys DE75 7PZ, England
POETRY REVIEW, 22 Betterton Street, London WC2H 9BU, England
THE POWYS JOURNAL, 82 Linden Road, Gloucester, Gloucestershire GL1 5HD, England
The Powys Society, Hamilton's, Kilmersdon, Bath, Somerset, U.K. BA3 5TE, Gloucester, Gloucestershire GL1 5HD, England, 0452-304539
Protean Publications, 34 Summerfield Crescent, Flat 4, Edgbaston, Birmingham B16 OER, England
PURPLE PATCH, 8 Beaconview House, Charlemont Farm, West Bromwich, West Midlands, England
QED, 1 Straylands Grove, York Y03 0EB, England, 904-424-381
Red Candle Press, 9 Milner Road, Wisbech, PE13 2LR, England, tel: 01945 581067
REFERENCE SERVICES REVIEW, MCB University Press, 60/63 Toller Lane, Bradford, W. Yorkshire BD8 9BY, England, 01274-777700; Fax 01274-785200 or 785201; www.mcb.co.uk
THE RIALTO, PO Box 309 Aylsham, Norwich NR11 6LN, England
Saqi Books Publisher, 26 Westbourne Grove, London W2 5RH, England, 071-221-9347; FAX 071-229-7692
SEPIA, Knill Cross House, Higher Anderton Road, Millbrook, Nr Torpoint, Cornwall, England
The Smallest County Press, 37 Northgate, Oakham, Rutland LE15 6QR, England, 01572-770011
SMOKE, 40 Canning Street, Liverpool L8 7NP, England
SPARE RIB, 27 Clerkenwell Close, London EC1 0AT, England
Spectacular Diseases, 83(b) London Road, Peterborough, Cambs, England
SPECTACULAR DISEASES, 83(b) London Road, Peterborough, Cambs, England
STAND MAGAZINE, 179 Wingrove Road, Newcastle-on-Tyne NE49DA, England, +44 011-273-3280
TANDEM, 13 Stephenson Road Barbourne, Worchester, WR1 3EB, England, 01705-28002
TEARS IN THE FENCE, 38 Hod View, Stourpaine, Blandford Forum, Dorset DT11 8TN, England
THE THIRD HALF, "Amikeco", 16, Fane Close, Stamford, Lincs., PE9 1HG, England, (01780) 754193
TIME HAIKU, 105, Kings Head Hill, London E4 7JG, England, 0181-529-6478
Trentham Books, Westview House, 734 London Road, Oakhill, Stoke-on-Trent, Staffordshire ST4 5NP, England, 01782-745567; Fax 01782-745553
Trigon Press, 117 Kent House Road, Beckenham, Kent BR3 1JJ, England, 081-778-0534; FAX 081-776-7525; trigon@easynet.co.uk
VARIOUS ARTISTS, 65, Springfield Avenue, Horfield, Bristol BS7 9QS, England
VERTICAL IMAGES, 10A Dickenson Road, Crouch End, London N8 9ET, England, 0181-340-5974
Wellcome Institute for the History of Medicine, 183 Euston Road, London NW1 2BE, England
The Wellsweep Press, 1 Grove End Ho., 150 Highgate Road, London HW5 1PD, England, (0171)267-3525, e-mail ws@shadoof.demon.co.uk
WEYFARERS, 9 White Rose Lane, Woking, Surrey GU22 7JA, England
Windows Project, 40 Canning Street, Liverpool L8 7NP, England
Working Press, 54 Sharsled Street, London SE17 4TN, England, 071-735-6221; FAX 071-582-7021
Writers & Scholars International Ltd., 33 Islington High Street, London N1 9LH, England, 171-278-2313, Fax 171-278-1878
Writers Forum, 89A Petherton Road, London N5 2QT, England, 0171-226-2657

FINLAND

BOOKS FROM FINLAND, PO Box 15 (Unioninkatu 36), FIN-00014 University of Helsinki, Finland, (358/g) 1357942; bff@helsinki.fi; http://linnea.helsinki.fi/bff
KOOMA, Huvilate 4A2, 96300 Rovaniemi, Finland
SIVULLINEN, Kaarelantie 86 B 28, 00420 Helsinki, Finland

FRANCE

Citeaux Commentarii Cistercienses, 17 rue Rabe, 89230 Pontigny, France, Pontigny, France, fax (33) 86.47.58.64
CITEAUX: COMMENTARII CISTERCIENSES, 17, rue Rabe, 89230 Pontigny France, Pontigny, France, e-mail 104124.3655@compuserve.com
FRANK: AN INTERNATIONAL JOURNAL OF CONTEMPORARY WRITING AND ART, 32 rue Edouard Vaillant, 93100 Montreuil Sous Bois, France, (33) 1 48596658; e-mail david@paris-anglo.com
Handshake Editions, Atelier A2, 83 rue de la Tombe-Issoire, Paris 75014, France, 4327-1767
J'ECRIS, 85, rue des Tennerolles, Saint-Cloud 92210, France, (1) 47-71-79-63
PARIS/ATLANTIC, The American University of Paris, 31, avenue Bosquet, 75007 Paris, France, 33-1-01 40 62 05 89; fax 33-1-01 45 51 89 13

GERMANY

Dreamboy Books, PO Box 910133, 12413 Berlin, Germany, 030-2472-5060
Edition Gemini, Juelichstrasse 7, Huerth-Efferen D-50354, Germany, 02233/63550; Fax: 02233/65866
Expanded Media Editions, PO Box 190136, Prinz Albert Str. 65, 53AA3 Bonn 1, Germany, Germany, 0228/22 95 83; FAX 0228/21 95 07
STRANGER THAN MADNESS, Zieglerstrasse 8, 01217 Dresden, Germany
TRAFIK - Internationales Journal zur Libertaren Kultur & Politik, EduardstraBe 40, Mulheim/Ruhr 45468, Germany
TRANVIA - Revue der Iberischen Halbinsel, PO Box 303626, D-0727 Berlin 19, Germany, 883-2561; tranvia@aol.com

GREAT BRITAIN

IOTA, 67 Hady Crescent, Chesterfield, Derbyshire S41 0EB, Great Britain, 01246-276532
Second Aeon Publications, 19 Southminster Road, Roath, Cardiff, Wales CF2 5AT, Great Britain, 01222-493093; peter.finch@dial.pipex.com
TRIVIUM, Dept. Of History, St. David's University College, Lampeter, Dyfed SA48 7ED, Great Britain, 0570-422351 ext 244

HOLLAND

AMSTERDAM CHRONICLE, Kanaalstraat 66 huis, 1054XK Amsterdam, Holland
PHILATELIC LITERATURE NEWS INTERNATIONAL, Brandespad 14, NL-3067 EB Rotterdam, Holland

HONG KONG

AREOPAGUS, Tao Fong Shan Christian Centre, PO Box 33, Shatin, New Territories, Hong Kong, 952-269-1904; FAX 852-269-9885

Philopsychy Press, PO Box 1224, Shatin Central, N.T., Hong Kong, phone/fax 852-26044403; email ppp@hkbu.edu.hk; www.hkbu.edu.hk/~ppp/ppp/intro.html

RENDITIONS, Chinese University of Hong Kong, Shatin, NT, Hong Kong, 26-097-400, 26-097-407; fax 26-035-149; e-Mail renditions@cuhk.hk

Research Centre for Translation, Chinese University of Hong Kong, Research Centre for Translation, Chinese University of Hong Kong, Shatin, NT, Hong Kong, 852-26097700/7407; e-Mail renditions@cuhk.hk

INDIA

THE INDIAN WRITER, 1-A, 59 Ormes Road, Chennai 600010, India, 6261370, 6284421

Jaffe Publishing Management Service, Kunnuparambil Buildings, Kurichy, Kottayam 686549, India, phone/fax 91-481-430470

MANUSHI - a journal about women & society, C-174 Lajpat Nagar - I, New Delhi, New Delhi 110024, India, 6833022 or 6839158

Prakalpana Literature, P-40 Nandana Park, Calcutta-700034, West Bengal, India, (91) (033) 478-2347

PRAKALPANA SAHITYA/PRAKALPANA LITERATURE, P-40 Nandana Park, Calcutta-700034, West Bengal, India, (91) (033) 478-2347

TIGER MOON, 3/677 Coconut Grove, Prasanthi Nilayam A.P. 515134, India

Tiger Moon, 3/677 Coconut Grove, Prasanthi Nilayam A.P., India

WORLD BOOK INDUSTRY, Kunnuparambil Buildings, Kurichy, Kottayam 686549, India, 91-481-430470; FAX 91-481-561190

IRELAND

THE BROBDINGNAGIAN TIMES, 96 Albert Road, Cork, Ireland, (21 311227)

CELTIC HISTORY REVIEW, 216 Falls Road, Belfast, BT12, Ireland, 0232-232608

THE CELTIC PEN, 36 Fruithill Park, Belfast, BT11 8GE, Ireland, 01232-232608

DOPE FRIENDS, Ivy Shields, Ballagh, Bushypark, Galway, Ireland, e-mail mmtaylor@iol.ie

Poetry Ireland, Bermingham Tower, Upper Yard, Dublin Castle, Dublin 2, Ireland

POETRY IRELAND REVIEW, Bermingham Tower, Upper yard, Dublin Castle, Dublin 2, Ireland, 6714632 + 353-1; fax 6714634 + 353-1

Sparkling Diamond Paperbacks, 66 St. Joseph's Place, Off Blessington Street, Dublin 7, Ireland

Wolfhound Press, 68 Mountjoy Square, Dublin 1, Ireland, 740354

ISRAEL

THE OTHER ISRAEL, PO Box 2542, Holon 58125, Israel, 972-3-5565804 (also fax)

STUDIO ART MAGAZINE, Studio, PO Box 23570, Tel Aviv, 61231, Israel, 03-5255701; fax 03-5255702; e-mail studio1@netvision.net.il

VOICES - ISRAEL, c/o Mark Levinson, PO Box 5780, Herzliya 46157, Israel, 09-9552411

ITALY

LO STRANIERO: The Stranger, Der Fremde, L'Etranger, Via Chiaia 149, Napoli 80121, Italy, ITALY/81/426052

JAPAN

Abiko Literary Press (ALP), 8-1-8 Namiki, Abiko, Chiba 270-1165, Japan, 0471-84-7904; alp@db3.so-net.or.jp

THE ABIKO QUARTERLY WITH JAMES JOYCE FW STUDIES, 8-1-8 Namiki, Abiko-shi, Chiba-ken 270-1165, Japan, 0471-84-7904; alp@db3.so-net.or.jp

BLUE BEAT JACKET, 1-5-54 Sugue-cho, Sanjo-shi, Niigata-ken 955, Japan, 0256-32-3301

Blue Jacket Press, 1-5-54 Sugu.-cho, Sanjo-shi, Niigata-ken 955, Japan, 0256-32-3301

THE LONSDALE - The International Quarterly of The Romantic Six, Trash City 3rd Floor, 6-18-16 Nishi-Gotanda, Shinagawa-ku, Tokyo 141, Japan, 03(5434)0729

POETRY KANTO, Kanto Gakuin University, Kamariya Minami 3-22-1, Kanazawa-Ku, Yokohama 236-8502, Japan

MALAWI

BWALO: A Forum for Social Development, PO Box 278, Zomba, Malawi, 265-522-916; Fax 265-522-578

JOURNAL OF HUMANITIES, Faculty of Humanities, Chancellor College, Box 280, Zomba, Malawi, 265-522-222; Fax 265-522-046

MALAYSIA

ENVIRONMENTAL NEWS DIGEST, 19 Kelawei Road, 10250 Penang, Malaysia

Sahabat Alam Malaysia (Friends of the Earth Malaysia), 19 Kelawei Road, 10250 Penang, Malaysia

MEXICO

Barking Dog Books, Centro De Mensajes, A.P. 48, Todos Santos, B.C.S. 23300, Mexico, fax 011-52-114-50288

NEPAL

Book Faith India, PO Box 3872, Kathmandu, Nepal, fax 977-1-424943; e-mail pilgrims@wlink.com.np

SARAGAM: A Musical Quarterly Magazine, PO Box 3872, Kathmandu, Nepal, Fax 977-1-229983

NEW ZEALAND

Brick Row Publishing Co. Ltd., PO Box 100-057, North Shore Mail Centre, Auckland 1310, New Zealand, 64-9-410-6993

POETRY NZ, PO Box 100-057, North Shore Mail Centre, Auckland 1310, New Zealand, 64-9-410-6993

SPIN, 7 Megan Avenue, Pakuranga, Auckland 1706, New Zealand, 006495768577

TAKAHE, PO Box 13-335, Christchurch 1, New Zealand, 03-5198133

NORTHERN IRELAND

WRITING ULSTER, U. of Ulster-Jordanstown, Shore Rd, Newtownabbey Co. Antrim, BT 370QB, Northern Ireland, 011-44-232-365131; fax 232-366824

NORWAY

GATEAVISA, Hjelmsgt 3, 0355 Oslo 3, Norway, +47 2 69 12 84

PEOPLE'S REPUBLIC OF CHINA

CHINESE LITERATURE, 24 Baiwanzhuang Road, Beijing 100037, People's Republic of China, 892554
Chinese Literature Press, 24 Baiwanzhuang Road, Beijing 100037, People's Republic of China

PORTUGAL

LA PERIPHERIE, Apartado 240, Portalegre, 7300, Portugal

REPUBLIC OF SOUTH AFRICA

AFRICAN STUDIES, WITS, 2050 Johannesburg, Republic of South Africa
Lionheart Publishing, Private Bag X5, Constantia, Cape Town 7848, Republic of South Africa, 002721-794-4923; Fax 002721-794-1487; cajmi@iafrica.com; www.toltec-foundation.org
Witwatersrand University Press, WITS, 2050 Johannesburg, Republic of South Africa, 011-716-2029

ROMANIA

SMARANDACHE NOTIONS, Department of Mathematics, University of Craiova, Craiova 1100, Romania, research37@aol.com

SCOTLAND

CHAPMAN, 4 Broughton Place, Edinburgh EH1 3RX, Scotland, 0131-557-2207
EDINBURGH REVIEW, 22 George Square, Edinburgh EH8 9LF, Scotland, 0315581117/8
The Gleniffer Press, 'Benvoir' Wigtown, NEWTON STEWART, Galloway, DG8 9EE, Scotland, 041-889-9579
NORTHWORDS, The Stable, Long Road, Avoch, Ross-shire IV9 8QR, Scotland, website www.cali.co.uk/highexp/nwords/
OBJECT PERMANENCE, Flat 3/2, 16 Ancroft Street, Glasgow G20 7HU, Scotland, 0141-332-7571
ONE EARTH, Findhorn Foundation, The Park, Forres, Morayshire 1V36 OTZ, Scotland, 44-1309-691128
THE ORCADIAN, The Orcadian Limited, PO Box 18, Kirkwall, Orkney, Scotland
WRITERS NEWS, PO Box 4, Nairn IV12 4HU, Scotland, 01667-454441
WRITING MAGAZINE, PO Box 4, Nairn IV12 4HU, Scotland, 01667-454441

SWEDEN

ALLA TIDERS BODER, Tumstocksvagen 19, Taby S-18304, Sweden, 08-7567445
Tryckeriforlaget, Tumstocksvagen 19, Taby S-18366, Sweden, 08-7567445
Vanitas Press, Platslagarevagen 4E1, 22730 Lund, Sweden

SWITZERLAND

BIBLIOTHEQUE D'HUMANISME ET RENAISSANCE, Librairie Droz S.A., 11r.Massot, 1211 Geneve 12, Switzerland
Librairie Droz S.A., 11r.Massot, 1211 Geneve 12, Switzerland
TRANSNATIONAL PERSPECTIVES, CP 161, CH-1211 Geneva 16, Switzerland

THE NETHERLANDS

YUMTZILOB: Tijdschrift over de Americas, PO Box 32077, 2303 DB Leiden, The Netherlands, 31-10-4131960; FAX 31-10-4045357; E-mail yumtzilob@freemail.nl

TRINIDAD & TOBAGO

MONEYMAKING NEWSLETTER, PO Box 3418, Maraval, Trinidad & Tobago, 809-657-3657; 809-638-3756
MYSTIC VOICES, PO Box 3418, Maraval, Trinidad & Tobago
Reyes Investment Enterprise Ltd., PO Box 3418, Maraval, Trinidad & Tobago, 809-638-3756; 809-657-3657

UNITED KINGDOM

AABYE (formerly New Hope International Writing), 20 Werneth Avenue, Gee Cross, Hyde, Cheshire SK14 5NL, United Kingdom, 061-351 1878
ANARCHIST STUDIES, 10 High Street, Knapwell, Cambridge CB3 8NR, United Kingdom
AVON LITERARY INTELLIGENCER, 20 Byron Place, Bristol, BS8 1JT, United Kingdom, 44-225-826105
B.A.D. Press, 43 Kingsdown House, Amhurst Road, London E8 2AS, United Kingdom, 0171-923-0734
Bowerdean Publishing Co. Ltd., 8 Abbotstone Road, London SW15 1QR, United Kingdom, Phone/Fax 44(0)181-7880938; E-mail 101467.1264@compuserve.com
BRANDO'S HAT, 14 Vine Street, Kersal, Salford M7 3PG, United Kingdom, e-mail tarantula-pubs@lineone.net
BREAKFAST ALL DAY, 43 Kingsdown House, Amhurst Road, London E8 2AS, United Kingdom, 0171-923-0734
BRITISH JOURNAL OF AESTHETICS, Journal Subscription Department, Pinkhill House, Southfield Road, Eynsham, Oxford, OX8 1JJ, United Kingdom
CAMBRENSIS: THE SHORT STORY QUARTERLY MAGAZINE OF WALES, 41 Heol Fach, Cornelly, Bridgend, Mid-Glamorgan, CF334LN South Wales, United Kingdom, 01656-741-994
Deborah Charles Publications, 173 Mather Avenue, Liverpool L18 6JZ, United Kingdom, fax 441-151-729-0371 from outside UK
Crescent Moon, PO Box 393, Maidstone, Kent ME14 5XU, United Kingdom
DIALOGOS: Hellenic Studies Review, Dept. of Byzantine & Modern Greek, Attn: David Ricks, King's College, London WC2R 2LS, United Kingdom
ECONOMIC AFFAIRS, 2 Lord North Street, London SW1P 3LB, United Kingdom
EUROPEAN JUDAISM, Leo Baeck College, 80 East End Rd., Sternberg Centre for Judaism, London N3 2SY, United Kingdom, 44-181-349-4525; Fax 44-181-343-2558; leo-baeck-college@mailbox.ulcc.ac.uk; www.lb-college.demon.co.uk

720

FEMINIST LEGAL STUDIES, 173 Mather Avenue, Liverpool L18 6JZ, United Kingdom
FEMINIST REVIEW, 52 Featherstone Street, Brecknock Road, London EC1Y 8RT, United Kingdom
FIGMENTS, 14 William Street, Donaghadee, Co. Down NI BT21 0HP, United Kingdom, 01247-884267
Figments Publishing, 14 William Street, Donaghadee, Co. Down N.I. BT21 0HP, United Kingdom, 01247-884267
FIRE, 3 Hollywell Mews, Holywell Road, Malvern WR14 4LF, United Kingdom
THE FROGMORE PAPERS, 42 Morehall Avenue, Folkestone, Kent CT19 4EF, United Kingdom
The Frogmore Press, 42 Morehall Avenue, Folkestone, Kent. CT19 4EF, United Kingdom
GREEN ANARCHIST, BM 1715, London WC1N 3XX, United Kingdom
HOAX!, 64 Beechgrove, Aberhonddu, Powys Cymru LD3 9ET, United Kingdom
INTERNATIONAL JOURNAL FOR THE SEMIOTICS OF LAW, 173 Mather Avenue, Liverpool L18 6JZ, United Kingdom
THE INTERPRETER'S HOUSE, 38 Verne Drive, Ampthill, MK45 2PS, United Kingdom, 01525-403018
Kozmik Press, 134 Elsenham Street, London SW18 5NP, United Kingdom, 44-81-874-8218
LAW AND CRITIQUE, 173 Mather Avenue, Liverpool L18 6JZ, United Kingdom
LINKS, 'Bude Haven' 18 Frankfield Rise, Tunbridge Wells TN2 5LF, United Kingdom, 01892-539800
LIVERPOOL LAW REVIEW, 173 Mather Avenue, Liverpool L18 6JZ, United Kingdom
MAIN STREET JOURNAL, 29 Princes Road, Ashford, Middlesex TW15 2LT, United Kingdom, 44-171-378-8809
New Hope International, 20 Werneth Avenue, Gee Cross, Hyde SK14 5NL, United Kingdom, 0161-351 1878; www.nhi.clara.net/online.htm
NEW HOPE INTERNATIONAL REVIEW, 20 Werneth Avenue, Gee Cross, Hyde, Cheshire SK14 5NL, United Kingdom, 061-351 1878
NEWS FROM THE SMALL PRESS CENTRE, BM BOZO, London W1N 3XX, United Kingdom
OASIS, 12 Stevenage Road, London SW6 6ES, United Kingdom
Oasis Books, 12 Stevenage Road, London, SW6 6ES, United Kingdom
OTTER, Parford Cottage, Chagford, Newton Abbot TQ13 8JR, United Kingdom
OUTLET, 33 Aintree Crescent, Barkingside, Ilford, Essex IG6 2HD, United Kingdom, 081-551-3346
OUTPOSTS POETRY QUARTERLY, 22, Whitewell Road, Frome, Somerset BA11 4EL, United Kingdom
Oxford University Press, Journal Subscriptions Department, Pinkhill House, Southfield Road, Eynsham, Oxford OX8 1JJ, United Kingdom
PAGAN AMERICA, PO Box 393, Maidstone, Kent ME14 5XU, United Kingdom
PANURGE, Crooked Home Farm Cottage, Brampton, Cumbria CA8 2AT, United Kingdom, 016977 41087
PASSION, PO Box 393, Maidstone, Kent ME14 5XU, United Kingdom
PERSPECTIVES, BM 6682, London WC1N 3XX, United Kingdom
Poetical Histories, 27 Sturton Street, Cambridge CB1 2QG, United Kingdom, 0223-327455
PSYCHOPOETICA, Department of Psychology, University of Hull, Hull HU6 7RX, United Kingdom, website www.fernhse.demon.co.uk/eastword/psycho
PULSAR, 34 Lineacre, Grange Park, Swindon, Wiltshire SN5 6DA, United Kingdom, 01793-875941; e-mail david.pike@virgin.net
Reality Street Editions, 4 Howard Court, Peckham Rye, London SE15 3PH, United Kingdom, 0171-639-7297
RES PUBLICA, 173 Mather aAvenue, Liverpool L18 6JZ, United Kingdom
Shearsman Books, c/o IPD (Independent Press Distribution), 12 Stevenage Road, London SW6 6ES, United Kingdom, 0752-779682
SHRIKE, 13 Primrose Way, Alperton, MDDX HA0 1DS, United Kingdom, 44-081-998-5707
Slab-O-Concrete Publications, PO Box 148, Hove BN3 3DQ, United Kingdom, 011-44-1273-739634; Fax 011-44-1273-205502
STAPLE, Tor Cottage, 81 Cavendish Road, Matlock, Derbyshire DE4 3HD, United Kingdom
SUPER TROUPER, 35 Kearsley Road, Sheffield, S2 4TE, United Kingdom
Tears in the Fence, 38 Hod View Stourpaine, Blandford Forum, Dorset DT11 8TN, United Kingdom
Transeuropa, BM 6682, London WC1N 3XX, United Kingdom
VIGIL, 12 Priory Mead, Bruton, Somerset BA10 0DZ, United Kingdom, Bruton 813349

WALES

ALT-J: Association for Learning Technology Journal, 6 Gwennyth Street, Cathays, Cardiff CF2 4YD, Wales
CONTEMPORARY WALES, 6 Gwennyth Street, Cathays, Cardiff CF2 4YD, Wales, 44-1222-231919; Fax 44-1222-230908; press@press.wales.ac.uk
EFRYDIAU ATHRONYDDOL, 6 Gwennyth St., Cathays, Cardiff CF2 4YD, Wales, 44-1222-231919; Fax 44-1222-230908; press@press.wales.ac.uk
JOURNAL OF CELTIC LINGUISTICS, 6 Gwennyth Street, Cathays, Cardiff CF2 4YD, Wales, 44-1222-231919; Fax 44-1222-230908; press@press.wales.ac.uk
LLEN CYMRU, 6 Gwennyth St., Cathays, Cardiff CF2 4YD, Wales, 44-1222-231919; Fax 44-1222-230908; press@press.wales.ac.uk
POETRY WALES, First Floor, 2 Wyndham Street, Bridgend, CF31 1EF, Wales
Poetry Wales Press, Ltd., First Floor, 2 Wyndham Street, Bridgend CF31 1EF, Wales
STUDIA CELTICA, University of Wales Press, 6 Gwennyth St., Cathays, Cardiff CF2 4YD, Wales, 44-1222-231919; Fax 44-1222-230908; press@press.wales.ac.uk
University Of Wales Press, 6 Gwennyth Street, Cathays, Cardiff CF2 4YD, Wales, +44-1222-231919; Fax +44-1222-230908; press@press.wales.ac.uk
WELSH HISTORY REVIEW, 6 Gwennyth Street, Cathays, Cardiff CF2 4YD, Wales, 44-1222-231919; Fax 44-1222-230908; press@press.wales.ac.uk
WELSH JOURNAL OF EDUCATION, 6 Gwennyth Street, Cathays, Cardiff CF2 4YD, Wales, 44-1222-231919; Fax 44-1222-230908; press@press.wales.ac.uk

WEST INDIES

Sandberry Press, PO Box 507, Kingston 10, Jamaica, West Indies, fax 809-968-4067, phone 809-929-8089

Subject Index

THE AFRICAN BOOK PUBLISHING RECORD
AFRICAN STUDIES
African Ways Publishing
AIM MAGAZINE
Ariko Publications
Autonomedia, Inc.
BELLES LETTRES
Between The Lines
Bicycle Books (Publishing) Inc.
THE BLACK SCHOLAR: Journal of Black Studies and
  Research
BLU
Brunswick Publishing Corporation
BWALO: A Forum for Social Development
CLASS ACT
Clover Park Press
THE COOL TRAVELER
Coteau Books
THE DIRTY GOAT
DRUMVOICES REVUE
Five Star Publications
Florida Academic Press
Four Walls Eight Windows
GATEAVISA
Good Hope Enterprises, Inc.
GrapeVinePress
Gumbs & Thomas Publishers, Inc.
Hans Zell Publishers
HAWAI'I REVIEW
Hope Publishing House
Host Publications, Inc.
IAAS Publishers, Inc.
Inner Traditions International
INTERCULTURAL WRITERS REVIEW
Interlink Publishing Group, Inc.
International Publishers Co. Inc.
THE JOURNAL OF AFRICAN TRAVEL-WRITING
JOURNAL OF HUMANITIES
Kenyette Productions
LFW Enterprises
LOST GENERATION JOURNAL
Lotus Press, Inc.
MAIN STREET JOURNAL
MESECHABE: The Journal of Surre(gion)alism
NEW HOPE INTERNATIONAL REVIEW
THE NEW RENAISSANCE, An International Magazine
  of Ideas & Opinions, Emphasizing Literature & The
  Arts
OBSIDIAN II: BLACK LITERATURE IN REVIEW
ORACLE STORY
Oyez
Paragon House Publishers
PASSAGER: A Journal of Remembrance and Discovery
Passeggiata Press, Inc.
Path Press, Inc.
Pathfinder Press
Poltroon Press
Redbird Press, Inc.
Semiotext Foreign Agents Books Series
SEMIOTEXT(E)
TitleWaves Publishing
Tombouctou Books
TOWARD FREEDOM
21ST CENTURY AFRO REVIEW
University of Calgary Press
White Cliffs Media, Inc.
Witwatersrand University Press
World Music Press
WORLD RAINFOREST REPORT
WRITER'S LIFELINE

AFRICAN-AMERICAN

African American Audio Press
AFRICAN AMERICAN AUDIOBOOK REVIEW
African Ways Publishing
Afrimax, Inc.
American Literary Press Inc./Noble House
Anacus Press, Inc.

Ananse Press
Baker Street Publications
Bancroft Press
BLACK LACE
BLACK TALENT NEWS (The Entertainment Industry
  Publication for African Americans)
BLACKFIRE
BLK
BLU
Blue Heron Publishing, Inc.
Bonus Books, Inc.
Bosck Publishing House
Burning Bush Publications
Clarity Press, Inc.
Common Courage Press
Conari Press
The Crossing Press
DRUMVOICES REVUE
Ecrivez!
The Feminist Press at the City College
The Fire!! Press
Fjord Press
GATEAVISA
GrapeVinePress
IAAS Publishers, Inc.
ICA Publishing
Innisfree Press
INTERCULTURAL WRITERS REVIEW
IRIS: A Journal About Women
J & J Consultants, Inc.
KUUMBA
LADYBUG, the Magazine for Young Children
LFW Enterprises
MESECHABE: The Journal of Surre(gion)alism
Minnesota Historical Society Press
MIXED BAG
THE NEW PRESS LITERARY QUARTERLY
New Spring Publications
Open Hand Publishing Inc.
Paint Rock Publishing, Inc.
PAPYRUS
Papyrus Literary Enterprises, Inc.
Passeggiata Press, Inc.
The Place In The Woods
Pomegranate Communications
POTOMAC REVIEW
QED Press
Schenkman Books
THE SCRIBIA
SILHOUETTE MAGAZINE
21ST CENTURY AFRO REVIEW
University of Massachusetts Press
Veracity Press
THE VINCENT BROTHERS REVIEW
Waverly House Publishing
Wright-Armstead Associates
Yucca Tree Press
Z MAGAZINE

AGING

American Source Books, a division of Impact Publishers
Anti-Aging Press
Arjay Associates
Beacon Point Press
BELLES LETTRES
Blue Dolphin Publishing, Inc.
Bonus Books, Inc.
Borderland Sciences Research Foundation
Conari Press
CRONE CHRONICLES: A Journal of Conscious Aging
The Crossing Press
Cyclone Books
EduCare Press
Elder Books
FOCUS: Library Service to Older Adults, People with
  Disabilities
FOREVER ALIVE
Gateway Books

THE GENTLE SURVIVALIST
HEALTH AND HAPPINESS
Human Kinetics Pub. Inc.
Hunter House Inc., Publishers
Impact Publishers, Inc.
Innisfree Press
JOURNAL OF AGING AND PHYSICAL ACTIVITY (JAPA)
The Leaping Frog Press
Mills & Sanderson, Publishers
North Star Books
Papier-Mache Press
Parabola
PenRose Publishing Company, Inc.
Peradam Press
The Place In The Woods
Potentials Development, Inc.
Queen of Swords Press
RED OWL
Saint Mary's Press
SMART DRUG NEWS
SO YOUNG!
Spinsters Ink
STONES IN MY POCKET
TAPROOT, a journal of older writers
Tide Book Publishing Company
Two Thousand Three Associates
Valiant Press, Inc.
VanderWyk & Burnham
Vista Publishing, Inc.
WHOLE EARTH
Wings of Fire Press
THE WISDOM CONSERVANCY NEWSLETTER
World Changing Books
XIB
Xib Publications

AGRICULTURE

AFFABLE NEIGHBOR
Affable Neighbor Press
AGRICULTURAL HISTORY
Alpine Press
ASSEMBLING
Assembling Press
THE AZOREAN EXPRESS
BLACK JACK & VALLEY GRAPEVINE
Cadmus Editions
THE CARETAKER GAZETTE
The Chicot Press
China Books & Periodicals, Inc.
CHRONICLE OF COMMUNITY
CJE NEWS (Newsletter of the Coalition for Jobs & the Environment)
COMMUNITY DEVELOPMENT JOURNAL
FARMER'S DIGEST
FARMING UNCLE
Food First Books
GRASS ROOTS
THE GROWING EDGE MAGAZINE
W.D. Hoard & Sons Company
HOARD'S DAIRYMAN
HORTIDEAS
The Independent Institute
KICK IT OVER
Kumarian Press, Inc.
La Alameda Press
Lahontan Images
Lessiter Publications
Lester Street Publishing
LOST GENERATION JOURNAL
THE MAD FARMERS' JUBILEE ALMANACK
MASSEY COLLECTORS NEWS—WILD HARVEST
MINIATURE DONKEY TALK iNC
NANCY'S MAGAZINE
THE NEW RENAISSANCE, An International Magazine of Ideas & Opinions, Emphasizing Literature & The Arts
Oasis Books

OLD ABE'S NEWS
The Rateavers
RED POWER
RFD
RURAL HERITAGE
Shallowater Press
Timber Press
THE TOWNSHIPS SUN
Two Eagles Press International
University of Calgary Press
Woodbridge Press
WORLD RAINFOREST REPORT

AIDS

A & U AMERICA'S AIDS MAGAZINE
Abiko Literary Press (ALP)
AFFAIR OF THE MIND: A Literary Quarterly
American Literary Press Inc./Noble House
ATL Press, Inc.
Bay Press
BLK
By-The-Book Publishing
COLLEGIUM NEWSLETTER
CROSS ROADS
The Crossing Press
Doctors Press, Inc.
Down There Press
Elysian Hills Publishing Company, Inc.
ETR Associates
THE EVERGREEN CHRONICLES
Focus Publications, Inc.
GATEAVISA
GERBIL: Queer Culture Zine
GREEN ANARCHIST
IRIS: A Journal About Women
The Leaping Frog Press
Lone Willow Press
LOVE AND RAGE, A Revolutionary Anarchist Newspaper
Nosukumo
Outrider Press
Rainbow's End
Signature Books
Skidmore-Roth Publishing, Inc.
Slate Press
TEENS IN MOTION NEWS
THE UNIT CIRCLE
Z MAGAZINE

AIRPLANES

Ancient City Press
R.J. Bender Publishing
THE BLAB
Cage Consulting, Inc.
CESSNA OWNER MAGAZINE
The Film Instruction Company of America
FLASHPOINT: Military Books Reviewed by Military Professionals
Foundation Books
Galde Press, Inc.
Golden Eagle Press
Mach 1, Inc.
NORTHERN PILOT
OUT YOUR BACKDOOR: The Magazine of Informal Adventure and Cheap Culture
PIPERS MAGAZINE
The Times Journal Publishing Co.
Westchester House
World Wide Publishing Corp.

ALASKA

Alaska Geographic Society
Alaska Native Language Center
Alaska Northwest Books
AMERICAN WRITING: A Magazine
Arrowstar Publishing
Baker Street Publications
Blue Heron Publishing, Inc.

Circumpolar Press
THE CLIMBING ART
Council For Indian Education
The Denali Press
DWELLING PORTABLY
Epicenter Press Inc.
Fathom Publishing Co.
Fireweed Press
Full Moon Publications
Golden Eagle Press
Heyday Books
HORIZONS
JOURNAL OF ALASKA WOMEN
Light, Words & Music
MIXED BAG
Moon Publications, Inc.
Mountain Automation Corporation
The Mountaineers Books
NORTHERN PILOT
POW-WOW
Pruett Publishing Company
Sasquatch Books
Umbrella Books
WESTERN SKIES
Windsong Press
Wizard Works

ALCOHOL, ALCOHOLISM

Al-Anon Family Group Headquarters, Inc.
CLUBHOUSE
Devil Mountain Books
DOPE FRIENDS
EAP DIGEST
FELL SWOOP
THE FORUM
Four Seasons Publishers
Gaff Press
GATEAVISA
GEORGE & MERTIE'S PLACE: Rooms With a View
Good Book Publishing Company
GRAFFITI OFF THE ASYLUM WALLS
Gurze Books
Haight-Ashbury Publications
HOAX!
Islewest Publishing
JOURNAL OF PSYCHOACTIVE DRUGS
THE LETTER PARADE
Newjoy Press
Paradise Research Publications, Inc.
PARTING GIFTS
Publitec Editions
PUCK: The Unofficial Journal of the Irrepressible
RedBrick Press
Schenkman Books
See Sharp Press
STONES IN MY POCKET
STREET VOICE
Tyro Publishing
WISEBLOOD

ALTERNATIVE MEDICINE

Baker Street Publications
Beekman Publishers, Inc.
EquiLibrium Press, Inc.
GATEAVISA
HEALTH AND HAPPINESS
Hohm Press
Midwifery Today Books
THE SALEM JOURNAL

AMERICANA

ACORN WHISTLE
AFFABLE NEIGHBOR
Affable Neighbor Press
ALWAYS JUKIN'
Always Jukin'
Ancient City Press
Avery Color Studios

Axelrod Publishing of Tampa Bay
Baker Street Publications
Bear & Company, Inc.
Blue Mouse Studio
BOOGLIT
Booksplus of Maine
THE BOOMERPHILE
The Borgo Press
Branden Publishing Company
The Brookfield Reader
Business Smarts, Inc.
CANADIAN REVIEW OF AMERICAN STUDIES
The Caxton Press
Cherokee Publishing Company
CLASS ACT
Colophon House
Commonwealth Press Virginia
Cottontail Publications
Crossroads Communications
DAYSPRING
Dead Metaphor Press
Devil Mountain Books
Devin-Adair Publishers, Inc.
Down The Shore Publishing
DREAM WHIP
Eagle's View Publishing
Eborn Books
EL PALACIO
Elliott & Clark Publishing
Emerald Ink Publishing
Excelsior Cee Publishing
EXIT 13 MAGAZINE
Foundation Books
Four Seasons Publishers
Fulcrum, Inc.
Full Moon Publications
Gabriel's Horn Publishing Co., Inc.
Gallery West Associates
Gallopade International
GEORGE & MERTIE'S PLACE: Rooms With a View
GLEN BURNIELAND
Glenbridge Publishing Ltd.
The Globe Pequot Press
Harbor House
Heritage Books, Inc.
HOAX!
Hollis Publishing Company
HOLLYWOOD NOSTALGIA
HORIZONS
House of the 9 Muses, Inc.
Huntington Library Press
Ice Cube Press
International Publishers Co. Inc.
The Philip Lesly Company
THE LETTER PARADE
Lexikos
Little Bayou Press
LPD Press
THE MASONIA ROUNDUP
Mayhaven Publishing
MIXED BAG
Mountain Press Publishing Co.
Museum of New Mexico Press
Mustang Publishing Co.
Noontide Press
NORTHWOODS JOURNAL, A Magazine for Writers
NYX OBSCURA MAGAZINE
Oregon State University Press
PASSAGER: A Journal of Remembrance and Discovery
THE PATRIOT
Peachtree Publishers, Ltd.
The Petrarch Press
The Place In The Woods
Pocahontas Press, Inc.
POTOMAC REVIEW
The Preservation Press
THE PRESIDENTS' JOURNAL
Pruett Publishing Company

THING (QECE)
RED AND BLACK
See Sharp Press
Semiotext Foreign Agents Books Series
SEMIOTEXT(E)
SHORT FUSE
Slab-O-Concrete Publications
Smyrna Press
SOCIAL ANARCHISM: A Journal of Practice and Theory
South End Press
SUB-TERRAIN
Times Change Press
TRAFIK - Internationales Journal zur Libertaren Kultur & Politik
Transeuropa
TURNING THE TIDE: A Journal of Anti-Racist Activism, Research & Education
THE UNIT CIRCLE
Vanity Press/Strolling Dog Press
THE VOLUNTARYIST
Wolf-Wise Press
Working Press
YUWITAYA LAKOTA
Z MAGAZINE

ANCIENT ASTRONAUTS

ANT ANT ANT ANT ANT
THE MONTHLY INDEPENDENT TRIBUNE TIMES JOURNAL POST GAZETTE NEWS CHRONICLE BULLETIN
New Paradigm Books
RED OWL

ANIMALS

Access Multimedia
Alaska Geographic Society
Alaska Northwest Books
Alpine Publications, Inc.
Anaphase II
ANIMAL ACTION
ANIMAL LIFE
ANIMAL PEOPLE
THE ANIMALS' AGENDA
ASC NEWSLETTER
Avery Color Studios
The Benefactory, Inc.
Blue Reef Publications, Inc.
Camino Bay Books
Capra Press
Catamount Press
THE CATBIRD SEAT
Chelsea Green Publishing Company
Child's Play
Circumpolar Press
THE CIVIL ABOLITIONIST
Civitas
CJE NEWS (Newsletter of the Coalition for Jobs & the Environment)
The Crossing Press
Cyclone Books
S. Deal & Assoc.
Dimi Press
Dog-Eared Publications
Doral Publishing
EBB AND FLOW
EZ Nature Books
Falcon Press Publishing Company
FARMING UNCLE
FISH DRUM MAGAZINE
Five Corners Publications, Ltd.
Flower Press
Foundation Books
Gahmken Press
THE GENTLE SURVIVALIST
GEORGE & MERTIE'S PLACE: Rooms With a View
Heritage Concepts Publishing Inc
Howln Moon Press

HUMANS & OTHER SPECIES
Inquiry Press
Island Publishers
JEWISH VEGETARIAN NEWSLETTER
Michael Kesend Publishing, Ltd.
Kindness Publications, Inc.
LADYBUG, the Magazine for Young Children
LAKE SUPERIOR MAGAZINE
THE LATHAM LETTER
Lester Street Publishing
LIVE AND LET LIVE
LLAMAS MAGAZINE
The Madson Group, Inc.
Mayhaven Publishing
Micah Publications Inc.
MINIATURE DONKEY TALK INC
Mountain Press Publishing Co.
NATURE SOCIETY NEWS
Naturegraph Publishers, Inc.
NEW METHODS JOURNAL (VETERINARY)
THE NEW PRESS LITERARY QUARTERLY
The Olive Press Publications
C. Olson & Company
Pangaea
Paw Print Publishing Co.
Peartree Books & Music
Peel Productions, Inc.
PenRose Publishing Company, Inc.
Pineapple Press, Inc.
Premium Press America
QECE: QUESTION EVERYTHING. CHALLENGE EVERYTHING.
QUESTION EVERYTHING CHALLENGE EVERYTHING (QECE)
RALPH'S REVIEW
Red Crane Books, Inc.
RED OWL
RESONANCE
Rhino Publishing
RURAL HERITAGE
Ryrich Publications
Sierra Club Books
Silver Seahorse Press
SJL Publishing Company
Skinny Lamb Publishing Company
Gibbs Smith, Publisher
SNOWY EGRET
Spirit Talk Press
George Sroda, Publisher
Stillpoint Publishing
Tilbury House, Publishers
Trouvere Company
Two Dog Press
Univelt, Inc.
VEGETARIAN JOURNAL
Venus Communications
Vonpalisaden Publications Inc.
WILD EARTH
Williamson Publishing Company, Inc.
WISCONSIN TRAILS
Words & Pictures Press
WORLD RAINFOREST REPORT
Zagier & Urruty Publicaciones

ANTHOLOGY

Bancroft Press
Blue Heron Publishing, Inc.
In Print Publishing
J. Mark Press
MARGIN: EXPLORING MODERN MAGICAL REALISM
Nightsun Books
Parabola
Ravenhawk Books
Scrivenery Press
Seal Press
The Spirit That Moves Us Press, Inc.

ANTHROPOLOGY, ARCHAELOGY

AFFAIR OF THE MIND: A Literary Quarterly
AFRICAN STUDIES
Alaska Native Language Center
AMERICAN WRITING: A Magazine
Ancient City Press
Arjuna Library Press
Axelrod Publishing of Tampa Bay
Baker Street Publications
Ballena Press
Bear & Company, Inc.
Blue Dolphin Publishing, Inc.
Cave Books
Celtic Heritage Books
Center for Japanese Studies
Center for South and Southeast Asian Studies Publications
Chandler & Sharp Publishers, Inc.
Circumpolar Press
Citeaux Commentarii Cistercienses
CITEAUX: COMMENTARII CISTERCIENSES
THE CLASSICAL OUTLOOK
The Compass Press
DAEDALUS, Journal of the American Academy of Arts and Sciences
THE DALHOUSIE REVIEW
The Denali Press
DIALOGOS: Hellenic Studies Review
DREAM NETWORK JOURNAL
Eborn Books
ECHOS DU MONDE CLASSIQUE/CLASSICAL VIEWS
EL PALACIO
FACES: The Magazine About People
Full Moon Publications
Galde Press, Inc.
Glenbridge Publishing Ltd.
The Heather Foundation
Hollis Publishing Company
Hope Publishing House
HORIZONS
Horned Owl Publishing
The Independent Institute
Inner Traditions International
Institute of Archaeology Publications
INTERCULTURE
ITALIAN AMERICANA
Jaguar Books
JOURNAL OF UNCONVENTIONAL HISTORY
KMT, A Modern Journal of Ancient Egypt
KMT Communications
Kumarian Press, Inc.
LAKE SUPERIOR MAGAZINE
THE MAD FARMERS' JUBILEE ALMANACK
McPherson & Company Publishers
Mehring Books, Inc.
The Menard Press
Minnesota Historical Society Press
Moon Publications, Inc.
Museum of New Mexico Press
NightinGale Resources
Noyce Publishing
Pangaea
Paragon House Publishers
POW-WOW
Protean Press
Pruett Publishing Company
Psychohistory Press
PUCK: The Unofficial Journal of the Irrepressible
Royal Purcell, Publisher
Q ZINE
THE READER'S REVIEW
REALM OF THE VAMPIRE
Red Crane Books, Inc.
REPORTS OF THE NATIONAL CENTER FOR SCIENCE EDUCATION
REPRESENTATIONS
Research & Discovery Publications

THE SALEM JOURNAL
SHAMAN'S DRUM: A Journal of Experiential Shamanism
SOUTHWEST JOURNAL
Theytus Books Ltd.
Thomas Jefferson University Press
Torchlight Publishing
TRADICION REVISTA
Treasure Chest Books LLC
THE UNDERGROUND FOREST - LA SELVA SUBTERRANEA
University of Calgary Press
WESTERN SKIES
Whalesback Books
White Cliffs Media, Inc.
THE WILD FOODS FORUM
Witwatersrand University Press
WORLD RAINFOREST REPORT
XCP: CROSS-CULTURAL POETICS
YUMTZILOB: Tijdschrift over de Americas
Zagier & Urruty Publicaciones
ZONE
Zone Books

ANTIQUES

ALWAYS JUKIN'
Always Jukin'
Astrion Publishing
Bonus Books, Inc.
C & T Publishing
Cattpigg Press
China Books & Periodicals, Inc.
ClockWorks Press
Cyclone Books
GemStone Press
THE ILLUSTRATOR COLLECTOR'S NEWS
IN PRINT
LAKE SUPERIOR MAGAZINE
MASSEY COLLECTORS NEWS—WILD HARVEST
Mosaic Press
NEW ENGLAND ANTIQUES JOURNAL
Paperweight Press
Passeggiata Press, Inc.
RED POWER
REFLECT
Sonoran Publishing
SOUTHERN QUARTERLY: A Journal of the Arts in the South
Tomart Publications
Vestal Press Ltd
Whalesback Books
White Plume Press

APPALACHIA

APPALACHIA JOURNAL
Appalachian Consortium Press
APPALACHIAN HERITAGE
THE AZOREAN EXPRESS
BLACK JACK & VALLEY GRAPEVINE
Bright Mountain Books, Inc.
CJE NEWS (Newsletter of the Coalition for Jobs & the Environment)
THE CLIMBING ART
Commonwealth Press Virginia
Great Elm Press
HABERSHAM REVIEW
House of the 9 Muses, Inc.
Institute for Southern Studies
KESTREL: A Journal of Literature and Art
Mountain State Press
THE NEW PRESS LITERARY QUARTERLY
Nightshade Press
NORTH CAROLINA LITERARY REVIEW
NORTHWOODS JOURNAL, A Magazine for Writers
NOW AND THEN
PIKEVILLE REVIEW
Pocahontas Press, Inc.
POTATO EYES

POTOMAC REVIEW
THE PURPLE MONKEY
Rowan Mountain Press
Signal Books
TRADITION

ARCHITECTURE

Ancient City Press
ART PAPERS
ASSEMBLAGE: A Critical Journal of Architecture and
    Design Culture
ASSEMBLING
Assembling Press
Astrion Publishing
Balcony Press
Bay Press
Capra Press
China Books & Periodicals, Inc.
Citeaux Commentarii Cistercienses
CITEAUX: COMMENTARII CISTERCIENSES
CJE NEWS (Newsletter of the Coalition for Jobs & the
    Environment)
THE COOPERATOR
Craftsman Book Company
DESIGN BOOK REVIEW
DREAM WHIP
Elliott & Clark Publishing
ENVIRONMENT AND ART LETTER
ENVIRONMENTAL & ARCHITECTURAL PHENO-
    MENOLOGY NEWSLETTER
GATEAVISA
GEORGE & MERTIE'S PLACE: Rooms With a View
Goodheart-Willcox Publisher
ILLINOIS ARCHITECTURAL & HISTORICAL RE-
    VIEW
Interalia/Design Books
Italica Press, Inc.
LAKE SUPERIOR MAGAZINE
Macrocosm USA, Inc.
MARQUEE
Midmarch Arts Press
MINISTRY & LITURGY
Minnesota Historical Society Press
Mosaic Press
Mount Ida Press
THE NEW CRITERION
NewSage Press
OLD-HOUSE JOURNAL
OUT YOUR BACKDOOR: The Magazine of Informal
    Adventure and Cheap Culture
Passeggiata Press, Inc.
Pendaya Publications, Inc.
Pineapple Press, Inc.
Pogo Press, Incorporated
The Preservation Press
Race Point Press
Really Great Books
SJL Publishing Company
Gibbs Smith, Publisher
SOUTHERN QUARTERLY: A Journal of the Arts in the
    South
Synergistic Press
Tailored Tours Publications, Inc.
THEATRE DESIGN AND TECHNOLOGY
Thirteen Colonies Press
Timber Press
Tuns Press
THE UNDERGROUND FOREST - LA SELVA SUB-
    TERRANEA
THE UNIT CIRCLE
University of Massachusetts Press
Vestal Press Ltd
WATERFRONT WORLD SPOTLIGHT
WE INTERNATIONAL (formerly WOMEN AND EN-
    VIRONMENTS)
Whalesback Books
Wisconsin Trails
ZONE

Zone Books

ARIZONA

Baker Street Publications
Eborn Books
Falcon Press Publishing Company
Four Peaks Press
Full Moon Publications
Law Mexico Publishing
LPD Press
MIXED BAG
Moon Publications, Inc.
Mountain Automation Corporation
The Patrice Press
POW-WOW
Primer Publishers
Pruett Publishing Company
SARU Press International
Gibbs Smith, Publisher
SOUTHWEST JOURNAL
Tamarack Books, Inc.
Tortilla Press
TRADICION REVISTA
Treasure Chest Books LLC
Turtle Island Press, Inc.
WEBER STUDIES: Voices and Viewpoints of the
    Contemporary West
WESTERN SKIES

ARKANSAS

MIXED BAG
Mountain Automation Corporation
Premium Press America
Rose Publishing Co.

ARMENIAN

AFFAIR OF THE MIND: A Literary Quarterly
ARARAT
Blue Crane Books
Griffon House Publications
THE NEW PRESS LITERARY QUARTERLY
Passeggiata Press, Inc.
PenRose Publishing Company, Inc.
Saqi Books Publisher
TRANSCAUCASUS: A Chronology
Zon International Publishing Co.

AROMATHERAPY

Inner Traditions International

ARTHURIAN

CLASS ACT
Full Moon Publications
GEORGE & MERTIE'S PLACE: Rooms With a View
THE HAUNTED JOURNAL
HORIZONS BEYOND
Horned Owl Publishing
KELTIC FRINGE
Pride & Imprints
RENAISSANCE MAGAZINE
THE SALEM JOURNAL
VIRTUTE ET MORTE MAGAZINE

ARTIFICIAL INTELLIGENCE

Ageless Press
DISSONANCE MAGAZINE
GATEAVISA
GEORGE & MERTIE'S PLACE: Rooms With a View
JACK MACKEREL MAGAZINE
THE LETTER PARADE
MAD SCIENTIST
Media Arts Publishing
META4: Journal of Object Oriented Poetics (OOPS)
Rowhouse Press
WHOLE EARTH
Z MAGAZINE

ARTS

A & U AMERICA'S AIDS MAGAZINE
Abiko Literary Press (ALP)
Acrobat Books
AERIAL
AFFABLE NEIGHBOR
Affable Neighbor Press
AFFAIR OF THE MIND: A Literary Quarterly
THE AFFILIATE
Airplane Books
AK Press
Alan Wofsy Fine Arts
Alicubi Publications
Allworth Press
Altamont Press, Inc.
American Canadian Publishers, Inc.
American Living Press
AMERICAN PHYSICIANS ART ASSOCIATION NEWSLETTER
AMERICAN WRITING: A Magazine
Americans for the Arts/ACA Books
AMNESIA
ANT ANT ANT ANT ANT
APOSTROPHE: USCB Journal of the Arts
ARISTOS
Arjuna Library Press
ARNAZELLA
ART CALENDAR
ART PAPERS
ART TIMES
ART-CORE
ART/LIFE
Art/Life Limited Editions
ART:MAG
ARTSLINK
ASSEMBLAGE: A Critical Journal of Architecture and Design Culture
ASSEMBLING
Assembling Press
ASSPANTS
Astrion Publishing
Asylum Arts
AUFBAU
Autonomedia, Inc.
AXE FACTORY REVIEW
Axelrod Publishing of Tampa Bay
BABYSUE MUSIC REVIEW
Backspace Ink
Baker Street Publications
Balcony Press
Banana Productions
Bancroft Press
Barking Dog Books
BARNABE MOUNTAIN REVIEW
William L. Bauhan, Publisher
Bay Press
BB Books
THE BEAR DELUXE
The Bear Wallow Publishing Company
BEHIND BARS
THE BENT
BGB Press, Inc.
Birdalone Books
Black Dress Press
Black Tie Press
BLACKFLASH
Bliss Publishing Company, Inc.
Blue Heron Publishing, Inc.
Blue Raven Publishing
BLUE UNICORN
BOMB MAGAZINE
BOOK/MARK SMALL PRESS QUARTERLY REVIEW
Booksplus of Maine
Borden Publishing Co.
BORDERLANDS: Texas Poetry Review
BOSTON REVIEW
BOULEVARD

Branden Publishing Company
THE BREAD AND BUTTER CHRONICLES
BREAKFAST ALL DAY
Brick Row Publishing Co. Ltd.
Bright Hill Press
The Brookfield Reader
BROWNBAG PRESS
Brownout Laboratories
Burning Books
BURNING CAR
C & T Publishing
CALYX: A Journal of Art and Literature by Women
Canterbury Press
THE CAPILANO REVIEW
A Cappella Books
Capra Press
Carrefour Press
CAVEAT LECTOR
Celestial Otter Press
THE CENTENNIAL REVIEW
CHANTEH, the Iranian Cross Cultural Qu'ly
CHAOS FOR THE CREATIVE MIND
THE CHEROTIC (r)EVOLUTIONARY
CHICAGO REVIEW
Chicago Review Press
CHILDREN, CHURCHES AND DADDIES, A Non Religious, Non Familial Literary Magazine
Child's Play
China Books & Periodicals, Inc.
Chiron Press
CHIRON REVIEW
CHRISTIANITY & THE ARTS
Citeaux Commentarii Cistercienses
CITEAUX: COMMENTARII CISTERCIENSES
Clamshell Press
CLASS ACT
CLOCKWATCH REVIEW
Community Resource Institute Press
CONFLICT OF INTEREST
The Consultant Press, Ltd.
THE COOL TRAVELER
CORONA
COTTONWOOD
Cottonwood Press
Council Oak Books
COVER MAGAZINE
THE CREATIVE WOMAN
Crescent Moon
CRIPES!
CROSSCURRENTS
CULTUREFRONT
CURMUDGEON
DAEDALUS, Journal of the American Academy of Arts and Sciences
THE DALHOUSIE REVIEW
DANDELION ARTS MAGAZINE
Dawn Sign Press
DENVER QUARTERLY
DESCANT
THE DIRTY GOAT
Dovehaven Press
DRASTIC LIVES
THE DROPLET JOURNAL
THE EDGE CITY REVIEW
Edgewise Press
EKPHRASIS
EL PALACIO
Elliott & Clark Publishing
EMERGING VOICES
Empire Publishing Service
ENOUGH IS ENOUGH!
Enthea Press
ENVIRONMENT AND ART LETTER
ENVIRONMENTAL & ARCHITECTURAL PHENO-MENOLOGY NEWSLETTER
EPM Publications, Inc.
ETCETERA
EUROPEAN JUDAISM

THE EVERGREEN CHRONICLES
Ex Machina Publishing Company
EXCLAIM!
EXPERIMENTAL MUSICAL INSTRUMENTS
EyeDEA Books
FAULTLINE, Journal of Art and Literature
The Feathered Serpent
FIBERARTS
Film-Video Publications
Five Corners Publications, Ltd.
FIVE POINTS
FODDERWING
Fotofolio, Inc.
Four Walls Eight Windows
4*9*1: Neo-Immanentist/Sursymbolist-Imagination
FRANK: AN INTERNATIONAL JOURNAL OF CON-
    TEMPORARY WRITING AND ART
FREEFALL
FROM THE MARGIN
Fromm International Publishing Corporation
Frontier Publishing, Inc.
FUEL MAGAZINE
FULL MOON DIRECTORY
FURTHER TOO
The Future Press
Gallery West Associates
GATEAVISA
Gateways Books And Tapes
GEORGE & MERTIE'S PLACE: Rooms With a View
THE GLASS CHERRY
The Glass Cherry Press
Glenbridge Publishing Ltd.
The Gleniffer Press
GRAFFITI OFF THE ASYLUM WALLS
GRAIN
GrapeVinePress
G'RAPH
The Green Hut Press
GULF COAST
Gumbs & Thomas Publishers, Inc.
H & C NEWSLETTER
Hands & Heart Books
Hard Press
Hard Press, Inc.
HAWAI'I REVIEW
HEAVEN BONE MAGAZINE
Heaven Bone Press
Helicon Nine Editions
THE HIGGINSVILLE READER
HOAX!
Homa & Sekey Books
Homestead Publishing
HOOTENANNY
The Hosanna Press
Host Publications, Inc.
THE HUDSON REVIEW
Huntington Library Press
HUNTINGTON LIBRARY QUARTERLY
Hyacinth House Publications/Caligula Editions
ICARUS WAS RIGHT
THE ILLUSTRATOR COLLECTOR'S NEWS
Images For Media/Sesquin
INNER JOURNEYS
Inner Traditions International
Interalia/Design Books
INTERBANG
Interlink Publishing Group, Inc.
INTERNATIONAL ART POST
INTERNATIONAL QUARTERLY
IRIS: A Journal About Women
ITALIAN AMERICANA
Italica Press, Inc.
Itidwitir Publishing
IWAN: INMATE WRITERS OF AMERICA NEWSLET-
    TER
THE J MAN TIMES
J P Publications
JACK MACKEREL MAGAZINE

JB Press
JEWISH LIFE
JOURNAL OF AESTHETICS AND ART CRITICISM
JOURNAL OF ALASKA WOMEN
JOURNAL OF REGIONAL CRITICISM
KALDRON, An International Journal Of Visual Poetry
KALLIOPE, A Journal of Women's Art
Kelsey St. Press
KMT, A Modern Journal of Ancient Egypt
KMT Communications
Knightraven Books
La Alameda Press
LADYBUG, the Magazine for Young Children
LAKE SUPERIOR MAGAZINE
LEFT CURVE
Left Hand Books
LEO Productions LLC.
LIES MAGAZINE
Light, Words & Music
LIGHTWORKS MAGAZINE
LINGO
LINQ
LITRAG
Locks Art Publications
LOST AND FOUND TIMES
Lowy Publishing
LPD Press
LULLWATER REVIEW
LUMMOX JOURNAL
Luna Bisonte Prods
LUZ EN ARTE Y LITERATURA
THE MAC GUFFIN
Macrocosm USA, Inc.
THE MAD FARMERS' JUBILEE ALMANACK
MAGIC CHANGES
Mandala Publishing Group
MANOA: A Pacific Journal of International Writing
Peter Marcan Publications
MATI
Maxima New Media
Mayhaven Publishing
McPherson & Company Publishers
ME MAGAZINE
MEANJIN
MEDIA SPOTLIGHT
Mehring Books, Inc.
METAL CURSE
Metamorphous Press
THE METAPHYSICAL REVIEW
Midmarch Arts Press
MIDWEST ART FAIRS
Miles & Miles
MINISTRY & LITURGY
MISSISSIPPI MUD
MIXED BAG
MOMMY AND I ARE ONE
Moon Publications, Inc.
Mortal Press
MUSE NATURA, A Sensual Journey of the Arts
Museum of New Mexico Press
MUSHROOM DREAMS
MUSICWORKS: The Journal of Sound Explorations
    (Audio-Visual)
MYSTERIOUS WYSTERIA
N D
NANCY'S MAGAZINE
NATURALLY
NERVE COWBOY
NEW ART EXAMINER
New Broom Private Press
THE NEW CRITERION
NEW ENGLAND ANTIQUES JOURNAL
NEW HOPE INTERNATIONAL REVIEW
NEW LETTERS
THE NEW RENAISSANCE, An International Magazine
    of Ideas & Opinions, Emphasizing Literature & The
    Arts
NEW YORK STORIES

NEWS FROM NATIVE CALIFORNIA
NewSage Press
NIGHT ROSES
NIGHTLORE
NIGHTSHADE
Nightshade Press
NITE-WRITER'S INTERNATIONAL LITERARY
ARTS JOURNAL
THE NOISE
Norton Coker Press
Not-For-Sale-Press or NFS Press
NWI National Writers Institute
Ocean View Books
OHIOANA QUARTERLY
OLD CROW
Old West Publishing Co.
ONE EARTH
OPEN EXCHANGE MAGAZINE
Ophelia Editions
ORNAMENT
The Overlook Press
OWEN WISTER REVIEW
THE PACIFIC REVIEW
PAGAN AMERICA
PAPERBACK PARADE
Paperweight Press
Papillon Publishing
Parabola
PASSION
Pebble Press, Inc.
PEOPLE'S CULTURE
Phelps Publishing Company
PHOEBE: A JOURNAL OF LITERARY ARTS
PHOTOBULLETIN
THE PHOTOLETTER
PIG IRON
Pig Iron Press
Pittore Euforico
PLAIN BROWN WRAPPER (PBW)
Players Press, Inc.
PLUME
PLUMTREES
POETRY MOTEL
Pogo Press, Incorporated
POINT OF CONTACT
Pomegranate Communications
The Porcupine's Quill, Inc.
Bern Porter Books
POTOMAC REVIEW
THE POWYS JOURNAL
PRAIRIE WINDS
The Preservation Press
Proper PH Publications
PROVINCETOWN ARTS
PSYCHOTRAIN
Purple Finch Press
Pygmy Forest Press
QECE: QUESTION EVERYTHING. CHALLENGE
EVERYTHING.
Quarterly Committee of Queen's University
QUEEN'S QUARTERLY: A Canadian Review
THE QUEST
QUESTION EVERYTHING CHALLENGE EVERY-
THING (QECE)
R & M Publishing Company
RADIANCE, The Magazine For Large Women
RARITAN: A Quarterly Review
RATTAPALLAX
THE READER'S REVIEW
Really Great Books
REALM OF THE VAMPIRE
Red Cedar Press
RED CEDAR REVIEW
Red Crane Books, Inc.
REFLECT
REPRESENTATIONS
Resource Publications, Inc.
RIVER STYX

THE ROTKIN REVIEW
Rowhouse Press
RUBBERSTAMPMADNESS
The Runaway Spoon Press
Running Press
St. Georges Press
SALMAGUNDI
SALOME: A Journal for the Performing Arts
SALON: A Journal of Aesthetics
SALT HILL
Salt Lick Press
SANDBOX MAGAZINE
SANTA BARBARA REVIEW
Saqi Books Publisher
Scarecrow Press
Scars Publications
Score
SCORE
SCRAWL MAGAZINE
SCRIVENER
SEMIGLOSS
SHATTERED WIG REVIEW
SHORT FUSE
SISTERSONG: Women Across Cultures
SIVULLINEN
SKYLARK
Skytop Publishing
Slab-O-Concrete Publications
Slate Press
SLIPSTREAM
SMALL PRESS CREATIVE EXPLOSION
Gibbs Smith, Publisher
Smyrna Press
SO TO SPEAK
SONAR MAP
Sound View Press
THE SOUNDS OF POETRY
SOUTHERN QUARTERLY: A Journal of the Arts in the
South
SPEAK UP
SPELUNKER FLOPHOUSE
Spirit Talk Press
Station Hill Press
Steamshovel Press
Stemmer House Publishers, Inc.
Studia Hispanica Editors
STUDIO ART MAGAZINE
STUDIO ONE
SUITCASE: A Journal of Transcultural Traffic
SULPHUR RIVER LITERARY REVIEW
SYCAMORE REVIEW
SYMPLOKE: A Journal for the Intermingling of Literary,
Cultural and Theoretical Scholarship
SYNCOPATED CITY
Synergistic Press
Syracuse Cultural Workers/Tools for Change
Teachers & Writers Collaborative
TEACHERS & WRITERS MAGAZINE
Ten Penny Players, Inc.
THEATRE DESIGN AND TECHNOLOGY
THIN COYOTE
THE THREEPENNY REVIEW
THRESHOLDS JOURNAL
Tiger Moon
Timber Press
TOLE WORLD
TRADICION REVISTA
TRADITION
Transcending Mundane
TRIVIUM
21st Century Publishing, Inc.
Twin Palms Publishers
UMBRELLA
THE UNDERGROUND FOREST - LA SELVA SUB-
TERRANEA
THE UNIT CIRCLE
University of Calgary Press
University of Massachusetts Press

UNIVERSITY OF WINDSOR PEVIEW
UNMUZZLED OX
UNO MAS MAGAZINE
Urban Legend Press
THE URBANITE
Urthona Press
VARIOUS ARTISTS
VEGGIE LIFE
Venus Communications
Vestal Press Ltd
THE VINCENT BROTHERS REVIEW
Vincent Laspina
VIRTUTE ET MORTE MAGAZINE
Visual Studies Workshop
Vitreous Group/Camp Colton
Voices From My Retreat
Volcano Press, Inc
WASHINGTON REVIEW
Water Mark Press
WATERWAYS: Poetry in the Mainstream
WAY STATION MAGAZINE
WEIRD POETRY
WESTART
Westgate Press
Whalesback Books
Whelks Walk Press
White Cliffs Media, Inc.
WHITEWALLS: A Journal of Language and Art
Wings of Fire Press
WISCONSIN REVIEW
WISCONSIN TRAILS
WISEBLOOD
WITNESS
Wolfhound Press
WOMAN'S ART JOURNAL
WOMEN ARTISTS NEWS BOOK REVIEW
WOMEN IN THE ARTS BULLETIN/NEWSLETTER
WOOD STROKES & WOODCRAFTS
Writers House Press
WRITER'S LIFELINE
WRITER'S WORKSHOP REVIEW
XIB
Xib Publications
X-RAY
Yatra Publications/11:11 Studio
YELLOW SILK: Journal Of Erotic Arts
YUMTZILOB: Tijdschrift over de Americas
Z MAGAZINE
Zon International Publishing Co.
ZUZU'S PETALS: QUARTERLY ONLINE

ASIA, INDOCHINA

AREOPAGUS
Arjay Associates
ASIAN SURVEY
Autonomedia, Inc.
AXE FACTORY REVIEW
BELLES LETTRES
The Bess Press
Between The Lines
Book Faith India
Center for South and Southeast Asian Studies Publications
China Books & Periodicals, Inc.
Chinese Literature Press
CICADA
Clover Park Press
Cynic Press
Florida Academic Press
GATEAVISA
Hoover Institution Press
HORIZONS
Images For Media/Sesquin
INDIA CURRENTS
Inner Traditions International
J P Publications
JOURNAL OF ASIAN MARTIAL ARTS
Kumarian Press, Inc.
Mandala Publishing Group

MANOA: A Pacific Journal of International Writing
MEANJIN
Moon Publications, Inc.
Nguoi Dan
NGUOI DAN
The Olive Press Publications
Open Court Publishing
THE OTHER ISRAEL
PACIFIC HISTORICAL REVIEW
Pacific View Press
Papillon Publishing
Passeggiata Press, Inc.
Redbird Press, Inc.
Salt Lick Press
Schenkman Books
SYMBIOTIC OATMEAL
TitleWaves Publishing
TOWARD FREEDOM
TRANSITIONS ABROAD: The Guide to Living,
    Learning, and Working Overseas
Vesta Publications Limited
Via Media Publishing Company
VIETNAM GENERATION: A Journal of Recent History
    and Contemporary Issues
George Wahr Publishing Company
White Pine Press
Wings of Fire Press
Wisdom Publications, Inc.
WORDS OF WISDOM
World Music Press
WORLD RAINFOREST REPORT
YEFIEF

ASIAN-AMERICAN

AFRICAN AMERICAN AUDIOBOOK REVIEW
THE ASIAN PACIFIC AMERICAN JOURNAL
AXE FACTORY REVIEW
Baker Street Publications
BAMBOO RIDGE, A HAWAI'I WRITERS JOURNAL
Bamboo Ridge Press
BELLES LETTRES
The Bess Press
Blue Heron Publishing, Inc.
BRAVO, THE POET'S MAGAZINE
BRILLIANT STAR
Buddhist Study Center Press
Burning Bush Publications
Carolina Wren Press/Lollipop Power Books
Chandler & Sharp Publishers, Inc.
China Books & Periodicals, Inc.
Comstock Bonanza Press
Cynic Press
HAWAI'I REVIEW
Heritage West Books
Hollis Publishing Company
Homa & Sekey Books
Images For Media/Sesquin
INDIA CURRENTS
JAPANOPHILE
Kelsey St. Press
Kodomo Press
MANOA: A Pacific Journal of International Writing
MOONRABBIT REVIEW
NEW ART EXAMINER
THE NEW PRESS LITERARY QUARTERLY
THE NEW RENAISSANCE, An International Magazine
    of Ideas & Opinions, Emphasizing Literature & The
    Arts
Nguoi Dan
NGUOI DAN
PACIFIC HISTORICAL REVIEW
Papillon Publishing
PASSAGER: A Journal of Remembrance and Discovery
Passeggiata Press, Inc.
The Place In The Woods
Polar Bear Productions & Company
Pygmy Forest Press
Red Crane Books, Inc.

Reference Service Press
Schenkman Books
SHEMP! The Lowlife Culture Magazine
Strawberry Hill Press
SYMBIOTIC OATMEAL
University of Massachusetts Press
Venus Communications
Vesta Publications Limited
VIETNAM GENERATION: A Journal of Recent History
 and Contemporary Issues
Ward Hill Press
Willendorf Press
YEFIEF
Z MAGAZINE

ASTROLOGY

ACS Publications
THE AFFILIATE
Altair Publications
ASTROFLASH
Bear & Company, Inc.
Blue Dolphin Publishing, Inc.
Blue River Publishing Inc.
BOTH SIDES NOW
Cassandra Press, Inc.
Cosmoenergetics Publications
CRCS Publications
CRONE CHRONICLES: A Journal of Conscious Aging
Golden Isis Press
GRAFFITI OFF THE ASYLUM WALLS
HECATE'S LOOM - A Journal of Magical Arts
Inner Traditions International
Intelligenesis Publications
INTUITIVE EXPLORATIONS
Llewellyn Publications
THE MAD FARMERS' JUBILEE ALMANACK
THE MOUNTAIN ASTROLOGER
NIGHT ROSES
Parabola
Quicksilver Productions
QUINTILE
Quintile
RADIANCE, The Magazine For Large Women
Rio Grande Press
SAGEWOMAN
SO YOUNG!
SPIRIT TO SPIRIT
STONES IN MY POCKET
TEC Publications
Three Pyramids Publishing
Tickerwick Publications
Top Of The Mountain Publishing
Torchlight Publishing
Samuel Weiser, Inc.
Whitford Press

ASTRONOMY

ABELexpress
ATL Press, Inc.
Catamount Press
GEORGE & MERTIE'S PLACE: Rooms With a View
HECATE'S LOOM - A Journal of Magical Arts
Lowy Publishing
THE MAD FARMERS' JUBILEE ALMANACK
Naturegraph Publishers, Inc.
New Spirit Press/The Poet Tree
ODYSSEY: Science Adventures in Science
Outer Space Press
Parabola
POEMS THAT THUMP IN THE DARK/SECOND
 GLANCE
RED OWL
SJL Publishing Company
STRUGGLE: A Magazine of Proletarian Revolutionary
 Literature
Torchlight Publishing
Univelt, Inc.
Visions Communications

WHOLE EARTH

ATHEISM

AXE FACTORY REVIEW
Brownout Laboratories
COLLEGIUM NEWSLETTER
FREE INQUIRY
GATEAVISA
GEORGE & MERTIE'S PLACE: Rooms With a View
GRAFFITI OFF THE ASYLUM WALLS
ICARUS WAS RIGHT
Itidwitir Publishing
QUESTION EVERYTHING CHALLENGE EVERY-
 THING (QECE)
See Sharp Press
SPIRIT TO SPIRIT
STRUGGLE: A Magazine of Proletarian Revolutionary
 Literature
THE TRUTH SEEKER
XIB
Xib Publications

AUDIO/VIDEO

COUNTERPOISE: For Social Responsibilities, Liberty
 and Dissent
GLASS AUDIO
Golden Eagle Press
LifeQuest Publishing Group
Turtle Island Press, Inc.

AUSTRALIA

Baker Street Publications
BELLES LETTRES
Child's Play
Content Communications
DAEDALUS, Journal of the American Academy of Arts
 and Sciences
EDDIE THE MAGAZINE
The Feminist Press at the City College
GATEAVISA
GEORGE & MERTIE'S PLACE: Rooms With a View
HORIZONS
House of the 9 Muses, Inc.
Inner Traditions International
J P Publications
Kali Press
Kells Media Group
Edward J. Lefkowicz, Inc.
MEANJIN
THE METAPHYSICAL REVIEW
Moon Publications, Inc.
THE NEW PRESS LITERARY QUARTERLY
Nosukumo
OVERLAND
Passeggiata Press, Inc.
STUDIO - A Journal of Christians Writing
ULITARRA
UNION RECORDER
University of Sydney Union
Visa Books (Division of South Continent Corporation Pty
 Ltd)
Wide World Publishing/TETRA
WORLD RAINFOREST REPORT

AUTOBIOGRAPHY

ACORN WHISTLE
Adaptive Living
African American Audio Press
AFRICAN AMERICAN AUDIOBOOK REVIEW
Alaska Native Language Center
Amador Publishers
American Literary Press Inc./Noble House
ANAIS: An International Journal
Ancient City Press
Arjay Associates
Axelrod Publishing of Tampa Bay
Beacon Point Press
Bear & Company, Inc.

BELLES LETTRES
Bonus Books, Inc.
BookPartners, Inc.
Bright Mountain Books, Inc.
Brunswick Publishing Corporation
Carrefour Press
Carrier Pigeon Press
Cave Books
Celo Valley Books
China Books & Periodicals, Inc.
CLASS ACT
Clover Park Press
COLLEGIUM NEWSLETTER
THE CREAM CITY REVIEW
CRONE CHRONICLES: A Journal of Conscious Aging
Crystal Clarity, Publishers
CURMUDGEON
DANDELION ARTS MAGAZINE
John Daniel and Company, Publishers
Devil Mountain Books
Elysian Hills Publishing Company, Inc.
Eros Publishing
FC-Izdat Publishing
The Feminist Press at the City College
Fromm International Publishing Corporation
FURTHER TOO
Galde Press, Inc.
Gay Sunshine Press, Inc.
Golden Eagle Press
GRANULATED TUPPERWARE
Happy Rock Press
Hobblebush Books
House of the 9 Muses, Inc.
THE HUNTED NEWS
In Print Publishing
Inner Traditions International
Innisfree Press
JACK MACKEREL MAGAZINE
JEWISH LIFE
JOURNAL OF ALASKA WOMEN
KARMA LAPEL
KESTREL: A Journal of Literature and Art
Leyland Publications
Limelight Editions
LITTLE FREE PRESS
Log Cabin Manuscripts
Lowy Publishing
MAIN STREET JOURNAL
MANOA: A Pacific Journal of International Writing
THE MASONIA ROUNDUP
Massey-Reyner Publishing
Minnesota Historical Society Press
NEW HOPE INTERNATIONAL REVIEW
The New Humanity Press
New World Press
North Country Books, Inc.
Nosukumo
NOT BORED!
The Overmountain Press
PALO ALTO REVIEW
THE PANNUS INDEX
Parabola
Passeggiata Press, Inc.
PEN & INK WRITERS JOURNAL
PenRose Publishing Company, Inc.
PLAIN BROWN WRAPPER (PBW)
POTOMAC REVIEW
Prudhomme Press
Red Apple Publishing
Rhino Publishing
Rowhouse Press
Seekers Press
Signal Books
Skinny Lamb Publishing Company
SLEUTH JOURNAL
Genny Smith Books
SOUTHWEST JOURNAL
Spelman Publishing, Inc.

STAPLE
The Subourbon Press
Swan Raven & Company
Tilbury House, Publishers
Times Change Press
Tyro Publishing
University of Massachusetts Press
URBAN GRAFFITI
VanderWyk & Burnham
W.E.C. Plant Publishing
George Wahr Publishing Company
Waverly House Publishing
Words & Pictures Press
Wright-Armstead Associates
WRITING FOR OUR LIVES
Xenos Books
Z MAGAZINE

AUTOS

AUTO-FREE TIMES
Bonus Books, Inc.
ELECTRIC VEHICLE NEWS
Fisher Books
Goodheart-Willcox Publisher
Premium Press America
Prestige Publishing
Swan Publishing Company

AVANT-GARDE, EXPERIMENTAL ART

A & U AMERICA'S AIDS MAGAZINE
ABRAXAS
AC
AD/VANCE
AFFABLE NEIGHBOR
Affable Neighbor Press
AFFAIR OF THE MIND: A Literary Quarterly
AMERICAN WRITING: A Magazine
ANT ANT ANT ANT ANT
Arjuna Library Press
ARNAZELLA
ART CALENDAR
ART PAPERS
ART/LIFE
Art/Life Limited Editions
ART'S GARBAGE GAZZETTE
ARTSLINK
ASSEMBLAGE: A Critical Journal of Architecture and
  Design Culture
Asylum Arts
ATELIER
ATROCITY
Autonomedia, Inc.
Baker Street Publications
BALL MAGAZINE
BATHTUB GIN
BLACK BEAR REVIEW
Black Sparrow Press
Black Tie Press
BOUILLABAISSE
Brownout Laboratories
Burning Books
BURNING CAR
Burning Llama Press
CASTAWAYS
Castle Peak Editions
THE CHEROTIC (r)EVOLUTIONARY
CHRONICLES OF DISORDER
CLWN WR
COKEFISH
Cokefish Press
CRIPES!
CURMUDGEON
Dead Metaphor Press
Depth Charge
DIRIGIBLE
THE DIRTY GOAT
DISSONANCE MAGAZINE
DISTURBED GUILLOTINE

736

Yatra Publications/11:11 Studio
YEFIEF
YELLOW SILK: Journal Of Erotic Arts
ZERO HOUR
Zombie Logic Press
ZOMBIE LOGIC REVIEW
ZONE
Zone Books
ZUZU'S PETALS: QUARTERLY ONLINE
ZYX

AVIATION

Acorn Publishing
Aeolus Press, Inc.
Alta Research
Associated Writing Programs
Aviation Book Company
The Bear Wallow Publishing Company
Beekman Publishers, Inc.
Burd Street Press
Butterfield Press
CESSNA OWNER MAGAZINE
CONTACT!
Eagle Publishing Company
The Film Instruction Company of America
Focus Publications, Inc.
Foundation Books
Galde Press, Inc.
GATEAVISA
Golden Eagle Press
HANG GLIDING
House of Hits, Inc.
KITE LINES
Mach 1, Inc.
Paul Maravelas
Mountain Press Publishing Co.
The Nautical & Aviation Publishing Co. of America, Inc.
NORTHERN PILOT
Para Publishing
PARACHUTIST
The Patrice Press
PIPERS MAGAZINE
Publitec Editions
SKYDIVING
Sunflower University Press
The Times Journal Publishing Co.
Words & Pictures Press
World Wide Publishing Corp.
WRITER'S CHRONICLE

AWARDS, FOUNDATIONS, GRANTS

Abiko Literary Press (ALP)
ART CALENDAR
Avisson Press, Inc.
Center Press
Cultivated Underground Press
ENTELECHY MAGAZINE
Film-Video Publications
FOLIO: A LITERARY JOURNAL
The Foundation Center
PHOENIX MAGAZINE
Phoenix Press
The Place In The Woods
POETIC SPACE: Poetry & Fiction
QUESTION EVERYTHING CHALLENGE EVERY-
THING (QECE)
Reference Service Press
WRITER'S LIFELINE

BEAT

AFFABLE NEIGHBOR
Affable Neighbor Press
Alpha Beat Press
ALPHA BEAT SOUP
ARTHUR'S COUSIN
AXE FACTORY REVIEW
Baker Street Publications
BATHTUB GIN

BLUE BEAT JACKET
Blue Jacket Press
Boog Literature
BOOGLIT
BOUILLABAISSE
BROWNBAG PRESS
BURNING CAR
THE CAFE REVIEW
THE CHEROTIC (r)EVOLUTIONARY
CHILDREN, CHURCHES AND DADDIES, A Non
Religious, Non Familial Literary Magazine
Chiron Press
CHIRON REVIEW
CHRONICLES OF DISORDER
Cokefish Press
Conari Press
CURMUDGEON
Cynic Press
Dead Metaphor Press
DHARMA BEAT
THE DIRTY GOAT
Drum
THE EVER DANCING MUSE
EXCLAIM!
Frozen Waffles Press/Shattered Sidewalks Press; 45th
Century Chapbooks
Full Moon Publications
FURTHER TOO
Gay Sunshine Press, Inc.
GEORGE & MERTIE'S PLACE: Rooms With a View
HAWAI'I REVIEW
HEELTAP/Pariah Press
THE HIGHWAY POET
Host Publications, Inc.
Hyacinth House Publications/Caligula Editions
IllumiNet Press
KARMA LAPEL
LA PERIPHERIE
LUMMOX JOURNAL
MACHINEGUN MAGAZINE: New Lit. Quarterly
MAIN STREET JOURNAL
MESECHABE: The Journal of Surre(gion)alism
MIXED BAG
NEW HOPE INTERNATIONAL REVIEW
Pariah Press
PEACE, The Magazine of the Sixties
Phony Lid Publications
PSYCHOTRAIN
Red Crane Books, Inc.
Scars Publications
SHOCKBOX
THE SPITTING IMAGE
THE BOBBY STAR NEWSLETTER
Steamshovel Press
STEAMSHOVEL PRESS
STOVEPIPE: A Journal of Little Literary Value
Sweet Lady Moon Press
SYNCOPATED CITY
THE UNIT CIRCLE
VAGABOND
VOICES - ISRAEL
Who Who Who Publishing
WINDOW PANES
XIB
Xib Publications

SAUL BELLOW

CLASS ACT
GEORGE & MERTIE'S PLACE: Rooms With a View
MAIN STREET JOURNAL
Moonbeam Publications, Inc.

JOHN BERRYMAN

Abiko Literary Press (ALP)
CLASS ACT
PHOENIX MAGAZINE
Phoenix Press
Pygmy Forest Press

BIBLIOGRAPHY

THE AFRICAN BOOK PUBLISHING RECORD
AMERICAN LITERATURE
Americana Books
ANQ: A Quarterly Journal of Short Articles, Notes, and Reviews
Appalachian Consortium Press
Arden Press, Inc.
ASSEMBLING
Assembling Press
Athanor Books (a division of ETX Seminars)
Bayley & Musgrave
Bicycle Books (Publishing) Inc.
Black Sparrow Press
Bluestocking Press
The Borgo Press
Carrefour Press
Center for Japanese Studies
THE CHRISTIAN LIBRARIAN
CLASS ACT
Confluence Press, Inc.
COUNTERPOISE: For Social Responsibilities, Liberty and Dissent
The F. Marion Crawford Memorial Society
The Denali Press
Dustbooks
Ecrivez!
ECW Press
Edition Gemini
Editions Ex Libris
ELT Press
ENGLISH LITERATURE IN TRANSITION, 1880-1920
ESSAYS ON CANADIAN WRITING
Ex Machina Publishing Company
Fallen Leaf Press
FEMINIST COLLECTIONS: A QUARTERLY OF WO-MEN'S STUDIES RESOURCES
FEMINIST PERIODICALS: A CURRENT LISTING OF CONTENTS
The Feminist Press at the City College
The Gleniffer Press
The Great Rift Press
Gryphon Publications
Hans Zell Publishers
Heresy Press
Hoover Institution Press
HUMANS & OTHER SPECIES
Ithaca Press
THE JOURNAL OF COMMONWEALTH LITERA-TURE
JOURNAL OF MODERN LITERATURE
KARMA LAPEL
Edward J. Lefkowicz, Inc.
THE LEFT INDEX
LEO Productions LLC.
Library Research Associates, Inc.
LINQ
THE LONSDALE - The International Quarterly of The Romantic Six
LOST GENERATION JOURNAL
Peter Marcan Publications
MARTHA'S KIDLIT NEWSLETTER
Mayhaven Publishing
Minnesota Historical Society Press
MUSICWORKS: The Journal of Sound Explorations (Audio-Visual)
Nevada Publications
NEW BOOKS ON WOMEN & FEMINISM
NEW HOPE INTERNATIONAL REVIEW
Norton Coker Press
NOVA EXPRESS
Noyce Publishing
Oak Knoll Press
Open Horizons Publishing Company
Palari Publishing
PAPERBACK PARADE
Passeggiata Press, Inc.

Poltroon Press
Bern Porter Books
The Press of the Nightowl
R & E Publishers
THE READER'S REVIEW
THE ROMANTIST
Saqi Books Publisher
Smyrna Press
SYNERJY: A Directory of Renewable Energy
THE UNDERGROUND FOREST - LA SELVA SUB-TERRANEA
University of Calgary Press
THE VINCENT BROTHERS REVIEW
WHITECHAPEL JOURNAL
Wings of Fire Press
Wise Owl Press
Witwatersrand University Press
Women's Studies Librarian, University of Wisconsin System
Wood River Publishing
YUMTZILOB: Tijdschrift over de Americas

BICYCLING

Acorn Publishing
ADVENTURE CYCLIST
Alchemist/Light Publishing
Anacus Press, Inc.
AUTO-FREE TIMES
Beachway Press
The Bess Press
Bicycle Books (Publishing) Inc.
BIG WORLD
DWELLING PORTABLY
EZ Nature Books
Fine Edge Productions
Footprint Press
The Globe Pequot Press
Good Life Publications
Heyday Books
Human Kinetics Pub. Inc.
THE LETTER PARADE
Menasha Ridge Press
The Mountaineers Books
New England Cartographics, Inc.
Nicolin Fields Publishing, Inc.
OUT YOUR BACKDOOR: The Magazine of Informal Adventure and Cheap Culture
Pruett Publishing Company
RAIN MAGAZINE
R-Squared Press
Trimarket
VELONEWS
WHOLE EARTH
Wilderness Adventure Books
WISCONSIN TRAILS
Wisconsin Trails

BILINGUAL

A.R.A. JOURNAL
Alaska Native Language Center
Arjay Associates
AXE FACTORY REVIEW
BabelCom, Inc.
Barking Dog Books
Bayley & Musgrave
Bilingual Review/Press
BILINGUAL REVIEW/Revista Bilingue
Blue Crane Books
Branden Publishing Company
BUENO
Carrefour Press
Chandler & Sharp Publishers, Inc.
Chardon Press
The Chicot Press
Child's Play
China Books & Periodicals, Inc.
DANDELION ARTS MAGAZINE
Dawn Publications

Dawn Sign Press
THE DIRTY GOAT
DWAN
EMPLOI PLUS
EVANSVILLE REVIEW
Exceptional Books, Ltd.
Helicon Nine Editions
Hope Publishing House
Host Publications, Inc.
ICA Publishing
In One Ear Publications
INTERBANG
Interlink Publishing Group, Inc.
INTERNATIONAL POETRY REVIEW
Italica Press, Inc.
Latin American Literary Review Press
LATINO STUFF REVIEW
LEO Productions LLC.
Lollipop Power Books
LOVE AND RAGE, A Revolutionary Anarchist News-paper
LUZ EN ARTE Y LITERATURA
Miles River Press
Mindfield Publications
Minor Heron Press
MoonFall Press
THE NEW PRESS LITERARY QUARTERLY
The Olivia and Hill Press, Inc.
Open Hand Publishing Inc.
OXYGEN
Pangaea
Passeggiata Press, Inc.
The Place In The Woods
Pocahontas Press, Inc.
POETRY NEW YORK: A Journal of Poetry and Translation
POTOMAC REVIEW
READ, AMERICA!
Red Crane Books, Inc.
Salt Lick Press
San Diego State University Press
Saqi Books Publisher
Serena Bay Books
Smyrna Press
The Speech Bin, Inc.
Spirit Talk Press
Station Hill Press
Studia Hispanica Editors
Synergistic Press
Tilbury House, Publishers
THE UNDERGROUND FOREST - LA SELVA SUB-TERRANEA
Writers Forum
Xenos Books

BIOGRAPHY

Acorn Books
Affinity Publishers Services
African American Audio Press
AFRICAN AMERICAN AUDIOBOOK REVIEW
African Ways Publishing
AK Press
Americana Books
ANAIS: An International Journal
Anderson Press
THE ANNALS OF IOWA
ANQ: A Quarterly Journal of Short Articles, Notes, and Reviews
Anubian Press
Appalachian Consortium Press
Arden Press, Inc.
ARTISTAMP NEWS
ASSEMBLING
Assembling Press
Astrion Publishing
AUFBAU
Avisson Press, Inc.
BAJA SUN

Bancroft Press
THE BAREFOOT POET: Journal of Poetry, Fiction, Essays, & Art
Barricade Books
Bayley & Musgrave
Beacon Point Press
Bear & Company, Inc.
BELLES LETTRES
BELLOWING ARK
Black Sparrow Press
Blue River Publishing Inc.
Bonus Books, Inc.
The Boxwood Press
The Bradford Book Company, Inc.
Branden Publishing Company
Brooke-Richards Press
Brunswick Publishing Corporation
Burd Street Press
Calliope Press
Cambric Press dba Emerald House
Camel Press
Canterbury Press
Capra Press
Carrefour Press
Carson Street Publishing Inc.
Celebrity Profiles Publishing
Celo Valley Books
THE CENTENNIAL REVIEW
Chandler & Sharp Publishers, Inc.
Chelsea Green Publishing Company
Cherokee Publishing Company
Cherubic Press
Chicago Spectrum Press
China Books & Periodicals, Inc.
CIN-DAV, Inc.
Clover Park Press
Colophon House
Community Service, Inc.
COMMUNITY SERVICE NEWSLETTER
The Compass Press
Comstock Bonanza Press
Conari Press
Coreopsis Books
COTTONWOOD
Cottonwood Press
The F. Marion Crawford Memorial Society
Crescent Moon
CRONE CHRONICLES: A Journal of Conscious Aging
Crossroads Communications
CURMUDGEON
Cypress House
DANDELION ARTS MAGAZINE
DAYSPRING
Devil Mountain Books
Discovery Enterprises, Ltd.
DOOR COUNTY ALMANAK
DorPete Press
DOUBLE BILL
Dovehaven Press
Duckworth Press
DUST (From the Ego Trip)
Earth Star Publications
Edition Stencil
ELT Press
Elysian Hills Publishing Company, Inc.
Encounter Books
ENGLISH LITERATURE IN TRANSITION, 1880-1920
Epicenter Press Inc.
EPM Publications, Inc.
Eros Publishing
ETC Publications
EUROPEAN JUDAISM
Evanston Publishing, Inc.
Ex Machina Publishing Company
EZ Nature Books
Fels and Firn Press
The Feminist Press at the City College
Feral House

FIDEI DEFENSOR: JOURNAL OF CATHOLIC APO-
LOGETICS
Finesse Publishing Company
FISICA
Five Star Publications
Foundation Books
Four Walls Eight Windows
THE FREEDONIA GAZETTE
Friends United Press
Fromm International Publishing Corporation
Fulcrum, Inc.
The Future Press
Galde Press, Inc.
Gay Sunshine Press, Inc.
Get In-Line! Publishing
Glenbridge Publishing Ltd.
The Gleniffer Press
Golden Eagle Press
Good Book Publishing Company
THE GREAT BLUE BEACON
Halo Books
Happy Rock Press
Harbor House
HAWAI'I REVIEW
Hawk Publishing Group
Heresy Press
Heritage House Publishers
Heritage West Books
Icarus Books
IMPRINT, A LITERARY JOURNAL
In Print Publishing
The Independent Institute
THE INDEPENDENT REVIEW: A Journal of Political
Economy
The Infinity Group
Inner Traditions International
Institute for Southern Studies
INTERBANG
International Publishers Co. Inc.
Ironweed Press
ISRAEL HORIZONS
Italica Press, Inc.
Ithaca Press
JACK MACKEREL MAGAZINE
JEWISH LIFE
JOURNAL OF MODERN LITERATURE
JOURNAL OF UNCONVENTIONAL HISTORY
KESTREL: A Journal of Literature and Art
Allen A. Knoll Publishers
THE KOSCIUSZKO PORTFOLIO
Kozmik Press
LAKE SUPERIOR MAGAZINE
The Latona Press
LEFTHANDER MAGAZINE
Libertarian Press, Inc./American Book Distributors
Library Research Associates, Inc.
Limelight Editions
LININGTON LINEUP
Log Cabin Manuscripts
THE LONSDALE - The International Quarterly of The
Romantic Six
LOST GENERATION JOURNAL
Mandala Publishing Group
Maryland Historical Press
Mayhaven Publishing
THE METAPHYSICAL REVIEW
Minnesota Historical Society Press
The Mountaineers Books
Naturegraph Publishers, Inc.
Network 3000 Publishing
NEW HOPE INTERNATIONAL REVIEW
The New Humanity Press
THE NEW PRESS LITERARY QUARTERLY
New World Press
NightinGale Resources
NORTH CAROLINA LITERARY REVIEW
North Country Books, Inc.
Nosukumo

The Olive Press Publications
Open Hand Publishing Inc.
Oregon State University Press
Organization for Equal Education of the Sexes, Inc.
The Overmountain Press
Oxford House Publishing
Paerdegat Park Publishing Co.
Palm Island Press
Pamlico Press
Paragon House Publishers
Passeggiata Press, Inc.
PASSION
Path Press, Inc.
Patria Press, Inc.
The Patrice Press
Pavlovsk Press
Peachtree Publishers, Ltd.
PEN & INK WRITERS JOURNAL
The Place In The Woods
THE PLOUGH
Pocahontas Press, Inc.
Poetry Wales Press, Ltd.
POTOMAC REVIEW
Protean Press
Pussywillow Publishing House, Inc.
QED Press
Quarterly Committee of Queen's University
QUEEN'S QUARTERLY: A Canadian Review
RADICAL AMERICA
REAL PEOPLE
Red Alder Books
Red Apple Publishing
Rockbridge Publishing Co.
THE ROMANTIST
Rowhouse Press
Sagapress, Inc.
St. Michael's Press
SALMAGUNDI
Saqi Books Publisher
Scentouri, Publishing Division
Scottwall Associates, Publishers
Scrivenery Press
Signature Books
Skyline Publications, Inc.
SLEUTH JOURNAL
Small Helm Press
Gibbs Smith, Publisher
Soundboard Books
SOUTH DAKOTA REVIEW
Steamshovel Press
Steerforth Press, L.C.
THE WALLACE STEVENS JOURNAL
Stewart Publishing & Printing
Strawberry Hill Press
Sherwood Sugden & Company, Publishers
The Sulgrave Press
Synergistic Press
Tailored Tours Publications, Inc.
Thirteen Colonies Press
Thomas Jefferson University Press
Tilbury House, Publishers
Times Change Press
The Times Journal Publishing Co.
Tomart Publications
Tudor Publishers, Inc.
University of Calgary Press
University of Massachusetts Press
Valiant Press, Inc.
Vestal Press Ltd
THE VINCENT BROTHERS REVIEW
Ward Hill Press
Waters Edge Press
White Cliffs Media, Inc.
White Mane Publishing Company, Inc.
Wolfhound Press
Words & Pictures Press
World Wide Publishing Corp.
Wright-Armstead Associates

Writers House Press
WRITER'S WORKSHOP REVIEW
Wynn Publishing

BIOLOGY

Access Multimedia
American Malacologists, Inc.
Anaphase II
ASC NEWSLETTER
Avery Publishing Group, Inc.
CANADIAN JOURNAL OF APPLIED PHYSIOLOGY
   (CJAP)
Cave Books
Child's Play
THE CIVIL ABOLITIONIST
dbS Productions
The Denali Press
Dimi Press
Doctors Press, Inc.
Dog-Eared Publications
ETR Associates
Flower Press
Gahmken Press
Genesis Publishing Company, Inc.
GEORGE & MERTIE'S PLACE: Rooms With a View
Happy Rock Press
Homestead Publishing
Human Kinetics Pub. Inc.
Humana Press
Island Press
JOURNAL OF APPLIED BIOMECHANICS (JAB)
KIDSCIENCE
THE LATHAM LETTER
The Latona Press
Lester Street Publishing
MEDIPHORS
MIND MATTERS REVIEW
Naturegraph Publishers, Inc.
THE NAUTILUS
Oregon State University Press
Pangaea
Parkway Publishers, Inc.
RESONANCE
SNOWY EGRET
SUPER TROUPER
Tell Publishing
Tiger Moon
Tortilla Press
VDT NEWS
VINEGAR   CONNOISSEURS   INTERNATIONAL
   NEWSLETTER
Weidner & Sons, Publishing
WHOLE EARTH
WILD EARTH
Witwatersrand University Press
WORLD RAINFOREST REPORT
Z MAGAZINE

BIOTECHNOLOGY

THE CIVIL ABOLITIONIST
Civitas
CJE NEWS (Newsletter of the Coalition for Jobs & the
   Environment)
DISSONANCE MAGAZINE
GATEAVISA
GEORGE & MERTIE'S PLACE: Rooms With a View
THE HUMANIST
MEDIPHORS
RESONANCE
SMART DRUG NEWS

BIRDS

Annedawn Publishing
Capra Press
Chelsea Green Publishing Company
CJE NEWS (Newsletter of the Coalition for Jobs & the
   Environment)
Cucumber Island Storytellers

Dimi Press
Drum
Gahmken Press
Light, Words & Music
The Mountaineers Books
Naturegraph Publishers, Inc.
New Spirit Press/The Poet Tree
Peartree Books & Music
PenRose Publishing Company, Inc.
Pineapple Press, Inc.
POTOMAC REVIEW
Pruett Publishing Company
SJL Publishing Company
SNOWY EGRET
WISCONSIN TRAILS
Zagier & Urruty Publicaciones

BIRTH, BIRTH CONTROL, POPULATION

AFFAIR OF THE MIND: A Literary Quarterly
THE AFFILIATE
AT-HOME DAD
Avery Publishing Group, Inc.
Cassandra Press, Inc.
Ceres Press
Children Of Mary
Child's Play
China Books & Periodicals, Inc.
CJE NEWS (Newsletter of the Coalition for Jobs & the
   Environment)
Emerald Wave
Feral House
FIDELIS ET VERUS
Fisher Books
FREE INQUIRY
GATEAVISA
GEORGE & MERTIE'S PLACE: Rooms With a View
Harvard Common Press
HAWAI'I REVIEW
HERBAL CHOICE
HIP MAMA
Humana Press
THE HUMANIST
Hunter House Inc., Publishers
ICEA
Interlink Publishing Group, Inc.
IRIS: A Journal About Women
LOVE AND RAGE, A Revolutionary Anarchist News-
   paper
Midwifery Today Books
More To Life Publishing
NEW ANGLICAN REVIEW
NEW CATHOLIC REVIEW
OFF OUR BACKS
RED OWL
SCIENCE/HEALTH ABSTRACTS
Skidmore-Roth Publishing, Inc.
WILD EARTH
WORLD RAINFOREST REPORT
XIB
Xib Publications

BISEXUAL

ANT ANT ANT ANT ANT
Broken Jaw Press
COLLEGIUM NEWSLETTER
DWAN
GATEAVISA
GIRLFRIENDS MAGAZINE
GLB Publishers
ON OUR BACKS MAGAZINE
Palm Drive Publishing
Pride & Imprints
RED OWL

BLACK

AAIMS Publishers
African American Audio Press
AFRICAN AMERICAN AUDIOBOOK REVIEW

African American Images
AFRICAN AMERICAN REVIEW
AFRICAN STUDIES
AFRO-HISPANIC REVIEW
AIM MAGAZINE
American Literary Press Inc./Noble House
Ariko Publications
ASSEMBLING
Assembling Press
Baker Street Publications
Beacon Press
Bicycle Books (Publishing) Inc.
BLACK LACE
Black Light Fellowship
THE BLACK SCHOLAR: Journal of Black Studies and
    Research
BLACKFIRE
BLK
Bonus Books, Inc.
The Borgo Press
BRILLIANT STAR
CALLALOO
Carolina Wren Press/Lollipop Power Books
Chardon Press
Chicago Spectrum Press
Clarity Press, Inc.
CODA: The Jazz Magazine
Content Communications
COTTONWOOD
Cottonwood Press
CROSS ROADS
Discovery Enterprises, Ltd.
The Edwin Mellen Press
EXCLAIM!
The Feminist Press at the City College
The Fire!! Press
GATEAVISA
Gay Sunshine Press, Inc.
GEORGE & MERTIE'S PLACE: Rooms With a View
GrapeVinePress
Gumbs & Thomas Publishers, Inc.
HAWAI'I REVIEW
Hope Publishing House
IAAS Publishers, Inc.
Inner Traditions International
Institute for Southern Studies
INTERCULTURAL WRITERS REVIEW
International Publishers Co. Inc.
KUUMBA
LFW Enterprises
Lotus Press, Inc.
LOVE AND RAGE, A Revolutionary Anarchist News-
    paper
LUMMOX JOURNAL
Maryland Historical Press
MESECHABE: The Journal of Surre(gion)alism
Middle Passage Press
THE MILITANT
MIM NOTES: Offcial Newsletter of the Maoist Interna-
    tionalist Movement
OBSIDIAN II: BLACK LITERATURE IN REVIEW
Open Hand Publishing Inc.
Organization for Equal Education of the Sexes, Inc.
Oxford House Publishing
OXYGEN
PAPYRUS
Papyrus Literary Enterprises, Inc.
Passeggiata Press, Inc.
Path Press, Inc.
Pathfinder Press
The Place In The Woods
PLENTY GOOD ROOM
POTOMAC REVIEW
Pygmy Forest Press
R & E Publishers
RADICAL AMERICA
Reference Service Press
Schenkman Books

SILHOUETTE MAGAZINE
Smyrna Press
SPARE RIB
SPIRIT TO SPIRIT
Strawberry Hill Press
STREET VOICE
STRUGGLE: A Magazine of Proletarian Revolutionary
    Literature
Syracuse Cultural Workers/Tools for Change
Times Change Press
TURNING THE TIDE: A Journal of Anti-Racist
    Activism, Research & Education
21ST CENTURY AFRO REVIEW
University of Massachusetts Press
VIETNAM GENERATION: A Journal of Recent History
    and Contemporary Issues
THE VINCENT BROTHERS REVIEW
Ward Hill Press
White Cliffs Media, Inc.
Witwatersrand University Press
Woman in the Moon Publications (W.I.M. Publications)
WOMEN ARTISTS NEWS BOOK REVIEW
Wright-Armstead Associates
XAVIER REVIEW
Yucca Tree Press

WILLIAM BLAKE

Abiko Literary Press (ALP)
CLASS ACT
Drum
GEORGE & MERTIE'S PLACE: Rooms With a View
ICARUS WAS RIGHT
Itidwitir Publishing
KELTIC FRINGE
Kosmos
THE LONSDALE - The International Quarterly of The
    Romantic Six
MESECHABE: The Journal of Surre(gion)alism
NEW HOPE INTERNATIONAL REVIEW
New Spirit Press/The Poet Tree
OXYGEN
THE RIVER
Station Hill Press

BOOK ARTS, CALLIGRAPHY

THE AFFILIATE
AMERICAN AMATEUR JOURNALIST
ART CALENDAR
ART PAPERS
Baker Street Publications
Blue Heron Publishing, Inc.
THE BOOK ARTS CLASSIFIED
BOOK MARKETING UPDATE
BOOK/MARK SMALL PRESS QUARTERLY REVIEW
Branden Publishing Company
Caliban Press
CHILDREN, CHURCHES AND DADDIES, A Non
    Religious, Non Familial Literary Magazine
Chiron Press
CHIRON REVIEW
CHRISTIANITY & THE ARTS
CLASS ACT
Cold-Drill Books
The F. Marion Crawford Memorial Society
DANDELION ARTS MAGAZINE
Drum
ENDING THE BEGIN
ETCETERA
The Feathered Serpent
FIGMENTS
FULL MOON DIRECTORY
FURTHER TOO
G'RAPH
HAND PAPERMAKING
THE HIGHWAY POET
The Hosanna Press
THE ILLUSTRATOR COLLECTOR'S NEWS
Images For Media/Sesquin

Interalia/Design Books
IT GOES ON THE SHELF
JEWISH LIFE
KALDRON, An International Journal Of Visual Poetry
LETTER ARTS REVIEW
LIGHTWORKS MAGAZINE
LPD Press
LUMMOX JOURNAL
MAINE IN PRINT
MARTHA'S KIDLIT NEWSLETTER
MIXED BAG
Mortal Press
NEW ART EXAMINER
NEW HOPE INTERNATIONAL REVIEW
The New Humanity Press
NIGHTSHADE
Now It's Up To You Publications
Oak Knoll Press
Open Horizons Publishing Company
Palari Publishing
PAPERBACK PARADE
PLOPLOP
The Poetry Center Press/Shoestring Press
POTOMAC REVIEW
The Press of the Nightowl
Rarach Press
THE READER'S REVIEW
REALM OF THE VAMPIRE
THE ROMANTIST
SALON: A Journal of Aesthetics
Saqi Books Publisher
Scars Publications
SCIENCE FICTION CHRONICLE
Strawberry Hill Press
STUDIO ART MAGAZINE
TITIVILLITIA: Studies of Illiteracy in the Private Press
21st Century Publishing, Inc.
UMBRELLA
THE UNIT CIRCLE
UNO MAS MAGAZINE
URBAN GRAFFITI
Visual Studies Workshop
Water Mark Press
WHITEWALLS: A Journal of Language and Art

BOOK COLLECTING, BOOKSELLING

AFRICAN AMERICAN AUDIOBOOK REVIEW
Algol Press
The Alternate Press
Americana Books
BAKER STREET GAZETTE
Baker Street Publications
Bluestocking Press
THE BOOK ARTS CLASSIFIED
BOOK DEALERS WORLD
BOOK MARKETING UPDATE
BOOK NEWS & BOOK BUSINESS MART
BOOK TALK
Chicago Spectrum Press
Children Of Mary
THE CIVIL WAR NEWS
CLASS ACT
The F. Marion Crawford Memorial Society
Evanston Publishing, Inc.
FIDELIS ET VERUS
FULL MOON DIRECTORY
Full Moon Publications
Gallopade International
The Gleniffer Press
Gryphon Publications
THE HAUNTED JOURNAL
HOLLYWOOD NOSTALGIA
THE ILLUSTRATOR COLLECTOR'S NEWS
INDEPENDENT PUBLISHER
INDY MAGAZINE
Jaffe Publishing Management Service
JEWISH LIFE
LIBRARIANS AT LIBERTY

THE LONSDALE - The International Quarterly of The
Romantic Six
Peter Marcan Publications
MARTHA'S KIDLIT NEWSLETTER
MIXED BAG
MYSTERY READERS JOURNAL
The New Humanity Press
NIGHTSHADE
NORTH CAROLINA LITERARY REVIEW
Oak Knoll Press
Open Horizons Publishing Company
ORTHODOX MISSION
Orthodox Mission in Belize
OUT YOUR BACKDOOR: The Magazine of Informal
Adventure and Cheap Culture
PAPERBACK PARADE
Para Publishing
PEN & INK WRITERS JOURNAL
THE PIPE SMOKER'S EPHEMERIS
Premier Publishers, Inc.
The Press of the Nightowl
PUBLISHING ENTREPRENEUR
RALPH'S REVIEW
READ, AMERICA!
REALM OF THE VAMPIRE
REFERRALS
THE ROMANTIST
SCIENCE FICTION CHRONICLE
Selective Books, Inc.
SLEUTH JOURNAL
SOUTHWEST JOURNAL
SPEX (SMALL PRESS EXCHANGE)
Stonehouse Publications
Tomart Publications
TOWERS CLUB, USA INFO MARKETING REPORT
Trigon Press
UMBRELLA
White Plume Press
Women's Studies Librarian, University of Wisconsin
System
WORLD BOOK INDUSTRY
WRITER'S WORKSHOP REVIEW

BOOK REVIEWING

Abiko Literary Press (ALP)
AC
Ad-Lib Publications
African American Audio Press
AFRICAN AMERICAN AUDIOBOOK REVIEW
AFRICAN STUDIES
AIM MAGAZINE
ALABAMA LITERARY REVIEW
Algol Press
ALIVE: Canadian Journal of Health and Nutrition
Amelia Press
Anderson Press
THE ANGRY THOREAUAN
THE ANNALS OF IOWA
ANQ: A Quarterly Journal of Short Articles, Notes, and
Reviews
Anti-Aging Press
THE ANTIGONISH REVIEW
APPALACHIAN HERITAGE
ARISTOS
ARTISTAMP NEWS
Arts End Books
AT-HOME DAD
AUFBAU
AXE FACTORY REVIEW
BACKBOARD
BAJA SUN
BAKER STREET GAZETTE
Baker Street Publications
Bancroft Press
THE BEAR DELUXE
BELLES LETTRES
BIBLIOTHEQUE D'HUMANISME ET RENAISSANCE
BIG WORLD

743

Black Rose Books Ltd.
BLK
THE BLOOMSBURY REVIEW
BLUE MESA REVIEW
Bluestocking Press
BOOGLIT
BOOK MARKETING UPDATE
THE BOOK REPORT: Journal for Junior & Senior High
  School Librarians
BOOK TALK
BOOK/MARK SMALL PRESS QUARTERLY REVIEW
BOOKS FROM FINLAND
THE BOOKWATCH
BOOMERANG! MAGAZINE
BORDERLANDS: Texas Poetry Review
THE BOSTON BOOK REVIEW
BRIDGES: An Interdisciplinary Journal of Theology,
  Philosophy, History, and Science
BURNING CAR
THE BURNING CLOUD REVIEW
C.S.P. WORLD NEWS
CAPITALISM, NATURE, SOCIALISM
CHELSEA
Children Of Mary
THE CHRISTIAN LIBRARIAN
CHRISTIANITY & THE ARTS
Citeaux Commentarii Cistercienses
CITEAUX: COMMENTARII CISTERCIENSES
THE CIVIL ABOLITIONIST
THE CIVIL WAR NEWS
Civitas
CJE NEWS (Newsletter of the Coalition for Jobs & the
  Environment)
CLASS ACT
THE CLASSICAL OUTLOOK
THE CLIMBING ART
COLLEGIUM NEWSLETTER
COMPUTER BOOK REVIEW
CONTEXT SOUTH
COTTONWOOD
Cottonwood Press
COUNTERPOISE: For Social Responsibilities, Liberty
  and Dissent
COVER MAGAZINE
CREATIVE NONFICTION
Crescent Moon
CRONE CHRONICLES: A Journal of Conscious Aging
CROSS ROADS
CULTUREFRONT
CUTBANK
Cynic Press
THE DALHOUSIE REVIEW
DANGER!
DAUGHTERS OF SARAH
The Denali Press
DESIGN BOOK REVIEW
DIRIGIBLE
DREAM NETWORK JOURNAL
THE DROOD REVIEW OF MYSTERY
THE EDGE CITY REVIEW
En Passant Poetry Press
EN PASSANT/POETRY
ENGLISH LITERATURE IN TRANSITION, 1880-1920
EXCLAIM!
FAMILY TIMES: The Newspaper for Chippewa Valley
  Parents
FARMER'S DIGEST
THE FEMINIST BOOKSTORE NEWS
FEMINIST COLLECTIONS: A QUARTERLY OF WO-
  MEN'S STUDIES RESOURCES
FIDEI DEFENSOR: JOURNAL OF CATHOLIC APO-
  LOGETICS
FIDELIS ET VERUS
FINE MADNESS
FORESIGHT MAGAZINE
FOURTH GENRE: EXPLORATIONS IN NONFICTION
FULL MOON DIRECTORY
Full Moon Publications

The Future Press
THE GALLEY SAIL REVIEW
GATEAVISA
Global Options
GRAFFITI OFF THE ASYLUM WALLS
G'RAPH
GRASS ROOTS
GRAY AREAS
THE GREAT BLUE BEACON
GREEN MOUNTAINS REVIEW
THE HAUNTED JOURNAL
HAWAI'I REVIEW
HEAVEN BONE MAGAZINE
Heaven Bone Press
HIP MAMA
HOLLYWOOD NOSTALGIA
HORIZONS BEYOND
THE HUNTED NEWS
ICARUS WAS RIGHT
THE ICONOCLAST
IMPETUS
The Independent Institute
INDEPENDENT PUBLISHER
THE INDEPENDENT REVIEW: A Journal of Political
  Economy
INDY MAGAZINE
INTERBANG
INTERCULTURAL WRITERS REVIEW
THE IOWA REVIEW
IRIS: A Journal About Women
IRISH FAMILY JOURNAL
IRISH LITERARY SUPPLEMENT
ISSUES
Itidwitir Publishing
THE J MAN TIMES
JACARANDA
JACK MACKEREL MAGAZINE
JACK THE RIPPER GAZETTE
JAMES JOYCE BROADSHEET
JARRETT'S JOURNAL
JEWISH LIFE
THE JOURNAL OF AFRICAN TRAVEL-WRITING
JOURNAL OF COURT REPORTING
JOURNAL OF HUMANITIES
KALDRON, An International Journal Of Visual Poetry
KALEIDOSCOPE: INTERNATIONAL MAGAZINE OF
  LITERATURE, FINE ARTS, AND DISABILITY
KARMA LAPEL
KLIATT
LAKE SUPERIOR MAGAZINE
LAMBDA BOOK REPORT
LEFT BUSINESS OBSERVER
LEFTHANDER MAGAZINE
Lester Street Publishing
LIBRARIANS AT LIBERTY
LIFTOUTS
LIGHTWORKS MAGAZINE
LINQ
Linworth Publishing, Inc.
Listen and Learn Home Education, Inc.
THE LITERARY QUARTERLY
LITERARY SKETCHES
LLAMAS MAGAZINE
THE LONSDALE - The International Quarterly of The
  Romantic Six
LUMMOX JOURNAL
LUZ EN ARTE Y LITERATURA
MARK
MARTHA'S KIDLIT NEWSLETTER
THE MATCH
MEANJIN
THE METAPHYSICAL REVIEW
MID-AMERICAN REVIEW
Midmarch Arts Press
MIXED BAG
MODERN HAIKU
MYSTERY READERS JOURNAL
NEDGE

NEW ART EXAMINER
NEW HOPE INTERNATIONAL REVIEW
The New Humanity Press
NEW THOUGHT JOURNAL
NIGHTLORE
NIGHTSHADE
NOCTURNAL REPORTER
NORTH CAROLINA LITERARY REVIEW
NORTH DAKOTA QUARTERLY
North Stone Press
NORTHWEST REVIEW
NORTHWOODS JOURNAL, A Magazine for Writers
NOSTOC MAGAZINE
NOVA EXPRESS
OBSIDIAN II: BLACK LITERATURE IN REVIEW
OHIO WRITER
OHIOANA QUARTERLY
ORTHODOX MISSION
Orthodox Mission in Belize
OUR TWO CENTS
PALO ALTO REVIEW
THE PANNUS INDEX
PAPERPLATES
PAPYRUS
Para Publishing
PASSION
PEN & INK WRITERS JOURNAL
PLAIN BROWN WRAPPER (PBW)
THE PLOUGH
POETIC SPACE: Poetry & Fiction
POETRY FLASH
POETRY INTERNATIONAL
POET'S FANTASY
POTATO EYES
POTOMAC REVIEW
POW-WOW
PRECISELY
PSYCHOANALYTIC BOOKS: A QUARTERLY JOUR-
NAL OF REVIEWS
THE PUCKERBRUSH REVIEW
PULSAR
PUNCTURE
Q ZINE
Quarterly Committee of Queen's University
QUEEN'S QUARTERLY: A Canadian Review
QUESTION EVERYTHING CHALLENGE EVERY-
THING (QECE)
Quiet Lion Press
RADIANCE, The Magazine For Large Women
RAG MAG
RAIN CITY REVIEW
RAIN TAXI REVIEW OF BOOKS
RARITAN: A Quarterly Review
THE READER'S REVIEW
REALM OF DARKNESS
REALM OF THE VAMPIRE
Red Cedar Press
RED CEDAR REVIEW
REDOUBT
RESOURCES FOR FEMINIST RESEARCH/DOCU-
MENTATION SUR LA RECHERCHE FEMINISTE
Rio Grande Press
THE ROMANTIST
Rowhouse Press
ST. CROIX REVIEW
ST. LOUIS JOURNALISM REVIEW
THE SALEM JOURNAL
SALMAGUNDI
SALOME: A Journal for the Performing Arts
SALT HILL
SCIENCE & SOCIETY
SCIENCE FICTION CHRONICLE
SCRIVENER
SE LA VIE WRITER'S JOURNAL
SEWANEE REVIEW
SF COMMENTARY
SHARE INTERNATIONAL
THE SIGNAL - Network International

SILHOUETTE MAGAZINE
SLEUTH JOURNAL
THE SMALL POND MAGAZINE OF LITERATURE
aka SMALL POND
THE SMALL PRESS BOOK REVIEW
THE SMALL PRESS REVIEW/SMALL MAGAZINE
REVIEW
SMALL PUBLISHER
SO TO SPEAK
SOCIAL JUSTICE: A JOURNAL OF CRIME, CON-
FLICT, & WORLD ORDER
SOUTHERN HUMANITIES REVIEW
SOUTHERN QUARTERLY: A Journal of the Arts in the
South
SOUTHWEST JOURNAL
Southwest Research and Information Center
SPEX (SMALL PRESS EXCHANGE)
STUDIO - A Journal of Christians Writing
The Subourbon Press
THE SUNDAY SUITOR POETRY REVIEW
SYCAMORE REVIEW
TALISMAN: A Journal of Contemporary Poetry and
Poetics
TEENS IN MOTION NEWS
Telos Press
THEATER
THEATRE DESIGN AND TECHNOLOGY
THEY WON'T STAY DEAD!
TITIVILLITIA: Studies of Illiteracy in the Private Press
TOLE WORLD
TOWARD FREEDOM
TRADITION
TRAVEL BOOKS WORLDWIDE
TRIVIUM
UMBRELLA
THE UNDERGROUND FOREST - LA SELVA SUB-
TERRANEA
THE UNIT CIRCLE
UNITED LUMBEE NATION TIMES
URBAN GRAFFITI
VEGGIE LIFE
VIETNAM GENERATION: A Journal of Recent History
and Contemporary Issues
THE VINCENT BROTHERS REVIEW
THE VIRGINIA QUARTERLY REVIEW
THE WASHINGTON MONTHLY
WESTERN SKIES
WHAT IS ENLIGHTENMENT?
WHITECHAPEL JOURNAL
WINDOW PANES
Witwatersrand University Press
Woman in the Moon Publications (W.I.M. Publications)
Women's Studies Librarian, University of Wisconsin
System
WOOD STROKES & WOODCRAFTS
THE WORKBOOK
WORLD OF FANDOM MAGAZINE
THE WRITE WAY
WRITER'S CAROUSEL
WRITERS GAZETTE
WRITER'S GUIDELINES: A Roundtable for Writers and
Editors
WRITERS INK
WRITER'S LIFELINE
WRITER'S WORKSHOP REVIEW
XAVIER REVIEW
YOUNG VOICES
YUWITAYA LAKOTA
Z MAGAZINE
Zagier & Urruty Publicaciones
ZYX

BOTANY

Baker Street Publications
Clover Park Press
Allen A. Knoll Publishers
MIXED BAG
RED OWL

RESONANCE
Venus Communications
THE WILD FOODS FORUM
Wilderness Adventure Books

BRITISH COLUMBIA

Epicenter Press Inc.
EXCLAIM!
Moon Publications, Inc.
THE NEW PRESS LITERARY QUARTERLY
New Star Books Ltd.
Open Hand Publishing Inc.
POW-WOW
Resolution Business Press, Inc.
Ronsdale Press
White Plume Press
WORLD RAINFOREST REPORT

BROADCASTING

Bonus Books, Inc.
Z W L Publishing, Inc.

BRONTES

CLASS ACT
GEORGE & MERTIE'S PLACE: Rooms With a View
ICARUS WAS RIGHT
NEW HOPE INTERNATIONAL REVIEW

BROWNING

CLASS ACT

BUDDHISM

AREOPAGUS
AXE FACTORY REVIEW
Beacon Point Press
Beacon Press
Blue Dove Press
Book Faith India
Buddhist Study Center Press
Center for Japanese Studies
Center for South and Southeast Asian Studies Publications
China Books & Periodicals, Inc.
ClearPoint Press
Cynic Press
Dharma Publishing
THE EVER DANCING MUSE
Frozen Waffles Press/Shattered Sidewalks Press; 45th Century Chapbooks
GATEAVISA
Gay Sunshine Press, Inc.
GEORGE & MERTIE'S PLACE: Rooms With a View
GESAR-Buddhism in the West
HEAVEN BONE MAGAZINE
Heaven Bone Press
Hohm Press
INDIA CURRENTS
Inner Traditions International
INTERCULTURAL WRITERS REVIEW
THE JOURNAL OF THE ORDER OF BUDDHIST CONTEMPLATIVES
LIVE AND LET LIVE
META4: Journal of Object Oriented Poetics (OOPS)
THE MINDFULNESS BELL
MYSTIC VOICES
nine muses books
Paragon House Publishers
Parallax Press
QUESTION EVERYTHING CHALLENGE EVERY-THING (QECE)
Reyes Investment Enterprise Ltd.
Shaolin Communications
Snow Lion Publications, Inc.
STONES IN MY POCKET
SYMBIOTIC OATMEAL
Theosophical Publishing House
Tiger Moon
Timeless Books
TRICYCLE: The Buddhist Review

TURNING WHEEL
WHAT IS ENLIGHTENMENT?
Who Who Who Publishing
Wings of Fire Press
Wisdom Publications, Inc.

CHARLES BUKOWSKI

CLUTCH
GATEAVISA
MACHINEGUN MAGAZINE: New Lit. Quarterly
PHOENIX MAGAZINE
Phoenix Press
Phony Lid Publications
VAGABOND

BUSINESS & ECONOMICS

Acclaim Publishing Co. Inc.
Actium Publishing, Inc.
Acton Circle Publishing Company
Adams-Blake Publishing
Adams-Hall Publishing
Addicus Books, Inc.
Ad-Lib Publications
Adolfo Street Publications
Advisory Press, Inc.
Aegis Publishing Group, Ltd.
Afcom Publishing
Afrimax, Inc.
Allworth Press
Alpine Guild, Inc.
The Alternate Press
Application Publishing, Inc.
Archipelago Publishing
ARTSLINK
AT-HOME DAD
ATL Press, Inc.
Axiom Press, Publishers
BAJA SUN
Beekman Publishers, Inc.
Behavioral Sciences Research Press, Inc.
Bell Publishing
Bell Springs Publishing
Benchmark Publications Inc.
BERKELEY JOURNAL OF INTERNATIONAL LAW
Best Sellers Publishing
Between The Lines
Black Rose Books Ltd.
Blue Bird Publishing
Bluestocking Press
Bonus Books, Inc.
BOOK MARKETING UPDATE
BOOK NEWS & BOOK BUSINESS MART
Bookhaven Press, LLC
Bookhome Publishing/Panda Publishing
THE BOOMERPHILE
BOOTSTRAPPIN' ENTREPRENEUR: The Newsletter For Individuals With Great Ideas and a Little Bit of Cash
Bowerdean Publishing Co. Ltd.
The Boxwood Press
Brenner Information Group
Brighton Publications, Inc.
BUSINESPIRIT JOURNAL
BUSINESS CONSUMER GUIDE
Business Resource Publishing
Business Smarts, Inc.
Byte Masters International
CANADIAN MONEYSAVER
CANADIAN PUBLIC POLICY- Analyse de Politiques
Capital Communications
Career Advancement Center, Inc.
Center for Japanese Studies
Center For Self-Sufficiency
Chandler & Sharp Publishers, Inc.
The Chicot Press
China Books & Periodicals, Inc.
CJE NEWS (Newsletter of the Coalition for Jobs & the Environment)

CLASS ACT
Cobra Publishing
Communication Creativity
COMMUNITY DEVELOPMENT JOURNAL
Community Resource Institute Press
Community Service, Inc.
COMMUNITY SERVICE NEWSLETTER
Consumer Education Research Center
COPING WITH TURBULENT TIMES
CPG Publishing Company
Craftsman Book Company
Creighton-Morgan Publishing Group
CROSS ROADS
Cypress Publishing Group, Inc.
D.B.A. Books
DAEDALUS, Journal of the American Academy of Arts and Sciences
Timothy A. Dimoff/SACS Consulting
THE DIPLOMAT
DIRECT RESPONSE
Dry Bones Press
ECONOMIC AFFAIRS
Emerald Ink Publishing
Encounter Books
Energeia Publishing, Inc.
ETC Publications
Film-Video Publications
FINANCIAL FOCUS
Fisher Books
The Foundation for Economic Education, Inc.
Franklin-Sarrett Publishers
THE FREEMAN: Ideas On Liberty
Frugal Marketer Publishing
Gain Publications
The P. Gaines Co., Publishers
Gallopade International
Gemstone House Publishing
GEORGE & MERTIE'S PLACE: Rooms With a View
Glenbridge Publishing Ltd.
Good Hope Enterprises, Inc.
Bruce Gould Publications
Great Western Publishing Company
Halle House Publishing
Harvard Common Press
Haverford Business Press
The Heather Foundation
Herbelin Publishing
HOARD'S DAIRYMAN
Hollis Publishing Company
Hoover Institution Press
Hoover's, Inc.
Human Kinetics Pub. Inc.
IAAS Publishers, Inc.
Image Industry Publications
The Independent Institute
THE INDEPENDENT REVIEW: A Journal of Political Economy
INFOCUS
INFORMATION ENTREPRENUER
Information International
Information Research Lab
Innovation Press
Institute for Contemporary Studies
International Publishers Co. Inc.
International University Line (IUL)
INVESTMENT COLUMN QUARTERLY (newsletter)
Jamenair Ltd.
JLA Publications, A Division Of Jeffrey Lant Associates, Inc.
JOURNAL OF COURT REPORTING
JOURNAL OF SPORT MANAGEMENT (JSM)
Keel Publications
Kells Media Group
Kent Information Services, Inc.
Kumarian Press, Inc.
LAKE SUPERIOR MAGAZINE
Lamp Light Press
LATIN AMERICAN PERSPECTIVES

Lawco Ltd./Moneytree Publications/Que-House
Leadership Education and Development, Inc.
LEFT BUSINESS OBSERVER
Libertarian Press, Inc./American Book Distributors
LIBERTY
Liberty Publishing Company, Inc.
Life Energy Media
LifeThread Publications
LITTLE FREE PRESS
LLAMAS MAGAZINE
Lone Eagle Publishing Co.
LONE STAR SOCIALIST
THE LONG TERM VIEW: A Journal of Informed Opinion
The Madson Group, Inc.
Mainstream Press
Mayhaven Publishing
Metamorphous Press
Miles River Press
MONEYMAKING NEWSLETTER
Morgan-Rand Publishing
MORNINGSTAR
Mountain Automation Corporation
Mountain Publishing
MUTUAL FUND SOURCEBOOK
NATURAL LIFE
New Management Publishing Company, Inc.
New World Library
North American Bookdealers Exchange
NP Press
Nunciata
Olde & Oppenheim Publishers
ONE EARTH
OPEN EXCHANGE MAGAZINE
Open Horizons Publishing Company
Osmyrrah Publishing
Park Place Publications
Passeggiata Press, Inc.
Perpetual Press
Piccadilly Books
Piggy Bank Press
Planning/Communications
Plympton Press International
THE PRAGMATIST
Princess Publishing
Prudhomme Press
PSI Research/The Oasis Press/Hellgate Press
PUBLISHING ENTREPRENEUR
Publitec Editions
Pyramid Publishing
QP Publishing
QUALITY QUIPS NEWSLETTER
Quarterly Committee of Queen's University
QUEEN'S QUARTERLY: A Canadian Review
RED OWL
Resolution Business Press, Inc.
Ronin Publishing, Inc.
Russian Information Services
ST. CROIX REVIEW
San Diego Publishing Company
Selah Publishing
SJL Publishing Company
THE SMALL BUSINESS ADVISOR
THE SMALL POND MAGAZINE OF LITERATURE aka SMALL POND
SOCIETY
Solution Publishing
Sourcebooks, Inc.
Stewart Publishing & Printing
Stone Bridge Press
Stonehouse Publications
Stones Point Press
Sylvan Books
Third Side Press, Inc.
TIMESHARE AND VACATION OWNERSHIP REVIEW
Tiptoe Literary Service
TitleWaves Publishing

747

Triumph Books
Tryckeriforlaget
21ST CENTURY AFRO REVIEW
University of Calgary Press
Upstart Publishing Company, Inc.
VanderWyk & Burnham
VDT NEWS
Vestal Press Ltd
Visions Communications
Vista Publishing, Inc.
WATERFRONT WORLD SPOTLIGHT
WEEKEND WOODCRAFTS
White Knight Press
WHOLE EARTH
Wildstone Media
Winslow Publishing
Witwatersrand University Press
WorkLife Publishing
World Wide Publishing Corp.
Wright-Armstead Associates
Writers Forum
Z MAGAZINE

CALIFORNIA

THE ACORN
AMELIA
Androgyne Books
Archipelago Publishing
THE AZOREAN EXPRESS
BAJA SUN
Ballena Press
Borden Publishing Co.
BOTTOMFISH
Carousel Press
Castle Peak Editions
Chandler & Sharp Publishers, Inc.
THE CLIMBING ART
Clover Park Press
Comstock Bonanza Press
Devil Mountain Books
Discovery Enterprises, Ltd.
DREAM WHIP
THE EAR
EZ Nature Books
Falcon Press Publishing Company
The Feathered Serpent
Foghorn Press
Golden Eagle Press
Good Life Publications
Heritage House Publishers
Heritage West Books
Heyday Books
HOLLYWOOD NOSTALGIA
Huntington Library Press
ICA Publishing
The Image Maker Publishing Co.
INTERBANG
Allen A. Knoll Publishers
Lahontan Images
Law Mexico Publishing
Lexikos
The Live Oak Press
MacAdam/Cage Publishing Inc.
McNally & Loftin, Publishers
Midmarch Arts Press
Miles & Miles
MIXED BAG
Moon Publications, Inc.
Naturegraph Publishers, Inc.
NORTHERN PILOT
Old West Publishing Co.
ORANGE COAST MAGAZINE
PHOENIX MAGAZINE
Phoenix Press
POW-WOW
Primer Publishers
Pygmy Forest Press
Quill Driver Books

Rayve Productions Inc.
Really Great Books
RedBrick Press
RELIX
Sand River Press
Sasquatch Books
Scottwall Associates, Publishers
Genny Smith Books
Gibbs Smith, Publisher
Steamshovel Press
Tamarack Books, Inc.
TURNING THE TIDE: A Journal of Anti-Racist
    Activism, Research & Education
Volcano Press, Inc
Waters Edge Press
WESTERN SKIES
Wide World Publishing/TETRA
WOODNOTES

CALLIGRAPHY

Abiko Literary Press (ALP)
THE BOOK ARTS CLASSIFIED
China Books & Periodicals, Inc.
G'RAPH
HOAX!
KELTIC FRINGE
LETTER ARTS REVIEW
NEW HOPE INTERNATIONAL REVIEW
The Overlook Press
POET'S FANTASY
The Square-Rigger Press

CANADA

Aardvark Enterprises (A Division of Speers Investments
    Ltd.)
The Alternate Press
AU NATUREL
Baker Street Publications
BELLES LETTRES
Betelgeuse Books
Between The Lines
Black Rose Books Ltd.
Borealis Press Limited
Broken Jaw Press
BROKEN PENCIL
CANADIAN CHILDREN'S LITERATURE
Canadian Educators' Press
CANADIAN LITERATURE
CANADIAN PUBLIC POLICY- Analyse de Politiques
CONNEXIONS DIGEST
Connexions Information Services, Inc.
Coteau Books
DESCANT
Epicenter Press Inc.
EXCLAIM!
Falcon Press Publishing Company
Full Moon Publications
Golden Meteorite Press
Grade School Press
HORIZONS
JOURNAL OF CANADIAN STUDIES/Revue d'etudes
    canadiennes
LAKE SUPERIOR MAGAZINE
LOVE AND RAGE, A Revolutionary Anarchist News-
    paper
MIXED BAG
Moon Publications, Inc.
Mountain Automation Corporation
NEW MUSE OF CONTEMPT
THE NEW PRESS LITERARY QUARTERLY
New Star Books Ltd.
NEWSLETTER (LEAGUE OF CANADIAN POETS)
NORTHERN PILOT
POTATO EYES
Pottersfield Press
POW-WOW
PRAIRIE FIRE
THE PRAIRIE JOURNAL OF CANADIAN LITERA-

TURE
Prairie Journal Press
Prairie Publishing Company
Resolution Business Press, Inc.
Rio Grande Press
SE LA VIE WRITER'S JOURNAL
Thirteen Colonies Press
TOWARD FREEDOM
THE TOWNSHIPS SUN
Tuns Press
Tyro Publishing
University of Calgary Press
Upney Editions
URBAN GRAFFITI
WEST COAST LINE: A Journal of Contemporary
  Writing and Criticism
WESTERN SKIES
Whole Person Associates Inc.
YUWITAYA LAKOTA

CAREERS

Acton Circle Publishing Company
Allworth Press
Bookhaven Press, LLC
Bookhome Publishing/Panda Publishing
Cage Consulting, Inc.
Capital Communications
Contemax Publishers
CPG Publishing Company
Cyclone Books
Timothy A. Dimoff/SACS Consulting
Edin Books, Inc.
Energeia Publishing, Inc.
Galen Press, Ltd.
Global Sports Productions, Ltd.
Golden Eagle Press
Goodheart-Willcox Publisher
Harvard Common Press
Impact Publishers, Inc.
Innisfree Press
Job Search Publishers
Lawco Ltd./Moneytree Publications/Que-House
The Madson Group, Inc.
The Neo Herramann Group
North Star Books
Organization for Equal Education of the Sexes, Inc.
Perpetual Press
Photo Data Research
Planning/Communications
PREP Publishing
Prosperity Press
Prudhomme Press
QED Press
The Saunderstown Press
Sovereignty Press
TECH DIRECTIONS
TEENS IN MOTION NEWS
Ticket to Adventure, Inc.

CARIBBEAN

Baker Street Publications
Blue Reef Publications, Inc.
CARIBBEAN NEWSLETTER
THE CARIBBEAN WRITER
Clover Park Press
Comparative Sedimentology Lab.
Cultivated Underground Press
Department of Romance Languages
Full Moon Publications
GOLD COAST NEWS
HORIZONS
HOT CALALOO
IAAS Publishers, Inc.
INTERCULTURAL WRITERS REVIEW
MESECHABE: The Journal of Surre(gion)alism
MIXED BAG
Moon Publications, Inc.
THE NEW PRESS LITERARY QUARTERLY

Pangaea
Passeggiata Press, Inc.
PLAY THE ODDS
POINT OF CONTACT
PREP Publishing
Sandberry Press
Schenkman Books
Smyrna Press
SOCIETE
TORRE DE PAPEL
Tortuga Books
21ST CENTURY AFRO REVIEW
Two Thousand Three Associates
University of Massachusetts Press
THE VORTEX
Wescott Cove Publishing Co.
White Cliffs Media, Inc.
XAVIER REVIEW

LEWIS CARROLL

Abiko Literary Press (ALP)
CLASS ACT
DAYSPRING
Hope Publishing House
NEW HOPE INTERNATIONAL REVIEW
NIGHT ROSES
Press Here
THE SPITTING IMAGE

CARTOONS

AC
AFFABLE NEIGHBOR
Affable Neighbor Press
AMELIA
Amelia Press
ARNAZELLA
ART-CORE
ATROCITY
AXE FACTORY REVIEW
Baker Street Publications
BLK
Bonus Books, Inc.
BOOGLIT
BREAKFAST ALL DAY
BURNING CAR
BUTTON
BUZZARD
THE CHEROTIC (r)EVOLUTIONARY
THE CIVIL ABOLITIONIST
COLLEGIUM NEWSLETTER
Coyote Publishing
CREEPY MIKE'S OMNIBUS OF FUN
CROSS ROADS
Doggerel Press
DOPE FRIENDS
DOUBLE BILL
DREAM WHIP
Eat Your Hair
EMERGING VOICES
ETCETERA
EXCLAIM!
Feral House
FUNNY PAGES
GATEAVISA
GRAFFITI OFF THE ASYLUM WALLS
G'RAPH
GRAY AREAS
THE GREAT BLUE BEACON
HEARTLAND (Australia)
House of the 9 Muses, Inc.
Ignite! Entertainment
IMPRINT, A LITERARY JOURNAL
INDY MAGAZINE
INTERBANG
JAPANOPHILE
Japanophile Press
JOURNAL OF ALASKA WOMEN
LAKE SUPERIOR MAGAZINE

Landwaster Books
LIES MAGAZINE
LIGHT: The Quarterly of Light Verse
THE LITERARY QUARTERLY
Long Wind Publishing
THE LONSDALE - The International Quarterly of The
  Romantic Six
Lowy Publishing
Mica Press
MIXED BAG
MOOSE BOUND PRESS JOURNAL/NEWSLETTER
NEW YORK STORIES
THE NOISE
NORTH CAROLINA LITERARY REVIEW
OFFICE NUMBER ONE
PAST TIMES: The Nostalgia Entertainment Newsletter
The Place In The Woods
The Press at Foggy Bottom
Pride & Imprints
QECE: QUESTION EVERYTHING. CHALLENGE
  EVERYTHING.
QUESTION EVERYTHING CHALLENGE EVERY-
  THING (QECE)
REALM OF THE VAMPIRE
Rio Grande Press
Rotten Pepper
SE LA VIE WRITER'S JOURNAL
SHORT FUSE
Signature Books
SIVULLINEN
SKINNYDIPPING
Slab-O-Concrete Publications
SMALL PRESS CREATIVE EXPLOSION
SO YOUNG!
StarLance Publications
T.V. HEADS
TWISTED IMAGE NEWSLETTER
UNDERGROUND SURREALIST MAGAZINE
UNO MAS MAGAZINE
UNWOUND
URBAN GRAFFITI
THE VINCENT BROTHERS REVIEW
W.E.C. Plant Publishing
WAY STATION MAGAZINE
THE WHITE DOT - Survival Guide for the TV-Free
WORLD OF FANDOM MAGAZINE
WRITER'S WORKSHOP REVIEW

CATHOLIC

ASSEMBLY
Beacon Point Press
Bear & Company, Inc.
CATECHUMENATE: A Journal of Christian Initiation
CHICAGO STUDIES
CHRISTIANITY & THE ARTS
ENVIRONMENT AND ART LETTER
EZ Nature Books
FIDEI DEFENSOR: JOURNAL OF CATHOLIC APO-
  LOGETICS
Franciscan University Press
GRANULATED TUPPERWARE
LITURGY 90
LPD Press
MUSIC NEWS
Open University of America Press
Palm Drive Publishing
PLENTY GOOD ROOM
Saint Mary's Press
St. Michael's Press
TRADICION REVISTA
VIRTUTE ET MORTE MAGAZINE
White Buck Publishing
Writers House Press

CAVES

Cave Books
Dimi Press
McNally & Loftin, Publishers

Pruett Publishing Company

EDGAR CAYCE

A.R.E. Press
ENLIGHTENMENTS
MYSTIC VOICES
Reyes Investment Enterprise Ltd.

CELTIC

Abiko Literary Press (ALP)
AFFABLE NEIGHBOR
Affable Neighbor Press
THE AFFILIATE
Baker Street Publications
Bardsong Press
Carpe Diem Publishing
Celtic Heritage Books
CELTIC HISTORY REVIEW
THE CELTIC PEN
CLASS ACT
THE COMPANY NORTH AMERICA
The F. Marion Crawford Memorial Society
DAYSPRING
DeerTrail Books
DIRTY LINEN
Dufour Editions Inc.
THE EDGE CITY REVIEW
FIGMENTS
Full Moon Publications
GATEAVISA
GEORGE & MERTIE'S PLACE: Rooms With a View
GOTHIX
GREEN EGG
THE HAUNTED JOURNAL
HAZEL GROVE MUSINGS
HORIZONS
Horned Owl Publishing
Inner Traditions International
IRISH FAMILY JOURNAL
Irish Genealogical Foundation
IRISH JOURNAL
IRISH LITERARY SUPPLEMENT
Kells Media Group
KELTIC FRINGE
Landwaster Books
LLEN CYMRU
MIXED BAG
MYSTIC VOICES
New Paradigm Books
THE NEW PRESS LITERARY QUARTERLY
NEW THOUGHT JOURNAL
NIGHTSHADE
Palm Drive Publishing
RENAISSANCE MAGAZINE
Reyes Investment Enterprise Ltd.
THE ROMANTIST
SAGEWOMAN
Saint Mary's Press
SPIRIT TO SPIRIT
STUDIA CELTICA
THIN COYOTE
THIRST (CYBERTHIRST)
University Of Wales Press
White Plume Press
Wolfhound Press
Writers Forum
Z MAGAZINE

CHANNELLING

Anti-Aging Press
The Crossing Press
Dream Street Publishing
Emerald Wave
Horus Publishing, Inc.
New Paradigm Books
Plus Publications

GEOFFREY CHAUCER

Abiko Literary Press (ALP)
CLASS ACT
GEORGE & MERTIE'S PLACE: Rooms With a View

CHICAGO

Bonus Books, Inc.
Chicago Review Press
Chicago Spectrum Press
CHILDREN, CHURCHES AND DADDIES, A Non
    Religious, Non Familial Literary Magazine
CHRISTIANITY & THE ARTS
Crossroads Communications
Evanston Publishing, Inc.
GEORGE & MERTIE'S PLACE: Rooms With a View
Lyceum Books, Inc.
MIXED BAG
NEW ART EXAMINER
Path Press, Inc.
ROCTOBER COMICS AND MUSIC
Scars Publications
Wright-Armstead Associates

CHICANO/A

Arte Publico Press
AZTLAN: A Journal of Chicano Studies
Baker Street Publications
BELLES LETTRES
Bilingual Review/Press
BILINGUAL REVIEW/Revista Bilingue
Bilingue Publications & Productions
Blue Heron Publishing, Inc.
BOOK TALK
THE BOTTOM LINE PUBLICATIONS
Burning Bush Publications
Carolina Wren Press/Lollipop Power Books
Chicano Studies Research Center Publications
Content Communications
CROSS ROADS
DAYS AND NIGHTS OF A SMALL PRESS PUB-
    LISHER
The Denali Press
The Feminist Press at the City College
HAWAI'I REVIEW
Hope Publishing House
ICA Publishing
MEXICAN STUDIES/ESTUDIOS MEXICANOS
MIXED BAG
NEW ART EXAMINER
PASSAGER: A Journal of Remembrance and Discovery
The Place In The Woods
Pocahontas Press, Inc.
POCKETS (Devotional Magazine for Children)
Pygmy Forest Press
R & E Publishers
READ, AMERICA!
Red Crane Books, Inc.
Reference Service Press
Strawberry Hill Press
STRUGGLE: A Magazine of Proletarian Revolutionary
    Literature
Treasure Chest Books LLC
TURNING THE TIDE: A Journal of Anti-Racist
    Activism, Research & Education
VIETNAM GENERATION: A Journal of Recent History
    and Contemporary Issues
Volcano Press, Inc
Ward Hill Press
White Cliffs Media, Inc.

CHILDREN, YOUTH

Acorn Books
Adirondack Mountain Club, Inc.
Ad-Lib Publications
Afcom Publishing
Alegra House Publishers
Alicubi Publications

The Alternate Press
Alyson Publications, Inc.
American Audio Prose Library (non-print)
Amherst Writers & Artists Press, Inc.
Ancient City Press
Annick Press Ltd.
Anteater Press
AT-HOME DAD
ATL Press, Inc.
Auromere Books and Imports
Avalon Writing Center, Inc.
Avery Publishing Group, Inc.
The B & R Samizdat Express
Bayley & Musgrave
The Benefactory, Inc.
The Bess Press
Blue Heron Publishing, Inc.
Blue Mouse Studio
Bluestocking Press
Bold Productions
Book Peddlers
THE BOOKWATCH
BOOMERANG! MAGAZINE
Borealis Press Limited
Boulevard Books, Inc. Florida
Bright Ring Publishing, Inc.
BRILLIANT STAR
The Brookfield Reader
CANADIAN CHILDREN'S LITERATURE
Carolina Wren Press/Lollipop Power Books
Carousel Press
CCM Publishing
CE CONNECTION COMMUNIQUE
Center for Public Representation
The Center Press
Chandler & Sharp Publishers, Inc.
Cherubic Press
Chicago Review Press
Chicken Soup Press, Inc.
CHILDREN'S LITERATURE IN EDUCATION
Child's Play
CLUBHOUSE
COBBLESTONE: The History Magazine for Young
    People
Coldwater Press
Colophon House
Commonwealth Press Virginia
Computer Press
Conari Press
Conscious Living
Coteau Books
Cougar Books
Council For Indian Education
Cove View Press
CPG Publishing Company
Creative With Words Publications (CWW)
CRICKET
CROSS ROADS
The Crossing Press
Cucumber Island Storytellers
Dawn Sign Press
Dharma Publishing
Discovery Enterprises, Ltd.
DISSONANCE MAGAZINE
Doctors Press, Inc.
Dolphin Books, Inc.
Dovehaven Press
Dovetail Publishing
Down There Press
Dream Street Publishing
Dufour Editions Inc.
Eagle's View Publishing
Ecrivez!
Wm.B. Eerdmans Publishing Co.
EMERGING VOICES
Epicenter Press Inc.
Excalibur Publishing Inc.
EXCEPTIONALITY EDUCATION CANADA

EXCLAIM!
Falcon Press Publishing Company
FAMILY TIMES: The Newspaper for Chippewa Valley Parents
The Feminist Press at the City College
Five Star Publications
Flatland Tales Publishing
Flower Press
Focus Publications, Inc.
Foghorn Press
Free Spirit Publishing Inc.
Front Row Experience
Future Horizons, Inc.
The Future Press
Galde Press, Inc.
The Galileo Press Ltd.
Gallaudet University Press
Gallopade International
Gan Publishing
Gazelle Publications
Gifted Education Press/The Reading Tutorium
The Gleniffer Press
Grade School Press
Grand Slam Press, Inc.
Grapevine Publications, Inc.
GrapeVinePress
Grayson Bernard Publishers, Inc.
THE GREAT IDEA PATCH
GROWING WITHOUT SCHOOLING
Gryphon House, Inc.
Guardian Press
Guarionex Press Ltd.
Hannacroix Creek Books, Inc
Harvest Hill Press
Heartsong Books
Herald Press
HIP MAMA
Hollis Publishing Company
HOME EDUCATION MAGAZINE
Homestead Publishing
Horned Owl Publishing
House of the 9 Muses, Inc.
Human Kinetics Pub. Inc.
Hungry Tiger Press
Hunter House Inc., Publishers
ICA Publishing
ICEA
Illumination Arts
Impact Publishers, Inc.
In Between Books
Indelible Inc.
Innerworks Publishing
INQ Publishing Co.
Interlink Publishing Group, Inc.
Intermountain Publishing
Jalmar Press
JOURNAL OF CHILD AND YOUTH CARE
Kar-Ben Copies, Inc.
Kenyette Productions
KID'S WORLD
KIDSCIENCE
Kindness Publications, Inc.
KLIATT
Allen A. Knoll Publishers
Kodomo Press
H J Kramer
La Alameda Press
La Casa Press
LADYBUG, the Magazine for Young Children
THE LATHAM LETTER
Libertarian Press, Inc./American Book Distributors
Liberty Publishing Company, Inc.
THE LION AND THE UNICORN: A Critical Journal of Children's Literature
Listen and Learn Home Education, Inc.
Literary Moments
Little Buckaroo Press
The Live Oak Press

Lollipop Power Books
Long Wind Publishing
The Love and Logic Press, Inc.
LOVE AND RAGE, A Revolutionary Anarchist Newspaper
LUNO
Magic Circle Press
Magical Music Express
Magnolia Publishing
Majestic Books
Mandala Publishing Group
MARTHA'S KIDLIT NEWSLETTER
Maxima New Media
Mayhaven Publishing
MERLYN'S PEN: Fiction, Essays, and Poems By America's Teens
Metamorphous Press
Miles River Press
Monroe Press
MOOSE BOUND PRESS JOURNAL/NEWSLETTER
Morning Glory Press
Mountain Automation Corporation
MUSIC NEWS
NATURAL LIFE
NEW ALTERNATIVES
New Canaan Publishing Company Inc.
THE NEW PRESS LITERARY QUARTERLY
New Seed Press
NightinGale Resources
No Starch Press
North Country Books, Inc.
ON THE LINE
Open Hand Publishing Inc.
Open Horizons Publishing Company
Our Child Press
Pacific View Press
Pangaea
Paper Chase Press
Papillon Publishing
Parabola
Parenting Press, Inc.
Partners In Publishing
Passport Press
Path Press, Inc.
Patria Press, Inc.
Peachtree Publishers, Ltd.
Peartree Books & Music
PEDIATRIC EXERCISE SCIENCE (PES)
Peel Productions, Inc.
Peerless Publishing
PenRose Publishing Company, Inc.
Perspectives Press
Philomel Books
Pinchgut Press
The Place In The Woods
Playground Books
THE PLOUGH
Pocahontas Press, Inc.
POCKETS (Devotional Magazine for Children)
Polar Bear Productions & Company
Portunus Publishing Company
Premium Press America
The Preservation Press
The Press at Foggy Bottom
Prestige Publications
Pride & Imprints
Purple Finch Press
RADIANCE, The Magazine For Large Women
Rama Publishing Co.
Raspberry Press Ltd.
THE RAVEN CHRONICLES
READ, AMERICA!
Real Life Storybooks
Red Crane Books, Inc.
Red Hen Press
Redbird Press, Inc.
Ronsdale Press
Roof Publishing Company

Running Press
Ryrich Publications
Salina Bookshelf
Sandberry Press
Sandcastle Publishing
Sasquatch Books
Scarf Press
SCHOOL MATES
Sea Fog Press, Inc.
Seed Center
Sheer Joy! Press
Shivam Publications
Sidran Foundation and Press
Silver Seahorse Press
Skinny Lamb Publishing Company
SMART DRUG NEWS
Gibbs Smith, Publisher
SPIDER
STONE SOUP, The Magazine By Young Writers and
  Artists
StoneBrook Publishing
STONES IN MY POCKET
Storytime Ink International
Summit Crossroads Press
Swan Raven & Company
TEACHING ELEMENTARY PHYSICAL EDUCATION
  (TEPE)
TEENS IN MOTION NEWS
Terra Nova Press
Theytus Books Ltd.
Thistledown Press Ltd.
Thunder & Ink
Tilbury House, Publishers
Torchlight Publishing
Tortuga Books
Treasure Chest Books LLC
Treehouse Micropress
Trellis Publishing, Inc.
Tug Press
TURNING THE TIDE: A Journal of Anti-Racist
  Activism, Research & Education
Turtle Island Press, Inc.
Twelve Star Publishing
Two Thousand Three Associates
Unity Books
University of Calgary Press
Valiant Press, Inc.
Vanitas Press
Veronica Lane Books
Volcano Press, Inc
VOYA (Voice of Youth Advocate)
Westport Publishers
What The Heck Press
White Mane Publishing Company, Inc.
Willendorf Press
Williamson Publishing Company, Inc.
B. L. Winch & Associates
Wisconsin Trails
Witwatersrand University Press
Wolfhound Press
WONDER TIME
Writers Forum
Writers House Press
YOUNG VOICES
Z MAGAZINE
Zino Press Children's Books

CHINA

AFFAIR OF THE MIND: A Literary Quarterly
AREOPAGUS
AXE FACTORY REVIEW
The Bess Press
China Books & Periodicals, Inc.
CHINA REVIEW INTERNATIONAL
Cynic Press
GATEAVISA
Images For Media/Sesquin
LEO Productions LLC.

The Olive Press Publications
Schenkman Books
Signal Books
Small Helm Press
SYMBIOTIC OATMEAL
THE TEMPLE
Venus Communications
The Wellsweep Press

SRI CHINMOY

INDIA CURRENTS

KATE CHOPIN

CLASS ACT
THE RIVER

CHRISTIANITY

Abiko Literary Press (ALP)
Acclaim Publishing Co. Inc.
American Literary Press Inc./Noble House
APKL Publications
AREOPAGUS
ART'S GARBAGE GAZZETTE
ASSEMBLY
Beacon Point Press
Beacon Press
BitterSweet Publishing Company
Blue Dolphin Publishing, Inc.
Blue Dove Press
By-The-Book Publishing
Candlestick Publishing
Carrier Pigeon Press
CATECHUMENATE: A Journal of Christian Initiation
CHICAGO STUDIES
Children Of Mary
CHRISTIANITY & THE ARTS
CHRISTIAN*NEW AGE QUARTERLY
Conari Press
CORNERSTONE
Crossway Books
Cultivated Underground Press
DAUGHTERS OF SARAH
DOVETAIL: A Journal by and for Jewish/Christian
  Families
Dovetail Publishing
Dunamis House
Eborn Books
Wm.B. Eerdmans Publishing Co.
ENVIRONMENT AND ART LETTER
Exhorter Publications International
FIDEI DEFENSOR: JOURNAL OF CATHOLIC APO-
  LOGETICS
FIDELIS ET VERUS
Fort Dearborn Press
Four Seasons Publishers
Friends United Press
GATEAVISA
Genesis Publishing Company, Inc.
GEORGE & MERTIE'S PLACE: Rooms With a View
The Glencannon Press
Good Book Publishing Company
The Heather Foundation
Infinite Passion Publishing
Innisfree Press
ISSUES
J & L Publications
Langmarc Publishing
The Leaping Frog Press
LFW Enterprises
LITURGY 90
LPD Press
Marlton Publishers, Inc.
MEDIA SPOTLIGHT
More To Life Publishing
Mountaintop Books
MUSIC NEWS
Network 3000 Publishing
New Canaan Publishing Company Inc.

NEW HOPE INTERNATIONAL REVIEW
THE NEW PRESS LITERARY QUARTERLY
New Regency Publishing
New Spirit Press/The Poet Tree
OFFICE NUMBER ONE
ORTHODOX MISSION
Orthodox Mission in Belize
OXYGEN
Papillon Publishing
Parabola
Paragon House Publishers
PenRose Publishing Company, Inc.
Philopsychy Press
PLENTY GOOD ROOM
POET'S PARK
QUARTZ HILL JOURNAL OF THEOLOGY
Quartz Hill Publishing House
Ragged Edge Press
Rainbow's End
Revive Publishing
Ridgeway Press of Michigan
Saint Mary's Press
St. Michael's Press
Selah Publishing
SelectiveHouse Publishers, Inc.
Sheer Joy! Press
Signature Books
Skinny Lamb Publishing Company
Small Helm Press
Sparrow Hawk Press
STUDENT LEADERSHIP JOURNAL
Sherwood Sugden & Company, Publishers
Thirteen Colonies Press
Tiger Moon
THE TRUTH SEEKER
WHAT IS ENLIGHTENMENT?
White Buck Publishing
White Plume Press
World Wide Publishing Corp.
Writers House Press

CHRISTMAS

American Literary Press Inc./Noble House
Blue Sky Marketing, Inc.
CHRISTIANITY & THE ARTS
Cucumber Island Storytellers
Enthea Press
THE GREAT IDEA PATCH
HOAX!
Innisfree Press
The Leaping Frog Press
LPD Press
Momentum Books, Ltd.
SJL Publishing Company
Gibbs Smith, Publisher
WRITER'S WORKSHOP REVIEW

CITIES

ABELexpress
ALLA TIDERS BODER
AMERICAN HIKER
ASSEMBLAGE: A Critical Journal of Architecture and
   Design Culture
Astrion Publishing
Baker Street Publications
Barney Press
Black Rose Books Ltd.
Bonus Books, Inc.
Career Publishing, Inc.
Carousel Press
CROSS ROADS
CURMUDGEON
DAYSPRING
DESIGN BOOK REVIEW
ENVIRONMENTAL & ARCHITECTURAL PHENO-
   MENOLOGY NEWSLETTER
FURTHER TOO
Gallopade International

Gemini Publishing Company
GEORGE & MERTIE'S PLACE: Rooms With a View
Heritage House Publishers
Italica Press, Inc.
JOURNAL OF UNCONVENTIONAL HISTORY
KICK IT OVER
LAKE SUPERIOR MAGAZINE
LANDSCAPE
Peter Marcan Publications
MIXED BAG
Moon Publications, Inc.
Mount Ida Press
New Spring Publications
POTOMAC REVIEW
Redbird Press, Inc.
Tailored Tours Publications, Inc.
THE UNDERGROUND FOREST - LA SELVA SUB-
   TERRANEA
URBAN GRAFFITI
THE URBAN REVIEW
VIRTUTE ET MORTE MAGAZINE
WATERFRONT WORLD SPOTLIGHT
WE INTERNATIONAL (formerly WOMEN AND EN-
   VIRONMENTS)
Writers Forum
Z MAGAZINE

CIVIL RIGHTS

The Advocado Press
AFFAIR OF THE MIND: A Literary Quarterly
THE AFFILIATE
African American Audio Press
AFRICAN AMERICAN AUDIOBOOK REVIEW
ART'S GARBAGE GAZZETTE
Baker Street Publications
BALLOT ACCESS NEWS
Beacon Press
BLK
Carolina Wren Press/Lollipop Power Books
Chardon Press
Child's Play
Clarity Press, Inc.
COLORLINES
CROSS ROADS
THE DISABILITY RAG & RESOURCE
FOCUS: Library Service to Older Adults, People with
   Disabilities
GATEAVISA
GAUNTLET: Exploring the Limits of Free Expression
GEORGE & MERTIE'S PLACE: Rooms With a View
Global Options
GRAFFITI OFF THE ASYLUM WALLS
ICARUS WAS RIGHT
IRIS: A Journal About Women
Itidwitir Publishing
The Leaping Frog Press
LFW Enterprises
THE LIBERATOR
LONE STAR SOCIALIST
Macrocosm USA, Inc.
MAIN STREET JOURNAL
MIXED BAG
NATURALLY
Nguoi Dan
NGUOI DAN
Open Hand Publishing Inc.
Organization for Equal Education of the Sexes, Inc.
THE OTHER ISRAEL
Path Press, Inc.
PEACE, The Magazine of the Sixties
The Place In The Woods
POTOMAC REVIEW
PRISON LEGAL NEWS
Pygmy Forest Press
QECE: QUESTION EVERYTHING. CHALLENGE
   EVERYTHING.
QUESTION EVERYTHING CHALLENGE EVERY-
   THING (QECE)

Schenkman Books
SKINNYDIPPING
SOCIAL JUSTICE: A JOURNAL OF CRIME, CON-
FLICT, & WORLD ORDER
Strata Publishing, Inc.
STRUGGLE: A Magazine of Proletarian Revolutionary
Literature
Tiger Moon
TRANSCAUCASUS: A Chronology
TURNING THE TIDE: A Journal of Anti-Racist
Activism, Research & Education
University of Massachusetts Press
WRITER'S WORKSHOP REVIEW
YUWITAYA LAKOTA
Z MAGAZINE

CIVIL WAR

AFFAIR OF THE MIND: A Literary Quarterly
Averasboro Press
Blacksmith Corporation
John F. Blair, Publisher
The Brookfield Reader
Brunswick Publishing Corporation
Burd Street Press
Cherokee Publishing Company
THE CIVIL WAR NEWS
EPM Publications, Inc.
Faded Banner Publications
FLASHPOINT: Military Books Reviewed by Military
Professionals
Galen Press, Ltd.
Hohm Press
Inheritance Press Inc.
MacDonald/Sward Publishing Company
Meyer Publishing
The New Humanity Press
North Country Books, Inc.
Paint Rock Publishing, Inc.
Premium Press America
Pride & Imprints
REALM OF THE VAMPIRE
Rockbridge Publishing Co.
Gibbs Smith, Publisher
White Mane Publishing Company, Inc.

CLASSICAL STUDIES

Abiko Literary Press (ALP)
AFFAIR OF THE MIND: A Literary Quarterly
The Aldine Press, Ltd.
Anderson Press
APOSTROPHE: USCB Journal of the Arts
Bandanna Books
Bliss Publishing Company, Inc.
Branden Publishing Company
CLASSICAL ANTIQUITY
THE CLASSICAL OUTLOOK
DAEDALUS, Journal of the American Academy of Arts
and Sciences
THE DALHOUSIE REVIEW
DIALOGOS: Hellenic Studies Review
Dovehaven Press
Dufour Editions Inc.
ECHOS DU MONDE CLASSIQUE/CLASSICAL
VIEWS
The Edwin Mellen Press
Erespin Press
HELLAS: A Journal of Poetry & the Humanities
Hollis Publishing Company
Horned Owl Publishing
Mandala Publishing Group
Moon Publications, Inc.
PERSEPHONE
QECE: QUESTION EVERYTHING. CHALLENGE
EVERYTHING.
THE READER'S REVIEW
Salt Lick Press
Spring Publications Inc.
Station Hill Press

University of Calgary Press
Witwatersrand University Press

CLOTHING

Eagle's View Publishing
Goodheart-Willcox Publisher
SKINNYDIPPING

COLLECTIBLES

Baker Street Publications
BLITZ
Bonus Books, Inc.
Borden Publishing Co.
C & T Publishing
Cattpigg Press
Celebrity Profiles Publishing
China Books & Periodicals, Inc.
ClockWorks Press
Cottontail Publications
FOLK ART MESSENGER
FULL MOON DIRECTORY
FURTHER TOO
GemStone Press
Gryphon Publications
HOLLYWOOD NOSTALGIA
THE ILLUSTRATOR COLLECTOR'S NEWS
IN PRINT
MARTHA'S KIDLIT NEWSLETTER
MIXED BAG
NEW ENGLAND ANTIQUES JOURNAL
NIGHTSHADE
THE OVERLOOK CONNECTION
PAPERBACK PARADE
PARA TROOP
THE PRESIDENTS' JOURNAL
RALPH'S REVIEW
SCIENCE FICTION CHRONICLE
Silver Print Press
Gibbs Smith, Publisher
Sonoran Publishing
THEY WON'T STAY DEAD!
Tomart Publications
Waters Edge Press
WORLDLINKS - FRIENDSHIP NEWS

COLOR

Anti-Aging Press
BORDERLANDS: A Quarterly Journal Of Borderland
Research
Child's Play
The Crossing Press
Epicenter Press Inc.
The Green Hut Press
LAKE SUPERIOR MAGAZINE
NP Press
OXYGEN
Ponderosa Publishers
Gibbs Smith, Publisher
Top Of The Mountain Publishing

COLORADO

CITY PRIMEVAL
Crossroads Communications
Custom Services
Falcon Press Publishing Company
Fulcrum, Inc.
Homestead Publishing
LPD Press
MIXED BAG
Moon Publications, Inc.
Mountain Automation Corporation
The Mountaineers Books
Old West Publishing Co.
PINYON POETRY
POW-WOW
Pruett Publishing Company
Tamarack Books, Inc.
TRADICION REVISTA

Transcending Mundane
Treasure Chest Books LLC
WEBER STUDIES: Voices and Viewpoints of the
Contemporary West
WESTERN SKIES

COMICS

AC
Alan Wofsy Fine Arts
Alternating Crimes Publishing
ANGELFLESH
Angelflesh Press
ASSEMBLING
Assembling Press
ATROCITY
Austen Press
BABYSUE
BABYSUE MUSIC REVIEW
BAKER STREET GAZETTE
Baker Street Publications
Bogg Publications
BONDAGE FANTASIES
Bonus Books, Inc.
BOUDOIR NOIR
BROKEN PENCIL
BURNING CAR
Carpe Diem Publishing
THE COMICS JOURNAL
COMICS REVUE
CON-TEMPORAL
Coyote Publishing
CREEPY MIKE'S OMNIBUS OF FUN
Dolphin-Moon Press
DOPE FRIENDS
DOUBLE BILL
DRASTIC LIVES
THE DUCKBURG TIMES
Eat Your Hair
EDDIE THE MAGAZINE
ENDING THE BEGIN
EXCLAIM!
Exclaim! Brand Comics
Fantagraphics Books
FAT TUESDAY
FETISH BAZAAR
FISH DRUM MAGAZINE
FROM THE MARGIN
Full Moon Publications
FUNNY PAGES
The Future Press
GATEAVISA
GAUNTLET: Exploring the Limits of Free Expression
GRAFFITI OFF THE ASYLUM WALLS
GRAY AREAS
THE HAUNTED JOURNAL
Headveins Graphics
HOAX!
HOTHEAD PAISAN, HOMICIDAL LESBIAN TER-
RORIST
House of the 9 Muses, Inc.
ICARUS WAS RIGHT
Ignite! Entertainment
IMPETUS
INDY MAGAZINE
INTERCULTURAL WRITERS REVIEW
Itidwitir Publishing
JACK MACKEREL MAGAZINE
KARMA LAPEL
KOMIC FANTASIES
KOOMA
Leyland Publications
LIFE ON PLANET EARTH, VOL III
LIGHT: The Quarterly of Light Verse
THE LONSDALE - The International Quarterly of The
Romantic Six
MANGAJIN
Manuscript Press
MIXED BAG

Mosaic Press
MOTORBOOTY MAGAZINE
MUSHROOM DREAMS
NANCY'S MAGAZINE
NBM Publishing Company
New Voice Media
NIGHTSHADE
OM
THE OVERLOOK CONNECTION
OZ-STORY
Phelps Publishing Company
PIG IRON
Pride & Imprints
QUESTION EVERYTHING CHALLENGE EVERY-
THING (QECE)
RABID ANIMAL KOMIX
REAL DEAL MAGAZINE
REALM OF THE VAMPIRE
ROCTOBER COMICS AND MUSIC
Rotten Pepper
Rowhouse Press
Royal Print
The Runaway Spoon Press
Scarf Press
SIVULLINEN
SLEUTH JOURNAL
SMALL PRESS CREATIVE EXPLOSION
STRANGE GROWTHS
T.V. HEADS
THEY WON'T STAY DEAD!
THIRST (CYBERTHIRST)
Tiptoe Literary Service
Treasure Chest Books LLC
UNDERGROUND SURREALIST MAGAZINE
URBAN GRAFFITI
VISUAL ASSAULT OMNIBUS
WISEBLOOD
WORLD OF FANDOM MAGAZINE
Writers Forum
WRITER'S WORKSHOP REVIEW
Z MAGAZINE

COMMUNICATION, JOURNALISM

Access Multimedia
THE AFFILIATE
ALTERNATIVE PRESS REVIEW
and books
Arjuna Library Press
ATROCITY
ATS Publishing
Autonomedia, Inc.
Baker Street Publications
Beekman Publishers, Inc.
Between The Lines
Bonus Books, Inc.
Branden Publishing Company
BROKEN PENCIL
BYLINE
Chicory Blue Press, Inc.
THE CHRISTIAN LIBRARIAN
CNW Publishing
Communication Creativity
Communicom Publishing Company
CREATIVITY CONNECTION
DAEDALUS, Journal of the American Academy of Arts
and Sciences
DAYSPRING
THE EDGE CITY REVIEW
ESPERANTIC STUDIES
Feral House
FREE INQUIRY
Freelance Communications
FREELANCE WRITER'S REPORT
The Future Press
Gallopade International
GATEAVISA
Global Sports Productions, Ltd.
Goodheart-Willcox Publisher

756

GRANULATED TUPPERWARE
G'RAPH
THE GREAT BLUE BEACON
Guarionex Press Ltd.
THE HIGHWAY POET
HOAX!
Hollis Publishing Company
ICARUS WAS RIGHT
INTERBANG
Intercultural Press, Inc.
Itidwitir Publishing
JARRETT'S JOURNAL
JLA Publications, A Division Of Jeffrey Lant Associates, Inc.
KALDRON, An International Journal Of Visual Poetry
KARMA LAPEL
Keel Publications
KETTERING REVIEW
The Philip Lesly Company
LIGHTWORKS MAGAZINE
LOST GENERATION JOURNAL
LUMMOX JOURNAL
Maupin House
The Media Institute
MEDIA SPOTLIGHT
Metamorphous Press
The Middleburg Press
MIND MATTERS REVIEW
MinRef Press
MIXED BAG
Multi Media Arts
New Spring Publications
OHIO WRITER
Open Horizons Publishing Company
Para Publishing
PASSAGES NORTH
The Place In The Woods
Pocahontas Press, Inc.
THE PUBLIC RELATIONS QUARTERLY
PUNCTURE
QECE: QUESTION EVERYTHING. CHALLENGE EVERYTHING.
REDOUBT
Rio Grande Press
THE ROTKIN REVIEW
S.E.T. FREE: The Newsletter Against Television
ST. LOUIS JOURNALISM REVIEW
SALON: A Journal of Aesthetics
SE LA VIE WRITER'S JOURNAL
Selah Publishing
SHADOW KNOWS MOVIEEYE
The Speech Bin, Inc.
Strata Publishing, Inc.
TEENS IN MOTION NEWS
TOWARD FREEDOM
THE TRIBUNE
Univelt, Inc.
University of Calgary Press
VIETNAM GENERATION: A Journal of Recent History and Contemporary Issues
THE VINCENT BROTHERS REVIEW
THE WASHINGTON MONTHLY
Winslow Publishing
WOMEN AND LANGUAGE
WRITER'S CAROUSEL
WRITER'S LIFELINE
Z W L Publishing, Inc.

COMMUNISM, MARXISM, LENINISM

AMERICAN JONES BUILDING & MAINTENANCE
Autonomedia, Inc.
Beekman Publishers, Inc.
BLUE COLLAR REVIEW
Children Of Mary
China Books & Periodicals, Inc.
CROSS ROADS
FIDELIS ET VERUS
FREE INQUIRY

FURTHER TOO
GATEAVISA
GEORGE & MERTIE'S PLACE: Rooms With a View
Heron Press
Hoover Institution Press
International Publishers Co. Inc.
LEFT BUSINESS OBSERVER
LEFT CURVE
LONE STAR SOCIALIST
LOVE AND RAGE, A Revolutionary Anarchist Newspaper
Mehring Books, Inc.
THE MILITANT
MIM NOTES: Offcial Newsletter of the Maoist Internationalist Movement
MIND MATTERS REVIEW
Missing Spoke Press
New International
NGUOI DAN
Partisan Press
Pathfinder Press
PEOPLE'S CULTURE
RADICAL AMERICA
RETHINKING MARXISM
SALMAGUNDI
Semiotext Foreign Agents Books Series
SEMIOTEXT(E)
Small Helm Press
STRUGGLE: A Magazine of Proletarian Revolutionary Literature
Telos Press
Times Change Press
TOWARD FREEDOM
TURNING THE TIDE: A Journal of Anti-Racist Activism, Research & Education
URBAN GRAFFITI
Walnut Publishing Co., Inc.

COMMUNITY

Adolfo Street Publications
THE AFFILIATE
AMERICAN JONES BUILDING & MAINTENANCE
ASSEMBLY
Bear & Company, Inc.
Black Rose Books Ltd.
Bottom Dog Press
Carrier Pigeon Press
THE CHEROTIC (r)EVOLUTIONARY
Child's Play
CHRONICLE OF COMMUNITY
CJE NEWS (Newsletter of the Coalition for Jobs & the Environment)
COMMUNITIES
COMMUNITY DEVELOPMENT JOURNAL
Community Service, Inc.
COMMUNITY SERVICE NEWSLETTER
CRONE CHRONICLES: A Journal of Conscious Aging
EUROPEAN JUDAISM
FAMILY TIMES: The Newspaper for Chippewa Valley Parents
FRIENDS OF PEACE PILGRIM
FURTHER TOO
Gan Publishing
GATEAVISA
GEORGE & MERTIE'S PLACE: Rooms With a View
Global Options
Golden Eagle Press
GRANULATED TUPPERWARE
GrapeVinePress
GRASS ROOTS
The Heather Foundation
Herald Press
HIP MAMA
Hollis Publishing Company
ICARUS WAS RIGHT
Ice Cube Press
Impact Publishers, Inc.
INFUSION

Innisfree Press
INNOVATING
Institute for Southern Studies
INTERCULTURE
ISRAEL HORIZONS
Itidwitir Publishing
JOURNAL OF CHILD AND YOUTH CARE
KETTERING REVIEW
KICK IT OVER
Kivaki Press
LAKE SUPERIOR MAGAZINE
LITURGY 90
LOVING ALTERNATIVES MAGAZINE
THE MAD FARMERS' JUBILEE ALMANACK
Missing Spoke Press
MIXED BAG
NATURAL LIFE
Naturist Foundation
NEW ENVIRONMENT BULLETIN
NEW THOUGHT JOURNAL
ONE EARTH
OTTER
OUT YOUR BACKDOOR: The Magazine of Informal
  Adventure and Cheap Culture
THE PLOUGH
POTOMAC REVIEW
R & E Publishers
RAIN MAGAZINE
Red Alder Books
RFD
RURAL NETWORK ADVOCATE
SILVER WINGS/MAYFLOWER PULPIT
SOCIAL ANARCHISM: A Journal of Practice and
  Theory
SOCIAL JUSTICE: A JOURNAL OF CRIME, CON-
  FLICT, & WORLD ORDER
SOCIAL POLICY
SYCAMORE ROOTS: New Native Americans
TEENS IN MOTION NEWS
Telos Press
Times Change Press
Trentham Books
TURNING WHEEL
THE UNIT CIRCLE
Volcano Press, Inc
WE INTERNATIONAL (formerly WOMEN AND EN-
  VIRONMENTS)
WHOLE EARTH
THE WISDOM CONSERVANCY NEWSLETTER
Witwatersrand University Press
Z MAGAZINE

COMPUTERS, CALCULATORS

Access Multimedia
Adams-Blake Publishing
THE AFFILIATE
AFTERTOUCH: New Music Discoveries
Ageless Press
Allworth Press
ALT-J: Association for Learning Technology Journal
and books
Application Publishing, Inc.
ATL Press, Inc.
Autonomedia, Inc.
Baker Street Publications
Bell Publishing
Benchmark Publications Inc.
THE BOOKWATCH
Bowerdean Publishing Co. Ltd.
Brenner Information Group
Byte Masters International
Career Publishing, Inc.
Carpe Diem Publishing
THE CHRISTIAN LIBRARIAN
THE COMPLEAT NURSE
COMPUTER BOOK REVIEW
Cove View Press
Cultivated Underground Press

Cypress Publishing Group, Inc.
DAEDALUS, Journal of the American Academy of Arts
  and Sciences
DISSONANCE MAGAZINE
Dry Bones Press
Easel Publishing Corporation
FISICA
Frontline Publications
Gallopade International
GATEAVISA
Grapevine Publications, Inc.
GRAY AREAS
HOAX!
HOBSON'S CHOICE
Hunter House Inc., Publishers
INFOCUS
Jamenair Ltd.
Kent Information Services, Inc.
Lexikon Services
Lion Press & Video
Mayhaven Publishing
META4: Journal of Object Oriented Poetics (OOPS)
Microdex Bookshelf
MODERN LOGIC: An International Journal for the
  History of Mathematical Logic, Set Theory, and
  Foundations of Mathematics
Mountain Automation Corporation
MULTIMEDIA REVIEWS FOR EDUCATION, MULTI-
  MEDIA REVIEWS FOR INDUSTRY
NEW HOPE INTERNATIONAL REVIEW
No Starch Press
NWI National Writers Institute
Online Training Solutions, Inc.
Paladin Enterprises, Inc.
PalmTree Publishers
Pikes Peak Press
PLAIN BROWN WRAPPER (PBW)
PRIVACY JOURNAL
Professional Resource Exchange, Inc.
PUCK: The Unofficial Journal of the Irrepressible
Purple Finch Press
Quale Press
Resolution Business Press, Inc.
Roof Publishing Company
Seacoast Information Services
Shallowater Press
Steamshovel Press
STONES IN MY POCKET
TECHNICALITIES
THIRST (CYBERTHIRST)
Tiptoe Literary Service
VDT NEWS
White Cliffs Media, Inc.
WHOLE EARTH
WRITER'S WORKSHOP REVIEW

JOSEPH CONRAD

Abiko Literary Press (ALP)
CLASS ACT
ENGLISH LITERATURE IN TRANSITION, 1880-1920
THE JOURNAL OF AFRICAN TRAVEL-WRITING
NIGHT ROSES
Passeggiata Press, Inc.

CONSERVATION

ADIRONDAC
Adirondack Mountain Club, Inc.
THE AFFILIATE
AMERICAN FORESTS
AMERICAN HIKER
American Hiking Society
THE AMICUS JOURNAL
THE ANIMALS' AGENDA
APPALACHIA JOURNAL
AQUATERRA, METAECOLOGY & CULTURE
Baker Street Publications
Beacon Press
Bear & Company, Inc.

THE BEAR DELUXE
Bliss Publishing Company, Inc.
The Boxwood Press
Catamount Press
Cave Books
Chelsea Green Publishing Company
Child's Play
CHRONICLE OF COMMUNITY
CJE NEWS (Newsletter of the Coalition for Jobs & the
 Environment)
CURRENTS
Dog-Eared Publications
DWELLING PORTABLY
ELECTRONIC GREEN JOURNAL
Emerald Ink Publishing
Envirographics
HIGH COUNTRY NEWS
Hollis Publishing Company
Homestead Publishing
ICARUS WAS RIGHT
Institute for Southern Studies
Island Press
Itidwitir Publishing
Keokee Co. Publishing, Inc.
Kivaki Press
Kumarian Press, Inc.
La Alameda Press
THE LATHAM LETTER
The Latona Press
THE LETTER PARADE
Lexikos
Macrocosm USA, Inc.
MIXED BAG
The Mountaineers Books
Naturist Foundation
New England Cartographics, Inc.
NORTHWOODS JOURNAL, A Magazine for Writers
Oak Knoll Press
Oregon State University Press
OUT YOUR BACKDOOR: The Magazine of Informal
 Adventure and Cheap Culture
Pangaea
Pineapple Press, Inc.
POW-WOW
Pygmy Forest Press
The Rateavers
RED OWL
THE RIVER
SANDPOINT MAGAZINE
SEED SAVERS EXCHANGE
SKINNYDIPPING
THE SMALL POND MAGAZINE OF LITERATURE
 aka SMALL POND
Genny Smith Books
Stone Wall Press, Inc
TURNING THE TIDE: A Journal of Anti-Racist
 Activism, Research & Education
University of Calgary Press
VIRTUTE ET MORTE MAGAZINE
WESTERN SKIES
WILD EARTH
THE WILD FOODS FORUM
Wineberry Press
WISCONSIN TRAILS
WORLD RAINFOREST REPORT
Zagier & Urruty Publicaciones

CONSTUCTION

CJE NEWS (Newsletter of the Coalition for Jobs & the
 Environment)
Construction Trades Press
Consumer Press
Goodheart-Willcox Publisher
NEW CIVILIZATION STAFF REPORT
The Olive Press Publications
PAVEMENT SAW
Pavement Saw Press
Swan Publishing Company

CONSULTING

PSI Research/The Oasis Press/Hellgate Press

CONSUMER

and books
Autumn Publishing Group, LLC.
Bayley & Musgrave
Best Sellers Publishing
Bluestocking Press
Bonus Books, Inc.
THE BOOKWATCH
Branden Publishing Company
Brenner Information Group
Brighton Publications, Inc.
CANADIAN MONEYSAVER
Center for Public Representation
Center For Self-Sufficiency
Consumer Education Research Center
Consumer Press
DWELLING PORTABLY
ENOUGH IS ENOUGH!
GemStone Press
The Globe Pequot Press
Guarionex Press Ltd.
HOAX!
HORIZONS
Kells Media Group
Liberty Publishing Company, Inc.
Macrocosm USA, Inc.
NUTRITION ACTION HEALTHLETTER
Pineapple Press, Inc.
PRIVACY JOURNAL
Race Point Press
Roblin Press
Silvercat Publications
THE SMALL POND MAGAZINE OF LITERATURE
 aka SMALL POND
Stratton Press
Swan Publishing Company
The Tonal Company
Upper Access Inc.
VEGETARIAN JOURNAL
THE WHITE DOT - Survival Guide for the TV-Free
Willendorf Press
Winslow Publishing
WRITER'S WORKSHOP REVIEW

COOKING

Acclaim Publishing Co. Inc.
Airplane Books
Alaska Northwest Books
Alchemist/Light Publishing
Alive Books
ALIVE: Canadian Journal of Health and Nutrition
The Alternate Press
Amador Publishers
American Cooking Guild
Anaphase II
Anteater Press
Avery Color Studios
Barnegat Light Press/Pine Barrens Press
Berkeley Hills Books
The Bess Press
Black Forest Press
Blue Dolphin Publishing, Inc.
Blue Heron Publishing, Inc.
Bonus Books, Inc.
BookPartners, Inc.
Bright Mountain Books, Inc.
BURNING CAR
Callawind Publications Inc.
Center for South and Southeast Asian Studies Publications
Cherubic Press
Chicago Review Press
China Books & Periodicals, Inc.
Circumpolar Press
Cole Publishing Group, Inc.

COLLEGIUM NEWSLETTER
Conari Press
COOKING CONTEST CHRONICLE
THE COOL TRAVELER
Corona Publishing Co.
Coyote Publishing
The Crossing Press
Crystal Clarity, Publishers
Culinary Arts Ltd.
S. Deal & Assoc.
DOUBLE BILL
Enthea Press
EPM Publications, Inc.
Explorer's Guide Publishing
EZ Nature Books
Fantail
Fisher Books
Five Star Publications
Foghorn Press
FOOD WRITER
Gabriel's Horn Publishing Co., Inc.
The Globe Pequot Press
Golden Eagle Press
GOOD COOKING SERIES
Teri Gordon, Publisher
Hands & Heart Books
Harvard Common Press
Harvest Hill Press
HIP MAMA
Hoffman Press
The Image Maker Publishing Co.
Inner Traditions International
Island Publishers
Jackson Harbor Press
JEWISH VEGETARIAN NEWSLETTER
JPS Publishing Company
Kar-Ben Copies, Inc.
H J Kramer
La Alameda Press
LAKE SUPERIOR MAGAZINE
Owen Laughlin Publishers
Liberty Publishing Company, Inc.
Life Lessons
Momentum Books, Ltd.
NATURAL LIFE
Naturegraph Publishers, Inc.
Nicolin Fields Publishing, Inc.
NightinGale Resources
George Ohsawa Macrobiotic Foundation
Page One
Pedestal Press
Penfield Press
PenRose Publishing Company, Inc.
Pickle Point Publishing
Prestige Publications
Pruett Publishing Company
Pura Vida Publishing Company
Quicksilver Productions
Red Crane Books, Inc.
RedBrick Press
R-Squared Press
Running Press
Sandpiper Press
Sasquatch Books
Scratch & Scribble Press
Sibyl Publications, Inc
SJL Publishing Company
Gibbs Smith, Publisher
SPECIALTY COOKING MAGAZINE
SPROUTLETTER
Strawberry Patchworks
The Sulgrave Press
Tamarack Books, Inc.
Tiger Press
Tilbury House, Publishers
Tiptoe Literary Service
Tudor Publishers, Inc.
Twin Peaks Press

Tyro Publishing
Upper Access Inc.
Valiant Press, Inc.
VEGETARIAN JOURNAL
The Vegetarian Resource Group
THE VINCENT BROTHERS REVIEW
VINEGAR CONNOISSEURS INTERNATIONAL
  NEWSLETTER
W.E.C. Plant Publishing
Wave Publishing
Westport Publishers
THE WILD FOODS FORUM
Williamson Publishing Company, Inc.
Windsong Press
WISCONSIN TRAILS
Wisconsin Trails
Woodbridge Press

CO-OPS

The Alternate Press
Carousel Press
CJE NEWS (Newsletter of the Coalition for Jobs & the
  Environment)
CLASS ACT
THE COOPERATOR
FURTHER TOO
GATEAVISA
KICK IT OVER
LOVE AND RAGE, A Revolutionary Anarchist News-
  paper
Macrocosm USA, Inc.
MEANDER QUARTERLY
PHOENIX MAGAZINE
Phoenix Press
The Place In The Woods
RAIN MAGAZINE
WRITER'S WORKSHOP REVIEW

COSMOLOGY

MAD SCIENTIST
Media Arts Publishing
New Paradigm Books
SunShine Press Publications, Inc.

COUNTER-CULTURE, ALTERNATIVES, COM-MUNES

AFFABLE NEIGHBOR
Affable Neighbor Press
AFFAIR OF THE MIND: A Literary Quarterly
ALADDIN'S WINDOW
ALTERNATIVE PRESS REVIEW
The American Dissident
and books
THE ANGRY THOREAUAN
AREOPAGUS
ARTISTAMP NEWS
Baker Street Publications
Bear & Company, Inc.
THE BLAB
BORDERLANDS: A Quarterly Journal Of Borderland
  Research
BOTH SIDES NOW
BREAKFAST ALL DAY
Breakout Productions
BROKEN PENCIL
BROWNBAG PRESS
Brownout Laboratories
Carrier Pigeon Press
Cassandra Press, Inc.
THE CHEROTIC (r)EVOLUTIONARY
CHILDREN, CHURCHES AND DADDIES, A Non
  Religious, Non Familial Literary Magazine
China Books & Periodicals, Inc.
CJE NEWS (Newsletter of the Coalition for Jobs & the
  Environment)
COMMUNITIES
Community Resource Institute Press
COUNTERPOISE: For Social Responsibilities, Liberty

and Dissent
CRIPES!
CRONE CHRONICLES: A Journal of Conscious Aging
Crystal Clarity, Publishers
THE DALHOUSIE REVIEW
The Denali Press
DISSONANCE MAGAZINE
DRASTIC LIVES
DROP FORGE
DWELLING PORTABLY
EBB AND FLOW
EDDIE THE MAGAZINE
The Edwin Mellen Press
FIRST CLASS
Four-Sep Publications
FULL MOON DIRECTORY
Full Moon Publications
FURTHER TOO
GATEAVISA
Gay Sunshine Press, Inc.
GEORGE & MERTIE'S PLACE: Rooms With a View
GRAFFITI OFF THE ASYLUM WALLS
GRASS ROOTS
GRAY AREAS
GREEN FUSE POETRY
THE GROWING EDGE MAGAZINE
THE HAUNTED JOURNAL
HERBAL CHOICE
HIP MAMA
HOAX!
Homeward Press
Hyacinth House Publications/Caligula Editions
IllumiNet Press
Index Publishing Group, Inc
INDY MAGAZINE
Inner Traditions International
INTERCULTURAL WRITERS REVIEW
INTERNATIONAL ART POST
THE J MAN TIMES
Jade Moon Publications
KARMA LAPEL
KASPAHRASTER
KICK IT OVER
Leyland Publications
THE (LIBERTARIAN) CONNECTION
LIBRARIANS AT LIBERTY
LIFE ON PLANET EARTH, VOL III
LIGHTWORKS MAGAZINE
LITTLE FREE PRESS
LOVE AND RAGE, A Revolutionary Anarchist News-
   paper
LOVING ALTERNATIVES MAGAZINE
LULLWATER REVIEW
MACHINEGUN MAGAZINE: New Lit. Quarterly
Macrocosm USA, Inc.
THE MAD FARMERS' JUBILEE ALMANACK
Mandala Publishing Group
MARGIN: EXPLORING MODERN MAGICAL REA-
   LISM
MEANDER QUARTERLY
MESECHABE: The Journal of Surre(gion)alism
MESHUGGAH
MIXED BAG
MSRRT NEWSLETTER: LIBRARY ALTERNATIVES
NATURALLY
NEW ENVIRONMENT BULLETIN
New Spring Publications
NIGHTSHADE
NOCTURNAL REPORTER
OPEN EXCHANGE MAGAZINE
OPTIONS IN LEARNING
THE OTHER ISRAEL
OUT YOUR BACKDOOR: The Magazine of Informal
   Adventure and Cheap Culture
Outrider Press
Paladin Enterprises, Inc.
Passing Through Publications
PEACE, The Magazine of the Sixties

PEOPLE'S CULTURE
Permeable Press
PERSPECTIVES
PIG IRON
THE PLOUGH
Pottersfield Press
Progressive Education
PROGRESSIVE PERIODICALS DIRECTORY/UPDATE
PSYCHOTRAIN
Pygmy Forest Press
QUESTION EVERYTHING CHALLENGE EVERY-
   THING (QECE)
RADICAL AMERICA
RAIN MAGAZINE
Really Great Books
REALM OF THE VAMPIRE
Red Eye Press
REMOTE JOCKEY DIGEST
RFD
Roam Publishing
ROCTOBER COMICS AND MUSIC
RURAL NETWORK ADVOCATE
THE SALEM JOURNAL
SANDBOX MAGAZINE
Savant Garde Workshop
Scars Publications
Schenkman Books
SCIENCE & SOCIETY
SCIENCE/HEALTH ABSTRACTS
Semiotext Foreign Agents Books Series
SEMIOTEXT(E)
SHORT FUSE
SKINNYDIPPING
Slab-O-Concrete Publications
SOCIAL ANARCHISM: A Journal of Practice and
   Theory
SONAR MAP
SPECTRUM—The Wholistic News Magazine
SPIRIT MAGAZINE
SPIRIT TO SPIRIT
THE SPITTING IMAGE
SPROUTLETTER
STARGREEN
Steamshovel Press
STEAMSHOVEL PRESS
STOVEPIPE: A Journal of Little Literary Value
Swan Raven & Company
Sweet Lady Moon Press
Syracuse Cultural Workers/Tools for Change
Tafford Publishing
Times Change Press
Transcending Mundane
Transeuropa
TURNING THE TIDE: A Journal of Anti-Racist
   Activism, Research & Education
THE UNDERGROUND
THE UNDERGROUND FOREST - LA SELVA SUB-
   TERRANEA
THE UNIT CIRCLE
Upper Access Inc.
URBAN GRAFFITI
URBANUS/RAIZIRR
VAMPIRE NIGHTS
VIETNAM GENERATION: A Journal of Recent History
   and Contemporary Issues
Ward Hill Press
WHOLE EARTH
Winchester/G. Ander Books
XIB
Z MAGAZINE
ZERO HOUR

CRAFTS, HOBBIES

Aeolus Press, Inc.
Affinity Publishers Services
Altamont Press, Inc.
AMERICAN AMATEUR JOURNALIST
AMERICAN MODELER, The Newspaper of Scale

Modeling
Americans for the Arts/ACA Books
Ancient City Press
APPALACHIAN HERITAGE
ART CALENDAR
Backcountry Publishing
Baker Street Publications
Bayley & Musgrave
Bear Creek Publications
Bonus Books, Inc.
Briarwood Publishing
BRIDAL CRAFTS
Bright Ring Publishing, Inc.
BUTTON
C & T Publishing
Canterbury Press
Capra Press
Cattpigg Press
Center For Self-Sufficiency
CHAOS FOR THE CREATIVE MIND
CHESS LIFE
Chicago Review Press
Child's Play
China Books & Periodicals, Inc.
ClockWorks Press
CLUBHOUSE
Cottontail Publications
Council For Indian Education
Coyote Publishing
CRAFTS 'N THINGS
THE CROSS STITCHER
Culinary Arts Ltd.
Cypress Publishing Group, Inc.
DWELLING PORTABLY
Eagle's View Publishing
EPM Publications, Inc.
ETC Publications
FIBERARTS
THE FRONT STRIKER BULLETIN
GemStone Press
The Gleniffer Press
Global Sports Productions, Ltd.
The Globe Pequot Press
Goodheart-Willcox Publisher
GRASS ROOTS
THE GREAT IDEA PATCH
Guarionex Press Ltd.
Hands & Heart Books
HOAX!
Hunter Publishing, Co.
IN PRINT
Interlink Publishing Group, Inc.
JARRETT'S JOURNAL
THE JOURNAL OF DESIGN AND TECHNOLOGY
  EDUCATION
JPS Publishing Company
KITE LINES
LADYBUG, the Magazine for Young Children
LAKE SUPERIOR MAGAZINE
Lester Street Publishing
Life Lessons
MAKING $$$ AT HOME
Mayhaven Publishing
Midmarch Arts Press
MIDWEST ART FAIRS
Miles & Miles
MIXED BAG
Moon Publications, Inc.
Naturegraph Publishers, Inc.
N-B-T-V
NEW HOPE INTERNATIONAL REVIEW
NightinGale Resources
No Starch Press
Open Hand Publishing Inc.
ORNAMENT
OUT YOUR BACKDOOR: The Magazine of Informal
  Adventure and Cheap Culture
PACK-O-FUN

PAINTING
Parabola
Pebble Press, Inc.
Penfield Press
PenRose Publishing Company, Inc.
Petroglyph Press, Ltd.
Ponderosa Publishers
Potentials Development, Inc.
POW-WOW
THE PRESIDENTS' JOURNAL
Profile Press
Prospect Hill Press
Red Crane Books, Inc.
Scentouri, Publishing Division
THE $ENSIBLE SOUND
Sierra Outdoor Products Co.
SJL Publishing Company
Storytime Ink International
Success Publishing
Sun Designs
Sunstone Press
Sylvan Books
Tamal Vista Publications
Thirteen Colonies Press
Timber Press
TIMBER TIMES
TOLE WORLD
Tomart Publications
TRADITION
Twin Peaks Press
UNITED LUMBEE NATION TIMES
VEGGIE LIFE
Venus Communications
Vestal Press Ltd
VINEGAR   CONNOISSEURS   INTERNATIONAL
  NEWSLETTER
Vitreous Group/Camp Colton
WEEKEND WOODCRAFTS
Wescott Cove Publishing Co.
WESTART
WHISPERING WIND MAGAZINE
WHOLE EARTH
Williamson Publishing Company, Inc.
WISCONSIN TRAILS
WOMEN ARTISTS NEWS BOOK REVIEW
WOOD STROKES & WOODCRAFTS
WOODWORKER'S JOURNAL
WORLDLINKS - FRIENDSHIP NEWS
YE OLDE NEWES

CREATIVITY

AFFABLE NEIGHBOR
Affable Neighbor Press
Anaphase II
THE ANGRY THOREAUAN
Arjay Associates
Baker Street Publications
CASTAWAYS
CHAOS FOR THE CREATIVE MIND
CLASS ACT
COMMON BOUNDARY MAGAZINE
COOKING CONTEST CHRONICLE
Crescent Moon
CRONE CHRONICLES: A Journal of Conscious Aging
Cultivated Underground Press
THE EMSHOCK LETTER
ETCETERA
FIGMENTS
FIRST DRAFT
Free Spirit Publishing Inc.
FURTHER TOO
Golden Eagle Press
GrapeVinePress
The Green Hut Press
The Heather Foundation
HOAX!
House of the 9 Muses, Inc.
Innisfree Press

INTERBANG
JOURNAL OF AESTHETICS AND ART CRITICISM
LIGHTWORKS MAGAZINE
Lowy Publishing
LULLWATER REVIEW
Manta Press
META4: Journal of Object Oriented Poetics (OOPS)
METAL CURSE
MIXED BAG
MONOZINE
NIGHTSHADE
Palari Publishing
Parabola
PASSAGER: A Journal of Remembrance and Discovery
PASSAGES NORTH
PASSION
Ponderosa Publishers
POTOMAC REVIEW
SALON: A Journal of Aesthetics
Savant Garde Workshop
Scrivenery Press
SHORT FUSE
SMALL PRESS CREATIVE EXPLOSION
SMART DRUG NEWS
SO TO SPEAK
SONAR MAP
SPELUNKER FLOPHOUSE
SPIRIT TO SPIRIT
STONES IN MY POCKET
THE SUNDAY SUITOR POETRY REVIEW
SYNCOPATED CITY
TRANSMOG
THE UNIT CIRCLE
Verve Press
THE VINCENT BROTHERS REVIEW
VIRTUTE ET MORTE MAGAZINE
WRITER'S CAROUSEL
WRITER'S EXCHANGE

CRIME

AC
Acclaim Publishing Co. Inc.
Addicus Books, Inc.
THE ANGRY THOREAUAN
BAKER STREET GAZETTE
Baker Street Publications
Barricade Books
BERKELEY WOMEN'S LAW JOURNAL
Breakout Productions
Briarwood Publishing
COALITION FOR PRISONERS' RIGHTS NEWSLET-
    TER
CORRECTIONS TODAY
CRIMINAL JUSTICE ABSTRACTS
Criminal Justice Press
DANGER!
DOUBLE BILL
The Dragon Press
Feral House
Full Moon Publications
FURTHER TOO
Galde Press, Inc.
GATEAVISA
Global Options
Golden Eagle Press
GRAY AREAS
Gryphon Publications
Guardian Press
HARDBOILED
HOAX!
Holbrook Street Press
ICA Publishing
ICARUS WAS RIGHT
Index Publishing Group, Inc
INTERCULTURAL WRITERS REVIEW
Itidwitir Publishing
THE J MAN TIMES
JACK THE RIPPER GAZETTE

Macrocosm USA, Inc.
MURDER CAN BE FUN
Mystery Notebook Editions
THE MYSTERY REVIEW
NOCTURNAL REPORTER
North Country Books, Inc.
Paladin Enterprises, Inc.
PAPERBACK PARADE
Paw Print Publishing Co.
POEMS THAT THUMP IN THE DARK/SECOND
    GLANCE
Primal Publishing
PRISON LEGAL NEWS
Really Great Books
RES PUBLICA
SHEMP! The Lowlife Culture Magazine
SISTERS IN CRIME BOOKS IN PRINT
SLEUTH JOURNAL
SOCIAL JUSTICE: A JOURNAL OF CRIME, CON-
    FLICT, & WORLD ORDER
Starbooks Press/FLF Press
THEY WON'T STAY DEAD!
Tudor Publishers, Inc.
TURNING THE TIDE: A Journal of Anti-Racist
    Activism, Research & Education
21ST CENTURY AFRO REVIEW
URBAN GRAFFITI
VIRTUTE ET MORTE MAGAZINE
WHITECHAPEL JOURNAL
Willow Tree Press, Inc.
Z MAGAZINE

CRITICISM

AABYE (formerly New Hope International Writing)
Abiko Literary Press (ALP)
ABRAXAS
Acclaim Publishing Co. Inc.
AFRICAN AMERICAN REVIEW
AGADA
ALABAMA LITERARY REVIEW
ALASKA QUARTERLY REVIEW
The Aldine Press, Ltd.
AMELIA
Amelia Press
American Canadian Publishers, Inc.
AMERICAN LITERATURE
THE ANGRY THOREAUAN
THE ANTIGONISH REVIEW
ARISTOS
Arjuna Library Press
ASSEMBLAGE: A Critical Journal of Architecture and
    Design Culture
Associated Writing Programs
Autonomedia, Inc.
AXE FACTORY REVIEW
BAKER STREET GAZETTE
Baker Street Publications
Bay Press
BELLES LETTRES
BIBLIOTHEQUE D'HUMANISME ET RENAISSANCE
Bilingual Review/Press
Black Sparrow Press
Black Tie Press
The Blue Oak Press
BOGG
BOOK/MARK SMALL PRESS QUARTERLY REVIEW
BORDERLANDS: Texas Poetry Review
Borealis Press Limited
The Borgo Press
BOULEVARD
THE BOUND SPIRAL
Bright Hill Press
Brownout Laboratories
Calypso Publications
CANADIAN CHILDREN'S LITERATURE
CANADIAN LITERATURE
Capra Press
Carrefour Press

763

Castle Peak Editions
Center for Japanese Studies
Chandler & Sharp Publishers, Inc.
CHILDREN'S LITERATURE IN EDUCATION
Chiron Press
CHIRON REVIEW
CIMARRON REVIEW
CINEASTE MAGAZINE
Clamshell Press
CLASS ACT
CLOCKWATCH REVIEW
Confluence Press, Inc.
CONTEMPORARY LITERATURE
CONTEXT SOUTH
Coteau Books
COUNTERPOISE: For Social Responsibilities, Liberty and Dissent
The F. Marion Crawford Memorial Society
Crescent Moon
CROSSCURRENTS
CUMBERLAND POETRY REVIEW
THE DALHOUSIE REVIEW
Manya DeLeon Booksmith
Department of Romance Languages
DESCANT
DIRIGIBLE
THE DIRTY GOAT
THE DROOD REVIEW OF MYSTERY
THE DURHAM UNIVERSITY JOURNAL
The Ecco Press
ECW Press
Edgewise Press
ELT Press
Encounter Books
ENGLISH LITERATURE IN TRANSITION, 1880-1920
Enitharmon Press
ENTELECHY MAGAZINE
ENTROPY NEGATIVE
ESSAYS ON CANADIAN WRITING
EUROPEAN JUDAISM
THE EVERGREEN CHRONICLES
Fels and Firn Press
Feral House
FIDEI DEFENSOR: JOURNAL OF CATHOLIC APO-LOGETICS
FIRST DRAFT
FLYING HORSE
From Here Press
FUGUE
Full Moon Publications
FURTHER TOO
The Future Press
THE GALLEY SAIL REVIEW
GATEAVISA
GEORGE & MERTIE'S PLACE: Rooms With a View
THE GEORGIA REVIEW
god is DEAD, publications
Gothic Press
GOTHIX
GrapeVinePress
Graywolf Press
GREEN MOUNTAINS REVIEW
GUARD THE NORTH
H & C NEWSLETTER
THE HAUNTED JOURNAL
HAWAI'I REVIEW
HELLAS: A Journal of Poetry & the Humanities
Hippopotamus Press
HOAX!
Hope Publishing House
Host Publications, Inc.
H2SO4
Indelible Inc.
Interalia/Design Books
INTERBANG
Interim Press
THE INTERNATIONAL FICTION REVIEW
THE IOWA REVIEW

IRISH LITERARY SUPPLEMENT
Ironweed Press
Itidwitir Publishing
THE J MAN TIMES
JAMES JOYCE BROADSHEET
JOURNAL OF AESTHETICS AND ART CRITICISM
JOURNAL OF CANADIAN POETRY
JOURNAL OF CANADIAN STUDIES/Revue d'etudes canadiennes
JOURNAL OF MODERN LITERATURE
JOURNAL OF NARRATIVE THEORY
JOURNAL OF REGIONAL CRITICISM
JUMP CUT, A Review of Contemporary Media
KALDRON, An International Journal Of Visual Poetry
KALEIDOSCOPE: INTERNATIONAL MAGAZINE OF LITERATURE, FINE ARTS, AND DISABILITY
KARMA LAPEL
THE KENYON REVIEW
LAW AND CRITIQUE
LEFT CURVE
Liberty Bell Press & Publishing Co.
LIES MAGAZINE
LIFTOUTS
Limelight Editions
LINQ
LITERARY MAGAZINE REVIEW
LITERARY SKETCHES
LOGIC LETTER
Lord John Press
LUMMOX JOURNAL
MAGNET MAGAZINE
Maisonneuve Press
MARK
MASSACRE
MEANJIN
The Menard Press
METAL CURSE
MID-AMERICAN REVIEW
THE MIDWEST QUARTERLY
Miles & Miles
MIND MATTERS REVIEW
MISSISSIPPI REVIEW
MIXED BAG
MODERN LANGUAGE QUARTERLY: A Journal of Literary History
Moon Publications, Inc.
MUDLARK
NEDGE
NEOLOGISMS
NEW ART EXAMINER
THE NEW ENGLAND QUARTERLY
NEW GERMAN REVIEW: A Journal of Germanic Studies
New Hope International
NEW HOPE INTERNATIONAL REVIEW
THE NEW PRESS LITERARY QUARTERLY
New Spring Publications
NIGHTSHADE
NORTH DAKOTA QUARTERLY
North Stone Press
NORTHEAST
Nosukumo
NOVA EXPRESS
ONE TRICK PONY
OUTPOSTS POETRY QUARTERLY
Oyez
THE PANNUS INDEX
PAPYRUS
PARTISAN REVIEW
Passeggiata Press, Inc.
PASSION
PenRose Publishing Company, Inc.
PHOEBE: A JOURNAL OF LITERARY ARTS
PIG IRON
PLOUGHSHARES
POETRY FLASH
THE POETRY MISCELLANY
POETRY NOTTINGHAM INTERNATIONAL

POETRY WALES
THE POWYS JOURNAL
THE PRAIRIE JOURNAL OF CANADIAN LITERA-
TURE
Prairie Journal Press
PRECISELY
Press Here
PSYCHOANALYTIC BOOKS: A QUARTERLY JOUR-
NAL OF REVIEWS
Pyncheon House
QUARTER AFTER EIGHT
Quarterly Committee of Queen's University
QUEEN'S QUARTERLY: A Canadian Review
Quiet Lion Press
RAIN CITY REVIEW
RARITAN: A Quarterly Review
RATTAPALLAX
THE READER'S REVIEW
REALM OF THE VAMPIRE
REPRESENTATIONS
REVUE CELFAN REVIEW
THE ROMANTIST
Ronsdale Press
Rowhouse Press
The Runaway Spoon Press
ST. CROIX REVIEW
ST. LOUIS JOURNALISM REVIEW
St. Michael's Press
SALMAGUNDI
SALOME: A Journal for the Performing Arts
SALON: A Journal of Aesthetics
SCIENCE & SOCIETY
SCRIVENER
SEMIGLOSS
Semiotext Foreign Agents Books Series
SEMIOTEXT(E)
SENECA REVIEW
SEWANEE REVIEW
SF EYE
THE SHAKESPEARE NEWSLETTER
SHORT FUSE
THE SIGNAL - Network International
Slate Press
SLEUTH JOURNAL
SOLO
SOUTH DAKOTA REVIEW
SOUTHERN HUMANITIES REVIEW
SOUTHERN QUARTERLY: A Journal of the Arts in the
South
Spectrum Press
SPILLWAY
THE STARLIGHT PAPERS
Station Hill Press
THE WALLACE STEVENS JOURNAL
Strata Publishing, Inc.
Studia Hispanica Editors
Sherwood Sugden & Company, Publishers
SYMPLOKE: A Journal for the Intermingling of Literary,
Cultural and Theoretical Scholarship
TALISMAN: A Journal of Contemporary Poetry and
Poetics
Talisman House, Publishers
TEARS IN THE FENCE
TELOS
THE TEMPLE
Texture Press
THALIA: Studies in Literary Humor
13TH MOON
Thomas Jefferson University Press
THE THREEPENNY REVIEW
TORRE DE PAPEL
THE TRUTH SEEKER
Turnstone Press
THE UNDERGROUND FOREST - LA SELVA SUB-
TERRANEA
THE UNIT CIRCLE
University of Calgary Press
URBAN GRAFFITI

Vesta Publications Limited
VIETNAM GENERATION: A Journal of Recent History
and Contemporary Issues
THE VINCENT BROTHERS REVIEW
WALT WHITMAN QUARTERLY REVIEW
WAY STATION MAGAZINE
WEST COAST LINE: A Journal of Contemporary
Writing and Criticism
WHELKS WALK REVIEW
WHITECHAPEL JOURNAL
WILLOW SPRINGS
Witwatersrand University Press
WOODNOTES
THE WORCESTER REVIEW
WORLD OF FANDOM MAGAZINE
WRITER'S CHRONICLE
Writers Forum
WRITERS GAZETTE
THE YALE REVIEW
Zoland Books
ZUZU'S PETALS: QUARTERLY ONLINE

CRYSTALS

Borderland Sciences Research Foundation
The Crossing Press
Galde Press, Inc.
THE J MAN TIMES
Llewellyn Publications
MetaGnosis
MYSTIC VOICES
Reyes Investment Enterprise Ltd.
SAGEWOMAN
SPIRIT TO SPIRIT
STONES IN MY POCKET
Three Pyramids Publishing

CUBA

Baker Street Publications
BLU
Full Moon Publications
GATEAVISA
LONE STAR SOCIALIST
LS Press, Inc.
MESECHABE: The Journal of Surre(gion)alism
THE MILITANT
MIXED BAG
THE NEW PRESS LITERARY QUARTERLY
Pangaea
Pathfinder Press
Smyrna Press
SOCIETE

CULTS

AFFABLE NEIGHBOR
Affable Neighbor Press
THE AFFILIATE
AXE FACTORY REVIEW
Baker Street Publications
Blue River Publishing Inc.
Carrier Pigeon Press
Feral House
FULL MOON DIRECTORY
Full Moon Publications
FURTHER TOO
GATEAVISA
GRAFFITI OFF THE ASYLUM WALLS
GRANULATED TUPPERWARE
THE HAUNTED JOURNAL
HOAX!
Hunter House Inc., Publishers
Hyacinth House Publications/Caligula Editions
IllumiNet Press
Inner Traditions International
THE J MAN TIMES
NOCTURNAL REPORTER
OFFICE NUMBER ONE
REALM OF THE VAMPIRE
THE SALEM JOURNAL

765

SOCIETE
STAGNANCY IS REVOLTING
URBAN GRAFFITI
VAMPIRE NIGHTS
VIRTUTE ET MORTE MAGAZINE
White Cliffs Media, Inc.

CURRENT AFFAIRS

ATL Press, Inc.
Bancroft Press
BLU
Bonus Books, Inc.
BOOK/MARK SMALL PRESS QUARTERLY REVIEW
Bowerdean Publishing Co. Ltd.
CHAOS FOR THE CREATIVE MIND
Clarity Press, Inc.
THE EDGE CITY REVIEW
Encounter Books
First Amendment Press International Company
The Foundation for Economic Education, Inc.
THE FREEMAN: Ideas On Liberty
GEORGE & MERTIE'S PLACE: Rooms With a View
Heron Press
Hollis Publishing Company
INFUSION
THE J MAN TIMES
THE KITHARA
The Leaping Frog Press
MAIN STREET JOURNAL
Manta Press
Marmot Publishing
McGregor Publishing
MIM NOTES: Offcial Newsletter of the Maoist Internationalist Movement
New Spring Publications
NGUOI DAN
The Pamphleeter's Press
READERS SPEAK OUT!
UNDER THE VOLCANO
THE UNIT CIRCLE
UTNE READER
Visions Communications
THE WHITE DOT - Survival Guide for the TV-Free

CULTURE

AERIAL
AFFABLE NEIGHBOR
Affable Neighbor Press
AFFAIR OF THE MIND: A Literary Quarterly
Alaska Geographic Society
Alaska Native Language Center
THE ANIMALS' AGENDA
Ariko Publications
ARISTOS
Arjay Associates
ART CALENDAR
ASSEMBLAGE: A Critical Journal of Architecture and Design Culture
ASSEMBLY
Autonomedia, Inc.
BACKSPACE: A QUEER POETS JOURNAL
Baker Street Publications
Balcony Press
Bay Press
Between The Lines
BIG WORLD
Birch Brook Press
BLUE COLLAR REVIEW
BOOK/MARK SMALL PRESS QUARTERLY REVIEW
THE BOOMERPHILE
Borealis Press Limited
BOSTON REVIEW
BRIDGES: An Interdisciplinary Journal of Theology, Philosophy, History, and Science
BROKEN PENCIL
Brownout Laboratories
Carrefour Press
Chandler & Sharp Publishers, Inc.

THE CHARIOTEER
THE CHEROTIC (r)EVOLUTIONARY
CHILDREN, CHURCHES AND DADDIES, A Non Religious, Non Familial Literary Magazine
Child's Play
CJE NEWS (Newsletter of the Coalition for Jobs & the Environment)
Clover Park Press
COLORLINES
COMMON BOUNDARY MAGAZINE
THE COOL TRAVELER
CORONA
Coteau Books
Crescent Moon
CRIPES!
CRONE CHRONICLES: A Journal of Conscious Aging
CULTUREFRONT
DAEDALUS, Journal of the American Academy of Arts and Sciences
Dawn Sign Press
Derrynane Press
DESCANT
THE DIRTY GOAT
DOWN UNDER MANHATTAN BRIDGE
THE DROPLET JOURNAL
Encounter Books
ENOUGH IS ENOUGH!
EXCLAIM!
Exile Press
FACES: The Magazine About People
Feral House
FIGMENTS
Five Fingers Press
FIVE FINGERS REVIEW
FLIPSIDE
Four Walls Eight Windows
FURTHER TOO
GATEAVISA
GEORGE & MERTIE'S PLACE: Rooms With a View
THE GEORGIA REVIEW
GERBIL: Queer Culture Zine
GIRLFRIENDS MAGAZINE
GREEN MOUNTAINS REVIEW
Gumbs & Thomas Publishers, Inc.
H & C NEWSLETTER
Heartsong Books
Heron Press
HOAX!
Hope Publishing House
HORIZON
Host Publications, Inc.
House of the 9 Muses, Inc.
HURRICANE ALICE
Inner Traditions International
Integral Publishing
Intercultural Press, Inc.
INTERCULTURAL WRITERS REVIEW
INTERCULTURE
Interlink Publishing Group, Inc.
IRIS: A Journal About Women
JEWISH LIFE
JOURNAL OF AESTHETICS AND ART CRITICISM
JOURNAL OF ALASKA WOMEN
KALDRON, An International Journal Of Visual Poetry
KARMA LAPEL
THE KITHARA
Kivaki Press
KMT, A Modern Journal of Ancient Egypt
KMT Communications
Kodiak Media Group
La Alameda Press
LAKE SUPERIOR MAGAZINE
LATINO STUFF REVIEW
The Leaping Frog Press
LEFT CURVE
THE LETTER PARADE
LO STRANIERO: The Stranger, Der Fremde, L'Etranger
LPD Press

LA PERIPHERIE
LIGHTWORKS MAGAZINE
LOST AND FOUND TIMES
LOST GENERATION JOURNAL
Luna Bisonte Prods
Lunar Offensive Publications
MASSACRE
MESECHABE: The Journal of Surre(gion)alism
META4: Journal of Object Oriented Poetics (OOPS)
NEW MUSE OF CONTEMPT
THE NEW SOUTHERN SURREALIST REVIEW
NIGHTSHADE
North Stone Press
NOT BORED!
Ocean View Books
OXYGEN
PANJANDRUM POETRY JOURNAL
Pariah Press
PAVEMENT SAW
Pavement Saw Press
PEAKY HIDE
Permeable Press
Phrygian Press
PIG IRON
Pig Iron Press
PLAIN BROWN WRAPPER (PBW)
The Press of the Third Mind
PSYCHOTRAIN
QUESTION EVERYTHING CHALLENGE EVERY-
THING (QECE)
RAG SHOCK
REALM OF THE VAMPIRE
Rowhouse Press
THE SALEM JOURNAL
SALT LICK
Salt Lick Press
Savant Garde Workshop
Scars Publications
Scopcraeft
SHOCKBOX
SHORT FUSE
SHRIKE
SMALL PRESS CREATIVE EXPLOSION
THE SPITTING IMAGE
Station Hill Press
TEXTURE
TRANSMOG
TWISTED TIMES
URBAN GRAFFITI
Urban Legend Press
THE URBANITE
THE VINCENT BROTHERS REVIEW
Vortex Editions
Who Who Who Publishing
XIB
Xib Publications
ZYX

DANCE

AMERICAN WRITING: A Magazine
Amherst Writers & Artists Press, Inc.
Anderson Press
ARISTOS
ARTSLINK
Bonus Books, Inc.
A Cappella Books
COVER MAGAZINE
FODDERWING
Fromm International Publishing Corporation
Golden Eagle Press
Human Kinetics Pub. Inc.
JACK MACKEREL MAGAZINE
JOURNAL OF ALASKA WOMEN
Life Energy Media
Limelight Editions
MINISTRY & LITURGY
Moon Publications, Inc.
MUSICWORKS: The Journal of Sound Explorations

(Audio-Visual)
THE NEW PRESS LITERARY QUARTERLY
NEW THOUGHT JOURNAL
NIGHT ROSES
Ommation Press
Princeton Book Company, Publishers
Purple Finch Press
Resource Publications, Inc.
Rowhouse Press
SALMAGUNDI
SALOME: A Journal for the Performing Arts
SOUTHERN QUARTERLY: A Journal of the Arts in the
South
Strawberry Hill Press
THEATRE DESIGN AND TECHNOLOGY
Thirteen Colonies Press
TRADITION
World Music Press
Writers Forum
YOUNG VOICES

DANISH

Blue Dolphin Publishing, Inc.
Lester Street Publishing
THE NEW PRESS LITERARY QUARTERLY
TRANSITIONS ABROAD: The Guide to Living,
Learning, and Working Overseas

AUGUST DERLETH

Algol Press
BAKER STREET GAZETTE
Baker Street Publications
The F. Marion Crawford Memorial Society
Embassy Hall Editions
Full Moon Publications
THE HAUNTED JOURNAL
NIGHTSHADE
RALPH'S REVIEW
SCIENCE FICTION CHRONICLE
SLEUTH JOURNAL
WISCONSIN TRAILS

DESIGN

Access Multimedia
Aegean Publishing Company
Allworth Press
APOSTROPHE: USCB Journal of the Arts
ART CALENDAR
ART/LIFE
ASSEMBLAGE: A Critical Journal of Architecture and
Design Culture
Balcony Press
Banana Productions
BREAKFAST ALL DAY
Brenner Information Group
Ceres Press
THE COOPERATOR
DeerTrail Books
DESIGN BOOK REVIEW
DRASTIC LIVES
ENVIRONMENTAL & ARCHITECTURAL PHENO-
MENOLOGY NEWSLETTER
ETCETERA
FURTHER TOO
GemStone Press
Goodheart-Willcox Publisher
HOAX!
Interalia/Design Books
KALDRON, An International Journal Of Visual Poetry
Dean Lem Associates, Inc.
MIXED BAG
Mortal Press
NIGHT ROSES
OUT YOUR BACKDOOR: The Magazine of Informal
Adventure and Cheap Culture
The Overlook Press
Pendaya Publications, Inc.
Poltroon Press

Ponderosa Publishers
THE RESOURCE
SJL Publishing Company
Slab-O-Concrete Publications
Stemmer House Publishers, Inc.
Stone Bridge Press
Sun Designs
Tuns Press
THE UNIT CIRCLE
Waterfront Books
WATERFRONT WORLD SPOTLIGHT
WE INTERNATIONAL (formerly WOMEN AND EN-
  VIRONMENTS)
WHOLE EARTH
ZONE
Zone Books

DESKTOP PUBLISHING

Cultivated Underground Press
THE GREAT BLUE BEACON
Dean Lem Associates, Inc.

DIARIES

ACORN WHISTLE
AFFAIR OF THE MIND: A Literary Quarterly
ANAIS: An International Journal
APHRODITE GONE BERSERK
BELLES LETTRES
Burd Street Press
Burning Bush Publications
CLASS ACT
Cold-Drill Books
DIARIST'S JOURNAL
The Feathered Serpent
First Amendment Press International Company
Fromm International Publishing Corporation
Galde Press, Inc.
god is DEAD, publications
Happy Rock Press
THE HUNTED NEWS
KESTREL: A Journal of Literature and Art
LEO Productions LLC.
Magic Circle Press
MESSAGES FROM THE HEART
THE METAPHYSICAL REVIEW
NEW HOPE INTERNATIONAL REVIEW
Nosukumo
OVERLAND JOURNAL
Paris Press, Inc.
PLAIN BROWN WRAPPER (PBW)
POTOMAC REVIEW
Signature Books
Skinny Lamb Publishing Company
The Subourbon Press
URBAN GRAFFITI
Writers House Press

CHARLES DICKENS

Abiko Literary Press (ALP)
Baker Street Publications
CLASS ACT
MIXED BAG
New Spirit Press/The Poet Tree

JAMES DICKEY

CLASS ACT
JAMES DICKEY NEWSLETTER

EMILY DICKINSON

Abiko Literary Press (ALP)
THE CENTENNIAL REVIEW
CLASS ACT
Crescent Moon
GEORGE & MERTIE'S PLACE: Rooms With a View
JEJUNE: america Eats its Young
Naturegraph Publishers, Inc.
New Spirit Press/The Poet Tree
PASSION

DICTIONARIES

Alaska Native Language Center
Anderson Press
Bandanna Books
Celo Valley Books
Center for South and Southeast Asian Studies Publications
China Books & Periodicals, Inc.
CLASS ACT
FURTHER TOO
Maledicta Press
Minnesota Historical Society Press
NEW HOPE INTERNATIONAL REVIEW
NEW WRITING
Nosukumo
OPTIMA Books
Top Of The Mountain Publishing
The Wordtree

DISABLED

ABILITY NETWORK
ADAPTED PHYSICAL ACTIVITY QUARTERLY
  (APAQ)
Adaptive Living
The Advocado Press
Alpine Guild, Inc.
BERKELEY WOMEN'S LAW JOURNAL
Cherubic Press
Child's Play
THE CIVIL ABOLITIONIST
COLLEGIUM NEWSLETTER
THE DISABILITY RAG & RESOURCE
EPM Publications, Inc.
The Feminist Press at the City College
FOCUS: Library Service to Older Adults, People with
  Disabilities
Future Horizons, Inc.
Human Kinetics Pub. Inc.
Hunter House Inc., Publishers
Impact Publishers, Inc.
THE INCLUSION NOTEBOOK
JARRETT'S JOURNAL
KALEIDOSCOPE: INTERNATIONAL MAGAZINE OF
  LITERATURE, FINE ARTS, AND DISABILITY
Kodiak Media Group
LOVE AND RAGE, A Revolutionary Anarchist News-
  paper
Macrocosm USA, Inc.
Massey-Reyner Publishing
THE MATURE TRAVELER
Mho & Mho Works
MOTOR CONTROL
MOUTH: Voice of the Disability Nation
NEW HOPE INTERNATIONAL REVIEW
The New Humanity Press
Organization for Equal Education of the Sexes, Inc.
Parabola
Pennycorner Press
PHOENIX MAGAZINE
Phoenix Press
The Place In The Woods
Potentials Development, Inc.
Publitec Editions
Rainbow Books, Inc.
Real Life Storybooks
The Saunderstown Press
SKYLARK
Spinsters Ink
TRANSITIONS ABROAD: The Guide to Living,
  Learning, and Working Overseas
Twin Peaks Press
WHOLE EARTH
Willendorf Press
Woodbine House

DISEASE

AFFAIR OF THE MIND: A Literary Quarterly
ATL Press, Inc.

THE CIVIL ABOLITIONIST
Civitas
THE COMPLEAT NURSE
Conari Press
Dry Bones Press
ELDERCARE FORUM
Elysian Hills Publishing Company, Inc.
Feral House
GATEAVISA
GEORGE & MERTIE'S PLACE: Rooms With a View
JARRETT'S JOURNAL
Kali Press
Ledero Press
MEDICAL HISTORY
MEDIPHORS
NEW WRITING
Parabola
Real Life Storybooks
SMART DRUG NEWS
SPROUTLETTER
STONES IN MY POCKET
STREET VOICE
The Tonal Company
URBAN GRAFFITI

DISNEY

Cultivated Underground Press
THE DUCKBURG TIMES
GOLD COAST NEWS
HOAX!
HOLLYWOOD NOSTALGIA
JEJUNE: america Eats its Young
Tomart Publications
WORLD OF FANDOM MAGAZINE

DIVORCE

Cherubic Press
Conari Press
The Crossing Press
Cyclone Books
Fillmore Publishing Company
GEORGE & MERTIE'S PLACE: Rooms With a View
Golden Eagle Press
HIP MAMA
Hunter House Inc., Publishers
Impact Publishers, Inc.
The Leaping Frog Press
THE LIBERATOR
PT Publications, Inc.
River Press
Single Parent Press
SINGLE SCENE

DRAMA

Admiral House Publishing
AFFAIR OF THE MIND: A Literary Quarterly
THE ALEMBIC
ALLEGHENY REVIEW
AMELIA
Amelia Press
ANQ: A Quarterly Journal of Short Articles, Notes, and
    Reviews
APOSTROPHE: USCB Journal of the Arts
ARISTOS
Arjuna Library Press
Arnold & Johnson, Publishers
Arte Publico Press
ARTSLINK
Asylum Arts
Walter H. Baker Company (Baker's Plays)
BATHTUB GIN
BELLES LETTRES
THE BELLINGHAM REVIEW
Bilingual Review/Press
BkMk Press
BOMB MAGAZINE
Borealis Press Limited
BOTTOMFISH

Branden Publishing Company
Broken Boulder Press
Brownout Laboratories
Canterbury Press
CAVEAT LECTOR
Center for Japanese Studies
Center for South and Southeast Asian Studies Publications
CLASS ACT
Coldwater Press
Coteau Books
Cottonwood Press, Inc.
COVER MAGAZINE
DAEDALUS, Journal of the American Academy of Arts
    and Sciences
THE DALHOUSIE REVIEW
Dawn Sign Press
DESCANT
DIALOGOS: Hellenic Studies Review
THE DIRTY GOAT
Dolphin-Moon Press
Dovehaven Press
Drama Publishers
Dramaline Publications
DRAMATIKA
Empire Publishing Service
ENGLISH LITERATURE IN TRANSITION, 1880-1920
THE EUGENE O'NEILL REVIEW
EVANSVILLE REVIEW
THE EVERGREEN CHRONICLES
Fall Creek Press
Gallopade International
GEORGE & MERTIE'S PLACE: Rooms With a View
Golden Eagle Press
GRAFFITI OFF THE ASYLUM WALLS
GRAIN
Griffon House Publications
Host Publications, Inc.
Howling Dog Press/Stiletto
IRISH LITERARY SUPPLEMENT
Irvington St. Press, Inc.
JOURNAL OF AESTHETICS AND ART CRITICISM
JOURNAL OF ALASKA WOMEN
THE KENYON REVIEW
Labor Arts Books
Left Hand Books
LEO Productions LLC.
LINQ
THE LITERARY QUARTERLY
THE LOUISIANA REVIEW
Lowy Publishing
Marathon International Book Company
MARK
Mellen Poetry Press
Midmarch Arts Press
MINISTRY & LITURGY
NEOTROPE
New Sins Press
Nextstep Books
Nightsun Books
NWI National Writers Institute
OBSIDIAN II: BLACK LITERATURE IN REVIEW
OXYGEN
THE PACIFIC REVIEW
Passeggiata Press, Inc.
PHOEBE: A JOURNAL OF LITERARY ARTS
PIG IRON
Players Press, Inc.
POEMS & PLAYS
Poetry Wales Press, Ltd.
Bern Porter Books
POTOMAC REVIEW
THE POTTERSFIELD PORTFOLIO
PRISM INTERNATIONAL
Questex Consulting Ltd.
RAMBUNCTIOUS REVIEW
Resource Publications, Inc.
Ridgeway Press of Michigan
THE ROCKFORD REVIEW

Ronsdale Press
The Runaway Spoon Press
SALOME: A Journal for the Performing Arts
THE SHAKESPEARE NEWSLETTER
SKYLARK
Slate Press
Smyrna Press
SO TO SPEAK
SOUTHERN QUARTERLY: A Journal of the Arts in the
  South
Spectrum Productions
SPINNING JENNY
STILETTO
STRUGGLE: A Magazine of Proletarian Revolutionary
  Literature
Studio Editions
SYCAMORE REVIEW
Ten Penny Players, Inc.
THEATER
THEATRE DESIGN AND TECHNOLOGY
32 PAGES
THE UNIT CIRCLE
University of Massachusetts Press
Valentine Publishing & Drama Co.
Vesta Publications Limited
WordWorkers Press
Writers Forum
Xenos Books

DREAMS

AFFAIR OF THE MIND: A Literary Quarterly
AMERICAN WRITING: A Magazine
ANAIS: An International Journal
Asylum Arts
AXE FACTORY REVIEW
Baker Street Publications
THE CATBIRD SEAT
Conari Press
Coteau Books
CRONE CHRONICLES: A Journal of Conscious Aging
The Crossing Press
Deerbridge Books
DREAM INTERNATIONAL QUARTERLY
DREAM NETWORK JOURNAL
DREAM SCENE MAGAZINE
DREAM WHIP
THE EMSHOCK LETTER
GEORGE & MERTIE'S PLACE: Rooms With a View
The Golden Sufi Center
GRAFFITI OFF THE ASYLUM WALLS
Innisfree Press
INTUITIVE EXPLORATIONS
J & L Publications
H J Kramer
Lao Tse Press, Ltd.
The Leaping Frog Press
LITERARY ROCKET
Llewellyn Publications
Lunar Offensive Publications
THE MAD FARMERS' JUBILEE ALMANACK
MARGIN: EXPLORING MODERN MAGICAL REA-
  LISM
MESECHABE: The Journal of Surre(gion)alism
META4: Journal of Object Oriented Poetics (OOPS)
MetaGnosis
METAL CURSE
THE METAPHYSICAL REVIEW
MYSTIC VOICES
New Spirit Press/The Poet Tree
THE NOCTURNAL LYRIC
NYX OBSCURA MAGAZINE
PARADOX
Philopsychy Press
PLAIN BROWN WRAPPER (PBW)
RAG SHOCK
RALPH'S REVIEW
REALM OF THE VAMPIRE
RED OWL

Reyes Investment Enterprise Ltd.
St. Georges Press
THE SALEM JOURNAL
SHAMAN'S DRUM: A Journal of Experiential Shaman-
  ism
SHORT FUSE
SHRIKE
Sigo Press
SOM Publishing, division of School of Metaphysics
SOMNIAL TIMES
SPIRIT TO SPIRIT
THE SPITTING IMAGE
STONES IN MY POCKET
SUPER TROUPER
Three Pyramids Publishing
THRESHOLDS JOURNAL
TRANSMOG
Venus Communications
Verity Press Publishing
THE VINCENT BROTHERS REVIEW
VIRTUTE ET MORTE MAGAZINE
WRITER'S GUIDELINES: A Roundtable for Writers and
  Editors
WRITER'S WORKSHOP REVIEW

DRUGS

Addicus Books, Inc.
AFFABLE NEIGHBOR
Affable Neighbor Press
AFFAIR OF THE MIND: A Literary Quarterly
THE AFFILIATE
Alegra House Publishers
ANT ANT ANT ANT ANT
ATL Press, Inc.
Black Forest Press
Chandler & Sharp Publishers, Inc.
THE CIVIL ABOLITIONIST
Civitas
Consumer Press
Devil Mountain Books
DOPE FRIENDS
EAP DIGEST
FELL SWOOP
Fisher Books
GATEAVISA
Global Options
GRAFFITI OFF THE ASYLUM WALLS
GRANULATED TUPPERWARE
GRAY AREAS
Haight-Ashbury Publications
Health Press
HOAX!
Human Kinetics Pub. Inc.
Hyacinth House Publications/Caligula Editions
JACK MACKEREL MAGAZINE
JOURNAL OF PSYCHOACTIVE DRUGS
The Leaping Frog Press
LIES MAGAZINE
LOVE AND RAGE, A Revolutionary Anarchist News-
  paper
Lunar Offensive Publications
MESECHABE: The Journal of Surre(gion)alism
METAL CURSE
NEW AGE PATRIOT
Newjoy Press
Paladin Enterprises, Inc.
PEACE, The Magazine of the Sixties
Phony Lid Publications
R & E Publishers
RAG SHOCK
Red Alder Books
Red Eye Press
Rowhouse Press
RUBBER DUCKY MAGAZINE
SCIENCE/HEALTH ABSTRACTS
Skidmore-Roth Publishing, Inc.
SMART DRUG NEWS
SOCIAL JUSTICE: A JOURNAL OF CRIME, CON-

FLICT, & WORLD ORDER
Station Hill Press
Steamshovel Press
STEAMSHOVEL PRESS
Steel Balls Press
STREET VOICE
TEENS IN MOTION NEWS
Tyro Publishing
URBAN GRAFFITI
VAGABOND
VIRTUTE ET MORTE MAGAZINE
WISEBLOOD

BOB DYLAN

Abiko Literary Press (ALP)
and books
EXCLAIM!
FURTHER TOO
GEORGE & MERTIE'S PLACE: Rooms With a View
GRAY AREAS
Limelight Editions
MAIN STREET JOURNAL
STEAMSHOVEL PRESS

EARTH, NATURAL HISTORY

ADIRONDAC
Adirondack Mountain Club, Inc.
AFFAIR OF THE MIND: A Literary Quarterly
Alaska Geographic Society
Alaska Northwest Books
Alpine Publications, Inc.
America West Publishers
AMERICAN FORESTS
AMERICAN HIKER
American Hiking Society
American Malacologists, Inc.
THE ANIMALS' AGENDA
APPALACHIA JOURNAL
AQUATERRA, METAECOLOGY & CULTURE
ASC NEWSLETTER
ATL Press, Inc.
BAJA SUN
Baker Street Publications
Beacon Press
Bliss Publishing Company, Inc.
THE BOOKWATCH
Borderland Sciences Research Foundation
BORDERLANDS: A Quarterly Journal Of Borderland
    Research
The Boxwood Press
Caliban Press
Camino Bay Books
Capra Press
The Carnation Press
Catamount Press
Chelsea Green Publishing Company
Child's Play
China Books & Periodicals, Inc.
Civitas
CJE NEWS (Newsletter of the Coalition for Jobs & the
    Environment)
Clover Park Press
Continuing Education Press
COTYLEDON
Dawn Publications
Desert Oasis Publishing Co.
Dimi Press
Dog-Eared Publications
EBB AND FLOW
Elliott & Clark Publishing
ETC Publications
EXIT 13 MAGAZINE
EZ Nature Books
Falcon Press Publishing Company
Five Corners Publications, Ltd.
Flower Press
GEORGE & MERTIE'S PLACE: Rooms With a View

The Globe Pequot Press
GRASS ROOTS
Great Elm Press
Green Eagle Press
GREEN WORLD: News and Views For Gardening Who
    Care About The Earth
Heartsong Books
Heyday Books
Hollis Publishing Company
Homestead Publishing
Inner Traditions International
Island Press
Michael Kesend Publishing, Ltd.
KIDSCIENCE
LAKE SUPERIOR MAGAZINE
The Latona Press
Lester Street Publishing
Light, Words & Music
LLEWELLYN'S NEW WORLDS OF MIND AND
    SPIRIT
MANOA: A Pacific Journal of International Writing
McDonald & Woodward Publishing Company
Milkweed Editions
MIXED BAG
Mountain Press Publishing Co.
The Mountaineers Books
Multi Media Arts
NATURE SOCIETY NEWS
Naturegraph Publishers, Inc.
THE NAUTILUS
New England Cartographics, Inc.
NEW THOUGHT JOURNAL
North Country Books, Inc.
Northern Rim Press
Oregon State University Press
Pangaea
Paper Chase Press
Philopsychy Press
Pineapple Press, Inc.
Pygmy Forest Press
Quarterly Committee of Queen's University
QUEEN'S QUARTERLY: A Canadian Review
Red Crane Books, Inc.
Ridge Times Press
Sand River Press
Sasquatch Books
Sea Challengers, Inc.
Sierra Club Books
SKINNYDIPPING
SKYWRITERS
Genny Smith Books
Gibbs Smith, Publisher
SNOWY EGRET
SOUTH AMERICAN EXPLORER
George Sroda, Publisher
Stained Glass Press
Stemmer House Publishers, Inc.
Stone Wall Press, Inc
Synapse-Centurion
Tiger Moon
Timber Press
Timberline Press
Tortilla Press
THE TOWNSHIPS SUN
Treasure Chest Books LLC
University of Calgary Press
University of Massachusetts Press
Weidner & Sons, Publishing
WHOLE EARTH
THE WILD FOODS FORUM
Williamson Publishing Company, Inc.
Wisconsin Trails
Witwatersrand University Press
Wood Thrush Books
WORLD RAINFOREST REPORT
YUWITAYA LAKOTA
Z MAGAZINE
Zagier & Urruty Publicaciones

EASTERN EUROPE

Full Moon Publications
JACK MACKEREL MAGAZINE
MESECHABE: The Journal of Surre(gion)alism
THE NEW PRESS LITERARY QUARTERLY
Papillon Publishing
Rowhouse Press

ECOLOGY, FOODS

ADIRONDAC
THE AFFILIATE
The Alternate Press
AMERICAN FORESTS
Anaphase II
Androgyne Books
THE ANIMALS' AGENDA
APPALACHIA JOURNAL
APPALACHIAN HERITAGE
AQUATERRA, METAECOLOGY & CULTURE
Ash Tree Publishing
BAJA SUN
Baker Street Publications
Beacon Press
Bear & Company, Inc.
Beekman Publishers, Inc.
Black Rose Books Ltd.
Bliss Publishing Company, Inc.
Blue Dolphin Publishing, Inc.
THE BOOKWATCH
Bookworm Publishing Company
BORDERLANDS: A Quarterly Journal Of Borderland
    Research
The Boxwood Press
Briarwood Publishing
Bull Publishing Co.
CAPITALISM, NATURE, SOCIALISM
Capra Press
Cassandra Press, Inc.
Catamount Press
Center for South and Southeast Asian Studies Publications
Chelsea Green Publishing Company
China Books & Periodicals, Inc.
City Lights Books
THE CIVIL ABOLITIONIST
Civitas
CJE NEWS (Newsletter of the Coalition for Jobs & the
    Environment)
COMMUNITY DEVELOPMENT JOURNAL
Consumer Education Research Center
Continuing Education Press
The Crossing Press
Culinary Arts Ltd.
Dawn Publications
Devin-Adair Publishers, Inc.
Dog-Eared Publications
DWELLING PORTABLY
EBB AND FLOW
ECOLOGY LAW QUARTERLY
ENVIRONMENTAL & ARCHITECTURAL PHENO-
    MENOLOGY NEWSLETTER
ETC Publications
Flower Press
Foghorn Press
GATEAVISA
THE GENTLE SURVIVALIST
Geraventure
GRASS ROOTS
Great Elm Press
GREEN ANARCHIST
GREEN FUSE POETRY
Hope Publishing House
Inner Traditions International
Institute for Southern Studies
Island Press
JAPANOPHILE
JEWISH VEGETARIAN NEWSLETTER
KICK IT OVER

Kivaki Press
La Alameda Press
THE LATHAM LETTER
The Latona Press
Lester Street Publishing
Lexikos
Library Research Associates
LITTLE FREE PRESS
LIVING OFF THE LAND, Subtropic Newsletter
LOVE AND RAGE, A Revolutionary Anarchist News-
    paper
MACROBIOTICS TODAY
Macrocosm USA, Inc.
MESECHABE: The Journal of Surre(gion)alism
THE MILITANT
MIND MATTERS REVIEW
MIXED BAG
More To Life Publishing
MYSTIC VOICES
NATURAL LIFE
Naturegraph Publishers, Inc.
NEW FRONTIER
New Spirit Press/The Poet Tree
NEW THOUGHT JOURNAL
NightinGale Resources
THE NORTH AMERICAN REVIEW
NUTRITION ACTION HEALTHLETTER
George Ohsawa Macrobiotic Foundation
ONE EARTH
Oregon State University Press
OUT YOUR BACKDOOR: The Magazine of Informal
    Adventure and Cheap Culture
Panjandrum Books
Peavine Publications
Petroglyph Press, Ltd.
Pineapple Press, Inc.
Polar Bear Productions & Company
Royal Purcell, Publisher
Pygmy Forest Press
QECE: QUESTION EVERYTHING. CHALLENGE
    EVERYTHING.
R & M Publishing Company
RADICAL AMERICA
RAIN MAGAZINE
Rama Publishing Co.
The Rateavers
Red Crane Books, Inc.
RED OWL
Reyes Investment Enterprise Ltd.
Rossi
SAGEWOMAN
Sandpiper Press
Sanguinaria Publishing
SCIENCE/HEALTH ABSTRACTS
Sierra Club Books
Silvercat Publications
The Smallest County Press
Southwest Research and Information Center
SPECTRUM—The Wholistic News Magazine
SPROUTLETTER
Stillpoint Publishing
Strawberry Patchworks
Survival News Service
Synapse-Centurion
Times Change Press
THE TOWNSHIPS SUN
TRANSITIONS ABROAD: The Guide to Living,
    Learning, and Working Overseas
TURNING THE TIDE: A Journal of Anti-Racist
    Activism, Research & Education
Twin Peaks Press
THE UNDERGROUND FOREST - LA SELVA SUB-
    TERRANEA
United Lumbee Nation
UNITED LUMBEE NATION TIMES
University of Calgary Press
Upper Access Inc.
VEGETARIAN JOURNAL

The Vegetarian Resource Group
THE VINCENT BROTHERS REVIEW
VINEGAR CONNOISSEURS INTERNATIONAL NEWSLETTER
WHOLE EARTH
Wide World Publishing/TETRA
THE WILD FOODS FORUM
Williamson Publishing Company, Inc.
Wise Owl Press
Woodbridge Press
THE WORKBOOK
WORLD RAINFOREST REPORT
Z MAGAZINE

EDITING

Aletheia Publications, Inc.
BAST Media, Inc.
Brenner Information Group
CLASS ACT
THE EDITORIAL EYE
EPM Publications, Inc.
Eros Publishing
ETCETERA
FOOD WRITER
Gan Publishing
THE GREAT BLUE BEACON
THE HELIOCENTRIC WRITER'S NETWORK
INTERCULTURAL WRITERS REVIEW
THE NEW PRESS LITERARY QUARTERLY
PEN & INK WRITERS JOURNAL
READERS SPEAK OUT!
Strata Publishing, Inc.
The Times Journal Publishing Co.
WRITER'S CAROUSEL
WRITER'S WORKSHOP REVIEW

EDUCATION

Accent on Music
Access Multimedia
Acclaim Publishing Co. Inc.
Adirondack Mountain Club, Inc.
AERO-GRAMME
Afcom Publishing
African American Images
Alaska Geographic Society
Alaska Native Language Center
Alicubi Publications
AltaMira Press
The Alternate Press
ALT-J: Association for Learning Technology Journal
AMBASSADOR REPORT
American Audio Prose Library (non-print)
The American Dissident
Anubian Press
APPALACHIAN HERITAGE
AQUATERRA, METAECOLOGY & CULTURE
Arch Grove Press
Arjay Associates
ARTSLINK
Ash Grove Press
Ash Lad Press
Associated Writing Programs
ATL Press, Inc.
Autumn Publishing Group, LLC.
B & B Publishing, Inc.
Bayhampton Publications
Between The Lines
BILINGUAL REVIEW/Revista Bilingue
Black Forest Press
Blue Bird Publishing
Blue Dolphin Publishing, Inc.
Bluestocking Press
Bold Productions
Bonus Books, Inc.
THE BOOK REPORT: Journal for Junior & Senior High School Librarians
Books for All Times, Inc.
BOOMERANG! MAGAZINE

Bowerdean Publishing Co. Ltd.
The Boxwood Press
BRAIN/MIND BULLETIN, Bulletin of Breakthroughs
Branden Publishing Company
Briarwood Publishing
Brick Row Publishing Co. Ltd.
Bright Ring Publishing, Inc.
Brook Farm Books
BUENO
Business Smarts, Inc.
Caddo Gap Press
Canadian Educators' Press
Canterbury Press
Capital Communications
CATECHUMENATE: A Journal of Christian Initiation
Center for Public Representation
Chandler & Sharp Publishers, Inc.
CHILDREN'S LITERATURE IN EDUCATION
Child's Play
Circumpolar Press
CLASS ACT
THE CLASSICAL OUTLOOK
COMMUNITY DEVELOPMENT JOURNAL
Community Resource Institute Press
Community Service, Inc.
COMMUNITY SERVICE NEWSLETTER
Computer Press
Conscious Living
Construction Trades Press
Consumer Education Research Center
Continuing Education Press
CORRECTIONS TODAY
Cottonwood Press, Inc.
Council For Indian Education
CPG Publishing Company
Creative Concern Publications
CROSS ROADS
Cucumber Island Storytellers
Cypress Publishing Group, Inc.
D.B.A. Books
DAEDALUS, Journal of the American Academy of Arts and Sciences
Dawn Publications
Dawn Sign Press
DAYSPRING
Discovery Enterprises, Ltd.
Doctors Press, Inc.
Dovehaven Press
DREAM NETWORK JOURNAL
Easel Publishing Corporation
Edge Publishing
EduCare Press
THE EDUCATION DIGEST
EDUCATION IN FOCUS
EDUCATIONAL FOUNDATIONS
EDUCATIONAL LEADERSHIP & ADMINISTRATION
Empire Publishing Service
THE EMSHOCK LETTER
Energeia Publishing, Inc.
ETC Publications
ETR Associates
EUROPEAN JUDAISM
EXCEPTIONALITY EDUCATION CANADA
The Feminist Press at the City College
Fisher Books
Five Star Publications
Flower Press
Four Seasons Publishing
FREE INQUIRY
Free Spirit Publishing Inc.
Friendly Oaks Publications
Front Row Experience
Gallaudet University Press
Gallopade International
Gan Publishing
Gazelle Publications
GCT Inc.
GEORGE & MERTIE'S PLACE: Rooms With a View

Gifted Education Press/The Reading Tutorium
Grade School Press
Grayson Bernard Publishers, Inc.
Green Stone Publications
Greencrest Press
GROWING WITHOUT SCHOOLING
Gryphon House, Inc.
Guarionex Press Ltd.
Heartsong Books
Highsmith Press
HIP MAMA
HISTORY NEWS
Holistic Education Press
HOLISTIC EDUCATION REVIEW
Hollis Publishing Company
HOME EDUCATION MAGAZINE
Hoover Institution Press
Hope Publishing House
House of the 9 Muses, Inc.
Human Kinetics Pub. Inc.
THE HUMANIST
Hunter House Inc., Publishers
ICA Publishing
Image Industry Publications
Impact Publishers, Inc.
In One Ear Publications
THE INCLUSION NOTEBOOK
The Independent Institute
THE INDEPENDENT REVIEW: A Journal of Political
    Economy
INFUSION
INNOVATING
Institute for Southern Studies
Intercultural Press, Inc.
INTERCULTURE
Interface Press
Intermountain Publishing
INTERVENTION IN SCHOOL AND CLINIC
J P Publications
Jalmar Press
Jamenair Ltd.
THE JOURNAL OF DESIGN AND TECHNOLOGY
    EDUCATION
JOURNAL OF TEACHING IN PHYSICAL EDUCA-
    TION (JTPE)
JOURNAL OF THOUGHT
K.T. Publications
Kells Media Group
Kettering Foundation
KETTERING REVIEW
KIDSCIENCE
Kodiak Media Group
H J Kramer
Lamp Light Press
THE LATHAM LETTER
LIBRARY TALK: The Magazine for Elementary School
    Librarians
Linworth Publishing, Inc.
Listen and Learn Home Education, Inc.
Log Cabin Publishers
THE LONG TERM VIEW: A Journal of Informed
    Opinion
LUMMOX JOURNAL
LUNO
Macrocosm USA, Inc.
The Madson Group, Inc.
Magical Music Express
Manta Press
Masefield Books
Massey-Reyner Publishing
Maupin House
MCS Publishing
MCT - MULTICULTURAL TEACHING
Metamorphous Press
Miles River Press
Milkweed Editions
MIND MATTERS REVIEW
MINISTRY & LITURGY

MIXED BAG
Monroe Press
Morning Glory Press
Mountain Meadow Press
Multi Media Arts
MULTICULTURAL EDUCATION
NAR Publications
NATURAL LIFE
The Neo Herramann Group
NEW ART EXAMINER
New Canaan Publishing Company Inc.
The New Humanity Press
New View Publications
NOTES AND ABSTRACTS IN AMERICAN AND
    INTERNATIONAL EDUCATION
Nova Press
Nunciata
Open Court Publishing
OPEN EXCHANGE MAGAZINE
Open University of America Press
OPTIMA Books
OPTIONS IN LEARNING
Organization for Equal Education of the Sexes, Inc.
Our Schools/Our Selves
OUR SCHOOLS/OUR SELVES
The Overmountain Press
PACIFIC ENTERPRISE
PALO ALTO REVIEW
Parabola
Parenting Press, Inc.
Parkway Publishers, Inc.
Partners In Publishing
Pennycorner Press
Photo Data Research
Pine Publications
The Place In The Woods
Players Press, Inc.
Playground Books
THE PLOUGH
Pocket of Sanity
Poetry Wales Press, Ltd.
PPT EXPRESS
Prakken Publications
The Press at Foggy Bottom
Prometheus Enterprises, Inc.
Royal Purcell, Publisher
Purple Finch Press
QED
Quarterly Committee of Queen's University
QUEEN'S QUARTERLY: A Canadian Review
QUEST
R & E Publishers
R & M Publishing Company
RADIANCE, The Magazine For Large Women
Rama Publishing Co.
Raven Rocks Press
Real Life Storybooks
Redbird Press, Inc.
Reference Desk Books
Reference Service Press
Nancy Renfro Studios, Inc.
REPORTS OF THE NATIONAL CENTER FOR
    SCIENCE EDUCATION
RESEARCH IN HIGHER EDUCATION
RESOURCES FOR FEMINIST RESEARCH/DOCU-
    MENTATION SUR LA RECHERCHE FEMINISTE
Roof Publishing Company
Rowan Mountain Press
ST. CROIX REVIEW
Sandcastle Publishing
The Saunderstown Press
Scarecrow Press
Scentouri, Publishing Division
Sea Challengers, Inc.
Sea Fog Press, Inc.
Selah Publishing
SKEPTICAL INQUIRER
Small Helm Press

SMART DRUG NEWS
SOCIAL POLICY
The Speech Bin, Inc.
STONE SOUP, The Magazine By Young Writers and
Artists
Storytime Ink International
Success Publishing
Sherwood Sugden & Company, Publishers
SUMMER ACADEME: A Journal of Higher Education
TEACHER EDUCATION QUARTERLY
TEACHER LIBRARIAN: The Journal for School Library
Professionals
Teachers & Writers Collaborative
TEACHERS & WRITERS MAGAZINE
TEACHING ELEMENTARY PHYSICAL EDUCATION
(TEPE)
TECH DIRECTIONS
TEXAS YOUNG WRITERS' NEWSLETTER
THRESHOLDS JOURNAL
Tilbury House, Publishers
TIME PILOT
Trentham Books
THE TRUTH SEEKER
TURNING THE TIDE: A Journal of Anti-Racist
Activism, Research & Education
TURNING WHEEL
21ST CENTURY AFRO REVIEW
Two Eagles Press International
Tyro Publishing
UNION RECORDER
UNITED LUMBEE NATION TIMES
University of Calgary Press
University of Massachusetts Press
THE URBAN REVIEW
VanderWyk & Burnham
Via God Publishing
Vista Publishing, Inc.
VITAE SCHOLASTICAE: The Journal of Educational
Biography
THE WASHINGTON MONTHLY
Waterfront Books
WE INTERNATIONAL (formerly WOMEN AND EN-
VIRONMENTS)
WELSH JOURNAL OF EDUCATION
Westgate Publishing & Entertainment, Inc.
WHOLE EARTH
Willendorf Press
Williamson Publishing Company, Inc.
B. L. Winch & Associates
Witwatersrand University Press
WOMEN'S STUDIES QUARTERLY
World Music Press
Wright-Armstead Associates
WRITER'S CHRONICLE
WRITER'S GUIDELINES: A Roundtable for Writers and
Editors
Z MAGAZINE
Z W L Publishing, Inc.

EGYPT

Inner Traditions International

ELECTRONICS

Access Multimedia
Acting World Books
AD/VANCE
AFRICAN AMERICAN REVIEW
AFTERIMAGE
THE AGENCIES-WHAT THE ACTOR NEEDS TO
KNOW
Allworth Press
APHRODITE GONE BERSERK
Arden Press, Inc.
ART CALENDAR
ART PAPERS
ATROCITY
Autonomedia, Inc.
Axiom Information Resources

BAKER STREET GAZETTE
Baker Street Publications
Bancroft Press
THE BENT
Between The Lines
BLACK MOON MAGAZINE
Black Moon Publishing
BLACK TALENT NEWS (The Entertainment Industry
Publication for African Americans)
BLK
Blue Arrow Books
BOMB MAGAZINE
BORDERLANDS: A Quarterly Journal Of Borderland
Research
CAMERA OBSCURA: Feminism, Culture, and Media
Studies
Children Of Mary
Child's Play
CINEASTE MAGAZINE
CLASS ACT
Communicom Publishing Company
Companion Press
COVER MAGAZINE
Creatures At Large Press
Crescent Moon
CULTUREFRONT
THE DALHOUSIE REVIEW
dbS Productions
THE DIRTY GOAT
DOUBLE BILL
DRASTIC LIVES
Empty Closet Enterprises, Inc.
Excalibur Publishing Inc.
FIDELIS ET VERUS
FILM
FILM QUARTERLY
FILM SCORE MONTHLY
Film-Video Publications
THE FREEDONIA GAZETTE
FULL MOON DIRECTORY
Full Moon Publications
Future Horizons, Inc.
The Future Press
GAUNTLET: Exploring the Limits of Free Expression
GEORGE & MERTIE'S PLACE: Rooms With a View
Goodheart-Willcox Publisher
GRAY AREAS
THE HAUNTED JOURNAL
THE HOLLYWOOD ACTING COACHES AND
TEACHERS DIRECTORY
Hollywood Film Archive
HORIZONS BEYOND
Host Publications, Inc.
THE HUNTED NEWS
INFORMATION ENTREPRENUER
IRIS: A Journal About Women
THE J MAN TIMES
JACK MACKEREL MAGAZINE
JACK THE RIPPER GAZETTE
THE JOE BOB REPORT
JOURNAL OF AESTHETICS AND ART CRITICISM
JOURNAL OF MODERN LITERATURE
JUMP CUT, A Review of Contemporary Media
Lake View Press
THE LAS VEGAS INSIDER
LEFT CURVE
Leyland Publications
LIGHTWORKS MAGAZINE
Limelight Editions
Lone Eagle Publishing Co.
LOVING ALTERNATIVES MAGAZINE
MACHINEGUN MAGAZINE: New Lit. Quarterly
McPherson & Company Publishers
MEANJIN
MEDIA SPOTLIGHT
META4: Journal of Object Oriented Poetics (OOPS)
METAL CURSE
THE METAPHYSICAL REVIEW

METASEX
Midmarch Arts Press
MIXED BAG
MOVIE CLUB
N-B-T-V
NEW ART EXAMINER
The New Humanity Press
NEW ORLEANS REVIEW
NEW THOUGHT JOURNAL
NIGHTSHADE
NOBODADDIES
NOCTURNAL REPORTER
Norton Coker Press
OUR TWO CENTS
THE OVERLOOK CONNECTION
P & K Stark Productions, Inc.
Palm Drive Publishing
PASSION
PAST TIMES: The Nostalgia Entertainment Newsletter
Pennycorner Press
Pittore Euforico
PLAIN BROWN WRAPPER (PBW)
POINT OF CONTACT
POW-WOW
Prudhomme Press
REAL PEOPLE
Really Great Books
REALM OF THE VAMPIRE
Reference Desk Books
Rhizome
Rowhouse Press
ST. LOUIS JOURNALISM REVIEW
THE SALEM JOURNAL
SALMAGUNDI
SALON: A Journal of Aesthetics
SF COMMENTARY
SHEMP! The Lowlife Culture Magazine
Slate Press
SLEUTH JOURNAL
THE SMALL PRESS BOOK REVIEW
Sonoran Publishing
SOUND PRACTICES
SOUTHERN QUARTERLY: A Journal of the Arts in the
   South
SOUTHWEST JOURNAL
STAGNANCY IS REVOLTING
Starbooks Press/FLF Press
Strawberry Hill Press
STUDIO ART MAGAZINE
The Subourbon Press
THEATRE DESIGN AND TECHNOLOGY
THEY WON'T STAY DEAD!
Theytus Books Ltd.
THE THREEPENNY REVIEW
TRIVIUM
THE UNIT CIRCLE
Vestal Press Ltd
Via God Publishing
VIETNAM GENERATION: A Journal of Recent History
   and Contemporary Issues
THE VINCENT BROTHERS REVIEW
Visa Books (Division of South Continent Corporation Pty
   Ltd)
WESTERN SKIES
WOMEN ARTISTS NEWS BOOK REVIEW
WORLD OF FANDOM MAGAZINE
YUWITAYA LAKOTA

EMPLOYMENT

Adolfo Street Publications
Autumn Publishing Group, LLC.
Black Forest Press
Bookhaven Press, LLC
Brenner Information Group
THE CARETAKER GAZETTE
CJE NEWS (Newsletter of the Coalition for Jobs & the
   Environment)
CORRECTIONS TODAY

CPG Publishing Company
Cyclone Books
Cypress Publishing Group, Inc.
Edge Publishing
Galen Press, Ltd.
Global Sports Productions, Ltd.
Golden Eagle Press
GRAFFITI OFF THE ASYLUM WALLS
Harvard Common Press
Information Research Lab
Jamenair Ltd.
Job Search Publishers
Manta Press
Parabola
Planning/Communications
Prakken Publications
Pro-Guides, Professional Guides Publications
Resolution Business Press, Inc.
The Saunderstown Press
Ticket to Adventure, Inc.
21ST CENTURY AFRO REVIEW
URBAN GRAFFITI
WRITER'S WORKSHOP REVIEW
Z MAGAZINE

ENERGY

aatec publications
The Alternate Press
Anti-Aging Press
AQUATERRA, METAECOLOGY & CULTURE
AUTO-FREE TIMES
Blue Dolphin Publishing, Inc.
Borderland Sciences Research Foundation
BORDERLANDS: A Quarterly Journal Of Borderland
   Research
The Borgo Press
The Boxwood Press
Capra Press
CJE NEWS (Newsletter of the Coalition for Jobs & the
   Environment)
DESIGN BOOK REVIEW
DWELLING PORTABLY
ELECTRIC VEHICLE NEWS
Emerald Ink Publishing
The Film Instruction Company of America
HIGH COUNTRY NEWS
Home Power, Inc.
HOME POWER MAGAZINE
Hope Publishing House
Institute for Southern Studies
Island Press
Macrocosm USA, Inc.
The Message Company
RED OWL
RESONANCE
SJL Publishing Company
THE SMALL POND MAGAZINE OF LITERATURE
   aka SMALL POND
Southwest Research and Information Center
SYNERJY: A Directory of Renewable Energy
University of Calgary Press
Visions Communications
THE WASHINGTON MONTHLY
THE WORKBOOK
XIB
Xib Publications
YUWITAYA LAKOTA

ENGINEERING

ADVANCES IN THE ASTRONAUTICAL SCIENCES
Aegean Publishing Company
AQUATERRA, METAECOLOGY & CULTURE
ATL Press, Inc.
Bayley & Musgrave
Borderland Sciences Research Foundation
BORDERLANDS: A Quarterly Journal Of Borderland
   Research
Brenner Information Group

Construction Trades Press
CONTACT!
THE COOPERATOR
GLASS AUDIO
HOBSON'S CHOICE
N-B-T-V
Pendaya Publications, Inc.
Quale Press
SCIENCE AND TECHNOLOGY
SJL Publishing Company
Univelt, Inc.
University of Calgary Press
Visions Communications
Wind River Institute Press/Wind River Broadcasting

ENGLAND

Baker Street Publications
CLASS ACT
THE EDGE CITY REVIEW
FURTHER TOO
GEORGE & MERTIE'S PLACE: Rooms With a View
GREEN ANARCHIST
KELTIC FRINGE
LABOUR & TRADE UNION REVIEW
THE LONSDALE - The International Quarterly of The
    Romantic Six
MIXED BAG
NEW HOPE INTERNATIONAL REVIEW
THE NEW PRESS LITERARY QUARTERLY
NightinGale Resources
North Stone Press
PLUME
Pride & Imprints
PULSAR
QED
RED OWL
RhwymBooks
Stewart Publishing & Printing
Three Pyramids Publishing
WHITECHAPEL JOURNAL

ENGLISH

American Audio Prose Library (non-print)
ANQ: A Quarterly Journal of Short Articles, Notes, and
    Reviews
APOSTROPHE: USCB Journal of the Arts
Arjay Associates
Bandanna Books
BLACKWATER
Bliss Publishing Company, Inc.
Borealis Press Limited
BREAKFAST ALL DAY
THE CENTENNIAL REVIEW
Chandler & Sharp Publishers, Inc.
Child's Play
CIMARRON REVIEW
CLASS ACT
COLLEGE ENGLISH
Cottonwood Press, Inc.
The F. Marion Crawford Memorial Society
CREATIVE NONFICTION
THE DALHOUSIE REVIEW
DAYSPRING
THE DIRTY GOAT
THE EDGE CITY REVIEW
THE EDITORIAL EYE
FAULTLINE, Journal of Art and Literature
FISH DRUM MAGAZINE
Fjord Press
FURTHER TOO
The Future Press
Galaxy Press
Gallaudet University Press
Gallopade International
GEORGE & MERTIE'S PLACE: Rooms With a View
Teri Gordon, Publisher
GRANTA
Green Stone Publications

H & C NEWSLETTER
Host Publications, Inc.
House of the 9 Muses, Inc.
In One Ear Publications
THE IOWA REVIEW
JOURNAL OF AESTHETICS AND ART CRITICISM
JOURNAL OF NARRATIVE THEORY
LA PERIPHERIE
Light, Words & Music
LULLWATER REVIEW
Maupin House
MEANJIN
MERLYN'S PEN: Fiction, Essays, and Poems By
    America's Teens
Miles & Miles
Multi Media Arts
THE NEBRASKA REVIEW
THE NEW CRITERION
THE NEW ENGLAND QUARTERLY
NEW HOPE INTERNATIONAL REVIEW
THE NEW PRESS LITERARY QUARTERLY
NOTES & QUERIES
PANOPTICON
Pennsylvania State University Press
POINT OF CONTACT
THE PRAIRIE JOURNAL OF CANADIAN LITERA-
    TURE
Prairie Journal Press
The Purchase Press
Purple Finch Press
REPRESENTATIONS
SALMAGUNDI
SALT LICK
SCRIVENER
Scrivenery Press
SEWANEE REVIEW
THE SHAKESPEARE NEWSLETTER
SHAW: THE ANNUAL OF BERNARD SHAW STU-
    DIES
Station Hill Press
Studia Hispanica Editors
Sherwood Sugden & Company, Publishers
SYCAMORE REVIEW
SYMPLOKE: A Journal for the Intermingling of Literary,
    Cultural and Theoretical Scholarship
Telos Press
University of Calgary Press
VIETNAM GENERATION: A Journal of Recent History
    and Contemporary Issues
THE VINCENT BROTHERS REVIEW
THE VIRGINIA QUARTERLY REVIEW
George Wahr Publishing Company
Waterfront Books
Weidner & Sons, Publishing
Witwatersrand University Press
The Wordtree
WRITER'S CAROUSEL
THE YALE REVIEW
Z W L Publishing, Inc.

ENTERTAINMENT

Acting World Books
THE AFFILIATE
AFRICAN AMERICAN AUDIOBOOK REVIEW
THE AGENCIES-WHAT THE ACTOR NEEDS TO
    KNOW
AK Press
ATROCITY
Axiom Information Resources
BAJA SUN
Baker Street Publications
BLACK TALENT NEWS (The Entertainment Industry
    Publication for African Americans)
BLK
Bonus Books, Inc.
THE BOOMERPHILE
Briarwood Publishing
CADENCE: THE REVIEW OF JAZZ & BLUES:

CREATIVE IMPROVISED MUSIC
Carson Street Publishing Inc.
Celebrity Profiles Publishing
CIN-DAV, Inc.
CREEPY MIKE'S OMNIBUS OF FUN
Cyclone Books
THE DROPLET JOURNAL
Empire Publishing Service
Empty Closet Enterprises, Inc.
THE EMSHOCK LETTER
Enthea Press
Excalibur Publishing Inc.
Feral House
Film-Video Publications
FLIPSIDE
FULL MOON DIRECTORY
Full Moon Publications
GEORGE & MERTIE'S PLACE: Rooms With a View
GOLD COAST NEWS
GRAFFITI OFF THE ASYLUM WALLS
Halo Books
THE HAUNTED JOURNAL
HOAX!
THE HOLLYWOOD ACTING COACHES AND
    TEACHERS DIRECTORY
HOLLYWOOD NOSTALGIA
THE J MAN TIMES
JAM RAG
KMJ Educational Programs
LOVING ALTERNATIVES MAGAZINE
MEDIA SPOTLIGHT
METAL CURSE
METASEX
MIXED BAG
MOBILE BEAT: The DJ Magazine
Monitor Publications AR
Mustang Publishing Co.
NIGHTLORE
NIGHTSHADE
THE OFFICIAL MCCALLUM OBSERVER
Open Horizons Publishing Company
PAST TIMES: The Nostalgia Entertainment Newsletter
Peachtree Publishers, Ltd.
Piccadilly Books
PLAY THE ODDS
Players Press, Inc.
REAL PEOPLE
REALM OF THE VAMPIRE
Rio Grande Press
RUBBER DUCKY MAGAZINE
SALOME: A Journal for the Performing Arts
SANDPOINT MAGAZINE
SE LA VIE WRITER'S JOURNAL
SLAM!
Sparkling Diamond Paperbacks
STAGNANCY IS REVOLTING
Starbooks Press/FLF Press
Strawberry Hill Press
Swan Publishing Company
TIME PILOT
TRADITION
Vestal Press Ltd
Words & Pictures Press
WORLD OF FANDOM MAGAZINE
WRESTLING - THEN & NOW
Wynn Publishing
YE OLDE NEWES
Z W L Publishing, Inc.

ENVIRONMENT

ADIRONDAC
AFTERTHOUGHTS
AK Press
The Alternate Press
AMERICAN HIKER
American Hiking Society
THE ANIMALS' AGENDA
AUTO-FREE TIMES

Beacon Press
THE BEAR DELUXE
The Benefactory, Inc.
Blue Bird Publishing
Blue Reef Publications, Inc.
Book Peddlers
Bookhaven Press, LLC
BORDERLINES
The Brookfield Reader
THE CARETAKER GAZETTE
CARIBBEAN NEWSLETTER
Catamount Press
Ceres Press
CHRONICLE OF COMMUNITY
Civitas
Comparative Sedimentology Lab.
THE COOL TRAVELER
Coreopsis Books
COTYLEDON
Dawn Publications
Ecopress
ELECTRONIC GREEN JOURNAL
Envirographics
ENVIRONMENT AND ART LETTER
ENVIRONMENTAL & ARCHITECTURAL PHENO-
    MENOLOGY NEWSLETTER
FARMING UNCLE
FOURTH WORLD REVIEW
Fulcrum, Inc.
GATEAVISA
GEORGE & MERTIE'S PLACE: Rooms With a View
GREEN ANARCHIST
Green Eagle Press
GREEN WORLD: News and Views For Gardening Who
    Care About The Earth
Heartsong Books
HIGH COUNTRY NEWS
Hollis Publishing Company
The Independent Institute
THE INDEPENDENT REVIEW: A Journal of Political
    Economy
INTERCULTURAL WRITERS REVIEW
Island Press
JAM RAG
Kali Press
Keokee Co. Publishing, Inc.
KICK IT OVER
Kumarian Press, Inc.
LAKE SUPERIOR MAGAZINE
LITTLE FREE PRESS
LONE STAR SOCIALIST
MANOA: A Pacific Journal of International Writing
The Media Institute
Mercury House
MIXED BAG
Moon Publications, Inc.
Naturegraph Publishers, Inc.
NEW AGE PATRIOT
New England Cartographics, Inc.
NEW ENVIRONMENT BULLETIN
NEW FRONTIER
New Star Books Ltd.
NEW THOUGHT JOURNAL
North Country Books, Inc.
Northern Rim Press
PEACE, The Magazine of the Sixties
Phantom Press Publications
Pineapple Press, Inc.
PLEASANT LIVING
POTOMAC REVIEW
Pruett Publishing Company
QECE: QUESTION EVERYTHING. CHALLENGE
    EVERYTHING.
Questex Consulting Ltd.
QUESTION EVERYTHING CHALLENGE EVERY-
    THING (QECE)
RAIN MAGAZINE
RALPH'S REVIEW

Red Crane Books, Inc.
RED OWL
RESONANCE
Rising Tide Press New Mexico
THE RIVER
SEA KAYAKER
SHARE INTERNATIONAL
SIGNPOST FOR NORTHWEST TRAILS
SJL Publishing Company
SKINNYDIPPING
Gibbs Smith, Publisher
SOCIAL ANARCHISM: A Journal of Practice and Theory
South End Press
Stillpoint Publishing
Stone Wall Press, Inc
Sulisa Publishing
Synapse-Centurion
Theosophical Publishing House
Tilbury House, Publishers
Timber Press
Tortilla Press
Tortuga Books
TOWARD FREEDOM
TRANSITIONS ABROAD: The Guide to Living, Learning, and Working Overseas
Two Eagles Press International
University of Calgary Press
University of Massachusetts Press
THE UNKNOWN WRITER
THE VINCENT BROTHERS REVIEW
WE INTERNATIONAL (formerly WOMEN AND ENVIRONMENTS)
WEBER STUDIES: Voices and Viewpoints of the Contemporary West
WHOLE EARTH
WHOLE TERRAIN - REFLECTIVE ENVIRONMENTAL PRACTICE
Wild Dove Studio and Press, Inc.
WILD DUCK REVIEW
WILD EARTH
WORLD RAINFOREST REPORT

EROTICA

Abiko Literary Press (ALP)
AC
AFFABLE NEIGHBOR
Affable Neighbor Press
AFFAIR OF THE MIND: A Literary Quarterly
THE AFFILIATE
Alicubi Publications
THE ANGRY THOREAUAN
ANT ANT ANT ANT ANT
APHRODITE GONE BERSERK
ART-CORE
ARTHUR'S COUSIN
Asylum Arts
ATROCITY
AXE FACTORY REVIEW
BabelCom, Inc.
THE BLOWFISH CATALOG
Blowfish Press
BONDAGE FANTASIES
BOUDOIR NOIR
(THE) BRAVE NEW TICK
BROWNBAG PRESS
BURNING CAR
THE CHEROTIC (r)EVOLUTIONARY
Chiron Press
CHIRON REVIEW
Circlet Press, Inc.
Cosmic Trend
THE DIRTY GOAT
Down There Press
DRASTIC LIVES
Dreamboy Books
Eidos
EIDOS: Sexual Freedom & Erotic Entertainment for

Consenting Adults
THE EMSHOCK LETTER
Eurotique Press
The Feathered Serpent
Feral House
FETISH BAZAAR
FUCK DECENCY
FURTHER TOO
GATEAVISA
Gay Sunshine Press, Inc.
GEORGE & MERTIE'S PLACE: Rooms With a View
GLB Publishers
THE GODDESS OF THE BAY
GRAFFITI OFF THE ASYLUM WALLS
GrapeVinePress
Host Publications, Inc.
THE HUNTED NEWS
Hyacinth House Publications/Caligula Editions
Inner Traditions International
INTERCULTURAL WRITERS REVIEW
JACK MACKEREL MAGAZINE
KOMIC FANTASIES
LA PERIPHERIE
Laocoon Books
Leyland Publications
LIBIDO: The Journal of Sex and Sensibility
LITERARY ROCKET
LONG SHOT
LOVING ALTERNATIVES MAGAZINE
LUMMOX JOURNAL
Lunar Offensive Publications
MESECHABE: The Journal of Surre(gion)alism
MIP Company
MUSE NATURA, A Sensual Journey of the Arts
MYSTIC VOICES
NEW HOPE INTERNATIONAL REVIEW
New Spirit Press/The Poet Tree
Nite-Owl Press
NORTHWOODS JOURNAL, A Magazine for Writers
OFF OUR BACKS
ON OUR BACKS MAGAZINE
Ophelia Editions
OXYGEN
Palm Drive Publishing
PARADOX
PARA*PHRASE
Parkhurst Press
PHOENIX MAGAZINE
Phoenix Press
PLAIN BROWN WRAPPER (PBW)
POEMS THAT THUMP IN THE DARK/SECOND GLANCE
The Press of the Third Mind
Pride & Imprints
PSYCHOTRAIN
RAG SHOCK
REALM OF THE VAMPIRE
Red Alder Books
RED OWL
REDEMPTION
Reyes Investment Enterprise Ltd.
Roam Publishing
Rowhouse Press
RUBBER DUCKY MAGAZINE
THE SALEM JOURNAL
Sheer Joy! Press
SHEILA-NA-GIG
SHORT FUSE
SKINNYDIPPING
Spectrum Press
SPIRIT TO SPIRIT
THE SPITTING IMAGE
SPSM&H
SQUARE ONE - A Magazine of Disturbing Fiction
STAGNANCY IS REVOLTING
THE BOBBY STAR NEWSLETTER
Starbooks Press/FLF Press
STILETTO

The Subourbon Press
SYMBIOTIC OATMEAL
SYNCOPATED CITY
Thunder Rain Publishing Corp.
TWISTED IMAGE NEWSLETTER
URBAN GRAFFITI
VAMPIRE NIGHTS
VIRTUTE ET MORTE MAGAZINE
X-it Press
YELLOW SILK: Journal Of Erotic Arts

ESSAYS

Abiko Literary Press (ALP)
THE ACORN
AERIAL
AFFAIR OF THE MIND: A Literary Quarterly
AFTERTHOUGHTS
Alicubi Publications
AMERICAN INDIAN CULTURE AND RESEARCH
    JOURNAL
American Indian Studies Center
AMERICAN JONES BUILDING & MAINTENANCE
AMERICAN LETTERS & COMMENTARY
AMERICAN LITERARY REVIEW
AMERICAN WRITING: A Magazine
Angelflesh Press
ARCHIPELAGO
ARISTOS
ART:MAG
Associated Writing Programs
Asylum Arts
ATELIER
AXE FACTORY REVIEW
Baker Street Publications
Bancroft Press
THE BAREFOOT POET: Journal of Poetry, Fiction,
    Essays, & Art
BARNABE MOUNTAIN REVIEW
BATHTUB GIN
THE BELLINGHAM REVIEW
BkMk Press
BLACK DIRT
BlackBox
Blue Heron Publishing, Inc.
BOGG
BORDERLANDS: Texas Poetry Review
BOTTOMFISH
Bright Hill Press
Broken Shadow Publications
Brownout Laboratories
BURNING CAR
Calypso Publications
Carolina Wren Press/Lollipop Power Books
Carrefour Press
CAVEAT LECTOR
Center for South and Southeast Asian Studies Publications
CHANTEH, the Iranian Cross Cultural Qu'ly
Chelsea Green Publishing Company
THE CHEROTIC (r)EVOLUTIONARY
CHICAGO STUDIES
CICADA
CIMARRON REVIEW
CLASS ACT
CLUTCH
Coffee House Press
CONFLUENCE
Confluence Press, Inc.
CONNECTICUT REVIEW
CONTEXT SOUTH
THE CREAM CITY REVIEW
CREATIVE NONFICTION
CRONE CHRONICLES: A Journal of Conscious Aging
Cynic Press
THE DALHOUSIE REVIEW
Devil Mountain Books
THE DIRTY GOAT
EASTGATE QUARTERLY REVIEW OF HYPERTEXT
THE EDGE CITY REVIEW

Edgewise Press
The Eighth Mountain Press
ELF: ECLECTIC LITERARY FORUM (ELF MAGA-
    ZINE)
EMERGING VOICES
ETCETERA
EVANSVILLE REVIEW
THE EVERGREEN CHRONICLES
Ex Machina Publishing Company
Exile Press
Factor Press
FAULTLINE, Journal of Art and Literature
The Feminist Press at the City College
FIRST DRAFT
Five Corners Publications, Ltd.
Five Fingers Press
FIVE FINGERS REVIEW
FkB Press
FLIPSIDE
FLYING HORSE
FODDERWING
FOLIO: A LITERARY JOURNAL
4*9*1: Neo-Immanentist/Sursymbolist-Imagination
FOURTH GENRE: EXPLORATIONS IN NONFICTION
Fromm International Publishing Corporation
Full Moon Publications
FURTHER TOO
Gaff Press
GAUNTLET: Exploring the Limits of Free Expression
Gay Sunshine Press, Inc.
GEORGE & MERTIE'S PLACE: Rooms With a View
THE GEORGIA REVIEW
THE GETTYSBURG REVIEW
Golden Eagle Press
GrapeVinePress
GULF COAST
H & C NEWSLETTER
THE HAUNTED JOURNAL
HAWAII PACIFIC REVIEW
HAWAI'I REVIEW
HAZEL GROVE MUSINGS
HEAVEN BONE MAGAZINE
Heaven Bone Press
Helicon Nine Editions
THE HIGGINSVILLE READER
HIP MAMA
HOBSON'S CHOICE
HOLLYWOOD NOSTALGIA
Honors Group
HORIZONS BEYOND
Host Publications, Inc.
THE HUNTED NEWS
Hyacinth House Publications/Caligula Editions
ICA Publishing
ICARUS WAS RIGHT
ICON
THE ICONOCLAST
IGNIS FATUUS REVIEW
Images For Media/Sesquin
IMPRINT, A LITERARY JOURNAL
Innisfree Press
INNOVATING
INTERCULTURAL WRITERS REVIEW
Ione Press
IRIS: A Journal About Women
Itidwitir Publishing
THE J MAN TIMES
JACK MACKEREL MAGAZINE
JACK THE RIPPER GAZETTE
JEWISH LIFE
THE JOURNAL OF AFRICAN TRAVEL-WRITING
KALEIDOSCOPE: INTERNATIONAL MAGAZINE OF
    LITERATURE, FINE ARTS, AND DISABILITY
KARMA LAPEL
KESTREL: A Journal of Literature and Art
Allen A. Knoll Publishers
Lakes & Prairies Press
LATINO STUFF REVIEW

THE LAUREL REVIEW
The Leaping Frog Press
LEAPINGS LITERARY MAGAZINE
LIGHT: The Quarterly of Light Verse
THE LISTENING EYE
LITERAL LATTE
THE LITERARY QUARTERLY
LONE STAR SOCIALIST
THE LONSDALE - The International Quarterly of The
  Romantic Six
Loonfeather Press
Lost Horse Press
THE LOWELL REVIEW
LUMMOX JOURNAL
LYNX EYE
MacMurray & Beck
MAIN STREET JOURNAL
MANOA: A Pacific Journal of International Writing
MANY MOUNTAINS MOVING
Marmot Publishing
MEANJIN
Mercury House
MESECHABE: The Journal of Surre(gion)alism
THE METAPHYSICAL REVIEW
MID-AMERICAN REVIEW
Missing Spoke Press
MIXED BAG
MOMMY AND I ARE ONE
MOOSE BOUND PRESS JOURNAL/NEWSLETTER
Mountain State Press
MUDLARK
MUSE NATURA, A Sensual Journey of the Arts
NANCY'S MAGAZINE
NATURAL BRIDGE
NEW DELTA REVIEW
NEW HOPE INTERNATIONAL REVIEW
THE NEW PRESS LITERARY QUARTERLY
THE NEW SOUTHERN SURREALIST REVIEW
New Spring Publications
NIGHTSHADE
NOCTURNAL REPORTER
NORTH CAROLINA LITERARY REVIEW
NORTHEAST
OASIS
Oasis Books
Oasis In Print
OFFICE NUMBER ONE
OLD CROW
THE ONSET REVIEW
Ortalda & Associates
OUR TWO CENTS
PACIFIC COAST JOURNAL
PALO ALTO REVIEW
THE PANNUS INDEX
PAPERPLATES
Parabola
Paris Press, Inc.
Passeggiata Press, Inc.
PEARL RIVER REVIEW
Pecan Grove Press
PEN & INK WRITERS JOURNAL
PenRose Publishing Company, Inc.
PEREGRINE
Permeable Press
Poetic License Press
Pogo Press, Incorporated
POTATO EYES
POTOMAC REVIEW
POTPOURRI: A Magazine of the Literary Arts
POW-WOW
PRAIRIE SCHOONER
The Press of the Nightowl
PRINCETON ARTS REVIEW
Pruett Publishing Company
Q ZINE
QUARTER AFTER EIGHT
QUESTION EVERYTHING CHALLENGE EVERY-
  THING (QECE)

RAIN TAXI REVIEW OF BOOKS
THE RAINTOWN REVIEW: A Forum for the Essayist's
  Art
THE RATIONAL FEMINIST
RATTAPALLAX
READERS SPEAK OUT!
REALM OF THE VAMPIRE
Red Crane Books, Inc.
Red Hen Press
RED ROCK REVIEW
REFLECTIONS
RHINO: THE POETRY FORUM
THE RIVER
Rose Alley Press
THE ROSWELL LITERARY REVIEW
S Press
Saint Mary's Press
St. Michael's Press
SALT HILL
SANDPOINT MAGAZINE
SANTA BARBARA REVIEW
Serena Bay Books
SEWANEE REVIEW
SFEST, LTD.
SHENANDOAH
SHORT FUSE
Signature Books
SKYLARK
Slough Press
The Smith (subsidiary of The Generalist Assn., Inc.)
THE SPIRIT THAT MOVES US
The Spirit That Moves Us Press, Inc.
SPIRIT TO SPIRIT
SPORT LITERATE, Honest Reflections on Life's Leisur-
  ely Diversions
SPOUT
Spout Press
SPSM&H
Steerforth Press, L.C.
Still Waters Poetry Press
Stones Point Press
STUDIO ONE
THE STYLUS
The Subourbon Press
SUITCASE: A Journal of Transcultural Traffic
SULPHUR RIVER LITERARY REVIEW
THE SUN, A MAGAZINE OF IDEAS
SYCAMORE REVIEW
THEATER
THIRD COAST
13TH MOON
32 PAGES
Tilbury House, Publishers
TURNSTILE
ULITARRA
THE UNIT CIRCLE
University of Massachusetts Press
URBAN GRAFFITI
THE VINCENT BROTHERS REVIEW
WAY STATION MAGAZINE
WEBER STUDIES: Voices and Viewpoints of the
  Contemporary West
The Wellsweep Press
WESTERN SKIES
WHELKS WALK REVIEW
White Pine Press
WHITECHAPEL JOURNAL
WILD EARTH
WIND
WINDOW PANES
Wood Thrush Books
WORDS OF WISDOM
WORLDLINKS - FRIENDSHIP NEWS
WRITER TO WRITER
WRITER'S CHRONICLE
Writers House Press
XAVIER REVIEW
YUWITAYA LAKOTA

ZUZU'S PETALS: QUARTERLY ONLINE

ETHICS

Aardvark Enterprises (A Division of Speers Investments Ltd.)
Acclaim Publishing Co. Inc.
AFFAIR OF THE MIND: A Literary Quarterly
THE AFFILIATE
THE ANIMALS' AGENDA
Baker Street Publications
Bandanna Books
BARNABE MOUNTAIN REVIEW
Beacon Press
CANADIAN JOURNAL OF PHILOSOPHY
CAPITALISM, NATURE, SOCIALISM
THE CHEROTIC (r)EVOLUTIONARY
CRONE CHRONICLES: A Journal of Conscious Aging
Wm.B. Eerdmans Publishing Co.
THE EMSHOCK LETTER
ETICA & CIENCIA
Free Spirit Publishing Inc.
FURTHER TOO
Galen Press, Ltd.
GATEAVISA
Genesis Publishing Company, Inc.
GEORGE & MERTIE'S PLACE: Rooms With a View
Heartsong Books
HOAX!
Humana Press
ICARUS WAS RIGHT
Images For Media/Sesquin
Itidwitir Publishing
JEWISH VEGETARIAN NEWSLETTER
KEREM: Creative Explorations in Judaism
THE LETTER PARADE
LIBERTY
LIVE AND LET LIVE
LOVE AND RAGE, A Revolutionary Anarchist Newspaper
Macrocosm USA, Inc.
MIXED BAG
Pipeline Press
POTOMAC REVIEW
THE RATIONAL FEMINIST
St. Michael's Press
Smyrna Press
Stone Wall Press, Inc
SYMPLOKE: A Journal for the Intermingling of Literary, Cultural and Theoretical Scholarship
TEENS IN MOTION NEWS
THE VINCENT BROTHERS REVIEW
VIRTUTE ET MORTE MAGAZINE
THE WISDOM CONSERVANCY NEWSLETTER
Writers House Press
XIB
Xib Publications
Zagier & Urruty Publicaciones

EUROPE

AFFAIR OF THE MIND: A Literary Quarterly
Bicycle Books (Publishing) Inc.
CIMARRON REVIEW
Citeaux Commentarii Cistercienses
CITEAUX: COMMENTARII CISTERCIENSES
CLASS ACT
THE COOL TRAVELER
Department of Romance Languages
THE DIRTY GOAT
EAST EUROPEAN POLITICS & SOCIETIES
GEORGE & MERTIE'S PLACE: Rooms With a View
GERMAN LIFE
Heron Press
Heyday Books
Host Publications, Inc.
THE JOURNAL OF HISTORICAL REVIEW
LA PERIPHERIE
LABOUR & TRADE UNION REVIEW
Lester Street Publishing

Midmarch Arts Press
The Mountaineers Books
Mustang Publishing Co.
THE NEW PRESS LITERARY QUARTERLY
NightinGale Resources
PASSAGER: A Journal of Remembrance and Discovery
PLUME
Thirteen Colonies Press
TOWARD FREEDOM
Travel Keys
Upney Editions
George Wahr Publishing Company
Zephyr Press

EUTHANASIA, DEATH

AFFABLE NEIGHBOR
Affable Neighbor Press
AFFAIR OF THE MIND: A Literary Quarterly
Baker Street Publications
Cherubic Press
CRONE CHRONICLES: A Journal of Conscious Aging
Dead Metaphor Press
FULL MOON DIRECTORY
Galen Press, Ltd.
GATEAVISA
GRAFFITI OFF THE ASYLUM WALLS
HEMLOCK TIMELINES
THE HUMANIST
JEWISH LIFE
LIVE AND LET LIVE
Lunar Offensive Publications
THE MONTHLY INDEPENDENT TRIBUNE TIMES JOURNAL POST GAZETTE NEWS CHRONICLE BULLETIN
MURDER CAN BE FUN
New Regency Publishing
NIGHTSHADE
THE NOCTURNAL LYRIC
NOCTURNAL REPORTER
PARADOX
RAG SHOCK
REALM OF DARKNESS
REALM OF THE VAMPIRE
THE SALEM JOURNAL
TIMELINES, Newsletter of the Hemlock Society U.S.A.
TURNING WHEEL
VAMPIRE NIGHTS
Westgate Press
WICKED MYSTIC

FAMILY

AAIMS Publishers
Aardvark Enterprises (A Division of Speers Investments Ltd.)
THE ACORN
THE AFFILIATE
African American Images
Al-Anon Family Group Headquarters, Inc.
Alegra House Publishers
The Alternate Press
AMERICAN JONES BUILDING & MAINTENANCE
American Source Books, a division of Impact Publishers
AT-HOME DAD
Autumn Publishing Group, LLC.
Avery Publishing Group, Inc.
Axelrod Publishing of Tampa Bay
BLU
Blue Sky Marketing, Inc.
Bolton Press
THE BOOMERPHILE
Bright Ring Publishing, Inc.
Carousel Press
CE CONNECTION COMMUNIQUE
Center for Public Representation
Chandler & Sharp Publishers, Inc.
Cherubic Press
Child's Play
Cold-Drill Books

Colophon House
Community Service, Inc.
COMMUNITY SERVICE NEWSLETTER
Conari Press
DOVETAIL: A Journal by and for Jewish/Christian Families
Dovetail Publishing
Elysian Hills Publishing Company, Inc.
Excalibur Publishing Inc.
FAMILY TIMES: The Newspaper for Chippewa Valley Parents
Family Works Publications
FIDEI DEFENSOR: JOURNAL OF CATHOLIC APO-LOGETICS
Fillmore Publishing Company
Fisher Books
Five Corners Publications, Ltd.
THE FORUM
Free Spirit Publishing Inc.
Front Row Experience
Future Horizons, Inc.
Gallopade International
Gan Publishing
GLEN BURNIELAND
Good Life Publishing
Goodheart-Willcox Publisher
Grade School Press
Greenlawn Press
Guarionex Press Ltd.
Gumbs & Thomas Publishers, Inc.
Halo Books
Harvard Common Press
HARVARD WOMEN'S LAW JOURNAL
Herald Press
HIP MAMA
HOME EDUCATION MAGAZINE
Hope Publishing House
Human Kinetics Pub. Inc.
Hunter House Inc., Publishers
Impact Publishers, Inc.
J. Mark Press
Jalmar Press
JOURNAL OF CHILD AND YOUTH CARE
Kivaki Press
LADYBUG, the Magazine for Young Children
Langmarc Publishing
LEO Productions LLC.
Liberty Bell Press & Publishing Co.
Log Cabin Manuscripts
Long Wind Publishing
The Love and Logic Press, Inc.
LOVING MORE
THE MASONIA ROUNDUP
Mayhaven Publishing
MESSAGES FROM THE HEART
Mills & Sanderson, Publishers
Missing Spoke Press
Monroe Press
Mountain Meadow Press
Naturist Foundation
NightinGale Resources
No Starch Press
NORTHWOODS JOURNAL, A Magazine for Writers
NOSTALGIA, A Sentimental State of Mind
The Olive Press Publications
OPTIONS IN LEARNING
Our Child Press
Parenting Press, Inc.
PenRose Publishing Company, Inc.
Perspectives Press
PLEASANT LIVING
THE PLOUGH
Quiet Tymes, Inc.
RADIANCE, The Magazine For Large Women
Rayve Productions Inc.
Rio Grande Press
Saint Mary's Press
SCIENCE/HEALTH ABSTRACTS

SILVER WINGS/MAYFLOWER PULPIT
Single Parent Press
Skinny Lamb Publishing Company
SKINNYDIPPING
Stillpoint Publishing
Strawberry Hill Press
Success Publishing
Summit Crossroads Press
Swan Publishing Company
TEENS IN MOTION NEWS
Terra Nova Press
Tide Book Publishing Company
Two Thousand Three Associates
VanderWyk & Burnham
Volcano Press, Inc
B. L. Winch & Associates
Wright-Armstead Associates

FANTASY, HORROR

ABERRATIONS
AC
Algol Press
Amador Publishers
American Literary Press Inc./Noble House
Anamnesis Press
Argo Press
ASTERISM: The Journal of Science Fiction, Fantasy, and Space Music
Baker Street Publications
BARDIC RUNES
Bereshith Publishing
BLACK MOON MAGAZINE
Black Moon Publishing
Black Tie Press
BLACKWATER
Booksplus of Maine
THE BOOKWATCH
The Borgo Press
Boulevard Books, Inc. Florida
Briarwood Publishing
Broken Mirrors Press
CHAOS FOR THE CREATIVE MIND
Chaos Warrior Productions
CLASS ACT
The F. Marion Crawford Memorial Society
Creatures At Large Press
DARK REGIONS: The Years Best Fantastic Fiction
DAYSPRING
The Design Image Group Inc.
DREAM INTERNATIONAL QUARTERLY
DREAMS AND NIGHTMARES
DREAMS OF DECADENCE: Vampire Poetry and Fiction
EASTGATE QUARTERLY REVIEW OF HYPERTEXT
ECLIPSE
Edgewood Press
Embassy Hall Editions
THE EMSHOCK LETTER
FELICITY
FLIPSIDE
Four Seasons Publishers
THE FRACTAL
FULL MOON DIRECTORY
Full Moon Publications
Galde Press, Inc.
GATEAVISA
GAUNTLET: Exploring the Limits of Free Expression
THE GENRE WRITER'S NEWS
THE GODDESS OF THE BAY
Gothic Press
GRAFFITI OFF THE ASYLUM WALLS
GRUE MAGAZINE
Gryphon Publications
THE HAUNTED JOURNAL
HAUNTS
HELIOCENTRIC NET/STIGMATA
HOBSON'S CHOICE
HOLLYWOOD NOSTALGIA

Conari Press
Coteau Books
THE CREATIVE WOMAN
Crescent Moon
CROSS ROADS
The Crossing Press
DAUGHTERS OF SARAH
DeeMar Communications
DOUBLE BILL
Down There Press
The Eighth Mountain Press
Empty Closet Enterprises, Inc.
THE FEMINIST BOOKSTORE NEWS
FEMINIST COLLECTIONS: A QUARTERLY OF WO-
    MEN'S STUDIES RESOURCES
FEMINIST LEGAL STUDIES
FEMINIST PERIODICALS: A CURRENT LISTING OF
    CONTENTS
The Feminist Press at the City College
FEMINIST STUDIES
FEMINIST VOICES NEWSJOURNAL
Four Walls Eight Windows
FRONTIERS: A Journal of Women Studies
FURTHER TOO
GATEAVISA
GAYELLOW PAGES
GEORGE & MERTIE'S PLACE: Rooms With a View
GIRLFRIENDS MAGAZINE
GLB Publishers
Golden Eagle Press
Golden Isis Press
GRAFFITI OFF THE ASYLUM WALLS
Guardian Press
HARVARD WOMEN'S LAW JOURNAL
HAZEL GROVE MUSINGS
HECATE'S LOOM - A Journal of Magical Arts
HERBAL CHOICE
HerBooks
HIP MAMA
Hohm Press
HOTHEAD PAISAN, HOMICIDAL LESBIAN TER-
    RORIST
H2SO4
HURRICANE ALICE
Hyacinth House Publications/Caligula Editions
HYPATIA: A Journal of Feminist Philosophy
ICARUS WAS RIGHT
III Publishing
Images For Media/Sesquin
Innisfree Press
Institute for Southern Studies
Interlink Publishing Group, Inc.
IRIS: A Journal About Women
ISSUES QUARTERLY
Itidwitir Publishing
Javelina Books
JEJUNE: america Eats its Young
JOURNAL OF AESTHETICS AND ART CRITICISM
KALLIOPE, A Journal of Women's Art
KICK IT OVER
La Alameda Press
THE LETTER PARADE
LOVE AND RAGE, A Revolutionary Anarchist News-
    paper
LOVING ALTERNATIVES MAGAZINE
Macrocosm USA, Inc.
Maisonneuve Press
MANY MOUNTAINS MOVING
MATRIARCH'S WAY: The Journal of Female Supre-
    macy
MEANJIN
MESECHABE: The Journal of Surre(gion)alism
MICHIGAN FEMINIST STUDIES
Midmarch Arts Press
THE MILITANT
MIM NOTES: Offcial Newsletter of the Maoist Interna-
    tionalist Movement
MIND MATTERS REVIEW

THE MINNESOTA REVIEW
THE MOTHER IS ME: Profiling the Cultural Aspects of
    Motherhood
National Council for Research on Women
NEW BOOKS ON WOMEN & FEMINISM
THE NEW ENGLAND QUARTERLY
New Spring Publications
NewSage Press
OF A LIKE MIND
OFF OUR BACKS
ON OUR BACKS MAGAZINE
Organization for Equal Education of the Sexes, Inc.
PAGAN AMERICA
Palm Drive Publishing
Papier-Mache Press
Parabola
Paris Press, Inc.
Partisan Press
Passeggiata Press, Inc.
PASSION
PEACE, The Magazine of the Sixties
PenRose Publishing Company, Inc.
The Place In The Woods
Plus Publications
POINT OF CONTACT
QECE: QUESTION EVERYTHING. CHALLENGE
    EVERYTHING.
Queen of Swords Press
RADIANCE, The Magazine For Large Women
RADICAL AMERICA
THE RATIONAL FEMINIST
READERS SPEAK OUT!
Red Alder Books
Red Letter Press
Relief Press
RESOURCES FOR FEMINIST RESEARCH/DOCU-
    MENTATION SUR LA RECHERCHE FEMINISTE
RETHINKING MARXISM
ROCTOBER COMICS AND MUSIC
SAGEWOMAN
THE SALEM JOURNAL
Sanguinaria Publishing
Saqi Books Publisher
Scars Publications
Seal Press
SHEILA-NA-GIG
Sibyl Publications, Inc
Signature Books
SIGNS: JOURNAL OF WOMEN IN CULTURE AND
    SOCIETY
SINISTER WISDOM
SISTERS IN CRIME BOOKS IN PRINT
SISTERSONG: Women Across Cultures
SKINNYDIPPING
Smyrna Press
SO TO SPEAK
SOCIAL ANARCHISM: A Journal of Practice and
    Theory
SOJOURNER, THE WOMEN'S FORUM
South End Press
SPARE RIB
Spectrum Press
Spinsters Ink
STRUGGLE: A Magazine of Proletarian Revolutionary
    Literature
Sulisa Publishing
SYMBIOTIC OATMEAL
SYMPLOKE: A Journal for the Intermingling of Literary,
    Cultural and Theoretical Scholarship
Syracuse Cultural Workers/Tools for Change
Tesseract Publications
Theosophical Publishing House
Third Side Press, Inc.
13TH MOON
Times Change Press
TOWARD FREEDOM
Trilogy Books
TURNING THE TIDE: A Journal of Anti-Racist

Activism, Research & Education
THE UNFORGETTABLE FIRE
University of Massachusetts Press
Vanessapress
VIETNAM GENERATION: A Journal of Recent History
and Contemporary Issues
VIRTUTE ET MORTE MAGAZINE
VIVA PETITES
Volcano Press, Inc
Ward Hill Press
WE INTERNATIONAL (formerly WOMEN AND EN-
VIRONMENTS)
Whole Person Associates Inc.
Wild Dove Studio and Press, Inc.
Willendorf Press
THE WISE WOMAN
WOMEN ARTISTS NEWS BOOK REVIEW
WOMEN'S RESEARCH NETWORK NEWS
THE WOMEN'S REVIEW OF BOOKS
Women's Studies Librarian, University of Wisconsin
System
WOMEN'S WORK
WOMENWISE
WRITING FOR OUR LIVES
XY: Men, Sex, Politics
YEFIEF

FESTIVALS

Eureka Publishing Group
Film-Video Publications
HOLLYWOOD NOSTALGIA
HORIZONS BEYOND
JACK MACKEREL MAGAZINE
JARRETT'S JOURNAL
LADYBUG, the Magazine for Young Children
THE MAD FARMERS' JUBILEE ALMANACK
POW-WOW
Rowhouse Press
THE SALEM JOURNAL
SKINNYDIPPING
VIRTUTE ET MORTE MAGAZINE
WISCONSIN TRAILS
THE WISDOM CONSERVANCY NEWSLETTER
YE OLDE NEWES

FICTION

ABBEY
ABERRATIONS
Abiko Literary Press (ALP)
AC
Acclaim Publishing Co. Inc.
ACM (ANOTHER CHICAGO MAGAZINE)
ACME Press
THE ACORN
ACORN WHISTLE
Acrobat Books
Admiral House Publishing
Aegina Press, Inc.
AFFAIR OF THE MIND: A Literary Quarterly
African American Audio Press
AFRICAN AMERICAN AUDIOBOOK REVIEW
AFRICAN AMERICAN REVIEW
AGADA
Ageless Press
AGNI
THE AGUILAR EXPRESSION
AIM MAGAZINE
AK Press
ALABAMA LITERARY REVIEW
Alchemist/Light Publishing
Alicubi Publications
ALLEGHENY REVIEW
Alternating Crimes Publishing
Amador Publishers
AMBIT
AMELIA
Amelia Press
American Audio Prose Library (non-print)

American Indian Studies Center
AMERICAN JONES BUILDING & MAINTENANCE
AMERICAN LETTERS & COMMENTARY
American Literary Press Inc./Noble House
AMERICAN SHORT FICTION
AMERICAN WRITING: A Magazine
AMERICAS REVIEW
Amherst Press
Ana Libri Press
Andmar Press
Androgyne Books
ANGELFLESH
Angelflesh Press
Angst World Library
ANQ: A Quarterly Journal of Short Articles, Notes, and
Reviews
THE ANTHOLOGY OF NEW ENGLAND WRITERS
ANTIETAM REVIEW
THE ANTIGONISH REVIEW
THE ANTIOCH REVIEW
APOSTROPHE: USCB Journal of the Arts
Arch Grove Press
ARCHIPELAGO
Ariadne Press
Arjuna Library Press
ARNAZELLA
ART-CORE
Arte Publico Press
ARTFUL DODGE
Artifact Press, Ltd.
ART:MAG
Associated Writing Programs
Asylum Arts
ATELIER
ATLANTA REVIEW
ATOM MIND
ATROCITY
Austen Press
Author's Partner in Publishing
Avery Color Studios
Avisson Press, Inc.
Avocet Press Inc.
AXE FACTORY REVIEW
THE AZOREAN EXPRESS
The B & R Samizdat Express
The Bacchae Press
BAKER STREET GAZETTE
Baker Street Publications
Balboa Books
Bancroft Press
Bank Street Press
Banks Channel Books
Bardsong Press
THE BAREFOOT POET: Journal of Poetry, Fiction,
Essays, & Art
Barking Dog Books
BARNABE MOUNTAIN REVIEW
THE BEAR DELUXE
BEGINNINGS - A Magazine for the Novice Writer
BEHIND BARS
Belle Terre Press, Inc.
THE BELLINGHAM REVIEW
BELLOWING ARK
Bellowing Ark Press
BELOIT FICTION JOURNAL
BGB Press, Inc.
BIG SCREAM
Big Star Press
Bigwater Publishing
Bilingual Review/Press
Birdalone Books
BITTER OLEANDER
BkMk Press
Black Diamond Book Publishing
BLACK DIRT
Black Dress Press
Black Forest Press
Black Heron Press

BLACK ICE
BLACK JACK & VALLEY GRAPEVINE
BLACK MOON MAGAZINE
Black Moon Publishing
Black Sparrow Press
Black Thistle Press
THE BLACK WARRIOR REVIEW
BlackBox
BLACKWATER
BLOOD & APHORISMS: A Journal of Literary Fiction
Blue Arrow Books
Blue Bird Publishing
BLUE HORSE
Blue Horse Publications
BLUELINE
BOMB MAGAZINE
BONE & FLESH
Boog Literature
BOOGLIT
Books for All Times, Inc.
BOOKS FROM FINLAND
Booksplus of Maine
Borealis Press Limited
BOTH COASTS BOOK REVIEW
Bottom Dog Press
BOTTOMFISH
BOULEVARD
Boulevard Books, Inc. Florida
Branden Publishing Company
Briarwood Publishing
BrickHouse Books, Inc.
THE BRIDGE: A Journal of Fiction and Poetry
Bright Hill Press
THE BROBDINGNAGIAN TIMES
Broken Boulder Press
BROKEN PENCIL
BROWNBAG PRESS
Brownout Laboratories
PTOLEMY
THE BROWNS MILLS REVIEW
Brunswick Publishing Corporation
Buckhead Press
BUFFALO SPREE
Burning Books
BURNING CAR
Burning Cities Press
Burning Deck Press
Business Smarts, Inc.
BUTTON
BYLINE
Cadmus Editions
Caliban Press
Calypso Publications
Capra Press
THE CAROLINA QUARTERLY
Carolina Wren Press/Lollipop Power Books
Carpenter Press
Castle Peak Editions
Catbird Press
Cave Books
CAVEAT LECTOR
CAYO, A MAGAZINE OF LIFE IN THE KEYS
CC600
Celo Valley Books
Center for Japanese Studies
Center Press
Chandler & Sharp Publishers, Inc.
CHANTEH, the Iranian Cross Cultural Qu'ly
Chaos Warrior Productions
CHARITON REVIEW
CHELSEA
THE CHEROTIC (r)EVOLUTIONARY
Chicory Blue Press, Inc.
CHILDREN, CHURCHES AND DADDIES, A Non Religious, Non Familial Literary Magazine
Child's Play
China Books & Periodicals, Inc.
Chiron Press

CHIRON REVIEW
CICADA
CIMARRON REVIEW
CITIES AND ROADS: A Collection of Short Stories for North Carolina Readers and Writers.
City Lights Books
CITY PRIMEVAL
CLASS ACT
Cleis Press
CLOCKWATCH REVIEW
CLUTCH
Coffee House Press
Coker Publishing House
COLD-DRILL
COLORADO REVIEW: A Journal of Contemporary Literature
Commonwealth Press Virginia
Communication Creativity
Company of Words Publishing
CONFLUENCE
Confluence Press, Inc.
CONJUNCTIONS
CONNECTICUT REVIEW
Context Publications
Copper Beech Press
Coreopsis Books
Corona Publishing Co.
CORRECTIONS TODAY
Coteau Books
COTTONWOOD
Cottonwood Press
Council Oak Books
CRAB CREEK REVIEW
CRAB ORCHARD REVIEW
CRAZYHORSE
THE CREAM CITY REVIEW
Creative Concern Publications
CREATIVITY CONNECTION
Crime and Again Press
CRIPES!
CROSSCURRENTS, A QUARTERLY
Crossway Books
CRUCIBLE
Curbstone Press
CURMUDGEON
CURRENT ACCOUNTS
CUTBANK
Cypress House
D.D.B. Press
THE DALHOUSIE REVIEW
Dalkey Archive Press
John Daniel and Company, Publishers
Dawnwood Press
DAYSPRING
December Press
Deerbridge Books
Delta-West Publishing, Inc.
Depth Charge
DESCANT
DESCANT
The Design Image Group Inc.
DEVIL BLOSSOMS
DIALOGOS: Hellenic Studies Review
Paul Dilsaver, Publisher
DIRIGIBLE
THE DIRTY GOAT
DISTURBED GUILLOTINE
Dolphin-Moon Press
Down The Shore Publishing
Down There Press
DOWN UNDER MANHATTAN BRIDGE
DREAM INTERNATIONAL QUARTERLY
Dreamboy Books
THE DROPLET JOURNAL
Duckworth Press
Dufour Editions Inc.
Duval-Bibb Publishing Company
E.M. Press, Inc.

THE EAR
Earth Star Publications
EARTH'S DAUGHTERS: Feminist Arts Periodical
EASTGATE QUARTERLY REVIEW OF HYPERTEXT
Eau Gallie Publishing, Inc.
The Ecco Press
Ecrivez!
THE EDGE CITY REVIEW
The Eighth Mountain Press
ELF: ECLECTIC LITERARY FORUM (ELF MAGA-
ZINE)
ELT Press
EMERGING VOICES
THE EMSHOCK LETTER
ENTELECHY MAGAZINE
Enthea Press
EPOCH
Paul S. Eriksson, Publisher
Eros Publishing
ETCETERA
Eurotique Press
EVANSVILLE REVIEW
EVENT
Event Horizon Press
Ex Machina Publishing Company
Excalibur Publishing Inc.
Exile Press
Expanded Media Editions
EyeDEA Books
Far Corner Books
FAR GONE
FAT TUESDAY
FAULTLINE, Journal of Art and Literature
FC2/Black Ice Books
The Feathered Serpent
FELICITY
The Feminist Press at the City College
FICTION
FICTION FORUM
FICTION INTERNATIONAL
FICTION WRITER'S GUIDELINE
FIDEI DEFENSOR: JOURNAL OF CATHOLIC APO-
LOGETICS
FIGMENTS
The Figures
Filibuster Press
FINE MADNESS
FIRM NONCOMMITTAL: An International Journal of
Whimsy
First Amendment Press International Company
FIRST DRAFT
FIRST INTENSITY
FISH DRUM MAGAZINE
Fithian Press
Five Fingers Press
FIVE FINGERS REVIEW
FIVE POINTS
Fjord Press
FkB Press
Flatland Tales Publishing
FLIPSIDE
FLOATING ISLAND
Floating Island Publications
THE FLORIDA REVIEW
FLYING HORSE
FLYWAY
FODDERWING
FOLIO: A LITERARY JOURNAL
Four Seasons Publishers
Four Walls Eight Windows
FOURTEEN HILLS: The SFSU Review
FRANK: AN INTERNATIONAL JOURNAL OF CON-
TEMPORARY WRITING AND ART
Free People Press
FREEFALL
THE FROGMORE PAPERS
Fromm International Publishing Corporation
Frozen Waffles Press/Shattered Sidewalks Press; 45th

Century Chapbooks
FUEL MAGAZINE
FUGUE
Fugue State Press
Full Moon Publications
FURTHER TOO
The Future Press
The Galileo Press Ltd.
Gallaudet University Press
Gallopade International
GARGOYLE
GATEAVISA
GAUNTLET: Exploring the Limits of Free Expression
Gay Sunshine Press, Inc.
Genesis Publishing Company, Inc.
GEORGE & MERTIE'S PLACE: Rooms With a View
GEORGETOWN REVIEW
THE GEORGIA REVIEW
GERBIL: Queer Culture Zine
Gesture Press
THE GETTYSBURG REVIEW
GINOSKO
THE GLASS CHERRY
The Glass Cherry Press
GLB Publishers
The Glencannon Press
THE GODDESS OF THE BAY
Golden Eagle Press
Golden Grove Books
Golden Meteorite Press
GoldenIsle Publishers, Inc.
Gothic Press
GRAFFITI OFF THE ASYLUM WALLS
GRAIN
GRANTA
GRANULATED TUPPERWARE
GrapeVinePress
Graywolf Press
THE GREAT BLUE BEACON
GREAT RIVER REVIEW
THE GREEN HILLS LITERARY LANTERN
GREEN MOUNTAINS REVIEW
GREEN'S MAGAZINE
THE GREENSBORO REVIEW
Greensleeve Editions
Gryphon Publications
Guardian Press
GULF COAST
Haley's
HANGING LOOSE
Hanging Loose Press
Harbor House
Hard Press, Inc.
THE HAUNTED JOURNAL
HAWAII PACIFIC REVIEW
HAWAI'I REVIEW
Hawk Publishing Group
HAYDEN'S FERRY REVIEW
HEARTLAND (Australia)
HEAVEN BONE MAGAZINE
Heaven Bone Press
Helicon Nine Editions
HELIOCENTRIC NET/STIGMATA
HELLP!
Hellp! Press
Herald Press
Hermes House Press, Inc.
Hermitage (Ermitazh)
The Heyeck Press
Hi Jinx Press
THE HIGGINSVILLE READER
HIP MAMA
HOBSON'S CHOICE
HOLLYWOOD NOSTALGIA
Homa & Sekey Books
HOME PLANET NEWS
HOOTENANNY
HORIZONS BEYOND

HOR-TASY
Host Publications, Inc.
House of the 9 Muses, Inc.
Howling Dog Press/Stiletto
Howling Wolf Publishing
Howln Moon Press
H2SO4
THE HUNTED NEWS
Hutton Publications
Hyacinth House Publications/Caligula Editions
IBIS REVIEW
ICON
THE ICONOCLAST
IDIOM 23
IDIOT WIND
IGNIS FATUUS REVIEW
ILLUMINATIONS
IllumiNet Press
ILLYA'S HONEY
The Image Maker Publishing Co.
The Imaginary Press
IMPRINT, A LITERARY JOURNAL
Indelible Inc.
INDIANA REVIEW
The Infinity Group
INNER VOICES: A New Journal of Prison Literature
Insomniac Press
Institute for Southern Studies
INTERBANG
Intercontinental Publishing, Inc
INTERCULTURAL WRITERS REVIEW
INTERIM
THE INTERNATIONAL FICTION REVIEW
INTERNATIONAL QUARTERLY
Intrigue Press
Ione Press
THE IOWA REVIEW
IPSISSIMA VERBA/THE VERY WORDS: Fiction &
  Poetry in the First Person
IRIS: A Journal About Women
Ironweed Press
Irvington St. Press, Inc.
Italica Press, Inc.
Ithaca Press
THE J MAN TIMES
JACARANDA
JACK MACKEREL MAGAZINE
JACK THE RIPPER GAZETTE
Jaguar Books
J'ECRIS
Jesus Pinata Press
JEWISH LIFE
JOURNAL OF AESTHETICS AND ART CRITICISM
THE JOURNAL OF EXPERIMENTAL FICTION
JOURNAL OF MODERN LITERATURE
Journey Books Publishing
K.T. Publications
KALEIDOSCOPE: INTERNATIONAL MAGAZINE OF
  LITERATURE, FINE ARTS, AND DISABILITY
KARAMU
KARAWANE
KARMA LAPEL
Karmichael Press
Kawabata Press
THE KELSEY REVIEW
Kelsey St. Press
THE KENYON REVIEW
Michael Kesend Publishing, Ltd.
KESTREL: A Journal of Literature and Art
Allen A. Knoll Publishers
KOJA
KOOMA
Kozmik Press
H J Kramer
La Alameda Press
La Casa Press
LADYBUG, the Magazine for Young Children
LAKE SUPERIOR MAGAZINE

Lakes & Prairies Press
THE LAUREL REVIEW
Leapfrog Press
LEO Productions LLC.
Leyland Publications
Library Research Associates, Inc.
LIFTOUTS
LIGHT: The Quarterly of Light Verse
LIGHTHOUSE
LIMESTONE: A LITERARY JOURNAL
LINGO
LINQ
Lintel
THE LISTENING EYE
LITERAL LATTE
THE LITERARY QUARTERLY
LITERARY ROCKET
LITRAG
THE LITTLE MAGAZINE
Logodaedalus
LONDON FOG
London Fog Publishing
THE LONG STORY
THE LONSDALE - The International Quarterly of The
  Romantic Six
LOONFEATHER: A magazine of poetry, short prose, and
  graphics
Loonfeather Press
Lord John Press
Lost Prophet Press
THE LOUISIANA REVIEW
THE LOUISVILLE REVIEW
THE LOWELL REVIEW
LOWLANDS REVIEW
Low-Tech Press
LS Press, Inc.
LUCKY HEART BOOKS
LULLWATER REVIEW
Lunar Offensive Publications
THE MAC GUFFIN
MacAdam/Cage Publishing Inc.
MacMurray & Beck
THE MADISON REVIEW
MAGIC REALISM
MAIN STREET JOURNAL
Majestic Books
MANGROVE MAGAZINE
MANOA: A Pacific Journal of International Writing
MANY MOUNTAINS MOVING
March Street Press
MARGIN: EXPLORING MODERN MAGICAL REA-
  LISM
MARK
THE MARLBORO REVIEW
Marlton Publishers, Inc.
MASSACRE
MATI
Mayhaven Publishing
McGregor Publishing
McPherson & Company Publishers
MEANJIN
Meanjin
Mercury House
MERLYN'S PEN: Fiction, Essays, and Poems By
  America's Teens
Merrimack Books
Merwood Books
MESHUGGAH
Metacom Press
THE METAPHYSICAL REVIEW
Micah Publications Inc.
MID-AMERICAN REVIEW
Mid-List Press
Milkweed Editions
Mindfield Publications
MINIMUS
Minor Heron Press
MIP Company

Missing Spoke Press
MISSISSIPPI MUD
MISSISSIPPI REVIEW
MIXED BAG
MOMMY AND I ARE ONE
THE MONTHLY (formerly THE BERKELEY MONTH-
   LY)
MoonFall Press
MOONRABBIT REVIEW
Mortal Press
Mountain State Press
Munsey Music
MUSE NATURA, A Sensual Journey of the Arts
MUSHROOM DREAMS
Mustang Publishing Co.
MYSTERIOUS WYSTERIA
Mystery Notebook Editions
MYSTERY TIME ANTHOLOGY
Nada Press
National Woodlands Publishing Company
NATURAL BRIDGE
Naturegraph Publishers, Inc.
NEBO
THE NEBRASKA REVIEW
NEDGE
NEOTROPE
Neshui Publishing
NEW AMERICAN WRITING
NEW ANGLICAN REVIEW
NEW CATHOLIC REVIEW
NEW DELTA REVIEW
NEW ENGLAND REVIEW
NEW HOPE INTERNATIONAL REVIEW
The New Humanity Press
NEW LETTERS
NEW MUSE OF CONTEMPT
NEW ORLEANS REVIEW
THE NEW PRESS LITERARY QUARTERLY
New Rivers Press, Inc.
New Star Books Ltd.
NEW STONE CIRCLE
THE NEW WRITER
NEW YORK STORIES
Newmark Publishing Company
Nextstep Books
NIGHTSHADE
Nightshade Press
Nightsun Books
NIMROD INTERNATIONAL
NITE-WRITER'S   INTERNATIONAL   LITERARY
   ARTS JOURNAL
NOBODADDIES
THE NORTH AMERICAN REVIEW
North Stone Press
NORTHEAST
NORTHERN PILOT
NORTHRIDGE REVIEW
NORTHWEST REVIEW
Northwoods Press
NOTRE DAME REVIEW
NOVA EXPRESS
NOW AND THEN
NOW HERE NOWHERE
NWI National Writers Institute
The O Press
OASIS
Oasis Books
OBSIDIAN II: BLACK LITERATURE IN REVIEW
Off the Cuff Books
OFFICE NUMBER ONE
OLD CROW
THE OLD RED KIMONO
Ommation Press
THE ONSET REVIEW
Oolichan Books
Orchises Press
Orloff Press
Ortalda & Associates

Osric Publishing
OTHER VOICES
OUR TWO CENTS
Outer Space Press
OUTERBRIDGE
THE OVAL MAGAZINE
The Overmountain Press
Owl Creek Press
Oxford House Publishing
OYSTER BOY REVIEW
O!!ZONE, A LITERARY-ART ZINE
OZ-STORY
P & K Stark Productions, Inc.
PACIFIC ENTERPRISE
THE PACIFIC REVIEW
Pahsimeroi Press
Palari Publishing
Palm Drive Publishing
PALO ALTO REVIEW
THE PANHANDLER
THE PANNUS INDEX
PANURGE
THE PAPER BAG
The Paper Bag Press
PAPERPLATES
Papier-Mache Press
Papillon Publishing
PAPYRUS
Papyrus Literary Enterprises, Inc.
Parabola
Paris Press, Inc.
Parkhurst Press
PARTING GIFTS
PASSAGES NORTH
Passeggiata Press, Inc.
Passing Through Publications
Path Press, Inc.
Pathway Books
Pathways Press, Inc.
Paycock Press
Peachtree Publishers, Ltd.
Pearl River Press
PEARL RIVER REVIEW
Pearl-Win Publishing Co.
Peartree Books & Music
Pecan Grove Press
THE PEGASUS REVIEW
PEMBROKE MAGAZINE
PEN & INK WRITERS JOURNAL
Pendragonian Publications
Peninhand Press
PEREGRINE
The Permanent Press/The Second Chance Press
Permeable Press
Phantom Press Publications
PHOEBE: A JOURNAL OF LITERARY ARTS
Phrygian Press
Picaro Press
Picturesque Publications
PIEDMONT LITERARY REVIEW
PIG IRON
Pig Iron Press
Pinchgut Press
Pineapple Press, Inc.
PIRATE WRITINGS
PLAY THE ODDS
Playground Books
Pleasure Boat Studio
PLOT
PLOUGHSHARES
Pocahontas Press, Inc.
Poetic License Press
POETIC SPACE: Poetry & Fiction
POETRY EAST
POETRY MOTEL
Poetry Wales Press, Ltd.
POETS & WRITERS MAGAZINE
Polar Bear & Company

Portals Press
Portmanteau Editions
THE POST
The Post-Apollo Press
POTATO EYES
POTOMAC REVIEW
POTPOURRI: A Magazine of the Literary Arts
Pottersfield Press
Samuel Powell Publishing Company
PRAIRIE FIRE
THE PRAIRIE JOURNAL OF CANADIAN LITERA-
TURE
Prairie Journal Press
PRAIRIE SCHOONER
PRAIRIE WINDS
Preludium Publishers
PREP Publishing
PrePress Publishing of Michigan
PRESS
The Press at Foggy Bottom
The Press of the Nightowl
Prestige Publications
Pride & Imprints
Primal Publishing
PRIMAVERA
PRIME
PRINCETON ARTS REVIEW
PRISM INTERNATIONAL
Prudhomme Press
PSYCHOTRAIN
PTOLEMY/BROWNS MILLS REVIEW
Publishers Syndication Int'l (PSI)
Puckerbrush Press
THE PUCKERBRUSH REVIEW
PUERTO DEL SOL
PURPLE
Purple Finch Press
PURPLE PATCH
Pygmy Forest Press
Pyncheon House
Pyx Press
Q ZINE
QED Press
QUARTER AFTER EIGHT
QUARTERLY WEST
Queen of Swords Press
Questex Consulting Ltd.
Quiet Lion Press
THE QUILL MAGAZINE QUARTERLY
Rabeth Publishing Company
RAFTERS
RAG MAG
RAG SHOCK
RAIN CITY REVIEW
Ram Press
RAMBUNCTIOUS REVIEW
RATTAPALLAX
Ravenhawk Books
Real Life Storybooks
Really Great Books
REALM OF THE VAMPIRE
Red Alder Books
Red Cedar Press
RED CEDAR REVIEW
Red Crane Books, Inc.
Red Dust
Red Hen Press
REDOUBT
REFLECT
REFLECTIONS
THE REJECTED QUARTERLY
THE REVIEW OF CONTEMPORARY FICTION
Revive Publishing
RFD
RhwymBooks
Ridgeway Press of Michigan
Rio Grande Press
THE RIVER

RIVER CITY
RIVER STYX
Roam Publishing
THE ROCKFORD REVIEW
ROMANTIC HEARTS
Ronsdale Press
Rose Shell Press
ROSEBUD
THE ROSWELL LITERARY REVIEW
THE ROUND TABLE: A Journal of Poetry and Fiction
Rowhouse Press
Royal Print
Ryrich Publications
S Press
Sachem Press
Saddle Mountain Press
St. Andrews Press
St. Augustine Society Press
St. Georges Press
Saint Mary's Press
St. Michael's Press
SALAMANDER
THE SALEM JOURNAL
SALMAGUNDI
SALOME: A Journal for the Performing Arts
SALT HILL
Sandberry Press
Sandpiper Press
SANTA BARBARA REVIEW
Saqi Books Publisher
Sarabande Books, Inc.
Raymond Saroff, Publisher
Savant Garde Workshop
Scars Publications
Scherf, Inc./Scherf Books
SCRIVENER
Scrivenery Press
SE LA VIE WRITER'S JOURNAL
Seed Center
Seekers Press
SEEMS
SelectiveHouse Publishers, Inc.
Senior Press
SEPIA
Serena Bay Books
Serendipity Systems
Seven Buffaloes Press
SEWANEE REVIEW
SFEST, LTD.
SHADES OF DECEMBER
Shann Press
Shaolin Communications
Shearer Publishing
SHEILA-NA-GIG
SHENANDOAH
Shivam Publications
SHOCKBOX
SHORT FUSE
SIDEWALKS
Sierra Club Books
Signal Books
THE SIGNAL - Network International
Signature Books
Silver Mountain Press
Silver Phoenix Press
Silver Seahorse Press
SILVERFISH REVIEW
SING HEAVENLY MUSE! WOMEN'S POETRY AND
PROSE
SISTERSONG: Women Across Cultures
SKYLARK
Skyline Publications, Inc.
Slate Press
SLEUTH JOURNAL
SLIGHTLY WEST
A Slow Tempo Press
THE SMALL POND MAGAZINE OF LITERATURE
aka SMALL POND

SMALL PRESS CREATIVE EXPLOSION
The Smallest County Press
Smiling Dog Press
The Smith (subsidiary of The Generalist Assn., Inc.)
Gibbs Smith, Publisher
SMOKE
Smyrna Press
SNAKE RIVER REFLECTIONS
SNOWY EGRET
SO TO SPEAK
SONGS OF INNOCENCE
Sorenson Books
SOUNDINGS EAST
SOUTH CAROLINA REVIEW
SOUTH DAKOTA REVIEW
THE SOUTHERN CALIFORNIA ANTHOLOGY
SOUTHERN HUMANITIES REVIEW
THE SOUTHERN REVIEW
Southern Star Publishing
SOUTHWEST JOURNAL
SOUTHWEST REVIEW
SOU'WESTER
SPEAK UP
Spectrum Press
SPELUNKER FLOPHOUSE
Spillway Publications
SPINNING JENNY
Spinsters Ink
THE SPIRIT THAT MOVES US
The Spirit That Moves Us Press, Inc.
SPIRIT TO SPIRIT
SPITBALL: The Literary Baseball Magazine
THE SPITTING IMAGE
SPOUT
Spout Press
SPSM&H
SQUARE ONE - A Magazine of Disturbing Fiction
The Square-Rigger Press
STANDARD DEVIATIONS
STAPLE
Starbooks Press/FLF Press
StarLance Publications
State Street Press
Station Hill Press
Stemmer House Publishers, Inc.
STILETTO
Stones Point Press
Stormline Press, Inc.
STORY
Story County Books
STORYQUARTERLY
STOVEPIPE: A Journal of Little Literary Value
STRUGGLE: A Magazine of Proletarian Revolutionary
    Literature
Studia Hispanica Editors
STUDIO - A Journal of Christians Writing
STUDIO ONE
THE STYLUS
The Subourbon Press
SUB-TERRAIN
SUITCASE: A Journal of Transcultural Traffic
Sulisa Publishing
SULPHUR RIVER LITERARY REVIEW
THE SUN, A MAGAZINE OF IDEAS
Sun Dog Press
Swallow's Tale Press
Swan Publishing Company
Sweet Lady Moon Press
SYCAMORE REVIEW
SYMPLOKE: A Journal for the Intermingling of Literary,
    Cultural and Theoretical Scholarship
Synapse-Centurion
SYNCOPATED CITY
Tafford Publishing
TAKAHE
Tal San Publishing/Distributors
Talisman House, Publishers
TAPROOT LITERARY REVIEW

TEAK ROUNDUP
TEENS IN MOTION NEWS
Tell Publishing
Ten Star Press
A THEATER OF BLOOD
THEMA
Theytus Books Ltd.
THIN COYOTE
THIRD COAST
THE THIRD HALF
Third Side Press, Inc.
13TH MOON
32 PAGES
Thistledown Press Ltd.
THORNY LOCUST
THE THREEPENNY REVIEW
THRESHOLDS JOURNAL
Thunder & Ink
Thunder Rain Publishing Corp.
Tickerwick Publications
Tiger Moon
The Times Journal Publishing Co.
Tiptoe Literary Service
TitleWaves Publishing
Tombouctou Books
TOUCHSTONE LITERARY JOURNAL
TREASURE HOUSE
TRIQUARTERLY
Tryckeriforlaget
TUCUMCARI LITERARY REVIEW
Tudor Publishers, Inc.
TURNSTILE
Turnstone Press
The Twickenham Press
2.13.61 Publications
Tyro Publishing
ULITARRA
THE UNDERGROUND
THE UNIT CIRCLE
University Editions, Inc.
University of Massachusetts Press
UNIVERSITY OF WINDSOR REVIEW
URBAN GRAFFITI
URBANUS/RAIZIRR
Urion Press
US1 Poets' Cooperative
US1 WORKSHEETS
VACUITY
VAMPIRE NIGHTS
Vanitas Press
Vehicule Press
VERVE
Vesta Publications Limited
VICTORY PARK: THE JOURNAL OF THE NEW
    HAMPSHIRE INSTITUTE OF ART
THE VINCENT BROTHERS REVIEW
VIRGIN MEAT E-ZINE
VIRGINIA LITERARY REVIEW
VIRTUTE ET MORTE MAGAZINE
Vista Publishing, Inc.
VISUAL ASSAULT OMNIBUS
VOLITION
Vortex Editions
WASHINGTON REVIEW
Water Row Press
Wave Publishing
WAY STATION MAGAZINE
WEBER STUDIES: Voices and Viewpoints of the
    Contemporary West
WELLSPRING
The Wellsweep Press
West Anglia Publications
WEST BRANCH
WESTERN SKIES
Whelks Walk Press
WHELKS WALK REVIEW
WHETSTONE
The White Cross Press

THE WHITE CROW
White Pine Press
White Wolf Publishing
WIDENER REVIEW
WILLOW SPRINGS
Winchester/G. Ander Books
WIND
WINDOW PANES
Windsong Press
Wineberry Press
WISCONSIN REVIEW
WITNESS
Wolfhound Press
THE WORCESTER REVIEW
Words & Pictures Press
WORDS OF WISDOM
THE WORLD
WORMWOOD REVIEW
WRITER TO WRITER
The Writers Block, Inc.
WRITER'S CHRONICLE
WRITERS' FORUM
Writers Forum
WRITERS GAZETTE
WRITER'S GUIDELINES: A Roundtable for Writers and
  Editors
Writers House Press
WRITER'S LIFELINE
WRITER'S WORLD
WRITING FOR OUR LIVES
XAVIER REVIEW
Xenos Books
YEFIEF
YELLOW SILK: Journal Of Erotic Arts
Yggdrasil Books
Zero Hour Publishing
ZOETROPE: All-Story
ZUZU'S PETALS: QUARTERLY ONLINE

FINANCES

Acclaim Publishing Co. Inc.
Acton Circle Publishing Company
Adams-Hall Publishing
Advisory Press, Inc.
Allworth Press
ATL Press, Inc.
Autumn Publishing Group, LLC.
Bancroft Press
Bluestocking Press
Brittain Communications
Capital Communications
Career Advancement Center, Inc.
THE COOPERATOR
COPING WITH TURBULENT TIMES
Garrett Publishing, Inc.
Gemstone House Publishing
Golden Eagle Press
INNOVATING
MONEY LINES
MOTHER EARTH JOURNAL: An International Quar-
  terly
Naturegraph Publishers, Inc.
PACIFIC ENTERPRISE
Paladin Enterprises, Inc.
Prometheus Enterprises, Inc.
Rhino Publishing

F. SCOTT FITZGERALD

Abiko Literary Press (ALP)
CLASS ACT
GEORGE & MERTIE'S PLACE: Rooms With a View
LOST GENERATION JOURNAL

FLORIDA

Baker Street Publications
Blue Reef Publications, Inc.
CAYO, A MAGAZINE OF LIFE IN THE KEYS
Comparative Sedimentology Lab.

Full Moon Publications
GOLD COAST NEWS
HORIZONS
Karmichael Press
Light, Words & Music
Long Wind Publishing
MIXED BAG
The New Humanity Press
Palm Island Press
Pineapple Press, Inc.
Pogo Press, Incorporated
POW-WOW
Premium Press America
Starbooks Press/FLF Press
Tailored Tours Publications, Inc.
Tortuga Books
Two Thousand Three Associates
Valiant Press, Inc.

FOLKLORE

THE ACORN
ACORN WHISTLE
AFRICAN STUDIES
Alaska Native Language Center
AMERICAN WRITING: A Magazine
Ancient City Press
Ariko Publications
Avery Color Studios
THE AZOREAN EXPRESS
Baker Street Publications
Ballena Press
John F. Blair, Publisher
Booksplus of Maine
Borealis Press Limited
The Brookfield Reader
Celtic Heritage Books
Center for South and Southeast Asian Studies Publications
CHAFFIN JOURNAL
Children's Book Press
Child's Play
China Books & Periodicals, Inc.
CLASS ACT
Commonwealth Press Virginia
Confluence Press, Inc.
Coteau Books
Council For Indian Education
Creative With Words Publications (CWW)
THE DIRTY GOAT
THE DRAGON CHRONICLE
EXIT 13 MAGAZINE
Foundation Books
FREEFALL
Full Moon Publications
FURTHER TOO
Galde Press, Inc.
GEORGE & MERTIE'S PLACE: Rooms With a View
GRASS ROOTS
GREEN EGG
THE HAUNTED JOURNAL
HAZEL GROVE MUSINGS
Historical Dimensions Press
HOAX!
HORIZONS
Host Publications, Inc.
House of the 9 Muses, Inc.
Ice Cube Press
IMPRINT, A LITERARY JOURNAL
Inheritance Press Inc.
Institute for Southern Studies
INTUITIVE EXPLORATIONS
IRISH LITERARY SUPPLEMENT
Jolly Roger Press
JOURNAL OF AESTHETICS AND ART CRITICISM
Kar-Ben Copies, Inc.
KELTIC FRINGE
KESTREL: A Journal of Literature and Art
Allen A. Knoll Publishers
LADYBUG, the Magazine for Young Children

LAKE SUPERIOR MAGAZINE
LEO Productions LLC.
Lexikos
The Lockhart Press
LORE AND LANGUAGE
Lost Horse Press
Luna Bisonte Prods
MAGIC REALISM
Maledicta Press
MALEDICTA: The International Journal of Verbal
Aggression
MARGIN: EXPLORING MODERN MAGICAL REA-
LISM
THE MASONIA ROUNDUP
The Middle Atlantic Press
MIXED BAG
Museum of New Mexico Press
Nashville House
Naturegraph Publishers, Inc.
THE NEW PRESS LITERARY QUARTERLY
NEW THOUGHT JOURNAL
NightinGale Resources
NIGHTSHADE
NOCTURNAL REPORTER
North Country Books, Inc.
NORTHWOODS JOURNAL, A Magazine for Writers
The Olive Press Publications
Parabola
PARABOLA MAGAZINE
Passeggiata Press, Inc.
PenRose Publishing Company, Inc.
PERSPECTIVES
Petroglyph Press, Ltd.
Pineapple Press, Inc.
Pocahontas Press, Inc.
Pocket of Sanity
POEMS THAT THUMP IN THE DARK/SECOND
GLANCE
Poetry Wales Press, Ltd.
POTOMAC REVIEW
POW-WOW
The Press at Foggy Bottom
Pyx Press
Rainy Day Press
Rarach Press
REALM OF THE VAMPIRE
Red Crane Books, Inc.
Research & Discovery Publications
THE RIVER
Rockbridge Publishing Co.
ROCTOBER COMICS AND MUSIC
THE SALEM JOURNAL
Salina Bookshelf
SEMIOTEXT(E)
Serpent & Eagle Press
SHORT FUSE
Signal Books
SING OUT! The Folk Song Magazine
SKYLARK
SOCIETE
SOUTHWEST JOURNAL
SPIRIT TO SPIRIT
STRANGE MAGAZINE
Strawberry Hill Press
SYCAMORE ROOTS: New Native Americans
Top Of The Mountain Publishing
TRADITION
Transeuropa
Treasure Chest Books LLC
Two Dog Press
THE UNDERGROUND FOREST - LA SELVA SUB-
TERRANEA
United Lumbee Nation
UNITED LUMBEE NATION TIMES
VAMPIRE NIGHTS
Victory Press
THE VINCENT BROTHERS REVIEW
VIRTUTE ET MORTE MAGAZINE

WESTERN AMERICAN LITERATURE
WESTERN SKIES
Westgate Press
White Cliffs Media, Inc.
THE WILD FOODS FORUM
Wildstone Media
Williamson Publishing Company, Inc.
WISCONSIN TRAILS
Wisconsin Trails
Witwatersrand University Press
XCP: CROSS-CULTURAL POETICS
Yellow Moon Press
Yggdrasil Books

FORENSIC SCIENCE

AFFAIR OF THE MIND: A Literary Quarterly
Galen Press, Ltd.

FRANCE, FRENCH

AU NATUREL
Bicycle Books (Publishing) Inc.
Capital Communications
Carrefour Press
Catbird Press
The Chicot Press
Citeaux Commentarii Cistercienses
CITEAUX: COMMENTARII CISTERCIENSES
Department of Romance Languages
FRANK: AN INTERNATIONAL JOURNAL OF CON-
TEMPORARY WRITING AND ART
GATEAVISA
INTERNATIONAL POETRY REVIEW
THE J MAN TIMES
LA PERIPHERIE
LEO Productions LLC.
LOST GENERATION JOURNAL
THE NEW PRESS LITERARY QUARTERLY
NightinGale Resources
OSIRIS
PLUME
REVUE CELFAN REVIEW
Rio Grande Press
SE LA VIE WRITER'S JOURNAL
SERIE D'ECRITURE
Station Hill Press
Synergistic Press
TRANSITIONS ABROAD: The Guide to Living,
Learning, and Working Overseas

FUNDRAISING

Bonus Books, Inc.
Chardon Press
GRASSROOTS FUNDRAISING JOURNAL
JARRETT'S JOURNAL
Pineapple Press, Inc.

FUTURISM

AFFABLE NEIGHBOR
Affable Neighbor Press
Angst World Library
ASTERISM: The Journal of Science Fiction, Fantasy, and
Space Music
Astrion Publishing
Cambric Press dba Emerald House
COPING WITH TURBULENT TIMES
Devin-Adair Publishers, Inc.
DIRIGIBLE
DISSONANCE MAGAZINE
DWELLING PORTABLY
FARM PULP MAGAZINE
FELL SWOOP
THE FUTURIST
Gallopade International
GATEAVISA
GEORGE & MERTIE'S PLACE: Rooms With a View
Golden Eagle Press
Heartsong Books
HORIZONS BEYOND

THE HUMANIST
JACK MACKEREL MAGAZINE
KALDRON, An International Journal Of Visual Poetry
LITERARY ROCKET
LITTLE FREE PRESS
LOVING MORE
MAD SCIENTIST
Masefield Books
Media Arts Publishing
ON COURSE
PERSPECTIVES
PIG IRON
POEMS THAT THUMP IN THE DARK/SECOND
  GLANCE
Pride & Imprints
RALPH'S REVIEW
RED OWL
Rowhouse Press
Savant Garde Workshop
SHARE INTERNATIONAL
SQUARE ONE - A Magazine of Disturbing Fiction
Steamshovel Press
Stillpoint Publishing
Swan Raven & Company
Transeuropa
UNARIUS LIGHT JOURNAL
THE UNIT CIRCLE
VACUITY
Vortex Editions

GAELIC

Abiko Literary Press (ALP)
THE ABIKO QUARTERLY WITH JAMES JOYCE FW
  STUDIES
Celtic Heritage Books
CLASS ACT
The F. Marion Crawford Memorial Society
Elder Books
HAZEL GROVE MUSINGS
Kells Media Group
KELTIC FRINGE
Palm Drive Publishing
Poetry Ireland
POETRY IRELAND REVIEW
THE ROMANTIST
SPIRIT TO SPIRIT
Wolfhound Press

GALAPAGOS ISLANDS

Light, Words & Music
New World Publications, Inc.

GAMES

The Alternate Press
BLACKJACK FORUM
Bonus Books, Inc.
Capra Press
Cardoza Publishing
Carousel Press
Chess Enterprises
CHESS LIFE
Child's Play
CLASS ACT
Commonwealth Press Virginia
CON-TEMPORAL
Dawn Sign Press
Dead Metaphor Press
DISC GOLF WORLD NEWS
EN PASSANT
Explorer's Guide Publishing
Front Row Experience
FULL MOON DIRECTORY
Gallopade International
GEORGE & MERTIE'S PLACE: Rooms With a View
GRAFFITI OFF THE ASYLUM WALLS
GRAY AREAS
Guarionex Press Ltd.
HOAX!

HORIZONS BEYOND
Human Kinetics Pub. Inc.
Hunter House Inc., Publishers
Huntington Press
Impact Publishers, Inc.
Jolly Roger Press
LADYBUG, the Magazine for Young Children
Lawco Ltd./Moneytree Publications/Que-House
Liberty Publishing Company, Inc.
MEDIA SPOTLIGHT
Mustang Publishing Co.
Naturist Foundation
NORTH CAROLINA LITERARY REVIEW
Piccadilly Books
PLAY THE ODDS
Potentials Development, Inc.
The Preservation Press
R.G.E. Publishing
REALM OF THE VAMPIRE
THE SALEM JOURNAL
Salt Lick Press
Sandwich Islands Publishing
SCHOOL MATES
SJL Publishing Company
SLEUTH JOURNAL
TEACHING ELEMENTARY PHYSICAL EDUCATION
  (TEPE)
Trimarket
Zookeeper Publications

GARDENING

Acton Circle Publishing Company
Alaska Northwest Books
The Alternate Press
Andmar Press
Annedawn Publishing
Arizona Master Gardener Press
Baker Street Publications
Banks Channel Books
Barnegat Light Press/Pine Barrens Press
Blue Dolphin Publishing, Inc.
Bookworm Publishing Company
BUTTERFLY GARDENERS' QUARTERLY
Center For Self-Sufficiency
Chelsea Green Publishing Company
Chicago Review Press
The Chicot Press
China Books & Periodicals, Inc.
CJE NEWS (Newsletter of the Coalition for Jobs & the
  Environment)
DESIGN BOOK REVIEW
Devin-Adair Publishers, Inc.
EBB AND FLOW
FARMING UNCLE
Fisher Books
Fulcrum, Inc.
Gallopade International
THE GENTLE SURVIVALIST
Geraventure
The Globe Pequot Press
GRASS ROOTS
THE GREAT IDEA PATCH
GREEN PRINTS, "The Weeder's Digest"
GREEN WORLD: News and Views For Gardening Who
  Care About The Earth
THE GROWING EDGE MAGAZINE
GROWING FOR MARKET
HORTIDEAS
Interlink Publishing Group, Inc.
KIDSCIENCE
Allen A. Knoll Publishers
La Alameda Press
LAKE SUPERIOR MAGAZINE
Lester Street Publishing
LIVING OFF THE LAND, Subtropic Newsletter
Llewellyn Publications
LLEWELLYN'S NEW WORLDS OF MIND AND
  SPIRIT

THE MAD FARMERS' JUBILEE ALMANACK
Mayhaven Publishing
Museum of New Mexico Press
Naturegraph Publishers, Inc.
No Starch Press
ON COURSE
OUT YOUR BACKDOOR: The Magazine of Informal
  Adventure and Cheap Culture
Paper Chase Press
PenRose Publishing Company, Inc.
Petroglyph Press, Ltd.
Pineapple Press, Inc.
PLEASANT LIVING
Ponderosa Publishers
POTOMAC REVIEW
Prospect Hill Press
The Rateavers
Red Crane Books, Inc.
Red Eye Press
RED OWL
RFD
Running Press
RURAL HERITAGE
Sagapress, Inc.
Saint Mary's Press
Sasquatch Books
SCIENCE/HEALTH ABSTRACTS
SEED SAVERS EXCHANGE
Shearer Publishing
Sierra Club Books
SJL Publishing Company
Gibbs Smith, Publisher
SPECTRUM—The Wholistic News Magazine
SPROUTLETTER
Strawberry Hill Press
Swan Publishing Company
Timber Press
Tortilla Press
Venus Communications
THE VINCENT BROTHERS REVIEW
Waters Edge Press
WESTERN SKIES
WHOLE EARTH
THE WILD FOODS FORUM
WISCONSIN TRAILS
Wisconsin Trails
Woodbridge Press

GAY

Abiko Literary Press (ALP)
Acclaim Publishing Co. Inc.
AD/VANCE
AFFABLE NEIGHBOR
Affable Neighbor Press
AFFAIR OF THE MIND: A Literary Quarterly
Alamo Square Press
THE ALEMBIC
Alyson Publications, Inc.
Alyson Wonderland
AMELIA
Amelia Press
APHRODITE GONE BERSERK
BACKSPACE: A QUEER POETS JOURNAL
Bay Press
BAY WINDOWS
Beacon Press
BLACK LACE
BLACKFIRE
BLK
THE BLOWFISH CATALOG
Blowfish Press
BOOGLIT
BOTH COASTS BOOK REVIEW
(THE) BRAVE NEW TICK
Broken Jaw Press
BROWNBAG PRESS
Burning Bush Publications
Carolina Wren Press/Lollipop Power Books

Chandler & Sharp Publishers, Inc.
THE CHEROTIC (r)EVOLUTIONARY
Chiron Press
CHIRON REVIEW
Circlet Press, Inc.
COLLEGIUM NEWSLETTER
Companion Press
Conari Press
Coteau Books
COUNTRY CHARM MAGAZINE
Curtis/Strongmen Publishing
DOUBLE BILL
DREAM WHIP
Dreamboy Books
DWAN
Elysian Hills Publishing Company, Inc.
THE EVERGREEN CHRONICLES
Factor Press
FAG RAG
FIRSTHAND
FURTHER TOO
GATEAVISA
Gay Sunshine Press, Inc.
GAYELLOW PAGES
GEORGE & MERTIE'S PLACE: Rooms With a View
GERBIL: Queer Culture Zine
GIRLFRIENDS MAGAZINE
GLB Publishers
Golden Isis Press
Good Gay Poets Press
GRAFFITI OFF THE ASYLUM WALLS
GrapeVinePress
Green Eagle Press
HECATE'S LOOM - A Journal of Magical Arts
HerBooks
HOTHEAD PAISAN, HOMICIDAL LESBIAN TER-
  RORIST
Hyacinth House Publications/Caligula Editions
Ignite! Entertainment
Institute for Southern Studies
JAMES WHITE REVIEW; A Gay Men's Literary
  Quarterly
Javelina Books
JEJUNE: america Eats its Young
KICK IT OVER
KUUMBA
LAMBDA BOOK REPORT
Landwaster Books
Lemieux International Ltd.
Leyland Publications
Lone Willow Press
LOVE AND RAGE, A Revolutionary Anarchist News-
  paper
MESECHABE: The Journal of Surre(gion)alism
Mho & Mho Works
MOM GUESS WHAT NEWSPAPER
MONADNOCK GAY MEN
MUSE NATURA, A Sensual Journey of the Arts
NAMBLA BULLETIN
NEW ART EXAMINER
THE NEW PRESS LITERARY QUARTERLY
New Star Books Ltd.
Nosukumo
Odysseus Enterprises Ltd.
OFF OUR BACKS
OFF OUR BACKS
OFF THE ROCKS
Outrider Press
Palari Publishing
Palm Drive Publishing
The Place In The Woods
The Preservation Press
Pride & Imprints
PSYCHOTRAIN
Q ZINE
QECE: QUESTION EVERYTHING. CHALLENGE
  EVERYTHING.
QUESTION EVERYTHING CHALLENGE EVERY-

THING (QECE)
RADICAL AMERICA
Red Crane Books, Inc.
Red Letter Press
RFD
SHEILA-NA-GIG
Spectrum Press
SPSM&H
THE BOBBY STAR NEWSLETTER
Starbooks Press/FLF Press
Strawberry Hill Press
Syracuse Cultural Workers/Tools for Change
Times Change Press
TURNING THE TIDE: A Journal of Anti-Racist
  Activism, Research & Education
Twelvetrees Press
Unified Publications
Union Park Press
THE UNIT CIRCLE
URBAN GRAFFITI
Urban Legend Press
THE URBANITE
VIETNAM GENERATION: A Journal of Recent History
  and Contemporary Issues
Volcano Press, Inc
White Wolf Publishing
Willendorf Press
THE WISHING WELL
Woman in the Moon Publications (W.I.M. Publications)
WOMENWISE
WORMWOOD REVIEW
Writers Forum
X-it Press
XY: Men, Sex, Politics

GENDER ISSUES

AFFAIR OF THE MIND: A Literary Quarterly
AXE FACTORY REVIEW
Blue Heron Publishing, Inc.
Chandler & Sharp Publishers, Inc.
COLLEGIUM NEWSLETTER
THE DALHOUSIE REVIEW
DWAN
Eros Publishing
GATEAVISA
Golden Eagle Press
HYPATIA: A Journal of Feminist Philosophy
Islewest Publishing
Kumarian Press, Inc.
MESECHABE: The Journal of Surre(gion)alism
Pavement Saw Press
Seal Press
WHAT IS ENLIGHTENMENT?

GENEALOGY

Alaska Native Language Center
Appalachian Log Publishing Company
Cottontail Publications
DeerTrail Books
DorPete Press
Genealogical Publishing Co., Inc.
Golden Eagle Press
Guarionex Press Ltd.
Heritage Books, Inc.
IRISH FAMILY JOURNAL
Irish Genealogical Foundation
KELTIC FRINGE
LFW Enterprises
Log Cabin Manuscripts
Meridional Publications
The Overmountain Press
R & M Publishing Company
Rayve Productions Inc.
THE SOUTHERN JOURNAL
Stewart Publishing & Printing
Tailored Tours Publications, Inc.
Tyro Publishing
The Urbana Free Library

WORLDLINKS - FRIENDSHIP NEWS
Wright-Armstead Associates

GEOGRAPHY

Alaska Geographic Society
American & World Geographic Publishing
APPALACHIA JOURNAL
The Bess Press
BIG WORLD
Center for South and Southeast Asian Studies Publications
Child's Play
The Denali Press
EduCare Press
EXIT 13 MAGAZINE
Falcon Press Publishing Company
Gallopade International
International University Line (IUL)
THE JOURNAL OF AFRICAN TRAVEL-WRITING
LAKE SUPERIOR MAGAZINE
LANDSCAPE
Lexikos
New England Cartographics, Inc.
Northern Rim Press
POW-WOW
STARGREEN
TIERRA DEL FUEGO MAGAZINE
TOWPATHS
THE UNDERGROUND FOREST - LA SELVA SUB-
  TERRANEA
University of Calgary Press
The Urbana Free Library
Utah Geographic Series
WE INTERNATIONAL (formerly WOMEN AND EN-
  VIRONMENTS)
WHOLE EARTH
Williamson Publishing Company, Inc.
Witwatersrand University Press
Zagier & Urruty Publicaciones

GEOLOGY

AFFAIR OF THE MIND: A Literary Quarterly
America West Publishers
ATL Press, Inc.
Cave Books
Comparative Sedimentology Lab.
FARM PULP MAGAZINE
GemStone Press
THE GENTLE SURVIVALIST
GEORGE & MERTIE'S PLACE: Rooms With a View
GOTTA WRITE NETWORK LITMAG
Mountain Press Publishing Co.
Naturegraph Publishers, Inc.
The Overmountain Press
PenRose Publishing Company, Inc.
RESONANCE
SEA KAYAKER
Genny Smith Books

GERMAN

AFFAIR OF THE MIND: A Literary Quarterly
AUFBAU
R.J. Bender Publishing
Dufour Editions Inc.
The Edwin Mellen Press
Fromm International Publishing Corporation
GATEAVISA
GERMAN LIFE
The Green Hut Press
INTERNATIONAL POETRY REVIEW
NEW GERMAN REVIEW: A Journal of Germanic
  Studies
Passeggiata Press, Inc.
Top Of The Mountain Publishing
TRANSITIONS ABROAD: The Guide to Living,
  Learning, and Working Overseas
Venus Communications

GLOBAL AFFAIRS

AFFAIR OF THE MIND: A Literary Quarterly
ATL Press, Inc.
GREEN ANARCHIST
Griffon House Publications
Hollis Publishing Company
Images For Media/Sesquin
The Independent Institute
THE INDEPENDENT REVIEW: A Journal of Political
    Economy
Kumarian Press, Inc.
MAIN STREET JOURNAL
THE NEW PRESS LITERARY QUARTERLY
New Spring Publications
NGUOI DAN
The Pamphleeter's Press
POTOMAC REVIEW
RED OWL
Schenkman Books
SJL Publishing Company
WORLDVIEWS: A Quarterly Review of Resources for
    Education and Action

GOVERNMENT

Adolfo Street Publications
AFFAIR OF THE MIND: A Literary Quarterly
Aletheia Publications, Inc.
American Literary Press Inc./Noble House
Benchmark Publications Inc.
Bluestocking Press
Bookhaven Press, LLC
Borealis Press Limited
Bowerdean Publishing Co. Ltd.
Brenner Information Group
BWALO: A Forum for Social Development
Chandler & Sharp Publishers, Inc.
Children Of Mary
Child's Play
CHRONICLE OF COMMUNITY
CJE NEWS (Newsletter of the Coalition for Jobs & the
    Environment)
Comstock Bonanza Press
THE CONSTANTIAN
CROSS ROADS
DISSONANCE MAGAZINE
FIDELIS ET VERUS
FLASHPOINT: Military Books Reviewed by Military
    Professionals
Florida Academic Press
The Foundation for Economic Education, Inc.
FPMI Communications, Inc.
THE FREEMAN: Ideas On Liberty
FURTHER TOO
GATEAVISA
GEORGE & MERTIE'S PLACE: Rooms With a View
Griffon House Publications
Heron Press
Hollis Publishing Company
IAAS Publishers, Inc.
The Independent Institute
THE INDEPENDENT REVIEW: A Journal of Political
    Economy
INNOVATING
Itidwitir Publishing
JARRETT'S JOURNAL
KETTERING REVIEW
THE KITHARA
Kumarian Press, Inc.
LABOUR & TRADE UNION REVIEW
LITTLE FREE PRESS
LONE STAR SOCIALIST
THE LONG TERM VIEW: A Journal of Informed
    Opinion
Manta Press
Marmot Publishing
New Regency Publishing
New Spring Publications

NGUOI DAN
PEACE, The Magazine of the Sixties
PenRose Publishing Company, Inc.
Planning/Communications
Ponderosa Publishers
PRISON LEGAL NEWS
Selah Publishing
SJL Publishing Company
Skyline Publications, Inc.
SMART DRUG NEWS
SOCIETY
The Tonal Company
THE TRUTH SEEKER
TURNING THE TIDE: A Journal of Anti-Racist
    Activism, Research & Education
21ST CENTURY AFRO REVIEW
University of Calgary Press
University of Massachusetts Press
The Urbana Free Library
VIRGINIA LIBERTY
George Wahr Publishing Company
THE WASHINGTON MONTHLY
White Plume Press
Wind River Institute Press/Wind River Broadcasting
YUWITAYA LAKOTA

GRAPHIC DESIGN

Abiko Literary Press (ALP)
Baker Street Publications
Brenner Information Group
ICARUS WAS RIGHT
Itidwitir Publishing
Dean Lem Associates, Inc.
MIXED BAG
NIGHTSHADE
Oak Knoll Press
The Press of the Nightowl
TEENS IN MOTION NEWS

GRAPHICS

ABRAXAS
AGADA
Allworth Press
AMERICAN AMATEUR JOURNALIST
ART-CORE
BACKBOARD
Baker Street Publications
Banana Productions
Barefoot Press
BOOK MARKETING UPDATE
Brenner Information Group
BrickHouse Books, Inc.
CHILDREN, CHURCHES AND DADDIES, A Non
    Religious, Non Familial Literary Magazine
CLOCKWATCH REVIEW
CONTEXT SOUTH
CROSSCURRENTS, A QUARTERLY
DESIGN BOOK REVIEW
THE DIRTY GOAT
DISSONANCE MAGAZINE
En Passant Poetry Press
EN PASSANT/POETRY
ENDING THE BEGIN
ETCETERA
FLOATING ISLAND
Full Moon Publications
The Future Press
GATEAVISA
Ghost Pony Press
Goodheart-Willcox Publisher
G'RAPH
THE HAUNTED JOURNAL
Headveins Graphics
HEARTLAND (Australia)
Heresy Press
HOAX!
The Hosanna Press
Host Publications, Inc.

Insomniac Press
INTERNATIONAL ART POST
INTERNATIONAL POETRY REVIEW
KALDRON, An International Journal Of Visual Poetry
KICK IT OVER
Dean Lem Associates, Inc.
LIGHT: The Quarterly of Light Verse
LIGHTWORKS MAGAZINE
LOST GENERATION JOURNAL
Lowy Publishing
Luna Bisonte Prods
MARK
MATI
Mr. Cogito Press
MIXED BAG
MOOSE BOUND PRESS JOURNAL/NEWSLETTER
Mortal Press
NANCY'S MAGAZINE
NIGHTSHADE
Oasis Books
PARA TROOP
PEN & INK WRITERS JOURNAL
PIG IRON
Pittore Euforico
Pleasure Dome Press (Long Island Poetry Collective Inc.)
Protean Publications
REALM OF THE VAMPIRE
Red Cedar Press
RED CEDAR REVIEW
REDOUBT
RIVER STYX
The Runaway Spoon Press
Salt Lick Press
Scars Publications
SKYLARK
Slab-O-Concrete Publications
SLEUTH JOURNAL
SLIPSTREAM
Smyrna Press
SOUTHWEST JOURNAL
SPELUNKER FLOPHOUSE
STILETTO
STUDIO - A Journal of Christians Writing
TEENS IN MOTION NEWS
13TH MOON
TIGHTROPE
THE UNIT CIRCLE
Univelt, Inc.
THE VINCENT BROTHERS REVIEW
WEST BRANCH
Westgate Press
THE WORCESTER REVIEW
Writers Forum
XANADU

GREAT LAKES

Cambric Press dba Emerald House
Canterbury Press
Wm.B. Eerdmans Publishing Co.
Jackson Harbor Press
LAKE SUPERIOR MAGAZINE
Palladium Communications
PASSAGES NORTH
Pfeifer-Hamilton
THE RIVER
SKYLARK
W.E.C. Plant Publishing
Wilderness Adventure Books

GREAT PLAINS

THE AZOREAN EXPRESS
Baker Street Publications
Coteau Books
DREAM WHIP
Eagle's View Publishing
Full Moon Publications
MANKATO POETRY REVIEW
NORTH DAKOTA QUARTERLY

OVERLAND JOURNAL
Point Riders Press
POW-WOW
THE PRAIRIE JOURNAL OF CANADIAN LITERA-
TURE
THE RIVER
Silver Print Press
Skyline West Press/Wyoming Almanac
SOUTHWEST JOURNAL
TRADITION
WESTERN AMERICAN LITERATURE
WESTERN SKIES

GREEK

Abiko Literary Press (ALP)
Bandanna Books
Bolchazy-Carducci Publishers, Inc.
THE CHARIOTEER
Child's Play
DIALOGOS: Hellenic Studies Review
Dovehaven Press
EduCare Press
JOURNAL OF THE HELLENIC DIASPORA
Kelsey St. Press
Pella Publishing Co
PERSEPHONE
University of Calgary Press
Wide World Publishing/TETRA

GRIEVING

AFFAIR OF THE MIND: A Literary Quarterly
American Literary Press Inc./Noble House
Cherubic Press
Conari Press
The Crossing Press
Dead Metaphor Press
Elder Books
Fisher Books
Free Spirit Publishing Inc.
Galen Press, Ltd.
GEORGE & MERTIE'S PLACE: Rooms With a View
Golden Eagle Press
Greeson & Boyle, Inc.
Islewest Publishing
MESSAGES FROM THE HEART
New Liberty Press
Saint Mary's Press
Two Bytes Publishing
White Buck Publishing
YOUR LIFE MATTERS

GUIDANCE

Black Forest Press
Briarwood Publishing
Capital Communications
Cherubic Press
COLLEGIUM NEWSLETTER
Coteau Books
Energeia Publishing, Inc.
Fisher Books
Golden Eagle Press
Hunter House Inc., Publishers
Impact Publishers, Inc.
International University Line (IUL)
H J Kramer
Langmarc Publishing
Organization for Equal Education of the Sexes, Inc.
Perpetual Press
Prosperity Press
Saint Mary's Press
The Saunderstown Press
Small Helm Press
Stillpoint Publishing
STONES IN MY POCKET
Twelve Star Publishing

HAIKU

Abiko Literary Press (ALP)

AFFABLE NEIGHBOR
Affable Neighbor Press
AHA Books
AMELIA
Amelia Press
American Literary Press Inc./Noble House
ANT ANT ANT ANT ANT
BACKBOARD
Baker Street Publications
BLACK BEAR REVIEW
BLACK BOUGH
BLITHE SPIRIT
Brooks Books
BURNING CAR
Chiron Press
CHIRON REVIEW
CICADA
CLASS ACT
COTYLEDON
DAYSPRING
DREAM INTERNATIONAL QUARTERLY
ELF: ECLECTIC LITERARY FORUM (ELF MAGA-
ZINE)
ENDING THE BEGIN
FREEDOM ISN'T FREE
FROGPOND: Quarterly Haiku Journal
From Here Press
Frozen Waffles Press/Shattered Sidewalks Press; 45th
Century Chapbooks
Golden Isis Press
Headveins Graphics
IDIOM 23
INTERCULTURAL WRITERS REVIEW
Irvington St. Press, Inc.
J. Mark Press
Jackson Harbor Press
JAPANOPHILE
Japanophile Press
Kenyette Productions
La Alameda Press
LILLIPUT REVIEW
Little River Press
LUMMOX JOURNAL
MATI
MAYFLY
MIXED BAG
MODERN HAIKU
New Hope International
NEW HOPE INTERNATIONAL REVIEW
THE NEW PRESS LITERARY QUARTERLY
NIGHTSHADE
Nite-Owl Press
NITE-WRITER'S   INTERNATIONAL   LITERARY
ARTS JOURNAL
NORTHEAST
PAPER WASP: A Journal of Haiku
PARNASSUS LITERARY JOURNAL
PenRose Publishing Company, Inc.
Persephone Press
PERSIMMON
PIEDMONT LITERARY REVIEW
PINE ISLAND JOURNAL OF NEW ENGLAND
POETRY
PIRATE WRITINGS
Poetic License Press
POETS' ROUNDTABLE
POETS'PAPER
POTPOURRI: A Magazine of the Literary Arts
Press Here
RATTAPALLAX
THE SALEM JOURNAL
SHORT FUSE
SKYLARK
SPIRIT TO SPIRIT
SPORT LITERATE, Honest Reflections on Life's Leisur-
ely Diversions
THE STARLIGHT PAPERS
STOVEPIPE: A Journal of Little Literary Value

THE SUNDAY SUITOR POETRY REVIEW
Sweet Lady Moon Press
TEXTSHOP
TIGHTROPE
TIME HAIKU
TitleWaves Publishing
THE UNDERGROUND FOREST - LA SELVA SUB-
TERRANEA
THE UNIT CIRCLE
VARIOUS ARTISTS
VERSE: A Journal of Poetry & Poetics
THE VINCENT BROTHERS REVIEW
West Anglia Publications
WINDOW PANES
WOODNOTES
WORDS OF WISDOM
XTRAS

HANDICAPPED

Alpine Guild, Inc.
The Brookfield Reader
COLLEGIUM NEWSLETTER
INTERCULTURAL WRITERS REVIEW
JARRETT'S JOURNAL
Massey-Reyner Publishing
THE NEW PRESS LITERARY QUARTERLY
The Place In The Woods
The Poetry Connection
THE POETRY CONNECTION
POW-WOW
The Saunderstown Press
University of Calgary Press

HANDWRITING/WRITTEN

Pavement Saw Press

HAWAII

BAMBOO RIDGE, A HAWAI'I WRITERS JOURNAL
Bamboo Ridge Press
The Bess Press
BEST OF MAUI
Beyond Words Publishing, Inc.
Falcon Press Publishing Company
GATEAVISA
Golden Eagle Press
HAWAI'I REVIEW
JAPANOPHILE
Kauai Press
Light, Words & Music
MANOA: A Pacific Journal of International Writing
MEANJIN
Moon Publications, Inc.
Mutual Publishing
Paradise Publications
Petroglyph Press, Ltd.
TURNING THE TIDE: A Journal of Anti-Racist
Activism, Research & Education
W.E.C. Plant Publishing
Wide World Publishing/TETRA

HEALTH

A.R.E. Press
ABELexpress
Addicus Books, Inc.
AFFAIR OF THE MIND: A Literary Quarterly
Ageless Press
Alive Books
ALIVE: Canadian Journal of Health and Nutrition
Allergy Publications
AlphaBooks, Inc.
Alpine Guild, Inc.
Amador Publishers
Anaphase II
THE ANIMALS' AGENDA
Anti-Aging Press
The Arthritis Trust of America/The Rheumatoid Disease
Foundation
Ash Tree Publishing

ATL Press, Inc.
Author's Partner in Publishing
Autumn Publishing Group, LLC.
Avery Publishing Group, Inc.
Axelrod Publishing of Tampa Bay
Barricade Books
Bear & Company, Inc.
Beekman Publishers, Inc.
Beyond Words Publishing, Inc.
Bio-Probe, Inc.
Blue Bird Publishing
Blue Poppy Press Inc.
Bonus Books, Inc.
BookPartners, Inc.
THE BOOMERPHILE
Borderland Sciences Research Foundation
BORDERLANDS: A Quarterly Journal Of Borderland
  Research
Branden Publishing Company
Bull Publishing Co.
By-The-Book Publishing
CANADIAN JOURNAL OF APPLIED PHYSIOLOGY
  (CJAP)
Capital Communications
Cassandra Press, Inc.
Center for Public Representation
Center Press
THE CIVIL ABOLITIONIST
Civitas
CLUBHOUSE
Commune-A-Key Publishing, Inc.
COMMUNITY DEVELOPMENT JOURNAL
Community Resource Institute Press
THE COMPLEAT NURSE
Conari Press
Conscious Living
Consumer Press
Cosmoenergetics Publications
Cougar Books
Beverly Cracom Publications
CRCS Publications
The Crossing Press
Cypress House
DAILY WORD
Devin-Adair Publishers, Inc.
Dharma Publishing
DIET & HEALTH MAGAZINE
Down There Press
Dry Bones Press
EAP DIGEST
EBB AND FLOW
Elder Books
Elysian Hills Publishing Company, Inc.
Emerald Wave
Envirographics
EquiLibrium Press, Inc.
ETR Associates
Factor Press
FELL'S HEALTH FITNESS MAGAZINE
Fisher Books
Focus Publications, Inc.
Foghorn Press
FORESIGHT MAGAZINE
FOREST: The Freedom Organization for the Right to
  Smoke Tobacco
FOREVER ALIVE
Four Walls Eight Windows
FREE CHOICE
Free Spirit Publishing Inc.
Front Row Experience
Future Horizons, Inc.
Galde Press, Inc.
Galen Press, Ltd.
Gallaudet University Press
THE GENTLE SURVIVALIST
Get In-Line! Publishing
Glenbridge Publishing Ltd.
Golden West Books

Good Book Publishing Company
GRASS ROOTS
Greeson & Boyle, Inc.
THE GROVE
Guardian Press
Gurze Books
Haight-Ashbury Publications
HEALTH AND HAPPINESS
Health Plus Publishers
Health Press
HEALTHY WEIGHT JOURNAL
Herald Press
HERBAL CHOICE
Heritage Global Publishing
Hill Country Books
Himalayan Institute Press
Hohm Press
Hope Publishing House
Howln Moon Press
Human Kinetics Pub. Inc.
Hunter House Inc., Publishers
HWD Publishing
IMPACC USA
Impact Publishers, Inc.
Inner Traditions International
Innisfree Press
Inquiry Press
INTEGRAL YOGA MAGAZINE
INTERNATIONAL JOURNAL OF SPORT NUTRITION
  (IJSN)
JARRETT'S JOURNAL
JEWISH VEGETARIAN NEWSLETTER
Joelle Publishing
JOURNAL OF PSYCHOACTIVE DRUGS
JOURNAL OF TEACHING IN PHYSICAL EDUCA-
  TION (JTPE)
JOURNAL OF VISION REHABILITATION
JPS Publishing Company
Kali Press
Michael Kesend Publishing, Ltd.
KIDSCIENCE
Kivaki Press
H J Kramer
La Alameda Press
La Casa Press
Lamp Light Press
Lao Tse Press, Ltd.
Lemieux International Ltd.
Lester Street Publishing
Library Research Associates
Life Energy Media
Lion Press & Video
Llewellyn Publications
LLEWELLYN'S NEW WORLDS OF MIND AND
  SPIRIT
MACROBIOTICS TODAY
MEDICAL HISTORY
MEDICAL REFORM
Medical Reform Group
MEDIPHORS
Metamorphous Press
Midwifery Today Books
MONOZINE
Moon Publications, Inc.
Morning Glory Press
MOTOR CONTROL
John Muir Publications, Inc.
N: NUDE & NATURAL
Naturegraph Publishers, Inc.
Naturist Foundation
New Sins Press
New World Library
Newmark Publishing Company
Nicolas-Hays, Inc.
Nicolin Fields Publishing, Inc.
Noontide Press
North Star Books
NUTRITION ACTION HEALTHLETTER

OFF OUR BACKS
George Ohsawa Macrobiotic Foundation
OPEN EXCHANGE MAGAZINE
OVERLAND JOURNAL
Pacific View Press
Palari Publishing
Papillon Publishing
Parabola
Pathway Books
Pathways Press, Inc.
Peanut Butter and Jelly Press
Pedestal Press
PEDIATRICS FOR PARENTS
Pennycorner Press
Personal Fitness Publishing
Perspectives Press
Petroglyph Press, Ltd.
Piccadilly Books
Pine Publications
Popular Medicine Press
Power Publications
Princess Publishing
Prometheus Enterprises, Inc.
Publitec Editions
Pura Vida Publishing Company
QED Press
Race Point Press
RADIANCE, The Magazine For Large Women
Rama Publishing Co.
THE RATIONAL FEMINIST
Real Life Storybooks
Reveal
RFD
Rossi
St. Georges Press
Sanguinaria Publishing
SCIENCE/HEALTH ABSTRACTS
Seacoast Information Services
Seal Press
SeaStar Publishing Company
Self Healing Press
Shallowater Press
Shaolin Communications
Sharp Publishing
Sigo Press
Silvercat Publications
SJL Publishing Company
Skidmore-Roth Publishing, Inc.
SKINNYDIPPING
SMART DRUG NEWS
SO YOUNG!
SOM Publishing, division of School of Metaphysics
Spelman Publishing, Inc.
SPROUTLETTER
Steel Balls Press
Stillpoint Publishing
STONES IN MY POCKET
Strawberry Hill Press
STREET VOICE
SunShine Press Publications, Inc.
Swan Publishing Company
Swan Raven & Company
TAI CHI
TEC Publications
Tell Publishing
Ten Star Press
Theosophical Publishing House
Third Side Press, Inc.
THRESHOLDS JOURNAL
Tide Book Publishing Company
Tiger Press
Tiptoe Literary Service
Toad Hall Press
The Tonal Company
Topping International Institute, Inc.
Turtle Island Press, Inc.
Twin Peaks Press
UC Books

Unity Books
UNITY MAGAZINE
University of Calgary Press
Upper Access Inc.
Vanitas Press
VDT NEWS
VEGETARIAN JOURNAL
Vestibular Disorders Association
VINEGAR CONNOISSEURS INTERNATIONAL NEWSLETTER
Vista Publishing, Inc.
Volcano Press, Inc
Waterfront Books
Wayfarer Publications
Samuel Weiser, Inc.
Westport Publishers
Wharton Publishing, Inc.
Whitford Press
Whole Person Associates Inc.
THE WILD FOODS FORUM
Willendorf Press
WIN NEWS
Women of Diversity Productions, Inc.
Woodbridge Press
World Changing Books
YOUR LIFE MATTERS

ERNEST HEMINGWAY

Abiko Literary Press (ALP)
AC
Broken Jaw Press
THE CENTENNIAL REVIEW
Clamp Down Press
CLASS ACT
GEORGE & MERTIE'S PLACE: Rooms With a View
LOST GENERATION JOURNAL
MAIN STREET JOURNAL
Palm Island Press
Pineapple Press, Inc.
THE STYLUS

HISTORY

A. Borough Books
Aardvark Enterprises (A Division of Speers Investments Ltd.)
AAS HISTORY SERIES
Acclaim Publishing Co. Inc.
THE ACORN
Acorn Books
ADAPTED PHYSICAL ACTIVITY QUARTERLY (APAQ)
Afcom Publishing
AFFAIR OF THE MIND: A Literary Quarterly
AFRICAN STUDIES
African Ways Publishing
AK Press
Alaska Geographic Society
ALBERTA HISTORY
AltaMira Press
AMERICAN AMATEUR JOURNALIST
Ana Libri Press
Anderson Press
THE ANNALS OF IOWA
Anubian Press
Appalachian Consortium Press
Appalachian Log Publishing Company
Arden Press, Inc.
ARTISTAMP NEWS
Autonomedia, Inc.
Averasboro Press
Avery Color Studios
Axios Newletter, Inc.
BAJA SUN
Baker Street Publications
Bandanna Books
The Battery Press, Inc.
William L. Bauhan, Publisher
The Bear Wallow Publishing Company

R.J. Bender Publishing
The Bess Press
Betelgeuse Books
Between The Lines
BIBLIOTHEQUE D'HUMANISME ET RENAISSANCE
Bigwater Publishing
Black Dome Press Corp.
Black Sparrow Press
Blacksmith Corporation
Blue Crane Books
Blue Unicorn Press, Inc.
Bluestocking Press
Bolchazy-Carducci Publishers, Inc.
BookPartners, Inc.
THE BOOMERPHILE
Borealis Press Limited
The Borgo Press
Branden Publishing Company
Brick Row Publishing Co. Ltd.
BRIDGES: An Interdisciplinary Journal of Theology,
    Philosophy, History, and Science
Broken Jaw Press
Broken Rifle Press
The Brookfield Reader
Burd Street Press
CALLIOPE: World History for Young People
Camel Press
Canadian Committee on Labour History
CANADIAN REVIEW OF AMERICAN STUDIES
Candlestick Publishing
CAPE FEAR JOURNAL
CAPITALISM, NATURE, SOCIALISM
Capra Press
The Carnation Press
Carrefour Press
Celtic Heritage Books
CELTIC HISTORY REVIEW
Center for Japanese Studies
Center for South and Southeast Asian Studies Publications
Chandler & Sharp Publishers, Inc.
Chelsea Green Publishing Company
Cherokee Publishing Company
CINEASTE MAGAZINE
Citeaux Commentarii Cistercienses
CITEAUX: COMMENTARII CISTERCIENSES
THE CIVIL WAR NEWS
Arthur H. Clark Co.
Clover Park Press
COBBLESTONE: The History Magazine for Young
    People
Coldwater Press
Commonwealth Press Virginia
Communication Creativity
Comparative Sedimentology Lab.
The Compass Press
Comstock Bonanza Press
Conari Press
THE CONSTANTIAN
Coreopsis Books
Coteau Books
Cottontail Publications
Creative Roots, Inc.
CROSS ROADS
Crossroads Communications
CULTUREFRONT
Cypress House
DAILY WORD
THE DALHOUSIE REVIEW
DANDELION ARTS MAGAZINE
DAUGHTERS OF SARAH
Dawnwood Press
December Press
DeerTrail Books
The Denali Press
Derrynane Press
Dharma Publishing
Discovery Enterprises, Ltd.
DOOR COUNTY ALMANAK

DorPete Press
Down The Shore Publishing
Duckworth Press
Dufour Editions Inc.
THE DURHAM UNIVERSITY JOURNAL
DUST (From the Ego Trip)
Eagle's View Publishing
EAST EUROPEAN QUARTERLY
Edition Gemini
Editorial El Sol De Baja
Editorial Review
EduCare Press
The Edwin Mellen Press
Wm.B. Eerdmans Publishing Co.
EL PALACIO
Epicenter Press Inc.
EPM Publications, Inc.
Erespin Press
EUROPEAN JUDAISM
Event Horizon Press
Exceptional Books, Ltd.
EZ Nature Books
Falcon Press Publishing Company
Fathom Publishing Co.
The Feminist Press at the City College
FIDEI DEFENSOR: JOURNAL OF CATHOLIC APO-
    LOGETICS
FISICA
Florida Academic Press
Foundation Books
The Foundation for Economic Education, Inc.
Four Peaks Press
Four Walls Eight Windows
THE FREEMAN: Ideas On Liberty
Friends United Press
Fromm International Publishing Corporation
Fulcrum, Inc.
Galde Press, Inc.
Gallaudet University Press
Gallopade International
Gay Sunshine Press, Inc.
Genealogical Publishing Co., Inc.
GEORGE & MERTIE'S PLACE: Rooms With a View
GERMAN LIFE
The Glencannon Press
Golden West Books
Golden West Historical Publications
Good Book Publishing Company
Good Life Publications
GORHAM
Green Eagle Press
Griffon House Publications
Gumbs & Thomas Publishers, Inc.
The Gutenberg Press
Halo Books
Happy Rock Press
Harbor House
Hawk Publishing Group
Heartsong Books
Heritage Books, Inc.
Heritage Concepts Publishing Inc
Heritage House Publishers
Heritage West Books
Hermitage (Ermitazh)
Heron Press
Heyday Books
High Plains Press
Hill Country Books
Historical Dimensions Press
Historical Society of Alberta
HISTORICAL STUDIES IN THE PHYSICAL & BIOLO-
    GICAL SCIENCES
HISTORY NEWS
Homeward Press
Hoover Institution Press
Hope Publishing House
Horned Owl Publishing
House of the 9 Muses, Inc.

H2SO4
Hunter Publishing, Co.
Huntington Library Press
HUNTINGTON LIBRARY QUARTERLY
IAAS Publishers, Inc.
Icarus Books
ILLINOIS ARCHITECTURAL & HISTORICAL REVIEW
Images For Media/Sesquin
IMPERIAL RUSSIAN JOURNAL
THE INDEPENDENT REVIEW: A Journal of Political Economy
The Infinity Group
Inheritance Press Inc.
Institute for Southern Studies
Institute of Archaeology Publications
Intelligenesis Publications
Interlink Publishing Group, Inc.
IOWA HERITAGE ILLUSTRATED (formerly The Palimpsest)
IRIS: A Journal About Women
Ironweed Press
Island Publishers
ISRAEL HORIZONS
ITALIAN AMERICANA
Italica Press, Inc.
JACK MACKEREL MAGAZINE
Jackson Harbor Press
Jaguar Books
JEWISH CURRENTS
JEWISH LIFE
JOURNAL OF CANADIAN STUDIES/Revue d'etudes canadiennes
THE JOURNAL OF HISTORICAL REVIEW
THE JOURNAL OF PSYCHOHISTORY
JOURNAL OF THE WEST
JOURNAL OF UNCONVENTIONAL HISTORY
Keokee Co. Publishing, Inc.
Michael Kesend Publishing, Ltd.
KMT, A Modern Journal of Ancient Egypt
KMT Communications
Allen A. Knoll Publishers
THE KOSCIUSZKO PORTFOLIO
LABOUR & TRADE UNION REVIEW
LABOUR/LE TRAVAIL
Lahontan Images
LAKE SUPERIOR MAGAZINE
LANDSCAPE
Landwaster Books
The Latona Press
Edward J. Lefkowicz, Inc.
Lemieux International Ltd.
LEO Productions LLC.
Lexikos
Library Research Associates, Inc.
LOVE AND RAGE, A Revolutionary Anarchist Newspaper
Lyceum Books, Inc.
MacDonald/Sward Publishing Company
THE MAD FARMERS' JUBILEE ALMANACK
MARATHON & BEYOND (M&B)
Paul Maravelas
Peter Marcan Publications
Maryland Historical Press
Masefield Books
Mayhaven Publishing
McNally & Loftin, Publishers
MEDICAL HISTORY
Mehring Books, Inc.
Meyer Publishing
THE MIDWEST QUARTERLY
Miles & Miles
Minnesota Historical Society Press
MODERN LANGUAGE QUARTERLY: A Journal of Literary History
Moon Publications, Inc.
Mount Ida Press
Mountain Automation Corporation

Mountain Meadow Press
Mountain State Press
Museum of New Mexico Press
N: NUDE & NATURAL
Nashville House
Nevada Publications
THE NEW ENGLAND QUARTERLY
THE NEW PRESS LITERARY QUARTERLY
New Spirit Press/The Poet Tree
New Star Books Ltd.
NEWS FROM NATIVE CALIFORNIA
NGUOI DAN
NightinGale Resources
Noontide Press
NORTH CAROLINA LITERARY REVIEW
North Country Books, Inc.
NORTHWOODS JOURNAL, A Magazine for Writers
NWI National Writers Institute
OLD ABE'S NEWS
Open Hand Publishing Inc.
Oregon State University Press
Organization for Equal Education of the Sexes, Inc.
THE OTHER ISRAEL
The Overmountain Press
Oxford House Publishing
Paint Rock Publishing, Inc.
Paladin Enterprises, Inc.
Pamlico Press
The Pamphleteer's Press
Paragon House Publishers
Parkway Publishers, Inc.
PASSAGER: A Journal of Remembrance and Discovery
Pathfinder Press
Patria Press, Inc.
The Patrice Press
Pavlovsk Press
PEACE, The Magazine of the Sixties
Peartree Books & Music
Penfield Press
Phillips Publications, Inc.
Photo Data Research
Pictorial Histories Pub. Co.
PIEDMONT LITERARY REVIEW
Pineapple Press, Inc.
The Place In The Woods
THE PLOUGH
Pocahontas Press, Inc.
Poetry Wales Press, Ltd.
Pogo Press, Incorporated
The Post-Apollo Press
POW-WOW
Prairie Publishing Company
Protean Press
Pruett Publishing Company
Psychohistory Press
THE PUBLIC HISTORIAN
QED
QED Press
Quarterly Committee of Queen's University
QUEEN'S QUARTERLY: A Canadian Review
Questex Consulting Ltd.
Quill Driver Books
RADIANCE, The Magazine For Large Women
RADICAL AMERICA
RAVEN - A Journal of Vexillology
Rayve Productions Inc.
THE READER'S REVIEW
Red Apple Publishing
Red Crane Books, Inc.
Reference Desk Books
REPRESENTATIONS
RhwymBooks
Ronsdale Press
Rose Publishing Co.
Rowhouse Press
Sagapress, Inc.
St. Michael's Press
San Diego State University Press

Sand River Press
Saqi Books Publisher
SCIENCE & SOCIETY
Scottwall Associates, Publishers
Sea Sports Publications
Signature Books
THE SMALL POND MAGAZINE OF LITERATURE
 aka SMALL POND
Genny Smith Books
Gibbs Smith, Publisher
Smyrna Press
Sonoran Publishing
Sorenson Books
THE SOUTHERN JOURNAL
SOUTHWEST JOURNAL
SPORT HISTORY REVIEW (SHR)
THE STARLIGHT PAPERS
Steerforth Press, L.C.
Stewart Publishing & Printing
Strawberry Hill Press
Sherwood Sugden & Company, Publishers
Summerthought Ltd.
Sun Books
Sunflower University Press
Sunstone Press
SYMPLOKE: A Journal for the Intermingling of Literary,
 Cultural and Theoretical Scholarship
TAIL SPINS
Tamarack Books, Inc.
Theytus Books Ltd.
Thirteen Colonies Press
Thomas Jefferson University Press
A Thousand Autumns Press
TIERRA DEL FUEGO MAGAZINE
Tilbury House, Publishers
Times Change Press
TOWPATHS
TRANVIA - Revue der Iberischen Halbinsel
Treasure Chest Books LLC
TRIVIUM
THE TRUTH SEEKER
Tsunami Inc.
Tuns Press
Umbrella Books
Unity Books
UNITY MAGAZINE
University of Calgary Press
University of Massachusetts Press
Upney Editions
The Urbana Free Library
Urion Press
Valiant Press, Inc.
Vestal Press Ltd
VIETNAM GENERATION: A Journal of Recent History
 and Contemporary Issues
THE VINCENT BROTHERS REVIEW
THE VIRGINIA QUARTERLY REVIEW
Volcano Press, Inc
THE VORTEX
W.E.C. Plant Publishing
Waterfront Books
Waters Edge Press
Wayfinder Press
WELSH HISTORY REVIEW
Wescott Cove Publishing Co.
WESTERN SKIES
The White Cross Press
White Mane Publishing Company, Inc.
Williamson Publishing Company, Inc.
Wisconsin Trails
Witwatersrand University Press
Wolfhound Press
Writers House Press
XIB
Xib Publications
Ye Galleon Press
YUMTZILOB: Tijdschrift over de Americas
Zagier & Urruty Publicaciones

ZONE
Zone Books

SHERLOCK HOLMES

BAKER STREET GAZETTE
Baker Street Publications
CLASS ACT
DAYS AND NIGHTS OF A SMALL PRESS PUB-
 LISHER
ENGLISH LITERATURE IN TRANSITION, 1880-1920
FULL MOON DIRECTORY
Gryphon Publications
HOLLYWOOD NOSTALGIA
JACK THE RIPPER GAZETTE
THE MYSTERY REVIEW
PAPERBACK PARADE
THE PIPE SMOKER'S EPHEMERIS
Polar Bear Productions & Company
SLEUTH JOURNAL

HOLOCAUST

AFFAIR OF THE MIND: A Literary Quarterly
Anubian Press
AUFBAU
BRIDGES: An Interdisciplinary Journal of Theology,
 Philosophy, History, and Science
Coteau Books
EUROPEAN JUDAISM
Full Moon Publications
GATEAVISA
JEWISH LIFE
THE JOURNAL OF HISTORICAL REVIEW
Lowy Publishing
MIXED BAG
THE NEW PRESS LITERARY QUARTERLY
Noontide Press
Paragon House Publishers
TRANSCAUCASUS: A Chronology
THE UNIT CIRCLE
University of Massachusetts Press

HOLOGRAPHY

Access Multimedia
JACK MACKEREL MAGAZINE
Reveal
Rowhouse Press
THEATRE DESIGN AND TECHNOLOGY

HOMELESSNESS

Calyx Books

HOMEMAKING

THE ACORN
Book Peddlers
Brighton Publications, Inc.
Center For Self-Sufficiency
COOKING CONTEST CHRONICLE
HIP MAMA
Nunciata
OUT YOUR BACKDOOR: The Magazine of Informal
 Adventure and Cheap Culture
Page One
PenRose Publishing Company, Inc.
Twin Peaks Press
VINEGAR   CONNOISSEURS   INTERNATIONAL
 NEWSLETTER

HORTICULTURE

Andmar Press
Arizona Master Gardener Press
Barnegat Light Press/Pine Barrens Press
GREEN WORLD: News and Views For Gardening Who
 Care About The Earth
Huntington Library Press
Allen A. Knoll Publishers
Naturegraph Publishers, Inc.
Park Place Publications
Ponderosa Publishers

Prospect Hill Press
Red Crane Books, Inc.
Red Eye Press
RED OWL
Gibbs Smith, Publisher
Venus Communications
THE VINCENT BROTHERS REVIEW

HOW-TO

A. Borough Books
Accent on Music
Acclaim Publishing Co. Inc.
Acting World Books
Actium Publishing, Inc.
Addicus Books, Inc.
Aeolus Press, Inc.
Afcom Publishing
AFFABLE NEIGHBOR
Affable Neighbor Press
Affinity Publishers Services
AFRICAN AMERICAN AUDIOBOOK REVIEW
Afrimax, Inc.
THE AGENCIES-WHAT THE ACTOR NEEDS TO
  KNOW
Airplane Books
Alaska Native Language Center
Aletheia Publications, Inc.
Allworth Press
Altamont Press, Inc.
American Literary Press Inc./Noble House
Amherst Media, Inc.
Anaphase II
and books
Annedawn Publishing
Anti-Aging Press
Arden Press, Inc.
ATL Press, Inc.
ATS Publishing
Autumn Publishing Group, LLC.
Avery Publishing Group, Inc.
BACKBOARD
Backcountry Publishing
Baker Street Publications
Barney Press
Bear Creek Publications
Bell Springs Publishing
Benchmark Publications Inc.
Beynch Press Publishing Company
Bicycle Books (Publishing) Inc.
Big Mouth Publications
Blue Bird Publishing
Blue Dolphin Publishing, Inc.
Blue Heron Publishing, Inc.
Blue Horizon Press
Blue Reef Publications, Inc.
Blue Sky Marketing, Inc.
Bluestocking Press
Bonus Books, Inc.
BOOK NEWS & BOOK BUSINESS MART
Bookhaven Press, LLC
Bookworm Publishing Company
Bottom Line Pre$$
Breakout Productions
Brenner Information Group
Briarwood Publishing
Bright Ring Publishing, Inc.
Brighton Publications, Inc.
Browder Springs
BYLINE
Byte Masters International
C & T Publishing
Cage Consulting, Inc.
Capital Communications
Capra Press
Cardoza Publishing
Career Advancement Center, Inc.
Carousel Press
Cassandra Press, Inc.

CCM Publishing
CE CONNECTION COMMUNIQUE
Center for Public Representation
Center For Self-Sufficiency
Chelsea Green Publishing Company
Chicago Review Press
Chicago Spectrum Press
The Chicot Press
ClockWorks Press
CLUBHOUSE
Communication Creativity
The Communication Press
Communicom Publishing Company
Consumer Press
Contemax Publishers
Courtyard Publishing Company
Coyote Publishing
CPG Publishing Company
Culinary Arts Ltd.
Cultivated Underground Press
Cyclone Books
Cypress House
Cypress Publishing Group, Inc.
Dalrymple Publishing Company
Devin-Adair Publishers, Inc.
The Dragon Press
Dumont Press
Dustbooks
DWELLING PORTABLY
Eagle's View Publishing
Ecrivez!
Edgeworth & North Books
Emerald Ink Publishing
THE EMSHOCK LETTER
Energeia Publishing, Inc.
Envirographics
EPM Publications, Inc.
ETC Publications
Eureka Publishing Group
Evanston Publishing, Inc.
FIBERARTS
Fisher Books
Five Star Publications
J. Flores Publications
Flower Press
Forbes/Wittenburg & Brown
Four Seasons Publishers
Four Walls Eight Windows
Franklin Multimedia, Inc.
Frugal Marketer Publishing
The P. Gaines Co., Publishers
Gazelle Publications
Gemini Publishing Company
GemStone Press
Get In-Line! Publishing
Gilgal Publications
GLASS AUDIO
Glenbridge Publishing Ltd.
The Globe Pequot Press
Golden Eagle Press
Good Life Products, Inc./DBA Beauty Ed
Good Times Publishing Co.
Goodheart-Willcox Publisher
Grade School Press
GRANULATED TUPPERWARE
GRASS ROOTS
THE GREAT IDEA PATCH
Great Western Publishing Company
Greeson & Boyle, Inc.
Guardian Press
Guarionex Press Ltd.
Gumbs & Thomas Publishers, Inc.
Halle House Publishing
Hands & Heart Books
Harvard Common Press
HERBAL CHOICE
HOAX!
HOBSON'S CHOICE

THE HOLLYWOOD ACTING COACHES AND TEACHERS DIRECTORY
Howln Moon Press
Human Kinetics Pub. Inc.
Hundman Publishing
Hunter Publishing, Co.
The Image Maker Publishing Co.
IN PRINT
In Print Publishing
INFOCUS
Information Research Lab
Infotrends Press
INQ Publishing Co.
Interlink Publishing Group, Inc.
Islewest Publishing
Jalmar Press
Jamenair Ltd.
JLA Publications, A Division Of Jeffrey Lant Associates, Inc.
J-Mart Press
JPS Publishing Company
Kali Press
Keel Publications
Kells Media Group
Michael Kesend Publishing, Ltd.
KITE LINES
KMJ Educational Programs
H J Kramer
Lamp Light Press
Landwaster Books
LAUGHING BEAR NEWSLETTER
Lawco Ltd./Moneytree Publications/Que-House
Ledero Press
LEFTHANDER MAGAZINE
Lemieux International Ltd.
Lester Street Publishing
Lexikos
Liberty Bell Press & Publishing Co.
Liberty Publishing Company, Inc.
Lion Press & Video
LITTLE FREE PRESS
Llewellyn Publications
LLEWELLYN'S NEW WORLDS OF MIND AND SPIRIT
Log Cabin Publishers
MAINLINE MODELER
MAKING $$$ AT HOME
Marinelli Publishing
Marmot Publishing
THE MASONIA ROUNDUP
Mayhaven Publishing
Metamorphous Press
Microdex Bookshelf
MIXED BAG
Moon Publications, Inc.
The Mountaineers Books
Mustang Publishing Co.
Naturegraph Publishers, Inc.
N-B-T-V
Nightsun Books
Nolo Press - Occidental
North American Bookdealers Exchange
Nunciata
OLD-HOUSE JOURNAL
Open Horizons Publishing Company
Osmyrrah Publishing
Page One
Paladin Enterprises, Inc.
Panjandrum Books
Paper Chase Press
Para Publishing
Pathway Books
Pennycorner Press
Perpetual Press
Photo Data Research
Piccadilly Books
Pineapple Press, Inc.
The Poetry Center Press/Shoestring Press

Poets & Writers, Inc.
Polar Bear Productions & Company
Premier Publishers, Inc.
PREP Publishing
The Preservation Press
Pride & Imprints
Progresiv Publishr
Prosperity Press
Pruett Publishing Company
PSI Research/The Oasis Press/Hellgate Press
PT Publications, Inc.
Publitec Editions
Pushcart Press
Pyramid Publishing
QED Press
Quill Driver Books
R & E Publishers
R & M Publishing Company
Rainbow Books, Inc.
Rainbow's End
Rainy Day Press
Ram Press
Red Crane Books, Inc.
Red Eye Press
RED HOT HOME INCOME REPORTER
Reference Desk Books
THE RESOURCE
Rio Grande Press
Roblin Press
Ronin Publishing, Inc.
Rossi
Running Press
St. Georges Press
Santa Monica Press/Offbeat Press
The Saunderstown Press
Scentouri, Publishing Division
SCIENCE/HEALTH ABSTRACTS
Scratch & Scribble Press
Scrivenery Press
SE LA VIE WRITER'S JOURNAL
SEA KAYAKER
Selah Publishing
Senay Publishing Inc.
Shaolin Communications
Silver Dollar Press
Six Strings Music Publishing
SJL Publishing Company
Solution Publishing
SOM Publishing, division of School of Metaphysics
Sourcebooks, Inc.
Southern Star Publishing
Southwest Research and Information Center
SPEX (SMALL PRESS EXCHANGE)
Steel Balls Press
Stewart Publishing & Printing
StoneBrook Publishing
Stonehouse Publications
Strawberry Hill Press
Success Publishing
Swan Publishing Company
Tamal Vista Publications
Tax Property Investor, Inc.
Three Pyramids Publishing
Ticket to Adventure, Inc.
Tide Book Publishing Company
Tiptoe Literary Service
TitleWaves Publishing
Top Of The Mountain Publishing
TOWERS CLUB, USA INFO MARKETING REPORT
Trafton Publising
Travel Keys
Triad Press
Tudor Publishers, Inc.
Twin Peaks Press
Tyro Publishing
THE UNDERGROUND FOREST - LA SELVA SUBTERRANEA
Upper Access Inc.

Verity Press Publishing
Vestal Press Ltd
Via God Publishing
VINEGAR CONNOISSEURS INTERNATIONAL
  NEWSLETTER
Visions Communications
Vista Mark Publications
Vitreous Group/Camp Colton
Waterfront Books
Waverly House Publishing
Wescott Cove Publishing Co.
Wharton Publishing, Inc.
WHISPERING WIND MAGAZINE
White Knight Press
White Plume Press
Whitmore Publishing Company
THE WILD FOODS FORUM
Wilderness Adventure Books
Williamson Publishing Company, Inc.
Winslow Publishing
Wordwrights Canada
THE WORKBOOK
WRITER TO WRITER
WRITERS GAZETTE
WRITER'S GUIDELINES: A Roundtable for Writers and
  Editors
WRITER'S WORKSHOP REVIEW
YOUR LIFE MATTERS
Z W L Publishing, Inc.

HUMAN RIGHTS

AFFAIR OF THE MIND: A Literary Quarterly
BAJA SUN
Baker Street Publications
Beacon Press
BLU
Candlestick Publishing
Chandler & Sharp Publishers, Inc.
Child's Play
Clarity Press, Inc.
Coteau Books
COUNTERPOISE: For Social Responsibilities, Liberty
  and Dissent
CROSS ROADS
DREAM NETWORK JOURNAL
Drum
Food First Books
FOREST: The Freedom Organization for the Right to
  Smoke Tobacco
The Foundation for Economic Education, Inc.
FOURTH WORLD REVIEW
FREE CHOICE
THE FREEMAN: Ideas On Liberty
GATEAVISA
GEORGE & MERTIE'S PLACE: Rooms With a View
GLB Publishers
Global Options
GRAFFITI OFF THE ASYLUM WALLS
Hollis Publishing Company
Howling Dog Press/Stiletto
Hunter House Inc., Publishers
ICARUS WAS RIGHT
Images For Media/Sesquin
The Independent Institute
THE INDEPENDENT REVIEW: A Journal of Political
  Economy
INTERCULTURE
IRIS: A Journal About Women
Itidwitir Publishing
JAM RAG
JEJUNE: america Eats its Young
JEWISH LIFE
KETTERING REVIEW
The Leaping Frog Press
LIBERTY
LIVE AND LET LIVE
LONE STAR SOCIALIST
MEANDER QUARTERLY

Mercury House
MESECHABE: The Journal of Surre(gion)alism
METAL CURSE
Mr. Cogito Press
MIXED BAG
NATURALLY
NGUOI DAN
PEACE & DEMOCRACY
PEACE MAGAZINE
Philopsychy Press
POW-WOW
PRISON LEGAL NEWS
Pygmy Forest Press
QECE: QUESTION EVERYTHING. CHALLENGE
  EVERYTHING.
QUESTION EVERYTHING CHALLENGE EVERY-
  THING (QECE)
RESONANCE
Reveal
Savant Garde Workshop
Schenkman Books
SHARE INTERNATIONAL
SHEILA-NA-GIG
SOCIAL JUSTICE: A JOURNAL OF CRIME, CON-
  FLICT, & WORLD ORDER
STILETTO
SUITCASE: A Journal of Transcultural Traffic
Syracuse Cultural Workers/Tools for Change
TRANSCAUCASUS: A Chronology
TURNING THE TIDE: A Journal of Anti-Racist
  Activism, Research & Education
TURNING WHEEL
21ST CENTURY AFRO REVIEW
THE UNDERGROUND
Willendorf Press
World Changing Books
WORLD RAINFOREST REPORT
XIB
Xib Publications

HUMANISM

Acclaim Publishing Co. Inc.
Baker Street Publications
Bandanna Books
BARNABE MOUNTAIN REVIEW
Black Rose Books Ltd.
Caliban Press
CAPITALISM, NATURE, SOCIALISM
THE CHEROTIC (r)EVOLUTIONARY
CIMARRON REVIEW
CULTUREFRONT
Dharma Publishing
DOWN UNDER MANHATTAN BRIDGE
Dufour Editions Inc.
Eagle Publishing
EMERGING
Erespin Press
FOURTH WORLD REVIEW
FREE INQUIRY
FURTHER TOO
GEORGE & MERTIE'S PLACE: Rooms With a View
The Gleniffer Press
Golden Eagle Press
GRAFFITI OFF THE ASYLUM WALLS
GrapeVinePress
The Green Hut Press
H & C NEWSLETTER
THE HUMANIST
Hyacinth House Publications/Caligula Editions
IASP NEWSLETTER
Jalmar Press
THE LATHAM LETTER
The Philip Lesly Company
LOGIC LETTER
LP Publications (Teleos Institute)
METAL CURSE
Metamorphous Press
MIXED BAG

Mountaintop Books
NATURALLY
The New Humanity Press
New Spirit Press/The Poet Tree
NEW THOUGHT JOURNAL
The Olive Press Publications
PEOPLE'S CULTURE
PIG IRON
POTOMAC REVIEW
THE PRAGMATIST
Royal Purcell, Publisher
R & E Publishers
RADIANCE, The Magazine For Large Women
REPORTS OF THE NATIONAL CENTER FOR SCIENCE EDUCATION
Reveal
The Saunderstown Press
Savant Garde Workshop
Shaolin Communications
SHARE INTERNATIONAL
SKYLARK
THE SMALL POND MAGAZINE OF LITERATURE aka SMALL POND
SNAKE RIVER REFLECTIONS
Steamshovel Press
Strawberry Hill Press
SYMPLOKE: A Journal for the Intermingling of Literary, Cultural and Theoretical Scholarship
Times Change Press
Top Of The Mountain Publishing
TOWARD FREEDOM
THE TRUTH SEEKER
THE UNFORGETTABLE FIRE
VanderWyk & Burnham
Waterfront Books
B. L. Winch & Associates
THE WISHING WELL
WITNESS
XIB
Xib Publications
Yes You Can Press

HUMOR

A. Borough Books
Acclaim Publishing Co. Inc.
ACME Press
ACORN WHISTLE
AFFABLE NEIGHBOR
Affable Neighbor Press
AFFAIR OF THE MIND: A Literary Quarterly
Ageless Press
AMELIA
American Literary Press Inc./Noble House
Anaphase II
and books
THE ANGRY THOREAUAN
Anti-Aging Press
Ariadne Press
ART'S GARBAGE GAZZETTE
Ashton Productions, Inc.
AT-HOME DAD
ATROCITY
Axelrod Publishing of Tampa Bay
BABYSUE
BAJA SUN
BAKER STREET GAZETTE
Baker Street Publications
Bancroft Press
BEGINNINGS - A Magazine for the Novice Writer
BELLES LETTRES
The Bess Press
Big Mouth Publications
THE BLAB
BLADES
Blue Dolphin Publishing, Inc.
BLUE HORSE
Blue Horse Publications
Blue Mouse Studio

Blue Sky Marketing, Inc.
Bogg Publications
Bonus Books, Inc.
THE BOOMERPHILE
BREAKFAST ALL DAY
Bright Mountain Books, Inc.
Brook Farm Books
BURNING CAR
BUZZARD
CASTAWAYS
Catbird Press
The Center Press
THE CHEROTIC (r)EVOLUTIONARY
Child's Play
Chiron Press
CHIRON REVIEW
CIMARRON REVIEW
Commune-A-Key Publishing, Inc.
The Communication Press
Conari Press
Coteau Books
Cottonwood Press, Inc.
Custom Services
Dawn Sign Press
DEANOTATIONS
Doggerel Press
DOPE FRIENDS
Down There Press
THE DUPLEX PLANET
THE EMSHOCK LETTER
Enthea Press
ETCETERA
Event Horizon Press
Ex Machina Publishing Company
Excalibur Publishing Inc.
EXCLAIM!
FAT TUESDAY
FINE MADNESS
FIRM NONCOMMITTAL: An International Journal of Whimsy
FIRST DRAFT
FLIPSIDE
Four Seasons Publishing
Franklin Multimedia, Inc.
FREDIAN SLIP: THE LEONARD ZELIG OF ZINES
THE FREEDONIA GAZETTE
Freelance Communications
Fulcrum, Inc.
Full Moon Publications
FUNNY PAGES
THE FUNNY TIMES
Gaff Press
Galde Press, Inc.
GATEAVISA
Gateways Books And Tapes
GEORGE & MERTIE'S PLACE: Rooms With a View
GLEN BURNIELAND
Golden Eagle Press
GoldenIsle Publishers, Inc.
GOTHIX
GRAFFITI OFF THE ASYLUM WALLS
GrapeVinePress
Green Stone Publications
Halo Books
THE HAUNTED JOURNAL
HEELTAP/Pariah Press
Herbelin Publishing
HIP MAMA
Hobblebush Books
HOTHEAD PAISAN, HOMICIDAL LESBIAN TERRORIST
House of the 9 Muses, Inc.
H2SO4
Hyacinth House Publications/Caligula Editions
IDIOT WIND
IGNIS FATUUS REVIEW
Ignite! Entertainment
IllumiNet Press

THE IMPLODING TIE-DYED TOUPEE
IMPRINT, A LITERARY JOURNAL
INDY MAGAZINE
Inner Traditions International
INTERBANG
THE J MAN TIMES
THE JOE BOB REPORT
Jolly Roger Press
JOURNAL OF AESTHETICS AND ART CRITICISM
JOURNAL OF ALASKA WOMEN
JOURNAL OF POLYMORPHOUS PERVERSITY
KALEIDOSCOPE: INTERNATIONAL MAGAZINE OF
  LITERATURE, FINE ARTS, AND DISABILITY
Keel Publications
Kimm Publishing, Inc.
Knightraven Books
Allen A. Knoll Publishers
KOOMA
KRAX
KUMQUAT MERINGUE
LADIES' FETISH & TABOO SOCIETY COMPEN-
  DIUM OF URBAN ANTHROPOLOGY
LADYBUG, the Magazine for Young Children
LAKE SUPERIOR MAGAZINE
Landwaster Books
LATEST JOKES NEWSLETTER
Lawco Ltd./Moneytree Publications/Que-House
The Leaping Frog Press
Ledero Press
Leyland Publications
LIES MAGAZINE
THE LITERARY QUARTERLY
THE LOST PERUKE
Lowy Publishing
MALEDICTA: The International Journal of Verbal
  Aggression
MARK
THE MASONIA ROUNDUP
MASSACRE
Mayhaven Publishing
MESHUGGAH
METAL CURSE
Metamorphous Press
Miles & Miles
MIXED BAG
Momentum Books, Ltd.
MOMMY AND I ARE ONE
Monitor Publications AR
MONOZINE
THE MONTHLY INDEPENDENT TRIBUNE TIMES
  JOURNAL POST GAZETTE NEWS CHRONICLE
  BULLETIN
MOOSE BOUND PRESS JOURNAL/NEWSLETTER
Mortal Press
Mosaic Press
MOTORBOOTY MAGAZINE
THE MOUNTAIN ASTROLOGER
MurPubCo
Mustang Publishing Co.
NANCY'S MAGAZINE
NANNY FANNY
NATURAL BRIDGE
Naturegraph Publishers, Inc.
NEW HOPE INTERNATIONAL REVIEW
THE NEW PRESS LITERARY QUARTERLY
New Spirit Press/The Poet Tree
New Victoria Publishers
New Voice Media
NEW YORK STORIES
NIGHTSHADE
No Starch Press
NORTHERN PILOT
NOSTALGIA, A Sentimental State of Mind
NUTHOUSE
NWI National Writers Institute
OFFICE NUMBER ONE
The Olive Press Publications
ON COURSE

Paladin Enterprises, Inc.
PALO ALTO REVIEW
Pariah Press
PARNASSUS LITERARY JOURNAL
PASSAGES NORTH
Peachtree Publishers, Ltd.
PEN & INK WRITERS JOURNAL
Piccadilly Books
Piggy Bank Press
PIRATE WRITINGS
Pittore Euforico
PLAIN BROWN WRAPPER (PBW)
Poetic License Press
The Poetry Center Press/Shoestring Press
Pogo Press, Incorporated
Portmanteau Editions
POTATO EYES
POTOMAC REVIEW
THE PRAIRIE JOURNAL OF CANADIAN LITERA-
  TURE
Prairie Journal Press
The Press at Foggy Bottom
Push/Pull/Press
QECE: QUESTION EVERYTHING. CHALLENGE
  EVERYTHING.
QUESTION EVERYTHING CHALLENGE EVERY-
  THING (QECE)
THE RAINTOWN REVIEW: A Forum for the Essayist's
  Art
THE RATIONAL FEMINIST
Raw Dog Press
RED OWL
REFERRALS
THE REJECTED QUARTERLY
Resource Publications, Inc.
Rio Grande Press
Ronin Publishing, Inc.
RUBBER DUCKY MAGAZINE
The Runaway Spoon Press
Saddle Mountain Press
SALON: A Journal of Aesthetics
SE LA VIE WRITER'S JOURNAL
SFEST, LTD.
SHEILA-NA-GIG
SHORT FUSE
Signature Books
SJL Publishing Company
SKINNYDIPPING
SKYLARK
Slab-O-Concrete Publications
SLEUTH JOURNAL
THE SMALL POND MAGAZINE OF LITERATURE
  aka SMALL POND
SMALL PRESS CREATIVE EXPLOSION
Gibbs Smith, Publisher
SO YOUNG!
SONAR MAP
SQUARE ONE - A Magazine of Disturbing Fiction
StoneBrook Publishing
STOVEPIPE: A Journal of Little Literary Value
STRUGGLE: A Magazine of Proletarian Revolutionary
  Literature
SUPER TROUPER
Synapse-Centurion
Synergistic Press
THALIA: Studies in Literary Humor
THEY WON'T STAY DEAD!
THOUGHTS FOR ALL SEASONS: The Magazine of
  Epigrams
THRESHOLDS JOURNAL
Times Change Press
Trafton Publising
Transcending Mundane
TURNSTILE
Twelve Star Publishing
TWISTED IMAGE NEWSLETTER
TWISTED TIMES
Two Thousand Three Associates

Tyro Publishing
THE UNDERGROUND FOREST - LA SELVA SUB-
    TERRANEA
URBAN GRAFFITI
Urban Legend Press
THE URBANITE
VAMPIRE NIGHTS
Vanity Press/Strolling Dog Press
Vestal Press Ltd
Via God Publishing
THE VINCENT BROTHERS REVIEW
VOICES - ISRAEL
Waterfront Books
THE WEIRD NEWS
WHAT IF...THE MAGAZINE OF THE MODERN
    PHILOSOPHER
WHOLE EARTH
Wildstone Media
WINDOW PANES
Words & Pictures Press
WORDS OF WISDOM
World Changing Books
WORLD DOMINATION REVIEW
Writers Forum
WRITER'S GUIDELINES & NEWS
XIB
Xib Publications
ZUZU'S PETALS: QUARTERLY ONLINE

HUNGER

AFFAIR OF THE MIND: A Literary Quarterly
Baker Street Publications
Food First Books
Howling Dog Press/Stiletto
Kumarian Press, Inc.
Lester Street Publishing
MIXED BAG
RED OWL
SHARE INTERNATIONAL
STILETTO

HYPNOSIS

Borden Publishing Co.
INTUITIVE EXPLORATIONS
JARRETT'S JOURNAL
LifeQuest Publishing Group
Llewellyn Publications
Metamorphous Press
RESONANCE
Shaolin Communications
SUPER TROUPER
Top Of The Mountain Publishing

IDAHO

Blue Heron Publishing, Inc.
COLD-DRILL
Cold-Drill Books
THE EMSHOCK LETTER
Falcon Press Publishing Company
Keokee Co. Publishing, Inc.
Moon Publications, Inc.
Mountain Meadow Press
Pahsimeroi Press
Resolution Business Press, Inc.
SANDPOINT MAGAZINE
Tamarack Books, Inc.
THE TEMPLE
WEBER STUDIES: Voices and Viewpoints of the
    Contemporary West
WESTERN SKIES

ILLINOIS

The Carnation Press
Chicago Review Press
Chicago Spectrum Press
CHILDREN, CHURCHES AND DADDIES, A Non
    Religious, Non Familial Literary Magazine
CHRISTIANITY & THE ARTS

Crossroads Communications
Evanston Publishing, Inc.
ILLINOIS ARCHITECTURAL & HISTORICAL RE-
    VIEW
Illinois Heritage Press
International University Line (IUL)
Mayhaven Publishing
NIGHT ROSES
Palm Drive Publishing
ST. LOUIS JOURNALISM REVIEW
Scars Publications
Stormline Press, Inc.
32 PAGES
The Urbana Free Library

IMMIGRATION

AFFAIR OF THE MIND: A Literary Quarterly
AXE FACTORY REVIEW
Banks Channel Books
Burning Bush Publications
COLORLINES
Content Communications
CROSS ROADS
Hollis Publishing Company
ICA Publishing
The Independent Institute
THE INDEPENDENT REVIEW: A Journal of Political
    Economy
INDIA CURRENTS
INTERCULTURE
Kumarian Press, Inc.
LOVE AND RAGE, A Revolutionary Anarchist News-
    paper
Palladium Communications
PRISON LEGAL NEWS
Wright-Armstead Associates

INDEXES & ABSTRACTS

ALTERNATIVE PRESS INDEX
Anderson Press
The Borgo Press
THE CHRISTIAN LIBRARIAN
CONNEXIONS DIGEST
Connexions Information Services, Inc.
THE DALHOUSIE REVIEW
The Denali Press
Fallen Leaf Press
FEMINIST PERIODICALS: A CURRENT LISTING OF
    CONTENTS
HORTIDEAS
THE LEFT INDEX
LEGAL INFORMATION MANAGEMENT INDEX
Little Buckaroo Press
NEW BOOKS ON WOMEN & FEMINISM
Passeggiata Press, Inc.
Resolution Business Press, Inc.
Univelt, Inc.
The Urbana Free Library
Volcano Press, Inc
Women's Studies Librarian, University of Wisconsin
    System
The Wordtree

INDIA

AFFAIR OF THE MIND: A Literary Quarterly
Baker Street Publications
Blue Dove Press
Center for South and Southeast Asian Studies Publications
Erespin Press
The Feminist Press at the City College
Full Moon Publications
GEORGE & MERTIE'S PLACE: Rooms With a View
Happy Rock Press
HORIZONS
INDIA CURRENTS
Mandala Publishing Group
Noyce Publishing
Passeggiata Press, Inc.

RhwymBooks
Schenkman Books
Tiger Moon

INDIANA

Frozen Waffles Press/Shattered Sidewalks Press; 45th
    Century Chapbooks
SJL Publishing Company
SKYLARK
SYCAMORE REVIEW

INDIANS

Abiko Literary Press (ALP)
Alaska Native Language Center
Baker Street Publications
Child's Play
Coyote Publishing
Eagle's View Publishing
Epicenter Press Inc.
EZ Nature Books
Galde Press, Inc.
GATEAVISA
GEORGE & MERTIE'S PLACE: Rooms With a View
Heyday Books
LAKE SUPERIOR MAGAZINE
Minnesota Historical Society Press
MIXED BAG
National Woodlands Publishing Company
Naturegraph Publishers, Inc.
New Spirit Press/The Poet Tree
Noyce Publishing
Oregon State University Press
Outer Space Press
Parabola
Pygmy Forest Press
SHENANDOAH NEWSLETTER
SOUTHWEST JOURNAL
STONES IN MY POCKET
Survival News Service
Swan Raven & Company
Tiger Moon
Treasure Chest Books LLC
WHISPERING WIND MAGAZINE
YUMTZILOB: Tijdschrift over de Americas
YUWITAYA LAKOTA

INDIGENOUS CULTURES

Inner Traditions International

INSPIRATIONAL

American Literary Press Inc./Noble House
AREOPAGUS
Ascension Publishing
THE AUROREAN, A POETIC QUARTERLY
Axelrod Publishing of Tampa Bay
Beacon Point Press
Blue Dove Press
Blue Star Press
The Book Department
Business Resource Publishing
Capital Communications
CHAOS FOR THE CREATIVE MIND
Cherubic Press
CHRISTIANITY & THE ARTS
Commune-A-Key Publishing, Inc.
Conari Press
Dawn Publications
Dharma Publishing
ELF: ECLECTIC LITERARY FORUM (ELF MAGA-
    ZINE)
Elysian Hills Publishing Company, Inc.
Enthea Press
Four Seasons Publishers
THE GENTLE SURVIVALIST
Golden Eagle Press
Good Book Publishing Company
GrapeVinePress
Greeson & Boyle, Inc.

Heartsong Books
The Heather Foundation
Himalayan Institute Press
HIP MAMA
Horus Publishing, Inc.
Illumination Arts
In Print Publishing
Innisfree Press
J & L Publications
JARRETT'S JOURNAL
Kells Media Group
H J Kramer
Lamp Light Press
Langmarc Publishing
Leadership Education and Development, Inc.
The Leaping Frog Press
Light, Words & Music
LITTLE FREE PRESS
LUNO
Mandala Publishing Group
MESSAGES FROM THE HEART
More To Life Publishing
Munsey Music
MYSTIC VOICES
Naturegraph Publishers, Inc.
Network 3000 Publishing
THE NEW PRESS LITERARY QUARTERLY
NEW THOUGHT JOURNAL
New World Library
Nicolin Fields Publishing, Inc.
Nite-Owl Press
PACIFIC ENTERPRISE
Picturesque Publications
The Poetry Center Press/Shoestring Press
Point Bonita Books
PREP Publishing
Pura Vida Publishing Company
QUINTILE
Quintile
REFERRALS
Reveal
Reyes Investment Enterprise Ltd.
The Saunderstown Press
Scherf, Inc./Scherf Books
Gibbs Smith, Publisher
Sovereignty Press
Sparrow Hawk Press
SPIRIT TO SPIRIT
SPIRITCHASER
Stillpoint Publishing
STONES IN MY POCKET
Sun-Scape Publications, a division of Sun-Scape Enter-
    prises Ltd.
Theosophical Publishing House
THRESHOLDS JOURNAL
Tiger Moon
Timeless Books
Top Of The Mountain Publishing
Twelve Star Publishing
Tyro Publishing
VanderWyk & Burnham
Via God Publishing
Visions Communications
WHAT IS ENLIGHTENMENT?
Yes You Can Press
YOUR LIFE MATTERS

INSURANCE

Maryland Historical Press
THE MONTHLY INDEPENDENT TRIBUNE TIMES
    JOURNAL POST GAZETTE NEWS CHRONICLE
    BULLETIN
Publitec Editions
Selah Publishing
THE SMALL BUSINESS ADVISOR
Stratton Press
The Tonal Company
VDT NEWS

815

CREATIVE NONFICTION
DAYS AND NIGHTS OF A SMALL PRESS PUB-
LISHER
DIARIST'S JOURNAL
DIRIGIBLE
DREAM NETWORK JOURNAL
THE DROPLET JOURNAL
FAULTLINE, Journal of Art and Literature
FREEDOM ISN'T FREE
Fromm International Publishing Corporation
FULL MOON DIRECTORY
Full Moon Publications
FURTHER TOO
GEORGE & MERTIE'S PLACE: Rooms With a View
Happy Rock Press
THE HAUNTED JOURNAL
Hyacinth House Publications/Caligula Editions
IMPRINT, A LITERARY JOURNAL
The Independent Institute
JACK MACKEREL MAGAZINE
JACK THE RIPPER GAZETTE
LA PERIPHERIE
THE LITERARY QUARTERLY
LULLWATER REVIEW
MAD SCIENTIST
Magic Circle Press
Media Arts Publishing
MESSAGES FROM THE HEART
MIXED BAG
MOOSE BOUND PRESS JOURNAL/NEWSLETTER
NIGHTSHADE
Nosukumo
PALO ALTO REVIEW
Paris Press, Inc.
PEACE, The Magazine of the Sixties
PEN & INK WRITERS JOURNAL
Poetic License Press
Rayve Productions Inc.
REALM OF THE VAMPIRE
RETHINKING MARXISM
Rowhouse Press
ST. LOUIS JOURNALISM REVIEW
Scars Publications
SCIENCE & SOCIETY
Signature Books
SJL Publishing Company
SLEUTH JOURNAL
SOMNIAL TIMES
THE SUN, A MAGAZINE OF IDEAS
13TH MOON
TORRE DE PAPEL
TOWERS CLUB, USA INFO MARKETING REPORT
WESTERN SKIES
WRITER'S WORKSHOP REVIEW
Ye Galleon Press

JAMES JOYCE

Abiko Literary Press (ALP)
THE ABIKO QUARTERLY WITH JAMES JOYCE FW
STUDIES
CHRONICLES OF DISORDER
CLASS ACT
GEORGE & MERTIE'S PLACE: Rooms With a View
HOAX!
JAMES JOYCE BROADSHEET
JAMES JOYCE QUARTERLY
KELTIC FRINGE
NOBODADDIES
PLAIN BROWN WRAPPER (PBW)
PORTLAND REVIEW
Scripta Humanistica
Station Hill Press
University of Tulsa

JUDAISM

AFFAIR OF THE MIND: A Literary Quarterly
AGADA
Alef Design Group

Beacon Press
Biblio Press
Blue Dove Press
BRIDGES: A Journal for Jewish Feminists and Our
Friends
Burning Bush Publications
Chicago Spectrum Press
COMMON BOUNDARY MAGAZINE
Coteau Books
DAYS AND NIGHTS OF A SMALL PRESS PUB-
LISHER
DOVETAIL: A Journal by and for Jewish/Christian
Families
Dovetail Publishing
The Edwin Mellen Press
The Eighth Mountain Press
EUROPEAN JUDAISM
Florida Academic Press
Full Moon Publications
Gan Publishing
GATEAVISA
Gloger Family Books
HerBooks
ISRAEL HORIZONS
ISSUES
J & L Publications
JEWISH LIFE
Jewish Publication Society
Jewish Radical Education Project
JEWISH VEGETARIAN NEWSLETTER
J-REP NEWS AND VIEWS
Judah Magnes Museum Publications
Kar-Ben Copies, Inc.
KEREM: Creative Explorations in Judaism
LILITH
Lowy Publishing
Micah Publications Inc.
MIXED BAG
Mountaintop Books
THE NEW PRESS LITERARY QUARTERLY
NightinGale Resources
No Starch Press
OXYGEN
Paragon House Publishers
The Press at Foggy Bottom
THE READER'S REVIEW
Real Life Storybooks
RECONSTRUCTIONIST
RESPONSE: A Contemporary Jewish Review
Rossi
Saint Mary's Press
SALMAGUNDI
Saqi Books Publisher
SHIRIM
THE TRUTH SEEKER
VOICES - ISRAEL
WHAT IS ENLIGHTENMENT?
Zagier & Urruty Publicaciones

JUVENILE FICTION

AFFABLE NEIGHBOR
Affable Neighbor Press
African American Audio Press
AFRICAN AMERICAN AUDIOBOOK REVIEW
The Brookfield Reader
Business Smarts, Inc.
Cherubic Press
Ecrivez!
GrapeVinePress
Hungry Tiger Press
Journey Books Publishing
Allen A. Knoll Publishers
LEO Productions LLC.
Naturegraph Publishers, Inc.
Nextstep Books
OZ-STORY
Pocket of Sanity
Premium Press America

817

Center for Japanese Studies
Center for South and Southeast Asian Studies Publications
Chandler & Sharp Publishers, Inc.
The Chicot Press
CHILDREN, CHURCHES AND DADDIES, A Non Religious, Non Familial Literary Magazine
Child's Play
China Books & Periodicals, Inc.
Circumpolar Press
Clamshell Press
CLASS ACT
THE CLASSICAL OUTLOOK
Cosmoenergetics Publications
THE DALHOUSIE REVIEW
S. Deal & Assoc.
Department of Romance Languages
ESPERANTIC STUDIES
ETCETERA
Gallaudet University Press
Gallopade International
GEORGE & MERTIE'S PLACE: Rooms With a View
Teri Gordon, Publisher
GRAIN
Grayson Bernard Publishers, Inc.
HEAVEN BONE MAGAZINE
Heaven Bone Press
HENNEPIN COUNTY LIBRARY CATALOGING BULLETIN
IBEX Publishers
Images For Media/Sesquin
In One Ear Publications
INTERNATIONAL JOURNAL FOR THE SEMIOTICS OF LAW
JACK MACKEREL MAGAZINE
JOURNAL OF CELTIC LINGUISTICS
JOURNAL OF COURT REPORTING
JOURNAL OF HUMANITIES
KALDRON, An International Journal Of Visual Poetry
LANGUAGE INTERNATIONAL: THE MAGAZINE FOR THE LANGUAGE PROFESSIONS
Liverpool University Press
LORE AND LANGUAGE
LULLWATER REVIEW
LUNO
LUZ EN ARTE Y LITERATURA
Maledicta Press
MALEDICTA: The International Journal of Verbal Aggression
MANGAJIN
MESECHABE: The Journal of Surre(gion)alism
META4: Journal of Object Oriented Poetics (OOPS)
Metamorphous Press
MIND MATTERS REVIEW
THE MODERN LANGUAGE JOURNAL
MOKSHA JOURNAL
Moon Publications, Inc.
Multi Media Arts
NANCY'S MAGAZINE
National Court Reporters Association Press
NEW HOPE INTERNATIONAL REVIEW
THE NEW PRESS LITERARY QUARTERLY
nine muses books
NOTES & QUERIES
The Olivia and Hill Press, Inc.
Open Horizons Publishing Company
OPTIMA Books
OSIRIS
Palladium Communications
THE PANNUS INDEX
Papillon Publishing
Petroglyph Press, Ltd.
POINT OF CONTACT
POSTCARD
Progresiv Publishr
Protean Press
Red Crane Books, Inc.
RHETORICA: A Journal of the History of Rhetoric
Rowhouse Press

Salt Lick Press
Saqi Books Publisher
Scars Publications
Score
SCORE
Serena Bay Books
Slate Press
SOCKS, DREGS AND ROCKING CHAIRS
Station Hill Press
Stone Bridge Press
Strata Publishing, Inc.
THE SUBTLE JOURNAL OF RAW COINAGE
SULPHUR RIVER LITERARY REVIEW
SYMPLOKE: A Journal for the Intermingling of Literary, Cultural and Theoretical Scholarship
THE UNDERGROUND FOREST - LA SELVA SUBTERRANEA
Univelt, Inc.
Vajra Printing an Publishing of Yoga Anand Ashram
Verbatim
A VOICE WITHOUT SIDES
George Wahr Publishing Company
Weidner & Sons, Publishing
WHOLE EARTH
Witwatersrand University Press
WOMEN AND LANGUAGE
The Wordtree
THE WRITE WAY
YUMTZILOB: Tijdschrift over de Americas

LAPIDARY

AFFAIR OF THE MIND: A Literary Quarterly
Cynic Press
GemStone Press

LATIN AMERICA

AFRO-HISPANIC REVIEW
ALCATRAZ
Autonomedia, Inc.
BAJA SUN
Barking Dog Books
Between The Lines
BLU
BUENO
CHALLENGE: A Journal of Faith and Action in the Americas
CHASQUI
Cleis Press
Clover Park Press
CROSS ROADS
DAYS AND NIGHTS OF A SMALL PRESS PUBLISHER
Department of Romance Languages
EPICA
The Feminist Press at the City College
Full Moon Publications
GATEAVISA
Gateway Books
Gay Sunshine Press, Inc.
GEORGE & MERTIE'S PLACE: Rooms With a View
Hoover Institution Press
Hope Publishing House
HORIZONS
In One Ear Publications
Information Research Lab
Interlink Publishing Group, Inc.
Jaguar Books
Kumarian Press, Inc.
LATIN AMERICAN LITERARY REVIEW
LATIN AMERICAN PERSPECTIVES
Law Mexico Publishing
MARGIN: EXPLORING MODERN MAGICAL REALISM
THE MILITANT
Mindfield Publications
MIXED BAG
Moon Publications, Inc.
Museum of New Mexico Press

New Earth Publications
NEW ORLEANS REVIEW
THE NEW PRESS LITERARY QUARTERLY
NewSage Press
Outer Space Press
Palladium Communications
Pangaea
Paragon House Publishers
Passeggiata Press, Inc.
Passport Press
Pathfinder Press
POINT OF CONTACT
Pyx Press
RESOURCE CENTER BULLETIN
SALMAGUNDI
Signal Books
SOCIETE
SOUTH AMERICAN EXPLORER
Studia Hispanica Editors
Syracuse Cultural Workers/Tools for Change
THE TEMPLE
Times Change Press
TORRE DE PAPEL
TOWARD FREEDOM
TRADICION REVISTA
Two Eagles Press International
THE UNDERGROUND FOREST - LA SELVA SUB-
TERRANEA
White Pine Press
World Music Press
WORLD RAINFOREST REPORT
Zagier & Urruty Publicaciones

LATINO

Baker Street Publications
BILINGUAL REVIEW/Revista Bilingue
BLU
BRAVO, THE POET'S MAGAZINE
BUENO
DAYS AND NIGHTS OF A SMALL PRESS PUB-
LISHER
Full Moon Publications
HORIZONS
ICA Publishing
JAPANOPHILE
LATINO STUFF REVIEW
The Leaping Frog Press
LOVE AND RAGE, A Revolutionary Anarchist News-
paper
LPD Press
LUMMOX JOURNAL
Mindfield Publications
MIXED BAG
Museum of New Mexico Press
NEW ART EXAMINER
New Sins Press
Outer Space Press
The Place In The Woods
POINT OF CONTACT
THE SOUNDS OF POETRY
TORRE DE PAPEL
TRADICION REVISTA
Treasure Chest Books LLC
TURNING THE TIDE: A Journal of Anti-Racist
Activism, Research & Education
Ward Hill Press

LATVIA

GATEAVISA

LAW

Allworth Press
AMBASSADOR REPORT
Archipelago Publishing
ART CALENDAR
BERKELEY JOURNAL OF EMPLOYMENT AND
LABOR LAW
BERKELEY JOURNAL OF INTERNATIONAL LAW

BERKELEY TECHNOLOGY LAW JOURNAL
Bluestocking Press
Bonus Books, Inc.
Calibre Press, Inc.
CALIFORNIA LAW REVIEW
Catbird Press
Center for Public Representation
Claitor's Law Books & Publishing Division, Inc.
Columbine Publishing Group
THE COOPERATOR
CRIMINAL JUSTICE ABSTRACTS
Criminal Justice Press
ECOLOGY LAW QUARTERLY
Edgeworth & North Books
Event Horizon Press
Fathom Publishing Co.
FEMINIST LEGAL STUDIES
FIJACTIVIST
Fillmore Publishing Company
The Fine Print Press, Ltd.
The P. Gaines Co., Publishers
Global Options
Grand River Press
GRAY AREAS
HARVARD WOMEN'S LAW JOURNAL
HOAX!
Impact Publishers, Inc.
The Independent Institute
THE INDEPENDENT REVIEW: A Journal of Political
Economy
INDEX TO FOREIGN LEGAL PERIODICALS
Institute for Southern Studies
INTERNATIONAL JOURNAL FOR THE SEMIOTICS
OF LAW
International University Line (IUL)
JOURNAL OF COURT REPORTING
LAW AND CRITIQUE
Law Mexico Publishing
LEGAL INFORMATION MANAGEMENT INDEX
LIVERPOOL LAW REVIEW
THE LONG TERM VIEW: A Journal of Informed
Opinion
The Media Institute
National Court Reporters Association Press
New Spring Publications
Nolo Press
Nolo Press - Occidental
Peartree Books & Music
Philopsychy Press
Pineapple Press, Inc.
PRISON LEGAL NEWS
PRIVACY JOURNAL
Professional Resource Exchange, Inc.
R & E Publishers
Reniets, Inc.
RES PUBLICA
SKINNYDIPPING
THE SMALL BUSINESS ADVISOR
SOCIAL JUSTICE: A JOURNAL OF CRIME, CON-
FLICT, & WORLD ORDER
Solution Publishing
Sourcebooks, Inc.
Strata Publishing, Inc.
Stratton Press
STUDENT LAWYER
The Survival Series Publishing Co.
Trace Publications
University of Calgary Press
Weidner & Sons, Publishing
White Knight Press
Willow Tree Press, Inc.
Wind River Institute Press/Wind River Broadcasting
Writers Forum

D.H. LAWRENCE

Abiko Literary Press (ALP)
ANAIS: An International Journal
Black Sparrow Press

LIBERAL ARTS

PSI Research/The Oasis Press/Hellgate Press

LIBERTARIAN

AFFAIR OF THE MIND: A Literary Quarterly
Autonomedia, Inc.
Axios Newletter, Inc.
Bluestocking Press
Books for All Times, Inc.
Candlestick Publishing
Capital Communications
THE CHEROTIC (r)EVOLUTIONARY
City Lights Books
Columbia Alternative Library
Michael E. Coughlin, Publisher
THE DANDELION
Feral House
Filibuster Press
FOREST: The Freedom Organization for the Right to Smoke Tobacco
The Foundation for Economic Education, Inc.
FREE CHOICE
FREE INQUIRY
THE FREEMAN: Ideas On Liberty
FURTHER TOO
GATEAVISA
GEORGE & MERTIE'S PLACE: Rooms With a View
Handshake Editions
The Heather Foundation
HOAX!
IllumiNet Press
The Independent Institute
THE INDEPENDENT REVIEW: A Journal of Political Economy
KICK IT OVER
Landwaster Books
THE (LIBERTARIAN) CONNECTION
Libertarian Press, Inc./American Book Distributors
LIBERTY
LITTLE FREE PRESS
LIVE AND LET LIVE
LIVING FREE
THE MAD FARMERS' JUBILEE ALMANACK
Marmot Publishing
Mustang Publishing Co.
The New Humanity Press
THE NEW SOUTHERN SURREALIST REVIEW
Reveal
SALON: A Journal of Aesthetics
SHORT FUSE
SKINNYDIPPING
SMART DRUG NEWS
Steamshovel Press
STEAMSHOVEL PRESS
THE TRUTH SEEKER
URBAN GRAFFITI
VIRGINIA LIBERTY
THE VOLUNTARYIST
THE VORTEX

LIBRARIES

Abiko Literary Press (ALP)
American Audio Prose Library (non-print)
Baker Street Publications
BkMk Press
Bluestocking Press
THE BOOK REPORT: Journal for Junior & Senior High School Librarians
BOOK TALK
BRAVO, THE POET'S MAGAZINE
Caliban Press
Canadian Library Association
THE CHRISTIAN LIBRARIAN
CLASS ACT
COUNTERPOISE: For Social Responsibilities, Liberty and Dissent
The Denali Press

Fallout Shelter Press
FELICITER
FEMINIST COLLECTIONS: A QUARTERLY OF WOMEN'S STUDIES RESOURCES
FEMINIST PERIODICALS: A CURRENT LISTING OF CONTENTS
FOCUS: Library Service to Older Adults, People with Disabilities
The Gleniffer Press
HENNEPIN COUNTY LIBRARY CATALOGING BULLETIN
Highsmith Press
INDEPENDENT PUBLISHER
KLIATT
L D A Publishers
LEGAL INFORMATION MANAGEMENT INDEX
LIBRARIANS AT LIBERTY
LIBRARY HI TECH
LIBRARY HIGH TECH NEWS
LIBRARY TALK: The Magazine for Elementary School Librarians
Linworth Publishing, Inc.
THE LONSDALE - The International Quarterly of The Romantic Six
Masefield Books
MIXED BAG
MSRRT NEWSLETTER: LIBRARY ALTERNATIVES
NEW BOOKS ON WOMEN & FEMINISM
Noyce Publishing
The Place In The Woods
THE PRAIRIE JOURNAL OF CANADIAN LITERATURE
PUBLISHING ENTREPRENEUR
R & E Publishers
Nancy Renfro Studios, Inc.
Rio Grande Press
THE ROTKIN REVIEW
Scarecrow Press
SE LA VIE WRITER'S JOURNAL
SJL Publishing Company
TEACHER LIBRARIAN: The Journal for School Library Professionals
TECHNICALITIES
THE U*N*A*B*A*S*H*E*D LIBRARIAN, THE "HOW I RUN MY LIBRARY GOOD" LETTER
University of Calgary Press
The Urbana Free Library
Willowood Press
Wings of Fire Press
Women's Studies Librarian, University of Wisconsin System
Writers Forum
WRITER'S LIFELINE

LIFESTYLES

AFFABLE NEIGHBOR
Affable Neighbor Press
ALIVE: Canadian Journal of Health and Nutrition
Baker Street Publications
BONDAGE FANTASIES
Bookhome Publishing/Panda Publishing
BOUDOIR NOIR
Cherubic Press
COLLEGIUM NEWSLETTER
DAYS AND NIGHTS OF A SMALL PRESS PUBLISHER
FETISH BAZAAR
ICARUS WAS RIGHT
IRIS: A Journal About Women
Itidwitir Publishing
JPS Publishing Company
KOMIC FANTASIES
Life Lessons
LifeThread Publications
Magical Blend
MIXED BAG
N: NUDE & NATURAL
NATURALLY

New Spring Publications
NEW YORK STORIES
NIGHTSHADE
NOCTURNAL REPORTER
Passing Through Publications
PEACE, The Magazine of the Sixties
PLEASANT LIVING
QECE: QUESTION EVERYTHING. CHALLENGE
  EVERYTHING.
REALM OF THE VAMPIRE
Saint Mary's Press
SANDPOINT MAGAZINE
SKINNYDIPPING
SO YOUNG!
URBAN GRAFFITI
VINEGAR   CONNOISSEURS   INTERNATIONAL
  NEWSLETTER
Visions Communications
VIVA PETITES

LIGHTHOUSES

Pineapple Press, Inc.

LITERARY REVIEW

AABYE (formerly New Hope International Writing)
Abiko Literary Press (ALP)
THE ABIKO QUARTERLY WITH JAMES JOYCE FW
  STUDIES
Acclaim Publishing Co. Inc.
AFFAIR OF THE MIND: A Literary Quarterly
African American Audio Press
AFRICAN AMERICAN AUDIOBOOK REVIEW
AFRICAN AMERICAN REVIEW
ALASKA QUARTERLY REVIEW
ALLEGHENY REVIEW
AMARANTH
THE AMERICAN BOOK REVIEW
The American Dissident
AMERICAN LETTERS & COMMENTARY
AMERICAN WRITING: A Magazine
ANQ: A Quarterly Journal of Short Articles, Notes, and
  Reviews
THE ANTIGONISH REVIEW
APOSTROPHE: USCB Journal of the Arts
ARCHIPELAGO
ARIEL—A Review of International English Literature
ARISTOS
ATELIER
AURA LITERARY/ARTS REVIEW
BACKBOARD
BAKER STREET GAZETTE
Baker Street Publications
THE BALTIMORE REVIEW
Bancroft Press
BARNWOOD
BELLES LETTRES
THE BELLINGHAM REVIEW
THE BENT
Black Dress Press
BLACK MOON
BLOOD & APHORISMS: A Journal of Literary Fiction
BOOK TALK
BOOK/MARK SMALL PRESS QUARTERLY REVIEW
BOOKS FROM FINLAND
THE BOSTON BOOK REVIEW
BOSTON REVIEW
Brick Row Publishing Co. Ltd.
BRITISH JOURNAL OF AESTHETICS
Brooding Heron Press
BURNING CAR
THE BURNING CLOUD REVIEW
CALYX: A Journal of Art and Literature by Women
CANADIAN LITERATURE
THE CAPILANO REVIEW
THE CELTIC PEN
CHAPMAN
CHARITON REVIEW
CHASQUI

THE CHATTAHOOCHEE REVIEW
CHICAGO REVIEW
CHILDREN, CHURCHES AND DADDIES, A Non
  Religious, Non Familial Literary Magazine
Chiron Press
CHIRON REVIEW
CLASS ACT
CLUTCH
CONFRONTATION
THE CONNECTICUT POETRY REVIEW
CORRECTIONS TODAY
COTTONWOOD
Cottonwood Press
COVER MAGAZINE
CRAB ORCHARD REVIEW
The F. Marion Crawford Memorial Society
THE CREAM CITY REVIEW
Crescent Moon
CRUCIBLE
CUTBANK
THE DALHOUSIE REVIEW
DAYSPRING
Manya DeLeon Booksmith
DESCANT
DIONYSIA
DIRIGIBLE
THE DROOD REVIEW OF MYSTERY
THE EDGE CITY REVIEW
EDINBURGH REVIEW
EVANSVILLE REVIEW
FACTSHEET FIVE
THE FIDDLEHEAD
FIGMENTS
FINE MADNESS
Five Fingers Press
FIVE FINGERS REVIEW
4*9*1: Neo-Immanentist/Sursymbolist-Imagination
FRANK: AN INTERNATIONAL JOURNAL OF CON-
  TEMPORARY WRITING AND ART
Full Moon Publications
The Future Press
THE GEORGIA REVIEW
THE GLASS CHERRY
The Glass Cherry Press
GLOBAL TAPESTRY
GRANTA
THE GREAT BLUE BEACON
HABERSHAM REVIEW
Hans Zell Publishers
Hard Press, Inc.
THE HARVARD ADVOCATE
THE HAUNTED JOURNAL
HIGH PLAINS LITERARY REVIEW
HOBSON'S CHOICE
THE HOLLINS CRITIC
HOME PLANET NEWS
Home Planet Publications
H2SO4
THE HUDSON REVIEW
ICARUS WAS RIGHT
THE ICONOCLAST
IMPETUS
INDEPENDENT PUBLISHER
INDIANA REVIEW
INTERBANG
THE IOWA REVIEW
IRISH LITERARY SUPPLEMENT
Itidwitir Publishing
THE J MAN TIMES
JAMES JOYCE BROADSHEET
JAMES JOYCE QUARTERLY
JAMES WHITE REVIEW; A Gay Men's Literary
  Quarterly
JEWISH LIFE
THE JOURNAL OF COMMONWEALTH LITERA-
  TURE
JOURNAL OF MODERN LITERATURE
KALDRON, An International Journal Of Visual Poetry

KARMA LAPEL
THE KELSEY REVIEW
THE KENYON REVIEW
LAMBDA BOOK REPORT
THE LANGSTON HUGHES REVIEW
LATINO STUFF REVIEW
THE LICKING RIVER REVIEW
Limberlost Press
LIMESTONE: A LITERARY JOURNAL
LINGO
LININGTON LINEUP
LINQ
LITERARY MAGAZINE REVIEW
THE LITERARY QUARTERLY
THE LITERARY REVIEW
LITERARY ROCKET
THE LONSDALE - The International Quarterly of The
    Romantic Six
THE LOWELL REVIEW
LULLWATER REVIEW
THE MALAHAT REVIEW
MARGIN: EXPLORING MODERN MAGICAL REA-
    LISM
THE MASSACHUSETTS REVIEW
MEANJIN
Mehring Books, Inc.
THE METAPHYSICAL REVIEW
METASEX
MICHIGAN QUARTERLY REVIEW
Middlebury College
THE MIDWEST QUARTERLY
THE MISSOURI REVIEW
MIXED BAG
MOCKINGBIRD
MOONRABBIT REVIEW
MYSTERY READERS JOURNAL
THE MYSTERY REVIEW
NEW ENGLAND REVIEW
New Hope International
NEW HOPE INTERNATIONAL REVIEW
NEW ORLEANS REVIEW
THE NEW PRESS LITERARY QUARTERLY
NIGHT ROSES
NOBODADDIES
NORTH DAKOTA QUARTERLY
North Stone Press
NORTHERN CONTOURS
NOTES & QUERIES
NOTRE DAME REVIEW
NOVA EXPRESS
NUDE BEACH
THE OHIO REVIEW
OHIO WRITER
OHIOANA QUARTERLY
ORBIS
Ortalda & Associates
OSIRIS
OTHER VOICES
Otherwind
PACIFIC ENTERPRISE
THE PACIFIC REVIEW
PANJANDRUM POETRY JOURNAL
THE PANNUS INDEX
PAPERPLATES
PARNASSUS: POETRY IN REVIEW
PARTISAN REVIEW
PASSAGES NORTH
PASSAIC REVIEW (MILLENNIUM EDITIONS)
PASSION
THE PATERSON LITERARY REVIEW
PEMBROKE MAGAZINE
PENNINE PLATFORM
Pennsylvania State University Press
PIG IRON
PIKEVILLE REVIEW
PIRATE WRITINGS
PLAINSONG
PLOUGHSHARES

POETRY EAST
POETRY INTERNATIONAL
POETRY MOTEL
THE POETRY PROJECT NEWSLETTER
POTATO EYES
POTOMAC REVIEW
THE PRAIRIE JOURNAL OF CANADIAN LITERA-
    TURE
PRAIRIE SCHOONER
PRAKALPANA SAHITYA/PRAKALPANA LITERA-
    TURE
PROBABLE CAUSE: A LITERARY REVUE
THE PUCKERBRUSH REVIEW
PULSAR
PURPLE PATCH
Pyx Press
RAIN TAXI REVIEW OF BOOKS
RALPH'S REVIEW
REALM OF THE VAMPIRE
REDOUBT
THE REVIEW OF CONTEMPORARY FICTION
Rio Grande Press
RIVERWIND
THE ROMANTIST
ROOM OF ONE'S OWN
ROSEBUD
ST. LOUIS JOURNALISM REVIEW
SANDHILLS REVIEW (formerly ST. ANDREWS RE-
    VIEW)
THE SANTA MONICA REVIEW
Scars Publications
SE LA VIE WRITER'S JOURNAL
SEWANEE REVIEW
SHAW: THE ANNUAL OF BERNARD SHAW STU-
    DIES
SLEUTH JOURNAL
SO TO SPEAK
SONORA REVIEW
SOUTHERN HUMANITIES REVIEW
THE SOUTHERN REVIEW
SOUTHWEST REVIEW
STAND MAGAZINE
STEAMSHOVEL PRESS
STROKER
STUDIO - A Journal of Christians Writing
THE STYLUS
SUITCASE: A Journal of Transcultural Traffic
SULFUR
SULPHUR RIVER LITERARY REVIEW
SYCAMORE REVIEW
SYMPLOKE: A Journal for the Intermingling of Literary,
    Cultural and Theoretical Scholarship
TAKAHE
TALISMAN: A Journal of Contemporary Poetry and
    Poetics
THE TEXAS REVIEW
TEXTURE
Texture Press
THALIA: Studies in Literary Humor
13TH MOON
THE THREEPENNY REVIEW
TORRE DE PAPEL
TRANSCENDENT VISIONS
TRANSLATION REVIEW
TULSA STUDIES IN WOMEN'S LITERATURE
TURNSTILE
TWO RIVERS REVIEW
THE UNDERGROUND FOREST - LA SELVA SUB-
    TERRANEA
University of Tulsa
UNIVERSITY OF WINDSOR REVIEW
UNMUZZLED OX
URBANUS/RAIZIRR
VIGIL
THE VINCENT BROTHERS REVIEW
VIRGINIA LITERARY REVIEW
THE VIRGINIA QUARTERLY REVIEW
VISIONS-INTERNATIONAL, The World Journal of

823

Illustrated Poetry
WATER ROW REVIEW
WAY STATION MAGAZINE
WESTERN AMERICAN LITERATURE
WESTERN HUMANITIES REVIEW
WHOLE EARTH
WILD DUCK REVIEW
WILLIAM AND MARY REVIEW
WINDHOVER: A Journal of Christian Literature
Witwatersrand University Press
Woman in the Moon Publications (W.I.M. Publications)
WOMENWISE
THE WORCESTER REVIEW
WORMWOOD REVIEW
WRITER'S EXCHANGE
WRITER'S GUIDELINES: A Roundtable for Writers and
    Editors
WRITER'S GUIDELINES & NEWS
WRITER'S WORKSHOP REVIEW
THE WRITING SELF
XAVIER REVIEW
THE YALE REVIEW
YELLOW SILK: Journal Of Erotic Arts
ZUZU'S PETALS: QUARTERLY ONLINE

LITERATURE (GENERAL)

A & U AMERICA'S AIDS MAGAZINE
Abiko Literary Press (ALP)
AERIAL
AFFAIR OF THE MIND: A Literary Quarterly
African American Audio Press
AFRICAN AMERICAN AUDIOBOOK REVIEW
AGADA
AK Press
ALCATRAZ
Alioth Press
AMARANTH
American Audio Prose Library (non-print)
THE AMERICAN VOICE
THE AMETHYST REVIEW
Angelflesh Press
Anhinga Press
ANQ: A Quarterly Journal of Short Articles, Notes, and
    Reviews
APOSTROPHE: USCB Journal of the Arts
Appalachian Consortium Press
ARIEL—A Review of International English Literature
ARISTOS
ASCENT
Associated Writing Programs
ASSPANTS
Asylum Arts
AUFBAU
AURA LITERARY/ARTS REVIEW
AXE FACTORY REVIEW
Baker Street Publications
BAMBOO RIDGE, A HAWAI'I WRITERS JOURNAL
Bamboo Ridge Press
Bandanna Books
BARNABE MOUNTAIN REVIEW
BATHTUB GIN
Beacon Press
THE BEAR DELUXE
BELLES LETTRES
Big Star Press
Bilingue Publications & Productions
Birch Brook Press
BkMk Press
Black Dress Press
Black Hat Press
Black Heron Press
Black Sparrow Press
Blind Beggar Press
BLOOD & APHORISMS: A Journal of Literary Fiction
BLOODJET LITERARY MAGAZINE
THE BLOOMSBURY REVIEW
Blue Heron Publishing, Inc.
Bluestocking Press

Bolton Press
BOOK/MARK SMALL PRESS QUARTERLY REVIEW
BORDERLANDS: Texas Poetry Review
Borealis Press Limited
THE BOSTON BOOK REVIEW
BOTTOMFISH
BOULEVARD
The Boxwood Press
Branden Publishing Company
Brick Row Publishing Co. Ltd.
THE BRIDGE: A Journal of Fiction and Poetry
BRILLIANT STAR
Broken Jaw Press
BROKEN PENCIL
THE BROWNSTONE REVIEW
Burning Books
Burning Bush Publications
THE BURNING CLOUD REVIEW
CALAPOOYA
Caliban Press
CALLALOO
CALYX: A Journal of Art and Literature by Women
Capra Press
THE CAROLINA QUARTERLY
Carolina Wren Press/Lollipop Power Books
Carrefour Press
Center for South and Southeast Asian Studies Publications
Chandler & Sharp Publishers, Inc.
Chaos Warrior Productions
CHELSEA
THE CHEROTIC (r)EVOLUTIONARY
Chicago Spectrum Press
CHILDREN, CHURCHES AND DADDIES, A Non
    Religious, Non Familial Literary Magazine
Chinese Literature Press
Chiron Press
CHIRON REVIEW
CHRISTIANITY & THE ARTS
CHRONICLES OF DISORDER
CIMARRON REVIEW
City Lights Books
CITY PRIMEVAL
CLASS ACT
Clover Park Press
Coffee House Press
COLD-DRILL
Company of Words Publishing
CONFLICT OF INTEREST
CONFLUENCE
Confluence Press, Inc.
CONJUNCTIONS
Coteau Books
CRAB CREEK REVIEW
The F. Marion Crawford Memorial Society
CREATIVE NONFICTION
Crescent Moon
CRICKET
CRIPES!
CROSSCURRENTS, A QUARTERLY
CRUCIBLE
Cumberland
CURRENT ACCOUNTS
Cypress House
Dalkey Archive Press
Dan River Press
John Daniel and Company, Publishers
DAYS AND NIGHTS OF A SMALL PRESS PUB-
    LISHER
DAYSPRING
December Press
Manya DeLeon Booksmith
Department of Romance Languages
DESCANT
DHARMA BEAT
DIALOGOS: Hellenic Studies Review
DIRIGIBLE
THE DIRTY GOAT
Down The Shore Publishing

DROP FORGE
DRUMVOICES REVUE
Dufour Editions Inc.
THE DUPLEX PLANET
THE DURHAM UNIVERSITY JOURNAL
EARTH'S DAUGHTERS: Feminist Arts Periodical
EASTGATE QUARTERLY REVIEW OF HYPERTEXT
THE EDGE CITY REVIEW
Edition Gemini
ELT Press
ENGLISH LITERATURE IN TRANSITION, 1880-1920
Eros Publishing
ETCETERA
Evanston Publishing, Inc.
EVANSVILLE REVIEW
THE EVER DANCING MUSE
THE EVERGREEN CHRONICLES
Exile Press
Far Corner Books
FAULTLINE, Journal of Art and Literature
The Feminist Press at the City College
FICTION
FINE MADNESS
FIRST CLASS
FISH DRUM MAGAZINE
Fithian Press
Fjord Press
THE FLORIDA REVIEW
Four Seasons Publishers
Four Walls Eight Windows
Four-Sep Publications
FOURTEEN HILLS: The SFSU Review
Fromm International Publishing Corporation
Full Moon Publications
The Future Press
The Galileo Press Ltd.
Gay Sunshine Press, Inc.
GEORGE & MERTIE'S PLACE: Rooms With a View
THE GETTYSBURG REVIEW
GINOSKO
The Gleniffer Press
GRAND STREET
GRANTA
Graywolf Press
Great Elm Press
Green Bean Press
Griffon House Publications
Growing Room Collective
Guernica Editions, Inc.
HABERSHAM REVIEW
HAIGHT ASHBURY LITERARY JOURNAL
THE HARVARD ADVOCATE
THE HAUNTED JOURNAL
Hermitage (Ermitazh)
Heyday Books
The Heyeck Press
Hi Jinx Press
Hobblebush Books
THE HOLLINS CRITIC
Holy Cow! Press
HORIZON
Host Publications, Inc.
Howling Dog Press/Stiletto
H2SO4
Humana Press
Huntington Library Press
HUNTINGTON LIBRARY QUARTERLY
HURRICANE ALICE
ICARUS WAS RIGHT
ICON
THE ICONOCLAST
IDIOM 23
ILLUMINATIONS
Images For Media/Sesquin
IMAGO
Indelible Inc.
THE INDIAN WRITER
The Institute of Mind and Behavior

INTERBANG
THE IOWA REVIEW
ITALIAN AMERICANA
Italica Press, Inc.
Itidwitir Publishing
IWAN: INMATE WRITERS OF AMERICA NEWSLETTER
THE J MAN TIMES
JACK MACKEREL MAGAZINE
Jade Moon Publications
Jahbone Press
JAMES JOYCE BROADSHEET
Javelina Books
J'ECRIS
JEJUNE: america Eats its Young
JOURNAL OF CANADIAN STUDIES/Revue d'etudes canadiennes
THE JOURNAL OF MIND AND BEHAVIOR
JOURNAL OF MODERN LITERATURE
July Blue Press
KALDRON, An International Journal Of Visual Poetry
KARMA LAPEL
Kelsey St. Press
Kenyette Productions
THE KENYON REVIEW
KEREM: Creative Explorations in Judaism
Michael Kesend Publishing, Ltd.
Allen A. Knoll Publishers
La Alameda Press
LATIN AMERICAN LITERARY REVIEW
Latin American Literary Review Press
Leapfrog Press
LEAPINGS LITERARY MAGAZINE
Leete's Island Books
LEFT CURVE
LIES MAGAZINE
LIGHT: The Quarterly of Light Verse
LIMESTONE: A LITERARY JOURNAL
Lincoln Springs Press
THE LION AND THE UNICORN: A Critical Journal of Children's Literature
THE LITERARY QUARTERLY
LITERARY ROCKET
THE LONSDALE - The International Quarterly of The Romantic Six
LOST GENERATION JOURNAL
Lost Horse Press
Lotus Press, Inc.
LUCKY HEART BOOKS
LULLWATER REVIEW
LUZ EN ARTE Y LITERATURA
LYNX EYE
MAIN STREET JOURNAL
MAINE IN PRINT
Maisonneuve Press
THE MANHATTAN REVIEW
MANOA: A Pacific Journal of International Writing
MARK
McPherson & Company Publishers
MEDIA SPOTLIGHT
MEDUSA'S HAIRDO
The Menard Press
Mercury House
MERLYN'S PEN: Fiction, Essays, and Poems By America's Teens
MESSAGES FROM THE HEART
THE METAPHYSICAL REVIEW
MICHIGAN QUARTERLY REVIEW
The Middleburg Press
Middlebury College
Mid-List Press
Midwest Villages & Voices
Miles & Miles
Milkweed Editions
MINNESOTA LITERATURE
THE MINNESOTA REVIEW
MIXED BAG
MODERN LANGUAGE QUARTERLY: A Journal of

THE SMALL POND MAGAZINE OF LITERATURE
  aka SMALL POND
SOUTH DAKOTA REVIEW
THE SOUTHERN REVIEW
SOUTHWEST REVIEW
Spectrum Press
SPIDER
THE SPITTING IMAGE
SPRING: A Journal of Archetype and Culture
The Square-Rigger Press
STAGNANCY IS REVOLTING
Station Hill Press
Steerforth Press, L.C.
THE WALLACE STEVENS JOURNAL
STILETTO
STONEFLOWER LITERARY JOURNAL
STORY
STORYQUARTERLY
STOVEPIPE: A Journal of Little Literary Value
STUDIO - A Journal of Christians Writing
THE STYLUS
Sherwood Sugden & Company, Publishers
Sulisa Publishing
SULPHUR RIVER LITERARY REVIEW
Sweet Lady Moon Press
SYCAMORE REVIEW
SYMPLOKE: A Journal for the Intermingling of Literary,
  Cultural and Theoretical Scholarship
SYNAESTHETIC
SYNCOPATED CITY
Synergistic Press
Tafford Publishing
TAKAHE
Talisman House, Publishers
TALKING RIVER REVIEW
TAPROOT, a journal of older writers
TAPROOT LITERARY REVIEW
THALIA: Studies in Literary Humor
THEMA
13TH MOON
32 PAGES
THE THREEPENNY REVIEW
Threshold Books
Tia Chucha Press
Tilbury House, Publishers
TORRE DE PAPEL
TRANVIA - Revue der Iberischen Halbinsel
TRIQUARTERLY
TRIVIUM
Turnstone Press
Tyro Publishing
ULITARRA
THE UNDERGROUND FOREST - LA SELVA SUB-
  TERRANEA
Underwhich Editions
THE UNIT CIRCLE
University of Calgary Press
University of Massachusetts Press
University of Sydney Union
UNO MÁS MAGAZINE
Urion Press
Vagabond Press
Valentine Publishing & Drama Co.
VERSE: A Journal of Poetry & Poetics
Via God Publishing
THE VINCENT BROTHERS REVIEW
THE VIRGINIA QUARTERLY REVIEW
WATER ROW REVIEW
Weidner & Sons, Publishing
The Wellsweep Press
West Anglia Publications
West End Press
WESTERN AMERICAN LITERATURE
WESTERN HUMANITIES REVIEW
Who Who Who Publishing
WIND
Wise Owl Press
WITNESS

WRITER'S CHRONICLE
WRITERS GAZETTE
WRITER'S GUIDELINES: A Roundtable for Writers and
  Editors
WRITER'S GUIDELINES & NEWS
Writers House Press
WRITERS IN PARADISE
WRITER'S LIFELINE
WRITING ULSTER
XAVIER REVIEW
X-RAY
YELLOW SILK: Journal Of Erotic Arts
Zoland Books
ZUZU'S PETALS: QUARTERLY ONLINE

LONDON

American Literary Press Inc./Noble House
BAKER STREET GAZETTE
Baker Street Publications
CLASS ACT
DAYS AND NIGHTS OF A SMALL PRESS PUB-
  LISHER
KELTIC FRINGE
THE LONSDALE - The International Quarterly of The
  Romantic Six
Peter Marcan Publications
MIXED BAG
SLEUTH JOURNAL
WHITECHAPEL JOURNAL

JACK LONDON

Abiko Literary Press (ALP)
ATOM MIND
CLASS ACT
The Live Oak Press
Mutual Publishing
Queen of Swords Press
THE STYLUS
WESTERN AMERICAN LITERATURE

LOS ANGELES

Baker Street Publications
Balcony Press
Clover Park Press
DAYS AND NIGHTS OF A SMALL PRESS PUB-
  LISHER
Happy Rock Press
HOLLYWOOD NOSTALGIA
Allen A. Knoll Publishers
LUMMOX JOURNAL
MIXED BAG
PLAIN BROWN WRAPPER (PBW)
Really Great Books
SHEILA-NA-GIG
Gibbs Smith, Publisher

LOUISIANA

Baker Street Publications
The Chicot Press
Claitor's Law Books & Publishing Division, Inc.
DAYS AND NIGHTS OF A SMALL PRESS PUB-
  LISHER
DESIRE STREET
Full Moon Publications
HORIZONS
THE LOUISIANA REVIEW
MESECHABE: The Journal of Surre(gion)alism
MIXED BAG
Thunder Rain Publishing Corp.
XAVIER REVIEW

H.P. LOVECRAFT

Algol Press
Baker Street Publications
CLASS ACT
The F. Marion Crawford Memorial Society
CURMUDGEON
Full Moon Publications

Gryphon Publications
THE HAUNTED JOURNAL
HORIZONS BEYOND
METAL CURSE
NIGHTSHADE
NOCTURNAL REPORTER
NOVA EXPRESS
THE OVERLOOK CONNECTION
PAPERBACK PARADE
POEMS THAT THUMP IN THE DARK/SECOND GLANCE
RALPH'S REVIEW
REALM OF DARKNESS
REALM OF THE VAMPIRE
RED OWL
THE ROMANTIST
THE SALEM JOURNAL
SCIENCE FICTION CHRONICLE
SOCIETE
VIRTUTE ET MORTE MAGAZINE

BULWER LYTTON

CLASS ACT
The F. Marion Crawford Memorial Society
THE ROMANTIST

MAGAZINES

Abiko Literary Press (ALP)
AFFABLE NEIGHBOR
Affable Neighbor Press
African American Audio Press
AFRICAN AMERICAN AUDIOBOOK REVIEW
ALTERNATIVE PRESS REVIEW
THE ANGRY THOREAUAN
ARCHIPELAGO
Astrion Publishing
THE AUCTION MAGAZINE
BABYSUE
BAKER STREET GAZETTE
Baker Street Publications
BOOK MARKETING UPDATE
BRAVO, THE POET'S MAGAZINE
CHILDREN, CHURCHES AND DADDIES, A Non Religious, Non Familial Literary Magazine
CLASS ACT
CONFRONTATION
COUNTERPOISE: For Social Responsibilities, Liberty and Dissent
CREEPY MIKE'S OMNIBUS OF FUN
CRICKET
CRIPES!
DAYS AND NIGHTS OF A SMALL PRESS PUBLISHER
DISSONANCE MAGAZINE
DRASTIC LIVES
DREAM NETWORK JOURNAL
THE DROPLET JOURNAL
ETCETERA
FAULTLINE, Journal of Art and Literature
FEMINIST PERIODICALS: A CURRENT LISTING OF CONTENTS
FIDELIS ET VERUS
FRANK: AN INTERNATIONAL JOURNAL OF CONTEMPORARY WRITING AND ART
FULL MOON DIRECTORY
Full Moon Publications
GATEAVISA
GRAFFITI OFF THE ASYLUM WALLS
GRAY AREAS
THE GREAT BLUE BEACON
Gryphon Publications
THE HAUNTED JOURNAL
Heidelberg Graphics
HELIOCENTRIC NET/STIGMATA
Himalayan Institute Press
HIP MAMA
HOAX!
HORIZONS BEYOND

ICARUS WAS RIGHT
THE ICONOCLAST
THE ILLUSTRATOR COLLECTOR'S NEWS
IMPETUS
INDY MAGAZINE
Itidwitir Publishing
JARRETT'S JOURNAL
JEWISH LIFE
JOTS (Journal of the Senses)
KALDRON, An International Journal Of Visual Poetry
KARMA LAPEL
LITERARY MAGAZINE REVIEW
THE LITERARY QUARTERLY
LOST GENERATION JOURNAL
Marinelli Publishing
MEDIA SPOTLIGHT
METAL CURSE
THE METAPHYSICAL REVIEW
Mindfield Publications
MIXED BAG
THE MONTHLY (formerly THE BERKELEY MONTHLY)
MSRRT NEWSLETTER: LIBRARY ALTERNATIVES
NEW HOPE INTERNATIONAL REVIEW
NEW THOUGHT JOURNAL
NIGHTSHADE
NOCTURNAL REPORTER
Nonsilent Press
OHIO WRITER
OTHER VOICES
PAPYRUS
Peartree Books & Music
PEN & INK WRITERS JOURNAL
PHOENIX MAGAZINE
Phoenix Press
PIG IRON
POETRY MOTEL
POETS' ROUNDTABLE
POETS' VOICE
POTATO EYES
THE PRAIRIE JOURNAL OF CANADIAN LITERATURE
Prakken Publications
Progressive Education
PROGRESSIVE PERIODICALS DIRECTORY/UPDATE
REALM OF THE VAMPIRE
RELIX
Reveal
Rio Grande Press
ST. LOUIS JOURNALISM REVIEW
THE SALEM JOURNAL
Scars Publications
SE LA VIE WRITER'S JOURNAL
SHEILA-NA-GIG
Slab-O-Concrete Publications
SLEUTH JOURNAL
THE SMALL PRESS BOOK REVIEW
SMALL PRESS CREATIVE EXPLOSION
THE SMALL PRESS REVIEW/SMALL MAGAZINE REVIEW
SMALL PUBLISHER
SNOW LION NEWSLETTER & CATALOG
SPIDER
STONE SOUP, The Magazine By Young Writers and Artists
THEY WON'T STAY DEAD!
13TH MOON
THRESHOLDS JOURNAL
THE UNDERGROUND FOREST - LA SELVA SUBTERRANEA
THE UNIT CIRCLE
URBAN GRAFFITI
Vagabond Press
WESTERN SKIES
WHOLE EARTH
WORLD OF FANDOM MAGAZINE
THE WRITE WAY
Writers Forum

WRITER'S GUIDELINES & NEWS
WRITER'S WORKSHOP REVIEW
Years Press

MAGIC

Baker Street Publications
THE CATBIRD SEAT
THE CHEROTIC (r)EVOLUTiONARY
Crescent Moon
The Crossing Press
DAYS AND NIGHTS OF A SMALL PRESS PUB-
LISHER
Earth Magic Productions, Inc.
THE EMSHOCK LETTER
FULL MOON DIRECTORY
GATEAVISA
GEORGE & MERTIE'S PLACE: Rooms With a View
HECATE'S LOOM - A Journal of Magical Arts
HOAX!
Horned Owl Publishing
INTUITIVE EXPLORATIONS
KMJ Educational Programs
Llewellyn Publications
MARGIN: EXPLORING MODERN MAGICAL REA-
LISM
MetaGnosis
METAL CURSE
MYSTIC VOICES
NIGHTSHADE
nine muses books
NOCTURNAL REPORTER
OF A LIKE MIND
PASSION
Piccadilly Books
Pride & Imprints
REALM OF DARKNESS
REALM OF THE VAMPIRE
RED OWL
Reyes Investment Enterprise Ltd.
SAGEWOMAN
SPIRIT TO SPIRIT
SQUARE ONE - A Magazine of Disturbing Fiction
Three Pyramids Publishing
Tiger Press
VAMPIRE NIGHTS
Samuel Weiser, Inc.
Willendorf Press

MAINE

Baker Street Publications
Booksplus of Maine
THE CLIMBING ART
DAYS AND NIGHTS OF A SMALL PRESS PUB-
LISHER
Falcon Press Publishing Company
Full Moon Publications
Heartsong Books
HORIZONS
The Latona Press
MAINE IN PRINT
MIXED BAG
New England Cartographics, Inc.
NORTHWOODS JOURNAL, A Magazine for Writers
Pocahontas Press, Inc.
Stones Point Press
Tilbury House, Publishers
University of Calgary Press
Wescott Cove Publishing Co.

MANAGEMENT

Acton Circle Publishing Company
Afcom Publishing
Alpine Guild, Inc.
Archipelago Publishing
Behavioral Sciences Research Press, Inc.
Benchmark Publications Inc.
BUSINESPIRIT JOURNAL
Canadian Educators' Press

Capital Communications
Timothy A. Dimoff/SACS Consulting
Fisher Books
Frugal Marketer Publishing
Haverford Business Press
Information Research Lab
INNOVATING
JOURNAL OF COURT REPORTING
Keel Publications
The Madson Group, Inc.
Manta Press
MCS Publishing
Metamorphous Press
Mountain Automation Corporation
New Management Publishing Company, Inc.
New View Publications
Pegasus Communications, Inc.
PREP Publishing
PT Publications, Inc.
THE RATIONAL FEMINIST
THE SMALL BUSINESS ADVISOR
Tell Publishing
Two Eagles Press International
VanderWyk & Burnham
WHOLE EARTH

MAPS

Bright Mountain Books, Inc.
MAP AFICIONADO
RED OWL
Winchester/G. Ander Books

MARINE LIFE

Baker Street Publications
Full Moon Publications
HORIZONS
MIXED BAG
Naturegraph Publishers, Inc.
New World Publications, Inc.
RESONANCE
Sea Challengers, Inc.
SEA KAYAKER
Tortuga Books
W.E.C. Plant Publishing

MARKETING

A Cappela Publishing
The Dragon Press
Eureka Publishing Group
Frugal Marketer Publishing
Golden Eagle Press
Infinite Corridor Publishing
JOURNAL OF COURT REPORTING
Page One
Pipeline Press
PSI Research/The Oasis Press/Hellgate Press
SJL Publishing Company
SUBSCRIBE, Ideas and Marketing Tips for Newsletter
Publishers
Tiptoe Literary Service
Trace Publications
WRITER'S WORKSHOP REVIEW

MARRIAGE

Axelrod Publishing of Tampa Bay
Beekman Publishers, Inc.
Blue Dolphin Publishing, Inc.
Brighton Publications, Inc.
Cherubic Press
Conari Press
Coteau Books
Cyclone Books
DAUGHTERS OF SARAH
The Dibble Fund for Marriage Education
DOVETAIL: A Journal by and for Jewish/Christian
Families
Dovetail Publishing
Fisher Books

Gateway Books
GEORGE & MERTIE'S PLACE: Rooms With a View
GLEN BURNIELAND
Greenlawn Press
Halo Books
HIP MAMA
Impact Publishers, Inc.
Innovanna Publishing Co., Inc.
Langmarc Publishing
MATRIARCH'S WAY: The Journal of Female Supremacy
New Regency Publishing
Nolo Press - Occidental
Papillon Publishing
Perspectives Press
THE PLOUGH
THE RATIONAL FEMINIST
River Press
Times Change Press
WHOLE EARTH

MARTIAL ARTS

Abiko Literary Press (ALP)
Arjuna Library Press
Galt Publishing
JOURNAL OF ASIAN MARTIAL ARTS
The Overlook Press
Paladin Enterprises, Inc.
Shaolin Communications
Synapse-Centurion
THEATER
Turtle Press, division of S.K. Productions Inc.
Via Media Publishing Company
Samuel Weiser, Inc.
WHOLE EARTH

MASSAGE

Anti-Aging Press
The Crossing Press
NEW FRONTIER
SCIENCE/HEALTH ABSTRACTS
SKINNYDIPPING
SO YOUNG!
STONES IN MY POCKET

MATHEMATICS

Applied Probability Trust
Arjuna Library Press
ATL Press, Inc.
BLACKJACK FORUM
Child's Play
Clearwater Publishing Co.
Construction Trades Press
Goodheart-Willcox Publisher
Huntington Press
JOURNAL OF REGIONAL CRITICISM
KIDSCIENCE
Lowy Publishing
MATHEMATICAL SPECTRUM
MODERN LOGIC: An International Journal for the History of Mathematical Logic, Set Theory, and Foundations of Mathematics
Modern Logic Publishing
Multi Media Arts
MUSIC PERCEPTION
NEW HOPE INTERNATIONAL REVIEW
Organization for Equal Education of the Sexes, Inc.
Polar Bear Productions & Company
Polygonal Publishing House
Prometheus Enterprises, Inc.
QED
R.G.E. Publishing
SJL Publishing Company
SMARANDACHE NOTIONS
SMARANDACHE NOTIONS JOURNAL
George Wahr Publishing Company
WHOLE EARTH
Wide World Publishing/TETRA

MEDIA

American Audio Prose Library (non-print)
AMERICAN JOURNALISM REVIEW
THE ANGRY THOREAUAN
ATROCITY
Baker Street Publications
Bay Press
BOOGLIT
BOOK MARKETING UPDATE
Crescent Moon
D.B.A. Books
DISSONANCE MAGAZINE
Film-Video Publications
FODDERWING
GEORGE & MERTIE'S PLACE: Rooms With a View
GRAFFITI OFF THE ASYLUM WALLS
GrapeVinePress
HOAX!
Images For Media/Sesquin
JARRETT'S JOURNAL
KARMA LAPEL
Keel Publications
KETTERING REVIEW
LEFT BUSINESS OBSERVER
LEFT CURVE
MEANJIN
The Media Institute
Mho & Mho Works
MIXED BAG
New Spirit Press/The Poet Tree
Open Horizons Publishing Company
PASSION
Progressive Education
PROGRESSIVE PERIODICALS DIRECTORY/UPDATE
QECE: QUESTION EVERYTHING. CHALLENGE EVERYTHING.
QUESTION EVERYTHING CHALLENGE EVERYTHING (QECE)
Reference Desk Books
S.E.T. FREE: The Newsletter Against Television
ST. LOUIS JOURNALISM REVIEW
SANDBOX MAGAZINE
Slab-O-Concrete Publications
Strata Publishing, Inc.
THE UNIT CIRCLE
THE WASHINGTON MONTHLY
THE WHITE DOT - Survival Guide for the TV-Free
WORLD OF FANDOM MAGAZINE

MEDICINE

ABELexpress
Adams-Blake Publishing
ADAPTED PHYSICAL ACTIVITY QUARTERLY (APAQ)
AFFAIR OF THE MIND: A Literary Quarterly
Alpine Guild, Inc.
America West Publishers
AMERICAN PHYSICIANS ART ASSOCIATION NEWSLETTER
THE ANIMALS' AGENDA
ATHLETIC THERAPY TODAY (ATT)
ATL Press, Inc.
Axelrod Publishing of Tampa Bay
Beekman Publishers, Inc.
Bonus Books, Inc.
Borderland Sciences Research Foundation
CANADIAN JOURNAL OF APPLIED PHYSIOLOGY (CJAP)
Carolina Academic Press
THE CIVIL ABOLITIONIST
Civitas
THE COMPLEAT NURSE
Consumer Press
dbS Productions
Devil Mountain Books
Dry Bones Press
EXERCISE IMMUNOLOGY REVIEW (EIR)

Fillmore Publishing Company
Fisher Books
FOREST: The Freedom Organization for the Right to Smoke Tobacco
FREE CHOICE
Future Horizons, Inc.
Galde Press, Inc.
Galen Press, Ltd.
GoldenIsle Publishers, Inc.
Health Press
HEALTHY WEIGHT JOURNAL
Human Kinetics Pub. Inc.
Humana Press
Images For Media/Sesquin
JOURNAL OF POLYMORPHOUS PERVERSITY
JOURNAL OF SCIENTIFIC EXPLORATION
JOURNAL OF SPORT REHABILITATION (JSR)
Kali Press
Ledero Press
Lester Street Publishing
Library Research Associates
MEDICAL HISTORY
MEDIPHORS
MedStudy Corporation
MIDWIFERY TODAY
Midwifery Today Books
MOTOR CONTROL
Papillon Publishing
Parabola
PEDIATRIC EXERCISE SCIENCE (PES)
Pine Publications
Plympton Press International
Popular Medicine Press
Power Publications
Real Life Storybooks
RESONANCE
Reveal
St. Georges Press
SCIENCE/HEALTH ABSTRACTS
Skidmore-Roth Publishing, Inc.
SMART DRUG NEWS
Smart Publications
STONES IN MY POCKET
Swan Publishing Company
The Tonal Company
Vanitas Press
Vista Publishing, Inc.
WHOLE EARTH
WOMENWISE

MEDIEVAL

Abiko Literary Press (ALP)
AFFAIR OF THE MIND: A Literary Quarterly
Baker Street Publications
Bolchazy-Carducci Publishers, Inc.
The Carnation Press
CLASS ACT
Conari Press
The F. Marion Crawford Memorial Society
DAYS AND NIGHTS OF A SMALL PRESS PUB-LISHER
Erespin Press
FULL MOON DIRECTORY
Full Moon Publications
GEORGE & MERTIE'S PLACE: Rooms With a View
Heron Press
HORIZONS BEYOND
Italica Press, Inc.
JOURNAL OF UNCONVENTIONAL HISTORY
LEO Productions LLC.
NEW HOPE INTERNATIONAL REVIEW
NOTES & QUERIES
NOTTINGHAM MEDIEVAL STUDIES
REALM OF DARKNESS
REALM OF THE VAMPIRE
RENAISSANCE MAGAZINE
Resource Publications, Inc.
THE ROMANTIST

VAMPIRE NIGHTS
VIRGIN MEAT E-ZINE
VIRTUTE ET MORTE MAGAZINE
YE OLDE NEWES

MEMOIRS

THE ACORN
ACORN WHISTLE
AFFAIR OF THE MIND: A Literary Quarterly
Alaska Native Language Center
Arjay Associates
Axelrod Publishing of Tampa Bay
Bancroft Press
BARNABE MOUNTAIN REVIEW
Beacon Point Press
Big Star Press
Bright Mountain Books, Inc.
Carrefour Press
Chandler & Sharp Publishers, Inc.
Chicory Blue Press, Inc.
CLASS ACT
Comstock Bonanza Press
THE CREAM CITY REVIEW
Cypress House
John Daniel and Company, Publishers
DAYS AND NIGHTS OF A SMALL PRESS PUB-LISHER
December Press
Eros Publishing
ETCETERA
Fithian Press
FOURTH GENRE: EXPLORATIONS IN NONFICTION
GEORGE & MERTIE'S PLACE: Rooms With a View
god is DEAD, publications
Golden Eagle Press
GrapeVinePress
Hollis Publishing Company
JEWISH LIFE
Leapfrog Press
MacMurray & Beck
MANGROVE MAGAZINE
THE METAPHYSICAL REVIEW
Orchises Press
Palm Island Press
PALO ALTO REVIEW
Paris Press, Inc.
PASSAGER: A Journal of Remembrance and Discovery
PEACE, The Magazine of the Sixties
POTOMAC REVIEW
Premium Press America
Pruett Publishing Company
QED Press
Red Apple Publishing
Red Crane Books, Inc.
Rockbridge Publishing Co.
SALAMANDER
Seal Press
SEWANEE REVIEW
Sherman Asher Publishing
SISTERSONG: Women Across Cultures
Steerforth Press, L.C.
Sun Dog Press
Turnstone Press

MEN

Acclaim Publishing Co. Inc.
AFFAIR OF THE MIND: A Literary Quarterly
ARTHUR'S COUSIN
AT-HOME DAD
Beacon Press
Bear & Company, Inc.
BLK
Blue Dolphin Publishing, Inc.
Chandler & Sharp Publishers, Inc.
Commune-A-Key Publishing, Inc.
Coteau Books
The Crossing Press
Down There Press

Ecrivez!
FIRSTHAND
FURTHER TOO
Gemini Publishing Company
GEORGE & MERTIE'S PLACE: Rooms With a View
GLB Publishers
Hunter House Inc., Publishers
ICON THOUGHTSTYLE MAGAZINE
Inner Traditions International
Islewest Publishing
JAMES WHITE REVIEW; A Gay Men's Literary
  Quarterly
THE LIBERATOR
Liberty Bell Press & Publishing Co.
NEW THOUGHT JOURNAL
C. Olson & Company
Palm Drive Publishing
The Place In The Woods
THE RATIONAL FEMINIST
Red Alder Books
RFD
SINGLE SCENE
SKINNYDIPPING
SO YOUNG!
Steel Balls Press
Swan Publishing Company
Tilbury House, Publishers
Times Change Press
Triad Press
Twelvetrees Press
Whole Person Associates Inc.
XIB
Xib Publications
XY: Men, Sex, Politics
Yellow Moon Press

H.L. MENCKEN

CLASS ACT
The Independent Institute
THE INDEPENDENT REVIEW: A Journal of Political
  Economy
Passeggiata Press, Inc.
SCIENCE FICTION CHRONICLE
THE STYLUS
THE TRUTH SEEKER

MENTAL HEALTH

Anti-Aging Press
Axelrod Publishing of Tampa Bay
BERKELEY WOMEN'S LAW JOURNAL
COMMON BOUNDARY MAGAZINE
Commune-A-Key Publishing, Inc.
Compact Clinicals
Consumer Press
Fillmore Publishing Company
GEORGE & MERTIE'S PLACE: Rooms With a View
Himalayan Institute Press
Holbrook Street Press
Intermountain Publishing
JACK MACKEREL MAGAZINE
JOURNAL OF PSYCHOACTIVE DRUGS
Lemieux International Ltd.
LFW Enterprises
LifeQuest Publishing Group
Meadow Mountain Press
THE MUSING PLACE
NEW ALTERNATIVES
Newjoy Press
PHOENIX MAGAZINE
Phoenix Press
QED Press
Sidran Foundation and Press
SO YOUNG!
STONES IN MY POCKET
Third Side Press, Inc.
Turtle Island Press, Inc.
URBAN GRAFFITI
Women of Diversity Productions, Inc.

METAPHYSICS

A.R.E. Press
Abiko Literary Press (ALP)
ACS Publications
AFFAIR OF THE MIND: A Literary Quarterly
Altair Publications
ANT ANT ANT ANT ANT
Anti-Aging Press
AREOPAGUS
Arjuna Library Press
Ascension Publishing
ASTROFLASH
AT-HOME DAD
Axelrod Publishing of Tampa Bay
Baker Street Publications
Balboa Books
Bear & Company, Inc.
Blue Dolphin Publishing, Inc.
Booksplus of Maine
Borden Publishing Co.
Borderland Sciences Research Foundation
BORDERLANDS: A Quarterly Journal Of Borderland
  Research
BOTH SIDES NOW
CANADIAN JOURNAL OF PHILOSOPHY
Cherubic Press
Cosmic Concepts
Cosmoenergetics Publications
CRONE CHRONICLES: A Journal of Conscious Aging
The Crossing Press
Desert Oasis Publishing Co.
Dharma Publishing
Divina (A MacMurray & Beck imprint)
Dream Street Publishing
Earth Magic Productions, Inc.
Edin Books, Inc.
Emerald Wave
EMERGING
THE EMSHOCK LETTER
ENLIGHTENMENTS
Free People Press
Galde Press, Inc.
Gateways Books And Tapes
Golden Eagle Press
Golden Isis Press
Great Western Publishing Company
Heartsong Books
HEAVEN BONE MAGAZINE
Heaven Bone Press
HECATE'S LOOM - A Journal of Magical Arts
HOAX!
Horned Owl Publishing
Hyacinth House Publications/Caligula Editions
IllumiNet Press
In Print Publishing
INNER JOURNEYS
Inner Traditions International
INTUITIVE EXPLORATIONS
J & L Publications
Jaguar Books
JOURNAL OF AESTHETICS AND ART CRITICISM
JOURNAL OF REGIONAL CRITICISM
H J Kramer
Llewellyn Publications
THE LONSDALE - The International Quarterly of The
  Romantic Six
LP Publications (Teleos Institute)
Magical Blend
Merging Worlds Publishers, Inc.
META4: Journal of Object Oriented Poetics (OOPS)
MetaGnosis
MYSTIC VOICES
Native Plant Publishing
NEW FRONTIER
The New Humanity Press
New Native Press
New Paradigm Books

New Spirit Press/The Poet Tree
New Vision Publishing
NOCTURNAL REPORTER
OFFICE NUMBER ONE
Omega Publications, Inc.
Parabola
PARABOLA MAGAZINE
Pathways Press, Inc.
Philopsychy Press
Picturesque Publications
POEMS THAT THUMP IN THE DARK/SECOND
GLANCE
Princess Publishing
Quantum Mind Publications
THE QUEST
Reyes Investment Enterprise Ltd.
Rio Grande Press
SAGEWOMAN
St. Georges Press
Savant Garde Workshop
SHAMAN'S DRUM: A Journal of Experiential Shaman-
ism
SHARE INTERNATIONAL
Sigo Press
Skytop Publishing
SOM Publishing, division of School of Metaphysics
Sparrow Hawk Press
SPIRIT TO SPIRIT
Steamshovel Press
Stillpoint Publishing
STONES IN MY POCKET
Sun-Scape Publications, a division of Sun-Scape Enter-
prises Ltd.
SunShine Press Publications, Inc.
Swan Raven & Company
Theosophical Publishing House
Three Pyramids Publishing
THRESHOLDS JOURNAL
Tickerwick Publications
Timeless Books
Toad Hall, Inc.
Top Of The Mountain Publishing
Torchlight Publishing
Unified Publications
Unity Books
UNITY MAGAZINE
Verity Press Publishing
Samuel Weiser, Inc.
Westgate Press
THE WISDOM CONSERVANCY NEWSLETTER
The Woodbridge Group
Yes You Can Press

MEXICO

AXE FACTORY REVIEW
BAJA SUN
Baker Street Publications
BORDERLINES
Editorial El Sol De Baja
HORIZONS
LOVE AND RAGE, A Revolutionary Anarchist News-
paper
MIXED BAG

MICHIGAN

Avery Color Studios
Wm.B. Eerdmans Publishing Co.
Grand River Press
JAM RAG
LAKE SUPERIOR MAGAZINE
Momentum Books, Ltd.
NORTH COAST REVIEW
Palladium Communications
PASSAGES NORTH
Poetic License Press
Poetry Harbor
SINCERE SINGLES
Wilderness Adventure Books

MIDDLE EAST

ALADDIN'S WINDOW
AUFBAU
Baker Street Publications
Between The Lines
The Borgo Press
Clarity Press, Inc.
Coyote Publishing
CRITICAL REVIEW
CROSS ROADS
EUROPEAN JUDAISM
Florida Academic Press
Full Moon Publications
Gay Sunshine Press, Inc.
Hoover Institution Press
HORIZONS
House of Hits, Inc.
IBEX Publishers
Interlink Publishing Group, Inc.
ISRAEL HORIZONS
JEWISH CURRENTS
JEWISH LIFE
THE JOURNAL OF HISTORICAL REVIEW
Judah Magnes Museum Publications
KMT, A Modern Journal of Ancient Egypt
KMT Communications
Kumarian Press, Inc.
Lake View Press
MIDDLE EAST REPORT
THE NEW PRESS LITERARY QUARTERLY
Noontide Press
Passeggiata Press, Inc.
The Post-Apollo Press
RECONSTRUCTIONIST
Saqi Books Publisher
Smyrna Press
Times Change Press
TOWARD FREEDOM
TRANSCAUCASUS: A Chronology
VOICES - ISRAEL

MIDWEST

Acorn Books
THE ANNALS OF IOWA
Avery Color Studios
B & B Publishing, Inc.
Blue Bird Publishing
Cardinal Press, Inc.
Wm Caxton Ltd
Chicago Review Press
CHILDREN, CHURCHES AND DADDIES, A Non
Religious, Non Familial Literary Magazine
CHRISTIANITY & THE ARTS
DRUMVOICES REVUE
Ex Machina Publishing Company
Foundation Books
Full Moon Publications
Gabriel's Horn Publishing Co., Inc.
Galde Press, Inc.
GEORGE & MERTIE'S PLACE: Rooms With a View
Homestead Publishing
HORIZONS
THE LETTER PARADE
THE LICKING RIVER REVIEW
MANKATO POETRY REVIEW
THE MAVERICK PRESS
Mayhaven Publishing
MIXED BAG
THE NEW PRESS LITERARY QUARTERLY
Palladium Communications
Palm Drive Publishing
Poetic License Press
POW-WOW
THE PRAIRIE JOURNAL OF CANADIAN LITERA-
TURE
THE RIVER
RIVERWIND

ST. LOUIS JOURNALISM REVIEW
Scars Publications
SKYLARK
SOUTHWEST JOURNAL
32 PAGES
TRADITION
The Urbana Free Library
THE VINCENT BROTHERS REVIEW
WESTERN SKIES
Wisconsin Trails
Words & Pictures Press

MILITARY, VETERANS

AAIMS Publishers
The Battery Press, Inc.
R.J. Bender Publishing
BkMk Press
Blacksmith Corporation
Bookhaven Press, LLC
The Borgo Press
Broken Rifle Press
THE CIVIL WAR NEWS
Consumer Education Research Center
Coteau Books
FLASHPOINT: Military Books Reviewed by Military
  Professionals
J. Flores Publications
Galde Press, Inc.
Golden Eagle Press
Griffon House Publications
Heritage Concepts Publishing Inc
Hope Publishing House
Karmichael Press
Lancer Militaria
Leyland Publications
Mach 1, Inc.
MESSAGES FROM THE HEART
MINERVA: Quarterly Report on Women and the Military
The Nautical & Aviation Publishing Co. of America, Inc.
Paladin Enterprises, Inc.
PEACE, The Magazine of the Sixties
Phillips Publications, Inc.
The Place In The Woods
Pogo Press, Incorporated
Premium Press America
RAVEN - A Journal of Vexillology
Red Apple Publishing
Reference Desk Books
Selah Publishing
Skinny Lamb Publishing Company
A Thousand Autumns Press
The Urbana Free Library
VIETNAM GENERATION: A Journal of Recent History
  and Contemporary Issues
White Mane Publishing Company, Inc.
Yucca Tree Press

HENRY MILLER

Abiko Literary Press (ALP)
ANAIS: An International Journal
Carrefour Press
CLASS ACT
Crescent Moon
GEORGE & MERTIE'S PLACE: Rooms With a View
GRANULATED TUPPERWARE
Happy Rock Press
THE HUNTED NEWS
OXYGEN
PASSION
Phony Lid Publications
PLAIN BROWN WRAPPER (PBW)
PLOPLOP
THE STYLUS
The Subourbon Press
VAGABOND

MINIATURE BOOKS

Abiko Literary Press (ALP)

AFFABLE NEIGHBOR
Affable Neighbor Press
Alicubi Publications
Clamp Down Press
DWELLING PORTABLY
ENDING THE BEGIN
The Feathered Serpent
FURTHER TOO
The Gleniffer Press
Headveins Graphics
THE HUNTED NEWS
Running Press
SALT LICK
Stewart Publishing & Printing
The Subourbon Press
Theosophical Publishing House
THE UNIT CIRCLE

MINNESOTA

Blue Sky Marketing, Inc.
THE BURNING CLOUD REVIEW
Falcon Press Publishing Company
Galde Press, Inc.
LAKE SUPERIOR MAGAZINE
MANKATO POETRY REVIEW
MIDWEST ART FAIRS
Minnesota Historical Society Press
MSRRT NEWSLETTER: LIBRARY ALTERNATIVES
NORTH COAST REVIEW
Open Horizons Publishing Company
Poetry Harbor
POETRY MOTEL
Pogo Press, Incorporated
THE RIVER
Suburban Wilderness Press
Tailored Tours Publications, Inc.
Whole Person Associates Inc.

MISSOURI

Crossroads Communications
Falcon Press Publishing Company
LEO Productions LLC.
The Patrice Press
Reveal
ST. LOUIS JOURNALISM REVIEW
White Oak Press
Wildstone Media
WRITER'S GUIDELINES: A Roundtable for Writers and
  Editors

MONTANA

Blue Heron Publishing, Inc.
CUTBANK
Editorial Review
Exceptional Books, Ltd.
Falcon Press Publishing Company
Keokee Co. Publishing, Inc.
MIXED BAG
Moon Publications, Inc.
Mountain Meadow Press
Mountain Press Publishing Co.
Old West Publishing Co.
Pruett Publishing Company
Spirit Talk Press
Tamarack Books, Inc.
WESTERN SKIES
YUWITAYA LAKOTA

MORMON

Abiko Literary Press (ALP)
THE DEFENDER - RUSH UTAH'S NEWSLETTER
Eborn Books
GEORGE & MERTIE'S PLACE: Rooms With a View
Signature Books
Gibbs Smith, Publisher

MOTIVATION, SUCCESS

Arden Press, Inc.

Autumn Publishing Group, LLC.
Axelrod Publishing of Tampa Bay
Baker Street Publications
Behavioral Sciences Research Press, Inc.
Big Mouth Publications
Blue River Publishing Inc.
Bottom Line Pre$$
Business Resource Publishing
Capital Communications
Cherubic Press
Child's Play
CLASS ACT
Company of Words Publishing
Contemax Publishers
CROSS ROADS
Cypress Publishing Group, Inc.
DAILY WORD
DREAM NETWORK JOURNAL
Emerald Ink Publishing
Free Spirit Publishing Inc.
Frugal Marketer Publishing
Golden Eagle Press
House of the 9 Muses, Inc.
INTUITIVE EXPLORATIONS
JARRETT'S JOURNAL
Keel Publications
Kells Media Group
H J Kramer
Life Lessons
LifeQuest Publishing Group
LITTLE FREE PRESS
Markowski International Publishers
Massey-Reyner Publishing
MONEYMAKING NEWSLETTER
More To Life Publishing
New Management Publishing Company, Inc.
New View Publications
Open Horizons Publishing Company
The Poetry Center Press/Shoestring Press
PREP Publishing
Princess Publishing
RED HOT HOME INCOME REPORTER
REFERRALS
St. Georges Press
SJL Publishing Company
TitleWaves Publishing
Top Of The Mountain Publishing
Unity Books
UNITY MAGAZINE
WRITER'S WORLD
Z W L Publishing, Inc.

MOVIES

Abiko Literary Press (ALP)
ARTHUR'S COUSIN
ATROCITY
BAKER STREET GAZETTE
Baker Street Publications
BOOGLIT
CREEPY MIKE'S OMNIBUS OF FUN
CURMUDGEON
Cyclone Books
DAYS AND NIGHTS OF A SMALL PRESS PUB-
   LISHER
December Press
DOUBLE BILL
DRASTIC LIVES
Excalibur Publishing Inc.
Film-Video Publications
FLIPSIDE
FODDERWING
FULL MOON DIRECTORY
Full Moon Publications
GAUNTLET: Exploring the Limits of Free Expression
GEORGE & MERTIE'S PLACE: Rooms With a View
GRAFFITI OFF THE ASYLUM WALLS
Greeson & Boyle, Inc.
THE HAUNTED JOURNAL

Hollywood Film Archive
HOLLYWOOD NOSTALGIA
HORIZONS BEYOND
ICARUS WAS RIGHT
INDY MAGAZINE
Itidwitir Publishing
THE J MAN TIMES
THE JOE BOB REPORT
METAL CURSE
THE METAPHYSICAL REVIEW
MIXED BAG
MOMMY AND I ARE ONE
MOVIE CLUB
The New Humanity Press
NIGHTLORE
NIGHTSHADE
NOCTURNAL REPORTER
NWI National Writers Institute
Open Horizons Publishing Company
PAST TIMES: The Nostalgia Entertainment Newsletter
POTOMAC REVIEW
Prudhomme Press
Push/Pull/Press
REALM OF THE VAMPIRE
REMOTE JOCKEY DIGEST
ROCTOBER COMICS AND MUSIC
SF COMMENTARY
SHEMP! The Lowlife Culture Magazine
SLEUTH JOURNAL
SMALL PRESS CREATIVE EXPLOSION
Starbooks Press/FLF Press
THEY WON'T STAY DEAD!
Vestal Press Ltd
Via God Publishing
THE VINCENT BROTHERS REVIEW
WESTERN SKIES
WORLD OF FANDOM MAGAZINE
YOUR LIFE MATTERS
YUWITAYA LAKOTA

MULTICULTURAL

Ananse Press
Anteater Press
ART PAPERS
Baker Street Publications
BkMk Press
BLUE COLLAR REVIEW
Blue Heron Publishing, Inc.
Bonus Books, Inc.
BOOK/MARK SMALL PRESS QUARTERLY REVIEW
Burning Bush Publications
Carolina Wren Press/Lollipop Power Books
COLLEGIUM NEWSLETTER
Dawn Sign Press
DAYS AND NIGHTS OF A SMALL PRESS PUB-
   LISHER
Deerbridge Books
DOVETAIL: A Journal by and for Jewish/Christian
   Families
Dovetail Publishing
FIRM NONCOMMITTAL: An International Journal of
   Whimsy
Five Fingers Press
FIVE FINGERS REVIEW
FRONTIERS: A Journal of Women Studies
Full Moon Publications
Heartsong Books
HORIZONS
ICA Publishing
Images For Media/Sesquin
INDIA CURRENTS
Intercultural Press, Inc.
INTERCULTURAL WRITERS REVIEW
INTERCULTURE
IRIS: A Journal About Women
Javelina Books
THE KENYON REVIEW
Allen A. Knoll Publishers

LOVE AND RAGE, A Revolutionary Anarchist News-
paper
MARGIN: EXPLORING MODERN MAGICAL REA-
LISM
THE NEW PRESS LITERARY QUARTERLY
New Seed Press
New Spring Publications
Open Hand Publishing Inc.
Palladium Communications
Papillon Publishing
Parabola
Paris Press, Inc.
Partisan Press
Peartree Books & Music
POINT OF CONTACT
POTOMAC REVIEW
Pride & Imprints
Really Great Books
Serena Bay Books
The Spirit That Moves Us Press, Inc.
SPIRIT TO SPIRIT
SYMPLOKE: A Journal for the Intermingling of Literary,
Cultural and Theoretical Scholarship
Turtle Island Press, Inc.
Victory Press
W.E.C. Plant Publishing
WEBER STUDIES: Voices and Viewpoints of the
Contemporary West
WEST COAST LINE: A Journal of Contemporary
Writing and Criticism
WESTERN SKIES
WHOLE EARTH
Williamson Publishing Company, Inc.

MUSIC

A G M Enterprises, Inc.
Accent on Music
AD/VANCE
AFTERTOUCH: New Music Discoveries
ALARM CLOCK
THE ALEMBIC
Allworth Press
ALWAYS JUKIN'
Always Jukin'
AMERICAN WRITING: A Magazine
and books
Anderson Press
THE ANGRY THOREAUAN
Anubian Press
ARISTOS
ARTHUR'S COUSIN
ASTERISM: The Journal of Science Fiction, Fantasy, and
Space Music
AUFBAU
BABYSUE
BABYSUE MUSIC REVIEW
Backspace Ink
BANAL PROBE
Bell Springs Publishing
THE BENT
Berkeley Hills Books
BIG WORLD
Birdalone Books
Black Dress Press
BLACK MOON MAGAZINE
Black Moon Publishing
BLACK SHEETS MAGAZINE
Bliss Publishing Company, Inc.
BLITZ
BLU
The Bold Strummer Ltd.
BOOGLIT
Burning Books
BUTTON
CADENCE: THE REVIEW OF JAZZ & BLUES:
CREATIVE IMPROVISED MUSIC
A Cappella Books
Carpe Diem Publishing

CAVEAT LECTOR
Celebrity Profiles Publishing
Center for Japanese Studies
Child's Play
CHRISTIANITY & THE ARTS
CHRONICLES OF DISORDER
CIN-DAV, Inc.
CLOCKWATCH REVIEW
CODA: The Jazz Magazine
THE COMPANY NORTH AMERICA
Cosmic Trend
Coteau Books
CREEPY MIKE'S OMNIBUS OF FUN
CROSSCURRENTS
Crystal Publishers, Inc.
DAYS AND NIGHTS OF A SMALL PRESS PUB-
LISHER
DIRTY LINEN
DISSONANCE MAGAZINE
DOUBLE BILL
DOWN UNDER MANHATTAN BRIDGE
Drum
THE EDGE CITY REVIEW
The Edwin Mellen Press
Empty Closet Enterprises, Inc.
EXCLAIM!
EXPERIMENTAL MUSICAL INSTRUMENTS
Fallen Leaf Press
FIDDLER MAGAZINE
FILM SCORE MONTHLY
FLIPSIDE
FODDERWING
FREEDOM OF EXPRESSION (FOE)
Fromm International Publishing Corporation
FULL MOON DIRECTORY
FURTHER TOO
GATEAVISA
GAUNTLET: Exploring the Limits of Free Expression
GEORGE & MERTIE'S PLACE: Rooms With a View
Glenbridge Publishing Ltd.
GRAFFITI OFF THE ASYLUM WALLS
GRANULATED TUPPERWARE
GRAY AREAS
HEARTSONG REVIEW
HOAX!
H2SO4
THE HUNTED NEWS
Hyacinth House Publications/Caligula Editions
ICARUS WAS RIGHT
Images For Media/Sesquin
Inner Traditions International
Intermountain Publishing
IRIS: A Journal About Women
Ironweed Press
ITALIAN AMERICANA
Itidwitir Publishing
JACK MACKEREL MAGAZINE
JAM RAG
JOURNAL OF AESTHETICS AND ART CRITICISM
JOURNAL OF HUMANITIES
JOURNAL OF MUSICOLOGY
Keyboard Workshop
LADYBUG, the Magazine for Young Children
Leyland Publications
LIES MAGAZINE
Light, Words & Music
LIGHTWORKS MAGAZINE
Limelight Editions
LINGO
LITURGY 90
LUMMOX JOURNAL
Magical Music Express
MAGNET MAGAZINE
Peter Marcan Publications
MARK
Merwood Books
METAL CURSE
Metamorphous Press

836

THE METAPHYSICAL REVIEW
MINISTRY & LITURGY
MOBILE BEAT: The DJ Magazine
MOMMY AND I ARE ONE
Moon Publications, Inc.
MOTORBOOTY MAGAZINE
Multi Media Arts
MUSIC AND LETTERS
MUSIC NEWS
MUSIC PERCEPTION
MUSICAL OPINION
MUSICWORKS: The Journal of Sound Explorations
  (Audio-Visual)
N D
NEW ART EXAMINER
THE NEW CRITERION
NEW HOPE INTERNATIONAL REVIEW
NEW THOUGHT JOURNAL
Nicolas-Hays, Inc.
19TH-CENTURY MUSIC
THE NOISE
Norton Coker Press
The O Press
Omega Publications, Inc.
OUTLET
Palladium Communications
PARA*PHRASE
Passeggiata Press, Inc.
PAST TIMES: The Nostalgia Entertainment Newsletter
PLAIN BROWN WRAPPER (PBW)
The Poetry Connection
THE POETRY CONNECTION
Pogo Press, Incorporated
Potentials Development, Inc.
Premium Press America
Pro Musica Press
Pro/Am Music Resources, Inc.
PUNCTURE
Push/Pull/Press
REALM OF THE VAMPIRE
REDISCOVER MUSIC CATALOG
RELIX
Resource Publications, Inc.
Reveal
ROCTOBER COMICS AND MUSIC
Rowhouse Press
St. Andrew Press
SALON: A Journal of Aesthetics
SANDBOX MAGAZINE
SARAGAM: A Musical Quarterly Magazine
Scarecrow Press
Schenkman Books
SCRAWL MAGAZINE
See Sharp Press
Selah Publishing Co. Inc.
THE $ENSIBLE SOUND
SHEMP! The Lowlife Culture Magazine
SING OUT! The Folk Song Magazine
Six Strings Music Publishing
Skytop Publishing
SMALL PRESS CREATIVE EXPLOSION
SONAR MAP
SOS JAZZ
SOUTHERN QUARTERLY: A Journal of the Arts in the
  South
The Spinning Star Press
STAGNANCY IS REVOLTING
Station Hill Press
STONES IN MY POCKET
The Subourbon Press
SUPER TROUPER
TAIL SPINS
THEY WON'T STAY DEAD!
THIRST (CYBERTHIRST)
Thirteen Colonies Press
TRADITION
Trafton Publising
Two Bytes Publishing

2.13.61 Publications
UNDER THE VOLCANO
Underwhich Editions
THE UNIT CIRCLE
UNO MAS MAGAZINE
Vestal Press Ltd
Via God Publishing
White Cliffs Media, Inc.
WHOLE EARTH
WICKED MYSTIC
Williamson Publishing Company, Inc.
Winchester/G. Ander Books
Witwatersrand University Press
World Music Press
WORLD OF FANDOM MAGAZINE
Writers Forum
Wynn Publishing
Yellow Moon Press
Z W L Publishing, Inc.
ZERO HOUR

MYSTERY

AC
AFFAIR OF THE MIND: A Literary Quarterly
African American Audio Press
Ageless Press
Ana Libri Press
Andrew Scott Publishers
Avocet Press Inc.
BAKER STREET GAZETTE
Baker Street Publications
BEGINNINGS - A Magazine for the Novice Writer
BELLES LETTRES
Blue Heron Publishing, Inc.
Borderland Sciences Research Foundation
Boulevard Books, Inc. Florida
Briarwood Publishing
CITY PRIMEVAL
CLASS ACT
Company of Words Publishing
COZY DETECTIVE MYSTERY MAGAZINE
Crime and Again Press
DAYS AND NIGHTS OF A SMALL PRESS PUB-
  LISHER
THE DROOD REVIEW OF MYSTERY
Ecrivez!
FULL MOON DIRECTORY
GAUNTLET: Exploring the Limits of Free Expression
Golden Eagle Press
Golden Meteorite Press
Gryphon Publications
HARDBOILED
HOAX!
HOLLYWOOD NOSTALGIA
Hutton Publications
The Imaginary Press
Intercontinental Publishing, Inc
Intrigue Press
JACK THE RIPPER GAZETTE
Kent Information Services, Inc.
Allen A. Knoll Publishers
Lemieux International Ltd.
LININGTON LINEUP
LONDON FOG
London Fog Publishing
Meager Ink Press
THE METAPHYSICAL REVIEW
MOOSE BOUND PRESS JOURNAL/NEWSLETTER
Mystery Notebook Editions
MYSTERY READERS JOURNAL
THE MYSTERY REVIEW
New Victoria Publishers
NOCTURNAL REPORTER
P & K Stark Productions, Inc.
Palari Publishing
PAPERBACK PARADE
PIRATE WRITINGS
PLOT

THE POST
Purple Finch Press
Questex Consulting Ltd.
Reveal
THE RIVER
Rowan Mountain Press
St Kitts Press
Scrivenery Press
SelectiveHouse Publishers, Inc.
SHERLOCKIAN TIDBITS
Silver Phoenix Press
SISTERS IN CRIME BOOKS IN PRINT
SLEUTH JOURNAL
Southern Star Publishing
Spinsters Ink
SQUARE ONE - A Magazine of Disturbing Fiction
Synapse-Centurion
Waverly House Publishing
White Wolf Publishing
WHITECHAPEL JOURNAL
Writers House Press

MYTH, MYTHOLOGY

Abiko Literary Press (ALP)
AFFAIR OF THE MIND: A Literary Quarterly
Agathon Books
Alaska Native Language Center
AMERICAN WRITING: A Magazine
Ana Libri Press
Arjuna Library Press
Baker Street Publications
Beacon Press
Bear & Company, Inc.
Bright Mountain Books, Inc.
China Books & Periodicals, Inc.
CLASS ACT
COMMON BOUNDARY MAGAZINE
Crescent Moon
DAYS AND NIGHTS OF A SMALL PRESS PUB-
   LISHER
Dovehaven Press
THE DRAGON CHRONICLE
DREAM NETWORK JOURNAL
ENLIGHTENMENTS
Exceptional Books, Ltd.
FkB Press
FULL MOON DIRECTORY
Full Moon Publications
Galde Press, Inc.
GEORGE & MERTIE'S PLACE: Rooms With a View
Golden Eagle Press
Golden Isis Press
GRAFFITI OFF THE ASYLUM WALLS
GREEN EGG
THE HAUNTED JOURNAL
Heyday Books
HOAX!
HORIZONS
HORIZONS BEYOND
Horned Owl Publishing
Inner Traditions International
INTERBANG
INTUITIVE EXPLORATIONS
JEWISH LIFE
KELTIC FRINGE
Llewellyn Publications
MAGIC REALISM
MARGIN: EXPLORING MODERN MAGICAL REA-
   LISM
MEDUSA'S HAIRDO
META4: Journal of Object Oriented Poetics (OOPS)
MetaGnosis
METAL CURSE
MIXED BAG
Naturegraph Publishers, Inc.
NEW FRONTIER
The New Humanity Press
New Native Press

New Spirit Press/The Poet Tree
NIGHTSHADE
nine muses books
NOCTURNAL REPORTER
OLD CROW
Oregon State University Press
Outer Space Press
PAGAN AMERICA
Parabola
PARABOLA MAGAZINE
Passeggiata Press, Inc.
PASSION
PERSPECTIVES
Pocket of Sanity
POEMS THAT THUMP IN THE DARK/SECOND
   GLANCE
Point Bonita Books
Polar Bear Productions & Company
POW-WOW
PUCK: The Unofficial Journal of the Irrepressible
Pyx Press
Quantum Mind Publications
THE RATIONAL FEMINIST
REALM OF DARKNESS
REALM OF THE VAMPIRE
Reveal
SAGEWOMAN
Sibyl Publications, Inc
Sigo Press
SOCIETE
SOUTHWEST JOURNAL
SPIRIT TO SPIRIT
Spring Publications Inc.
SULPHUR RIVER LITERARY REVIEW
The Teitan Press, Inc.
Theosophical Publishing House
Three Pyramids Publishing
Top Of The Mountain Publishing
Transeuropa
VAMPIRE NIGHTS
THE VINCENT BROTHERS REVIEW
VIRTUTE ET MORTE MAGAZINE
Samuel Weiser, Inc.
WESTERN SKIES
THE WISDOM CONSERVANCY NEWSLETTER
Yggdrasil Books
YUWITAYA LAKOTA

NATIVE AMERICAN

Abiko Literary Press (ALP)
ABRAXAS
Access Multimedia
Alaska Geographic Society
Alaska Native Language Center
Alaska Northwest Books
ALBERTA HISTORY
American Audio Prose Library (non-print)
AMERICAN INDIAN CULTURE AND RESEARCH
   JOURNAL
American Indian Studies Center
Ancient City Press
Arrowstar Publishing
Avery Color Studios
Backcountry Publishing
Baker Street Publications
Ballena Press
Beacon Press
Bear & Company, Inc.
BELLES LETTRES
Between The Lines
Blue Bird Publishing
Blue Heron Publishing, Inc.
Blue Horizon Press
BOOK TALK
Borealis Press Limited
Bright Mountain Books, Inc.
BRILLIANT STAR
The Brookfield Reader

Burning Bush Publications
Burning Llama Press
Capra Press
Carolina Wren Press/Lollipop Power Books
CJE NEWS (Newsletter of the Coalition for Jobs & the Environment)
Clarity Press, Inc.
Commune-A-Key Publishing, Inc.
Comstock Bonanza Press
Confluence Press, Inc.
Content Communications
Council For Indian Education
The Crossing Press
DAYS AND NIGHTS OF A SMALL PRESS PUBLISHER
Deerbridge Books
The Denali Press
DREAM NETWORK JOURNAL
Eagle's View Publishing
Epicenter Press Inc.
ETC Publications
EZ Nature Books
Five Star Publications
Frozen Waffles Press/Shattered Sidewalks Press; 45th Century Chapbooks
Fulcrum, Inc.
Full Moon Publications
Galde Press, Inc.
GATEAVISA
THE GENTLE SURVIVALIST
GEORGE & MERTIE'S PLACE: Rooms With a View
Ghost Pony Press
Golden Eagle Press
Golden Isis Press
Heartsong Books
Heidelberg Graphics
Heyday Books
HIGH COUNTRY NEWS
Historical Society of Alberta
HOAX!
HORIZONS
Institute for Southern Studies
INTERCULTURAL WRITERS REVIEW
INTERCULTURE
Jaguar Books
Karmichael Press
KICK IT OVER
Kiva Publishing, Inc.
La Alameda Press
LADYBUG, the Magazine for Young Children
LAKE SUPERIOR MAGAZINE
Lost Horse Press
LOVE AND RAGE, A Revolutionary Anarchist Newspaper
LPD Press
MARGIN: EXPLORING MODERN MAGICAL REALISM
Maryland Historical Press
McDonald & Woodward Publishing Company
McNally & Loftin, Publishers
The Middle Atlantic Press
Miles River Press
MIM NOTES: Offcial Newsletter of the Maoist Internationalist Movement
Minnesota Historical Society Press
Minor Heron Press
MIXED BAG
MOCCASIN TELEGRAPH
Mountain Meadow Press
Museum of New Mexico Press
National Woodlands Publishing Company
Naturegraph Publishers, Inc.
NEW ART EXAMINER
NEW ENGLAND ANTIQUES JOURNAL
THE NEW ENGLAND QUARTERLY
New Native Press
THE NEW PRESS LITERARY QUARTERLY
THE NEW SOUTHERN SURREALIST REVIEW

New Spirit Press/The Poet Tree
New Star Books Ltd.
NEW THOUGHT JOURNAL
NEWS FROM NATIVE CALIFORNIA
NORTH COAST REVIEW
North Country Books, Inc.
NORTH DAKOTA QUARTERLY
Noyce Publishing
Oregon State University Press
Organization for Equal Education of the Sexes, Inc.
Outer Space Press
Outrider Press
Oxford House Publishing
Palari Publishing
Palladium Communications
Parabola
Paragon House Publishers
Passeggiata Press, Inc.
The Place In The Woods
Pocahontas Press, Inc.
Poetic License Press
Poetry Harbor
Pogo Press, Incorporated
Point Riders Press
Polar Bear Productions & Company
POTOMAC REVIEW
POW-WOW
Pruett Publishing Company
Pygmy Forest Press
QUESTION EVERYTHING CHALLENGE EVERYTHING (QECE)
Red Apple Publishing
Red Crane Books, Inc.
Reference Service Press
THE RIVER
SAGEWOMAN
Salina Bookshelf
Sand River Press
Sasquatch Books
SHAMAN'S DRUM: A Journal of Experiential Shamanism
Shaolin Communications
SHENANDOAH NEWSLETTER
Genny Smith Books
Gibbs Smith, Publisher
SOUTH DAKOTA REVIEW
SOUTHWEST JOURNAL
Spirit Talk Press
SPIRIT TO SPIRIT
STONES IN MY POCKET
STRUGGLE: A Magazine of Proletarian Revolutionary Literature
Swan Raven & Company
Sweetlight Books
Syracuse Cultural Workers/Tools for Change
Tamarack Books, Inc.
Theosophical Publishing House
Theytus Books Ltd.
TOWARD FREEDOM
Treasure Chest Books LLC
TURNING THE TIDE: A Journal of Anti-Racist Activism, Research & Education
Two Bytes Publishing
United Lumbee Nation
UNITED LUMBEE NATION TIMES
University of Massachusetts Press
Venus Communications
VIETNAM GENERATION: A Journal of Recent History and Contemporary Issues
W.E.C. Plant Publishing
Ward Hill Press
WESTERN SKIES
WHISPERING WIND MAGAZINE
Whitford Press
THE WILD FOODS FORUM
World Music Press
Ye Galleon Press
YUMTZILOB: Tijdschrift over de Americas

839

YUWITAYA LAKOTA
Zagier & Urruty Publicaciones

NATURE

Abiko Literary Press (ALP)
THE ACORN
ACORN WHISTLE
Acton Circle Publishing Company
Adirondack Mountain Club, Inc.
AMERICAN FORESTS
ATL Press, Inc.
AU NATUREL
Baker Street Publications
Blue Reef Publications, Inc.
BUTTERFLY GARDENERS' QUARTERLY
CALIFORNIA EXPLORER
Catamount Press
THE CATBIRD SEAT
Coreopsis Books
Corona Publishing Co.
COTYLEDON
Cucumber Island Storytellers
Dawn Publications
DAYS AND NIGHTS OF A SMALL PRESS PUB-
LISHER
Dog-Eared Publications
Down The Shore Publishing
Ecopress
Envirographics
EZ Nature Books
Falcon Press Publishing Company
Footprint Press
Fulcrum, Inc.
Golden Eagle Press
GREEN WORLD: News and Views For Gardening Who
Care About The Earth
Harvard Common Press
Ice Cube Press
IMPRINT, A LITERARY JOURNAL
Kodomo Press
Mercury House
MIXED BAG
NATURALLY
Naturegraph Publishers, Inc.
THE NEW PRESS LITERARY QUARTERLY
New Spirit Press/The Poet Tree
North Country Books, Inc.
Omega Publications, Inc.
Pangaea
Peartree Books & Music
Primer Publishers
Pruett Publishing Company
RALPH'S REVIEW
THE RATIONAL FEMINIST
THE RIVER
Sasquatch Books
Seekers Press
SIGNPOST FOR NORTHWEST TRAILS
SKINNYDIPPING
SKYLARK
Gibbs Smith, Publisher
Stillpoint Publishing
Stone Wall Press, Inc
STONES IN MY POCKET
Sulisa Publishing
Sweetlight Books
SYCAMORE ROOTS: New Native Americans
Synapse-Centurion
Tilbury House, Publishers
Treasure Chest Books LLC
THE UNKNOWN WRITER
VanderWyk & Burnham
Venus Communications
THE VINCENT BROTHERS REVIEW
WESTERN SKIES
WHOLE TERRAIN - REFLECTIVE ENVIRONMEN-
TAL PRACTICE
Wild Dove Studio and Press, Inc.

WILD DUCK REVIEW
WILD EARTH
THE WILD FOODS FORUM
Williamson Publishing Company, Inc.
Wood Thrush Books

NEBRASKA

Lone Willow Press

NETWORKING

The Alternate Press
AQUATERRA, METAECOLOGY & CULTURE
BACKBOARD
BANAL PROBE
Black Forest Press
Center for Public Representation
THE CHRISTIAN LIBRARIAN
CJE NEWS (Newsletter of the Coalition for Jobs & the
Environment)
CONNEXIONS DIGEST
Connexions Information Services, Inc.
DAYS AND NIGHTS OF A SMALL PRESS PUB-
LISHER
DISSONANCE MAGAZINE
Full Moon Publications
FURTHER TOO
Golden Eagle Press
THE HAUNTED JOURNAL
HOAX!
HOLLYWOOD NOSTALGIA
Hyacinth House Publications/Caligula Editions
ICA Publishing
LIGHTWORKS MAGAZINE
LUNO
Lycanthrope Press
MSRRT NEWSLETTER: LIBRARY ALTERNATIVES
NETWORK
NYX OBSCURA MAGAZINE
OUT YOUR BACKDOOR: The Magazine of Informal
Adventure and Cheap Culture
PEN & INK WRITERS JOURNAL
The Poetry Connection
THE POETRY CONNECTION
READERS SPEAK OUT!
Rio Grande Press
RURAL NETWORK ADVOCATE
SE LA VIE WRITER'S JOURNAL
SLUG & LETTUCE
SOCIETE
SPROUTLETTER
WHOLE EARTH
WRITER'S WORKSHOP REVIEW

NEW AGE

A.R.E. Press
ACS Publications
Afcom Publishing
AFFAIR OF THE MIND: A Literary Quarterly
Al-Galaxy Publishing Company
American Literary Press Inc./Noble House
Amethyst & Emerald
Anti-Aging Press
AREOPAGUS
Ascension Publishing
ASTROFLASH
Athanor Books (a division of ETX Seminars)
AXE FACTORY REVIEW
Axelrod Publishing of Tampa Bay
Baker Street Publications
Beacon Press
Bear & Company, Inc.
Berkeley Hills Books
Big Mouth Publications
Black Diamond Book Publishing
Blue Dolphin Publishing, Inc.
Booksplus of Maine
BORDERLANDS: A Quarterly Journal Of Borderland
Research

BOTH SIDES NOW
Brason-Sargar Publications
A Cappella Books
Cherubic Press
CHILDREN, CHURCHES AND DADDIES, A Non
   Religious, Non Familial Literary Magazine
Chiron Press
CHIRON REVIEW
CHRISTIAN*NEW AGE QUARTERLY
COMMUNITIES
Conari Press
Cosmic Concepts
Cosmic Trend
Cosmoenergetics Publications
CRONE CHRONICLES: A Journal of Conscious Aging
The Crossing Press
Crystal Clarity, Publishers
D.B.A. Books
DREAM NETWORK JOURNAL
Edin Books, Inc.
Emerald Ink Publishing
Emerald Wave
Encircle Publications
Enthea Press
Excalibur Publishing Inc.
Free People Press
FULL MOON DIRECTORY
Full Moon Publications
Galde Press, Inc.
GEORGE & MERTIE'S PLACE: Rooms With a View
Golden Isis Press
Great Western Publishing Company
GREEN EGG
Guarionex Press Ltd.
Halo Books
Harbor House
THE HAUNTED JOURNAL
HEAVEN BONE MAGAZINE
Heaven Bone Press
Hohm Press
HORIZONS BEYOND
Horus Publishing, Inc.
Hunter House Inc., Publishers
Illumination Arts
IllumiNet Press
In Print Publishing
Inner Traditions International
INTUITIVE EXPLORATIONS
J & L Publications
Jalmar Press
H J Kramer
LifeQuest Publishing Group
Llewellyn Publications
LOVING ALTERNATIVES MAGAZINE
LOVING MORE
Lycanthrope Press
Macrocosm USA, Inc.
MAGICAL BLEND MAGAZINE
MARGIN: EXPLORING MODERN MAGICAL REA-
   LISM
Master Key Inc.
Merging Worlds Publishers, Inc.
MetaGnosis
Mho & Mho Works
THE MOUNTAIN ASTROLOGER
MYSTIC VOICES
N: NUDE & NATURAL
Native Plant Publishing
Naturegraph Publishers, Inc.
NEW ENVIRONMENT BULLETIN
NEW FRONTIER
New Paradigm Books
New Spirit Press/The Poet Tree
New World Library
NIGHTSHADE
NOCTURNAL REPORTER
OFFICE NUMBER ONE
Omega Publications, Inc.

ONE EARTH
Origin Press
PAGAN PRIDE
Palm Drive Publishing
Paragon House Publishers
PARA*PHRASE
Pathways Press, Inc.
Phantom Press Publications
The Place In The Woods
Plus Publications
POEMS THAT THUMP IN THE DARK/SECOND
   GLANCE
Polar Bear Productions & Company
Princess Publishing
Pura Vida Publishing Company
Quantum Mind Publications
QUINTILE
Quintile
REALM OF THE VAMPIRE
Reyes Investment Enterprise Ltd.
RFD
Rio Grande Press
SAGEWOMAN
St. Georges Press
Scars Publications
SCIENCE/HEALTH ABSTRACTS
SelectiveHouse Publishers, Inc.
Sigo Press
SKINNYDIPPING
Skytop Publishing
Gibbs Smith, Publisher
SOM Publishing, division of School of Metaphysics
Sparrow Hawk Press
SPECTRUM—The Wholistic News Magazine
SPIRIT MAGAZINE
SPIRIT TO SPIRIT
SPROUTLETTER
Station Hill Press
Steamshovel Press
STEAMSHOVEL PRESS
Stewart Publishing & Printing
Stillpoint Publishing
STONES IN MY POCKET
Sun-Scape Publications, a division of Sun-Scape Enter-
   prises Ltd.
Swan Raven & Company
TAI CHI
TEC Publications
Theosophical Publishing House
Three Pyramids Publishing
Toad Hall, Inc.
Top Of The Mountain Publishing
THE TRUTH SEEKER
Turtle Island Press, Inc.
Twelve Star Publishing
Unified Publications
Universal Unity
UP CLOSE, A Quarterly Review of New Age &
   Alternative Publication Newsletter
Upper Access Inc.
Verity Press Publishing
Victory Press
Samuel Weiser, Inc.
Westgate Press
White Phoenix Publishing
Whitford Press
B. L. Winch & Associates
The Woodbridge Group

NEW ENGLAND

THE AUROREAN, A POETIC QUARTERLY
Baker Street Publications
Beacon Press
Bliss Publishing Company, Inc.
Chelsea Green Publishing Company
THE CLIMBING ART
Devin-Adair Publishers, Inc.
Full Moon Publications

The Globe Pequot Press
Hollis Publishing Company
HORIZONS
The Latona Press
Midmarch Arts Press
MIXED BAG
MONADNOCK GAY MEN
New England Cartographics, Inc.
THE NEW ENGLAND QUARTERLY
Nicolin Fields Publishing, Inc.
THE NOISE
NORTHWOODS JOURNAL, A Magazine for Writers
PINE ISLAND JOURNAL OF NEW ENGLAND
  POETRY
Pocahontas Press, Inc.
Silver Print Press
Stones Point Press
Thirteen Colonies Press
Union Park Press
University of Massachusetts Press
Wescott Cove Publishing Co.
THE WORCESTER REVIEW

NEW HAMPSHIRE

New England Cartographics, Inc.
Nicolin Fields Publishing, Inc.

NEW MEXICO

Ancient City Press
Baker Street Publications
BLACKWATER
Cave Books
DAYS AND NIGHTS OF A SMALL PRESS PUB-
  LISHER
DREAM WHIP
Duckworth Press
Elysian Hills Publishing Company, Inc.
Falcon Press Publishing Company
Kiva Publishing, Inc.
KUMQUAT MERINGUE
La Alameda Press
Lao Tse Press, Ltd.
LIES MAGAZINE
LPD Press
MIXED BAG
Moon Publications, Inc.
The Mountaineers Books
Old West Publishing Co.
Poetic License Press
POW-WOW
Primer Publishers
Pruett Publishing Company
Red Crane Books, Inc.
SOUTHWEST JOURNAL
Tamarack Books, Inc.
Tortilla Press
TRADICION REVISTA
Treasure Chest Books LLC
TUCUMCARI LITERARY REVIEW
WEBER STUDIES: Voices and Viewpoints of the
  Contemporary West
WESTERN SKIES
YEFIEF
Yucca Tree Press

NEW YORK

Adirondack Mountain Club, Inc.
AUFBAU
Baker Street Publications
Black Dome Press Corp.
Chelsea Green Publishing Company
DAYS AND NIGHTS OF A SMALL PRESS PUB-
  LISHER
Footprint Press
Four Walls Eight Windows
Full Moon Publications
Happy Rock Press
HORIZONS

JEWISH LIFE
McBooks Press
MIXED BAG
Mount Ida Press
NEW ART EXAMINER
New England Cartographics, Inc.
North Country Books, Inc.
Paerdegat Park Publishing Co.
PHOTOGRAPHY IN NEW YORK, INTERNATIONAL
SEMIGLOSS
SITUATION
SKINNYDIPPING
Gibbs Smith, Publisher
UNDER THE VOLCANO
Wright-Armstead Associates

NEW ZEALAND

Baker Street Publications
Brick Row Publishing Co. Ltd.
GATEAVISA
MEANJIN
Moon Publications, Inc.

NEWSLETTER

Abiko Literary Press (ALP)
Acclaim Publishing Co. Inc.
The Alternate Press
Anti-Aging Press
AQUATERRA, METAECOLOGY & CULTURE
ARTISTAMP NEWS
ASC NEWSLETTER
Autumn Publishing Group, LLC.
AVON LITERARY INTELLIGENCER
BACKBOARD
BAKER STREET GAZETTE
Baker Street Publications
Black Forest Press
THE BOOKWATCH
The Boxwood Press
THE BREAD AND BUTTER CHRONICLES
By-The-Book Publishing
CARIBBEAN NEWSLETTER
Center For Self-Sufficiency
CLASS ACT
Community Service, Inc.
COMMUNITY SERVICE NEWSLETTER
THE COMPANY NORTH AMERICA
COOKING CONTEST CHRONICLE
COPING WITH TURBULENT TIMES
Coyote Publishing
CURRENTS
DAYS AND NIGHTS OF A SMALL PRESS PUB-
  LISHER
Eborn Books
THE EDITORIAL EYE
THE EUGENE O'NEILL REVIEW
FELICITY
FIDELIS ET VERUS
FOCUS: Library Service to Older Adults, People with
  Disabilities
FULL MOON DIRECTORY
The Gleniffer Press
G'RAPH
THE GREAT BLUE BEACON
THE GREAT IDEA PATCH
Great Western Publishing Company
GREEN WORLD: News and Views For Gardening Who
  Care About The Earth
THE HAUNTED JOURNAL
HORIZONS BEYOND
INNER JOURNEYS
JARRETT'S JOURNAL
THE JOE BOB REPORT
KARMA LAPEL
Kells Media Group
Kodiak Media Group
LAUGHING BEAR NEWSLETTER
LOCUS: The Newspaper of the Science Fiction Field

NEWSPAPERS

NICARAGUA

ANAIS NIN

NON-FICTION

THE BELLINGHAM REVIEW
Benchmark Publications Inc.
R.J. Bender Publishing
Best Sellers Publishing
BGB Press, Inc.
Big Mouth Publications
BitterSweet Publishing Company
BLACK DIRT
Black Dome Press Corp.
Black Dress Press
Black Forest Press
Black Thistle Press
John F. Blair, Publisher
Blue Crane Books
Blue Heron Publishing, Inc.
Blue River Publishing Inc.
Bluestocking Press
Bolchazy-Carducci Publishers, Inc.
Bonus Books, Inc.
Boog Literature
Book Faith India
Bookhome Publishing/Panda Publishing
Books for All Times, Inc.
Booksplus of Maine
Bowerdean Publishing Co. Ltd.
Breakout Productions
Brenner Information Group
Bright Mountain Books, Inc.
Broken Rifle Press
The Brookfield Reader
Brownout Laboratories
Brunswick Publishing Corporation
BUFFALO SPREE
Burd Street Press
BURNING CAR
Burning Cities Press
Business Smarts, Inc.
Butterfield Press
BYLINE
Calypso Publications
Canterbury Press
Carousel Press
Carson Street Publishing Inc.
Catbird Press
Cave Books
The Caxton Press
Wm Caxton Ltd
THE CENTENNIAL REVIEW
Chandler & Sharp Publishers, Inc.
Chelsea Green Publishing Company
THE CHEROTIC (r)EVOLUTIONARY
Cherubic Press
Chicago Spectrum Press
Children Of Mary
China Books & Periodicals, Inc.
Chiron Press
CHIRON REVIEW
CIMARRON REVIEW
CLASS ACT
Clover Park Press
CLUTCH
Colophon House
Commune-A-Key Publishing, Inc.
Company of Words Publishing
Comstock Bonanza Press
Conari Press
Confluence Press, Inc.
Consumer Press
Continuing Education Press
Coreopsis Books
CORRECTIONS TODAY
Cosmoenergetics Publications
Coteau Books
CPG Publishing Company
CRAB ORCHARD REVIEW
THE CREAM CITY REVIEW
CREATIVE NONFICTION
CRIPES!

CRONE CHRONICLES: A Journal of Conscious Aging
The Crossing Press
Crossway Books
Cultivated Underground Press
CURRENT ACCOUNTS
Custom Services
Cyclone Books
DAILY WORD
DAYS AND NIGHTS OF A SMALL PRESS PUB-
    LISHER
Delta-West Publishing, Inc.
Dimension Engineering Press
Down There Press
Duckworth Press
Dufour Editions Inc.
E.M. Press, Inc.
Eagle's View Publishing
EAP DIGEST
THE EAR
Eau Gallie Publishing, Inc.
Ecopress
Ecrivez!
Editions Ex Libris
Wm.B. Eerdmans Publishing Co.
ELF: ECLECTIC LITERARY FORUM (ELF MAGA-
    ZINE)
EMORY EDGE
ENTELECHY MAGAZINE
Paul S. Eriksson, Publisher
Eros Publishing
ETCETERA
Eurotique Press
Evanston Publishing, Inc.
THE EVERGREEN CHRONICLES
Ex Machina Publishing Company
Excalibur Publishing Inc.
Fantail
FAULTLINE, Journal of Art and Literature
Feral House
FIDELIS ET VERUS
Fillmore Publishing Company
The Fine Print Press, Ltd.
FIRM NONCOMMITTAL: An International Journal of
    Whimsy
FIVE POINTS
Florida Academic Press
FLYWAY
FODDERWING
FOLIO: A LITERARY JOURNAL
Footprint Press
Four Seasons Publishers
Franklin Multimedia, Inc.
Franklin-Sarrett Publishers
Free Spirit Publishing Inc.
Fromm International Publishing Corporation
Front Row Experience
FUGUE
Fulcrum, Inc.
Full Moon Publications
FURTHER TOO
Gaff Press
Galde Press, Inc.
Galen Press, Ltd.
The Galileo Press Ltd.
Galt Publishing
Gateways Books And Tapes
GAUNTLET: Exploring the Limits of Free Expression
Gay Sunshine Press, Inc.
THE GEORGIA REVIEW
Get In-Line! Publishing
GLB Publishers
The Glencannon Press
The Globe Pequot Press
Golden Eagle Press
Golden Isis Press
Golden Meteorite Press
Good Book Publishing Company
Graywolf Press

Ponderosa Publishers
Popular Medicine Press
POTOMAC REVIEW
POTPOURRI: A Magazine of the Literary Arts
POW-WOW
Premium Press America
Prestige Publications
PRISM INTERNATIONAL
Prudhomme Press
Pruett Publishing Company
PT Publications, Inc.
Publitec Editions
PURPLE
Purple Finch Press
THE PURPLE MONKEY
Pyramid Publishing
Quiet Lion Press
THE QUILL MAGAZINE QUARTERLY
Rabeth Publishing Company
RAFTERS
Ragged Edge Press
RAIN CITY REVIEW
THE RAINTOWN REVIEW: A Forum for the Essayist's
   Art
Ram Press
RATTAPALLAX
Ravenhawk Books
REALM OF THE VAMPIRE
Red Apple Publishing
Reference Desk Books
Reveal
Reyes Investment Enterprise Ltd.
Rio Grande Press
THE RIVER
Rockbridge Publishing Co.
ROMANTIC HEARTS
Ronsdale Press
Saddle Mountain Press
St. Augustine Society Press
St. Georges Press
Saint Mary's Press
Santa Monica Press/Offbeat Press
Saqi Books Publisher
Raymond Saroff, Publisher
Schenkman Books
Scrivenery Press
SE LA VIE WRITER'S JOURNAL
Seekers Press
Selah Publishing
Serena Bay Books
SEWANEE REVIEW
Shallowater Press
Shaolin Communications
Signal Books
Silver Phoenix Press
SISTERSONG: Women Across Cultures
SJL Publishing Company
SKYLARK
SLEUTH JOURNAL
Small Helm Press
The Smith (subsidiary of The Generalist Assn., Inc.)
Genny Smith Books
Gibbs Smith, Publisher
SO YOUNG!
Solution Publishing
SOUTHWEST JOURNAL
Sovereignty Press
Spectrum Press
Spinsters Ink
SPIRIT TO SPIRIT
SPORT LITERATE, Honest Reflections on Life's Leisur-
   ely Diversions
SPOUT
Spout Press
Starbooks Press/FLF Press
Stone Wall Press, Inc
Stones Point Press
Storm Peak Press

SUB-TERRAIN
SULPHUR RIVER LITERARY REVIEW
Summer Stream Press
THE SUN, A MAGAZINE OF IDEAS
Sun-Scape Publications, a division of Sun-Scape Enter-
   prises Ltd.
SunShine Press Publications, Inc.
SYCAMORE REVIEW
SYMPLOKE: A Journal for the Intermingling of Literary,
   Cultural and Theoretical Scholarship
Tal San Publishing/Distributors
Tamarack Books, Inc.
TEAK ROUNDUP
TEENS IN MOTION NEWS
Tell Publishing
Ten Star Press
Terra Nova Press
:THAT:
Theosophical Publishing House
Third Side Press, Inc.
Tickerwick Publications
Times Change Press
The Times Journal Publishing Co.
TIMESHARE AND VACATION OWNERSHIP RE-
   VIEW
TitleWaves Publishing
Top Of The Mountain Publishing
Tortuga Books
TOWERS CLUB, USA INFO MARKETING REPORT
TUCUMCARI LITERARY REVIEW
Turtle Island Press, Inc.
Two Eagles Press International
Tyro Publishing
ULITARRA
THE UNDERGROUND
THE UNDERGROUND FOREST - LA SELVA SUB-
   TERRANEA
THE UNIT CIRCLE
Unity Books
UNITY MAGAZINE
Universal Unity
University Editions, Inc.
Upney Editions
Upper Access Inc.
URBAN GRAFFITI
URBANUS/RAIZIRR
Urthona Press
Valiant Press, Inc.
VanderWyk & Burnham
Vehicule Press
Verity Press Publishing
Vestal Press Ltd
THE VINCENT BROTHERS REVIEW
VIRTUTE ET MORTE MAGAZINE
Visions Communications
Vista Publishing, Inc.
George Wahr Publishing Company
Ward Hill Press
THE WASHINGTON MONTHLY
WEBER STUDIES: Voices and Viewpoints of the
   Contemporary West
The Wellsweep Press
WESTERN SKIES
Westgate Press
Westport Publishers
Wharton Publishing, Inc.
White Mane Publishing Company, Inc.
Whitford Press
WHOLE TERRAIN - REFLECTIVE ENVIRONMEN-
   TAL PRACTICE
Williamson Publishing Company, Inc.
WINDOW PANES
Wisconsin Trails
Wood Thrush Books
WORDS OF WISDOM
WRITER TO WRITER
WRITERS GAZETTE
Writers House Press

WRITER'S WORKSHOP REVIEW
WRITER'S WORLD
Xenos Books
Yes You Can Press
YOUNG VOICES
Z W L Publishing, Inc.
Zoland Books

NON-VIOLENCE

THE AFFILIATE
THE ANIMALS' AGENDA
Beacon Point Press
Broken Rifle Press
Child's Play
DAUGHTERS OF SARAH
Ex Machina Publishing Company
Fallout Shelter Press
Free People Press
FRIENDS OF PEACE PILGRIM
GATEAVISA
GEORGE & MERTIE'S PLACE: Rooms With a View
GRAFFITI OFF THE ASYLUM WALLS
HARMONY: VOICES FOR A JUST FUTURE
Heartsong Books
HOAX!
ICARUS WAS RIGHT
The Independent Institute
THE INDEPENDENT REVIEW: A Journal of Political
    Economy
Innisfree Press
Itidwitir Publishing
J & L Publications
KICK IT OVER
THE MINDFULNESS BELL
MOKSHA JOURNAL
The New Humanity Press
THE NONVIOLENT ACTIVIST
Parallax Press
Path Press, Inc.
PEACE MAGAZINE
Philopsychy Press
The Place In The Woods
THE PLOUGH
POEMS THAT THUMP IN THE DARK/SECOND
    GLANCE
The Press at Foggy Bottom
SOCIAL ANARCHISM: A Journal of Practice and
    Theory
TEENS IN MOTION NEWS
TURNING THE TIDE: A Journal of Anti-Racist
    Activism, Research & Education
TURNING WHEEL
THE UNIT CIRCLE
Vajra Printing an Publishing of Yoga Anand Ashram
THE VINCENT BROTHERS REVIEW
VOICES - ISRAEL
THE VOLUNTARYIST
Ward Hill Press
Wild Dove Studio and Press, Inc.
THE WRITE WAY
Yes You Can Press

THE NORTH

Betelgeuse Books
Coteau Books
Mountain Automation Corporation
NORTH COAST REVIEW
Northern Rim Press
Poetry Harbor
THE RIVER

NORTH AMERICA

THE NEW PRESS LITERARY QUARTERLY
Palladium Communications
Poetic License Press
RAVEN - A Journal of Vexillology
SKINNYDIPPING
University of Calgary Press

WILD EARTH

NORTH CAROLINA

AC
Averasboro Press
Banks Channel Books
John F. Blair, Publisher
Bright Mountain Books, Inc.
CAPE FEAR JOURNAL
CITIES AND ROADS: A Collection of Short Stories for
    North Carolina Readers and Writers.
Explorer Press
The Feminist Press at the City College
NORTH CAROLINA LITERARY REVIEW
OYSTER BOY REVIEW
Pamlico Press
PREP Publishing
REFLECTIONS
THE RESOURCE
Signal Books
Starfish Press
Tailored Tours Publications, Inc.

NOVELS

A & M Books
Abiko Literary Press (ALP)
ACME Press
Amelia Press
American Audio Prose Library (non-print)
American Literary Press Inc./Noble House
Angelflesh Press
Asylum Arts
Avisson Press, Inc.
The Backwaters Press
Baker Street Publications
Banks Channel Books
Bardsong Press
Barking Dog Books
Barney Press
Bayhampton Publications
BELLES LETTRES
Black Heron Press
Black Sparrow Press
Blue Heron Publishing, Inc.
Bosck Publishing House
Boulevard Books, Inc. Florida
Briarwood Publishing
Brunswick Publishing Corporation
Cambric Press dba Emerald House
Catbird Press
Cave Books
Celo Valley Books
China Books & Periodicals, Inc.
CLASS ACT
Cleis Press
Coffee House Press
Company of Words Publishing
Confluence Press, Inc.
Coteau Books
Cultivated Underground Press
John Daniel and Company, Publishers
DAYS AND NIGHTS OF A SMALL PRESS PUB-
    LISHER
Depth Charge
The Design Image Group Inc.
THE DIRTY GOAT
EduCare Press
Eros Publishing
Excalibur Publishing Inc.
FIRST DRAFT
Fithian Press
FREEFALL
Fromm International Publishing Corporation
FULL MOON DIRECTORY
Full Moon Publications
FURTHER TOO
Galde Press, Inc.
The Galileo Press Ltd.

Gay Sunshine Press, Inc.
Golden Eagle Press
GoldenIsle Publishers, Inc.
GrapeVinePress
Green Bean Press
THE HAUNTED JOURNAL
Hi Jinx Press
Host Publications, Inc.
House of the 9 Muses, Inc.
Ignite! Entertainment
ILLUMINATIONS
INTERBANG
Italica Press, Inc.
THE J MAN TIMES
Jackson Harbor Press
Journey Books Publishing
Allen A. Knoll Publishers
Leyland Publications
LFW Enterprises
THE LITERARY QUARTERLY
LULLWATER REVIEW
MANOA: A Pacific Journal of International Writing
Mercury House
THE METAPHYSICAL REVIEW
Millennium Press
MIXED BAG
Mountain State Press
The New Humanity Press
New Victoria Publishers
NWI National Writers Institute
The O Press
Orloff Press
Outer Space Press
The Overmountain Press
Oxford House Publishing
OXYGEN
Paint Rock Publishing, Inc.
Papillon Publishing
Papyrus Literary Enterprises, Inc.
PEN & INK WRITERS JOURNAL
Pennycorner Press
Permeable Press
Polar Bear & Company
POTOMAC REVIEW
PREP Publishing
Primal Publishing
PRINCETON ARTS REVIEW
Pyncheon House
QUESTION EVERYTHING CHALLENGE EVERY-
  THING (QECE)
Ravenhawk Books
Red Crane Books, Inc.
Saqi Books Publisher
Scrivenery Press
SelectiveHouse Publishers, Inc.
SF COMMENTARY
Shaolin Communications
Signal Books
Signature Books
SILHOUETTE MAGAZINE
Silver Mountain Press
SLEUTH JOURNAL
Slough Press
The Smith (subsidiary of The Generalist Assn., Inc.)
Gibbs Smith, Publisher
Spectrum Press
The Spirit That Moves Us Press, Inc.
Steerforth Press, L.C.
Stones Point Press
Sulisa Publishing
SYMPLOKE: A Journal for the Intermingling of Literary,
  Cultural and Theoretical Scholarship
Talisman House, Publishers
Tell Publishing
Ten Star Press
Third Side Press, Inc.
Thunder Rain Publishing Corp.
Turnstone Press

2.13.61 Publications
Tyro Publishing
THE UNIT CIRCLE
URBAN GRAFFITI
THE VINCENT BROTHERS REVIEW
The White Cross Press
White Pine Press
White Wolf Publishing
Xenos Books
Zephyr Press
Zoland Books

NUCLEAR ENERGY

AFFAIR OF THE MIND: A Literary Quarterly
THE BLAB
CJE NEWS (Newsletter of the Coalition for Jobs & the
  Environment)
LOVE AND RAGE, A Revolutionary Anarchist News-
  paper
RED OWL
RESONANCE
Rising Tide Press New Mexico

NUMISMATICS

Bonus Books, Inc.
FELL'S U.S. COINS INVESTMENT QUARTERLY
GATEAVISA

NURSING

Commune-A-Key Publishing, Inc.
THE COMPLEAT NURSE
Dry Bones Press
Galen Press, Ltd.
Midwifery Today Books
Power Publications
REVOLUTION
Skidmore-Roth Publishing, Inc.
Sovereignty Press
The Tonal Company

OCCULT

THE AFFILIATE
Alamo Square Press
Athanor Books (a division of ETX Seminars)
Auromere Books and Imports
AXE FACTORY REVIEW
Baker Street Publications
Bennett Books
Borden Publishing Co.
Borderland Sciences Research Foundation
BOTH SIDES NOW
BROWNBAG PRESS
Cassandra Press, Inc.
Cosmoenergetics Publications
The F. Marion Crawford Memorial Society
CRCS Publications
Crescent Moon
Dalrymple Publishing Company
DANGER!
DAYS AND NIGHTS OF A SMALL PRESS PUB-
  LISHER
THE DRAGON CHRONICLE
Earth Magic Productions, Inc.
EMERGING
THE EMSHOCK LETTER
Eros Publishing
Feral House
Free People Press
FULL MOON DIRECTORY
Full Moon Publications
Galde Press, Inc.
GATEAVISA
Golden Isis Press
GRAFFITI OFF THE ASYLUM WALLS
GREEN EGG
THE HAUNTED JOURNAL
Heartsong Books
HECATE'S LOOM - A Journal of Magical Arts

HELIOCENTRIC NET/STIGMATA
HOAX!
Horned Owl Publishing
Hyacinth House Publications/Caligula Editions
IllumiNet Press
INCREDIBLE INQUIRY REPORTS
Inner Traditions International
INTUITIVE EXPLORATIONS
THE J MAN TIMES
LifeQuest Publishing Group
Llewellyn Publications
LLEWELLYN'S NEW WORLDS OF MIND AND
  SPIRIT
LP Publications (Teleos Institute)
LUMMOX JOURNAL
THE MAD FARMERS' JUBILEE ALMANACK
Magical Blend
MAGICAL BLEND MAGAZINE
MARGIN: EXPLORING MODERN MAGICAL REA-
  LISM
MetaGnosis
METAL CURSE
MIXED BAG
MYSTIC VOICES
NEW FRONTIER
The New Humanity Press
New Spirit Press/The Poet Tree
NIGHTSHADE
nine muses books
THE NOCTURNAL LYRIC
NOCTURNAL REPORTER
NORTHWOODS JOURNAL, A Magazine for Writers
NYX OBSCURA MAGAZINE
PAGAN PRIDE
Palm Drive Publishing
PASSION
POEMS THAT THUMP IN THE DARK/SECOND
  GLANCE
PSYCHOTRAIN
Quicksilver Productions
RALPH'S REVIEW
THE READER'S REVIEW
REALM OF DARKNESS
REALM OF THE VAMPIRE
REFLECT
RENAISSANCE MAGAZINE
Reyes Investment Enterprise Ltd.
Rio Grande Press
THE ROMANTIST
SAGEWOMAN
The Smallest County Press
SOCIETE
SPIRIT TO SPIRIT
SQUARE ONE - A Magazine of Disturbing Fiction
Station Hill Press
STRANGE MAGAZINE
Strawberry Hill Press
SUPER TROUPER
TEC Publications
Technicians of the Sacred
The Teitan Press, Inc.
Three Pyramids Publishing
Toad Hall, Inc.
Top Of The Mountain Publishing
2AM MAGAZINE
2AM Publications
Tyro Publishing
VAMPIRE NIGHTS
Verity Press Publishing
VIRGIN MEAT E-ZINE
VIRTUTE ET MORTE MAGAZINE
Samuel Weiser, Inc.
Westgate Press
Whitford Press
WICKED MYSTIC
THE WISE WOMAN

OCEANOGRAPHY

American Malacologists, Inc.
Baker Street Publications
Blue Reef Publications, Inc.
Commonwealth Press Virginia
DAYS AND NIGHTS OF A SMALL PRESS PUB-
  LISHER
Galde Press, Inc.
LAKE SUPERIOR MAGAZINE

OHIO

The Bacchae Press
Enthea Press
Gabriel's Horn Publishing Co., Inc.
GEORGE & MERTIE'S PLACE: Rooms With a View
ICON
Kenyette Productions
Mountain Automation Corporation
OHIO WRITER
RIVERWIND
TOWPATHS
THE VINCENT BROTHERS REVIEW
Wright-Armstead Associates

OLD WEST

The Bear Wallow Publishing Company
Discovery Enterprises, Ltd.
Full Moon Publications
GATEAVISA
Tamarack Books, Inc.
Venus Communications
WESTERN SKIES

OREGON

Blue Heron Publishing, Inc.
Castle Peak Editions
Epicenter Press Inc.
Flying Pencil Publications
Gahmken Press
LEO Productions LLC.
MIXED BAG
Moon Publications, Inc.
The Mountaineers Books
NORTHERN PILOT
Resolution Business Press, Inc.
Tamarack Books, Inc.
WESTERN SKIES

PACIFIC NORTHWEST

Access Multimedia
Alaska Northwest Books
Baker Street Publications
Ballena Press
Blue Heron Publishing, Inc.
BookPartners, Inc.
Castle Peak Editions
THE CLIMBING ART
Confluence Press, Inc.
Continuing Education Press
DAYS AND NIGHTS OF A SMALL PRESS PUB-
  LISHER
The Denali Press
Dog-Eared Publications
Dunamis House
DWELLING PORTABLY
Editorial Review
Epicenter Press Inc.
Falcon Press Publishing Company
Far Corner Books
FERRY TRAVEL GUIDE
FINE MADNESS
Flying Pencil Publications
Full Moon Publications
Gaff Press
Gahmken Press
GEORGE & MERTIE'S PLACE: Rooms With a View
Homestead Publishing

HORIZONS
ICARUS WAS RIGHT
Island Publishers
Itidwitir Publishing
Keokee Co. Publishing, Inc.
Edward J. Lefkowicz, Inc.
Light, Words & Music
THE MAD FARMERS' JUBILEE ALMANACK
MARGIN: EXPLORING MODERN MAGICAL REALISM
MIXED BAG
Moon Publications, Inc.
The Mountaineers Books
Naturegraph Publishers, Inc.
NORTHERN PILOT
Open Hand Publishing Inc.
Oregon State University Press
Perpetual Press
POETIC SPACE: Poetry & Fiction
POW-WOW
Pruett Publishing Company
Pygmy Forest Press
QED Press
Red Apple Publishing
Resolution Business Press, Inc.
SANDPOINT MAGAZINE
Sasquatch Books
SIGNPOST FOR NORTHWEST TRAILS
Timber Press
TIMBER TIMES
Tiptoe Literary Service
Trace Publications
Umbrella Books
UNWOUND
Waters Edge Press
WESTERN SKIES
White Plume Press
WOMEN ARTISTS NEWS BOOK REVIEW
Ye Galleon Press

PACIFIC REGION

NORTHERN PILOT
STORYBOARD

PARENTING

THE AFFILIATE
American Literary Press Inc./Noble House
Ascension Publishing
AT-HOME DAD
Autumn Publishing Group, LLC.
Bancroft Press
Bayhampton Publications
Bear Creek Publications
Blue Bird Publishing
Bluestocking Press
Book Peddlers
Bright Ring Publishing, Inc.
Cherubic Press
Circumpolar Press
Conari Press
Consumer Press
Coteau Books
The Crossing Press
Cyclone Books
DAUGHTERS OF SARAH
DOVETAIL: A Journal by and for Jewish/Christian Families
Dovetail Publishing
Down There Press
Elder Books
Excalibur Publishing Inc.
Family Works Publications
Fillmore Publishing Company
Fisher Books
Free Spirit Publishing Inc.
FURTHER TOO
Future Horizons, Inc.
Gan Publishing

GEORGE & MERTIE'S PLACE: Rooms With a View
GLB Publishers
GLEN BURNIELAND
Goodheart-Willcox Publisher
Grayson Bernard Publishers, Inc.
Gurze Books
Harvard Common Press
Heritage Global Publishing
HIP MAMA
Human Kinetics Pub. Inc.
Hunter House Inc., Publishers
Impact Publishers, Inc.
Inner Traditions International
INQ Publishing Co.
Intermountain Publishing
Islewest Publishing
Kimm Publishing, Inc.
Kivaki Press
Kodiak Media Group
LADYBUG, the Magazine for Young Children
Langmarc Publishing
Long Wind Publishing
The Love and Logic Press, Inc.
Macrocosm USA, Inc.
MAMA'S LITTLE HELPER
THE MASONIA ROUNDUP
McBooks Press
Midwifery Today Books
Mills & Sanderson, Publishers
Monroe Press
THE MOTHER IS ME: Profiling the Cultural Aspects of Motherhood
New Regency Publishing
New Spring Publications
OPTIONS IN LEARNING
Parabola
Parenting Press, Inc.
PEDIATRICS FOR PARENTS
Perspectives Press
THE PLOUGH
PPT EXPRESS
Purple Finch Press
Quiet Tymes, Inc.
Real Life Storybooks
St. John's Publishing, Inc.
SCIENCE/HEALTH ABSTRACTS
Sibyl Publications, Inc
Sigo Press
Studio 4 Productions
Summit Crossroads Press
Swan Publishing Company
TEENS IN MOTION NEWS
VanderWyk & Burnham
Westport Publishers
THE WHITE DOT - Survival Guide for the TV-Free
WHOLE EARTH
Williamson Publishing Company, Inc.
Women of Diversity Productions, Inc.

PEACE

THE ADVOCATE
THE AFFILIATE
American Literary Press Inc./Noble House
Astarte Shell Press
Atrium Society Publications/DBA Education For Peace Publications
Beacon Point Press
BLUE COLLAR REVIEW
Branden Publishing Company
Broken Rifle Press
Child's Play
COKEFISH
Cosmic Concepts
CRONE CHRONICLES: A Journal of Conscious Aging
CROSS ROADS
CURMUDGEON
DAUGHTERS OF SARAH
Deerbridge Books

The Denali Press
Dry Bones Press
EPICA
Free People Press
FRIENDS OF PEACE PILGRIM
GATEAVISA
GEORGE & MERTIE'S PLACE: Rooms With a View
GRAFFITI OFF THE ASYLUM WALLS
GREEN FUSE POETRY
HARMONY: VOICES FOR A JUST FUTURE
Heartsong Books
The Heather Foundation
Herald Press
HOAX!
Impact Publishers, Inc.
INFUSION
International Publishers Co. Inc.
ISRAEL HORIZONS
Jalmar Press
KICK IT OVER
H J Kramer
Kumarian Press, Inc.
LITTLE FREE PRESS
LONE STAR SOCIALIST
THE MILITANT
THE MINDFULNESS BELL
NEW HOPE INTERNATIONAL REVIEW
New Spirit Press/The Poet Tree
Nolo Press - Occidental
THE NONVIOLENT ACTIVIST
ONE EARTH
ORTHODOX MISSION
Orthodox Mission in Belize
Partisan Press
PEACE MAGAZINE
PEACE, The Magazine of the Sixties
PEACEWORK
THE PLOUGH
RADICAL AMERICA
RAIN MAGAZINE
RED OWL
RFD
Sandpiper Press
Schenkman Books
South End Press
STONES IN MY POCKET
Syracuse Cultural Workers/Tools for Change
Tilbury House, Publishers
TOWARD FREEDOM
TRANSNATIONAL PERSPECTIVES
THE UNDERGROUND FOREST - LA SELVA SUB-
  TERRANEA
VIETNAM GENERATION: A Journal of Recent History
  and Contemporary Issues
THE VINCENT BROTHERS REVIEW
VOICES - ISRAEL
Ward Hill Press
B. L. Winch & Associates

PERFORMING ARTS

Anacus Press, Inc.
ART PAPERS
Dovehaven Press
Griffon House Publications
JOURNAL OF HUMANITIES
KARAWANE
Mercury House
NEW ART EXAMINER
NIGHTSHADE
nine muses books
Palladium Communications
Prudhomme Press
University of Massachusetts Press
Z W L Publishing, Inc.

PETS

Conari Press
Dimension Engineering Press

Howln Moon Press
JPS Publishing Company
Kali Press
MINIATURE DONKEY TALK INC
Two Dog Press

PHILATELY, NUMISMATICS

Ana Libri Press
ARTISTAMP NEWS
Banana Productions
COLLECTORS CLUB PHILATELIST
INTERNATIONAL ART POST
PHILATELIC LITERATURE NEWS INTERNATIONAL
RALPH'S REVIEW
TOPICAL TIME
Vestal Press Ltd

PHILOSOPHY

A.R.E. Press
Abiko Literary Press (ALP)
Acclaim Publishing Co. Inc.
AFFAIR OF THE MIND: A Literary Quarterly
THE AFFILIATE
Agathon Books
AK Press
THE ANGRY THOREAUAN
THE ANIMALS' AGENDA
ARISTOS
Auromere Books and Imports
Autonomedia, Inc.
AXE FACTORY REVIEW
BARNABE MOUNTAIN REVIEW
Beacon Press
Bennett Books
Birdalone Books
Black Rose Books Ltd.
BOTH SIDES NOW
The Boxwood Press
Brason-Sargar Publications
BRIDGES: An Interdisciplinary Journal of Theology,
  Philosophy, History, and Science
BRITISH JOURNAL OF AESTHETICS
Brownout Laboratories
Burning Books
C.S.P. WORLD NEWS
Camino Bay Books
CANADIAN JOURNAL OF PHILOSOPHY
Carrefour Press
CAVEAT LECTOR
Chandler & Sharp Publishers, Inc.
Chaos Warrior Productions
THE CHEROTIC (r)EVOLUTIONARY
Children Of Mary
Community Service, Inc.
COMMUNITY SERVICE NEWSLETTER
Cosmoenergetics Publications
Crescent Moon
CRITICAL REVIEW
CRONE CHRONICLES: A Journal of Conscious Aging
THE DALHOUSIE REVIEW
Dalrymple Publishing Company
Manya DeLeon Booksmith
Desert Oasis Publishing Co.
Dharma Publishing
Dufour Editions Inc.
THE DURHAM UNIVERSITY JOURNAL
Edition Gemini
EduCare Press
The Edwin Mellen Press
EFRYDIAU ATHRONYDDOL
THE EMSHOCK LETTER
Encircle Publications
ETCETERA
ETICA & CIENCIA
THE EVER DANCING MUSE
Exile Press
FAT TUESDAY
FIDELIS ET VERUS

Vajra Printing an Publishing of Yoga Anand Ashram
Verity Press Publishing
VIRTUTE ET MORTE MAGAZINE
Samuel Weiser, Inc.
Westgate Press
WHAT IS ENLIGHTENMENT?
Whitford Press
Whitmore Publishing Company
Who Who Who Publishing
THE WISDOM CONSERVANCY NEWSLETTER
Wisdom Publications, Inc.
Witwatersrand University Press
Wood Thrush Books
World Wisdom Books, Inc.
Writers House Press
ZONE
Zone Books

PHOTOGRAPHY

Abiko Literary Press (ALP)
ACM (ANOTHER CHICAGO MAGAZINE)
ACORN WHISTLE
THE AFFILIATE
AFTERIMAGE
ALABAMA LITERARY REVIEW
Alicubi Publications
ALLEGHENY REVIEW
Allworth Press
American & World Geographic Publishing
THE AMERICAN VOICE
Amherst Media, Inc.
ANT ANT ANT ANT ANT
ANTIETAM REVIEW
APHRODITE GONE BERSERK
Appalachian Consortium Press
Arjuna Library Press
ARNAZELLA
ART CALENDAR
ART/LIFE
Art/Life Limited Editions
Avery Color Studios
BAJA SUN
Baker Street Publications
Banana Productions
THE BAREFOOT POET: Journal of Poetry, Fiction,
 Essays, & Art
Barefoot Press
BATHTUB GIN
Bay Press
The Bear Wallow Publishing Company
BEHIND BARS
Beyond Words Publishing, Inc.
BITTER OLEANDER
THE BLACK WARRIOR REVIEW
BlackBox
BLACKFLASH
Blue Heron Publishing, Inc.
Blue Unicorn Press, Inc.
THE BREAD AND BUTTER CHRONICLES
THE CAPE ROCK
Capra Press
The Carnation Press
CAVEAT LECTOR
Center Press
THE CHEROTIC (r)EVOLUTIONARY
CHILDREN, CHURCHES AND DADDIES, A Non
 Religious, Non Familial Literary Magazine
Conari Press
The Consultant Press, Ltd.
COTTONWOOD
Cottonwood Press
CURARE
CURMUDGEON
Dawn Sign Press
DAYS AND NIGHTS OF A SMALL PRESS PUB-
 LISHER
DESCANT
Devin-Adair Publishers, Inc.

Down There Press
THE DROPLET JOURNAL
Elliott & Clark Publishing
THE EMSHOCK LETTER
ENTELECHY MAGAZINE
Epicenter Press Inc.
ETCETERA
EyeDEA Books
Falcon Press Publishing Company
Film-Video Publications
Five Corners Publications, Ltd.
FLOATING ISLAND
FOLIO: A LITERARY JOURNAL
Fotofolio, Inc.
FOTOTEQUE
4*9*1: Neo-Immanentist/Sursymbolist-Imagination
Gesture Press
Ghost Pony Press
Goodheart-Willcox Publisher
GRAFFITI OFF THE ASYLUM WALLS
GrapeVinePress
Happy Rock Press
HOLLYWOOD NOSTALGIA
Hundman Publishing
ILLYA'S HONEY
The Image Maker Publishing Co.
Images For Media/Sesquin
INDEFINITE SPACE
INTERNATIONAL ART POST
J P Publications
JOTS (Journal of the Senses)
JOURNAL OF REGIONAL CRITICISM
JPS Publishing Company
Kenyette Productions
KESTREL: A Journal of Literature and Art
Allen A. Knoll Publishers
LEFT CURVE
Lessiter Publications
LIBIDO: The Journal of Sex and Sensibility
Light, Words & Music
LIGHTWORKS MAGAZINE
LIMESTONE: A LITERARY JOURNAL
Lincoln Springs Press
THE LISTENING EYE
LITRAG
LOST GENERATION JOURNAL
Lost Prophet Press
Lunar Offensive Publications
LUZ EN ARTE Y LITERATURA
MAINLINE MODELER
MARK
Midmarch Arts Press
Mr. Cogito Press
MIXED BAG
MOOSE BOUND PRESS JOURNAL/NEWSLETTER
MUSE NATURA, A Sensual Journey of the Arts
Mutual Publishing
N: NUDE & NATURAL
NEW ORLEANS REVIEW
NewSage Press
NIGHTSHADE
NORTH CAROLINA LITERARY REVIEW
North Country Books, Inc.
Not-For-Sale-Press or NFS Press
THE ONSET REVIEW
Ophelia Editions
Papier-Mache Press
PHOEBE: A JOURNAL OF LITERARY ARTS
Photo Data Research
PHOTOBULLETIN
PHOTOGRAPHY IN NEW YORK, INTERNATIONAL
THE PHOTOLETTER
PIG IRON
PLAY THE ODDS
Pomegranate Communications
POW-WOW
PRAIRIE WINDS
The Preservation Press

PUNCTURE
THE PURPLE MONKEY
RAG SHOCK
Really Great Books
REALM OF THE VAMPIRE
Red Alder Books
Red Crane Books, Inc.
Reference Desk Books
RIVER STYX
Ronsdale Press
THE ROTKIN REVIEW
S Press
St. Georges Press
SALT HILL
Salt Lick Press
Scars Publications
Sierra Club Books
Signal Books
Signature Books
SKYLARK
SLIPSTREAM
Gibbs Smith, Publisher
SO TO SPEAK
SPILLWAY
THE SPIRIT THAT MOVES US
The Spirit That Moves Us Press, Inc.
THE SPITTING IMAGE
Station Hill Press
STONES IN MY POCKET
Stormline Press, Inc.
Studia Hispanica Editors
STUDIO ART MAGAZINE
STUDIO ONE
THE SUN, A MAGAZINE OF IDEAS
THIN COYOTE
Tilbury House, Publishers
The Times Journal Publishing Co.
TOLE WORLD
TURNSTILE
Twelvetrees Press
Twin Palms Publishers
ULITARRA
UMBRELLA
THE UNIT CIRCLE
UNO MAS MAGAZINE
URBAN GRAFFITI
The Urbana Free Library
VACUITY
VEGGIE LIFE
Venom Press
VICTORY PARK: THE JOURNAL OF THE NEW
   HAMPSHIRE INSTITUTE OF ART
THE VINCENT BROTHERS REVIEW
Visual Studies Workshop
Voices From My Retreat
WEST BRANCH
WESTERN SKIES
Whalesback Books
WHITEWALLS: A Journal of Language and Art
WHOLE EARTH
Wisconsin Trails
WOOD STROKES & WOODCRAFTS
THE WORCESTER REVIEW
Writers Forum
Writers House Press
XIB
Xib Publications
Yatra Publications/11:11 Studio
YEFIEF
YELLOW SILK: Journal Of Erotic Arts
Zoland Books
Zon International Publishing Co.

PICTURE BOOKS

Abiko Literary Press (ALP)
Alicubi Publications
Barefoot Press
Bradley Publishing

The Brookfield Reader
Cherubic Press
FOTOTEQUE
Illumination Arts
Allen A. Knoll Publishers
Light, Words & Music
Long Wind Publishing
Papillon Publishing
Parabola
Peerless Publishing
Positive Press - Star Bear Books
Gibbs Smith, Publisher
Tortuga Books
Treasure Chest Books LLC
Trellis Publishing, Inc.
Turtle Island Press, Inc.
Waters Edge Press

PHYSICS

Abiko Literary Press (ALP)
AFFAIR OF THE MIND: A Literary Quarterly
THE AFFILIATE
Al-Galaxy Publishing Company
Astrion Publishing
Borderland Sciences Research Foundation
BORDERLANDS: A Quarterly Journal Of Borderland
   Research
Dimension Engineering Press
DISSONANCE MAGAZINE
THE EMSHOCK LETTER
Exceptional Books, Ltd.
FISICA
GATEAVISA
Genesis Publishing Company, Inc.
GEORGE & MERTIE'S PLACE: Rooms With a View
JACK MACKEREL MAGAZINE
JOURNAL OF REGIONAL CRITICISM
JOURNAL OF SCIENTIFIC EXPLORATION
THE MAD FARMERS' JUBILEE ALMANACK
MAD SCIENTIST
Media Arts Publishing
Outer Space Press
Polar Bear Productions & Company
RESONANCE
Rowhouse Press
Scopcraeft
SunShine Press Publications, Inc.
VACUITY
Zagier & Urruty Publicaciones

POETRY

A.L.I.
AABYE (formerly New Hope International Writing)
ABBEY
Abiko Literary Press (ALP)
THE ABIKO QUARTERLY WITH JAMES JOYCE FW
   STUDIES
ABRAXAS
AC
ACM (ANOTHER CHICAGO MAGAZINE)
THE ACORN
ACORN WHISTLE
Acre Press
Adastra Press
Aegina Press, Inc.
AERIAL
AFFAIR OF THE MIND: A Literary Quarterly
THE AFFILIATE
AFRICAN AMERICAN REVIEW
AFTERTHOUGHTS
AGADA
Agathon Books
AGNI
THE AGUILAR EXPRESSION
Ahsahta
ALABAMA DOGSHOE MOUSTACHE
ALABAMA LITERARY REVIEW
ALBATROSS

The Aldine Press, Ltd.
THE ALEMBIC
Alice James Books
ALLEGHENY REVIEW
Ally Press
Alms House Press
Alpha Beat Press
ALPHA BEAT SOUP
Alternating Crimes Publishing
AMARANTH
AMBIT
AMELIA
Amelia Press
AMERICAN INDIAN CULTURE AND RESEARCH
  JOURNAL
American Indian Studies Center
AMERICAN JONES BUILDING & MAINTENANCE
AMERICAN LETTERS & COMMENTARY
American Literary Press Inc./Noble House
AMERICAN LITERARY REVIEW
American Living Press
AMERICAN POETRY MONTHLY
AMERICAN POETRY REVIEW
THE AMERICAN SCHOLAR
AMERICAN TANKA
AMERICAN WRITING: A Magazine
AMERICAS REVIEW
Amethyst & Emerald
THE AMETHYST REVIEW
THE AMICUS JOURNAL
AMNESIA
Anamnesis Press
ANGELFLESH
Angelflesh Press
Anhinga Press
ANT ANT ANT ANT ANT
THE ANTHOLOGY OF NEW ENGLAND WRITERS
Anti-Aging Press
ANTIETAM REVIEW
THE ANTIOCH REVIEW
APKL Publications
APOSTROPHE: USCB Journal of the Arts
APPALACHIA JOURNAL
AQUARIUS
ARCHIPELAGO
Arctos Press
Arjuna Library Press
The Ark
Arnold & Johnson, Publishers
ART-CORE
Arte Publico Press
ARTFUL DODGE
ARTHUR'S COUSIN
Artifact Press, Ltd.
ART/LIFE
Art/Life Limited Editions
ART:MAG
Arts End Books
ART'S GARBAGE GAZZETTE
ARTWORD QUARTERLY
The Ashland Poetry Press
Associated Writing Programs
ASSPANTS
Astro Black Books
ATELIER
ATLANTA REVIEW
ATOM MIND
AURA LITERARY/ARTS REVIEW
Avocet Press Inc.
AVON LITERARY INTELLIGENCER
AXE FACTORY REVIEW
THE AZOREAN EXPRESS
BABYSUE
The Bacchae Press
BACKBOARD
Backspace Ink
The Backwaters Press
THE BADGER STONE CHRONICLES

BAKER STREET GAZETTE
Baker Street Publications
THE BALTIMORE REVIEW
Banshee Press
Bard Press
Bardsong Press
THE BAREFOOT POET: Journal of Poetry, Fiction,
  Essays, & Art
Barking Dog Books
BARNABE MOUNTAIN REVIEW
BARNWOOD
The Barnwood Press
BATHTUB GIN
BB Books
THE BEAR DELUXE
Bear Star Press
Bearhouse Publishing
BEGINNINGS - A Magazine for the Novice Writer
BEHIND BARS
THE BELLINGHAM REVIEW
BELLOWING ARK
Bellowing Ark Press
BELOIT POETRY JOURNAL
Bennett & Kitchel
BERKELEY POETRY REVIEW
BEYOND DOGGEREL
BGB Press, Inc.
BGS Press
BIG SCREAM
Big Star Press
Bilingual Review/Press
BIRMINGHAM POETRY REVIEW
BITTER OLEANDER
BkMk Press
Black Bear Publications
BLACK BEAR REVIEW
Black Buzzard Press
BLACK BUZZARD REVIEW
BLACK CROSS
BLACK DIRT
Black Dirt Press
Black Dress Press
Black Forest Press
BLACK JACK & VALLEY GRAPEVINE
BLACK MOON
Black Sparrow Press
Black Thistle Press
Black Tie Press
THE BLACK WARRIOR REVIEW
BlackBox
BLACKWATER
BLADES
Blind Beggar Press
THE BLIND HORSE REVIEW
BLITHE SPIRIT
BLOCK'S MAGAZINE
BLOOD & FEATHERS: Poems of Survival
BLOODJET LITERARY MAGAZINE
Bloody Someday Press
Blue Heron Publishing, Inc.
BLUE HORSE
Blue Horse Publications
BLUE MESA REVIEW
The Blue Oak Press
BLUE SATELLITE
Blue Star Press
BLUE UNICORN
BLUE VIOLIN
BLUEBOOK
BLUELINE
BOA Editions, Ltd.
BOGG
Bogg Publications
Bombshelter Press
BONE & FLESH
Boog Literature
BOOGLIT
The Book Department

BOOKS FROM FINLAND
Booksplus of Maine
BORDERLANDS: Texas Poetry Review
Borealis Press Limited
Bosck Publishing House
BOTH COASTS BOOK REVIEW
Bottom Dog Press
BOTTOMFISH
BOUILLABAISSE
BOULEVARD
THE BOUND SPIRAL
Branch Redd Books
BRANCH REDD REVIEW
BRANDO'S HAT
BRAVO, THE POET'S MAGAZINE
BrickHouse Books, Inc.
THE BRIDGE: A Journal of Fiction and Poetry
Bright Hill Press
THE BROBDINGNAGIAN TIMES
Broken Boulder Press
Broken Jaw Press
Broken Shadow Publications
Brooding Heron Press
Brooks Books
Browder Springs
BROWNBAG PRESS
Brownout Laboratories
PTOLEMY
THE BROWNS MILLS REVIEW
THE BROWNSTONE REVIEW
Brunswick Publishing Corporation
BUFFALO SPREE
The Bunny & The Crocodile Press/Forest Woods Media
  Productions, Inc
BURNING CAR
Burning Cities Press
THE BURNING CLOUD REVIEW
Burning Deck Press
Burning Llama Press
BUTTON
BYLINE
Cadmus Editions
CALAPOOYA
CALIFORNIA STATE POETRY QUARTERLY (CQ)
Calypso Publications
CALYX: A Journal of Art and Literature by Women
Cambric Press dba Emerald House
CANADIAN LITERATURE
CANDELABRUM POETRY MAGAZINE
THE CAPE ROCK
Cardinal Press, Inc.
THE CAROLINA QUARTERLY
Carolina Wren Press/Lollipop Power Books
Carpenter Press
Carrefour Press
Catamount Press
CAVEAT LECTOR
CAYO, A MAGAZINE OF LIFE IN THE KEYS
CC. Marimbo Communications
Cedar Hill Publications
CEDAR HILL REVIEW
CELEBRATION
Celestial Otter Press
Celo Valley Books
THE CENTENNIAL REVIEW
Center for Japanese Studies
Center Press
CHACHALACA POETRY REVIEW
CHAFFIN JOURNAL
CHANCE MAGAZINE
CHANTEH, the Iranian Cross Cultural Qu'ly
CHARITON REVIEW
CHELSEA
THE CHEROTIC (r)EVOLUTIONARY
Chicago Spectrum Press
Chicory Blue Press, Inc.
CHILDREN, CHURCHES AND DADDIES, A Non
  Religious, Non Familial Literary Magazine

Chili Verde
Chiron Press
CHIRON REVIEW
CHRISTIANITY & THE ARTS
CICADA
Cider Mill Press
CIMARRON REVIEW
Circumpolar Press
City Lights Books
Clamp Down Press
Clamshell Press
CLASS ACT
Cleveland State Univ. Poetry Center
CLOCKWATCH REVIEW
CLUTCH
CLWN WR
Coffee House Press
COKEFISH
Cokefish Press
COLD-DRILL
COLORADO REVIEW: A Journal of Contemporary
  Literature
THE COMSTOCK REVIEW
CONFLICT OF INTEREST
CONFLUENCE
Confluence Press, Inc.
CONJUNCTIONS
THE CONNECTICUT POETRY REVIEW
CONNECTICUT REVIEW
CONNECTICUT RIVER REVIEW: A National Poetry
  Journal
CONTEXT SOUTH
Copper Beech Press
Copper Canyon Press
Coreopsis Books
Cosmic Trend
Coteau Books
COTTONWOOD
Cottonwood Press
Cottonwood Press, Inc.
COVER MAGAZINE
John Edwin Cowen/Bravo Editions
CRAB CREEK REVIEW
CRAB ORCHARD REVIEW
The F. Marion Crawford Memorial Society
CRAZYHORSE
THE CREAM CITY REVIEW
Creative Arts & Science Enterprises
Creative With Words Publications (CWW)
Crescent Moon
CRIPES!
CROSSCURRENTS, A QUARTERLY
CRUCIBLE
Cultivated Underground Press
CUMBERLAND POETRY REVIEW
THE CUP
CURARE
Curbstone Press
CURMUDGEON
CURRENT ACCOUNTS
CUTBANK
Cynic Press
D.D.B. Press
THE DALHOUSIE REVIEW
DANDELION ARTS MAGAZINE
John Daniel and Company, Publishers
DAYS AND NIGHTS OF A SMALL PRESS PUB-
  LISHER
Dead Metaphor Press
DEANOTATIONS
DeeMar Communications
Manya DeLeon Booksmith
DENVER QUARTERLY
Depth Charge
DESCANT
DESCANT
DESIRE STREET
THE DESK

DEVIL BLOSSOMS
THE DEVIL'S MILLHOPPER
The Devil's Millhopper Press (TDM Press)
DIALOGOS: Hellenic Studies Review
DIE YOUNG
Paul Dilsaver, Publisher
DIRIGIBLE
THE DIRTY GOAT
DISTURBED GUILLOTINE
Doctor Jazz Press
Dolphin-Moon Press
Dovehaven Press
Down There Press
DOWN UNDER MANHATTAN BRIDGE
DREAM INTERNATIONAL QUARTERLY
DREAM NETWORK JOURNAL
DREAMS AND NIGHTMARES
THE DROPLET JOURNAL
Drum
DRY CRIK REVIEW
Dufour Editions Inc.
DWAN
THE EAR
EARTH'S DAUGHTERS: Feminist Arts Periodical
The Ecco Press
THE EDGE CITY REVIEW
Edgewise Press
Editorial Review
The Edwin Mellen Press
Ehrman Entertainment Press
The Eighth Mountain Press
EKPHRASIS
THE ELEVENTH MUSE, a publication by Poetry West
ELF: ECLECTIC LITERARY FORUM (ELF MAGA-
ZINE)
ELT Press
Embassy Hall Editions
Emerald Ink Publishing
EMERGING VOICES
EMPLOI PLUS
THE EMSHOCK LETTER
En Passant Poetry Press
EN PASSANT/POETRY
ENDING THE BEGIN
Enitharmon Press
ENTELECHY MAGAZINE
Enthea Press
EPOCH
Erespin Press
ETCETERA
EVANSVILLE REVIEW
EVENT
THE EVER DANCING MUSE
THE EVERGREEN CHRONICLES
Ex Machina Publishing Company
Excelsior Cee Publishing
EXIT 13 MAGAZINE
Expanded Media Editions
Fallout Shelter Press
Far Corner Books
FAR GONE
FAT TUESDAY
FAULTLINE, Journal of Art and Literature
FC-Izdat Publishing
The Feathered Serpent
FELICITY
FELL SWOOP
The Feminist Press at the City College
FENICE BROADSHEETS
THE FIDDLEHEAD
FIDEI DEFENSOR: JOURNAL OF CATHOLIC APO-
LOGETICS
FIELD
FIGMENTS
The Figures
FINE MADNESS
FIRM NONCOMMITTAL: An International Journal of
Whimsy

FIRST CLASS
FIRST DRAFT
FIRST INTENSITY
FISH DRUM MAGAZINE
FISH STORIES
Fithian Press
5 AM
Five Fingers Press
FIVE FINGERS REVIEW
FIVE POINTS
FkB Press
FLIPSIDE
Floating Bridge Press
FLOATING ISLAND
Floating Island Publications
THE FLORIDA REVIEW
FLYING HORSE
FLYWAY
FODDERWING
FOLIO: A LITERARY JOURNAL
THE FORMALIST
Four Seasons Publishers
Four Seasons Publishing
Four Way Books
4*9*1: Neo-Immanentist/Sursymbolist-Imagination
Four-Sep Publications
FOURTEEN HILLS: The SFSU Review
FRANK: AN INTERNATIONAL JOURNAL OF CON-
TEMPORARY WRITING AND ART
FREE LUNCH
FREEDOM ISN'T FREE
FREEFALL
French Bread Publications
FRESH GROUND
Frith Press
THE FROGMORE PAPERS
The Frogmore Press
From Here Press
FROM THE MARGIN
Frozen Waffles Press/Shattered Sidewalks Press; 45th
Century Chapbooks
FUEL MAGAZINE
FUGUE
Full Moon Publications
The Future Press
Gaff Press
Galaxy Press
The Galileo Press Ltd.
THE GALLEY SAIL REVIEW
Gallopade International
Garden St Press
GARGOYLE
Gay Sunshine Press, Inc.
Gearhead Press
Geekspeak Unique Press
THE GENRE WRITER'S NEWS
THE GENTLE SURVIVALIST
GEORGE & MERTIE'S PLACE: Rooms With a View
GEORGETOWN REVIEW
THE GEORGIA REVIEW
GERBIL: Queer Culture Zine
Gesture Press
THE GETTYSBURG REVIEW
Ghost Pony Press
Gild of Saint George
THE GLASS CHERRY
The Glass Cherry Press
GLB Publishers
The Gleniffer Press
Goats & Compasses
god is DEAD, publications
THE GODDESS OF THE BAY
Golden Isis Press
Good Gay Poets Press
Gothic Press
GRAFFITI OFF THE ASYLUM WALLS
GRAIN
GrapeVinePress

GRASSLANDS REVIEW
Gravity Presses, Inc.
Graywolf Press
THE GREAT BLUE BEACON
Great Elm Press
GREAT RIVER REVIEW
Great Western Publishing Company
Green Bean Press
GREEN FUSE POETRY
THE GREEN HILLS LITERARY LANTERN
The Green Hut Press
GREEN MOUNTAINS REVIEW
Green River Writers, Inc./Grex Press
The Greenfield Review Press/Ithaca House
Greenhouse Review Press
GREEN'S MAGAZINE
THE GREENSBORO REVIEW
Greensleeve Editions
Griffon House Publications
The Groundwater Press
Guildford Poets Press
GULF COAST
H & C NEWSLETTER
HAIGHT ASHBURY LITERARY JOURNAL
Haley's
HAMMERS
HANGING LOOSE
Hanging Loose Press
Hannacroix Creek Books, Inc
Hard Press
HARP-STRINGS
THE HAUNTED JOURNAL
HAWAII PACIFIC REVIEW
HAWAI'I REVIEW
Hawk Publishing Group
HAYDEN'S FERRY REVIEW
Headveins Graphics
HEARTLAND (Australia)
Heat Press
HEAVEN BONE MAGAZINE
Heaven Bone Press
Helicon Nine Editions
Helikon Press
HELIOCENTRIC NET/STIGMATA
HELLAS: A Journal of Poetry & the Humanities
HELLP!
Hellp! Press
Hermes House Press, Inc.
The Heyeck Press
THE HIGGINSVILLE READER
THE HIGHWAY POET
Hippopotamus Press
HIRAM POETRY REVIEW
Hobblebush Books
HOBO POETRY & HAIKU MAGAZINE
Hohm Press
Holy Cow! Press
HOME PLANET NEWS
Home Planet Publications
Homeward Press
Honors Group
HOOTENANNY
HORIZONS
Horse & Buggy Press
The Hosanna Press
Host Publications, Inc.
HOT FLASHES
Howling Dog Press/Stiletto
HQ POETRY MAGAZINE (The Haiku Quarterly)
HSC Publications
H2SO4
HUBBUB
Humana Press
THE HUNTED NEWS
Huntsville Literary Association
Hutton Publications
Hyacinth House Publications/Caligula Editions
Ibbetson St. Press

IBIS REVIEW
Icarus Books
ICON
THE ICONOCLAST
IDIOM 23
IGNIS FATUUS REVIEW
ILLINOIS ARCHITECTURAL & HISTORICAL REVIEW
ILLUMINATIONS
ILLYA'S HONEY
Images For Media/Sesquin
IMAGO
IMPETUS
THE IMPLODING TIE-DYED TOUPEE
Implosion Press
INDEFINITE SPACE
Indelible Inc.
THE INDIAN WRITER
INDIANA REVIEW
Infinite Passion Publishing
INNER VOICES: A New Journal of Prison Literature
Insomniac Press
INTERBANG
INTERCULTURAL WRITERS REVIEW
INTERIM
Interim Press
INTERNATIONAL OLYMPIC LIFTER
INTERNATIONAL POETRY REVIEW
INTERNATIONAL QUARTERLY
THE INTERPRETER'S HOUSE
Intertext
INVISIBLE CITY
Ione Press
IOTA
IPSISSIMA VERBA/THE VERY WORDS: Fiction & Poetry in the First Person
IRIS: A Journal About Women
IRISH JOURNAL
IRISH LITERARY SUPPLEMENT
Irvington St. Press, Inc.
Island Publishers
ISSUES
J & J Consultants, Inc.
THE J MAN TIMES
J. Mark Press
JACARANDA
JACK MACKEREL MAGAZINE
JACK THE RIPPER GAZETTE
Jackson Harbor Press
Jahbone Press
Jalmar Press
JAPANOPHILE
JB Press
JEJUNE: america Eats its Young
Jesus Pinata Press
JEWISH LIFE
JOURNAL OF CANADIAN POETRY
JOURNAL OF HUMANITIES
JOURNAL OF NEW JERSEY POETS
Judah Magnes Museum Publications
Juggernaut
Junction Press
Jungle Man Press
K.T. Publications
KALDRON, An International Journal Of Visual Poetry
KALEIDOSCOPE: INTERNATIONAL MAGAZINE OF LITERATURE, FINE ARTS, AND DISABILITY
Kaleidoscope Road Publications
KARAMU
KARAWANE
Karmichael Press
Katydid Books
Kawabata Press
THE KELSEY REVIEW
Kelsey St. Press
Kenyette Productions
THE KENYON REVIEW
THE KERF

KESTREL: A Journal of Literature and Art
KICK IT OVER
Kings Estate Press
Knightraven Books
KOJA
Konocti Books
THE KOSCIUSZKO PORTFOLIO
Kosmos
Kozmik Press
KRAX
KUMQUAT MERINGUE
KUUMBA
La Alameda Press
La Jolla Poets Press
LADYBUG, the Magazine for Young Children
Lakes & Prairies Press
LATINO STUFF REVIEW
LAUREATE LETTER
THE LAUREL REVIEW
Leapfrog Press
LEAPINGS LITERARY MAGAZINE
Ledero Press
THE LEDGE
LEFT CURVE
Left Hand Books
LEO Productions LLC.
L'Epervier Press
LFW Enterprises
THE LICKING RIVER REVIEW
LIFTOUTS
LIGHT: The Quarterly of Light Verse
LIGHTHOUSE
LILLIPUT REVIEW
Limberlost Press
LIME GREEN BULLDOZERS (AND OTHER RELAT-
ED SPECIES)
LIMESTONE: A LITERARY JOURNAL
Lincoln Springs Press
LINKS
LINQ
Lintel
LIPS
Liquid Paper Press
THE LISTENING EYE
LITERAL LATTE
Literary Moments
LITERARY ROCKET
LITRAG
THE LITTLE MAGAZINE
Little River Press
The Lockhart Press
Logodaedalus
LOGODAEDALUS
London Fog Publishing
LONE STARS MAGAZINE
Lone Willow Press
LONGHOUSE
Longhouse
THE LONSDALE - The International Quarterly of The
Romantic Six
Loom Press
LOONFEATHER: A magazine of poetry, short prose, and
graphics
Loonfeather Press
LOS
LOST AND FOUND TIMES
Lost Horse Press
Lost Prophet Press
Lost Roads Publishers
Lotus Press, Inc.
THE LOUISIANA REVIEW
THE LOUISVILLE REVIEW
THE LOWELL REVIEW
LOWLANDS REVIEW
Low-Tech Press
LS Press, Inc.
LUCIDITY
LUCKY HEART BOOKS

LULLWATER REVIEW
LUMMOX JOURNAL
Luna Bisonte Prods
Lunar Offensive Publications
LUZ EN ARTE Y LITERATURA
LYNX EYE
THE LYRIC
THE MAC GUFFIN
THE MAD FARMERS' JUBILEE ALMANACK
Mad River Press
THE MADISON REVIEW
MAGIC CHANGES
Magic Circle Press
MAGIC REALISM
MAIN STREET RAG POETRY JOURNAL
MALACHITE AND AGATE
MANGROVE MAGAZINE
THE MANHATTAN REVIEW
MANKATO POETRY REVIEW
MANOA: A Pacific Journal of International Writing
MANY MOUNTAINS MOVING
Marathon International Book Company
March Street Press
MARK
THE MARLBORO REVIEW
MATCHBOOK
MATI
MATRIX
THE MAVERICK PRESS
MAYFLY
MCS Publishing
ME MAGAZINE
MEANJIN
Meanjin
MEDUSA'S HAIRDO
Mellen Poetry Press
The Menard Press
Meridional Publications
MERLYN'S PEN: Fiction, Essays, and Poems By
America's Teens
Merrimack Books
Merwood Books
MESECHABE: The Journal of Surre(gion)alism
MESSAGES FROM THE HEART
Metacom Press
META4: Journal of Object Oriented Poetics (OOPS)
METAL CURSE
THE METAPHYSICAL REVIEW
Miami University Press
Mica Press
MICROPRESS YATES
MID-AMERICAN REVIEW
Mid-List Press
Midmarch Arts Press
MIDWEST POETRY REVIEW
THE MIDWEST QUARTERLY
Midwest Villages & Voices
Milkweed Editions
Mille Grazie Press
MINIMUS
Minor Heron Press
MIP Company
Missing Spoke Press
MISSISSIPPI MUD
MISSISSIPPI REVIEW
Mr. Cogito Press
MIXED BAG
MOCKINGBIRD
MOKSHA JOURNAL
Monographics Press
MOODY STREET IRREGULARS: A Jack Kerouac
Magazine
Moody Street Irregulars, Inc.
MOONRABBIT REVIEW
MOOSE BOUND PRESS JOURNAL/NEWSLETTER
Mortal Press
MOTHER EARTH JOURNAL: An International Quar-
terly

Moving Parts Press
MUDFISH
MUDLARK
Multi Media Arts
Mundus Artium Press
MUSE NATURA, A Sensual Journey of the Arts
MUSE OF FIRE
MUSHROOM DREAMS
MUSICWORKS: The Journal of Sound Explorations
(Audio-Visual)
THE MUSING PLACE
MY LEGACY
Nada Press
NANNY FANNY
National Poetry Association Publishers
NATURAL BRIDGE
NEBO
THE NEBRASKA REVIEW
NEDGE
NEGATIVE CAPABILITY
Negative Capability Press
NEOLOGISMS
NERVE COWBOY
NEW ALTERNATIVES
NEW AMERICAN WRITING
NEW COLLAGE MAGAZINE
New Collage Press
THE NEW CRITERION
NEW DELTA REVIEW
New Earth Publications
NEW ENGLAND REVIEW
New Hope International
NEW HOPE INTERNATIONAL REVIEW
New Issues Press
THE NEW LAUREL REVIEW
NEW LETTERS
THE NEW MOON REVIEW
NEW MUSE OF CONTEMPT
New Native Press
NEW ORLEANS REVIEW
THE NEW PRESS LITERARY QUARTERLY
New Rivers Press, Inc.
THE NEW SOUTHERN SURREALIST REVIEW
New Spirit Press/The Poet Tree
NEW STONE CIRCLE
NEW THOUGHT JOURNAL
New World Press
THE NEW WRITER
NEWSLETTER INAGO
NEWSLETTER (LEAGUE OF CANADIAN POETS)
Nextstep Books
Nicolin Fields Publishing, Inc.
NIGHT ROSES
NIGHTSHADE
Nightshade Press
Nightsun Books
NIMROD INTERNATIONAL
nine muses books
Ninety-Six Press
Nite-Owl Press
NITE-WRITER'S   INTERNATIONAL   LITERARY
ARTS JOURNAL
THE NORTH AMERICAN REVIEW
NORTH COAST REVIEW
North Stone Press
NORTHEAST
NORTHRIDGE REVIEW
NORTHWEST REVIEW
NORTHWOODS JOURNAL, A Magazine for Writers
Northwoods Press
NORTHWORDS
NOSTALGIA, A Sentimental State of Mind
NOSTOC MAGAZINE
Nosukumo
NOTRE DAME REVIEW
NOW AND THEN
NOW HERE NOWHERE
Now It's Up To You Publications

O.ARS, Inc.
OASIS
Oasis Books
Oasis In Print
Oberlin College Press
OBJECT PERMANENCE
OBSIDIAN II: BLACK LITERATURE IN REVIEW
OF UNICORNS AND SPACE STATIONS
Off the Cuff Books
THE OHIO REVIEW
OLD CROW
THE OLD RED KIMONO
The Olive Press Publications
Ommation Press
ON COURSE
ONE TRICK PONY
Oolichan Books
Open University of America Press
ORACLE POETRY
ORBIS
Orchises Press
Ortalda & Associates
OSIRIS
Osric Publishing
Otherwind
OTTER
OUTERBRIDGE
OUTPOSTS POETRY QUARTERLY
THE OVAL MAGAZINE
Owl Creek Press
OXYGEN
Oyez
OYSTER BOY REVIEW
O!!ZONE, A LITERARY-ART ZINE
The O!!Zone Press
OZ-STORY
P & K Stark Productions, Inc.
PACIFIC COAST JOURNAL
PACIFIC ENTERPRISE
THE PACIFIC REVIEW
PAGAN AMERICA
PAGAN PRIDE
Palanquin Press
Palladium Communications
PalmTree Publishers
PALO ALTO REVIEW
Pancake Press
PANDALOON
THE PANHANDLER
Panjandrum Books
PANJANDRUM POETRY JOURNAL
THE PANNUS INDEX
THE PAPER BAG
The Paper Bag Press
PAPERPLATES
Papier-Mache Press
PAPYRUS
Parabola
PARADOX
PARA*PHRASE
Paris Press, Inc.
PARNASSUS LITERARY JOURNAL
PARNASSUS: POETRY IN REVIEW
PARTING GIFTS
PASSAGES NORTH
PASSAIC REVIEW (MILLENNIUM EDITIONS)
Passeggiata Press, Inc.
PASSION
THE PATERSON LITERARY REVIEW
THE PATRIOT
PAVEMENT SAW
Pavement Saw Press
Paycock Press
PEACE, The Magazine of the Sixties
PEAKY HIDE
PEARL
Pearl Editions
Pearl River Press

860

PEARL RIVER REVIEW
Pearl-Win Publishing Co.
Pecan Grove Press
PEGASUS
THE PEGASUS REVIEW
PEMBROKE MAGAZINE
PEMMICAN
Pemmican Press
PEN & INK WRITERS JOURNAL
Pendragonian Publications
Peninhand Press
PENNINE PLATFORM
PENNY DREADFUL: Tales and Poems of Fantastic
  Terror
PenRose Publishing Company, Inc.
PEREGRINE
PERSEPHONE
Persephone Press
Perugia Press
The Petrarch Press
PHOEBE: A JOURNAL OF LITERARY ARTS
PHOENIX MAGAZINE
Phoenix Press
Picaro Press
PIEDMONT LITERARY REVIEW
PIG IRON
Pig Iron Press
Pinched Nerves Press
Pinchgut Press
Pine Grove Press
PINE ISLAND JOURNAL OF NEW ENGLAND
  POETRY
Pine Press
PINYON POETRY
PIRATE WRITINGS
Pittore Euforico
PLAINSONG
THE PLASTIC TOWER
PLEASANT LIVING
Pleasure Boat Studio
Pleasure Dome Press (Long Island Poetry Collective Inc.)
Plinth Books
PLOUGHSHARES
THE PLOWMAN
Pluma Productions
PLUME
POEM
POEMS & PLAYS
POEMS THAT THUMP IN THE DARK/SECOND
  GLANCE
POET LORE
Poetic License Press
Poetic Page
POETIC SPACE: Poetry & Fiction
Poetical Histories
POETRY
POETRY AND AUDIENCE
POETRY BONE
The Poetry Center Press/Shoestring Press
The Poetry Connection
THE POETRY CONNECTION
POETRY EAST
THE POETRY EXPLOSION NEWSLETTER (THE
  PEN)
POETRY FLASH
Poetry Harbor
POETRY INTERNATIONAL
Poetry Ireland
POETRY IRELAND REVIEW
POETRY KANTO
THE POETRY MISCELLANY
POETRY MOTEL
POETRY NEW YORK: A Journal of Poetry and
  Translation
POETRY NOTTINGHAM INTERNATIONAL
Poetry Nottingham Society Publications
Poetry Now, Sacramento's Literary Calendar and Review
POETRY NZ

The Poetry Project
THE POETRY PROJECT NEWSLETTER
POETRY REVIEW
POETRY USA
POETRY WALES
Poetry Wales Press, Ltd.
POETS & WRITERS MAGAZINE
POETS AT WORK
POET'S FANTASY
POET'S FORUM
POETS ON THE LINE
POET'S PARK
POETS' ROUNDTABLE
POETS' VOICE
POETS'PAPER
POETSWEST LITERARY JOURNAL
Point Bonita Books
Point Riders Press
Polar Bear & Company
Poltroon Press
The Porcupine's Quill, Inc.
Portals Press
Bern Porter Books
Portmanteau Editions
The Post-Apollo Press
POSTCARD
Pot Shard Press
POTATO EYES
Potes & Poets Press Inc.
POTOMAC REVIEW
POTPOURRI: A Magazine of the Literary Arts
THE POTTERSFIELD PORTFOLIO
PRAIRIE FIRE
THE PRAIRIE JOURNAL OF CANADIAN LITERA-
  TURE
Prairie Journal Press
PRAIRIE SCHOONER
PRAIRIE WINDS
Prakalpana Literature
PRAKALPANA SAHITYA/PRAKALPANA LITERA-
  TURE
Preludium Publishers
PrePress Publishing of Michigan
PRESS
Press Here
The Press of Appletree Alley
Prickly Pear Press
Pride & Imprints
Primal Publishing
PRIMAVERA
PRIME
PRINCETON ARTS REVIEW
PRISM INTERNATIONAL
PROOF ROCK
Proper PH Publications
THE PROSE POEM: An International Journal
PROSODIA
Protean Press
Protean Publications
PROVINCETOWN ARTS
PSYCHOPOETICA
PSYCHOTRAIN
PTOLEMY/BROWNS MILLS REVIEW
Puckerbrush Press
THE PUCKERBRUSH REVIEW
Pudding House Publications
PUDDING MAGAZINE: THE INTERNATIONAL
  JOURNAL OF APPLIED POETRY
PUERTO DEL SOL
PULSAR
The Purchase Press
PURPLE
Purple Finch Press
THE PURPLE MONKEY
PURPLE PATCH
Pygmy Forest Press
Pyncheon House
Pyx Press

QRL POETRY SERIES
Quarterly Review of Literature Press
QUARTERLY WEST
Queen of Swords Press
Rabeth Publishing Company
RAFTERS
RAG MAG
RAG SHOCK
RAIN CITY REVIEW
Rainbow's End
THE RAINTREE REVIEW: Poetry Edition
RALPH'S REVIEW
RAMBUNCTIOUS REVIEW
Rarach Press
RATTAPALLAX
RATTLE
Raw Dog Press
RAZOR WIRE
THE READER'S REVIEW
Reality Street Editions
REALM OF DARKNESS
REALM OF THE VAMPIRE
Red Alder Books
Red Apple Publishing
Red Candle Press
Red Cedar Press
RED CEDAR REVIEW
Red Crane Books, Inc.
Red Dragon Press
Red Dust
Red Hen Press
Red Hill Press, San Francisco + Los Angeles
Red Letter Press
RED OWL
RED ROCK REVIEW
REDOUBT
REFLECT
REFLECTIONS
Relief Press
RFD
Rhiannon Press
RHINO: THE POETRY FORUM
Rhizome
RHYME TIME POETRY NEWSLETTER
THE RIALTO
Ridgeway Press of Michigan
Rio Grande Press
THE RIVER
RIVER CITY
RIVER KING POETRY SUPPLEMENT
RIVER STYX
Riverstone, A Press for Poetry
THE ROCKFORD REVIEW
ROMANTIC HEARTS
THE ROMANTIST
Ronsdale Press
ROOM
Rose Alley Press
Rose Shell Press
ROSEBUD
THE ROSWELL LITERARY REVIEW
Roth Publishing, Inc.
THE ROUND TABLE: A Journal of Poetry and Fiction
Rowan Mountain Press
Rowhouse Press
Runaway Publications
The Runaway Spoon Press
S Press
S.
Sachem Press
The Sacred Beverage Press
St. Andrews Press
St. John's Publishing, Inc.
Saint Mary's Press
St. Michael's Press
SALAMANDER
SALMAGUNDI
SALOME: A Journal for the Performing Arts

SALT HILL
SALT LICK
Salt Lick Press
San Diego Poet's Press
Sandberry Press
SANDHILLS REVIEW (formerly ST. ANDREWS RE-
    VIEW)
Sandpiper Press
SANTA BARBARA REVIEW
Saqi Books Publisher
Sarabande Books, Inc.
SARU Press International
Saturday Press, Inc.
Savant Garde Workshop
Scars Publications
Scopcraeft
Score
SCORE
Scots Plaid Press
THE SCRIBIA
Scripta Humanistica
SCRIVENER
SE LA VIE WRITER'S JOURNAL
Second Aeon Publications
Second Coming Press
Sedna Press
SEEMS
SENECA REVIEW
SEPIA
SERIE D'ECRITURE
Serpent & Eagle Press
Seven Buffaloes Press
SEWANEE REVIEW
SFEST, LTD.
SHADES OF DECEMBER
Shadowlight Press
Shaolin Communications
SHATTERED WIG REVIEW
Shearsman Books
The Sheep Meadow Press
SHEILA-NA-GIG
SHENANDOAH
Sherman Asher Publishing
SHIRIM
SHOCKBOX
SHORT FUSE
SIDEWALKS
THE SIGNAL - Network International
Signature Books
Signpost Press Inc.
SILHOUETTE MAGAZINE
Silver Mountain Press
SILVERFISH REVIEW
SING HEAVENLY MUSE! WOMEN'S POETRY AND
    PROSE
Singular Speech Press
SISTERSONG: Women Across Cultures
SITUATION
SIVULLINEN
69 FLAVORS OF PARANOIA
Skinny Lamb Publishing Company
SKYLARK
SLANT: A Journal of Poetry
Slapering Hol Press
Slate Press
SLEUTH JOURNAL
SLIGHTLY WEST
SLIPSTREAM
A Slow Tempo Press
THE SMALL POND MAGAZINE OF LITERATURE
    aka SMALL POND
SMELT MONEY (A Poetics Newsletter from the KAW
    River Bottoms)
Smiling Dog Press
The Smith (subsidiary of The Generalist Assn., Inc.)
Gibbs Smith, Publisher
SMOKE
Smyrna Press

Underwhich Editions
Unfinished Monument Press
THE UNIT CIRCLE
Uniting the World Press, Inc.
University Editions, Inc.
University of Massachusetts Press
UNIVERSITY OF WINDSOR REVIEW
THE UNKNOWN WRITER
UNWOUND
URBAN GRAFFITI
Urban Legend Press
THE URBANITE
URBANUS/RAIZIRR
Urthona Press
US1 Poets' Cooperative
US1 WORKSHEETS
VACUITY
Vajra Printing an Publishing of Yoga Anand Ashram
VARIOUS ARTISTS
Vehicule Press
Venom Press
Veracity Press
VERANDAH
VERSE: A Journal of Poetry & Poetics
VERTICAL IMAGES
VERVE
Vesta Publications Limited
VICTORY PARK: THE JOURNAL OF THE NEW
  HAMPSHIRE INSTITUTE OF ART
VIGIL
THE VINCENT BROTHERS REVIEW
Vincent Laspina
VIRGIN MEAT E-ZINE
VIRGINIA LITERARY REVIEW
THE VIRGINIA QUARTERLY REVIEW
VIRTUTE ET MORTE MAGAZINE
VISIONS-INTERNATIONAL, The World Journal of
  Illustrated Poetry
A VOICE WITHOUT SIDES
Voices From My Retreat
VOICES - ISRAEL
VOL. NO. MAGAZINE
VOLITION
Warthog Press
WASHINGTON REVIEW
Washington Writers' Publishing House
Water Mark Press
Water Row Press
WATER ROW REVIEW
WATERWAYS: Poetry in the Mainstream
WAY STATION MAGAZINE
WEBER STUDIES: Voices and Viewpoints of the
  Contemporary West
WEIRD POETRY
West Anglia Publications
WEST BRANCH
West End Press
WESTERN SKIES
WEYFARERS
Whelks Walk Press
WHELKS WALK REVIEW
WHETSTONE
White Buck Publishing
THE WHITE CROW
White Pine Press
White Plume Press
Who Who Who Publishing
WHOLE NOTES
Whole Notes Press
WICKED MYSTIC
WIDENER REVIEW
Wild Dove Studio and Press, Inc.
WILD EARTH
WILLOW SPRINGS
WIND
WINDOW PANES
Windows Project
Windsong Press

Wineberry Press
WISCONSIN REVIEW
WISEBLOOD
THE WISHING WELL
WITNESS
Wolf Angel Press
Wolf-Wise Press
Woman in the Moon Publications (W.I.M. Publications)
WOMAN POET
Women-in-Literature, Inc.
WOODNOTES
Woods Hole Press
THE WORCESTER REVIEW
The Word Works, Inc.
Words & Pictures Press
Wordwrights Canada
THE WORLD
WORLD LETTER
WORMWOOD REVIEW
THE WRITE WAY
WRITER TO WRITER
WRITER'S CHRONICLE
WRITER'S EXCHANGE
WRITERS' FORUM
Writers Forum
WRITERS GAZETTE
WRITER'S GUIDELINES & NEWS
Writers House Press
Writers Ink Press
WRITER'S LIFELINE
Writers Unlimited Agency, Inc
WRITER'S WORLD
WRITES OF PASSAGE
WRITING FOR OUR LIVES
WRITING ULSTER
XANADU
XAVIER REVIEW
Xenos Books
XIB
Xib Publications
X-it Press
XTRAS
YARROW, A JOURNAL OF POETRY
Ye Olde Font Shoppe
Years Press
YEFIEF
Yellow Moon Press
YELLOW SILK: Journal Of Erotic Arts
YOUNG VOICES
Zephyr Press
Zerx Press
Zoland Books
Zombie Logic Press
ZOMBIE LOGIC REVIEW
ZONE 3
ZUZU'S PETALS: QUARTERLY ONLINE

POLAND

AFFAIR OF THE MIND: A Literary Quarterly
THE DIRTY GOAT
Host Publications, Inc.
JACK MACKEREL MAGAZINE
THE KOSCIUSZKO PORTFOLIO
Mr. Cogito Press
THE NEW PRESS LITERARY QUARTERLY
Rowhouse Press
World Music Press

POLITICAL SCIENCE

AK Press
THE ANIMALS' AGENDA
BALLOT ACCESS NEWS
Between The Lines
The Borgo Press
BOSTON REVIEW
Branden Publishing Company
Brunswick Publishing Corporation
CANADIAN PUBLIC POLICY- Analyse de Politiques

864

Capital Communications
Center for South and Southeast Asian Studies Publications
Chandler & Sharp Publishers, Inc.
Circa Press
Clarity Press, Inc.
COMMUNITY DEVELOPMENT JOURNAL
The Compass Press
CRITICAL REVIEW
CROSS ROADS
THE DALHOUSIE REVIEW
The Denali Press
DorPete Press
EAST EUROPEAN POLITICS & SOCIETIES
EAST EUROPEAN QUARTERLY
FLASHPOINT: Military Books Reviewed by Military
    Professionals
Florida Academic Press
The Foundation for Economic Education, Inc.
FOURTH WORLD REVIEW
THE FREEMAN: Ideas On Liberty
FURTHER TOO
GEORGE & MERTIE'S PLACE: Rooms With a View
Gild of Saint George
Glenbridge Publishing Ltd.
Golden West Historical Publications
The Heather Foundation
Hollis Publishing Company
Hoover Institution Press
H2SO4
IAAS Publishers, Inc.
ICARUS WAS RIGHT
The Independent Institute
THE INDEPENDENT REVIEW: A Journal of Political
    Economy
International University Line (IUL)
ITALIAN AMERICANA
Itidwitir Publishing
Ken and Scatter Publications
KETTERING REVIEW
KICK IT OVER
Kumarian Press, Inc.
Libertarian Press, Inc./American Book Distributors
LITTLE FREE PRESS
LIVERPOOL NEWSLETTER
THE LONG TERM VIEW: A Journal of Informed
    Opinion
Maisonneuve Press
Manta Press
MEXICAN STUDIES/ESTUDIOS MEXICANOS
MIDDLE EAST REPORT
THE MILITANT
Mindfield Publications
NEW CIVILIZATION STAFF REPORT
New International
New Spring Publications
Open Hand Publishing Inc.
Paragon House Publishers
Parkway Publishers, Inc.
Pathfinder Press
PEACE, The Magazine of the Sixties
PEACEWORK
Poetry Wales Press, Ltd.
QED Press
RADICAL AMERICA
RAVEN - A Journal of Vexillology
ST. CROIX REVIEW
Saqi Books Publisher
SCIENCE AND TECHNOLOGY
Selous Foundation Press
SJL Publishing Company
SOCIAL POLICY
SOCIETY
STATE AND LOCAL GOVERNMENT REVIEW
Strata Publishing, Inc.
Telos Press
TOWARD FREEDOM
TRANSCAUCASUS: A Chronology
TRANSNATIONAL PERSPECTIVES

Tsunami Inc.
21ST CENTURY AFRO REVIEW
THE UNDERGROUND FOREST - LA SELVA SUB-
    TERRANEA
Univelt, Inc.
University of Calgary Press
University of Massachusetts Press
VIETNAM GENERATION: A Journal of Recent History
    and Contemporary Issues
THE VIRGINIA QUARTERLY REVIEW
George Wahr Publishing Company
THE WASHINGTON MONTHLY
Witwatersrand University Press
Writers House Press
YUWITAYA LAKOTA

POLITICS

Aardvark Enterprises (A Division of Speers Investments
    Ltd.)
Acclaim Publishing Co. Inc.
ACM (ANOTHER CHICAGO MAGAZINE)
THE AFFILIATE
African Ways Publishing
ALCATRAZ
Aletheia Publications, Inc.
America West Publishers
Arden Press, Inc.
ART'S GARBAGE GAZZETTE
Astarte Shell Press
AUFBAU
Autonomedia, Inc.
BAJA SUN
BALLOT ACCESS NEWS
BARNABE MOUNTAIN REVIEW
Bay Press
Beacon Press
Beekman Publishers, Inc.
Benchmark Publications Inc.
BERKELEY WOMEN'S LAW JOURNAL
Between The Lines
Blue Crane Books
Blue Heron Publishing, Inc.
THE BOOMERPHILE
BORDERLANDS: Texas Poetry Review
BORDERLINES
BOTH SIDES NOW
Brick Row Publishing Co. Ltd.
BROKEN PENCIL
Brownout Laboratories
CANADIAN PUBLIC POLICY- Analyse de Politiques
CANADIAN REVIEW OF AMERICAN STUDIES
Capital Communications
CAPITALISM, NATURE, SOCIALISM
A Cappella Books
CARIBBEAN NEWSLETTER
Cassandra Press, Inc.
CASTAWAYS
Center for Public Representation
CHALLENGE: A Journal of Faith and Action in the
    Americas
Chandler & Sharp Publishers, Inc.
Chelsea Green Publishing Company
Chicago Review Press
Children Of Mary
China Books & Periodicals, Inc.
CINEASTE MAGAZINE
City Lights Books
COLORLINES
Common Courage Press
COMMUNITY DEVELOPMENT JOURNAL
The Compass Press
Comstock Bonanza Press
THE CONSTANTIAN
CRITICAL REVIEW
CROSS ROADS
The Denali Press
Devin-Adair Publishers, Inc.
Drum

865

Dufour Editions Inc.
THE DURHAM UNIVERSITY JOURNAL
Editorial Research Service
Encounter Books
ENOUGH IS ENOUGH!
EPICA
FAG RAG
FEMINIST REVIEW
FICTION INTERNATIONAL
FIDELIS ET VERUS
FIFTH ESTATE
Filibuster Press
The Film Instruction Company of America
Four Walls Eight Windows
FOURTH WORLD REVIEW
Free People Press
Free Spirit Publishing Inc.
FULL DISCLOSURE
THE FUNNY TIMES
Gain Publications
GATEAVISA
Gay Sunshine Press, Inc.
GEORGE & MERTIE'S PLACE: Rooms With a View
Glenbridge Publishing Ltd.
Good Hope Enterprises, Inc.
GRAFFITI OFF THE ASYLUM WALLS
GRANTA
GREEN ANARCHIST
GREEN FUSE POETRY
Greenlawn Press
Guernica Editions, Inc.
HARMONY: VOICES FOR A JUST FUTURE
Heron Press
Heyday Books
HOAX!
Hollis Publishing Company
Hoover Institution Press
Howling Dog Press/Stiletto
IllumiNet Press
The Independent Institute
THE INDEPENDENT REVIEW: A Journal of Political
  Economy
Institute for Southern Studies
International Publishers Co. Inc.
International University Line (IUL)
IRIS: A Journal About Women
ISRAEL HORIZONS
JAM RAG
JARRETT'S JOURNAL
JEWISH CURRENTS
Ken and Scatter Publications
Kettering Foundation
KETTERING REVIEW
KICK IT OVER
THE KITHARA
Kumarian Press, Inc.
LABOUR & TRADE UNION REVIEW
LATIN AMERICAN PERSPECTIVES
LEFT BUSINESS OBSERVER
LEFT CURVE
THE (LIBERTARIAN) CONNECTION
Library Research Associates, Inc.
LIES MAGAZINE
LifeThread Publications
LITTLE FREE PRESS
LO STRANIERO: The Stranger, Der Fremde, L'Etranger
LONE STAR SOCIALIST
THE LONG TERM VIEW: A Journal of Informed
  Opinion
LOVE AND RAGE, A Revolutionary Anarchist News-
  paper
Lunar Offensive Publications
Macrocosm USA, Inc.
Manta Press
Marmot Publishing
Mehring Books, Inc.
The Menard Press
THE MILITANT

MIM NOTES: Offcial Newsletter of the Maoist Interna-
  tionalist Movement
MIND MATTERS REVIEW
Monitor Publications AR
Moon Publications, Inc.
More To Life Publishing
MOUTH: Voice of the Disability Nation
Moving Parts Press
MSRRT NEWSLETTER: LIBRARY ALTERNATIVES
NAMBLA BULLETIN
THE NEW ENGLAND QUARTERLY
THE NEW PRESS LITERARY QUARTERLY
New Regency Publishing
New Spring Publications
New Star Books Ltd.
NEWS FROM NATIVE CALIFORNIA
Nguoi Dan
NGUOI DAN
nine muses books
THE NONVIOLENT ACTIVIST
OFF OUR BACKS
Open Hand Publishing Inc.
The Pamphleeter's Press
Paragon House Publishers
Path Press, Inc.
Pathfinder Press
PEACE & DEMOCRACY
PEACE, The Magazine of the Sixties
PEACEWORK
PERSPECTIVES
Philopsychy Press
PHOENIX MAGAZINE
Phoenix Press
Pig Iron Press
Poetry Wales Press, Ltd.
THE PRAGMATIST
PUNCTURE
QECE: QUESTION EVERYTHING. CHALLENGE
  EVERYTHING.
Quarterly Committee of Queen's University
QUEEN'S QUARTERLY: A Canadian Review
RAG SHOCK
RAIN MAGAZINE
THE RAINTOWN REVIEW: A Forum for the Essayist's
  Art
THE RATIONAL FEMINIST
Red Letter Press
RESOURCE CENTER BULLETIN
RETHINKING MARXISM
RFD
THE ROTKIN REVIEW
ST. CROIX REVIEW
Saqi Books Publisher
SCANDINAVIAN REVIEW
SCIENCE & SOCIETY
Semiotext Foreign Agents Books Series
SEMIOTEXT(E)
Skyline Publications, Inc.
THE SMALL POND MAGAZINE OF LITERATURE
  aka SMALL POND
SMART DRUG NEWS
Solution Publishing
South End Press
SOUTHERN EXPOSURE
SPECTRUM—The Wholistic News Magazine
STILETTO
SUITCASE: A Journal of Transcultural Traffic
SYMPLOKE: A Journal for the Intermingling of Literary,
  Cultural and Theoretical Scholarship
Syracuse Cultural Workers/Tools for Change
TAIL SPINS
Tilbury House, Publishers
Times Change Press
Tiptoe Literary Service
The Tonal Company
TOWARD FREEDOM
TRAFIK - Internationales Journal zur Libertaren Kultur &
  Politik

Transeuropa
TRANVIA - Revue der Iberischen Halbinsel
TURNING THE TIDE: A Journal of Anti-Racist
  Activism, Research & Education
TWISTED TIMES
University of Calgary Press
University of Massachusetts Press
VIETNAM GENERATION: A Journal of Recent History
  and Contemporary Issues
VIRGINIA LIBERTY
THE VIRGINIA QUARTERLY REVIEW
George Wahr Publishing Company
Walnut Publishing Co., Inc.
THE WASHINGTON MONTHLY
THE WASHINGTON REPORT
THE WEIRD NEWS
West End Press
Witwatersrand University Press
Wright-Armstead Associates
Writers House Press
YUWITAYA LAKOTA
ZERO HOUR

PORTUGAL

Bandanna Books
FILM SCORE MONTHLY
LA PERIPHERIE
THE NEW PRESS LITERARY QUARTERLY
TORRE DE PAPEL
TRANSITIONS ABROAD: The Guide to Living,
  Learning, and Working Overseas
TRANVIA - Revue der Iberischen Halbinsel

POST MODERN

Abiko Literary Press (ALP)
AD/VANCE
AFFABLE NEIGHBOR
Affable Neighbor Press
AFFAIR OF THE MIND: A Literary Quarterly
Alicubi Publications
AMERICAN WRITING: A Magazine
Asylum Arts
AXE FACTORY REVIEW
Baker Street Publications
THE BLAB
Brownout Laboratories
THE COOL TRAVELER
CURMUDGEON
DAYS AND NIGHTS OF A SMALL PRESS PUB-
  LISHER
Dead Metaphor Press
DIRIGIBLE
THE DIRTY GOAT
DISSONANCE MAGAZINE
DISTURBED GUILLOTINE
DOWN UNDER MANHATTAN BRIDGE
ENOUGH IS ENOUGH!
FICTION INTERNATIONAL
FIRST CLASS
Four-Sep Publications
FURTHER TOO
GRAFFITI OFF THE ASYLUM WALLS
Host Publications, Inc.
Jahbone Press
JEWISH LIFE
JOURNAL OF AESTHETICS AND ART CRITICISM
KOJA
LEFT CURVE
THE MAD FARMERS' JUBILEE ALMANACK
MEANJIN
MESECHABE: The Journal of Surre(gion)alism
MIXED BAG
New Native Press
NEW WRITING
NOBODADDIES
PEAKY HIDE
PLAIN BROWN WRAPPER (PBW)
The Press of the Third Mind

THE READER'S REVIEW
Savant Garde Workshop
SHRIKE
THE SPITTING IMAGE
THE WALLACE STEVENS JOURNAL
TEXTSHOP
THE UNIT CIRCLE
University of Massachusetts Press
URBANUS/RAIZIRR
WEST COAST LINE: A Journal of Contemporary
  Writing and Criticism
Wordcraft of Oregon
XIB
Xib Publications
ZYX

POSTCARDS

AFFABLE NEIGHBOR
Affable Neighbor Press
Baker Street Publications
Barefoot Press
DAYS AND NIGHTS OF A SMALL PRESS PUB-
  LISHER
Deltiologists of America
Drum
ETCETERA
The Feathered Serpent
Gesture Press
NEW ENGLAND ANTIQUES JOURNAL
Now It's Up To You Publications
PLAIN BROWN WRAPPER (PBW)
POSTCARD CLASSICS
Running Press
Slab-O-Concrete Publications
Vestal Press Ltd
Waters Edge Press
Westgate Press
WORLDLINKS - FRIENDSHIP NEWS

PRESIDENTS

THE PRESIDENTS' JOURNAL

ELVIS PRESLEY

EXCLAIM!
FURTHER TOO
GRAFFITI OFF THE ASYLUM WALLS
LONG SHOT
New Spirit Press/The Poet Tree
PLAIN BROWN WRAPPER (PBW)
POEMS THAT THUMP IN THE DARK/SECOND
  GLANCE
SHEMP! The Lowlife Culture Magazine

PRINTING

Ad-Lib Publications
AFFABLE NEIGHBOR
Affable Neighbor Press
THE AFFILIATE
Alpine Guild, Inc.
AMERICAN AMATEUR JOURNALIST
BACKBOARD
Baker Street Publications
THE BOOK ARTS CLASSIFIED
BOOK DEALERS WORLD
BOOK MARKETING UPDATE
BOOK NEWS & BOOK BUSINESS MART
BOOK TALK
Brenner Information Group
Caliban Press
Commonwealth Press Virginia
Communication Creativity
DAYS AND NIGHTS OF A SMALL PRESS PUB-
  LISHER
The Denali Press
FEMINIST COLLECTIONS: A QUARTERLY OF WO-
  MEN'S STUDIES RESOURCES
FULL MOON DIRECTORY
FURTHER TOO

867

The Gleniffer Press
G'RAPH
INFOCUS
J'ECRIS
Jessee Poet Publications
JLA Publications, A Division Of Jeffrey Lant Associates, Inc.
Dean Lem Associates, Inc.
LOST GENERATION JOURNAL
MIXED BAG
NIGHTSHADE
Oak Knoll Press
OHIO WRITER
Para Publishing
PEN & INK WRITERS JOURNAL
The Poetry Center Press/Shoestring Press
Poltroon Press
Premier Publishers, Inc.
The Press of the Nightowl
PUBLISHING POYNTERS
PUCK: The Unofficial Journal of the Irrepressible
QED Press
REALM OF THE VAMPIRE
Rio Grande Press
THE ROMANTIST
ST. LOUIS JOURNALISM REVIEW
Selective Books, Inc.
SPEX (SMALL PRESS EXCHANGE)
Stewart Publishing & Printing
Stonehouse Publications
Success Publishing
TITIVILLITIA: Studies of Illiteracy in the Private Press
Trigon Press
Twin Peaks Press
UMBRELLA
THE UNDERGROUND FOREST - LA SELVA SUB-TERRANEA
Univelt, Inc.
Winslow Publishing
Woman in the Moon Publications (W.I.M. Publications)
Women's Studies Librarian, University of Wisconsin System

PRISON

THE AFFILIATE
Center for Public Representation
Chardon Press
COALITION FOR PRISONERS' RIGHTS NEWSLETTER
Coker Publishing House
COLLEGIUM NEWSLETTER
CORRECTIONS TODAY
FLORIDA PRISON LEGAL PERSPECTIVES
FURTHER TOO
GATEAVISA
Gay Sunshine Press, Inc.
Global Options
GRAFFITI OFF THE ASYLUM WALLS
GrapeVinePress
GRAY AREAS
Herald Press
Howling Dog Press/Stiletto
INNER VOICES: A New Journal of Prison Literature
Institute for Southern Studies
INTERCULTURAL WRITERS REVIEW
IWAN: INMATE WRITERS OF AMERICA NEWSLETTER
Ledero Press
Leyland Publications
LOVE AND RAGE, A Revolutionary Anarchist Newspaper
MIM NOTES: Offcial Newsletter of the Maoist Internationalist Movement
Nextstep Books
Nite-Owl Press
Oline Publishing
Palm Drive Publishing
PHOENIX MAGAZINE

Phoenix Press
The Place In The Woods
THE PLOUGH
PRISON LEGAL NEWS
Pygmy Forest Press
R & E Publishers
RFD
The Saunderstown Press
Signal Books
SOCIAL JUSTICE: A JOURNAL OF CRIME, CONFLICT, & WORLD ORDER
SPIRIT TO SPIRIT
Starbooks Press/FLF Press
STILETTO
STROKER
TURNING THE TIDE: A Journal of Anti-Racist Activism, Research & Education
Volcano Press, Inc

PROSE

Abiko Literary Press (ALP)
AFFABLE NEIGHBOR
Affable Neighbor Press
AFFAIR OF THE MIND: A Literary Quarterly
THE AFFILIATE
AGADA
THE ALEMBIC
American Audio Prose Library (non-print)
AMERICAN LETTERS & COMMENTARY
American Living Press
Amethyst & Emerald
ARCHIPELAGO
ART/LIFE
Art/Life Limited Editions
ASSPANTS
Asylum Arts
AXE FACTORY REVIEW
BAKER STREET GAZETTE
Baker Street Publications
THE BAREFOOT POET: Journal of Poetry, Fiction, Essays, & Art
BARNABE MOUNTAIN REVIEW
Bearhouse Publishing
BkMk Press
THE BLIND HORSE REVIEW
BLOOD & APHORISMS: A Journal of Literary Fiction
The Book Department
BOOKS FROM FINLAND
Brownout Laboratories
BURNING CAR
Carolina Wren Press/Lollipop Power Books
CAYO, A MAGAZINE OF LIFE IN THE KEYS
Cedar Hill Publications
CEDAR HILL REVIEW
THE CHEROTIC (r)EVOLUTIONARY
CIMARRON REVIEW
Confluence Press, Inc.
Coteau Books
Creative Arts & Science Enterprises
Crescent Moon
CRIPES!
CURARE
CURMUDGEON
DAYS AND NIGHTS OF A SMALL PRESS PUBLISHER
Manya DeLeon Booksmith
DIRIGIBLE
THE DIRTY GOAT
DREAM INTERNATIONAL QUARTERLY
THE EDGE CITY REVIEW
The Eighth Mountain Press
ELF: ECLECTIC LITERARY FORUM (ELF MAGAZINE)
EMERGING VOICES
ETCETERA
EVANSVILLE REVIEW
THE EVER DANCING MUSE
FAULTLINE, Journal of Art and Literature

FINE MADNESS
FIRST DRAFT
FODDERWING
FOLIO: A LITERARY JOURNAL
FOURTEEN HILLS: The SFSU Review
FREEFALL
Full Moon Publications
FURTHER TOO
THE GLASS CHERRY
The Glass Cherry Press
GRAFFITI OFF THE ASYLUM WALLS
Graywolf Press
THE GREAT BLUE BEACON
THE HAUNTED JOURNAL
HAWAI'I REVIEW
THE HIGGINSVILLE READER
HIP MAMA
HOLLYWOOD NOSTALGIA
HORIZONS BEYOND
Host Publications, Inc.
Hyacinth House Publications/Caligula Editions
IDIOM 23
IGNIS FATUUS REVIEW
INTERBANG
INTERCULTURAL WRITERS REVIEW
Irvington St. Press, Inc.
JACK MACKEREL MAGAZINE
JEWISH LIFE
KALEIDOSCOPE: INTERNATIONAL MAGAZINE OF
    LITERATURE, FINE ARTS, AND DISABILITY
KOJA
KUMQUAT MERINGUE
Lakes & Prairies Press
LIGHT: The Quarterly of Light Verse
Lincoln Springs Press
LONE STARS MAGAZINE
THE LOWELL REVIEW
LULLWATER REVIEW
LUMMOX JOURNAL
MANGROVE MAGAZINE
MASSACRE
THE METAPHYSICAL REVIEW
Milkweed Editions
MIXED BAG
Monographics Press
NATURAL BRIDGE
NEW HOPE INTERNATIONAL REVIEW
THE NEW PRESS LITERARY QUARTERLY
New Rivers Press, Inc.
Nite-Owl Press
NITE-WRITER'S   INTERNATIONAL   LITERARY
    ARTS JOURNAL
NORTHEAST
Oasis Books
ORBIS
OXYGEN
PAGAN AMERICA
THE PANNUS INDEX
PASSAGES NORTH
Passing Through Publications
PASSION
PAVEMENT SAW
Pavement Saw Press
PEN & INK WRITERS JOURNAL
PenRose Publishing Company, Inc.
Poetic License Press
POET'S FANTASY
POETS'PAPER
POSTCARD
POTOMAC REVIEW
POTPOURRI: A Magazine of the Literary Arts
THE POTTERSFIELD PORTFOLIO
The Press of Appletree Alley
THE PURPLE MONKEY
QUARTER AFTER EIGHT
RATTAPALLAX
RAZOR WIRE
THE RIVER

THE ROCKFORD REVIEW
ROSEBUD
Rowhouse Press
SANTA BARBARA REVIEW
SFEST, LTD.
SHADES OF DECEMBER
SILHOUETTE MAGAZINE
SKYLARK
SLEUTH JOURNAL
The Smith (subsidiary of The Generalist Assn., Inc.)
SPELUNKER FLOPHOUSE
Spillway Publications
SPIRIT TO SPIRIT
THE SPITTING IMAGE
STARBURST
STONES IN MY POCKET
SULPHUR RIVER LITERARY REVIEW
THE SUNDAY SUITOR POETRY REVIEW
Sun-Scape Publications, a division of Sun-Scape Enter-
    prises Ltd.
TEAK ROUNDUP
Tears in the Fence
TEARS IN THE FENCE
TEXTSHOP
32 PAGES
Thunder Rain Publishing Corp.
2.13.61 Publications
Tyro Publishing
ULITARRA
THE UNIT CIRCLE
Urthona Press
VAMPIRE NIGHTS
Venom Press
VERANDAH
THE VINCENT BROTHERS REVIEW
VIRGINIA LITERARY REVIEW
WEIRD POETRY
WESTERN SKIES
Westgate Press
Who Who Who Publishing
Windsong Press
WISEBLOOD
THE WRITE WAY
Writers Forum
WRITERS GAZETTE
Writers House Press
WRITER'S WORKSHOP REVIEW
Xenos Books
XIB
Xib Publications
YELLOW SILK: Journal Of Erotic Arts
Zerx Press

PSYCHIATRY

AFFAIR OF THE MIND: A Literary Quarterly
BREAKFAST ALL DAY
Brittain Communications
Compact Clinicals
Consumer Press
GEORGE & MERTIE'S PLACE: Rooms With a View
Holbrook Street Press
INTERCULTURAL WRITERS REVIEW
JOURNAL OF PSYCHOACTIVE DRUGS
Meadow Mountain Press
PHOENIX MAGAZINE
Phoenix Press
PSYCHOANALYTIC BOOKS: A QUARTERLY JOUR-
    NAL OF REVIEWS
RESONANCE
STONES IN MY POCKET
Turtle Island Press, Inc.

PSYCHOLOGY

A.R.E. Press
ADOLESCENCE
AFFAIR OF THE MIND: A Literary Quarterly
THE AFFILIATE
ALADDIN'S WINDOW

Alamo Square Press
Alegra House Publishers
Aletheia Publications, Inc.
AlphaBooks, Inc.
Alpine Guild, Inc.
Altair Publications
AMBASSADOR REPORT
America West Publishers
THE AMERICAN JOURNAL OF PSYCHOANALYSIS
Anderson Press
THE ANGRY THOREAUAN
AREOPAGUS
ART CALENDAR
Ash Lad Press
Atrium Society Publications/DBA Education For Peace
  Publications
Axelrod Publishing of Tampa Bay
Baker Street Publications
BARNABE MOUNTAIN REVIEW
Bayhampton Publications
Bear & Company, Inc.
Behavioral Sciences Research Press, Inc.
Best Sellers Publishing
Beynch Press Publishing Company
BGB Press, Inc.
Birth Day Publishing Company
Blue Dolphin Publishing, Inc.
The Boxwood Press
BRAIN/MIND BULLETIN, Bulletin of Breakthroughs
Brason-Sargar Publications
BREAKFAST ALL DAY
Brittain Communications
Brunswick Publishing Corporation
Capital Communications
Celo Valley Books
The Center Press
Chandler & Sharp Publishers, Inc.
THE CHEROTIC (r)EVOLUTIONARY
Cherubic Press
COMMON BOUNDARY MAGAZINE
Community Resource Institute Press
Compact Clinicals
Conscious Living
Consumer Press
Content Communications
Coreopsis Books
CORRECTIONS TODAY
Cosmoenergetics Publications
Courtyard Publishing Company
CRCS Publications
Creative Roots, Inc.
CRONE CHRONICLES: A Journal of Conscious Aging
Dalrymple Publishing Company
DeeMar Communications
Dharma Publishing
Down There Press
DREAM INTERNATIONAL QUARTERLY
DREAM NETWORK JOURNAL
Ecrivez!
Elder Books
Emerald Wave
THE EMSHOCK LETTER
ETC Publications
FAMILY THERAPY
Fisher Books
Five Corners Publications, Ltd.
Fort Dearborn Press
Free Spirit Publishing Inc.
Fromm International Publishing Corporation
Gateways Books And Tapes
Gay Sunshine Press, Inc.
GEORGE & MERTIE'S PLACE: Rooms With a View
Gifted Education Press/The Reading Tutorium
Gilgal Publications
GLB Publishers
Glenbridge Publishing Ltd.
Golden Eagle Press
The Golden Sufi Center

The Green Hut Press
Greeson & Boyle, Inc.
Gurze Books
Halo Books
Health Press
Himalayan Institute Press
HOAX!
Hohm Press
Holbrook Street Press
Howln Moon Press
Human Kinetics Pub. Inc.
Humana Press
Hunter House Inc., Publishers
IAAS Publishers, Inc.
Ice Cube Press
Impact Publishers, Inc.
Inner City Books
Innisfree Press
The Institute of Mind and Behavior
Interface Press
Intermountain Publishing
INTERVENTION IN SCHOOL AND CLINIC
Islewest Publishing
ITALIAN AMERICANA
J & J Consultants, Inc.
Jalmar Press
Joelle Publishing
JOTS (Journal of the Senses)
JOURNAL OF MENTAL IMAGERY
THE JOURNAL OF MIND AND BEHAVIOR
JOURNAL OF POLYMORPHOUS PERVERSITY
JOURNAL OF PROCESS ORIENTED PSYCHOLOGY
JOURNAL OF PSYCHOACTIVE DRUGS
THE JOURNAL OF PSYCHOHISTORY
JOURNAL OF SPORT AND EXERCISE PSYCHO-
  LOGY (JSEP)
Keel Publications
H J Kramer
Lao Tse Press, Ltd.
Libra Publishers, Inc.
Life Energy Media
LifeQuest Publishing Group
The Lockhart Press
LOGIC LETTER
The Love and Logic Press, Inc.
THE MAD FARMERS' JUBILEE ALMANACK
Markowski International Publishers
Master Key Inc.
Meadow Mountain Press
META4: Journal of Object Oriented Poetics (OOPS)
Metamorphous Press
Monroe Press
Mother Courage Press
MUSIC PERCEPTION
THE MUSING PLACE
MYSTIC VOICES
Myth Breakers
The Neo Herramann Group
Network 3000 Publishing
New Liberty Press
NEW THOUGHT JOURNAL
New View Publications
New World Library
Nicolas-Hays, Inc.
Nightsun Books
Northern Star Press
Obsessive Compulsive Anonymous
Omega Publications, Inc.
ON COURSE
Open Court Publishing
OPEN EXCHANGE MAGAZINE
Origin Press
OXYGEN
PalmTree Publishers
Parabola
Paragon House Publishers
Pathway Books
Paw Print Publishing Co.

Pedestal Press
Peradam Press
Perspectives Press
Philopsychy Press
Plus Publications
POEMS THAT THUMP IN THE DARK/SECOND
  GLANCE
Ponderosa Publishers
Princess Publishing
Professional Resource Exchange, Inc.
Progresiv Publishr
PSYCHOANALYTIC BOOKS: A QUARTERLY JOUR-
  NAL OF REVIEWS
Psychohistory Press
PSYCHOLOGY OF WOMEN QUARTERLY
PSYCHOPOETICA
Pudding House Publications
PUDDING MAGAZINE: THE INTERNATIONAL
  JOURNAL OF APPLIED POETRY
Quarterly Committee of Queen's University
QUEEN'S QUARTERLY: A Canadian Review
THE QUEST
R & E Publishers
RADIANCE, The Magazine For Large Women
Raven Rocks Press
THE READER'S REVIEW
REALM OF THE VAMPIRE
Red Alder Books
Reyes Investment Enterprise Ltd.
Rio Grande Press
River Press
The Runaway Spoon Press
St. Georges Press
The Saunderstown Press
Schenkman Books
See Sharp Press
Shaolin Communications
Shimoda Publishing
Sibyl Publications, Inc
Sidran Foundation and Press
Sigo Press
SKEPTICAL INQUIRER
Skidmore-Roth Publishing, Inc.
SOCIETY
Sorenson Books
SPECTRUM—The Wholistic News Magazine
Spinsters Ink
SPIRIT TO SPIRIT
THE SPORT PSYCHOLOGIST (TSP)
SPRING: A Journal of Archetype and Culture
Spring Publications Inc.
Starbooks Press/FLF Press
Station Hill Press
Steamshovel Press
Stillpoint Publishing
STONES IN MY POCKET
SunShine Press Publications, Inc.
Swan Raven & Company
SYCAMORE ROOTS: New Native Americans
Theosophical Publishing House
Third Side Press, Inc.
Tomar House Publishers
Top Of The Mountain Publishing
Topping International Institute, Inc.
Training Systems, Inc.
Tudor Publishers, Inc.
Turtle Island Press, Inc.
UNARIUS LIGHT JOURNAL
Unfoldment Publications
University of Calgary Press
VanderWyk & Burnham
Visions Communications
VIVA PETITES
Volcano Press, Inc
Waterfront Books
Samuel Weiser, Inc.
Westport Publishers
WHAT IS ENLIGHTENMENT?

Whitford Press
Whole Person Associates Inc.
WillowBrook Publishing
B. L. Winch & Associates
Wisdom Publications, Inc.
Witwatersrand University Press
WOMEN & THERAPY
Women of Diversity Productions, Inc.
WORLDLINKS - FRIENDSHIP NEWS
Writers House Press
Yes You Can Press
YOUR LIFE MATTERS

PUBLIC AFFAIRS

THE ANIMALS' AGENDA
THE ANTIOCH REVIEW
AXIOS
Beacon Press
Borealis Press Limited
The Borgo Press
Camel Press
CANADIAN JOURNAL OF PROGRAM EVALUA-
  TION/LA REVUE CANADIENNE D'EVALUATION
  DE PROGRAMME
CANADIAN PUBLIC POLICY- Analyse de Politiques
Capra Press
Center for Public Representation
Chandler & Sharp Publishers, Inc.
CHRONICLE OF COMMUNITY
CJE NEWS (Newsletter of the Coalition for Jobs & the
  Environment)
The Compass Press
Continuing Education Press
CROSS ROADS
The Denali Press
DUST (From the Ego Trip)
Editorial Research Service
The Foundation for Economic Education, Inc.
FOURTH WORLD REVIEW
THE FREEMAN: Ideas On Liberty
Frugal Marketer Publishing
FULL DISCLOSURE
Gain Publications
GEORGE & MERTIE'S PLACE: Rooms With a View
Hoover Institution Press
IAAS Publishers, Inc.
The Independent Institute
THE INDEPENDENT REVIEW: A Journal of Political
  Economy
Institute for Contemporary Studies
Institute for Southern Studies
International Publishers Co. Inc.
Jewish Radical Education Project
J-REP NEWS AND VIEWS
Ken and Scatter Publications
KETTERING REVIEW
LABOUR & TRADE UNION REVIEW
LEFT BUSINESS OBSERVER
The Philip Lesly Company
LITTLE FREE PRESS
LOGIC LETTER
THE LONG TERM VIEW: A Journal of Informed
  Opinion
Manta Press
New Spring Publications
NGUOI DAN
Noontide Press
Occam Publishers
The Olive Press Publications
THE OTHER ISRAEL
The Pamphleteer's Press
PARTISAN REVIEW
Planning/Communications
POTOMAC REVIEW
THE PRAGMATIST
Progressive Education
PROGRESSIVE PERIODICALS DIRECTORY/UPDATE
THE PUBLIC RELATIONS QUARTERLY

RETHINKING MARXISM
Small Helm Press
THE SMALL POND MAGAZINE OF LITERATURE
  aka SMALL POND
SOCIAL POLICY
SPECTRUM—The Wholistic News Magazine
TAPROOT, a journal of older writers
The Tonal Company
TRANSCAUCASUS: A Chronology
21ST CENTURY AFRO REVIEW
University of Calgary Press
University of Massachusetts Press
VDT NEWS
Volcano Press, Inc
THE WASHINGTON MONTHLY

PUBLIC RELATIONS/PUBLICITY

PSI Research/The Oasis Press/Hellgate Press

PUBLISHING

Abiko Literary Press (ALP)
Ad-Lib Publications
THE AFFILIATE
THE AFRICAN BOOK PUBLISHING RECORD
Algol Press
Alpine Guild, Inc.
Avisson Press, Inc.
Baker Street Publications
BAST Media, Inc.
Blue Heron Publishing, Inc.
Bold Productions
BOOK MARKETING UPDATE
Bookhome Publishing/Panda Publishing
Brenner Information Group
BROKEN PENCIL
A Cappela Publishing
Cardoza Publishing
Chiron Press
CHIRON REVIEW
Columbine Publishing Group
COUNTERPOISE: For Social Responsibilities, Liberty
  and Dissent
CREATIVITY CONNECTION
Cultivated Underground Press
D.B.A. Books
DAYS AND NIGHTS OF A SMALL PRESS PUB-
  LISHER
DISSONANCE MAGAZINE
Ecrivez!
Editions Ex Libris
Editorial El Sol De Baja
THE EDITORIAL EYE
EEI Press
THE ELECTRONIC PUBLISHING FORUM
ETCETERA
FACTSHEET FIVE
Fisher Books
FULL MOON DIRECTORY
Full Moon Publications
Gan Publishing
G'RAPH
THE GREAT BLUE BEACON
Hans Zell Publishers
THE HELIOCENTRIC WRITER'S NETWORK
IASP NEWSLETTER
ICARUS WAS RIGHT
INDEPENDENT PUBLISHER
INTERCULTURAL WRITERS REVIEW
INTERLIT
Itidwitir Publishing
IWAN: INMATE WRITERS OF AMERICA NEWSLET-
  TER
Jaffe Publishing Management Service
Kells Media Group
LAUGHING BEAR NEWSLETTER
Dean Lem Associates, Inc.
LIBRARIANS AT LIBERTY
LOCUS: The Newspaper of the Science Fiction Field

MAINE IN PRINT
MARTHA'S KIDLIT NEWSLETTER
THE METAPHYSICAL REVIEW
MIXED BAG
Morgan-Rand Publishing
Multi Media Arts
Myriad Press
The New Humanity Press
NIGHTSHADE
NOCTURNAL REPORTER
North American Bookdealers Exchange
Oak Knoll Press
Oasis In Print
Open Horizons Publishing Company
Page One
PEN & INK WRITERS JOURNAL
The Press of the Nightowl
PUBLISHER'S REPORT
PUBLISHING ENTREPRENEUR
READ, AMERICA!
REALM OF THE VAMPIRE
RED HOT HOME INCOME REPORTER
REFERRALS
Rio Grande Press
SCIENCE FICTION CHRONICLE
SMALL PRESS CREATIVE EXPLOSION
THE SMALL PRESS REVIEW/SMALL MAGAZINE
  REVIEW
SMALL PUBLISHER
SUBSCRIBE, Ideas and Marketing Tips for Newsletter
  Publishers
TEXAS YOUNG WRITERS' NEWSLETTER
Tiptoe Literary Service
Toad Hall Press
TOWERS CLUB, USA INFO MARKETING REPORT
THE UNIT CIRCLE
Visions Communications
WORLD BOOK INDUSTRY
WORLDLINKS - FRIENDSHIP NEWS
THE WRITE WAY
WRITER'S CAROUSEL
WRITER'S GUIDELINES & NEWS
WRITER'S WORKSHOP REVIEW
ZUZU'S PETALS: QUARTERLY ONLINE

PUERTO RICO

GEORGE & MERTIE'S PLACE: Rooms With a View
LOVE AND RAGE, A Revolutionary Anarchist News-
  paper
MESECHABE: The Journal of Surre(gion)alism
THE NEW PRESS LITERARY QUARTERLY
Open Hand Publishing Inc.
Pangaea
The Place In The Woods
POINT OF CONTACT
TORRE DE PAPEL
Tortuga Books
TURNING THE TIDE: A Journal of Anti-Racist
  Activism, Research & Education

QUILTING, SEWING

Altamont Press, Inc.
C & T Publishing
Eagle's View Publishing
FIBERARTS
Law Mexico Publishing
Mayhaven Publishing
MIDWEST ART FAIRS
Miles & Miles
NEW WRITING
PenRose Publishing Company, Inc.
Silver Dollar Press
Success Publishing
Twin Peaks Press
Williamson Publishing Company, Inc.

QUOTATIONS

AFFABLE NEIGHBOR

Affable Neighbor Press
American Literary Press Inc./Noble House
Anderson Press
Brason-Sargar Publications
CLASS ACT
DOUBLE BILL
ETCETERA
INTERCULTURAL WRITERS REVIEW
Light, Words & Music
Miles & Miles
Momentum Books, Ltd.
Naturegraph Publishers, Inc.
THE NEW PRESS LITERARY QUARTERLY
Nicolin Fields Publishing, Inc.
Open Horizons Publishing Company
PULSAR
THE QUILL MAGAZINE QUARTERLY
R & E Publishers
Red Eye Press
VIRTUTE ET MORTE MAGAZINE
THE WRITE WAY

RACE

AFFAIR OF THE MIND: A Literary Quarterly
African American Audio Press
AFRICAN AMERICAN AUDIOBOOK REVIEW
Beacon Press
BLK
BLUE COLLAR REVIEW
Child's Play
COLORLINES
Comstock Bonanza Press
Content Communications
THE COOL TRAVELER
CROSS ROADS
Ecrivez!
The Feminist Press at the City College
FURTHER TOO
GATEAVISA
GrapeVinePress
IAAS Publishers, Inc.
ICA Publishing
IRIS: A Journal About Women
THE J MAN TIMES
KICK IT OVER
LFW Enterprises
MAIN STREET JOURNAL
MCT - MULTICULTURAL TEACHING
Open Hand Publishing Inc.
Papyrus Literary Enterprises, Inc.
Partisan Press
PenRose Publishing Company, Inc.
The Place In The Woods
PRIME
Schenkman Books
SOCIAL JUSTICE: A JOURNAL OF CRIME, CON-
    FLICT, & WORLD ORDER
South End Press
SYMPLOKE: A Journal for the Intermingling of Literary,
    Cultural and Theoretical Scholarship
TEEN VOICES MAGAZINE
TURNING THE TIDE: A Journal of Anti-Racist
    Activism, Research & Education
University of Massachusetts Press
Ward Hill Press
WEST COAST LINE: A Journal of Contemporary
    Writing and Criticism
Wright-Armstead Associates
YUWITAYA LAKOTA

RADIO

American Audio Prose Library (non-print)
BOOK MARKETING UPDATE
Coteau Books
Crescent Moon
DAYS AND NIGHTS OF A SMALL PRESS PUB-
    LISHER
DOUBLE BILL

HOLLYWOOD NOSTALGIA
Index Publishing Group, Inc
JACK MACKEREL MAGAZINE
The Media Institute
MESECHABE: The Journal of Surre(gion)alism
THE METAPHYSICAL REVIEW
MIXED BAG
NIGHTSHADE
THE NOISE
PASSION
PAST TIMES: The Nostalgia Entertainment Newsletter
QUESTION EVERYTHING CHALLENGE EVERY-
    THING (QECE)
Rowhouse Press
Sonoran Publishing
Tiare Publications
THE UNIT CIRCLE
Vestal Press Ltd
W.E.C. Plant Publishing
THE WHITE DOT - Survival Guide for the TV-Free
WHOLE EARTH
Wind River Institute Press/Wind River Broadcasting
Z W L Publishing, Inc.

READING

THE ANGRY THOREAUAN
ARCHIPELAGO
Baker Street Publications
BOOMERANG! MAGAZINE
Child's Play
CLASS ACT
Computer Press
Coteau Books
DAYS AND NIGHTS OF A SMALL PRESS PUB-
    LISHER
FURTHER TOO
GEORGE & MERTIE'S PLACE: Rooms With a View
Grayson Bernard Publishers, Inc.
House of the 9 Muses, Inc.
Maupin House
THE METAPHYSICAL REVIEW
MIXED BAG
Multi Media Arts
NEW HOPE INTERNATIONAL REVIEW
PEN & INK WRITERS JOURNAL
The Place In The Woods
READ, AMERICA!
SYMPLOKE: A Journal for the Intermingling of Literary,
    Cultural and Theoretical Scholarship
George Wahr Publishing Company
WHOLE EARTH
Williamson Publishing Company, Inc.

REAL ESTATE

Acclaim Publishing Co. Inc.
Adams-Blake Publishing
Ancient City Press
Axiom Press, Publishers
BAJA SUN
Bottom Line Pre$$
Brenner Information Group
CANADIAN MONEYSAVER
Capital Communications
Consumer Education Research Center
Consumer Press
THE COOPERATOR
Gemstone House Publishing
GRANULATED TUPPERWARE
The Heather Foundation
LAKE SUPERIOR MAGAZINE
Mesa House Publishing
Myth Breakers
Pro-Guides, Professional Guides Publications
REFERRALS
Reniets, Inc.
Reveal
Rhino Publishing
SJL Publishing Company

Sourcebooks, Inc.
Swan Publishing Company
Tax Property Investor, Inc.
TEC Publications
Upper Access Inc.

REFERENCE

Affinity Publishers Services
Alan Wofsy Fine Arts
Alaska Geographic Society
Allworth Press
Anderson Press
Appalachian Consortium Press
Arden Press, Inc.
Ariko Publications
Axiom Information Resources
B & B Publishing, Inc.
Bacchus Press Ltd.
BAKER STREET GAZETTE
Baker Street Publications
Biblio Press
Black Forest Press
Blue Heron Publishing, Inc.
Bluestocking Press
Bonus Books, Inc.
The Borgo Press
Brenner Information Group
Brunswick Publishing Corporation
Center for Japanese Studies
Center For Self-Sufficiency
Center for South and Southeast Asian Studies Publications
THE CHRISTIAN LIBRARIAN
CONNEXIONS DIGEST
Connexions Information Services, Inc.
COUNTERPOISE: For Social Responsibilities, Liberty
  and Dissent
Dawn Sign Press
DAYS AND NIGHTS OF A SMALL PRESS PUB-
  LISHER
The Denali Press
Dustbooks
Earth-Love Publishing House LTD
ECW Press
Edgeworth & North Books
THE EDUCATION DIGEST
Energeia Publishing, Inc.
Eureka Publishing Group
Fallen Leaf Press
Film-Video Publications
Fisher Books
Foghorn Press
The Foundation Center
Frontier Publishing, Inc.
Fulcrum, Inc.
Full Moon Publications
Galen Press, Ltd.
GATEAVISA
Global Sports Productions, Ltd.
Good Book Publishing Company
Grayson Bernard Publishers, Inc.
THE HAUNTED JOURNAL
Highsmith Press
Hollywood Film Archive
Hoover's, Inc.
Howln Moon Press
Human Kinetics Pub. Inc.
Innovanna Publishing Co., Inc.
J P Publications
JEWISH LIFE
Jolly Roger Press
Kali Press
L D A Publishers
Landwaster Books
Lester Street Publishing
Lexikos
LIBRARY HI TECH
LIBRARY HIGH TECH NEWS
Maledicta Press

Peter Marcan Publications
Menasha Ridge Press
Microdex Bookshelf
MinRef Press
MIXED BAG
National Court Reporters Association Press
National Woodlands Publishing Company
Network 3000 Publishing
NEW HOPE INTERNATIONAL REVIEW
Next Decade, Inc. (formerly New Decade Inc.)
NIGHTSHADE
NOCTURNAL REPORTER
Nolo Press
Nolo Press - Occidental
Open Horizons Publishing Company
The Overmountain Press
P E N American Center
Paradise Publications
Paragon House Publishers
PEN & INK WRITERS JOURNAL
Photo Data Research
Pine Publications
Pineapple Press, Inc.
Pipeline Press
Poetry Wales Press, Ltd.
Poets & Writers, Inc.
Popular Medicine Press
Prakken Publications
The Preservation Press
Progressive Education
PROGRESSIVE PERIODICALS DIRECTORY/UPDATE
Push/Pull/Press
Pyramid Publishing
R & E Publishers
Rainbow Books, Inc.
Rayve Productions Inc.
REALM OF THE VAMPIRE
Red Eye Press
Reference Desk Books
Reference Service Press
REFERENCE SERVICES REVIEW
THE RESOURCE
Running Press
Saddle Mountain Press
Santa Monica Press/Offbeat Press
Scarecrow Press
Scentouri, Publishing Division
Scratch & Scribble Press
Selah Publishing Co. Inc.
Senay Publishing Inc.
Signature Books
SILVER WINGS/MAYFLOWER PULPIT
Silvercat Publications
SLEUTH JOURNAL
Sound View Press
SOUTHWEST JOURNAL
Southwest Research and Information Center
Twin Peaks Press
Univelt, Inc.
Upper Access Inc.
Vestal Press Ltd
Volcano Press, Inc
WASHINGTON INTERNATIONAL ARTS LETTER
Weidner & Sons, Publishing
Wescott Cove Publishing Co.
WHOLE EARTH
Willowood Press
Wings of Fire Press
The Wordtree
THE WORKBOOK
WRITER'S WORKSHOP REVIEW
ZUZU'S PETALS: QUARTERLY ONLINE

RELATIONSHIPS

A.R.E. Press
AFFABLE NEIGHBOR
Affable Neighbor Press
AFFAIR OF THE MIND: A Literary Quarterly

874

Free People Press
FREETHOUGHT HISTORY
Friends United Press
Galaxy Press
Galde Press, Inc.
Genesis Publishing Company, Inc.
THE GENTLE SURVIVALIST
GEORGE & MERTIE'S PLACE: Rooms With a View
Gilgal Publications
Gloger Family Books
Good Book Publishing Company
Good Life Publishing
GREEN EGG
Greenlawn Press
HECATE'S LOOM - A Journal of Magical Arts
Herald Press
HOAX!
Hohm Press
Hope Publishing House
Horned Owl Publishing
THE HUMANIST
In Print Publishing
Inner Traditions International
Innisfree Press
THE INQUIRER
Integral Publishing
INTERCULTURE
ISSUES
THE J MAN TIMES
JEWISH CURRENTS
THE JOURNAL OF THE ORDER OF BUDDHIST
  CONTEMPLATIVES
Kar-Ben Copies, Inc.
KEREM: Creative Explorations in Judaism
Landwaster Books
Langmarc Publishing
The Leaping Frog Press
LITURGY 90
LIVE AND LET LIVE
Llewellyn Publications
LLEWELLYN'S NEW WORLDS OF MIND AND
  SPIRIT
Lone Willow Press
LPD Press
Lycanthrope Press
THE MAD FARMERS' JUBILEE ALMANACK
Magnus Press
Peter Marcan Publications
Massey-Reyner Publishing
MASTER THOUGHTS
MEDIA SPOTLIGHT
MIND MATTERS REVIEW
MINISTRY & LITURGY
MOKSHA JOURNAL
Moksha Press
Moon Publications, Inc.
More To Life Publishing
Mountaintop Books
Multnomah Publishers, Inc.
MUSIC NEWS
Naturegraph Publishers, Inc.
Network 3000 Publishing
Nevada Publications
NEW ANGLICAN REVIEW
NEW CATHOLIC REVIEW
THE NEW PRESS LITERARY QUARTERLY
NEW THOUGHT
NEW THOUGHT JOURNAL
New World Library
NEW YORK STORIES
NightinGale Resources
NOCTURNAL REPORTER
Noyce Publishing
OBLATES
Occam Publishers
OFFICE NUMBER ONE
The Olive Press Publications
Omega Publications, Inc.

ON COURSE
Open Court Publishing
PAGAN AMERICA
Palm Drive Publishing
PalmTree Publishers
Parabola
PARABOLA MAGAZINE
Paragon House Publishers
Parallax Press
PASSION
Penfield Press
PenRose Publishing Company, Inc.
The Petrarch Press
Philopsychy Press
PLENTY GOOD ROOM
THE PLOUGH
Plus Publications
Polebridge Press
PREP Publishing
The Press at Foggy Bottom
Progresiv Publishr
QUARTZ HILL JOURNAL OF THEOLOGY
Quartz Hill Publishing House
QUEEN OF ALL HEARTS
THE QUEST
R & E Publishers
Rabeth Publishing Company
Ragged Edge Press
THE READER'S REVIEW
RECONSTRUCTIONIST
REPORTS OF THE NATIONAL CENTER FOR
  SCIENCE EDUCATION
Resource Publications, Inc.
Reveal
Rhino Publishing
RhwymBooks
Rowan Mountain Press
SAGEWOMAN
St. Andrew Press
St. Augustine Society Press
ST. CROIX REVIEW
Saint Mary's Press
St. Matthew's Press
St. Michael's Press
Sandpiper Press
Saqi Books Publisher
SAT SANDESH: THE MESSAGE OF THE MASTERS
Scarf Press
SCP NEWSLETTER
SelectiveHouse Publishers, Inc.
SHAMAN'S DRUM: A Journal of Experiential Shaman-
  ism
Sheed & Ward
Sheer Joy! Press
Signature Books
Sigo Press
Skytop Publishing
Smyth & Helwys Publishing, Inc.
SOCIETE
Sparrow Hawk Press
SPECTRUM—The Wholistic News Magazine
THE SPIRIT GARDEN
Spring Publications Inc.
STUDENT LEADERSHIP JOURNAL
STUDIO - A Journal of Christians Writing
Sherwood Sugden & Company, Publishers
Technicians of the Sacred
THEOLOGIA 21
Theosophical Publishing House
Thirteen Colonies Press
Threshold Books
THRESHOLDS JOURNAL
TOLE WORLD
Top Of The Mountain Publishing
Torchlight Publishing
THE TRUTH SEEKER
THE UNDERGROUND FOREST - LA SELVA SUB-
  TERRANEA

876

Unity Books
UNITY MAGAZINE
Universal Unity
University of Calgary Press
Vajra Printing an Publishing of Yoga Anand Ashram
Vedanta Press
VEGGIE LIFE
Vesta Publications Limited
Via God Publishing
VIRTUTE ET MORTE MAGAZINE
VOICES - ISRAEL
George Wahr Publishing Company
West Anglia Publications
Westhaven Publishing
WHAT IS ENLIGHTENMENT?
Wheat Forders/Trabuco Books
White Buck Publishing
White Plume Press
WHOLE EARTH
THE WISDOM CONSERVANCY NEWSLETTER
Wisdom Publications, Inc.
Witwatersrand University Press
WONDER TIME
WOOD STROKES & WOODCRAFTS
Words & Pictures Press
World Wide Publishing Corp.
World Wisdom Books, Inc.
Writers House Press
YUWITAYA LAKOTA
ZONE

RENAISSANCE

Abiko Literary Press (ALP)
AFFAIR OF THE MIND: A Literary Quarterly
Baker Street Publications
CLASS ACT
GEORGE & MERTIE'S PLACE. Rooms With a View
Heron Press
Italica Press, Inc.
JOURNAL OF UNCONVENTIONAL HISTORY
Laureate Press
MIXED BAG
RENAISSANCE MAGAZINE
University of Massachusetts Press
VIRTUTE ET MORTE MAGAZINE
YE OLDE NEWES

REPRINTS

Abiko Literary Press (ALP)
AFFABLE NEIGHBOR
Affable Neighbor Press
Alan Wofsy Fine Arts
ALTERNATIVE PRESS REVIEW
Ancient City Press
Anderson Press
Avery Color Studios
BAKER STREET GAZETTE
Baker Street Publications
BELLES LETTRES
Black Sparrow Press
Bliss Publishing Company, Inc
Blue Heron Publishing, Inc.
BOTH SIDES NOW
Carousel Press
Center for Japanese Studies
Cherokee Publishing Company
China Books & Periodicals, Inc.
CLASS ACT
COZY DETECTIVE MYSTERY MAGAZINE
The Crossing Press
DAYS AND NIGHTS OF A SMALL PRESS PUB-
LISHER
Dry Bones Press
Eagle's View Publishing
Ecrivez!
Edition Stencil
The Feminist Press at the City College
Free People Press

Fromm International Publishing Corporation
Frugal Marketer Publishing
FULL MOON DIRECTORY
Full Moon Publications
GATEAVISA
THE HAUNTED JOURNAL
Heritage Books, Inc.
HOLLYWOOD NOSTALGIA
Indelible Inc.
Irish Genealogical Foundation
Ironweed Press
JACK THE RIPPER GAZETTE
JEWISH LIFE
Allen A. Knoll Publishers
Libertarian Press, Inc./American Book Distributors
Macrocosm USA, Inc.
Meager Ink Press
Mercury House
Mid-List Press
MIXED BAG
Mountain Press Publishing Co.
Munklinde Vestergaard
Mutual Publishing
NIGHTSHADE
NOCTURNAL REPORTER
Oregon State University Press
OUT YOUR BACKDOOR: The Magazine of Informal
Adventure and Cheap Culture
Paladin Enterprises, Inc.
PEN & INK WRITERS JOURNAL
Poets & Writers, Inc.
THE RAINTOWN REVIEW: A Forum for the Essayist's
Art
REALM OF THE VAMPIRE
RhwymBooks
SALOME: A Journal for the Performing Arts
Saqi Books Publisher
Signature Books
SLEUTH JOURNAL
Genny Smith Books
Gibbs Smith, Publisher
SOCIETE
SPILLWAY
Graham Stone
Sherwood Sugden & Company, Publishers
32 PAGES
TIMESHARE AND VACATION OWNERSHIP RE-
VIEW
THE UNDERGROUND FOREST - LA SELVA SUB-
TERRANEA
UNITED LUMBEE NATION TIMES
University of Calgary Press
Vestal Press Ltd
THE VIRGINIA QUARTERLY REVIEW
WESTERN SKIES

RESEARCH

Eros Publishing

REVIEWS

Abiko Literary Press (ALP)
ACM (ANOTHER CHICAGO MAGAZINE)
Aeolus Press, Inc.
AFFABLE NEIGHBOR
Affable Neighbor Press
AFRICAN STUDIES
THE ALEMBIC
Algol Press
ALTERNATIVE PRESS REVIEW
AMERICAN LETTERS & COMMENTARY
AMUSING YOURSELF TO DEATH
Anderson Press
ANGELFLESH
Angelflesh Press
THE ANGRY THOREAUAN
APPALACHIA JOURNAL
ARCHIPELAGO
ARISTOS

ATOM MIND
AXE FACTORY REVIEW
BAKER STREET GAZETTE
Baker Street Publications
THE BENT
BLACK MOON MAGAZINE
Black Moon Publishing
BLACK SHEETS MAGAZINE
BLOCK'S MAGAZINE
BOGG
Boog Literature
BOOGLIT
BOOK MARKETING UPDATE
BOOK/MARK SMALL PRESS QUARTERLY REVIEW
BORDERLANDS: Texas Poetry Review
BOTH COASTS BOOK REVIEW
THE BOUND SPIRAL
BURNING CAR
BUSINESPIRIT JOURNAL
Calypso Publications
CE CONNECTION COMMUNIQUE
CEDAR HILL REVIEW
Chiron Press
CHIRON REVIEW
CIMARRON REVIEW
CLASS ACT
THE COMPANY NORTH AMERICA
THE COOL TRAVELER
CORRECTIONS TODAY
COUNTERPOISE: For Social Responsibilities, Liberty
and Dissent
THE CREAM CITY REVIEW
CREEPY MIKE'S OMNIBUS OF FUN
Crescent Moon
CRONE CHRONICLES: A Journal of Conscious Aging
THE DALHOUSIE REVIEW
DAYS AND NIGHTS OF A SMALL PRESS PUB-
LISHER
DIRIGIBLE
DISSONANCE MAGAZINE
DREAM NETWORK JOURNAL
THE EDGE CITY REVIEW
ENGLISH LITERATURE IN TRANSITION, 1880-1920
THE EVERGREEN CHRONICLES
FACTSHEET FIVE
FIGMENTS
FLYFISHER
FOOD WRITER
The Foundation for Economic Education, Inc.
FREEDOM OF EXPRESSION (FOE)
THE FREEMAN: Ideas On Liberty
FULL MOON DIRECTORY
Full Moon Publications
FURTHER TOO
GAUNTLET: Exploring the Limits of Free Expression
THE GENRE WRITER'S NEWS
GEORGE & MERTIE'S PLACE: Rooms With a View
THE GEORGIA REVIEW
GERBIL: Queer Culture Zine
G'RAPH
GRAY AREAS
THE GREAT BLUE BEACON
Gryphon Publications
THE HAUNTED JOURNAL
HELIOCENTRIC NET/STIGMATA
HIP MAMA
HOAX!
HOBSON'S CHOICE
HOLLYWOOD NOSTALGIA
HORIZONS
HORIZONS BEYOND
H2SO4
HUMANS & OTHER SPECIES
Hyacinth House Publications/Caligula Editions
IDIOM 23
ILLUMINATIONS
The Independent Institute
INDEPENDENT PUBLISHER

THE INDEPENDENT REVIEW: A Journal of Political
Economy
INNER JOURNEYS
INNOVATING
INTERCULTURAL WRITERS REVIEW
IOTA
IRIS: A Journal About Women
IRISH JOURNAL
THE J MAN TIMES
JACK THE RIPPER GAZETTE
JAMES JOYCE BROADSHEET
JEWISH LIFE
THE JOURNAL OF AFRICAN TRAVEL-WRITING
KALEIDOSCOPE: INTERNATIONAL MAGAZINE OF
LITERATURE, FINE ARTS, AND DISABILITY
KARMA LAPEL
KITE LINES
KLIATT
LAKE SUPERIOR MAGAZINE
LAMBDA BOOK REPORT
LAUGHING BEAR NEWSLETTER
LIFE ON PLANET EARTH, VOL III
LIGHT: The Quarterly of Light Verse
LINKS
LITERARY MAGAZINE REVIEW
THE LITERARY QUARTERLY
LITRAG
THE LONSDALE - The International Quarterly of The
Romantic Six
LOVE AND RAGE, A Revolutionary Anarchist News-
paper
LUMMOX JOURNAL
Lunar Offensive Publications
MANOA: A Pacific Journal of International Writing
THE MARLBORO REVIEW
THE MASONIA ROUNDUP
MATCHBOOK
METAL CURSE
THE METAPHYSICAL REVIEW
Mica Press
MIXED BAG
MOCKINGBIRD
MSRRT NEWSLETTER: LIBRARY ALTERNATIVES
THE MYSTERY REVIEW
NEW DELTA REVIEW
THE NEW ENGLAND QUARTERLY
NEW HOPE INTERNATIONAL REVIEW
THE NEW SOUTHERN SURREALIST REVIEW
NIGHTSHADE
NOCTURNAL REPORTER
North Stone Press
NORTHEAST
NOTRE DAME REVIEW
OASIS
OBJECT PERMANENCE
OLD CROW
ONE TRICK PONY
THE ONSET REVIEW
OYSTER BOY REVIEW
PACIFIC COAST JOURNAL
PASSION
PEN & INK WRITERS JOURNAL
PENNINE PLATFORM
PEREGRINE
PINYON POETRY
PLAY THE ODDS
PLEASANT LIVING
POET LORE
Poetry Now, Sacramento's Literary Calendar and Review
POETS' VOICE
POTATO EYES
POTOMAC REVIEW
POTPOURRI: A Magazine of the Literary Arts
POW-WOW
PRAIRIE SCHOONER
Progressive Education
PROGRESSIVE PERIODICALS DIRECTORY/UPDATE
PSYCHOANALYTIC BOOKS: A QUARTERLY JOUR-

PHILOSOPHER
WORDS OF WISDOM
WORLD DOMINATION REVIEW
Writers House Press
WRITER'S WORKSHOP REVIEW

SCANDINAVIA

Culinary Arts Ltd.
Fjord Press
Friends United Press
GATEAVISA
Lester Street Publishing
THE NEW PRESS LITERARY QUARTERLY
Penfield Press
SCANDINAVIAN REVIEW
TRANSITIONS ABROAD: The Guide to Living, Learning, and Working Overseas
World Wide Publishing Corp.
Years Press

SCIENCE

AAS HISTORY SERIES
ABELexpress
Abiko Literary Press (ALP)
Access Multimedia
ADVANCES IN THE ASTRONAUTICAL SCIENCES
Anaphase II
THE ANIMALS' AGENDA
ASC NEWSLETTER
Astrion Publishing
ATL Press, Inc.
BAJA SUN
BARNABE MOUNTAIN REVIEW
Bear & Company, Inc.
Beaudoin Publishing Co.
Berkeley Hills Books
BIOLOGY DIGEST
THE BOOKWATCH
Borderland Sciences Research Foundation
BORDERLANDS: A Quarterly Journal Of Borderland Research
The Boxwood Press
BRAIN/MIND BULLETIN, Bulletin of Breakthroughs
Brenner Information Group
BRIDGES: An Interdisciplinary Journal of Theology, Philosophy, History, and Science
CANADIAN JOURNAL OF APPLIED PHYSIOLOGY (CJAP)
Catamount Press
THE CENTENNIAL REVIEW
Center Press
Chandler & Sharp Publishers, Inc.
Chaos Warrior Productions
Chicago Review Press
Clearwater Publishing Co.
Comparative Sedimentology Lab.
Continuing Education Press
COTYLEDON
DAEDALUS, Journal of the American Academy of Arts and Sciences
The Denali Press
Desert Oasis Publishing Co.
Dimension Engineering Press
Discovery Enterprises, Ltd.
Dog-Eared Publications
ETICA & CIENCIA
Flower Press
Frontline Publications
Genesis Publishing Company, Inc.
THE GENTLE SURVIVALIST
GEORGE & MERTIE'S PLACE: Rooms With a View
HEALTH AND HAPPINESS
The Heather Foundation
HOBSON'S CHOICE
Human Kinetics Pub. Inc.
Humana Press
IASP NEWSLETTER
Inquiry Press

Interface Press
Intermountain Publishing
International University Line (IUL)
Island Press
Island Publishers
JOURNAL OF POLYMORPHOUS PERVERSITY
JOURNAL OF SCIENTIFIC EXPLORATION
JOURNAL OF STRENGTH AND CONDITIONING RESEARCH (JSCR)
JOURNAL OF VISION REHABILITATION
Jupiter Scientific Publishing
KETTERING REVIEW
KIDSCIENCE
LADYBUG, the Magazine for Young Children
Lester Street Publishing
Library Research Associates
MAD SCIENTIST
Marmot Publishing
Media Arts Publishing
Medical Physics Publishing Corp.
The Message Company
MIND MATTERS REVIEW
Mission Press
Multi Media Arts
Naturegraph Publishers, Inc.
N-B-T-V
Network 3000 Publishing
Orchises Press
Organization for Equal Education of the Sexes, Inc.
Outer Space Press
PABLO LENNIS
Parabola
Parkway Publishers, Inc.
Peavine Publications
Plexus Publishing, Inc.
POEMS THAT THUMP IN THE DARK/SECOND GLANCE
Polar Bear Productions & Company
Popular Medicine Press
Progresiv Publishr
PSYCHOANALYTIC BOOKS: A QUARTERLY JOURNAL OF REVIEWS
PSYCHOLOGY OF WOMEN QUARTERLY
QED
Quale Press
Quarterly Committee of Queen's University
QUEEN'S QUARTERLY: A Canadian Review
THE QUEST
REPORTS OF THE NATIONAL CENTER FOR SCIENCE EDUCATION
RESONANCE
Reveal
St. Georges Press
SANTA BARBARA REVIEW
SCIENCE AND TECHNOLOGY
SCIENCE BOOKS & FILMS
SCIENCE/HEALTH ABSTRACTS
Sea Challengers, Inc.
Shadowlight Press
SJL Publishing Company
SKEPTICAL INQUIRER
SMART DRUG NEWS
TAIL SPINS
Timber Press
TIME PILOT
Torchlight Publishing
Univelt, Inc.
University of Calgary Press
VDT NEWS
Weidner & Sons, Publishing
WHAT IS ENLIGHTENMENT?
Wheat Forders/Trabuco Books
WHOLE EARTH
Woods Hole Press
XIB
Xib Publications
Zagier & Urruty Publicaciones

SCIENCE FICTION

AAS HISTORY SERIES
ABERRATIONS
Abiko Literary Press (ALP)
ABSOLUTE MAGNITUDE
Access Multimedia
African American Audio Press
AFRICAN AMERICAN AUDIOBOOK REVIEW
Algol Press
AMELIA
Anamnesis Press
Angst World Library
Argo Press
ASTERISM: The Journal of Science Fiction, Fantasy, and
    Space Music
Astrion Publishing
AXE FACTORY REVIEW
BALL MAGAZINE
Bear & Company, Inc.
Bereshith Publishing
BOMB MAGAZINE
THE BOOKWATCH
The Bradford Press
Broken Mirrors Press
Cambric Press dba Emerald House
Catamount Press
Chaos Warrior Productions
Circlet Press, Inc.
CLASS ACT
A COMPANION IN ZEOR
CON-TEMPORAL
COTYLEDON
The F. Marion Crawford Memorial Society
DARK REGIONS: The Years Best Fantastic Fiction
Dimension Engineering Press
THE DIRTY GOAT
DNA Publications, Inc.
Dolphin Books, Inc.
DREAM INTERNATIONAL QUARTERLY
DREAMS AND NIGHTMARES
Earth Star Publications
EASTGATE QUARTERLY REVIEW OF HYPERTEXT
ECLIPSE
Ecrivez!
Edgewood Press
EMPLOI PLUS
ENTROPY NEGATIVE
Event Horizon Press
The Feminist Press at the City College
FISH DRUM MAGAZINE
Four Seasons Publishers
Four Walls Eight Windows
THE FRACTAL
Full Moon Publications
The Future Press
Gallopade International
GATEAVISA
THE GENRE WRITER'S NEWS
Golden Eagle Press
Gryphon Publications
GUARD THE NORTH
THE HAUNTED JOURNAL
HAUNTS
HAWAI'I REVIEW
Heresy Press
HOBSON'S CHOICE
HOLLYWOOD NOSTALGIA
HORIZONS BEYOND
Host Publications, Inc.
III Publishing
INTERBANG
IT GOES ON THE SHELF
Journey Books Publishing
KASPAHRASTER
KOOMA
LAKE SUPERIOR MAGAZINE
Landwaster Books

Leyland Publications
LOCUS: The Newspaper of the Science Fiction Field
MAD SCIENTIST
Manuscript Press
MATI
Mayhaven Publishing
Meager Ink Press
Media Arts Publishing
METAL CURSE
Munsey Music
Network 3000 Publishing
New Fantasy Publications
The New Humanity Press
THE NEW PRESS LITERARY QUARTERLY
New Victoria Publishers
NITE-WRITER'S   INTERNATIONAL   LITERARY
    ARTS JOURNAL
THE NOCTURNAL LYRIC
NOVA EXPRESS
Ocean View Books
OF UNICORNS AND SPACE STATIONS
ON SPEC: More Than Just Science Fiction
Open Hand Publishing Inc.
Outer Space Press
THE OVERLOOK CONNECTION
Owlswick Press
P & K Stark Productions, Inc.
PABLO LENNIS
PAPERBACK PARADE
Paw Print Publishing Co.
Phantom Press Publications
PIG IRON
Pig Iron Press
PIRATE WRITINGS
PLOT
Portals Press
Pottersfield Press
Pride & Imprints
Purple Mouth Press
Q ZINE
RALPH'S REVIEW
RED OWL
THE REJECTED QUARTERLY
Rio Grande Press
RISING STAR
RIVERSIDE QUARTERLY
THE ROMANTIST
THE ROSWELL LITERARY REVIEW
Savant Garde Workshop
SCAVENGER'S NEWSLETTER
SCIENCE FICTION CHRONICLE
SelectiveHouse Publishers, Inc.
SF COMMENTARY
SF EYE
SF**3
Shadowlight Press
THE SILVER WEB
69 FLAVORS OF PARANOIA
SJL Publishing Company
SOM Publishing, division of School of Metaphysics
SPACE AND TIME
Space and Time Press
SQUARE ONE - A Magazine of Disturbing Fiction
StarLance Publications
Steamshovel Press
STEAMSHOVEL PRESS
Graham Stone
Tafford Publishing
THRESHOLDS JOURNAL
TIME PILOT
TRANSVERSIONS
2AM MAGAZINE
2AM Publications
Univelt, Inc.
Urban Legend Press
THE URBANITE
Via God Publishing
VISUAL ASSAULT OMNIBUS

Waverly House Publishing
White Wolf Publishing
Wolf-Wise Press
Wordcraft of Oregon
WORLD OF FANDOM MAGAZINE
WWW.TOMORROWSF.COM
YOUNG VOICES

SCOTLAND

AFFABLE NEIGHBOR
Affable Neighbor Press
Averasboro Press
Celtic Heritage Books
CLASS ACT
DeerTrail Books
Dufour Editions Inc.
Full Moon Publications
GATEAVISA
HORIZONS
KELTIC FRINGE
NEW HOPE INTERNATIONAL REVIEW
NORTHWORDS
OBJECT PERMANENCE
Penfield Press
Rowan Mountain Press
Stewart Publishing & Printing

SCOUTING

dbS Productions
GEORGE & MERTIE'S PLACE: Rooms With a View
New Regency Publishing

SELF-HELP

Acclaim Publishing Co. Inc.
Afcom Publishing
Al-Anon Family Group Headquarters, Inc.
Al-Galaxy Publishing Company
AlphaBooks, Inc.
American Source Books, a division of Impact Publishers
Amethyst & Emerald
Anti-Aging Press
Arden Press, Inc.
Ascension Publishing
Ashton Productions, Inc.
Astrion Publishing
THE AUROREAN, A POETIC QUARTERLY
Author's Partner in Publishing
Axelrod Publishing of Tampa Bay
Baker Street Publications
Bayhampton Publications
Beacon Point Press
Bear & Company, Inc.
Behavioral Sciences Research Press, Inc.
Best Sellers Publishing
Big Mouth Publications
Black Diamond Book Publishing
Black Forest Press
Blue Dolphin Publishing, Inc.
Blue Horizon Press
Blue River Publishing Inc.
Blue Sky Marketing, Inc.
Bonus Books, Inc.
BookPartners, Inc.
Bottom Line Pre$$
Brason-Sargar Publications
Brenner Information Group
Briarwood Publishing
Broken Jaw Press
Buckhorn Books
Business Resource Publishing
Cage Consulting, Inc.
Capital Communications
Cherubic Press
Chicago Spectrum Press
Cobra Publishing
COLLEGIUM NEWSLETTER
COMMON BOUNDARY MAGAZINE
Commune-A-Key Publishing, Inc.

Company of Words Publishing
Conari Press
Contemax Publishers
COPING WITH TURBULENT TIMES
Coreopsis Books
Courtyard Publishing Company
CREATIVITY CONNECTION
The Crossing Press
Cultivated Underground Press
Cyclone Books
Cypress House
Cypress Publishing Group, Inc.
D.B.A. Books
DAILY WORD
Dakota Books
Dawn Sign Press
DAYS AND NIGHTS OF A SMALL PRESS PUB-
LISHER
DOVETAIL: A Journal by and for Jewish/Christian
Families
Dovetail Publishing
Down There Press
Earth Magic Productions, Inc.
Ecrivez!
Elder Books
ELDERCARE FORUM
Emerald Wave
Encircle Publications
Enthea Press
Envirographics
Evanston Publishing, Inc.
The Fine Print Press, Ltd.
Fisher Books
FOREVER ALIVE
THE FORUM
Four Seasons Publishers
Free Spirit Publishing Inc.
Fulcrum, Inc.
Future Horizons, Inc.
GATEAVISA
Gateway Books
GEORGE & MERTIE'S PLACE: Rooms With a View
Golden Eagle Press
GrapeVinePress
THE GREAT IDEA PATCH
Greenlawn Press
Halo Books
Hannacroix Creek Books, Inc
HEALTH AND HAPPINESS
Health Press
Heartsong Books
HERBAL CHOICE
Himalayan Institute Press
Hohm Press
Holbrook Street Press
Human Kinetics Pub. Inc.
Humana Press
Hunter House Inc., Publishers
Impact Publishers, Inc.
Infinite Passion Publishing
Information Research Lab
Inner Traditions International
Innerworks Publishing
Innisfree Press
Innovation Press
Intermountain Publishing
INTUITIVE EXPLORATIONS
Islewest Publishing
JOURNAL OF PSYCHOACTIVE DRUGS
JPS Publishing Company
Keel Publications
Kells Media Group
H J Kramer
Life Lessons
LIVING CHEAP NEWS
Llewellyn Publications
The Love and Logic Press, Inc.
Markowski International Publishers

Master Key Inc.
Meadow Mountain Press
MetaGnosis
Metamorphous Press
Mills & Sanderson, Publishers
MIXED BAG
Monroe Press
More To Life Publishing
Naturegraph Publishers, Inc.
The Neo Herramann Group
Network 3000 Publishing
New Liberty Press
New World Library
Newjoy Press
Nicolin Fields Publishing, Inc.
Nunciata
Obsessive Compulsive Anonymous
Open Horizons Publishing Company
Osmyrrah Publishing
PACIFIC ENTERPRISE
Pathways Press, Inc.
Paw Print Publishing Co.
Peachtree Publishers, Ltd.
Pedestal Press
Perpetual Press
Perspectives Press
Philopsychy Press
Piggy Bank Press
Pipeline Press
Plus Publications
The Poetry Center Press/Shoestring Press
POETS' VOICE
Ponderosa Publishers
Positive Publishing
Pride & Imprints
Princess Publishing
Prosperity Press
Prudhomme Press
Publitec Editions
QED Press
Quantum Mind Publications
Quill Driver Books
QUINTILE
Quintile
Rainbow Books, Inc.
Rainbow's End
Ravenhawk Books
RED HOT HOME INCOME REPORTER
River Press
Roam Publishing
RURAL NETWORK ADVOCATE
St. Georges Press
Sandpiper Press
Santa Monica Press/Offbeat Press
The Saunderstown Press
Scherf, Inc./Scherf Books
SCIENCE/HEALTH ABSTRACTS
Seal Press
Shaolin Communications
Sharp Publishing
Shimoda Publishing
Sigo Press
Silvercat Publications
SJL Publishing Company
Small Helm Press
SMART DRUG NEWS
Smart Publications
SO YOUNG!
SOMNIAL TIMES
Steel Balls Press
Stewart Publishing & Printing
Stillpoint Publishing
Studio 4 Productions
SunShine Press Publications, Inc.
Swan Publishing Company
TEC Publications
Terra Nova Press
Timeless Books

Tiptoe Literary Service
TitleWaves Publishing
Tomar House Publishers
Top Of The Mountain Publishing
Torchlight Publishing
TOWERS CLUB, USA INFO MARKETING REPORT
Tudor Publishers, Inc.
Turtle Island Press, Inc.
Twelve Star Publishing
Tyro Publishing
Unity Books
UNITY MAGAZINE
Upper Access Inc.
VanderWyk & Burnham
Samuel Weiser, Inc.
Westport Publishers
WHOLE EARTH
Wildstone Media
Wisdom Publications, Inc.
Women of Diversity Productions, Inc.
World Wide Publishing Corp.
Wright-Armstead Associates
Yes You Can Press
Z W L Publishing, Inc.

SENIOR CITIZENS

Adams-Blake Publishing
American Source Books, a division of Impact Publishers
Anti-Aging Press
Arjay Associates
Autumn Publishing Group, LLC.
Blue River Publishing Inc.
Bonus Books, Inc.
Brenner Information Group
Center for Public Representation
Creative With Words Publications (CWW)
DeerTrail Books
Duckworth Press
THE DUPLEX PLANET
Elder Books
FOCUS: Library Service to Older Adults, People with Disabilities
Gateway Books
GEORGE & MERTIE'S PLACE: Rooms With a View
Golden Eagle Press
Guarionex Press Ltd.
Heritage West Books
Human Kinetics Pub. Inc.
Impact Publishers, Inc.
Institute for Southern Studies
JARRETT'S JOURNAL
Lester Street Publishing
THE MATURE TRAVELER
Parabola
Pineapple Press, Inc.
The Place In The Woods
The Poetry Center Press/Shoestring Press
Potentials Development, Inc.
Quill Driver Books
Red Apple Publishing
St. Georges Press
SO YOUNG!
TAPROOT, a journal of older writers
Tide Book Publishing Company
Tudor Publishers, Inc.
Twin Peaks Press
Volcano Press, Inc
WHOLE EARTH

SEX, SEXUALITY

Afcom Publishing
AFFABLE NEIGHBOR
Affable Neighbor Press
AK Press
Al-Galaxy Publishing Company
THE ANGRY THOREAUAN
APHRODITE GONE BERSERK
Arrowstar Publishing

ARTHUR'S COUSIN
ATROCITY
Autonomedia, Inc.
AXE FACTORY REVIEW
Axelrod Publishing of Tampa Bay
BabelCom, Inc.
Barricade Books
THE BLAB
BLACK LACE
BLACK SHEETS MAGAZINE
BLACKFIRE
BLK
THE BLOWFISH CATALOG
Blowfish Press
Blue Dolphin Publishing, Inc.
BONDAGE FANTASIES
BOUDOIR NOIR
Brownout Laboratories
Capital Communications
Carpe Diem Publishing
Center Press
Chandler & Sharp Publishers, Inc.
Child's Play
Chiron Press
CHIRON REVIEW
COKEFISH
Cokefish Press
COLLEGIUM NEWSLETTER
Conari Press
Cosmoenergetics Publications
Courtyard Publishing Company
Crescent Moon
The Crossing Press
Cyclone Books
Cynic Press
Daedalus Publishing Company
Down There Press
DRASTIC LIVES
DREAM WHIP
Eidos
EIDOS: Sexual Freedom & Erotic Entertainment for
   Consenting Adults
THE EMSHOCK LETTER
Factor Press
FELL SWOOP
Feral House
FETISH BAZAAR
The Fine Print Press, Ltd.
Fort Dearborn Press
FURTHER TOO
Garrett County Press
GATEAVISA
Gay Sunshine Press, Inc.
GLB Publishers
god is DEAD, publications
GRAFFITI OFF THE ASYLUM WALLS
GRAY AREAS
GREEN EGG
Guardian Press
Happy Rock Press
HARVARD WOMEN'S LAW JOURNAL
HIP MAMA
Hunter House Inc., Publishers
Hyacinth House Publications/Caligula Editions
IMPACC USA
Impact Publishers, Inc.
IMPETUS
Inner Traditions International
IRIS: A Journal About Women
THE J MAN TIMES
JACK MACKEREL MAGAZINE
JPS Publishing Company
Kells Media Group
Kivaki Press
KOMIC FANTASIES
KOOMA
Laocoon Books
Leyland Publications

LIBIDO: The Journal of Sex and Sensibility
LITERARY ROCKET
LOVING ALTERNATIVES MAGAZINE
LOVING MORE
Lunar Offensive Publications
MALEDICTA: The International Journal of Verbal
   Aggression
MESECHABE: The Journal of Surre(gion)alism
METASEX
MIND MATTERS REVIEW
MIP Company
Mother Courage Press
NAMBLA BULLETIN
NEW FRONTIER
New Spring Publications
NOT BORED!
ON OUR BACKS MAGAZINE
PAGAN AMERICA
Palm Drive Publishing
PASSION
PLAIN BROWN WRAPPER (PBW)
Plexus
POEMS THAT THUMP IN THE DARK/SECOND
   GLANCE
Pride & Imprints
RAG SHOCK
Red Alder Books
RED OWL
REDEMPTION
Rowhouse Press
RUBBER DUCKY MAGAZINE
Salt Lick Press
Semiotext Foreign Agents Books Series
SEMIOTEXT(E)
Sheer Joy! Press
SKINNYDIPPING
SMART DRUG NEWS
SPECTRUM—The Wholistic News Magazine
Spelman Publishing, Inc.
STANDARD DEVIATIONS
Starbooks Press/FLF Press
Steel Balls Press
Swan Publishing Company
THIRST (CYBERTHIRST)
Times Change Press
Transcending Mundane
UNO MAS MAGAZINE
URBAN GRAFFITI
VIRTUTE ET MORTE MAGAZINE
WHITECHAPEL JOURNAL
WHOLE EARTH
XIB
Xib Publications
XY: Men, Sex, Politics
YELLOW SILK: Journal Of Erotic Arts

SEXUAL ABUSE

American Literary Press Inc./Noble House
Bear & Company, Inc.
BLK
Coteau Books
GEORGE & MERTIE'S PLACE: Rooms With a View
Greeson & Boyle, Inc.
Impact Publishers, Inc.
IRIS: A Journal About Women
Islewest Publishing
THE J MAN TIMES
JOURNAL OF CHILD AND YOUTH CARE
Kodiak Media Group
Queen of Swords Press
Rainbow's End
Seal Press
Sidran Foundation and Press
STILETTO
STONES IN MY POCKET
TEEN VOICES MAGAZINE
TEENS IN MOTION NEWS
University of Calgary Press

YOUR LIFE MATTERS

SHAKER

GEORGE & MERTIE'S PLACE: Rooms With a View
NEW ENGLAND ANTIQUES JOURNAL

SHAKESPEARE

Abiko Literary Press (ALP)
Anderson Press
APOSTROPHE: USCB Journal of the Arts
CLASS ACT
Crescent Moon
Empire Publishing Service
Five Star Publications
Gallopade International
GEORGE & MERTIE'S PLACE: Rooms With a View
Griffon House Publications
New Spirit Press/The Poet Tree
C. Olson & Company
PASSION
Players Press, Inc.
THE SHAKESPEARE NEWSLETTER
SPSM&H
Valentine Publishing & Drama Co.
Westchester House

SHIPWRECKS

Premium Press America
Wilderness Adventure Books
Ye Galleon Press

G.B. SHAW

CLASS ACT
ENGLISH LITERATURE IN TRANSITION, 1880-1920
GEORGE & MERTIE'S PLACE: Rooms With a View
THE INDEPENDENT SHAVIAN
IRISH LITERARY SUPPLEMENT
KELTIC FRINGE
Limelight Editions
Pennsylvania State University Press
The Press of Appletree Alley
SHAW: THE ANNUAL OF BERNARD SHAW STU-
    DIES

SHORT STORIES

A.L.I.
Abiko Literary Press (ALP)
ACORN WHISTLE
AFFABLE NEIGHBOR
Affable Neighbor Press
AFFAIR OF THE MIND: A Literary Quarterly
AGADA
Ageless Press
THE ALEMBIC
Amelia Press
American Audio Prose Library (non-print)
AMERICAN LETTERS & COMMENTARY
AMERICAN LITERARY REVIEW
American Living Press
THE AMETHYST REVIEW
ANGELFLESH
Angelflesh Press
THE ANTHOLOGY OF NEW ENGLAND WRITERS
ARCHIPELAGO
ARTHUR'S COUSIN
ART:MAG
Ashton Productions, Inc.
Asylum Arts
Avisson Press, Inc.
AVON LITERARY INTELLIGENCER
AXE FACTORY REVIEW
The Backwaters Press
BAKER STREET GAZETTE
Baker Street Publications
BALL MAGAZINE
THE BALTIMORE REVIEW
BANANAFISH
THE BAREFOOT POET: Journal of Poetry, Fiction,

Essays, & Art
BARNABE MOUNTAIN REVIEW
BAST Media, Inc.
THE BEAR DELUXE
BELOIT FICTION JOURNAL
Big Star Press
BkMk Press
Black Bile Press
Black Forest Press
Black Heron Press
Black Sparrow Press
BLOOD & APHORISMS: A Journal of Literary Fiction
Blue Crane Books
BLUE MESA REVIEW
Borealis Press Limited
BOTTOMFISH
Boulevard Books, Inc. Florida
THE BOUND SPIRAL
The Bradford Press
Briarwood Publishing
Broken Jaw Press
Broken Shadow Publications
Browder Springs
BROWNBAG PRESS
PTOLEMY
THE BROWNS MILLS REVIEW
BUFFALO SPREE
Castle Peak Editions
CHAOS FOR THE CREATIVE MIND
Child's Play
Chiron Press
CHIRON REVIEW
CIMARRON REVIEW
CITIES AND ROADS: A Collection of Short Stories for
    North Carolina Readers and Writers.
CLASS ACT
CLUTCH
Coffee House Press
COLD-DRILL
CONFLUENCE
Confluence Press, Inc.
Coteau Books
CRAB CREEK REVIEW
CRAB ORCHARD REVIEW
THE CREAM CITY REVIEW
THE CRESCENT REVIEW
CRIPES!
CUTBANK
DANDELION ARTS MAGAZINE
John Daniel and Company, Publishers
December Press
DeeMar Communications
The Design Image Group Inc.
Devil Mountain Books
DIRIGIBLE
Down There Press
DOWNSTATE STORY
DREAM INTERNATIONAL QUARTERLY
Ecrivez!
EDDIE THE MAGAZINE
THE EDGE CITY REVIEW
ELF: ECLECTIC LITERARY FORUM (ELF MAGA-
    ZINE)
EMERGING VOICES
EMPLOI PLUS
ENTELECHY MAGAZINE
Eros Publishing
EVANSVILLE REVIEW
THE EVERGREEN CHRONICLES
Exile Press
Factor Press
FAR GONE
FIRST DRAFT
FIRST INTENSITY
FISH STORIES
Fithian Press
Five Fingers Press
FIVE FINGERS REVIEW

FODDERWING
FOLIO: A LITERARY JOURNAL
Four Way Books
FOURTEEN HILLS: The SFSU Review
FREEFALL
French Bread Publications
THE FROGMORE PAPERS
Fromm International Publishing Corporation
Full Moon Publications
THE FUNNY TIMES
Galde Press, Inc.
The Galileo Press Ltd.
Gay Sunshine Press, Inc.
THE GENRE WRITER'S NEWS
GEORGE & MERTIE'S PLACE: Rooms With a View
THE GEORGIA REVIEW
GERBIL: Queer Culture Zine
GINOSKO
GRAFFITI OFF THE ASYLUM WALLS
GrapeVinePress
GRASSLANDS REVIEW
Graywolf Press
THE GREAT BLUE BEACON
Gryphon Publications
GULF COAST
HARDBOILED
THE HAUNTED JOURNAL
HAWAII PACIFIC REVIEW
HEARTLAND (Australia)
Helicon Nine Editions
HELIOCENTRIC NET/STIGMATA
Hi Jinx Press
HIP MAMA
HOBSON'S CHOICE
HOLLYWOOD NOSTALGIA
Homa & Sekey Books
HORIZONS
HORIZONS BEYOND
Horse & Buggy Press
THE HUNTED NEWS
Hyacinth House Publications/Caligula Editions
IBIS REVIEW
ICARUS WAS RIGHT
THE ICONOCLAST
IDIOM 23
IGNIS FATUUS REVIEW
ILLYA'S HONEY
IMAGO
IMPRINT, A LITERARY JOURNAL
Insomniac Press
INTERBANG
INTERCULTURAL WRITERS REVIEW
THE INTERPRETER'S HOUSE
Ione Press
IRIS: A Journal About Women
IRISH JOURNAL
Irvington St. Press, Inc.
ITALIAN AMERICANA
Itidwitir Publishing
THE J MAN TIMES
JACK MACKEREL MAGAZINE
JACK THE RIPPER GAZETTE
JAPANOPHILE
Japanophile Press
JEWISH LIFE
THE JOURNAL OF AFRICAN TRAVEL-WRITING
July Blue Press
KARMA LAPEL
THE KENYON REVIEW
KESTREL: A Journal of Literature and Art
Kings Estate Press
Allen A. Knoll Publishers
KOJA
KUMQUAT MERINGUE
LADYBUG, the Magazine for Young Children
LATINO STUFF REVIEW
LEFT CURVE
LEO Productions LLC.

Leyland Publications
THE LICKING RIVER REVIEW
LIES MAGAZINE
THE LISTENING EYE
LITERAL LATTE
Literary Moments
THE LITERARY QUARTERLY
LONDON FOG
LOONFEATHER: A magazine of poetry, short prose, and
  graphics
Lost Horse Press
LULLWATER REVIEW
LUZ EN ARTE Y LITERATURA
LYNX EYE
MAD SCIENTIST
MAGIC REALISM
Majestic Books
MANGROVE MAGAZINE
MANOA: A Pacific Journal of International Writing
MANY MOUNTAINS MOVING
MARGIN: EXPLORING MODERN MAGICAL REA-
  LISM
MASSACRE
MEANJIN
Media Arts Publishing
Mercury House
THE METAPHYSICAL REVIEW
Mid-List Press
MIP Company
MIXED BAG
MOOSE BOUND PRESS JOURNAL/NEWSLETTER
Mountain State Press
Multi Media Arts
MY LEGACY
NATURAL BRIDGE
NEOLOGISMS
THE NEW PRESS LITERARY QUARTERLY
New Rivers Press, Inc.
NEW YORK STORIES
Nextstep Books
NIGHTLORE
NIGHTSHADE
Nite-Owl Press
NITE-WRITER'S   INTERNATIONAL   LITERARY
  ARTS JOURNAL
NORTHWORDS
NYX OBSCURA MAGAZINE
The O Press
ORACLE STORY
Orloff Press
OTHER VOICES
OZ-STORY
P & K Stark Productions, Inc.
PACIFIC COAST JOURNAL
Paint Rock Publishing, Inc.
Palari Publishing
Palm Drive Publishing
PANGOLIN PAPERS
PANURGE
PAPERPLATES
Papier-Mache Press
PASSAGES NORTH
Passing Through Publications
PAVEMENT SAW
Paw Print Publishing Co.
PEARL
PEN & INK WRITERS JOURNAL
PENNY DREADFUL: Tales and Poems of Fantastic
  Terror
Phantom Press Publications
Phony Lid Publications
Pine Grove Press
PLAY THE ODDS
PLEASANT LIVING
PLUME
Poetic License Press
Poetic Page
Poetry Wales Press, Ltd.

POET'S FANTASY
POTATO EYES
POTOMAC REVIEW
POTPOURRI: A Magazine of the Literary Arts
THE POTTERSFIELD PORTFOLIO
POW-WOW
PRAIRIE SCHOONER
PRESS
The Press at Foggy Bottom
The Press of Appletree Alley
The Press of the Nightowl
PRINCETON ARTS REVIEW
PSYCHOTRAIN
Purple Finch Press
Pygmy Forest Press
Pyncheon House
Pyx Press
Queen of Swords Press
Questex Consulting Ltd.
QUESTION EVERYTHING CHALLENGE EVERY-
    THING (QECE)
THE QUILL MAGAZINE QUARTERLY
RAFTERS
RALPH'S REVIEW
RATTAPALLAX
REALM OF THE VAMPIRE
Red Cedar Press
RED CEDAR REVIEW
Red Crane Books, Inc.
Red Dragon Press
RED ROCK REVIEW
REDOUBT
REFLECTIONS
Rio Grande Press
THE RIVER
THE ROSWELL LITERARY REVIEW
Rowan Mountain Press
Rowhouse Press
St. Georges Press
Saint Mary's Press
SALAMANDER
SALT HILL
SANTA BARBARA REVIEW
Sarabande Books, Inc.
SE LA VIE WRITER'S JOURNAL
SEMIGLOSS
SEWANEE REVIEW
SF COMMENTARY
SHADES OF DECEMBER
SHEILA-NA-GIG
SHORT FUSE
Signal Books
Signature Books
SILHOUETTE MAGAZINE
SKYLARK
SLEUTH JOURNAL
Slough Press
The Smith (subsidiary of The Generalist Assn., Inc.)
Gibbs Smith, Publisher
SNAKE RIVER REFLECTIONS
SOUTHWEST JOURNAL
Spectrum Press
SPELUNKER FLOPHOUSE
THE SPIRIT THAT MOVES US
The Spirit That Moves Us Press, Inc.
SPIRIT TO SPIRIT
THE SPITTING IMAGE
SQUARE ONE - A Magazine of Disturbing Fiction
STAPLE
StarLance Publications
Stones Point Press
STORY
STOVEPIPE: A Journal of Little Literary Value
STRUGGLE: A Magazine of Proletarian Revolutionary
    Literature
STUDIO ONE
THE STYLUS
The Subourbon Press

Sulisa Publishing
SULPHUR RIVER LITERARY REVIEW
SWEET ANNIE & SWEET PEA REVIEW
Sweet Annie Press
Sweet Lady Moon Press
SYCAMORE REVIEW
SYNCOPATED CITY
TAPROOT LITERARY REVIEW
TEENS IN MOTION NEWS
The Teitan Press, Inc.
TEXAS YOUNG WRITERS' NEWSLETTER
TEXTSHOP
A THEATER OF BLOOD
THIRD COAST
13TH MOON
32 PAGES
Thunder Rain Publishing Corp.
Tiptoe Literary Service
TRANSVERSIONS
TREASURE HOUSE
TURNSTILE
Turnstone Press
2AM MAGAZINE
2AM Publications
2.13.61 Publications
ULITARRA
Underwhich Editions
THE UNFORGETTABLE FIRE
THE UNIT CIRCLE
University of Massachusetts Press
URBAN GRAFFITI
Urban Legend Press
THE URBANITE
URBANUS/RAIZIRR
VAGABOND
VAMPIRE NIGHTS
VICTORY PARK: THE JOURNAL OF THE NEW
    HAMPSHIRE INSTITUTE OF ART
THE VINCENT BROTHERS REVIEW
VIRGINIA LITERARY REVIEW
VIRTUTE ET MORTE MAGAZINE
Voices From My Retreat
WEBER STUDIES: Voices and Viewpoints of the
    Contemporary West
WEIRD POETRY
WELLSPRING
WESTERN SKIES
White Pine Press
WICKED MYSTIC
WISEBLOOD
WORDS OF WISDOM
WORLD LETTER
WORLDLINKS - FRIENDSHIP NEWS
WRITER'S GUIDELINES & NEWS
WRITER'S WORKSHOP REVIEW
WRITES OF PASSAGE
WRITING FOR OUR LIVES
XAVIER REVIEW
XIB
Xib Publications
YELLOW SILK: Journal Of Erotic Arts
Yggdrasil Books
YOUNG VOICES
Zerx Press
Zoland Books
ZUZU'S PETALS: QUARTERLY ONLINE

SINGLES

Afcom Publishing
Anti-Aging Press
BabelCom, Inc.
Blue Sky Marketing, Inc.
Capital Communications
COLLEGIUM NEWSLETTER
FURTHER TOO
Gateway Books
GEORGE & MERTIE'S PLACE: Rooms With a View
JACK MACKEREL MAGAZINE

JPS Publishing Company
Nunciata
Reveal
Rowhouse Press
RURAL NETWORK ADVOCATE
SINCERE SINGLES
SINGLE SCENE
SINGLE TODAY
SKINNYDIPPING
SO YOUNG!
Steel Balls Press

SNORKELING

ANGLE
Blue Reef Publications, Inc.
New World Publications, Inc.

SOCIAL SECURITY

AFFAIR OF THE MIND: A Literary Quarterly
The Foundation for Economic Education, Inc.

SOCIAL WORK

Baker Street Publications
DAYS AND NIGHTS OF A SMALL PRESS PUB-
    LISHER
DeeMar Communications
INTERCULTURE
Islewest Publishing
JOURNAL OF CHILD AND YOUTH CARE
JOURNAL OF PSYCHOACTIVE DRUGS
Lyceum Books, Inc.
MIXED BAG
Peradam Press
The Press at Foggy Bottom
QUESTION EVERYTHING CHALLENGE EVERY-
    THING (QECE)
University of Calgary Press
VanderWyk & Burnham

SOCIALIST

AFFAIR OF THE MIND: A Literary Quarterly
AIM MAGAZINE
AMERICAN JONES BUILDING & MAINTENANCE
Autonomedia, Inc.
Between The Lines
BLUE COLLAR REVIEW
Cardinal Press, Inc.
Children Of Mary
China Books & Periodicals, Inc.
Clarity Press, Inc.
CROSS ROADS
Dufour Editions Inc.
FIDELIS ET VERUS
FURTHER TOO
GATEAVISA
GEORGE & MERTIE'S PLACE: Rooms With a View
Global Options
GOTTA WRITE NETWORK LITMAG
Homeward Press
Institute for Southern Studies
International Publishers Co. Inc.
International University Line (IUL)
ISRAEL HORIZONS
JEWISH CURRENTS
LABOUR & TRADE UNION REVIEW
LEFT CURVE
LITTLE FREE PRESS
LONE STAR SOCIALIST
LOVE AND RAGE, A Revolutionary Anarchist News-
    paper
Mehring Books, Inc.
MIDDLE EAST REPORT
THE MILITANT
Missing Spoke Press
New International
NEW UNIONIST
Partisan Press
PEOPLE'S CULTURE

PERSPECTIVES
QUESTION EVERYTHING CHALLENGE EVERY-
    THING (QECE)
RADICAL AMERICA
Red Letter Press
RETHINKING MARXISM
Schenkman Books
SCIENCE & SOCIETY
SLEUTH JOURNAL
Smyrna Press
SOCIAL JUSTICE: A JOURNAL OF CRIME, CON-
    FLICT, & WORLD ORDER
South End Press
STRUGGLE: A Magazine of Proletarian Revolutionary
    Literature
SUB-TERRAIN
Times Change Press
Transeuropa
TURNING THE TIDE: A Journal of Anti-Racist
    Activism, Research & Education
THE WEIRD NEWS

SOCIETY

Acclaim Publishing Co. Inc.
ADOLESCENCE
AFTERTHOUGHTS
THE ANIMALS' AGENDA
Arjay Associates
AZTLAN: A Journal of Chicano Studies
Baker Street Publications
Between The Lines
Blue Bird Publishing
BLUE COLLAR REVIEW
BORDERLANDS: Texas Poetry Review
Borealis Press Limited
Brownout Laboratories
Carrefour Press
Center for Public Representation
Chandler & Sharp Publishers, Inc.
Chelsea Green Publishing Company
Cherubic Press
Chicano Studies Research Center Publications
Child's Play
COMMON BOUNDARY MAGAZINE
Community Service, Inc.
COMMUNITY SERVICE NEWSLETTER
Cumberland
DAYS AND NIGHTS OF A SMALL PRESS PUB-
    LISHER
The Denali Press
The Edwin Mellen Press
ETC Publications
FAMILY THERAPY
FLORIDA PRISON LEGAL PERSPECTIVES
FOURTH WORLD REVIEW
FURTHER TOO
GATEAVISA
GLB Publishers
Global Options
god is DEAD, publications
The Heather Foundation
Hollis Publishing Company
The Independent Institute
THE INDEPENDENT REVIEW: A Journal of Political
    Economy
Institute for Southern Studies
The Institute of Mind and Behavior
INTERCULTURE
International University Line (IUL)
THE JOURNAL OF MIND AND BEHAVIOR
Ken and Scatter Publications
Kettering Foundation
KETTERING REVIEW
Kumarian Press, Inc.
The Philip Lesly Company
Libra Publishers, Inc.
LOGIC LETTER
THE LONG TERM VIEW: A Journal of Informed

Opinion
LUNO
Manta Press
MEDICAL HISTORY
MESHUGGAH
THE MIDWEST QUARTERLY
MIXED BAG
THE MUSING PLACE
The New South Company & Boson Books
New Spirit Press/The Poet Tree
New Spring Publications
NEW THOUGHT JOURNAL
NEW YORK STORIES
Occam Publishers
Partisan Press
PEACE, The Magazine of the Sixties
POEMS THAT THUMP IN THE DARK/SECOND
 GLANCE
Ragged Edge Press
THE RAINTOWN REVIEW: A Forum for the Essayist's
 Art
Red Alder Books
Reveal
SCANDINAVIAN REVIEW
SHARE INTERNATIONAL
SOCIAL JUSTICE: A JOURNAL OF CRIME, CON-
 FLICT, & WORLD ORDER
SOCIAL POLICY
SOCIAL PROBLEMS
SOCIETY
Southwest Research and Information Center
STARGREEN
TEENS IN MOTION NEWS
THOUGHTS FOR ALL SEASONS: The Magazine of
 Epigrams
TIME PILOT
Times Change Press
The Tonal Company
TWISTED TIMES
UTNE READER
Volcano Press, Inc
THE VORTEX
THE WASHINGTON MONTHLY
THE WORKBOOK
XIB
Xib Publications

SOCIOLOGY

Adaptive Living
African American Images
AIM MAGAZINE
Aletheia Publications, Inc.
Appalachian Consortium Press
AREOPAGUS
Author's Partner in Publishing
Baker Street Publications
BARNABE MOUNTAIN REVIEW
Bear & Company, Inc.
Black Rose Books Ltd.
The Borgo Press
Broken Rifle Press
Brownout Laboratories
Canadian Educators' Press
CANADIAN REVIEW OF AMERICAN STUDIES
Carrier Pigeon Press
Center for Public Representation
Chandler & Sharp Publishers, Inc.
CINEASTE MAGAZINE
Circa Press
Coker Publishing House
COLORLINES
COMMUNITY DEVELOPMENT JOURNAL
Community Service, Inc.
COMMUNITY SERVICE NEWSLETTER
The Compass Press
CONTEMPORARY WALES
Content Communications
CRIMINAL JUSTICE ABSTRACTS

Criminal Justice Press
CRITICAL REVIEW
THE DALHOUSIE REVIEW
DeeMar Communications
DeerTrail Books
DorPete Press
Dumont Press
ESPERANTIC STUDIES
Feral House
Five Corners Publications, Ltd.
Gain Publications
Gallaudet University Press
GEORGE & MERTIE'S PLACE: Rooms With a View
Global Options
god is DEAD, publications
GRAY AREAS
Gumbs & Thomas Publishers, Inc.
Haight-Ashbury Publications
The Heather Foundation
Hollis Publishing Company
Human Kinetics Pub. Inc.
IAAS Publishers, Inc.
Impact Publishers, Inc.
The Independent Institute
THE INDEPENDENT REVIEW: A Journal of Political
 Economy
Institute for Southern Studies
The Institute of Mind and Behavior
INTERCULTURE
Interlink Publishing Group, Inc.
ITALIAN AMERICANA
Jalmar Press
JAPANOPHILE
JOTS (Journal of the Senses)
THE JOURNAL OF MIND AND BEHAVIOR
JOURNAL OF PSYCHOACTIVE DRUGS
KAIROS, A Journal of Contemporary Thought and
 Criticism
KETTERING REVIEW
Kumarian Press, Inc.
LO STRANIERO: The Stranger, Der Fremde, L'Etranger
The Love and Logic Press, Inc.
Lyceum Books, Inc.
Maisonneuve Press
Manta Press
Metamorphous Press
MIXED BAG
Multi Media Arts
NEW CIVILIZATION STAFF REPORT
THE NEW ENGLAND QUARTERLY
NEW ENVIRONMENT BULLETIN
Nguoi Dan
NGUOI DAN
Open Court Publishing
Polar Bear Productions & Company
Progresiv Publishr
Royal Purcell, Publisher
R & E Publishers
R & M Publishing Company
Reveal
Saqi Books Publisher
SCIENCE AND TECHNOLOGY
Selah Publishing
SKINNYDIPPING
Slate Press
Small Helm Press
SOCIAL JUSTICE: A JOURNAL OF CRIME, CON-
 FLICT, & WORLD ORDER
SOCIAL POLICY
SOCIAL PROBLEMS
SOCIETY
SOCIOLOGY OF SPORT JOURNAL (SSJ)
Thomas Jefferson University Press
Tide Book Publishing Company
21ST CENTURY AFRO REVIEW
Two Bytes Publishing
Univelt, Inc.
University of Massachusetts Press

VIETNAM GENERATION: A Journal of Recent History and Contemporary Issues
Waterfront Books
Willendorf Press
Willow Tree Press, Inc.
B. L. Winch & Associates
Witwatersrand University Press
WORLDLINKS - FRIENDSHIP NEWS
XIB
Xib Publications
ZONE
Zone Books
ZUZU'S PETALS: QUARTERLY ONLINE

SOLAR

CJE NEWS (Newsletter of the Coalition for Jobs & the Environment)
The Film Instruction Company of America
Macrocosm USA, Inc.
NATURAL LIFE
Polar Bear Productions & Company
WHOLE EARTH

SOUTH

Appalachian Consortium Press
Baker Street Publications
John F. Blair, Publisher
Bright Mountain Books, Inc.
Cherokee Publishing Company
The F. Marion Crawford Memorial Society
DAYS AND NIGHTS OF A SMALL PRESS PUB-LISHER
Full Moon Publications
GEORGE & MERTIE'S PLACE: Rooms With a View
GRAFFITI OFF THE ASYLUM WALLS
Gut Punch Press
HABERSHAM REVIEW
HORIZONS
Institute for Southern Studies
Midmarch Arts Press
MIXED BAG
Ninety-Six Press
Papyrus Literary Enterprises, Inc.
Peachtree Publishers, Ltd.
PIKEVILLE REVIEW
Premium Press America
Redbird Press, Inc.
Rockbridge Publishing Co.
THE ROMANTIST
Rose Publishing Co.
Signal Books
SOUTHERN EXPOSURE
SOUTHERN QUARTERLY: A Journal of the Arts in the South
Sherwood Sugden & Company, Publishers
Tailored Tours Publications, Inc.
TRADITION
THE VIRGINIA QUARTERLY REVIEW
XAVIER REVIEW

SOUTH AMERICA

Anteater Press
Baker Street Publications
BUENO
Full Moon Publications
HORIZONS
MIXED BAG
The Mountaineers Books
THE NEW PRESS LITERARY QUARTERLY
ON PARAGUAY
Palladium Communications
Pangaea

SOUTH CAROLINA

Pineapple Press, Inc.

SOUTHWEST

Amador Publishers

Ancient City Press
Baker Street Publications
Balcony Press
Ballena Press
Bear & Company, Inc.
BLUE MESA REVIEW
BOOK TALK
BOOKS OF THE SOUTHWEST
BORDERLANDS: Texas Poetry Review
Cardinal Press, Inc.
Coldwater Press
CONCHO RIVER REVIEW
DREAM WHIP
Duende Press
EL PALACIO
FISH DRUM MAGAZINE
Fisher Books
Four Peaks Press
Full Moon Publications
Gallery West Associates
THE GENTLE SURVIVALIST
Golden Eagle Press
Hill Country Books
HORIZONS
Javelina Books
Kiva Publishing, Inc.
KUMQUAT MERINGUE
La Alameda Press
Law Mexico Publishing
LPD Press
Minor Heron Press
MIXED BAG
Moon Publications, Inc.
Museum of New Mexico Press
Naturegraph Publishers, Inc.
Old West Publishing Co.
Point Riders Press
POW-WOW
Primer Publishers
Pruett Publishing Company
Red Crane Books, Inc.
Research & Discovery Publications
Rio Grande Press
SE LA VIE WRITER'S JOURNAL
Gibbs Smith, Publisher
SOUTHWEST JOURNAL
SOUTHWEST REVIEW
Studia Hispanica Editors
Sunstone Press
Tortilla Press
TRADICION REVISTA
Treasure Chest Books LLC
TUCUMCARI LITERARY REVIEW
Two Eagles Press International
WEBER STUDIES: Voices and Viewpoints of the Contemporary West
WESTERN AMERICAN LITERATURE
WESTERN SKIES
Yucca Tree Press

SPACE

AAS HISTORY SERIES
ADVANCES IN THE ASTRONAUTICAL SCIENCES
ASTERISM: The Journal of Science Fiction, Fantasy, and Space Music
Borderland Sciences Research Foundation
BORDERLANDS: A Quarterly Journal Of Borderland Research
Brenner Information Group
Caliban Press
Catamount Press
DISSONANCE MAGAZINE
THE EMSHOCK LETTER
GATEAVISA
GEORGE & MERTIE'S PLACE: Rooms With a View
GRANULATED TUPPERWARE
HOBSON'S CHOICE
JACK MACKEREL MAGAZINE

KIDSCIENCE
Lowy Publishing
Mach 1, Inc.
MAD SCIENTIST
Media Arts Publishing
New Spirit Press/The Poet Tree
ODYSSEY: Science Adventures in Science
POEMS THAT THUMP IN THE DARK/SECOND
    GLANCE
RED OWL
Rowhouse Press
SCIENCE AND TECHNOLOGY
THE STAR BEACON
Steamshovel Press

SPAIN

BUENO
Child's Play
Department of Romance Languages
LA PERIPHERIE
THE NEW PRESS LITERARY QUARTERLY
OXYGEN
Pocahontas Press, Inc.
TORRE DE PAPEL
TRANVIA - Revue der Iberischen Halbinsel

SPEAKING

Adolfo Street Publications
Bonus Books, Inc.
Child's Play
CLASS ACT
Foundation Books
Golden Eagle Press
Grayson Bernard Publishers, Inc.
REFERRALS
Strata Publishing, Inc.
Z W L Publishing, Inc.

SPIRITUAL

Abiko Literary Press (ALP)
Acclaim Publishing Co. Inc.
AGADA
Alamo Square Press
Altair Publications
America West Publishers
Amethyst & Emerald
APPALACHIAN HERITAGE
AREOPAGUS
Ascension Publishing
Ash Grove Press
Ash Tree Publishing
Ashton Productions, Inc.
ASSEMBLY
Astarte Shell Press
Athanor Books (a division of ETX Seminars)
Auromere Books and Imports
Avery Publishing Group, Inc.
AXE FACTORY REVIEW
Barney Press
Beacon Point Press
Beacon Press
Bear & Company, Inc.
Beekman Publishers, Inc.
BEGINNINGS - A Magazine for the Novice Writer
Bennett Books
Beyond Words Publishing, Inc.
Birth Day Publishing Company
Black Diamond Book Publishing
THE BLOWFISH CATALOG
Blowfish Press
Blue Bird Publishing
Blue Dove Press
Borderland Sciences Research Foundation
BORDERLANDS: A Quarterly Journal Of Borderland
    Research
BOTH SIDES NOW
Brason-Sargar Publications
BRILLIANT STAR

Brunswick Publishing Corporation
Buddhist Study Center Press
Burning Books
BUSINESPIRIT JOURNAL
Cassandra Press, Inc.
Center Press
Cherubic Press
Children Of Mary
CHRISTIANITY & THE ARTS
CHRISTIAN*NEW AGE QUARTERLY
COMMON BOUNDARY MAGAZINE
Commune-A-Key Publishing, Inc.
Cosmic Concepts
Cosmoenergetics Publications
CRONE CHRONICLES: A Journal of Conscious Aging
The Crossing Press
Crystal Clarity, Publishers
Cultivated Underground Press
CURMUDGEON
DAILY WORD
Dalrymple Publishing Company
DAUGHTERS OF SARAH
Deerbridge Books
Dharma Publishing
Divina (A MacMurray & Beck imprint)
DOVETAIL: A Journal by and for Jewish/Christian
    Families
Dovetail Publishing
DREAM INTERNATIONAL QUARTERLY
Dream Street Publishing
Earth Magic Productions, Inc.
Earth Star Publications
Elysian Hills Publishing Company, Inc.
Emerald Ink Publishing
EMERGING
THE EMSHOCK LETTER
Ex Machina Publishing Company
Factor Press
FIDEI DEFENSOR: JOURNAL OF CATHOLIC APO-
    LOGETICS
FIDELIS ET VERUS
Flax Press, Inc.
FORESIGHT MAGAZINE
Fort Dearborn Press
Four Seasons Publishers
Friends United Press
Gateways Books And Tapes
GEORGE & MERTIE'S PLACE: Rooms With a View
GINOSKO
Gloger Family Books
Golden Isis Press
The Golden Sufi Center
Good Book Publishing Company
GrapeVinePress
Great Western Publishing Company
Greenlawn Press
Guarionex Press Ltd.
Happy Rock Press
HAZEL GROVE MUSINGS
HEALTH AND HAPPINESS
Heartsong Books
HEARTSONG REVIEW
HEAVEN BONE MAGAZINE
Heaven Bone Press
Herald Press
Himalayan Institute Press
Hohm Press
Hope Publishing House
Horus Publishing, Inc.
HSC Publications
Hunter House Inc., Publishers
Illumination Arts
In Print Publishing
Infinite Passion Publishing
INNER JOURNEYS
Inner Traditions International
Innisfree Press
Integral Publishing

INTEGRAL YOGA MAGAZINE
INTUITIVE EXPLORATIONS
IRIS: A Journal About Women
J & L Publications
THE J MAN TIMES
J. Mark Press
THE JOURNAL OF THE ORDER OF BUDDHIST CONTEMPLATIVES
Journey Publications
Kauai Press
KEREM: Creative Explorations in Judaism
Kivaki Press
H J Kramer
Lamp Light Press
Lemieux International Ltd.
LEO Productions LLC.
Life Energy Media
Light, Words & Music
Llewellyn Publications
LLEWELLYN'S NEW WORLDS OF MIND AND SPIRIT
LP Publications (Teleos Institute)
Magical Blend
MAGICAL BLEND MAGAZINE
MARGIN: EXPLORING MODERN MAGICAL REALISM
MATRIARCH'S WAY: The Journal of Female Supremacy
MEDIA SPOTLIGHT
MetaGnosis
MIND MATTERS REVIEW
MINISTRY & LITURGY
Moksha Press
Moon Publications, Inc.
More To Life Publishing
Mortal Press
Munsey Music
MUSICWORKS: The Journal of Sound Explorations (Audio-Visual)
MYSTIC VOICES
NEW ANGLICAN REVIEW
NEW CATHOLIC REVIEW
New Earth Publications
NEW FRONTIER
New Native Press
THE NEW PRESS LITERARY QUARTERLY
New Spirit Press/The Poet Tree
NEW THOUGHT
NEW THOUGHT JOURNAL
New Vision Publishing
New World Library
Nicolas-Hays, Inc.
NOSTALGIA, A Sentimental State of Mind
NP Press
OBLATES
OF A LIKE MIND
Omega Publications, Inc.
ON COURSE
ONE EARTH
Origin Press
PalmTree Publishers
Parabola
PARABOLA MAGAZINE
Paragon House Publishers
Pathways Press, Inc.
PenRose Publishing Company, Inc.
Peradam Press
Picturesque Publications
Plexus
THE PLOUGH
Plus Publications
POEMS THAT THUMP IN THE DARK/SECOND GLANCE
Polar Bear Productions & Company
PREP Publishing
Pura Vida Publishing Company
Quantum Mind Publications
THE QUEST

RADIANCE, The Magazine For Large Women
Resource Publications, Inc.
Reveal
Reyes Investment Enterprise Ltd.
RFD
Rhino Publishing
Rio Grande Press
S.I.R.S. Caravan Publications
SAGEWOMAN
St. Andrew Press
Saint Mary's Press
St. Michael's Press
SANDBOX MAGAZINE
Sandpiper Press
SAT SANDESH: THE MESSAGE OF THE MASTERS
Scherf, Inc./Scherf Books
SCP NEWSLETTER
Seed Center
SelectiveHouse Publishers, Inc.
Serena Bay Books
SHAMAN'S DRUM: A Journal of Experiential Shamanism
Shaolin Communications
SHARE INTERNATIONAL
Sibyl Publications, Inc
Skytop Publishing
SO YOUNG!
SOCIETE
SOM Publishing, division of School of Metaphysics
Sparrow Hawk Press
SPECTRUM—The Wholistic News Magazine
SPIRIT MAGAZINE
SPIRIT TO SPIRIT
SPIRITCHASER
STAGNANCY IS REVOLTING
THE STAR BEACON
Station Hill Press
Stewart Publishing & Printing
Stillpoint Publishing
STONES IN MY POCKET
STUDENT LEADERSHIP JOURNAL
Sun-Scape Publications, a division of Sun-Scape Enterprises Ltd.
SunShine Press Publications, Inc.
Swan Raven & Company
TAI CHI
Theosophical Publishing House
Three Pyramids Publishing
Threshold Books
THRESHOLDS JOURNAL
Tickerwick Publications
Tiger Moon
Timeless Books
Times Change Press
TitleWaves Publishing
Top Of The Mountain Publishing
Torchlight Publishing
Turtle Island Press, Inc.
Twelve Star Publishing
UNARIUS LIGHT JOURNAL
Unfoldment Publications
Unity Books
UNITY MAGAZINE
Universal Unity
Upper Access Inc.
Verity Press Publishing
Via God Publishing
VIRTUTE ET MORTE MAGAZINE
Visions Communications
Wayfarer Publications
Samuel Weiser, Inc.
WHAT IS ENLIGHTENMENT?
Wheat Forders/Trabuco Books
White Buck Publishing
White Phoenix Publishing
Whitford Press
THE WISDOM CONSERVANCY NEWSLETTER
Wisdom Publications, Inc.

THE WISE WOMAN
Writers Forum
YUWITAYA LAKOTA

SPORTS, OUTDOORS, BOATING

Access Multimedia
Acorn Publishing
ADAPTED PHYSICAL ACTIVITY QUARTERLY (APAQ)
ADIRONDAC
Adirondack Mountain Club, Inc.
Aeolus Press, Inc.
THE AFFILIATE
AMERICAN HIKER
American Hiking Society
Anacus Press, Inc.
APPALACHIA JOURNAL
Appalachian Mountain Club Books
Apples & Oranges, Inc.
Armchair Publishing
AU NATUREL
Avery Color Studios
Backcountry Publishing
BAJA SUN
Bicycle Books (Publishing) Inc.
Blacksmith Corporation
John F. Blair, Publisher
Bliss Publishing Company, Inc.
BLITZ
Blue Reef Publications, Inc.
Bonus Books, Inc.
The Bradford Book Company, Inc.
Bright Mountain Books, Inc.
Brooke-Richards Press
Brunswick Publishing Corporation
Capra Press
CATAMARAN SAILOR
Cave Books
Celo Valley Books
The Center Press
Chicago Review Press
Child's Play
THE CLIMBING ART
CURRENTS
dbS Productions
S. Deal & Assoc.
DISC GOLF JOURNAL
DISC GOLF WORLD NEWS
Dunamis House
DWELLING PORTABLY
Ecopress
Edgeworth & North Books
ETC Publications
Explorer's Guide Publishing
Falcon Press Publishing Company
FERRY TRAVEL GUIDE
Fine Edge Productions
J. Flores Publications
FLYFISHER
Flying Pencil Publications
Foghorn Press
Footprint Press
Front Row Experience
Fulcrum, Inc.
GATEAVISA
Gemini Marine Publications
GEORGE & MERTIE'S PLACE: Rooms With a View
The Glencannon Press
Global Sports Productions, Ltd.
The Globe Pequot Press
Good Life Publications
Grand Slam Press, Inc.
The Great Rift Press
THE GROVE
Halo Books
HANG GLIDING
Heyday Books
Hill Country Books

Hope Publishing House
HSC Publications
Human Kinetics Pub. Inc.
Impact Publishers, Inc.
INTERNATIONAL JOURNAL OF SPORT NUTRITION (IJSN)
JOTS (Journal of the Senses)
JOURNAL OF APPLIED BIOMECHANICS (JAB)
JOURNAL OF ASIAN MARTIAL ARTS
JOURNAL OF SPORT AND EXERCISE PSYCHOLOGY (JSEP)
JOURNAL OF SPORT MANAGEMENT (JSM)
JOURNAL OF SPORT REHABILITATION (JSR)
JOURNAL OF STRENGTH AND CONDITIONING RESEARCH (JSCR)
JOURNAL OF TEACHING IN PHYSICAL EDUCATION (JTPE)
JOURNAL OF THE PHILOSOPHY OF SPORT (JPS)
Keel Publications
Keokee Co. Publishing, Inc.
Michael Kesend Publishing, Ltd.
KITE LINES
LADYBUG, the Magazine for Young Children
LAKE SUPERIOR MAGAZINE
Laureate Press
Ledero Press
Liberty Publishing Company, Inc.
Life Adventures Publishing
THE LISTENING EYE
LLAMAS MAGAZINE
A LOAD OF BULL
McBooks Press
McGregor Publishing
McNally & Loftin, Publishers
Menasha Ridge Press
Mission Press
Momentum Books, Ltd.
More To Life Publishing
MOTOR CONTROL
Mountain Press Publishing Co.
The Mountaineers Books
NATIONAL MASTERS NEWS
Naturegraph Publishers, Inc.
Naturist Foundation
New England Cartographics, Inc.
THE NEW PRESS LITERARY QUARTERLY
Nicolin Fields Publishing, Inc.
OUT WEST
OUT YOUR BACKDOOR: The Magazine of Informal Adventure and Cheap Culture
Outdoor Enterprises, Inc.
Pahsimeroi Press
Paladin Enterprises, Inc.
Para Publishing
PARACHUTIST
Pavement Saw Press
Peartree Books & Music
PEDIATRIC EXERCISE SCIENCE (PES)
PenRose Publishing Company, Inc.
Perpetual Press
Premium Press America
Primer Publishers
Pruett Publishing Company
Publitec Editions
QUEST
Ram Press
Running Press
SANDPOINT MAGAZINE
Schafer's Publishing
SEA KAYAKER
Sea Sports Publications
Seal Press
Sierra Outdoor Products Co.
SIGNPOST FOR NORTHWEST TRAILS
SKINNYDIPPING
SKYDIVING
Genny Smith Books
SOCIOLOGY OF SPORT JOURNAL (SSJ)

MIXED BAG
THE MONTHLY INDEPENDENT TRIBUNE TIMES
  JOURNAL POST GAZETTE NEWS CHRONICLE
  BULLETIN
The New Humanity Press
NIGHTSHADE
NOCTURNAL REPORTER
North Country Books, Inc.
NYX OBSCURA MAGAZINE
Picturesque Publications
POEMS THAT THUMP IN THE DARK/SECOND
  GLANCE
Pruett Publishing Company
REALM OF DARKNESS
REALM OF THE VAMPIRE
Reveal
Rio Grande Press
Rockbridge Publishing Co.
THE ROMANTIST
SCIENCE FICTION CHRONICLE
Shadowlight Press
THE SILVER WEB
69 FLAVORS OF PARANOIA
SPIRIT TO SPIRIT
THE SPITTING IMAGE
SQUARE ONE - A Magazine of Disturbing Fiction
STONES IN MY POCKET
STRANGE MAGAZINE
Three Pyramids Publishing
Tiger Moon
Toad Hall, Inc.
Tyro Publishing
VAMPIRE NIGHTS
Verity Press Publishing
THE VINCENT BROTHERS REVIEW
VIRGIN MEAT E-ZINE
VIRTUTE ET MORTE MAGAZINE
Westgate Press
WICKED MYSTIC

SURREALISM

Abiko Literary Press (ALP)
AFFAIR OF THE MIND: A Literary Quarterly
AK Press
AMERICAN WRITING: A Magazine
ANAIS: An International Journal
ANT ANT ANT ANT ANT
Arjuna Library Press
Asylum Arts
AXE FACTORY REVIEW
Baker Street Publications
BLACK MOON
Black Tie Press
BLACKWATER
Burning Llama Press
THE CATBIRD SEAT
CHAOS FOR THE CREATIVE MIND
DIRIGIBLE
THE DIRTY GOAT
ETCETERA
Full Moon Publications
FURTHER TOO
THE GENRE WRITER'S NEWS
GEORGE & MERTIE'S PLACE: Rooms With a View
GRAFFITI OFF THE ASYLUM WALLS
GRANULATED TUPPERWARE
HOAX!
Host Publications, Inc.
Hyacinth House Publications/Caligula Editions
THE IMPLODING TIE-DYED TOUPEE
Indelible Inc.
JACK MACKEREL MAGAZINE
Jolly Roger Press
JOURNAL OF AESTHETICS AND ART CRITICISM
JOURNAL OF REGIONAL CRITICISM
LITERARY ROCKET
Lunar Offensive Publications
THE MAD FARMERS' JUBILEE ALMANACK

MARGIN: EXPLORING MODERN MAGICAL REA-
  LISM
MASSACRE
MESECHABE: The Journal of Surre(gion)alism
META4: Journal of Object Oriented Poetics (OOPS)
METAL CURSE
MIXED BAG
THE MONTHLY INDEPENDENT TRIBUNE TIMES
  JOURNAL POST GAZETTE NEWS CHRONICLE
  BULLETIN
New Native Press
THE NEW SOUTHERN SURREALIST REVIEW
New Spirit Press/The Poet Tree
NEW WRITING
NIGHTSHADE
NOCTURNAL REPORTER
O!!ZONE, A LITERARY-ART ZINE
The O!!Zone Press
PASSAGES NORTH
PAVEMENT SAW
Pavement Saw Press
PEAKY HIDE
Phrygian Press
PLOPLOP
POEMS THAT THUMP IN THE DARK/SECOND
  GLANCE
The Press of the Third Mind
RAG SHOCK
THE READER'S REVIEW
REALM OF DARKNESS
THE REJECTED QUARTERLY
Ridgeway Press of Michigan
THE RIVER
THE ROSWELL LITERARY REVIEW
Rowhouse Press
THE SALEM JOURNAL
Savant Garde Workshop
Scopcraeft
Shadowlight Press
THE SILVER WEB
SKYLARK
THE SPITTING IMAGE
Transcending Mundane
TRANSMOG
TRANSVERSIONS
Urban Legend Press
THE URBANITE
VAMPIRE NIGHTS
THE VINCENT BROTHERS REVIEW
VIRTUTE ET MORTE MAGAZINE
Westgate Press
WICKED MYSTIC
WINDOW PANES
Wordcraft of Oregon
Xenos Books
XIB
Xib Publications
Zombie Logic Press
ZOMBIE LOGIC REVIEW
ZYX

T'AI CHI

Baker Street Publications
JOURNAL OF ASIAN MARTIAL ARTS
MIXED BAG
THE SALEM JOURNAL
Shaolin Communications
STONES IN MY POCKET
Venus Communications
Via Media Publishing Company

TAPES & RECORDS

ALWAYS JUKIN'
Always Jukin'
AMELIA
American Audio Prose Library (non-print)
THE ANGRY THOREAUAN
Anti-Aging Press

AXE FACTORY REVIEW
BAKER STREET GAZETTE
Baker Street Publications
Black Forest Press
BLACK MOON MAGAZINE
Black Moon Publishing
BLITZ
BOOGLIT
BOOMERANG! MAGAZINE
Cardinal Press, Inc.
Center For Self-Sufficiency
China Books & Periodicals, Inc.
CLASS ACT
THE COMPANY NORTH AMERICA
Conscious Living
CREEPY MIKE'S OMNIBUS OF FUN
Cynic Press
DAYS AND NIGHTS OF A SMALL PRESS PUB-
   LISHER
DIRTY LINEN
DISSONANCE MAGAZINE
Drum
Duende Press
FISH DRUM MAGAZINE
FREEDOM OF EXPRESSION (FOE)
FULL MOON DIRECTORY
Full Moon Publications
FURTHER TOO
Gallopade International
Gateways Books And Tapes
Global Options
Golden Eagle Press
GRAFFITI OFF THE ASYLUM WALLS
GrapeVinePress
GRAY AREAS
THE HAUNTED JOURNAL
HEARTSONG REVIEW
HOAX!
HOLLYWOOD NOSTALGIA
HORIZONS BEYOND
THE HUNTED NEWS
ICARUS WAS RIGHT
IllumiNet Press
Impact Publishers, Inc.
In Print Publishing
INNER JOURNEYS
Itidwitir Publishing
J & L Publications
JACK MACKEREL MAGAZINE
Jalmar Press
JAM RAG
Light, Words & Music
Listen and Learn Home Education, Inc.
LUMMOX JOURNAL
MAIN STREET JOURNAL
METAL CURSE
Metamorphous Press
MIXED BAG
MOBILE BEAT: The DJ Magazine
Momentum Books, Ltd.
Multi Media Arts
MUSICWORKS: The Journal of Sound Explorations
   (Audio-Visual)
NEW HOPE INTERNATIONAL REVIEW
New World Library
nine muses books
NOCTURNAL REPORTER
North Country Books, Inc.
Norton Coker Press
PARADOX
PAST TIMES: The Nostalgia Entertainment Newsletter
PLANTAGENET PRODUCTIONS, Libraries of Spoken
   Word Recordings and of Stagescripts
THE PLOUGH
POW-WOW
Pride & Imprints
PUNCTURE
Pygmy Forest Press

Quiet Tymes, Inc.
REALM OF THE VAMPIRE
RELIX
Resource Publications, Inc.
Reveal
Rowhouse Press
St. Andrew Press
Selah Publishing
SEMIGLOSS
Shaolin Communications
SHEMP! The Lowlife Culture Magazine
SLEUTH JOURNAL
THE SMALL PRESS BOOK REVIEW
SMALL PRESS CREATIVE EXPLOSION
SONAR MAP
STAGNANCY IS REVOLTING
Station Hill Press
The Subourbon Press
SUPER TROUPER
THEY WON'T STAY DEAD!
Timeless Books
UMBRELLA
Underwhich Editions
THE UNIT CIRCLE
Vestal Press Ltd
VIRGIN MEAT E-ZINE
WHOLE EARTH
World Music Press
WORLD OF FANDOM MAGAZINE
World Wide Publishing Corp.
Writers Forum
Yellow Moon Press

TAROT

Abiko Literary Press (ALP)
Bear & Company, Inc.
The Crossing Press
Golden Isis Press
GRAFFITI OFF THE ASYLUM WALLS
HECATE'S LOOM - A Journal of Magical Arts
HOAX!
Inner Traditions International
INTUITIVE EXPLORATIONS
J & L Publications
Llewellyn Publications
MYSTIC VOICES
Reyes Investment Enterprise Ltd.
SAGEWOMAN
SPIRIT TO SPIRIT
Three Pyramids Publishing
Samuel Weiser, Inc.

TAXES

Avery Publishing Group, Inc.
BERKELEY JOURNAL OF INTERNATIONAL LAW
CANADIAN MONEYSAVER
Claitor's Law Books & Publishing Division, Inc.
MIXED BAG
NEW WRITING
THE PRAGMATIST
PSI Research/The Oasis Press/Hellgate Press
Tax Property Investor, Inc.
THE TRUTH SEEKER
Upper Access Inc.
VIRGINIA LIBERTY
WRITER'S WORKSHOP REVIEW

TECHNOLOGY

Aegean Publishing Company
APDG, Publishing
Goodheart-Willcox Publisher
Kent Information Services, Inc.
MAD SCIENTIST
Media Arts Publishing
Mission Press
Open University of America Press
Prakken Publications
Roam Publishing

897

TELEVISION

BAKER STREET GAZETTE
Baker Street Publications
Between The Lines
BLACK TALENT NEWS (The Entertainment Industry Publication for African Americans)
Blue Arrow Books
BOOK MARKETING UPDATE
CREEPY MIKE'S OMNIBUS OF FUN
Crescent Moon
DAYS AND NIGHTS OF A SMALL PRESS PUBLISHER
DOUBLE BILL
DREAM WHIP
Explorer Press
Film-Video Publications
Full Moon Publications
GRAFFITI OFF THE ASYLUM WALLS
THE HAUNTED JOURNAL
HOAX!
HOLLYWOOD NOSTALGIA
THE J MAN TIMES
The Leaping Frog Press
The Media Institute
MIXED BAG
The New Humanity Press
NIGHTSHADE
NOCTURNAL REPORTER
PASSION
Prudhomme Press
REALM OF THE VAMPIRE
ROCTOBER COMICS AND MUSIC
S.E.T. FREE: The Newsletter Against Television
SLEUTH JOURNAL
TEENAGE GANG DEBS
WESTERN SKIES
THE WHITE DOT - Survival Guide for the TV-Free
WHOLE EARTH

TENNESSEE

Abiko Literary Press (ALP)
CJE NEWS (Newsletter of the Coalition for Jobs & the Environment)
ENTELECHY MAGAZINE
MIXED BAG
Premium Press America

TENNYSON, ALFRED LORD

Abiko Literary Press (ALP)
CLASS ACT

TEXAS

ARTHUR'S COUSIN
Baker Street Publications
BORDERLANDS: Texas Poetry Review
Coldwater Press
Colophon House
CONCHO RIVER REVIEW
Corona Publishing Co.
Discovery Enterprises, Ltd.
DREAM WHIP
Duckworth Press
Falcon Press Publishing Company
Full Moon Publications
HORIZONS
Law Mexico Publishing
Ledero Press
Life Adventures Publishing
LONE STAR SOCIALIST
LPD Press
Midmarch Arts Press
Moon Publications, Inc.
Outer Space Press
Rio Grande Press
SALT LICK
SE LA VIE WRITER'S JOURNAL
Shearer Publishing

Studia Hispanica Editors
TRADICIÓN REVISTA
WESTERN AMERICAN LITERATURE

TEXTBOOKS

Acada Books
Accent on Music
Adams-Blake Publishing
Afcom Publishing
Alaska Native Language Center
Ariko Publications
ATL Press, Inc.
Black Forest Press
Blue Heron Publishing, Inc.
Bonus Books, Inc.
Buddhist Study Center Press
Calibre Press, Inc.
Canadian Educators' Press
Center for South and Southeast Asian Studies Publications
Chandler & Sharp Publishers, Inc.
Chicago Spectrum Press
Children Of Mary
China Books & Periodicals, Inc.
Circumpolar Press
Claitor's Law Books & Publishing Division, Inc.
CLASS ACT
Communicom Publishing Company
Construction Trades Press
Crystal Publishers, Inc.
DAYS AND NIGHTS OF A SMALL PRESS PUBLISHER
Desert Oasis Publishing Co.
Dimension Engineering Press
Doctors Press, Inc.
Evanston Publishing, Inc.
FIDELIS ET VERUS
Finesse Publishing Company
Five Star Publications
Free Spirit Publishing Inc.
Front Row Experience
Galen Press, Ltd.
Gallaudet University Press
Gan Publishing
Genesis Publishing Company, Inc.
Goodheart-Willcox Publisher
The Green Hut Press
Human Kinetics Pub. Inc.
Jamenair Ltd.
Dean Lem Associates, Inc.
Lester Street Publishing
Lintel
LS Press, Inc.
Microdex Bookshelf
Multi Media Arts
The Neo Herramann Group
Nunciata
OPTIMA Books
Organization for Equal Education of the Sexes, Inc.
Palari Publishing
Paragon House Publishers
PenRose Publishing Company, Inc.
Philopsychy Press
Pikes Peak Press
Pine Publications
Prakken Publications
Princeton Book Company, Publishers
Professional Resource Exchange, Inc.
Pruett Publishing Company
Reference Desk Books
St. Georges Press
Saint Mary's Press
Sandberry Press
The Saunderstown Press
Scentouri, Publishing Division
Serena Bay Books
Shallowater Press
Signal Books
Gibbs Smith, Publisher

Stewart Publishing & Printing
Sherwood Sugden & Company, Publishers
Trimarket
University of Calgary Press
VanderWyk & Burnham
Via God Publishing
Visions Communications
Witwatersrand University Press
Wordwrights Canada

TEXTILES

Goodheart-Willcox Publisher
Mount Ida Press
NEW HOPE INTERNATIONAL REVIEW
Open Hand Publishing Inc.
ORNAMENT
TRADICION REVISTA
WHOLE EARTH

THEATRE

A & U AMERICA'S AIDS MAGAZINE
Abiko Literary Press (ALP)
Acting World Books
AFFAIR OF THE MIND: A Literary Quarterly
THE AGENCIES-WHAT THE ACTOR NEEDS TO KNOW
Anacus Press, Inc.
Anderson Press
ANQ: A Quarterly Journal of Short Articles, Notes, and Reviews
ARISTOS
AUFBAU
Walter H. Baker Company (Baker's Plays)
BLACK TALENT NEWS (The Entertainment Industry Publication for African Americans)
BOMB MAGAZINE
Branden Publishing Company
Brownout Laboratories
CALLBOARD
Center for Japanese Studies
CLASS ACT
COVER MAGAZINE
Crescent Moon
THE DALHOUSIE REVIEW
Drama Publishers
DRAMATIKA
DRAMATISTS GUILD NEWSLETTER
Empire Publishing Service
THE EUGENE O'NEILL REVIEW
Excalibur Publishing Inc.
Fall Creek Press
GEORGE & MERTIE'S PLACE: Rooms With a View
GRAFFITI OFF THE ASYLUM WALLS
Gumbs & Thomas Publishers, Inc.
HAWAI'I REVIEW
THE HOLLYWOOD ACTING COACHES AND TEACHERS DIRECTORY
IDIOM 23
Indelible Inc.
Institute for Southern Studies
IRISH LITERARY SUPPLEMENT
KMJ Educational Programs
Labor Arts Books
Laureate Press
LEO Productions LLC.
Limelight Editions
Magic Circle Press
MARQUEE
MEANJIN
MEDIA SPOTLIGHT
Moon Publications, Inc.
Passeggiata Press, Inc.
PASSION
PAST TIMES: The Nostalgia Entertainment Newsletter
PenRose Publishing Company, Inc.
Piccadilly Books
Players Press, Inc.
Pogo Press, Incorporated

THE PRAIRIE JOURNAL OF CANADIAN LITERATURE
Preludium Publishers
The Press at Foggy Bottom
Prudhomme Press
Questex Consulting Ltd.
Resource Publications, Inc.
SALOME: A Journal for the Performing Arts
THE SHAKESPEARE NEWSLETTER
SKINNYDIPPING
Slate Press
SOUTHERN QUARTERLY: A Journal of the Arts in the South
Station Hill Press
SUB-TERRAIN
THEATER
THEATRE DESIGN AND TECHNOLOGY
THE THREEPENNY REVIEW
Tomart Publications
University of Massachusetts Press
Waterfront Books
WordWorkers Press

THEOSOPHICAL

Altair Publications
Baker Street Publications
Light, Words & Music
MetaGnosis
THE QUEST
THE SALEM JOURNAL
Theosophical Publishing House
Universal Unity
WHAT IS ENLIGHTENMENT?
White Buck Publishing

THIRD WORLD, MINORITIES

Acclaim Publishing Co. Inc.
AFFAIR OF THE MIND: A Literary Quarterly
AGADA
Aunt Lute Books
AXE FACTORY REVIEW
Baker Street Publications
Between The Lines
BIG WORLD
Blind Beggar Press
Book Faith India
BORDERLANDS: Texas Poetry Review
BRILLIANT STAR
Broken Rifle Press
CHALLENGE: A Journal of Faith and Action in the Americas
Chandler & Sharp Publishers, Inc.
Children's Book Press
China Books & Periodicals, Inc.
Clarity Press, Inc.
Clover Park Press
COMMUNITY DEVELOPMENT JOURNAL
CROSS ROADS
DAUGHTERS OF SARAH
DAYS AND NIGHTS OF A SMALL PRESS PUBLISHER
The Denali Press
EPICA
THE FEMINIST BOOKSTORE NEWS
The Feminist Press at the City College
Florida Academic Press
FOURTH WORLD REVIEW
Frozen Waffles Press/Shattered Sidewalks Press; 45th Century Chapbooks
Full Moon Publications
GATEAVISA
Gay Sunshine Press, Inc.
Global Options
Heyday Books
Hope Publishing House
IAAS Publishers, Inc.
IASP NEWSLETTER
INDIA CURRENTS

INFUSION
Institute for Southern Studies
INTERCULTURE
INTERLIT
Kumarian Press, Inc.
Lake View Press
LEFT CURVE
Lotus Press, Inc.
MEANJIN
Mehring Books, Inc.
THE MILITANT
MIM NOTES: Offcial Newsletter of the Maoist Internationalist Movement
Mindfield Publications
Mr. Cogito Press
MIXED BAG
Noyce Publishing
OBSIDIAN II: BLACK LITERATURE IN REVIEW
OFF OUR BACKS
THE OTHER ISRAEL
Paragon House Publishers
Passeggiata Press, Inc.
Path Press, Inc.
The Place In The Woods
Pocahontas Press, Inc.
PUCK: The Unofficial Journal of the Irrepressible
RADICAL AMERICA
RAIN MAGAZINE
THE RAVEN CHRONICLES
Red Letter Press
REVUE CELFAN REVIEW
Ridge Times Press
Saqi Books Publisher
Schenkman Books
SHARE INTERNATIONAL
SISTERSONG: Women Across Cultures
Smyrna Press
SOCIAL JUSTICE: A JOURNAL OF CRIME, CONFLICT, & WORLD ORDER
SPARE RIB
Spinsters Ink
STRUGGLE: A Magazine of Proletarian Revolutionary Literature
Syracuse Cultural Workers/Tools for Change
Telos Press
Times Change Press
TOWARD FREEDOM
TRANSITIONS ABROAD: The Guide to Living, Learning, and Working Overseas
TRANSNATIONAL PERSPECTIVES
TURNING THE TIDE: A Journal of Anti-Racist Activism, Research & Education
University of Massachusetts Press
Volcano Press, Inc
White Cliffs Media, Inc.
Woman in the Moon Publications (W.I.M. Publications)
WOMEN'S STUDIES QUARTERLY
WORLD RAINFOREST REPORT
Writers Forum
YUWITAYA LAKOTA

DYLAN THOMAS

Abiko Literary Press (ALP)
CLASS ACT
GEORGE & MERTIE'S PLACE: Rooms With a View
KELTIC FRINGE
PHOENIX MAGAZINE
Phoenix Press

H.D. THOREAU

Abiko Literary Press (ALP)
CLASS ACT
THE CLIMBING ART
DIARIST'S JOURNAL
Drum
FREE INQUIRY
GEORGE & MERTIE'S PLACE: Rooms With a View
Lester Street Publishing

MAIN STREET JOURNAL
THE RIVER
Sierra Club Books
SISTERS IN CRIME BOOKS IN PRINT
WRITER'S GUIDELINES: A Roundtable for Writers and Editors

J.R.R. TOLKIEN

Abiko Literary Press (ALP)
Algol Press
CLASS ACT
HORIZONS BEYOND
MINAS TIRITH EVENING-STAR
Polar Bear Productions & Company
SCIENCE FICTION CHRONICLE
W.W. Publications

TRADE

PSI Research/The Oasis Press/Hellgate Press

TRANSLATION

THE ABIKO QUARTERLY WITH JAMES JOYCE FW STUDIES
ABRAXAS
AFFAIR OF THE MIND: A Literary Quarterly
AGADA
ALCATRAZ
Alcatraz Editions
Ariko Publications
The Ark
ARTFUL DODGE
Ash Tree Publishing
Asylum Arts
AXE FACTORY REVIEW
B & B Publishing, Inc.
BAJA SUN
Baker Street Publications
Bandanna Books
BARNABE MOUNTAIN REVIEW
Birdalone Books
BkMk Press
BLACKWATER
BOA Editions, Ltd.
Branden Publishing Company
Buddhist Study Center Press
BUENO
CALYX: A Journal of Art and Literature by Women
Catbird Press
THE CELTIC PEN
Center for Japanese Studies
Center for South and Southeast Asian Studies Publications
CHARITON REVIEW
CHELSEA
Clamshell Press
Clover Park Press
COLORADO REVIEW: A Journal of Contemporary Literature
CONNECTICUT REVIEW
Copper Beech Press
COTTONWOOD
Cottonwood Press
CRAB CREEK REVIEW
Curbstone Press
Cynic Press
THE DIRTY GOAT
DWAN
The Edwin Mellen Press
ELLIPSE
Erespin Press
Eros Publishing
EVANSVILLE REVIEW
Fantail
FIELD
FINE MADNESS
Five Fingers Press
FIVE FINGERS REVIEW
Fjord Press
FOLIO: A LITERARY JOURNAL

THE FORMALIST
FRANK: AN INTERNATIONAL JOURNAL OF CONTEMPORARY WRITING AND ART
Frozen Waffles Press/Shattered Sidewalks Press; 45th Century Chapbooks
Gay Sunshine Press, Inc.
Goats & Compasses
Happy Rock Press
HAWAI'I REVIEW
Hope Publishing House
Host Publications, Inc.
IBIS REVIEW
ILLUMINATIONS
Interim Press
INTERNATIONAL POETRY REVIEW
INTERNATIONAL QUARTERLY
Italica Press, Inc.
JAMES JOYCE BROADSHEET
Katydid Books
THE KENYON REVIEW
KESTREL: A Journal of Literature and Art
KOJA
Kosmos
Leete's Island Books
Lester Street Publishing
LIFTOUTS
LONGHOUSE
Longhouse
LUZ EN ARTE Y LITERATURA
MANOA: A Pacific Journal of International Writing
MARK
THE MARLBORO REVIEW
MATCHBOOK
MATI
MEANJIN
Mellen Poetry Press
The Menard Press
Mercury House
Mr. Cogito Press
MIXED BAG
MUDLARK
Mundus Artium Press
Munklinde Vestergaard
NATURAL BRIDGE
NEW AMERICAN WRITING
NEW HOPE INTERNATIONAL REVIEW
THE NEW PRESS LITERARY QUARTERLY
New Rivers Press, Inc.
Nguoi Dan
NGUOI DAN
Norton Coker Press
Oberlin College Press
ORBIS
Palladium Communications
The Pamphleteer's Press
Parabola
PASSAGER: A Journal of Remembrance and Discovery
Passeggiata Press, Inc.
Pearl River Press
PEARL RIVER REVIEW
PENNINE PLATFORM
PERSEPHONE
PHOEBE: A JOURNAL OF LITERARY ARTS
PHOENIX MAGAZINE
Phoenix Press
Pleasure Boat Studio
POETRY EAST
THE POETRY MISCELLANY
POETRY NEW YORK: A Journal of Poetry and Translation
POETRY WALES
POINT OF CONTACT
POTOMAC REVIEW
Preludium Publishers
PRISM INTERNATIONAL
Pygmy Forest Press
QRL POETRY SERIES
Queen of Swords Press

Red Hill Press, San Francisco + Los Angeles
REFLECTIONS
RENDITIONS
Research Centre for Translation, Chinese University of Hong Kong
SALAMANDER
SALMAGUNDI
SALOME: A Journal for the Performing Arts
SALT HILL
San Diego State University Press
SARU Press International
SCANDINAVIAN REVIEW
Scopcraeft
Serena Bay Books
Singular Speech Press
SKYLARK
Spectacular Diseases
SPECTACULAR DISEASES
THE SPIRIT THAT MOVES US
THE SPITTING IMAGE
STAPLE
THE STARLIGHT PAPERS
Station Hill Press
Stone Bridge Press
Studia Hispanica Editors
32 PAGES
Threshold Books
Top Of The Mountain Publishing
TORRE DE PAPEL
TOUCHSTONE LITERARY JOURNAL
TRANSLATION REVIEW
TWO LINES
Universal Unity
University of Massachusetts Press
Vehicule Press
VISIONS-INTERNATIONAL, The World Journal of Illustrated Poetry
White Pine Press
WILLOW SPRINGS
The Wordtree
WORLD LETTER
WRITER'S GUIDELINES: A Roundtable for Writers and Editors
Writers House Press
Xenos Books
Yellow Moon Press
Zephyr Press
ZONE
Zone Books
ZONE 3

TRANSPORTATION, TRAVEL

Alaska Northwest Books
American & World Geographic Publishing
BabelCom, Inc.
Bain-Dror International Travel, Inc. (BDIT)
BAJA SUN
Bear Creek Publications
Beekman Publishers, Inc.
The Bess Press
Bicycle Books (Publishing) Inc.
BIG WORLD
BLADES
John F. Blair, Publisher
Book Faith India
BUS TOURS MAGAZINE
Carousel Press
Catbird Press
Chandler & Sharp Publishers, Inc.
China Books & Periodicals, Inc.
CJE NEWS (Newsletter of the Coalition for Jobs & the Environment)
Comstock Bonanza Press
THE COOL TRAVELER
Cottage Publications, Inc.
Crossroads Communications
Custom Services
DWELLING PORTABLY

The Eighth Mountain Press
EPM Publications, Inc.
EXIT 13 MAGAZINE
The Feminist Press at the City College
FERRY TRAVEL GUIDE
Five Corners Publications, Ltd.
Foghorn Press
Four Seasons Publishing
Fulcrum, Inc.
Gabriel's Horn Publishing Co., Inc.
Galde Press, Inc.
GATEAVISA
The Glencannon Press
The Globe Pequot Press
GOLD COAST NEWS
Golden West Books
Gumbs & Thomas Publishers, Inc.
Halle House Publishing
Harvard Common Press
Heritage House Publishers
THE INDEPENDENT REVIEW: A Journal of Political
   Economy
Interlink Publishing Group, Inc.
Italica Press, Inc.
J P Publications
JOTS (Journal of the Senses)
THE JOURNAL OF AFRICAN TRAVEL-WRITING
Keokee Co. Publishing, Inc.
Kozmik Press
LAKE SUPERIOR MAGAZINE
THE LAS VEGAS INSIDER
Law Mexico Publishing
Lexikos
Lion Press & Video
THE MATURE TRAVELER
McDonald & Woodward Publishing Company
Monitor Publications AR
Moon Publications, Inc.
Mountain Automation Corporation
Mountain Press Publishing Co.
The Mountaineers Books
Mustang Publishing Co.
NATIONAL BUS TRADER
Nevada Publications
NEW HOPE INTERNATIONAL REVIEW
NORTHERN PILOT
The Olivia and Hill Press, Inc.
OUT WEST
Pamlico Press
Paradise Publications
Passing Through Publications
Passport Press
PenRose Publishing Company, Inc.
Peradam Press
Perpetual Press
PLAY THE ODDS
Plympton Press International
Pride-Frost Publishing
RAIN MAGAZINE
Redbird Press, Inc.
RedBrick Press
Sasquatch Books
Sierra Club Books
SJL Publishing Company
Small Helm Press
Genny Smith Books
SPECIALTY TRAVEL INDEX
Stone Bridge Press
Summerthought Ltd.
Synergistic Press
Ticket to Adventure, Inc.
TIMBER TIMES
TOWPATHS
TRANSITIONS ABROAD: The Guide to Living,
   Learning, and Working Overseas
Transportation Trails
TRAVEL BOOKS WORLDWIDE
Travel Keys

Twin Peaks Press
Umbrella Books
University of Massachusetts Press
The Urbana Free Library
VIRTUTE ET MORTE MAGAZINE
Wayfinder Press
WE INTERNATIONAL (formerly WOMEN AND EN-
   VIRONMENTS)
Wescott Cove Publishing Co.
WHOLE EARTH
Wide World Publishing/TETRA
Windsong Press
WISCONSIN TRAILS
World Travel Institute, Inc.
World Wide Publishing Corp.

TRAVEL

Adirondack Mountain Club, Inc.
AFFABLE NEIGHBOR
Affable Neighbor Press
Afrimax, Inc.
Alaska Geographic Society
Anacus Press, Inc.
Archipelago Publishing
Arjay Associates
Ash Lad Press
Averasboro Press
Baker Street Publications
Barking Dog Books
Barnegat Light Press/Pine Barrens Press
Berkeley Hills Books
BIG WORLD
Blue Heron Publishing, Inc.
Blue Reef Publications, Inc.
CALIFORNIA EXPLORER
Callawind Publications Inc.
CAPE FEAR JOURNAL
The Center Press
Conari Press
Cucumber Island Storytellers
Cultivated Underground Press
Dimi Press
Footprint Press
Fulcrum, Inc.
GERMAN LIFE
GOLD COAST NEWS
Golden Eagle Press
Huntington Press
Innovanna Publishing Co., Inc.
Insider Publications
Ione Press
THE JOURNAL OF AFRICAN TRAVEL-WRITING
Life Adventures Publishing
The Live Oak Press
MARATHON & BEYOND (M&B)
Menasha Ridge Press
MIXED BAG
Mountain Meadow Press
The Mountaineers Books
John Muir Publications, Inc.
Museon Publishing
N: NUDE & NATURAL
NATURALLY
Newjoy Press
Nystrom Publishing Co.
Palladium Communications
Pangaea
Pineapple Press, Inc.
Pogo Press, Incorporated
POTOMAC REVIEW
THE PRESIDENTS' JOURNAL
Pruett Publishing Company
RED OWL
Roam Publishing
Rockbridge Publishing Co.
Russian Information Services
SANDPOINT MAGAZINE
Sasquatch Books

SEA KAYAKER
Seal Press
Seekers Press
Signature Books
SKINNYDIPPING
SPECIALTY TRAVEL INDEX
STARGREEN
Swan Publishing Company
Tortuga Books
Turnstone Press
Two Thousand Three Associates
THE UNKNOWN WRITER
Upney Editions
Venus Communications
W.E.C. Plant Publishing
Wisconsin Trails
WORDS OF WISDOM
WORLDLINKS - FRIENDSHIP NEWS

TREASURE

Foundation Books
Jolly Roger Press
Research & Discovery Publications

TRIVIA

Pineapple Press, Inc.

MARK TWAIN

CLASS ACT
Dovehaven Press
Passeggiata Press, Inc.
Genny Smith Books
Writers Forum

U.S. HISPANIC

Ancient City Press
Baker Street Publications
Barking Dog Books
BILINGUAL REVIEW/Revista Bilingue
BUENO
Carolina Wren Press/Lollipop Power Books
Content Communications
Full Moon Publications
HORIZONS
ICA Publishing
LADYBUG, the Magazine for Young Children
LATINO STUFF REVIEW
The Leaping Frog Press
LOVE AND RAGE, A Revolutionary Anarchist Newspaper
LPD Press
Museum of New Mexico Press
THE NEW PRESS LITERARY QUARTERLY
Organization for Equal Education of the Sexes, Inc.
Outer Space Press
OXYGEN
The Place In The Woods
POINT OF CONTACT
Red Crane Books, Inc.
Serena Bay Books
Treasure Chest Books LLC
Ward Hill Press
WESTERN SKIES

U.S.S.R.

Autonomedia, Inc.
Capra Press
CROSS ROADS
Hoover Institution Press
International Publishers Co. Inc.
Kozmik Press
Mehring Books, Inc.
MIP Company
Moon Publications, Inc.
Paragon House Publishers
Pathfinder Press
Russian Information Services
Semiotext Foreign Agents Books Series

TRANSCAUCASUS: A Chronology
TRANSNATIONAL PERSPECTIVES
Writers Forum
Xenos Books

UTAH

Falcon Press Publishing Company
Signature Books
Gibbs Smith, Publisher
WEBER STUDIES: Voices and Viewpoints of the Contemporary West
WESTERN SKIES

VEGETARIANISM

AFTERTHOUGHTS
Alive Books
ALIVE: Canadian Journal of Health and Nutrition
The Alternate Press
THE ANIMALS' AGENDA
Beekman Publishers, Inc.
Blue Dolphin Publishing, Inc.
Brownout Laboratories
Capital Communications
Center For Self-Sufficiency
Civitas
CJE NEWS (Newsletter of the Coalition for Jobs & the Environment)
The Crossing Press
Dawn Publications
Fisher Books
GATEAVISA
GREEN ANARCHIST
Himalayan Institute Press
INDIA CURRENTS
JEWISH VEGETARIAN NEWSLETTER
JPS Publishing Company
H J Kramer
LIVE AND LET LIVE
Macrocosm USA, Inc.
McBooks Press
Micah Publications Inc.
MYSTIC VOICES
Naturegraph Publishers, Inc.
NEW FRONTIER
Pura Vida Publishing Company
QECE: QUESTION EVERYTHING. CHALLENGE EVERYTHING.
Reyes Investment Enterprise Ltd.
SCIENCE/HEALTH ABSTRACTS
SPECTRUM—The Wholistic News Magazine
Stillpoint Publishing
VEGETARIAN JOURNAL
The Vegetarian Resource Group
THE VINCENT BROTHERS REVIEW
VOICES - ISRAEL

JULES VERNE

CLASS ACT
HORIZONS BEYOND

VIETNAM

AFFAIR OF THE MIND: A Literary Quarterly
AXE FACTORY REVIEW
Burning Cities Press
Galen Press, Ltd.
GATEAVISA
Griffon House Publications
Islewest Publishing
Open Hand Publishing Inc.
THE RAINTOWN REVIEW: A Forum for the Essayist's Art

VIRGINIA

The Brookfield Reader
Brunswick Publishing Corporation
CJE NEWS (Newsletter of the Coalition for Jobs & the Environment)
Falcon Press Publishing Company

GATEAVISA
PLEASANT LIVING
POTOMAC REVIEW
Premium Press America
Rockbridge Publishing Co.
Signal Books
VIRGINIA LIBERTY
Wright-Armstead Associates

VISUAL ARTS

A & U AMERICA'S AIDS MAGAZINE
Abiko Literary Press (ALP)
AFFABLE NEIGHBOR
Affable Neighbor Press
AGADA
Alicubi Publications
Allworth Press
Altamont Press, Inc.
AMERICAN WRITING: A Magazine
ANT ANT ANT ANT ANT
ARCHIPELAGO
ARISTOS
ART CALENDAR
ARTISTAMP NEWS
ART/LIFE
Art/Life Limited Editions
ASSEMBLAGE: A Critical Journal of Architecture and
   Design Culture
AXE FACTORY REVIEW
Axelrod Publishing of Tampa Bay
Baker Street Publications
Black Sparrow Press
BlackBox
BLADES
BLOOD & FEATHERS: Poems of Survival
Blue Raven Publishing
BOMB MAGAZINE
Brick Row Publishing Co. Ltd.
Burning Books
China Books & Periodicals, Inc.
Chiron Press
CHIRON REVIEW
CHRISTIANITY & THE ARTS
Crescent Moon
DAYS AND NIGHTS OF A SMALL PRESS PUB-
   LISHER
THE DIRTY GOAT
DOWN UNDER MANHATTAN BRIDGE
DRASTIC LIVES
Edgewise Press
ENDING THE BEGIN
ETCETERA
FIBERARTS
FISH DRUM MAGAZINE
FOLIO: A LITERARY JOURNAL
FOLK ART MESSENGER
FROM THE MARGIN
FULL MOON DIRECTORY
FURTHER TOO
GemStone Press
GEORGE & MERTIE'S PLACE: Rooms With a View
Gesture Press
G'RAPH
The Green Hut Press
GULF COAST
Gumbs & Thomas Publishers, Inc.
HAND PAPERMAKING
Helicon Nine Editions
Hollywood Film Archive
HOME PLANET NEWS
HORIZONS BEYOND
The Hosanna Press
Host Publications, Inc.
ICARUS WAS RIGHT
Interalia/Design Books
INTERNATIONAL ART POST
Itidwitir Publishing
J P Publications

JACK MACKEREL MAGAZINE
JAMES JOYCE BROADSHEET
JOURNAL OF AESTHETICS AND ART CRITICISM
JOURNAL OF ALASKA WOMEN
KALDRON, An International Journal Of Visual Poetry
KESTREL: A Journal of Literature and Art
Kiva Publishing, Inc.
Allen A. Knoll Publishers
KOJA
LEFT CURVE
LEFTHANDER MAGAZINE
Dean Lem Associates, Inc.
LIGHTWORKS MAGAZINE
LO STRANIERO: The Stranger, Der Fremde, L'Etranger
Luna Bisonte Prods
MANOA: A Pacific Journal of International Writing
Mayhaven Publishing
MEDIA SPOTLIGHT
META4: Journal of Object Oriented Poetics (OOPS)
Midmarch Arts Press
MIXED BAG
Mortal Press
Multi Media Arts
MYSTERIOUS WYSTERIA
NATURALLY
N-B-T-V
NEW ART EXAMINER
THE NEW RENAISSANCE, An International Magazine
   of Ideas & Opinions, Emphasizing Literature & The
   Arts
NIGHTSHADE
Nightsun Books
NOCTURNAL REPORTER
Norton Coker Press
OM
Ommation Press
THE ORIGINAL ART REPORT (TOAR)
O!!ZONE, A LITERARY-ART ZINE
PASSION
PEAKY HIDE
Peel Productions, Inc.
Peninhand Press
PIG IRON
POINT OF CONTACT
The Post-Apollo Press
POW-WOW
PRISM INTERNATIONAL
PROVINCETOWN ARTS
Purple Finch Press
RATTAPALLAX
REALM OF THE VAMPIRE
Reference Desk Books
Reveal
Rowhouse Press
RUBBERSTAMPMADNESS
The Runaway Spoon Press
S Press
THE SALEM JOURNAL
SALOME: A Journal for the Performing Arts
SALON: A Journal of Aesthetics
SANDBOX MAGAZINE
SANTA BARBARA REVIEW
THE SIGNAL - Network International
SISTERSONG: Women Across Cultures
SKYLARK
SO TO SPEAK
SOUTHERN QUARTERLY: A Journal of the Arts in the
   South
THE SOW'S EAR POETRY REVIEW
THE SPIRIT THAT MOVES US
SULPHUR RIVER LITERARY REVIEW
Syracuse Cultural Workers/Tools for Change
13TH MOON
TRIVIUM
Twelvetrees Press
UMBRELLA
THE UNIT CIRCLE
University of Calgary Press

904

VAMPIRE NIGHTS
Venus Communications
VICTORY PARK: THE JOURNAL OF THE NEW
  HAMPSHIRE INSTITUTE OF ART
THE VINCENT BROTHERS REVIEW
Waterfront Books
WESTERN AMERICAN LITERATURE
Westgate Press
WHITEWALLS: A Journal of Language and Art
WOMEN ARTISTS NEWS BOOK REVIEW
Working Press
Yatra Publications/11:11 Studio
YELLOW SILK: Journal Of Erotic Arts
ZUZU'S PETALS: QUARTERLY ONLINE

HUNCE VOELCKER

Jolly Roger Press
Writers Forum

WALES

Access Multimedia
CLASS ACT
Dufour Editions Inc.
GATEAVISA
GEORGE & MERTIE'S PLACE: Rooms With a View
HOAX!
KELTIC FRINGE
Writers Forum

WAR

Acclaim Publishing Co. Inc.
AFFAIR OF THE MIND: A Literary Quarterly
Burd Street Press
CROSS ROADS
The Glencannon Press
GREEN ANARCHIST
JEJUNE: america Eats its Young
Karmichael Press
LOVE AND RAGE, A Revolutionary Anarchist News-
  paper
Lunar Offensive Publications
Open Hand Publishing Inc.
Oxford House Publishing
Paladin Enterprises, Inc.
Premium Press America
RAG SHOCK
THE RAINTOWN REVIEW: A Forum for the Essayist's
  Art
Red Apple Publishing
Rowan Mountain Press
Visions Communications
THE VORTEX
White Mane Publishing Company, Inc.
Yucca Tree Press

WASHINGTON

Blue Heron Publishing, Inc.
The Brookfield Reader
Light, Words & Music
MARGIN: EXPLORING MODERN MAGICAL REA-
  LISM
NORTHERN PILOT

WASHINGTON, D.C.

Blue Unicorn Press, Inc.
Elliott & Clark Publishing
EPM Publications, Inc.
FOLIO: A LITERARY JOURNAL
Gut Punch Press
KETTERING REVIEW
NUTRITION ACTION HEALTHLETTER
POTOMAC REVIEW
Redbird Press, Inc.
THE WASHINGTON MONTHLY
White Mane Publishing Company, Inc.

WATER

AQUATERRA, METAECOLOGY & CULTURE

Blue Reef Publications, Inc.
CJE NEWS (Newsletter of the Coalition for Jobs & the
  Environment)
Coteau Books
Envirographics
FLYFISHER
THE GENTLE SURVIVALIST
Human Kinetics Pub. Inc.
Island Press
Kali Press
LAKE SUPERIOR MAGAZINE
Macrocosm USA, Inc.
Oregon State University Press
Ram Press
SEA KAYAKER
Genny Smith Books
SPROUTLETTER
Two Eagles Press International
WESTERN WATER

WEAPONS

THE ANGRY THOREAUAN
Blacksmith Corporation
Custom Services
GRANULATED TUPPERWARE
Heritage Concepts Publishing Inc
HOAX!
Index Publishing Group, Inc
Lunar Offensive Publications
Marmot Publishing
Paladin Enerprises, Inc.
RAG SHOCK
Tamarack Books, Inc.
Varro Press

WEATHER

APPALACHIA JOURNAL
Child's Play
Coteau Books
Fisher Books
The Mountaineers Books
C. Olson & Company
Peavine Publications
SJL Publishing Company
SKINNYDIPPING

WEAVING

Altamont Press, Inc.
ART CALENDAR
FIBERARTS
LLAMAS MAGAZINE
Open Hand Publishing Inc.
ORNAMENT
TRADICION REVISTA
TRADITION

WEDDINGS

Innovanna Publishing Co., Inc.

H.G. WELLS

ENGLISH LITERATURE IN TRANSITION, 1880-1920
HOAX!
HORIZONS BEYOND
Polar Bear Productions & Company
SF COMMENTARY

THE WEST

THE ACORN
Acorn Books
Alta Research
Ancient City Press
Andmar Press
Baker Street Publications
Ballena Press
The Bear Wallow Publishing Company
Blue Heron Publishing, Inc.
Blue River Publishing Inc.
Borderland Sciences Research Foundation

Carousel Press
CHRONICLE OF COMMUNITY
THE CLIMBING ART
Clover Park Press
Cold-Drill Books
Comstock Bonanza Press
Coteau Books
Devil Mountain Books
DREAM WHIP
DRY CRIK REVIEW
Eagle's View Publishing
Exceptional Books, Ltd.
Falcon Press Publishing Company
Flying Pencil Publications
Foundation Books
Fulcrum, Inc.
Full Moon Publications
The Glencannon Press
Golden Eagle Press
Heritage Concepts Publishing Inc
HIGH COUNTRY NEWS
High Plains Press
Homestead Publishing
HORIZONS
House of the 9 Muses, Inc.
Lahontan Images
Meager Ink Press
Mesa House Publishing
MIXED BAG
Mountain Automation Corporation
Mountain Meadow Press
Mountain Press Publishing Co.
Museum of New Mexico Press
Naturegraph Publishers, Inc.
Old West Publishing Co.
Oregon State University Press
OUT WEST
OVERLAND JOURNAL
PACIFIC COAST JOURNAL
PACIFIC HISTORICAL REVIEW
Point Riders Press
POW-WOW
Primer Publishers
Research & Discovery Publications
Sand River Press
Signature Books
Skyline West Press/Wyoming Almanac
Genny Smith Books
Gibbs Smith, Publisher
SOUTH DAKOTA REVIEW
SOUTHWEST JOURNAL
Spirit Talk Press
Tamarack Books, Inc.
Tortilla Press
Treasure Chest Books LLC
TUCUMCARI LITERARY REVIEW
UNWOUND
Utah Geographic Series
WEBER STUDIES: Voices and Viewpoints of the Contemporary West
WESTERN AMERICAN LITERATURE
WESTERN SKIES
WRITERS' FORUM
YUWITAYA LAKOTA
Zon International Publishing Co.

WHALING

THE ANIMALS' AGENDA
EZ Nature Books
JAPANOPHILE
Edward J. Lefkowicz, Inc.

WALT WHITMAN

Abiko Literary Press (ALP)
Bandanna Books
CLASS ACT
Drum
Gay Sunshine Press, Inc.

GEORGE & MERTIE'S PLACE: Rooms With a View
MESECHABE: The Journal of Surre(gion)alism
The Petrarch Press
WALT WHITMAN QUARTERLY REVIEW
WINDOW PANES
WRITER'S GUIDELINES: A Roundtable for Writers and Editors

WICCA

Baker Street Publications
The Crossing Press
THE DRAGON CHRONICLE
FULL MOON DIRECTORY
Full Moon Publications
Golden Isis Press
THE HAUNTED JOURNAL
HAZEL GROVE MUSINGS
HECATE'S LOOM - A Journal of Magical Arts
HOAX!
Horned Owl Publishing
Hyacinth House Publications/Caligula Editions
MATRIARCH'S WAY: The Journal of Female Supremacy
MYSTIC VOICES
NOCTURNAL REPORTER
OF A LIKE MIND
PAGAN PRIDE
REALM OF DARKNESS
REALM OF THE VAMPIRE
Reyes Investment Enterprise Ltd.
THE SALEM JOURNAL
SPIRIT TO SPIRIT
Tilbury House, Publishers
VAMPIRE NIGHTS

WINE, WINERIES

BAJA SUN
Berkeley Hills Books
Enthea Press
The Feathered Serpent
GOLD COAST NEWS
NEW WRITING
North Country Books, Inc.
OUT YOUR BACKDOOR: The Magazine of Informal Adventure and Cheap Culture
Pruett Publishing Company
SJL Publishing Company
VINEGAR CONNOISSEURS INTERNATIONAL NEWSLETTER

WISCONSIN

AT THE LAKE MAGAZINE
Blue Sky Marketing, Inc.
Center for Public Representation
Crossroads Communications
DOOR COUNTY ALMANAK
Explorer's Guide Publishing
FAMILY TIMES: The Newspaper for Chippewa Valley Parents
FEMINIST COLLECTIONS: A QUARTERLY OF WOMEN'S STUDIES RESOURCES
Galde Press, Inc.
Jackson Harbor Press
LAKE SUPERIOR MAGAZINE
NORTH COAST REVIEW
Open Horizons Publishing Company
Poetry Harbor
THE RIVER
SQUARE ONE - A Magazine of Disturbing Fiction
Whole Person Associates Inc.
WISCONSIN ACADEMY REVIEW
WISCONSIN TRAILS
Wisconsin Trails
Women's Studies Librarian, University of Wisconsin System
Wright-Armstead Associates

LLEWELLYN'S NEW WORLDS OF MIND AND SPIRIT
Lollipop Power Books
Lotus Press, Inc.
LOVE AND RAGE, A Revolutionary Anarchist Newspaper
Lunar Offensive Publications
Macrocosm USA, Inc.
Magic Circle Press
Malafemmina Press
MANUSHI - a journal about women & society
MARGIN: EXPLORING MODERN MAGICAL REALISM
MATI
MATRIARCH'S WAY: The Journal of Female Supremacy
MEANJIN
Mercury House
Midmarch Arts Press
Midwifery Today Books
Mills & Sanderson, Publishers
MIND MATTERS REVIEW
MINERVA: Quarterly Report on Women and the Military
Minnesota Historical Society Press
MIXED BAG
Morning Glory Press
THE MOTHER IS ME: Profiling the Cultural Aspects of Motherhood
The Naiad Press, Inc.
National Council for Research on Women
NEW ART EXAMINER
NEW BOOKS ON WOMEN & FEMINISM
New Victoria Publishers
New World Library
NewSage Press
OF A LIKE MIND
OFF OUR BACKS
The Olive Press Publications
Ommation Press
ON OUR BACKS MAGAZINE
Open Hand Publishing Inc.
Organization for Equal Education of the Sexes, Inc.
Outrider Press
PAGAN AMERICA
Palm Drive Publishing
Papier-Mache Press
Parabola
Paris Press, Inc.
PARTING GIFTS
PASSAGER: A Journal of Remembrance and Discovery
Passing Through Publications
PASSION
PEACE, The Magazine of the Sixties
PenRose Publishing Company, Inc.
Perugia Press
The Place In The Woods
Plain View Press, Inc.
Plus Publications
POETS'PAPER
Pomegranate Communications
Pot Shard Press
Power Publications
THE PRAIRIE JOURNAL OF CANADIAN LITERATURE
Prairie Journal Press
Premium Press America
PRIMAVERA
Pruett Publishing Company
PSYCHOLOGY OF WOMEN QUARTERLY
PUCK: The Unofficial Journal of the Irrepressible
QED Press
Queen of Swords Press
RADICAL AMERICA
RAG SHOCK
Rama Publishing Co.
THE READER'S REVIEW
Red Alder Books
Reference Service Press

RESOURCES FOR FEMINIST RESEARCH/DOCUMENTATION SUR LA RECHERCHE FEMINISTE
Reveal
Rhiannon Press
RHINO: THE POETRY FORUM
RhwymBooks
ROOM OF ONE'S OWN
Rose Shell Press
SAGEWOMAN
Saint Mary's Press
THE SALEM JOURNAL
Sandberry Press
SANDBOX MAGAZINE
Sanguinaria Publishing
Scars Publications
Schenkman Books
SCIENCE & SOCIETY
Seal Press
Sedna Press
SF**3
Sibyl Publications, Inc
Signature Books
SIGNS: JOURNAL OF WOMEN IN CULTURE AND SOCIETY
Sigo Press
SING HEAVENLY MUSE! WOMEN'S POETRY AND PROSE
SINGLE SCENE
SINISTER WISDOM
SISTERSONG: Women Across Cultures
SKINNYDIPPING
SKYLARK
THE SMALL POND MAGAZINE OF LITERATURE aka SMALL POND
Genny Smith Books
Smyrna Press
SO TO SPEAK
SO YOUNG!
SOJOURNER, THE WOMEN'S FORUM
Spinsters Ink
STRUGGLE: A Magazine of Proletarian Revolutionary Literature
Swan Raven & Company
Sylvan Books
Tamarack Books, Inc.
TAPROOT LITERARY REVIEW
TEEN VOICES MAGAZINE
Third Side Press, Inc.
13TH MOON
Ticket to Adventure, Inc.
Tide Book Publishing Company
Tilbury House, Publishers
Times Change Press
TOLE WORLD
TORRE DE PAPEL
Triad Press
THE TRIBUNE
Trilogy Books
TULSA STUDIES IN WOMEN'S LITERATURE
THE UNFORGETTABLE FIRE
Universal Unity
University of Massachusetts Press
VanderWyk & Burnham
Vanessapress
VARIOUS ARTISTS
VEGGIE LIFE
VIETNAM GENERATION: A Journal of Recent History and Contemporary Issues
Visions Communications
Vista Publishing, Inc.
Volcano Press, Inc
WE INTERNATIONAL (formerly WOMEN AND ENVIRONMENTS)
Wild Dove Studio and Press, Inc.
WIN NEWS
THE WISHING WELL
Woman in the Moon Publications (W.I.M. Publications)
WOMAN POET

WOMAN'S ART JOURNAL
WOMEN AND LANGUAGE
WOMEN & THERAPY
WOMEN ARTISTS NEWS BOOK REVIEW
WOMEN IN THE ARTS BULLETIN/NEWSLETTER
Women of Diversity Productions, Inc.
Women-in-Literature, Inc.
WOMEN'S RESEARCH NETWORK NEWS
THE WOMEN'S REVIEW OF BOOKS
Women's Studies Librarian, University of Wisconsin
System
WOMEN'S STUDIES QUARTERLY
WOMEN'S WORK
WOMENWISE
WOOD STROKES & WOODCRAFTS
WORLDLINKS - FRIENDSHIP NEWS
WRITER'S CHRONICLE
WRITER'S GUIDELINES: A Roundtable for Writers and
Editors
WRITING FOR OUR LIVES
XIB
Xib Publications
XY: Men, Sex, Politics
YEFIEF
Yellow Moon Press
YOUR LIFE MATTERS
Z W L Publishing, Inc.
Zephyr Press

WOOD ENGRAVING

Naturegraph Publishers, Inc.
Vestal Press Ltd

WORKER

AFFABLE NEIGHBOR
Affable Neighbor Press
AMERICAN JONES BUILDING & MAINTENANCE
Autonomedia, Inc.
Baker Street Publications
Between The Lines
Black Forest Press
BLUE COLLAR REVIEW
EAP DIGEST
Garrett County Press
GEORGE & MERTIE'S PLACE: Rooms With a View
Herbelin Publishing
Hope Publishing House
Institute for Southern Studies
International Publishers Co. Inc.
The Leaping Frog Press
LEFT CURVE
LITTLE FREE PRESS
Mehring Books, Inc.
MESECHABE: The Journal of Surre(gion)alism
Mindfield Publications
Missing Spoke Press
MIXED BAG
Open Hand Publishing Inc.
Partisan Press
Prakken Publications
SKYLARK
STRUGGLE: A Magazine of Proletarian Revolutionary
Literature
TECH DIRECTIONS
VDT NEWS
Working Press
WorkLife Publishing

WORLD WAR II

A. Borough Books
AFFAIR OF THE MIND: A Literary Quarterly
AUFBAU
Avalon Writing Center, Inc.
R.J. Bender Publishing
Black Forest Press
Branden Publishing Company
Brunswick Publishing Corporation
Burd Street Press

Coteau Books
Cypress House
EZ Nature Books
FLASHPOINT: Military Books Reviewed by Military
Professionals
Galde Press, Inc.
The Glencannon Press
THE JOURNAL OF HISTORICAL REVIEW
Log Cabin Manuscripts
Meyer Publishing
Momentum Books, Ltd.
Noontide Press
Parabola
Path Press, Inc.
Premium Press America
QED Press
Red Apple Publishing
White Mane Publishing Company, Inc.
Yucca Tree Press

WRITERS/WRITING

Abiko Literary Press (ALP)
Ad-Lib Publications
AFFABLE NEIGHBOR
Affable Neighbor Press
ALLA TIDERS BODER
Allworth Press
AMERICAN AMATEUR JOURNALIST
American Audio Prose Library (non-print)
Anaphase II
ARCHIPELAGO
Arden Press, Inc.
Avisson Press, Inc.
AXE FACTORY REVIEW
BAKER STREET GAZETTE
Baker Street Publications
BAST Media, Inc.
Blue Heron Publishing, Inc.
Bonus Books, Inc.
BOOK MARKETING UPDATE
Bookhome Publishing/Panda Publishing
BOOK/MARK SMALL PRESS QUARTERLY REVIEW
THE BOUND SPIRAL
BURNING CAR
BYLINE
A Cappela Publishing
Capra Press
Carrefour Press
The Center Press
CHILDREN, CHURCHES AND DADDIES, A Non
Religious, Non Familial Literary Magazine
Chiron Press
CHIRON REVIEW
CIMARRON REVIEW
CLASS ACT
Coteau Books
CREATIVITY CONNECTION
CRIPES!
Cultivated Underground Press
THE ELECTRONIC PUBLISHING FORUM
EMERGING VOICES
EUROPEAN JUDAISM
FAULTLINE, Journal of Art and Literature
FICTION WRITER'S GUIDELINE
FIRST DRAFT
FOOD WRITER
Foundation Books
FREEFALL
FULL MOON DIRECTORY
Full Moon Publications
Gan Publishing
GEORGE & MERTIE'S PLACE: Rooms With a View
Golden Eagle Press
G'RAPH
THE GREAT BLUE BEACON
H & C NEWSLETTER
Hard Press, Inc.
THE HAUNTED JOURNAL

THE HELIOCENTRIC WRITER'S NETWORK
HORIZONS
Impact Publishers, Inc.
INTERBANG
Ironweed Press
JACK MACKEREL MAGAZINE
J'ECRIS
JEJUNE: america Eats its Young
JEWISH LIFE
JOURNAL OF HUMANITIES
KARAWANE
KARMA LAPEL
Allen A. Knoll Publishers
THE LITERARY QUARTERLY
THE LONSDALE - The International Quarterly of The
   Romantic Six
LULLWATER REVIEW
MAINE IN PRINT
MAKING $$$ AT HOME
MANGROVE MAGAZINE
MESSAGES FROM THE HEART
MIXED BAG
MOCCASIN TELEGRAPH
Myriad Press
New Hope International
NEW HOPE INTERNATIONAL REVIEW
THE NEW PRESS LITERARY QUARTERLY
THE NEW WRITER
Nextstep Books
NIGHTLORE
NIGHTSHADE
NOCTURNAL REPORTER
North Stone Press
Open Horizons Publishing Company
Page One
PAPERBACK PARADE
PAPYRUS
PEN & INK WRITERS JOURNAL
PLUME
POET'S FANTASY
POETS'PAPER
POTPOURRI: A Magazine of the Literary Arts
Quill Driver Books
REALM OF THE VAMPIRE
REDOUBT
Rio Grande Press
Roblin Press
ROMANTIC HEARTS
ROSEBUD
Rowhouse Press
SALON: A Journal of Aesthetics
Scars Publications
SE LA VIE WRITER'S JOURNAL
SEWANEE REVIEW
SF COMMENTARY
SHEILA-NA-GIG
SISTERS IN CRIME BOOKS iN PRINT
SLEUTH JOURNAL
SMALL PUBLISHER
SNAKE RIVER REFLECTIONS
SO TO SPEAK
SOUTHWEST JOURNAL
SPIRIT TO SPIRIT
SPORT LITERATE, Honest Reflections on Life's Leisur-
   ely Diversions
Starbooks Press/FLF Press
Steamshovel Press
Strata Publishing, Inc.
THE STYLUS
SUBSCRIBE, Ideas and Marketing Tips for Newsletter
   Publishers
THE SUNDAY SUITOR POETRY REVIEW
SYCAMORE REVIEW
TEENS IN MOTION NEWS
TEXAS YOUNG WRITERS' NEWSLETTER
TORRE DE PAPEL
TOWERS CLUB, USA INFO MARKETING REPORT
Tudor Publishers, Inc.

ULITARRA
VAMPIRE NIGHTS
Verve Press
WAY STATION MAGAZINE
WILD DUCK REVIEW
WORLDLINKS - FRIENDSHIP NEWS
THE WRITE WAY
WRITER'S EXCHANGE
WRITERS GAZETTE
WRITER'S GUIDELINES: A Roundtable for Writers and
   Editors
WRITER'S GUIDELINES & NEWS
WRITERS NEWS
WRITER'S NEWS
WRITER'S WORKSHOP REVIEW
WRITER'S WORLD
WRITES OF PASSAGE
WRITING MAGAZINE
THE WRITING SELF
ZUZU'S PETALS: QUARTERLY ONLINE
ZYX

WYOMING

Andmar Press
Avalon Writing Center, Inc.
The Bear Wallow Publishing Company
Golden Eagle Press
High Plains Press
MIXED BAG
Moon Publications, Inc.
The Mountaineers Books
Old West Publishing Co.
Pruett Publishing Company
Skyline West Press/Wyoming Almanac
Tamarack Books, Inc.
UNWOUND
WEBER STUDIES: Voices and Viewpoints of the
   Contemporary West
WESTERN SKIES
YUWITAYA LAKOTA

YOGA

Airplane Books
AREOPAGUS
Beacon Point Press
Borderland Sciences Research Foundation
Crystal Clarity, Publishers
THE EMSHOCK LETTER
Himalayan Institute Press
INDIA CURRENTS
Inner Traditions International
INTEGRAL YOGA MAGAZINE
LifeQuest Publishing Group
Llewellyn Publications
Mandala Publishing Group
MetaGnosis
MOKSHA JOURNAL
MYSTIC VOICES
NEW FRONTIER
Pathways Press, Inc.
Plus Publications
Polar Bear Productions & Company
Reyes Investment Enterprise Ltd.
SAT SANDESH: THE MESSAGE OF THE MASTERS
Ten Star Press
Theosophical Publishing House
Timeless Books
Torchlight Publishing
Vajra Printing an Publishing of Yoga Anand Ashram
Samuel Weiser, Inc.

YOUNG ADULT

ATL Press, Inc.
Austen Press
Avisson Press, Inc.
Baker Street Publications
Blue Heron Publishing, Inc.
The Brookfield Reader

Chicken Soup Press, Inc.
Conari Press
Cucumber Island Storytellers
Discovery Enterprises, Ltd.
Dolphin Books, Inc.
THE DROPLET JOURNAL
EMERGING VOICES
Free Spirit Publishing Inc.
Heartsong Books
Horned Owl Publishing
ICA Publishing
ICARUS WAS RIGHT
INFUSION
Itidwitir Publishing
J-Mart Press
The Leaping Frog Press
LEO Productions LLC.
MOOSE BOUND PRESS JOURNAL/NEWSLETTER
Munsey Music
Naturegraph Publishers, Inc.
Neshui Publishing
THE NEW PRESS LITERARY QUARTERLY
North Country Books, Inc.
The Place In The Woods
Polar Bear & Company
Pride & Imprints
THE RATIONAL FEMINIST
READERS SPEAK OUT!
Saint Mary's Press
Seal Press
SEMIGLOSS
SPEAK UP
Speak Up Press
THE SUNDAY SUITOR POETRY REVIEW
TEEN VOICES MAGAZINE
TEENS IN MOTION NEWS
TEXAS YOUNG WRITERS' NEWSLETTER
Visions Communications
VOYA (Voice of Youth Advocate)
Ward Hill Press
WORLDLINKS - FRIENDSHIP NEWS
WRITER'S WORKSHOP REVIEW
WRITES OF PASSAGE

ZEN

Abiko Literary Press (ALP)
Alamo Square Press
AREOPAGUS
AXE FACTORY REVIEW
Beacon Point Press
Beacon Press
BLITHE SPIRIT
Blue Dolphin Publishing, Inc.
Bottom Dog Press
Brooks Books
COMMON BOUNDARY MAGAZINE
THE EMSHOCK LETTER
THE EVER DANCING MUSE
FAT TUESDAY
FISH DRUM MAGAZINE
Flax Press, Inc.
Frozen Waffles Press/Shattered Sidewalks Press; 45th
   Century Chapbooks
GEORGE & MERTIE'S PLACE: Rooms With a View
HOAX!
Hohm Press
IllumiNet Press
Inner Traditions International
JAPANOPHILE
La Alameda Press
LIES MAGAZINE
LifeQuest Publishing Group
META4: Journal of Object Oriented Poetics (OOPS)
THE MINDFULNESS BELL
MOKSHA JOURNAL
NEW FRONTIER
PalmTree Publishers
Parallax Press

PARTING GIFTS
Polar Bear Productions & Company
Press Here
Reveal
Shaolin Communications
Theosophical Publishing House
TURNING WHEEL
Turtle Press, division of S.K. Productions Inc.
Vajra Printing an Publishing of Yoga Anand Ashram
Venus Communications
Samuel Weiser, Inc.
West Anglia Publications
WHAT IS ENLIGHTENMENT?
White Pine Press
Who Who Who Publishing
WINDOW PANES
Wings of Fire Press

ZINES

AMUSING YOURSELF TO DEATH
AXE FACTORY REVIEW
BROKEN PENCIL
CHRONICLES OF DISORDER
COLLEGIUM NEWSLETTER
DEAD FUN
DEANOTATIONS
Full Moon Publications
GATEAVISA
GREEN ANARCHIST
HORIZONS
INTERBANG
THE J MAN TIMES
MESECHABE: The Journal of Surre(gion)alism
PHOENIX MAGAZINE
Phoenix Press
READERS SPEAK OUT!